TABLE OF CONTENTS—Continued

"The data reported herein has been compiled from authoritative sources. While every effort is made by the editors to attain accuracy, manufacturing changes as well as typographical errors and omissions may occur. The publisher then cannot be responsible nor does it assume responsibility for such omissions, errors or changes."

MOTOR
LIGHT TRUCK & VAN
REPAIR MANUAL

2nd Edition

First Printing

Michael J. Kromida, SAE
Editor

Warren Schildknecht, SAE
Managing Editor

Dan Irizarry, SAE
Senior Editor

Michael E. Pallien, SAE • Mark E. Flynn, SAE
Patrick Peyton, SAE • Robert R. Savasta, SAE • John R. Lypen, SAE
Associate Editors

Daniel E. Doku • Denver Steele • James M. Garripoli
John E. DeGroat • Thomas G. Gaeta
Assistant Editors

Published by

MOTOR

HEARST Books/Business Publishing Group,
A Division of The Hearst Corp.

Frank A. Bennack, Jr.
President

Gordon L. Jones
Vice President,
Hearst Books/Business
Publishing Group

Philip D. Shalala
Vice President,
Automotive Group

Louis C. Forier, SAE
Editorial Director
Motor Books

555 West 57th St., New York, N.Y. 10019

Printed in the U.S.A. © Copyright 1985 by The Hearst Corporation
ISBN 0-87851-603-4

DECIMAL & MILLIMETER EQUIVALENTS

INCH	INCH	MM
1/64	.015625	.397
1/32	.03125	.794
3/64	.046875	1.191
1/16	.0625	1.587
5/64	.078125	1.984
3/32	.09375	2.381
7/64	.109375	2.778
1/8	.125	3.175
9/64	.140625	3.572
5/32	.15625	3.969
11/64	.171875	4.366
3/16	.1875	4.762
13/64	.203125	5.159
7/32	.21875	5.556
15/64	.234375	5.953
1/4	.25	6.350
17/64	.265625	6.747
9/32	.28125	7.144
19/64	.296875	7.541
5/16	.3125	7.937
21/64	.328125	8.334
11/32	.34375	8.731

INCH	INCH	MM
23/64	.359375	9.128
3/8	.375	9.525
25/64	.390625	9.922
13/32	.40625	10.319
27/64	.421875	10.716
7/16	.4375	11.113
29/64	.453125	11.509
15/32	.46875	11.906
31/64	.484375	12.303
1/2	.5	12.700
33/64	.515625	13.097
17/32	.53125	13.494
35/64	.546875	13.890
9/16	.5625	14.287
37/64	.578125	14.684
19/32	.59375	15.081
39/64	.609375	15.478
5/8	.625	15.875
41/64	.640625	16.272
21/32	.65625	16.669
43/64	.671875	17.065

INCH	INCH	MM
11/16	.6875	17.462
45/64	.703125	17.859
23/32	.71875	18.265
47/64	.734375	18.653
3/4	.75	19.050
49/64	.765625	19.447
25/32	.78125	19.884
51/64	.796875	20.240
13/16	.8125	20.637
53/64	.828125	21.034
27/32	.84375	21.431
55/64	.859375	21.828
7/8	.875	22.225
57/64	.890625	22.622
29/32	.90625	23.019
59/64	.921875	23.415
15/16	.9375	23.812
61/64	.953125	24.209
31/32	.96875	24.606
63/64	.984375	25.003
1		25.400

Special Service Tools

Throughout this manual references are made to and illustrations may depict the use of special tools required to perform certain jobs. These special tools can generally be ordered through the dealers of the make vehicle being serviced. It is also suggested that you check with local automotive supply firms as they also supply tools manufactured by other firms that will assist in the performance of these jobs. The vehicle manufacturers special tools are supplied by:

American Motors & General Motors . . . . Service Tool Division
Kent-Moore Corporation
29784 Little Mack
Roseville, Michigan 48066

Chrysler Corp. . . . . Miller Special Tools
A Division of Utica Tool Co.
32615 Park Lane
Garden City, Michigan 48135

Ford Motor Co. . . . . Owatonna Tool Company
Owatonna, Minnesota 55060

1

GASOLINE ENGINE TUNE UP SPECIFICATIONS

TABLE OF CONTENTS

AMERICAN MOTORS/JEEP
Except 1984—85 Cherokee & Wagoneer

The following specifications are published from the latest information available. This data should be used only in the absence of a decal affixed in the engine compartment.

★ When checking ignition timing, disconnect vacuum hose at distributor and plug opening in hose so idle speed will not be affected. Also, on some computer controlled ignition systems, it may be necessary to disconnect certain vacuum hoses and/or electrical connectors. Refer to vehicle emission decal.

▲ Before removing wires from distributor cap, determine location of the No. 1 wire in cap, as distributor position may have been altered from that shown at the end of this chart.

Year & Engine	Spark Plug Gap	Firing Order Fig. ▲	Ignition Timing BTDC①★ Man. Trans.	Auto. Trans.	Mark Location	Curb Idle Speed② Man. Trans.	Auto. Trans.	Fast Idle Speed Man. Trans.	Auto. Trans.	Fuel Pump Pressure Psi.
1984—85										
4-150 Exc. High Alt.	.035	D	12°	12°	Damper	⑤	⑥	2000⑦	2300⑦	4—5
4-150 High Alt.	.035	D	19°	19°	Damper	⑤	⑥	2000⑦	2300⑦	4—5
6-258 Exc. High Alt.	.035	A	9°	9°	Damper	680③	600D④	1700⑦	1850⑦	4—5
6-258 High Alt.	.035	A	16°	16°	Damper	700③	650D④	1700⑦	1850⑦	4—5
V8-360, Exc. High Alt.	.035	B	10°	10°	Damper	600	600	1500⑦	1600⑦	5—6½
V8-360 High Alt.	.035	B	16°	16°	Damper	600	600	1550⑦	1550⑦	5—6½
1983										
4-150 Exc. High Alt.	.035	D	12°	12°	Damper	500⑤	500D⑥	2000⑦	2300⑦	4—5
4-150 High Alt.	.035	D	19°	19°	Damper	500⑤	500D⑥	2000⑦	2300⑦	4—5
4-151	.060	C	12°	—	Damper	500/900	—	2500⑦	—	6½—8
6-258 Exc. Calif. & High Alt.	.035	A	6°	6°	Damper	600⑤	500D⑧	1700⑦	1850⑦	4—5
6-258 Calif.	.035	A	6°	6°	Damper	650⑤	550D⑧	1700⑦	1850⑦	4—5
6-258 High Alt.	.035	A	13°	13°	Damper	700⑨	650D⑩	1700⑦	1850⑦	4—5
V8-360 Exc. High Alt.	.035	B	10°	10°	Damper	500/600	500/600D	1500⑦	1600⑦	5—6½
V8-360 High Alt.	.035	B	16°	16°	Damper	500/600	500/600D	1500⑦	1600⑦	5—6½
1982										
4-151 Exc. Calif. & High Alt.	.060	C	12°	—	Damper	500/900	—	2400⑦	—	6½—8
4-151 Calif.	.060	C	8°	—	Damper	500/900	—	2400⑦	—	6½—8
4-151 High Alt.	.060	C	17°	—	Chemper	500/900	—	2400⑦	—	6½—8
6-258 Exc. Calif.⑪	.035	A	8°	8°	Damper	650⑫	550D⑬	1700⑦	1850⑦	4—5
6-258 Calif.⑪	.035	A	15°	15°	Damper	650⑫	550D⑬	1700⑦	1850⑦	4—5
6-258 Exc. High Alt.⑭	.035	A	15°	15°	Damper	600⑫	500D⑬	1700⑦	1850⑦	4—5
6-258 High Alt.	.035	A	19°	21°	Damper	600⑫	500D⑬	1700⑦	1850⑦	4—5
V8-360 Exc. High Alt.	.035	B	10°	10°	Damper	500/600	500/600D	1500⑦	1600⑦	5—6½
V8-360 High Alt.	.035	B	16°	16°	Damper	500/600	500/600D	1500⑦	1600⑦	5—6½
1981										
4-151 Exc. Calif.	.060	C	10°	12°	Damper	500/900	500/700D	2400⑦	2600⑦	6½—8
4-151 Calif.	.060	C	10°	10°	Damper	500/900	500/700D	2400⑦	2600⑦	6½—8
6-258 Exc. Calif.	.035	A	8°	8°	Damper	650⑫	550D⑬	1700⑦	1850⑦	4—5
6-258 Calif.	.035	A	4°	6°	Damper	650⑫	550D⑬	1700⑦	1850⑦	4—5
V8-304	.035	B	8°⑮	10°	Damper	600⑯	600D	1500⑦	1600⑦	5—6½
V8-360	.035	B	10°	10°	Damper	600	600D	1500⑦	1600⑦	5—6½

continued

AMERICAN MOTORS/JEEP—Continued

The following specifications are published from the latest information available. This data should be used only in the absence of a decal affixed in the engine compartment.

★ When checking ignition timing, disconnect vacuum hose at distributor and plug opening in hose so idle speed will not be affected. Also, on some computer controlled ignition systems, it may be necessary to disconnect certain vacuum hoses and/or electrical connectors. Refer to vehicle emission decal.

▲ Before removing wires from distributor cap, determine location of the No. 1 wire in cap, as distributor position may have been altered from that shown at the end of this chart.

Year & Engine	Spark Plug Gap	Firing Order Fig. ▲	Ignition Timing BTDC①★ Man. Trans.	Auto. Trans.	Mark Location	Curb Idle Speed② Man. Trans.	Auto. Trans.	Fast Idle Speed Man. Trans.	Auto. Trans.	Fuel Pump Pressure Psi.
Except 1984–85 Cherokee & Wagoneer—Continued										
1980										
4-151	.060	C	12°	—	Damper	500/900	—	2400⑦	—	6½–8
6-258 Exc. Calif.⑪	.035	A	8°	10°	Damper	700	500/600D	1700⑦	1850⑦	4–5
6-258 Calif.⑪	.035	A	6°	8°	Damper	700	500/600D	1700⑦	1850⑦	4–5
6-258⑭	.035	A	8°	8°	Damper	700	700D	1700⑦	1850⑦	4–5
V8-304 Exc. Calif.	.035	B	8°⑮	10°	Damper	700	500/600D	1500⑦	1600⑦	5–6½
V8-304 Calif.	.035	B	5°	5°	Damper	700	500/600D	1500⑦	1600⑦	5–6½
V8-360	.035	B	8°	8°	Damper	800	600D	1500⑦	1600⑦	5–6½
1979										
6-258⑪	.035	A	6°	4°	Damper	700	600D	1500⑦	1600⑦	4–5
6-258⑭	.035	A	8°	8°	Damper	700	600D	1500⑦	1600⑦	4–5
V8-304 Exc. Calif.	.035	B	5°	8°	Damper	700	600D	1500⑦	1600⑦	5–6½
V8-304 Calif.	.035	B	5°	—	Damper	750	—	1500⑦	—	5–6½
V8-360	.035	B	8°	8°	Damper	800	600D	1500⑦	1600⑦	5–6½

①—B.T.D.C.—Before top dead center.
②—Idle speed on man. trans. vehicles is adjusted in Neutral & on auto. trans. equipped vehicles is adjusted in Drive unless otherwise specified. When two idle speeds are listed, the higher speed is with the A/C or Idle solenoid energized.
③—With holding solenoid energized, 900 RPM; with vacuum actuator energized, 1100 RPM.
④—With holding solenoid energized, 800D RPM; with vacuum actuator energized, 900D RPM.
⑤—With holding solenoid energized, 750 RPM; with vacuum actuator energized, 950 RPM.
⑥—With holding solenoid energized, 700D RPM; with vacuum actuator energized, 850D RPM.
⑦—With fast idle adjusting screw on second step of fast idle cam, engine at operating temperature & EGR vacuum hose disconnected & plugged.
⑧—with holding solenoid energized, 650D RPM; with vacuum actuator energized, 850D RPM.
⑨—With holding solenoid energized, 950 RPM; with vacuum actuator energized, 1000 RPM.
⑩—With holding solenoid energized, 750D RPM; with vacuum actuator energized, 850D RPM.
⑪—CJ Models.
⑫—With holding solenoid energized, 750 RPM; with vacuum actuator energized, 900 RPM.
⑬—With holding solenoid energized, 650D RPM; with vacuum actuator energized, 800D RPM.
⑭—Cherokee, Wagoneer, J-10 & J-20.
⑮—On hilly terrain, set at 12° BTDC.
⑯—On hilly terrain, set at 700 RPM.

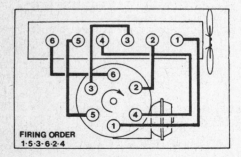

Fig. A

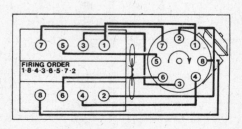

Fig. B

continued

AMERICAN MOTORS/JEEP—Continued
Exc. 1984-85 Cherokee & Wagoneer

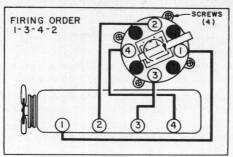

Fig. C   Fig. D

1984-85 Cherokee & Wagoneer

The following specifications are published from the latest information available. This data should be used only in the absence of a decal affixed in the engine compartment.

★ When checking ignition timing, disconnect vacuum hose at distributor and plug opening in hose so idle speed will not be affected. Also, on some computer controlled ignition systems, it may be necessary to disconnect certain vacuum hoses and/or electrical connectors. Refer to vehicle emission decal.

▲ Before removing wires from distributor cap, determine location of the No. 1 wire in cap, as distributor position may have been altered from that shown at the end of this chart.

Year & Engine	Spark Plug Gap	Ignition Timing BTDC①★				Curb Idle Speed		Fast Idle Speed		Fuel Pump Pressure
		Firing Order Fig. ▲	Man. Trans.	Auto. Trans.	Mark Fig.	Man. Trans.	Auto. Trans.	Man. Trans.	Auto. Trans.	
1984-85										
4-150, 2.5L	.035	B	②	②	B	750	700D	2000④	2300④	4-5
V6-173, 2.8L	.041	C	③	12°	D	700	700D	2000④	2300④	6-7½

①—Before top dead center.
②—Exc. high altitude, 12°; high altitude, 19° BTDC.
③—Exc. Calif., 8°; Calif., 10° BTDC.
④—With engine warm and EGR valve disconnected.

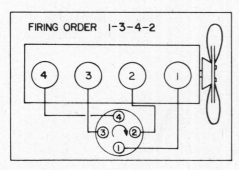

Fig. A

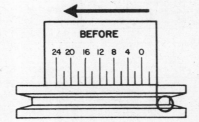

Fig. B

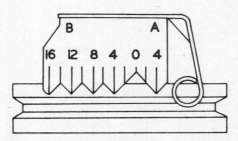

Fig. D

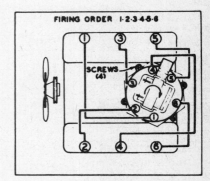

Fig. C

continued

CHRYSLER CORP.
Dodge & Plymouth
Except Rampage, Scamp & Mini Vans

The following specifications are published from the latest information available. This data should be used only in the absence of a decal affixed in the engine compartment.

★ When checking ignition timing, disconnect vacuum hose at distributor and plug opening in hose so idle speed will not be affected. Also, on some computer controlled ignition systems, it may be necessary to disconnect certain vacuum hoses and/or electrical connectors. Refer to vehicle emission decal.

▲ Before removing wires from distributor cap, determine location of the No. 1 wire in cap, as distributor position may have been altered from that shown at the end of this chart.

Year & Engine	Spark Plug Gap	Firing Order Fig. ▲	Ignition Timing BTDC①★ Man. Trans.	Auto. Trans.	Mark Location	Curb Idle Speed② Man. Trans.	Auto. Trans.	Fast Idle Speed Man. Trans.	Auto. Trans.	Fuel Pump Pressure Psi.
1985										
6-225, 1 Bbl Exc. Calif.	.035	A	12°	16°	Damper	725/825	750/850	1600	1600	3–4¼
6-225, 1 Bbl Calif.	.035	A	12°	16°	Damper	775/825	775/850	1600	1600	3–4¼
V8-318, 2 Bbl Fed.	.035	B	12°	12°	Damper	700/850	700/850	1600	1600	4¾–6¼
V8-318, 2 Bbl High. Alt.	.035	B	8°	8°	Damper	650/750	650/750	1400	1400	4¾–6¼
V8-318, 2 Bbl Calif.	.035	B	8°	8°	Damper	725/850	650/800	1625	1450	4¾–6¼
V8-360, 4 Bbl Exc. High Alt.	.035	B	6°	6°	Damper	800/840	800/900	1350	1350	4¾–6¼
V8-360, 4 Bbl High Alt.	.035	B	—	16°	Damper	—	750	—	1600	4¾–6¼
1984										
6-225, 1 Bbl[20]	.035	A	12°	16°	Damper	700/800	725/800	1600	1600	3–4½
V8-318, 2 Bbl Exc. Calif.[20][21]	.035	B	16°	16°	Damper	800/850	800/850	1400	1400	4¾–6¼
V8-318, 2 Bbl Calif.[20][21]	.035	B	16°	16°	Damper	740/850	700/850	1400	1400	4¾–6¼
V8-318, 2 Bbl Exc. Calif.[20][22]	.035	B	12°	12°	Damper	760	760	1500	1500	4¾–6¼
V8-360, 4 Bbl Exc. Calif.[5][20]	.035	B	—	14°	Damper	—	760	—	1500	4¾–6¼
V8-360, 4 Bbl Exc. Calif.[5][19]	.035	B	—	14°	Damper	—	725	—	1600	4¾–6¼
V8-360, 4 Bbl Exc. Calif.[4][19]	.035	B	—	4°	Damper	—	700	1500	1500	4¾–6¼
V8-360, 4 Bbl Calif.[4][20]	.035	B	—	10°	Damper	—	—	1700	1700	4¾–6¼
1983										
6-225, 1 Bbl Exc. Calif.	.035	A	12°	16°	Damper	600/800	650/800	1600	1600	3–4½
6-225, 1 Bbl Calif.	.035	A	12°	16°	Damper	750/850	750/850	1600	1600	3–4½
6-225, 2 Bbl Exc. Calif.	.035	A	12°	—	Damper	700/850	—	1600	—	3–4½
V8-318, 2 Bbl Exc. Calif.	.035	B	12°	12°	Damper	750/850	750/850	1500	1500	4¾–6¼
V8-318, 2 Bbl Calif.	.035	B	16°	16°	Damper	700/850	700/850	1400	1400	4¾–6¼
V8-318, 2 Bbl High Alt.	.035	B	16°	16°	Damper	700/850	700/850	1400	1400	4¾–6¼
V8-318, 4 Bbl Exc. Calif.[5]	.035	B	12°	16°	Damper	750	750	1600	1600	4¾–6¼
V8-318, 4 Bbl Calif.[5]	.035	B	12°	—	Damper	750	—	1800	—	4¾–6¼
V8-318, 4 Bbl[4]	.035	B	8°	8°	Damper	750	750	1800	1800	4¾–6¼
V8-360, 4 Bbl Exc. Calif.	.035	B	4°	4°	Damper	700	700	1500	1500	4¾–6¼
V8-360, 4 Bbl Calif.[4]	.035	B	10°	10°	Damper	750	750	1700	1700	4¾–6¼
1982										
6-225, Exc. Calif.	.035	A	12°	16°	Damper	600/800	600/800	1800	1600	3½–5
6-225, Calif.	.035	A	12°	16°	Damper	800	800	1800	1600	3½–5
6-225-2, 2 Bbl	.035	A	12°	—	Damper	700	—	1600	—	3½–5
V8-318, 2 Bbl Exc. Calif.	.035	B	12°	12°	Damper	750	750	1500	1600	5–7
V8-318, 4 Bbl	.035	B	12°	16°	Damper	750	750	[23]	[23]	5–7

continued

CHRYSLER CORP.—Continued

The following specifications are published from the latest information available. This
data should be used only in the absence of a decal affixed in the engine compartment.

★ When checking ignition timing, disconnect vacuum hose at distributor and plug opening in hose so idle speed will not be affected.
Also, on some computer controlled ignition systems, it may be necessary to disconnect certain vacuum hoses and/or electrical
connectors. Refer to vehicle emission decal.

▲ Before removing wires from distributor cap, determine location of the No. 1 wire in cap, as distributor position may have been
altered from that shown at the end of this chart.

Year & Engine	Spark Plug Gap	Firing Order Fig. ▲	Ignition Timing BTDC①★ Man. Trans.	Auto. Trans.	Mark Location	Curb Idle Speed② Man. Trans.	Auto. Trans.	Fast Idle Speed Man. Trans.	Auto. Trans.	Fuel Pump Pressure Psi.
DODGE & PLYMOUTH EXCEPT RAMPAGE, SCAMP & MINI VANS—Continued										
1982—Continued										
V8-318, 4 Bbl ④	.035	B	8°	8°	Damper	750	750	㉓	㉓	5–7
V8-360, 4 Bbl Exc. Calif. ④	.035	B	4°	4°	Damper	700	700	—	—	5–7
V8-360, 4 Bbl Calif. ④	.035	B	10°	10°	Damper	750	750	1700	1700	5–7
1981										
6-225 Exc. Calif.	.035	A	12°	16°	Damper	600/800	600/800	1600	1600	3½–5
6-225 Calif.	.035	A	12°	16°	Damper	800	800	1800	1600	3½–5
V8-318 2 Barrel Carb.	.035	B	10°	16°	Damper	650/800	650/800	1500	1500	5–7
V8-318 4 Barrel Carb. Exc. Calif. ⑤	.035	B	—	16°	Damper	—	750/800	1800	1800	5–7
V8-318 4 Barrel Carb. Calif. ⑤⑮	.035	B	12°	16°	Damper	750/800	750/800	1500	1600	5–7
V8-318 4 Barrel Carb. Calif. ⑤⑯	.035	B	16°	16°	Damper	700/800	700/800	1500	1600	5–7
V8-318 4 Barrel Carb. ④	.035	B	12°	12°	Damper	750/800	750/800	1800	1800	5–7
V8-360-1 Exc. Calif. ⑤	.035	B	12°	16°	Damper	600/800	625/800	1500	1500	5–7
V8-360-1 Calif. ⑤⑰	.035	B	12°	16°	Damper	750/800	750/800	1700	1700	5–7
V8-360-1 Calif. ⑤⑱	.035	B	16°	16°	Damper	700/800	700/1800	1700	1700	5–7
V8-360-1 ④	.035	B	—	4°	Damper	—	700/800	—	1500	5–7
V8-360-3 ⑲	.035	B	—	4°	Damper	—	700/800	—	1500	5–7
V8-360-3 ⑳	.035	B	—	10°	Damper	—	750/800	—	1700	5–7
1980										
6-225 Exc. Calif.	.035	A	12°	12°	Damper	600	600	1600	1600	3½–5
6-225 Calif.	.035	A	12°	12°	Damper	800	800	1600	1700	3½–5
V8-318 2 Barrel Carb.	.035	B	12°	12°	Damper	600	600	1600	1600	5–7
V8-318 4 Barrel Carb. ③	.035	B	6°	6°	Damper	750	750	1500	1500	5–7
V8-318 4 Barrel Carb. ④	.035	B	8°	8°	Damper	750	750	1800	1800	5–7
V8-360-1 4 Barrel Carb. Exc. Calif. ⑤	.035	B	12°	12°	Damper	650	650	1600	1600	5–7
V8-360-1 4 Barrel Carb. Exc. Calif. ④	.035	B	4°	4°	Damper	700	700	1600	1600	5–7
V8-360-1 4 Barrel Carb. Calif.	.035	B	10°	10°	Damper	750	750	1600	1600	5–7
V8-360-3 4 Barrel Carb. Exc. Calif.	.035	B	4°	4°	Damper	700	700	—	1600	5–7
V8-360-3 4 Barrel Carb. Calif. ⑥	.035	B	10°	10°	Damper	750	750	1800	1800	5–7
V8-360-3 4 Barrel Carb. Calif. ⑦	.035	B	4°	4°	Damper	700	700	1600	1600	5–7
MV-446	.035	⑧	5°⑨	5°⑨	Damper	525/575	625/675	2400	2400	4½–5¾
1979										
6-225 Exc. Calif.	.035	A	12°	12°	Damper	675	675	1600	1600	3½–5
6-225 Calif.	.035	A	8°	8°	Damper	800	800	1400	1600	3½–5
V8-318 Exc. Calif.	.035	B	12°	12°	Damper	680	680	1400	1500	5–7
V8-318 Calif. ⑩	.035	B	6°	8°	Damper	750	750	1600	1600	5–7
V8-318 Calif. ③	.035	B	6°	6°	Damper	750	750	1600	1600	5–7
V8-360 2 Barrel Carb. Exc. Calif. ⑪	.035	B	10°	10°	Damper	750	750	1600	1600	5–7

continued

CHRYSLER CORP.—Continued

The following specifications are published from the latest information available. This data should be used only in the absence of a decal affixed in the engine compartment.

★ When checking ignition timing, disconnect vacuum hose at distributor and plug opening in hose so idle speed will not be affected. Also, on some computer controlled ignition systems, it may be necessary to disconnect certain vacuum hoses and/or electrical connectors. Refer to vehicle emission decal.

▲ Before removing wires from distributor cap, determine location of the No. 1 wire in cap, as distributor position may have been altered from that shown at the end of this chart.

Year & Engine	Spark Plug	Ignition Timing BTDC①★			Curb Idle Speed②		Fast Idle Speed		Fuel Pump Pressure Psi.
	Gap	Firing Order Fig. ▲	Man. Trans.	Auto. Trans.	Mark Location	Man. Trans.	Auto. Trans.	Man. Trans.	Auto. Trans.	

Year & Engine	Gap	Firing Order Fig. ▲	Man. Trans.	Auto. Trans.	Mark Location	Man. Trans.	Auto. Trans.	Man. Trans.	Auto. Trans.	Fuel Pump Pressure Psi.
DODGE & PLYMOUTH EXCEPT RAMPAGE, SCAMP & MINI VANS—Continued										
1979—Continued										
V8-360-3 2 Barrel Carb.⑫	.035	B	—	TDC	Damper	—	⑬	1600	1600	5–7
V8-360 4 Barrel Carb. Exc. Calif.⑤	.035	B	—	4°	Damper	—	750	1600	1600	5–7
V8-360 4 Barrel Carb. Calif.⑤	.035	B	10°	10°	Damper	750	750	1600	1600	5–7
V8-360 4 Barrel Carb.④	.035	B	4°	4°	Damper	700	700	1600	1600	5–7
V8-440⑪	.035	C	—	8°	Damper⑭	—	700	—	1400	5–7
V8-440-3⑫	.035	C	—	8°	Damper⑭	—	700	—	1400	5–7

①—B.T.D.C.—Before top dead center.
②—Idle speed on Man. Trans. vehicles is adjusted in Neutral. Where two idle speeds are listed, the higher speed is with the Electric Throttle Control (ETC) or idle solenoid energized.
③—Medium duty emissions, GVWR 6001 to 8500 lbs.
④—Heavy duty emissions, GVWR 8501 lbs. & above.
⑤—Light duty emissions, GVWR, 8500 lbs & under.
⑥—Exc. models with carburetor No. TQ-9261S.
⑦—Models with carburetor No. TQ-9261S.
⑧—Cylinder numbering (front to rear), right bank, 1-3-5-7; left bank, 2-4-6-8. Firing order, 1-2-7-3-4-5-6-8.
⑨—There are two timing mark plates located on the engine front cover. If the upper timing plate is to be used to check timing, connect timing light to No. 1 cylinder. If the lower timing plate is used to check timing, connect timing light to No. 7 cylinder.
⑩—Light duty emissions, GVWR 6000 lbs. & under.
⑪—Except motor home chassis.
⑫—Motor home chassis.
⑬—Except Calif., 750N RPM; California, 700N RPM.
⑭—On B series, Voyager & motor home chassis models, timing mark located on torque converter
⑮—Models w/distributor No. 4111501 for man. trans., No. 4145602 for auto. trans.
⑯—Models w/distributor No. 4145753.
⑰—Models w/distributor No. 4145364 for man. trans., No. 4145604 for auto. trans.
⑱—Models w/distributor No. 4145350.
⑲—Models less catalytic converter.
⑳—Models w/catalytic converter.
㉑—With electronic spark advance.
㉒—Exc. electronic spark advance.
㉓—W/carb. No. 4287013, 1600 RPM; W/carb. No. 4241752, 1800 RPM; W/carb. No. 4287016, 1500 RPM; W/carb. No. 4241753, 1700 RPM.

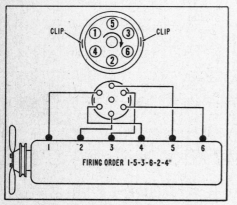

Fig. A

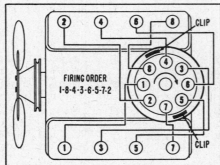

Fig. B

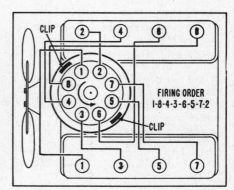

Fig. C

CHRYSLER CORP.—Continued

Dodge Rampage & Plymouth Scamp

The following specifications are published from the latest information available. This data should be used only in the absence of a decal affixed in the engine compartment.

★ When checking ignition timing, disconnect vacuum hose at distributor and plug opening in hose so idle speed will not be affected. Also, on some computer controlled ignition systems, it may be necessary to disconnect certain vacuum hoses and/or electrical connectors. Refer to vehicle emission decal.

▲ Before removing wires from distributor cap, determine location of the No. 1 wire in cap, as distributor position may have been altered from that shown at the end of this chart.

Year & Engine	Spark Plug	Ignition Timing BTDC①★				Curb Idle Speed②		Fast Idle Speed		Fuel Pump Pressure Psi.
	Gap	Firing Order Fig. ▲	Man. Trans.	Auto. Trans.	Mark Location	Man. Trans.	Auto. Trans.	Man. Trans.	Auto. Trans.	
1984										
4-135	.035	A	10°	10°	Flywheel	800	900N	—	—	4.5—6
1983										
4-135 Exc. Calif. & High Alt.	.035	A	10°③	10°③	Flywheel	775	900N	1300	1500	4.5—6
4-135 Calif.	.035	A	10°③	10°③	Flywheel	775	900N	1400	1500	4.5—6
4-135 High Alt.	.035	A	6°③	6°③	Flywheel	900	900N	1350	1275	4.5—6
1982										
4-135	.035	A	12°	12°	Flywheel	850	900N	—	—	4½—6

①—B.T.D.C.—Before top dead center. ②—N: Neutral. ③—Basic Timing set with vacuum line disconnected—do not readjust curb idle.

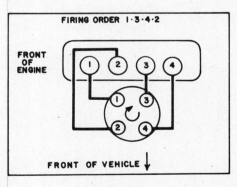

FIRING ORDER 1·3·4·2

FRONT OF ENGINE

FRONT OF VEHICLE ↓

Fig. A

continued

Dodge Caravan & Mini Ram Van • Plymouth Voyager

The following specifications are published from the latest information available. This data should be used only in the absence of a decal affixed in the engine compartment.

★ When checking ignition timing, disconnect vacuum hose at distributor and plug opening in hose so idle speed will not be affected. Also, on some computer controlled ignition systems, it may be necessary to disconnect certain vacuum hoses and/or electrical connectors. Refer to vehicle emission decal.

▲ Before removing wires from distributor cap, determine location of the No. 1 wire in cap, as distributor position may have been altered from that shown at the end of this chart.

Year & Engine	Spark Plug Gap	Firing Order Fig. ▲	Ignition Timing BTDC①★ Man. Trans.	Ignition Timing BTDC①★ Auto. Trans.	Mark Location	Curb Idle Speed② Man. Trans.	Curb Idle Speed② Auto. Trans.	Fast Idle Speed Man. Trans.	Fast Idle Speed Auto. Trans.	Fuel Pump Pressure Psi.
1985										
4-135	.035	A	10°	10°	Flywheel	800	900N	1700	1850N	4.5—6
4-156 Exc. Calif. & High Alt.	.035—.040	B	—	7°	Damper	—	800N	—	1300N	4.5—6
4-156 Calif.	.035—.040	B	—	7°	Damper	—	850N	—	950N	4.5—6
4-156 High Alt.	.035—.040	B	—	7°	Damper	—	800N	—	950N	4.5—6
1984										
4-135	.035	A	12°	12°	Flywheel	800	900N	1500N	1700N	4.5—6
4-156	.035—.040	B	—	7°	Damper	—	800N	—	②	4.5—6

①—BTDC—Before top dead center.
②—California, 950N; exc. California, 1300N.
③—850 w/carburetor model No. R-40143A; 800 Exc. carburetor model No. R-40143A

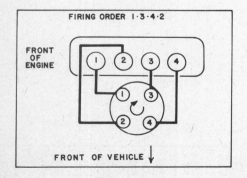

Fig. A

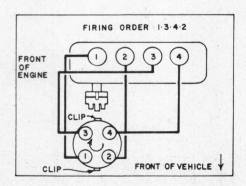

Fig. B

continued

FORD MOTOR COMPANY Except 1983–85 Ranger & 1984–85 Bronco II

The following specifications are published from the latest information available. This data should be used only in the absence of a decal affixed in the engine compartment.

★ When checking ignition timing, disconnect vacuum hose at distributor and plug opening in hose so idle speed will not be affected. Also, on some computer controlled ignition systems, it may be necessary to disconnect certain vacuum hoses and/or electrical connectors. Refer to vehicle emission decal.

▲ Before removing wires from distributor cap, determine location of the No. 1 wire in cap, as distributor position may have been altered from that shown at the end of this chart.

Year & Engine	Spark Plug Gap	Ignition Timing BTDC①★				Curb Idle Speed②		Fast Idle Speed		Fuel Pump Pressure
		Firing Order Fig. ▲	Man. Trans.	Auto. Trans.	Mark Location	Man. Trans.	Auto. Trans.	Man. Trans.	Auto. Trans.	
1985										
6-300(50)	.044	㊽	10°	10°	Damper	650	600D	1600(78)	1600(78)	5–7
6-300(51)	.044	㊽	12°	12°	Damper	500/700	500/550D	1600(78)	1600(78)	5–7
V8-302 2 Bbl.	.044	A	—	10°	Damper	—	575D	—	2000(79)	6–8
V8-302 E.F.I.	.044	A	㉕	10°	Damper	㉖	㉖	㉖	㉖	—
V8-351 Exc. Calif. & High Alt.(50)	.044	B	10°	10°	Damper	700	700D	2000(79)	1900(79)	6–8
V8-351 Calif.(50)	.044	B	—	10°	Damper	—	600D	—	2000(79)	6–8
V8-351 High Alt.(50)	.044	B	14°	14°	Damper	700	700D	2000(79)	1900(79)	6–8
V8-351(51)	.044	B	8°	8°	Damper	700	525/650D	1500(78)	1500(78)	6–8
V8-460	.044	㊾	8°	8°	Damper	800	650D	1600(78)	1600(78)	6–8
1984										
6-300(50)	.044	㊽	10°	10°	Damper	650	600D	1600(78)	1600(78)	5–7
6-300(51)	.044	㊽	12°	12°	Damper	500/700	550D	1600(78)	1600(78)	5–7
V8-302 Exc. Calif. & High Alt.	.044	A	8°	8°	Damper	700/800	600/675D	2100(79)	2100(79)	6–8
V8-302 Calif.	.044	A	—	10°	Damper	—	575D	—	2000(79)	6–8
V8-302 High Alt.	.044	A	12°	12°	Damper	700/800	600/675D	2100(79)	2100(79)	6–8
V8-351 Exc. Calif. & High Alt.(50)(91)	.044	B	10°	10°	Damper	750	600D	2000(79)	2000(79)	6–8
V8-351 Exc. Calif. & High Alt.(50)(92)	.044	B	—	10°	Damper	—	650/700D	—	1900(79)	6–8
V8-351 Calif.(50)	.044	B	—	10°	Damper	—	600D	—	2000(79)	6–8
V8-351 High Alt. (50)(93)	.044	B	—	10°	Damper	—	600D	—	2000(79)	6–8
V8-351 High Alt. (50)(94)	.044	B	—	10°	Damper	—	650/700D	—	1900(79)	6–8
V8-351(51)	.044	B	8°	8°	Damper	700	650D	1500(78)	1500(78)	6–8
V8-460	.044	㊾	8°	8°	Damper	800	650D⑥(77)	1600(78)	1600(78)	6–8
1983										
V6-232	.044	C	2°	10°	Damper	700/850	650/750D	1300(78)	2200(79)	6–8
6-300 Exc. Calif. & High Alt.(50)	.044	㊽	6°⑥(70)	10°	Damper	600/700 ⑥㉔	550/600D ⑥(72)	1600(78)	1600(78)	5–7
6-300 Calif.(50)	.044	㊽	6°	10°	Damper	600/700	550/600D	1600(78)	1600(78)	5–7
6-300 High Alt.(50)	.044	㊽	10°	14°	Damper	600/700	550/600D	1600(78)	1600(78)	5–7
6-300(51)	.044	㊽	12°⑥(71)	12°	Damper	500/700	550D	1600(78)	1600(78)	5–7
V8-302 Exc. Calif. & High Alt.	.044	A	8°	8°	Damper	700/800	600/675D	2100(79)	2250(79)	6–8
V8-302 Calif.	.044	A	—	—	Damper	—	575D	—	2000(79)	6–8
V8-302 High Alt.	.044	A	12°	12°	Damper	700/800	600/675D	2100(79)	2250(79)	6–8
V8-351 Exc. Calif. & High Alt.(50)	.044	B	—	10°	Damper	750/850 ⑥(73)	550/625D	1700⑥(80)(81)	2000(79)	6–8

continued

The following specifications are published from the latest information available. This data should be used only in the absence of a decal affixed in the engine compartment.

★ When checking ignition timing, disconnect vacuum hose at distributor and plug opening in hose so idle speed will not be affected. Also, on some computer controlled ignition systems, it may be necessary to disconnect certain vacuum hoses and/or electrical connectors. Refer to vehicle emission decal.

▲ Before removing wires from distributor cap, determine location of the No. 1 wire in cap, as distributor position may have been altered from that shown at the end of this chart.

| Year & Engine | Spark Plug Gap | Ignition Timing BTDC①★ | | | | Curb Idle Speed② | | Fast Idle Speed | | Fuel Pump Pressure |
		Firing Order Fig. ▲	Man. Trans.	Auto. Trans.	Mark Location	Man. Trans.	Auto. Trans.	Man. Trans.	Auto. Trans.	
EXC. 1983–85 RANGER & 1984–85 BRONCO II—Continued										
1983—Continued										
V8-351 Exc. High Alt.⑤⓪	.044	B	—	—	Damper	600/900	—	2000⑧⓪	—	6–8
V8-351 High Alt.⑤⓪	.044	B	—	14°	Damper	750/850 ⑥⑦④	550/625D	1700⑥⑧⓪⑧②	2000⑦⑨	6–8
V8-351⑤①	.044	B	8°	8°	Damper	700	650D	1500⑦⑧	1500⑦⑧	6–8
V8-460	.044	⑨	⑥⑦⑤	⑥⑦⑤	Damper	800	⑥⑦⑤	1500⑦⑧	1600⑦⑧	6–8
1982										
V6-232	.044	C	10°	12°	Damper	650/750	⑥⑧③	2100⑦⑨	2200⑦⑨	6–8
V8-255	.044	A	8°	8°	Damper	750	625/700D	2250⑦⑧	2000⑦⑨	6–8
6-300 Exc. Calif. & High Alt.⑤⓪	.044	⑧	6°⑥⑧④	10°	Damper	600/700 ⑥⑧⑤	550D	1400⑥⑦⑧⑥⑥	1400⑦⑧	5–7
6-300 Calif.⑤⓪	.044	⑧	6°	10°	Damper	600/700	⑥⑧⑦	1600⑦⑧	1400⑦⑧	5–7
6-300 High Alt.⑤⓪	.044	⑧	10°	14°	Damper	500/600	500N/550D	1400⑦⑧	1400⑦⑧	5–7
6-300⑤①	.044	⑧	⑧⑧	12°	Damper	500/700	500N/550D	1600⑦⑧	1600⑦⑧	5–7
V8-302 Exc. Calif. & High Alt.	.044	A	8°	8°	Damper	700	575/650D⑥ ⑧⑨	2000⑦⑨	2000⑦⑨	6–8
V8-302 Calif.	.044	A	—	—	Damper	—	575/650D	—	1350⑨⓪	6–8
V8-302 High Alt.	.044	A	12°	12°	Damper	730	575/650D	2000⑦⑨	2100⑦⑨	6–8
V8-351⑥②⑦⑤⓪	.044	B	10°	10°	Damper	550/625	550/625D	2000⑦⑨	2000⑦⑨	6–8
V8-351⑥③⓪⑤⓪	.044	B	14°	14°	Damper	550/625	550/625D	2000⑦⑨	2000⑦⑨	6–8
V8-351⑥③①⑤⓪	.044	B	—	—	Damper	750/850	600D	③②	1650⑧⓪	6–8
V8-351⑥⑤①⑤②	.044	B	5°⑥③③	6°⑥③④	Damper	700⑥③⑤	525N/650D	1500⑦⑧	1500⑥③⑥⑦⑧	6–8
V8-351⑥⑤①⑤③	.044	B	12°	—	Damper	500	—	1600⑦⑧	—	6–8
V8-400	.044	B	6°	6°	Damper	600	500N/600D	1750⑦⑨	2000⑦⑨	6–8
V8-460	.044	A	8°	—	Damper	650	—	1600⑦⑨	—	6–8
1981										
6-300 Exc. E & F-350	.044	⑧	6°	10°	Damper	600/700⑥⑤	550D⑥⑤	1400⑦⑧	1400⑦⑧	5–7
6-300 E & F-350 Exc. Calif.	.044	⑧	12°	12°	Damper	500/700	500/550D	1600⑦⑨	③⑦	5–7
6-300 F-350 Calif.	.044	⑧	10°	—	Damper	500/700	—	1600⑦⑨	—	5–7
V8-255	.044	A	4°	10°	Damper	750⑥⑤	575/650D⑥⑤	2200⑦⑨	2000⑦⑨	6–8
V8-302	.044	A	8°	8°	Damper	700⑥⑤	575/650D⑥⑤	2200⑦⑨	2000③⑧⑦⑨	6–8
V8-351W Exc. Calif. & High Alt.⑩⑥⑥	.044	B	—	10°	Damper	—	550/625D	—	2000⑦⑨	6–8
V8-351W Exc. Calif.⑩⑥⑦	.044	B	—	6°	Damper	—	525/600D	—	1700⑦⑨	6–8
V8-351W Calif.	.044	B	—	—	Damper	—	600D⑥⑤	—	1650⑧⓪	6–8
V8-351W High Alt.	.044	B	—	8°	Damper	—	550/625D	—	2000⑦⑨	6–8
V8-351M⑥⑮⑥⑧	.044	B	10°	6°	Damper	650	550/625D	2000⑦⑨	2000⑦⑨③⑨	6–8
V8-351M⑥⑮⑥⑨	.044	B	10°	10°	Damper	600	500/600D	1750⑦⑨	1750⑦⑨	6–8
V8-400 Exc. Calif.	.044	B	6°	3°	Damper	500/600	500/600D	1750⑦⑨	2000⑦⑨	6–8
V8-400 Calif.	.044	B	6°	6°	Damper	600	500/600D	1750⑦⑨	2000⑦⑨	6–8
V8-460	.044	A	—	8°	Damper	650	650D	1600⑦⑨	1600⑦⑨	6–8

continued

FORD MOTOR COMPANY—Continued

The following specifications are published from the latest information available. This data should be used only in the absence of a decal affixed in the engine compartment.

★ When checking ignition timing, disconnect vacuum hose at distributor and plug opening in hose so idle speed will not be affected. Also, on some computer controlled ignition systems, it may be necessary to disconnect certain vacuum hoses and/or electrical connectors. Refer to vehicle emission decal.

▲ Before removing wires from distributor cap, determine location of the No. 1 wire in cap, as distributor position may have been altered from that shown at the end of this chart.

Year & Engine	Spark Plug Gap	Firing Order Fig. ▲	Ignition Timing BTDC[1]★		Mark Location	Curb Idle Speed[2]		Fast Idle Speed		Fuel Pump Pressure
			Man. Trans.	Auto. Trans.		Man. Trans.	Auto. Trans.	Man. Trans.	Auto. Trans.	
EXC. 1983–85 RANGER & 1984–85 BRONCO II—Continued										
1980										
6-300 Bronco, E & F-100, 150, 250 Exc. Calif.	.044	[48]	6°	10°	Damper	600/700	550D	1400 [6][40][78]	1400 [6][40][78]	5–7
6-300 Bronco, E & F-100, 150, 250 Calif.	.044	[48]	6°	[3][6]	Damper	500/700	550D	1400 [6][40][41][78]	1400 [6][40][42][78]	5–7
6-300 E & F350 Exc. Calif.	.044	[48]	12°	12°	Damper	500/700	550D	1400[78]	1400[78]	5–7
6-300 F350 Calif.	.044	[48]	10°	10°	Damper	500/700	550D	1400[78]	1400[78]	5–7
V8-302 E100, 150 Exc. Calif.	.044	A	8°	10°	Damper	700	575D	2000[79]	2000[79]	6–8
V8-302 E100 Calif.	.044	A	—	6°	Damper	—	650D	—	2400	6–8
V8-302 E150 Calif.	.044	A	—	[6][7]	Damper	—	600D	—	2000	6–8
V8-302 E250 Calif.	.044	A	—	10°	Damper	—	575D	—	2100	6–8
V8-302 F100	.044	A	6°	8°	Damper	700	575D	[43]	[44]	6–8
V8-302 F150 Exc. Calif.[4]	.044	A	2°	8°	Damper	550/800	575D	2000[79]	2000[79]	6–8
V8-302 F150 Calif.[4]	.044	A	[8]	8°	Damper	[9]	650D	2500[79]	2400[79]	6–8
V8-302 F150 & Bronco Exc. Calif.[5]	.044	A	8°	[6][11]	Damper	700	575D	2000[79]	2000 [6][45][79]	6–8
V8-302 F150 & Bronco Calif.[5]	.044	A	4°	[6][12]	Damper	750	575D	2500[79]	2100[79]	6–8
V8-302 F250 Exc. Calif.[4]	.044	A	[13]	8°	Damper	700	575D	2000[79]	2000[79]	6–8
V8-302 F250 Calif.[4]	.044	A	—	10°	Damper	—	575D	—	2000[79]	6–8
V8-302 F250[5]	.044	A	8°	8°	Damper	700	575D	2000[79]	2000 [6][46][79]	6–8
V8-351W E100, 150 Exc. Calif. [6][10][14]	.044	B	—	6°	Damper	—	525/650D	—	—	6–8
V8-351W E100, 150 Exc. Calif. [6][10][16][17]	.044	B	—	16°	Damper	—	500/600D	—	1750[78]	6–8
V8-351W E100, 150 Exc. Calif. [6][10][16][18]	.044	B	—	14°	Damper	—	500/600D	—	1750[78]	6–8
V8-351W E100, 150 Calif.[6][10][19]	.044	B	—	8°	Damper	—	500/600D	—	—	6–8
V8-351W E100, 150 High Alt. [6][10][20]	.044	B	—	14°	Damper	—	500/600D	—	—	6–8
V8-351W E100, 150[6][10][21]	.044	B	—	10°	Damper	—	500/600D	—	1750[78]	6–8
V8-351W E100, 150[6][10][22]	.044	B	—	8°	Damper	—	500/600D	—	1750[78]	6–8
V8-351M E250, 350[6][15][23]	.044	B	—	6°	Damper	—	550/625D	—	2000[79]	6–8
V8-351M E250, 350[6][15][54]	.044	B	—	4°	Damper	—	550/625D	—	2000[79]	6–8

continued

GASOLINE ENGINE TUNE UP SPECIFICATIONS

FORD MOTOR COMPANY—Continued

The following specifications are published from the latest information available. This data should be used only in the absence of a decal affixed in the engine compartment.

★ When checking ignition timing, disconnect vacuum hose at distributor and plug opening in hose so idle speed will not be affected. Also, on some computer controlled ignition systems, it may be necessary to disconnect certain vacuum hoses and/or electrical connectors. Refer to vehicle emission decal.

▲ Before removing wires from distributor cap, determine location of the No. 1 wire in cap, as distributor position may have been altered from that shown at the end of this chart.

Year & Engine	Spark Plug Gap	Ignition Timing BTDC[1]★				Curb Idle Speed[2]		Fast Idle Speed		Fuel Pump Pressure
		Firing Order Fig. ▲	Man. Trans.	Auto. Trans.	Mark Location	Man. Trans.	Auto. Trans.	Man. Trans.	Auto. Trans.	
EXC. 1983–85 RANGER & 1984–85 BRONCO II—Continued										
1980—Continued										
V8-351M F100-350 & Bronco[6][15][55]	.044	B	10°[56]	10°[56]	Damper	600	500/600D	1750[79]	2000[79]	6–8
V8-351M F100-350 & Bronco[6][15][57]	.044	B	16°[56]	14°[56]	Damper	650	550/625D	2000[79]	2000[79]	6–8
V8-351M F100-350 & Bronco[6][15][58]	.044	B	10°	12°[56]	Damper	650	550/625D	2000[79]	2000[79]	6–8
V8-351M F100-350 & Bronco[6][15][59]	.044	B	10°	8°[56]	Damper	550/800	550/625D	2000[79]	1750[79]	6–8
V8-351M F100-350 & Bronco[6][15][60]	.044	B	—	6°[56]	Damper	—	550/625D	—	2000[79]	6–8
V8-351M F100-350 & Bronco[6][15][61]	.044	B	—	4°[56]	Damper	—	550/625D	—	—	6–8
V8-400 E250, 350	.044	B	—	4°	Damper	—	550/625D	—	2000[79]	6–8
V8-400 F100-350 Exc. Calif.[6][62]	.044	B	6°[56]	3°[56]	Damper	600	500/600D	1750[79]	2000[79]	6–8
V8-400 F100-350[6][63]	.044	B	6°[56]	6°[56]	Damper	600	500/600D	1750[79]	2000[79]	6–8
V8-400 F100-350[6][64]	.044	B	—	4°[56]	Damper	—	550/625D	—	2000[79]	6–8
V8-460	.044	A	—	8°	Damper	—	650D	—	1600[79]	6–8
1979										
6-300 E & F-100, 150 & 250	.044	[48]	6°	10°	Damper	500/700	500/550D	1600[78]	1600[78]	5–7
6-300 E & F-350	.044	[48]	12°	12°	Damper	500/700	500/550D	1600[6][41][78]	1600[78]	5–7
V8-302 Ranchero Exc. Calif.	.050	A	—	8°	Damper	—	600/675D	—	2100[79]	6–8
V8-302 Ranchero Calif.	.050	A	—	12°	Damper	—	600/675D	—	1800[79]	6–8
V8-302 E-100, 150, 250	.044	A	4°	6°	Damper	700	550/600D[28]	2000[79]	2000[79]	6–8
V8-302 F-100, 150 Exc. Calif.	.044	A	6°	8°	Damper	700	550/600D	2000[79]	2000[79]	6–8
V8-302 F-100 Calif.	.044	A	—	8°	Damper	—	550/650D	—	2400[79]	6–8
V8-302 F-150 Calif.	.044	A	—	6°	Damper	—	550/600D	—	2000[6][47][79]	6–8
V8-351W Ranchero[10]	.050	B	—	15°	Damper	—	600/650D	—	2100[79]	6–8
V8-351W E-100[10]	.044	B	—	10°	Damper	—	500/600D	—	2200[79]	6–8
V8-351W E-150 Exc. Calif.[10]	.044	B	4°	10°	Damper	500/800	500/600D	1500[78]	2200[79]	6–8
V8-351W E-150 Calif.[10]	.044	B	—	8°	Damper	—	500/650D	—	2200[79]	6–8
V8-351W E-250[10]	.044	B	4°	12°	Damper	500/800	500/600D	1500[78]	2200[79]	6–8
V8-351W E-350[10]	.044	B	—	6°	Damper	—	525/650D	—	1700[78]	6–8
V8-351M Ranchero Exc. Calif.[15]	.050	B	—	12°	Damper	—	600/650D	—	2200[79]	6–8

continued

FORD MOTOR COMPANY—Continued

The following specifications are published from the latest information available. This data should be used only in the absence of a decal affixed in the engine compartment.

★ When checking ignition timing, disconnect vacuum hose at distributor and plug opening in hose so idle speed will not be affected. Also, on some computer controlled ignition systems, it may be necessary to disconnect certain vacuum hoses and/or electrical connectors. Refer to vehicle emission decal.

▲ Before removing wires from distributor cap, determine location of the No. 1 wire in cap, as distributor position may have been altered from that shown at the end of this chart.

Year & Engine	Spark Plug Gap	Firing Order Fig. ▲	Ignition Timing BTDC①★		Mark Location	Curb Idle Speed②		Fast Idle Speed		Fuel Pump Pressure
			Man. Trans.	Auto. Trans.		Man. Trans.	Auto. Trans.	Man. Trans.	Auto. Trans.	

EXC. 1983–85 RANGER & 1984–85 BRONCO II—Continued
1979—Continued

Year & Engine	Spark Plug Gap	Firing Order Fig.	Man. Trans.	Auto. Trans.	Mark Location	Man. Trans.	Auto. Trans.	Man. Trans.	Auto. Trans.	Fuel Pump Pressure
V8-351M Ranchero Calif.⑮	.050	B	—	14°	Damper	—	600/650D	—	2200⑦⑨	6–8
V8-351M F-100 Exc. Calif.⑮	.044	B	10°	6°	Damper	650	550D	2000⑦⑨	2000⑦⑨	6–8
V8-351M F-100 Calif.⑮	.044	B	—	10°	Damper	—	550D	—	2100⑦⑨	6–8
V8-351M F-150, 250 & Bronco⑮	.044	B	㉙	6°	Damper	650	550D	2000⑦⑨	2000⑦⑨	6–8
V8-351M F-350⑮	.044	B	6°	12°	Damper	600	500/600D	1750⑦⑨	2000⑦⑨	6–8
V8-400 F-150, 250 & Bronco	.044	B	10°	6°	Damper	650	550D	2000⑦⑨	1900⑦⑨	6–8
V8-400 F-350	.044	B	3°	3°	Damper	600	600D	1750⑦⑨	2000⑦⑨	6–8
V8-460 E-250	.044	A	—	14°	Damper	—	650/800D	—	1600⑦⑧	6–8
V8-460 E-350	.044	A	—	8°	Damper	—	650D	—	1600⑦⑧	6–8

① B.T.D.C.—Before top-dead center.
② Idle speed on man. trans. vehicles is adjusted in Neutral & on auto. trans. vehicles is adjusted in Drive unless otherwise specified. Where two idle speeds are listed, the higher speed is with the A/C or idle solenoid energized.
③ Except calibration code 0-52S-R10, 10° BTDC; calibration code 0-52S-R10, 6° BTDC.
④ Except 4 wheel drive models.
⑤ 4 wheel drive models.
⑥ Refer to engine calibration code on engine identification label, located at rear of left valve cover on V8 engines, on front of valve cover on 6 cylinder engines. The calibration code is located on the label after the engine code number and is preceded by the letter C and the revision code is located below the calibration code and is preceded by the letter R.
⑦ Calibration code 0-54T-R0, 12° BTDC; calibration code 0-54T-R10, 8° BTDC.
⑧ Models w/3 spd. & 4 spd. overdrive man. trans., 2° BTDC; models w/4 spd. man. trans., 4° BTDC.
⑨ Models w/3 spd. or 4 spd. overdrive man. trans., 550/800 RPM; models w/4 spd. man. trans., 750 RPM.
⑩ Windsor engine.
⑪ Calibration code 0-54D-R0, 14° BTDC; 0-54D-R11, 12° BTDC; 0-54F-R0 & 0-54M-R0, 8° BTDC.
⑫ Calibration code 0-54M-R0 8° BTDC; 0-54R-R0, 10° BTDC.
⑬ Models w/3 spd. or 4 spd. overdrive man. trans., 6° BTDC; models w/4 spd. man. trans., 8° BTDC.
⑭ Calibration code 7-76J-R11.
⑮ Modified engine.

⑯ Except high altitude.
⑰ Calibration codes 0-64A-R0, R10 & R11.
⑱ Calibration codes 0-64B-R0 & R10.
⑲ Calibration codes 0-64T-R0, R10 & R11.
⑳ Calibration code 0-64B-R11.
㉑ Calibration codes 0-64G-R0, R10 & R11.
㉒ Calibration codes 0-64H-R0, R10 & R11.
㉓ Calibration codes 0-60D-R0 & R10.
㉔ Calibration code 3-51P-R00, 475/500 RPM; calibration code 3-51T-R10, 500/600 RPM.
㉕ Calibration codes 5-53D-R00, 5-53F-R00, 5-53F-R00 & 5-53H-R00, 10°; calibration codes 5-53D-R01, 5-53F-R01 & 5-53H-R01, 8°.
㉖ Idle speed controlled by an electronic control module.
㉗ Calibration code 1-64H-R2.
㉘ E-100 California models w/2.75 rear axle ratio, set at 500/650D.
㉙ Man. trans., except Calif. models w/ 3.50 or 3.54 axle ratio 10° BTDC; California models w/3.50 or 3.54 axle ratio, 8° BTDC.
㉚ Calibration code 2-64X-R0.
㉛ Except calibration codes 1-64H-R2 & 2-64X-R0.
㉜ Except Calif., 1700 RPM; Calif., 1650 RPM.
㉝ Calibration code 7-75J-R14, 6°; calibration codes 2-75A-R10 & 2-75J-R20, 8°.
㉞ Calibration codes 2-76A-R10 & 2-76J-R20, 8°; calibration codes 2-76J-R17 & 2-76J-R18, 5°.
㉟ Calibration code 2-75A-R10, 800 RPM.

㊱ Calibration codes 7-76J-R11, 7-76J-R14 & 7-76J-R15, 1700 RPM.
㊲ Calibration code 9-78J-R0, 1500 RPM on kickdown step of cam; calibration code 9-78J-R11, 1600 RPM on high step of fast idle cam.
㊳ Calibration codes 1-54P-R0 & 1-54R-R0, 1350 on high step of fast idle cam.
㊴ Calibration codes 1-60A-R0 & 1-60B-R0, 2200 RPM.
㊵ Calibration code 0-51F-R0, 1600 RPM on kickdown step of cam.
㊶ Calibration codes 0-51S-R0 & 0-51T-R0, 1600 RPM on kickdown step of cam.
㊷ Calibration code 0-52S-R0, 1600 RPM on kickdown step of cam.
㊸ Except Calif., 2000 RPM on high step of fast idle cam; Calif., 2500 RPM on high step of fast idle cam.
㊹ Except Calif., 2000 RPM on high step of fast idle cam; Calif., 2400 RPM on high step of fast idle cam.
㊺ Calibration code 0-54M-R0, 2100 RPM on high step of fast idle cam.
㊻ Calibration code 9-77M-R0, 2550 RPM on high step of fast idle cam.
㊼ Calibration code 9-54U-R0, 2400 RPM on high step of fast idle cam.
㊽ Cylinder numbering front to rear, firing order 1-5-3-6-2-4.
㊾ Cylinder numbering (front to rear), right bank 1-2-3-4, left bank 5-6-7-8, firing order 1-5-4-2-6-3-7-8.
㊿ Light duty models.
51 Heavy duty models.
52 Exc. calibration code 7-76J-R13.
53 Calibration code 7-76J-R13.
54 Calibration code 0-62D-R10.
55 Calibration codes, man. trans. 9-71J-

continued

FORD MOTOR COMPANY—Continued
Exc. 1983–85 Ranger & 1984–85 Bronco II Notes

R10; auto. trans. 9-72J-R11.

⑤⑥—On early 1980 Bronco & F Series, a sight hole located at the upper right hand corner of the fan shroud is used for viewing the pointer when adjusting ignition timing. It is recommended that the timing be set 2° less than the value observed on the engine damper through the sight hole, due to the angle employed when viewing the pointer.

⑤⑦—Calibration codes, man. trans. 0-59C-R0 & R10; auto. trans. 0-60A-R0 & R10.

⑤⑧—Calibration codes, man. trans. 0-59G-R0 & R10, 0-59H-R0 & R10 & 0-59J-R0 & R10: auto. trans. 0-60B-R0 & R10 & 0-60C-R0 & R10.

⑤⑨—Calibration codes, man. trans. 0-59S-R0: auto. trans. 0-60G-R0, 0-60H-R11 & 0-60H-R13.

⑥⓪—Calibration codes 0-60H-R0, 0-60H-R12, 0-60K-R0, R10, R11, R12 & 0-60J-R0.

⑥①—Calibration code 0-60L-R10.

⑥②—Calibration codes, man. trans. 9-73J-R11; auto. trans. 9-74J-R11.

⑥③—Calibration codes, man. trans. 9-73J-R12; auto. trans. 9-74J-R12.

⑥④—Calibration code 0-62L-R0.

⑥⑤—If mileage on vehicle is less than 100 mi., set idle speed 50 RPM less than specified.

⑥⑥—Models with G.V.W.R less than 8500 lbs.

⑥⑦—Models with G.V.W.R 8500 lbs. & above.

⑥⑧—Except calibration code 9-72J-R10.

⑥⑨—Calibration code 9-71J-R10.

⑦⓪—Except calibration code 3-51P-R00, 10°.

⑦①—Except calibration code 9-77S-R10, 10°.

⑦②—Calibration code 3-51Z-R00, 600/700D RPM.

⑦③—Calibration code 1-64T-R15B, 600/900 RPM.

⑦④—Calibration codes 2-63Y-R14B & 2-64Y-R14B, 600/900 RPM.

⑦⑤—Calibration code 3-98S-R00, 6°; calibration code 9-97J-R13, 8°.

⑦⑥—Calibration code 3-98S-R00, 600D RPM; calibration code 9-97J-R13, 650D RPM.

⑦⑦—Calibration code 3-98S-R10, 600D RPM.

⑦⑧—On kickdown step of cam.

⑦⑨—On high step of fast idle cam.

⑧⓪—On second highest step of fast idle cam.

⑧①—Calibration codes 1-64T-R12 & 1-64T-R13, 1650 RPM on second highest step of fast idle cam.

⑧②—Calibration codes 2-64Y-R11 & 1-64Y-R12, 1650 RPM on second highest step of fast idle cam.

⑧③—Calibration code 2-56D-R0, 550/600D RPM; calibration code 2-56D-R10, 600/700D RPM.

⑧④—Calibration code 2-51P-R0, 10°; calibration code 2-51P-R10, 12°.

⑧⑤—Calibration codes 2-51P-R0 & 2-51P-R10, 500 RPM.

⑧⑥—Calibration codes 2-51P-R0 & 2-51P-R10, 1600 RPM.

⑧⑦—Calibration code 2-52S-R0, 550/600D RPM; calibration code 2-52T-R0 550D RPM.

⑧⑧—Calibration code 9-77J-R12, 12°; calibration code 9-77S-R10, 10°.

⑧⑨—Calibration codes 2-54F-R0 & 2-54F-R10, 575D RPM.

⑨⓪—On third highest step of fast idle cam.

⑨①—Calibration codes 4-63H-R0, 4-64H-R0 & 4-64H-R00.

⑨②—Calibration codes 4-64G-R00 & 4-64G-R02.

⑨③—Calibration code 4-64Y-R00.

⑨④—Calibration code 4-64Z-R00.

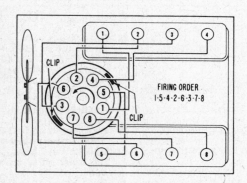

Fig. A

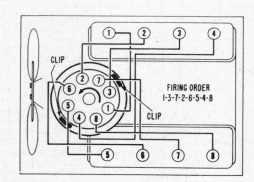

Fig. B

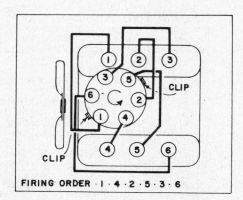

Fig. C

continued

FORD MOTOR COMPANY—Continued

1983-85 Ranger & 1984-85 Bronco II

The following specifications are published from the latest information available. This data should be used only in the absence of a decal affixed in the engine compartment.

★ When checking ignition timing, disconnect vacuum hose at distributor and plug opening in hose so idle speed will not be affected. Also, on some computer controlled ignition systems, it may be necessary to disconnect certain vacuum hoses and/or electrical connectors. Refer to vehicle emission decal.

▲ Before removing wires from distributor cap, determine location of the No. 1 wire in cap, as distributor position may have been altered from that shown at the end of this chart.

Year & Engine	Spark Plug Gap	Firing Order Fig. ▲	Ignition Timing BTDC①★			Curb Idle Speed②		Fast Idle Speed		Fuel Pump Pressure
			Man. Trans.	Auto. Trans.	Mark Fig.	Man. Trans.	Auto. Trans.	Man. Trans.	Auto. Trans.	
1985										
4-122	.044	A	6°	—	B	800	—	1700	—	5–7
4-140	.044	A	10°	10°	B	⑪⑮	⑪⑮	—	—	—
V6-171 Exc. Calif.	.044	C	14°	10°	D	850⑪	750⑪	3000	3000	4.5–6.5
V6-171 Calif.	.044	C	14°	10°	D	850⑪	750⑪	3200	3000	4.5–6.5
1984										
4-122	.034	A	⑭	—	B	800	—	2000	—	5–7
4-140 Exc. High Alt.	.034	A	6°	6°	B	④	800	2000	2000	5–7
4-140 High Alt.	.044	A	10°	10°	B	④	800	2000	2000	5–7
V6-171	.044	C	10°	10°	D	③⑪	750⑪	3000	3000	4.5–6.5
1983										
4-122	.034	A	6°	—	B	800	—	2000	—	5–7
4-140 Exc. Calif. & High Alt.	.044	A	6°	6°	B	④	800	2000	2000	5–7
4-140 Calif.⑤	.044	A	6°	6°	B	④	800	2000	2000	5–7
4-140 Calif.⑥	.034	A	6°	8°	B	④	⑦	2000	2000	5–7
4-140 High Alt.⑧	.044	A	10°	10°	B	④	800	2000	2000	5–7
4-140 High Alt.⑨	.034	A	10°	⑩	B	850	800	2000	2000	5–7

①—Before top dead center
②—Idle speed on man. trans. vehicles is adjusted in Neutral and on auto. trans. vehicles in Drive unless otherwise specified. Adjustment should be made with all vacuum hoses connected.
③—Calibration codes 4-61G-R00 & 4-61G-R10, 750 RPM; calibration codes 4-61K-R01 & 4-61K-R10, 900 RPM; all others, 850 RPM.
④—With power steering, 850 RPM; less power steering, 800 RPM.

⑤—Calibration codes 3-49S-R16, 3-49T-R20 & 3-50S-R18.
⑥—Exc. calibration codes 3-49S-R16, 3-49T-R20 & 3-50S-R18.
⑦—Calibration code 3-50S-R11, 800 RPM; calibration code 3-50S-R01, 750 RPM.
⑧—Calibration codes 3-49Y-R19 & 3-50Y-R18.
⑨—Exc. calibration codes 3-49Y-R19 & 3-50Y-R18.
⑩—Calibration code 3-50X-R10, 8°; calibration code 3-50X-R11, 10°.

⑪—Controlled by automatic idle speed control.
⑫—Calibration code 4-62S-R01, 875 RPM; calibration code 4-62S-R10, 850 RPM.
⑬—Calibration code 4-62S-R01, 775 RPM; calibration code 4-62S-R10, 750 RPM.
⑭—Calibration code 3-41P-R15, 8°; calibration code 3-41S-R18, 9°.
⑮—Calibration codes 5-50H-R02 and 5-50S-R02, 700 RPM; except calibration codes 5-50H-R02 and 5-50S-R02, 650 RPM.

continued

FORD MOTOR COMPANY—Continued
1983—85 Ranger & 1984—85 Bronco II

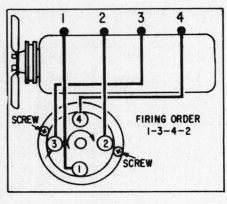

FIRING ORDER
1-3-4-2

Fig. A

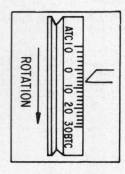

Fig. B

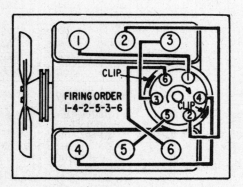

FIRING ORDER
1-4-2-5-3-6

Fig. C

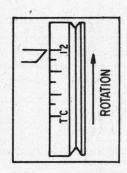

Fig. D

continued

GENERAL MOTORS CORP.
Chevrolet & GMC Except S/T-10 & 15 & Astro Van & Safari Van

The following specifications are published from the latest information available. This data should be used only in the absence of a decal affixed in the engine compartment.

★ When checking ignition timing, disconnect vacuum hose at distributor and plug opening in hose so idle speed will not be affected. Also, on some computer controlled ignition systems, it may be necessary to disconnect certain vacuum hoses and/or electrical connectors. Refer to vehicle emission decal.

▲ Before removing wires from distributor cap, determine location of the No. 1 wire in cap, as distributor position may have been altered from that shown at the end of this chart.

Year & Engine	Spark Plug Gap	Firing Order Fig.▲	Ignition Timing BTDC①★			Curb Idle Speed②		Fast Idle Speed		Fuel Pump Pressure
			Man. Trans.	Auto. Trans.	Location	Man. Trans.	Auto. Trans.	Man. Trans.	Auto. Trans.	
1985										
6-292	—	C	—	—	Damper	—	—	—	—	4–6.5
V6-262, Exc. Caballero & El Camino	—	A	—	—	—	—	—	—	—	4–6.5
V6-262, Caballero & El Camino	—	A	—	—	—	—	—	—	—	9–13
V8-305, Series 10–30 & 1500–3500	—	D	—	—	Damper	—	—	—	—	4–6.5
V8-305, Caballero & El Camino	—	D	—	—	Damper	—	—	—	—	4–6.5
V8-350	—	D	—	—	Damper	—	—	—	—	4–6.5
V8-454	—	D	—	—	Damper	—	—	—	—	4–6.5
1984										
V6-229	.045	A	—	TDC	Damper	—	⑰	—	2200N	5½–6½
V6-231	.060	B	—	15°	Damper	—	525D	—	2200N	5½–6½
6-250	—	C	6°	10°	Damper	700/850	525/650D	2000	2000	4½–6
6-292	—	C	8°	8°	Damper	700	700N	2400N	2400N	4½–6
V8-305⑤	.045	D	—	6°	Damper	—	500/650D	—	2200	④
V8-305 Series 10–30 & 1500–3500⑨	.045	D	4°	4°	Damper	700/800	500/650D	⑪	1600N	④
V8-305 Series 10–30 & 1500–3500 Calif.	.045	D	—	6°	Damper	—	550/650D	—	1800N	④
V8-305 Series 10–30 & 1500–3500 High Alt.	.045	D	4°	4°	Damper	700	600D	1200	1400N	④
V8-350 Exc. Calif. & High Alt.㉒	.045	D	8°	8°	Damper	700/800	⑫	1300	1600N	④
V8-350 Calif.㉒	.045	D	—	6°	Damper	—	550/650D	—	1800N	④
V8-350 High Alt.㉒	.045	D	8°	8°	Damper	700/800	600/650	1400	1400N	④
V8-350⑥	.045	D	⑬	⑬	Damper	700/1600⑩	700/1600N⑩	1900	1900N	④
V8-454	.045	D	4°	4°	Damper	700/1500⑩	700/1500N⑩	1900	1900N	7½–9
1983										
V6-229	.045	A	—	TDC	Damper	—	⑰	—	2200N	4½–6
V6-231	.080	B	—	15°	Damper	—	500D	—	2200N	5½–6½
6-250 Exc. Calif. & High Alt.	.035	C	10°	10°	Damper	550/750	525/650D	2000	2200N	4½–6
6-250 Calif.	.035	C	6°	6°	Damper	700/850	㉖	2000	2200N	4½–6
6-250 High Alt.	.035	C	10°	6°	Damper	600/750	550/650D	2000	2200N	4½–6
6-292	.035	C	8°	—	Damper	700/1500⑩	—	2400	—	4–5
V8-305⑤	.045	D	—	6°	Damper	—	500/650D	—	2200N	7½–9
V8-305 Exc. Calif. & High Alt.	.045	D	4°	4°	Damper	⑭	500/600D	1300	1600N	④
V8-305 Calif.	.045	D	—	8°	Damper	—	550/600D	—	1600N	④
V8-305 High Alt.	.045	D	4°	4°	Damper	700	600D	1300	1600N	④
V8-350 Exc. Calif. & High Alt.㉒	.045	D	8°	8°	Damper	600/750	500/600D	1300	1600N	④

continued

GENERAL MOTORS CORP.—Continued

The following specifications are published from the latest information available. This data should be used only in the absence of a decal affixed in the engine compartment.

★ When checking ignition timing, disconnect vacuum hose at distributor and plug opening in hose so idle speed will not be affected. Also, on some computer controlled ignition systems, it may be necessary to disconnect certain vacuum hoses and/or electrical connectors. Refer to vehicle emission decal.

▲ Before removing wires from distributor cap, determine location of the No. 1 wire in cap, as distributor position may have been altered from that shown at the end of this chart.

Year & Engine	Spark Plug Gap	Firing Order Fig.▲	Ignition Timing BTDC① ★ Man. Trans.	Auto. Trans.	Location	Curb Idle Speed② Man. Trans.	Auto. Trans.	Fast Idle Speed Man. Trans.	Auto. Trans.	Fuel Pump Pressure
CHEVROLET & GMC EXCEPT S/T-10 & 15 & ASTRO VAN & SAFARI VAN, 1983—Continued										
V8-350 Calif.㉒	.045	D	—	8°	Damper	—	500/600D	—	1800N	④
V8-350 High Alt.㉒	.045	D	8°	8°	Damper	700	600D	1600	1600N	④
V8-350 Exc. Calif.⑥	.045	D	4°	4°	Damper	700/1600⑩	700/1600N⑩	1900	1900N	④
V8-350 Calif.⑥	.045	D	6°	6°	Damper	700/1500⑩	⑩㉙	1900	1900N	④
V8-454	.045	D	4°	4°	Damper	700/1500⑩	700/1500N⑩	1900	1900N	④
1982										
V6-229	.045	A	—	TDC	Damper	—	⑰	—	2200N	4½–6
V6-231	.080	A	—	15°	Damper	—	500D	—	2200N	3 Min.
6-250 C10 Exc. Calif. & High Alt.	.035	C	10°	10°	Damper	450/625	550/600D	2000	2200N	4½–6
6-250 C10 Calif.	.035	C	10°	10°	Damper	450/700	450/650D	2000	2000N	4½–6
6-250 C10 High Alt.	.035	C	—	10°	Damper	—	550/650D	—	2200N	4½–6
6-250 K10 Exc. High Alt.	.035	C	10°	10°	Damper	550/700	525/650D	2000	2200N	4½–6
6-250 K10 High Alt.	.035	C	—	10°	Damper	—	550/650D	—	2200N	4½–6
6-250 C20	.035	C	10°	10°	Damper	550/700	525/650D	2000	2200N	4½–6
6-250 G Series	.035	C	10°	10°	Damper	550/700	550/650D	2000	2200N	4½–6
6-292	.035	C	8°	8°	Damper	450/700	450/700	2400	2400N	4–5
V8-267	.045	D	—	2°	Damper	—	500/600D	—	2200N	7½–9
V8-305⑤	.045	D	—	6°	Damper	—	500/600D	—	2200N	7½–9
V8-305 Exc. Calif. & High Alt.	.045	D	4°	4°	Damper	600/750	500/600D	1300	1600N	④
V8-305 Calif.	.045	D	—	8°	Damper	—	500/600D	—	1800N	④
V8-305 High Alt.	.045	D	4°	4°	Damper	700	600D	1300	1600N	④
V8-350 Exc. Calif. & High Alt.㉒	.045	D	8°	8°	Damper	600/750	500/600D	1300	1600N	④
V8-350 Calif.㉒	.045	D	—	8°	Damper	—	550/650D	—	1800N	④
V8-350 High Alt.㉒	.045	D	8°	8°	Damper	700	600D	1600	1600N	④
V8-350 Exc. Calif.⑥	.045	D	4°	4°	Damper	700	700N	1900	1900N	④
V8-350 Calif.⑥	.045	D	6°	6°	Damper	700	700N	1900	1900N	④
V8-454	.045	D	4°	4°	Damper	700	700N	1900	1900N	④
1981										
V6-229	.045	A	6°	6°	Damper	⑰	⑰	2200	2200N	4½–6
V6-231	.080	B	—	15°	Damper	—	⑰	—	1800N	3 Min.
6-250	.035	C	10°	10°	Damper	450/750⑱	450/650D⑲	2000	2200N	4½–6
6-292	.035	C	8°	8°	Damper	450/700	450/700N	2400	2400N	4½–6
V8-267	.045	D	—	6°	Damper	—	500/600D	—	2200N	7½–9
V8-305⑤	.045	D	6°	6°	Damper	700/800	500/600D	2200	2200N	7½–9
V8-305 2 Barrel Carb. Series 10–30	.045	D	8°	8°	Damper	600/700	500/600D	1300	1600N	④
V8-305 4 Barrel Carb. C10–20, K10 Exc. Calif.	.045	D	4°	⑳	Damper	㉑	500D	㉗	1600N	④
V8-305 4 Barrel Carb. C10–20 Calif.	.045	D	—	8°	Damper	—	550/650D	—	1800N	④
V8-305 4 Barrel Carb. G10–20	.045	D	6°	4°	Damper	700	500D	1300	1600N	④

continued

GENERAL MOTORS CORP.—Continued

The following specifications are published from the latest information available. This data should be used only in the absence of a decal affixed in the engine compartment.

★ When checking ignition timing, disconnect vacuum hose at distributor and plug opening in hose so idle speed will not be affected. Also, on some computer controlled ignition systems, it may be necessary to disconnect certain vacuum hoses and/or electrical connectors. Refer to vehicle emission decal.

▲ Before removing wires from distributor cap, determine location of the No. 1 wire in cap, as distributor position may have been altered from that shown at the end of this chart.

Year & Engine	Spark Plug Gap	Firing Order Fig.▲	Ignition Timing BTDC①★ Man. Trans.	Auto. Trans.	Location	Curb Idle Speed② Man. Trans.	Auto. Trans.	Fast Idle Speed Man. Trans.	Auto. Trans.	Fuel Pump Pressure
CHEVROLET & GMC EXCEPT S/T-10 & 15 & ASTRO VAN & SAFARI VAN, 1981—Continued										
V8-350 Exc. Calif.㉒	.045	D	8°	8°	Damper	700	500/600D	1300	1600N	④
V8-350 C, K10 Calif.㉒	.045	D	—	6°	Damper	—	550/650D	—	1800N	④
V8-350 C, K20 Calif.㉒	.045	D	—	㉕	Damper	—	550/650D	—	1600N	④
V8-350 G10—20 Calif.㉒	.045	D	—	8°	Damper	—	550/650D	—	1800N	④
V8-350 C, K20—30 Exc. Calif.⑥	.045	D	4°	6°	Damper	700/1600⑩	700/1600N	1900	1900N	④
V8-350 G30, P20—30 Exc. Calif.⑥	.045	D	4°	4°	Damper	700/1600⑩	700/1600N⑩	1900	1900N	④
V8-350 Calif.⑥	.045	D	6°	6°	Damper	700/1500⑩	700/1500N⑩	1900	1900N	④
V8-454	.045	D	4°	4°	Damper	700/1500⑩	700/1500N⑩	1900	1900N	7½—9
1980										
V6-229	.045	A	8°	12°	Damper	700/800	600/675D	1300	1750N	4½—6
V6-231 Exc. Calif.	.060	B	—	15°	Damper	—	560/670D	—	2200N	3 Min.
V6-231 Calif.	.060	B	—	15°	Damper	—	600D	—	2200N	3 Min.
6-250 Exc. Calif.	.035	C	10°	10°	Damper	450/750	450/650D	2000	2200N	4½—6
6-250 C, G-10 Calif.	.035	C	10°	10°	Damper	425/750	425/600D	2000	2200N	4½—6
6-250 C, G-20 Calif.	.035	C	10°	8°	Damper	425/750	425/600D	2000	2200N	4½—6
6-292	.035	C	8°	8°	Damper	700	700N	2400	2400N	4—5
V8-267	.045	D	—	4°	Damper	—	500/600D	—	1850N	7½—9
V8-305 Exc. Calif.⑤	.045	D	4°	4°	Damper	700	500/600D	1500	1850N	7½—9
V8-305 Calif.⑤	.045	D	—	4°	Damper	—	550/650D	—	2200N	7½—9
V8-305 Series 10—30	.045	D	⑮	8°	Damper	600/700	500/600D	1300	1600N	④
V8-350	.045	D	8°⑯	8°⑯	Damper	700	500/600D	1600	1600N	④
V8-350 Exc. Calif.⑧	.045	D	4°	4°	Damper	700	700N	1900	1900N	④
V8-350 Calif.⑧	.045	D	6°	6°	Damper	700	700N	1900	1900N	④
V8-400 G-20	.045	D	—	4°	Damper	—	500/600D	—	1600N	④
V8-400 K-20, G & K-30 Exc. Calif.	.045	D	—	4°	Damper	—	700N	—	1900N	④
V8-400 K-20, G & K-30 Calif.	.045	D	—	6°	Damper	—	700N	—	1900N	④
V8-454 C-20 & C, P-30	.045	D	4°	4°	Damper	700/1500⑩	700/1500N⑩	1900	1900N	7½—9
1979										
V6-200	.045	A	8°	12°	Damper	700/800	600/700D	1300	1600N	4¼—5¾
V6-231 Exc. Calif. & High Alt.	.060	B	—	15°	Damper	—	③	—	2200N	3 Min.
V6-231 Calif. & High Alt.	.060	B	—	15°	Damper	—	600D	—	2200N	3 Min.
6-250 C, G & K-10	.035	C	10°	10°	Damper	425/750	425/600D	1800	2000N	4½—6
6-250 C, G-20 & G-30 Exc. Calif.	.035	C	10°	10°	Damper	425/750	425/600D	1800	2000N	4½—6
6-250 C, G-20 & G-30 Calif.	.035	C	6°	8°	Damper	425/750	425/600D	2100	2100N	4½—6
6-292	.035	C	8°	8°	Damper	700	700N	2400	2400N	4½—6
V8-267	.045	D	4°	8°	Damper	600/700	500/600D	1300	1600N	7½—9
V8-305 Exc. High Alt.	.045	D	4°	4°	Damper	700	500/600D	1300	1600N	7½—9
V8-305 High Alt.⑤	.045	D	—	4°	Damper	—	600/650D	—	1750N	7½—9

continued

GENERAL MOTORS CORP.—Continued

The following specifications are published from the latest information available. This data should be used only in the absence of a decal affixed in the engine compartment.

★ When checking ignition timing, disconnect vacuum hose at distributor and plug opening in hose so idle speed will not be affected. Also, on some computer controlled ignition systems, it may be necessary to disconnect certain vacuum hoses and/or electrical connectors. Refer to vehicle emission decal.

▲ Before removing wires from distributor cap, determine location of the No. 1 wire in cap, as distributor position may have been altered from that shown at the end of this chart.

| Year & Engine | Spark Plug Gap | Ignition Timing BTDC①★ | | | | Curb Idle Speed② | | Fast Idle Speed | | Fuel Pump Pressure |
		Firing Order Fig.▲	Man. Trans.	Auto. Trans.	Location	Man. Trans.	Auto. Trans.	Man. Trans.	Auto. Trans.	
CHEVROLET & GMC EXCEPT S/T-10 & 15 & ASTRO VAN & SAFARI VAN, 1979—Continued										
V8-305 C, G, K-10 & C-20	.045	D	6°	6°	Damper	600/700	500/600D	1300	1600N	④
V8-350 High Alt.⑤	.045	D	—	8°	Damper	—	600/650D	—	1750N	7½—9
V8-350⑦	.045	D	8°	8°	Damper	700	500/600D	㉓	1600N	④
V8-350⑧	.045	D	4°	4°	Damper	700	700N	1900	1900N	④
V8-400 K-10, 20 & C-20, 30	.045	D	—	4°	Damper	—	500/600D	—	1600N	④
V8-400 G, K-30	.045	D	—	4°	Damper	—	700N	—	1900N	④
V8-454⑦	.045	D	8°	8°	Damper	700	550/600D	1600	1600N	7½—9
V8-454⑧	.045	D	4°	4°	Damper	700	700N	1900	1900N	7½—9

①—B.T.D.C.—Before top dead center.
②—Idle speed on Man. Trans. vehicles is adjusted in Neutral & on Auto. Trans. vehicles is adjusted in Drive (D) or Neutral (N) as specified. Where two idle speeds are listed, the higher speed is with the A/C or idle solenoid energized.
③—Less A/C, 550D RPM; with A/C, 560/670D RPM.
④—With vapor return line, 5½—7 psi.; less vapor return line, 7½—9 psi.
⑤—Caballero, El Camino or Sprint.
⑥—Series 10-30 heavy duty emissions, GVWR 8501 lbs. & above.
⑦—Series 10-30 light duty emissions, GVWR 6000 lbs. & under.
⑧—Series 10-30 heavy duty emissions, GVWR 6001 lbs. & above.
⑨—Exc. Calif. & high altitude.

⑩—Higher speed is throttle return control speed.
⑪—C series, 1500 RPM; G & K series, 1600 RPM.
⑫—C & K series, 500/650D RPM; G series, 550/650D RPM.
⑬—Exc. Calif., 4° BTDC; Calif. 6° BTDC.
⑭—Exc. C-10/1500, 600/700 RPM; C-10/1500, 600/750 RPM.
⑮—Distributor model No. 1103381, set at 8° BTDC; distributor model No. 1103369, set at 6° BTDC.
⑯—C-10 & 20 series with distributor model No. 1103339, set at 6° BTDC.
⑰—Equipped w/idle speed control motor.
⑱—G-10-20 w/emission control label code ADA, set at 450/800 RPM.
⑲—G-10-20 w/emission control label code AAC, set at 450/700D RPM.

⑳—Emission control label code AAH, 4° BTDC; AAN, 6° BTDC; AAS, 2° BTDC.
㉑—Except emission control label code AUS, 700 RPM; emission control label code AUS, 600 RPM.
㉒—Series 10-30 light duty emissions, GVWR 8500 lbs. & under.
㉓—Exc. Calif., 1300 RPM; Calif. 1600 RPM.
㉔—Exc. P-30/3500, 700/1600N RPM; P-30/3500, 700/1500N RPM.
㉕—Except emission control label code AAZ, 6° BTDC; emission control label code AAZ, 8° BTDC.
㉖—Less A/C, 500/650D RPM; with A/C, 500/700D RPM.
㉗—Except emission control label code AUS, 1300 RPM; emission control label AUS, 1500 RPM.

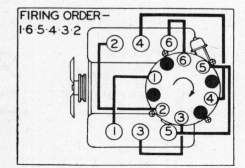

Fig. A

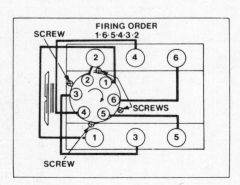

Fig. B

continued

Chevrolet & GMC Except S/T-10 & 15 & Astro Van & Safari Van

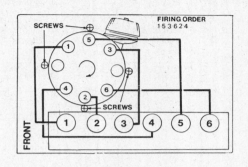

Fig. C

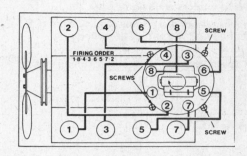

Fig. D

Chevrolet & GMC S/T-10 & 15

The following specifications are published from the latest information available. This data should be used only in the absence of a decal affixed in the engine compartment.

★ When checking ignition timing, disconnect vacuum hose at distributor and plug opening in hose so idle speed will not be affected. Also, on some computer controlled ignition systems, it may be necessary to disconnect certain vacuum hoses and/or electrical connectors. Refer to vehicle emission decal.

▲ Before removing wires from distributor cap, determine location of the No. 1 wire in cap, as distributor position may have been altered from that shown at the end of this chart.

Year & Engine	Spark Plug Gap	Firing Order Fig. ▲	Ignition Timing BTDC①★ Man. Trans.	Auto. Trans.	Mark Fig.	Curb Idle Speed Man. Trans.	Auto. Trans.	Fast Idle Speed Man. Trans.	Auto. Trans.	Fuel Pump Pressure
1982										
4-119	.043	A	6°	6°	Damper	800/900	900/1900P	—	—	3.6
V6-173 Exc. Calif. & High Alt.③	.045	B	6°	④	Damper	650/850	650/850D	1800	2100	6–7.5
V6-173 Exc. Calif. & High Alt.⑤	.045	B	8°	16°	Damper	650/850	650/850D	1800	2100	6–7.5
V6-173 Calif.	.045	B	10°	10°	Damper	750/950	650/850D	2100	2100	6–7.5
V6-173 High Alt.	.045	B	10°	④	Damper	750/850	650/850D	1800	2100	6–7.5
1983										
4-119 Exc. Calif.	.043	A	6°	6°	Damper	800/900	900/1900P	—	—	3.6
4-119 Calif.	.043	A	6°	6°	Damper	800/900	900/1900P	—	—	3.6
4-121	.035	C	—	2°	Damper	—	800/925D	—	2600	4.5
V6-173 Exc. Calif. & High Alt.	.045	B	8°	12°	Damper	650/850	650/850D	1800	2100	6–7.5
V6-173 Calif.	.045	B	10°	10°	Damper	750/950	650/850D	2100	2100	6–7.5
V6-173 High Alt.	.045	B	10°	12°	Damper	700/850	700/850D	1800	2100	6–7.5
1984										
4-119 Exc. Calif.	.043	A	6°	—	Damper	800/900	—	—	—	3.6
4-119 Calif.	.043	A	6°	6°	Damper	900	900/1900N	—	—	3.6
4-121	.035	C	2°	2°	Damper	800/1075	800/925D	3000	2600N	4.5
V6-173 Exc. Calif. & High Alt.	.045	B	8°	12°	Damper	700/850	650/850D	2100	2100N	6–7.5
V6-173 Calif.	.045	B	10°	10°	Damper	750/950	650/850D	2100	2100N	6–7.5
V6-173 High Alt.	.045	B	10°	14°	Damper	700/850	700/850D	2100	2100N	6–7.5

continued

GENERAL MOTORS CORP.—Continued

The following specifications are published from the latest information available. This
data should be used only in the absence of a decal affixed in the engine compartment.

★ When checking ignition timing, disconnect vacuum hose at distributor and plug opening in hose so idle speed will not be affected.
Also, on some computer controlled ignition systems, it may be necessary to disconnect certain vacuum hoses and/or electrical
connectors. Refer to vehicle emission decal.

▲ Before removing wires from distributor cap, determine location of the No. 1 wire in cap, as distributor position may have been
altered from that shown at the end of this chart.

Year & Engine	Spark Plug Gap	Ignition Timing BTDC①★				Curb Idle Speed		Fast Idle Speed		Fuel Pump Pressure
		Firing Order Fig. ▲	Man. Trans.	Auto. Trans.	Mark Fig.	Man. Trans.	Auto. Trans.	Man. Trans.	Auto. Trans.	
CHEVROLET & GMC S/T-10 & 15—Continued										
1985										
4-119	.043	A	—	—	Damper	—	—	—	—	4–6.5
4-151 Exc. Calif.	—	—	—	—	Damper	—	—	—	—	9–13
4-151 Calif.	—	—	—	—	Damper	—	—	—	—	9–13
V6-173 Exc. Calif.	.045	B	—	—	Damper	—	—	—	—	4–6.5
V6-173 Calif.	.045	B	—	—	Damper	—	—	—	—	4–6.5

①—BTDC—Before top dead center.
②—Idle speed on man. trans. vehicles is
adjusted in Neutral & on auto. trans.
vehicles is adjusted in Drive (D) or
Park (P) as specified. Where two idle
speeds are listed, the higher speed is
with the A/C or idle solenoid energized.

③—Except cab-chassis & utility.
④—Less A/C, 16° BTDC; with A/C, 14°
BTDC.
⑤—Cab-chassis & utility.

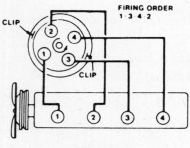

Fig. A

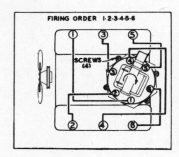

Fig. B

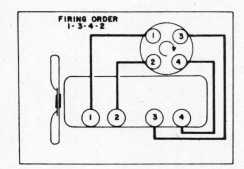

Fig. C

GENERAL MOTORS CORP.

Chevrolet Astro Van & GMC Safari Van

The following specifications are published from the latest information available. This data should be used only in the absence of a decal affixed in the engine compartment.

★ When checking ignition timing, disconnect vacuum hose at distributor and plug opening in hose so idle speed will not be affected. Also, on some computer controlled ignition systems, it may be necessary to disconnect certain vacuum hoses and/or electrical connectors. Refer to vehicle emission decal.

▲ Before removing wires from distributor cap, determine location of the No. 1 wire in cap, as distributor position may have been altered from that shown at the end of this chart.

Year & Engine	Spark Plug Gap	Ignition Timing BTDC①★				Curb Idle Speed②		Fast Idle Speed		Fuel Pump Pressure
		Firing Order Fig. ▲	Man. Trans.	Auto. Trans.	Mark Location	Man. Trans.	Auto. Trans.	Man. Trans.	Auto. Trans.	
1985										
4-151	—	—	—	—	Damper	—	—	—	—	—
V6-262	—	—	—	—	Damper	—	—	—	—	—

①—BTDC—Before top dead center.
②—Idle speed on man. trans. vehicles is adjusted in Neutral & on auto. trans. vehicles is adjusted in Drive (D) or Park (P) as specified.

DIESEL ENGINE PERFORMANCE SPECIFICATIONS

TABLE OF CONTENTS

DIESEL ENGINE PERFORMANCE SPECIFICATIONS

AMERICAN MOTORS/JEEP

Year	Engine	Firing Order	Injection Timing B.T.D.C. (Static)
1985	4-126 (2.1L)	1-3-4-2	TDC①

①—At .032 inch injection pump piston lift.

CHRYSLER CORP.

Year	Engine	Firing Order	Injection Timing B.T.D.C.①	Cylinder Compression Pressure @ 170 RPM	Injection Nozzle Opening Pressure Psi	Curb Idle Speed	Governed Speed
1979	D-243-6	1-5-3-6-2-4	18°	425	1705	550–600	3700

①—B.T.C.D.—Before top dead center.

FORD MOTOR COMPANY
Except 1983–85 Ranger

Year	Engine	Compression Ratio	Firing Order	Injection Timing B.T.D.C.①	Injection Nozzle Opening Pressure Psi	Idle Speed
1983–84	V8-420	20.7	1-2-7-3-4-5-6-8	②	③	600–700

①—B.T.D.C.—Before top dead center.
②—Marks aligned.
③—Early 1984 & all 1983 calibration codes 3-68J-R10 & 3-68X-R10, 2000–2150 psi; 1984 calibration codes 4-68J-R00 & 4-68X-R00, 1800–1950 psi.

1983–85 Ranger

Year	Engine	Firing Order	Injection Timing A.T.D.C.①②	Cylinder Compression Pressure psi @ RPM	Injection Nozzle Opening Pressure psi	Curb Idle Speed	Fast Idle Speed
1983–84	4-135	1-3-4-2	2°	427 @ 200	1957	780–830	1150–1250

①—A.T.D.C.—After top dead center.
②—Engine static.

GENERAL MOTORS CORP.
Chevrolet & GMC S/T-10 & 15

Year	Engine	Firing Order	Injection Timing B.T.D.C.①	Cylinder Compression Pressure Psi @ R.P.M.	Fuel Injection Starting Pressure Psi	Idle Speed
1984–85	4-137	1-3-4-2	15°②	441 @ 220	1493	800

①—Plunger lift (inches) at degrees Before Top Dead Center (BTDC).
②—Exc. Calif. .020 inch @ 15°; Calif. .020 inch @ 13°.

continued

GENERAL MOTORS CORP.—Continued
Chevrolet & GMC Except S/T-10 & 15

Year	Engine	Injection Timing①	Curb Idle Speed	Fast Idle Speed
1979—80	V8-350②	4½°④⑤	575D	650D
1979—80	V8-350③	5½°④⑤	575D	650D
1981	V8-350②	4°④⑤	⑥	⑦
1981	V8-350③	5°④⑤	⑥	⑦
1982	V8-379⑧	—	575N	700N
1982	V8-379⑨	—	550D	700N
1982	V8-379⑩	—	600D	700N
1982	V8-379⑪	—	625N	700N
1983—84	V8-350	4°⑤⑫	600D	750D
1983—85	V8-379	—	650N	800N

①—ATDC—After top dead center.
②—Exc. high altitude.
③—High altitude.
④—At 1200 RPM.
⑤—Using diesel timing meter J-33075 or equivalent

⑥—Exc. California, 575D; California, 600D.
⑦—Exc. California, 650D; California, 750D.
⑧—Engine codes CAF, CAH, CAK, CBK, CBN & CBS.
⑨—Engine codes CBM, CBR & CBT.
⑩—Engine codes CYF, CYJ & CYM.
⑪—Engine codes CYC, CYD, CYH & CYK.
⑫—At 1250 RPM.

TROUBLESHOOTING
TABLE OF CONTENTS

Introduction

STARTING A STALLED ENGINE

When an engine fails to start the chances are that 90 per cent of the cases will involve the ignition system and seldom the fuel system or other miscellaneous reasons. If a systematic procedure is followed the trouble can almost always be found without the use of special equipment.

To begin with, turn on the ignition switch and if the ammeter shows a slight discharge (or if the telltale lamp lights) it indicates that current is flowing. A glance at the gas gauge will indicate whether or not there is fuel in the tank.

Operate the starter and if the engine turns over freely, both the battery and starter are functioning properly. On the other hand, if the starter action is sluggish it may be due to a discharged or defective battery, loose, corroded or dirty battery terminals, mechanical failure in the starter, starter switch or starter drive. If the starter circuit is okay, skip this phase of the discussion and proceed to ignition.

STARTER CIRCUIT CHECKOUT

To determine which part of the starter circuit is at fault, turn on the light switch and again operate the starter. Should the lights go out or become dim, the trouble is either in the battery, its connections or cables. A hydrometer test of the battery should indicate better than 1.250 specific gravity, while a voltmeter, placed across the positive and negative posts, should indicate about 12 volts. If either of these tests prove okay, clean and tighten the battery connections and cable terminals or replace any cable which seems doubtful.

If the lights remain bright when the starter is operated, the trouble is between the battery and the starter, or the starter switch is at fault, since it is evident that there is no electrical connection between these points. If these connections are clean and tight, it is safe to assume that the starter or starter switch is defective.

NEUTRAL SAFETY SWITCH

If the ammeter shows a slight discharge (or if the telltale lamp lights) when the ignition is turned on, but the system goes dead when the starting circuit is closed, the neutral safety switch may be at fault. To check, bypass the switch with a suitable jumper. If the engine now starts, adjust or replace the switch.

CAUTION: With the safety switch bypassed, the truck can be started in any gear. Be sure the transmission is in neutral or park and the parking brake is applied.

SEDONDARY IGNITION CHECKOUT

First of all, remove the wire from one of the spark plugs, turn on the ignition and operate the starter. While the engine is cranking, hold the terminal of the spark plug wire about ¼″ away from the engine or spark plug base. If the spark is strong and jumps the gap, the trouble is confined to either the spark plugs or lack of fuel. Before going any further, wipe the outside of the plugs to remove any dirt or dampness which would create an easy path for the current to flow, then try to start the engine again. If it still fails to start, remove one of the spark plugs and if it is wet around the base, it indicates that the fuel system is okay, so it naturally follows that the spark plugs are at fault. Remove all the plugs, clean them and set the gaps. An emergency adjustment of spark plug gaps can be made by folding a piece of newspaper into 6 or 7 layers. When changing the gap, always bend the side (ground) electrode and never the center one as there is danger of breaking the insulation.

FUEL SYSTEM CHECKOUT

If the spark plug that was removed showed no indication of dampness on its base, check the fuel system. A quick check can be made by simply removing the carburetor air cleaner and looking down into the carburetor. Open and close the throttle manually and if fuel is present in the carburetor, the throttle will operate the accelerating pump, causing it to push gasoline through the pump jet. If it does, check the choke valve. If the engine is cold, the choke valve should be closed. If the choke won't close, the engine can be started by covering the carburetor throat while the engine is cranking, provided, of course, that fuel is reaching the carburetor.

Check the operation of the fuel pump by disconnecting the fuel lines from the pump to the carburetor. Crank the engine and if the pump is working, fuel will pulsate out of the line. If not, either the pump isn't working or the line from the tank to the pump is clogged. Before blaming the pump, however, disconnect the line at the inlet side of the pump which leads to the tank and, while a companion listens at the tank blow through the line. If a gurgling sound is heard back in the tank, the line is open and the trouble is in the pump. Remove the sediment bowl, if so equipped and clean the screen, then replace the bowl and screen, being sure that you have an airtight fit. If the pump still refuses to function, it should be removed and repaired.

The foregoing discussion will, in most cases, uncover the cause of why an engine won't start. However, if further diagnosis is necessary, the following list will undoubtedly provide the answer.

ENGINE NOISE TESTS
LOOSE MAIN BEARING

A loose main bearing is indicated by a powerful but dull thud or knock when the engine is pulling. If all main bearings are loose a noticeable clatter will be audible.

The thud occurs regularly every other revolution. The knock can be confirmed by shorting spark plugs on cylinders adjacent to the bearing. Knock will disappear or be less when plugs are shorted. This test should be made at a fast idle equivalent to 15 mph in high gear. If bearing is not quite loose enough to produce a knock by itself, the bearing may knock if oil is too thin or if there is no oil at the bearing.

LOOSE FLYWHEEL

A loose flywheel is indicated by a thud or click which is usually irregular. To test, idle the engine at about 20 mph and shut off the ignition. If thud is heard, the flywheel may be loose.

LOOSE ROD BEARING

A loose rod bearing is indicated by a metallic knock which is usually loudest at about 30 mph with throttle closed. Knock can be reduced or even eliminated by shorting spark plug. If bearing is not loose enough to produce a knock by itself, the bearing may knock if oil is too thin or if there is no oil at the bearing.

PISTON PIN

Piston pin, piston and connecting rod noises are difficult to tell apart.

A loose piston pin causes a sharp double knock which is usually heard when engine is idling. Severity of knock should increase when spark plug to this cylinder is short-circuited. However, on some engines the knock becomes more noticable at 25 to 35 mph on the road.

Piston pin rubs against cylinder wall, caused by lock screw being loose or snap ring broken.

HYDRAULIC LIFTERS

The malfunctioning of a hydraulic valve lifter is almost always accompanied by a clicking or tapping noise. More or less hydraulic lifter noise may be expected when the engine is cold but if lifters are functioning properly the noise should disappear when the engine warms up.

If all or nearly all lifters are noisy, they may be stuck because of dirty or gummy oil.

If all lifters are noisy, oil pressure to them may be inadequate. Foaming oil may also cause this trouble. If oil foams there will be bubbles on the oil level dipstick. Foaming may be caused by water in the oil or by too high an oil level or by a very low oil level.

If the hydraulic plungers require an initial adjustment, they will be noisy if this adjustment is incorrect.

If one lifter is noisy the cause may be:
1. Plunger too tight in lifter body.
2. Weak or broken plunger spring.
3. Ball valve leaks.
4. Plunger worn.
5. Lock ring (if any) improperly installed or missing.
6. Lack of oil pressure to this plunger.

If ball valve leaks, clean plunger in special solvent such as acetone and reinstall. Too often, plungers are condemned as faulty when all they need is a thorough cleaning.

Gum and dirty oil are the most common causes of hydraulic valve lifter trouble. Engine oil must be free of dirt. Select a standard brand of engine oil and use no other. Mixing up one standard brand with another may cause gummy oil and sticking plungers. Do not use any special oils unless recommended by the truck manufacturer and change oil filter or element at recommended intervals.

LOOSE ENGINE MOUNTINGS

Occasional thud with truck in operation. Most likely to be noticed at the moment the throttle is opened or closed.

EXCESSIVE CRANKSHAFT END PLAY

A rather sharp rap which occurs at idling speed but may be heard at higher speeds also. The noise should disappear when clutch is disengaged.

FUEL PUMP NOISE

Diagnosis of fuel pumps suspected as noisy requires that some form of sounding device be used. Judgment by ear alone is not sufficient, otherwise a fuel pump may be needlessly replaced in attempting to correct noise contributed by some other component. Use of a stethoscope, a long screwdriver, or a sounding rod is recommended to locate the area or component causing the noise. The sounding rod can easily be made from a length of copper tubing ¼ to ⅜ inch in diameter.

If the noise has been isolated to the fuel pump, remove the pump and run the engine with the fuel remaining in the carburetor bowl. If the noise level does not change, the source of the noise is elsewhere and the original fuel pump should be reinstalled. On models using a fuel pump push rod, check for excessive wear and/or galling of the push rod.

VAPOR LOCK

The term vapor lock means the flow of fuel to the mixing chamber in the carburetor has been stopped (locked) by the formation of vaporized fuel pockets or bubbles caused by overheating the fuel by hot fuel pump, hot fuel lines or hot carburetor.

The more volatile the fuel the greater the tendency for it to vapor lock. Vapor lock is encouraged by high atmospheric temperature, hard driving, defective engine cooling and high altitude.

A mild case of vapor lock will cause missing and hard starting when engine is warm. Somewhat more severe vapor lock will stop the engine which cannot be started again until it has cooled off enough so that any vaporized fuel has condensed to a liquid.

PERCOLATION

Percolation means simply that gasoline in the carburetor bowl is boiling over into the intake manifold. This condition is most apt to occur immediately after a hot engine is shut off. Most carburetors have a provision for relieving the vapor pressure of overheated fuel in the carburetor bowl by means of ports. If, however, percolation should take place, the engine may be started by allowing it to cool slightly and then holding the throttle wide open while cranking to clear the intake manifold of excess fuel.

SPARK KNOCK, PING, DETONATION

All three expressions mean the same thing. It is a sharp metallic knock caused by vibration of the cylinder head and block. The vibration is due to split-second high-pressure waves resulting from almost instantaneous abnormal combustion instead of the slower normal combustion.

The ping may be mild or loud. A mild ping does no harm but a severe ping will reduce power. A very severe ping may shatter spark plugs, break valves or crack pistons.

Pinging is most likely to occur on open throttle at low or moderate engine speed. Pinging is encouraged by:
1. Overheated engine.
2. Low octane fuel.
3. Too high compression.
4. Spark advanced too far.
5. Hot mixture due to hot engine or hot weather.
6. Heavy carbon deposit which increases the compression pressure.
7. Clogged or restricted EGR passages.

Tendency to ping increases with mixture temperature including high atmospheric temperature; intake manifold heater valve "on" when engine is warm; hot cooling water; hot interior engine surfaces due to sluggish water circulation or water jackets clogged with rust or dirt especially around exhaust valves. Some of these troubles may be confined to one or two cylinders.

If an engine pings objectionably even when using the highest octane fuel available, retard the spark setting, but first be sure the EGR system is functioning, the cooling system is in good condition, the mixture is not too lean, and the combustion chambers are free of carbon deposits.

PRE-IGNITION

Pre-ignition means that the mixture is set on fire before the spark occurs, being ignited by a red hot spot in the combustion chamber such as an incandescent particle of carbon; a thin piece of protruding metal; an overheated spark plug, or a bright red hot exhaust valve. The result is reduction of power and overheating accompanied by pinging. The bright red hot exhaust valve may be due to a leak, to lack of tappet clearance, to valve sticking, or to a weak or broken spring.

Pre-ignition may not be noticed if not severe. Severe pre-ignition results in severe pinging. The most common cause of pre-ignition is a badly overheated engine.

When the engine won't stop when the ignition is shut off, the cause is often due to red hot carbon particles resting on heavy carbon deposit in a very hot engine.

AFTER-BURNING

A subdued put-putting at the exhaust tail pipe may be due to leaky exhaust valves which permit the mixture to finish combustion in the muffler. If exhaust pipe or muffler is red hot, better let it cool, as there is some danger of setting the car on fire. Most likely to occur when mixture is lean.

ENGINE CONTINUES TO RUN AFTER IGNITION IS TURNED OFF

This condition, known as "dieseling," "run on," or "after running," is caused by improper idle speed and/or high temperature. Idle speed and engine temperature are affected by:

Carburetor Adjustment: High idle speed will increase the tendency to diesel because of the inertia of the engine crankshaft and flywheel. Too low an idle speed, particularly with a lean mixture, will result in an increase in engine temperature, especially if the engine is allowed to idle for long periods of time.

Ignition Timing: Because advanced ignition timing causes a corresponding increase in idle speed and retarded timing reduces idle speed, ignition timing influences the tendency to diesel in the same manner as Carburetor Adjustment.

Fuel Mixture: Enriching the idle fuel mixture decreases the tendency to diesel by

TROUBLESHOOTING

causing the engine to run cooler.

Fuel Content: High octane fuels tend to reduce dieseling. Increased fuel content of lead alkyl increases the tendency to diesel. Phosphates and nickel fuel additives help prevent dieseling.

Spark Plugs: Plugs of too high a heat range for the engine in question can cause dieseling.

Throttle Plates: If the throttle plates are not properly aligned in the carburetor bore,

a resulting leanness in fuel mixture occurs, contributing to dieseling.

Electrical System: Normally, during dieseling, ignition is self-supplied by a "hot spot," self-igniting fuel, etc. However, there is a possibility of the vehicle's electrical system supplying the necessary ignition. When the ignition switch is turned off, a small amount of current can flow from the generator into the primary of the ignition coil through the generator tell-tale light. This is particularly true when the warning light bulb has been changed for one of increased wattage.

NOTE: "Run on" is more prevalent in an engine when the ignition is turned off before the engine is allowed to return to idle. Therefore, it can be reduced by letting the engine return to idle before shutting off the ignition. "Run on" incidence can be reduced on automatic transmission units by turning off the engine when in gear.

A certain amount of "run on" can be expected from any gasoline engine regardless of make, size or configuration. (Diesel engines operate on this principle.) However, if the above suggestions are correctly employed, "Run on" will be reduced to an unnoticeable level.

Gasoline Engine

NOTE: Refer to the appropriate truck chapters for diesel engine trouble shooting.

ENGINE PERFORMANCE, LUBRICATION & NOISES

Condition	Possible Cause	Correction
ENGINE WILL NOT START	1. Weak battery.	1. Test battery specific gravity. Recharge or replace as necessary.
	2. Corroded or loose battery connections.	2. Clean and tighten battery connections. Apply a coat of petroleum to terminals.
	3. Faulty starter.	3. Repair starter motor.
	4. Moisture on ignition wires and distributor cap.	4. Wipe wires and cap clean and dry.
	5. Faulty ignition cables.	5. Replace any cracked or shorted cables.
	6. Open or shorted primary ignition circuit.	6. Trace primary ignition circuit and repair as necessary.
	7. Malfunctioning ignition points or condensor.	7. Replace ignition points & condensor as necessary.
	8. Faulty coil.	8. Test and replace if necessary.
	9. Incorrect spark plug gap.	9. Set gap correctly.
	10. Incorrect ignition timing.	10. Reset timing.
	11. Dirt or water in fuel line or carburetor.	11. Clean lines and carburetor. Replace filter.
	12. Carburetor flooded.	12. Adjust float level—check seats.
	13. Incorrect carburetor float setting.	13. Adjust float level—check seats.
	14. Faulty fuel pump.	14. Install new fuel pump.
	15. Carburetor percolating. No fuel in the carburetor.	15. Measure float level. Adjust bowl vent. Inspect operation of manifold heat control valve.
ENGINE STALLS	1. Idle speed set too low.	1. Adjust carburetor.
	2. Incorrect choke adjustment.	2. Adjust choke.
	3. Idle mixture too lean or too rich.	3. Adjust carburetor.
	4. Incorrect carburetor float setting.	4. Adjust float setting.
	5. Leak in intake manifold.	5. Inspect intake manifold gasket and replace if necessary.
	6. Worn or burned distributor rotor.	6. Install new rotor.
	7. Incorrect ignition wiring.	7. Install correct wiring.
	8. Faulty coil.	8. Test and replace if necessary.
	9. Incorrect tappet lash.	9. Adjust to specifications.
ENGINE LOSS OF POWER	1. Incorrect ignition timing.	1. Reset timing.
	2. Worn or burned distributor rotor.	2. Install new rotor.
	3. Worn distributor shaft.	3. Remove and repair distributor.
	4. Dirty or incorrectly gapped spark plugs.	4. Clean plugs and set gap.
	5. Dirt or water in fuel line, carburetor or filter.	5. Clean lines, carburetor and replace filter.
	6. Incorrect carburetor float setting.	6. Adjust float level.
	7. Faulty fuel pump.	7. Install new pump.

ENGINE PERFORMANCE, LUBRICATION & NOISES—Continued

Condition	Possible Cause	Correction
ENGINE LOSS OF POWER, Continued	8. Incorrect valve timing.	8. Check and correct valve timing.
	9. Blown cylinder head gasket.	9. Install new head gasket.
	10. Low compression.	10. Test compression of each cylinder.
	11. Burned, warped or pitted valves.	11. Install new valves.
	12. Plugged or restricted exhaust system.	12. Install new parts as necessary.
	13. Faulty ignition cables.	13. Replace any cracked or shorted cables.
	14. Faulty coil.	14. Test and replace as necessary.
ENGINE MISSES ON ACCELERATION	1. Dirty, or gap too wide in spark plugs.	1. Clean spark plugs and set gap.
	2. Incorrect ignition timing.	2. Reset timing.
	3. Dirt in carburetor.	3. Clean carburetor and replace filter.
	4. Acceleration pump in carburetor.	4. Install new pump.
	5. Burned, warped or pitted valves.	5. Install new valves.
	6. Faulty coil.	6. Test and replace if necessary.
ENGINE MISSES AT HIGH SPEED	1. Dirty or gap set too wide in spark plug.	1. Clean spark plugs and set gap.
	2. Worn distributor shaft.	2. Remove and repair distributor.
	3. Worn or burned distributor rotor.	3. Install new rotor.
	4. Faulty coil.	4. Test and replace if necessary.
	5. Incorrect ignition timing.	5. Reset timing.
	6. Dirty jets in carburetor.	6. Clean carburetor, replace filter.
	7. Dirt or water in fuel line, carburetor or filter.	7. Clean lines, carburetor and replace filter.
NOISY VALVES	1. High or low oil level in crankcase.	1. Check for correct oil level.
	2. Thin or diluted oil.	2. Change oil.
	3. Low oil pressure.	3. Check engine oil level.
	4. Dirt in valve lifters.	4. Clean lifters.
	5. Bent push rod.	5. Install new push rods.
	6. Worn rocker arms.	6. Inspect oil supply to rockers.
	7. Worn tappets.	7. Install new tappets.
	8. Worn valve guides.	8. Ream and install new valves with O/S Stems.
	9. Excessive run-out of valve seats or valve faces.	9. Grind valve seats and valves.
	10. Incorrect tappet lash.	10. Adjust to specifications.
CONNECTING ROD NOISE	1. Insufficient oil supply.	1. Check engine oil level.
	2. Low oil pressure.	2. Check engine oil level. Inspect oil pump relief valve and spring.
	3. Thin or diluted oil.	3. Change oil to correct viscosity.
	4. Excessive bearing clearance.	4. Measure bearings for correct clearance.
	5. Connecting rod journals out-of-round.	5. Replace crankshaft or regrind journals.
	6. Misaligned (bent) connecting rods.	6. Replace bent connecting rods.
MAIN BEARING NOISE	1. Insufficient oil supply.	1. Check engine oil level.
	2. Low oil pressure.	2. Check engine oil level. Inspect oil pump relief valve and spring.
	3. Thin or diluted oil.	3. Change oil to correct viscosity.
	4. Excessive bearing clearance.	4. Measure bearings for correct clearances.
	5. Excessive end play.	5. Check thrust bearing for wear on flanges.
	6. Crankshaft journal worn out-of-round.	6. Replace crankshaft or regrind journals.
	7. Loose flywheel or torque converter.	7. Tighten to correct torque.
OIL PUMPING AT RINGS	1. Worn, scuffed, or broken rings.	1. Hone cylinder bores and install new rings.
	2. Carbon in oil ring slot.	2. Install new rings.
	3. Rings fitted too tight in grooves.	3. Remove the rings. Check grooves. If groove is not proper width, replace piston.

ENGINE PERFORMANCE, LUBRICATION & NOISES—Continued

Condition	Possible Cause	Correction
OIL PRESSURE DROP	1. Low oil level.	1. Check engine oil level.
	2. Faulty oil pressure sending unit.	2. Install new sending unit.
	3. Clogged oil filter.	3. Install new oil filter.
	4. Worn parts in oil pump.	4. Replace worn parts or pump.
	5. Thin or diluted oil.	5. Change oil to correct viscosity.
	6. Excessive bearing clearance.	6. Measure bearings for correct clearance.
	7. Oil pump relief valve stuck.	7. Remove valve and inspect, clean, and reinstall.
	8. Oil pump suction tube loose, bent or cracked.	8. Remove oil pan and install new tube if necessary.
NO OIL PRESSURE	1. Low oil level.	1. Add oil to correct level.
	2. Oil pressure gauge or sending unit inaccurate.	2. Replace defective unit.
	3. Oil pump malfunction.	3. Repair oil pump.
	4. Oil pressure relief valve sticking.	4. Remove and inspect oil pressure relief valve assembly.
	5. Oil passages on pressure side of pump obstructed.	5. Inspect oil passages for obstructions.
	6. Oil pickup screen or tube obstructed.	6. Inspect oil pickup for obstructions.
LOW OIL PRESSURE	1. Low oil level.	1. Add oil to correct level.
	2. Oil excessively thin due to dilution, poor quality, or improper grade.	2. Drain and refill crankcase with recommended oil.
	3. Oil pressure relief spring weak or sticking.	3. Remove and inspect oil pressure relief valve assembly.
	4. Oil pickup tube and screen assembly has restriction or air leak.	4. Remove and inspect oil inlet tube and screen assembly. (Fill pickup with lacquer thinner to find leaks.)
	5. Excessive oil pump clearance.	5. Check clearances.
	6. Excessive main, rod, or camshaft bearing clearance.	6. Measure bearing clearances, repair as necessary.
HIGH OIL PRESSURE	1. Improper grade oil.	1. Drain and refill crankcase with correct grade oil.
	2. Oil pressure gauge or sending unit inaccurate.	2. Replace defective unit.
	3. Oil pressure relief valve sticking closed.	3. Remove and inspect oil pressure relief valve assembly.
EXTERNAL OIL LEAK	1. Fuel pump gasket broken or improperly seated.	1. Replace gasket.
	2. Cylinder head cover gasket broken or improperly seated.	2. Replace gasket; check cylinder head cover gasket flange and cylinder head gasket surface for distortion.
	3. Oil filter gasket broken or improperly seated.	3. Replace oil filter.
	4. Oil pan side gasket broken or improperly seated.	4. Replace gasket; check oil pan gasket flange for distortion.
	5. Oil pan front oil seal broken or improperly seated.	5. Replace seal; check timing chain cover and oil pan seal flange for distortion.
	6. Oil pan rear oil seal broken or improperly seated.	6. Replace seal; check oil pan rear oil seal flange; check rear main bearing cap for cracks, plugged oil return channels, or distortion in seal groove.
	7. Timing chain cover oil seal broken or improperly seated.	7. Replace seal.
	8. Oil pan drain plug loose or has stripped threads.	8. Repair as necessary and tighten.
	9. Rear oil gallery plug loose.	9. Use appropriate sealant on gallery plug and tighten.
	10. Rear camshaft plug loose or improperly seated.	10. Seat camshaft plug or replace and seal, as necessary.

ENGINE PERFORMANCE, LUBRICATION & NOISES—Continued

Condition	Possible Cause	Correction
EXCESSIVE OIL CONSUMPTION	1. Oil level too high.	1. Lower oil level to specifications.
	2. Oil too thin.	2. Replace with specified oil.
	3. Valve stem oil seals are damaged, missing, or incorrect type.	3. Replace valve stem oil seals.
	4. Valve stems or valve guides worn.	4. Check stem-to-guide clearance and repair as necessary.
	5. Piston rings broken, missing.	5. Replace missing or broken rings.
	6. Piston rings incorrect size.	6. Check ring gap, repair as necessary.
	7. Piston rings sticking or excessively loose in grooves.	7. Check ring side clearance, repair as necessary.
	8. Compression rings installed upside down.	8. Repair as necessary.
	9. Cylinder walls worn, scored, or glazed.	9. Repair as necessary.
	10. Piston ring gaps not properly staggered.	10. Repair as necessary.
	11. Excessive main or connecting rod bearing clearance.	11. Check bearing clearance, repair as necessary.

OIL PRESSURE INDICATOR

Condition	Possible Cause	Correction
LIGHT NOT LIT, IGNITION ON AND ENGINE NOT RUNNING.	1. Bulb burned out.	1. Replace bulb.
	2. Open in light circuit.	2. Locate and correct open.
	3. Defective oil pressure switch.	3. Replace oil pressure switch.
LIGHT ON, ENGINE RUNNING ABOVE IDLE SPEED.	1. Grounded wiring between light and switch.	1. Locate and repair ground.
	2. Defective oil pressure switch.	2. Replace oil pressure switch.
	3. Low oil pressure.	3. Locate cause of low oil pressure and correct.

IGNITION, STARTER & FUEL

Condition	Possible Cause	Correction
NOTHING HAPPENS WHEN START ATTEMPT IS MADE	1. Undercharged or defective battery.	1. Check condition of battery and recharge or replace as required.
	2. Loose battery cables.	2. Clean and tighten cable connections.
	3. Burned fusible link in starting circuit.	3. Check for burned fusible link. Correct wiring problem.
	4. Incorrectly positioned or defective neutral start switch.	4. Check neutral start switch adjustment. If O.K., replace switch.
	5. Loose or defective wiring between neutral start switch and ignition switch.	5. Check for loose connections and opens between battery, horn relay, ignition switch, and solenoid "S" terminal. Check battery ground cable. Replace or repair defective item.
	6. Defective starter motor.	6. Repair or replace starter motor.
	7. Defective starter interlock system.	7. Use emergency button under hood. If car starts, repair circuit in interlock system. If car does not start, check and repair starter circuit.
SOLENOID SWITCH CLICKS BUT STARTER DOES NOT CRANK	1. Undercharged or defective battery.	1. Test battery. Recharge or replace battery.
	2. Loose battery cables.	2. Check and tighten battery connections.
	3. Loose or defective wiring at starter.	3. Tighten connections or repair wiring as required.
	4. Defective solenoid.	4. Replace solenoid.
	5. "Hot stall" condition.	5. Check engine cooling system.
	6. Excessive engine rotational torque caused by mechanical problem within engine.	6. Check engine torque for excessive friction.
	7. Defective starter motor.	7. Repair or replace starter motor.

Condition	Possible Cause	Correction
SLOW CRANKING	1. Vehicle is overheating.	1. Check engine cooling system and repair as required.
	2. Undercharged or defective battery.	2. Recharge or replace battery.
	3. Loose or defective wiring between battery and engine block.	3. Repair or replace wiring.
	4. Loose or defective wiring between battery and solenoid "Bat" terminal.	4. Repair or replace wiring.
	5. Defective starter motor.	5. Repair or replace starter.
STARTER SPINS AND/OR MAKES LOUD GRINDING NOISE BUT DOES NOT TURN ENGINE	1. Defective starter motor.	1. Repair or replace starter motor.
	2. Defective ring gear.	2. Replace ring gear.
STARTER KEEPS RUNNING AFTER IGNITION SWITCH IS RELEASED— FROM "START" TO "RUN" POSITION	1. Defective ignition switch.	1. Replace ignition switch.
	2. Defective solenoid.	2. Replace solenoid.
STARTER ENGAGES ("Clunks") BUT ENGINE DOES NOT CRANK	1. Open circuit in solenoid armature or field coils.	1. Repair or replace solenoid or starter motor.
	2. Short or ground in field coil or armature.	2. Repair or replace starter motor.
HARD STARTING (Engine Cranks Normally)	1. Binding linkage, choke valve or choke piston.	1. Repair as necessary.
	2. Restricted choke vacuum and hot air passages.	2. Clean passages.
	3. Improper fuel level.	3. Adjust float level.
	4. Dirty, worn or faulty needle valve and seat.	4. Repair as necessary.
	5. Float sticking.	5. Repair as necessary.
	6. Exhaust manifold heat valve stuck.	6. Repair as necessary.
	7. Faulty fuel pump.	7. Replace fuel pump.
	8. Incorrect choke cover adjustment.	8. Adjust choke cover.
	9. Inadequate unloader adjustment.	9. Adjust unloader.
	10. Faulty ignition coil.	10. Test and replace as necessary.
	11. Improper spark plug gap.	11. Adjust gap.
	12. Incorrect initial timing.	12. Adjust timing.
	13. Incorrect valve timing.	13. Check valve timing; repair as necessary.
ROUGH IDLE OR STALLING	1. Incorrect curb or fast idle speed.	1. Adjust curb or fast idle speed.
	2. Incorrect initial timing.	2. Adjust timing to specifications.
	3. Improper idle mixture adjustment.	3. Adjust idle mixture.
	4. Damaged tip on idle mixture screw(s).	4. Replace mixture screw(s).
	5. Improper fast idle cam adjustment.	5. Adjust fast idle.
	6. Faulty PCV valve air flow.	6. Test PCV valve and replace as necessary.
	7. Exhaust manifold heat valve inoperative.	7. Lubricate or replace heat valve as necessary.
	8. Choke binding.	8. Locate and eliminate binding condition.
	9. Improper choke setting.	9. Adjust choke.
	10. Vacuum leak.	10. Check manifold vacuum and repair as necessary.
	11. Improper fuel level.	11. Adjust fuel level.
	12. Faulty distributor rotor or cap.	12. Replace rotor or cap.
	13. Leaking engine valves.	13. Check cylinder leakdown rate or compression and repair as necessary.
	14. Incorrect ignition wiring.	14. Check wiring and correct as necessary.
	15. Faulty coil.	15. Test coil and replace as necessary.
	16. Clogged air bleed or idle passages.	16. Clean passages.
	17. Restricted air cleaner.	17. Clean or replace air cleaner.
	18. Faulty EGR valve operation if equipped.	18. Test EGR system and replace as necessary if equipped.

IGNITION, STARTER & FUEL—Continued

Condition	Possible Cause	Correction
FAULTY LOW-SPEED OPERATION	1. Clogged idle transfer slots.	1. Clean transfer slots.
	2. Restricted idle air bleeds and passages.	2. Clean air bleeds and passages.
	3. Restricted air cleaner.	3. Clean or replace air cleaner.
	4. Improper fuel level.	4. Adjust fuel level.
	5. Faulty spark plugs.	5. Clean or replace spark plugs.
	6. Dirty, corroded, or loose secondary circuit connections.	6. Clean or tighten secondary circuit connections.
	7. Faulty ignition cable.	7. Replace ignition cable.
	8. Faulty distributor cap.	8. Replace cap.
FAULTY ACCELERATION	1. Improper pump stroke.	1. Adjust pump stroke.
	2. Incorrect ignition timing.	2. Adjust timing.
	3. Inoperative pump discharge check ball or needle.	3. Clean or replace as necessary.
	4. Worn or damaged pump diaphragm or piston.	4. Replace diaphragm or piston.
	5. Leaking main body cover gasket.	5. Replace gasket.
	6. Engine cold and choke too lean.	6. Adjust choke.
	7. Faulty spark plug(s).	7. Clean or replace spark plug(s).
	8. Leaking engine valves.	8. Check cylinder leakdown rate or compression, repair as necessary.
	9. Faulty coil.	9. Test coil and replace as necessary.
FAULTY HIGH-SPEED OPERATION	1. Incorrect ignition timing.	1. Adjust timing.
	2. Faulty distributor centrifugal advance.	2. Check centrifugal advance and repair as necessary.
	3. Faulty distributor vacuum advance.	3. Check vacuum advance and repair as necessary.
	4. Low fuel pump volume.	4. Replace fuel pump.
	5. Improper spark plug gap.	5. Adjust gap.
	6. Faulty choke operation.	6. Adjust choke.
	7. Partially restricted exhaust manifold, exhaust pipe, muffler, or tailpipe.	7. Eliminate restriction.
	8. Clogged vacuum passages.	8. Clean passages.
	9. Improper size or obstructed main jets.	9. Clean or replace as necessary.
	10. Restricted air cleaner.	10. Clean or replace as necessary.
	11. Faulty distributor rotor or cap.	11. Replace rotor or cap.
	12. Worn distributor shaft.	12. Replace shaft.
	13. Faulty coil.	13. Test coil and replace as necessary.
	14. Leaking engine valve(s).	14. Check cylinder leakdown or compression and repair as necessary.
	15. Faulty valve spring(s).	15. Inspect and test valve spring tension and replace as necessary.
	16. Incorrect valve timing.	16. Check valve timing and repair as necessary.
	17. Intake manifold restricted.	17. Pass chain through passages.
MISFIRE AT ALL SPEEDS	1. Faulty spark plug(s).	1. Clean or replace spark plug(s).
	2. Faulty spark plug cable(s).	2. Replace as necessary.
	3. Faulty distributor cap or rotor.	3. Replace cap or rotor.
	4. Faulty coil.	4. Test coil and replace as necessary.
	5. Primary circuit shorted or open intermittently.	5. Trace primary circuit and repair as necessary.
	6. Leaking engine valve(s).	6. Check cylinder leakdown rate or compression and repair as necessary.
	7. Faulty hydraulic tappet(s).	7. Clean or replace tappet(s).
	8. Faulty valve spring(s).	8. Inspect and test valve spring tension, repair as necessary.
	9. Worn lobes on camshaft.	9. Replace camshaft.
	10. Vacuum leak.	10. Check manifold vacuum and repair as necessary.
	11. Improper carburetor settings.	11. Adjust carburetor.
	12. Fuel pump volume or pressure low.	12. Replace fuel pump.
	13. Blown cylinder head gasket.	13. Replace gasket.
	14. Intake or exhaust manifold passage(s) restricted.	14. Pass chain through passages.

TROUBLESHOOTING

Condition	Possible Cause	Correction
POWER NOT UP TO NORMAL	1. Incorrect ignition timing. 2. Faulty distributor rotor. 3. Worn distributor shaft. 4. Incorrect spark plug gap. 5. Faulty fuel pump. 6. Incorrect valve timing. 7. Faulty coil. 8. Faulty ignition cables. 9. Leaking engine valves. 10. Blown cylinder head gasket. 11. Leaking piston rings.	1. Adjust timing. 2. Replace rotor. 3. Replace shaft. 4. Adjust gap. 5. Replace fuel pump. 6. Check valve timing and repair as necessary. 7. Test coil and replace as necessary. 8. Test cables and replace as necessary. 9. Check cylinder leakdown rate or compression and repair as necessary. 10. Replace gasket. 11. Check compression and repair as necessary.
INTAKE BACKFIRE	1. Improper ignition timing. 2. Faulty accelerator pump discharge. 3. Improper choke operation. 4. Lean fuel mixture.	1. Adjust timing. 2. Repair as necessary. 3. Repair as necessary. 4. Check float level or manifold vacuum for vacuum leak.
EXHAUST BACKFIRE	1. Vacuum leak. 2. Faulty A.I.R. diverter valve. 3. Faulty choke operation. 4. Exhaust leak.	1. Check manifold vacuum and repair as necessary. 2. Test diverter valve and replace as necessary. 3. Repair as necessary. 4. Locate and eliminate leak.
PING OR SPARK KNOCK	1. Incorrect ignition timing. 2. Distributor centrifugal or vacuum advance malfunction. 3. Excessive combustion chamber deposits. 4. Carburetor set too lean. 5. Vacuum leak. 6. Excessively high compression. 7. Fuel octane rating excessively low. 8. Heat riser stuck in heat on position. 9. Insufficient EGR flow.	1. Adjust timing. 2. Check advance and repair as necessary. 3. Use combustion chamber cleaner. 4. Adjust carburetor. 5. Check manifold vacuum and repair as necessary. 6. Check compression and repair as necessary. 7. Try alternate fuel source. 8. Free-up or replace heat riser. 9. Check EGR system operation.
SURGING (Cruising Speeds To Top Speeds)	1. Low fuel level. 2. Low fuel pump pressure or volume. 3. Improper PCV valve air flow. 4. Vacuum leak. 5. Dirt in carburetor. 6. Undersize main jets. 7. Clogged fuel filter screen. 8. Restricted air cleaner. 9. Excessive EGR valve flow.	1. Adjust fuel level. 2. Replace fuel pump. 3. Test PCV valve and replace as necessary. 4. Check manifold vacuum and repair as necessary. 5. Clean carburetor, replace filter. 6. Replace main jet(s). 7. Replace fuel filter. 8. Clean or replace air cleaner. 9. Check EGR system operation.

CHARGING SYSTEM

Condition	Possible Cause	Correction
ALTERNATOR FAILS TO CHARGE (No Output or Low Output)	1. Alternator drive belt loose. 2. Regulator base improperly grounded. 3. Worn brushes and/or slip rings. 4. Sticking brushes. 5. Open field circuit. 6. Open charging circuit.	1. Adjust drive belt to specifications. 2. Connect regulator to a good ground. 3. Install new brushes and/or slip rings. 4. Clean slip rings and brush holders. Install new brushes if necessary. 5. Test all the field circuit connections, and correct as required. 6. Inspect all connections in charging circuit, and correct as required.

CHARGING SYSTEM—Continued

Condition	Possible Cause	Correction
ALTERNATOR FAILS TO CHARGE (No Output or Low Output), continued	7. Open circuit in stator windings.	7. Remove alternator and disassemble. Test stator windings. Install new stator if necessary.
	8. Open rectifiers.	8. Remove alternator and disassemble. Test the rectifiers. Install new rectifier assemblies if necessary.
LOW, UNSTEADY CHARGING RATE	1. High resistance in body to engine ground lead.	1. Tighten ground lead connections. Install new ground lead if necessary.
	2. Alternator drive belt loose.	2. Adjust alternator drive belt.
	3. High resistance at battery terminals.	3. Clean and tighten battery terminals.
	4. High resistance in charging circuit.	4. Test charging circuit resistance. Correct as required.
	5. Open stator winding.	5. Remove and disassemble alternator. Test stator windings. Install new stator if necessary.
LOW OUTPUT AND A LOW BATTERY	1. High resistance in charging circuit.	1. Test charging circuit resistance and correct as required.
	2. Shorted rectifier. Open rectifier.	2. Perform current output test. Test the rectifiers and install new rectifier heat sink assembly as required. Remove and disassemble the alternator.
	3. Grounded stator windings.	3. Remove and disassemble alternator. Test stator windings. Install new stator if necessary.
	4. Faulty voltage regulator.	4. Test voltage regulator. Replace as necessary.
EXCESSIVE CHARGING RATE TO A FULLY CHARGED BATTERY	1. Faulty ignition switch.	1. Install new ignition switch.
	2. Faulty voltage regulator.	2. Test voltage regulator. Replace as necessary.
NOISY ALTERNATOR	1. Alternator mounting loose.	1. Properly install and tighten alternator mounting.
	2. Worn or frayed drive belt.	2. Install a new drive belt and adjust to specifications.
	3. Worn bearings.	3. Remove and disassemble alternator. Install new bearings as required.
	4. Interference between rotor fan and stator leads.	4. Remove and disassemble alternator. Correct interference as required.
	5. Rotor or rotor fan damaged.	5. Remove and disassemble alternator. Install new rotor.
	6. Open or shorted rectifer.	6. Remove and disassemble alternator. Test rectifers. Install new rectifier heat sink assemble as required.
	7. Open or shorted winding in stator.	7. Remove and disassemble alternator. Test stator windings. Install new stator if necessary.
EXCESSIVE AMMETER FLUCTUATION	1. High resistance in the alternator and voltage regulator circuit.	1. Clean and tighten all connections as necessary.

CHARGING SYSTEM INDICATOR

LIGHT ON, IGNITION OFF	1. Shorted positive diode.	1. Locate and replace shorted diode.
LIGHT NOT ON, IGNITION ON AND ENGINE NOT RUNNING	1. Bulb burned out.	1. Replace bulb.
	2. Open in light circuit.	2. Locate and correct open.
	3. Open in field.	3. Replace rotor.
LIGHT ON, ENGINE RUNNING ABOVE IDLE SPEED	1. No generator output.	1. Check and correct cause of no output.
	2. Shorted negative diode.	2. Locate and replace shorted diode.
	3. Loose or broken generator belt.	3. Tighten or replace and tighten generator belt.

TROUBLESHOOTING

COOLING SYSTEM

Condition	Possible Cause	Correction
HIGH TEMPERATURE INDICATION— OVERHEATING	1. Coolant level low.	1. Replenish coolant level.
	2. Fan belt loose.	2. Adjust fan belt.
	3. Radiator hose(s) collapsed.	3. Replace hose(s).
	4. Radiator blocked to airflow.	4. Remove restriction.
	5. Faulty radiator cap.	5. Replace cap.
	6. Car overloaded.	6. Reduce load.
	7. Ignition timing incorrect.	7. Adjust ignition timing.
	8. Idle speed low.	8. Adjust idle speed.
	9. Air trapped in cooling system.	9. Purge air.
	10. Car in heavy traffic.	10. Operate at fast idle intermittently to cool engine.
	11. Incorrect cooling system component(s) installed.	11. Install proper component(s).
	12. Faulty thermostat.	12. Replace thermostat.
	13. Water pump shaft broken or impeller loose.	13. Replace water pump.
	14. Radiator tubes clogged.	14. Flush radiator.
	15. Cooling system clogged.	15. Flush system.
	16. Casting flash in cooling passages.	16. Repair or replace as necessary. Flash may be visible by removing cooling system components or removing core plugs.
	17. Brakes dragging.	17. Repair brakes.
	18. Excessive engine friction.	18. Repair engine.
	19. Car working beyond cooling system capacity.	19. Install heavy-duty cooling fan and/or radiator.
	20. Antifreeze concentration over 68%.	20. Lower antifreeze content.
	21. Low anti-freeze concentration.	21. Add anti-freeze to provide a minimum 50% concentration.
LOW TEMPERATURE INDICATION— OVERCOOLING	1. Improper fan being used.	1. Install proper fan.
	2. Improper radiator.	2. Install proper radiator.
	3. Thermostat stuck open.	3. Replace thermostat.
	4. Improper fan pulley (too small).	4. Install proper pulley.
COOLANT LOSS—BOILOVER	Refer to Overheating Causes in addition to the following:	
NOTE: Immediately after shutdown, the engine enters a period known as heat soak. This is caused because the cooling system is inoperative but engine temperature is still high. If coolant temperature rises above boiling point, it may push some coolant out of the radiator overflow tube. If this does not occur frequently, it is considered normal.	1. Overfilled cooling system.	1. Reduce coolant level to proper specification.
	2. Quick shutdown after hard (hot) run.	2. Allow engine to run at fast idle prior to shutdown.
	3. Air in system resulting in occasional "burping" of coolant.	3. Purge system.
	4. Insufficient antifreeze allowing coolant boiling point to be too low.	4. Add antifreeze to raise boiling point.
	5. Antifreeze deteriorated because of age or contamination.	5. Replace coolant.
	6. Leaks due to loose hose clamps, loose nuts, bolts, drain plugs, faulty hoses, or defective radiator.	6. Pressure test system to locate leak then repair as necessary.
	7. Faulty head gasket.	7. Replace head gasket.
	8. Cracked head, manifold, or block.	8. Replace as necessary.
COOLANT ENTRY INTO CRANKCASE OR CYLINDER	1. Faulty head gasket.	1. Replace head gasket.
	2. Crack in head, manifold or block.	2. Replace as necessary.
COOLANT RECOVERY SYSTEM INOPERATIVE	1. Coolant level low.	1. Replenish coolant.
	2. Leak in system.	2. Pressure test to isolate leak and repair as necessary.
	3. Pressure cap not tight or gasket missing or leaking.	3. Repair as necessary.
	4. Pressure cap defective.	4. Replace cap.
	5. Overflow tube clogged or leaking.	5. Repair as necessary.
	6. Recovery bottle vent plugged.	6. Remove restriction.
NOISE	1. Fan contacting shroud.	1. Reposition shroud and check engine mounts.
	2. Loose water pump impeller.	2. Replace pump.
	3. Dry fan belt.	3. Apply belt dressing or replace belt.

COOLING SYSTEM—Continued

Condition	Possible Cause	Correction
NOISE, continued	4. Loose fan belt.	4. Adjust fan belt.
	5. Rough surface on drive pulley.	5. Replace pulley.
	6. Water pump bearing worn.	6. Remove belt to isolate. Replace pump.
NO COOLANT FLOW THROUGH HEATER CORE	1. Plugged return pipe in water pump.	1. Remove obstruction.
	2. Heater hose collapsed or plugged.	2. Remove obstruction or replace hose.
	3. Plugged heater core.	3. Remove obstruction or replace core.
	4. Plugged outlet in thermostat housing.	4. Remove flash or obstruction.
	5. Heater bypass hole in cylinder head plugged.	5. Remove obstruction.

COOLANT TEMPERATURE INDICATOR

Condition	Possible Cause	Correction
"HOT" INDICATOR; LIGHT NOT LIT WHEN CRANKING ENGINE	1. Bulb burned out.	1. Replace bulb.
	2. Open in light circuit.	2. Locate and correct open.
	3. Defective ignition switch.	3. Replace ignition switch.
LIGHT ON, ENGINE RUNNING	1. Wiring grounded between light and switch.	1. Locate and correct grounded wiring.
	2. Defective temperature switch.	2. Replace temperature switch.
	3. Defective ignition switch.	3. Replace ignition switch.
	4. High coolant temperature.	4. Locate and correct cause of high coolant temperature.

EXHAUST SYSTEM

Condition	Possible Cause	Correction
LEAKING EXHAUST GASES	1. Leaks at pipe joints.	1. Tighten U-bolt nuts at leaking joints.
	2. Damaged or improperly installed seals or packing.	2. Replace seals or packing as necessary.
	3. Loose exhaust pipe heat tube extension connections.	3. Replace seals or packing as required. Tighten stud nuts or bolts.
	4. Burned or rusted out exhaust pipe heat tube extensions.	4. Replace heat tube extensions as required.
EXHAUST NOISES	1. Leaks at manifold or pipe connections.	1. Tighten clamps at leaking connections to specified torque. Replace gasket or packing as required.
	2. Burned or blown out muffler.	2. Replace muffler assembly.
	3. Burned or rusted out exhaust pipe.	3. Replace exhaust pipe.
	4. Exhaust pipe leaking at manifold flange.	4. Tighten attaching bolt nuts.
	5. Exhaust manifold cracked or broken.	5. Replace manifold.
	6. Leak between manifold and cylinder head.	6. Tighten manifold to cylinder head stud nuts or bolts.
LOSS OF ENGINE POWER AND/OR INTERNAL RATTLES IN MUFFLER	1. Dislodged turning tubes and or baffles in muffler.	1. Replace muffler.
LOSS OF ENGINE POWER	1. Imploding (inner wall collapse) of exhaust pipe.	1. Replace exhaust pipe.
ENGINE HARD TO WARM UP OR WILL NOT RETURN TO NORMAL IDLE	1. Heat control valve frozen in the open position.	1. Free up manifold heat control using a suitable manifold heat control solvent.
MANIFOLD HEAT CONTROL VALVE NOISE	1. Thermostat broken.	1. Replace thermostat.
	2. Broken, weak or missing anti-rattle spring.	2. Replace spring.

TROUBLESHOOTING
Clutch & Manual Transmission

Condition	Possible Cause	Correction
CLUTCH CHATTER	1. Worn or damaged disc assembly.	1. Replace disc assembly.
	2. Grease or oil on disc facings.	2. Replace disc assembly and correct cause of contamination.
	3. Improperly adjusted cover assembly.	3. Replace cover assembly.
	4. Broken or loose engine mounts.	4. Replace or tighten mounts.
	5. Misaligned clutch housing.	5. Align clutch housing.
CLUTCH SLIPPING	1. Insufficient pedal free play.	1. Adjust release fork rod.
	2. Burned, worn, or oil soaked facings.	2. Replace disc assembly and correct cause of contamination.
	3. Weak or broken pressure springs.	3. Replace cover assembly.
DIFFICULT GEAR SHIFTING	1. Excessive pedal free play.	1. Adjust release fork rod.
	2. Excessive deflection in linkage or firewall.	2. Repair or replace linkage.
	3. Worn or damaged disc assembly.	3. Replace disc assembly.
	4. Improperly adjusted cover assembly.	4. Replace cover assembly.
	5. Clutch disc splines sticking.	5. Remove disc assembly and free up splines or replace disc.
	6. Worn or dry pilot bushing.	6. Lubricate or replace bushing.
	7. Clutch housing misaligned.	7. Align clutch housing.
CLUTCH NOISY	1. Dry clutch linkage.	1. Lubricate where necessary.
	2. Worn release bearing.	2. Replace release bearing.
	3. Worn disc assembly.	3. Replace disc assembly.
	4. Worn release levers.	4. Replace cover assembly.
	5. Worn or dry pilot bushing.	5. Lubricate or replace bushing.
	6. Dry contact-pressure plate lugs in cover.	6. Lubricate very lightly.
TRANSMISSION SHIFTS HARD	1. Incorrect clutch adjustment.	1. Adjust clutch pedal free-play.
	2. Clutch linkage binding.	2. Lubricate or repair linkage as required.
	3. Gearshift linkage incorrectly adjusted, bent, or binding.	3. Adjust linkage—correct any bind. Replace bent parts.
	4. Bind in steering column, or column is misaligned.	4. Disconnect shift rods at column. Check for bind/misalignment between tube and jacket by shifting lever into all positions. Correct as required.
	5. Incorrect lubricant.	5. Drain and refill transmission.
	6. Internal bind in transmissions—e.g. shift rails, interlocks, shift forks, synchronizer teeth.	6. Remove transmission and inspect shift mechanism. Repair as required.
	7. Clutch housing misalignment.	7. Check runout at rear face of clutch housing.
GEAR CLASH WHEN SHIFTING FROM ONE FORWARD GEAR TO ANOTHER	1. Incorrect clutch adjustment.	1. Adjust clutch.
	2. Clutch linkage binding.	2. Lubricate or repair linkage as required.
	3. Gear shift linkage incorrectly adjusted, bent, or binding.	3. Adjust linkage, correct binds, replace bent parts.
	4. Clutch housing misalignment.	4. Check runout at rear face of clutch housing.
	5. Damaged or worn transmission components: shift forks, synchronizers, shift rails and interlocks. Excessive end play due to worn thrust washers.	5. Inspect components. Repair or replace as required.
TRANSMISSION NOISY	1. Insufficient lubricant.	1. Check lubricant level and replenish as required.
	2. Incorrect lubricant.	2. Replace with proper lubricant.
	3. Clutch housing to engine or transmission to clutch housing bolts loose.	3. Check and correct bolt torque as required.
	4. Dirt, chips in lubricant.	4. Drain and flush transmission.
	5. Gearshift linkage incorrectly adjusted, or bent or binding.	5. Adjust linkage, correct binds, replace bent parts.
	6. Clutch housing misalignment.	6. Check runout at rear face of clutch housing.

CLUTCH & MANUAL TRANSMISSION—Continued

Condition	Possible Cause	Correction
TRANSMISSION NOISY, continued	7. Worn transmission components: front-rear bearings, worn gear teeth, damaged gear teeth or synchronizer components.	7. Inspect components and repair as required.
JUMPS OUT OF GEAR	1. Gearshift linkage incorrectly adjusted.	1. Adjust linkage.
	2. Gearshift linkage bent or binding.	2. Correct bind, replace bent parts.
	3. Clutch housing misaligned.	3. Check runout at rear face of clutch housing.
	4. Worn pilot bushing.	4. Replace bushing.
	5. Worn or damaged clutch shaft roller bearings.	5. Replace bearings.
	6. Worn, tapered gear teeth; synchronizer parts worn.	6. Inspect and replace as required.
	7. Shifter forks, shift rails, or detent-interlock parts worn, missing, etc.	7. Inspect and replace as required.
	8. Excessive end play of output shaft gear train, countershaft gear or reverse idler gear.	8. Replace thrust washers, and snap rings (output shaft gear train).
WILL NOT SHIFT INTO ONE GEAR— ALL OTHERS OK	1. Gearshift linkage not adjusted correctly.	1. Adjust linkage.
	2. Bent shift rod at transmission.	2. Replace rod.
	3. Transmission shifter levers reversed.	3. Correctly position levers.
	4. Worn or damaged shift rails, shift forks, detent-interlock plugs, loose setscrew in shifter fork, worn synchronizer parts.	4. Inspect and repair or replace parts as required.
LOCKED IN ONE GEAR—CANNOT BE SHIFTED OUT OF THAT GEAR	1. Gearshift linkage binding or bent.	1. Correct bind, replace bent components.
	2. Transmission shifter lever attaching nuts loose or levers are worn at shifter fork shaft hole.	2. Tighten nuts, replace worn levers.
	3. Shift rails worn or broken, shifter fork bent, setscrew loose, detent-interlock plug missing or worn.	3. Inspect and replace worn or damaged parts.
	4. Broken gear teeth on countershaft gear, clutch shaft, or reverse idler gear.	4. Inspect and replace damaged part.

Transfer Case

Condition	Possible Cause	Correction
TRANSFER CASE NOISY **NOTE:** If the vehicle has not been driven for a week or more, noise may occur during initial operation. This is a normal condition and the noise will usually stop after continued operation.	1. Incorrect tire inflation pressures and/or tire and wheel size.	1. Check that all tire and wheel assemblies are the same size and inflation pressures are correct.
	2. Incorrect lubricant level.	2. Check and fill lubricant as required.
	3. Worn or damaged bearings.	3. Inspect and replace as required.
	4. Worn or damaged drive chain.	4. Inspect and replace as required.
	5. Incorrectly aligned driveshafts or universal joints.	5. Inspect and align as required.
	6. Loose adapter bolts.	6. Check and correct bolt torque as required.
SHIFTER LEVER DIFFICULT TO MOVE	1. Dirty or contaminated linkage.	1. Clean and lubricate as required.
	2. Internal component damage.	2. Inspect and replace as required.
JUMPS OUT OF GEAR	1. Incorrectly adjusted or loose shift linkage.	1. Adjust and/or tighten linkage bolts.
	2. Loose mounting bolts.	2. Check and correct bolt torque as required
	3. Front and rear driveshaft slip yokes dry or loose.	3. Lubricate and repair slip yokes as required. Correct bolt torque as required.
	4. Internal case component damage.	4. Inspect and replace worn and/or damaged case components as required.

TRANSFER CASE—Continued

Condition	Possible Cause	Correction
FRONT AXLE SLIPS OUT OF ENGAGEMENT	1. Spring loose or broken. 2. Incorrect shift linkage or cable adjustment.	1. Inspect and replace as required. 2. Adjust linkage or cable as required.
TRANSFER CASE LEAKING	1. Excessive lubricant in case. 2. Worn and/or damaged seals or gaskets. 3. Loose mounting case bolts. 4. Scored yoke in seal contact area.	1. Correct lubricant level as required. 2. Inspect and replace as required. 3. Check and correct bolt torque as required 4. Repair or replace as required.

Brakes

LOW BRAKE PEDAL (Excessive pedal travel required to apply brake)	1. Excessive clearance between linings and drums caused by inoperative automatic adjusters. 2. Worn brake lining. 3. Bent, distorted brakeshoes. 4. Caliper pistons corroded. 5. Power unit push rod height incorrect.	1. Make 10 to 15 firm forward and reverse brake stops to adjust brakes. If brake pedal does not come up, repair or replace adjuster parts as necessary. 2. Inspect and replace lining if worn beyond minimum thickness specification. 3. Replace brakeshoes in axle sets. 4. Repair or replace calipers. 5. Check height with gauge (only). Replace power unit if push rod height is not within specifications.
LOW BRAKE PEDAL (Pedal may go to floor under steady pressure)	1. Leak in hydraulic system. 2. Air in hydraulic system. 3. Incorrect or non-recommended brake fluid (fluid boils away at below normal temp.).	1. Fill master cylinder to within ¼-inch of rim; have helper apply brakes and check calipers, wheel cylinders combination valve, tubes, hoses and fittings for leaks. Repair or replace parts as necessary. 2. Bleed air from system. Refer to Brake Bleeding. 3. Flush hydraulic system with clean brake fluid. Refill with correct-type fluid.
LOW BRAKE PEDAL (Pedal goes to floor on first application—OK on subsequent applications)	1. Disc brakeshoe (pad) knock back; shoes push caliper piston back into bore. Caused by loose wheel bearings or excessive lateral runout of rotor (rotor wobble). 2. Calipers sticking on mounting surfaces of caliper and anchor. Caused by buildup of dirt, rust, or corrosion on abutment.	1. Adjust wheel bearings and check lateral runout of rotor(s). Refinish rotors if runout is over limits. Replace rotor if refinishing would cause rotor to fall below minimum thickness limit. 2. Clean mounting surfaces and lubricate surfaces with molydisulphide grease or equivalent.
FADING BRAKE PEDAL (Pedal falls away under steady pressure)	1. Leak in hydraulic system. 2. Master cylinder piston cups worn, or master cylinder bore is scored, worn or corroded.	1. Fill master cylinder reservoirs to within ¼-inch of rim; have helper apply brakes, check master cylinder, calipers, wheel cylinders combination valve, tubes, hoses, and fittings for leaks. Repair or replace parts as necessary. 2. Repair or replace master cylinder.

BRAKES—Continued

Condition	Possible Cause	Correction

DECREASING BRAKE PEDAL TRAVEL (Pedal travel required to apply brakes decreases, may be accompanied by hard pedal)	1. Caliper or wheel cylinder pistons sticking or seized.
	2. Master cylinder compensator ports blocked (preventing fluid return to reservoirs) or pistons sticking or seized in master cylinder bore.
	3. Power brake unit binding internally.
		1. Repair or replace calipers, or wheel cylinders.
		2. Repair or replace master cylinder.
		
		3. Test unit as follows:
		  a. Raise hood, shift transmission into neutral and start engine.
		  b. Increase engine speed to 1500 RPM, close throttle and fully depress brake pedal.
		  c. Slowly release brake pedal and stop engine.
		  d. Remove vacuum check valve and hose from power unit. Observe for backward movement of brake pedal or power unit-to-brake pedal push rod.
		  e. If pedal or push rod moves backward, power unit has internal bind—replace power brake unit.

	4. Incorrect power unit push rod height.	4. Adjust push rod height.
SPONGY BRAKE PEDAL (Pedal has abnormally soft, springy, spongy feel when depressed)	1. Air in hydraulic system. 2. Brakeshoes bent or distorted. 3. Brake lining not yet seated to drums and rotors.	1. Bleed brakes. 2. Replace brakeshoes. 3. Burnish brakes.
HARD BRAKE PEDAL (Excessive pedal pressure required to stop car. May be accompanied by brake fade)	1. Loose or leaking power brake unit vacuum hose. 2. Brake lining contaminated by grease or brake fluid. 3. Incorrect or poor quality brake lining. 4. Bent, broken, distorted brakeshoes. 5. Calipers binding or dragging on anchor. Rear brakeshoes dragging on support plate.	1. Tighten connections or replace leaking hose. 2. Determine cause of contaminations and correct. Replace contaminated brake lining in axle sets. 3. Replace lining in axle sets. 4. Replace brakeshoes and lining. 5. Sand or wire brush anchors and caliper mounting surfaces and lubricate surfaces lightly. Clean rust or burrs from rear brake support plate ledges and lubricate ledges.
		NOTE: If ledges are deeply grooved or scored, do not attempt to sand or grind them smooth—replace support plate.

	6. Rear brake drum(s) bell mouthed, flared or barrel shaped (distorted).
	7. Caliper, wheel cylinder, or master cylinder pistons sticking or seized.
	8. Power brake unit vacuum check valve malfunction.
		6. Replace rear drum(s).
		
		7. Repair or replace parts as necessary.
		8. Test valve as follows:
		  a. Start engine, increase engine speed to 1500 RPM, close throttle and immediately stop engine.
		  b. Wait at least 90 seconds then try brake action.
		  c. If brakes are not vacuum assisted for 2 or more applications, check valve is faulty.

BRAKES—Continued

Condition	Possible Cause	Correction
HARD BRAKE PEDAL, continued	9. Power brake unit has internal bind or incorrect push rod height (too long).	9. Test unit as follows: a. With engine stopped, apply brakes several times to exhaust all vacuum in system. b. Shift transmission into neutral, depress brake pedal and start engine. c. If pedal falls away under foot pressure and less pressure is required to hold pedal in applied position, power unit vacuum system is working. Test power unit as outlined in item (3) under "Decreasing Brake Pedal Travel." If power unit exhibits bind condition, replace power unit. d. If power unit does not exhibit bind condition, disconnect master cylinder and check push rod height with appropriate gauge. If height is not within specifications, replace power unit.
	10. Master cylinder compensator ports (at bottom of reservoirs) blocked by dirt, scale, rust, or have small burrs (blocked ports prevent fluid return to reservoirs).	10. Repair or replace master cylinder. **CAUTION:** Do not attempt to clean blocked ports with wire, pencils, or similar implements.
	11. Brake hoses, tubes, fittings clogged or restricted.	11. Use compressed air to check or unclog parts. Replace any damaged parts.
	12. Brake fluid contaminated with improper fluids (motor oil, transmission fluid, or poor quality brake fluid) causing rubber components to swell and stick in bores.	12. Replace all rubber components and hoses. Flush entire brake system. Refill with recommended brake fluid.
GRABBING BRAKES **(Severe reaction to brake pedal pressure)**	1. Brake lining(s) contaminated by grease or brake fluid.	1. Determine and correct cause of contamination and replace brakeshoes and linings in axle sets.
	2. Parking brake cables incorrectly adjusted or seized.	2. Adjust cables. Free up or replace seized cables.
	3. Power brake unit binding internally or push rod height incorrect.	3. Test unit as outlined in item (3) under Decreasing Brake Pedal Travel. If O.K., check push rod height. If unit has internal bind or incorrect push rod height, replace unit.
	4. Incorrect brake lining or lining loose on brakeshoes.	4. Replace brakeshoes in axle sets.
	5. Brakeshoes bent, cracked, distorted.	5. Replace brakeshoes in axle sets.
	6. Caliper anchor plate bolts loose.	6. Tighten bolts.
	7. Rear brakeshoes binding on support plate ledges.	7. Clean and lubricate ledges. Replace support plate(s) if ledges are deeply grooved. Do not attempt to smooth ledges by grinding.
	8. Rear brake support plates loose.	8. Tighten mounting bolts.
	9. Caliper or wheel cylinder piston sticking or seized.	9. Repair or replace parts as necessary.
	10. Master cylinder pistons sticking or seized in bore.	10. Repair or replace master cylinder.
BRAKES GRAB, PULL, OR WON'T HOLD IN WET WEATHER	1. Brake lining water soaked.	1. Drive car with brakes lightly applied to dry out lining. If problem persists after lining has dried, replace brakeshoe lining in axle sets.
	2. Rear brake support plate bent allowing excessive amount of water to enter drum.	2. Replace support plate.

BRAKES—Continued

Condition	Possible Cause	Correction
DRAGGING BRAKES **(Slow or incomplete release of brakes)**	1. Brake pedal binding at pivot.	1. Free up and lubricate.
	2. Power brake unit push rod height incorrect (too high) or unit has internal bind.	2. Replace unit if push rod height is incorrect. If height is O.K., check for internal bind as outlined in item (3) under "Decreasing Brake Pedal Travel."
	3. Parking brake cables incorrectly adjusted or seized.	3. Adjust cables. Free up or replace seized cables.
	4. Brakeshoe return springs weak or broken.	4. Replace return springs. Replace brakeshoe if necessary in axle sets.
	5. Automatic adjusters malfunctioning.	5. Repair or replace adjuster parts as required.
	6. Caliper, wheel cylinder or master cylinder pistons sticking or seized.	6. Repair or replace parts as necessary.
	7. Master cylinder compensating ports blocked (fluid does not return to reservoirs).	7. Use compressed air to clear ports. Do not use wire, pencils, or similar objects to open blocked ports.
CAR PULLS TO ONE SIDE WHEN BRAKES ARE APPLIED	1. Incorrect front tire pressure.	1. Inflate to recommended cold (reduced load) inflation pressures.
	2. Incorrect front wheel bearing adjustment or worn—damaged wheel bearings.	2. Adjust wheel bearings. Replace worn, damaged bearings.
	3. Brakeshoe lining on one side contaminated.	3. Determine and correct cause of contamination and replace brakeshoe lining in axle sets.
	4. Brakeshoes on one side bent, distorted, or lining loose on shoe.	4. Replace brakeshoes in axle sets.
	5. Support plate bent or loose on one side.	5. Tighten or replace support plate.
	6. Brake lining not yet seated to drums and rotors.	6. Burnish brakes.
	7. Caliper anchor plate loose on one side.	7. Tighten anchor plate bolts.
	8. Caliper or wheel cylinder piston sticking or seized.	8. Repair or replace caliper or wheel cylinder.
	9. Brakeshoe linings watersoaked.	9. Drive car with brakes lightly applied to dry linings. Replace brakeshoes in axle sets if problem persists.
	10. Loose suspension component attaching or mounting bolts, incorrect front end alignment. Worn suspension parts.	10. Tighten suspension bolts. Replace worn suspension components. Check and correct alignment as necessary.
CHATTER OR SHUDDER WHEN BRAKES ARE APPLIED **(Pedal pulsation and roughness may also occur)**	1. Front wheel bearings loose.	1. Adjust wheel bearings.
	2. Brakeshoes distorted, bent, contaminated, or worn.	2. Replace brakeshoes in axle sets.
	3. Caliper anchor plate or support plate loose.	3. Tighten mounting bolts.
	4. Excessive thickness variation or lateral rim out of rotor.	4. Refinish or replace rotor.
	5. Rear drum(s) out of round, sharp spots.	5. Refinish or replace drum.
	6. Loose suspension component attaching or mounting bolts, incorrect front end alignment. Worn suspension parts.	6. Tighten suspension bolts. Replace worn suspension components. Check and correct alignment as necessary.
NOISY BRAKES **(Squealing, clicking, scraping sound when brakes are applied)**	1. Bent, broken, distorted brakeshoes.	1. Replace brakeshoes in axle sets.
	2. Brake lining worn out—shoes contacting drum or rotor.	2. Replace brakeshoes and lining in axle sets. Refinish or replace drums or rotors.
	3. Foreign material imbedded in brake lining.	3. Replace brake lining.
	4. Broken or loose hold-down or return springs.	4. Replace parts as necessary.
	5. Rough or dry drum brake support plate ledges.	5. Lubricate support plate ledges.
	6. Cracked, grooved, or scored rotor(s) or drum(s).	6. Replace rotor(s) or drum(s). Replace brakeshoes and lining in axle sets if necessary.

BRAKES—Continued

Condition	Possible Cause	Correction
PULSATING BRAKE PEDAL	1. Out of round drums or excessive thickness variation or lateral runout in disc brake rotor(s).	1. Refinish or replace drums or rotors.
	2. Bent rear axle shaft.	2. Replace axle shaft.

Steering

Condition	Possible Cause	Correction
EXCESSIVE PLAY OR LOOSENESS IN STEERING	1. Incorrectly adjusted front wheel bearings.	1. Adjust bearings.
	2. Worn steering shaft couplings.	2. Inspect and replace as required.
	3. Steering wheel loose on shaft, loose pitman arm, tie rods, steering arms or steering linkage ball studs.	3. Check and correct steering attachment torques as required.
	4. Worn ball joints.	4. Inspect and replace as required.
	5. Worn intermediate rod or tie rod sockets.	5. Inspect and replace as required.
HARD OR ERRATIC STEERING	1. Incorrect tire pressure.	1. Inflate tires to recommended pressure.
	2. Insufficient or incorrect lubrication.	2. Lubricate as required.
	3. Steering or linkage parts damaged or misaligned.	3. Repair or replace parts as required.
	4. Incorrect front wheel alignment.	4. Adjust wheel alignment angles.
	5. Incorrect steering gear adjustment.	5. Adjust steering gear.
POOR STEERING RETURNABILITY	1. Insufficient ball joint or linkage lubrication.	1. Lubricate as required.
	2. Steering gear adjusted too tightly.	2. Adjust over center and thrust bearing preload.
	3. Steering gear to column misaligned.	3. Align steering column.
	4. Incorrect front wheel alignment (caster).	4. Check alignment and correct as required.
WHEEL SHIMMY OR TRAMP	1. Improper tire pressure.	1. Inflate tires to recommended pressures.
	2. Wheels, tires, or brake drums out-of-balance or out-of-round.	2. Inspect parts and replace unacceptable out-of-round parts. Rebalance parts.
	3. Inoperative, worn, or loose shock absorbers or mounting parts.	3. Repair or replace shocks or mountings.
	4. Loose or worn steering or suspension parts.	4. Tighten or replace as necessary.
	5. Loose or worn wheel bearings.	5. Adjust or replace bearings.
	6. Incorrect steering gear adjustments.	6. Adjust steering gear.
	7. Incorrect front wheel alignment.	7. Correct front wheel alignment.
TIRE WEAR	1. Improper tire pressure.	1. Inflate tires to recommended pressures.
	2. Failure to rotate tires.	2. Rotate tires.
	3. Brakes grabbing.	3. Adjust or repair brakes.
	4. Incorrect front wheel alignment.	4. Align incorrect angles.
	5. Broken or damaged steering and suspension parts.	5. Repair or replace defective parts.
	6. Wheel runout.	6. Replace faulty wheel.
	7. Excessive speed on turns.	7. Make driver aware of condition.
TRUCK LEADS TO ONE SIDE	1. Improper tire pressures.	1. Inflate tires to recommended pressures.
	2. Front tires with uneven tread depth, wear pattern, or different cord design (i.e., one bias ply and one belted tire on front wheels).	2. Install tires of same cord construction and reasonably even tread depth and wear pattern.
	3. Incorrect front wheel alignment.	3. Align incorrect angles.
	4. Brakes dragging.	4. Adjust or repair brakes.
	5. Faulty power steering gear valve assembly.	5. Replace valve assembly.
	6. Pulling due to uneven tire construction.	6. Replace faulty tire.

Suspension

Condition	Possible Cause	Correction
FRONT BOTTOMING OR RIDING LOW	1. Incorrect tire pressure.	1. Inflate tires to recommended pressure.
	2. Incorrect tire and wheel usage.	2. Install correct tire and wheel assembly.
	3. Truck overloaded or unevenly loaded.	3. Correct as required.
	4. Broken or incorrectly installed front springs.	4. Repair or replace as required.
	5. Loose or broken shock absorbers.	5. Tighten or replace as required.
	6. Loose or broken shackles.	6. Tighten or replace as required.
	7. Incorrect truck ride height.	7. Measure vertical distance between axle(s) and spring tower flange/frame rail. If below ride, install shims.
	8. Incorrect springs.	8. Check springs and replace if necessary.
DOG TRACKING OF REAR WHEELS	1. Loose or damaged front and/or rear suspension parts.	1. Inspect, repair or replace as required.
	2. Loose rear spring U-bolts.	2. Check and correct bolt torque as required.
	3. Rear springs incorrectly installed on axle.	3. Repair as required.
	4. Incorrectly installed front coil or leaf springs.	4. Repair as required.
SWAY OR ROLL	1. Unequal load distribution (side to side).	1. Correct as required.
	2. Excessive load or body height.	2. Correct as required.
	3. Incorrect tire pressure.	3. Correct tire inflation pressure.
	4. Loose wheel lug nuts.	4. Torque lug nuts as required.
	5. Worn or loose stabilizer bar assembly.	5. Tighten or replace as required.
	6. Loose or defective shock absorbers.	6. Torque mounting bolts or replace as required.
	7. Broken or sagging spring.	7. Replace spring as required.
FRONT END NOISE	1. Insufficient ball joint or linkage lubricant.	1. Lubricate parts as required.
	2. Worn bushings or loose shock absorber.	2. Tighten bolts and/or replace bushings.
	3. Worn control arm bushings.	3. Replace bushings.
	4. Worn tie rod ends.	4. Replace tie rod ends.
	5. Worn or loose wheel bearings.	5. Adjust or replace wheel bearings.
	6. Loose stabilizer bar.	6. Torque all stabilizer bar attachments as required.
	7. Loose wheel lug nuts.	7. Torque lug nuts as required.
	8. Incorrectly positioned spring.	8. Correctly install spring.
	9. Loose suspension bolts.	9. Check and correct bolt torque as required.
FRONT AXLE NOISE	1. Incorrect lubricant level.	1. Check and fill lubricant as required.
	2. Excessive pinion end-play.	2. Check and adjust end play as required.
	3. Incorrect pinion bearing preload.	3. Check and adjust pinion bearing preload.
	4. Worn and/or damaged pinion or differential bearings.	4. Inspect and replace worn and/or damaged bearings.
	5. Excessive differential bearing preload.	5. Check and adjust differential bearing preload.
	6. Damaged pinion gears.	6. Replace gears.

NOTE: A knocking noise heard at low speed or when coasting may be caused by loose differential side gears. If this is encountered, operate vehicle at speed where noise is loudest and apply brakes lightly. If loose gears are causing the problem, noise level should decrease as brakes are applied.

TROUBLESHOOTING

Exterior Lighting

HEADLAMPS

Condition	Possible Cause	Correction
ONE HEADLAMP INOPERATIVE OR INTERMITTENT	1. Loose connection.	1. Secure connections to sealed beam including ground.
	2. Defective sealed beam.	2. Replace sealed beam.
ONE OR MORE HEADLIGHTS ARE DIM	1. Open ground connection at headlight.	1. Repair ground wire connection between sealed beam and body ground.
	2. Ground wire mislocated in headlight connector (type 2 sealed beam).	2. Relocate ground wire in connector.
ONE OR MORE HEADLIGHTS SHORT LIFE	1. Voltage regulator maladjusted.	1. Readjust regulator to specifications.
ALL HEADLIGHTS INOPERATIVE OR INTERMITTENT	1. Loose connection.	1. Check and secure connections at dimmer switch and light switch.
	2. Defective dimmer switch.	2. Check voltage at dimmer switch with test lamp. If test lamp bulb lights only at switch "Hot" wire terminal, replace dimmer switch.
	3. Open wiring—light switch to dimmer switch.	3. Check wiring with test lamp. If bulb lights at light switch wire terminal, but not at dimmer switch, repair open wire.
	4. Open wiring—light switch to battery.	4. Check "Hot" wire terminal at light switch with test lamp. If lamp does not light, repair open wire circuit to battery (possible open fusible link).
	5. Shorted ground circuit.	5. If, after a few minutes operation, headlights flicker "ON" and "OFF" and/or a thumping noise can be heard from the light switch (circuit breaker opening and closing), repair short to ground in circuit between light switch and headlights. After repairing short, check for headlight flickering after one minute operation. If flickering occurs, the circuit breaker has been damaged and light switch must be replaced.
	6. Defective light switch.	6. Check light switch. Replace light switch, if defective.
UPPER OR LOWER BEAM WILL NOT LIGHT OR INTERMITTENT	1. Open connection or defective dimmer switch.	1. Check dimmer switch terminals with test lamp. If bulb lights at all wire terminals, repair open wiring between dimmer switch and headlights. If bulb will not light at one of these terminals, replace dimmer switch.
	2. Short circuit to ground.	2. Follow diagnosis above (all headlights inoperative or intermittent).

SIDE MARKER LAMPS

Condition	Possible Cause	Correction
ONE LAMP INOPERATIVE	1. Turn signal bulb burnt out (front lamp).	1. Switch turn signals on. If signal bulb does not light, replace bulb.
	2. Side marker bulb burnt out.	2. Replace bulb.
	3. Loose connection or open in wiring.	3. Using test lamp, check "Hot" wire terminal at bulb socket. If test lamp lights, repair open ground circuit. If lamp does not light, repair open "Hot" wire circuit.

SIDE MARKER LAMPS—Continued

Condition	Possible Cause	Correction
FRONT OR REAR LAMPS INOPERATIVE	1. Loose connection or open ground connection.	1. If associated tail or park lamps do not operate, secure all connectors in "Hot" wire circuit. If park and turn lamps operate, repair open ground connections.
	2. Multiple bulbs burnt out.	2. Replace burnt out bulbs.
ALL LAMPS INOPERATIVE	1. Blown fuse.	1. If park and tail lamps do not operate, replace blown fuse. If new fuse blows, check for short to ground between fuse panel and lamps.
	2. Loose connection.	2. Secure connector to light switch.
	3. Open in wiring.	3. Check tail light fuse with test lamp. If test lamp lights, repair open wiring between fuse and light switch. If not, repair open wiring between fuse and battery (possible open fusible link).
	4. Defective light switch.	4. Check light switch. Replace light switch, if defective.

TAIL, PARK AND LICENSE LAMPS

Condition	Possible Cause	Correction
ONE SIDE INOPERATIVE	1. Bulb burnt out.	1. Replace bulb.
	2. Open ground connection at bulb socket or ground wire terminal.	2. Jump bulb base socket connection to ground. If lamp lights, repair open ground circuit.
BOTH SIDES INOPERATIVE	1. Tail lamp fuse blown.	1. Replace fuse. If new fuse blows, repair short to ground in "Hot" wire circuit between fuse panel through light switch to lamps.
	2. Loose connection.	2. Secure connector at light switch.
	3. Open wiring.	3. Using test light, check circuit on both sides of fuse. If lamp does not light on either side, repair open circuit between fuse panel and battery (possible open fusible link). If test lamp lights at light switch terminal, repair open wiring between light switch and lamps.
	4. Multiple bulb burnout.	4. If test lamp lights at lamp socket "Hot" wire terminal, replace bulbs.
	5. Defective light switch.	5. Check light switch. Replace light switch, if defective.

TURN SIGNAL AND HAZARD WARNING LAMP

Condition	Possible Cause	Correction
TURN SIGNALS INOPERATIVE ONE SIDE	1. Bulb(s) burnt out (flasher cannot be heard).	1. Turn hazard warning system on. If one or more bulbs are inoperative replace necessary bulbs.
	2. Open wiring or ground connection.	2. Turn hazard warning system on. If one or more bulbs are inoperative, use test lamp and check circuit at lamp socket. If test lamp lights, repair open ground connection. If not, repair open wiring between bulb socket and turn signal switch.
	3. Improper bulb or defective turn signal switch.	3. Turn hazard warning system on. If all front and rear lamps operate, check for improper bulb. If bulbs are O.K., replace defective turn signal switch.
	4. Short to ground (flasher can be heard, no bulbs operate).	4. Locate and repair short to ground by disconnecting front and rear circuits separately.

TROUBLESHOOTING

TURN SIGNAL AND HAZARD WARNING LAMP—Continued

Condition	Possible Cause	Correction
TURN SIGNALS INOPERATIVE	1. Blown turn signal fuse.	1. Turn hazard warning system on. If all lamps operate, replace blown fuse. If new fuse blows, repair short to ground between fuse and lamps.
	2. Defective flasher.	2. If turn signal fuse is O.K. and hazard warning system will operate lamps, replace defective turn signal flasher.
	3. Loose connection.	3. Secure steering column connector.
HAZARD WARNING LAMPS INOPERATIVE	1. Blown fuse.	1. Switch turn signals on. If lamps operate, replace fuse if blown. If new fuse blows, repair short to ground. (could be in stop light circuit).
	2. Defective hazard warning flasher.	2. If fuse is O.K., switch turn signals on. If lamps operate, replace defective hazard flasher.
	3. Open in wiring or defective turn signal switch.	3. Using test lamp, check hazard switch feed wire in turn signal steering column connector. If lamp does not light on either side of connector, repair open circuit between flasher and connector. If lamp lights only on feed side of connector, clean connector contacts. If lamp lights on both sides of connector, replace defective turn signal switch assembly.

BACK-UP LAMP

Condition	Possible Cause	Correction
ONE LAMP INOPERATIVE OR INTERMITTENT	1. Loose or burnt out bulb.	1. Secure or replace bulb.
	2. Loose connection.	2. Tighten connectors.
	3. Open ground connections.	3. Repair bulb ground circuit.
BOTH LAMPS INOPERATIVE OR INTERMITTENT	1. Neutral start or back-up lamp switch maladjusted.	1. Readjust or replace bulb.
	2. Loose connection or open circuit.	2. Secure all connectors. If O.K., check continuity of circuit from fuse to lamps with test lamp. If lamp does not light on either side of fuse, correct open circuit from battery to fuse.
	3. Blown fuse.	3. Replace fuse. If new fuse blows, repair short to ground in circuit from fuse through neutral start switch to back-up lamps.
	4. Defective neutral start or back-up lamp switch.	4. Check switch. Replace neutral start or back-up lamp switch, if defective.
	5. Defective ignition switch.	5. If test lamp lights at ignition switch battery terminal but not at output terminal, replace ignition switch.
LAMP WILL NOT TURN OFF	1. Neutral start or back-up switch maladjusted.	1. Readjust neutral start or back-up lamp switch.
	2. Defective neutral start or back-up lamp switch.	2. Check switch. Replace neutral start or back-up lamp switch, if defective.

STOP LIGHTS

Condition	Possible Cause	Correction
ONE BULB INOPERATIVE	1. Bulb burnt out.	1. Replace bulb.
ONE SIDE INOPERATIVE	1. Loose connection, open wiring or defective bulbs.	1. Turn on directional signal. If lamp does not operate, check bulbs. If bulbs are O.K., secure all connections. If lamp still does not operate, use test lamp and check for open wiring.

STOP LIGHTS—Continued

Condition	Possible Cause	Correction
ONE SIDE INOPERATIVE, continued	2. Defective directional signal switch or cancelling cam.	2. If lamp will operate by turning directional signal on, the switch is not centering properly during cancelling operation. Replace defective cancelling cam or directional signal switch.
ALL INOPERATIVE	1. Blown fuse.	1. Replace fuse. If new fuse blows, repair short to ground in circuit between fuse and lamps.
	2. Stop-switch maladjusted or defective.	2. Check stop switch. Adjust or replace stop switch, if required.
WILL NOT TURN OFF	1. Stop switch maladjusted or defective.	1. Readjust switch. If switch still malfunctions, replace.

Horns

Condition	Possible Cause	Correction
HORNS WILL NOT OPERATE	1. Loose connections in circuit.	1. Check and tighten connections. Be sure to check ground straps.
	2. Defective horn switch.	2. Replace defective parts.
	3. Defective horn relay.	3. Replace relay.
	4. Defects within horn.	4. Replace horn.
HORNS HAVE POOR TONE	1. Low available voltage at horn, or defects within horn.	1. Check battery and charging circuit. Although horn should blow at any voltage above 7.0 volts, a weak or poor tone may occur at operating voltage below 11.0 volts. If horn has weak or poor tone at operating voltage of 11.0 volts or higher, remove horn and replace.
HORNS OPERATE INTERMITTENTLY	1. Loose or intermittent connections in horn relay or horn switch.	1. Check and tighten connections.
	2. Defective horn switch.	2. Replace switch.
	3. Defective relay.	3. Replace relay.
	4. Defects within horn.	4. Replace horn.
HORNS BLOW CONSTANTLY	1. Sticking horn relay.	1. Replace relay.
	2. Horn relay energized by grounded or shorted wiring.	2. Check and adjust wiring.
	3. Horn button can be grounded by sticking closed.	3. Adjust or replace damaged parts.

Speedometer

Condition	Possible Cause	Correction
SPEEDOMETER NOT OPERATING PROPERLY	1. Noisy speedometer cable.	1. Loosen over-tightened casing nuts and snap-on at speedometer head. Replace housing and core. Replace broken cable.
	2. Pointer and odometer inoperative. Inaccurate reading.	2. Check tire size. Check for correct speedometer driven gear.
	3. Kinked cable.	3. Replace cable. Reroute casing so that bends have no less than 6″ radius.
	4. Defective speedometer head.	4. Replace speedometer.
	5. Casing connector loose on speedometer case.	5. Tighten connector.

Noise, Vibration & Harshness

ROAD TEST

A road test and customer interview can provide much of the information needed to identify the specific condition which must be dealt with.

1. Make notes during diagnosis routine. This will ensure diagnosis is complete and systematic. Take care not to overlook details.
2. Road test vehicle and study condition by reproducing it several times during test.
3. When condition is reproduced, perform road test checks immediately. Refer to "Road Test Quick Checks" to identify proper section of diagnostic procedure. Perform checks several times to ensure valid conclusions. While the quick checks may not locate the problem, they will indicate the areas where there are no problems.
4. Do not make changes or adjustments before a road test and inspection of vehicle are performed. Any changes made can hide problems or add additional problems. Check and note tire pressures, any leaks, loose nuts or bolts, shiny spots where components may be rubbing, and if any unusually heavy items are loaded onto truck.

ROAD TEST QUICK CHECKS

1. **25–50 mph**—Under light acceleration, a moaning noise can be heard possibly accompanied by a vibration in floor. Refer to "Tip-In Moan" diagnostic procedure.
2. **25–45 mph**—Under steady to heavy acceleration, a rumbling noise can be heard. Refer to "Incorrect Driveline Angle" diagnostic procedure.
3. **High Speed**—Under slow acceleration and deceleration, shaking is noticeable in steering column or wheel, seats, floor pan, trim panels, or front end sheet metal. Refer to "High Speed Shake" procedure.
4. **High Speed**—Vibration can be felt in floor pan or seats, with no visible shaking but with rumble, buzz, hum, or booming noise. Refer to "Driveline Vibration" procedure.
5. **High Speed**—Coast with clutch disengaged or with automatic transmission in neutral and engine idling. If vibration is present, refer to "Driveline Vibration" procedure. If vibration is no longer present, refer to "Engine and Accessory Vibration" or "High Speed Shake" procedures.
6. **0–High Speed**—Vibration can be felt when engine reaches particular RPM. Vibration can also be felt when vehicle

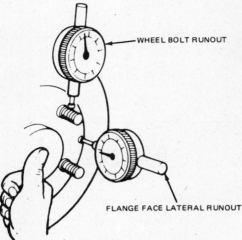

WHEEL BOLT RUNOUT

FLANGE FACE LATERAL RUNOUT

Fig. 1   Checking axle flange & wheel bolt run-out

is stationary. Refer to "Engine and Accessory Vibration."

TYPES OF CONDITIONS

HIGH SPEED SHAKE (35 MPH)

This condition involves a visible shake and pumping feeling in steering column, seats, or floor pan. The vibration is of low frequency (about 9–15 cycles per second) and may be seen as front end sheet metal shake. The condition may or may not be intensified by lightly applying brakes.

TIP-IN MOAN (15–50 MPH)

Acceleration between 15–50 mph is accompanied by vibration which causes moan or high frequency resonance in floor pan. This condition is usually worse at a particular engine speed and at a particular throttle opening during acceleration at that speed. A moaning sound may also be caused depending on which component is producing the noise.

DRIVELINE VIBRATION (50 MPH)

This condition does not involve a visible vibration, but is felt in floor pan as rumble, buzz, hum, drone, or boom. This condition is independent of engine speed and will occur at same speed in any gear, and is not sensitive to acceleration or deceleration and cannot be reduced by coasting in neutral. The condition can be duplicated by supporting vehicle on axle-type hoist and operating driveline in gear at appropriate speed.

ENGINE OR ACCESSORY VIBRATION (ALL SPEEDS)

This condition can occur at any vehicle speed but always at same engine RPM. Vibration will disappear during neutral coast and can be duplicated by operating engine at problem RPM with vehicle stationary. The condition can be caused by any component turning at engine speed when vehicle is stationary.

HIGH SPEED SHAKE

1. Apply brakes gently. If shake increases, proceed to step 2; if shake does not increase, proceed to step 10.
2. Lightly apply parking brake. If shake increases, proceed to step 3; if shake does not increase, proceed to step 6.
3. Check clearance between rear drum and brake shoe. Loosen cable tension if necessary. If clearance is correct, proceed to step 4; if clearance is not correct, proceed to step 7.
4. Using dial indicator, check axle flange run-out, **Fig. 1.** If run-out is acceptable, proceed to step 5. If run-out is unacceptable, proceed to step 8.
5. Check run-out of rear brake drum or disc. If run-out is acceptable, proceed to step 10. If run-out is unacceptable, proceed to step 9.
6. Check run-out of front brake disc. If run-out is acceptable, proceed to step 10. If run-out is unacceptable, proceed to step 9.
7. Adjust parking brake cable tension and road test vehicle. If shake is not eliminated, proceed to step 4.
8. Replace axle shaft and road test vehicle. If shake is not eliminated, proceed to step 5.
9. Replace or machine brake drums or discs and road test vehicle. If shake is not eliminated, proceed to step 10.
10. Raise and support vehicle. Turn wheels by hand and check for abnormal wear, damage, wheel bearing play or roughness. If abnormal wear or damage is found, proceed to step 12. If wheel bearing displays excessive play or roughness, proceed to step 13. If brakes drag, proceed to steps 5 and 6.
11. Road test vehicle, noting carefully which area of vehicle is shaking. If front end sheet metal is shaking heavily, proceed to step 14. If shaking is felt more in floor pan, seat and steering column, proceed to step 15.
12. Replace worn or damaged tires and

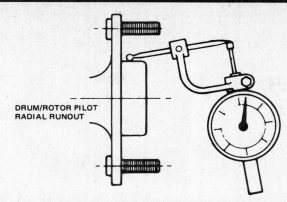

Fig. 2 Checking drum/rotor pilot radial run-out

check for any other damaged components such as shock absorbers. Road test vehicle. If vehicle still shakes, proceed to step 15.

13. Check and adjust wheel bearings. Replace damaged wheel bearings and road test vehicle. If shake is not eliminated, proceed to step 15.

14. Check and tighten all major front end sheet metal attaching bolts and adjust hood rests. Road test vehicle. If shake is not eliminated, proceed to step 15.

15. Balance wheels on vehicle and check tires and rims for run-out. If wheel balancing is not necessary, proceed to step 16. If wheel and tire run-out are found, proceed to step 19.

16. Road test vehicle at speed at which condition was most apparent. If shake is not eliminated, proceed to step 17.

17. Install a known good set of wheels and tires on vehicle and road test. If shake is eliminated, proceed to step 18. If shake is not eliminated, proceed to step 23.

18. If one or more of the tires has a construction irregularity which causes tire to contact the road in an irregular manner, substitute known good tires until irregular tires are located.

19. Attempt to reduce run-out by mounting wheel in different position in relation to axle. If run-out is now acceptable, proceed to step 16. If run-out is still excessive, proceed to step 17. If repositioning indicates axle shaft run-out, proceed to step 22. If repositioning indicates tire and wheel run-out, proceed to step 20.

20. Attempt to correct run-out by repositioning tire on rim. If run-out is acceptable, proceed to step 15. If run-out is still excessive, proceed to step 21.

21. Replace component shown to be unserviceable and recheck run-out. If run-out is acceptable, proceed to step 15. If run-out is excessive, proceed to step 22.

22. Measure axle shaft run-out, **Fig. 2.** Replace shaft if run-out is excessive and check run-out of new shaft. Install wheel and check run-out again. If run-out is acceptable, proceed to step 15. If run-out is excessive, proceed to step 20.

23. Raise and support vehicle. Remove rear wheels and tires. Check all axle and brake rotor run-out measurements if not already checked. If axle and brake run-out are acceptable, proceed to step 24. If axle run-out is excessive, proceed to step 8. If brake disc run-out is excessive, proceed to step 9.

24. Check driveshaft run-out. If run-out is acceptable, proceed to step 25. If run-out is excessive, proceed to step 27.

25. Remove driveshaft and inspect universal joints. If joints are O.K., proceed to step 26. If joints are defective, replace joints.

26. Install driveshaft and check for vibration. If vibration is unacceptable, proceed to step 27.

27. Measure ring gear run-out. If run-out is excessive, proceed to step 28.

28. Install new ring and pinion. Check run-out to ensure parts are within specifications. Recheck for vibration.

MOANING NOISE DURING LIGHT ACCELERATION

1. Inspect air cleaner for correct positioning of gasket, lid and gasket, element and duct. Correct if necessary and check condition. If noise is unacceptable, proceed to step 2.

2. On vehicles where a transmission extension housing damper is specified, ensure damper is installed. Recheck condition, if noise is unacceptable, proceed to step 3.

3. Loosen engine mounts, start engine, and shift from Neutral to Drive and back to normalize engine mounts. Tighten engine mounts and check condition; if noise is unacceptable, proceed to step 4.

4. With exhaust system hot, loosen hangers, and operate engine while shifting from Neutral to Drive and back to normalize exhaust system. Tighten hangers and recheck condition; if noise is unacceptable, proceed to step 5.

5. Inspect accessory drive belts for prop-

er tension and accessory brackets for proper bolt torques. Adjust or tighten if necessary and check condition, if noise is unacceptable, proceed to step 6.

6. Loosen all bell housing bolts ¾ turn to test if noise is reduced. If noise is reduced, recheck step 2.

DRIVELINE VIBRATION

NOTE: Driveline vibration is a higher frequency, lower amplitude vibration than high speed shake, directly related to road speeds of 45 mph and higher. This type of vibration will be felt in the floor pan or heard as a rumble, hum, buzz or boom and will be present in all driving modes. The vibration may vary during acceleration, deceleration or coasting conditions. A driveline vibration can usually be duplicated with the axle supported, through light braking applications while accelerating and decelerating to simulate road load resistance.

1. Raise and support vehicle with drive wheels free. Operate driveline at problem speed. If vibration is present, proceed to step 3; if vibration is not present, proceed to step 2.

2. Retest vehicle to observe reported condition.

3. Evaluate noise and vibration by operating driveline at problem speed. If audible boom or rumble occurs above 45 mph, proceed to step 4. If buzzy feel occurs in floor pan above 45 mph, proceed to step 5. If a gravelly feel or grinding sound occurs at low speeds, proceed to step 4.

4. Install rear spring dampers if available for vehicle. If condition is still unacceptable or dampers are not available, proceed to step 5.

5. Scribe a line to index rear axle companion flange to driveshaft flange. Inspect drive shaft for dents, undercoating, proper seating of U-joint bearing caps, and tight U-joints. If driveshaft is in acceptable condition, proceed to step 6. Replace driveshaft if damaged. Replace U-joints if worn or improperly positioned.

6. Inspect wheel bearings. If bearings are O.K., proceed to step 10; if wheel bearings are not in acceptable condition, proceed to step 7.

7. Replace wheel bearings and retest for vibration. If vibration is unacceptable proceed to step 10.

8. Repair or replace driveshaft. If vibration is unacceptable proceed to step 10.

9. Reposition U-joint bearing caps or replace U-joints. If vibration is unacceptable, proceed to step 10.

10. Disconnect driveshaft from rear axle companion flange and reconnect 180° from original position. Operate driveline at problem speed. If vibration is unacceptable, install rear axle pinion nose damper if available for vehicle. If

pinion damper is not available or vibration is still unacceptable, proceed to step 11.

11. Disconnect driveshaft and return to original position. Refer to "Driveshaft Run-out," procedure and check run-out at front, center, and rear of driveshaft. If run-out is less than .035 inch at all positions, proceed to step 15 of "High Speed Shake" diagnosis. If run-out at front and/or center of driveshaft exceeds .035 inch while rear of shaft is acceptable, proceed to step 8. If run-out at rear of driveshaft exceeds .035 inch, proceed to "Driveshaft Run-out Check" procedure.

12. Balance driveshaft on vehicle and test vehicle at problem speed. If vibration is still unacceptable, proceed to step 17 of "High Speed Shake" diagnosis.

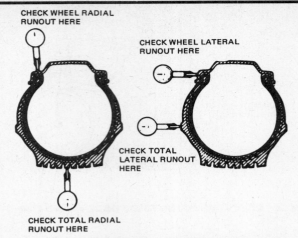

Fig. 3   Checking tire/wheel radial run-out

INCORRECT PINION ANGLE

1. Ensure U-joints are tight and all bearing caps are in plate. If U-joints are in good condition, proceed to step 3; if not, proceed to step 2.
2. Make an index mark on driveshaft and rear axle companion flange. Remove driveshaft and replace U-joints. Retest vehicle; if vibration is unacceptable, proceed to step 3.
3. Refer to "Driveline Pinion Angle Check" procedure to check pinion angle.
4. If pinion angle is correct, proceed to step 1 of "Driveline Vibration."

ENGINE OR ACCESSORY VIBRATION

1. With vehicle stationary, run engine at problem speed to check for condition. If vibration is present, proceed to step 2; if not, proceed to step 1 of "Driveline Vibration" diagnosis.
2. Inspect drive belts to check for wear or fraying. Ensure pulleys are not damaged or bent. Replace any damaged components and operate engine at problem speed. If vibration is present, proceed to step 3.
3. Check drive belt tension and adjust if necessary. Operate engine at problem speed. If vibration is still present, proceed to step 4.
4. Check torque of all accessory bracket bolts and retorque as necessary. Operate engine at problem speed; if vibration is still present, proceed to step 5.
5. Check pulley alignment and run-out visually at idle. Realign or replace pulleys if necessary. Operate engine at problem speed; if condition is still present, proceed to step 6.
6. Inspect belts for severe whipping at problem speed. If whip cannot be cor-

rected by adjusting tension, replace belts. Operate engine at problem speed; if condition is still present, proceed to step 7.
7. Check engine accessories for noise while operating engine at problem speed. If vibration is still present, proceed to step 9. If vibration is not present, proceed to step 8.
8. Repair or replace noisy accessory. Connect and tension drive belt. Operate engine at problem speed; if vibration is still present, proceed to step 9.
9. Remove accessory from bracket. Inspect all hardware and bracket. Repair or replace as necessary.

CHECKS & ADJUSTMENTS
TIRE/WHEEL RUN-OUT

1. After road test, promptly raise car on hoist to prevent flat spots in tires. Spin front wheels by hand to check for rough wheel bearings. Ensure bearings are not loose and adjust if necessary. If bearings are O.K., proceed to step 2. If bearings have rough feel, proceed to step 2.
2. Check total radial and lateral run-out of tire and wheel assembly, **Fig. 3**. If both run-out measurements are less than .070 inch, balance tires. If lateral run-out exceeds .070 inch, proceed to step 3. If radial run-out exceeds .070 inch, proceed to step 4.
3. Check wheel rim lateral run-out. If run-out is less than .045 inch, replace tire and proceed to step 2. If run-out exceeds .045 inch, replace wheel and proceed to step 2.
4. Mark point of maximum run-out on tire thread. Check radial run-out of wheel. If radial run-out of wheel exceeds .045 inch, replace wheel and proceed to step 2. If radial run-out of wheel is less than .045 inch, proceed to step 5.

5. Mark point of least run-out on wheel. Remove tire from wheel and match point of maximum tire run-out with point of least run-out on wheel. Mount tire in this position and check total radial run-out of wheel and tire assembly. If total radial run-out is less than .070 inch, balance tires. If run-out exceeds .070 inch, replace tire and proceed to step 2.

DRIVESHAFT RUNOUT

1. Raise and support vehicle. Mark position of drive wheels or hub lugs for installation, then remove wheels.
2. On one piece driveshafts, proceed as follows:
   a. Using a suitable dial indicator, measure driveshaft run-out at front, center and rear of driveshaft. Rotate driveshaft by turning brake drum or brake rotor.
   b. If measured run-out exceeds .035 inch at front or center, replace driveshaft.
   c. If front and center run-out measurements are within specified amount and rear is not, mark rear run-out high point and proceed to step 4.
   d. If run-out exceeds specified amount at all test points, proceed to "Driveshaft Balance."
3. On two piece driveshafts, proceed as follows:
   a. Using a suitable dial indicator, measure run-out at areas A through F as shown in **Fig. 4**. Rotate coupling shaft or driveshaft by turning rear wheel or drum.
   b. Mark run-out high points on coupling shaft and driveshaft.
   c. If run-out exceeds .035 inch at areas A, B or C, replace coupling shaft.
   d. If run-out exceeds .035 inch at areas D or E, replace driveshaft.
   e. If run-out at front, center or rear is less than .035 inch, proceed to

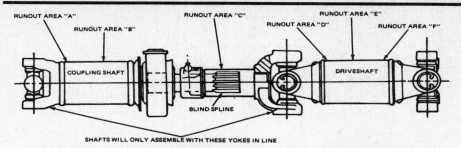

Fig. 4   Two piece driveshaft run-out check areas

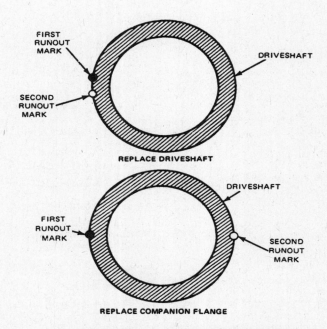

Fig. 5   Checking driveshaft run-out

"Driveshaft Balance."

f. If run-out at area F exceeds .035 inch, mark run-out high point on shaft.

4. Note or mark indexing of driveshaft to rear axle pinion flange. Disconnect driveshaft, turn 180° and reconnect. Check run-out at rear of shaft. If run-out exceeds .035 inch, mark run-out high point and proceed to step 5. If run-out is within specified amount, check for vibration at road test speed. If vibration is still present proceed to "Driveshaft Balance."

5. Excessive driveshaft run-out may originate in the driveshaft, pinion yoke or flange. To determine which, compare the two run-out high points marked in steps 2, 3 and 4, **Fig. 5.** If the marks are within 1 inch of each other, replace driveshaft and recheck for vibration. If the marks are on opposite sides of the driveshaft, approximately 180° apart, the yoke or flange is worn and/or damaged.

NOTE: During replacement of a yoke type flange, driveshaft run-out should not exceed .035 inch when reconnected. When run-out is within specified amount, check for vibration at road speed and road test if vibration is not present or substantially reduced. if vibration persists, proceed to "Driveshaft Balance."

DRIVESHAFT BALANCE

Two methods are possible depending on the method of connecting the driveshaft to the differential. Some vehicles are equipped with a drilled companion flange at the differential which allows re-indexing of the driveshaft in 45° increments. Driveshafts not equipped with this style flange can be balanced using worm-drive hose clamps, **Fig. 6.**

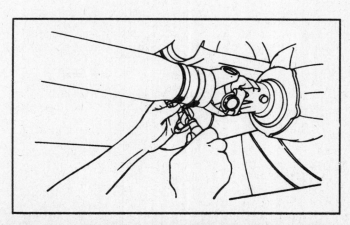

Fig. 6   Balancing driveshaft using hose clamps

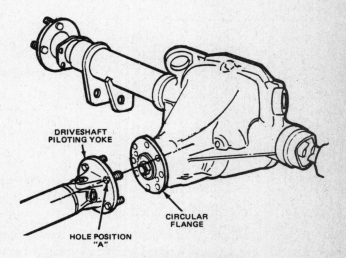

Fig. 7   Driveshaft indexing

TROUBLESHOOTING

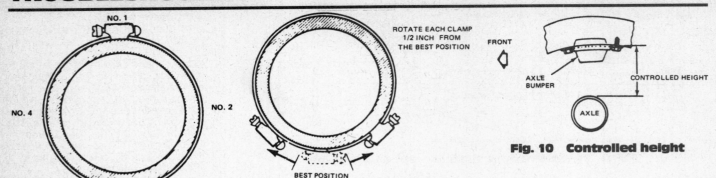

Fig. 8　Installing hose clamp

Fig. 9　Optimizing clamp location

Fig. 10　Controlled height

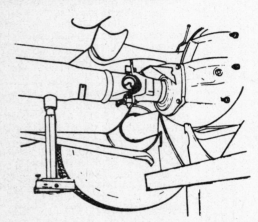

Fig. 11　Positioning driveline angle gauge on driveshaft

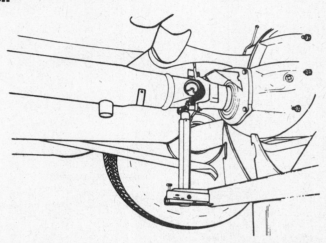

Fig. 12　Positioning driveline angle gauge on pinion U-joint cap

Re-indexing Method

1. Mark one hole of rear U-joint yoke flange with letter A. Number rear axle pinion flange holes 1 through 8 starting with hole opposite yoke flange hole A, **Fig. 7**. Position A-1 will be considered original index position.

NOTE: Check U-joints for binding while re-indexing.

2. Index driveshaft 180° to position A-5. Road test vehicle. If condition is still unsatisfactory, check condition in position A-3 and position A-7.
3. If further improvement is necessary, evaluate remaining positions that are located between best of previous positions A-3 and A-7.
4. Coat flange bolts with suitable thread locking compound and torque to 70–95 ft. lbs.

Hose Clamp Method

1. Make a mark to index rear axle companion flange to driveshaft. Disconnect driveshaft at flange, turn 180° and reconnect. If vibration increases, return driveshaft to original position. If

vibration is reduced, proceed to step 2.

2. Mark rear of driveshaft with 4 equal sections numbered 1 through 4. Install a worm-drive hose clamp with screw at position 1 on driveshaft, **Fig. 8**. Operate driveline at problem speed. Check with clamp in each position. If vibration is worse in each position, proceed to step 5. If vibration is reduced in any one position, proceed to step 3. If vibration is reduced in any 2 positions, turn clamp between those positions and proceed to step 3.
3. Install additional clamp with screw in same position as first clamp in its best position. Operate driveline at problem speed. If vibration is same or increased, proceed to step 4.
4. Rotate each clamp screw ½ inch away in opposite directions, **Fig. 9**. If vibration is reduced, continue to move clamp screws apart until vibration is minimal. If vibration is still excessive, proceed to step 5.
5. Install wheels and road test vehicle to check if vibration might be acceptable on road. If vibration is unacceptable, proceed to step 17 of "High Speed Shake" diagnosis procedure.

DRIVELINE PINION ANGLE CHECKING

1. Raise vehicle on drive-on hoist, ensuring vehicle is at proper controlled height, **Fig. 10**.
2. Turn driveshaft so pinion U-joint bearing cap is facing down.
3. Place Vee magnet from pinion angle measuring tool T68P-4602-A or equivalent on driveshaft. Working from left side of vehicle, position pinion angle gauge on Vee magnet with adjusting screw towards front of vehicle. Adjust screw so bubble just contacts zero line, **Fig. 11**.
4. Move gauge to U-joint bearing cap with tool in same relative position as it was on Vee magnet, **Fig. 12**.
5. Read position on left edge of bubble on scale to determine driveshaft pinion angle. If pinion angle is not correct, adjust. Recheck and proceed to step 6.
6. Position Vee magnet on front of driveshaft and position gauge on magnet. Zero bubble and move gauge to downward facing U-joint bearing cap at rear of transmission. Read driveline angle and compare with specification.

Electrical

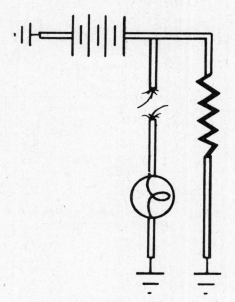

Fig. 1   Open circuit

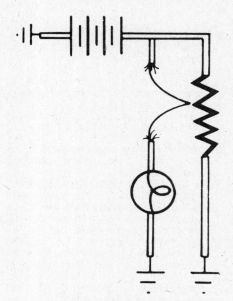

Fig. 2   Short circuit

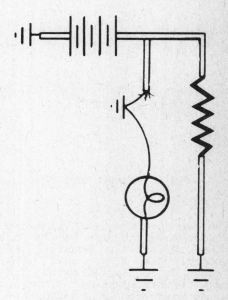

Fig. 3   Grounded circuit

CIRCUIT MALFUNCTIONS

There are three types of electrical malfunctions that cause an inoperative circuit. They are the open circuit, short circuit and grounded circuit.

OPEN CIRCUIT

When there is a complete break in the normal current patch such as a broken wire, **Fig. 1,** it prevents the flow of electricity from the source of power to the electrical unit or from the electrical unit to the ground. In the automotive electrical circuit, the current usually flows through wires or cables, through switches and an electrical component. The component may be grounded through its mounting attachments or another wire to ground and back to the source. A break anywhere along this route results in an open circuit and a complete loss of power. A break in the circuit is an infinite high resistance. However, symptoms will appear different than the typical high resistance circuit. For example, there will be no heat created by this type of malfunction since there is no current flow. An ammeter will not produce a reading since there is no current flow. A voltmeter, depending on where it is placed in the circuit in relation to the "Open", may or may not register a reading.

A high resistance in a circuit reduces current flow and causes the unit to operate intermittently or not at all. An open or high resistance circuit may be caused by a broken wire in the wiring harness, loose connections at terminals, broken leads or wiring within the units or poor ground connections between the unit and the ground.

SHORT CIRCUIT

A short circuit, **Fig. 2,** is basically one that is completed the wrong way, such as two bare wires contacting each other so the current bypasses part of the circuit. When the current bypasses part of the circuit, it has found the path of least resistance and a higher current flow results. This causes blown fuses, wiring and component overheating, burned components and insulation, and inoperative components.

A short circuit causes more current flow through the conductor than the conductor can handle. This causes the conductor to overheat and, if the overload is severe or lasts long enough, will melt the wire and burn the insulation. If the wire melts through, there is no path for the current to flow and the circuit becomes an open circuit.

GROUNDED CIRCUIT

A grounded circuit, **Fig. 3,** is similar to the short circuit since a grounded circuit also bypasses part of the normal circuit. However, the current flows directly to ground. A grounded circuit may be caused by a bare wire contacting the ground, or part of the circuit within a component contacting the frame or housing of the component. A grounded circuit may also be caused by deposits of dirt, oil or moisture around the connections or terminals since these deposits provide a path for the current to flow to ground. The current follows the path of least resistance to complete the circuit back to ground.

CIRCUIT PROTECTION
FUSES

The most common circuit protector in the automotive electrical system is the fuse. The fuse consists of a thin wire or strip of metal enclosed in a glass tube. Some vehicles use a new type fuse where the wire is enclosed in plastic. The wire or metal strip melts when there is an overload caused by a short or grounded circuit. The fuse is designed to melt before the wiring or electrical components are damaged. The cause of the overload must be located and repaired before the new fuse is installed since the new fuse will also blow.

Fuses are rated in amperes. Since different circuits carry various amounts of current, depending upon load components and wire gauge, the properly rated fuse must be installed in the circuit. Never install a fuse with a higher amperage rating than the original.

CIRCUIT BREAKERS

Circuit breakers incorporate a bimetallic

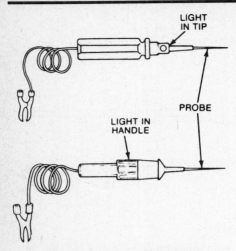

Fig. 4   12 volt test light

strip which, when heated by an overloaded circuit, moves and opens the contacts to break the circuit. When the bimetallic strip cools, it returns to the original position, closing the contacts and completing the circuit. The circuit breaker will open and close the circuit until the overload is located and repaired or the circuit is opened with a switch.

FUSIBLE LINK

A fusible link is a short length of wire connected into a heavy feed circuit of the wiring system. The wire is generally four gauge sizes smaller than the circuit being protected and is used when the circuit is not protected by a fuse or circuit breaker. The fusible link is designed to melt in event of an overload before damage can occur to the circuit. Fusible links are marked on the insulation with the wire gauge size since the heavy insulation causes the link to appear heavier in wire size. Engine compartment wiring harnesses incorporate fusible links. When replacing a fusible link, the overload must be located and repaired and the same size fusible link installed in the circuit.

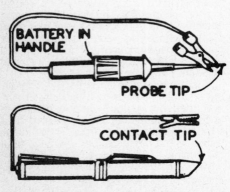

Fig. 6   Self powered test light

TEST LAMP
UNPOWERED TYPE

A test light consists of a 12 volt lamp bulb fitted with a pair of convenient test leads or one lead and a probe, **Fig. 4**. This test light is used with the power "On."

Check for Power
1. Connect one of the leads to a good ground or the battery negative terminal, **Fig. 5**.
2. Use the other test lead to check for power at the suspected wires, connectors or components.
3. If the light illuminates, power exists at the location being tested.

Blown Fuse Condition Check
1. Turn off all equipment powered through the fuse.
2. Disconnect all load items powered through the fuse. If a motor is present in the circuit, disconnect the motor connector. If a light is present in the circuit, remove the lamp bulb.
3. Turn ignition switch to "Run" position if necessary to supply power to the fuse, then turn "On" the equipment switches.
4. Connect one test lead to the "Hot" end of the blown fuse and the other lead to a good ground. The light should illuminate, indicating power to the fuse.
5. Disconnect the test lead connected to ground and connect lead to the other end of the blown fuse. If the light does not illuminate, it indicates that the short circuit has been removed by disconnecting the equipment. If the light illuminates, it indicates that a ground is present in the wiring. Isolate the ground by disconnecting the connectors in the circuit one at a time. Refer to the "Power Check".

SELF-POWERED TYPE

The self-powered test light is a light and battery holder assembly fitted with test leads, or a test lead and a probe, **Fig. 6**. The light battery and test leads are connected in series so when the test leads are connected to two points of a continuous circuit, the light will illuminate, **Fig. 7**. This test light is used with the power "Off".

Continuity Check
Connect test leads to the ends of the suspected circuit. If the light illuminates, it indicates that the circuit is continuous and not broken. This test light may also be used to test a switch or other component. Connect the test leads to the switch terminals. If the light illuminates, the switch contacts are closed. At least one of the switch terminals should be disconnected from the normal switch circuit, so that only the switch is checked.

Ground Check
Connect one test lead to the suspected point and the other lead to the ground. If the light illuminates, it indicates that the

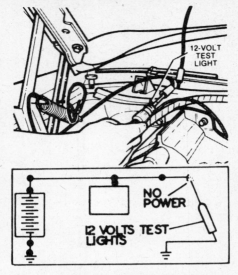

Fig. 5   Checking for power with 12 volt test light

point is grounded.

JUMPER WIRE

A jumper wire is simply a length of wire with terminals at both ends, usually alligator clips, and is used to connect two points of a circuit or component, **Fig. 8**. The jumper wire is used for bypassing a portion of the circuit to temporarily prevent it from causing an open circuit. The jumper wire is used with the power "On".

In an open circuit consisting of a switch in series with a light or other load compo-

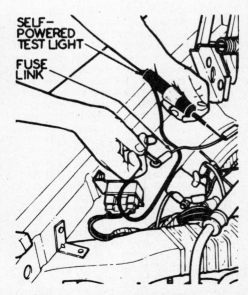

Fig. 7   Checking for continuity with self powered test light

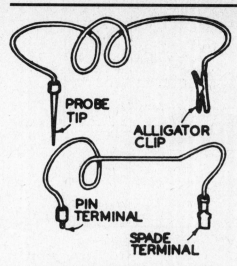

Fig. 8   Typical jumper wires

nent, connect the jumper wire to the switch terminals and apply power to the circuit, **Fig. 9**. If the connection of the jumper wire causes the circuit to operate, this indicates that the switch is open.

TEST EQUIPMENT
VOLTMETER

A DC voltmeter is used to measure DC voltage to ground. Connect the negative lead of the voltmeter to the ground and the positive lead to the point where voltage is to be measured, **Fig. 10**. This is called a parallel connection. The voltmeter is used with the power "On".

CAUTION: Do not use the jumper wire as a substitute for high resistance loads such as motors that are connected between the hot circuit and the ground.

OHMMETER

The ohmmeter is used to measure resistance between two points in a circuit. Connect one lead of the ohmmeter to one point in the circuit and the other lead to the second point in the circuit being checked, **Fig. 11**. The ohmmeter is also used to check continuity of a circuit. For example, if you connect the ohmmeter leads to both ends of a length of wire, the reading will indicate some resistance or simply, a reading will be obtained. Now if the same length of wire is cut in half, the circuit is broken or open and no reading will be obtained, indicating an open circuit. The ohmmeter is used with the power "Off".

AMMETER

A DC ammeter indicates current flow in amperes. The ammeter is connected into the circuit in series. Connect the positive lead of the ammeter to the power source and the negative lead into the remaining circuit so that all current must flow through the ammeter, **Fig. 12**. The ammeter is used with the power "On".

Some ammeters are equipped with a clamp-on probe. These ammeters are used to measure starter current.

DIGITAL MULTIMETER

This test instrument, **Fig. 13**, combines the functions of all the above analog style instruments. The digital reading ensures more accurate voltage read out, which is especially important when testing low voltage circuits often used in microprocessor systems. When using such a device to test voltage or current of an unknown magnitude, be sure to set the range selector to the highest range first. Reduce setting as necessary to obtain satisfactory reading.

SHORT CIRCUIT TESTER

A home-made short circuit tester can be made with a sealed beam, flasher or 7 amp. circuit breaker, wire and/or a buzzer as follows:
1. Connect test lead to two lengths of wire.
2. Connect one wire to the ground terminal of the sealed beam, **Fig. 14**.

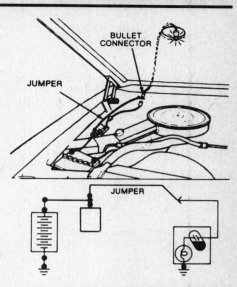

Fig. 9   Bypassing part of circuit with jumper wire

NOTE: It is desirable that a sealed beam connector be obtained since it will be easier to replace the sealed beam when it fails.

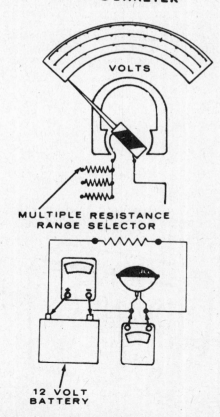

Fig. 10   Voltmeter & connection into circuit

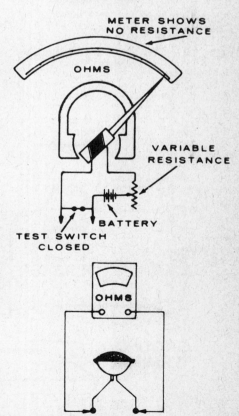

Fig. 11   Ohmmeter & connection into circuit

TROUBLESHOOTING

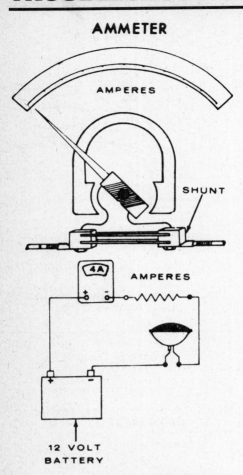

AMMETER

AMPERES

SHUNT

4A

AMPERES

12 VOLT
BATTERY

**Fig. 12   Ammeter & connection
into circuit**

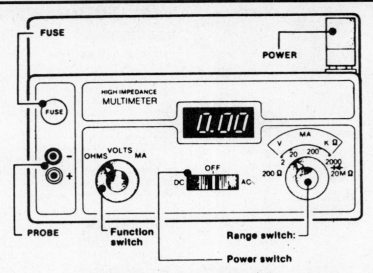

FUSE

POWER

HIGH IMPEDANCE
MULTIMETER

0.00

FUSE

OHMS VOLTS MA

OFF

DC   AC

V   MA
K Ω

PROBE

**Function
switch**

Range switch:

Power switch

Fig. 13   Digital multimeter

3. Wire the high and low beam terminals and attach a length of wire to them.
4. Connect the flasher or circuit breaker in series with the sealed beam.
5. It is desirable but not necessary to connect a buzzer in parallel with the flasher. Also, an "On-Off" switch installed in one of the buzzer leads will make the signal optional during testing.
6. Various adapters can be made from old wiring harnesses so the tester leads can be connected at various points of the circuit such as fuse panel, connectors, etc.

To Use the Tester
Connect the tester in series with the cir-

cuit being tested, using battery power as feed current, **Fig. 15.** When the circuit is closed and full power is supplied, the sealed beam will flash brightly and also, the buzzer will sound intermittently if connected in the circuit.

COMPASS

An ordinary magnetic compass may be used for locating grounded circuits. The use of the compass utilizes the principle that a current carrying conductor creates a magnetic field.

In circuits protected by a circuit breaker, a short or ground can be located quickly. Activate the circuit and follow the conduc-

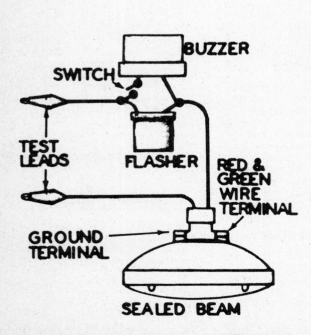

BUZZER

SWITCH

TEST
LEADS

FLASHER

RED &
GREEN
WIRE
TERMINAL

GROUND
TERMINAL

SEALED BEAM

Fig. 14   Short circuit tester construction

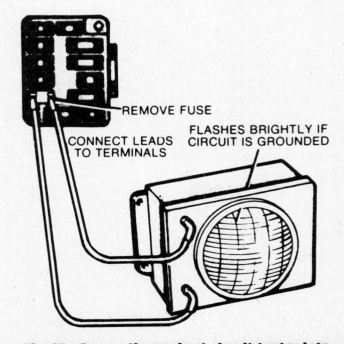

REMOVE FUSE

CONNECT LEADS
TO TERMINALS

FLASHES BRIGHTLY IF
CIRCUIT IS GROUNDED

**Fig. 15   Connecting a short circuit tester into
circuit**

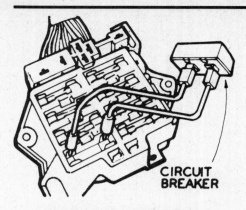

Fig. 16   Connecting circuit breaker into circuit in place of fuse

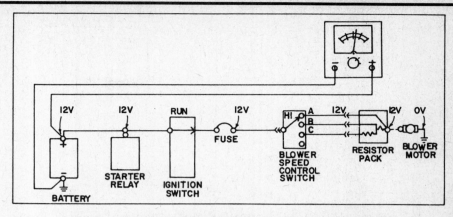

Fig. 17   Three speed blower motor circuit. Typical

tor with the compass. The compass will oscillate each time the circuit breaker closes. When the compass passes the point of the short or ground, the compass will stop oscillating, indicating the location of the malfunction.

The compass can be used without removing trim, cover plates or tape. If the circuit is protected by a fuse, the defect can be found with the compass by substituting a circuit breaker for the fuse.

FUSE SUBSTITUTION

By using a circuit breaker in place of the fuse in the circuit being tested, **Fig. 16,** other tools can be effectively used. A turn signal flasher may be used as a circuit breaker. Solder a lead to each terminal of the flasher, solder the leads to each end cap of blown fuse. This unit may be installed in the fuse block in place of the fuse normally used. However, when attempting to locate a short or ground when using a magnetic compass, the flasher may operate too quickly to produce satisfactory needle deflection. To slow the flasher operation, insert a generator field control rheostat in series in one flasher lead. By adding additional resistance, the rate of flasher operation may be reduced to produce satisfactory compass needle deflection.

CURRENT DRAW & VOLTAGE DROP

AVAILABLE VOLTAGE & VOLTAGE DROP

Voltage drop is the amount of voltage lost as electricity passes through a resistance (lamp bulb, blower motor, resistor) and is measured using a voltmeter. The principle of voltage drop can best be demonstrated using a heater blower circuit where resistors are used to deliberately create voltage drops. In a typical three speed blower circuit the blower motor is

powered through a speed control switch. The switch has three wires leading to the resistor pack, **Fig. 17.** The amount of voltage available to the motor depends on which wire is fed from the switch. Resistors in the blower circuit allow for a change in blower speed by causing a voltage drop ahead of the motor. It must be remembered that available voltage and voltage drop must be measured under load; that is, with the circuit operating a load component such as a motor, or light bulb. In **Fig. 17** power to the blower is through wire A, by-passing the resistors. The blower is now operating at maximum speed. Available voltage may be measured by connecting a voltmeter negative lead to a ground and moving the positive lead various points along the blower circuit, **Fig. 17.** Battery voltage is available at the motor because there is little resistance in the circuit up to this point. Available voltage from the motor is zero volts because the circuit has used up the full 12 volts to operate the motor.

VOLTAGE DROP IN A SERIES CIRCUIT

If the blower switch is positioned for medium speed, power to the motor must travel through wire B and through one of the resistors in the resistor pack, **Fig. 18.** A resistor has now been placed in series with the motor. The voltage drop is four volts through the resistor and eight volts through the motor for a total voltage drop of 12 volts. The motor now operates slower because there are only eight volts available to operate it.

NOTE: When resistances are connected in series, the voltage drops add up to the total available voltage at the source. Each voltage drop is proportional to the resistance of component the electricity flows through.

When the blower switch is positioned for low speed, the switch feeds wire C and there are now two resistors in series with the motor, **Fig. 19.** The available voltages are 12 volts into the resistor block, eight

volts into resistor B and 4 volts into the motor. The voltage drops are four volts at resistor A, four volts at resistor B and four volts at the motor for a total voltage drop of 12 volts. In each case zero volts are available out of the motor because the ground circuit has no resistance. If the ground circuit had resistance caused by a faulty ground connection, there would be a positive reading out of the motor. Also, each of the resistors would have proportionately lower voltage drops.

Measuring Voltage Drop Directly

Voltage drop may be read directly from the meter by connecting the meter across the component or segment of the circuit, **Fig. 20.** Check that the voltmeter positive lead is connected to the battery side of the circuit and the negative lead is connected to the ground side. **Fig. 20** shows voltmeter connections for reading voltage drop across the resistor pack on the low blower circuit. The combined voltage drop through both resistors is eight volts.

No Load Voltage

With the blower circuit operating on low blower and the motor disconnected from the circuit, connect two voltmeters as shown in **Fig. 21.** Meter A is connected as if to read resistor pack voltage drop. It will read zero because there is no voltage drop in a non-operating circuit. Meter B is connected as if to read available voltage. It is actually reading battery no load voltage. The circuit must be operating, that is, under load, to read voltage drop directly and to read available voltage in order to compute voltage drop. If the circuit is not under load, there will be no voltage drop.

CURRENT DRAW

Current draw, or current, is the amount of electrical flow or volume and is measured using an ammeter. The ammeter is connected into the circuit, in series with the load, switch or resistor. It will measure current draw only when the circuit is closed and electricity is flowing. In **Fig. 22,** the ammeter is connected as if to read current draw from the battery. The positive battery cable is disconnected so that any current

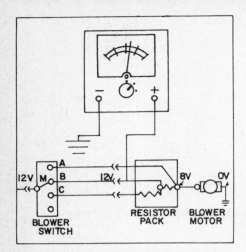

Fig. 18 Measuring voltage drop through one resistor

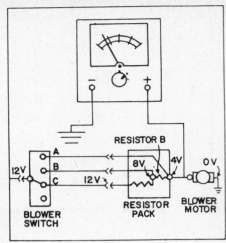

Fig. 19 Measuring voltage drop through two resistors

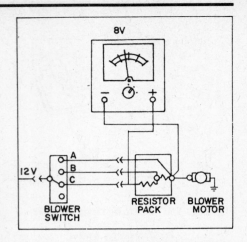

Fig. 20 Measuring voltage drop directly

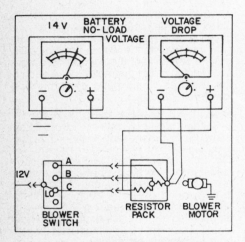

Fig. 21 Measuring no-load voltage

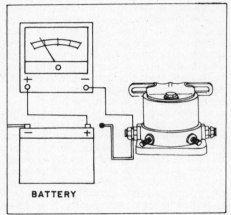

Fig. 22 Measuring current draw from battery

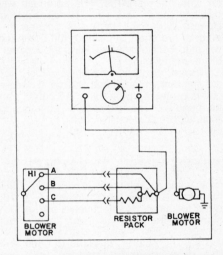

Fig. 23 Measuring blower motor current draw

flowing must go through the meter. If the vehicle's electrical systems were turned on one at a time, the meter would measure how much current each draws. The ammeter may be connected anywhere in a circuit, even between load and ground, as long as it is connected in series and correct polarity is observed.

High Resistance Short To Ground

When a short circuit occurs and the current draw is not sufficient to cause the fuse to blow, but does cause a drain on the battery, an ammeter may be used to locate the short. If a current draw exists with everything off, then there is a short to ground.

NOTE: On some vehicles equipped with an electric clock, there will be a slight current draw at all times with all accessories off. This current draw should be taken into consideration when diagnosing a short circuit with an ammeter.

To locate the short, remove fuses one at a time until the meter reads zero. If this occurs, trouble shoot that circuit for a short to ground.

Electric Motor Current Draw

Using the previous example of a blower circuit, an ammeter connected in series between the resistor pack and blower motor with the blower switch on high, **Fig. 23,** will show a reading of eight amps. This is a typical current draw for this type of motor. When the blower switch is moved to the medium position, the blower is being fed through a resistor and this reduces available voltage to the motor. The motor now draws about six amps and the motor operates slower. On low blower speed, the draw would decrease to 3 or 4 amps. If the switch were turned off, the ammeter would read zero.

NOTE: Current draw is highest with no

resistance and reduces as resistances are added in series.

If a second blower motor were connected in parallel and both were operated from the same switch, the electrical load would be doubled. The current draw, in the high speed position, would be 16 amps. Whenever electrical loads are added in parallel, the current draw increases. The effective resistance of the circuit decreases as parallel loads are added. If the two motors were connected in series, both would operate at reduced speed because one would act as a resistor for the other.

When an electric motor or solenoid has to work harder due to mechanical resistance, it draws more current. If the resistance is great, the motor will draw more current than that which can be safely handled by the circuit's fuse or circuit breaker. In this case the fuse blows or circuit breaker opens and interrupts the flow of current.

FUEL, IGNITION & GENERAL MAINTENANCE

TABLE OF CONTENTS

Fuel System Service

INDEX

DESCRIPTION

The fuel system receives gasoline from the fuel pump and combines it with air to form an explosive substance. This air/fuel mixture is then drawn through the induction system into the combustion chamber by the downward movement of the piston on the intake stroke. The ideal air/fuel ratio is approximately fifteen parts air to each part gasoline. The fuel system constantly adjusts the air/fuel ratio which varies as the engine operates over a range of loads, speeds, and temperatures.

Most of the work performed by the carburetor is done internally, but there are several simple external adjustments that will provide easier starts, smoother running, and better gas mileage. All vehicles use both an air filter and a gas filter. If these filters are not changed at regular intervals, the vehicle will lose power and waste gasoline. The choke changes the air/fuel mixture when the engine is cold. It should be periodically cleaned and checked for proper adjustment. The fast idle speed works in conjunction with the choke, and must be set so that engine does not stall when cold.

There are several emission control devices that may also affect operation of the fuel system. The PCV (positive crankcase ventilation) valve meters gasses from the engine crankcase back through the induction system to be burned. If the PCV valve is not working properly, it can alter the air/fuel ratio and cause the vehicle to idle rough. Gasoline vapors from the fuel tank and carburetor are directed to a charcoal canister. Some of these canisters contain a filter that should be changed at manufacturer's recommended intervals. Exhaust gasses are recycled through an EGR (exhaust gas recirculation) valve back into the intake manifold. The EGR valve should be serviced at manufacturer's recommended intervals.

AIR FILTER

All gasoline powered vehicles use dry type air filters that should be changed periodically to maintain optimum engine performance. Consult owner's manual for proper replacement intervals. The air filter is contained inside of the air filter housing. To gain access to the air filter, remove air filter housing cover. Depending on make and model of vehicle, the housing cover is retained by bolt(s), nut(s), wing nut(s), or spring clips. Many air filter housings also contain other filters, such as vent filters, which can be replaced when replacing air filter.

FUEL SYSTEM ADJUSTMENTS

NOTE: Fuel system adjustments on fuel injected engines, require the use of sophisticated testing, metering and adjustment equipment, and should not be performed unless this equipment is available.

While the carburetor is generally assumed to be the cause of poor engine performance or rough idle, there are other factors to be considered before attempting to adjust the carburetor:
1. Faulty distributor.
2. Misadjusted timing.

3. Faulty spark plugs and/or wires.
4. Faulty air cleaner.
5. Defective evaporative emission system.
6. Defective early fuel evaporative emission system.
7. Defective positive crankcase ventilation system.
8. Defective exhaust gas recirculation valve.
9. Insufficient engine compression.
10. Leaking vacuum at intake manifold, vacuum hoses, or connections.
11. Loose carburetor mounting bolts or nuts.

It is advisable to seek professional advice before assuming the carburetor is at fault.

While various carburetor adjusting specifications and some adjusting procedures are given on the vehicle emission control information label, it is advisable not to attempt adjustment. Most carburetors in use today have various limiting devices installed on them as required by Federal law. As a general rule, these limiting devices should only be removed when overhauling carburetor, and then only by a qualified technician. While various settings can be checked against specifications, it is advisable to seek professional advice whenever carburetor adjustments are required.

CARBURETOR
REPLACE

NOTE: The carburetor identification number is found on a tag attached to the carburetor or stamped on the carburetor body.

REMOVAL

NOTE: Although many different carburetor/engine applications are used, carburetor removal, cleaning, inspection and installation procedures for all vehicles are basically the same. The following carburetor replacement procedure is generalized around the major steps required to remove the carburetor assembly from the vehicle.

1. Disconnect battery ground cable.
2. Remove air cleaner and duct assembly from carburetor.
3. Mark (identify), then disconnect all vacuum lines, carburetor heat lines, if equipped, and electrical connectors from carburetor assembly.
4. Disconnect, then cap fuel line from carburetor fuel inlet fitting.
5. Disconnect throttle linkage(s), choke linkage and downshift cable or linkage from carburetor, if equipped.
6. Disconnect cruise control linkage or cable from carburetor assembly, if equipped.
7. Remove carburetor attaching bolts, then the carburetor, gasket(s) or insulator from engine.

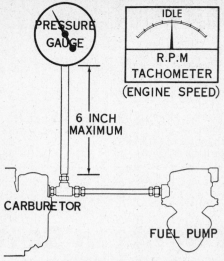

Fig. 1 Pressure testing fuel pump. Dodge & Plymouth

INSTALLATION

1. Thoroughly clean carburetor throttle body and intake manifold gasket surfaces.
2. Install gasket(s) or insulator and carburetor assembly onto engine. Install attaching bolts.

NOTE: Some carburetors require the use of a spacer plate positioned between two new gaskets.

3. Identify, then connect all linkages, vacuum lines, heat lines and electrical connectors to carburetor assembly. Ensure proper connection of all lines and electrical connectors.
4. Connect fuel line, air cleaner assembly and battery ground cable.
5. Crank engine and check for leaks.

CHARCOAL CANISTER

Most gasoline powered vehicles have an evaporative emission system to control the escape of gasoline vapors into the atmosphere. All evaporative emission systems use charcoal canisters. Most charcoal canisters are nonserviceable. A few canisters of the open bottom type are used on vehicles such as Chevrolet and GMC. These open bottom type canisters require periodic filter replacement. Consult owners manual for filter replacement intervals and applicability and change filter as described below.

1. Mark all canister hoses for proper assembly, then remove all hoses from top of canister.

CAUTION: Charcoal canisters are usually made of plastic and are easily subject to breakage. When removing hoses from canister, use extreme care to avoid damaging canister.

2. Carefully remove canister from vehicle.
3. Remove filter element by squeezing it out from under lip surface at bottom of canister, and from under retainer bar, if applicable.
4. Squeeze new element under retainer bar, if applicable, and position it evenly around entire bottom of canister, tucking edges under lip of canister.
5. Install canister in original position in vehicle.
6. Connect canister hoses to proper locations on top of canister.

FUEL FILLER CAP

The fuel filler cap used on vehicles without an evaporative emission system incorporates an anti-surge mechanism that prevents fuel spillage through the cap due to surge when cornering. Atmospheric air and fuel vapor are normally allowed to pass into and out of the fuel system, preventing tank collapse and/or excess pressure build up. In some cases the anti-surge mechanism can prevent fuel vapor from passing through the cap but pressure cannot build to excess levels.

The fuel filler cap used on vehicles with an evaporative emission system has a pressure-vacuum valve that vents air into the tank as fuel is consumed to prevent fuel tank collapse. Fuel vapor will not vent into the atmosphere until a predetermined pressure above atmospheric has been reached.

Use of an improper filler cap can result in damage to the fuel system or poor vehicle performance.

FUEL PUMP PRESSURE TEST
CARBURETED ENGINES

CHEVROLET & GMC
1. Disconnect fuel line at pump and connect suitable pressure gauge.
2. Start engine and note pressure with engine running at slow idle speed. On vehicles equipped with vapor return system, squeeze off return hose.
3. Refer to individual truck chapter for specifications.

DODGE & PLYMOUTH
1. Insert T-fitting in fuel line at carburetor, **Fig. 1.**
2. Connect a piece of hose, six inches maximum length, between T-fitting and suitable pressure gauge, then vent pump for a few seconds.
3. Connect a tachometer, then start engine and run at 500 RPM, noting pressure reading. Refer to individual truck chapter for specifications.

FORD
Electric Pump
1. Ensure that there is fuel in tank and check for leaks at all lines and fit-

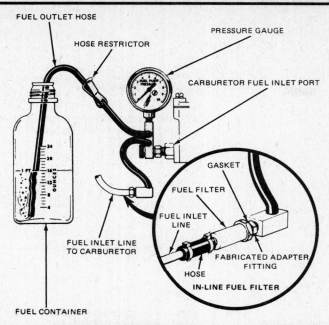

Fig. 2 Pressure testing fuel pump. Ford & Jeep

tings.
2. Check for electrical continuity to fuel pump as follows:
   a. Disconnect electrical connector just forward of fuel tank.
   b. Connect voltmeter to body wiring harness.
   c. Turn ignition key to "ON" while observing voltmeter. Voltage should rise to battery voltage, then return to zero voltage after approximately one second.
   d. Turn key to "START" momentarily while observing voltmeter. Voltage should rise to approximately eight volts while cranking.
3. If voltage is not as described, check electrical system.
4. Check pump operation as follows:
   a. Disconnect return fuel line at throttle body.
   b. Connect hose from throttle body fitting to a calibrated container of at least one quart capacity.
   c. Connect suitable pressure gauge to fuel diagnostic valve on fuel charging system.
   d. Disconnect electrical connector to fuel pump located just forward of fuel tank.
   e. Connect auxiliary wiring harness to connector to fuel pump.
   f. Connect auxiliary wiring harness to 12 volt battery for ten seconds and observe pressure.

NOTE: If fuel pump does not run, check connection directly at fuel pump before replacing pump.

   g. Allow fuel to drain from hose into container.
5. If fuel pressure reaches 35–45 psi,

fuel flow is at least ten ounces in ten seconds, and fuel pressure remains above 30 psi immediately after de-energization, fuel pump operation is normal.

Mechanical Pump
1. Remove air cleaner assembly and disconnect fuel inlet line or fuel filter at carburetor.
2. Connect pressure gauge, restrictor, and flexible hose between fuel filter and carburetor, **Fig. 2.**

NOTE: Inside diameter of smallest passage in test flow circuit must not be smaller than .220 inch.

3. Position flexible fuel outlet hose and restrictor so that fuel can be discharged into a suitable graduated container.
4. Operate engine at idle and vent system into container by momentarily opening hose restrictor.
5. Close restrictor, allow pressure to stabilize, and note reading. Refer to individual truck chapter for specifications.

JEEP
1. Remove air cleaner assembly.
2. Disconnect fuel inlet line or fuel filter at carburetor.
3. Disconnect fuel return line at fuel filter and plug nipple on filter.
4. Connect pressure gauge, restrictor, and flexible hose between fuel filter and carburetor, **Fig. 2.**
5. Position flexible hose with restrictor so that fuel can be discharged into suitable graduated container.
6. Operate engine at curb idle speed and

vent system into container by momentarily opening restrictor.
7. Close restrictor, allow pressure to stabilize, and note reading. Refer to individual truck chapter for specifications.

GAS FILTER

All gasoline powered vehicles use a gas filter to prevent the entry of dirt into the carburetor. These filters should be changed periodically as a clogged gas filter will cause stalling or hesitation. Some gas filters are in line between the carburetor and the fuel pump while others are installed at the carburetor inlet. To change in-line filters, proceed as follows:
1. Loosen spring clips or clamps at outer ends of hoses and slide toward gas filter until they clear flanges on fuel line.
2. Remove filter with hoses and clamps attached.

NOTE: If replacement hoses and clamps are provided with replacement filter, removal of old filter assembly can be facilitated by slicing original hoses lengthwise to prevent unnecessary distortion of fuel line.

3. If replacement hoses and clamps are not provided with replacement filter, loosen spring clips or clamps on hoses and slide them past flanges of gas filter, remove hoses from old filter and install them on replacement filter, and secure with spring clips or clamps, ensuring that spring clips or clamps are inboard of filter flanges.
4. Install replacement filter assembly in gas line, ensuring that arrow on filter points toward carburetor. Secure with spring clips or clamps, ensuring that they are outboard of gas line flanges.

To change gas filters installed externally at carburetor inlet, proceed as follows:
1. Loosen spring clip or clamp at fuel line end of hose and slide upward over flange of fuel line.
2. Unscrew filter from carburetor and remove filter with hose from vehicle.
3. Screw new filter into carburetor.

CAUTION: Screw new filter in only until snug. Filter usually will not fit flush against carburetor. Overtightening of filter will cause breakage with neck of filter becoming lodged in carburetor.

4. Install new hose, if provided, or original hose on filter and insert fuel line into other end of hose, securing with spring clips or clamps.

To change gas filters installed internally at carburetor inlet, proceed as follows, **Fig. 3:**
1. Hold large nut with suitable wrench and loosen small nut.

CAUTION: Use a flare nut wrench on small nut. Use of a conventional wrench

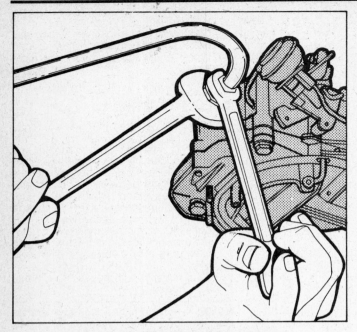

Fig. 3   Disconnecting fuel line

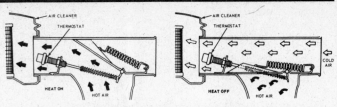

Fig. 4   Thermostatically operated heated air intake system (Typical)

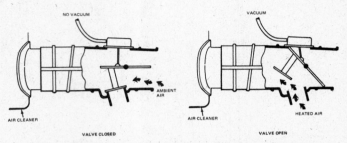

Fig. 5   Vacuum operated heated air intake system (typical)

will distort nut. Break nut lose by manually rapping wrench rather than pushing or pulling it.

2. Remove large nut together with gas filter, spring, and gaskets, noting installed direction of filter.
3. Install paper gasket in large nut, then the replacement filter, ensuring that filter is installed in correct direction.
4. Insert spring into carburetor inlet, then the nut with filter. Ensure that gasket is properly positioned on nut.
5. Tighten nut until snug.
6. Hand start fuel line flare nut into large nut.
7. Hold large nut with suitable wrench, and tighten flare nut until snug.

After changing any gas filter, start the engine and check for leaks.

HEATED AIR INTAKE SYSTEM

All gasoline powered vehicles use a heated air intake system to improve driveability and maximize gas mileage. This system is either thermostatically or vacuum controlled, **Figs. 4 and 5.** There are several visual checks that can be made to check for proper system operation.

1. Disconnect air cleaner duct system as necessary to allow viewing of air door, usually located in air cleaner snorkel.
2. With engine cold, check position of air door, using a flashlight and/or mirror to facilitate viewing as necessary. Air door should be in up position, blocking entry of outside air and allowing entry of heated air from exhaust manifold.
3. Start engine and run at idle. As engine warms up, air door should lower gradually until it is in a fully down position when engine reaches operating temperature.
4. If air door does not work as described in steps 2 and 3, check air door for sticking or binding and check spring for weakness or distortion.
5. If air door is free and spring is satisfactory, check duct work for leaks or loose connections and, on vacuum operated systems, check vacuum hoses for cracks, leaks, or loose connections.
6. If system still does not work, seek professional advice.

PCV VALVE

The PCV valve is part of the positive crankcase ventilation system. This system regulates the venting of engine crankcase gasses back into the intake manifold where they are burned. A malfunctioning valve will cause the engine to idle rough or stall.

The PCV valve should be changed at recommended intervals. The PCV system can be checked as follows:

1. Remove PCV from intake manifold and rocker arm cover.
2. Run engine at idle.
3. Place thumb over end of valve and check for vacuum.
4. If there is no vacuum, check for clogged hoses or valve.
5. Shut off engine.
6. Shake valve. If valve does not rattle, replace it.
7. When installing new PCV valve, check engine idle and adjust as necessary.

VACUUM HOSES

Many problems encountered in the fuel system can be caused by the vacuum hoses. All vacuum hoses should be checked for cracks, leaks, breakage, or faulty connections. Replace any suspect vacuum hoses. Check the vacuum hose routings referring to the emission control sticker, if available. This sticker is usually located on a valve cover, adjacent to the radiator, on the underside of the hood, or on a shock tower. The vacuum hose routing is color coded and, for the most part, the actual hose colors correspond to the color coding. However, an individual hose color may differ from the color coding.

General Maintenance

INDEX

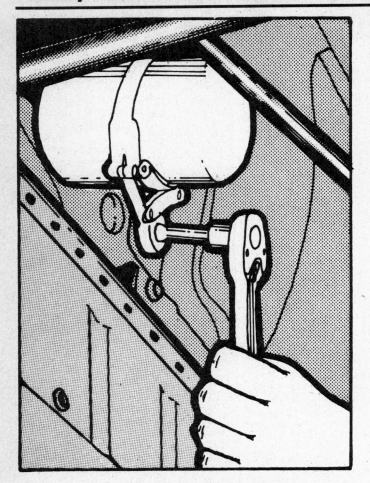

Fig. 1   Oil filter removal (typical)

Coat Gasket With Engine Oil

Fig. 2   Oil filter installation (typical)

LUBRICATION & OIL CHANGE

ENGINE OIL & FILTER CHANGE

NOTE: Engine oil and filter should be changed at intervals recommended by the vehicle manufacturer.

1. Operate engine and allow to reach operating temperature, then turn ignition off.
2. Place drain pan under engine oil pan, then using a suitable wrench remove drain plug.
3. Allow engine oil to thoroughly drain into pan, then replace drain plug.

NOTE: Do not overtighten drain plug, as this can strip the threads in oil pan.

4. If oil filter is to be replaced, position drain pan under filter, then install oil filter wrench and remove filter by turning counterclockwise, **Fig. 1.**

NOTE: Ensure old oil filter gasket is not on the filter adapter on the engine. Clean adapter before installing new filter.

5. Coat new oil filter gasket with engine oil, then position filter on adapter, **Fig. 2.** Hand tighten filter until gasket contacts adapter face, then tighten filter one additional turn. Wipe filter and adapter with a clean cloth.

NOTE: Ensure gasket is in position on filter before tightening. Do not use oil filter wrench to tighten filter. Hand tighten only.

6. Remove oil filler cap and add quantity of oil specified by manufacturer, then install filler cap.

NOTE: Only add oil which meets the vehicle manufacturer's specifications.

7. Start engine and check to ensure oil filter and drain plug are not leaking, then turn ignition off.
8. Check oil level to ensure crankcase is full but not overfilled. Add oil as necessary.

NOTE: Do not bring oil level above "Full" mark on dipstick. Overfilling could result in damage to engine gaskets or seals causing leaks.

CHASSIS LUBRICATING

The first time you perform a grease job, you will spend much of the time looking for the fittings, **Figs. 3 and 4.**

As you find a fitting, wipe it off with a clean rag. This will help you spot it later and also prevent you from injecting dirt with the grease.

The injection tip of the grease gun should be a catch fit on the fitting nipple. That is, once in place it will not slip off. Slight, straight-on pressure is all that is necessary for the gun tip to engage the fitting. Once that is done, pump the handle. Follow the recommendations below to ensure proper lubrication and also prevent damage to the seals:

Ford and Jeep

Pump slowly until the rubber boot can be felt or seen to swell slightly.

Chrysler Corp., General Motors

Pump slowly until grease starts to flow from bleed holes at the base of the seals, or until the seals start to swell.

NOTE: If the fitting fails to take grease, the lubricant will ooze out between fitting and top of the gun. Do not just keep pumping, hoping some grease is getting in, or you will have a mess. It is normal for a bit of grease to seep out. However, if the fitting is obviously not taking grease, it should be replaced.

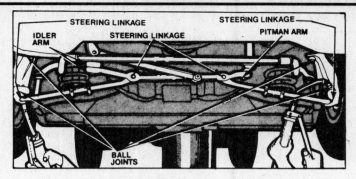

Fig. 3   Fitting locations (typical)

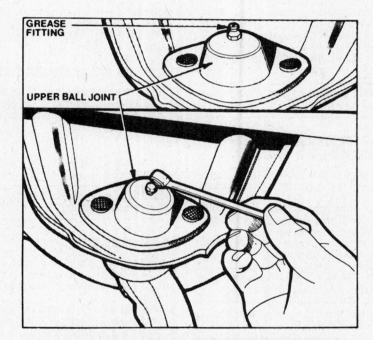

Fig. 4   Identifying grease fittings (typical). If vehicle is equipped with plugs, the plugs must be removed and a grease fitting installed prior to lubricating

REPACKING FRONT WHEEL BEARINGS

1. Remove inner and outer bearings as outlined in truck chapters.
2. Clean old lubricant from hub and spindle.
3. Clean inner and outer bearings and bearing races with kerosene.

NOTE: Ensure all old lubricant is removed before repacking. Allow bearings and races to dry thoroughly. Do not use compressed air to clean bearings.

4. Inspect cones, rollers and races for cracks, nicks and wear, and replace as necessary.

NOTE: Bearings and race must be replaced as a unit.

5. Place a small amount of wheel bearing grease in palm of hand, then force grease into large end of roller cage until grease protrudes from small end.

NOTE: Use only wheel bearing grease which meets the vehicle manufacturer's specifications.

6. Lubricate remaining bearings in the same manner, then install and adjust bearings as outlined in truck chapter.

NOTE: Apply a light film of grease to lips of grease retainer before installing.

CHECKING & MAINTAINING FLUID LEVELS

NOTE: When checking fluid levels, ensure vehicle is on a level surface. If vehicle is not level, an accurate fluid level reading cannot be obtained.

ENGINE OIL LEVEL

1. Warm up engine, then turn ignition off and allow a few minutes for oil to return to crankcase.
2. Remove dipstick and wipe off.
3. Replace dipstick and ensure it is seated in tube.
4. Remove dipstick and inspect to see if oil level is between "Add" and "Full" marks.

NOTE: Add oil only if level is at or below "Add" mark.

5. If oil level is at "Add" mark, one quart of oil will bring level to "Full" mark. If oil level is below "Add" mark, add sufficient amount of oil to bring level between "Add" & "Full" marks.

NOTE: Do not bring oil level above "Full" mark, as overfilling of crankcase could result in damage to engine gaskets and seals and cause leaks. Only add oil meeting the vehicle manufacturer's specifications.

6. Replace dipstick.

BATTERY

1. Remove filler cap and check fluid level in each cell.

NOTE: Keep flame and sparks away from top of battery as combustible gases present may explode. Do not allow battery electrolyte to contact skin, eyes, fabric or painted surfaces. Flush contacted area with water immediately and thoroughly and seek medical attention if necessary. Wear eye protection when working on or near battery. Do not wear rings or other metal jewelry when working on or near battery.

2. Add water as required to bring fluid level of each cell up to split ring located at bottom of filler well.

NOTE: In areas where water is known to be hard or have a high mineral or alkali content, distilled water must be used. If water is added during freezing temperatures, the vehicle should be driven several miles afterwards to mix the water and battery electrolyte.

3. Install filler caps.

COOLING SYSTEM

NOTE: Add only permanent type antifreeze which meets the vehicle manufacturer's specifications.

CAUTION: Never add large quantities of water into radiator if truck has overheated before engine has cooled off. If necessary to service at this time, start engine and add water to coolant slowly. This will avoid damage to the engine.

Less Coolant Recovery System

NOTE: Avoid checking coolant level if engine is hot. If coolant level must be checked when engine is hot, muffle radiator cap with a thick cloth, then turn cap counterclockwise until pressure starts to escape. After pressure has been completely relieved, finish removing cap.

1. With engine cold, remove radiator cap and inspect coolant level.
2. Coolant level should be approximately 1 inch below bottom of filler neck.
3. Add solution of 50% water–50% antifreeze as required.
4. Install radiator cap.

With Coolant Recovery System

NOTE: On these type systems, do not remove radiator cap to check coolant level.

1. Start engine and allow to reach operating temperature.
2. Visually inspect coolant level in plastic reservoir.
3. On all models except Chrysler Corp. vehicles, coolant level should be between "Full" and "Add" marks or at "Full Hot" mark, depending on reservoir. On Chrysler Corp. vehicles, coolant level should be between the one and two quart marks with engine operating at idle speed.
4. Remove reservoir filler cap and add solution of 50% water-50% antifreeze as required.
5. Install reservoir filler cap.

BRAKE MASTER CYLINDER RESERVOIR

1. Clean master cylinder reservoir cover, then using a screwdriver, unsnap

retainer(s) and remove cover.

NOTE: Do not hold cover over vehicle, as brake fluid may damage finish.

2. Brake fluid level should be ¼ inch from top of master cylinder reservoir.

NOTE: If brake fluid level is excessively low, the brake linings should be inspected for wear and brake system checked for leaks. Fluid level in reservoirs servicing disc brakes will decrease as disc brake pads wear.

3. Add brake fluid as required.

NOTE: Only add brake fluid which meets the vehicle manufacturer's specifications. Use only brake fluid which has been in a tightly closed container to prevent contamination from dirt and moisture. Do not allow petroleum base fluids to contaminate brake fluid, as seal damage may result.

4. Install cover and snap retainer into place.

NOTE: Ensure retainer is locked into cover grooves.

POWER STEERING PUMP RESERVOIR

1. Start engine and allow to reach operating temperature, then turn ignition off.
2. Clean area around filler cap or dipstick, then remove filler cap or dipstick and inspect fluid level.
3. Fluid level should be between "Full" mark and end of dipstick.

NOTE: On models without dipstick, fluid level should be half way up filler neck.

4. Add fluid as necessary, then install filler cap or dipstick.

NOTE: Only add fluid recommended by the vehicle manufacturer.

AUTOMATIC TRANSMISSION

1. Firmly apply parking brake, then start and run engine for approximately 10 minutes to bring transmission fluid to operating temperature.

NOTE: Do not run engine in unventilated area. Exhaust gases contain carbon monoxide which could be deadly in unventilated areas.

2. With engine running at idle speed, shift selector lever through all positions, then place lever in Neutral on Chrysler Corp. and Jeep vehicles, and in Park on Ford Motor Co. and General Motors Corp.
3. Clean dipstick cap, then remove dipstick and wipe off.

4. Replace dipstick and ensure it is seated in tube.
5. Remove dipstick and inspect to see if fluid level is between "Add" and "Full" marks.

NOTE: Add fluid only if level is at or below "Add" mark.

6. If fluid level is at "Add" mark, one pint of transmission fluid will bring level to "Full" mark. If fluid level is below "Add" mark, add sufficient amount of fluid to bring level between "Add" and "Full" marks. Transmission fluid is added through the dipstick tube.

NOTE: Do not bring level above "Full" mark, as overfilling could result in damage to transmission. Only add automatic transmission fluid of type and specification recommended by the vehicle manufacturer.

7. Replace dipstick and ensure it is seated in tube.

MANUAL TRANSMISSION

1. Set parking brake and block wheels.
2. Clean area around filler plug, then using a suitable wrench or ratchet, remove filler plug.
3. Fluid should be level with bottom of filler plug hole.
4. Add fluid as required, then install filler plug.

NOTE: Only add lubricant recommended by the vehicle manufacturer.

REAR AXLE

1. Set parking brake and block wheels.
2. Clean area around filler plug, then using a suitable ratchet, remove filler plug.
3. Fluid level should be approximately ½ inch below bottom of filler plug hole.
4. Add fluid as required, then install filler plug.

NOTE: Only add lubricant recommended by vehicle manufacturer.

COOLING SYSTEM SERVICE

CAUTION: Do not attempt to perform any system servicing when the engine is hot or the cooling system is pressurized. Even a simple operation such as removing the radiator cap should be avoided since personal injury and loss of coolant may result.

DRAINING THE SYSTEM

Most cooling systems incorporate a radiator petcock usually located on the engine side of the radiator at either of the lower corners. Some radiator petcocks are locat-

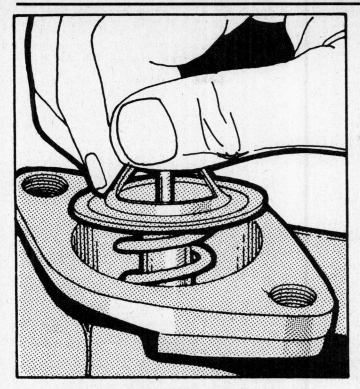

Fig. 5   Replacing thermostat (typical)

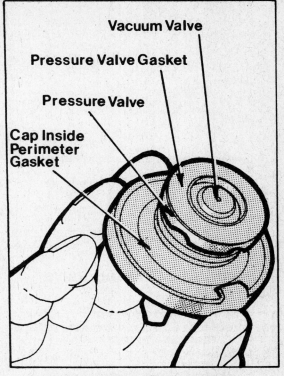

Vacuum Valve

Pressure Valve Gasket

Pressure Valve

Cap Inside Perimeter Gasket

Fig. 6   Radiator cap (typical)

ed on the side of the radiator. Not all cooling systems are equipped with a radiator petcock.

1. Place a suitable container under radiator to catch coolant.
2. On systems equipped with a radiator petcock, turn the tangs (ears) to open the petcock. However, do not apply excessive pressure in either direction as damage to the petcock may result because some petcocks turn clockwise and others counterclockwise to open.
3. On systems not equipped with a radiator petcock, it will be necessary to remove the lower hose from the radiator.
4. Dispose of coolant.

FLUSHING THE SYSTEM

There are two flushing methods which can be performed without the use of special equipment. One method outlined below requires the use of a garden hose only. The second method requires the use of the garden hose and a "Tee" fitting spliced into one of the heater hoses. The "Tee" fitting and other items and instructions needed to perform this type of flushing are available through aftermarket manufacturers.

1. With coolant system drained, remove thermostat as outlined below:
   a. To locate the thermostat housing on most engines follow the upper radiator hose from the radiator to the engine block. On some engines, follow the lower radiator

hose from the radiator to the engine block. The point at which these hoses connect is the thermostat housing.
   b. The thermostat housing is usually retained by two bolts or nuts. Remove these bolts or nuts and remove the housing.
   c. Lift the thermostat from the mounting flange, **Fig. 5,** noting the position in which it was installed. This is important to avoid reinstalling the thermostat upside down.
   d. Reinstall thermostat housing, however do not reinstall thermostat. Tighten retaining bolts.
2. Insert garden hose into radiator filler opening, open radiator petcock and turn on water.
3. Start engine and run engine for a few minutes. This should flush out any loose particles in the system.
4. Turn off engine and remove the garden hose.
5. Remove thermostat housing. Thoroughly clean the thermostat housing and engine surfaces of old gasket and sealer. This is necessary to prevent leakage between the housing and engine surfaces.
6. Install new thermostat housing gasket and the thermostat. Make certain the thermostat is installed exactly in the same position as it was removed.
7. Install thermostat housing and tighten retaining bolts and nuts.
8. Allow radiator to drain.
9. Close radiator petcock, if equipped.
10. Remove coolant overflow tank, if

equipped. Thoroughly clean the inside of the tank and reinstall.

REFILLING THE SYSTEM

1. Determine the amount of anti-freeze required to achieve a 50/50 solution in the cooling system. Refer to the "Cooling System & Capacity Data" tables in the individual truck chapters. Take the total number of quarts listed in the tables and divide by two. This number is the amount of anti-freeze, in quarts, required to achieve the 50/50 solution. This solution will generally provide protection to −35 degrees F.
2. Add the amount of anti-freeze to the radiator determined in the preceding step. If radiator fills before required amount of anti-freeze is installed, start engine and turn on heater. Add the anti-freeze as the coolant level sinks in the radiator.
3. Continue to run engine with the radiator cap removed until the upper radiator hose becomes hot to the touch.
4. Top up the coolant level in the radiator to the bottom of the filler neck with a 50/50 mixture of anti-freeze and water.
5. If equipped with an overflow tank, add a 50/50 mixture of anti-freeze and water to the cold level as marked on the side of the tank.

RADIATOR CAP

The radiator filler cap contains a pressure relief valve and a vacuum relief valve, **Fig. 6.** The pressure relief valve is held

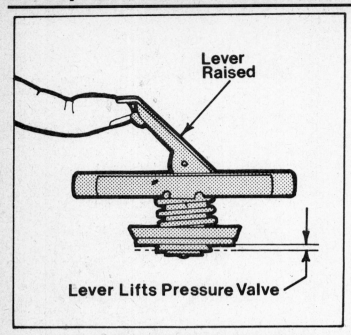

Fig. 7 Radiator cap with pressure release mechanism (typical)

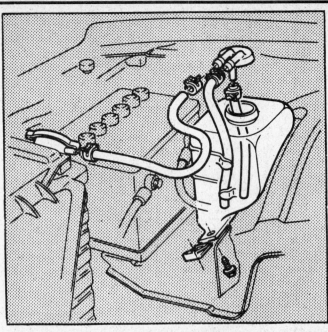

Fig. 8 Factory installed coolant recovery system (typical)

against its seat by a spring, which when compressed relieves excessive pressure out the radiator overflow. The vacuum valve is also held against its seat by a spring which when compressed opens the valve to relieve the vacuum created when the system cools.

NOTE: Some aftermarket radiator caps incorporate a pressure release mechanism to relieve cooling system pressure before rotating cap, **Fig. 7.**

The radiator cap should be washed with clean water and pressure checked at regular tune-up intervals. Inspect rubber seal on cap for tears or cracks. If the pressure cap will not hold pressure or does not release at the proper pressure, replace the cap.

COOLANT RECOVERY SYSTEM

The coolant recovery system supplements the standard cooling system in that additional coolant is available from a plastic reservoir, **Fig. 8.**

As the coolant is heated it expands within the cooling system and overflows into the plastic reservoir. As the engine cools, the coolant contracts and is drawn back into the radiator by vacuum. In this way, the radiator is filled to capacity at all times, resulting in increased cooling efficiency.

Air or vapor entering the system will be forced to the reservoir under the coolant and will exit through the reservoir cap.

A special radiator cap is designed to discourage inadvertent removal. The finger grips have been eliminated, replaced by a round configuration.

Fig. 9 Aftermarket coolant recovery system installation (typical)

Overflow Kit

If your truck does not have an overflow reservoir, it is easy to fit it with one, **Fig. 9.** A kit should include the following:
1. A clear plastic reservoir with quart markings to indicate fluid level.
2. A replacement radiator cap, with an air sealing gasket in the cap's inside perimeter.
3. Necessary hoses and fittings.

HOSE REPLACEMENT

The radiator, heater and the coolant bypass hoses are held at each end by a clamp. All clamps but the spring design can be loosened with a screwdriver. To save yourself time after you have removed the hose from your radiator or heater, buy the replacement hose and any necessary clamps before starting the job.

Removal

1. Drain the radiator as outlined previously. Use a clean container, large enough to hold the coolant from your cooling system to save for refilling the system after replacing the hose. If you

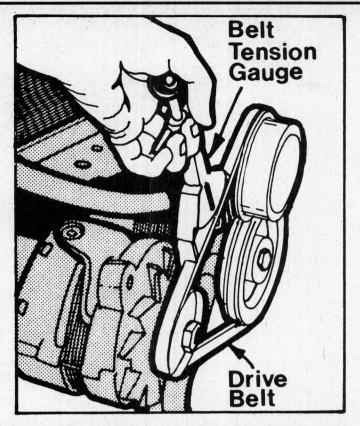

Fig. 10   Checking belt tension with a tension gauge

are removing the radiator upper hose or heater hoses, you need only drain the radiator. If you are removing the lower hose, also drain the block as follows: disconnect the lower hose at the radiator, bend it down and use it as a drain spout.

2. Loosen the clamps with a screwdriver at each end of the hose to be removed. If the clamps are old and corroded, they may be stuck to the hose. Loosening the screw may not be enough on some designs, in which case you'll have to pry the clamp.

CAUTION: Be very careful when prying under the clamp. The fittings are extremely fragile and might bend or break if too much force is exerted.

If the hose is held by spring clamps, you may be in for a struggle unless you have spring clamp pliers. There are many types of pliers designed for these clamps, including ordinary slip-joint pliers with recesses cut into the jaws to grip each end of the clamp. To release the clamp you must squeeze the ends together, and if you try to use ordinary pliers, the ends may slip off. The best procedure is to discard the spring type and install a wormdrive band clamp, but if you insist on reusing the one you have, at least invest in a pair of special pliers.

3. Twist the hose back and forth to loosen it from the connector. Slide the hose off the connections. If the hose is stuck, shove in a screwdriver and try to pry loose. If the working angle is poor for the screwdriver, or if the hose is really stuck, cut the hose off the neck with a single-edge razor blade. If the hose being removed is dried and cracked and remnants of it remain on either connection, clean the connection thoroughly with a scraper or putty knife.

Installation

1. With the old hose removed, wire brush the hose connections to remove foreign material.
2. To ease installation, coat hose neck with a soap solution.
3. Slide the hose in position so it is completely on the neck at each end, to avoid possibility of kinking and to provide room for proper positioning of the clamp. Except for the wormdrive clamp, which can be opened completely, the clamp must be loosely placed over the hose prior to fitting its end on the neck.
4. Make sure the clamps are beyond the head and placed in the center of the clamping surface of the connections.
5. Tighten the clamps.
6. Refill the cooling system as outlined previously.

COOLING SYSTEM LEAKS

If the coolant level must be adjusted frequently, the cooling system may be leaking either internally or externally. To determine if the system is leaking internally, special equipment must be used such as a pressure tester. To determine if the system is leaking externally, check for leakage in the following locations: radiator and its seams, hoses and their connections, heater core, water pump, coolant temperature sending unit, thermostat housing, hot water choke housing, heater water valve, coolant recovery tank and core plugs.

DRIVE BELTS

Proper belt tension is important not only to minimize noise and prolong belt life, but also to protect the accessories being driven.

Belts which are adjusted too tight may cause failure to the bearing of the accessory which it drives. Premature wear and breakage of the belt may also result. Belts which are too loose will slip on their pulleys and cause a screeching sound. Loose belts can also cause the battery to go dead, the engine to overheat, steering to become hard (if equipped with power steering) and air conditioner to malfunction.

DRIVE BELT TENSION GAUGE

The use of a belt tension gauge will quickly indicate whether a belt is properly adjusted or not. Low cost tension gauges give spot readings while the more expensive ones give continuous readings as the belt tension is adjusted, **Fig. 10**.

DRIVE BELT INSPECTION

All belts should be inspected at regular intervals for uneven wear, fraying and glazing.

CAUTION: Do not inspect belts while engine is running.

Small cracks on the underside of the belt can be enlarged for inspection by flexing the belt. Cracks expose the interior to damage, leading to breakage without warning.

Grease rots ordinary rubber belts. It also causes the belts to slip.

Glazed belts, indicated with a shiny friction surface cause the belts to slip. This can cause overheating, a low charging rate, and hard steering in the case of vehicles with power steering.

Always make sure to inspect the underside of belts. Belts that appear sound from the top, may be severely split on the sides and bottom, ready to fail.

DRIVE BELT TENSION ADJUSTMENT

1. Run engine until it reaches normal operating temperature, then turn engine off.

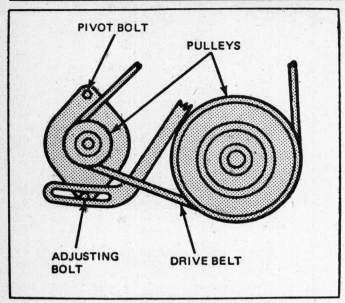

Fig. 11   Pivot bolt and adjusting bolt arrangement

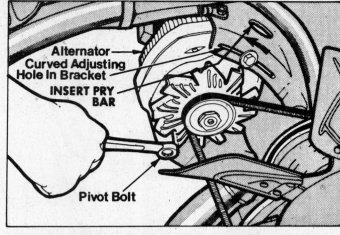

Fig. 12   Loosening adjusting bolt and pivot bolt

CAUTION: Do not attempt to check or adjust any drive belt while engine is running. Turn engine off.

2. Using belt tension gauge following manufacturer's instructions, check tension of each belt, individually. Refer to individual vehicle chapter for belt tension specifications.
3. If adjustment is necessary, proceed as follows:
   a. Pivot Bolt and Adjusting Bolt, **Figs. 11 and 12:** using a suitable wrench, loosen adjusting bolt and pivot bolt, then using a pry bar, move accessory toward or away from engine until tension gauge reaches specified reading. Make sure to tighten bolts before reliev-

ing force applied to pry bar.

CAUTION: Do not pry against power steering housing or air pump housing.

   b. Adjusting Bolt and Adjusting Bolt Slots, **Fig. 13,** loosen adjusting slot bolts, then loosen or tighten adjusting bolt until tension gauge reaches specified reading. Make sure to tighten adjusting slot bolts.
   c. Idler Pulley Pivot Bolt and Adjusting Bolt: loosen idler pulley pivot bolt and adjusting bolt, then insert a ½ inch flex handle into pulley arm slot and apply force on handle until tension gauge reaches specified reading. Make sure to tighten pivot

and adjusting bolt before relieving force on handle.
4. To check tension on a belt without a belt tension gauge, proceed as follows:
   a. Place a straight edge along the belt from pulley to pulley, **Fig. 14.**
   b. Using a ruler, depress belt at midpoint between pulleys. Measure amount of deflection. For belt with a free span of less than 12 inches between pulleys, amount of deflection should be ¼ inch. For belts with a free span of more than 12 inches between pulleys, amount of deflection should be ½ inch.
   c. Adjust belt tension, if necessary, as described previously.
5. Recheck belt tension, and readjust if necessary.

DRIVE BELT REPLACEMENT

To replace a belt, loosen the adjusting bolt and pivot bolt. Move accessory as required to obtain maximum slack on belt.

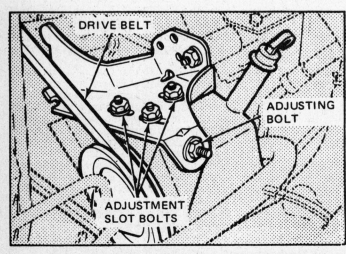

Fig. 13   Adjustment bolt and adjustment slot arrangement

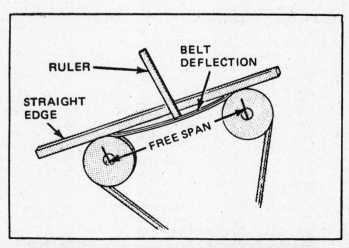

Fig. 14   Checking belt tension without belt tension gauge

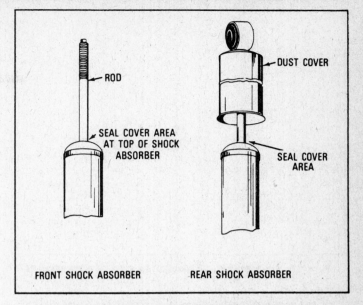

Fig. 16 Possible source of shock absorber leakage

Fig. 15 Disconnecting lower shock absorber mount (typical)

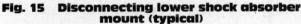

Remove belt by lifting off the pulleys and working it around the fan or other accessories, as necessary. Occasionally on multiple belt arrangements, it will be necessary to remove one or more additional belts in order to remove the defective belt. To install belt, reverse the removal procedure and adjust belt tension as described previously.

NOTE: On accessories which are driven by dual belts, it is advisable to replace both belts even if only one needs replacement.

SHOCK ABSORBERS
ON VEHICLE CHECKS
Bounce Test

Check each shock absorber by bouncing each corner of vehicle. This is best accomplished by alternately lifting up and pushing down at corner of vehicle until maximum up and down movement is reached. Let go of vehicle and ensure movement stops very quickly. Relative damping of shocks should be compared side to side but not front to rear.

Shock Mounts

If noise appears to come from shock mounts, raise vehicle on hoist that supports wheels and check mountings for the following:
1. Worn or defective grommets.
2. Loose mounting nuts or bolts.
3. Possible interference condition.

4. Missing bump stops.

If no apparent faults can be found but noise condition exists when vehicle is bounced, proceed to next check.

Leak Inspection & Manual Operation Check

1. Disconnect each shock lower mount, **Fig. 15,** and pull down on shock absorber until fully extended.
2. Check for leaks in seal cover area, **Fig. 16.** Shock absorber oil is a very thin hydraulic fluid that has a characteristic odor and dark brown color.

NOTE: Shock absorber seals are intended to allow slight seepage to lubricate rod. A trace of oil around seal cover area is not cause for shock absorber replacement since the unit has sufficient reserve fluid to compensate for this seepage.

Ensure oil spray is not from some other source. To check, wipe wet area clean and manually operate shock absorber as described in following step. Fluid will reappear if shock absorber is leaking.

NOTE: Air line must be disconnected from air adjustable shocks before they are manually operated.

3. If necessary, fabricate bracket or handle to enable a secure grip on shock absorber end, **Fig. 17.**
4. Check for internal binding, leakage, and improper or defective valving by

pulling down and pushing up shock absorber. Compare rebound resistance (downward) of both shock absorbers, then compression resistance. If any noticeable difference is detected during either stroke, the weaker unit is usually at fault.

5. If shock absorber operates noisily, it should be replaced. Noise conditions that require shock absorber replacement are as follows:
   a. Grunt or squeal after full stroke in both directions.
   b. Clicking noise during fast direction reversal.
   c. Skip or lag when reversing direction in mid-stroke.

BENCH CHECKS

If a suitable hoist is not available to perform on-vehicle shock absorber checks, or there is still doubt as to whether the units are defective, the following bench test can be performed.

Spiral Groove Reservoir Shock Absorbers

NOTE: If this style shock absorber is stored or left to lie in a horizontal position for any length of time, an air pocket will form in pressure chamber. If air pocket is not purged, shock absorber may be misdiagnosed as faulty. Purge air from pressure chamber as follows:
a. Extend shock absorber while holding it vertically and right side up, **Fig. 18.**
b. Invert shock absorber and fully compress unit.
c. Repeat steps a and b at least 5 times to ensure air is completely purged.

1. Obtain known good shock absorber with same part number.
2. Hold both shock absorbers in vertical

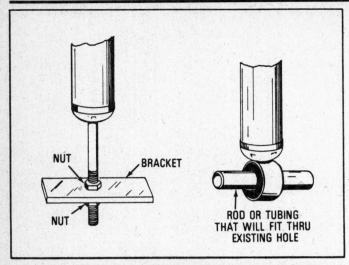

Fig. 17   Methods of gripping shock absorbers

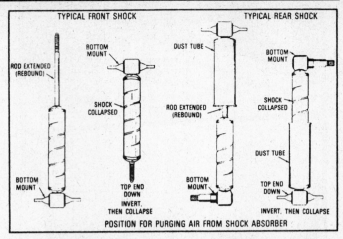

Fig. 18   Purging air from shock absorbers

Fig. 19   Supporting control arm on vehicles with spring on lower control arm

position and clamp bottom mounts in vise. Do not clamp on mounting threads or on reservoir tube.
3. Operate shock absorbers by hand at different speeds and compare resistance of known good shock to the other. Rebound resistance (extension) is usually greater than compression resistance (about 2:1). Resistance should be smooth and consistent for each stroke rate.
4. Check for the following conditions which indicate a defective shock absorber:
   a. Skip or lag when reversing direction in mid-stroke.
   b. Seizing or binding except at extreme end of stroke.
   c. Noises such as grunt or squeal after completing full stroke in either direction.
   d. Clicking noise at fast reversal.
   e. Fluid leakage.
5. Check for loose piston by extending shock absorber to full rebound position, then give an extra hard pull. If any give is present, piston is loose and unit must be replaced.

Gas Cell Shock Absorbers

These shock absorbers are equipped with a gas-filled cell which takes the place of air in the reservoir. Foaming of the fluid is eliminated since air and fluid cannot mix. Because of this feature, these style shock absorbers must be tested in an upside down position. If a lag is noticed when unit is stroked, gas cell has ruptured and unit must be replaced.

Air Adjustable Shock Absorbers

These shock absorbers have an air chamber similar to the spiral groove reservoir type which must be purged. Refer to note under "Spiral Groove Reservoir Shock Absorbers" to purge air from shock absorbers.
1. Place shock absorber in vise in vertical position with larger diameter tube at top, and clamp at lower mounting

ring.
2. Operate unit manually at different speeds. A consistent degree of resistance should be felt through length of stroke. A gurgling noise is normal since unit is normally pressurized.
3. Refer to "Spiral Groove Reservoir Shock Absorbers" test procedure for remainder of bench checks.

FRONT SUSPENSION & STEERING CHECKS

To perform the following wear checks, tension must be removed from the suspension parts. Raise the vehicle and support with jack stands. Relieve load from suspension as follows: on vehicles with the spring or torsion bar on the lower control arm, place a floor jack or single piston hydraulic jack under lower arm control as close to ball joint as possible, **Fig. 19,** and raise control arm until vehicle chassis is about to lift off jack stand, then stop; on vehicles with spring on upper control arm, jack up lower control arm as described previously, place block of wood between upper control arm and frame, **Fig. 20,** and slowly lower jack from lower control arm,

making sure that neither upper control nor wooden block move. Wooden block must be removed after inspection is completed.

UPPER & LOWER CONTROL ARM BUSHINGS CHECK

1. Have assistant sit in vehicle and apply brake to lock front wheels.
2. Grasp front wheel with both hands and vigorously attempt to rotate it forward and backward. Observe control arms for excessive front-to-rear movement.
3. Repeat procedure on other front wheel.

UPPER BALL JOINT CHECK

1. Grasp front wheel at top with one hand and at bottom with other.
2. Pull wheel out at bottom while simultaneously pushing in at top. Have assistant watch for play in upper ball joint.
3. Repeat on other front wheel.

LOWER BALL JOINT CHECK

1. Place suitable bar or pipe directly under center of tire.
2. Wedge pipe against ground and lift. Several tries may be necessary to get

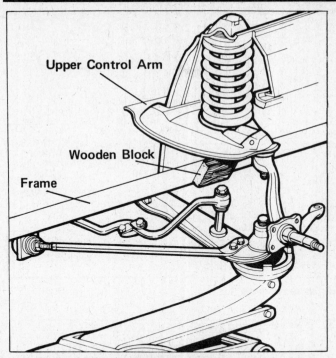

Fig. 20 Blocking control arm of vehicles with spring on upper control arm

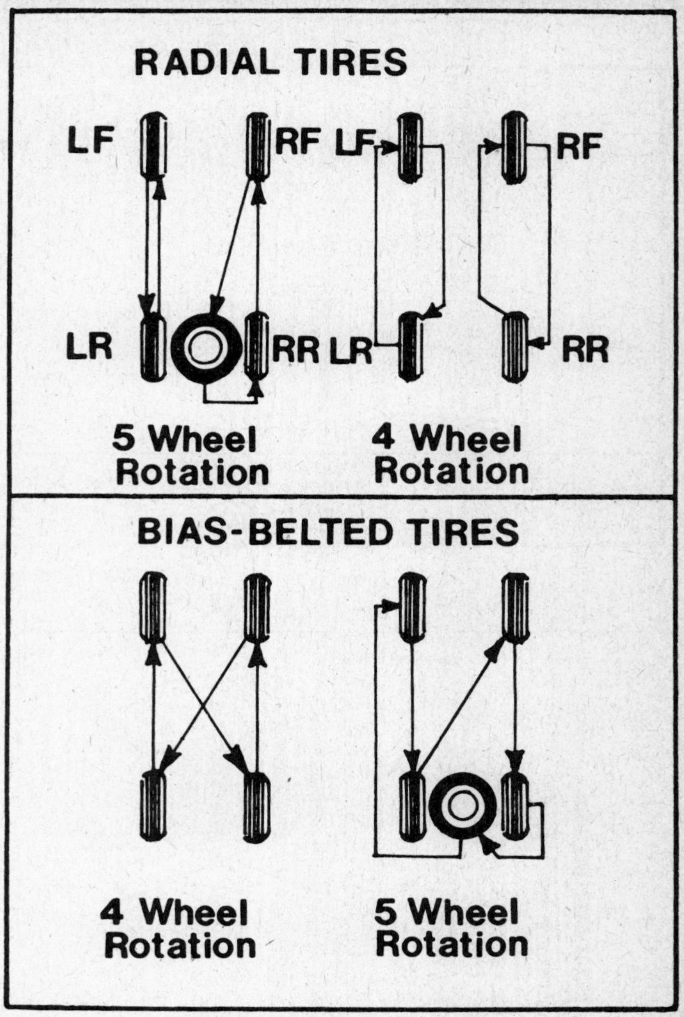

RADIAL TIRES

5 Wheel Rotation

4 Wheel Rotation

BIAS-BELTED TIRES

4 Wheel Rotation

5 Wheel Rotation

Fig. 21 Tire rotation chart

a good check.

3. Repeat procedure on other wheel.

STEERING LINKAGE CHECK

1. Grasp wheel with both hands and vigorously shake tire from right to left. Have assistant check for wear in tie-rod ends, center link, and idler arm. Idler arm should not move up and down.
2. Repeat procedure on other wheel.

TIRE CARE

TIRE ROTATION

The purpose of tire rotation is to equalize normal wear. By equalizing this wear evenly over the entire tread surface, you extend tire life. Recommended rotation patterns are shown in **Fig. 21**.

It is wise to provide snow tires with rims of their own, so they do not have to be removed from rims in the late fall. They can be kept on rims of their own during both storage and use. In this way, you will protect tires from the bead damage which becomes a possibility when you break a tire away from a rim.

A studded snow tire should always be mounted on the same wheel of the car year after year. When storing studded snow tires, mark tire in chalk for either Right or Left, depending upon which side of the car the tire was mounted.

When storing tires, lay them flat, off the tread to prevent flat spots from developing. Keep tires away from electricity-producing machinery which creates ozone and can damage rubber.

TIRE MAINTENANCE

Tires should be inspected regularly for excessive or abnormal tread wear, fabric breaks, cuts or other damage, **Fig. 22**. A bulge or bump in the sidewall or tread is reason for discarding a tire. A bulge indicates that the tread or sidewall has separated from the tire body. The tire is a candidate for a blowout. Look also for small stones or other foreign bodies wedged in the tread. These can be removed by prying them out carefully with a screwdriver.

BATTERY SERVICE

CONSTRUCTION & OPERATION

To understand why batteries malfunction, some knowledge of batteries is important. Simply stated, the battery is constructed of two unlike materials, a positive plate and a negative plate with a porous separator between the two plates, **Fig. 23**. This assembly placed in a suitable battery case and filled slightly above the top of the plates with electrolyte (sulphuric acid and distilled water) forms a cell. The 12 volt battery is composed of 6 cells interconnected by plate straps. Note that batteries have varying number of plates per cell, but each cell in any given battery has the same number of plates.

The battery performs the following four basic functions in a vehicle:

1. Supplies electrical energy to the starter motor to crank and start the engine and also to the ignition system while the engine is being started.
2. Supplies electrical energy for accessories such as radio, tape deck, heater, and lights when engine is not running and the ignition switch is in the "OFF" or the "Accessory" position.
3. Supplies additional electrical energy for accessories while the engine is running when the output alternator is exceeded by the various accessories.

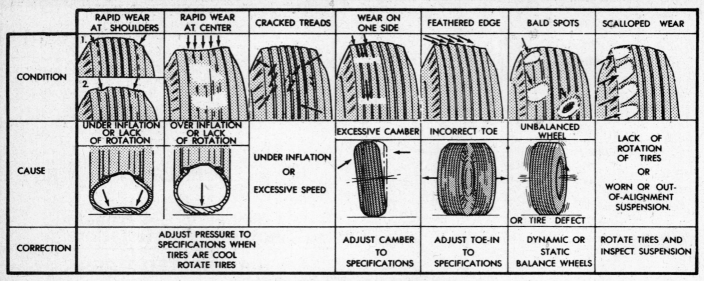

Fig. 22   Tire tread wear patterns

	RAPID WEAR AT SHOULDERS	RAPID WEAR AT CENTER	CRACKED TREADS	WEAR ON ONE SIDE	FEATHERED EDGE	BALD SPOTS	SCALLOPED WEAR
CONDITION	1. ___ 2. ___						
CAUSE	UNDER INFLATION OR LACK OF ROTATION	OVER INFLATION OR LACK OF ROTATION	UNDER INFLATION OR EXCESSIVE SPEED	EXCESSIVE CAMBER	INCORRECT TOE	UNBALANCED WHEEL OR TIRE DEFECT	LACK OF ROTATION OF TIRES OR WORN OR OUT-OF-ALIGNMENT SUSPENSION.
CORRECTION	ADJUST PRESSURE TO SPECIFICATIONS WHEN TIRES ARE COOL ROTATE TIRES			ADJUST CAMBER TO SPECIFICATIONS	ADJUST TOE-IN TO SPECIFICATIONS	DYNAMIC OR STATIC BALANCE WHEELS	ROTATE TIRES AND INSPECT SUSPENSION

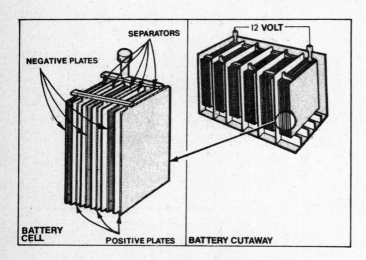

Fig. 23   Battery construction

4. Stabilizes voltage in the electrical system. Satisfactory operation of the ignition system and any other electrical device is impossible with a damaged, weak or even underpowered (low rating) battery.

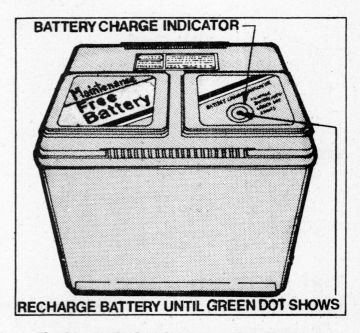

Fig. 24   Typical maintenance free battery

SEALED BATTERIES

Sealed batteries, called "Maintenance Free" or "Freedom" batteries, **Fig. 24**, are available on some vehicles, and can also be purchased from other sources.

The sealed batteries have unique chemistry and construction methods which provide advantages.

Water never needs to be added to the battery.

The battery is completely sealed except for two small vent holes on the side. The vent holes allow what small amount of gases are produced in the battery to escape. The special chemical composition inside the battery reduces the production of gas to an extremely small amount at normal

charging voltages.

The battery has a very strong ability to withstand damaging effects of overcharge, and the terminals are tightly sealed to minimize leakage. A charge indicator in the cover indicates state of charge.

Compared to a conventional battery in which performance decreases steadily with age, the sealed battery delivers more available power at any time during its life. The battery has a reduced tendency to self-discharge as compared to a conventional battery.

SAFETY PRECAUTIONS

CAUTION: Electrolyte solution in the battery is a strong and dangerous acid. It is extremely harmful to eyes, skin and clothing. If acid contacts any part of the body, flush immediately with water for a period not less than 15 minutes. If acid is accidentally swallowed, drink large quantities of milk or water, followed by milk of magnesia, a beaten raw egg or vegetable oil. Call physician immediately.

When batteries are being charged, highly explosive hydrogen and oxygen gases form in each battery cell. Some of this gas escapes through the vent holes in the plugs on top of battery case and forms an explosive atmosphere surrounding the battery. This explosive gas will remain in and/or around the battery for several hours

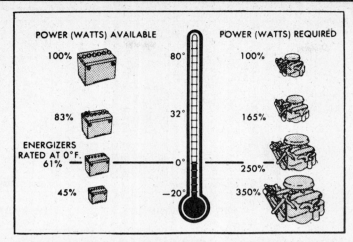

Fig. 25   Battery energy versus falling temperature comparison chart

after the battery has been charged. Sparks or flames can ignite this gas and cause a dangerous battery explosion.

The following precautions must be observed to avoid battery explosion, personal harm and damage to the vehicle's electrical system.

1. Do not smoke near batteries being charged or those which have been recently charged. It is a good practice never to smoke near a battery even though the battery is in the vehicle.
2. Always shield your eyes when working with batteries.
3. Do not disconnect live (working) circuits (lights or accessories operating) at the terminals of batteries since sparking usually occurs at a point where such a circuit is disconnected.
4. Use extreme caution when connecting or disconnecting booster leads or cable clamps from battery chargers. Make sure live (working) circuits are disconnected before connecting or disconnecting the booster leads or cable clamps. Poor booster lead connections are a common cause of electrical arcing causing battery explosions.

CAUSES OF DISCHARGED BATTERIES

There are numerous reasons that could cause a battery to discharge and appear to be defective, therefore the battery should not be targeted as the primary source of electrical and/or starting problems before it has been tested.

The following are some common conditions that could discharge a good battery:

1. Lights left "ON" or doors not closed properly, leaving dome light "ON."
2. Excessive use of accessories with the engine not running.
3. Improper installation of aftermarket accessories.
4. Alternator belt loose or damaged.
5. Dirty battery case causing a self-dis-

charge condition.
6. Loose battery cable terminals.
7. Low alternator output.
8. High resistance in charging circuits caused by other loose electrical connections.

BATTERY RATING & CAPACITY

The two most commonly used ratings are the 20 hour rating of 80° F and the cold cranking load capacity of the battery at 0° F, specified in amps. Batteries are also rated by watts in the Peak Watt Rating (PWR) which is actually the cold cranking ability of the battery at 0° F.

Another battery rating method is the reserve capacity rating in minutes. The purpose of this rating is to determine the length of time a vehicle can be operated with a faulty charging system (malfunctioning alternator or regulator). Batteries are normally marketed by the Ampere-Hour rating which is based on the 20 hour rating. The Ampere-Hour rating is also normally stamped on the battery case or on a label attached to the battery. A battery capable of furnishing 4 amps for a period of 20 hours is classified as an 80 ampere hour battery (4 amps × 20 hours = 80).

The Ampere-Hour rating should not be confused with the cranking performance of a battery at 0° F. Batteries with the same Ampere-Hour ratings can have various 0° F cranking capacities. The higher quality battery will have a higher Ampere-Hour rating and a higher cranking capacity rating at 0° F. Note that battery capacity will increase with larger number of plates per cell, larger size of plates, and larger battery case size allowing for more electrolyte solution.

SELECTING A REPLACEMENT BATTERY

Long and troublefree service can be better assured when the capacity or wattage rating of the replacement battery is at least

equal to the wattage rating of the battery originally engineered for the application by the manufacturer.

The use of an undersized battery may result in poor performance and early failure. **Fig. 25** shows how battery power shrinks while the need for engine cranking power increases with falling temperatures. Sub-zero temperatures reduce capacity of a fully charged battery to 45% of its normal power and at the same time increase cranking load to 3½ times the normal warm weather load.

Hot weather can also place excessive electrical loads on the battery. Difficulty in starting may occur when cranking is attempted shortly after a hot engine has been turned off or stalls. High compression engines can be as difficult to start under such conditions as on the coldest day. Consequently, good performance can be obtained only if the battery has ample capacity to cope with these conditions.

A battery of greater capacity should be considered if the electrical load has been increased through the addition of accessories, or if driving conditions are such that the generator cannot keep the battery charged.

On applications where heavy electrical loads are encountered, a higher output generator that will supply a charge during low speed operation may be required to increase battery life and improve battery performance.

TESTING BATTERY (SPECIFIC GRAVITY)

NOTE: The specific gravity of a sealed battery cannot be checked.

A hydrometer can be used to measure the specific gravity of the electrolyte in each cell. There are several types of hydrometers available, the least expensive consisting of a glass tube, a rubber bulb at the end of the tube and several balls within the tube. To use this type, the specific gravity of the battery must be interpreted by the number of balls which float to the surface of the electrolyte, according to the manufacturer's instructions.

The hydrometer indicates the concentration of the electrolyte.

BOOST STARTING A VEHICLE WITH A DISCHARGED BATTERY

1. Be sure the ignition key is in the off position and all accessories and lights are off.
2. Shield eyes. Use goggles or similar eye protection.
3. Connect the booster cables from the positive (+) battery terminal of the discharged battery (vehicle to be started) to the positive (+) battery terminal of the vehicle used as the booster.
4. Connect one end of the other cable to negative (−) terminal of the good battery.
5. Connect one end of the other cable to

Watt Rating	5 Amperes	10 Amperes	20 Amperes	30 Amperes	40 Amperes	50 Amperes
Below 2450	10 Hours	5 Hours	2½ Hours	2 Hours		
2450–2950	12 Hours	6 Hours	3 Hours	2 Hours	1½ Hours	
Above 2950	15 Hours	7½ Hours	3¼ Hours	2 Hours	1¾ Hours	1½ Hours

Fig. 26   Battery charging guide

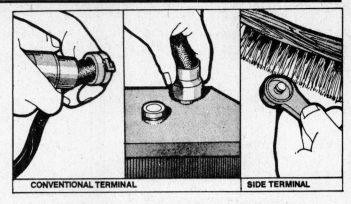

CONVENTIONAL TERMINAL   SIDE TERMINAL

Fig. 27   Cleaning battery terminals

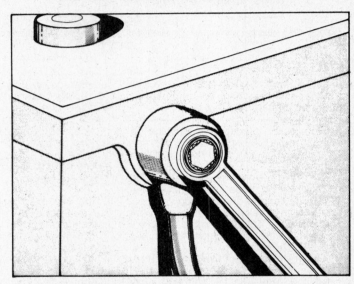

Fig. 28   Removing side type battery terminal

engine bolthead or similar good contact spot on the vehicle being started.

CAUTION: Never connect to negative terminal of dead battery.

NOTE: To prevent damage to other electrical components on the vehicle being started, make certain engine is at idle speed before disconnecting jumper cables.

CHARGING THE BATTERY

There are two separate methods of recharging batteries which differ basically in the rate of charge.

Slow Charging Method

Slow charging is the best and only method of completely recharging a battery. This method, when properly applied, may be used safely under all possible conditions providing the electrolyte is at proper level and the battery is capable of being fully charged. The normal charging rate is 5 amperes.

A fully charged battery is indicated when all cell specific gravities do not increase when checked at three one-hour intervals and all cells are gassing freely.

Charge periods of 24 hours or more may be required because of the low charging rate. See charging guide, **Fig. 26.**

Quick Charging Method

In order to get a car back on the road in the least amount of time, it is sometimes necessary to quick charge a battery. The battery cannot be brought up to full charged condition by the quick charge method. It can, however, be substantially recharged or boosted but, in order to bring it to a fully charged condition, the charging cycle must be finished by charging at a low or normal rate. Some quick chargers have a provision for finishing the charging cycle at a low rate to bring the battery up to a fully charged condition.

CAUTION: Too high a current during quick charging will damage battery plates.

BATTERY CABLE SERVICE

NOTE: At regular intervals, perform a visual inspection of the battery.

This inspection should be performed when any of the underhood maintenance items such as engine oil, transmission fluid or radiator coolant level are checked.

1. Clean any heavy accumulation of dirt or corrosion on the battery terminals and battery tray with a wire brush, **Fig. 27.** Finish cleaning with a solution of baking soda and water. Diluted ammonia can also be used as a washing agent. Thoroughly flush battery with clean water.

NOTE: Baking soda and ammonia neutralize battery acid. Therefore make sure these agents are kept out of the battery by keeping the battery caps tightly in place.

2. Check for damaged cable insulation. Damaged insulation can cause the cable to short out against the body of the vehicle or other accessories. Cables in this condition should be replaced immediately.
3. Check level of electrolyte. If required, add water as described further on.
4. Make sure battery is securely held in place. A loose or broken bracket can result in battery damage (both internally and externally) from excessive vibration.

BATTERY CABLE, REPLACE

NOTE: When disconnecting battery cables, first make sure all accessories are off, disconnect the negative battery cable and then the positive cable. Make sure to reconnect cables in the reverse order of removal.

1. On side terminal batteries, loosen the retaining bolts using a ⁵⁄₁₆-inch wrench, and disconnect the cable from the battery, **Fig. 28.**
2. On all other type batteries, loosen the cable retaining bolt using a ½ inch or ⁹⁄₁₆ inch box wrench, **Fig. 29,** and lift the cable off the battery posts. Some cables can be removed by squeezing the tabs on the cable terminal using a pair of pliers, **Fig. 30,** and lifting the cable off the battery posts.
3. If the battery terminals are difficult to remove, use a terminal puller, **Fig. 31.** Place the legs of the puller underneath the terminal and tighten the puller screw until the terminal is removed.
4. Clean the cable terminals and battery

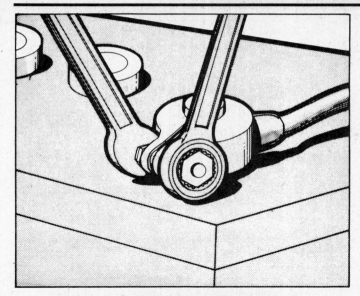

Fig. 29   Removing bolt type terminal

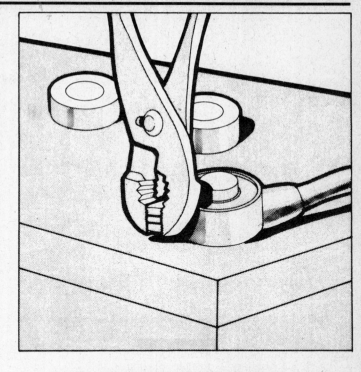

Fig. 30   Removing spread type terminal

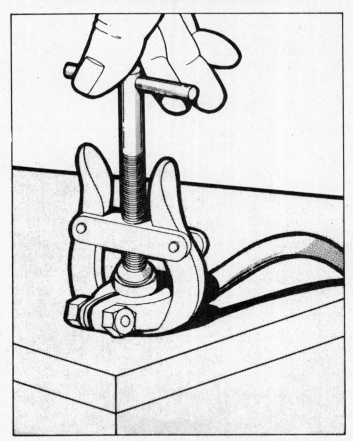

Fig. 31   Removing battery cable terminal using cable terminal puller

7. To install the cables on all other types of batteries, place the cables on the battery post and force them all the way down. If the cable is not completely bottomed, spread the cable terminal slightly with a screwdriver, until the terminal is properly positioned.
8. Tighten the terminal bolts using a ½ inch or ⁹⁄₁₆ inch box wrench.
9. Coat the outside of the terminals with petroleum jelly to prevent corrosion.

BATTERY, REPLACE

Careless installation of a new battery can ruin the battery. In removing the old battery, note the location of the positive battery post so the new battery can be installed in the same position. Always remove the negative (ground) cable first.

Use an open-end wrench to loosen the clamp. If the nut is very tight, use one wrench on the head of the bolt and the other on the nut to avoid straining and possibly cracking the battery cover. A pair of battery pliers can be used to loosen the nut, but a wrench should always be used on the head of the bolt.

If a cable terminal is corroded to the post, do not try to loosen it by hammering, or by resting a tool on the battery and prying—either method can break the battery container. Use a screw type terminal puller, **Fig. 31,** or spread the cable terminals slightly with a screwdriver.

Clean any corrosion from the cables, battery case, or hold-downs, and inspect them. Paint any corroded steel parts with acid-proof paint. Make sure the cable is of the correct size and that its insulation and

posts using a terminal and post wire brush, **Fig. 27.**
5. Clean the battery top using a solution of soda and water. Ensure the battery is thoroughly cleaned and dried. Make sure you cover the battery caps to

avoid entry of the soda and water solution into the battery.
6. To install the cables on a side terminal battery, place the cables onto the battery and tighten the retaining screws using a ⁵⁄₁₆ inch wrench.

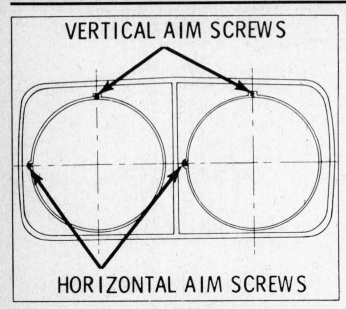

Fig. 32 Headlamp adjusting screws (typical)

clamp terminal are in good condition.

Put the new battery in position, making sure it sits level, and tighten the hold-downs a little at a time, alternately, to avoid distorting and breaking the battery case. The hold-downs should be snug enough to prevent bouncing, but should not be too tight.

NOTE: Before connecting the cables, check the battery terminals to be sure the battery is not reversed.

Clean the battery post bright with sandpaper or a wire brush.

Don't hammer the terminals down on the posts, as the battery case may crack. Spread the terminals slightly if necessary. Connect the starter cable first and the negative (ground) cable last, tightening the terminal bolts after making sure the cables don't interfere with the vent plugs or rub against the hold-downs.

HEADLAMP AIMING

It is recommended that headlamps be

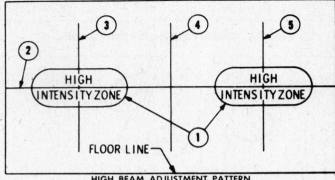

Fig. 33 Headlamp aiming

checked for proper aim every 12 months or whenever front body work is repaired. On most vehicles, aiming can be performed without removing headlamp bezels. Vertical adjustment is usually accomplished with a screw at the top of the sealed beam retaining ring (12 o'clock position). Horizontal adjustment is provided by a screw at the right or left (3 or 9 o'clock position) of the sealed beam unit, **Fig. 32**. Headlamp aiming can be performed visually with a screen as follows:

1. Vehicle should be on level floor so headlamps are 25 ft. from screen or light colored wall. Fuel tank should be ½ full. Any heavy loads that are normally in vehicle should remain there. Driver and passengers should not be in vehicle during aiming. Tires should be inflated to specified pressures and headlamps lenses should be cleaned.
2. Mark screen or wall with four lines as shown in **Fig. 33**.
3. Adjust low beam pattern only as shown in top diagram in **Fig. 33**.
4. On vehicles with four headlamp systems, cover low beam (outboard or upper lamps) and adjust high beam lamp pattern as shown in bottom diagram of **Fig. 33**.

Ignition System Service

INDEX

BASIC OPERATION

Combustion of air/fuel mixtures in gasoline engines is initiated by spark ignition. Complete burning (combustion) of the air/fuel mixtures is essential for proper engine performance, acceptable driveability and fuel economy, and exhaust emission control. In order to ensure that the air/fuel mixtures burn completely, the spark that begins combustion must be of sufficient heat (voltage) and duration, and it must be applied at exactly the right moment during each cylinder's operating cycle.

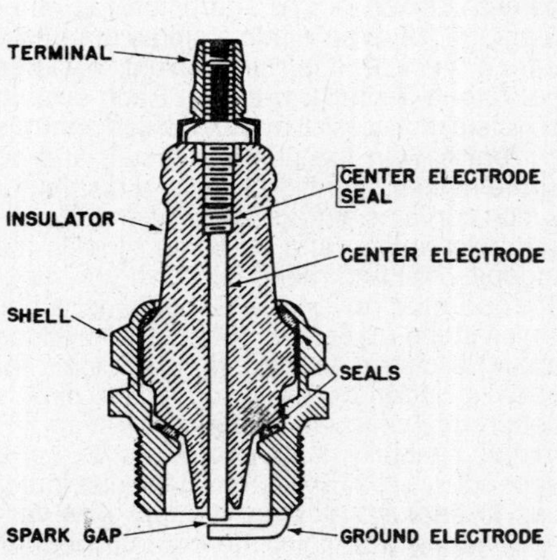

The part of the vehicle electrical system that produces spark to ignite the air/fuel mixtures is the ignition system. Spark is created by producing an electric arc between electrodes of the spark plug, **Fig. 1**, which is installed in the combustion chamber of each cylinder. Depending upon engine design and operating conditions, 5000 to 30,000 volts of electricity are required to produce a spark of sufficient energy to ensure proper combustion of air/fuel mixtures.

The ignition system receives energy to produce spark from the vehicle battery and charging system. Since the nominal voltage of most automotive electrical systems is 12 volts, one of the main functions of the ignition system is to increase battery voltage to the voltage required to produce an arc across the spark plug of sufficient heat and duration. The other main function of ignition systems is to deliver these "stepped-up" voltages to the spark plug of each cylinder at exactly the right time to ensure that air/fuel mixtures burn completely and transfer the maximum amount of energy to produce power.

Ignition systems are broken down into two main sub-systems which relate to the two main system functions. The primary (low voltage) side of the system performs the function of increasing battery voltage to the levels necessary to produce spark. The secondary side of the system delivers the high voltage to the spark plugs.

The ignition coil is the transformer that steps-up battery voltage to produce spark, and also the division point between primary and secondary ignition circuits. The coil consists of two coils of wire, insulated from each other, which are wound around an iron core, **Fig. 2**. The primary windings consist of a few turns of large diameter wire, while the secondary windings consist of many turns of fine wire. The coil creates

Fig. 1   Spark plug, cross-sectional view. (Typical)

TERMINAL

CENTER ELECTRODE SEAL

INSULATOR

CENTER ELECTRODE

SHELL

SEALS

SPARK GAP

GROUND ELECTRODE

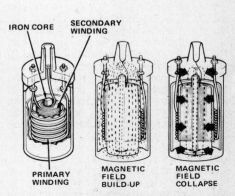

Fig. 2   Ignition coil construction & operation. (Typical)

IRON CORE

SECONDARY WINDING

PRIMARY WINDING

MAGNETIC FIELD BUILD-UP

MAGNETIC FIELD COLLAPSE

high voltages necessary to produce spark through magnetic induction.

As battery voltage (current) flows through the coil primary windings, a magnetic field is produced. When current flow through the primary windings is momentarily interrupted, the magnetic field instantly collapses and high voltage is induced in the coil secondary windings. This induced voltage is discharged through the spark plug, creating spark to initiate combustion.

Secondary voltage strength is determined by the strength of the magnetic field created by current flow in the primary windings, the speed with which the magnetic field collapses and the difference between the number of turns of wire in the primary and secondary sides of the coil. The longer current flows in the primary windings (dwell period), the stronger the magnetic field created will be. The stronger the magnetic field is and the quicker it collapses, the higher the voltages in the secondary circuit will be. In addition, secondary voltages increase as the difference between the number of turns of wire in the primary and secondary windings increases.

The ignition distributor, **Fig. 3,** acts as both the switch that turns current flow on and off in the primary circuit, and as the mechanism that delivers secondary (high) voltages to each spark plug at the right time. The distributor is driven by the engine and synchronized to the engine's mechanical operation. When the distributor is properly installed and adjusted, it will momentarily stop current flow in the primary circuit and connect the coil secondary windings to the spark plug of each cylinder just as the piston in that cylinder is reaching top dead center on the compression stroke. This synchronization between ignition system electrical operation and engine mechanical operation is referred to as ignition timing.

Common practice is to relate the ignition firing point to the rotation of the crankshaft, and to express this relationship in degrees. The point of crankshaft rotation where the piston is at Top Dead Center (TDC) is expressed as zero degrees. Generally, the ignition system is adjusted so that the firing point will occur before TDC, which is referred to as ignition advance. If the firing point is set to occur after TDC, it is referred to as spark retard.

In order for air/fuel mixtures to transfer maximum energy to the engine, the mixture must reach the point of complete combustion just after each piston has reached TDC on its compression stroke. Because there is a slight lag between the time that the mixture begins to burn (ignition) and the time that complete combustion is achieved, ignition must occur before the piston has reached TDC and begun its downward travel. If the spark occurs too late, energy is lost because the piston is already moving downward when the mixture reaches its maximum explosive force. If spark occurs too early, the piston must fight against the explosive force in order to rise, which absorbs energy and ultimately causes damage to engine components. Therefore, correct timing of the ignition

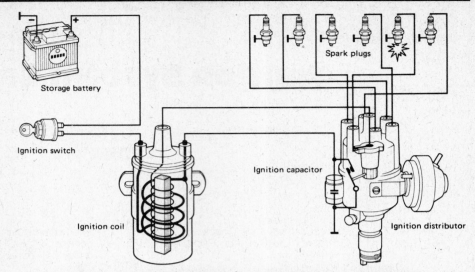

Fig. 3   Conventional coil ignition system schematic

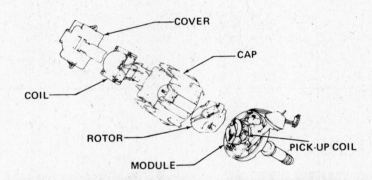

Fig. 4   GM-Delco High Energy Ignition (HEI) distributor. W/integral coil

system is essential for efficient engine operation.

Basic ignition timing is determined by the installation position of the distributor. However, ideal ignition timing to ensure proper combustion varies constantly with changing engine operating conditions. Ignition systems have built in electronic, mechanical and/or vacuum operated devices which advance or retard ignition timing from the basic setting to compensate for changing loads, air/fuel mixtures and engine speeds.

ELECTRONIC IGNITION SYSTEMS

In order to properly ignite air/fuel mixtures required for exhaust emission control under all operating conditions, vehicles covered in this manual use electronic ignition systems. On electronic systems, the breaker points, operating cam and condenser used on older systems to control primary circuit voltage have been replaced by a non-mechanical triggering mechanism and an electronic control unit (module). This allows the electronic systems to control current flow through the ignition pri-

mary circuit with more flexibility and precision, resulting in higher secondary voltages and more precise ignition timing. In addition, because there is no mechanical triggering mechanism to wear out, electronic systems require less maintenance.

Although electronic ignition components differ in design from manufacturer to manufacturer, or even within a single manufacturer's vehicle line, all current systems operate in a similar manner. Each system consists of a control module which controls current flow in the primary circuit, and on some systems a distributor which contains a magnetic trigger and sensor mechanism, and on some models the module, coil and mechanical and/or vacuum operated advance mechanisms; a coil which steps-up battery voltages to produce spark; a distributor cap with terminals for each cylinder and a rotor which directs secondary voltages to the proper cap terminal; specially insulated wires to carry secondary voltages from the distributor cap to each spark plug; primary (low voltage) wiring that links the control module, trigger sensor, ignition coil and the vehicle electrical system. Installation and mounting of these components varies from vehi-

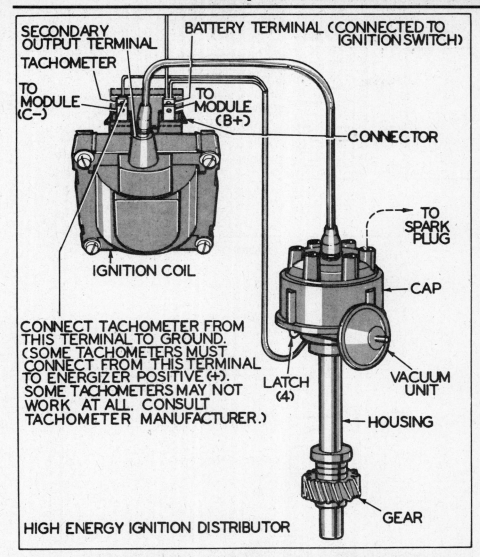

SECONDARY OUTPUT TERMINAL

TACHOMETER

TO MODULE (C–)

BATTERY TERMINAL (CONNECTED TO IGNITION SWITCH)

TO MODULE (B+)

CONNECTOR

IGNITION COIL

TO SPARK PLUG

CAP

CONNECT TACHOMETER FROM THIS TERMINAL TO GROUND. (SOME TACHOMETERS MUST CONNECT FROM THIS TERMINAL TO ENERGIZER POSITIVE (+). SOME TACHOMETERS MAY NOT WORK AT ALL. CONSULT TACHOMETER MANUFACTURER.)

VACUUM UNIT

LATCH (4)

HOUSING

GEAR

HIGH ENERGY IGNITION DISTRIBUTOR

Fig. 5   GM-Delco High Energy Ignition (HEI) distributor. W/remote coil

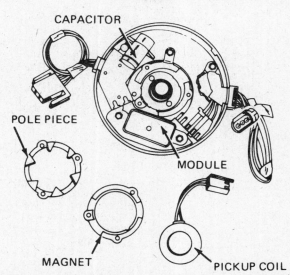

CAPACITOR

POLE PIECE

MODULE

MAGNET

PICKUP COIL

Fig. 6   Magnetic pick-up assembly exploded view. GM-HEI type systems

cle to vehicle.

The electronic ignition coil consists of primary and secondary windings like coils used with breaker point systems. Current flow through the coil primary windings is switched on and off by the electronic control module, which on most systems, has the ability to vary the "on" time (dwell period) to match secondary voltages to engine operating conditions. Module operation is controlled by a magnetic "impulse" type mechanism which consists of a trigger wheel mounted on the distributor shaft and a sensor coil which detects trigger wheel position.

CHEVROLET & GMC

All models except S/T series equipped with the 4-119 (1.9L) engine use the GM-Delco High Energy Ignition (HEI) ignition system. Models equipped with the 4-119 (1.9L) engine use an HEI system manufactured by Nippondenso. The module, magnetic trigger and pick-up, and ignition coil are contained within the distributor on most models, **Fig. 4.** On 4 cylinder engines the ignition coil is remotely mounted, **Fig. 5.**

High Energy Ignition (HEI)

The HEI system uses an all electronic module, timer core and pick-up coil to control current flow through the primary ignition circuit. The timer core is integral with the distributor shaft. The pick-up assembly, **Fig. 6,** consisting of a permanent magnet, coil and an internally toothed pole piece, and the control module are mounted on the distributor body.

When the distributor shaft rotates, the teeth on the timer core pass very close to the teeth on the pick-up pole piece. As the teeth pass, voltage is induced in the pick-up coil and transmitted to the electronic control module. At the instant that timer core teeth begin to pass the pole piece teeth, the module opens the ignition primary circuit, inducing high voltage in the secondary circuit.

HEI is a 12 volt system that does not use a ballast resistor in the coil primary circuit. This allows the coil to develop higher secondary voltages, while simplifying the ignition feed circuit. A current limiting circuit within the module protects electronic components from overload.

Ignition timing advance on conventional HEI systems is controlled by centrifugal advance weights and by a vacuum diaphragm. The vacuum diaphragm is connected to the magnetic pick-up assembly. When vacuum acting against the diaphragm overcomes spring tension, the diaphragm rotates the pick-up assembly, advancing the pole pieces in relation to the timer core. The timer core position is controlled by conventional advance weights which allow it to advance in relation to the pole piece as engine speed increases.

Electronic Spark Control (ESC)

1980–85 models with a V8-305 engine and 4 barrel carburetor (except models with California emission controls) are equipped with the ESC system. ESC is a closed-loop system that constantly adjusts

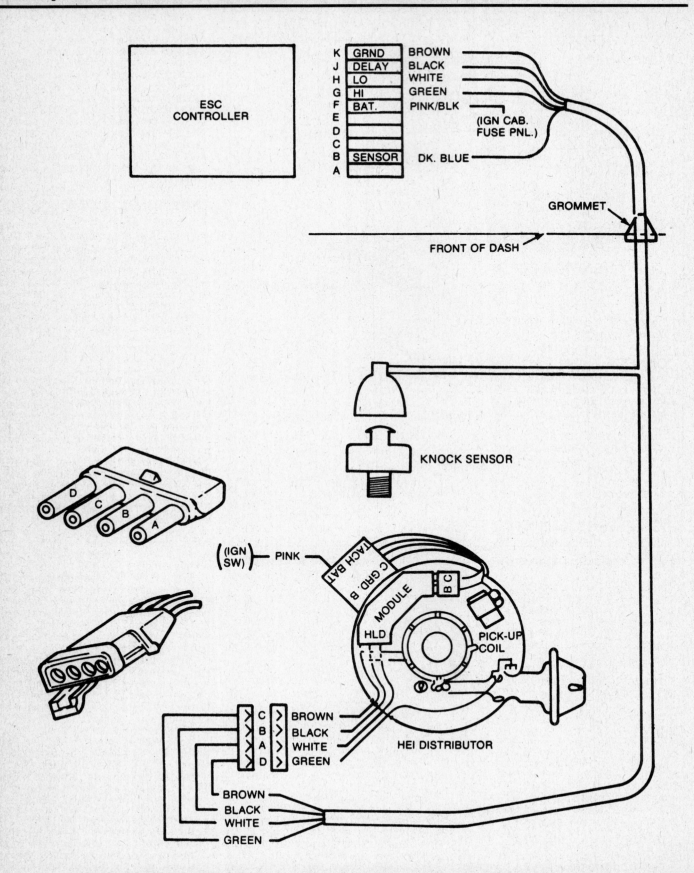

Fig. 7 Electronic Spark Control (ESC) system schematic. GM-HEI type systems

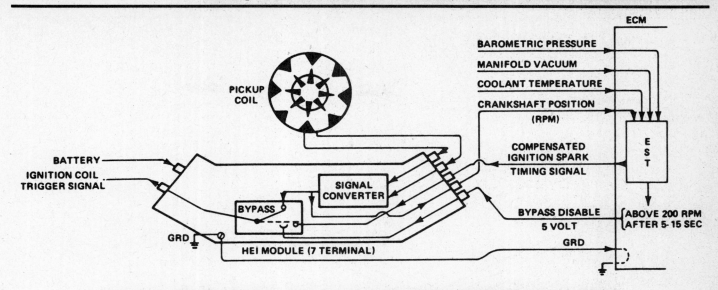

Fig. 8 Electronic Spark Timing (EST) system schematic. GM-HEI type systems

ignition timing in order to eliminate detonation. The system allows ignition timing to be advanced for increased efficiency during normal vehicle operation, but electronically retards the spark if the engine begins to detonate (knock). The degree of detonation determines the amount that the spark is retarded.

The ESC system, **Fig. 7,** consists of a modified HEI control module, an engine mounted knock sensor, a separate ESC controller and a wiring to link components. Vibrations produced by engine detonation are sensed by the knock sensor and converted into an electrical signal; the stronger the vibration, the higher signal voltage signal will be. The ESC controller evaluates signals from the knock sensor and sends a command signal to the special HEI module to control ignition timing. The HEI module is capable of retarding spark timing up to 15° from the existing mechanical setting (combination of base, centrifugal and vacuum advance settings) by delaying the primary current switching.

Electronic Spark Timing (EST)

Ignition timing and spark advance on some models with a full function Computer Command Control (C-3) system are controlled by the EST section of the C-3 control module. Models equipped with EST use a 7 pin HEI module, **Fig. 8,** which converts signals from the pick-up coil into crankshaft position information. Crankshaft position information is transmitted to the C-3 control module which computes optimum spark timing based on input from other engine and vehicle sensors. The C-3 module controls ignition timing under all operating conditions except during cranking or when the system is bypassed. The distributor on EST controlled models does

not have centrifugal or vacuum advance mechanisms.

DODGE & PLYMOUTH

1979—80 MODELS

These models use a conventional electronic ignition system, **Fig. 9,** which consists of a remote mounted electronic control unit (module) and conventional ignition coil, external ballast resistor and a distributor in which breaker points, cam and condenser have been replaced by a magnetic pick-up and reluctor (trigger wheel). During normal operation, battery voltage is supplied to the ignition coil through the ballast resistor, which acts as a voltage stabilizer. However, during cranking the ballast resistor is by-passed and the coil receives full battery voltage. On 1979 models, control module operating voltage is also supplied through a second ballast resistor circuit. On 1980 models, the module has a built-in current regulator, and receives full battery voltage.

The ignition coil primary circuit is completed to ground through a switching transistor in the control module. The single pole magnetic pick-up controls operation of the module switching transistor. As the reluctor rotates with the distributor shaft, the reluctor poles pass the pick-up pole each time a spark plug should be fired. As the reluctor poles pass the pick-up, a voltage signal is produced in the pick-up coil which is transmitted to the control module. Each time the module receives this signal, the transistor momentarily interrupts current flow through the coil primary circuit, causing high voltage to be induced in the secondary circuit. Secondary voltages are distributed to the spark plugs through a conventional distributor cap and rotor, and

specially insulated spark plug wires.

Spark advance is controlled by both a centrifugal advance mechanism and a vacuum diaphragm. The centrifugal advance, located under the breaker plate, advances the position of the reluctor (trigger wheel) in relation to the magnetic pick-up as engine speed increases. The vacuum diaphragm operates the magnetic pick-up mounting plate (breaker plate), changing the position of the pick-up in relation to the reluctor, depending upon the strength of the vacuum signal.

1981—85 6-225 & V8 ENGINES

All 1981—84 models except V8 models with manual transmissions use a dual pick-up distributor, **Fig. 10,** in which one magnetic pick-up provides signal voltage to the electronic control module only during starting, and signals from the other pick-up are used only during normal running. In addition, all models with the 6-225 engine and some 1983—85 models with the V8-318 engine are equipped with the Electronic Spark Control (ESC) system. The ignition system used on V8 models with manual transmissions operates the same way as the 1980 system.

Dual Pick-Up Distributor

The dual pick-up distributor allows basic ignition timing during normal running to be advanced for improved performance, while allowing the spark advance to be reduced during cranking for easier starting. On models with ESC, the dual pick-up distributor operation is controlled by a spark control computer. On models without ESC, the signal pulses from the two magnetic pick-up assemblies are controlled by a relay. When the ignition switch is in the start position, the dual pick-up relay is ener-

FUEL, IGNITION & GENERAL MAINTENANCE

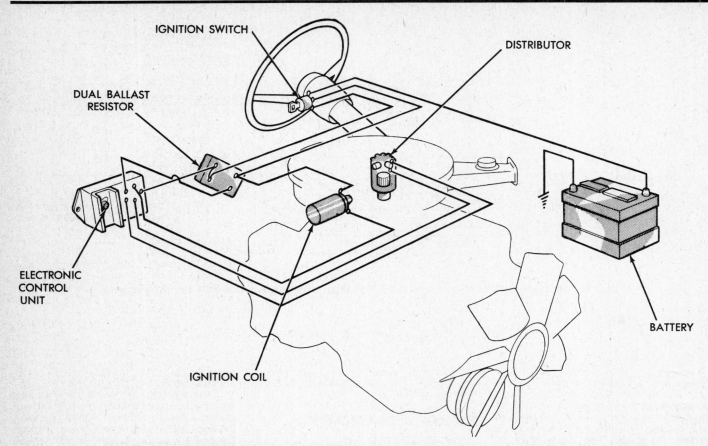

Fig. 9   Electronic ignition system schematic. 1979 Dodge & Plymouth (1980 models similar)

gized through the starter solenoid, and the control module is operated by pulse signals from the start pick-up. When the ignition switch is in the on (run) position, the relay is de-energized and module operation is controlled by the run pick-up. The remainder of the ignition system on models without ESC operates the same way as the 1980 system.

Electronic Spark Control (ESC)

The ESC system uses a micro-processor control module (computer) to control ignition timing, and air/fuel mixtures and Exhaust Gas Recirculation (EGR) in order to ensure optimum engine performance under all operating conditions. ESC system components include the spark control computer with an integral vacuum transducer (sensor), a dual pick-up distributor, coolant and charge (air/fuel mixture) temperature sensors, and a throttle position sensor. The distributor used with ESC systems does not have centrifugal or vacuum advance mechanisms, as all ignition timing functions are controlled by the computer.

The spark control computer assembly, **Fig. 11,** consists of a printed circuit board, vacuum sensor and an electronic control module (computer) which are contained in a housing attached to the air cleaner. The module computes optimum ignition timing for all operating conditions, based on input from the various sensors. Ignition timing is controlled by the module by controlling cur-

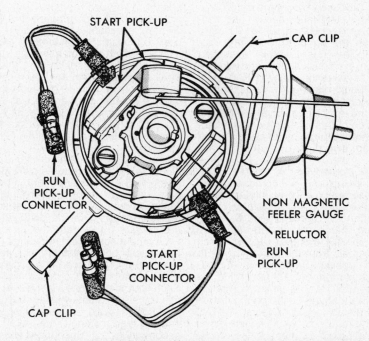

Fig. 10   Dual pick-up distributor. Dodge & Plymouth V8 engines (6 cylinder engines similar)

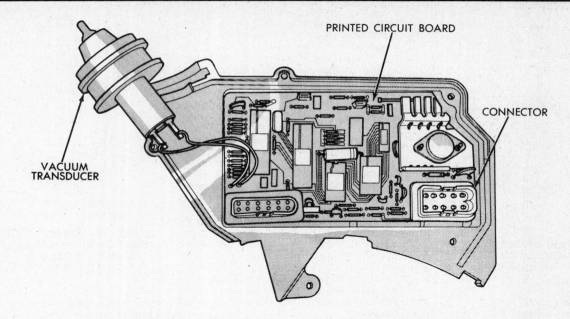

Fig. 11   Spark Control Computer (SCC). Dodge & Plymouth

rent switching in the ignition coil primary circuit.

The computer operates in two basic modes, start and run. The start mode only functions when the ignition switch is in the start position or when the run mode is disabled. The run mode only functions when the ignition switch is in the on (run) position. The two operating modes cannot function at the same time.

During cranking, computer operation is controlled by pulse signals from the distributor start pick-up and the run mode is by-passed. Ignition timing remains fixed at the value determined by start pick-up installation position. The amount of spark advance available in this mode is determined by distributor installation position.

During normal running, the start mode is by-passed, and the computer uses pulse signals from the distributor run pick-up as a reference signal and to compute engine RPM and crankshaft position. Whenever the throttle is moved away from idle position (throttle position switch open), the computer constantly alters ignition timing based on input from vehicle sensors. When the throttle is returned to idle position (throttle position switch closed), ignition timing is maintained at a fixed value.

If there is a malfunction in the computer run circuit, the system will switch to the start mode but performance and fuel economy will be reduced. However, if the start pick-up is defective, or if there is a failure in the computer start circuit, the engine will not start or run.

4-135 (2.2L) ENGINE

Ignition system operation and spark timing on Rampage, Scamp and 1984–85 Mini-Vans equipped with the 4-135 (2.2L) engine is controlled by the Electronic Fuel Control (EFC) system. Ignition system

components include the spark control computer, Hall effect distributor, conventional type ignition coil, specially insulated distributor cap, rotor and spark plug wires, and various sensors that provide vehicle operating information to the computer. The spark control computer controls both ignition timing and air/fuel mixtures to ensure proper combustion under all operating conditions.

The spark control computer assembly, **Fig. 11,** consists of a printed circuit board, vacuum sensor and electronic control module (computer). It controls ignition timing under all operating conditions, based on information from vehicle sensors. The computer controls ignition timing by controlling current switching in the ignition coil primary circuit.

System operation on these models is similar to the operation of the ESC system used on six and eight cylinder engines, but the control signals are generated by a Hall effect sensor in the distributor, rather than by separate pick-up coils. During cranking, the computer maintains ignition timing at a fixed value, based on distributor installation position. During normal running, the computer uses distributor signals as a reference to compute engine RPM and crankshaft position. As long as the throttle position switch is open (off-idle position), the computer adjusts ignition timing based on sensor signals. When the throttle switch is closed (idle position), the computer maintains ignition timing at a fixed value.

Hall Effect Distributor

The Hall effect sensor consists of a small integrated circuit and semi-conductor sensor assembly, and a permanent magnet which is mounted facing the sensor and separated by an air gap, **Fig. 12.** Four metal "shutter" plates attached to the dis-

tributor rotor pass through this air gap as the distributor rotates. When the semi-conductor sensor is exposed to the magnetic field (no plate in the air gap), a voltage signal is generated on the sensor. When the magnetic field is blocked by the presence of a plate in the air gap, no voltage signal is generated. The voltage signal cycle is converted to a sharp "on/off" signal by the integrated circuit attached to the sensor. This on/off signal is used by the spark control computer to control ignition system operation and compute RPM and crankshaft position.

4-156 (2.6L) ENGINE

This system consists of a conventional ignition coil, specially insulated distributor cap, rotor and spark plug wires, and a distributor, **Fig. 13,** which contains an electronic control module (IC igniter), magnetic pick-up assembly, and centrifugal and vacuum advance mechanisms. Ignition coil primary current is controlled by the module in response to timing signals generated by the magnetic pick-up. System and component operation is typical of conventional electronic ignition systems.

FORD

Ford trucks covered in this manual use three different electronic ignition systems. All models that do not use the Electronic Engine Control (EEC-III or EEC-IV) emission control system use Dura Spark II. Models equipped with the EEC-III system use Dura Spark III, while 1984–85 models with EEC-IV use the Thick Film Ignition (TFI-IV) system.

Dura Spark II

The Dura Spark II system consists of a remotely mounted electronic control module and oil filled ignition coil, a two-piece

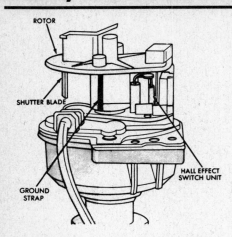

Fig. 12 Hall effect distributor. Dodge & Plymouth 4-135 (2.2L) engines

System operation is typical of conventional electronic ignition systems. As the distributor rotates, poles on the shaft mounted armature pass the single pole stator assembly, **Fig. 15,** inducing voltage in the stator windings. These voltage pulses are transmitted to the control module as timing signals. The module momentarily interrupts current flow in the ignition coil primary circuit whenever it receives a timing pulse, which causes spark voltage to be induced in the coil secondary windings. Secondary voltages are distributed to the spark plugs through the distributor cap, rotor and specially insulated plug wires.

Spark advance is controlled by a centrifugal advance mechanism and by a dual or single diaphragm vacuum capsule. The centrifugal advance mechanism allows the position of the distributor armature to advance in relation to the stator as engine speed increases, advancing ignition timing. The vacuum capsule rotates the stator mounting plate position in relation to the armature, advancing or retarding ignition timing depending upon the vacuum signal received.

Two different electronic control modules are used with Dura Spark II systems, depending upon vehicle application. The standard module, identified by a blue wiring grommet and two electrical connectors, performs as outlined, controlling primary circuit current in response to stator signals. The Unitized Integrated Circuit (UIC) module, identified by a yellow wiring grommet and three electrical connectors, is used on some 1981–85 models calibrated for high

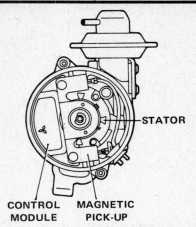

Fig. 13 Electronic ignition distributor w/integral control module. Dodge & Plymouth 4-156 (2.6L) engines

altitude operation and some models with micro-processor controlled (MCU) fuel systems. The UIC module controls primary current based on stator signals, but also includes a provision for external control of ignition timing. The third module connector receives a signal from a barometric pressure switch, ignition timing vacuum switch or the MCU system controlled under certain operating conditions. When the module receives this signal it delays switching of the ignition coil primary circuit to retard ignition timing.

distributor cap and specially designed rotor, silicone jacketed spark plug wires and a distributor which contains a stator (magnetic pick-up), armature (trigger wheel), centrifugal advance mechanism and a vacuum advance/retard diaphragm, **Fig. 14.** Battery voltage is supplied to the ignition coil primary windings through a resistance wire for normal running, but a by-pass circuit in the control module allows full battery voltage to be applied to the coil for increased spark voltage during cranking.

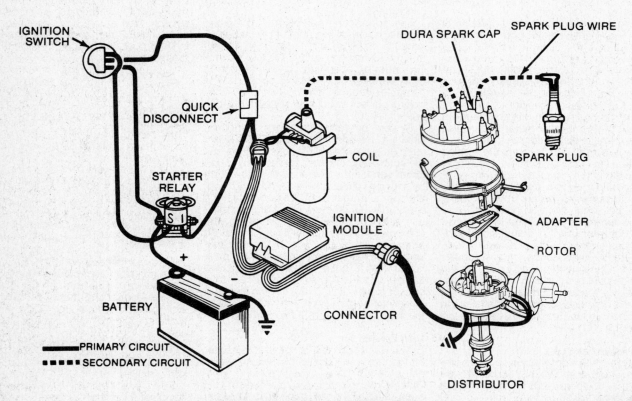

Fig. 14 Dura Spark II schematic

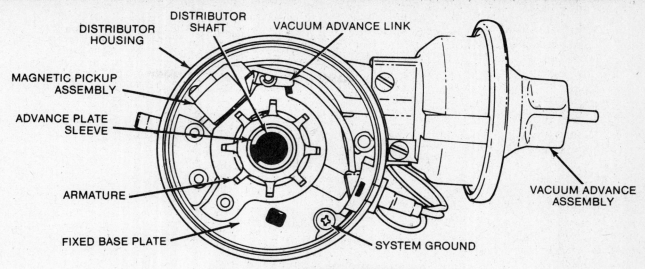

Fig. 15   Dura Spark II distributor

Dura Spark III

Ignition timing on models with Dura Spark III is electronically controlled by the EEC III computer. The EEC computer monitors signals from various engine and vehicle sensors, including a crankshaft position sensor, and computes the ideal ignition timing for operating conditions. The EEC computer provides timing signals to the ignition module which controls current switching in the primary ignition circuit.

The Dura Spark III distributor, **Fig. 16,** has been modified by the elimination of the centrifugal advance mechanism, vacuum advance diaphragm, and the stator and armature. The Dura Spark III distributor is secured to the engine and serves only to distribute secondary voltage to the spark plugs. Ignition timing is not adjusted by repositioning the distributor.

Thick Film Ignition (TFI-IV)

TFI-IV is a universal distributor ignition system in which the EEC-IV computer controls all ignition timing functions. Ignition system components include a distributor which provides mounting for the ignition module, and includes the crankshaft position sensor and a special provision for tailoring ignition timing to various fuel octane levels, a specially designed ignition module, E-core ignition coil, two piece distributor cap, rotor and silicone jacketed spark plug wires, **Fig. 17.**

The ignition module supplies current to the Profile Ignition Pick-up (PIP) which then provides crankshaft position information to the module. The ignition module transmits crankshaft position information to the EEC-IV computer which determines optimum ignition timing based on input from various sensors. The EEC-IV computer transmits a timing signal (spout) to the ignition module, and the module momentarily interrupts current flow in the

primary circuit in response to this spout. The ignition module determines dwell time and limits primary current to a "safe" value, and in addition can use the PIP signal to trigger primary switching if there is an open in the "spout" signal circuit.

The Profile Ignition Pick-up (PIP) consists of a semi-conductor Hall effect sensor

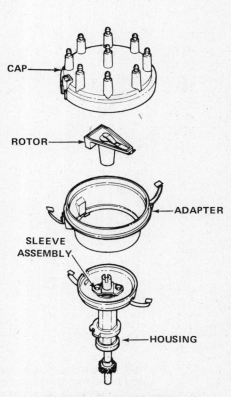

Fig. 16   Dura Spark III distributor. Exc. V6-232 (3.8L) engines

and a permanent magnet that are mounted in the distributor facing each other and separated by an air gap, **Fig. 18.** A rotary cup which has a proportionally spaced vanes is attached to the distributor shaft, and the vanes pass through the gap between the sensor and magnet. The action of the vanes passing through the air gap causes voltage pulses to be generated by the Hall sensor. These voltage pulses are used by the EEC-IV computer to determine engine RPM and crankshaft position.

The distributor does not include centrifugal or vacuum advance mechanisms, and ignition timing is not adjusted by altering distributor position. Adjustments to compensate for fuel octane can be made by replacing calibration rods in the distributor base, but these rods are only available to technicians in factory authorized service centers.

JEEP

1979–85 models, except models equipped with the 4-151 engine and 1984–85 models with the V8-173 (2.8L) engine standards, use the Solid State Ignition (SSI) system. Models equipped with the 4-151 engine use the GM-Delco HEI system, and 1984–85 models equipped with V6-173 (2.8L) engines use an HEI/EST type system. For descriptions and operation of these HEI based systems, refer to the "Chevrolet and GMC" section.

Solid State Ignition (SSI)

The SSI system consists of a distributor, remotely mounted electronic control module and ignition coil with weather-proof electrical connectors, and a distributor cap, rotor and spark plug wires, **Fig. 19.** In addition, the control module used on 1982–85 models with electronic fuel control systems includes an input connector to allow the

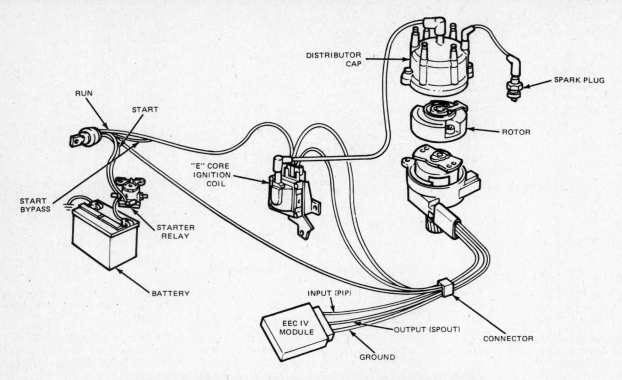

Fig. 17   Thick Film Ignition (TFI-IV) system schematic

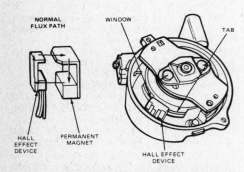

Fig. 18   Profile Ignition Pick-Up (PIP). Ford TFI-IV system

fuel control computer to retard ignition timing under certain operating conditions. The distributor contains a shaft mounted trigger wheel with one pole for each cylinder, a magnetic pick-up assembly, and centrifugal and vacuum advance mechanisms.

The pick-up assembly consists of a coil of fine wire wound around a permanent magnet. As the trigger wheel poles pass the magnetic pick-up pole, the magnetic field strength is increased and a voltage pulse is induced which is transmitted to the control module. Each time the module receives a pulse signal it momentarily interrupts current flow in the ignition coil primary windings and spark voltage is induced in the coil secondary windings.

Battery voltage is supplied directly to the ignition coil during cranking, and through a resistance wire when the ignition switch is in the on (run) position. Primary circuit

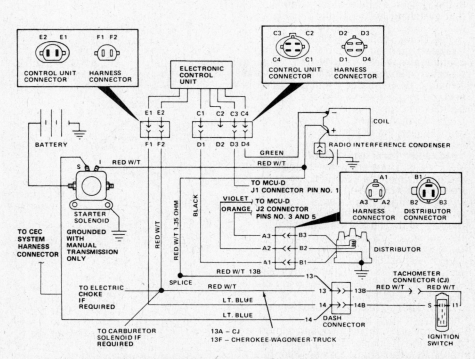

Fig. 19   Solid State Ignition (SSI) system schematic. Jeep models less fuel control computer (models w/fuel control computer similar)

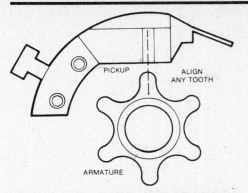

Fig. 20 Magnetic pick-up air gap

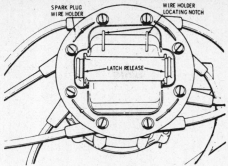

Fig. 21 Spark plug wire retainer. GM-HEI type systems

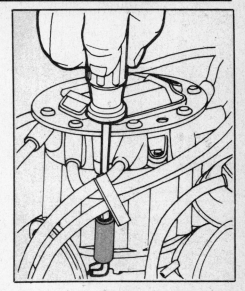

Fig. 22 Distributor cap removal. GM-HEI type systems

dwell time is controlled by the electronic control module. A timing circuit within the module opens the primary circuit just long enough to allow secondary voltage to be induced, then the timer closes the circuit.

Basic ignition timing is set by adjusting the distributor position, but the timing can be modified in three possible ways. The centrifugal advance mechanism advances the position of the trigger wheel in relation to the pick-up in direct proportion to engine speed. The vacuum capsule advances the position of the pick-up in relation to the trigger wheel in response to vacuum signals. On 1982–85 models with electronically controlled fuel systems, the fuel control computer can retard ignition timing to compensate for vehicle operating conditions. The fuel control computer monitors signals from an engine mounted knock sensor. When the knock sensor indicates engine detonation (spark knock), the fuel control computer generates an electrical signal that is transmitted to the ignition module. Depending upon the strength of this timing signal, the module can retard timing by as much as 12° by delaying current switching in the primary circuit.

ELECTRONIC IGNITION SERVICE

IGNITION SYSTEM TUNE-UP

The following is an outline of the visual inspections and repair procedures necessary to ensure proper operation of the ignition systems described previously. Refer to appropriate headings for actual repair, replacement and inspection procedures for each component or sub-assembly. Follow all listed precautions to ensure successful repairs.

1. Inspect battery, cables and connections.
2. Ensure that battery is fully charged, connections are tight and free from corrosion, and that cables are not frayed or damaged.

NOTE: Refer to "General Maintenance Section" for battery service procedures.

3. Inspect wiring and connections be-

tween the distributor and remotely mounted ignition coil, control module and fuel control computer, if equipped.
4. Ensure that all connections are tight and free from corrosion, and that wiring is properly routed and not pinched or damaged.

NOTE: An electrically conductive silicone grease is used in the wiring connectors of most electronic ignition systems. Do not remove this grease from the connectors.

5. Inspect spark plug wires. Ensure that wires are properly retained in the clamps provided to keep them away from other engine components.
6. Spark plug wires that are cracked, broken, burned or saturated with oil should be replaced.
7. Inspect distributor cap and rotor for cracks, burned terminals and insulation, and carbon tracking.
8. Check air gap between the magnetic pick-up and trigger wheel, if equipped, using a non-magnetic feeler gauge as shown in **Fig. 20.**

NOTE: Although the distributor air gap is not adjustable on many models, the correct air gap is essential for proper ignition system operation.

CAUTION: Using a ferrous metal (steel, iron etc.) gauge to check the distributor air gap will damage ignition system components.

9. Inspect ignition coil, noting the following:
   a. Coil should be replaced if terminals are burned or damaged.
   b. Oil filled coils should be replaced if there are signs of leakage or cracks around the high tension tower or primary terminals.
   c. On open type coils, used on GM-HEI and Ford TFI-IV, replace coil if windings are burned or terminals are loose.

NOTE: Slight play in the windings of open type coils is normal, and does not indicate a defective coil.

10. Remove and inspect spark plugs, and replace as needed.
11. Check basic ignition timing.
12. Check operation of centrifugal, vacuum and/or electronic ignition timing control mechanisms.

DISTRIBUTOR CAP & ROTOR, REPLACE

Observe the following precautions when replacing the cap and rotor:
1. Note installation position of the No. 1 spark plug wire on the distributor cap.
2. Mark each spark plug wire with the corresponding cylinder number, using tape, paint etc. If wiring positions become confused, refer to the "Tune Up Specifications" section in the individual truck chapters.
3. Note the installation position of the cap on the distributor housing, and ensure that the cap is properly seated during installation.
4. Note the rotor installation position on the distributor shaft, and ensure that the rotor is properly indexed and seated during installation.

CAUTION: If the cap and/or rotor are improperly installed, cranking the engine will damage distributor components. If the ignition wires are incorrectly installed, the engine may back-fire, resulting in component damage and a possible engine compartment fire.

Removal
1. Disconnect battery ground cable.
2. On models equipped with GM-Delco

HEI type systems, proceed as follows:

a. If spark plug wires are secured by a retainer, **Fig. 21,** release retainer latches and remove retainer and plug wires from cap as an assembly.

b. On models with an integral coil, release latches securing battery lead and distributor connector, then disconnect electrical connectors from cap.

CAUTION: Release plug wire retainer and electrical connector latches carefully to avoid breakage.

3. Release distributor cap from housing as follows:

a. On models with GM-HEI type systems, press each latch down with a flat blade screw driver, then turn latch counterclockwise ¼–½ turn, **Fig. 22.**

b. On Dodge and Plymouth V8 and 6 cylinder models, and all International models, insert a flat blade screw driver between each bale clip and the cap, **Fig. 23,** and pry clips away from cap.

c. On Dodge and Plymouth 4 cylinder models and Jeep models with BID or SSI, turn retaining screws counterclockwise until they are released

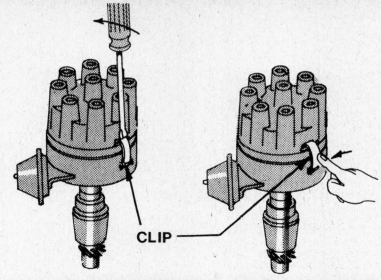

CLIP

Fig. 23   Distributor cap removal. W/bale type retainers

from the distributor housing.

d. On Ford models with a two piece cap, release bale clips holding cap to adapter. On models with a one piece cap, turn screws counterclockwise until they are released from the distributor housing.

4. Lift cap from distributor housing, tak-

ing care not to damage rotor or carbon button in center of cap.

5. If spark plug wires are still connected to cap, invert cap for inspection, taking care not to stretch or dislodge wires.

6. Remove screws securing rotor, if equipped, then remove rotor from distributor shaft.

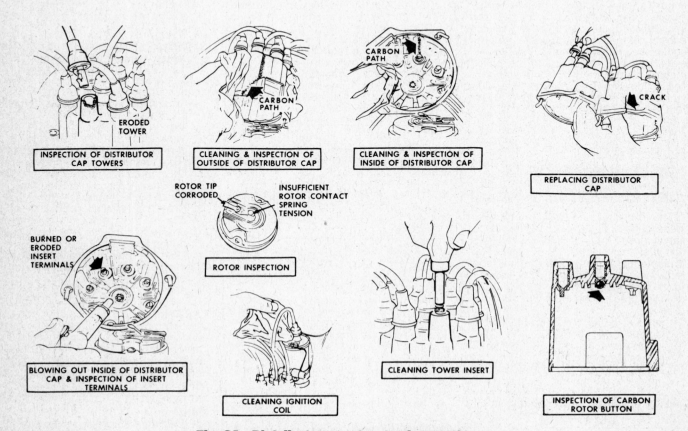

INSPECTION OF DISTRIBUTOR CAP TOWERS

ERODED TOWER

CLEANING & INSPECTION OF OUTSIDE OF DISTRIBUTOR CAP

CARBON PATH

CLEANING & INSPECTION OF INSIDE OF DISTRIBUTOR CAP

CARBON PATH

REPLACING DISTRIBUTOR CAP

CRACK

BURNED OR ERODED INSERT TERMINALS

BLOWING OUT INSIDE OF DISTRIBUTOR CAP & INSPECTION OF INSERT TERMINALS

ROTOR TIP CORRODED

INSUFFICIENT ROTOR CONTACT SPRING TENSION

ROTOR INSPECTION

CLEANING IGNITION COIL

CLEANING TOWER INSERT

INSPECTION OF CARBON ROTOR BUTTON

Fig. 24   Distributor cap & rotor inspection

GAP BRIDGED

IDENTIFIED BY DEPOSIT BUILD-UP CLOSING GAP BETWEEN ELECTRODES. CAUSED BY OIL OR CARBON FOULING. IF DEPOSITS ARE NOT EXCESSIVE, THE PLUG CAN BE CLEANED.

OIL FOULED

IDENTIFIED BY WET BLACK DEPOSITS ON THE INSULATOR SHELL BORE ELECTRODES CAUSED BY EXCESSIVE OIL ENTERING COMBUSTION CHAMBER THROUGH WORN RINGS AND PISTONS, EXCESSIVE CLEARANCE BETWEEN VALVE GUIDES AND STEMS, OR WORN OR LOOSE BEARINGS. CAN BE CLEANED IF ENGINE IS NOT REPAIRED, USE A HOTTER PLUG.

CARBON FOULED

IDENTIFIED BY BLACK, DRY FLUFFY CARBON DEPOSITS ON INSULATOR TIPS, EXPOSED SHELL SURFACES AND ELECTRODES. CAUSED BY TOO COLD A PLUG, WEAK IGNITION, DIRTY AIR CLEANER, DEFECTIVE FUEL PUMP, TOO RICH A FUEL MIXTURE, IMPROPERLY OPERATING HEAT RISER OR EXCESSIVE IDLING. CAN BE CLEANED.

WORN

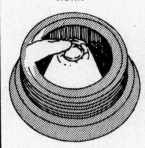

IDENTIFIED BY SEVERELY ERODED OR WORN ELECTRODES. CAUSED BY NORMAL WEAR. SHOULD BE REPLACED

NORMAL

IDENTIFIED BY LIGHT TAN OR GRAY DEPOSITS ON THE FIRING TIP. CAN BE CLEANED.

LEAD FOULED

IDENTIFIED BY DARK GRAY, BLACK, YELLOW OR TAN DEPOSITS OR A FUSED GLAZED COATING ON THE INSULATOR TIP. CAUSED BY HIGHLY LEADED GASOLINE. CAN BE CLEANED.

PRE-IGNITION

IDENTIFIED BY MELTED ELECTRODES AND POSSIBLY BLISTERED INSULATOR. METALLIC DEPOSITS ON INSULATOR INDICATE ENGINE DAMAGE. CAUSED BY WRONG TYPE OF FUEL, INCORRECT IGNITION TIMING OR ADVANCE, TOO HOT A PLUG, BURNT VALVES OR ENGINE OVERHEATING. REPLACE THE PLUG.

OVERHEATING

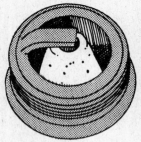

IDENTIFIED BY A WHITE OR LIGHT GRAY INSULATOR WITH SMALL BLACK OR GRAY BROWN SPOTS AND WITH BLUISH-BURNT APPEARANCE OF ELECTRODES, CAUSED BY ENGINE OVERHEATING. WRONG TYPE OF FUEL, LOOSE SPARK PLUGS, TOO HOT A PLUG, LOW FUEL PUMP PRESSURE OR INCORRECT IGNITION TIMING. REPLACE THE PLUG.

FUSED SPOT DEPOSIT

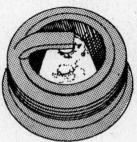

IDENTIFIED BY MELTED OR SPOTTY DEPOSITS RESEMBLING BUBBLES OR BLISTERS. CAUSED BY SUDDEN ACCELERATION. CAN BE CLEANED.

Fig. 25 Spark plug inspection

Inspection

1. Inspect cap as shown in **Fig. 24**. Cap should be replaced if it is cracked, carbon tracked, burnt, or if terminals are excessively worn or corroded.
2. Inspect rotor contacts and replace rotor if contacts are damaged or severely pitted.
3. Inspect rotor body and replace rotor if plastic is cracked or if there are signs of burning (indicated by gray-white spots).

Installation

1. Install rotor on distributor shaft, ensuring that all locating tabs and notches are aligned, and that rotor is fully seated. Tighten retaining screws evenly, if equipped.
2. If cap is to be replaced, transfer spark plug wires, one at a time, to proper terminals on replacement cap.
3. Position cap on distributor housing, ensuring that all locating tabs are engaged in their respective slots and that cap is fully seated.
4. Secure cap to distributor as follows:
   a. On GM-HEI type systems, depress each retainer with a flat blade screw driver, then turn retainer clockwise until it contacts distributor housing. Ensure that retainers are engaged in slots on housing.
   b. On caps retained with bale clips, press each clip into its slot by hand, while holding cap in position.
   c. On caps retained with screws, tighten screws securely and evenly, but do not over tighten screws as cap may be damaged.
5. Check installation position of cap and wires against firing order diagram shown in "Tune-Up Specifications" section before starting engine.

SPARK PLUGS, REPLACE

1. Mark each spark plug wire with the corresponding cylinder number, using tape, paint, etc. Refer to "Tune-Up Specifications" for cylinder numbering.
2. Disconnect wires from each spark plug as follows:
   a. Grasp wire boot firmly and twist boot back and forth approximately ½ turn to free boot from plug.
   b. Still holding boot, pull wire away from plug with a slight twisting motion.
   c. Pull wires off by the boot only. Pulling on the wires may cause internal breakage.
3. Blow out loose dirt adjacent to spark plugs before loosening each plug.

NOTE: If compressed air is not available, remove dirt by blowing through a straw or short length of hose.

4. Install a suitable spark plug socket ($^{13}/_{16}$ inch or $^{5}/_{8}$ inch) over spark plug.
5. Connect ratchet to spark plug socket

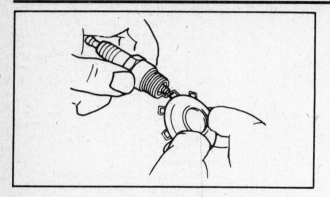

Fig. 26   Spark plug gap measurement

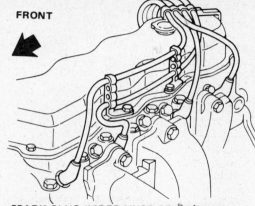

FRONT

SPARK PLUG WIRES MUST BE ROUTED
TO AVOID CONTACT OR RUBBING AGAINST
EACH OTHER OR OTHER OBJECT.

**Fig. 27   Spark plug wire installation.
4 cyl. engine (Typical)**

using extensions, if necessary, to allow ratchet handle to swing, then turn plug counterclockwise until loose (approximately 1 full turn).

6. Loosen each plug as outlined in steps 4 and 5, then briefly crank engine to "blow out" loosened carbon.
7. Remove spark plugs by hand, using plug socket and a suitable extension to reach plugs.
8. If a spark plug cannot be turned by hand after performing steps 4–6, proceed as follows:
   a. Apply penetrating oil to plug threads and retighten plug with ratchet.
   b. Wait 1–2 minutes, then attempt to remove plug as outlined previously.
   c. If plug is still too tight to be unscrewed by hand, alternately tighten and loosen plug (steps "a" and "b") until it becomes free.

CAUTION: If spark plug does not loosen after performing steps "a" and "b" a few times, plug may be incorrectly installed, siezed, or damaged. Retighten plug and have plug removed by a professional technician.

9. Inspect plugs, referring to **Fig. 25,** and replace as needed. Correct any problem causing abnormal spark plug condition.
10. Adjust gaps for each spark plug to be installed using a round, wire type feeler gauge, **Fig. 26,** and a suitable bending tool.

CAUTION: Always use a suitable tool to adjust spark plug gap. Tapping ground electrode against a hard surface or prying against the center electrode may damage spark plug. Never install a spark plug without first checking the electrode gap.

11. Install spark plugs, using the plug socket and extension to turn each plug clockwise, by hand, until plug is seated against cylinder head.

NOTE: If plugs cannot be installed by hand, ensure that threads in cylinder head are free from dirt and damage. If threads

are damaged, have engine repaired by a competent technician.

12. Torque spark plugs to specifications found in individual truck chapters. If torque wrench is not available, turn each taper-seat type plug $\frac{1}{16}$ turn clockwise from hand tight position; turn each gasket seat plug $\frac{1}{4}$ turn.
13. Lightly coat inside of each plug wire boot with a suitable silicone grease to prevent boots from seizing on plugs, then reconnect wires.
14. Check installation position of plug wires against engine firing order. Ensure that wires are properly connected before starting engine.

SPARK PLUG WIRES, REPLACE

1. Remove spark plug wires individually, even if the entire set is being replaced, to ensure that each wire is routed properly.
2. On GM-HEI type systems where wires are held in a retainer, release clips securing retainer to cap, free wires from cap terminals by turning boot back and forth, and allow assembly to rest in position on distributor.
3. On all models, disconnect spark plug wire at distributor, noting installation position.
4. Release wire from all looms and clamps between distributor and spark plug, then disconnect wire from plug.
5. Select a replacement wire of the same length and type, and having the same type terminals (straight, angled, etc.) as the wire that was removed.
6. Lightly coat inside of spark plug terminal boot with a suitable silicone grease to prevent wire from seizing on plug,

then connect new wire to plug.

NOTE: Ensure that wire is fully seated on spark plug terminal end.

7. Route replacement wire through all looms and clamps installed to prevent wire from contacting hot or moving engine components, **Figs. 27 through 29.**
8. Lightly lubricate inside of distributor terminal boot with suitable silicone grease, then connect wire to distributor cap terminal.

NOTE: On GM-HEI type systems so equipped, engage wire in proper retainer hole.

9. Repeat procedure with remaining wires that must be replaced.
10. Check installation position of all wires against engine firing order.
11. Ensure that wires are properly installed and fully seated before starting engine.
12. On GM-HEI type system with a wire retainer, press retainer and wire assembly onto cap evenly until latches "click" into place.

DISTRIBUTOR, REPLACE

The following is a general procedure which includes many of the precautions that must be observed whenever an ignition distributor is removed and installed on a gasoline engine. Steps 1 through 7 of the removal procedure can be used to check whether distributor installation position is correct, or to properly index the engine for distributor installation if the engine has been rotated with the distributor removed. However, because distributor installation position is critical to proper engine perfor-

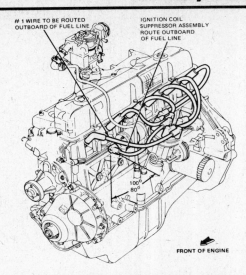

Fig. 28   Spark plug wire installation. Inline 6 cyl. engines (Typical)

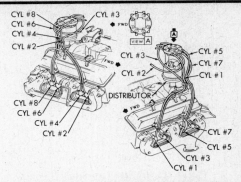

Fig. 29   Spark plug wire installation. V8 engine (Typical)

mance, and because there are many possible mistakes that can result in severe engine damage and even personal injury, removal and installation of the distributor should not be attempted by the beginner.

Read the procedure and included precautions carefully, noting each step that may (or may not) apply to your vehicle. If there is any doubt as to whether your possess the required mechanical skills or the proper tools to perform the steps as outlined, seek the assistance of a professional technician.

Removal

1. Disconnect spark plug wire and remove No. 1 spark plug on all except International models with V8 engines. On International V8 engines, remove No. 8 spark plug.

NOTE: Refer to "Tune-Up Specifications" in individual truck chapters for firing order and cylinder numbering.

2. Disable ignition system to prevent engine from starting as follows:
   a. Disconnect ignition coil secondary lead from distributor cap, if equipped, then ground lead to engine using a suitable jumper wire.
   b. On GM-HEI type systems with an integral coil, release latch and disconnect battery lead (heavy gauge red wire) from distributor cap.
3. Crank engine in short bursts, holding thumb over spark plug opening, until compression pressure can be felt at opening.
4. When compression pressure can be felt at opening, disengage starter and observe timing marks.

NOTE: Refer to "Tune-Up Specifications" in individual truck chapters for timing mark locations.

5. Stationary and movable marks should be quite close to each other. Rotate engine by hand, as needed, to align timing marks at 0° (TDC) position.
6. Mark position of No. 1 spark plug wire terminal (No. 8 on International V8) on distributor housing, then remove distributor cap.
7. If rotor contact is pointing at mark made in step 6, proceed to next step; if not, proceed as follows:
   a. If contact is pointing directly away from mark (180° out), rotate engine exactly 1 full revolution, until timing marks are aligned at TDC, then proceed to step 8.
   b. If rotor contact is not pointing at or directly away from housing reference mark with timing marks aligned at TDC, distributor is incorrectly installed or defective, or engine timing chain may be defective. Engine should be checked by a professional technician.
8. Disconnect battery ground cable, then mark position of rotor contact and housing reference mark on engine using chalk, paint, etc.
9. Disconnect electrical connectors to distributor, then remove hold-down bolt and clamp.

NOTE: Special hold down bolts are used on some models to prevent distributor position adjustment. Do not attempt to remove these bolts unless you have the proper tool.

10. Lift distributor straight out of engine while observing rotor. Rotor may move away from reference position due to design of distributor drive gear. Note position of rotor when distributor is fully withdrawn.

CAUTION: Do not rotate engine with distributor removed. If engine is rotated, it will be necessary to return engine to TDC on

the compression stroke of the reference cylinder before the distributor can be reinstalled.

Installation

1. Ensure that engine position has not changed while distributor was removed.
2. If distributor is being replaced, temporarily install cap on replacement distributor and mark position of cap reference terminal on housing.
3. Rotate distributor shaft so that rotor contact is pointing at reference mark on distributor housing.

NOTE: If rotor positioned changed as distributor was removed from engine, position rotor as noted in step 10 of removal procedure.

4. Align mark on distributor housing with mark on engine, then insert distributor into engine.
5. Distributor should seat fully in engine, and rotor contact mark on engine and mark on distributor housing should be aligned.

NOTE: If so equipped, ensure that oil pump driveshaft is properly engaged with distributor shaft. It may be necessary to crank engine with starter after distributor drive gear is partially engaged in order to engage oil pump shaft and allow distributor to seat.

6. Install distributor hold down clamp and retaining bolts.

NOTE: If it was necessary to rotate engine to allow full engagement of distributor shaft, recheck that distributor housing reference mark and rotor contact are aligned with reference cylinder at TDC on the compression stroke.

7. Reconnect electrical connectors and reinstall distributor cap.
8. Check basic ignition timing and adjust as needed.

NOTE: On Ford Models with Dura Spark III

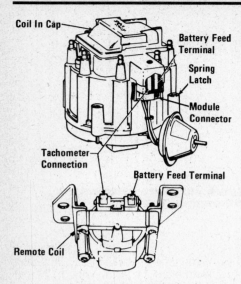

Fig. 30 Tachometer connections. GM-HEI type systems

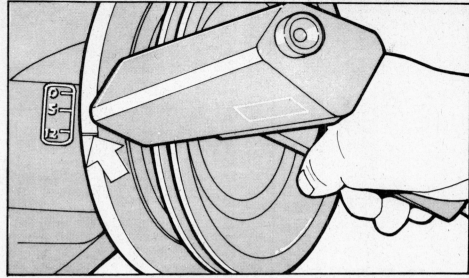

Fig. 31 Strobe action of timing light "stopping" moving timing mark

or TFI-IV, ensure that rotor is properly indexed to distributor.

IGNITION TIMING, ADJUSTMENT

During normal service, engines sparked by electronic ignition systems do not require ignition timing adjustments. Because there are no mechanical control components in the ignition system to wear out, ignition timing cannot change unless it is altered by adjustment or there is a component failure. However, as an aid to vehicle performance diagnosis, basic ignition timing should be checked to ensure that the ignition system is operating within specifications.

Observe the following precautions when checking or adjusting ignition timing on engines equipped with electronic ignition:

1. Always use a timing light recommended by the manufacturer as suitable for use with electronic ignition systems.
2. Never pierce the spark plug wire insulation when connecting the timing light. Once the insulation has been broken, voltage will jump to ground and the spark plug will not fire properly.
3. Since timing must be checked with the engine running at normal operating temperature, keep test equipment leads, clothing and your hands away from hot or moving engine components.

NOTE: Suitable eye protection should be worn when working around a running engine.

4. Refer to "Tune-Up Specifications" and the underhood Emission Control Information label when performing adjustments.
5. Clean movable and stationary timing marks with a suitable solvent, then "highlight" the fixed reference mark and the specified adjustment value with chalk, white or yellow paint, etc.
6. Always adjust ignition timing to manufacturer's specifications. If there is any doubt about the correct specifications, or if vehicle performance is unsatisfactory with timing adjusted to specifications, seek assistance of a professional technician.

CHEVROLET & GMC
Exc. Models with Electronic Spark Timing (EST)

1. Connect timing light sensor lead to No. 1 spark plug wire and power leads to battery following manufacturer's instructions.
2. Connect a suitable tachometer to the "TACH" terminal of the ignition coil, **Fig. 30,** following manufacturer's instructions.

CAUTION: Use of an unsuitable tachometer or grounding of the system "TACH" terminal will damage ignition system components.

3. Disconnect and plug hose at distributor vacuum advance capsule.
4. Start engine and run until it reaches normal operating temperature.
5. Adjust engine to specified curb idle speed (or ignition timing adjustment speed) following instructions or underhood emissions label.
6. Aim timing light at timing marks. Strobe action of light will act to "stop" the movable indicator, **Fig. 31.**

7. If indicator does not appear to stop at number of line corresponding to specified timing value, adjust distributor position as follows:
   a. Loosen distributor hold down bolt just enough to allow distributor to be rotated.
   b. If ignition timing is retarded, advance distributor by rotating it opposite to the direction of rotor rotation.
   c. If ignition timing is advanced, retard distributor by rotating it in the direction of rotor rotation.

NOTE: Move the distributor in small amounts and recheck timing marks after each adjustment.

   d. When timing marks are aligned at the specified value, tighten distributor hold down and recheck timing to ensure that distributor has not moved.
8. If ignition timing cannot be adjusted to specifications within the normal adjustment range of distributor, recheck installation of test equipment.
9. If test equipment is properly connected, check for malfunctioning centrifugal or vacuum advance mechanisms.
10. If advance systems are satisfactory, but ignition timing cannot be adjusted to specifications, have engine checked by a professional technician.

With Electronic Spark Timing (EST)
On models with EST, only the base ignition timing (distributor position) can be adjusted, as ignition timing is controlled by the C-3 system computer. To check base ignition timing, proceed as follows:

1. Connect a suitable timing light and

tachometer to engine as outlined for models without EST.

2. By-pass C-3 computer control of ignition timing as follows:
   a. On all engines except the V6-229 (3.8L), disconnect 4 wire EST connector between distributor and C-3 computer.
   b. On V229 (3.9L) engines, connect a jumper wire between EST test terminal, **Fig. 32,** and ground.

3. Start engine and run until it reaches normal operating temperature, then set engine to run at idle speed specified on underhood emissions label.

4. Check ignition timing and adjust distributor position as outlined in steps 6 through 8 for models without EST.

NOTE: If base timing cannot be adjusted to specifications within normal adjustment range of distributor, have system checked by a professional.

5. Remove jumper wire or reconnect EST connector, disconnect and remove test equipment, then road test vehicle.

DODGE & PLYMOUTH

1. Connect sensor lead of timing light to No. 1 spark plug wire and power leads to battery following manufacturer's instructions.

2. Connect suitable tachometer following manufacturer's instructions, start engine and run until it reaches normal operating temperature.

3. On models with a Spark Control Computer, disconnect and plug vacuum hose at transducer and connect a jumper wire between carburetor switch (throttle position sensor) and ground, **Fig. 33.**

4. On models without a spark control computer, disconnect and plug vacuum hose at distributor.

5. On all models, ensure that curb idle speed is within specifications.

6. Aim timing lamp at timing marks. Strobe action of light will "stop" the movable indicator, **Fig. 31.**

NOTE: Refer to "Tune-Up Specifications"

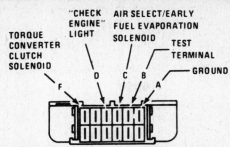

ASSEMBLY LINE COMMUNICATION
LINK (ALCL) CONNECTOR

Fig. 32   Computer command control (C-3) system underdash test connector

for timing mark locations.

7. If movable indicator does not appear to "stop" at line or number corresponding to specified timing value, adjust distributor position as follows:
   a. Loosen distributor hold down bolt just enough to allow distributor to be rotated.
   b. If movable indicator "stops" after specified timing value (timing retarded), advance distributor by rotating it opposite the direction of rotor rotation.
   c. If movable indicator "stops" before the specified value (timing advanced), retard distributor by rotating it in the direction of rotor rotation.

NOTE: Move distributor in small amounts and check timing marks after each adjustment.

   d. When timing marks are aligned at the specified value, tighten distributor hold down and recheck timing to ensure that distributor has not moved.

8. If base ignition timing cannot be set within the normal adjustment range of the distributor, recheck test equipment installation.

9. If test equipment is properly installed,

check for a malfunction in the mechanical or electronic spark advance mechanisms.

10. Disconnect test equipment and reconnect vacuum hoses to proper fittings. If idle speed changes, reset curb idle speed to specifications, but do not readjust ignition timing.

FORD

Dura Spark II Systems

1. Connect sensor lead of timing light to No. 1 spark plug wire and power leads to battery following manufacturer's instructions.

2. Connect tachometer to coil "TACH TEST" terminal, **Fig. 34,** following manufacturer's instructions, start engine and run until it reaches normal operating temperature.

3. Ensure that engine is operating at specified curb idle speed, then disconnect and plug vacuum hoses at distributor.

4. Aim timing light at timing marks. Strobe action of light will "stop" the movable indicator, **Fig. 31.**

5. If movable indicator does not appear to "stop" at line or number corresponding to the specified timing value, adjust distributor position as follows:
   a. Loosen distributor hold down bolt just enough to allow distributor to be rotated.
   b. If movable indicator "stops" after specified timing value (timing retarded), advance distributor by rotating it in the opposite direction of rotor rotation.
   c. If movable indicator "stops" before the specified value (timing advanced), retard distributor by rotating it in the direction of rotor rotation.

NOTE: Move distributor in small amounts and check timing marks after each adjustment.

   d. Tighten distributor hold down, then recheck timing to ensure that distributor position has not changed.

6. If ignition timing can not be adjusted to specifications within the normal ad-

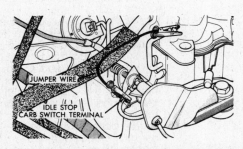

Fig. 33   Grounding carburetor switch. Dodge & Plymouth w/Spark Control Computer (SCC)

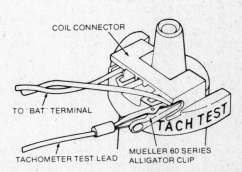

Fig. 34   Tachometer connection. Ford Dura Spark & Jeep SSI systems

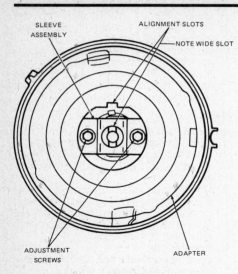

Fig. 35 Rotor position alignment. Ford Dura Spark III

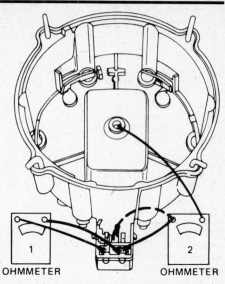

Fig. 36 HEI distributor ignition coil ohmmeter tests. Integral coil models

alignment tool can be inserted in slots of sleeve and adapter.

7. Tighten sleeve assembly adjusting screws and remove alignment tool.

8. Install rotor, and cap asembly, then ensure that wires are fully seated in cap.

TFI-IV Systems

Ignition timing on engines equipped with TFI-IV ignition is not adjustable.

JEEP

For adjustment procedures on GM-HEI type systems, refer to procedures outlined under "Chevrolet and GMC."

SSI Systems

1. Connect sensor lead of timing light to No. 1 spark plug wire and power leads to battery following manufacturer's instructions.

2. Connect suitable tachometer to "TACH TEST" terminal on coil, **Fig. 34,** following manufacturer's instructions, start engine and run until it reaches normal operating temperature.

3. Disconnect and plug vacuum hose at distributor and ensure that engine is running at specified adjustment speed.

4. Aim timing light at timing marks. Strobe action of light will "stop" movable indicator, **Fig. 31.**

5. If movable indicator does not appear to "stop" at line or number corresponding to specified timing value, adjust distributor position as follows:

   a. Loosen distributor hold down bolt just enough to allow distributor to be rotated.

   b. If movable indicator "stops" after specified timing value (timing retarded), rotate distributor in the direction opposite rotor rotation.

   c. If movable indicator stops before specified timing value (timing advanced), rotate distributor in the direction of rotor rotation.

   d. When timing marks are aligned, tighten distributor hold down bolt, then recheck timing to ensure that distributor has not moved.

6. If ignition timing cannot be adjusted to specifications within the normal adjustment range of distributor, recheck installation of test equipment.

7. If test equipment is properly connected, check for malfunction in the centrifugal or vacuum advance mechanisms.

8. If advance mechanisms are satisfactory, but ignition timing cannot be adjusted to specifications, have engine checked by a professional technician.

CENTRIFUGAL ADVANCE CHECK

1. Remove distributor cap, leaving wires connected, and position aside.

justment range of distributor, recheck installation of test equipment.

7. If test equipment is properly connected, check for malfunctioning centrifugal or vacuum advance mechanisms.

8. If advance mechanisms are satisfactory, but ignition timing cannot be adjusted to specifications, have engine checked by a professional technician.

Dura Spark III Systems

Basic ignition timing cannot be adjusted by altering distributor position. If distributor is removed, ensure that during installation, distributor is installed so that the rotor is properly aligned to fire the No. 1 cylinder. To check and adjust rotor alignment, proceed as follows:

NOTE: Rotor alignment check requires the use of alignment tool T79P-12200-A or equivalent.

1. Remove distributor cap with wires attached and position assembly aside, then remove rotor.

2. Rotate engine until No. 1 cylinder is on the compression stroke as outlined in "Distributor, Replace."

3. Continue to rotate engine, slowly, until alignment tool can be inserted into slots in sleeve assembly and adapter, **Fig. 35.**

4. Inspect timing marks. If marks are aligned within the 4° before or after Top Dead Center (TDC), rotor alignment is acceptable.

5. If timing marks are not aligned within specified range, remove alignment tool and rotate engine until No. 1 cylinder is at TDC on compression stroke.

6. Loosen sleeve assembly adjusting screws and position sleeve so that

2. Rotate distributor rotor toward normal direction of rotation, then release rotor.

NOTE: Rotor should move with relative ease against spring tension. Do not force rotor to move.

3. Rotor should move approximately 15° in direction of rotation, then "snap" back into position when released.

4. Reinstall distributor cap, then prepare vehicle for ignition timing check as outlined.

5. Aim timing lamp at timing marks, then increase engine speed to approximately 2000 RPM.

6. Ignition timing should advance progressively as engine speed is increased.

7. If advance mechanism fails to operate as outlined, distributor should be repaired by a professional technician.

VACUUM ADVANCE CHECK

1. Remove distributor cap, leaving wires connected, and position aside.

2. Disconnect and plug vacuum hoses to distributor.

3. Apply suction to vacuum advance unit using a section of vacuum hose or a vacuum pump. On dual diaphragm units, apply suction to both fittings.

4. When suction is applied to vacuum advance diaphragm, breaker plate or magnetic pick-up, assembly should move in the opposite direction of rotor rotation.

5. When suction is applied to retard diaphragm, if equipped, breaker plate or magnetic pick-up should move in the direction of rotor rotation.

6. When suction is removed from either

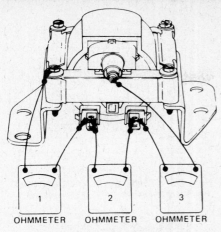

Fig. 37 HEI ignition coil ohmmeter tests. Remote coil models

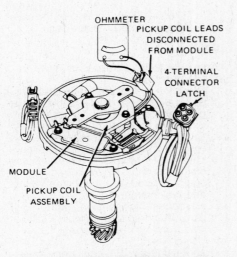

Fig. 39 HEI distributor pickup coil test

diaphragm, breaker plate or pick-up should return to original position.
7. If mechanism fails to perform as outlined, distributor should be repaired by a professional technician.

SYSTEM DIAGNOSIS & TESTING

NOTE: Electronic ignition systems are usually controlled and are a part of an electronic engine control system such as Chrysler's Electronic Fuel Control (EFC) system, Ford's EEC-III and EEC-IV systems and General Motors and in some Jeep applications, the C-3, C-4 systems.

Indepth ignition system diagnosis and testing procedures cannot be accomplished on a vehicle using such a system, without the aid of sophisticated metering, testing and adjustment equipment. The following procedures are generalized around common engine and/or component conditions.

CHEVROLET & GMC

Engine Cranks Normally, But Will Not Start

1. Connect suitable voltmeter between distributor cap "Bat" terminal on integral coil models, or coil connector "Bat" terminal on remote coil and engine ground. Turn ignition "On".
2. If voltage is zero, there is an open circuit between the distributor or coil and the 12 volt power source. Check wiring connections to the ignition switch and from the ignition switch to the starter solenoid. Check ignition switch operation. Repair as necessary.
3. If reading is battery voltage, hold one spark plug lead with insulated pliers approximately ¼ inch away from a dry area of engine block and crank engine. If a spark is visible, the distributor has been eliminated as source of trouble. Check spark plugs and fuel system.
4. If there is no visible spark, perform the "Component Checkout" and proceed as described further on.

Engine Starts But Runs Rough

1. Check for proper fuel delivery to carburetor.
2. Check all vacuum hoses for leakage.
3. Visually inspect and listen for sparks jumping to ground.
4. Check ignition timing.
5. Check centrifugal advance mechanism for proper operation (if equipped).
6. Remove spark plugs and check for unusual defects, such as very wide gap, abnormal fouling, cracked insulators (inside and out), etc.
7. If no defects are found, perform the "Component Checkout" procedure as described below.

Component Checkout

1. Remove cap and coil assembly on integral coil models, or cap only on remote coil models.
2. Inspect cap, coil and rotor for spark arcover.
3. On integral coil models:
   a. Connect ohmmeter, **Fig. 36**, step 1. If ohmmeter reading is other than zero or very near to zero, the ignition coil must be replaced.
   b. If no ohmmeter reading was observed in step 1, reconnect ohmmeter both ways, **Fig. 36**, step 2. If both ohmmeter readings are infinite on high scale, replace ignition coil.
4. On remote coil models:
   a. Connect ohmmeter, **Fig. 37**, step 1. If reading is not infinite, replace coil.
   b. Connect ohmmeter, **Fig. 37**, step 2. If reading is not zero or near zero, replace coil.
   c. Connect ohmmeter, **Fig. 37**, step 3. If reading is infinite, replace coil.
5. Connect an external vacuum source to the vacuum advance unit (if

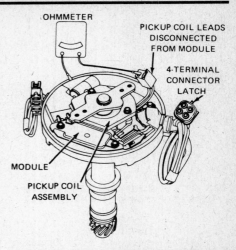

Fig. 38 HEI distributor pick-up coil test

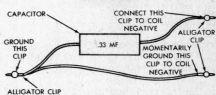

Fig. 40 Special coil negative to ground jumper wire

equipped). Replace vacuum unit if inoperative.
6. If vacuum unit is operating properly, connect ohmmeter, **Fig. 38**. If ohmmeter reading on middle scale is not infinite at all times, pick-up coil must be replaced.
7. With ohmmeter connected, **Fig. 39**. Reading should be within 500 to 1500 ohms.

NOTE: Tester J-24624 is required to test the module. If this tester is not available, and malfunction still exists after performing the above checks, replace module.

DODGE & PLYMOUTH

Engine Will Not Start

1. Turn ignition Off and disconnect connector from ignition control unit.
2. Turn ignition On, then hold end of coil wire approximately ¼ inch away from a good ground and momentarily short coil negative wire to ground with jumper wire as shown in **Fig. 40**.
3. If a spark is obtained, the control unit or electrical connector is faulty. Repair or replace as necessary.
4. If no spark is obtained, measure voltage at coil positive terminal. If voltage is zero, check wiring between battery and coil and repair as necessary. If reading is battery voltage, refer to "Component Checkout".

Engine Starts But Runs Rough

1. Check for proper fuel delivery to carburetor.

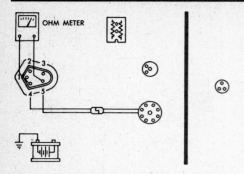

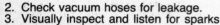

Fig. 41 Pickup coil test. Models less Electronic Spark Control

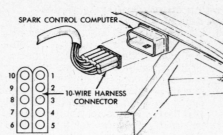

Fig. 42 Pickup coil test. Models w/Electronic Spark Control

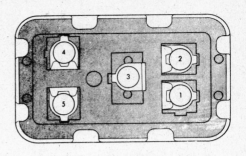

Fig. 43 Dual pickup start run relay terminal identification

2. Check vacuum hoses for leakage.
3. Visually inspect and listen for sparks jumping to ground.
4. Check ignition timing.
5. Remove and inspect spark plugs.
6. If no defects are found, refer to "Component Checkout".

Component Checkout

1. Remove cap and coil assembly. Inspect cap, coil and rotor for arc-over.
2. Measure voltage at coil negative terminal. If voltage is not within 1 volt of battery voltage, replace coil. If voltage is satisfactory, but no spark is obtained when grounding coil negative terminal, replace coil.
3. On models equipped less electronic spark control, measure resistance between pick-up coil connector terminals 4 and 5, **Fig. 41**. If resistance is not 150–900 ohms, disconnect distributor dual lead connector and measure resistance between two leads on distributor side of connector. If resistance is still not 150–900 ohms, replace pick-up coil.
4. On models equipped with electronic spark control, measure resistance between terminals 5 and 9 for run pick-up coil and terminals 3 and 9 for start pick-up coil, **Fig. 42**. If resistance is not 150–900 ohms, disconnect pick-up coil leads from distributor and measure resistance at leads going into distributor. If resistance is still not 150–900 ohms, replace pick-up coil.
5. On models equipped with dual pick-up start run relay, disconnect two-way connector from relay and measure resistance between pins 4 and 5, **Fig. 43**. If resistance does not measure 20–30 ohms, replace relay.

FORD

ENGINE CRANKS NORMALLY, BUT WILL NOT START

1. Visually inspect engine electrical wiring and connectors for breaks, chafing, burns, etc. and repair as necessary.
2. Using a spark plug with the side electrode removed, test for spark by inserting the modified spark plug into a

spark plug cable. Ground the modified plug shell and crank the engine while checking for spark. If spark is visible, distributor has been eliminated at source of trouble. Check spark plugs and fuel system.
3. If a spark was not visible during step 2 above, install the modified spark plug in the coil lead and repeat test. If spark is now visible, check distributor cap and rotor for carbon tracking, burns and moisture. If spark is not visible, perform "Component Checkout" as outlined below.

ENGINE STARTS BUT RUNS ROUGH

1. Check for proper fuel delivery to carburetor.
2. Check vacuum hoses for leakage.
3. Visually inspect and listen for sparks jumping to ground.
4. Check ignition timing.
5. Remove and inspect spark plugs.
6. If no defects are found, refer to "Component Checkout".

COMPONENT CHECKOUT

Checking Stator (Pick-Up Coil)

1. Disconnect distributor 3 wire connector.
2. Connect suitable ohmmeter between parallel blades of distributor connector. Resistance should be 400–1000 ohms. If reading obtained is outside specifications, replace stator.
3. With ignition switch "Off", measure resistance between distributor connector orange wire and ground and purple wire and ground. Reading at each wire should exceed 70,000 ohms.

Checking Ignition Coil

1. Disconnect and inspect ignition coil electrical connector.
2. To measure ignition coil primary resistance, proceed as follows:
   a. Connect ohmmeter across coil "Batt" and "Tach" (or "Dec") terminals while observing ohmmeter reading.
   b. If reading obtained is 1–2 ohms, coil is satisfactory. If not, replace coil.
3. To measure ignition coil secondary

resistance, proceed as follows:
   a. Connect ohmmeter between coil "Batt" terminal and high tension lead terminal while observing ohmmeter reading.
   b. If reading obtained is between 7700–10,500 ohms, coil is satisfactory. If not, replace coil.

JEEP

ENGINE CRANKS NORMALLY, BUT WILL NOT START

1. Disconnect high tension wire from one spark plug, then using suitable insulated pliers, hold wire approximately ½ inch from engine ground.
2. Crank engine while observing end of wire for sparks. If no spark occurs, proceed to step 3. If spark occurs, distributor has been eliminated as source of trouble. Check spark plugs and fuel system.
3. Reconnect high tension lead to spark plug, then remove coil high tension lead from distributor cap.
4. Using insulated pliers, hold wire approximately ½ inch from engine ground. Crank engine and observe end of wire for sparks. If sparks occur, check distributor cap and rotor for carbon tracking, burns and moisture. If spark does not occur, perform "Component Checkout" as outlined below.

COMPONENT CHECKING

Checking Ignition Coil

1. Disconnect ignition coil connector.
2. To measure ignition coil primary resistance, proceed as follows:
   a. Connect ohmmeter across coil positive and negative terminals while observing ohmmeter reading.
   b. If reading obtained is 1.13–1.23 ohms on SSI systems, coil is satisfactory. If not, replace coil.
3. To measure ignition coil secondary resistance, proceed as follows:
   a. Connect ohmmeter between coil positive terminal and high tension lead terminal while observing ohmmeter reading.
   b. If reading obtained is 7,700–9,300 on SSI systems, coil is satisfactory. If not, replace coil.

LUBRICATION DIAGRAMS

INDEX

Chevrolet & GMC

LUBRICATION POINTS
A-1 CHASSIS — SEE MAINTENANCE SCHEDULE
A-2 ENGINE OIL AND FILTER
A-4 COOLING SYSTEM
A-5 WHEEL BEARINGS
A-6 AUTO. TRANSMISSION FLUID

UPPER CONTROL ARM BALL JOINTS
LOWER CONTROL ARM BALL JOINTS

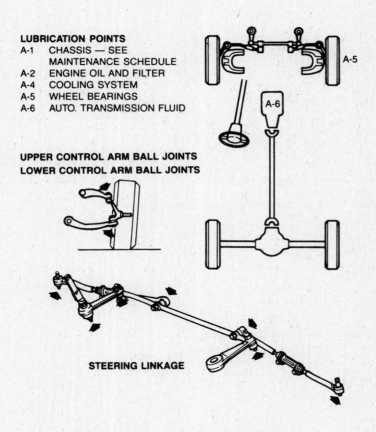

STEERING LINKAGE

ENGINE COMPARTMENT

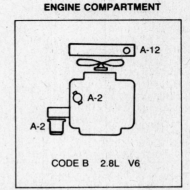

CODE B   2.8L V6

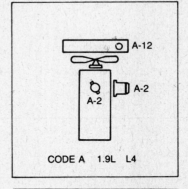

CODE A   1.9L L4

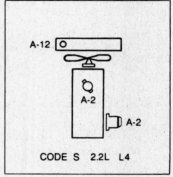

CODE S 2.2L L4

1982–85 Chevrolet & GMC S/T-10 & 15

LUBRICATION DIAGRAMS

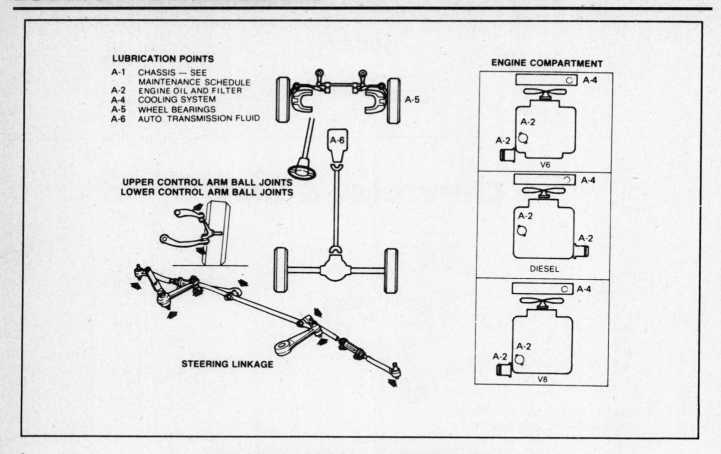

LUBRICATION POINTS

A-1 CHASSIS — SEE
 MAINTENANCE SCHEDULE
A-2 ENGINE OIL AND FILTER
A-4 COOLING SYSTEM
A-5 WHEEL BEARINGS
A-6 AUTO. TRANSMISSION FLUID

UPPER CONTROL ARM BALL JOINTS
LOWER CONTROL ARM BALL JOINTS

STEERING LINKAGE

ENGINE COMPARTMENT

V6

DIESEL

V8

1979—85 Chevrolet El Camino & GMC Caballero

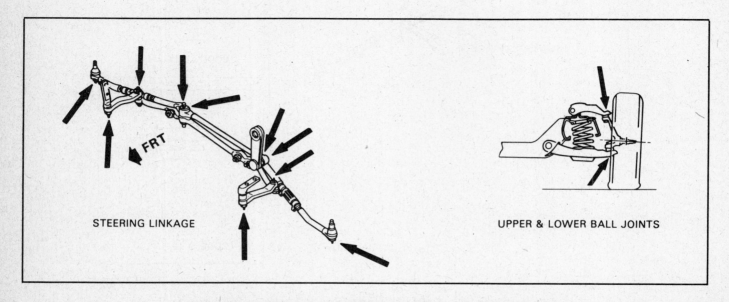

FRT

STEERING LINKAGE

UPPER & LOWER BALL JOINTS

Front suspension lubrication points. Astro Van & Safari

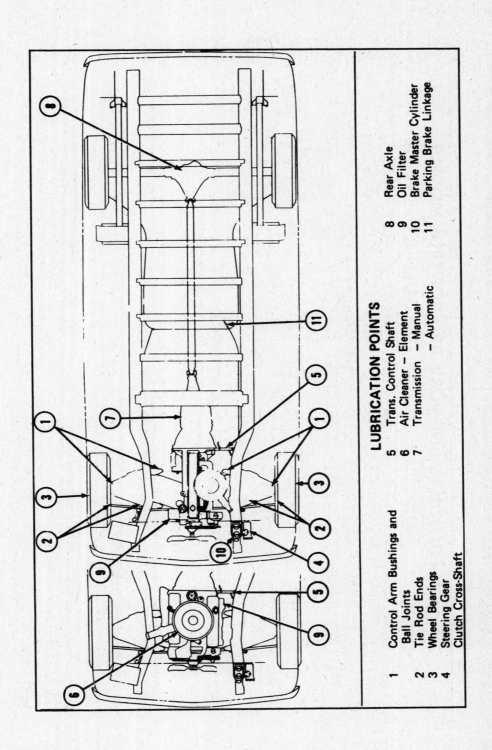

LUBRICATION POINTS

1 Control Arm Bushings and
  Ball Joints
2 Tie Rod Ends
3 Wheel Bearings
4 Steering Gear
  Clutch Cross-Shaft

5 Trans. Control Shaft
6 Air Cleaner – Element
7 Transmission – Manual
               – Automatic

8 Rear Axle
9 Oil Filter
10 Brake Master Cylinder
11 Parking Brake Linkage

1979—85 Chevrolet & GMC G Series

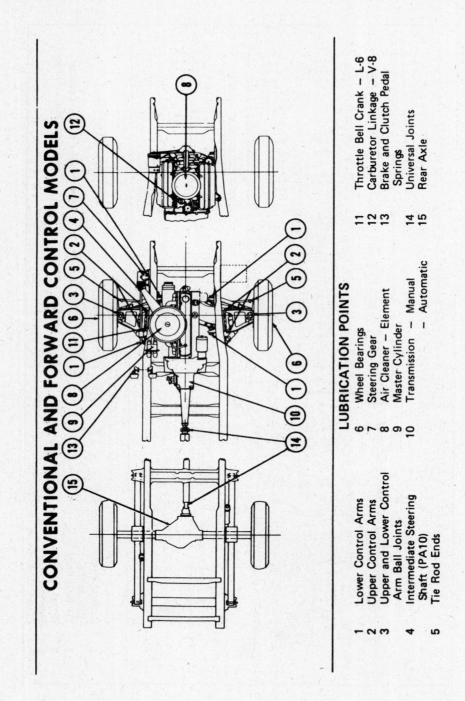

CONVENTIONAL AND FORWARD CONTROL MODELS

LUBRICATION POINTS

1 Lower Control Arms
2 Upper Control Arms
3 Upper and Lower Control
   Arm Ball Joints
4 Intermediate Steering
   Shaft (PA10)
5 Tie Rod Ends

6 Wheel Bearings
7 Steering Gear
8 Air Cleaner – Element
9 Master Cylinder
10 Transmission – Manual
              – Automatic

11 Throttle Bell Crank – L-6
12 Carburetor Linkage – V-8
13 Brake and Clutch Pedal
    Springs
14 Universal Joints
15 Rear Axle

**1979–85 Chevrolet & GMC C Series, Blazer (Exc. S-10) &
Jimmy (Exc. S-15) 2 wheel drive models**

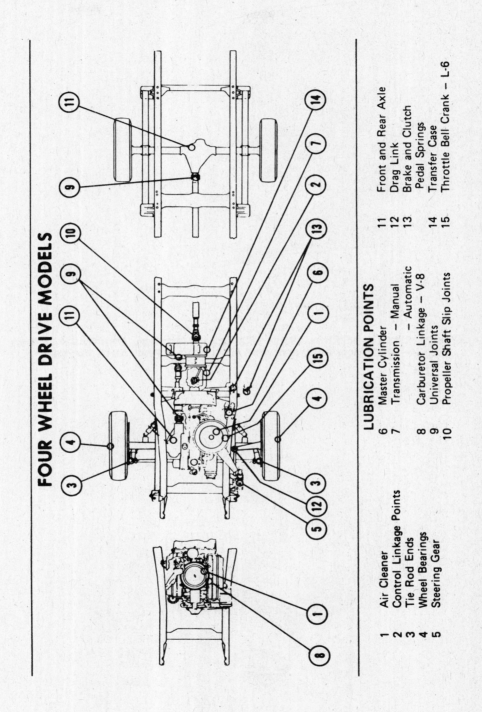

FOUR WHEEL DRIVE MODELS

LUBRICATION POINTS

1	Air Cleaner	6	Master Cylinder	11	Front and Rear Axle
2	Control Linkage Points	7	Transmission – Manual	12	Drag Link
3	Tie Rod Ends		– Automatic	13	Brake and Clutch
4	Wheel Bearings	8	Carburetor Linkage – V-8		Pedal Springs
5	Steering Gear	9	Universal Joints	14	Transfer Case
		10	Propeller Shaft Slip Joints	15	Throttle Bell Crank – L-6

**1979—85 Chevrolet & GMC C/K Series & Blazer (Exc. S-10) &
Jimmy (Exc. S-15) 4 wheel drive models**

Dodge & Plymouth

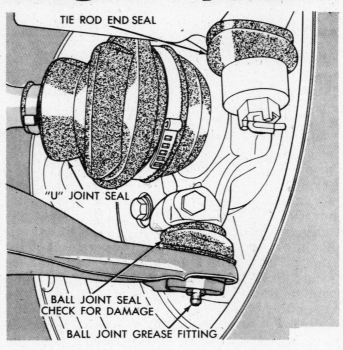

Ball joint fitting location. 1982—84 Dodge Rampage, Plymouth Scamp & 1984—85 Dodge Caravan, Mini Ram Van & Plymouth Voyager

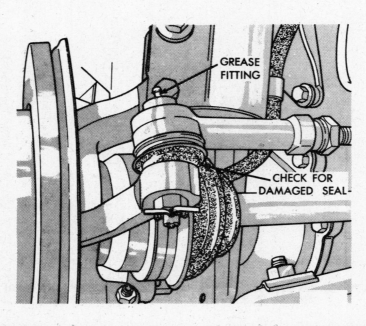

Tie rod fitting location. 1982—84 Dodge Rampage, Plymouth Scamp & 1984—85 Dodge Caravan, Mini Ram Van & Plymouth Voyager

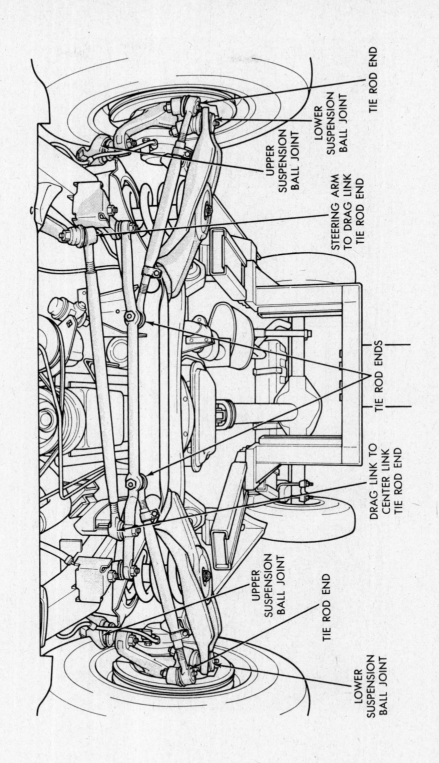

UPPER
SUSPENSION
BALL JOINT

LOWER
SUSPENSION
BALL JOINT

TIE ROD END

STEERING ARM
TO DRAG LINK
TIE ROD END

TIE ROD ENDS

DRAG LINK TO
CENTER LINK
TIE ROD END

UPPER
SUSPENSION
BALL JOINT

TIE ROD END

LOWER
SUSPENSION
BALL JOINT

1979—83 Plymouth Voyager & 1979—85 Dodge B Series

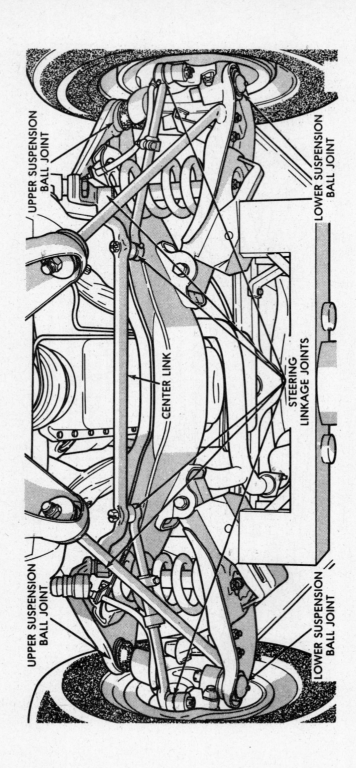

1979—85 D & W 100—400 & Ramcharger (Typical)

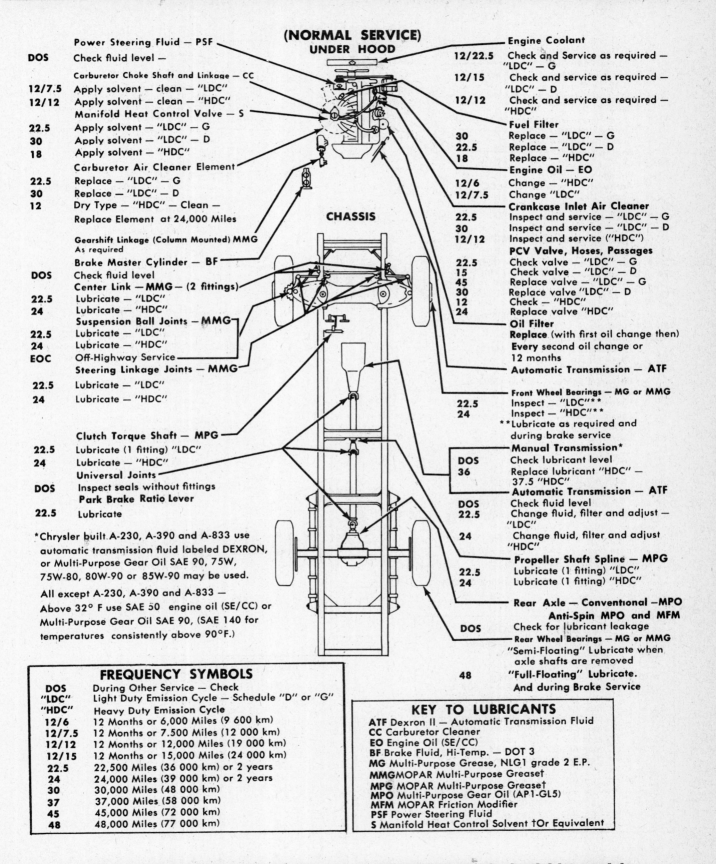

(NORMAL SERVICE)
UNDER HOOD

Power Steering Fluid — PSF
DOS — Check fluid level —

Carburetor Choke Shaft and Linkage — CC
12/7.5 — Apply solvent — clean — "LDC"
12/12 — Apply solvent — clean — "HDC"

Manifold Heat Control Valve — S
22.5 — Apply solvent "LDC" — G
30 — Apply solvent "LDC" — D
18 — Apply solvent "HDC"

Carburetor Air Cleaner Element
22.5 — Replace — "LDC" — G
30 — Replace — "LDC" — D
12 — Dry Type — "HDC" — Clean —
Replace Element at 24,000 Miles

Gearshift Linkage (Column Mounted) MMG
As required

Brake Master Cylinder — BF
DOS — Check fluid level

Center Link — MMG — (2 fittings)
22.5 — Lubricate — "LDC"
24 — Lubricate — "HDC"

Suspension Ball Joints — MMG
22.5 — Lubricate — "LDC"
24 — Lubricate — "HDC"
EOC — Off-Highway Service

Steering Linkage Joints — MMG
22.5 — Lubricate — "LDC"
24 — Lubricate — "HDC"

Clutch Torque Shaft — MPG
22.5 — Lubricate (1 fitting) "LDC"
24 — Lubricate — "HDC"

Universal Joints
DOS — Inspect seals without fittings
Park Brake Ratio Lever
22.5 — Lubricate

*Chrysler built A-230, A-390 and A-833 use automatic transmission fluid labeled DEXRON, or Multi-Purpose Gear Oil SAE 90, 75W, 75W-80, 80W-90 or 85W-90 may be used.

All except A-230, A-390 and A-833 —
Above 32° F use SAE 50 engine oil (SE/CC) or Multi-Purpose Gear Oil SAE 90, (SAE 140 for temperatures consistently above 90°F.)

CHASSIS

Engine Coolant
12/22.5 — Check and Service as required — "LDC" — G
12/15 — Check and service as required — "LDC" — D
12/12 — Check and service as required — "HDC"

Fuel Filter
30 — Replace — "LDC" — G
22.5 — Replace — "LDC" — D
18 — Replace — "HDC"

Engine Oil — EO
12/6 — Change — "HDC"
12/7.5 — Change "LDC"

Crankcase Inlet Air Cleaner
22.5 — Inspect and service — "LDC" — G
30 — Inspect and service — "LDC" — D
12/12 — Inspect and service ("HDC")

PCV Valve, Hoses, Passages
22.5 — Check valve — "LDC" — G
15 — Check valve — "LDC" — D
45 — Replace valve — "LDC" — G
30 — Replace valve "LDC" — D
12 — Check — "HDC"
24 — Replace valve "HDC"

Oil Filter
Replace (with first oil change then)
Every second oil change or
12 months

Automatic Transmission — ATF

Front Wheel Bearings — MG or MMG
22.5 — Inspect — "LDC"**
24 — Inspect — "HDC"**
**Lubricate as required and during brake service

Manual Transmission*
DOS — Check lubricant level
36 — Replace lubricant "HDC" — 37.5 "HDC"

Automatic Transmission — ATF
DOS — Check fluid level
22.5 — Change fluid, filter and adjust — "LDC"
24 — Change fluid, filter and adjust "HDC"

Propeller Shaft Spline — MPG
22.5 — Lubricate (1 fitting) "LDC"
24 — Lubricate (1 fitting) "HDC"

Rear Axle — Conventional — MPO
Anti-Spin MPO and MFM
DOS — Check for lubricant leakage

Rear Wheel Bearings — MG or MMG
"Semi-Floating" Lubricate when axle shafts are removed
48 — "Full-Floating" Lubricate. And during Brake Service

FREQUENCY SYMBOLS

DOS	During Other Service — Check
"LDC"	Light Duty Emission Cycle — Schedule "D" or "G"
"HDC"	Heavy Duty Emission Cycle
12/6	12 Months or 6,000 Miles (9 600 km)
12/7.5	12 Months or 7,500 Miles (12 000 km)
12/12	12 Months or 12,000 Miles (19 000 km)
12/15	12 Months or 15,000 Miles (24 000 km)
22.5	22,500 Miles (36 000 km) or 2 years
24	24,000 Miles (39 000 km) or 2 years
30	30,000 Miles (48 000 km)
37	37,000 Miles (58 000 km)
45	45,000 Miles (72 000 km)
48	48,000 Miles (77 000 km)

KEY TO LUBRICANTS

ATF Dexron II — Automatic Transmission Fluid
CC Carburetor Cleaner
EO Engine Oil (SE/CC)
BF Brake Fluid, Hi-Temp. — DOT 3
MG Multi-Purpose Grease, NLG1 grade 2 E.P.
MMG MOPAR Multi-Purpose Grease†
MPG MOPAR Multi-Purpose Grease†
MPO Multi-Purpose Gear Oil (AP1-GL5)
MFM MOPAR Friction Modifier
PSF Power Steering Fluid
S Manifold Heat Control Solvent †Or Equivalent

1979 Dodge D100–400, Ramcharger & Plymouth Trail Duster 2 wheel drive models

LUBRICATION DIAGRAMS

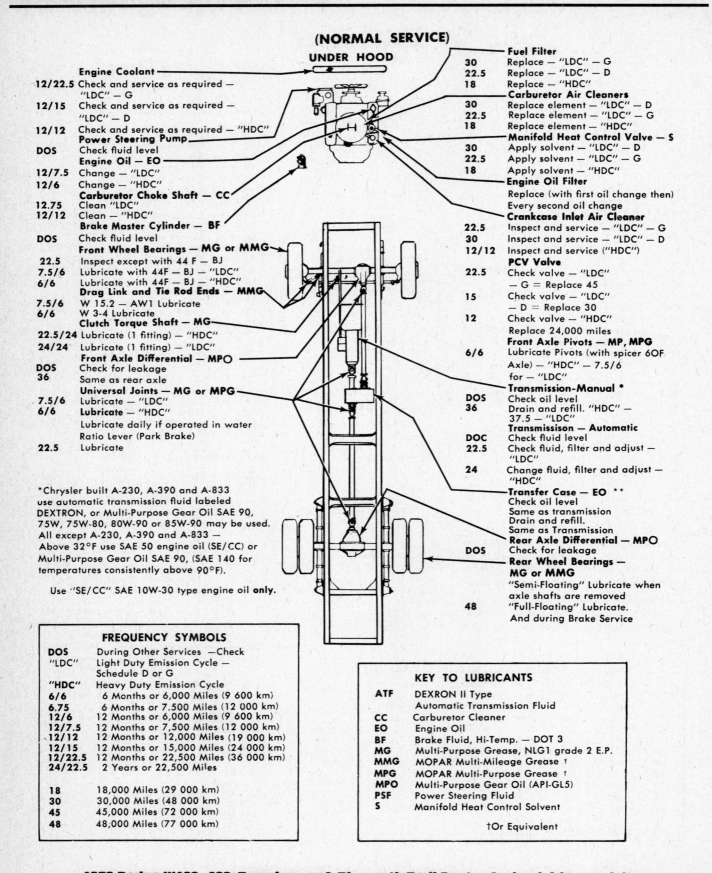

(NORMAL SERVICE)

UNDER HOOD

Engine Coolant
12/22.5   Check and service as required — "LDC" — G
12/15   Check and service as required — "LDC" — D
12/12   Check and service as required — "HDC"
Power Steering Pump
DOS   Check fluid level
Engine Oil — EO
12/7.5   Change — "LDC"
12/6   Change — "HDC"
Carburetor Choke Shaft — CC
12.75   Clean "LDC"
12/12   Clean — "HDC"
Brake Master Cylinder — BF
DOS   Check fluid level
Front Wheel Bearings — MG or MMG
22.5   Inspect except with 44 F — BJ
7.5/6   Lubricate with 44F — BJ — "LDC"
6/6   Lubricate with 44F — BJ — "HDC"
Drag Link and Tie Rod Ends — MMG
7.5/6   W 15.2 — AW1 Lubricate
6/6   W 3-4 Lubricate
Clutch Torque Shaft — MG
22.5/24   Lubricate (1 fitting) — "HDC"
24/24   Lubricate (1 fitting) — "LDC"
Front Axle Differential — MPO
DOS   Check for leakage
36   Same as rear axle
Universal Joints — MG or MPG
7.5/6   Lubricate — "LDC"
6/6   Lubricate — "HDC"
   Lubricate daily if operated in water
   Ratio Lever (Park Brake)
22.5   Lubricate

Fuel Filter
30   Replace — "LDC" — G
22.5   Replace — "LDC" — D
18   Replace — "HDC"
Carburetor Air Cleaners
30   Replace element — "LDC" — D
22.5   Replace element — "LDC" — G
18   Replace element — "HDC"
Manifold Heat Control Valve — S
30   Apply solvent — "LDC" — D
22.5   Apply solvent — "LDC" — G
18   Apply solvent — "HDC"
Engine Oil Filter
   Replace (with first oil change then)
   Every second oil change
Crankcase Inlet Air Cleaner
22.5   Inspect and service — "LDC" — G
30   Inspect and service — "LDC" — D
12/12   Inspect and service ("HDC")
PCV Valve
22.5   Check valve — "LDC"
   — G = Replace 45
15   Check valve — "LDC"
   — D = Replace 30
12   Check valve — "HDC"
   Replace 24,000 miles
Front Axle Pivots — MP, MPG
6/6   Lubricate Pivots (with spicer 6OF
   Axle) — "HDC" — 7.5/6
   for — "LDC"
Transmission-Manual *
DOS   Check oil level
36   Drain and refill. "HDC" —
   37.5 — "LDC"
Transmisison — Automatic
DOC   Check fluid level
22.5   Check fluid, filter and adjust — "LDC"
24   Change fluid, filter and adjust — "HDC"
Transfer Case — EO **
   Check oil level
   Same as transmission
   Drain and refill.
   Same as Transmission
Rear Axle Differential — MPO
DOS   Check for leakage
Rear Wheel Bearings — MG or MMG
   "Semi-Floating" Lubricate when axle shafts are removed
48   "Full-Floating" Lubricate.
   And during Brake Service

*Chrysler built A-230, A-390 and A-833 use automatic transmission fluid labeled DEXTRON, or Multi-Purpose Gear Oil SAE 90, 75W, 75W-80, 80W-90 or 85W-90 may be used. All except A-230, A-390 and A-833 — Above 32°F use SAE 50 engine oil (SE/CC) or Multi-Purpose Gear Oil SAE 90, (SAE 140 for temperatures consistently above 90°F).

Use "SE/CC" SAE 10W-30 type engine oil **only**.

FREQUENCY SYMBOLS

DOS	During Other Services —Check
"LDC"	Light Duty Emission Cycle — Schedule D or G
"HDC"	Heavy Duty Emission Cycle
6/6	6 Months or 6,000 Miles (9 600 km)
6.75	6 Months or 7,500 Miles (12 000 km)
12/6	12 Months or 6,000 Miles (9 600 km)
12/7.5	12 Months or 7,500 Miles (12 000 km)
12/12	12 Months or 12,000 Miles (19 000 km)
12/15	12 Months or 15,000 Miles (24 000 km)
12/22.5	12 Months or 22,500 Miles (36 000 km)
24/22.5	2 Years or 22,500 Miles
18	18,000 Miles (29 000 km)
30	30,000 Miles (48 000 km)
45	45,000 Miles (72 000 km)
48	48,000 Miles (77 000 km)

KEY TO LUBRICANTS

ATF	DEXRON II Type Automatic Transmission Fluid
CC	Carburetor Cleaner
EO	Engine Oil
BF	Brake Fluid, Hi-Temp. — DOT 3
MG	Multi-Purpose Grease, NLG1 grade 2 E.P.
MMG	MOPAR Multi-Mileage Grease †
MPG	MOPAR Multi-Purpose Grease †
MPO	Multi-Purpose Gear Oil (API-GL5)
PSF	Power Steering Fluid
S	Manifold Heat Control Solvent

†Or Equivalent

1979 Dodge W100—400, Ramcharger & Plymouth Trail Duster 4 wheel drive models

NORMAL SERVICE

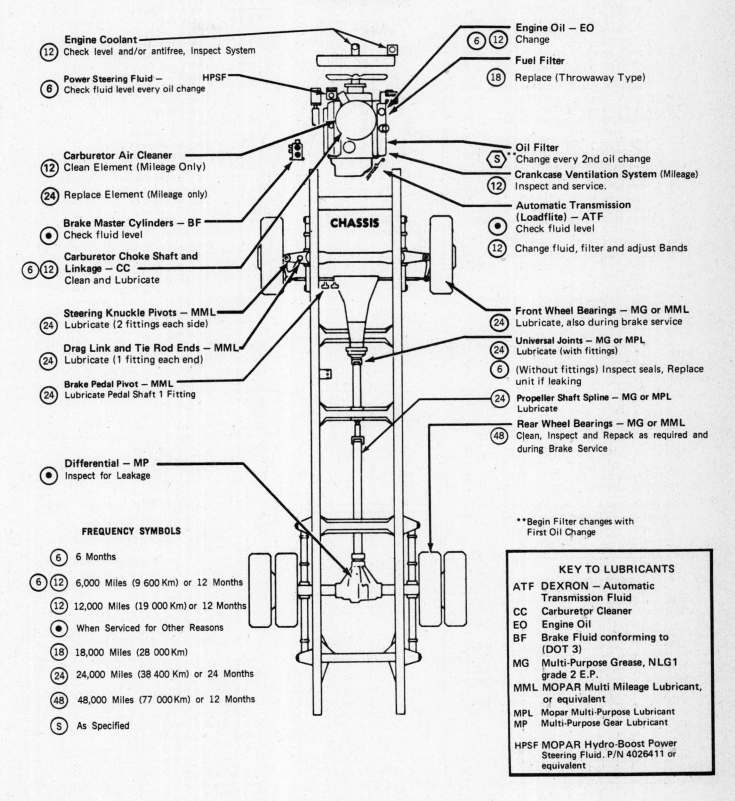

Engine Coolant
(12) Check level and/or antifree, Inspect System

Power Steering Fluid — HPSF
(6) Check fluid level every oil change

Carburetor Air Cleaner
(12) Clean Element (Mileage Only)

(24) Replace Element (Mileage only)

Brake Master Cylinders — BF
(•) Check fluid level

Carburetor Choke Shaft and Linkage — CC
(6)(12) Clean and Lubricate

Steering Knuckle Pivots — MML
(24) Lubricate (2 fittings each side)

Drag Link and Tie Rod Ends — MML
(24) Lubricate (1 fitting each end)

Brake Pedal Pivot — MML
(24) Lubricate Pedal Shaft 1 Fitting

Differential — MP
(•) Inspect for Leakage

Engine Oil — EO
(6)(12) Change

Fuel Filter
(18) Replace (Throwaway Type)

Oil Filter
(S)** Change every 2nd oil change

Crankcase Ventilation System (Mileage)
(12) Inspect and service.

Automatic Transmission (Loadflite) — ATF
(•) Check fluid level

(12) Change fluid, filter and adjust Bands

Front Wheel Bearings — MG or MML
(24) Lubricate, also during brake service

Universal Joints — MG or MPL
(24) Lubricate (with fittings)

(6) (Without fittings) Inspect seals, Replace unit if leaking

Propeller Shaft Spline — MG or MPL
(24) Lubricate

Rear Wheel Bearings — MG or MML
(48) Clean, Inspect and Repack as required and during Brake Service

CHASSIS

FREQUENCY SYMBOLS

(6) 6 Months

(6)(12) 6,000 Miles (9 600 Km) or 12 Months

(12) 12,000 Miles (19 000 Km) or 12 Months

(•) When Serviced for Other Reasons

(18) 18,000 Miles (28 000 Km)

(24) 24,000 Miles (38 400 Km) or 24 Months

(48) 48,000 Miles (77 000 Km) or 12 Months

(S) As Specified

**Begin Filter changes with First Oil Change

KEY TO LUBRICANTS	
ATF	DEXRON — Automatic Transmission Fluid
CC	Carburetor Cleaner
EO	Engine Oil
BF	Brake Fluid conforming to (DOT 3)
MG	Multi-Purpose Grease, NLG1 grade 2 E.P.
MML	MOPAR Multi Mileage Lubricant, or equivalent
MPL	Mopar Multi-Purpose Lubricant
MP	Multi-Purpose Gear Lubricant
HPSF	MOPAR Hydro-Boost Power Steering Fluid. P/N 4026411 or equivalent

1979–80 Dodge Motor Home chassis

LUBRICATION DIAGRAMS

(NORMAL SERVICE)

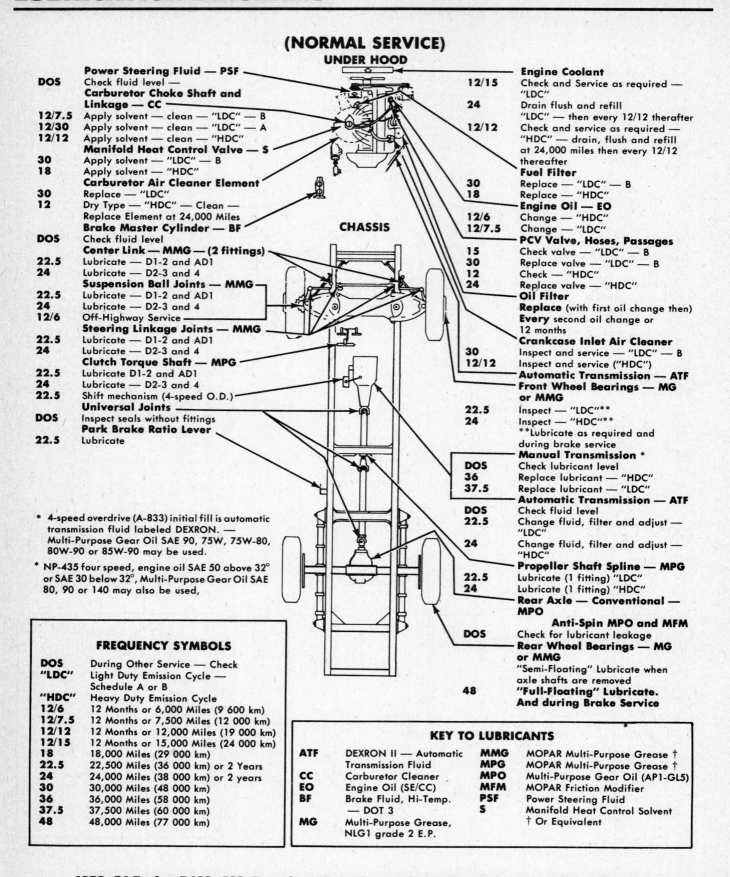

UNDER HOOD

DOS	**Power Steering Fluid — PSF**
	Check fluid level —
	Carburetor Choke Shaft and Linkage — CC
12/7.5	Apply solvent — clean — "LDC" — B
12/30	Apply solvent — clean — "LDC" — A
12/12	Apply solvent — clean — "HDC"
	Manifold Heat Control Valve — S
30	Apply solvent — "LDC" — B
18	Apply solvent — "HDC"
	Carburetor Air Cleaner Element
30	Replace — "LDC"
12	Dry Type — "HDC" — Clean — Replace Element at 24,000 Miles
	Brake Master Cylinder — BF
DOS	Check fluid level
	Center Link — MMG — (2 fittings)
22.5	Lubricate — D1-2 and AD1
24	Lubricate — D2-3 and 4
	Suspension Ball Joints — MMG
22.5	Lubricate — D1-2 and AD1
24	Lubricate — D2-3 and 4
12/6	Off-Highway Service
	Steering Linkage Joints — MMG
22.5	Lubricate — D1-2 and AD1
24	Lubricate — D2-3 and 4
	Clutch Torque Shaft — MPG
22.5	Lubricate D1-2 and AD1
24	Lubricate — D2-3 and 4
22.5	Shift mechanism (4-speed O.D.)
	Universal Joints
DOS	Inspect seals without fittings
	Park Brake Ratio Lever
22.5	Lubricate

CHASSIS

12/15	**Engine Coolant**
	Check and Service as required — "LDC"
24	Drain flush and refill "LDC" — then every 12/12 therafter
12/12	Check and service as required — "HDC" — drain, flush and refill at 24,000 miles then every 12/12 thereafter
	Fuel Filter
30	Replace — "LDC" — B
18	Replace — "HDC"
	Engine Oil — EO
12/6	Change — "HDC"
12/7.5	Change — "LDC"
	PCV Valve, Hoses, Passages
15	Check valve — "LDC" — B
30	Replace valve — "LDC" — B
12	Check — "HDC"
24	Replace valve — "HDC"
	Oil Filter
	Replace (with first oil change then) Every second oil change or 12 months
	Crankcase Inlet Air Cleaner
30	Inspect and service — "LDC" — B
12/12	Inspect and service ("HDC")
	Automatic Transmission — ATF
	Front Wheel Bearings — MG or MMG
22.5	Inspect — "LDC"**
24	Inspect — "HDC"**
	**Lubricate as required and during brake service
	Manual Transmission *
DOS	Check lubricant level
36	Replace lubricant — "HDC"
37.5	Replace lubricant — "LDC"
	Automatic Transmission — ATF
DOS	Check fluid level
22.5	Change fluid, filter and adjust — "LDC"
24	Change fluid, filter and adjust — "HDC"
	Propeller Shaft Spline — MPG
22.5	Lubricate (1 fitting) "LDC"
24	Lubricate (1 fitting) "HDC"
	Rear Axle — Conventional — MPO
	Anti-Spin MPO and MFM
DOS	Check for lubricant leakage
	Rear Wheel Bearings — MG or MMG
	"Semi-Floating" Lubricate when axle shafts are removed
48	"Full-Floating" Lubricate. And during Brake Service

* 4-speed overdrive (A-833) initial fill is automatic transmission fluid labeled DEXRON. — Multi-Purpose Gear Oil SAE 90, 75W, 75W-80, 80W-90 or 85W-90 may be used.

* NP-435 four speed, engine oil SAE 50 above 32° or SAE 30 below 32°, Multi-Purpose Gear Oil SAE 80, 90 or 140 may also be used.

FREQUENCY SYMBOLS

DOS	During Other Service — Check
"LDC"	Light Duty Emission Cycle — Schedule A or B
"HDC"	Heavy Duty Emission Cycle
12/6	12 Months or 6,000 Miles (9 600 km)
12/7.5	12 Months or 7,500 Miles (12 000 km)
12/12	12 Months or 12,000 Miles (19 000 km)
12/15	12 Months or 15,000 Miles (24 000 km)
18	18,000 Miles (29 000 km)
22.5	22,500 Miles (36 000 km) or 2 Years
24	24,000 Miles (38 000 km) or 2 years
30	30,000 Miles (48 000 km)
36	36,000 Miles (58 000 km)
37.5	37,500 Miles (60 000 km)
48	48,000 Miles (77 000 km)

KEY TO LUBRICANTS

ATF	DEXRON II — Automatic Transmission Fluid	MMG	MOPAR Multi-Purpose Grease †
CC	Carburetor Cleaner	MPG	MOPAR Multi-Purpose Grease †
EO	Engine Oil (SE/CC)	MPO	Multi-Purpose Gear Oil (AP1-GL5)
BF	Brake Fluid, Hi-Temp. — DOT 3	MFM	MOPAR Friction Modifier
		PSF	Power Steering Fluid
MG	Multi-Purpose Grease, NLG1 grade 2 E.P.	S	Manifold Heat Control Solvent
		†	Or Equivalent

1980—81 Dodge D100—400, Ramcharger & Plymouth Trail Duster 2 wheel drive models

(NORMAL SERVICE)
UNDER HOOD

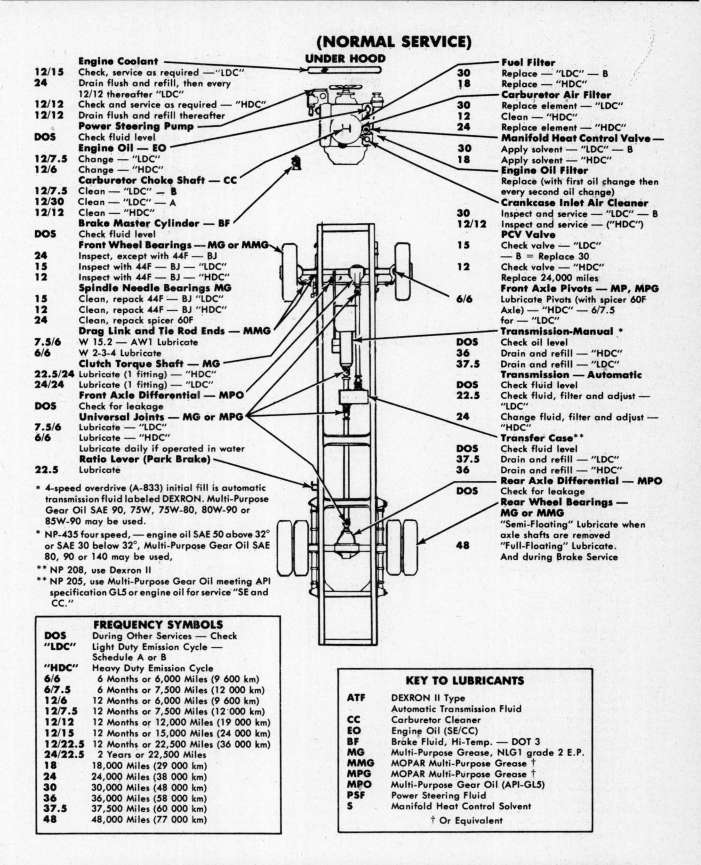

	Engine Coolant
12/15	Check, service as required — "LDC"
24	Drain flush and refill, then every 12/12 thereafter "LDC"
12/12	Check and service as required — "HDC"
12/12	Drain flush and refill thereafter
	Power Steering Pump
DOS	Check fluid level
	Engine Oil — EO
12/7.5	Change — "LDC"
12/6	Change — "HDC"
	Carburetor Choke Shaft — CC
12/7.5	Clean — "LDC" — B
12/30	Clean — "LDC" — A
12/12	Clean — "HDC"
	Brake Master Cylinder — BF
DOS	Check fluid level
	Front Wheel Bearings — MG or MMG
24	Inspect, except with 44F — BJ
15	Inspect with 44F — BJ "LDC"
12	Inspect with 44F — BJ "HDC"
	Spindle Needle Bearings MG
15	Clean, repack 44F — BJ "LDC"
12	Clean, repack 44F — BJ "HDC"
24	Clean, repack spicer 60F
	Drag Link and Tie Rod Ends — MMG
7.5/6	W 15.2 — AW1 Lubricate
6/6	W 2-3-4 Lubricate
	Clutch Torque Shaft — MG
22.5/24	Lubricate (1 fitting) — "HDC"
24/24	Lubricate (1 fitting) — "LDC"
	Front Axle Differential — MPO
DOS	Check for leakage
	Universal Joints — MG or MPG
7.5/6	Lubricate — "LDC"
6/6	Lubricate — "HDC"
	Lubricate daily if operated in water
	Ratio Lever (Park Brake)
22.5	Lubricate

	Fuel Filter
30	Replace — "LDC" — B
18	Replace — "HDC"
	Carburetor Air Filter
30	Replace element — "LDC"
12	Clean — "HDC"
24	Replace element — "HDC"
	Manifold Heat Control Valve
30	Apply solvent — "LDC" — B
18	Apply solvent — "HDC"
	Engine Oil Filter
	Replace (with first oil change then every second oil change)
	Crankcase Inlet Air Cleaner
30	Inspect and service — "LDC" — B
12/12	Inspect and service — ("HDC")
	PCV Valve
15	Check valve — "LDC" — B = Replace 30
12	Check valve — "HDC" Replace 24,000 miles
	Front Axle Pivots — MP, MPG
6/6	Lubricate Pivots (with spicer 60F Axle) — "HDC" — 6/7.5 for — "LDC"
	Transmission-Manual *
DOS	Check oil level
36	Drain and refill — "HDC"
37.5	Drain and refill — "LDC"
	Transmission — Automatic
DOS	Check fluid level
22.5	Check fluid, filter and adjust — "LDC"
24	Change fluid, filter and adjust — "HDC"
	Transfer Case**
DOS	Check fluid level
37.5	Drain and refill — "LDC"
36	Drain and refill — "HDC"
	Rear Axle Differential — MPO
DOS	Check for leakage
	Rear Wheel Bearings — MG or MMG
	"Semi-Floating" Lubricate when axle shafts are removed
48	"Full-Floating" Lubricate. And during Brake Service

* 4-speed overdrive (A-833) initial fill is automatic transmission fluid labeled DEXRON. Multi-Purpose Gear Oil SAE 90, 75W, 75W-80, 80W-90 or 85W-90 may be used.

* NP-435 four speed, — engine oil SAE 50 above 32° or SAE 30 below 32°, Multi-Purpose Gear Oil SAE 80, 90 or 140 may be used,

** NP 208, use Dexron II

** NP 205, use Multi-Purpose Gear Oil meeting API specification GL5 or engine oil for service "SE and CC."

FREQUENCY SYMBOLS

DOS	During Other Services — Check
"LDC"	Light Duty Emission Cycle — Schedule A or B
"HDC"	Heavy Duty Emission Cycle
6/6	6 Months or 6,000 Miles (9 600 km)
6/7.5	6 Months or 7,500 Miles (12 000 km)
12/6	12 Months or 6,000 Miles (9 600 km)
12/7.5	12 Months or 7,500 Miles (12 000 km)
12/12	12 Months or 12,000 Miles (19 000 km)
12/15	12 Months or 15,000 Miles (24 000 km)
12/22.5	12 Months or 22,500 Miles (36 000 km)
24/22.5	2 Years or 22,500 Miles
18	18,000 Miles (29 000 km)
24	24,000 Miles (38 000 km)
30	30,000 Miles (48 000 km)
36	36,000 Miles (58 000 km)
37.5	37,500 Miles (60 000 km)
48	48,000 Miles (77 000 km)

KEY TO LUBRICANTS

ATF	DEXRON II Type Automatic Transmission Fluid
CC	Carburetor Cleaner
EO	Engine Oil (SE/CC)
BF	Brake Fluid, Hi-Temp. — DOT 3
MG	Multi-Purpose Grease, NLG1 grade 2 E.P.
MMG	MOPAR Multi-Purpose Grease †
MPG	MOPAR Multi-Purpose Grease †
MPO	Multi-Purpose Gear Oil (API-GL5)
PSF	Power Steering Fluid
S	Manifold Heat Control Solvent
	† Or Equivalent

1980—81 Dodge W100—400, Ramcharger & Plymouth Trail Duster 4 wheel drive models

LUBRICATION DIAGRAMS

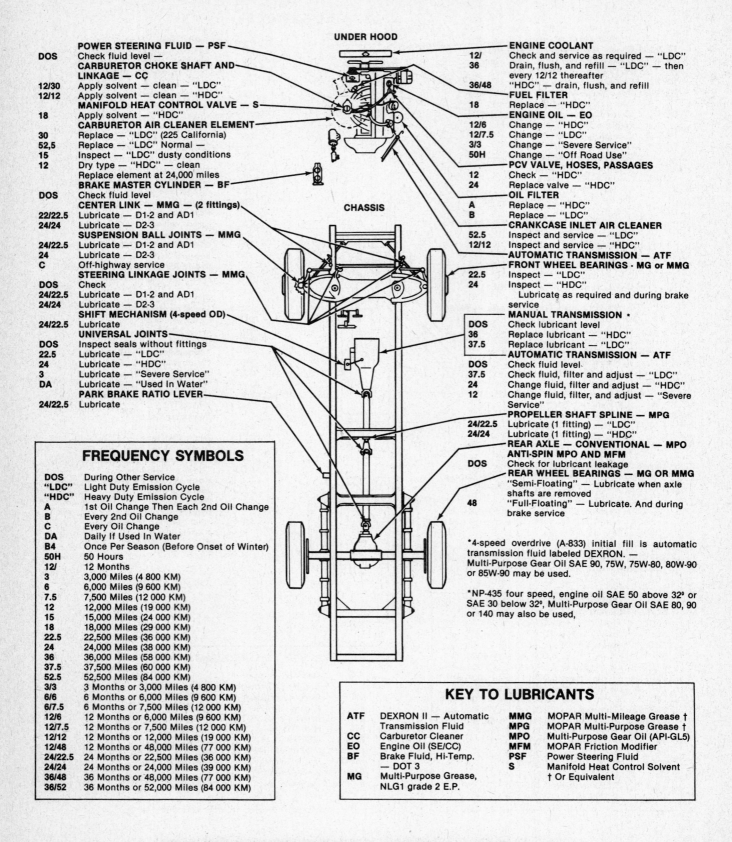

UNDER HOOD

	POWER STEERING FLUID — PSF
DOS	Check fluid level —
	CARBURETOR CHOKE SHAFT AND LINKAGE — CC
12/30	Apply solvent — clean — "LDC"
12/12	Apply solvent — clean — "HDC"
	MANIFOLD HEAT CONTROL VALVE — S
18	Apply solvent — "HDC"
	CARBURETOR AIR CLEANER ELEMENT
30	Replace — "LDC" (225 California)
52,5	Replace — "LDC" Normal —
15	Inspect — "LDC" dusty conditions
12	Dry type — "HDC" — clean
	Replace element at 24,000 miles
	BRAKE MASTER CYLINDER — BF
DOS	Check fluid level
	CENTER LINK — MMG — (2 fittings)
22/22.5	Lubricate — D1-2 and AD1
24/24	Lubricate — D2-3
	SUSPENSION BALL JOINTS — MMG
24/22.5	Lubricate — D1-2 and AD1
24	Lubricate — D2-3
C	Off-highway service
	STEERING LINKAGE JOINTS — MMG
DOS	Check
24/22.5	Lubricate — D1-2 and AD1
24/24	Lubricate — D2-3
	SHIFT MECHANISM (4-speed OD)
24/22.5	Lubricate
	UNIVERSAL JOINTS
DOS	Inspect seals without fittings
22.5	Lubricate — "LDC"
24	Lubricate — "HDC"
3	Lubricate — "Severe Service"
DA	Lubricate — "Used In Water"
	PARK BRAKE RATIO LEVER
24/22.5	Lubricate

CHASSIS

	ENGINE COOLANT
12/	Check and service as required — "LDC"
36	Drain, flush, and refill — "LDC" — then every 12/12 thereafter
36/48	"HDC" — drain, flush, and refill
	FUEL FILTER
18	Replace — "HDC"
	ENGINE OIL — EO
12/6	Change — "HDC"
12/7.5	Change — "LDC"
3/3	Change — "Severe Service"
50H	Change — "Off Road Use"
	PCV VALVE, HOSES, PASSAGES
12	Check — "HDC"
24	Replace valve — "HDC"
	OIL FILTER
A	Replace — "HDC"
B	Replace — "LDC"
	CRANKCASE INLET AIR CLEANER
52.5	Inspect and service — "LDC"
12/12	Inspect and service — "HDC"
	AUTOMATIC TRANSMISSION — ATF
	FRONT WHEEL BEARINGS · MG or MMG
22.5	Inspect — "LDC"
24	Inspect — "HDC"
	Lubricate as required and during brake service
	MANUAL TRANSMISSION ·
DOS	Check lubricant level
36	Replace lubricant — "HDC"
37.5	Replace lubricant — "LDC"
	AUTOMATIC TRANSMISSION — ATF
DOS	Check fluid level
37.5	Check fluid, filter and adjust — "LDC"
24	Change fluid, filter and adjust — "HDC"
12	Change fluid, filter, and adjust — "Severe Service"
	PROPELLER SHAFT SPLINE — MPG
24/22.5	Lubricate (1 fitting) — "LDC"
24/24	Lubricate (1 fitting) — "HDC"
	REAR AXLE — CONVENTIONAL — MPO ANTI-SPIN MPO AND MFM
DOS	Check for lubricant leakage
	REAR WHEEL BEARINGS — MG OR MMG
	"Semi-Floating" — Lubricate when axle shafts are removed
48	"Full-Floating" — Lubricate. And during brake service

*4-speed overdrive (A-833) initial fill is automatic transmission fluid labeled DEXRON. — Multi-Purpose Gear Oil SAE 90, 75W, 75W-80, 80W-90 or 85W-90 may be used.

*NP-435 four speed, engine oil SAE 50 above 32º or SAE 30 below 32º, Multi-Purpose Gear Oil SAE 80, 90 or 140 may also be used,

FREQUENCY SYMBOLS

DOS	During Other Service
"LDC"	Light Duty Emission Cycle
"HDC"	Heavy Duty Emission Cycle
A	1st Oil Change Then Each 2nd Oil Change
B	Every 2nd Oil Change
C	Every Oil Change
DA	Daily If Used In Water
B4	Once Per Season (Before Onset of Winter)
50H	50 Hours
12/	12 Months
3	3,000 Miles (4 800 KM)
6	6,000 Miles (9 600 KM)
7.5	7,500 Miles (12 000 KM)
12	12,000 Miles (19 000 KM)
15	15,000 Miles (24 000 KM)
18	18,000 Miles (29 000 KM)
22.5	22,500 Miles (36 000 KM)
24	24,000 Miles (38 000 KM)
36	36,000 Miles (58 000 KM)
37.5	37,500 Miles (60 000 KM)
52.5	52,500 Miles (84 000 KM)
3/3	3 Months or 3,000 Miles (4 800 KM)
6/6	6 Months or 6,000 Miles (9 600 KM)
6/7.5	6 Months or 7,500 Miles (12 000 KM)
12/6	12 Months or 6,000 Miles (9 600 KM)
12/7.5	12 Months or 7,500 Miles (12 000 KM)
12/12	12 Months or 12,000 Miles (19 000 KM)
12/48	12 Months or 48,000 Miles (77 000 KM)
24/22.5	24 Months or 22,500 Miles (36 000 KM)
24/24	24 Months or 24,000 Miles (39 000 KM)
36/48	36 Months or 48,000 Miles (77 000 KM)
36/52	36 Months or 52,000 Miles (84 000 KM)

KEY TO LUBRICANTS

ATF	DEXRON II — Automatic Transmission Fluid	MMG	MOPAR Multi-Mileage Grease †
CC	Carburetor Cleaner	MPG	MOPAR Multi-Purpose Grease †
EO	Engine Oil (SE/CC)	MPO	Multi-Purpose Gear Oil (API-GL5)
BF	Brake Fluid, Hi-Temp. — DOT 3	MFM	MOPAR Friction Modifier
MG	Multi-Purpose Grease, NLG1 grade 2 E.P.	PSF	Power Steering Fluid
		S	Manifold Heat Control Solvent
		†	Or Equivalent

1982—83 Dodge D100—350 & Ramcharger 2 wheel drive models

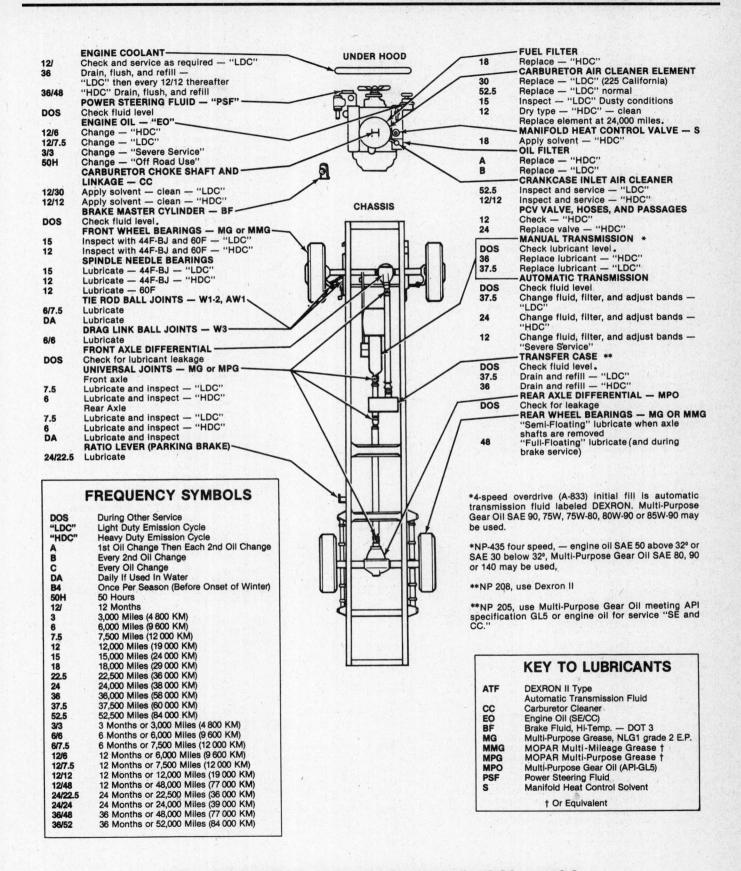

UNDER HOOD

ENGINE COOLANT
12/	Check and service as required — "LDC"
36	Drain, flush, and refill — "LDC" then every 12/12 thereafter
36/48	"HDC" Drain, flush, and refill

POWER STEERING FLUID — "PSF"
| DOS | Check fluid level |

ENGINE OIL — "EO"
12/6	Change — "HDC"
12/7.5	Change — "LDC"
3/3	Change — "Severe Service"
50H	Change — "Off Road Use"

CARBURETOR CHOKE SHAFT AND LINKAGE — CC
| 12/30 | Apply solvent — clean — "LDC" |
| 12/12 | Apply solvent — clean — "HDC" |

BRAKE MASTER CYLINDER — BF
| DOS | Check fluid level. |

FRONT WHEEL BEARINGS — MG or MMG
| 15 | Inspect with 44F-BJ and 60F — "LDC" |
| 12 | Inspect with 44F-BJ and 60F — "HDC" |

SPINDLE NEEDLE BEARINGS
15	Lubricate — 44F-BJ — "LDC"
12	Lubricate — 44F-BJ — "HDC"
12	Lubricate — 60F

TIE ROD BALL JOINTS — W1-2, AW1
| 6/7.5 | Lubricate |
| DA | Lubricate |

DRAG LINK BALL JOINTS — W3
| 6/6 | Lubricate |

FRONT AXLE DIFFERENTIAL
| DOS | Check for lubricant leakage |

UNIVERSAL JOINTS — MG or MPG
Front axle
| 7.5 | Lubricate and inspect — "LDC" |
| 6 | Lubricate and inspect — "HDC" |
Rear Axle
7.5	Lubricate and inspect — "LDC"
6	Lubricate and inspect — "HDC"
DA	Lubricate and inspect

RATIO LEVER (PARKING BRAKE)
| 24/22.5 | Lubricate |

CHASSIS

FUEL FILTER
| 18 | Replace — "HDC" |

CARBURETOR AIR CLEANER ELEMENT
30	Replace — "LDC" (225 California)
52.5	Replace — "LDC" normal
15	Inspect — "LDC" Dusty conditions
12	Dry type — "HDC" — clean Replace element at 24,000 miles.

MANIFOLD HEAT CONTROL VALVE — S
| 18 | Apply solvent — "HDC" |

OIL FILTER
| A | Replace — "HDC" |
| B | Replace — "LDC" |

CRANKCASE INLET AIR CLEANER
| 52.5 | Inspect and service — "LDC" |
| 12/12 | Inspect and service — "HDC" |

PCV VALVE, HOSES, AND PASSAGES
| 12 | Check — "HDC" |
| 24 | Replace valve — "HDC" |

MANUAL TRANSMISSION *
DOS	Check lubricant level.
36	Replace lubricant — "HDC"
37.5	Replace lubricant — "LDC"

AUTOMATIC TRANSMISSION
DOS	Check fluid level
37.5	Change fluid, filter, and adjust bands — "LDC"
24	Change fluid, filter, and adjust bands — "HDC"
12	Change fluid, filter, and adjust bands — "Severe Service"

TRANSFER CASE **
DOS	Check fluid level.
37.5	Drain and refill — "LDC"
36	Drain and refill — "HDC"

REAR AXLE DIFFERENTIAL — MPO
| DOS | Check for leakage |

REAR WHEEL BEARINGS — MG OR MMG
"Semi-Floating" lubricate when axle shafts are removed
| 48 | "Full-Floating" lubricate (and during brake service) |

FREQUENCY SYMBOLS

DOS	During Other Service
"LDC"	Light Duty Emission Cycle
"HDC"	Heavy Duty Emission Cycle
A	1st Oil Change Then Each 2nd Oil Change
B	Every 2nd Oil Change
C	Every Oil Change
DA	Daily If Used In Water
B4	Once Per Season (Before Onset of Winter)
50H	50 Hours
12/	12 Months
3	3,000 Miles (4 800 KM)
6	6,000 Miles (9 600 KM)
7.5	7,500 Miles (12 000 KM)
12	12,000 Miles (19 000 KM)
15	15,000 Miles (24 000 KM)
18	18,000 Miles (29 000 KM)
22.5	22,500 Miles (36 000 KM)
24	24,000 Miles (38 000 KM)
36	36,000 Miles (58 000 KM)
37.5	37,500 Miles (60 000 KM)
52.5	52,500 Miles (84 000 KM)
3/3	3 Months or 3,000 Miles (4 800 KM)
6/6	6 Months or 6,000 Miles (9 600 KM)
6/7.5	6 Months or 7,500 Miles (12 000 KM)
12/6	12 Months or 6,000 Miles (9 600 KM)
12/7.5	12 Months or 7,500 Miles (12 000 KM)
12/12	12 Months or 12,000 Miles (19 000 KM)
12/48	12 Months or 48,000 Miles (77 000 KM)
24/22.5	24 Months or 22,500 Miles (36 000 KM)
24/24	24 Months or 24,000 Miles (39 000 KM)
36/48	36 Months or 48,000 Miles (77 000 KM)
36/52	36 Months or 52,000 Miles (84 000 KM)

*4-speed overdrive (A-833) initial fill is automatic transmission fluid labeled DEXRON. Multi-Purpose Gear Oil SAE 90, 75W, 75W-80, 80W-90 or 85W-90 may be used.

*NP-435 four speed, — engine oil SAE 50 above 32° or SAE 30 below 32°, Multi-Purpose Gear Oil SAE 80, 90 or 140 may be used.

**NP 208, use Dexron II

**NP 205, use Multi-Purpose Gear Oil meeting API specification GL5 or engine oil for service "SE and CC."

KEY TO LUBRICANTS

ATF	DEXRON II Type Automatic Transmission Fluid
CC	Carburetor Cleaner
EO	Engine Oil (SE/CC)
BF	Brake Fluid, Hi-Temp. — DOT 3
MG	Multi-Purpose Grease, NLG1 grade 2 E.P.
MMG	MOPAR Multi-Mileage Grease †
MPG	MOPAR Multi-Purpose Grease †
MPO	Multi-Purpose Gear Oil (API-GL5)
PSF	Power Steering Fluid
S	Manifold Heat Control Solvent

† Or Equivalent

1982—83 Dodge W100—350 & Ramcharger 4 wheel drive models

LUBRICATION DIAGRAMS

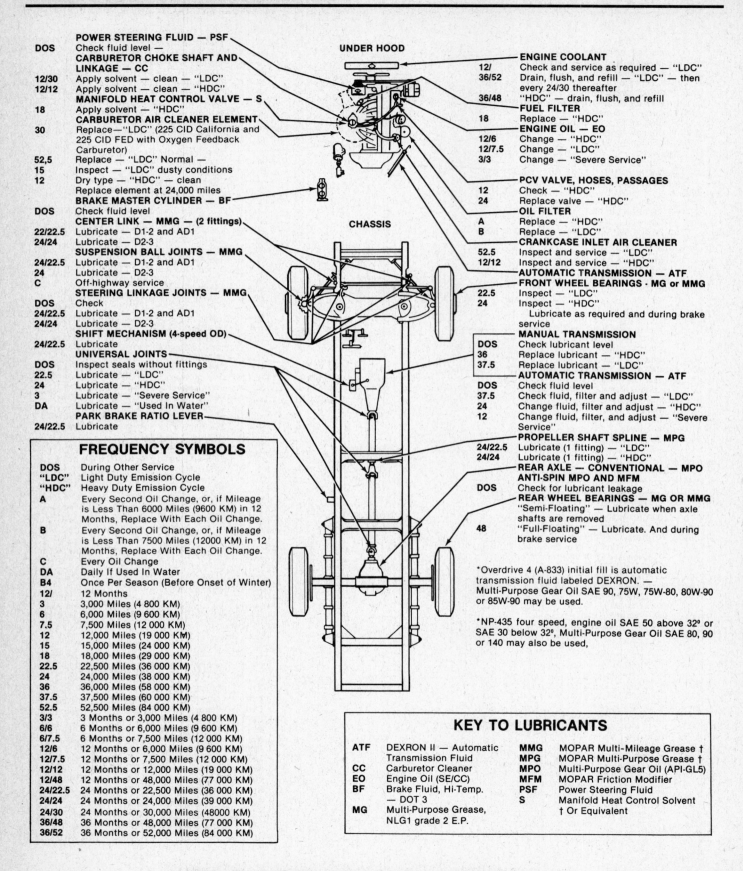

POWER STEERING FLUID — PSF
DOS — Check fluid level —

CARBURETOR CHOKE SHAFT AND LINKAGE — CC
12/30 — Apply solvent — clean — "LDC"
12/12 — Apply solvent — clean — "HDC"

MANIFOLD HEAT CONTROL VALVE — S
18 — Apply solvent — "HDC"

CARBURETOR AIR CLEANER ELEMENT
30 — Replace—"LDC" (225 CID California and 225 CID FED with Oxygen Feedback Carburetor)
52,5 — Replace — "LDC" Normal —
15 — Inspect — "LDC" dusty conditions
12 — Dry type "HDC" — clean
Replace element at 24,000 miles

BRAKE MASTER CYLINDER — BF
DOS — Check fluid level

CENTER LINK — MMG — (2 fittings)
22/22.5 — Lubricate — D1-2 and AD1
24/24 — Lubricate — D2-3

SUSPENSION BALL JOINTS — MMG
24/22.5 — Lubricate — D1-2 and AD1
24 — Lubricate — D2-3
C — Off-highway service

STEERING LINKAGE JOINTS — MMG
DOS — Check
24/22.5 — Lubricate — D1-2 and AD1
24/24 — Lubricate — D2-3

SHIFT MECHANISM (4-speed OD)
24/22.5 — Lubricate

UNIVERSAL JOINTS
DOS — Inspect seals without fittings
22.5 — Lubricate — "LDC"
24 — Lubricate — "HDC"
3 — Lubricate — "Severe Service"
DA — Lubricate — "Used In Water"

PARK BRAKE RATIO LEVER
24/22.5 — Lubricate

UNDER HOOD

CHASSIS

ENGINE COOLANT
12/ — Check and service as required — "LDC"
36/52 — Drain, flush, and refill — "LDC" — then every 24/30 thereafter
36/48 — "HDC" — drain, flush, and refill

FUEL FILTER
18 — Replace — "HDC"

ENGINE OIL — EO
12/6 — Change — "HDC"
12/7.5 — Change — "LDC"
3/3 — Change — "Severe Service"

PCV VALVE, HOSES, PASSAGES
12 — Check — "HDC"
24 — Replace valve — "HDC"

OIL FILTER
A — Replace — "HDC"
B — Replace — "LDC"

CRANKCASE INLET AIR CLEANER
52.5 — Inspect and service — "LDC"
12/12 — Inspect and service — "HDC"

AUTOMATIC TRANSMISSION — ATF
FRONT WHEEL BEARINGS - MG or MMG
22.5 — Inspect — "LDC"
24 — Inspect — "HDC"
Lubricate as required and during brake service

MANUAL TRANSMISSION
DOS — Check lubricant level
36 — Replace lubricant — "HDC"
37.5 — Replace lubricant — "LDC"

AUTOMATIC TRANSMISSION — ATF
DOS — Check fluid level
37.5 — Check fluid, filter and adjust — "LDC"
24 — Change fluid, filter and adjust — "HDC"
12 — Change fluid, filter, and adjust — "Severe Service"

PROPELLER SHAFT SPLINE — MPG
24/22.5 — Lubricate (1 fitting) — "LDC"
24/24 — Lubricate (1 fitting) — "HDC"

REAR AXLE — CONVENTIONAL — MPO ANTI-SPIN MPO AND MFM
DOS — Check for lubricant leakage

REAR WHEEL BEARINGS — MG OR MMG
"Semi-Floating" — Lubricate when axle shafts are removed
48 — "Full-Floating" — Lubricate. And during brake service

FREQUENCY SYMBOLS

DOS	During Other Service
"LDC"	Light Duty Emission Cycle
"HDC"	Heavy Duty Emission Cycle
A	Every Second Oil Change, or, if Mileage is Less Than 6000 Miles (9600 KM) in 12 Months, Replace With Each Oil Change.
B	Every Second Oil Change, or, if Mileage is Less Than 7500 Miles (12000 KM) in 12 Months, Replace With Each Oil Change.
C	Every Oil Change
DA	Daily If Used In Water
B4	Once Per Season (Before Onset of Winter)
12/	12 Months
3	3,000 Miles (4 800 KM)
6	6,000 Miles (9 600 KM)
7.5	7,500 Miles (12 000 KM)
12	12,000 Miles (19 000 KM)
15	15,000 Miles (24 000 KM)
18	18,000 Miles (29 000 KM)
22.5	22,500 Miles (36 000 KM)
24	24,000 Miles (38 000 KM)
36	36,000 Miles (58 000 KM)
37.5	37,500 Miles (60 000 KM)
52.5	52,500 Miles (84 000 KM)
3/3	3 Months or 3,000 Miles (4 800 KM)
6/6	6 Months or 6,000 Miles (9 600 KM)
6/7.5	6 Months or 7,500 Miles (12 000 KM)
12/6	12 Months or 6,000 Miles (9 600 KM)
12/7.5	12 Months or 7,500 Miles (12 000 KM)
12/12	12 Months or 12,000 Miles (19 000 KM)
12/48	12 Months or 48,000 Miles (77 000 KM)
24/22.5	24 Months or 22,500 Miles (36 000 KM)
24/24	24 Months or 24,000 Miles (39 000 KM)
24/30	24 Months or 30,000 Miles (48000 KM)
36/48	36 Months or 48,000 Miles (77 000 KM)
36/52	36 Months or 52,000 Miles (84 000 KM)

*Overdrive 4 (A-833) initial fill is automatic transmission fluid labeled DEXRON. — Multi-Purpose Gear Oil SAE 90, 75W, 75W-80, 80W-90 or 85W-90 may be used.

*NP-435 four speed, engine oil SAE 50 above 32⁰ or SAE 30 below 32⁰, Multi-Purpose Gear Oil SAE 80, 90 or 140 may also be used,

KEY TO LUBRICANTS

ATF	DEXRON II — Automatic Transmission Fluid	MMG	MOPAR Multi-Mileage Grease †
CC	Carburetor Cleaner	MPG	MOPAR Multi-Purpose Grease †
EO	Engine Oil (SE/CC)	MPO	Multi-Purpose Gear Oil (API-GL5)
BF	Brake Fluid, Hi-Temp. — DOT 3	MFM	MOPAR Friction Modifier
		PSF	Power Steering Fluid
MG	Multi-Purpose Grease, NLG1 grade 2 E.P.	S	Manifold Heat Control Solvent
			† Or Equivalent

1984 Dodge D100—350 & Ramcharger 2 wheel drive models

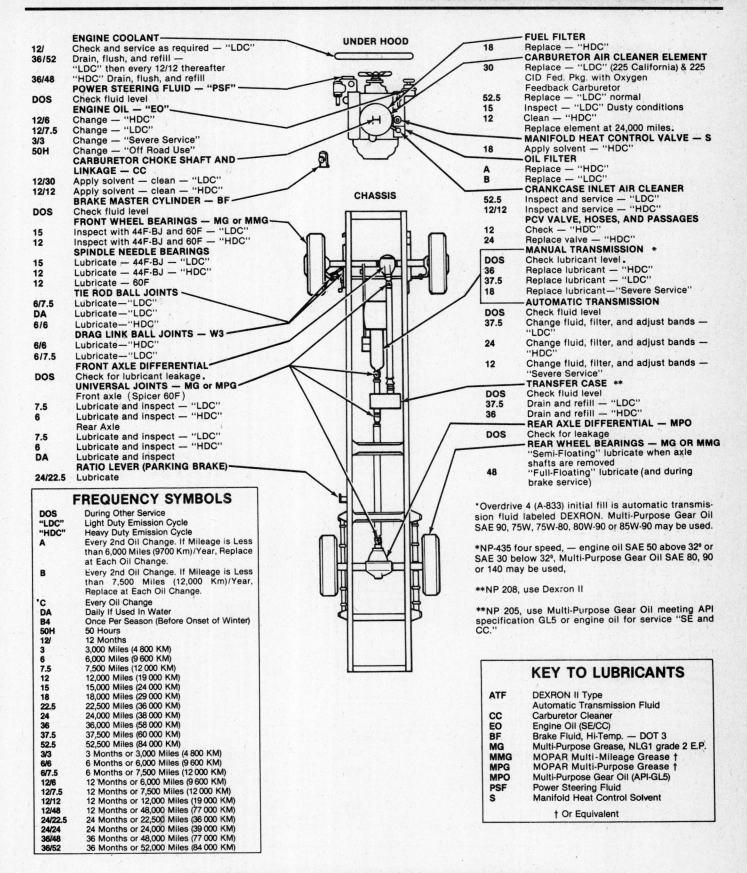

UNDER HOOD

ENGINE COOLANT
12/	Check and service as required — "LDC"
36/52	Drain, flush, and refill — "LDC" then every 12/12 thereafter
36/48	"HDC" Drain, flush, and refill

POWER STEERING FLUID — "PSF"
DOS	Check fluid level

ENGINE OIL — "EO"
12/6	Change — "HDC"
12/7.5	Change — "LDC"
3/3	Change — "Severe Service"
50H	Change — "Off Road Use"

CARBURETOR CHOKE SHAFT AND LINKAGE — CC
12/30	Apply solvent — clean — "LDC"
12/12	Apply solvent — clean — "HDC"

BRAKE MASTER CYLINDER — BF
DOS	Check fluid level

FRONT WHEEL BEARINGS — MG or MMG
15	Inspect with 44F-BJ and 60F — "LDC"
12	Inspect with 44F-BJ and 60F — "HDC"

SPINDLE NEEDLE BEARINGS
15	Lubricate — 44F-BJ — "LDC"
12	Lubricate — 44F-BJ — "HDC"
12	Lubricate — 60F

TIE ROD BALL JOINTS
6/7.5	Lubricate — "LDC"
DA	Lubricate — "LDC"
6/6	Lubricate — "HDC"

DRAG LINK BALL JOINTS — W3
6/6	Lubricate — "HDC"
6/7.5	Lubricate — "LDC"

FRONT AXLE DIFFERENTIAL
DOS	Check for lubricant leakage.

UNIVERSAL JOINTS — MG or MPG
Front axle (Spicer 60F)
7.5	Lubricate and inspect — "LDC"
6	Lubricate and inspect — "HDC"

Rear Axle
7.5	Lubricate and inspect — "LDC"
6	Lubricate and inspect — "HDC"
DA	Lubricate and inspect

RATIO LEVER (PARKING BRAKE)
24/22.5	Lubricate

CHASSIS

FUEL FILTER
18	Replace — "HDC"

CARBURETOR AIR CLEANER ELEMENT
30	Replace — "LDC" (225 California) & 225 CID Fed. Pkg. with Oxygen Feedback Carburetor
52.5	Replace — "LDC" normal
15	Inspect — "LDC" Dusty conditions
12	Clean — "HDC"
	Replace element at 24,000 miles.

MANIFOLD HEAT CONTROL VALVE — S
18	Apply solvent — "HDC"

OIL FILTER
A	Replace — "HDC"
B	Replace — "LDC"

CRANKCASE INLET AIR CLEANER
52.5	Inspect and service — "LDC"
12/12	Inspect and service — "HDC"

PCV VALVE, HOSES, AND PASSAGES
12	Check — "HDC"
24	Replace valve — "HDC"

MANUAL TRANSMISSION *
DOS	Check lubricant level.
36	Replace lubricant — "HDC"
37.5	Replace lubricant — "LDC"
18	Replace lubricant — "Severe Service"

AUTOMATIC TRANSMISSION
DOS	Check fluid level
37.5	Change fluid, filter, and adjust bands — "LDC"
24	Change fluid, filter, and adjust bands — "HDC"
12	Change fluid, filter, and adjust bands — "Severe Service"

TRANSFER CASE **
DOS	Check fluid level
37.5	Drain and refill — "LDC"
36	Drain and refill — "HDC"

REAR AXLE DIFFERENTIAL — MPO
DOS	Check for leakage

REAR WHEEL BEARINGS — MG OR MMG
	"Semi-Floating" lubricate when axle shafts are removed
48	"Full-Floating" lubricate (and during brake service)

FREQUENCY SYMBOLS

DOS	During Other Service
"LDC"	Light Duty Emission Cycle
"HDC"	Heavy Duty Emission Cycle
A	Every 2nd Oil Change. If Mileage is Less than 6,000 Miles (9700 Km)/Year, Replace at Each Oil Change.
B	Every 2nd Oil Change. If Mileage is Less than 7,500 Miles (12,000 Km)/Year, Replace at Each Oil Change.
C	Every Oil Change
DA	Daily If Used In Water
B4	Once Per Season (Before Onset of Winter)
50H	50 Hours
12/	12 Months
3	3,000 Miles (4 800 KM)
6	6,000 Miles (9 600 KM)
7.5	7,500 Miles (12 000 KM)
12	12,000 Miles (19 000 KM)
15	15,000 Miles (24 000 KM)
18	18,000 Miles (29 000 KM)
22.5	22,500 Miles (36 000 KM)
24	24,000 Miles (38 000 KM)
36	36,000 Miles (58 000 KM)
37.5	37,500 Miles (60 000 KM)
52.5	52,500 Miles (84 000 KM)
3/3	3 Months or 3,000 Miles (4 800 KM)
6/6	6 Months or 6,000 Miles (9 600 KM)
6/7.5	6 Months or 7,500 Miles (12 000 KM)
12/6	12 Months or 6,000 Miles (9 600 KM)
12/7.5	12 Months or 7,500 Miles (12 000 KM)
12/12	12 Months or 12,000 Miles (19 000 KM)
12/48	12 Months or 48,000 Miles (77 000 KM)
24/22.5	24 Months or 22,500 Miles (36 000 KM)
24/24	24 Months or 24,000 Miles (39 000 KM)
36/48	36 Months or 48,000 Miles (77 000 KM)
36/52	36 Months or 52,000 Miles (84 000 KM)

*Overdrive 4 (A-833) initial fill is automatic transmission fluid labeled DEXRON. Multi-Purpose Gear Oil SAE 90, 75W, 75W-80, 80W-90 or 85W-90 may be used.

*NP-435 four speed, — engine oil SAE 50 above 32° or SAE 30 below 32°, Multi-Purpose Gear Oil SAE 80, 90 or 140 may be used,

**NP 208, use Dexron II

**NP 205, use Multi-Purpose Gear Oil meeting API specification GL5 or engine oil for service "SE and CC."

KEY TO LUBRICANTS

ATF	DEXRON II Type Automatic Transmission Fluid
CC	Carburetor Cleaner
EO	Engine Oil (SE/CC)
BF	Brake Fluid, Hi-Temp. — DOT 3
MG	Multi-Purpose Grease, NLG1 grade 2 E.P.
MMG	MOPAR Multi-Mileage Grease †
MPG	MOPAR Multi-Purpose Grease †
MPO	Multi-Purpose Gear Oil (API-GL5)
PSF	Power Steering Fluid
S	Manifold Heat Control Solvent

† Or Equivalent

1984 Dodge W100—350 & Ramcharger 4 wheel drive models

LUBRICATION DIAGRAMS

DOS — **POWER STEERING FLUID — PSF**
Check fluid level —

DOS — **BRAKE MASTER CYLINDER — BF**
Check fluid level

CENTER LINK — MMG — (2 fittings)
24/22.5   Lubricate — "LDC"
24/24   Lubricate — "HDC"

SUSPENSION BALL JOINTS — MMG
24/22.5   Lubricate — "LDC"
24   Lubricate — "HDC"
C   Off-highway service

STEERING LINKAGE JOINTS — MMG
DOS   Check
24/22.5   Lubricate — "LDC"
24/24   Lubricate — "HDC"

SHIFT MECHANISM (4-speed OD)
24/22.5   Lubricate

UNIVERSAL JOINTS
DOS   Inspect seals without fittings
22.5   Lubricate — "LDC"
24   Lubricate — "HDC"
3   Lubricate — "Severe Service"
DA   Lubricate — "Used In Water"

PARK BRAKE RATIO LEVER
24/22.5   Lubricate

UNDER HOOD

CHASSIS

ENGINE COOLANT
12/   Check and service as required — "LDC"
36/52   Drain, flush, and refill — "LDC" — then every 24/30 thereafter
36/48   "HDC" — drain, flush, and refill - then every 24/30 thereafter

AUTOMATIC TRANSMISSION — ATF
FRONT WHEEL BEARINGS · MG or MMG
22.5   Inspect — "LDC"
24   Inspect — "HDC"
   Lubricate as required and during brake service

MANUAL TRANSMISSION
DOS   Check lubricant level
36   Replace lubricant — "HDC"
37.5   Replace lubricant — "LDC"

AUTOMATIC TRANSMISSION — ATF
DOS   Check fluid level
37.5   Check fluid, filter and adjust — "LDC"
24   Change fluid, filter and adjust — "HDC"
12   Change fluid, filter, and adjust — "Severe Service"

PROPELLER SHAFT SPLINE — MPG
24/22.5   Lubricate (1 fitting) — "LDC"
24/24   Lubricate (1 fitting) — "HDC"
3   Lubricate - "Severe Service"
DA   Lubricate - "Used in Water"

REAR AXLE — CONVENTIONAL — MPO
ANTI-SPIN MPO AND MFM
DOS   Check for lubricant leakage

REAR WHEEL BEARINGS — MG OR MMG
"Semi-Floating" — Lubricate when axle shafts are removed
"Full-Floating" — Lubricate during brake service

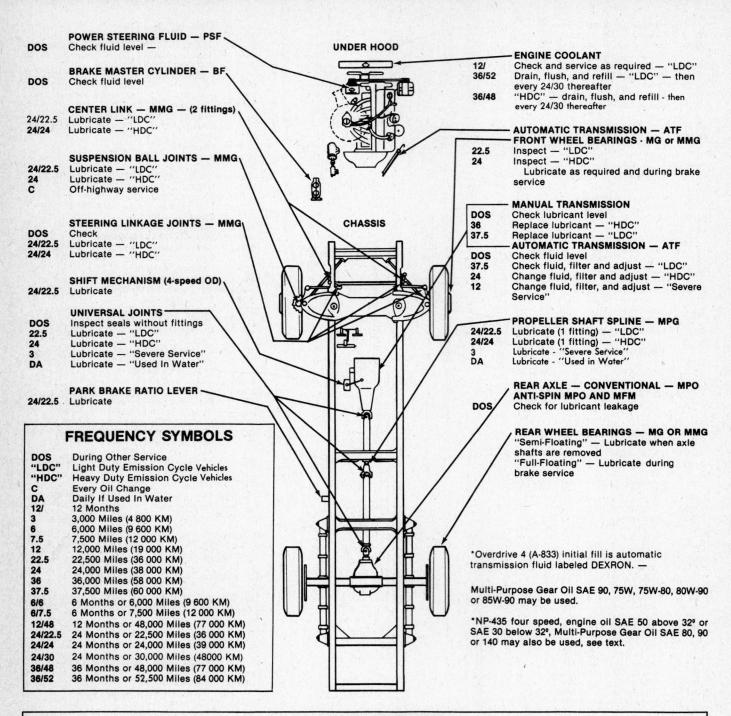

FREQUENCY SYMBOLS

DOS	During Other Service
"LDC"	Light Duty Emission Cycle Vehicles
"HDC"	Heavy Duty Emission Cycle Vehicles
C	Every Oil Change
DA	Daily If Used In Water
12/	12 Months
3	3,000 Miles (4 800 KM)
6	6,000 Miles (9 600 KM)
7.5	7,500 Miles (12 000 KM)
12	12,000 Miles (19 000 KM)
22.5	22,500 Miles (36 000 KM)
24	24,000 Miles (38 000 KM)
36	36,000 Miles (58 000 KM)
37.5	37,500 Miles (60 000 KM)
6/6	6 Months or 6,000 Miles (9 600 KM)
6/7.5	6 Months or 7,500 Miles (12 000 KM)
12/48	12 Months or 48,000 Miles (77 000 KM)
24/22.5	24 Months or 22,500 Miles (36 000 KM)
24/24	24 Months or 24,000 Miles (39 000 KM)
24/30	24 Months or 30,000 Miles (48000 KM)
36/48	36 Months or 48,000 Miles (77 000 KM)
36/52	36 Months or 52,500 Miles (84 000 KM)

*Overdrive 4 (A-833) initial fill is automatic transmission fluid labeled DEXRON. —

Multi-Purpose Gear Oil SAE 90, 75W, 75W-80, 80W-90 or 85W-90 may be used.

*NP-435 four speed, engine oil SAE 50 above 32° or SAE 30 below 32°, Multi-Purpose Gear Oil SAE 80, 90 or 140 may also be used, see text.

KEY TO LUBRICANTS

ATF   DEXRON II — Automatic Transmission Fluid
1 qt (0.95 L), P/N 4271243
55 gal (208L), P/N 4271245

CC   Carburetor Cleaner
EO   Engine Oil (SF/CC)
BF   Brake Fluid, Hi-Temp. — DOT 3
MG   Multi-Purpose Grease, NLG1 grade 2 E.P. (P/N 4318063)

MMG   MOPAR Multi-Mileage Grease (P/N 4318062)
MPO   Multi-Purpose Gear Oil MOPAR Hypoid Lubricant
1 qt (0.95 L), P/N 4318058
16 gal (60.6 L), P/N 4318059
MFM   MOPAR Friction Modifier
PSF   Power Steering Fluid (see text)
S   Manifold Heat Control Valve Solvent Or Equivalent

1985 Dodge D100—350 & Ramcharger 2 wheel drive models

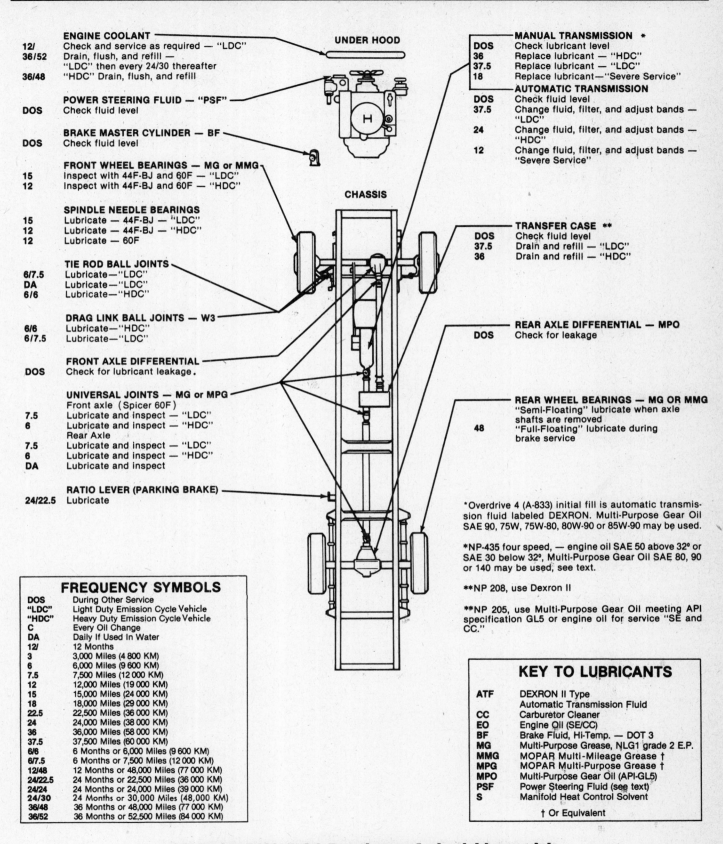

ENGINE COOLANT
12/	Check and service as required — "LDC"
36/52	Drain, flush, and refill — "LDC" then every 24/30 thereafter
36/48	"HDC" Drain, flush, and refill

POWER STEERING FLUID — "PSF"
| DOS | Check fluid level |

BRAKE MASTER CYLINDER — BF
| DOS | Check fluid level |

FRONT WHEEL BEARINGS — MG or MMG
| 15 | Inspect with 44F-BJ and 60F — "LDC" |
| 12 | Inspect with 44F-BJ and 60F — "HDC" |

SPINDLE NEEDLE BEARINGS
15	Lubricate — 44F-BJ — "LDC"
12	Lubricate — 44F-BJ — "HDC"
12	Lubricate — 60F

TIE ROD BALL JOINTS
6/7.5	Lubricate—"LDC"
DA	Lubricate—"LDC"
6/6	Lubricate—"HDC"

DRAG LINK BALL JOINTS — W3
| 6/6 | Lubricate—"HDC" |
| 6/7.5 | Lubricate—"LDC" |

FRONT AXLE DIFFERENTIAL
| DOS | Check for lubricant leakage. |

UNIVERSAL JOINTS — MG or MPG
Front axle (Spicer 60F)
| 7.5 | Lubricate and inspect — "LDC" |
| 6 | Lubricate and inspect — "HDC" |

Rear Axle
7.5	Lubricate and inspect — "LDC"
6	Lubricate and inspect — "HDC"
DA	Lubricate and inspect

RATIO LEVER (PARKING BRAKE)
| 24/22.5 | Lubricate |

UNDER HOOD

CHASSIS

MANUAL TRANSMISSION *
DOS	Check lubricant level
36	Replace lubricant — "HDC"
37.5	Replace lubricant — "LDC"
18	Replace lubricant—"Severe Service"

AUTOMATIC TRANSMISSION
DOS	Check fluid level
37.5	Change fluid, filter, and adjust bands — "LDC"
24	Change fluid, filter, and adjust bands — "HDC"
12	Change fluid, filter, and adjust bands — "Severe Service"

TRANSFER CASE **
DOS	Check fluid level
37.5	Drain and refill — "LDC"
36	Drain and refill — "HDC"

REAR AXLE DIFFERENTIAL — MPO
| DOS | Check for leakage |

REAR WHEEL BEARINGS — MG OR MMG
"Semi-Floating" lubricate when axle shafts are removed
| 48 | "Full-Floating" lubricate during brake service |

*Overdrive 4 (A-833) initial fill is automatic transmission fluid labeled DEXRON. Multi-Purpose Gear Oil SAE 90, 75W, 75W-80, 80W-90 or 85W-90 may be used.

*NP-435 four speed, — engine oil SAE 50 above 32° or SAE 30 below 32°, Multi-Purpose Gear Oil SAE 80, 90 or 140 may be used, see text.

**NP 208, use Dexron II

**NP 205, use Multi-Purpose Gear Oil meeting API specification GL5 or engine oil for service "SE and CC."

FREQUENCY SYMBOLS

DOS	During Other Service
"LDC"	Light Duty Emission Cycle Vehicle
"HDC"	Heavy Duty Emission Cycle Vehicle
C	Every Oil Change
DA	Daily If Used In Water
12/	12 Months
3	3,000 Miles (4 800 KM)
6	6,000 Miles (9 600 KM)
7.5	7,500 Miles (12 000 KM)
12	12,000 Miles (19 000 KM)
15	15,000 Miles (24 000 KM)
18	18,000 Miles (29 000 KM)
22.5	22,500 Miles (36 000 KM)
24	24,000 Miles (38 000 KM)
36	36,000 Miles (58 000 KM)
37.5	37,500 Miles (60 000 KM)
6/6	6 Months or 6,000 Miles (9 600 KM)
6/7.5	6 Months or 7,500 Miles (12 000 KM)
12/48	12 Months or 48,000 Miles (77 000 KM)
24/22.5	24 Months or 22,500 Miles (36 000 KM)
24/24	24 Months or 24,000 Miles (39 000 KM)
24/30	24 Months or 30,000 Miles (48 000 KM)
36/48	36 Months or 48,000 Miles (77 000 KM)
36/52	36 Months or 52,500 Miles (84 000 KM)

KEY TO LUBRICANTS

ATF	DEXRON II Type Automatic Transmission Fluid
CC	Carburetor Cleaner
EO	Engine Oil (SE/CC)
BF	Brake Fluid, Hi-Temp. — DOT 3
MG	Multi-Purpose Grease, NLG1 grade 2 E.P.
MMG	MOPAR Multi-Mileage Grease †
MPG	MOPAR Multi-Purpose Grease †
MPO	Multi-Purpose Gear Oil (API-GL5)
PSF	Power Steering Fluid (see text)
S	Manifold Heat Control Solvent

† Or Equivalent

1985 Dodge D100—350 & Ramcharger 4 wheel drive models

Ford

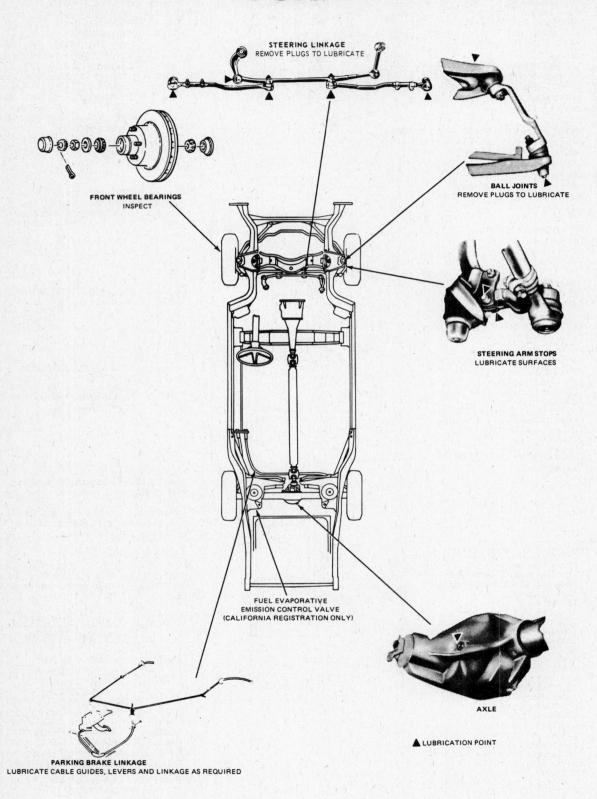

STEERING LINKAGE
REMOVE PLUGS TO LUBRICATE

BALL JOINTS
REMOVE PLUGS TO LUBRICATE

FRONT WHEEL BEARINGS
INSPECT

STEERING ARM STOPS
LUBRICATE SURFACES

FUEL EVAPORATIVE
EMISSION CONTROL VALVE
(CALIFORNIA REGISTRATION ONLY)

AXLE

▲ LUBRICATION POINT

PARKING BRAKE LINKAGE
LUBRICATE CABLE GUIDES, LEVERS AND LINKAGE AS REQUIRED

1979 Ford Ranchero chassis lubrication diagram

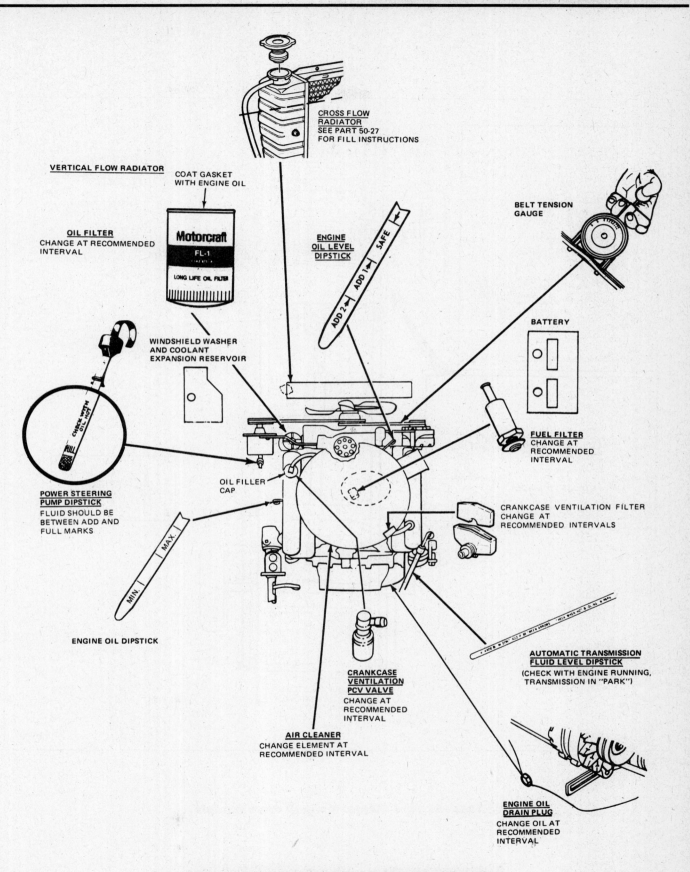

CROSS FLOW
RADIATOR
SEE PART 50-27
FOR FILL INSTRUCTIONS

VERTICAL FLOW RADIATOR

COAT GASKET
WITH ENGINE OIL

OIL FILTER
CHANGE AT RECOMMENDED
INTERVAL

Motorcraft
FL-1
LONG LIFE OIL FILTER

ENGINE
OIL LEVEL
DIPSTICK

SAFE
ADD 1
ADD 2

BELT TENSION
GAUGE

BATTERY

WINDSHIELD WASHER
AND COOLANT
EXPANSION RESERVOIR

FUEL FILTER
CHANGE AT
RECOMMENDED
INTERVAL

CHECK WITH
OIL HOT
FULL

OIL FILLER
CAP

POWER STEERING
PUMP DIPSTICK
FLUID SHOULD BE
BETWEEN ADD AND
FULL MARKS

CRANKCASE VENTILATION FILTER
CHANGE AT
RECOMMENDED INTERVALS

MAX.

MIN.

AUTOMATIC TRANSMISSION
FLUID LEVEL DIPSTICK
(CHECK WITH ENGINE RUNNING,
TRANSMISSION IN "PARK")

ENGINE OIL DIPSTICK

CRANKCASE
VENTILATION
PCV VALVE
CHANGE AT
RECOMMENDED
INTERVAL

AIR CLEANER
CHANGE ELEMENT AT
RECOMMENDED INTERVAL

ENGINE OIL
DRAIN PLUG
CHANGE OIL AT
RECOMMENDED
INTERVAL

1979 Ford Ranchero engine lubrication diagram

LUBRICATION DIAGRAMS

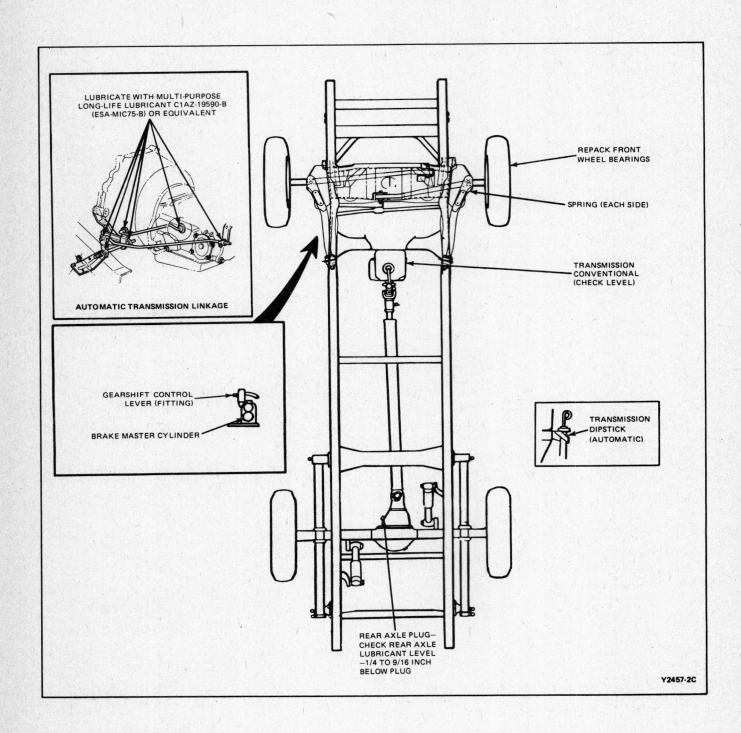

LUBRICATE WITH MULTI-PURPOSE
LONG-LIFE LUBRICANT C1AZ-19590-B
(ESA-MIC75-B) OR EQUIVALENT

AUTOMATIC TRANSMISSION LINKAGE

GEARSHIFT CONTROL
LEVER (FITTING)

BRAKE MASTER CYLINDER

REPACK FRONT
WHEEL BEARINGS

SPRING (EACH SIDE)

TRANSMISSION
CONVENTIONAL
(CHECK LEVEL)

TRANSMISSION
DIPSTICK
(AUTOMATIC)

REAR AXLE PLUG—
CHECK REAR AXLE
LUBRICANT LEVEL
—1/4 TO 9/16 INCH
BELOW PLUG

Y2457-2C

1983—85 Ford Ranger 2 wheel drive models

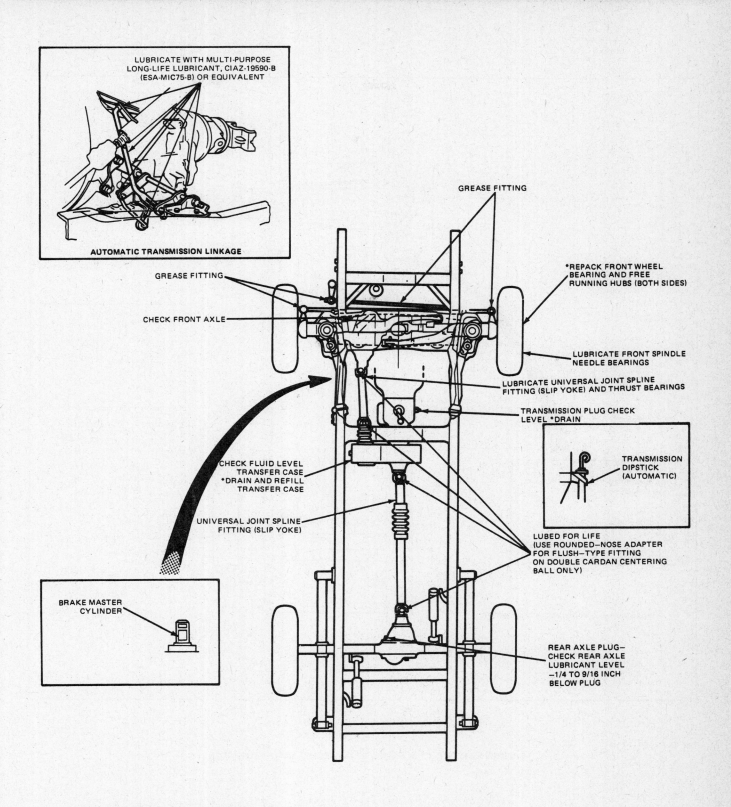

LUBRICATE WITH MULTI-PURPOSE
LONG-LIFE LUBRICANT, CIAZ-19590-B
(ESA-MIC75-B) OR EQUIVALENT

AUTOMATIC TRANSMISSION LINKAGE

GREASE FITTING

GREASE FITTING

CHECK FRONT AXLE

*REPACK FRONT WHEEL
BEARING AND FREE
RUNNING HUBS (BOTH SIDES)

LUBRICATE FRONT SPINDLE
NEEDLE BEARINGS

LUBRICATE UNIVERSAL JOINT SPLINE
FITTING (SLIP YOKE) AND THRUST BEARINGS

TRANSMISSION PLUG CHECK
LEVEL *DRAIN

CHECK FLUID LEVEL
TRANSFER CASE
*DRAIN AND REFILL
TRANSFER CASE

TRANSMISSION
DIPSTICK
(AUTOMATIC)

UNIVERSAL JOINT SPLINE
FITTING (SLIP YOKE)

LUBED FOR LIFE
(USE ROUNDED-NOSE ADAPTER
FOR FLUSH-TYPE FITTING
ON DOUBLE CARDAN CENTERING
BALL ONLY)

BRAKE MASTER
CYLINDER

REAR AXLE PLUG—
CHECK REAR AXLE
LUBRICANT LEVEL
—1/4 TO 9/16 INCH
BELOW PLUG

*DAILY WHEN OPERATING IN DEEP WATER

1983–84 Ford Ranger & 1984 Bronco II 4 wheel drive models

LUBRICATION DIAGRAMS

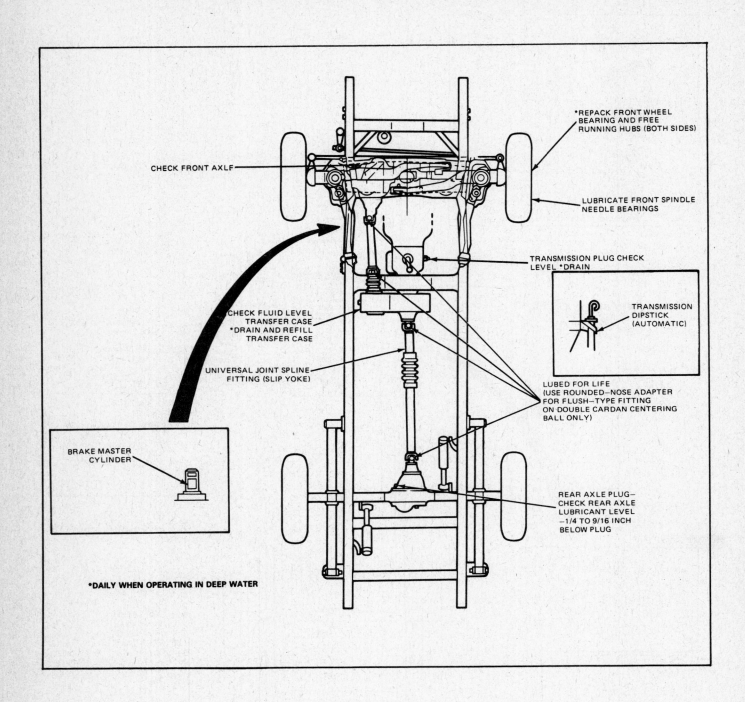

CHECK FRONT AXLE

*REPACK FRONT WHEEL BEARING AND FREE RUNNING HUBS (BOTH SIDES)

LUBRICATE FRONT SPINDLE NEEDLE BEARINGS

TRANSMISSION PLUG CHECK LEVEL *DRAIN

TRANSMISSION DIPSTICK (AUTOMATIC)

CHECK FLUID LEVEL TRANSFER CASE *DRAIN AND REFILL TRANSFER CASE

UNIVERSAL JOINT SPLINE FITTING (SLIP YOKE)

LUBED FOR LIFE (USE ROUNDED–NOSE ADAPTER FOR FLUSH–TYPE FITTING ON DOUBLE CARDAN CENTERING BALL ONLY)

BRAKE MASTER CYLINDER

REAR AXLE PLUG– CHECK REAR AXLE LUBRICANT LEVEL –1/4 TO 9/16 INCH BELOW PLUG

*DAILY WHEN OPERATING IN DEEP WATER

1985 Bronco II & Ranger 4 wheel drive models

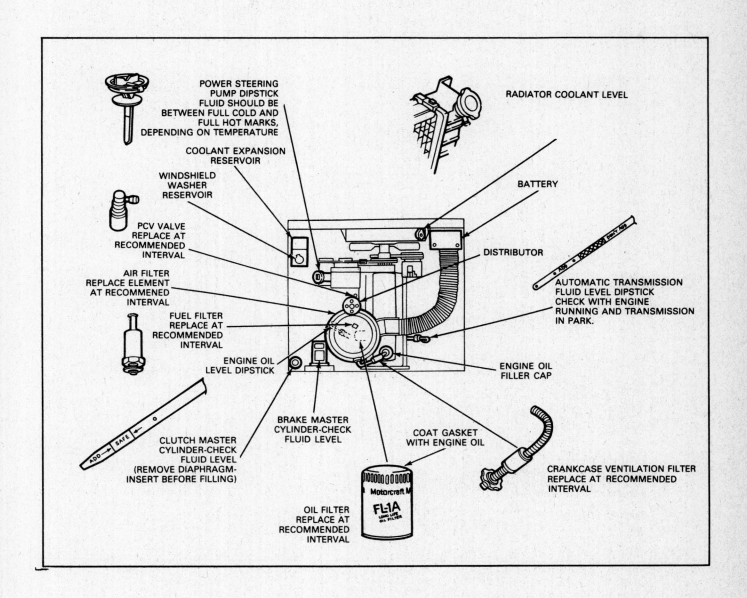

POWER STEERING PUMP DIPSTICK FLUID SHOULD BE BETWEEN FULL COLD AND FULL HOT MARKS, DEPENDING ON TEMPERATURE

RADIATOR COOLANT LEVEL

COOLANT EXPANSION RESERVOIR

WINDSHIELD WASHER RESERVOIR

BATTERY

PCV VALVE REPLACE AT RECOMMENDED INTERVAL

DISTRIBUTOR

AIR FILTER REPLACE ELEMENT AT RECOMMENED INTERVAL

AUTOMATIC TRANSMISSION FLUID LEVEL DIPSTICK CHECK WITH ENGINE RUNNING AND TRANSMISSION IN PARK.

FUEL FILTER REPLACE AT RECOMMENDED INTERVAL

ENGINE OIL LEVEL DIPSTICK

ENGINE OIL FILLER CAP

CLUTCH MASTER CYLINDER-CHECK FLUID LEVEL (REMOVE DIAPHRAGM-INSERT BEFORE FILLING)

BRAKE MASTER CYLINDER-CHECK FLUID LEVEL

COAT GASKET WITH ENGINE OIL

CRANKCASE VENTILATION FILTER REPLACE AT RECOMMENDED INTERVAL

OIL FILTER REPLACE AT RECOMMENDED INTERVAL

Motorcraft M

FL-1A
LONG LIFE OIL FILTER

1985 Bronco II & Ranger w/4-122 or 4-140 gasoline engine

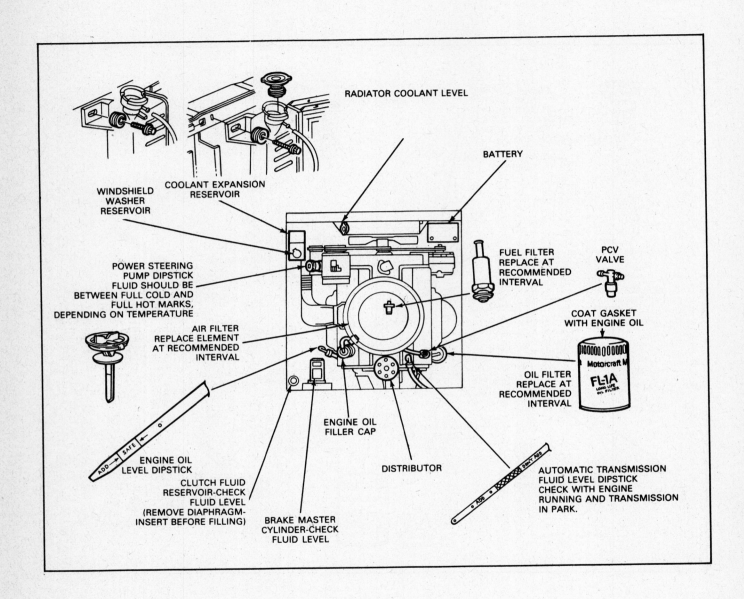

RADIATOR COOLANT LEVEL

BATTERY

COOLANT EXPANSION
RESERVOIR

WINDSHIELD
WASHER
RESERVOIR

FUEL FILTER
REPLACE AT
RECOMMENDED
INTERVAL

PCV
VALVE

POWER STEERING
PUMP DIPSTICK
FLUID SHOULD BE
BETWEEN FULL COLD AND
FULL HOT MARKS,
DEPENDING ON TEMPERATURE

COAT GASKET
WITH ENGINE OIL

AIR FILTER
REPLACE ELEMENT
AT RECOMMENDED
INTERVAL

Motorcraft
FL-1A

OIL FILTER
REPLACE AT
RECOMMENDED
INTERVAL

ENGINE OIL
LEVEL DIPSTICK

ENGINE OIL
FILLER CAP

DISTRIBUTOR

AUTOMATIC TRANSMISSION
FLUID LEVEL DIPSTICK
CHECK WITH ENGINE
RUNNING AND TRANSMISSION
IN PARK.

CLUTCH FLUID
RESERVOIR-CHECK
FLUID LEVEL
(REMOVE DIAPHRAGM-
INSERT BEFORE FILLING)

BRAKE MASTER
CYLINDER-CHECK
FLUID LEVEL

1985 Bronco II & Ranger w/V6-171 gasoline engine

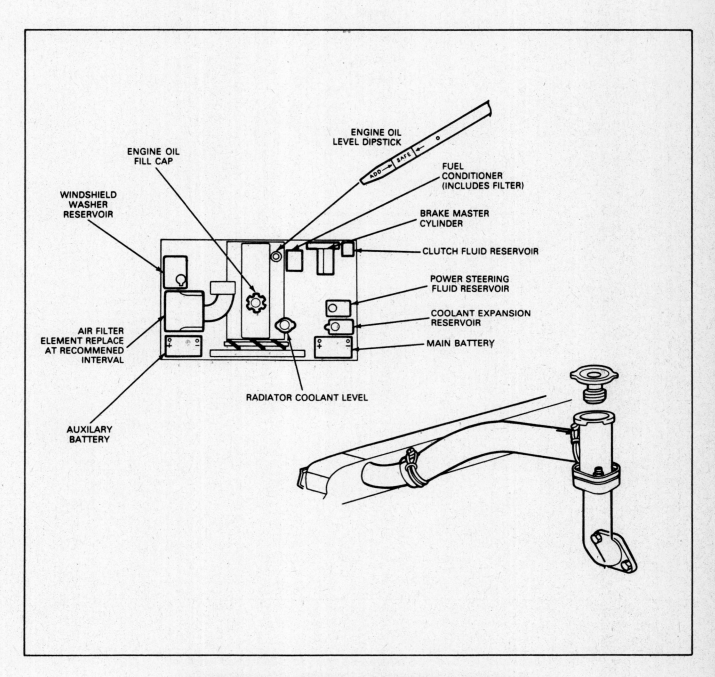

ENGINE OIL
LEVEL DIPSTICK

ENGINE OIL
FILL CAP

FUEL
CONDITIONER
(INCLUDES FILTER)

WINDSHIELD
WASHER
RESERVOIR

BRAKE MASTER
CYLINDER

CLUTCH FLUID RESERVOIR

POWER STEERING
FLUID RESERVOIR

COOLANT EXPANSION
RESERVOIR

AIR FILTER
ELEMENT REPLACE
AT RECOMMENED
INTERVAL

MAIN BATTERY

RADIATOR COOLANT LEVEL

AUXILARY
BATTERY

1985 Bronco II & Ranger w/4-143 turbo diesel engine

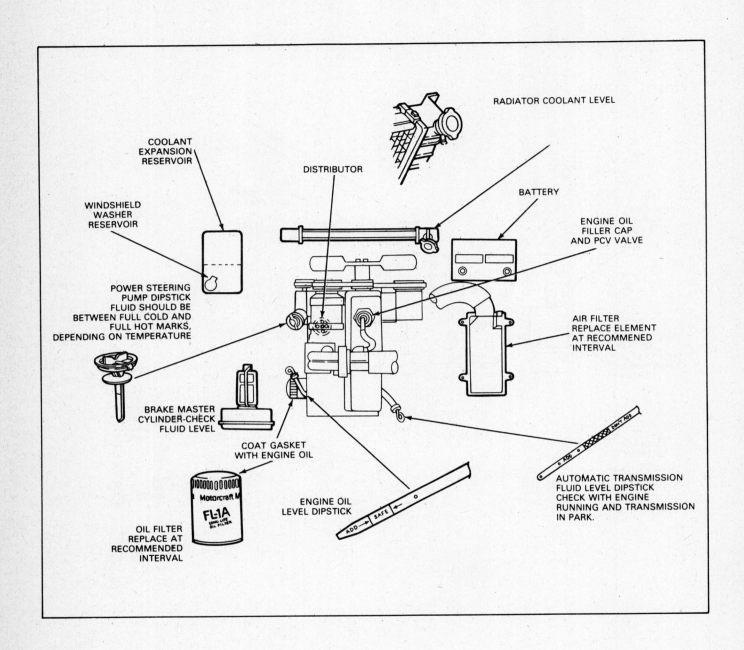

RADIATOR COOLANT LEVEL

COOLANT
EXPANSION
RESERVOIR

DISTRIBUTOR

BATTERY

WINDSHIELD
WASHER
RESERVOIR

ENGINE OIL
FILLER CAP
AND PCV VALVE

POWER STEERING
PUMP DIPSTICK
FLUID SHOULD BE
BETWEEN FULL COLD AND
FULL HOT MARKS,
DEPENDING ON TEMPERATURE

AIR FILTER
REPLACE ELEMENT
AT RECOMMENED
INTERVAL

BRAKE MASTER
CYLINDER-CHECK
FLUID LEVEL

COAT GASKET
WITH ENGINE OIL

Motorcraft

FL-1A
LONG LIFE
OIL FILTER

ENGINE OIL
LEVEL DIPSTICK

ADD   SAFE

AUTOMATIC TRANSMISSION
FLUID LEVEL DIPSTICK
CHECK WITH ENGINE
RUNNING AND TRANSMISSION
IN PARK.

OIL FILTER
REPLACE AT
RECOMMENDED
INTERVAL

1985 Ranger w/4-140 overhead cam fuel injected engine

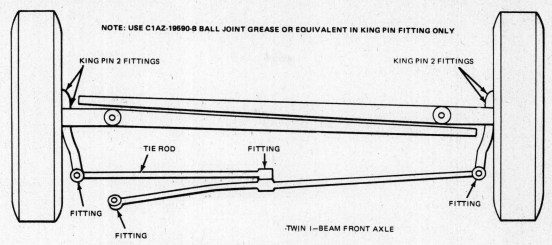

NOTE: USE C1AZ-19590-B BALL JOINT GREASE OR EQUIVALENT IN KING PIN FITTING ONLY

KING PIN 2 FITTINGS

KING PIN 2 FITTINGS

TIE ROD

FITTING

FITTING

FITTING

FITTING

-TWIN I—BEAM FRONT AXLE

NOTE: USE D4AZ-19590-A STEERING LINKAGE LUBRICANT OR EQUIVALENT

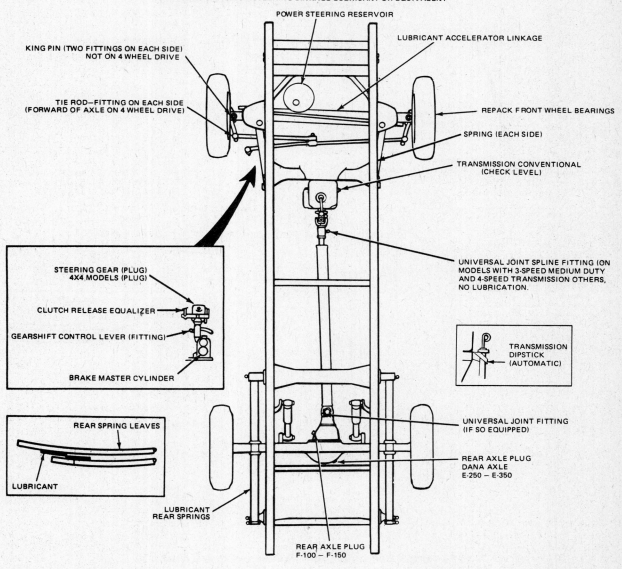

POWER STEERING RESERVOIR

LUBRICANT ACCELERATOR LINKAGE

KING PIN (TWO FITTINGS ON EACH SIDE)
NOT ON 4 WHEEL DRIVE

TIE ROD—FITTING ON EACH SIDE
(FORWARD OF AXLE ON 4 WHEEL DRIVE)

REPACK FRONT WHEEL BEARINGS

SPRING (EACH SIDE)

TRANSMISSION CONVENTIONAL
(CHECK LEVEL)

STEERING GEAR (PLUG)
4X4 MODELS (PLUG)

CLUTCH RELEASE EQUALIZER

GEARSHIFT CONTROL LEVER (FITTING)

BRAKE MASTER CYLINDER

UNIVERSAL JOINT SPLINE FITTING (ON
MODELS WITH 3-SPEED MEDIUM DUTY
AND 4-SPEED TRANSMISSION OTHERS,
NO LUBRICATION.

TRANSMISSION
DIPSTICK
(AUTOMATIC)

REAR SPRING LEAVES

LUBRICANT

UNIVERSAL JOINT FITTING
(IF SO EQUIPPED)

REAR AXLE PLUG
DANA AXLE
E-250 — E-350

LUBRICANT
REAR SPRINGS

REAR AXLE PLUG
F-100 — F-150

1979 Ford F Series 2 wheel drive models

LUBRICATION DIAGRAMS

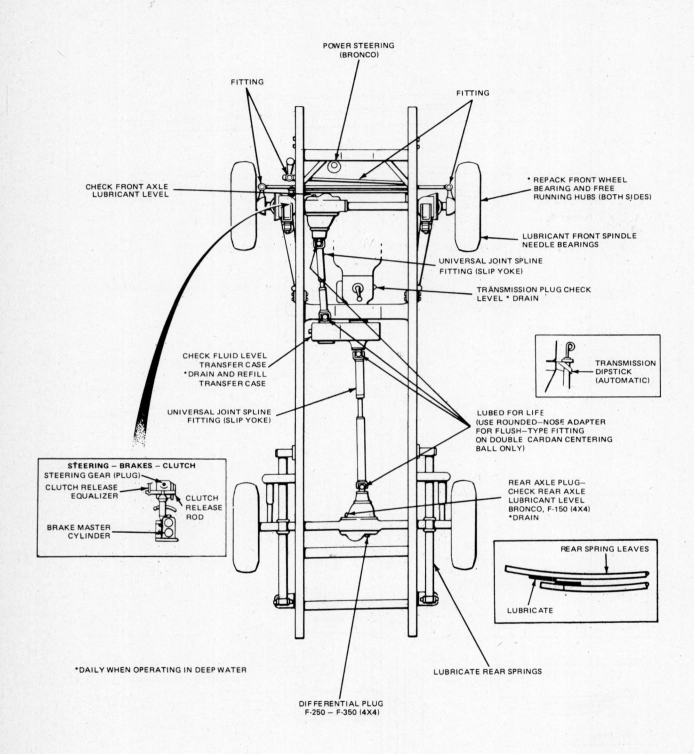

POWER STEERING
(BRONCO)

FITTING

FITTING

CHECK FRONT AXLE
LUBRICANT LEVEL

* REPACK FRONT WHEEL
BEARING AND FREE
RUNNING HUBS (BOTH SIDES)

LUBRICANT FRONT SPINDLE
NEEDLE BEARINGS

UNIVERSAL JOINT SPLINE
FITTING (SLIP YOKE)

TRANSMISSION PLUG CHECK
LEVEL * DRAIN

CHECK FLUID LEVEL
TRANSFER CASE
*DRAIN AND REFILL
TRANSFER CASE

UNIVERSAL JOINT SPLINE
FITTING (SLIP YOKE)

TRANSMISSION
DIPSTICK
(AUTOMATIC)

LUBED FOR LIFE
(USE ROUNDED—NOSE ADAPTER
FOR FLUSH—TYPE FITTING
ON DOUBLE CARDAN CENTERING
BALL ONLY)

STEERING – BRAKES – CLUTCH
STEERING GEAR (PLUG)
CLUTCH RELEASE
EQUALIZER
CLUTCH
RELEASE
ROD
BRAKE MASTER
CYLINDER

REAR AXLE PLUG—
CHECK REAR AXLE
LUBRICANT LEVEL
BRONCO, F-150 (4X4)
*DRAIN

REAR SPRING LEAVES

LUBRICATE

*DAILY WHEN OPERATING IN DEEP WATER

LUBRICATE REAR SPRINGS

DIFFERENTIAL PLUG
F-250 – F-350 (4X4)

1979 Ford F Series & Bronco 4 wheel drive models

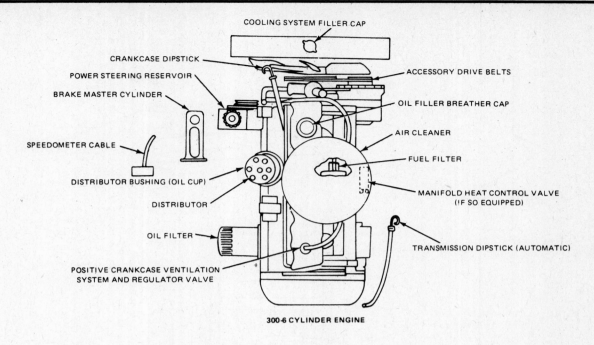

COOLING SYSTEM FILLER CAP

CRANKCASE DIPSTICK

POWER STEERING RESERVOIR

BRAKE MASTER CYLINDER

SPEEDOMETER CABLE

DISTRIBUTOR BUSHING (OIL CUP)

DISTRIBUTOR

OIL FILTER

POSITIVE CRANKCASE VENTILATION
SYSTEM AND REGULATOR VALVE

ACCESSORY DRIVE BELTS

OIL FILLER BREATHER CAP

AIR CLEANER

FUEL FILTER

MANIFOLD HEAT CONTROL VALVE
(IF SO EQUIPPED)

TRANSMISSION DIPSTICK (AUTOMATIC)

300-6 CYLINDER ENGINE

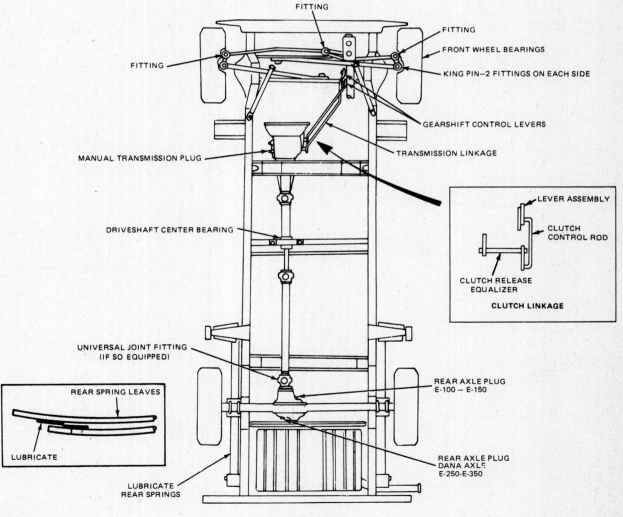

FITTING

FITTING

FITTING

FRONT WHEEL BEARINGS

KING PIN—2 FITTINGS ON EACH SIDE

GEARSHIFT CONTROL LEVERS

MANUAL TRANSMISSION PLUG

TRANSMISSION LINKAGE

LEVER ASSEMBLY

CLUTCH
CONTROL ROD

CLUTCH RELEASE
EQUALIZER

CLUTCH LINKAGE

DRIVESHAFT CENTER BEARING

UNIVERSAL JOINT FITTING
(IF SO EQUIPPED)

REAR SPRING LEAVES

LUBRICATE

REAR AXLE PLUG
E-100 — E-150

REAR AXLE PLUG
DANA AXLE
E-250-E-350

LUBRICATE
REAR SPRINGS

1979 Ford E Series

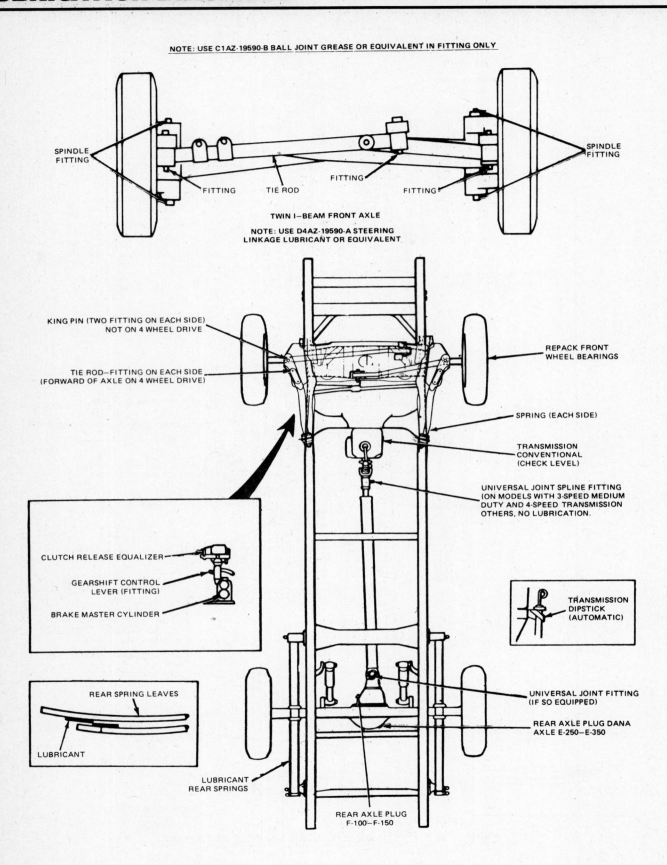

NOTE: USE C1AZ-19590-B BALL JOINT GREASE OR EQUIVALENT IN FITTING ONLY

SPINDLE FITTING

SPINDLE FITTING

FITTING

TIE ROD

FITTING

FITTING

TWIN I—BEAM FRONT AXLE

NOTE: USE D4AZ-19590-A STEERING LINKAGE LUBRICANT OR EQUIVALENT

KING PIN (TWO FITTING ON EACH SIDE) NOT ON 4 WHEEL DRIVE

TIE ROD—FITTING ON EACH SIDE (FORWARD OF AXLE ON 4 WHEEL DRIVE)

REPACK FRONT WHEEL BEARINGS

SPRING (EACH SIDE)

TRANSMISSION CONVENTIONAL (CHECK LEVEL)

UNIVERSAL JOINT SPLINE FITTING (ON MODELS WITH 3-SPEED MEDIUM DUTY AND 4-SPEED TRANSMISSION OTHERS, NO LUBRICATION.

CLUTCH RELEASE EQUALIZER

GEARSHIFT CONTROL LEVER (FITTING)

BRAKE MASTER CYLINDER

TRANSMISSION DIPSTICK (AUTOMATIC)

REAR SPRING LEAVES

LUBRICANT

UNIVERSAL JOINT FITTING (IF SO EQUIPPED)

REAR AXLE PLUG DANA AXLE E-250—E-350

LUBRICANT REAR SPRINGS

REAR AXLE PLUG F-100—F-150

1980 Ford F Series 2 wheel drive models

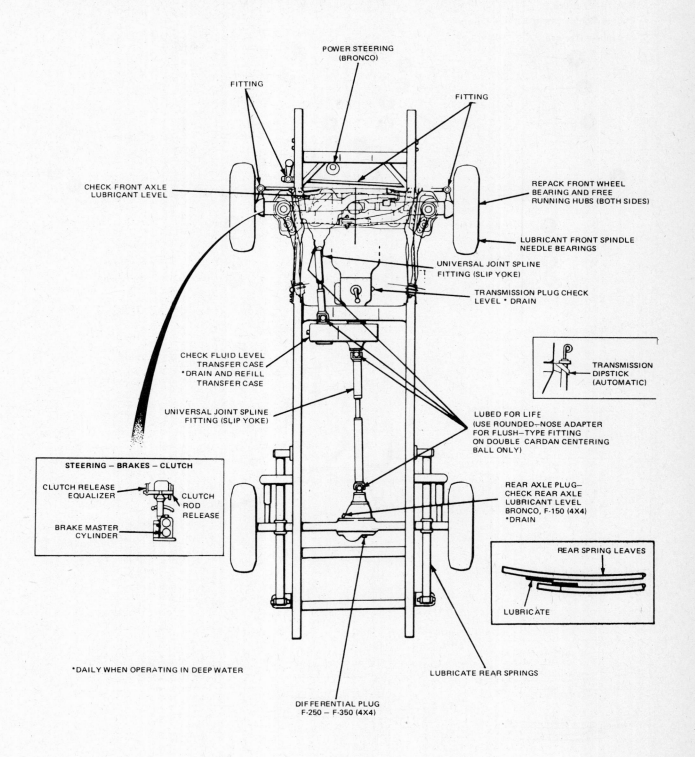

POWER STEERING
(BRONCO)

FITTING

FITTING

CHECK FRONT AXLE
LUBRICANT LEVEL

REPACK FRONT WHEEL
BEARING AND FREE
RUNNING HUBS (BOTH SIDES)

LUBRICANT FRONT SPINDLE
NEEDLE BEARINGS

UNIVERSAL JOINT SPLINE
FITTING (SLIP YOKE)

TRANSMISSION PLUG CHECK
LEVEL * DRAIN

CHECK FLUID LEVEL
TRANSFER CASE
*DRAIN AND REFILL
TRANSFER CASE

TRANSMISSION
DIPSTICK
(AUTOMATIC)

UNIVERSAL JOINT SPLINE
FITTING (SLIP YOKE)

LUBED FOR LIFE
(USE ROUNDED–NOSE ADAPTER
FOR FLUSH–TYPE FITTING
ON DOUBLE CARDAN CENTERING
BALL ONLY)

STEERING – BRAKES – CLUTCH

CLUTCH RELEASE
EQUALIZER

CLUTCH
ROD
RELEASE

BRAKE MASTER
CYLINDER

REAR AXLE PLUG–
CHECK REAR AXLE
LUBRICANT LEVEL
BRONCO, F-150 (4X4)
*DRAIN

REAR SPRING LEAVES

LUBRICATE

*DAILY WHEN OPERATING IN DEEP WATER

LUBRICATE REAR SPRINGS

DIFFERENTIAL PLUG
F-250 – F-350 (4X4)

1980 Ford F Series & Bronco 4 wheel drive models

LUBRICATION DIAGRAMS

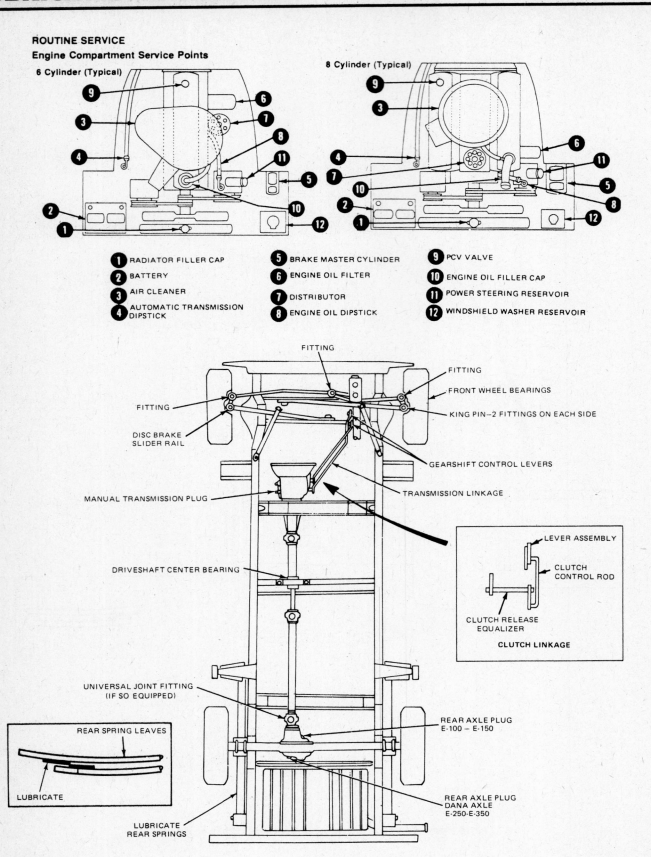

ROUTINE SERVICE

Engine Compartment Service Points

6 Cylinder (Typical)

8 Cylinder (Typical)

1 RADIATOR FILLER CAP

2 BATTERY

3 AIR CLEANER

4 AUTOMATIC TRANSMISSION DIPSTICK

5 BRAKE MASTER CYLINDER

6 ENGINE OIL FILTER

7 DISTRIBUTOR

8 ENGINE OIL DIPSTICK

9 PCV VALVE

10 ENGINE OIL FILLER CAP

11 POWER STEERING RESERVOIR

12 WINDSHIELD WASHER RESERVOIR

FITTING

FITTING

FITTING

FRONT WHEEL BEARINGS

FITTING

KING PIN—2 FITTINGS ON EACH SIDE

DISC BRAKE SLIDER RAIL

GEARSHIFT CONTROL LEVERS

MANUAL TRANSMISSION PLUG

TRANSMISSION LINKAGE

DRIVESHAFT CENTER BEARING

LEVER ASSEMBLY

CLUTCH CONTROL ROD

CLUTCH RELEASE EQUALIZER

CLUTCH LINKAGE

UNIVERSAL JOINT FITTING (IF SO EQUIPPED)

REAR AXLE PLUG E-100 – E-150

REAR SPRING LEAVES

LUBRICATE

REAR AXLE PLUG DANA AXLE E-250-E-350

LUBRICATE REAR SPRINGS

1980 Ford F Series

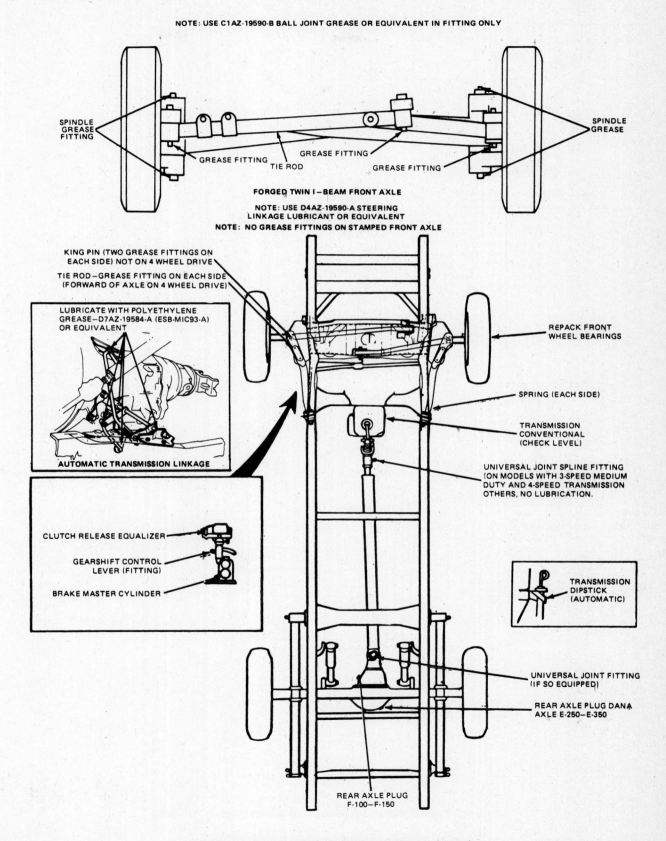

NOTE: USE C1AZ-19590-B BALL JOINT GREASE OR EQUIVALENT IN FITTING ONLY

SPINDLE GREASE FITTING

SPINDLE GREASE

GREASE FITTING

GREASE FITTING

TIE ROD

GREASE FITTING

FORGED TWIN I-BEAM FRONT AXLE

NOTE: USE D4AZ-19590-A STEERING LINKAGE LUBRICANT OR EQUIVALENT

NOTE: NO GREASE FITTINGS ON STAMPED FRONT AXLE

KING PIN (TWO GREASE FITTINGS ON EACH SIDE) NOT ON 4 WHEEL DRIVE

TIE ROD—GREASE FITTING ON EACH SIDE (FORWARD OF AXLE ON 4 WHEEL DRIVE)

LUBRICATE WITH POLYETHYLENE GREASE—D7AZ-19584-A (ESB-MIC93-A) OR EQUIVALENT

AUTOMATIC TRANSMISSION LINKAGE

REPACK FRONT WHEEL BEARINGS

SPRING (EACH SIDE)

TRANSMISSION CONVENTIONAL (CHECK LEVEL)

UNIVERSAL JOINT SPLINE FITTING (ON MODELS WITH 3-SPEED MEDIUM DUTY AND 4-SPEED TRANSMISSION OTHERS, NO LUBRICATION.

CLUTCH RELEASE EQUALIZER

GEARSHIFT CONTROL LEVER (FITTING)

BRAKE MASTER CYLINDER

TRANSMISSION DIPSTICK (AUTOMATIC)

UNIVERSAL JOINT FITTING (IF SO EQUIPPED)

REAR AXLE PLUG DANA AXLE E-250—E-350

REAR AXLE PLUG F-100—F-150

1981—82 Ford F Series 2 wheel drive models

LUBRICATION DIAGRAMS

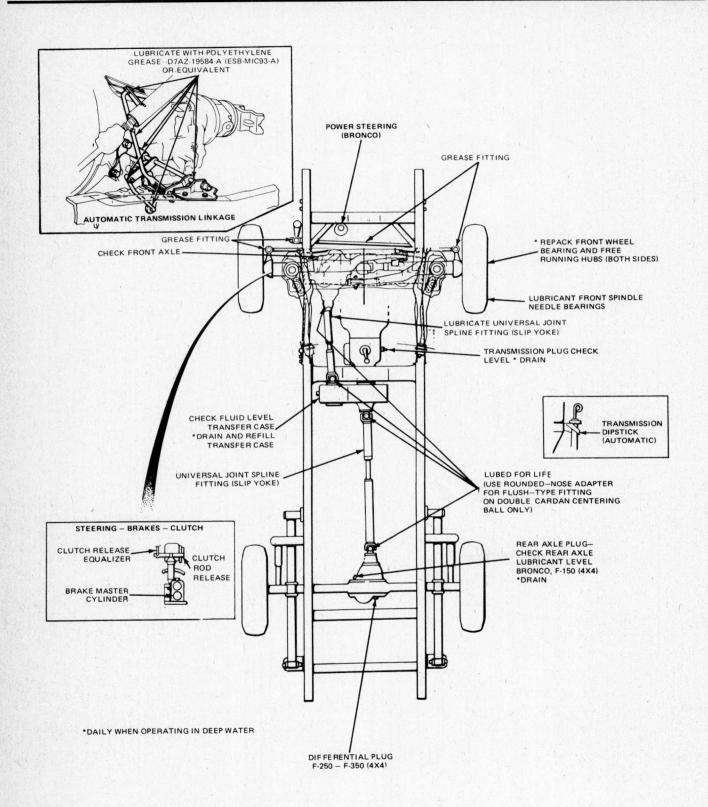

LUBRICATE WITH POLYETHYLENE GREASE · D7AZ-19584-A (ESB-MIC93-A) OR EQUIVALENT

AUTOMATIC TRANSMISSION LINKAGE

POWER STEERING (BRONCO)

GREASE FITTING

GREASE FITTING

CHECK FRONT AXLE

* REPACK FRONT WHEEL BEARING AND FREE RUNNING HUBS (BOTH SIDES)

LUBRICANT FRONT SPINDLE NEEDLE BEARINGS

LUBRICATE UNIVERSAL JOINT SPLINE FITTING (SLIP YOKE)

TRANSMISSION PLUG CHECK LEVEL * DRAIN

CHECK FLUID LEVEL TRANSFER CASE *DRAIN AND REFILL TRANSFER CASE

UNIVERSAL JOINT SPLINE FITTING (SLIP YOKE)

LUBED FOR LIFE (USE ROUNDED—NOSE ADAPTER FOR FLUSH—TYPE FITTING ON DOUBLE CARDAN CENTERING BALL ONLY)

TRANSMISSION DIPSTICK (AUTOMATIC)

REAR AXLE PLUG— CHECK REAR AXLE LUBRICANT LEVEL BRONCO, F-150 (4X4) *DRAIN

STEERING – BRAKES – CLUTCH

CLUTCH RELEASE EQUALIZER

CLUTCH ROD RELEASE

BRAKE MASTER CYLINDER

*DAILY WHEN OPERATING IN DEEP WATER

DIFFERENTIAL PLUG F-250 – F-350 (4X4)

1981—82 Ford F Series & Bronco 4 wheel drive models

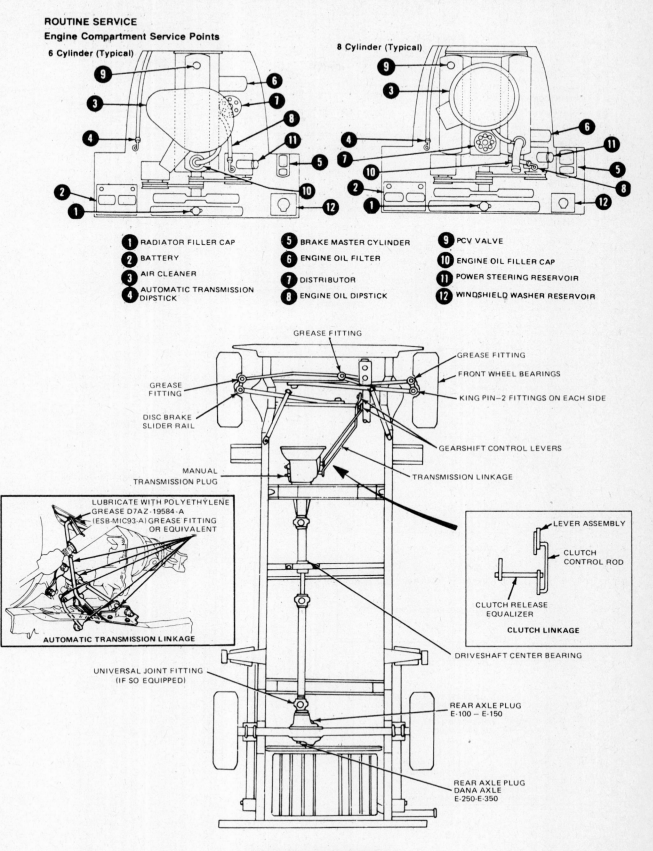

ROUTINE SERVICE
Engine Compartment Service Points

6 Cylinder (Typical)

8 Cylinder (Typical)

1. RADIATOR FILLER CAP
2. BATTERY
3. AIR CLEANER
4. AUTOMATIC TRANSMISSION DIPSTICK
5. BRAKE MASTER CYLINDER
6. ENGINE OIL FILTER
7. DISTRIBUTOR
8. ENGINE OIL DIPSTICK
9. PCV VALVE
10. ENGINE OIL FILLER CAP
11. POWER STEERING RESERVOIR
12. WINDSHIELD WASHER RESERVOIR

GREASE FITTING

GREASE FITTING

FRONT WHEEL BEARINGS

GREASE FITTING

KING PIN—2 FITTINGS ON EACH SIDE

DISC BRAKE SLIDER RAIL

GEARSHIFT CONTROL LEVERS

MANUAL TRANSMISSION PLUG

TRANSMISSION LINKAGE

LUBRICATE WITH POLYETHYLENE GREASE D7AZ-19584-A (ESB-MIC93-A) GREASE FITTING OR EQUIVALENT

LEVER ASSEMBLY

CLUTCH CONTROL ROD

CLUTCH RELEASE EQUALIZER

AUTOMATIC TRANSMISSION LINKAGE

CLUTCH LINKAGE

DRIVESHAFT CENTER BEARING

UNIVERSAL JOINT FITTING (IF SO EQUIPPED)

REAR AXLE PLUG
E-100 — E-150

REAR AXLE PLUG
DANA AXLE
E-250-E-350

1981—82 Ford E Series

LUBRICATION DIAGRAMS

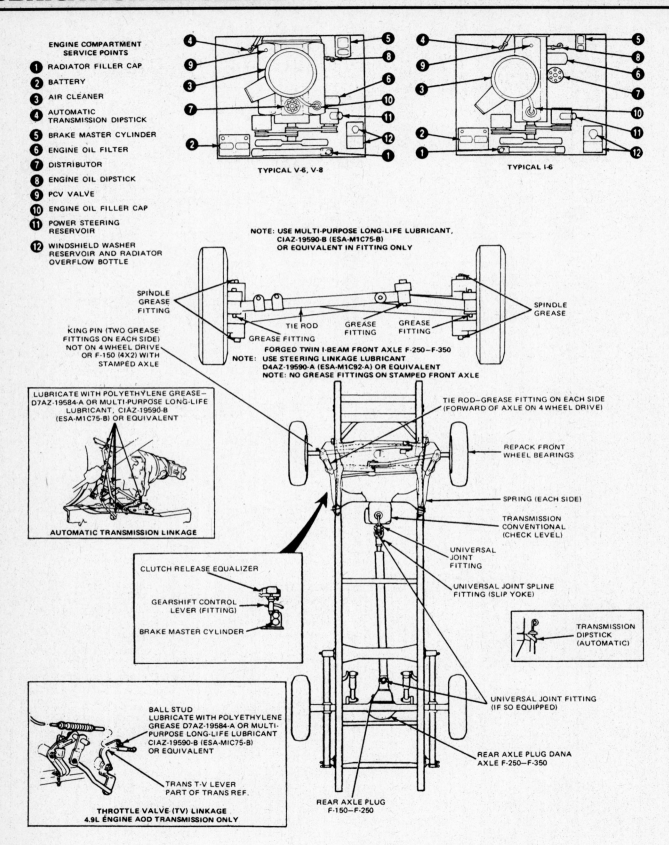

ENGINE COMPARTMENT SERVICE POINTS

1. RADIATOR FILLER CAP
2. BATTERY
3. AIR CLEANER
4. AUTOMATIC TRANSMISSION DIPSTICK
5. BRAKE MASTER CYLINDER
6. ENGINE OIL FILTER
7. DISTRIBUTOR
8. ENGINE OIL DIPSTICK
9. PCV VALVE
10. ENGINE OIL FILLER CAP
11. POWER STEERING RESERVOIR
12. WINDSHIELD WASHER RESERVOIR AND RADIATOR OVERFLOW BOTTLE

TYPICAL V-6, V-8

TYPICAL I-6

NOTE: USE MULTI-PURPOSE LONG-LIFE LUBRICANT, CIAZ-19590-B (ESA-M1C75-B) OR EQUIVALENT IN FITTING ONLY

SPINDLE GREASE FITTING

SPINDLE GREASE

KING PIN (TWO GREASE FITTINGS ON EACH SIDE) NOT ON 4 WHEEL DRIVE OR F-150 (4X2) WITH STAMPED AXLE

TIE ROD

GREASE FITTING

GREASE FITTING

GREASE FITTING

FORGED TWIN I-BEAM FRONT AXLE F-250—F-350
NOTE: USE STEERING LINKAGE LUBRICANT D4AZ-19590-A (ESA-M1C92-A) OR EQUIVALENT
NOTE: NO GREASE FITTINGS ON STAMPED FRONT AXLE

LUBRICATE WITH POLYETHYLENE GREASE—D7AZ-19584-A OR MULTI-PURPOSE LONG-LIFE LUBRICANT, CIAZ-19590-B (ESA-M1C75-B) OR EQUIVALENT

AUTOMATIC TRANSMISSION LINKAGE

TIE ROD—GREASE FITTING ON EACH SIDE (FORWARD OF AXLE ON 4 WHEEL DRIVE)

REPACK FRONT WHEEL BEARINGS

SPRING (EACH SIDE)

TRANSMISSION CONVENTIONAL (CHECK LEVEL)

UNIVERSAL JOINT FITTING

UNIVERSAL JOINT SPLINE FITTING (SLIP YOKE)

CLUTCH RELEASE EQUALIZER

GEARSHIFT CONTROL LEVER (FITTING)

BRAKE MASTER CYLINDER

TRANSMISSION DIPSTICK (AUTOMATIC)

UNIVERSAL JOINT FITTING (IF SO EQUIPPED)

BALL STUD LUBRICATE WITH POLYETHYLENE GREASE D7AZ-19584-A OR MULTI-PURPOSE LONG-LIFE LUBRICANT CIAZ-19590-B (ESA-MIC75-B) OR EQUIVALENT

TRANS T-V LEVER PART OF TRANS REF.

THROTTLE VALVE (TV) LINKAGE 4.9L ENGINE AOD TRANSMISSION ONLY

REAR AXLE PLUG DANA AXLE F-250—F-350

REAR AXLE PLUG F-150—F-250

1983—84 Ford F Series 2 wheel drive models

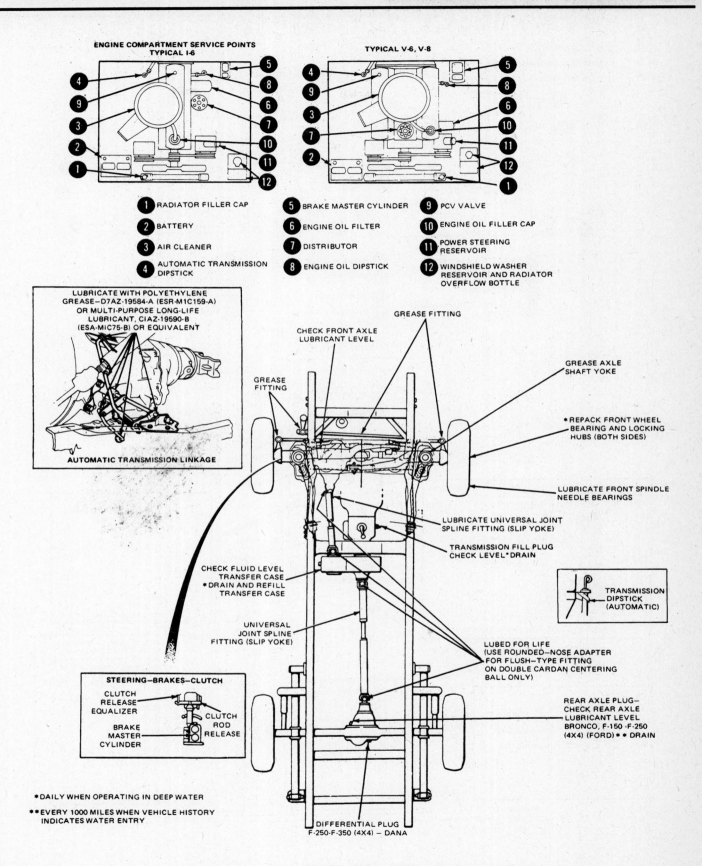

ENGINE COMPARTMENT SERVICE POINTS
TYPICAL I-6

TYPICAL V-6, V-8

1. RADIATOR FILLER CAP
2. BATTERY
3. AIR CLEANER
4. AUTOMATIC TRANSMISSION DIPSTICK
5. BRAKE MASTER CYLINDER
6. ENGINE OIL FILTER
7. DISTRIBUTOR
8. ENGINE OIL DIPSTICK
9. PCV VALVE
10. ENGINE OIL FILLER CAP
11. POWER STEERING RESERVOIR
12. WINDSHIELD WASHER RESERVOIR AND RADIATOR OVERFLOW BOTTLE

LUBRICATE WITH POLYETHYLENE GREASE—D7AZ-19584-A (ESR-M1C159-A) OR MULTI-PURPOSE LONG-LIFE LUBRICANT, C1AZ-19590-B (ESA-MIC75-B) OR EQUIVALENT

AUTOMATIC TRANSMISSION LINKAGE

CHECK FRONT AXLE LUBRICANT LEVEL

GREASE FITTING

GREASE FITTING

GREASE AXLE SHAFT YOKE

*REPACK FRONT WHEEL BEARING AND LOCKING HUBS (BOTH SIDES)

LUBRICATE FRONT SPINDLE NEEDLE BEARINGS

LUBRICATE UNIVERSAL JOINT SPLINE FITTING (SLIP YOKE)

TRANSMISSION FILL PLUG CHECK LEVEL*DRAIN

CHECK FLUID LEVEL TRANSFER CASE
*DRAIN AND REFILL TRANSFER CASE

UNIVERSAL JOINT SPLINE FITTING (SLIP YOKE)

TRANSMISSION DIPSTICK (AUTOMATIC)

LUBED FOR LIFE (USE ROUNDED-NOSE ADAPTER FOR FLUSH-TYPE FITTING ON DOUBLE CARDAN CENTERING BALL ONLY)

STEERING—BRAKES—CLUTCH
CLUTCH RELEASE EQUALIZER
CLUTCH ROD RELEASE
BRAKE MASTER CYLINDER

REAR AXLE PLUG—CHECK REAR AXLE LUBRICANT LEVEL BRONCO, F-150 -F-250 (4X4) (FORD) * * DRAIN

*DAILY WHEN OPERATING IN DEEP WATER

**EVERY 1000 MILES WHEN VEHICLE HISTORY INDICATES WATER ENTRY

DIFFERENTIAL PLUG F-250-F-350 (4X4) — DANA

1983—84 Ford F Series & Bronco 4 wheel drive models

LUBRICATION DIAGRAMS

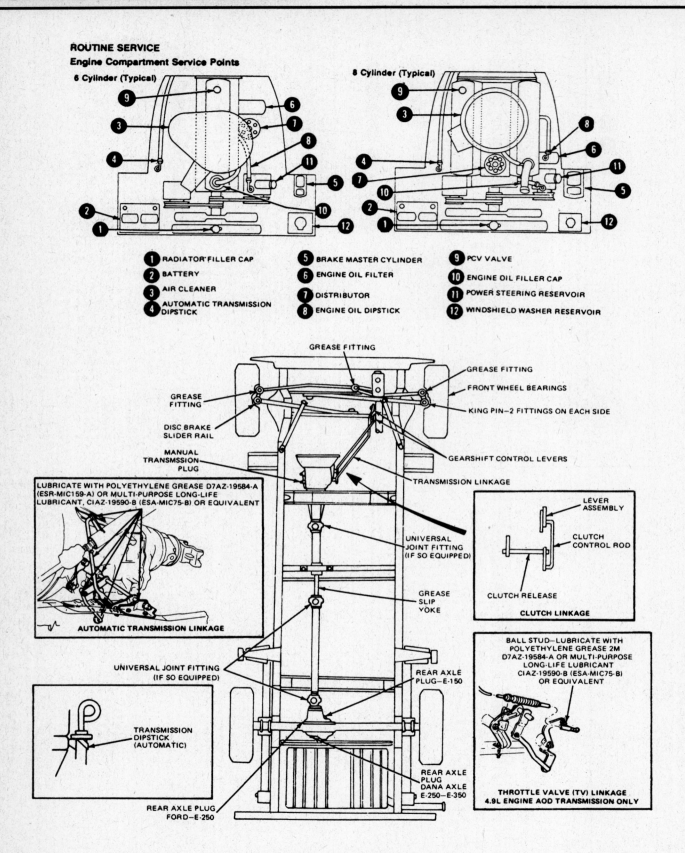

ROUTINE SERVICE
Engine Compartment Service Points

6 Cylinder (Typical)

8 Cylinder (Typical)

1	RADIATOR FILLER CAP	5	BRAKE MASTER CYLINDER	9	PCV VALVE
2	BATTERY	6	ENGINE OIL FILTER	10	ENGINE OIL FILLER CAP
3	AIR CLEANER	7	DISTRIBUTOR	11	POWER STEERING RESERVOIR
4	AUTOMATIC TRANSMISSION DIPSTICK	8	ENGINE OIL DIPSTICK	12	WINDSHIELD WASHER RESERVOIR

GREASE FITTING

GREASE FITTING

GREASE FITTING

FRONT WHEEL BEARINGS

DISC BRAKE SLIDER RAIL

KING PIN—2 FITTINGS ON EACH SIDE

MANUAL TRANSMSSION PLUG

GEARSHIFT CONTROL LEVERS

TRANSMISSION LINKAGE

LUBRICATE WITH POLYETHYLENE GREASE D7AZ-19584-A (ESR-MIC159-A) OR MULTI-PURPOSE LONG-LIFE LUBRICANT, CIAZ-19590-B (ESA-MIC75-B) OR EQUIVALENT

AUTOMATIC TRANSMISSION LINKAGE

UNIVERSAL JOINT FITTING (IF SO EQUIPPED)

GREASE SLIP YOKE

LEVER ASSEMBLY

CLUTCH CONTROL ROD

CLUTCH RELEASE

CLUTCH LINKAGE

UNIVERSAL JOINT FITTING (IF SO EQUIPPED)

TRANSMISSION DIPSTICK (AUTOMATIC)

REAR AXLE PLUG—E-150

REAR AXLE PLUG DANA AXLE E-250—E-350

REAR AXLE PLUG FORD—E-250

BALL STUD—LUBRICATE WITH POLYETHYLENE GREASE 2M D7AZ-19584-A OR MULTI-PURPOSE LONG-LIFE LUBRICANT CIAZ-19590-B (ESA-MIC75-B) OR EQUIVALENT

THROTTLE VALVE (TV) LINKAGE 4.9L ENGINE AOD TRANSMISSION ONLY

1983—84 Ford E Series

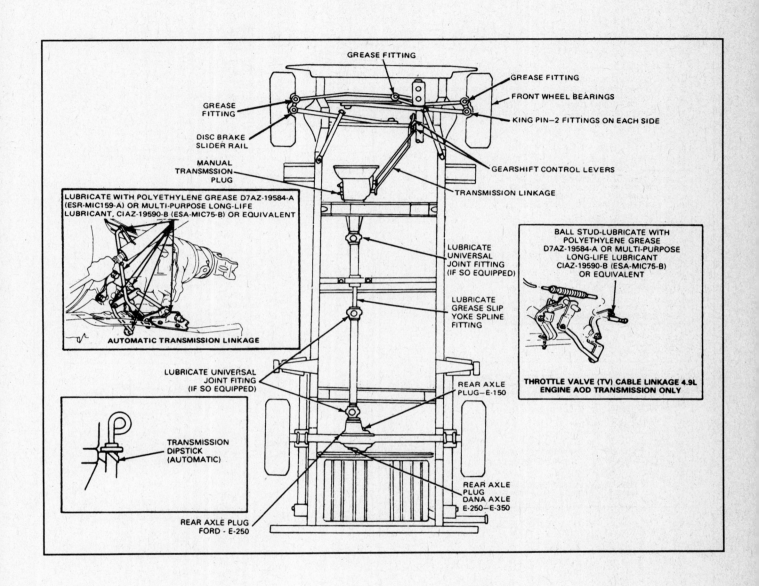

GREASE FITTING

GREASE FITTING

FRONT WHEEL BEARINGS

GREASE FITTING

KING PIN—2 FITTINGS ON EACH SIDE

DISC BRAKE SLIDER RAIL

GEARSHIFT CONTROL LEVERS

MANUAL TRANSMSSION PLUG

TRANSMISSION LINKAGE

LUBRICATE WITH POLYETHYLENE GREASE D7AZ-19584-A (ESR-MIC159-A) OR MULTI-PURPOSE LONG-LIFE LUBRICANT, CIAZ-19590-B (ESA-MIC75-B) OR EQUIVALENT

LUBRICATE UNIVERSAL JOINT FITTING (IF SO EQUIPPED)

LUBRICATE GREASE SLIP YOKE SPLINE FITTING

BALL STUD-LUBRICATE WITH POLYETHYLENE GREASE D7AZ-19584-A OR MULTI-PURPOSE LONG-LIFE LUBRICANT CIAZ-19590-B (ESA-MIC75-B) OR EQUIVALENT

AUTOMATIC TRANSMISSION LINKAGE

LUBRICATE UNIVERSAL JOINT FITING (IF SO EQUIPPED)

REAR AXLE PLUG—E-150

THROTTLE VALVE (TV) CABLE LINKAGE 4.9L ENGINE AOD TRANSMISSION ONLY

TRANSMISSION DIPSTICK (AUTOMATIC)

REAR AXLE PLUG DANA AXLE E-250—E-350

REAR AXLE PLUG FORD - E-250

1985 Ford E Series

LUBRICATION DIAGRAMS

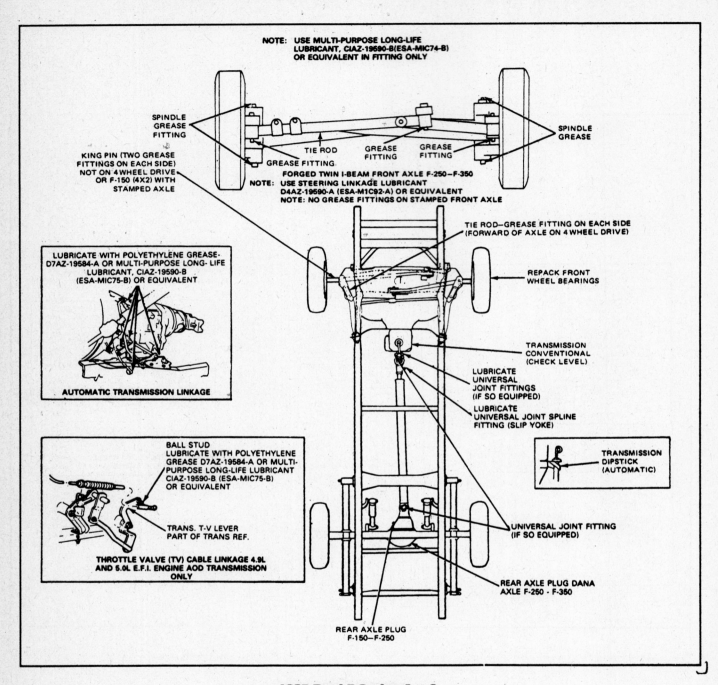

NOTE: USE MULTI-PURPOSE LONG-LIFE LUBRICANT, CIAZ-19690-B(ESA-MIC74-B) OR EQUIVALENT IN FITTING ONLY

SPINDLE GREASE FITTING

SPINDLE GREASE

KING PIN (TWO GREASE FITTINGS ON EACH SIDE) NOT ON 4 WHEEL DRIVE OR F-150 (4X2) WITH STAMPED AXLE

TIE ROD

GREASE FITTING

GREASE FITTING

GREASE FITTING

FORGED TWIN I-BEAM FRONT AXLE F-250–F-350
NOTE: USE STEERING LINKAGE LUBRICANT D4AZ-19590-A (ESA-M1C92-A) OR EQUIVALENT
NOTE: NO GREASE FITTINGS ON STAMPED FRONT AXLE

TIE ROD—GREASE FITTING ON EACH SIDE (FORWARD OF AXLE ON 4 WHEEL DRIVE)

REPACK FRONT WHEEL BEARINGS

LUBRICATE WITH POLYETHYLENE GREASE-D7AZ-19584-A OR MULTI-PURPOSE LONG-LIFE LUBRICANT, CIAZ-19590-B (ESA-MIC75-B) OR EQUIVALENT

AUTOMATIC TRANSMISSION LINKAGE

TRANSMISSION CONVENTIONAL (CHECK LEVEL)

LUBRICATE UNIVERSAL JOINT FITTINGS (IF SO EQUIPPED)

LUBRICATE UNIVERSAL JOINT SPLINE FITTING (SLIP YOKE)

BALL STUD
LUBRICATE WITH POLYETHYLENE GREASE D7AZ-19584-A OR MULTI-PURPOSE LONG-LIFE LUBRICANT CIAZ-19590-B (ESA-MIC75-B) OR EQUIVALENT

TRANS. T-V LEVER PART OF TRANS REF.

THROTTLE VALVE (TV) CABLE LINKAGE 4.9L AND 5.0L E.F.I. ENGINE AOD TRANSMISSION ONLY

TRANSMISSION DIPSTICK (AUTOMATIC)

UNIVERSAL JOINT FITTING (IF SO EQUIPPED)

REAR AXLE PLUG DANA AXLE F-250 - F-350

REAR AXLE PLUG F-150—F-250

1985 Ford F Series 4 × 2

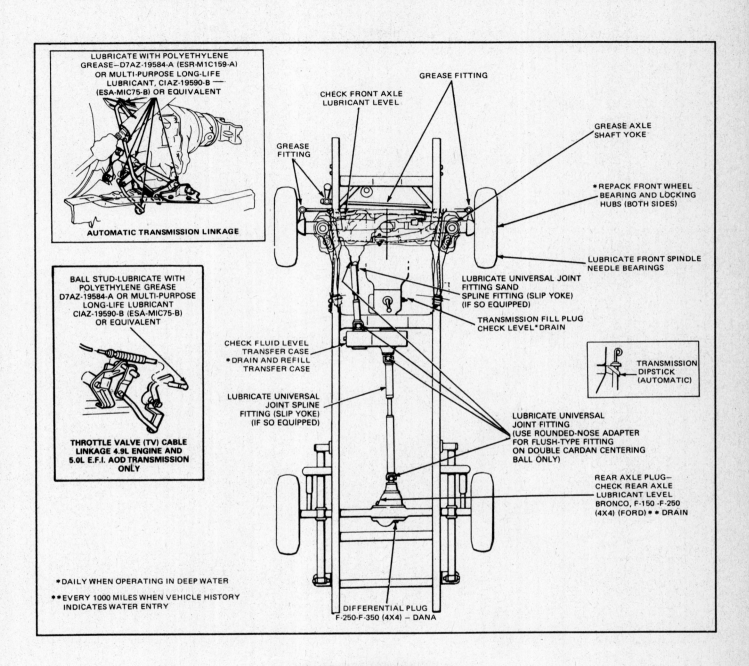

LUBRICATE WITH POLYETHYLENE GREASE—D7AZ-19584-A (ESR-M1C159-A) OR MULTI-PURPOSE LONG-LIFE LUBRICANT, CIAZ-19590-B (ESA-MIC75-B) OR EQUIVALENT

AUTOMATIC TRANSMISSION LINKAGE

BALL STUD-LUBRICATE WITH POLYETHYLENE GREASE D7AZ-19584-A OR MULTI-PURPOSE LONG-LIFE LUBRICANT CIAZ-19590-B (ESA-MIC75-B) OR EQUIVALENT

THROTTLE VALVE (TV) CABLE LINKAGE 4.9L ENGINE AND 5.0L E.F.I. AOD TRANSMISSION ONLY

GREASE FITTING

CHECK FRONT AXLE LUBRICANT LEVEL

GREASE FITTING

GREASE AXLE SHAFT YOKE

*REPACK FRONT WHEEL BEARING AND LOCKING HUBS (BOTH SIDES)

LUBRICATE FRONT SPINDLE NEEDLE BEARINGS

LUBRICATE UNIVERSAL JOINT FITTING SAND SPLINE FITTING (SLIP YOKE) (IF SO EQUIPPED)

TRANSMISSION FILL PLUG CHECK LEVEL*DRAIN

CHECK FLUID LEVEL TRANSFER CASE
*DRAIN AND REFILL TRANSFER CASE

LUBRICATE UNIVERSAL JOINT SPLINE FITTING (SLIP YOKE) (IF SO EQUIPPED)

TRANSMISSION DIPSTICK (AUTOMATIC)

LUBRICATE UNIVERSAL JOINT FITTING (USE ROUNDED-NOSE ADAPTER FOR FLUSH-TYPE FITTING ON DOUBLE CARDAN CENTERING BALL ONLY)

REAR AXLE PLUG— CHECK REAR AXLE LUBRICANT LEVEL BRONCO, F-150 -F-250 (4X4) (FORD) * * DRAIN

DIFFERENTIAL PLUG F-250-F-350 (4X4) — DANA

*DAILY WHEN OPERATING IN DEEP WATER

**EVERY 1000 MILES WHEN VEHICLE HISTORY INDICATES WATER ENTRY

1985 Ford F Series 4 × 4

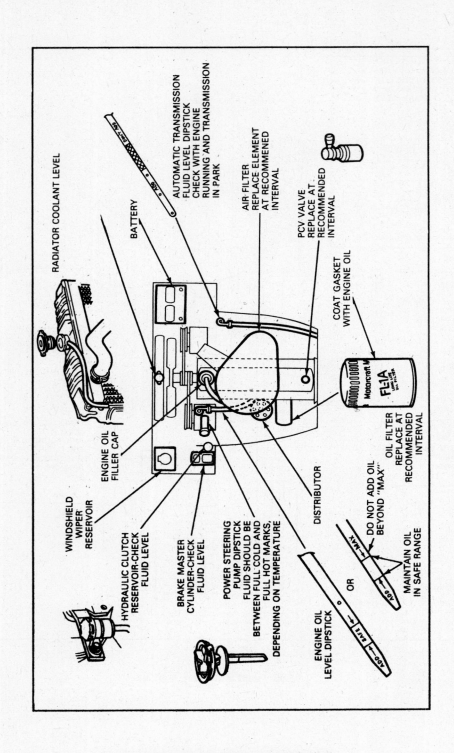

1985 Ford E Series w/6-300 engine

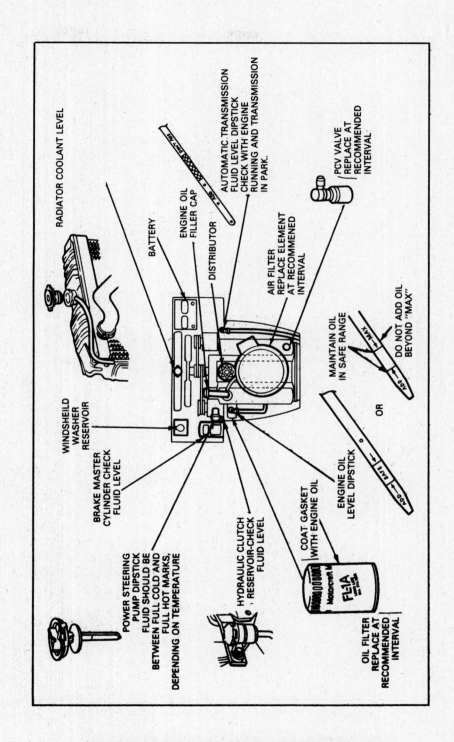

1985 Ford E Series w/V8-302 or V8-351 engine

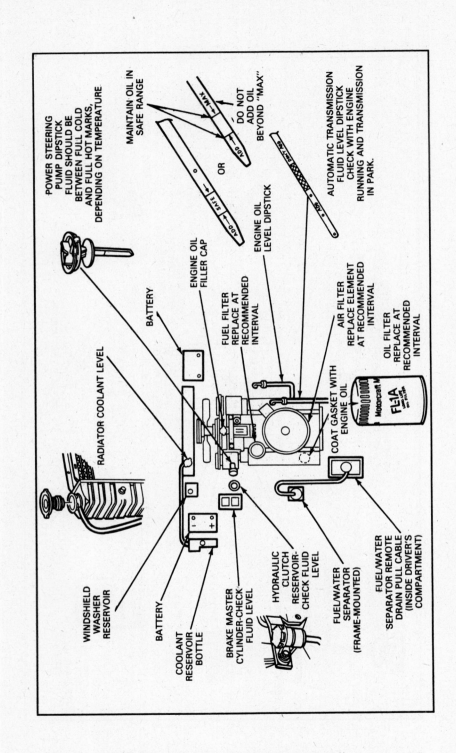

1985 Ford E Series w/V8-420 diesel engine

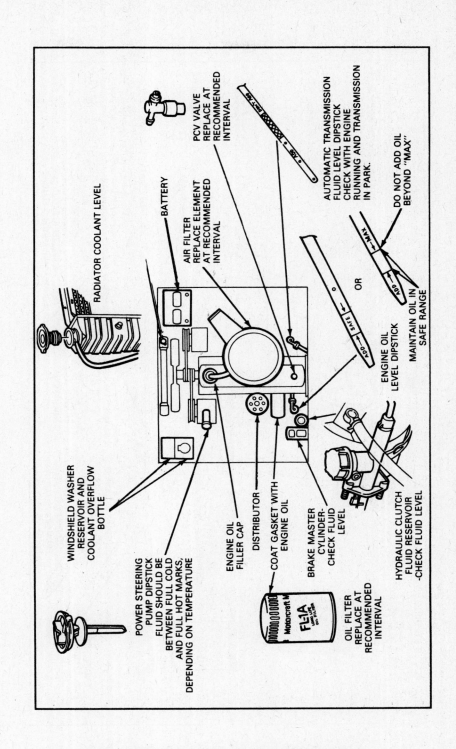

1985 Ford F Series & Bronco w/6-300 engine

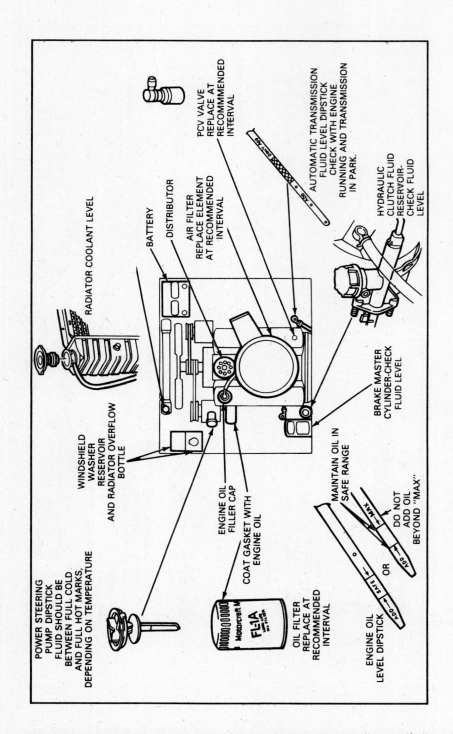

1985 Ford F Series & Bronco w/V8-302 or V8-351 gasoline engine

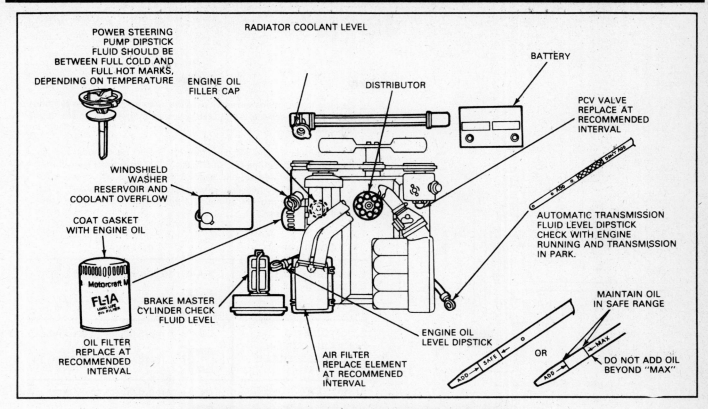

1985 Ford F Series w/V8-302 fuel injected engine

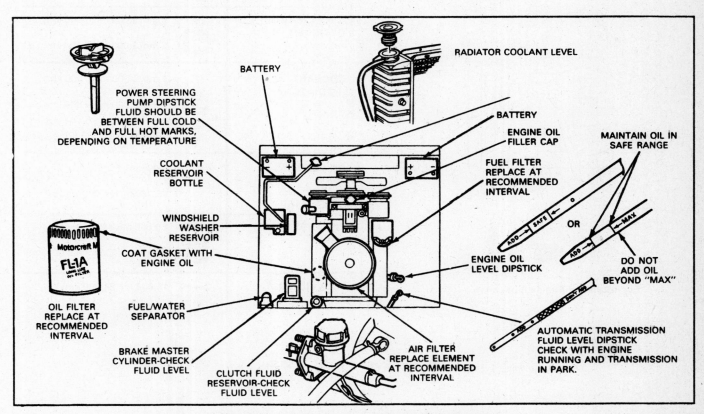

1985 Ford F Series w/V8-420 diesel engine

Jeep

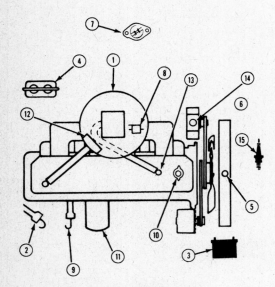

Six-Cylinder Engine Illustration

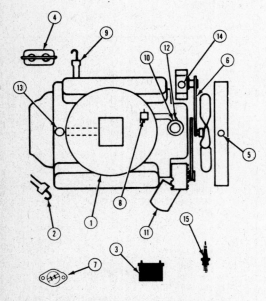

Eight-Cylinder Engine Illustration

Perform the maintenance services at the intervals shown. The symbol tells you what service is required followed by the time and/or distance interval.

For example: Engine Oil (Number 10) should be drained and replaced every 5 months or 5,000 miles (8 000 km), whichever comes first, under normal use, and every 3 months or 3,000 miles (4 800 km), whichever comes first, under heavy-duty operation. (The lettered footnotes provide additional information about certain components or services.)

COMPONENT	INTERVAL	
1. AIR CLEANER (FILTER)	🔧	30,000 mi (48 000 km)
	🚙	15 mo/15,000 mi (24 000 km)
2. AUTOMATIC TRANSMISSION DIPSTICK/FILLER	✔	5 mo/5,000 mi (8 000 km)
	🚙	3 mo/3,000 mi (4 800 km)
3. BATTERY	✔	5 mo/5,000 mi (8 000 km)
	🚙	3 mo/3,000 mi (4 800 km)
4. BRAKE MASTER CYLINDER	✔	5 mo/5,000 mi (8 000 km)
	🚙	3 mo/3,000 mi (4 800 km)
5. COOLANT (RADIATOR)	✔	5 mo/5,000 mi (8 000 km)
	🚙	3 mo/3,000 mi (4 800 km)
	▼	25 mo/25,000 mi (40 000 km) **a.**
6. DRIVE BELTS	✔	5,000 mi (8 000 km)
		15,000 mi (24 000 km) **b.**
7. EXHAUST HEAT VALVE		30,000 mi (48 000 km)
	🚙	30 mo/30,000 mi (48 000 km)
8. FUEL FILTER	🔧	15,000 mi (24 000 km)

1979–81 Jeep (Part 1 of 2)

9. OIL DIPSTICK	✔	At Each Fuel Fill
10. OIL (FILLER CAP)	⊤	5 mo/5,000 mi (8 000 km) **c.**
	🚐	3 mo/3,000 mi (4 800 km)
11. OIL FILTER	🔧	5 mo/5,000 mi (8 000 km)
	🚐	3 mo/3,000 mi (4 800 km)
12. PCV FILTER	✔	30,000 mi (48 000 km) **d.**
	🚐	30 mo/30,000 mi (48 000 km)
13. PCV VALVE	🔧	30,000 mi (48 000 km)
	🚐	30 mo/30,000 mi (48 000 km)
14. POWER STEERING PUMP	✔	5 mo/5,000 mi (8 000 km)
	🚐	3 mo/3,000 mi (4 800 km)
15. TUNE-UP	✔	5,000 mi (8 000 km) Check and adjust curb and high idle speeds, as required. **e.**
	✔	15,000 mi (24 000 km) Check the following items and correct as required (CJ models with eight-cylinder only): choke system, idle mixture, ignition timing, and vacuum fittings, hoses and connections. **f.**
	⟵	30,000 mi (48 000 km) Complete engine tune-up. **g.**
	🚐	30mo/30,000 mi (48 000 km)

Legend of Symbols

✔	CHECK OR INSPECTION
⊤	DRAIN AND REPLACE FLUID
⟵	ENGINE TUNE-UP
🚐	HEAVY-DUTY OPERATION
	LUBRICATION
🔧	SERVICE COMPONENT REPLACEMENT

a. Change engine coolant initially at 25 months or 25,000 miles (40 000 km), whichever comes first then at the start of each winter season.

b. Check drive belts initially at 5,000 miles (8 000 km), then at 15,000 miles (24 000 km) and every 15,000 miles (24 000 km) thereafter.

c. When most driving is on paved roads with trips of less than six miles (10 km), change engine oil every 2,500 miles (4 000 km) and oil filter every 5,000 miles (8 000 km).

d. On six-cylinder models, clean PCV filter. On eight-cylinder models, clean oil filler cap filter.

e. Perform service initially at 5,000 miles (8 000 km) then at 30,000 miles (48 000 km) and every 30,000 miles (48 000 km) thereafter.

f. Not required on California vehicles.

g. Tune-up consists of examining the components listed under each system for proper assembly, condition and operation. Correct, adjust or service to specifications if necessary:

Engine Mechanical Systems
Inspect:
Air Guard system hoses.
Condition and tension of fan/alternator, power steering, air pump and air conditioning drive belts.
Vacuum lines and fittings, Exhaust Gas Recirculation (EGR) lines, hoses and connections.

Ignition System
Coil and spark plug wires.
Distributor—cap and rotor, vacuum and centrifugal advance mechanisms.
Transmission controlled spark system (TCS).
Replace spark plugs.
Fuel System
Inspect:
Fuel tank, cap, lines and connections.
Air cleaner thermostatic control system (TAC).
Choke linkage for free movement.
PCV system hoses.
Replace charcoal canister air inlet filter.

Final Adjustments
Ignition timing.
Idle mixture.
Curb and high idle speeds.

1979–81 Jeep (Part 2 of 2)

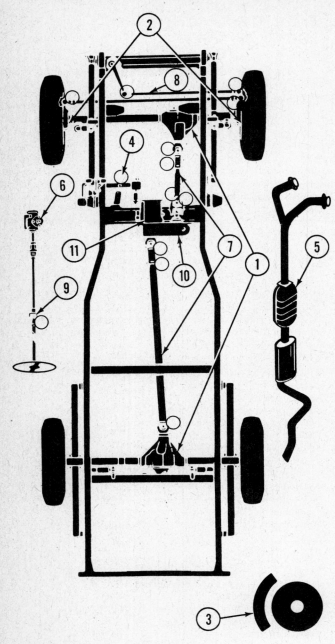

Lubrication points

Chassis Illustration

Legend of Symbols

✓	CHECK OR INSPECTION
⊤	DRAIN AND REPLACE FLUID
↔	ENGINE TUNE-UP
🚐	HEAVY-DUTY OPERATION
⊏	LUBRICATION
🔧	SERVICE COMPONENT REPLACEMENT

Perform the maintenance services at the intervals shown. The symbol tells you what service is required, followed by the time and/or distance interval.

For example: Front Wheel Bearings (Number 2) should be lubricated every 25,000 miles (40 000 km) under normal use, and every 25 months or 25,000 miles (40 000 km) under heavy-duty operation. (The lettered footnotes provide additional information about certain components and services.

COMPONENT		INTERVAL
1. AXLE DIFFERENTIALS (FRONT AND REAR)	✓	5,000 mi (8 000 km)
	🚐	3 mo/3,000 mi (4 800 km)
	⊤	30,000 mi (48 000 km)
	🚐	30 mo/30,000 mi (48 000 km)
2. BEARINGS, FRONT WHEEL	⊏	25,000 mi (40 000 km) **a.**
	🚐	25 mo/25,000 mi (40 000 km)
3. BRAKE AND CHASSIS INSPECTION	✓	15,000 mi (24 000 km) **b.**
	🚐	5 mo/5,000 mi (8 000 km)
BODY LUBRICATION	⊏	15,000 mi (24 000 km) **b.**
	🚐	5 mo/5,000 mi (8 000 km)
4. CLUTCH LEVER AND LINKAGE CJ	⊏	5,000 mi (8 000 km)
	🚐	3 mo/3,000 mi (4 800 km)
CHEROKEE, WAGONEER, TRUCK	⊏	15,000 mi (24 000 km)
	🚐	5 mo/5,000 mi (8 000 km)
5. EXHAUST SYSTEM INSPECTION	✓	5,000 mi (8 000 km) **c.**
	🚐	5 mo/5,000 mi (8 000 km)
6. MANUAL STEERING GEAR	✓	5,000 mi (8 000 km)
	🚐	3 mo/3,000 mi (4 800 km)
7. PROPELLER SHAFTS (FRONT AND REAR) CJ	⊏	5,000 mi (8 000 km) **d.**
	🚐	3 mo/3,000 mi (4 800 km)
CHEROKEE, WAGONEER, TRUCK	⊏	10,000 mi (16 000 km) **d.**
	🚐	5 mo/5,000 mi (8 000 km)
8. STEERING LINKAGE CJ	✓ ⊏	5,000 mi (8 000 km) **e.**
	🚐	3 mo/3,000 mi (4 800 km)
CHEROKEE, WAGONEER, TRUCK	✓ ⊏	15,000 mi (24 000 km) **e.**
	🚐	5 mo/5,000 mi (8 000 km)
9. STEERING SHAFT U-JOINT	⊏	10,000 mi (16 000 km)
	🚐	5 mo/5,000 mi (8 000 km)

1979–81 Jeep (Part 1 of 2)

10. TRANSFER CASE ALL	(symbol)	5,000 mi (8 000 km)	
		3 mo/3,000 mi (4 800 km)	
MODEL 20	(symbol)	30,000 mi (48 000 km)	
		30 mo/30,000 mi (48 000 km)	
QUADRA-TRAC	(symbol)	15,000 mi (24 000 km)	
		10 mo/10,000 mi (16 000 km)	
11. TRANSMISSION MANUAL	(symbol)	5,000 mi (8 000 km)	
		3 mo/3,000 mi (4 800 km)	
	(symbol)	30,000 mi (48 000 km)	
		30 mo/30,000 mi (48 000 km)	
AUTOMATIC	(symbol)	30,000 mi (48 000 km) f.	
		10 mo/10,000 mi (16 000 km)	

Footnotes

a. Rear wheel bearings do not require periodic or scheduled lubrication.

b. Check the following items as indicated. Correct to specifications as necessary:

Brakes

    Front and rear brake linings for wear.
    Rear brake self-adjusting mechanism for proper
        operation.
    Master cylinder, calipers, wheel cylinders and differentials
        warning valves for leaks.
    Brake lines, fittings and hoses for condition and leaks.
    Parking brake for proper operation.
    Overall brake condition and action.

Steering/Suspension

    Manual or power steering gear and linkage for leaks,
        looseness or wear.
    Springs, shock absorbers, steering damper and bushings
        for leaks, looseness or wear.
    Tire condition.
    Overall steering/suspension condition and action.

Also:

Adjust parking brake, if necessary.
Adjust tire pressures to specifications.
Adjust manual transmission clutch free play, if necessary.
Lubricate Model 20 transfer case linkage.

Body Lubrication

Lubricate the following items with the recommended lubricants:

    Ashtray slides.
    Courtesy light buttons.
    Door, hood, liftgate, tailgate latches and hinges.
    Front seat tracks.
    Glove box door latch and hinge.
    Locks.
    Windshield hinges and holddown knobs (CJ only).

c. Check exhaust system for leaks, damage, misalignment or grounding against body sheet metal or frame. Check catalytic converter for bulging or heat damage.

d. Lubricate sleeve yokes (splines) and single and double cardan U-joints.

e. Inspect and replace torn or ruptured grease seals, replace damaged steering components, and lubricate ball joints.

f. Also replace automatic transmission filter.

MAINTENANCE BY MILEAGE INTERVALS

Recommended Interval (miles)	(km)	Engine Component	Engine Service	Chassis Component	Chassis Service	Model
5,000	(8 000)	2.	(symbol)	1.	(symbol)	All
		3.	(symbol)	4.	(symbol)	CJ
		4.	(symbol)	5.	(symbol)	All
		5.	(symbol)	6.	(symbol)	All
		6.	(symbol)	7.	(symbol)	CJ
		10.	(symbol)	8.	(symbol)	CJ
		11.	(symbol)	10.	(symbol)	All
		14.	(symbol)	11.	(symbol)	All
		15.	(symbol)			
10,000	(16 000)			7.	(symbol)	C,W,T
				9.	(symbol)	All
15,000	(24 000)	8.	(symbol)	3.	(symbol)	All
		15.	(symbol) a.	4.	(symbol)	C,W,T
				7.	(symbol)	C,W,T
				8.	(symbol)	C,W,T
				10.	(symbol)	All b.
25,000	(40 000)	5.	(symbol) c.	2.	(symbol)	All
30,000	(48 000)	1.	(symbol)	1.	(symbol)	All
		7.	(symbol)	10.	(symbol)	All d
		12.	(symbol)	11.	(symbol)	All
		13.	(symbol)			
		15.	(symbol)			

Footnotes

a. CJ models with 8-cylinder only (except California vehicles)

b. Quadra-Trac Only

c. Change coolant initially at 25 months or 25,000 miles (40 000 km), whichever comes first, then at the start of each winter season.

d. Model 20 Transfer case only

1979—81 Jeep (Part 2 of 2)

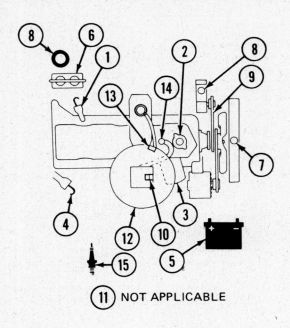

Four-Cylinder Engine

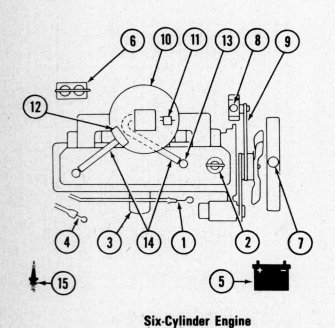

Six-Cylinder Engine

Eight-Cylinder Engine

1982—83 Jeep (Part 1 of 2)

	Each Fuel Fill	5	12.5	20	27.5	30	35	42.5	50
Miles (Thousands)		5	12.5	20	27.5	30	35	42.5	50
Kilometers (Thousands)		8	20	32	44	48	56	68	80
Months		5	12.5	20	27.5	30	35	42.5	50
1) Check Engine Oil Level	●								
2) Change Engine Oil		●	●	●	●		●	●	●
3) Change Engine Oil Filter (4-Cylinder California)		●	◆	●	◆		●	◆	●
3) Change Engine Oil Filter (Except 4-Cylinder California)		●	◆	●	◆		●	●	●
4) Check Automatic Transmission Fluid		●	●	●	●		●	●	●
5) Check Battery		●	●	●	●		●	●	●
6) Check Brake Master Cylinder Fluid Level		●	●	●	●		●	●	●
7) Check Cooling System Fluid Level		●	●	●	●		●	●	●
7) Drain and Change Coolant ①					●				
8) Check Hydraulic Clutch Reservoir Fluid Level		●	●	●	●		●	●	●
8) Check Power Steering Pump Fluid Level		●	●	●	●		●	●	●
9) Check Drive Belt Tension		◆		◆③		●	◆③	◆	◆③
9) Check Drive Belt Tension (8-Cyl.)		●				●		●	
10) Replace Fuel Filter (4- and 6-Cyl.)			◆		◆			◆	
10) Replace Fuel Filter (8-Cyl.)				●		●		●	
11) Lubricate Exhaust Heat Valve (8-Cylinder only)						●			
12) Replace Air Cleaner Filter ②						●			
13) Replace PCV Filter (4-Cylinder California)						●			
13) Clean PCV Filter (8-, 6- and 4-Cylinder except 4-Cyl. California) ④						●			
14) Replace PCV Valve						◆			
14) Replace PCV Valve (8-Cyl.)						●			
14) Inspect PCV Hoses and Connections						◆			
14) Inspect PCV Hoses and Connections (8-Cylinder)						●			
15) Tune Up									
Check and Adjust Curb and Fast Idle Speed		●				◆			
Check and Adjust Curb and Fast Idle Speed (8-Cylinder)						●			
Check Distributor Vacuum and Centrifugal Advance Mechanism						◆			
Check Distributor Vacuum and Centrifugal Advance Mechanism (8 Cylinder)						●			
Check Distributor Cap and Rotor						◆			
Check Distributor Cap and Rotor (8-Cyl.)						●			
Check and Adjust Carburetor Mounting Bolts (4-Cylinder)		●							
Clean Choke System						●			
Check TAC Control System						◆			
Check TAC Control System (8-Cyl.)						●			
Check Fuel System, Filler Cap, Tank, Lines, Hoses and Connections (4- and 6 Cyl.)			●		●			●	
Check Air System Hoses (8-Cylinder)						●			
Check Fuel System, Filler Cap, Tank, Lines and Connections (8-Cylinder)						●			
Check Vacuum Fittings, Hoses and Connections						◆			
Check Vacuum Fittings, Hoses and Connections (8-Cylinder)						●			
Check Coil and Spark Plug Wires			◆		◆			◆	
Check Coil and Spark Plug Wires (8-Cyl.)			◆			●		◆	
Check Exhaust System		●	●	●	●		●	●	●
Check Ignition Timing						◆			
Check Ignition Timing (8-Cyl.)						●			
Replace Spark Plugs						●			
Replace Oxygen Sensor (4-Cylinder California)						●			
Reset Oxygen Sensor Signal (4-Cylinder California)						●			
Replace Charcoal Canister Air Inlet Filter (8-Cylinder)						●			

● Required   ◆ Recommended, But Not Required

① Change coolant initially at 20,000 mi (32 000 km) or 20 months, whichever comes first, then at the start of each winter season. Maintain a 50/50 mixture of coolant and clean water (−34°F/−36°C Freezing Point) for cooling system corrosion protection during the summer season.

② Replace air cleaner element once in between each normally scheduled change under heavy duty conditions - particularly driving predominantly on dusty roads.

③ 4-Cylinder only.

④ On 6-Cylinder models, clean PCV filter in air cleaner. On 8-Cylinder models, clean PCV filter in oil filler cap.

1982—83 Jeep (Part 2 of 2)

LUBRICATION DIAGRAMS

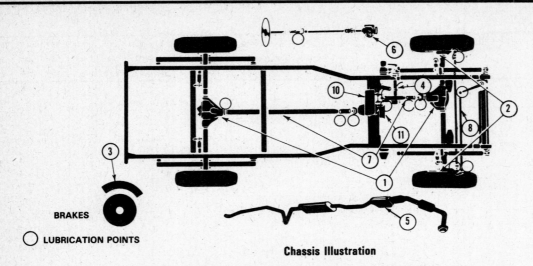

BRAKES

◯ **LUBRICATION POINTS**

Chassis Illustration

Jeep Combined (Heavy-Duty & Regular) Maintenance Schedule

		2,500	5,000	8,750	12,500	16,250	20,000	23,750	27,500	30,000	32,500	35,000	38,750	42,500	46,250	50,000
Miles — EACH																
Kilometers — FUEL		4 000	8 000	14 000	20 000	26 000	32 000	38 000	44 000	48 000	52 000	56 000	62 000	68 000	74 000	80 000
Months — FILL		2.5	5	9	12½	16	20	24	27½	30	32	35	39	42½	46	50
1) Check Axle Differentials (Front & Rear)		HD	HD•	HD	HD•	HD	HD•	HD	HD•		HD	HD•	HD	HD•	HD	HD•
1) Replace Axle Differential Fluid (Front & Rear)										•						
2) Lubricate Front Wheel Bearings [a]					HD				HD•					HD		
2) Lubricate Manual Locking Hubs					HD				HD•					HD		
3) Check Brakes & Chassis [b]			HD		HD•		HD		HD•			HD		HD•		HD
3) Lubricate Body Components [b]			HD		HD•		HD		HD•			HD		HD•		HD
4) Lubricate Clutch Lever & Linkage (CJ)		HD	HD•	HD	HD•	HD	HD•	HD	HD•	HD	HD	HD•	HD	HD•	HD	HD•
4) Lubricate Clutch Lever & Linkage (Cherokee, Wagoneer, Truck)			HD		HD•		HD		HD•			HD		HD•		HD
5) Inspect Exhaust System [c]		HD	HD•		HD•		HD•		HD•		HD	HD•		HD•		HD•
6) Check Manual Steering Gear		HD	HD•	HD	HD•	HD	HD•	HD	HD•	HD	HD	HD•	HD	HD•	HD	HD•
7) Lubricate Propeller Shafts (Front and Rear) (CJ) [d]		HD	HD•	HD	HD•	HD	HD•	HD	HD•	HD	HD	HD•	HD	HD•	HD	HD•
7) Lubricate Propeller Shafts (Front & Rear) (Cherokee, Wagoneer, Truck) [d]			HD		HD•				HD•			HD•		HD•		HD•
8) Check and Lubricate Steering Linkage (CJ) [e]		HD	HD•	HD	HD•	HD	HD•	HD	HD•	HD	HD	HD•	HD	HD•	HD	HD•
8) Check and Lubricate Steering Linkage (Cherokee, Wagoneer, Truck) [e]			HD		HD•				HD•			HD•		HD•		HD•
9) Check Windshield Washer Level Fluid	•															
10) Check Transfer Case Fluid		HD	HD•	HD	HD•	HD	HD•	HD	HD•		HD	HD•	HD	HD•	HD	HD•
10) Replace Transfer Case Fluid										•						
11) Check Manual Transmission Fluid		HD	HD•	HD	HD•	HD	HD				HD	HD•	HD	HD•	HD	HD•
11) Replace Manual Transmission Fluid										•						
11) Replace Automatic Transmission Fluid & Filter					HD		HD			•		HD		HD		

[a] Replace spindle oil and bearing seals on front wheel bearings (rear wheel bearings do not require periodic or scheduled lubrication).

[b] Check the following items as indicated. Correct to specifications as necessary: BRAKES - Front and rear brake linings for wear; rear brake self-adjusting mechanism for proper operation; master cylinder, calipers, wheel cylinders and differential warning valves for leaks; brake lines, fittings and hoses for condition and leaks; parking brake for proper operation; overall brake condition and action. STEERING/SUSPENSION - Manual or power steering gear and linkage for leaks, looseness or wear; springs, shock absorbers, steering damper and bushings for leaks, looseness or wear; tire condition; overall steering/suspension condition and action. BODY LUBRICATION - Lubricate the following items with the recommended lubricants: ashtry slides; courtesy light buttons; door, hood, liftgate, tailgate latches and hinges; front seat tracks; glove box door latch and hinge; locks; windshield hinges and holddown knobs (CJ/Scrambler only.) ALSO - Adjust parking brake and manual transmission clutch free play, if necessary; adjust tire pressures to specifications; lubricate Model 300 transfer case linkage.

[c] Check exhaust system for leaks, damage, misalignment or grounding against body sheet metal or frame. Check catalytic converter for bulging or heat damage.

[d] Lubricate sleeve yokes (splines) and single and double cardan U-joints.

[e] Inspect and replace torn or ruptured grease seals, replace damaged steering components, and lubricate ball joints.

1982–83 Jeep

AMERICAN MOTORS/JEEP

SECTION INDEX

1984-85 JEEP CHEROKEE & WAGONEER

INDEX OF SERVICE OPERATIONS

NOTE: Refer to page 1 of this manual for vehicle manufacturer's special service tool suppliers.

General Engine Specifications

Year	Engine CID①/Liters	Carburetor	Bore and Stroke	Compression Ratio	Net H.P. @ R.P.M.	Maximum Torque Lbs. Ft. @ R.P.M.	Normal Oil Pressure Pounds
1984-85	4-150, 2.5L	YFA, 1 Bbl.②	3.88 × 3.19	9.2	—	132 @ 2800	37-75
	V6-173, 2.8L	2 Bbl.③④	3.50 × 2.99	8.5	110 @ 4800	145 @ 2100	50-65
1985	4-126, 2.1L⑤	Fuel Inj.	3.38 × 3.50	21.5	85 @ 3750	132 @ 2750	43.5

①—Cubic Inch Displacement.
②—Carter feedback carburetor.
③—Rochester.
④—Exc. Calif., 2SE; Calif. models, E2SE
fuel feedback carburetor.
⑤—Diesel engine.

Valve Specifications

Year	Engine	Valve Lash Int.	Valve Lash Exh.	Valve Angles Seat	Valve Angles Face	Valve Spring Installed Height	Valve Spring Pressure Lbs. @ In.	Stem Clearance Intake	Stem Clearance Exhaust	Stem Diameter, Standard Intake	Stem Diameter, Standard Exhaust
1984-85	4-150, 2.5L	Hydraulic①	Hydraulic①	45	44	1.62	212 @ 1.20	.0010-.0030	.0010-.0030	.3110-.3120	.3110-.3120
	V6-173, 2.8L	Hydraulic②	Hydraulic②	46	45	1.57	195 @ 1.18	.0010-.0030	.0010-.0030	.3410-.3420	.3410-.3420
1985	4-126, 2.1L③	—	—	90	45	1.779④	135 @ 1.17	—	—	.314	.314

①—No adjustment.
②—Turn rocker arm stud nut until all lash is eliminated, then tighten nut an additional 1½ turns.
③—Diesel engine.
④—Free length.

Pistons, Pins, Rings, Crankshaft & Bearings

Year	Engine	Piston Clearance	Ring End Gap① Comp.	Ring End Gap① Oil	Wristpin Diameter	Rod Bearings Shaft Diameter	Rod Bearings Bearing Clearance	Main Bearings Shaft Diameter	Main Bearings Bearing Clearance	Thrust on Bear. No.	Shaft End Play
1984-85	4-126, 2.1L④	—	—	—	1.102	—	—	—	—	—	.001-.005
	4-150, 2.5L	.0009-.0017	.010	.010	.9307	2.0934-2.0955	.001-.003	2.4996-2.5001	.0010-.0025	2	.0015-.0065
	V6-173, 2.8L	.0006-.0016	.010	.020	.9054	1.9980-1.9990	.001-.003	②	③	3	.0020-.0060

①—Fit rings in tapered bores for clearance listed in tightest portion of ring travel.
②—Nos. 1, 2, 4; 2.4937-2.4946. No. 3; 2.4930-2.4941.
③—Nos. 1, 2, 4; .0016-.0032. No. 3; .0020-.0030.
④—Diesel engine.

continued

Engine Tightening Specifications★

★Torque specifications are for clean and lightly lubricated threads only. Dry or dirty threads produce increased friction which prevents accurate measurement of tightness.

Year	Engine	Spark Plugs Ft. Lbs.	Cylinder Head Bolts Ft. Lbs.	Intake Manifold Ft. Lbs.	Exhaust Manifold Ft. Lbs.	Rocker Arm Shaft Bracket Ft. Lbs.	Rocker Arm Cover Ft. Lbs.	Connecting Rod Cap Bolts Ft. Lbs.	Main Bearing Cap Bolts Ft. Lbs.	Flywheel to Crank-shaft Ft. Lbs.	Vibration Damper or Pulley Ft. Lbs.
1984 -85	4-126, 2.1L⑤	—	⑦	—	—	15①	35–53②	44–48	65–72	⑥	96
	4-150, 2.5L	22–33	80	18–28	18–28	16–26①	28②	30–35	70–85	③	70–100
	V6-173, 2.8L	7–15	65–75	20–25	22–28	43–49④	6–9	34–40	63–74	45–55	66–84

①—Rocker arm cap screw.
②—Inch pounds.
③—Torque bolts to 50 ft. lbs., then tighten bolts an additional 60°.
④—Rocker arm stud.

⑤—Diesel engine.
⑥—With manual trans., 41 ft. lbs.; with auto. trans., 52 ft. lbs.
⑦—Torque bolts in four steps, first to 22

ft. lbs., next to 37 ft. lbs., then to 70–77 ft. lbs. Finally recheck bolt torque and ensure bolt torque is 70–77 ft. lbs.

Alternator Specifications

Year	Make	Engine	Ground Polarity	Alternator Rated Output Amperes	Alternator Rated Output Volts	Field Current Amperes @ 80° F.	Field Current Volts	Regulator Model ①	Regulator Volts @ 120° F.
1984–85	Delco	4-150, 2.5L	Negative	56	—	4–5	12	1116387	13.4–14.4
	Delco	4-150, 2.5L	Negative	68	—	4–5	12	1116387	13.4–14.4
	Delco	4-150, 2.5L	Negative	78	—	4–5	12	1116387	13.4–14.4
	Delco	V6-173, 2.8L	Negative	56	—	4–5	12	1116387	13.4–14.4
	Delco	V6-173, 2.8L	Negative	68	—	4–5	12	1116387	13.4–14.4
	Delco	V6-173, 2.8L	Negative	78	—	4–5	12	1116387	13.4–14.4
1985	Paris Rhone	4-126, 2.1L②	—	—	—	—	—	—	—

①—Solid state integral assembly, no adjustment required.
②—Diesel engine.

Starting Motor Specifications

Year	Engine Model	Starter Number	Free Speed Test Amps.	Free Speed Test Volts	Free Speed Test R.P.M.
1984–85	4-150, 2.5L	—	67	12	7380–9356
	V6-173, 2.8L	1109526	45–70	9	7000–11000
1985	4-126, 2.1L①	—	—	—	—

①—Diesel engine.

continued

Brake Specifications

Year	Model	Rear Drum I.D.	Wheel Cyl. Bore		Disc Brake Rotor					Master Cyl. I.D.
			Front Disc	Rear Drum	Nominal Thickness	Minimum Thickness	Thickness Variation (Parallelism)	Run Out (TIR)	Finish (microinch)	
1984-85	All	10	2.60	.875	.880	.815	—	.004	—	.937

Drive Axle Specifications

Year	Axle	Carrier Type	Ring Gear & Pinion Backlash		Pinion Bearing Preload			Differential Bearing Preload
			Method	Adjustment	Method	New Bearings Inch-Lbs.	Used Bearings Inch-Lbs.	
1984-85	Front	Integral	Shims	.005–.010	Shims	20–40	15–25	①
	Rear	Integral	Shims	.005–.009	Spacer	15–25	15–25	.008

①—Case spread with new bearings, .015 inch.

Wheel Alignment Specifications

Year	Model	Caster Deg.	Camber Deg.	Toe-In (Inches)
1984-85	Cherokee, Wagoneer	7 to 8	−½ to +½	−1/32 to +1/32

Cooling System & Capacity Data

Year	Model or Engine	Cooling Capacity Qts.		Radiator Cap Relief Pressure, Lbs.	Thermo. Opening Temp.	Fuel Tank Gals.	Engine Oil Refill Qts. ①	Transmission Oil				Axle Oil Pints
		Less A/C	With A/C					4 Speed Pints	5 Speed Pints	Auto. Trans. Qts. ②	Trans. Case Pints	
1984-85	4-150, 2.5L	10③	10③	15	195	13.5	4	④	⑤	6.5	⑥	⑦
	V6-173, 2.8L	12③	12③	15	195	13.5	4	④	⑤	6.5	⑥	⑦
1985	4-126, 2.1L⑧	9	9	—	—	13.5	6.3⑨	④	⑤	6.5	⑥	⑦

①—With or without filter change.
②—Approximate. Make final check with dipstick.
③—Includes coolant recovery bottle.
④—Borg Warner, 3.9 pts.; Aisin, 7.4 pts.
⑤—Borg Warner, 4.5 pts.; Aisin, 7.0 pts.
⑥—New Process 207, 4.5 pts.; New Process 229, 6.0 pts.
⑦—Front or rear, 2.5 pts.; models with
Selec-Trac add 5 oz. for front axle disconnect housing.
⑧—Diesel engine.
⑨—With filter.

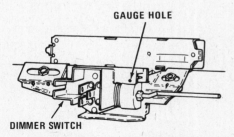

Fig. 1   **Adjusting dimmer switch**

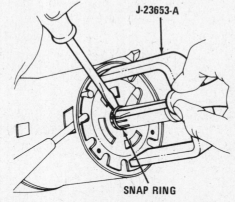

Fig. 2   **Removing steering shaft snap ring**

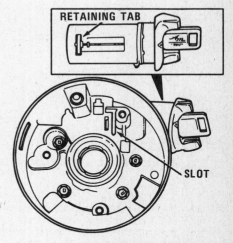

Fig. 3   **Lock cylinder removal**

STARTER, REPLACE

4-126 DIESEL

1. Disconnect battery ground cable.
2. Disconnect starter motor wiring.
3. Remove starter motor mounting bolts and nuts.
4. Remove starter assembly.
5. Reverse procedure to install.

4-150

1. Disconnect battery ground cable.
2. Raise and support vehicle, then remove support bracket to starter retaining bolt and washer.
3. Remove starter motor attaching bolts and the starter motor. Remove shims, if used.
4. Reverse procedure to install. Reinstall any shims that were removed.

V6-173

1. Disconnect battery ground cable.
2. Raise and support vehicle, then disconnect wiring from starter solenoid.
3. Remove starter motor attaching bolts and the starter motor. Remove shims, if used.
4. Reverse procedure to install. Reinstall any shims that were removed.

HORN SOUNDER & STEERING WHEEL
REPLACE

1. Disconnect battery ground cable.
2. Remove horn button and ring.
3. Remove steering wheel retaining nut, then scribe alignment marks on steering shaft and wheel to aid installation.
4. Using a suitable puller, remove steering wheel from shaft.
5. Reverse procedure to install. Torque steering wheel retaining nut to 25 ft. lbs.

DIMMER SWITCH
REPLACE

1. Disconnect battery ground cable.
2. Remove instrument panel lower shroud.
3. Remove steering column to instrument panel retaining bolts, then lower steering column as necessary.
4. Tape actuator rod to column, then remove dimmer switch retaining screws and pull switch from actuator rod.
5. Reverse procedure to install, then adjust dimmer switch as follows:
   a. Depress switch slightly, then insert a ³⁄₃₂ inch drill bit into switch gauge hole, **Fig. 1.**
   b. Move switch toward steering wheel to remove excess lash from actuator rod, then torque switch retaining screws to 35 inch lbs.
   c. Remove drill bit, then test dimmer switch function by operating actuator lever.

TURN SIGNAL SWITCH
REPLACE

1. Disconnect battery ground cable, then remove steering wheel as outlined previously.
2. Remove lockplate cover.
3. On models with tilt column, remove tilt lever. On all models, depress hazard warning knob, turn counterclockwise, then remove from steering column.

4. Compress lockplate using tool J-23653-A or equivalent, then remove steering shaft snap ring, **Fig. 2.**
5. Remove lockplate, canceling cam, upper bearing preload spring, spring seat and bearing race.
6. Disengage turn signal/wiper lever by pulling it straight out, then disconnect turn signal switch harness connector from steering column lower bracket.

NOTE: Wrap tape around switch harness connector to prevent snagging during removal.

7. Remove turn signal switch retaining screws and actuator, then remove switch and harness by pulling switch straight up and out of column.
8. Reverse procedure to install.

IGNITION LOCK
REPLACE

1. Remove turn signal switch as outlined previously.
2. Turn ignition to "ON" position, then remove key warning buzzer and contacts using a needlenose pliers.

NOTE: Do not attempt to remove switch and contacts separately, as contacts may fall into steering column.

3. Turn ignition to OFF-LOCK (tilt col-

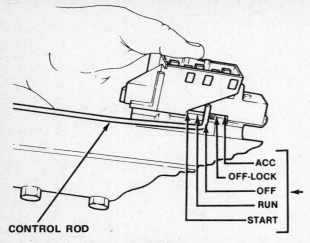

Fig. 4   Ignition switch installation (Typical)

CONTROL ROD

ACC
OFF-LOCK
OFF
RUN
START

INSTRUMENT CLUSTER
ATTACHING SCREWS

SWITCH
HOUSING

CIGAR
LIGHTER
HOUSING

Fig. 5   Removing instrument cluster

umn) or two detents clockwise from OFF-LOCK (standard column) position, then depress retaining tab and pull lock cylinder from steering column.

NOTE: The retaining tab is accessible through the slot adjacent to the turn signal switch mounting boss, **Fig. 3.**

4. To install lock cylinder, insert key into lock, then hold cylinder sleeve and rotate key clockwise until key stops. Insert lock cylinder into housing bore, ensuring cylinder tab is aligned with keyway in housing. Push cylinder inward until it bottoms in housing, then rotate key counterclockwise until drive section of cylinder mates with sector. Push cylinder in fully until retaining tab engages housing groove.

IGNITION SWITCH
REPLACE

1. Disconnect battery ground cable, then place ignition lock in OFF-LOCK position.
2. Remove instrument panel lower shroud.
3. Remove steering column to instrument panel retaining bolts, then lower steering column as necessary.
4. Disconnect control rod and electrical connector from switch, then remove switch attaching screws and the switch.
5. Position switch slider to the ACCESSORY position as shown, **Fig. 4.** Place ignition key in ACCESSORY position, then insert control rod into switch and install attaching screws.

NOTE: On standard column vehicles, the accessory position is to the extreme left, with the left side of the ignition switch facing toward the steering wheel. On tilt column vehicles, the accessory position is to

the extreme right, with the right side of the switch facing downward from the steering wheel.

6. Move switch downward to remove excess control rod lash, then torque attaching screws to 35 inch lbs.
7. Reconnect switch electrical connector.

LIGHT SWITCH
REPLACE

1. Disconnect battery ground cable, then pull control knob fully outward.
2. Working from underneath instrument panel, depress light switch shaft retainer button, then pull shaft from switch.
3. Remove light switch ferrule nut from front of instrument panel.
4. Disconnect switch electrical connector, then remove switch from vehicle.
5. Reverse procedure to install.

STOP LIGHT SWITCH
REPLACE

1. Disconnect battery ground cable.
2. Disconnect electrical connector from switch.
3. Remove brake pedal pivot bolt, nylon retaining rings, sleeve and switch.
4. Reverse procedure to install.

NEUTRAL START/ BACK-UP LIGHT SWITCH
REPLACE

AUTOMATIC TRANSMISSION VEHICLES

NOTE: The neutral start and back-up light

switches are an integral assembly and cannot be replaced separately.

1. Raise and support vehicle.
2. Disconnect electrical connector from switch.
3. Unscrew switch from transmission and allow fluid to drain into a suitable container.
4. Move shift linkage to PARK and NEUTRAL positions and observe switch operating fingers for proper positioning.
5. Reverse procedure to install. Correct transmission fluid as required, then check back up lights for proper operation.

BACK-UP LIGHT SWITCH
REPLACE

MANUAL TRANSMISSION VEHICLES

1. Raise and support vehicle.
2. Disconnect electrical connector from switch.
3. Unscrew switch from transmission housing and remove from vehicle.
4. Reverse procedure to install. Correct transmission fluid level as required, then check back-up lights for proper operation.

INSTRUMENT CLUSTER
REPLACE

1. Disconnect battery ground cable.
2. Remove the four instrument cluster bezel attaching screws, then carefully snap bezel from instrument panel.
3. Remove cigar lighter housing, switch housing and instrument cluster attaching screws, **Fig. 5.**
4. Disconnect speedometer cable.
5. Pull cluster out slightly, then discon-

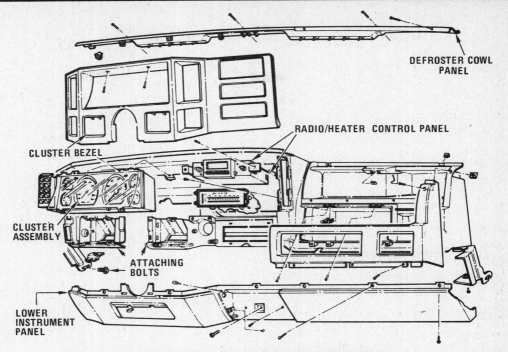

Fig. 6   Instrument panel exploded view

nect electrical connectors and remove cluster from vehicle.

6. Reverse procedure to install.

INSTRUMENT PANEL
REPLACE

1. Disconnect battery ground cable.

2. Remove lower instrument panel attaching screws, then the lower instrument panel, **Fig. 6.**
3. Remove instrument cluster as outlined previously.
4. Remove radio and heater control panel attaching screws, then the control panel.
5. Remove instrument panel switches.
6. Remove defroster cowl panel to instrument panel attaching screws, then

the defroster cowl panel.
7. Remove instrument panel attaching bolts, then the instrument panel assembly.
8. Reverse procedure to install.

NOTE: The instrument panel wiring harness is attached to the rear of the instrument panel and must be installed in similar fashion to facilitate installation.

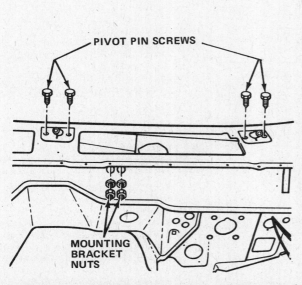

Fig. 7   Windshield wiper motor replacement

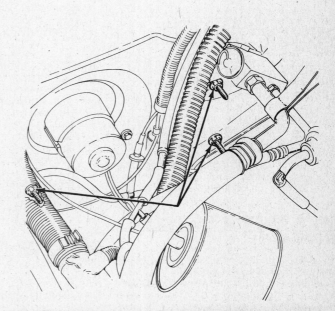

Fig. 8   Removing evaporator/blower housing

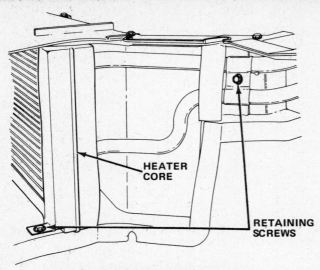

Fig. 9   Removing heater core

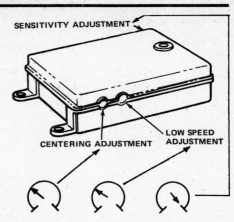

Fig. 10   Speed control regulator adjustments

W/S WIPER MOTOR
REPLACE

1. Disconnect battery ground cable, then remove wiper arm assemblies.
2. Remove cowl trim panel attaching screws and the trim panel.
3. Disconnect washer hose, then remove mounting bracket attaching nuts and pivot pin attaching screws, **Fig. 7**.
4. Disconnect wiper motor electrical connector, then remove wiper motor and linkage assembly.

NOTE: The wiper motor is shrouded in a rubber protective boot. Exercise caution when removing or replacing wiper motor to avoid damaging boot.

5. Reverse procedure to install.

LIFTGATE WIPER MOTOR
REPLACE

1. Disconnect battery ground cable, then remove wiper arm assembly.
2. Disconnect washer hose, then remove pin retaining nut.
3. Remove liftgate interior trim panel attaching screws and the trim panel.
4. Disconnect electrical connector from wiper motor.
5. Remove wiper motor attaching bolts and the wiper motor.
6. Reverse procedure to install.

W/S WIPER SWITCH
REPLACE

1. Remove horn sounder and steering wheel as outlined previously.
2. Remove turn signal switch as outlined in "Turn Signal Switch, Replace" procedure.
3. Disconnect electrical connector, then

remove pivot pin.
4. Remove wiper switch assembly.
5. Reverse procedure to install.

LIFTGATE WIPER SWITCH
REPLACE

1. Disconnect battery ground cable.
2. Remove instrument cluster bezel, then the switch housing panel.
3. Disconnect switch electrical connector.
4. Depress switch mounting tabs and remove switch from instrument panel.
5. Reverse procedure to install.

RADIO
REPLACE

NOTE: When installing radio, adjust antenna trimmer for peak performance.

1. Disconnect battery ground cable.
2. Remove instrument cluster bezel attaching screws, then gently snap bezel from instrument panel.
3. Remove the two radio retaining screws, then pull radio out gently and disconnect electrical connector and antenna lead.
4. Remove radio from vehicle.
5. Reverse procedure to install.

HEATER CORE
REPLACE

1. Disconnect battery ground cable, then drain cooling system.
2. Disconnect hoses from heater core.
3. If equipped with A/C, remove evapora-

tor/blower housing as follows:
   a. Discharge A/C system, then disconnect hoses from expansion valve.
   b. Disconnect electrical connector and vent tube from blower motor.
   c. Remove console, if equipped.
   d. Remove lower instrument panel attaching screws, then the lower panel.
   e. Disconnect electrical connections from A/C relay, blower motor resistors and A/C thermostat.
   f. Disconnect vacuum hose from vacuum motor.
   g. Cut evaporator/blower housing to heater core housing retaining strap, then disconnect heater control cable.
   h. Pry retaining clip from rear of blower housing flange, then remove the three retaining screws.
   i. Working from engine compartment, remove evaporator/blower housing attaching nuts, then the evaporator drain tube, **Fig. 8**.
   j. Remove right kick panel, then the instrument panel support bolt.
   k. Pull right side of dash outward, then rotate housing downward and towards rear of vehicle until studs clear dash panel. Remove housing from vehicle.
4. Remove heater core to housing retaining screws, then the heater core, **Fig. 9**.
5. Reverse procedure to install.

BLOWER MOTOR
REPLACE

1. Disconnect battery ground cable.
2. Disconnect electrical connectors from blower motor.
3. Remove blower motor and fan assembly attaching nuts, then blower motor and fan.
4. Remove fan retaining clip from fan hub.
5. Remove fan from the motor shaft.
6. Reverse procedure to install.

SPEED CONTROL
ADJUST

REGULATOR ADJUSTMENTS

The regulator adjustments are pre-set by the manufacturer. However, if all of the other components of the system appear to be functioning normally and the speed control system remains inoperative, perform the adjustments below to determine if the regulator is working properly.

Pre-Adjustment

Turn the sensitivity adjustment screw fully clockwise, and the low speed and centering adjusting screws to the 10 o'clock position as shown in **Fig. 10.**

NOTE: The adjustment screws are extremely delicate. Insert the screwdriver into the slots carefully to avoid damaging regulator.

Centering Adjustment

Road test vehicle and observe engagement speed. If speed control engages at 2 mph or greater than the selected road speed, turn centering adjusting screw counterclockwise in small increments. If engagement speed is 2 or more mph below selected speed, turn adjusting screw clockwise in small increments. Check for proper centering adjustment by engaging speed control system on a level road after each adjustment is completed. If adjustments have no effect on system operation, replace the regulator.

Gasoline Engine Section

ENGINE MOUNTS, REPLACE
FRONT MOUNT

1. Disconnect battery ground cable.
2. Remove through bolt retaining nut (1), **Fig. 1.** Do not remove through bolt at this time.
3. Remove engine mount upper retaining bolt (3), then raise and support vehicle.
4. Support engine with a suitable jack, then remove engine mount lower retaining nut (4) and through bolt (2).

NOTE: On six cylinder engines, it may be necessary to remove the air pump and hose assembly to allow removal of through bolt.

5. Raise engine slightly and remove engine mount (5).
6. Reverse procedure to install. Torque all nuts and bolts to 32 ft. lbs.

REAR MOUNT

1. Raise and support vehicle and transmission.
2. Remove rear mount to crossmember retaining nuts (1), **Fig. 2,** then the crossmember to frame retaining nuts and bolts (2). Remove crossmember from vehicle.
3. Remove rear mount to support bracket retaining nuts (4), then the rear mount.
4. Reverse procedure to install. Torque crossmember to frame retaining nuts and bolts to 35 ft. lbs., mount to support bracket retaining nuts to 30 ft. lbs., and mount to crossmember retaining nuts to 18 ft. lbs.

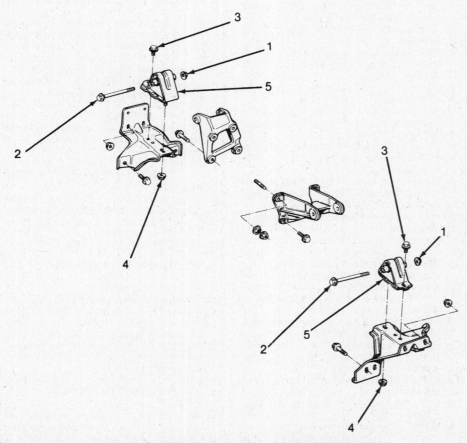

Fig. 1   Front engne mount replacement

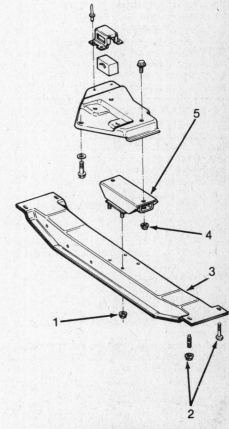

Fig. 2   Rear engine mount replacement

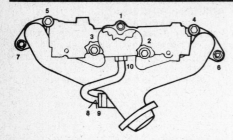

Fig. 3 Intake manifold bolt tightening sequence. 4-150

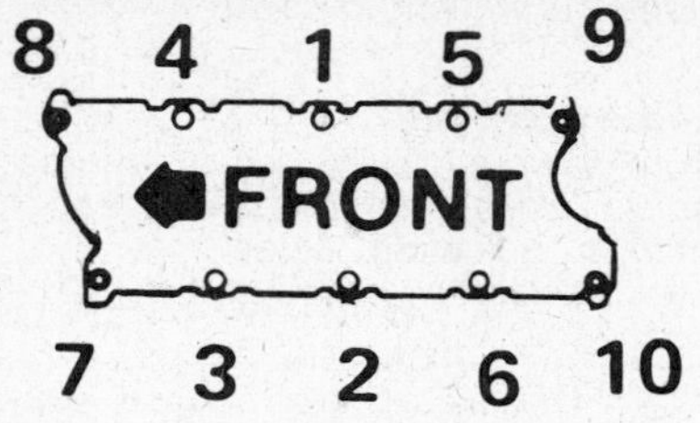

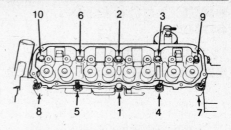

Fig. 4 Intake manifold bolt tightening sequence. V6-173

Fig. 5 Cylinder head bolt tightening sequence. 4-150

ENGINE
REPLACE

4-150

1. Disconnect battery ground cable, then remove air cleaner and hood.
2. Drain cooling system and remove upper and lower radiator hoses.
3. Remove fan shroud.
4. On vehicles equipped with automatic transmission, disconnect transmission cooling lines from radiator.
5. Remove radiator. On vehicles equipped with A/C, remove A/C condenser.
6. Remove fan assembly, then install a $5/16 \times 1/2$ inch bolt to retain fan pulley to water pump flange.
7. Disconnect heater hoses, throttle linkages, throttle valve rod and cruise control cable, if equipped.
8. Disconnect wires from starter motor.
9. Disconnect CEC wiring harness connector.
10. Disconnect fuel line from fuel pump and fuel return line from fuel filter.
11. On vehicles equipped with A/C, remove service valves and cap compressor ports.
12. If equipped with power brakes, remove vacuum check valve from brake booster.
13. If equipped with power steering, disconnect and plug hoses from steering gear, then drain power steering pump reservoir.
14. Disconnect all wires and vacuum hoses which will interfere with engine removal. Label wires and hoses to aid installation.
15. Raise and support vehicle, then remove starter motor.
16. Disconnect exhaust pipe from manifold.
17. Remove transmission housing inspection cover.
18. On automatic transmission equipped vehicles, mark torque converter to drive plate location, then remove converter to drive plate attaching bolts.
19. On all vehicles, remove upper transmission housing to engine attaching bolts and loosen bottom bolts.
20. Remove engine mount to support bracket attaching bolts, then install a suitable engine hoist.

21. Raise engine and support transmission with a suitable jack.
22. Remove the remaining transmission to engine attaching bolts.
23. Raise engine and remove from vehicle.
24. Reverse procedure to install.

V6-173

1. Disconnect battery ground cable, then remove air cleaner and hood.
2. Drain cooling system and remove upper and lower radiator hoses.
3. Remove fan shroud, then disconnect automatic transmission cooling lines from radiator, if equipped.
4. Remove radiator and, if equipped with A/C, the A/C condenser.
5. Remove fan assembly.
6. Disconnect heater hoses, throttle linkage, throttle valve cable and cruise control cable, if equipped.
7. Disconnect hose from power brake booster.
8. Disconnect and label all wires and vacuum hoses which will interfere with engine removal.
9. Remove power steering pump and position aside.
10. Disconnect fuel line from fuel pump.
11. Disconnect hoses from A/C compressor, if equipped.
12. Raise and support vehicle, then disconnect exhaust pipes from exhaust manifolds.
13. Disconnect exhaust pipe from catalytic converter flange and allow pipe to drop to floor.
14. Remove transmission housing inspection cover.
15. If equipped with automatic transmission, mark torque converter to drive plate location, then remove converter to drive plate attaching bolts.
16. Disconnect wires from starter motor, then remove transmission housing to engine retaining bolts.
17. Lower vehicle and support transmission with suitable jack.
18. Remove air pump to support bracket retaining bolts, then position air pump aside.
19. Install a suitable engine hoist, then remove engine mount through bolts.
20. Disconnect ground strap at left side cylinder head.
21. Raise engine and remove from vehicle.
22. Reverse procedure to install.

INTAKE MANIFOLD
REPLACE

4-150

1. Disconnect battery ground cable and drain cooling system.
2. Remove air cleaner.
3. Disconnect fuel line, air horn vent hose and idle speed control hose and wire connector from carburetor.
4. Disconnect coolant hoses from manifold and throttle cable from carburetor bellcrank.
5. Disconnect PCV hose from manifold, then remove vacuum advance CTO valve vacuum hose.
6. Disconnect fuel feedback coolant temperature sender wire connector from manifold.
7. Disconnect vacuum hose from EGR valve.
8. If equipped with automatic transmission, disconnect throttle valve linkage from carburetor.
9. If equipped with power steering, remove power steering pump mounting bracket, then position pump and bracket aside. Do not disconnect hoses from pump.
10. Remove carburetor.
11. Disconnect intake manifold heater wire connector, then remove EGR valve tube.
12. Remove intake manifold attaching nuts, bolts and clamps, then the intake manifold.
13. Reverse procedure to install. Torque manifold nuts and bolts to specification in sequence shown in **Fig. 3.**

V6-173

1. Disconnect battery ground cable and remove air cleaner.
2. Drain cooling system.
3. Disconnect wire connectors, vacuum hoses, fuel line and control linkage from carburetor, then remove carburetor attaching nuts and the carburetor.
4. Remove A/C compressor, if equipped, and position aside. Do not disconnect hoses from compressor.
5. Disconnect wires from spark plugs and ignition coil, then remove distributor cap.
6. Mark distributor position in relation to cylinder block, then remove distributor hold-down bolt and the distributor.
7. Remove EGR valve retaining bolts

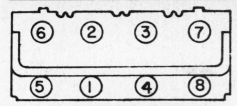

Fig. 6 Cylinder head bolt tightening sequence. V6-173

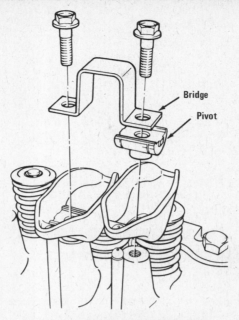

Bridge

Pivot

Fig. 7 Rocker arm assembly. 4-150

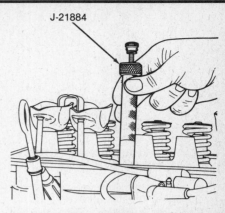

J-21884

Fig. 8 Valve lifter replacement. 4-150

and the EGR valve.

8. Disconnect air injection and charcoal canister hoses.
9. Remove air injection pipe bracket from left valve cover.
10. Remove left valve cover and the diverter valve.
11. Remove diverter valve and coil retaining bracket, then the right valve cover.
12. Remove upper radiator hose, then disconnect heater hose.
13. Disconnect coolant temperature switch wire connectors.
14. Remove intake manifold retaining bolts, then the intake manifold.
15. Reverse procedure to install. Torque manifold bolts to specification in sequence shown in **Fig. 4.**

NOTE: When installing new intake manifold gaskets, note gaskets are marked right side and left side. Install them as indicated to maintain proper engine operation.

CYLINDER HEAD
REPLACE

4-150

1. Disconnect battery ground cable.
2. Drain cooling system and disconnect hoses from thermostat housing.
3. Remove air cleaner, then the valve cover.
4. Remove rocker arm cap screws, bridges and pivots, then the rocker arms and push rods.

NOTE: Retain push rods, bridge, pivot and rocker arms in the same order as removed to facilitate installation in the original positions.

5. If equipped with power steering, remove power steering pump retaining bracket, then position bracket and pump assembly aside. Do not disconnect hoses from pump.
6. Remove intake and exhaust manifolds from cylinder head.
7. If equipped with A/C, remove compressor drive belt and loosen alternator belt.
8. Remove A/C compressor/alternator

bracket to cylinder head mounting screw, if equipped.
9. Remove remaining bolts and position alternator and A/C compressor aside.
10. Disconnect ignition wires and remove spark plugs.
11. Disconnect temperature sender wire connector, then remove cylinder head retaining bolts.
12. Remove cylinder head and gasket.
13. Reverse procedure to install. Torque cylinder head bolts to specification in sequence shown in **Fig. 5.**

V6-173

1. Remove intake manifold as outlined previously.
2. Drain coolant from cylinder block.
3. If removing left cylinder head, remove oil dipstick tube retaining nut and power steering pump and bracket assembly, if equipped.
4. Disconnect exhaust pipe from exhaust manifold, then remove exhaust manifold.
5. Loosen rocker arm retaining nuts, position rocker arms aside, then remove push rods.
6. If removing right cylinder head, remove alternator/air pump retaining bracket assembly.
7. Remove cylinder head retaining bolts, then the cylinder head.
8. Reverse procedure to install. Torque cylinder head bolts to specification in sequence shown in **Fig. 6.**

ROCKER ARM
SERVICE

4-150

Remove rocker arm cap screws, bridge, pivot and rocker arms as shown in **Fig. 7.** Inspect pivot and rocker arm for excessive wear or scoring. Replace if necessary. To install, lubricate rocker arm and pivot, then position rocker arm, pivot and bridge onto cylinder head. Install cap screws, then tighten alternately one turn at a time until proper torque specification is reached.

V6-173

Remove stud nut, pivot and rocker arm. Inspect pivot and rocker arm for excessive wear or scoring. Replace if necessary. Coat rocker arm and pivot friction surfaces with Molycote or equivalent, then install rocker arm, pivot and stud nut. Tighten stud nut until all lash is eliminated, ensuring push rod is correctly seated in lifter and rocker arm socket. Adjust valves as outlined in "Valve Adjustment" procedure.

VALVE ARRANGEMENT
FRONT TO REAR

4-150	E-I-I-E-E-I-I-E
V6-173	E-I-I-E-I-E

VALVES
ADJUST

V6-173

1. Crank engine until mark on torsional damper is aligned with TDC mark on timing tab. Ensure engine is in No. 1 cylinder firing position by placing fingers on No. 1 cylinder rocker arms as mark on damper comes near TDC mark on timing tab. If valves are not moving, engine is in No. 1 firing position. If valves move as damper mark nears TDC mark on timing tab, engine

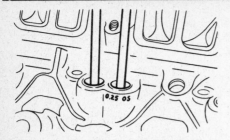

Fig. 9 Oversize valve lifter stamping. V6-173

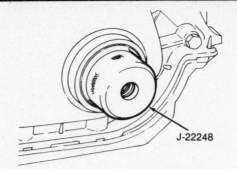

Fig. 10 Timing case cover alignment tool. 4-150

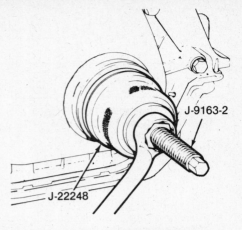

Fig. 11 Installing front seal. 4-150

is in No. 4 cylinder firing position and should be rotated one revolution to reach No. 1 cylinder firing position.

2. With engine in No. 1 cylinder firing position, adjust the following valves: exhaust: 1, 2, 3; intake: 1, 5, 6. To adjust valves, back off adjusting nut until lash is felt at push rod, then tighten adjusting nut until all lash is removed. This can be determined by rotating push rod while tightening adjusting nut. When all lash has been eliminated, turn adjusting nut the additional number of turns listed under "Valve Specifications."

3. Crank engine one revolution until mark on torsional damper and TDC mark are again aligned. This is No. 4 cylinder firing position. With engine in this position, the following valves can be adjusted: exhaust: 4, 5, 6; intake: 2, 3, 4.

4. Install rocker arm covers, then start engine and check timing and idle speed.

VALVE LIFTERS
REPLACE

4-150

1. Remove rocker arms as previously outlined.
2. Remove push rods.
3. Working through push rod openings, remove valve lifters using tool J-21884 or equivalent, **Fig. 8.**
4. Reverse procedure to install, using service tool outlined above.

V6-173

NOTE: This engine may be equipped with both standard and .25mm. oversize valve lifters. Where oversized valve lifters are installed, the valve lifter boss will be marked by a dab of white paint and a ".25 OS" stamping as shown, **Fig. 9.**

1. Remove intake manifold and rocker arms as previously outlined.
2. Remove push rods.
3. Using a suitable tool, remove valve lifters from cylinder block.
4. Reverse procedure to install. Coat base of lifter with Molycote or equivalent to prevent damage to lifter and/or camshaft.

VALVE TIMING SPECS.
INTAKE OPENS BEFORE TDC

Engine	Year	Degrees
4-150	1984-85	12°
V6-173	1984-85	7°

VALVE LIFT SPECS.

Engine	Year	Intake	Exhaust
4-150	1984-85	.424	.424
V6-173	1984-85	.347	.394

VALVE GUIDES
ALL ENGINES

The valve guides are an integral part of the cylinder head. If valve stem to guide clearance is excessive, the guide should be reamed to the next oversize and the appropriate oversized valve installed. Valves are available in .003 and .015 inch oversizes for 4-150 engines, while .0035, .0155, and .0305 inch oversizes are available for V6-173 engines.

TIMING CASE COVER & SEAL
REPLACE

4-150

1. Disconnect battery ground cable.
2. Remove drive belts, then the vibration damper and pulley.
3. Remove cooling fan and hub assembly, then the fan shroud.
4. Remove A/C compressor (if equipped) and alternator bracket assembly from cylinder head, and position aside.
5. Remove oil pan to cover retaining screws and cover to cylinder block retaining bolts.
6. Remove timing case cover, front seal and gasket.
7. Cut off oil pan side gasket end tabs and front seal tabs until they are flush with front face of cylinder block.
8. Clean timing case cover, oil pan and cylinder block sealing surfaces, then remove front crankshaft seal from timing cover.
9. Apply sealing compound to both sides of timing case cover gasket, then position gasket onto cylinder block.
10. Cut off end tabs from replacement oil pan side gaskets, then cement tabs to corresponding points on oil pan.
11. Coat front cover seal end tab recesses with RTV sealant, then position seal on timing case cover.
12. Apply engine oil to seal/oil pan contact surface, then position timing case cover onto cylinder block.
13. Install timing case cover alignment tool J-22248 or equivalent into opening in timing case cover as shown, **Fig. 10.**
14. Install cover to cylinder block retaining bolts and oil pan to cover retaining screws. Torque retaining bolts to 5 ft. lbs. and retaining screws to 11 ft. lbs.
15. Remove alignment tool, then position a new crankshaft seal onto tool, ensuring lip on seal faces outward. Apply a light coat of sealing compound to outside diameter of crankshaft seal, then coat crankshaft snout with engine oil.
16. Position alignment tool and seal over crankshaft snout, then insert installation tool J-9163-2 or equivalent into alignment tool as shown, **Fig. 11.** Tighten nut on installation tool until alignment tool contacts timing cover. Remove tool.
17. Install vibration damper and pulley. Torque vibration damper retaining nut to specification.

NOTE: If engine is equipped with a serpentine drive belt, the pulley is integral with the vibration damper.

18. Install A/C compressor (if equipped) and alternator bracket assembly, then the cooling fan, hub, and fan shroud.
19. Install drive belts, then reconnect battery ground cable.

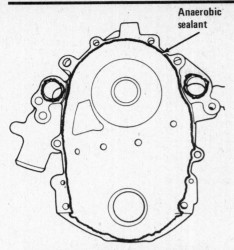

Fig. 12   Applying sealant to timing case cover. V6-173

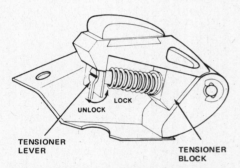

Fig. 14   Timing chain tensioner. 4-150

V6-173

1. Disconnect battery ground cable and drain cooling system.
2. Remove drive belts, then the radiator fan shroud.
3. Remove cooling fan and pulley.
4. If equipped with A/C, disconnect compressor from mounting bracket, position compressor aside and remove mounting bracket. Do not disconnect hoses from compressor.
5. Remove water pump retaining bolts and the water pump.
6. Remove vibration damper, then disconnect lower radiator hose from timing cover.
7. Remove timing cover attaching bolts, then the timing cover.
8. Pry crankshaft seal from timing cover, then position new seal so open end of seal faces towards inside of cover. Drive seal into position using tool J-23042 or equivalent.
9. Clean old sealant from timing cover and cylinder block.
10. Apply a continuous 3/32 inch bead of anaerobic sealant to timing cover sealing surface as shown, **Fig. 12,** then position cover onto cylinder block. Install bolts, then torque M8 × 1.25 bolts to 15 ft. lbs. and M10 × 1.50 bolts to 25 ft. lbs.

11. Install water pump.
12. Connect lower radiator hose, then install vibration damper.
13. Install A/C compressor mounting bracket, if equipped, then the cooling fan, pulley and fan shroud.
14. Install drive belts and fill cooling system.
15. Reconnect battery ground cable.

TIMING CHAIN & SPROCKETS
REPLACE

4-150

1. Remove timing case cover as previously outlined.
2. Rotate crankshaft until timing marks on camshaft and crankshaft sprockets align as shown in **Fig. 13.**
3. Remove oil slinger from crankshaft snout.
4. Remove camshaft sprocket retaining bolt, then lift off sprockets and timing chain as an assembly.
5. Turn timing chain tensioner lever, **Fig. 14,** to its unlocked position, then pull tensioner block towards lever, to compress spring. While holding tensioner block in this position, lock tensioner lever as shown.
6. Install timing chain and sprockets, ensuring timing marks are properly aligned.
7. Install camshaft sprocket retaining bolt and torque to 80 ft. lbs.

NOTE: To verify correct installation of timing chain, rotate crankshaft until camshaft sprocket timing mark is in one o'clock position. This should place crankshaft sprocket timing mark in three o'clock position. Count number of chain pins between timing marks. If valve timing is correct, there should be 20 chain pins between timing marks of both sprockets.

8. Install oil slinger, then the timing case cover.

V6-173

1. Remove timing case cover as outlined previously, then position No. 1 piston at TDC until marks on camshaft and crankshaft sprockets align as shown in **Fig. 15.**
2. Remove camshaft sprocket retaining bolts, then the sprockets and timing chain.
3. Install timing chain on sprockets, then hold camshaft sprocket vertically to allow timing chain to hang downward. Align timing marks on sprockets as shown in **Fig. 15.**
4. Align dowel pin on camshaft with dowel pinhole on camshaft sprocket, then install sprockets onto camshaft and crankshaft.
5. Install camshaft sprocket retaining bolts and torque to 17 ft. lbs.
6. Lubricate timing chain, then install tim-

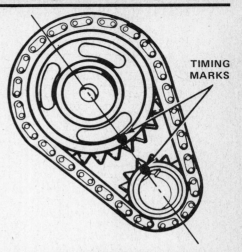

Fig. 13   Aligning valve timing marks. 4-150

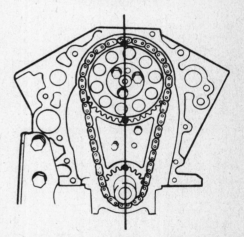

Fig. 15   Aligning valve timing marks. V6-173

ing case cover as previously outlined.

CAMSHAFT
REPLACE

4-150

1. Disconnect battery ground cable and drain cooling system.
2. Remove radiator and if equipped with A/C, the condenser.
3. Remove fuel pump, distributor and ignition wires.
4. Remove rocker arms, push rods and valve lifters as previously outlined.
5. Remove timing case cover, then the timing chain and sprocket.
6. Carefully slide camshaft out of cylinder block.
7. Reverse procedure to install.

V6-173

1. Disconnect battery ground cable and drain cooling system.

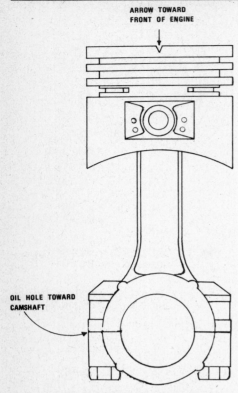

Fig. 16   Piston & rod assembly. 4-150

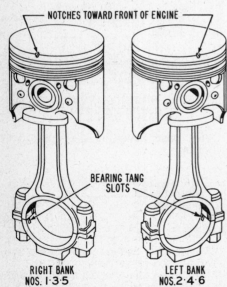

Fig. 17   Piston & rod assembly. V6-173

2. Remove radiator and if equipped with A/C, the condenser.
3. Remove intake manifold as previously outlined.
4. Remove fuel pump, push rods and valve lifters.
5. Remove timing case cover as previously outlined.
6. Remove timing chain and sprockets as outlined in "Timing Chain & Sprockets, Replace" procedure.

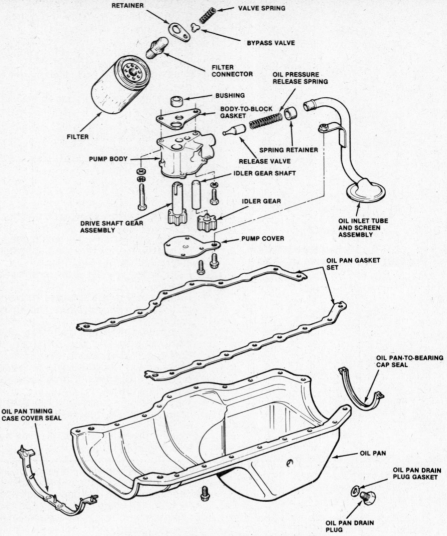

Fig. 18   Oil pan & pump. 4-150

7. Carefully slide camshaft out of cylinder block.
8. Reverse procedure to install.

PISTONS & RODS
ASSEMBLE

4-150

Pistons are marked with an arrow on the top perimeter. When assembling piston to rod, ensure arrow faces front of engine and oil spurt hole on connecting rod faces toward camshaft, as shown in **Fig. 16**. Check side clearance between connecting rod and crankshaft journal. Clearance should be .010 to .019 inch.

V6-173

Assemble piston to connecting rod with notch on top of piston facing toward front of engine and connecting rod bearing tang opposite camshaft, as shown in **Fig. 17**. Check side clearance between connecting rod and crankshaft journal. Side clearance should be .006 to .017 inch.

OIL PAN
REPLACE

4-150

1. Disconnect battery ground cable.
2. Raise and support vehicle, then drain oil pan.
3. Disconnect exhaust pipe at manifold, then remove hanger at catalytic converter and allow pipe to drop to floor.
4. Remove starter motor, then the transmission housing inspection cover.
5. Remove oil pan retaining bolts, then the oil pan and gaskets, **Fig. 18**.
6. Reverse procedure to install.

V6-173

1. Disconnect battery ground cable.
2. Disconnect right side exhaust pipe from manifold, then raise and support

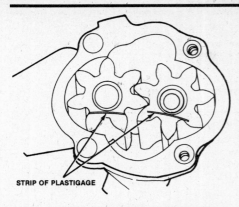

Fig. 19 Checking oil pump gear end clearance. 4-150

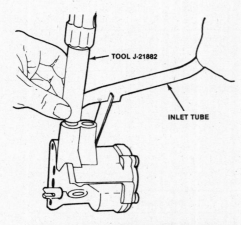

Fig. 21 Installing oil pump pickup tube and screen assembly. 4-150

vehicle.
3. Drain oil pan.
4. Disconnect left side exhaust pipe from manifold, then remove starter motor.
5. Remove transmission housing inspection cover.
6. Disconnect exhaust pipe at catalytic converter flange, then lower "Y" pipe onto upper control arms.
7. Remove oil pan retaining bolts, then the oil pan and gasket.
8. Reverse procedure to install.

NOTE: Before installing oil pan thoroughly clean all sealing surfaces, then apply a ⅛ inch bead of RTV sealant or equivalent to entire oil pan sealing flange.

OIL PUMP REPLACE & SERVICING

4-150

Removal
1. Remove oil pan as previously outlined.
2. Remove oil pump to cylinder block

retaining bolts, then the oil pump and gasket.

NOTE: Do not disturb positioning of oil pump strainer and tube. If tube is moved, a replacement tube and screen assembly must be installed to prevent pump cavitation.

Inspection
1. Remove pump cover to body retaining screws, then the pump cover.
2. Measure gear end clearance by positioning Plastigage across the full width of each gear as shown in **Fig. 19.** Reinstall pump cover and torque cover retaining bolts to 70 inch lbs. Remove cover and determine clearance by comparing compressed Plastigage with scale on Plastigage envelope. Clearance should be .002 to .006 inch. If clearance is excessive, replace oil pump.
3. Measure gear to pump body clearance by inserting a feeler gauge between each gear tooth and the pump body inner wall as shown in **Fig. 20.** Clearance should be .002 to .004 inch. If clearance is excessive, replace idler gear, shaft and drive gear assembly.
4. If checking pressure relief valve, remove pickup tube and screen assembly and position aside. Remove cotter pin, then slide spring retainer, spring and pressure relief valve plunger out of pump body. If plunger binds during removal, clean or replace plunger as necessary.

NOTE: Relief valve plungers are available in standard or .010 inch oversizes. When replacing plunger, ensure correct size is installed.

Assembly
1. Install relief valve plunger, spring, retainer and cotter pin.
2. If pickup tube and screen assembly was removed, install replacement assembly as follows:
   a. Apply a light coat of Permatex No. 2 sealant or equivalent, to end of pickup tube.
   b. Using tool J-21882 or equivalent, drive tube into pump body as shown in **Fig. 21.** Ensure support bracket is aligned properly.
3. Before installing pump cover, fill pump with petroleum jelly.
4. Install pump cover and torque retaining screws to 70 inch lbs.

Installation
Install oil pump and new gasket onto cylinder block. Torque retaining bolts to 13 ft. lbs, then install oil pan.

V6-173

Removal
1. Remove oil pan as described under "Oil Pan, Replace."
2. Remove pump to rear main bearing

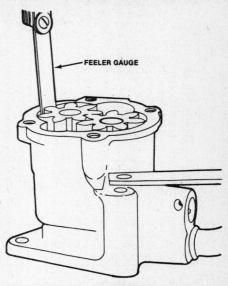

Fig. 20 Checking oil pump gear to body clearance. 4-150

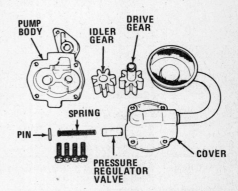

Fig. 22 Oil pump disassembled view. V6-173

cap bolt, and pump and extension shaft.

Disassembly
1. Remove pump cover attaching bolts and pump cover, **Fig. 22.**
2. Mark drive and idler gear teeth so they can be installed in the same position, then remove idler and drive gear and shaft from pump body.
3. Remove pin, spring and pressure regulator valve from pump cover.
4. If pick-up tube and screen assembly are to be replaced, mount pump cover in a soft jawed vise and remove pickup tube from cover. Do not remove screen from pick-up tube, as these components are serviced as an assembly.

Inspection
1. Inspect pump body and cover for excessive wear and cracks.
2. Inspect pump gear for damage or excessive wear. If pump gears are damaged or worn, the entire pump assembly must be replaced.
3. Check drive gear shaft for looseness

Crankshaft No. 1 Main Bearing Journal Color Codes and Diameter in Inches (mm)	Cylinder Block No. 1 Main Bearing Bore Color Code and Size in Inches (mm)		Bearing Insert Color Code	
			Upper Insert Size	Lower Insert Size
Yellow — 2.5001 to 2.4996 (Standard) (63.5025 to 63.4898 mm)	Yellow —	2.6910 to 2.6915 (68.3514 to 68.3641 mm)	Yellow — Standard	Yellow — Standard
	Black —	2.6915 to 2.6920 (68.3641 to 68.3768 mm)	Yellow — Standard	Black — 0.001-inch Undersize (0.025 mm)
Orange — 2.4996 to 2.4991 (0.0005 Undersize) (63.4898 to 63.4771 mm)	Yellow —	2.6910 to 2.6915 (68.3514 to 68.3641 mm)	Yellow — Standard	Black — 0.001-inch Undersize — (0.001 mm)
	Black —	2.6915 to 2.6920 (68.3461 to 68.3768 mm)	Black — 0.001-inch Undersize (0.025 mm)	Black — 0.001-inch Undersize (0.025 mm)
Black — 2.4991 to 2.4986 (0.001 Undersize) (63.4771 to 63.4644 mm)	Yellow —	2.6910 to 2.6915 (68.3514 to 68.3641 mm)	Black — 0.001-inch Undersize — (0.025 mm)	Black — 0.001-inch Undersize — (0.025 mm)
	Black —	2.6915 to 2.6920 (68.3461 to 68.3768 mm)	Black — 0.001-inch Undersize (0.025 mm)	Green — 0.002-inch Undersize (0.051 mm)
Green — 2.4986 to 2.4981 (0.0015 Undersize) (63.4644 to 63.4517 mm)	Yellow —	2.6910 to 2.6915 (68.3514 to 68.3641 mm)	Black — 0.001-inch Undersize — (0.025 mm)	Green — 0.002-inch Undersize (0.051 mm)
Red — 2.4901 to 2.4896 (0.010 Undersize) (63.2485 to 63.2358 mm)	Yellow —	2.6910 to 2.6915 (68.3514 to 68.3641 mm)	Red — 0.010-inch Undersize (0.254 mm)	Red — 0.010-inch Undersize — (0.254 mm)

Fig. 23 Main bearing selection chart. 4-150, No. 1 main bearing

Crankshaft Main Bearing Journal 2-3-4-5 Color Code and Diameter in Inches (Journal Size)	Bearing Insert Color Code	
	Upper Insert Size	Lower Insert Size
Yellow — 2.5001 to 2.4996 (Standard) (63.5025 to 63.4898 mm)	Yellow — Standard	Yellow — Standard
Orange — 2.4996 to 2.4991 (0.0005 Undersize) (63.4898 to 63.4771 mm)	Yellow — Standard	Black — 0.001-inch Undersize (0.025mm)
Black — 2.4991 to 2.4986 (0.001 Undersize) (63.4771 to 63.4644 mm)	Black — 0.001-inch Undersize (0.025 mm)	Black — 0.001-inch Undersize (0.025 mm)
Green — 2.4986 to 2.4981 (0.0015 Undersize) (63.4644 to 63.4517 mm)	Black — 0.001-inch Undersize (0.025 mm)	Green — 0.002-inch Undersize (0.051 mm)
Red — 2.4901 to 2.4896 (0.010 Undersize) (63.2485 to 63.2358 mm)	Red — 0.010-inch Undersize (0.054 mm)	Red — 0.010-inch Undersize (0.254 mm)

Fig. 24 Main bearing selection chart. 4-150, Nos. 2, 3, 4, & 5 main bearings

Crankshaft Connecting Rod Journal Color Code and Diameter in Inches (Journal Size)	Bearing Insert Color Code	
	Upper Insert Size	Lower Insert Size
Yellow — 2.0955 to 2.0948 (53.2257 - 53.2079 mm) (Standard) Orange — 2.0948 to 2.0941 (53.2079 - 53.1901 mm) (0.0007 Undersize) Black — 2.0941 to 2.0943 (53.1901 to 53.1723 mm) (0.0014 Undersize) Red — 2.0855 to 2.0848 (53.9717 to 53.9539 mm) (0.010 Undersize)	Yellow — Standard Yellow — Standard Black — 0.001-inch (0.025 mm) Undersize Red — 0.010-inch (0.254 mm) Undersize	Yellow — Standard Black — 0.001-inch (0.025 mm) Undersize Black — 0.001-inch (0.025 mm) Undersize Red — 0.010-inch (0.245 mm) Undersize

Fig. 25 Connecting rod bearing selection chart. 4-150

in pump body.

4. Inspect pump cover for wear that would allow oil to leak past gear teeth.
5. Inspect pick-up tube and screen assembly for damage.
6. Check pressure regulator valve for fit in pump cover.

Assembly

1. If pick-up tube and screen were removed, apply sealer to end of pick-up tube, mount pump cover in a soft-jawed vise and using tool No. J-21882, tap pick-up tube into position using a plastic mallet.

NOTE: Whenever the pick-up tube and screen assembly has been removed, a new assembly should be installed. Use care when installing assembly so tube does not twist, shear or collapse. Loss of a press fit condition could result in an air leak and a loss of oil pressure.

2. Install pressure regulator valve, spring and pin, **Fig. 22.**
3. Install drive gear and shaft in pump body.
4. Align marks made during disassembly, then install idler gear.
5. Install pump cover gasket, cover and attaching bolts. Torque bolts to 6 to 9 ft. lbs.
6. Rotate pump drive shaft by hand and check pump for smooth operation.

Installation

1. Assemble pump and extension shaft with retainer to rear main bearing cap, aligning top end of hexagon extension shaft with hexagon socket on lower end of distributor shaft.
2. Install pump to rear main bearing cap bolt.
3. Install oil pan as described under "Oil Pan, Replace."

MAIN BEARINGS

4-150

The main bearing journal diameter is identified by a color-coded paint mark located on the adjacent cheek toward the rear (flanged) end of the crankshaft, except for the rear main journal mark which is located on the crankshaft rear flange. Color codes used to indicate journal and corresponding bearing sizes are listed in **Figs. 23 and 24.**

V6-173

Main bearings are available in standard size and undersizes of .013 and .026mm.

CONNECTING ROD BEARINGS

4-150

The connecting rod journal is identified by a color coded paint mark on the adja-

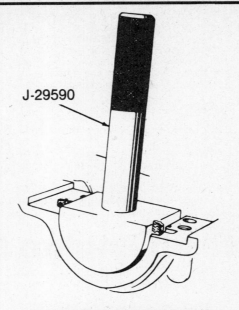

Fig. 26   Rear main oil seal repair. V6-173

cent counterweight near the rear of the crankshaft. Color codes used to indicate journal sizes and corresponding bearing sizes are listed in **Fig. 25.**

V6-173

Connecting rod bearings are available in standard size and undersizes of .013 and .026mm.

REAR MAIN OIL SEAL

4-150

1. Remove transmission as outlined in the "Clutch & Manual Transmission" section of this chapter.
2. Remove flywheel or converter drive plate.
3. Carefully pry seal out from around crankshaft flange.
4. Coat inner lip of replacement seal with engine oil, then carefully position seal around flange.
5. Using a plastic or rubber mallet, tap seal until flush with cylinder block.
6. Install flywheel or converter drive plate, then the transmission.

V6-173

NOTE: The rear main seal on this engine may be repaired without removing the crankshaft. To repair seal with crankshaft installed, follow the procedure below.

1. Remove oil pan and oil pump as previously described.
2. Remove rear main bearing cap.
3. Using tool No. J-29114-2, gently drive upper seal into groove approximately 1/4 in.
4. Repeat step 3 for other end of seal.
5. Measure the amount that was driven

in on one side and add 1/16 in. Using a suitable cutting tool, cut this length from the oil rear main bearing cap lower seal using the main bearing cap as a guide. Repeat this step for the other end of seal.

6. Place piece of cut seal into groove of seal installer tool guide No. J-29114-1 and install tool guide onto engine block.
7. Using seal packing tool No. J-29114-2, drive piece of seal into block. Drive seal in until packing tool contacts machined stop.
8. Remove tool guide and repeat steps 6 and 7 for other end of seal.
9. Install new seal in bearing cap.
10. Cut ends of seal flush with cap using tool J-29590, **Fig. 26.**
11. Place a piece of plastic gauging material on rear main journal, then install rear main bearing cap and torque to 70 ft. lbs.
12. Remove rear cap and check plastic gauge for bearing clearance. If clearance is not within specifications, recheck seal ends for fraying which may prevent cap from fully seating, and repair as necessary.
13. Clean plastic gauge from journal and bearing.
14. Apply a thin film of sealant No. 1052357 or equivalent to rear cap, then install cap. Use care not to allow sealant to contact the seal and bearing.

FUEL PUMP

REPLACE

4-150

1. Disconnect fuel lines from pump.
2. Remove retaining screws and fuel pump.
3. Remove all gasket material from the pump and block gasket surfaces. Apply sealer to both sides of new gasket.
4. Position gasket on pump flange and hold pump in position against its mounting surface. Ensure rocker arm is riding on camshaft eccentric.
5. Press pump tight against its mounting. Install retaining screws and tighten them alternately.
6. Connect fuel lines. Then operate engine and check for leaks.

NOTE: When installing pump, crank engine to place camshaft eccentric in a position which will place the least amount of tension on fuel pump rocker arm. This will ease pump installation.

V6-173

1. Disconnect battery ground cable.
2. Disconnect inlet and outlet hoses from fuel pump.
3. Remove fuel pump attaching bolts, then the fuel pump and gasket.
4. Reverse procedure to install.

NOTE: Before installing pump, rotate camshaft to "down stroke" position. When installation is completed, start engine and check for fuel leaks.

WATER PUMP
REPLACE

4-150

1. Drain cooling system, then disconnect hoses from pump.
2. Remove drive belts.
3. If equipped with power steering, remove power steering pump bracket from water pump boss.
4. Remove fan assembly and, if equipped, the radiator fan shroud.
5. Remove water pump retaining bolts, then the water pump and gasket.
6. Reverse procedure to install.

V6-173

1. Drain cooling system, then remove drive belts.
2. Remove fan assembly and, if equipped, the radiator shroud attaching screws and shroud.
3. Disconnect heater hose from pump, then remove water pump attaching bolts and nut and the water pump.
4. Reverse procedure to install.

BELT TENSION DATA

	New Lbs.	Used Lbs.
V Type Belts		
A/C Comp.	120-160	90-115
Air Pump	120-160	90-115
Alternator	120-160	90-115
Power Steer.	120-140	90-115
Serpentine Drive Belt	180-200	140-160

4-126 Diesel Engine Section

ENGINE
REPLACE

1. Scribe hood hinge locations and remove hood.
2. Disconnect battery cables and remove battery.
3. Remove skid plate, if equipped.
4. Drain cooling system and remove air cleaner assembly.
5. On models with A/C, seat service valve and remove them from the compressor.
6. On all models, disconnect radiator hoses and remove "E" clip from bottom of radiator.
7. Raise and support vehicle.
8. On models equipped with automatic transmission, disconnect cooler lines.
9. Remove splash shield from the oil pan, then lower vehicle.
10. Loosen radiator shroud, then remove the radiator fan.
11. Remove shroud and splash shield.
12. Remove radiator.
13. On models equipped with A/C, remove condenser.
14. Remove intercooler.
15. On all models, remove the exhaust shield from manifold.
16. Disconnect oil hoses from filter, then remove oil filter.
17. Tag and disconnect all vacuum hoses and electrical connections.
18. Disconnect and plug the fuel inlet and return lines.
19. Disconnect throttle cable, then raise vehicle.
20. On models equipped with power steering, disconnect power steering hoses, then drain power steering pump.
21. On all models, disconnect exhaust pipe at exhaust manifold.
22. Remove motor mount retaining nuts.
23. Mark and remove the converter to drive plate bolts.
24. Remove the transmission to engine retaining bolts, then lower vehicle.

1. Cylinder Head Cover
2. Cylinder Head Cover Gasket
3. Rocker Arm and Shaft Assembly
4. Camshaft
5. Valve Spring Locks
6. Valve Spring Retainer
7. Valve Spring
8. Valve Spring Washer
9. Valve
10. Injector
11. Glow Plug
12. Cylinder Head Gasket
13. Pre-Combustion Chamber
14. Cylinder Head
15. Camshaft Oil Seal
16. Camshaft Sprocket
17. Turbocharger

Fig. 1 Cylinder head exploded view

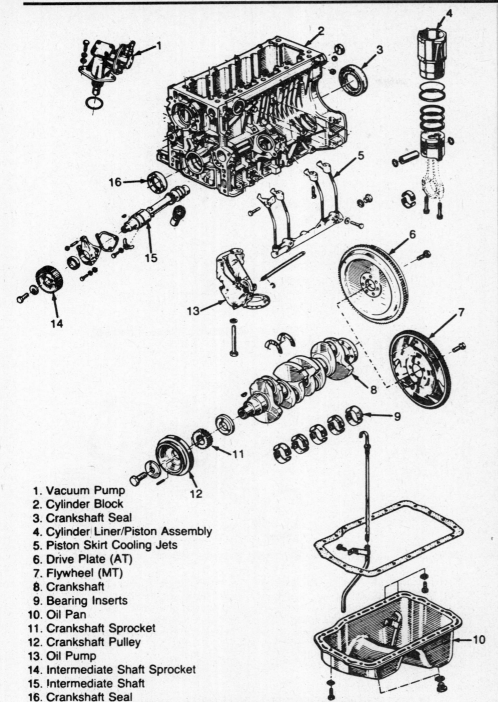

1. Vacuum Pump
2. Cylinder Block
3. Crankshaft Seal
4. Cylinder Liner/Piston Assembly
5. Piston Skirt Cooling Jets
6. Drive Plate (AT)
7. Flywheel (MT)
8. Crankshaft
9. Bearing Inserts
10. Oil Pan
11. Crankshaft Sprocket
12. Crankshaft Pulley
13. Oil Pump
14. Intermediate Shaft Sprocket
15. Intermediate Shaft
16. Crankshaft Seal

Fig. 2 Cylinder block exploded view

25. Remove the motor mount retaining bolts.
26. On models equipped with power steering, remove power steering reservoir.
27. On all models, remove the oil separator.
28. Disconnect heater hoses.
29. Remove the reference pressure regulator from dash panel. Attach suitable engine lifting equipment to engine. Support transmission with a suitable jack.

30. Remove engine from vehicle.
31. Reverse procedure to install.

ENGINE DISASSEMBLY

NOTE: Refer to **Figs. 1 and 2** for disassembled view of engine.

1. Remove drive belts, alternator, starter and A/C compressor, if equipped.
2. Remove oil supply line and oil return hose from turbocharger.
3. Remove turbocharger attaching bolts, then the turbocharger.
4. Remove valve cover attaching bolts, then the cover and gasket.
5. Remove TDC inspection plug, **Fig. 3.** Rotate the crankshaft into position and insert TDC rod Mot. 861 into TDC slot in crankshaft countershaft.

NOTE: Ensure rod is not inserted into crankshaft counterweight balance hole.

6. Remove fan and water pump pulley assembly.
7. Drain cooling system and engine oil.
8. Remove timing belt cover attaching screws, then the cover.
9. Install sprocket holding tool Mot. 854 or equivalent, then remove the camshaft sprocket retaining bolt.
10. Loosen belt tensioner bolts and position tensioner away from belt. Tighten tensioner bolts, then remove belt.
11. Disconnect fuel pipe fittings from injectors and injection pump. Cap all openings.
12. Disconnect and cap all hoses from fuel injection pump.
13. Remove mounting brackets and attaching bolts, then the injection pump assembly.
14. Remove cylinder head attaching nuts and bolts, then loosen pivot bolt, **Fig. 4.**
15. Remove the remaining cylinder head attaching bolts. Place a block of wood against the cylinder head and tap it lightly with a hammer to loosen cylinder head gasket.
16. Remove the pivot bolt and rocker arm shaft attaching bolts, then the rocker arm shaft assembly.

NOTE: Do not lift cylinder head from the cylinder block until gasket is completely loosened from the cylinder liners, since liner seals could be damaged.

17. Remove the cylinder head and gasket, then install cylinder liner clamps, Mot. 521-01 or equivalent, onto cylinder block.
18. Remove camshaft sprocket attaching bolt.
19. Install tool B.Vi 28-01 or equivalent, onto camshaft sprocket, then remove sprocket.
20. Disconnect fuel return hose fittings from injectors, then remove holders and injectors. Cap all openings.

NOTE: Mark each injector with the corresponding cylinder number to facilitate installation.

21. Remove copper washers and heat shields.

NOTE: Copper washers and heat shields must be replaced when injectors are installed.

22. Remove wire harness and glow plugs.
23. Remove intake and exhaust mani-

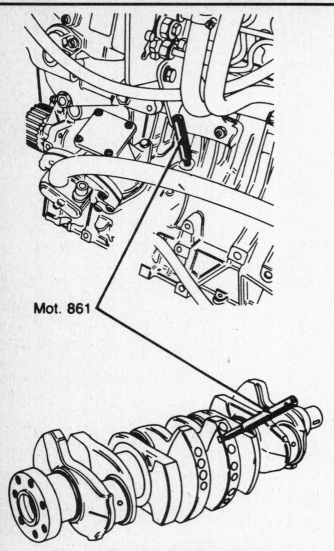

Mot. 861

Fig. 3   TDC inspection plug location

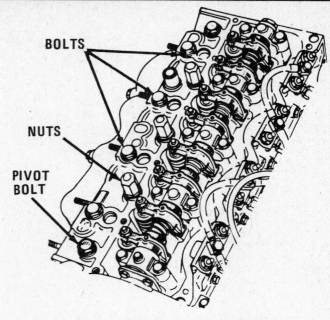

BOLTS

NUTS

PIVOT BOLT

Fig. 4   Cylinder head removal

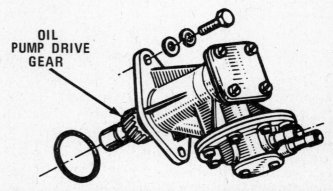

OIL PUMP DRIVE GEAR

Fig. 5   Vacuum pump with oil pump drive gear

folds, then gaskets from the cylinder head.

24. Remove camshaft oil seal using a suitable puller, then remove camshaft from cylinder head.
25. Remove thermostat housing and gasket.
26. Remove vacuum pump along with pump drive gear, **Fig. 5.**
27. Loosen intermediate shaft drive sprocket bolt using sprocket holding tool Mot. 855 or equivalent, and suitable wrench.
28. Remove intermediate shaft bolt, sprocket, cover attaching screws, cover, clamp plate and intermediate shaft, **Fig. 6.**
29. Remove oil pan attaching screws, then the oil pan.
30. Remove oil pump assembly attaching screws, then the oil pump.
31. Using a long strap and clip, **Fig. 7,** retain timing belt tensioner plunger, then remove water pump attaching screws, water pump, inlet housing and gasket.

32. Remove crankshaft pulley attaching bolt, washer and pulley.

NOTE: Remove pins from the crankshaft pulley.

33. Using a suitable puller, remove the crankshaft sprocket and washer as follows:
    a. Position sprocket removal tool B.Vi 28-01 (with shaft end protector tool 15-01), with jaws inserted behind sprocket washer.
    b. Force sprocket washer and sprocket away from crankshaft until washer stops against woodruff key. Do not force washer beyond this position.
    c. Remove tools installed in step (a), then install tools with jaws inserted between the sprocket washer and sprocket assembly.
    d. Force sprocket from crankshaft assembly.
    e. If there is not enough clearance between the washer and sprocket

to insert sprocket removal tool jaws, insert two .078 inch metal strips between the washer and sprocket.
    f. Insert the removal tool jaws behind the washer and force the washer and sprocket assembly from crankshaft until the washer stops at the woodruff key. Then repeat step (c).
34. Remove connecting rod bearing cap bolts, connecting rod bearing caps and bearing inserts.
35. Remove cylinder liner clamps.
36. Remove connecting rods, cylinder liners and pistons as an assembly.

NOTE: Each piston and cylinder liner are a matched set. Mark each piston and liner to ensure installation in their original positions.

37. Install holding plate Mot. 582 or equivalent to prevent the crankshaft from turning, then remove flywheel or drive plate from crankshaft.

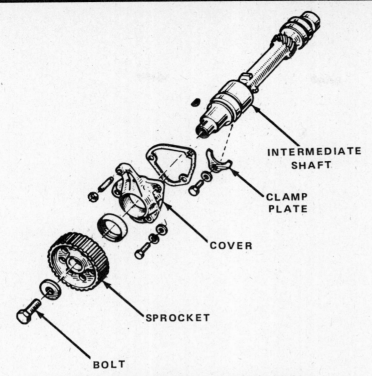

Fig. 6 Intermediate shaft assembly

Labels: INTERMEDIATE SHAFT, CLAMP PLATE, COVER, SPROCKET, BOLT

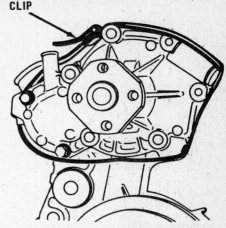

Fig. 7 Water pump removal

Label: CLIP

38. Remove the crankshaft main bearing caps.

NOTE: Mark the crankshaft main bearing caps according to their position, to facilitate installation in their original positions.

39. Remove bearing inserts from the caps, then crankshaft and bearing upper inserts.
40. Using a suitable puller, remove clutch pilot bearing from the crankshaft, if equipped.

ROCKER ARM SHAFT DISASSEMBLY

1. Remove camshaft thrust plate, **Fig. 8.**
2. Remove end plug and filter.
3. Remove No. 1 shaft bearing.
4. Remove set bolt and No. 5 shaft bearing.
5. Remove springs, rocker arms and remaining shaft bearings.
6. Retain all components in order removed to facilitate installation.

CYLINDER HEAD DISASSEMBLY

1. Compress valve spring, then remove valve collets.
2. Release valve spring compressor, then remove spring retainer, spring, oil seal, spring seat and valve.
3. Place valve train components in their original order to facilitate installation.

PISTON & ROD DISASSEMBLY

1. Remove piston rings.
2. Remove piston pin retaining clips, then the piston pin.
3. Keep disassembled parts in their original order to facilitate installation.

ASSEMBLY
CYLINDER HEAD ASSEMBLY

1. Insert valve into valve guide.
2. Install valve spring seat and stem oil seal.
3. Install spring and valve spring retainer.
4. Compress valve spring and install valve collets.

PISTON & ROD ASSEMBLY

1. Insert piston pin through piston and connecting rod, then install retaining clips.
2. Install piston rings.
3. Ensure that pistons, rods and cylinder liners for each cylinder assembly are installed in their original positions.

NOTE: When installing rods, ensure that each connecting rod lubrication hole is adjacent to the oil pump side of the cylinder block.

ROCKER ARM SHAFT ASSEMBLY

1. Install No. 5 shaft bearing, then the set

bolt in the bearing so that shaft oil holes face downward, **Fig. 9.**

NOTE: The intake and exhaust valve rocker arms are identical.

2. Install valve rocker arm, spring and another rocker arm.
3. Install intermediary shaft bearing with the offset facing toward the flywheel, or drive plate end of the cylinder head. Continue with the installation of the remaining components.
4. Install the No. 1 shaft bearing, filter and end plug.
5. Install thrust plate. Torque set bolts to 20 ft. lbs. and end plug to 15 ft. lbs.

ENGINE ASSEMBLY

NOTE: If main bearing inserts are being fitted to an out-of-round journal, ensure that the inserts are large enough for the maximum diameter of the journal. If inserts are fitted to the minimum diameter and the journal is out-of-round 0.001 inch or more, interference between bearing inserts and journal will result in rapid bearing failure.

1. Position crankshaft in cylinder block, then install main bearing cap Nos. 2, 3 and 4 with the replacement lower inserts in position.
2. Install the No. 1 main bearing cap, with a replacement lower insert, without the side seals. Tighten bolts and check end-play.

NOTE: If end play is not within specification, install thrust washers as necessary to obtain the correct end play.

3. Install No. 5 main bearing cap, with a replacement lower insert. Rotate crankshaft and ensure that it rotates smoothly.
4. Measure distance between the No. 1 main bearing cap and cylinder block, and No. 5 main bearing cap and cylinder block. If distance is .197 inch or less, use a .201 inch thick side seal. If distance is more than .197 inch, use a .212 inch thick side seal.

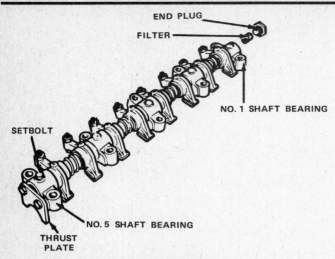

Fig. 8   Rocker arm shaft assembly

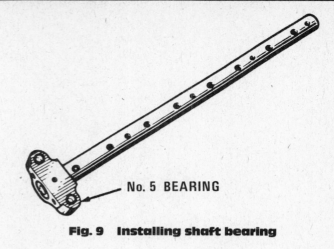

Fig. 9   Installing shaft bearing

Fig. 10   Foil installation

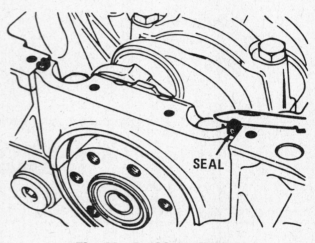

Fig. 11   Seal installation

5. Remove the No. 1 and No. 5 main bearing caps, then insert side seals in the main bearing cap slots, with grooves facing outward.

NOTE: Each side seal should protrude approximately 0.008 inch outward from cap. Lubricate contact surfaces of side seals lightly with clean engine oil.

6. Position a strip of suitable foil, **Fig. 10,** on each side of the main bearing caps. Torque caps to specifications.
7. Cut side seal ends so they protrude .020–.028 inch above the cylinder block surface, **Fig. 11.**
8. Using oil seal installation tool Mot. 788 or equivalent, for the seal at the flywheel/drive plate end and Mot. 789 or equivalent, for seal at the crankshaft sprocket end of cylinder block, install main bearing oil seals.

NOTE: If oil seal lip has excessively worn the contact surface at either end of the crankshaft, a .06 inch washer must be placed between installation tool and replacement oil seal to position seal further inward on crankshaft.

9. Install a replacement O-ring seal and plastic ring on each cylinder liner and ensure that O-ring is not damaged, **Fig. 12.**

NOTE: If a connecting rod bearing upper insert is being fitted to an out-of-round journal, ensure that insert is large enough for the maximum diameter of the journal. If bearing insert is fitted to the minimum diameter and journal is out-of-round 0.001 inch or more, interference between the bearing insert and journal will result in rapid bearing failure. The bearing upper inserts have lubrication holes and the lower inserts do not. Ensure that the holes in upper insert are aligned with lubrication holes in the connecting rod.

10. Install piston, connecting rod and cylinder liner assemblies into cylinder block with bearing upper inserts and rods positioned on crankshaft journals, **Fig. 13.** Ensure that cylinder liners are installed correctly. No. 1 cylinder liner assembly is adjacent to flywheel/drive plate end of block and liner flat surfaces are parallel. Ensure cylinder number stamped on each connecting rod and bearing cap is adjacent to the intermediate shaft side of block, and the combustion chamber in each piston crown faces toward the intermediate shaft side of block.
11. Install liner clamp tool Mot. 521-01 or equivalent, to cylinder head and torque bolts to 37 ft. lbs. to compress the liner seals to prevent liner seals from shifting.
12. Install each connecting rod bearing cap on its original connecting rod. Torque bearing cap bolts to 44–48 ft. lbs.

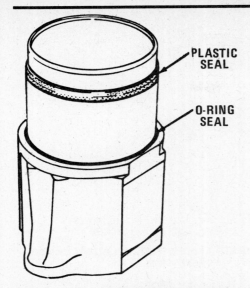

Fig. 12 Installing seals on liners

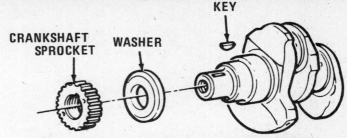

Fig. 14 Crankshaft sprocket installation

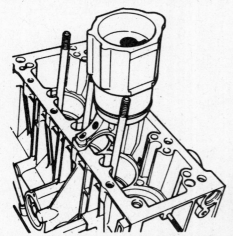

Fig. 13 Piston, connecting rod and liner installation

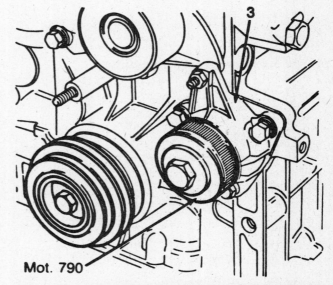

Fig. 15 Aligning intermediate shaft cover

NOTE: Tap each connecting rod lightly (parallel to the crankshaft) and ensure that there is adequate clearance. Rotate crankshaft and ensure that the pistons, connecting rods and crankshaft function normally.

13. Install oil pump assembly and gasket. Ensure that locating dowels are in place. Torque oil pump retaining bolts to 30–33 ft. lbs.

14. Install oil pan and gasket. Torque bolts to 70–88 inch-lbs.

15. Install water pump assembly. Continue to retain the timing belt tensioner plunger along with long strap and clip. Connect coolant hose and release strap, clip and timing belt tensioner.

16. Install clutch pilot bearing into end of crankshaft, if equipped. Seat bearing by gently tapping with a rubber mallet.

17. Apply Loctite 549, or equivalent, onto crankshaft to flywheel/drive plate mating surface.

18. Position flywheel/drive plate on to crankshaft and install holding tool Mot.

582 or equivalent.

NOTE: The original flywheel/drive plate self-locking bolts are not reusable. Use replacement bolts for each installation.

19. Lubricate threads of the replacement flywheel/drive plate bolts with Loctite 242, or equivalent, and torque flywheel bolts to 41 ft. lbs., and drive plate bolts to 52 ft. lbs. Bend locking plate tabs over flywheel/drive plate bolts. Remove holding tool.

20. Install washer, key and crankshaft sprocket, **Fig. 14.** The chamfered side of washer must face cylinder block and chamfered edge of sprocket bore faces washer.

21. Install the intermediate shaft, clamp plate, gasket and cover. Loosely install retaining bolt and nut.

22. Install intermediate shaft oil seal and align cover with installation tool Mot. 790, **Fig. 15.**

NOTE: If oil seal lip contact surface on the intermediate shaft has been excessively worn by the original seal, insert a .04 inch washer between the seal and installation tool to position seal further inward on shaft. The intermediate shaft cover retaining bolt extends through cylinder block and oil could seep out around bolt unless properly sealed.

23. Apply Loctite 242, or equivalent, to bolt threads, then install and tighten intermediate shaft cover retaining bolt and nut.

24. Install intermediate shaft sprocket, washer and bolt. Install sprocket with wider offset facing cylinder block.

25. Using holding tool Mot. 855 or equivalent, torque sprocket bolt to 37 ft. lbs.

26. Install oil pump drive shaft, gear, washer, and vacuum pump, **Fig. 16.**

NOTE: Clearance between the intermediate shaft cover and the timing belt tensioner must be adjusted to prevent lateral movement of the timing belt when belt is tightened. The correct clearance is .004 inch. Adjust clearance by turning adjustment screw, **Fig. 17.**

27. Before the cylinder head can be installed, piston protrusion measurement must be done to determine correct size replacement gasket to be used. To determine piston protrusion, proceed as follows:

NOTE: The piston protrusion measurement, (A), **Fig. 18,** procedure is necessary whenever major engine components have been replaced.

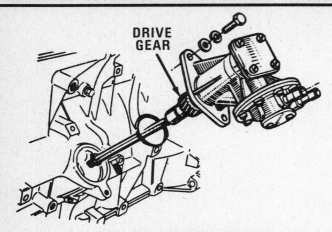

Fig. 16   Oil pump assembly installation

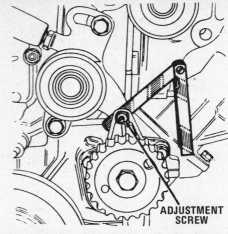

Fig. 17   Adjusting intermediate shaft cover clearance

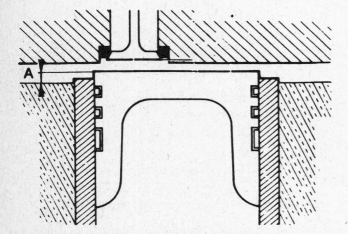

Fig. 18   Piston protrusion measurement

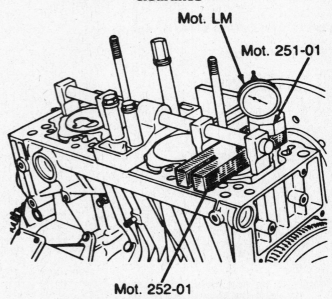

Fig. 19   Dial indicator installation

a. Rotate crankshaft one complete revolution and position No. 1 piston near (before) TDC of compression stroke.

b. Place thrust plate tool Mot. 252-01 or equivalent, on top of piston, then insert dial indicator Mot. LM in block gauge Mot. 251-01 or equivalent. Tighten screw clamp and place assembly on one side of thrust plate. Zero dial indicator pointer with stem located on cylinder block face, **Fig. 19.** Place dial indicator stem on piston crown and rotate crankshaft clockwise until piston is at TDC.

NOTE: Do not press on tools or piston since incorrect readings will result.

c. Record stem travel distance indicated by the dial indicator pointer. Repeat measurement procedure with dial indicator placed on the opposite side of thrust plate. Record stem travel distance indicated by dial indicator pointer.

d. Calculate the average amount of piston protrusion from the two

measurements. Note the following example: If protrusion at one side of piston is .033 inch and protrusion at the other side of piston is .043 inch, add .033 and .043 and divide by 2. Average piston protrusion is .038 inch.

e. Use the same procedure described to determine average amount of protrusion for the remaining pistons. Use piston that has the largest amount of average protrusion to determine required thickness of replacement cylinder head gasket.

f. If the largest amount of piston average protrusion is less than .038 inch, use gasket (A) that is .063 inch thick or has 2 holes, **Fig. 20.** If between .038 and .041 inch, use gasket (B) that is .067 inch thick or has one hole. If more than .041 inch, use gasket (C) that is .071 inch thick or has three holes.

28. Remove cylinder liner clamps Mot.

588 and install cylinder head locating tool Mot. 720 or equivalent, at (A), **Fig. 21,** for alignment.

29. Position replacement gasket onto cylinder block and ensure that gasket has the correct thickness for piston protrusion.

30. Position camshaft in cylinder head, then install cylinder head and gasket onto block. Torque cylinder head bolts in 4 steps in sequence shown in **Fig. 22,** as follows:
   a. First, torque bolts to 22 ft. lbs.
   b. Second, torque bolts to 37 ft. lbs.
   c. Third, torque bolts to 70–77 ft. lbs.
   d. Finally, torque bolts again to 70–77 ft. lbs. Remove tool Mot. 720 or equivalent.

NOTE: The cylinder head bolts must be retightened after engine is installed in vehicle. Operate engine for a minimum of 20 minutes. Allow engine to cool for a mini-

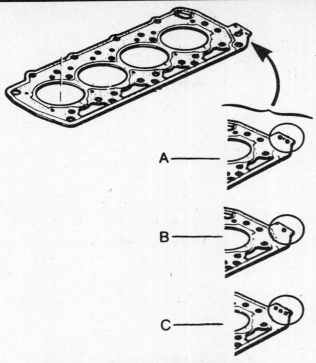

Fig. 20 Head gasket identification

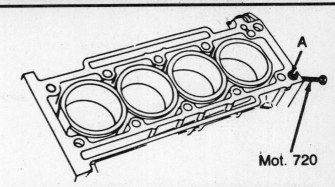

Fig. 21 Cylinder head locating tool installation

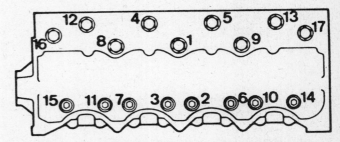

Fig. 22 Cylinder head tightening sequence

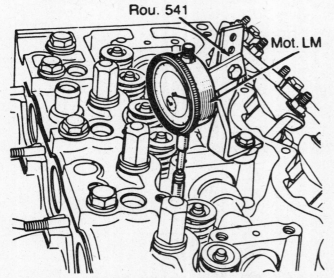

Fig. 23 Piston to cylinder head clearance

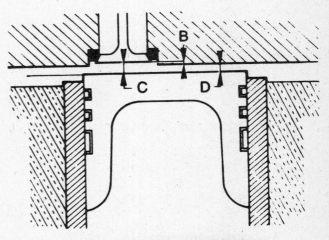

Fig. 24 Valve travel distance

mum of 2.5 hours, then loosen each cylinder head bolt (in sequence) ½ turn and then torque in sequence to 70–77 ft. lbs. For final torquing, torque bolts again in sequence to 70–77 ft. lbs.

31. Check piston-to-cylinder head clearance. Clearance must be greater than .023 inch for proper operation.
32. Select a valve and use the following procedure to measure clearance between valve face (when seated) and the corresponding piston crown:
   a. Rotate crankshaft clockwise and move selected piston to BTDC

position. Compress valve spring using valve spring compressor Mot. 382 or equivalent, and remove locks and spring.
   b. Push down on valve stem and ensure that piston is near TDC position. Attach bracket tool Rou. 541 or equivalent, to an adjacent rocker arm shaft bearing pedestal with a bearing hold-down bolt, **Fig. 23.**
   c. Attach dial indicator Mot. LM or equivalent to bracket tool and align it so that the stem rests on valve stem selected for measurement.

With valve resting on piston crown, use dial indicator as a reference and rotate crankshaft to move piston up exactly to TDC position, then set dial indicator pointer to zero.
   d. Lift valve up into its seat in the cylinder head and observe dial indicator valve travel distance between piston crown and valve seat. Record valve travel distance (C), **Fig. 24.**
   e. Calculate piston-to-cylinder head clearance according to the following procedure: Subtract valve recess (B) dimension, **Fig. 24,** from valve travel distance (C) measured

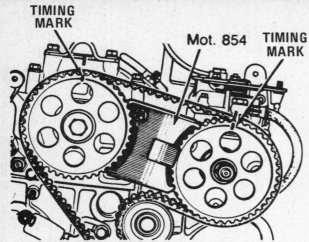

Fig. 25   Retaining timing mark position

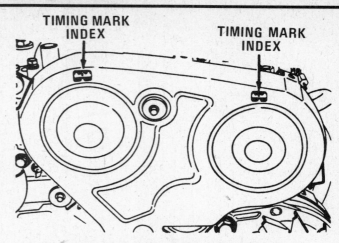

Fig. 26   Timing mark index location

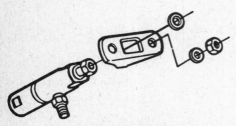

Fig. 27   Injector clamp installation

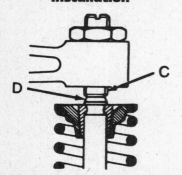

Fig. 28   Aligning adjustment screw with valve stem

EXHAUST VALVE OPEN	ADJUST INTAKE VALVE	ADJUST EXHAUST VALVE
1	3	4
3	4	2
4	2	1
2	1	3

Fig. 29   Adjusting rocker arm clearance

above. The result should be greater than .023 inch.

f. Note the following example: If intake valve recess is .036 inch, and exhaust valve recess is .034 inch, both valve recess dimensions are within the valve recess tolerance of .031–.045 inch. The smallest valve recess dimension should always be used for the piston to cylinder head clearance calculation. Valve travel distance (C) is .061 inch, the clearance (D) equals (C) minus (B). (D) equals .061 inch minus .034 inch. (D) equals .027 inch and is an acceptable clearance.

g. Position valve spring over valve stem, compress spring with a compressor tool and install valve collets.

33. Install rocker arm shaft assembly into cylinder head. Torque shaft bearing hold-down bolts to specifications.
34. Install replacement camshaft oil seal, then measure camshaft end-play.
35. Install camshaft sprocket and retaining bolt. Using sprocket holding tool Mot. 855 or equivalent, torque camshaft sprocket bolt to 37 ft. lbs. Rotate camshaft until sprocket timing marks are at the 12 o'clock position.
36. Attach fuel injection pump mounting brackets and pump to cylinder head with the retaining bolts.
37. Remove inspection plug from cylinder block and install TDC rod Mot. 861 or equivalent into hole against crankshaft counterweight. Rotate crankshaft clockwise until TDC rod enters TDC slot in the crankshaft countershaft.
38. Install sprocket holding tool Mot. 854 or equivalent, to retain camshaft and

fuel injection pump sprocket timing marks in place, **Fig. 25**.
39. Install timing belt on the sprockets.

NOTE: There should be a total of 19 timing belt cogs (teeth) between camshaft sprocket timing mark and the fuel injection pump sprocket timing mark. Temporarily position timing belt cover over the sprockets and check camshaft and fuel injection pump sprocket timing marks with indexes on cover, **Fig. 26**.

40. Remove timing belt cover and sprocket holding tool Mot. 854 or equivalent.
41. Adjust timing belt tension as follows:
   a. Ensure that timing belt is correctly positioned around all the sprockets and loosen belt tensioner bolts ½ of a turn (maximum). The spring loaded belt tensioner, in contact with belt, will automatically adjust to the correct position.
   b. Tighten tensioner bolts and remove TDC rod Mot. 861 or equiva-

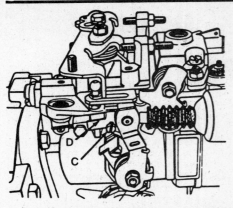

Fig. 30   Adjusting control cable

lent, and install inspection plug into cylinder block.

c. Rotate crankshaft clockwise, two complete revolutions and loosen timing belt tensioner bolts ½ of a turn, then tighten.

d. Measure timing belt tension. Belt deflection should be .118 to .197 inch. Install timing belt cover.

42. Install replacement copper washers and heat shields into cylinder head injector bores.
43. Install injectors in their original bores in the cylinder head. Place injector clamps over injectors and install retaining washers and nuts, **Fig. 27.** Torque clamp nuts to 12.5 ft. lbs.
44. Install glow plugs and connect injector fuel return hoses with replacement washers at each fitting.
45. Install glow plug wire harness.

NOTE: Do not install injector high pressure fuel pipes at this time.

46. Apply loctite 549 or equivalent, to crankshaft sprocket mating surface on the crankshaft pulley. Position crankshaft pulley on end of crankshaft.
47. Insert pins through the pulley and into the crankshaft sprocket.
48. Apply a small amount of Loctite 242 or equivalent, to the threads of crankshaft pulley bolt.
49. Install crankshaft pulley washer and bolt. Torque bolt to 96 ft. lbs.
50. Install water pump pulley and fan assembly.
51. Install starter, alternator, drive belts and, if equipped, A/C compressor. Check belt tension.
52. Install intake and exhaust manifolds with replacement gaskets.
53. Install turbocharger with replacement nuts. Connect all hoses and the oil supply line.

54. Install thermostat housing assembly with a replacement gasket.

VALVES
ADJUST

1. With engine cold, rotate crankshaft clockwise (as viewed from the front of the engine) until No. 1 cylinder exhaust valve is completely open.

NOTE: The No. 1 cylinder is located at the flywheel or drive plate assembly end of the engine. As each adjustment screw (C), **Fig. 28** is tightened, ensure that the bottom of the screw is aligned with the valve stem (D). If the adjustment screw is not aligned with the stem when tightened, stem damage can result.

2. Using adjustment tool Mot. 647 or equivalent, adjust rocker arm clearance for the No. 3 cylinder intake valve and No. 4 cylinder exhaust valve.
3. Rocker arm intake valve clearance should be .008 inch, rocker arm exhaust valve clearance should be .010 inch.
4. Refer to **Fig. 29** and adjust rocker arm valve clearance to specification and in cylinder sequence shown.

INJECTION PUMP TIMING
ADJUST

1. Loosen screw (C), **Fig. 30,** and turn injection pump control cable clevis pin (D) ¼ turn, then disconnect cold start system control assembly.
2. Rotate crankshaft clockwise 2 revolutions (as viewed from the front of the engine) and align camshaft and injection pump sprocket timing marks with the timing belt cover (Y) indexes, **Fig. 26.**
3. Install TDC rod tool Mot. 861 or equivalent, into crankshaft counterweight TDC slot, **Fig. 3.**
4. Remove screw plug (1), **Fig. 31,** located between the 4 high pressure fuel outlets at the rear of the injection pump assembly.
5. Remove copper washer (2), then install dial indicator support tool Mot. 856 or equivalent into screw plug bore on injection pump assembly.
6. Insert stem of dial indicator tool Mot. LM, or equivalent, into support tool previously installed on injection pump.
7. Remove TDC rod tool Mot. 861 from

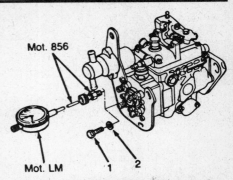

Fig. 31   Install dial indicator & indicator support into screw plug

crankshaft counterweight TDC slot.
8. Slowly turn crankshaft counterclockwise until dial indicator pointer stops moving.
9. Zero dial indicator pointer.
10. Slowly turn crankshaft clockwise until TDC rod Mot. 861 can be inserted into TDC slot in crankshaft counterweight.
11. At TDC, the dial indicator pointer should indicate a piston lift travel distance of .032 inch.
12. If dial indicator reading obtained is not as specified, proceed as follows:
    a. Loosen pump adjustment bolts.
    b. Check dial indicator reading.
    c. To increase piston lift, rotate pump toward engine and then away from engine.
    d. To decrease piston lift, rotate pump away from engine.

NOTE: Always adjust piston lift by rotating pump away from engine. This is the normal direction of pump rotation. When increasing the piston lift, rotate pump toward the engine until piston lift is greater than the specified tolerance and then rotate pump away from engine until the correct piston lift is indicated on the dial indicator.

13. After adjustment is completed, tighten adjustment bolts and remove TDC rod from the crankshaft counterweight.

BELT TENSION DATA

	New Lbs.	Used Lbs.
Alternator	155	115
Power Steering	155	115
Water Pump	155	115

Clutch & Manual Transmission Section

CLUTCH
ADJUST

These vehicles are equipped with an hydraulic actuated clutch which requires no adjustment.

CLUTCH ASSEMBLY
REPLACE

REMOVAL

1. Raise and support vehicle.
2. Remove transmission as outlined in "Transmission, Replace" procedure.
3. Scribe marks on pressure plate and flywheel to aid installation, then loosen pressure plate attaching bolts one turn at a time to relieve spring tension.

NOTE: The pressure plate bolts must be loosened evenly and in rotation to prevent distortion.

4. Remove pressure plate attaching bolts, then the pressure plate and clutch disc.
5. Remove throwout bearing and clutch release lever from clutch housing.
6. Remove pilot bushing lubricating wick from crankshaft.

INSTALLATION

1. Lubricate and install pilot bushing lubricating wick.
2. Install clutch disc and pressure plate onto flywheel, then align disc and plate using alignment tool J-33169 or equivalent.

NOTE: Ensure side of clutch disc marked "flywheel" is positioned against flywheel.

3. Install attaching bolts, then torque bolts evenly to 23 ft. lbs. on 4-150 engines or 16 ft. lbs. on V6-173 engines.
4. Install throwout bearing and clutch release lever into clutch housing.
5. Install transmission, then lower vehicle.

CLUTCH MASTER CYLINDER
REPLACE

1. Disconnect hydraulic line from master cylinder, then plug opening to prevent dirt from entering line.
2. Remove cylinder push rod to clutch pedal cotter pin and washer, then slide rod off pedal pivot.
3. Remove master cylinder to dash panel attaching nuts, then the master cylinder.
4. Reverse procedure to install. Torque cylinder attaching nuts to 19 ft. lbs., then bleed hydraulic system.

CLUTCH SLAVE CYLINDER
REPLACE

1. Raise and support vehicle.
2. Disconnect hydraulic line from slave cylinder.
3. Remove slave cylinder to clutch housing attaching bolts, then the slave cylinder.
4. Reverse procedure to install, then bleed hydraulic system.

CLUTCH SYSTEM
BLEED

1. Ensure fluid reservoir is full. If reservoir is not full, replenish with brake fluid.
2. Raise and support vehicle.
3. Remove slave cylinder to clutch housing attaching bolts, then the slave cylinder.
4. Compress slave cylinder plunger using tool J-24420-A or equivalent.
5. Attach one end of suitable hose to slave cylinder bleed screw nipple. Place the other end in a jar filled halfway with clean brake fluid.

NOTE: Ensure end of hose is submerged in brake fluid.

6. Loosen bleeder screw, then have an assistant depress and hold clutch pedal at end of travel.
7. Tighten bleeder screw, then have assistant release clutch pedal.
8. Repeat steps 6 and 7 until fluid entering jar is free of bubbles.

NOTE: While bleeding clutch system, constantly check master cylinder fluid level and replenish as necessary to prevent master cylinder from running out of fluid.

9. Remove tool from slave cylinder, then install slave cylinder.
10. Lower vehicle and check master cylinder level.

TRANSMISSION
REPLACE

REMOVAL

1. Remove outer gear shift lever boot, then remove upper console attaching screws and the upper console.
2. Remove lower console attaching screws and the lower console.
3. Remove shift lever inner boot.
4. Using tool J-34635 or equivalent, remove gearshift lever.
5. Raise and support vehicle, then drain transmission and transfer case lubricant.
6. Scribe alignment marks on rear propeller shaft and axle yoke, then remove propeller shaft.
7. Position a suitable jack under transfer case to support transmission and transfer case.
8. Remove rear crossmember to frame rail attaching bolts and nuts, then the rear crossmember.
9. Disconnect speedometer cable, back up light switch connector and transfer case vent hose.
10. Disconnect transfer case vacuum hoses and linkage.
11. Remove slave cylinder to clutch housing attaching nuts and position slave cylinder aside.
12. Scribe alignment marks on front propeller shaft and transfer case yoke, then disconnect propeller shaft and secure to underbody with suitable wire.
13. Install a suitable transmission jack to transmission and transfer case.
14. Remove clutch housing to engine attaching bolts, then the transmission and transfer case assembly.
15. Remove transmission to transfer case attaching bolts, then separate transfer case from transmission.

INSTALLATION

1. Shift transmission into gear using shift lever or suitable screwdriver.
2. Install transmission onto transmission jack, then raise jack and align transmission input shaft with clutch disc splines.
3. Install transmission clutch housing to engine, then torque attaching bolts to 28 ft. lbs.
4. Install slave cylinder.
5. Position transfer case onto transmission jack, then raise jack and connect transfer case to transmission. Torque attaching nuts to 26 ft. lbs.
6. Reconnect transfer case vent hose, back up light switch connector and speedometer cable.
7. Install transfer case linkage and vacuum hoses, then connect front propeller shaft to transfer case yoke, aligning scribe marks made during removal.
8. Install rear crossmember, then torque attaching nuts and bolts to 30 ft. lbs.
9. Remove transmission jack, then connect rear propeller shaft to axle yoke, aligning scribe marks made during removal.
10. Fill transfer case and transmission with proper lubricant, then lower vehicle.
11. Install gearshift lever, inner boot, lower and upper consoles, then the outer boot.

Transfer Case Section

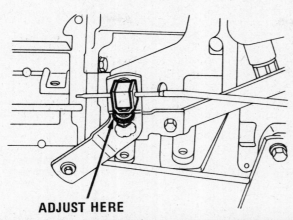

ADJUST HERE

Fig. 1   Transfer case range control linkage adjustment (Typical)

TRANSFER CASE
REPLACE

NEW PROCESS 207

NOTE: The New Process Model 207 transfer case is a part-time four-wheel drive unit used with the Command-Trac system.

1. Shift transfer case into 4-High position.
2. Raise and support vehicle, then drain lubricant from case.
3. Scribe alignment marks on rear axle yoke and propeller shaft, then remove rear propeller shaft.
4. Disconnect speedometer cable, vacuum hoses and vent hose.
5. Raise transmission and transfer case, then remove crossmember attaching bolts and the crossmember.
6. Scribe alignment marks on front output shaft flange and propeller shaft, then disconnect front propeller shaft from transfer case.
7. Disconnect shift lever linkage rod, then remove shift lever bracket bolts.
8. Support transfer case, then remove attaching bolts.
9. Remove transfer case from vehicle.
10. Reverse procedure to install. Torque transfer case attaching bolts to 26 ft. lbs. and crossmember to frame attaching nuts and bolts to 30 ft. lbs.

NEW PROCESS 229

NOTE: The New Process Model 229 transfer case is a full-time four-wheel drive unit used with the Selec-trac system.

1. Raise and support vehicle, then drain lubricant from case.
2. Disconnect speedometer cable and vent hose.
3. Disconnect transfer case shift lever link from operating lever.
4. Support transmission, then remove rear crossmember attaching bolts and the rear crossmember.
5. Scribe alignment marks on transfer case yokes and propeller shafts, then disconnect propeller shafts from transfer case.
6. Disconnect shift motor vacuum hoses.
7. Disconnect transfer case shift linkage, then remove transfer case to transmission attaching bolts.
8. Move transfer case rearward until clear of transmission output shaft and remove from vehicle.
9. Reverse procedure to install. Torque transfer case attaching bolts to 40 ft. lbs. and crossmember to frame attaching nuts and bolts to 30 ft. lbs.

TRANSFER CASE RANGE CONTROL LINKAGE ADJUSTMENT

1. Position range control lever in 2WD (Model 207) or High (Model 229).
2. Install a 1/8 inch spacer between gate and lever while holding lever in position.
3. Position range control lever as noted in step 1, then adjust link as shown, **Fig. 1,** until a free pin fit is achieved at transfer case outer layer.

Rear Axle, Suspension & Brakes Section

AXLE HOUSING ASSEMBLY
REPLACE

1. Raise and support vehicle, then remove wheels and brake drums.
2. Support axle, then disconnect shock absorbers at lower mount.
3. Disconnect brake hoses at frame rails and parking brake cables at equalizer.
4. Scribe alignment marks, then disconnect propeller shaft from axle.
5. Remove axle to spring U-bolts, then lower axle and remove from vehicle.

6. Reverse procedure to install. Torque U-bolt nuts to 52 ft. lbs., then bleed brake system.

AXLE SHAFT, BEARING & SEAL
REMOVAL

1. Raise and support vehicle, then remove wheel and brake drum.
2. Working through holes in axle shaft flange, remove brake support plate attaching nuts.

3. Using a suitable slide hammer type puller, remove axle shaft from housing.

DISASSEMBLY

1. Position axle shaft in a vise.
2. Drill a 1/4 inch hole approximately 3/4 of the way through bearing retaining ring, then chisel a deep groove in ring and remove from axle shaft, **Fig. 1.**
3. Using tool J-23674 or equivalent, press bearing from shaft, **Fig. 2.**
4. Remove seal, gasket and retainer plate from axle shaft.

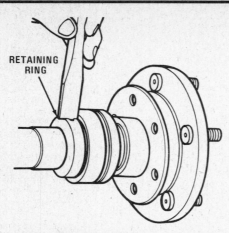

Fig. 1   Removing retaining ring from axle shaft

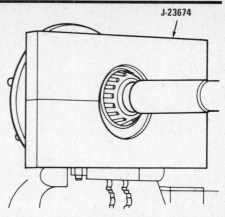

Fig. 2   Replacing axle shaft bearing

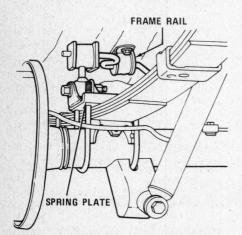

Fig. 3   Stabilizer bar mounting locations

ASSEMBLY

1. Lubricate seal, then install retainer plate, gasket and seal onto axle shaft.
2. Lubricate bearing, then using tool J-23674 and a suitable press, install bearing and retaining ring onto axle shaft. Ensure bearing and ring are properly seated against axle shaft shoulder.

INSTALLATION

1. Clean axle housing bearing bore, then apply a thin coat of grease to outer diameter of bearing cup.
2. Install axle shaft, then alternately torque brake support plate attaching nuts to 32 ft. lbs.
3. Install brake drum and wheel, then lower vehicle.

SHOCK ABSORBER
REPLACE

1. Raise vehicle and support rear axle

with a suitable jack.
2. Raise jack slightly, then remove upper shock mount to body retaining bolts.
3. Remove lower retaining nut and washer, then the shock absorber.
4. Reverse procedure to install. Torque upper retaining bolts to 15 ft. lbs. and lower retaining nut to 44 ft. lbs.

NOTE: If vehicle is equipped with Automatic Load Leveling System, disconnect lines from shock absorber before removing.

STABILIZER BAR
REPLACE

1. Raise and support vehicle.
2. Disconnect stabilizer bar at spring plates and frame rails, **Fig. 3.**
3. Remove stabilizer bar from vehicle.
4. Reverse procedure to install. Torque retaining bolts and nuts to 55 ft. lbs.

LEAF SPRING & BUSHING
REPLACE

1. Raise vehicle and support at side sills.
2. Position with a suitable jack under axle assembly, then raise jack slightly to relieve tension.
3. Disconnect shock absorber at lower mount, then remove wheel.
4. Disconnect stabilizer bar from spring plate.
5. Remove U-bolt attaching nuts, then the U-bolts and spring plate.
6. Remove front and rear spring eye to bracket retaining nuts and bolts, then lower axle and remove spring from vehicle.
7. To replace bushing, position spring on an arbor press and press bushing from spring using a suitable rod or pipe.
8. Reverse procedure to install. Torque U-bolt attaching nuts to 52 ft. lbs. and front and rear spring eye retaining nuts to 110 ft. lbs.

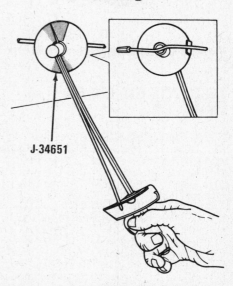

Fig. 4   Adjusting parking brake using tool J-34651

SERVICE BRAKES
ADJUST

1. Raise and support vehicle.
2. Remove access slot cover at rear of brake support plate.
3. Rotate adjuster screw until wheel locks, then back off screw approximately one turn.
4. Install access slot cover, then lower vehicle and check for proper brake operation.
5. Drive vehicle in Reverse, making 10 to 15 firm brake applications with one forward stop between each reverse application to equalize adjustment.

PARKING BRAKE
ADJUST

NOTE: Service brakes must be properly

adjusted before adjusting parking brake mechanism.

1. Fully apply and release parking brake lever approximately five times.
2. Pull parking brake lever up to 5th click, then raise and support vehicle.
3. Install adjustment gauge tool J-34651 onto an inch lb. torque wrench, **Fig. 4**, then apply a 45–50 inch lb. load to cable.
4. Adjust equalizer nut until gauge pointer is in Green range, then repeat Step 1.
5. Recheck adjustment. If adjustment is

MASTER CYLINDER
REPLACE

1. Disconnect and plug lines from master cylinder.
2. Remove master cylinder to brake booster retaining nuts.
3. Remove master cylinder from vehicle.
4. Reverse procedure to install, then bleed brake hydraulic system.

correct, stake nut to maintain setting, then lower vehicle.

POWER BRAKE UNIT
REPLACE

1. Disconnect power brake unit push rod from brake pedal assembly.
2. Disconnect vacuum hose from booster check valve.
3. Remove master cylinder retaining nuts and position master cylinder aside. Do not disconnect brake lines from cylinder.
4. Remove power brake unit to dash panel retaining nuts.
5. Remove power brake unit from vehicle.
6. Reverse procedure to install. Torque retaining nuts to 30 ft. lbs.

Front Suspension & Steering Section

DESCRIPTION

The front suspension, **Fig. 1**, consists of a solid axle, four control arms, two coil springs, a stabilizer bar, dual action shock absorbers and a track bar.

SHOCK ABSORBER
REPLACE

1. Remove shock absorber upper attaching nut and washer.
2. Raise and support vehicle.
3. Remove lower attaching nuts and bolts, then the shock absorber.
4. Reverse procedure to install. Torque upper attaching nut to 8 ft. lbs. and lower attaching nuts and bolts to 14 ft. lbs.

TRACK BAR
REPLACE

1. Raise and support vehicle.
2. Remove track bar to frame rail bracket cotter pin and retaining nut.
3. Remove track bar to axle bracket retaining nut and bolt, then the track bar.
4. Reverse procedure to install. Torque track bar to frame rail bracket retaining nut to 35 ft. lbs. and track bar to axle bracket retaining nut and bolt to 74 ft. lbs.

CONTROL ARM
REPLACE

UPPER ARM

1. On V6 equipped vehicles, disconnect right side engine mount, then raise engine until rear bolt is clear of exhaust pipe.
2. On all vehicles, raise and support vehicle, then remove control arm to axle attaching nuts and bolts.

3. Remove control arm to frame rail attaching bolt.
4. Remove control arm from vehicle.
5. Reverse procedure to install. Torque attaching nuts and bolts onto axle to 55 ft. lbs. and frame rail attaching nuts and bolts to 66 ft. lbs.

LOWER ARM

1. Raise and support vehicle.
2. Remove control arm to axle and control arm to rear bracket attaching nuts and bolts.
3. Remove control arm from vehicle.
4. Reverse procedure to install. Torque attaching nuts and bolts to 133 ft. lbs.

STABILIZER BAR
REPLACE

1. Raise and support vehicle.
2. Remove stabilizer bar to link attaching nuts, then the rubber bushings.
3. Remove stabilizer bar bracket to side sill retaining bolts.
4. Remove stabilizer bar.
5. Reverse procedure to install. Torque stabilizer bar to link attaching nuts to 27 ft. lbs. and stabilizer bar bracket to side sill retaining bolts to 55 ft. lbs.

STEERING DAMPER
REPLACE

1. Place front wheels in straight ahead position.
2. Remove cotter pin and retaining nut at center link.
3. Remove steering damper to axle bracket retaining nut and bolt, then the steering damper.
4. Reverse procedure to install. Torque steering damper to axle bracket retaining nut and bolt to 55 ft. lbs. and damper to center link retaining nut to 35 ft. lbs.

COIL SPRING
REPLACE

1. Raise and support vehicle.
2. Remove wheel, then position a suitable jack under axle.
3. Scribe alignment marks, then disconnect front propeller shaft from axle.
4. Disconnect lower control arm, stabilizer bar link and shock absorber from axle, then the track bar from side sill.
5. Disconnect center steering link from pitman arm.
6. Carefully lower axle assembly, then loosen spring retainer attaching nut and remove coil spring from vehicle.
7. Reverse procedure to install. Torque lower control arm retaining bolts and nuts to 133 ft. lbs., stabilizer bar link attaching nut to 70 ft. lbs., track bar to side sill retaining bolt to 35 ft. lbs. and center steering link to pitman arm retaining nut to 35 ft. lbs.

WHEEL ALIGNMENT

NOTE: Refer to "Wheel Alignment Specification Chart" at the beginning of this chapter for correct wheel alignment settings.

CAMBER

Camber is pre-set at the factory and is not adjustable. If the camber angle is not within specifications, replace the suspension components responsible for the incorrect angles.

CASTER

Caster is adjusted by adding or subtracting shims at the rear of the lower control arms.

TOE ADJUSTMENT

To adjust toe setting, center steering

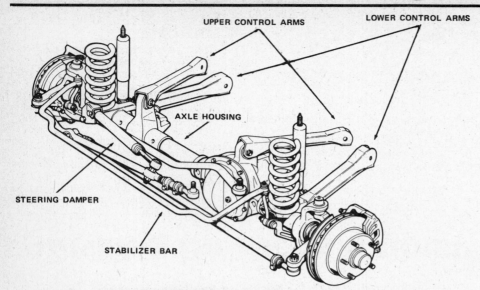

Fig. 1   Front suspension. 1984-85 Cherokee & Wagoneer

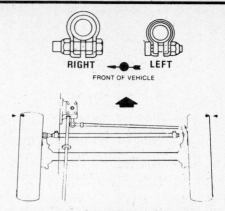

Fig. 2   Positioning adjusting tube clamps

gear, then lock steering wheel to hold in position. Adjust right wheel toe setting by loosening clamp bolt and rotating center link connecting pitman arm to right wheel. Adjust left wheel toe setting by loosening clamp bolt and rotating the tie rod connecting the center link to the left wheel.

After adjustments are completed, position clamps as shown, **Fig. 2.** Torque clamp bolts to 14 ft. lbs.

STEERING KNUCKLE
REPLACE

1. Remove axle shaft as outlined in "Front Wheel Drive Section."
2. Remove caliper anchor plate from knuckle, then the knuckle to ball joint cotter pins and retaining nuts.
3. Strike steering knuckle with a suitable mallet and remove from vehicle.

NOTE: A split ring seat is located in the bottom end of steering knuckle. Before installing knuckle, set split ring seat to a depth of .206 inch, using tool J-23447 or equivalent. Measure depth to top of ring seat as shown, **Fig. 3.**

4. Reverse procedure to install. Torque steering knuckle retaining nuts to 75 ft. lbs. and anchor plate retaining bolts to 77 ft. lbs.

BALL JOINTS
REPLACE

UPPER BALL JOINT

1. Remove steering knuckle as previously outlined.
2. Position receiver tool J-34503-1 over top part of ball joint and adapter tool J-34503-3 onto C-clamp as shown, **Fig. 4.**
3. Tighten clamp and press ball joint from steering knuckle.
4. To install, place tool J-34503-5 over replacement ball joint and receiver

tool J-34503-2 onto C-clamp. Position tool against yoke shoulder, then tighten clamp and press ball joint into knuckle.
5. Install steering knuckle.

LOWER BALL JOINT

1. Remove steering knuckle as previously outlined.
2. Position receiver tool J-34503-1 over ball joint stud and adapter tool J-34503-3 onto C-clamp as shown, **Fig. 5.**
3. Tighten clamp and press ball joint from steering knuckle.
4. To install, place tool J-34503-4 over replacement ball joint and receiver tool J-34503-2 onto C-clamp. Position tool against yoke shoulder, then tighten clamp and press ball joint into knuckle.
5. Install steering knuckle.

STEERING GEAR
REPLACE

MANUAL STEERING GEAR

1. Disconnect steering shaft from gear, then raise and support vehicle.
2. Disconnect center link from pitman arm.
3. Remove stabilizer bar as previously outlined.
4. Remove pitman arm retaining nut, then scribe alignment marks on sector shaft and arm.
5. Using tool J-6632-01 or equivalent, remove pitman arm from shaft.
6. Remove steering gear retaining bolts, then the steering gear.
7. Reverse procedure to install. Torque steering gear retaining bolts to 65 ft. lbs., pitman arm retaining nut to 185 ft. lbs. and center link retaining nut to 35 ft. lbs. Stake pitman arm retaining nut to sector shaft for proper retention.

POWER STEERING GEAR

1. Place front wheels in straight ahead position.
2. Disconnect hoses from steering gear, then plug hoses to prevent dirt from entering.
3. Disconnect intermediate shaft from stub shaft.
4. Raise and support vehicle, then disconnect center link from pitman arm.
5. Remove stabilizer bar as outlined previously.
6. Remove pitman arm retaining nut, then scribe alignment marks on arm and sector shaft.
7. Using tool J-6632-01 or equivalent, remove pitman arm from shaft.
8. Remove steering gear retaining bolts, then the steering gear.
9. Reverse procedure to install. Torque steering gear retaining bolts to 65 ft. lbs., pitman arm retaining nut to 185 ft. lbs. and center link retaining nut to 35 ft. lbs. Stake pitman arm retaining nut to sector shaft for proper retention, then bleed hydraulic system as outlined in "Power Steering Pump, Replace" procedure.

POWER STEERING PUMP
REPLACE

1. Loosen pump adjusting bolt, then remove drive belt.
2. Remove air cleaner, if necessary.
3. Disconnect hoses from pump, then plug hoses to prevent dirt from entering.
4. Remove front bracket to engine retaining bolts and pump to rear bracket retaining nuts.
5. Remove power steering pump together with front bracket.
6. Reverse procedure to install, then bleed hydraulic system as follows:
a. Fill pump reservoir, then start engine and allow to reach normal operating temperature.
b. Turn wheels to full left lock, stop engine, then add fluid to COLD mark on dipstick.

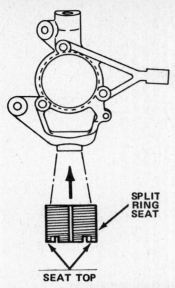

Fig. 3 Steering knuckle split ring seat depth measurement

c. Restart engine, then bleed system by turning wheels side to side until all air bubbles are eliminated. Do not allow wheels to hit stops.

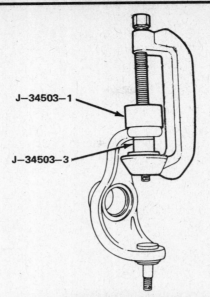

Fig. 4 Removing upper ball joint

d. Return wheels to straight ahead position, allow engine to idle for approximately three minutes, then stop engine.

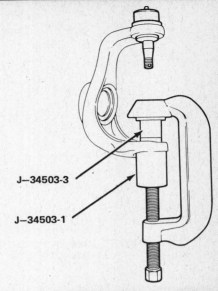

Fig. 5 Removing lower ball joint

e. Check fluid level. Fluid level should be at HOT mark on dipstick. If level is not at HOT, fill reservoir as necessary.

Front Wheel Drive Section

AXLE HOUSING ASSEMBLY
REPLACE

NOTE: 1984–85 Cherokee and Wagoneer models use the Spicer Model 30 type drive axle. The axle code number is attached to a tag located on the differential housing cover.

1. Raise and support vehicle.
2. Remove tire/wheel assemblies, then the brake calipers and rotors.
3. Disconnect vacuum harness from shift motor and vent hose from axle housing.
4. Disconnect stabilizer bar, rod and center links, then the front propeller shaft, shock absorbers, steering damper and track bar from axle.
5. Position a suitable jack under axle, then disconnect upper and lower control arms at axle.
6. Carefully lower axle housing and remove from vehicle.
7. Reverse procedure to install. Torque upper control arm attaching bolts to 55 ft. lbs., lower control arm attaching bolts to 133 ft. lbs., stabilizer bar link to 70 ft. lbs., and steering damper and track bar attaching nuts to 74 ft. lbs.

NOTE: When installing vent hose, secure hose away from the steering shaft U-joint.

AXLE HUB & BEARING SERVICE

Removal
1. Raise and support front of vehicle, then remove wheel, brake caliper and rotor.
2. Remove cotter pin, lock nut, axle hub retaining nut and washer.
3. Remove hub/carrier assembly to steering knuckle attaching bolts, then the hub/carrier assembly.

Disassembly
1. Press hub from carrier, then remove

bearings and seals, **Fig. 1.**
2. Inspect bearing cups for wear or scoring. If replacement is necessary, drive bearing cups from carrier with a suitable drift.

NOTE: If replacement is required, replace bearings and cups in matched sets only.

Assembly
1. Press new bearing cups into carrier, if applicable.
2. Fill steering knuckle and carrier cavities and coat seals with lithium base wheel bearing grease.
3. Repack, then install bearings into carrier.
4. Install new seal on hub side of carrier, then press hub through carrier.

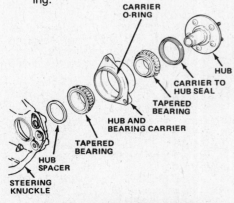

Fig. 1 Axle hub & bearing assembly (Typical)

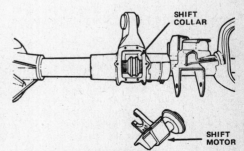

Fig. 2 Axle shift motor & housing collar

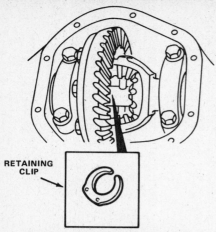

Fig. 3 Intermediate shaft retaining clip

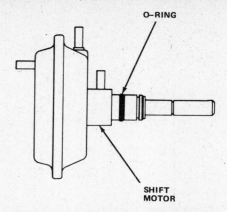

Fig. 4 Front axle shift motor & o-ring

Installation

1. Fill steering knuckle hub cavity with chassis grease, then install hub/carrier assembly. Torque hub/carrier assembly to steering knuckle attaching bolts to 75 ft. lbs.
2. Install washer and axle hub retaining nut, torque retaining nut to 175 ft. lbs., then install lock nut and cotter pin.
3. Install rotor, caliper and wheel, then lower vehicle.

AXLE SHAFT
REPLACE

REMOVAL

1. Remove axle hub as outlined previously.
2. Remove splash shield from steering knuckle.
3. If replacing left axle shaft, pull shaft from housing using a suitable puller.
4. If replacing right axle shaft, disconnect vacuum harness from shift motor, then disengage and remove motor from housing shift collar, **Fig. 2.** Pull axle shaft from housing.

INSTALLATION

1. If replacing left axle shaft, install axle shaft into housing, then install splash shield and axle hub.
2. If replacing right axle shaft, install shaft into housing, ensuring shaft is fully engaged over intermediate shaft end and shift collar is properly positioned in housing. Install shift motor so fork engages collar, then torque retaining bolts to 8 ft. lbs. Reconnect vacuum harness to shift motor, then install splash shield and axle hub.

INTERMEDIATE SHAFT
REPLACE

1. Raise and support vehicle.
2. Remove axle housing cover and drain lubricant from housing.
3. Remove right axle shaft as outlined previously.
4. Remove intermediate shaft retaining clip, **Fig. 3,** then the intermediate shaft.
5. Reverse procedure to install.

AXLE TUBE BEARING
REPLACE

1. Remove intermediate shaft as previously outlined.
2. Insert tools J-34659-3 and 4 or equivalents through outer end of axle tube, then working from access hole in shift motor housing, connect tool J-34659-1 to tools previously mentioned.
3. Position remover tool behind bearing, then tighten nut and remove bearing through access hole in shift motor housing.
4. Position new bearing into housing, then drive bearing into position using tool J-34659-2.
5. Install intermediate shaft.

AXLE TUBE SEAL & GUARD
REPLACE

1. Remove intermediate shaft as previously outlined.
2. Using tool J-34659-5 or equivalent, insert tool through outer end of axle tube, then drive seal and guard into shift motor housing and remove through access hole.
3. Position new seal and guard into shift motor housing, then using tool J-34659-2 or equivalent, tighten nut and pull seal and guard into position.
4. Install intermediate shaft.

AXLE SHIFT MOTOR SERVICE

Removal

1. Raise and support vehicle.
2. Drain lubricant from pan, then disconnect vacuum harness from shift motor.
3. Remove shift motor housing retaining bolts, then the housing, shift motor and fork assembly.

Disassembly

1. Scribe alignment marks on shift fork and housing to aid in assembly.
2. Rotate shift motor, then remove shift fork and motor retaining rings.
3. Remove shift motor from housing.
4. Remove O-ring from shift motor, **Fig. 4.**

Assembly

1. Install replacement O-ring onto shift motor.
2. Install shift motor into housing, then slide shift fork onto shaft, aligning scribe marks made previously.
3. Install shift fork and motor retaining rings.

Installation

1. Engage shift fork into collar, then install shift motor housing retaining bolts. Torque bolts to 8 ft. lbs.
2. Reconnect vacuum harness to shift motor, then add lubricant to proper level.
3. Lower vehicle.

INDEX OF SERVICE OPERATIONS

NOTE: Refer to page 1 of this manual for vehicle manufacturer's special service tool suppliers.

General Engine Specifications

Year	Engine Model	Engine V.I.N. Code ①	Carb. Type	Bore × Stroke	Comp. Ratio	Horsepower @ R.P.M.	Torque Ft. Lbs. @ R.P.M.	Normal Oil Pressure Lbs.
1979	6-258	C	2 Bore	3.75 × 3.895	8.0	—	—	37–75
	V8-304	H	2 Bore	3.75 × 3.44	8.4	—	—	37–75
	V8-360	N	2 Bore	4.08 × 3.44	8.25	—	—	37–75
1980–81	4-151	B	2 Bore	4.00 × 3.00	8.24	—	—	36–41
	6-258	C	2 Bore	3.75 × 3.895	8.0	—	—	37–75
	V8-304	H	2 Bore	3.75 × 3.44	8.4	150 @ 4200	245 @ 2500	37–75
	V8-360	N	2 Bore	4.08 × 3.44	8.25	175	285	37–75
1982	4-151	B	2 Bore	4.00 × 3.00	8.24	—	—	36–41
	6-258	C	2 Bore	3.75 × 3.895	8.6	—	—	37–75
	V8-360	N	2 Bore	4.08 × 3.44	8.25	175	—	37–75
1983	4-150	U	1 Bore	3.88 × 3.19	9.2	—	132 @ 3200	37–75
	4-151	B	2 Bore	4.00 × 3.00	8.24	—	—	36–41
	6-258	C	2 Bore	3.75 × 3.895	9.2	110	—	37–75
	V8-360	N	2 Bore	4.08 × 3.44	8.25	175	—	37–75
1984–85	4-150	U	1 Bore	3.88 × 3.19	9.2	—	132 @ 3200	37–75
	6-258	C	2 Bore	3.75 × 3.895	9.2	110	—	37–75
	V8-360	N	2 Bore	4.08 × 3.44	8.25	175	—	37–75

①—On vehicle identification plate located on left hand side of dash panel under the hood. On 1979–80 models, the sixth digit of the Vehicle Identification Number (V.I.N.) denotes engine code. On 1981–85 models, the fourth digit of the Vehicle Identification Number (V.I.N.) denotes engine code.

Pistons, Pins, Rings, Crankshaft & Bearings

Year	Engine Model	Piston Clearance	Ring End Gap ①		Wrist-pin Diameter	Rod Bearings		Main Bearings			Shaft End Play
			Comp.	Oil		Shaft Diameter	Bearing Clearance	Shaft Diameter	Bearing Clearance	Thrust on Bear. No.	
1979–80	6-258	.0009–.0017	.010	.010	.9307	2.0934–2.0955	.0010–.0025	2.4986–2.5001	.001–.003	3	.0015–.0065
1977–81	V8-304	.0010–.0018	.010	.010	.9311	2.0934–2.0955	.001–.003	②	④	3	.003–.008
1977–81	V8-360	.0012–.0020	.010	.015	.9311	2.0934–2.0955	.001–.003	②	④	3	.003–.008
1980–83	4-151	.0025–.0033	.010	.015	.927	2.000	.0005–.0026	2.2998	.0005–.0022	5	.0035–.0085
1981	6-258	.0009–.0017	.010	.010	.9307	2.0934–2.0955	.0010–.0025	2.4986–2.5001	③	3	.0015–.0065
1982–85	6-258	.0009–.0017	.010	.010	.9307	2.0934–2.0955	.001–.003	2.4996–2.5001	.001–.0025	3	.0015–.0065
	V8-360	.0012–.0020	.010	.015	.9311	2.0934–2.0955	.001–.003	②	④	3	.003–.008
1983–85	4-150	.0009–.0017	.010	.010	.9307	2.0934–2.0955	.001–.003	2.4996–2.5001	.0010–.0025	2	.0015–.0065

①—Fit rings in tapered bores for clearance listed in tightest portion of ring travel.

②—Rear, 2.7464–2.7479"; others, 2.7474–2.7489".

③—No. 1, .0005–.0026; No. 2, 3, 4, 5, & 6, .0005–.0030; No. 7, .0011–.0035.

④—Rear, .002–.004"; others, .001–.003".

continued

Valve Specifications

Year	Engine Model	Valve Lash		Valve Angles		Valve Spring Installed Height	Valve Spring Pressure Lbs. @ In.	Stem Clearance		Stem Diameter	
		Int.	Exh.	Seat	Face			Intake	Exhaust	Intake	Exhaust
1979-80	6-258	Zero	Zero	④	②	1 13/16	195 @ 1 13/32	.001-.003	.001-.003	.3715-.3725	.3715-.3725
1979-80	V8-304	Zero	Zero	④	②	1 13/16	213 @ 1 23/64	.001-.003	.001-.003	.3715-.3725	.3715-.3725
1979-80	V8-360	Zero	Zero	④	②	1 13/16	213 @ 1 23/64	.001-.003	.001-.003	.3715-.3725	.3715-.3725
1980-81	4-151	Zero	Zero	46	45	1.66	172 @ 1.25	.0010-.0027	.0010-.0027	.3418-.3425	.3418-.3425
1981	6-258	Zero	Zero	④	②	①	③	.001-.003	.001-.003	.3715-.3725	.3715-.3725
1981	V8-304	Zero	Zero	④	②	1.78	211 @ 1.356	.001-.003	.001-.003	.3715-.3725	.3715-.3725
1981	V8-360	Zero	Zero	④	②	1.78	211 @ 1.356	.001-.003	.001-.003	.3715-.3725	.3715-.3725
1982-83	4-151	Zero	Zero	46°	45°	1.66	176 @ 1.25	.0010-.0027	.0010-.0027	.3418-.3425	.3418-.3425
1982-85	6-258	Zero	Zero	④	②	1.786	195 @ 1.411	.001-.003	.001-.003	.3715-.3725	.3715-.3725
1982-85	V8-360	Zero	Zero	④	②	1.786	211 @ 1.356	.001-.003	.001-.003	.3715-.3725	.3715-.3725
1983-85	4-150	Zero	Zero	44½	44	1.625	213 @ 1.20	.001-.003	.001-.003	.3110-.3120	.3110-.3120

①—Intake valve 1.625, exhaust valve 1.786.
②—Intake 29°, exhaust 44°.
③—Intake 188-202 lbs. @ 1.411", exhaust 210-226 lbs. @ 1.188".
④—Intake 30°, exhaust 44½°.

Engine Tightening Specifications★

★ Torque specifications are for clean and lightly lubricated threads only. Dry or dirty threads produce increased friction which prevents accurate measurement of tightness.

Year	Engine	Spark Plug Ft. Lbs.	Cylinder Head Bolts Ft. Lbs.	Intake Manifold Ft. Lbs.	Exhaust Manifold Ft. Lbs.	Rocker Arm Cap Screw Ft. Lbs.	Rocker Arm Cover Inch Lbs.	Connecting Rod Cap Bolts Ft. Lbs.	Main Bearing Cap Bolts Ft. Lbs.	Flywheel to Crankshaft Ft. Lbs.	Vibration Damper or Pulley Ft. Lbs.
1979-80	6-258	28	105	23	23	19	50	33	80	105	80①
	V8-304, 360	28	110	43	②	19	50	33	100	105	90①
1980	4-151	7-15	92	37	39	③	84	30	65	68	160
1981	4-151	7-15	92	37	39	20	84	30	65	68	160
	6-258	11	85	23	23	19	28	33	65	105	80①
	V8-304, 360	28	110	43	②	19	50	33	100	105	90①
1982	4-151	7-15	92	37	37	20	84	30	65	68	160
	6-258	11	85	23	23	19	28	33	80	105	80①
	V8-360	28	110	43	②	19	50	33	100	105	90①
1983	4-150	27	85	23	23	19	55	33	80	④	80①
	4-151	7-15	92	26	37	20	84	30	65	68	162
	6-258	11	85	23	23	19	28	33	80	105	80①
	V8-360	28	110	43	②	19	50	33	100	105	90①
1984-85	4-150	27	85	23	23	19	55	33	80	④	80
	6-258	11	85	23	23	19	28	33	80	105	80①
	V8-360	28	110	43	②	19	50	33	100	105	90①

①—Lubricate bolts with engine oil.
②—Center two bolts, 25 ft. lbs.; outer four bolts, 15 ft. lbs.
③—Rocker arm stud to cylinder head, 60 ft. lbs; rocker arm stud nut, 20 ft. lbs.
④—Torque bolts to 50 ft. lbs., then tighten bolts an additional 60 degrees.

continued

Starting Motor Specifications

Year	Engine Model	Brush Spring Tension Oz.	Free Speed Test		
			Amps.	Volts	RPM
1979–81	All	—	77	12	8900–9600
1980–83	4-151	—	45–70	9	7000–11900
1982–85	6-258, V8-360	—	67	12	7380–9356
1983–85	4-150	—	67	12	7380–9356

Alternator Specifications

Year	Make	Alternator		Regulator	
		Field Current @ 80°F	Rated Output Amps.①	Model	Voltage @ 80°F
1979–80	Delco	4.0–4.5	37	Integral	14.1–14.6
	Delco	4.0–4.5	63	Integral	14.1–14.6
1981–82	Delco	4.0–5.0	42	Integral	13.9–14.9
	Delco	4.0–5.0	63	Integral	13.9–14.9
	Delco	4.0–5.0	70	Integral	13.9–14.9
	Delco	4.0–5.0	85	Integral	13.9–14.9
1983–85	Delco	4.0–5.0	42	Integral	13.9–14.9
	Delco	4.0–5.0	56	Integral	13.9–14.9
	Delco	4.0–5.0	78	Integral	13.9–14.9

①—Stamped on alternator frame.

Brake Specifications

Year	Model	Rear Drum I.D.①	Wheel Cyl. Bore		Disc Brake Rotor				Master Cyl. Bore Dia.
			Front Disc	Rear Drum	Minimum Thickness	Thickness Variation (Parallelism)	Run Out (TIR)	Finish (Microinch)	
1979–83	Cherokee, Wagoneer	11.06	2.937	.937	1.215	.0010	.005	20–60	1.125
1979–85	CJ Models	10.06	2.6	.875	.815	.0010	.005	15–80	1.0
	J-10	11.06	2.937	.937	1.215	.0010	.005	20–60	1.125
	J-20	12.06	2.937	1.125	1.215	.0010	.005	20–60	1.125
1982–85	Scrambler	10.06	2.6	.875	.815	.0010	.005	15–80	1.0
1984–85	Grand Wagoneer	11.06	2.937	.937	1.215	.0010	.005	15–80	1.125

①—Maximum.

Wheel Alignment Specifications

Year	Model	Caster Deg.	Camber Deg.	Toe-in Inch	Kingpin Inclination Deg.
1979–80	CJ Models	+3°	+1½°	³⁄₆₄–³⁄₃₂	8½°
	Exc. CJ Models	+4°	+1½°	³⁄₆₄–³⁄₃₂	8½°
1981	CJ	+6°	+1½°	³⁄₆₄–³⁄₃₂	8½°
1981–85	Exc. CJ & Scrambler	+4°	Zero	³⁄₆₄–³⁄₃₂	8½°
1982–83	CJ & Scrambler	+6°	Zero	³⁄₆₄–³⁄₃₂	8½°
1984–85	CJ & Scrambler	+6°	Zero	³⁄₃₂	10°

continued

Drive Axle Specifications

Year	Model	Carrier Type	Ring Gear & Pinion Backlash		Pinion Bearing Preload			Differential Bearing Preload		
			Method	Adjustment	Method	New Bearings Inch Lbs.	Used Bearings Inch Lbs.	Method	New Bearings Inch Lbs.	Used Bearings Inch Lbs.
1979	Exc CJ Models①	Integral	Shims	.005–.010	Shims	20–40	10–20	Shims	③	③
1979–81	CJ Models①	Integral	Shims	.005–.009	Sleeve	17–25	17–25	Shims	④	④
1979–85	All②	Integral	Shims	.005–.010	Shims	20–40	10–20	Shims	③	③
1980–83	Cherokee, Wagoneer①	Integral	Shims	.005–.009	Sleeve	17–25	17–25	Shims	④	④
1980–85	J-10①	Integral	Shims	.005–.009	Sleeve	17–25	17–25	Shims	④	④
1980–85	J-20①	Integral	Shims	.005–.010	Shims	20–40	10–20	Shims	③	③
1982–85	CJ, Scrambler①	Integral	Shims	.005–.009	Sleeve	17–25	17–25	Shims	④	④
1984–85	Grand Wagoneer①	Integral	Shims	.005–.009	Sleeve	17–25	17–25	Shims	④	④

①—Rear drive axle.
②—Front drive axle.
③—Slip fit in case (zero preload) plus .015   ④—Slip fit in case (zero preload) plus .004

inch additional preload added to gear tooth side shim pack.

inch additional preload added to each side.

Cooling System & Capacity Data

Year	Model or Engine	Cooling Capacity, Qts.		Radiator Cap Relief Pressure Lbs.	Thermo. Opening Temp.	Fuel Tank Gals.	Engine Oil Refill Qts. ①	Transmission Oil			Drive Axle Oil Pints
		Less A/C	With A/C					3 Speed Pints	4 & 5 Speed Pints	Auto. Trans. Qts. ②	
1979	6-258 CJ Models	10.5	10.5	15	195	14.8	5	2.8③	6.5③	⑤⑥	4.8④
	6-258 Cherokee	10.5	10.5	15	195	21.5	5	2.8③	6.5③	⑤⑥	3⑦
	6-258 J-10 Truck	10.5	10.5	15	195	18.2	5	2.8③	6.5③	⑤⑥	3⑦
	V8-304 CJ Models	13	13	15	195	14.8	4	2.8③	6.5③	⑤⑥	4.8④
	V8-360 Cherokee	14	14	15	195	21.5	4	2.8③	6.5③	⑤⑥	3⑦
	V8-360 Wagoneer	14	14	15	195	21.5	4	—	—	⑤⑥	3⑦
	V8-360 J-10 Truck	14	14	15	195	18.2	4	2.8③	6.5③	⑤⑥	3⑦
	V8-360 J-20 Truck	14	14	15	195	18.2	4	2.8③	6.5③	⑤⑥	6⑧
1980	4-151 CJ Models	7.8	7.8	15	195	14.8	3⑨	—	3⑩	—	4.8④
	6-258 CJ Models	10.5	10.5	15	195	14.8	5	—	⑩⑪	⑩⑫	4.8④
	6-258 Cherokee & Wagoneer	10.5	10.5	15	195	20.3	5	—	3.5⑬	⑩⑫	4.8⑧
	6-258 J-10 Truck	10.5	10.5	15	195	19	5	—	3.5⑬	⑩⑫	4.8⑧
	V8-304 CJ Models	13	13	15	195	14.8	4	—	3.5⑩	⑩⑫	4.8④
	V8-360 Cherokee & Wagoneer	14	14	15	195	20.3	4	—	3.5⑬	⑩⑫	4.8⑧
	V8-360 J-10 Truck	14	14	15	195	19	4	—	3.5⑬	⑩⑫	4.8⑧
	V8-360 J-20 Truck	14	14	15	195	19	4	—	6.5⑬	⑩⑫	6⑧
1981	4-151 CJ Models	7.8	7.8	15	195	14.8	3⑨	—	3⑩	⑩⑫	4.8④
	6-258 CJ Models	10.5	10.5	15	195	14.8	5	—	3⑩	⑩⑫	4.8④
	6-258 Cherokee & Wagoneer	10.5	10.5	15	195	20.3	5	—	3.5⑬	⑩⑫	4.8⑧
	6-258 J-10 Truck	10.5	10.5	15	195	19	5	—	3.5⑬	⑩⑫	4.8③
	V8-304 CJ Models	13	13	15	195	14.8	4	—	3⑩	⑩⑫	4.8④
	V8-360 Cherokee & Wagoneer	14	14	15	195	20.3	4	—	3.5⑬	⑩⑫	4.8③
	V8-360 J-10 Truck	14	14	15	195	19	4	—	3.5⑬	⑩⑫	4.8③
	V8-360 J-20 Truck	14	14	15	195	19	4	—	6.5⑬	⑩⑫	6⑧

continued

COOLING SYSTEM & CAPACITY DATA—Continued

Year	Model or Engine	Cooling Capacity, Qts.		Radiator Cap Relief Pressure Lbs.	Thermo. Opening Temp.	Fuel Tank Gals.	Engine Oil Refill Qts. [1]	Transmission Oil			Drive Axle Oil Pints
		Less A/C	With A/C					3 Speed Pints	4 & 5 Speed Pints	Auto. Trans. Qts. [2]	
1982	4-151 CJ & Scrambler	7.8	7.8	15	195	14.8[14]	3[9]	—	[10][15]	[10][12]	4.8[4]
	6-258 CJ & Scrambler	10.5	10.5	15	195	14.8[14]	5	—	[10][15]	[10][12]	4.8[4]
	6-258 Cherokee & Wagoneer	10.5	10.5	15	195	20.3	5	—	[13][15]	[10][12]	4.8[8]
	6-258 J-10 Truck	10.5	10.5	15	195	18.2	5	—	[13][15]	[10][12]	4.8[8]
	V8-360 Cherokee & Wagoneer	14	14	15	195	20.3	4	—	3.5[13]	[10][12]	4.8[8]
	V8-360 J-10 Truck	14	14	15	195	18.2	4	—	3.5[13]	[10][12]	4.8[8]
	V8-360 J-20 Truck	14	14	15	195	18.2	4	—	6.5[13]	[10][12]	6[8]
1983	4-150 CJ & Scrambler	—	—	15	195	14.8[14]	4[9]	—	[10][15]	[10][12]	4.8[4]
	4-151 CJ & Scrambler	7.8	7.8	15	195	14.8[14]	3[9]	—	[10][15]	[10][12]	4.8[4]
	6-258 CJ & Scrambler	10.5	10.5	15	195	14.8[14]	5	—	[10][15]	[10][12]	4.8[4]
	6-258 Cherokee & Wagoneer	10.5	10.5	15	195	20.3	5	—	[13][15]	[12][13]	4.8[16]
	6-258 J-10 Truck	10.5	10.5	15	195	18.2	5	—	[13][15]	[12][13]	4.8[16]
	V8-360 Cherokee & Wagoneer	14	14	15	195	20.3	4	—	3.5[13]	[12][13]	4.8[16]
	V8-360 J-10 Truck	14	14	15	195	18.2	4	—	3.5[13]	[12][13]	4.8[16]
	V8-360 J-20 Truck	14	14	15	195	18.2	4	—	6.5[13]	[12][13]	6[8]
1984–85	4-150 CJ & Scrambler	9	9	14	195	14.8[14]	4[9]	—	[10][15]	[10][12]	4.8[4]
	6-258 CJ & Scrambler	10.5	10.5	14	195	14.8[14]	6[9]	—	[10][15]	[10][12]	4.8[4]
	6-258 Grand Wagoneer	10.5	10.5	15	195	20.3	6[9]	—	3.5[13]	[12][13]	4.8[16]
	6-258 J-10 Truck	10.5	10.5	15	195	18.2	6[9]	—	3.5[13]	[12][13]	4.8[16]
	V8-360 Grand Wagoneer	14.8	14.8	15	195	20.3	5[9]	—	3.5[13]	[12][13]	4.8[16]
	V8-360 J-10 Truck	14.8	14.8	15	195	18.2	5[9]	—	3.5[13]	[12][13]	4.8[16]
	V8-360 J-20 Truck	14.8	14.8	15	195	18.2	5[9]	—	3.5[13]	[12][13]	6[16]

[1]—Add one quart with filter change, unless otherwise noted.
[2]—Approximate. Make final check with dipstick.
[3]—Transfer case, 3.2 pts.
[4]—Front axle, 2.5 pts.
[5]—Oil pan only, 5 qts.; total capacity, 11 qts.
[6]—Transfer case, Quadra Trac less reduction unit, 4 pts.; Quadra Trac w/ reduction unit, 5 pts.
[7]—Front & rear axle.
[8]—Front axle, 3 pts.
[9]—With or without filter change.
[10]—Transfer case, 4 pts.
[11]—SR-4 trans., 3 pts.; T-176 trans., 3.5 pts.
[12]—Oil pan only, 4¼ qts.; total capacity, 8½ qts.
[13]—Transfer case, 6 pts.
[14]—Optional gasoline tanks, 20 gals.
[15]—4 spd. trans., 3.5 pts.; 5 spd. trans., 4 pts.
[16]—Front axle, less Selec Trac, 3 pts.; w/ Selec Trac, 4.5 pts.

Electrical Section

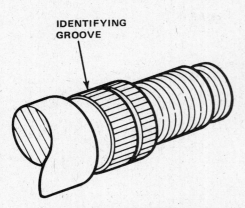

Fig. 1   Metric steering shaft identification

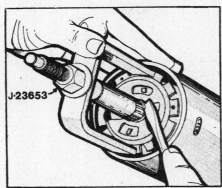

Fig. 2   Compressing lock plate & removing snap ring

Fig. 3   Lock cylinder removal

STARTER
REPLACE

1. Disconnect battery ground cable.
2. Disconnect cable from starter motor terminal.
3. Remove bracket and mounting bolts, starter motor and shims, as equipped.
4. Reverse procedure to install.

NOTE: On 4-150 engines, shims are used to properly center starter in relation to flywheel ring gear. Shims are available in .015 inch and .045 inch sizes, with .045 inch being the nominal design shim dimension. If noisy starter engagement is observed, shims should be removed or installed, as needed to correct the problem. However, the total shim pack thickness cannot exceed .090 inch.

IGNITION LOCK
REPLACE

1. Disconnect battery ground cable.
2. Apply tape to painted areas of steering column.
3. Remove steering wheel nut and washer.
4. Paint or scribe an alignment mark on steering wheel and steering column.
5. Using a suitable puller, remove steering wheel.
6. Using screwdrivers, pry lock plate cover from steering column.
7. Compress lock plate and remove steering shaft snap ring as follows:
   a. Check and identify steering shaft nut thread type. Metric type steering shafts have an identifying groove in the steering wheel locating splines, **Fig. 1.**
   b. If steering shaft is not a metric type, use lock plate compressor tool No.

J-23653 to compress lock plate and remove snap ring, **Fig. 2.**
   c. If the steering shaft is of the metric type, replace compressor tool bolt with metric forcing bolt J-23653-4 before installing compressor tool onto steering shaft.

NOTE: The lock plate is under strong spring tension. Do not attempt to remove the steering shaft snap ring without using the specified lock plate compressor tool.

8. Remove compressor tool and snap ring.
9. Remove lock plate, canceling cam, and upper bearing preload spring.
10. Remove turn signal lever.
11. Press hazard warning knob inward, turn knob counterclockwise and remove from steering shaft.
12. Remove turn signal switch attaching screws and position switch aside.
13. On manual transmission models, position lock cylinder into "ON" position. On automatic transmission models, position lock cylinder into "OFF-LOCK" position.
14. Using a thin blade screwdriver, compress lock cylinder retaining tab and remove lock cylinder from steering column, **Fig. 3.**
15. Reverse procedure to install.

IGNITION SWITCH
REPLACE

The ignition switch is mounted on the lower portion of the steering column and is connected to the steering lock by a remote control actuator rod.

REMOVAL

1. Disconnect battery ground cable.
2. Place ignition in "OFF-UNLOCK"

position and remove switch attaching screws.
3. Disconnect switch from control rod and electrical connector from switch, then remove switch from steering column.

INSTALLATION

1. Move switch slider to "ACCESSORY" position.
2. Move switch slider back 2 clicks to "OFF-UNLOCK" position.
3. Engage remote actuator rod into switch slider and position ignition switch onto steering column.

NOTE: Do not move switch slider when positioning ignition switch onto steering column jacket.

4. Install and torque switch retaining screws to 35 inch lbs.
5. Connect electrical connector onto switch.
6. Connect battery ground cable and check ignition switch for proper operation.

STOP LIGHT SWITCH
REPLACE

The stop light switch is retained in its mounting bracket by a spring clip which engages the threaded portion of the switch housing, **Fig. 4.** To remove the stop light switch, pull switch straight out of the mounting bracket and retainer.

NEUTRAL SAFETY SWITCH
REPLACE

1979-80 MODELS

1. Disconnect battery ground cable.
2. Disconnect electrical switch harness from switch.
3. Remove neutral safety switch attaching screws, then the switch from steering column.
4. Reverse procedure to install.

1981-85 MODELS

1. Disconnect battery ground cable.
2. Raise and support vehicle.
3. Disconnect electrical connector from switch and remove switch from transmission. Allow transmission fluid to drain into a suitable container.
4. Move selector lever to Park and Neutral positions. Check switch operating fingers for proper operation.
5. Reverse procedure to install. Correct transmission fluid level as required.

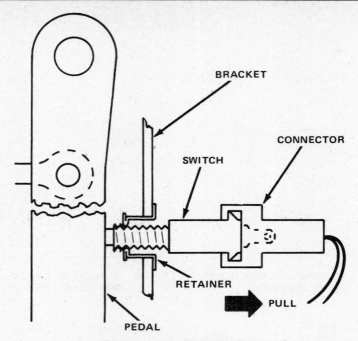

Fig. 4   Stop light switch

TURN SIGNAL SWITCH
REPLACE

1. Disconnect battery ground cable.
2. Remove horn center button.
3. Remove screws, bushing, receiver and spring.
4. Place alignment marks on steering wheel and steering column for installation.
5. Remove steering wheel retaining nut.
6. Using a suitable puller, remove steering wheel from column.
7. Pry cover from lock plate using 2 screwdrivers, then remove lock plate as follows:
   a. Identify steering shaft thread type. Metric shafts have an identifying groove on steering wheel locating splines as shown in **Fig. 1.**
   b. Mount lock plate compressor J-23653 or equivalent on steering shaft, using forcing bolt J-23653-4 on models with metric steering shafts.
   c. Tighten nut on tool to compress upper bearing preload spring, then remove and discard lock plate retaining ring, **Fig. 2.**
   d. Loosen nut on tool, then remove tool and lock plate.
8. Remove turn signal canceling cam, upper bearing preload spring and thrust washer from steering shaft.
9. Move turn signal actuating lever in right turn position and remove lever.
10. Depress hazard warning light switch and remove button by turning counterclockwise.
11. Remove turn signal electrical connector harness from column

mounting bracket and disconnect connector.
12. Remove turn signal switch attaching screws, then pull switch and electrical connector harness from steering column.
13. Reverse procedure to install.

HORN SOUNDER & STEERING WHEEL
REPLACE

NOTE: Some steering shafts have metric steering wheel nut threads. Check and identify shaft thread type before installing a replacement steering wheel nut. Metric steering shafts have an identifying groove in the steering wheel splines.

CJ & SCRAMBLER MODELS

1. Disconnect battery ground cable.
2. Ensure front wheels are in straight-ahead position.
3. Remove rubber boot, if equipped, and horn from steering wheel. Rotate button until lock tabs on button align with notches in contact cup, then pull upward and remove from steering wheel.
4. Remove steering wheel nut and washer.
5. Remove horn button receiver bushing attaching screws, then the bushing.
6. Remove horn button receiver and contact plate.
7. Paint or scribe an alignment mark on steering wheel and steering shaft for installation.
8. Using a suitable puller, remove steering wheel from steering shaft.

1979-83 CHEROKEE, WAGONEER & 1984-85 GRAND WAGONEER

1. Disconnect battery ground cable.
2. Ensure front wheels are in straight-ahead position.
3. On models with standard steering wheel, remove horn cover attaching screws from underside of steering wheel, then the cover. On models with sport type steering wheel, disconnect horn wire, then remove retainer and spring assembly.
4. Remove steering wheel nut and washer.
5. On models with sport type steering wheel, remove receiver bushing attaching screws, then the bushing, horn button receiver and contact plate.
6. Paint or scribe an alignment mark on steering wheel and steering shaft for installation.
7. Using a suitable puller, remove steering wheel from steering shaft.
8. Reverse procedure to install.

INSTRUMENT CLUSTER
REPLACE

CJ & SCRAMBLER MODELS

1. Disconnect battery ground cable.
2. On models equipped with air conditioning, remove evaporator assembly bolts, then lower evaporator assembly

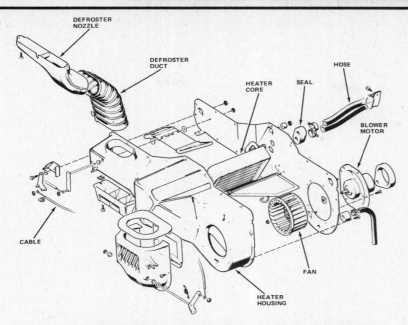

Fig. 5 Heater assembly. CJ & Scrambler models

from instrument panel.
3. Disconnect speedometer cable from cluster.
4. Remove instrument cluster retaining screws, then the cluster.
5. Reverse procedure to install.

1979–83 CHEROKEE, WAGONEER & 1984–85 GRAND WAGONEER

1. Disconnect battery ground cable.
2. Disconnect speedometer cable from cluster.
3. Remove cluster retaining screws, tilt top of cluster outward, then disconnect electrical connectors from cluster and ammeter.

NOTE: Mark installation position of ammeter wires, if equipped, to ensure proper assembly.

4. Disconnect electrical connectors and vacuum hoses from heater assembly.
5. Disconnect blend air door control cable.
6. Remove cluster from instrument panel.
7. Reverse procedure to install.

W/S WIPER MOTOR
REPLACE

CJ & SCRAMBLER MODELS

1. Disconnect battery ground cable.
2. Remove necessary top components from windshield frame.
3. Remove right and left windshield hold down knobs, then fold windshield down.

4. On models without crash pad assembly, remove wiper motor cover.
5. Remove left access hold cover.
6. Disconnect drive link from left wiper pivot.
7. Disconnect wiper motor electrical connector from switch.
8. Remove wiper motor retaining bolts, then the wiper motor.
9. Reverse procedure to install.

1979–83 CHEROKEE, WAGONEER & 1984–85 GRAND WAGONEER

1. Disconnect battery ground cable.
2. Remove bolts retaining wiper motor adapter plate to dash panel.
3. Disconnect wiper motor electrical connector from motor.
4. Pull wiper motor and linkage outward to expose drive link to crank pin retaining clip.
5. Using a suitable screwdriver, raise locking tab up and slide retaining clip off of crank pin.
6. Remove wiper motor assembly from vehicle.
7. Reverse procedure to install.

W/S WIPER SWITCH
REPLACE

1. On models equipped with air conditioning, remove screws retaining evaporator assembly to instrument panel and lower assembly.
2. Remove switch control knob, nut and switch from instrument panel.
3. Mark wire color locations on switch, then disconnect electrical connector from wiper switch.
4. Reverse procedure to install.

RADIO
REPLACE

CJ & SCRAMBLER MODELS

1. Disconnect battery ground cable.
2. On models equipped with air conditioning, remove screws retaining evaporator assembly to instrument panel and lower assembly.
3. Remove radio control knobs, nuts and bezel.
4. Remove radio support bracket from instrument panel.
5. Pull and tilt radio downward toward steering wheel.
6. Disconnect antenna lead, speaker and power electrical connectors.
7. Remove radio from instrument panel.
8. Reverse procedure to install.

1979–83 CHEROKEE, WAGONEER & 1984–85 GRAND WAGONEER

1. Disconnect battery ground cable.
2. Remove glove compartment liner and lock striker.
3. Disconnect microphone lead connector from radio, if equipped.
4. Disconnect antenna lead(s).
5. Disconnect power wire connector from fuse panel.
6. Disconnect speaker electrical connectors from radio.
7. Remove rear support bracket from radio.
8. Remove radio control knobs and nuts.
9. Push radio back to clear instrument panel and remove radio through glove compartment.
10. Reverse procedure to install.

HEATER CORE
REPLACE

CJ & SCRAMBLER MODELS

1. Disconnect battery ground cable and drain cooling system.
2. Disconnect heater core hoses.
3. Disconnect damper door control cables.
4. Disconnect blower motor electrical connector.
5. Disconnect water drain hose and defroster hose.
6. Remove nuts retaining heater housing assembly to instrument panel. Remove heater housing assembly by tilting heater downward to disengage it from air inlet duct and pulling toward rear of vehicle.
7. Remove heater core from heater housing, **Fig. 5.**
8. Reverse procedure to install.

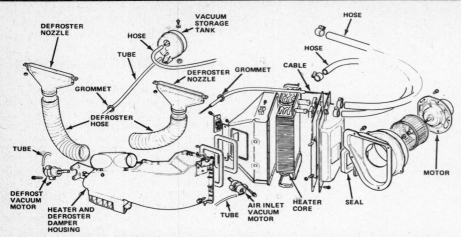

Fig. 6   Heater assembly. 1979—83 Cherokee, Wagoneer & 1984—85 Grand Wagoneer

1979—83 CHEROKEE, WAGONEER & 1984—85 GRAND WAGONEER

1. Disconnect battery ground cable.
2. Drain cooling system, then disconnect hose from heater.
3. Disconnect temperature control cable from blend air door.
4. Disconnect resistor harness electrical connector.
5. Remove heater core housing to cowl panel retaining nuts, then the housing assembly.
6. Separate heater halves, **Fig. 6**.
7. Remove heater core retaining screws, then the heater core.
8. Reverse procedure to install.

BLOWER MOTOR
REPLACE

CJ & SCRAMBLER MODELS

Less Air Conditioning
1. Disconnect battery ground cable.
2. Remove heater core as described previously.
3. Remove blower motor assembly retaining screws, then the blower motor.
4. Reverse procedure to install.

With Air Conditioning
1. Disconnect battery ground cable.
2. Remove screws retaining evaporator assembly to instrument panel and position aside.
3. Disconnect blower motor electrical connector.
4. Remove blower motor retaining screws, then the blower motor.
5. Reverse procedure to install.

1979—83 CHEROKEE, WAGONEER & 1984—85 GRAND WAGONEER

Less Air Conditioning
1. Disconnect battery ground cable.

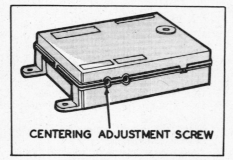

Fig. 8   Centering adjusting screw location. 1981—85 all except 1981 models with V8 engine

2. Remove blower motor to housing retaining screws, then the blower motor.
3. Reverse procedure to install.

With Air Conditioning
1. Disconnect battery ground cable.
2. Remove screws retaining evaporator assembly to instrument panel and position aside.
3. Disconnect blower motor electrical connector.
4. Remove blower motor to housing retaining screws, then the blower motor.
5. Reverse procedure to install.

SPEED CONTROL
ADJUST

1979—80 ALL & 1981 MODELS WITH V8 ENGINE

Before adjusting bellows chain, the carburetor throttle must be at idle position, ignition off and choke valve fully open.

Ensure bellows bracket screws are tight. Adjust chain at bellows hook, one bead at

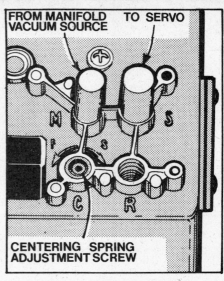

Fig. 7   Centering spring adjustment. 1979—80 all & 1981 models with V8 engine

a time until a free pin fit is obtained at throttle lever. After adjustment, there should be a slight deflection in the chain without moving either the throttle lever or bellows. Bend the bellows hook tabs together. The chain must be free in the hook after bending the bellows hook tabs.

Centering Spring Adjustment

NOTE: The centering spring adjustment is extremely sensitive and eccentric must never be turned more than 1/8 turn in either direction.

If speed control system engages at 2 or more mph higher than selected speed, turn centering spring adjustment screw (C) toward (S) 1/32 inch or less, **Fig. 7**. If engagement speed is below selected speed, turn centering spring adjustment screw (C) toward (F) 1/32 inch or less.

1981—85 ALL EXCEPT 1981 MODELS WITH V8 ENGINE

Centering Adjustment
This adjustment is made by turning the centering adjusting screw on the regulator, **Fig. 8**. If speed control engages at 2 or more mph higher than selected speed, turn centering adjusting screw counterclockwise a small amount. If engagement speed is 2 or more mph below selected speed, turn centering adjusting screw clockwise a small amount. Check for proper centering adjustment on a level road after each adjustment.

Vacuum Dump Or Vent Valve
While holding brake pedal in the depressed position, move vacuum dump valve toward pedal bracket as far as possible, then release brake pedal.

ENGINE MOUNTS
REPLACE

Removal or replacement of any cushion can be accomplished by supporting the weight of the engine or transmission at the area of the cushion to be replaced. If it is necessary to remove front mounts and/or crossmember an engine support fixture can be fabricated as shown in **Fig. 1,** and installed prior to raising vehicle.

ENGINE
REPLACE

1. Disconnect cables from battery, remove battery and drain cooling system.
2. Mark position of hood hinges for assembly, disconnect electrical connector to hood lamp if equipped, then remove hood.
3. Disconnect electrical connectors from alternator, ignition coil and distributor, oil pressure switch and starter motor, then separate CEC system engine harness connector.
4. Disconnect supply pipe to fuel pump and plug pipe and pump fitting.
5. Remove air cleaner and disconnect engine ground strap.
6. Disconnect vacuum purge and bowl vent hoses from canister, throttle linkage, idle speed control and MC solenoid electrical connectors, fuel return hose (at filter), and remove vacuum check valve from brake booster.
7. Disconnect coolant temperature and oxygen sensor electrical connectors.
8. Disconnect coolant hoses from radiator, rear of intake manifold and thermostat housing.
9. Remove fan shroud and radiator mounting bolts, then the fan shroud and radiator assembly.
10. Remove fan and spacer or thermostatic clutch, as equipped.
11. Install 5/16 × 1/4 inch SAE bolt through fan pulley and thread into water pump in order to maintain pulley alignment as crankshaft is rotated.
12. On models with power steering, disconnect hoses from steering gear, drain fluid into suitable container, then plug hoses and open fittings.
13. On models with A/C (aftermarket system), disconnect hoses or remove compressor, following manufacturer's instructions.
14. Raise and support vehicle and remove starter motor, flywheel housing cover and front motor mount through bolts.
15. Disconnect exhaust pipe from manifold, remove upper flywheel housing bolts and loosen lower bolts.
16. Lower vehicle and attach suitable lift-

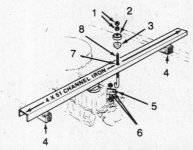

1 - 9/16-Inch – 12 Nuts
2 - Upper Trunnion Bearing
3 - Pivot or Sleeve
4 - 2 × 2 × 6-Inch Hardwood Block
5 - 1¼-Inch Angle Iron
6 - 1/2-Inch Holes
7 - 1-Inch Hole
8 - 9/16-Inch – 12 Trunnion

Fig. 1   Engine support tool fabrication dimensions

ing equipment to engine.
17. Raise engine off mounts, place suitable support under flywheel housing and remove lower flywheel housing to engine bolts.
18. Separate engine from flywheel housing and remove from vehicle.
19. Reverse procedure to install.

CYLINDER HEAD
REPLACE

1. Disconnect battery ground cable, drain coolant and disconnect hoses from thermostat housing.
2. Remove air cleaner, then the rocker cover, using following procedure:
   a. Remove PCV hose, shut-off valve and PCV valve.
   b. Disconnect fuel pipe from fuel pump, loosen carburetor fitting and position pipe aside.
   c. Disconnect necessary vacuum and AIR hoses, noting position for assembly.
   d. Remove rocker cover nuts and the cover, breaking RTV seal with suitable putty knife or cutter.

NOTE: Do not pry on cover until seal has been completely broken, and only pry cover at locations marked, or cover will be damaged.

3. Remove rocker arm, bridge and pivot assemblies, then the push rods, keeping all components in order for assembly.

NOTE: Loosen retaining bolts alternately, 1 turn at a time, to avoid damaging bridges.

4. Disconnect power steering pump

bracket and position aside.
5. Remove intake and exhaust manifolds as outlined.
6. Disconnect plug wires, temperature sensor lead and battery ground strap.
7. Remove cylinder head bolts, cylinder head and gasket, **Fig. 2.**
8. Reverse procedure to install, noting the following:
   a. Apply suitable sealing compound to head gasket and install gasket over dowel pins with "TOP" mark facing up.
   b. Install head and retaining bolts and torque bolts to specifications in sequence shown in **Fig. 3.**

NOTE: Coat threads of stud bolt in No. 8 position with suitable sealer and only torque this bolt to 75 ft. lbs.

   c. Apply continuous bead of RTV sealer, 3/16 inch wide, to rocker cover, install cover and torque nuts to specifications.
   d. Remove temperature sensor and leave removed until cooling system is filled, allowing air to escape from block and head.

INTAKE MANIFOLD
REPLACE

NOTE: Mark installation position of all components, hoses and wiring prior to removal to aid reassembly.

1. Disconnect battery ground cable, drain coolant and remove air cleaner.
2. Disconnect fuel line, air horn vent hose, idle speed control hose and electrical connector, choke heater connector and throttle linkages from carburetor.
3. Disconnect coolant hoses from intake manifold.
4. Disconnect vacuum hoses from vacuum advance control valve and EGR valve, and electrical connectors from coolant sensor and intake manifold heater.
5. Remove carburetor from manifold.
6. On models with power steering, remove mounting bracket and position pump aside without disconnecting hoses.
7. On all models, disconnect EGR tube from intake manifold, then remove mounting bolts and the manifold, **Fig. 2.**
8. Reverse procedure to install, using new gaskets on manifold and carburetor, and torque manifold bolts to specifications in sequence shown in **Fig. 4.**

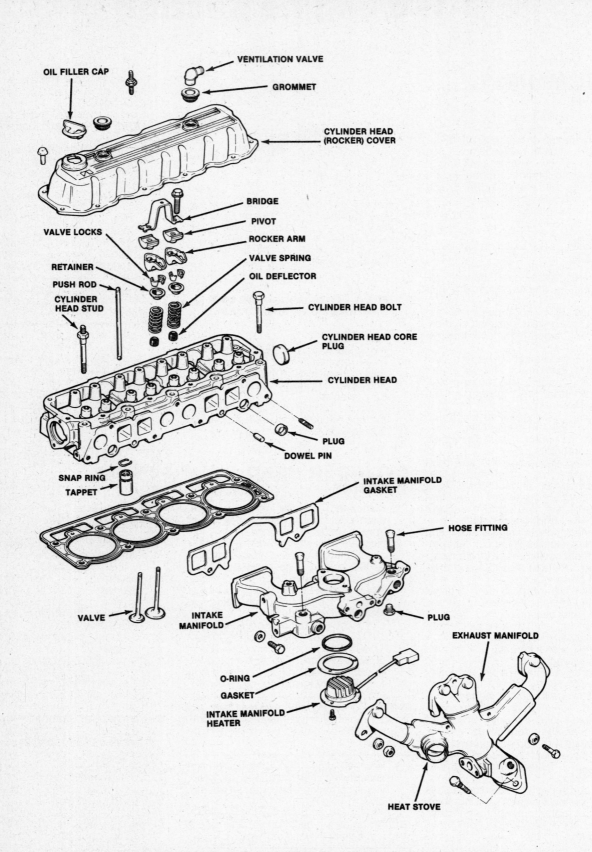

OIL FILLER CAP

VENTILATION VALVE

GROMMET

CYLINDER HEAD (ROCKER) COVER

BRIDGE

PIVOT

VALVE LOCKS

ROCKER ARM

VALVE SPRING

RETAINER

OIL DEFLECTOR

PUSH ROD

CYLINDER HEAD STUD

CYLINDER HEAD BOLT

CYLINDER HEAD CORE PLUG

CYLINDER HEAD

PLUG

DOWEL PIN

SNAP RING

TAPPET

INTAKE MANIFOLD GASKET

HOSE FITTING

VALVE

INTAKE MANIFOLD

PLUG

EXHAUST MANIFOLD

O-RING

GASKET

INTAKE MANIFOLD HEATER

HEAT STOVE

Fig. 2 Cylinder head and manifold assemblies exploded view

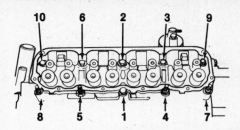

Fig. 3 Cylinder head tightening sequence

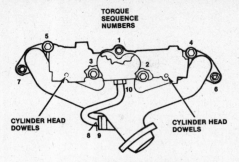

Fig. 4 Intake manifold tightening sequence

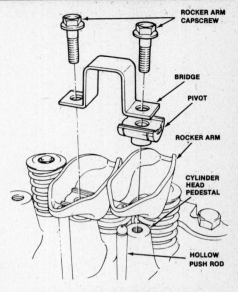

Fig. 5 Rocker arm, bridge & pivot assembly

Fig. 6 Hydraulic lifter removal

EXHAUST MANIFOLD
REPLACE

1. Remove intake manifold as outlined.
2. Disconnect EGR tube and exhaust pipe from exhaust manifold.
3. Disconnect oxygen sensor electrical connector and remove sensor from exhaust pipe.
4. Remove manifold mounting nuts and the manifold, **Fig. 2.**
5. Reverse procedure to install.

VALVE ARRANGEMENT
FRONT TO REAR

4-150 . . . . E-I-I-E-E-I-I-E

VALVE LIFT SPECS.

Engine	Year	Intake	Exhaust
4-150	1983–85	.424	.424

VALVE TIMING SPECS.
INTAKE OPENS BEFORE TDC

Engine	Year	Degrees
4-150	1983–85	12

ROCKER ARMS
REPLACE

1. Remove rocker arm cover attaching screws, then remove rocker arm cover as outlined in "Cylinder Head, Replace."

NOTE: RTV sealant is used between rocker arm cover and cylinder head mating surfaces. To avoid damaging rocker arm cover, do not pry cover upward until seal has been completely broken. When prying cover upward, pry only in areas marked "Pry Here," which are located near rocker arm cover bolt holes.

2. Alternately loosen the rocker arm cap screws one turn at a time to prevent damage to bridge, **Fig. 5.**
3. After removing rocker arm cap screws, remove bridge, pivots, rocker arms and push rods.

NOTE: Tag all components so they can be reinstalled in the same position as removed.

4. Reverse procedure to install. When installing rocker arm cap screws, tighten each screw alternately and evenly approximately one turn at a time to prevent damage to bridge.

VALVE GUIDES

The valve guides are an integral part of the cylinder head. If valve system to guide clearance is excessive, the guide should be reamed to the next oversize and the approximate oversize valve installed. Valves are available in standard size and oversizes of .003 inch and .015 inch.

VALVE LIFTERS
REPLACE

Valve lifters can be removed after removing rocker arm assemblies and push rods, using tool J-21884 or equivalent, **Fig. 6.** Failure of hydraulic lifters used in these engines, **Fig. 7,** is generally caused by dirt or insufficient lubrication due to low oil levels, oil contamination or foaming.

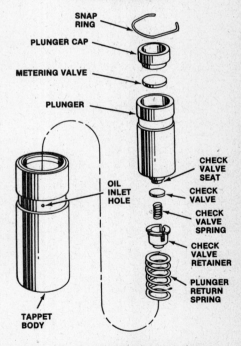

Fig. 7 Hydraulic valve lifter assembly

TIMING CASE COVER, TIMING CHAIN & GEARS
REPLACE

Removal

1. Disconnect battery ground cable and remove accessory drive belts.
2. Remove engine cooling fan, fan hub and fan shroud.
3. Remove crankshaft damper hub bolt, then the damper, using suitable puller.

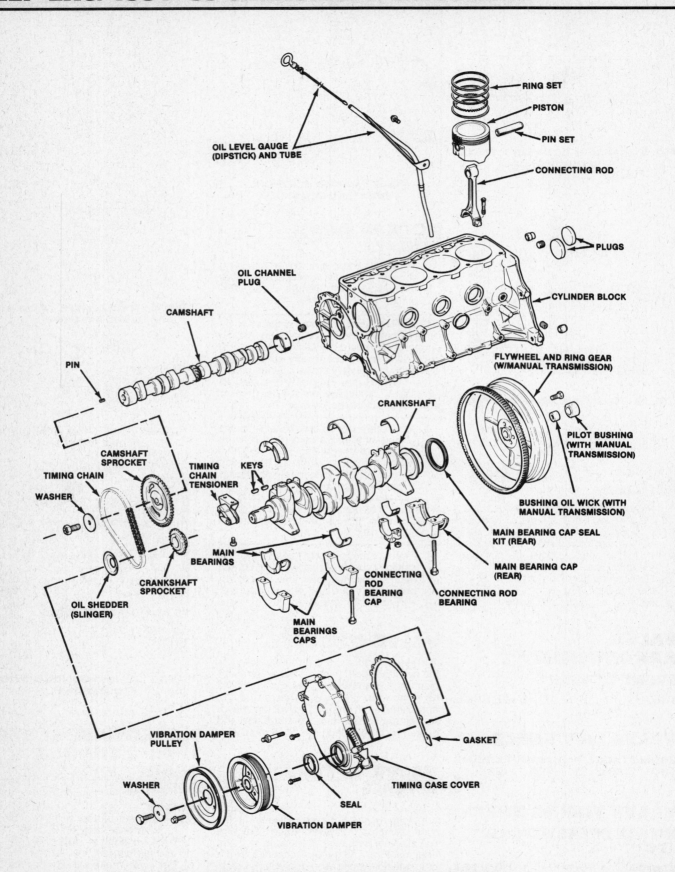

Fig. 8 Cylinder block components exploded view

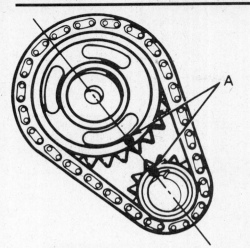

Fig. 9   Valve timing mark alignment

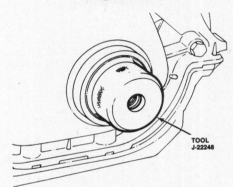

Fig. 12   Using tool J-22248 to align timing case cover

4. Remove alternator bracket assembly and position alternator aside.
5. Remove bolts securing oil pan to timing cover and timing cover to block, then the timing cover and crankshaft oil slinger, **Fig. 8.**
6. Rotate crankshaft until zero degree mark on crankshaft sprocket is aligned with timing mark on camshaft sprocket (A), **Fig. 9.**
7. Remove camshaft sprocket retaining bolt, then remove timing chain and sprockets as an assembly.
8. Cut off oil pan side gaskets flush with engine block and remove ends of gaskets.
9. Pry oil seal from timing cover using suitable lever.
10. Clean all old gasket material from block, timing cover and front of oil pan.

Installation

1. Rotate lever on timing chain tensioner, **Fig. 10,** to unlocked position, pull tensioner block toward tensioner to compress spring, then rotate lever up to locked position.
2. Position cam and crankshaft sprockets in timing chain with timing marks aligned, then mount assembly on engine. Install camshaft sprocket retaining bolt and torque bolt to 50 ft. lbs.

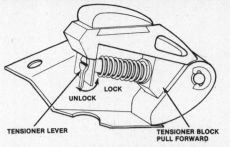

Fig. 10   Positioning timing chain tensioner in the unlock position

NOTE: To verify proper installation of timing chain and gears, rotate crankshaft to position camshaft sprocket timing mark approximately at 1:00 o'clock position, which should position the tooth adjacent to the crankshaft sprocket mark in mesh with the chain at the 3:00 o'clock position, **Fig. 11.** With sprockets aligned in this position, count the number of chain pins between the timing marks on both sprockets. If assembly is properly installed, there will be 20 pins between the timing marks.

3. Apply suitable sealing compound to both sides of timing cover gasket and position gasket on block.
4. Cut end tabs off replacement oil pan side gaskets to correspond to those cut from original gasket, then cement end tabs to oil pan.
5. Coat front pan seal end tabs with RTV sealer and apply sealer to pan side rail gasket joints, then install end seal on timing case cover.
6. Apply engine oil to the end seal/oil pan contact surface, install oil slinger, then position timing cover on block and install retaining bolts hand tight.
7. Install alignment tool J-22248 or equivalent in the timing cover seal opening, **Fig. 12,** then torque cover to block bolts to 5 ft. lbs. and oil pan bolts to 7 ft. lbs.
8. Remove alignment tool from cover, mount new oil seal on tool with seal lip facing out and coat outer surface of seal with suitable sealer.
9. Lightly coat crankshaft with engine oil, position tool over end of crankshaft and install screw J-9163-2 into tool and thread screw into crankshaft, **Fig. 13.**
10. Hold screw and tighten nut until body of installer contacts timing cover, then remove tool assembly.
11. Reverse remaining procedure to complete installation.

CAMSHAFT
REPLACE

1. Remove distributor, ignition wires and fuel pump.
2. Remove radiator from vehicle. If equipped with A/C, remove condenser and receiver with refrigerant lines at-

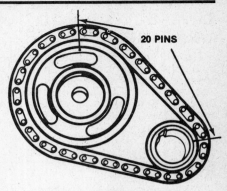

Fig. 11   Timing chain installation check

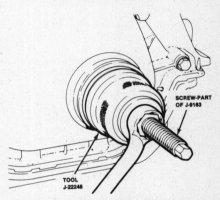

Fig. 13   Installing timing case cover front seal

tached and position out of way.
3. Remove cylinder head and valve lifters.
4. Remove timing chain cover.
5. Rotate crankshaft until timing marks on sprockets are aligned, **Fig. 9.**
6. Remove sprockets and chain.
7. Remove front bumper or grille as required to remove camshaft.
8. Remove camshaft.
9. Reverse procedure to install.

PISTON & ROD ASSEMBLE

Pistons are marked with an arrow on the top perimeter, **Fig. 14.** When installing piston in engine, the arrow must face toward front of engine. Always assemble rods and caps with oil spurt holes facing camshaft. Check side clearance between connecting rod and crankshaft journal. Clearance should be .010 to .019 inch.

MAIN BEARINGS

The main bearing journal size (diameter) is identified by a color coded paint mark on adjacent cheek toward flanged (rear) end of crankshaft, except for rear main journal which is on crankshaft rear flange. Color codes used to indicate journal and corresponding bearing sizes are listed in **Figs. 15 and 16.**

CONNECTING ROD BEARINGS

The connecting rod journal is identified by a color coded paint mark on adjacent cheek or counterweight toward flanged (rear) end of crankshaft. Color codes used to indicate journal sizes and corresponding bearing sizes are listed in **Fig. 17**.

OIL PAN
REPLACE

1. Disconnect battery ground cable, raise vehicle and support at side sills.
2. Drain engine oil, then remove starter motor and flywheel housing cover.
3. Remove oil pan retaining screws, then lower pan and slide to the rear to gain clearance for removal.
4. Clean all old gasket material and sealer from oil pan, engine block and timing cover.
5. Install new oil pan front seal into timing case cover and liberally apply RTV sealer to recesses in ends of seal.
6. Install rear pan seal into recess in rear main bearing cap, ensuring that seal is fully seated.
7. If gasket is being used on pan side rails, coat both sides of gaskets with suitable "Hi-Tack" sealer and cement gaskets to block side rails, ensuring that gasket tabs are properly engaged in seal recesses.

NOTE: If RTV sealer is used in place of pan rail gaskets, apply a continuous bead of sealer to pan side rails, ³⁄₁₆ inch wide, circling all bolt holes.

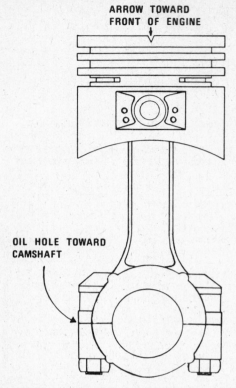

ARROW TOWARD FRONT OF ENGINE

OIL HOLE TOWARD CAMSHAFT

Fig. 14   Piston & rod assembly

7. Install oil pan and torque retaining bolts to 11 ft. lbs.
8. Reverse remaining procedure to complete installation.

OIL PUMP
REPLACE

1. Drain crankcase, then remove oil pan.
2. Remove bolts attaching oil pump to cylinder block, then remove oil pump and gasket.

NOTE: Do not disturb positioning of oil pump strainer and tube. If tube is moved, a replacement tube and screen assembly must be installed.

3. Reverse procedure to install. Torque short attaching bolts to 10 ft. lbs. and long attaching bolts to 17 ft. lbs.

OIL PUMP SERVICE

1. Remove oil pump cover retaining screws, then remove cover from pump body.
2. Check gear end clearance as follows:
   a. Place straight edge across ends of gears and pump body, **Fig. 18**.
   b. Check clearance using a suitable feeler gauge.
   c. Clearance should be .002 to .006 inch. If clearance is not within limits, replace oil pump assembly.
3. Check gear to pump body clearance as follows:
   a. Insert a suitable feeler gauge between gear tooth and pump body, **Fig. 19**.
   b. Clearance should be .002 to .004 inch. If clearance is not within limits, replace idler gear, idler shaft and drive gear assembly.
4. If pressure relief valve is to be checked, move pickup tube and

Crankshaft No. 1 Main Bearing Journal Color Codes and Diameter in Inches (mm)	Cylinder Block No. 1 Main Bearing Bore Color Code and Size in Inches (mm)		Bearing Insert Color Code	
			Upper Insert Size	Lower Insert Size
Yellow — 2.5001 to 2.4996 (Standard) (63.5025 to 63.4898 mm)	Yellow —	2.6910 to 2.6915 (68.3514 to 68.3641 mm)	Yellow — Standard	Yellow — Standard
	Black —	2.6915 to 2.6920 (68.3641 to 68.3768 mm)	Yellow — Standard	Black — 0.001-inch Undersize (0.025 mm)
Orange — 2.4996 to 2.4991 (0.0005 Undersize) (63.4898 to 63.4771 mm)	Yellow —	2.6910 to 2.6915 (68.3514 to 68.3641 mm)	Yellow — Standard	Black — 0.001-inch Undersize — (0.001 mm)
	Black —	2.6915 to 2.6920 (68.3461 to 68.3768 mm)	Black — 0.001-inch Undersize (0.025 mm)	Black — 0.001-inch Undersize (0.025 mm)
Black — 2.4991 to 2.4986 (0.001 Undersize) (63.4771 to 63.4644 mm)	Yellow —	2.6910 to 2.6915 (68.3514 to 68.3641 mm)	Black — 0.001-inch Undersize — (0.025 mm)	Black — 0.001-inch Undersize (0.025 mm)
	Black —	2.6915 to 2.6920 (68.3461 to 68.3768 mm)	Black — 0.001-inch Undersize (0.025 mm)	Green — 0.002-inch Undersize (0.051 mm)
Green — 2.4986 to 2.4981 (0.0015 Undersize) (63.4644 to 63.4517 mm)	Yellow —	2.6910 to 2.6915 (68.3514 to 68.3641 mm)	Black — 0.001-inch Undersize — (0.025 mm)	Green — 0.002-inch Undersize (0.051 mm)
Red — 2.4901 to 2.4896 (0.010 Undersize) (63.2485 to 63.2358 mm)	Yellow —	2.6910 to 2.6915 (68.3514 to 68.3641 mm)	Red — 0.010-inch Undersize (0.254 mm)	Red — 0.010-inch Undersize (0.254 mm)

Fig. 15   Main bearing selection chart. 4-150 No. 1 main bearing

Crankshaft Main Bearing Journal 2-3-4-5 Color Code and Diameter in Inches (Journal Size)	Bearing Insert Color Code	
	Upper Insert Size	Lower Insert Size
Yellow — 2.5001 to 2.4996 (Standard) (63.5025 to 63.4898 mm)	Yellow — Standard	Yellow — Standard
Orange — 2.4996 to 2.4991 (0.0005 Undersize) (63.4898 to 63.4771 mm)	Yellow — Standard	Black — 0.001-inch Undersize (0.025mm)
Black — 2.4991 to 2.4986 (0.001 Undersize) (63.4771 to 63.4644 mm)	Black — 0.001-inch Undersize (0.025 mm)	Black — 0.001-inch Undersize (0.025 mm)
Green — 2.4986 to 2.4981 (0.0015 Undersize) (63.4644 to 63.4517 mm)	Black — 0.001-inch Undersize (0.025 mm)	Green — 0.002-inch Undersize (0.051 mm)
Red — 2.4901 to 2.4896 (0.010 Undersize) (63.2485 to 63.2358 mm)	Red — 0.010-inch Undersize (0.054 mm)	Red — 0.010-inch Undersize (0.254 mm)

Fig. 16   Main bearing selection chart. 4-150 Nos. 2, 3, 4, 5 main bearings

Connecting Rod Bearing Journal 2-3-4-5 Color Code and Diameter in Inches (Journal Size)	Bearing Insert Color Code	
	Upper Insert Size	Lower Insert Size
Yellow — 2.0955 to 2.0948 (53.2257 - 53.2079 mm) (Standard) Orange — 2.0948 to 2.0941 (53.2079 - 53.1901 mm) (0.0007 Undersize) Black — 2.0941 to 2.0943 (53.1901 to 53.1723 mm) (0.0014 Undersize) Red — 2.0855 to 2.0848 (53.9717 to 53.9539 mm) (0.010 Undersize)	Yellow — Standard Yellow — Standard Black — 0.001-inch (0.025 mm) Undersize Red — 0.010-inch (0.254 mm) Undersize	Yellow — Standard Black — 0.001-inch (0.025 mm) Undersize Black — 0.001-inch (0.025 mm) Undersize Red — 0.010-inch (0.245 mm) Undersize

Fig. 17   Connecting rod bearing chart. 4-150

screen assembly out of way. Remove spring retainer, spring and oil pressure relief valve plunger. Check pressure relief valve components for binding and clean or replace as necessary. After reinstalling relief valve components, install a replacement pickup tube and screen assembly.

NOTE: When replacing relief valve plunger, ensure correct size is installed. Plungers are available in standard size and .010 inch oversize.

5. If a replacement pickup tube is to be installed, apply a light coating of Permatex No. 2 sealant or equivalent to end of tube. Install pickup tube and screen using tool No. J-21882, **Fig. 20.**
6. Before installing pump cover, fill pump with petroleum jelly.
7. When installing pump cover, torque attaching screws to 70 inch lbs.

BELT TENSION DATA

	New	Used Lbs.
V Type Belts		
A/C Comp.	125–155	90–155
Air Pump		
Less Power Steer.	125–155	90–115
W/Power Steer.	65–75	60–70
Alternator	125–155	90–115
Power Steer.	125–155	90–115
Serpentine Type Belt	180–200	140–160

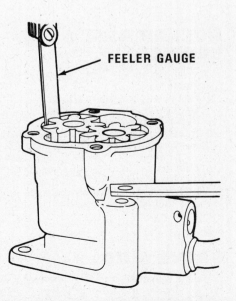

Fig. 19   Checking oil pump gear to body clearance

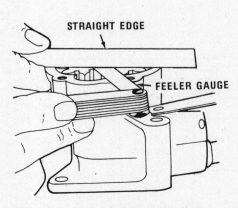

Fig. 18   Checking oil pump gear end clearance

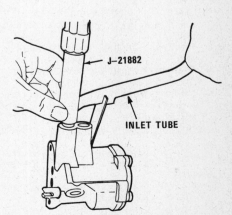

Fig. 20   Installing oil pump pickup screen & tube assembly

WATER PUMP
REPLACE

1. Drain cooling system.
2. Disconnect radiator and heater hoses from water pump.
3. Remove drive belts.
4. If equipped, remove fan shroud attaching screws, then remove fan and fan shroud.
5. Remove water pump attaching bolts, then remove water pump and gasket.
6. Reverse procedure to install. Torque water pump attaching bolts to 13 ft. lbs.

FUEL PUMP
REPLACE

1. Disconnect fuel lines from pump.
2. Remove retaining screws and fuel pump.
3. Remove all gasket material from the pump and block gasket surfaces. Apply sealer to both sides of new gasket.
4. Position gasket on pump flange and hold pump in position against its mounting surface. Make sure rocker arm is riding on camshaft eccentric.
5. Press pump tight against its mounting. Install retaining screws and tighten them alternately.
6. Connect fuel lines. Then operate engine and check for leaks.

NOTE: When installing pump, crank engine to place camshaft eccentric in a position as to place the least amount of tension on fuel pump rocker arm. This will ease pump installation.

4-151 Engine Section

ENGINE MOUNTS
REPLACE

NOTE: Remove fan shroud to radiator attaching screws to prevent damage to shroud.

Removal or replacement of any cushion, **Fig. 1** can be accomplished by supporting the weight of the engine at the area of the cushion to be replaced.

ENGINE
REPLACE

1. Disconnect battery ground cable and body ground strap from firewall.
2. Remove air cleaner assembly.
3. Raise and support vehicle.
4. Disconnect electrical connector from oxygen sensor and exhaust pipe from exhaust manifold.
5. Disconnect battery cable and solenoid electrical connector from starter motor.
6. Remove starter motor attaching bolts, rear bracket nut, then the starter motor.
7. Disconnect electrical connectors from distributor and oil pressure sending unit.
8. Remove engine mount attaching nuts.
9. Remove hydraulic clutch slave cylinder and flywheel inspection plate.
10. Remove transmission clutch housing to engine attaching bolts.
11. Lower vehicle.
12. Support transmission using a suitable floor jack.
13. Mark and disconnect all vacuum hoses and electrical connector from engine.
14. Remove inlet and outlet heater hoses from heater core.
15. Drain radiator and remove lower radiator hose.
16. Remove upper radiator hose, fan shroud and radiator from vehicle.
17. Disconnect and cap power steering lines at power steering pump.
18. Install suitable engine lifting equipment to engine lifting eyes.
19. Remove engine from vehicle.

NOTE: If necessary, raise transmission slightly to provide a smooth engine from transmission separation.

20. Reverse procedure to install.

CYLINDER HEAD
REPLACE

1. Disconnect battery ground cable, then the cylinder head cover.
2. Drain coolant from radiator and engine block.
3. Disconnect electrical connector from oxygen sensor and exhaust pipe from exhaust manifold.
4. Mark and disconnect all vacuum hoses from cylinder head.
5. Remove alternator and position aside, then disconnect fuel line from carburetor.
6. Disconnect rear heater and upper radiator hoses from cylinder head.
7. Remove power steering pump and bracket and position aside. Do not disconnect power steering hoses.
8. Remove dipstick, rocker arm and push rod assemblies.

NOTE: Tag rocker arms and push rods so they can be installed in their original positions.

9. Remove cylinder head attaching bolts.
10. Remove cylinder head by inserting a suitable tool into alternator bracket and prying upward.
11. Reverse procedure to install. On 1980 models, torque cylinder head bolts to 92 ft. lbs. in sequence shown in **Fig. 2**. On 1981–83 models, torque cylinder head bolts to 92 ft. lbs. in sequence shown in **Fig. 3**.

VALVE ARRANGEMENT
FRONT TO REAR

4-151 . . . . I-E-I-E-I-E-I

CAM LOBE LIFT SPECS

4-151 230

VALVE TIMING
INTAKE OPENS BEFORE TDC

4-151	1980	33 Degrees
4-151	1981–83	25 Degrees

ROCKER ARM SERVICE

To remove rocker arm assembly, proceed as follows:
1. Remove cylinder head cover.
2. Remove rocker arm nut and ball.
3. Remove rocker arm.
4. Reverse procedure to install. Clean all parts using a suitable cleaning solvent. Blow dry parts using compressed air. Inspect the pivot contact surface of each rocker arm, pivot ball and push rod assembly. Replace any part that has been found unserviceable.

VALVE GUIDES

Valves with oversize stems are available for both intake and exhaust valves. Valve guides should be reamed and replacement oversize valves installed whenever clearances exceed specification.

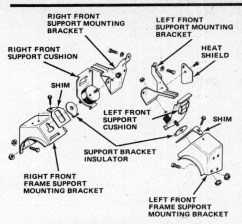

Fig. 1 Engine mounts. 4-151

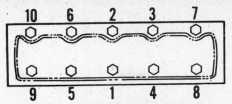

Fig. 2 Cylinder head bolt tightening sequence. 1980 4-151

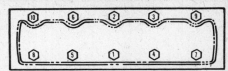

Fig. 3 Cylinder head bolt tightening sequence. 1981-83 4-151

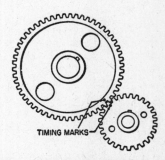

Fig. 5 Aligning valve timing marks. 4-151

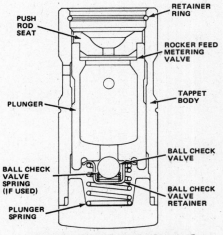

Fig. 4 Sectional view of hydraulic valve lifter. 4-151

HYDRAULIC LIFTERS

Failure of a hydraulic valve lifter, **Fig. 4**, is generally caused by an inadequate oil supply or dirt. An air leak at the intake side of the oil pump or excessive oil in the engine will cause air bubbles in the oil supply to the lifters causing them to collapse. This is a probable cause of trouble if several lifters fail to function, but air in oil is an unlikely cause of failure of a single unit.

Valve lifters can be removed after removing rocker arm cover, intake manifold and push rod cover. Loosen rocker arm stud nut and rotate rocker arm so that push rod can be removed, then remove valve lifter. If necessary, use tool No. J-3049 to facilitate valve lifter removal.

TIMING CASE COVER

1. Disconnect battery ground cable.
2. Remove crankshaft pulley hub, then remove alternator bracket.
3. Remove fan and shroud attaching nuts, then loosen drive belts and remove fan and shroud.
4. Remove oil pan to timing case cover attaching screws, then pull cover slightly forward to permit cutting of oil pan front seal.
5. Using a suitable cutting tool, cut oil pan front seal flush with engine block at both sides of cover.
6. Remove front cover with attached portion of oil pan front seal.
7. Clean timing case cover and cylinder block gasket surfaces.
8. Cut tabs from a replacement oil pan front oil seal.
9. Install seal on timing case cover, inserting tips into holes provided in cover.
10. Coat gasket with gasket sealer, then position gasket on cover.
11. Apply a 1/8 inch bead of RTV sealer to joint surface formed at oil pan and cylinder block.
12. Position centering tool J-23042 into timing case cover oil seal, then position cover on block and install and partially tighten two oil pan to timing case cover attaching screws.
13. Install timing case cover to cylinder block attaching screws.
14. Tighten all timing case cover attaching screws, then remove centering tool.
15. Install alternator bracket, crankshaft pulley hub, fan and shroud.
16. Tighten all drive belts, then connect battery ground cable.

TIMING GEARS

The camshaft is driven by an iron crankshaft gear meshed with a fiber gear attached to the camshaft, **Fig. 5**. To remove the fiber timing gear requires the removal of the camshaft. Position camshaft and timing gear assembly in suitable press plate and press camshaft out of gear using appropriate size socket and arbor press.

NOTE: Thrust plate must be properly aligned with camshaft woodruff key when pressing shaft out of gear or damage to thrust plate may result.

Reverse procedure to install timing gear. End clearance of thrust plate should be .0015–.0050 inch. If clearance is less than .0015 inch, replace spacer ring. If clearance is more than .0050 inch, replace thrust plate.

CAMSHAFT
REPLACE

To remove camshaft, remove timing case cover as outlined previously and proceed as follows:
1. Remove air cleaner.

WARNING: Do not remove block drain plugs or loosen radiator draincock with system under pressure. Scalding can occur from the hot coolant.

2. Drain radiator.
3. Disconnect radiator hoses at radiator. Refer to radiator removal procedure and remove radiator.
4. Remove camshaft thrust plate screws in camshaft gear.
5. Refer to the appropriate removal procedures and remove distributor, oil and fuel pumps.
6. Remove camshaft and gear assembly, withdraw assemblies through front of block. Secure shaft carefully when removing to prevent camshaft bearing damage.
7. Reverse procedure to install, aligning timing marks, **Fig. 5**. Thoroughly clean and inspect all parts. Any component found to be unserviceable should be replaced.

PISTONS & RODS
ASSEMBLE

Assemble piston to rod with notch on piston facing toward front of engine and the raised notch side of rod at bearing end facing toward rear of engine, **Fig. 6**.

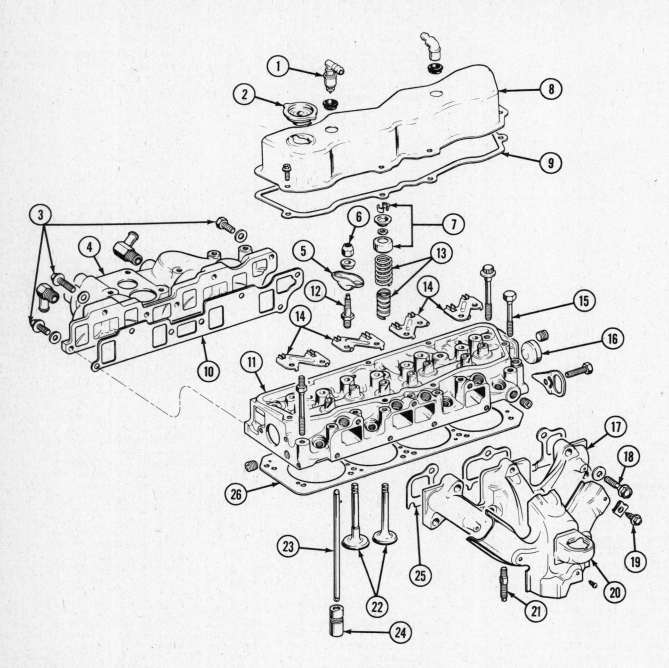

1. PCV VALVE
2. OIL FILLER CAP
3. INTAKE MANIFOLD ATTACHING BOLTS
4. INTAKE MANIFOLD
5. ROCKER ARM
6. ROCKER ARM PIVOT BALL AND NUT
7. VALVE SPRING RETAINER ASSEMBLY
8. CYLINDER HEAD COVER (ROCKER COVER)

9. CYLINDER HEAD COVER GASKET
10. INTAKE MANIFOLD GASKET
11. CYLINDER HEAD
12. ROCKER ARM STUD
13. VALVE SPRING
14. PUSH ROD GUIDE
15. CYLINDER HEAD BOLTS
16. CYLINDER HEAD CORE PLUG
17. EXHAUST MANIFOLD
18. EXHAUST MANIFOLD BOLT

19. OIL LEVEL INDICATOR TUBE ATTACHING SCREW
20. EXHAUST MANIFOLD HEAT SHROUD (HEAT SHIELD)
21. EXHAUST MANIFOLD TO EXHAUST PIPE STUD
22. VALVES
23. PUSH ROD
24. LIFTER
25. EXHAUST MANIFOLD GASKET
26. CYLINDER HEAD GASKET

Exploded view of cylinder head, intake & exhaust manifolds. 4-151

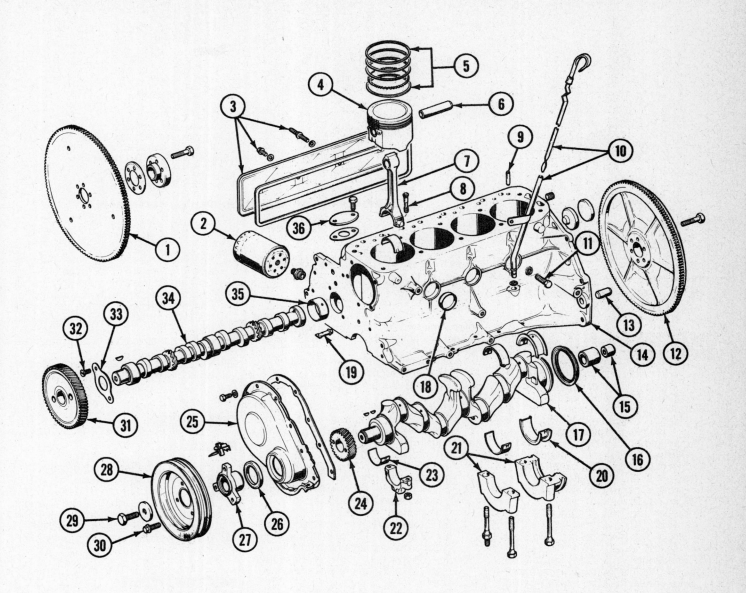

Exploded view of cylinder block & components. 4-151

1. DRIVE PLATE AND RING (AUTO-
   MATIC TRANS)
2. OIL FILTER
3. PUSH ROD COVER AND BOLTS
4. PISTON
5. PISTON RING
6. PISTON PIN
7. CONNECTING ROD
8. CONNECTING ROD BOLT
9. DOWEL
10. OIL LEVEL INDICATOR AND TUBE
11. BLOCK DRAIN
12. FLYWHEEL AND RING GEAR (MAN-
    UAL TRANS)

13. DOWEL
14. CYLINDER BLOCK
15. PILOT AND/OR CONVERTER
    BUSHING
16. REAR OIL SEAL
17. CRANKSHAFT
18. BLOCK CORE PLUG
19. TIMING CHAIN OILER
20. MAIN BEARINGS
21. MAIN BEARING CAPS
22. CONNECTING ROD BEARING CAP
23. CONNECTING ROD BEARING
24. CRANKSHAFT GEAR

25. TIMING COVER (FRONT)
26. TIMING COVER OIL SEAL
27. CRANKSHAFT PULLEY HUB
28. CRANKSHAFT PULLEY
29. CRANKSHAFT PULLEY HUB BOLT
30. CRANKSHAFT PULLEY BOLT
31. CRANKSHAFT TIMING GEAR
32. CAMSHAFT THRUST PLATE SCREW
33. CAMSHAFT THRUST PLATE
34. CAMSHAFT
35. CAMSHAFT BEARING
36. OIL PUMP DRIVESHAFT RETAINER
    PLATE, GASKET AND BOLT

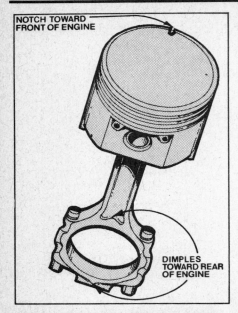

Fig. 6   Piston & rod assembly. 4-151

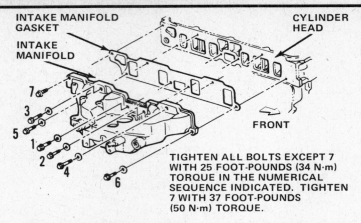

TIGHTEN ALL BOLTS EXCEPT 7 WITH 25 FOOT-POUNDS (34 N·m) TORQUE IN THE NUMERICAL SEQUENCE INDICATED. TIGHTEN 7 WITH 37 FOOT-POUNDS (50 N·m) TORQUE.

Fig. 7   Intake manifold bolt tightening sequence. 4-151

INTAKE MANIFOLD
REPLACE

1. Disconnect battery ground cable.
2. Remove air cleaner assembly and disconnect PCV valve hose.
3. Drain cooling system.
4. Mark and disconnect all vacuum lines and electrical connectors from intake manifold and carburetor.
5. Disconnect fuel line from carburetor.
6. Disconnect throttle linkage from carburetor.
7. Remove carburetor and spacer plate from intake manifold.
8. Remove bellcrank and throttle linkage brackets and position aside.
9. Disconnect heater hose from intake manifold.
10. Remove alternator and position aside.
11. Remove intake manifold to cylinder head bolts, then the intake manifold.
12. Reverse procedure to install. Torque cylinder head bolts in sequence shown in **Fig. 7.** Torque all bolts except bolt No. 7 to 25 ft. lbs. Torque bolt No. 7 to 37 ft. lbs.

PISTONS, PINS & RINGS

Pistons are available in standard size and oversizes of .005, .010, .020 and .030 inch. Piston pins are available in oversizes of .001 and .003 inch.

MAIN & ROD BEARINGS

Main and rod bearings are available in standard size and undersizes of .001, .002 and .010 inch.

CRANKSHAFT REAR OIL SEAL
REPLACE

The rear main bearing oil seal is a one piece unit and can be removed or installed without removing the oil pan or the crankshaft.

1. Disconnect battery ground cable and raise and support vehicle.
2. Remove transmission and transfer case as a unit.
3. Remove starter motor.
4. On manual transmissions only, remove inspection plate from flywheel housing.
5. On manual transmissions only, remove hydraulic clutch slave cylinder from flywheel housing.
6. On all models, remove flywheel/drive plate housing from engine.
7. On manual transmissions, remove clutch pressure plate and disc assembly by loosening bolts ¼ turn in equal amounts until pressure is relieved.
8. On all models, mark flywheel/drive plate location to ensure correct assembly.
9. Remove flywheel/drive plate.
10. Using a small screwdriver, pry out rear main oil seal, using care not to damage seating groove or crankshaft.
11. Center replacement seal over crankshaft with lip facing toward front of engine. Using a soft hammer, tap around perimeter of seal until it seats in groove taking care to prevent seal from binding on crankshaft and not seating properly.
12. Install flywheel/drive plate on crankshaft and torque to 68 ft. lbs.
13. On manual transmissions only, install clutch pressure plate and disc assembly. Alternately tighten bolts ¼ turn at a time until assembly is flush against flywheel. Torque bolts to 18 ft. lbs.

NOTE: Using alignment tool J-5824-01 or equivalent align clutch disc prior to tightening bolts.

14. Install flywheel/drive plate housing and torque bolts to 35 ft. lbs.
15. On manual transmissions only, install inspection plate on flywheel housing, and install hydraulic clutch slave cylinder on flywheel housing. Torque bolts to 18 ft. lbs.
16. Install transmission/transfer case assembly.
17. Install starter motor, lower vehicle, and connect battery ground cable.

OIL PAN
REMOVAL

1. Disconnect battery ground cable.
2. Raise and support vehicle.
3. Drain engine oil from oil pan.
4. Disconnect battery cable and solenoid electrical connector from starter, then remove starter motor from vehicle.
5. Remove oil pan attaching bolts, then the oil pan.

INSTALLATION

1. Thoroughly clean oil pan and cylinder block gasket surfaces.
2. Install rear oil pan gasket into rear main bearing cap. Apply a suitable sealant to depression where pan gasket contacts cylinder block.
3. Position gasket onto oil pan. Apply a ⅛ × ¼ inch bead of suitable sealer to split lines of front and side gasket.
4. Position oil pan onto cylinder block. Insert and torque pan side bolts to 75 inch lbs. Insert and torque oil pan to timing case cover bolts to 90 inch lbs.
5. Install starter motor. Torque ⅜ inch bolts to 27 ft. lbs. Torque No. 10 nut to 40 inch lbs.
6. Connect battery cable and solenoid electrical connector onto starter motor.
7. Lower vehicle.
8. Connect battery ground cable and add oil to engine.

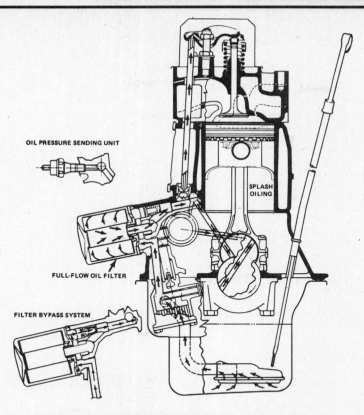

Fig. 8 Engine lubrication system. 4-151

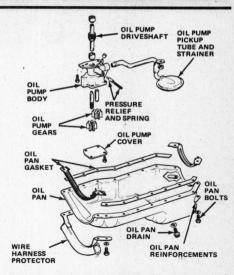

Fig. 9 Oil pan & pump assembly. 4-151

OIL PUMP SERVICE

Engine lubrication is accomplished with a gear type pump that pumps engine oil from the oil pan sump through the full flow oil filter and into an oil passage that runs along the right side of the block and intersects the hydraulic valve tappet bores, **Fig. 8.** Oil from this passage is directed to the crankshaft and camshaft bearings. Oil reaches the rocker arms through holes in the hydraulic valve tappets which force oil up through the tubular push rods to the rocker arms.

A bypass valve in the oil filter mounting boss and a pressure regulator valve in the oil pump body ensure the proper flow of oil. The full flow oil filter is mounted on the right side of the engine.

REMOVAL

1. Drain oil and remove oil pan.
2. Remove flange mounting bolts and nut from main bearing cap bolt and remove pump and pickup assembly as a unit.

DISASSEMBLY

1. Remove oil pump cover, idler gear and drive gear and shaft, **Fig. 9.**
2. Remove pressure regulator valve and parts.

NOTE: The oil pickup pipe is attached during factory assembly and should not be disturbed.

3. The complete pump assembly should be replaced if any of the following conditions are observed during inspection:
   a. Pump body is cracked or shows excessive wear.
   b. Pump gears have cracks, excessive wear, and damage.
   c. Shaft is loose in housing.
   d. Inside of cover is worn enough to allow oil to leak past end of gears.
   e. Oil pickup assembly has damaged strainer screen or relief grommet.

NOTE: Remove any debris found on strainer screen surface.

   f. Pressure regulator valve plunger does not fit properly in body.

ASSEMBLY

1. Place drive gear and shaft in oil pump body.
2. Install idler gear so smooth side of gear will face cover.
3. Install cover and torque attaching screws to 9 ft. lbs. Make sure that shaft turns freely.
4. Install regulator valve plunger, spring, retainer, and pin.

INSTALLATION

1. Position oil pump gear shaft tang so it aligns with oil pump drive shaft slot.

Install oil pump to block positioning flange over oil pump drive shaft lower bushing. Do not use gasket. Torque bolts to 18 ft. lbs.

NOTE: If oil pump does not slide easily into place, remove shaft and relocate slot.

2. Install oil pan with new gaskets and seals.

WATER PUMP
REPLACE

1. Disconnect battery ground cable.
2. Drain cooling system.
3. Remove drive belt and fan.
4. Disconnect lower radiator and heater hoses from water pump.
5. Remove water pump attaching bolts, then the water pump.
6. Reverse procedure to install. Torque water pump attaching bolts to 25 ft. lbs.

BELT TENSION DATA

	New lbs.	Used lbs.
Drive belt	125–155	90–115

FUEL PUMP
REPLACE

1. Disconnect battery ground cable.
2. Disconnect and cap fuel lines from fuel pump.
3. Remove fuel pump attaching bolts, then the fuel pump and gasket.
4. Reverse procedure to install.

6-258 Engine Section

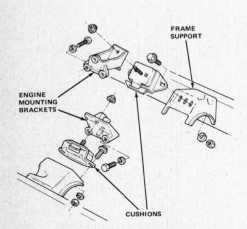

Fig. 1   Engine mounts

ENGINE MOUNTS

Removal or replacement of any cushion or bracket, **Fig. 1** can be accomplished by fabricating an engine holding fixture to support the engine, **Fig. 2**. The engine may also be supported by a suitable jack positioned under the oil pan skid plate. Use a board between the jack and oil pan skid plate to distribute engine weight evenly.

ENGINE
REPLACE

1. Disconnect battery ground cable and drain cooling system.
2. Mark position of hood hinges, disconnect hood lamp if equipped, then remove hood.
3. Disconnect remaining cable and remove battery.
4. Remove air cleaner.
5. Disconnect fuel inlet pipe at pump and plug pipe and pump fitting.
6. Disconnect fuel return hose from pipe on frame or fuel filter, as equipped.
7. Disconnect heater hoses from engine and core fittings, remove fan shroud retaining screws, then disconnect hoses from radiator.
8. Disconnect electrical connectors and ground straps from engine, and remove vacuum switch and bracket from valve cover, if equipped.
9. Mark and disconnect all vacuum hoses from engine.
10. Disconnect throttle linkages and cables from throttle lever and engine mounted brackets.
11. Disconnect transmission cooler lines

from radiator, if equipped, and plug lines and open fittings.
12. Remove radiator mounting bolts, radiator and fan shroud.
13. Remove fan and spacer or fan clutch, then install bolt through pulley and thread bolt into water pump hub to maintain pulley alignment.
14. On models with A/C proceed as follows:
    a. Remove service valve caps and rotate service valves fully clockwise to the front seated position.
    b. Slowly discharge refrigerant from compressor through service valve cores.
    c. Disconnect service valve assemblies from compressor and secure hoses aside. Plug open ports in compressor and service valves.
15. On models with power steering, disconnect hoses from steering gear and plug hose and gear fittings.
16. On all models, remove nut securing right front mount cushion to bracket and the bolt securing transmission filler tube, if equipped.
17. Raise and support vehicle and remove remaining mount cushion to bracket nuts.
18. Disconnect electrical connector to oxygen sensor, if equipped, then disconnect exhaust pipe from manifold.
19. Remove starter motor.
20. On models with manual transmission, remove flywheel shield and disconnect clutch linkage.
21. On models with automatic transmission, proceed as follows:
    a. Remove converter access cover and converter bolts, rotating crankshaft as needed to gain access to bolts.
    b. Remove oil pan bolts securing cooler line brackets to engine.
    c. Remove brace between converter housing and exhaust pipe, if equipped.
22. On all models, remove upper bell housing to engine bolts and loosen lower bolts, then lower vehicle.
23. Remove A/C idler pulley and bracket, if equipped, then attach suitable lifting equipment to engine.
24. Raise engine off mounts, place suitable support under bell housing, then remove lower bell housing bolts.
25. Separate engine from bell housing and remove from vehicle.
26. Reverse procedure to install.

NOTE: Prior to refilling cooling system, remove coolant temperature sending unit to allow air to escape from engine block. When system is filled, reinstall sending unit.

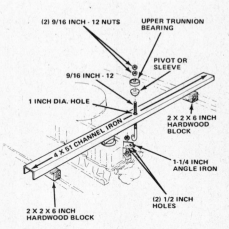

Fig. 2   Engine holding fixture

CYLINDER HEAD
REPLACE

1. Disconnect battery ground cable and drain cooling system.
2. Remove air cleaner, fuel pipe between carburetor and pump, and vacuum advance hose.
3. Remove rocker cover as follows:
    a. Remove PCV valve and molded hose, and disconnect hose from PCV shut-off valve, if equipped.
    b. Remove vacuum switch and bracket, and diverter valve and bracket assemblies from cover, if equipped.
    c. Mark and disconnect necessary air and vacuum hoses to provide clearance for cover removal.
    d. Remove cover bolts and break gasket/sealer seal using putty knife or suitable cutter.

NOTE: Do not pry on cover to break seal, as sealing surface may be damaged.

    e. Rotate cover toward passenger side of vehicle and remove cover.
4. Remove rocker arms, bridges and pivots, and the push rods, keeping components in order for assembly.

NOTE: Alternately loosen rocker arm bolts, one turn at a time, to prevent damaging bridges.

5. Remove power steering and air pump mounting bolts, as equipped, and secure pumps aside.
6. Refer to "Intake and Exhaust Manifold, Replace," and disconnect manifolds from cylinder head.
7. On models with A/C, proceed as follows:

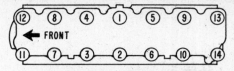

Fig. 3 Rocker arm, bridge & pivot assembly

a. Remove compressor belt idler pulley and bracket.
b. Loosen alternator belt and disconnect alternator bracket from cylinder head.
c. Remove compressor mounting bolts and position compressor aside.

8. On all models, disconnect spark plug wires and temperature sending unit electrical connector.
9. Remove spark plugs, ignition coil and coil bracket.
10. Remove cylinder head bolts, cylinder head and gasket.
11. Ensure that head and block gasket surfaces are clean and free from old gasket material, coat both sides of replacement gasket with suitable sealer and position gasket on block with "TOP" mark facing up.
12. Ensure that gasket is properly seated on block, install cylinder head and head bolts, and torque bolts to specifications in sequence shown in **Fig. 3**.

NOTE: Apply suitable sealer to threads of left front head bolt (11), prior to installation.

13. Remove temperature sending unit and leave removed until cooling system is filled to allow air to escape from engine block.
14. Reverse remaining procedure to complete installation.

INTAKE & EXHAUST MANIFOLDS
REPLACE

1979—80

1. Disconnect battery ground cable and remove air cleaner.
2. Disconnect fuel line, bowl vent hose and solenoid electrical connector from carburetor.
3. Disconnect throttle cable and throttle valve rod, as equipped.
4. Remove molded PCV hose, then disconnect spark advance CTO and EGR valve vacuum hoses, and TCS solenoid electrical connector.
5. Disconnect AIR hoses from pump and check valve, then remove diverter valve and hoses as an assembly.
6. Remove AIR/power steering pump lower bracket and the air pump.
7. Remove power steering pump and secure aside, leaving hoses connected.

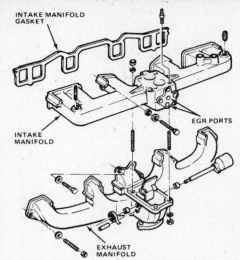

Fig. 4 Manifold installation. 1979—80

8. Remove A/C compressor belt idler pulley and bracket, if equipped.
9. Disconnect exhaust pipe from manifold.
10. Remove manifold mounting bolts, nuts and clamps, then the manifold assembly and intake manifold gasket, **Fig. 4.**
11. Remove carburetor and insulator from intake manifold.
12. Remove throttle control bracket and bolts securing exhaust manifold to intake manifold, separate manifolds and discard gasket.
13. Transfer necessary components and mounting studs to replacement manifold and thoroughly clean all sealing surfaces.
14. Join intake and exhaust manifolds using new gasket, and torque bolts to 2–4 ft. lbs.

NOTE: Do not overtighten bolts as manifolds must be loose enough to slide during installation on cylinder head.

15. Position new intake manifold gasket on cylinder head, install manifold assembly and tighten nuts and bolts hand tight.
16. Torque manifold fasteners to specifications in sequence shown in **Fig. 5**.
17. Install carburetor on intake manifold using new base gasket and torque nuts to 14 ft. lbs.
18. Reverse remaining procedure to complete installation.

1981—85
Intake Manifold

1. Disconnect battery ground cable, drain coolant and remove air cleaner.
2. Disconnect fuel line, bowl vent and idle speed control hoses, and idle speed control and choke heater electrical connectors, as equipped.
3. Disconnect coolant and PCV hoses

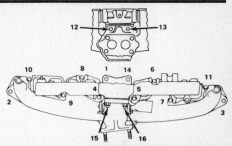

Fig. 5 Manifold tightening sequence. 1979—80

from manifold, and vacuum hoses from spark advance CTO valve.
4. Disconnect electrical connectors to manifold heater, temperature sensing unit and carburetor, as equipped.
5. Disconnect throttle cable and throttle valve rod, if equipped.
6. Disconnect EGR tube from manifolds and vacuum hose from EGR valve.
7. On models with AIR, disconnect hoses from pump and check valves, then remove diverter valve and hoses as an assembly.
8. On all models, remove carburetor along with vacuum hoses and base gasket.
9. Remove AIR/power steering pump lower bracket, if equipped, then the AIR pump.
10. Remove power steering pump and secure aside, leaving hoses connected.
11. Remove A/C compressor belt idler pulley and bracket, if equipped.
12. Remove intake manifold retaining bolts, intake manifold and gasket, **Fig. 6.**
13. Ensure that sealing surfaces are clean and free from old gasket material, then loosen end nuts securing exhaust manifold.
14. Position new gasket on cylinder head, install intake manifold and torque bolts to specifications in sequence shown in **Fig. 7**.
15. Reverse procedure to complete installation, using new base gasket when installing carburetor.

NOTE: Remove coolant temperature sensor and leave removed until cooling system is filled to allow air to escape from block. When cooling system is filled, reinstall temperature sensor.

Exhaust Manifold

1. Remove intake manifold as outlined.
2. Disconnect exhaust pipe from manifold.
3. Disconnect electrical connector from oxygen sensor and remove sensor, if equipped.
4. Remove nuts from end studs, then the exhaust manifold.
5. Mount manifold on end studs and tighten retaining nuts hand tight.
6. Clean threads in oxygen sensor bore, coat sensor threads with suitable antiseize compound, install sensor and

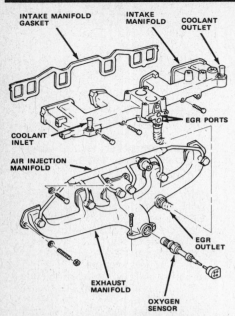

Fig. 6 **Manifold installation. 1981–85**

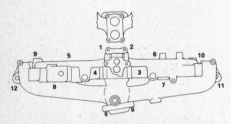

Fig. 7 **Manifold tightening sequence. 1981–85**

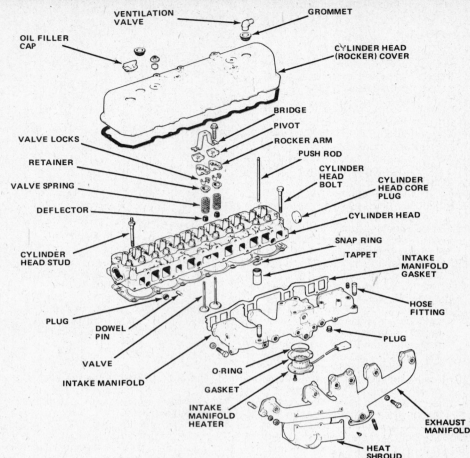

Exploded view of cylinder head, intake & exhaust manifold (Typical)

torque to 35 ft. lbs.
7. Connect exhaust pipe to manifold.
8. Reinstall intake manifold and torque retaining bolts and nuts to specifications as outlined.

ROCKER ARM SERVICE

The intake and exhaust rocker arms of each cylinder pivot on a bridge and pivot assembly that is secured with two capscrews as shown in **Fig. 8.** Each rocker arm is actuated by a hollow push rod with a hardened ball at each end. The hallow push rods route engine oil to the rocker arm assembly.

REMOVAL

1. Disconnect battery ground cable.
2. Remove cylinder head cover and gasket.
3. Remove the two capscrews at each bridge and pivot assembly.

NOTE: Alternately loosen capscrews one turn at a time to avoid damaging bridge.

4. Remove bridge and pivot assemblies with their rocker arms and push rods and position aside.

NOTE: Bridge, pivot, rocker arms and push rods must be installed in their original locations.

INSTALLATION

1. Clean all parts with a suitable solvent.
2. Using compressed air blow out rocker arm and push rod oil passages.
3. Check rocker arms and push rods for wear or damage. Replace as required.
4. Install push rods into their original locations.

NOTE: Ensure bottom end of each push rod is centered into hydraulic valve lifter plunger cap.

5. Install rocker arms, bridge and pivot assemblies into their original locations.
6. Loosely install bridge capscrews on each bridge and pivot assembly.
7. Torque capscrews alternately one turn

at a time at each bridge and pivot assembly to 19 ft. lbs.
8. Install cylinder head cover and gasket.
9. Connect battery ground cable.

VALVE ARRANGEMENT
FRONT TO REAR

6-232, 258 . . . . E-I-I-E-I-E-E-I-E-I-I-E

VALVE GUIDES

Valve guides are an integral part of the cylinder head and are not replaceable. When valve stem to guide clearance exceeds specification, ream the valve guide bores to accommodate the next larger oversize valve stem. Oversize valves are available with .003, .015 and .030 inch stem diameter sizes.

NOTE: Ream valve guides in steps, starting with the .003 inch oversize reamer and progressing to size required.

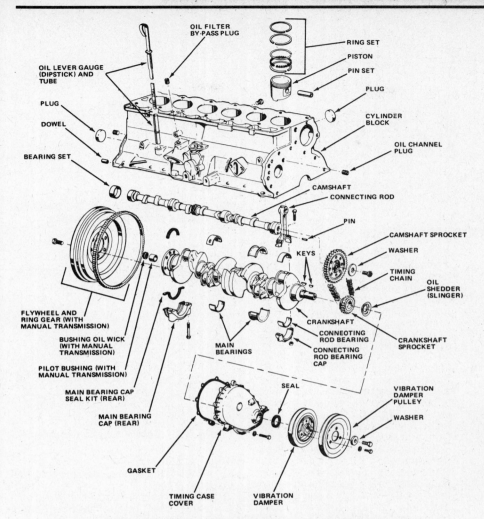

Exploded view of cylinder block & components

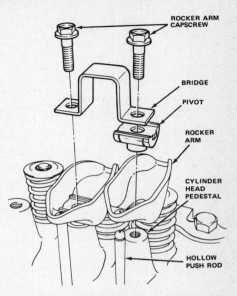

Fig. 8   Rocker arm, bridge & pivot assembly

HYDRAULIC VALVE LIFTERS

Valve lifters, **Fig. 9** may be removed from their bores after the cylinder head assembly is removed by using tool No. J-21884.

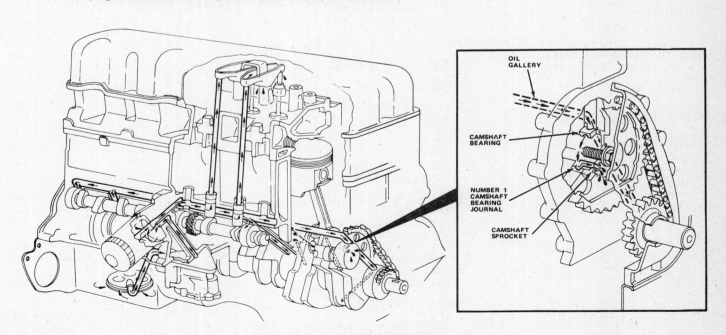

6-258 engine lubrication system

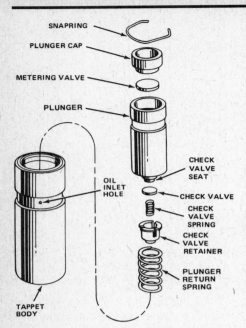

Fig. 9 Hydraulic valve lifter assembly

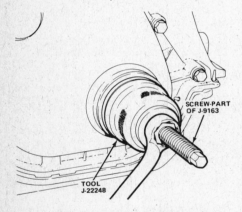

Fig. 12 Installing timing case cover front seal

TIMING CASE COVER
REMOVAL

1. Disconnect battery ground cable.
2. Remove drive belt(s), engine fan, hub assembly, damper pulley and vibration damper.
3. Remove oil pan to timing case cover and timing case cover to cylinder block bolts.
4. Remove timing case cover and gasket from engine, **Fig. 10**.
5. Using a suitable tool, cut oil pan gasket end tabs flush with front face of engine cylinder block and remove gasket tabs.
6. Clean timing case cover, oil pan and cylinder block gasket surfaces.
7. Remove crankshaft oil seal from timing case cover.

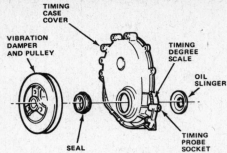

Fig. 10 Timing case cover

INSTALLATION

1. Apply a suitable sealer to timing case cover gasket and install onto cylinder block.
2. Cut end tabs off of replacement oil pan gasket corresponding to pieces cut from original gasket. Using a suitable sealer install cut pieces onto oil pan.
3. Coat oil pan seal end tabs with a suitable sealer and install seal onto timing case cover.
4. Install timing case cover onto engine. Position timing case cover alignment tool and seal installer J-22248 into crankshaft opening of case cover as shown in **Fig. 11**.
5. Install case cover to cylinder block bolts and oil pan to case cover bolts. Torque bolts to 5 ft. lbs. Torque oil pan to case cover bolts to 11 ft. lbs.
6. Remove case cover aligning tool and position oil seal onto tool with seal lip facing outward. Apply a suitable sealer to outer diameter to seal.
7. Insert tool screw No. J-9163 into seal tool. Tighten tool nut until tool contacts timing case cover, **Fig. 12**.
8. Remove tool and apply clean engine oil to seal lip.

TIMING CHAIN
REMOVAL

1. Disconnect battery ground cable.
2. Remove engine fan and hub assembly.
3. Remove vibration damper pulley and vibration damper.
4. Remove timing case cover.
5. Remove oil seal from timing case cover.
6. Remove camshaft sprocket retaining bolt and washer.
7. Rotate crankshaft until crankshaft sprocket timing marks is closest to and aligned with timing mark on camshaft sprocket, **Fig. 13**.
8. Remove timing chain and sprockets as an assembly.

INSTALLATION

1. Assemble timing chain, crankshaft and camshaft sprockets with timing marks aligned as shown in **Fig. 13**.

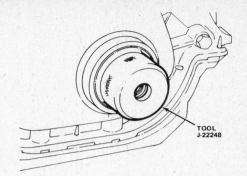

Fig. 11 Using tool No. J-22248 to align timing case cover

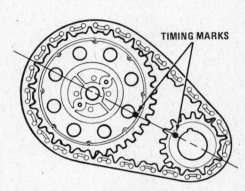

Fig. 13 Valve timing marks

2. Install timing chain assembly onto engine.
3. Install camshaft sprocket retaining bolt and washer. Torque retaining bolt to 50 ft. lbs.

NOTE: To verify correct installation of timing chain, position timing mark of the camshaft sprocket at approximately the one o'clock position. This positions crankshaft sprocket timing mark at a location where the adjacent tooth meshes with the timing chain, **Fig. 14**. Count the number of timing chain pins between timing marks of both crankshaft and camshaft sprockets. There must be 15 pins.

4. Install timing case cover and oil seal.
5. Install vibration damper. Torque damper bolt to 80 ft. lbs.
6. Install vibration damper pulley. Torque bolts to 20 ft. lbs.
7. Install engine fan and hub assembly.
8. Connect battery ground cable.

CAMSHAFT
REPLACE

1. Disconnect battery ground cable.
2. Drain cooling system.
3. Remove air conditioner condenser and receiver assembly as a unit if equipped.
4. Remove radiator and fan assembly.

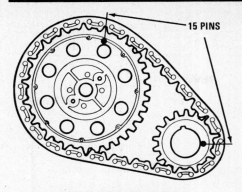

15 PINS

Fig. 14 Timing chain installation check

5. Remove fuel pump, distributor and spark plug wires.
6. Remove cylinder head cover.
7. Remove rocker arm, bridge and pivot assembly.
8. Remove push rods.

NOTE: Ensure to install rocker arms, bridge, pivot and push rod assemblies in their original locations.

9. Remove cylinder head and gasket.
10. Remove valve lifters.
11. Remove timing case cover, timing chain and sprockets.
12. Remove front bumper or grille.
13. Remove camshaft front engine.
14. Reverse procedure to install.

NOTE: During installation of distributor, rotate crankshaft until No. 1 piston is at TDC of compression stroke. Install distributor with rotor aligned with No. 1 terminal on distributor cap when distributor is completely seated on block.

PISTON & ROD
ASSEMBLE

Pistons are marked with a depression notch on the top perimeter, **Fig. 15.** When installed in the engine this notch must face toward the front of engine. Always assemble rods and caps with the cylinder numbers or oil squirt holes facing the camshaft side of engine.

MAIN BEARINGS

The main bearing journal size (diameter) is identified by a color coded paint mark on adjacent cheek toward flanged (rear) end of crankshaft, except for rear main journal which is on crankshaft rear flange. Color codes used to indicate journal and corresponding bearing sizes are listed in **Fig. 16** for 1979-80 models and **Figs. 17 through 19** for 1981-85 models.

CONNECTING ROD BEARINGS

The connecting rod journal is identified by a color coded paint mark on adjacent cheek or counterweight toward flanged (rear) end of crankshaft. Color codes used to indicate journal sizes and corresponding bearing sizes are listed in **Fig. 20.**

CRANKSHAFT REAR OIL SEAL
REMOVAL

1. Disconnect battery ground cable.
2. Drain oil from engine.
3. Remove oil pan attaching bolts, then the oil pan.
4. Remove rear main bearing cap and lower oil seal.
5. Loosen all remaining main bearing caps.
6. Using a brass drift and hammer, tap oil seal until seal protrudes from groove. Pull oil seal from groove.
7. Remove oil pan front and rear oil seals and oil pan side gaskets.
8. Clean oil pan and engine block gasket surfaces.
9. Clean main bearing cap.

INSTALLATION

1. Clean sealing surface of crankshaft, then apply clean engine oil to crankshaft sealing surface.
2. Coat lip of upper seal with engine oil, **Fig. 21.**
3. Install upper seal into engine block.

NOTE: Lip of seal must face toward front of engine.

4. Coat both sides of lower seal end tabs with RTV sealer or equivalent.

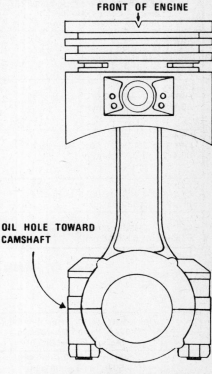

ARROW TOWARD FRONT OF ENGINE

OIL HOLE TOWARD CAMSHAFT

Fig. 15 Piston and rod assembly

NOTE: Do not apply RTV to lip of seal.

5. Coat outer curved surface of lower seal with soap and seal lip with clean engine oil, **Fig. 21.**
6. Install seal completely into cap recess.
7. Coat both chamfered edges of rear main bearing cap with RTV or equivalent.
8. Install rear main bearing cap. Torque all main bearing cap bolts a little at a time to specification.
9. Install oil pan, add engine oil and connect battery ground cable.

OIL PAN
REPLACE

1. Disconnect battery ground cable.

Crankshaft Main Bearing Journal Color Code and Diameter in Inches (Journal Size)		Bearing Color Code			
		Upper Insert Size		Lower Insert Size	
Yellow	−2.5001 to 2.4996 (Standard)	Yellow	— Standard	Yellow	— Standard
Orange	−2.4996 to 2.4991 (0.0005 Undersize)	Yellow	— Standard	Black	— .001-inch Undersize
Black	−2.4991 to 2.4986 (0.001 Undersize)	Black	— .001-inch Undersize	Black	— .001-inch Undersize
Green	−2.4986 to 2.4981 (0.0015 Undersize)	Black	— .001-inch Undersize	Green	— .002-inch Undersize
Red	−2.4901 to 2.4896 (0.010 Undersize)	Red	— .010-inch Undersize	Red	— .010-inch Undersize

Fig. 16 Main bearing selection chart. 1979-80

Crankshaft No. 1 Main Bearing Journal Color Code and Diameter In Inches (mm)	Cylinder Block No. 1 Main Bearing Bore Color Code and Size In Inches (mm)	Bearing Insert Color Code	
		Upper Insert Size	Lower Insert Size
Yellow — 2.5001 to 2.4996 (Standard) (63.5025 to 63.4898mm)	Yellow — 2.6910 to 2.6915 (68.3514 to 68.3641mm)	Yellow — Standard	Yellow — Standard
	Black — 2.6915 to 2.6920 (68.3641 to 68.3768mm)	Yellow — Standard	Black — 0.001-inch Undersize (0.025mm)
Orange — 2.4996 to 2.4991 (0.0005 Undersize) (63.4898 to 63.4771mm)	Yellow — 2.6910 to 2.6915 (68.3514 to 68.3641mm)	Yellow — Standard	Black — 0.001-inch Undersize (0.025mm)
	Black — 2.6915 to 2.6920 (68.3641 to 68.3768mm)	Black — 0.001-inch Undersize (0.025mm)	Green — 0.002-inch Undersize (0.051mm)
Black — 2.4991 to 2.4986 (0.001 Undersize) (63.4771 to 63.4644mm)	Yellow — 2.6910 to 2.6915 (68.3514 to 68.3641mm)	Black — 0.001-inch Undersize (0.025mm)	Black — 0.001-inch Undersize (0.025mm)
	Black — 2.6915 to 2.6920 (68.3641 to 68.3768mm)	Black — 0.001-inch Undersize (0.025mm)	Green — 0.002-inch Undersize (0.051mm)
Green — 2.4986 to 2.4981 (0.0015 Undersize) (63.4644 to 63.4517mm)	Yellow — 2.6910 to 2.6915 (68.3514 to 68.3641mm)	Black — 0.001-inch Undersize (0.025mm)	Green — 0.002-inch Undersize (0.051mm)
Red — 2.4901 to 2.4986 (0.010 Undersize) (63.2485 to 63.2358mm)	Yellow — 2.6910 to 2.6915 (68.3541 to 68.3641mm)	Red — 0.010-inch Undersize (0.254mm)	Red — 0.010-inch Undersize (0.254mm)

Fig. 17   Main bearing selection chart. 1981–85 main bearing No. 1

Crankshaft Main Bearing Journal 2-6 Color Code and Diameter in Inches (Journal Size)	Bearing Insert Color Code	
	Upper Insert Size	Lower Insert Size
Yellow — 2.5001 to 2.4996 (Standard) (63.5025 to 63.4898 mm)	Yellow — Standard	Yellow — Standard
Orange — 2.4996 to 2.4991 (0.0005 Undersize) (63.4898 to 63.4771 mm)	Yellow — Standard	Black — 0.001-inch Undersize (0.025mm)
Black — 2.4991 to 2.4986 (0.001 Undersize) (63.4771 to 63.4644 mm)	Black — 0.001-inch Undersize (0.025mm)	Black — 0.001-inch Undersize (0.025mm)
Green — 2.4986 to 2.4981 (0.0015 Undersize) (63.4644 to 63.4517 mm)	Black — 0.001-inch Undersize (0.025mm)	Green — 0.002-inch Undersize (0.051mm)
Red — 2.4901 to 2.4986 (0.010 Undersize) (63.2485 to 63.2358 mm)	Red — 0.010-inch Undersize (0.254mm)	Red — 0.010-inch Undersize (0.254mm)

Fig. 18   Main bearing selection chart. 1981–85 main bearing Nos. 2 through 6

Crankshaft Main Bearing Journal 7 Color Code and Diameter in Inches (Journal Size)	Bearing Insert Color Code	
	Upper Insert Size	Lower Insert Size
Yellow — 2.4995 to 2.4990 (Standard) (63.4873 to 63.4746 mm)	Yellow — Standard	Yellow — Standard
Orange — 2.4990 to 2.4985 (0.0005 Undersize) (63.4746 to 63.4619 mm)	Yellow — Standard	Black — 0.001-inch Undersize (0.025mm)
Black — 2.4985 to 2.4980 (0.001 Undersize) (63.4619 to 63.4492 mm)	Black — 0.001-inch Undersize (0.025mm)	Black — 0.001-inch Undersize (0.025mm)
Green — 2.4980 to 2.4975 (0.0015 Undersize) (63.4492 to 63.4365 mm)	Black — 0.001-inch Undersize (0.025mm)	Green — 0.002-inch Undersize (0.051mm)
Red — 2.4895 to 2.4890 (0.010 Undersize) (63.2333 to 63.2206 mm)	Red — 0.010-inch Undersize (0.254mm)	Red — 0.010-inch Undersize (0.254mm)

Fig. 19   Main bearing selection chart. 1981–85 main bearing No. 7

Crankshaft Connecting Rod Journal Color and Diameter in Inches (Journal Size)	Bearing Color Code	
	Upper Insert Size	Lower Insert Size
Yellow −2.0955 to 2.0948 (Standard) Orange −2.0948 to 2.0941 (0.0007 Undersize) Black −2.0941 to 2.0934 (0.0014 Undersize) Red −2.0855 to 2.0848 (0.010 Undersize)	Yellow − Standard Yellow − Standard Black − .001-Inch Undersize Red − .010-Inch Undersize	Yellow − Standard Black − .001-inch Undersize Black − .001-inch Undersize Red − .010-inch Undersize

Fig. 20 Connecting rod bearing selection chart

2. Raise and support vehicle.
3. Drain oil from engine.
4. On CJ and Scrambler models, position a suitable jack under transmission. Remove right engine support cushion bracket from engine block. Raise engine slightly.
4. Remove starter motor attaching bolts, then the starter motor.
5. Remove oil pan attaching bolts, then the oil pan.
6. Reverse procedure to install.

OIL PUMP

REMOVAL

1. Disconnect battery ground cable.
2. Raise and support vehicle.
3. Drain oil from engine.
4. Remove oil pan attaching bolts, then the oil pan.
5. Remove oil pump attaching bolts, then the oil pump, **Fig. 22.**

SERVICE

1. Remove cover retaining bolts, cover and gasket.
2. Using the preferred method, check gear end clearance as follows:
   a. Place a strip of Plastigage across full width of each gear end, **Fig. 23.**
   b. Apply a bead of locktite 515 or equivalent, around perimeter of oil pump cover and install onto oil pump.
   c. Torque cover bolts to 70 inch lbs.
   d. Remove oil pump cover and determine amount of end clearance by measuring width of compressed Plastigage.
   e. Clearance should be .002–.006 inch.
3. Using the alternate method, check gear end clearance as follows:
   a. Place a straightedge across ends of gears and pump body.
   b. Using a feeler gauge, measure gear end clearance. Clearance should be .004–.008 inch.
   c. If clearance obtained exceeds specified amount, replace oil pump assembly.
4. Using a feeler gauge, measure clearance between gear tooth and oil pump body inner wall directly opposite point of gear mesh. Rotate pump gears and measure each gear tooth clearance. Clearance should be .0005–.0025 inch.

5. If clearance obtained exceeds specified amount, replace idler gear, idler shaft and drive gear assembly.
6. Remove cotter pin and slide spring retainer, spring and oil pressure release valve plunger out of oil pump body. Check parts for wear or damage.
7. Install oil pressure release valve plunger, spring retainer and cotter pin.
8. Install idler shaft, idler gear and drive gear assembly.
9. Apply a suitable sealer to oil pump cover and install onto pump. Torque cover bolts to 70 inch lbs.

INSTALLATION

1. Install oil pump gasket onto engine. Torque oil pump short bolts to 10 ft. lbs. Torque oil pump long bolts to 17 ft. lbs.
2. Install oil pan and gasket.
3. Lower vehicle.
4. Add oil to engine and connect battery ground cable.

Fig. 21 Crankshaft rear main oil seal & cap installation

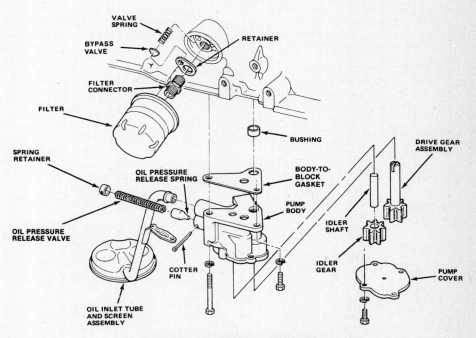

Fig. 22 Oil pump assembly

A−67

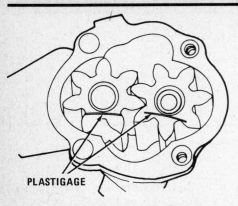

PLASTIGAGE

Fig. 23   Installing Plastigage across oil pump gears

BELT TENSION DATA

	New lbs.	Used lbs.
A/C Comp.	125–155	90–115
Air Pump	65–75	60–70
Fan & Alternator	125–155	90–115
Power Steering Pump	125–155	90–115
Drive Belt (Serpentine)	180–200	140–160

WATER PUMP
REPLACE

1. Disconnect battery ground cable.
2. Drain cooling system.
3. Disconnect radiator and heater hoses from water pump, **Fig. 24.**
4. Remove drive belts.
5. Remove fan shroud and fan.
6. Remove water pump attaching bolts, then the water pump and gasket.
7. Reverse procedure to install.

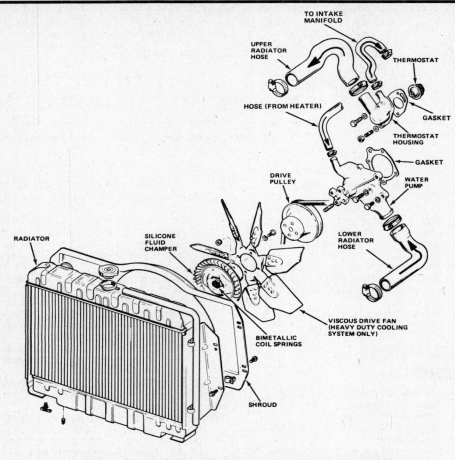

Fig. 24   Water pump & cooling system components

FUEL PUMP
REPLACE

1. Disconnect battery ground cable.
2. Disconnect and cap fuel lines from fuel pump.
3. Remove fuel pump attaching bolts, then the fuel pump and gasket.
4. Reverse procedure to install.

V8 Engine Section

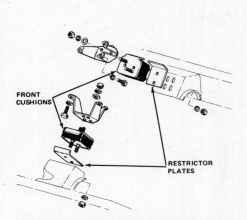

FRONT CUSHIONS

RESTRICTOR PLATES

Fig. 1   Engine mounts. V8 engine

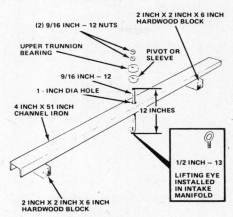

(2) 9/16 INCH – 12 NUTS

2 INCH X 2 INCH X 6 INCH HARDWOOD BLOCK

UPPER TRUNNION BEARING

PIVOT OR SLEEVE

9/16 INCH – 12

1 - INCH DIA HOLE

4 INCH X 51 INCH CHANNEL IRON

12 INCHES

2 INCH X 2 INCH X 6 INCH HARDWOOD BLOCK

1/2 INCH – 13
LIFTING EYE INSTALLED IN INTAKE MANIFOLD

Fig. 2   Engine holding fixture. V8 engine

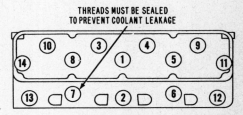

THREADS MUST BE SEALED TO PREVENT COOLANT LEAKAGE

Fig. 3   Cylinder head tightening sequence. V8 engine

ENGINE MOUNTS

Removal or replacement of any cushion or bracket, **Fig. 1,** can be accomplished by fabricating an engine holding fixture to support the engine, **Fig. 2.**

ENGINE
REPLACE

1. Disconnect cables from battery and remove battery.
2. On Cherokee, Wagoneer and Grand Wagoneer models, mark hood hinge location and remove hood.
3. Remove air cleaner assembly from carburetor.
4. Drain cooling system, then disconnect upper, lower and heater hoses.
5. On models equipped with automatic transmission, disconnect fluid cooler lines from radiator and engine retaining brackets.
6. Remove fan shroud, if equipped.
7. Remove radiator and fan assembly from vehicle.
8. Disconnect and cap power steering lines from power steering pump, if equipped.
9. On models equipped with air conditioning, proceed as follows:
   a. Turn compressor service fitting valve stem to the front seated position.
   b. Loosen service fitting.
   c. Carefully and gradually discharge refrigerant from compressor

NOTE: Do not allow refrigerant to contact eyes or skin.

   d. Remove service valve fitting from compressor.
10. Remove speed control vacuum servo bellows and mounting bracket as an assembly, if equipped.

11. Mark and disconnect all vacuum lines and electrical connectors from engine.
12. Disconnect fuel lines from frame hoses.
13. On models equipped with automatic transmission, disconnect filler tube bracket from engine.
14. Raise and support vehicle.
15. Remove both engine front support cushion to frame retaining nuts.
16. Disconnect exhaust pipe from manifolds and front bracket.
17. Remove starter motor.
18. On models equipped with automatic transmission, proceed as follows:
   a. Remove flywheel inspection cover and scribe matching mark between flex plate and torque converter.
   b. Remove torque converter bolts, rotating crankshaft as needed to gain access to bolts.
   c. Remove support for lower throttle valve and inner manual linkage, then disconnect throttle valve rod from lower bell crank.
19. On all models, remove upper bell housing to engine bolts and loosen lower bolts.
20. Lower vehicle and attach suitable lifting equipment to engine.
21. Raise engine to remove weight from mounts, place suitable support under transmission, and remove lower bell housing bolts.
22. Separate engine from transmission and remove engine, taking care not to damage brake booster.
23. Reverse procedure to install.

CYLINDER HEAD
REPLACE

1. Remove air cleaner and drain cooling system, then if equipped with Air Guard emission system, disconnect

air hose from injection manifold.
2. Disconnect all hoses and electrical leads from intake manifold.
3. Remove valve covers, bridged pivot assemblies, rocker arms and push rods.

NOTE: Loosen each bridged pivot bolt one turn at a time to avoid breaking the bridged pivot. Also, keep rocker arms, bridged pivot and push rods in same order as removed so that they can be reinstalled in their original locations.

4. Disconnect spark plug wires and remove spark plugs.
5. Remove intake manifold and disconnect exhaust manifolds from cylinder head.
6. Loosen all drive belts, then if equipped with air conditioning, remove compressor bracket attaching bolts and set compressor aside.
7. Disconnect alternator support brace, power steering mounting bracket and Air Guard pump (if used) mounting bracket from cylinder head.
8. Remove cylinder head bolts and cylinder head.
9. Reverse removal procedure to install. First torque the cylinder head bolts to 80 ft. lbs. and in the sequence shown in **Fig. 3,** then finally torque the cylinder head bolts to the specifications given in the "Engine Tightening" chart.

NOTE: The cylinder block has two locating dowels on each bank to assist in lining up and holding the cylinder head and gasket in position during installation.

CAUTION: The No. 7 bolt shown in **Fig. 3,** second from front on the left bank, must have the threads sealed to prevent coolant leakage. Permatex No. 2 or equivalent is recommended.

ROCKER ARM SERVICE

The intake and exhaust rocker arms of each cylinder pivot on a bridge and pivot

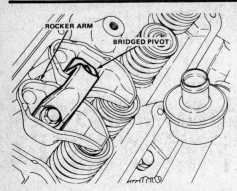

Fig. 4 Rocker arm, bridge and pivot assembly. V8 engine

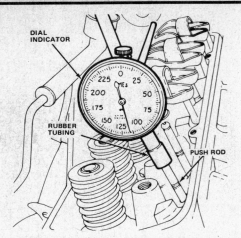

Fig. 5 Measuring cam lobe lift. V8 engine

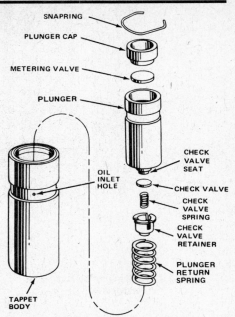

Fig. 6 Hydraulic valve lifter assembly. V8 engine

assembly which is secured with two capscrews as shown in **Fig. 4.** Each rocker arm is actuated by a hollow push rod with a hardened ball at each end. The hollow push rods route engine oil to the rocker arm assembly.

REMOVAL

1. Disconnect battery ground cable.
2. Remove cylinder head cover and gasket.
3. Remove the two capscrews at each bridge and pivot assembly.

NOTE: Alternately loosen capscrews one turn at a time to avoid damaging bridge.

4. Remove bridge and pivot assemblies with their rocker arms and push rods and position aside.

NOTE: Bridge, pivot, rocker arms and push rods must be installed in their original locations.

INSTALLATION

1. Clean all parts with a suitable solvent.
2. Using compressed air, blow out rocker arm and push rod oil passages.
3. Check rocker arms and push rods for wear or damage. Replace as required.
4. Install push rods into their original locations.

NOTE: Ensure bottom end of each push rod is centered into the hydraulic valve lifter plunger cap.

5. Install rocker arms, bridge and pivot assemblies into their original locations.
6. Loosely install bridge capscrews on each bridge and pivot assembly.
7. Torque capscrews alternately one turn at a time at each bridge and pivot assembly to 19 ft. lbs.
8. Install cylinder head cover and gasket.
9. Connect battery ground cable.

VALVE ARRANGEMENT
FRONT TO REAR

All V8s.................. E-I-I-E-E-I-I-E

VALVE GUIDES

Valve guides are an integral part of the cylinder head. When valve stem to guide clearance is excessive, ream valve guide bores to the next larger valve stem size. Valves are available with .003, .015 and .030 inch oversize stems. Ream valve guide bores in steps, starting with the .003 inch reamer and progressing to the size required.

CAM LOBE LIFT MEASUREMENT

1. Disconnect battery ground cable.
2. Remove cylinder head cover, bridge and pivot assembly and rocker arms.
3. Remove spark plugs.
4. Position a suitable piece of rubber tubing over push rod end, then install a dial indicator into other end of hose as shown in **Fig. 5.**
5. Rotate crankshaft until cam lobe base circle (push rod down) is under valve tappet.
6. Set dial indicator to zero, then rotate crankshaft until point of maximum push rod upward movement is obtained. Note dial indicator reading.
7. Refer to Cam Lobe Lift Specs for specifications.

CAM LOBE LIFT SPECS

V8-304, 360 .266 inch

VALVE TIMING
Intake Opens Before TDC

V8-304, 360 .... 14.75 Degrees

HYDRAULIC VALVE LIFTERS

The hydraulic valve lifters may be removed from their bores after removing cylinder head cover, bridge and pivot assembly, rocker arms, push rods and intake manifold. Tool NO. J-21884 may be used to remove valve lifters from their bores, **Fig. 6.**

TIMING CASE COVER
REPLACE

The timing chain cover is a die casting incorporating an oil seal at the vibration damper hub, **Fig. 7.**

The front oil seal can be installed from either side of the cover, and the seal can be replaced after removing the damper. The timing cover does not have to be removed to replace the oil seal.

REMOVAL

1. Disconnect battery ground cable and drain cooling system.
2. Disconnect lower radiator and bypass hoses from engine, then remove drive belts, cooling fan, and clutch or hub.
3. On models with A/C, remove compressor from bracket and secure aside, leaving hoses connected.
4. On all models, remove alternator, mounting bracket and rear idler pul-

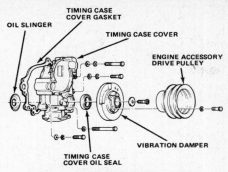

Fig. 7   Timing case cover assembly. V8 engine

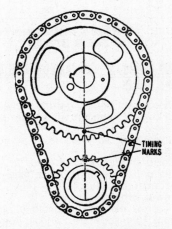

Fig. 9   Valve timing. V8-304

ley.
5. Remove power steering and AIR pumps, and the mounting brackets, as equipped. Leave power steering hoses connected and secure pumps aside.
6. Remove vibration damper assembly using suitable puller.
7. Remove distributor cap and disconnect electrical connectors from distributor.
8. Mark position fo distributor rotor and body, then remove distributor and fuel pump from front cover.
9. Remove 2 front oil pan bolt and bolts securing front cover to block, noting installation position for assembly.
10. Remove front cover, gasket and crankshaft oil slinger, then drive seal from cover using suitable drift and discard seal.

INSTALLATION

1. Remove lower dowel pin from front of block and trim both protruding oil pan side gaskets flush with face of block. Retain gasket ends.
2. Apply suitable sealer to replacement front cover gasket, cement gasket to engine block, then install crankshaft oil slinger.
3. Apply suitable sealer to outer diameter

of oil seal and install seal in cover using J-26562 or equivalent to ensure that seal is properly seated.
4. On models with oil pan gasket, proceed as follows:
   a. Using original pieces as guide, trim ends off replacement gasket which correspond to gaskets removed previously.
   b. Install oil pan front seal onto timing case cover, align tabs of replacement pan gasket ends with oil pan seal and cement gaskets onto front cover.
   c. Apply suitable sealer to oil pan/engine block joint where pan gaskets were cut, mount cover in position on engine, then install front oil pan bolts.
   d. Tighten oil pan bolts slowly and evenly until front cover aligns with upper locating dowel, insert lower dowel through cover and drive dowel into place in engine block.
   e. Install remaining front cover bolts and torque all bolts to 25 ft. lbs.
5. On models where RTV sealer is used to seal oil pan, proceed as follows:
   a. Ensure that cover and oil pan sealing flanges are clean and free from oil, then apply a ⅛ inch wide bead of RTV sealer to cover flanges.
   b. Mount front cover on engine, aligning it with top locating dowel, then loosely install cover to block retaining bolts.
   c. Insert lower locating dowel through cover and drive into place in block, then torque cover bolts to 25 ft. lbs.
   d. Apply a small bead of RTV sealer to joint between pan and front cover and press sealer into place with finger.
   e. Apply suitable thread locking compound to front oil pan bolts, then install bolts and tighten until snug.

NOTE: Do not overtighten front oil pan bolts as pan will be distorted.

6. Reverse remaining procedure to complete installation.

TIMING CHAIN
REMOVAL

1. Disconnect battery ground cable.
2. Remove vibration damper pulley, damper, timing case cover and gasket.
3. Remove crankshaft oil slinger.
4. Remove camshaft sprocket retaining screw and washer.
5. Remove distributor drive gear and fuel pump eccentric, **Fig. 8.**
6. Rotate crankshaft until timing mark on crankshaft sprocket aligns with timing mark on camshaft sprocket, **Figs. 9 and 10.**
7. Remove crankshaft sprocket, camshaft sprocket and timing chain as an assembly.

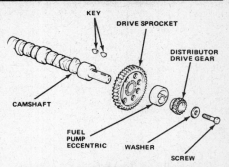

Fig. 8   Camshaft assembly. V8 engine

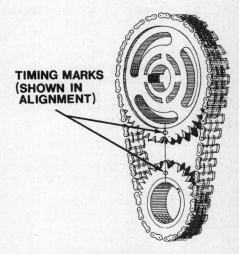

Fig. 10   Valve timing. V8-360

INSTALLATION

1. Assemble timing chain, crankshaft sprocket and camshaft sprocket with timing marks positioned as shown in **Figs. 9 and 10.**
2. Install timing chain and sprocket assembly onto engine.
3. Install fuel pump eccentric and distributor drive gear.

NOTE: Install fuel pump eccentric with word "REAR" on eccentric facing toward camshaft.

4. Install camshaft washer and retaining bolt. Torque bolt to 30 ft. lbs.
5. To verify correct installation of timing chain, proceed as follows:
   a. Rotate crankshaft until timing mark on camshaft is at the three o'clock position.
   b. Starting with the pin directly adjacent to camshaft sprocket timing mark, count the number of pins downward to timing mark on crankshaft sprocket.
   c. There must be 20 pins between these two points.
6. Install crankshaft oil slinger.
7. Remove original oil seal from timing case cover.
8. Install new seal into timing case cover, then position cover onto engine.

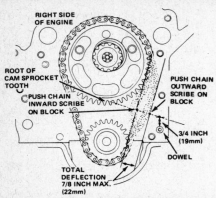

Fig. 11 Measuring timing chain wear. V8 engine

Torque case cover bolts to 25 ft. lbs.
9. Install vibration damper and pulley.
10. Install battery ground cable.

TIMING CHAIN WEAR MEASUREMENT

1. Disconnect battery ground cable.
2. Remove timing case cover.
3. Rotate camshaft or crankshaft sprocket until right side of timing chain is taut.
4. Determine a reference point for timing chain deflection measurement as follows:
   a. Measure ¾ of an inch up from dowel pin located on right side of engine and mark location, **Fig. 11.**
   b. Position a suitable straight edge across timing chain from point at lowest root of camshaft sprocket to point obtained (marked) in step 4a, **Fig. 11.**
   c. Grasp timing chain at point where straight edge dissects (cuts across) timing chain and use this point as a reference.
   d. Move timing chain inward toward centerline of engine and mark engine block at point of maximum inward chain deflection, **Fig. 11.**
   e. Move timing chain outward from centerline of engine and mark engine block at point of maximum outward chain deflection.
   f. Measure distance between inward and outward chain deflection marks placed on engine block.
   g. Replace timing chain assembly if deflection (wear) exceeds ⅞ inch.
5. Install timing case cover and connect battery ground cable.

CAMSHAFT
REPLACE

1. Disconnect battery ground cable.
2. Drain cooling system.
3. Remove radiator and fan assembly.
4. On models equipped with air conditioning, remove condenser and receiver assembly and position aside.

5. Remove cylinder head covers and gaskets.
6. Remove bridge and pivot assembly, rocker arms and push rods.

NOTE: During removal of bridge and pivot assembly, loosen capscrews one turn at a time to avoid damaging bridge.

7. Remove intake manifold assembly from engine.
8. Remove valve lifters.
9. Remove distributor.
10. Remove damper pulley and vibration damper.
11. Remove timing case cover.
12. Rotate crankshaft until timing mark on crankshaft sprocket aligns with timing mark on camshaft sprocket.
13. Remove camshaft and crankshaft sprocket retaining bolts.
14. Remove distributor drive gear and fuel pump eccentric from camshaft, **Fig. 8.**
15. Remove timing chain, camshaft and crankshaft sprockets as an assembly.
16. Remove hood latch support bracket, front bumper or grille, as required.
17. Remove camshaft from engine.
18. Reverse procedure to install. During installation of distributor, rotate crankshaft until No. 1 piston is at TDC of compression stroke. Install distributor with rotor aligned with No. 1 terminal on distributor cap when distributor is completely seated on engine block. During installation of timing chain, assemble crankshaft sprocket, camshaft sprocket with timing marks positioned as shown in **Figs. 9 and 10.**

INTAKE MANIFOLD
REPLACE

1. Disconnect battery ground cable.
2. Drain cooling system.
3. Remove air cleaner assembly from carburetor.
4. Mark and disconnect ignition wires from spark plugs.
5. Disconnect upper radiator hose and bypass hose from intake manifold.
6. Disconnect electrical connectors from coolant temperature gauge valve.
7. Remove ignition coil bracket and position aside.
8. Disconnect heater hoses from intake manifold.
9. Mark and disconnect all vacuum hoses and electrical connectors from carburetor.
10. Disconnect throttle and throttle valve linkage from carburetor and intake manifold.
11. Disconnect air lines from air injection manifold.
12. Disconnect diverter valve from air pump output line and position aside.
13. Remove carburetor from engine.
14. Remove intake manifold attaching bolts, then the intake manifold.
15. Reverse procedure to install. Torque intake manifold bolts to 43 ft. lbs.

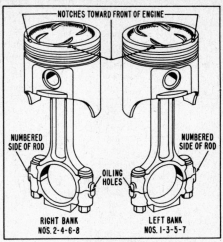

Fig. 12 Piston & rod assembly. V8-304 & 360

EXHAUST MANIFOLD
REPLACE

1. Disconnect battery ground cable.
2. Disconnect ignition wires from spark plugs.
3. Disconnect air lines from air manifold.
4. Raise and support vehicle.
5. Disconnect front exhaust pipe from exhaust manifold.
6. Lower vehicle.
7. Remove exhaust manifold attaching bolts, then separate manifold from cylinder head.
8. Remove air injection manifold, service fittings and washers.
9. Reverse procedure to install. During installation of exhaust manifold, torque manifold center attaching bolts to 25 ft. lbs. Torque manifold outer bolts to 15 ft. lbs.

PISTON & ROD
ASSEMBLE

Pistons and rods should be assembled and installed as shown in **Fig. 12.**

MAIN BEARINGS

The main bearing journal size (diameter) is identified by a color coded paint mark on adjacent cheek toward flanged (rear) end of crankshaft, except for rear main journal which is on crankshaft rear flange. Color codes used to indicate journal and corresponding bearing sizes are listed in **Fig. 13.**

CONNECTING ROD BEARINGS

The connecting rod journal is identified by a color coded paint mark on adjacent cheek or counterweight toward flanged (rear) end of crankshaft. Color codes used to indicate journal sizes and corresponding bearing sizes are listed in **Fig. 14.**

Crankshaft Main Bearing Journal Color Code and Diameter in Inches (Journal Size)		Bearing Color Code			
		Upper Insert Size		Lower Insert Size	
Yellow	−2.7489 to 2.7484 (Standard)	Yellow	— Standard	Yellow	— Standard
Orange	−2.7484 to 2.7479 (0.0005 Undersize)	Yellow	— Standard	Black	— .001-inch Undersize
Black	−2.7479 to 2.7474 (0.001 Undersize)	Black	— .001-inch Undersize	Black	— .001-inch Undersize
Green	−2.7474 to 2.7469 (0.0015 Undersize)	Black	— .001-inch Undersize	Green	— .002-inch Undersize
Red	−2.7389 to 2.7384 (0.010 Undersize)	Red	— .010-inch Undersize	Red	— .010-inch Undersize

Fig. 13   Main bearing selection chart. V8 engine

Crankshaft Main Bearing Journal Color Code and Diameter in Inches (mm)		Bearing Color Code			
		Upper Insert Size		Lower Insert Size	
Yellow	−2.7489 to 2.7484 (69.8220-69.8093mm)(Standard)	Yellow	—Standard	Yellow	—Standard
Orange	−2.7484 to 2.7479 (69.8093-69.7966mm)(0.0005 Undersize)	Yellow	—Standard	Black	0.001-inch(0.025mm) Undersize
Black	−2.7479 to 2.7474 (69.7966-69.7839mm)(0.001 Undersize)	Black	0.001-inch (0.025mm) Undersize	Black	0.001-inch(0.025mm) Undersize
Green	−2.7474 to 2.7469 (69.7839-69.7712mm)(0.0015 Undersize)	Black	0.001-inch (0.025mm) Undersize	Green	0.002-inch(0.051mm) Undersize
Red	−2.7389 to 2.7384 (69.5680-69.5553mm)(0.010 Undersize)	Red	0.010-inch (0.254mm) Undersize	Red	0.010-inch(0.254mm) Undersize

Fig. 14   Connecting rod bearing selection chart. V8 engines

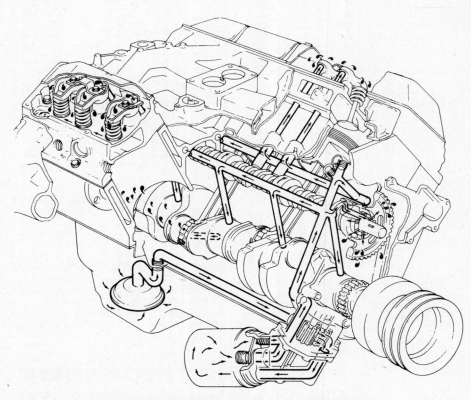

Engine lubrication system. V8 engine

CRANKSHAFT REAR OIL SEAL

1. To replace the seal, **Fig. 15,** remove oil pan and scrape oil pan surfaces clean.
2. Remove rear main bearing cap.
3. Remove and discard oil seals.
4. Clean cap thoroughly.
5. Loosen all remaining main bearing cap screws.
6. With a brass drift and hammer, tap upper seal until sufficient seal is protruding to permit pulling seal out completely with pliers.
7. Wipe seal surface of crankshaft clean, then oil lightly.
8. Coat back surface of upper seal with soap, and lip of seal with No. 40 engine oil.
9. Install upper seal into cylinder block. Lip of seal must face to front of engine.
10. Coat cap and cylinder block mating surface portion of seal with Permatex No. 2 or equivalent, being careful not to apply sealer on lip of seal.
11. Coat back surface of lower seal with soap, and lip of seal with No. 40 engine oil. Place into cap, seating seal firmly into seal recess in cap.
12. Place Permatex No. 2 or equivalent on both chamfered edges of rear main bearing cap.
13. Install main bearing and cap. Torque cap to 100 ft. lbs.
14. Cement oil pan gasket to cylinder block with tongue of gasket at each end coated with Permatex or equiva-

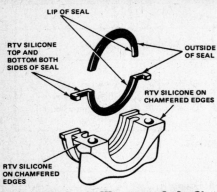

Fig. 15 Installing crankshaft rear oil seal. V8 engine

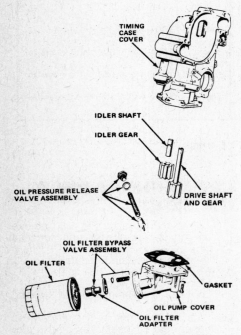

Fig. 17 Oil pump & filter assembly. V8 engine

lent before installing into rear main bearing cap at joint of tongue and oil pan front neoprene seal.

15. Coat oil pan rear seal with soap. Place into recess of rear main bearing cap, making certain seal is firmly and evenly seated.

16. Install oil pan and tighten drain plug securely.

OIL PAN
REPLACE

1. Disconnect battery ground cable.
2. Raise and support vehicle.
3. Drain oil from engine.
4. On vehicles equipped with manual transmission, bend dust shield tabs downward.
5. Remove oil pan attaching bolts, then the oil pan.

6. Reverse procedure to install.

OIL PUMP
REMOVAL

1. Disconnect battery ground cable.
2. Refer to "Oil Pan, Replace" and remove oil pan.
3. Remove attaching bolts, then remove oil pump cover gasket and oil filter assembly, **Fig. 16**.

SERVICE

1. Remove drive gear and idler gear assembly from pump body, **Fig. 17**.
2. Remove oil pressure relief, retaining cap and spring assembly.
3. Using the preferred method, measure gear end clearance as follows:
   a. Place a strip of Plastigage across full width of each oil pump gear.
   b. Install oil pump cover and gasket. Torque cover bolts to 55 inch lbs.
   c. Remove pump cover and measure width of compressed plastigage.
   d. Gear end clearance should be .002–.008 inch.
4. Using the alternate method, measure gear end clearance as follows:
   a. Place a suitable straight edge across gears and oil pump body.
   b. Place a feeler gauge between gears and straight edge.
   c. Gear end clearance should be .004–.008 inch.
   d. If gear end clearance is excessive measure gear length. If gear length is correct install a thinner oil pump cover gasket. If gear length is incorrect, replace gears and idler shaft.
5. Measure gear tooth to pump body clearance as follows:
   a. Place a suitable feeler gauge between gear tooth and pump body inner wall directly opposite point of gear mesh.
   b. Rotate gears and measure each gear tooth clearance.
   c. Clearance should be .0005–.0025 inch.
   d. If gear tooth to body clearance exceeds specified limit, use a micrometer and measure gear diameter. If gear diameter is correct and gear clearance is correct, replace cover. If gear diameter is incorrect, replace gears and idler shaft.

INSTALLATION

1. Install oil pressure relief valve into pump cover.

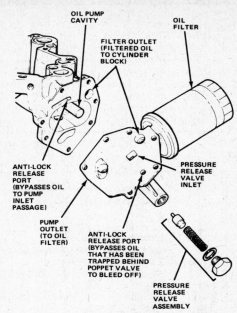

Fig. 16 Oil pump cover assembly. V8 engine

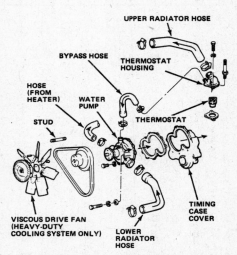

Fig. 18 Engine cooling system components. V8 engine

2. Install spring and retaining cap into pump cover.
3. Install idler shaft, idler gear and drive gear assembly into pump body.
4. Install pump cover and oil filter assembly. Torque pump cover screws to 55 inch lbs.

BELT TENSION DATA

	New lbs.	Used lbs.
A/C Compressor, Air pump, Fan, Alternator & Power Steering Pump	125–155	90–115

WATER PUMP
REPLACE

1. Disconnect battery ground cable.
2. Drain cooling system, then disconnect upper hose from radiator.
3. Loosen drive belts and remove fan shroud, if equipped.
4. Remove fan and hub assembly from water pump, **Fig. 18.**
5. On models equipped air conditioning, remove compressor bracket to water pump stud.
6. Remove alternator and mounting bracket assembly and position aside.
7. Remove power steering pump to rear mounting bracket nuts.
8. Remove front and rear power steering bracket to water pump mounting stud.
9. Disconnect heater hose, bypass hose and lower radiator hose from water pump.
10. Remove water pump and gasket from timing case cover.
11. Reverse procedure to install.

FUEL PUMP
REPLACE

1. Disconnect battery ground cable.
2. Disconnect and cap fuel lines from fuel pump.
3. Remove fuel pump attaching bolts, then the fuel pump.
4. Reverse procedure to install.

Clutch & Manual Transmission Section

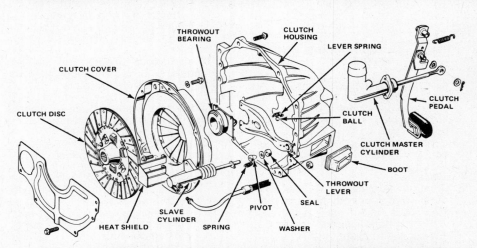

Fig. 1 Hydraulic clutch release mechanism. 4 cylinder models

CLUTCH PEDAL
ADJUST

NOTE: Some 1980–85 models equipped with four cylinder engines use a hydraulic clutch mechanism, **Fig. 1,** which is self adjusting. Free play adjustments are not necessary and there is no provision for such an adjustment.

1. Position clutch pedal against pedal support bracket stop.
2. On Cherokee, Wagoneer, Grand Wagoneer and all truck models, adjust pedal to bellcrank push rod until bellcrank inner lever is parallel to front face of clutch housing and slightly forward from the vertical position.
3. On all models, loosen jam nut on release rod adjuster and rotate adjuster as needed to obtain the following pedal free play: ⅜–⅝ inch on all models with V-8 engines and 1979–81 Cherokee, Wagoneer and Truck models with 6 cylinder engines; 1¼ inches on CJ, Scrambler, Grand Wagoneer, 1982–83 Cherokee and Wagoneer, and 1982–85 Truck models with 6 cylinder engines.
4. Tighten release rod adjuster jam nut and ensure that pedal free play is still within specification.

CLUTCH HYDRAULIC SYSTEM
BLEED

1. Ensure that clutch master cylinder is adequately filled, then raise and support vehicle.
2. Remove slave cylinder from clutch housing and disconnect push rod from cylinder.
3. Compress slave cylinder plunger using clamp J-24420-A or equivalent.
4. Attach suitable flexible tubing to slave cylinder bleed screw and immerse other end of tube in container filled half-way with clean brake fluid, ensuring that hose end remains submerged in fluid.
5. Loose bleed screw, have assistant fully depress and hold clutch pedal, tighten bleed screw, then release clutch pedal.

NOTE: Do not allow clutch pedal to be released while bleed screw is open, and do not allow master cylinder to run out of fluid during bleeding.

6. Repeat step 5 until all air is purged from system, then reinstall slave cylinder, ensure that clutch master cylinder is adequately filled and check clutch release mechanism operation.

CLUTCH MASTER CYLINDER
REPLACE

1. Disconnect hydraulic line at clutch cylinder.
2. Cap hydraulic line and master cylinder opening to prevent entry of dirt.
3. Remove cotter pin and washer retaining cylinder push rod on clutch pedal and slide rod off pedal pivot.
4. Remove nuts attaching clutch cylinder to firewall and remove cylinder.
5. Reverse procedure to install. Torque cylinder attaching nuts to 11 ft. lbs.

CLUTCH SLAVE CYLINDER
REPLACE

1. Raise vehicle and disconnect hydraulic line at cylinder.
2. Remove throwout lever-to-cylinder push rod retaining spring.
3. Remove slave cylinder, heat shield, throwout lever pivot, washer and seal from clutch housing.

CLUTCH ASSEMBLY
REPLACE

REMOVAL

1. Raise and support vehicle.
2. Remove transmission as outlined, then the starter motor.
3. On models with hydraulic release mechanism, remove slave cylinder bolts, disconnect push rod from release fork and secure cylinder aside leaving hoses connected.
4. On all models, remove throwout bearing and clutch housing assembly, noting position of clutch housing shims, if equipped.
5. Mark position of pressure plate on flywheel for assembly reference.
6. Alternately loosen the pressure plate attaching bolts to relieve spring tension.

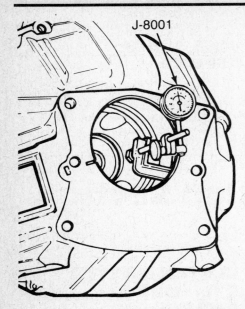

Fig. 2 **Clutch housing alignment check**

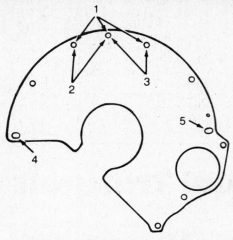

Fig. 3 **Clutch housing shim locations**

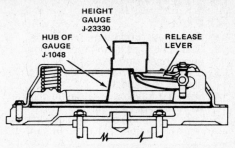

Fig. 4 **Pressure plate release lever height measurement**

NOTE: The pressure plate bolts must be loosened evenly to prevent distortion of cover.

7. Remove pressure plate bolts, then the pressure plate and driven plate from flywheel.

NOTE: Place a mark on the side of the driven plate facing the flywheel for assembly reference.

8. Remove pilot bushing lubricating wick and soak wick in engine oil.

CLUTCH HOUSING ALIGNMENT CHECK

Clutch housing misalignment is caused by excessive face or bore runout of the clutch housing or transmission adapter. Misalignment causes improper clutch release, clutch noise and vibration, clutch plate and front transmission bearing failure, premature pilot bearing wear, and in severe cases, gear jumpout on deceleration. If these malfunctions are evident, clutch housing alignment should be checked and corrected, as needed, using the following procedure.
1. With clutch housing assembly, pressure plate and clutch disc removed, remove one flywheel bolt.
2. Obtain a ½-20 bolt and nut to use as dial indicator support. Bolt should be 9 inches long for models less transmission adapter or 15 inches long for models with transmission adapter.
3. Install nut on bolt, thread bolt into crankshaft by hand, then tighten nut against flywheel to secure bolt.
4. Install clutch housing assembly, positioning shims as noted during removal, and torque bolts to 54 ft. lbs. for 4

cylinder engines, 30 ft. lbs. for V8 engines, or 35 ft. lbs. top and 45 ft. lbs. bottom for 6 cylinder engines.
5. Mount suitable dial indicator on support bolt with pointer bearing against transmission mounting face of clutch housing or adapter, approximately ⅛ inch from edge of bore, **Fig. 2.** Zero indicator.
6. Rotate crankshaft a full 360° while observing dial indicator and note readings. Face runout must not exceed .010 inch (total indicator reading) at any point in rotation.

NOTE: Crankshaft end play must be held at zero to obtain accurate readings. Move and hold crankshaft with suitable lever to eliminate end play.

7. Reposition dial indicator so that pointer bears against center of transmission front bearing adapter bore in clutch housing or adapter, then zero indicator.
8. Holding end play at zero, rotate crankshaft a full 360° while observing indicator and note readings. Bore runout must not exceed .010 inch (total indicator reading).
9. If either face or bore runout exceed .010 inch on models without transmission adapter, proceed as follows:
   a. Move dial indicator aside and loosen clutch housing retaining bolts.
   b. Insert shims between clutch housing and engine or engine adapter to correct misalignment. When inserting shims, note that a change in face alignment will also change bore alignment.
   c. Shims inserted at point 1, **Fig. 3,** affect top to bottom alignment.
   d. Shims inserted at points 2 and 3, **Fig. 3,** affect side to side alignment.
   e. Shims inserted at points 4 and 5, **Fig. 3,** affect both top to bottom and side to side alignment.
   f. After inserting shims, torque housing bolts to specifications given in

step 4, then recheck face and bore runout.
   g. If both bore and face alignment cannot be brought within specifications, housing should be replaced.
10. If face runout exceeds .010 inch on models with transmission adapter, adjust as outlined in step 9.
11. If both face and bore runout exceed specifications, correct face alignment, then recheck and correct bore alignment as outlined in step 12.
12. On models with transmission adapter, adjust adapter bore alignment as follows:
   a. Move dial indicator aside, then loosen bolts securing adapter to clutch housing.
   b. Reposition adapter on housing, moving adapter up or down, left or right, as needed.
   c. Torque adapter bolts to 35 ft. lbs., then recheck bore runout.
13. On all models, replace clutch housing and transmission adapter, if equipped, if face and bore runout cannot be brought within specifications.

NOTE: Ensure that face and bore runout of replacement components is within specifications during installation.

14. When housing alignment has been set, remove dial indicator, then the housing assembly, noting installation position of shims.
15. Remove support bolt from crankshaft, install flywheel bolt and torque to specifications.
16. Install clutch disc and pressure plate assembly, then the clutch housing, insert housing shims in proper positions, then torque clutch housing bolts to specifications listed in step 4.

PRESSURE PLATE (CLUTCH COVER) RELEASE LEVER ADJUSTMENT

1979-83

NOTE: This procedure applies to all models not equipped with diaphragm spring type pressure plate (clutch cover).

1. Remove flywheel and position on flat surface with drive face up, then install gauge plate J-1048 on flywheel in

position normally occupied by clutch disc.

2. Position pressure plate assembly over gauge plate, rotate plate to align machined lands with pressure plate release levers and ensure that gauge plate hub is centered.
3. Install pressure plate bolts and torque bolts alternately and evenly to 40 ft. lbs.
4. Compress each release lever several times to seat levers in operating position.
5. Measure height of each lever above gauge plate hub using height gauge J-23330, **Fig. 4.**
6. If release levers are not specified height above gauge plate hub, **Fig. 5,** adjust by turning lever height adjusting nuts until specified dimension is obtained.
7. After each lever is adjusted, compress lever several times, recheck adjustment and correct as needed.
8. When all levers are at specified height, stake position of adjusting nuts to secure adjustment.

Year	Model	Lever Height
1979—82	CJ, Scrambler①	.093—.1093
	Cherokee, Wagoneer Truck	.1875
1980—83	All②	1.595—1.720
1982—83	6 cyl.③	2.04—2.16
	V8	.1875

①—Exc. 4 cyl. engines.   ②—4 Cyl. engines.
③—Using .305 gauge.

Fig. 5 Pressure plate release lever height specifications

INSTALLATION

1. Lightly lubricate release lever pivots.
2. Install pilot bushing lubricating wick into crankshaft bore.
3. Install a suitable clutch alignment tool or a spare clutch shaft into driven plate hub.
4. Install assembled plate and tool on flywheel. Ensure that tool is seated fully in the pilot bushing.

NOTE: Ensure that the proper side of the driven plate faces the flywheel.

5. Place pressure plate on flywheel and over driven plate and alignment tool. Align pressure plate and flywheel using the marks made during removal. Install pressure plate attaching bolts finger tight.
6. Torque pressure plate evenly and alternately to 40 ft. lbs. except on CJ & Scrambler models with four cylinder engine. Torque these pressure plate bolts to 23 ft. lbs.
7. Install clutch housing and starter motor.
8. Install throwout bearing and waved washer, if used.
9. Install transmission.

MANUAL TRANSMISSION
REPLACE

1980—85 ALL

1. Remove transmission shift lever boot

attaching screws and slide boot upward.
2. On models with SR-4, T4 or T5 transmissions, remove bolts attaching transmission shift lever housing to transmission. Lift shift lever and housing upward and out of transmission.
3. On models with T-18A transmission, remove shift lever cap, gasket, spring seat, spring and shift lever as an assembly, then remove shift lever locating pins from housing.
4. On models with T-176 transmission, press and rotate transmission shift lever retainer, then remove lever, boot, spring and seat as an assembly.
5. Raise vehicle, then place alignment marks on propeller shaft and transfer case yoke. Disconnect propeller shaft at transfer case yoke and secure to underbody with wire.
6. On Cherokee and truck models, disconnect front parking brake cable at equalizer, then remove clip that retains rear cable to rear crossmember and position cable out of way.
7. Support engine by positioning a jack stand under clutch housing.
8. Remove bolts and nuts attaching rear crossmember to frame side rails and support cushion, then remove crossmember.
9. Disconnect speedometer cable, back-up lamp switch wire and four-wheel drive indicator switch wire.
10. Disconnect transfer case vent hose at transfer case.
11. Place alignment marks on front propeller shaft and transfer case yoke, then disconnect propeller shaft and secure to underbody with wire.
12. On CJ models, remove transfer case shifter shaft retaining nut and control link pins, then remove shifter shaft and disengage shift lever from shift control links. Slide shift lever upward into boot to position lever out of way.

NOTE: On some units, it may be necessary to unthread shifter shaft to remove.

13. On Cherokee and truck models, re-

move cotter pin and washer that connect link to shift lever, then disconnect link.
14. Using a suitable jack, support transmission and transfer case assembly.
15. Remove transmission to clutch housing attaching bolts, then remove transmission and transfer case assembly.
16. Reverse procedure to install. Soak pilot bushing lubricating wick in engine oil before installing.

1979 ALL

1. Remove floor lever knob, trimming boot, floor covering and pan.
2. On three-speed transmissions, remove shift control lever housing assembly and on four-speed transmissions, remove shift cap, spring retainer, spring, shift lever and pin.
3. Remove transfer case shift lever and bracket assembly.
4. Raise vehicle, remove front propeller shaft and disconnect rear propeller shaft from transfer case.
5. Disconnect speedometer cable, back-up lamp switch and TCS switch wires, and brake cable.
6. On vehicles with V8 engines, disconnect exhaust pipes from manifolds.
7. Support transmission and engine with jacks and remove frame center crossmember.
8. Remove transmission to bell housing bolts and lower transmission slightly, then slide transmission and transfer case toward rear of vehicle until clutch shaft clears bell housing.

MANUAL TRANSMISSION SHIFT MECHANISM

The shift mechanism, **Figs. 6 and 7,** on all manual transmission models is located within the shift control housing which also serves as the transmission top cover. The shift mechanism does not require adjustment and can be serviced separately from the transmission.

Transfer Case Section

TRANSFER CASE
REPLACE

1979 EXC. QUADRA-TRAC

1. Remove shift lever knob, trim ring and boot from transmission.
2. Remove transfer case shift levers.
3. Remove floor covering, if equipped, then the transmission access cover from floorpan.
4. Raise and support vehicle.
5. Drain transfer case lubricant. On CJ models, drain transmission lubricant.
6. Disconnect torque reaction bracket from crossmember, if equipped.
7. On CJ models, place a jack stand under clutch housing to support engine and transmission, then remove rear crossmember.
8. On all models, disconnect front and rear propeller shafts from output shaft yokes.
9. Disconnect speedometer cable from transfer case.
10. On Cherokee and truck models, disconnect parking brake cable at equalizer and the exhaust pipe support bracket from transfer case.
11. On all models, remove transfer case to transmission attaching bolts.

NOTE: One attaching bolt is located at the front of the transfer case at the lower right corner of the transmission.

12. Remove transfer case from vehicle. Remove and discard transfer case to transmission gasket.
13. Install new transfer case to transmission gasket.
14. Reverse steps 1 through 12 to install.

1979 QUADRA-TRAC

1. Raise and support vehicle.
2. On Cherokee, Wagoneer and Truck models equipped with low range reduction unit, remove reduction unit as follows:
   a. Loosen reduction unit to transfer case cover attaching bolts, then move reduction unit rearward just far enough to allow oil to drain from unit.
   b. Disconnect shift linkage at reduction unit control lever.
   c. Remove reduction unit to transfer case cover attaching bolts.
   d. Move reduction unit rearward to clear transmission output shaft and pinion cage.
3. On all models, scribe alignment marks on transfer case front and rear output shaft yokes and propeller shafts for proper assembly.
4. Mark Emergency Drive control dia-

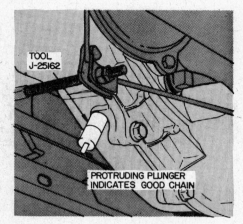

Fig. 1 Warner Quadra-Trac, drive chain tension check

TOOL J-25162

PROTRUDING PLUNGER INDICATES GOOD CHAIN

phragm vacuum hoses for proper assembly, then disconnect hoses.
5. Disconnect electrical connector at Emergency Drive indicator, then the speedometer cable.
6. On CJ-7 models, place suitable support under transmission and remove rear crossmember.
7. On all models, disconnect front and rear propeller shafts at transfer case yokes and secure shafts out of way.
8. Disconnect parking brake cable guide from pivot on right frame rail.
9. Remove exhaust pipe support bracket to transfer case attaching bolts.
10. Remove two transfer case to transmission mounting bolts that enter from front side of vehicle.
11. Remove two transfer case to transmission mounting bolts that enter from rear of vehicle and install ⁷⁄₁₆-14 by 5 inch long guide pin in each hole.

NOTE: If guide pins are difficult to install, the transfer case attaching bolts may have created burrs on the bolt hole edges. Remove burrs with small file.

12. Move transfer case assembly rearward until free of transmission output shaft and guide pins and remove assembly.
13. Remove all gasket material from rear of transmission.
14. Reverse procedure to install.

1980—85 EXC. QUADRA-TRAC & 1980—82 QUADRA-TRAC

CJ & Scrambler Models
1. Remove shift lever knob, trim ring and boot from transmission and transfer case shift levers.
2. On all models, remove floor covering,

if equipped, then the transmission access cover from floorpan.
3. Raise and support vehicle. Drain lubricant from transfer case.
4. Place a jack stand under clutch housing to support engine and transmission, then remove rear crossmember.
5. Disconnect front and rear propeller shafts from output shaft yokes.
6. Disconnect speedometer cable from transfer case.
7. Disconnect parking brake cable at equalizer, if necessary.
8. Disconnect exhaust pipe support bracket from transfer case, if equipped.
9. Remove transfer case to transmission attaching bolts.
10. Remove transfer case from vehicle.
11. Remove and discard transfer case to transmission gasket.
12. Install new transfer case to transmission gasket.
13. Reverse steps 1 through 11 to install.

Cherokee, Wagoneer, Grand Wagoneer & Truck Models
1. Raise and support vehicle.
2. Drain transfer case lubricant.
3. Mark alignment of transfer case front and rear output shaft yokes and propeller shafts, then disconnect front and rear propeller shafts from output shaft yokes.
4. Disconnect speedometer cable and indicator switch wires from transfer case.
5. Support transmission with a suitable jack and remove rear crossmember.
6. Disconnect parking brake cable guide from pivot, located at right frame rail, if necessary.
7. Remove bolts attaching exhaust pipe support bracket to transfer case, if necessary.
8. Remove transfer case to transmission attaching bolts.
9. Remove transfer case from vehicle.
10. Remove transfer case to transmission gasket and discard.
11. Install new transfer case to transmission gasket.
12. Reverse steps 1 through 9 to install.

1983 QUADRA-TRAC

1. Raise and support vehicle and drain lubricant from transfer case.
2. Disconnect speedometer cable and indicator switch wires, then the transfer case shift lever link at operating lever.
3. Disconnect parking brake cable guide from pivot on right frame rail, if necessary.
4. Place suitable support under transmission and remove rear crossmember.

5. Scribe alignment marks on transfer case front and rear output shafts at transfer case yokes and propeller shafts for proper assembly.
6. Disconnect front and rear propeller shafts at transfer case yokes and secure out of way.
7. Disconnect shift motor vacuum lines and the transfer case shift linkage.
8. Remove exhaust pipe support bracket to transfer case attaching bolts, if necessary.
9. Remove transfer case to transmission attaching bolts, then move transfer case assembly rearward until free of transmission output shaft and remove assembly.
10. Remove all gasket material from rear of transmission adapter housing.
11. Reverse procedure to install.

1984–85 QUADRA-TRAC

1. Raise and support vehicle and drain lubricant from transfer case.
2. Disconnect speedometer cable and vent hose, then the transfer case shift lever link at the operating lever.
3. Place suitable support under transmission and remove rear crossmember.
4. Scribe alignment marks on transfer case front and rear output shafts at transfer case yokes and propeller shafts for proper assembly.
5. Disconnect front and rear propeller shafts at transfer case yokes and secure shafts out of way.
6. Disconnect shift motor vacuum hoses and the transfer case shift linkage.
7. Remove transfer case to transmission attaching bolts.
8. Move transfer case rearward until clear of transmission output shaft and remove assembly.
9. Remove all gasket material from rear of transmission adapter housing.
10. Reverse procedure to install.

DRIVE CHAIN TENSION CHECK

1979 QUADRA-TRAC TRANSFER CASE

Drain lubricant from transfer case and reinstall drain plug. Remove chain inspection plug and install chain tension gauge into hole. If chain tension is satisfactory, plunger will protrude past end of tool, **Fig. 1**. If plunger is flush or is recessed within tool, the drive chain has lost tension, requiring replacement.

FRONT/REAR OUTPUT SHAFT SEAL REPLACE

1979 QUADRA-TRAC TRANSFER CASE

1. Raise and support vehicle.

2. When replacing front output shaft seal, place suitable jack under transmission and remove rear crossmember.
3. Scribe alignment marks on pertinent propeller shaft and transfer case yoke for proper assembly, then disconnect shaft at yoke.
4. Using suitable tools, remove yoke retaining nut, then the yoke.
5. Using suitable tools, remove oil seal and install new oil seal.
6. Install yoke, washer and new retaining nut on shaft, torquing nut to 120 ft. lbs.
7. Connect propeller shaft to yoke, then install crossmember, if removed.

FRONT/REAR YOKE OIL SEAL REPLACE

MODEL 20 TRANSFER CASE

1. Raise and support vehicle.
2. Place suitable jack under transmission and remove rear crossmember.
3. Scribe alignment marks on pertinent propeller shaft and transfer case yoke, then disconnect propeller shaft at transfer case yoke.
4. Using suitable tools, remove transfer case yoke nut washer, then the yoke.
5. Using suitable tools, remove oil seal and install new oil seal.
6. Install yoke, washer and nut, torquing nut to 140 ft. lbs.

MODEL 300 TRANSFER CASE

1. Raise and support vehicle.
2. Place suitable jack under transmission and remove rear crossmember.
3. Scribe alignment marks on pertinent propeller shaft and transfer case yoke for proper assembly, then disconnect shaft from yoke.
4. Using suitable tools, remove transfer case yoke nut and washer, then the yoke.
5. Using suitable tools, remove oil seal and install new oil seal.
6. Install yoke, washer and nut, torquing nut to 120 ft. lbs.

SHIFT ROD OIL SEAL REPLACE

MODEL 20 TRANSFER CASE

CJ Models
1. When placing left side shift rod seal, shift transfer case to 4L position.
2. Raise and support vehicle.
3. Remove pins connecting control links to transfer case shift rods.
4. Using suitable tool, remove shift rod oil seal and install new seal.

Exc. CJ Models
1. If equipped with 3 speed transmission, shift transfer case into 2H position and remove shift lever knob and boot.
2. Remove transfer case shift lever housing to support tube attaching bolts and pull shift lever straight back to 4H position.
3. Raise and support vehicle.
4. On models equipped with 8 cylinder engine, place suitable jack under transmission and remove rear crossmember.
5. On all models, scribe alignment marks on front propeller shaft and yoke for proper assembly, then disconnect shaft at transfer case yoke.
6. Remove pins connecting control links to transfer case shift rods.
7. On models equipped with 3 speed transmission, remove transfer case shift housing from support tool.
8. Using suitable tools, remove shift rod seal and install new seal.
9. On models equipped with 3 speed transmission, install transfer case shift housing on support tube.
10. On all models, install pins connecting control links to transfer case shift rods and secure with new cotter pins.
11. Connect propeller shaft to transfer case yoke.
12. On models equipped with 8 cylinder engine, install rear crossmember, then remove jack.
13. On all models, lower vehicle.
14. On all models equipped with 3 speed transmission, install shift housing to support tube attaching bolts and the shift lever boot and knob.

MODEL 300 TRANSFER CASE

1. When replacing left side shift rod seal, shift transfer case into 4L position.
2. Raise and support vehicle.
3. Remove pins connecting control links to transfer case shift rods.
4. Using suitable tools, remove shift rod oil seal and install new seal.
5. Install pins connecting control links to transfer case shift rods, securing with new cotter pins.

REAR BEARING CAP/SPEEDOMETER DRIVE GEAR REPLACE

MODEL 300 TRANSFER CASE

1. Disconnect rear propeller shaft at transfer case yoke and support out of way.
2. Disconnect speedometer cable, then remove speedometer driven gear sleeve and driven gear.
3. Remove transfer case vent hose.
4. Using suitable tools, remove output

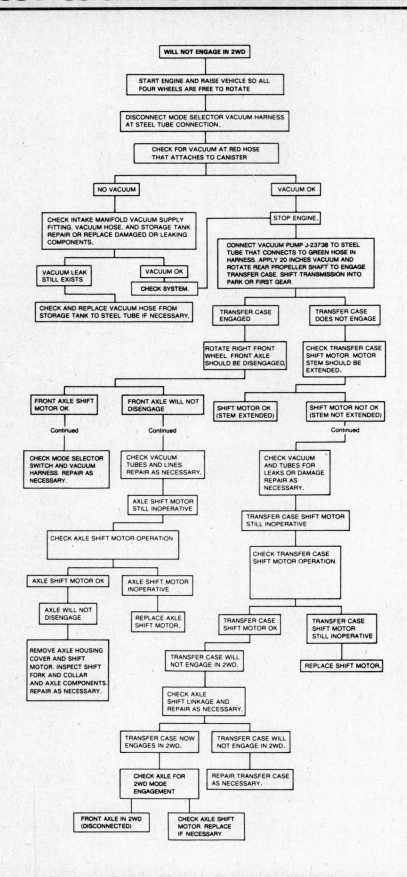

Fig. 2   Selec-Trac diagnosis. Model 229 transfer case (Part 1 of 2)

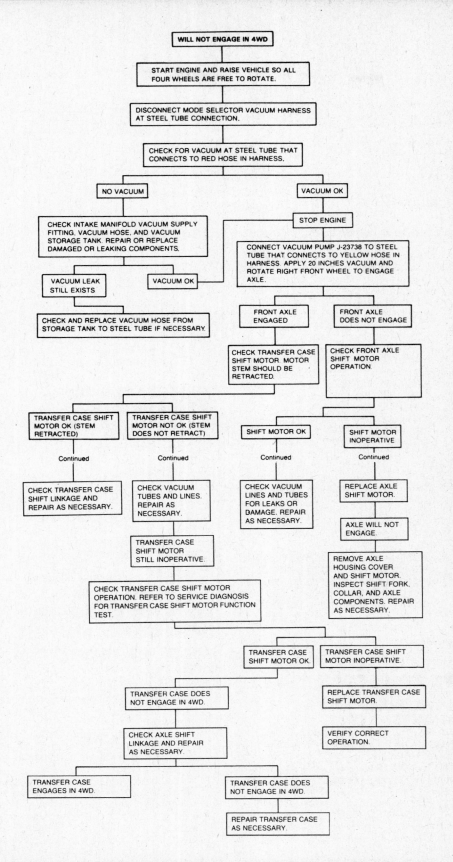

Fig. 2   Selec-Trac diagnosis. Model 229 transfer case (Part 2 of 2)

shaft yoke.

5. Remove bearing cap to transfer case bolts and remove bearing cap.
6. Remove shims and speedometer driven gear from output shaft, then the speedometer driven gear bushing from the bearing cap.
7. Using suitable tool, install speedometer driven gear bushing.
8. Install speedometer driven gear and shims on shaft.
9. Apply bead of suitable sealant to mating surface of cap and install cap, using two screws to align bolt holes, and tap cap into position with plastic mallet.
10. Torque bearing cap bolts to 35 ft. lbs.
11. Using suitable tools, install output shaft yoke, torquing lock nut to 12 ft. lbs.
12. Check rear output shaft end play as follows:
    a. Attach suitable dial indicator to bearing cap and position indicator stylus against output shaft.
    b. Pry output shaft back and forth to check end play.
    c. If end play is not .001–.005 inches, remove or add shims between speedometer drive gear and output shaft rear bearing.
13. Install transfer case vent hose and the speedometer driven gear sleeve and driven gear.
14. Install speedometer cable.
15. Install rear propeller shaft, torquing clamp strap bolts to 15 ft. lbs.

SPEEDOMETER GEAR, SHAFT SEAL, REAR BEARING & RETAINER, OIL PUMP & PUMP SEAL
REPLACE

MODEL 208 TRANSFER CASE

1. Raise and support vehicle.
2. Remove fill and drain plugs and drain oil from transfer case.
3. Scribe alignment marks on propeller shaft and transfer case yoke for proper assembly, then disconnect propeller shaft.
4. Using suitable tools, remove and discard transfer case yoke retaining nut and yoke seal washer.
5. Remove yoke, using suitable tools as necessary.
6. Remove speedometer driven gear sleeve and driven gear from rear retainer.
7. Scribe alignment marks on rear retainer for proper assembly, then remove retainer attaching bolts and the retainer.

CAUTION: Do not attempt to pry retainer off rear case. Tap retainer loose using only a rawhide or plastic mallet.

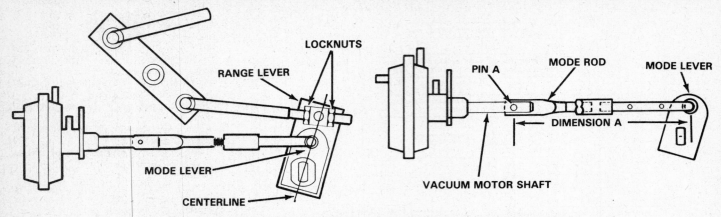

Fig. 3 Adjusting mode & range rods. Model 229 transfer case

8. Remove speedometer drive gear, then the pump housing from retainer and seal from housing.
9. When replacing bearing or retainer, remove bearing retaining snap ring from rear retainer, and tap bearing out of retainer.
10. Remove oil pump from mainshaft, then remove output shaft seal.
11. Install oil pump on mainshaft, the seal into pump housing and the speedometer driven gear.
12. Install rear output bearing in rear retainer and install snap ring, ensuring that shielded side of bearing faces interior of transfer case.
13. Install pump housing in rear retainer, then apply suitable sealant to rear retainer mating surface and install retainer on case.
14. Install retainer attaching bolts, torquing to 23 ft. lbs., and install output shaft seal, then install yoke, yoke seal washer and yoke nut, torquing nut to 120 ft. lbs.
15. Install speedometer driven gear and sleeve, then the drain plug.
16. Fill transfer case to edge of fill plug with suitable lubricant, then install fill plug.
17. Contact propeller shaft, torquing clamp strap bolts to 14 ft. lbs.

SPEEDOMETER GEAR, REAR BEARING, REAR SEAL & SHAFT YOKE
REPLACE

MODEL 219 TRANSFER CASE

1. Raise and support vehicle, then remove fill and drain plugs and drain oil from transfer case.
2. Scribe alignment marks on propeller shaft and transfer case yoke for proper assembly, then disconnect shaft from yoke.

3. Using suitable tools, remove and discard transfer case yoke nut and seal washer, then remove yoke.
4. Remove speedometer cable from retainer, then scribe alignment marks on rear retainer for proper assembly and remove retainer.
5. Remove differential shims and speedometer driven gear.
6. Remove rear output bearing snap ring and remove bearing from retainer.
7. Using suitable tool, remove rear seal from retainer.
8. Install bearing in retainer, ensuring that shielded side of bearing faces case interior, then install bearing snap ring.
9. Using suitable tool, install rear yoke seal.
10. Install speedometer gear and differential shim.
11. Apply suitable sealant to mating surface of rear retainer and install retainer, torquing attaching bolts to 23 ft. lbs.
12. Install yoke seal, washer and yoke nut, torquing nut to 120 ft. lbs.
13. Install speedometer cable and connect propeller shaft.
14. Install drain plug and fill transfer case to bottom edge of fill plug hole with suitable lubricant.
15. Install fill plug.

TORQUE BIAS TEST

1979 QUADRA-TRAC TRANSFER CASE

NOTE: The torque bias test is a method for checking differential brake cone preload. This test measures the torque at which the differential brake cones will release.

1. Ensure that Emergency Drive is not engaged, then shift transmission into Neutral.
2. Disconnect rear propeller shaft at transfer case yoke.
3. Install suitable torque wrench on transfer case rear yoke retaining nut.

4. With service brakes firmly applied, apply torque to retaining nut in clockwise direction.
5. If brake cones release at a torque value of 80 ft. lbs. or less, the differential unit may have to be replaced.
6. If cones do not release when 170 ft. lbs. torque or more is applied, improper lubricant may be the cause.

MODELS 219 & 229 TRANSFER CASES

1. Place vehicle on level surface, then shut off engine.
2. Place transmission shift lever in Neutral and transfer case shift lever in 4-HIGH position.
3. Raise and support vehicle so that one front wheel is off ground.
4. Remove hub cap from raised wheel.
5. Install torque wrench on a lug nut of raised wheel and rotate wheel with torque wrench to measure torque required to rotate wheel.
6. If required torque is at least 45 ft. lbs., viscous coupling is satisfactory.

TESTING TRANSFER CASE SHIFT MOTOR

MODEL 229 TRANSFER CASE

1. Disconnect vacuum harness from transfer case shift motor and connect suitable vacuum pump to shift motor front port.
2. Apply 15 inches vacuum to shift motor and rotate rear propeller shaft to fully engage transfer case in 4 wheel drive mode.
3. If shift motor does not retain vacuum for at least 30 seconds, replace motor.
4. Disconnect vacuum pump from front port of shift motor and connect to rear port, plug front axle connecting port and apply 15 inches vacuum to motor.
5. Place automatic transmission in Park or manual transmission in 1st gear.
6. If shift motor does not maintain vacu-

um for at least 30 seconds, replace motor.

7. Remove cap from shift motor axle connecting port and check for vacuum at port. If there is no vacuum, rotate rear propeller shaft as necessary to ensure total transfer case engagement.

NOTE: The transfer case must be fully engaged before shift motor stem will extend fully and open axle interconnecting port.

8. If vacuum is now present at shift motor axle connecting port, refer to **Fig. 2.**
9. If vacuum is still not present, slide boot away from shift motor stem and measure distance stem has extended. Stem should extend 5/8 inch as measured from edge of shift motor housing to E-ring on stem.
10. If shift motor stem does not extend specified distance, refer to **Fig. 2.**
11. If shift motor stem extends specified distance but there is still no vacuum at axle connecting port, replace motor.

TESTING FRONT AXLE SHIFT MOTOR

Model 229 Transfer Case

1. Disconnect vacuum harness from front axle shift motor and connect suitable vacuum pump to shift motor front port.
2. Apply 15 inches vacuum to shift motor and rotate right front wheel to fully

disengage axle.

3. If shift motor does not maintain vacuum for at least 30 seconds, replace motor.
4. Disconnect vacuum pump from shift motor front port and connect pump to shift motor rear port, cap transfer case connecting port and apply 15 inches vacuum to motor.
5. If shift motor does not maintain vacuum for at least 30 seconds, replace motor.
6. Remove cap from shift motor transfer case connecting port and check for vacuum at port.
7. If vacuum is not present, rotate right front wheel as necessary to ensure that axle has disengaged completely.
8. Check vacuum at shift motor transfer case connecting port again. If vacuum is now present, refer to **Fig. 2.**

MODE ROD

ADJUST

MODEL 229 TRANSFER CASE

NOTE: With transfer case in 2WD/HI, both mode lever and range lever must be aligned on the same centerline, **Fig. 3,** prior to mode rod adjustment. If levers are not properly aligned, the transfer case may not fully engage 2WD/HI, resulting in damage to the transfer case viscous coupling.

1. Ensure that all vacuum hoses are cor-

rectly routed and not loose or disconnected.

2. Adjust mode rod to approximately 5.9 inches, dimension A, **Fig. 3.**
3. Drive vehicle a short distance, shifting into 4WD and back to 2WD/HI.
4. Check mode lever position after test drive. If mode lever is not aligned with range lever, increase mode rod length one turn and repeat steps 1 and 2.
5. With transfer case vacuum motor shaft fully extended and transfer case in 2WD/HI, adjust mode rod so that pin "A" moves freely in hole through vacuum motor shaft and mode rod.

RANGE ROD

ADJUST

MODEL 229 TRANSFER CASE

NOTE: After adjusting mode rod, check position of range lever inside vehicle. Range lever should be positioned 1/2 to 1 inch above floor when it is in 2WD/HI range. This ensures sufficient travel for complete range engagement. Adjustment should be made at transfer case end of linkage.

1. Loosen lock nuts and shorten or lengthen rod to correctly position floor lever.
2. Tighten lock nuts to maintain rod adjustment.

Rear Axle, Suspension & Brake Section

AXLE SHAFT
REMOVE
SEMI-FLOATING-TAPERED SHAFT

The hub and drum are separate units, and the hub and axle shaft are serrated to mate and fit together on the taper. Both are marked to insure correct assembly. The axle shaft and bearing assembly may be removed as follows:

1. Remove rear wheel, drum and hub, then disconnect parking brake cable at equalizer.

CAUTION: Do not use a slide hammer or knockout type puller to remove hub from axle shaft. Damage to the axle bearings or other components will result.

2. Disconnect brake tube from wheel cylinder and remove brake support plate assembly, oil seal and axle shims from axle shaft.

NOTE: Axle shaft end play shims are located on the left side only.

3. Using suitable puller, pull axle shaft and bearing from axle tube, **Fig. 1.**

CAUTION: On models equipped with Trak-Lok differential, do not rotate differential unless both axle shafts are in place.

SEMI-FLOATING-FLANGED SHAFT

1. Raise and support vehicle and remove rear wheels.
2. Remove drum, **Fig. 2.**
3. Remove axle retainer nuts using access hole in axle shaft flange.
4. Remove axle shaft from housing using suitable slide hammer. Remove bearing cup from housing.

FULL-FLOATING

NOTE: It is not necessary to remove rear wheels to facilitate axle shaft replacement.

1. Remove axle flange nuts, lockwashers, and split washers retaining axle shaft flange.

2. Remove axle shaft from housing, **Fig. 3.**

BEARING OR OIL SEAL
REPLACE
SEMI-FLOATING-TAPERED SHAFT

Remove and install axle shaft bearing using a suitable arbor press. Remove old oil seal from axle housing bore, clean bore and install new seal.

SEMI-FLOATING-FLANGED SHAFT

1. Remove oil seal from housing bore, clean bore and install new seal.
2. To remove bearing, drill 1/4 inch hole in retainer ring. Hole depth should be 3/4 of the ring thickness. Do not allow drill to contact axle shaft.
3. Use a large chisel to deeply nick the retaining ring. This will enlarge the

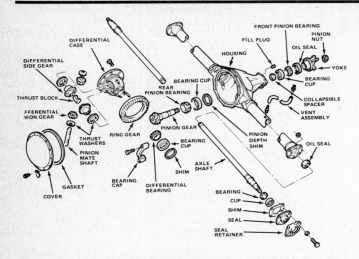

Fig. 1   Semi-floating axle with tapered shaft

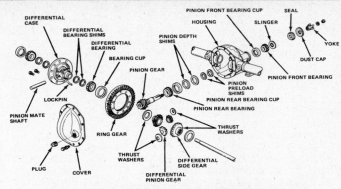

Fig. 2   Semi-floating flanged axle shaft

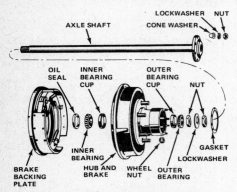

Fig. 3   Full-floating axle with wheel bearing

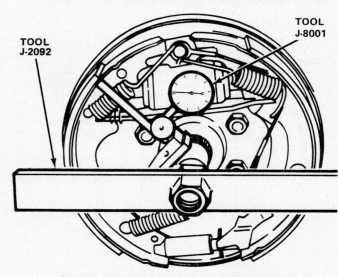

Fig. 4   Measuring axle shaft end play

ring, or split it, allowing it to be removed.

NOTE: Be certain not to damage axle shaft.

4. Cut through outer oil seal using a hacksaw, then remove seal from shaft.
5. Using suitable press, remove bearing from axle shaft. Remove retainer plate.
6. Reverse procedure to install. When installing new bearing, pack bearing with wheel bearing grease and install with cup rib ring facing axle flange.

FULL-FLOATING AXLE

1. Remove axle shaft.
2. Bend lip of lockwasher and remove locknut and lockwasher.
3. Raise and support vehicle.
4. Remove adjusting nut, outer wheel bearing and pull the wheel straight off the axle.
5. Service wheel bearings as required.
6. Reverse procedure to install. Adjust wheel bearings as described in "Wheel Bearings, Adjust".

AXLE SHAFT
INSTALL

SEMI-FLOATING-TAPERED SHAFT

NOTE: Tapered shaft bearings do not have any provision for lubrication after assembly and must be packed with a high quality wheel bearing lubricant before installation.

1. If axle shaft bearing is replaced, pack bearing with generous amount of wheel bearing lubricant and press bearing onto shaft, ensuring that small diameter of bearing faces toward outer tapered end of shaft.
2. Coat inner seal with light lubricating oil, coat outer surface of seal metal retainer with nonhardening sealer, and install seal using suitable tool.
3. Install axle shafts, aligning shaft splines with differential side gear splines, and insert shaft into gear.
4. Install outer bearing cup, then inspect brake support plate for elongated bolt holes or other damage, replacing as necessary.

NOTE: During assembly, apply suitable

sealant to axle tube flange and brake support plate mounting area to prevent entry of water and dust.

5. Install original axle end play shims, oil seal assembly and brake support plate, torquing attaching bolts to 35 ft. lbs.

NOTE: The oil seal and retainer are located on the outside of the brake support plate.

6. Connect brake line to wheel cylinder, then bleed and adjust brakes.
7. Check and adjust axle shaft end play as follows:

NOTE: Axle shaft end play is adjusted at the left side axle shaft only.

a. Strike end of each axle shaft with lead hammer to seat bearing cups against support plate.
b. Attach axle shaft end play tool J-2092 or equivalent to end of left side axle shaft and mount dial indicator on support plate or tool, **Fig. 4,** then check end play while pushing or pulling on axle shaft. End play should be .004–.008 inch.

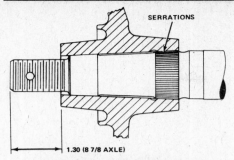

Fig. 5 Replacement hub installation measurement. 1979–85 with tapered shaft

c. Adjust shim pack as necessary, adding shims to increase end play or removing shims to decrease end play.
8. When installing original hub, proceed as follows:
   a. Align keyway in hub with axle shaft key and slide hub onto axle shaft as far as possible.
   b. Install axle shaft nut and washer, then the brake drum, drum retaining screws and wheel assembly.
   c. Lower vehicle to ground, then torque axle shaft nut to 250 ft. lbs. and install cotter pin. If cotter pin hole is not aligned, tighten nut to next castellation, do not loosen nut to align cotter pin hole.

NOTE: When a replacement axle shaft is installed, a replacement hub must also be installed. A replacement hub may be installed on an original axle shaft if the serrations on the shaft are not worn or damaged.

9. When installing replacement hub, proceed as follows:
   a. Align keyway in hub with axle shaft key and slide hub onto shaft as far as possible.
   b. Lubricate two thrust washers with liberal amount of chassis grease and install washers on axle shaft.
   c. Install axle shaft nut, then the brake drum, drum retaining screws and wheel assembly.
   d. Lower vehicle to ground, then tighten axle shaft nut until distance from hub outer face to axle shaft outer end is 1 5/16 inches, **Fig. 5**.
   e. Remove axle shaft nut and one thrust washer.
   f. Install axle shaft nut and torque to 250 ft. lbs.
   g. Install new cotter pin. If cotter pin hole is not aligned, tighten nut to next castellation, do not loosen nut to align cotter pin hole.

SEMI-FLOATING-FLANGED SHAFT

1. Lubricate outer diameter of bearing cup and install axle shaft and bearing assembly into axle housing using care

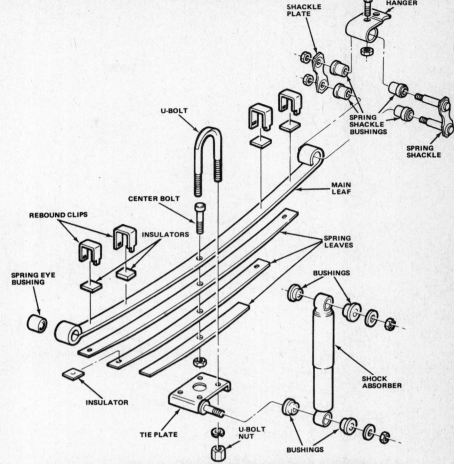

Fig. 6 Rear spring and shock absorber assembly. CJ & Scrambler models

not to damage oil seal.
2. Install axle shaft retainer and backing plate to housing. Torque retainer nuts to 30 ft. lbs.
3. Install cup plug into axle flange hole if required.
4. Install brake drum and wheel. Lower vehicle.

FULL-FLOATING AXLE SHAFT

1. Install new gasket on hub.
2. Install axle shaft and tighten nuts securely.

NOTE: It may be necessary to rotate wheel hub to align axle shaft splines with differential splines.

WHEEL BEARING
ADJUST

FULL-FLOATING AXLE

1. Remove axle shaft as described in "Axle Shaft, Remove".
2. Straighten lip of lockwasher and remove locknut and lockwasher.

3. Raise and support vehicle.
4. Rotate wheel and torque adjusting nut to 50 ft. lbs. to seat bearings. Back off nut 1/6 turn or until wheel rotates freely without lateral movement.
5. Install locknut, torquing to 50 ft. lbs., and bend over lockwasher lip.

AXLE ASSEMBLY
REPLACE

1979–83

1. Raise and support vehicle and remove rear wheels.
2. Scribe alignment marks on propeller shaft and axle for proper assembly, then disconnect propeller shaft from axle.
3. Disconnect shock absorbers at axle tubes.
4. Disconnect hydraulic brake hose at rear axle tee fitting, taping ends of hose and fitting.
5. Disconnect parking brake cable at equalizer.
6. Support axle with suitable jack.
7. Remove U-bolts and, on vehicles with spring mounted above axle, disconnect spring at rear shackle, then slide

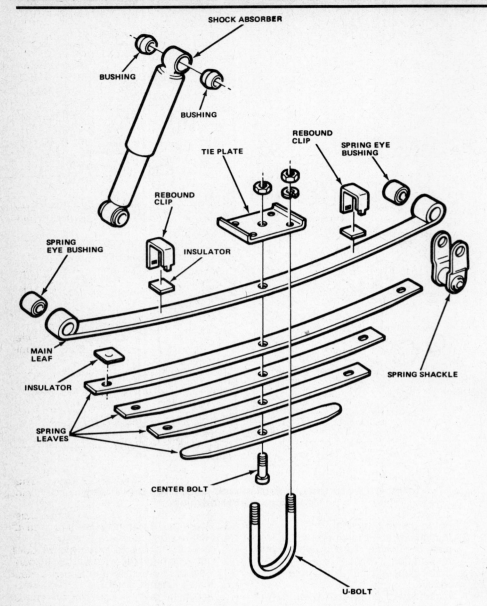

Fig. 7 **Rear spring and shock absorber assembly. 1979–83 Cherokee, Wagoneer, 1984–85 Grand Wagoneer & all truck models**

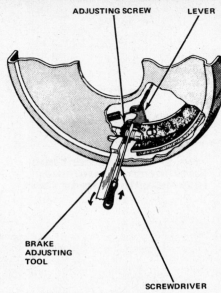

Fig. 8 **Brake adjustment**

16. Reverse procedure to install.

SHOCK ABSORBER
REPLACE

1. Disconnect battery ground cable.
2. Raise and support vehicle.
3. Position a suitable jack under axle assembly, then raise axle slightly.
4. Remove washers and lock nuts attaching shock absorber to upper and lower mounting pins.
5. Remove shock absorber and bushings from shock mounting eyes, **Figs. 6 and 7.**
6. Reverse procedure to install.

LEAF SPRING
REPLACE

LEAF SPRING MOUNTED ABOVE AXLE

1. Disconnect battery ground cable.
2. Raise and support vehicle.
3. Position a suitable jack under axle, then raise axle slightly.
4. Remove tie plate U bolts, **Figs. 5 and 6.**
5. Remove bolt attaching spring rear eye to shackle.
6. Remove bolt attaching spring front eye to frame mounting bracket.
7. Remove spring from vehicle.
8. Reverse procedure to install.

LEAF SPRING MOUNTED BELOW AXLE

1. Disconnect battery ground cable.
2. Raise and support vehicle.
3. If left side leaf spring requires service, remove fuel tank skid plate.

axle from under vehicle.
8. Reverse procedure to install.

1984-85

1. Apply parking brake and place manual transmission in 1st gear, or automatic transmission in Park.
2. Remove and discard cotter pins, then remove axle shaft nuts.
3. Raise and support rear of vehicle and remove rear wheels.
4. Remove brake drum retaining screws, then release parking brake and remove brake drums.
5. Using suitable puller, remove axle hub.
6. Disconnect brake lines at wheel cylinders, then remove support plates, oil seals and retainers and the end play

shims.
7. Using suitable tool, remove axle shafts.
8. Remove axle housing cover and drain lubricant, then reinstall cover.
9. Disconnect parking brake cables at equalizer.
10. Scribe alignment marks on propeller shaft and axle yokes for proper assembly, then disconnect propeller shaft at axle yoke.
11. Disconnect flexible brake hose at body floorpan bracket, then the vent hose at the axle tube.
12. Support rear axle with suitable jack.
13. Disconnect shock absorbers at spring tie plates.
14. Remove spring U-bolts, spring plates and spring clip plate, if equipped.
15. Lower jack and remove axle.

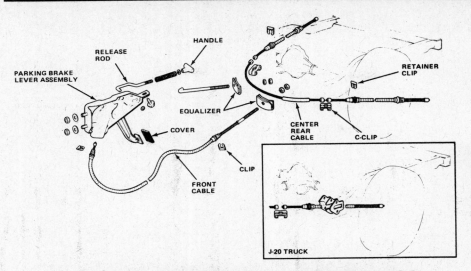

Fig. 9 Parking brake assembly. CJ & Scrambler models

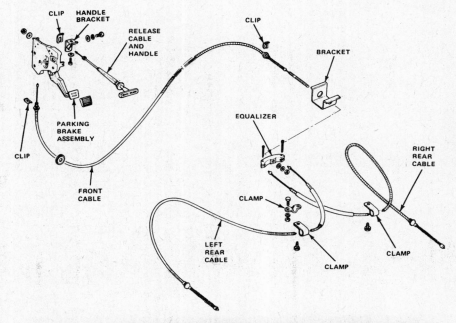

Fig. 10 Parking brake assembly. Cherokee, Wagoneer, Grand Wagoneer & all truck models

4. Position a suitable jack under axle, then raise axle slightly.
5. Disconnect shock absorber from mounting bracket.
6. Remove wheel assembly.
7. Remove tie plate U bolts and tie plate.
8. Remove bolt attaching spring rear eye to shackle.
9. Remove bolt attaching spring front eye to frame rail bracket.
10. Remove spring from vehicle.
11. Reverse procedure to install.

SERVICE BRAKE ADJUSTMENTS

Two different rear drum brake designs are used. They are similar in construction and operation but differ in method of automatic adjustment. Rear drum brakes on CJ and Scrambler models have cable operated automatic adjusters while rear drum brakes on Cherokee, Wagoneer, Grand Wagoneer and all truck models have linkage operated automatic adjusters.

If the rear brakes are serviced, an initial adjustment must be performed before installing brake drums.

ADJUSTMENT

1. Remove access slot covers from brake support plates.
2. Using brake adjusting tool, rotate adjusting screw clockwise direction until

brakes are locked.
3. Rotate brake adjuster screw counterclockwise until wheel turns freely, **Fig. 8.**

NOTE: The automatic adjuster lever must be disconnected from the adjuster screw before screw can be turned.

PARKING BRAKE
ADJUST

NOTE: Adjust service brakes before adjusting parking brake.

1. Release parking brakes.
2. Loosen equalizer locknuts to release tension on cables, **Figs. 9 and 10.**
3. Check cables for wear or damage. Replace damaged cables.
4. Tighten equalizer locknuts until a slight drag is obtained at wheels.
5. Loosen equalizer locknuts until wheel turns freely and brake drag is eliminated.
6. Tighten equalizer locknuts.

BRAKE MASTER CYLINDER
REPLACE

1. Disconnect brake lines from master cylinder. Cap lines and master cylinder ports.
2. On models with manual brakes, disconnect master cylinder push rod at brake pedal.
3. On all models, remove nuts or bolts attaching master cylinder to dash panel or brake booster and remove master cylinder.
4. Install in the reverse order of removal and bleed the brake system.

POWER BRAKE UNIT
REPLACE

1. Disconnect booster push rod from brake pedal.
2. Remove vacuum hose from check valve.
3. Remove nuts and washers securing master cylinder to booster unit, then separate master cylinder from booster unit.

NOTE: Do not disconnect brake lines from master cylinder.

4. Remove booster unit to firewall attaching nuts and remove booster unit.
5. Reverse procedure to install.

Front Suspension & Steering Section

CAMBER & CASTER
SOLID AXLE MODELS

Camber is set into the axle assembly at time of manufacture and cannot be adjusted.

Caster may be adjusted by installing new front end components or caster shims between the axle pad and the springs.

TOE-IN
ADJUST

Position the wheels to a true straight-ahead position with the steering gear also in a straight-ahead driving position. Then turn both tie rod adjusting sleeves an equal amount until the desired toe-in setting is obtained.

WHEEL BEARINGS
REPLACE & ADJUST

Refer to Front Wheel Drive Section under "Axle Shaft, Replace" for wheel bearing replacement and adjustment procedure.

STEERING KNUCKLE
REPLACE

OPEN KNUCKLE TYPE, REMOVAL

1. Remove axle shaft as described in Front Wheel Drive Section under "Axle Shaft, Replace".
2. Disconnect tie rod from knuckle arm.
3. Remove lower ball stud jamnut and discard, **Fig. 1.** Loosen upper ball stud nut until top of nut is flush with top of stud.
4. Unseat ball studs using suitable hammer. Remove upper ball stud nut and steering knuckle.
5. Remove upper ball stud split ring seat using suitable nut wrench.

OPEN KNUCKLE TYPE, INSTALLATION

1. Install upper ball split ring seat until top of seat is flush with top of yoke.
2. Install steering knuckle on yoke then a new lower ball stud jamnut finger tight.
3. On 1979–80 models position Nut Wrench J-25158, Button J-25211-3, Plate J-25211-3 and Puller J-25215. On 1981–85 models, position Nut Wrench J-23447, Button J-25211-3, Plate J-25211-1 and Puller J-25212 as shown, **Fig. 2.**

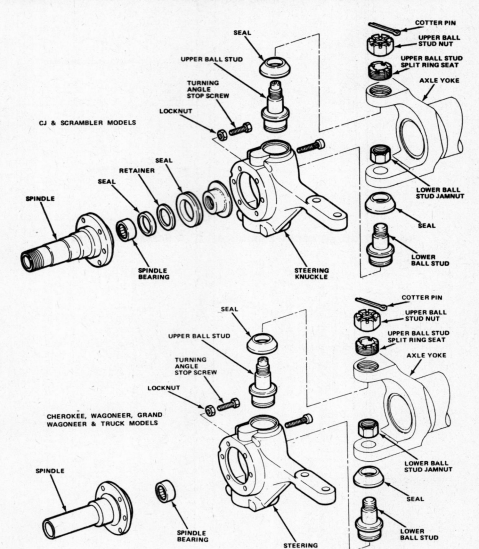

Fig. 1 Exploded view of steering knuckle & components

4. Tighten puller screw until lower ball stud is held firmly seated. Torque jamnut to 85 ft. lbs. on CJ and Scrambler models, and 75 ft. lbs. on all other models. Remove puller and plate.
5. Torque upper ball stud split ring seat to 50 ft. lbs.
6. Install upper ball stud nut and torque to 100 ft. lbs. Install cotter pin.
7. Install tie rod to steering knuckle. Torque tie rod end nuts to 50 ft. lbs.
8. Install axle shaft as described in Front Wheel Drive Section under "Axle Shaft, Replace".

BALL STUDS
REPLACE

1. Remove steering knuckle as described in "Steering Knuckle, Replace".
2. Remove lower ball stud snap ring.
3. Using suitable tools, press lower and upper ball studs from steering knuckle.
4. Reverse procedure to install. Install a new replacement snap ring on the lower ball stud.

BALL STUD PRELOAD MEASUREMENT

NOTE: Ball stud preload is measured when vehicle exhibits high steering effort or slow return of the steering mechanism after turns. If this condition occurs and all other items affecting steering effort are normal, ball stud preload should be checked.

1. Raise and support vehicle. Remove front wheels.
2. Disconnect steering damper at tie rod if equipped.
3. Unlock steering column. Disconnect steering connecting rod at right-side of steering knuckle on CJ and Scrambler models; and on all other models, at right side of tie rod.
4. Remove cotter pin and nut attaching tie rod to right side steering knuckle.
5. Rotate both steering knuckles completely several times, working from right side of vehicle.
6. Assemble a socket and 0-50 ft. lb. torque wrench onto right tie rod attaching nut.

NOTE: Torque wrench must be positioned parallel with the steering knuckle arm on 1979-80 vehicles, or perpendicular to arm on 1981-85 vehicles.

7. Rotate steering knuckles slowly and steadily through a complete arc and measure torque required to rotate knuckles.
   a. If reading is less than 25 ft. lbs., turning effort at knuckles is normal. Check other steering components for defects or binding.
   b. If reading is greater than 25 ft. lbs., proceed to step 8.
8. Disconnect tie rod from both steering knuckles. Install a ½ × 1 inch bolt, flat washer and nut in tie rod mounting hole in each of the steering knuckles.
9. Measure torque required to rotate each steering knuckle as described previously.
   a. If torque is less than 10 ft. lbs., steering effort is within specifications.
   b. If torque is more than 10 ft. lbs., perform "Ball Stud Preload, Adjust" procedure.
10. If both steering knuckles are within specification, check for damaged or tight tie rod ends.

BALL STUD PRELOAD
ADJUST

1. Remove front axle shafts as described in Front Wheel Drive Section under "Axle Shaft, Replace".
2. Loosen lower ball stud jamnut, then remove upper ball stud nut.
3. Unseat ball studs from yoke using suitable hammer.
4. Remove upper ball stud split ring seat and discard.
5. Remove lower ball stud jamnut and steering knuckle. Discard jamnut.
6. Clean upper ball stud split ring seat threads, lower ball stud taper in steering knuckle, threads and tapered surfaces of ball studs, and upper ball stud retaining nut threads.

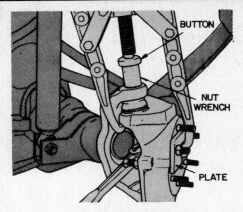

Fig. 2 Steering knuckle installation tools

7. Position steering knuckle on axle and install a new lower ball stud jamnut finger tight.
8. Install upper ball stud nut and torque 10-20 ft. lbs. to draw upper ball stud into yoke.

NOTE: Do not install upper ball stud split ring seat at this time.

9. Torque lower ball stud jamnut to 80 ft. lbs.
10. Remove upper ball stud nut and install a new split ring seat. Torque split ring seat to 50 ft. lbs. Install upper ball stud nut and torque to 100 ft. lbs. Align and install cotter pin.

NOTE: Do not loosen nut to align cotter pin holes. Tighten only enough to align the holes and install cotter pin.

11. Install front axle shafts and steering spindles loosely and measure turning effort of each steering knuckle as described in "Ball Stud Preload, Measurement".
   a. If turning effort is less than 10 ft. lbs., proceed to next step.
   b. If turning effort is more than 10 ft. lbs., replace upper and lower ball studs as described in "Ball Studs, Replace".
12. Install front axle shafts and connect tie rod to steering knuckle arms. Torque tie rod end retaining nuts to 45 ft. lbs.
13. Attach connecting rod to tie rod. Torque connecting rod nut to 60 ft. lbs. on CJ and Scrambler models; and 75 ft. lbs. on all other models. Install steering damper if equipped.
14. Install front wheels and lower vehicle.

MANUAL STEERING GEAR
REPLACE

1. Remove intermediate shaft to worm-shaft coupling clamp bolt and disconnect intermediate shaft.
2. Remove pitman arm nut and lock-washer, then separate pitman arm

from steering gear shaft using a puller.
3. On all except CJ models, remove steering gear to frame bolts and remove steering gear.
4. On CJ and Scrambler models:
   a. Slightly raise left side of vehicle to relieve tension on left front spring, then place support stand under frame.
   b. Remove steering gear lower bracket to frame bolts.
   c. Remove steering gear upper bracket to crossmember bolts and remove gear.
   d. Remove bolts attaching upper bracket to tie plate and lower bracket to steering gear and remove brackets.
5. Reverse procedure to install. Apply Locktite 271 or equivalent to the steering gear to frame bolts, the bracket to gear bolts and the bracket to tie plate bolt. Torque steering gear to frame bolts and bracket to gear bolts to 70 ft. lbs., the bracket to tie plate bolt to 55 ft. lbs., the coupling pinch bolt and nut to 45 ft. lbs., and pitman arm nut to 185 ft. lbs.

NOTE: If there is a slightly rough feel after the steering gear is installed, turn the steering wheel completely to the left and then to the right for 10 to 15 complete cycles.

POWER STEERING GEAR
REPLACE

1. Disconnect lines from gear. Plug lines to prevent entry of dirt and keep lines raised to avoid excessive fluid loss.
2. On all except CJ and Scrambler models, remove clamp bolt and nut attaching flex coupling to steering gear shaft and disconnect intermediate shaft.
3. On CJ and Scrambler models, remove clamp bolt and nut attaching intermediate shaft coupling to steering gear shaft and disconnect intermediate shaft.
4. Paint alignment marks on pitman shaft and pitman arm for assembly reference, then remove and discard the pitman arm nut and lockwasher. Use new nut and lockwasher.
5. Remove pitman using a puller.
6. On all except CJ and Scrambler models, remove steering gear to frame mounting bolts and remove steering gear.
7. On CJ and Scrambler models:
   a. Raise left side of vehicle to relieve tension on left front spring and place support stand under the frame.
   b. Remove the three lower steering gear mounting brackets to frame bolts.
   c. Remove the two upper steering gear mounting brackets to crossmember bolts and remove steering

gear and mounting brackets.

d. Remove mounting bracket to gear attaching bolts and remove upper and lower mounting brackets from steering gear.

8. Reverse procedure to install. Apply Locktite 271 or equivalent to mounting bracket to steering gear bolts and to steering gear to frame bolts. Torque steering gear to frame bolts to 70 ft. lbs. on all except CJ and Scrambler models, and 55 ft. lbs. on CJ and Scrambler models, the mounting bracket to steering gear bolts to 70 ft. lbs., the flex coupling clamp bolt to 30 ft. lbs., the intermediate shaft coupling to steering gear bolt to 45 lbs. and the pitman arm nut to 185 ft. lbs.

Front Wheel Drive Section

AXLE SHAFT
REPLACE

CJ & SCRAMBLER MODELS

1. Raise and support vehicle, then remove wheel.
2. Remove brake caliper.
3. Remove hub cap and drive flange snap ring, **Fig. 1.**
4. Remove rotor hub bolts, hub cover and gasket.
5. Remove axle flange.
6. Straighten lip of lockwasher and remove outer nut, lockwasher, inner adjusting nut and bearing lockwasher.
7. Remove outer bearing and drum/rotor assembly.

NOTE: Do not damage oil seal.

8. Remove brake support plate or caliper adapter and splash shield as equipped.
9. Remove spindle and spindle bearing, then slide out axle shaft assembly.
10. Reverse procedure to install. Torque inner adjusting nut to 50 ft. lbs. while rotating hub to seat bearings. Back off adjusting nut ⅓ turn on 1979 models and ⅛ turn on 1980–85 models. Install outer lockwasher and locknut. Torque locknut to 50 ft. lbs. and bend lip of washer over nut. On 1980–85 models, torque hub body bolts to 30 ft. lbs.

MODELS LESS SELEC-TRAC EXCEPT CJ & SCRAMBLER

1. Raise and support vehicle.
2. Remove disc brake caliper(s).
3. On models less front hubs, remove rotor hub cap, then the axle shaft snap ring, drive gear, pressure spring and spring retainer, **Fig. 1.**
4. On models with front hubs, proceed as follows:
   a. Remove socket head screws from hub body, then remove the body and large retaining ring.
   b. Remove small retaining ring from axle shaft.
   c. Remove hub clutch assembly from axle.
5. On all models, remove outer lock nut, washer and inner lock nut.
6. Remove rotor. The spring retainer and outer bearing are removed with the rotor.

7. Remove nuts and bolts attaching spindle and support shield and remove spindle and shield, tapping spindle with suitable mallet as necessary to remove it from knuckle.
8. Remove axle shaft.
9. Reverse procedure to install. Torque inner wheel bearing adjusting nut to 50 ft. lbs. while rotating wheel to seat bearings, then back off nut ⅓ turn on 1979 models or ⅛ turn on 1980–85 models. Turn inner adjusting lock nut until peg engages nearest hole in lock washer. Install outer lock nut and torque to 50 ft. lbs. Torque socket head screws to 30 inch lbs.

NOTE: Install spring retainer with cupped side facing toward center of vehicle.

1983–85 MODELS WITH SELEC-TRAC, EXC. CJ & SCRAMBLER

NOTE: To remove right side axle shaft refer to "Models Less Selec-Trac, Except CJ & Scrambler" for procedure. To remove left side axle shaft refer to "Models Less Selec-Trac, Except CJ & Scrambler" steps 1–8, then use following procedure.

1. Disconnect vacuum hoses from axle shift motor, then loosen axle housing cover bolts, allowing lubricant to drain from housing.
2. Remove axle housing cover and shift motor as an assembly, **Fig. 2.**
3. Remove retaining clip from inner axle shaft, then, using a suitable magnet remove inner axle shaft from axle

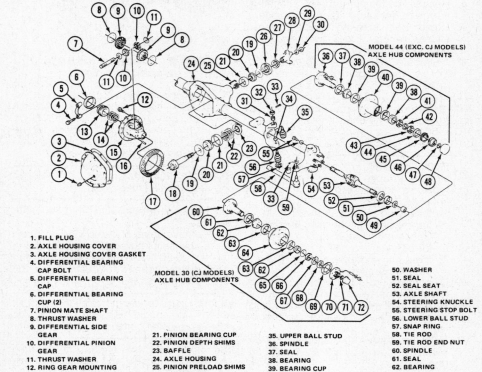

MODEL 44 (EXC. CJ MODELS) AXLE HUB COMPONENTS

MODEL 30 (CJ MODELS) AXLE HUB COMPONENTS

1. FILL PLUG
2. AXLE HOUSING COVER
3. AXLE HOUSING COVER GASKET
4. DIFFERENTIAL BEARING CAP BOLT
5. DIFFERENTIAL BEARING CAP
6. DIFFERENTIAL BEARING CUP (2)
7. PINION MATE SHAFT
8. THRUST WASHER
9. DIFFERENTIAL SIDE GEAR
10. DIFFERENTIAL PINION GEAR
11. THRUST WASHER
12. RING GEAR MOUNTING BOLTS
13. DIFFERENTIAL BEARING (2)
14. DIFFERENTIAL BEARING PRELOAD SHIMS
15. DIFFERENTIAL CASE
16. PINION MATE SHAFT PIN
17. RING GEAR
18. PINION GEAR
19. SLINGER
20. PINION BEARING

21. PINION BEARING CUP
22. PINION DEPTH SHIMS
23. BAFFLE
24. AXLE HOUSING
25. PINION PRELOAD SHIMS
26. OIL SEAL
27. DUST CAP
28. YOKE
29. WASHER
30. PINION NUT
31. UPPER BALL STUD SPLIT RING SEAT
32. UPPER BALL STUD NUT
33. COTTER PIN
34. LOWER BALL STUD JAMNUT

35. UPPER BALL STUD
36. SPINDLE
37. SEAL
38. BEARING
39. BEARING CUP
40. HUB
41. INNER LOCKNUT
42. WASHER
43. OUTER LOCKNUT
44. SPRING CUP
45. PRESSURE SPRING
46. DRIVE GEAR
47. SNAP RING
48. HUB CAP
49. SPINDLE BEARING

50. WASHER
51. SEAL
52. SEAL SEAT
53. AXLE SHAFT
54. STEERING KNUCKLE
55. STEERING STOP BOLT
56. LOWER BALL STUD
57. SNAP RING
58. TIE ROD
59. TIE ROD END NUT
60. SPINDLE
61. SEAL
62. BEARING
63. BEARING CUP
64. HUB
65. TABBED WASHER
66. INNER LOCKNUT
67. LOCK WASHER
68. OUTER LOCKNUT
69. GASKET
70. DRIVE FLANGE
71. SNAP RING
72. HUB CAP

Fig. 1 Front axle assembly. Open knuckle type

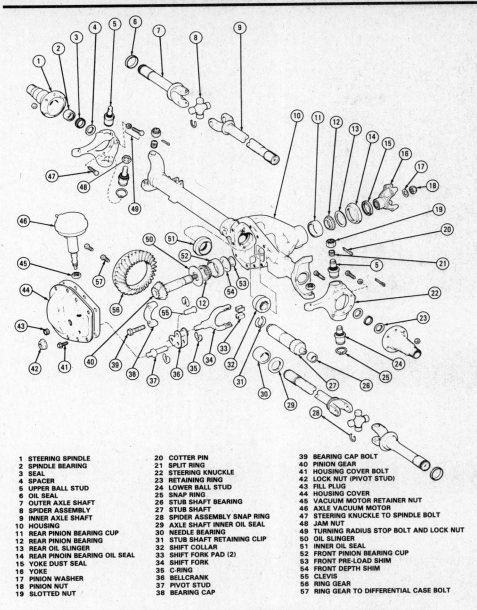

Fig. 2 Selec-Trac front axle assembly. Open knuckle type

1 STEERING SPINDLE	20 COTTER PIN	39 BEARING CAP BOLT
2 SPINDLE BEARING	21 SPLIT RING	40 PINION GEAR
3 SEAL	22 STEERING KNUCKLE	41 HOUSING COVER BOLT
4 SPACER	23 RETAINING RING	42 LOCK NUT (PIVOT STUD)
5 UPPER BALL STUD	24 LOWER BALL STUD	43 FILL PLUG
6 OIL SEAL	25 STUB SHAFT	44 HOUSING COVER
7 OUTER AXLE SHAFT	26 STUB SHAFT BEARING	45 VACUUM MOTOR RETAINER NUT
8 SPIDER ASSEMBLY	27 STUB SHAFT	46 AXLE VACUUM MOTOR
9 INNER AXLE SHAFT	28 SPIDER ASSEMBLY SNAP RING	47 STEERING KNUCKLE TO SPINDLE BOLT
10 HOUSING	29 AXLE SHAFT INNER OIL SEAL	48 JAM NUT
11 REAR PINION BEARING CUP	30 NEEDLE BEARING	49 TURNING RADIUS STOP BOLT AND LOCK NUT
12 REAR PINION BEARING	31 STUB SHAFT RETAINING CLIP	50 OIL SLINGER
13 REAR OIL SLINGER	32 SHIFT COLLAR	51 INNER OIL SEAL
14 REAR PINOIN BEARING OIL SEAL	33 SHIFT FORK PAD (2)	52 FRONT PINION BEARING CUP
15 YOKE DUST SEAL	34 SHIFT FORK	53 FRONT PRE-LOAD SHIM
16 YOKE	35 C-RING	54 FRONT DEPTH SHIM
17 PINION WASHER	36 BELLCRANK	55 CLEVIS
18 PINION NUT	37 PIVOT STUD	56 RING GEAR
19 SLOTTED NUT	38 BEARING CAP	57 RING GEAR TO DIFFERENTIAL CASE BOLT

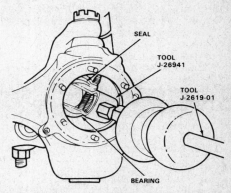

Fig. 3 Inner axle shaft retaining clip & shift collar

Fig. 4 Outer axle shaft bearing & seal removal

tube. Remove shift collar from housing, **Fig. 3.**

4. Remove outer axle shaft bearing and seal using Tool J-26941 and J2619-01, **Fig. 4.**

5. Reverse procedure to install. Torque inner wheel bearing adjusting nut to 50 ft. lbs. while rotating wheel to seat bearings, then back nut off ⅛ turn. Install lockwasher with inner tab aligned with keyway in spindle. Turn inner adjusting nut until the peg engages nearest hole in lockwasher. Install outer locknut and torque to 50 ft. lbs.

NOTE: Install spring retainer with cupped side facing toward center of vehicle.

AXLE SHIFT MOTOR SERVICE
1983-85 MODELS WITH SELEC-TRAC

Removal
1. Raise and support front of vehicle, then drain lubricant from front axle.
2. Disconnect vacuum lines from shift motor.
3. Remove axle housing cover, shift motor and shift fork as an assembly, **Fig. 5.**

Disassembly
1. Remove shift fork to pivot pin retaining E-clip, **Fig. 5.**
2. Disconnect shift fork pivot from shift

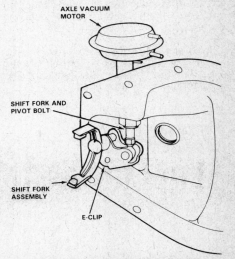

Fig. 5 Axle vacuum motor & shift fork assembly

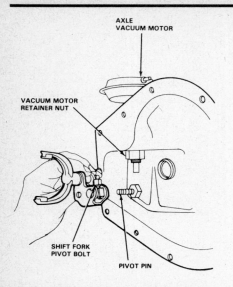

Fig. 6 Removal & installation of shift fork assembly

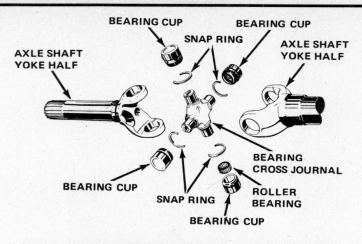

Fig. 7 Axle shaft & universal joint assembly

motor shaft by threading pivot out of shaft.

3. Remove shift fork assembly from pivot pin, **Fig. 6.**
4. Remove shift motor retaining nut and remove shift motor from axle housing cover.
5. Remove O-ring from shift motor.

Assembly

1. Install new O-ring on motor.
2. Apply small amount of sealer around shift motor mounting hole and install shift motor and retaining nut, **Fig. 5.**
3. Install shift fork assembly on pivot pin and thread shift fork pivot into shift motor shaft. Install E-clip on shift fork pivot pin, **Fig. 5.**

Installation

1. Apply RTV sealant to axle cover sealing surfaces and install on axle.

NOTE: Shift fork and fork tabs must be engaged in shift collar before installing cover bolts.

2. Torque axle housing cover bolts to 20 ft. lbs. Fill axle to bottom of fill plug hole with suitable gear lubricant and reconnect vacuum lines.

FRONT AXLE ASSEMBLY
REPLACE

1. Raise and support vehicle. Support at frame behind front springs.
2. Remove front wheels.
3. Scribe alignment marks on propeller shaft and axle yoke for proper assembly, then disconnect propeller shaft at axle yoke.
4. Disconnect connecting rod at steering knuckles.
5. Disconnect shock absorbers at axle housing.

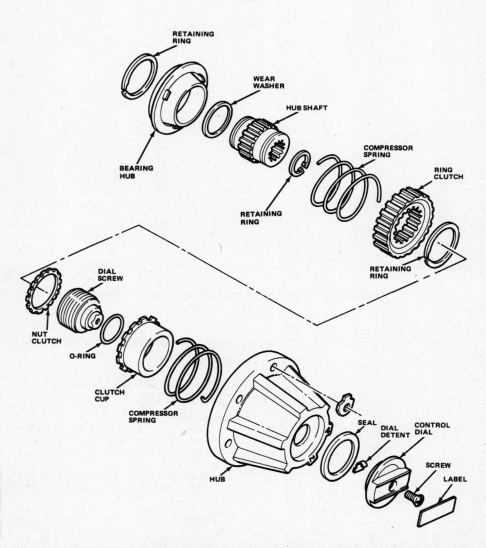

Fig. 8 Front drive hub model M243. 1980–81 CJ & Scrambler models

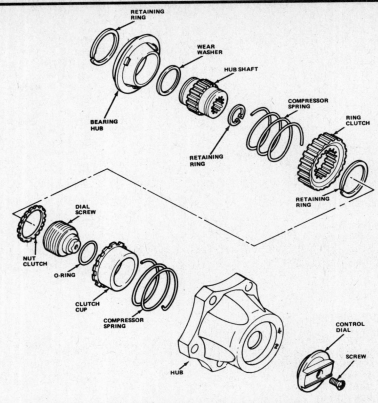

Fig. 9   Front drive hub model M253. 1982–85 CJ & Scrambler models

6. Remove stabilizer bar connecting links to spring tie plates attaching bolts, if equipped.
7. Disconnect breather tube at axle housing.
8. Disconnect stabilizer bar link bolts at spring clips.
9. Remove disc brake calipers, rotors and brake shields.
10. Remove U-bolts and tie plates.
11. Support axle assembly with suitable jack to relieve spring tension.
12. Loosen rear spring shackle to spring attaching bolts.
13. Remove front spring shackle to spring attaching bolts and lower spring to floor.
14. Remove axle from under vehicle.
15. Reverse procedure to install.

AXLE SHAFT UNIVERSAL JOINT

1. Remove axle shaft as described under "Axle Shaft, Replace".
2. Remove snap rings from universal joint bearing cups, **Fig. 7.**
3. Press on one end of bearing cup to remove opposite bearing cup from yoke half.
4. Press on exposed end of bearing cross journal and remove remaining bearing cup from yoke.
5. Repeat steps 3 and 4 for remaining bearing cups.

6. Clean universal joint components in a suitable solvent. Check parts for wear or damage. Replace damaged parts as required.
7. Pack bearing cups ⅓ full of suitable lubricant and install bearing rollers.
8. Install bearing cross journal.
9. Install bearing cups into axle shaft yoke halves. Ensure bearing cups are completely seated against bearing shoulders.
10. Install bearing cups onto journal.
11. Install bearing cup snap rings.

NOTE: If universal joint binds when assembled, gently tap on yoke to relieve tension on bearing cups at each end of journal.

FRONT DRIVE HUBS

Manual front drive hubs are used on models 208 or 300 part-time front wheel drive transfer case assemblies only.

Three different front drive hub assemblies are used. Hub assembly model M243, **Fig. 8,** is used on 1980–81 CJ and Scrambler models, hub model M253, **Fig. 9,** is used on 1981–85 CJ and Scrambler models, hub model M247, **Fig. 10,** is used on 1980–85 Cherokee, Wagoneer, Grand Wagoneer and all truck models.

All three hub assembly models are manually locked or unlocked. These hubs are serviced as an assembly or sub-assembly only. Do not attempt to disassemble these

units. If an entire hub or sub-assembly is defective, replace the entire assembly or sub-assembly. The hubs may be removed for cleaning and inspection purposes and for periodic lubrication only.

MODELS M243 & 253

Removal

1. Remove bolts and lock washers securing hub body to axle hub, **Figs. 8 and 9.**
2. Remove gasket and hub body.

CAUTION: Do not turn hub control dial after removing hub body.

3. Remove retaining ring, hub clutch and bearing assembly.
4. Clean and inspect all components for wear or damage. Replace as necessary.

Installation

CAUTION: Do not turn hub control dial until after hub control dial is installed. The hub clutch nut and cup can be damaged if dial is rotated while the hub is off the vehicle.

1. Apply a light coat of suitable lubricant to all hub components.
2. Install bearing assembly and hub clutch with retaining ring on axle shaft.
3. Install hub body and gasket. Install tabbed lockwashers and bolts into hub

body and axle. Torque bolts to 30 ft. lbs.

4. Raise and support front of vehicle, with dial in free position, rotate wheels. If wheels drag, check hub for correct installation.
5. Lower vehicle.

MODEL M247

Removal

1. Remove socket head screws, axle hub retaining ring and axle shaft retaining ring.
2. Remove hub clutch assembly, **Fig. 10.**
3. Clean and inspect all components for wear or damage. Replace as necessary.

Installation

1. Apply a light coat of suitable lubricant to all hub components.
2. Install hub clutch, axle hub retaining ring and axle shaft retaining ring.
3. Install new O-ring into hub body and position into clutch. Install socket head screw and torque to 30 inch lbs.
4. Raise and support front of vehicle, turn dial to free position and rotate wheels. If wheels drag, check hub for correct installation.
5. Lower vehicle.

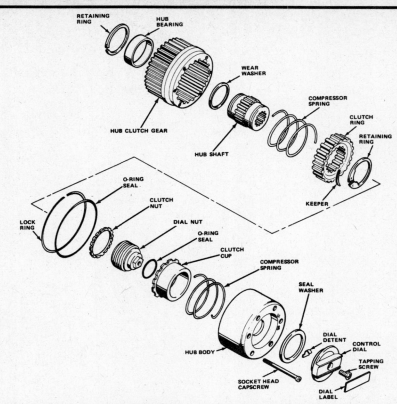

Fig. 10 Front drive hub model M247. 1980—85 Cherokee, Wagoneer, Grand Wagoneer & all truck models

AIR CONDITIONING

TABLE OF CONTENTS

A/C System Testing

INDEX

GENERAL PRECAUTIONS

The Freon refrigerant used is also known as R-12 or F-12. It is colorless and odorless both as a gas and a liquid. Since it boils (vaporizes) at −21.7° F., it will usually be in a vapor state when being handled in a repair shop. But if a portion of the liquid coolant should come in contact with the hands or face, note that its temperature momentarily will be at least 22° below zero.

Protective goggles should be worn when opening any refrigerant lines. If liquid coolant does touch the eyes, bathe the eyes quickly in cold water, then apply a bland disinfectant oil to the eyes. See an eye doctor.

When checking a system for leaks with a torch type leak detector, do not breathe the vapors coming from the flame. Do not discharge refrigerant in the area of a live flame. A poisonous phosgene gas is produced when R-12 or F-12 is burned. While the small amount of this gas produced by a leak detector is not harmful unless inhaled directly at the flame, the quantity of refrigerant released into the air when a system is purged can be extremely dangerous if allowed to come in contact with an open flame. Thus, when purging a system, be sure that the discharge hose is routed to a well ventilated place where no flame is present. Under these conditions the refrigerant will be quickly dissipated into the surrounding air.

Never allow the temperature of refrigerant drums to exceed 125° F. The resultant increase in temperature will cause a corresponding increase in pressure which may cause the safety plug to release or the drum to burst.

If it is necessary to heat a drum of refrigerant when charging a system, the drum should be placed in water that is no hotter than 125° F. Never use a blowtorch, or other open flame. If possible, a pressure release mechanism should be attached before the drum is heated.

When connecting and disconnecting service gauges on A/C system, ensure that gauge hand valves are fully closed and that compressor service valves, if equipped, are in the back-seated (fully counterclockwise) position. Do not disconnect gauge hoses from service port adapters, if used, while gauges are connected to A/C system. To disconnect hoses, always remove adapter from service port. Do not disconnect hoses from gauge manifold while connected to A/C system, as refrigerant will be rapidly discharged.

After disconnecting gauge lines, check the valve areas to be sure service valves are correctly seated and Schraeder valves, if used, are not leaking.

EXERCISE SYSTEM

An important fact most owners ignore is that A/C units must be used periodically. Manufacturers caution that when the air conditioner is not used regularly, particularly during cold months, it should be turned on for a few minutes once every two or three weeks while the engine is running. This keeps the system in good operating condition.

Checking out the system for the effects of disuse before the onset of summer is one of the most important aspects of A/C servicing.

First clean out the condenser core, mounted in all cases at the front of the radiator. All obstructions, such as leaves, bugs, and dirt, must be removed, as they will reduce heat transfer and impair the efficiency of the system. Make sure the space between the condenser and the radiator also is free of foreign matter.

Make certain the evaporator water drain is open. Certain systems have two evaporators, one in the engine compartment and one toward the rear of the vehicle. The evaporator cools and dehumidifies the air before it enters the passenger compartment; there, the refrigerant is changed from a liquid to a vapor. As the core cools the air, moisture condenses on it but is prevented from collecting in the evaporator by the water drain.

PERFORMANCE TEST

The system should be operated for at least 15 minutes to allow sufficient time for all parts to become completely stabilized. Determine if the system is fully charged by the use of test gauges and sight glass if one is installed on system. Head pressure will read from 180 psi to 220 psi or higher, depending upon ambient temperature and the type unit being tested. The sight glass should be free of bubbles if a glass is used in the system. Low side pressures should read approximately 15 psi to 30 psi, again depending on the ambient temperature and the unit being tested. It is not feasible to give a definite reading for all types of systems used, as the type control and component installation used on a particular system will directly influence the pressure readings on the high and low sides, **Fig. 1.**

The high side pressure will definitely be affected by the ambient or outside air temperature. A system that is operating normally will indicate a high side gauge reading between 150–170 psi with an 80°F ambient temperature. The same system will register 210–230 psi with an ambient temperature of 100°F. No two systems will register exactly the same, which requires that allowance for variations in head pressures must be considered. Following are the most important normal readings likely to be encountered during the season.

Ambient Temp.	High Side Pressure
80	150–170
90	175–195
95	185–205
100	210–230
105	230–250
110	250–270

RELATIVE TEMPERATURE OF HIGH AND LOW SIDES

The high side of the system should be uniformly hot to the touch throughout. A difference in temperature will indicate a partial blockage of liquid or gas at this point.

The low side of the system should be uniformly cool to the touch with no excessive sweating of the suction line or low side service valve. Excessive sweating or frosting of the low side service valve usually indicates an expansion valve is allowing an excessive amount of refrigerant into the evaporator.

EVAPORATOR OUTPUT

At this point, provided all other inspection tests have been performed, and components have been found to operate as they should, a rapid cooling down of the interior of the vehicle should result. The use of a thermometer is not necessary to determine evaporator output. Bringing all units to the correct operating specifications will insure that the evaporator performs as intended.

LEAK TEST

Testing the refrigerant system for leaks is one of the most important phases of troubleshooting. Several types of leak detectors are available that are suitable for detecting A/C system leaks. One or more of the following procedures will prove useful for detecting leaks and checking connections after service work has been performed. Prior to performing any leak test, prepare the vehicle as follows:

1. Attach a suitable gauge manifold to system and observe pressure readings.
2. If little or no pressure is indicated, the system must be partially charged.
3. If gauges indicate pressure, set engine to run at fast idle and operate system at maximum cooling for 10–15 minutes, then stop engine and perform leak tests.

Evaporator Pressure Gauge Reading	Evaporator Temperature F°	High Pressure Gauge Reading	Ambient Temperature
0	-21°	45	20°
0.6	-20°	55	30°
2.4	-15°	72	40°
4.5	-10°	86	50°
6.8	-5°	105	60°
9.2	0°	126	70°
11.8	5°	140	75°
14.7	10°	160	80°
17.1	15°	185	90°
21.1	20°	195	95°
22.5	22°	220	100°
23.9	24°	240	105°
25.4	26°	260	110°
26.9	28°	275	115°
28.5	30°	290	120°
37.0	40°	305	125°
46.7	50°	325	130°
57.7	60°		
70.1	70°		
84.1	80°		
99.6	90°		
116.9	100°		
136.0	110°		
157.1	120°		
179.0	130°		

Fig. 1   A/C system pressure/temperature relationship (Typical). Equivalent to 1750 RPM (30 mph)

FLAME TYPE (HALIDE) LEAK DETECTORS

CAUTION: Avoid inhaling fumes produced by burning refrigerant when using flame-type detectors. Use caution when using detector near flammable materials such as interior trim components. Do not use flame-type detector where concentrations of combustible or explosive gasses, dusts or vapors may exist.

1. Light leak detector and adjust flame as low as possible to obtain maximum sensitivity.
2. Allow detector to warm until copper element is cherry-red. Flame should be almost colorless.
3. Test reaction plate sensitivity by passing end of sensor hose near an opened can of refrigerant. Flame should react violently, turning bright blue.
4. If flame does not change color, replace reaction plate following manufacturer's instructions.
5. Allow flame to clear, then slowly move sensor hose along areas suspected of leakage while observing flame.

NOTE: Position sensor hose under areas of suspected leakage, as R-12 refrigerant is heavier than air.

6. Move sensor hose under all lines, fittings and components. Insert hose into evaporator case, if possible, and check compressor shaft seal.
7. The presence of refrigerant will cause flame to change color as follows: Pale blue, no refrigerant; yellow-yellow/green, slight leak; bright blue-purple/blue, major leak or concentration of refrigerant.
8. If detector indicates a large leak or heavy concentration of refrigerant, ventilate area using a small fan in order to pinpoint leak.
9. Repair leaks as needed, evacuate and recharge system, then recheck system for leaks.

ELECTRONIC LEAK DETECTORS

The procedure for using an electronic leak detector is similar to the procedure for

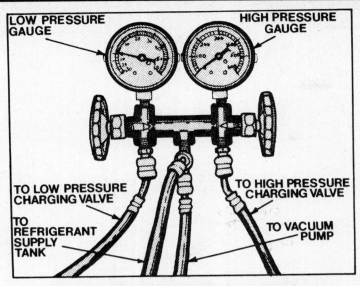

Fig. 2 Gauge manifold hose connections

Labels in figure: LOW PRESSURE GAUGE, HIGH PRESSURE GAUGE, TO LOW PRESSURE CHARGING VALVE, TO HIGH PRESSURE CHARGING VALVE, TO REFRIGERANT SUPPLY TANK, TO VACUUM PUMP

flame-type leak detectors, except that the presence of refrigerant is indicated by an audible tone or flashing light. Refer to operating instructions for unit being used, and observe the following procedures:

1. Move detector probe 1 inch per second along areas of suspected leakage.
2. Position probe under area to be tested as refrigerant is heavier than air.
3. Check gauge manifold, hoses and service ports for leakage.

FLUID LEAK DETECTORS

Apply leak detector solution around joints to be tested. A cluster of bubbles will form immediately if there is a leak. A white foam that forms after a short while will indicate an extremely small leak. In some confined areas such as sections of the evaporator and condenser, electronic leak detectors will be more useful.

DISCHARGING & EVACUATING SYSTEM

DISCHARGING

1. Ensure that all gauge manifold or charging station hand valves are closed and that compressor service valves, if equipped, are in the backseated (fully counterclockwise) position.
2. Connect compound (low) side gauge hose to the low (suction) side service port, and the high pressure gauge hose to the high (discharge) side port, **Figs. 2 and 3**, then open compressor service valves to mid-position, if equipped.

NOTE: Refer to "Charging Valve Location" in the "A/C System Servicing" section for service port locations.

3. If charging station is being used, disconnect hose from vacuum pump inlet and ensure that vacuum valve is open.
4. Insert charging station vacuum hose or gauge manifold center hose into a suitable container that is vented to shop exhaust system.
5. If system is operational, set engine to run at fast idle and operate A/C system in maximum cooling position, with blower on high, for 10–15 minutes to return oil to compressor, then reduce idle and stop engine.
6. Slightly open low side control valve on manifold or charging station, and allow refrigerant to discharge slowly into container.

NOTE: Do not allow refrigerant to discharge rapidly. Too rapid purging will draw the system oil charge out with the refrigerant.

7. When system is nearly discharged, slightly open high side control valve on manifold to discharge remaining refrigerant from compressor and lines.
8. When system is completely discharged (gauges read zero), close high and low side control valves and measure amount of oil in discharge container.
9. If more than ½ ounce of refrigeration oil is trapped in container, perform "Oil Level Check."

NOTE: If addition of refrigeration oil is necessary, oil should be added prior to evacuating system.

EVACUATING SYSTEM WITH VACUUM PUMP

Vacuum pumps suitable for removing air

and moisture from A/C systems are commercially available. The pump should be capable of drawing the system down to 28–29½ inches Hg at sea level. For each 1000 foot increase in altitude, this specification should be decreased by 1 inch Hg. As an example, at 5000 feet elevation, only 23–24½ inches Hg can be obtained.

1. Connect suitable gauge manifold and discharge system as outlined previously.

NOTE: System must be completely discharged prior to evacuation. If pressurized refrigerant is allowed to enter vacuum pump, pump will be damaged.

2. Connect hose from gauge manifold center port to vacuum pump inlet.
3. Fully open both gauge manifold hand valves.
4. Operate vacuum pump while observing low side compound gauge. If system does not "pump-down" to 28–29½ inches Hg (at sea level) within approximately 5 minutes, recheck connections and leak test system.
5. Continue to operate vacuum pump for 15–30 minutes, longer if system was open for an extended period of time, then close both manifold valves and stop pump.
6. Check ability of system to hold vacuum. Watch low side compound gauge and ensure that reading does not rise at a rate faster than 1 inch Hg every 4–5 minutes.
7. If system fails to hold vacuum, recheck fittings and connections, and leak test system.
8. If system holds vacuum, charge system with refrigerant.

EVACUATING SYSTEM WITH CHARGING STATION

A vacuum pump is built into the charging station that is constructed to withstand repeated and prolonged use without damage. Complete moisture removal from the A/C system is possible only with a pump of this type.

1. Connect charging station and discharge system as outlined previously.

NOTE: System must be completely discharged prior to evacuation. If pressurized refrigerant is allowed to enter vacuum pump, pump will be damaged.

2. Reconnect vacuum hose to vacuum pump and ensure that vacuum control valve is closed.
3. Fully open low and high pressure control valves.
4. Connect station to a suitable voltage source and operate vacuum pump.
5. Slowly open vacuum control valve and observe low side compound gauge. If system does not "pump down" to 28–29½ inches Hg (at sea level) within approximately 5 minutes, recheck connections and leak test system.
6. Continue to operate vacuum pump for

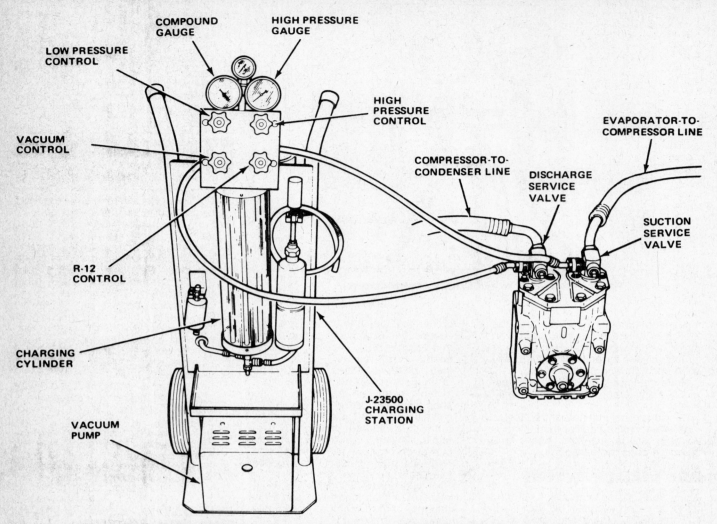

Fig. 3 Charging station J-23500-01 hose connections. Shown with York type compressor

15–30 minutes, longer if system was open for an extended period of time, then close all control valves and stop pump.

7. Check ability of system to hold vacuum. Watch low side compound gauge and ensure that reading does not rise at a rate faster than 1 inch Hg every 4–5 minutes.

8. If system fails to hold vacuum, recheck fittings and connections, and leak test system.

9. If system holds vacuum, charge system with refrigerant.

CHARGING THE SYSTEM

NOTE: Refer to "A/C Data Table" in the "A/C System Servicing" section, for refrigerant capacities.

DISPOSABLE CAN METHOD

1. Connect pressure gauge and manifold assembly J-23575 or equivalent. Keep both service valves in mid-position.

2. Close both gauge hand valves and disconnect service hose from vacuum pump.

3. Connect service hose to center of refrigerant can opener. Close valves on dispenser.

4. Attach refrigerant cans to opener. Refer to A/C Data Table in the "A/C System Servicing" section, for proper weight of refrigerant for vehicle being serviced.

5. Open one petcock valve and loosen center service hose at gauge to allow refrigerant to purge air from hose. Tighten hose and close petcock valve.

6. Open suction gauge hand valve and one petcock valve. Do not open high pressure gauge hand valve.

7. Start engine and set A/C system controls to maximum cooling position. Compressor will help pull refrigerant gas into suction side of system.

NOTE: Refrigerant cans can be placed in pan of water no hotter than 125° F to aid charging process.

8. When first can is empty, open next valve to continue charging until specified amount of refrigerant is in system. Frost line on can may be used as a guide when specifications call for using part of full can. If a scale is available, weigh cans before and during charging procedure to ensure accurate filling.

9. When system is fully charged, close suction gauge hand valve and all petcock valves.

10. Operate system for 5–10 minutes to

allow it to stabilize and to determine if system cycles properly.

11. After checking operation of system, back-seat suction and discharge service valves to normal operating position by turning valves fully counterclockwise.

12. Loosen pressure gauge and manifold assembly service hoses to release refrigerant trapped in hoses. Remove pressure gauge and manifold assembly and install dust caps on fittings.

CHARGING STATION J-23500-01 METHOD

1. After discharging and evacuating system, close low pressure valve on charging station. Fully open left hand refrigerant control valve at base of cylinder and high pressure valve on charging station and allow required charge of refrigerant to enter high side of system. When full charge has entered system, close refrigerant control valve and high pressure valve on charging station, **Fig. 3.**

CAUTION: Do not permit level of liquid to drop below zero mark on cylinder sight glass.

2. After charging is completed, close manifold gauges and check high and low pressures and system operation.

CAUTION: Read gauges with high and low pressure valves closed on charging station. Low pressure gauge can be damaged if both high and low pressure valves are opened.

3. Close all valves on charging station and close refrigerant drum valve when all operations are finished.

4. After completing operational check, back-seat suction and discharge service valves to their normal operating position by turning them fully counterclockwise.

5. Disconnect high and low pressure charging hoses from compressor.

6. Open valve on top of cylinder to remove remaining refrigerant as charging cylinder is not designed to store refrigerant.

7. Replace quick seal caps on compressor service valves.

A/C System Servicing

INDEX

COMPRESSOR SERVICE VALVES

Most models are equipped with manual valves to isolate the compressor from the refrigerant system. These valves allow the compressor to be removed, or opened for oil level checks, without discharging the A/C system. Refrigerant system service access fittings are also included on most models.

During normal system operation, the manual valves are in the back-seated (fully counterclockwise) position, **Fig. 1.** To isolate the compressor, the valves are rotated to the front-seated (fully clockwise) position, closing off the refrigerant line passage to the compressor. To allow refrigerant system service access, the valves are rotated to the mid-position, **Fig. 1,** which opens the service port while still allowing refrigerant to flow through the system.

NOTE: Manual compressor service valves should be in the back-seated (fully counterclockwise) position whenever service gauges are being connected or disconnected on the A/C system. Always install protective caps over manual valve stems and service ports, if equipped, after completing A/C service.

ISOLATING COMPRESSOR

1. Connect suitable gauge manifold to system and remove protective caps from manual valve stems.

2. Slightly open both service valves toward mid-position, then start engine and operate air conditioning.

3. Slowly rotate suction (low) side service valve clockwise toward front-seated position.

4. When suction (low) side gauge reads zero, stop engine, then rotate both low and high side valves to the fully clockwise (front-seated) position, **Fig. 1.**

5. Relieve internal compressor pressure as follows:

NOTE: A suitable face shield should be worn when relieving compressor pressure.

a. On Sankyo 5 cylinder and York 2 cylinder compressors, slightly loosen oil sump filler plug.

PURGING COMPRESSOR

The compressor must be purged of air whenever it has been isolated from the system for service.

1. Install oil plugs or reconnect refrigerant lines and manual valves to compressor as needed.

2. Cap service access ports on both manual valves, then rotate low (suction) side service valve counterclockwise to the back-seated position.

3. Rotate high (discharge) side manual valve to mid-position, then slightly loosen cap on high side gauge port to allow refrigerant to force air out of compressor.

4. Back seat high side manual valve, then tighten gauge port cap.

OIL LEVEL CHECK

NOTE: Refer to "A/C Data Table" for oil level specifications.

SANKYO COMPRESSOR

1. Isolate compressor as outlined in "Compressor Service Valves."

2. Remove compressor drive belt and rotate compressor so that filler plug faces straight up.

3. Slowly loosen, then remove oil filler plug.

NOTE: A suitable face shield should be worn when removing filler plug.

4. Rotate front clutch plate to position piston connecting rod in center of oil filler opening, **Fig. 2.**

5. Flush dipstick J-29642-12 or equivalent with refrigerant, then insert dipstick through opening to right of piston, **Fig. 3,** until stop bottoms against compressor housing.

6. Remove dipstick and note number of increments covered by oil. When properly filled, oil level should be between 4 and 6 increments.

7. Add suitable refrigeration oil, as needed, to obtain specified level.

8. Install oil filler plug and compressor

A/C Data Table

Year	Model	Refrigerant Capacity Lbs.	Refrigeration Oil				Compressor Clutch Air Gap Inches
			Viscosity	Total System Capacity Ounces	Compressor Oil Level Check Inches		
1979–80	Exc. CJ Series	2¼	500	7	①		—
	CJ Series	2½	500	7	①		—
1981–83	Exc. CJ Series	2¼	500	②	③		④
	CJ Series	2½	500	②	③		④
1984–85	CJ Series	2	500	6½	⑤		④
	Grand Wagoneer & Truck	⑥	500	6½	⑦		④
	Cherokee & Wagoneer	—	500	6½	⑤		④

①—Horizontal mount, ¹³⁄₁₆–1³⁄₁₆ in.; Vertical mount, ⅞–1⅛ in.
②—Sankyo 5 cyl. comp., 7–8 oz.; York 2 cyl. comp., 7 oz.
③—York 2 cyl. comp.: Horizontal mount, ¹³⁄₁₆–1³⁄₁₈ in.; Vertical mount, ⅞–1⅛ in. Sankyo 5 cyl. comp., note that "Oil Level Inches" cannot be checked. Refer to total capacity and see text for checking procedure.
④—Sankyo 5 cyl. comp., .016–.031 in.
⑤—Note that "Oil Level Inches" can not be checked. Refer to total capacity and see text for checking procedure.
⑥—In-Line 6 cyl. engines, 2 lbs.; V8 engines, 2¼ lbs.
⑦—York compressor, .8125–1.1865 inch.; Sankyo 5 cyl. compressor, note that "Oil Level Inches" cannot be checked. Refer to total capacity and see text for checking procedure.

drive belt, if removed, then purge air from compressor.

YORK COMPRESSOR

NOTE: Compressor oil level should be checked whenever system is discharged for service part replacement or after rapid loss of refrigerant.

1. Isolate compressor as outlined previously.

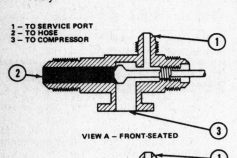

1 – TO SERVICE PORT
2 – TO HOSE
3 – TO COMPRESSOR

VIEW A – FRONT-SEATED

VIEW B – BACK-SEATED

VIEW C – MIDPOSITIONED

Fig. 1 Compressor service valves, cross sectional view

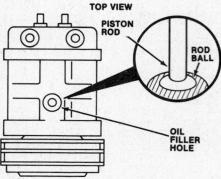

TOP VIEW
PISTON ROD
ROD BALL
OIL FILLER HOLE

Fig. 2 Positioning compressor piston rod for oil level check. Sankyo compressor

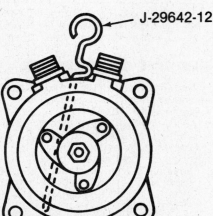

J-29642-12

Fig. 3 Compressor oil level check. Sankyo compressor

2. Slowly loosen crankcase oil check plug to relieve internal pressures, then after pressure is released, remove plug.
3. Hold dipstick, tool No. J-29642-12 in a vertical position, **Fig. 4,** then insert into check plug opening until dipstick bottoms in compressor.

NOTE: If necessary, slightly rotate crankshaft to clear dipstick path.

4. Remove dipstick and count number of dipstick increments covered with oil.
5. When properly filled, compressor should contain 7–10 increments of oil.
6. Add or remove oil as necessary.

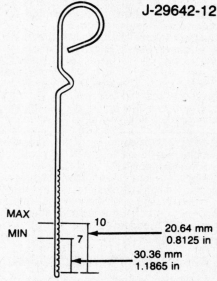

J-29642-12

MAX
MIN
10
7
20.64 mm
0.8125 in
30.36 mm
1.1865 in

Fig. 4 Compressor oil level check. York compressor

OIL CHARGE

Compressor oil level should be checked whenever the A/C system is discharged for repair or due to a malfunction. To ensure proper oil level after system service, proceed as follows:

1. Discharge system and repair as needed.

NOTE: If compressor is replaced, ensure that oil level in replacement compressor is the same as the oil level in the defective compressor. If the evaporator or condenser is replaced, add 1 ounce of oil to each component prior to installation.

2. Evacuate and recharge system, then operate A/C until pressure gauge readings stabilize (approximately 10 minutes).

3. Stop engine and perform "Oil Level Check."

CHARGING VALVE LOCATION

Both high pressure and low pressure fittings are located on the compressor service valves.

VARIABLE SPEED FANS

INDEX

CAUTION: Do not operate engine until fan has first been inspected for cracks and/or separations. If a fan blade is found to be bent or damaged in any way, do not attempt to repair or reuse damaged part. Proper balance is essential in fan assembly operation. Balance cannot be assured once a fan assembly has been found to be bent or damaged and failure may occur during operation, creating an extremely dangerous condition. Always replace damaged fan assembly.

DESCRIPTION

The fan drive clutch, **Fig. 1**, is a fluid coupling containing silicone oil. Fan speed is regulated by the torque-carrying capacity of the silicone oil. The more silicone oil in the coupling, the greater the fan speed, and the less silicone oil, the slower the fan speed.

The fan drive clutch uses a heat sensitive, coiled bi-metallic spring connected to an opening plate which brings about similar results, **Fig. 2**. This causes the fan speed to increase with a rise in temperature and to decrease as temperature decreases.

TROUBLESHOOTING

FAN DRIVE CLUTCH TEST

CAUTION: Do not operate the engine until the fan has been first checked for possible cracks and separations.

To check the clutch fan, disconnect the bi-metal spring, **Fig. 3,** and rotate 90° counter-clockwise. This disables the temperature-controlled, free-wheeling feature and the clutch performs like a conventional fan. If this cures the overheating condition, replace the clutch fan.

FAN CLUTCH NOISE

Fan clutch noise can sometimes be noticed when clutch is engaged for maximum cooling. Clutch noise is also noticeable within the first few minutes after starting engine while clutch is redistributing the silicone fluid back to its normal, disengaged operating condition after settling for long periods of time (over night). However, continuous fan noise or an excessive roar indicates the clutch assembly is locked-up due to internal failure. This condition can be checked by attempting to manually rotate fan. If fan cannot be rotated manually or there is a rough, abrasive feel as fan is rotated, the clutch should be replaced.

FAN LOOSENESS

Lateral movement can be observed at the fan blade tip under various temperature conditions because of the type bearing used. This movement should not exceed ¼ inch (6.5mm) as measured at the fan tip. If this lateral movement does not exceed specifications, there is no cause for replacement.

CLUTCH FLUID LEAK

Small fluid leaks do not generally affect

Fig. 1   Fan drive clutch assembly, 1984–85. 1979–83 similar

Fig. 2   Variable speed fan with coiled bi-metallic thermostatic spring

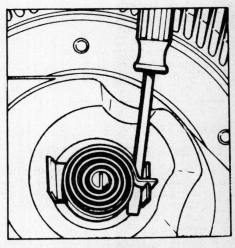

Fig. 3   Bi-metallic coiled spring removal

the operation of the unit. These generally occur around the area of the bearing assembly, but if the leaks appear to be excessive, engine overheating may occur. Check for clutch and fan free-wheeling by attempting to rotate fan and clutch assembly by hand five times. If no drag is felt, replace clutch.

FAN BLADE INSPECTION

Place fan on flat surface with leading edge facing down. If there is a clearance between fan blade touching surface and opposite blade of more than .090 inch (2mm), replace fan. (See caution at beginning of chapter.)

ALTERNATOR SYSTEMS
Delco-Remy Alternators

NOTE: For service procedures on these alternators, refer to "Alternator Systems" section of the Chevrolet/GMC chapter.

STARTER MOTORS & SWITCHES
TABLE OF CONTENTS

Delco-Remy Starters

NOTE: For service procedures on this starter, refer to "Delco-Remy Starters" section in "Chevrolet & GMC" chapter.

Ford Motorcraft Starters

NOTE: For description, diagnosis and starter overhaul procedures on these starters, refer to "Ford Motorcraft Starters" section in "Ford" chapter. For testing, refer to this section.

INDEX

ON-VEHICLE TESTING
SOLENOID GROUND TEST

1. Connect one ohmmeter test probe to battery negative post and other probe to sheet metal adjacent to solenoid on manual transmission, or ground terminal on automatic transmission, and note resistance.
2. Move test probe to solenoid S terminal. If resistance increases by more than 5 ohms, check solenoid ground.

SOLENOID PULL-IN COIL WINDING TEST

1. Disconnect S terminal wire from solenoid.
2. Connect ohmmeter leads to S terminal and the mounting bracket on manual transmission, or ground terminal on automatic transmission.
3. If there is no continuity, replace solenoid.

STARTER MOTOR FULL-LOAD CURRENT TEST

1. Ensure that battery is fully charged, then disconnect and ground ignition coil secondary wire.
2. Connect remote control starter switch between positive battery terminal and S terminal on solenoid.
3. Connect circuit tester, **Fig. 1,** then actuate remote starter switch and note voltmeter reading.

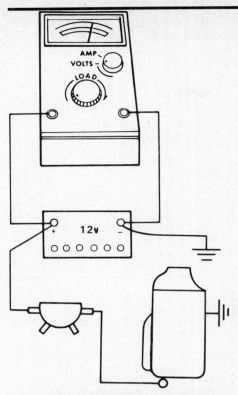

Fig. 1   Full-load current test connections

NOTE: Note voltage after starter has reached maximum RPM.

4. Turn off remote starter switch, then turn load control knob clockwise until indicated voltage is exactly the same as when starter was running.
5. If ammeter does not read as follows, bench test starter:
   a. All 1981–83 & 1984–85 Grand Wagoneer and Truck models w/6 cylinder engine, 150–180 amps.
   b. All 1981–83 & 1984–85 Grand Wagoneer and Truck models w/8 cylinder engine, 160–210 amps.
   c. All 1979–80 & 1984–85 exc. Grand Wagoneer and Truck models, 180–220 amps.

OFF-VEHICLE TESTING

ARMATURE BALANCE TEST

1. Place armature in growler and turn power switch to "GROWLER" position.
2. Place contact fingers of meter test probe across adjacent commutator bars, then adjust voltage control until pointer indicates highest voltage on scale.
3. Test each commutator bar with adja-

cent bar. If any reading of zero volts is obtained, replace armature.

ARMATURE GROUND TEST

1. Place armature in growler and turn power switch to "TEST" position.
2. Place one lead of test lamp on armature core and other lead to each commutator bar.
3. If test lamp lights at any time, replace armature.

ARMATURE SHORT TEST

1. Place armature in growler and turn power switch to "GROWLER" position.
2. Hold steel blade parallel to and touching armature core, then slowly rotate armature at least one full turn.
3. If steel blade vibrates, replace armature.

FIELD WINDING TERMINAL-TO-BRUSH CONTINUITY TEST

1. Insert a piece of paper between contact points.
2. Touch ohmmeter leads to field winding terminal and insulated brush.
3. If resistance is greater than zero ohms, determine which solder joints have excessive resistance and repair with 600 watt soldering iron.

HOLD-IN COIL WINDING RESISTANCE TEST

1. Insert piece of paper between contact points.
2. Using ohmmeter, measure resistance between S terminal and starter motor frame.
3. If resistance is not 2.0–3.5 ohms, replace field winding assembly.

INSULATED BRUSH CONNECTION TEST

1. Using ohmmeter, test resistance through solder joint by touching leads to brush and the copper bus bar.
2. If resistance is more than zero ohms, resolder joint with 600 watt soldering iron.

NO-LOAD CURRENT TEST

1. Connect test equipment as shown, **Fig. 2,** and turn tester load control knob fully counterclockwise, then operate starter and note voltage.
2. Using mechanical tachometer, determine exact motor RPM. Connect tachometer by removing seal from end of drive end housing and clean grease from end of armature shaft.
3. Disconnect battery cable from starter.

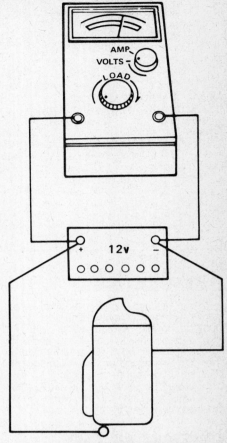

Fig. 2   No-load current test connections

4. Turn load control knob clockwise until voltage reading is exactly that obtained in step 1.
5. If ammeter does not read 77 amps with a starter motor RPM of 8900–9600 on 1979–81 models, or 67 amps with a starter motor RPM of 7380–9356 on 1982–85 models, repair or replace starter as necessary.

SOLENOID CONTACT POINT TEST

1. Using ohmmeter, test resistance through solder joint.
2. If resistance is more than zero ohms, resolder joint using 600 watt soldering iron.

TERMINAL BRACKET INSULATION TEST

1. Using ohmmeter, test resistance between terminal bracket and end cap.
2. If resistance is less than infinite, replace end cap.

DASH GAUGES & GRAPHIC DISPLAYS

INDEX

DASH GAUGES

Gauge failures are often caused by defective wiring or grounds. The first step in locating trouble should be a thorough inspection of all wiring, terminals and printed circuits. If wiring is secured by clamps, check to see whether the insulation has been severed, thereby grounding the wire. In the case of a fuel gauge installation, rust may cause failure by corrosion at the ground connection of the tank unit.

CONSTANT VOLTAGE REGULATOR TYPE (CVR)

The Constant Voltage Regulator (CVR) type indicator is a bimetal-resistance type system consisting of an Instrument Voltage Regulator (IVR), an indicator gauge, and a variable resistance sending unit. Current to the system is applied to the gauge terminals by the IVR, which maintains an average-pulsating value of 5 volts.

The indicator gauge consists of a pointer which is attached to a wire-wound bimetal strip. Current passing through the coil heats the bimetal strip, causing the pointer to move. As more current passes through the coil, heat increases, moving the pointer farther.

The circuit is completed through a sending unit which contains a variable resistor. When resistance is high, less current is allowed to pass through the gauge, and the pointer moves very little. As resistance decreases due to changing conditions in system being monitored, more current passes through gauge coil, causing pointer to move farther.

OPERATIONAL TEST

1. Disconnect wiring harness connector at sending unit. Connect a test lamp or voltmeter between terminal in wiring harness connector and ground.
2. With ignition switch in ON position, light should pulse or meter reading should fluctuate.
3. If lamp lights but does not pulse, or if meter reading remains steady, check ground to IVR. If ground is satisfactory, IVR is defective.
4. If lamp fails to light, or if meter reads 0 volts, check for open circuit across IVR terminals, indicator gauge terminals, or open circuit in wiring harness and printed circuit between components.
5. Connect test lamp or voltmeter ground lead to ground terminal in sending unit wiring harness connector. Light should pulse or meter reading should fluctuate as in step 2. If not, locate open in ground circuit.

NOTE: Do not apply battery voltage to system or ground output terminals of IVR, as damage to system components or wiring circuits may result.

SENDING UNIT TESTS

Fuel Tank Gauge

1. Disconnect wiring harness connector at sending unit and connect ohmmeter between ground terminal and resistor terminal on sending unit.
2. Meter should read 1–88 ohms on 1984–85 Cherokee and Wagoneer, 10–63 ohms on 1984–85 Grand Wagoneer and Truck, or 10–63 ohms on all other models. If reading shows no continuity (infinite reading), check ground connection to tank gauge.
3. If ground is satisfactory, but reading is not within specification, tank unit is defective.
4. If reading is within specification, remove fuel tank gauge from vehicle and connect ohmmeter between resistor terminal and ground terminal (metal housing on single terminal units).
5. Observe meter while slowly moving float rod between empty and full stops. Meter should read at high end of specifications listed in step 2 at empty stop and at low end of specifications listed in step 2 at full stop. Change in readings should be smooth, without hesita-

tion or jumping.
6. If tank unit fails to operate as outlined, unit is defective.

NOTE: Before installing fuel tank gauge, connect wiring harness connector to gauge and move float rod from empty to full position with ignition key in ON position. If dash gauge reading is incorrect, check IVR and dash gauge. If system tests prove satisfactory, but system still does not operate correctly, check that tank gauge rod is not bent or binding and that float is not damaged, loose or filled with fuel.

Oil & Temperature Sending Units

1. Test dash gauge and IVR as outlined above.
2. If system is satisfactory, start engine and allow it to reach operating temperature.
3. If no reading is indicated on the gauge, check the sending unit-to-gauge wire by removing the wire from the sending unit and momentarily ground this wire to a clean, unpainted portion of the engine.
4. If the gauge still does not indicate, the wire is defective. Repair or replace the wire.
5. If grounding the new or repaired wire causes the dash gauge to indicate, the sending unit is faulty.

VARIABLE VOLTAGE TYPE

The variable voltage type dash gauge consists of two magnetic coils to which battery voltage is applied. The coils act on the gauge pointer and pull in opposite directions. One coil is grounded directly to the chassis, while the other coil is grounded through a variable resistor within the sending unit. Resistance through the sending unit determines current flow through its coil, and therefore pointer position.

When resistance is high in the sending unit, less current is allowed to flow through its coil, causing the gauge pointer to move toward the directly grounded coil. When

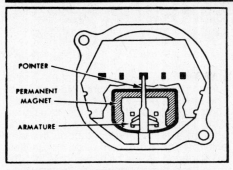

Fig. 1 Conventional type ammeter

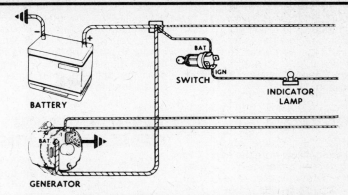

Fig. 2 Charge indicator lamp wiring system. Delco S1 type charging system

resistance in the sending unit decreases, more current is allowed to pass through its coil, increasing the magnetic field. The gauge pointer is then attracted toward the coil which is grounded through the sending unit.

A special tester is required to diagnose this type gauge. Follow instructions included with the tester.

AMMETERS

The ammeter is an instrument used to indicate current flow into and out of the battery. When electrical accessories in the vehicle draw more current than the alternator can supply, current flows from the battery and the ammeter indicates a discharge (−) condition. When electrical loads of the vehicle are less than alternator output, current is available to charge the battery, and the ammeter indicates a charge (+) condition. If battery is fully charged, the voltage regulator reduces alternator output to meet only immediate vehicle electrical loads. When this happens, ammeter reads zero.

CONVENTIONAL AMMETER

A conventional ammeter must be connected between the battery and alternator in order to indicate current flow. This type ammeter, **Fig. 1**, consists of a frame to which a permanent magnet is attached. The frame also supports an armature and pointer assembly. Current in this system flows from the alternator through the ammeter, then to the battery or from the battery through the ammeter into the vehicle electrical system, depending on vehicle operating conditions.

When no current flows through the ammeter, the magnet holds the pointer armature so that the pointer stands at the center of the dial. When current passes in either direction through the ammeter, the resulting magnetic field attracts the armature away from the effect of the permanent magnet, thus giving a reading proportional to the strength of the current flowing.

Troubleshooting

When the ammeter apparently fails to register correctly, there may be trouble in the wiring which connects the ammeter to the alternator and battery or in the alternator or battery itself.

To check the connections, first tighten the two terminal posts on the back of the ammeter. Then, following each wire from the ammeter, tighten all connections on the ignition switch, battery and alternator. Chafed, burned or broken insulation can be found by following each ammeter wire from end to end.

All wires with chafed, burned or broken insulation should be repaired or replaced. After this is done, and all connections are tightened, connect the battery cable and turn on the ignition switch. The needle should point slightly to the discharge (−) side.

Start the engine and run slightly above idling speed. The needle should move slowly to the charge side (+).

If the pointer does not move as indicated, the ammeter is out of order and should be replaced.

SHUNT TYPE AMMETER

The shunt type ammeter is actually a specifically calibrated voltmeter. If it connected to read voltage drop across a resistance wire (shunt) between the battery and alternator. The shunt is located either in the vehicle wiring or within the ammeter itself.

When voltage is higher at the alternator end of the shunt, the meter indicates a charge (+) condition. When voltage is higher at the battery end of the shunt, the meter indicates a discharge (−) condition. When voltage is equal at both ends of the shunt, the meter reads zero.

Troubleshooting

Ammeter accuracy can be determined by comparing reading with an ammeter of known accuracy.

1. With engine stopped and ignition switch in RUN position, switch on headlamps and heater fan. Meter should indicate a discharge (−) condition.
2. If ammeter pointer does not move, check ammeter terminals for proper connection and check for open circuit in wiring harness. If connections and wiring harness are satisfactory, ammeter is defective.
3. If ammeter indicates a charge (+) condition, wiring harness connections are reversed at ammeter.

ALTERNATOR INDICATOR LIGHT
DELCOTRON SI INTEGRAL CHARGING SYSTEM

This system features an integral solid state regulator mounted inside the alternator slip ring end frame. The alternator indicator lamp is installed in the field wire circuit connected between the ignition "Ign." terminal and alternator No. 1 terminal, **Fig. 2**. The resistance provided by the alternator warning light circuit is needed to protect the diode trio. The alternator indicator lamp should light when the ignition switch is turned on before engine is started. If lamp does not light, either lamp is burned out or indicator lamp wiring has an open circuit. After engine is started, the indicator lamp should be out at all times. If indicator lamp comes on, alternator belt may be loose, alternator or regulator may be defective, charging circuit may be defective or fuse may be blown.

Troubleshooting

1. Switch Off, lamp On:
   a. Disconnect electrical connector from alternator terminals 1 and 2.
   b. If indicator light remains lit, repair short circuit between leads.
   c. If indicator light goes out, replace alternator rectifier bridge.
2. Switch On, lamp Off, engine not running:
   a. Perform tests described in step 1.
   b. If problem still exists, there may be an open circuit.
   c. To locate open circuit, check for blown fuse or fusible link, burned out bulb, defective bulb socket or an open in No. 1 lead circuit between alternator and ignition switch.
   d. If no faults are found, check charging system for proper operation.

3. Switch On, lamp On, engine running:
   a. On models so equipped, check condition of fuse between indicator light and ignition switch and fuse in A/C circuit.
   b. Check charging system for proper operation.

VOLTMETER

The voltmeter is a gauge which measures the electrical flow from the battery to indicate whether the battery output is within tolerances. The voltmeter reading can range from 13.5–14.0 volts under normal operating conditions. If an undercharge or overcharge condition is indicated for an extended period, the battery and charging system should be checked.

TROUBLESHOOTING

To check voltmeter, turn key and headlights on with engine off. Pointer should move to 12.5 volts. If no needle movement is observed, check connections from battery to circuit breaker. If connections are tight and meter shows no movement, check wire continuity. If wire continuity is satisfactory, the meter is inoperative and must be replaced.

OIL PRESSURE INDICATOR LIGHT

Many trucks utilize a warning light on the instrument panel in place of the conventional dash indicating gauge to warn the driver when the oil pressure is dangerously low. The warning light is wired in series with the ignition switch and the engine unit—which is an oil pressure switch.

The oil pressure switch contains a diaphragm and a set of contacts. When the ignition switch is turned on, the warning light circuit is energized and the circuit is completed through the closed contacts in the pressure switch. When the engine is started, build-up of oil pressure compresses the diaphragm, opening the contacts, thereby breaking the circuit and putting out the light.

TROUBLESHOOTING

The oil pressure warning light should go on when the ignition is turned on. If it does not light, disconnect the wire from the engine unit and ground the wire to the frame or cylinder block. Then if the warning light still does not go on with the ignition switch on, replace the bulb.

If the warning light goes on when the wire is grounded to the frame or cylinder block, the engine unit should be checked for being loose or poorly grounded. If the unit is found to be tight and properly grounded, it should be removed and a new one installed. (The presence of sealing compound on the threads of the engine unit will cause a poor ground).

If the warning light remains lit when it normally should be out, replace the engine unit before proceeding further to determine the cause for a low pressure indication.

The warning light will sometimes light up or flicker when the engine is idling, even though the oil pressure is adequate. However, the light should go out when the engine speed is increased.

TEMPERATURE INDICATOR LIGHT

A bimetal temperature switch located in the cylinder head control the operation of a temperature indicator light with a red lens. If the engine cooling system is not functioning properly and coolant temperature exceeds a predetermined value, the warning light will illuminate.

TROUBLESHOOTING

If the red light is not lit when the engine is being cranked, check for a burned out bulb, an open in the light circuit, or a defective ignition switch.

If the red light is lit when the engine is running, check the wiring between light and switch for a ground, defective temperature switch, or overheated cooling system.

NOTE: As a test circuit to check whether the red bulb is functioning properly, a wire which is connected to the ground terminal of the ignition switch is tapped into its circuit. When the ignition is in the "Start" (engine cranking) position, the ground terminal is grounded inside the switch and the red bulb will be lit. When the engine is started and the ignition switch is in the "On" position, the test circuit is opened and the bulb is then controlled by the temperature switch.

ELECTRICAL TEMPERATURE GAUGES

This temperature indicating system consists of a sending unit, located on the cylinder head, electrical temperature gauge and an instrument voltage regulator. As engine temperature increases or decreases, the resistance of the sending unit changes, in turn controlling current flow to the gauge. When engine temperature is low, the resistance of the sending unit is high, restricting current flow to the gauge, in turn indicating low engine temperature. As engine temperature increases, the resistance of the ending unit decreases, permitting an increased current flow to the gauge, resulting in an increased temperature reading.

TROUBLESHOOTING

Troubleshooting for the electrical temperature indicating system is the same as for the electrical oil pressure indicating system.

ELECTRICAL OIL PRESSURE GAUGES

This oil pressure indicating system incorporates an instrument voltage regulator, electrical oil pressure gauge and a sending unit which are connected in series. The sending unit consists of a diaphragm, contact and a variable resistor. As oil pressure increases or decreases, the diaphragm actuated the contact on the variable resistor, in turn controlling current flow to the gauge. When oil pressure is low, the resistance of the variable resistor is high, restricting current flow to the gauge, in turn indicating low oil pressure. As oil pressure increases, the resistance of the variable resistor is lowered, permitting an increased current flow to the gauge, resulting in an increased gauge reading.

TROUBLESHOOTING

Disconnect the oil pressure gauge lead from the sending unit, connect a 12 volt test lamp between the gauge lead and the ground and turn ignition ON. If test lamp flashes, the instrument voltage regulator is functioning properly and the gauge circuit is not broken. If the test lamp remains lit, the instrument voltage regulator is defective and must be replaced. If the test lamp does not light, check the instrument voltage regulator for proper ground or an open circuit. Also, check for an open in the instrument voltage regulator to oil pressure gauge wire or in the gauge itself.

NOTE: If test lamp flashes and gauge is not accurate, the gauge may be out of calibration, requiring replacement.

SPEEDOMETERS

The following material covers only that service on speedometers which is feasible to perform. Repairs on the units themselves are not included as they require special tools and extreme care when making repairs and adjustments that only an experienced speedometer technician should attempt.

The speedometer has two main parts—the speedometer head and the speedometer drive cable. When the speedometer fails to indicate speed or mileage, the cable or cable housing is probably broken.

SPEEDOMETER CABLE

Most cables are broken due to lack of lubrication, or a sharp bend or kink in the housing.

A cable might break because of the speedometer head mechanism binds. In such cases, the speedometer head should be repaired or replaced before a new cable or housing is installed.

A "jumpy" pointer condition, together with a scraping noise, is due, in most instances, to a dry or kinked speedometer cable. The kinked cable rubs on the housing and winds up, slowing down the pointer. The cable then unwinds and the pointer "jumps."

To check for kinks, remove the cable, lay it on a flat surface and twist one end with the fingers. If it turns over smoothly the cable is not kinked. But if part of the cable flops over as it is twisted, the cable is kinked and should be replaced.

LUBRICATION

The speedometer cable should be lubricated with special cable lubricant. Fill the ferrule on the upper end of the housing with the cable lubricant. Insert the cable in the housing, starting at the upper end. Turn the cable around carefully while feeding it into the housing. Repeat filling the ferrule except for the last six inches of cable. Too much lubricant at this point may cause the lubricant to work into the speedometer head.

INSTALLING CABLE

During installation, if the cable sticks when inserted in the housing and will not go through, the housing is damaged inside or kinked. Be sure to check the housing from one end to the other. Straighten any sharp bends by relocating clamps or elbows. Replace housing if it is badly kinked or broken. Position the cable and housing so that they lead into the head as straight as possible.

Check the new cable for kinks before installing it. Use wide, sweeping, gradual curves where the cable comes out of the transmission and connects to the head so the cable will not be damaged during installation.

Arrange the housing so it does not lean against the engine because heat from the engine may dry out the lubricant.

If inspection indicates that the cable and housing are in good condition, yet pointer action is erratic, check the speedometer head for possible binding.

The speedometer drive pinion should also be checked. If the pinion is dry or its teeth are stripped, the speedometer may not register properly.

VACUUM GAUGE

This gauge, **Fig. 3**, measures intake manifold vacuum. The intake manifold vacuum varies with engine operating conditions, carburetor adjustments, valve timing, ignition timing and general engine condition.

Since the optimum fuel economy is directly proportional to a properly functioning engine, a high vacuum reading on the gauge relates to fuel economy. Most gauges have colored sectors the green sector being the "Economy" range and the red the "Power" range. Therefore, the vehicle should be operated with gauge registering in the green sector or a high numerical number, **Fig. 3**, for maximum economy.

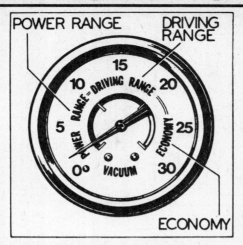

Fig. 3   Typical vacuum gauge

FUEL ECONOMY WARNING SYSTEM

This system actually monitors the engine vacuum just like the vacuum gauge, but all it registers is a low vacuum. The light on the instrument panel warns the vehicle operator when engine manifold vacuum drops below the economical limit. Switch operation is similar to that of the oil pressure indicating light, except that the switch opens when vacuum , rather than oil pressure, is applied.

TROUBLESHOOTING

Fuel Economy Warning Light

The fuel economy warning light should go on when the ignition is turned on. If it does not light, disconnect the wire from the fuel economy vacuum switch connector and ground the wire to the frame or cylinder block. If the warning light still does not go on, check for burned out indicating bulb or an open in the harness between the vacuum switch and instrument panel. If warning light goes on, circuit is functioning and the vacuum switch should be checked for proper ground. Remove and clean the mounting bracket screws and the mounting surfaces.

If system still does not operate, perform the following:

With the electrical connector and vacuum tube disconnected from the switch, connect a self-powered test light to the switch electrical connector and to the vacuum gauge mountng bracket. Attach a vacuum pump to gauge. If the following conditions are not met the switch has to be replaced:

1. With vacuum applied test light should be "Off".
2. With no vacuum to the vacuum switch test light should be "On".

If the warning light remains lit when it normally should be out, check vacuum hose to vacuum switch for damage or plugged condition.

ELECTRIC CLOCKS

Regulation of electric clocks is accomplished automatically by resetting the time. If the clock is running fast, the action of turning the hands back to correct the time will automatically cause the clock to run slightly slower. If the clock is running slow, the action of turning the hands forward to correct the time will automatically cause the clock to run slightly faster (10 to 15 seconds day).

A lock-out feature prevents the clock regulator mechanism from being reset more than once per wind cycle, regardless of the number ot times the time is reset. After the clock rewinds, if the time is then reset, automatic regulation will take place. If a clock varies over 10 minutes per day, it will never adjust properly and must be repaired or replaced.

WINDING CLOCK WHEN CONNECTING BATTERY OR CLOCK WIRING

The clock requires special attention when reconnecting a battery that has been disconnected for any reason, a clock that has been disconnected, or when replacing a blown clock fuse. It is very important that the initial wind be fully made. The procedure is as follows:

1. Make sure that all other instruments and lights are turned off.
2. Connect positive cable to battery.
3. Before connecting the negative cable, press the terminal to its post on the battery. Immediately afterward, strike the terminal against the battery post to see if there is a spark. If there is a spark, allow the clock to run down until it stops ticking, and repeat as above until there is no spark. Then immediately make the permanent connection before the clock can again run down. The clock will run down in approximately two minutes.
4. Reset clock after all connections have been made. The foregoing procedure should also be followed when reconnecting the clock after it has been disconnected, or if it has stopped because of a blown fuse. Be sure to disconnect battery before installing a new fuse.

TROUBLESHOOTING

If clock does not run, check for blown "clock" fuse. If fuse is blown, check for short in wiring. If fuse is not blown, check for open circuit.

With an electric clock, the most frequent cause of clock fuse blowing is voltage at the clock which will prevent a complete wind and allow clock contacts to remain closed. This may be caused by any of the following: discharged battery, corrosion on contact surface of battery terminals, loose connections at battery terminals, at junction block, at fuse clips, or at terminal connection of clock. Therefore, if in reconnecting battery or clock it is noted that the clock

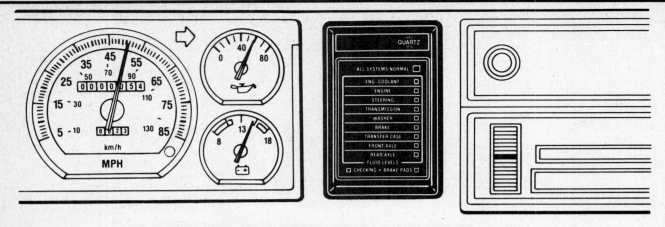

Fig. 4   Systems Sentry System warning light display module

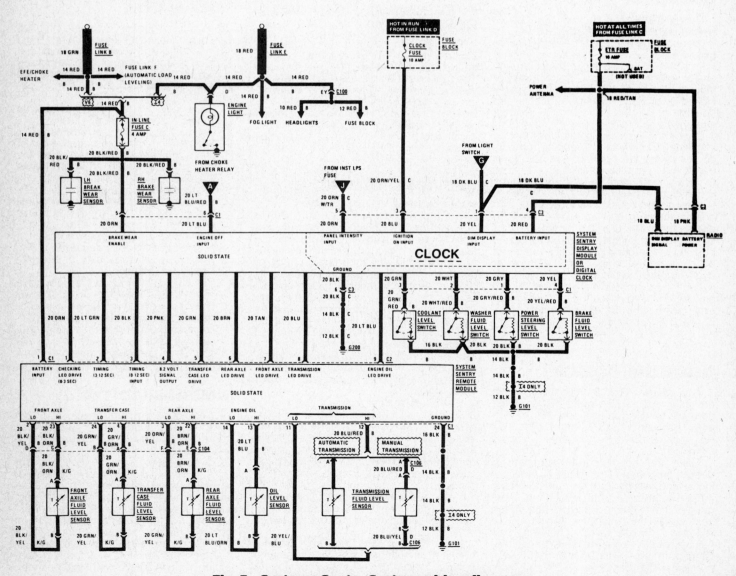

Fig. 5   Systems Sentry System wiring diagram

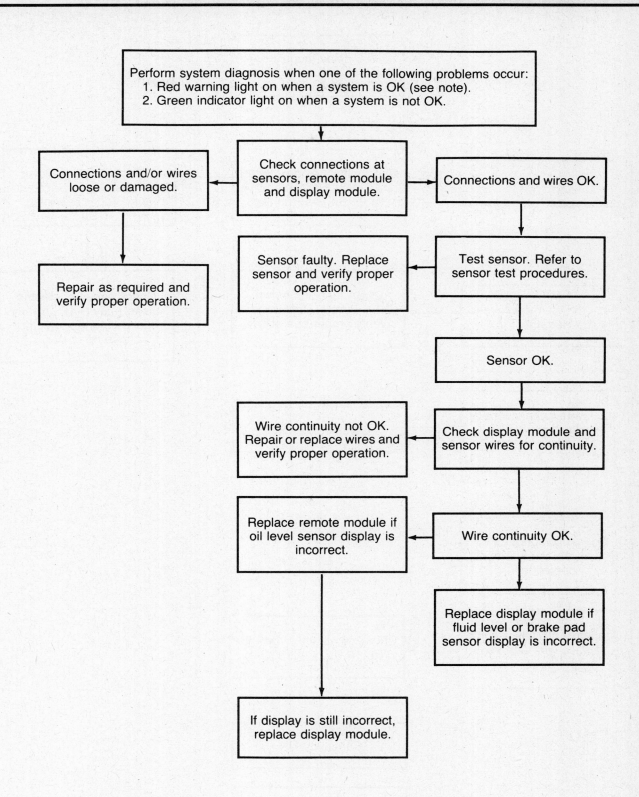

Perform system diagnosis when one of the following problems occur:
1. Red warning light on when a system is OK (see note).
2. Green indicator light on when a system is not OK.

Check connections at sensors, remote module and display module.

Connections and/or wires loose or damaged.

Connections and wires OK.

Repair as required and verify proper operation.

Sensor faulty. Replace sensor and verify proper operation.

Test sensor. Refer to sensor test procedures.

Sensor OK.

Wire continuity not OK. Repair or replace wires and verify proper operation.

Check display module and sensor wires for continuity.

Replace remote module if oil level sensor display is incorrect.

Wire continuity OK.

Replace display module if fluid level or brake pad sensor display is incorrect.

If display is still incorrect, replace display module.

NOTE: Front disc brake pad replacement alone will not turn off the brake wear warning light. The wear warning sensor and the 4-amp signal fuse must also be replaced.

Fig. 6 Systems Sentry System diagnostic chart (Part 1 of 2)

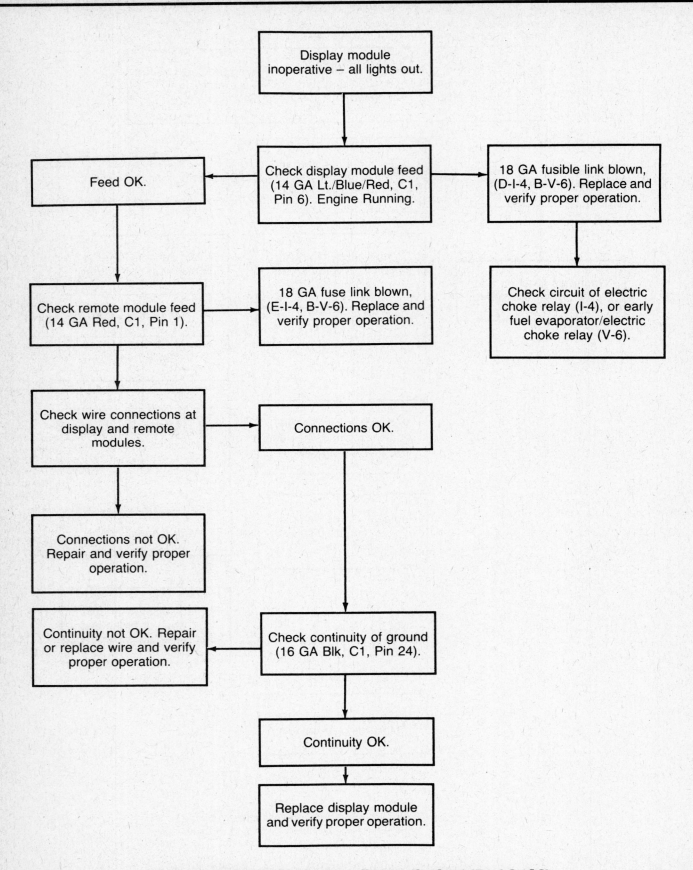

Fig. 6   Systems Sentry System diagnostic chart (Part 2 of 2)

is not ticking, always check for blown fuse, or examine the circuits at the points indicated above to determine and correct the cause.

SYSTEMS SENTRY SYSTEM

DESCRIPTION & OPERATION

This system, available on 1985 Cherokee and Wagoneer models, is a diagnostic warning system used to monitor vital fluid levels and disc brake pad wear.

The system consists of a warning light display module, **Fig. 4,** mounted on right side of instrument cluster, a remote module under the dash, various fluid level and wear sensors and the necessary interconnecting wiring.

The warning light display module in the instrument cluster contains three different color lights. The amber checking lights indicate that each system is being checked. The green lights indicate that fluid level or brake pads are satisfactory. The red lights indicate that fluid level or brake pads should be checked and corrected as necessary. It should be noted that disconnected fluid level sensor wires or open circuits will cause a red warning light, however, disconnected brake pad wear sensor wires will not create any indication.

The remote module monitors and analyzes electrical current flow through the sensors connected to it. Because current varies with fluid level, the module is able to energize the appropriate warning light on the display module. The engine, transmission, transfer case and rear axle oil level sensors are connected to the remote module.

The various sensors and their locations are as follows: engine coolant, located in the coolant recovery bottle; engine oil, located in the oil pan; power steering fluid, located in the pump reservoir; manual transmission oil, located in the transmission fill plug; automatic transmission fluid, located on the transmission dipstick; windshield washer fluid, located in the washer reservoir; brake fluid, located in the master cylinder; transfer case oil, located in the rear section of the transfer case; front and rear axle oil, located in front and rear axle housings; front disc brake pads, located on each inboard brake pad.

The engine, transfer case, transmission and axle oil level sensors operate on the principle of changes in resistance in relation to contact with oil and are connected to the remote module. The power steering, brake fluid, windshield washer and engine coolant sensors are float-type sensors affected by changes in fluid level and are wired directly to the display module. The brake pad wear sensor is also wired directly to the display module and is an electro-mechanical device actuated by contact with the rotor surface. When the pad is worn enough to allow sensor to contact rotor, the sensor grounds against the rotor. This creates a brief current surge on the pad warning circuit and shorts the 4 amp in-line signal fuse, resulting in illumination of the red warning light.

CHECKING FLUID LEVELS AND/OR BRAKE PAD WEAR

1. Operate vehicle until fluids reach normal operating temperature.
2. Park vehicle on a level surface.
3. Turn ignition to Off position and observe display module indicator lights, noting the following:
   a. Amber lights indicate that all systems are being checked.
   b. A green light indicates that the fluid level or pad wear is satisfactory.
   c. A red light indicates that the fluid level or pad wear should be checked.
4. To repeat warning light display, restart engine and idle for 30 seconds, then turn ignition to Off position.

DIAGNOSIS

In a properly functioning system, a red light caused by a low fluid condition will go out when the fluid level has been corrected. If a warning light remains lit after correcting the fluid level, or if the fluid level was actually satisfactory when the warning light was energized, refer to wiring diagram, **Fig. 5,** and diagnostic charts, **Fig. 6** to pinpoint and correct the malfunction.

In the case of front disc brake pads, replacement of the pads alone will not turn off the brake pad warning light. The 4 amp signal fuse and brake pad wear sensors must also be replaced.

TESTING

Engine, Front Axle, Transfer Case, Transmission & Rear Axle Sensors

NOTE: These sensors may be tested while installed in vehicle.

1. Disconnect sensor electrical connectors.
2. Measure resistance across pins in sensor electrical connector using a suitable ohmmeter.
3. If ohmmeter reads 6–20 ohms resistance, sensor is satisfactory.
4. If ohmmeter indicates no resistance, sensor is defective and must be replaced.

Brake, Engine Coolant, Power Steering & Windshield Washer Sensors

NOTE: These sensors must be removed from vehicle for testing.

1. Remove sensor from vehicle.
2. Connect a suitable ohmmeter to terminal pins in sensor connector.
3. Invert sensor to simulate a full reservoir condition and note ohmmeter reading. If ohmmeter does not read 2640–3960 ohms, sensor is defective and must be replaced.
4. Turn sensor right side up to simulate an empty reservoir condition and note ohmmeter reading. If any resistance is indicated, sensor is defective and must be replaced.

Front Disc Brake Pad Wear Sensor

This sensor cannot be tested. It is a single wire one-time use component that is activated only when grounded against the rotor surface.

DISC BRAKES

TABLE OF CONTENTS

General Information

INDEX

TROUBLESHOOTING

EXCESSIVE PEDAL TRAVEL

1. Worn brake lining.
2. Shoe and lining knock back after cornering or rough road travel.
3. Piston and shoe and lining assembly not properly seated or positioned.
4. Air leak or insufficient fluid in system or caliper.
5. Loose wheel bearing adjustment.
6. Damaged or worn caliper piston seal.
7. Improper booster push rod adjustment.
8. Shoe out of flat more than .005".
9. Rear brake automatic adjusters inoperative.
10. Improperly ground rear brake shoe and lining assemblies.

BRAKE ROUGHNESS OR CHATTER; PEDAL PUMPING

1. Excessive lateral run-out of rotor.
2. Rotor excessively out of parallel.

EXCESSIVE PEDAL EFFORT

1. Frozen or seized pistons.
2. Brake fluid, oil or grease on linings.
3. Shoe and lining worn below specifications.
4. Proportioning valve malfunction.
5. Booster inoperative.
6. Leaking booster vacuum check valve.

PULL, UNEVEN OR GRABBING BRAKES

1. Frozen or seized pistons.
2. Brake fluid, oil or grease on linings.
3. Caliper out of alignment with rotor.
4. Loose caliper attachment.
5. Unequalized front tire pressure.
6. Incorrect front end alignment.
7. Lining protruding beyond end of shoe.

BRAKE RATTLE

1. Excessive clearance between shoe and caliper or between shoe and splash shield.
2. Shoe hold-down clips missing or improperly positioned.

HEAVY BRAKE DRAG

1. Frozen or seized pistons.
2. Operator riding brake pedal.
3. Incomplete brake pedal return due to linkage interference.
4. Faulty booster check valve holding pressure in hydraulic system.
5. Residual pressure in front brake hydraulic system.

CALIPER BRAKE FLUID LEAK

1. Damaged or worn caliper piston seal.
2. Scores in cylinder bore.
3. Corrosion build-up in cylinder bore or on piston surface.
4. Metal clip in seal groove.

NO BRAKING EFFECT WHEN PEDAL IS DEPRESSED

1. Piston and shoe and lining assembly not properly seated or positioned.
2. Air leak or insufficient fluid in system or caliper.
3. Damaged or worn caliper piston seal.
4. Bleeder screw open.
5. Air in hydraulic system or improper bleeding.

REAR BRAKES LOCKING ON APPLICATION

On brake system equipped with a proportioning or rear pressure regulator valve, should the valve malfunction, rear brakes may receive excess pressure, resulting in wheel lock-up.

SERVICE PRECAUTIONS

BRAKE LINES & LININGS

Remove one of the front wheels and inspect the brake disc, caliper and linings. (The wheel bearings should be inspected at this time and repacked if necessary.)

Do not get any oil or grease on the linings. It is recommended that both front wheel sets be replaced whenever a respective shoe and lining is worn or damaged. Inspect and, if necessary, replace rear brake linings also.

If the caliper is cracked or fluid leakage through the casting is evident, it must be replaced as a unit.

BRAKE ROUGHNESS

The most common cause of brake chatter on disc brakes is a variation in thickness of the disc. If roughness or vibration is encountered during highway operation or if pedal pumping is experienced at low speeds, the disc may have excessive thickness variation. To check for this condition, measure the disc at 12 points with a micrometer at a radius approximately one inch from edge of disc. If thickness measurements vary more than specifications allow, the disc should be replaced with a new one.

Excessive lateral runout of braking disc may cause a "knocking back" of the pistons, possibly creating increased pedal travel and vibration when brakes are applied.

Before checking the runout, wheel bearings should be adjusted. Be sure to make the adjustment according to the recommendations given in the individual truck chapters.

BRAKE DISC SERVICE

Servicing of disc brakes is extremely critical due to the close tolerances required in machining the brake disc to insure proper brake operation.

The maintenance of these close controls on the friction surfaces is necessary to prevent brake roughness. In addition, the surface finish must be non-directional and maintained at a micro-inch finish. This close control of the rubbing surface finish is necessary to avoid pulls and erratic performance and promote long lining life and equal lining wear of both left and right brakes.

In light of the foregoing remarks, refinishing of the rubbing surfaces should not be attempted unless precision equipment, capable of measuring in micro-inches is available.

To check runout of a disc, mount a dial indicator on a convenient part (steering knuckle, tie rod, disc brake caliper housing) so that the plunger of the dial indicator contacts the disc at a point one inch from the outer edge. If the total indicated runout

exceeds specifications, install a new disc.

GENERAL PRECAUTIONS

1. Grease or any other foreign material must be kept off the caliper, surfaces of the disc and external surfaces of the hub, during service procedures. Handling the brake disc and caliper should be done in a way to avoid deformation of the disc and nicking or scratching brake linings.
2. If inspection reveals rubber piston seals are worn or damaged, they should be replaced immediately.
3. During removal and installation of a wheel assembly, exercise care so as not to interfere with or damage the caliper splash shield, the bleeder screw or the transfer tube, (if equipped).
4. Front wheel bearings should be adjusted to specifications.
5. Be sure vehicle is centered on hoist before servicing any of the front end components to avoid bending or damaging the disc splash shield on full right or left wheel turns.
6. Before the vehicle is moved after any brake service work, be sure to obtain a firm brake pedal.
7. The assembly bolts of the two caliper housings (if equipped) should not be disturbed unless the caliper requires service.

INSPECTION OF CALIPER

Should it become necessary to remove the caliper for installation of new parts, clean all parts in alcohol, wipe dry using lint-free cloths. Using an air hose, blow out

drilled passages and bores. Check dust boots for punctures or tears. If punctures or tears are evident, new boots should be installed upon reassembly.

Inspect piston bores in both housings for scoring or pitting. Bores that show light scratches or corrosion can usually be cleaned with crocus cloth. However, bores that have deep scratches or scoring may be honed, provided the diameter of the bore is not increased more than .002". If the bore does not clean up within this specification, a new caliper housing should be installed (black stains on the bore walls are caused by piston seals and will do no harm).

When using a hone, be sure to install the hone baffle before honing bore. The baffle is used to protect the hone stones from damage. Use extreme care in cleaning the caliper after honing. Remove all dust and grit by flushing the caliper with alcohol. Wipe dry with clean lint-less cloth and then clean a second time in the same manner.

BLEEDING DISC BRAKES

The disc brake hydraulic system can be bled manually or with pressure bleeding equipment. On vehicles with disc brakes, the brake pedal will require more pumping and frequent checking of fluid level in master cylinder during bleeding operation.

Never use brake fluid that has been drained from hydraulic system when bleeding the brakes. Be sure the disc brake pistons are returned to their normal positions and that the shoe and lining assemblies are properly seated. Before driving the vehicle, check brake operation to be sure that a firm pedal has been obtained.

Bendix Single Piston Sliding Caliper

INDEX

DESCRIPTION

The disc brake is of the sliding caliper, single piston design. On 1979–81 CJ models, the caliper is positioned into abutment surfaces machined into the leading and trailing edges of the caliper anchor bracket, **Fig. 1.** On 1979–83 Cherokee, Wagoneer and Truck and 1984–85 Grand Wagoneer

and Truck models, the caliper is positioned on mounting bolts located in the caliper support bracket, **Fig. 2.** On 1982–85 CJ and Scrambler and 1984–85 Cherokee and Wagoneer models, the caliper is positioned over the rotor and slides on two mounting pins which maintain caliper position relative to rotor and caliper anchor plate, **Fig. 3.** Although caliper designs dif-

fer in construction, operation and service procedures remain the same.

All models are equipped with an integral type hub and rotor. The caliper is a one-piece casting containing a piston, piston bore, bleeder screw and inlet ports. A rubber dust boot with integral metal retainer is used on all models except 1979–81 CJ models, which use a solid rubber boot. The dust boot is positioned in a counterbore machined in the upper edge of the piston bore and in a groove machined in the exterior surface of the piston.

Lining wear is compensated for by the lateral sliding movement of the caliper and by increased piston extension.

CALIPER REMOVAL

1979—81 CJ

1. Drain and discard ⅔ of brake fluid from largest master cylinder reservoir.
2. Raise and support vehicle.
3. Remove front wheel and tire assemblies.
4. Press caliper piston to bottom of bore using suitable screwdriver or C-clamp.
5. Remove caliper support key retaining screw using a ¼ inch hex wrench.
6. Remove caliper support key and spring using punch and hammer.
7. Lift caliper up and out of anchor plate and off rotor.

1979—83 CHEROKEE, TRUCK & WAGONEER; 1984—85 GRAND WAGONEER & TRUCK

1. Drain and discard ⅔ of brake fluid from master cylinder front reservoir.
2. Raise and support vehicle.
3. Remove front wheel and tire assemblies.
4. Press caliper piston to bottom of bore using suitable screwdriver or C-clamp.
5. Remove caliper mounting bolts.
6. Remove caliper by lifting upward and out of shield and support.

1982—85 CJ & SCRAMBLER; 1984—85 CHEROKEE & WAGONEER

1. Remove and discard ⅔ of brake fluid from largest master cylinder reservoir.
2. Raise and support vehicle.
3. Remove front wheel and tire assemblies.
4. Press caliper piston to bottom of bore using suitable screwdriver or C-clamp.
5. Remove caliper mounting pins.
6. Lift caliper up and out of anchor plate and off rotor.

BRAKE SHOE REMOVAL

1979—81 CJ

1. Unfasten caliper as previously described, leaving brake hose attached to caliper.

NOTE: Suspend caliper from suspension

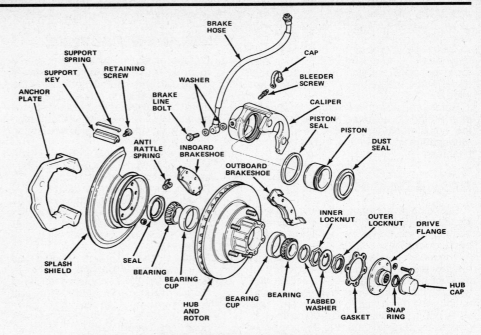

Fig. 1 Exploded view of disc brake assembly. 1979—81 CJ

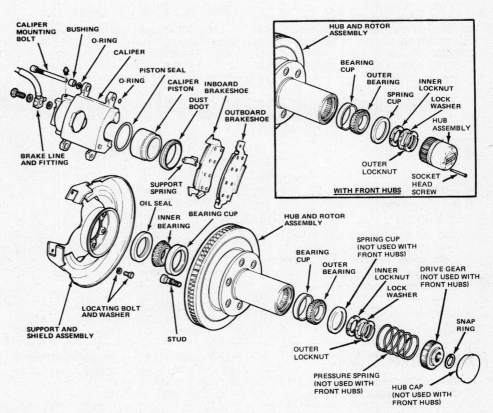

Fig. 2 Exploded view of disc brake assembly. 1979—83 Cherokee, Truck & Wagoneer; 1984—85 Grand Wagoneer & Truck

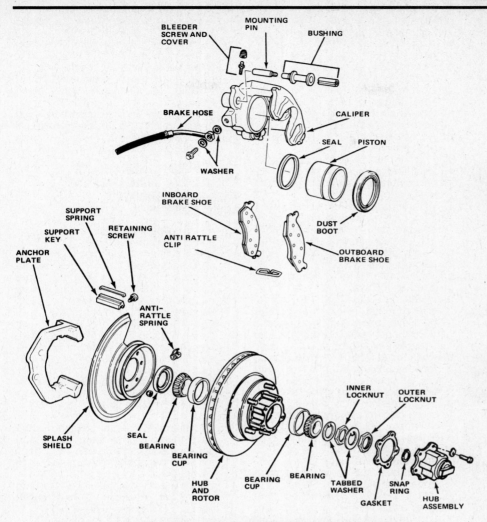

**Fig. 3   Exploded view of disc brake assembly.
1982–85 CJ & Scrambler; 1984–85 Cherokee & Wagoneer**

spring. Do not let caliper hang by hydraulic line.

2. Remove inboard brake shoe from anchor plate.
3. Remove anti-rattle spring from inboard shoe, noting position of spring for assembly reference.
4. Remove outboard brake shoe from caliper.
5. Clean caliper interior using clean shop cloths. Do not use compressed air, as damage to dust boot may result.

1979–83 CHEROKEE, TRUCK & WAGONEER; 1984–85 GRAND WAGONEER & TRUCK

1. Unfasten caliper as previously described, leaving brake hose attached to caliper.

NOTE: Suspend caliper from suspension spring. Do not let caliper hang by hydraulic line.

2. Remove inboard and outboard brake shoes from caliper.
3. Remove support spring from inboard shoe, noting position of spring for assembly reference.
4. Remove sleeves and rubber bushings from mounting bolt bores in caliper mounting ears.
5. Clean mounting bolts, bolt core and bushing grooves in caliper mounting ears with suitable solvent. Do not use abrasives to clean or polish the mounting bolts.
6. Clean caliper interior and dust boot using clean shop cloths. Do not use compressed air, as damage to boot may result.

1982–85 CJ & SCRAMBLER; 1984–85 CHEROKEE & WAGONEER

1. Unfasten caliper as previously described, leaving brake hose attached to caliper.

NOTE: Suspend caliper from suspension

spring. Do not let caliper hang by hydraulic line.

2. Remove outboard brake shoe from anchor plate while holding anti-rattle clip.
3. Remove inboard brake shoe and anti-rattle clip.
4. Clean caliper interior using clean shop cloths. Do not use compressed air, as damage to dust boot may result.

BRAKE SHOE INSTALLATION

1979–81 CJ

1. Install inboard brake shoe anti-rattle spring on rear flange of shoe. Ensure looped section of spring faces away from rotor.
2. Install inboard brake shoe with spring in caliper anchor plate.
3. Install outboard brake shoe in caliper.
4. Install caliper as described under "Caliper Installation."

1979–83 CHEROKEE, TRUCK & WAGONEER; 1984–85 GRAND WAGONEER & TRUCK

1. Apply suitable silicone lubricant to replacement bushings, sleeves, bushing grooves and small ends of mounting bolts.
2. Install new rubber bushings in caliper mounting ears.
3. Install new sleeves in inboard mounting ears of caliper. Ensure sleeve end faces shoe and lining is flush with machined surface of mounting ear.
4. Install support spring on inboard brake shoe. Position single tang end of spring over notch in shoe.
5. Install inboard shoe in caliper. Ensure shoe is flush against piston and support spring is fully seated in piston.
6. Install outboard shoe until shoe is fully seated. Ensure shoe ears rest on upper surface of caliper mounting ears and lower shoe tab fits into cutout in caliper.

NOTE: Outboard shoes with formed ears are meant for original installation only and are fitted to the caliper. Shoes of this type must never be relined or reconditioned.

7. Install caliper as described under "Caliper Installation."

1982–85 CJ & SCRAMBLER; 1984–85 CHEROKEE & WAGONEER

1. Install anti-rattle clip on trailing edge of anchor plate, ensuring split end of clip faces away from rotor.
2. Install inboard, then the outboard shoes while holding anti-rattle clip.

3. Install caliper as described under "Caliper Installation."

DISASSEMBLING CALIPER

1. Clean outside of caliper with suitable solvent.
2. Drain fluid from caliper and place clean shop cloths in caliper opposite piston.
3. Slowly apply compressed air to caliper inlet port until piston pops out of bore.
4. Remove and discard dust boot, using a suitable screwdriver. Use care to avoid scratching caliper piston bore.
5. Remove and discard piston seal, using a suitable wooden or plastic tool.
6. Remove bleeder screw and protective cap, if equipped.
7. Remove and discard inner and outer bushings and plastic sleeves, if equipped.
8. Clean all components with clean brake fluid and compressed air.

ASSEMBLING CALIPER

1. Lubricate piston bore and new piston seal with clean brake fluid.
2. Install seal in bore groove by hand and lubricate piston with clean brake fluid.
3. On 1979–81 CJ models, install bleeder screw and protective cap.
4. On 1979–81 CJ models, if piston dust boot installation tool No. J-24837 is available, install boot and piston as follows:
   a. Apply clean brake fluid to piston and new dust boot.
   b. Position dust boot on installation tool with approximately ¼ inch of tool extending beyond small lip of dust boot.
   c. Place boot and tool assembly over piston bore, then reach through tool and work large lip of boot into boot groove in upper edge of piston bore until boot is fully seated.
   d. Apply clean brake fluid to caliper piston, then insert piston through tool and center piston in bore.
   e. Press piston half way into bore using steady pressure on a hammer handle.
   f. Remove boot installer tool, then seat dust boot rubber lip in piston groove.
   g. Press piston to bottom of bore using hammer handle.
5. On 1979–81 CJ models, if piston dust

boot installation tool is not available, install boot and piston as follows:
   a. Apply clean brake fluid to piston bore.
   b. Position dry dust boot on piston bore.
   c. Reach through top of boot and work large lip of boot into boot groove at upper edge of bore until boot is fully seated.
   d. Apply clean brake fluid to piston and small lip of dust boot.
   e. Position piston over small lip of boot and apply approximately 15 psi compressed air into caliper fluid inlet port.
   f. With air pressure expanding boot, work piston into boot until boot lip seats in piston groove. When lip is fully seated, release air pressure.
   g. Press piston to bottom of bore using hammer handle.
6. On all except 1979–81 CJ models, proceed as follows:
   a. Install new dust boot on piston, sliding metal retainer portion of boot over open end of piston and pulling boot rearward until boot lip seats in piston groove.
   b. Push metal retainer portion of boot forward until retainer is flush with rim at open end of piston, then snap boot fold into place.
   c. Install piston into caliper bore, using care to avoid unseating piston seal.
   d. Press piston to bottom of bore, then using tool No. J-33028 or equivalent, seat metal retainer portion of dust boot in counterbore at upper end of bore.
   e. Install bleeder screw, then new inner and outer bushings and plastic sleeves, if equipped, in caliper mounting ears.

CALIPER INSTALLATION

1979–81 CJ

1. Install caliper over rotor and in anchor plate.
2. Align caliper and anchor plate, then install support key and spring between abutment surfaces at trailing edge of caliper.
3. Complete installation of support key and spring using a hammer and punch.
4. Install support key retaining screw. Ensure screw is properly seated in support key notch, then torque screw to 15 ft. lbs.
5. Install new washers on brake line connector or fitting and connect brake line to caliper. Torque brake line bolt to

160 inch lbs. or brake line fitting to 25 ft. lbs.
6. Fill master cylinder to within ¼ inch of reservoir rims.
7. Depress brake pedal several times to seat brake shoes, then refill master cylinder, if necessary, and bleed brakes.
8. Install wheel and tire assembly, then lower vehicle and check operation of brake system.

1979–83 CHEROKEE, TRUCK & WAGONEER; 1984–85 GRAND WAGONEER & TRUCK

1. Install caliper over rotor and in support shield and bracket.
2. Install caliper mounting bolts, ensuring bolts pass under inboard shoe retaining ears. Insert bolts until they enter bores in outboard shoe and caliper mounting ears, then thread bolts into support bracket and torque to 35 ft. lbs.
3. Install new copper gaskets on brake line, then connect brake line to caliper and torque brake line bolt to 160 inch lbs.
4. Fill master cylinder to within ¼ inch of reservoir rims, then depress brake pedal several times to seat brake shoes.
5. Clinch upper ears of outboard shoe until there is no radial clearance between shoe and caliper.
6. Install wheel and tire assemblies, then lower vehicle.
7. Check master cylinder fluid level and correct as necessary, then check operation of brake system.

1982–85 CJ & SCRAMBLER; 1984–85 CHEROKEE & WAGONEER

1. Install caliper over rotor and in anchor plate.
2. Align caliper and anchor plate, then install caliper mounting pins and torque to 30 ft. lbs.
3. Install new washers on brake line connector or fitting and connect brake line to caliper. Torque brake line bolt to 160 inch lbs. or brake line fitting to 25 ft. lbs. (23 ft. lbs. on 1984–85 Cherokee and Wagoneer).
4. Fill master cylinder to within ¼ inch of reservoir rims, then depress brake pedal several times to seat brake shoes.
5. Install wheel and tire assemblies, then lower vehicle.
6. Check master cylinder fluid level and correct as necessary, then check operation of brake system.

DRUM BRAKES

TABLE OF CONTENTS

General Information

INDEX

SERVICE PRECAUTIONS

When working on or around brake assemblies, care must be taken to prevent breathing asbestos dust, as many manufacturers incorporate asbestos fibers in the production of brake linings. During routine service operations, the amount of asbestos dust from brake lining wear is at a low level due to a chemical breakdown during use, and a few precautions will minimize exposure.

CAUTION: Do not sand or grind brake linings unless suitable local exhaust ventilation equipment is used to prevent excessive asbestos exposure.

1. Wear a suitable respirator approved for asbestos dust use during all repair procedures.
2. When cleaning brake dust from brake parts, use a vacuum cleaner with a highly efficient filter system. If a suitable vacuum cleaner is not available, use a water soaked rag.

NOTE: Do not use compressed air or dry brush to clean brake parts.

3. Keep work area clean, using same equipment as for cleaning brake parts.
4. Properly dispose of rags and vacuum cleaner bags by placing them in plastic bags.
5. Do not smoke or eat while working on brake systems.

GENERAL INSPECTION

BRAKE DRUMS

Any time the brake drums are removed for brake service, the braking surface diameter should be checked with a suitable brake drum micrometer at several points to determine if they are within the safe oversize limit stamped on the brake drum outer surface. If the braking surface diameter exceeds specifications, the drum must be replaced. If the braking surface diameter is within specifications, drums should be cleaned and inspected for cracks, scores, deep grooves, taper, out of round and heat spotting. If drums are cracked or heat spotted, they must be replaced. Minor scores should be removed with sandpaper. Grooves and large scores can only be removed by machining with special equipment, as long as the braking surface is within specifications stamped on brake drum outer surface. Any brake drum sufficiently out of round to cause vehicle vibration or noise while braking, or showing taper should also be machined, removing only enough stock to true up the brake drum.

After a brake drum is machined, wipe the braking surface diameter with a cloth soaked in denatured alcohol. If one brake drum is machined, the other should also be machined to the same diameter to maintain equal braking forces.

BRAKE LININGS & SPRINGS

Inspect brake linings for excessive wear, damage, oil, grease or brake fluid contamination. If any of the above conditions exists, brake linings should be replaced. Do not attempt to replace only one set of brake shoes; they should be replaced as an axle set only to maintain equal braking forces. Examine brake shoe webbing, hold down and return springs for signs of overheating indicated by a slight blue color. If any component exhibits signs of overheating, replace hold down and return springs with new ones. Overheated springs lose their pull and could cause brake linings to wear out prematurely. Inspect all springs for sags, bends and external damage, and replace as necessary.

Inspect hold down retainers and pins for bends, rust and corrosion. If any of the above conditions exist, replace retainers and pins.

BACKING PLATE

Inspect backing plate shoe contact surface for grooves that may restrict shoe movement and cannot be removed by lightly sanding with emery cloth or other suitable abrasive. If backing plate exhibits above condition, it should be replaced. Also inspect for signs of cracks, warpage and excessive rust, indicating need for replacement.

ADJUSTER MECHANISM

Inspect all components for rust, corrosion, bends and fatigue. Replace as necessary. On adjuster mechanism equipped with adjuster cable, inspect cable for kinks, fraying or elongation of eyelet and replace as necessary.

PARKING BRAKE CABLE

Inspect parking brake cable end for kinks, fraying and elongation, and replace as necessary. Use a small hose clamp to compress clamp where it enters backing plate to remove.

1979–83 Cherokee & Wagoneer;
1984–85 Grand Wagoneer;
All J-10 & J-20

INDEX

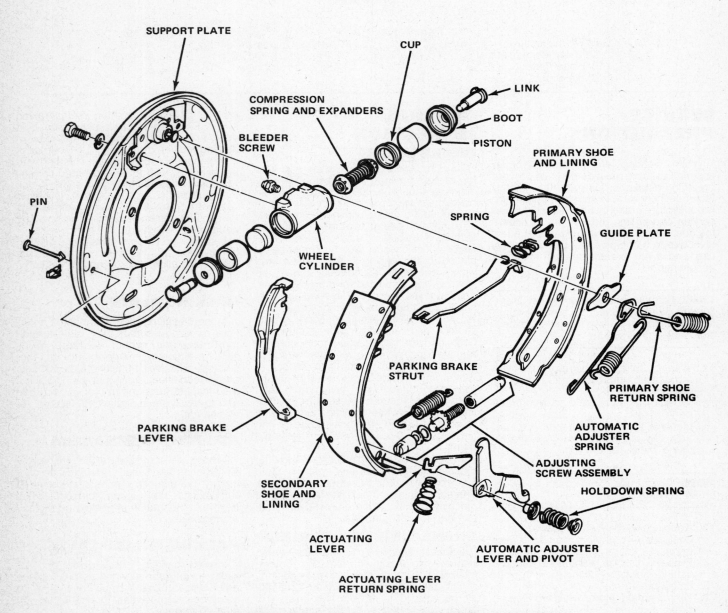

Fig. 1   Drum brake assembly. 1983–84 Cherokee & Wagoneer;
1984–85 Grand Wagoneer; All J-10 & J-20

REMOVAL

1. Raise and support vehicle.
2. Remove wheel and tire assemblies.
3. Release parking brake and loosen lock nuts at parking brake equalizer.
4. Remove rear drum-to-hub locating screws, if equipped.
5. Remove drums.
6. Remove primary return spring, then the automatic adjuster actuating spring and secondary shoe return spring, **Fig. 1**.
7. Remove hold down springs and brake shoe assemblies.
8. On rear brakes, disengage parking brake cable from parking brake lever.
9. Place suitable clamp over ends of wheel cylinder.

INSTALLATION

1. Using suitable lubricant, lubricate support plate edges, anchor pin, adjusting screw threads and pivot, and adjuster lever to secondary brake shoe contact surface.
2. Using suitable lubricant, lubricate parking brake lever pivot and portion of lever that contacts secondary brake shoe.
3. On rear brakes, attach parking brake cable to parking lever on secondary shoe.
4. Install secondary shoe and automatic adjuster lever and pivot as an assembly and secure assembly to support plate with hold down spring.
5. Install actuating and adjusting levers, then the return spring on actuating lever tang with large end of spring resting on brake shoe.
6. Install primary shoe and hold down spring, then the guide plate onto anchor pin.
7. On rear brakes, install parking brake strut.
8. Install adjusting screw and spring.
9. Install adjuster spring, secondary shoe return spring and primary shoe return spring.
10. Turn adjusting screw until brake drum slides over shoes with slight drag, then back off adjusting screw 30 notches and install drums.
11. If any hydraulic lines were opened, bleed brake system.
12. Install wheel and tire assemblies and lower vehicle.
13. Check master cylinder fluid level, filling as necessary.
14. Check brake pedal for proper feel and return.
15. Drive vehicle and make 10–15 forward and reverse stops until satisfactory brake pedal height is obtained.

1984–85 Cherokee, CJ, Scrambler & Wagoneer

INDEX

REMOVAL

1. Raise and support vehicle.
2. Remove wheel and tire assemblies, then the brake drums.
3. Install suitable clamps over ends of wheel cylinders.
4. Remove U-clip and washer (1) from parking brake lever pivot pin, **Fig. 1**, and discard clip.
5. Using suitable tool, remove primary and secondary return springs (2).
6. Remove spring retainers, hold down springs, and retaining pins (3).
7. Remove adjuster lever, adjuster screw, and spring (4) from brake shoes (5).
8. Remove brake shoes.

INSTALLATION

1. Using suitable lubricant, lubricate support plate ledges, anchor pins, adjuster cable guides, adjuster screw and pivot, and parking brake lever and lever pivot pin.
2. Attach parking brake lever (6) to secondary brake shoe and secure with washer and new U-clip.
3. Remove clamps from wheel cylinders.
4. Install brake shoes and secure with hold down springs, pins, and retainers.
5. Install parking brake lever strut and

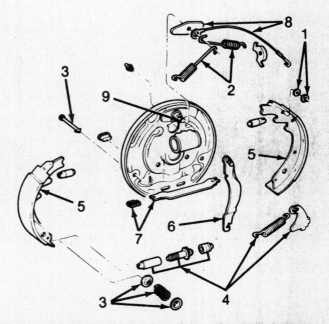

Fig. 1 Drum brake assembly. 1984–85 Cherokee, CJ, Scrambler & Wagoneer

spring (7).

6. Install guide plate and adjuster cable (8) on anchor pin (9).
7. Install primary and secondary return springs with cable guide.
8. Install adjuster screw, spring, and

lever, then connect adjuster cable at adjuster lever.
9. If any hydraulic lines were opened, bleed brake system.
10. Install drums.
11. Install wheel and tire assemblies, and

lower vehicle.
12. Check master cylinder fluid level, filling as necessary.
13. Check brake pedal for proper feel and return, then road test vehicle.

1979—83 CJ & Scrambler

INDEX

REMOVAL

1. Raise and support vehicle.
2. Remove wheel and tire assemblies, then the brake drums. If brake lining is dragging on drum, back off brake adjustment by rotating adjustment screw.
3. Using suitable pliers, grasp adjusting lever and remove lever tang from hole in secondary shoe, **Fig. 1.**
4. Place suitable clamp over ends of wheel cylinder.
5. Remove brake return springs.
6. Remove secondary return spring, adjuster cable, primary return spring, cable guide, adjuster lever, and adjuster springs.
7. Remove hold down springs and brake shoes.
8. On rear brake shoes, disengage parking brake cable from parking brake lever.

INSTALLATION

1. Using suitable lubricant, lubricate support plate edges, anchor pin, self-adjusting cable guide adjuster screw threads, pivot, and parking brake cable lever.
2. Position brake shoes on support plate and install hold down springs.
3. On rear brakes, install parking brake lever, then the parking brake cable on lever, and install strut and spring.
4. Install adjuster cable end on anchor pin.
5. Install primary return spring.
6. Install cable guide and secondary return spring.
7. Install adjusting screw assembly, then place small hooked end of adjuster

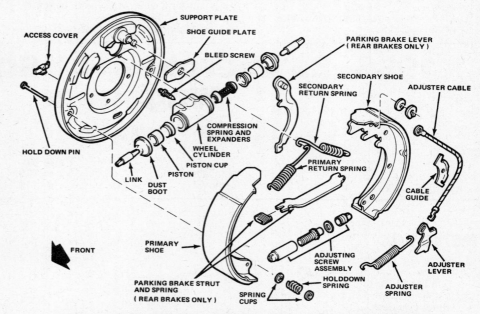

Fig. 1   Drum brake assembly. 1979—83 CJ & Scrambler

spring in large hole in primary shoe and large hooked end in adjuster lever.
8. Place hooked end of adjuster cable over cable guide.
9. Using suitable pliers, grasp adjuster lever and hook adjuster lever tang in large hole in bottom of secondary shoe.
10. Set adjusting screws so that approximately ⅜ inch of thread is exposed between adjuster screw and adjuster screw nut.

11. Install drums.
12. If any hydraulic lines were opened, bleed brake system.
13. Install wheel and tire assemblies and lower vehicle.
14. Check master cylinder fluid level, filling as necessary.
15. Check brake pedal for proper feel and return.
16. Drive vehicle in reverse and forward, making 10 to 15 brake applications, alternating forward and reverse stops, then road test vehicle.

UNIVERSAL JOINTS

INDEX

SERVICE NOTES

Before disassembling any universal joint, examine the assembly carefully and note the position of the grease fitting (if used). Also, be sure to mark the yokes with relation to the propeller shaft so they may be reassembled in the same relative position. Failure to observe these precautions may produce rough vehicle operation which results in rapid wear and failure of parts, and place an unbalanced load on transmission, engine and rear axle.

When universal joints are disassembled for lubrication or inspection, and the old parts are to be reinstalled, special care must be exercised to avoid damage to universal joint spider or cross and bearing cups.

NOTE: Some driveshafts use an injected nylon retainer on the universal joint bearings. When service is necessary, pressing the bearings out will sheer the nylon retainer, **Fig. 1.** Replacement with the conventional steel snap ring type is then necessary, **Fig. 2.**

CROSS & ROLLER TYPE

Figs. 3 and 4 illustrate typical examples of universal joints of this type. They all operate on the same principle and similar service and replacement procedures may be applied to all.

SERVICING WITHOUT UNIVERSAL JOINT REPLACEMENT TOOL

Disassembly

1. Remove snap rings (or retainer plates) that retain bearings in yoke and drive shaft.
2. Place U-joint in a vise.
3. Select a wrench socket with an outside diameter slightly smaller than the U-joint bearings. Select another wrench socket with an inside diameter slightly larger than the U-joint bearings.
4. Place the sockets at opposite bearings in the yoke so that the smaller socket becomes a bearing pusher and the larger socket becomes a bearing

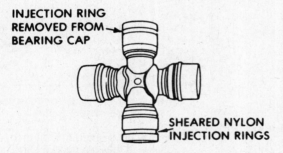

Fig. 1   Production type universal joints which use nylon injection rings in place of snap rings

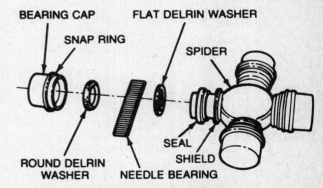

Fig. 2   Service type universal joint (internal snap ring type)

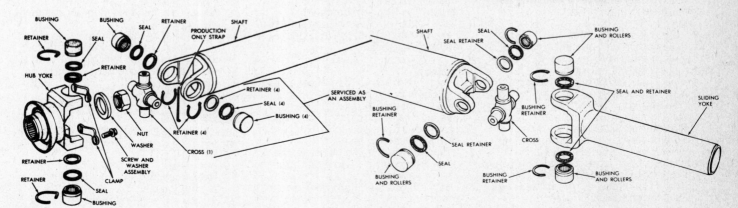

Fig. 3   Cross & roller type universal joints

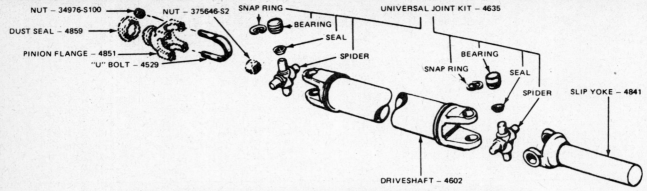

Fig. 4   Cross & roller type universal joints & propeller shaft

Fig. 5   Removing bearings from yoke using a small socket as a driver & large socket as a receiver

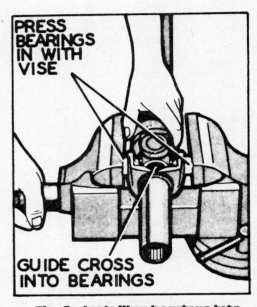

Fig. 6   Installing bearings into drive shaft yoke

receiver when the vise jaws come together, **Fig. 5.** Close vise jaws until both bearings are free of yoke and remove bearings from the cross or spider.

5. If bearings will not come all the way out, close vise until bearing in receiver socket protrudes from yoke as much as possible without using excessive force. Then remove from vise and place that portion of bearing which protrudes from yoke between vise jaws. Tighten vise to hold bearing and drive yoke off with a soft hammer.

6. To remove opposite bearing from yoke, replace in vise with pusher socket on exposed cross journal with receiver socket over bearing cup. Then tighten vise jaws to press bearing back through yoke into receiving socket.

7. Remove yoke from drive shaft and

again place protruding portion of bearing between vise jaws. Then tighten vise to hold bearing while driving yoke off bearing with soft hammer.

8. Turn spider or cross ¼ turn and use the same procedure to press bearings out of drive shaft.

Assembly

1. If old parts are to be reassembled, pack bearing cups with universal joint grease. Do not fill cups completely or use excessive amounts as over-lubrication may damage seals during reassembly. Use new seals.

2. If new parts are being installed, check new bearings for adequate grease before assembling.

3. With the pusher (smaller) socket, press one bearing part way into drive shaft. Position spider into the partially installed bearing. Place second bear-

ing into drive shaft. Fasten drive shaft in vise so that bearings are in contact with faces of vise jaws, **Fig. 6.** Some spiders are provided with locating lugs which must face toward drive shaft when installed.

4. Press bearings all the way into position and install snap rings or retainer plates.

5. Install bearings in yoke in same manner. When installation is completed, check U-joint for binding or roughness. If free movement is impeded, correct the condition before installation in vehicle.

SERVICING USING UNIVERSAL JOINT REPLACEMENT TOOL

Disassembly

1. Place driveshaft in a vise using care to avoid damaging it.

2. Remove bearing retaining snap rings.

NOTE: Some universal joints use injected

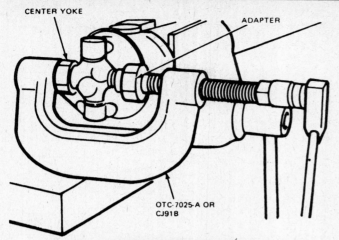

Fig. 7   Removing bearing caps using tool & adapter

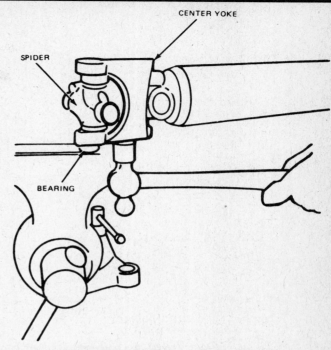

Fig. 8   Removing bearing cap by holding cap in vise & striking center yoke with hammer

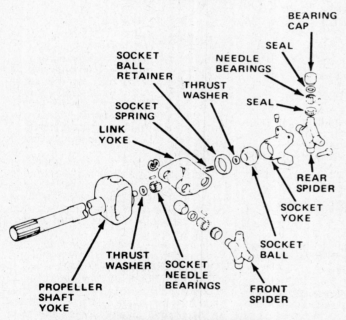

Fig. 9   Double cardan universal joint exploded view

nylon retainers in place of snap rings. During servicing, the snap rings supplied with the replacement universal joint assembly must be used.

3. Position tool on shaft and press bearing out of yoke, **Fig. 7**. If bearing cannot be pressed all the way out, remove it using vise grips or channel lock pliers or position driveshaft as shown and strike center yoke with hammer, **Fig. 8**. Mark yoke and shaft to make sure they will be reassembled in their same relative positions.
4. Reposition tool so that it presses on the spider in order to press other bearing from opposite side of flange.
5. If used, remove flange from spider.

Assembly
1. Start new bearing into yoke, then position spider into yoke and press bearing until it is ¼ inch below surface.
2. Remove tool and install a new snap ring.
3. Start new bearing in opposite side of yoke, then install tool and press on bearing until opposite bearing contacts snap ring.
4. Remove tool and install remaining snap ring.

DOUBLE CARDAN TYPE

The double cardan type joint, **Fig. 9**, incorporates two universal joints, a centering socket yoke, and center yoke at one end of the shaft. A single universal joint is used at the other end.

DISASSEMBLY

1. Remove all bearing cap retainers.
2. Mark bearing caps, spiders, propeller shaft yoke, link yoke and socket yoke for assembly alignment reference, **Fig. 9.**
3. Remove bearing caps attaching from spider to propeller shaft yoke as follows:
   a. Use a ⅝ inch socket to drive the bearing cap and a 1¹⁄₁₆ inch socket to receive the opposite bearing cap as it is driven out.
   b. Place ⅝ inch socket on one bearing cap and 1¹⁄₁₆ inch socket on opposite bearing.
   c. Position assembly in vise so vise jaws bear directly against sockets.
   d. Tighten vise to press first bearing cap out of link yoke.
   e. Loosen vise, reposition sockets and press opposite bearing cap out of link yoke.
4. Disengage propeller shaft yoke from link yoke.
5. Remove bearing caps attaching front spider to propeller shaft as described in step 3 above.
6. Remove front spider from yoke.
7. Remove bearing caps attaching rear spider to link yoke as outlined in step 3 above and remove spider and socket yoke from link yoke.
8. Clean all parts in solvent and wipe dry. Inspect assembly for damage or wear. If any component is worn or damaged, the entire assembly must be replaced.

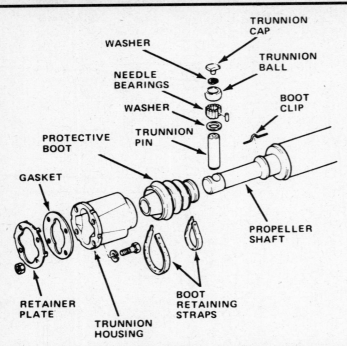

Fig. 10   Ball & trunnion universal joint exploded view

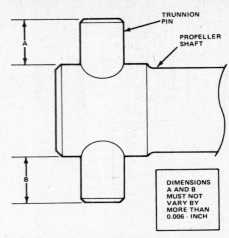

Fig. 11   Centering trunnion pin in shaft bore

ASSEMBLY

NOTE: When assembling universal joint, make sure to align spiders and yokes according to marks made during disassembly.

1. Lubricate all bearings and contact surfaces with lithium base chassis grease.
2. Install bearing caps on yoke ends of rear spider and secure caps with tape, **Fig. 9.**
3. Assemble socket yoke and rear spider.
4. Position rear spider in link yoke and install bearing caps. Press caps into yoke using ⅝ inch socket until bearing cap retainer grooves are exposed.
5. Install rear spider-to-link yoke bearing cap retainers.
6. Position front spider in propeller shaft yoke and install bearing caps. Press caps into yoke using a ⅝ inch socket until bearing cap retainer grooves are exposed.
7. Install front spider-to-propeller shaft yoke bearing cap retainers.
8. Install thrust washer and socket spring in ball socket bearing bore, if removed.
9. Install thrust washer on ball socket bearing boss (located on propeller shaft yoke), if removed.
10. Align ball socket bearing boss on propeller shaft yoke with ball socket bearing bore and insert boss into bore.
11. Align front spider with link yoke bearing cap bores and install bearing caps.

Press caps into yoke using a ⅝ inch socket until bearing cap retainer grooves are exposed.
12. Install front spider-to-link yoke bearing cap retainers.

BALL & TRUNNION TYPE

The ball and trunnion universal joint, **Fig. 10,** is a combination unit functioning as both a slip yoke and universal joint. It is used on some models on the transfer case to propeller shaft. A flange is used to connect one end while a conventional universal joint is used to connect the other.

DISASSEMBLY

1. Straighten retainer plate locktabs and remove plate and gasket from trunnion housing.
2. Cut and remove protective boot retaining straps.
3. Push trunnion housing and protective boot rearward to expose ball and trunnion assembly.
4. Remove trunnion cap and cap washer, **Fig. 10.**
5. Remove trunnion ball, trunnion ball needle bearings and trunnion ball washer.
6. Remove trunnion pin from pin bore in shaft using an arbor press and suitable adapter.
7. Remove trunnion housing, protective boot and boot clip from shaft.
8. Clean all parts in solvent and wipe dry.

ASSEMBLY

1. Lubricate shaft trunnion pin bore, trunnion pin, trunnion ball and needle bearings and trunnion cap with chassis grease. Also, liberally apply grease to interior of trunnion housing.
2. Place boot clip on raised, semi-circular boss on shaft. Use rubber bands or string to retain clip during installation, **Fig. 10.**
3. Install protective boot onto shaft and install one boot retaining strap. Make sure boot is seated on raised shaft boss and boot clip before installing strap. Also make sure strap is seated in strap groove in boot before tightening.
4. Install trunnion housing on shaft, then seat protective boot in housing and install remaining boot retaining strap. Make sure boot is fully seated in housing and strap is seated in strap groove in boot before tightening.
5. Place shaft in arbor press and start trunnion pin in bore. Carefully press pin into bore until pin is centered in shaft to within .006 inch, **Fig. 11.**

CAUTION: Pin must project an equal amount from each side of shaft pin bore. If pin is not centered within .006 inch, propeller shaft vibration may result.

6. Install trunnion ball washer on pin and install trunnion ball and needle bearings on pin.
7. Install trunnion cap washer and trunnion cap on pin.
8. Move housing forward and over ball and trunnion assembly. Make sure assembly is properly and completely seated in housing.
9. Install gasket and plate on housing and bend plate locktabs into housing slots to retain plate and gasket.

MANUAL SHIFT TRANSMISSIONS

NOTE: See individual truck chapters for procedures on removing the transmission and adjusting the gearshift linkage.

TABLE OF CONTENTS

Warner T-14A & T-15A 3 Speed Manual Transmission

INDEX

DISASSEMBLE

TRANSMISSION

1. Remove housing cover and gasket from top of transmission case.
2. Remove nut and flat washer securing transfer case drive gear on the mainshaft. Remove transfer case drive gear, adapter and spacer.
3. Remove main drive gear bearing retainer and gasket, **Fig. 1.**
4. Remove main drive gear and mainshaft bearing snap rings.
5. Using suitable puller, remove main drive gear and mainshaft bearings, **Fig. 2.**
6. Remove main drive gear from case.

NOTE: Transmission must be shifted into second gear to permit removal of the mainshaft and gear assembly.

7. Remove mainshaft and gears as an assembly through the case cover opening, **Fig. 3.**
8. On remote shift units, remove the shifter forks by removing the roll pins from the shift lever shafts and housing. From inside the transmission case, slide the shift levers and interlock assembly toward the outside of the case and remove shifter forks and lever assemblies.

9. Remove lockplate by tapping lightly on the front end of the countershaft and reverse idler shaft. Remove lockplate from the slots in the shafts.
10. Using a suitable drift, drive countershaft rearward out of case. Remove countergear assembly, thrust washers and bearings.
11. Drive reverse idler shaft rearward out of case. Remove idler gear.

MAINSHAFT

1. Remove clutch hub snap ring and 2-3 synchronizer assembly from the mainshaft.
2. Remove 2nd speed gear.
3. Remove reverse gear from mainshaft.
4. Remove clutch hub, snap ring, and low synchronizer assembly from the mainshaft.
5. Remove first speed gear from mainshaft.

ASSEMBLE

1. Install reverse idler gear assembly, making sure that the slot end of the idler shaft is aligned to receive the lockplate.
2. Assemble countershaft center spacer, bearing spacers and rollers in the countergear. Using a suitable dummy

shaft to retain rollers, install gear in case and with thrust washers in place, install countershaft through rear of case with the lockplate slot toward the rear and aligned to receive lockplate.
3. Locate the lockplate in the two shafts and tapping alternately, drive shafts in until lockplate is tight against case.
4. Install mainshaft and gear assembly as a unit through the top cover opening of the transmission case.

NOTE: On remote shift units, the shifter forks and levers must be installed at this time. Interlock levers are stamped and must be installed in the respective locations.

5. Using a screwdriver, depress interlock lever while installing shift fork into shifter lever and synchronizer clutch sleeve. Be sure poppet spring is properly installed. Install tapered pins securing lever shafts in case.
6. Install main drive gear and oil retainer into case with the cutaway part of the gear downward. Guide main drive gear onto mainshaft using care not to drop the rollers.
7. Install main bearings and snap rings.
8. Install main drive gear bearing retainer. Make sure oil drain holes are aligned.
9. Install transmission cover.

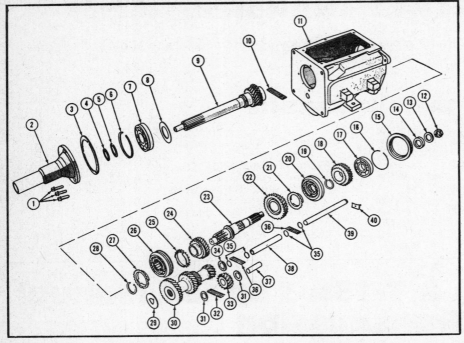

1. Screws
2. Retainer
3. Gasket
4. Seal
5. Snap ring
6. Snap ring
7. Main drive bearing
8. Oil slinger
9. Main drive gear
10. Rollers
11. Case
12. Nut
13. Flatwasher
14. Spacer
15. Bearing adapter
16. Snap ring
17. Mainshaft bearing
18. Reverse gear
19. Snap ring
20. Low synchronizer assembly
21. Blocking ring
22. Low gear
23. Mainshaft
24. Second gear
25. Blocking ring
26. 2-3 synchronizer assembly
27. Blocking ring
28. Snap ring
29. Thrust washer
30. Countergear
31. Washer
32. Rollers
33. Reverse idler gear
34. Thrust washer
35. Spacer washer
36. Rollers
37. Reverse idler shaft
38. Spacer
39. Countershaft
40. Lockplate

Fig. 1   Disassembled view of Warner T-14A & T-15A 3 speed manual transmission

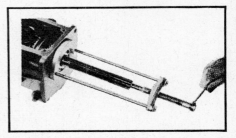

Fig. 2   Main drive gear removal

Fig. 3   Mainshaft removal

Warner T-150 3 Speed Manual Transmission

INDEX

DISASSEMBLE

TRANSMISSION

1. Remove transfer case to transmission attaching bolts, then separate transfer case from transmission, **Fig. 1.**
2. Remove shift control housing, **Fig. 2.**
3. Move 2-3 synchronizer sleeve forward and the 1st.-reverse sleeve rearward to lock the mainshaft.
4. Remove transfer case gear lock nut, flat washer and drive gear.
5. Move both synchronizers back to the Neutral position.
6. Remove fill plug.
7. Remove countershaft roll pin with a ³⁄₁₆ inch punch. The roll pin is accessible through fill plug opening.
8. Remove countershaft and access plug using tool J-25232. Remove countershaft from rear of case. Permit countershaft gear to remain at bottom of case after countershaft removal.
9. Punch alignment marks in front bearing cap and transmission case for assembly reference.

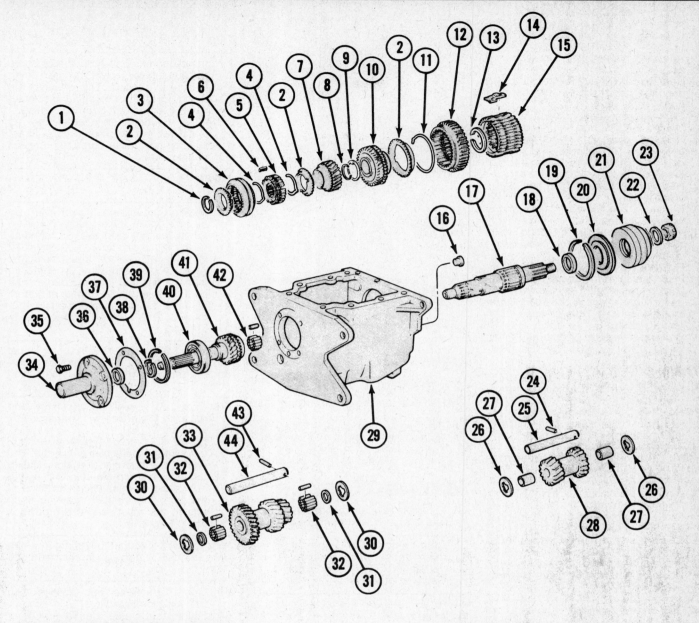

1. MAINSHAFT RETAINING SNAP RING
2. SYNCHRONIZER BLOCKING RINGS (3)
3. SECOND-THIRD SYNCHRONIZER SLEEVE
4. SECOND-THIRD SYNCHRONIZER INSERT SPRING (2)
5. SECOND-THIRD HUB
6. SECOND-THIRD SYNCHRONIZER INSERT (3)
7. SECOND GEAR
8. FIRST GEAR RETAINING SNAP RING
9. FIRST GEAR TABBED THRUST WASHER
10. FIRST GEAR
11. FIRST-REVERSE SYNCHRONIZER INSERT SPRING
12. FIRST-REVERSE SLEEVE AND GEAR
13. FIRST-REVERSE HUB RETAINING SNAP RING
14. FIRST-REVERSE SYNCHRONIZER INSERT (3)
15. FIRST-REVERSE HUB
16. COUNTERSHAFT ACCESS PLUG
17. MAINSHAFT
18. MAINSHAFT SPACER
19. REAR BEARING ADAPTER LOCK RING
20. OIL SLINGER/SPACER
21. REAR BEARING AND ADAPTER ASSEMBLY
22. WASHER

23. LOCKNUT
24. ROLL PIN
25. REVERSE IDLER GEAR SHAFT
26. THRUST WASHER
27. BUSHING (PART OF IDLER GEAR)
28. REVERSE IDLER GEAR
29. TRANSMISSION CASE
30. THRUST WASHER (2)
31. BEARING RETAINER (2)
32. COUNTERSHAFT NEEDLE BEARINGS (50)
33. COUNTERSHAFT GEAR
34. FRONT BEARING CAP
35. BOLT (4)
36. FRONT BEARING CAP OIL SEAL
37. GASKET
38. FRONT BEARING RETAINER SNAP RING
39. FRONT BEARING LOCKRING
40. FRONT BEARING
41. CLUTCH SHAFT
42. MAINSHAFT PILOT ROLLER BEARINGS
43. ROLL PIN
44. COUNTERSHAFT

Fig. 1   Disassembled view of Warner T-150 3 speed manual transmission

10. Remove front bearing cap and gasket.
11. Remove large lock ring from front bearing.
12. Remove clutch shaft and front bearing assembly with tool J-6654-01.
13. Remove 2-3 synchronizer blocking ring from clutch shaft or synchronizer hub.
14. Remove rear bearing and adapter using a suitable drift and hammer.
15. Remove mainshaft and geartrain assembly. Tilt splined end of shaft downward and lift the forward end of the shaft up and out from case.
16. Remove countershaft gear and tool as an assembly.
17. Remove countershaft gear thrust washers, countershaft roll pin and any mainshaft pilot roller bearings which may have fallen into the case during clutch shaft removal.
18. Remove reverse idler gear shaft. Insert a brass drift through clutch shaft bore in front of case and tap shaft until end of shaft with roll pin clears countershaft bore in rear of case, then remove shaft.
19. Remove reverse idler gear and thrust washers.

MAINSHAFT

1. Remove retaining snap ring from front of mainshaft.
2. Remove 2-3 synchronizer assembly and the second gear. Mark hub and sleeve for assembly reference.

NOTE: Observe position of insert springs and inserts for assembly reference.

3. Remove insert springs from 2-3 synchronizer. Remove the three inserts and separate sleeve from synchronizer hub.
4. Remove snap ring and tabbed thrust washer from shaft.
5. Remove first gear and blocking ring.
6. Remove 1st.-reverse hub retaining snap ring.

NOTE: Observe position of inserts and spring for assembly reference.

7. Remove sleeve and gear, insert spring and three inserts from hub.
8. Remove oil slinger and spacer from rear of mainshaft.
9. Remove hub from output shaft using a suitable press.

NOTE: Do not attempt to hammer the press-fit hub from the shaft since damage to the hub and shaft will occur.

CLUTCH SHAFT

1. Remove front bearing retaining snap ring and any remaining roller bearings.
2. Press front bearing from shaft.

NOTE: Do not attempt to hammer the bearing from the shaft since damage to the

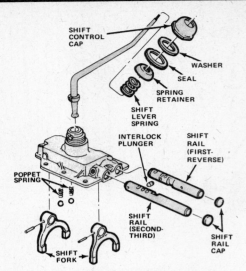

Fig. 2 Disassembled view of shift control housing

shaft and bearing will occur.

REAR BEARING & ADAPTER

1. Clamp rear bearing adapter in a soft-jawed vise.
2. Remove rear bearing retaining snap ring.
3. Remove bearing adapter from vise.
4. Press bearing from adapter with a suitable press.
5. Remove bearing adapter lock ring.

ASSEMBLE

1. Lubricate reverse idler gear shaft bore and bushings with transmission lubricant.
2. Coat transmission case reverse idler gear thrust washer surfaces with petroleum jelly, then install thrust washers into case.

NOTE: Ensure that the locating tabs on the thrust washers are engaged into case slots.

3. Install reverse idler gear. Align gear bore, thrust washers and case bores, then install reverse idler gear shaft from rear of case. Align and seat roll pin in shaft in counterbore in rear of case.
4. Measure reverse idler gear end play by inserting a feeler gauge between thrust washer and gear. End play should be .004—.018 inch. If not, replace thrust washers.
5. Coat needle bearings and bearing bores in countershaft gear with petroleum jelly. Insert tool J-25232 in bore of gear and install 25 needle bearings and one retainer in each end of gear.
6. Coat countershaft gear thrust washer surfaces with petroleum and place thrust washers in the case.

NOTE: Ensure that the locating tabs on the thrust washers are engaged into case slots.

7. Insert countershaft into rear case bore far enough to secure the rear thrust washer in position. This prevents the thrust washer from being displaced when countershaft gear is installed.
8. Install countershaft gear but do not install roll pin. Align gear bore, thrust washers and case bores, then install countershaft.

NOTE: Do not remove tool J-25232 completely.

9. Measure countershaft gear end play by inserting a feeler gauge between thrust washer and the countershaft gear. End play should be .004—.018 inch. If not, replace thrust washers. After proper end play is obtained, install arbor tool fully in countershaft gear. Permit gear to remain at bottom of case. Leave countershaft in rear case bore to secure thrust washer in position.

NOTE: The countershaft gear must remain at bottom of case to provide clearance for installation of the mainshaft and clutch shaft assemblies.

10. Coat all mainshaft splines and machined surfaces with transmission lubricant.
11. Start 1st-reverse synchronizer hub onto output shaft splines by hand. The end of the hub with the slots should face toward front of shaft. Use a suitable press to complete installation of the hub, then install retaining snap ring in the most rearward groove in shaft, **Fig. 3.**

NOTE: Do not attempt to hammer the hub onto shaft since damage to shaft and hub will occur.

12. Coat 1st-reverse hub splines with transmission lubricant.
13. Install 1st-reverse sleeve and gear half-way onto hub. The gear end of the sleeve must face toward rear of shaft. Align sleeve and hub using alignment marks made during disassembly.
14. Install insert springs into 1st-reverse hub. Ensure the spring is bottomed in hub and covers all three insert slots. Position the three "T" shaped inserts into hub with small ends in hub slots, **Fig. 3.** Push the inserts fully into hub so the inserts seat on the insert spring, then slide 1-reverse sleeve and gear over inserts until inserts engage in sleeve, **Fig. 4.**
15. Coat bore and blocking ring surface of first gear with transmission lubricant and place first gear blocking ring on tapered surface of gear.
16. Install first gear on mainshaft. Rotate gear until notches in blocking ring engage inserts in 1st-reverse hub, then install tabbed thrust washer, with

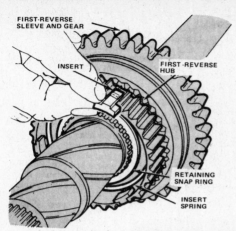

Fig. 3   1st-reverse hub insert

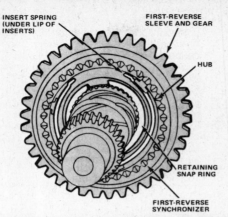

Fig. 4   Snap ring & insert spring positioning in 1st-reverse hub

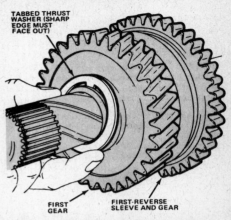

Fig. 5   1st gear thrust washer installation

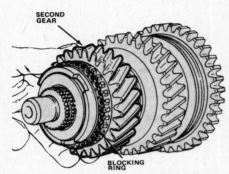

Fig. 6   2nd gear installation

Fig. 8   Measuring mainshaft end-play

hub.

20. Place three inserts into hub slots and on top of insert spring, then push sleeve fully onto hub to engage inserts in sleeve, **Fig. 7**. Install remaining insert spring in the exact same position as the first spring. The ends of both springs must cover same slots in hub and not be staggered.

NOTE: The inserts have a small lip on each end. When properly installed, this lip will fit over the insert spring.

21. Install 2-3 synchronizer assembly on mainshaft. Rotate second gear until notches in blocking ring engage inserts in 2-3 synchronizer assembly.
22. Install retaining snap ring on mainshaft and measure end play between snap ring and 2-3 synchronizer hub with a feeler gauge, **Fig. 8**. End play should be .004–.014 inch. If not, replace thrust washer and all snap rings on output shaft assembly.
23. Install spacer and oil slinger on rear of mainshaft.
24. Install mainshaft assembly into case. Ensure 1st.-reverse sleeve and gear is in Neutral (centered) position on hub so gear end of sleeve will clear top of case when output shaft assembly is installed.
25. Press rear bearing into rear bearing adapter using a suitable press.
26. Install rear bearing retaining ring and bearing adapter lock ring in adapter.
27. Support mainshaft assembly and install rear bearing and adapter assembly into case. Use a mallet to seat adapter into case.
28. Press front bearing onto clutch shaft. Install bearing retaining snap ring on clutch shaft and lock ring in front bearing groove.

NOTE: When properly installed, the snap ring groove in the front bearing will be nearest to the front of the clutch shaft.

29. Coat bearing bore of clutch shaft with petroleum jelly.

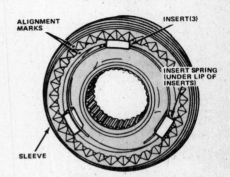

Fig. 7   2nd-3rd synchronizer assembly

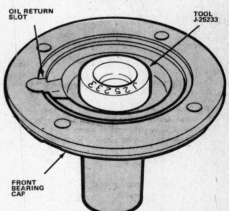

Fig. 9   Front bearing cap oil seal installation

30. Install 15 roller bearings in clutch shaft bore.
31. Coat blocking ring surface of clutch shaft with transmission lubricant and place blocking ring on shaft.
32. Support mainshaft assembly and install clutch shaft through front bearing bore in case. Seat mainshaft pilot in clutch shaft roller bearings and tap front bearing into place with a mallet.
33. Apply a thin film of sealer to front bearing cap gasket and place gasket on case. Ensure that the gasket notch is aligned with the oil return hole in

sharp edge facing outward, and retaining snap on mainshaft, **Fig. 5**.
17. Coat bore and blocking ring surface of second gear with transmission lubricant and place second gear blocking ring on tapered surface of gear.
18. Install second gear on mainshaft with tapered surface of gear facing toward front of shaft, **Fig. 6**.
19. Install one insert spring into 2-3 hub. Ensure that the spring covers all three insert slots in hub. Align 2-3 sleeve to hub using alignment marks made during disassembly, and start sleeve onto

case.

34. Replace front bearing cap oil seal. Remove old seal with a screwdriver and drive new seal into bearing cap with tool J-25233, **Fig. 9**.
35. Install front bearing cap and torque attaching bolts to 33 ft. lbs.

NOTE: When installing the front bearing cap, align the cap and case index marks. Also, ensure that the cap oil return slot and case oil return hole are aligned.

36. Fabricate a wire loop approximately 18 to 20 inches long. Pass the wire loop under the countershaft gear assembly, then raise countershaft gear with loop. Align countershaft gear bore with front thrust washer and countershaft and start countershaft into gear. Align roll pin hole in countershaft and roll pin holes in case, then complete countershaft installation.
37. Install countershaft access plug in rear of case, seating plug with a mallet.
38. Install countershaft roll pin in case. Use a magnet or pair of needlenose pliers to insert pin in case. Use a ½ inch diameter punch to seat pin. Install fill plug.

39. Shift synchronizer sleeves into all gear positions to check for proper operation. If clutch shaft and mainshaft binds in Neutral position, check for sticking blocking rings on the first or second speed gear tapers.
40. Shift both synchronizers into gear to prevent gear rotation.
41. Install transfer case drive gear. Install and torque retaining nut to 150 ft. lbs.
42. Shift synchronizers into Neutral position.
43. Attach transmission to transfer case. Torque attaching bolts to 30 ft. lbs.

Aisin AX4 4 Speed Manual Transmission

INDEX

DISASSEMBLE

1. Remove clutch release fork and throwout bearing from clutch housing.
2. Remove back up light switch, shift lever retainer and the restrictor pins. Note difference in pins to aid in reassembly.
3. Remove clutch housing retaining bolts, then the housing.
4. Remove screw plug from side of adapter housing, **Fig. 1**.
5. Using a magnet, remove spring and detent ball.
6. Remove the five adapter housing retaining bolts and the one nut.
7. Remove shift lever housing set bolt, then the lock plate.
8. Remove plug at rear of shift fork shaft, then pull shaft from housing.

9. Rotate and remove select lever.
10. Remove extension housing retaining bolts and nuts, then the extension housing.

NOTE: Leave gasket attached to intermediate plate.

11. Remove the front bearing retainer and outer snap rings from transmission case.
12. Using a plastic mallet or equivalent, separate transmission case from intermediate plate.
13. Mount intermediate plate in a vise using bolts, washers and nuts as shown, **Fig. 2**. Increase or decrease the number of washers so that bolt tip and outer surface of nuts are flush.
14. Remove screw plug, locking balls and springs from intermediate plate, **Fig. 3**.
15. Using hammer and punch, drive out the slotted spring pins, then remove

the E-rings from the shift rails with suitable pliers, **Fig. 4**.

NOTE: The locking ball from the reverse shift head and the locking ball and pin from the intermediate housing will drop out from their respective holes.

16. Pull No. 4. shift fork from intermediate plate, then disengage locking ball and remove shaft, **Fig. 5**.
17. Remove reverse shift head and interlock pins.
18. Remove No. 3 shift fork shaft and interlock pins, **Fig. 6**.
19. Remove No. 1 shift fork shaft and the interlock pin, **Fig. 7**.
20. Remove No. 2 shift fork shaft, then the No. 1 and No. 2 shift forks, **Fig. 8**.
21. Remove reverse idler gear shaft stopper, reverse idler gear and shaft, then the reverse shift arm from shift arm bracket, **Fig. 9**.
22. Lock output shaft, then remove coun-

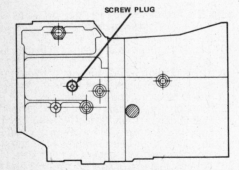

Fig. 1   Screw plug location. Aisin AX4 4 speed manual transmission

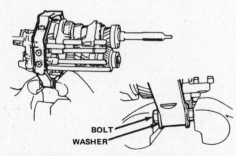

Fig. 2   Mounting intermediate plate

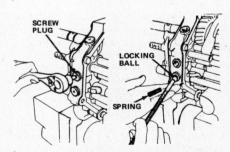

Fig. 3   Replacing screw plug, locking balls & springs

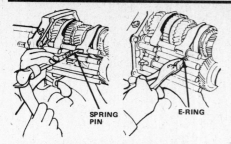

Fig. 4　Replacing spring pins & E-rings

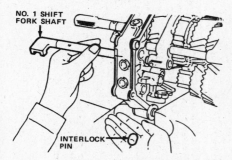

Fig. 7　Replacing No. 1 shift fork shaft & interlock pin

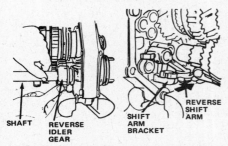

Fig. 9　Replacing reverse idler gear shaft stopper, reverse idler gear, shaft & reverse shift arm

tershaft lock nut.
23. Remove spacer and ball, then the reverse shift arm bracket.
24. Remove rear bearing retainer bolts, then the snap ring.
25. Remove output shaft, input shaft and countershaft from intermediate plate by pulling on countershaft while tapping on intermediate plate, **Fig. 10.**
26. Separate input shaft from output shaft, then remove countershaft rear bearing from intermediate plate.

SUB-ASSEMBLY SERVICE

OUTPUT SHAFT

Disassemble
1. Remove snap ring, **Fig. 11.**
2. Press rear bearing, first gear and inner race from shaft, then remove needle bearing, synchronizer ring and locking ball.

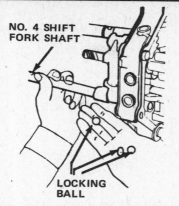

Fig. 5　Replacing No. 4 shift fork shaft & locking ball

3. Press No. 1 hub sleeve, synchronizer ring and second gear from shaft. Remove needle bearing.
4. Remove snap ring from opposite side of shaft, then press No. 2 hub sleeve, synchronizer ring and third gear from shaft. Remove needle bearing.

Inspect
1. Measure output shaft and inner race flange thickness as shown, **Fig. 12.** The minimum thickness for the output shaft flange should be no less than .189 inch., while the inner race flange thickness should be no less than .157 inch. If thickness is less than specified, replace effected parts.
2. Measure output shaft journal diameter at second and third gear locations. Second gear journal surface diameter should be at least 1.495 inch., while third gear journal diameter should be 1.377 inch. If measurements are not as specified, replace output shaft.
3. Measure outer diameter of inner race. Minimum diameter should be 1.535 inch. If diameter is not as specified, replace inner race.
4. Mount output shaft in "V" blocks, then measure shaft runout with a dial indicator. Maximum allowable runout is .002 inch. If runout exceeds specification, replace output shaft.

Assemble
1. Apply gear lubricant to output shaft and the third gear needle bearing, then position third gear synchronizer ring onto gear, ensuring that ring slots align with shifting keys.
2. Install needle bearing between third gear and No. 2 hub sleeve, then press gear and hub sleeve onto output shaft.
3. Select a new snap ring from chart, **Fig. 13,** that will allow minimum axial play, then install snap ring onto output shaft.
4. Measure third gear thrust clearance with a feeler gauge. Clearance should be .004–.010 inch.
5. Apply gear lubricant to output shaft and second gear needle bearing, then position second gear synchronizer ring onto gear, ensuring that ring slots

---

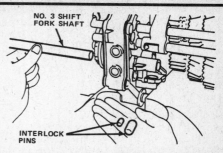

Fig. 6　Replacing No. 3 shift fork shaft & interlock pins

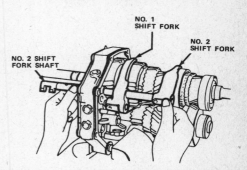

Fig. 8　Replacing No. 2 shift fork shaft & Nos. 1 & 2 shift forks

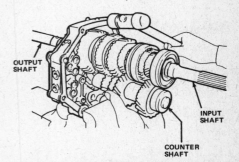

Fig. 10　Replacing input, output & countershafts

align with shifting keys.
6. Install needle bearing into second gear, then press gear and No. 1 hub sleeve onto output shaft.
7. Insert first gear locking ball into output shaft, then apply gear lubricant to needle bearing.
8. Assemble first gear, synchronizer ring, needle bearing and inner race.
9. Install assembly onto output shaft, ensuring that synchronizer ring slots align with shifting keys.
10. Turn inner race until it aligns with locking ball, then press rear bearing onto shaft so that outer race snap ring groove faces rearward.

NOTE: When pressing rear bearing onto shaft, hold first gear in place with a screwdriver.

11. Measure first and second gear thrust clearance with a feeler gauge. Clearance should be .004–.010 inch.
12. Select a snap ring from chart, **Fig. 14,**

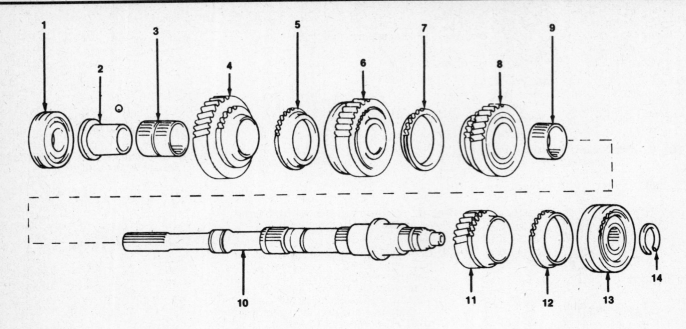

1. Rear Bearing
2. Inner Race
3. Needle Roller Bearing 1st Gear
4. 1st Gear
5. Synchronizer Ring 1st Gear
6. Hub Sleeve No. 1
7. Synchronizer Ring 2nd Gear

8. 2nd Gear
9. Needle Roller Bearing 2nd Gear
10. Output Shaft
11. 3rd Gear
12. Synchronizer Ring 3rd Gear
13. Hub Sleeve No. 2
14. Snap Ring

Fig. 11 Output shaft & components

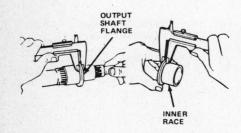

Fig. 12 Measuring output shaft & inner flange thickness

Mark	Thickness mm (in.)	
C-1	1.75-1.80	(0.0689-0.0709)
D	1.80-1.85	(0.0709-0.0728)
D-1	1.85-1.90	(0.0728-0.0748)
E	1.90-1.95	(0.0748-0.0768)
E-1	1.95-2.00	(0.0768-0.0787)
F	2.00-2.05	(0.0788-0.0807)
F-1	2.05-2.10	(0.0807-0.0827)

Fig. 13 Snap ring identification chart (input shaft side)

Mark	Thickness mm (in.)	
A	2.67-2.72	(0.1051-0.1071)
B	2.73-2.78	(0.1075-0.1094)
C	2.79-2.84	(0.1098-0.1118)
D	2.85-2.90	(0.1122-0.1142)
E	2.91-2.96	(0.1146-0.1165)
F	2.97-3.02	(0.1169-0.1189)
G	3.03-3.08	(0.1193-0.1213)
H	3.09-3.14	(0.1217-0.1236)
J	3.15-3.20	(0.1240-0.1260)
K	3.21-3.26	(0.1264-0.1283)
L	3.27-3.32	(0.1287-0.1307)

Fig. 14 Snap ring identification chart (rear bearing side)

that will allow minimum axial play. Install snap ring.

ASSEMBLE

1. Apply suitable grease to input shaft needle bearings, then install bearings on shaft.
2. Install output shaft into intermediate plate by pulling on shaft while tapping on plate with a plastic mallet.

3. Connect input and output shafts, ensuring synchronizer ring slots align with shifting keys.
4. Install countershaft into intermediate plate, then drive bearing into plate.
5. Install output shaft rear bearing retainer and snap ring. Torque bearing retainer attaching screws to 13 ft. lbs.
6. Install reverse shift arm bracket onto intermediate plate, **Fig. 15,** and torque attaching bolts to 13 ft. lbs.
7. Install ball and spacer onto countershaft.

8. Lock output shaft and install locknut onto countershaft. Torque locknut to 90 ft. lbs. and stake to prevent movement.
9. Install reverse shift arm into reverse shift arm bracket, then the reverse idler gear onto shaft, **Fig. 9.**
10. Align reverse shift arm shoe to reverse idler gear groove, then insert reverse idler gear shaft into intermediate plate.
11. Install reverse idler gear shaft stopper

and torque retaining bolt to 13 ft. lbs.

12. Position No. 1 and 2 shift forks into grooves of hub sleeves, then insert No. 2 shift fork shaft through intermediate plate and into shift forks, **Fig. 8.**

13. Apply suitable grease to interlock pins, then install pins into intermediate plate and No. 2 shift fork shaft hole.

14. Install No. 1 shift fork shaft through intermediate plate and into No. 1 shift fork.

15. Apply suitable grease to interlock pins, then install pins into intermediate plate and No. 1 shift fork shaft hole.

16. Install No. 3 shift fork shaft through intermediate plate and into reverse shift arm.

17. Insert shaft through intermediate plate, ensuring No. 3 shift fork shaft engages reverse shift head.

18. Install locking ball into reverse shift head hole.

19. Position No. 3 shift fork into No. 3 hub sleeve groove, then insert No. 4 shift fork shaft into No. 3 shift fork and the reverse shift arm.

20. Install locking ball into intermediate plate, then insert No. 4 shift fork shaft through intermediate plate.

21. Pull No. 1 shift fork shaft into first speed position, then check interlock by trying to move all other shafts. Shafts should not move.

22. Install new slotted spring pins into each shift fork, the reverse shift arm

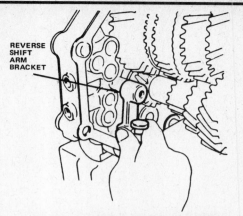

Fig. 15   Installing reverse shift arm bracket

and the reverse shift head, then install the two shift fork shaft E-rings, **Fig. 4.**

23. Install locking balls and springs into intermediate plate, then apply sealer to screw plugs and install into intermediate plate. Torque screw plugs to 14 ft. lbs.

NOTE: Install short spring into tower of intermediate plate.

24. Remove intermediate plate from vise. Remove bolts, washer and nuts.

25. Align each bearing outer race, each shift fork end and the reverse idler gear with the holes in the transmission case, then connect case to intermediate plate.

26. Install two new snap rings, then the front bearing retainer and gasket. Apply sealer to bearing retainer bolts, then install bolts and torque to 12 ft. lbs.

27. Install new gasket onto intermediate plate, then install adapter housing and bolts. Torque bolts to 27 ft. lbs.

28. Install shift lever housing.

29. Insert shift lever into housing, then install shift lever housing bolt and lock plate. Torque bolt to 28 ft. lbs. and lock the locking plate.

30. Install plug at rear of shift fork shaft. Torque plug to 13 ft. lbs.

31. Install detent ball and spring, then apply sealer to screw plug and install into side of adapter housing, **Fig. 1.** Torque screw plug to 14 ft. lbs.

32. Check to ensure input and output shafts can be rotated and that shifting can be done smoothly.

33. Install restrictor pins and torque to 20 ft. lbs.

34. Install shift lever retainer, gasket and attaching bolts. Torque bolts to 13 ft. lbs.

35. Install back-up light switch and torque to 27 ft. lbs.

36. Install clutch housing and retaining bolts, then torque bolts to 27 ft. lbs.

Warner SR4 4 Speed Manual Transmission

INDEX

DISASSEMBLE

1. Remove transfer case from transmission, then drain transmission fluid.

2. Remove offset lever from shift rail, then remove adapter housing from transmission, **Fig. 1.**

3. Remove shift control housing and gasket from transmission. Note position of two dowel type bolts for reference during assembly.

4. Remove spring clip securing reverse lever to reverse lever pivot bolt, then remove reverse lever pivot bolt, reverse lever and reverse lever fork as an assembly.

5. Scribe alignment marks on front bearing cap and transmission case for reference during assembly, then remove

bearing cap and gasket.

6. Remove snap rings from front and rear bearings, then remove front bearing clutch shaft using suitable tool. Remove clutch shaft from case.

7. Remove rear bearing from output shaft using suitable puller.

8. Remove output shaft and gear train as an assembly. Check that synchronizer sleeves do not separate from hubs during removal.

9. Remove reverse idler gear and shaft from rear of case, then remove countershaft from rear of case using tool J26624 or equivalent.

10. Remove countershaft gear and tool used to remove countershaft as an assembly, then remove countershaft gear thrust washers and all clutch

shaft pilot bearings from case.

11. Remove needle bearing retainer and 50 needle bearings from countershaft gear.

SUB-ASSEMBLY SERVICE

OUTPUT SHAFT

Disassemble

1. Place reference marks on 3rd-4th synchronizer hub and sleeve for reference during assembly.

2. Remove output shaft snap ring, then remove 3rd-4th synchronizer assembly.

3. Remove 3rd gear, 2nd gear snap ring,

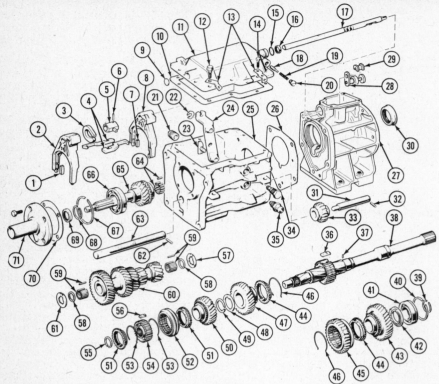

Fig. 1   Disassembled view of Warner SR4 4 Speed manual transmission

1. THIRD — FOURTH SHIFT INSERT
2. THIRD — FOURTH SHIFT FORK
3. SELECTOR INTERLOCK PLATE
4. SELECTOR ARM PLATE (2)
5. SELECTOR ARM
6. SELECTOR ARM ROLL PIN
7. FIRST — SECOND SHIFT FORK INSERT
8. FIRST — SECOND SHIFT FORK
9. SHIFT RAIL PLUG
10. TRANSMISSION COVER GASKET
11. TRANSMISSION COVER
12. TRANSMISSION COVER DOWEL BOLT (2)
13. CLIP
14. TRANSMISSION COVER BOLT (8)
15. SHIFT RAIL O-RING SEAL
16. SHIFT RAIL OIL SEAL
17. SHIFT RAIL
18. DETENT PLUNGER
19. DETENT SPRING
20. DETENT PLUG
21. FILL PLUG
22. REVERSE LEVER PIVOT BOLT C-CLIP
23. REVERSE LEVER FORK
24. REVERSE LEVER
25. TRANSMISSION CASE
26. GASKET
27. ADAPTER HOUSING
28. OFFSET LEVER
29. OFFSET LEVER INSERT

30. EXTENSION HOUSING OIL SEAL
31. REVERSE IDLER SHAFT
32. REVERSE IDLER SHAFT ROLL PIN
33. REVERSE IDLER GEAR
34. REVERSE LEVER PIVOT BOLT
35. BACKUP LAMP SWITCH
36. FIRST — SECOND SYNCHRONIZER INSERT (3)
37. FIRST GEAR ROLL PIN
38. OUTPUT SHAFT AND HUB ASSEMBLY
39. REAR BEARING RETAINING SNAP RING
40. REAR BEARING LOCATING SNAP RING
41. REAR BEARING
42. FIRST GEAR THRUST WASHER
43. FIRST GEAR
44. FIRST — SECOND SYNCHRONIZER BLOCKING RING (2)
45. FIRST — REVERSE SLEEVE AND GEAR
46. FIRST — SECOND SYNCHRONIZER INSERT SPRING (2)
47. SECOND GEAR
48. SECOND GEAR THRUST WASHER (TABBED)
49. SECOND GEAR SNAP RING
50. THIRD GEAR
51. THIRD — FOURTH SYNCHRONIZER BLOCKING RING (2)

52. THIRD — FOURTH SYNCHRONIZER SLEEVE
53. THIRD — FOURTH SYNCHRONIZER INSERT SPRING (2)
54. THIRD — FOURTH SYNCHRONIZER HUB
55. OUTPUT SHAFT SNAP RING
56. THIRD — FOURTH SYNCHRONIZER INSERT (3)
57. COUNTERSHAFT GEAR REAR THRUST WASHER (METAL)
58. COUNTERSHAFT NEEDLE BEARING RETAINER (2)
59. COUNTERSHAFT NEEDLE BEARING (50)
60. COUNTERSHAFT GEAR
61. COUNTERSHAFT GEAR FRONT THRUST WASHER (PLASTIC)
62. COUNTERSHAFT ROLL PIN
63. COUNTERSHAFT
64. CLUTCH SHAFT ROLLER BEARINGS (15)
65. CLUTCH SHAFT
66. FRONT BEARING
67. FRONT BEARING LOCATING SNAP RING
68. FRONT BEARING RETAINING SNAP RING
69. FRONT BEARING CAP OIL SEAL
70. FRONT BEARING CAP GASKET
71. FRONT BEARING CAP

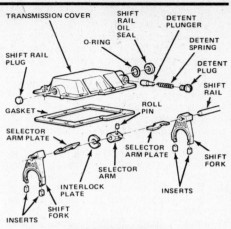

Fig. 2   Disassembled view of shift control housing

thrust washer, 2nd gear and blocking ring.

4. Remove 1st gear thrust washer and roll pin, then remove 1st gear and blocking ring. Thrust washer has oil groove and roll pin has locating slot on one side. This side must face 1st gear when assembled.
5. Place alignment marks on 1st-2nd synchronizer sleeve and output shaft hub for reference during assembly.
6. Remove insert spring and inserts from 1st-2nd sleeve, then remove sleeve from output shaft hub.

NOTE: Do not attempt to remove 1st-2nd-reverse hub from output shaft. Hub and shaft are machined and matched as an assembly.

Assemble

1. Lubricate output shaft and gear bores with transmission fluid.
2. Install 1st-2nd synchronizer sleeve on output shaft hub using reference marks made during disassembly.
3. Install three 1st-2nd synchronizer inserts and two insert springs into 1st-2nd synchronizer sleeve. Engage tang end of each insert spring into same synchronizer insert but position open ends of spring so that they face away from each other.
4. Install blocking ring onto 1st gear, then install gear and ring onto output shaft. Ensure that synchronizer inserts engage notches in 1st gear blocking ring.
5. Install 1st gear roll pin into output shaft, then install gear and ring onto

output shaft. Ensure that sharp edge of washer faces outward and that tab engages output shaft notch.

6. Measure 2nd gear end play by inserting feeler gauge between gear and thrust washer. End play should be .004–.014 inch. If end play is greater than .0014 inch, replace thrust washer and snap ring and inspect synchronizer hub for damage or wear.

NOTE: If any output shaft gear must be replaced, the countershaft gear must also be replaced to maintain proper gear mesh and avoid excessive noise during operation.

7. Install blocking ring onto 3rd gear, then install gear and ring onto output shaft.
8. Install 3rd-4th synchronizer sleeve onto 3rd-4th synchronizer hub and align marks made during disassembly.
9. Refer to step 3 for assembly of synchronizer.
10. Measure 3rd-4th synchronizer end play using feeler gauge inserted between output shaft snap ring and 3rd-4th synchronizer hub. End play should be .004–.014 inch.
11. If end play is greater than .014 inch, replace snap ring and inspect synchronizer hub for damage and wear.

SHIFT CONTROL HOUSING

Disassemble

1. Remove detent plug, spring and plunger, **Fig. 2.**
2. Position selector arm plates and shift rail in Neutral. Rotate shift rail counterclockwise until selector arm disengages from selector arm plates and selector arm roll pin is accessible.
3. Position shift rail rearward until selector arm contacts 1st-2nd shift fork.
4. Remove selector arm roll pin, then remove shift rail. Remove shift forks, selector arm plates, selector arm, roll pin and interlock plate.

5. Remove shift rail oil seal and O-ring, then remove shift rail plug.
6. Remove nylon inserts and selector arm plates from shift forks. Note position of inserts and plates for reference during assembly.

Assemble

1. Install nylon inserts and selector arm plates into shift forks, then install shift rail plug.
2. Lubricate shift rail and shift rail bores with vaseline and install shift rail into cover until end of rail is flush with inside edge of cover.
3. Position 1st-2nd shift fork in cover with fork offset facing rear of cover, then install shift rail through fork.

NOTE: 1st-2nd shift fork is larger of two forks.

4. Position selector arm and C shaped interlock plate in cover, then insert shift rail through arm. Ensure that widest part of interlock plate faces away from cover and that selector arm roll pin hole faces downward and toward rear of cover.
5. Position 3rd-4th shift fork in cover with fork offset facing rear of cover. 3rd-4th shift fork selector arm plate must be positioned under 1st-2nd shift fork selector arm plate.
6. Install shift rail through 3rd-4th shift fork and into front shift rail bore in cover.
7. Rotate shift rail until selector arm plate at rail forward end faces away from, but is parallel to, cover.
8. Align roll pin holes in selector arm and shift rail, then install roll pin.

9. Install detent plunger, spring and plug. Install O-ring in groove of shift rail oil seal. Install shift rail oil seal using suitable tools.

ASSEMBLE

1. Lubricate countershaft gear thrust washers with vaseline, then position in case.

NOTE: Install plastic washer at front of case and metal washer at rear.

2. Install tool J26624 or equivalent into countershaft gear, then install 50 needle bearings into bearing bores at front and rear of gear. Install needle bearing retainers.
3. Position assembled countershaft gear into case, then install countershaft from rear of case. Check that thrust washers are not disturbed during installation.
4. Position reverse idler gear into case with shift lever groove facing front of case. Install reverse idler shaft from rear of case.
5. Install output shaft and gear train assembly into case using caution not to disturb synchronizer assemblies.
6. Install 4th gear blocking ring into 3rd-4th synchronizer sleeve. Lubricate 15 roller bearings and clutch shaft roller bearing bore with vaseline, then install bearings into shaft bore.
7. Install shaft into case and engage into 3rd-4th synchronizer sleeve and blocking ring.
8. Install front bearing using tool J22697 or equivalent. Position front bearing

onto clutch shaft, then position output shaft 1st gear against rear of case. Align bearing with case bearing bore and install bearing. Install bearing retainer and snap ring.
9. Install front bearing cap oil seal in front bearing cap using tool J26625 or equivalent.
10. Install front bearing cap onto case. Check that groove in cap aligns with oil hole in case. Torque retaining bolts to 13 ft. lbs.
11. Install 1st gear thrust washer onto output shaft, then install rear bearing using J22697 or equivalent. Install retaining ring and snap ring.
12. Position reverse lever in case, then install reverse lever pivot bolt into case. Install reverse lever onto bolt, install spring clip, then torque bolt to 20 ft. lbs.

NOTE: Check that reverse lever fork engages reverse idler gear.

13. Rotate clutch shaft and output shaft gears. If blocking rings stick to gear cones separate rings from cones by prying them off with a screwdriver.
14. Replace adapter housing oil seal, if necessary, the position reverse lever in Neutral and install transmission cover gasket and cover assembly into case. Torque bolts evenly to 10 ft. lbs. Ensure that cover dowel bolts are installed in proper location.
15. Position adapter housing gasket onto case, then install adapter housing.
16. Fill transmission with 3 pints of fluid, then torque drain plug to 23 ft. lbs.
17. Install transfer case onto transmission.

Warner T-4 4 Speed Manual Transmission

INDEX

DISASSEMBLE

NOTE: Except for filler plug and gearshift lever attaching bolts, all bolts and threaded holes in the transmission case have metric threads. If replacement bolts are necessary, use only those of the same size and length as the originals.

1. Remove drain plug on transmission and drain lubricant.
2. Using pin punch and hammer, remove roll pin attaching offset lever to shift

rail, **Fig. 1.**
3. Remove adapter housing-to-transmission case bolts, then remove housing and offset lever as assembly.

CAUTION: Do not attempt to remove offset lever while the adapter housing is still bolted in place. The lever has a positioning lug engaged in the housing detent plate that prevents moving the lever far enough back for removal.

4. Remove detent ball and spring from offset lever, then remove roll pin from

adapter housing or offset lever.
5. Remove and retain countershaft rear thrust bearing and race.
6. Remove transmission cover, shift fork assembly attaching bolts, then transmission cover.

NOTE: Two shift control housing cover bolts are dowel-type alignment bolts. Note their location for assembly reference.

7. Remove "C" clip attaching reverse lever to reverse lever pivot bolt, then remove pivot bolt and remove reverse

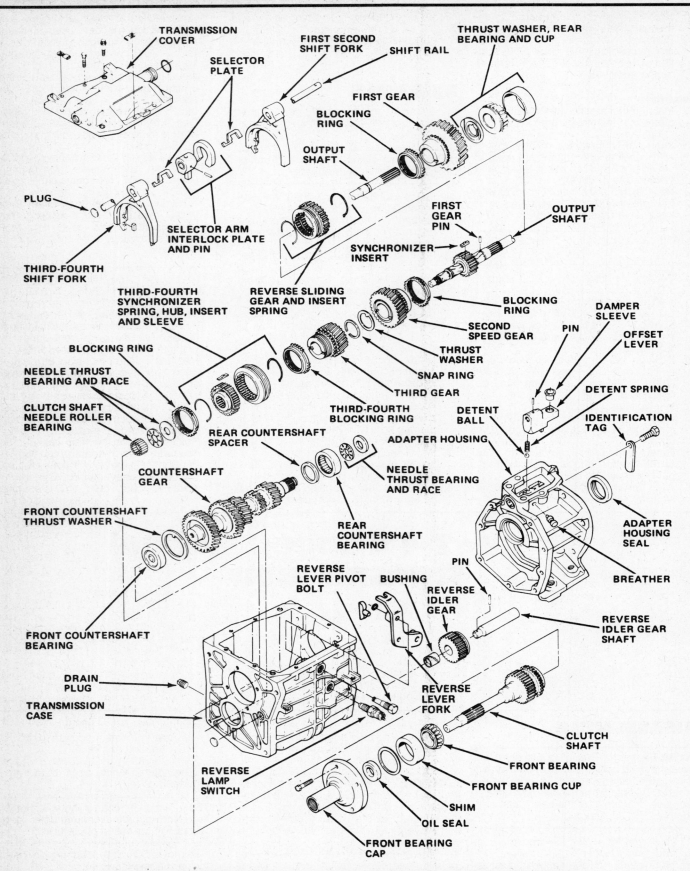

Fig. 1   Disassembled view of Warner T-4 4 speed manual transmission

lever and reverse lever fork as assembly.

8. Using center punch, mark position of front bearing cap on transmission, then remove front bearing cap bolts and cap.
9. Remove front bearing race and end play shims from cap, then remove oil seal from cap using screwdriver.
10. Rotate clutch shaft so that flat on gear teeth is facing countershaft, remove shaft, then remove thrust bearing and 15 roller bearings from clutch shaft.
11. Remove output shaft bearing race, tapping front of output shaft with suitable mallet, if necessary.
12. Tilt output shaft assembly upward and remove transmission from case.
13. Using brass drift and arbor press, remove countershaft rear bearing, noting position of bearing for assembly reference. Bearing identification numbers face outward when bearing is installed correctly.
14. Move countershaft rearward, tilt shaft upward and remove from case. Noting position for assembly reference, remove countershaft front thrust washer from case.
15. Remove countershaft rear bearing spacer, then remove reverse idler shaft roll pin using pin punch and hammer.
16. Remove reverse idler shaft and gear, noting position of gear for assembly reference, then remove countershaft front bearing using arbor press.
17. Using removal tool J-29721 and J-22912 or equivalent, remove clutch shaft front bearing, then remove rear adapter housing seal using flat drift and hammer.
18. Remove backup lamp switch from transmission case.

SUB-ASSEMBLY SERVICE

OUTPUT SHAFT SERVICE

1. Remove thrust bearing washer from front end of output shaft, then scribe alignment marks on third-fourth synchronizer hub and sleeve for assembly reference.
2. Remove third-fourth synchronizer blocking ring, sleeve and hub assembly, noting position of hub and sleeve for assembly reference.
3. Remove third-fourth synchronizer and insert springs, then remove inserts and remove sleeve from hub.
4. Remove third gear from shaft, then remove snap ring retaining second gear on shaft and remove tabbed second gear thrust washer and second gear.
5. Using puller set J-29721 and adapters 293-39 or equivalents, remove output shaft bearing.
6. Remove first gear thrust washer, first gear roll pin, first gear and blocking ring.
7. Scribe alignment marks on first-sec-

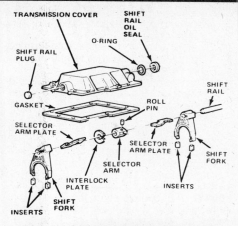

Fig. 2 Disassembled view of shift control housing

ond gear synchronizer sleeve and output shaft hub for assembly reference and remove insert spring and inserts from first-reverse sliding gear, then remove gear from output shaft hub.

CAUTION: Do not attempt to remove the first-second-reverse hub from output shaft. The hub and shaft are assembled and machined as a matched set during manufacture to insure concentricity. If any output shaft gear is replaced, the countershaft gear must also be replaced to maintain proper gear mesh and avoid noisy operation.

8. Lubricate output shaft and gear bores, then install and align first-second synchronizer sleeve on output shaft hub using reference marks.
9. Install three first-second synchronizer inserts and two insert springs in first-reverse synchronizer sleeve, engaging tang end of springs in same synchronizer insert but positioning open ends of springs to face 180 degrees from each other. Align sleeve and hub using reference marks.
10. Install blocking ring and second gear on mainshaft, then install tabbed thrust washer and second gear snap ring on mainshaft, being sure washer tab is properly seated in mainshaft notch.
11. Install blocking ring and first gear on output shaft, then install first gear roll pin in output shaft.
12. Using tool J-2995 or equivalent, and arbor press, install rear bearing on output shaft.
13. Install first gear thrust washer, then install third gear, third and fourth gear synchronizer hub inserts and sleeve on shaft, making sure hub offset faces forward.
14. Install thrust bearing washer on forward end of output shaft.

SHIFT CONTROL HOUSING
Disassemble

1. Place selector arm plates and shift rail in neutral position, then turn shift rail

counterclockwise until selector arm disengages from selector arm plates and selector arm roll pin is accessible, **Fig. 2.**
2. Pull shift rail rearward until selector contacts first-second shift fork and remove selector arm roll pin using pin punch, then remove shift rail.
3. Remove shift forks, selector arm plates, selector arm, and roll pin and interlock plate, then remove shift rail oil seal and "O" ring using suitable tool.
4. Using punch and hammer, remove shift rail plug.
5. Remove nylon inserts and selector arm plates from shift forks, noting position of inserts and plates for assembly reference.

Assemble

1. Install nylon inserts and selector arm plates in shift forks.
2. Coat edges of shift rail plug with sealer and install, then lubricate shift rail and bores and insert shift rail in cover. Install rail until end of rail is flush with inside edge of cover.
3. Position first-second shift fork (larger of the two forks) in cover with offset facing rear of cover and push shift rail through fork.
4. Position selector arm and C-shaped interlock plate in cover and insert shift rail through arm with widest part of interlock plate facing away from cover and selector arm roll pin hole facing downward and toward rear of cover.
5. Position third-fourth shift fork in cover with offset facing rear of cover, being sure third-fourth shift fork selector arm plate is positioned under first-second shift fork selector arm plate.
6. Insert shift rail through third-fourth shift fork and into front shift rail bore in cover, then rotate shift rail until selector arm plate at forward end of rail faces away from, but is parallel to cover.
7. Align roll pin holes in selector arm and shift rail, then install roll pin, being sure it is flush with surface of selector arm to prevent contact between pin and selector arm plates during shifting.
8. Install "O" ring in groove of shift rail oil seal, then install shift rail oil seal:
   a. Install tool J-26628-2 or equivalent over threaded end of shift rail.
   b. Lubricate lip of oil seal and slide over tool and onto shift rail.
   c. Seat seal in transmission cover using tool J-26628-1 or equivalent.

ASSEMBLE

1. Coat countershaft front bearing outer cage with suitable sealer and install countershaft front bearing flush with case using arbor press.
2. Lubricate countershaft tabbed thrust washer and install so that tab engages proper depression in case.
3. Tipping case on end, install countershaft in front bearing bore, then insert

countershaft rear bearing spacer.

4. Using tool J-29895 or equivalent, and suitable mallet, lubricate and install countershaft rear bearing so that it extends .125 in. (3 mm.) beyond case surface.

5. Position reverse idler gear in case with shift lever groove facing rear of case. Install reverse idler shaft from rear of case and install retaining roll pin in shaft.

6. Install assembled output shaft in case.

7. Using tool J-2995 or equivalent, and arbor press, install front clutch shaft bearing on clutch shaft.

8. Lubricate pilot roller bearings and install in clutch shaft.

9. Install thrust bearing and race in clutch shaft.

10. Install fourth gear blocker ring on output shaft, then install rear output shaft bearing race.

11. Install clutch shaft in case and engage shaft in third-fourth synchronizer sleeve and blocking ring.

12. Using tool J-26625 or equivalent, install replacement oil seal in front bearing cap.

13. Using tool J-29184 or equivalent install new oil seal in rear adapter housing.

14. Install front bearing race in cap and install cap.

15. Install reverse lever, pivot pin, and retaining "C" clip, being sure that reverse lever fork is engaged in reverse idler gear. Coat pivot pin threads with sealer.

16. Lubricate countershaft rear bearing race and thrust bearing and install in adapter housing.

17. Install adapter housing temporarily. Do not seal housing or torque bolts at this time.

18. Turn transmission case on end and mount dial indicator on adapter housing with indicator stylus on end of output shaft.

19. Turn clutch and output shaft and zero dial indicator.

20. Pull upward on output shaft to remove end play. Read end play dimension on indicator.

NOTE: To completely eliminate output shaft and clutch shaft end play, bearings must be preloaded from .001–.005 in. (0.03–0.13 mm.)

21. Select shim package measuring .001–.005 in. thicker than measured end play.

22. Place transmission on work bench horizontally and remove front bearing cap and race, then add shims to bearing cap to obtain preload and install clutch shaft bearing race in cap.

23. Install sealant on case mating surface of front bearing cap and install cap noting alignment marks, and torque retaining bolts to 15 ft. lbs.

24. Recheck end play. There must be no end play.

25. Remove adapter housing.

26. Move shift forks on transmission cover and synchronizer rings inside transmission to the neutral position.

27. Apply suitable sealant to cover mating surface of transmission.

28. Lower cover assembly onto case while aligning shift forks and synchronizer sleeves. Center cover to engage reverse relay lever and install dowel bolts in cover. Install remaining bolts in cover and torque all cover bolts to 9 ft. lbs.

NOTE: The offset lever-to-shift rail roll pin is in a vertical position when steps 26 and 28 are performed properly.

29. Apply sealant to adapter housing-to-transmission case mating surface.

30. Install adapter housing over output shaft and shift rail so that the shift rail just enters shift cover opening.

31. Install detent spring into offset lever. Place ball in neutral guide plate detent. Apply pressure on ball with detent spring and offset lever and slide offset lever on shift rail and seat adapter housing against transmission case.

NOTE: The offset lever and shift rail roll pin holes should be aligned in a vertical position following step 31.

32. Install adapter housing retaining bolts and torque to 25 ft. lbs.

33. Install roll pin in shift rail and offset lever and install damper sleeve in offset lever, then coat backup lamp switch threads with suitable sealant and install switch in case.

Warner T-18 & T-18A 4 Speed Manual Transmission

INDEX

DISASSEMBLE

1. Remove gear shift housing from transmission, **Figs. 1 and 2,** then the parking brake drum. With the transmission locked in two gears, remove U-joint flange and oil seal.

2. Remove speedometer driven gear and bearing assembly.

3. Remove output shaft bearing retainer and speedometer drive gear and spacer, then remove output bearing retainer studs from case.

4. Remove output shaft bearing snap ring, then using suitable tool remove bearing.

5. Remove countershaft and idler shaft retainer and power take-off cover.

6. Remove input shaft bearing snap ring and bearing.

7. Remove oil baffle.

8. Remove roll pin from reverse gear shifter arm shaft, then remove shaft from shifter and lift shifter from case.

9. Remove output shaft and gear assembly from case.

10. Using a dummy shaft, drive countershaft out from front of transmission.

NOTE: Keep dummy shaft in contact with countershaft to avoid dropping rollers.

11. Remove input shaft and synchronizer blocking ring, then using a suitable puller remove idler shaft.

12. Remove idler gear and countershaft gear, use care not to lose rollers.

SUB-ASSEMBLY SERVICE
OUTPUT SHAFT

Disassemble

1. Remove 3-4 speed synchronizer hub snap ring from output shaft. Slide syn-

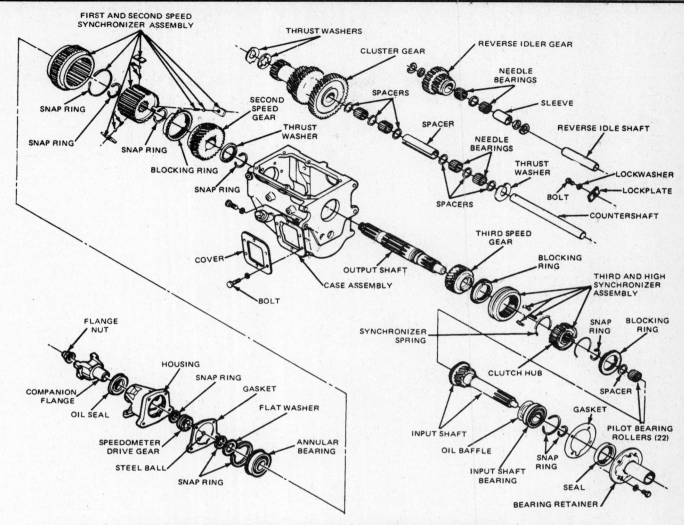

Fig. 1 Disassembled view of Warner T-18 & T-18A 4 speed manual transmission

chronizer assembly and 3rd gear from shaft.
2. Press reverse gear from output shaft.
3. Remove 1st speed gear snap ring, then slide gear from shaft.
4. Remove 1st-2nd speed synchronizer snap ring, then slide synchronizer from shaft.
5. Remove snap ring from rear of 2nd speed gear, then remove gear and thrust washer.

Assemble
1. Install 2nd speed gear thrust washer and snap ring on shaft, then hold shaft in vertical position and install 2nd speed gear.
2. Install snap ring at rear of 2nd speed gear, then position blocking ring on gear.
3. Press 1st-2nd speed synchronizer onto shaft and install snap ring.
4. Install 1st speed gear and snap ring on shaft.
5. Press reverse gear onto shaft, then remove shaft from press and install 3rd speed gear and synchronizer blocking

ring.
6. Install snap ring with openings staggered at both ends 3rd-4th speed synchronizer hub.
7. Place inserts into synchronizer sleeve and position sleeve on hub.
8. Slide synchronizer assembly onto output shaft and install snap ring at front of synchronizer assembly.

NOTE: Slots in blocking ring must be aligned with synchronizer inserts.

COUNTERSHAFT GEAR

Disassemble
Remove dummy shaft; pilot bearing rollers, bearing spacers and center spacer from countershaft gear.

Assemble
1. Position long bearing spacer into countershaft gear bore, then insert dummy shaft in spacer.
2. Position gear in vertical position, then install spacer and place 22 pilot roller bearings in gear bore.

3. Position bearing spacer on top of rollers, then install 2 more roller bearings and another bearing spacer.
4. Place a large washer against end of countershaft gear to prevent rollers from dropping out then turn assembly over.
5. Install rollers and spacers in other end of countershaft gear.

REVERSE IDLER GEAR

Disassemble
Remove snap ring from end of gear, then remove bearing rollers thrust washers, bearing spacer and bushing.

Assemble
1. Install snap ring in one end of idler gear, then set gear on end with snap ring on bottom.
2. Position thrust washer and bushing in gear bore, then install 37 bearing rollers between bushing and gear bore.
3. Install spacer on top of rollers then install 37 more bearing rollers.
4. Place remaining thrust washer on

A—139

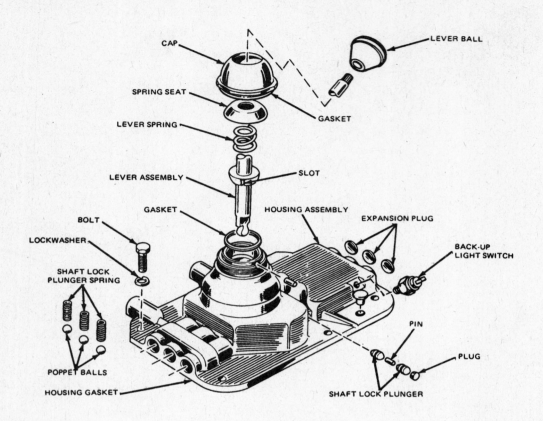

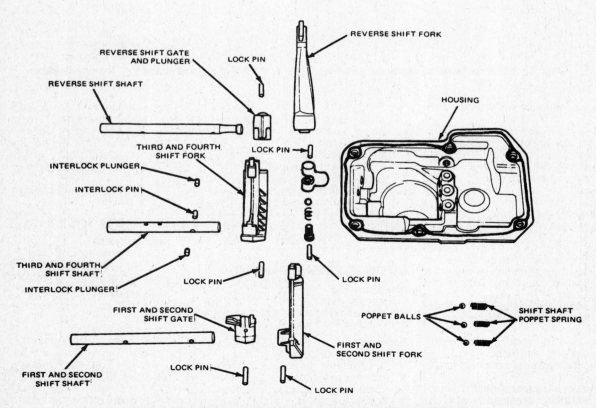

Fig. 2   Disassembled view of shift control housing

rollers and install snap ring.

ASSEMBLE

1. Lubricate all parts with transmission oil, then position countershaft gear assembly in case.
2. Position idler gear assembly in case, then install idler shaft and shifter arm.

NOTE: Position idler shaft so that slot at rear will engage retainer.

3. Drive countershaft in through rear of case forcing dummy shaft out through front.

NOTE: Position countershaft so that slot at rear will engage retainer.

4. Install thrust washers as necessary to obtain countershaft end play of .006 to .020 inch.
5. Install countershaft and idler shaft retainer.
6. Position oil baffle and input shaft pilot rollers so that baffle will not rub on bearing race, then position input shaft in case and install blocking ring.
7. Install output shaft assembly in case.
8. Using a suitable tool drive input shaft bearing onto shaft then install thickest select fit snap ring that will fit on bearing. Snap ring is available in thicknesses of, .117–.119, .120–.122, .123–.125 and .127–.129 inch. Install input shaft snap ring.

9. Install output shaft bearing.
10. Install input shaft bearing retainer without gasket and tighten bolts only enough to bottom retainer on bearing snap ring. Measure distance between retainer and case and select a gasket that will seal and also prevent end play retainer and snap ring. Gaskets are available in thicknesses of, .008–.011, .0135–.0165, .018–.022 and .0225–.0275 inch. Install gasket and tighten bolts.
11. Position speedometer drive gear and spacer, then install output shaft bearing retainer and gasket.
12. Install brake drum then lubricate extension housing bushing, seal and U joint flange with ball joint grease.
13. Install U joint flange and tighten bolt.

Warner T-176 4 Speed Manual Transmission

INDEX

DISASSEMBLE

1. Remove transfer case from transmission. Drain lubricant from transmission.
2. Remove shift control housing.

NOTE: Two of the housing attaching bolts are of the dowel pin type. Note location of the bolts during disassembly.

3. Using arbor tool J-29342, tap countershaft from rear of case, **Fig. 1.**
4. Remove rear bearing locating ring and snap ring. Using a suitable puller, remove rear bearing from case, **Fig. 2.**
5. Scribe alignment marks on front bearing cap and transmission case, then remove front bearing cap and gasket and oil seal from cap.
6. Remove locating ring and retaining snap ring from front bearing, **Fig. 3.**
7. Using suitable puller, remove clutch shaft and front bearing from case, **Fig. 4.**
8. Remove 3rd-4th gear blocking ring from clutch shaft or synchronizer hub.
9. Press front bearing from clutch shaft,

Fig. 5.
10. Remove mainshaft pilot bearing rollers from clutch shaft, **Fig. 3.**
11. Move 3rd-4th gear synchronizer sleeve rearward to 3rd gear position. Tilt rear end of mainshaft downward and lift front upward and remove mainshaft and geartrain assembly.
12. Remove countershaft gear and arbor tool as an assembly.
13. Remove countershaft gear thrust washers and any fallen mainshaft pilot bearing rollers from the case.
14. Remove reverse gear idler shaft from rear of case. Remove gear assembly

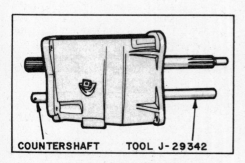

Fig. 1 Countershaft replacement. Warner T-176 4 speed manual transmission

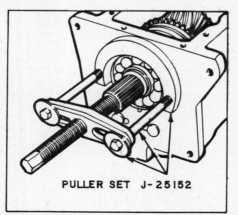

Fig. 2 Rear bearing removal

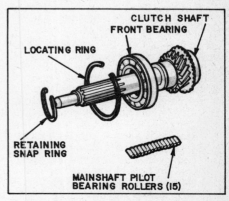

Fig. 3 Clutch shaft & front bearing assembly

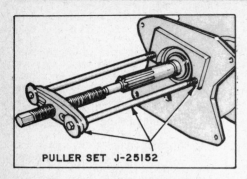

Fig. 4   Clutch shaft & front bearing removal

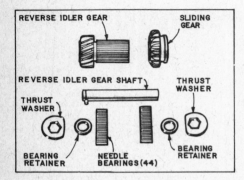

Fig. 7   Reverse idler gear assembly

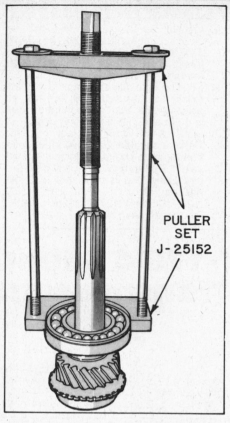

Fig. 5   Removing front bearing from clutch shaft

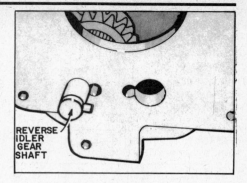

Fig. 6   Reverse idler gear shaft replacement

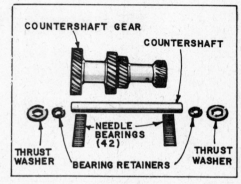

Fig. 8   Countershaft gear assembly

and thrust washers, **Fig. 6.**

15. Remove needle bearings and retainers from gear assembly, **Fig. 7.** Note position of sliding gear and remove from reverse idler gear.
16. Remove arbor shaft tool from countershaft gear and remove needle bearing and retainers, **Fig. 8.**

MAINSHAFT, DISASSEMBLE

1. Remove 3rd-4th synchronizer snap ring from front of mainshaft, **Fig. 9.**
2. Remove 3rd-4th assembly from shaft, then slide hub from sleeve. Remove insert springs and three inserts and blocking ring. Note position of insert springs for reassembly.
3. Remove 3rd gear from shaft.
4. Remove 2nd gear snap ring, gear, blocking ring and tabbed washer from shaft, **Fig. 9.**
5. Remove snap ring from 1st-2nd gear synchronizer hub. Remove hub, reverse gear and sleeve as an assembly. Mark hub and sleeve for assembly reference. Remove insert springs, inserts, sleeve and gear from hub.
6. Remove first gear thrust washer, then the first gear and blocking ring from shaft.

ASSEMBLE

1. Lubricate and assemble reverse idler gear and sliding gear, **Fig. 7.**
2. Install arbor tool J-29343 in reverse idler gear. Install 22 needle bearings and one retainer at each end of gear, **Fig. 10.**
3. Lubricate reverse idler gear thrust washers with petroleum jelly and install in case.

NOTE: Install thrust washers with flats facing the mainshaft and engage the washer locating tabs into slots of case.

4. Install reverse idler gear assembly into case, **Fig. 11.** Install reverse idler shaft from rear of case, **Fig. 6.** Ensure that roll pin seats in case recess.
5. Measure reverse idler gear end play by inserting a feeler gauge between thrust washer and gear. End play should be 0.004 to 0.018 inch. If not, replace thrust washers.
6. Lubricate countershaft gear bore, needle bearings and bearing bores in gear with petroleum jelly. Install arbor tool in bore of gear and install 21 needle bearings and one retainer in each end of gear.

7. Lubricate countershaft gear thrust washers with petroleum jelly and position in case.

NOTE: Install thrust washers with the locating tabs in slots of case.

8. Insert countershaft into rear case bore just enough to hold rear thrust washer in position. This will prevent thrust washer from being displaced during countershaft gear installation.
9. Install countershaft gear. Align gear bore, thrust washers, bores in case and install countershaft partially into case. Ensure arbor tool enters shaft bore at front of case.

NOTE: Do not remove countershaft arbor tool completely.

10. Measure countershaft gear end play with a feeler gauge inserted between gear and thrust washer. End play should be 0.004 to 0.018 inch. If not, replace the thrust washers. After correct end play has been obtained, reinstall arbor tool in counter shaft gear and allow gear to remain at bottom of case. Leave countershaft in rear case

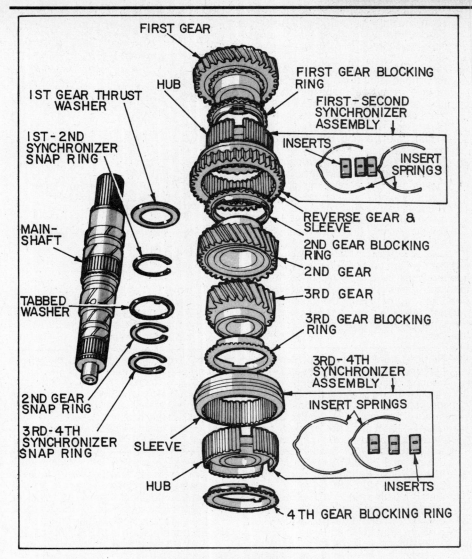

Fig. 9 **Mainshaft assembly**

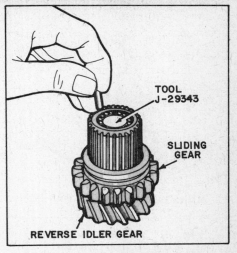

Fig. 10 **Reverse idler gear needle bearing installation**

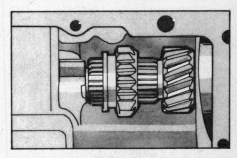

Fig. 11 **Reverse idler gear installation**

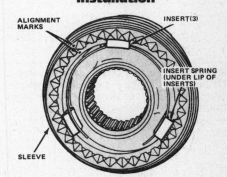

Fig. 12 **Synchronizer insert spring installation**

bore to retain thrust washer in position.

NOTE: Countershaft gear must remain at bottom of case to allow clearance for main-shaft and clutch shaft installation.

11. Lubricate mainshaft, synchronizer assemblies and gear bores with trans-mission lubricant.
12. Assemble 1st-2nd synchronizer hub and reverse gear and sleeve, **Fig. 9**:
   a. Install gear and sleeve on hub and place assembly flat on bench.
   b. Install the inserts into the hub slots.
   c. Install the insert spring. Position loop-end of spring in one insert, compress spring ends and insert the spring ends under lips of remaining two inserts, **Fig. 12**.
   d. Turn assembly over and install remaining insert spring as de-scribed in previous step. However, install this spring so open end is

180° opposite first spring.
13. Install assembled 1st-2nd synchroniz-er hub and reverse gear and sleeve on mainshaft, **Fig. 9**.
14. Install 1st-2nd synchronizer snap ring on mainshaft.
15. Install 1st gear and blocking ring on rear of mainshaft and the first gear thrust washer, **Fig. 13**.
16. Install new tabbed washer on main-shaft. Ensure that washer tab is seated in mainshaft tab bore, **Fig. 14**.
17. Install 2nd gear and blocking ring on mainshaft, then a new 2nd gear snap ring.
18. Install 3rd gear and blocking ring on mainshaft.
19. Assemble 3rd-4th synchronizer, **Fig. 9**:
   a. Install sleeve on synchronizer hub. Align parts using reference marks.
   b. Place assembled hub and sleeve flat on bench.

   c. Install the inserts into the hub slots.
   d. Install insert spring. Position loop-end of spring in one insert, com-press spring ends and insert under lips of remaining two inserts, **Fig. 12**.
   e. Turn assembly over and install remaining insert spring as de-scribed in previous step. However, position this spring so open end faces 180° opposite first spring.
20. Install 3rd-4th synchronizer assembly on mainshaft.
21. Install new 3rd-4th synchronizer re-

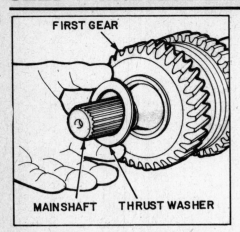

Fig. 13 1st gear & thrust washer installation

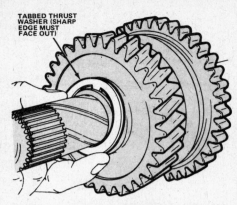

Fig. 14 Tabbed thrust washer installation

taining snap ring on mainshaft and measure end play between hub and snap ring. End play should be 0.004 to 0.014 inch. If not, replace snap rings and thrust washers.

22. Install mainshaft assembly into case. The synchronizers must be in neutral position so sleeves will clear top of case.
23. Install locating snap ring on front bearing, then install the front bearing partially onto clutch shaft.

NOTE: Do not install bearing completely since the shaft will not clear the countershaft gear during installation.

24. Lubricate bearing bore in clutch shaft and mainshaft roller bearings with petroleum jelly. Install 15 roller bearings in clutch shaft bearing bore.

CAUTION: Do not use chassis grease or other heavy grease in the clutch shaft bore since improper lubrication of the roller bearings may result.

25. Lubricate blocking ring surface of clutch shaft with transmission lubricant and position blocking ring on shaft.
26. Support mainshaft assembly and insert clutch shaft through front bearing bore in case. Seat mainshaft pilot hub in clutch shaft roller bearings and tap front bearing and clutch shaft into case using suitable mallet.
27. Install front bearing cap and tighten bolts finger tight.
28. Position rear bearing on mainshaft. Do not install bearing locating snap ring at this time. Start bearing onto shaft and into case bore using tool J-29345. Remove tool and finish bearing installation using suitable mallet. Install retaining snap ring when bearing is fully seated.

NOTE: To seat bearing on mainshaft, the bearing must be driven into case deeper than the locating snap ring would allow. Therefore, do not install the locating snap ring until after the bearing is fully seated on the shaft and the retaining snap ring is installed.

29. Remove front bearing cap, seat front bearing fully on clutch shaft and install bearing retaining snap ring.
30. Apply a thin film of sealer to front bearing cap gasket and position on case. Ensure that notch in gasket and oil return hole in case are aligned.
31. Remove front bearing cap oil seal using suitable tool. Install new seal using tool J-25233.
32. Install front bearing cap and torque cap bolts to 12 ft. lbs.
33. Install locating ring on rear bearing. Reseat bearing in case if necessary.
34. Install countershaft as follows:
    a. Turn transmission case on end. Position case at edge of workbench with clutchshaft facing downward. Ensure that countershaft bore in front of case is accessible.
    b. Have an assistant hold case in position.
    c. Align countershaft gear bores with thrust washers and case bores and tap shaft into place.

NOTE: The arbor tool will be driven through opposite end of case.

CAUTION: Do not damage thrust washers during installation of countershaft. Ensure that the washers, case bores and gear bores are aligned when installing countershaft.

35. Check operation of synchronizer sleeves in all gear positions. If clutch shaft or mainshaft appear to bind in neutral position, check for blocking rings sticking on gears. Use a screwdriver to free any sticking rings.
36. Fill transmission with 3.5 pints of SAE 85W-90 gear lubricant.
37. Install shift control housing with new gasket. Torque housing bolts to 12 ft. lbs.
38. Install transmission on transfer case.

Aisin AX5 5 Speed Manual Transmission

INDEX

DISASSEMBLE

1. Remove clutch release fork and throwout bearing from clutch housing.
2. Remove back-up light switch, shift retainer and restrictor pins. Note difference in pins to aid in reassembly.
3. Remove clutch housing attaching bolts and the clutch housing.
4. Remove screw plug from side of adapter housing, **Fig. 1.**
5. Remove spring and detent ball, using a suitable magnet.
6. Remove 5 adapter housing attaching bolts and one nut.
7. Remove shift lever housing set bolt, then the lock plate.
8. Remove plug from rear of shift fork shaft, then pull shaft from housing.
9. Rotate and remove select lever.

10. Remove extension housing retaining bolts and nuts, then the extension housing.

NOTE: Leave gasket attached to intermediate plate.

11. Remove the front bearing retainer and outer snap rings from transmission case.
12. Using a plastic mallet or equivalent, separate transmission case from intermediate plate.
13. Mount intermediate plate in a vise using bolts, washers and nuts as shown, **Fig. 2.** Increase or decrease the number of washers so that bolt tip and outer surface of nuts are flush.
14. Remove screw plug, locking balls and springs from intermediate plate, **Fig. 3.**

15. Using a hammer and punch, drive out the slotted spring pins, then remove the E-rings from the shift rails with suitable pliers, **Fig. 4.**

NOTE: The locking ball from the reverse shift head and the locking ball and pin from the intermediate housing will drop out from their respective holes.

16. Pull No. 4 shift fork shaft from intermediate plate, disengage locking ball, then remove shaft and 5th gear fork, **Fig. 5.**
17. Remove No. 5 shift fork shaft and the reverse shift head, **Fig. 6.** Remove interlock pins.
18. Remove No. 3 shift fork shaft and interlock pins, **Fig. 7.**
19. Remove No. 1 shift fork shaft and the interlock pin, **Fig. 8.**

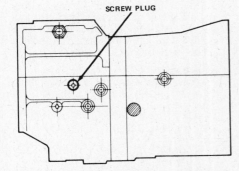

Fig. 1   Screw plug location. Aisin AX5 5 speed manual transmission

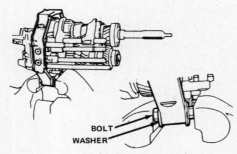

Fig. 2   Mounting intermediate plate

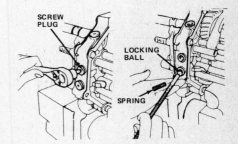

Fig. 3   Replacing screw plug, locking balls & springs

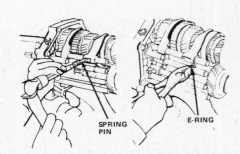

Fig. 4   Replacing spring pins & E-rings

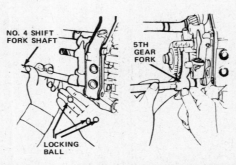

Fig. 5   Replacing No. 4 shift fork shaft, locking ball & 5th gear fork

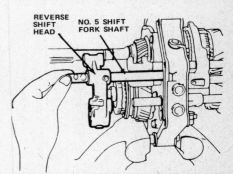

Fig. 6   Replacing No. 5 shift fork shaft & reverse shift head

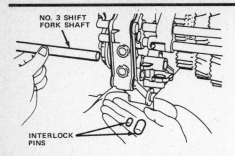

Fig. 7   Replacing No. 3 shift fork shaft & interlock pins

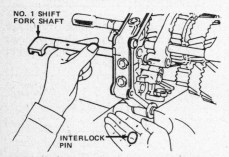

Fig. 8   Replacing No. 1 shift fork shaft & interlock pin

20. Remove No. 2 shift fork shaft, then the No. 2 and No. 1 shift forks, **Fig. 9.**
21. Remove reverse idle gear shaft stopper, reverse idler gear and shaft, then the reverse shift arm from shift arm bracket, **Fig. 10.**
22. Measure counter fifth gear thrust clearance with a feeler gauge as shown, **Fig. 11.** Clearance should be .004–.012 inch.
23. Lock output shaft, then remove counter shaft lock nut.
24. Use puller J-22888 or equivalent to remove No. 5 gear spline piece, synchronizer ring, needle bearings and counter fifth gear and hub sleeve, **Fig. 12.**
25. Remove spacer and ball, then the reverse shift arm bracket.
26. Remove rear bearing retainer bolts, then the snap ring.
27. Remove output shaft, input shaft and counter shaft from intermediate plate by pulling on countershaft, while tapping on intermediate plate, **Fig. 13.**

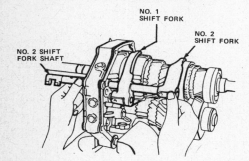

Fig. 9   Replacing No. 2 shift fork shaft & Nos. 1 and 2 shift forks

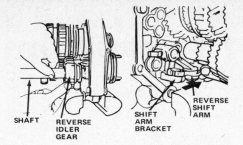

Fig. 10   Replacing reverse idler gear shaft stopper, reverse idler gear, shaft & reverse shift arm

28. Separate input shaft from output shaft, then remove counter shaft rear bearing from intermediate plate.

SUB-ASSEMBLY SERVICE

OUTPUT SHAFT

Disassemble
1. Remove snap ring, **Fig. 14.**
2. Press fifth gear, rear bearing, first gear and inner race from shaft, then remove needle bearing, synchronizer ring and locking ball.
3. Press No. 1 hub sleeve, synchronizer ring and second gear from shaft. Remove needle bearing.
4. Remove snap ring from opposite side of shaft, then press No. 2 hub sleeve, synchronizer ring and third gear from shaft. Remove needle bearing.

Inspect
1. Measure output shaft and inner race flange thickness as shown, **Fig. 15.** The minimum thickness for the output shaft flange should be no less than .189 inch, while the inner race flange

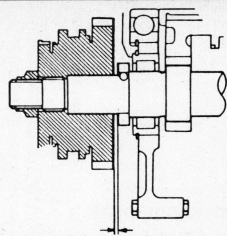

Fig. 11   Checking counter 5th gear thrust clearance

thickness should be no less than .157 inch. If thickness is less than specified, replace effected parts.
2. Measure output shaft journal diameter at second and third gear locations. Second gear journal surface diameter should be at least 1.495 inch, while third gear journal diameter should be 1.377 inch. If measurements are not as specified, replace output shaft.
3. Measure outer diameter of inner race. Minimum diameter should be 1.535 inch. If diameter is not as specified, replace inner race.
4. Mount output shaft in "V" blocks, then measure shaft runout with a dial indicator. Maximum allowable runout is .002 inch. If runout exceeds specification, replace output shaft.

Assemble
1. Apply gear lubricant to output shaft

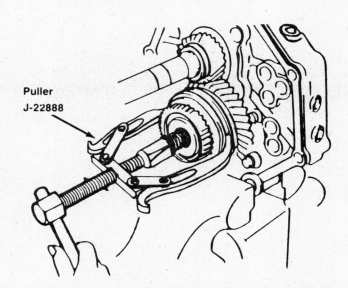

Puller J-22888

Fig. 12   Replacing No. 5 gear spline piece, synchronizer ring, needle bearing & counter 5th gear & hub

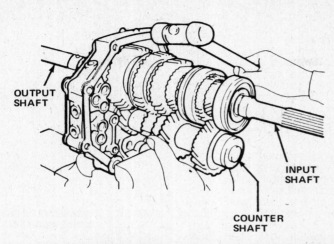

OUTPUT SHAFT

INPUT SHAFT

COUNTER SHAFT

Fig. 13   Replacing input, output & countershafts

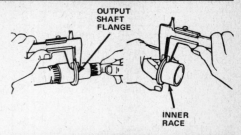

OUTPUT SHAFT FLANGE

INNER RACE

Fig. 15   Measuring output shaft & inner race flange thickness

Mark	Thickness mm (in.)	
C-1	1.75-1.80	(0.0689-0.0709)
D	1.80-1.85	(0.0709-0.0728)
D-1	1.85-1.90	(0.0728-0.0748)
E	1.90-1.95	(0.0748-0.0768)
E-1	1.95-2.00	(0.0768-0.0787)
F	2.00-2.05	(0.0788-0.0807)
F-1	2.05-2.10	(0.0807-0.0827)

Fig. 16   Snap ring identification chart (input shaft side)

and third gear needle bearing, then position third gear synchronizer ring onto gear, ensuring that ring slots align with shifting keys.

2. Install needle bearing between third gear and No. 2 hub sleeve, then press gear and hub sleeve onto output shaft.

3. Select a new snap ring from chart, **Fig. 16,** that will allow minimum axial play, then install snap ring onto output shaft.

4. Measure third gear thrust clearance with a feeler gauge. Clearance should be .004—.010 inch.

5. Apply gear lubricant to output shaft and second gear needle bearing, then position second gear synchronizer ring onto gear, ensuring that ring slots align with shifting keys.

6. Install needle bearing into second gear, then press gear and No. 1 hub sleeve onto output shaft.

7. Insert first gear locking ball into output shaft, then apply gear lubricant to needle bearing.

8. Assemble first gear, synchronizer ring,

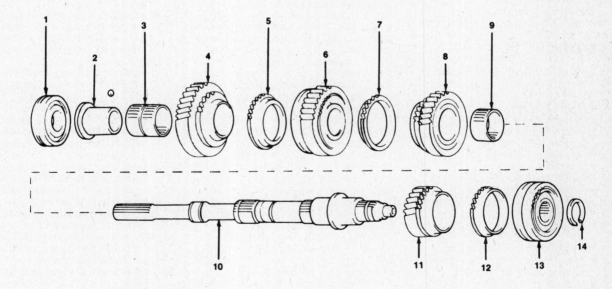

1. Rear Bearing
2. Inner Race
3. Needle Roller Bearing 1st Gear
4. 1st Gear
5. Synchronizer Ring 1st Gear
6. Hub Sleeve No. 1
7. Synchronizer Ring 2nd Gear
8. 2nd Gear
9. Needle Roller Bearing 2nd Gear
10. Output Shaft
11. 3rd Gear
12. Synchronizer Ring 3rd Gear
13. Hub Sleeve No. 2
14. Snap Ring

Fig. 14   Disassembled view of output shaft

Mark	Thickness mm (in.)	
A	2.67-2.72	(0.1051-0.1071)
B	2.73-2.78	(0.1075-0.1094)
C	2.79-2.84	(0.1098-0.1118)
D	2.85-2.90	(0.1122-0.1142)
E	2.91-2.96	(0.1146-0.1165)
F	2.97-3.02	(0.1169-0.1189)
G	3.03-3.08	(0.1193-0.1213)
H	3.09-3.14	(0.1217-0.1236)
J	3.15-3.20	(0.1240-0.1260)
K	3.21-3.26	(0.1264-0.1283)
L	3.27-3.32	(0.1287-0.1307)

Fig. 17   Snap ring identification chart (rear bearing side)

needle bearing and inner race.
9. Install assembly onto output shaft, ensuring that synchronizer ring slots align with shifting keys.
10. Turn inner race until it aligns with locking ball, then press rear bearing onto shaft so that outer race snap ring groove faces rearward.

NOTE: When pressing rear bearing onto shaft, hold first gear in place with a screwdriver.

11. Measure first and second gear thrust clearance with a feeler gauge. Clearance should be .004–.010 inch.
12. Press fifth gear onto shaft, then select a snap ring from chart, **Fig. 17,** that will allow minimum axial play. Install snap ring.

ASSEMBLE

1. Apply grease to input shaft needle bearings, then install bearings into shaft.
2. Install output shaft into intermediate plate by pulling on shaft while tapping on plate with a plastic mallet.
3. Connect input and output shafts, ensuring that synchronizer ring slots align with shifting keys.
4. Install counter shaft into intermediate plate, then drive bearing into plate.
5. Install output shaft rear bearing retainer and snap ring. Torque bearing retainer attaching screws to 13 ft. lbs.
6. Install reverse shift arm bracket onto intermediate plate, **Fig. 18,** then torque retaining bolts to 13 ft. lbs.
7. Install ball and spacer onto counter shaft.
8. Install shifting keys and No. 3 hub sleeve onto counter fifth gear. Install shifting key springs under keys, ensuring that end gaps are not in alignment.
9. Apply gear lubricant to needle bear-

ing, then install counter fifth gear, hub sleeve and needle bearing onto counter shaft.
10. Assemble synchronizer ring to No. 5 gear spline piece, ensuring that ring slots align with shifting keys, then install assembly onto counter shaft.
11. Lock output shaft and install lock nut onto counter shaft. Torque lock nut to 90 ft. lbs. and stake nut to prevent movement.
12. Measure counter fifth gear thrust clearance with a feeler gauge, **Fig. 11.** Clearance should be .004–.012 inch.
13. Install reverse shift arm into reverse shift arm bracket, then the reverse idler gear onto shaft, **Fig. 10.**
14. Align reverse shift arm shoe to reverse idler gear groove, then insert reverse idler gear shaft into intermediate plate.
15. Install reverse idler gear shaft stopper and torque retaining bolt to 13 ft. lbs.
16. Position No. 1 and 2 shift forks into grooves of hub sleeves, then insert No. 2 shift fork shaft through intermediate plate and into shift forks, **Fig. 9.**
17. Apply grease to interlock pins, then install pins into intermediate plate and No. 2 shift fork shaft hole.
18. Install No. 1 shift fork shaft through intermediate plate and into No. 1 shift fork.
19. Apply grease to interlock pins, then install pins into intermediate plate and No. 1 shift fork shaft hole.
20. Install No. 3 shift fork shaft through intermediate plate and into reverse shift arm.
21. Install reverse shift head onto No. 5 shift fork shaft, then insert shaft through intermediate plate, ensuring that No. 3 shift fork shaft engages reverse shift head, **Fig. 6.**
22. Install locking ball into reverse shift head hole, then shift No. 3 hub sleeve into fifth gear position.
23. Position No. 3 shift fork into No. 3 hub sleeve groove, then insert No. 4 shift fork shaft into No. 3 shift fork and the reverse shift arm.
24. Install locking ball into intermediate plate, then insert No. 4 shift fork shaft through intermediate plate.
25. Pull No. 1 shift fork shaft into first speed position, then check interlock by trying to move all other shafts. Shafts should not move.
26. Install new slotted spring pins into each shift fork, the reverse shift arm and the reverse shift head, then install the two shift fork shaft E-rings, **Fig. 4.**
27. Install locking balls and springs into intermediate plate, then apply sealer to screw plugs and install into interme-

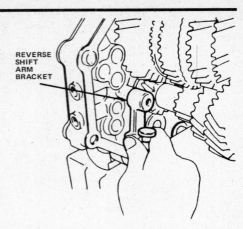

Fig. 18   Installing reverse shift arm bracket

diate plate. Torque screw plugs to 14 ft. lbs.

NOTE: Install short spring into tower of intermediate plate.

28. Remove intermediate plate from vise. Remove bolts, washers and nuts.
29. Align each bearing outer race, each shift fork end and the reverse idler gear with the holes in the transmission case, then connect case to intermediate plate.
30. Install two new snap rings, then the front bearing retainer and gasket. Apply sealer to bearing retainer bolts, then install bolts and torque to 12 ft. lbs.
31. Install new gasket onto intermediate plate, then install adapter housing and bolts. Torque bolts to 27 ft. lbs.
32. Install shift lever housing.
33. Insert shift lever into housing, then install shift lever housing bolt and lock plate. Torque bolt to 28 ft. lbs. and lock the locking plate.
34. Install plug at rear of shift fork shaft. Torque plug to 13 ft. lbs.
35. Install detent ball and spring, then apply sealer to screw plug and install into side of adapter housing, **Fig. 1.** Torque screw plug to 14 ft. lbs.
36. Check to ensure that input and output shafts can be rotated and that shifting can be done smoothly.
37. Install restrictor pins and torque to 20 ft. lbs.
38. Install shift lever retainer, gasket and attaching bolts. Torque bolts to 13 ft. lbs.
39. Install back up light switch and torque to 27 ft. lbs.
40. Install clutch housing and retaining bolts, then torque bolts to 27 ft. lbs.

Warner T-5 5 Speed Manual Transmission

INDEX

DISASSEMBLE

1. Remove drain plug and drain lubricant.

CAUTION: Except for fill plug and gearshift lever attaching bolts, all threaded holes and bolts used in the transmission case have metric threads. When using replacement bolts be sure they are the same size and length as the originals.

2. Using pin punch and hammer, remove offset lever to shift rail attaching roll pin, **Fig. 1.**
3. Remove adapter housing-to-transmission case bolts, then remove housing and offset lever as assembly.

NOTE: Do not attempt to remove offset lever while adapter housing is still bolted in place. The lever has a positioning lug engaged in the housing detent plate which prevents moving the lever far enough forward for removal.

4. Remove detent ball and spring from offset lever and remove roll pin from adapter housing or offset lever, then remove plastic funnel, thrust bearing race, and thrust bearing from rear of countershaft. (The countershaft rear thrust bearing, washer, and plastic funnel may be found either on the end of countershaft or inside adapter housing.)
5. Remove transmission cover and shift fork assembly attaching bolts, noting location of the two alignment type dowel bolts for assembly reference, and remove cover.
6. Using hammer and punch, remove roll pin from fifth gear shift fork, being sure to place wood block under the fork during removal of roll pin to prevent damage to fifth gear/reverse shift rail.
7. Remove fifth gear synchronizer snap ring, shift fork, fifth gear synchronizer sleeve, blocking ring, and fifth speed drive gear from rear of countershaft.
8. Remove fifth gear insert retainer synchronizer springs and inserts from sleeve and hub, marking position of sleeve and hub for assembly reference.
9. Using tool J-25215 or equivalent, remove snap ring and fifth speed driven gear from rear of output shaft.
10. Using suitable tool, mark position of front bearing cap on front of transmission case for assembly reference.
11. Remove front bearing cap bolts and front bearing cap, then remove front race and end play shim(s) from cap and remove oil seal from cap using screwdriver.
12. Turn clutch shaft so that flat surface on main drive gear faces countershaft and remove clutch shaft from transmission case, then remove 15 clutch shaft needle bearings, thrust bearing, and race.
13. Remove output shaft rear bearing race, then tilt output shaft assembly upward and remove assembly from transmission case.
14. Using suitable tool, unhook over center link spring from rear of transmission case.
15. Remove "C" clip attaching reverse lever and fork assembly-to-reverse lever pivot pin.
16. Turn fifth gear-reverse shift rail clockwise (as viewed from top of transmission) to disengage rail from reverse lever assembly, then remove rail from rear of case.
17. Remove fork assembly and reverse lever pivot pin and detach reverse lever from reverse idler gear, then remove reverse lever and fork assembly from transmission case.
18. Remove rear countershaft snap ring and spacer, then, inserting brass drift through clutch shaft opening in front of transmission case and using arbor press, press countershaft assembly rearward to remove rear countershaft bearing. When properly installed, bearing identification numbers face outward.
19. Move countershaft assembly rearward inside case, then tilt upward and remove from case. Remove front countershaft thrust washer from case, noting washer position for assembly reference.
20. Remove countershaft rear bearing spacer, then remove roll pin from forward end of reverse idler shaft using hammer and punch.
21. Remove reverse idler shaft and gear from transmission case, noting gear position for assembly reference.
22. Using arbor press, remove countershaft front bearing from transmission case.
23. Using tool J-29721 and J-22912-01 or equivalent, remove clutch shaft front bearing.
24. Using suitable tool, remove rear adapter housing seal.

SUB-ASSEMBLY SERVICE
OUTPUT SHAFT
Disassemble

1. Remove thrust bearing washer from front end of output shaft.
2. Mark third-fourth synchronizer hub and sleeve for assembly reference, then remove blocking ring, sleeve, and hub as assembly.
3. Remove third-fourth synchronizer insert springs and remove inserts, then remove sleeves from hubs.
4. Remove third gear from shaft, then remove snap ring retaining second gear on shaft and remove tabbed second gear thrust washer and second gear.
5. Using tool J-29721 and adapters 293-39 or equivalent, remove output shaft rear bearing.
6. Remove first gear thrust washer, first gear roll pin, first gear, and blocking ring.
7. Mark alignment of first-second gear synchronizer sleeve and output shaft hub for assembly reference, then remove insert spring and inserts from first-reverse sliding gear and remove gear from output shaft hub.

CAUTION: Do not try to remove the first-second-reverse hub from the output shaft as the hub and shaft are assembled and machined as a matched set during manufacture to insure concentricity.

Assemble

NOTE: If any output shaft gear is replaced, the countershaft gear must also be replaced to maintain proper gear mesh and avoid noisy operation.

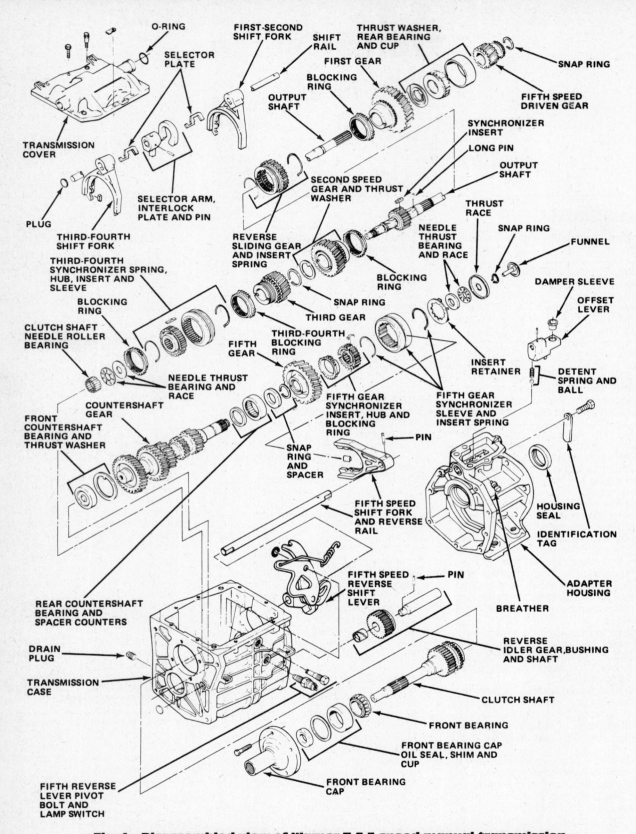

O-RING

SELECTOR PLATE

FIRST-SECOND SHIFT FORK

SHIFT RAIL

THRUST WASHER, REAR BEARING AND CUP

FIRST GEAR

BLOCKING RING

OUTPUT SHAFT

SNAP RING

FIFTH SPEED DRIVEN GEAR

TRANSMISSION COVER

PLUG

SECOND SPEED GEAR AND THRUST WASHER

SYNCHRONIZER INSERT

LONG PIN

OUTPUT SHAFT

THRUST RACE

SNAP RING

FUNNEL

THIRD-FOURTH SHIFT FORK

SELECTOR ARM, INTERLOCK PLATE AND PIN

REVERSE SLIDING GEAR AND INSERT SPRING

NEEDLE THRUST BEARING AND RACE

DAMPER SLEEVE

THIRD-FOURTH SYNCHRONIZER SPRING, HUB, INSERT AND SLEEVE

BLOCKING RING

BLOCKING RING

SNAP RING

THIRD GEAR

OFFSET LEVER

CLUTCH SHAFT NEEDLE ROLLER BEARING

FIFTH GEAR

THIRD-FOURTH BLOCKING RING

INSERT RETAINER

DETENT SPRING AND BALL

NEEDLE THRUST BEARING AND RACE

FIFTH GEAR SYNCHRONIZER INSERT, HUB AND BLOCKING RING

FIFTH GEAR SYNCHRONIZER SLEEVE AND INSERT SPRING

COUNTERSHAFT GEAR

FRONT COUNTERSHAFT BEARING AND THRUST WASHER

SNAP RING AND SPACER

PIN

FIFTH SPEED SHIFT FORK AND REVERSE RAIL

HOUSING SEAL

IDENTIFICATION TAG

REAR COUNTERSHAFT BEARING AND SPACER COUNTERS

FIFTH SPEED REVERSE SHIFT LEVER

PIN

BREATHER

ADAPTER HOUSING

DRAIN PLUG

TRANSMISSION CASE

REVERSE IDLER GEAR, BUSHING AND SHAFT

CLUTCH SHAFT

FRONT BEARING

FIFTH REVERSE LEVER PIVOT BOLT AND LAMP SWITCH

FRONT BEARING CAP OIL SEAL, SHIM AND CUP

FRONT BEARING CAP

Fig. 1   Disassembled view of Warner T-5 5 speed manual transmission

1. Lubricate output shaft and gear bores, then install and align first-second synchronizer sleeve on output shaft hub using assembly reference marks.
2. Install 3 first-second synchronizer inserts and 2 insert springs in first-reverse synchronizer sleeve. Engage tang end of each spring in same synchronizer insert but position open ends of insert springs to face 180 degrees from each other. Check alignment of sleeve and hub using assembly reference marks.
3. Install blocking ring and second gear on mainshaft, then install tabbed thrust washer and second gear retaining snap ring on mainshaft, making sure washer tab is properly seated in mainshaft notch.
4. Install blocking ring and first gear on output shaft and install first gear roll pin in output shaft.
5. Using tool J-2995 or equivalent, and suitable press, install rear bearing on output shaft and install first gear thrust washer.
6. Install third gear, third and fourth gear synchronizer hub inserts, and sleeve on shaft with hub offset facing forward, then install thrust bearing washer on forward end of shaft.

SHIFT CONTROL HOUSING

Disassemble

1. Place selector arm plates and shift rail in neutral position.
2. Turn shift rail counterclockwise until selector arm disengages from selector arm plates and selector arm roll pin is accessible, then pull shift rail rearward until selector arm contacts first-second shift fork, **Fig. 2.**
3. Using suitable punch, remove selector arm roll pin and remove shift rail.
4. Remove shift forks, selector arm plates, selector arm, roll pin, and interlock plate, then remove shift rail oil seal and O-ring using screwdriver.
5. Using hammer and punch, remove shift rail plug, then remove selector arm plates and nylon inserts from shift forks, noting position of plates and inserts for assembly reference.

Assemble

1. Install selector arm plates and nylon inserts in shift forks, then coat edges of shift rail plug with suitable sealer and install plug.
2. Lubricate shift rail and bores and insert shift rail in cover so that end of rail is flush with inside edge of cover.
3. Position first-second shift fork (larger of two forks) in cover with offset facing rear of cover and push shift rail through fork.
4. Position selector arm and C-shaped interlock plate in cover and insert shift rail in cover with widest part of interlock plate facing away from cover and selector arm roll pin hole facing downward and toward rear of cover.
5. Position third-fourth shift fork in cover with offset facing rear of cover. Third-fourth shift fork selector arm plate

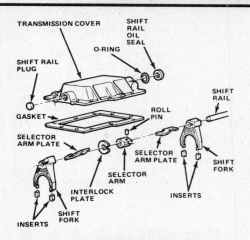

Fig. 2   Disassembled view of shift control housing

must be positioned under first-second shift fork selector arm plate.
6. Insert shift rail through third-fourth shift fork and into front shift rail bore in cover, then turn shift rail until selector arm plate at forward end of rail faces away from, but is parallel to cover.
7. Align roll pin holes in selector arm and shift rail, then install roll pin flush with surface of selector arm to prevent contact between pin and selector arm plates during shifts.
8. Install O-ring in groove of shift rail oil seal and install shift rail oil seal in the following manner:
   a. Install tool J-26628-2 over threaded end of shift rail.
   b. Lubricate lip of oil seal and slide seal over tool and onto shift rail.
   c. Using tool J-26628-1 or equivalent, seat oil seal in transmission cover.

ASSEMBLE

1. Coat countershaft front bearing with suitable sealant and, using arbor press, install countershaft front bearing flush with case.
2. Lubricate countershaft tabbed thrust washer and install so tab engages proper depression in case.
3. Tip transmission case on end and install countershaft in front of bearing bore, then install countershaft rear bearing spacer.
4. Lubricate rear bearing and, using tool J-29895 and J-33032 or equivalent, install bearing so that it extends .125 in. (3 mm.) beyond case surface. Proper tool must be used to prevent needles from catching on countershaft shoulder.
5. Position reverse idler gear in case with shift lever groove facing rear of case and install reverse idler shaft from rear of case. Install retaining roll pin in shaft.
6. Install output shaft assembly in case.
7. Using tool J-2995 or equivalent and arbor press, install front clutch shaft bearing on clutch shaft, then lubricate

pilot roller bearings and install in clutch shaft.
8. Install thrust bearing and race in clutch shaft, then install rear output shaft bearing race cap.
9. Install fourth gear blocking ring on output shaft, then install clutch shaft in case and engage in third-fourth synchronizer sleeve and blocking ring.
10. Using tool J-26625 or equivalent, install new oil seal in front bearing cap.
11. Install front bearing race in cap and temporarily install front bearing cap.
12. Coat pivot bolt threads with sealer, then install fifth speed-reverse lever, pivot bolt, and retaining "C" clip. Engage reverse lever fork in reverse idler gear.
13. Install fifth speed driven gear and retaining snap ring on rear of output shaft, then install countershaft rear bearing spacer and retaining snap ring.
14. Install fifth speed gear on countershaft, then insert fifth speed-reverse rail through opening in rear of case and install in reverse fifth speed lever, turning rail during installation to facilitate engagement with lever.
15. Install fifth speed-reverse lever over center spring, then assemble fifth gear synchronizer sleeve, insert springs, and insert retainer using assembly reference marks.
16. Install plastic inserts in notches on either side of fifth speed shift fork, then put assembled fifth gear synchronizer sleeve on fifth speed shift fork and slide onto countershaft and fifth speed-reverse rail, making sure roll pin holes in fifth-reverse rail and fifth speed shift fork are aligned.
17. Placing assembled fifth speed-reverse rail and shift fork on block of wood, install retaining roll pin, then install thrust race against fifth speed synchronizer hub and install retaining snap ring.
18. Lubricate needle type thrust bearing and thrust race and install bearing against race on countershaft.
19. Install thrust race over thrust bearing and insert plastic funnel into hole in end of countershaft gear.
20. Install adapter housing temporarily without sealing or torquing bolts, then turn transmission case on end and mount dial indicator on adapter housing with stylus on end of output shaft.
21. Turn clutch and output shaft to zero dial indicator, then pull upward on output shaft until end play is eliminated. To completely eliminate end play, bearings must be preloaded from .001−.005 in. (0.03−0.13 mm.)
22. Select shim pack measuring .001−.005 in. thicker than measured end play and, placing transmission horizontally on workbench, remove front bearing cap and race, then add shim to bearing cap and install clutch shaft bearing race cap.
23. Apply suitable sealant on case mating

surface of front bearing cap, then align assembly reference marks and install front bearing cap, torquing retaining bolts to 15 ft. lbs.

24. Recheck end play to make sure there is no end play.
25. Remove adapter housing and, using tool J-29184 or equivalent, install adapter housing rear seal.
26. Move shift forks on transmission cover and synchronizer rings inside transmission to the neutral position.
27. Apply suitable sealant to cover mating surface of transmission and lower cover assembly onto case, aligning shift forks and synchronizer sleeves, then center cover on case to engage reverse relay lever and install dowel bolts in cover.
28. Install remaining bolts and torque all cover bolts to 9 ft. lbs.

NOTE: The offset lever-to-shift rail roll pin hole should be in a vertical position after completion of steps 26 through 28.

29. Apply suitable sealant to adapter housing-to-transmission case mating surface and install adapter housing over output shaft and shift rail so that shift rail just enters shift cover opening.
30. Install detent spring into offset lever and place ball in neutral guide plate detent. Applying pressure on ball with detent spring and offset lever, slide offset lever on shift rail and seat adapter housing against transmission case so that the offset lever and shift rail roll pin holes are aligned and in a vertical position.
31. Install and torque adapter housing retaining bolts to 25 ft. lbs.
32. Install roll pin in offset lever and shift rail, then install damper sleeve in offset lever.
33. Coat backup lamp switch threads with suitable sealant and install switch in case.

TRANSFER CASES

TABLE OF CONTENTS

Borg Warner Transfer Cases

INDEX

WARNER QUADRA-TRAC

CASE DISASSEMBLY

1. Remove front and rear output shaft yokes.
2. If unit is not equipped with reduction unit, remove power take-off cover and the sealing ring from transfer case rear cover, **Fig. 1.**
3. Remove cover from transfer case. Position cover with drive chain downward and place a 2 × 4 × 6 inch block of wood under sprocket.
4. If not equipped with reduction unit, expand snap ring securing drive hub and sleeve to drive sprocket rear splines and remove hub and sleeve.
5. If equipped with reduction unit, remove pinion cage from drive sprocket rear splines.
6. Remove cover from drive sprocket and differential, slide drive sprocket toward differential and remove chain.

SUB-ASSEMBLY SERVICE

Differential Disassembly

1. Apply identification markings on case sprocket and end caps to ensure proper assembly.
2. Remove screws attaching front end cap to case sprocket, then remove end cap, thrust washers, preload springs, brake cone and side gear from case sprocket. Repeat for rear end cap, **Fig. 1.**
3. Remove pinion shaft lock pin and drive out the pinion shaft from case sprocket with a suitable drift.

Inspection

Clutch, thrust surfaces and shaft bores may be polished. Small smooth score marks and machine marks are acceptable. Case sprocket teeth will show a polished wear pattern, whereas pinion and side gears will have a "rough machined" appearance. The pinion shaft should be straight and fit snugly into case sprocket. The thrust washers should be flat and preload springs should be dished approximately 3/32 inch. Clean all parts of differential before assembly.

Differential Reassembly

During reassembly, bearing and thrust surfaces must be coated with lubricant, Jeep P/N 8123004.

1. Install pinion shaft sprocket approximately 3 inches into case and place pinion thrust washers and gears on shaft in proper sequence. Fully drive shaft into sprocket, aligning lock pin holes in shaft and case.
2. Slide pinion gears apart and mesh either front or rear side gear with pinion gears. Install brake cone over side gear followed by large thrust washer, preload springs, small thrust washer and end cap, **Fig. 1.**
3. Install pinion shaft lock pin and mesh remaining side gear with pinion gears. Install brake cone over side gear followed by large thrust washer, preload springs, small thrust washer and end cap.

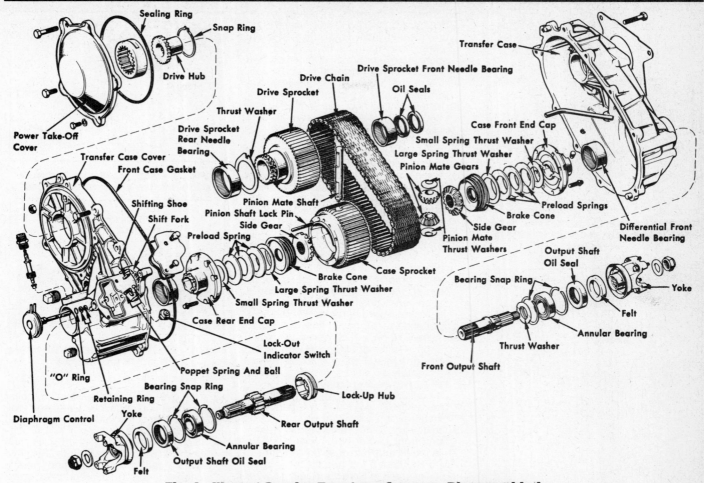

Fig. 1 Warner Quadra-Trac transfer case. Disassembled

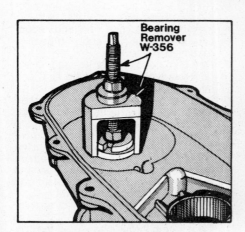

Fig. 2 Warner Quadra-Trac differential drive sprocket needle bearings removal

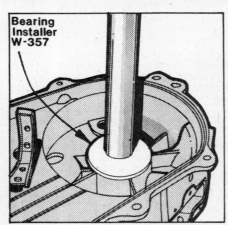

Fig. 3 Warner Quadra-Trac differential needle bearings installation

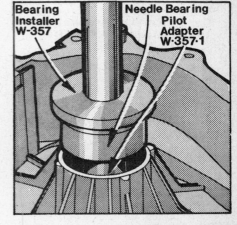

Fig. 4 Warner Quadra-Trac drive sprocket front needle bearing installation

4. Install front and rear output shafts into differential and rotate shafts so both shafts are aligned having entered the brake cone splines and tighten end cap screws.

Bearing Replacement

Refer to **Figs. 2 through 5** when replacing differential or drive sprocket needle bearings. Install drive sprocket rear needle bearings with removal tools, **Fig. 5**, with tool #W361-1 installed into the case bore.

Front and rear output shaft annular bearings are retained by selected thickness snap rings. The outer snap ring is available in the following thickness ranges: .060"–.063", .064"–.066", .067"–.069" and .070"–.072". The inner snap ring is available only in a thickness of .060–.063 inch. These bearings can be removed by hand or with a brass drift, if necessary. When removing the rear output shaft bearing, remove speedometer gear, then the outer snap

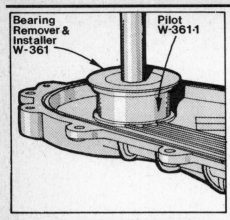

Fig. 5 Warner Quadra-Trac drive sprocket rear needle bearing removal

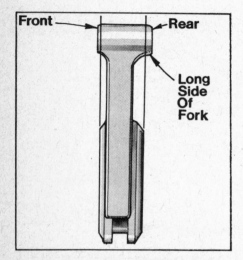

Fig. 7 Warner Quadra-Trac lock-up hub & shift fork assembly

ring and bearing. When installing outer snap ring, install proper snap ring to provide .001–.003 inch bearing end play.

Diaphragm Control, Shift Fork & Lock-Up Hub Disassembly

1. Remove vent cover and sealing ring.
2. Remove shift fork retaining rings from diaphragm control rod.
3. Remove dowel pin and insert a small magnet into dowel pin hole, **Fig. 6**. Remove diaphragm control from case cover, detent ball and spring.

NOTE: The diaphragm control is held by the detent ball and spring.

4. Remove shift fork, shifting shoes and lock-up hub.

Diaphragm Control, Shift Fork & Lock-Up Hub Reassembly

1. Lubricate and install shifting shoes and lock-up hub into shift fork.
2. Install fork and hub assembly into case cover with care not to separate lock-up hub from fork, **Fig. 7**.

3. Slide diaphragm control into case cover, past the fork but not further than the detent ball hole. Insert detent spring and ball into hole, using a ¼ inch punch, depress detent ball and slide diaphragm control rod past ball.
4. Install shift fork retaining rings and diaphragm control retaining dowel pin.
5. Install sealing ring and vent cover.

CASE REASSEMBLY

1. Place drive sprocket on a 2 × 4 × 6 inch block of wood with differential assembly about 2 inches from sprocket with front end down. Place drive chain around sprocket and differential, ensuring chain is engaged with sprocket and differential teeth. Remove slack from chain, **Fig. 8.**
2. Install rear output shaft into differential and shift lock-up hub to rear of case cover.
3. With grease holding drive sprocket thrust washer in position on cover, align and position cover on drive sprocket and differential. Rotate output shaft to align with lock-up hub.
4. Assemble drive hub, drive sleeve and snap ring. If not equipped with reduction unit, install drive hub and sleeve assembly on drive sprocket, ensuring snap ring seats properly.
5. If equipped with reduction unit, ensure oil baffle is positioned properly and install pinion cage and snap ring.
6. Install front output shaft, thrust washer and front gasket onto case.
7. Insert oil tube into case bore located at front output shaft bearing boss, then insert a ⁵⁄₁₆ × 6 inch rod into oil tube.
8. Position case onto drive sprocket and differential assembly. Using the ⁵⁄₁₆ × 6 inch rod to align oil tube with case cover, install and torque case to cover screws to 15–25 ft. lbs.

NOTE: Rotate drive sleeve to ensure drive sprocket thrust washer is correctly positioned. Sleeve should turn without binding.

9. Install power take-off sealing ring and cover.
10. Install speedometer gear onto rear output shaft and the front and rear output shaft oil seals into case bores.
11. Install front yoke and torque nut to 90–150 ft. lbs.

WARNER QUADRA-TRAC REDUCTION UNIT

DISASSEMBLY

1. Remove power take-off cover and gasket.
2. Remove reduction mainshaft snap ring and spacer, pull reduction mainshaft and sun gear assembly forward out of housing. Remove mainshaft needle bearings, **Fig. 9.**

Fig. 6 Warner Quadra-Trac diaphragm control removal

Fig. 8 Warner Quadra-Trac drive chain installation

3. Remove ring gear, reduction collar plate, pinion cage lock plate, shift collar hub and the reduction collar hub assembly from housing.
4. Using a mallet, tap shift collar hub from pinion cage lock plate. Remove pinion cage lock plate and needle bearing, ring gear, reduction collar plate and shift collar hub.
5. Remove reduction collar hub and needle bearings from shift collar hub.
6. Remove snap rings retaining reduction collar plate hub and ring gear to reduction collar plate.
7. Remove needle bearing and direct drive sleeve from reduction shift collar.
8. With the control lever move reduction shift collar to center detent, move collar away from shift fork and disengage fork. Move fork rearward to direct drive detent and collar toward fork, align outer teeth on collar and inner teeth on reduction holding plate. Move fork and collar forward to reduction detent and remove reduction shift collar.
9. Remove rear snap ring and annular bearing.
10. Remove shift fork locating spring pin, large expansion plug and shift rail taper plugs.
11. Remove control lever from shift lever.
12. Drive spring pin out from shift fork and rail with a ³⁄₁₆ inch punch, slide rail out of fork and remove fork.
13. Remove shift rail poppet ball, drive poppet taper plug into rail bore and remove plug and poppet spring.
14. Remove shift lever retaining pin and lever assembly.
15. Remove snap ring and reduction hold-

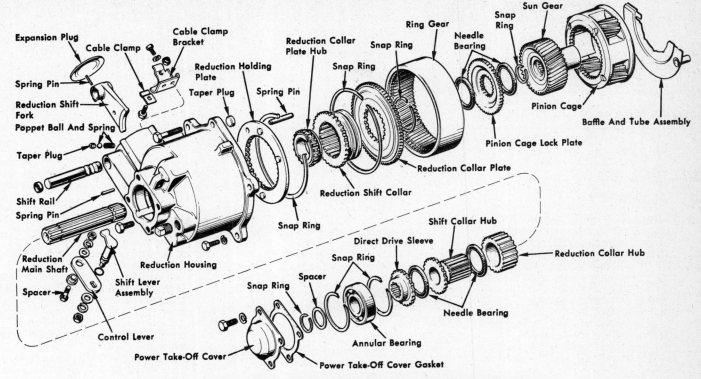

Fig. 9 Warner Quadra-Trac reduction unit. Disassembled

ing plate.

REASSEMBLY

1. Install reduction holding plate with locating pin indexed in reduction housing shift fork locating spring pin holes in plate aligned with holes in the housing, **Fig. 10**. Install holding plate snap ring with tabs forward.
2. Install shift lever assembly into housing with lever and rearward. Place O-ring in groove on shift lever shaft and move shift lever assembly inward to a position allowing installation of shift lever locating taper pin.
3. Install shift rail with grooved end first into rail rear bore and rotate rail so flat side is adjacent to poppet spring. Slide rail so shift fork is meshed with shift lever assembly and rail, move rail through fork so end of rail is even with edge of poppet bore.
4. Place poppet ball on end of spring and with a spring pin, depress ball and slide shift rail over ball as far as possible. Remove pin, slide rail to first detent position and rotate rail flat side facing shift lever assembly and spring bore aligning with spring pin bore in shift fork. Align spring pin holes in shift rail and fork, install spring pin flush with fork.
5. Install shift rail taper plugs, poppet bore taper plug and rail cover expansion plug.

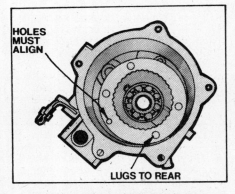

Fig. 10 Warner Quadra-Trac reaction unit holding plate installation

6. Install shift fork locating spring pin and control lever.
7. Place shift fork in center detent. Mesh reduction shift collar outer teeth with reduction holding plate inner teeth. Move fork to rear detent and shift collar away from fork, aligning groove in collar with shift fork. Move collar toward fork, engaging collar groove with fork.
8. Install direct drive sleeve into reduction shift collar with needle bearing surface and pointed ends of outer teeth forward. Adequately lubricate needle bearing and install against direct drive sleeve.

9. Install needle bearing and reduction collar hub onto shift collar hub. Install ring gear, reduction collar plate and hub assembly onto shift collar hub.

NOTE: A needle bearing is not used between reduction collar plate hub and reduction collar hub.

10. Install needle bearing onto shift collar hub and between reduction collar plate hub. Install pinion cage lock plate on shift collar hub so lock plate is snug against needle bearing. Install assembly into housing, rotating ring gear or pinion cage lock plate to align splines. Place needle bearing on shift collar hub and pinion cage lock plate.
11. Install reduction mainshaft and sun gear assembly into shift collar hub through the direct drive sleeve and annular bearing, rotating assembly to align splines. Use a drift to tap mainshaft fully rearward.
12. Install rear spacer and snap ring. Snap rings are available in various thickness ranges of .089"–.091", .092"–.094", .095"–.097", .099"–.101" and .103"–.105". Install appropriate snap ring to provide .004–.009 inch spacer clearance.
13. Install power take-off gasket and cover and torque cover screws to 15–25 ft. lbs.

Dana/Spicer Transfer Cases

INDEX

MODEL 20
DISASSEMBLY

1. Remove shift lever assembly, then remove bottom cover and gasket.
2. Remove rear bearing cap attaching bolts, then the bearing cap, **Fig. 1**.
3. Remove intermediate shaft lock plate, then drive intermediate shaft out rear of case using arbor tool J-25142 and suitable soft faced hammer.
4. Align arbor tool J-25142 in intermediate shaft assembly and remove gear assembly and thrust washers.
5. Remove front output shaft nut and washer, then the output shaft yoke and oil seal.
6. Remove cover plate attaching screws, then the cover plate, **Fig. 1**.

NOTE: When removing cover plate, do not damage the shims and gaskets.

7. Remove front output shaft rear bearing, then move rear output shaft shift rod towards rear of transfer case.
8. Remove rear output shaft shift fork setscrew, then the poppet ball and spring plugs.
9. Insert suitable punch through rear output shaft shift rod pin hole, then rotate shift rod ¼ turn counterclockwise and pull rod free of case.

NOTE: Do not lose shift rod poppet ball and spring when shift fork is free of shift rod.

10. Remove front bearing cap attaching bolts, then slide bearing cap off transfer case and shift rod.
11. Remove rear output shaft sliding gear and shaft fork.
12. Support transfer case on suitable wood blocks, then using a hammer and brass drift, drive front output shaft out rear of case.
13. Remove gears, bearings and spacers from transfer case.
14. Remove front output shaft shift fork setscrew, then pull shift rod out of shift fork.
15. Remove shift rod thimbles using a ⅜ inch drive, ⁷⁄₁₆ inch socket and extension.
16. Disassemble intermediate shaft.
17. Remove front output shaft bearing cup using suitable brass drift and hammer.

18. Remove front output shaft rear bearing by using the following procedure:
    a. Mount sliding gear in suitable vise with shaft lever groove facing downward.
    b. Insert output shaft through gear splines.
    c. Drive bearing from shaft using hammer and suitable brass drift.

REAR BEARING CAP-SPEEDOMETER DRIVE SERVICE
Disassembly

1. Remove speedometer driven gear sleeve and gear from bearing cap.
2. Mount bearing cap in suitable vise.
3. Remove output shaft yoke nut, then the yoke.
4. Remove bearing cap bore seal using tool J-25180.
5. Remove bearing cap assembly from vise, then using rear face of cap for support, drive output shaft from bearing cap using hammer and suitable brass drift.
6. Lift tapered bearing and drive bearing cup from bearing cap front bore.
7. Remove speedometer drive gear and shims from shaft.

NOTE: Retain shims for reassembly.

8. Remove front bearing from shaft. If necessary, remove speedometer driven gear bushing from bearing cap.

Assembly

1. If removed, install speedometer driven gear with suitable bushing installer.
2. Install front bearing cup in bore, then the front bearing on shaft.
3. Install rear bearing cup in bore, then the speedometer drive gear and shims on shaft.
4. Place output shaft in bearing cap, then install rear cone and roller and drive bearing onto shaft, seating against shims.
5. Install yoke seal, yoke, flat washer and nut. Torque nut to 140 ft. lbs.
6. Clamp dial indicator on bearing cap, then position indicator stylus against output shaft. Pry shaft in and out while checking end play. End play should be .002–.005 inch. If reading exceeds specifications, it can be corrected by adding or removing shims between speedometer drive gear and output

shaft front bearing. Install speedometer driven gear and sleeve in bearing cap.

ASSEMBLY

1. Install front output shaft bearing cup in case. Ensure cup is flush with exterior surface of case, **Fig. 1**.
2. Install shaft rail thimbles, then the front bearing cap. Torque front bearing cap attaching bolts to 30 ft. lbs.
3. Position front output shaft rear bearing on 1¼ inch socket, then install shaft in bearing using suitable brass drift and hammer.
4. Install poppet ball and spring into front output shaft shift rail, then compress poppet ball and spring and install front output shaft rod partially into case.
5. Install front output shaft shift fork, positioning fork so setscrew offset faces front of case.
6. Install front output shaft shift rod through shift fork.
7. Align fork and rod setscrew holes, then install setscrew and torque to 14 ft. lbs.
8. Install front output shaft front bearing, bearing spacer, front output shaft sliding gear and front output shaft gear.

NOTE: Ensure shift fork groove in sliding gear faces rear of transfer case.

9. Install front output shaft through gears, spacers and bearings, then support transfer case on suitable wood blocks and drive front output shaft into front housing using suitable brass drift and hammer.

NOTE: Ensure bearing is seated against front output shaft shoulder.

10. Install front output shaft rear bearing cup using suitable wood block and hammer.
11. Install rear bearing, cover plate and shims. Torque cover plate attaching screws to 30 ft. lbs.
12. Check front output shaft end play as follows:
    a. Strike end of front output shaft with lead hammer to seat rear bearing cup.
    b. Mount suitable dial indicator in front bearing cap, then position indicator stylus against end of output shaft.

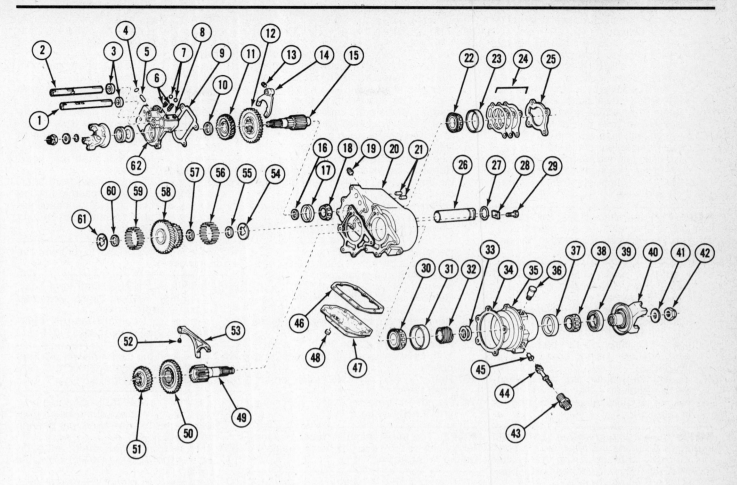

1. SHIFT ROD - REAR OUTPUT SHAFT SHIFT FORK
2. SHIFT ROD - FRONT OUTPUT SHAFT SHIFT FORK
3. SHIFT ROD OIL SEAL
4. INTERLOCK PLUG
5. INTERLOCK
6. POPPET BALL SPRING
7. POPPET BALL
8. FRONT BEARING CAP
9. FRONT BEARING CAP GASKET
10. FRONT OUTPUT SHAFT THRUST WASHER
11. FRONT OUTPUT SHAFT GEAR
12. FRONT OUTPUT SHAFT SLIDING GEAR
13. SETSCREW
14. FRONT OUTPUT SHAFT SHIFT FORK
15. FRONT OUTPUT SHAFT
16. FRONT OUTPUT SHAFT SPACER
17. FRONT OUTPUT SHAFT FRONT BEARING CUP
18. FRONT OUTPUT SHAFT FRONT BEARING
19. FILLER PLUG
20. TRANSFER CASE
21. THIMBLE COVER
22. FRONT OUTPUT SHAFT REAR BEARING
23. FRONT OUTPUT SHAFT REAR BEARING CUP
24. FRONT OUTPUT SHAFT REAR BEARING CUP SHIMS
25. COVER PLATE
26. INTERMEDIATE SHAFT
27. INTERMEDIATE SHAFT O-RING
28. LOCK PLATE
29. LOCK PLATE BOLT
30. REAR OUTPUT SHAFT FRONT BEARING

31. REAR OUTPUT SHAFT FRONT BEARING CUP
32. SPEEDOMETER DRIVE GEAR
33. REAR OUTPUT SHAFT BEARING SHIM
34. REAR BEARING CAP GASKET
35. REAR BEARING CAP
36. BREATHER
37. REAR OUTPUT SHAFT REAR BEARING CUP
38. REAR OUTPUT SHAFT REAR BEARING
39. REAR BEARING CAP OIL SEAL
40. REAR YOKE
41. REAR YOKE WASHER
42. REAR YOKE NUT
43. SPEEDOMETER SLEEVE
44. SPEEDOMETER DRIVEN GEAR
45. SPEEDOMETER BUSHING
46. BOTTOM COVER GASKET
47. BOTTOM COVER
48. DRAIN PLUG
49. REAR OUTPUT SHAFT
50. REAR OUTPUT SHAFT SLIDING GEAR
51. MAINSHAFT GEAR
52. SETSCREW
53. REAR OUTPUT SHAFT SHIFT FORK
54. INTERMEDIATE GEAR THRUST WASHER
55. INTERMEDIATE GEAR BEARING SPACER
56. INTERMEDIATE GEAR SHAFT NEEDLE BEARINGS
57. INTERMEDIATE GEAR BEARING SPACER
58. INTERMEDIATE GEAR
59. INTERMEDIATE GEAR SHAFT NEEDLE BEARINGS
60. INTERMEDIATE GEAR BEARING SPACER
61. INTERMEDIATE GEAR THRUST WASHER
62. FRONT BEARING CAP

Fig. 1   Exploded view of Dana/Spicer model 20 transfer case

c. Pry output shaft rearward and zero dial indicator.

d. Pry shaft forward while observing dial indicator. End play should be .001–.003 inch. If end play is not within specifications, adjust end play by adding or subtracting shims between cover plate and case. If shims are added, seat rear bearing cap by striking end of front output shaft with lead hammer.

13. Install rear output shaft shift rail poppet ball and spring in shift rod housing, then compress ball and spring and install rear output shaft shift rail partially into case.

NOTE: Prior to installing shift rail, ensure front output shaft shift rail is in neutral position and the interlock is seated in housing bore.

14. Install rear output shaft shift fork and sliding gear. Ensure shift fork groove in gear faces rear of case.
15. Align fork and rail setscrew holes, then install setscrew and torque to 14 ft. lbs.
16. Assemble intermediate gear rollers and spacers using arbor tool J-25142.
17. Install intermediate gear thrust washers in transfer case. Ensure thrust washer tangs are aligned with grooves in case.

NOTE: The rear thrust washer can be held in place by starting the intermediate shaft into the case and positioning the washer on the shaft. The front washer can be positioned using petroleum jelly.

18. Install O-ring on intermediate shaft, then insert intermediate gear in case. Drive intermediate shaft into case and intermediate gear until shaft forces arbor tool out front of case. Use only a soft-faced mallet or hammer to drive shaft into place.
19. Install intermediate shaft lock plate, identification tag, lockwasher and lock plate bolt. Torque lock plate bolt to 14 ft. lbs.
20. Install rear bearing cap and gasket assembly and slide rear output shaft through gear. Torque bearing cap bolts to 30 ft. lbs.
21. Install new front yoke seal, then the yoke. Torque yoke lock nut to 240 ft. lbs.
22. Install bottom cover and gasket. Torque attaching bolts to 14 ft. lbs.
23. Install shift rod oil seals using tool set J-25167.

MODEL 300
DISASSEMBLY

1. Remove shift lever assembly.
2. Remove bottom cover, **Fig. 2.** The bottom cover is coated with a sealant. Use a putty knife to break the seal, then work the knife around the edge to loosen and remove cover.
3. Remove front and rear yokes. Discard yoke nuts.
4. Remove socket head screws attaching the input shaft support to the case, then the support, rear output shaft gear and input shaft as an assembly, **Fig. 3.** The support is coated with a sealant. Use a putty knife to break the seal, then work knife around the edge to loosen and remove support.
5. Remove rear output shaft clutch sleeve from case.
6. Remove and discard snap ring retaining the rear output shaft gear on input shaft. Remove the gear.
7. Remove and discard input shaft bearing snap ring.
8. Remove input shaft and bearing from support. Tap end of input shaft with a mallet to aid removal.
9. Remove input shaft bearing and end play shims from shaft using a suitable press.
10. Remove input shaft oil seal from support. Discard the seal.
11. Remove intermediate shaft lock plate bolt and lock plate.
12. Remove intermediate shaft. Tap shaft from case using a suitable mallet and punch.
13. Remove and discard intermediate shaft O-ring.
14. Remove intermediate gear assembly and thrust washers.

NOTE: The thrust washers have locating tabs which must fit into notches in the case during reassembly.

15. Remove needle bearings and bearing spacers from intermediate gear.

NOTE: There are 48 needle bearings and 3 bearing spacers in the intermediate gear.

16. Remove rear bearing cap attaching bolts, then the cap. Tap on the output shaft to aid cap removal. The rear bearing cap is coated with a sealant. Use a putty knife to break the seal, then work knife around edge to loosen and remove cap.
17. Remove end play shims and speedometer drive gear from rear output shaft.
18. Remove and discard rear output shaft oil seal. Remove bearings and races from rear bearing cap.
19. Remove setscrews, retaining front and rear output shaft shift forks on shift rods, **Fig. 4.**
20. Remove shift rods. Insert a punch through clevis pin holes in rods and rotate rods while pulling out from case.

NOTE: When the shift rods are free of the front cap, avoid losing the shift rod poppet balls and springs.

21. Remove shift forks from case.
22. Remove bolts attaching front cap to case, then the cap. The front cap is coated with a sealant. Use a putty knife to break the seal, then work knife around edge to loosen and remove cap.
23. Remove front output shaft and shift rod oil seals from front cap.
24. Remove front bearing race from front bearing cap with tool J-29168.
25. Remove cover plate bolts, then the plate and end play shims from case.
26. Move front output shaft toward front of case.
27. Remove front output shaft rear bearing race from case.
28. Remove rear output shaft front bearing, **Fig. 5.** Position case on wood blocks. Seat clutch gear on case interior surface and tap shaft from bearing with a suitable mallet.

NOTE: If bearing is difficult to remove, use a suitable press.

29. Remove rear output shaft front bearing, thrust washer, clutch gear and output shaft from case.
30. Remove front output shaft rear bearing using a suitable press, **Fig. 6.**

NOTE: Support the case with wood blocks located at either side of case core to prevent damage to case.

31. Remove transfer case from press.
32. Remove front output shaft, clutch gear and sleeve, and the shaft rear bearing from case.
33. Remove front output shaft front bearing with tool J-22192-01 and a suitable press.
34. Remove front output shaft gear from shaft.
35. Remove input shaft rear needle bearing from rear output shaft with tool J-29369-1. Support output shaft in a vise during bearing removal.
36. Remove shift rod thimbles.

ASSEMBLY

1. Apply Loctite 220 sealer or equivalent to shift rod thimbles, then install the thimbles, **Fig. 2.**
2. Install front output shaft gear onto front output shaft. Ensure that the clutch teeth on the gear face toward shaft gear teeth.
3. Install front bearing on front output shaft using a suitable press. Ensure that the bearing is seated against the gear.
4. Install front output shaft into case, then the clutch sleeve and clutch gear on shaft.
5. Install front output shaft rear bearing with a suitable press, **Fig. 7.**

NOTE: Install an old yoke nut on the shaft to prevent thread damage.

6. Install input shaft rear needle bearing in rear output shaft with tool J-19179.
7. Place rear output shaft clutch gear in case and insert rear output shaft into gear.

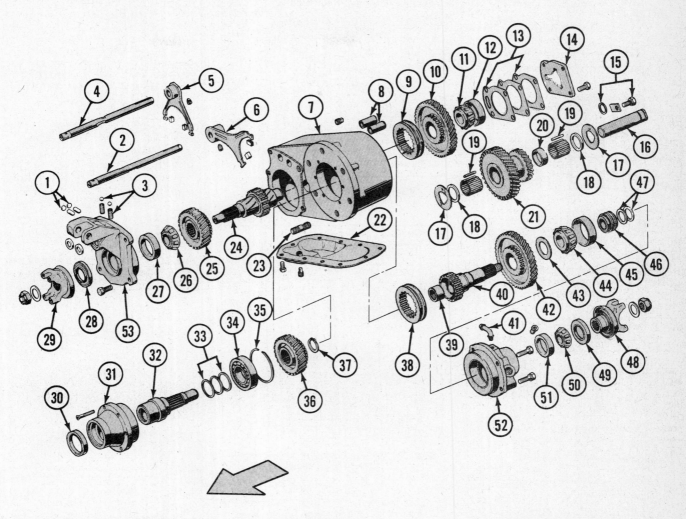

Fig. 2   Exploded view of Dana/Spicer model 300 transfer case

1. INTERLOCK PLUGS AND INTERLOCKS
2. SHIFT ROD – REAR OUTPUT SHAFT FORK
3. POPPET BALLS AND SPRINGS
4. SHIFT ROD – FRONT OUTPUT SHAFT FORK
5. FRONT OUTPUT SHAFT SHIFT FORK
6. REAR OUTPUT SHAFT SHIFT FORK
7. TRANSFER CASE
8. THIMBLE COVERS
9. CLUTCH SLEEVE – FRONT OUTPUT SHAFT
10. CLUTCH GEAR – FRONT OUTPUT SHAFT
11. BEARING – FRONT OUTPUT SHAFT REAR
12. RACE – FRONT OUTPUT SHAFT BEARING
13. END PLAY SHIMS – FRONT OUTPUT SHAFT
14. COVER PLATE
15. LOCK PLATE, BOLT AND WASHER
16. INTERMEDIATE GEAR SHAFT

17. THRUST WASHER
18. BEARING SPACER (THIN)
19. INTERMEDIATE GEAR SHAFT NEEDLE BEARINGS
20. BEARING SPACER (THICK)
21. INTERMEDIATE GEAR
22. BOTTOM COVER
23. STUD (CASE-TO-TRANS.)
24. FRONT OUTPUT SHAFT
25. FRONT OUTPUT SHAFT GEAR
26. FRONT OUTPUT SHAFT BEARING (FRONT)
27. FRONT OUTPUT SHAFT BEARING RACE
28. OIL SEAL
29. FRONT YOKE
30. SEAL
31. SUPPORT – INPUT SHAFT
32. INPUT SHAFT
33. SHIMS
34. INPUT SHAFT BEARING
35. INPUT SHAFT BEARING SNAP RING
36. REAR OUTPUT SHAFT GEAR

37. SNAP RING
38. CLUTCH SLEEVE – REAR OUTPUT SHAFT
39. INPUT SHAFT REAR BEARING (NEEDLE) (OR PILOT BEARING)
40. REAR OUTPUT SHAFT
41. VENT
42. CLUTCH GEAR – REAR OUTPUT SHAFT
43. THRUST WASHER
44. BEARING – REAR OUTPUT SHAFT FRONT
45. RACE – REAR OUTPUT SHAFT BEARING
46. SPEEDOMETER DRIVE GEAR
47. END PLAY SHIMS
48. REAR YOKE
49. REAR OUTPUT SHAFT OIL SEAL
50. BEARING – REAR OUTPUT SHAFT REAR
51. BEARING RACE
52. REAR BEARING CAP
53. FRONT BEARING CAP

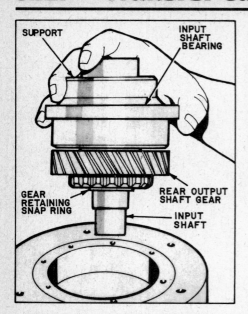

Fig. 3 Front support, input shaft & rear output shaft gear replacement

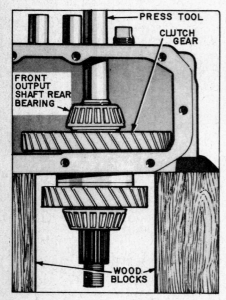

Fig. 6 Front output shaft front bearing removal

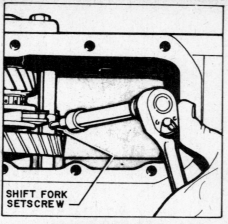

Fig. 4 Shift fork set screw replacement

Fig. 7 Front output shaft rear bearing installation

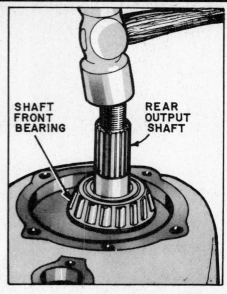

Fig. 5 Rear output shaft front bearing removal

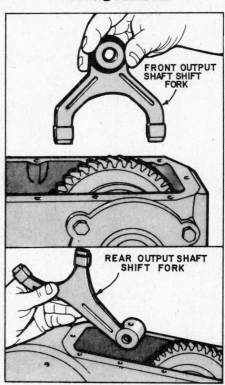

Fig. 8 Shift fork installation

8. Install thrust washer and front bearing on rear output shaft using a suitable press.
9. Install shims and bearing on input shaft using a suitable press.
10. Install new input shaft oil seal into input shaft support using tool J-19184.
11. Install input shaft and bearing in support. Install new bearing snap ring.
12. Install rear output shaft gear on input gear. Install new gear retaining snap ring.
13. Using a feeler gauge, measure clearance between input gear and the gear retaining snap ring. Clearance should

not exceed .003 inch. If clearance exceeds specification, disassemble input shaft and add shims between input shaft and shaft bearing.
14. Install clutch sleeve on rear output shaft.
15. Apply Loctite 515 sealer or equivalent to mating surface of input shaft support and install assembled support, shaft and gear into case. Use two support bolts to align the support on case and tap support into position with a mallet.
16. Install and torque socket head screws in support to 10 ft. lbs.
17. Install rear bearing cap front bearing race using tool J-9276-3.
18. Install rear bearing cap rear bearing using tool J-29182.
19. Position rear output shaft rear bearing in rear bearing cap.
20. Install rear output shaft yoke oil seal with tool J-25160.
21. Install speedometer gear and end play shims on rear output shaft.
22. Apply Loctite 515 sealer or equivalent to mating surface of rear bearing cap, then install the cap. Use two cap bolts to align bolt holes and tap rear cap into

place with a suitable mallet. Install and torque cap bolts to 35 ft. lbs.
23. Install rear output shaft yoke. Torque new lock nut to 120 ft. lbs.
24. Check rear output shaft end play as follows:
   a. Install a dial indicator onto bearing cap and position indicator so the plunger contacts end of shaft.
   b. Move output shaft back and forth to check end play. End play should be

.001–.005 inch.

c. If end play is not within specifications, remove or add shims between speedometer drive gear and output shaft rear bearing.

25. Install front output shaft rear bearing race.

26. Install front output shaft end play shims and cover plate. Install and torque cover plate bolts to 35 ft. lbs.

NOTE: Apply Loctite 220 sealer or equivalent to bolt threads prior to installation.

27. Install front output shaft front bearing race using tools J-8092 and J-29181.

28. Install front output shaft yoke oil seal using tool J-25160.

29. Install shift rod oil seals using tool J-25167.

30. Apply Loctite 515 sealer or equivalent to mating surface of front bearing cap, then install the cap. Use two bolts to align cap and case bolt holes and tap cap into position with a mallet. Torque cap bolts to 35 ft. lbs.

31. Check front output shaft end play as follows:
    a. Seat rear bearing cup against cover plate by tapping end of front output shaft with a mallet.
    b. Install a dial indicator on front bearing cap so the plunger contacts end of output shaft.
    c. Move output shaft back and forth to check end play. End play should be .001–.005 inch.
    d. If end play is not within specifications, remove or add shims between cover plate and case. If shims are added, seat rear bearing cup as outlined previously before rechecking end play.

32. Install front output shaft yoke. Install and torque new lock nut to 120 ft. lbs.

33. Insert front and rear output shaft shift forks into case, **Fig. 8.**

34. Install front output shaft shift rod poppet ball and spring into front bearing cap.

35. Compress poppet ball and spring and install front output shaft shift rod partially into case. Insert from output shaft shift rod through shift fork. Align setscrew hole in shift fork, then install and torque setscrew to 14 ft. lbs.

36. Install rear output shaft shift rod poppet ball and spring into front bearing cap.

37. Compress poppet ball and spring and install rear output shaft shift rail partially into case.

NOTE: Before installing shift rail, ensure that the front output shaft shift rod is in the neutral position and that the interlocks are seated in the front bearing cap bore.

38. Insert rear output shaft shift rod through shift fork. Align setscrew holes in fork and rod. Install and torque setscrew to 14 ft. lbs.

39. Insert tool J-25142 in intermediate gear and install needle bearings and spacers into gear.

40. Install intermediate gear thrust washers into case. Ensure that the washer tangs are aligned with grooves in case. Secure thrust washers in position with petroleum jelly.

41. Install new O-ring seal on intermediate shaft.

42. Position intermediate gear into case.

43. Install intermediate shaft in case core. Tap shaft into gear until shaft forces tool J-25142 from case.

44. Install intermediate shaft lock plate and bolt. Torque bolt to 23 ft. lbs.

45. Install bottom cover. Apply Loctite 515 sealer or equivalent to mating surface of cover. Install and torque cover bolts to 15 ft. lbs.

New Process Transfer Cases

INDEX

MODEL 207

NOTE: For service procedures on this transfer case, refer to "Chevrolet & GMC" chapter and note following service bulletin below.

SERVICE BULLETIN Some 1984 Cherokee and Wagoneer models equipped with a model 207 transfer case may experience an occasional, mild gear clash when shifting from 2-wheel to 4 wheel drive at speeds above 30 mph. This condition can be corrected as follows:

1. Check transfer case range control linkage adjustment and condition, adjusting or repairing linkage as necessary. If condition still exists, proceed to step 2.
2. Remove and disassemble transfer case.
3. Note serial number on transfer case I.D. tag and proceed as follows:
    a. On transfer cases after serial number 1-9-84, disassemble and inspect synchronizer assembly components replacing damaged parts as necessary.
    b. On transfer cases built before serial number 1-9-84, replace synchronizer assembly, synchronizer ring and drive sprocket.
4. Assemble and install transfer case.
5. Adjust range control linkage, then ensure that transfer case shifts properly at speeds up to 55 mph.

MODEL 208

NOTE: For service procedures on this transfer case, refer to "Chevrolet & GMC" chapter.

MODEL 219
DISASSEMBLY

1. Remove fill and drain plugs. Drain lubricant from transfer case.
2. Remove front and rear output shaft yokes. Discard yoke seal washers and yoke nuts.
3. Mark relationship between rear retainer and rear case for alignment at reassembly, **Fig. 1.**
4. Remove rear retainer attaching bolts, then the rear retainer. If necessary use a mallet to loosen retainer. Do not pry from case.
5. Remove differential shim and speedometer drive gear from rear output shaft, **Fig. 2.** Tag the shim or shims for assembly reference.

NOTE: The speedometer drive gear is installed with the long end facing toward the case. Note the gear position for assembly.

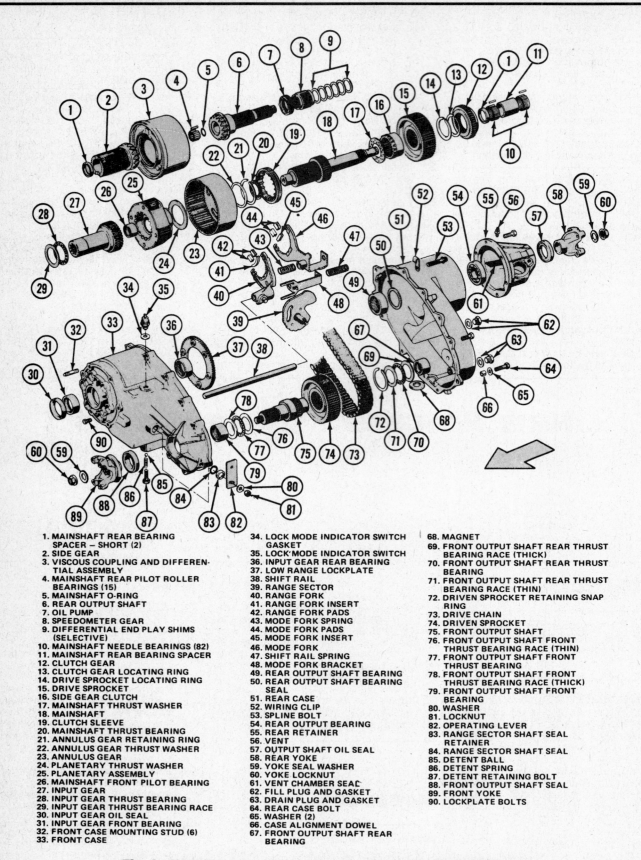

Fig. 1 New Process model 219 transfer case, disassembled.

1. MAINSHAFT REAR BEARING SPACER – SHORT (2)
2. SIDE GEAR
3. VISCOUS COUPLING AND DIFFERENTIAL ASSEMBLY
4. MAINSHAFT REAR PILOT ROLLER BEARINGS (15)
5. MAINSHAFT O-RING
6. REAR OUTPUT SHAFT
7. OIL PUMP
8. SPEEDOMETER GEAR
9. DIFFERENTIAL END PLAY SHIMS (SELECTIVE)
10. MAINSHAFT NEEDLE BEARINGS (82)
11. MAINSHAFT REAR BEARING SPACER
12. CLUTCH GEAR
13. CLUTCH GEAR LOCATING RING
14. DRIVE SPROCKET LOCATING RING
15. DRIVE SPROCKET
16. SIDE GEAR CLUTCH
17. MAINSHAFT THRUST WASHER
18. MAINSHAFT
19. CLUTCH SLEEVE
20. MAINSHAFT THRUST BEARING
21. ANNULUS GEAR RETAINING RING
22. ANNULUS GEAR THRUST WASHER
23. ANNULUS GEAR
24. PLANETARY THRUST WASHER
25. PLANETARY ASSEMBLY
26. MAINSHAFT FRONT PILOT BEARING
27. INPUT GEAR
28. INPUT GEAR THRUST BEARING
29. INPUT GEAR THRUST BEARING RACE
30. INPUT GEAR OIL SEAL
31. INPUT GEAR FRONT BEARING
32. FRONT CASE MOUNTING STUD (6)
33. FRONT CASE

34. LOCK MODE INDICATOR SWITCH GASKET
35. LOCK MODE INDICATOR SWITCH
36. INPUT GEAR REAR BEARING
37. LOW RANGE LOCKPLATE
38. SHIFT RAIL
39. RANGE SECTOR
40. RANGE FORK
41. RANGE FORK INSERT
42. RANGE FORK PADS
43. MODE FORK SPRING
44. MODE FORK PADS
45. MODE FORK INSERT
46. MODE FORK
47. SHIFT RAIL SPRING
48. MODE FORK BRACKET
49. REAR OUTPUT SHAFT BEARING
50. REAR OUTPUT SHAFT BEARING SEAL
51. REAR CASE
52. WIRING CLIP
53. SPLINE BOLT
54. REAR OUTPUT BEARING
55. REAR RETAINER
56. VENT
57. OUTPUT SHAFT OIL SEAL
58. REAR YOKE
59. YOKE SEAL WASHER
60. YOKE LOCKNUT
61. VENT CHAMBER SEAL
62. FILL PLUG AND GASKET
63. DRAIN PLUG AND GASKET
64. REAR CASE BOLT
65. WASHER (2)
66. CASE ALIGNMENT DOWEL
67. FRONT OUTPUT SHAFT REAR BEARING

68. MAGNET
69. FRONT OUTPUT SHAFT REAR THRUST BEARING RACE (THICK)
70. FRONT OUTPUT SHAFT REAR THRUST BEARING
71. FRONT OUTPUT SHAFT REAR THRUST BEARING RACE (THIN)
72. DRIVEN SPROCKET RETAINING SNAP RING
73. DRIVE CHAIN
74. DRIVEN SPROCKET
75. FRONT OUTPUT SHAFT
76. FRONT OUTPUT SHAFT FRONT THRUST BEARING RACE (THIN)
77. FRONT OUTPUT SHAFT FRONT THRUST BEARING
78. FRONT OUTPUT SHAFT FRONT THRUST BEARING RACE (THICK)
79. FRONT OUTPUT SHAFT FRONT BEARING
80. WASHER
81. LOCKNUT
82. OPERATING LEVER
83. RANGE SECTOR SHAFT SEAL RETAINER
84. RANGE SECTOR SHAFT SEAL
85. DETENT BALL
86. DETENT SPRING
87. DETENT RETAINING BOLT
88. FRONT OUTPUT SHAFT SEAL
89. FRONT YOKE
90. LOCKPLATE BOLTS

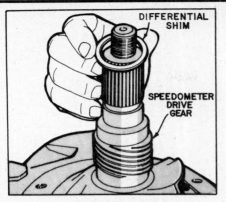

Fig. 2 Differential shim & speedometer drive gear replacement

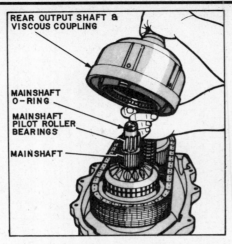

Fig. 3 Rear output shaft & viscous coupling replacement

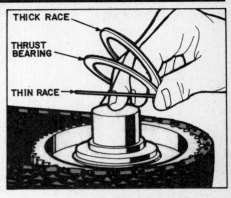

Fig. 4 Front output shaft rear thrust bearing assembly replacement

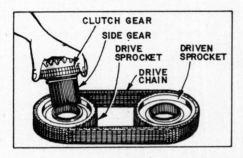

Fig. 5 Side gear, clutch gear, sprockets & chain assembly

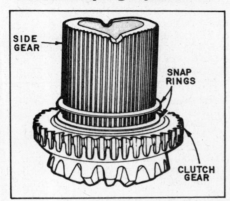

Fig. 6 Side gear components

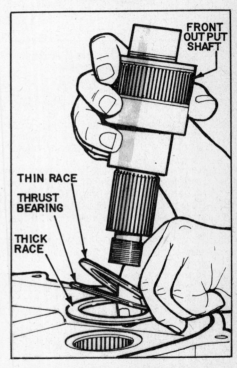

Fig. 7 Front output shaft & shaft front thrust bearing replacement

6. Remove rear output bearing snap ring, then the bearing from retainer with a mallet.

NOTE: The rear output bearing has one shielded side. Note position for assembly.

7. Remove rear output shaft seal from rear retainer using a suitable screwdriver or a punch.
8. Position transfer case on wood blocks with the front case resting on the wood. If necessary, cut "V" notches in the blocks so the front case rests squarely on the blocks.
9. Remove rear case to front case attaching bolts, then the rear case from front case. To remove, insert suitable screwdrivers into notches at case ends to pry rear case from front case.

NOTE: The two case end bolts have flat washers and alignment dowels. Note bolt, dowel and washer locations for assembly.

10. Remove rear output shaft and viscous coupling as an assembly, **Fig. 3**. If necessary, tap shaft with a plastic mallet to remove.
11. Remove O-ring seal and pilot roller bearings from mainshaft.
12. Remove rear output shaft from viscous coupling.
13. Remove shift rail spring from rail.

14. Remove plastic oil pump from shaft bore in rear case. Note pump position for reassembly. The side of the pump with the recess must face toward shaft bore when installed.
15. Remove rear output shaft bearing seal from case using a suitable screwdriver to pry seal from seal bore.
16. Remove front output shaft thrust bearing assembly, **Fig. 4**. Tag the assembly for installation reference.
17. Remove driven sprocket retaining snap ring.
18. Remove drive sprocket, drive chain, driven sprocket, side gear clutch and clutch gear as an assembly, **Fig. 5**. Place assembly on bench and mark components for reassembly reference.
19. Remove needle bearings and bearing spacers from mainshaft or side gear bore. A total of 82 needle bearings and three spacers are used.
20. Remove side gear/clutch gear assembly from drive sprocket, **Fig. 5**. Remove two snap rings, then the clutch gear from the side gear, **Fig. 6**. Note position of snap rings and gears for reassembly.
21. Remove side gear clutch, mainshaft thrust washer and the remaining (short) mainshaft needle bearing

spacer.
22. Remove front output shaft and shaft thrust bearing assembly, **Fig. 7**. Note installation sequence of thrust bearing assembly. The proper sequence is: thin race, bearing, then thick race.
23. Remove front output shaft seal from front case using a suitable screwdriver or punch.
24. Remove shaft rail spring from shaft rail if not previously removed.
25. Remove clutch sleeve, mode fork and mode fork spring as an assembly, **Fig. 8**.
26. Remove mainshaft thrust washer, then the mainshaft. Pull mainshaft straight up to remove.
27. Move range operating lever downward to the last detent position, then disen-

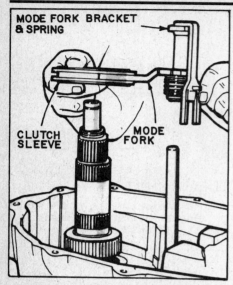

Fig. 8   Clutch sleeve & mode fork replacement

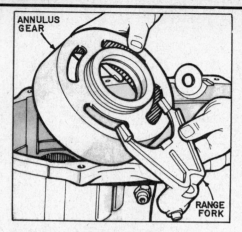

Fig. 9   Annulus gear & range fork replacement

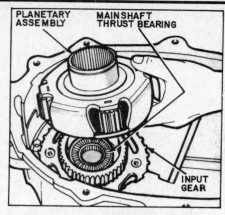

Fig. 10   Planetary assembly replacement

gage range fork lug from range sector slot.

28. Remove annulus gear retaining snap ring and thrust washer, then the annulus gear and range fork as an assembly, **Fig. 9.**
29. Remove planetary thrust washer from planetary assembly hub, then the planetary assembly, **Fig. 10.**
30. Remove mainshaft thrust bearing from input gear, then the input gear, thrust bearing and race.
31. Remove range sector detent ball and spring retaining bolt, then the ball and spring.
32. Remove range sector and operating lever attaching nut and lock washer, then the lever.
33. Remove sector, then the range sector shaft O-ring and retainer.
34. Remove input gear oil seal from front case using a suitable screwdriver or punch.

SUB-ASSEMBLY SERVICE

LOCK PLATE, REPLACE

1. Remove and discard lock plate attaching bolts.
2. Remove lock plate from case.
3. Coat case and lock plate surfaces around bolt holes with Loctite 515 sealer or equivalent.
4. Place new lock plate surfaces around bolt holes in lock plate and case.
5. Coat new lock plate attaching bolts with Loctite 271 sealer or equivalent.
6. Install and torque lock plate attaching bolts to 30 ft. lbs.

BEARING & BUSHING REPLACEMENT

NOTE: The following bearings and bushings are replaced using special service tools. However, they may also be replaced using suitable equivalent tooling and when using these tools, care should be taken so as not to damage any components.

Also, all the bearings used must be correctly positioned to prevent covering the bearing oil feed holes. After replacing any bearing, check position of bearing to ensure that the oil feed hole is not obstructed or blocked by the bearing.

Rear Output Shaft Bearing, Replace

1. Remove bearing using tools J-8092 and J-29165.
2. Install new bearing with tools J-8092 and J-29166.
3. Remove tools and check position of bearing to ensure that the oil feed hole is clear.

Front Output Shaft Front Bearing, Replace

1. Remove bearing with tools J-8082 and J-29168.
2. Install new bearing with tools J-8092 and J-29167.
3. Remove tools and check position of bearing to ensure that the oil feed hole is clear.

Front Output Shaft Rear Bearing, Replace

1. Remove bearing with tools J-26941 and J-2619-01.
2. Install new bearing with tools J-8092 and J-29163.
3. Remove tools and check position of bearing to ensure that oil feed hole is clear and that the bearing is seated flush with the edge of the bore in the case to permit clearance for thrust bearing assembly.

Input Gear Front & Rear Bearings, Replace

1. Remove both bearings simultaneously with tools J-8092 and J-29170.
2. Install new bearings one at a time. First, install the rear bearing, then the front bearing. Bearings are installed with tools J-8092 and J-29169.
3. Remove tools and check position of bearings to ensure that the oil feed holes are clear and that the bearings are flush with the case bore surfaces.

Mainshaft Front Pilot Bearing, Replace

1. If bearing cannot be removed by hand, use tools J-2619-01 and J-29369. A similar internal type blind hold bearing puller may also be used.
2. If necessary, install new bearing with tools J-8092 and J-29174.
3. Remove tools and check position of bearing to ensure that the oil feed hole is clear and that the bearing is seated flush with edge of bearing bore.

Rear Output Bearing, Replace

1. Remove snap ring, then the bearing using a mallet or brass punch.
2. Install new bearing with tools J-8092 and J-7818.

NOTE: Ensure that the shielded side of the bearing faces toward the inside of the transfer case after installation.

3. Install bearing snap ring.
4. Install new seal with tool J-29162.

Annulus Gear Bushing, Replace

1. Remove bushing with tools J-8092 and J-29185.
2. Install new bushing using the same tools.
3. Remove any metal chips caused by bushing replacement.

ASSEMBLY

NOTE: During assembly, lubricate all components with 10W-30 engine oil or petroleum jelly where indicated only. Do not use any other types of lubricant.

1. Install new input gear and rear output shaft bearing oil seals. Seat the seals flush with the edge of seal bore or in seal groove in the case. Coat seal lips with petroleum jelly after installation.
2. Install input gear thrust bearing race in the case counterbore, **Fig. 1.**
3. Install input thrust bearing on input gear, then install the gear and bearing assembly into case.
4. Install mainshaft thrust bearing into bearing recess in input gear.

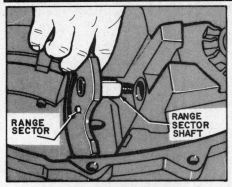

Fig. 11   Range sector installation

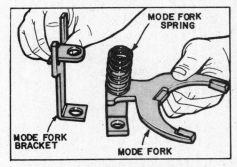

Fig. 14   Mode fork, spring & bracket assembly

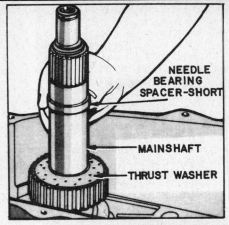

Fig. 12   Mainshaft installation

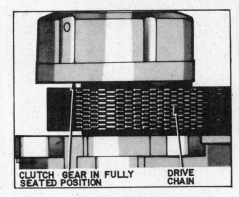

Fig. 15   Seating viscous coupling on clutch gear

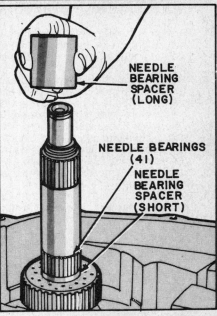

Fig. 13   Mainshaft needle bearings & spacer installation

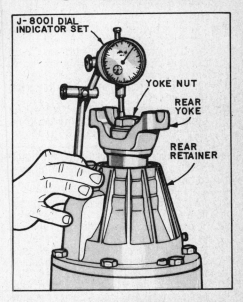

Fig. 16   Checking differential end play

5. Install planetary assembly on input gear. Ensure that the planetary pinion teeth mesh fully with the input gear.
6. Install planetary thrust washer on planetary hub.
7. Install new sector shaft O-ring and retainer in shaft bore in the case.
8. Install range sector in front case, **Fig. 11.** Install operating lever on sector shaft, then the lever attaching washer and lock nut on shaft. Torque lock nut to 17 ft. lbs.
9. Install detent ball, spring and retaining bolt into front case detent bore. Torque retaining bolt to 22 ft. lbs.
10. Move range sector to last detent position.
11. Assemble annulus gear and range fork. Install the assembly on and over planetary assembly. Ensure that the annulus gear is meshed fully with planetary pinions.
12. Insert range fork lug in range sector detent slot.
13. Install annulus thrust washer and annulus retaining ring on annulus gear hub.
14. Align mainshaft thrust washer in input gear, if necessary.
15. Install mainshaft and ensure that the shaft is seated fully in the input gear, **Fig. 12.**
16. Install mainshaft thrust washer on mainshaft.
17. Install short mainshaft needle bearing spacer on the shaft, **Fig. 13.**
18. Liberally coat mainshaft needle bearing surface and all 82 needle bearings with petroleum jelly. Install 41 needle bearings on the shaft, **Fig. 13.** Ensure that bearings are in the vertical position and seated on the short spacer.
19. Install the long mainshaft needle bearing spacer on the shaft, **Fig. 13.** Lower the spacer onto previously installed needle bearings. Avoid displacing bearings.
20. Align shift rail bore in the case with bore in range fork and install shift rail.

NOTE: The shift rail bore in the case must be dry and not contain any oil. A small amount of oil may prevent the shift rail from seating completely and also may prevent rear case installation.

21. Assemble mode fork, mode fork spring and mode fork bracket, **Fig. 14.**
22. Install clutch sleeve in mode fork. Ensure that the sleeve is positioned so the I.D. numbers on the sleeve face upward after the sleeve is installed.
23. Align clutch sleeve and mode fork assembly with shift rail and install assembly onto shift rail and mainshaft. Ensure that the clutch sleeve is meshed with the mainshaft gear.
24. Install remaining 41 mainshaft needle bearings on shaft.
25. Install side gear clutch on mainshaft with clutch gear teeth facing downward. Ensure that the gear teeth mesh with the clutch sleeve.
26. Install the remaining short mainshaft needle bearing spacer. Avoid displacing the bearings.
27. Install front output shaft front thrust bearing assembly into front case. The correct assembly sequence is: thick race, thrust bearing, then thin race.
28. Install front output shaft into front case.
29. Install clutch gear on side gear. The tapered side of the clutch gear teeth must face toward side gear teeth.
30. Install clutch gear and drive sprocket locating snap rings on side gear.

A—165

Install the snap rings so the rings face each other.

31. Position drive and driven sprockets in drive chain and install the assembled side and clutch gears in the drive sprocket.
32. Install assembled drive chain, sprockets and side gear on mainshaft and front output shaft. Align sprockets with shafts, then, keeping the assembly level, lower the assembly onto both shafts simultaneously. Avoid displacing mainshaft needle bearings during chain and sprockets installation.
33. Install driven sprocket retaining snap ring.
34. Install front output shaft rear thrust bearing assembly onto front output shaft. The proper installation sequence is: thin race, thrust bearing, then thick race.
35. Install shift rail spring on shift rail.
36. Install new O-ring on mainshaft pilot bearing hub.
37. Thickly coat mainshaft pilot roller bearing hub and pilot roller bearings with petroleum jelly. Install rollers onto shaft.
38. Install rear output shaft in viscous coupling. Ensure that the shaft is seated fully.
39. Install assembled viscous coupling and rear output shaft on mainshaft. Align mainshaft pilot hub with pilot bearing bore in rear output shaft and lower assembly onto mainshaft. Avoid displacing pilot roller bearings during installation.
40. Align clutch gear teeth with viscous coupling teeth and seat the coupling fully onto the clutch gear, **Fig. 15.**

NOTE: When properly installed, the clutch gear teeth will not be visible or extend past the coupling.

41. Install magnet into front case, if removed.
42. Thoroughly clean mating surfaces of front and rear cases. Apply Loctite 515 sealer or equivalent to mating surface of front case and to all case attaching bolts.
43. Install rear case onto front case. Align case dowels and install case attaching bolts. Torque attaching bolts to 22 ft. lbs.

NOTE: The two case end bolts require flat washers.

44. Install oil pump on rear output shaft and seat into case. Install the pump so the recessed side faces toward inside of case.
45. Install speedometer drive gear and differential shim on output shaft.
46. Install vent chamber seal in rear retainer, if removed.
47. Align and install rear retainer on rear case. Install retainer bolts finger tight only.
48. Install yoke onto rear output shaft. Install yoke nut finger tight only.
49. Install a dial indicator onto retainer

with the plunger contacting the top of the yoke nut, **Fig. 16.**
50. Install yoke on front output shaft and rotate the front shaft 10 complete revolutions.
51. Rotate front output shaft again and note end play reading on dial indicator. End play should be .002 to .010 inch. If end play is not within specifications, remove rear retainer and add or remove differential shims as required. Recheck end play.
52. Remove both output shaft yokes.
53. Install new front and rear yoke seals if not previously installed.
54. Remove rear retainer bolts and apply Loctite 515 sealer or equivalent to mating surface of retainer and to the bolts. Install and torque retainer bolts to 22 ft. lbs.
55. Install new yoke seal washers on output shafts, then the yokes. Install and torque new yoke nuts to 110 ft. lbs.
56. Install and torque drain plug to 18 ft. lbs.
57. Install 4 pints of 10W-30 engine oil into transfer case through fill plug.
58. Install and torque fill plug to 18 ft. lbs.

MODEL 229
DISASSEMBLY

1. Remove fill and drain plugs and drain lubricant from transfer case.
2. Remove front and rear yoke nuts and seal washers. Discard washers.
3. Mark relationship between front and rear yokes and propeller shafts for reference during reassembly, then remove yokes, **Fig. 17.**
4. Support transfer case on wood blocks with V-notches cut in blocks to provide clearance for front case mounting studs.
5. Mark relationship between rear retainer and rear case for reference during reassembly, then remove rear retainer attaching bolts and pry retainer off case by inserting screwdrivers in slots provided in case.
6. Remove differential shim(s) and speedometer drive gear from rear output shaft, **Fig. 18.**
7. Remove rear case to front case attaching bolts, then separate the case halves by prying with screwdrivers in slots at case ends.
8. Remove thrust bearing and races from front output shaft, **Fig. 19.** Note position of bearing and races for reference during reassembly.
9. Remove oil pump from rear output shaft, noting position of oil pump for reference during reassembly.
10. Remove mainshaft pilot bearing rollers (15) from shaft, or from coupling if rollers fell off during rear output shaft removal.
11. Remove O-ring from end of mainshaft, then the viscous coupling from mainshaft and side gear, **Fig. 20.**
12. Remove front output shaft, driven

sprocket and drive chain assembly. To ease removal, lift the assembly upward, tilt front shaft towards mainshaft and slide chain off drive sprocket.
13. Remove front output shaft front thrust bearing from case or shaft, then the drive chain from front output shaft and sprocket.
14. Remove snap ring retaining driven sprocket to front output shaft, then remove sprocket from shaft. Mark relationship between shaft and sprocket for reference during reassembly.
15. Remove mainshaft, side gear, clutch gear, drive sprocket and spline gear as an assembly, **Fig. 21.**
16. Remove mode fork, shift rail and clutch sleeve as an assembly, **Fig. 22.** Mark relationship between sleeve and fork for reference during reassembly and remove sleeve from fork.
17. Remove locking fork, clutch sleeve, fork brackets and fork springs as an assembly, then disassemble components for cleaning and inspection.
18. Remove range sector detent screw, spring, plunger and ball.
19. Disengage low range fork lug from range sector slot.
20. Remove annulus gear snap ring and thrust washer, then the annulus gear, range fork and rail as an assembly. Disassemble components for cleaning and inspection.
21. Remove thrust washer from planetary assembly hub, then remove planetary gear assembly.
22. Remove mainshaft thrust bearing from input gear, then the input gear and the input gear thrust bearing and race.
23. Remove range sector and operating lever attaching nut and lockwasher, then remove lever, the range sector and shaft, range sector O-ring and retainer.
24. Remove sprocket clutch gear and side gear from mainshaft.
25. Remove needle bearings (82) and two bearing spacers from mainshaft. Note position of spacers for reference during reassembly.
26. Remove spline gear and thrust washer, side gear, and clutch gear and thrust washer from sprocket carrier and sprocket, **Fig. 23.**
27. Remove clutch gear and thrust washer from side gear.
28. Remove one sprocket carrier snap ring, then remove drive sprocket from carrier.
29. Remove three bearing spacers and all sprocket carrier needle bearings from carrier.

NOTE: The sprocket carrier and mainshaft needle bearings are different sizes and care must be taken to avoid mixing them.

30. Remove rear output bearing and rear yoke seal from retainer. Note position of bearing for reference during reassembly.
31. Remove input gear and front yoke seals from case. Pry seals from case using a screwdriver.

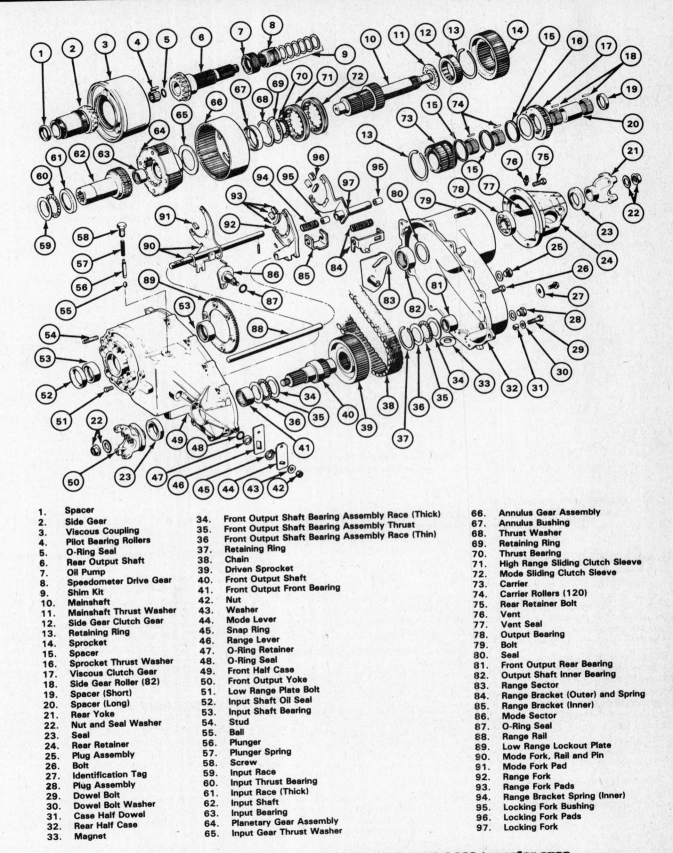

Fig. 17 Exploded view of New Process model 229 transfer case

1.	Spacer
2.	Side Gear
3.	Viscous Coupling
4.	Pilot Bearing Rollers
5.	O-Ring Seal
6.	Rear Output Shaft
7.	Oil Pump
8.	Speedometer Drive Gear
9.	Shim Kit
10.	Mainshaft
11.	Mainshaft Thrust Washer
12.	Side Gear Clutch Gear
13.	Retaining Ring
14.	Sprocket
15.	Spacer
16.	Sprocket Thrust Washer
17.	Viscous Clutch Gear
18.	Side Gear Roller (82)
19.	Spacer (Short)
20.	Spacer (Long)
21.	Rear Yoke
22.	Nut and Seal Washer
23.	Seal
24.	Rear Retainer
25.	Plug Assembly
26.	Bolt
27.	Identification Tag
28.	Plug Assembly
29.	Dowel Bolt
30.	Dowel Bolt Washer
31.	Case Half Dowel
32.	Rear Half Case
33.	Magnet

34.	Front Output Shaft Bearing Assembly Race (Thick)
35.	Front Output Shaft Bearing Assembly Thrust
36.	Front Output Shaft Bearing Assembly Race (Thin)
37.	Retaining Ring
38.	Chain
39.	Driven Sprocket
40.	Front Output Shaft
41.	Front Output Front Bearing
42.	Nut
43.	Washer
44.	Mode Lever
45.	Snap Ring
46.	Range Lever
47.	O-Ring Retainer
48.	O-Ring Seal
49.	Front Half Case
50.	Front Output Yoke
51.	Low Range Plate Bolt
52.	Input Shaft Oil Seal
53.	Input Shaft Bearing
54.	Stud
55.	Ball
56.	Plunger
57.	Plunger Spring
58.	Screw
59.	Input Race
60.	Input Thrust Bearing
61.	Input Race (Thick)
62.	Input Shaft
63.	Input Bearing
64.	Planetary Gear Assembly
65.	Input Gear Thrust Washer

66.	Annulus Gear Assembly
67.	Annulus Bushing
68.	Thrust Washer
69.	Retaining Ring
70.	Thrust Bearing
71.	High Range Sliding Clutch Sleeve
72.	Mode Sliding Clutch Sleeve
73.	Carrier
74.	Carrier Rollers (120)
75.	Rear Retainer Bolt
76.	Vent
77.	Vent Seal
78.	Output Bearing
79.	Bolt
80.	Seal
81.	Front Output Rear Bearing
82.	Output Shaft Inner Bearing
83.	Range Sector
84.	Range Bracket (Outer) and Spring
85.	Range Bracket (Inner)
86.	Mode Sector
87.	O-Ring Seal
88.	Range Rail
89.	Low Range Lockout Plate
90.	Mode Fork, Rail and Pin
91.	Mode Fork Pad
92.	Range Fork
93.	Range Fork Pads
94.	Range Bracket Spring (Inner)
95.	Locking Fork Bushing
96.	Locking Fork Pads
97.	Locking Fork

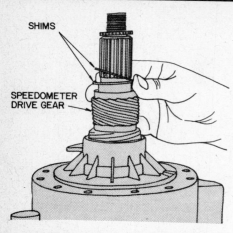

Fig. 18   Differential shims & speedometer drive gear replacement

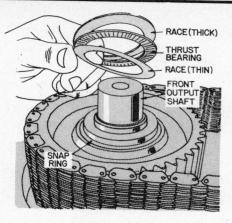

Fig. 19   Front output shaft thrust bearing replacement

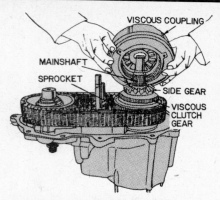

Fig. 20   Viscous coupling replacement

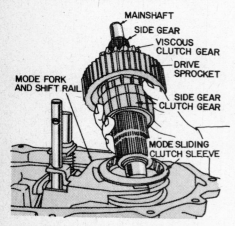

Fig. 21   Mainshaft assembly replacement

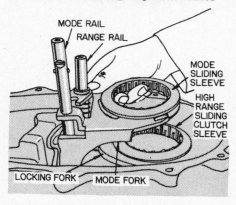

Fig. 22   Mode fork, shift fork & clutch sleeve removal

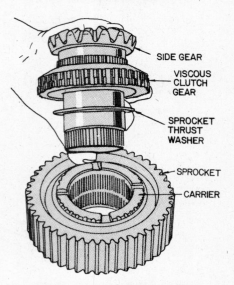

Fig. 23   Side & clutch gear replacement

SUB-ASSEMBLY SERVICE

NOTE: All bearings used in the transfer case must be properly aligned to avoid blocking the oil passages. After installing bearings, check their position to make sure that oil passages are clear.

Rear Output Shaft Bearing, Replace
1. Remove bearing using tools J-26941 and J-2619-01.
2. Remove rear output lip seal with a small screwdriver.
3. Install a new lip seal, then the new bearing using tools J-8092 and J-29166.
4. Remove tools and check that oil feed hold is not blocked.

Front Output Shaft Front Bearing, Replace
1. Remove bearing using tools J-8092 and J-29168.
2. Install new bearing using tools J-8092 and J-29167.
3. Remove tools and check that oil feed hole is not blocked.

Front Output Shaft Rear Bearing, Replace
1. Remove bearing using tools J-26941 and J-2619-01.
2. Install new bearing using tools J-8092 and J29163.
3. Remove tools and check that oil feed hole is not blocked and that bearing is seated flush with edge of bore in case to permit clearance for thrust bearing assembly.

Input Gear Front & Rear Bearings, Replace
1. Remove both bearings simultaneously using tools J-8092 and J-29170.
2. Install bearings one at a time, rear bearing first, using tools J-8092 and J-29169.
3. Remove tools and check that oil feed hole is not blocked and that bearings are flush with case bore surfaces.
4. Install new oil seal using tool J-29162.

Mainshaft Pilot Bushing, Replace
1. Remove bushing using tools J-2619-01 and J-29369-1.
2. Install new bushing using tools J-8092 and J-29174.
3. Remove tool and check that oil feed hole is not blocked.

Rear Output Bearing & Rear Yoke Seal
1. Remove bearing and seal using a brass drift and hammer.
2. Install new bearing using tools J-8092 and J-7818.

NOTE: The shielded side of the bearing must face the case interior.

3. Install new seal in retainer using tool J-29162.

ASSEMBLY

NOTE: During assembly, lubricate all internal components with Dexron II or petroleum jelly if specified. Do not use any other types of lubricant.

1. Install new input gear and rear output shaft bearing seals and apply petroleum jelly to seals. Seals must seat flush with edge of seal bore or in seal groove in case.
2. Install input gear thrust bearing race in case counterbore and thrust bearing on input gear, then install gear and

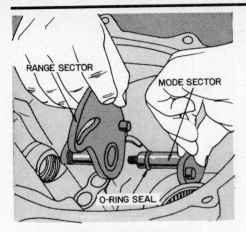

Fig. 24 Range sector installation

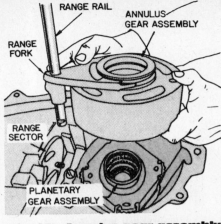

Fig. 25 Annulus gear assembly installation

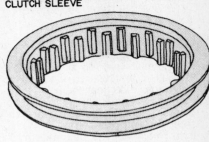

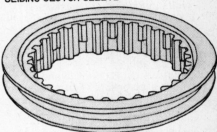

Fig. 26 Mode & locking clutch sleeve identification

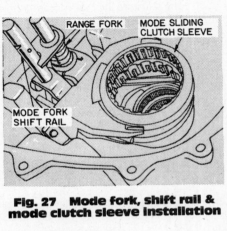

Fig. 27 Mode fork, shift rail & mode clutch sleeve installation

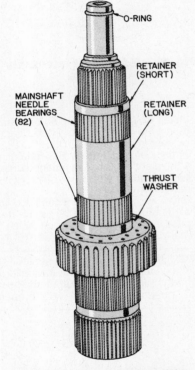

Fig. 28 Mainshaft needle bearing installation

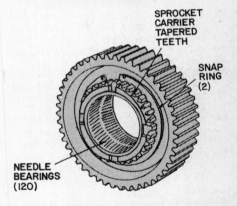

Fig. 29 Sprocket carrier & drive sprocket assembly

bearing in case.

3. Install mainshaft thrust bearing in bearing recess in input gear.
4. Install planetary assembly on input gear. Ensure that planetary pinion teeth are fully meshed with input gear.
5. Install new sector shaft O-ring on mode sector shaft.
6. Install mode sector through range sector.
7. Install range sector in front case, **Fig. 24.**
8. Install operating lever and snap ring on range sector shaft, then the lever attaching washer and locknut on mode sector shaft. Torque locknut to 17 ft. lbs.
9. Assemble annulus gear, range fork and rail, then install the assembly on and over planetary assembly, **Fig. 25.** Ensure annulus gear is fully meshed with planetary pinions.
10. Install annulus thrust washer and annulus retaining ring on annulus gear hub.
11. Install detent spring, plunger, ball and screw in front case detent bore. Torque screw to 22 ft. lbs.
12. Assemble and install locking fork, fork brackets, fork springs and clutch sleeve. Ensure that lug on fork is fully seated in range sector detent.

NOTE: The splines in the locking clutch sleeve and the mode clutch sleeve are different, **Fig. 26.** Make sure that the correct sleeve is installed in the corresponding shift fork.

13. Install range fork lug in range sector detent notch, then place range sector in high range position.
14. Assemble and install mode fork, shift rail and mode clutch sleeve, **Fig. 27.**
15. Install thrust washer, new O-ring, needle bearings and bearing spacers on mainshaft, **Fig. 28.**
16. Coat shaft bearing surface and all 82 needle bearings with petroleum jelly.
17. Install 41 needle bearings and the

long bearing spacer, then install remaining 41 bearings and the short spacer, **Fig. 28.**
18. Install spline gear on mainshaft, using care not to displace bearings.
19. Install sprocket carrier in drive sprocket using reference marks made during disassembly.

NOTE: Assemble the sprocket carrier and drive sprocket so that the tapered teeth on the carrier are on the same side as the recess in the drive sprocket, **Fig. 29.**

20. Install sprocket carrier bearings and spacers, **Fig. 29.**
21. Coat carrier bore and all 120 needle bearings with petroleum jelly.
22. Install center spacer and position 60 bearings in each end of carrier, then install the two remaining spacers, one on each side of carrier.

23. Install sprocket carrier and drive shaft on mainshaft, **Fig. 30.** Ensure recessed side of drive sprocket faces downward.
24. Install clutch gear thrust washer on mainshaft, **Fig. 30.**
25. Install clutch gear on side gear, **Fig. 23.** Ensure that tapered edge of clutch gear faces side gear teeth.
26. Install side and clutch gear assembly on mainshaft. Ensure side gear is fully seated in sprocket carrier.
27. Install mainshaft and gear assembly in case, **Fig. 21.** Ensure mainshaft is fully seated in input gear.
28. Install driven sprocket and snap ring on front output shaft using reference marks made during disassembly.
29. Install front output shaft front thrust bearing, then the thick race, bearing and thick race in case.
30. Install drive chain on driven sprocket, then lift and tilt driven sprocket and chain and install opposite end of chain on drive sprocket. Align front output shaft with shaft bore in front case and install shaft in case. Ensure shaft thrust bearing is seated in case.
31. Install front output shaft rear thrust bearing assembly on front output shaft, **Fig. 19.** Install thin race first, then the bearing and thick race.
32. Install viscous coupling on side gear and clutch gear, **Fig. 18.** Ensure coupling is fully seated on clutch gear, clutch gear is flush with coupling and gear teeth are visible.
33. Apply petroleum jelly to mainshaft pilot bearing surface and all 15 pilot roller bearings, then install bearings on shaft.
34. Install rear output shaft on mainshaft and into viscous coupling. Shaft must be completely seated in coupling. If not, tap into position with a rubber mallet. Use caution not to displace pilot bearings during shaft installation.

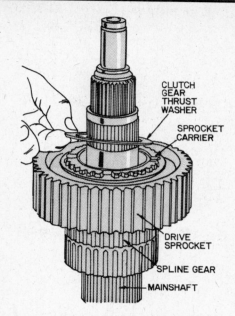

CLUTCH GEAR THRUST WASHER

SPROCKET CARRIER

DRIVE SPROCKET

SPLINE GEAR

MAINSHAFT

Fig. 30   Mainshaft assembly

35. Install oil pump on rear output shaft, then a new rear output shaft bearing oil seal in rear case.
36. Apply bead of Loctite 515 sealer or equivalent to rear case mating surface and install magnet in case, if removed.
37. Install rear case on front case. Ensure alignment dowels on ends of front case are lined up with bolt holes in rear case.

NOTE: If the rear case will not seat fully in the front case, check for the following: oil in range fork rail bore; front output shaft rear thrust bearing assembly not properly aligned with rear case; mainshaft not fully seated; rear case and oil pump misaligned.

38. Install case attaching bolts and torque to 23 ft. lbs. Ensure that flat washers are used on bolts at case ends with alignment dowels.
39. Install speedometer drive gear and differential shims on rear output shaft, **Fig. 16.**
40. Install rear retainer on rear case. Tighten bolts securely but not to final torque.
41. Install front and rear output shaft yokes and original yoke nuts. Tighten nuts finger tight only.
42. Install a dial indicator onto rear retainer so that plunger contacts rear yoke nut, **Fig. 14.**
43. Rotate front output shaft 10–12 revolutions and zero the dial indicator, then rotate shaft one more revolution and note dial indicator reading.
44. End play should be .002–.010 inch. If not, remove retainer and add or remove shims as necessary to bring end play within limits.
45. Remove front and rear yokes and rear retainer. Discard original yoke nuts.
46. Apply Loctite 515 sealer or equivalent to retainer mating surface and retainer bolts, then install retainer and torque bolts to 23 ft. lbs.
47. Install yokes with new seal washers and nuts. Torque nuts to 120 ft. lbs. Hold yokes with tool J-8614-01 while tightening nuts.
48. Apply sealer to detent bolt, then install ball, spring and bolt. Torque bolt to 23 ft. lbs.
49. Install drain plug and washer and torque plug to 18 ft. lbs.
50. Fill transfer case with 6 pints of Dexron II transmission fluid and install fill plug with washer. Torque fill plug to 18 ft. lbs.

AUTOMATIC TRANSMISSIONS

TABLE OF CONTENTS

Chrysler 727, 904 & 999 Torque Command Automatic Transmissions

NOTE: For service procedures not found in this section, refer to A-727, A-904, A-904T & A-999 Loadflite automatic transmission section in the Dodge & Plymouth chapter.

INDEX

DESCRIPTION

These transmissions, **Figs. 1 and 2** combine a torque converter with a fully automatic three speed gear system. The converter housing and transmission case are an integral aluminum casting. The transmission consists of two multiple disc clutches, an overrunning (one-way) clutch, two servos and bands and two planetary gear sets to provide three forward speeds and reverse, **Fig. 3.**

The common sun gear of the planetary gear sets is connected to the front clutch by a driving shell that is splined to the sun gear and to the front clutch retainer.

The hydraulic system consists of a single oil pump and a valve body that contains all the valves except the governor valve.

Venting of the transmission is accomplished by a drilled passage through the upper part of the front pump housing.

The torque converter is attached to the engine crankshaft through a flexible driving plate. The converter is cooled by circulating the transmission fluid through an oil-to-water type cooler located in the radiator lower tank. The converter is a sealed assembly that cannot be disassembled.

A lock-up clutch, **Fig. 4,** (torque converter clutch) is incorporated in some transmission applications.

The lock-up mode is activated only in direct drive above a minimum preset vehicle speed. At wider throttle openings, where the 2-3 upshift occurs above the minimum lock-up speed, the lock-up shift will occur immediately after the 2-3 upshift.

IN-VEHICLE ADJUSTMENTS

SHIFT LINKAGE, ADJUST

1. Loosen shift rod trunnion nuts.
2. Remove shift rod trunnion to bellcrank retaining lock pin, then disconnect trunnion and shift rod assembly from bell crank.
3. Place gearshift lever into Park position, then lock steering column.
4. Move valve body manual lever rearward into Park.
5. Check for positive engagement of park lock by attempting to rotate drive shaft.
6. Adjust shift rod trunnion to obtain free pin fit in bellcrank arm and tighten trunnion nuts.

KICKDOWN BAND, ADJUST

The kickdown band adjusting screw is located on the left side of the transmission case, **Fig. 5.**
1. Loosen adjusting screw locknut, then back off nut approximately 5 turns.
2. Turn adjusting screw and check for binding. If screw binds, lubricate threads as required.
3. Torque adjusting screw to 72 inch lbs., then back off adjusting screw 2 turns on CJ and Scrambler with 6 or 8 cylinder engine, or 2½ turns on other models.
4. While holding adjusting screw in position, torque lock nut to 35 ft. lbs.

LOW AND REVERSE BAND, ADJUST

Except 1984–85 Cherokee & Wagoneer
1. Raise vehicle, drain transmission and remove oil pan.
2. Loosen adjusting screw lock nut and back off nut approximately five turns, **Fig. 6.** Check adjusting screw for free turning in the lever.
3. Using an inch-pound torque wrench, tighten band adjusting screw to a reading of 72 inch lbs.
4. On 1981 Jeep CJ-7 models with 4-151 engine (model 904 transmission) back off adjusting screw 7 turns from 41 inch lbs. On 1980–83 CJ-7 & Scrambler models (model 999 transmission) back off adjusting screw 4 turns from 72 inch lbs. On 1980–83 Jeep Cherokee and Wagoneer, 1980–85 Truck models (model 727 transmission) and 1984–85 Grand Wagoneer, back off adjusting screw 2 turns, or on 999

A–171

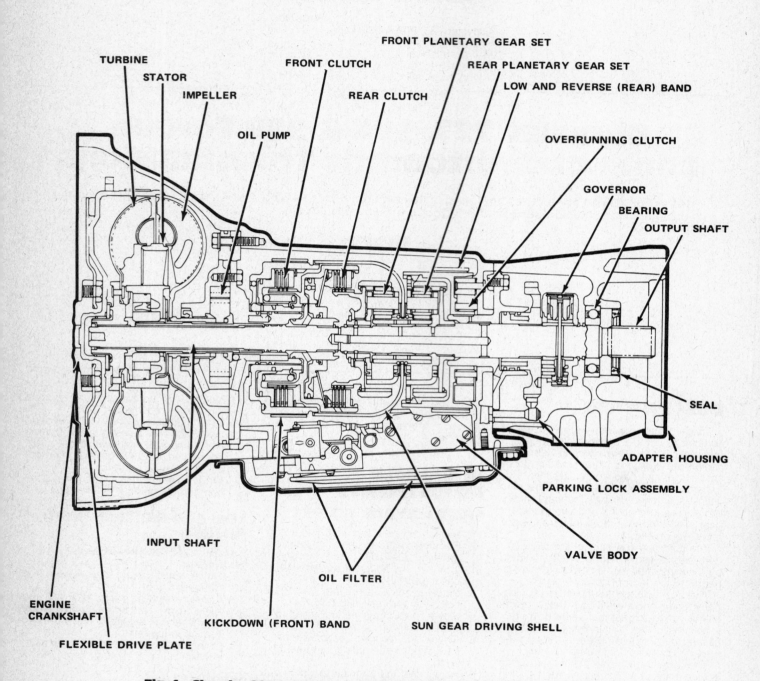

Fig. 1   Chrysler 904 & 999 Torque-Command automatic transmission

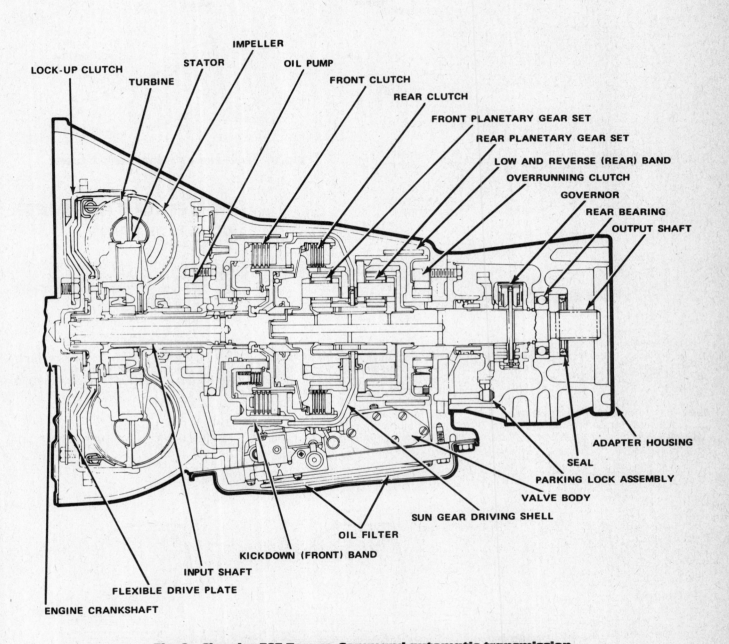

LOCK-UP CLUTCH

TURBINE

STATOR

IMPELLER

OIL PUMP

FRONT CLUTCH

REAR CLUTCH

FRONT PLANETARY GEAR SET

REAR PLANETARY GEAR SET

LOW AND REVERSE (REAR) BAND

OVERRUNNING CLUTCH

GOVERNOR

REAR BEARING

OUTPUT SHAFT

ADAPTER HOUSING

SEAL

PARKING LOCK ASSEMBLY

VALVE BODY

SUN GEAR DRIVING SHELL

OIL FILTER

KICKDOWN (FRONT) BAND

INPUT SHAFT

FLEXIBLE DRIVE PLATE

ENGINE CRANKSHAFT

Fig. 2 Chrysler 727 Torque-Command automatic transmission

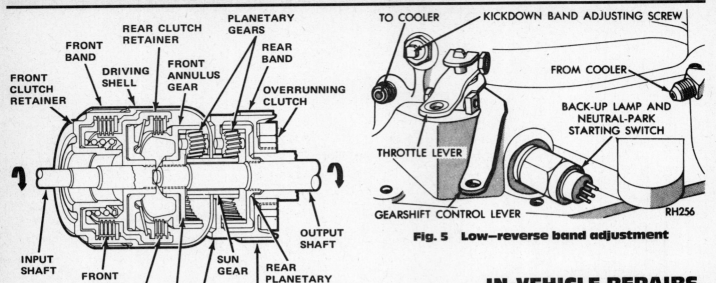

Fig. 3 Clutch, band & gear system

Fig. 5 Low—reverse band adjustment

models, 4 turns from 72 inch lbs. On all models, tighten locknut while holding adjusting screw in position.
5. Install oil pan and fill transmission with fluid.

1984—85 Cherokee & Wagoneer
1. Raise and support vehicle, then remove oil pan and drain transmission fluid.
2. Remove adjusting screw locknut.
3. Torque adjusting screw to 41 inch lbs., then back off. 7 turns.
4. Install locknut and torque to 35 ft. lbs. While tightening locknut, ensure adjusting screw does not rotate.
5. Install oil pan and gasket, then lower vehicle and fill transmission to capacity.

IN-VEHICLE REPAIRS
GOVERNOR VALVE, REPLACE
1. Disconnect battery ground cable.
2. Raise and support vehicle.
3. Mark propeller shaft yokes for assembly reference.
4. Disconnect front and rear propeller shafts from transmission assembly.
5. Disconnect speedometer cable from transfer case.
6. Position a suitable jack under transmission converter housing.
7. Remove rear crossmember assembly.
8. Disconnect parking brake cable at equalizer, then exhaust pipe support brackets, if equipped.
9. Remove transfer case to transmission

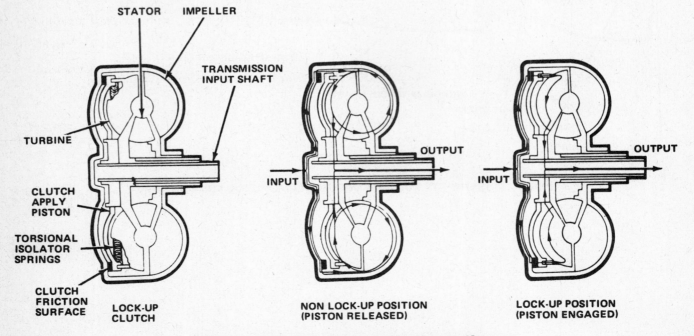

Fig. 4 Lock-up torque converter operation

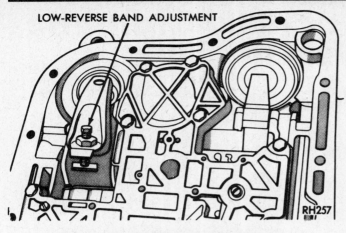

Fig. 6 Kickdown band adjustment

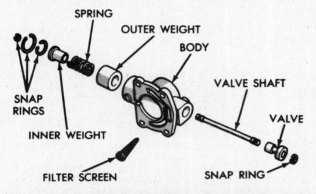

Fig. 8 Exploded view of governor assembly

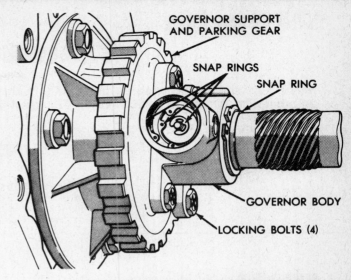

Fig. 7 Governor shaft & weight snap rings

adapter housing attaching bolts, then the transfer case.
10. Rotate transmission output shaft until governor weight faces downward.
11. Remove E-clip from weight end of governor valve shaft assembly, **Fig. 7.**
12. Remove governor valve and shaft from governor body, **Fig. 8.**
13. Remove snap ring retaining governor body parking gear assembly on to output shaft.
14. Remove governor body-park gear assembly from output shaft.
15. Reverse procedure to install.

TRANSMISSION
REPLACE

1. Disconnect battery ground cable.
2. Disconnect transmission filler tube from upper bracket.
3. Raise and support vehicle.
4. Remove inspection cover from torque converter housing.
5. Remove starter motor attaching bolts, then the starter motor.
6. Mark propeller shafts and axle yokes for installation.
7. Disconnect propeller shafts from transfer case yokes.
8. On models equipped with V8 engine, disconnect front exhaust pipes from exhaust manifolds.
9. On Cherokee, Wagoneer and truck models, drain fluid from transfer case assembly. Disconnect speedometer cable from transfer case assembly.
10. Disconnect gearshift and throttle linkages.
11. Disconnect electrical connectors from neutral start switch.
12. Mark torque converter and drive plate for installation, then remove torque converter to drive plate bolts.
13. Position a suitable jack under transmission. Secure transmission onto jack using a safety chain.
14. Remove rear crossmember from vehicle.
15. Disconnect and cap transmission fluid lines.
16. Remove transmission to engine attaching bolts.
17. Lower transmission from vehicle.
18. Reverse procedure to install.

GM Turbo Hydra-Matic 400 Automatic Transmission

NOTE: For service procedures not found in this section, refer to Turbo Hydra-Matic 400 & 475 automatic transmission section in the Chevrolet & GMC chapter.

INDEX

IN-VEHICLE ADJUSTMENTS

SHIFT LINKAGE, ADJUST

1. Place steering column shift lever into neutral position.
2. Raise and support vehicle.
3. Loosen locknut on gearshift rod trunnion enough to permit movement of gearshift rod in trunnion.
4. Place transmission outer range selector lever completely into Neutral detent position, then tighten trunnion locknut to 9 ft. lbs.
5. Lower vehicle and operate steering column gearshift lever in all ranges. Vehicle should start in Park and Neutral detent positions only. Column gearshift lever should engage properly in all detent positions.

NEUTRAL SWITCH, ADJUST

1. Apply parking brake.
2. Check and adjust shift linkage, if necessary.
3. Remove neutral switch from steering column assembly.
4. Place gearshift selector lever in Park position and lock steering column.
5. Move switch actuating lever until it is aligned with letter "P" stamped on back face of switch.
6. Insert a ³⁄₃₂ inch drill into hole located below letter "N" stamped on back face of switch.

TRANSMISSION
REPLACE

1. Disconnect battery ground cable.
2. Remove transmission fluid dipstick.
3. Remove fan shroud, if equipped.
4. Raise and support vehicle.
5. On Cherokee, Wagoneer and truck models, remove parking brake cable nut and adjuster locknut. Remove clip securing parking brake cable to crossmember.
6. On Cherokee, Wagoneer and truck models equipped with low range reduction unit, remove reduction unit shift lever from shift shaft, then the reduction unit.
7. On CJ models with low range reduction unit, disconnect shift rod from reduction unit, then remove reduction unit from vehicle.
8. Disconnect speedometer cable from transmission.
9. Mark then disconnect emergency drive control vacuum line from assembly. Disconnect emergency drive control indicator lamp electrical connector.
10. Remove bolt securing vacuum line from rear of transfer case assembly, if equipped.
11. Disconnect detent solenoid electrical connector from transmission.
12. Remove starter attaching bolts, then the starter motor from vehicle.
13. Remove torque converter housing inspection cover.
14. Mark torque converter and flywheel for installation.
15. Remove torque converter to flywheel attaching nuts.
16. Remove rear support cushion to crossmember attaching nuts.
17. Position a suitable jack under transmission assembly.
18. Raise transmission slightly, then remove crossmember from vehicle.
19. Disconnect gearshift rod and trunnion from outer range selector lever.
20. Disconnect front propeller shaft from transfer case yoke, if equipped.
21. Remove propeller shaft from vehicle.
22. Disconnect and cap transmission fluid cooler lines.
23. Disconnect vacuum hose from vacuum modulator.
24. Position a suitable jack under engine and remove transmission to engine attaching bolts.
25. Remove dipstick tube.
26. Carefully separate transmission assembly from engine.
27. Remove transmission from vehicle.
28. Reverse procedure to install.

CHRYSLER CORP.

SECTION INDEX

DODGE RAMPAGE & PLYMOUTH SCAMP

INDEX OF SERVICE OPERATIONS

NOTE: Refer to page 1 of this manual for vehicle manufacturer's special service tool suppliers.

General Engine Specifications

Year	Engine	Carb.	Bore & Stroke	Comp. Ratio	Horsepower @ R.P.M.	Torque Ft. @ R.P.M.	Normal Oil Pressure psi.
1982	4-135	2 Bbl.	3.44 × 3.62	8.5:1	84 @ 4800	111 @ 2400	45–50
1983–84	4-135	2 Bbl.	3.44 × 3.62	9:1	94 @ 5200	117 @ 3200	50

Alternator & Regulator Specifications

I.D. Tag Color	Ground Polarity	Field Coil Draw Amperes @ 12 Volts	Current Output			Operating Voltage		
			Engine R.P.M.	Amperes	Volts	Engine R.P.M.	Volts	Voltage @ 140°F
Yellow Tag	Neg.	4.5 to 6.5	1250	45	15	1250	15	13.3 to 13.9
Brown Tag	Neg.	4.5 to 6.5	1250	56	15	1250	15	13.3 to 13.9

Starting Motor Specifications

Engine	Model	Ident. No.②	Brush Spring Tension Oz.	Free Speed Test		
				Amps.③	Volts	R.P.M.④
4-135	Bosch	5213045	—	47	11	6600
4-135①	Bosch	5213395	—	47	11	6600
4-135	Nippondenso	5213645	—	47	11	6600

①—Manual Trans.
②—Number located on plate riveted to starter housing.
③—Maximum current drawn.
④—Minimum speed.

Piston, Pin, Ring, Crankshaft & Bearing Specifications

Year	Engine Model	Wristpin Diameter	Piston Clearance, Inch	Ring End Gap, Inch (Minimum)①		Crankpin Diameter, Inch	Rod Bearing Clearance, Inch	Main Bearing Journal Diameter, Inch	Main Bearing Clearance, Inch	End Thrust on Bearing No.	Shaft End Play
				Comp.	Oil						
1982–84	4-135	.9008	.0005–.0015	.011	.015	1.968–1.969	.0008–.0034	2.362–2.363	.0003–.0031	3	.002 to .007

①—Fit rings in tapered bores for clearance listed in tightest portion of ring travel.

continued

Valve Specifications

Year	Engine Model	Valve Lash		Valve Angle		Valve Spring		Valve Stem Clearance		Stem Diameter, Std.	
		Int.	Exh.	Seat	Face	Installed Height	Pressure Lbs. @ In.	Intake	Exhaust	Intake	Exhaust
1982	4-135	Hydraulic①	Hydraulic①	45°	45°	1.65	175 @ 1.22	.0009–.0026	.0028–.0044	.3124	.3103
1983–84	4-135	Hydraulic①	Hydraulic①	45°	45°	1.65	175 @ 1.22	.0009–.0026	.0030–.0047	.3124	.3103

①—No adjustment.

Engine Tightening Specifications★

★ Torque specifications are for clean and lightly lubricated threads only. Dry or dirty threads produce increased friction which prevents accurate measurement of tightness.

Year	Engine Model	Spark Plug Ft. Lbs.	Cylinder Head Bolts Ft. Lbs.	Intake Manifold Inch Lbs.	Exhaust Manifold Inch Lbs.	Camshaft Cover Inch Lbs.	Connecting Rod Cap Bolts Ft. Lbs.	Main Bearing Cap Bolts Ft. Lbs.	Flywheel to Crankshaft Ft. Lbs.	Crankshaft Pulley Ft. Lbs.
1982–84	4-135	26	45①	200	200	105	40①	30①	65②	20.8

①—Turn torque wrench an additional ¼ turn after the specified torque has been achieved.
②—Manual trans.

Wheel Alignment Specifications

Year	Model	Caster Angle, Degrees		Camber Angle, Degrees				Toe In. Inch
		Limits	Desired	Limits		Desired		
				Left	Right	Left	Right	
1982–84	Rampage & Scamp①	—	—	−¼ to +¾	−¼ to +¾	+5/16	+5/16	③
1982–84	Rampage & Scamp②	—	—	−1¼ to −¼	−1¼ to −¼	−¾	−¾	3/32

①—Front wheel alignment.
②—Rear wheel alignment.
③—Toe-out, 1/16 inch.

Brake Specifications

Year	Model	Rear Drum I.D.	Wheel Cyl. Bore		Disc Brake Rotor					Master Cyl. I.D.
			Front Disc	Rear Drum	Nominal Thickness	Minimum Thickness	Thickness Variation (Parallelism)	Run Out (TIR)	Finish (microinch)	
1982	Rampage	7.87	1.893–1.895	.625	.490–.505	.431	.0005	.004	15–80	.875
1983–84	Rampage & Scamp	7.87	2.130	.625	.490–.505	.431	.0005	.004	15–80	.827

continued

Cooling System & Capacity Data

Year	Engine & Model	Cooling Capacity		Radiator Cap Relief Pressure, Lbs.	Thermo-Opening Temp. Degrees F. (Centigrade)	Fuel Tank Gals. (Liters)	Engine Oil Refill Qts. (Liters)	Transaxle Oil		Auto. Trans. Qts. (Liters)
		Less A/C Qts. (Liters)	With A/C Qts. (Liters)					4-Speed Pts. (Liters)	5-Speed Pts. (Liters)	
1982	Rampage 4-135	7 (6.6)	7 (6.6)	14—17	195 (91)	13① (49)	4② (3.8)	4 (1.8)	—	7.5③ (7.1)
1983	Rampage & Scamp 4-135	9 (8.5)	9 (8.5)	10—14	195 (91)	13① (49)	4② (3.8)	4 (1.8)	4.6 (2.1)	8.9 (8.4)
1984	Rampage 4-135	9 (8.5)	9 (8.5)	14—18	195 (91)	13① (49)	4② (3.8)	4 (1.8)	4.6 (2.1)	8.9 (8.4)

①—Approximate.
②—With or without filter.
③—Some 1982 transaxles were manufactured with 1983 oil pans, therefore some 1982 capacities are increased to 8.9 qts. Use dipstick for final check.

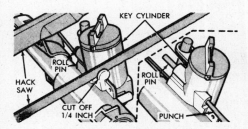

Fig. 1   Ignition lock replacement

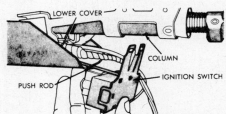

Fig. 2   Ignition switch replacement

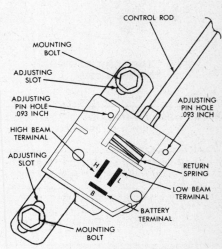

Fig. 3   Dimmer switch replacement

STARTER
REPLACE

1982–84 MODELS

1. Disconnect battery ground cable.
2. Remove starter to flywheel housing and rear bracket to engine or transaxle attaching bolts.
3. Loosen air pump tube at exhaust manifold, then position tube bracket away from starter motor.
4. If equipped, remove heat shield clamp and heat shield.
5. Disconnect battery cable at starter motor and solenoid leads at solenoid, then remove starter motor.
6. Reverse procedure to install.

IGNITION LOCK
REPLACE

1982–84 MODELS

NOTE: Removal and installation of ignition lock must be done with key removed.

1. Disconnect battery ground cable.
2. Remove steering wheel, column covers and turn signal switch, refer to "Steering Wheel, Replace" and "Turn Signal Switch, Replace" procedures.
3. Cut upper ¼ inch from key cylinder retainer pin boss, using a hack saw blade, **Fig. 1.**
4. Remove roll pin from housing, using a suitable punch, then remove key cylinder.
5. Install new cylinder, ensuring it engages the lug or ignition switch driver.
6. Install roll pin and check for proper operation of lock.

STEERING WHEEL & HORN SOUNDER
REPLACE

1982–84 MODELS

1. Disconnect battery ground cable.
2. Remove horn button by carefully lifting with fingers, then the steering wheel nut and horn switch.
3. Remove steering wheel using puller No. C-3428B.
4. To install, align master spline in wheel hub with missing tooth of shaft.
5. Install horn switch, then the steering wheel nut. Torque to 45 ft. lbs.

NOTE: Do not torque steering wheel nut against column lock mechanism, or damage may occur.

6. Install horn button and check for proper operation.

IGNITION SWITCH
REPLACE

1982–84 MODELS

1. Disconnect battery ground cable.
2. Remove electrical connector from ignition switch.
3. Place ignition lock in "Lock" position and remove key.
4. Remove two ignition switch attaching screws and permit switch and push rod to drop below column jacket, **Fig. 2.**
5. Rotate the switch 90° for removal of switch from push rod.
6. To install, position ignition switch in "Lock" position, second detent from top of switch.
7. Place switch at right angle to column and insert push rod.
8. Align switch on bracket and loosely install screws.
9. Apply light rearward force to switch, then tighten attaching screws.

10. Connect ignition switch electrical connector and battery ground cable.
11. Check for proper operation of switch.

LIGHT SWITCH
REPLACE

1982–84 MODELS

1. Disconnect battery ground cable.
2. Reach under instrument panel and depress light switch knob release button, then pull light switch knob and shaft from switch.
3. Remove four bezel attaching screws, then the bezel.
4. Remove switch attaching screws and disconnect electrical connectors from switch.
5. Remove switch from panel.
6. Reverse procedure to install.

DIMMER SWITCH
REPLACE

1982–84 MODELS

1. Disconnect battery ground cable, then the electrical connector from switch.
2. Remove two switch mounting screws, then disengage switch from push rod, **Fig. 3.**
3. To install switch, firmly seat push rod into switch, then compress switch until two .093 inch drill shanks can be inserted into alignment holes. Position upper end of push rod in pocket of wash/wipe switch.

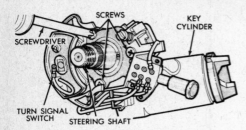

Fig. 4   Turn signal switch replacement

NOTE: This can be done by feel, or if necessary, by removing lower column cover.

4. Apply light rearward force to switch, then install screws and remove drills.

NOTE: Switch should click when lever is lifted, and again as lever returns, just before it reaches its stop in down position.

5. Connect dimmer switch electrical connector, then the battery ground cable.

TURN SIGNAL SWITCH
REPLACE

1982—84 MODELS

1. Disconnect battery ground cable.
2. Remove horn button, three screws and the horn switch.
3. Remove steering wheel nut, then the steering wheel using a suitable puller.
4. Remove lower steering column cover attaching screws, then the column cover.
5. Remove wipe/wash switch attaching screw and position switch aside.
6. Disconnect turn signal and hazard warning switch electrical connector, then disengage wiring harness from support bracket.
7. Remove three turn signal switch attaching screws, **Fig. 4.**
8. Remove turn signal and hazard warning switch while guiding wire harness out from column.
9. Reverse procedure to install.

INSTRUMENT CLUSTER
REPLACE

1982—83 MODELS

1. Disconnect battery ground cable.
2. Remove two mask-lens assembly lower attaching spring pins by pulling rearward with suitable pliers.

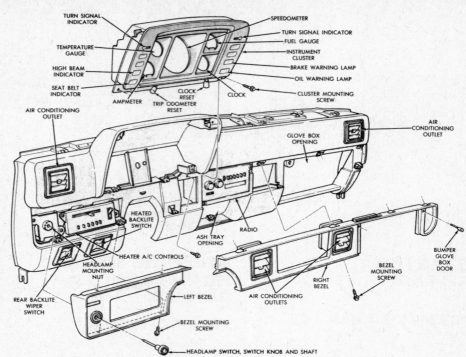

Fig. 5   Instrument panel, exploded view (Typical). 1982—83 models

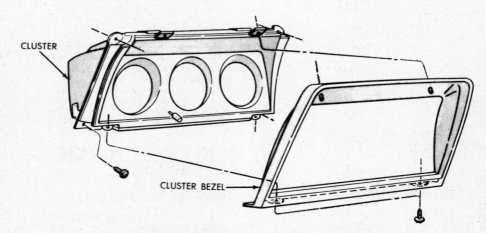

Fig. 6   Instrument cluster & bezel. 1984 models

3. Pull mask-lens rearward, lower slightly and remove from cluster.
4. Remove two speedometer attaching screws, then the speedometer.
5. Disconnect wire harness electrical connectors.
6. Remove cluster attaching screws, **Fig. 5,** and pull cluster from dash.
7. Reach behind cluster and disconnect clock and tachometer wiring, if equipped.
8. Remove cluster from vehicle.
9. Reverse procedure to install.

1984 MODELS

1. Disconnect battery ground cable.
2. Remove two lower cluster bezel attaching screws, **Fig. 6.**
3. Allow bezel to drop slightly, then remove bezel.
4. Remove four screws securing instrument cluster and pull cluster away from dash.
5. Disconnect electrical connectors and speedometer cable, then remove cluster.
6. Reverse procedure to install.

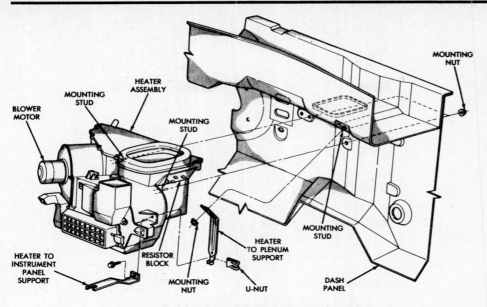

Fig. 7   Heater assembly. Models less A/C

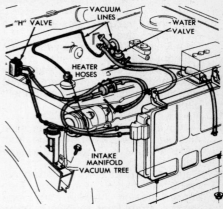

Fig. 8   Air conditioning & heater hose routing

WIPER SWITCH
REPLACE

1982–84 MODELS

1. Disconnect battery ground cable.
2. Disconnect wiper switch and turn signal switch wiring harness connectors.
3. Remove lower column cover, then the horn button.
4. Place ignition switch in "Off" position and turn steering wheel so access hole in hub area is at 9 o'clock position on 1983–84 models, and in 3 o'clock position on 1982 models.
5. Loosen turn signal lever screw through access hole using a suitable screwdriver.
6. Disengage dimmer push rod from wiper switch.
7. Unsnap wiring clip and remove wiper switch.
8. Reverse procedure to install.

WINDSHIELD WIPER MOTOR
REPLACE

1982–84 MODELS

1. Disconnect battery ground cable.
2. Remove wiper arm assemblies.
3. Remove nuts from right and left pivots.
4. Open hood, then remove wiper motor plastic cover and washer hose attaching clip.
5. Disconnect wiper motor electrical connector.
6. Remove three bolts from wiper motor mounting bracket.

7. Disengage pivots from cowl top mounting positions.
8. Remove wiper motor, cranks, pivots and drive link assembly from cowl plenum chamber.
9. Remove wiper motor from drive crank linkage.
10. Reverse procedure to install.

RADIO
REPLACE

1982–84 MODELS

1. Disconnect battery ground cable.
2. Remove right bezel attaching screws, then the bezel. On 1982–83 models, open glove box and guide bezel around glove box as needed.
3. Remove radio attaching screws.
4. Pull radio from panel and disconnect wiring ground strap and antenna lead from radio.
5. Remove radio from vehicle.
6. Reverse procedure to install.

HEATER CORE
REPLACE

LESS A/C

1982–84 Models

1. Disconnect battery ground cable, then drain cooling system.
2. Disconnect blower motor electrical connector, then remove ash tray.
3. Depress red color coded tab on end of temperature control cable, and pull control cable out of receiver on heater assembly.
4. Remove glove box and door assembly.

5. Disconnect heater hoses and plug heater core tube openings.
6. Remove two heater assembly to dash panel attaching nuts, **Fig. 7**.
7. Disconnect blower resistor electrical connector, then remove heater support brace to instrument panel attaching screws.
8. Remove heater support bracket nut, then disconnect strap from plenum stud and lower heater assembly from under instrument panel.
9. Depress yellow color coded tab on end of mode door control cable out of receiver on heater assembly.
10. Move heater unit towards right side of vehicle, then out from under instrument panel.
11. Remove left heater outlet duct attaching screws, then the heater outlet duct.
12. Remove four blower motor mounting plate attaching screws, then the blower motor assembly.
13. Remove four outside air and defroster door cover attaching screws, then the door cover.
14. Remove defroster door assembly, then lift defroster door control rod out of heater assembly.
15. Remove 8 heater core cover attaching screws, then the core cover.
16. Slide heater core up and out of heater assembly.
17. Reverse procedure to install.

WITH A/C

1984 Models

1. Disconnect battery ground cable, then drain cooling system and discharge A/C system.
2. Disconnect blend air door cable and disengage from clip on heater air duct.
3. Remove glove box and door assembly.
4. Remove center bezel attaching screws, then the center bezel.
5. Remove center distribution duct and defroster duct adapter.
6. Disconnect heater hoses and A/C

lines. Plug heater core tube openings.

7. Disconnect vacuum lines at engine and water valve, **Fig. 8.**
8. Remove four dash retaining nuts, then the right side cowl trim panel.
9. Remove right instrument panel pivot bracket attaching screw, then the two screws attaching lower instrument panel at steering column.
10. Remove panel top cover.
11. Remove all but left panel to fenceline attaching screw, then pull carpet from under A/C unit as far rearward as possible.
12. Remove support strap attaching nut and blower motor ground cable, then support heater unit with hands and remove strap from its plenum stud, **Fig. 9.**
13. Lift and pull evaporator heater assembly rearward to clear dash panel and liner. The panel will also have to be pulled rearward to allow assembly clearance.
14. Remove evaporator heater assembly from dash panel, taking care to prevent dash panel attaching studs from hanging up in dash liner.
15. Place evaporator heater assembly on work bench, then remove nut from mode door actuator arm on top cover.
16. Remove two retaining clips from front edge of cover, then the mode door actuator to cover attaching screws and mode door actuator.
17. Remove 15 heater unit cover attaching screws, then the cover. Lift mode door out of heater assembly.
18. Remove heater core tube retaining bracket attaching screw, then lift core from heater assembly.
19. Reverse procedure to install.

1982—83 Models

1. Disconnect battery ground cable, then drain cooling system and discharge A/C system.
2. Disconnect heater hose at heater core. Plug heater core tube opening.
3. Disconnect vacuum lines at engine intake manifold and water valve, **Fig. 8.**
4. Remove expansion valve ("H" valve), **Fig. 8,** as follows:
   a. Disconnect low pressure cut-off switch electrical connector, located on side of "H" valve.
   b. Remove hex head bolt from center of plumbing sealing plate.
   c. Pull refrigerant line assembly towards front of vehicle.
   d. Remove two allen head cap screws, then carefully remove the disassembled valve.
5. Remove hose clamp, then the condensate drain tube from evaporator heater assembly.
6. Remove evaporator heater assembly to dash panel attaching nuts, then depress red color coded tab on end of temperature control cable and pull control cable out of receiver on heater

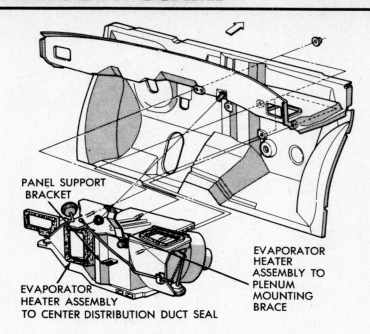

PANEL SUPPORT BRACKET

EVAPORATOR HEATER ASSEMBLY TO CENTER DISTRIBUTION DUCT SEAL

EVAPORATOR HEATER ASSEMBLY TO PLENUM MOUNTING BRACE

Fig. 9 Heater assembly. Models with A/C

assembly.

7. Remove glove box and door assembly, then disconnect vacuum harness from heater A/C control, located under instrument panel.
8. Disconnect blower motor electrical connector.
9. Remove right trim bezel to instrument panel attaching screws, then the right trim bezel.
10. Remove center distribution duct to instrument panel attaching screws, then the distribution duct.
11. Remove defroster duct adapter, then the panel support bracket.
12. Remove right side cowl lower panel, then the right side instrument panel pivot bracket screw.
13. Remove screws attaching lower instrument panel to steering column, then pull carpet from under evaporator heater assembly as far rearward as possible.
14. Remove nut attaching evaporator heater assembly to plenum mounting brace and blower motor ground cable, then support heater assembly with hands and remove mounting brace from its stud, **Fig. 9.**
15. Lift and pull evaporator heater assembly rearward to clear dash panel and liner. The panel will also have to be pulled rearward to allow assembly clearance.
16. Remove evaporator heater assembly from dash panel, taking care to prevent dash panel attaching studs from hanging up in dash liner.
17. Place evaporator assembly on work bench, then remove nut from mode door actuator arm on top cover.
18. Remove two retaining clips from front edge of cover, then the mode door actuator to cover attaching screws and mode door actuator.

19. Remove 15 heater assembly cover attaching screws, then lift cover door out of heater assembly.
20. Remove heater core tube retaining bracket attaching screw, then lift core from heater assembly.
21. Reverse procedure to install.

BLOWER MOTOR
REPLACE

LESS A/C

1. Disconnect battery ground cable.
2. Disconnect blower motor wiring connector.
3. Remove left heater outlet duct.
4. Remove five blower mounting plate to heater assembly attaching screws.
5. Remove blower motor assembly.
6. Reverse procedure to install.

WITH A/C

1. Disconnect battery ground cable.
2. Remove three glove box to instrument panel attaching screws, then the glove box.
3. Disconnect blower motor wiring connector. Remove wires from retaining clip on recirculating housing.
4. Disconnect blower motor vent tube from A/C unit.
5. Loosen recirculation door actuator from bracket and remove actuator from housing. Do not disconnect vacuum lines.
6. Remove seven recirculating housing to A/C unit attaching screws, then the recirculating housing.
7. Remove three blower motor mounting flange nuts, then the blower motor.
8. Reverse procedure to install.

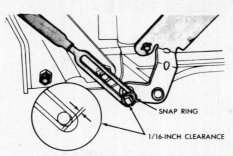

Fig. 10 Throttle control cable

SNAP RING

1/16-INCH CLEARANCE

SPEED CONTROL
LOCK-IN SCREW ADJUSTMENT

NOTE: Lock-in accuracy can be affected by poor engine performance, overloading of vehicle, or improper slack in throttle control cable.

1. If the above note has been taken into consideration and vehicle speed still varies or drops more than 2–3 mph when speed control is activated, proceed as follows:
   a. Turn lock-in adjusting screw counterclockwise approximately ¼ turn for every 1 mph out of adjustment.
2. If vehicle speed increases more than 2–3 mph when speed control is activated, proceed as follows:
   a. Turn lock-in adjusting screw clockwise approximately ¼ turn for every 1 mph out of adjustment.

NOTE: The above adjustments should not exceed two turns in either direction, or damage to unit may occur.

STOP LIGHT SWITCH
REPLACE

1982–84 MODELS

1. Disconnect battery ground cable.
2. Disconnect stop light switch electrical connector, then remove switch assembly attaching screw and switch from brake pedal bracket.
3. Install new switch and connect switch electrical connector. Torque attaching bolt to 75 inch lbs.
4. If adjustment is required, proceed as follows:
   a. Loosen switch assembly to brake pedal bracket attaching screw and slide switch assembly away from brake pedal blade.
   b. Depress brake pedal and allow it to return freely.

NOTE: Do not pull brake pedal back at any time.

   c. Place a .130 inch (3.275mm) spacer gauge on brake pedal blade.
   d. Slide switch assembly toward pedal blade until switch plunger is fully depressed against spacer gauge without moving the pedal.
   e. Torque stop light switch attaching screw to 75 inch lbs.
   f. Remove spacer and ensure stop light switch does not prevent full brake pedal return.

NEUTRAL START & BACK-UP LIGHT SWITCH
REPLACE

1982–84 MODELS

NOTE: The following procedure applies to automatic transaxle equipped models only. On manual transaxle equipped models, a back-up light switch is mounted on transaxle case.

1. Disconnect battery ground cable.
2. Disconnect switch wiring connector.
3. Remove switch from transaxle case, allow fluid to drain into a suitable container.
4. Install switch with new seal into transaxle case and connect switch wiring connector. Torque switch to 24 ft. lbs.

THROTTLE CONTROL CABLE ADJUSTMENT

1. Start engine and allow to reach normal operating temperature.
2. Remove snap ring, then check clearance between throttle stud and cable clevis, **Fig. 10**.
3. If adjustment is required, proceed as follows:
   a. Loosen cable clamp attaching nut.
   b. Pull all slack out of cable, using head of throttle stud as a gauge.

NOTE: Do not pull cable so tight that it moves throttle away from curb idle position.

   c. Torque cable clamp attaching nut to 45 inch lbs. and move cable clevis back on round portion of stud.
4. Install snap ring and check for proper operation.

Engine Section

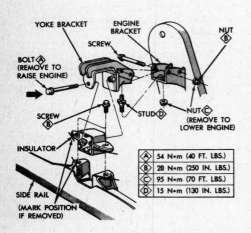

A	54 N•m (40 FT. LBS.)
B	28 N•m (250 IN. LBS.)
C	95 N•m (70 FT. LBS.)
D	15 N•m (130 IN. LBS.)

Fig. 1   Engine mount. 1982–83, right side

| A | 54 N•m (40 FT. LBS.) |
| B | 95 N•m (70 FT. LBS.) |

Fig. 2   Front engine mount. 1982–83

| A | 54 N•m (40 FT. LBS.) |
| B | 75 N•m (55 FT. LBS.) |

Fig. 3   Engine mount. 1982–83, left side w/automatic transaxle

ENGINE MOUNTS
REPLACE

NOTE: Before removing engine mounts on 1982–83 models, driveshaft length should be measured to ensure correct engine and driveshaft positioning during installation. When positioning the engine on 1984 models, check driveshaft length as outlined in the "Front Suspension & Steering Section" under "Driveshaft Length, Adjust." On all models, the engine mounts incorporate slotted bolt holes and permit side-to-side positioning of the engine, thereby affecting the length of the driveshaft. Failure to properly position the engine may result in extensive damage to the engine.

Refer to **Figs. 1 through 7** when replacing engine mounts.

NOTE: On 1982–83 vehicles, the left engine mount is attached with two types of mounting screws. Two of the three are of the pilot type with extended tips. Extended tip screws must be installed in proper position, **Fig. 8.** Damage to shift cover or difficult shifting may occur if screws are incorrectly installed.

ENGINE
REPLACE

1982–83 MODELS

1. Disconnect battery ground cable.
2. Scribe alignment marks on hood and hood hinge, then remove hood.
3. Drain cooling system, then disconnect radiator hoses at radiator and engine.
4. Remove radiator and fan shroud, then remove air cleaner.
5. If equipped with A/C, remove compressor from the mounting bracket

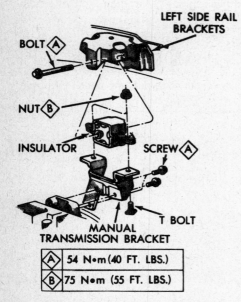

| A | 54 N•m (40 FT. LBS.) |
| B | 75 N•m (55 FT. LBS.) |

Fig. 4   Engine mount. 1982–83, left side w/manual transaxle

Fig. 5   Engine mount. 1984, right side

A–28 N•m (250 IN. LBS.)
B–95 N•m (70 FT. LBS.)

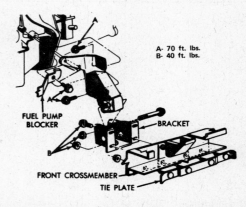

A– 70 ft. lbs.
B– 40 ft. lbs.

Fig. 6   Front engine mount. 1984

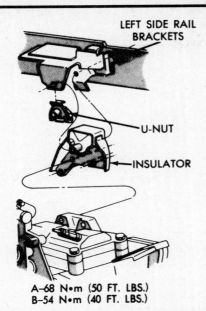

Fig. 7 Engine mount. 1984, left side

A–68 N•m (50 FT. LBS.)
B–54 N•m (40 FT. LBS.)

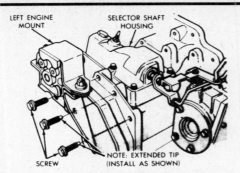

Fig. 8 Correct positioning of extended tip screws

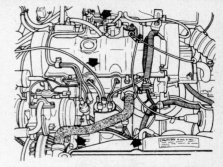

Fig. 9 Position of electrical connectors

Fig. 10 Fuel line, heater hose and accelerator connections

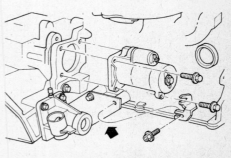

Fig. 11 Starter motor removal

and position aside with the hoses attached.

6. Remove power steering pump from mounting bracket and position aside with the hoses attached, if equipped.
7. Drain crankcase and remove the oil filter.
8. Disconnect the wire connectors at the alternator, carburetor and engine, **Fig. 9.**
9. Disconnect fuel line, heater hose and the accelerator cable, **Fig. 10.**
10. Remove alternator from mounting bracket and position aside.
11. On models equipped with manual transmission, disconnect clutch cable, then remove transmission lower cover.
12. Disconnect exhaust pipe at the manifold, then remove the starter motor, **Fig. 11.**
13. On models equipped with automatic transmission, remove transmission case lower cover and place alignment

marks on the flex plate and torque converter. Remove converter to flex plate attaching screws. Attach a C-clamp to the front lower position of the housing so as to retain the torque converter in the housing when removing the engine.

14. On all models, install a suitable transmission holding fixture and attach a suitable lifting device, **Fig. 12.**
15. Remove right hand inner splash shield, then disconnect ground strap, **Fig. 13.**
16. Remove right hand engine mount through bolts.
17. Remove transmission case-to-engine-block attaching bolts.
18. Remove front engine mount bolt.
19. On 1983 vehicles with manual transmission, remove anti-roll strut, **Fig. 14.**
20. On all models, carefully lift engine from vehicle.
21. Reverse procedure to install.

1984 MODELS

1. Perform steps 1 through 15 for 1982–83 models.
2. Remove long bolt through yoke bracket and insulator.

NOTE: If insulator screws are to be removed, mark position on side rail for exact reinstallation.

3. Remove transmission case to cylinder block mounting screws.
4. Remove front engine mount screw and nut.
5. On vehicles with manual transmission, remove anti-roll strut, **Fig. 14.**
6. On vehicles with manual transmission, remove insulator through bolt from inside wheel house, or the insulator bracket to transmission screws.
7. On all vehicles, carefully remove engine from vehicle.
8. Reverse procedure to install.

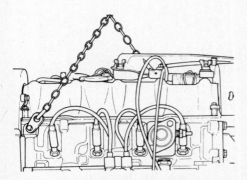

Fig. 12 Engine lifting device attached

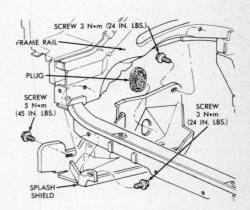

Fig. 13 Right inner splash shield

A–22 N•m (16 FT. LBS.)
B–28 N•m (250 IN. LBS.)
C–54 N•m (40 FT. LBS.)

TORQUE	
A	54 N•m	40 FT. LBS.
B	41 N•m	30 FT. LBS.
C	23 N•m	200 IN. LBS.

TORQUES	
A	54 N•m	40 FT. LBS.
B	41 N•m	30 FT. LBS.

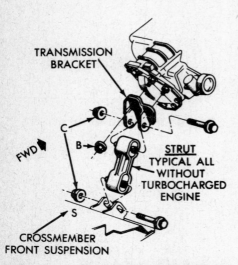

Fig. 14   Anti-roll strut (Typical)

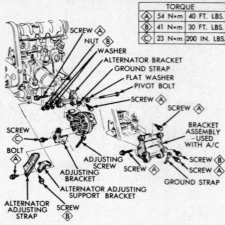

Fig. 15   Alternator & compressor mounting bracket removal

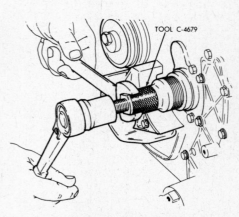

Fig. 16   Power steering pump mounting bracket

TIMING SPROCKETS & OIL SEAL REPLACE

ALTERNATOR BELT REMOVAL

1. Disconnect battery ground cable.
2. Loosen alternator locking screw, then loosen adjusting screw and remove the alternator belt.
3. Reverse procedure to install.

ALTERNATOR & COMPRESSOR MOUNTING BRACKET REMOVAL

For replacement of alternator and compressor mounting bracket, refer to **Fig. 15**.

POWER STEERING PUMP MOUNTING BRACKET REMOVAL

1. Remove pump locking screw, **Fig. 16**.
2. Remove pivot bolt and pivot nut, then the drive belt.
3. Remove power steering pump and lay aside.
4. Remove mounting bracket bolts, then the bracket.
5. Reverse procedure to install.

CRANKSHAFT PULLEY & WATER PUMP PULLEY REMOVAL

1. Remove screws retaining water pump pulley to pump shaft, **Fig. 17**.

2. Remove bolts retaining crankshaft pulley.
3. Raise and support front of vehicle, then remove right inner splash shield and remove crankshaft pulley.
4. Reverse procedure to install.

TIMING BELT COVER REMOVAL

1. Remove nuts securing timing belt cover to the cylinder head, **Fig. 18**.
2. Remove screws securing the cover to the cylinder head, then remove both halves of the timing belt cover.
3. Position a suitable jack under engine, then remove right hand engine mount-bolt and raise engine slightly.
4. Loosen timing belt tensioner, then remove timing belt.
5. Reverse procedure to install.

NOTE: On 1983–84 models, torque all attaching hardware to 40 inch lbs.

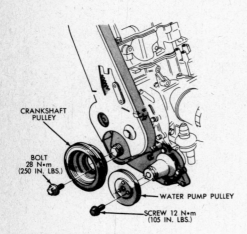

Fig. 17   Crankshaft and water pump pulley removal

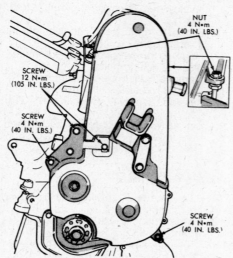

Fig. 18   Timing belt cover removal

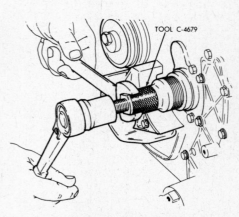

Fig. 19   Crankshaft, intermediate shaft & camshaft oil seal removal

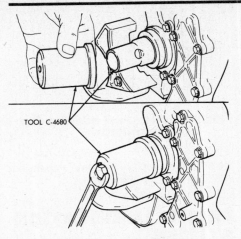

Fig. 20 Crankshaft, intermediate shaft & camshaft oil seal installation

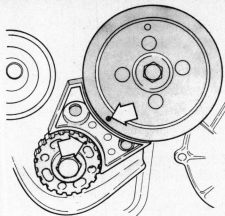

Fig. 21 Aligning crankshaft & intermediate shaft timing marks

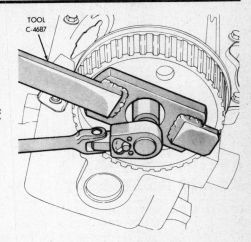

Fig. 22 Camshaft & intermediate shaft replacement

CRANKSHAFT SPROCKET REMOVAL

1. With the timing belt removed from engine, remove the crankshaft sprocket bolt.
2. Remove crankshaft sprocket using a suitable puller.

CRANKSHAFT, INTERMEDIATE SHAFT & CAMSHAFT OIL SEAL SERVICE

Refer to **Figs. 19 and 20,** for removal and installation of crankshaft, intermediate shaft or camshaft seals.

CRANKSHAFT & INTERMEDIATE SHAFT TIMING

1. Rotate crankshaft and intermediate shaft until markings on sprockets are aligned, **Fig. 21.**

CAMSHAFT TIMING

1. Rotate camshaft until arrows on hub are aligned with No. 1 camshaft cap to cylinder head line. Small hole must be located along vertical centerline.
2. Install timing belt. Refer to "Adjusting Drive Belt Tension" described elsewhere, for proper drive belt adjustment.
3. Rotate crankshaft two full revolutions and recheck timing.

NOTE: Do not allow oil or solvents to contact the timing belt, since they will deteriorate the rubber and cause tooth slippage.

CAMSHAFT & INTERMEDIATE SHAFT REMOVAL & INSTALLATION

Refer to **Fig. 22,** for removal and installation of camshaft and intermediate shaft sprocket.

ADJUSTING DRIVE BELT TENSION

1. Remove spark plugs, then rotate crankshaft to TDC position.
2. Using a suitable tool, loosen tensioner lock nut, **Fig. 23.**
3. Reset tension so that belt tensioning tool's axis is within 15° of horizontal.
4. Rotate crankshaft two revolutions in a clockwise direction and position at TDC, then tighten tensioner lock nut.

INTAKE & EXHAUST MANIFOLD
REPLACE

1. Disconnect battery ground cable and drain coolant system.
2. Remove air cleaner and disconnect all vacuum and fuel lines, and electrical connectors from carburetor.
3. Disconnect throttle linkage, and remove power steering pump drive belt.
4. Disconnect power brake vacuum hose from carburetor, if equipped.
5. Disconnect hose from water crossover, then raise and support vehicle and disconnect exhaust pipe from exhaust manifold.
6. Remove power steering pump and position aside, then remove intake manifold support bracket.
7. Remove EGR tube, then remove intake manifold retaining screws.
8. Lower vehicle and remove intake manifold.
9. Remove exhaust manifold retaining nuts, then the exhaust manifold.
10. Reverse procedure to install.

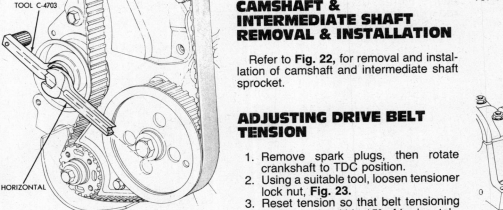

Fig. 23 Adjusting drive belt tension

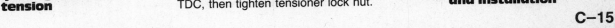

Fig. 24 Valve spring removal and installation

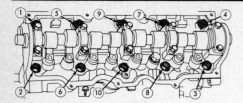

Fig. 25   Cylinder head bolt removal sequence

Fig. 26   Cylinder head bolt tightening sequence

Fig. 27   Camshaft bearing cap installation

CYLINDER HEAD & VALVE ASSEMBLY

SERVICE BULLETIN Some engines may be equipped with cylinder heads which have oversize journals. When servicing the cylinder head on these engines, proper replacement components must be installed. To identify over size cylinder head journals, the top of the bearing caps are painted green and "O/S J" is stamped on air pump end of head.

REMOVING & INSTALLING VALVE SPRINGS

Cylinder Head-On Engine

1. Rotate crankshaft until piston is at TDC on compression stroke.
2. Apply 90–120 psi of compressed air into spark plug hole of valve spring being removed.
3. Using tool 4682, compress valve spring enough to remove valve stem locks, **Fig. 24**.
4. Remove valve spring and spring seat.
5. Remove valve seal.

CYLINDER HEAD BOLT REMOVAL SEQUENCE

SERVICE BULLETIN On 1982 models, oil leaks in the left front head gasket area may be found. If oil leakage is found, loosen cylinder head bolts ¼ turn and retorque according to specifications.

When removing cylinder head, remove cylinder head bolts in proper sequence, **Fig. 25**.

CYLINDER HEAD BOLT TIGHTENING SEQUENCE

Refer to **Fig. 26** for cylinder head bolt tightening sequence.

CAMSHAFT BEARING CAPS

SERVICE BULLETIN Some engines may be equipped with camshafts which have oversize journals. When servicing the camshaft on these engines, proper replacement components must be installed. To identify oversize camshaft journals, the barrel of the cam is painted green and "O/S J" is stamped on the air pump end of the camshaft. Never install an oversize journal camshaft in a cylinder head with standard size bores, or cam cap breakage could result.

1. With caps removed from engine, check oil holes for obstructions.
2. With caps aligned in proper sequence, make sure arrow on caps 1, 2, 3 and 4 point toward timing belt, **Fig. 27**.
3. Apply suitable sealant to No. 1 and 5 bearing caps.
4. Install caps before installing camshaft seals, then torque cap bolts to 165 inch lbs.

PISTON & ROD ASSEMBLY

When installing the piston and rod assembly, the indentation on the top of piston must face the timing belt side of the engine, **Fig. 28**. The oil hole on connecting rod must also face the timing belt side of the engine and be on the same side as the indented mark on the piston.

ENGINE LUBRICATION SYSTEM

SERVICE BULLETIN Some 1982 engines may exhibit a knock sound similar to a diesel engine. This noise occurs after a previously warmed up engine has sat for 4 hours or longer and been restarted. To alleviate this condition, a new oil filter adapter has been released which has an integral check valve. The new part No. is 4273323, and is used on all later models. When installing this adapter, inspect the check valve for proper operation by inserting a screwdriver in the oil filter end of the adapter and lightly pushing on the check valve. Under very light pressure, the valve should freely move ¼ inch. If the valve sticks or binds, replace the oil filter adapter. A sticking valve may restrict oil pressure, possibly resulting in engine damage.

OIL PUMP ASSEMBLY

1. With oil pan removed, remove the screw securing oil pump to the cylinder block, **Fig. 29**.
2. Reverse procedure to install. Torque oil pump attaching screw to 200 inch lbs.

OIL PUMP SERVICE

1. Measure the following oil pump clearances:

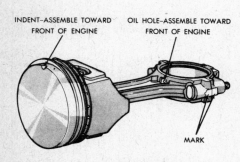

INDENT—ASSEMBLE TOWARD FRONT OF ENGINE

OIL HOLE—ASSEMBLE TOWARD FRONT OF ENGINE

MARK

Fig. 28   Piston & connecting rod assembly

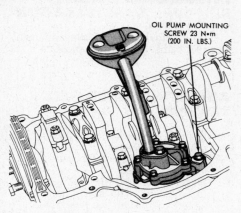

OIL PUMP MOUNTING SCREW 23 N•m (200 IN. LBS.)

Fig. 29   Oil pump assembly

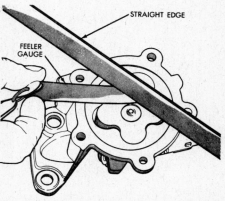

STRAIGHT EDGE

FEELER GAUGE

Fig. 30   Checking oil pump end play

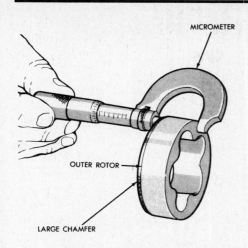

Fig. 31 Measuring oil pump outer rotor thickness

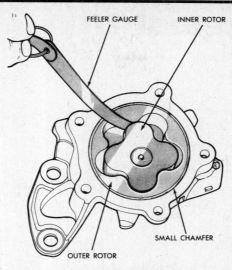

Fig. 32 Measuring clearance between oil pump rotors

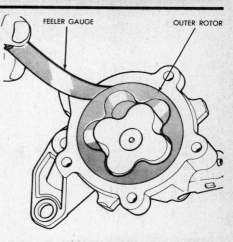

Fig. 33 Measuring oil pump outer rotor clearance

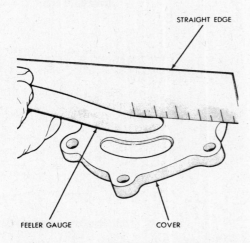

Fig. 34 Measuring oil pump cover clearance

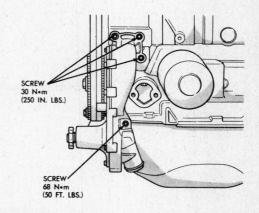

Fig. 35 Water pump to cylinder block attaching bolts

a. End play, **Fig. 30.** End play should be .001–.006 inch on 1982 vehicles, or .001–.004 inch on 1983–84 vehicles.

b. Outer rotor thickness, **Fig. 31.** Thickness should be .825 inch, minimum. Install outer rotor with chamfered edge in pump body.

c. Clearance between rotors, **Fig. 32,** should be .010 inch, maximum.

d. Outer rotor clearance, **Fig. 33.** Clearance should be .014 inch, maximum.

e. Oil pump cover clearance, **Fig. 34,** should be no greater than .015 inch on 1982 vehicles, or .003 inch on 1983–84 vehicles.

f. Oil pressure relief valve spring length should be 1.95 inches.

WATER PUMP
REPLACE

1. Disconnect battery ground cable.
2. Drain cooling system, then remove upper radiator hose.
3. Remove A/C compressor from mounting brackets and position aside with refrigerant lines attached, if equipped.
4. Remove alternator.
5. Disconnect lower radiator hose, bypass hose and four water pump to engine attaching screws, **Fig. 35,** then remove water pump from engine.
6. Reverse procedure to install.

BELT TENSION DATA

		NEW	USED
1982–84	Air Cond.	95	80
	Alternator	115	80
	Power Steer.	95	80

Clutch & Manual Transaxle Section

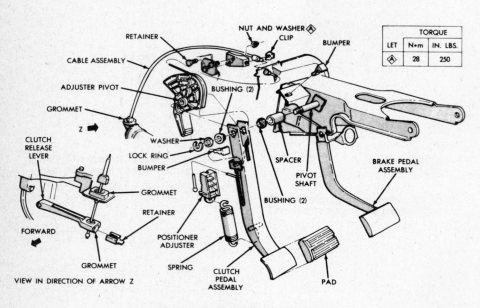

TORQUE		
LET	N•m	IN. LBS.
◊	28	250

Fig. 1   Clutch cable routing

VIEW IN DIRECTION OF ARROW Z

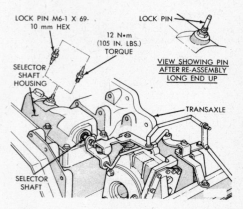

Fig. 2   Lock pin removal & installation

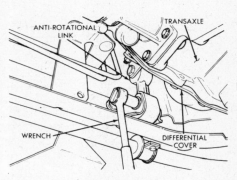

Fig. 4   Removing anti-rotational link

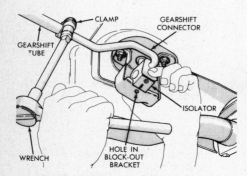

Fig. 3   Adjusting gear shift linkage

CLUTCH
ADJUST

The clutch release cable, **Fig. 1**, on these models cannot be adjusted. When the cable is properly routed, the spring between the clutch pedal and positioner adjuster will hold the clutch cable in the proper position. An adjuster pivot is used to hold release cable in place to ensure complete clutch release when the clutch pedal is depressed.

CLUTCH
REPLACE

1. Remove transmission as outlined under "Manual Transaxle, Replace" procedure.
2. Mark relationship between clutch cover and flywheel for reference during reassembly, then insert suitable clutch disc aligning tool through clutch disc hub.
3. Gradually loosen clutch cover attaching bolts, then remove pressure plate and cover assembly and disc from flywheel.
4. Remove clutch release shaft and slide release bearing assembly off input shaft seal retainer. Remove fork from release bearing thrust plate.
5. Reverse procedure to install. Align reference marks made during reassembly. Using clutch disc alignment tool, install disc, plate and cover to flywheel and torque bolts to 21 ft. lbs.

GEARSHIFT LINKAGE
ADJUST

1. Remove lock pin from transaxle selec-

tor shaft housing, **Fig. 2.**
2. Reverse lock pin, so long end is facing downward, and insert pin into same threaded hole while pushing selector shaft into selector housing.
3. Raise and support vehicle, then loosen clamp bolt that secures gearshift tube to gearshift rod.
4. Check that gearshift connector slides and rotates freely in gearshift tube.
5. Position shifter mechanism connector assembly so that isolater is spaced .050 inch away from upstanding flange. Align holes in block-out bracket, then hold connector isolater in this position while torquing nut on gearshift tube to 170 inch lbs. Excessive force should not be used on linkage during this procedure, **Fig. 3.**
6. Lower vehicle, remove lock pin from selector shaft housing and reinstall lock pin in reversed position. Torque pin to 105 inch lbs.
7. Check for proper operation.

MANUAL TRANSAXLE
REPLACE

1. Disconnect battery ground cable.
2. Raise and support vehicle and install suitable engine support fixture.
3. Disconnect gearshift linkage and clutch cable from transaxle.
4. Remove front wheel and tire assemblies.
5. Remove left front splash shield, then the impact bracket from transaxle if so equipped.
6. Refer to "Driveshafts, Replace" to disconnect driveshafts.
7. Support transaxle and remove upper clutch housing bolts.
8. Remove left engine mount from transaxle noting location of bolts.
9. Remove anti-rotational link, if equipped, **Fig. 4**.
10. Move engine to transaxle toward left side of vehicle until mainshaft clears clutch, then lower and remove transaxle.
12. Reverse procedure to install. When installing left engine mount, refer to "Engine Mounts, Replace" in "Engine Section."

Rear Axle, Rear Suspension & Brakes Section

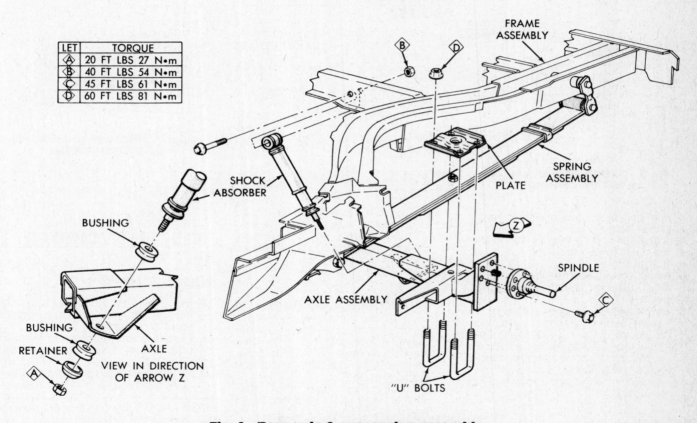

LET	TORQUE	
A	20 FT LBS	27 N•m
B	40 FT LBS	54 N•m
C	45 FT LBS	61 N•m
D	60 FT LBS	81 N•m

Fig. 1   Rear axle & suspension assembly

REAR AXLE & SPRING
REPLACE

REMOVAL

1. Raise and support vehicle, then position suitable floor jack under axle assembly and raise axle assembly to relieve weight on rear springs.
2. Disconnect rear brake proportioning valve spring, then the lower ends of rear shock absorbers at axle brackets, **Fig. 1**.
3. Remove U-bolt attaching nuts, then the U-bolt and spring plate.
4. Lower rear axle assembly, allowing rear spring to hang free.
5. Remove front pivot bolt from front spring hanger.
6. Remove rear spring shackle attaching nuts, then the shackles from the spring.
7. Remove springs from vehicle.

INSTALLATION

1. Assemble shackle and bushings in rear of spring and rear spring hanger, then install shackle bolt, **Figs. 1 and 2**. Do not tighten nut at this point.
2. Raise front of spring, then install pivot bolt and attaching nut. Do not tighten nut at this point.
3. Raise axle assembly into correct posi-

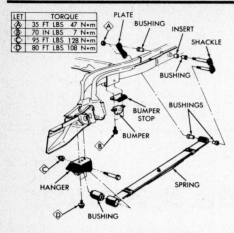

LET	TORQUE	
Ⓐ	35 FT LBS	47 N·m
Ⓑ	70 IN LBS	7 N·m
Ⓒ	95 FT LBS	128 N·m
Ⓓ	80 FT LBS	108 N·m

Fig. 2 Rear spring installation

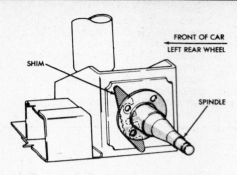

Fig. 3 Shim installation for toe-out

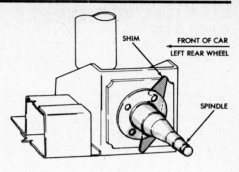

Fig. 4 Shim installation for toe-in

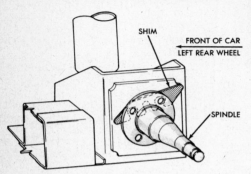

Fig. 5 Shim installation for positive camber

tion with axle centered under spring center bolt.
4. Install spring plate, U-bolts and attaching nuts. Torque attaching nuts to 60 ft. lbs.
5. Install shock absorbers and attaching nuts. Do not tighten nuts at this point.
6. Lower vehicle to floor, allowing full weight of vehicle on wheels, then torque the following fasteners: front pivot bolt, 95 ft. lbs.; shackle nuts, 35 ft. lbs.; upper shock absorber attaching nut, 40 ft. lbs.
7. Connect rear brake proportioning valve spring.

REAR WHEEL ALIGNMENT

Due to the design of the rear suspension and the incorporation of stub axles or wheel spindles, it is possible to adjust camber and toe of the rear wheels on these vehicles. Adjustment is controlled by adding shims approximately .010 inch thick between the spindle mounting surface and spindle mounting plate. The amount of adjustment is approximately 0° 18' per shim for 1982 vehicles, and 3° per shim for 1983–84 vehicles. Refer to **Figs. 3 through 6** for proper replacement of shims.

REAR WHEEL BEARING
ADJUST

1. Raise and support rear of vehicle.
2. Torque adjusting nut to 270 inch lbs. while rotating wheel.
3. Stop wheel and loosen adjusting nut, **Fig. 7.**
4. Tighten adjusting nut finger tight. End play should be .001–.003 inch.
5. Install castle lock with slots aligned with cotter pin hole.
6. Install cotter pin and grease cap.

SERVICE BRAKES
ADJUST

The rear brakes on 1983–84 models are self-adjusting and no adjustment is necessary. On 1982 models, the rear brakes are not self-adjusting and periodic adjustment is required as follows:
1. Raise and support vehicle.
2. Remove adjusting hole covers from brake supports.
3. Release parking brake and back off cable adjustment to slacken cable.
4. Insert a narrow screwdriver into adjusting nut hole. Move screwdriver handle downward on left side or upward on right side until wheels are locked, **Fig. 8.**
5. Back off nut ten clicks, then adjust parking brake, refer to "Parking Brake, Adjust" procedure.

PARKING BRAKE
ADJUST

1. Raise and support vehicle.
2. Release parking brake and back off cable adjustment to slacken cable.
3. Tighten cable adjusting nut until a slight drag is obtained while rotating wheels.
4. Loosen cable adjusting nut until the wheels rotate freely, then an additional two turns.
5. Apply and release parking brake to check for proper operation. The rear

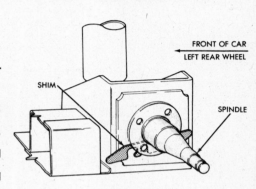

Fig. 6 Shim installation for negative camber

wheels should rotate without dragging.

MASTER CYLINDER
REPLACE

MANUAL BRAKES

1. Disconnect and plug brake tubes from master cylinder. Cap master cylinder ports to prevent fluid leakage.
2. Disconnect stop lamp switch mounting bracket from beneath instrument panel.
3. Pull brake pedal rearward to disengage push rod from master cylinder.

NOTE: Pulling the brake pedal rearward will destroy the grommet. Install a new grommet when installing the push rod.

4. Remove master cylinder attaching nuts, then the master cylinder from vehicle.
5. Reverse procedure to install.

NOTE: Master cylinder should be bench bled before installation using tool No. C-4546 or equivalent.

POWER BRAKES

1. Disconnect and plug brake tubes from master cylinder. Cap master cylinder

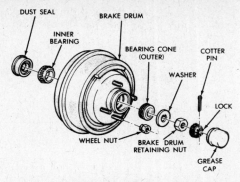

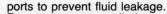

Fig. 7 Wheel bearing assembly

Fig. 8 Adjusting service brake

ports to prevent fluid leakage.
2. Remove master cylinder attaching nuts, then master cylinder from power brake unit.
3. Reverse procedure to install.

NOTE: Master cylinder should be bench bled before installation using tool No. C-4546 or equivalent.

POWER BRAKE UNIT
REPLACE

1. Remove master cylinder attaching nuts, slide master cylinder from mounting studs and support on fender shield. Do not disconnect brake tubes from master cylinder.
2. Disconnect vacuum hose from power brake unit.
3. Install a suitable screwdriver between center tang on retainer clip and the brake pedal pin, located under instrument panel. Rotate screwdriver so retainer clip center tang will pass over brake pedal pin.
4. Pull retainer clip from pin.
5. Remove power brake unit attaching nuts, then the power brake unit from vehicle.
6. Reverse procedure to install. Torque power brake unit and master cylinder unit attaching nuts to 200—300 inch lbs. for 1983—84 models, and 200—250 inch lbs. for 1982 models.

Front Suspension & Steering Section

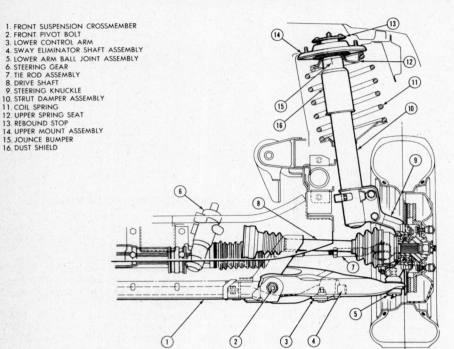

1. FRONT SUSPENSION CROSSMEMBER
2. FRONT PIVOT BOLT
3. LOWER CONTROL ARM
4. SWAY ELIMINATOR SHAFT ASSEMBLY
5. LOWER ARM BALL JOINT ASSEMBLY
6. STEERING GEAR
7. TIE ROD ASSEMBLY
8. DRIVE SHAFT
9. STEERING KNUCKLE
10. STRUT DAMPER ASSEMBLY
11. COIL SPRING
12. UPPER SPRING SEAT
13. REBOUND STOP
14. UPPER MOUNT ASSEMBLY
15. JOUNCE BUMPER
16. DUST SHIELD

Fig. 1   Front suspension (Typical)

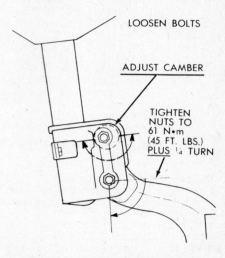

Fig. 2   Camber adjustment

DESCRIPTION

These vehicles use a MacPherson-type front suspension with the vertical shock absorber struts attached to the upper fender reinforcement and the steering knuckle, **Fig. 1.** The lower control arms are attached inboard to a crossmember and outboard to the steering knuckle through a ball joint to provide lower steering knuckle position. During steering maneuvers, the strut and steering knuckle rotate as an assembly.

The drive shafts are attached inboard to the transaxle output drive flanges and outboard to the driven wheel hub.

WHEEL ALIGNMENT

NOTE: Prior to wheel alignment, ensure tires are at recommended pressure, are of equal size and have approximately the same wear pattern. Check front wheel and tire assembly for radial runout and inspect lower ball joints and steering linkage for looseness. Check front and rear springs for sagging or damage. Front suspension inspections should be performed on a level floor or alignment rack with fuel tank at capacity and vehicle free of luggage and passenger compartment load.

Prior to each alignment reading, the vehicle should be bounced an equal number of times from the center of the bumper alternately, first from the rear, then the front, releasing at bottom of down cycle.

CASTER

The caster angle on these vehicles cannot be adjusted.

CAMBER

To adjust camber, loosen the cam and through bolts, **Fig. 2.** Rotate the upper cam bolt to move the top of the wheel in or out to achieve the specified camber angle. Torque cam bolts to 45 ft. lbs., then advance bolts an additional ¼ turn (90 degrees).

TOE-IN

To adjust toe-in, center the steering wheel and hold in position with a suitable tool. Loosen the tie rod lock nuts and rotate the rod, **Fig. 3,** to adjust toe-in to specifications. Use care not to twist the steering gear rubber boots. Torque the tie rod lock nuts to 55 ft. lbs. (75 Nm). Adjust position of steering gear rubber boots. Remove steering wheel holding tool.

STRUT DAMPER ASSEMBLY
REPLACE

REMOVAL

1. Raise and support vehicle, then remove front wheels.
2. Mark position of camber adjusting cam, then remove the camber adjusting bolt, the through bolt and the brake hose to damper bracket retaining screw, **Figs. 4 and 5.**
3. Remove strut damper to fender shield mounting nut and washer assemblies.
4. Remove strut damper from vehicle.

INSTALLATION

1. Position strut assembly into fender reinforcement, then install retaining nuts and washers and torque to 20 ft. lbs.
2. Position steering knuckle and washer plate to strut, then install upper cam and lower through bolts.
3. Install brake hose retainer on damper, then index cam bolt to alignment mark made during removal.
4. Position a 4-inch or larger, C-clamp on steering knuckle and strut, **Fig. 6.** Tighten clamp just enough to eliminate any looseness between strut and knuckle. Check alignment of marks made during removal, then tighten bolts to 45 ft. lbs. plus an additional ¼ turn beyond the specified torque.
5. Remove C-clamp, then install wheel and tire assembly.

COIL SPRING
REPLACE

1. Remove strut damper assembly as outlined previously.
2. Using a suitable tool, compress coil spring.
3. Remove strut rod nut while holding strut rod to prevent rotation.
4. Remove the mount assembly, **Fig. 7.**
5. Remove coil spring from strut damper.
6. Inspect mount assembly for deterioration of rubber isolator, retainers for cracks and distortion and bearings for binding.
7. Install the bumper dust shield assembly.
8. Install spring and seat, upper spring retainer, bearing and spacer, mount assembly and the rebound bumper, retainer and rod nut upper.

NOTE: Position the spring retainer alignment notch parallel to the damper lower attaching brackets.

9. Torque strut rod nut to 60 ft. lbs. (81 Nm). Do not release spring compressor before torquing nut.
10. Remove spring compressor.

BALL JOINTS

The ball joint is pressed into the lower control arm. On these models, the ball joint can be pressed from the lower control arm using a 1 1/16 inch deep socket and tool No. C-4699-2. When pressing ball joint into lower control arm, use tools Nos. C-4699-1 and C-4699-2. Install ball joint seal using a 1 1/2 inch deep socket and tool No. C-4699-2.

NOTE: On some models the ball joint is welded to the lower control arm. On these models, the ball joint and lower control arm must be replaced as an assembly.

CHECKING BALL JOINTS

With weight of vehicle resting on wheel and tire assembly, attempt to move grease fitting with fingers, **Fig. 8.** Do not use a tool or added force to attempt to move grease fitting. If grease fitting moves freely, ball joint is worn and should be replaced.

LOWER CONTROL ARM
REPLACE

REMOVAL

1. Raise and support vehicle.
2. Remove the front inner pivot through bolt, the rear stub strut nut, retainer and bushing and the ball joint to steering knuckle clamp bolt, **Fig. 9.**
3. Separate the ball joint from the steer-

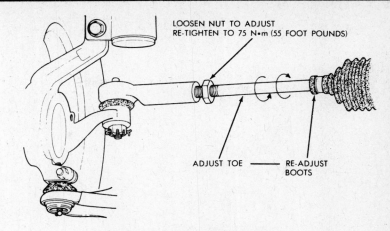

Fig. 3   Toe-in adjustment

ing knuckle by prying between the ball stud retainer and the lower control arm.

NOTE: Pulling the steering knuckle "Out" from vehicle after releasing from ball joint can separate inner C/V joint.

4. Remove sway bar to control arm nut and reinforcement and rotate control arm over sway bar. Remove rear stub strut bushing, sleeve and retainer.

INSTALLATION

1. Install retainer, bushing and sleeve on stub strut.
2. Position control arm over sway bar and install rear stub strut and front pivot into crossmember.
3. Install front pivot bolt and loosely assemble nut, **Fig. 9.**
4. Install stub strut bushing and retainer and loosely assemble nut.
5. Install ball joint stud into steering knuckle, then the clamp bolt. Torque clamp bolt to 50 ft. lbs. (67 N.m) for 1982–83 models, 70 ft. lbs. (95 N.m) for 1984 models.
6. Place sway bar end bushing retainer to control arm, then install retainer bolts. Torque retainer bolts to 22 ft.

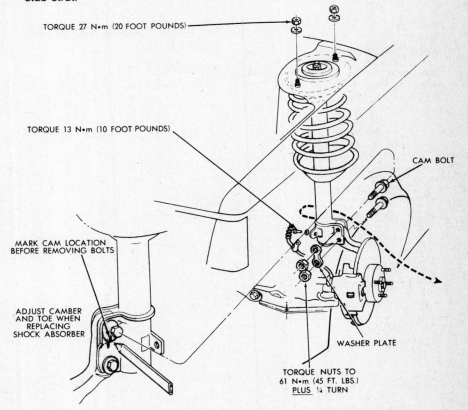

Fig. 4   Strut damper replacement. 1982–83 models

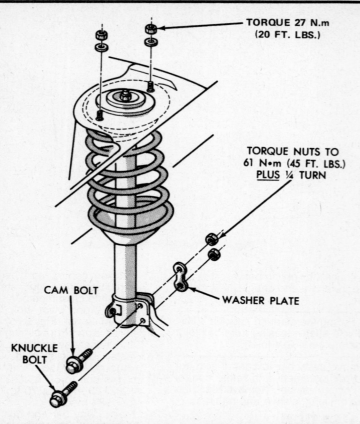

Fig. 5 Strut damper replacement. 1984 models

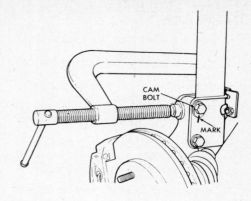

Fig. 6 Strut damper installation

lbs. (30 N.m) for 1982–83 models, 25 ft. lbs. (34 N.m) for 1984 models.
7. Lower vehicle so suspension fully supports vehicle, then torque front pivot bolt to 105 ft. lbs. (142 N.m) and stub strut nut to 70 ft. lbs. (95 N.m).

STEERING KNUCKLE
REPLACE
REMOVAL
1. Remove cotter pin and nut lock.

2. Loosen hub nut with brakes applied, **Fig. 10.**

NOTE: The hub and driveshaft are splined together through the knuckle (bearing) and retained by the hub nut.

3. Raise and support vehicle, then remove front wheel.
4. Remove hub nut. Ensure that the splined driveshaft is free to separate from spline in hub during knuckle removal. A pulling force on the shaft can separate the inner C/V joint. Tap lightly with a brass drift, if required.
5. Disconnect the tie rod end from steering arm with a suitable puller.
6. Disconnect brake hose retainer from strut damper.
7. Remove clamp bolt securing ball joint stud into steering knuckle and brake caliper adapter screw and washer assemblies.
8. Support caliper with a piece of wire. Do not hang by brake hose.
9. Remove rotor.
10. Mark position of camber cam upper adjusting bolt and loosen both bolts.
11. Support steering knuckle and remove cam adjusting and through bolts. Move upper knuckle "neck" from strut damper bracket and lift knuckle from ball joint stud.

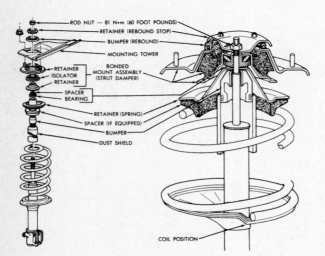

Fig. 7 Strut damper assembly

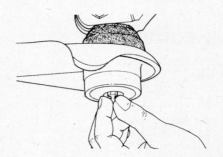

Fig. 8 Checking ball joint for wear

3. Install and torque ball joint to steering knuckle clamp bolt to 50 ft. lbs. (68 Nm).
4. Install tie rod end into steering arm and torque nut to 35 ft. lbs. (47 Nm). Install cotter pin.
5. Install rotor.
6. Install caliper over rotor and position adapter to steering knuckle. Install adapter to knuckle bolts and torque to 85 ft. lbs. (115 Nm). For 1982 vehicles, or 160 ft. lbs. (216 Nm) for 1983–84 vehicles.
7. Attach brake hose retainer to strut damper and torque screw to 10 ft. lbs. (13 Nm).
8. a. Install washer and hub nut.
   b. With brakes applied, torque hub nut to 180 ft. lbs. (245 Nm).
   c. Install nut lock and new cotter pin, **Fig. 10.**

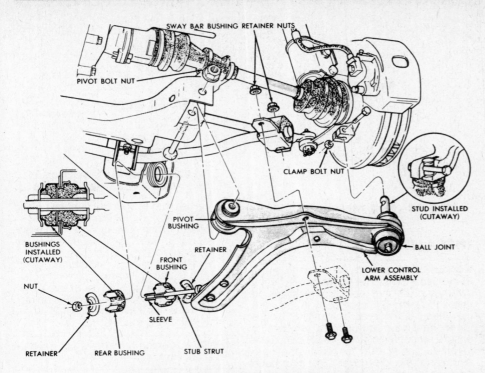

Fig. 9 Lower control arm assembly

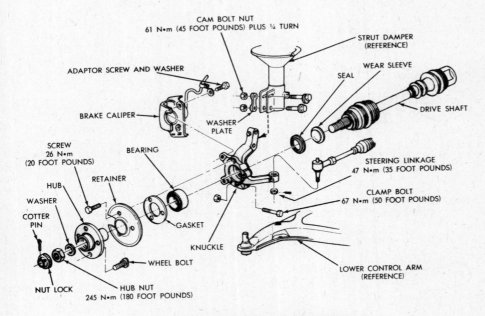

Fig. 10 Steering knuckle assembly

NOTE: Support driveshaft during knuckle removal. Do not permit driveshaft to hang after separating steering knuckle from vehicle.

INSTALLATION

1. Place steering knuckle on lower ball joint stud and the driveshaft through hub.
2. Position upper "neck" of knuckle into strut damper bracket and install cam and through bolts. Place cam in original position. Place a 4-inch or larger C-clamp on strut and steering knuckle, then tighten clamp just enough to eliminate looseness between knuckle and strut. Check to ensure that cam alignment marks made during removal are aligned, then tighten bolts to 45 ft. lbs. plus an additional ¼ turn beyond specified torque. Remove C-clamp.

HUB & BEARING
REPLACE

REMOVAL

1. Remove steering knuckle as outlined previously.
2. Remove hub using tool No. L-4539 on 1982–83 vehicles, or tool No. C-4811 on 1984 vehicles, **Figs. 11 and 12.**

NOTE: On 1982–83 models, the bearing inner races will separate and the outer race will remain in the hub.

3. On 1982–83 models, remove bearing outer race from hub using suitable puller, **Fig. 13,** then remove brake dust shield, if equipped.
4. On all models, remove bearing retainer attaching screws, then the retainer.
5. Remove bearing from knuckle using press and suitable socket for 1982–83 models, or tool No. C-4811 for 1984 models, **Figs. 14 and 15.**

INSTALLATION

1. Press new bearing into knuckle using tool No. L-4463 and a suitable press for 1982–83 models, or tool No. C-4811 for 1984 models, **Figs. 16 and 17.**
2. Install bearing retainer. Torque retainer screws to 20 ft. lbs. (27 N.m).
3. Press hub into bearing using suitable press and socket for 1982–83 models, or tool No. C-4811 for 1984 models, **Figs. 18 and 19.**
4. Install steering knuckle as described under "Steering Knuckle, Replace."

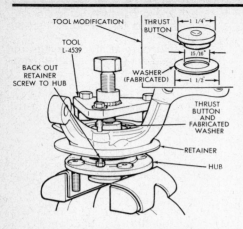

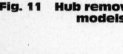

Fig. 11   Hub removal. 1982–83 models

SWAY BAR
REPLACE

REMOVAL

1. Raise and support vehicle.
2. Remove nuts, bolts and retainers at the control arms, **Fig. 20.**
3. Remove crossmember clamp attaching bolts, then the crossmember clamps.
4. Remove sway bar from vehicle.

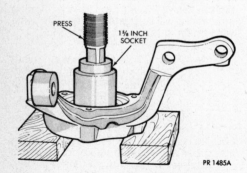

Fig. 14   Removing bearing from knuckle. 1982–83 models

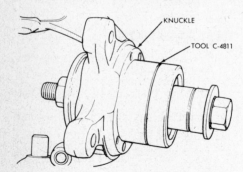

Fig. 17   Installing bearing into knuckle. 1984 models

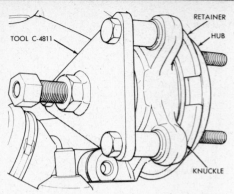

Fig. 12   Hub removal. 1984 models

INSTALLATION

NOTE: A linkless sway bar is used in the front suspension. The sway bar is nearly symmetric looking, and it is possible to install the sway bar improperly in the vehicle when it is removed for service. Always mark the sway bar prior to removal to ensure proper installation. Sway bars used for production and service replacement are marked on the left (driver side) by a daub or stripe of paint.

1. Position crossmember bushings on

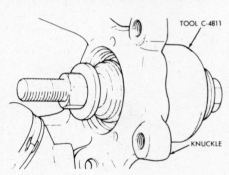

Fig. 15   Removing bearing from knuckle. 1984 models

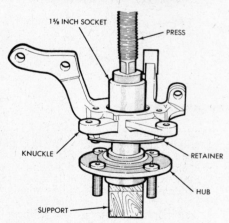

Fig. 18   Installing hub into knuckle. 1982–83 models

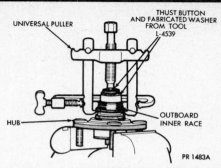

Fig. 13   Removing outboard inner race. 1982–83 models

the bar with the curved surface up and split to front of vehicle.
2. Position bar assembly onto crossmember, then install clamps and attaching bolts.
3. Position retainers at control arms, then install bolts and attaching nuts.
4. Raise lower control arm to correct position, then torque attaching bolts to 25 ft. lbs. for 1984 models, or 22 ft. lbs. for 1982–83 models.

NOTE: A bushing retainer is not used on 1984 models.

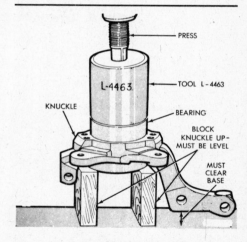

Fig. 16   Installing bearing into knuckle. 1982–83 models

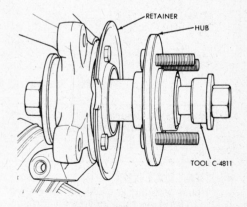

Fig. 19   Installing hub into knuckle. 1984 models

DRIVESHAFT IDENTIFICATION

Driveshafts are identified as "A.C.I." or "G.K.N." assemblies, **Fig. 21.** Vehicles can be equipped with either of these assemblies, however they should not be intermixed. Procedures for installation and removal of driveshafts are essentially the same for either type assembly used.

DRIVESHAFTS
REPLACE

REMOVAL

NOTE: On early 1982 models, the inboard C/V joints have stub shafts splined into the differential side gears and are retained with circlips, **Fig. 22.** The circlip "Tangs" are located on a machined surface on the inner end of the stub shafts and are removed and installed with the shaft. On late 1982–84 models, the driveshafts are spring loaded and are retained to the side gears by constant spring pressure provided by the spring contained in the C/V joints, **Fig. 23.**

1. On early 1982 models, drain transaxle differential unit and remove cover.
2. If removing the right hand driveshaft, the speedometer pinion must be removed prior to driveshaft removal, **Fig. 24.**
3. On early 1982 models, rotate driveshaft to expose circlip tangs, **Fig. 25.** Using needle nose pliers, compress circlip tangs while prying shaft into side gear splined cavity, **Fig. 26.** The circlip will be compressed in the cavity with the shaft.
4. Remove clamp bolt securing ball joint stud to steering knuckle, then, separate ball joint stud from steering knuckle. Do not damage ball joint or C/V joint boots.
5. Separate outer C/V joint splined shaft from hub by holding C/V housing while moving knuckle hub assembly away from C/V joint.

NOTE: Do not damage slinger on outer C/V joint. Do not attempt to remove, repair or replace.

6. Support assembly at C/V joint housings and remove by pulling outward on the inner C/V joint housing. Do not pull on the shaft.

NOTE: If removing left hand driveshaft assembly, the removal may be aided by inserting a screwdriver blade between the differential pinion shaft and carefully prying against the end face of stub.

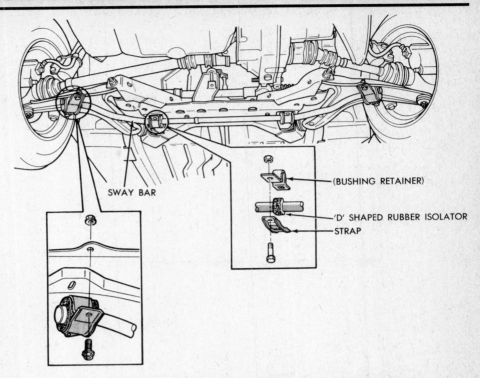

SWAY BAR

(BUSHING RETAINER)

'D' SHAPED RUBBER ISOLATOR

STRAP

Fig. 20   Sway bar assembly. 1982—83 (Typical of 1984)

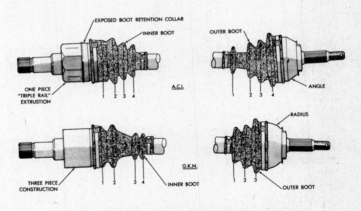

EXPOSED BOOT RETENTION COLLAR

INNER BOOT

OUTER BOOT

ONE PIECE "TRIPLE RAIL" EXTRUSTION

A.C.I.

ANGLE

THREE PIECE CONSTRUCTION

G.K.N.

INNER BOOT

RADIUS

OUTER BOOT

Fig. 21   Driveshaft identification

7. Remove driveshaft assembly from vehicle.

INSTALLATION

NOTE: On early 1982 models, install new circlips on inner joint shaft before installation, **Fig. 27.**

1. On early 1982 units, be sure tangs on circlips are aligned with flattened end of shaft before inserting shaft into transaxle. If not, jamming or component damage may result.
2. Hold inner joint assembly at housing while aligning and guiding the inner joint spline into transaxle.
3. While holding the inner joint housing, quickly thrust the shaft into the differential. This will complete the lock-up of the driveshaft to the axle side gear.

NOTE: On early 1982 models, inspect circlip positioning in side gears to verify lock-up.

4. Push knuckle/hub assembly out and install splined outer C/V joint shaft into hub.
5. Install knuckle assembly on ball joint stud.

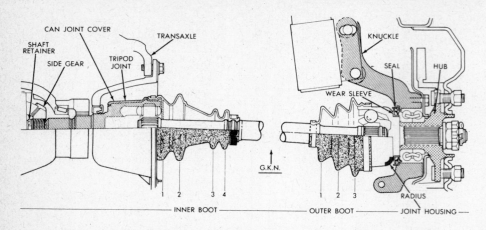

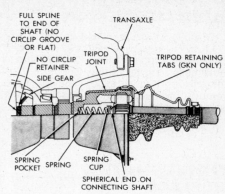

Fig. 22 Driveshaft assembly. Early 1982

Fig. 23 Driveshaft assembly. Late 1982–84 G.K.N. axles. (similar to 1984 A.I.S. axles)

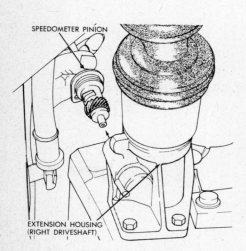

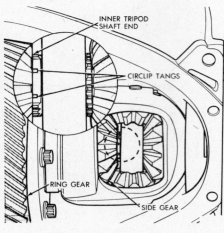

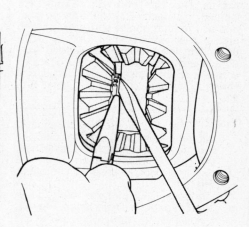

Fig. 24 Speedometer pinion replacement

Fig. 25 Circlips exposed. Early 1982 models

Fig. 26 Compressing circlips. Early 1982 models

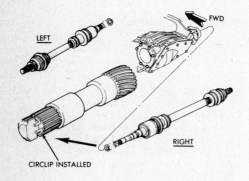

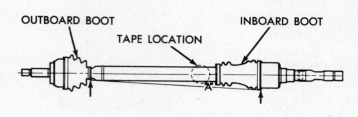

Fig. 27 Circlips installation. Early 1982 models

Fig. 28 Measuring driveshaft

Driveshaft Identification			"A" Dimension	
Type	Side	Tape Color	M.M	Inch
G.K.N.	Right	Yellow	498–509	19.6–20
G.K.N.	Left	Yellow	240–253	9.5–10
A.C.I.	Right	Red	469–478	18.5–19
A.C.I.	Left	Red	208–218	8.2–8.6

Fig. 29 Driveshaft length specification

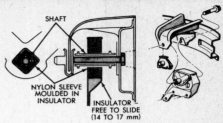

Fig. 30 Left engine mount, adjust

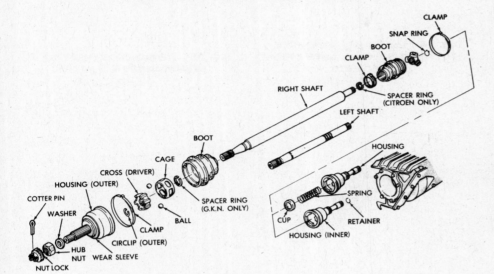

Fig. 31 Driveshaft components. 1982–83 (Similar to 1984)

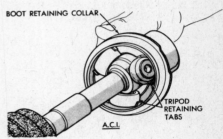

Fig. 32 Removing inner C/V joint tripod housing. A.C.I. units

6. Install and torque clamp bolt to 50 ft. lbs. (68 Nm).
7. Install speedometer pinion, Fig. 24.
8. On early 1982 models, apply a 1/16 inch bead of silicone sealant, part number 4026070, to differential cover sealing surface and mating surface of transaxle case after both have been properly cleaned and inspected.
9. On early 1982 models, install differential cover and torque retaining screws to 165 inch lbs. (19 Nm), then fill differential to bottom of filler plug hole with Dexron automatic transmission fluid.
10. Install washer and hub nut. Torque hub nut to 180 ft. lbs. (245 Nm). Install nut lock and cotter pin.
11. If, after attaching driveshaft assembly in vehicle the inboard boot appears collapsed or deformed, vent the inner boot by inserting a round tipped, small diameter rod between the boot and shaft. As venting occurs, the boot will return to the normal shape.

DRIVESHAFT LENGTH
ADJUST
1983

1. Position vehicle with wheels straight ahead and body weight distributed on all four tires.
2. Measure direct distance between inner edge of outboard boot to inner edge of inboard boot on both driveshafts. This measurement (dimension

"A") should be taken at the bottom (6 o'clock position) of driveshafts, Fig. 28.

NOTE: Damper weights are used on left driveshaft assembly. Before measuring driveshaft length, damper should be removed from shaft. After specified measurement is completed, install damper weight and torque damper weight attaching bolts to 8 ft. lbs. (11 N.m).

3. Driveshaft length (dimension "A") must be within specifications in chart, Fig. 29. If measurement is not within specifications, engine position must be corrected as follows:
   a. Remove load from engine mounts by carefully supporting engine and transaxle assembly using a suitable jack.
   b. Loosen right engine mount vertical bolts, then the front engine mount bracket-to-crossmember attaching bolts.
   c. Pry engine to the right or left as necessary to bring driveshaft length within specifications.

NOTE: The left engine mount is sleeved over long support bolt and shaft, Fig. 30, to provide lateral adjustment whether or not engine weight is removed.

   d. Torque engine mount vertical bolts to 250 inch lbs. and front engine mount bolts to 40 ft. lbs.

   e. Center left engine mount, then recheck driveshaft length.

INNER CONSTANT VELOCITY JOINT SERVICE
DISASSEMBLE, FIG. 31

NOTE: Driveshaft assembly should be identified before starting service procedure. Refer to "Driveshaft Identification."

1. Remove clamp and boot from joint and discard.
2. On A.C.I. units, position tripod housing so all three rollers are flush with retaining tabs. Pull housing out by hand at a slight angle to pop one roller at a time out of the retaining tabs, Fig. 32. Do not hold joint at too severe an angle, as rollers may be damaged.

NOTE: The retaining tabs must not be bent during removal or installation of tripod housing.

3. On early 1982 G.K.N. nonspring loaded units, slide tripod from housing, Fig. 33. On late 1982–84 G.K.N. spring loaded units, bend tabs on joint cover using needle nose pliers, then remove tripod from housing, Fig. 34.
4. Remove snap ring from end of shaft, then remove tripod using brass punch, Fig. 35.

INSPECTION

Remove grease from assembly and

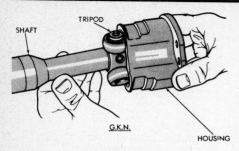

Fig. 33 Removing inner C/V joint tripod housing. Early model G.K.N. units

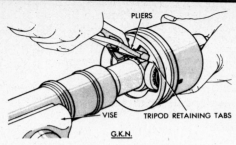

Fig. 34 Removing inner C/V joint tripod housing. Late model G.K.N. units

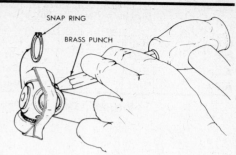

Fig. 35 Removing snap ring & tripod inner C/V joints

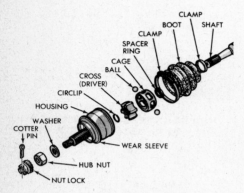

Fig. 36 Outer C/V joint disassembled

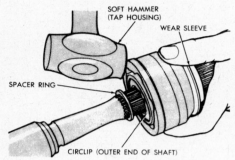

Fig. 37 Removing joint from shaft. Outer C/V joints

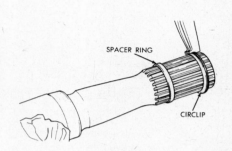

Fig. 38 Circlip removal. Outer C/V joints

inspect bearing race and tripod components for wear and damage and replace as necessary. On late 1982–84 spring loaded joints inspect spring, spring cup and spherical end of connecting shaft for wear and damage and replace as necessary.

NOTE: Components of spring loaded and nonspring loaded inner C/V joints cannot be interchanged.

ASSEMBLE

1. Slide small end of boot over shaft. On tubular type shafts, align boot lip with mark on shaft outer diameter. On solid type shafts, position small end of boot in groove on shaft.
2. Place rubber clamp over groove on boot.
3. Install tripod on shaft with non-chamfered face of tripod body facing shaft retainer groove.
4. Lock tripod assembly on shaft by installing retaining ring in shaft groove.
5. Distribute packets of special grease provided in boot and clamp kit as follows:
   a. On early 1982 G.K.N. units, distribute one packet of grease in housing before positioning housing over tripod.
   b. On late 1982–84 G.K.N. units, distribute one packet of grease in housing, then position spring with

spring cup attached to exposed end into spring pocket. Place a small amount of grease on spring cup.
   c. On A.C.I. units, distribute one packet of grease in boot and remaining packet in housing.
6. On early 1982 G.K.N. units, slip tripod into housing, then install boot over housing groove.
7. On late 1982–84 G.K.N. units, slip tripod into housing and bend retaining tabs down to their original position. Install boot over housing and ensure retaining tabs hold tripod in housing.
8. On A.C.I. units, align tripod roller with retaining tabs and housing tracks. Install one roller at a time through retaining tabs, and bend retaining tabs down into their original position. Install boot over housing and ensure retaining tabs hold tripod in housing.

NOTE: On all spring loaded joints, check to ensure spring remains in pocket and centered in housing. Also ensure spring cup contacts spherical end of connecting shaft.

9. On all models, install boot clamp.

OUTER CONSTANT VELOCITY JOINT SERVICE
DISASSEMBLY
Figs. 31 & 36

NOTE: Driveshaft assembly should be identified before starting service procedure. Refer to "Driveshaft Identification."

1. Cut boot clamps from boot and discard.
2. Clean grease from joint.
3. Support shaft in a soft-jawed vise. Support the outer joint, and tap with a mallet to dislodge joint from internal circlip installed in a groove at the outer end of the shaft, **Fig. 37.** Do not remove slinger from housing.
4. Remove circlip from shaft groove and discard, **Fig. 38.**
5. Unless the shaft requires replacement, do not remove the heavy lock ring from shaft, **Fig. 38.**
6. If constant velocity joint was operating satisfactorily and grease does not appear contaminated, proceed to "Assembly" procedure, step 7.
7. If the constant velocity joint is noisy or

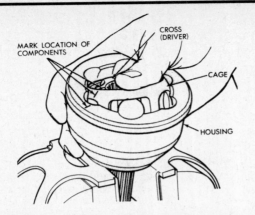

Fig. 39   Ball removal. Outer C/V joints

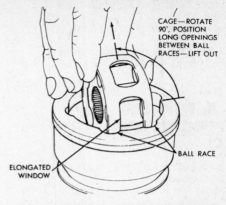

Fig. 40   Cage & cross assembly removal. Outer C/V joints

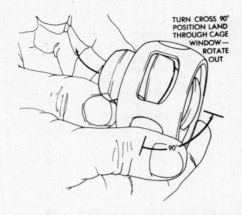

Fig. 41   Removing cross from cage. Outer C/V joints

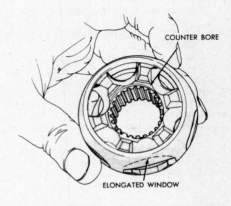

Fig. 42   Cage & cross assembly. Outer C/V joints

badly worn, replace entire unit. The repair kit will include boot, clamps, circlip and lubricant. Clean and inspect the joint outlined in the following steps.

8. Clean surplus grease and mark relative position of inner cross, cage and housing with a dab of paint.
9. Hold joint vertically in a soft jawed vise.
10. Press downward on one side of the inner race to tilt cage and remove ball from opposite side, **Fig. 39**. If joint is tight, use a hammer and a brass drift to tap inner race. Do not strike the cage. Repeat this step until all six balls are removed. A screwdriver may be used to pry the balls loose.
11. Tilt the cage assembly vertically and position the two opposing, elongated cage windows in area between ball grooves. Remove cage and inner race assembly by pulling upward from the housing, **Fig. 40**.
12. Rotate inner cross 90 degrees to cage and align one of the race spherical lands with an elongated cage window. Raise land into cage window and remove inner race by swinging outward, **Fig. 41**.

INSPECTION

1. Check housing ball races for excessive wear.
2. Check splined shaft and nut threads for damage.
3. Inspect the balls for pitting, cracks, scouring and wearing. Dulling of the surface is normal.
4. Inspect cage for excessive wear on inner and outer spherical surfaces, heavy brinelling of cage, window cracks and chipping.
5. Inspect inner race (Cross) for excessive wear or scoring of ball races.
6. If any of the defects listed in steps 1 through 5, are found, replace the C/V assembly as a unit.

NOTE: Polished areas in races (Cross and housing) and on cage spheres are normal and do not indicate a need for joint replacement unless they are suspected of causing noise and vibration.

ASSEMBLY

Figs. 31 & 36

1. If removed, position wear sleeve on joint housing, then tap sleeve onto housing, using tool No. C-4698.
2. Lightly oil components, then align marks made during disassembly.
3. Align one of the inner race lands with elongated window of cage, then insert race into cage and pivot 90°, **Fig. 42**.
4. Align elongated cage windows with housing land, then pivot cage 90°. The curved side of the elongated cage windows and inner race counterbore should face outward from joint, **Fig. 43**.
5. Lubricate ball races with one packet of grease from kit.
6. Tilt cage and inner race assembly and insert balls.
7. With shaft supported in a soft-jawed vise, install boot.
8. Slide small end of boot over spacer ring and shaft, then position boot end in machined groove.
9. Install snap ring on shaft. When installing use care not to overexpand snap ring.
10. Position joint housing on shaft, then engage by tapping sharply with a soft-faced mallet.
11. Check to ensure that snap ring is prop-

erly seated, by attempting to pull joint from shaft.
12. Locate large end of boot over housing.
13. On G.K.N. units, secure boot clamps using tool No. C-4124.

RACK & PINION STEERING GEAR
REPLACE

1. Raise and support vehicle, then remove front wheels.
2. Remove tie rod ends with a suitable puller.
3. Remove splash shields and boot seal shields.
4. Drive out lower roll pin attaching pinion shaft to lower universal joint.
5. Support front suspension crossmember with a suitable jack.
6. On power steering units, disconnect hoses from steering gear.
7. Disconnect tie rod ends from steering knuckles.
8. On all models, remove bolts attaching steering gear to front suspension crossmember. Loosen crossmember from vehicle frame.

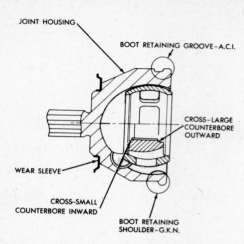

JOINT HOUSING

BOOT RETAINING GROOVE-A.C.I.

CROSS-LARGE COUNTERBORE OUTWARD

WEAR SLEEVE

CROSS-SMALL COUNTERBORE INWARD

BOOT RETAINING SHOULDER-G.K.N.

Fig. 43 Cage & cross assembly installed in housing. Outer C/V joints

9. Remove steering gear from left side of vehicle.
10. Reverse procedure to install.

POWER STEERING PUMP
REPLACE

1. Remove power steering pump drive belt adjusting bolt and nut, then remove nut attaching pump end hose bracket, if equipped.
2. Raise and support vehicle, then remove nut attaching pump pressure hose locating bracket to crossmember.
3. Disconnect pressure hose from steering gear and allow fluid to drain into a suitable container.
4. Remove drive belt splash shield, then disconnect both pressure and return hoses at power steering pump. Cap hoses and fitting to prevent entry of dirt.
5. Remove lower stud nut and pivot bolt from power steering pump, then lower vehicle.
6. Remove drive belt pulley from pump, then move pump rearward to clear mounting bracket, and remove adjusting bracket.
7. Rotate pump so pulley faces rear of vehicle, then lift pump assembly from vehicle.
8. Reverse procedure to install.

DODGE CARAVAN & MINI RAM VAN • PLYMOUTH VOYAGER

INDEX OF SERVICE OPERATIONS

NOTE: Refer to page 1 of this manual for the manufacturer's special service tool suppliers.

General Engine Specifications

Year	Engine	Carb.	Bore & Stroke inch (millimeters)	Comp. Ratio	Horsepower @ R.P.M.	Torque Ft. @ R.P.M.	Normal Oil Pressure Pounds
1984	4-135	2 Bbl.	3.44 × 3.62 (87.5 × 92)	9.6	101 @ 5600	121 @ 3600	40①
	4-156	2 Bbl.	3.59 × 3.86 (91.1 × 98)	8.7	99 @ 4800	143 @ 2000	85②
1985	4-135	2 Bbl.	3.44 × 3.62 (87.5 × 92)	9.5	101 @ 5600	121 @ 3600	25–90③
	4-156	2 Bbl.	3.59 × 3.86 (91.1 × 98)	8.7	104 @ 4800	142 @ 2800	45–90③

①—At 2000 R.P.M. ②—At 2500 R.P.M. ③—At 3000 R.P.M.

Alternator & Regulator Specifications

| Year | Identification | Alternator | | | Regulator | |
		Rated Hot Output Amps.	Field Current 12 Volts @ 80° F.	Output @ 15 Volts 1250 R.P.M.	Part Number	Voltage @ 80° F.
1984–85	Yellow①	60	2.5–5	47	—	13.9–14.4
	Brown①	78	2.5–5	56	—	13.9–14.4
	A4T25191②	75	—	63–70④	Integral	14.1–14.7③

①—Chrysler alternators are identified by tag color.
②—Mitsubishi alternator.
③—68°F (20°C).
④—Output @ 13.5 volts, 1000 R.P.M.

Starting Motor Specifications

| Engine | Model | Ident. No. | Cranking Amperage Draw Test① | Free Speed Test | | |
				Amps.②	Volts	R.P.M.③
4-135	Bosch	5213045	120–160	47	11	6600
	Nippondenso	5213645	120–160	47	11	6600
4-156	Nippondenso	5213235	150–210	85	11	3700

①—Engine should be at normal operating temperature.
②—Maximum current drawn.
③—Minimum speed.

Pistons, Pins, Rings, Crankshaft & Bearings Specifications

Year	Engine Model	Wristpin Diameter	Piston Clearance, Inch	Ring End Gap, Inch (Minimum) Comp.	Ring End Gap, Inch (Minimum) Oil	Crankpin Diameter, Inch	Rod Bearing Clearance, Inch	Main Bearing Journal Diameter, Inch	Main Bearing Clearance, Inch	End Thrust on Bearing No.	Shaft End Play
1984–85	4-135	.9008	.0005–.0015	.011	.015	1.968–1.969	.0008–.0034	2.362–2.363	.0003–.0031	3	.002–.007
	4-156	.866	.0008–.0016	.010	.0078	2.0866	.0008–.0028	2.3622	.0008–.0028	3	.002–.007

continued

Valve Specifications

Year	Engine Model	Valve Lash Int.	Valve Lash Exh.	Valve Angle Seat	Valve Angle Face	Valve Spring Installed Height	Valve Spring Pressure Lbs. @ In.	Valve Stem Clearance Intake	Valve Stem Clearance Exhaust	Stem Diameter, Std. Intake	Stem Diameter, Std. Exhaust
1984–85	4-135	Hydraulic		45°	45°	1.65	②	.0009–.0026	.0030–.0047	.3124	.3103
	4-156	.006①	.010①	45°	45°	1.59	61 @ 1.59	.0012–.0024	.0020–.0035	.300	.300

①—Engine at normal operating temperature.
②—1984, 135 lbs. @ 1.22 in.; 1985, 150 lbs. @ 1.22 in.

Engine Tightening Specifications★

★ Torque specifications are for clean and lightly lubricated threads only. Dry or dirty threads produce increased friction which prevents accurate measurement of tightness.

Year	Engine Model	Spark Plug Ft. Lbs.	Cylinder Head Bolts Ft. Lbs.	Intake Manifold Inch Lbs.	Exhaust Manifold Inch Lbs.	Camshaft Cover Inch Lbs.	Connecting Rod Cap Bolts Ft. Lbs.	Main Bearing Cap Bolts Ft. Lbs.	Flywheel to Crankshaft Ft. Lbs.	Crankshaft Pulley Ft. Lbs.
1984–85	4-135	26	45①	200	200	105	40①	30①	65	21
	4-156	18	②	150	150	53	34	58	100	87

①—Turn torque wrench an additional ¼ turn after the specified torque has been achieved.
②—Cold engine, 69 ft. lbs.; warm engine, 76 ft. lbs.

Wheel Alignment Specifications

Year	Model	Caster Angle, Degrees Limits	Caster Angle, Degrees Desired	Camber Angle, Degrees Limits Left	Camber Angle, Degrees Limits Right	Camber Angle, Degrees Desired Left	Camber Angle, Degrees Desired Right	Toe In. Inch
1984–85	ALL①	—	—	−¼ to +¾	−¼ to +¾	+5/16	+5/16	③
	ALL②	—	—	−1⅛ to −⅛	−1⅛ to −⅛	−½	−½	④

①—Front wheel alignment.
②—Rear wheel alignment.
③—0 to ⅛″ out.
④—1984, 3/32″; 1985, zero.

Brake Specifications

Year	Model	Rear Drum I.D.	Wheel Cyl. Bore Front Disc	Wheel Cyl. Bore Rear Drum	Disc Brake Rotor Nominal Thickness	Disc Brake Rotor Minimum Thickness	Disc Brake Rotor Thickness Variation (Parallelism)	Disc Brake Rotor Run Out (TIR)①	Disc Brake Rotor Finish (microinch)	Master Cyl. I.D.
1984–85	ALL	9	2.362	.748	.861–.870	.803	.0005	.004	15–80	.944

①—T.I.R.—Total indicator reading.

continued

Cooling System & Capacity Data

Year	Engine	Cooling Capacity		Radiator Cap Relief Pressure, Lbs.	Thermo. Opening Temp. Degrees F. (Centi-grade)	Fuel Tank Gals. (Litres)	Engine Oil Refill Qts. (Litres)	Transaxle Oil		
		Less A/C Qts. (Litres)	With A/C Qts. (Litres)					4 Speed Pints (Litres)	5 Speed Pints (Litres)	Auto. Trans. Qts. (Litres)
1984–85	4-135	8.5 (8.1)	8.5 (8.1)	14–18	195 (91)	15 (56.8)	4① (3.8)	2 (1.8)	2.3 (2.1)	8.9③ (8.4)
	4-156	9.5 (9)	9.5 (9)	14–18	④	15 (56.8)	5② (4.8)	—	—	8.9③ (8.4)

①—With or without filter change.
②—Includes 1 pint (.47 liter) for filter.
③—Replacement volume is approximately 4 qts. (3.8 liters). Make final check
   with dipstick.
④—Except California, 190°F (87°C); California, 180°F (84°C).

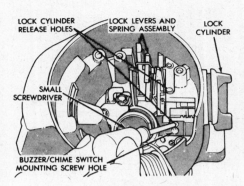

Fig. 1   Ignition lock removal. Models w/standard column

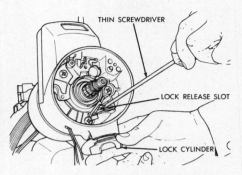

Fig. 2   Ignition lock removal. Models w/tilt column

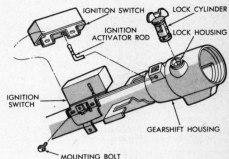

Fig. 3   Ignition switch replacement

STARTER
REPLACE

4-135

1. Disconnect battery ground cable.
2. Remove heatshield clamp, then the heatshield if equipped.
3. Loosen air pump tube at exhaust manifold, then position tube bracket away from starter motor.
4. Disconnect battery cable at starter motor and solenoid leads at solenoid.
5. Remove starter to flywheel housing and rear bracket to engine or transaxle attaching bolts.
6. Remove starter.
7. Reverse procedure to install.

4-156

1. Disconnect battery ground cable.
2. Disconnect battery cable at starter motor and solenoid leads at solenoid.
3. Remove starter to flywheel housing attaching bolts, then the starter.
4. Reverse procedure to install.

IGNITION LOCK
REPLACE

MODELS LESS TILT COLUMN

1. Disconnect battery ground cable.
2. Remove turn signal switch as described under "Turn Signal/Hazard Warning Switch, Replace."
3. Disconnect horn and ignition key lamp ground wires, then remove ignition key lamp attaching screw and lamp.
4. Remove four screws attaching upper bearing housing to lock housing, then remove snap ring from upper end of steering shaft and remove upper bearing housing.
5. Remove lock plate spring and lock plate from steering shaft.
6. Position lock cylinder in Lock position and remove ignition key.
7. Remove key warning buzzer attaching screws, then remove buzzer.
8. Remove two screws attaching ignition switch to steering column, then remove switch by rotating it 90° and sliding from rod.
9. Remove two screws attaching dimmer switch, then disengage dimmer switch from actuator rod.
10. Remove two bellcrank attaching screws, then slide bellcrank up into lock housing until it can be disconnected from ignition switch actuator rod.
11. With lock cylinder in Lock position, insert a small diameter screwdriver into lock cylinder release holes and push inward until spring loaded lock cylinder retainers release, **Fig. 1.**
12. Grasp lock cylinder and pull from lock housing bore.
13. Reverse procedure to install. The lock cylinder and ignition switch must be in the Lock position.

MODELS W/TILT COLUMN

1. Disconnect battery ground cable.
2. Remove turn signal switch as described under "Turn Signal Switch, Replace."
3. Remove ignition key lamp.
4. Position ignition lock cylinder in the Lock position, then remove ignition key.
5. Insert a thin screwdriver into lock cylinder release slot and depress spring latch which releases lock cylinder, then grasp lock cylinder and remove from column, **Fig. 2.**
6. Reverse procedure to install.

IGNITION SWITCH
REPLACE

1. Disconnect battery ground cable.
2. Remove left lower instrument panel cover.
3. Position gear selector to "D" and disconnect indicator cable, if equipped with automatic transaxle.
4. Remove lower panel reinforcement, then five steering column to support bracket attaching nuts.
5. Lower column and disconnect ignition switch electrical connector.
6. Position ignition lock cylinder in the Lock position.
7. Tape ignition switch rod to steering column to prevent rod from falling out of lock cylinder assembly.
8. Remove two ignition switch attaching screws, then the switch, **Fig. 3.**
9. Reverse procedure to install.

STEERING WHEEL
REPLACE

1. Disconnect battery ground cable.
2. On standard steering wheels, remove two horn pad assembly attaching screws.
3. On premium steering wheels, pry off horn pad using suitable screwdriver.
4. On all models, remove steering wheel nut.
5. Remove steering wheel using puller No. C-3428B or equivalent.
6. Reverse procedure to install. Torque

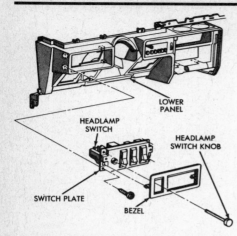

Fig. 4 Light switch removal

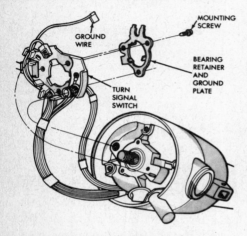

Fig. 7 Turn signal switch replacement

steering wheel attaching nut to 45 ft. lbs.

LIGHT SWITCH
REPLACE

1. Disconnect battery ground cable.
2. Remove headlight and accessory switch trim bezel, **Fig. 4.**
3. Remove four switch plate to lower panel attaching screws.
4. Pull switch assembly rearward, then disconnect switch electrical connectors.
5. Remove switch knob and stem by depressing button on switch.
6. Remove two headlight switch plate to switch plate assembly attaching screws, then the headlight switch retainer and switch.
7. Reverse procedure to install.

DIMMER SWITCH
REPLACE

1. Disconnect battery ground cable.

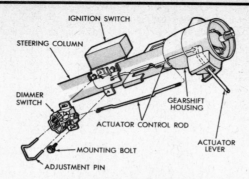

Fig. 5 Dimmer switch replacement

2. Remove left lower instrument panel cover, then tape dimmer switch rod to steering column to prevent rod from falling out of notch in actuator lever.
3. Remove switch to column attaching screws.
4. Disconnect switch electrical connector, then remove switch from steering column, **Fig. 5.**
5. Reverse procedure to install. During installation, gently push up on switch to take up slack on rod.

TURN SIGNAL/ HAZARD WARNING SWITCH
REPLACE

1. Remove steering wheel. Refer to "Steering Wheel, Replace" procedure.
2. Remove steering column cover, silencer and lower reinforcement, **Fig. 6.**
3. Pry off wiring trough from steering column, then disconnect turn signal/hazard warning switch electrical connector.
4. On models equipped with standard column, proceed as follows:
   a. Remove wiper/washer switch-to-turn signal switch pivot attaching screw. Leave turn signal lever in its installed position.
   b. Remove 3 bearing retainer and turn signal switch-to-upper bearing housing attaching screws, **Fig. 7.**
5. On models equipped with tilt column, proceed as follows:
   a. Remove plastic cover, if equipped, from lock plate.
   b. Depress lock plate using tool No. C-4156 and pry retaining ring out of groove with a suitable screwdriver, **Fig. 8.**

NOTE: The full load of the upper bearing spring should not be relieved. If the full load is relieved, the retaining ring will turn too easily and make removal difficult.

   c. Remove lock plate, cancelling cam and upper bearing spring, then place turn signal switch in right turn position.

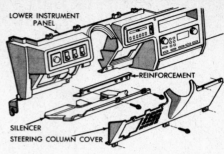

Fig. 6 Steering column cover, silencer & reinforcement removal

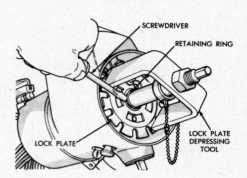

Fig. 8 Lock plate removal. Models w/tilt column

   d. Remove screw attaching link between turn signal switch and wiper/washer switch pivot.
   e. Remove hazard warning switch knob attaching screw, then the 3 turn signal switch-to-steering column attaching screws.
6. On all models, remove turn signal/hazard warning switch assembly by gently pulling switch up from column while straightening and guiding wires up through column opening, **Fig. 7.**
7. Reverse procedure to install.

INSTRUMENT CLUSTER
REPLACE

1. Disconnect battery ground cable.
2. Remove instrument cluster bezel, then disconnect speedometer cable in engine compartment.
3. On models with automatic transaxle, remove instrument panel lower left cover, then disconnect shift indicator wire.
4. On all models, remove five instrument cluster to instrument panel attaching screws, **Fig. 9,** then disconnect speedometer cable from speedometer.
5. Disconnect cluster electrical connectors, then remove cluster from right side of steering column.
6. Reverse procedure to install.

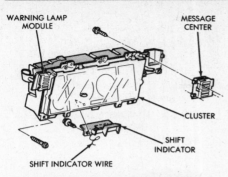

Fig. 9   Instrument cluster removal

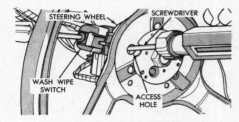

Fig. 11   Access hole for turn signal lever

WASH/WIPE SWITCH
REPLACE

FRONT

Standard Column
1. Disconnect battery ground cable.
2. On standard steering wheels, remove two horn pad assembly attaching screws.
3. On premium steering wheels, pry off horn pad using suitable screwdriver.
4. On all models, remove steering column cover, silencer and lower reinforcement, **Fig. 6.**
5. Pry off wiring trough from steering column, then remove wash/wipe switch cover attaching bolts and rotate cover upward.
6. Disconnect wash/wipe switch electrical connector, then the intermittent wipe switch and speed control electrical connectors if equipped, **Fig. 10.**
7. Place ignition in "Off" position and turn steering wheel so access hole in hub area is at 9 o'clock position. Using screwdriver, loosen turn signal lever screw through this access hole, **Fig. 11.**

NOTE: Use tape to secure dimmer switch rod in place.

8. Remove wash/wipe assembly.
9. Pull hider up control lever, then remove two control lever sleeve to wash/wipe switch attaching screws, **Fig. 12.**
10. Remove wash/wipe switch control knob from end of control lever.
11. Rotate control lever shaft clockwise and pull shaft straight out of switch.

12. Reverse procedure to install.

Tilt Column
1. Remove steering wheel. Refer to "Steering Wheel, Replace" procedure.
2. Remove steering column cover, silencer and lower reinforcement, **Fig. 6.**
3. Pry off wiring trough from steering column, then remove plastic cover from lock plate, if equipped.
4. Depress lock plate using tool No. C-4156 and pry retaining ring out of groove with screwdriver, **Fig. 8.**

NOTE: Full load of upper bearing spring should not be relieved. If full load is relieved, retaining ring will turn too easily, making removal more difficult.

5. Remove lock plate, cancelling cam and upper bearing spring, then remove switch lever actuator attaching screw and lever.
6. Push in hazard warning knob, then remove by turning knob counterclockwise.
7. Disconnect wash/wipe switch electrical connector, then the intermittent wipe switch and speed control electrical connectors if equipped, **Fig. 10.**
8. Remove three turn signal switch attaching screws, then place selector lever in "1" position. Wrap a piece of tape around electrical connector and wires to prevent snagging during switch removal.
9. Remove turn signal switch and wiring, then the ignition key lamp.
10. Position ignition lock cylinder in the Lock position, then insert a small diameter screwdriver into lock cylinder release holes and push inward until spring loaded lock cylinder retainers release, **Fig. 2.**
11. Remove buzzer/chime switch by inserting a bent piece of stiff wire into the exposed loop of the switch and pull straight out.

NOTE: Use caution not to drop switch into steering column.

12. Remove three switch housing cover attaching screws, then the housing cover.
13. Remove wash/wipe switch pivot pin using a suitable punch, then remove wash/wipe switch assembly.
14. Pull hider up control lever, then remove control lever sleeve to wash/wipe switch attaching screws, **Fig. 12.**

NOTE: Use tape to secure dimmer switch rod in place.

15. Remove wash/wipe switch control knob from end of control lever.
16. Rotate control lever shaft clockwise and pull shaft straight out of switch.
17. Reverse procedure to install.

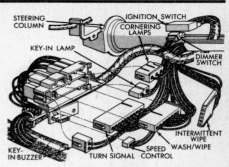

Fig. 10   Steering column electrical connectors

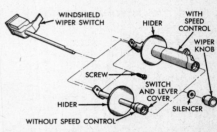

Fig. 12   Control lever assembly

REAR
1. Disconnect battery ground cable.
2. Remove headlight and accessory switch trim bezel.
3. Remove four switch plate to lower panel attaching screws.
4. Pull switch assembly rearward, then disconnect switch electrical connectors.
5. Remove switch lamp assembly attaching screw.
6. Remove two switch to switch plate assembly attaching screws, then the switch.
7. Reverse procedure to install.

WIPER MOTOR
REPLACE

FRONT
1. Disconnect battery ground cable.
2. Remove wiper arms and blades, then disconnect fluid hoses from wiper arms.
3. Open hood assembly, then remove cowl top plenum grill and disconnect fluid hose from connector.
4. Remove cowl plenum chamber plastic screen, then the wiper pivot screws.
5. Disconnect pivots from cowl top mounting positions, then push pivots down into plenum chamber.
6. Disconnect wiper motor electrical connector, then remove three wiper motor attaching nuts.
7. Remove wiper motor assembly and linkage.
8. Remove cranks and linkage by clamping crank in vise and removing nut from end of motor shaft, then remove

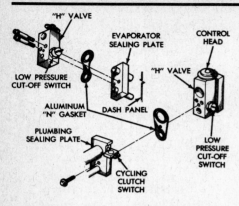

Fig. 13   H-valve assembly

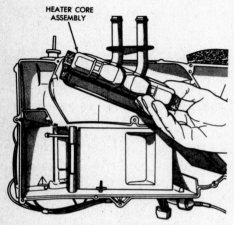

Fig. 15   Heater core replacement

cranks and linkage from motor.
9. Reverse procedure to install.

REAR

1. Disconnect battery ground cable.
2. Remove wiper arm assembly from output shaft using tool No. C-3982.
3. Open lift gate and remove lift gate trim panel.
4. Remove 4 wiper motor attaching screws, then disconnect wiper motor electrical connector.
5. Remove motor assembly from lift gate.
6. Reverse procedure to install.

RADIO
REPLACE

1. Disconnect battery ground cable.
2. Remove three attaching screws from top of bezel, then remove ash tray.
3. Remove two attaching screws at lower edge of bezel, then pull bezel rearward to release clip at left side of bezel.
4. Remove two radio to instrument panel attaching screws, then pull radio through front face of panel.
5. Disconnect radio electrical connector,

---

antenna lead and ground strap.
6. Reverse procedure to install.

HEATER CORE & BLOWER MOTOR
REPLACE

1. Disconnect battery ground cable, drain cooling system and discharge refrigerant from A/C system if equipped.
2. Disconnect heater hoses at heater core. Plug heater core tube openings to prevent coolant leakage.
3. Disconnect vacuum lines at brake booster and water valve, if equipped.
4. On models with A/C, remove expansion valve (H-valve) as follows:
   a. Disconnect low pressure cut-off switch electrical connector located on side of H-valve.
   b. Remove hex head bolt from center of plumbing sealing plate.
   c. Pull refrigerant line assembly towards front of vehicle.
   d. Remove two allen head cap screws, then carefully remove the disassembled valve, **Fig. 13**.
5. Remove condensate drain tube, then the evaporator heater assembly to dash attaching nuts.
6. Remove resistor block electrical connector, push out grommet, then feed wire through grommet hole into passenger compartment.
7. Remove steering wheel. Refer to "Steering Wheel, Replace" procedure.
8. Remove lower instrument panel as follows:
   a. Remove left lower instrument panel cover, then the side cowl and sill moulding.
   b. Loosen side cowl attaching bolts, then place selector lever in "N" position and disconnect shift indicator cable if equipped with automatic transaxle.
   c. Remove instrument panel lower reinforcement, then the five steering column to support bracket attaching nuts. Lower steering column onto seat.
   d. Remove right instrument panel trim moulding, then nine lower panel to upper panel and mid-reinforcement attaching screws.
   e. Drop lower panel down approximately six inches, then disconnect park brake release cable.
   f. Disconnect heater control cable, then the A/C control cable if equipped.
   g. Disconnect antenna and electrical connector from radio, then the electrical connections at cluster, bulkhead disconnect, side cowl, heater or A/C unit, blower motor and steering column.
   h. Disconnect fresh air duct, then remove garnish moulding and

---

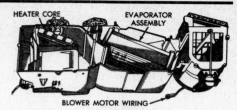

Fig. 14   Evaporator heater assembly

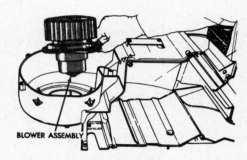

Fig. 16   Blower motor replacement. (Typical)

weatherstrip.
   i. Remove lower instrument panel from vehicle.
9. Remove evaporator heater unit hanger strap, then pull assembly rearward and out of vehicle, **Fig. 14**.
10. Place evaporator heater assembly on work bench, then remove vacuum harness attaching screw. Feed harness through hole in cover.
11. Remove thirteen cover attaching screws, then the cover. Temperature control door will come out with cover.
12. Remove heater core tube retaining bracket attaching screw, then the heater core, **Fig. 15**.
13. Remove 5 sound helment attaching screws, then the blower wheel by removing retainer clamp from blower wheel hub and sliding blower wheel from blower motor shaft.
14. Remove blower motor attaching screws, then the blower motor, **Fig. 16**.
15. Reverse procedure to install.

STOP LIGHT SWITCH
REPLACE

1. Disconnect battery ground cable.
2. Disconnect stop light switch electrical connector, then remove switch assembly.
3. Install new switch and connect switch electrical connector. If adjustment of switch is required, proceed as follows:
   a. Push switch forward until fully

seated. This will move brake pedal slightly forward.

b. Pull back on brake pedal until it will go back no further. This will cause the switch to ratchet backward into correct position.

NEUTRAL START & BACK-UP LIGHT SWITCH
REPLACE

NOTE: The following procedure applies to automatic transaxle equipped models only. On manual transaxle equipped models, a back-up switch is mounted on the transaxle case.

1. Disconnect battery ground cable.
2. Disconnect switch electrical connector.
3. Remove switch from transaxle case and allow fluid to drain into suitable container.
4. Install switch with new seal into transcase and connect switch electrical connector. Torque switch to 24 ft. lbs.

SPEED CONTROL
LOCK-IN SCREW ADJUSTMENT

NOTE: Lock-in accuracy can be affected

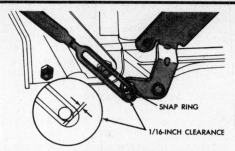

Fig. 17 Throttle control cable adjustment

by poor engine performance, overloaded vehicle, or improper slack in throttle control cable.

1. If the above note has been taken into consideration and vehicle speed still varies or drops more than 2–3 mph when speed control is activated, proceed as follows:
   a. Turn lock-in adjusting screw counterclockwise approximately ¼ turn for every 1 mph out of adjustment.
2. If vehicle speed increases more than 2–3 mph when speed control is activated, proceed as follows:
   a. Turn lock-in adjusting screw clockwise approximately ¼ turn for every 1 mph out of adjustment.

NOTE: The above adjustments should not exceed two turns in either direction, or damage to unit may occur.

THROTTLE CONTROL CABLE ADJUSTMENT

1. Start engine and allow to reach normal operating temperature.
2. Remove snap ring, then check clearance between throttle stud and cable clevis, **Fig. 17.**
3. If adjustment is required, proceed as follows:
   a. Loosen cable clamp attaching nut.
   b. Pull all slack out of cable, using head of throttle stud as a gauge.

NOTE: Do not pull cable so tight that it moves the throttle away from curb idle position.

   c. Torque cable clamp attaching nut to 45 inch lbs. and move cable clevis back on round portion of stud.
4. Install snap ring and check for proper operation.

4-135 Engine Section

ENGINE MOUNTS
REPLACE

NOTE: When positioning the engine, check driveshaft length as outlined in the "Front Suspension & Steering Section" under "Driveshaft Length, Adjust." The engine mounts incorporate slotted bolt holes and permit side-to-side positioning of the engine, thereby affecting the length of the driveshaft. Failure to properly position the engine may result in extensive damage to the engine.

Refer to **Figs. 1 through 3** when replacing engine mounts.

ENGINE
REPLACE

1. Disconnect battery ground cable.
2. Scribe hood hinge locations and remove hood.
3. Drain cooling system, then disconnect coolant hoses from radiator and engine.

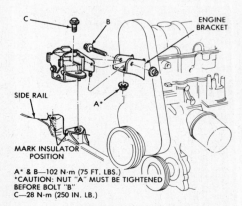

A* & B—102 N·m (75 FT. LBS.)
*CAUTION: NUT "A" MUST BE TIGHTENED BEFORE BOLT "B"
C—28 N·m (250 IN. LB.)

Fig. 1 Right side engine mount

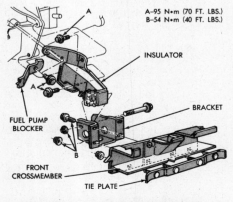

A—95 N·m (70 FT. LBS.)
B—54 N·m (40 FT. LBS.)

Fig. 2 Front engine mount

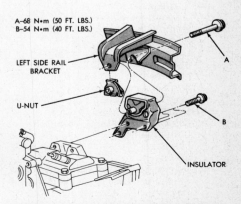

A—68 N·m (50 FT. LBS.)
B—54 N·m (40 FT. LBS.)

Fig. 3 Left side engine mount

Fig. 4 Electrical connector locations

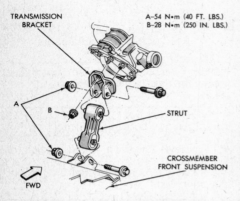

TRANSMISSION BRACKET

A–54 N•m (40 FT. LBS.)
B–28 N•m (250 IN. LBS.)

STRUT

CROSSMEMBER FRONT SUSPENSION

FWD

Fig. 6 Engine anti-roll strut

4. Remove radiator and fan assembly, then the air cleaner and hoses.
5. On models equipped with A/C, unfasten A/C compressor and position aside, leaving refrigerant hoses attached.
6. On models equipped with power steering, unfasten power steering pump and position aside.
7. On all models, drain oil pan and remove oil filter.
8. Disconnect electrical connectors from alternator, carburetor and engine, **Fig. 4.**
9. Disconnect fuel line, heater hose and accelerator cable, **Fig. 5.**
10. On models equipped with manual transaxle, proceed as follows:
    a. Disconnect clutch cable.
    b. Remove transaxle case lower cover.
    c. Disconnect exhaust pipe from exhaust manifold.
    d. Unfasten starter motor and position aside.
11. On models equipped with automatic transaxle, proceed as follows:
    a. Disconnect exhaust pipe from exhaust manifold.
    b. Unfasten starter motor and position aside.
    c. Remove transaxle case lower cover, then mark flex plate to torque converter for assembly reference.
    d. Remove torque converter-to-flex plate attaching bolts.

e. Position a C-clamp on front bottom of torque converter housing to prevent torque converter from falling out.
12. On all models, install a suitable transaxle holding fixture and attach a suitable lifting device.
13. Remove right side inner splash shield, then disconnect ground strap.
14. Remove long bolt through yoke bracket and insulator.

NOTE: If yoke screws are to be removed, mark position on side rail for assembly reference.

15. Remove transaxle case-to-cylinder block attaching bolts.
16. Remove front engine mount screw and nut.
17. On models equipped with manual transaxle, proceed as follows:
    a. Remove anti-roll strut, **Fig. 6.**
    b. Remove insulator through bolt from inside wheel housing or the insulator bracket-to-transaxle attaching bolts.
18. Reverse procedure to install.

INTAKE & EXHAUST MANIFOLD
REPLACE

1. Disconnect battery ground cable.
2. Drain cooling system, then disconnect all vacuum lines, electrical connectors and fuel lines from carburetor.
3. Remove throttle linkage, then the power steering pump drive belt, if equipped.
4. Disconnect power brake vacuum hose, if equipped, from intake manifold.
5. Remove coolant hoses from water crossover.
6. Raise and support vehicle.
7. Remove exhaust pipe from exhaust manifold.
8. On models equipped with power steering, unfasten power steering pump and position aside.
9. On all models, remove intake manifold support bracket, then the EGR tube.
10. Remove intake manifold attaching bolts, then lower vehicle.
11. Remove intake and exhaust manifold assembly from engine, **Fig. 7.**
12. Remove exhaust manifold retaining nuts and separate exhaust manifold from intake manifold.
13. Reverse procedure to install, noting the following:
    a. Discard gaskets and clean gasket surfaces on both manifolds and cylinder head.
    b. Use a straightedge to ensure gasket surfaces on manifolds are flat within .006 inch per foot of manifold length.
    c. Install new gaskets with suitable sealant on manifold side.
    d. Torque exhaust manifold retaining nuts and intake manifold attaching

Fig. 5 Fuel line, heater hose & accelerator cable connector locations

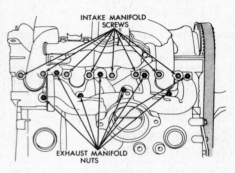

INTAKE MANIFOLD SCREWS

EXHAUST MANIFOLD NUTS

Fig. 7 Intake & exhaust manifold replacement

bolts to 200 inch lbs., starting at center and working outward in both directions.

TIMING SPROCKETS & OIL SEAL
ALTERNATOR BELT REMOVAL

1. Disconnect battery ground cable.
2. Loosen alternator locking screw, then loosen adjusting screw and remove the alternator belt.
3. Reverse procedure to install.

ALTERNATOR & COMPRESSOR MOUNTING BRACKET REMOVAL

For replacement of alternator and compressor mounting bracket, refer to **Figs. 8 and 9.**

POWER STEERING PUMP MOUNTING BRACKET REMOVAL

1. Remove pump locking screw, **Fig. 10.**
2. Remove pivot bolt and pivot nut, then the drive belt.
3. Remove power steering pump and lay aside.
4. Remove mounting bracket bolts, then the bracket.
5. Reverse procedure to install.

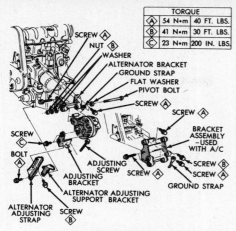

TORQUE		
A	54 N•m	40 FT. LBS.
B	41 N•m	30 FT. LBS.
C	23 N•m	200 IN. LBS.

Fig. 8 Alternator & A/C compressor mounting bracket removal. 1984

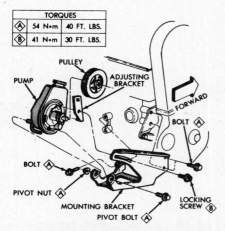

TORQUES		
A	54 N•m	40 FT. LBS.
B	41 N•m	30 FT. LBS.

Fig. 10 Power steering mounting bracket removal

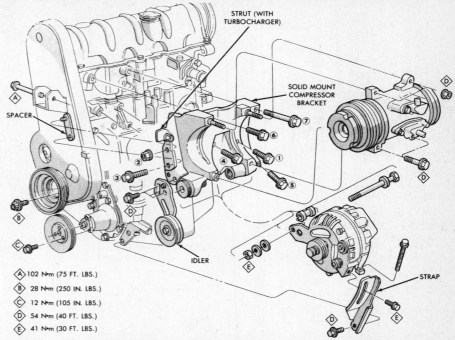

A	102 N•m	(75 FT. LBS.)
B	28 N•m	(250 IN. LBS.)
C	12 N•m	(105 IN. LBS.)
D	54 N•m	(40 FT. LBS.)
E	41 N•m	(30 FT. LBS.)

Fig. 9 Alternator & A/C compressor mounting bracket removal. 1985

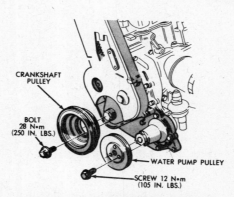

Fig. 11 Crankshaft & water pump pulley removal

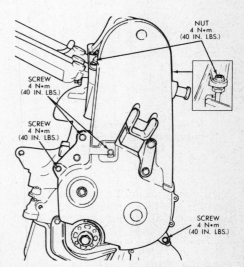

Fig. 12 Timing belt cover removal

CRANKSHAFT PULLEY & WATER PUMP PULLEY REMOVAL

1. Remove screws retaining water pump pulley to pump shaft, **Fig. 11.**
2. Remove bolts retaining crankshaft pulley.
3. Raise and support front of vehicle, then remove right inner splash shield and remove crankshaft pulley.
4. Reverse procedure to install.

TIMING BELT COVER REMOVAL

1. Remove nuts securing timing belt cover to the cylinder head, **Fig. 12.**
2. Remove screws securing the cover to the cylinder head, then remove both halves of the timing belt cover.
3. Position a suitable jack under engine, then remove right hand engine mount-bolt and raise engine slightly.
4. Loosen timing belt tensioner, then remove timing belt.
5. Reverse procedure to install.

CRANKSHAFT SPROCKET REMOVAL

1. With the timing belt removed from engine, remove the crankshaft sprocket bolt.
2. Remove crankshaft sprocket using a suitable puller.

CRANKSHAFT, INTERMEDIATE SHAFT & CAMSHAFT OIL SEAL SERVICE

Refer to **Figs. 13 and 14,** for removal and installation of crankshaft, intermediate shaft or camshaft seals.

CRANKSHAFT & INTERMEDIATE SHAFT TIMING

1. Rotate crankshaft and intermediate

shaft until markings on sprockets are aligned, **Fig. 15.**

CAMSHAFT TIMING

1. Rotate camshaft until arrows on hub are aligned with No. 1 camshaft cap to cylinder head line. Small hole must be located along vertical centerline.
2. Install timing belt. Refer to "Adjusting Drive Belt Tension" described elsewhere, for proper drive belt adjustment.
3. Rotate crankshaft two full revolutions and recheck timing.

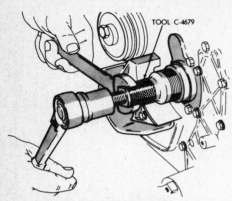

Fig. 13 Crankshaft, intermediate shaft & camshaft oil seal removal

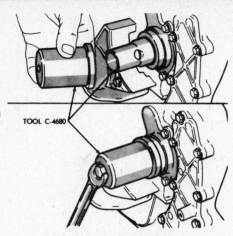

Fig. 14 Crankshaft, intermediate shaft & camshaft oil seal installation

Fig. 15 Aligning crankshaft & intermediate shaft timing marks

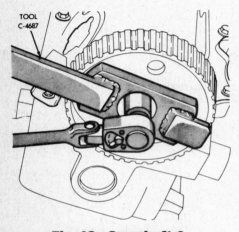

Fig. 16 Camshaft & intermediate shaft sprocket replacement

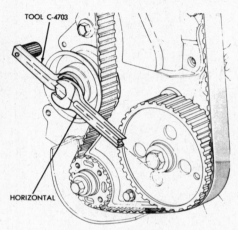

Fig. 17 Adjusting drive belt tension

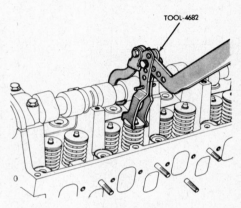

Fig. 18 Valve spring removal & installation

NOTE: Do not allow oil or solvents to contact the timing belt, since they will deteriorate the rubber and cause tooth slippage.

CAMSHAFT & INTERMEDIATE SHAFT SPROCKET REMOVAL & INSTALLATION

Refer to **Fig. 16,** for removal and installation of camshaft and intermediate shaft sprocket.

ADJUSTING DRIVE BELT TENSION

1. Remove spark plugs, then rotate crankshaft to TDC position.
2. Using a suitable tool, loosen tensioner lock nut, **Fig. 17.**
3. Reset tension so that belt tensioning tool's axis is within 15° of horizontal.
4. Rotate crankshaft two revolutions in a clockwise direction and position at

TDC, then tighten tensioner lock nut.

CYLINDER HEAD & VALVE ASSEMBLY

SERVICE BULLETIN Some engines may be equipped with cylinder heads which have oversize journals. When servicing the cylinder head on these engines, proper replacement components must be installed. To identify oversize cylinder head journals, the top of the bearing caps are painted green and "O/S J" is stamped on air pump end of head.

REMOVING & INSTALLING VALVE SPRINGS

Cylinder Head On Engine
1. Rotate crankshaft until piston is at TDC on compression stroke.
2. Apply 90–120 psi of compressed air into spark plug hole of valve spring

being removed.
3. Using tool 4682, compress valve spring enough to remove valve stem locks, **Fig. 18.**
4. Remove valve spring and spring seat.
5. Remove valve seal.

CYLINDER HEAD BOLT REMOVAL SEQUENCE

When removing cylinder head, remove cylinder head bolts in proper sequence, **Fig. 19.**

CYLINDER HEAD BOLT TIGHTENING SEQUENCE

Refer to **Fig. 20** for cylinder head bolt tightening sequence.

CAMSHAFT BEARING CAPS

SERVICE BULLETIN Some engines may be equipped with camshafts which have

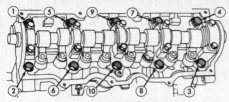

Fig. 19 Cylinder head bolt removal sequence

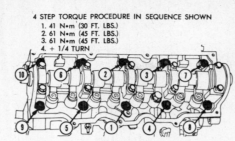

4 STEP TORQUE PROCEDURE IN SEQUENCE SHOWN
1. 41 N•m (30 FT. LBS.)
2. 61 N•m (45 FT. LBS.)
3. 61 N•m (45 FT. LBS.)
4. + 1/4 TURN

Fig. 20 Cylinder head bolt tightening sequence

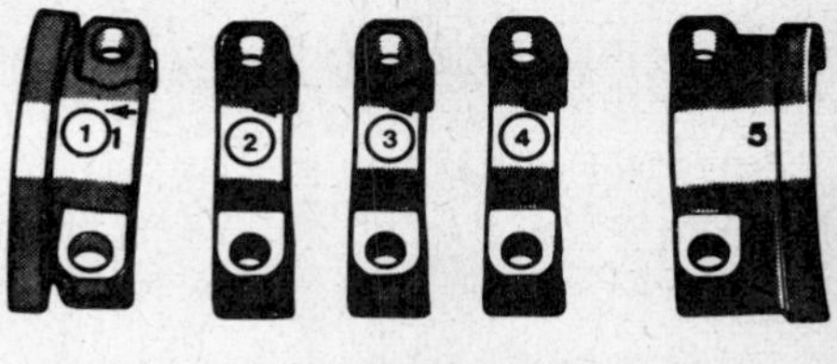

Fig. 21 Camshaft bearing cap installation

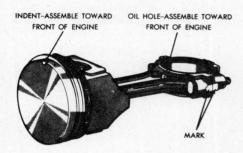

INDENT–ASSEMBLE TOWARD FRONT OF ENGINE

OIL HOLE–ASSEMBLE TOWARD FRONT OF ENGINE

MARK

Fig. 22 Piston & connecting rod assembly

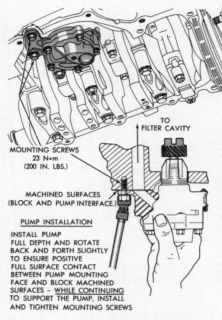

TO FILTER CAVITY

MOUNTING SCREWS
23 N•m
(200 IN. LBS.)

MACHINED SURFACES
(BLOCK AND PUMP INTERFACE.)

PUMP INSTALLATION

INSTALL PUMP FULL DEPTH AND ROTATE BACK AND FORTH SLIGHTLY TO ENSURE POSITIVE FULL SURFACE CONTACT BETWEEN PUMP MOUNTING FACE AND BLOCK MACHINED SURFACES – WHILE CONTINUING TO SUPPORT THE PUMP, INSTALL AND TIGHTEN MOUNTING SCREWS

Fig. 23 Oil pump assembly

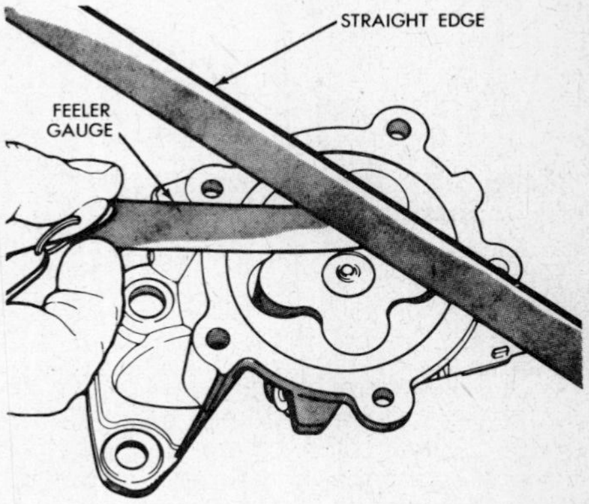

STRAIGHT EDGE

FEELER GAUGE

Fig. 24 Checking oil pump end play

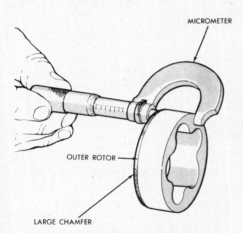

MICROMETER

OUTER ROTOR

LARGE CHAMFER

Fig. 25 Measuring oil pump outer rotor thickness

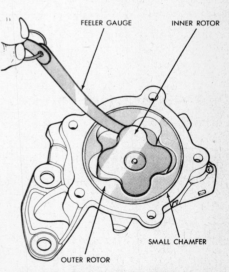

FEELER GAUGE

INNER ROTOR

SMALL CHAMFER

OUTER ROTOR

Fig. 26 Measuring clearance between oil pump rotors

oversize journals. When servicing the camshaft on these engines, proper replacement components must be installed. To identify oversize camshaft journals, the barrel of the cam is painted green and "O/S J" is stamped on the air pump end of the camshaft. Never install an oversize journal camshaft in a cylinder head with standard size bores, or cam cap breakage could result.

1. With caps removed from engine, check oil holes for obstructions.
2. With caps aligned in proper sequence, make sure arrow on caps 1, 2, 3 and 4 point toward timing belt, **Fig. 21.**
3. Apply suitable sealant to No. 1 and 5 bearing caps.
4. Install caps before installing camshaft seals, then torque cap bolts to 165 inch lbs.

PISTON & ROD ASSEMBLY

When installing the piston and rod assembly, the indentation on the top of piston must face the timing belt side of the engine, **Fig. 22.** The oil hole on connecting rod must also face the timing belt side of the engine and be on the same side as the indented mark on the piston.

ENGINE LUBRICATION SYSTEM

OIL PUMP ASSEMBLY

1. With oil pan removed, remove the screw securing oil pump to the cylinder block, **Fig. 23.**
2. Reverse procedure to install. Torque oil pump attaching screw to 200 inch lbs.

OIL PUMP SERVICE

1. Measure the following oil pump clearances:
   a. End play, **Fig. 24.** End play should be .001–.004 inch.
   b. Outer rotor thickness, **Fig. 25.** Thickness should be .825 inch, minimum. Install outer rotor with chamfered edge in pump body.

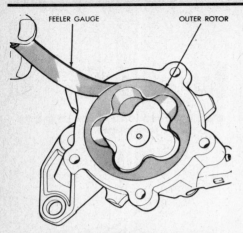

Fig. 27 Measuring oil pump outer rotor clearance

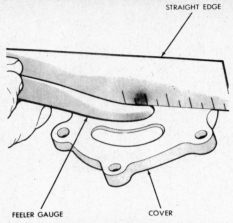

Fig. 28 Measuring oil pump cover clearance

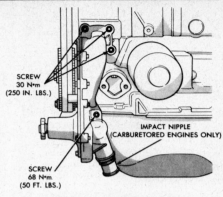

Fig. 29 Water pump replacement

c. Clearance between rotors, **Fig. 26**, should be .010 inch, maximum.
d. Outer rotor clearance, **Fig. 27**. Clearance should be .014 inch, maximum.
e. Oil pump cover clearance, **Fig. 28**, should be no greater than .003 inch.
f. Oil pressure relief valve spring length should be 1.95 inches.

WATER PUMP
REPLACE

1. Disconnect battery ground cable.
2. Drain cooling system, then remove upper radiator hose.
3. Remove A/C compressor from mounting brackets and position aside with refrigerant lines attached, if equipped.
4. Remove alternator.
5. Disconnect lower radiator hose, bypass hose and four water pump to engine attaching screws, **Fig. 29**, then remove water pump from engine.
6. Reverse procedure to install.

BELT TENSION DATA

		NEW	USED
1984	Air Cond.	95	80
	Alternator	115	80
	Power Steer.	95	80
1985	Air Cond.	105	80
	Alternator	115	80
	Power Steer.	105	80

4-156 Engine Section

ENGINE MOUNTS
REPLACE

NOTE: When positioning the engine, check driveshaft length as outlined in the "Front Suspension & Steering Section" under "Driveshaft Length, Adjust." The engine mounts incorporate slotted bolt holes and permit side-to-side positioning of the engine, thereby affecting the length of the driveshaft. Failure to properly position the engine may result in extensive damage to the engine.

Refer to **Figs. 1 through 3** when replacing engine mounts.

ENGINE
REPLACE

1. Disconnect battery ground cable.
2. Scribe alignment marks on hood and

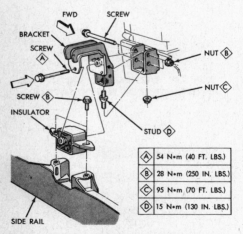

A	54 N•m (40 FT. LBS.)
B	28 N•m (250 IN. LBS.)
C	95 N•m (70 FT. LBS.)
D	15 N•m (130 IN. LBS.)

Fig. 1 Right side engine mount. 1984

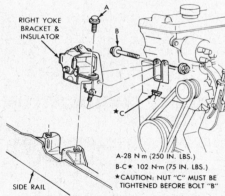

A-28 N•m (250 IN. LBS.)
B-C ★ 102 N•m (75 FT. LBS.)
★CAUTION: NUT "C" MUST BE TIGHTENED BEFORE BOLT "B"

Fig. 1A Right side engine mount. 1985

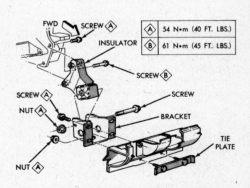

| A | 54 N•m (40 FT. LBS.) |
| B | 61 N•m (45 FT. LBS.) |

Fig. 2 Front engine mount

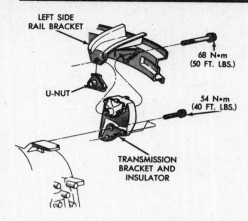

Fig. 3   Left side engine mount

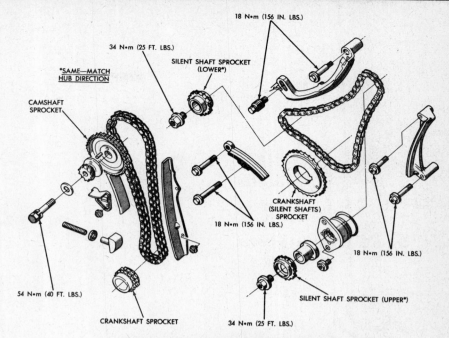

Timing gears & chain assembly

hood hinge, then remove hood.
3. Drain cooling system, then disconnect radiator hoses at radiator and engine.
4. Remove radiator and fan shroud, then remove air cleaner.
5. On models equipped with A/C, remove A/C compressor from mounting bracket and position aside with hoses attached.
6. On models equipped with power steering, remove power steering pump from mounting bracket and position aside with hoses attached.
7. On all models, drain crankcase and remove oil filter.
8. Disconnect electrical connectors at alternator, carburetor and engine.
9. Disconnect fuel line, heater hose and accelerator cable.
10. Remove alternator from mounting bracket and position aside.
11. Disconnect exhaust pipe from exhaust manifold, then remove starter motor.
12. Remove transaxle case lower cover and place alignment marks on flex plate and torque converter, then remove converter to flex plate attaching screws. Attach a C-clamp to front lower portion of converter housing to retain torque converter in housing when engine is being removed.
13. Install a suitable transmission holding fixture and attach a suitable engine lifting device.
14. Remove right hand inner splash shield, then disconnect ground strap.
15. Remove right hand engine mount to insulator through bolt. Mark insulator position on side rail to assure correct positioning during installation.
16. Remove transmission case to engine block attaching bolts.
17. Remove front engine mount to bracket attaching bolt, then carefully lift engine from vehicle.
18. Reverse procedure to install.

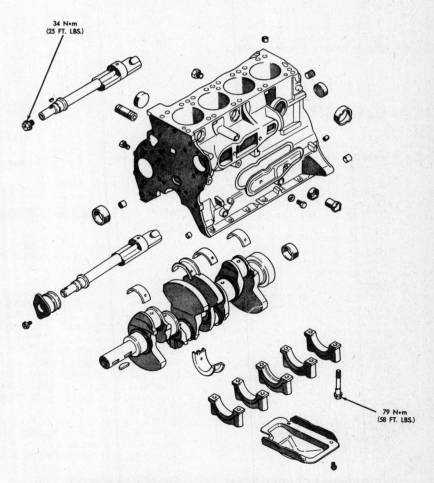

Crankshaft, bearings & silent shaft assembly

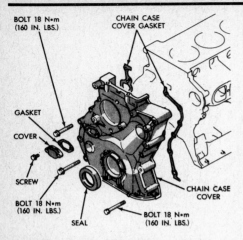

Fig. 4 Chain case cover removal

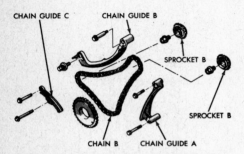

Fig. 5 Silent shaft drive chain, replace

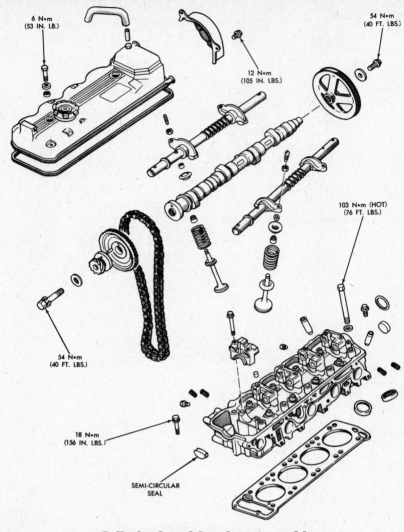

Cylinder head & valve assembly

TIMING GEARS & OIL SEALS

SERVICE BULLETIN A rattle from the camshaft and silent shaft chain area at the front of the engine accompanied by a broken camshaft timing chain guide may be caused by a blocked oil feed hole to the timing chain tensioner in the oil pump housing. This blockage occurs when a portion of the oil pump mounting gasket collapses into the channel in the pump cover which directs oil from the main gallery in the block to the chain tensioner feed hole. The lockwasher between silent shaft chain guide B pivot bolt and timing chain guide may also be missing. This problem may be corrected as follows:

1. Remove chain case cover, silent shaft chain, camshaft chain and broken chain guide.
2. Remove engine oil pump, then clean all gasket material from pump and engine block.
3. Install new gasket (part No. MD060521), then the oil pump and new timing chain guide. Ensure gasket has hole cut in it.
4. Install timing chain, silent shaft chain, guides and chain case cover. Ensure chain guide B pivot bolt lock washer is in place before installing cover.

TIMING CHAIN CASE COVER, REMOVAL

1. Disconnect battery ground cable.
2. Remove alternator locking screw, then loosen jam nut and adjusting screw. Remove drive belt.
3. Remove distributor attaching nut, then the distributor from cylinder head and position aside.
4. On models equipped with A/C, remove front and rear A/C compressor to bracket attaching screws, then the A/C compressor and position aside.
5. On models equipped with power steering, remove power steering pump pivot and lock screws, then the drive belt.
6. Remove power steering pump attaching screw and nut, then position power steering pump aside.
7. Remove power steering pump bracket to engine attaching screws, then the bracket.
8. On all models, raise and support vehi-

cle, then remove right inner splash shield.
9. Drain crankcase, then remove crankshaft drive pulley.
10. Lower vehicle and position a suitable jack under engine.
11. Remove engine mount to frame side rail through bolt, then remove engine oil dipstick.
12. Remove air cleaner assembly, then the spark plug wires.
13. Disconnect vacuum hoses from cylinder head cover.
14. Remove cylinder head cover attaching screws, then the cylinder head cover.
15. Remove two front cylinder head attaching bolts. Do not disturb any other cylinder head bolts.
16. Remove oil pan attaching bolts, then the oil pan.
17. Remove timing indicator plate from timing chain case cover.
18. Remove engine mounting plate from timing chain case cover.

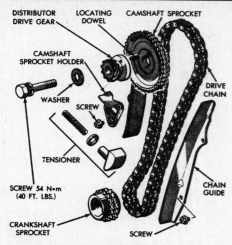

Fig. 6 Camshaft drive chain, replace

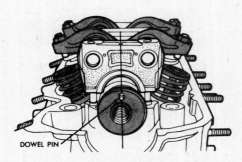

Fig. 7 Camshaft timing mark alignment

19. Refer to **Fig. 4** and remove remaining screws securing chain case cover to engine.

SILENT SHAFT DRIVE CHAIN, REMOVAL

1. Remove timing chain case cover as previously described.
2. Remove sprocket screws, then the drive chain, crankshaft sprocket and silent shaft sprocket, **Fig. 5**.

CAMSHAFT DRIVE CHAIN, REMOVAL

1. Remove timing chain case cover as previously described.
2. Remove camshaft sprocket holder, then the left and right timing chain guides, **Fig. 6**.
3. Depress tensioner to remove drive chain.
4. Remove crankshaft and camshaft sprockets.

CAMSHAFT INSTALLATION

1. With camshaft bearing caps installed, rotate camshaft until timing marks are aligned as shown in **Fig. 7**.

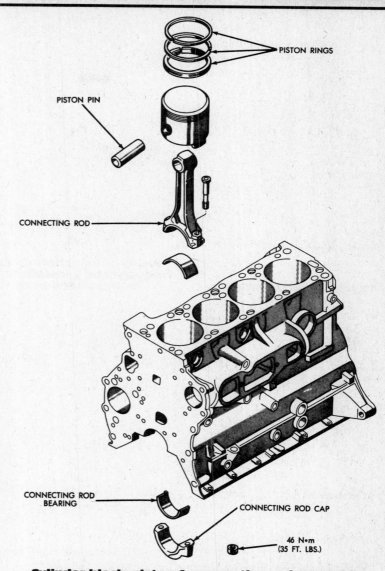

Cylinder block, piston & connecting rod assembly

TIMING CHAIN INSTALLATION

1. Install sprocket holder, and the left and right chain guides, **Fig. 5**.
2. Rotate crankshaft until No. 1 piston is at TDC on compression stroke.
3. Install tensioner spring assembly onto oil pump body, **Fig. 6**.
4. Install timing chain on camshaft sprocket and crankshaft sprocket. Ensure timing marks are aligned, **Fig. 8**. Timing marks on sprockets are punch marks on the teeth, while timing marks on chain are plated links.
5. Align crankshaft sprocket to crankshaft keyway and slide into place. Align camshaft sprocket dowel hole to camshaft dowel hole.
6. Install dowel pin, then the distributor drive gear. Install sprocket attaching screw onto camshaft and torque to 40 ft. lbs.

SILENT SHAFT CHAIN INSTALLATION & ADJUSTMENT

1. Install silent shaft chain drive pulley onto crankshaft.
2. Install silent shaft chain onto oil pump sprocket and silent shaft sprocket, **Fig. 9**.
3. Ensure timing marks are aligned. Timing marks on the sprockets are punch marks on the teeth, while marks on the chain are plated links.
4. Align crankshaft sprocket plated link with punch mark on sprocket.
5. Position chain on crankshaft sprocket, then install oil pump sprocket and silent shaft sprockets on their respective shafts.
6. Install oil pump and silent shaft sprocket attaching bolts. Torque attaching bolts to 25 ft. lbs.
7. Install three chain guides. Tighten snug retaining bolts.

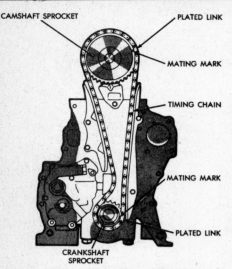

Fig. 8   Timing chain installation

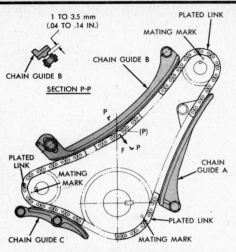

Fig. 9   Silent shaft chain adjustment & installation w/engine removed

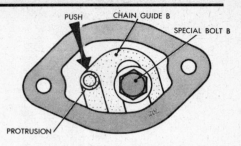

Fig. 10   Silent shaft chain adjustment w/engine installed

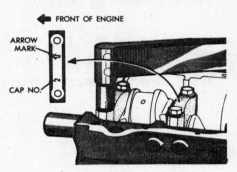

Fig. 13   Main bearing cap installation

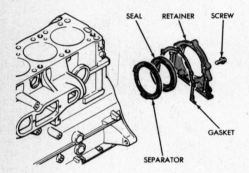

Fig. 11   Rear oil seal, replace

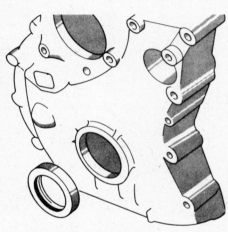

Fig. 12   Front oil seal, replace

8. Refer to **Fig. 9** and adjust silent shaft chain tension as follows:
   a. Tighten chain guide "A" mounting screws.
   b. Tighten chain guide "C" mounting screws.
   c. Shake oil pump and silent shaft sprockets to collect slack at point "P."
   d. Adjust position of chain guide "B" so when the chain is pulled in direction of arrow "F," clearance between chain guide "B" and chain links will be .04–.14 inch. Tighten chain guide "B" mounting screws.
9. Install new gasket on chain case, coat gasket with suitable sealant, then install chain case to block and torque attaching screws to 156 inch lbs.

TENSION ADJUSTMENT W/ ENGINE INSTALLED

1. Remove cover over access hole in chain case cover, **Fig. 10**.
2. Loosen bolt "B," **Fig. 10**.
3. Apply pressure by hand on boss indicated in **Fig. 10**, then torque bolt "B" to 160 inch lbs.

CRANKSHAFT, BEARINGS & SILENT SHAFT

REAR OIL SEAL, REPLACE

1. Remove screws attaching crankshaft rear oil seal retainer, then the retainer, **Fig. 11**.
2. Remove separator from retainer, then the oil seal.
3. Install new oil seal into retainer, then the separator. Ensure oil hole is positioned at separator bottom.

FRONT OIL SEAL, REPLACE

1. Remove crankshaft pulley, then pry out oil seal, **Fig. 12**. Use caution not to nick or damage sealing surface.
2. Lightly apply suitable locking compound to outside portion of new oil seal, then install oil seal.
3. Install crankshaft drive pulley. Torque attaching bolt to 87 ft. lbs.

MAIN BEARING CAPS

1. Install main bearing caps in sequence starting with cap nearest timing chain. Ensure arrows on caps are pointed in direction of timing chain, **Fig. 13**.

OIL PUMP & SILENT SHAFT

1. Refer to **Fig. 14** and remove silent shaft screw, then the silent shaft.
2. Remove oil pump to cylinder block attaching screw, then the oil pump.

LEFT SILENT SHAFT THRUST PLATE, REPLACE

1. Install two .31 inch screws into tapped holes in thrust plate, **Fig. 15**.
2. Turn both screws evenly until thrust plate loosens, then pull thrust plate from silent shaft.

SILENT SHAFT CLEARANCES

Before installing silent shaft, measure outer diameter to outer bearing clearance. Clearance should be .0008–.0024 inch (.02–.06mm). Measure inner diameter to inner bearing clearance. Clearance should be .0020 to .0035 inch (.05–.09mm).

PISTON & ROD ASSEMBLY

During installation of piston and rod assembly, arrow at top of piston must face toward front of engine (timing chain), **Fig. 16**. Refer to **Fig. 17** for correct piston ring installation.

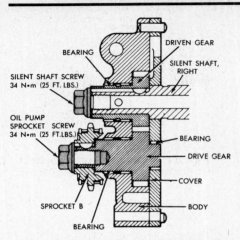

Fig. 14 Oil pump & silent shaft, removal

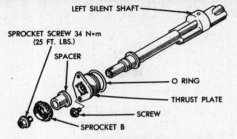

Fig. 15 Left silent shaft thrust plate, removal

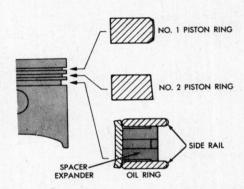

Fig. 17 Piston ring installation

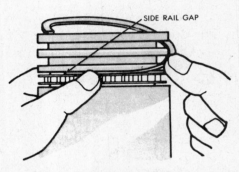

Fig. 18 Installing oil ring side rail

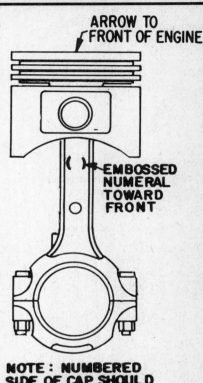

Fig. 16 Piston & rod assembly

1. Note the following ring groove clearances:
   a. No. 1 upper: .0024–.0039 inch (.06–.10mm); wear limit, .004 inch (.1mm).
   b. No. 2 intermediate: .0008–.0024 inch (.02–.06mm); wear limit, .004 inch (.1mm).
   c. Oil ring: oil ring side rails must be free to rotate after assembly.
2. Note the following end gap clearances:
   a. No. 1 upper: .010–.018 inch (.25–.45mm); wear limit, .039 inch (.1mm).
   b. No. 2 intermediate: .010–.018 inch (.25–.45 mm); wear limit, .039 inch (.1mm).
   c. Oil ring side rail: .008–.035 inch (.2–.4mm); wear limit .059 inch (1.5mm).
3. Connecting rod side clearance should be .004–.010 inch (.1–.25mm).

INSTALLING PISTON RING SIDE RAIL

1. Place one end of side rail between piston ring groove and spacer expander, **Fig. 18.**
2. Hold end of ring firmly and press downward on portion to be installed until side rail is in position. Do not use piston ring extender.
3. Install upper side rail first, then the lower side rail.

PISTON RING END GAP LOCATION

1. Position piston ring end gaps as shown in **Fig. 19.**
2. Position oil ring expander gap at least 45° from side rail gaps, but not on the piston pin center line or in thrust direction.

CYLINDER HEAD & VALVE ASSEMBLY

CYLINDER HEAD, REPLACE

1. Disconnect battery ground cable and drain cooling system.
2. Remove upper radiator hose, then disconnect heater hoses.
3. Disconnect spark plug wires at spark plugs, then remove distributor.
4. Remove carburetor to valve cover bracket.
5. Disconnect fuel lines from fuel pump, then remove fuel pump.
6. Remove cylinder head cover attaching bolts, then the cylinder head cover.
7. Disconnect all electrical connectors and vacuum lines from cylinder head.
8. Disconnect throttle linkage from carburetor, then remove water pump belt and pulley.
9. Rotate crankshaft until No. 1 piston is at TDC.
10. Paint a white reference mark on the timing chain in line with timing mark on camshaft sprocket.
11. Remove camshaft sprocket bolt, sprocket and distributor drive gear.
12. Raise and support vehicle, then disconnect air feed lines.
13. Remove power steering pump and position aside.
14. Disconnect ground strap and remove dipstick tube.
15. Remove exhaust manifold heat shield, then disconnect exhaust pipe from catalytic converter and lower vehicle.
16. Remove cylinder head bolts in sequence shown in **Fig. 20.**
17. Reverse procedure to install. Refer to cylinder head bolt tightening sequence, **Fig. 21,** and torque cylinder head bolts in two steps as follows:
    a. Torque all bolts to 35 ft. lbs.
    b. Torque all bolts except No. 11 to 69 ft. lbs. on a cold engine or 75 ft. lbs. on a hot engine.
    c. Torque cylinder head to chain case cover bolts, No. 11, to 156 inch lbs.

CAMSHAFT BEARING CAP

1. Align camshaft bearing caps with arrows pointing toward timing chain, **Fig. 22.** Install bearing caps in numerical order.

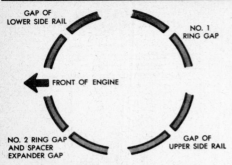

Fig. 19   Piston ring end gap location

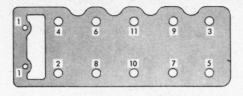

Fig. 20   Cylinder head bolt removal sequence

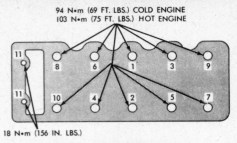

94 N•m (69 FT. LBS.) COLD ENGINE
103 N•m (75 FT. LBS.) HOT ENGINE

18 N•m (156 IN. LBS.)

Fig. 21   Cylinder head bolt tightening sequence

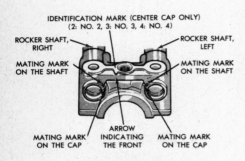

Fig. 22   Camshaft bearing cap installation

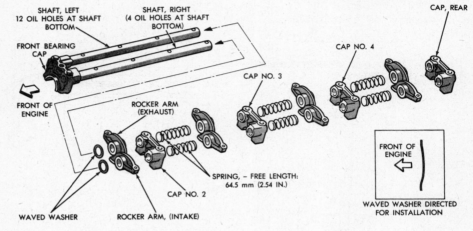

Fig. 23   Rocker arm shaft assembly

ROCKER ARM SHAFT ASSEMBLY

1. Refer to **Fig. 23** and install bolts in front bearing caps.
2. Install wave washers, rocker arms, bearing caps and spring in order shown, **Fig. 23.**
3. Place rocker shaft assembly into position, then rotate camshaft until dowel pin hole is in vertical centerline, **Fig. 7.**
4. Torque camshaft bearing cap bolts to 85 inch lbs., following the sequence listed below:
   a. No. 3 cap bolts
   b. No. 2 cap bolts
   c. No. 4 cap bolts
   d. Front cap bolts
   e. Rear cap bolts
5. Repeat step 4, increasing torque to 175 inch lbs.

INSTALLED VALVE SPRING HEIGHT

1. Measure installed height of valve spring between spring seat and spring retainer, **Fig. 24.** Installed height should be 1.590 inches (40.4mm). If height is greater than 1.629 inches (41.4mm), replace spring.

VALVE CLEARANCE ADJUSTMENT

NOTE: Check hot engine torque on cylinder head bolts before performing valve adjustments.

1. Allow engine to reach normal operating temperature, then position piston at TDC on compression stroke.
2. Loosen valve adjuster lock nut, then adjust valve clearance by rotating adjusting screw while measuring with a feeler gauge, **Fig. 25.**
3. Valve clearance should be as follows: intake, .006 inch; exhaust, .010 inch.
4. Tighten lock nut securely while holding adjusting screw with screwdriver.

INTAKE MANIFOLD, REPLACE

1. Disconnect battery ground cable and drain cooling system.
2. Disconnect hose between water pump and intake manifold.
3. Disconnect carburetor air horn and position aside.
4. Disconnect carburetor and intake manifold vacuum hoses, throttle linkage and fuel line.
5. Remove fuel filter and fuel pump and position aside.
6. Remove mounting nuts and washers securing intake manifold, then the intake manifold.
7. Reverse procedure to install.

EXHAUST MANIFOLD, REPLACE

1. Disconnect battery ground cable and drain cooling system.
2. Remove air cleaner, then the power steering pump drive belt, if equipped.
3. Raise and support vehicle.
4. Disconnect exhaust pipe from exhaust manifold.
5. Disconnect air injection tube assembly from exhaust manifold, then lower vehicle.
6. Disconnect air injection tube assembly from air pump and position tube assembly aside.
7. Unfasten power steering pump, if equipped, and position aside.
8. Remove heat cowl from exhaust manifold.
9. Remove exhaust manifold retaining nuts and the exhaust manifold.
10. Reverse procedure to install.

VALVE TIMING
INTAKE OPENS BEFORE TDC

Engine	Year	Degrees
4-156	1984–85	25

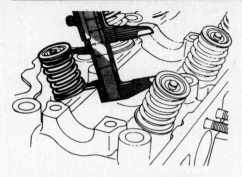

Fig. 24 Measuring installed valve spring height

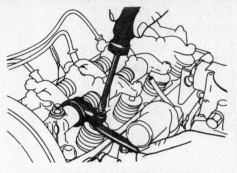

Fig. 25 Adjusting valve clearance

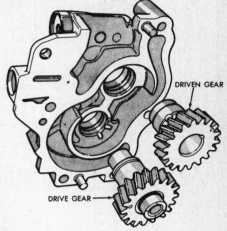

Fig. 26 Oil pump bearing clearance

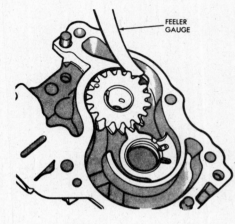

Fig. 27 Driven gear to housing clearance

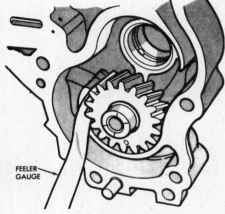

Fig. 28 Drive gear to housing clearance

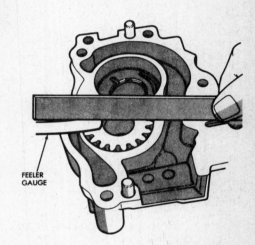

Fig. 29 Driven gear end play

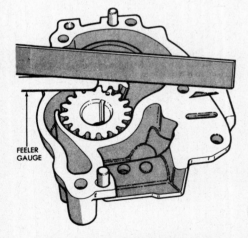

Fig. 30 Drive gear end play

ENGINE LUBRICATION SYSTEM

OIL PAN, REPLACE

1. Drain crankcase oil from engine.
2. Remove oil pan attaching screws, then the oil pan.
3. Clean oil pan rail and oil pan.
4. Install oil pan using new gasket. Torque oil pan attaching screws to 60 inch lbs.

OIL PUMP SERVICE

1. Measure drive gear to bearing clearance, **Fig. 26.** Clearance should be .0008–.0020 inch (.02–.05mm).
2. Measure driven gear to bearing clearance, **Fig. 26.** Clearance should be .0008–.0020 inch (.02–.05mm).
3. Measure driven gear to housing clearance, **Fig. 27.** Clearance should be .0043–.0059 inch (.11–.15mm).
4. Measure drive gear to housing clearance, **Fig. 28.** Clearance should be .0043–.0059 inch (.11–.15mm).
5. Measure driven gear end play, **Fig. 29.** End play should be .0016–.0039 inch (.04–.10mm).
6. Measure drive gear end play., **Fig. 30.** End play should be .0020–.0043 inch (.05–.11mm).

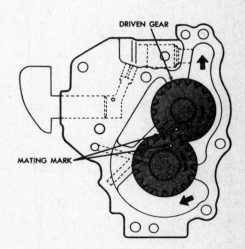

Fig. 31 Oil pump gear alignment

7. Measure relief valve spring free length. Free length should be 1.850 inch (47mm).
8. Measure relief valve spring load. Spring load should be 9.5 lbs. @ 1.575 inch (42.2N @ 40mm).
9. Refer to **Fig. 31** and align mating marks of drive and driven gears, then prime pump with clean oil and install on engine.

WATER PUMP
REPLACE

1. Disconnect battery ground cable.
2. Drain cooling system.
3. Disconnect radiator hose, bypass hose, and heater hose from water pump.
4. Remove drive pulley shield.
5. Remove locking screw and pivot screws.
6. Remove drive belt, then the water pump from engine.
7. Reverse procedure to install.

BELT TENSION DATA

	New	Used
Air Cond.	115	80
Alternator	115	80
Power Steer	95	80

Clutch & Manual Transaxle Section

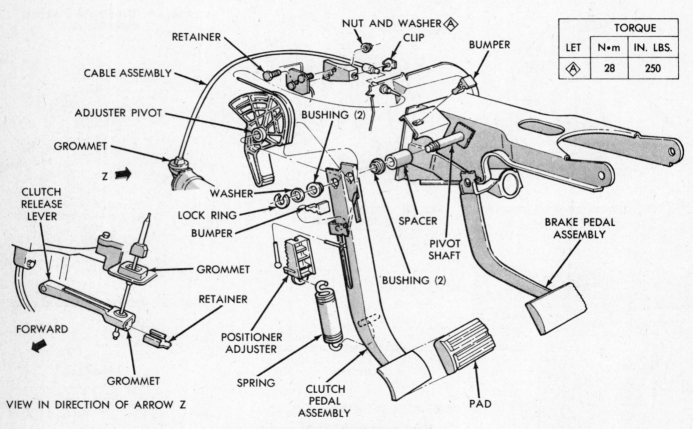

TORQUE		
LET	N•m	IN. LBS.
⬩A⬩	28	250

Fig. 1 Clutch cable routing

VIEW IN DIRECTION OF ARROW Z

CLUTCH
ADJUST

The clutch release cable, **Fig. 1**, cannot be adjusted on these models. When the cable is properly routed, the spring between the clutch pedal and positioner adjuster will hold the clutch cable in proper position. An adjuster pivot is used to hold release cable in place to ensure complete clutch release when clutch pedal is depressed.

SERVICE BULLETIN A broken clutch cable, slow clutch action or high clutch pedal effort on 1984 models may be the result of an improperly routed clutch cable. The transaxle cable mounting shelf contains two holes, **Fig. 2**. One hole is for clutch cable retention and the other is for manufacturing purposes. If the cable is not routed as shown in **Fig. 2**, reroute as necessary, replacing cable if damaged.

CLUTCH
REPLACE

1. Remove transaxle as outlined under "Manual Transaxle, Replace" procedure.
2. Mark relationship between clutch cover and flywheel for reference during assembly, then install a suitable clutch disc aligning tool through clutch disc

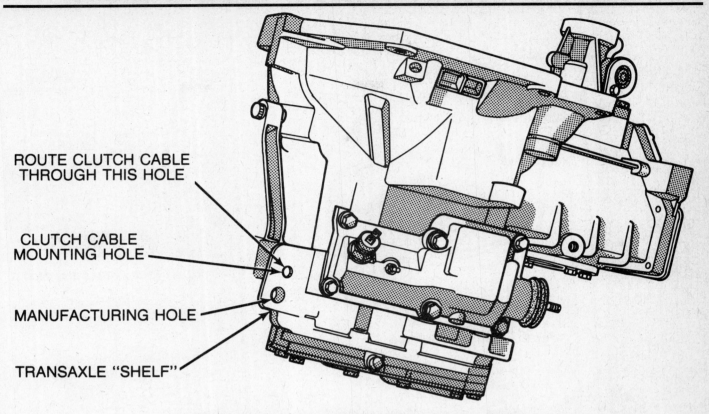

ROUTE CLUTCH CABLE THROUGH THIS HOLE

CLUTCH CABLE MOUNTING HOLE

MANUFACTURING HOLE

TRANSAXLE "SHELF"

Fig. 2   Clutch cable mounting hole identification

hub to prevent clutch disc from falling and damaging faces.
3. Gradually loosen clutch cover attaching bolts, then remove pressure plate, cover assembly and disc from flywheel.
4. Remove clutch release shaft and slide release bearing assembly off input shaft seal retainer. Remove fork from release bearing thrust plate.
5. Reverse procedure to install. Align ref-

erence marks made during disassembly, then using a clutch disc alignment tool, install disc, plate and cover to flywheel. Refer to **Fig. 3** for torque specifications.

GEARSHIFT LINKAGE
ADJUST

1. Remove lock pin from transaxle selec-

tor shaft housing, **Fig. 4.**
2. Reverse lock pin so long end is facing downward, then insert lock pin into same threaded hole while pushing selector shaft into selector housing. This locks selector in 1-2 neutral position, **Fig. 4.**
3. Remove gearshift knob, retaining nut and pull-up ring, **Fig. 5.**
4. Remove boot assembly from console, then the console.
5. Fabricate two cable adjusting pins as shown in **Fig. 6.**
6. Adjust selector cable and torque adjusting screw to 55 inch lbs., **Fig. 7.**

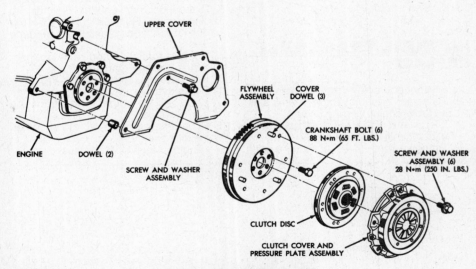

UPPER COVER

FLYWHEEL ASSEMBLY

COVER DOWEL (3)

CRANKSHAFT BOLT (6) 88 N•m (65 FT. LBS.)

SCREW AND WASHER ASSEMBLY (6) 28 N•m (250 IN. LBS.)

ENGINE

DOWEL (2)

SCREW AND WASHER ASSEMBLY

CLUTCH DISC

CLUTCH COVER AND PRESSURE PLATE ASSEMBLY

Fig. 3   Clutch assembly

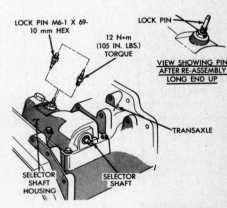

LOCK PIN M6-1 X 69-10 mm HEX

LOCK PIN

12 N•m (105 IN. LBS.) TORQUE

VIEW SHOWING PIN AFTER RE-ASSEMBLY LONG END UP

TRANSAXLE

SELECTOR SHAFT HOUSING

SELECTOR SHAFT

Fig. 4   Lock pin removal & installation

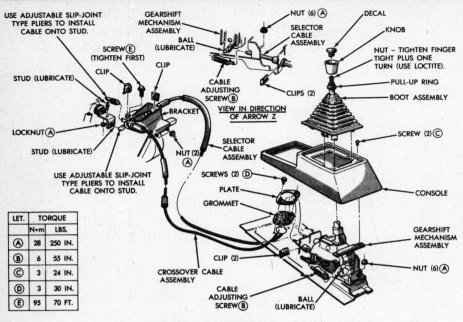

LET.	TORQUE	
	N•m	LBS.
Ⓐ	28	250 IN.
Ⓑ	6	55 IN.
Ⓒ	3	24 IN.
Ⓓ	3	30 IN.
Ⓔ	95	70 FT.

Fig. 5   Gear shift linkage

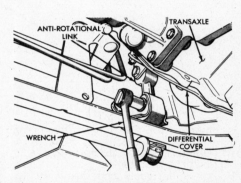

Fig. 6   Cable adjusting pins

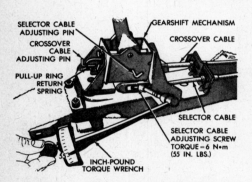

Fig. 7   Adjusting selector cable

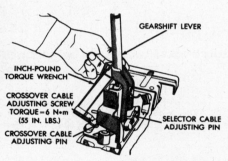

Fig. 8   Adjusting crossover cable

Fig. 9   Removing anti-rotational link

NOTE: The selector cable adjusting screw must be properly torqued.

7. Adjust crossover cable and torque adjusting screw to 55 inch lbs., **Fig. 8.**

NOTE: The crossover cable adjusting screw must be properly torqued.

8. Install console and boot assembly, then the pull-up ring, retaining nut and gearshift knob. Apply suitable locking compound to retaining nut and tighten finger tight plus one turn.
9. Remove lock pin from selector shaft housing, then reinstall lock pin so long

end is up in selector shaft housing, **Fig. 4.** Torque lock pin to 105 inch lbs.
10. Check for proper operation.

MANUAL TRANSAXLE
REPLACE

1. Disconnect battery ground cable.
2. Raise and support vehicle, then install suitable engine support fixture.
3. Disconnect gearshift linkage and clutch cable from transaxle.
4. Remove front wheel and tire assem-

blies.
5. Remove left front splash shield, then the left engine mount from transaxle.
6. Disconnect driveshafts. Refer to "Driveshaft, Replace" procedure under "Front Suspension & Steering Section."
7. Support transaxle and remove upper clutch housing attaching bolts.
8. Remove anti-rotational link, **Fig. 9.**
9. Pry transaxle rearward until mainshaft clears clutch, then lower transaxle from vehicle.
10. Reverse procedure to install. When installing left engine mount, refer to "Engine Mounts" procedure.

Rear Axle, Suspension & Brake Section

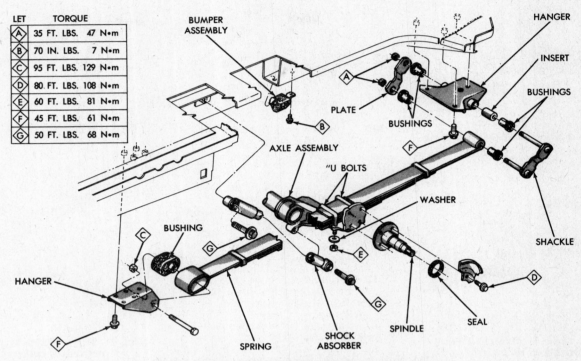

LET	TORQUE	
A	35 FT. LBS.	47 N•m
B	70 IN. LBS.	7 N•m
C	95 FT. LBS.	129 N•m
D	80 FT. LBS.	108 N•m
E	60 FT. LBS.	81 N•m
F	45 FT. LBS.	61 N•m
G	50 FT. LBS.	68 N•m

Fig. 1   Rear axle & suspension assembly

REAR AXLE & SPRING
REPLACE

REMOVAL

1. Raise and support vehicle, then position suitable floor jack under axle assembly and raise axle assembly to relieve weight on rear springs.
2. Disconnect rear brake proportioning valve spring, then the lower ends of the rear shock absorbers at axle brackets, **Fig. 1.**
3. Remove U-bolt attaching nuts and washers, then the U-bolt.
4. Lower rear axle assembly, allowing rear spring to hang free.
5. Remove four attaching bolts from front spring hanger.
6. Remove rear spring shackle attaching nuts and plate, then the shackle from the spring.
7. Remove front pivot bolt from front spring hanger.
8. Remove springs from vehicle.

INSTALLATION

1. Assemble shackle, bushings and plate on rear of spring and rear spring hanger, then install shackle bolt, **Fig. 1.** Do not tighten nut at this point.
2. Assemble front spring hanger to front of spring eye, then install pivot bolt. Do not tighten nut at this point.

NOTE: Pivot bolt must face inboard to prevent structural damage during installation of spring.

3. Raise front spring, then install four hanger attaching bolts. Torque bolts to 45 ft. lbs.
4. Raise axle assembly with axle centered under spring center bolt, then install U-bolt and washer. Torque U-bolt attaching nut to 60 ft. lbs.
5. Install shock absorbers and attaching nuts. Do not tighten nuts at this point.
6. Lower vehicle to floor, allowing full weight of vehicle on wheels, then torque the following fasteners: front pivot bolt, 95 ft. lbs.; shackle nuts, 35 ft. lbs.; 1984 shock absorber bolts, 50 ft. lbs.; 1985 shock absorber upper bolts, 85 ft. lbs.; 1985 shock absorber lower bolts, 80 ft. lbs.
7. Connect rear brake proportioning valve spring.

REAR WHEEL ALIGNMENT

Due to the design of the rear suspension and the incorporation of stub axles or wheel spindles, it is possible to adjust camber and toe of the rear wheels on these vehicles. Adjustment is controlled by adding shims approximately .010 inch thick between spindle mounting surface and spindle mounting plate. The amount of adjustment is approximately 3° per shim. Refer to **Figs. 3 through 6** for proper replacement of shims.

REAR WHEEL BEARING
ADJUST

1. Raise and support rear of vehicle.
2. Torque adjusting nut to 270 inch lbs. while rotating wheel.
3. Stop wheel and loosen adjusting nut, **Fig. 2.**
4. Tighten adjusting nut finger tight. End play should be .0001–.0020 inch.
5. Install castle lock with slots aligned with cotter pin hole.
6. Install cotter pin and grease cap.

SERVICE BRAKES
ADJUST

The rear brakes are self-adjusting. An initial adjustment is necessary after the brake shoes have been relined or replaced, or when the length of the star wheel adjuster has been changed during other service operations. To adjust the rear brakes, proceed as follows:

1. Raise and support vehicle.

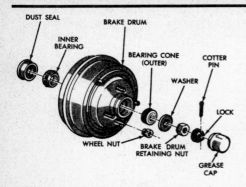

Fig. 2   Wheel bearing assembly

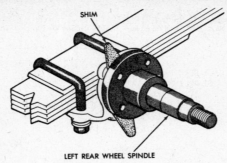

Fig. 3   Shim installation for toe-out

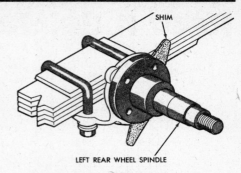

Fig. 4   Shim installation for toe-in

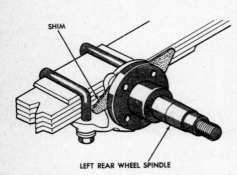

Fig. 5   Shim installation for positive camber

1. Raise and support vehicle.
2. Release parking brake, then tighten adjusting nut until both rear wheels drag and are difficult to turn.
3. Loosen adjusting nut until both wheels turn freely. From this point, loosen adjusting nut an additional 25 turns.
4. Apply parking brake two times to seat all components.
5. Start engine and apply parking brake 15 clicks. With automatic transaxle in Drive or manual transaxle in 1st gear, both rear wheels should slide under engine torque.
6. Apply and release parking brake with ignition on to verify that instrument panel warning light shuts off. If light remains lit, tighten adjusting nut one turn at a time until system operates properly.

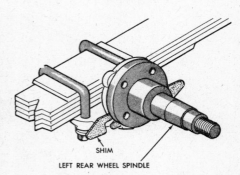

Fig. 6   Shim installation for negative camber

2. Remove adjusting hole covers from brake supports.
3. Release parking brake and back off adjustment to slacken cable.
4. Insert adjusting tool C-3784 or equivalent into star wheel of adjusting screw. Move handle of tool upward until a slight drag is felt.
5. Insert a suitable tool into brake adjusting hole and push adjusting lever out of engagement with star wheel, then back off star wheel to ensure there is no brake shoe drag.

NOTE: Use caution not to bend adjusting lever or distort lever spring.

6. Adjust parking brake, referring to "Parking Brake, Adjust" procedure.

PARKING BRAKE
ADJUST

SERVICE BULLETIN Vehicles built prior to July 11, 1984 may experience high pedal effort when applying the parking brake. On these models, the following parking brake adjustment procedure should be used.

1. Raise and support vehicle.
2. Release parking brake and back off cable adjustment to slacken cable.
3. Tighten cable adjusting nut until a slight drag is obtained while rotating wheels.
4. Loosen cable adjusting nut until rear wheels rotate freely, then an additional two turns.
5. Apply and release parking brake to check for proper operation. The rear wheels should rotate without dragging.

MASTER CYLINDER
REPLACE

1. Disconnect and plug brake tubes from master cylinder. Cap master cylinder ports.
2. Remove master cylinder attaching nuts.
3. Remove master cylinder from power brake unit.
4. Reverse procedure to install.

NOTE: Master cylinder should be bench

bled before installation, using tool No. C-4546 or equivalent.

POWER BRAKE UNIT
REPLACE

1. Remove master cylinder attaching nuts, slide master cylinder from mounting studs and support on fender shield. Do not disconnect brake tubes from master cylinder.
2. Disconnect vacuum hose from power brake unit.
3. Install suitable screwdriver between center tang on retainer clip and the brake pedal pin located under instrument panel. Rotate screwdriver so retainer clip center tang will pass over brake pedal pin.
4. Pull retainer clip from pin.
5. Remove power brake unit attaching nuts, then the power brake unit from vehicle.
6. Reverse procedure to install. Torque power brake unit and master cylinder unit attaching nuts to 200–300 inch lbs.

Front Suspension & Steering Section

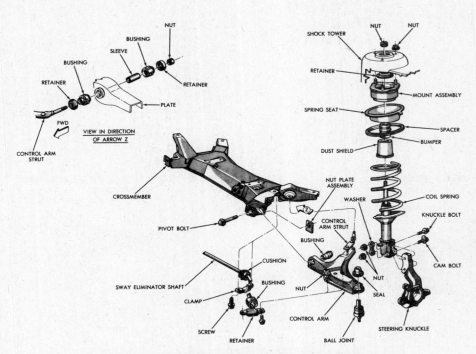

Fig. 1 Front suspension exploded view

Fig. 2 Camber adjustment

DESCRIPTION

These vehicles use a MacPherson type front suspension with vertical shock absorber struts attached to upper fender reinforcement and steering knuckle, **Fig. 1.** The lower control arms are attached inboard to a crossmember and outboard to steering knuckle through a ball joint to provide lower steering knuckle position. During steering maneuvers, strut and steering knuckle rotate as an assembly.

The driveshafts are attached inboard to transaxle output drive flanges, and outboard to driven wheel hub.

WHEEL ALIGNMENT

NOTE: Prior to wheel alignment, ensure tires are at recommended pressure, are of equal size and have approximately the same wear pattern. Check front wheel and tire assembly for radial runout and inspect lower ball joints and steering linkage for looseness. Check front and rear springs for sagging or damage. Front suspension inspections should be performed on a level floor or alignment rack with fuel tank at capacity and vehicle free of luggage and passenger compartment load.

Prior to each alignment reading, the vehicle should be bounced an equal number of times from the center of the bumper alternating first from the rear, then the front, and releasing at bottom of down cycle.

CASTER

The caster angle on these vehicles cannot be adjusted.

CAMBER

To adjust camber, loosen cam and through bolts, **Fig. 2.** Rotate upper cam bolt to move top of wheel in or out to achieve specified camber angle. Torque attaching nuts to 75 ft. lbs. plus an additional 1/4 turn.

TOE-IN

To adjust toe-in, center steering wheel and hold in position with a suitable tool. Loosen tie rod lock nuts and rotate rod, **Fig. 3,** to adjust toe-in to specifications. Use care not to twist steering gear rubber boots. Torque tie rod lock nuts to 55 ft. lbs. (75Nm). Adjust position of steering gear rubber boots. Remove steering wheel holding tool.

STRUT DAMPER ASSEMBLY
REPLACE

REMOVAL

1. Raise and support vehicle, then remove front wheels.
2. Mark position of camber adjusting cam, then remove camber adjusting bolt, through bolt and brake hose to damper bracket retaining screw, **Fig. 4.**
3. Remove strut damper to fender shield mounting nut and washer assemblies.
4. Remove strut damper from vehicle.

INSTALLATION

1. Position strut assembly into fender reinforcement, then install retaining nut and washer assemblies. Torque retaining nut to 20 ft. lbs.
2. Position steering knuckle into strut, then install washer plate, cam bolts and knuckle bolts.
3. Attach brake hose retainers to damper. Torque to 10 ft. lbs.
4. Index cam bolt to alignment mark made during removal.
5. Position a 4 inch or larger C-clamp on steering knuckle and strut, **Fig. 5,** then tighten clamp just enough to eliminate any looseness between strut and knuckle. Torque cam bolts to 75 ft. lbs. plus an additional 1/4 turn.
6. Remove C-clamp, then install wheel and tire assembly.

COIL SPRING
REPLACE

1. Remove strut damper assembly as previously outlined.
2. Compress coil spring using suitable tool.

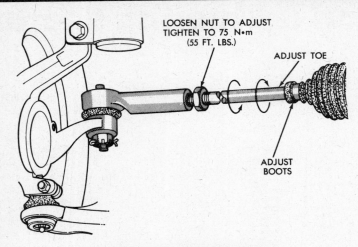

Fig. 3   Toe-in adjustment

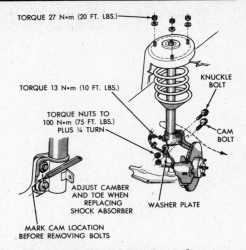

Fig. 4   Removing strut damper assembly

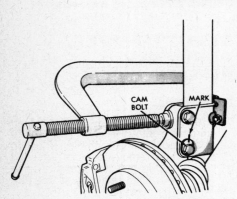

Fig. 5   Installing strut damper assembly

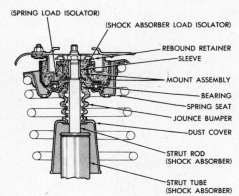

Fig. 6   Strut damper mount assembly

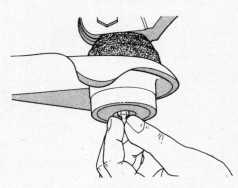

Fig. 7   Checking ball joint for wear

3. Remove strut rod nut while holding strut rod to prevent rotation.
4. Remove the mount assembly, **Fig. 6.**
5. Remove coil spring from strut damper.
6. Inspect mount assembly for deterioration of rubber isolator, retainers for cracks and distortion, and bearings for blinding.
7. Install dust shield, jounce bumper, spacer and seat to top of spring. Mount assembly to rod, then install retainer and rod nut.
8. Position spring retainer alignment notch parallel to damper lower attaching bracket.
9. Torque strut rod nut to 60 ft. lbs., using suitable tool, then release spring compressor.
10. With weight of vehicle off front wheels, turn both strut rod and strut rod nut in same direction until upper spring seat is properly positioned, then recheck torque of strut rod nut.

BALL JOINTS
CHECKING BALL JOINTS

With weight of vehicle resting on wheel and tire assembly, attempt to move grease fitting with fingers, **Fig. 7.** Do not use tool or added force to attempt to move grease fitting. If grease fitting moves freely, ball joint is worn and should be replaced.

REPLACE

The ball joint is pressed into the lower control arm. On these models, the ball joint can be pressed from the lower control arm using a 1 1/16 inch deep socket and tool No. C-4699-2. When pressing ball joint into lower control arm, use tool Nos. C-4699-1 and C-4699-2. Install ball joint seal using a 1 1/2 inch socket and tool No. C-4699-2.

LOWER CONTROL ARM
REPLACE

REMOVAL

1. Raise and support vehicle.
2. Remove front inner pivot through bolt, rear stub strut nut, retainer and bushing, then the ball joint to steering knuckle clamp bolt, **Fig. 8.**
3. Separate ball joint from steering knuckle by prying between ball stud retainer and lower control arm.

NOTE: Pulling steering knuckle out from vehicle after releasing from ball joint can separate inner C/V joint.

4. Remove sway bar to control arm nut, then rotate control arm over sway bar.
5. Remove rear stub strut bushing, sleeve and retainer.

INSTALLATION

1. Install retainer, bushing and sleeve on stub strut.
2. Position control arm over sway bar and install rear stub strut and front pivot into crossmember.
3. Install front pivot bolt and loosely assemble nut, **Fig. 8.**
4. Install stub strut bushing and retainer and loosely assemble nut.
5. Install ball joint stud into steering knuckle, then the clamp bolt. Torque clamp bolt to 70 ft. lbs. (95 Nm)
6. Place sway bar end bushing retainer to control arm, then install retainer bolts. Torque retainer bolts to 25 ft. lbs. (34 Nm).
7. Lower vehicle so suspension fully sup-

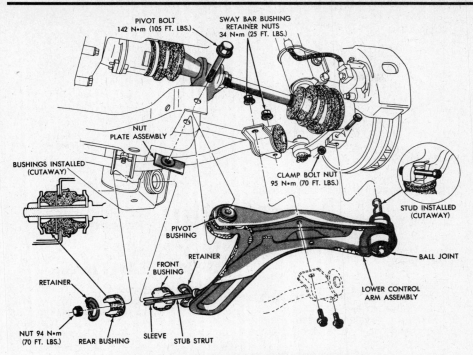

Fig. 8 Lower control arm assembly

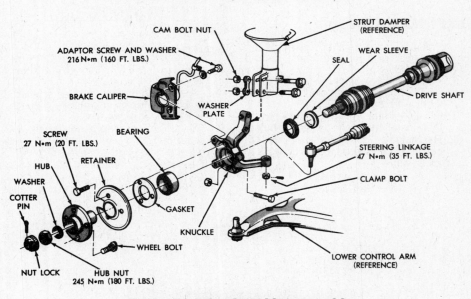

Fig. 9 Steering knuckle assembly

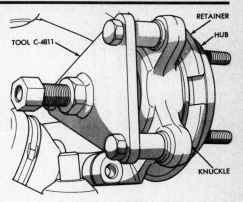

Fig. 10 Hub removal

6. Disconnect brake hose retainer from strut damper.
7. Remove clamp bolt securing ball joint stud into steering knuckle, then the brake caliper adapter screw and washer assemblies.
8. Support caliper with a piece of wire. Do not hang by brake hose.
9. Remove rotor, then separate ball joint stud from knuckle assembly.
10. Remove knuckle assembly from vehicle.

NOTE: Support driveshaft during knuckle removal. Do not permit driveshaft to hang after separating steering knuckle from vehicle.

INSTALLATION

1. Place steering knuckle on lower ball joint stud and the driveshaft through hub.
2. Install and torque ball joint to steering knuckle clamp bolt to 70 ft. lbs. (95 Nm).
3. Install tie rod end into steering arm and torque nut to 35 ft. lbs. (47 Nm). Install cotter pin, **Fig. 9**.
4. Install rotor.
5. Install caliper over rotor and position adapter to steering knuckle. Install adapter to knuckle attaching bolts and torque to 160 ft. lbs. (216 Nm).
6. Attach brake hose retainer to strut damper and torque attaching screw to 10 ft. lbs. (13 Nm).
7. Install hub nut assembly as follows:
   a. With brakes applied, install hub nut and torque to 180 ft. lbs. (245 Nm).
   b. Install spring washer, nut lock and new cotter pin.

HUB & BEARING
REPLACE

REMOVAL

1. Remove steering knuckle as previously outlined.
2. Remove hub using tool No. C-4811, **Fig. 10**.

ports vehicle, then torque front pivot bolt to 105 ft. lbs. (142 Nm) and stub strut nut to 70 ft. lbs. (95 Nm).

STEERING KNUCKLE
REPLACE

REMOVAL

1. Remove cotter pin, nut lock and spring washer.
2. Loosen hub nut with brakes applied, **Fig. 9**.

NOTE: The hub and driveshaft are splined together through the knuckle (bearing) and retained by the hub nut.

3. Raise and support vehicle, then remove front wheel and tire assembly.
4. Remove hub nut. Ensure splined driveshaft is free to separate from spline in hub during knuckle removal. A pulling force on shaft can separate inner C/V joint. Tap lightly with brass drift, if required.
5. Disconnect tie rod end from steering arm with a suitable puller.

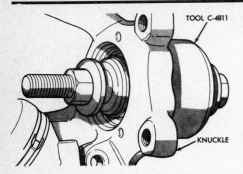

Fig. 11   Removing bearing from knuckle

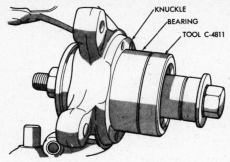

Fig. 12   Installing bearing into knuckle

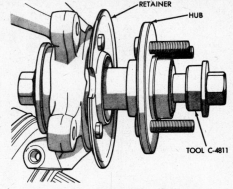

Fig. 13   Installing hub into knuckle

3. Remove three bearing retainer to knuckle attaching screws, then the bearing retainer.
4. Pry bearing seal from machined recess in knuckle assembly.
5. Remove bearing from knuckle using tool No. C-4811, **Fig. 11**.

INSTALLATION

1. Press new bearing into knuckle using tool No. C-4811, **Fig. 12**.
2. Install bearing retainer. Torque retainer attaching screws to 20 ft. lbs.
3. Press hub into bearing using tool No. C-4811, **Fig. 13**.
4. Position new seal in recess, then install using tool No. C-4698 or equivalent.
5. Install steering knuckle as described under "Steering Knuckle, Replace."

SWAY BAR
REPLACE

SERVICE BULLETIN 1984 models may experience a low pitched squeak at the sway bar bushings and mounting cushions in ambient temperatures below 32°F. This noise will occur when the vehicle is bounced up and down, such as when hitting dips, bumps, etc. This problem can be corrected as follows:
1. Remove sway bar as described below.
2. Remove and discard sway bar cushions.
3. Install new cushions (part No. 4322677, color coded beige), without using any type of lubricant.
4. Remove outer bushings using a hammer or other suitable tool. Do not cut bushings.
5. Clean inner diameter of bushing and bushing mating surface on sway bar.
6. Apply suitable sealant to inner surface of bushing and bushing mating surface on sway bar.
7. Install bushings onto sway bar until approximately ½ inch of bar protrudes at each end.
8. Install sway bar as described below.

REMOVAL

1. Raise and support vehicle.
2. Remove nuts, bolts and retainers at the control arms, **Fig. 14**.
3. Remove crossmember clamp attaching bolts, then the crossmember clamps.
4. Remove sway bar from vehicle.

INSTALLATION

1. Position crossmember bushings on sway bar with curved surface up and split to front of vehicle.
2. Position bar assembly onto crossmember, then install clamps and attaching bolts, **Fig. 14**.
3. Position retainers at control arms, then install bolts and attaching nuts.
4. Raise lower control arm to correct position, then torque attaching bolts to 25 ft. lbs.

DRIVESHAFT IDENTIFICATION

Driveshafts are identified as "Citroen" or "G.K.N." assemblies, **Fig. 15**. Vehicles can be equipped with either of these assemblies, however they should not be intermixed. Procedures for installation and removal of driveshafts are essentially the same for either type assembly used.

DRIVESHAFTS
REPLACE

REMOVAL

1. Remove cotter pin, nut lock and spring washer from wheel hub.
2. Loosen hub nut with brakes applied.
3. Raise and support vehicle, then remove wheel and tire assembly.
4. If removing the right driveshaft, the speedometer pinion must be removed prior to driveshaft removal, **Fig. 16**.
5. Remove ball joint stud to steering

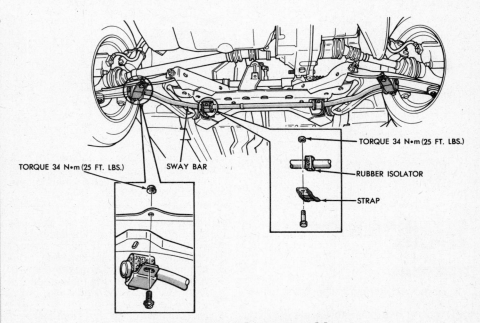

TORQUE 34 N•m (25 FT. LBS.)

TORQUE 34 N•m (25 FT. LBS.)

RUBBER ISOLATOR

STRAP

SWAY BAR

Fig. 14   Sway bar assembly

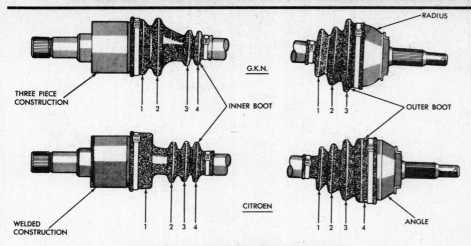

Fig. 15 Driveshaft identification

knuckle clamp bolt, then separate ball joint stud from steering knuckle using a suitable pry bar.

NOTE: Use caution not to damage ball joint or C/V joint boots.

6. Separate outer C/V joint splined shaft from hub by holding C/V housing while moving knuckle/hub assembly away.

NOTE: Do not use pry bar to separate hub from shaft or damage to outer wear sleeve on C/V joint may occur.

7. Support driveshaft assembly at C/V joint housing and remove by pulling outward on the inner C/V joint housing. Do not pull on the shaft.
8. Remove driveshaft assembly from vehicle.

INSTALLATION

1. Hold inner joint assembly at housing while aligning and guiding the inner joint spline into transaxle.
2. Push knuckle/hub assembly out and

install outer C/V joint shaft into hub.
3. Install knuckle assembly on ball joint stud, then the clamp bolt. Torque bolt to 70 ft. lbs.

NOTE: Steering knuckle clamp bolt is "prevailing torque type." Original or equivalent bolt must be installed during assembly.

4. Install speedometer pinion, right driveshaft only, **Fig. 16.**
5. Fill transaxle with suitable transaxle fluid.
6. Install washer and hub nut, then torque hub nut to 180 ft. lbs. Install nut lock and cotter pin.
7. If after installing driveshaft assembly in vehicle the inboard boot appears collapsed or deformed, vent the inner boot by inserting a round tipped, small diameter rod between boot and shaft. As venting occurs, the boot will return to its normal shape.
8. Install wheel and tire assembly.

NOTE: After installation of driveshaft, check the driveshaft length as outlined in

"Driveshaft Length, Adjust" procedure.

DRIVESHAFT LENGTH
ADJUST

1. Position vehicle with wheels straight ahead and body weight distributed on all four tires.
2. Measure direct distance between inner edge of outboard boot to inner edge of inboard boot on both driveshafts. This measurement (dimension "A") should be taken at the bottom (six o'clock position) of driveshafts, **Fig. 17.**

NOTE: Damper weights are used on left driveshaft assembly. Before measuring driveshaft length, damper should be removed from shaft. After specified measurement is completed, install damper weight and torque damper weight attaching bolts to 21 ft. lbs. (28 Nm).

3. Driveshaft length (dimension "A") must be within specifications in chart, **Fig. 18.** If measurement is not within specifications, engine position must be corrected as follows:
   a. Remove load from engine mounts by carefully supporting engine and transaxle assembly using a suitable jack.
   b. Loosen right engine mount vertical bolts, then the front engine mount bracket-to-crossmember attaching bolts.
   c. Pry engine to right or left as necessary to bring driveshaft length within specifications.

NOTE: The left engine mount is sleeved over long support bolt and shaft, **Fig. 19,** to provide lateral adjustment whether or not engine weight is removed.

   d. Torque engine mount vertical bolts to 250 inch lbs. and front engine

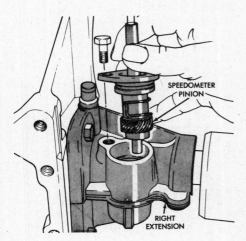

Fig. 16 Speedometer pinion removal

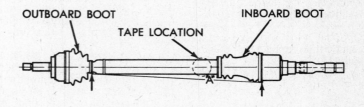

Fig. 17 Measuring driveshaft

Driveshaft Identification			"A" Dimension	
Type	Side	Tape Color	M.M.	Inch
G.K.N.	Right	Green	542–549	21.3–21.6
G.K.N.	Left	Green	270–285	10.6–11.2
A.C.I.	Right	Blue	520–532	20.5–20.9
A.C.I.	Left	Blue	255–270	10.0–10.6

Fig. 18 Driveshaft length specifications

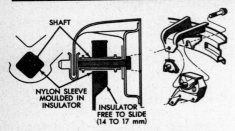

Fig. 19   Left engine mount adjust

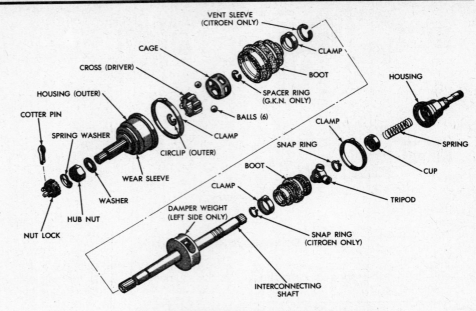

Fig. 20   Driveshaft components

mount bolts to 40 ft. lbs.
e. Center left engine mount, then re-check driveshaft length.

INNER CONSTANT VELOCITY JOINT SERVICE

DISASSEMBLE

NOTE: Driveshaft assembly should be identified before starting service procedure. Refer to "Driveshaft Identification" procedure.

1. Remove boot clamps, then pull back boot to gain access to the tripod, **Fig. 20.**
2. On G.K.N. units, place driveshaft assembly in vise and hold housing as shown in **Fig. 21.** Lightly compress C/V joint retention spring while bending tabs back with suitable pliers, then remove tripod from housing.
3. On Citroen units, separate tripod from housing by slightly deforming retaining ring at three locations, **Fig. 22.** If necessary, cut retaining ring from housing and install replacement retaining ring by rolling the edge into machined groove in housing with suitable punch.

NOTE: When removing tripod from housing, secure rollers. After tripod has been removed, secure assembly with tape.

4. On all models, remove snap ring from end of shaft, then remove tripod using brass punch.

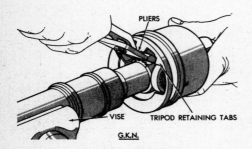

Fig. 21   Removing inner C/V joint tripod. G.K.N. units

INSPECTION

Remove grease from assembly and inspect bearing race, tripod components, spring, spring cup and spherical end of connecting shaft for excessive wear or damage and replace if necessary.

ASSEMBLE

1. Slide small end of boot over shaft, then place clamp over groove on boot, **Fig. 20.**
2. Install tripod on shaft, then lock tripod assembly on shaft by installing retaining ring in shaft groove.

NOTE: On G.K.N. units, slide tripod on shaft with non-chamfered end facing tripod retainer ring groove.

3. Distribute packets of special grease provided in boot clamp kit as follows:
   a. On G.K.N. units, distribute one packet of grease in the housing and remaining packets into the boot.
   b. On Citroen units, distribute ⅔ of a packet of grease into the boot and remaining amount in the housing.
4. Position spring, with spring cup attached to exposed end, into spring pocket. Place a small amount of grease on spring cup.
5. Install tripod into housing as follows:
   a. On G.K.N. units, slip tripod into housing and bend retaining tabs down to their original position. Ensure retaining tabs hold tripod in housing.
   b. On Citroen units, remove tape holding rollers and needle bearings in place, then install tripod assembly into housing. Reform or install new retainer ring. Ensure retaining collar holds tripod in housing.

NOTE: If new retainer ring is installed, hold ring in position with two C-clamps and roll the edge into machined groove in housing using a suitable punch.

6. On all models, ensure proper spring positioning. The spring must remain centered in the housing spring pocket when tripod is installed and seated in the spring cup.
7. Position boot over boot groove in housing, then install clamp.

OUTER CONSTANT VELOCITY JOINT SERVICE

DISASSEMBLY

NOTE: Driveshaft assembly should be identified before starting service proce-

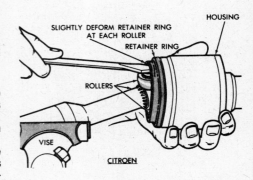

Fig. 22   Removing inner C/V joint tripod. Citroen units

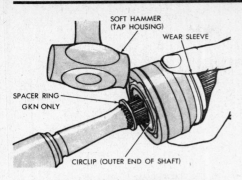

Fig. 23   Removing outer C/V joint from shaft

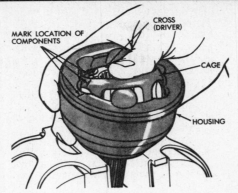

Fig. 24   Ball removal. Outer C/V joint

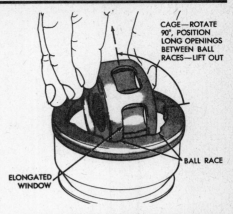

Fig. 25   Cage & cross assembly removal. Outer C/V joint

dure. Refer to "Driveshaft Identification" procedure.

1. Remove boot clamps, then pull back boot to gain access to joint, **Fig. 20.**
2. Clean grease from joint.
3. Place driveshaft assembly in suitable vise and support outer joint. Remove outer joint from shaft by tapping top of joint body with a soft hammer, **Fig. 23.**
4. Remove circlip from shaft groove and discard.
5. On G.K.N. units, remove heavy lock ring from shaft only if shaft needs replacement.
6. On all units, if constant velocity joint is operating satisfactorily and grease does not appear contaminated, proceed to "Assembly" procedure, step 7.
7. If constant velocity joint is noisy or badly worn, replace entire unit. The repair kit will include boot, clamps, circlip and lubricant. Clean and inspect joint outlined in the following steps.
8. Clean surplus grease and mark relative position of inner cross, cage and housing with a dab of paint, **Fig. 24.**
9. Hold joint vertically in a soft jawed vise.
10. Press downward on one side of the inner race to tilt cage and remove ball from opposite side, **Fig. 24.** If joint is tight, use a hammer and brass drift to

tap inner race. Do not strike the cage. Repeat this step until all balls have been removed. A screwdriver may be used to pry balls loose.
11. Tilt cage assembly vertically and position the two opposing, elongated cage windows in area between ball grooves. Remove cage and inner race assembly by pulling upward from the housing, **Fig. 25.**
12. Rotate inner cross 90° to cage and align one of the race spherical lands with an elongated cage window. Raise land into cage window and remove inner race by swinging outward, **Fig. 26.**

INSPECTION

1. Check housing ball races for excessive wear.
2. Check splined shaft and nut threads for damage.
3. Inspect the balls for pitting, cracks, scouring and wearing. Dulling of the surface is normal.
4. Inspect cage for excessive wear on inner and outer spherical surfaces, heavy brinelling of the cage, window cracks and chipping.
5. Inspect inner race (cross) for excessive wear or scoring of ball races.
6. If any of the defects listed in steps 1 through 5 are found, replace the C/V joint assembly as a unit.

NOTE: Polished areas in races (cross and housing) and cage spheres are normal and do not indicate a need for joint replacement unless they are suspected of causing noise and vibration.

ASSEMBLY

1. If removed, position wear sleeve on joint housing, then tap sleeve onto housing using tool No. C-4698.
2. Lightly oil components, then align marks made during disassembly.
3. Align one of the inner race (cross) lands into cage window, then insert race into cage and pivot 90°, **Figs. 27 and 28.**
4. Align opposite elongated cage windows with housing land and insert cage assembly into housing. Pivot cage 90° to complete installation, **Fig. 29.**

NOTE: When properly assembled, the cross counter bore should be facing outward from the joint on G.K.N. units, **Figs. 27 and 30.** On Citroen units, the cross and cage chamfers will be facing outward from the joint, **Figs. 28 and 31.**

5. Apply lubricant to ball races between

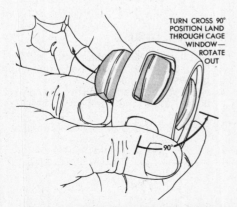

Fig. 26   Removing cross from cage. Outer C/V joint

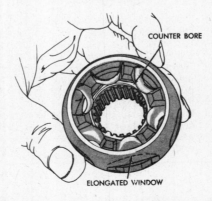

Fig. 27   Cage & cross assembled. G.K.N. units

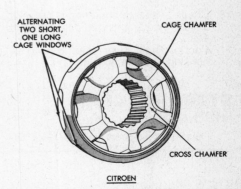

Fig. 28   Cage & cross assembled. Citroen units

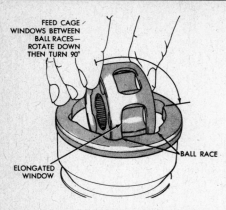

Fig. 29 Installing cage & cross assembly into housing. Outer C/V joint

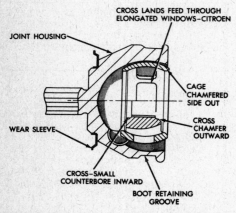

Fig. 31 Cage & cross installed in housing. Citroen units

all sides of ball grooves.

6. Insert balls into raceway by tilting cage and inner race assembly.
7. Slide small end of boot over shaft, then place clamp over groove on boot, **Fig. 20.**
8. Insert new circlip in shaft groove. Do not over expand or twist circlip during assembly, **Fig. 32.**
9. Position joint housing on shaft, then engage by tapping sharply with a soft faced mallet.
10. Check to ensure snap ring is properly seated by attempting to pull joint from shaft.
11. Position boot over boot groove in housing, then install clamp.

STEERING GEAR
REPLACE

1. Raise and support vehicle, then re-

move front wheels.
2. Remove tie rod ends using a suitable puller.
3. Remove steering column as follows:
   a. Disconnect battery ground cable.
   b. On column shift vehicles, disconnect cable rod by prying rod out of grommet in shift lever, then remove cable clip from lower bracket.
   c. Disconnect all wiring connectors at steering column jacket and remove steering wheel center pad.
   d. Disconnect horn electrical connector and horn switch, then remove steering wheel using suitable puller.
   e. Expose steering column bracket, then remove instrument panel steering column cover and lower reinforcement. Remove bezel.
   f. Remove indicator set screw and shift indicator pointer from shift housing.
   g. Remove nuts attaching steering column bracket to instrument panel support, then lower bracket support to floor.
   h. Remove four front suspension crossmember attaching bolts, then lower crossmember using suitable jack.
   i. Remove coupling assembly to steering gear retaining pin.
   j. Remove anti-rotational link from crossmember and air diverter valve bracket from left side of crossmember, if equipped.
   k. Pull steering column and steering coupling rearward.
4. Remove splash shields and boot seal shields, then the fluid lines to the pump on power steering gear only.
5. Disconnect tie rod ends from steering knuckles.
6. Remove crossmember to steering gear attaching bolts, then the steering gear from left side of vehicle.

POWER STEERING PUMP
REPLACE

4-135 ENGINES

1. Disconnect battery ground cable.
2. Disconnect vapor separator hose from carburetor, then electrical connector from A/C cycling switch, if equipped.
3. Remove drive belt adjustment locking screw from front of pump, then the pump end hose bracket attaching nut, if equipped.
4. Raise and support vehicle, then disconnect return hose from gear tube and drain oil from pump through open end of hose.

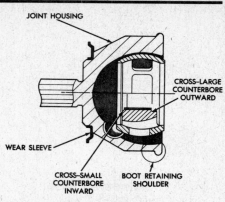

Fig. 30 Cage & cross installed in housing. G.K.N. units

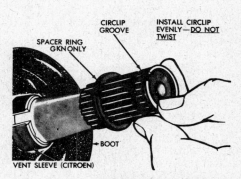

Fig. 32 Installing circlip. Outer C/V joint

NOTE: Do not allow hoses to touch hot exhaust manifold or catalyst.

5. Remove right side splash shield, then disconnect remaining fluid hoses from pump. Plug pump ports and hose ends to prevent contamination.
6. Remove pump lower stud nut and pivot screw.
7. Lower vehicle and remove belt from pulley, then move pump rearward to clear mounting bracket.
8. Remove pump adjustment bracket.
9. Rotate pump clockwise so pump faces rear of vehicle, then remove pump.
10. Reverse procedure to install.

4-156 ENGINES

1. Disconnect fluid hoses from pump. Plug pump ports and hose ends to prevent contamination.
2. Remove belt adjustment and pivot bolts, then the belt from pulley groove.
3. Remove pump and mounting bracket from vehicle as an assembly.
4. Reverse procedure to install.

DODGE & PLYMOUTH EXC. RAMPAGE, SCAMP & MINI-VANS

INDEX OF SERVICE OPERATIONS

NOTE: Refer to page 1 of this manual for vehicle manufacturer's special service tool suppliers.

Engine Identification

ENGINE NUMBER LOCATION: The engine serial number is located on a machined surface on the cylinder block. The engine serial number prefix denotes the series letter, followed by engine model, followed by serial number.

General Engine Specifications

Year	Engine Code	Engine Model	Carb. Type	Bore & Stroke	Comp. Ratio	Horsepower @ R.P.M.	Torque Ft. Lbs. @ R.P.M.	Governed Speed R.P.M.	Normal Oil Pressure Lbs.
1979	225-1	6-225①	1 Bore	3.40 × 4.125	8.4	110 @ 3600	175 @ 1600	—	30–70
	225-1	6-225②	1 Bore	3.40 × 4.125	8.4	115 @ 3600	175 @ 2000	—	30–70
	225-1	6-225⑤	2 Bore	3.40 × 4.125	8.4	110 @ 3600	—	—	30–70
	243	D-243-6⑧	⑨	3.62 × 3.94	20	100 @ 3700	163 @ 2200	3700	42.7
	318-1	V8-318①	2 Bore	3.91 × 3.31	8.7	150 @ 4000	250 @ 2000	—	30–80
	318-1	V8-318②	2 Bore	3.91 × 3.31	8.7	150 @ 4000	230 @ 2400	—	30–80
	318-1	V8-318①⑤	4 Bore	3.91 × 3.31	8.7	150 @ 3600	—	—	30–80
	318-1	V8-318③⑤	4 Bore	3.91 × 3.31	8.7	155 @ 3800	—	—	30–80
	360-1	V8-360①	2 Bore	4.00 × 3.58	8.6	160 @ 3600	290 @ 2000	—	30–80
	360-1	V8-360②	2 Bore	4.00 × 3.58	8.6	180 @ 3600	270 @ 2000	—	30–80
	360-1	V8-360①	4 Bore	4.00 × 3.58	8.6	215 @ 4000	300 @ 3200	—	30–80
	360-1	V8-360②	4 Bore	4.00 × 3.58	8.6	175 @ 3600	280 @ 2000	—	30–80
	360-3	V8-360②	2 Bore	4.00 × 3.58	8.0	180 @ 3600	260 @ 2400	—	30–80
	360-1	V8-360③⑤	4 Bore	4.00 × 3.58	8.6	175 @ 3600	—	—	30–80
	360-1	V8-360②⑤	4 Bore	4.00 × 3.58	8.6	180 @ 3600	—	—	30–80
	440-1	V8-440②	4 Bore	4.32 × 3.75	8.2	220 @ 4000	320 @ 4000	—	30–80
	440-3	V8-440②	4 Bore	4.32 × 3.75	8.1	225 @ 2400	320 @ 2400	—	30–80
1980	225	6-225①	1 Bore	3.40 × 4.125	8.4	95 @ 3600	170 @ 1600	—	30–80
	225	6-225③⑤	1 Bore	3.40 × 4.125	8.4	90 @ 3600	150 @ 2000	—	30–80
	318	V8-318①	2 Bore	3.91 × 3.31	8.7	135 @ 4000	240 @ 2000	—	30–80
	318	V8-318①	2 Bore	3.91 × 3.31	8.7	140 @ 4000	240 @ 2400	—	30–80
	318	V8-318③	4 Bore	3.91 × 3.31	8.7	160 @ 4000	245 @ 2000	—	30–80
	318	V8-318②⑤	4 Bore	3.91 × 3.31	8.0	155 @ 4000	240 @ 2000	—	30–80
	360-1	V8-360①	4 Bore	4.00 × 3.58	8.6	170 @ 4000	270 @ 2000	—	30–80
	360-1	V8-360③	4 Bore	4.00 × 3.58	8.6	170 @ 4000	270 @ 2000	—	30–80
	360-1	V8-360①	4 Bore	4.00 × 3.58	8.6	205 @ 4000	295 @ 3200	—	30–80
	360-1	V8-360①③	4 Bore	4.00 × 3.58	8.6	175 @ 3600	260 @ 2800	—	30–80
	360-1	V8-360②	4 Bore	4.00 × 3.58	8.2	180 @ 3600	270 @ 2000	—	30–80
	360-3	V8-360②	4 Bore	4.00 × 3.58	8.0	180 @ 4000	260 @ 2400	—	30–80
	360-3	V8-360②	4 Bore	4.00 × 3.58	8.0	210 @ 4000	285 @ 3200	—	30–80
	360-3	V8-360②⑤	4 Bore	4.00 × 3.58	8.0	175 @ 3600	260 @ 2800	—	30–80
	360-3	V8-360②⑤	4 Bore	4.00 × 3.58	8.0	200 @ 4000	280 @ 3200	—	30–80
	446⑥	V8-446②	4 Bore	4.125 × 4.18	8.0	230 @ 3600	360 @ 2800	—	15–50
1981–82	225	6-225①④	1 Bore	3.40 × 4.125	8.4	95 @ 3600	170 @ 1600	—	30–70
	225	6-225③⑤	1 Bore	3.40 × 4.125	8.4	90 @ 3600	165 @ 1200	—	30–70
	318	V8-318①④	2 Bore	3.91 × 3.31	8.6	140 @ 3600	240 @ 2400	—	30–80
	318	V8-318①④	2 Bore	3.91 × 3.31	8.6	135 @ 4000	240 @ 2000	—	30–80
	318	V8-318①④	4 Bore	3.91 × 3.31	8.6	170 @ 4000	245 @ 2000	—	30–80
	318	V8-318②	4 Bore	3.91 × 3.31	8.6	160 @ 4000	220 @ 3200	—	30–80
	318	V8-318③⑤	4 Bore	3.91 × 3.31	8.6	160 @ 4000	245 @ 2000	—	30–80
	360	V8-360①④	4 Bore	4.00 × 3.58	8.5	175 @ 4000	260 @ 2000	—	30–80
	360	V8-360①⑤	4 Bore	4.00 × 3.58	8.5	180 @ 4000	260 @ 2000	—	30–80
	360	V8-360②⑤	4 Bore	4.00 × 3.58	8.5	170 @ 4000	265 @ 2400	—	30–80
	360	V8-360②④	4 Bore	4.00 × 3.58	8.5	180 @ 3600	270 @ 2000	—	30–80

continued

GENERAL ENGINE SPECIFICATIONS—Continued

Year	Engine Code	Engine Model	Carb. Type	Bore & Stroke	Comp. Ratio	Horsepower @ R.P.M.	Torque Ft. Lbs. @ R.P.M.	Governed Speed R.P.M.	Normal Oil Pressure Lbs.
1983	225	6-225①	1 Bore	3.40 × 4.125	8.4	95 @ 3600	170 @ 1200	—	30–70
	225	6-225①	2 Bore	3.40 × 4.125	8.4	100 @ 3600	175 @ 1600	—	30–70
	225	6-225③⑤	1 Bore	3.40 × 4.125	8.4	84 @ 3600	162 @ 1600	—	30–70
	318	V8-318①	2 Bore	3.91 × 3.31	8.6	150 @ 4400	255 @ 2000	—	30–80
	318	V8-318 ③⑤⑦	2 Bore	3.91 × 3.31	8.6	143 @ 3600	253 @ 1600	—	30–80
	318	V8-318 ①⑤⑦	2 Bore	3.91 × 3.31	8.6	143 @ 4000	250 @ 1600	—	30–80
	318	V8-318①	4 Bore	3.91 × 3.31	8.6	167 @ 4000	245 @ 2000	—	30–80
	318	V8-318②	4 Bore	3.91 × 3.31	8.6	158 @ 4000	240 @ 4000	—	30–80
	360	V8-360②	4 Bore	4.00 × 3.58	8.5	190 @ 4000	265 @ 3200	—	30–80
	360	V8-360②⑤	4 Bore	4.00 × 3.58	8.5	169 @ 4000	265 @ 3200	—	30–80
1984	225	6-225①④	1 Bore	3.40 × 4.125	8.4	95 @ 3600	170 @ 1600	—	30–70
	225	6-225③⑤	1 Bore	3.40 × 4.125	8.4	85 @ 3600	170 @ 1600	—	30–70
	318	V8-318 ③⑤⑦	2 Bore	3.91 × 3.31	8.6	135 @ 4000	240 @ 2000	—	30–80
	318	V8-318①④	2 Bore	3.91 × 3.31	8.6	150 @ 4000	250 @ 1600	—	30–80
	360	V8-360①④	4 Bore	4.0 × 3.58	8.5	175 @ 4000	280 @ 2000	—	30–80
	360	V8-360②⑤	4 Bore	4.0 × 3.58	8.5	175 @ 4000	225 @ 1600	—	30–80
	360	V8-360②④	4 Bore	4.0 × 3.58	8.5	180 @ 3600	270 @ 2000	—	30–80
1985	225	6-225①④	1 Bore	3.40 × 4.125	8.4	90 @ 3600	165 @ 1600	—	30–70
	225	6-225③⑤	1 Bore	3.40 × 4.125	8.4	90 @ 3600	160 @ 1600	—	30–70
	318	V8-318①④	2 Bore	3.91 × 3.31	9.0	145 @ 4000	255 @ 2000	—	30–80
	318	V8-318③⑤	2 Bore	3.91 × 3.31	9.0	145 @ 3600	250 @ 1600	—	30–80
	360	V8-360①④	4 Bore	4.0 × 3.58	8.5	175 @ 4000	280 @ 2000	—	30–80
	360	V8-360②④	4 Bore	4.0 × 3.58	8.5	180 @ 3600	270 @ 2000	—	30–80
	360	V8-360②⑤	4 Bore	4.0 × 3.58	8.5	175 @ 4000	255 @ 1600	—	30–80

①—Light duty emissions.　　④—Exc. Calif.　　⑦—High alt.
②—Heavy duty emissions.　　⑤—Calif.　　⑧—Diesel engine.
③—Medium duty emissions.　　⑥—Motor home.　　⑨—Injection pump.

Piston, Pin, Ring, Crankshaft & Bearing Specifications

Year	Engine Model ①	Wristpin Diameter	Piston Clearance, Inch	Ring End Gap In. (Minimum) Comp.	Ring End Gap In. (Minimum) Oil	Crankpin Diameter, Inch	Rod Bearing Clearance, Inch	Main Bearing Journal Diameter, Inch	Main Bearing Clearance, Inch	End Thrust On Bearing No.	Shaft End Play
1979–85	6-225	.9008	.0015	.010	.015	2.1865–2.1875	.0010–.0022	2.7495–2.7505	.0010–.0025	3	.0035–.0095
1979	D-243-6②	1.1022	.007	.0015	.016	2.281–2.282	.0015–.0044	2.754–2.755	.0012–.0035	7	.004–.010
1979	V8-318	.9842	.0015	.010	.015	2.124–2.125	.0005–.0025	2.4995–2.5005	.0005–.0020	3	.002–.007
1980	V8-318	.9842	.0015	.010	.015	2.124–2.125	.0005–.0025	2.4995–2.5005	③	3	.002–.007
1981–85	V8-318	.9842	.0015	.010	.015	2.124–2.125	.0005–.0022	2.4995–2.5005	③	3	.002–.007
1979	V8-360	.9842	.0015	.010	.015	2.124–2.125	.0005–.0025	2.8095–2.8105	.0005–.0020	3	.002–.009
1980	V8-360	.9842	.0015	.010	.015	2.124–2.125	.0005–.0025	2.8095–2.8105	③	3	.002–.009
1981–85	V8-360	.9842	.0015	.010	.015	2.124–2.125	.0005–.0022	2.8095–2.8105	③	3	.002–.009
1979	V8-440	1.0936	.0013	.013	.015	2.375–2.376	.0005–.0030	2.7495–2.7505	.0001–.0022	3	.002–.009
1980	V8-446	1.020	.0017	.013	.013	2.498–2.499	.0011–.0036	3.1228–3.1236	.0010–.0036	3	.0025–.0085

①—Engine size—cubic inch displacement and number of cylinders.　　②—Diesel.　　③—No. 1, .0005–.0015; Nos. 2, 3, 4 & 5, .0005–.0020.

Valve Specifications

Engine Model	Year	Valve Lash		Valve Angles		Valve Springs		Valve Stem Clearance		Stem Diameters, Std.	
		Int.	Exh.	Seat	Face	Installed Height	Pressure Lbs. @ In.	Intake	Exhaust	Intake	Exhaust
6-225	1979–80	.010H	.020H	45	①	1²¹/₃₂	144 @ 1⁵/₁₆	.001–.003	.002–.004	.372–.373	.371–.372
6-225	1981–85	Zero	Zero	45	①	1¹¹/₁₆	144 @ 1⁵/₁₆	.001–.003	.002–.004	.372–.373	.371–.372
D-243-6 ②	1979	.012C	.012C	45	45	③	④	.002–.003	.003–.004	—	.314–.315
8-318	1979–85	Zero	Zero	45	45	⑦	⑧	.001–.003	.002–.004	.372–.373	.371–.372
8-360	1979	Zero	Zero	45	45	⑦	⑧	.001–.003	.002–.004	.372–.373	.371–.372
8-360	1980–85	Zero	Zero	45	45	⑦	⑨	.001–.003	.002–.004	.372–.373	.371–.372
8-440	1979	Zero	Zero	45	45	1⁵⁵/₆₄	200 @ 1⁷/₁₆	.0011–.0028	⑤	.3723–.3730	⑥
8-446	1980	Zero	Zero	45	45	—	188 @ 1.429	.00115–.00285	.00165–.00235	.37215–.37285	.37165–.37235

①—Intake 45, exhaust 43.
②—Diesel.
③—Free length—Outer, 2.01 inch; Inner, 1.71 inch.
④—Outer, 37.26 @ 1.772; Inner, 15.87 @ 1.530.
⑤—Hot end, .0021–.0038; Cold end, .0011–.0028.
⑥—Hot end, .3713–.372; Cold end, .3723–.373.
⑦—Intake or exhaust without rotator, 1¹¹/₁₆"; Exhaust with rotator, 1³³/₆₄".
⑧—Intake or exhaust without rotator; 177 @ 1⁵/₁₆", exhaust with rotator; 187 @ 1⁵/₆₄".
⑨—Intake, 177 @ 1⁵/₁₆; exhaust with rotator, 189 @ 1¹/₁₆.

Engine Tightening Specifications★

★ Torque specifications are for clean and lightly lubricated threads only. Dry or dirty threads produce increased friction which prevents accurate measurement of tightness.

Year	Engine	Spark Plugs Ft. Lbs.	Cylinder Head Bolts Ft. Lbs.	Intake Manifold Ft. Lbs.	Exhaust Manifold Ft. Lbs.	Rocker Arm Shaft Bracket Ft. Lbs.	Rocker Arm Cover In. Lbs.	Connecting Rod Cap Bolts Ft. Lbs.	Main Bearing Cap Bolts Ft. Lbs.	Flywheel to Crankshaft Ft. Lbs.	Vibration Damper to Pulley Ft. Lbs.
1979	6-225	10	70	120①	120①	25	40	45	85	55	②
	6-243④	—	90.4	—	—	—	—	57.9	79.5	65.1	289.3
	V8-318, V8-360	30	⑤	40	③	200①	40	45	85	55	100
	V8-440	30	70	45	30	25	40	45	85	55	135
1980	6-225	10	70	120①	120①	25	40	45	85	55	②
	V8-318, V8-360	30	⑥	40	③	200①	40	45	85	55	100
	V8-446	15	105	—	18	20	72	41	95	—	90
1981–85	6-225	10	70	120①	120①	25	80	45	85	55	②
	V8-318, V8-360	30	⑥	40	③	200①	80	45	85	55	100

①—Inch Lbs.
②—Press fit.
③—Screw, 20 ft. lbs.; Nut, 15 ft. lbs.
④—Diesel.
⑤—V8-360, 105 ft. lbs. Some V8-318 engine blocks have cylinder head bolt holes drilled through the block into the water jacket. Insert a screwdriver into the block head bolt holes. If it goes in at least 2 inches, head bolt must be sealed with a suitable sealer and torqued to 95 ft. lbs.; All other V8-318 head bolts, 105 ft. lbs.
⑥—1981–84 V8-318, 95 ft. lbs.; 1981–84 V8-360, 105 ft. lbs.; All 1985, 105 ft. lbs.

Alternator & Regulator Specifications

Year	I.D. Tag Color	Ground Polarity	Field Coil Draw Amperes ①	Current Output			Operating Voltage		
				Engine R.P.M.	Amperes ②	Volts	Engine R.P.M.	Volts	Voltage @ 140° F ③
1979	Violet 41 Amp	Neg.	4.5–6.5	1250	40	15	1250	15	13.3–13.9
	Yellow 60 Amp	Neg.	4.5–6.5	1250	57	15	1250	15	13.3–13.9
	Yellow 100 Amp	Neg.	4.5–6.5	900	72	13	900	13	13.3–13.9
	Yellow 117 Amp	Neg.	4.75–6.0	900	72	13	900	13	13.3–13.9
1980	Violet 41 Amp	Neg.	4.5–6.5	1250	40	15	1250	15	13.3–13.9
	Yellow 60 Amp	Neg.	4.5–6.5	1250	57	15	1250	15	13.3–13.9
	Yellow 117 Amp	Neg.	4.5–6.5	900	72	13	900	13	13.3–13.9
1981	Violet 41 Amp	Neg.	4.5–6.5	1250	40	15	1250	15	13.3–13.9
	Yellow 60 Amp	Neg.	4.5–6.5	1250	57	15	1250	15	13.3–13.9
	Yellow 117 Amp	Neg.	4.5–6.5	900	72	13	900	13	13.3–13.9
1982	Violet 41 Amp	Neg.	4.5–6.5	1250	40	15	1250	15	13.3–13.9
	Yellow 60 Amp	Neg.	4.5–6.5	1250	57	15	1250	15	13.3–13.9
	Yellow 117 Amp	Neg.	4.5–6.5	900	72	13	900	13	13.3–13.9
1983	Violet 41 Amp	Neg.	4.5–6.5	1250	40	15	1250	15	13.3–13.9
	Yellow 60 Amp	Neg.	4.5–6.5	1250	57	15	1250	15	13.3–13.9
	Yellow 117 Amp	Neg.	4.5–6.5	900	72	13	900	13	13.3–13.9
1984	Violet 41 Amp	Neg.	2.5–5.0	1250	32	15	1250	15	13.0–13.7
	Yellow 60 Amp	Neg.	2.5–5.0	1250	47	15	1250	15	13.0–13.7
	Brown 78 Amp	Neg.	2.5–5.0	1250	57	15	1250	15	13.0–13.7
	Yellow 114 Amp	Neg.	2.5–5.0	900	97	13	900	13	13.0–13.7
1985	Violet 41 Amp	Neg.	2.5–5.0	1250	32	15	1250	15	13.3–13.9
	Yellow 60 Amp	Neg.	2.5–5.0	1250	47	15	1250	15	13.3–13.9
	Brown 78 Amp	Neg.	2.5–5.0	1250	57	15	1250	15	13.3–13.9
	Yellow 114 Amp	Neg.	2.5–5.0	900	97	13	900	13	13.3–13.9

①—Current draw at 12 volts while turning rotor shaft by hand.
②—If output is low, stator or rectifier is shorted.
③—Temperature is checked with a thermometer ¼ inch from voltage regulator.

Starting Motor Specifications

Model Number ①	Year	Brush Spring Tension, Oz.	No Load Test			Torque Test		
			Amperes	Volts	R.P.M.	Amperes	Volts	Torque Ft. Lbs.
4091975	1979	32–36	90	11	3700	475–550	4	—
4111855	1980–85	32–36	90	11	3700	475–550	4	—
4111860	1984–85	32–36	90	11	5700	475–550	4	—
ME007293 ②	1979	37	180	11	3300	—	3.5	—

①—Stamped on plate riveted to housing.
②—Mitsubishi.

Brake Specifications

Year	Model	Rear Drum I.D.	Wheel Cyl. Bore		Disc Brake Rotor					Master Cyl. I.D.	
			Front Disc	Rear Drum	Nominal Thickness	Minimum Thickness	Thickness Variation (Parallelism)	Run Out (TIR)	Finish (microinch)	Manual Brakes	Power Brakes
VANS, WAGONS & FRONT SECTIONS											
1979–80	100	10	3.10	.938	1.250	1.180	.0005	.004	15–80	1.125	1.125
	200	10	3.10	.938	1.250	1.180	.0005	.004	15–80	1.125	1.125
	300②	12	3.10	.875	1.250	1.180	.0005	.004	15–80	1.125	1.125
	300, 400③	12	3.10	1.00	1.190	1.125	.0005	.004	15–80	1.125	1.125
	400①	13	3.10	1.125	1.190	1.125	.0005	.004	15–80	1.31	1.31
1981	B-150	10	3.10	.938	1.250	1.180	.0005	.004	15–80	1.125	1.125
	B-250	10	3.10	.938	1.250	1.180	.0005	.004	15–80	1.125	1.125
	B-350②	12	3.10	1.00	1.250	1.180	.0005	.004	15–80	1.125	1.125
	B-350③	12	3.10	1.06	1.190	1.125	.0005	.004	15–80	1.125	1.125
1982	B-150	10	3.10	.938	1.250	1.180	.0005	.004	15–80	1.125	1.125
	B-250	10	3.10	.938	1.250	1.180	.0005	.004	15–80	1.125	1.125
	B-350②	12	3.10	1.00	1.250	1.180	.0005	.004	15–80	1.125	1.125
	B-350③	12	3.10	1.06	1.190	1.125	.0005	.004	15–80	1.125	1.125
1983	B-150	10	3.10	.938	1.250	1.180	.0005	.004	15–80	1.125	1.125
	B-250	10	3.10	.938	1.250	1.180	.0005	.004	15–80	1.125	1.125
	B-350②	12	3.10	1.00	1.250	1.180	.0005	.004	15–80	1.125	1.125
	B-350③	12	3.10	1.06	1.190	1.125	.0005	.004	15–80	1.125	1.125
1984	B-150	11	3.10	.938	1.250	1.180	.0005	.004	15–80	1.125	1.125
	B-250	11	3.10	.938	1.250	1.180	.0005	.004	15–80	1.125	1.125
	B-350②	12	3.10	1.00	1.250	1.180	.0005	.004	15–80	1.125	1.125
	B-350③	12	3.10	1.06	1.190	1.125	.0005	.004	15–80	1.125	1.125
1985	B-150	11	3.10	.938	1.250	1.180	.0005	.004	15–80	1.125	1.125
	B-250	11	3.10	.938	1.250	1.180	.0005	.004	15–80	1.125	1.125
	B-350②	12	3.10	.875	1.250	1.180	.0005	.004	15–80	1.125	1.125
	B-350③	12	3.10	1.00	1.190	1.125	.0005	.004	15–80	1.125	1.125
RAMCHARGER & TRAIL DUSTER											
1979	ALL	10	3.10	.938	1.250	1.180	.0005	.004	15–80	1.03	1.03
1980	ALL④	10	3.10	.938	1.250	1.180	.0005	.004	15–80	1.125	1.125
	ALL⑤	10	3.10	.938	1.250	1.180	.001	.005	15–80	1.125	1.125
1981	ALL④	10	3.10	.938	1.250	1.180	.0005	.004	15–80	1.125	1.125
	ALL⑤	10	3.10	.938	1.250	1.180	.001	.005	15–80	1.125	1.125
1982	ALL④	10	3.10	.938	1.250	1.180	.0005	.004	15–80	1.125	1.125
	ALL⑤	10	3.10	.938	1.250	1.180	.001	.005	15–80	1.125	1.125
1983	ALL④	10	3.10	.938	1.250	1.180	.0005	.004	15–80	1.125	1.125
	ALL⑤	10	3.10	.938	1.250	1.180	.001	.005	15–80	1.125	1.125
1984–85	ALL④	11	3.10	.938	1.250	1.180	.0005	.004	15–80	—	1.125
	ALL⑤	11	3.10	.938	1.250	1.180	.001	.005	15–80	—	1.125
CONVENTIONAL CAB											
1979	D-100	10	3.10	.938	1.250	1.180	.0005	.004	15–80	⑩	⑩
	W-150	10	3.10	.938	1.250	1.180	.001	.005	15–80	⑩	⑩
	D-200	⑧	⑪	⑨	⑫	⑬	.001	.005	15–80	⑩	⑩
	W-200⑥	12	3.10	1.00	1.190	1.125	.001	.005	15–80	⑩	⑩
	W-200⑦	12	3.38	1.00	1.190	1.125	.001	.005	15–80	⑩	⑩
	D-300	12	3.10	1.00	1.190	1.125	.001	.005	15–80	1.03	1.03
	W-300	12	3.38	1.06	1.190	1.125	.001	.005	15–80	1.125	1.125
	D-400	12	3.10	1.06	1.190	1.125	.001	.005	15–80	1.03	1.03
	W-400	12	3.38	1.06	1.190	1.125	.001	.005	15–80	1.125	1.125
1980	D-150	10	3.10	.938	1.250	1.180	.0005	.004	15–80	1.125	1.125
	W-150	10	3.10	.938	1.250	1.180	.001	.005	15–80	1.125	1.125
	D-200	⑧	3.10	⑨	⑫	⑬	.001	.005	15–80	1.125	1.125

continued

BRAKE SPECIFICATIONS—Continued

Year	Model	Rear Drum I.D.	Wheel Cyl. Bore		Disc Brake Rotor					Master Cyl. I.D.	
			Front Disc	Rear Drum	Nominal Thickness	Minimum Thickness	Thickness Variation (Parallelism)	Run Out (TIR)	Finish (microinch)	Manual Brakes	Power Brakes
CONVENTIONAL CAB—Continued											
1980	W-200⑥	12	3.10	1.00	1.190	1.125	.001	.005	15–80	1.125	1.125
	W-200⑦	12	3.38	1.00	1.190	1.125	.001	.005	15–80	1.125	1.125
	D-300	12	3.10	1.00	1.190	1.125	.001	.005	15–80	1.125	1.125
	W-300	12	3.38	1.06	1.190	1.125	.001	.005	15–80	1.125	1.125
	D-400	12	3.10	1.06	1.190	1.125	.001	.005	15–80	1.125	1.125
	W-400	12	3.38	1.06	1.190	1.125	.001	.005	15–80	1.125	1.125
1981	D-150	10	3.10	.938	1.250	1.180	.0005	.004	15–80	1.125	1.125
	W-150	10	3.10	.938	1.250	1.180	.001	.005	15–80	1.125	1.125
	D-250	12	3.10	1.00	⑫	⑬	.001	.005	15–80	1.125	1.125
	W-250⑥	12	3.10	1.00	1.190	1.125	.001	.005	15–80	1.125	1.125
	W-250⑦	12	3.38	1.00	1.190	1.125	.001	.005	15–80	1.125	1.125
	D-350	12	3.10	1.00	1.190	1.125	.001	.005	15–80	1.125	1.125
	W-350	12	3.38	1.06	1.190	1.125	.001	.005	15–80	1.125	1.125
	D-450	12	3.10	1.00	1.190	1.125	.001	.005	15–80	1.125	1.125
	W-450	12	3.38	1.06	1.190	1.125	.001	.005	15–80	1.125	1.125
1982	D-150	10	3.10	.938	1.250	1.180	.0005	.004	15–80	1.125	1.125
	W-150	10	3.10	.938	1.250	1.180	.001	.005	15–80	1.125	1.125
	D-250	12	3.10	1.00	⑫	⑬	.001	.005	15–80	1.125	1.125
	W-250⑥	12	3.10	1.00	1.190	1.125	.001	.005	15–80	1.125	1.125
	W-250⑦	12	3.38	1.00	1.190	1.125	.001	.005	15–80	1.125	1.125
	D-350	12	3.10	1.00	1.190	1.125	.001	.005	15–80	1.125	1.125
	W-350	12	3.38	1.06	1.190	1.125	.001	.005	15–80	1.125	1.125
1983	D-150	10	3.10	.938	1.250	1.180	.0005	.004	15–80	1.125	1.125
	W-150	10	3.10	.938	1.250	1.180	.001	.005	15–80	1.125	1.125
	D-250	12	3.10	1.00	⑫	⑬	.001	.005	15–80	1.125	1.125
	W-250⑥	12	3.10	1.00	1.190	1.125	.001	.005	15–80	1.125	1.125
	W-250⑦	12	3.38	1.00	1.190	1.125	.001	.005	15–80	1.125	1.125
	D-350	12	3.10	1.00	1.190	1.125	.001	.005	15–80	1.125	1.125
	W-350	12	3.38	1.06	1.190	1.125	.001	.005	15–80	1.125	1.125
1984	D-150	11	3.10	.938	1.250	1.180	.0005	.004	15–80	—	1.125
	W-150	11	3.10	.938	1.250	1.180	.001	.005	15–80	—	1.125
	D-250	12	3.10	⑭	⑫	⑬	.001	.005	15–80	—	1.125
	W-250⑥	12	3.10	1.00	1.190	1.125	.001	.005	15–80	—	1.125
	W-250⑦	12	3.38	1.00	1.190	1.125	.001	.005	15–80	—	1.125
	D-350	12	3.10	1.00	1.190	1.125	.001	.005	15–80	—	1.125
	W-350	12	3.38	1.06	1.190	1.125	.001	.005	15–80	—	1.125
1985	D-150	11	3.10	.938	1.250	1.180	.0005	.004	15–80	—	1.125
	W-150	11	3.10	.938	1.250	1.180	.001	.005	15–80	—	1.125
	D-250	12	3.10	1.00	⑫	⑬	.001	.005	15–80	—	1.125
	W-250⑥	12	3.10	1.00	1.190	1.125	.001	.005	15–80	—	1.125
	W-250⑦	12	3.38	1.00	1.190	1.125	.001	.005	15–80	—	1.125
	D-350	12	3.10	1.125	1.190	1.125	.001	.005	15–80	—	1.125
	W-350	12	3.38	1.125	1.190	1.125	.001	.005	15–80	—	1.125
MOTOR HOME											
1979–80	M-300	12	2.38	1.06	1.550	—	.0008	.005	15–80	—	1.25
	M-400	12	2.38	1.06	1.550	—	.0008	.005	15–80	—	1.31
	M-500	15	2.38	1.375	1.550	—	.0008	.005	15–80	—	1.31
	M-600	15	2.38	1.50	1.550	—	.0008	.005	15–80	—	1.31

continued

BRAKE SPECIFICATIONS—Continued

①—Models with 163 inch wheel base.
②—Models with 3600 lb. front axle.
③—Models with 4000 lb. front axle.
④—Models less 4 wheel drive.
⑤—Models with 4 wheel drive.
⑥—Less Spicer 60 front axle.
⑦—With Spicer 60 front axle.
⑧—6200 G.V.W. exc. 165 inch wheel base crew cabs, 12.12 inches; others, 12 inches.
⑨—6200 G.V.W. exc. 165 inch wheel base crew cabs, .875 inch; others, 1.00 inch.
⑩—All exc. Chrysler master cylinder with power brakes, 1.125 inch; Chrysler master cylinder with power brakes, 1.03 inch.
⑪—With Spicer 60 front axle, 3.38 inches; less Spicer 60 front axle, 3.10 inches.
⑫—With 3300 lb. front axle, 1.25 inches; with 4000 lb. front axle, 1.19 inches.
⑬—With 3300 lb. front axle, 1.180 inches; with 4000 lb. front axle, 1.125 inches.
⑭—With Spicer 60 rear axle, 1.00 inch; with Spicer 60 HD rear axle, 1.125 inch.

Wheel Alignment Specifications

Model	Caster, Deg.	Camber, Deg.	Toe-In, Inch	Kingpin Inclination, Deg.
1979				
AD-100, PD-100	+½	+¼	⅛	—
AW-100, PW-100④	—	—	—	—
B-100, B-200, B-300	+½③⑦	+½⑧	⅛⑨	—
PB-100, PB-200, PB-300	+½③⑦	+½⑧	⅛⑨	—
CB-300, CB-400	+½③	+½	⅛	—
MB-300, MB-400	+½③	+½	⅛	—
M-300	+3	+2	⅛	7
M-400, M-500	+2½	+1	1/16	7
M-600	+2	+1	1/16	7
D-100, D-150, D-200, D-300, D-400	+½②	+¼	⅛	—
W-150, W-200①④⑩	+3	+1½	0	8½
W-200, W-300, W-400①⑤⑩	+3	+½	0	8½
1980				
AD-100, PD-100	+½②	+¼	⅛	—
AW-100, PW-100④	—	—	—	—
B-100, B-200, B-300	+2¼⑦	+½⑧	⅛⑨	—
PB-100, PB-200, PB-300	+2¼⑦	+½⑧	⅛⑨	—
CB-300, CB-400	+2¼	+½	⅛	—
MB-300, MB-400	+2¼	+½	⅛	—
M-300	—	—	—	—
M-400, M-500	—	—	—	—
M-600	—	—	—	—
D-100, D-150, D-200, D-300, D-400	+½②	+¼	⅛	—
W-150, W-200	+3①	+1½	0	8½
W-200, W-300, W-400①④⑤⑩	+3①	+½	0	8½
1981				
AD-150	+½	+¼	⅛	—
B-150, B-250, B-350	+2¼	+½	⅛	—
CB-350, CB-450	+2¼	+½	⅛	—
D-150, D-250, D-350, D-450	+½	+¼	⅛	—

Model	Caster, Deg.	Camber, Deg.	Toe-In, Inch	Kingpin Inclination, Deg.
MB-250, MB-350, MB-450	+2¼	+½	⅛	—
PB-150, PB-250, PB-350	+2¼	+½	⅛	—
PD-150	+½	+¼	⅛	—
W-150, W-250⑩	+3	+1½	0	8½
1982				
AD-150, D-150, D-250, D-350	+½	+¼	⅛	—
B-150, B-250, B-350	+2¼	+½	⅛	—
PB-150, PB-250, PB-350	+2¼	+½	⅛	—
W-150, W-250, W-350⑪	+3	+1½	⅛	8½
W-250, W-350⑥⑩	+3	+½	⅛	8½
1983				
AD-150, D-150, D-250, D-350	+½	+½	⅛	—
B-150, B-250, B-350	+2¼	+½	⅛	—
PB-150, PB-250, PB-350	+2¼	+½	⅛	—
W-150, W-250, W-350	+2⑩	+1	¼	8½
1984				
AD-150, D-150, D-250, D-350	+½⑩	+½	⅛	—
B-150, B-250, B-350	+2½	+⅜	⅛	—
PB-150, PB-250, PB-350	+2½	+⅜	⅛	—
W-150, W-250, W-350	+2⑩	+1	¼	8½
1985				
AD-150, D-150, D-250, D-350	+½⑩	+½	⅕	—
B-150, B-250, B-350	+2½	+⅜	⅛	—
PB-150, PB-250, PB-350	+2½	+⅜	⅛	—
W-150, W-250, W-350	+2⑩	+1	⅕	8½

①—No load.
②—Loaded.
③—Power Steering +2¼.
④—Four wheel drive.
⑤—4500 lb. axle.
⑥—Models with 135" W.B. and 149" W.B.
⑦—Heavy front axle load applications, +1½.
⑧—Heavy front axle load applications, +⅝.
⑨—Heavy front axle load applications, 0.
⑩—Caster should be checked with vehicle loaded. If vehicle wanders caster should be increased. If steering effort is very high, especially when cornering, caster should be decreased.
⑪—Models less 135" W.B. and 149" W.B.

Drive Axle Specifications

Year	Application	Ring Gear Size	Carrier Type	Ring Gear & Pinion Backlash		Pinion Bearing Preload			Differential Bearing Preload		
				Method	Adjustment	Method	New Bearings Inch Lbs.	Used Bearings Inch Lbs.	Method	New Bearings Inch Lbs.	Used Bearings Inch Lbs.
VANS, WAGONS & FRONT SECTIONS											
1979–83	ALL	8⅜	Integral	①	.006–.008	②	20–35	10–25③	①	⑤	⑤
	ALL	9¼	Integral	①	.006–.008	②	20–35	10–25③	①	⑤	⑤
	ALL	9¾④	Integral	Shims	.004–.009	Shims	10–20	10–20	Shims	.015	.015
	ALL	10½④	Integral	Shims	.004–.009	Shims	10–20	10–20	Shims	.015	.015
1984–85	ALL	8⅜	Integral	①	.006–.008	②	20–35	10–25③	①	⑤	⑤
	ALL	9¼	Integral	①	.006–.008	②	20–35	10–25③	①	⑤	⑤
	ALL	9¾④	Integral	Shims	.004–.009	Shims	10–20	10–20	Shims	.015	.015
RAMCHARGER & TRAIL DUSTER											
1979–85	ALL⑥	8⅜	Integral	①	.006–.008	②	20–35	10–25③	①	⑤	⑤
	ALL⑥	9¼	Integral	①	.006–.008	②	20–35	10–25③	①	⑤	⑤
	ALL⑦	8½④	Integral	Shims	.005–.009	Shims	20–40	10–20	Shims	.015	.015
CONVENTIONAL CAB											
1979	D-100, W-100⑥	8⅜	Integral	①	.006–.008	②	20–35	10–25③	①	⑤	⑤
	D-100, W-100⑥	9¼	Integral	①	.006–.008	②	20–35	10–25③	①	⑤	⑤
	D-200, W-200, D-300⑥	9¾④	Integral	Shims	.004–.009	Shims	10–20	10–20	Shims	.015	.015
	D-300, W-300, D-400, W-400⑥	10½④	Integral	Shims	.004–.009	Shims	10–20	10–20	Shims	.015	.015
	W-100, W-200⑦	8½④	Integral	Shims	.005–.009	Shims	20–40	10–20	Shims	.015	.015
	W-200, W-300, W-400⑦	9¾④	Integral	Shims	.004–.009	Shims	10–20	10–20	Shims	.015	.015
1980	D-150, W-100⑥	8⅜	Integral	①	.006–.008	②	20–35	10–25③	①	⑤	⑤
	D-150, W-100⑥	9¼	Integral	①	.006–.008	②	20–35	10–25③	①	⑤	⑤
	D-200, W-200, D-300⑥	9¾④	Integral	Shims	.004–.009	Shims	10–20	10–20	Shims	.015	.015
	D-300, W-300, D-400, W-400⑥	10½④	Integral	Shims	.004–.009	Shims	10–20	10–20	Shims	.015	.015
	W-150, W-200⑦	8½④	Integral	Shims	.005–.009	Shims	20–40	10–20	Shims	.015	.015
	W-200, W-300, W-400⑦	9¾④	Integral	Shims	.004–.009	Shims	10–20	10–20	Shims	.015	.015
1981	D-150, W-150⑥	8⅜	Integral	①	.006–.008	②	20–35	10–25③	①	⑤	⑤
	D-150, W-150⑥	9¼	Integral	①	.006–.008	②	20–35	10–25③	①	⑤	⑤
	D-250, W-250, D-350⑥	9¾④	Integral	Shims	.004–.009	Shims	10–20	10–20	Shims	.015	.015
	D-350, W-350, D-450, W-450⑥	10½④	Integral	Shims	.004–.009	Shims	10–20	10–20	Shims	.015	.015
	W-150, W-250⑦	8½④	Integral	Shims	.005–.009	Shims	20–40	10–20	Shims	.015	.015
	W-250, W-350, W-450⑦	9¾④	Integral	Shims	.004–.009	Shims	10–20	10–20	Shims	.015	.015
1982–83	D-150, W-150⑥	8⅜	Integral	①	.006–.008	②	20–35	10–25③	①	⑤	⑤
	D-150, W-150⑥	9¼	Integral	①	.006–.008	②	20–35	10–25③	①	⑤	⑤
	D-250, W-250, D-350⑥	9¾④	Integral	Shims	.004–.009	Shims	10–20	10–20	Shims	.015	.015
	D-350, W-350⑥	10½④	Integral	Shims	.004–.009	Shims	20–40	10–20	Shims	.015	.015
	⑦⑧	8½④	Integral	Shims	.005–.009	Shims	20–40	10–20	Shims	.015	.015
	⑦⑨	9¾④	Integral	Shims	.004–.009	Shims	10–20	10–20	Shims	.015	.015
1984	D-150, W-150⑥	8⅜	Integral	①	.006–.008	②	20–35	10–25③	①	⑤	⑤
	D-150, W-150, D-250, W-250⑥	9¼	Integral	①	.006–.008	②	20–35	10–25③	①	⑤	⑤

continued

DRIVE AXLE SPECIFICATIONS—Continued

Year	Application	Ring Gear Size	Carrier Type	Ring Gear & Pinion Backlash		Pinion Bearing Preload			Differential Bearing Preload		
				Method	Adjustment	Method	New Bearings Inch Lbs.	Used Bearings Inch Lbs.	Method	New Bearings Inch Lbs.	Used Bearings Inch Lbs.
CONVENTIONAL CAB—Continued											
1984	D-250, W-250, D-350⑥	9¾④	Integral	Shims	.004–.009	Shims	10–20	10–20	Shims	.015	.015
	D-350, W-350⑥	10½④	Integral	Shims	.004–.009	Shims	10–20	10–20	Shims	.015	.015
	⑦⑧	8½④	Integral	Shims	.005–.009	Shims	20–40	10–20	Shims	.015	.015
	⑦⑨	9¾④	Integral	Shims	.004–.009	Shims	10–20	10–20	Shims	.015	.015
1985	D-150⑥	8⅜	Integral	①	.006–.008	②	20–35	10–25③	①	⑤	⑤
	D-150, W-150, D-250, W-250⑥	9¼	Integral	①	.006–.008	②	20–35	10–25③	①	⑤	⑤
	D-250, W-250, W-350⑥	9¾④	Integral	Shims	.004–.009	Shims	10–20	10–20	Shims	.015	.015
	D-350, W-350⑥	10½④	Integral	Shims	.004–.009	Shims	10–20	10–20	Shims	.015	.015
	⑦⑧	8½④	Integral	Shims	.005–.009	Shims	20–40	10–20	Shims	.015	.015
	⑦⑨	9¾④	Integral	Shims	.004–.009	Shims	10–20	10–20	Shims	.015	.015
MOTOR HOME											
1979–80	M-300, M-400, M-500	10½④	Integral	Shims	.004–.009	Shims	10–20	10–20	Shims	.015	.015
	M-600	12½⑩	Integral	①⑪	.006–.012	Shims	5–15	5–15	①	⑫	⑫

①—Threaded adjuster.
②—Collapsible spacer.
③—With new front and used rear bearings.
④—Spicer axle.
⑤—Preload is correct when ring gear and pinion backlash is properly adjusted.
⑥—Rear axle.
⑦—Front axle.
⑧—W-150, W-250, W-350 with 131 inch wheel base and 149 inch wheel base.
⑨—W-250, W-350 with 135 inch wheel base and 149 inch wheel base.
⑩—Rockwell axle.
⑪—Low limit preferred for original bearings and high limit preferred for new bearings.
⑫—Tighten each adjusting nut one notch.

Cooling System & Capacity Data

Year	Model	Engine	Cooling Capacity, Qts.		Radiator Cap Relief Pressure, Lbs.	Thermo. Opening Temp.	Fuel Tank Gals.	Engine Oil Refill Qts.①	Transmission Oil			Transfer Case Pints	Rear Axle Oil Pints
			Less A/C	With A/C					3 Speed Pints	4 Speed Pints	Auto Trans. Qts.⑳		
VANS, WAGONS & FRONT SECTIONS													
1979	ALL	225	12	14	16	195	22	5	②	7½	8.3	—	③
	ALL	243	13	13	7	180	22	7	②	7½	8.3	—	③
	ALL	318	16	18	16	195	22	5	②	7½	8.3	—	③
	ALL	360	14½	④	16	195	⑥	5	②	7½	8.3	—	③
	ALL	440	14½	⑤	16	185	⑥	⑦	②	7½	8.3	—	③
1980	ALL	225	12	13	16	195	22	5	—	7½	8.3	—	③
	ALL	318	16	17	16	195	⑧	5	—	7½	8.3	—	③
	ALL	360	14½	15½	16	195	⑧	5	—	7½	8.3	—	③
1981	ALL	225	12	13	16	195	22	5	—	7½	8.3	—	③
	ALL	318	16	17	16	195	⑧	5	—	7½	8.3	—	③
	ALL	360	14½	15½	16	195	⑧	5	—	7½	8.3	—	③
1982	ALL	225	12	13	16	195	22	5	—	7½	8.3	—	③
	ALL	318	16	17	16	195	22	5	—	7½	8.3	—	③
	ALL	360	14½	15½	16	195	22	5	—	7½	8.3	—	③
1983	ALL	225	12	13	16	195	22	5	—	7½	8.3	—	③
	ALL	318	16	17	16	195	22	5	—	7½	8.3	—	③
	ALL	360	14½	15½	16	195	22	5	—	7½	8.3	—	③

continued

COOLING SYSTEM & CAPACITY DATA—Continued

Year	Model	Engine	Cooling Capacity, Qts. Less A/C	Cooling Capacity, Qts. With A/C	Radiator Cap Relief Pressure, Lbs.	Thermo. Opening Temp.	Fuel Tank Gals.	Engine Oil Refill Qts.(1)	Transmission Oil 3 Speed Pints	Transmission Oil 4 Speed Pints	Transmission Oil Auto Trans. Qts.(20)	Transfer Case Pints	Rear Axle Oil Pints
VANS, WAGONS & FRONT SECTIONS—Continued													
1984	ALL	225	12	13	16	195	22	5	—	7½	8.5	—	(3)
	ALL	318	16	17	16	195	22	5	—	7½	6.5	—	(3)
	ALL	360	14½	15½	16	195	22	5	—	7½	6.5	—	(3)
1985	ALL	225	12	14	16	195	22	5	—	7½	6.5	—	(3)
	ALL	318	16	18	16	195	22	5	—	7½	6.5	—	(3)
	ALL	360	14½	16½	16	195	22	5	—	7½	6.5	—	(3)
RAMCHARGER & TRAIL DUSTER													
1979	ALL	225	12	13	16	195	24	5	(10)	(11)	2(9)	—	(3)
	ALL	318	16	17	16	195	24	5	(10)	(11)	2(9)	9	(3)(4)
	ALL	360	14½	15½	16	195	24	5	(10)	(11)	2(9)	9	(3)(14)
1980	ALL	225	12	13	16	195	24	5	—	(11)	3.8(9)	—	(3)
	ALL	318	16	17	16	195	24	5	—	(11)	3.8(9)	(12)	(3)(15)
	ALL	360	14½	15½	16	195	24	5	—	(11)	3.8(9)	(12)	(3)(15)
1981	ALL	318	16	17	16	195	35	5	—	(11)	(13)	(12)	(15)(17)
	ALL	360	14½	15½	16	195	35	5	—	(11)	(13)	(12)	(15)(17)
1982	ALL	318	16	17	16	195	35	5	—	(11)	(13)	(12)	(15)(17)
	ALL	360	14½	15½	16	195	35	5	—	(11)	(13)	(12)	(15)(17)
1983	ALL	318	16	17	16	195	35	5	—	—	(13)	(6)	(15)(17)
1984	ALL	318	16	17	16	195	35	5	—	—	(13)	(6)	(15)(17)
	ALL	360	14½	15½	16	195	35	5	—	—	(13)	(6)	(15)(17)
1985	ALL	318	(21)	(21)	16	195	35	5	—	7	(13)	(6)	(17)(23)
	ALL	360	(22)	(22)	16	195	35	5	—	7	(13)	(6)	(17)(23)
CONVENTIONAL CAB													
1979	ALL	225	12	13	16	195	(16)	5	(10)	(11)	2(9)	9	(3)(14)
	ALL	243	13	14	7	180	(16)	7	(10)	(11)	2(9)	9	(3)(14)
	ALL	318	16	17	16	195	(16)	5	(10)	(11)	2(9)	9	(3)(14)
	ALL	360	14½	15½	16	195	(16)	5	(10)	(11)	2(9)	9	(3)(14)
1980	ALL	225	12	13	16	195	(16)	5	—	(11)	3.8(9)	(12)	(3)(15)
	ALL	318	16	17	16	195	(16)	5	—	(11)	3.8(9)	(12)	(3)(15)
	ALL	360	14½	15½	16	195	(16)	5	—	(11)	3.8(9)	(12)	(3)(15)
1981	ALL	225	12	13	16	195	20	5	—	(11)	(13)	(12)	(15)(17)
	ALL	318	16	17	16	195	20	5	—	(11)	(13)	(12)	(15)(17)
	ALL	360	14½	15½	16	195	20	5	—	(11)	(13)	(12)	(15)(17)
1982	ALL	225	12	13	16	195	20	5	—	(11)	(13)	(12)	(15)(17)
	ALL	318	16	17	16	195	20	5	—	(11)	(13)	(12)	(15)(17)
	ALL	360	14½	15½	16	195	20	5	—	(11)	(13)	(12)	(15)(17)
1983	ALL	225	12	13	16	195	20	5	—	(11)	(13)	(12)	(15)(17)
	ALL	318	16	17	16	195	20	5	—	(11)	(13)	(12)	(15)(17)
	ALL	360	14½	15½	16	195	20	5	—	(11)	(13)	(12)	(15)(17)
1984	ALL	225	12	13	16	195	20	5	—	(11)	(13)	(12)	(15)(17)
	ALL	318	16	17	16	195	20	5	—	(11)	(13)	(12)	(15)(17)
	ALL	360	14½	15½	16	195	20	5	—	(11)	(13)	(12)	(15)(17)
1985	ALL	225	(24)	(24)	16	195	20	5	—	(11)	(13)	(12)	(17)(23)
	ALL	318	(25)	(25)	16	195	20	5	—	(11)	(13)	(12)	(17)(23)
	ALL	360	(26)	(26)	16	195	20	5	—	(11)	(13)	(12)	(17)(23)

continued

COOLING SYSTEM & CAPACITY DATA—Continued

Year	Model	Engine	Cooling Capacity, Qts.		Radiator Cap Relief Pressure, Lbs.	Thermo. Opening Temp.	Fuel Tank Gals.	Engine Oil Refill Qts.[1]	Transmission Oil			Transfer Case Pints	Rear Axle Oil Pints
			Less A/C	With A/C					3 Speed Pints	4 Speed Pints	Auto Trans. Qts.[20]		
MOTOR HOME													
1979	ALL	360-3	21	—	16	195	[19]	6	—	—	8.5	—	[18]
	ALL	440-3	23	—	16	185	[19]	6	—	—	8.5	—	[18]
1980	ALL	360-3	21	—	16	195	75	6	—	—	8.5	—	[18]
	ALL	446	24½	—	16	180	75	6	—	—	8.5	—	[18]

[1]—Add one qt. with filter change.

[2]—A-230 transmission, 4¼ pts.; A-390 transmission, 3½ pts.

[3]—8⅜ inch ring gear, 4½ pts.; 9¼ inch ring gear, 4½ pts.; 9¾ inch ring gear, 6 pts.; 10½ inch ring gear, 6½ pts.

[4]—360-1 engine, 16½ qts.; 360-3 engine, 15½ qts.

[5]—440-1 engine, 16½ qts.; 440-3 engine, 15½ qts.

[6]—All 400 series front sections, 50 gals.; others, 22 gals.

[7]—All 400 series front sections, 5 qts.; others, 6 qts.

[8]—All 300 & 400 series front sections, 45 gals.; others, 22 gals.

[9]—Without torque converter drain.

[10]—A-230 trans. with short extension, 5 pts.; A-230 trans. with long extension, 4¼ pts.; A-390 trans., 3.6 pts.

[11]—A-833 trans., 7½ pts.; New Process 435 trans., 7 pts.; New Process 445 trans., 7½ pts.

[12]—New Process 208 transfer case, 6 pts.; New Process 205 transfer case, 4½ pts.

[13]—A-904T/A999 trans., 17.1 pts.; A-727 trans. (without torque converter drain), 7.7 pts.

[14]—Models equipped with 4 wheel drive, front axle 44 FBJ, 3½ pts.; front axle 60-F, 6 pts.

[15]—Models equipped with 4 wheel drive, front axle 44 FBJ, 3½ pts.; front axle 60-F, 6½ pts.

[16]—Frame mount ahead of rear axle, 18 gals.; Frame mount rear of rear axle, 21 gals.

[17]—8¼ inch ring gear, 4½ pts.; 9¼ inch ring gear, 4½ pts.; 9¾ inch ring gear, 6 pts.; 10½ inch ring gear, 6½ pts.

[18]—9¾ inch ring gear, 6 pts.; 10½ inch ring gear, 6½ pts.; 12½ inch ring gear, 14 pts.

[19]—M-300, M-400 & M-500 with 159 inch wheel base, 36 gals.; M-500 with 178 inch wheel base & M-600 models, 45 gals.

[20]—Approximate. Make final check with dipstick.

[21]—With 22 × 18 inch radiator, 16 qts.; With 26 × 18 inch radiator, 17 qts. If equipped with A/C or increased cooling package, add one qt. to above capacities.

[22]—With 22 × 18 inch radiator, 14.5 qts.; With 26 × 18 inch radiator, 15.5 qts. If equipped with A/C or increased cooling package, add one qt. to above capacities.

[23]—Models equipped with 4 wheel drive, front axle 44-8FD, 5.6 pts.; front axle 60-F, 6.5 pts.

[24]—With 19 × 18 inch radiator, 12 qts.; With 22 × 18 inch radiator, 12 qts.; With 26 × 18 inch radiator, 13 qts. If equipped with A/C or increased cooling package, add one qt. to above capacities.

[25]—With 22 × 18 inch radiator, 16 qts.; With 26 × 18 inch radiator, 17 qts.; With 26 × 20 inch radiator, 17.5 qts. If equipped with A/C or increased cooling package, add one qt. to above capacities.

[26]—With 22 × 18 inch radiator, 14.5 qts.; With 26 × 18 inch radiator, 15.5 qts.; With 26 × 20 inch radiator, 16 qts. If equipped with A/C or increased cooling package, add one qt. to above capacities.

Electrical Section

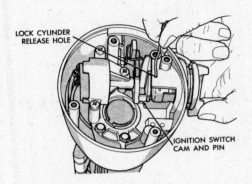

LOCK CYLINDER RELEASE HOLE

IGNITION SWITCH CAM AND PIN

Fig. 1 Lock cylinder removal. Less tilt steering wheel

STARTER
REPLACE

GASOLINE ENGINES

1. Disconnect battery ground cable.
2. Disconnect starter cable at starter, then the solenoid lead wire from solenoid.
3. Remove heat shield attaching bolt, then the heat shield if equipped.
4. Remove starter motor attaching bolts, then the oil cooler tube bracket, if equipped with automatic transmission.
5. Remove starter from vehicle.
6. Reverse procedure to install.

DIESEL ENGINES

1. Disconnect battery ground cable.
2. Raise and support vehicle, then disconnect starter cable at starter and solenoid lead wire from solenoid.
3. Remove starter motor attaching bolts, then the starter.
4. Reverse procedure to install.

IGNITION SWITCH & LOCK
REPLACE

MODELS LESS TILT STEERING WHEELS

1. Disconnect battery ground cable and remove turn signal switch as outlined in this chapter.
2. Remove ignition key lamp assembly attaching screws, then the assembly.
3. Remove snap ring from upper end of steering shaft.

4. Remove bearing housing to lock housing attaching screws, then the bearing housing from the shaft.
5. Remove buzzer switch attaching screws, then the buzzer switch, if equipped.
6. Remove lock lever guide plate attaching screws, then the lock plate.
7. Place lock cylinder in the "Lock" position and remove key. Using a suitable tool, depress spring loaded lock retainer and pull lock cylinder from housing bore, **Fig. 1.**
8. Remove ignition switch attaching screws, then the ignition switch.
9. Reverse procedure to install.

MODELS W/TILT STEERING WHEEL

NOTE: The ignition switch and lock assembly are separate units and must be replaced individually.

Ignition Lock, Replace

1. Disconnect battery ground cable and remove turn signal switch as outlined in this chapter.
2. Place lock cylinder in the "Lock" position and remove key. Insert suitable tool into slot next to switch mounting screw boss, **Fig. 2.**
3. Depress spring latch at bottom of slot, then remove lock.
4. To install ignition lock, place lock cylinder in the "Lock" position and remove key. Install lock cylinder assembly into housing, then press inward and move switch actuator rod up and down to align parts.

NOTE: When parts align, the lock cylinder will move inward and a spring loaded retainer will snap into place, locking cylinder into housing.

Ignition Switch, Replace

The ignition switch is located on the top of the steering column under the instrument panel. To replace it, the steering column should be lowered as follows:

1. Disconnect shift indicator link.
2. Remove nuts securing bracket to dash panel and carefully lower column.
3. Disconnect electrical connector from switch. Ensure switch is in "Accessory" position.
4. Remove switch attaching screws, then the switch.
5. To install ignition switch, place switch slider and lock in the "Accessory" position.
6. Fit actuator rod into switch and assemble to column.
7. Complete assembly in reverse of removal procedure.

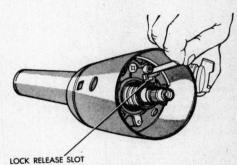

LOCK RELEASE SLOT

Fig. 2 Lock cylinder removal. W/tilt steering wheel

LIGHT SWITCH
REPLACE

1979—85 VANS, WAGONS & FRONT SECTIONS

1. Disconnect battery ground cable.
2. Depress knob and stem release button located on bottom of switch housing, and pull knob and stem assembly from switch.
3. Remove instrument panel hood and bezel assembly.
4. Remove switch bezel attaching screws, then the switch bezel.
5. Remove switch attaching nut, then disconnect switch electrical connector and remove switch.
6. Reverse procedure to install.

1979—80 RAMCHARGER, TRAIL DUSTER & CONVENTIONAL CABS

1. Disconnect battery ground cable.
2. Remove left air conditioner and air outlet assembly, if equipped.
3. Depress knob and stem release button located on bottom of switch housing, and pull knob and stem assembly from switch.
4. Remove switch attaching nut, then disconnect switch electrical connector and remove switch.
5. Reverse procedure to install.

1981—85 RAMCHARGER, TRAIL DUSTER & CONVENTIONAL CABS

1. Disconnect battery ground cable, then remove cluster faceplate.
2. Depress knob and stem release button located on bottom of switch housing, and pull knob and stem assembly from switch.
3. Remove wiper switch knob, then the bezel.

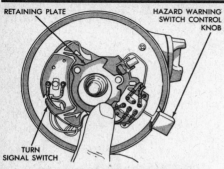

Fig. 3   Turn signal switch retainer removal. Standard columns

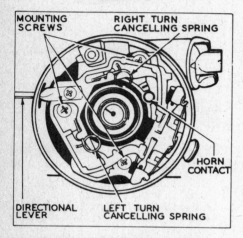

Fig. 5   Turn signal switch removal. Tilt columns

4. Remove switch attaching nut, then disconnect switch electrical connector and remove switch.
5. Reverse procedure to install.

STOP LIGHT SWITCH
REPLACE

EXC. MOTOR HOME

1. Disconnect battery ground cable.
2. Disconnect wiring from switch and remove switch from brake pedal bracket.
3. Reverse procedure to install.
4. To adjust, proceed as follows:
   a. Loosen switch assembly to pedal bracket attaching screw and slide assembly away from pedal blade or striker plate.
   b. Push brake pedal down and allow to return to free position.

NOTE: Do not pull brake pedal back at any time.

   c. Place spacer gauge on pedal blade.

NOTE: Models with speed control use a .070 inch spacer, 1979–83 models less speed control use a .130 inch spacer and

---

1984–85 models less speed control use a .140 inch spacer.

   d. Slide switch assembly toward pedal blade until switch plunger is fully depressed against spacer gauge without moving the pedal.
   e. Tighten the switch bracket attaching screw and remove spacer. Ensure stop light switch does not prevent full pedal return.

MOTOR HOME

1. Disconnect battery ground cable.
2. Disconnect wiring from switch and remove switch from bracket.
3. Reverse procedure to install.
4. To adjust, proceed as follows:
   a. Loosen switch lock nut, then the switch until plunger is no longer in contact with pedal blade.
   b. Disconnect pedal return spring and loosen push rod lock nut.
   c. Remove push rod end bolt and pedal return spring bracket assembly.
   d. Position a .010–.015 inch spacer between pedal blade and pedal stop.
   e. Turn push rod in or out until push rod end bolt can be inserted through pedal blade. Ensure push rod operates smoothly.
   f. Install pedal return spring bracket and torque attaching nut to 30 ft. lbs. Torque push rod lock nut to 120 inch lbs.
   g. Remove spacer and connect pedal return spring, then tighten stop light switch until it contacts pedal blade. Continue to tighten switch 2½ complete turns.
   h. Tighten switch lock nut and ensure proper switch operation.

NEUTRAL SAFETY & BACK-UP SWITCH
REPLACE

1. Unscrew switch from transmission case, allowing fluid to drain into container.
2. Move shift lever to "Park" and then to "Neutral" positions and inspect to ensure switch operating lever is centered in switch opening in case.
3. Screw switch into transmission case, then add fluid to the proper level.
4. Check to ensure proper switch operation.

HORN SOUNDER & STEERING WHEEL
REPLACE

1979 BUTTON TYPE STEERING WHEELS

1. Disconnect battery ground cable.
2. Lift horn button off wheel, then discon-

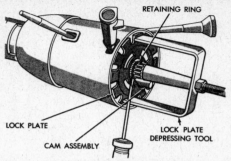

Fig. 4   Lock plate retaining ring removal

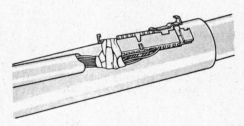

Fig. 6   Taping turn signal connector and wires

nect horn switch electrical connector.
3. Remove horn switch to steering wheel attaching screws, then the switch.
4. Remove screws mounting retainer to horn switch.
5. Remove steering wheel nut, then the steering wheel using a suitable puller.

NOTE: Do not bump or hammer on steering shaft to remove wheel, as damage to shaft may result.

6. Reverse procedure to install.

LUXURY TYPE PADDED STEERING WHEEL

1. Disconnect battery ground cable.
2. Pry off pad, then disconnect electrical connector from horn ring terminal.
3. Remove each horn switch to steering wheel retaining screw and lift out horn button switches from wheel.
4. Remove steering wheel nut, then the wheel using a suitable puller.

NOTE: Do not bump or hammer on steering shaft to remove wheel, as damage to shaft may result.

5. Reverse procedure to install.

PADDED TYPE EXC. LUXURY TYPE STEERING WHEEL

1. Disconnect battery ground cable.
2. On models with horn pad mounting screws located behind steering wheel spokes, remove screws and the pad. On all other models equipped with horn pad, pry horn pad from wheel.

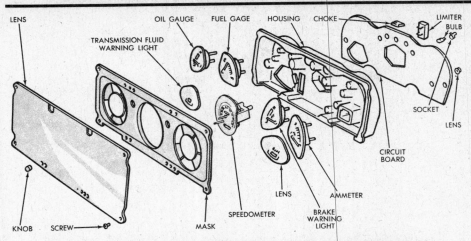

LENS · TRANSMISSION FLUID WARNING LIGHT · OIL GAUGE · FUEL GAGE · HOUSING · CHOKE · LIMITER · BULB · INSTRUMENT PANEL · MOUNTING SCREW · INSTRUMENT CLUSTER PANEL · MOUNTING SCREWS · SOCKET · LENS · CIRCUIT BOARD · MOUNTING SCREWS · KNOB · SCREW · MASK · SPEEDOMETER · LENS · AMMETER · BRAKE WARNING LIGHT

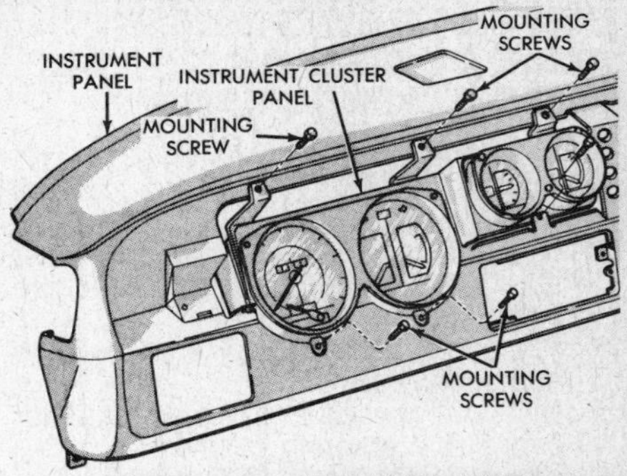

Fig. 8   Instrument cluster removal. 1979—85 Vans, Wagons & Front Sections

Fig. 7   Instrument cluster removal. 1979—80 Motor Home

3. Disconnect horn switch electrical connector.
4. Remove horn switch to retainer attaching screws, then the switch from retainer.
5. Remove steering wheel nut, then the steering wheel using a suitable puller.

NOTE: Do not bump or hammer on steering shaft to remove wheel, as damage to shaft may result.

6. Reverse procedure to install.

SPORT STEERING WHEEL

1. Disconnect battery ground cable.
2. Lift horn button off wheel, then disconnect switch electrical connector.
3. Remove steering wheel nut.
4. Remove horn switch to steering wheel attaching screw, then the horn switch.
5. Remove steering wheel using suitable puller.

NOTE: Do not bump or hammer on steering shaft to remove wheel, as damage to shaft may result.

6. Reverse procedure to install.

TURN SIGNAL/ HAZARD WARNING SWITCH
REPLACE

1. Disconnect battery ground cable.
2. On 1983—85 models, remove lower bezel from instrument panel.
3. On all models, remove horn sounder and steering wheel. Refer to "Horn Sounder & Steering Wheel, Replace" procedure.
4. On standard columns proceed as follows:
   a. Remove turn signal lever to switch attaching screw, then the lever.

NOTE: If equipped with speed control, allow lever to hang free.

   b. Remove switch retainer attaching screws, then the retainer, **Fig. 3.**
5. On tilt columns, proceed as follows:
   a. Remove plastic cover from lock plate, if equipped.
   b. Depress lock plate using tool C-4156 or equivalent, **Fig. 4,** then pry retaining ring out of groove using screwdriver.

NOTE: The full load of the cancelling cam spring should not be relieved. If full load is relieved, retaining ring will turn too easily, making removal more difficult.

   c. Remove lock plate, cancelling cam and spring, then place turn signal lever in right turn position.
   d. Remove turn signal lever to switch attaching screw, then the lever.

NOTE: If equipped with speed control, allow lever to hang free.

   e. Remove hazard warning switch knob attaching screw, then the turn signal switch attaching screws, **Fig. 5.**
6. On all models, position steering wheel in mid-point position.
7. On models equipped with column shift, place selector lever in first or third gear position.
8. On all models, remove wire cover attaching clips, then the cover if equipped.
9. Disconnect turn signal electrical connector. Wrap a piece of tape around the connector and wire to prevent snagging during switch removal, **Fig. 6.**
10. Remove turn signal/hazard warning switch assembly by pulling switch up from column while straightening and guiding wires up through column opening.
11. Reverse procedure to install.

INSTRUMENT CLUSTER
REPLACE

1979—80 MOTOR HOME

1. Disconnect battery ground cable.
2. Remove six instrument cluster to instrument panel attaching screws, then disconnect speedometer cable.
3. Disconnect instrument cluster electrical connectors, then remove cluster, **Fig. 7.**
4. Reverse procedure to install.

1979—85 VANS, WAGONS & FRONT SECTIONS

1. Disconnect battery ground cable.
2. Remove instrument panel hood and bezel assembly attaching screws, then pull bezel off upper retaining clips.
3. Remove cluster attaching screws, then pull cluster forward and disconnect speedometer cable.
4. Disconnect instrument cluster electrical connectors, then remove cluster, **Fig. 8.**
5. Reverse procedure to install.

1979—80 RAMCHARGER, TRAIL DUSTER & CONVENTIONAL CABS

1. Disconnect battery ground cable.
2. Cover steering column to prevent damage to paint.
3. Remove bezel attaching screws, then the bezel.
4. Remove radio and left air conditioner duct if equipped.
5. Disconnect speedometer cable from cluster.
6. Remove cluster assembly attaching screws, then pull cluster forward and disconnect cluster electrical connectors.
7. Remove cluster assembly from panel, **Fig. 9.**
8. Reverse procedure to install.

1981—85 RAMCHARGER, TRAIL DUSTER & CONVENTIONAL CABS

1. Disconnect battery ground cable.
2. Cover steering column to prevent damage to paint.
3. Remove face plate, then four lower steering column cover attaching screws, **Fig. 10.**
4. Pry out upper steering column cover and slide downward.
5. Disconnect selector lever actuator cable from steering column.
6. Loosen heater and A/C control. Pull rearward to clear forward mount on cluster housing.
7. Remove six cluster retaining screws, then pull cluster forward and disconnect speedometer cable.
8. Disconnect instrument cluster electrical connectors, then remove cluster.
9. Reverse procedure to install.

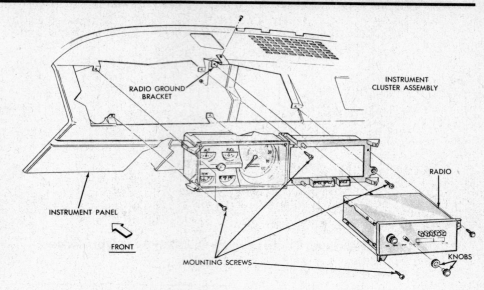

Fig. 9   Instrument cluster removal. 1979—80 Ramcharger, Trail Duster & Conventional Cabs

W/S WIPER MOTOR
REPLACE

1. Disconnect battery ground cable.
2. Disconnect wiper motor electrical connectors, then remove motor attaching screws.
3. Lower motor down far enough to gain access to crank arm to drive link retainer bushing.
4. Remove crank arm from drive link by prying retainer bushing from crank arm pin using a suitable screwdriver.
5. Remove motor from vehicle.

W/S WIPER TRANSMISSION
REPLACE

1979—85 VANS, WAGONS & FRONT SECTIONS
Drive Link, Replace
1. Remove wiper arms and washer hoses, then the cowl cover grille.
2. Remove drive link from crank arm and connecting link pins by prying retainer bushing apart using a suitable screwdriver, **Fig. 11.**
3. Remove drive link through access hole.
4. Reverse procedure to install.

Connecting Link, Replace
1. Remove cowl cover grille.
2. Remove connecting link from drive

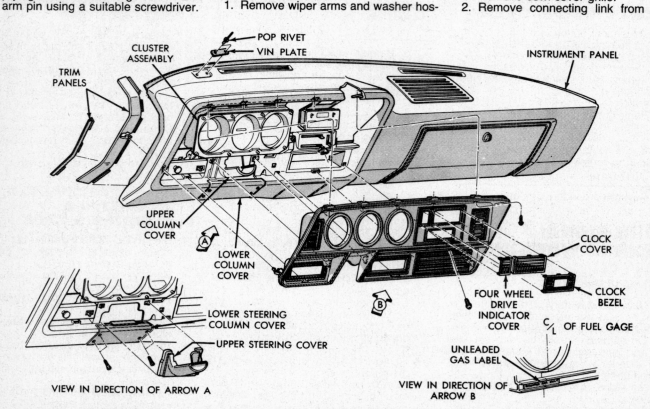

Fig. 10   Instrument cluster removal. 1981—85 Ramcharger, Trail Duster & Conventional Cabs

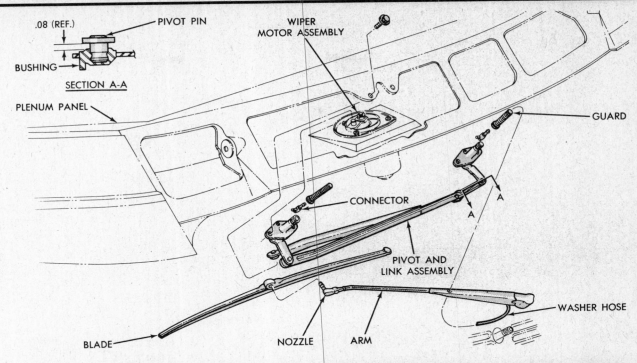

.08 (REF.)
PIVOT PIN
BUSHING
SECTION A-A
PLENUM PANEL
WIPER MOTOR ASSEMBLY
GUARD
CONNECTOR
A
A
PIVOT AND LINK ASSEMBLY
WASHER HOSE
BLADE
NOZZLE
ARM

Fig. 11 Windshield wiper transmission assembly. 1979—85 Vans, Wagons & Front Sections

link and pivot pins by prying retainer bushings apart using a suitable screwdriver, **Fig. 11.**
3. Remove connecting link through access hole.
4. Reverse procedure to install.

Crank Arm, Replace
1. Remove wiper arms and washer hoses.
2. Remove cowl cover grille.
3. Remove drive link from crank arm pin by prying retainer bushing apart using a suitable screwdriver, **Fig. 11.**
4. Remove crank arm to motor attaching nut, then the crank arm through access hole.
5. Reverse procedure to install.

Right Or Left Pivot, Replace
1. Remove wiper arms and washer hoses.
2. Remove cowl cover grille.
3. Remove connecting link from pivot pins by prying retainer bushing apart using a suitable screwdriver, **Fig. 11.**
4. Remove pivot attaching bolts, then lower pivot and remove through access hole.
5. Reverse procedure to install.

1979—85 RAMCHARGER, TRAIL DUSTER & CONVENTIONAL CAB

Crank Arm, Replace
1. Remove wiper motor. Refer to "W/S Wiper Motor, Replace" procedure.
2. Remove crank arm to motor drive shaft attaching nut, then the crank arm, **Fig. 12.**
3. Reverse procedure to install.

Drive Link & Left Pivot Assembly, Replace
1. Remove wiper arms, then the cowl cover attaching screws and cover.
2. Remove drive link from right pivot by prying retainer bushing apart using a suitable screwdriver, **Fig. 12.**
3. Remove crank arm from drive link by prying retainer bushing from crank arm pin using a suitable screwdriver.
4. Remove left pivot attaching screws and allow pivot to hang free.
5. Remove drive links and left pivot as an assembly.
6. Remove drive link from left pivot by prying retainer bushing from pivot pin using a suitable screwdriver.
7. Reverse procedure to install.

Right Pivot Assembly, Replace
1. Remove wiper arms, then the cowl cover attaching screws and cover.
2. Remove drive link from right pivot by prying retainer bushing from pivot pin using suitable screwdriver, **Fig. 12.**
3. Remove right pivot attaching screws, then the pivot through access hole.
4. Reverse procedure to install.

W/S WIPER SWITCH REPLACE

1979—85 VANS, WAGONS & FRONT SECTIONS
1. Disconnect battery ground cable.
2. Remove steering column cover, if equipped.
3. Remove two switch housing to instrument panel attaching screws.
4. Disconnect switch and bezel assembly electrical connectors.

5. Disconnect illumination lamp, then remove switch housing assembly from under instrument panel.
6. Remove switch to housing retaining screws, then the switch.
7. Reverse procedure to install.

1979—80 RAMCHARGER, TRAIL DUSTER & CONVENTIONAL CABS
1. Disconnect battery ground cable.
2. Remove ash tray housing.
3. Loosen knob attaching screw, then the knob from switch.
4. Remove switch to panel attaching nut, then working through ash tray opening, lower switch and disconnect switch electrical connector.
5. Remove lighting bracket, then the switch.
6. Reverse procedure to install.

1981—85 RAMCHARGER, TRAIL DUSTER & CONVENTIONAL CAB
1. Disconnect battery ground cable, then remove cluster faceplate.
2. Depress head light knob and stem release button located on bottom of switch housing and pull knob and stem assembly from switch.
3. Pull wiper switch knob off wiper switch.
4. Remove bezel attaching screws, then the bezel.
5. Remove four wiper switch attaching screws.
6. Disconnect switch electrical connectors, then remove switch.
7. Reverse procedure to install.

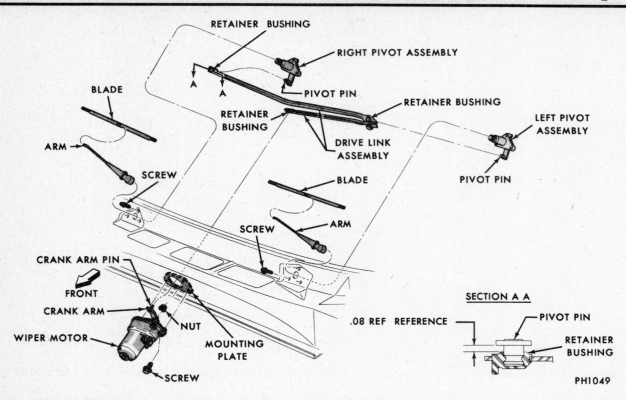

Fig. 12 Windshield wiper transmission assembly. 1979—85 Ramcharger, Trail Duster & Conventional Cabs

RADIO
REPLACE

NOTE: Do not operate radio with speaker leads detached, as damage to transistors may result.

1979—85 VANS, WAGONS & FRONT SECTIONS

1. Disconnect battery ground cable.
2. Remove cluster bezel attaching screws, then the bezel.
3. Remove radio attaching screws and ground strap screw.
4. Pull radio from panel, then disconnect antenna lead, speaker leads and electrical connectors.
5. Remove radio.
6. Reverse procedure to install.

1979—85 RAMCHARGER, TRAIL DUSTER & CONVENTIONAL CABS

1. Disconnect battery ground cable.
2. Remove instrument cluster bezel attaching screws, then the bezel.
3. Remove left air conditioner duct if equipped.
4. Disconnect antenna lead, speaker leads and electrical connectors, then remove radio to mounting bracket attaching nut.
5. Remove radio to cluster attaching bolts, then remove radio through clus-

ter housing opening.
6. Reverse procedure to install.

HEATER CORE
REPLACE

VANS, WAGONS & FRONT SECTIONS

LESS A/C

1979—85 Models

1. Disconnect battery ground cable and drain cooling system.
2. Disconnect heater core hoses.
3. Disconnect temperature control cable from heater core cover and blend air door crank.
4. Disconnect blower motor feed wire from resistor block located on distribution duct in cab.
5. Set coolant overflow tank aside.
6. Remove nuts retaining heater assembly to side cowl and nuts retaining heater assembly to dash panel, then remove heater assembly from vehicle, **Fig. 13.**
7. Remove heater core cover, then remove the two heater core retaining screws and remove heater core.
8. Reverse procedure to install.

WITH A/C

1979—85 Models

1. Discharge refrigerant from system.

2. Disconnect battery ground cable and drain cooling system.
3. Place a waterproof cover over alternator to prevent coolant from spilling over it, then disconnect and plug heater core hoses.
4. Disconnect refrigerant lines at H-valve, then remove two screws from filter drier bracket and position lines aside. Cap all refrigerant lines. Disconnect temperature control cable from cover.
5. From inside vehicle, remove glove box, spot cooler bezel and appearance shield.
6. Through glove box opening and under instrument panel, remove screws and nuts retaining evaporator housing to dash panel.
7. Remove the two screws from flange connection to blower housing. Separate evaporator housing from blower housing and carefully remove evaporator housing from vehicle, **Fig. 14.**
8. Remove cover from housing, then remove heater core strap retaining screw and remove heater core.
9. Reverse procedure to install.

RAMCHARGER, TRAIL DUSTER & CONVENTIONAL CAB

LESS A/C

1979—80 Models

1. Disconnect battery ground cable.
2. Drain cooling system and disconnect

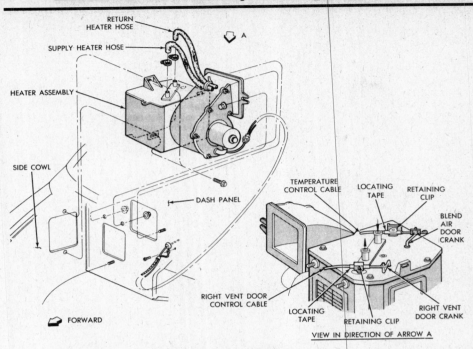

Fig. 13 Heater assembly. 1979–85 Vans, Wagons & Front Sections. Less A/C

hoses from heater core.
3. Disconnect electrical connector from resistor.
4. Disconnect control cables and remove defroster ducts.
5. Disconnect ground wire and cooling tube from blower motor.
6. Remove bracket from right end of instrument panel and pull toward rear of cab.
7. Remove the seven retaining nuts from engine side of firewall and from inside of cab near right hand kick panel.
8. Remove heater from vehicle, **Fig. 15.**
9. Remove screws and separate heater housing.
10. Remove core retaining screws and carefully slide core out of heater housing.
11. Reverse procedure to install.

1981–85 Models
1. Disconnect battery ground cable.

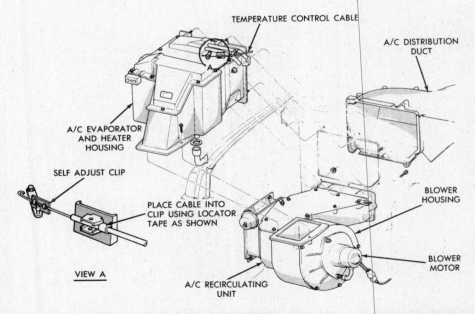

Fig. 14 Heater assembly. 1979–85 Vans, Wagons & Front Sections. With A/C

2. Disconnect heater hoses on engine side and plug heater outlets.
3. Remove right side cowl trim if so equipped.
4. Remove glovebox, then structural brace through glovebox opening.
5. Remove right half of instrument panel lower reinforcement, making sure to disconnect ground strap.
6. Disconnect control cables, then blower motor wires on engine side.
7. Disconnect wires from resistor block, **Fig. 16.**
8. Remove screw holding heater to cowl side sheet metal.
9. Remove 6 heater retaining nuts on firewall, then remove heater.
10. Remove mode door crank and 15 screws to remove cover from housing, then slide heater core out.
11. Reverse procedure to install.

WITH A/C

1979–80 Models
1. Disconnect battery ground cable.
2. Drain cooling system and disconnect hoses from heater core.
3. Remove glove box and ash tray.
4. Remove right and left A/C ducts, distribution duct and center air outlet and duct.
5. Disconnect wiring harness from resistor and vacuum lines from rear housing.
6. Remove the 24 retaining screws, then while holding defroster toward heat position, separate the units.
7. Remove one screw from engine side and two screws from each end of core and slide core out, **Fig. 17.**
8. Reverse procedure to install.

1981–85 Models
1. Disconnect battery ground cable.
2. Discharge A/C system and disconnect refrigerant and heater lines from unit.
3. Move shift levers away from dash.
4. Remove right side cowl trim panel, if equipped.
5. Remove 4 screws at base and remove glovebox, **Fig. 18.**
6. Remove brace through glovebox opening and remove ash tray.
7. Remove right half of lower reinforcement (7 screws to instrument panel and 1 to cowl side of trim panel).
8. Disconnect radio ground strap.
9. Remove right upper air duct by removing mounting screw and pulling duct out through glovebox opening.
10. Remove instrument panel center brace and right instrument panel cluster pivot bolt.
11. Remove instrument panel cluster, disconnect shift indicator cable and lower steering column.
12. Remove steering column studs and radio.
13. Remove scoop connecting heater to center distribution duct (2 screws).
14. Remove center distribution duct by pulling bottom of dash out to gain clearance.

15. Remove floor air distribution duct.
16. Disconnect temperature control cable through glovebox.
17. Remove 7 retaining nuts from firewall and screw that retains assembly to cowl side sheetmetal.
18. Flex dash out and remove heater assembly.
19. Remove nuts from door arms and remove door arms.
20. Remove 7 screws to remove cover from housing.
21. Remove evaporator core.
22. Reverse procedure to install.

BLOWER MOTOR
REPLACE

VANS, WAGONS & FRONT SECTIONS

LESS A/C

1979—85 Models
1. Disconnect battery ground cable and blower motor wires.
2. Remove 7 screws holding back plate to heater housing and remove blower assembly.
3. Remove spring clip holding blower wheel to motor and pull off blower wheel.
4. Remove vent tube from motor.
5. Remove 2 nuts holding blower motor to back plate and remove blower motor.
6. Reverse procedure to install.

WITH A/C

1979 Models
1. Disconnect battery ground cable.
2. Raise and support vehicle.
3. Remove blower motor cooler tube.
4. Disconnect lead wire at connector and ground wire at retaining screw.
5. Remove three blower motor to housing attaching nuts, then the blower motor.
6. Reverse procedure to install.

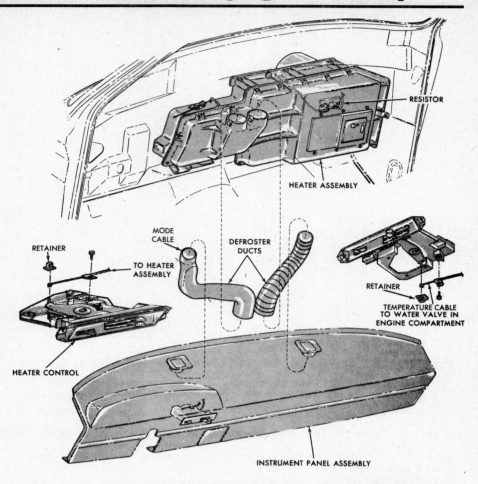

Fig. 15   Heater assembly. 1979—80 Ramcharger, Trail Duster & Conventional Cabs. Less A/C

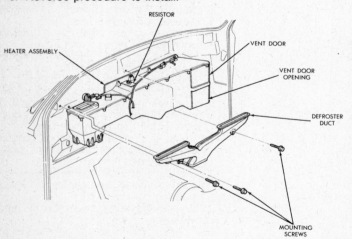

Fig. 16   Heater assembly. Ramcharger, Trail Duster & Conventional Cabs less A/C. 1981—84 shown, 1985 similar

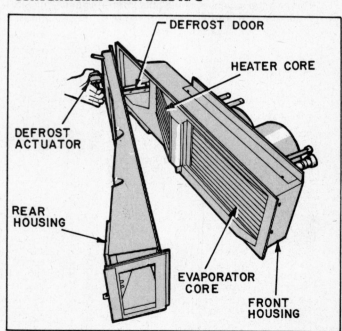

Fig. 17   Heater assembly. 1979—80 Ramcharger, Trail Duster & Conventional Cabs. With A/C

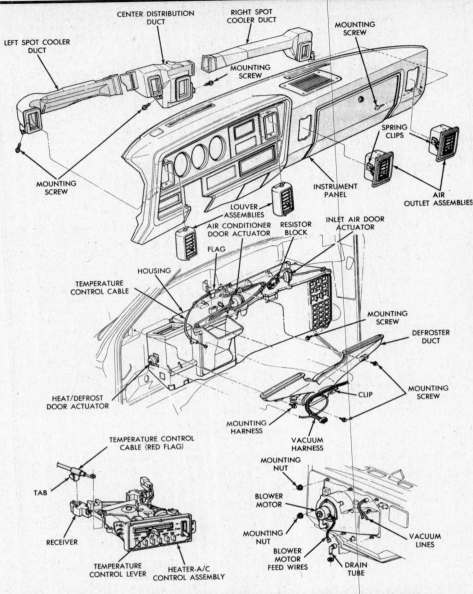

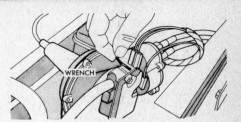

Fig. 19   Speed control lock-in screw adjustment

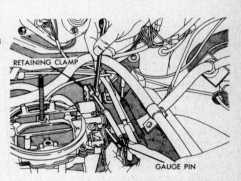

Fig. 20   Speed control servo throttle cable adjustment

Fig. 18   Heater assembly. 1981—85 Ramcharger, Trail Duster & Conventional Cabs. With A/C

1980—85 Models

1. Disconnect battery ground cable.
2. Remove top half of shroud by removing 2 screws from shroud to radiator support and two screws holding the halves of the shroud together. Top right screw on vehicles with six cylinder engine is hidden behind discharge line muffler. Move top half of shroud out of the way.
3. Disconnect blower motor electrical connector and remove blower motor cooling tube.
4. Remove the three retaining nuts from studs holding blower motor.
5. Pull A/C suction and discharge lines inboard and upward while pulling blower motor assembly from housing.
6. Remove blower motor.
7. Reverse procedure to install.

RAMCHARGER, TRAIL DUSTER & CONVENTIONAL CABS

LESS A/C

1979—80 Models

1. Disconnect battery ground cable and blower motor wiring.
2. Disconnect blower motor vent tube.
3. Remove blower assembly mounting screws and blower assembly.
4. Separate wheel from motor, noting position of wheel on shaft.
5. Remove blower mounting plate from motor.
6. Reverse procedure to install.

1981—85 Models

1. Disconnect battery ground cable and blower motor wiring.
2. Remove screws holding blower motor to heater housing on firewall.
3. Remove blower.
4. Reverse procedure to install.

WITH A/C

1979—80 Models

1. Disconnect battery ground cable and blower motor wiring.
2. Disconnect blower motor vent tube.
3. Remove blower assembly mounting screws and blower assembly.
4. Separate wheel from motor, noting position of wheel on shaft.
5. Remove blower mounting plate from motor.
6. Reverse procedure to install.

1981—85 Models

1. Disconnect battery ground cable and blower motor wiring.
2. Remove screws holding blower motor to heater housing on firewall, **Fig. 18.**
3. Remove blower.
4. Reverse procedure to install.

SPEED CONTROL
ADJUST

LOCK-IN SCREW ADJUSTMENT

Lock-in accuracy will be affected by poor engine performance (need for tune-up), loaded gross weight of car (trailering), or improper slack in control cable. After the foregoing items have been considered and the speed sags or drops more than 2 to 3 mph when the speed control is activated, the lock-in adjusting screw should be turned counter-clockwise approximately ¼ turn per one mph correction required.

If a speed increase of more than 2 to 3 mph occurs, the lock-in adjusting screw should be turned clockwise ¼ turn per one mph correction required, **Fig. 19.**

CAUTION: This adjustment must not exceed two turns in either direction or damage to the unit may occur.

THROTTLE CABLE ADJUSTMENT

Optimum servo performance is obtained with a given amount of free play in the throttle control cable. To obtain proper free play, insert a ¹⁄₁₆" diameter pin between forward end of slot in cable end of carburetor linkage pin (hair pin clip removed from linkage pin), **Fig. 20.** With choke in full open position and carburetor at curb idle, pull cable back toward dash until all free play is removed. Tighten cable clamp bolt to 45 inch lbs., remove ¹⁄₁₆" pin and install hair pin clip.

Gasoline Engine Section

ENGINE MOUNTS
REPLACE

1. Remove engine mount to frame attaching nuts.
2. Support engine, then remove mount to bracket attaching bolts and nuts.
3. Raise engine slightly, then remove mounts.

NOTE: Some models incorporate a insulator between the engine mount and engine mount attaching bracket.

4. Reverse procedure to install.

ENGINE
REPLACE

1979—85 VANS, WAGONS & FRONT SECTIONS

6-225 Engine

NOTE: If vehicle is equipped with manual transmission, transmission must be removed prior to engine removal. Refer to "Clutch & Manual Transmission Section" for transmission removal procedure.

1. Disconnect battery ground cable and remove oil dipstick.
2. Raise and support vehicle, then remove air pump tube from exhaust pipe.
3. Remove exhaust pipe, then the inspection cover from transmission.
4. Drain engine oil and remove engine to transmission strut.
5. Remove engine oil pan attaching screws, then the oil pan. It may be necessary to turn crankshaft to clear front of oil pan.
6. Turn pickup tube upward to protect from damage while removing engine, then remove flex plate to torque converter attaching bolts.
7. Remove lower transmission bell housing attaching bolts, then the lower right engine mount insulator attaching nut.
8. Lower vehicle and drain cooling system.
9. Remove engine cover, then the carburetor air cleaner and carburetor.
10. On models equipped with A/C, discharge refrigerant from system and disconnect condenser lines.
11. On all models, remove fan shroud, windshield washer and over flow reservoirs, then the front bumper, grille and support brace.
12. Disconnect radiator hoses, then remove radiator and support as an assembly.
13. Remove power steering pump with hoses attached and position aside, then remove air pump.
14. Disconnect throttle linkage, vacuum hoses and all engine electrical connectors.
15. Remove alternator with brackets, fan blade, pulley and all drive belts, then disconnect fuel line from fuel pump.
16. Remove starter attaching bolts, then the starter.
17. Remove distributor cap with spark plug wires attached.
18. Remove upper left engine mount insulator attaching nut.
19. Attach suitable chain to cylinder heads to provide as an engine lifting fixture.
20. Install suitable engine hoist to lifting fixture, then place suitable floor jack under transmission.
21. Remove upper bell housing attaching bolts.
22. Remove engine from front of vehicle.
23. Reverse procedure to install.

V8-318, 360 & 440 Engines

NOTE: On V8-318 & 360 engines equipped with manual transmission, transmission must be removed prior to engine removal. Refer to "Clutch & Manual Transmission Section" for transmission removal procedure.

1. Disconnect battery ground cable and remove oil dipstick.
2. Raise and support vehicle, then remove exhaust crossover pipe.
3. Remove inspection cover from transmission.
4. Drain engine oil and remove engine to transmission strut.
5. Remove engine oil pan attaching screws, then the oil pan. It may be necessary to turn crankshaft to clear front of oil pan.
6. Remove oil pump and pickup tube assembly, then the flex plate to torque converter attaching bolts.
7. Remove starter attaching bolts, then the starter.
8. Remove lower transmission bell housing attaching bolts, then the engine mount insulator lower attaching nuts.
9. Lower vehicle and drain cooling system.
10. Remove engine cover, then the carburetor air cleaner and carburetor.
11. On models equipped with A/C, discharge refrigerant from system and disconnect condenser lines.
12. On all models, remove front bumper, grill and support brace.
13. Disconnect radiator hoses, then remove radiator, condenser and support as an assembly.
14. Remove air conditioning compressor, if equipped, then plug all openings to keep out moisture and dirt.
15. Remove power steering pump with hoses attached and position aside, then remove air pump.
16. Disconnect throttle linkage, vacuum hoses and all engine electrical connectors.
17. Remove alternator, fan blade, pulley and all drive belts, then disconnect fuel line from fuel pump.
18. Remove left exhaust manifold and heat shield, then the distributor cap with spark plug wires attached.
19. Attach suitable chain to intake manifold to provide as an engine lifting fixture.
20. Install suitable engine hoist to lifting fixture, then place suitable floor jack under transmission.
21. Remove upper bell housing attaching bolts.
22. Remove engine from vehicle.
23. Reverse procedure to install.

1979—85 RAMCHARGER, TRAIL DUSTER & CONVENTIONAL CAB

NOTE: If vehicle is equipped with manual transmission, transmission must be removed prior to engine removal. Refer to "Clutch & Manual Transmission Section" for transmission removal procedure.

1. Disconnect battery cables and remove battery, then drain cooling system.
2. Mark position of hinges for reassembly, then remove hood.
3. Remove radiator and heater hoses,

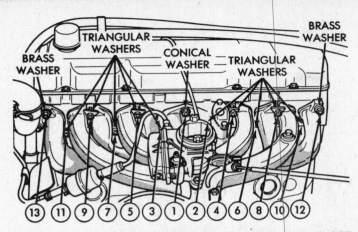

Fig. 1 Intake manifold tightening sequence. 6-225

then the radiator. Position fan shroud aside.
4. On models equipped with A/C, discharge refrigerant from system.
5. On all models, remove vacuum lines, then the distributor with spark plug wires attached.
6. Remove throttle linkage, then the carburetor.
7. Remove all engine electrical connectors.
8. Remove air conditioning hoses and power steering hoses, if equipped.
9. Remove starter motor, alternator, charcoal canister and horns.
10. Disconnect exhaust pipe at manifold.
11. Remove bell housing attaching bolts and inspection plate.
12. Attach C-clamp on bottom of transmission torque converter housing to prevent torque converter from falling out.
13. Remove torque converter drive plate attaching bolts from torque converter drive plate. Mark converter and drive plate to aid in reassembly.
14. Support transmission using suitable floor jack, then disconnect engine from torque converter drive plate.
15. Install suitable lifting fixture to cylinder head.
16. Install suitable engine hoist to lifting fixture, then remove engine front mount bolts.
17. Remove engine from vehicle.
18. Reverse procedure to install.

MOTOR HOME

1. Disconnect battery ground cable and drain cooling system.
2. Disconnect radiator hoses, then remove radiator.
3. Remove engine cover, passenger seat and other fixtures that may limit access to top of engine.
4. Disconnect heater hoses and all engine electrical connectors.
5. Remove air cleaner, fuel lines and carburetor.
6. Install engine lifting adapter to carburetor mounting pad on intake manifold.

7. Disconnect throttle linkage at transmission, then the exhaust pipes at both manifolds.
8. Remove line to fuel pump inlet.
9. Support engine using tool No. C-3487A or equivalent. With engine and transmission slightly raised, disconnect transmission rear mount, speedometer cable and hand brake.
10. Remove front bumper and frame front crossmember.
11. Install suitable engine hoist to lifting fixture, then disconnect front engine mounts from frame.
12. Remove engine from vehicle.
13. Reverse procedure to install.

INTAKE MANIFOLD
REPLACE

6-225
Removal
1. Disconnect battery ground cable.
2. Disconnect air cleaner vacuum line from carburetor, then the flexible connector between air cleaner and carburetor air heater.
3. Disconnect air cleaner line breather cap, then remove air cleaner.
4. Disconnect distributor vacuum control line, crankcase ventilator valve hose and carburetor bowl vent line, if equipped.
5. Remove carburetor air heater.
6. Disconnect fuel line, automatic choke rod and throttle linkage from carburetor, then remove carburetor.
7. Disconnect exhaust pipe from exhaust manifold.
8. Remove manifold assembly to cylinder head attaching nuts and washers, then the manifold assembly.
9. Remove three intake manifold to exhaust manifold attaching screws, then separate manifolds.

Installation
1. Install new gasket between the exhaust and intake manifolds, then the three long screws holding the manifolds together.

NOTE: Do not tighten the three intake and exhaust manifold attaching screws at this point.

2. Install new manifold to cylinder head gasket. Coat both sides of gasket with suitable sealing compound.
3. Install manifold assembly then the washers as specified in **Fig. 1**. Install steel conical washer with cup side facing nut and brass washer with flat side facing manifold.

NOTE: Ensure all washers spanning intake and exhaust flanges are flat and free from distortion.

4. Install nuts with cone side facing the washers, then torque all intake to exhaust manifold screws and manifold to cylinder head nuts to approximately 10 inch lbs.
5. Torque inboard intake to exhaust manifold screw to 20 ft. lbs., then the outboard intake to exhaust manifold screws to 20 ft. lbs.
6. Repeat step 5 until all three manifold screws are torqued to 20 ft. lbs.
7. Torque manifold to cylinder head nuts to 120 inch lbs. in sequence shown in **Fig. 1**.
8. Attach exhaust pipe to manifold flange, using a new gasket, then torque stud nuts to 35 ft. lbs.
9. Install carburetor air heater, then the air injection tube, if equipped. Torque tube to 200 inch lbs.
10. Install carburetor and connect fuel line, automatic choke rod and throttle linkage.
11. Install distributor vacuum control line and carburetor bowl vent line.
12. Install air cleaner, then connect breather cap to air cleaner line.
13. Install air cleaner vacuum line to carburetor, then the flexible connector between air cleaner and carburetor air heater.

V8-318, 360
1. Disconnect battery ground cable, then drain cooling system.
2. Remove alternator, carburetor air cleaner and fuel line, then disconnect accelerator linkage.
3. Remove vacuum control hose between carburetor and distributor.
4. Remove distributor cap with wires attached, then disconnect coil wires, heat indicator sending unit wire, heater hoses and bypass hose.
5. Remove closed ventilation system, evaporation control system and cylinder head covers.
6. Remove intake manifold attaching bolts, then the intake manifold.
7. Reverse procedure to install, noting the following:
   a. On V8-318 engines, coat intake manifold side gaskets with suitable sealer.
   b. On V8-360 engines, do not use any sealer on side composition gaskets.

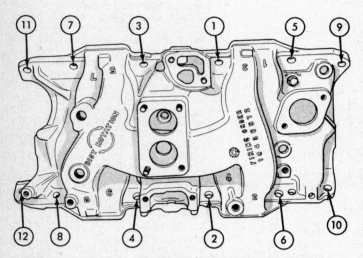

Fig. 2   Intake manifold tightening sequence. V8-318 & 360

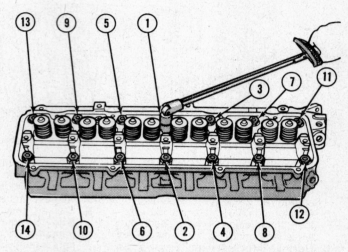

Fig. 3   Cylinder head tightening sequence. 6-225

c. Apply a thin coating of suitable sealer to the intake manifold front and rear gaskets and cylinder block gasket surface.

d. When installing front and rear gaskets, ensure center holes in gasket engage dowels in block and end holes in seals are locked into tangs of head gasket.

e. Place a drop of suitable sealer onto each of the four manifold to cylinder head gasket corners.

f. Tighten intake manifold bolts in sequence shown in **Fig. 2**.

V8-440

1. Disconnect battery ground cable, then drain cooling system.
2. Remove air cleaner, then disconnect diverter valve vacuum line from intake manifold, air pump from exhaust manifolds and diverter valve on the high mount air pump, if equipped.
3. Remove alternator, carburetor fuel line and accelerator linkage.
4. Remove closed ventilation system and evaporation control system.
5. Remove vacuum control tube at carburetor and distributor.
6. Remove distributor cap with wires attached, then disconnect coil wires and heater hose.
7. Disconnect heat indicator sending wire.

8. Remove intake manifold attaching bolts, then the intake manifold.
9. Reverse procedure to install.

EXHAUST MANIFOLD REPLACE

6-225

Refer to "Intake Manifold, Replace" procedure.

V8-318, 360

1. Remove bolts and nuts attaching exhaust pipe to manifold.
2. Remove bolts, nuts and washers attaching manifold to cylinder head.
3. Remove manifold from cylinder head.
4. Reverse procedure to install, noting the following:
   a. If exhaust manifold studs came out with nuts, install new studs, applying suitable sealer on coarse thread ends.

NOTE: If sealer is not applied to stud threads, water leaks may develop at the studs.

   b. Install two bolts and conical washers at inner ends of outboard arms

of manifold, then two bolts without washers on center arm of manifold.

V8-440

1. Disconnect battery ground cable.
2. Remove spark plugs and alternator.
3. Remove air injection tubes and gaskets, if equipped.
4. Disconnect exhaust pipe from exhaust manifolds.
5. Remove exhaust manifold to cylinder head attaching nuts, then slide manifolds off studs and away from cylinder heads.

NOTE: It may be necessary to bend oil lever indicator to facilitate manifold removal.

6. Reverse procedure to install, noting the following:
   a. If exhaust manifold studs came out with nuts, install new studs, applying suitable sealer on coarse thread ends.

NOTE: If sealer is not applied to stud threads, water leaks may develop at the studs.

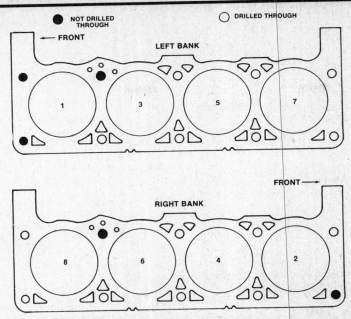

Fig. 4   Cylinder head bolt hole identification. Some 1979 & all 1980–85 Chrysler Corp. V8-318 engines

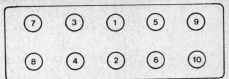

Fig. 5   Cylinder head tightening sequence. V8-318 & 360

7. Remove closed ventilation system, evaporation control system and cylinder head covers.
8. Remove intake manifold, ignition coil and carburetor as an assembly.
9. Remove exhaust manifolds.
10. Remove rocker shaft assembly and push rods.

NOTE: During disassembly note location of push rods so they can be installed in the same position.

11. Remove cylinder head attaching bolts, then the cylinder heads.
12. Reverse procedure to install noting the following:
    a. Tighten head bolts in sequence shown in **Fig. 5**.
    b. Tighten intake manifold bolts in sequence shown in **Fig. 2**.

V8-440

1. Disconnect battery ground cable and drain cooling system, then remove air cleaner.
2. On models equipped with high mount air pump, disconnect diverter valve vacuum line from intake manifold and air pump line from exhaust manifold.
3. On all models, remove alternator, carburetor fuel line and accelerator linkage.
4. Remove closed ventilation system and evaporation control system, if equipped.
5. Remove vacuum control tube at carburetor and distributor, then disconnect distributor cap, coil wires and heater hose.
6. Disconnect heat indicator sending unit electrical connector.
7. Remove spark plugs.
8. Remove intake manifold, ignition coil and carburetor as an assembly.
9. Remove tappet chamber cover, then the cylinder head cover and gasket.
10. Remove exhaust manifold attaching nuts, then the exhaust manifold.
11. Remove rocker shaft assembly and push rods.

NOTE: During disassembly note location of push rods so they can be installed in the same position.

12. Remove cylinder head attaching bolts, then the cylinder head.

NOTE: On some models equipped with A/C, it may be necessary to raise rear of

CYLINDER HEAD
REPLACE

6-225

1. Disconnect battery ground cable and drain cooling system.
2. Remove carburetor air cleaner and fuel line.
3. Disconnect accelerator linkage, then remove vacuum control tube at carburetor and distributor.
4. Disconnect spark plug wires from the spark plugs.
5. Disconnect heater hose, then the clamp attaching bypass hose.
6. Disconnect heat indicator sending unit electrical connector.
7. Disconnect exhaust pipe at exhaust manifold flange.
8. Disconnect diverter valve vacuum line from intake manifold, then remove air tube assembly from cylinder head, if equipped.
9. Remove closed ventilation system, evaporation control system and cylinder head cover.
10. Remove rocker shaft assembly and push rods.

NOTE: During disassembly note location of push rods so they can be installed in the same position.

11. Remove 14 cylinder head attaching bolts, then the cylinder head, intake and exhaust manifold as an assembly.
12. Reverse procedure to install noting the following:
    a. Tighten head bolts in sequence shown in **Fig. 3**.
    b. Loosen bolts and nuts holding

intake manifold to exhaust manifold. This is required to obtain proper alignment.
    c. Install intake and exhaust manifold and carburetor assembly to cylinder head with cup side of conical washers against manifold.

V8-318, 360

SERVICE BULLETIN Some 1979 and all 1980–85 V8-318 engines have cylinder head bolt holes drilled through the block into the water jacket in certain locations, **Fig. 4**. On 1979 models, this type cylinder block is identified by engine numbers beginning with 9M3180702 or 4104230-318. If engine number cannot be determined, refer to **Fig. 4** and insert a screwdriver into the head bolt holes. If the screwdriver can be inserted at least two inches into a hole, that hole is open to the water jacket. Cylinder head bolts in these locations must have sealer 4057989 or equivalent applied to the threads to prevent engine coolant leakage. Be sure old sealer is cleaned from the threads before applying new sealer.

1. Disconnect battery ground cable and drain cooling system.
2. Remove alternator, then the carburetor air cleaner and fuel line.
3. Disconnect accelerator linkage.
4. Remove vacuum control hoses between carburetor and distributor.
5. Remove distributor cap with spark plug wires attached, then disconnect coil wires and heat indicator sending unit electrical connector.
6. Remove heater hoses and by-pass hose.

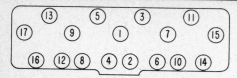

Fig. 6 Cylinder head tightening sequence. V8-440

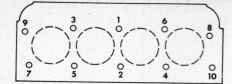

Fig. 7 Cylinder head tightening sequence. V8-446

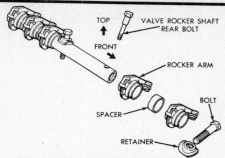

Fig. 8 Rocker arms and shaft. 6-225

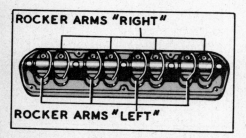

Fig. 9 Rocker arm and shaft assembly installed. V8-318 & 360

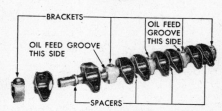

Fig. 10 Rocker arms and shaft. V8-400 & 440 (Typical)

compressor and place block of wood between bracket and engine block. This will allow enough clearance for cylinder head to clear dowel pins.

13. Reverse procedure to install noting the following:
   a. Tighten head bolts in sequence shown in **Fig. 6**.

V8-446

Cylinder heads should be tightened down by starting from the center, working outward from side to side and to the ends in the sequence shown in **Fig. 7**.

ROCKER ARM SERVICE

NOTE: When disassembling rocker arms, place all parts on the work bench in their proper sequence to insure correct assembly.

Clean all sludge and gum formation from the inside and outside of the shafts. Clean oil holes and passages in the rocker arms and shafts. Inspect the shafts for wear.

6-225

Stamped steel rocker arms are arranged on a single rocker arm shaft, **Fig. 8**. Hardened steel spacers are used between the pairs of rocker arms. The rocker shaft is held in place by bolts and stamped steel retainers attached to the seven brackets on the cylinder head.

Install rocker assembly to cylinder head in the following order:

1. Rocker arms and shaft assembly should be installed so the oil hole is positioned as shown in **Fig. 8**.
2. Install rocker shaft retainers between rocker arms. Ensure long retainer is

installed in center position only.
3. Install rocker shaft bolts, then the special bolt at rear of engine. Torque to specifications.
4. Inspect cylinder head cover gasket flange for scratches or distortion, straighten if necessary.
5. Install new cylinder head cover gasket, then the cylinder head cover.
6. Install closed ventilation system and evaporation control system.

V8-318 & 360

To provide proper lubrication of the rocker arms, the rocker shafts have a small notch machined at one end. Install rocker arm and shaft assemblies with notch on end of rocker shaft pointing to centerline of engine and toward front of engine on the left bank and to the rear on the right bank. If rocker arms are removed from shaft, care must be taken to ensure proper reassembly. Some exhaust rocker arms have a relieved area on the underside for rotator clearance. Refer to **Fig. 9** for proper positioning of rocker arms. Note placement of long stamped steel retainers in the number two and four positions between the rocker arms.

V8-440

The rocker arms are of stamped steel and are arranged on one rocker arm shaft, per cylinder head. The push rod angularity tends to force the pairs of rocker arms toward each other where oilite spacers carry the side thrust at the rocker arms, **Fig. 10**.

1. Install rocker shafts so that the ³⁄₁₆″ diameter rocker arm lubrication holes point downward into rocker arm, and so that the 15 degree angle of these holes point outward toward valve end of rocker arm, **Fig. 11**. The 15 degree angle is determined from the center line of the bolt holes through the shaft which are used to attach the shaft assembly to the cylinder head.
2. On all engines, install rocker arms and shaft assembly, making sure to install long stamped steel retainers in No. 2 and 4 positions.

NOTE: Use extreme care in tightening the bolts so that valve lifters have time to bleed down to their operating length. Bulged lifter bodies, bent push rods and permanent noisy operation may result if lifters are forced down too rapidly.

V8-446

The rocker arms on these engines are individually mounted and are retained by flange head bolts and pivot balls. Install the rocker arm components in original position, **Fig. 12**.

Inspect the pivot surfaces of the rocker arms and pivot balls for signs of scuffing, pitting or excessive wear. Inspect the valve stem contact surface of the rocker arms for pitting. Replace any component found unsatisfactory.

VALVE TIMING
INTAKE OPENS BEFORE TDC

Engine	Year	Degrees
6-225	1979–80	16
6-225	1981–85	6
V8-318	1979–85	10
V8-360	1979–85	18
V8-440	1979	18
V8-446	1980	14

VALVES
ADJUST

6-225 1979–80

If the cylinder head has been removed it is a good practice to make an initial valve adjustment before starting the engine. Make two chalk marks spaced 120 degrees apart (⅓ of circumference) on the vibration damper so that with the timing mark, the damper is divided into thirds. With the crankshaft at TDC, temporarily set the intake valve lash for No. 1 cylinder at .012 inch and the exhaust at .028 inch. Repeat the procedure for the remaining

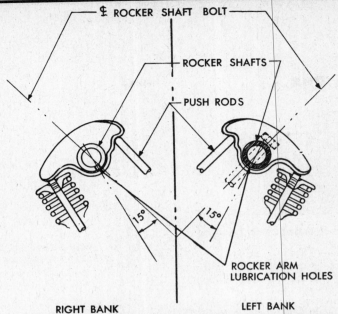

Fig. 11   Rocker arm shaft installation. V8-440

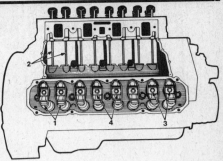

1. Rocker arms   3. Bolts
2. Push rods   4. Pivots

Fig. 12   Rocker arm and shaft assembly. V8-446

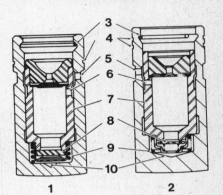

1. Type A   6. Plunger oil hole
2. Type B   7. Plunger
3. Snap ring   8. Check valve
4. Identification rules 9. Spring
5. Tappet oil hole 10. Oil Chamber

Fig. 14   Hydraulic valve lifter. V8-446

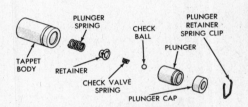

Fig. 13   Hydraulic valve lifter. 1979—85 exc. V8-446

valves, turning the crankshaft ⅓ turn in the direction of normal rotation while adjusting the valves in the firing order sequence of 1-5-3-6-2-4. For final adjustment, start and run engine at 550 RPM idle until normal operating temperature is reached. Then adjust valve lash to clearance listed in "Valve Specifications".

1981—85 6-225 & ALL 1979—85 V8 ENGINES

These engines are equipped with hydraulic lifters. No provisions for adjustment is provided.

VALVE GUIDES
V8-318, 360, 440 & 6-225

These engines do not have removable valve guides. The valves operate in guide holes bored in the cylinder head. Valves with oversize valve stems are available for service replacement when necessary to ream the guide holes.

Standard production stem diameter should be .372—.373 inch for intake valves and .371—.372 inch for exhaust valves. If stem wear exceeds .002 inch, replace valve. When reaming guides for oversize valve stems do not attempt to ream from

standard to .030" oversize. If necessary to ream to that size, use the step procedure of .005", .015" and .030". This must be done in order to maintain a true relationship of the guide to the valve seat. The following chart indicates reamer size and valve stem size.

Reamer Oversize	Valve Stem Size
.005"	.379—.380"
.015"	.389—.390"
.030"	.404—.405"

V8-446

Clean valve guides with a suitable cleaning tool. Then check each valve guide with a "GO" and "NO-GO" gauge, if available; otherwise, use a new valve to check the fit. If the "NO-GO" portion of the gauge enters, the guide must be replaced.

Replacement is recommended for valve guides with diameters exceeding specifications, bell-mouthed more than .0005 inch or guides which are out-of-round.

New guides should be installed so that the distance from the cylinder head to the top of the guide is ²⁷⁄₃₂ inches for intake and 1⅛ inch for exhaust.

When guides are properly installed, they should be reamed to .374—.375 inch.

HYDRAULIC VALVE LIFTERS

Figs. 13 and 14 illustrate the type of hydraulic valve lifters used. Before disassembling any part of the engine to check for noise, check the oil pressure at the gauge and the oil level in the oil pan. The oil level in the pan should never be above the "full" mark on the dipstick, nor below the "add oil" mark. Either of the two conditions could be responsible for noisy lifters.

LIFTER, REPLACE

Worn valve guides or cocked springs are sometimes mistaken for noisy lifters. Determine which lifter is noisy. If the application of side thrust on the valve spring fails to noticeably reduce the noise, the lifter is probably faulty and should be removed for inspection. Removal of stuck lifters requires a special tool, **Fig. 15.** When installing hydraulic lifters in the engine, fill them with light engine oil to avoid excessive time required to quiet them during initial operation of engine.

TIMING CHAIN COVER
6-225

1. To remove cover, drain cooling system and remove radiator and fan.
2. Remove vibration damper with a puller.
3. Loosen oil pan bolts to allow clearance and remove chain case cover.
4. Reverse above procedure to install cover.

Fig. 15   Removing stuck hydraulic lifter with special tool. Typical

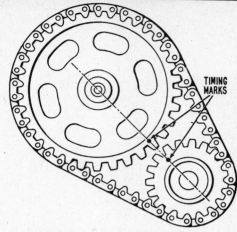

Fig. 16   Valve timing. All six cylinder engines

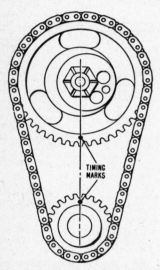

Fig. 17   Valve Timing. V8 Engines exc. V8-446

V8 ENGINES

To remove cover, first drain cooling system, remove radiator, fan belt, power steering pump and water pump assembly. Then, remove pulley from vibration damper and after removing bolt and washer. use puller to remove damper. Next, remove fuel lines and fuel pump. Loosen oil pan bolts and after removing front bolt at each side, timing cover may be removed. Reverse procedure to install cover, using new oil seal.

TIMING GEARS OR CHAIN
REPLACE

6-225

1. After removing timing chain cover as outlined above, remove camshaft sprocket lock bolt, then remove timing chain and sprocket.
2. Clean all parts and inspect chain for broken or damaged links. Inspect sprockets for cracks and chipped, worn or damaged teeth.
3. Turn crankshaft so sprocket timing mark is toward and directly in line with centerline of camshaft.
4. Temporarily install camshaft sprocket. Rotate camshaft to position sprocket timing mark toward and directly in line with centerline of crankshaft: then remove camshaft sprocket.
5. Place chain on crankshaft sprocket and position camshaft sprocket in chain so sprocket can be installed with timing marks aligned and without moving camshaft, **Fig. 16.**
6. Install remaining components in reverse order of removal.

V8 ENGINES EXC. V8-446

To install chain and sprockets, lay both camshaft and crankshaft sprockets on bench. Position sprockets so that the timing marks are next to each other. Place chain on both sprockets, then push sprockets apart as far as the chain will permit. Use a straightedge to form a line through the exact centers of both gears. The timing marks must be on this line.

Slide the chain with both sprockets on the camshaft and crankshaft at the same time, then recheck the alignment, **Fig. 17.**

NOTE: Use Tool C-3509 to prevent camshaft from contacting welch plug in rear of engine block. Remove distributor and oil pump-distributor drive gear. Position tool against rear side of camshaft gear and attach with distributor retainer plate bolt.

V8-446

When valves are correctly timed, the timing marks on the gears or sprockets should be adjacent to each other, **Fig. 18.**

CAMSHAFT
REPLACE

NOTE: When removing camshaft or bear-

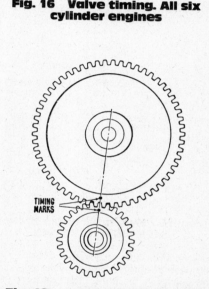

Fig. 18   Valve Timing. V8-446

ings, it is recommended that the engine be removed from chassis.

6-225

1. Remove lifters and push rod using tool No. C-4129. Identify lifters to ensure correct position during installation.
2. Remove timing sprockets, distributor and oil pump.
3. Remove fuel pump.
4. Install long bolt into front of camshaft to facilitate removal, then remove camshaft from engine, **Fig. 19.**
5. Reverse procedure to install.

NOTE: Whenever new camshaft or lifters have been installed, add one pint of suitable crankcase conditioner to engine oil to aid lubrication during break-in. Lifters should be inspected for crown using suitable straight edge. If negative crown (dishing) is observed, lifter should be replaced.

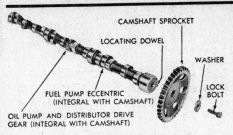

Fig. 19 Camshaft assembly. 6-225

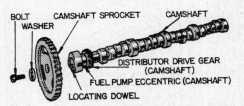

Fig. 22 Camshaft assembly. V8-440

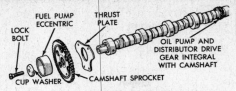

Fig. 20 Camshaft assembly. V8-318 & 360

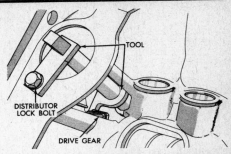

Fig. 21 Install camshaft holding tool

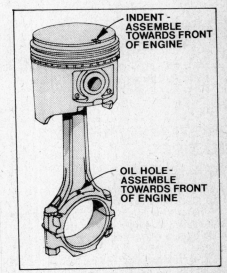

Fig. 23 Piston & rod assembly. 1979—85 6-225

V8-318 & 360

Removal

1. Remove intake manifold, cylinder head covers, timing chain cover and timing chain.
2. Remove rocker arm and shaft assemblies.
3. Remove push rods and lifters using suitable tool. Identify lifters to ensure correct position during installation.
4. Remove distributor, then lift out oil pump and distributor drive shaft.
5. Remove camshaft thrust plate noting location of oil tab.
6. Install long bolt into front of camshaft to facilitate removal, then remove camshaft from engine, **Fig. 20.**

Installation

1. Lubricate camshaft lobes and bearing journals, then install camshaft within two inches of final position in cylinder block.
2. Install tool No. C-3509 as shown in **Fig. 21.**
3. Hold tool in position with distributor lock plate screw.

NOTE: Tool should remain installed until camshaft, crankshaft sprockets and timing chain have been installed.

4. Install camshaft thrust plate and chain oil tab attaching screws, ensuring tang enters lower right hole in thrust plate, then torque attaching screws to 210 inch lbs.

NOTE: Top edge of tab should be flat against thrust plate in order to catch oil for chain lubrication.

5. Install timing chain, refer to "Timing Gears Or Chain" procedure.
6. Install fuel pump eccentric, cup washer and camshaft bolt. Torque bolt to 35 ft. lbs.
7. Reverse remaining procedure to assemble.

V8-440

Removal

1. Remove lifters, timing chain and sprockets.
2. Remove distributor, then lift out oil pump and distributor drive shaft.
3. Remove fuel pump, allowing fuel pump push rod to drop away from cam eccentric.
4. Remove camshaft from engine, **Fig. 22.**

Installation

1. Lubricate camshaft lobes and bearing journals, then install camshaft within two inches of final position in cylinder block.
2. Install suitable tool in place of distributor drive gear and shaft.
3. Hold tool in position with distributor lock plate screw.

NOTE: Tool should remain installed until camshaft, crankshaft sprockets and timing chain have been installed.

4. Reverse remaining procedure to install. To align timing marks refer to "Timing Gears Or Chain" procedure.

V8-446

1. Remove oil pump and distributor.
2. Remove valve lifters, water pump, crankshaft pulley and damper, then the timing case cover.
3. Remove camshaft thrust flange attaching bolts, then the camshaft.

NOTE: Use caution when handling camshaft assembly to prevent chipping distributor gear teeth.

4. Reverse procedure to install. To align timing marks refer to "Timing Gears Or Chain, Replace" procedure.

PISTON & ROD
ASSEMBLE

6-225

Piston and rod assemblies should be installed as shown in **Fig. 23.**

ALL V8 ENGINES EXC. V8-446

When installing piston and rod assemblies in the cylinders, the compression ring gaps should be diametrically opposite one another and not in line with the oil ring gap. The oil ring expander gap should be toward the outside of the "V" of the engine. The oil ring gap should be turned toward the inside of the engine "V".

Immerse the piston head and rings in clean engine oil and, with a suitable piston ring compressor, insert the piston and rod assembly into the bore. Tap the piston down into the bore, using the handle of a hammer.

Assemble and install the pistons and rods as shown in **Fig. 24.**

V8-446

Before disassembling, mark piston on same side as large chamfer on connecting rod, so they can be assembled in the same position. New pistons may be installed either way on connecting rod, **Fig. 25.**

When installing piston in engine the large chamfered side of each connecting rod must be located against the crankshaft face. The chamfer provides clearance at the crankshaft fillet.

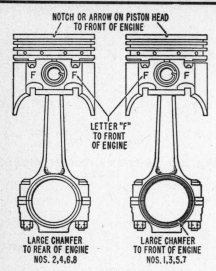

Fig. 24 Correct assembly of pistons and rods. V8 engines exc. V8-446

PISTONS, PINS & RINGS

EXC. V8-446

Pistons are available in standard sizes and .020 inch oversize.

Pins are available in the following oversizes: V8-318 & 360, .003, .008 inch. Oversize pins are not available on other engines.

Rings are available in the following oversizes: std. to .009, .020—.029, .040—.049 inch.

V8-446

Pistons are available in standard sizes and the following oversizes: .010, .020, .030 inch.

Oversize pins are not available.

Rings are available in the following oversizes: .010, .020, .030 inch.

MAIN & ROD BEARINGS

EXC. V8-446

Main bearings are furnished in standard sizes and the following undersizes: .001, .002, .003, .010, .012".

Rod bearings are furnished in standard sizes and the following undersizes: .001, .002, .003, .010, .012".

V8-446

Main and rod bearings are furnished in standard sizes and the following undersizes: .010, .020, .030 inch.

CRANKSHAFT OIL SEAL
REPLACE

6-225

Replacement seals are of two piece rubber type composition which make possible the replacement of upper rear seal without removing crankshaft. Both halves must be used. After removing oil pan, rear main bearing cap and seal retainer, pry lower seal from retainer with small screwdriver. On models with rope type seal, screw a special tool into upper seal and carefully pull to remove seal while rotating crankshaft. On models with rubber type seal, remove upper seal by pressing with a suitable screwdriver on end of seal, being careful not to damage crankshaft. Wipe crankshaft surface clean, then oil lightly before installing new upper seal. After oiling seal lip, hold seal with paint stripe to rear tightly against crankshaft with thumb. Carefully slide seal into groove in block making sure sharp edge does not shave or nick seal. Crankshaft may be rotated to ease seal into groove but sealing lip must not be damaged. Install other half of seal into lower seal retainer again with paint stripe to rear, then install rear main bearing

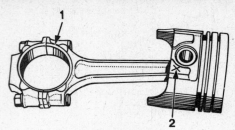

1 LARGE CHAMFER
2 PLACE MARK HERE

Fig. 25 Piston & rod assembly. V8-446

cap and torque to specifications. Before installing seal retainer, apply a small amount of gasket sealer to mating surface of retainer but not on seal ends or seal lip, Fig. 26. Install retainer and torque to 30 ft. lbs.

V8-318 & 360

Replacement of rear main bearing oil seals is similar to procedure given above for 6 cylinder engines. A seal retainer is not found on these engines; lower half of seal is installed into groove in rear main bearing cap.

The 318 engine has capseals in addition to lower seal secured by rear main bearing cap. Cap seal with yellow paint is installed, narrow sealing edge up, into right side with bearing cap in engine position. Cap seals must be flush with shoulder of bearing cap to prevent oil leakage.

The 360 engine requires sealer to be applied adjacent to rear main bearing oil seal as cap seals are not used, Fig. 27. After applying sealer, quickly assemble rear main bearing cap to block and torque to specifications.

V8-440

Replacement seals are of two piece rubber type composition which make possible the replacement of upper rear seal without removing crankshaft. Both halves must be used. After removing oil pan, seal retainer and rear main bearing cap, pry lower rope seal and side seals from lower seal retain-

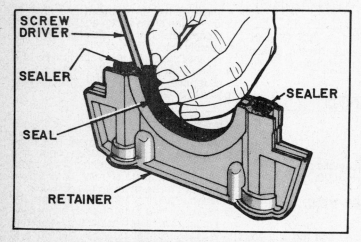

Fig. 26 Lower oil seal and retainer. 6-225

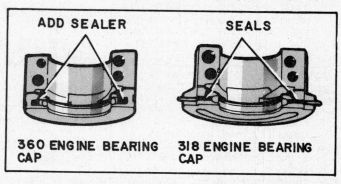

ADD SEALER — 360 ENGINE BEARING CAP

SEALS — 318 ENGINE BEARING CAP

Fig. 27 Rear main bearing caps. V8-318 & 360

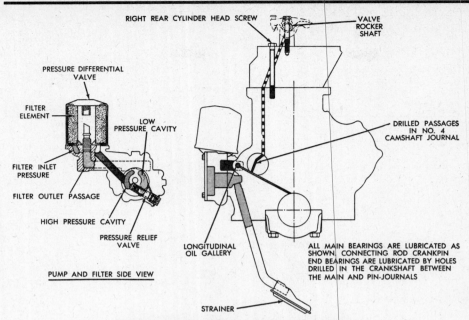

Engine lubrication. 6-225 (Typical)

V8-466

Crankshaft rear bearing oil seal consists of two pieces of special packing. One piece is installed in the groove in the rear bearing cap and the other piece is installed in a similar groove in the cylinder block.

Position the rear bearing seal in the groove in the cylinder block. Lay an improvised mandrel in the bearing bore and strike the mandrel with a hammer to drive the seal into the groove. Install the seal in the bearing cap in a similar manner. Using a sharp knife, cut off both ends of each seal which project out of the grooves. When cutting off the ends of the seals, do not leave frayed ends which would prevent proper seating of the bearing cap if the ends should extend between cap and cylinder block.

er with small screwdriver. Thoroughly clean seal retainer grooves. Screw a special tool into upper rope seal and carefully pull to remove seal while rotating crankshaft. Wipe crankshaft surface clean, then oil lightly before installing new upper seal. After oiling seal lip, hold seal with paint stripe to rear tightly against crankshaft with thumb. Carefully slide seal into groove in block making sure sharp edge does not shave or nick seal. Crankshaft may be rotated to ease seal into groove but sealing lip must not be damaged. Install other half of seal with paint stripe to rear into seal retainer. Install rear main bearing cap and torque to specifications. The side seals used with the rear seal retainer should be installed in the retainer and then into the engine as quickly as possible. These seals are made from a material that expands rapidly when oiled. Apply sealer to mating face of seal retainer but not to side seals or main bearing seal ends, then oil side seals with mineral spirits or diesel fuel. Install seals in sealer retainer grooves then quickly install retainer and torque to 30 ft. lbs. Failure to pre-oil seals will result in an oil leak.

OIL PAN
REPLACE

V8-318, 360, 440 & 446

1. Drain engine oil and remove oil dipstick.
2. On 318 and 360 engines, disconnect cross-over pipe from both manifolds. On Sport Utility vehicles, remove the left engine to transmission support only.
3. On all engines, remove the oil pan attaching screws and oil pan.
4. Reverse the procedure to install. Clean the oil pan in solvent and inspect the oil strainer alignment. On engines exc. V8-446, use a new pan gasket set and add a drop of sealant 4026070 or equivalent at corners of rubber and cork. On V8-446 engines, a liquid gasket material is used. Apply 1/8 inch bead of sealer at corners and both ends and 1/16 inch bead of sealer on both sides.

1979–85 6-225

1. Disconnect battery ground cable, then remove engine oil dipstick, dipstick tube, engine cover, and air cleaner.
2. Raise and support front of vehicle, then drain crankcase and remove engine to transmission strut, if equipped.
3. On models equipped with automatic transmission, remove torque converter inspection cover.
4. Remove frame reinforcement if so equipped.
5. Remove oil pan attaching screws and position the crankshaft to permit clearance for oil pan removal. Remove oil pan.
6. Reverse procedure to install. On California models, left side gasket is of high temperature type. On all models, apply 1/8 inch drop of suitable sealer to all four corners of rubber seal and cork gasket.

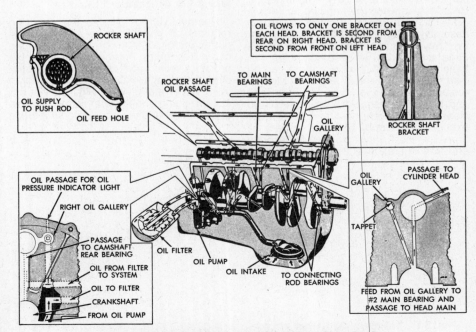

Engine lubrication. V8-318 & 360 (Typical)

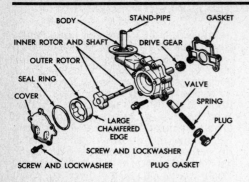

Fig. 28 Oil pump exploded view. 6-225

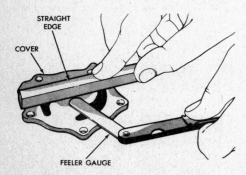

Fig. 29 Checking oil pump cover flatness. Typical

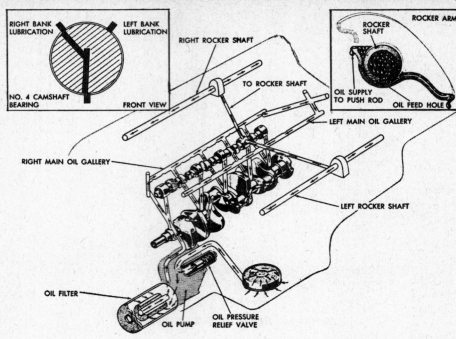

Engine lubrication. V8-440 (Typical)

OIL PUMP REPAIRS

6-225

Remove pump from side of engine by first unbolting oil pump cover, **Fig. 28.** Outer rotor will drop out when cover is removed. Do not allow rotor to be damaged by dropping it. Oil pump can now be unbolted and disassembled for inspection. Press off drive gear, supporting gear to keep load off aluminum body. Inner rotor and shaft can now be removed. Remove oil pressure relief valve plug and lift out spring and plunger. Clean all parts thoroughly. If mating surface of oil pump cover is scratched or grooved, replace pump assembly. Lay a straightedge across pump cover surface, **Fig. 29.** If a .0015 inch feel-er gauge can be inserted between cover and straightedge, replace pump assembly. If outer rotor thickness measures .649 inch on 1979–80 or .825 inch or less on 1981–85 engines, and the diameter is 2.469 inches or less, replace shaft and both rotors, **Fig. 30.** Shaft and both rotors should also be replaced if inner rotor thickness measures .649 inch or less on 1979–80, or .825 or less on 1981–85 engines, **Fig. 31.** With outer rotor inserted into pump body, press rotor to one side with fingers. If clearance between rotor and pump body is .014 inch or more, replace oil pump assembly, **Fig. 32.** With inner rotor inserted into pump body, place a straightedge across face between bolt holes. If a feeler gauge of .004 inch or more can be inserted between rotors and straightedge, replace oil pump assembly, **Fig. 33.** Shaft and both rotors should be replaced if tip clearance between inner and outer rotor exceeds .010 inch, **Fig. 34.** Inspect oil pressure relief valve plunger for scoring and free operation in its bore. The relief valve spring has a free length of 2¼ inches and should test between 22.3 and 23.3 lbs. when compressed to 1¹⁹/₃₂ inch. Replace spring that fails to meet specifications.

Using new parts as required, assemble pump except for outer rotor and cover. Install oil pump on engine then coat inside of pump with oil to assure priming. Install outer rotor and cover using new seal ring.

V8-318 & 360

Removal of oil pump for servicing requires oil pan to be removed and oil pump unbolted from rear main bearing cap. With pump removed, disassemble pressure relief valve by pulling out cotter pins and drilling a ⅛ inch hole into center of relief valve retainer cap, **Fig. 35.** Insert a self-threading sheet metal screw into cap and secure head in vise. While supporting

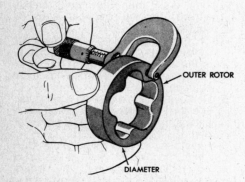

Fig. 30 Measuring outer rotor thickness

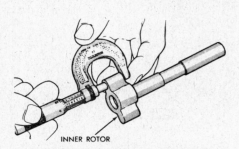

Fig. 31 Measuring inner rotor thickness

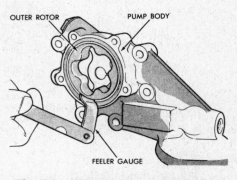

Fig. 32 Measuring outer rotor clearance in pump body

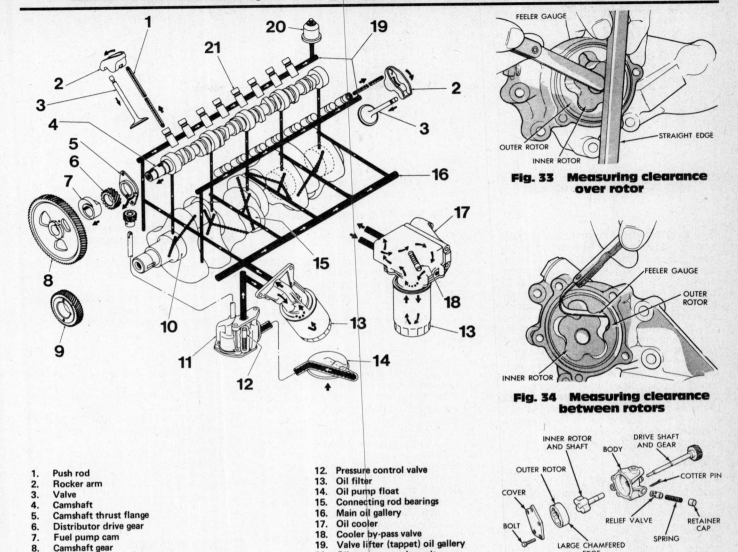

Fig. 33 Measuring clearance over rotor

FEELER GAUGE — OUTER ROTOR — INNER ROTOR — STRAIGHT EDGE

Fig. 34 Measuring clearance between rotors

FEELER GAUGE — OUTER ROTOR — INNER ROTOR

Fig. 35 Oil pump. V8-318 & 360

INNER ROTOR AND SHAFT — DRIVE SHAFT AND GEAR — BODY — COTTER PIN — OUTER ROTOR — COVER — BOLT — RELIEF VALVE — SPRING — RETAINER CAP — LARGE CHAMFERED EDGE

1. Push rod
2. Rocker arm
3. Valve
4. Camshaft
5. Camshaft thrust flange
6. Distributor drive gear
7. Fuel pump cam
8. Camshaft gear
9. Crankshaft gear
10. Main Bearing
11. Oil pump

12. Pressure control valve
13. Oil filter
14. Oil pump float
15. Connecting rod bearings
16. Main oil gallery
17. Oil cooler
18. Cooler by-pass valve
19. Valve lifter (tappet) oil gallery
20. Oil pressure sender unit
21. Hydraulic valve lifter (tappet)

Engine lubrication. V8-466

pump body, remove cap by tapping body with soft hammer. Discard retainer cap and remove spring and relief valve. Relief valve spring has a free length of 2¹/₃₂ to 2³/₆₄ inch and should test between 16.2 and 17.2 lbs. when compressed to 1¹¹/₃₂ inch. Replace spring that fails to meet specifications. Unbolt oil pump cover and discard oil seal ring. Inner rotor and shaft can now be removed as well as outer rotor. Clean all parts thoroughly and inspect for damage or wear. If mating surface of oil pump cover is scratched or grooved, replace pump assembly. Lay a straightedge across pump cover surface. If a .0015 inch feeler gauge can be inserted between cover and straightedge, replace pump assembly, **Fig. 29.** If outer rotor thickness measures .825 inch or less on 318 engine, or less than .943 inch on 360 engine, or the diameter is 2.469 inches or less, replace the outer rotor, **Fig. 30.** If inner rotor measures .825

inch or less on 318 engine or less than .943 on 360 engine, replace inner rotor and shaft assembly, **Fig. 31.** With outer rotor inserted into pump body, press rotor to one side with fingers. If clearance between rotor and pump body is .014 inch or more, replace oil pump assembly, **Fig. 32.** With inner rotor inserted into pump body, place a straightedge across face between bolt holes. If a feeler gauge of .004 inch can be inserted between rotors and straightedge, replace oil pump assembly, **Fig. 33.** Shaft and both rotors should be replaced if tip clearance between inner and outer rotor exceeds .010 inch, **Fig. 34.** Using new parts as required, assemble pump. Prime pump before installation by filling rotor cavity with engine oil.

V8-440

After removing oil filter element unbolt oil pump and filter base assembly. Remove

filter base and discard oil seal ring, **Fig. 36.** Inner rotor and shaft can now be removed as well as outer rotor. Remove pressure relief valve plug and lift out the spring and relief valve plunger. Clean all parts thoroughly and inspect for damage or wear. If mating surface of filter base (oil pump cover) is scratched or grooved, replace filter base. Lay a straightedge across oil pump filter base surface, **Fig. 29.** If a .0015 inch feeler gauge can be inserted between base and straightedge, filter base should be replaced. If outer rotor thickness measures .943 inch or less and diameter measures 2.469 inches or less, replace shaft and both rotors, **Fig. 30.** If inner rotor thickness measures .943 inch or less, replace shaft and both rotors, **Fig. 31.** With outer rotor inserted into pump body, press rotor to one side with fingers. If clearance between rotor and pump body is .014 inch or more, replace pump body, **Fig. 32.** With

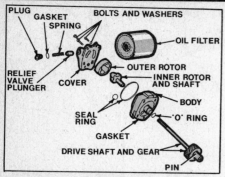

Fig. 36 Oil pump. V8-440

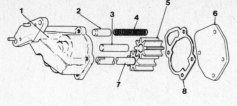

1. Body
2. Valve
3. Idler shaft
4. Spring
5. Idler gear
6. Cover
7. Drive shaft and gear
8. Gasket

Fig. 37 Oil pump. V8-446

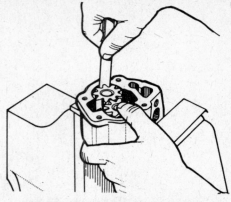

Fig. 38 Measuring oil pump gear to body clearance. V8-446

inner rotor inserted into pump body, place a straightedge across face between bolt holes. If a feeler gauge of .004 inch or more can be inserted between rotors and straightedge, replace pump body, **Fig. 33.** If the top clearance between inner and outer rotor is .010 inch or more, replace shaft and both rotors, **Fig. 34.** Inspect oil pressure relief valve plunger for scoring and free operation in its bore. The relief valve spring has a free length of 2¼ inches and should test between 22.3 and 23.3 lbs. when compressed to 1¹⁹⁄₃₂ inch. Replace spring that fails to meet specifications.

Using new parts as required, assemble pump and fill rotor cavity with engine oil to prime. Before bolting oil pump to engine, install new O-ring seal on pilot.

V8-446

The oil pump, **Fig. 37,** consists of two gears and a pressure relief valve enclosed in the body. The pump is driven from the distributor drive gear. The body is equipped with a regulator valve that limits oil pressure to approximately 50 psi.

After removing the oil pan, the pump may be removed from its mounting and disassembled for repairs. With the pump cover removed, exert pressure against gear with the thumb so as to push gear from outlet side of pump. Measure clearance between outside diameter of gear and bore of housing, **Fig. 38.** If clearance is not between .0014–.0054 inch, replace worn parts. Check pump shaft clearance in bore. If clearance is not between .001–.0025 inch, replace pump. Check backlash between pump body and gears. If clearance is more than .0107 inch, replace gear. Check body gear end clearance. Clearance should be .0015–.0065 inch. If end play is not within specifications, add or remove oil pump cover gaskets to obtain specified clearance.

WATER PUMP
REPLACE

CAUTION: When it becomes necessary to remove a fan clutch of the silicone type,

the assembly must be supported in the vertical position to prevent leaks of silicone fluid from the clutch mechanism. This loss of fluid will render the fan clutch inoperative.

6-225

1. Drain cooling system, then remove battery from vehicle.
2. Loosen alternator, air pump, power steering pump or idler pulley, if equipped, then remove all drive belts.
3. Remove fan, spacer or fluid unit, pulley and bolts as an assembly.
4. Remove fan shroud if equipped.
5. Remove A/C compressor and air pump bracket to water pump attaching bolts, if equipped, then position compressor and air pump aside. Keep compressor in upright position.
6. Disconnect heater hoses.
7. Remove water pump attaching bolts, then the water pump.
8. Reverse procedure to install.

V8-318 & 360

1. Drain cooling system, then remove battery from vehicle.
2. Remove radiator, if equipped with A/C.
3. Loosen alternator adjusting strap bolt and pivot bolt.
4. Loosen power steering and air pumps, if equipped, then remove all drive belts.
5. On engines without A/C, remove alternator bracket attaching bolts from water pump, then swing alternator out of way.
6. On engines with A/C, remove alternator, adjusting bracket and power steering pump attaching bolts and position aside.
7. On all models, remove fan blade, spacer or fluid unit, pulley and bolts as an assembly.
8. Disconnect heater and bypass hoses, then remove A/C compressor pulley and field coil assembly, if equipped.

9. Remove water pump to compressor front mount bracket attaching bolts and bracket.
10. Remove water pump attaching bolts, then the water pump.
11. Reverse procedure to install.

V8-440

1. Drain cooling system, then remove battery from vehicle.
2. Loosen all drive belts, then remove heater hoses, if necessary.
3. Remove fan shroud attaching screws and set shroud back over water pump housing.
4. Remove fan, spacer or fluid unit, pulley and bolts as an assembly.
5. Remove water pump attaching bolts, then the water pump.
6. Reverse procedure to install.

FUEL PUMP
REPLACE

NOTE: Before installing the pump, it is good practice to crank the engine so that the nose of the camshaft eccentric is out of the way of the fuel pump rocker arm when the pump is installed. In this way there will be the least amount of tension on the rocker arm, thereby easing the installation of the pump.

1. Disconnect fuel lines from fuel pump.
2. Remove fuel pump attaching bolts and fuel pump.
3. Remove all gasket material from the pump and block gasket surfaces. Apply sealer to both sides of new gasket.
4. Position gasket on pump flange and hold pump in position against its mounting surface. Make sure rocker arm is riding on camshaft eccentric.
5. Press pump tight against its mounting. Install retaining screws and tighten them alternately.
6. Connect fuel lines. Then operate engine and check for leaks.

Diesel Engine Diagnosis Section

Service Diagnosis

Condition	Possible Cause	Correction
HARD STARTING **Starter will not turn, or turns but fails to start engine**	1. Weak battery 2. Defective starter motor switch contacts 3. Magnetic switch contact plate arced or defective 4. Magnetic switch pull-in coil open 5. Bad brush contact 6. Burned starter motor commutator 7. High commutator mica 8. Starter motor field coil grounded 9. Starter motor armature grounded 10. Insufficient brush spring tension 11. Improperly soldered field coil 12. Worn starter motor bearing bushing 13. Open wiring between starter switch and magnet switch terminal 14. Faulty contact between battery and ground strap 15. Engine oil too thick	1. Test battery specific gravity and recharge or replace as necessary 2. Replace switch 3. Polish or replace contact plate 4. Replace 5. Correct brush contact 6. Repair commutator 7. Undercut commutator 8. Replace coil 9. Replace armature 10. Replace brush spring 11. Repair 12. Replace bushing 13. Repair or replace 14. Clean and correct 15. Change to specified oil
Starter turns but pinion fails to mesh with ring gear	1. Worn starter motor clutch pinion tip 2. Starter clutch races 3. Starter clutch drive spring defective 4. Starter fails to rotate in overrun direction 5. Splines meshing improperly 6. Worn starter bushing 7. Drive lever setting bolt missing 8. Magnetic switch pinion moves out to improper position 9. Worn bearing bushing 10. Worn ring gear	1. Replace pinion tip 2. Replace clutch 3. Replace drive spring 4. Replace starter 5. Lap, clean, and correct splines 6. Replace bushing 7. Replace bolt 8. Adjust stud bolt 9. Replace bushing 10. Replace ring gear
Starter turns but fails to stop	1. Magnetic switch coil layer shorted 2. Magnetic switch contact plate arced 3. Starter switch fails to disengage	1. Replace switch 2. Replace switch 3. Replace switch
Engine	1. Burned valve 2. Intake manifold gasket loose 3. Worn piston, piston rings, and cylinder sleeve 4. Defective head gasket	1. Lap or replace valve 2. Tighten manifold bolts or replace gasket 3. Overhaul engine 4. Replace head gasket
Fuel	1. Damaged air horn gasket or loose set-screw	1. Replace gasket or tighten set-screw
Ignition	1. Faulty glow plug operation	1. Check glow plug connections and glow plug operation
INADEQUATE IDLING **Valves**	1. Improper valve clearance 2. Valve and valve seat not properly fitted 3. Excessive clearance—valve stem to valve guide	1. Adjust valve clearance 2. Lap valve 3. Replace valve and valve guide
Cylinder Head	1. Head gasket leaking	1. Replace head gasket
Injection System	1. Improper injection timing 2. Dirty or worn fuel injection pump or injector nozzles 3. Leaking fuel lines	1. Adjust timing 2. See "Diesel Fuel Injection System" 3. Tighten connections or replace line

Condition	Possible Cause	Correction
ABNORMAL COMBUSTION Fuel	1. Dirty or clogged fuel pipe 2. Air leak into intake manifold	1. Clean or replace fuel pipe 2. Tighten manifold bolts or replace gasket
Valves	1. Improper valve clearance 2. Valve sticking 3. Valve spring defective	1. Adjust valve clearance 2. Disassemble and repair or replace valve 3. Replace valve spring
Cylinder Head	1. Carbon deposits in combustion chamber 2. Clogged cylinder head water tube 3. Gas leaking through head gasket	1. Remove carbon 2. Clean or replace water tube 3. Replace head gasket
Injection System	1. Improper injection timing 2. Dirty or worn fuel injection pump or fuel injection nozzles	1. Adjust injection timing 2. See "Diesel Fuel Injection System"
Cooling System	1. Overcooling	1. Check cooling system components
ENGINE NOISE	1. Excessive main bearing clearance 2. Main bearing scored 3. Excessive connecting rod bearing clearance 4. Bent connecting rod 5. Rod bearing scored 6. Excessive piston clearance from worn cylinder sleeve 7. Worn piston and piston pin 8. Piston seizure 9. Damaged piston rings 10. Excessive camshaft end play 11. Worn crankshaft thrust bearing 12. Worn timing gear 13. Excessive valve clearance 14. Defective water pump bearing 15. Loose or bent fan 16. Defective fan belt	1. Replace bearing 2. Replace bearing and check lubrication system 3. Replace bearing 4. Replace rod 5. Replace bearing and check lubrication system 6. Rebore and hone cylinder sleeve and fit oversize piston 7. Replace piston and piston pin 8. Replace piston 9. Replace piston rings 10. Replace camshaft thrust plate 11. Replace bearing 12. Replace timing gear 13. Adjust valve clearance 14. Replace bearing 15. Tighten or replace fan 16. Replace fan belt
INSUFFICIENT ACCELERATION	1. Burnt or misadjusted valve 2. Insufficient compression 3. Leaking head gasket 4. Improper injection timing 5. Improper fuel injection adjustment 6. Dirty air filter element	1. Replace or adjust valve 2. Disassemble and repair engine 3. Replace head gasket 4. Adjust injection timing 5. See "Diesel Fuel Injection System" 6. Replace air filter element
INSUFFICIENT POWER Insufficient Compression	1. Improper valve clearance 2. Compression leaks at valve seat 3. Valve stem seizure 4. Defective or broken valve spring 5. Leaking head gasket 6. Sticking or worn piston rings 7. Worn piston rings or cylinder	1. Adjust valve clearance 2. Remove cylinder head and lap valve 3. Correct or replace valve 4. Replace valve spring 5. Replace head gasket and tighten head bolts to specifications 6. Replace piston rings 7. Disassemble and repair engine
Injection System	1. Improper injection timing	1. Adjust injection timing
Fuel System	1. Clogged fuel pipe 2. Air in fuel system 3. Loose fuel pipe connection 4. Fuel pipe cracked 5. Clogged fuel filter 6. Clogged air cleaner	1. Clean pipe 2. Check each pipe connection Tighten connections and bleed fuel system 3. Tighten connection 4. Replace fuel pipe 5. Clean or replace filter element 6. Clean or replace air cleaner element

Condition	Possible Cause	Correction
Overheating	1. Insufficient coolant 2. Radiator leaking 3. Loose or damaged radiator connection 4. Water pump leaking 5. Loose or damaged heater hose 6. Head gasket leaking coolant 7. Cracked cylinder head or block 8. Loose fan belt 9. Worn or broken fan belt 10. Oil on fan belt 11. Defective thermostat 12. Defective water pump 13. Clogged radiator 14. Improper engine oil 15. Improper valve clearance 16. Excessive back pressure in exhaust system	1. Add coolant and check for leaks 2. Repair or replace radiator 3. Tighten clamp or replace hose 4. Repair or replace pump 5. Tighten or replace hose 6. Tighten head bolts to specifications 7. Repair or replace damaged component 8. Adjust or replace fan belt 9. Replace fan belt 10. Replace fan belt 11. Replace thermostat 12. Replace water pump 13. Clean radiator and water jacket 14. Change to specified oil 15. Adjust valve clearance 16. Clean or replace exhaust system
Overcooling	1. Faulty thermostat 2. Extremely low outside temperature	1. Replace thermostat 2. Decrease radiator air passage area
EXCESSIVE FUEL CONSUMPTION **Engine**	1. Improper valve clearance 2. Compression leaks at valve seat 3. Seized valve stem 4. Defective or broken valve spring 5. Leaking head gasket 6. Sticking or worn piston rings 7. Worn piston rings or cylinder sleeve	1. Adjust valve clearance 2. Remove cylinder head and lap valve 3. Correct or replace valve stem 4. Replace valve spring 5. Replace head gasket and tighten head bolts to specifications 6. Replace piston rings 7. Disassemble and repair engine
Injection System	1. Improper injection timing 2. Injection system leaks 3. Injection nozzles dribbling	1. Adjust injection timing 2. Tighten connections and replace leaking pipes 3. See "Diesel Fuel Injection System" group
EXCESSIVE ENGINE OIL CONSUMPTION **Oil Leaks**	1. Loose oil pan drain plug 2. Loose oil pan bolts 3. Defective pan gasket 4. Loose timing gear cover or defective cover gasket 5. Defective crankshaft front oil seal 6. Defective crankshaft rear oil seal 7. Defective cylinder head cover gasket 8. Loose oil filter or defective gasket	1. Tighten drain plug 2. Tighten pan bolts to specifications 3. Replace pan gasket 4. Tighten bolts or replace gasket 5. Replace oil seal 6. Replace oil seal 7. Replace gasket 8. Replace oil filter
Oil in Combustion Chamber	1. Improper piston ring gap position 2. Worn or sticking rings or ring grooves 3. Plugged oil return hole in oil ring 4. Excessively worn piston and cylinder sleeve 5. Excessively worn valve guide and/or valve stem 6. Clogged air filter element	1. Adjust ring position 2. Replace piston or rings 3. Replace oil ring 4. Replace piston or rebore sleeve 5. Replace valve guide insert and valve 6. Replace air filter element

Driveability Diagnosis

Condition	Cold Engine Symptom	Corrective Action
ENGINE CRANKS, BUT WILL NOT START **No fuel reaching injection pump**	1. Air trapped in fuel system	1. Bleed air from fuel filter and injection pump
	2. Fuel line drawing air	2. Replace cracked line or tighten loose connector
	3. No fuel in tank	3. Fill tank with specified fuel
	4. Gauze filter (strainer) at feed pump inlet clogged	4. Remove filter, clean, and replace
	5. Fuel line clogged	5. Disassemble and clean line
	6. Fuel filter clogged	6. Clean filter case and replace element
	7. Feed pump not delivering fuel	7. Valve inoperative or plunger stuck. Disassemble and repair
Fuel reaches injection pump	8. Injection pump seized	8. Replace injection pump
	9. Injection pump loose on mountings	9. Tighten injection pump mounting bolts
	10. Pump control rack seized Plunger stuck to barrel Control sleeve stuck	10. Replace injection pump
	11. Delivery valve stuck or spring broken	11. Replace injection pump
Slight smoke in exhaust; insufficient fuel injected	12. Air trapped in fuel system	12. See 1 above
	13. Gauze filter (strainer) at feed pump inlet clogged	13. See 4 above
	14. Fuel line clogged	14. See 5 above
	15. Fuel filter clogged	15. See 6 above
	16. Feed pump delivering insufficient fuel	16. See 7 above
	17. Pump control rack movement restricted	17. Adjust governor
	18. Accelerator linkage binding	18. Free and adjust accelerator linkage
	19. Injector line connector loose	19. Tighten connector
	20. Injection pump tappet sticking	20. Replace injection pump
	21. Injection pump tappet roller or cam excessively worn	21. Replace injection pump
	22. Injection pump tappet plunger stuck or spring broken	22. Replace injection pump
	23. Injection pump plunger excessively worn	23. Replace injection pump
	24. Injection pump control pinion setscrew loose	24. Align control pinion with line on control sleeve and tighten screw
	25. Fuel too viscous to flow freely	25. If weather is cold, heat fuel. If temperatures are normal, fuel is improper. Drain fuel and replace with specified grade
	26. Fuel leak or dribble at nozzle.	26. Replace faulty nozzle. Check injection cycle following manual procedures
Thick smoke in exhaust; incorrect injection timing	27. Injection pump improperly installed and timed	27. Reinstall pump and time properly. Refer to "Injection Timing"
	28. Injection pump tappet or cam worn excessively, throwing timing off	28. Replace injection pump and check timing
	29. Injection pump adjusting bolt loose, throwing timing off	29. Adjust injection timing and tighten adjusting bolt
Nozzle does not spray fuel properly	30. Needle valve stuck in nozzle body—nozzle remains open	30. Disassemble nozzle. Replace if necessary
	31. Nozzle valve does not seat properly and allows fuel to leak	31. Disassemble nozzle. Replace if necessary
	32. Injection pressure too low	32. Use nozzle tester. Adjust injection pressure to 1705 psi with adjusting screw
	33. Nozzle holder spring broken	33. Replace spring—adjust injection pressure
	34. Nozzle packing clogged	34. Remove packing and carbon deposits

Condition	Cold Engine Symptom	Corrective Action
ENGINE POWER OUTPUT INSUFFICIENT **Exhaust smoke thin; insufficient fuel supply**	35. Gauze filter (strainer) in feed pump inlet clogged	35. See 4 above
	36. Feed valve clogged; insufficient fuel feed	36. See 5 above
	37. Fuel feed pump delivering insufficient fuel	37. See 7 above
	38. Injector line connector leaking fuel	38. Tighten connector on injector line
	39. Injection pump tappet stuck	39. Replace injection pump
	40. Injection pump tappet roller or cam excessively worn	40. Replace injection pump
	41. Injection pump plunger stuck or spring broken	41. Replace injection pump
	42. Injection pump control pinion set-screw loose	42. See 24 above
	43. Injection pump delivery valve damaged or spring broken	43. Replace injection pump
	44. Nozzle leaking fuel	44. Replace defective nozzle
Thick white smoke in exhaust; injection timing late	45. Fuel too viscous to flow freely	45. See 25 above
	46. Injection interval improperly timed	46. Reset injection timing
	47. Injection pump tappet roller or cam excessively worn	47. Replace injection pump
	48. Injection pump tappet adjusting bolt loose throwing timing off	48. Adjust injection timing and tighten adjusting bolt
Thick black smoke in exhaust; injection timing early	49. Injection interval improperly timed	49. Reinstall pump and time properly Refer to "Injection Timing"
	50. Air cleaner clogged	50. Replace air cleaner element
	51. Air intake restricted	51. Clean air intake path
Thick black smoke in exhaust; fuel charge between cylinders non-uniform	52. Worn tappet roller or cam timing	52. Replace injection pump and recheck
	53. Loose tappet adjusting bolts	53. Set timing and tighten adjusting bolts
	54. Stuck tappets; poor tappet return	54. Replace injection pump
	55. Worn plungers; stuck plungers; broken springs	55. Replace injection pump
	56. Control pinion set-screws loose	56. Align control pinion with line on control sleeve and tighten set-screws
	57. Delivery valves damaged or springs broken	57. Replace injection pump
Improper nozzle spray pattern	58. Needle valve stuck in nozzle body; nozzle stays open	58. Disassemble nozzle; replace if necessary
	59. Nozzle valve does not seat; fuel leaks	59. Disassemble nozzle; replace if necessary
	60. Injection pressure too low	60. Use nozzle tester. Adjust injection pressure to 1705 psi with adjusting screw
	61. Nozzle holder spring broken	61. Replace spring; adjust injection pressure to specifications
	62. Nozzle packing clogged	62. Remove packing and carbon deposits
ENGINE KNOCKS	63. Injection too early. Engine knocks hard and produces black smoke	63. Remove and reinstall injection pump. Time properly. Refer to "Injection Timing"
	64. Injection timing retarded. Engine knocks weakly and produces white smoke	64. Remove and reinstall injection pump. Time properly. Refer to "Injection Timing"
	65. Cylinders into which too much fuel is injected are knocking	65. See 52 through 57 above
	66. Improper fuel spray from nozzles	66. See 58 through 62 above

Condition	Cold Engine Symptom	Corrective Action
EXCESSIVE SMOKE EMITTED DURING OPERATION **Thick white smoke in exhaust**	67. Injection timing retarded 68. Water in fuel	67. Remove and reinstall injection pump. Time properly. Refer to "Injection Timing" 68. Drain fuel filter. Drain fuel system. Replace with specified fuel
Thick black smoke in exhaust	69. Injection timing advanced 70. Excessive fuel delivery from injection pump 71. Non-uniform fuel delivery from injection pump 72. Nozzle spray non-uniform 73. Clogged air cleaner	69. See 67 above 70. Replace injection pump 71. See 52 through 57 above 72. See 58 through 62 above 73. Replace air cleaner element
ENGINE SPEED NOT SMOOTHLY CONTROLLED **Engine runs at high speed and will not stop**	74. Accelerator linkage binding between pedal and injection pump 75. Defective governor linkage 76. Injection pump rack binding 77. Injection pump control pinion set-screw loose	74. Check accelerator linkage and ensure free operation 75. Replace injection pump 76. Replace injection pump 77. Align control pinion with line on control sleeve and tighten set-screw

Diesel Engine Repair Section

ENGINE MOUNTS
REPLACE

1. Remove engine mount to frame attaching nuts, **Fig. 1.**
2. Support engine, then remove mount to bracket attaching bolts and nuts.
3. Raise engine slightly, then remove mounts.

NOTE: D-100 & D-200 models incorporate a spacer between the engine mount and engine mount attaching bracket.

4. Reverse procedure to install.

ENGINE
REPLACE

1. Disconnect battery cables and remove battery.
2. Remove air cleaner.
3. Scribe hood hinge locations on hood, then remove hood.
4. Drain cooling system and disconnect radiator hoses from engine.
k. Remove coolant reserve tank.
6. Raise and support vehicle.
7. Disconnect transmission oil cooler lines from radiator, if equipped.
8. Disconnect the lower radiator and fan shroud attaching screws.
9. Lower vehicle and remove upper radiator and fan shroud attaching screws. Remove radiator and fan shroud.
10. Disconnect heater hoses and position aside.
11. Disconnect speedometer cable housing from engine.
12. Disconnect all electrical wiring from engine that may interfere with engine removal. Position wiring harnesses aside.
13. Disconnect and cap fuel line at transfer pump inlet.
14. Disconnect and plug return line at injector lines bleed-back connection.
15. Disconnect and remove injector pump linkage. Disconnect and remove accelerator and throttle cable linkage.
16. Disconnect starter motor wiring and remove starter motor.
17. Disconnect battery ground cable from cylinder block. Remove engine ground strap.
18. Disconnect and plug power steering hoses from gear and position aside.
19. Raise and support vehicle.
20. Disconnect exhaust pipe from manifold.
21. Drain oil pan and remove dipstick tube.
22. Remove oil cooler lines, if equipped, and the road draft tube bracket from oil pan.
23. Remove oil pan bolts. Support engine under A/C compressor bracket.
24. Remove transmission inspection plate, then the oil pan.
25. Remove torque converter to flywheel bolts.
26. Remove exhaust pipe bracket and lower bell housing bolts.
27. Remove engine support placed under A/C compressor bracket.
28. Support transmission with a suitable jack.
29. Remove rocker arm cover.
30. Attach suitable engine lifting equipment to engine lift points.
31. Remove bolts and nuts from engine mounts, **Fig. 1.**
32. Remove upper bell housing bolts.
33. Pull engine forward to separate from transmission, then lift engine from vehicle.
34. Reverse procedure to install.

CYLINDER HEAD
REPLACE

1. Disconnect battery ground cable and drain cooling system.
2. Remove air cleaner.
3. Disconnect hoses from fuel filter at transfer pump and injection pump. Drain fuel filter and remove from rear of air manifold.
4. Remove nuts securing air manifold and air cleaner mounting brackets.
5. Disconnect the No. 3 and No. 6 fuel injection lines from injection pump.
6. Remove air intake manifold and gaskets from cylinder head.
7. Push exhaust manifold shield aside.
8. Disconnect bypass hose and heater hoses from engine.
9. Remove thermostat housing and upper radiator hose from water manifold. Remove spray gasket.
10. Disconnect fuel line mounting brackets from cylinder head and push fuel lines aside.
11. Remove three exhaust manifold bridges, then the water manifold and gasket from cylinder head.
12. Raise and support vehicle.
13. Remove exhaust pipe from exhaust

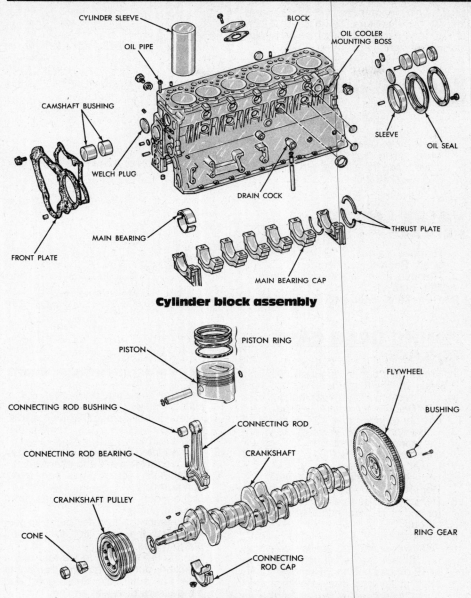

Cylinder block assembly

Crankshaft, piston & connecting rod assembly

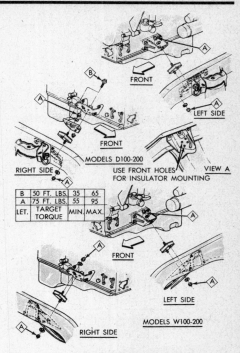

Fig. 1   Engine mounts

B	50 FT. LBS.	35	65
A	75 FT. LBS.	55	95
LET.	TARGET TORQUE	MIN.	MAX.

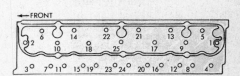

Fig. 2   Cylinder head bolt removal sequence

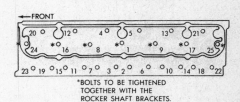

*BOLTS TO BE TIGHTENED TOGETHER WITH THE ROCKER SHAFT BRACKETS.

Fig. 3   Cylinder head bolt tightening sequence

manifold.

14. Lower vehicle and remove exhaust manifold, heat shield and gasket.
15. Disconnect wiring from glow plug buss bar.
16. Disconnect injection lines from fuel injection pump.
17. Disconnect fuel injection line and fuel injection line bracket and ground strap from cylinder head.
18. Disconnect alternator bracket and engine lifting fixture and position aside.
19. Loosen and remove cylinder head bolts in sequence, **Fig. 2.**
20. Remove rocker arm and shaft assembly.
21. Remove push rods. Mark location of push rods to ensure installation in original position.
22. Remove injector tubes, injector holders and injectors.
23. Remove glow plug buss bar and the glow plugs.
24. Remove cylinder head from engine.
25. Reverse procedure to install. Torque cylinder head bolts in sequence, **Fig. 3,** to specifications.

INTAKE MANIFOLD
REPLACE

Refer to steps 2 through 6 in "Cylinder Head, Replace" procedure.

EXHAUST MANIFOLD
REPLACE

1. Disconnect battery ground cable, then remove air cleaner.
2. Remove exhaust manifold heat shield assembly, then disconnect exhaust pipe.
3. Remove exhaust manifold bridges and exhaust manifold attaching bolts.
4. Remove exhaust manifold and gaskets from cylinder head.
5. Reverse procedure to install.

ROCKER ARMS
REPLACE

NOTE: Dimensions of the intake and exhaust rocker arms are different since a different dimension exists between the rocker shaft centerline and the intake and exhaust push rods, **Fig. 4.**

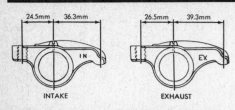

Fig. 4   Rocker arm identification

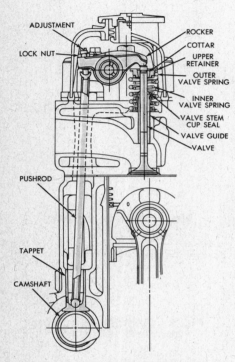

Fig. 6   Valve train

1. Remove cylinder head cover and gasket.
2. Remove nozzle holders and glow plugs.
3. Remove rocker shaft bracket retaining bolts.
4. Remove rocker arm and shaft assembly, **Fig. 5.**
5. Reverse procedure to install.

VALVE ARRANGEMENT

6-243 . . . . E-I-E-I-E-I-E-I-E-I-E-I

VALVE TIMING
Intake Opens Before TDC

Engine	Year	Degrees
6-243	1979	32

VALVES
ADJUST

The valves are adjusted with the engine cold. Adjust clearance between rocker arm and top of valve stem, **Fig. 6,** to .012 inch at top dead center of compression stroke of each cylinder.

VALVE GUIDES
REPLACE

1. Remove valve guide using suitable tool, **Fig. 7.**
2. Press new valve guide into cylinder head using suitable installer. The valve guide installed length should be .6968–.7250 inch.

VALVE LIFTER
REPLACE

1. Remove camshaft. Refer to "Camshaft, Replace" procedure.
2. Remove valve lifters from bottom of lifter bore.
3. Reverse procedure to install.

TIMING GEAR CASE
REPLACE

1. Disconnect battery ground cable and drain cooling system.
2. Remove upper and lower radiator hoses. Disconnect overflow line from coolant reserve tank.
3. Raise and support vehicle.
4. Disconnect transmission oil cooler lines from radiator.
5. Lower vehicle.
6. Loosen radiator mounting bolts.
7. Remove fan.
8. Remove rubber shield between radiator and grille, then the radiator and fan shroud.
9. Remove drive belts and idler pulley.
10. Remove crankshaft pulley retaining nut. Rotate crankshaft until keyway is at 12 o'clock position. Remove crankshaft pulley and damper with a suitable puller.
11. Remove timing gear case, gasket and idler pulley bracket, **Fig. 8.**
12. Reverse procedure to install.

FRONT OIL SEAL
REPLACE

The front oil seal may be replaced after removing the timing gear case.

TIMING GEAR ASSEMBLY
REPLACE
REMOVAL

1. Remove timing gear case, gasket, front oil seal and idler pulley bracket.
2. Align timing marks on gearset, **Fig. 9.**

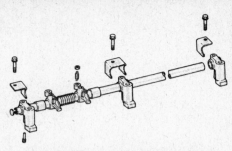

Fig. 5   Rocker shaft assembly

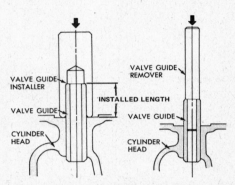

Fig. 7   Valve guide replacement

3. Remove camshaft drive gear with a suitable puller.
4. Rotate injection pump drive gear to allow notch in drive gear to pass idler gear teeth.
5. Loosen idler gear mounting bolt, then remove thrust plate and idler gear.
6. Disconnect injector pipes from injection pump.
7. Disconnect and cap fuel line from transfer pump.
8. Disconnect the transfer pump to fuel filter and the fuel filter to injection pump hoses.
9. Loosen the stay bolt in the rear of the injection pump. Remove the pump with the automatic timer gear and flange toward rear of engine.

INSTALLATION

1. Ensure engine is placed at top dead center of compression stroke, No. 1 cylinder.
2. Install idler shaft with a suitable drift and hammer, if removed.
3. Install idler gear on shaft so the marks on camshaft drive gear mate with marks on idler gear, **Fig. 9.** Install thrust plate and attaching bolt.
4. Install camshaft gear and thrust plate on camshaft with the marks on camshaft gear meshed properly with marks on idler gear, **Fig. 9.**
5. Place injection pump into position. Mesh the pump drive gear with idler gear, ensuring marks are properly aligned, **Fig. 9.** Also, ensure that the injection pump mounting flange scale is set at the injection timing point.
6. Install mounting bolts to timing gear case and flange mount.

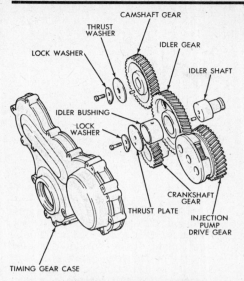

Fig. 8   Timing gear assembly

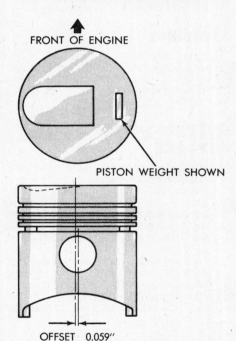

Fig. 10   Piston identification

CAMSHAFT
REPLACE

1. Remove engine from vehicle, and place in a suitable workstand.
2. Remove cylinder head.
3. Remove crankshaft pulley and damper.
4. Remove flywheel housing and flywheel.
5. Remove timing gear case.
6. Rotate crankshaft until No. 1 cylinder is at top dead center, compression stroke.
7. Remove injection pump.
8. Remove idler gear mounting bolt, thrust plate and idler gear.
9. Remove crankshaft gear and baffle.
10. Remove camshaft gear, then the oil pan.
11. Remove oil pickup tube and strainer. Loosen joint bolt and remove oil pump.
12. Remove thrust plate, then the camshaft from front of engine. Use care not to damage camshaft bearings.
13. Reverse procedure to install.

PISTON & ROD ASSEMBLY

The aluminum alloy piston has a top recess which forms a combustion chamber, **Fig. 10**. Assemble piston to rod with combustion chamber (recess) side of piston facing the side of the connecting rod having the weight stamping.

MAIN BEARINGS

Main bearings are furnished in standard size and the following undersizes: .010, .020 and .030 inch.

CYLINDER SLEEVES
REPLACE

REMOVAL

1. Mount a portable boring bar to top of cylinder block.
2. Align boring bar with center of cylinder sleeve at bottom where eccentric wear is minimum.
3. Bore sleeve wall out to a thickness of .02 inch.
4. Extract sleeve from cylinder block with suitable equipment. Use caution not to damage cylinder block inner surface.
5. Check block bottom hole condition after sleeve has been removed. Bottom hole must be rebored before installing new sleeve if damaged or other defects are noted.

INSTALLATION

If Bottom Hole Is Not Rebored
1. Measure inside diameter of bottom

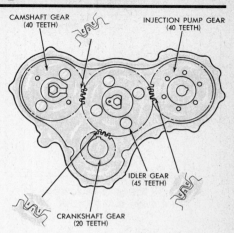

Fig. 9   Timing mark alignment

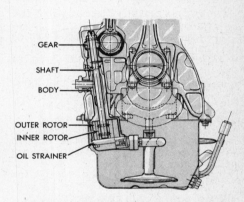

Fig. 11   Oil pump installation

hole and outside diameter of sleeve being installed. Sleeve to bottom hole clearance must be .003–.006 inch after installation.
2. Press cylinder sleeve into cylinder block until sleeve top surface is flush with cylinder block.
3. Bore the sleeve and finish to an inside diameter of 3.620–3.623 inch by honing.

If Bottom Hole Must Be Rebored
1. The standard bottom hole in the block is 3.738–3.739 inch. Select an oversize sleeve with an outside diameter .02 inch larger.
2. Bore hole in bottom of block with a diameter of 3.738–3.739 inch if a standard sleeve is being used. If an oversize sleeve is being used, the bottom hole should have an inside diameter of 3.758–3.759 inch. This ensures clearance between bottom hole and sleeve outside diameter of .003–.006 inch.
3. Press sleeve into cylinder block until sleeve top surface is flush with cylinder block.
4. Bore the sleeve and finish to an inside diameter of 3.620–3.623 inch by honing.

7. Connect fuel feed pipe and filter hoses to pump assembly.
8. Operate primer pump and bleed air from fuel filter and injection pump.
9. Connect injection pipes to injection pump.
10. Check idler gear end play with a feeler gauge placed between gear and thrust plate. End play should be .002–.006 inch. If end play exceeds repair limit of .014 inch, replace thrust plate and recheck end play.
11. Check gear camshaft backlash with a dial indicator. Backlash should be .004–.009 inch. If backlash exceeds repair limit of .01 inch, replace gear.
12. Install new front seal.
13. Install timing gear case and gasket.

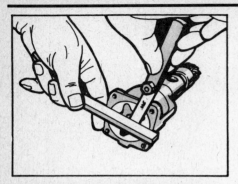

Fig. 12 Measuring rotor to cover clearance

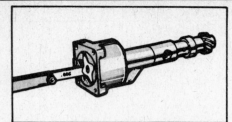

Fig. 13 Measuring inner to outer rotor clearance

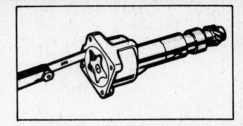

Fig. 14 Measuring outer rotor to body clearance

OIL PAN
REPLACE

1. Disconnect battery ground cable and remove oil dipstick.
2. Raise and support vehicle. Drain oil pan.
3. Remove oil dipstick tube from oil pan.
4. Disconnect transmission oil cooler lines and road draft tube.
5. Remove oil pan attaching bolts.
6. Lower vehicle.
7. Remove nuts from engine mounts.
8. Raise and support vehicle. Support engine with a stand under compressor bracket, if equipped.
9. Remove transmission inspection plate.
10. Remove oil pan from vehicle.
11. Reverse procedure to install.

OIL PUMP
REPLACE

1. Remove oil pan.
2. Remove oil pickup tube, strainer and gasket, **Fig. 11.**
3. Remove oil pump joint bolt.
4. Remove oil pump.

5. Reverse procedure to install.

OIL PUMP SERVICE
DISASSEMBLY

1. Loosen bolts and remove strainer (cover) from oil pump.
2. Remove inner rotor and shaft.
3. Lift out outer rotor from pump.

INSPECTION

1. Clean all parts of pump. The cover mating face should be smooth. Replace cover if scratched or grooved.
2. Install outer rotor into pump body. Install inner rotor into outer rotor and seat in pump body.
3. Place a straightedge across pump body face. Insert a feeler gauge between straightedge and rotors, **Fig. 12.** Clearance should be .0014–.004 inch. If clearance exceeds .006 inch, replace inner and outer rotors as an assembly.
4. Check clearance between inner and outer rotors, **Fig. 13.** Clearance should be .007 inch or less. If clearance exceeds .010 inch, replace inner and outer rotor as an assembly.
5. Check clearance between outer rotor and pump body, **Fig. 14.** Clearance

should be .008–.010 inch. If clearance exceeds .020 inch, replace outer rotor.
6. Measure rotor shaft outside diameter and pump body inside diameter. Clearance between shaft and body should be .001–.003 inch. If clearance exceeds .006 inch, replace inner rotor and shaft and/or pump body. Replace all parts showing excessive wear.

ASSEMBLY

1. Install outer rotor in pump body.
2. Install inner rotor and shaft in outer rotor.
3. Install strainer (cover) on pump body.

WATER PUMP
REPLACE

1. Disconnect battery ground cable and drain cooling system.
2. Disconnect radiator hoses from engine.
3. Loosen alternator attaching bolts, then remove fan drive belt.
4. Remove cooling fan, spacer and drive pulley assembly.
5. Remove water pump attaching bolts, then the water pump from engine block.
6. Reverse procedure to install.

Diesel Fuel Injection System

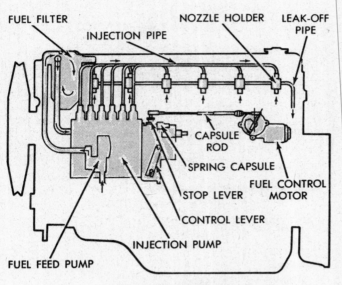

FUEL FILTER
INJECTION PIPE
NOZZLE HOLDER
LEAK-OFF PIPE
CAPSULE ROD
SPRING CAPSULE
STOP LEVER
CONTROL LEVER
FUEL CONTROL MOTOR
INJECTION PUMP
FUEL FEED PUMP

Fig. 1   Fuel system

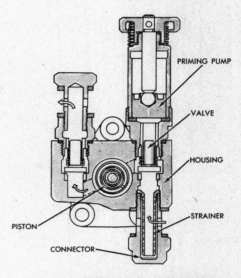

PRIMING PUMP
VALVE
HOUSING
STRAINER
PISTON
CONNECTOR

Fig. 2   Feed pump inlet fuel filter (strainer)

DESCRIPTION

The fuel system consists of the fuel tank, fuel line, feed pump, fuel filter, injection pump, injector lines, nozzle holders and nozzles, leak-off lines and the fuel return line, **Fig. 1.**

The feed pump draws fuel from the tank through the fuel line. The fuel then passes through the fuel filter, mounted at the rear of the intake manifold, and enters the injection pump. At the proper intervals, the injection pump forces the fuel under high pressure into the injector lines. This high pressure fuel is sprayed into the combustion chambers by the injector nozzles. Fuel not used during operation is drawn off by the leak-off lines and returned to the fuel tank by the fuel return line.

This fuel system utilizes three fuel filters. One filter is part of the gauge sending unit assembly immersed in the fuel tank at the end of the fuel line. This filter does not normally need service, however, it can be replaced if necessary. The second filter (strainer) is a gauze type filter located at the inlet port of the feed pump, **Fig. 2.** It operates under suction and removes large size particles of dirt and foreign matter. This filter should be removed and cleaned every 12,000 miles. Clean the wire gauze in a suitable solvent. After cleaning, reinstall filter and fuel line connector and bleed air from fuel system. The third filter is a paper element type, **Fig. 3,** mounted at the rear of the intake manifold, located between the feed pump and injection pump in the system.

The injection pump is a fixed stroke, plunger type pump. Fuel is injected at high pressure into the injector lines by movement of the plungers in the plunger barrels. Delivery valves at the top of the plunger barrels prevent fuel injection until sufficient injector pressure has built up in the injection pump and "After-drip" from the nozzle tips after injection has ended.

The amount of fuel delivered to the engine is controlled by an RU type maximum-minimum mechanical governor, **Fig. 4,** mounted at the rear of the injection pump housing. The governor regulates the amount of fuel injected by controlling the movement of the injection pump control rack and sleeve proportional to engine speed. The governor operates only at engine idle and at high speed operation. It is inoperative at intermediate engine speeds.

A gear type automatic timer, **Fig. 5,** mounted to the front of the injection pump camshaft, advances injection timing as engine speed increases to ensure injection of fuel at the proper intervals.

The nozzle tip is installed in the nozzle holder, **Fig. 6,** and is secured by a retaining nut. Fuel from the injection pump enters the upper part of the nozzle holder and flows into the fuel reservoir in the nozzle through a fuel passageway. The nozzle tip atomizes the high pressure fuel and sprays the fuel into the precombustion chamber.

When no high pressure fuel is present at the nozzle holder input, the needle valve holds the nozzle tip orifice closed. Fuel delivered at the specified injection pressure overcomes spring pressure and the needle valve opens. Fuel is then injected into the precombustion chamber. When injection pressure drops, the spring closes the needle valve. Fuel remaining in the nozzle reservoir is bled off to the fuel return line through the leak off line.

OPERATION

Fuel system operation during starting, stopping and at high speed is controlled by the Electrical Diesel Injection Control (EDIC) system. The EDIC system consists of the key switch, fuel control relay operated by the key switch signal, fuel control motor, capsule rod and injection pump.

The key switch position determines fuel control relay input. The fuel control relay passes current to the fuel control motor in accordance with key switch position. This current actuates the control motor which operates the injection pump stop lever through the capsule rod.

When the key switch is turned from "Off" to "Start", the starter motor begins to crank the engine. The fuel control relay actuates the control motor which pulls the injection pump stop lever to the "Start" position, compressing the spring in the spring capsule located at the top of the governor. With the key switch at "Start", the control motor continues to revolve, transmitting this movement to the stop lever.

When the stop lever is moved to the "Start" position by compressing the spring capsule, it restricts movement of the capsule rod, drive lever and stopper. The motor continues to rotate through the con-

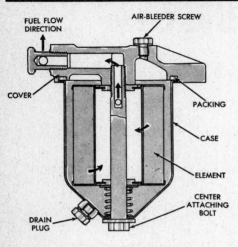

Fig. 3   Fuel filter

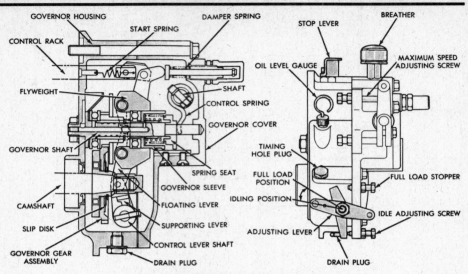

Fig. 4   Mechanical governor

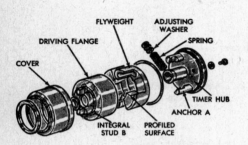

Fig. 5   Automatic timer

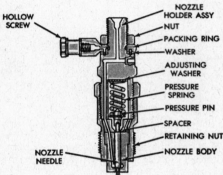

Fig. 6   Injection nozzle & holder

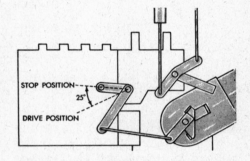

Fig. 7   Start operational check

trol assembly clutch which prevents damage to the rotating parts.

When the engine starts, the key switch is returned to the "On" position. The "On" signal at the fuel control relay reverses the rotation of the control motor, returning the stop lever to the "Drive" position.

When the key switch is turned from "On" to "Off", the fuel control relay senses the "Off" signal and actuates the control motor to push the injection pump lever to the "Stop" position. When the control motor limiter plate reaches the "Stop" position, current to the motor is cut off and the motor stops.

The capsule rod with the enclosed spring permits the drive lever to push the rod after the stop lever to push the road after the stop lever reaches the "Stop" position. The motor "Stop" position may overrun the stop lever "Stop" position to ensure a positive stop.

EDIC OPERATIONAL CHECKS

START POSITION CHECK

Turn key switch to the "Start" position. The control motor should move the injection pump stop lever to the "Start" position, **Fig. 7.**

DRIVE POSITION CHECK

After the engine starts, observe position of drive lever. The end of the drive lever at the motor should be positioned between the two machined marks, **Fig. 8.**

STOP ACTION CHECK

Turn the key switch to "Off" position. The injection pump lever should move to the "Stop" position and the engine should stop, **Fig. 9.**

FUEL CONTROL RELAY TEST

1. Disconnect electrical connector from fuel control relay.
2. Measure resistance between the following terminals on the relay connector socket, **Fig. 10:** 1 and 8, 4 and 6, 5 and 6, 6 and 7, 2 and 6, 3 and 6. All readings should be zero ohms.
3. If any readings indicate more than zero ohms in step 2, replace fuel control relay.
4. If readings are satisfactory in step 2, apply battery voltage (12 volts) between terminals 4 and 6, **Fig. 10.**

Measure resistance between terminals 1 and 8. Reading should be infinite. If not, replace fuel control relay. If resistance is infinite, apply the battery voltage to terminals 5 and 6, **Fig. 10.**
5. Measure resistance between terminals 1 and 3, **Fig. 10.** Reading should be zero ohms. If not, replace fuel control relay. If resistance is zero ohms, connect the battery voltage to terminals 6 and 7, **Fig. 10.**
6. Measure resistance between terminals 3 and 6, **Fig. 10.** Reading should be zero ohms. If not, replace fuel control relay. If all readings are satisfactory, the fuel control relay is satisfactory.

BLEEDING AIR FROM SYSTEM

1. Loosen fuel filter petcock or valve, **Fig. 3,** and operate the priming pump on the feed pump. If the filter is filled with fuel, fuel containing air bubbles will be discharged from the petcock or valve. Continue pumping until the discharged fuel contains no air bubbles. Tighten the petcock or valve securely.
2. Loosen the air bleeder screw at the

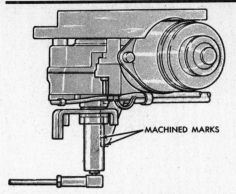

Fig. 8   Drive lever position check

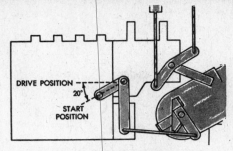

Fig. 9   Stop action check

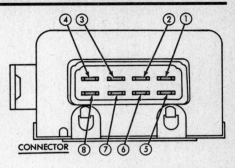

Fig. 10   Fuel control relay connector

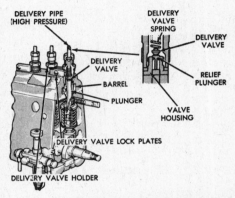

Fig. 11   Delivery valve assembly

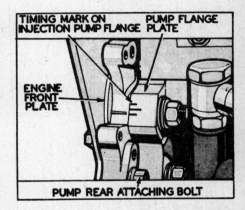

Fig. 12   Injection pump timing marks & attachment

top of the injection pump and operate the priming pump. Continue pumping until all air is bled from the fuel in the pump reservoir. Tighten bleeder screw securely.

NOTE: Approximately ¼ pint of fuel should be drained from the fuel filter daily to remove dirt and water accumulation. Remove drain plug or open petcock, if equipped, at bottom of filter and drain fuel into container.

FUEL CONTROL MOTOR
REPLACE

1. Disconnect motor connector.
2. Disconnect capsule rod at control motor and injection pump stop lever and remove rod.
3. Remove the three motor mounting bolts.
4. Remove motor from side of block.
5. Reverse procedure to install.

INJECTION TIMING
PRIMARY METHOD

1. Disconnect battery ground cable.

2. Disconnect fuel shutoff rod at injection pump stop lever.
3. Clean dirt and foreign material from No. 1 delivery valve, injection pipe and adjacent pump area.
4. Rotate crankshaft to place No. 1 cylinder at top dead center, compression stroke. Crankshaft position is identified by alignment of the degree marks on the crankshaft damper rear face with pointer on bottom of timing gear case.
5. Rotate crankshaft 1¾ revolutions.
6. Disconnect No. 1 injection pipe from delivery valve.
7. Remove lock plates from No. 1 delivery valve holder and unscrew delivery valve holder from pump carefully to prevent loss of delivery valve spring and any shims, **Fig. 11**.
8. Remove delivery valve springs and any shims. Reinstall delivery valve holder snugly.
9. Connect a clean plastic tube into open end of delivery valve holder and place the other end in a container.
10. Rotate crankshaft to approximately 30 degrees before top dead center. Unscrew handle of priming pump on fuel feed pump to unlock. Operate the pump until fuel flow is observed through the plastic tube.
11. Rotate crankshaft one degree and operate priming pump and observe fuel flow. Continue to rotate crankshaft in one degree increments and operate the priming pump until fuel no longer flows through plastic tube. This is the existing injection timing point.
12. If the existing timing point is not 18° before top dead center, loosen the four pump to flange plate nuts and rotate pump to adjust pump to specified timing point, **Fig. 12**. Turn the pump toward the cylinder block to advance timing or away from cylinder block to retard timing. The crankshaft angle varies by six degrees per division on pump flange plate scale, **Fig. 12**.
13. Tighten pump to flange plate nuts, **Fig. 12**.
14. Repeat step 5 and steps 10 through 12.
15. Remove plastic tube. Ensure that delivery valve spring and shims are clean and reinstall in holder. Tighten delivery valve holder and reinstall lock plates, **Fig. 11**.

16. Connect No. 1 injection pipe to delivery valve holder.
17. Install oil fill cap and lock the priming pump handle.
18. Connect fuel shutoff rod and the battery ground cable.
19. Start engine and check for leaks and proper operation.

ALTERNATE METHOD

1. Perform steps 1 through 6 as outlined under "Primary Method."
2. After removing the No. 1 injection pipe from the delivery valve, rotate the crankshaft in small increments. Stop when fuel begins to flow from the delivery valve holder. Fuel injection begins at this point.
3. Injection timing should be 18° before top dead center minus 2 degrees. When using the alternate timing method, 2 degrees of crankshaft rotation will be taken up in delivery valve delay. Therefore, the timing point should be 18° before top dead center minus 2 degrees or 16° before top dead center. Adjust injection timing as necessary and recheck.

INJECTION PUMP
REPLACE

REMOVAL

1. Disconnect battery ground cable.

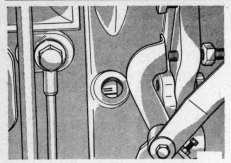

Fig. 13 Camshaft bushing timing mark

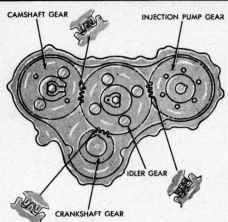

CAMSHAFT GEAR

INJECTION PUMP GEAR

IDLER GEAR

CRANKSHAFT GEAR

Fig. 14 Timing marks

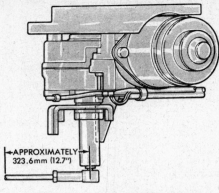

←APPROXIMATELY→
323.6mm (12.7")

Fig. 15 Adjusting capsule rod

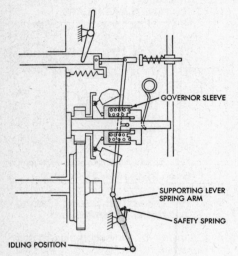

GOVERNOR SLEEVE

SUPPORTING LEVER SPRING ARM

SAFETY SPRING

IDLING POSITION

Fig. 16 Idling control

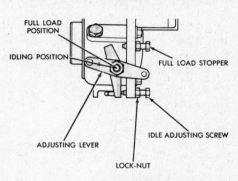

FULL LOAD POSITION

IDLING POSITION

FULL LOAD STOPPER

IDLE ADJUSTING SCREW

ADJUSTING LEVER

LOCK-NUT

Fig. 17 Idle speed adjustment

12. Disconnect injection pump lube line at block fitting near starter motor forward end.
13. The injection pump assembly is secured to the engine by five screws and one bolt. The front screws extend through the timing case and engine front plate into the pump flange plate. The rear bolt secures the flange plate to the engine front plate, **Fig. 12**. Remove the screws and bolt.
14. Pull injection pump rearward to disengage from engine front plate and timing gear case. Twist pump toward cylinder block and pull rearward until automatic timer is free of case.

INSTALLATION

1. Loosen four nuts attaching injection pump to mounting flange plate. Align center timing mark on pump flange with pointer on plate.
2. Ensure that the O-ring seal is in place on forward face of pump mounting flange.
3. Remove threaded timing port plug on governor housing behind control lever to expose pump camshaft bushing timing mark, **Fig. 13**. Turn pump drive gear to align timing mark on camshaft bushing with pointer on governor. The guide plate notch on drive gear will be approximately at the 8 o'clock position as viewed from the front.
4. Ensure that the crankshaft is still positioned as in step 10 in "Removal" procedure.
5. Insert automatic timer into timing gear case. Turn injection pump inward until against block. Then turn pump drive gear clockwise or counterclockwise to mesh drive and idler gears. Push pump forward into timing gear case and rotate away from block to align mounting holes.

NOTE: Correct gear mesh is assured by drive gear guide plate. If pump cannot be pushed forward manually until flange plate

seal diameter contacts engine front plate, the gear mesh is incorrect. Do not force pump into position. Retract the pump and turn drive gear as necessary to achieve correct gear mesh. Refer to **Fig. 14** for correct gear mesh.

6. Attach pump to timing gear case. Turn crankshaft in opposite direction of normal rotation until it reaches the specified timing point. The governor pointer and pump camshaft bushing timing marks should be aligned. If not, the pump is installed improperly and must be removed and reinstalled.
7. When timing marks are aligned, install governor housing timing port plug.
8. Reverse removal procedure but do not connect the No. 1 injection pipe or the battery ground cable.
9. Fill oil pan with specified oil.
10. Bleed air from fuel filter and injection pump as outlined previously.
11. Connect No. 1 injection pipe and the battery ground cable.
12. Check injection timing point and adjust as necessary as previously outlined.
13. Start engine and check for leaks and proper operation.

INJECTION NOZZLE SERVICE

REMOVAL

1. Disconnect injector line from nozzle

2. Disconnect fuel shutoff rod at stop lever.
3. Remove power steering pump and bracket assembly from engine and position aside.
4. Clean dirt and foreign material from fuel line, hose fittings and injection pipes at injection pump.
5. Drain oil pan and remove dipstick and tube.
6. Disconnect throttle cable and linkage from injection pump control lever.
7. Remove throttle control bracket assembly from cylinder block and the control motor bracket and position aside.
8. Disconnect fuel supply line to feed pump, loosening anchor clamps as necessary.
9. Disconnect filter hoses from feed pump and injection pump.
10. Rotate crankshaft until No. 1 piston is positioned between 7° before top dead center and top dead center of compression stroke. Check timing pointer. It should be located approximately midpoint between the TDC and 14 degree line on the damper.
11. Disconnect injection pipes from delivery valves and position away from cylinder block.

holder at cylinder.
2. Remove nozzle holder and nozzle assembly.

DISASSEMBLY

1. Place nozzle holder in a soft jawed vise. Tighten the vise against the retaining nut.
2. Remove nozzle holder body from retaining nut, **Fig. 6.**
3. Lift pressure pin, spring, washer, spacer and nozzle tip from nozzle holder, **Fig. 6.**

ASSEMBLY

1. Secure nozzle holder retaining nut in a vise.
2. Immerse nozzle tip and needle valve assembly in clean fuel oil.
3. Assemble spacer, pressure pin and pressure spring onto nozzle tip, **Fig. 6.**
4. Install adjusting shim into nozzle holder body.
5. Assemble nozzle holder and tip to retaining nut and torque nozzle holder to 43.4–57.9 ft. lbs.

INSTALLATION

1. Install nozzle holder and nozzle assembly.
2. Connect injector line to nozzle holder.

CAPSULE ROD
ADJUST

1. Check capsule rod installation at motor drive lever. With injection pump lever in "Drive" position, the drive lever at the motor should be between the two machined marks.
2. Turn drive lever with a screwdriver until it points to the 12 o'clock position.
3. Disconnect the capsule rod. Ensure that the injection pump stop lever is in the "Drive" position.
4. Loosen capsule rod lock nut and adjust rod length until the drive lever is positioned between the two machined marks.
5. Tighten the lock nut and connect capsule rod to drive lever. The nominal length of the capsule rod is 12.7 inches, **Fig. 15.**

IDLE SPEED
ADJUST

1. Remove cover and gasket from tachometer take-off on right side of engine in front of the oil filter assembly. Install mechanical tachometer adapter and attach mechanical tachometer and drive cable.

2. Turn hand throttle counterclockwise and pull fully outward. Depress accelerator pedal to floor and hold until engine starts. Permit engine to warm up and release accelerator slowly until engine runs smoothly. When engine begins to warm up, turn hand throttle clockwise to reduce engine speed to idle speed.

CAUTION: If a new accelerator pump has been installed, do not allow engine speed to rise above 1300 RPM. If engine overspeeds, serious damage may result.

3. Ensure that governor control is at idling position before adjusting idle speed, **Fig. 16.**
4. Observe tachometer. Idle speed should be 550–600 RPM.
5. If idle speed is not within specification, loosen idle adjusting screw lock nut. Adjust screws as necessary to obtain specified idle setting. Turn screw inward to raise idle speed or outward to lower idle speed, **Fig. 17.**
6. With idle speed at specified RPM, tighten idle adjusting screw lock nut. Recheck idle speed after tightening lock nut.
7. Remove tachometer, drive cable and adapter.
8. Install tachometer take-off gasket and cover.

Clutch & Manual Transmission Section

CLUTCH PEDAL
ADJUST

Adjust fork rod by turning self-locking adjusting nut to provide free movement at end of fork. Adjustment should be 3/32 inch. This movement will provide approximately 1–1½ inches of free play at pedal.

CLUTCH
REPLACE

REMOVAL

1. Remove transfer case, if equipped.
2. Remove transmission assembly.
3. Remove clutch housing pan, if equipped.
4. Disconnect return spring from clutch release fork and clutch housing.
5. Remove fork rod assembly spring washer from pin, then the rod with adjusting nut, washer and insulator.
6. Remove clutch release bearing and carrier assembly from clutch release fork, then the release fork and boot from clutch housing.
7. Mark clutch cover and flywheel to ensure correct position during installation.
8. Loosen clutch cover attaching bolts

one or two turns at a time to avoid bending cover flange.
9. Remove clutch assembly and disc from clutch housing.

INSTALLATION

NOTE: The pilot bushing requires a grease which will stay in place during high temperature operation. A small amount of grease should be placed in front of bushing and inner surface should be lightly coated.

Clean the surfaces of the flywheel and pressure plate, making certain no oil or grease remains on these parts. Hold the cover plate and disc in place and insert a special clutch aligning tool or a spare clutch shaft through the hub of the disc and into the pilot bearing in the crankshaft. Bolt the clutch cover loosely to the flywheel, being sure that punch marks previously made are lined up.

To avoid distortion of the clutch cover, tighten the cover bolts a few turns each in progression until all are tight.

Guide the transmission into place, using care to ensure the driven disc is not bent. Use a floor jack to support the transmission so that the clutch shaft may be guided through the driven disc safely. Finally, adjust the clutch pedal free travel.

TRANSMISSION
REPLACE

THREE SPEED UNITS

Disconnect propeller shaft, speedometer cable, speedometer pinion sleeve, gearshift control rods and hand brake cable. Remove transmission-to-clutch housing bolts and pull transmission straight back until input shaft clears clutch disc and release levers before lowering transmission out of truck. Do not disengage clutch or otherwise move clutch or clutch disc unless it is to be removed for service.

FOUR SPEED OVERDRIVE

1. Remove gear shift components, then drain fluid from transmission.
2. Disconnect propeller shaft at rear universal joint. Mark parts for reinstallation in same position, then carefully pull shaft yoke out of transmission housing.
3. Disconnect speedometer cable and back-up light switch.
4. Install engine lifting fixture and raise engine slightly.
5. Using a suitable jack, support transmission, then remove center crossmember.

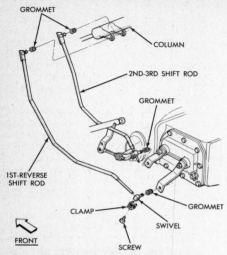

Fig. 1 Disassembled view of gearshift linkage. Except B-Series & Voyager w/A-230 transmission

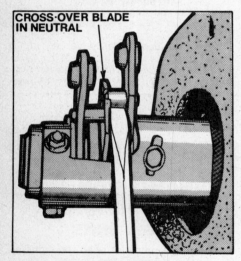

Fig. 2 Gearshift lever adjustments. Three speed transmission

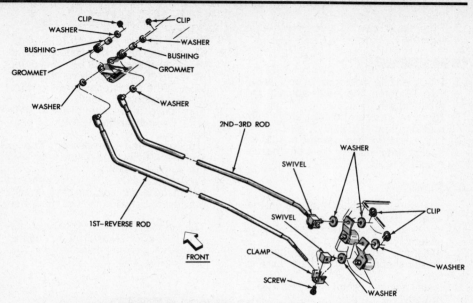

Fig. 3 Disassembled view of column shift linkage. B-Series & Voyager w/A-230 transmission

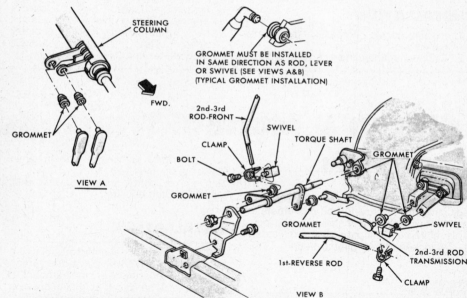

Fig. 4 Disassembled view of column shift linkage. B-Series & Voyager w/A-390 transmission

6. Remove transmission to clutch housing bolts, then slide transmission rearward until drive pinion shaft clears clutch disc.
7. Lower transmission and remove from vehicle.

NEW PROCESS 4-SPEED

1. Remove transfer case, if equipped, as described under "Transfer Case, Replace."
2. Disconnect back-up light switch.
3. Install engine support fixture, then, using a suitable jack, support transmission and remove transmission crossmember.
4. Remove transmission to clutch housing attaching bolts.
5. Slide transmission rearward until drive pinion shaft clears clutch disc, then

lower transmission and remove from vehicle.

GEARSHIFT
ADJUST

THREE SPEED

EXCEPT A-390 UNITS

1979 Exc. "B" Series & Voyager

1. Disconnect shift rod swivels from transmission levers, then place transmission levers in the neutral position, **Fig. 1.**
2. Move shift lever to align locating slots in column shift housing and bearing

housing. Then install a screwdriver or similar tool between cross-over blade and 2–3 shift lever, engaging both lever pins with cross-over blade, **Fig. 2.**
3. Place transmission 1st reverse shift lever in reverse position and adjust 1st reverse rod swivel to enter transmission shift lever. Tighten swivel bolt.
4. Remove gearshift housing locating tool and place column lever in neutral position.
5. Adjust 2-3 rod swivel to enter transmission shift lever and tighten swivel bolt.
6. Remove screwdriver or tool from crossover and check adjustment.

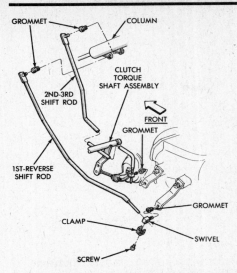

Fig. 5 Disassembled view of gearshift linkage. Except B-Series & Voyager w/A-390 transmission

1979 "B" Series & Voyager

Adjust length of 2–3 shift rod to properly position shift lever on steering column, then proceed as follows:

1. Install both shift rods and secure at each lever with a clip, then loosen swivel clamp bolts, **Fig. 3.**
2. Place transmission 2–3 shift lever in 3rd position and place steering column shift lever into a position approximately five degrees above the horizontal position, then tighten swivel clamp bolt.
3. Shift transmission into neutral and install a screwdriver or other suitable tool between cross-over blade and 2–3 lever at steering column, engaging both lever pins and cross-over blade, **Fig. 2.**
4. Place transmission 1st-reverse lever in neutral position and tighten swivel clamp bolt.
5. Remove screwdriver or tool from cross-over and check adjustment.

A-390 UNITS

1. Loosen both shift rod swivels, **Figs. 4 and 5.**
2. Place transmission shift levers in neutral (middle detent) position.
3. Move shift lever to align locating slots in bottom of steering column shift housing and bearing housing. Install a suitable tool into slot.
4. Place a screwdriver or other suitable tool between cross-over blade and 2–3 lever at steering column so both lever pins are engaged by the cross-over blade, **Fig. 2.**
5. Tighten both shift rod swivel bolts.
6. Remove gearshift housing locating tool.
7. Remove tool from cross-over blade at steering column.
8. Shift through gears to check adjustment and cross-over smoothness.
9. Check for proper operation of steering column lock in reverse. With proper adjustment, the ignition should lock in the reverse position only.

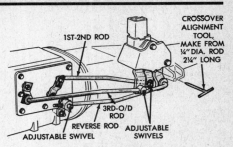

Fig. 6 Gearshift linkage adjustment. Four-speed overdrive

FOUR SPEED OVERDRIVE

1. Install gear shift lever aligning tool, **Fig. 6,** to hold levers in neutral cross-over position.
2. With all rods removed from transmission shift levers, place levers in neutral detent position.
3. Adjust threaded shift rod levers so they enter transmission levers freely without any rearward or forward movement.

NOTE: Start with 1–2 shift rod. It may be necessary to pull clip at shifter end to rotate this rod.

4. Install washers and clips, then remove aligning tool and check linkage operation.

Transfer Case Section

TRANSFER CASE
REPLACE

1. Remove skid plate, if equipped, and drain transfer case.
2. Disconnect speedometer cable and indicator switch electrical connector, then the parking brake cable guide from pivot, if necessary.
3. Disconnect input and output shafts then support and position shafts aside.

NOTE: Some 1979–81 models equipped with a single piece propeller shaft were assembled with the propeller shaft slip yoke positioned toward the rear axle assembly. When servicing these vehicles, the slip yoke should be positioned as assembled in production whether at the rear axle or at the transfer case.

4. Disconnect shift rods and de-clutch rod from transfer case.
5. Support transfer case with a suitable jack.
6. If transfer case is supported by crossmember, or a support bracket, remove crossmember or the support bracket bolts, then lower transfer case from vehicle.
7. If transfer case is secured to an adapter, remove transfer case to adapter mounting bolts. Slide transfer case rearward to disengage front input spline and lower transfer case from vehicle.
8. Reverse procedure to install.

TRANSFER CASE LINKAGE
ADJUST

NEW PROCESS 203

1. Loosen lock screws in both swivel rod clamps at shifter assembly, **Fig. 1.**
2. Place selector lever in Neutral position and insert suitable alignment rod through alignment holes in shifting housing, **Fig. 2.**
3. Place range shift lever on transfer case into Neutral position, then place lockout shift lever in Unlock position.
4. Tighten rod swivel lock screws, then remove alignment rod from shifter housing.

NEW PROCESS 205

NOTE: On 1980–83 models, there is no provision for transfer case linkage adjustment.

Refer to **Fig. 3** for adjustment procedure.

NEW PROCESS 208

NOTE: On 1980–83 models, there is no provision for transfer case linkage adjustment.

Refer to **Figs. 4 and 5** for adjustment procedure.

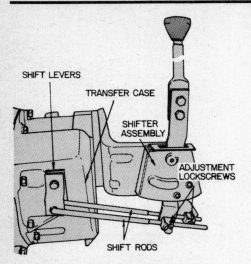

Fig. 1   Transfer case shifter assembly and linkage. NP-203

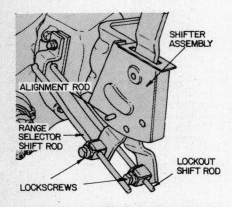

Fig. 2   Positioning alignment rod

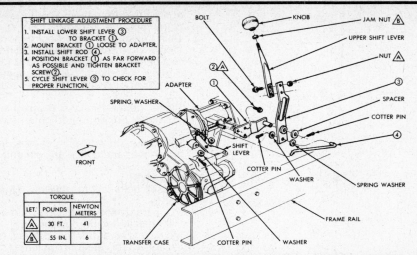

SHIFT LINKAGE ADJUSTMENT PROCEDURE
1. INSTALL LOWER SHIFT LEVER ③ TO BRACKET ①.
2. MOUNT BRACKET ① LOOSE TO ADAPTER.
3. INSTALL SHIFT ROD ④.
4. POSITION BRACKET ① AS FAR FORWARD AS POSSIBLE AND TIGHTEN BRACKET SCREW ②.
5. CYCLE SHIFT LEVER ③ TO CHECK FOR PROPER FUNCTION.

TORQUE		
LET.	POUNDS	NEWTON METERS
A	30 FT.	41
B	55 IN.	6

Fig. 3   Transfer case shifter assembly and linkage adjustment. 1984–85 NP-205

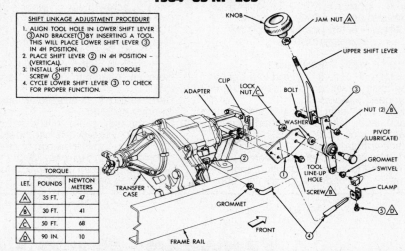

SHIFT LINKAGE ADJUSTMENT PROCEDURE
1. ALIGN TOOL HOLE IN LOWER SHIFT LEVER ③ AND BRACKET ① BY INSERTING A TOOL. THIS WILL PLACE LOWER SHIFT LEVER ③ IN 4H POSITION.
2. PLACE SHIFT LEVER ② IN 4H POSITION – (VERTICAL).
3. INSTALL SHIFT ROD ④ AND TORQUE SCREW ⑤
4. CYCLE LOWER SHIFT LEVER ③ TO CHECK FOR PROPER FUNCTION.

TORQUE		
LET.	POUNDS	NEWTON METERS
A	35 FT.	47
B	30 FT.	41
C	50 FT.	68
D	90 IN.	10

Fig. 4   Transfer case shifter assembly and linkage adjustment. 1984 NP-208

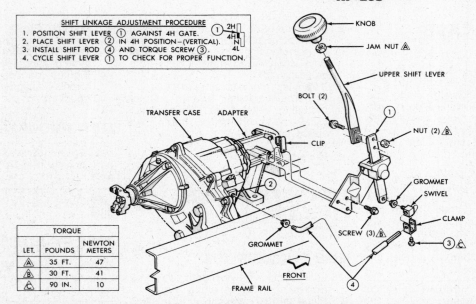

SHIFT LINKAGE ADJUSTMENT PROCEDURE
1. POSITION SHIFT LEVER ① AGAINST 4H GATE.
2. PLACE SHIFT LEVER ② IN 4H POSITION – (VERTICAL).
3. INSTALL SHIFT ROD ④ AND TORQUE SCREW ③.
4. CYCLE SHIFT LEVER ① TO CHECK FOR PROPER FUNCTION.

TORQUE		
LET.	POUNDS	NEWTON METERS
A	35 FT.	47
B	30 FT.	41
C	90 IN.	10

Fig. 5   Transfer case shifter assembly & linkage adjustment. 1985 NP-208

Rear Axles, Suspension & Brakes Section

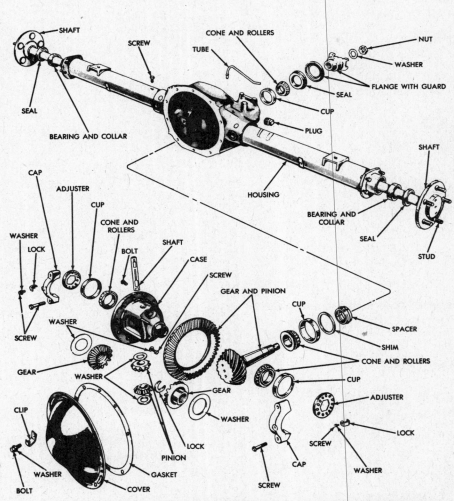

Fig. 1 8⅜" & 9¼" integral carrier rear axle assembly. The 8⅜ inch unit is equipped with a vent tube mounted on the carrier housing while the 9¼ inch unit has a vent located on the left leg of the housing

DESCRIPTION

These axle assemblies, **Figs. 1 through 3,** are of the integral carrier housing hypoid gear type with the centerline of the drive pinion mounted below the centerline of the ring gear. The drive pinion is supported by two preloaded taper roller bearings and the front and rear pinion bearing cones are pressed on the pinion stem. The front and rear pinion bearing cups are pressed against a shoulder that is recessed within the carrier casting. Drive pinion depth of mesh adjustment is controlled by installing metal shims between the rear pinion bearing cup and carrier casting.

REAR AXLE
REPLACE

1. Raise and support vehicle, then block brake pedal in the up position using a suitable block of wood.
2. Remove rear wheels.
3. Disconnect hydraulic brake lines at wheel cylinder. Cap fittings to prevent loss of brake fluid.
4. Disconnect parking brake cables, if necessary.
5. Scribe alignment marks on the propeller shaft universal joint and pinion flange to ensure correct position dur-

ing installation. Disconnect propeller shaft at differential pinion flange and secure to one side.
6. Remove shock absorbers from spring plate studs, then the rear spring U-bolts.
7. Remove axle assembly from vehicle.
8. Reverse procedure to install.

AXLE SHAFTS & BEARINGS
REPLACE

8⅜ & 9¼ INCH

1. Raise and support vehicle and remove brake drum.
2. Clean area around housing cover, then loosen housing cover and allow lubricant to drain. Remove cover.
3. Turn differential case until pinion shaft lock screw is accessible and remove lock screw and pinion shaft, **Fig. 4.**
4. Push axle shaft inward and remove C-washer locks from axle shaft, **Fig. 5,** then pull axle shaft from housing being careful not to damage axle shaft bearing.

NOTE: Inspect axle shaft bearing surfaces for signs of spalling or pitting. If any of these conditions exist, both shaft and bearing should be replaced. Normal bearing contact on shaft should be a dull gray and may appear lightly dented.

5. Remove axle shaft bearing and seal from axle housing using tools C-4167 and C-637 on all models except 1984—85 9¼ inch HD axle, **Fig. 6,** or tool C-4828 on 1984—85 9¼ inch HD axle, **Fig. 7.** If bearing shows no sign of excessive wear or damage, it can be reused along with a new seal. Never reuse an axle shaft seal.

NOTE: Remove any burrs that may be present in housing bearing shoulder, as bearing could become cocked during installation.

6. Using suitable tools, install bearing, making sure it does not become cocked. Drive bearing until it bottoms against shoulder.

NOTE: Do not use seal to position or bottom bearing as this will damage seal.

7. Using tool C-4130 or equivalent, **Fig. 8,** install axle shaft bearing seal until outer flange of tool bottoms against housing flange face. This will position seal to the proper depth.
8. Reverse disassembly procedure to reassemble axle.

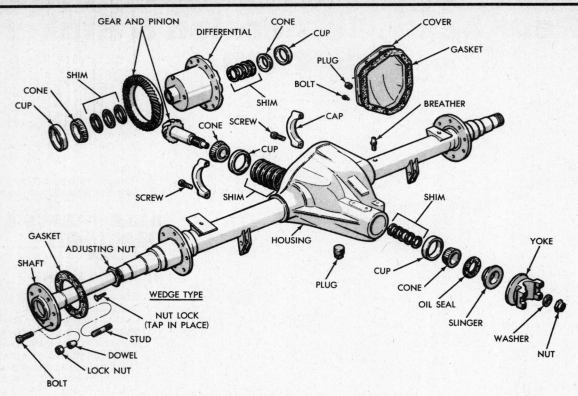

Fig. 2   Spicer 60 (9¾ inch) rear axle assembly

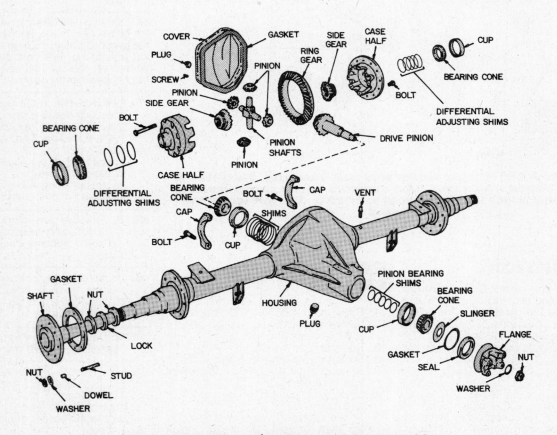

Fig. 3   Spicer 70 (10½ inch) rear axle assembly

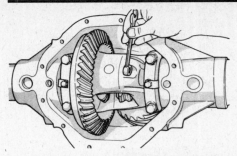

Fig. 4   Removing differential pinion shaft lock pin

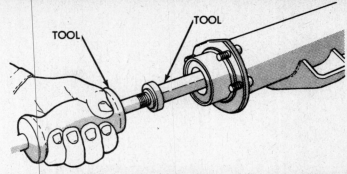

Fig. 6   Removing axle shaft bearing and seal. Exc. 9¼ inch HD axle

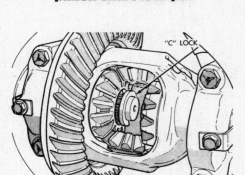

Fig. 5   Removing "C" lock washers

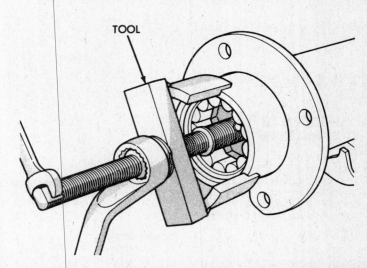

Fig. 7   Removing axle shaft & bearing seal. 1984—85 9¼ inch HD axle

AXLE SHAFT
REPLACE

SPICER TYPE

1. Remove axle shaft flange nuts and lockwashers.
2. Remove tapered dowels and axle shaft assembly by tapping axle shaft sharply in center of flange with a suitable hammer.
3. Reverse procedure to install.

SERVICE BRAKE
ADJUST

1979—85 SELF ADJUSTING BRAKES

These brakes have self-adjusting shoe mechanisms that assure correct lining-to-drum clearances at all times. The automatic adjusters operate only when the brakes are applied as the car is moving rearward.

Although the brakes are self-adjusting, an initial adjustment is necessary when the brake shoes have been relined or replaced, or when the length of the star wheel adjuster has been changed during some other service operation.

Frequent usage of an automatic transmission forward range to halt reverse vehicle motion may prevent the automatic adjusters from functioning, thereby inducing low pedal heights. Should low pedal heights be encountered, it is recommended that numerous forward and reverse stops be made until satisfactory pedal height is obtained.

NOTE: If a low pedal height condition cannot be corrected by making numerous reverse stops (provided the hydraulic system is free of air) it indicates that the self-adjusting mechanism is not functioning. Therefore, it will be necessary to remove the drum, clean, free up and lubricate the adjusting mechanism. Then adjust the brakes, being sure the parking brake is fully released.

Adjustment

1. Raise vehicle so wheels are free to turn, then remove rear adjusting hole cover.
2. Back off parking brake cable adjustment so there is slack in the cable. Ensure parking brake lever is fully released.
3. On models equipped with release type adjuster, **Fig. 9**, insert adjusting tool into star wheel of adjusting screw. Move tool handle downward until slight drag is felt when wheel is rotated.
4. On models equipped with application type adjuster, **Fig. 10**, insert adjusting tool into star wheel of adjusting screw. Move tool handle upward until slight drag is felt when wheel is rotated.

5. On all models, insert a suitable screwdriver into brake adjusting hole and push adjusting lever out of engagement with star wheel.

NOTE: Care should be taken not to bend adjusting lever.

6. Back off star wheel 10 to 12 notches until wheel rotates freely with no drag.
7. Install adjusting hole cover. Adjust brakes on remaining wheels in the same manner.

PARKING BRAKE
ADJUST

1. Release parking brake lever and loosen cable adjusting nut to be sure cable is slack.
2. With rear wheel brakes properly adjusted tighten cable adjusting nut until a slight drag is felt when the rear wheels are rotated. Then loosen the cable adjusting nut until both rear wheels can be rotated freely.
3. To complete the operation, back off an additional two turns of the cable adjusting nut.
4. Apply and release parking brake several times to be sure rear wheels are

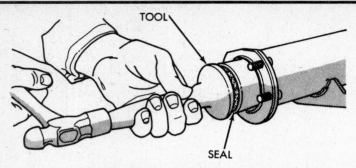

Fig. 8   Installing axle shaft oil seal

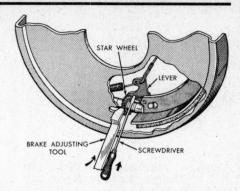

Fig. 9   Release type brake adjuster

not dragging when cable is in released position.

MASTER CYLINDER
REPLACE

EXC. 1979—85 WITH ALUMINUM MASTER CYLINDER

1. Disconnect brake lines from master cylinder. Install plugs in outlets to prevent fluid leakage.
2. Remove nuts that attach master cylinder to cowl panel or power brake unit, if equipped.
3. Disconnect pedal push rod (manual brakes) from brake pedal.
4. Slide master cylinder straight out from cowl panel and/or power brake unit.
5. Reverse procedure to install.

1979—85 WITH ALUMINUM MASTER CYLINDER

Manual Brakes
1. Disconnect brake lines from master cylinder. Install plugs in outlets to prevent fluid leakage.
2. From under instrument panel, disconnect stop lamp switch mounting bracket and position aside.
3. Grasp brake pedal and pull backward to disengage push rod from master cylinder piston.

NOTE: This will require a pull of about 50 lbs. Also, the retention grommet will be destroyed.

4. Remove master cylinder to cowl retaining nuts and remove master cylinder by pulling straight out.

CAUTION: Make sure to remove all traces of old grommet from push rod groove and master cylinder piston.

5. Reverse procedure to install. Install new grommet on push rod, then lubricate grommet with water and align push rod with master cylinder piston. Using brake pedal, apply pressure to fully seat push rod into piston.

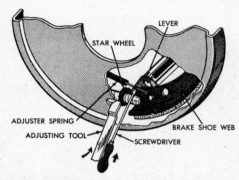

Fig. 10   Application type brake adjuster

Power Brakes
1. Disconnect primary and secondary brake tubes from master cylinder, then cap lines and master cylinder fitting.
2. Remove nuts attaching master cylinder to power brake unit, then slide master cylinder from power brake unit.
3. Reverse procedure to install.

POWER BOOSTER
REPLACE

EXC. HYDRO-BOOST

Transverse Mount
1. Disconnect vacuum hose from power booster.
2. Remove master cylinder to booster attaching nuts, then the master cylinder.
3. Remove booster push rod to pivot attaching bolts.
4. Remove power booster attaching nuts, then the power booster assembly.
5. Reverse procedure to install.

Inline Mount
1. Disconnect vacuum hose from check valve.
2. Remove master cylinder to booster attaching nuts.
3. Working from under instrument panel, position a suitable screwdriver between center tang on retainer clip and pin in brake pedal. Rotate screwdriver

enough to allow retainer clip center tang to pass over end of brake pedal pin, then pull retainer clip from pin.
4. Remove power booster attaching nuts, then slide booster away from dash panel.
5. Reverse procedure to install.

HYDRO-BOOST

1. Pump brake pedal several times to ensure that all pressure is discharged from the accumulator prior to disconnecting hoses from booster.
2. Remove master cylinder attaching nuts and position master cylinder aside.
3. Disconnect and plug all fluid lines from booster ports, then disconnect brake pedal spring.
4. Remove push rod to pedal attaching bolt.
5. Remove booster attaching nuts, then the booster.
6. Reverse procedure to install.

SHOCK ABSORBER
REPLACE

MOTOR HOME

1. Remove shock absorber to frame attaching bolts.
2. Remove shock absorber lower bracket attaching nut, rubber bushing and washers.
3. Remove shock absorber and bracket assembly from vehicle, then the bracket from the shock.
4. Reverse procedure to install.

RAMCHARGER, TRAIL DUSTER & CONVENTIONAL CAB

1. Remove two shock absorber bracket to frame attaching bolts.
2. On models equipped with 4-wheel drive, remove lower bracket attaching bolt, loosen upper attaching bolt, then rotate bracket until shock absorber clears upper bolt and remove.
3. On all models, remove shock absorb-

er lower bracket attaching nut, rubber bushings and washers.

4. Remove shock absorber and bracket assembly from vehicle, then the bracket from the shock.
5. Reverse procedure to install.

VANS, WAGONS & FRONT SECTIONS

1. Remove upper shock absorber attaching nut, bolt and washers.
2. Remove lower attaching nut at bushing end.
3. Swing shock absorber down, pivoting around lower bolt.
4. Remove shock absorber lower attaching bolt and washers, then the shock absorber from vehicle.
5. Reverse procedure to install.

LEAF SPRING
REPLACE

RAMCHARGER, TRAIL DUSTER, CONVENTIONAL CAB & MOTOR HOME

1. Raise vehicle until weight is removed from springs and wheels are just touching ground, then support vehicle using suitable safety stands.
2. Remove nuts, lock washers and U-bolts attaching spring to axle.
3. Remove spring shackle attaching bolts, shackle and spring front bolt, then remove spring.
4. Reverse procedure to install.

VANS, WAGONS & FRONT SECTIONS

1. Raise and support vehicle.

2. Remove U-bolt attaching nuts, U-bolts and plate.
3. Remove front pivot attaching bolt, then the rear shackle attaching nuts.
4. Remove outer shackle and bolt from hanger, then the spring. Some vehicles are equipped with one piece shackles.
5. Reverse procedure to install.

SWAY BAR
REPLACE

1. Remove link rod attaching nut from each end of sway bar.
2. Remove retainers and rubber bushings from sway bar link rods.
3. Remove sway bar support bracket attaching bolts, then the sway bar.
4. Reverse procedure to install.

Front Suspension & Steering Section

NOTE: Refer to "Front Wheel Drive Section" for 4 × 4 front axle service procedures not covered in this section.

DESCRIPTION
INDEPENDENT FRONT SUSPENSION

These vehicles are equipped with a coil spring front suspension system, **Figs. 1 through 4.** The upper control arms are mounted on longitudinal rails and the lower control arms are mounted on a removable crossmember. Both control arms have replaceable bushings on the inner ends and ball joints on the outer ends. The upper control arms also control caster and camber adjustments through eccentric pivot bolts at the inner ends or through slots in the upper control arm mounting bracket.

EXC. INDEPENDENT FRONT SUSPENSION

The front axle assembly, **Figs. 5 and 6,** may be divided into three assemblies; axle "I" beam, steering knuckles and steering linkage assemblies. It is unnecessary to remove the complete front axle assembly unless the "I" beam is to be replaced.

WHEEL ALIGNMENT
CASTER & CAMBER, ADJUST

Independent Front Suspension

NOTE: Front suspension height must be checked and corrected as necessary prior to checking wheel alignment.

1. Remove all foreign material from exposed threads of cam adjusting bolt nuts or pivot bar adjusting bolt nuts.

2. Record initial camber and caster readings before loosening cam bolt nuts or pivot bar bolt nuts, **Figs. 7 and 8.**
3. On vehicles using cam bolts, the camber and caster is adjusted by loosening the cam bolt nuts and turning the cam bolts as necessary until the desired setting is obtained. On vehicles using pivot bars, tool C-4581 or equivalent is required to adjust caster and camber. When performing adjustments, the camber settings should be held as close as possible to the "desired" setting, and the caster setting should be held as nearly equal as possible on both wheels.

Exc. Independent Front Suspension

NOTE: No adjustment is provided for camber. If camber is not within specifications, axle or steering knuckle is bent and should be replaced.

Caster may be adjusted by inserting a wedge between the spring and axle, **Fig. 9.** To increase caster insert wedge so that the thick part faces rear of vehicle. To decrease caster insert wedge so that the thick end is toward front of vehicle.

TOE-IN, ADJUST

With the front wheels in straight ahead position, loosen the clamps at each end of both adjusting tubes. Adjust toe-in by turning the tie rod sleeve which will "center" the steering wheel spokes. If the steering wheel was centered, make the toe-in adjustment by turning both sleeves an equal amount. Position sleeve clamps so ends do not align in the sleeve slot.

WHEEL BEARINGS
ADJUST

EXC. MOTOR HOME & 4-WHEEL DRIVE

1. Torque adjusting nut to 360–480 inch lbs. for Vans, Wagons and Front Sections or 90 inch lbs. for Ramcharger, Trail Duster and Conventional Cabs while rotating wheel.
2. Stop wheel from rotating, then back off adjusting nut to completely release bearing preload.
3. Tighten adjusting nut finger tight, then install lock nut and cotter key. End play should be .0001–.003 inch.
4. Clean grease cap, coat inside with suitable wheel bearing grease and install cap. Do not fill cap with grease.

MOTOR HOME

1. Rotate wheel and tighten adjusting nut until a slight binding is felt.
2. Back off adjusting nut so that the nearest slot indexes with the cotter pin hole in the spindle.

NOTE: Never back off adjusting nut less than half the distance from one slot to the next slot.

3. Install cotter pin to lock nut and ensure that wheel rotates freely.

4-WHEEL DRIVE

Spicer 44FBJ & 44-8FD Axle

1. Raise and support vehicle.
2. Remove locking hub assembly, then the wheel bearing locking nut and washer.

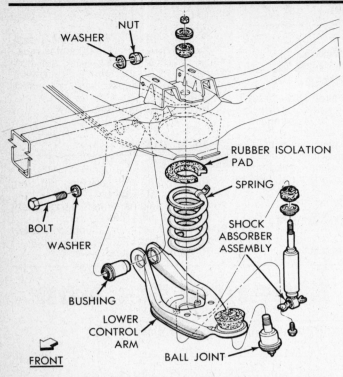

Fig. 1 **Lower control arm and coil spring. 1979–85 Vans, Wagons & Front Sections**

Fig. 2 **Upper control arm. 1979–85 Vans, Wagons & Front Sections**

3. Torque adjusting nut to 50 ft. lbs., using tool No. C-4170 or equivalent, to seat the bearing.
4. Loosen adjusting nut and retorque to 30–40 ft. lbs. while rotating hub, then back off adjusting nut 135°–150°.
5. Install retaining washer and bearing lock nut. Torque lock nut to 50 ft. lbs. End play should be .001–.010 inch.

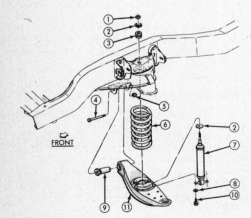

Fig. 3 **Lower control arm and coil spring. Ramcharger, Trail Duster & Conventional Cab except four wheel drive.**

1—Nut
2—Retainer
3—Bushing
4—Bolt
5—Nut
6—Coil Spring
7—Shock Absorber
8—Washer
9—Bushing Assembly
10—Capscrew
11—Lower Control Arm

Spicer 60 Axle

1. Raise and support vehicle.
2. Remove hub cap, then the snap ring using suitable pliers.
3. Remove flange nuts and lock washers, then the drive flange or locking hub if equipped.
4. Straighten tang on lock ring, then using tool No. DD-1241-JD or equivalent, remove outer lock nut and lock ring.
5. Torque lock nut to 50 ft. lbs. to seat the bearing, loosen lock nut and retorque to 30–40 ft. lbs. Back off lock nut 135°–150°.
6. Install lock ring and outer lock nut. Torque lock nut to 65 ft. lbs.
7. Bend tangs of long ring over both lock nuts. End play should be .001–.010 inch.

BALL JOINTS
REPLACE

EXC. 4-WHEEL DRIVE

Upper Ball Joint

1. Place ignition switch in the "Off" position.
2. Using a suitable jack raise front of vehicle and position a jack stand under lower control arm as close to wheel and tire assembly as possible.
3. Remove wheel and tire assembly.
4. Remove cotter pin and nut from upper ball joint stud. Position tool No. C3564-A or equivalent over lower ball joint stud, allowing tool to rest on knuckle arm, then set tool securely against upper ball joint stud.
5. Tighten tool to apply pressure against upper ball joint stud, then strike knuckle with hammer to loosen stud.
6. Remove tool, then detach upper ball joint from knuckle.

NOTE: Support knuckle and brake assembly to prevent damage to lower ball joint and brake hoses.

7. Remove upper ball joint from upper control arm, using tool No. C3561.
8. Reverse procedure to install. Thread

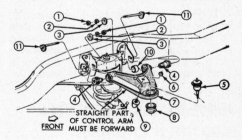

1—Nut
2—Lockwasher
3—Cam
4—Bushing Assembly
5—Ball Joint
6—Lock Nut
7—Upper Control Arm
8—Upper Ball Joint
9—Bumper Assembly
10—Sleeve
11—Cam and Bolt Assembly

Fig. 4 **Upper control arm. Ramcharger, Trail Duster & Conventional Cab except four wheel drive**

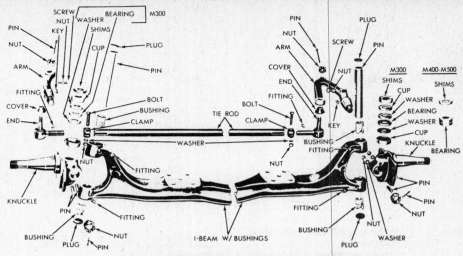

Fig. 5   Elliot type front axle assembly

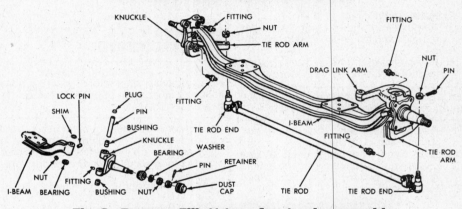

Fig. 6   Reverse Elliott type front axle assembly

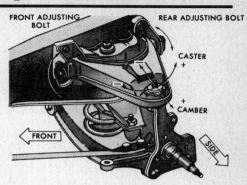

Fig. 7   Alignment adjustment locations & directions. Cam bolt type

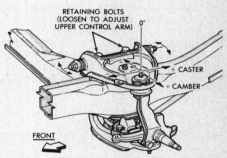

Fig. 8   Alignment adjustment locations & directions. Pivot bolt type

upper ball joint into control arm as far as possible by hand. Torque upper ball joint into control arm to 125 ft. lbs. Install ball joint into steering knuckle, then torque attaching bolts to 135 ft. lbs.

NOTE: Ball joint seals should be replaced whenever they have been removed.

Lower Ball Joint
1. Remove coil spring, refer to "Coil Spring, Replace" procedure.
2. Remove ball joint seal, then press ball joint out of lower control arm using tool No. C-4212 or equivalent.
3. Reverse procedure to install.

SHOCK ABSORBER
REPLACE
1. Raise and support vehicle.
2. Turn wheel as needed to gain access to upper shock absorber mount, then remove upper nut and retainer.
3. Remove two lower attaching bolts, then the shock.
4. Reverse procedure to install.

COIL SPRING
REPLACE

VANS, WAGONS & FRONT SECTIONS
1. Block brake pedal in up position.
2. Raise and support vehicle.
3. Remove front wheels, then the caliper retainer and anti-rattle spring assemblies.
4. Remove caliper from disc and position caliper aside, then remove inboard shoe.

NOTE: Do not allow caliper to hang or be supported by hydraulic brake hose.

5. Remove shock absorber, upper bushing and sleeve, then the strut.
6. Install spring compressor tool No. DD-1278 finger tight, then back off one half turn.
7. Remove cotter keys and ball joint nuts.
8. Install ball joint breaker tool No. C-3564-A or equivalent over lower ball joint stud, then set tool securely against upper ball joint stud.

9. Tighten tool to apply pressure against upper ball joint stud, then strike knuckle with hammer to loosen stud.
10. Remove tool, then slowly loosen coil spring compressor until all tension is relieved from spring.
11. Remove spring compressor and spring.
12. Reverse procedure to install, noting the following:
    a. Torque ball joint nuts to 135 ft. lbs. for upper and lower $11/16-16$ inch nuts or 175 ft. lbs. for $3/4-16$ inch nuts.
    b. Inboard shoe anti-rattle spring should be installed on top of retainer spring plate. Torque retaining clips to 180 inch lbs.

RAMCHARGER, TRAIL DUSTER & CONVENTIONAL CABS
1. Raise and support vehicle.
2. Remove front wheels, then the caliper retainer.
3. Remove caliper from disc and position caliper aside, then remove inboard shoe.

NOTE: Do not allow caliper to hang or be supported by hydraulic brake hose.

4. On 1979–84 models, proceed as follows:
    a. Remove grease cap, cotter key, lock nut, adjusting nut, washer and

b. Slide rotor from steering knuckle. Use caution not to damage steering knuckle thread, bearing or oil seal when removing rotor.

c. Remove splash shield attaching screws, then the splash shield, if equipped.

5. On all models, remove shock absorber, then disconnect sway bar at link, if equipped.

6. Remove spring pin from strut, then loosen strut attaching nut.

7. Install spring compressor tool No. DD-1278 finger tight, then back off half turn.

8. Remove cotter keys and ball joint nuts.

9. Install ball joint breaker tool No. C-3564-A or equivalent over lower ball joint stud, then set tool securely against upper ball joint stud.

10. Tighten tool to apply pressure against upper ball joint stud, then strike knuckle with hammer to loosen stud.

11. Remove tool, then slowly loosen coil spring compressor until all tension is relieved from spring.

12. Remove spring compressor and spring.

13. Reverse procedure to install noting the following:
    a. Torque ball joint nuts to 135 ft. lbs.
    b. Torque sway bar attaching bolt to 100 inch. lbs.

LEAF SPRING
REPLACE

MOTOR HOME & 4-WHEEL DRIVE MODELS

1. Raise vehicle until weight is removed from springs, then support spring using suitable jack.
2. Remove nuts, lock washers, U-bolts and U-bolt seat securing spring to axle.
3. Remove spring shackle attaching bolts, shackles and spring front eye bolt.
4. Remove spring from vehicle.
5. Reverse procedure to install.

SWAY BAR
REPLACE

1. Disconnect bar from right and left end links.
2. Disconnect attaching bolts from frame mounting brackets.
3. Remove bar assembly from vehicle.
4. Reverse procedure to install.

STEERING KNUCKLE
REPLACE

EXC. MOTOR HOME & 4-WHEEL DRIVE

1. Block brake pedal in up position.

Fig. 9   Caster angle adjustment. Exc. independent front suspension

2. Raise and support vehicle.
3. Remove front wheels, then the caliper retainer and anti-rattle spring assembly.
4. Remove caliper from disc and position disc aside, then remove inboard shoe.

NOTE: Do not allow caliper to hang or be supported by hydraulic brake hose.

5. Remove hub cap, cotter key, nut, washer and outer bearing.
6. Slide disc from steering knuckle. Use caution not to damage steering knuckle thread, bearing or oil seal when removing disc.
7. Position suitable jack under outer end of lower control arm, then disconnect tie rod at steering knuckle arm using tool No. C-3894-A or equivalent.
8. Separate steering knuckle and steering knuckle arm from ball joints.
9. Remove splash shield attaching bolts, if equipped, then the brake adapter attaching bolts, steering knuckle arm and steering knuckle together.
10. Reverse procedure to install noting the following:
    a. Torque steering knuckle arm to steering knuckle attaching bolts to 215 ft. lbs. for 5/8—19 bolts or 225 ft. lbs. for 3/4—16 inch bolts.
    b. Torque ball joint nuts to 135 ft. lbs. for upper and lower 11/16—16 inch nuts or 175 ft. lbs. for 3/4—16 inch nuts.
    c. Torque tie rod end attaching nut to 45 ft. lbs. for 1/2—20 nuts, 55 ft. lbs. for 9/16—18 nuts or 75 ft. lbs. for 5/8—18 nuts.
    d. Torque anti-rattle spring fasteners to 180 inch lbs.

MOTOR HOME

1. Raise and support vehicle.
2. Remove wheel, rotor and hub.
3. Remove disc brake adapter attaching bolts, then the adapter from steering knuckle.
4. Remove steering knuckle arm from steering knuckle, then the pivot pin

lock.

5. Remove upper pivot pin oil seal plug, then drive pivot pin down and out of assembly using suitable drift punch and hammer.

6. Remove steering knuckle and pivot pin thrust washer.

7. Reverse procedure to install noting the following:
    a. Torque steering knuckle arm attaching nut to 200 ft. lbs.
    b. Torque disc brake adapter attaching bolts to: 175—245 ft. lbs. on all M-600 models; 85—135 ft. lbs. on 1979—80 M-300 and all M-400 and M-500 models; 140—180 ft. lbs. for lower front bolts and 90—140 ft. lbs. for upper front bolts.

MANUAL STEERING GEAR
REPLACE

1979—85 VANS, WAGONS & FRONT SECTIONS

NOTE: It is recommended that the steering column be completely detached from floor and instrument panel before steering gear is removed.

1. Disconnect battery ground cable, then remove steering column.
2. Remove steering arm attaching nut and lock washer, located under vehicle.
3. Remove steering arm using tool No. C-4150.
4. Remove gear to frame attaching bolts or nuts, then the gear from vehicle.
5. Reverse procedure to install.

1979—85 RAMCHARGER, TRAIL DUSTER & CONVENTIONAL CAB

1. Disconnect battery ground cable.
2. Remove two wormshaft coupling attaching bolts.
3. Remove steering arm from steering gear using tool No. C-4150.
4. Remove steering gear to frame attaching bolts, then the gear from vehicle.
5. Reverse procedure to install.

POWER STEERING GEAR
REPLACE

1979—85 VANS, WAGONS & FRONT SECTIONS

NOTE: It is recommended that the steering column be completely detached from floor and instrument panel before steering gear is removed.

1. Disconnect battery ground cable, then

remove steering column.

2. Disconnect power steering hoses at gear. Cap all hoses and fluid ports to prevent oil leakage.
3. Remove steering arm attaching nut and lock washer, located under vehicle.
4. Remove steering arm using tool No. C-4150.
5. Remove three gear to frame attaching bolts or nuts, then the gear from vehicle.
6. Reverse procedure to install.

1979—85 EXC. VANS, WAGONS & FRONT SECTIONS

1. Center steering gear.

2. Remove steering gear arm to shaft attaching bolt, then the steering gear arm using suitable tool.
3. Disconnect power steering hoses at gear. Cap all hoses and fluid ports to prevent oil leakage.
4. Disconnect shaft coupling from steering gear.
5. Remove steering gear to frame attaching bolts, then the gear from vehicle.

NOTE: On some Motor Homes, body location may require steering gear and bracket be removed as an assembly. If gear and bracket is removed as an assembly, support assembly with suitable transmission jack and remove frame to bracket attaching bolts.

POWER STEERING PUMP
REPLACE

1. Loosen pump locking and attaching bolts, then remove drive belt.
2. Disconnect both fluid hoses from pump.
3. Remove pump locking and attaching bolts, then remove pump and bracket assembly.
4. Reverse procedure to install.

Front Wheel Drive Section

SPICER 44FBJ & 44-8FD, FRONT AXLE

AXLE ASSEMBLY, REPLACE

1. Secure brake pedal in the up position, then raise vehicle.
2. Disconnect front driveshaft at drive pinion yoke.
3. Disconnect drag link at steering knuckle arm (left side only).
4. Disconnect and plug brake line at frame crossmember.
5. Disconnect shock absorbers at lower mounts then disconnect sway bar link assembly, if equipped, from spring plates.
6. Remove nuts and washers from "U" bolt spring clips, then remove axle from vehicle.

7. Reverse procedure to install axle assembly. Lubricate all fittings, free brake pedal and bleed brakes.
8. Lower vehicle and check front wheel alignment.

SERVICING ROTOR, HUB OR BEARINGS

MODELS W/FULL TIME 4 WD

Removal & Inspection

1. Remove axle shaft cotter pin and loosen outer axle shaft nut.
2. Raise vehicle then remove wheel assembly.
3. After removing caliper retainer and anti-rattle spring assembly, slide caliper out and away from rotor. Hang caliper out of the way. Do not allow caliper to hang by hydraulic brake

hose. Remove inboard brake pad.
4. Remove outer axle shaft nut and washer. Secure a suitable puller to wheel studs and tighten main screw of tool to remove hub and rotor assembly, **Fig. 1.**
5. Remove puller from hub and rotor assembly.
6. Assemble Modified Bearing Press, Tool C-293-PA, Extension, Tool C-293-3, and Adapters, Tool No. C-293-49, to hub and rotor assembly and position in a vise. Pull outer bearing cone from hub and rotor and discard outer seal, **Fig. 2.**
7. Remove the six retainer bolts and retainer, **Fig. 3,** then remove brake caliper adapter from knuckle, if required.
8. Place a pry bar behind inner axle shaft yoke and push bearings out of knuck-

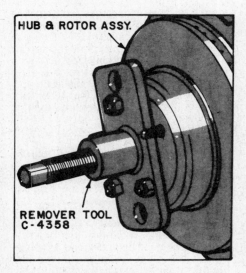

Fig. 1   Using puller to remove hub & rotor. 44 FBJ Units w/disc brakes. Models w/full time 4 WD

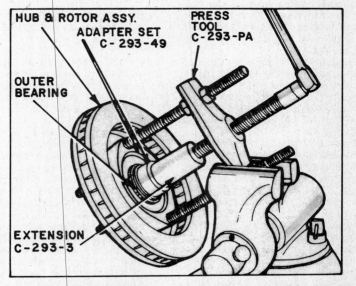

Fig. 2   Removing outer bearing cone. 44 FBJ Units w/disc brakes. Models w/full time 4 WD

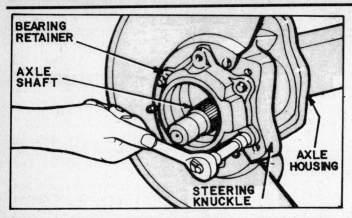

Fig. 3 Removing bearing retainer. 44 FBJ Units w/disc brakes. Models w/full time 4 WD

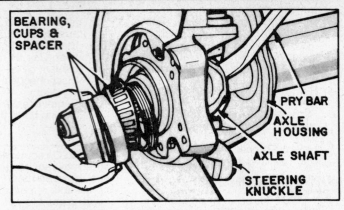

Fig. 4 Using pry bar to remove bearing from knuckle. 44 FBJ Units w/disc brakes. Models w/full time 4 WD

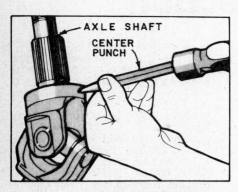

Fig. 5 Sizing axle shaft seal surface. 44 FBJ Units w/disc brakes. Models w/full time 4 WD

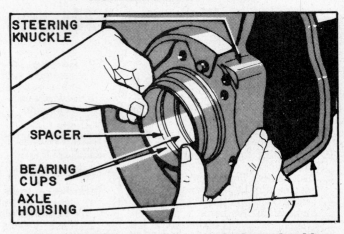

Fig. 6 Installing bearing cups before checking bearing clamp. 44 FBJ Units w/disc brakes. Models w/full time 4 WD

le, **Fig. 4.**

9. Remove and discard O-ring from knuckle, if equipped, then carefully remove axle shaft assembly.

Examine inner seal surface and knuckle bore for wear or damage and replace knuckle if required. If outer axle shaft seal surface is grooved, repair as follows:

a. Measure in from yoke shoulder of axle approximately 3/8 inch. Use a center punch and stake at 1/4 inch intervals around circumference of shaft. This will size shaft and ensure a tight fit of inner seal slinger, **Fig. 5.**

b. Proper bearing clamp should be checked by installing bearing cups and spacer into knuckle bore and bolting bearing retainer to knuckle, **Figs. 6 and 7.** If a .004 inch feeler gauge can not be inserted between knuckle and retainer at the six places midway between retainer mounting ears, the knuckle must be replaced, **Fig. 8.** The brake dust shield may have to be removed to complete this check. If knuckle is serviceable, remove retainer, bearing cups and spacer and install dust shield if removed.

Assembly & Installation

1. Apply RTV sealer or equivalent to seal surface of axle shaft.
2. Using driver, Tool No. C-4398-1, install seal slinger with lip toward splines onto outer axle shaft, **Figs. 9 and 10.**
3. Carefully insert axle shaft into housing so as not to damage differential seal at side gears. After sliding axle shaft completely in, wedge a pry bar through universal joint to retain shaft, **Fig. 11.**
4. Install seal cup using adapter, Tool C-4398-2, and driver, Tool No. C-4398-1. Use a small amount of wheel bearing grease on adapter face to hold cup in position, then drive up until bottomed in knuckle, **Figs. 12 and 13.** Do not remove tool at this time.
5. Using a suitable tool, install new outer seal in retainer plate, then locate retainer plate over hub of rotor.
6. Thoroughly pack wheel bearings with Multi-Purpose grease and press outer bearing onto hub using Tool No. C-4246-A and adapters, **Fig. 14.** Remove tool and place grease coated outer bearing cup over bearing cone

followed by spacer, grease coated inner bearing cup and inner bearing cone. Again use Tool No. C-4246-A and adapters to press components into position, **Fig. 14.** Remove tool.

7. Apply a 1/4 inch bead of RTV sealer to retainer face on the chamfer, **Fig. 15.** This replaces O-ring discarded during disassembly.
8. Carefully remove seal installing tool from knuckle bore so that outer axle shaft remains centered. If shaft is moved, be sure that lip seal is still riding inside cup. Correct if necessary.
9. Before assembling hub and rotor to knuckle, position bearing retainer in hub so that grease fitting is facing forward, if equipped. Using a criss-cross method, torque retainer plate bolts to 30 ft. lbs.

NOTE: Bearing retainers that have a grease fitting must be positioned on knuckle so that fitting is facing directly forward, **Fig. 16.**

10. Install brake adapter and remove pry bar from universal joint.

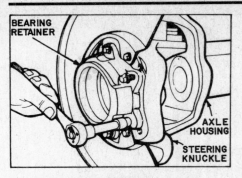

Fig. 7   Installing bearing retainer to check bearing clamp. 44 FBJ Units w/disc brakes. Models w/full time 4 WD

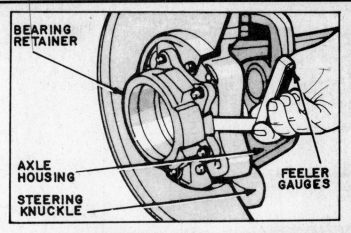

Fig. 8   Checking bearing clamp. 44 FBJ Units w/disc brakes. Models w/full time 4 WD

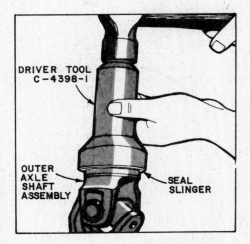

Fig. 9   Installing seal slinger on outer axle shaft. 44 FBJ Units w/disc brakes. Models w/full time 4 WD

11. Install axle shaft washer and nut. Torque nut to 100 ft. lbs. and continue to tighten nut until next slot in nut aligns with hole in axle shaft. Install cotter pin.
12. Through the access hole in hub, lubricate fitting in bearing retainer with Multi-Purpose grease until grease flows through new inner seal. Seal may be viewed at the universal joint area. Spin hub several times and lubricate fitting again. Grease must flow from ½ of seal diameter.
13. Replace brake caliper assembly and wheel, then lower truck and test operation.

MODELS LESS FULL TIME 4 WD

Removal & Inspection
1. Remove locking hub assembly, if equipped.
2. Raise and support vehicle, then remove wheel assembly.
3. Remove caliper retainer and anti-rattle assemblies.
4. Remove caliper from disc and support

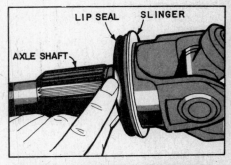

Fig. 10   Installing lip seal on outer axle shaft. 44 FBJ Units w/disc brakes. Models w/full time 4 WD

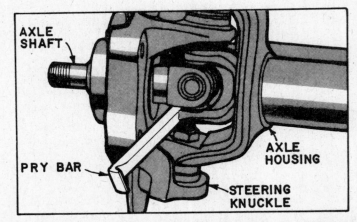

Fig. 11   Using pry bar to retain axle shaft. 44 FBJ Units w/disc brakes. Models w/full time 4 WD

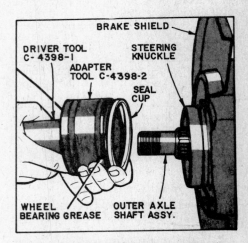

Fig. 12   Using driving & adapter to install seal cup into knuckle. 44 FBJ Units w/disc brakes. Models w/full time 4 WD

caliper to prevent damage to brake line.

5. Remove inboard brake shoe.

6. On 1985 models, remove grease cap and driving hub snap ring, then the driving hub and retaining spring.

7. On all models, remove wheel bearing adjusting lock nut using tool C-4170 or equivalent, then the washer and adjusting nut.

8. Remove rotor assembly. The outer wheel bearing and retainer spring plate will slide out as rotor is removed.

9. Pry inner wheel bearing grease seal from hub, then remove bearing cone and the inner and outer bearing cups.

Assembly & Installation

1. Install inner and outer bearing cups in rotor.

2. Lubricate and install inner bearings, then install the grease seal using suitable tools.

3. Install rotor, then the outer wheel bearing.

4. Install inner lock nut and torque to 50 ft. lbs., using tool C-4170, to seat bearings.

5. Loosen inner lock nut, then retorque to 30—40 ft. lbs. while rotating hub. Back off lock nut 135° to 150°. Set retaining washer in position by turning nut so that the pin pressed into lock nut will engage nearest hole in washer.

6. Install outer lock nut and torque to 50 ft. lbs. End play after final bearing adjustment should be .001—.010 inch.

7. On 1985 models, install retaining spring plate, retaining spring with large end first, driving hub, snap ring and grease cap.

8. On all models, install inboard brake shoe on adapter with shoe flanges in adapter slots, then install caliper assembly.

NOTE: Use care not to pull dust boot out of its grooves while sliding piston and boot over the inboard shoe.

9. Install anti-rattle springs and retaining clips and torque to 180 inch lbs.

NOTE: The inboard shoe anti-rattle spring must be installed on top of the retainer spring plate.

10. Install wheel assembly, then lower truck and test operation.

STEERING KNUCKLE & BALL JOINT

MODELS W/FULL TIME 4 WD
Removal & Disassembly

1. Remove axle shaft cotter pin and loosen outer axle shaft nut.

2. Raise vehicle, then remove wheel assembly.

3. After removing caliper retainer and anti-rattle spring assembly, slide caliper out and away from rotor. Hang

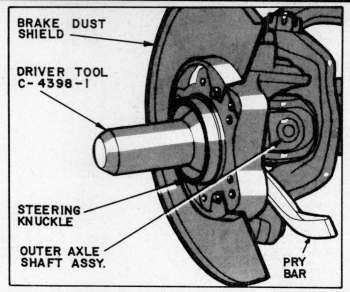

Fig. 13   Tools in place after seal cup is installed. 44 FBJ Units w/disc brakes. Models w/full time 4 WD

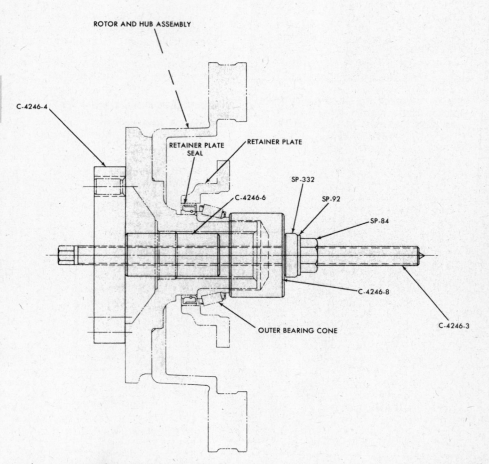

Fig. 14   Tools positioned to press outer bearing onto hub. 44 FBJ Units w/disc brakes. Models w/full time 4 WD

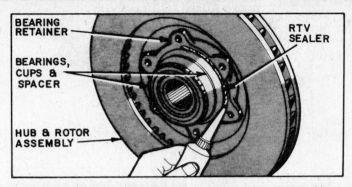

Fig. 15   Forming a seal on bearing retainer face. 44 FBJ Units w/disc brakes. Models w/full time 4 WD

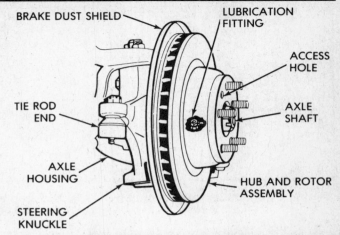

Fig. 16   Bearing retainer positioned with grease fitting facing forward. 44 FBJ Units w/disc brakes. Models w/full time 4 WD

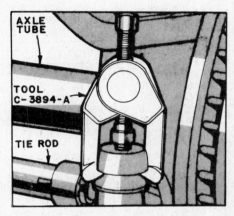

Fig. 17   Using puller to remove tie rod (Typical)

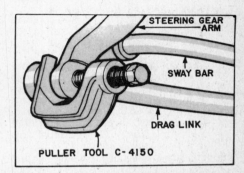

Fig. 18   Using puller to remove drag link from steering arm. (Typical)

12. Separate steering knuckle from axle housing yoke using a brass drift and a hammer, then, using a suitable tool, remove and discard sleeve from upper ball joint yoke on axle housing.
13. Secure steering knuckle upside down in a vise and remove snap ring from lower ball joint.
14. Use proper tools to press upper and lower ball joints from steering knuckle. Replace ball joints if any looseness or end play exists.

Assembly & Installation

1. Secure steering knuckle right side up in a vise and press upper and lower ball joints into position using proper tools. Install snap ring on lower joint and new boots on both joints.
2. Thread new sleeve into ball joint yoke on axle housing ensuring that two threads are exposed at the top.
3. Position steering knuckle on axle housing yoke, then install a new lower ball joint nut and torque to 80 ft. lbs.
4. Use Tool No. C-4169 and a torque wrench to torque sleeve in upper ball joint yoke to 40 ft. lbs., then install upper ball joint nut and torque to 100 ft. lbs. Install cotter pin if slot in nuts and hole in stud align. If not, tighten, do not loosen nut to align.
5. On left side only, position steering knuckle arm over studs on steering knuckle. Install tapered dowels and nuts, then torque nuts to 90 ft. lbs. Secure drag link to steering knuckle arm and torque nut to 60 ft. lbs.
6. Secure tie rod end to steering knuckle. Torque nut to 45 ft. lbs.
7. Install brake dust shield, if removed.
8. Inspect outer axle shaft seal surface for grooving. If surface is grooved, repair as described in "Servicing Rotor Hub or Bearings".
9. Apply RTV sealer to seal surface of axle shaft then using driver, C-4398-1, install seal slinger with lip toward splines onto outer axle shaft, **Figs. 9 and 10.**
10. Carefully insert axle shaft into housing

caliper out of the way. Do not allow caliper to hang by hydraulic brake hose. Remove inboard brake pad.
4. Remove outer axle shaft nut and washer and through access hole in rotor assembly; remove the six bearing retainer bolts.
5. Secure a suitable puller to wheel studs and tighten main screw of tool to remove hub, rotor, bearings, retainer and outer seal as an assembly. Remove puller from rotor.
6. Remove brake caliper adapter from knuckle, then remove and discard O-ring from knuckle, if equipped.
7. Carefully pull axle shaft assembly out and remove seal and slinger from shaft.
8. Disconnect tie rod from steering knuckle using a suitable tool, **Fig. 17,** so as not to damage seal.
9. On left side only, disconnect drag link from steering knuckle arm again using a suitable tool to avoid seal damage, **Fig. 18.**
10. Remove nuts from steering knuckle arm on left side only. Tap arm to loosen tapered dowels. Remove dowels and arm.
11. Remove cotter pin from upper ball joint nut then remove upper and lower ball joint nuts. Discard lower nut.

so as not to damage differential seal at side gears. After sliding axle shaft completely in, wedge a pry bar through universal joint to retain shaft, **Fig. 11.**
11. Install seal cup using adapter C-4398-2, and driver C-4398-1. Use a small amount of wheel bearing grease on adapter face to hold cup in position, then drive cup until bottomed in knuckle, **Figs. 12 and 13.** Do not remove tool at this time.
12. Apply a ¼ inch bead of RTV sealer to retainer face on the chamfer, **Fig. 15.** This replaces the O-ring discarded during disassembly.
13. Carefully remove seal installing tool from knuckle bore so that outer axle shaft remains centered. If shaft is moved, ensure that lip seal is still riding inside cup. Correct if necessary.
14. Before installing hub, rotor, retainer and bearing assembly on knuckle, position bearing retainer in hub so that grease fitting is facing forward, if equipped. Use a criss-cross method and torque retainer plate bolts to 30 ft. lbs.

NOTE: Bearing retainers that have a grease fitting must be positioned on knuck-

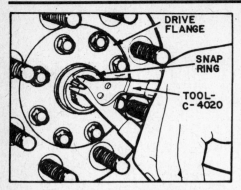

Fig. 19 Removing snap ring. 60 Front Axle

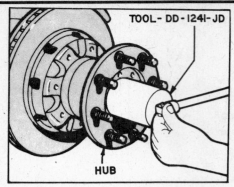

Fig. 20 Removing hub lock nut. 60 Front Axle

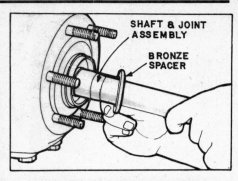

Fig. 21 Removing or replacing axle shaft. 60 Front Axle

le so that fitting is facing directly forward, **Fig. 16.**

15. Install brake adapter and remove any pry bar from universal joint.
16. Install axle shaft washer and nut. Torque nut to 100 ft. lbs. and continue to tighten nut until next slot in nut aligns with hole in axle shaft. Install cotter pin.
17. Through the access hole in hub, lubricate fitting in bearing retainer with Multi-Purpose grease until grease flows through new inner seal. Seal may be viewed through universal joint area. Spin hub several times and lubricate fitting again. Grease must flow from ½ of seal diameter.
18. Replace brake caliper assembly and wheel, then lower vehicle and test operation.

MODELS LESS FULL TIME 4 WD
Removal & Disassembly
1. Remove locking hub assembly, if equipped.
2. Raise vehicle and remove wheel assembly.
3. Remove caliper retainer and anti-rattle spring assemblies.
4. Remove caliper from disc and support caliper to prevent damage to brake line.
5. Remove the inboard brake pad and disc.
6. Remove the caliper adapter from knuckle.
7. Remove the six nuts and washers from spindle to steering knuckle attaching bolts.
8. Remove brake splash shield.
9. Tap spindle lightly with soft faced hammer to free from steering knuckle.
10. Upon removal, examine bronze spacer between needle bearing and shaft joint assembly. If wear is evident, replace.
11. Clamp spindle in vise avoiding bearing carrying surfaces. Remove needle bearing grease seal.
12. Using a suitable puller remover inner axle needle bearings.

NOTE: On 1985 models, left spindle does not have needle bearings.

13. Carefully remove axle shaft, axle seal and stone shield, if equipped.
14. Remove the tie rod from the steering knuckle.
15. On the left side only, remove drag link from steering knuckle.
16. On the left side only, remove the nuts and cone washers from steering knuckle arm. Tap the steering knuckle arm to free knuckle. Remove arm.
17. Remove cotter pin from upper ball joint nut. Remove upper and lower ball joint nut. Discard lower nut.
18. Using a brass drift and hammer separate steering knuckle from axle housing yoke. Remove sleeve from upper ball joint using tool C-4169. Discard sleeve.
19. Install steering knuckle in vise and remove snap ring from lower ball joint with suitable snap ring pliers.
20. Using tool C-4212-1 and adapter set C-4288, press lower ball joint from steering knuckle.
21. Reposition tool, and press upper ball joint from steering knuckle.

NOTE: Replace ball joints if any looseness or end play exists.

Cleaning & Inspection
1. Clean all parts using a suitable solvent.
2. Blow dry parts using compressed air.
3. Inspect all parts for cracks, wear, chips, burrs and distortion.
4. Replace any parts not suitable for further service.

Assembly & Installation
1. Position steering knuckle right side up in a vise. Using tool C-4212-1 and adapter set C-428, press the lower ball joint into position.
2. Using the same tool and adapter set as above, install the upper ball joint.
3. Install new boots on the ball joints and remove the steering knuckle from the vise.
4. Screw a new sleeve into the upper ball joint yoke leaving two threads showing at the top.
5. Position steering knuckle on axle housing yoke and torque new lower ball joint nut to 80 ft. lbs.
6. Using tool C-4169 and a torque wrench, torque sleeve in upper ball

joint to 40 ft. lbs. Install upper ball joint and torque to 100 ft. lbs. Align slot in nut with hole in stud and install cotter pin.

NOTE: Do not loosen to align.

7. On left side only, position steering knuckle arm over studs on steering knuckle. Install cone washers and nuts and torque to 90 ft. lbs.
8. Install drag link on steering knuckle arm and torque to 60 ft. lbs. Install cotter pin.
9. Install the rod end to steering knuckle. Torque nut to 45 ft. lbs. and install cotter pin.
10. Install lip seal on stone shield with lip toward axle shaft spline.
11. Carefully insert axle shaft into housing. Avoid damaging differential seal at side gears.
12. Using tools D-122 and C-4171, install new needle bearings into spindle.
13. Fill seal area with NLG1 grease or equivalent, and install seal with tools D-155 and C-4171.
14. Install new bronze spacer on axle shaft, install spindle and brake splash shield.
15. Install new nuts and torque to 25–35 ft. lbs.
16. Mount braking disc assembly and outer wheel bearing cone onto spindle.
17. Install wheel bearing nuts and locking washer.
18. Install locking hub assembly.
19. Install brake adapter and torque attaching bolts to 85 ft. lbs.
20. Install the assembled brake caliper assembly.
21. Install the wheel and torque the nuts to 110 ft. lbs. Lower vehicle and test operation.

1985 AXLE DISCONNECT HOUSING ASSEMBLY
Removal & Disassembly
1. Disconnect battery ground cable, then raise and support vehicle.
2. Disconnect vacuum lines and switch electrical connector.
3. Remove disconnect housing assembly, gasket and shield from axle housing.
4. Remove shift motor shaft E-clips, then

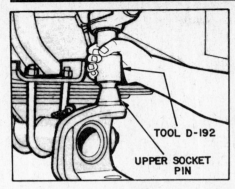

Fig. 22 Removing or replacing upper socket pin. 60 Front Axle

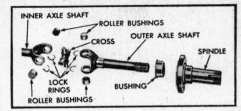

Fig. 23 Universal joint, spindle and bushing assembly. (Typical)

Fig. 24 Correct alignment of upper socket pin to steering knuckle. 60 Front Axle

the shift motor and shift fork.
5. Remove O-ring from shift motor shaft.

Assembly & Installation
1. Install new O-ring on shift motor.
2. Install shift motor into disconnect housing and through shift fork.
3. Install shift motor shaft E-clips.
4. Install disconnect housing assembly and gasket, ensuring shift fork engages groove of shift collar.
5. Install disconnect housing assembly shield and attaching bolts. Torque attaching bolts to 10 ft. lbs.

AXLE SHAFT ASSEMBLY

1979
Removal
1. Remove wheel cover and cotter key, then loosen outer axle shaft nut.
2. Raise and support vehicle, then remove wheel and tire assembly.
3. Remove caliper retainer and anti-rattle assemblies.
4. Remove caliper from disc and support caliper to prevent damage to brake line.
5. Remove inboard brake shoe.
6. Remove outer axle shaft nut and washer.
7. Working through hole in rotor assembly, remove six rotor attaching bolts. Secure a suitable puller to wheel studs and tighten main screw of tool to remove hub, rotor, bearings, retainer and outer seal as an assembly.
8. Remove puller from hub and rotor assembly, then the brake caliper adapter from the knuckle.
9. Remove bearings from knuckle using a suitable pry bar.
10. Remove O-ring from knuckle, if equipped.
11. Remove axle shaft assembly, then the seal and slinger from shaft.

Installation
1. Inspect outer axle shaft seal surface for damage. Replace damaged components as required.
2. Install brake dust shield, if removed. Torque mounting bolts to 160 inch lbs.

3. Apply suitable sealant to axle shaft seal surface. Using tool C-4398-1 or equivalent, install seal slinger on outer axle shaft.
4. Install lip seal on slinger with lip facing toward axle shaft spline.
5. Carefully insert assembly into housing.
6. Insert a suitable pry bar through axle shaft U-joint and wedge so that axle shaft is in all the way in and cannot be moved outward.
7. Using tools C-4398-2 and C-4398-1 or equivalents, carefully install seal cup until it bottoms in the knuckle assembly. A small amount of wheel bearing grease on the tool face will aid in holding the cup in position. Do not remove the tool.
8. Apply a ¼ inch bead of suitable sealer to retainer face on chamfer.
9. Carefully remove seal installer tool from knuckle bore.
10. Position bearing retainer on knuckle so that lubrication fitting is facing directly forward.
11. Install hub, rotor, retainer and bearing assembly on knuckle and tighten retainer plate bolts in a criss-cross pattern to 30 ft. lbs.
12. Install brake adapter and torque mounting bolts to 85 ft. lbs.
13. Remove pry bar from U-joint and install axle shaft washer and nut assembly.
14. Torque nut to 100 ft. lbs. and continue to tighten the nut until the next slot in nut aligns with cotter key hole in axle shaft. Install cotter key into hole.
15. Fill hub and rotor assembly with suitable lubricant, then rotate hub and rotor assembly several times and apply more lubricant until grease flows from at least 50% of the seal diameter.
16. Install inboard brake shoe on adapter with shoe flanges in adapter key holes.
17. Slowly slide caliper assembly into position in adapter and over disc. Align caliper on machined keyways of adapter.

NOTE: Be careful not to pull the dust boot from its grooves as the piston and boot slide over the inboard shoe.

18. Install anti-rattle springs and retaining clips, then torque to 180 inch lbs.

NOTE: The inboard shoe and anti-rattle spring must always be installed on top of the retainer spring plate.

19. Install tire and wheel assembly. Torque wheels nuts to 110 ft. lbs.

1980—84
Removal
1. Remove locking hub assembly from vehicle.
2. Raise and support vehicle.
3. Remove tire and wheel assembly.
4. Remove caliper retainer and anti-rattle spring assemblies. Remove caliper from disc by sliding outward and away from disc. Hang caliper away from assembly.

NOTE: Do not allow caliper to hang or be supported by the brake lines.

5. Remove inboard shoe.
6. Remove outer axle shaft locknut washer and nut assembly.
7. Remove rotor and bearing assembly.
8. Remove six nuts attaching splash shield and spindle to knuckle assembly, if equipped.
9. Remove splash shield and spindle.
10. Remove brake caliper adapter from knuckle.
11. Carefully remove axle shaft assembly. Remove seal and stone shield from shaft.

Installation
1. Install lip seal on axle shaft stone shield with lip of seal toward axle shaft spline.
2. Carefully insert axle shaft into housing.
3. Install spindle and brake splash shield. Install the six nuts and torque to 25—30 ft. lbs.
4. Install rotor, outer bearing nut, washer and locknut on spindle.
5. Install brake adapter and torque to 85 ft. lbs.

6. Install inboard brake shoe on adapter with shoe flanges located in adapter keyways. Slowly slide caliper assembly into position in adapter.
7. Install anti-rattle springs and retaining clips. Torque to 180 inch lbs.
8. Install locking hub assembly.
9. Install tire and wheel assembly. Torque attaching nuts to 110 ft. lbs.

1985

Right Axle Shaft, Removal
1. Raise and support vehicle.
2. Remove wheel and tire assembly.
3. Remove caliper retainer and anti-rattle spring assemblies.
4. Remove caliper from brake disc. Hang caliper aside.

NOTE: Do not allow caliper to hang from brake lines.

5. Remove braking disc.
6. Remove six nuts attaching splash shield and spindle to knuckle assembly.
7. Remove brake caliper adapter from knuckle.
8. Carefully remove axle shaft assembly from vehicle. Remove seal and stone shield.

Right Axle Shaft, Installation
1. Install lip seal on axle shaft stone shield with lip toward axle shaft spline.
2. Carefully insert axle shaft into the housing.
3. Install spindle and splash shield. Install, then torque nuts to 25–30 ft. lbs.
4. Install braking disc, outer bearing, nut, washer and locknut onto spindle.
5. Install spring retainer, spring, drive gear and drive gear snap ring.
6. Apply RTV sealant or equivalent to seating edge of grease cap, then install the cap.
7. Install brake adapter and torque mounting bolts to 85 ft. lbs.
8. Position inboard brake shoe on adapter with shoe flanges in adapter keyways. Slowly slide caliper assembly into position in adapter and over braking disc. Align caliper on machined ways of adapter.
9. Install anti-rattle springs and retaining clips. Torque to 180 inch lbs.
10. Install tire and wheel assembly.

Left Axle Shaft, Removal
1. Raise and support vehicle.
2. Remove wheel and tire assembly.
3. Remove caliper retainer and anti-rattle spring assemblies.
4. Remove caliper from brake disc.
5. Hang caliper aside.

NOTE: Do not allow brake caliper to hang from brake lines.

6. Remove inboard brake shoe.
7. Remove brake disc, splash shield and spindle.
8. Disconnect vacuum lines and electrical connector from disconnect hous-

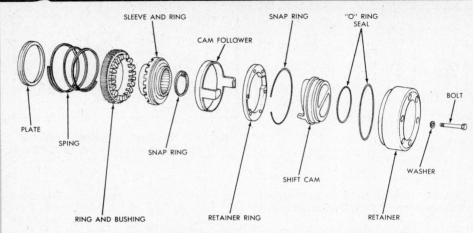

Fig. 25   Manual locking hub assembly exploded view. Exc. Dualmatic

ing assembly switch.
9. Remove disconnect housing assembly from vehicle as previously described.
10. Remove intermediate axle shaft assembly.

NOTE: Carefully slide shaft through axle shaft seal to avoid damaging the seal assembly.

11. Using tool D-330 or equivalent, remove needle bearing from intermediate axle shaft.
12. Remove shift collar from axle housing.
13. Loosen, then remove differential cover attaching screws. Remove cover and drain lubricant.
14. Push inner axle shaft toward center of vehicle and remove C-lock form shaft groove recess.
15. Using tools D-354-4 and D-354-1 or equivalents, remove inner axle shaft bearing.
16. Remove outer axle shaft bearing and seal from housing bore.

Left Axle Shaft, Installation
1. Using tools D-354-4, D-354-2 and C-367 or equivalents, install inner axle shaft bearing.
2. Using a suitable tool, install inner axle shaft. Install C-lock into axle shaft groove recess.
3. Install shift collar on splined end of inner axle shaft.
4. Install axle shaft bearing and seal.
5. Install needle bearing into intermediate axle shaft.
6. Install intermediate axle shaft through seal.
7. Install disconnect housing assembly and gasket as previously described.
8. Install disconnect housing assembly shield and bolts. Torque bolts to 10 ft. lbs.
9. Connect vacuum lines and electrical connectors to switch assembly.
10. Install splash shield and spindle.

Torque nuts to 25–30 ft. lbs.
11. Install brake disc, outer bearing, nut, washer and locknut on spindle assembly.
12. Install spring retainer, spring, drive gear and drive gear snap ring.
13. Apply RTV sealant to seating edge of grease cap, then install the cap.
14. Position inboard brake shoe on adapter with shoe flanges in adapter keyways. Slowly slide caliper assembly into position in adapter and over brake disc.
15. Install anti-rattle springs and retaining clips. Torque to 180 inch lbs.
16. Apply a 1/16 inch bead of suitable sealant along bolt circle of cover.
17. Allow sealant to cure and install on axle. Torque attaching bolts to 420 inch lbs.
18. Remove fill plug and fill axle with suitable lubricant.
19. Install tire and wheel assembly.

SPICER 60 FRONT AXLE

AXLE ASSEMBLY

Remove & Replace
1. Secure brake pedal in the up position, then raise vehicle.
2. Disconnect front drive shaft at drive pinion yoke.
3. Disconnect drag link at steering knuckle arm (left side only).
4. Disconnect and plug brake line at frame crossmember.
5. Disconnect shock absorbers at lower mounts then disconnect sway bar link assembly, if equipped, from spring plates.
6. Remove nuts and washers from universal bolt spring clips, then remove axle from vehicle.
7. Reverse procedure to install axle assembly. Lubricate all fittings, free

brake pedal and bleed brakes.

8. Lower vehicle and check front wheel alignment.

AXLE SHAFT, BALL JOINT & STEERING KNUCKLE REPAIRS

Removal & Disassembly

1. Block brake pedal in "Up" position.
2. Raise and support vehicle.
3. Remove wheel.
4. Remove brake caliper from adapter and, using a piece of wire, suspend caliper. Do not hang caliper by brake hose. The inner brake pad will remain on adapter.
5. Remove hub cap and snap ring, **Fig. 19.**
6. Remove flange nuts and lock washers.
7. Remove drive flange and discard gasket, or remove locking hub, if equipped.
8. Straighten tang on lock ring, then remove outer lock nut, lock ring, inner lock nut and outer-bearing, **Fig. 20.** Slide hub and rotor assembly from spindle.
9. Remove inner brake pad from adapter.
10. Remove nuts and washers securing brake splash shield, brake adapter and spindle to steering knuckle.
11. Remove spindle from knuckle. Slide inner and outer axle shaft with bronze spacer, seal and slinger from axle, **Fig. 21.**
12. Remove cotter key and nut from tie rod. Disconnect tie rod from steering knuckle.
13. On left side only, remove cotter key and nut from drag link. Disconnect drag link from steering knuckle arm. Also, remove nuts and upper knuckle cap. Discard gasket. Remove spring and upper socket sleeve.
14. Remove capscrews from lower knuckle cap and free cap from knuckle and housing.
15. To remove knucke from housing, swing outward at bottom, then lift up and off upper socket pin.
16. Using a suitable tool, loosen and remove upper socket pin, then the seal, **Fig. 22.**
17. Press lower ball socket from axle housing with suitable tools.
18. Referring to **Fig. 23,** disassemble shaft.

Assembly & Installation

1. Lubricate lower ball socket assembly with suitable grease.
2. With suitable tools, press seal and lower bearing cup into axle housing. Then, press lower bearing and seal into axle housing.
3. Using a suitable tool and torque wrench, install and torque upper socket pin to 500–600 ft. lbs, **Fig. 22.** Install seal over socket pin.
4. Place steering knuckle over socket

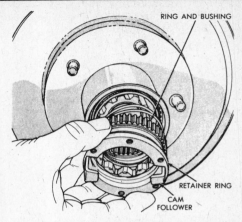

Fig. 26   Retaining ring and cam follower removal

pin. Fill lower socket cavity with suitable grease. Work lower knuckle cap into place on knuckle and housing. Install capscrews and torque to 70–90 ft. lbs.
5. Lubricate upper socket pin with suitable grease. Align upper socket sleeve in keyway of steering knuckle and slide into position, **Fig. 24.**
6. Install new gasket over upper steering knuckle studs. Place spring over sleeve. Install cap on left side steering knuckle arm. Install nuts and torque to 70–90 ft. lbs.
7. On left side only, attach drag link to steering knuckle arm and install and torque nut to 60 ft. lbs.
8. Connect tie rod to steering knuckle and install and torque nut to 45 ft. lbs. Install cotter key.
9. Referring to **Fig. 23,** assemble shaft.
10. Slide axle shaft into position. Place bronze spacer on axle shaft with chamfer facing toward universal joint, **Fig. 21.**
11. Install spindle, brake adapter and splash shield. Install and torque nuts to 50–70 ft. lbs.
12. Place inner brake pad on adapter.
13. Install hub and rotor assembly onto spindle. Install outer bearing and inner lock nut. Using tool DD-1241-JD and tool C-3952, torque lock nut to 50 ft. lbs. to seat bearings. Then, back off locknut and retorque to 30–40 ft. lbs. while rotating hub and rotor. Back off nut 135 to 150 degrees. Assemble lock ring and outer lock nut. Torque lock nut to 65 ft. lbs. minimum. Bend one tang of lock ring over inner lock nut and another tang over outer lock nut. Bearing end play should be .001–.010 inch.
14. Install new gasket on hub, then the drive flange, lock washers and nuts. Torque nuts to 30–40 ft. lbs. Install snap ring and hub cap, or locking hub, if equipped, **Fig. 19.**
15. Position caliper on adapter and torque Allen screw to 12–18 ft. lbs.
16. Install wheel and lower vehicle.
17. Remove block from brake pedal.

FRONT WHEEL LOCKING HUB SERVICE

MANUAL LOCKING HUB, EXC. DUALMATIC

DESCRIPTION

As shown in **Fig. 25,** the splines on the inside diameter of the axle shaft sleeve and ring assembly mesh with the axle shaft splines. The assembly is retained on the axle shaft with a snap ring. The splines on the outside diameter of the inner clutch ring assembly mesh with the wheel hub splines. Therefore, when the actuator knob is turned towards the "L" position, the actuating cam body is forced outward towards the hub end, allowing the inner clutch to be forced under spring tension towards the axle shaft sleeve and ring assembly until the inner clutch assembly teeth are engaged in the axle shaft sleeve and ring assembly teeth, locking the axle and hub.

OPERATION

"L" Position

When the transfer case is shifted into the position for driving the front axle, turn the actuating knob so that it is aligned with the letter L. If the clutch teeth do not engage with the knob turned to this position, the clutch teeth are butted and a slight movement of the wheel in either direction complete the lock. The front axle will now drive the wheel.

"F" Position

When the transfer case is to be shifted into the position for driving the rear axle only, turn the actuating knob so that it is aligned with the letter F. This will disengage the clutch teeth and thus unlock the wheel hub from the axle shaft. The wheel will now turn free on the axle.

NOTE: Be certain that the transfer case is shifted into two-wheel drive position before disengaging the Hub-Lok.

REMOVAL

1. Place hub in lock position, then remove six attaching bolts and washers from retainer using a suitable Allen wrench, **Fig. 25.**
2. Remove retainer and shift cam, then separate shift cam from retainer and discard O-rings.
3. Pry snap ring from hub internal groove, then slide retainer ring and cam follower from hub, **Fig. 26.**
4. Remove snap ring from axle shaft using suitable pliers.
5. Remove sleeve and ring, ring and bushing, spring and spring plate.
6. Inspect all parts for nicks, burrs or wear. Replace parts as necessary.

ASSEMBLY

1. Install spring plate and spring, large coils first, into wheel hub housing.
2. Assemble ring and bushing, and sleeve and ring into one assembly, then slide into housing.
3. Install snap ring in axle shaft groove.

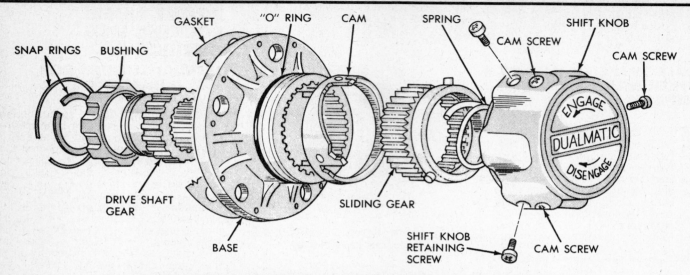

Fig. 27   Manual locking hub assembly exploded view. Dualmatic

4. Position cam follower and retainer ring into housing, then lock into place with large internal snap ring.
5. Install small O-ring seal in shift cam groove, lubricate using suitable lubricant, then install retainer at lock position.
6. Install large O-ring seal in retainer groove, lubricate using suitable lubricant, then position assembly in hub.
7. Install washers and six attaching screws, then check for proper operation.

DUALMATIC MANUAL LOCKING HUB

Removal & Disassembly

NOTE: Do not remove cam (outer) screws from cover. If cam screws are removed, misalignment could occur causing damage to cam.

1. Turn to engage position.
2. Apply pressure to the face of the shift knob, remove three shift knob retaining screws, **Fig. 27.**
3. Pull shift knob from mounting base and remove snap ring from axle shaft.
4. Remove capscrews and lockwashers from mounting flange.
5. Remove locking hub assembly from rotor hub and discard gasket.
6. Wash parts in mineral spirits and blow dry with compressed air. Inspect components for damage.

Assembly & Installation

1. Lubricate parts with multi-purpose lubricant part no. 2932524 or equivalent.
2. Install new gasket and locking hub onto rotor hub.
3. Install capscrews and lockwashers and torque to 30–40 ft. lbs.
4. Install axle shaft snap ring and shift knob on mounting base.
5. Align the splines by pushing inward on

shift knob and turning it clockwise to lock it in position.
6. Install and tighten three shift knob retaining screws.

AUTOMATIC LOCKING HUB

SERVICE BULLETIN Complaints of automatic locking hubs not engaging or disengaging on 1981 vehicles can be caused by the installation of the incorrect drag sleeve retainer washer, **Fig. 28.** To determine if the incorrect washer was installed, remove the automatic locking hub, then inspect the drag sleeve retainer washer located behind the wheel bearing lock nut. There are four tabs on the drag sleeve retainer washer that should be visible, **Fig. 28.** If the four tabs are not visible, the incorrect drag sleeve retainer washer is installed and should be replaced with the correct part.

Description

The Automatic Locking Hub, shown in **Fig. 28**, engages or disengages to lock the front axle shaft to the hub of the front wheel. Engagement occurs whenever the vehicle is operated in 4WD. Disengagement occurs whenever 2WD has been selected and the vehicle is moving rearward. Disengagement will not occur when the vehicle is moved rearward if 4WD is selected and the hub has already been engaged.

Before disassembling a unit for a complaint of abnormal noise, note the following:
a. To obtain all-wheel drive, the transfer case lever must be placed in 4L or 4H, at which time the hub locks will automatically engage.
b. To unlock the hubs, shift the transfer case lever to 2H, then slowly reverse the vehicle direction approximately 10 feet.
c. An incomplete shift from 2WD to 4WD, or disengagement of only one hub lock may cause an abnormal sound from the front axle. Shift to 4WD to stop the

noise, then unlock the hubs as previously stated.

Removal

1. Remove 5 screws retaining the cover to outer clutch housing.
2. Remove cover, seal, seal bridge and bearing components.
3. Compress the wire retaining ring and remove the remaining components from the hub.

Disassembly

NOTE: Before disassembly, the hub must be unlocked. If hub is locked when removed from wheel, hold hub outer housing and rotate drag sleeve in either direction to unlock.

1. Remove snap ring from groove in hub sleeve, then turn clutch gear until it falls into disengagement with the outer clutch housing. Lift and tilt the drag sleeve to unlock the tangs of the brake band from window of inner cage, **Fig. 29,** then remove the drag sleeve and brake assembly.

NOTE: The brake band must never be removed from the drag sleeve. The spring tension of the brake band can be changed if the coils are over-expanded and could affect hub operation.

2. Remove snap ring from groove in outer clutch housing, then pry plastic outer cage free from inner cage while inner cage is being removed.
3. Pry plastic outer cage tabs free from groove in outer clutch housing, then remove outer cage.
4. Remove clutch sleeve and attached components from outer clutch housing.
5. Compress return spring and hold the spring with clamps, **Fig. 30,** then position the assembly in a vise so that the vise holds both ends of the clutch sleeve. Remove retaining ring.
6. Remove clamps holding the return

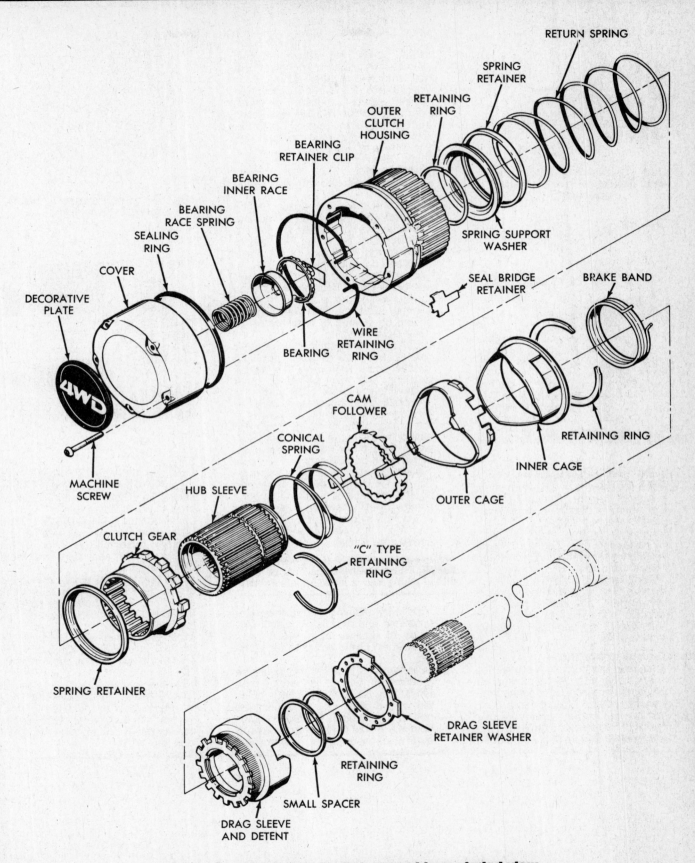

Fig. 28 Automatic locking hub assembly exploded view

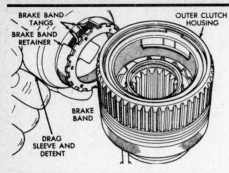

Fig. 29   Removing drag sleeve and detent & brake band assembly

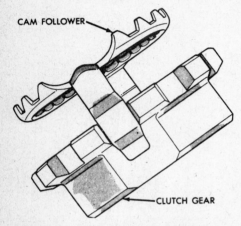

Fig. 31   Installing cam follower

spring, then slowly open the vise to permit the release of the return spring in a safe manner. Remove retainer seat, spring and spring support washers from the hub sleeve.

7. Remove C-ring from clutch sleeve. It is necessary to position sleeve assembly so that the C-ring ends are aligned with legs of cam follower, allowing removal between the legs.

8. Remove conical spring from between cam follower and clutch gear, then separate cam follower from clutch gear. Do not pry the legs of the cam follower apart.

Assembly & Installation

1. Install tangs of cam follower over flats of clutch gear, **Fig. 31,** then compress conical spring and position with large diameter located against clutch gear.

2. Position clutch gear assembly over splines of hub sleeve. The teeth of the cam follower should be located at the end of the hub sleeve with no splines, and the clutch gear and spring should slide freely over splines of hub sleeve.

3. Install C-ring into groove of hub sleeve, then install a spring retainer over each end of return spring.

4. Position one end of return spring with retainer against shoulder of clutch gear, then place support washer on end of the return spring. Compress return spring and install retainer ring into groove of hub sleeve.

5. Place assembled components into outer housing. The cam follower should be positioned with legs facing outward.

6. Install 3 of the cover screws into 3 holes of the outer clutch housing. These screws will support the component to permit the clutch hub to drop down so that the tangs of the brake band can be assembled.

7. Carefully install the plastic outer cage into outer clutch housing with ramps facing toward cam follower. The small external tabs of the plastic cage should be located in wide groove of outer clutch housing.

8. Install steel inner cage into the outer cage aligning tab of outer cage with window of the inner cage, then install retaining ring into groove of outer clutch housing above outer cage.

9. The brake band and drag are serviced as a complete assembly. Install one of the 2 tangs of the brake band on each side of the lug of the outer cage, located in the window of the steel inner cage. It will be necessary to tilt these parts to engage the tangs in this position as the drag sleeve is positioned against the face of the cam follower.

10. Remove the 3 screws and rest the end of the hub sleeve on a suitable support, then install washer and snap ring above drag sleeve.

NOTE: The following steps may be completed as the hub is installed into vehicle.

11. Install wire retaining ring into groove of unsplined end of clutch housing. The tangs of retainer ring should point away from splined end of clutch housing.

12. Hold the tangs together and install the 2 bent down tabs of seal bridge over tangs, **Fig. 32.** The seal bridge holds the wire retainer ring in a clamped position in groove of outer clutch housing. Install O-ring into groove of outer clutch housing and over the seal

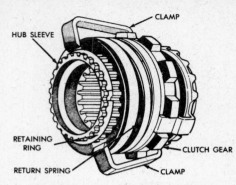

Fig. 30   Clutch gear & hub sleeve assembly

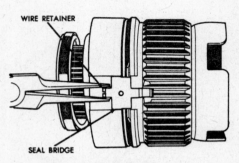

Fig. 32   Install seal bridge

bridge.

13. Lubricate and install the bearing over the inner race. The steel ball bearing should be visible when the bearing is properly installed.

14. Install bearing retainer clip into hole in outer race, then install bearing and retainer assembly in end of hub sleeve. Install seal ring over outer clutch housing.

15. Install bearing race spring into bore of cover, then install cover and spring assembly. Align holes in cover to holes in outer clutch housing and install 5 screws.

16. Install O-ring over seal bridge to prevent it from dislodging during handling prior to the hub bearing being installed into the vehicle.

17. The hub and attached parts should turn freely after installation. The 5 cover screws must be loosened to install the hub into the vehicle. After installation, torque the cover screws to 40—50 inch lbs.

AIR CONDITIONING

TABLE OF CONTENTS

A/C System Testing

INDEX

GENERAL PRECAUTIONS

The Freon refrigerant used is also known as R-12 or F-12. It is colorless and odorless both as a gas and a liquid. Since it boils (vaporizes) at −21.7° F., it will usually be in a vapor state when being handled in a repair shop. But if a portion of the liquid coolant should come in contact with the hands or face, note that its temperature momentarily will be at least 22° below zero.

Protective goggles should be worn when opening any refrigerant lines. If liquid coolant does touch the eyes, bathe the eyes quickly in cold water, then apply a bland disinfectant oil to the eyes. See an eye doctor.

When checking a system for leaks with a torch type leak detector, do not breathe the vapors coming from the flame. Do not discharge refrigerant in the area of a live flame. A poisonous phosgene gas is produced when R-12 or F-12 is burned. While the small amount of this gas produced by a leak detector is not harmful unless inhaled directly at the flame, the quantity of refrigerant released into the air when a system is purged can be extremely dangerous if allowed to come in contact with an open flame. Thus, when purging a system, be sure that the discharge hose is routed to a well ventilated place where no flame is present. Under these conditions the refrigerant will be quickly dissipated into the surrounding air.

Never allow the temperature of refrigerant drums to exceed 125° F. The resultant increase in temperature will cause a corresponding increase in pressure which may cause the safety plug to release or the drum to burst.

If it is necessary to heat a drum of refrigerant when charging a system, the drum should be placed in water that is no hotter than 125° F. Never use a blowtorch, or other open flame. If possible, a pressure release mechanism should be attached before the drum is heated.

When connecting and disconnecting service gauges on A/C system, ensure that gauge hand valves are fully closed and that compressor service valves, if equipped, are in the back-seated (fully counterclockwise) position. Do not disconnect gauge hoses from service port adapters, if used, while gauges are connected to A/C system. To disconnect hoses, always remove adapter from service port. Do not disconnect hoses from gauge manifold while connected to A/C system, as refrigerant will be rapidly discharged.

After disconnecting gauge lines, check the valve areas to be sure service valves are correctly seated and Schraeder valves, if used, are not leaking.

EXERCISE SYSTEM

An important fact most owners ignore is that A/C units must be used periodically. Manufacturers caution that when the air conditioner is not used regularly, particularly during cold months, it should be turned on for a few minutes once every two or three weeks while the engine is running.

This keeps the system in good operating condition.

Checking out the system for the effects of disuse before the onset of summer is one of the most important aspects of A/C servicing.

First clean out the condenser core, mounted in all cases at the front of the radiator. All obstructions, such as leaves, bugs, and dirt, must be removed, as they will reduce heat transfer and impair the efficiency of the system. Make sure the space between the condenser and the radiator also is free of foreign matter.

Make certain the evaporator water drain is open. Certain systems have two evaporators, one in the engine compartment and one toward the rear of the vehicle. The evaporator cools and dehumidifies the air before it enters the passenger compartment; there, the refrigerant is changed from a liquid to a vapor. As the core cools the air, moisture condenses on it but is prevented from collecting in the evaporator by the water drain.

PERFORMANCE TEST

The system should be operated for at least 15 minutes to allow sufficient time for all parts to become completely stabilized. Determine if the system is fully charged by the use of test gauges and sight glass if one is installed on system. Head pressure will read from 180 psi to 220 psi or higher, depending upon ambient temperature and the type unit being tested. The sight glass should be free of bubbles if a glass is used in the system. Low side pressures should read approximately 15 psi to 30 psi, again depending on the ambient temperature and the unit being tested. It is not feasible to give a definite reading for all types of systems used, as the type control and component installation used on a particular system will directly influence the pressure readings on the high and low sides, **Fig. 1**.

The high side pressure will definitely be affected by the ambient or outside air temperature. A system that is operating normally will indicate a high side gauge reading between 150–170 psi with an 80° F ambient temperature. The same system will register 210–230 psi with an ambient temperature of 100° F. No two systems will register exactly the same, which requires that allowance for variations in head pressures must be considered. Following are the most important normal readings likely to be encountered during the season.

Ambient Temp.	High Side Pressure
80	150–170
90	175–195
95	185–205
100	210–230
105	230–250
110	250–270

RELATIVE TEMPERATURE OF HIGH AND LOW SIDES

The high side of the system should be uniformly hot to the touch throughout. A difference in temperature will indicate a partial blockage of liquid or gas at this point.

The low side of the system should be uniformly cool to the touch with no excessive sweating of the suction line or low side service valve. Excessive sweating or frosting of the low side service valve usually indicates an expansion valve is allowing an excessive amount of refrigerant into the evaporator.

EVAPORATOR OUTPUT

At this point, provided all other inspection tests have been performed, and components have been found to operate as they should, a rapid cooling down of the interior of the vehicle should result. The use of a thermometer is not necessary to determine evaporator output. Bringing all units to the correct operating specifications will insure that the evaporator performs as intended.

LEAK TEST

Testing the refrigerant system for leaks is one of the most important phases of troubleshooting. Several types of leak detectors are available that are suitable for detecting A/C system leaks. One or more of the following procedures will prove useful for detecting leaks and checking connections after service work has been performed. Prior to performing any leak test,

Evaporator Pressure Gauge Reading	Evaporator Temperature F°	High Pressure Gauge Reading	Ambient Temperature
0	-21°	45	20°
0.6	-20°	55	30°
2.4	-15°	72	40°
4.5	-10°	86	50°
6.8	- 5°	105	60°
9.2	0°	126	70°
11.8	5°	140	75°
14.7	10°	160	80°
17.1	15°	185	90°
21.1	20°	195	95°
22.5	22°	220	100°
23.9	24°	240	105°
25.4	26°	260	110°
26.9	28°	275	115°
28.5	30°	290	120°
37.0	40°	305	125°
46.7	50°	325	130°
57.7	60°		
70.1	70°		
84.1	80°		
99.6	90°		
116.9	100°		
136.0	110°		
157.1	120°		
179.0	130°		

Fig. 1 A/C system pressure/temperature relationship (Typical). Equivalent to 1750 RPM (30 mph)

prepare the vehicle as follows:
1. Attach a suitable gauge manifold to system and observe pressure readings.
2. If little or no pressure is indicated, the system must be partially charged.
3. If gauges indicate pressure, set engine to run at fast idle and operate system at maximum cooling for 10–15 minutes, then stop engine and perform leak tests.

FLAME TYPE (HALIDE) LEAK DETECTORS

CAUTION: Avoid inhaling fumes produced by burning refrigerant when using flame-type detectors. Use caution when using detector near flammable materials such as interior trim components. Do not use flame-type detector where concentrations of combustible or explosive gasses, dusts or vapors may exist.

1. Light leak detector and adjust flame as low as possible to obtain maximum sensitivity.
2. Allow detector to warm until copper element is cherry-red. Flame should be almost colorless.
3. Test reaction plate sensitivity by passing end of sensor hose near an opened can of refrigerant. Flame should react violently, turning bright blue.
4. If flame does not change color, replace reaction plate following manufacturer's instructions.
5. Allow flame to clear, then slowly move sensor hose along areas suspected of leakage while observing flame.

NOTE: Position sensor hose under areas of suspected leakage, as R-12 refrigerant is heavier than air.

6. Move sensor hose under all lines, fittings and components. Insert hose into evaporator case, if possible, and check compressor shaft seal.
7. The presence of refrigerant will cause flame to change color as follows: Pale blue, no refrigerant; yellow-yellow/green, slight leak; bright blue-purple/blue, major leak or concentration of refrigerant.
8. If detector indicates a large leak or heavy concentration of refrigerant, ventillate area using a small fan in order to pinpoint leak.
9. Repair leaks as needed, evacuate and recharge system, then recheck system for leaks.

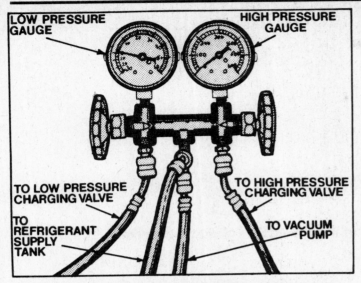

Fig. 2   Gauge manifold hose connections. Exc. RV-2 compressor

Fig. 3   Gauge manifold hose connections. RV-2 compressor

ELECTRONIC LEAK DETECTORS

The procedure for using an electronic leak detector is similar to the procedure for flame-type leak detectors, except that the presence of refrigerant is indicated by an audible tone or flashing light. Refer to operating instructions for unit being used, and observe the following procedures:
1. Move detector probe 1 inch per second along areas of suspected leakage.
2. Position probe under area to be tested as refrigerant is heavier than air.
3. Check gauge manifold, hoses and service ports for leakage.

FLUID LEAK DETECTORS

Apply leak detector solution around joints to be tested. A cluster of bubbles will form immediately if there is a leak. A white foam that forms after a short while will indicate an extremely small leak. In some confined areas such as sections of the evaporator and condenser, electronic leak detectors will be more useful.

DISCHARGING & EVACUATING SYSTEM
DISCHARGING

1. Ensure that all gauge manifold or charging station hand valves are closed.
2. Connect compound (low) side gauge hose to the low (suction) side service port, and the high pressure gauge hose to the high (discharge) side port, **Figs. 2 and 3.**

NOTE: Refer to "Charging Valve Location" chart in the "A/C System Servicing" section for service port locations.

3. If charging station is being used, disconnect hose from vacuum pump inlet and ensure that vacuum valve is open.
4. Insert charging station vacuum hose or gauge manifold center hose into a suitable container that is vented to shop exhaust system.
5. If system is operational, set engine to run at fast idle and operate A/C system in maximum cooling position, with blower on high, for 10–15 minutes to return oil to compressor, then reduce idle and stop engine.
6. Slightly open low side control valve on manifold or charging station, and allow refrigerant to discharge slowly into container.

NOTE: Do not allow refrigerant to discharge rapidly. Too rapid purging will draw the system oil charge out with the refrigerant.

7. When system is nearly discharged, slightly open high side control valve on manifold to discharge remaining refrigerant from compressor and lines.
8. When system is completely discharged (gauges read zero), close high and low side control valves and measure amount of oil in discharge container.
9. If more than ½ ounce of refrigeration oil is trapped in container, perform "Oil Level Check" as outlined in the "A/C System Servicing" section.

NOTE: If addition of refrigeration oil is necessary, oil should be added prior to evacuating system.

EVACUATING SYSTEM WITH VACUUM PUMP

Vacuum pumps suitable for removing air and moisture from A/C systems are commercially available. The pump should be capable of drawing the system down to 28–29½ inches Hg at sea level. For each 1000 foot increase in altitude, this specification should be decreased by 1 inch Hg. As an example, at 5000 feet elevation, only 23–24½ inches Hg can be obtained.
1. Connect suitable gauge manifold and discharge system as outlined previously.

NOTE: System must be completely discharged prior to evacuation. If pressurized refrigerant is allowed to enter vacuum pump, pump will be damaged.

2. Connect hose from gauge manifold center port to vacuum pump inlet.
3. Fully open both gauge manifold hand valves.
4. Operate vacuum pump while observing low side compound gauge. If system does not "pump-down" to 28–29½ inches Hg (at sea level) within approximately 5 minutes, recheck connections and leak test system.
5. Continue to operate vacuum pump for 15–30 minutes, longer if system was open for an extended period of time, then close both manifold valves and stop pump.
6. Check ability of system to hold vacuum. Watch low side compound gauge and ensure that reading does not rise at a rate faster than 1 inch Hg every 4–5 minutes.
7. If system fails to hold vacuum, recheck fittings and connections, and leak test system.
8. If system holds vacuum, charge system with refrigerant.

CHARGING THE SYSTEM

NOTE: Refer to "A/C Data Table" in the "A/C System Servicing" section for refrigerant capacities.

CHARGING WITH 14 OUNCE CANS

CAUTION: Never use cans to charge into high pressure side of system (compressor discharge port) or into system at high temperature, as high system pressure transferred into charging can may cause it to explode.

1. Attach center hose from manifold gauge set to refrigerant dispensing manifold. Turn refrigerant manifold valves completely counterclockwise to open fully, and remove protective caps from refrigerant manifold.
2. Screw refrigerant cans into manifold, ensuring gasket is in place and in good condition. Torque can and manifold nuts to 6–8 ft. lbs.
3. Turn refrigerant manifold valves clockwise to puncture cans, and close manifold valves, **Fig. 4.**
4. Loosen charging hose at gauge set manifold and turn a refrigerant valve counterclockwise to release refrigerant and purge air from charging hose. When refrigerant gas escapes from loose connection, retighten hose.
5. Fully open all refrigerant manifold valves being used and place refrigerant cans into pan of hot water at 125° F to aid transfer of refrigerant gas.

CAUTION: Do not heat refrigerant cans over 125° F as the may explode.

Place water pan and refrigerant cans on scale and note weight.
6. Connect jumper wire across terminals of cycling clutch switch connector located near "H" valve, if equipped, so that compressor clutch will remain engaged.
7. Start engine and set controls to A/C low blower position. Low pressure cutout switch will prevent clutch from engaging until refrigerant is added to system. If clutch does engage, replace

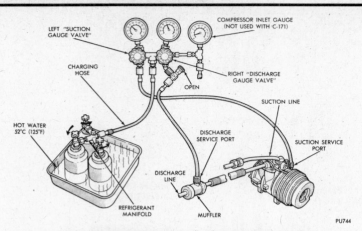

Fig. 4 A/C system charging (Typical)

switch before continuing.
8. Charge through suction side of system by slowly opening suction manifold valve. Adjust valve so charging pressure does not exceed 50 psig.
9. Adjust engine speed to fast idle of 1400 RPM.
10. After specified refrigerant charge has entered system, close gauge set manifold valves, refrigerant manifold valves, and reconnect wiring.

CHARGING WITH BULK REFRIGERANT SUPPLY

CAUTION: Only a charging bottle may be used to charge liquid refrigerant through the compressor discharge muffler. Never charge with liquid through compressor inlet or suction line ports, as damage to compressor is likely to occur. Do not run compressor while adding liquid refrigerant.

1. Warm charging bottle in pan of 125° F

water. Do not heat R-12 with a torch, as it may explode.
2. Loosen charging hose at gauge set manifold and slowly open refrigerant supply valve until refrigerant has purged air from hose. Retighten the hose.
3. Place refrigerant container upside down on scale and note weight.
4. Open refrigerant supply valve and compressor discharge gauge valve to charge system. When scale indicates proper amount of charge has entered system, close valves.

If required amount of refrigerant does not enter system, close compressor discharge valve on manifold gauge set. Turn charging bottle right side up so gas, not liquid, will enter system. Start engine and set A/C control in A/C position. Slowly open suction line valve on manifold gauge set. The compressor will draw refrigerant into system. Charging line valve should be set so suction pressure does not exceed 50 psig.

A/C System Servicing

INDEX

OIL LEVEL CHECK

NOTE: Refer to "A/C Data Table" for oil level specifications.

RV-2 COMPRESSOR

1. Connect gauge manifold and dis-

charge system as outlined.
2. When system is nearly discharged, flush compressor dipstick with remaining refrigerant to ensure that dipstick is clean and at approximately the same temperature as oil in compressor sump.
3. Slowly loosen, then remove oil filler plug, **Fig. 1.**

NOTE: A suitable face shield should be worn when removing oil filler plug, as refrigerant dissolved in compressor oil may force oil out through plug opening.

4. Allow refrigerant vapors to clear and oil surface to stabilize, then measure oil level with dipstick.
5. Add oil to compressor, as needed, to bring level to within specifications

A/C Data Table

Year	Model	Refrigerant Capacity Lbs.	Refrigeration Oil			Compressor Clutch Air Gap Inches
			Viscosity	Total System Capacity Ounces	Compressor Oil Level Check Inches	
1979–81	Exc. Van & Forward Control	2⅝	500	①	②	③
	Van & Forward Control④	3⅜	500	①	②	③
	Van & Forward Control⑤	4	500	①	②	③
1981	Van & Forward Control④	3	500	①	②	③
	Van & Forward Control⑤	4	500	①	②	③
1982–84	Exc. Van & Forward Control	2⅝	500	9–10	⑥	.020–.035
1982–83	Van & Forward Control④	3	500	9–10	⑥	.020–.035
	Van & Forward Control⑤	4	500	9–10	⑥	.020–.035
1984	Van & Forward Control④⑦	3	500	9–10	⑥	.020–.035
	Van & Forward Control⑤⑦	4	500	9–10	⑥	.020–.035
	Van & Wagon⑧	2⅓	500	9–10	⑥	.020–.035
1985	Van & Forward Control④⑦	3	500	7–7¼	⑥	.020–.035
	Van & Forward Control⑤⑦	4	500	7–7¼	⑥	.020–.035
	Van & Wagon⑧	2⅜	500	7–7¼	⑥	.020–.035

①—RV-2 comp., 10–12 oz.; C-171 comp., 9–10 oz.
②—RV-2 comp., 3–3.4 in.; C-171 comp., note that "Oil Level Inches" can not be checked. Refer to total capacity and see text for checking procedure.
③—C-171 comp., .020–.035 in.
④—Models less auxiliary (rear, overhead etc.) system.
⑤—Models with auxiliary (rear, overhead etc.) system.
⑥—Note that "Oil Level Inches" can not be checked. Refer to total capacity and see text for checking procedure.
⑦—Rear wheel drive.
⑧—Front wheel drive.

Charging Valve Location

Year	Model	High Pressure Fitting	Low Pressure Fitting
1979–81	Exc. Van & Front Section①	Discharge Line Muffler	Suction Line at Compressor
	Van & Front Section①	Discharge Line Muffler	Suction Hose
	All②	Discharge Line Muffler	Compressor
1982–85	All	Discharge Line Muffler	Compressor

①—RV-2 Compressor.
②—C-171 Compressor.

listed in "A/C Data Table."

NOTE: If other system components are replaced, refer to "Oil Charge."

6. Install filler plug, then evacuate and recharge system.

C-171 COMPRESSOR

This compressor must be removed from vehicle and drained to check the oil level. Refer to "Oil Charge" for service procedures.

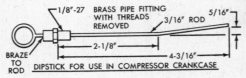

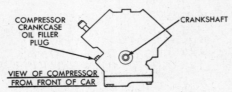

Fig. 1 Dipstick fabrication & oil filler plug location. RV-2 compressor

OIL CHARGE

OIL CHARGE—COMPONENT REPLACEMENT

If there are no signs of external oil leakage, proceed as follows to add oil to system during component replacement.

1. Discharge system, as outlined, and measure amount of oil collected in discharge container.

NOTE: The amount of oil collected when discharging system must be replaced with new refrigeration oil to maintain proper oil charge.

2. Remove defective components. Measure amount of oil remaining in compressor, if removed.

3. Add proper amount of new refrigera-

tion oil to each replacement component as follows:

a. If compressor is replaced, drain replacement compressor and add the same amount of oil as was drained from defective compressor.

b. If condenser is replaced, add 1 ounce of oil to replacement condenser.

c. If evaporator is replaced, add 2 ounces of oil to replacement evaporator.

d. If filter/drier is replaced, add 1 ounce of oil to replacement filter/drier.

4. Install replacement components, then evacuate and recharge system.

OIL LEVEL CHECK—LEAK CONDITION

RV-2 Compressor

Refer to "Oil Level Check" for service procedures.

C-171 Compressor

Compressor oil level need only be checked when there is evidence of oil loss from the system as in the case of a broken line, leaking fitting or component, defective compressor seal or collision damage to system. A wet, shiny surface around a leak point is evidence of oil loss.

1. Discharge system as outlined, and repair leak as needed.

2. Disconnect suction and discharge lines from compressor, then remove compressor and clutch assembly from vehicle.

3. Invert compressor and drain oil through suction and discharge ports.

4. Add 5 ounces of new refrigeration oil to compressor through suction port.

5. Reinstall compressor using new gaskets on refrigerant line fittings, then evacuate and recharge system.

ELECTRIC ENGINE COOLING FANS

INDEX

DESCRIPTION

The fan is controlled by a fan switch which is located on the radiator, **Figs. 1 and 2.** The switch will automatically turn on when coolant temperature reaches 200° F. On models with A/C, when the A/C system is in operation, the fan motor will operate continually regardless of engine coolant temperature. When the ignition switch is turned off, the fan motor will stop operating, except on some 1984—85 Chrysler models equipped with 2.6 L engines w/air conditioning. On some 1984—85 Chrysler models equipped with 2.6 L engines and air conditioning, the fan will remain operating with ignition off for approximately 5 minutes if ambient temperature at radiator is above a predetermined level.

The radiator fan switch is located on the left side of the radiator tank. The switch is normally open and incorporates a bimetallic disc which pushes a plunger when coolant temperature reaches 200° F. Normal operation is indicated when fan motor turns on and off at appropriate temperatures.

The ambient temperature switch, used on some 2.6 L Chrysler engines w/air conditioning, is located on the radiator cooling fan mounting bracket and is used in conjunction with a time delay to activate the radiator cooling fan for approximately 5 minutes with engine off during periods of radiator ambient temperature of 105° F or above.

TROUBLESHOOTING
RADIATOR FAN SWITCH

To check switch continuity, drain coolant until level is below switch. The switch can be viewed by looking downward through the radiator filler neck. Disconnect electrical connector from switch and remove switch from radiator. Bring switch to a temperature of 208° F or higher using a suitable oil bath, then check for switch continuity using an ohmmeter or suitable test lamp. If continuity is not indicated, replace

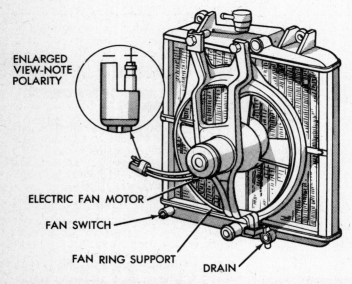

Fig. 1 Electric fan. 1984—85 Dodge & Plymouth Mini Vans

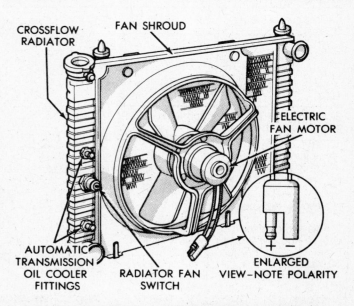

Fig. 2 Electric fan. 1984 Rampage (1982—83 Rampage & 1983 Scamp similar)

switch.

AMBIENT TEMPERATURE SWITCH

Test switch using a suitable ohmmeter. When switch is cold, continuity should not exist. When switch is warmed to 105° F or above, continuity should be present. Replace if defective.

ELECTRIC FAN MOTOR

Disconnect wire connector from fan motor terminal, then connect a 14 gauge jumper wire from battery to fan motor terminal. If fan motor does not operate properly, replace fan motor.

ELECTRIC FAN MOTOR RELAY

The fan motor relay is used on Chrysler F.W.D. models equipped with A/C. The relay is located on the front left-hand shock absorber housing. If radiator fan switch and fan motor test results are satisfactory, but fan motor will not operate, the fan motor relay is suspected. Replace relay, then disconnect wire connector from radiator fan switch and connect a 14 gauge jumper wire between wire connector terminals. Place ignition switch in Accessory position. Fan motor should operate.

VARIABLE SPEED FANS

INDEX

CAUTION: Do not operate engine until fan has first been inspected for cracks and/or separations. If a fan blade is found to be bent or damaged in any way, do not attempt to repair or reuse damaged part. Proper balance is essential in fan assembly operation. Balance cannot be assured once a fan assembly has been found to be bent or damaged and failure may occur during operation, creating an extremely dangerous condition. Always replace damaged fan assembly.

DESCRIPTION

The fan drive clutch, **Fig. 1,** is a fluid coupling containing silicone oil. Fan speed is regulated by the torque-carrying capacity of the silicone oil. The more silicone oil in the coupling, the greater the fan speed, and the less silicone oil, the slower the fan speed.

The fan drive clutch uses a heat-sensitive, coiled bi-metallic spring connected to an opening plate, **Fig. 2.** This unit causes the fan speed to increase with a rise in temperature and to decrease as temperature decreases.

TROUBLESHOOTING
FAN DRIVE CLUTCH TEST

CAUTION: Do not operate the engine until the fan has been first checked for possible cracks and separations.

To check the clutch fan, disconnect the bi-metal spring, **Fig. 3,** and rotate 90° counter-clockwise. This disables the temperature-controlled, free-wheeling feature and the clutch performs like a conventional fan. If this cures the overheating condition, replace the clutch fan.

FAN CLUTCH NOISE

Fan clutch noise can sometimes be noticed when clutch is engaged for maximum cooling. Clutch noise is also noticeable within the first few minutes after starting engine while clutch is redistributing the silicone fluid back to its normal, disengaged operating condition after settling for long periods of time (overnight). However, continuous fan noise or an excessive roar indicates the clutch assembly is locked-up due to internal failure. This condition can be checked by attempting to manually rotate fan. If fan cannot be rotated manually or there is a rough, abrasive feel as fan is rotated, the clutch should be replaced.

FAN LOOSENESS

Lateral movement can be observed at the fan blade tip under various temperature

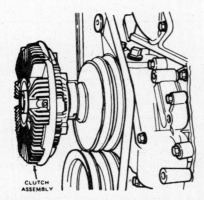

Fig. 1 Fan drive clutch assembly, 1984–85. 1979–83 similar

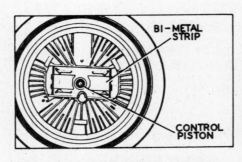

Fig. 2 Variable speed fan with flat bi-metallic thermostatic spring

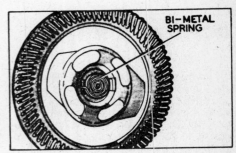

Fig. 3 Variable speed fan with coiled bi-metallic thermostatic spring

conditions because of the type bearing used. This movement should not exceed ¼ inch (6.5mm) as measured at the fan tip. If this lateral movement does not exceed specifications, there is no cause for replacement.

CLUTCH FLUID LEAK

Small fluid leaks do not generally affect the operation of the unit. These leaks generally occur around the area of the bearing assembly, but if the leaks appear to be excessive, engine overheating may occur. Check for clutch and fan free-wheeling by attempting to rotate fan and clutch assembly by hand five times. If no drag is felt, replace clutch.

FAN BLADE INSPECTION

Place fan on flat surface with leading edge facing down. If there is a clearance between fan blade touching surface and opposite blade of more than .090 inch (2mm), replace fan. (See caution at beginning of chapter.)

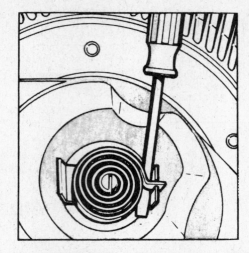

Fig. 4 Bi-metallic coiled spring removal

ALTERNATORS
TABLE OF CONTENTS

Chrysler Alternators
INDEX

DESCRIPTION

The main components of the alternator are the rotor, stator, diodes, end shields and drive pulley, **Figs. 1 through 4.** Direct current is available at the output "BAT" terminal. The function of the voltage regulator is to limit output voltage. This is accomplished by controlling the current flow in the rotor field coil, in turn controlling the strength of the rotor magnetic field. The electronic voltage regulator is a sealed, non-adjustable unit.

TESTING SYSTEM ON VEHICLE
CHARGING CIRCUIT SYSTEM RESISTANCE TEST

Testing
1. Disconnect battery ground cable.
2. Disconnect "Bat" lead at alternator output terminal.
3. Connect a 0–150 amp D.C. ammeter in series between alternator "Bat" terminal and disconnected "Bat" lead wire, **Fig. 5.**
4. Connect positive lead wire of a suitable voltmeter to disconnected "Bat"

lead wire, then connect negative lead to battery positive post.
5. Disconnect light green regulator field wire from alternator, then connect green regulator field wire to a suitable ground.

NOTE: On some 1984–85 units, disconnect electrical harness from voltage regulator, then connect jumper wire from harness connector green wire to suitable ground.

6. Connect a suitable engine tachometer, then reconnect battery ground cable.
7. Connect a variable carbon pile rheo-

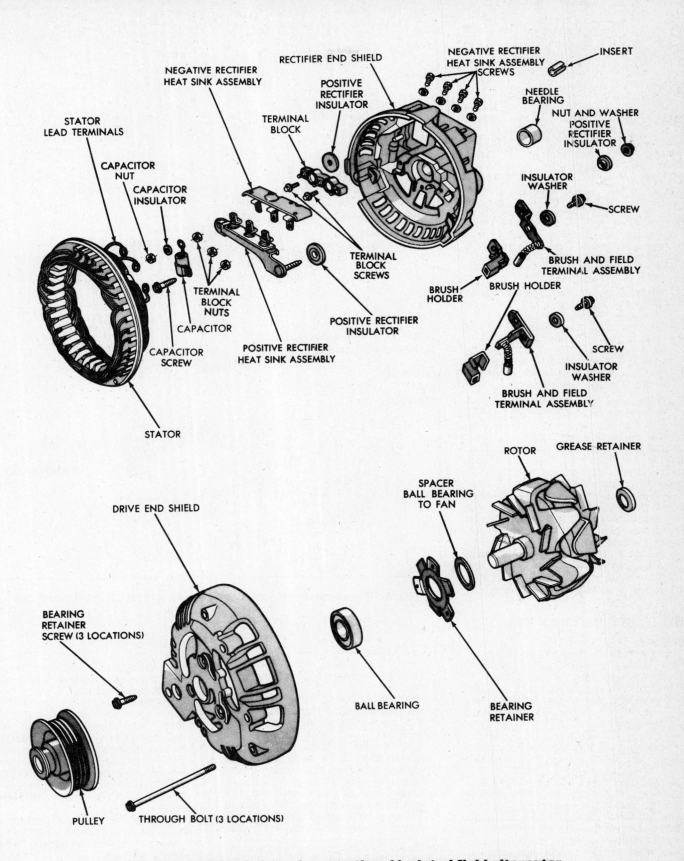

Fig. 1 Disassembled view of conventional isolated field alternator

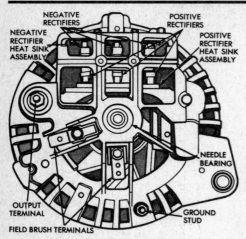

Fig. 2 Rear view of conventional isolated field alternator

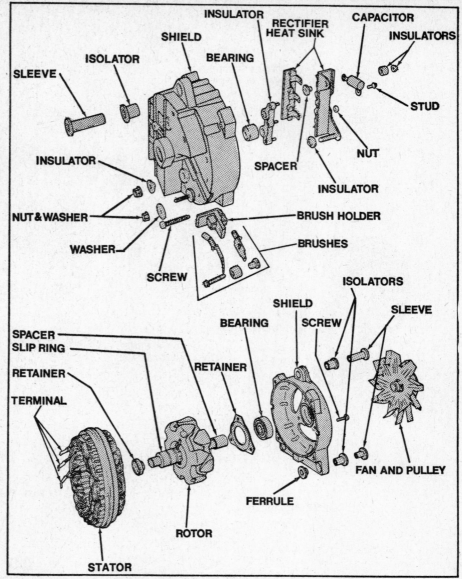

Fig. 3 Disassembled view of 100, 114 & 117 amp alternators

stat to battery terminals, ensuring carbon piles are in "open" or "off" position.

8. Start engine and operate at idle speed, then adjust carbon pile and engine speed to maintain a 20 amp circuit flow. Note voltmeter reading. Voltmeter reading should not exceed .7 volt (.5 volt on 1984–85 units).

Test Results

1. If a higher than specified voltage drop is indicated, clean and tighten all connectors in charging circuit.

NOTE: A voltage drop test may be performed at each connector to locate point of excessive resistance.

2. If charging circuit resistance test was satisfactory, disconnect battery ground cable, then the ammeter, voltmeter and carbon pile.
3. Remove jumper wire, then connect light green field wire to alternator field terminal or voltage regulator.
4. Connect battery ground cable.

CURRENT OUTPUT TEST

Testing

1. Disconnect battery ground cable.
2. Disconnect "Bat" lead at alternator output terminal.
3. Connect a 0–150 amp D.C. ammeter in series between alternator "Bat" terminal and disconnected "Bat" lead wire, **Fig. 6.**
4. Connect positive lead of a suitable voltmeter to "Bat" terminal of alternator, then connect negative lead to a suitable ground.
5. Disconnect green voltage regulator field wire at alternator, then connect it to a suitable ground.

NOTE: On some 1984–85 units, disconnect electrical harness from voltage regulator, then connect jumper wire from harness connector green wire to suitable

ground.

6. Connect a suitable engine tachometer, then reconnect battery ground cable.
7. Connect a variable carbon pile rheostat between battery terminals, ensuring carbon piles are in "open" or "off" position.
8. Start engine and operate at idle speed, then adjust carbon pile and engine speed in increments until a speed of 1250 RPM at 15 volts is obtained on all units except 100, 114 and 117 amp units. On 100, 114 and 117 amp units, adjust carbon pile and engine speed to 900 RPM at 13 volts.

NOTE: Do not allow voltmeter range to exceed 16 volts during testing.

Test Results

1. Note ammeter reading. Ammeter reading should be within specified limits noted in specification charts in individual truck chapters.
2. If reading is less than specified, remove alternator from vehicle and perform "Bench Test."
3. After completion of current output test, turn off carbon pile and ignition switch, then disconnect battery ground cable.
4. Remove ammeter, voltmeter, tachometer and carbon pile, then reconnect "Bat" lead to alternator output terminal.
5. Disconnect lead wire from ground, then reconnect green field wire to alternator terminal or voltage regulator.
6. Connect battery ground cable.

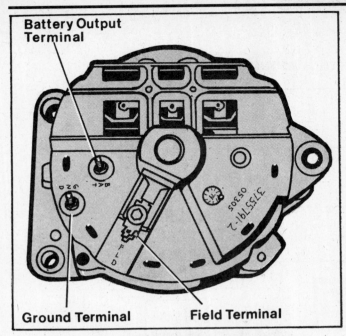

Fig. 4 Rear view of 100, 114 & 117 amp alternators

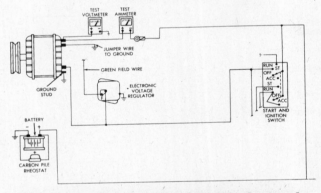

Fig. 6 Current output test with electronic regulator (Typical)

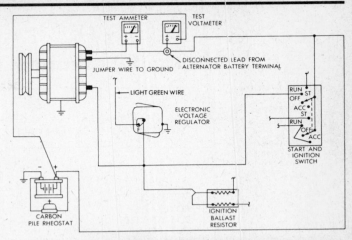

Fig. 5 Charging circuit resistance test with electronic regulator (Typical)

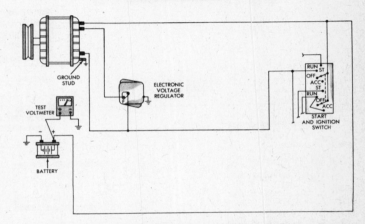

Fig. 7 Electronic voltage regulator test (Typical)

Ambient Temperature Near Regulator	−20° F.	80° F.	140° F.	Above 140° F.
1979–83	14.9–15.9	13.9–14.6	13.3–13.9	Less than 13.6
1984–85	14.6–15.8	13.9–14.4	13.0–13.7	Less than 13.6

Fig. 8 Regulator test specification chart

VOLTAGE REGULATOR TEST

Testing

NOTE: Battery must be fully charged for test to be accurate.

1. Clean battery terminals, then connect positive lead of a suitable voltmeter to battery positive post and the negative lead to a suitable ground, **Fig. 7.**
2. Connect an engine tachometer, then start and operate engine at 1250 RPM with all lights and accessories in the "off" position.
3. Note voltmeter readings, then refer to voltage chart, **Fig. 8.**

NOTE: An ammeter reading registering an immediate charge, then gradually returning to normal, is normal. The duration the ammeter remains positioned to the right depends on cranking time.

Test Results

1. If voltage is fluctuating or below limits, proceed as follows:
   a. Ensure voltage regulator has a proper ground through regulator case, mounting screws and chassis.
   b. Place ignition switch in "off" position, then disconnect voltage regulator connector and inspect for a possible open circuit.
   c. Place ignition switch in "on" position.

NOTE: Do not start engine or distort terminals with voltmeter probe.

   d. Inspect blue and green leads at wiring harness terminal for proper battery voltage, then place ignition switch in "off" position.

NOTE: If steps a through d are satisfactory, replace voltage regulator.

2. If voltage is above limits, **Fig. 8**, proceed as follows:
   a. Place ignition switch in "off" position, then disconnect voltage regulator connector.
   b. Place ignition switch in "on" position.

NOTE: Do not start engine or distort terminals with voltmeter probe.

   c. Inspect blue and green leads at wiring harness terminal for proper battery voltage, then place ignition switch in "off" position.

NOTE: If results of steps a, b and c are not satisfactory, replace voltage regulator.

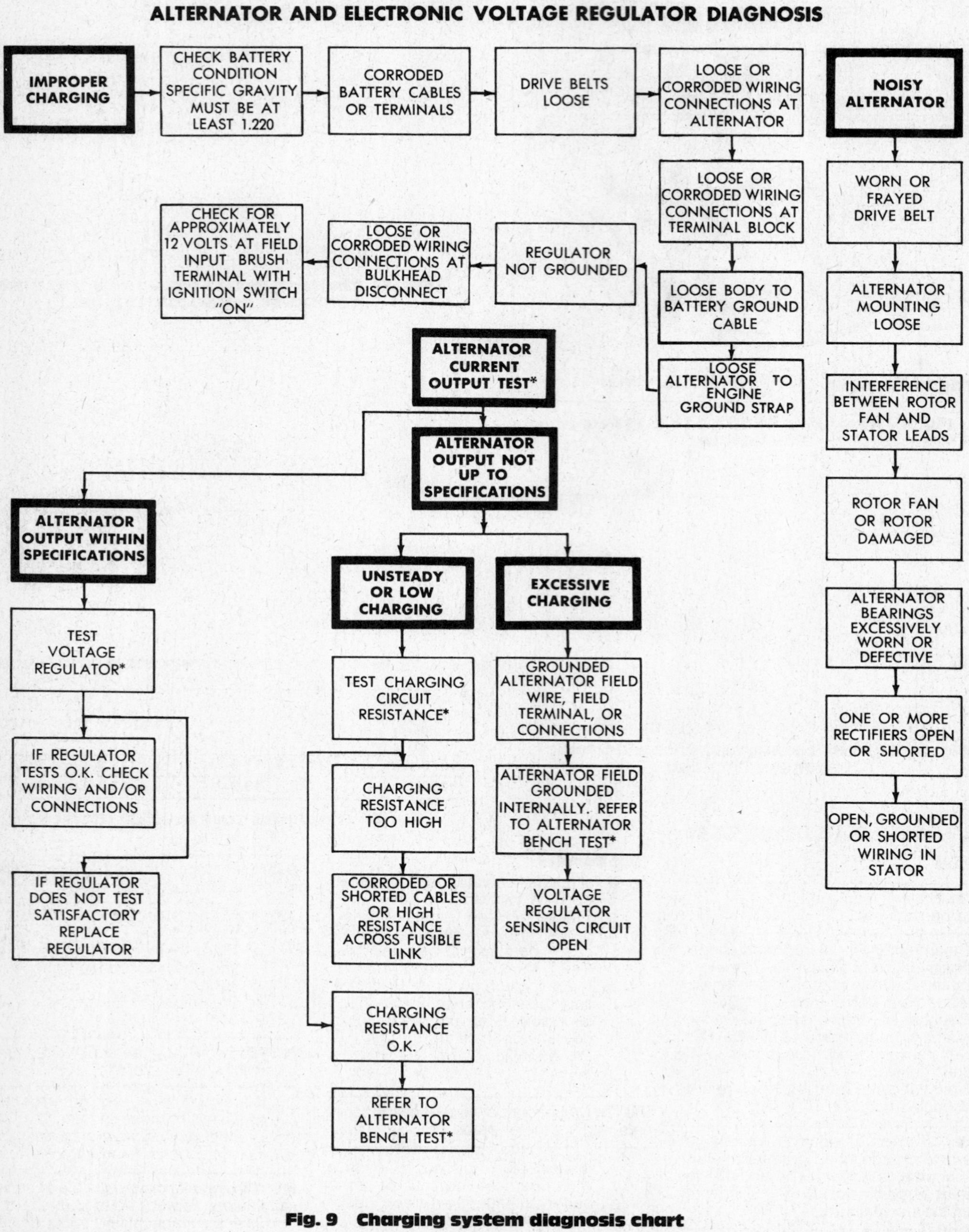

ALTERNATOR AND ELECTRONIC VOLTAGE REGULATOR DIAGNOSIS

IMPROPER CHARGING → CHECK BATTERY CONDITION SPECIFIC GRAVITY MUST BE AT LEAST 1.220 → CORRODED BATTERY CABLES OR TERMINALS → DRIVE BELTS LOOSE → LOOSE OR CORRODED WIRING CONNECTIONS AT ALTERNATOR

NOISY ALTERNATOR

LOOSE OR CORRODED WIRING CONNECTIONS AT TERMINAL BLOCK

WORN OR FRAYED DRIVE BELT

CHECK FOR APPROXIMATELY 12 VOLTS AT FIELD INPUT BRUSH TERMINAL WITH IGNITION SWITCH "ON" ← LOOSE OR CORRODED WIRING CONNECTIONS AT BULKHEAD DISCONNECT ← REGULATOR NOT GROUNDED

LOOSE BODY TO BATTERY GROUND CABLE

ALTERNATOR MOUNTING LOOSE

LOOSE ALTERNATOR TO ENGINE GROUND STRAP

INTERFERENCE BETWEEN ROTOR FAN AND STATOR LEADS

ALTERNATOR CURRENT OUTPUT TEST*

ALTERNATOR OUTPUT NOT UP TO SPECIFICATIONS

ROTOR FAN OR ROTOR DAMAGED

ALTERNATOR OUTPUT WITHIN SPECIFICATIONS

UNSTEADY OR LOW CHARGING

EXCESSIVE CHARGING

ALTERNATOR BEARINGS EXCESSIVELY WORN OR DEFECTIVE

TEST VOLTAGE REGULATOR*

TEST CHARGING CIRCUIT RESISTANCE*

GROUNDED ALTERNATOR FIELD WIRE, FIELD TERMINAL, OR CONNECTIONS

ONE OR MORE RECTIFIERS OPEN OR SHORTED

IF REGULATOR TESTS O.K. CHECK WIRING AND/OR CONNECTIONS

CHARGING RESISTANCE TOO HIGH

ALTERNATOR FIELD GROUNDED INTERNALLY. REFER TO ALTERNATOR BENCH TEST*

OPEN, GROUNDED OR SHORTED WIRING IN STATOR

IF REGULATOR DOES NOT TEST SATISFACTORY REPLACE REGULATOR

CORRODED OR SHORTED CABLES OR HIGH RESISTANCE ACROSS FUSIBLE LINK

VOLTAGE REGULATOR SENSING CIRCUIT OPEN

CHARGING RESISTANCE O.K.

REFER TO ALTERNATOR BENCH TEST*

Fig. 9   Charging system diagnosis chart

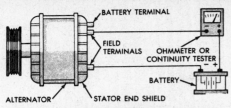

Fig. 10   Rotor field coil current draw test

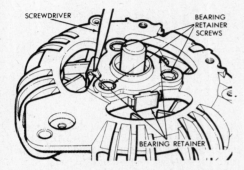

Fig. 13   Disengaging bearing retainer from end shield

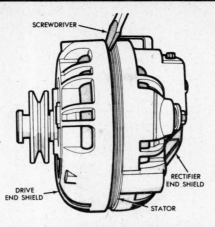

Fig. 11   Separating drive end shield from stator

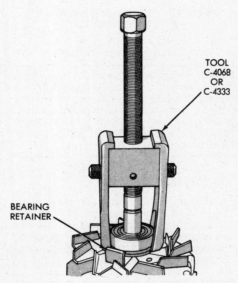

Fig. 14   Removing bearing from rotor shaft

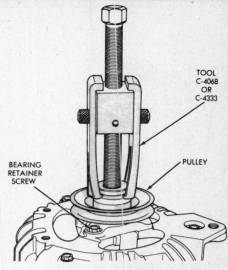

Fig. 12   Removing pulley

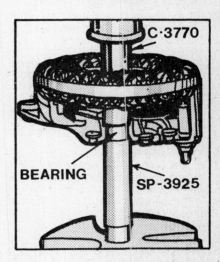

Fig. 15   Removing diode end shield bearing

3. Remove voltmeter and tachometer.

ALTERNATOR & REGULATOR DIAGNOSIS

Refer to **Fig. 9** for alternator and regulator diagnosis.

BENCH TESTS

If the alternator performance does not meet current output specification limits, it will have to be removed and disassembled for further tests and servicing.

To remove the alternator, disconnect the battery ground cable and the leads at the alternator. Then unfasten and remove the alternator from the vehicle.

FIELD COIL DRAW

1. Place alternator on an insulated surface.
2. Connect a jumper wire between one alternator field terminal and the negative terminal of a fully charged battery, **Fig. 10.**
3. Connect test ammeter positive lead to the other alternator field terminal and the ammeter negative lead to the positive battery terminal.
4. On 1979–83 units except 100, 114 and 117 amp, connect a jumper wire between alternator end shield and negative terminal of battery.
5. On all units, slowly rotate rotor by hand and note ammeter reading. On all units except 100, 114 and 117 amp, field current at 12 volts should be 4.5–6.5 (1979–83) or 2.5–5.5 (1984–85) amps. On 100 and 117 amp units, field current at 12 volts should be 4.75–6.0

amps. On 114 amp units, field current at 12 volts should be 2.5–5.0 amps.
6. A low rotor coil draw is an indication of high resistance in the field coil circuit, (brushes, slip rings or rotor coil). A high rotor coil draw indicates shorted rotor coil or grounded rotor. No reading indicates an open rotor or defective brushes.

ALTERNATOR REPAIRS, EXCEPT 100, 114 & 117 AMP UNITS

DISASSEMBLY

To prevent possible damage to the brush assemblies, they should be removed before disassembling the alternator. Both brushes are insulated and mounted in plastic holders.

1. Remove both brush screws, insulating

nylon washers and remove brush assemblies.

NOTE: The stator is laminated; do not burr it or the end shield.

2. Remove through bolts and pry between stator and drive end shield with a screwdriver. Carefully separate drive end shield, pulley and rotor from stator and diode rectifier shield, **Fig. 11.**
3. The pulley is an interference fit on the rotor shaft; therefore, a suitable puller must be used to remove it, **Fig. 12.**
4. Pry drive end bearing spring retainer from end shield with a screwdriver, **Fig. 13.**
5. Support end shield and tap rotor shaft with a plastic hammer to separate rotor from end shield.
6. The drive end ball bearing is an interference fit with the rotor shaft; therefore, a suitable puller must be used to

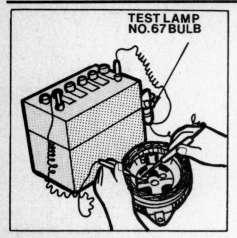

Fig. 16 Testing diodes with test lamp

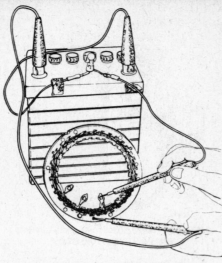

Fig. 17 Testing stator for grounds

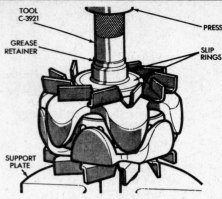

Fig. 18 Installing bearing grease retainer

remove it, **Fig. 14.**

7. To remove rectifiers and heat sinks, loosen screws securing negative rectifier and heat sink asembly to end shield, remove the two outer screws and lift assembly from end shield. Remove nuts securing positive rectifier and heat sink assembly to insulated terminals in end shield. Then, remove capacitor ground screw and lift insulated washer, capacitor and positive rectifier and heat sink assembly from end shield.

8. The needle roller bearing in the rectifier end shield is a press fit. If it is necessary to remove the rectifier end frame needle bearing, protect the end shield by supporting the shield when pressing out the bearing as shown in **Fig. 15.**

TESTING DIODE RECTIFIERS

A special Rectifier Tester Tool C-3829A provides a quick, simple and accurate method to test the rectifiers without the necessity of disconnecting the soldered rectifier leads. This instrument is commercially available and full instructions for its use are provided. Lacking this tool, the rectifiers may be tested with a 12 volt battery and a test lamp having a No. 67 bulb. The procedure is as follows:

1. Remove nuts securing stator windings, positive and negative rectifier straps to terminal block. Remove stator winding terminals and pry stator from end shield.

2. Connect one side of test lamp to positive battery post and the other side of the test lamp to a test probe. Connect another test probe to the negative battery post, **Fig. 16.**

3. Contact heat sink with one probe and strap on top of rectifier with the other probe.

4. Reverse position of probes. If test lamp lights in one direction only, the rectifier is satisfactory. If test lamp lights in both directions, the rectifier is shorted. If test lamp lights in neither

direction, the rectifier is open.

NOTE: Possible cause of an open or a blown rectifier is a faulty capacitor or a battery that has been installed on reverse polarity. If the battery is installed properly and the rectifiers are open, test the capacitor capacity, which should be .50 microfarad plus or minus 20%.

TESTING STATOR

1. Separate stator from end shields.

2. Using a 12 volt test lamp, **Fig. 17,** test stator for grounds. Contact one test probe to any pin on stator frame and the other to each stator lead. If lamp lights, stator is grounded.

NOTE: Remove varnish from stator frame pin to ensure proper electrical connection.

3. Use a 12-volt test lamp to test stator for continuity. Contact one stator lead with one probe and the remaining two leads with the other probe. If test lamp does not light, the stator has an open circuit.

4. Install new stator if one tested is defective.

TESTING ROTOR

The rotor may be tested electrically for grounded, open or shorted field coils as follows:

Grounded Field Coil Test: Connect an ohmmeter between each slip ring and the rotor shaft. The ohmmeter should indicate infinite resistance. If reading is zero or higher, rotor is grounded.

Open or shorted Field Coil Test: Connect an ohmmeter between the slip rings. A resistance of 1.5 to 2 ohms at room temperature indicates the field coils are satisfactory. A reading of 2.5 to 3 ohms indicates the alternator was operated at high underhood temperature, however, rotor is still satis-

factory. Resistance below 1.5 ohms indicates a shorted field coil. Resistances above 3.5 ohms indicates a high resistance in the field coils and further testing or rotor replacement is required.

REPLACING SLIP RINGS

NOTE: On 1979–85 units, slip rings and rotor are serviced as an assembly.

ALTERNATOR ASSEMBLY

1. Press grease retainer onto rotor shaft using tool No. C-3921, **Fig. 18.** The grease retainer is properly positioned when the inner bore of the installed tool bottoms on the rotor shaft.

2. Install diode end shield bearing, **Fig. 19.**

3. Install drive end bearing in end shield with bearing retainer plate to hold bearing in position. Place assembly on rotor shaft and press into position, **Fig. 20.**

NOTE: If a metal spacer is provided with replacement rotor to ball bearings, position this spacer on pulley end of rotor shaft first.

4. Press pulley onto rotor shaft until it contacts inner race of bearing.

NOTE: Do not exceed 6800 lbs.

5. Install output terminal stud and insulator through end shield. Place positive heat sink assembly over studs, guiding rectifier straps over studs.

6. Place capacitor terminal over heat sink stud, then insert insulator, ensuring insulator is properly seated in heat sink bore. Attach capacitor bracket to end shield with a metal screw, then torque screw to 30 to 40 inch lbs. Complete assembly by installing positive heat sink nut and lock washer, then torque nut to 30 inch lbs.

7. Turn end shield over, then install round plastic insulator over battery insulator, flat side up. Install nut and washer assembly, then torque to 30 to

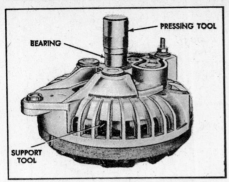

Fig. 19 Installing diode end shield bearing

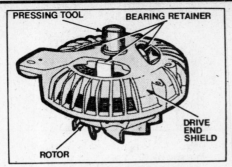

Fig. 20 Installing drive end shield bearing

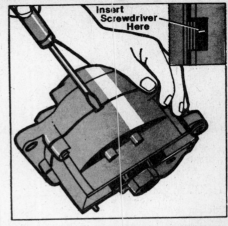

Fig. 21 Separating end shields. 100, 114 & 117 amp units

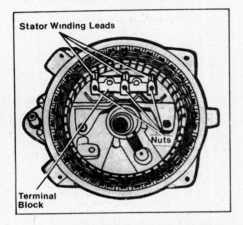

Fig. 22 Removing stator winding leads. 100, 114 & 117 amp units

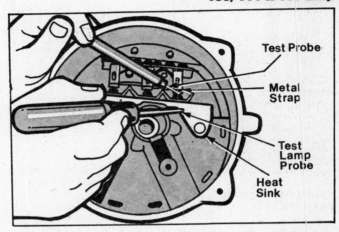

Fig. 23 Testing rectifiers with test lamp. 100, 114 & 117 amp units

50 inch lbs.

8. Slide negative rectifier and heat sink assembly into end shield, then install three diode straps onto terminal blocks. Install hex head screws through end shield and into negative heat sink, then torque screws to 19 to 29 inch lbs.

9. Position stator over rectifier end shield, then install stator leads over terminal block. Place stator into end shield, then install winding terminal nuts. Torque nuts to 11 to 17 inch lbs.

NOTE: Ensure leads are routed so as not to interfere with rotor or edge of negative heat sink.

10. Position rotor and drive end shield on stator and diode end shield.
11. Align through bolt holes in stator, diode end shield and drive end shield.
12. Compress stator and both end shields by hand and install through bolts, washers and nuts. Torque nuts to 25 to 55 inch lbs.
13. Install field brush into vertical and horizontal holders. Place an insulating washer on each field brush terminal and install lock-washers and attaching screws.

NOTE: Ensure brushes are not grounded.

14. Rotate pulley slowly by hand to be sure rotor fans do not touch diodes, capacitor lead and stator connections.
15. Install alternator and adjust drive belt.
16. Connect leads to alternator.
17. Connect battery ground cable.
18. Start and operate engine and observe alternator operation.
19. If necessary, test current output and regulator voltage setting.

ALTERNATOR REPAIRS, 100, 114 & 117 AMP UNITS
DISASSEMBLY & TESTING

NOTE: To prevent possible damage to brush assembly, they must be removed before separating end shields. Field brushes are mounted in plastic holders which retain brushes against rotor slip rings.

Separating End Shields
1. Remove brush holder screw and insu-lating washer, then lift brush holder from end shield.
2. Remove the through bolts, then using a screwdriver, pry between the stator and end shield in the slot provided to separate end shields, **Fig. 21.**

Rectifier Testing
1. Remove stator winding leads to terminal block stud nuts, **Fig. 22.**
2. Lift stator winding leads and pry stator from end shield.
3. Using a 12 volt battery and a test lamp equipped with a #67 bulb, test rectifiers as follows:
   a. Connect one test probe to rectifier heat sink and the other test probe to the metal strap on top of rectifier, **Fig. 23.** Reverse the probes.
   b. If test lamp lights in one direction and does not light in the other, rectifier is satisfactory. If test lamp lights in both directions, rectifier is shorted. If test lamp does not light in either direction, rectifier is open.

Rectifier & Heat Sink Assembly Removal
1. Remove nut and insulator securing positive heat sink assembly to end

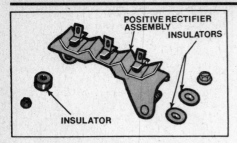

Fig. 24 Positive rectifier assembly. 100, 114 & 117 amp units

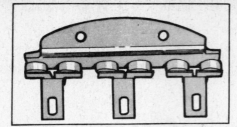

Fig. 25 Negative rectifier assembly. 100, 114 & 117 amp units

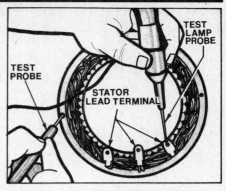

Fig. 26 Testing stator winding. 100, 114 & 117 amp units

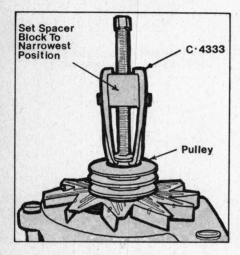

Fig. 27 Removing pulley. 100 amp unit

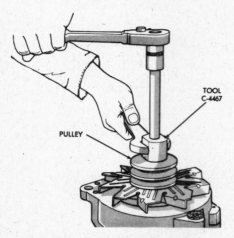

Fig. 28 Removing pulley. 114 & 117 amp units

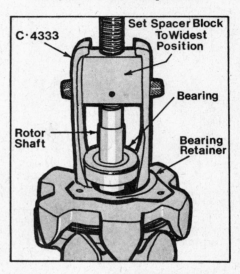

Fig. 29 Removing bearing from rotor shaft. 100, 114 & 117 amp units

shield stud.
2. Remove capacitor attaching screw.
3. Remove nut and insulator securing positive heat sink assembly stud to end shield, then remove positive heat sink assembly, **Fig. 24,** noting locating of the insulators.
4. Remove screws securing negative heat sink assembly to end shield, then the negative heat sink assembly, **Fig. 25.**
5. Remove terminal block, then the capacitor and insulator.

Stator Testing
1. Contact one test lamp probe to outer diameter of stator frame and the other probe to each of the stator lead terminals, one at a time, **Fig. 26.**
2. If test lamp lights, the stator lead is grounded, requiring replacement.

NOTE: The stator windings are Delta Wound therefore the windings cannot be tested for opens or shorts using a test lamp. If the stator is not grounded, and all other electrical circuits and alternator components test satisfactory, the stator may be open or shorted.

Pulley & Bearing Removal
1. On 100 amp alternators, remove pulley using tool No. C-4333, **Fig. 27.** On 114 and 117 amp alternators, remove

pulley with tool C-4467, **Fig. 28.**
2. Insert tool into hub of pulley, then rotate to lock into place.
3. Retain base of tool, then turn bolt clockwise until pulley is free from shaft.
4. Remove bearing retainer to drive end shield attaching screws.
5. Support end shield, then separate rotor from end shield using a suitable plastic mallet.
6. Drive end shield bearing is an interference fit with rotor shaft. Remove bearing using tool No. C-4333, then position spacer block of tool in widest position, **Fig. 29.**
7. Needle roller bearing in rectifier end shield is press fit. Remove bearing using tool No. C-4330, **Fig. 30.**

Rotor Testing
Grounded Field Coil Test: Connect a test lamp between each slip ring and the rotor shaft, **Fig. 31.** If test lamp lights, the rotor is grounded, requiring replacement.
Open Field Coil Test: Connect a test lamp between the slip rings, **Fig. 32.** If test lamp does not light, the rotor is open, requiring replacement.
Shorted Field Coil Test: Connect an ohmmeter between the slip rings, **Fig. 32.** If reading is below 1.7 ohms, the rotor is shorted.
High Resistance Test: with an ohmmeter connected across the slip rings, reading should be between 1.7 and 2.1 ohms at 80° F. If not, replace rotor.

ASSEMBLY
1. Press grease retainer onto rotor shaft, if applicable.
2. Place rectifier end shield bearing on base of tool C-4330-1, **Fig. 30.** (Omit tool C-4330-3), then place rectifier end shield on top of bearing. Using tool C-4330-2, press end shield onto bearing until end shield contacts press base.
3. Install new drive end bearing and retainer in drive end shield.
4. Position bearing and drive end shield on rotor shaft supporting base of shaft, then press bearing end shield into position on rotor using tool No. C-3858 and a suitable press, **Fig. 33.**
5. Press pulley onto rotor shaft until it contacts inner race of bearing.

NOTE: Do not exceed 6800 lbs. force.

6. Place insulator and capacitor on positive heat sink attaching stud, then install capacitor attaching screw and torque to 30 to 40 inch lbs.
7. Place terminal block into position in rectifier end shield, then insert attach-

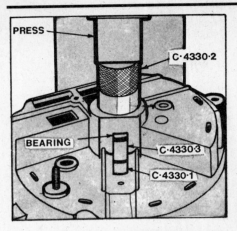

Fig. 30   Removing rectifier end shield bearing. 100, 114 & 117 amp units

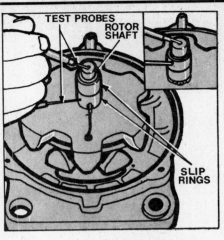

Fig. 31   Testing rotor for grounds. 100, 114 & 117 amp units

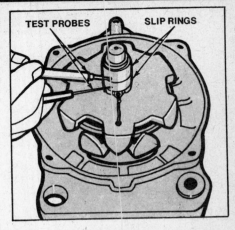

Fig. 32   Testing rotor for open or short circuits. 100, 114 & 117 amp units

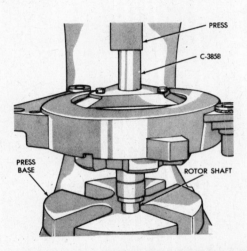

Fig. 33   Installing drive end shield bearing. 100, 114 & 117 amp units

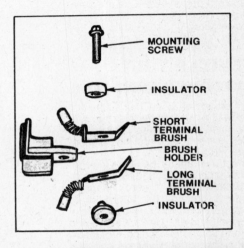

Fig. 34   Assembling field brushes. 100, 114 & 117 amp units

ing screws and torque to 30 to 40 inch lbs.

8. Place negative heat sink into position, ensuring metal straps are properly located over studs on terminal block, then install negative heat sink attaching screws and torque to 30 to 40 inch lbs.

9. Place insulator over positive heat sink stud and install positive heat sink assembly into position in end shield, ensuring metal straps are properly located over terminal block studs. From inside end shield, place insulator on positive heat sink mounting stud, then

install mounting nut and torque to 30 to 50 inch lbs. From outside end shield, place insulator on positive heat sink stud, then install mounting nut.

10. Place stator over rectifier end shield and install terminals on terminal block. Then, press stator pins into end shield and install terminal nuts. Torque nuts to 11 to 17 inch lbs.

NOTE: Route leads to avoid contact with rotor or sharp edge of negative heat sink.

11. Place rotor and drive end shield as-

sembly over stator and rectifier end shield assembly, aligning bolt holts. Compress stator and both end shields, then install and torque through bolts to 40–60 inch lbs.

12. Install field brushes into brush holder with long terminal on bottom and the short terminal on top, **Fig. 34.** Then, install insulators and mounting screw.

13. Place brush holder on end shield, ensure it is properly seated and tighten mounting screw.

14. Slowly rotate pulley to ensure rotor poles do not contact stator winding leads.

Mitsubishi Alternators

INDEX

DESCRIPTION

On these units, the regulator is incorporated into the alternator rear housing, **Figs. 1 and 2.** The electronic voltage regulator has the ability to vary regulated system voltage upward or downward as temperature changes. No voltage regulated adjustments are required on these units.

IN-VEHICLE TESTS

VOLTAGE REGULATOR TEST

1. With ignition switch in Off position, disconnect alternator battery lead at output terminal and connect ammeter in series between alternator and disconnected lead, **Fig. 3.**
2. Connect a voltmeter between alternator L terminal and ground, **Fig. 3.** Voltmeter should indicate zero voltage. If voltage is present, the alternator or charging system wiring is defective.
3. Place ignition switch in the On position and note voltmeter reading. Voltmeter reading should be 1 volt or less. If a higher reading is indicated, the alternator should be removed for bench tests.
4. Connect a tachometer to engine, then start and operate engine at approximately 2000 to 3000 RPM and note ammeter reading.

NOTE: When starting engine, ensure no starting current is applied to ammeter.

5. If ammeter reading is 5 amps or less on 1981–83 units, or 10 amps or less on 1984–85 models, check voltmeter reading with engine operating at 2000 to 3000 RPM. The charging voltage should be 14.4 volts at 68° F.
6. If ammeter reading is above 5 amps on 1981–83 models or above 10 amps on 1984–85 models, continue to charge battery until reading drops to less than 5 amps on 1981–83 models, or to less than 10 amps on 1984–85 models. If voltage is not within limits, remove alternator for bench tests.

NOTE: An alternative method to limiting charging current is to connect a ¼ ohm (25 watt) resistor in series with battery.

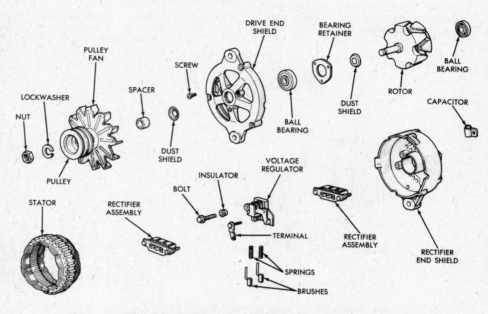

Fig. 1 Disassembled view of Mitsubishi alternator

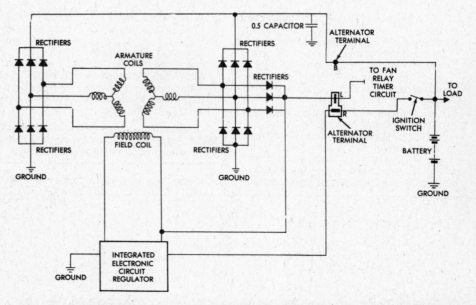

Fig. 2 Wiring diagram of Mitsubishi alternator charging system

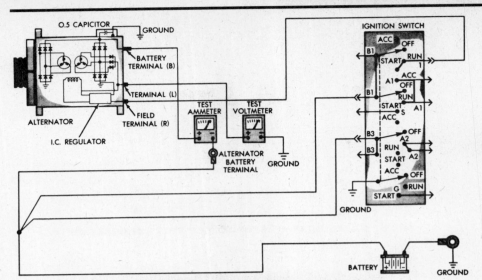

Fig. 3 Voltage regulator test connections

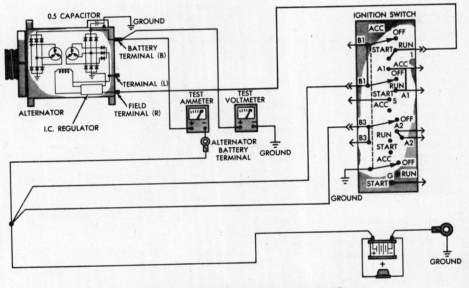

Fig. 4 Current output test connections

CURRENT OUTPUT CHART

Output current (Hot or Cold) at Engine RPM	17-25A at 13.5 Volts and 500 RPM 63-70A at 13.5 Volts and 1000 RPM 74A at 13.5 Volts and 2000 RPM

Fig. 5 Alternator test specifications

CURRENT OUTPUT TEST

1. With ignition switch in the Off position, disconnect battery ground cable, then disconnect battery lead from alternaor output terminal.
2. Connect an ammeter set at the 0 to 100 amp scale between alternator output terminal and the disconnected bat-tery lead, **Fig. 4.**
3. Connect positive lead of voltmeter to alternator output terminal and nega-tive lead to ground, **Fig. 4.**
4. Connect suitable tachometer to en-gine and reconnect battery ground cable.
5. Connect a variable carbon pile regula-tor between battery terminals. When

installing carbon pile regulator, ensure regulator is in Open or Off position.
6. Adjust carbon pile regulator and accel-erate engine to the specified RPM, noting ammeter and voltmeter read-ings, **Fig. 5.**
7. If ammeter reading is less than speci-fied, the alternator should be removed for bench tests.

CHARGING CIRCUIT RESISTANCE TEST

1. Disconnect battery ground cable.
2. Disconnect "BAT" lead at alternator output terminal.
3. Connect an ammeter set at 0 to 100 amp scale in series between alterna-tor output terminal and disconnected lead wire, **Fig. 6.** Connect positive lead to "BAT" terminal and negative lead to disconnected "BAT" lead.
4. Connect positive lead of a suitable voltmeter to disconnected "BAT" lead wire, then connect negative lead to battery positive post.
5. Connect a suitable tachometer to en-gine, then reconnect battery ground cable.
6. Connect a variable carbon pile regula-tor between battery terminals. When installing regulator, ensure it is in "open" or "off" position.
7. Start engine, then adjust engine speed and carbon pile regulator to maintain 20 amp circuit flow. Ensure voltmeter reading does not exceed .5 volts. If a higher voltage drop is indi-cated, proceed as follows:
   a. Tighten all connections to locate possible source of resistance.
   b. Inspect and clean each connec-tion.
8. If test proves satisfactory, disconnect battery ground cable, then remove ammeter, voltmeter and carbon pile.
9. Connect battery ground cable.

ALTERNATOR & ELECTRONIC VOLTAGE REGULATOR DIAGNOSIS

For "Alternator and Electronic Voltage Regulator Diagnosis," refer to **Fig. 7.**

ALTERNATOR DISASSEMBLY

1. Position alternator with mounting lug in a soft-jawed vise, then remove three alternator through bolts, **Fig. 1.**
2. Using a screwdriver, pry between sta-tor and drive end frame, then carefully separate drive end frame and rotor from stator and rectifier end frame.
3. Remove pulley nut, pulley, fan and pulley spacer from rotor shaft, then lift drive end shield from rotor.
4. Remove front and rear dust shields from drive end shield.
5. Remove drive end shield bearing re-tainer, then using a suitable socket, tap bearing from housing.
6. Unsolder six stator leads from rectifier

terminals, then remove stator assembly from rectifier end shield.

7. Remove four screws attaching rectifiers to end shield, then remove brush holder and screw attaching regulator to end housing.
8. Remove nut from alternator B terminal and disconnect capacitor lead.
9. Remove rectifier and regulator assembly.
10. Unsolder joint attaching one of the rectifiers to the regulator, then remove the other rectifier by sliding the battery stud out of the regulator.

BENCH TESTS

ROTOR TEST

Check for continuity between field coil and slip rings. If continuity does not exist, the rotor assembly must be replaced. Check for continuity between slip rings and rotor shaft. If continuity exists, the rotor assembly should be replaced.

STATOR COIL TEST

Using an ohmmeter, check for continuity between stator leads. If continuity does not exist, replace stator. Check for continuity between stator leads and stator coil frame. If continuity exists, stator is grounded and must be replaced.

RECTIFIER TEST

Using an ohmmeter, check for continuity between positive heat sink and stator coil lead terminals, **Fig. 8,** then reverse ohmmeter leads. Continuity should exist in one direction only. If continuity exists in both directions, replace rectifier assembly. Repeat procedure above for negative heat sink as shown in **Fig. 9,** then reverse ohmmeter leads. Continuity should exist in one

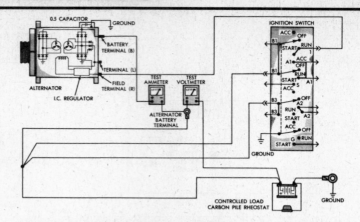

Fig. 6   Charging circuit resistance test connections

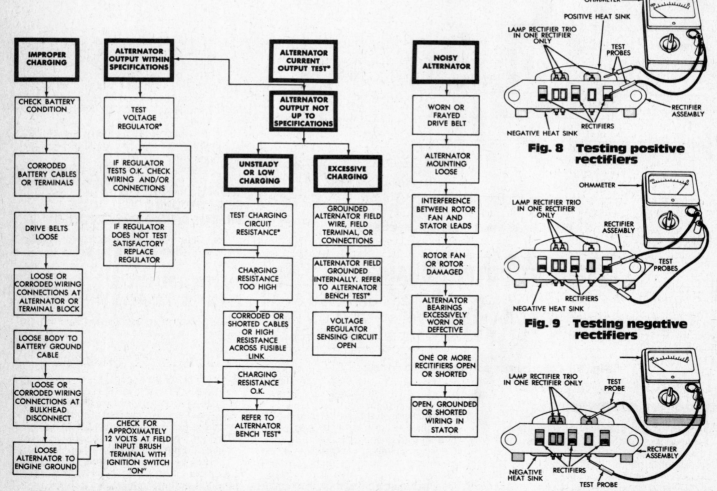

Fig. 7   Alternator & electronic voltage regulator diagnosis chart

Fig. 8   Testing positive rectifiers

Fig. 9   Testing negative rectifiers

Fig. 10   Lamp rectifier trio test

direction only. If continuity exists in both directions, replace rectifier assembly. Check the three lamp rectifiers for continuity, **Fig. 10.** Continuity should exist in one direction only. If continuity or open circuits exist in both directions, replace rectifier assembly.

BRUSH & BRUSH SPRING INSPECTION

Check brush length. A brush worn to .315 inch or less should be replaced.

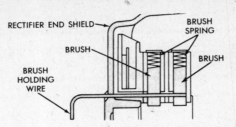

Fig. 11   Brush installation

Check brush spring tension. Brush spring tension should be .7 to 1 lb.

ALTERNATOR ASSEMBLY

Refer to "Alternator Disassembly" and reverse procedure to assemble. When installing rotor, push brushes into holder and insert a suitable piece of wire, **Fig. 11.** After rotor has been installed, remove wire from brushes.

STARTER MOTORS & SWITCHES

TABLE OF CONTENTS

Bosch Starters

INDEX

DESCRIPTION

The Bosch starter is a direct drive starter motor with an overrunning clutch type starter drive. A solenoid switch is mounted on the starter motor.

DIAGNOSIS

Refer to **Fig. 1** when diagnosing starter.

IN-VEHICLE TESTING

NOTE: Before starting any tests, ensure that battery is fully charged and that all connections are good.

AMPERAGE DRAW TEST

1. Run engine until it reaches operating temperature, then turn engine off.
2. Connect a suitable battery-starter tester according to manufacturer's instructions.
3. Turn battery-starter tester control knob to "OFF" position.
4. Turn voltmeter selector knob to "16 VOLT" position.
5. Turn battery-starter function selector to "STARTER SYSTEM TEST" (0–500 amp scale).
6. Connect red positive ammeter lead to positive battery terminal and the black negative ammeter lead to negative battery terminal.
7. Connect red positive voltmeter lead to positive battery terminal and the black negative voltmeter lead to the negative battery terminal.
8. Connect a remote starter jumper according to manufacturer's instructions.

CAUTION: Do not crank engine excessively during testing.

9. Disconnect coil wire from distributor cap center tower and secure to good ground.
10. Crank engine with remote starter switch and observe exact voltmeter reading, then stop cranking engine.
11. Turn tester control knob clockwise until voltmeter reads exactly the same as when engine was being cranked. Ammeter should read 120–160 amps.

STARTER RESISTANCE TEST

1. Disconnect positive battery cable and connect a 0–300 scale ammeter between disconnected lead and battery terminal post.
2. Connect a voltmeter, graduated in tenths, between positive post on battery and starter relay terminal on starter solenoid.
3. Crank engine while observing reading on voltmeter and ammeter. A voltage reading exceeding .3 volt indicates high resistance caused by loose circuit connections, a faulty cable, burned starter relay or solenoid switch contacts. A high current combined with slow cranking speed indicates need for starter repair.
4. Reconnect positive battery lead to battery.

INSULATED CIRCUIT TEST

1. Turn voltmeter selector knob to 4 volt position.
2. Disconnect ignition coil secondary cable.
3. Connect voltmeter positive lead to battery positive post and voltmeter negative lead to solenoid connector that connects to starter field coils.

NOTE: It may be necessary to peel back rubber boot on solenoid to reach solenoid

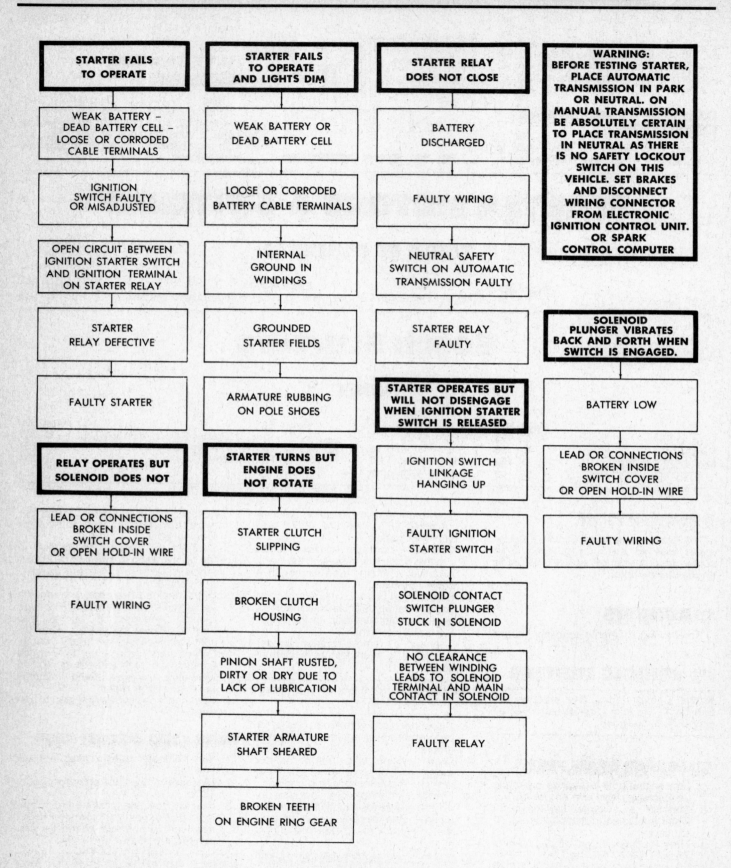

Fig. 1   Starter motor diagnosis

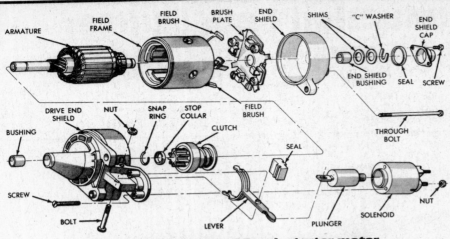

Fig. 2 Exploded view of Bosch starter motor

Fig. 3 Brush plate removal

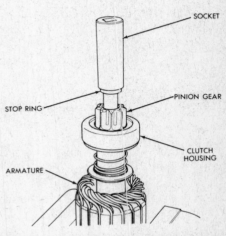

Fig. 4 Pressing stop collar from snap ring

connection. Voltmeter will read off scale to right until starter is actuated.

4. Connect remote control starter switch to battery solenoid terminal of starter relay.
5. Crank engine with remote control starter switch while observing voltmeter reading. If voltmeter reading exceeds .3 volt, there is high resistance in starter insulated circuit, proceed as follows:
   a. Remove voltmeter lead from solenoid connector and connect to following points, repeating test at each connection. Starter terminal of solenoid, battery terminal of solenoid, battery cable terminal at solenoid, starter relay and cable clamp at battery.
   b. A small change will occur each time a normal portion of circuit is removed from test. A definite change in voltmeter reading indicates that last part eliminated in test is at fault.

STARTER GROUND TEST

1. Connect voltmeter positive lead to starter through bolt and negative voltmeter lead to battery negative post.
2. Crank engine with remote control starter switch and observe voltmeter reading.
3. If voltmeter reading exceeds .2 volt, make following tests to isolate point of excessive voltage loss, repeating test at each connection; starter drive housing, cable terminal at engine, cable clamp at battery.
4. A small change will occur each time a normal portion of circuit is removed from test. A definite change in voltmeter reading indicates last part eliminated in test is at fault.

STARTER SOLENOID TEST

1. Connect heavy jumper wire on starter

relay between battery and solenoid terminals. If engine cranks, perform starter relay test.
2. If engine does not crank or solenoid chatters, check wiring and connectors from relay to starter for loose or corroded connections.
3. Repeat test and, if engine still does not crank properly, repair or replace starter as necessary.

STARTER SOLENOID BENCH TEST

1. Disconnect field coil wire from field coil terminal.
2. Check for continuity between solenoid terminal and field coil terminal. There should be continuity.
3. Check for continuity between solenoid terminal and solenoid housing. There should be continuity.
4. If there is no continuity in either test, place solenoid assembly.
5. Connect field coil wire to field coil terminal.

STARTER RELAY TEST

1. Place transmission in Neutral and apply parking brake.
2. Check for battery voltage between starter relay battery terminal and ground.
3. Connect jumper wire on starter relay between battery and ignition terminals.
4. If engine does not crank, connect a second jumper wire to starter relay between ground terminal and good ground and repeat test.
5. If engine cranks in step 4, transmission linkage is misadjusted or neutral safety switch is defective.
6. If engine does not crank in step 4, starter relay is defective.

STARTER OVERHAUL

1. Remove nut from solenoid field coil

terminal, then remove field coil strap from terminal, **Fig. 2.**
2. Remove solenoid attaching screws, then work solenoid from shift fork and remove solenoid.
3. Remove starter motor end shield bearing cap attaching screws and remove end shield cap, C-washer and bearing washer, **Fig. 2.**
4. Remove starter motor through bolts, then remove starter motor brush end shield.
5. Remove two starter motor brushes by prying the brush retaining springs back, then remove brush plate, **Fig. 3.**
6. Slide field frame from armature, then remove armature and clutch assembly from drive end housing.
7. Remove rubber seal and clutch lever bolt from drive end frame, then remove clutch lever.
8. Position armature in a suitable vise, then using a socket, press collar from pinion gear stop snap ring, **Fig. 4.** Remove snap ring from armature shaft using snap ring pliers.
9. Remove stop collar and clutch assembly from armature shaft.
10. Reverse procedure to assemble.

Chrysler Reduction Gear Starter

INDEX

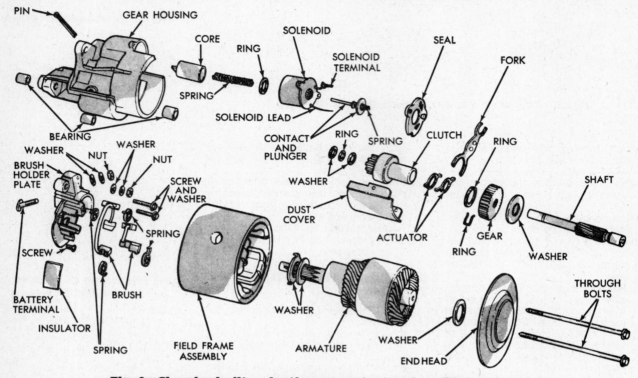

Fig. 1   Chrysler built reduction gear starter. Gasoline engines

DESCRIPTION
EXCEPT 6-243 DIESEL

This reduction gear starting motor, **Fig. 1,** has an armature-to-engine crankshaft ratio of 45 to 1; a 2 to 1 or 3½ to 1 reduction gear set is built into the motor assembly. The starter utilizes a solenoid shift. The housing of the solenoid is integral with the starter drive end housing.

DIAGNOSIS

Refer to **Fig. 2** when diagnosing starter.

IN-VEHICLE TESTING
1979–82 MODELS

Starter Current Draw Test
1. Run engine until it reaches operating temperature, then shut engine off.
2. Connect suitable battery-starter tester according to manufacturer's instructions.

3. Turn variable resistor control knob to off or zero position.
4. Connect remote starter jumper according to manufacturer's instructions.
5. Crank engine just long enough to read cranking voltage on voltmeter.
6. Stop cranking engine, then turn variable resistor control knob until voltmeter reads cranking voltage previously noted. Ammeter should read 180–200 amps on V8-360 engine or 165–180 amps on other engines.

Circuit Resistance Test
1. Connect voltmeter leads across each connection shown in circuit resistance chart, **Fig. 3.**
2. If readings are higher than specified, clean or repair connection, then repeat test.

Starter Solenoid Test
1. Connect heavy jumper wire on starter relay between battery and solenoid terminals.
2. If starter does not crank, or solenoid chatters, check wiring and connectors from relay to starter for loose or cor-

roded connections, then repeat test.
3. If engine still will not crank, repair or replace starter as necessary.

Starter Solenoid Bench Test
1. Remove solenoid assembly.
2. Connect solenoid to 6 volt DC power supply with an ammeter in series. Connect positive lead of power supply to solenoid terminal, positive lead of ammeter to solenoid sleeve and negative lead of power supply to other ammeter terminal.
3. Turn on circuit and check current draw for hold-in coil.
4. Transfer positive ammeter lead to solenoid lead terminal and check current draw for pull-in coil.
5. If current draw for hold-in coil is not 8–9 amps @ 77°F., current draw for pull-in coil is not 13–15 amps @ 77°F. or winding appears burnt or damaged, replace solenoid assembly.

Starter Relay Test
1. Place transmission in Neutral, then connect jumper wire on starter relay between battery and ignition terminals.

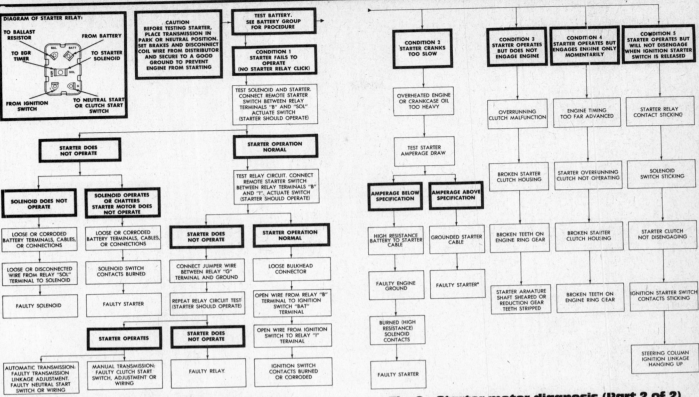

Fig. 2 Starter motor diagnosis (Part 1 of 2)

Fig. 2 Starter motor diagnosis (Part 2 of 2)

CIRCUIT RESISTANCE CHART			
Connection	Voltmeter Lead Connection		Voltmeter Reading
	Positive	Negative	
Positive post on battery to cable clamp	To post	To clamp	0
Negative post on battery to cable clamp	To post	To clamp	0
Battery ground cable to engine block.	To bolt	To cable connector	Not to exceed 0.2 volts
Battery cable to starter	To battery positive post	To battery terminal on starter	Not to exceed 0.2 volts
Starter housing to ground	To starter housing	To negative post on battery	Not to exceed 0.2 volts

Fig. 3 Circuit resistance chart

2. If engine does not crank, connect a second jumper wire on starter relay between ground terminal and good ground.
3. Repeat test. If engine cranks, transmission linkage is misadjusted or neutral safety switch is defective. If engine does not crank, starter relay is defective.

1983–85 MODELS

When performing amperage draw test, refer to "Bosch Starter" section. The circuit resistance test, starter solenoid test, starter solenoid bench test and starter relay test on 1983–85 models are the same as for 1979–82 models.

STARTER OVERHAUL
EXC. DIESEL STARTER

Disassembly

1. Place gear housing of starter in a vise with soft jaws. Use vise as a support fixture only; do not clamp.
2. Remove through bolts and starter end head assembly.
3. Carefully remove armature, then pull field frame assembly from gear housing to expose terminal screw.
4. Support terminal screw with a finger, then remove terminal screw, **Fig. 4.**
5. Remove field frame assembly, then the nuts attaching solenoid and brush holder plate assembly to gear housing, then the solenoid and brush plate assembly.
6. Remove nut, steel washer and insulating washer from solenoid terminal.
7. Unwind solenoid lead wire from brush terminal, **Fig. 5,** and remove screws securing solenoid to brush plate, then the solenoid from brush plate.
8. Remove nut from battery terminal on brush plate, then the battery terminal.
9. Remove solenoid contact and plunger assembly from solenoid, **Fig. 6,** then the return spring from the solenoid moving core.
10. Remove dust cover from gear housing, **Fig. 7.**
11. Release retainer clip positioning driven gear on pinion shaft, **Fig. 8.**

NOTE: The retainer clip is under tension. Therefore, it is recommended that a cloth be placed over the retainer clip when released, preventing it from springing away.

12. Remove pinion shaft "C" clip, **Fig. 9.**
13. Push pinion shaft toward rear of housing, **Fig. 10,** then remove retainer ring and thrust washers, clutch and pinion assembly, with the two shift fork nylon actuators as an assembly, **Fig. 11.**
14. Remove driven gear and thrust washer.
15. Pull shifting fork forward and remove solenoid moving core, **Fig. 12.**
16. Remove shifting fork retainer pin, **Fig. 13,** and remove clutch shifting fork assembly.

Reassembly

NOTE: The shifter fork consists of two spring steel plates assembled with two rivets, **Fig. 14.** There should be about 1/16" side movement to insure proper pinion gear engagement. Lubricate between plates sparingly with SAE 10 engine oil.

1. Position shift fork in drive housing and

Fig. 4   Terminal screw replacement

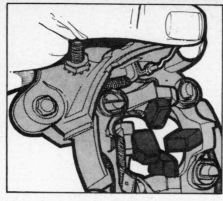

Fig. 5   Unwinding solenoid lead wire

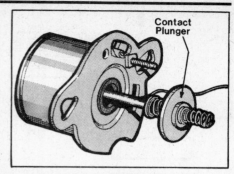

Fig. 6   Solenoid contact & plunger

Fig. 7   Dust cover removal

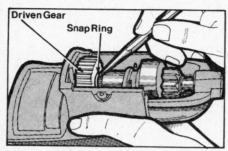

Fig. 8   Drive gear snap ring replacement

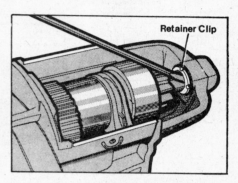

Fig. 9   Pinion shaft "C" clip replacement

Fig. 10   Removing pinion shaft

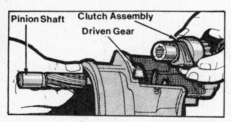

Fig. 11   Clutch assembly replacement

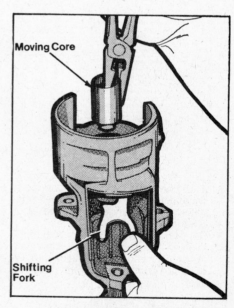

Fig. 12   Solenoid core replacement

install fork retaining pin, **Fig. 13.** One tip of pin should be straight, the other tip should be bent at a 15 degree angle away from housing. Fork and pin should operate freely after bending tip of pin.
2. Install solenoid moving core and engage shifting fork, **Fig. 12.**
3. Enter pinion shaft in drive housing and install friction washer and driven gear.
4. Install clutch and pinion assembly, **Fig. 11,** thrust washer, retaining ring, and thrust washer.
5. Complete installation of pinion shaft, engaging fork with clutch actuators, **Fig. 15.** Friction washer must be positioned on shoulder of splines of pinion shaft before driven gear is positioned.

6. Install driven gear snap ring, **Fig. 8,** then the pinion shaft retaining ring or "C" clip, **Fig. 9.**
7. Install starter solenoid return spring into movable core bore.

NOTE: Inspect starter solenoid switch contacting washer. If top of washer is burned, disassemble contact switch plunger assembly and reverse the washer.

8. Install solenoid contact plunger assembly into solenoid, **Fig. 6.** Ensure contact spring is properly positioned on shaft of solenoid contact plunger assembly.
9. Install battery terminal stud in brush holder.

NOTE: Inspect contacts in brush holder. If contacts are badly burned, replace brush holder with brushes and contacts as an assembly.

10. Position seal on brush holder plate.
11. Install solenoid lead wire through hole in brush holder, **Fig. 16,** then the solenoid stud, insulating washer, flat washer and nut.
12. Wrap solenoid lead wire around brush terminal post, **Fig. 5,** and solder with a high temperature resin core solder and resin flux.
13. Install brush holder attaching screws.

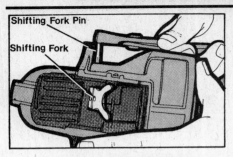

Fig. 13 Shifter fork pin replacement

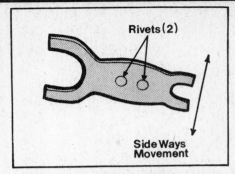

Fig. 14 Shifter fork assembly

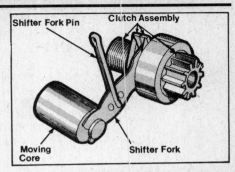

Fig. 15 Shifter fork & clutch assembly

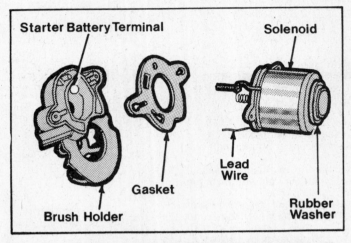

Fig. 16 Solenoid to brush holder plate assembly

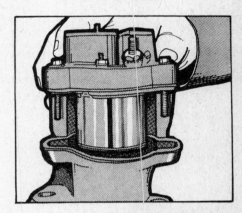

Fig. 17 Solenoid & brush installation

Fig. 18 Installation of brushes & armature

14. Install solenoid coil and brush plate assembly into gear housing bore and position brush plate assembly into starter gear housing, **Fig. 17**. Then install and tighten housing attaching nuts.

15. Install brushes with armature thrust washer, **Fig. 18**. This holds brushes out and facilitates proper armature installation.

16. On all units, install brush terminal screws, **Fig. 4**.

17. Position field frame on gear housing and install armature into field frame and starter gear housing, **Fig. 19**, carefully engaging splines of shaft with reduction gear by rotating armature slightly to engage splines.

18. Install thrust washer on armature shaft.

19. Install starter end head assembly, then the through bolts.

DIESEL STARTER

Disassembly

1. Remove through bolts and brush plate retaining screws from end plate, **Fig. 20**, then separate end plate from field frame and discard seal ring.

2. Separate brush springs from holders using a suitable tool, then remove brush plate from commutator.

3. Remove field terminal nut and washer, then separate field lead from solenoid terminal, **Fig. 21**.

4. Remove field frame from center bracket, then discard seal ring between frame and bracket.

5. Remove solenoid to drive end housing attaching screws, then lift rear of solenoid and pull outward to separate plunger from shift fork. Remove solenoid from drive end housing.

6. Remove center bracket to drive end housing attaching bolt, then separate center bracket and armature from drive end housing, **Fig. 22**.

7. Separate armature from center bracket assembly, then remove drive end housing gasket. Remove front shift fork metal retainer and plastic spacer.

8. Remove reduction gear bearing retainer attaching screws from drive end housing, then pull forward on reduction gear to separate gear, shaft shift fork pivot pin retainers, shift fork and pivot pin from drive end housing.

9. Disengage shift fork from clutch as-

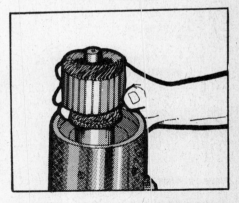

Fig. 19 Armature installation

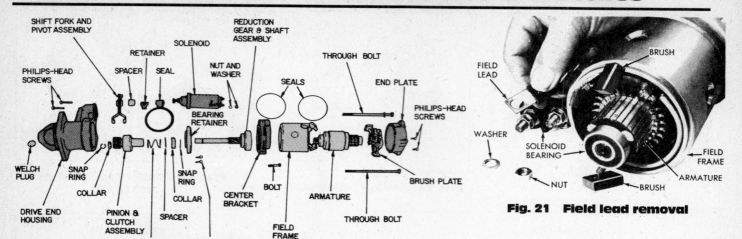

Fig. 20 **Chrysler built reduction gear starter. Diesel engines**

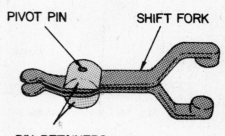

Fig. 21   Field lead removal

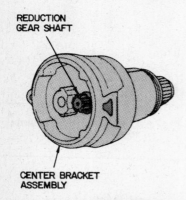

Fig. 22   Center bracket & armature removal

sembly, then remove pivot pin retainers and pivot pin, **Fig. 23.**

10. Remove welch plug from back of drive end housing using a suitable tool.

Reassembly

1. Install drive end housing welch plug, then the clutch spring and spring retainer onto clutch assembly and retain with snap ring.
2. Assemble reduction bearing retainer, clutch assembly and collar onto reduction gear and shaft assembly.

3. Install snap ring on reduction gear shaft, then secure snap ring with collar.
4. Install shift fork over clutch assembly, then assemble pivot pin and pivot pin retainers on shift fork.
5. Insert gear and shaft assembly, shift fork and pivot pin retainers in drive end housing, then slide end of pinion shaft into drive end housing. Install reduction gear retainer and attaching screws in housing, then tighten screws.
6. Install plastic spacer and metal retainer in front of shift fork retainers, then drive end housing gasket.
7. Insert armature assembly into center bracket bearing retainer, then engage armature pinion gear with reduction gear. Install center bracket to drive end housing and retain with bolt and washer.
8. Engage solenoid plunger with shift fork, then attach solenoid to housing with attaching screws. Ensure spacers are installed behind solenoid.
9. Install new seal ring on center bracket, then install field frame assembly.

NOTE: Ensure field frame assembly is installed as to permit connection to solenoid terminal.

Fig. 23   **Pinion pin & retainer removal**

10. Slide brush plate over armature commutator, then lift brush springs and install brush holders ensuring springs are squarely seated on brushes.
11. Install new field frame seal ring, then position end plate on field frame assembly. Place new fiber sealing washers onto brush plate retaining screws, then insert and tighten screws. Install through bolts and tighten securely.

Nippondenso Starter

INDEX

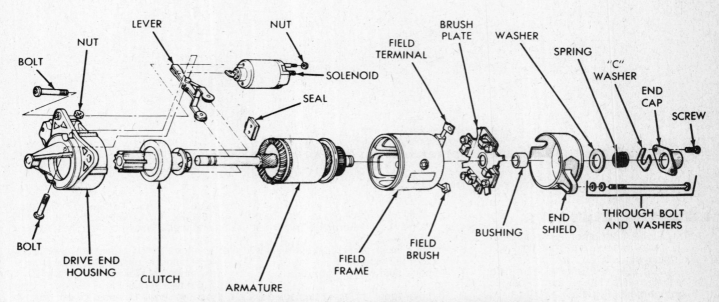

Fig. 1   Exploded view of Nippondenso direct drive starter

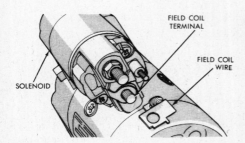

Fig. 2   Field coil terminal removal

DESCRIPTION

Nippondenso starters are either direct drive or reduction gear types. The direct drive starter has an overrunning clutch type starter drive and a solenoid switch is mounted on the starter motor. The structure of the reduction gear type starter differs from that of the direct drive type, but the electrical wiring is the same for both types.

DIAGNOSIS & TESTING

When diagnosing or testing Nippondenso starters, refer to "Bosch Starter" section.

STARTER OVERHAUL
DIRECT DRIVE TYPE

1. Remove nut from solenoid field coil terminal, then remove field coil strap, **Figs. 1 and 2.**
2. Remove nuts attaching solenoid to starter housing, then work solenoid from shift fork and remove solenoid.
3. Remove attaching screws end shield bearing cap, then remove end shield cap, C-washer, bearing spring and bearing washer, **Fig. 3.**
4. Remove starter motor through bolts, then remove starter motor brush end shield.
5. Pry back on brush spring and remove field brushes, then remove brush plate, **Fig. 4.**
6. Remove field frame from armature,

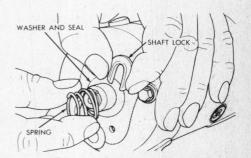

Fig. 3   Armature assembly removal

then remove rubber seal from drive end housing, **Fig. 5.**
7. Remove armature and clutch assembly from drive end frame, **Fig. 6.**
8. Remove clutch lever retainer from drive end frame, then remove clutch lever, **Fig. 7.**
9. Press stop collar from snap ring, then remove snap ring, stop collar and clutch, **Fig. 8.**
10. Reverse procedure to assemble.

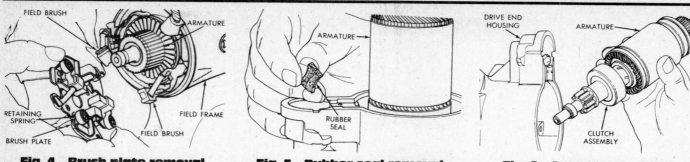

Fig. 4 Brush plate removal

Fig. 5 Rubber seal removal

Fig. 6 Armature & clutch assembly

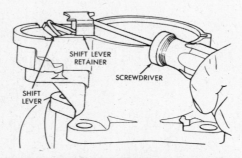

Fig. 7 Clutch shift lever retainer

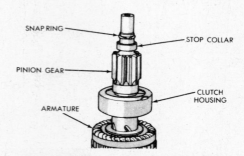

Fig. 8 Stop collar, snap ring & clutch assembly

REDUCTION GEAR TYPE

1. Pull rubber boot off of field coil terminal, then remove nut from field coil terminal stud.
2. Remove field coil terminal from field coil terminal stud, then remove through bolts, **Fig. 9.**
3. Remove two end shield screws, then the upper left solenoid screw securing field coil wire retainer, **Fig. 10.**
4. Remove field coil wire retainer, then the starter end shield.
5. Carefully pry retaining springs back and slide two field brushes from their brush holders, **Fig. 11.**
6. Remove brush plate, then slide armature out of field frame.
7. Remove field frame from gear housing.
8. Remove gear housing to solenoid attaching screws, then, using soft mallet, separate gear housing from solenoid.
9. Remove reduction gear pinion roller retainer, then remove reduction gear and clutch assembly from gear housing.
10. Remove pinion gear from gear housing, then the pinion gear rollers.
11. Remove solenoid ball and spring.
12. Remove remaining solenoid cover screws from solenoid, then remove solenoid cover.
13. Remove solenoid plunger from solenoid housing.
14. Reverse procedure to assemble.

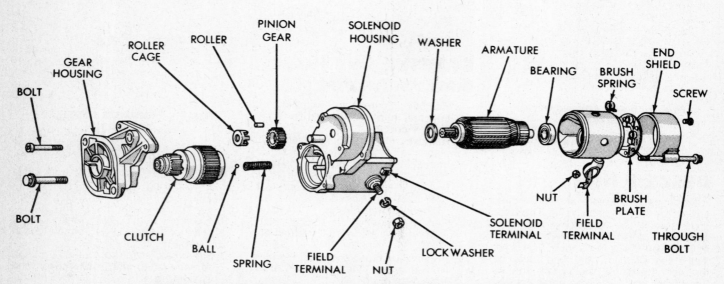

Fig. 9 Exploded view of Nippondenso reduction gear starter

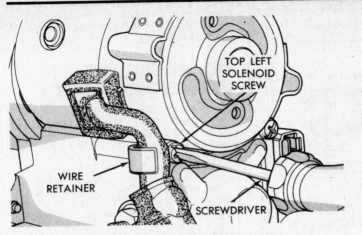

Fig. 10   Removing field coil wire retainer

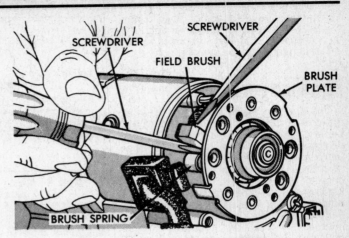

Fig. 11   Removing field brushes

DASH GAUGES & GRAPHIC DISPLAYS

INDEX

DASH GAUGES

Gauge failures are often caused by defective wiring or grounds. The first step in locating trouble should be a thorough inspection of all wiring, terminals and printed circuits. If wiring is secured by clamps, check to see whether the insulation has been severed, thereby grounding the wire. In the case of a fuel gauge installation, rust may cause failure by corrosion at the ground connection of the tank unit.

CONSTANT VOLTAGE REGULATOR TYPE (CVR)

The Constant Voltage Regulator (CVR) type indicator is a bimetal-resistance type system consisting of an Instrument Voltage Regulator (IVR), an indicator gauge, and a variable resistance sending unit. Current to the system is applied to the gauge terminals by the IVR, which maintains an average-pulsating value of 5 volts.

The indicator gauge consists of a pointer which is attached to a wire-wound bimetal strip. Current passing through the coil heats the bimetal strip, causing the pointer to move. As more current passes through the coil, heat increases, moving the pointer farther.

The circuit is completed through a sending unit which contains a variable resistor. When resistance is high, less current is allowed to pass through the gauge, and the pointer moves very little. As resistance decreases due to changing conditions in system being monitored, more current passes through gauge coil, causing pointer to move farther.

Voltage Limiter Test
1. Connect one lead of a voltmeter to temperature sending unit and other lead to a good ground. Do not disconnect sending unit lead from sending unit.
2. Turn ignition switch to On position and observe voltmeter.
3. A fluctuating voltmeter indicates that voltage limiter is operating.

VARIABLE VOLTAGE TYPE

The variable voltage type dash gauge consists of two magnetic coils to which battery voltage is applied. The coils act on the gauge pointer and pull in opposite directions. One coil is grounded directly to the chassis, while the other coil is grounded through a variable resistor within the sending unit. Resistance through the sending unit determines current flow through its coil, and therefore pointer position.

When resistance is high in the sending unit, less current is allowed to flow through its coil, causing the gauge pointer to move toward the directly grounded coil. When resistance in the sending unit decreases, more current is allowed to pass through its coil, increasing the magnetic field. The gauge pointer is then attracted toward the coil which is grounded through the sending unit.

Dash Gauge Test
1. Disconnect electrical connector from sending unit.
2. Turn ignition to On position.
3. Ground sending unit lead and observe

C–169

gauge. If gauge does not move to high side of scale, the gauge or wiring is defective. If gauge responds when grounded, replace sending unit.

AMMETERS

The ammeter is an instrument used to indicate current flow into and out of the battery. When electrical accessories in the vehicle draw more current than the alternator can supply, current flows from the battery and the ammeter indicates a discharge (−) condition. When electrical loads of the vehicle are less than alternator output, current is available to charge the battery, and the ammeter indicates a charge (+) condition. If battery is fully charged, the voltage regulator reduces alternator output to meet only immediate vehicle electrical loads. When this happens, ammeter reads zero.

CONVENTIONAL AMMETER

A conventional ammeter must be connected between the battery and alternator in order to indicate current flow. This type ammeter, **Fig. 1,** consists of a frame to which a permanent magnet is attached. The frame also supports an armature and pointer assembly. Current in this system flows from the alternator through the ammeter, then to the battery or from the battery through the ammeter into the vehicle electrical system, depending on vehicle operating conditions.

When no current flows through the ammeter, the magnet holds the pointer armature so that the pointer stands at the center of the dial. When current passes in either direction through the ammeter, the resulting magnetic field attracts the armature away from the effect of the permanent magnet, thus giving a reading proportional to the strength of the current flowing.

Troubleshooting

When the ammeter apparently fails to register correctly, there may be trouble in the wiring which connects the ammeter to the alternator and battery or in the alternator or battery itself.

To check the connections, first tighten the two terminal posts on the back of the ammeter. Then, following each wire from the ammeter, tighten all connections on the ignition switch, battery and alternator. Chafed, burned or broken insulation can be found by following each ammeter wire from end to end.

All wires with chafed, burned or broken insulation should be repaired or replaced. After this is done, and all connections are tightened, connect the battery cable and turn on the ignition switch. The needle should point slightly to the discharge (−) side.

Start the engine and run slightly above idling speed. The needle should move slowly to the charge side (+).

If the pointer does not move as indicated, the ammeter is out of order and should be replaced.

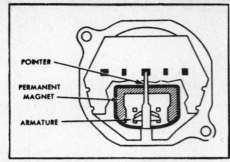

Fig. 1   Conventional type ammeter

SHUNT TYPE AMMETER

The shunt type ammeter is actually a specifically calibrated voltmeter. If it connected to read voltage drop across a resistance wire (shunt) between the battery and alternator. The shunt is located either in the vehicle wiring or within the ammeter itself.

When voltage is higher at the alternator end of the shunt, the meter indicates a charge (+) condition. When voltage is higher at the battery end of the shunt, the meter indicates a discharge (−) condition. When voltage is equal at both ends of the shunt, the meter reads zero.

Troubleshooting

Ammeter accuracy can be determined by comparing reading with an ammeter of known accuracy.

1. With engine stopped and ignition switch in RUN position, switch on headlamps and heater fan. Meter should indicate a discharge (−) condition.

2. If ammeter pointer does not move, check ammeter terminals for proper connection and check for open circuit in wiring harness. If connections and wiring harness are satisfactory, ammeter is defective.

3. If ammeter indicates a charge (+) condition, wiring harness connections are reversed at ammeter.

VOLTMETER

The voltmeter is a gauge which measures the electrical flow from the battery to indicate whether the battery output is within tolerances. The voltmeter reading can range from 13.5−14.0 volts under normal operating conditions. If an undercharge or overcharge condition is indicated for an extended period, the battery and charging system should be checked.

TROUBLESHOOTING

To check voltmeter, turn key and headlights on with engine off. Pointer should move to 12.5 volts. If no needle movement is observed, check connections from battery to circuit breaker. If connections are tight and meter shows no movement;

check wire continuity. If wire continuity is satisfactory, the meter is inoperative and must be replaced.

OIL PRESSURE INDICATOR LIGHT

Many trucks utilize a warning light on the instrument panel in place of the conventional dash indicating gauge to warn the driver when the oil pressure is dangerously low. The warning light is wired in series with the ignition switch and the engine unit—which is an oil pressure switch.

The oil pressure switch contains a diaphragm and a set of contacts. When the ignition switch is turned on, the warning light circuit is energized and the circuit is completed through the closed contacts in the pressure switch. When the engine is started, build-up of oil pressure compresses the diaphragm, opening the contacts, thereby breaking the circuit and putting out the light.

TROUBLESHOOTING

The oil pressure warning light should go on when the ignition is turned on. If it does not light, disconnect the wire from the engine unit and ground the wire to the frame or cylinder block. Then if the warning light still does not go on with the ignition switch on, replace the bulb.

If the warning light goes on when the wire is grounded to the frame or cylinder block, the engine unit should be checked for being loose or poorly grounded. If the unit is found to be tight and properly grounded, it should be removed and a new one installed. (The presence of sealing compound on the threads of the engine unit will cause a poor ground).

If the warning light remains lit when it normally should be out, replace the engine unit before proceeding further to determine the cause for a low pressure indication.

The warning light will sometimes light up or flicker when the engine is idling, even though the oil pressure is adequate. However, the light should go out when the engine speed is increased.

TEMPERATURE INDICATOR LIGHT

A bimetal temperature switch located in the cylinder head control the operation of a temperature indicator light with a red lens. If the engine cooling system is not functioning properly and coolant temperature exceeds a predetermined value, the warning light will illuminate.

TROUBLESHOOTING

If the red light is not lit when the engine is being cranked, check for a burned out bulb, an open in the light circuit, or a defective ignition switch.

If the red light is lit when the engine is running, check the wiring between light and switch for a ground, defective temperature switch, or overheated cooling system.

NOTE: As a test circuit to check whether the red bulb is functioning properly, a wire which is connected to the ground terminal of the ignition switch is tapped into its circuit. When the ignition is in the "Start" (engine cranking) position, the ground terminal is grounded inside the switch and the red bulb will be lit. When the engine is started and the ignition switch is in the "On" position, the test circuit is opened and the bulb is then controlled by the temperature switch.

ELECTRICAL TEMPERATURE GAUGES

CONSTANT VOLTAGE REGULATOR (CVR) TYPE

This temperature indicating system consists of a sending unit, located on the cylinder head, electrical temperature gauge and an instrument voltage regulator. As engine temperature increases or decreases, the resistance of the sending unit changes, in turn controlling current flow to the gauge. When engine temperature is low, the resistance of the sending unit is high, restricting current flow to the gauge, in turn indicating low engine temperature. As engine temperature increases, the resistance of the ending unit decreases, permitting an increased current flow to the gauge, resulting in an increased temperature reading.

TROUBLESHOOTING

A special tester is required to diagnose this type gauge. Follow instructions included with the tester.

ELECTRICAL OIL PRESSURE GAUGES

CONSTANT VOLTAGE REGULATOR (CVR) TYPE

This oil pressure indicating system incorporates an instrument voltage regulator, electrical oil pressure gauge and a sending unit which are connected in series. The sending unit consists of a diaphragm, contact and a variable resistor. As oil pressure increases or decreases, the diaphragm actuated the contact on the variable resistor, in turn controlling current flow to the gauge. When oil pressure is low, the resistance of the variable resistor is high, restricting current flow to the gauge, in turn indicating low oil pressure. As oil pressure increases, the resistance of the variable resistor is lowered, permitting an increased current flow to the gauge, resulting in an increased gauge reading.

TROUBLESHOOTING

A special tester is required to diagnose

this type gauge. Follow instructions included with the tester.

FUEL LEVEL INDICATING SYSTEM

A hinged float arm in the fuel tank contacts a variable resistor in the gauge sending unit. The varying resistance in the fuel gauge circuit registers on the instrument panel gauge. Resistance in the circuit is lowest when the fuel tank is full and float arm is raised. The resulting high current flow causes the instrument panel gauge to indicate Full.

TROUBLESHOOTING

1. Disconnect electrical connector from fuel tank sending unit and attach connector to a known good sending unit.
2. Connect a jumper wire between sending unit fuel pick-up tube and a good ground.
3. Secure sending unit float arm in the empty stop position and turn ignition On. Within two minutes, the gauge should read Empty, plus one pointer width or minus two pointer widths.
4. Move float arm and secure in the full stop position. Within two minutes, the gauge should read Full, plus two pointer widths, or minus one pointer width.
5. If fuel gauge does not operate as specified, check the following:
   a. Wiring and electrical connections between sending unit and connector.
   b. Wiring and electrical connections between connector and printed circuit board terminals.
   c. Circuit continuity between printed circuit board terminals and gauge terminals.
   d. Voltage limiter performance.
6. If fuel gauge operates as specified with known good sending unit, check fuel tank and original sending unit as follows:
   a. Remove sending unit from fuel tank.
   b. Connect sending unit wire and jumper wire as previously described.
   c. If fuel gauge now operates as specified, check sending unit for damage, obstructions or improper installation and correct as necessary.

SPEEDOMETERS

The following material covers only that service on speedometers which is feasible to perform. Repairs on the units themselves are not included as they require special tools and extreme care when making repairs and adjustments that only an experienced speedometer mechanic should attempt.

The speedometer has two main parts—the speedometer head and the speedome-

ter drive cable. When the speedometer fails to indicate speed or mileage, the cable or cable housing is probably broken.

SPEEDOMETER CABLE

Most cables are broken due to lack of lubrication, or a sharp bend or kink in the housing.

A cable might break because of the speedometer head mechanism binds. In such cases, the speedometer head should be repaired or replaced before a new cable or housing is installed.

A "jumpy" pointer condition, together with a scraping noise, is due, in most instances, to a dry or kinked speedometer cable. The kinked cable rubs on the housing and winds up, slowing down the pointer. The cable then unwinds and the pointer "jumps."

To check for kinks, remove the cable, lay it on a flat surface and twist one end with the fingers. If it turns over smoothly the cable is not kinked. But if part of the cable flops over as it is twisted, the cable is kinked and should be replaced.

LUBRICATION

The speedometer cable should be lubricated with special cable lubricant. Fill the ferrule on the upper end of the housing with the cable lubricant. Insert the cable in the housing, starting at the upper end. Turn the cable around carefully while feeding it into the housing. Repeat filling the ferrule except for the last six inches of cable. Too much lubricant at this point may cause the lubricant to work into the speedometer head.

INSTALLING CABLE

During installation, if the cable sticks when inserted in the housing and will not go through, the housing is damaged inside or kinked. Be sure to check the housing from one end to the other. Straighten any sharp bends by relocating clamps or elbows. Replace housing if it is badly kinked or broken. Position the cable and housing so that they lead into the head as straight as possible.

Check the new cable for kinks before installing it. Use wide, sweeping, gradual curves where the cable comes out of the transmission and connects to the head so the cable will not be damaged during installation.

Arrange the housing so it does not lean against the engine because heat from the engine may dry out the lubricant.

If inspection indicates that the cable and housing are in good condition, yet pointer action is erratic, check the speedometer head for possible binding.

The speedometer drive pinion should also be checked. If the pinion is dry or its teeth are stripped, the speedometer may not register properly.

VACUUM GAUGE

This gauge, **Fig. 2,** measures intake

manifold vacuum. The intake manifold vacuum varies with engine operating conditions, carburetor adjustments, valve timing, ignition timing and general engine condition.

Since the optimum fuel economy is directly proportional to a properly functioning engine, a high vacuum reading on the gauge relates to fuel economy. For this reason some manufacturers call the vacuum gauge a "Fuel Economy Indicator." Most gauges have colored sectors the green sector being the "Economy" range and the red the "Power" range. Therefore, the vehicle should be operated with gauge registering in the green sector or a high numerical number, **Fig. 2,** for maximum economy.

FUEL ECONOMY WARNING SYSTEM

This system actually monitors the engine vacuum just like the vacuum gauge, but all it registers is a low vacuum. The light on the instrument panel warns the vehicle operator when engine manifold vacuum drops below the economical limit. Switch operation is similar to that of the oil pressure indicating light, except that the switch opens when vacuum , rather than oil pressure, is applied.

TROUBLESHOOTING

Fuel Economy Warning Light

The fuel economy warning light should go on when the ignition is turned on. If it does not light, disconnect the wire from the fuel economy vacuum switch connector and ground the wire to the frame or cylinder block. If the warning light still does not go on, check for burned out indicating bulb or an open in the harness between the vacuum switch and instrument panel. If the warning light goes on, circuit is functioning and the vacuum switch should be checked for proper ground. Remove and clean the mounting bracket screws and the mounting surfaces.

If system still does not operate, perform the following:

With the electrical connector and vacuum tube disconnected from the switch, connect a self-powered test light to the switch electrical connector and to the vacuum gauge mountng bracket. Attach a vacuum pump to gauge (Rotunda Model No. ZRE-10662 hand operated). If the following conditions are not met the switch has to be replaced:

1. With vacuum applied test light should be "Off".
2. With no vacuum to the vacuum switch test light should be "On".

If the warning light remains lit when it normally should be out, check vacuum hose to vacuum switch for damage or plugged condition.

ELECTRIC CLOCKS

Regulation of electric clocks is accomplished automatically by resetting the time.

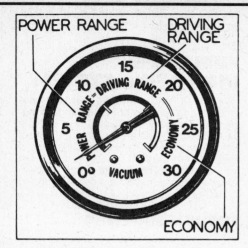

Fig. 2   Typical vacuum gauge

If the clock is running fast, the action of turning the hands back to correct the time will automatically cause the clock to run slightly slower. If the clock is running slow, the action of turning the hands forward to correct the time will automatically cause the clock to run slightly faster (10 to 15 seconds day).

A lock-out feature prevents the clock regulator mechanism from being reset more than once per wind cycle, regardless of the number of times the time is reset. After the clock rewinds, if the time is then reset, automatic regulation will take place. If a clock varies over 10 minutes per day, it will never adjust properly and must be repaired or replaced.

WINDING CLOCK WHEN CONNECTING BATTERY OR CLOCK WIRING

The clock requires special attention when reconnecting a battery that has been disconnected for any reason, a clock that has been disconnected, or when replacing a blown clock fuse. It is very important that the initial wind be fully made. The procedure is as follows:

1. Make sure that all other instruments and lights are turned off.
2. Connect positive cable to battery.
3. Before connecting the negative cable, press the terminal to its post on the battery. Immediately afterward, strike the terminal against the battery post to see if there is a spark. If there is a spark, allow the clock to run down until it stops ticking, and repeat as above until there is no spark. Then immediately make the permanent connection before the clock can again run down. The clock will run down in approximately two minutes.
4. Reset clock after all connections have been made. The foregoing procedure should also be followed when reconnecting the clock after it has been disconnected, or if it has stopped because of a blown fuse. Be sure to dis-

connect battery before installing a new fuse.

TROUBLESHOOTING

If clock does not run, check for blown "clock" fuse. If fuse is blown, check for short in wiring. If fuse is not blown, check for open circuit.

With an electric clock, the most frequent cause of clock fuse blowing is voltage at the clock which will prevent a complete wind and allow clock contacts to remain closed. This may be caused by any of the following: discharged battery, corrosion on contact surface of battery terminals, loose connections at battery terminals, at junction block, at fuse clips, or at terminal connection of clock. Therefore, if in reconnecting battery or clock it is noted that the clock is not ticking, always check for blown fuse, or examine the circuits at the points indicated above to determine and correct the cause.

RECREATIONAL VEHICLE SENSOR PACKAGE

The recreational vehicle sensor package consists of a separate instrument cluster, **Figs. 3 and 4,** which allows the driver to monitor the following conditions: engine oil level, engine coolant level, transmission fluid level and transmission fluid temperature.

TROUBLESHOOTING

Voltage Limiter Test

1. Connect voltmeter between temperature sending unit (locating in fitting in bottom radiator tank) and a suitable ground. Do not disconnect electrical connector from sending unit.
2. Turn ignition switch to On position and observe voltmeter.
3. If voltmeter needle fluctuates, the voltage limiter is operating properly.
4. If voltmeter does not fluctuate, replace voltage limiter.

NOTE: The voltage limiter is located on the sensor panel. To gain access to the limiter, remove panel and unsnap the back cover.

Temperature Gauge Test

1. Disconnect electrical connector from temperature sending unit in lower radiator tank.
2. Connect tester No. C-3826 or equivalent between temperature sending unit and a suitable ground.
3. Move tester pointer to "C" position, then turn ignition switch On and observe temperature gauge. Temperature gauge should read within 1/8 inch of "C".
4. Move tester pointer to "M" position. Temperature gauge should now advance to normal range left of 1/2 position on dial.
5. Move tester pointer to "H" position.

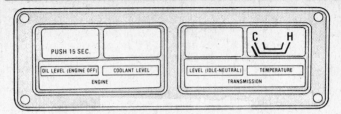

Fig. 3 Recreational vehicle sensor package instrument cluster. 1979—80

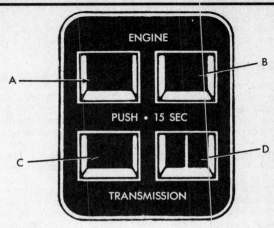

Fig. 4 Recreational vehicle sensor package instrument cluster. 1981—82

Temperature gauge should now advance to "H" position on dial.

6. If temperature gauge responds to tests described in steps 3, 4 and 5, but does not operate when sending unit electrical connector is attached, the sending unit is defective and should be replaced.
7. If temperature gauge does not respond to tests described in steps 3, 4 and 5, check for loose connections, broken wire, open printed circuit or faulty gauge.

Oil Level Push Button Switch

1. Inspect switch for poor solder connections and repair or replace as necessary.
2. Test each circuit for continuity using an ohmmeter or test lamp. If any open circuits are found, the switch should be replaced.

NOTE: To replace switch, remove circuit board and push switch toward back of sensor housing.

Printed Circuit Board

1. Inspect conductors for cracks or damaged circuits.
2. Test each circuit for continuity using an ohmmeter or test lamp. If any open circuits are found, the sensor panel assembly should be replaced.

DISC BRAKES
TABLE OF CONTENTS

General Information
INDEX

TROUBLESHOOTING
EXCESSIVE PEDAL TRAVEL

1. Worn brake lining.
2. Shoe and lining knock back after cornering or rough road travel.
3. Piston and shoe and lining assembly not properly seated or positioned.
4. Air leak or insufficient fluid in system or caliper.
5. Loose wheel bearing adjustment.
6. Damaged or worn caliper piston seal.
7. Improper booster push rod adjustment.
8. Shoe out of flat more than .005".
9. Rear brake automatic adjusters inoperative.
10. Improperly ground rear brake shoe and lining assemblies.

BRAKE ROUGHNESS OR CHATTER; PEDAL PUMPING

1. Excessive lateral run-out of rotor.
2. Rotor excessively out of parallel.

EXCESSIVE PEDAL EFFORT

1. Frozen or seized pistons.
2. Brake fluid, oil or grease on linings.
3. Shoe and lining worn below specifications.
4. Proportioning valve malfunction.
5. Booster inoperative.
6. Leaking booster vacuum check valve.

PULL, UNEVEN OR GRABBING BRAKES

1. Frozen or seized pistons.
2. Brake fluid, oil or grease on linings.
3. Caliper out of alignment with rotor.
4. Loose caliper attachment.
5. Unequalized front tire pressure.

6. Incorrect front end alignment.
7. Lining protruding beyond end of shoe.

BRAKE RATTLE

1. Excessive clearance between shoe and caliper or between shoe and splash shield.
2. Shoe hold-down clips missing or improperly positioned.

HEAVY BRAKE DRAG

1. Frozen or seized pistons.
2. Operator riding brake pedal.
3. Incomplete brake pedal return due to linkage interference.
4. Faulty booster check valve holding pressure in hydraulic system.
5. Residual pressure in front brake hydraulic system.

CALIPER BRAKE FLUID LEAK

1. Damaged or worn caliper piston seal.
2. Scores in cylinder bore.
3. Corrosion build-up in cylinder bore or on piston surface.
4. Metal clip in seal groove.

NO BRAKING EFFECT WHEN PEDAL IS DEPRESSED

1. Piston and shoe and lining assembly not properly seated or positioned.
2. Air leak or insufficient fluid in system or caliper.
3. Damaged or worn caliper piston seal.
4. Bleeder screw open.
5. Air in hydraulic system or improper bleeding.

REAR BRAKES LOCKING ON APPLICATION

On brake system equipped with a proportioning or rear pressure regulator valve, should the valve malfunction, rear brakes may receive excess pressure, resulting in wheel lock-up.

SERVICE PRECAUTIONS

BRAKE LINES & LININGS

Remove one of the front wheels and inspect the brake disc, caliper and linings. (The wheel bearings should be inspected at this time and repacked if necessary).

Do not get any oil or grease on the linings. It is recommended that both front wheel sets be replaced whenever a respective shoe and lining is worn or damaged. Inspect and, if necessary, replace rear brake linings also.

If the caliper is cracked or fluid leakage through the casting is evident, it must be replaced as a unit.

BRAKE ROUGHNESS

The most common cause of brake chatter on disc brakes is a variation in thickness of the disc. If roughness or vibration is encountered during highway operation or if pedal pumping is experienced at low speeds, the disc may have excessive thickness variation. To check for this condition, measure the disc at 12 points with a micrometer at a radius approximately one inch from edge of disc. If thickness measurements vary more than specifications allow, the disc should be replaced with a new one.

Excessive lateral runout of braking disc may cause a "knocking back" of the pistons, possibly creating increased pedal travel and vibration when brakes are applied.

Before checking the runout, wheel bearings should be adjusted. Be sure to make the adjustment according to the recommendations given in the individual truck chapters.

BRAKE DISC SERVICE

Servicing of disc brakes is extremely critical due to the close tolerances required in machining the brake disc to insure proper brake operation.

The maintenance of these close controls on the friction surfaces is necessary to prevent brake roughness. In addition, the surface finish must be non-directional and maintained at a micro-inch finish. This close control of the rubbing surface finish is necessary to avoid pulls and erratic performance and promote long lining life and equal lining wear of both left and right brakes.

In light of the foregoing remarks, refinishing of the rubbing surfaces should not be attempted unless precision equipment, capable of measuring in micro-inches (millionths of an inch) is available.

To check runout of a disc, mount a dial indicator on a convenient part (steering knuckle, tie rod, disc brake caliper housing) so that the plunger of the dial indicator contacts the disc at a point one inch from the outer edge. If the total indicated runout exceeds specifications, install a new disc.

GENERAL PRECAUTIONS

1. Grease or any other foreign material must be kept off the caliper, surfaces of the disc and external surfaces of the hub, during service procedures. Handling the brake disc and caliper should be done in a way to avoid deformation of the disc and nicking or scratching brake linings.
2. If inspection reveals rubber piston seals are worn or damaged, they should be replaced immediately.
3. During removal and installation of a wheel assembly, exercise care so as not to interfere with or damage the caliper splash shield, the bleeder screw or the transfer tube (if equipped).
4. Front wheel bearings should be adjusted to specifications.
5. Be sure vehicle is centered on hoist before servicing any of the front end components to avoid bending or damaging the disc splash shield on full right or left wheel turns.
6. Before the vehicle is moved after any brake service work, be sure to obtain a firm brake pedal.
7. The assembly bolts of the two caliper housings (if equipped) should not be disturbed unless the caliper requires service.

INSPECTION OF CALIPER

Should it become necessary to remove the caliper for installation of new parts, clean all parts in alcohol, wipe dry using lint-free cloths. Using an air hose, blow out drilled passages and bores. Check dust boots for punctures or tears. If punctures or tears are evident, new boots should be installed upon reassembly.

Inspect piston bores in both housings for scoring or pitting. Bores that show light scratches or corrosion can usually be cleaned with crocus cloth. However, bores that have deep scratches or scoring may be honed, provided the diameter of the bore is not increased more than .002". If the bore does not clean up within this specification, a new caliper housing should be installed (black stains on the bore walls are caused by piston seals and will do no harm).

When using a hone, be sure to install the hone baffle before honing bore. The baffle is used to protect the hone stones from damage. Use extreme care in cleaning the caliper after honing. Remove all dust and grit by flushing with alcohol. Wipe dry with clean lint-less cloth and then clean a second time in the same manner.

BLEEDING DISC BRAKES

The disc brake hydraulic system can be bled manually or with pressure bleeding equipment. On vehicles with disc brakes the brake pedal will require more pumping and frequent checking of fluid level in master cylinder during bleeding operation.

Never use brake fluid that has been drained from hydraulic system when bleeding the brakes. Be sure the disc brake pistons are returned to their normal positions and that the shoe and lining assemblies are properly seated. Before driving the vehicle, check brake operation to be sure that a firm pedal has been obtained.

A.T.E. Floating Caliper

INDEX

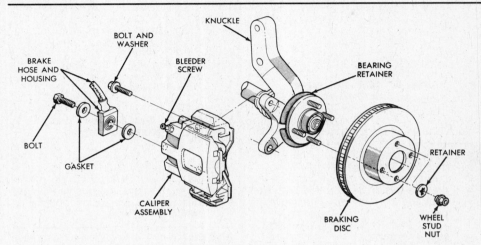

Fig. 1 Exploded view of disc brake assembly

3. Carefully slide caliper assembly away from disc. Support caliper assembly to prevent damage to brake hose.
4. Remove outboard shoe and lining assembly from adapter.
5. Remove rotor from drive axle flange and studs.
6. Remove inboard shoe and lining assembly from adapter.
7. Carefully push piston into caliper bore.

NOTE: Remove some brake fluid from reservoir to prevent overflowing when pushing piston into caliper bore.

8. Position inboard shoe and lining on adapter. Ensure metal portion of shoe is properly positioned in recess of adapter.
9. Install rotor over studs and drive flange.
10. While holding outboard shoe in position on adapter, carefully position adapter over disc brake rotor.
11. Carefully lower caliper over disc brake rotor and adapter.
12. Install guide pins through bushings, caliper and adapter.
13. Press in on guide pins and thread pin into adapter. Torque pins to 25 to 40 ft. lbs.
14. Install wheel and tire assembly, then lower vehicle.

DESCRIPTION

The single piston floating caliper disc brake assembly consists of the hub and disc brake rotor assembly, caliper, shoes and linings, splash shield and adapter, **Fig. 1.**

The caliper assembly floats on two rubber bushings riding on two steel guide pins threaded into the adapter. The bushings are inserted on the inboard portion of the caliper. Two machined abutments on the adapter position and align the caliper fore and aft. Guide pins and bushings control caliper and piston seal movement to assist in maintaining proper shoe clearance.

All braking force is taken directly by the adapter.

BRAKE SHOE & LINING
REPLACE

1. Raise and support front of vehicle, then remove wheel and tire assembly.
2. Remove caliper guide pins and anti-rattle spring.

CALIPER OVERHAUL
DISASSEMBLE

1. Remove caliper assembly as described under "Brake Shoe & Lining, Replace".
2. With brake hose attached to caliper, carefully depress brake pedal to push piston out of caliper bore. Prop brake pedal to any position below first inch of brake pedal travel to prevent brake fluid loss.
3. If pistons are to be removed from both calipers, disconnect brake hose at frame bracket after removing piston, then cap brake line and repeat procedure to remove piston from other caliper.
4. Disconnect brake hose from caliper.
5. Mount caliper, **Fig. 2,** in a soft jawed vise.
6. Support caliper and remove dust boot and discard.
7. Using a small wooden or plastic stick, remove seal from groove in piston bore and discard.

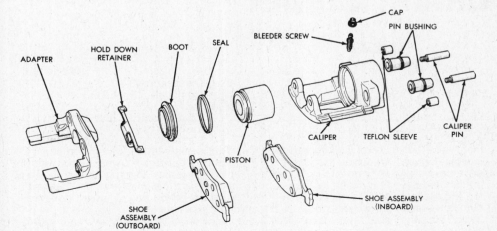

Fig. 2 Exploded view of disc brake caliper assembly

C–175

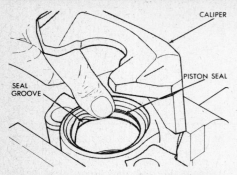

Fig. 3   Piston seal installation

8. Using a suitable tool, remove bushings from caliper.

INSPECTION

1. Clean all components using alcohol or other suitable cleaning solvent, then blow dry using compressed air. With compressed air blow out drilled passages and bores.
2. Inspect piston bore for pitting or scoring. Light scratches or corrosion can usually be cleared with crocus cloth. Bores that have deep scratches or scoring should be honed with tool No. C-4095, providing bore diameter is not increased by more than .001 in. If scratches or scoring cannot be cleared up, or if caliper bore is increased by more than .001 in., replace caliper housing.

NOTE: When using hone C-4095, coat hone and caliper bore with clean brake fluid. After honing, carefully clean boot and seal grooves with a stiff non-metallic brush. Flush caliper with clean brake fluid and wipe dry with a clean lintless cloth, then

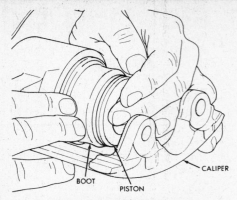

Fig. 4   Caliper piston installation

flush and wipe caliper dry again.

3. Replace piston if found to be scored, pitted or if plating is severely worn or if caliper bore was honed. Black stains on steel piston are caused by piston seal and are not cause for replacing piston.

ASSEMBLE

1. Mount caliper, **Fig. 2,** in a soft jawed vise.
2. Lubricate piston seal with clean brake fluid and install seal in caliper bore groove, **Fig. 3.** Ensure seal is properly seated.
3. Position dust boot over piston.
4. Install piston into bore by pushing it evenly past piston seal until it bottoms in bore, **Fig. 4.**
5. Position dust boot in counterbore, then using a hammer and tools C-4682 and C-4171 or equivalent, drive boot into counterbore, **Fig. 5.**

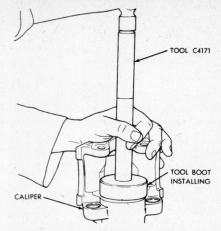

Fig. 5   Piston dust boot installation

6. Compress flanges of guide pin bushings and install bushings on caliper housing. Ensure that bushing flanges extend evenly over caliper housing on both sides.

NOTE: Remove teflon sleeves from guide pin bushings prior to installing bushings into caliper. After bushings are installed into caliper, reinstall teflon sleeves into bushings.

7. Connect brake hose to brake line at frame bracket.
8. Install caliper on vehicle as described under "Brake Shoe & Lining, Replace".
9. Check brake fluid level of master cylinder reservoir, then open caliper bleed screw and bleed brake system. Continue bleeding procedure until firm pedal is obtained.

Kelsey-Hayes Single Piston Sliding Caliper

INDEX

DESCRIPTION

This sliding caliper single piston system uses a one or two piece hub and is actuated by the hydraulic system and disc assembly, **Fig. 1.** Alignment and positioning of the caliper is achieved by two machined guides or "ways" on the adaptor, while caliper retaining clips allow lateral movement of the caliper, **Fig. 2.** Outboard shoe flanges are used to position and locate the shoe on the caliper fingers, **Fig. 3,** while the inboard shoe is retained by the adaptor, **Fig. 4.** Braking force applied onto the outboard shoe is transferred to the caliper, while braking force applied onto the inboard shoe is transferred directly to the adaptor.

A square cut piston seal provides a hydraulic seal between the piston and the cylinder bore, **Fig. 1.** A dust boot with a wiping lip installed in a groove in the cylinder bore and piston prevents contamination in the piston and cylinder bore area. Adjustment between the disc and the shoe is obtained automatically by the outward relocation of the piston as the inboard lining wears and inward movement of the caliper as the outboard lining wears.

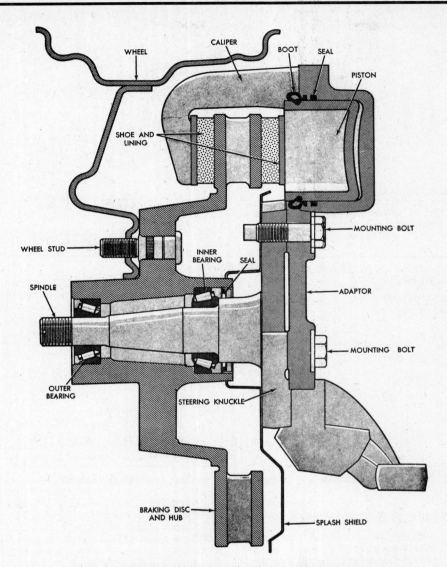

Fig. 1   Sectional view of disc brake assembly

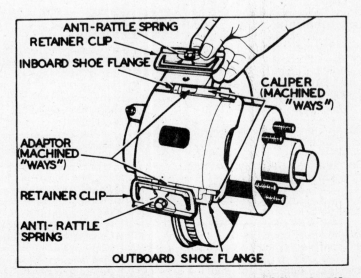

Fig. 2   Caliper mounted "ways" & assembly retention

Fig. 3   Fitting outboard shoe retaining flange

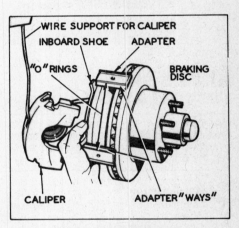

Fig. 4   Inboard shoe replacement

CALIPER REMOVAL

1. Raise the vehicle and remove front wheel.
2. Remove caliper retaining clips and anti-rattle springs, **Fig. 2.**
3. Remove caliper from disc by slowly sliding caliper assembly out and away from disc.

NOTE: Use some means to support caliper. Do not let caliper hang from hydraulic line.

BRAKE SHOE REMOVAL

1. Remove caliper assembly as outlined above.
2. Remove outboard shoe by prying between the shoe and the caliper fingers, **Fig. 5,** since flanges on outboard shoe retain caliper firmly.

NOTE: Caliper should be supported to avoid damage to the flexible brake hose.

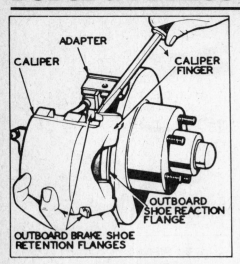

Fig. 5   Outboard shoe removal

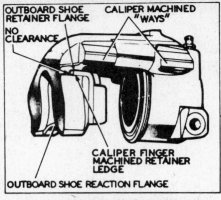

Fig. 6   Positioning outboard shoe onto caliper machined retainer ledge

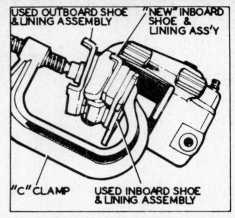

Fig. 7   Installing outboard shoe using C-clamp

3. Remove inboard brake shoe from the adaptor, **Fig. 4.**

BRAKE SHOE INSTALLATION

NOTE: Remove approximately ⅓ of the brake fluid out of the reservoir to prevent overflow when pistons are pushed back into the bore.

1. With care, push piston back into bore until bottomed.
2. Install new outboard shoe in recess of caliper.

NOTE: No free play should exist between brake shoe flanges and caliper fingers, **Fig. 6.**

If up and down movement of the shoe shows free play, shoe must be removed and flanges bent to provide a slight interference fit, **Fig. 3.** Reinstall shoe after modification, if shoe can not be finger snapped into place, use light "C" clamp pressure, **Fig. 7.**

3. Position inboard shoe with flanges inserted in adaptor "ways," **Fig. 4.**
4. Carefully slide caliper assembly into adaptor and over the disc while aligning caliper on machined "ways" of adaptor.

NOTE: Make sure dust boot is not pulled out from groove when piston and boot slide over the inboard shoe.

5. Install anti-rattle springs and retaining clips and torque retaining screws to 180 inch lbs. on 1984–85 Vans and Wagons, 235 inch lbs. on Motor Homes, or 200 inch lbs. on all other models.

NOTE: The inboard shoe anti-rattle spring is to be installed on top of the retainer spring plate, **Fig. 2.**

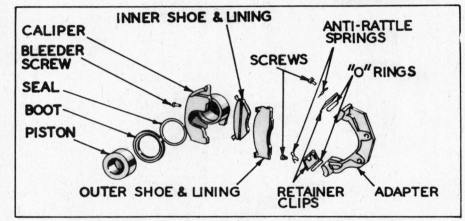

Fig. 8   Exploded view of disc brake caliper assembly

CALIPER DISASSEMBLY

1. With caliper and shoes removed as described previously, place the caliper onto the upper control arm and slowly depress brake pedal, in turn hydraulically pushing piston out of bore.
2. Support pedal below first inch of pedal travel to prevent excessive fluid loss.
3. To remove piston from the opposite caliper, disconnect flexible brake line at frame bracket, from vehicle side where piston has been removed previously and plug tube to prevent pressure loss. By depressing brake pedal this piston can also be hydraulically pushed out.

CAUTION: Air pressure should never be used to remove piston from bore.

4. Mount caliper in a vise equipped with protector jaws.

CAUTION: Excessive vise pressure will distort caliper bore.

5. Remove the dust boot, **Fig. 8.**
6. Insert a suitable tool such as a small, pointed wooden or plastic object between the cylinder bore and the seal and work seal out of the groove in the piston bore.

NOTE: A metal tool such as a screwdriver should not be used since it can cause damage to the piston bore or burr the edges of the seal groove.

CALIPER ASSEMBLY
1979–80

1. Before installing the new piston seal in groove of bore, dip seal in Ucon LB1145Y24 lubricant or equivalent. Work seal gently into the groove (using clean fingers) until seal is properly seated, making sure that seal is not twisted or rolled.

NOTE: Old seals should never be reused.

2. Lubricate new piston boot with Ucon LB1145Y24 or equivalent. Using finger pressure, install into caliper by pushing into outer groove of the caliper bore. When properly positioned in groove boot will snap into place. Double check to make sure boot is properly installed and seated by running finger around the inside of the boot.
3. Plug high pressure inlet to caliper and

bleeder screw hole and coat piston with a generous amount of lubricant. Spread boot with finger and work piston into boot while pressing down on piston. As piston is depressed, entrapped air below piston will force boot around piston and into its groove.

4. Remove the plug and apply uniform force to the piston (avoid cocking piston) until piston bottoms in bore.
5. Install caliper and shoes as described under "Brake Shoe Installation."

1981—85

1. Dip new piston seal in clean brake fluid, then work seal gently into groove (using clean fingers) until seal is properly seated, ensuring seal is not twisted or rolled.

NOTE: Old seals should never be reused.

2. Coat new piston dust boot with clean brake fluid, leaving generous amount inside boot.
3. Position dust boot over piston.
4. Install piston into bore, pushing piston past seal until piston bottoms in bore.
5. Position dust boot in counterbore, and using suitable tools, drive boot into counterbore.
6. Install caliper and shoes as described under "Brake Shoe Installation."

Kelsey-Hayes Dual Piston Sliding Caliper

INDEX

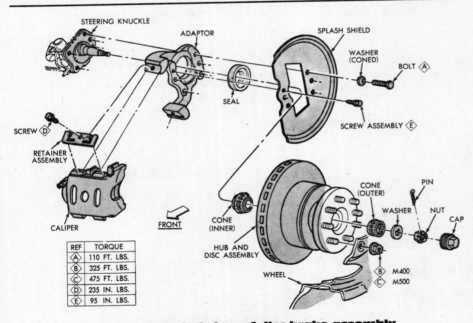

REF	TORQUE
Ⓐ	110 FT. LBS.
Ⓑ	325 FT. LBS.
Ⓒ	475 FT. LBS.
Ⓓ	235 IN. LBS.
Ⓔ	95 IN. LBS.

Fig. 1   Exploded view of disc brake assembly

DESCRIPTION

This sliding caliper dual piston system, **Fig. 1,** uses a two-piece hub. The caliper is held in position and aligned by two machined abutments on the adapter. Retainers hold the caliper in machined guides on the adapter and allow lateral movement of caliper. Outboard shoe flanges are used to position and locate the shoe on caliper fingers, while the inboard shoe is retained by the adapter. Braking force applied onto the outboard shoe is transferred to the caliper, while braking force applied onto the inboard shoe is transferred directly to the adapter.

A square cut piston seal provides an hydraulic seal between the piston and the cylinder bore. A dust boot with a wiping lip installed in a groove in the cylinder bore and piston prevents contamination in the piston and cylinder bore area. Adjustment between the disc and the shoe is obtained automatically by the outward relocation of the piston as the inboard lining wears, and inward movement of the caliper as the outboard lining wears.

CALIPER REMOVAL

1. Raise and support vehicle and remove front wheels.
2. Remove retaining screws, retaining

clips, and anti-rattle springs, **Fig. 2,** then carefully slide caliper out and away from disc and adapter.

NOTE: Use some means to support caliper. Do not let caliper hang from hydraulic line.

BRAKE SHOE REMOVAL

1. Remove caliper assembly as previously described.
2. Remove outboard shoe by prying between shoe and caliper fingers, as flanges on outboard shoe retain caliper firmly.

NOTE: Caliper should be supported to avoid damage to flexible brake hose.

3. Remove inboard brake shoe from adapter.

BRAKE SHOE INSTALLATION

NOTE: Remove approximately ⅓ of the brake fluid from reservoir to prevent overflow when pistons are pushed back into bore.

1. Carefully push pistons back into bore until bottomed.
2. Install new outboard shoe in recess of caliper.

NOTE: No free play should exist between brake shoe flanges and caliper fingers.

If up and down movement of shoe

shows free play, shoe must be removed and flanges bent to provide a slight interference fit. Reinstall shoe after modification and, if shoe cannot be finger snapped into place, use light C-clamp pressure.

3. Position inboard shoe with flanges inserted in adapter "ways."
4. Carefully slide caliper assembly into adapter and over disc while aligning caliper on machined "ways" of adapter.

NOTE: Ensure dust boot is not pulled out from groove when piston and boot slide over inboard shoe.

5. Install anti-rattle springs and retaining clips and torque retaining screws to 235 inch lbs.

CALIPER DISASSEMBLY

1. Remove caliper and brake shoes as previously described.
2. With caliper supported on axle or steering linkage, place 2×4×10 inch wood block between caliper fingers and pistons.

NOTE: Ensure wood block is a full 2 inches thick, as this is allowable limit piston can be pushed out of bore without loosening hydraulic seal.

3. Carefully depress brake pedal until both pistons contact wood block, then remove pistons.
4. pistons from other caliper.
5. Prop brake pedal to any position below one inch of pedal travel to prevent loss of fluid.

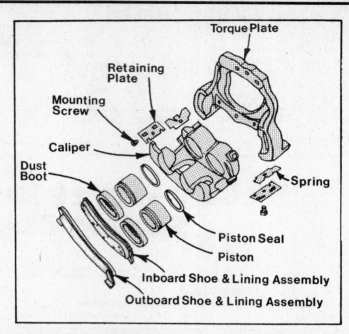

Fig. 2   Exploded view of disc brake caliper assembly

NOTE: Air pressure should never be used to remove piston from bores.

6. Disconnect flexible brake hose from caliper.
7. Mount caliper in a vise equipped with protector jaws.

CAUTION: Excessive vise pressure will distort caliper bores.

8. Remove dust boot.
9. Using a small pointed wooden or plastic stick, work piston seal out of groove in piston bore.

NOTE: A metal tool such as a screwdriver should not be used, as it can cause damage to the piston bore or burr the edges of the seal groove.

CALIPER ASSEMBLY

For caliper assembly, refer to "Kelsey-Hayes Single Piston Sliding Caliper" for procedure.

Kelsey-Hayes Single Pin Floating Caliper

INDEX

DESCRIPTION

The caliper assembly consists of a rotor, caliper, shoes and linings, and adapter, **Fig. 1.** The single piston caliper assembly floats through a rubber bushing on a single pin threaded into the adapter. The bushing is inserted into the inboard portion of the caliper. Two machined abutments on the adapter position and align the caliper fore

and aft. The guide pin and bushing controls the movement of the caliper and the piston seal to assist in maintaining proper shoe clearance.

This assembly has three anti-rattle clips. One is on top of the inboard shoe, one clip is on the bottom of the outboard shoe, and one clip is on top of the caliper.

All of the braking force is taken directly by the adapter. The caliper is a one-piece casting with the inboard side containing a

single piston cylinder bore. The phenolic piston is 2.13 inches in diameter.

A square cut rubber piston seal is located in a machined groove in the caliper bore and provides a seal between piston and caliper bore.

A molded rubber dust boot installed in a groove in the cylinder bore and piston keeps contamination from the caliper bore and piston. The boot mounts in the caliper bore and in a groove in the piston.

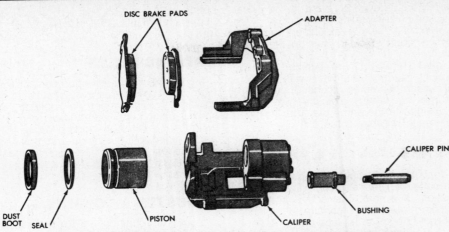

Fig. 1 Exploded view of disc brake caliper assembly

BRAKE SHOE & LINING
REPLACE

REMOVAL

1. Remove brake fluid until reservoir is half full.
2. Raise and support front of vehicle, then remove wheel and tire assembly.
3. Remove caliper guide pin and anti-rattle clips.
4. Remove caliper from disc by sliding caliper assembly out and away from braking disc. Suspend caliper with wire to avoid damaging flexible brake hose.
5. Remove outboard brake lining, then lift off rotor and remove inboard brake lining.

INSTALLATION

1. Push piston back into cylinder bore with uniform pressure until it is bottomed.
2. Position inboard shoe and lining on adapter, then install rotor.
3. While holding outboard shoe in position on adapter, carefully position caliper over disc brake rotor.
4. Lower caliper over rotor and adapter.
5. Install guide pin through bushing caliper and adapter.
6. Press in on guide pin and thread pin into adapter. Torque pin to 25 to 35 ft. lbs.
7. Install wheel and tire assembly, then lower vehicle.

CALIPER OVERHAUL

Refer to "Caliper Overhaul" under "A.T.E. Floating Caliper" for procedure.

DRUM BRAKES

TABLE OF CONTENTS

General Information

INDEX

SERVICE PRECAUTIONS

When working on or around brake assemblies, care must be taken to prevent breathing asbestos dust, as many manufacturers incorporate asbestos fibers in the production of brake linings. During routine service operations, the amount of asbestos dust from brake lining wear is at a low level due to a chemical breakdown during use, and a few precautions will minimize exposure.

CAUTION: Do not sand or grind brake linings unless suitable local exhaust ventilation equipment is used to prevent excessive asbestos exposure.

1. Wear a suitable respirator approved for asbestos dust use during all repair procedures.
2. When cleaning brake dust from brake parts, use a vacuum cleaner with a highly efficient filter system. If a suitable vacuum cleaner is not available, use a water soaked rag.

NOTE: Do not use compressed air or dry brush to clean brake parts.

3. Keep work area clean, using same equipment as for cleaning brake parts.

4. Properly dispose of rags and vacuum cleaner bags by placing them in plastic bags.
5. Do not smoke or eat while working on brake systems.

GENERAL INSPECTION

BRAKE DRUMS

Any time the brake drums are removed for brake service, the braking surface diameter should be checked with a suitable brake drum micrometer at several points to determine if they are within the safe oversize limit stamped on the brake drum outer surface. If the braking surface diameter exceeds specifications, the drum must be replaced. If the braking surface diameter is within specifications, drums should be cleaned and inspected for cracks, scores, deep grooves, taper, out of round and heat spotting. If drums are cracked or heat spotted, they must be replaced. Minor scores should be removed with sandpaper. Grooves and large scores can only be removed by machining with special equipment, as long as the braking surface is within specifications stamped on brake drum outer surface. Any brake drum sufficiently out of round to cause vehicle vibration or noise while braking, or showing taper should also be machined, removing only enough stock to true up the brake drum.

After a brake drum is machined, wipe the braking surface diameter with a cloth soaked in denatured alcohol. If one brake drum is machined, the other should also be machined to the same diameter to maintain equal braking forces.

BRAKE LININGS & SPRINGS

Inspect brake linings for excessive wear, damage, oil, grease or brake fluid contamination. If any of the above conditions exists, brake linings should be replaced. Do not attempt to replace only one set of brake shoes; they should be replaced as an axle set only to maintain equal braking forces. Examine brake shoe webbing, hold down and return springs for signs of overheating indicated by a slight blue color. If any component exhibits signs of overheating, replace hold down and return springs with new ones. Overheated springs lose their pull and could cause brake linings to wear out prematurely. Inspect all springs for sags, bends and external damage, and replace as necessary.

Inspect hold down retainers and pins for bends, rust and corrosion. If any of the above conditions exist, replace retainers and pins.

BACKING PLATE

Inspect backing plate shoe contact surface for grooves that may restrict shoe movement and cannot be removed by lightly sanding with emery cloth or other suitable abrasive. If backing plate exhibits above condition, it should be replaced. Also inspect for signs of cracks, warpage and excessive rust, indicating need for replacement.

ADJUSTER MECHANISM

Inspect all components for rust, corrosion, bends and fatigue. Replace as necessary. On adjuster mechanism equipped with adjuster cable, inspect cable for kinks, fraying or elongation of eyelet and replace as necessary.

PARKING BRAKE CABLE

Inspect parking brake cable end for kinks, fraying and elongation, and replace as necessary. Use a small hose clamp to compress clamp where it enters backing plate to remove.

1982 Models w/7.87 Inch Drums

INDEX

REMOVAL

1. Raise and support rear of vehicle, then remove tire and wheel assembly.
2. Remove brake drum. If brake lining is dragging on brake drum, back off brake adjustment by rotating adjustment screw.
3. Disconnect parking brake cable from parking brake lever, **Fig. 1.**
4. Using suitable pliers, remove brake shoe to anchor springs and hold down springs.
5. Fully seat adjuster nut, then spread shoes apart and remove adjuster screw assembly.
6. Raise parking brake lever, then pull trailing shoe away from support to ease return spring tension and disengage spring end from support. Remove trailing shoe.
7. Pull leading shoe away from support to ease return spring tension and disengage spring end from support. Remove leading shoe.
8. Remove parking brake lever from trailing shoe.
9. Clean dirt from brake drum, support

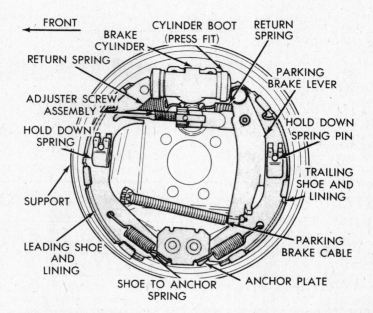

Fig. 1   Drum brake assembly. 1982 models w/7.87 inch drums

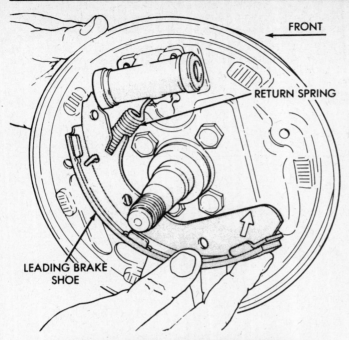

FRONT

RETURN SPRING

LEADING BRAKE SHOE

Fig. 2 Installing leading brake shoe

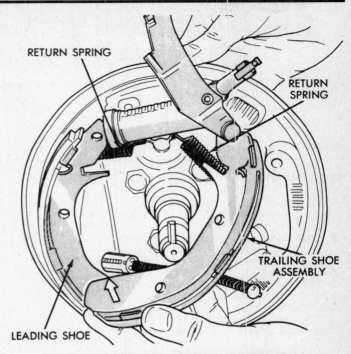

RETURN SPRING

RETURN SPRING

TRAILING SHOE ASSEMBLY

LEADING SHOE

Fig. 3 Installing trailing brake shoe

plate and all other components.

CAUTION: Do not use compressed air or dry brush to clean brake parts. Many brake parts contain asbestos fibers which, if inhaled, can cause serious injury. To clean brake parts, use a water soaked rag or a suitable vacuum cleaner to minimize airborne dust.

INSPECTION

1. Inspect components for damage and unusual wear. Replace as necessary.
2. Inspect wheel cylinders. Any torn, cut or heat damaged boots indicate need for wheel cylinder replacement. Peel back lower edge of boot. If fluid spills out, cup leakage is indicated and wheel cylinder should be replaced.

NOTE: A slight amount of fluid is always present and is considered normal. Fluid acts as a lubricant for the cylinder pistons.

3. Inspect support plate attaching bolts, and ensure they are tight.
4. Inspect adjuster screw assembly

operation. If satisfactory, lightly lubricate threads with suitable brake lube. If operation is unsatisfactory, replace.
5. Using fine emery cloth or other suitable abrasive, clean rust and dirt from shoe contact surfaces on support plate.

INSTALLATION

1. Lightly lubricate support plate shoe contact surfaces with suitable brake lube.
2. Remove brake drum hub grease seal and bearings, then clean and repack bearings and reinstall. Install new grease seal.
3. Position leading shoe return spring on shoe, then while holding shoe away from support, engage return spring in support plate, **Fig. 2,** and swing shoe end into position under anchor.
4. Install parking brake lever on trailing shoe.
5. Install trailing shoe return spring on shoe, then while holding shoe away from support, engage return spring in support plate, **Fig. 3,** and swing shoe end into position under anchor.
6. Spread shoes apart and install adjus-

ter screw assembly. Ensure forked end enters the leading shoe with curved tines facing down, **Fig. 1.**
7. Using a suitable pair of pliers, install hold down springs and shoe to anchor springs.
8. Pull back parking brake cable return spring slightly to expose cable, then slide parking brake cable into parking brake lever and release spring.
9. Install brake drum and bearings. Refer to individual truck chapter for wheel bearing adjustment procedure.
10. Adjust brakes. Refer to individual truck chapter for procedure.
11. Install tire and wheel assembly.
12. If any hydraulic connections have been opened, bleed brake system.
13. Check master cylinder level and replenish as necessary.
14. Check brake pedal for proper feel and return.
15. Lower vehicle and road test.

NOTE: Do not severely apply brakes immediately after installation of new brake linings or permanent damage may occur to linings and/or brake drums may become scored. Brakes must be used moderately during first several hundred miles of operation to ensure proper burnishing of linings.

1983—84 Models w/7.87 Inch Drums & All Models w/8.66 Inch Drums

INDEX

REMOVAL

1. Raise and support rear of vehicle, then remove tire and wheel assembly.
2. Remove brake drum. If brake lining is dragging on brake drum, back off brake adjustment by rotating adjustment screw.
3. Using suitable pliers, remove adjuster lever spring, **Fig. 1.**
4. Remove adjuster lever.
5. Turn automatic adjuster screw out to expand shoes past wheel cylinder boot.
6. Using suitable tool, remove hold down springs.
7. Pull brake shoe assembly down and away from anchor plate.
8. Remove "C" clip retaining parking brake lever to trailing brake shoe webbing.
9. Disassemble shoe assembly.
10. Clean dirt from brake drum, anchor plate and all other components.

CAUTION: Do not use compressed air or dry brush to clean brake parts. Many brake parts contain asbestos fibers which, if inhaled, can cause serious injury. To clean brake parts, use a water soaked rag or a suitable vacuum cleaner to minimize airborne dust.

INSPECTION

1. Inspect components for damage and unusual wear. Replace as necessary.
2. Inspect wheel cylinders. Any torn, cut or heat damaged boot indicates need of wheel cylinder replacement. Peel back lower edge of boot. If fluid spills out, cup leakage is indicated and wheel cylinder should be replaced.

NOTE: A slight amount of fluid is always present and is considered normal. Fluid acts as a lubricant for the cylinder pistons.

3. Inspect anchor plate attaching bolts, and ensure they are tight.
4. Inspect automatic adjuster screw assembly operation. If satisfactory, lightly lubricate threads with suitable brake lube. If operation is unsatisfac-

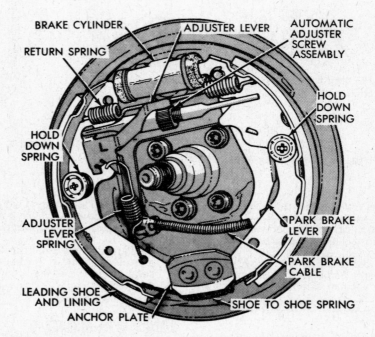

Fig. 1   Drum brake assembly. 1983—84 models w/7.87 inch drums & all models w/8.66 inch drums

tory, replace.
5. Using fine emery cloth or other suitable abrasive, clean rust and dirt from shoe contact surfaces on anchor plate.

INSTALLATION

1. Lightly lubricate anchor plate shoe contact surfaces with suitable brake lube.
2. Remove brake drum hub grease seal and bearings, then clean and repack bearings and reinstall. Install new grease seal.
3. Assemble automatic adjuster screw assembly, return spring and shoe-to-shoe spring to brake shoe assembly.
4. Position lining assembly near anchor plate, then assemble parking brake lever to trailing shoe webbing. Secure with "C" clip.
5. Install lining assembly onto anchor plate. When positioned, back off adjuster nut to seat brake shoe ends in wheel cylinder.
6. Install hold down springs.
7. Position adjuster lever, then using suitable pliers, install adjuster lever spring.
8. Install brake drum and bearings. Refer to individual truck chapter for wheel bearing adjustment procedure.
9. Adjust brakes. Refer to individual truck chapter for procedure.
10. Install tire and wheel assembly.
11. If any hydraulic connections have been opened, bleed brake system.
12. Check master cylinder level and replenish as necessary.
13. Check brake pedal for proper feel and return.
14. Lower vehicle and road test.

NOTE: Do not severely apply brakes immediately after installation of new brake linings or permanent damage may occur to linings and/or brake drums may become scored. Brakes must be used moderately during first several hundred miles of operation to ensure proper burnishing.

Models w/9, 10 & 11 Inch Drums

INDEX

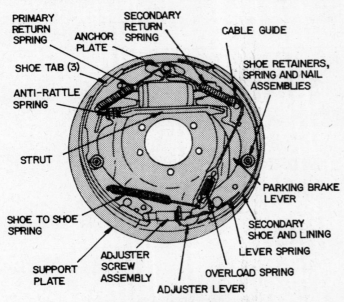

PRIMARY RETURN SPRING
SECONDARY RETURN SPRING
ANCHOR PLATE
CABLE GUIDE
SHOE TAB (3)
SHOE RETAINERS, SPRING AND NAIL ASSEMBLIES
ANTI-RATTLE SPRING
STRUT
PARKING BRAKE LEVER
SHOE TO SHOE SPRING
SECONDARY SHOE AND LINING
LEVER SPRING
SUPPORT PLATE
ADJUSTER SCREW ASSEMBLY
OVERLOAD SPRING
ADJUSTER LEVER

Fig. 1 Drum brake assembly. Models w/9, 10 & 11 inch drums

REMOVAL

1. Raise and support rear of vehicle, then remove tire and wheel assembly.
2. Remove brake drum. If brake lining is dragging on brake drum, back off brake adjustment by rotating adjustment screw.

NOTE: If brake drum is rusted or corroded to axle flange and cannot be removed, lightly tap axle flange to drum mounting surface with a suitable hammer.

3. Using brake spring pliers or equivalent, remove primary and secondary shoe return springs, **Fig. 1.**
4. Remove automatic adjuster cable from anchor plate, then unhook from adjuster lever.
5. Remove adjuster cable, overload spring, cable guide and anchor plate.
6. Unhook adjuster lever spring from lever, then remove spring and lever.
7. Remove shoe to shoe spring from secondary shoe web, then primary shoe.
8. Spread shoes apart and remove parking brake strut and spring.
9. Using suitable tool, remove shoe retainers, then springs and nails.
10. Disconnect parking brake cable from lever, then remove brake shoes.
11. Remove parking brake lever from secondary shoe.
12. Clean dirt from brake drum, backing plate and all other components.

CAUTION: Do not use compressed air or dry brush to clean brake parts. Many brake parts contain asbestos fibers which, if inhaled, can cause serious injury. To clean brake parts, use a water soaked rag or a suitable vacuum cleaner to minimize airborne dust.

INSPECTION

1. Inspect components for damage and unusual wear. Replace as necessary.
2. Inspect wheel cylinders. Boots which are torn, cut or heat damaged indicate need for wheel cylinder replacement. Peel back lower edge of boot. If fluid spills out, cup leakage is indicated and wheel cylinder should be replaced.

NOTE: A slight amount of fluid is always present and considered normal, acting as a lubricant for the cylinder pistons.

3. Inspect backing plate for evidence of seal leakage. If leakage exists, refer to individual truck chapter for axle seal replacement procedure.
4. Inspect backing plate attaching bolts, and ensure they are tight.
5. Inspect adjuster screw operation. If satisfactory, lightly lubricate adjusting screw and washer with suitable brake lube. If operation is unsatisfactory, replace.
6. Using fine emery cloth or other suitable abrasive, clean rust and dirt from shoe contact surfaces on backing plate.

INSTALLATION

1. Lubricate parking brake lever fulcrum with suitable brake lube, then attach lever to secondary brake shoe. Ensure lever operates smoothly.
2. Lightly lubricate backing plate shoe contact surfaces with suitable brake lube.
3. Connect parking brake lever to cable, then slide secondary brake shoe into position.
4. Connect wheel cylinder link to brake shoe (if equipped).
5. Slide parking brake lever strut behind axle flange and into parking brake lever slot, then place parking brake anti-rattle spring over strut.
6. Position primary brake shoe on backing plate, then connect wheel cylinder link (if equipped) and parking brake strut.
7. Install anchor plate, then position adjuster cable eye over anchor pin.
8. Install primary shoe return spring using brake spring pliers or equivalent.
9. Place protruding hole rim of cable guide in secondary shoe web hole, then holding guide in position, install secondary shoe return spring through cable guide and secondary shoe. Install spring on anchor pin using brake spring pliers or equivalent.

NOTE: Ensure cable guide remains flat against secondary shoe web during and after return spring installation. Also ensure secondary spring end overlaps primary spring end on anchor pin.

10. Using suitable pliers, squeeze spring ends around anchor pin until parallel.
11. Install adjuster screw assembly between primary and secondary brake

shoes with star wheel on secondary shoe side.

NOTE: The left side adjuster assembly stud is stamped "L" and is cadmium-plated. The right side adjuster assembly is not stamped and is colored black.

12. Install shoe to shoe spring, then position adjusting lever spring over pivot pin on shoe web.
13. Install adjusting lever under spring and over pivot pin, then slide lever slightly rearward.

14. Install nails, springs and retainers.
15. Thread adjuster cable over guide and hook end of overload spring in lever. Ensure eye of cable is pulled tight against anchor and in a straight line with guide.
16. Install brake drum, tire and wheel assembly.
17. Adjust brakes. Refer to individual truck chapters for procedure.
18. If any hydraulic connections have been opened, bleed brake system.
19. Check master cylinder fluid level, and replenish as necessary.

20. Check brake pedal for proper feel and return.
21. Lower vehicle and road test.

NOTE: Do not severely apply brakes immediately after installation of new brake linings or permanent damage may occur to linings, and/or brake drums may become scored. Brakes must be used moderately during first several hundred miles of operation to ensure proper burnishing of linings.

Models w/12 & 13 Inch Drums, Exc. Motor Home

INDEX

REMOVAL

1. Raise and support vehicle.
2. Remove wheel and tire assembly.
3. Remove axle shaft nuts, washers, and cones, then the axle shaft.

NOTE: If cones do not release, rap axle shaft sharply at center.

4. Remove outer hub nut, then straighten lock washer and remove washer, inner nut, and bearing.
5. Remove brake drum. If brake lining is dragging on brake drum, back off brake adjustment by rotating adjusting screw.
6. Unhook adjusting lever return spring from lever, remove lever and return spring from lever pivot pin, and unhook adjuster lever from adjuster cable assembly, **Fig. 1.**
7. Using suitable pliers, unhook upper shoe-to-shoe spring, then unhook and remove shoe hold down springs.
8. Disconnect parking brake cable from parking brake lever.
9. Remove shoes, lower shoe-to-shoe spring and star wheel as an assembly.

INSPECTION

1. Using suitable solvent, clean support, then inspect for burrs and remove as necessary.

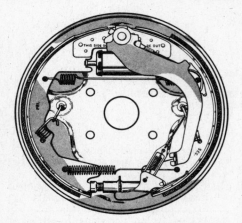

Fig. 1   Drum brake assembly. Models w/12 & 13 inch drums, exc. motor home

2. Clean and lubricate threads of adjusting screws, then inspect for pulled or stripped threads.
3. If spring paint shows discoloration, end coils are distorted, or spring strength is questionable, replace spring.

INSTALLATION

NOTE: Pivot screw and adjusting nut have

left hand threads on left side brakes and right hand threads on right side brakes.

1. Using suitable lubricant, lubricate and assemble star wheel assembly, then lubricate guide pads on support plates.
2. Assemble star wheel, lower shoe-to-shoe spring, and brake shoes and position assembly on support plate.
3. Connect parking brake cable to parking brake lever.
4. Install and hook hold down springs.
5. Install upper shoe-to-shoe spring.
6. Position adjuster lever return springs on pivots.
7. Install adjuster lever and route adjuster cable and connector to adjuster.
8. Position drum on axle housing.
9. Install bearing and inner nut. Refer to individual truck chapter for bearing adjustment procedure.
10. Install lock washer and outer nut, bending washer to lock in place.
11. Place new gasket on hub and install axle shaft, cones, lock washers, and nuts.
12. Adjust brakes. Refer to individual truck chapter for procedure.
13. Install tire and wheel assembly.
14. If any hydraulic connections have been opened, bleed brake system.
15. Check fluid level in master cylinder, filling as necessary.
16. Check brake pedal for proper feel and return.
17. Lower vehicle and road test.

Models w/12.12 Inch Drums

INDEX

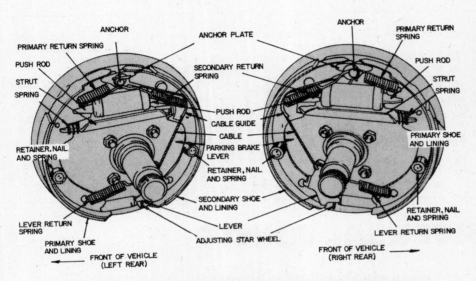

Fig. 1   Drum brake assembly. Models w/12.12 inch drums

REMOVAL

1. Raise and support vehicle.
2. Remove wheel and tire assemblies.
3. Remove axle shaft nuts, washers, and cones, then the axle shaft.

NOTE: If cones do not release, rap axle shaft sharply at center.

4. Using suitable tool, remove outer hub nut.
5. Straighten lock washer and remove lock washer, inner nut, and bearing, then the drum. If brake lining is dragging on brake drum, back off brake adjustment by rotating adjusting screw.
6. Using suitable tool, remove brake shoe return springs, **Fig. 1.**
7. Remove brake shoe retainers, springs, and nails.
8. Remove end of automatic adjuster cable from anchor, then other end from lever.
9. Remove automatic adjuster cable, cable guide, and anchor plate.
10. Disengage lever spring at both ends, then remove spring and lever.
11. Spread anchor ends of shoes and remove parking brake strut with spring.
12. Disconnect parking brake cable from parking brake lever and remove brake assembly.
13. Remove brake shoes with adjusting star wheel from support.

INSPECTION

1. Using suitable solvent, clean support, then inspect for burrs and remove as necessary.
2. Clean and lubricate threads of adjusting screws, then inspect for pulled or stripped threads.

INSTALLATION

1. Apply thin coat of suitable lubricant to shoe contact area of support platforms.
2. Attach parking brake lever to back side of secondary shoe.
3. Place brake shoes in their relative position on workbench.
4. Lubricate threads of adjusting screw and install screw between shoes with star wheel toward secondary shoe.

NOTE: Star wheels are stamped with an "R" or "L" to indicate whether they go on right or left side of vehicle.

5. Overlap anchor ends of shoes and install adjusting spring and lever.
6. Hold brake shoes in their relative position and attach parking brake cable to parking brake lever.
7. Install parking brake strut with spring between parking brake lever and primary shoe.
8. Position brake shoes on support and install retainer nails, springs, and retainers.
9. Install anchor plate.
10. Install end of adjusting cable on anchor, then install return spring between primary shoe and anchor.
11. Install cable guide in secondary shoe, then install secondary return spring.

NOTE: Ensure that secondary spring overlaps primary spring and that spring does not slip between adjuster cable end and anchor.

12. Place adjuster cable in groove of cable guide and engage hook of cable into adjusting lever, ensuring that cable guide lays flat against shoe web.
13. Position drum on axle housing.
14. Install bearing and inner nut. Refer to individual truck chapter for bearing adjustment procedure.
15. Install locking washer and outer nut, bending washer to lock in place.
16. Place new gasket on hub and install axle shaft, cones, lock washers, and nuts.
17. Adjust brakes. Refer to individual truck chapter for procedure.
18. Install tire and wheel assembly.
19. If any hydraulic connections have been opened, bleed brake system.
20. Check fluid level in master cylinder, filling as necessary.
21. Check brake pedal for proper feel and return.
22. Lower vehicle and road test.

Motor Home

INDEX

REMOVAL

1. Raise and support vehicle.
2. Remove wheels and drums, then install wheel cylinder clamps to hold pistons in cylinders.
3. Using suitable pliers, remove four shoe retracting springs.
4. Remove shoe hold down lock wires or cotter pins and castellated nuts, and remove shoes, then pull anchor pins out of anchor support.
5. Dismantle adjusting mechanism. To remove adjuster lock springs, loosen hold down screws or remove snap rings.
6. Thread each adjusting screw from shoe side of support.
7. Lift star wheels from slot.
8. Clean dirt and grease from drum, backing plate, and components.

INSTALLATION

1. Reverse removal procedure to install, noting the following:
   a. Apply a thin coat of suitable lubricant to one side of hold down washer and install washer with lubricated side contacting shoe web.
   b. Place a .025 inch feeler gauge between center shoe edge and rim of shoe.
   c. Hold shoe in position against anchor bracket and adjusting screw pad and install hold down nut finger tight.
   d. Back off hold down nut one castellation, install cotter pin, and remove feeler gauge.

UNIVERSAL JOINTS

INDEX

SERVICE NOTES

Before disassembling any universal joint, examine the assembly carefully and note the position of the grease fitting (if used). Also, be sure to mark the yokes with relation to the propeller shaft so they may be reassembled in the same relative position. Failure to observe these precautions may produce rough vehicle operation which results in rapid wear and failure of parts, and place an unbalanced load on transmission, engine and rear axle.

When universal joints are disassembled for lubrication or inspection, and the old parts are to be reinstalled, special care must be exercised to avoid damage to universal joint spider or cross and bearing cups.

NOTE: Some driveshafts use an injected nylon retainer on the universal joint bearings. When service is necessary, pressing the bearings out will sheer the nylon retainer, **Fig. 1.** Replacement with the conventional steel snap ring type is then necessary, **Fig. 2.**

CROSS & ROLLER TYPE

Figs. 3 and 4 illustrate typical examples of universal joints of this type. They all operate on the same principle and similar service and replacement procedures may be applied to all.

WITHOUT UNIVERSAL JOINT REPLACEMENT TOOL
Disassembly
1. Remove snap rings (or retainer plates) that retain bearings in yoke and drive shaft.
2. Place U-joint in a vise.
3. Select a wrench socket with an outside diameter slightly smaller than the U-joint bearings. Select another wrench socket with an inside diameter slightly larger than the U-joint bearings.
4. Place the sockets at opposite bearings in the yoke so that the smaller socket becomes a bearing pusher and the larger socket becomes a bearing receiver when the vise jaws come

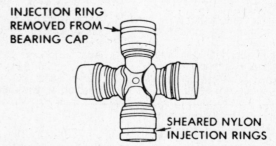

Fig. 1 Production type universal joints which use nylon injection rings in place of snap rings

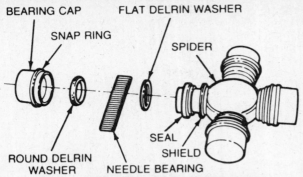

Fig. 2 Service type universal joints (internal snap ring type)

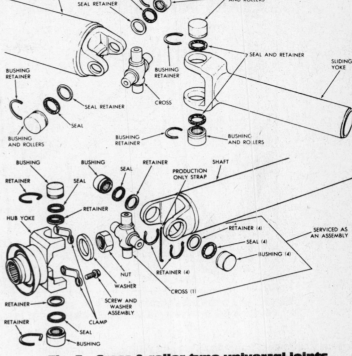

Fig. 3 Cross & roller type universal joints

together, **Fig. 5.** Close vise jaws until both bearings are free of yoke and remove bearings from the cross or spider.

5. If bearings will not come all the way out, close vise until bearing in receiver socket protrudes from yoke as much as possible without using excessive force. Then remove from vise and place that portion of bearing which protrudes from yoke between vise jaws. Tighten vise to hold bearing and drive yoke off with a soft hammer.

6. To remove opposite bearing from yoke, replace in vise with pusher socket on exposed cross journal with receiver socket over bearing cup. Then tighten vise jaws to press bearing back through yoke into receiving socket.

7. Remove yoke from drive shaft and again place protruding portion of bearing between vise jaws. Then tighten vise to hold bearing while driving yoke off bearing with soft hammer.

8. Turn spider or cross ¼ turn and use the same procedure to press bearings out of drive shaft.

Assembly

1. If old parts are to be reassembled, pack bearing cups with universal joint grease. *Do not fill cups completely or use excessive amounts as over-lubrication may damage seals during reassembly.* Use new seals.

2. If new parts are being installed, check new bearings for adequate grease before assembling.

3. With the pusher (smaller) socket, press one bearing part way into drive shaft. Position spider into the partially installed bearing. Place second bearing into drive shaft. Fasten drive shaft in vise so that bearings are in contact with faces of vise jaws, **Fig. 6.** Some spiders are provided with locating lugs which must face toward drive shaft when installed.

4. Press bearings all the way into position and install snap rings or retainer plates.

5. Install bearings in yoke in same manner. When installation is completed, check U-joint for binding or roughness. If free movement is impeded, correct the condition before installation in vehicle.

USING UNIVERSAL JOINT REPLACEMENT TOOL

Disassembly

1. Place driveshaft in a vise using care to avoid damaging it.

2. Remove bearing retaining snap rings.

NOTE: Some universal joints use injected nylon retainers in place of snap rings. Dur-

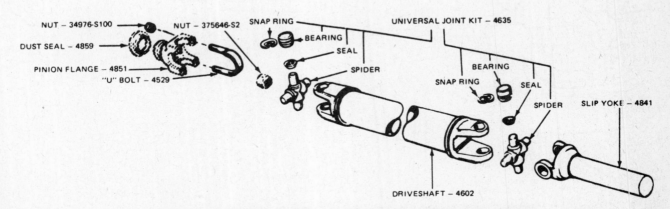

Fig. 4 Cross & roller type universal joints & propeller shaft

Fig. 5   Removing bearings from yoke using a small socket as a driver & large socket as a receiver

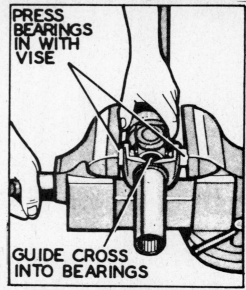

Fig. 6   Installing bearings into driveshaft yoke

ing servicing, the snap rings supplied with the replacement universal joint assembly must be used.

3. Position tool on shaft and press bearing out of yoke, **Fig. 7.** If bearing cannot be pressed all the way out, remove it using vise grips or channel lock pliers or position driveshaft as shown and strike center yoke with hammer, **Fig. 8.** Mark yoke and shaft to make sure they will be reassembled in their same relative positions.
4. Reposition tool so that it presses on the spider in order to press other bearing from opposite side of flange.
5. If used, remove flange from spider.

Assembly
1. Start new bearing into yoke, then posi-

tion spider into yoke and press bearing until it is ¼ inch below surface.
2. Remove tool and install a new snap ring.
3. Start new bearing in opposite side of yoke, then install tool and press on bearing until opposite bearing contacts snap ring.
4. Remove tool and install remaining snap ring.

CONSTANT VELOCITY TYPE

This type of universal joint, **Fig. 9,** consists of two conventional cross and roller joints connected with a special link yoke. Because the two joint angles are the same, even though the usual universal joint fluctuation is present within the unit, the acceleration of the front joint (within the yoke) is

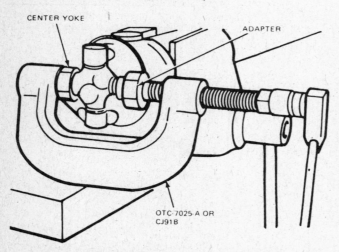

Fig. 7   Removing bearing caps using tool & adapter

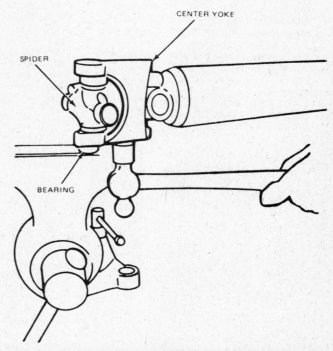

Fig. 8   Removing bearing cap by holding cap in vise & striking center yoke with hammer

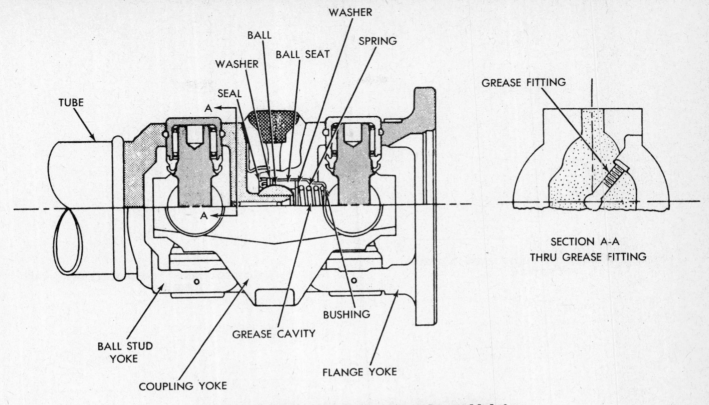

Fig. 9   Constant velocity (CV) universal joint

always neutralized by the deceleration of the rear joint (within the yoke) and vice versa. The end result is the front and rear propeller shafts always turn at a constant velocity.

DISASSEMBLY

Constant Velocity Joint

NOTE: To disassemble the constant velocity joint, the bearings should be removed in sequence shown in **Fig. 10**. This method requires the least amount of work.

1. Mark all yokes before disassembly as shown in **Fig. 11,** so that they can be reassembled in their original relationship to maintain driveshaft balance.

NOTE: The following procedure can be performed in a vise and a cross press tool, **Fig. 12,** can be used in place of the socket used to drive the bearings.

2. Support the driveshaft horizontally in line with the base plate of a press.

Place rear end of coupling yoke over a 1⅛ inch socket to accept the bearing. Place a socket slightly smaller than the bearing on the opposite side of the spider.

3. Press bearing cup out of coupling yoke ear. If bearing cup is not completely removed, insert spacer C-4365-4 or equivalent, **Fig. 13,** and complete removal of bearing cup.

4. Rotate driveshaft 180° and shear the opposite retaining ring, and press the

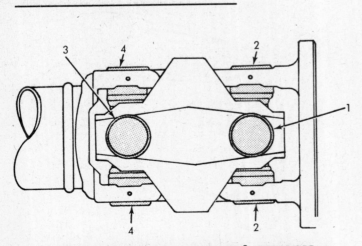

Fig. 10   Bearing cap removal sequence

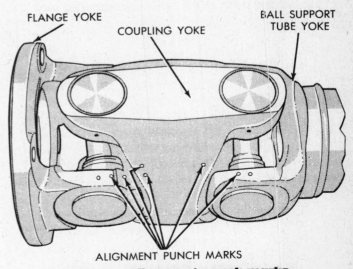

Fig. 11   Alignment punch marks

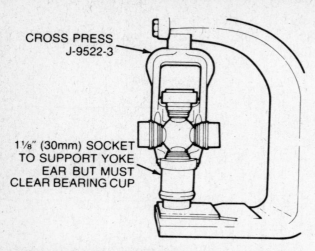

CROSS PRESS
J-9522-3

1⅛" (30mm) SOCKET
TO SUPPORT YOKE
EAR BUT MUST
CLEAR BEARING CUP

Fig. 12   Cross press being used in place of socket

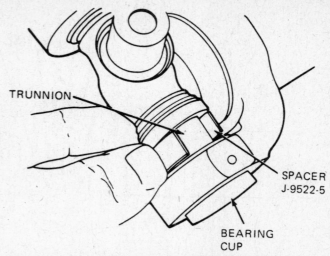

TRUNNION

SPACER
J-9522-5

BEARING
CUP

Fig. 13   Using spacer to completely drive out bearing

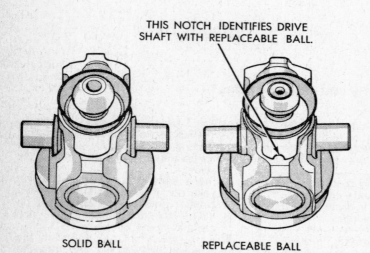

THIS NOTCH IDENTIFIES DRIVE
SHAFT WITH REPLACEABLE BALL.

SOLID BALL

REPLACEABLE BALL

Fig. 14   Solid ball & replaceable balls. Notch identifies driveshaft with replaceable ball

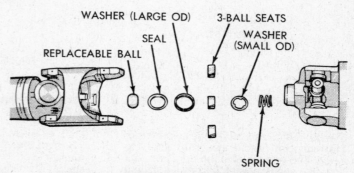

WASHER (LARGE OD)   3-BALL SEATS

SEAL   WASHER
                    (SMALL OD)
REPLACEABLE BALL

SPRING

Fig. 15   Ball & seat exploded view

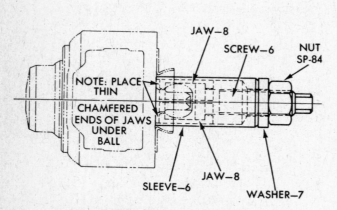

JAW—8

SCREW—6   NUT
                 SP-84

NOTE: PLACE
THIN

CHAMFERED
ENDS OF JAWS
UNDER
BALL

SLEEVE—6   JAW—8   WASHER—7

Fig. 16   Removing centering ball

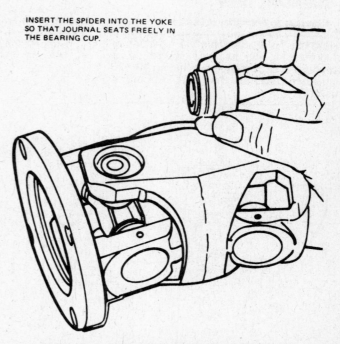

INSERT THE SPIDER INTO THE YOKE
SO THAT JOURNAL SEATS FREELY IN
THE BEARING CUP.

Fig. 17   Inserting cross into yoke

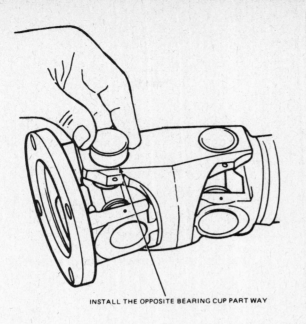

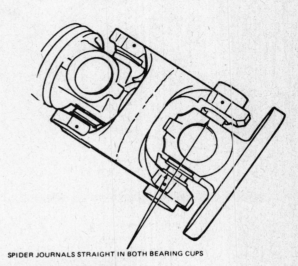

INSTALL THE OPPOSITE BEARING CUP PART WAY

SPIDER JOURNALS STRAIGHT IN BOTH BEARING CUPS

Fig. 18   Aligning bearing cups & journals

bearing cup out of the coupling yoke as described previously, using spacer C-4365-4 or equivalent.

5. Disengage cross trunnions, still attached to flange yoke, from coupling yoke. Pull flange yoke and cross from centering ball on ball support tube yoke. The ball socket is part of the flange yoke.

NOTE: The ball on some joints is not replaceable. The joints with a replaceable ball can be recognized as shown in **Fig. 14.** Do not attempt to remove solid ball, as removal tool may be damaged.

6. Pry seal from ball cavity, then remove

washers, spring and shoes, **Fig. 15.**

Ball Socket

1. To remove ball, separate universal joint between coupling yoke and flange yoke by pressing out trunnion bearing in coupling yoke. Pull flange yoke and cross with ball socket from centering ball as a unit.
2. Clean and inspect ball seat insert bushing for wear. If worn, replace flange yoke and cross assembly.
3. Pry seal from ball cavity, then remove washers, spring and ball seats.
4. Clean and inspect centering ball surface, seal, ball seats, spring and washer. If parts are worn or broken,

replace with a service kit.

5. Remove centering ball as shown in **Fig. 16,** using components of tool C-4365 or equivalent. Install components as shown, and draw ball off ball stud.

ASSEMBLY
Ball Socket & Constant Velocity Joint

NOTE: During assembly, make sure that marks made during disassembly, **Fig. 11,** are aligned to maintain balance.

1. To install centering ball onto stud, use

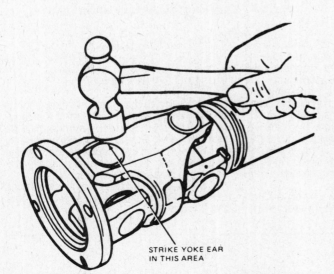

STRIKE YOKE EAR IN THIS AREA

Fig. 19   Relieving binding condition at point A

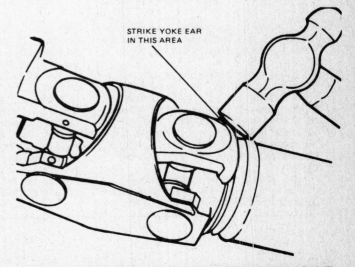

STRIKE YOKE EAR IN THIS AREA

Fig. 20   Relieving binding condition at point B

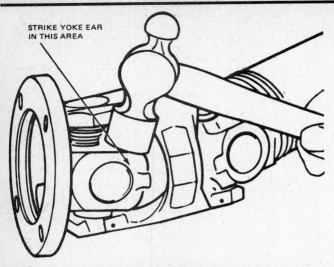

Fig. 21   Relieving binding condition at point C

STRIKE YOKE EAR IN THIS AREA

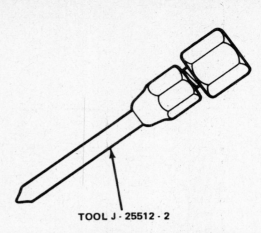

TOOL J - 25512 - 2

Fig. 22   Lubrication fitting adapter

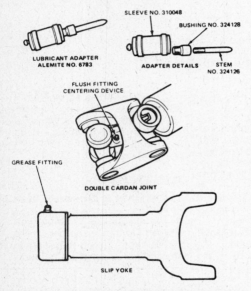

SLEEVE NO. 310048
BUSHING NO. 324128
LUBRICANT ADAPTER ALEMITE NO. 6783
ADAPTER DETAILS
STEM NO. 324126
FLUSH FITTING CENTERING DEVICE
GREASE FITTING
DOUBLE CARDAN JOINT

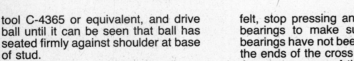

SLIP YOKE

Fig. 23   Lubrication fitting adapter & fitting location

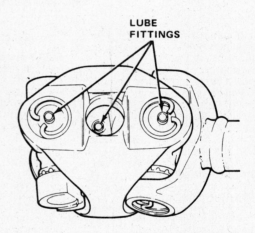

LUBE FITTINGS

Fig. 24   Lubrication fitting locations

tool C-4365 or equivalent, and drive ball until it can be seen that ball has seated firmly against shoulder at base of stud.

2. To install cross assembly, install one bearing cup part way into one side of yoke and turn this yoke to the bottom. Insert cross into yoke so that the trunnion seats into bearing, **Fig. 17.** Install opposite bearing cup part way, **Fig. 18.** Make sure that both cross journals are started straight into both bearing cups.

3. Press bearing cups, while moving cross to ensure free movement of trunnions in bearing. If any binding is felt, stop pressing and check needle bearings to make sure that needle bearings have not been trapped under the ends of the cross journals.

4. As soon as one of the retaining ring grooves clears the inside of yoke, stop pressing and install retaining ring.

5. Continue to press until opposite retaining ring can be snapped into place. If difficulty is encountered, strike the yoke firmly in locations shown in **Figs. 19, 20 and 21,** to spring the yoke ears slightly.

6. Relube center ball and socket, and assemble other half universal joint, if disassembled.

LUBRICATION

Lubrication of the constant velocity joints should not be overlooked during the regular service intervals recommended by the manufacturer. During lubrication, use only the type of lubricant recommended by the manufacturer. This lubricant is usually lithium type chassis grease.

Lubrication fitting adapters and locations of the lubrication fittings are shown in **Figs. 22, 23 and 24.**

MANUAL TRANSMISSIONS/TRANSAXLES

NOTE: See individual truck chapters for procedures on removing the transmission and adjusting the gearshift linkage.

TABLE OF CONTENTS

Chrysler A-230 3 Speed Manual Transmission

INDEX

DISASSEMBLE

TRANSMISSION

1. Shift transmission into 2nd gear for shift fork clearance and remove side cover and shifter assembly.
2. Remove front bearing retainer, **Fig. 1.**
3. Tap drive pinion forward with brass drift as far as possible to provide clearance for mainshaft removal.
4. Rotate cut away part of second gear next to countergear for mainshaft removal clearance. Shift 2–3 synchronizer sleeve forward.
5. Remove speedometer gear.
6. Remove rear extension housing.
7. Using dummy shaft, push reverse idler shaft and key out of case.
8. Remove idler gear with dummy shaft in place to retain rollers. Remove thrust washers.
9. Remove mainshaft through rear case opening, **Fig. 2.**
10. Using dummy shaft to retain rollers, tap countershaft out rear of case and lower countergear to bottom of case to permit removal of drive pinion.
11. Remove snap ring from pinion bearing outer race, drive pinion into case and remove through rear case opening.
12. Remove countergear through rear case opening.

MAINSHAFT

1. Remove 2–3 synchronizer clutch gear retaining ring from front of mainshaft.
2. Slide 2–3 synchronizer and 2nd gear stop ring off of shaft. Remove 2nd gear.
3. Spread snap ring in mainshaft bearing retainer and slide retainer off bearing race.
4. Remove snap ring securing bearing to mainshaft.
5. Support front side of the reverse gear in press and press bearing off shaft. When bearing clears shaft, do not allow parts to drop through.
6. Remove 1st-Reverse synchronizer assembly from mainshaft, **Fig. 3.**
7. Remove 1st gear and stop ring.
8. Reverse procedure to assemble mainshaft.

ASSEMBLE

1. Using dummy shaft to hold rollers in place and heavy grease to hold thrust washers, carefully place countergear assembly in bottom of case. Do not finish installation until drive pinion is installed.
2. Load rollers and retaining ring in drive pinion bore and install drive pinion through rear case opening and into case bore. Install large snap ring on bearing and install front bearing retainer.
3. Align countergear with its shaft bore and install countershaft through gear, driving dummy shaft out as countershaft is installed. Install countershaft key.
4. Carefully tap drive pinion forward to provide mainshaft installation clearance.
5. With 2–3 synchronizer sleeve fully forward and cut out on 2nd gear turned so it is toward countershaft, insert mainshaft assembly through rear case opening.

NOTE: If installation is correct, the bearing retainer will bottom in the case without force. If not, check for out of position strut, roller or stop ring.

6. Using dummy shaft to hold rollers,

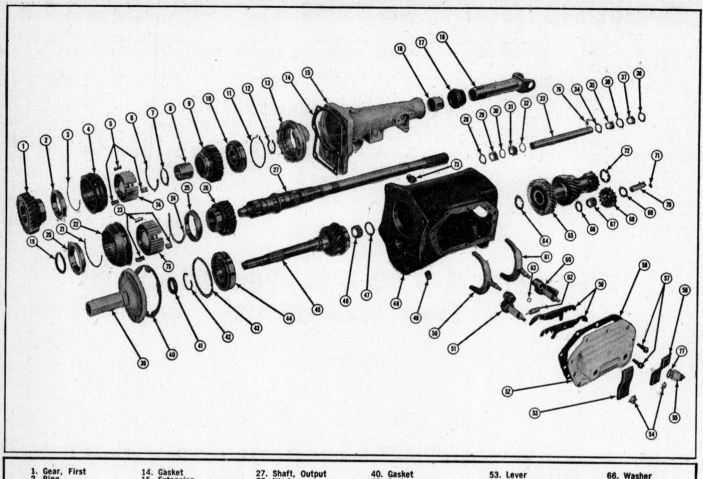

1. Gear, First	14. Gasket	27. Shaft, Output	40. Gasket
2. Ring	15. Extension	28. Washer	41. Seal
3. Spring	16. Bushing	29. Roller	42. Snap Ring
4. Sleeve	17. Seal	30. Washer	43. Snap Ring
5. Struts (3)	18. Yoke	31. Roller	44. Bearing
6. Spring	19. Snap Ring	32. Washer	45. Pinion, Drive
7. Snap Ring	20. Ring	33. Countershaft	46. Roller
8. Bushing	21. Spring	34. Washer	47. Snap Ring
9. Gear, Reverse	22. Sleeve	35. Roller	48. Case
10. Bearing	23. Struts (3)	36. Washer	49. Plug, Drain
11. Snap Ring	24. Spring	37. Roller	50. Fork
12. Snap Ring	25. Ring	38. Washer	51. Lever
13. Retainer	26. Gear, Second	39. Retainer	52. Housing

53. Lever	66. Washer
54. Nut Locking	67. Roller
55. Switch	68. Gear, Idler
56. Lever	69. Washer
57. Bolt	70. Shaft
58. Gasket	71. Key
59. Lever, Interlock	72. Washer
60. Lever	73. Plug, Filler
61. Fork	74. Gear, Clutch
62. Spring	75. Gear, Clutch
63. Snap Ring	76. Key
64. Washer	77. Gasket
65. Gear, Countershaft	

Fig. 1   Disassembled view of Chrysler A-230 3 speed manual transmission

Fig. 2   Removing mainshaft assembly from case

install reverse idler in case and install idler shaft and key.

7. Install rear extension housing, speedometer gear and with transmission shifted into 2nd gear, install cover and shifter assembly.

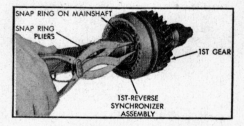

Fig. 3   Removing 1st—reverse synchronizer snap ring

Chrysler A-460 4 Speed & A-465/A-525 5 Speed Manual Transaxles

INDEX

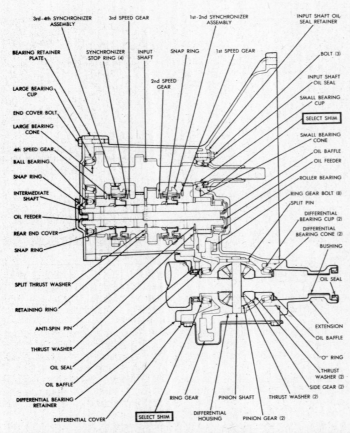

Fig. 1 Sectional view of Chrysler A-460 4 speed manual transaxle

SERVICE BULLETIN: Beginning with 1983 production, five speed units incorporate a threaded input shaft and a press fit 5th speed input gear. These changes make it possible to remove and install 5th speed input gear without removing transaxle from vehicle.

To replace 5th speed input gear with transaxle installed in vehicle, use the following procedure:
1. Raise and support front of vehicle, then remove left front tire and wheel assembly.

2. Remove transaxle end cover, 5th speed synchonizer strut retainer plate snap ring and the retainer plate.
3. Remove 5th speed synchonizer assembly, fork and input gear snap ring.
4. Remove 5th input gear, using a suitable puller.
5. Remove bearing support plate and bearing retainer plate. Clean sealant from mating surfaces, then apply RTV sealant and reinstall plate.
6. Draw input gear fully onto shaft splines, using tool No. C-4810 or

equivalent.
7. Install new copper colored 5th gear snap ring (No. 6500837).
8. Install 5th speed synchonizer assembly and fork.
9. Install strut retainer plate and new snap ring.
10. Apply bead of RTV sealant to end cover and install the cover.
11. Add transaxle fluid as necessary.
12. Install wheel and tire assembly, then lower vehicle and check transaxle for proper operation.

DISASSEMBLE

1. Remove differential cover bolts and differential cover, **Figs. 1 and 2.**
2. Remove differential bearing retainer bolts, then rotate differential bearing retainer using tool L-4435, or equivalent. Remove retainer.
3. Remove extension housing bolts, then remove differential assembly and extension housing.
4. Remove selector shaft housing and, on model A-460, rear end cover.
5. On 5-speed models A-465 and A-525, proceed as follows:
   a. Remove 5th speed shifter pin, detent ball and spring.
   b. Remove fill plug and rear end cover.
   c. Remove 5th speed synchronizer strut retainer plate snap ring, then the retainer plate.
   d. Remove 5th speed synchronizer assembly, shift fork with shift rail, and the intermediate 5th speed gear, **Fig. 3.**
   e. Remove input shaft 5th speed gear snap ring and the gear.
   f. Remove bearing support plate bolts and the support plate, **Fig. 4.**
6. On model A-460, remove large snap ring from intermediate shaft rear bearing.
7. On all models, remove bearing retainer plate by tapping with plastic hammer, **Fig. 5.**
8. On model A-460, remove 3-4 shift fork rail. On all models, remove reverse

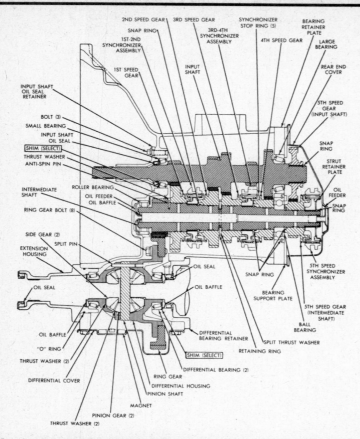

Fig. 2   Sectional view of Chrysler A-465 & A-525 5 speed manual transaxle

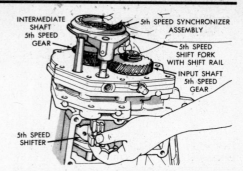

Fig. 3   5th speed synchronizer & shift fork removal. A-465 & A-525 transaxles

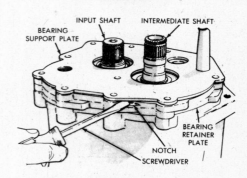

Fig. 4   Bearing support plate removal. A-465 & A-525 transaxles

idler gear shaft and reverse idler gear, **Fig. 6.**

9. Remove intermediate gear shaft and input gear shaft assemblies.
10. Remove shift forks and pads from intermediate gear shaft assembly.
11. Remove clutch release bearing shaft E clip, then remove clutch release shaft, **Fig. 7.**
12. Remove input shaft retainer and seal.
13. Remove reverse shift lever "E" clip and reverse shift lever.

SUB-ASSEMBLY SERVICE

TRANSAXLE CASE

1. Remove input shaft front bearing cup using tools C-4171, C-4656 and suitable press.
2. Remove intermediate shaft bearing strap, then remove intermediate shaft bearing using tool C-4660, or equivalent.
3. Install intermediate shaft bearing using tools C-4657, C-4171 and suitable press.
4. Install input shaft front bearing cup using tools C-4171, C-4655, or equivalents and suitable press.

INTERMEDIATE SHAFT ASSEMBLY

NOTE: The 1-2 and 3-4 shift forks and synchronizer stop rings are interchangeable. If original parts are to be reused, install in original positions.

1. Remove intermediate shaft rear bearing snap ring, **Fig. 8.**
2. Remove intermediate shaft rear bearing, using suitable puller.
3. Remove 3-4 synchronizer hub snap ring, then 3-4 synchronizer hub and third speed gear, using suitable puller.

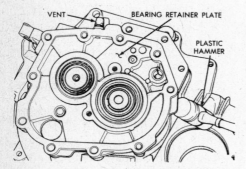

Fig. 5   Bearing retainer plate removal

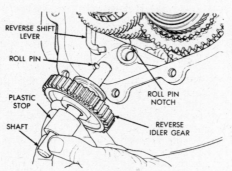

Fig. 6   Reverse idler gear, shaft & stop removal

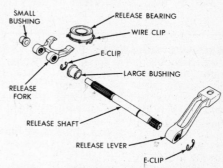

Fig. 7   Clutch release shaft components

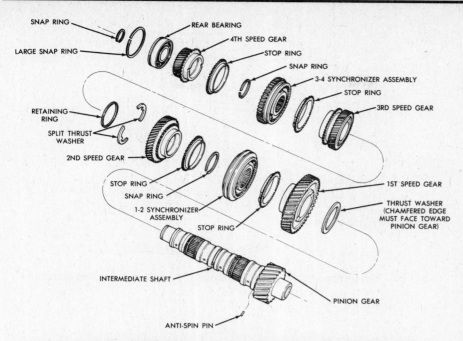

Fig. 8   Disassembled view of intermediate shaft assembly

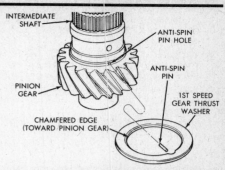

Fig. 9   1st speed gear thrust washer removal

4. Remove retaining ring and split thrust washer.
5. Remove second speed gear and stop ring, then the 1-2 synchronizer hub snap ring.
6. Remove first speed gear, stop ring and 1-2 synchronizer assembly.
7. Remove first speed gear thrust washer, **Fig. 9.**
8. Install first speed gear thrust washer, first speed gear, stop ring and 1-2 synchronizer assembly.
9. Install 1-2 synchronizer hub snap ring, second speed gear stop ring and second speed gear.
10. Install split thrust washer and retaining ring.

11. Install 3-4 synchronizer hub, using suitable press, and install third speed gear.
12. Install 3-4 synchronizer hub snap ring and intermediate shaft rear bearing, using tool C-4672, or equivalent and suitable press.
13. Install intermediate shaft rear bearing snap ring.

NOTE: Check to ensure that all gears rotate freely and have a minimum of .003 inch (.076 mm) end play.

SELECTOR SHAFT HOUSING

1. Remove selector shaft oil seal.

2. Remove selector shaft E clips, **Figs. 10 and 11,** then remove selector shaft. Disassemble remaining components of housing shown in **Figs. 10 and 11.**
3. Assemble selector shaft housing components in reverse order of removal, then install selector shaft.
4. Install selector shaft E clips, then install selector shaft oil seal, using tool C-4662 or equivalent.

SYNCHRONIZER ASSEMBLIES

Refer to **Figs. 12, 13, and 14** for servicing of synchronizer assemblies.

DIFFERENTIAL BEARING RETAINER

1. Remove differential bearing retainer oil seal, **Fig. 15.**
2. Remove differential bearing retainer cup and oil baffle using tool L-4518 or equivalent.
3. Install oil baffle, then install shim and bearing retainer cup, using tools C-4171 and L-4520, or equivalents. Shim is a select fit. To determine required shim thickness, refer to "Bearing Adjustments."
4. Install bearing retainer oil seal.

EXTENSION HOUSING

1. Remove extension housing oil seal, **Fig. 16,** then remove extension housing and oil baffle, using tool L-4518, or equivalent.
2. Install oil baffle, using tools C-4171 and L-4520, or equivalents and suitable press.
3. Install bearing cup using same tools and suitable press.

INPUT SHAFT

NOTE: Input shaft bearing shim thickness must be checked if any of the following parts are replaced: transaxle case input shaft seal retainer, bearing retainer plate, rear end cover, input shaft or input shaft bearings. Refer to "Bearing Adjustments" for procedure.

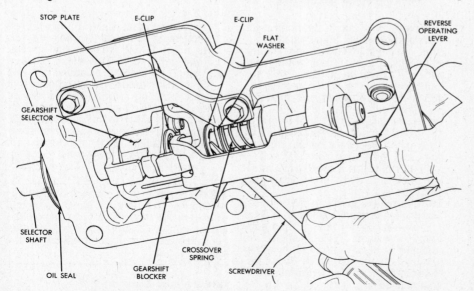

Fig. 10   Selector shaft disassembled. A-460 transaxle

1. Remove input shaft rear bearing cone, using tool C-293 and adapter C-293-45, or equivalents.
2. Remove input shaft front bearing cone, usng tool C-293, or equivalent.
3. Remove input shaft bearing rear bearing cup from bearing retainer plate, using tool C-4171 and L-4520 and suitable press.
4. Install input shaft rear bearing cone, using tool C-4652, or equivalent on A-460 model or L-4507 on A-465 and A-525 models.
5. Install input shaft front bearing cone, using tool C-4662, or equivalent.
6. Install rear end cover on model A-460, or bearing support plate on models A-465 and A-525 onto bearing retainer plate, then support plate on blocks of wood. Install input shaft rear bearing cup into bearing retainer plate using tools L-4520, C-4171 and suitable press. Check to ensure that bearing cone bottoms on rear end cover.

DIFFERENTIAL

NOTE: Differential bearing shim thickness must be checked if any of the following parts are replaced: transaxle case, differential bearing retainer, differential case or differential bearings. Refer to "Bearing Adjustment" for procedure.

1. Remove differential bearing cones, using tools L-4406-1 and L-4406-3, or equivalents, **Fig. 17.**
2. Remove ring gear from differential case.
3. Using suitable punch, remove pinion shaft split pin.
4. Remove pinion shaft, then remove pinion gears, side gears and thrust washers from differential case.
5. Reverse procedure to assemble. Use tools C-4171 and L-4410 and suitable press to install differential bearing cones.

BEARING ADJUSTMENTS
Input Shaft Bearing Endplay

NOTE: If input shaft bearing shim was reinstalled, press input shaft front bearing cup forward, using tools L-4656 and C-4171 or equivalents, then press bearing cup back into case using tools L-4655 and C-4171. This is necessary to properly position bearing cup and must be performed prior to endplay adjustment.

1. Select a shim that will allow .001–.010 inch endplay. This shim size may be determined by measuring original shim in input shaft seal retainer and selecting a shim .010 inch thinner than original.
2. Install shim selected onto bearing cap, then install input shaft seal retainer.

NOTE: Tighten input shaft seal retainer bolts alternately and evenly until input shaft seal retainer is bottomed against case. Torque bolts to 21 ft. lbs.

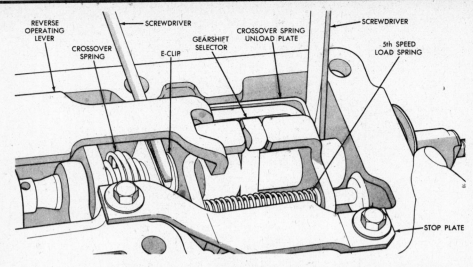

Fig. 11   Selector shaft disassembled. A-465 & A-525 transaxle

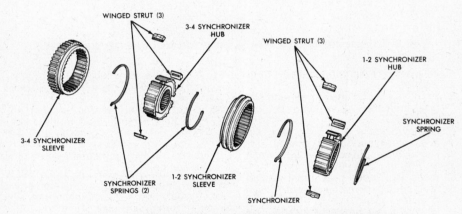

Fig. 12   Synchronizer assembly. Exploded view

3. Lubricate input shaft bearings with transmission fluid, then install input shaft into case. Install bearing retainer plate with input shaft rear bearing cup and end cover on model A-460, or bearing support plate on models A-465 and A-525 installed, and torque all retaining bolts to 21 ft. lbs.
4. Install dial indicator as shown in **Fig. 18,** to check input shaft endplay. Push input shaft rearward while rotating back and forth, then zero dial indicator. Pull input shaft forward while rotating back and forth, and record dial indicator reading.
5. To determine required shim thickness, add thickness of shim selected in Step 1 to dial indicator reading, then subtract .002 inch. Select shims as required to obtain shim that is within .0016 inch of required thickness. Refer to chart in **Fig. 19** for available shim thickness.
6. Remove input shaft seal retainer and shim selected in step 1. Install shim or shims selected in step 5, then install input shaft seal retainer with a 1/16 inch bead of R.T.V. sealant and torque retaining bolts to 21 ft. lbs.
7. Using tool L-4508, or equivalent and an inch lb. torque wrench, check input shaft rotating torque. Torque should be one to five inch lbs. for new bearings or one inch lb. for used bearings. If rotating torque is greater than specified, install .0016 inch thinner shim. If rotating torque is lower than specified, install .0016 inch thicker shim.

NOTE: Refer to note at beginning of this procedure and perform steps described whenever a thinner shim is installed. This will insure that the input shaft front bearing cup is installed the proper distance into the case.

Differential Bearing Preload
1. Remove bearing cup and shim from differential bearing retainer.

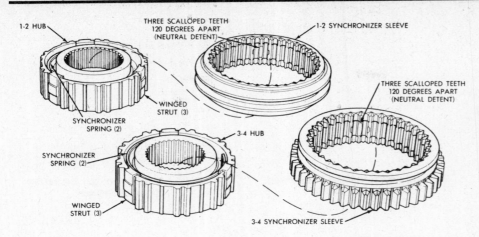

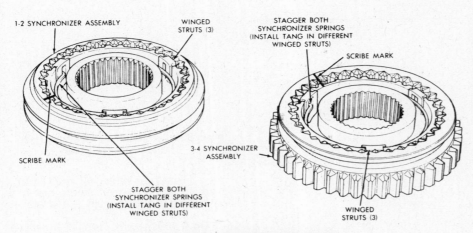

Fig. 13 Synchronizer assembly

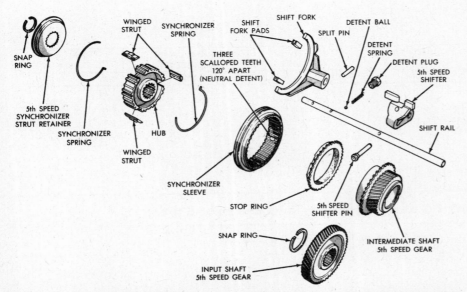

Fig. 14 5th speed synchronizer assembly. A-465 & A-525 transaxle

2. Select a shim that will allow .001–.010 inch endplay. This shim size may be determined by measuring thickness of original shim in differential bearing retainer and selecting a shim .015 inch thinner than original.
3. Install shim into differential bearing retainer, then install bearing cup.

NOTE: It is not necessary to install oil baffle when performing this adjustment.

4. Lubricate differential bearings with transmission fluid and install differential assembly into transaxle case. Install extension housing and differential bearing retainer and torque all bolts to 21 ft. lbs.
5. Position transaxle onto suitable work bench with bellhousing facing downward. Install dial indicator as shown in **Fig. 20.**
6. Press downward on ring gear while rotating ring gear back and forth to seat bearings. Zero dial indicator, then push upward on ring gear while rotating ring gear back and forth. Note dial indicator reading.
7. To determine required shim thickness, add thickness of shim selected in step 2 to dial indicator reading, then add .010 inch. Select shims as required to obtain shim thickness that is within .002 inch of required thickness. Refer to chart in **Fig. 21** for available shim thicknesses.
8. Remove differential bearing retainer, bearing cup and shim. Install oil baffle and selected shim or shims, then install bearing cup into differential bearing retainer.
9. Install differential bearing retainer with a 1/16 inch bead of R.T.V. sealant, then the extension housing and torque all bolts to 21 ft. lbs. Apply suitable sealer to housing prior to installing.
10. Using tool L-4436, or equivalent and an inch lb. torque wrench, check rotating torque of differential assembly. Rotating torque should be 9–14 inch lbs. for new bearings, or 6 inch lbs. for used bearings. If rotating torque is greater than specified, install a shim .002 inch thinner. If rotating torque is lower than specified, install a shim .002 inch thicker.

ASSEMBLE

1. Install reverse shift lever and "E" clip.
2. Install input shaft oil seal using tool C-4674, or equivalent.
3. Install input shaft retainer and clutch release shaft. Install clutch release shaft "E" clip.
4. Install shift forks onto intermediate shaft assembly, then install intermediate shaft assembly and input shaft assembly into transaxle case.
5. Install reverse idler gear and shaft.
6. On A-460 models, install 3-4 shift fork rail. On all models, install bearing retainer plate.

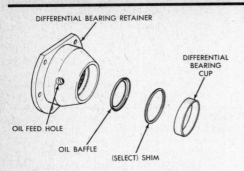

Fig. 15 Differential bearing retainer. Disassembled

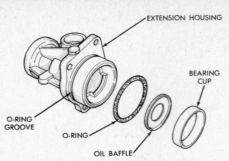

Fig. 16 Extension housing. Disassembled

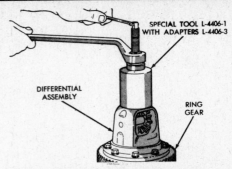

Fig. 17 Differential bearing cone removal

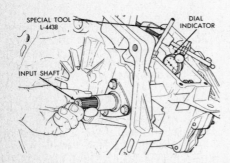

Fig. 18 Measuring input shaft end-play

7. On A-465 and A-525 models, proceed as follows:
   a. Install bearing support plate, then the input shaft 5th speed gear with snap ring.
   b. Install intermediate shaft 5th speed gear, 5th speed synchronizer assembly and shift fork with shift rail.
   c. Install 5th speed synchronizer strut retainer plate with snap ring, then

INPUT SHAFT SHIM CHART

mm	mm	inch
.62		.024
.66		.026
.70		.028
.74		.029
.78		.031
.82		.032
.86		.034
.90		.035
.94		.037
.98		.039
1.02		.040
1.06		.042
1.10		.043
1.14		.045
1.18		.046
1.22		.048
1.26		.050
1.30		.051
1.34		.053
1.36	(.66 + .70)	.054
1.40	(.66 + .74)	.055
1.44	(.70 + .74)	.057
1.48	(.70 + .78)	.059
1.52	(.74 + .78)	.060
1.56	(.74 + .82)	.061
1.60	(.78 + .82)	.063
1.64	(.78 + .86)	.065
1.68	(.82 + .86)	.066
1.72	(.82 + .90)	.068
1.76	(.86 + .90)	.069

Fig. 19 Input shaft bearing selective shim chart

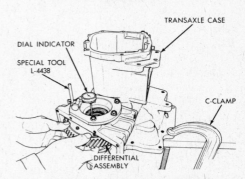

Fig. 20 Measuring differential bearing end-play

   install rear end cover and fill plug.
   d. Install 5th speed detent ball and spring and the 5th speed shifter pin.
8. On A-460 models, install intermediate shaft rear bearing large snap ring.
9. On A-460 models, install rear end cover. On all models, install selected shaft housing, differential assembly and extension housing.
10. On all models, install differential bearing retainer and cover.

Required Shim Combination		Total Thickness		Required Shim Combination		Total Thickness		Required Shim Combination		Total Thickness	
mm		mm	Inch	mm		mm	Inch	mm		mm	Inch
.50		.50	.020	.50 + .70		1.20	.047	1.00 + .70		1.70	.067
.75		.75	.030	.50 + .75		1.25	.049	1.00 + .75		1.75	.069
.80		.80	.032	.50 + .80		1.30	.051	1.00 + .80		1.80	.071
.85		.85	.034	.50 + .85		1.35	.053	1.00 + .85		1.85	.073
.90		.90	.035	.50 + .90		1.40	.055	1.00 + .90		1.90	.075
.95		.95	.037	.50 + .95		1.45	.057	1.00 + .95		1.95	.077
1.00		1.00	.039	.50 + 1.00		1.50	.059	1.00 + 1.00		2.00	.079
1.05		1.05	.041	.50 + 1.05		1.55	.061	1.00 + 1.05		2.05	.081
.50 + .60		1.10	.043	1.00 + .60		1.60	.063	1.05 + 1.05		2.10	.083
.50 + .65		1.15	.045	1.00 + .65		1.65	.065				

Fig. 21 Differential bearing end-play selective shim chart

New Process 435 4 Speed Manual Transmission

INDEX

DISASSEMBLE

1. With transmission in neutral, remove gearshift housing.
2. Lock transmission in two gears and remove output flange nut, yoke and brake drum.
3. Remove speedometer drive pinion and mainshaft rear bearing retainer, **Fig. 1.**
4. Remove drive pinion bearing retainer.
5. Rotate drive pinion gear to align space in pinion gear teeth with countershaft drive gear teeth and remove drive pinion gear and tapered roller bearing from transmission.
6. Remove snap ring, washer and pilot roller bearing from recess in drive pinion gear.
7. Using a brass drift placed in front center of mainshaft, drive mainshaft to rear, then when mainshaft rear bearing clears case, remove rear bearing and speedometer gear (with spacer) using a puller.
8. Move mainshaft assembly rearward and tilt front of mainshaft up.
9. Remove roller thrust bearing, synchronizer and stop rings, and mainshaft.
10. Remove reverse idler lock screw and lockplate.
11. Using a brass drift, drive idler gear rearward, then pull shaft and lift reverse idler gear from case.
12. Remove gearing retainer at rear end of countershaft.
13. Tilt cluster gear assembly and work it out of case.
14. Using a suitable driver, remove front bearings from case.

SUB-ASSEMBLIES SERVICE

DISASSEMBLE

Mainshaft

1. Remove clutch gear snap ring, then remove clutch gear, synchronizer outer stop ring to third speed gear shim(s) and third gear.
2. Using two screwdrivers, remove split lock ring, then remove second speed gear and synchronizer.
3. Remove first and reverse sliding gear.

Reverse Idler Gear

Do not disassemble idler gear. If satisfactory operation is doubtful, replace entire assembly complete with bearings.

Drive Pinion & Bearing Retainer

1. Using a suitable tool, remove roller bearing from pinion shaft.
2. Remove snap ring, washer and pilot rollers from gear bore.
3. Using a puller, remove bearing race from front bearing retainer.
4. Remove pinion shaft seal.

Shifter Housing

1. Remove roll pins from first and second speed shift fork and gate.
2. Push shift rail out through front to force expansion plug out of cover and remove rail, fork and gate.

NOTE: Cover detent ball access hole in cover to prevent ball and spring from flying out as rail clears hole.

3. Remove third and fourth speed rails, then remove reverse rail.
4. Compress reverse gear plunger, then remove retaining clip, plunger and spring from gate.

ASSEMBLE

When assembling sub-assemblies, use new expansion plugs, gaskets and seals. Lubricate all parts with clean transmission lubricant. Where grease is recommended, use oil soluble grease. Make certain that oil return passages are not obstructed with grease.

Mainshaft

1. Place mainshaft in soft jawed vise with rear end up and install first and reverse gear making sure that two spline springs (if used) are inside of gear.
2. Reverse mainshaft in vise with forward end up.
3. Assemble second speed synchronizer spring and synchronizer brake to second speed gear, then install snap ring making sure that snap ring tangs are facing away from gear.
4. Slide second speed gear onto front of output shaft making sure that synchronizer brake is toward rear, then install the two piece lock ring and install third speed gear.
5. Install shim(s) between third speed gear and third and fourth speed synchronizer stop ring. Check end play. If end play is not within .050–.070 inch, add or remove shims as necessary to bring end play to specifications.

Drive Pinion & Bearing Retainer

1. Using an arbor press and a wooden block placed on pinion gear, press gear into bearing until it contacts bearing inner race.
2. Coat roller bearings with a light coat of grease to hold rollers in place and insert into pocket of drive pinion.
3. Install washer and snap ring.
4. Press seal into bearing retainer making sure that lip of seal is toward mounting plate.
5. Press bearing race into retainer.

Shifter Housing

1. Install spring on reverse gear plunger, then compress spring into reverse shift gate and install retaining clip, **Fig. 2.**
2. Install reverse shift rail into cover and place detent spring and ball in position, then depress ball and slide rail over it.
3. Install gate and fork on rail, then install a new roll pin in gate and fork.
4. With reverse fork in neutral position, install the two interlock plungers in their bores.
5. Install interlock pin in third and fourth speed shift rail, then install rail in same manner as reverse shift rail.
6. Install first and second speed shift rail in same manner as reverse shift rail, making certain that interlock plunger is in place.

NOTE: Check interlocks by shifting reverse shift rail into reverse position. It should be impossible to shift all other rails when this rail is shifted.

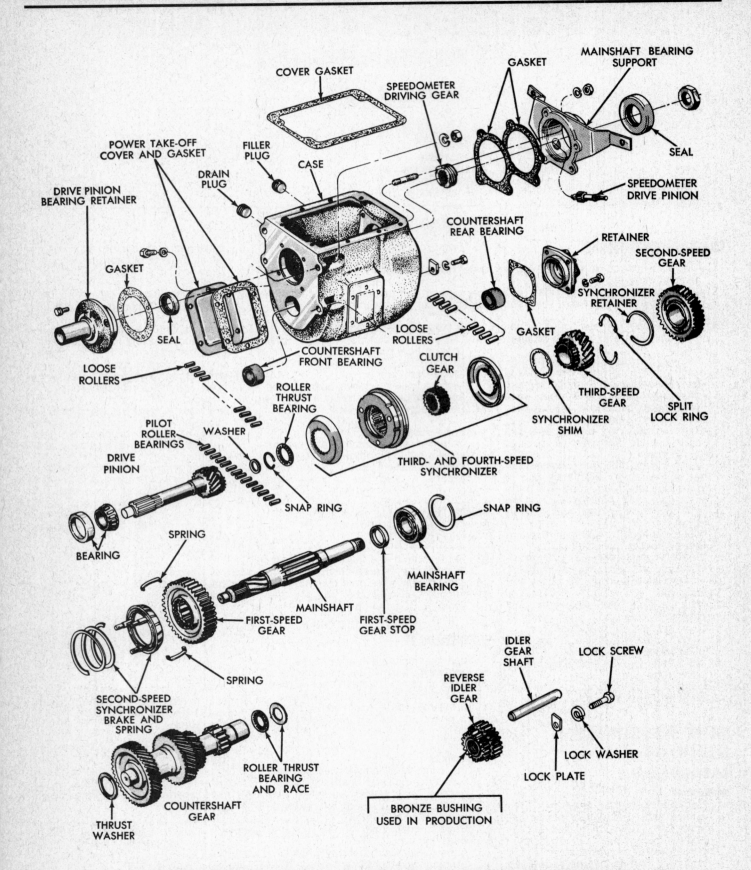

Fig. 1   Disassembled view of New Process 435 4 speed manual transmission

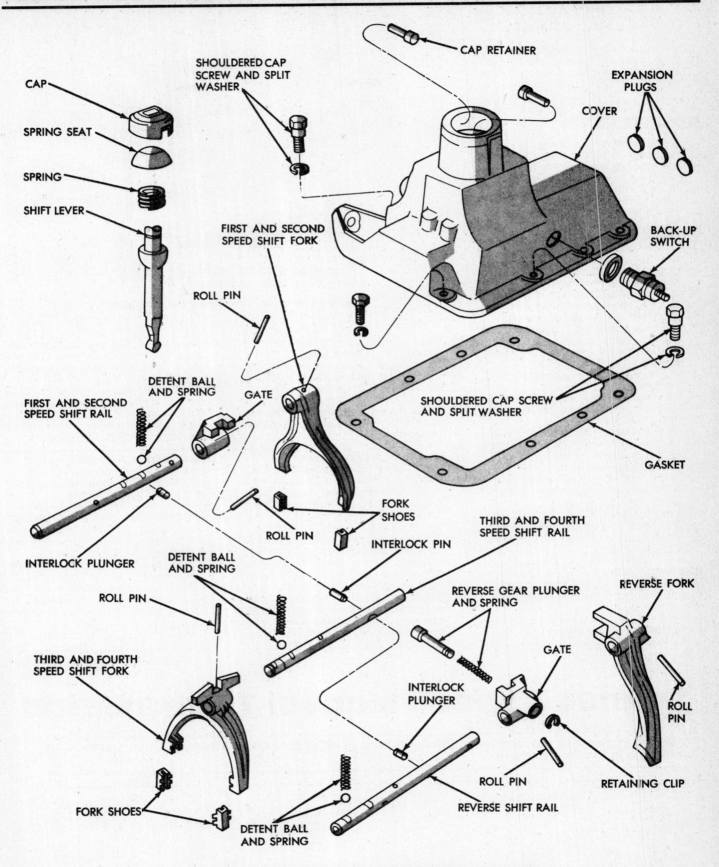

CAP RETAINER

SHOULDERED CAP SCREW AND SPLIT WASHER

EXPANSION PLUGS

CAP

SPRING SEAT

SPRING

SHIFT LEVER

COVER

BACK-UP SWITCH

FIRST AND SECOND SPEED SHIFT FORK

ROLL PIN

DETENT BALL AND SPRING

GATE

SHOULDERED CAP SCREW AND SPLIT WASHER

FIRST AND SECOND SPEED SHIFT RAIL

GASKET

INTERLOCK PLUNGER

DETENT BALL AND SPRING

ROLL PIN

FORK SHOES

INTERLOCK PIN

THIRD AND FOURTH SPEED SHIFT RAIL

REVERSE FORK

ROLL PIN

REVERSE GEAR PLUNGER AND SPRING

GATE

ROLL PIN

THIRD AND FOURTH SPEED SHIFT FORK

INTERLOCK PLUNGER

ROLL PIN

RETAINING CLIP

FORK SHOES

DETENT BALL AND SPRING

REVERSE SHIFT RAIL

Fig. 2 Disassembled view of shifter housing assembly

7. If installing shift lever, lubricate spherical ball seat and place cap in position.
8. Install back-up light switch, if used.
9. Install new expansion plugs in bores of rail holes and install interlock hole plug.

ASSEMBLE

1. Press front roller bearing into case until cage is flush with front of case and lubricate bearings with a light coat of grease.
2. Position transmission with front of case facing down. If uncaged roller bearings are being re-used, hold rollers in place with a light coat of grease.
3. Lower countershaft assembly into case, placing thrust washer tangs in slots in case and inserting front end of shaft into bearing.
4. Place countershaft rear roller thrust bearing on countershaft and hold in place with a light coat of grease.
5. Align countershaft assembly and install retainer gasket, retainer and bearing, then install and tighten screws.
6. Place reverse idler gear and bearing assembly in case.
7. Align reverse idler shaft so lock plate groove in shaft is properly aligned to install lock plate.
8. Tap reverse idler shaft far enough into case to start reverse gear, then while holding gear in position, tap shaft through case and gear.
9. Install lock plate, washer and screw. Make certain that gear turns freely on shaft.
10. Lower rear end of mainshaft into case, then while holding first speed gear on shaft, maneuver shaft through rear bearing opening.

NOTE: With shaft assembly moved to rear of case, make sure that third and fourth speed synchronizer and preselected shims remain in place.

11. Install roller thrust bearing.

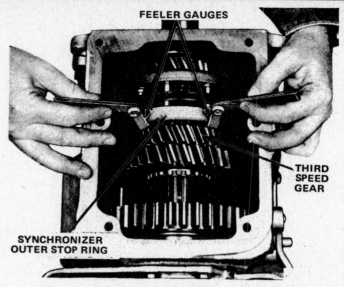

Fig. 3   Checking synchronizer end-play

12. Place a wood block between front of case and front of mainshaft.
13. Using a suitable size sleeve against inner race of bearing, install rear bearing onto shaft and into case until snap ring is flush against case.
14. Install drive pinion shaft and bearing assembly making sure pilot rollers remain in place.
15. Install spacer, speedometer gear, gasket and bearing retainer.
16. Place drive pinion bearing retainer over pinion shaft without gasket, then while holding retainer tight against bearing, measure clearance between retainer and case using a feeler gauge. Install a gasket shim pack .010–.015 inch greater than clearance measured between retainer and case to obtain the required .007–.017 inch pinion shaft end play. After retainer bolts are tightened, recheck end play.
17. Check for .050–.070 inch synchronizer end play after all mainshaft components are in place and properly tightened, using two sets of equal size feeler gauges **Fig. 3.** If necessary, disassemble mainshaft and change shims to retain end play within specifications.
18. Install speedometer drive pinion, yoke flange, drum and brake assembly and output flange nut.
19. Shift gears into all speed positions and check for freedom of operation.

NOTE: Before installing shifter housing, fill transmission with lubricant, then oil all exposed transmission parts to avoid damage to transmission at start up.

20. Move gears into neutral position, then lower cover and new gasket over transmission, engaging forks into proper gears.
21. Install one shouldered alignment screw in each of the holes on each side of cover located next to the front hole. Check gears for freedom by shifting gears with a long screwdriver inserted in cover tower.
22. Install remaining cover screws.

Tremec 3 Speed Manual Transmission

NOTE: For service procedures on this transmission, refer to Tremec 3 Speed Manual Transmission section in the Ford Chapter.

New Process 445D 4 Speed Manual Transmission

INDEX

DISASSEMBLE

1. Drain lubricant from transmission and remove gearshift cover.

NOTE: The two bolts opposite the tower are shouldered to properly position cover and are provided with lockwashers. Make certain that these alignment bolts are correctly located and tightened before installing cover.

2. Lock transmission in two gears and remove mainshaft nut and yoke.

3. Remove mainshaft rear extension housing and speedometer drive gear.
4. Remove pinion front bearing retainer and gasket, **Fig. 1,** then rotate drive pinion gear to align pinion gear with countershaft drive gear teeth and remove drive pinion gear and tapered roller bearing from transmission, **Fig. 2.**
5. Remove thrust bearing, then push mainshaft assembly rearward of transmission and tilt front of mainshaft up, **Fig. 3,** and remove mainshaft from case.

6. Remove reverse idler lock plate, then using tool C-603, pull idler shaft from case and lift out reverse idler gear.

NOTE: If tool C-603 is not available, the reverse idler shaft may be driven out the rear of the case with a hammer and brass drift. DO NOT ATTEMPT TO DRIVE IDLER SHAFT FORWARD, as it is a shouldered shaft and a broken case will result.

7. Remove countershaft rear bearing retainer, then slide countershaft rearward, up and out of case, **Fig. 4.**
8. Drive countershaft from bearing as-

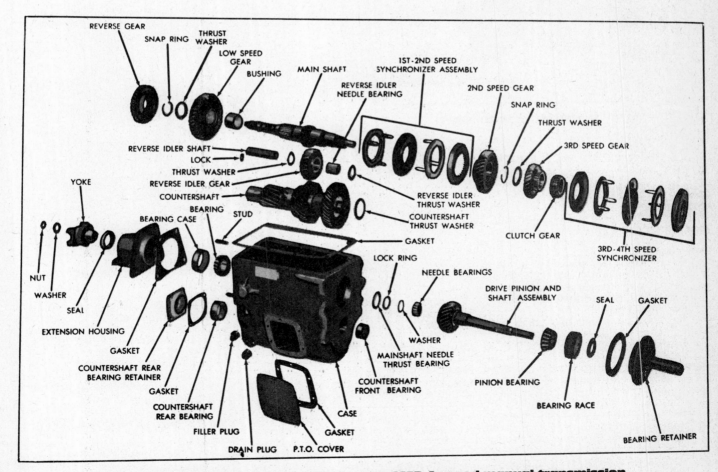

Fig. 1   Disassembled view of New Process 445D 4 speed manual transmission

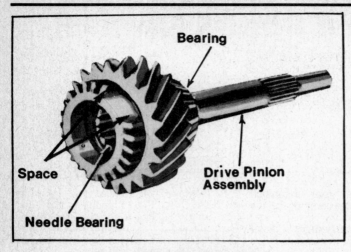

Fig. 2   Drive gear assembly

Fig. 3   Removing mainshaft from transmission case

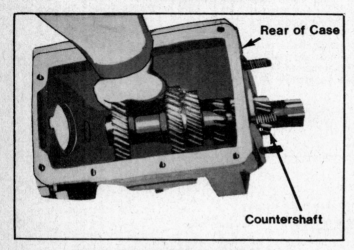

Fig. 4   Removing countershaft

sembly forward and out of transmission case.

SUB ASSEMBLY SERVICE

DISASSEMBLE

Mainshaft

1. Place mainshaft vertically in soft jawed vise with front end up, then lift 3rd-4th synchronizer and high speed clutch gear off mainshaft and remove third speed gear.
2. Remove 2nd speed gear snap ring with snap ring pliers and lift off thrust washer, **Fig. 5.**

NOTE: The thrust washer must be positioned with ground surface toward 2nd speed gear when the mainshaft is reassembled.

3. Remove 2nd speed gear and lift off low speed synchronizer and clutch gear from mainshaft.
4. Using a gear puller, remove tapered bearing from rear of mainshaft, then remove 1st speed gear snap ring and thrust washer and lift off 1st speed gear.

Cover & Shift Fork Assembly

NOTE: The shift cover should be disassembled only if it is necessary to replace a shift fork, a shaft or the cover.

1. Using a square type or spiral wound "easy out" mounted in a tap handle, remove roll pin from 1st-2nd speed shift fork and roll pin from shift gate, **Fig. 6.**
2. Push 1st-2nd speed shift rail out of

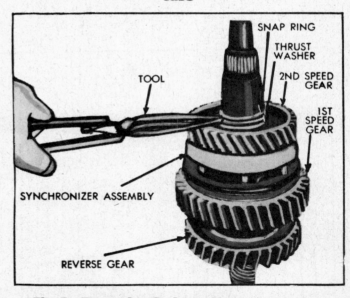

Fig. 5   Removing 2nd speed gear snap ring

rear of cover, driving out expansion plug and remove shift fork and gate. Be sure to cover detent hole to prevent loss of detent ball and spring.
3. Remove 3rd-4th speed shift rail in same manner as in steps 1 and 2.
4. Compress reverse gear plunger and remove retaining clip. Remove plunger and spring from gate.

CLEANING & INSPECTION

Wash all bearings in clean solvent and check all rollers and races for wear, pitting and spalled areas. Replace parts as necessary.

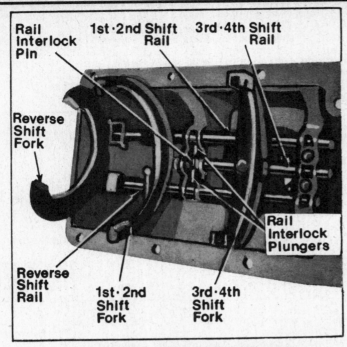

Fig. 6 Cover & shift fork assembly

Check operating gear teeth for wear or pitting on tooth faces. Gears which have been shortened or tapered from clashing during gear shifts should be replaced. If excessive axial gear clearance is found, check snap rings, washers, spacers and gear hubs for excessive wear. Proper axial clearance must be maintained on all mainshaft gears. Replace parts as necessary.

Check splines on mainshaft for excessive wear. If sliding gears, clutch hubs or flanges have been worn into the sides of the splines, the shaft should be replaced.

Check reverse idler gear shaft and rollers for wear and replace as necessary.

Check synchronizer for burrs and uneven or excessive wear at contact surfaces. Check blocker pins for excessive wear or looseness. Check synchronizer contact surfaces on all affected gears for excessive wear.

Check shift bar housing forks and gates for wear at pad and lever slot, check all forks for alignment, check roll pin fit in forks and gates and check neutral notches of shift shafts for wear from interlock balls. Shafts which are indented at points adjacent to neutral notches should be replaced. Replace all worn or damaged parts.

Check all other parts for cracks and fractures. Replace or repair as necessary. Cracked castings may be welded or brazed as long as cracks do not extend into bearing bores or bolting surfaces.

ASSEMBLE

Mainshaft

NOTE: Prior to assembly, lubricate all parts with clean transmission lubricant and replace all expansion plugs, gaskets and seals.

1. Place mainshaft in vertical position with rear end up and lubricate with transmission oil.
2. Slide 1st speed gear over mainshaft with clutch facing down and install thrust washer and snap ring.
3. Install reverse gear over end of mainshaft with fork groove down, then install mainshaft rear bearing and using appropriate size sleeve and tool C-4040, press bearing on inner race.
4. Reverse mainshaft in vise.
5. Install low speed synchronizer and slide 2nd speed gear over mainshaft, then install keyed thrust washer over mainshaft, with ground side facing 2nd gear. Secure with snap ring.
6. Install 3rd speed gear and one shim on mainshaft, then install 3rd-4th synchronizer over mainshaft, making certain that slotted end of clutch gear is positioned toward 3rd speed gear.

Gear Shift Cover

1. Grease interlock slugs and slide into openings in shift rail supports, **Fig. 6.**
2. Insert and slide reverse shift rail through reverse shift plate and shift fork.
3. Secure reverse shift plate and shift fork with roll pin, then install interlock pin into 3rd-4th shift rail and secure with grease.
4. Slide 3rd-4th shift rail into rail support from rear of cover, through 3rd-4th speed shift fork and over poppet ball and spring, then secure 3rd-4th speed shift fork to rail with roll pin.
5. Making sure interlock slug is in place, slide 1st-2nd speed shift rail into case

through shift fork and shift gate. Hold poppet ball and spring down until shift rail passes and secure 1st-2nd speed shift fork and shift gate with roll pins.

ASSEMBLE

1. Using a 1⅜ inch socket as driver, install countershaft front bearing in case. Grease needle bearings prior to installation. Hold bearings in place in bearing retainer with socket of appropriate diameter while seating retainer. Drive retainer until flush with front of case.
2. Install tanged thrust washer on countershaft with tangs facing out and install countershaft into case.
3. Install countershaft rear bearing retainer over countershaft rear bearing and using new washer, position retainer with curved segment toward bottom of case.
4. Install reverse idler gear with chamfer toward rear of case, then while holding thrust washers and needle bearings in position, slide reverse idler shaft into case through idler gear. Make certain that shaft lock notch is down and at rear of shaft and install shaft lock and bolt.
5. Place mainshaft vertically in a soft jawed vise with front end up.
6. Mount drive gear on top of mainshaft, then measure clearance between high speed synchronizer and drive gear with two feeler gauges. If clearance is greater than .043—.053 inch, install synchronizer shims between third speed gear and synchronizer brake drum of the thickness required to bring clearance within specifications. After required shim thickness has been determined, remove drive gear from mainshaft.
7. Insert assembled mainshaft into case and place thrust washer over pilot end of mainshaft.
8. Position drive gear so that the cutaway portion of gear is facing down, then slide drive gear into front of case engaging mainshaft pilot in pocket of drive gear.
9. Slide drive gear front bearing retainer over shaft with no gasket or bolts, then install mainshaft rear bearing retainer and tighten retainer bolts.
10. Hold retainer against front of transmission case and measure clearance between front bearing retainer and front of case with feeler gauge. Remove front bearing retainer.
11. Install a gasket pack on front bearing retainer which is .010—.015 inch thicker than the clearance measured in above step. Install front bearing retainer and tighten bolts. This will insure the required .007—.017 inch gear end play.
12. The front synchronizer end play float must be checked before installation of transmission cover. Measure end play float by inserting two feeler gauges diametrically opposite one another

between 3rd speed gear and synchronizer stop ring. Accurate measurement can be made only after all mainshaft components are in place and tightened securely. If front synchronizer end play is not within .050–.070 inch, shims should be added or removed as required between 3rd

speed gear and synchronizer stop ring.

13. Install yoke and retaining nut on mainshaft, then lock transmission in two gears and torque yoke nut to 125 ft. lbs.

14. Shift transmission into neutral and install cover gasket, then shift trans-

mission and cover into 2nd and carefully lower cover into position. It may be necessary to position reverse gear to permit shift fork to engage groove.

15. Install and tighten cover aligning screws, then install remaining cover screws and tighten all screws evenly and securely.

New Process A-833 4 Speed Overdrive Manual Transmission

INDEX

DISASSEMBLE
GEARSHIFT HOUSING

1. Remove reverse shift lever from shaft, **Fig. 1,** then the gearshift housing attaching bolts, **Fig. 2.**
2. With levers in neutral detent position, pull housing away from case. Remove forks from sleeves.
3. If oil leakage is present around gearshift lever shafts or the interlock levers are cracked, perform the following:
   a. Remove nuts and the shift operating levers from shafts.
   b. Remove gearshift lever shafts from housing.
   c. Remove "E" ring from interlock lever pivot pin, then the interlock levers and spring from housing.

EXTENSION HOUSING & MAINSHAFT

1. Remove bolt and retainer securing speedometer pinion adapter in extension housing, then the adapter and pinnion from housing.
2. Remove extension housing attaching bolts.
3. Rotate extension housing on output shaft to expose the rear of countershaft. Clearance is provided on extension housing flange to permit one bolt to be reinstalled to hold the extension housing in the inverted position for access to countershaft.
4. Drill a hole in the countershaft expansion plug at front of case. Then, working through hole, push countershaft rearward until woodruff key is exposed and remove key. Push countershaft forward against expansion plug and, using a brass drift, tap countershaft forward until expansion plug is driven from case.
5. With a dummy shaft, drive countershaft through rear of case, using caution so the countershaft washers do

not fall out of position. Lower cluster gear to bottom of case.
6. Rotate extension housing back to normal position.
7. Remove drive pinion bearing retainer attaching bolts, then slide retainer and gasket from pinion shaft. Pry pinion or seal from retainer. Use caution not to nick or scratch seal bore in retainer or the surface on which the seal bottoms.
8. With a brass drift, drive the pinion and bearing assembly through the front of case.
9. Slide third-fourth synchronizer sleeve slightly forward, slide reverse idler gear to center of shaft, then using a mallet, tap extension housing rearward. Slide extension housing and mainshaft assembly from case.
10. Remove snap ring retainer third-fourth synchronizer clutch gear and sleeve assembly, then slide the assembly from mainshaft.
11. Slide third speed gear and stop ring from mainshaft.
12. Compress snap ring retaining mainshaft ball bearing in extension housing and pull mainshaft assembly and bearing from extension housing, **Fig. 3.**
13. Remove mainshaft bearing retaining snap ring. Remove bearing by installing steel plates on the first speed gear, then press or drive mainshaft through bearing. Use caution not to damage gear teeth.
14. Remove bearing, bearing retainer ring, first speed gear and first speed stop ring from shaft.
15. Remove first-second clutch gear and sleeve assembly snap ring, **Fig. 4,** then slide assembly and the second speed gear from shaft.

DRIVE PINION & COUNTERSHAFT GEAR

1. Remove pinion bearing inner snap

ring, then press pinion from bearing.
2. Remove snap ring and roller bearings from drive pinion cavity.
3. Remove countershaft gear from bottom of case, **Fig. 5.**
4. Remove dummy shaft, needle bearings, thrust washers and spacer from countershaft gear.

REVERSE GEAR, LEVER & FORK

1. Remove reverse gearshift lever detent spring retainer, gasket, plug and detent ball spring from rear of case, **Fig. 6.**
2. Press reverse idler gear shaft from case and remove woodruff key.
3. If oil leakage is present around the reverse gearshift lever shaft, remove any burrs from the shaft. Carefully push reverse gearshift lever shaft inward and remove from case, **Fig. 7.** Remove detent ball from bottom of case, then the shift fork from shaft and detent plate.

ASSEMBLE
REVERSE GEAR, LEVER & FORK

1. Install new O-ring on reverse gearshift lever shaft. Lubricate lever shaft and install lever shaft into case bore, then the reverse fork in lever.
2. Install reverse detent spring retainer and gasket and torque to 50 ft. lbs. Insert ball and spring, then install and torque gasket and plug to 24 ft. lbs.
3. Place reverse idler gearshaft in position in end of case and drive into case to position reverse idler gear on the protruding end of shaft with shift slot facing toward rear and engine slot with reverse shift fork.
4. With reverse idler gear properly positioned, drive reverse idler gearshaft

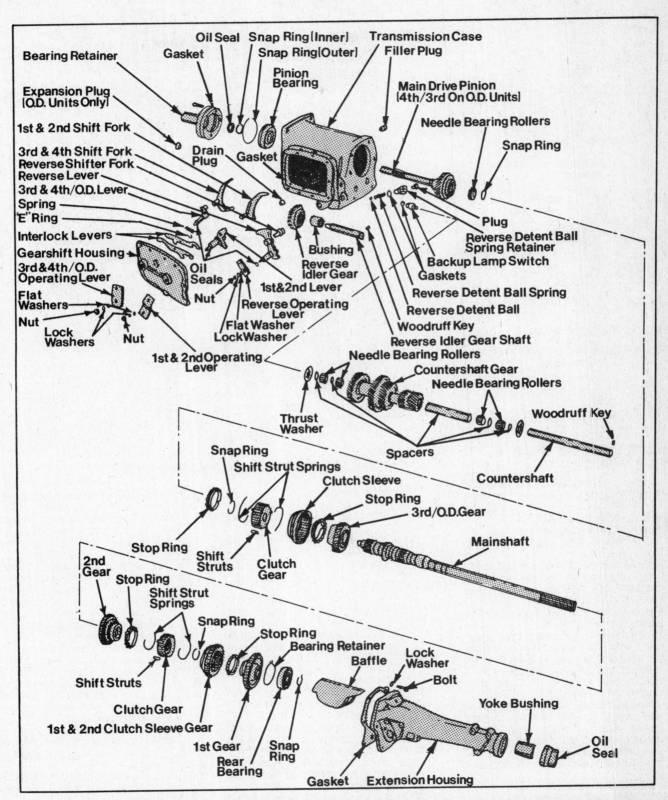

Fig. 1   Disassembled view of New Process A-833 4 speed manual overdrive transmission

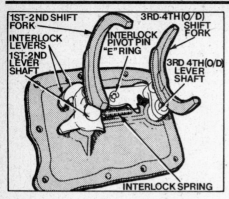

Fig. 2 Gearshift housing assembly

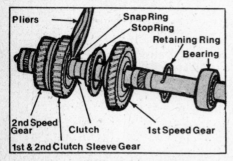

Fig. 4 Removing clutch gear snap ring

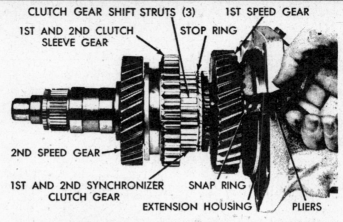

Fig. 3 Compressing center bearing snap ring

Fig. 5 Replacing countergear

into case and install woodruff key. Ensure shaft is flush with surface of case.

5. Install and torque back-up light switch and gasket to 15 ft. lbs. if removed.

COUNTERSHAFT GEAR & DRIVE PINION

1. Lubricate countershaft gear bore and install roller bearing spacer with dummy shaft into gear. Center the spacer and dummy shaft.
2. Install 19 rollers, a spacer ring, 19 more rollers and spacer ring into gear.
3. Lubricate and install new thrust washers, if needed, on dummy shaft with tanged side facing toward case boss.
4. Place countershaft gear assembly on bottom of case, **Fig. 5.**
5. Press drive pinion bearing onto pinion shaft with outer snap ring groove facing front of transmission. Fully seat the bearing against gear shoulder.
6. Install new bearing retainer snap ring.
7. With pinion shaft held in a soft jawed vise, install 16 roller bearings in shaft cavity. Coat bearing with heavy grease and install bearing retaining snap ring in groove.
8. Install new oil seal in retainer bore.

EXTENSION HOUSING BUSHING, REPLACE

1. Remove extension housing yoke seal.
2. Drive bushing from housing.
3. Drive new bushing into housing, aligning bushing oil hole with housing oil slot.
4. Install new extension housing yoke seal.

MAINSHAFT

1. Partially assemble synchronizer components as follows:
   a. Place a stop ring flat on bench, then the clutch sleeve and gear.
   b. Place struts into slots and snap a strut spring into place with the tang inside one strut.
   c. Turn assembly over and install second strut spring with the tang in a different strut.
2. Slide second speed gear onto mainshaft with synchronized cone facing toward rear against shoulder.
3. Slide first-second synchronizer with stop ring lugs indexed in slots onto mainshaft against second gear cone and secure with new snap ring. Slide next stop ring onto shaft and index lugs into clutch hub slots.
4. Slide first speed gear with synchroniz-

er cone facing forward into position against clutch sleeve gear.
5. Install mainshaft bearing retaining ring, then the mainshaft rear bearing. Press bearing into place and install new snap ring to retain bearing.
6. Install partially assembled mainshaft into extension housing and compress bearing retaining ring so mainshaft ball bearing can move inward and bottom against thrust shoulder in extension housing. Release and seat ring in groove in the housing.
7. Slide overdrive gear onto mainshaft with synchronizer cone facing forward, then the overdrive gear stop ring.
8. Install third-overdrive synchronizer clutch gear assembly on mainshaft with shift fork slot facing rearward against overdrive gear.
9. Install retaining snap ring then, with grease, position front stop ring over clutch gear, indexing ring lugs with shift struts.
10. Coat new extension housing to case gasket with grease, then place gasket on housing.
11. Slide reverse idler gear to center of the shaft, then move the third-fourth synchronizer sleeve or the third-overdrive

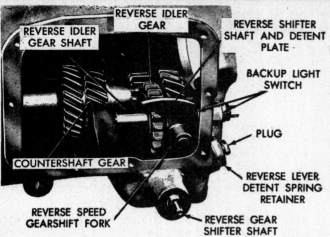

Fig. 6   Reverse gearing and countergear

Fig. 7   Removing reverse gear fork & lever

synchronizer sleeve forward.

12. Slowly insert mainshaft assembly into case, tilting the shaft as necessary to clear idler and cluster gears.

13. Place third-overdrive synchronizer sleeve in neutral position.

14. Rotate extension housing on mainshaft to expose countershaft rear and install one extension housing attaching bolt, while holding housing in inverted position and preventing housing from moving rearward.

15. Install drive pinion and bearing assembly through front of case and into front bore. Install outer snap ring in bearing groove. Tap lightly into position with a mallet. If all components are positioned properly, the bearing outer snap ring will bottom onto case face without force. If not, check position of struts, pinion rollers and stop rings.

16. Turn transmission upside down while holding countershaft gear assembly to prevent damage.

17. Lower countershaft gear assembly into position with teeth meshed with drive pinion gear. Ensure thrust washers are positioned properly with the tangs aligned with case slots.

18. Start countershaft into bore at rear of case and push until approximately halfway into case, then install woodruff key. Push shaft forward until end is flush with case surface. Remove dummy shaft.

19. Properly align extension housing on case and install and torque extension housing attaching bolts to 50 ft. lbs.

20. Install drive pinion bearing retainer and gasket. Coat attaching bolt threads with a suitable sealing compound, then install and torque bolts to 30 ft. lbs.

21. Install new expansion plug in countershaft bore at front of case.

GEARSHIFT HOUSING

1. Install interlock levers on pivot pin and retain with "E" ring, **Fig. 2.** Use pliers to install spring on interlock lever hangers.

2. Lubricate and install new O-rings on shift lever shafts. Lubricate housing bores and push shafts into proper bore.

3. Install operating levers and torque retaining nuts to 18 ft. lbs. Ensure the third-overdrive lever points downward.

4. Rotate shift fork bores to neutral position and install the third-overdrive shift fork in proper bore and under both interlock levers.

5. Position both synchronizer sleeves in neutral and place first-second shift fork in the first-second synchronizer sleeve groove.

6. Lay transmission on its right side and place gearshift housing gasket on case with grease to hold in position.

7. Lower gearshift housing into place, guiding the third-overdrive shift fork into synchronizer groove, and lead the first-second shift fork shaft into the first-second shift lever bore. Raise interlock lever against its spring tension with a screwdriver, allowing first-second shift fork shaft to slip under the levers. The gearshift housing should now seat against case gasket.

8. Install gearshift housing attaching bolts finger tight and shift transmission through all gears to insure proper operation.

NOTE: Eight gearshift housing attaching bolts are shoulder bolts used to accurately locate the mechanism on the transmision. One bolt shoulder is longer and acts as a dowel, passing through the cover and into the case at center of rear flange. Two bolts are of standard design, located at the lower rear of cover.

9. Torque gearshift housing attaching bolts to 15 ft. lbs.

10. The reverse shift lever and the first-second shift lever incorporate cam surfaces which mate in the reverse position to lock the first-second lever, fork and synchronizer in the neutral position. To check, place transmission in reverse, then, while turning input shaft, move first-second lever in each direction. If input shaft lock becomes difficult to turn, the synchronizer is partially engaged, caused by excessive cam clearance. Install a new first-second shift lever of different size. If insufficient cam clearance exists, it is difficult or impossible to shift into reverse.

11. Lubricate reverse shaft and install operating lever, then torque attaching nut to 18 ft. lbs.

12. Install speedometer drive pinion gear and adapter, ensuring range number (indicating number of teeth) is in the six o'clock position.

TRANSFER CASES
New Process Transfer Cases

INDEX

MODEL 203

CASE DISASSEMBLY

1. Remove front output rear cover located on side of range selector and drain lubricant, **Figs. 1 and 2**.
2. Remove rear output shaft retaining nut, washer and flange, **Fig. 3**.

NOTE: Tap dust cover shield rearward on shaft to gain clearance to remove bolts and install tool.

3. Remove front bearing retainer, **Fig. 4**, then using a hoist, position assembly on blocks in an upright position.
4. Remove rear output shaft retaining bolts then disengage assembly from transfer case and slide carrier unit from shaft.

NOTE: Install a suitable size band type hose clamp on input shaft to prevent losing bearings when removing input shaft assembly.

5. Raise shift rail, then drive out pin retaining shift fork to rail and remove shift rail poppet ball plug, gasket spring and ball from case, **Figs. 2 and 4**.

NOTE: Use a small magnet to remove ball from case.

6. Push shift rail down, lift up on lockout clutch and remove shift fork from clutch assembly.
7. Remove front output shaft rear bearing retainer bolts and tap on front of shaft or carefully pry retainer from shaft and discard gasket. Recover any roller bearings which may fall from rear cover.

NOTE: If replacing bearing, press bearing out. Press new bearing in until it is flush with output bearing rear cover.

8. Pry out output shaft front bearing then disengage front output shaft from chain and remove shaft from transfer case, **Fig. 4**.
9. Remove intermediate chain housing bolts and remove intermediate housing from range box.
10. Remove chain from intermediate housing, then remove lockout clutch, drive gear and input shaft from range box.

NOTE: Install a suitable size band type hose clamp on end of input shaft to prevent losing roller bearings which may fall out if clutch assembly is pulled off input shaft.

11. Pull up on shift rail and disconnect rail from link then remove input shaft assembly from range box.

Inspection

With the transfer case totally disassembled into sub-assemblies, the sub-assemblies should be further disassembled for cleaning and inspection.

Place all bearings, rollers, shafts and gears in cleaning solution and allow to remain long enough to loosen all accumulated lubricant. Bearings should be moved up and down and turned slowly in solvent. Dry all parts with compressed air. When drying bearings, direct air so as to avoid spinning the bearings. When cleaning transfer case, cover or housing, make certain that all traces of gasket are removed from surfaces.

Inspect all bearings and rollers for evi-

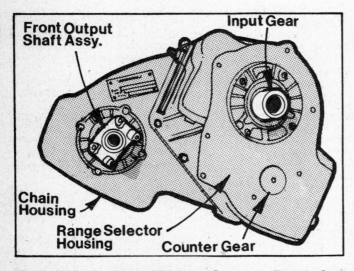

Fig. 1   New Process 203 transfer case. Front view

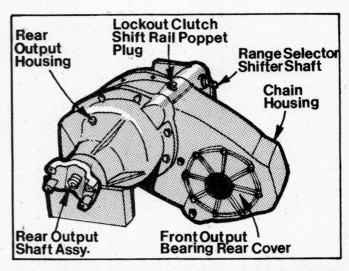

Fig. 2   New Process 203 transfer case. Rear view

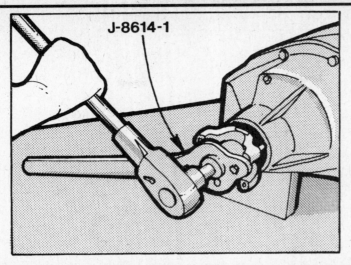

J-8614-1

Fig. 3   Removing rear output flange. New Process 203 transfer case

dence of chipping, cracking, or worn spots that would render bearing unfit for further use. Bearings are non-adjustable and if worn or damaged, must be replaced. Inspect shaft splines, drive chain and gears.

SUB-ASSEMBLY SERVICE

Differential Carrier Disassemble
1. Remove carrier assembly bolts and separate carrier sections, then lift pinion gear and spider assembly from carrier.

NOTE: Make certain that undercut side of pinion gear spider faces toward front side gear.

2. Remove pinion thrust washers, pinion roller washers, pinion gears and roller bearings from spider unit.
3. Clean, inspect and replace parts as necessary.

Differential Carrier Reassembly
1. Using petroleum jelly, insert roller bearings into pinion gears.

NOTE: A total of 132 bearings are required with 33 bearings in each pinion.

2. Install pinion roller washer, pinion gear, roller washer and thrust washer on each leg of spider.
3. Install spider assembly in front half of carrier with undercut surface of spider thrust spacer facing toward gear teeth.
4. Align marks on carrier sections and position carrier halves together, then install retaining bolts and torque to 45 ft. lbs.

Lockout Clutch Disassembly
1. Remove front side gear from input shaft assembly and remove thrust washer, roller bearings (123 total) and spacers from front side gear bore.

Note position of spacers to facilitate reassembly
2. Remove the snap ring retaining the drive sprocket to the clutch assembly, then slide the drive sprocket out from the front side gear and remove the the front side gear and remove the lower snap ring.
3. Remove sliding gear, spring and spring cup washer from front side gear.
4. Clean, inspect and replace parts as necessary.

Lockout Clutch Reassembly
1. Install spring cup washer, spring and sliding gear on front side gear.
2. Install snap ring retaining sliding clutch to front side gear.
3. Using petroleum jelly, load (123) roller bearings and spacers in front side gear.
4. Install thrust washer in gear end of the front side gear, then slide sprocket onto clutch splines and install retaining ring.

Input Shaft Disassembly
1. Slide thrust washer and spacer from shaft, then remove snap ring retaining input bearing retainer assembly to shaft. Remove bearing retainer assembly from shaft.
2. Support low speed gear and tap shaft out from the gear and thrust washer.

NOTE: Observe thrust washer pin locations in shaft.

3. Remove snap ring retaining input bearing in bearing retainer, then tap bearing out from the retainer.
4. Remove pilot roller bearings (15 total) and O-ring from input shaft.
5. Clean, inspect and replace parts as necessary.

Input Shaft Reassembly
1. Press bearing into retainer with ball

loading slots toward concave side of retainer.
2. Install large snap ring retaining bearing in the retainer.

NOTE: Use size A, B, C, or D snap ring to provide tightest fit.

3. Install low speed gear on shaft with clutch end facing toward gear end of shaft and position thrust washers onto shaft, aligning slot in washer with pin in shaft. Slide or tap washer into place.
4. Position input bearing retainer onto shaft and install snap ring, holding bearing in position on shaft.

NOTE: Use size A, B, C, or D snap ring to provide tightest fit.

5. Slide spacer and thrust washer onto shaft and align spacer with locator pin.
6. Using heavy grease, install (15) roller bearings and O-ring on end of shaft.

Removing Shifter Assembly
1. Remove poppet plate spring, plug and gasket, then disengage sliding clutch gear from input gear. Remove clutch fork and sliding gear from case.
2. Remove shift lever retaining nut, upper shift lever, shift lever snap ring and lower lever.
3. Push shifter shaft assembly down and remove locknut clutch connector link.

NOTE: Long end of connector link engages poppet plate.

4. Remove shifter shaft assembly and separate the inner and outer shifter shafts. Remove and discard O-rings.
5. Inspect poppet plate for damage. If necessary drive pivot shaft from case and remove poppet plate and spring from case.

Removing Input Gear Assembly
1. Remove input gear bearing and remove large snap ring from bearing.
2. Tap input gear and bearing out from the case then remove snap ring retaining input shaft bearing with the shaft and remove bearing from input gear.

Removing Countergear Assembly
1. Using tool J-24745, remove countershaft from cluster gear and remove cluster gear assembly.

NOTE: Recover roller bearings (72 total) from gear case and shaft.

2. Remove countergear thrust washers.
3. Clean, inspect and replace parts as necessary.

Installing Countergear Assembly
1. Using tool J-24745 and heavy grease, install (72) roller bearings and spacers in countergear bore.
2. Using heavy grease, position countershaft thrust washers in case. Engage tab on washers with slot in case thrust surface.

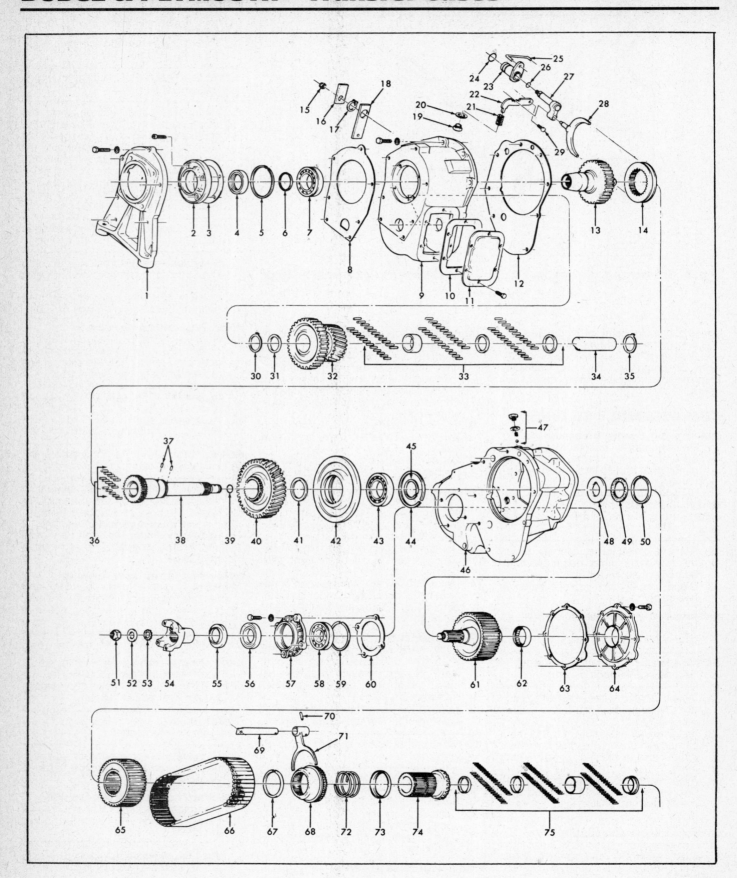

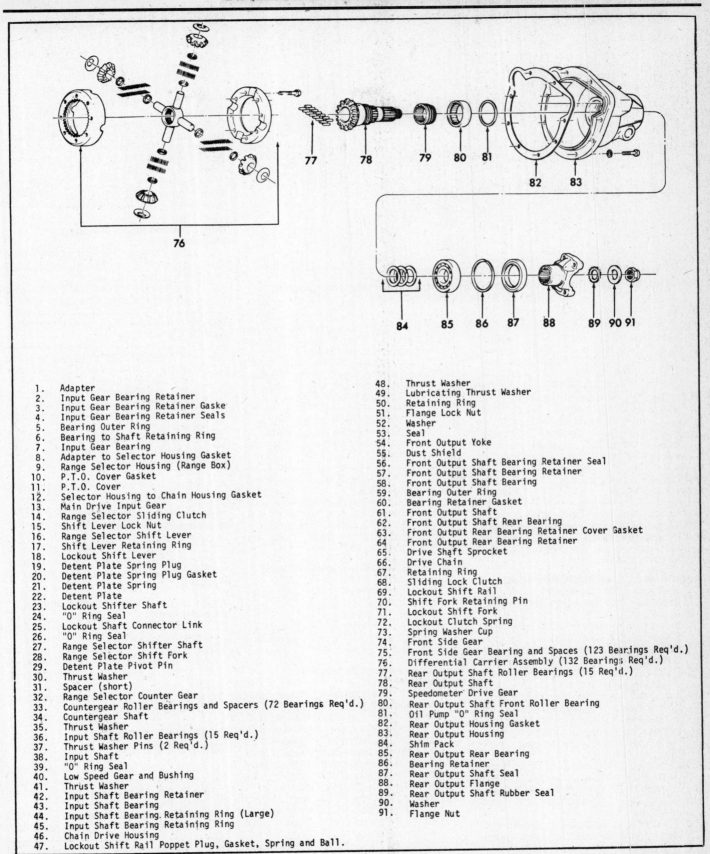

1. Adapter
2. Input Gear Bearing Retainer
3. Input Gear Bearing Retainer Gasket
4. Input Gear Bearing Retainer Seals
5. Bearing Outer Ring
6. Bearing to Shaft Retaining Ring
7. Input Gear Bearing
8. Adapter to Selector Housing Gasket
9. Range Selector Housing (Range Box)
10. P.T.O. Cover Gasket
11. P.T.O. Cover
12. Selector Housing to Chain Housing Gasket
13. Main Drive Input Gear
14. Range Selector Sliding Clutch
15. Shift Lever Lock Nut
16. Range Selector Shift Lever
17. Shift Lever Retaining Ring
18. Lockout Shift Lever
19. Detent Plate Spring Plug
20. Detent Plate Spring Plug Gasket
21. Detent Plate Spring
22. Detent Plate
23. Lockout Shifter Shaft
24. "O" Ring Seal
25. Lockout Shaft Connector Link
26. "O" Ring Seal
27. Range Selector Shifter Shaft
28. Range Selector Shift Fork
29. Detent Plate Pivot Pin
30. Thrust Washer
31. Spacer (short)
32. Range Selector Counter Gear
33. Countergear Roller Bearings and Spacers (72 Bearings Req'd.)
34. Countergear Shaft
35. Thrust Washer
36. Input Shaft Roller Bearings (15 Req'd.)
37. Thrust Washer Pins (2 Req'd.)
38. Input Shaft
39. "O" Ring Seal
40. Low Speed Gear and Bushing
41. Thrust Washer
42. Input Shaft Bearing Retainer
43. Input Shaft Bearing
44. Input Shaft Bearing Retaining Ring (Large)
45. Input Shaft Bearing Retaining Ring
46. Chain Drive Housing
47. Lockout Shift Rail Poppet Plug, Gasket, Spring and Ball.

48. Thrust Washer
49. Lubricating Thrust Washer
50. Retaining Ring
51. Flange Lock Nut
52. Washer
53. Seal
54. Front Output Yoke
55. Dust Shield
56. Front Output Shaft Bearing Retainer Seal
57. Front Output Shaft Bearing Retainer
58. Front Output Shaft Bearing
59. Bearing Outer Ring
60. Bearing Retainer Gasket
61. Front Output Shaft
62. Front Output Shaft Rear Bearing
63. Front Output Rear Bearing Retainer Cover Gasket
64. Front Output Rear Bearing Retainer
65. Drive Shaft Sprocket
66. Drive Chain
67. Retaining Ring
68. Sliding Lock Clutch
69. Lockout Shift Rail
70. Shift Fork Retaining Pin
71. Lockout Shift Fork
72. Lockout Clutch Spring
73. Spring Washer Cup
74. Front Side Gear
75. Front Side Gear Bearing and Spaces (123 Bearings Req'd.)
76. Differential Carrier Assembly (132 Bearings Req'd.)
77. Rear Output Shaft Roller Bearings (15 Req'd.)
78. Rear Output Shaft
79. Speedometer Drive Gear
80. Rear Output Shaft Front Roller Bearing
81. Oil Pump "O" Ring Seal
82. Rear Output Housing Gasket
83. Rear Output Housing
84. Shim Pack
85. Rear Output Rear Bearing
86. Bearing Retainer
87. Rear Output Shaft Seal
88. Rear Output Flange
89. Rear Output Shaft Rubber Seal
90. Washer
91. Flange Nut

Fig. 4 New Process 203 transfer case legend & exploded view of differential carrier assembly & rear output housing (first design)

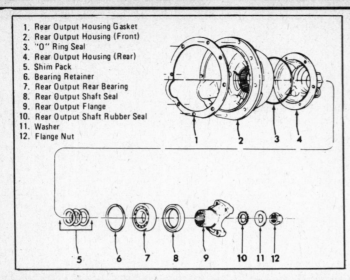

1. Rear Output Housing Gasket
2. Rear Output Housing (Front)
3. "O" Ring Seal
4. Rear Output Housing (Rear)
5. Shim Pack
6. Bearing Retainer
7. Rear Output Rear Bearing
8. Rear Output Shaft Seal
9. Rear Output Flange
10. Rear Output Shaft Rubber Seal
11. Washer
12. Flange Nut

Fig. 5 New Process 203 transfer case rear output housing (second design) exploded view

3. Position countergear assembly in case and install countershaft through front face of range box and into gear assembly. Flat on countershaft face should face forward and must be aligned with case gasket.

Installing Input Gear Assembly

1. Install bearing (without large snap ring) on input gear shaft positioning snap ring groove outward and install new retaining ring on shaft. Position input gear and bearing in housing.

NOTE: Use size A, B, C, or D snap ring to provide tightest fit.

2. Install snap ring onto bearing.
3. Align oil slot in retainer with drain hole in case and install input gear bearing retainer, gasket and bolts. Torque bolts to 30 ft. lbs.

Installing Shifter Shaft Assembly

1. Install poppet plate and pivot pin assembly into housing. Use sealant on pin.
2. Install new O-rings on inner and outer shifter shafts then lubricate O-rings and assemble inner shaft into the outer shaft.
3. Push shifter shafts into housing, engaging long end of locknut clutch connector link to the outer shifter shaft before the shaft assembly bottoms out in housing.
4. Install lower shift lever, retaining ring, upper shift lever and shifter shaft retaining nut.
5. Install shift fork and sliding clutch gear. Push fork up into shifter shaft assembly to engage poppet plate, sliding gear forward onto the input shaft gear.
6. Install poppet plate spring, gasket and plug into top of housing. Check spring engagement with poppet plate.

Input Gear Bearing Replacement

1. Remove bearing retainer and gasket.

2. Remove snap ring retaining bearing on the shaft. Pry bearing from case and remove it from shaft.

NOTE: Inspect input gear for burrs, scoring, heat discoloration etc. and inspect seal in retainer. Replace as necessary.

3. Install bearing and snap ring onto input gear shaft. Position bearing to case and tap into place using a small hammer.

NOTE: Use size A, B, C, or D snap ring to provide tightest fit.

4. Install new snap ring on shaft and position new gasket and bearing retainer to housing. Install bolts and torque to 30 ft. lbs.

Input Gear Bearing Retainer Seal Replacement

1. Remove bearing retainer bolts, retainer and gasket.
2. Pry seal out of retainer.
3. Install seal using tool J-21359.
4. Install bearing retainer and gasket and torque bolts to 30 ft. lbs.

Rear Output Shaft Housing Disassembly

1. Remove speedometer driven gear from housing and if not already removed, remove flange nut, washer and flange from shaft, **Figs. 4 and 5.**
2. Using a soft hammer, tap on flange end of pinion and remove pinion from carrier. If speedometer drive gear is not on the pinion shaft, reach into carrier and remove it from housing.
3. Using a screwdriver, pry seal out and pry behind open ends of snap ring retaining rear bearing in housing and remove snap ring.
4. Tap rear bearing out, then using a long drift inserted through rear opening drive the front bearing out of housing.

TORQUE SPECIFICATIONS

Intermediate Case to Range Box Bolts	30 ft. lbs.
Front Output Bearing Retainer Bolts	30 ft. lbs.
Output Shaft Yoke Nuts	150 ft. lbs.
Front Output Rear Bearing Retainer Bolts	30 ft. lbs.
Differential Assembly Screws	45 ft. lbs.
Rear Output Shaft Housing	30 ft. lbs.
Poppet Ball Retainer Nut	15 ft. lbs.
Power Take Off Cover Bolts	15 ft. lbs.
Front Input Bearing Retainer Bolts	20 ft. lbs.
Filler Plug	25 ft. lbs.

Rear Output Shaft Housing Reassembly

1. Using grease, position seal in bore and press roller bearing into place until it bottoms in housing.
2. Tap rear bearing into place and install snap ring retaining bearing in case.

NOTE: Use size A, B, C, or D snap ring to provide tightest fit.

3. Using tool J-22388, drive rear seal into housing until it is about 1/8—3/8 inch below housing face.
4. Install speedometer drive gear and shims (approximately .050 inch thick), install shaft into carrier through front opening.
5. Install flange, washer and nut. Leave nut loose until shim requirements are determined (approximately .060 inch thick).
6. Install speedometer driven gear into housing.

Front Output Shaft Bearing Retainer Seal, Replacement

1. Pry out seal from retainer.
2. Clean and inspect retainer.
3. Apply sealer to outer diameter of seal and install using tool J-22836 into retainer.

Front Output Shaft Rear Bearing, Replacement

1. Remove rear cover and gasket from transfer case.
2. Press out old bearing and press in new bearing until it is flush with opening. Use a block of wood over bearing.
3. Install cover and gasket and torque bolts to 30 ft. lbs.

TRANSFER CASE REASSEMBLY

1. Place range box on blocks with input gear side facing down and position range box to transfer case gasket on input housing.
2. Install lockout clutch and drive sprocket assembly on input shaft assembly.

NOTE: Install a 2 inch band type clamp on end of shaft to prevent losing bearings from clutch assembly.

3. Install input shaft, lockout clutch and drive sprocket assembly into range box, aligning tab on bearing retainer with notch in gasket.
4. Connect lockout clutch shift rail to the connector link and position rail in housing bore. Rotate the shifter shaft while lowering shift rail into the housing, to prevent the link and rail from being disconnected.
5. Install chain into housing, positioning chain around outer wall of housing then install chain housing onto range box, engaging the shift rail channel of the housing to the shift rail. Position chain onto input drive sprocket.
6. Install front output sprocket into case, engaging drive chain with sprocket. Rotate drive gear to aid in positioning chain onto drive sprocket.
7. Install shift fork onto clutch assembly and shift rail, then push clutch assembly into drive sprocket. Install roll pin retaining shift fork to shift rail.
8. Install front output shaft bearing, retainer, gasket and bolts.
9. Install front output shaft flange, gasket, seal, washer and nut. Install bolts in flange and tap dust shield into place.
10. Install front output shaft rear bearing retainer, gasket and bolts.

NOTE: If rear bearing was removed, place new bearing on outside face of cover and press into cover until bearing is flush with opening.

11. Install front output shaft flange, gasket, seal, washer and retaining nut. Tap dust shield back into place after installing flange bolts.
12. Install front output shaft rear bearing retainer, gasket and retaining bolts.
13. Install differential carrier assembly on input shaft with bolt heads facing rear of shaft.
14. Install rear output housing, gasket and bolts. Load bearings in pinion shaft.
15. Install speedometer gear and shims (about .050 inch) onto the output shaft.
16. Position the rear output of the rear assembly onto the rear output housing of the front assembly. Make sure that O-ring is properly positioned on the front section of the output housing.

NOTE: Make sure that vent is in the upward position.

17. Install flange, washer and retaining nut. Leave nut loose until shim requirements are determined.
18. Check shim requirements as follows:
    a. Make sure that output shaft retaining nut is loose about .060 inch.
    b. Install a dial indicator in such a manner as to contact the end of the output shaft.
    c. Push in rear output shaft to its full travel while rotating front output yoke and holding rear output yoke stationary. Set dial indicator to zero on the highest reading obtained.

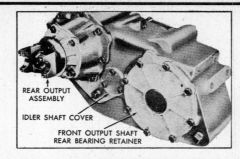

Fig. 6 Rear view of transfer case. New Process 205

    d. Pry out rear output shaft yoke until the maximum reading is obtained on the dial indicator. The allowable end play is .001–.010 inch. Add or remove shims as required to obtain the allowable end play.
    e. Check to make sure that end play is not too tight after the nut has been tightened, by holding the rear yoke stationary and rotating the front yoke. If the yoke can be rotated by hand and the "bumps" are felt, the end play is acceptable.
19. Install the speedometer driven gear into the housing.
20. Install lockout clutch shift rail poppet ball, spring and plug.
21. Install poppet plate spring, gasket and plug, if not installed previously.
22. Install shift levers on shifter shafts.
23. Torque all bolts, lock nuts and plugs to specifications listed above.

MODEL 205
DISASSEMBLY

1. Loosen rear output shaft yoke nut, then remove rear output shaft housing bolts, housing and retainer assembly from case, **Fig. 6.**
2. Remove rear output shaft retaining yoke and nut then remove shaft assembly from housing, **Fig. 7.**
3. Remove and discard snap ring using tool J-23432, then remove thrust washer and washer pin.
4. Remove tanged bronze washer, gear needle bearing (32 per row), spacer and second row of needle bearings from rear output shaft.
5. Remove tanged bronze thrust washer, pilot rollers (15), retainer ring, washer, oil seal retainer, ball bearing, speedometer gear and spacer from rear shaft.
6. Discard all gaskets and press out bearing from rear output shaft.
7. Remove locknut, washer and yoke from front output shaft.
8. Remove front bearing retainer attaching bolts and retainer, then the rear bearing retainer attaching bolts from front output shaft.
9. Tap output shaft, gear assembly and rear bearing retainer from case with a rubber mallet, **Fig. 8.**
10. Remove synchronizer from output

high gear, then the washer and bearing from case.
11. Remove and discard gear retaining ring from shaft, **Fig. 9.**
12. Remove thrust washer, pin, gear, needle bearings (32 per row) and spacer from shaft.

NOTE: If front output shaft rear bearing must be replaced, remove bearing by supporting the cover and pressing out the bearing. Press new bearing into position using a piece of pipe or wood until bearing is flush with opening.

13. Remove two poppet nuts, springs and, using a magnet, the poppet balls from top of transfer case.
14. Using a ¼ inch punch, drive cup plugs into case.
15. Place both shift rails in the neutral position and drive shift fork pins into case, **Fig. 10.**
16. Remove clevis pins, shift rail link and shift rails, **Fig. 11.** Remove upper (range) rail first, then the lower (4-wheel) rail.
17. Remove shift forks, sliding clutch, front output high gear, washer, bearing, shift rail cup plugs and pins from case.
18. Remove snap ring in front of bearing, then, using a rubber mallet, tap shaft and bearing out of case.
19. Tip case on power takeoff opening and remove two interlock pins from inside of case.
20. Remove idler gear shaft nut and rear cover.
21. Remove idler gear shaft using a rubber mallet and tool J-23429, **Fig. 12.**
22. Roll idler gear to front output shaft opening and remove gear from case, then remove bearing cups from gear.

ASSEMBLY

1. Press bearing cups in idler gear using tools J-9276-2 and J-8092.
2. Install the two bearing cones, spacer, shims and idler gear on dummy shaft J-23429 with bore up. Check that gear end play is .001–.002 inch.
3. Install idler gear assembly, large end first, with dummy shaft into case through front output bore, **Fig. 7.**
4. Install idler shaft from large bore side and drive through using a rubber mallet.
5. Install washer and new locknut. Torque locknut to 150 ft. lbs. Check for end play and free rotation.
6. Install idler shaft cover and gasket. Torque bolts to 20 ft. lbs. Flat on cover must be adjacent to front output shaft rear cover.
7. Press the two rail seals, with metal lip outward, into case, then install interlock pins through large bore or power takeoff opening.
8. Install front output drive shift rail into case from back, slotted end first, with poppet notches up.
9. Install shift fork, with long end inward, into rail, then push rail through to neu-

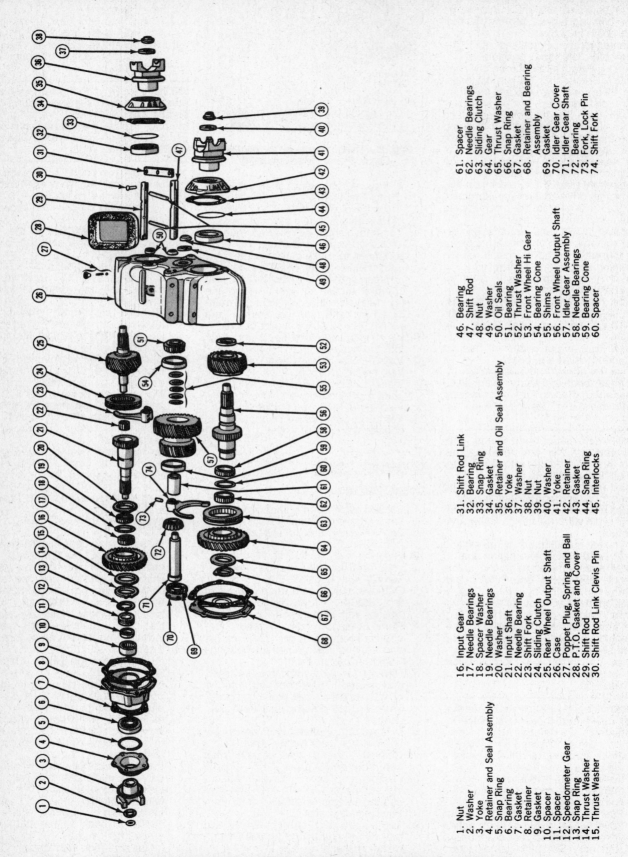

1. Nut
2. Washer
3. Yoke
4. Retainer and Seal Assembly
5. Snap Ring
6. Bearing
7. Gasket
8. Retainer
9. Gasket
10. Gasket
11. Spacer
12. Speedometer Gear
13. Snap Ring
14. Thrust Washer
15. Thrust Washer
16. Input Gear
17. Needle Bearings
18. Spacer Washer
19. Needle Bearings
20. Washer
21. Input Shaft
22. Needle Bearing
23. Shift Fork
24. Sliding Clutch
25. Rear Wheel Output Shaft
26. Case
27. Poppet Plug, Spring and Ball
28. P.T.O. Gasket and Cover
29. Shift Rod
30. Shift Rod Link Clevis Pin
31. Shift Rod Link
32. Bearing
33. Snap Ring
34. Gasket
35. Retainer and Oil Seal Assembly
36. Yoke
37. Washer
38. Nut
39. Yoke
40. Washer
41. Yoke
42. Retainer
43. Gasket
44. Snap Ring
45. Interlocks
46. Bearing
47. Shift Rod
48. Nut
49. Washer
50. Oil Seals
51. Bearing
52. Thrust Washer
53. Front Wheel Hi Gear
54. Bearing Cone
55. Shims
56. Front Wheel Output Shaft
57. Idler Gear Assembly
58. Needle Bearings
59. Bearing Cone
60. Spacer
61. Spacer
62. Needle Bearings
63. Sliding Clutch
64. Gear
65. Thrust Washer
66. Snap Ring
67. Gasket
68. Retainer and Bearing Assembly
69. Gasket
70. Idler Gear Cover
71. Idler Gear Shaft
72. Bearing
73. Fork, Lock Pin
74. Shift Fork

Fig. 7   Exploded view of New Process model 205 transfer case

Fig. 8 Removing front output shaft rear bearing retainer. New Process 205

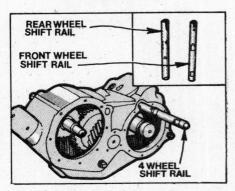

Fig. 11 Shift rail removed. New Process 205

Fig. 9 Removing gear retaining ring. New Process 205

Fig. 10 Removing shift fork pins. New Process 205

Fig. 12 Removing idler gear shaft. New Process 205

tral position.

10. Install input shaft bearing and shaft into case, then install range rail into case from front with poppet notches up.
11. Install sliding clutch onto fork and place over input shaft in case, then push range rail through to neutral position.
12. Install new lock pins through holes at top of case and drive them into the forks.

NOTE: When installing range rail lock pin, tip case on power takeoff opening.

13. Install two rows of needle bearings (32 each), separated by a spacer, in the front low output gear and apply an adequate amount of grease to hold in place.
14. Secure front output shaft in a soft-jawed vise, spline end down.
15. Install front low gear over shaft with clutch gear facing down, then install thrust washer pin, thrust washer and a new snap ring using tool J-23432. The snap ring opening should be opposite the pin.
16. Install front wheel high gear and washer in case.
17. Install synchronizer in shift fork, then place fork and rail in front wheel drive (4-H) position with clutch teeth meshed with teeth of front wheel high gear.
18. Line up washer, high gear and syn-

chronizer with bearing bore, then install front output shaft and low gear assembly through high gear assembly.
19. Install new seal in bearing retainer using tool J-22836, then install front output bearing and retainer in case.
20. Thoroughly clean and grease rollers in front output rear bearing retainer and install onto case with one gasket. Apply suitable sealant to bolts, then install them and torque to 30 ft. lbs.
21. Install front output yoke, washer and locknut. Torque locknut to 150 ft. lbs.
22. Install two rows of needle bearings (32 each), separated by a spacer, into low output gear and apply an adequate amount of grease to hold in place.
23. Install thrust washer, with tang down, onto rear output shaft in clutch gear groove.
24. Install output low gear onto shaft with clutch teeth facing down, then install thrust washer over gear with tab pointing up and away from gear.
25. Install washer pin and large thrust washer over shaft and pin. Rotate washer until tab fits into slot approximately 90° away from pin, then install snap ring using tools J-23423 and J-23423-1. Check that end play is .002–.027 inch.
26. Grease pilot bore or rear output shaft and install the 15 needle bearings, then the thrust washer and new snap ring in bore.
27. Clean, grease and install new bearing in retainer housing using tool J-23431.
28. Install housing onto output shaft assembly, then install spacer, speedometer gear and bearing.
29. Install rear bearing retainer seal using tool J-21359 or J-22834-2.
30. Install bearing retainer assembly with one or two gaskets. Torque bolts to 30 ft. lbs.
31. Install yoke, washer and locknut on output shaft, then place range rail in high and install output shaft and retainer assembly on case. Torque housing bolts to 30 ft. lbs.
32. Install power takeoff cover and gasket. Torque bolts to 15 ft. lbs.
33. Install and seal cup plugs at rail pin holes.
34. Install drain and filler plugs and torque to 30 ft. lbs.
35. Install shift rail cross link, clevis pins

and lock pins.

MODEL 208
DISASSEMBLY

1. Remove fill and drain plugs. Drain lubricant from transfer case.
2. Remove front and rear yokes. Discard the yoke seal washers and yoke nuts.
3. Rotate transfer case and position on wood blocks with the front case resting on the wood. If necessary, cut "V" notches in the blocks so the front case rests squarely on the blocks.
4. Remove lock mode indicator switch and washer, **Fig. 13**.
5. Remove detent bolt, spring and ball.
6. Mark relationship between rear retainer and case for alignment at reassembly.
7. Remove rear retainer attaching bolts, then the rear retainer and pump housing as an assembly. Do not pry retainer from case. If necessary, use a plastic mallet to tap retainer.
8. Remove pump housing from retainer then the pump seal from housing. Discard the seal.
9. Remove speedometer drive gear from mainshaft.
10. Remove oil pump from mainshaft noting position of pump for reassembly. The side of the pump facing toward inside of case is recessed.

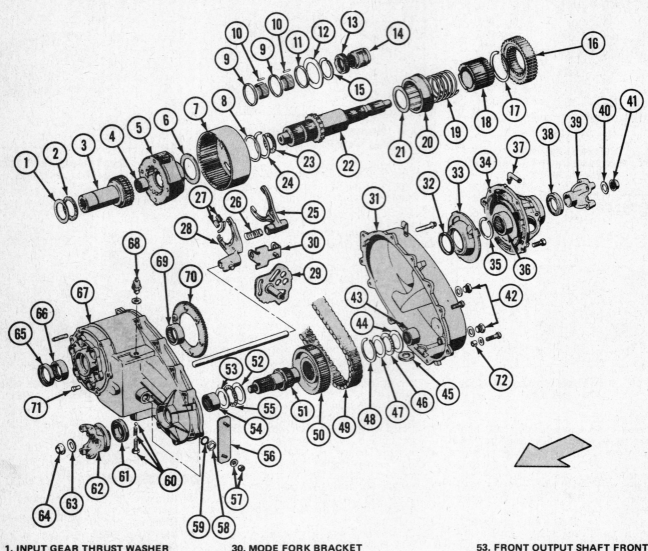

1. INPUT GEAR THRUST WASHER
2. INPUT GEAR THRUST BEARING
3. INPUT GEAR
4. MAINSHAFT PILOT BEARING
5. PLANETARY ASSEMBLY
6. PLANETARY THRUST WASHER
7. ANNULUS GEAR
8. ANNULUS GEAR THRUST WASHER
9. NEEDLE BEARING SPACERS
10. MAINSHAFT NEEDLE BEARINGS (120)
11. NEEDLE BEARING SPACER
12. THRUST WASHER
13. OIL PUMP
14. SPEEDOMETER GEAR
15. DRIVE SPROCKET RETAINING RING
16. DRIVE SPROCKET
17. SPROCKET CARRIER STOP RING
18. SPROCKET CARRIER
19. CLUTCH SPRING
20. SLIDING CLUTCH
21. THRUST WASHER
22. MAINSHAFT
23. MAINSHAFT THRUST BEARING
24. ANNULUS GEAR RETAINING RING
25. MODE FORK
26. MODE FORK SPRING
27. RANGE FORK INSERTS
28. RANGE FORK
29. RANGE SECTOR

30. MODE FORK BRACKET
31. REAR CASE
32. SEAL
33. PUMP HOUSING
34. REAR RETAINER
35. REAR OUTPUT BEARING
36. BEARING SNAP RING
37. VENT TUBE
38. REAR SEAL
39. REAR YOKE
40. YOKE SEAL WASHER
41. YOKE NUT
42. DRAIN AND FILL PLUGS
43. FRONT OUTPUT SHAFT REAR BEARING
44. FRONT OUTPUT SHAFT REAR THRUST BEARING RACE (THICK)
45. CASE MAGNET
46. FRONT OUTPUT SHAFT REAR THRUST BEARING
47. FRONT OUTPUT SHAFT REAR THRUST BEARING RACE (THIN)
48. DRIVEN SPROCKET RETAINING RING
49. DRIVE CHAIN
50. DRIVEN SPROCKET
51. FRONT OUTPUT SHAFT
52. FRONT OUTPUT SHAFT FRONT THRUST BEARING RACE (THIN)

53. FRONT OUTPUT SHAFT FRONT THRUST BEARING RACE (THICK)
54. FRONT OUTPUT SHAFT FRONT BEARING
55. FRONT OUTPUT SHAFT FRONT THRUST BEARING
56. OPERATING LEVER
57. WASHER AND LOCKNUT
58. RANGE SECTOR SHAFT SEAL RETAINER
59. RANGE SECTOR SHAFT SEAL
60. DETENT BALL, SPRING AND RETAINER BOLT
61. FRONT SEAL
62. FRONT YOKE
63. YOKE SEAL WASHER
64. YOKE NUT
65. INPUT GEAR OIL SEAL
66. INPUT GEAR FRONT BEARING
67. FRONT CASE
68. LOCK MODE INDICATOR SWITCH AND WASHER
69. INPUT GEAR REAR BEARING
70. LOCKPLATE
71. LOCKPLATE BOLTS
72. CASE ALIGNMENT DOWELS

Fig. 13   New Process model 208 transfer case, disassembled

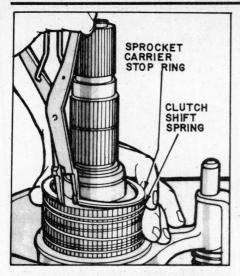

Fig. 14 Sprocket carrier stop ring & clutch spring replacement

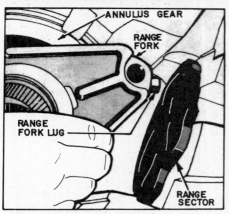

Fig. 17 Annulus gear & range fork replacement

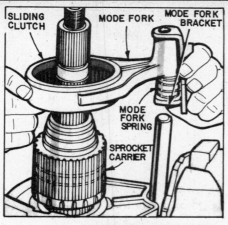

Fig. 15 Mode fork, spring, bracket & sliding clutch replacement

Fig. 18 Planetary thrust washer & planetary assembly replacement

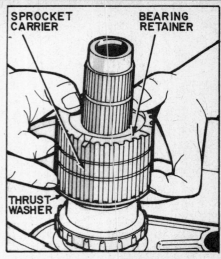

Fig. 16 Sprocket carriers, bearing retainers, thrust washer & needle bearing replacement

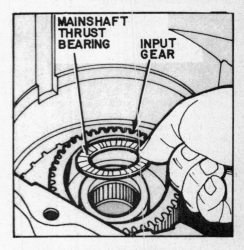

Fig. 19 Mainshaft thrust bearing & input gear replacement

11. Remove rear case to front case retaining bolts, then the rear case from front case.

NOTE: To remove rear case, insert a suitable screwdriver into the slots in the case ends and gently pry upward. Do not attempt to wedge the case halves apart at any point on the mating surfaces.

12. Remove front output shaft rear thrust bearing assembly. Note position of bearing and races for reassembly.
13. Remove driven sprocket retaining snap ring.
14. Remove drive sprocket retaining snap ring, then the thrust washer and spacer washer, if equipped.
15. Remove drive and driven sprockets and the drive chain as an assembly. Lift evenly on both sprockets to remove.
16. Remove front output shaft and front thrust bearing assembly.
17. Remove sprocket carrier stop ring and clutch spring, **Fig. 14.**
18. Remove sliding clutch, mode fork and mode fork spring as an assembly, **Fig. 15.** Then remove shift rail.
19. Remove sprocket carrier, needle bearing upper retainer, thrust washer and mainshaft needle bearings as an assembly, **Fig. 16.**
20. Remove mainshaft.
21. Remove annulus gear retaining ring and thrust washer, then the annulus gear and range fork as an assembly. Rotate fork counter-clockwise to disengage fork lug from range sector and lift assembly from case, **Fig. 17.**
22. Remove planetary thrust washer and planetary assembly, **Fig. 18.**
23. Remove mainshaft thrust bearing from input gear, then the input gear, **Fig. 19.** Lift the gear straight up and out from case.
24. Remove input gear thrust bearing and race, **Fig. 20.** Note position of bearing and race for reassembly.
25. Remove range sector operating lever attaching nut and washer, then the lever. Remove sector shaft seal and seal retainer.
26. Remove range sector.
27. Inspect lock plate. If lock plate is loose, worn or damaged, remove lock plate.
28. Remove output shaft seals from front and rear case seal bores.

SUB-ASSEMBLY SERVICE

LOCK PLATE, REPLACE:

1. Remove and discard lock plate attaching bolts.
2. Remove lock plate from case, **Fig. 13.**
3. Coat the case and lock plate surfaces around the bolt holes with Loctite 515 sealer or equivalent.
4. Position new lock plate in the case and align bolt holes in lock plate and case.
5. Coat new lock plate attaching bolts with Loctite 271 sealer or equivalent.
6. Install and torque lock plate attaching bolts to 30 ft. lbs.

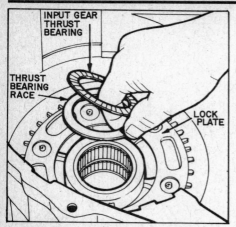

Fig. 20 Input gear thrust bearing & race replacement

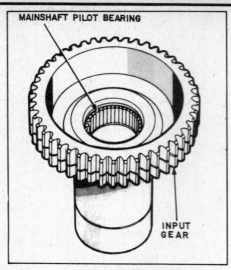

Fig. 21 Mainshaft pilot bearing installation

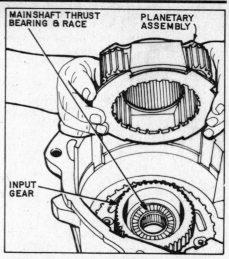

Fig. 22 Input gear, mainshaft thrust bearing & planetary installation

BEARING, BUSHING & SEAL REPLACEMENT

NOTE: The following bearings, bushings and seals are replaced using special service tools. However, they may also be replaced using suitable equivalent tooling and when using these tools, care should be taken as not to damage any components.

Also, all the bearings used must be correctly positioned to prevent covering the bearing oil feed holes. After replacing any bearing, check position of bearing to ensure that the oil feed hole is not obstructed or blocked by the bearing.

Rear Output Bearing & Seal, Replace

1. Remove bearing retaining snap ring and tap bearing from retainer with a mallet.
2. Remove rear seal using a suitable screwdriver or drift.
3. Install new bearing using tool J-7818. Ensure that shielded side of bearing faces toward inside of case.
4. Install bearing retaining snap ring.
5. Install new rear seal using tools J-8092 and J-29162.

Front Output Shaft Front Bearing, Replace

1. Remove bearing using tools J-8092 and J-29168.
2. Install new bearing using tools J-8092 and J-29167.
3. Remove tools and check bearing position to ensure that oil feed hole is clear.

Front Output Shaft Rear Bearing, Replace

1. Remove bearing using tools J-26941 and slide hammer J-2619-01.
2. Install new bearing using tools J-8092 and J-29163.
3. Remove tools and ensure that oil feed hole is clear and that the bearing is seated flush with edge of case bore to permit space for the thrust bearing assembly.

Input Gear Front & Rear Bearing, Replace

1. Remove both bearings simultaneously with tools J-8092 and J-28170.
2. Install new bearings one at a time. Install the rear bearing first, then the front bearing. Use tools J-8092 and J-29169.
3. Remove tools and check position of bearing to ensure that the oil feed hole is clear and that the bearings are flush with the case bore surfaces.

Mainshaft Pilot Bearing, Replace

1. If bearing cannot be removed by hand, remove by using slide hammer J-2619-01 and J-29369-1. A similar internal type blind hole bearing puller may also be used.
2. Install new bearing using tools J-8092 and J-29174.
3. Remove tools and check position of bearing to ensure that the oil feed hole is clear and that the bearing is seated flush with edge of bearing bore, **Fig. 21.**

Annulus Gear Bushing, Replace

1. Remove bushing with tools J-8092 and J-29185.
2. Install new bushing with tools J-8092 and J-29185-2.
3. Remove any metal chips made by bushing replacement.

ASSEMBLY

NOTE: During assembly, lubricate all components with 10W-30 engine or petroleum jelly where indicated only. Do not use any other types of lubricant.

1. Install input gear race and thrust bearing into front case, then the input gear, **Fig. 22.**
2. Install mainshaft thrust bearing in input gear, **Fig. 22.**
3. Install range sector shaft seal and seal retainer, then the range sector.

4. Install operating lever on range sector shaft. Install and torque shaft washer and lock nut to 18 ft. lbs.
5. Install planetary assembly over input gear and ensure that the assembly is fully seated and meshed with the gear.
6. Install planetary thrust washer on planetary hub.
7. Install inserts into range fork, if removed.
8. Engage range fork into annulus gear and install annulus gear over planetary assembly. Ensure that the range fork lug is inserted fully into range sector slot.
9. Install annulus gear thrust washer and retaining snap ring.
10. Align shift rail bores in the case and range fork and install shift rail.

NOTE: The shift rail bore in the case must be dry and not contain any oil. A small amount of oil may prevent the shift rail from seating completely and also may prevent front case installation.

11. Install mainshaft. Ensure that the mainshaft thrust bearing is seated properly in the input gear before installing mainshaft.
12. Thickly coat sprocket carrier bore with petroleum jelly and position bearing retainer at center of carrier bore.
13. Coat mainshaft needle bearings with petroleum jelly and install 60 needle bearings in each end of sprocket carrier bore. 120 needle bearings are used.
14. Install bearing retainer in each end of sprocket carrier bore and position the thrust washer on the bottom of the carrier, **Fig. 23.**
15. Align the assembled carrier and needle bearings with the mainshaft and install the assembly on the mainshaft. Use caution as not to dislodge the needle bearings.

16. Assemble the mode fork, fork spring and bracket. Engage the fork in the sliding clutch and install the assembly onto the shift rail and mainshaft.
17. Install clutch spring and stop ring on sprocket carrier.

NOTE: If the sprocket carrier has two ring grooves, install the stop ring in the upper groove only.

18. Install front output shaft front thrust bearing assembly in front case. The proper installation sequence is: thick race, thrust bearing, then thin race.
19. Install front output shaft.
20. Install sprockets and drive chain as an assembly. Position the sprockets in the chain, aligning the sprockets with the shafts and install the assembly.

NOTE: Ensure that the drive sprocket is installed with the recessed side of the sprocket facing toward the inside of the case.

21. Install spacer and thrust washer on drive sprocket, then the sprocket retaining snap ring.
22. Install driven sprocket retaining snap ring.
23. Install front output shaft rear thrust bearing assembly on front output shaft. The proper installation sequence is: thin race, thrust bearing, then thick race.
24. Install oil pump on mainshaft. Ensure that the recessed side of the pump faces toward inside of case.
25. Install speedometer drive gear on mainshaft.

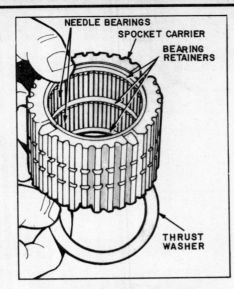

NEEDLE BEARINGS
SPOCKET CARRIER
BEARING RETAINERS
THRUST WASHER

Fig. 23 Sprocket carrier components assembly

26. Install magnet in front case, if removed.
27. Apply Loctite 515 sealer or equivalent to mating surface of front case. Then, install rear case onto front case.

NOTE: Ensure that the front output shaft rear thrust bearing assembly is properly seated in the rear case.

28. Align case bolt holes and alignment dowels and install retaining bolts. Alternately torque bolts to 23 ft. lbs.

NOTE: Flat washers are installed on the two bolts at opposite ends of the case.

29. Install rear output bearing in rear retainer, then install retaining snap ring.
30. Install seal into pump housing. Apply petroleum jelly to pump housing tabs. Install housing to rear retainer.
31. Apply Loctite 515 sealer or equivalent to mating surface of rear retainer. Align rear retainer and case alignment marks made during disassembly and install retainer.
32. Install and torque retainer bolts to 23 ft. lbs.
33. Install oil seal into rear retainer bore. Coat the seal lip with petroleum jelly prior to installation.
34. Install washer and indicator switch. Torque switch to 18 ft. lbs.
35. Lightly apply Loctite 515 sealer or equivalent to detent retainer bolt, then install detent ball, spring and bolt. Torque bolt to 23 ft. lbs.
36. Install drain plug and gasket. Torque drain plug to 18 ft. lbs.
37. Install oil seal in front case output shaft bore.
38. Install front and rear yokes.

NOTE: The yoke with the collar is installed on the front output shaft.

39. Install yoke seal washer and yoke nuts. Torque yoke nuts to 120 ft. lbs.
40. Install 6 pints of 10W-30 engine oil into transfer case through fill plug.
41. Install and torque fill plug to 18 ft. lbs.

AUTOMATIC TRANSMISSIONS/TRANSAXLES

TABLE OF CONTENTS

A-413 & A-470 Torqueflite Automatic Transaxles

INDEX

DESCRIPTION

These transaxles combine a torque converter, automatic 3 speed transmission, final drive gearing and differential combined into one unit. The torque converter, transaxle and differential assemblies are housed in an integral aluminum die cast housing, **Fig. 1.**

NOTE: On 1982 models, the differential oil sump is separate from the transaxle pump. Be sure differential oil level is $\frac{1}{8}$ to $\frac{3}{8}$ inch below the oil filler hole on the differential cover. On 1983–85 models, the differential oil sump is integral with the transaxle sump, and separate filling of the differential is not necessary.

The torque converter is connected to the crankshaft through a flexible drive plate. Converter cooling is accomplished by an oil-to-water type cooler, located in the radiator side tank. The torque converter cannot be disassembled. The transaxle consists of two multiple disc clutches, an overrunning clutch, two servos, a hydraulic accumulator, two bands and two planetary gear assemblies to provide three forward and one reverse gear. The sun gear is connected to the front clutch retainer. The hydraulic system consists of an oil pump, and a single valve body which contains all of the valves except the governor valves. Output torque from the main drive gears is transferred through helical gears to the transfer shaft. An integral ring gear on the transfer shaft drives the differential ring gear.

TROUBLESHOOTING GUIDE

HARSH ENGAGEMENT FROM N TO D OR R

1. High idle speed.
2. Defective or leaking valve body.
3. High hydraulic pressure.
4. Worn or damaged rear clutch.

DELAYED ENGAGEMENT FROM N TO D OR R

1. Low hydraulic pressure.
2. Defective or leaking valve body.
3. Low-reverse servo, band or linkage malfunction.
4. Low fluid level.
5. Incorrect gearshift linkage adjustment.
6. Clogged transmission oil filter.
7. Faulty oil pump.
8. Worn or damaged input shaft seal rings.
9. Aerated fluid.
10. Low idle speed.
11. Worn or damaged reaction shaft support seal rings.
12. Worn or defective front clutch.
13. Worn or defective rear clutch.

RUNAWAY UPSHIFTS

1. Low hydraulic pressure.
2. Defective or leaking valve body.
3. Low fluid level.
4. Clogged transmission oil filter.
5. Aerated fluid.
6. Incorrect throttle linkage adjustment.
7. Worn or damaged reaction shaft support seal rings.
8. Kickdown servo, band or linkage malfunction.
9. Worn or faulty front clutch.

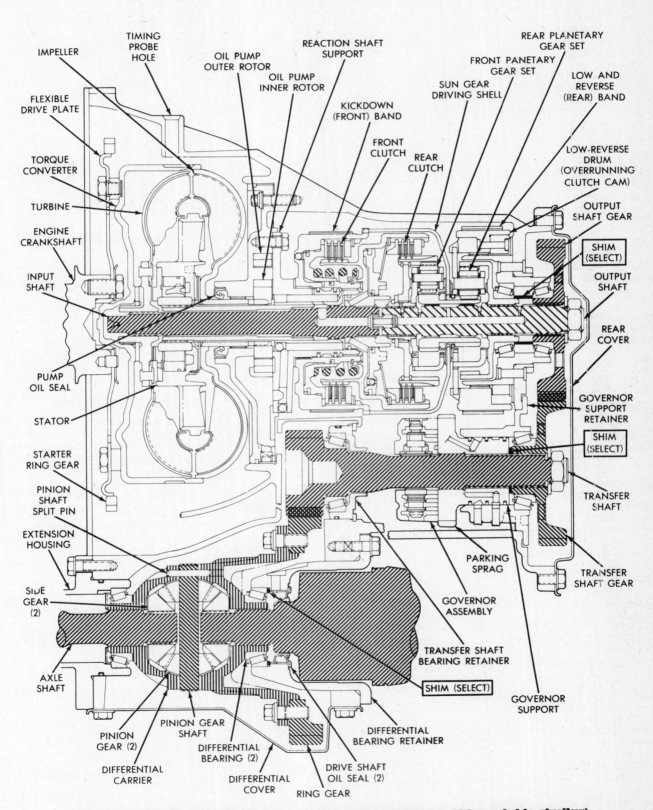

Fig. 1 Sectional view of A-413 automatic transaxle. (A-470 model is similar)

NO UPSHIFT
1. Low hydraulic pressure.
2. Defective or leaking valve body.
3. Low fluid level.
4. Incorrect gearshift linkage adjustment.
5. Incorrect throttle linkage adjustment.
6. Worn or damaged governor support seal rings.
7. Faulty governor.
8. Kickdown servo, band or linkage malfunction.
9. Worn or faulty front clutch.

3-2 KICKDOWN RUNAWAY
1. Low hydraulic pressure.
2. Defective or leaking valve body.
3. Low fluid level.
4. Aerated fluid.
5. Incorrect throttle linkage adjustment.
6. Kickdown band adjustment.
7. Worn or damaged reaction shaft support seal rings.
8. Kickdown servo, band or linkage malfunction.
9. Worn or faulty front clutch.

NO KICKDOWN OR NORMAL DOWNSHIFT
1. Defective or leaking valve body.
2. Incorrect throttle linkage adjustment.
3. Faulty governor.
4. Kickdown servo, band or linkage malfunction.

ERRATIC SHIFTS
1. Low hydraulic pressure.
2. Defective or leaking valve body.
3. Low fluid level.
4. Incorrect gearshift linkage adjustment.
5. Clogged transmission oil filter.
6. Faulty oil pump.
7. Aerated fluid.
8. Incorrect throttle linkage adjustment.
9. Worn or damaged governor support seal rings.
10. Worn or damaged reaction shaft support seal rings.
11. Faulty governor.
12. Kickdown servo, band or linkage malfunction.
13. Worn or faulty front clutch.

SLIPS IN 1, 2 OR D
1. Low hydraulic pressure.
2. Defective or leaking valve body.
3. Low fluid level.
4. Incorrect gearshift linkage adjustment.
5. Clogged transmission oil filter.
6. Faulty oil pump.
7. Worn or damaged input shaft seal rings.
8. Aerated fluid.
9. Incorrect throttle linkage adjustment.
10. Overrunning clutch not holding.
11. Worn or faulty rear clutch.
12. Overrunning clutch worn, damaged or seized.

SLIPS IN R ONLY
1. Low hydraulic pressure.
2. Low-reverse band adjustment.
3. Defective or leaking valve body.
4. Low-reverse servo, band or linkage

Fig. 2   Gearshift linkage. Rampage & Scamp

malfunction.
5. Low fluid level.
6. Incorrect gearshift linkage adjustment.
7. Faulty oil pump.
8. Aerated fluid.
9. Worn or damaged reaction shaft seal rings.
10. Worn or faulty front clutch.

SLIPS IN ALL RANGES
1. Low hydraulic pressure.
2. Defective or leaking valve body.
3. Low fluid level.
4. Clogged transmission oil filter.
5. Faulty oil pump.
6. Worn or damaged input shaft seal rings.
7. Aerated fluid.

NO DRIVE IN ANY RANGE
1. Low hydraulic pressure.
2. Defective or leaking valve body.
3. Low fluid level.
4. Clogged transmission oil filter.
5. Faulty oil pump.
6. Planetary gear sets damaged or seized.

NO DRIVE 1, 2 OR D
1. Low hydraulic pressure.
2. Defective or leaking valve body.
3. Low fluid level.
4. Worn or damaged input shaft seal rings.
5. Overrunning clutch not holding.
6. Worn or faulty rear clutch.
7. Planetary gear sets damaged or seized.
8. Overrunning clutch worn, damaged or seized.

NO DRIVE IN R
1. Low hydraulic pressure.
2. Low-reverse band adjustment.

3. Defective or leaking valve body.
4. Low-reverse servo, band or linkage malfunction.
5. Incorrect gearshift linkage adjustment.
6. Worn or damaged reaction shaft support seal rings.
7. Worn or faulty front clutch.
8. Worn or faulty rear clutch.
9. Planetary gear sets damaged or seized.

DRIVE IN NEUTRAL
1. Defective or leaking valve body.
2. Incorrect gearshift linkage adjustment.
3. Insufficient clutch plate clearance.
4. Worn or faulty rear clutch.
5. Rear clutch dragging.

DRAGS OR LOCKS
1. Low-reverse band adjustment.
2. Kickdown band adjustment.
3. Planetary gear sets damaged or seized.
4. Overrunning clutch worn, damaged or seized.

HARD TO FILL (OIL BLOWS OUT FILLER TUBE)
1. Clogged transmission oil filter.
2. Aerated fluid.
3. High fluid level.
4. Breather clogged.

TRANSMISSION OVERHEATS
1. Stuck switch valve.
2. High idle speed.
3. Low hydraulic pressure.
4. Low fluid level.
5. Incorrect gearshift adjustment.
6. Faulty oil pump.
7. Kickdown band adjustment too tight.
8. Faulty cooling system.
9. Insufficient clutch plate clearance.

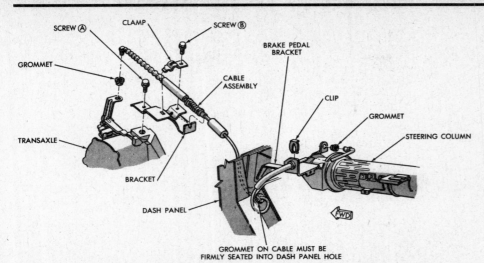

Fig. 3   Gearshift linkage. Ram Van, Caravan & Voyager mini van models

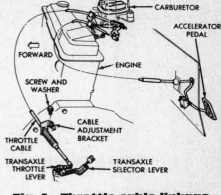

Fig. 4   Throttle cable linkage

HARSH UPSHIFTS

1. Low hydraulic pressure.
2. Incorrect throttle linkage adjustment.
3. Kickdown band adjustment.
4. High hydraulic pressure.

DELAYED UPSHIFT

1. Incorrect throttle linkage adjustment.
2. Kickdown band adjustment.
3. Worn or damaged governor support seal rings.
4. Worn or damaged reaction shaft support seal rings.
5. Faulty governor.
6. Kickdown servo, band or linkage malfunction.
7. Worn or faulty front clutch.

GRATING, SCRAPING OR GROWLING NOISE

1. Low-reverse band out of adjustment.
2. Kickdown band adjustment.
3. Output shaft bearing or bushing damaged.
4. Planetary gear sets damaged or seized.
5. Overrunning clutch worn, damaged or seized.

BUZZING NOISE

1. Defective or leaking valve body.
2. Low fluid level.
3. Aerated fluid.
4. Overrunning clutch inner race damaged.

MAINTENANCE

ADDING OIL

To check fluid level, apply the parking brake and operate engine at idle speed with transmission in Neutral or Park position. Add fluid as necessary.

CHANGING OIL

Fluid and filter changes are not required for average vehicle use. Severe usage such as commercial type usage or prolonged operation in city traffic requires that fluid be changed and bands adjusted every 15,000 miles.

Whenever factory fill fluid is changed, only fluid of the type labeled Dexron II should be used.

1. Raise vehicle and place a suitable drain pan under transmission oil pan.
2. Loosen transmission oil pan attaching bolts and allow fluid to drain, then remove oil pan.
3. Replace oil filter and adjust bands, if necessary, and install oil pan and gasket.
4. Add four quarts of approved automatic transmission fluid through the filler tube.
5. Start engine and allow to idle for at least two minutes on 1982 models, or at least six minutes on 1983–85 models, then with parking brake applied, move selector lever momentarily to each position. Place selector lever in Neutral or Park and check fluid level. Add fluid to bring level to Add mark.
6. Recheck fluid level after transmission has reached operating temperature. The level should be between Add and Full marks.

IN-VEHICLE ADJUSTMENTS

SHIFT LINKAGE, ADJUST

Rampage, Scamp & Mini Vans

NOTE: When linkage cable must be disconnected from levers which use plastic grommets as retainers, the grommets must be replaced.

1. Place selector lever into "P" position.
2. Pull shift lever, **Figs. 2 and 3** to front detent (Park) position.
3. While maintaining pressure on shift lever, torque locknut to 90 inch lbs. on Rampage and Scamp models and 105 inch lbs. on Mini Vans.
4. Check adjustment.

THROTTLE CABLE, ADJUST

1. Perform adjustment with engine at operating temperature, other wise ensure carburetor is not on fast idle cam by disconnecting choke.
2. Loosen adjusting bracket lock screw, **Fig. 4.**
3. Hold transmission lever rearward against internal stop and tighten adjusting bracket lock screw to 105 inch lbs.

KICKDOWN BAND, ADJUST

1. Loosen locknut and back off nut approximately 5 turns, **Fig. 5.**
2. Using tool No. C-3380-A and C-3705, torque band adjusting screw to 47–50 inch lbs. If tool No. C-3705 is not used, torque adjusting screw to 72 inch lbs.
3. On 1982–83 models, back off adjusting screw 2¾ turns. On 1984–85 models, back off adjusting screw 2½ turns.
4. Hold adjusting screw in this position and tighten locknut to 35 ft. lbs.

LOW-REVERSE BAND, ADJUST

1. Loosen, then back off locknut approximately 5 turns.
2. Torque adjusting screw to 41 inch lbs.
3. Back off adjusting screw 3½ turns and torque locknut to 14 ft. lbs.

IN-VEHICLE REPAIRS

VALVE BODY, REPLACE

1. Loosen transmission oil pan attaching

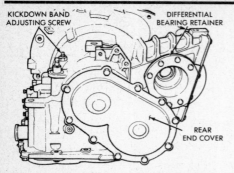

Fig. 5 Kickdown band adjusting screw location

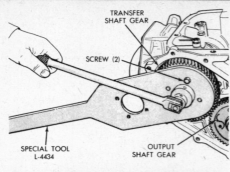

Fig. 6 Loosening transfer shaft gear retaining nut

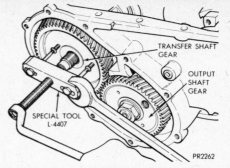

Fig. 7 Removing transfer shaft gear

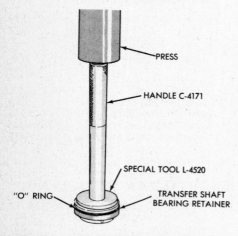

Fig. 8 Installing oil seal into shaft retainer

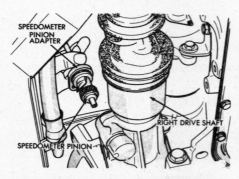

Fig. 9 Removing speedometer adapter, cable & pinion

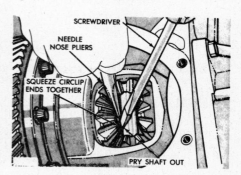

Fig. 10 Prying drive shaft out of side gear. 1982 models

bolts and allow transmission to drain, then remove oil pan.
2. Remove oil filter attaching screws and oil filter.
3. Using a screwdriver, remove E-clip, then remove parking rod.
4. Remove seven valve body attaching bolts, valve body and governor oil tubes.

GOVERNOR & TRANSFER SHAFT OIL SEAL, REPLACE

1. Remove rear cover attaching bolts and rear cover.
2. Using tool No. L-4434, remove transfer shaft gear retaining nut, **Fig. 6.**
3. Using tool No. L-4407, remove transfer shaft gear and shim, **Fig. 7.**
4. Remove governor support retainer, then low-reverse band anchor pin.
5. Remove governor assembly.
6. Remove transfer shaft retainer snap ring. Using tool No. L-4512 and a suitable puller, remove transfer shaft and retainer assembly.
7. Remove transfer shaft retainer from shaft.
8. Using a screwdriver, remove oil seal from transfer shaft retainer.

9. Using tools Nos. L-4520 and C-4171, press oil seal into shaft retainer, **Fig. 8.**
10. Reverse procedure to install. Torque transfer shaft gear retaining nut to 200 ft. lbs.

TRANSAXLE
REPLACE

NOTE: The transaxle and converter must be removed as an assembly.

1. Disconnect battery ground cable.
2. Disconnect transaxle shift control and throttle cables from transaxle and position aside.
3. On 1982 models, disconnect upper oil cooler hose. On 1983–85 models, disconnect both upper and lower oil cooler hoses.
4. Support engine with suitable engine lifting equipment.
5. Remove upper bell housing bolts.
6. Raise and support vehicle, then remove front wheels and left splash shield.
7. On 1982 models, remove differential cover.
8. Remove speedometer adapter, cable and pinion as an assembly, **Fig. 9.**
9. Remove sway bar and both lower ball

joint to steering knuckle bolts, then, using a suitable pry bar, remove lower ball joint.
10. Remove drive shaft from hub.
11. On 1982 models, rotate both drive shafts until circlip ends are visible. Compress circlip and pry drive shaft out of side gear, **Fig. 10.**
12. Remove both drive shafts.
13. Remove dust cover, then mark position of torque converter on drive plate and remove torque converter mounting bolts. Remove plug from access hole in right splash shield to rotate crankcase for bolt removal.
14. Disconnect Neutral/Park safety switch electrical connector and, on 1982 models, disconnect lower oil cooler hose.
15. Remove engine mount bracket from front crossmember, front mount insulator through-bolt and remaining bell housing bolts.
16. Support transaxle with a suitable jack.
17. Remove left side engine mount.
18. Move transaxle away from engine and lower from vehicle. It may be necessary to pry transaxle away from engine between extension housing and engine block for proper clearance.
19. Reverse procedure to install. When installing differential cover on 1982 models, apply a ⅛ inch bead of RTV sealant to cover.

Loadflite A-727, A-904, A-904T & A-999 Automatic Transmissions

INDEX

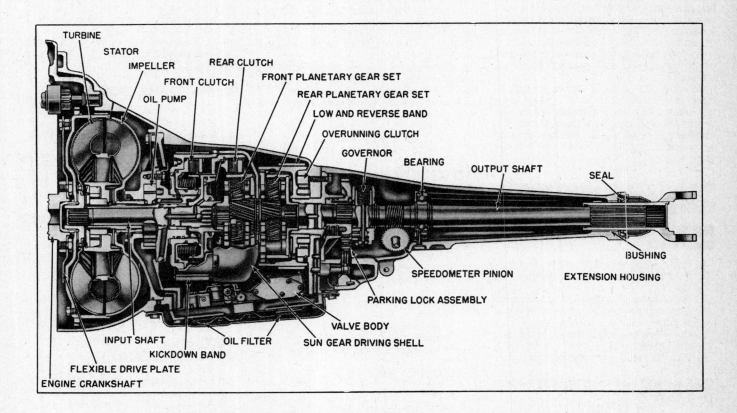

Fig. 1 Loadflite 727 automatic transmission without lockup torque converter

DESCRIPTION

These transmissions, **Figs. 1 through 3** combine a torque converter with a fully automatic three speed gear system. The converter housing and transmission case are an integral aluminum casting. The transmission consists of two multiple disc clutches, an overrunning (one-way) clutch, two servos and bands and two planetary gear sets to provide three forward speeds and reverse.

The common sun gear of the planetary gear sets is connected to the front clutch by a driving shell that is splined to the sun gear and to the front clutch retainer.

All A-904T and A-999 transmissions, **Fig. 4,** are equipped with a wide ratio gearset. Low gear ratio is 2.74 to 1. The sun gear and front planetary gearset is unique to the wide ratio transmission. The rear planetary gearset remains the same as previous A-904 and A-999 transmission models.

The hydraulic system consists of a single oil pump and a valve body that contains all the valves except the governor valve.

Venting of the transmission is accomplished by a drilled passage through the upper part of the front pump housing.

The torque converter is attached to the engine crankshaft through a flexible driving plate. The converter is cooled by circulating the transmission fluid through an oil-to-water type cooler located in the radiator lower tank. The converter is a sealed assembly that cannot be disassembled.

A lock-up clutch (torque converter clutch) is incorporated in some transmission applications.

The lock-up mode is activated only in direct drive above a minimum preset vehicle speed. At wider throttle openings, where the 2-3 upshift occurs above the minimum lock-up speed, the lock-up shift will occur immediately after the 2-3 upshift.

TROUBLESHOOTING GUIDE

HARSH ENGAGEMENT IN D-1-2-R

1. Engine idle speed too high.
2. Hydraulic pressures too high or too low.
3. Low-reverse band out of adjustment.
4. Accumulator sticking, broken rings or spring.
5. Low-reverse servo, band or linkage malfunction.
6. Worn or faulty front and/or rear clutch.

DELAYED ENGAGEMENT IN D-1-2-R

1. Lower fluid level.
2. Incorrect manual linkage adjustment.
3. Oil filter clogged.
4. Hydraulic pressures too high or low.
5. Valve body malfunction or leakage.
6. Accumulator sticking, broken rings or spring.

7. Clutches or servos sticking or not operating.
8. Faulty front oil pump.
9. Worn or faulty front and/or rear clutch.
10. Worn or broken input shaft and/or reaction shaft support seal rings.
11. Aerated fluid.

RUNAWAY OR HARSH UPSHIFT AND 3-2 KICKDOWN

1. Low fluid level.
2. Incorrect throttle linkage adjustment.
3. Hydraulic pressures too high or low.
4. Kickdown band out of adjustment.
5. Valve body malfunction or leakage.
6. Governor malfunction.
7. Accumulator sticking, broken rings or spring.
8. Clutches or servos sticking or not operating.
9. Kickdown servo, band or linkage malfunction.
10. Worn or faulty front clutch.
11. Worn or broken input shaft and/or reaction shaft support seal rings.

NO UPSHIFT

1. Low fluid level.
2. Incorrect throttle linkage adjustment.
3. Kickdown band out of adjustment.
4. Hydraulic pressures too high or low.
5. Governor sticking.
6. Valve body malfunction or leakage.
7. Accumulator sticking, broken rings or spring.
8. Clutches or servos sticking or not operating.
9. Faulty oil pump.
10. Kickdown servo, band or linkage malfunction.
11. Worn or faulty front clutch.
12. Worn or broken input shaft and/or reaction shaft support seal rings.

NO KICKDOWN OR NORMAL DOWNSHIFT

1. Incorrect throttle linkage adjustment.
2. Incorrect gearshift linkage adjustment.
3. Kickdown band out of adjustment.
4. Hydraulic pressure too high or low.
5. Governor sticking.
6. Valve body malfunction or leakage.
7. Accumulator sticking, broken rings or spring.
8. Clutches or servos sticking or not operating.
9. Kickdown servo, band or linkage malfunction.
10. Overrunning clutch not holding.

ERRATIC SHIFTS

1. Low fluid level.
2. Aerated fluid.
3. Incorrect throttle linkage adjustment.
4. Incorrect gearshift control linkage adjustment.
5. Hydraulic pressures too high or low.
6. Governor sticking.
7. Oil filter clogged.
8. Valve body malfunction or leakage.

9. Clutches or servos sticking or not operating.
10. Faulty oil pump.
11. Worn or broken input shaft and/or reaction shaft support seal rings.

SLIPS IN FORWARD DRIVE POSITIONS

1. Low oil level.
2. Aerated fluid.
3. Incorrect throttle linkage adjustment.
4. Incorrect gearshift control linkage adjustment.
5. Hydraulic pressures too low.
6. Valve body malfunction or leakage.
7. Accumulator sticking, broken rings or spring.
8. Clutches or servos sticking or not operating.
9. Worn or faulty front and/or rear clutch.
10. Overrunning clutch not holding.
11. Worn or broken input shaft and/or reaction shaft support seal rings.

SLIPS IN REVERSE ONLY

1. Low fluid level.
2. Aerated fluid.
3. Incorrect gearshift control linkage adjustment.
4. Hydraulic pressures too high or low.
5. Low-reverse band out of adjustment.
6. Valve body malfunction or leakage.
7. Front clutch or rear servo sticking or not operating.
8. Low-reverse servo, band or linkage malfunction.
9. Faulty oil pump.

SLIPS IN ALL POSITIONS

1. Low fluid level.
2. Hydraulic pressures too low.
3. Valve body malfunction or leakage.
4. Faulty oil pump.
5. Clutches or servos sticking or not operating.
6. Worn or broken input shaft and/or reaction shaft support seal rings.

NO DRIVE IN ANY POSITION

1. Low fluid level.
2. Hydraulic pressures too low.
3. Oil filter clogged.
4. Valve body malfunction or leakage.
5. Faulty oil pump.
6. Clutches or servos sticking or not operating.

NO DRIVE IN FORWARD DRIVE POSITIONS

1. Hydraulic pressures too low.
2. Valve body malfunction or leakage.
3. Accumulator sticking, broken rings or spring.
4. Clutches or servos, sticking or not operating.
5. Worn or faulty rear clutch.
6. Overrunning clutch not holding.
7. Worn or broken input shaft and/or reaction shaft support seal rings.

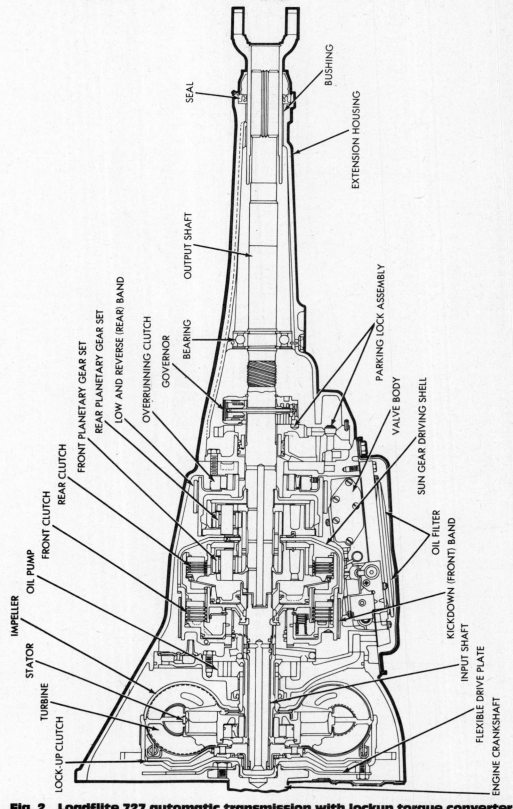

Fig. 2   Loadflite 727 automatic transmission with lockup torque converter

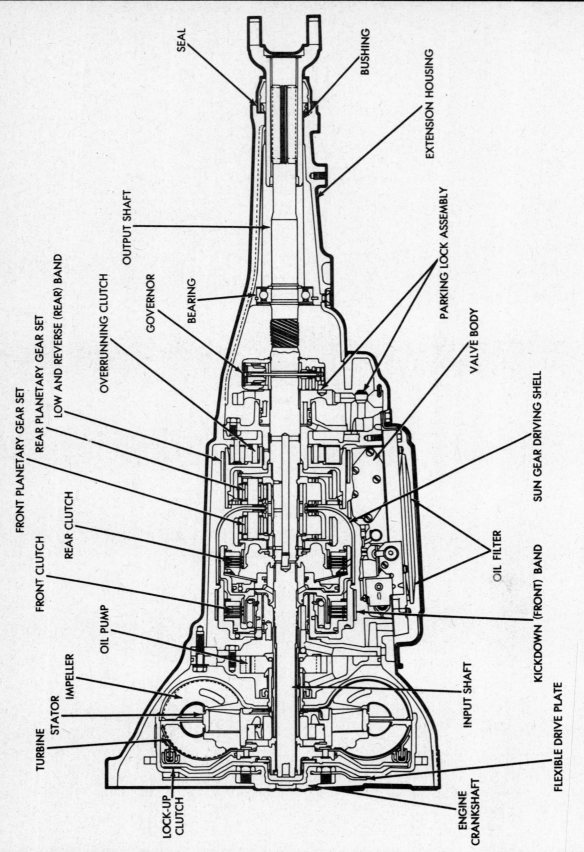

Fig. 3 Loadflite A-904T & A-999 automatic transmission with lockup torque converter

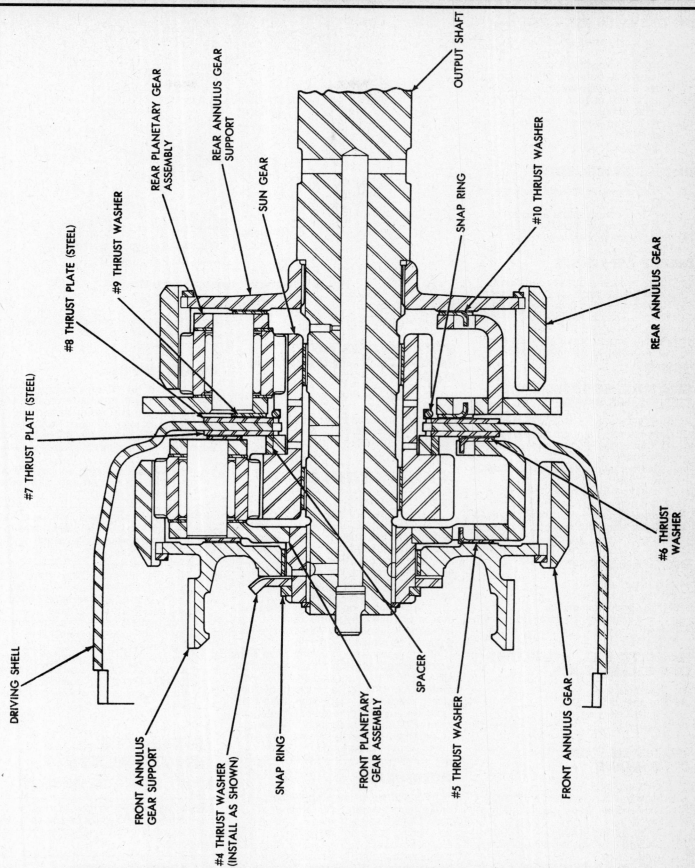

Fig. 4   Wide ratio planetary gearset used on A-904T & A-999 transmissions

NO DRIVE IN REVERSE

1. Incorrect gearshift control linkage adjustment.
2. Hydraulic pressures too low.
3. Low-reverse band out of adjustment.
4. Valve body malfunction or leakage.
5. Front clutch or rear servo sticking or not operating.
6. Low-reverse servo, band or linkage malfunction.
7. Worn or faulty front clutch.

DRIVES IN NEUTRAL

1. Incorrect gearshift control linkage adjustment.
2. Incorrect control cable adjustment.
3. Valve body malfunction or leakage.
4. Rear clutch inoperative.

DRAGS OR LOCKS

1. Kickdown band out of adjustment.
2. Low-reverse band out of adjustment.
3. Kickdown and/or low-reverse servo, band or linkage malfunction.
4. Front and/or rear clutch faulty.
5. Planetary gear sets broken or seized.
6. Overrunning clutch worn, broken or seized.

GRATING, SCRAPING OR GROWLING NOISE

1. Kickdown band out of adjustment.
2. Low-reverse band out of adjustment.
3. Output shaft bearing and/or bushing damaged.
4. Governor support binding or broken seal rings.
5. Oil pump scored or binding.
6. Front and/or rear clutch faulty.
7. Planetary gear sets broken or seized.
8. Overrunning clutch worn, broken or seized.

BUZZING NOISE

1. Low fluid level.
2. Pump sucking air.
3. Valve body malfunction.
4. Overrunning clutch inner race damaged.

HARD TO FILL, OIL FLOWS OUT FILLER TUBE

1. High fluid level.
2. Breather clogged.
3. Oil filter clogged.
4. Aerated fluid.

TRANSMISSION OVERHEATS

1. Low fluid level.
2. Kickdown band adjustment tight.
3. Low-reverse band adjustment too tight.
4. Faulty cooling system.
5. Cracked or restricted oil cooler line or fitting.
6. Faulty oil pump.
7. Insufficient clutch plate clearance in front and/or rear clutches.

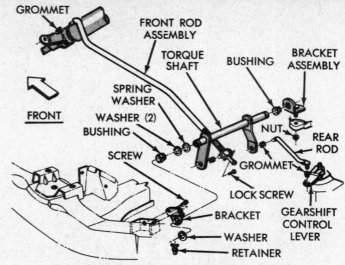

Fig. 5 Gearshift linkage adjustment

STARTER WILL NOT ENERGIZE IN NEUTRAL OR PARK

1. Incorrect gearshift control linkage adjustment.
2. Faulty or incorrectly adjusted neutral starting switch.
3. Broken lead to neutral switch.

MAINTENANCE

SERVICE BULLETIN

It has been determined that an occasional "no-drive" condition, generally occuring after making the first stop when a vehicle is cold can be caused by incorrect transmission fluid level. In cases where this condition is encountered, it is essential that the transmission fluid level be checked and corrected as outlined below.

If the no-drive condition still exists with the correct fluid level, the selector lever adjustment should be checked and/or adjusted as required.

After the above corrections have been accomplished and the no-drive condition still exists, it is suggested that the transmission be removed and the front pump disassembled for inspection before attempting any further repairs. Check pump inner rotor and front support for wear and/or damage, especially where the pinion rubs against the support.

ADDING OIL

To check the oil level, apply the parking brake and operate the engine at idle speed. Move selector lever into each position ending in the neutral position. A properly filled transmission should read near the "add one pint" mark when the fluid temperature is 70° F., and near but not over the "full" mark at 180° F. which is normal operating temperature. Then add oil as necessary to bring the oil to the prescribed level.

CHANGING OIL

Oil should be changed every 24,000 miles. Vehicles that operate continuously with abnormal loads should have more frequent periodic maintenance. Transmission should not be idled in gear for long periods. When refilling, use only fluids labeled Dexron II.

1. Remove drain plug (if equipped) from transmission oil pan and allow oil to drain.

NOTE: If the oil pan does not have a drain plug, loosen pan bolts and tap pan with a soft mallet to break it loose, permitting fluid to drain.

2. Remove transmission oil pan, clean intake screen and pan, and reinstall.
3. Add 4 quarts of automatic transmission fluid through filler tube.
4. Start engine and add approximately one quart while engine is idling.
5. Allow engine to idle for about two minutes. Then with parking brake applied, select each range momentarily, ending with the "N" position.
6. Add oil as necessary to bring to proper level.

IN-VEHICLE ADJUSTMENTS

SHIFT LINKAGE, ADJUST

NOTE: When linkage rod must be disconnected from levers which use plastic grommets as retainers, the grommets must be replaced.

1. Ensure adjustment swivel is free to turn on shift rod.

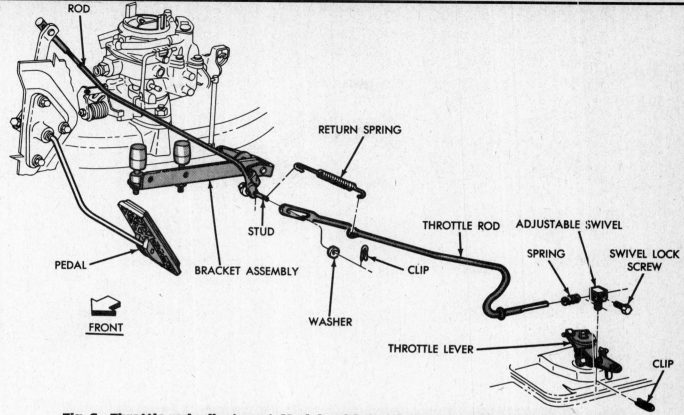

Fig. 6 Throttle rod adjustment. Models with 6 cylinder engine & 1 barrel carburetor

2. Place gearshift lever into Park position, **Fig. 5.**
3. With linkage assembled and adjustable swivel lock bolt loose, move transmission shift lever all the way to the rear detent (Park).
4. Tighten adjusting swivel lock bolt to 90 inch lbs.

THROTTLE LINKAGE, ADJUST

1. Support vehicle on hoist and loosen swivel lock screw, **Figs. 6, 7, and 8.**

NOTE: To insure correct adjustment, swivel must be free to slide along flat end of throttle rod so that preload spring action is not restricted. If necessary, disassemble and clean or repair parts to assure free action.

2. Hold transmission lever firmly forward against its internal stop and tighten swivel lock screw to 100 inch lbs., **Figs. 6, 7 and 8.**

NOTE: Adjustment is now finished. Linkage backlash was automatically removed by the preload spring.

3. Lower vehicle and test linkage operation by moving throttle rod rearward and slowly releasing it making certain that it returns fully.

KICKDOWN BAND, ADJUST

The kickdown band adjusting screw is located on the left side of the transmission case, **Fig. 9.**

1. Loosen adjusting screw locknut, then back off nut approximately 5 turns.
2. Turn adjusting screw and check for binding. If screw binds, lubricate threads as required.
3. Torque adjusting screw to 72 inch lbs., then back off adjusting screw the number of turns listed in **Fig. 10.**
4. While holding adjusting screw in position, tighten lock nut to 35 ft. lbs.

LOW AND REVERSE BAND, ADJUST

1. Raise vehicle, drain transmission and remove oil pan.
2. Loosen adjusting screw lock nut and back off nut approximately five turns, **Fig. 11.** Check adjusting screw for free turning in the lever.
3. Using an inch-pound torque wrench, tighten band adjusting screw to a reading of 72 inch lbs.
4. Backoff adjusting screw 2 turns, except on 1981–85 A-904T and A-999 model transmissions, back off screw 4 turns.
5. Install oil pan and fill transmission with fluid.

IN-VEHICLE REPAIRS

EXTENSION HOUSING, REPLACE

1. Disconnect battery ground cable.

2. Raise and support vehicle.
3. Mark propeller shaft flange and transmission extension housing for installation, then disconnect propeller shaft from transmission.
4. Remove speedometer pinion and adapter assembly.
5. Drain approximately 2 quarts of fluid from transmission.
6. Position a suitable jack under transmission assembly.
7. Remove extension housing to crossmember attaching bolts. Raise transmission slightly, then remove crossmember and support assembly from vehicle.
8. Place gearshift lever into 1 (low) position.
9. Remove extension housing to transmission attaching bolts.
10. Remove bolts, plate and gasket from bottom of extension housing mounting pad.
11. Using snap ring pliers, spread large snap ring as far as possible from output shaft, **Fig. 12,** then tap extension housing off of output shaft.
12. Carefully pull extension housing rearward from transmission assembly and out of vehicle.
13. Reverse procedure to install. Torque extension housing to transmission attaching bolts to 24 ft. lbs. Torque extension housing to crossmember bolts

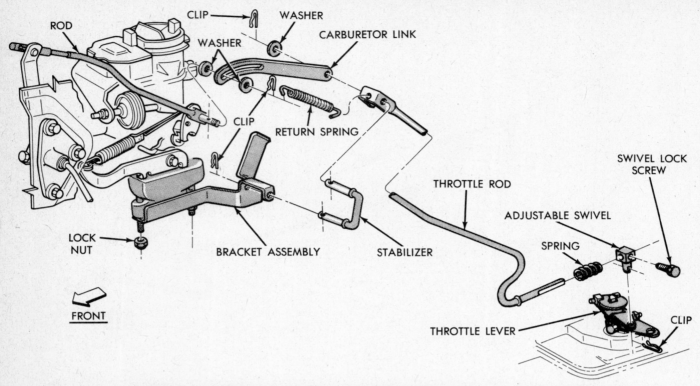

Fig. 7 Throttle rod adjustment. Models with 6 cylinder engine & 2 barrel carburetor

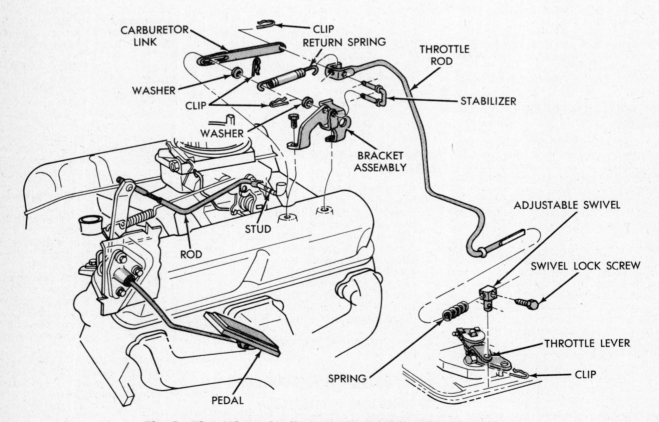

Fig. 8 Throttle rod adjustment. Models with V8 engine

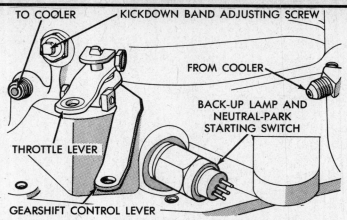

Fig. 9   Kickdown band adjusting screw location

Model	Year	Engine	Number of Turns
DODGE & PLYMOUTH			
Vans, Wagons & Front Sections	1979–80	6 Cyl.	2½
		V8	2
	1981–85	All	2½
Ramcharger & Trail Duster	1979	Except V8-440	2½
		V8-440	2
	1980	6 Cyl.	2½
		V8	2
	1981–85	All	2½
Conventional Cabs	1979	Except 6-243 Diesel & V8-440	2½
		6-243 Diesel & V8-440	2
	1980	6 Cyl.	2½
		V8	2
	1981–85	All	2½
Motor Home	1979	V8-318 & 360	2½
		V8-413 & 440	2
	1980	6 Cyl.	2½
		V8	2

Fig. 10   Kickdown band adjustment chart

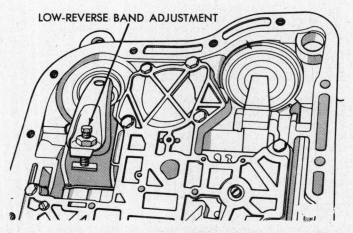

Fig. 11   Low-reverse band adjusting screw location

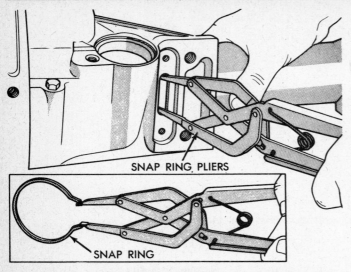

Fig. 12 Removing extension housing snap ring

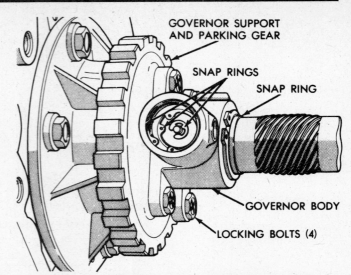

Fig. 13 Governor shaft & weight snap rings

to 50 ft. lbs.

VALVE BODY, REPLACE

1. Disconnect battery ground cable.
2. Raise and support vehicle.
3. Loosen oil pan bolts, then tap oil pan and drain fluid from transmission.
4. Loosen clamp bolts, then disconnect throttle and shift levers from transmission.
5. Disconnect back-up light and/or neutral start switch electrical connector(s) from transmission.
6. Position a suitable container under transmission and remove valve body to transmission attaching bolts. Remove valve body from transmission.
7. Reverse procedure to install.

GOVERNOR & PARKING GEAR, REPLACE

1. Disconnect battery ground cable.
2. Raise and support vehicle.
3. Remove extension housing as described under "Extension Housing, Replace."
4. Carefully pry snap ring from weight end of governor valve shaft, **Fig. 13**, then slide valve and shaft assembly from governor body.
5. Remove large snap ring from weight end of governor body, then the weight assembly.
6. Remove snap ring from inside governor weight. Remove inner weight and spring from outer weight, **Fig. 14.**
7. Remove snap ring from behind governor body, then slide governor and support assembly from output shaft.
8. Remove bolts, then separate governor body and screen from parking gear.
9. Reverse procedure to install.

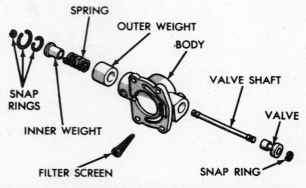

Fig. 14 Governor assembly exploded view

TRANSMISSION
REPLACE

1. Disconnect battery ground cable.
2. Raise and support vehicle.
3. Drain fluid from transmission.
4. Disconnect front exhaust pipe(s) from exhaust manifold(s).
5. Remove engine to transmission struts, if equipped.
6. Disconnect and cap transmission fluid lines.
7. Remove transmission fluid cooler line bracket.
8. Remove starter motor attaching bolts, then the starter motor.
9. Remove torque converter access cover.
10. Mark torque converter and drive plate for installation, then remove torque converter to drive plate attaching bolts.
11. Remove propeller shaft from vehicle.
12. Disconnect back-up light and neutral start switch electrical connector(s).
13. Disconnect gearshift rod and torque shaft assembly from transmission.
14. Disconnect throttle rod from transmission lever, then remove bellcrank linkage from transmission, if equipped.
15. Remove oil filler tube, then disconnect speedometer cable from transmission.
16. Position a suitable engine holding fixture onto engine.
17. Position a suitable jack under transmission, then raise transmission slightly.
18. Remove transmission mount to crossmember and crossmember to frame attaching bolts.
19. Remove transmission to engine attaching bolts.
20. Carefully separate transmission from engine, and install a suitable C clamp onto bellhousing to secure torque converter in place.
21. Lower transmission from vehicle.
22. Reverse procedure to install.

FORD MOTOR CO.

SECTION INDEX

BRONCO II & 1983-85 RANGER
INDEX OF SERVICE OPERATIONS

NOTE: Refer to page 1 of this manual for vehicle manufacturer's special service tool suppliers.

General Engine Specifications

Year	Engine CID①/Liter	Carburetor	Bore and Stroke	Compression Ratio	Net H.P. @ R.P.M.	Maximum Torque Lbs. Ft. @ R.P.M.	Normal Oil Pressure Pounds
1983–84	4-122, 2.0 L	YFA, 1 Bbl②	3.52 × 3.13	9.0	73 @ 4000	107 @ 2400	40–60
	4-135, 2.2 L⑦	Fuel Injection	3.50 × 3.50	22.0	59 @ 4000	90 @ 2500	57⑧
	4-140, 2.3 L④	YFA, 1 Bbl②③	3.78 × 3.13	9.0	79 @ 3800	124 @ 2200	40–60
	4-140, 2.3 L⑤	YFA, 1 Bbl②③	3.78 × 3.13	9.0	82 @ 4200	126 @ 2200	40–60
	V6-171, 2.8 L	2150, 2 Bbl⑥	3.65 × 2.70	8.7	115 @ 4600	150 @ 2600	40–60
1985	4-122, 2.0 L	YFA, 1 Bbl②	3.52 × 3.13	—	—	—	40–60
	4-140, 2.3 L	EFI	3.78 × 3.13	—	—	—	40–60
	4-143, 2.3 L⑦⑨	Fuel Injection	3.59 × 3.54	21.0	86 @ 4200	134 @ 2000	⑩
	V6-171, 2.8 L	2150, 2 Bbl⑥	3.65 × 2.70	—	—	—	40–60

①—Cubic Inch Displacement.
②—Carter.
③—Feedback carburetor, California only.
④—Manual Trans.
⑤—Automatic Trans.
⑥—Motorcraft.
⑦—Diesel engine.
⑧—At 3600 RPM.
⑨—Turbocharged engine.
⑩—11.3 psi at idle speed.

Pistons, Pins, Rings, Crankshaft & Bearings

Year	Engine	Piston Clearance	Ring End Gap① Comp.	Ring End Gap① Oil	Wristpin Diameter	Rod Bearings Shaft Diameter	Rod Bearings Bearing Clearance	Main Bearings Shaft Diameter	Main Bearings Bearing Clearance	Thrust on Bear. No.	Shaft End Play
1983–84	4-122	.0014–.0022	.010	.015	.9121	2.0462–2.0472	.0008–.0015	2.3982–2.3990	.0008–.0015	3	.0040–.0080
	4-135②	.0021–.0031	③	.014	1.1024	2.0861–2.0871	.0014–.0032	2.5586–2.5596	.0016–.0036	—	.0055–.0154
	4-140	.0014–.0022	.010	.015	.9121	2.0462–2.0472	.0008–.0015	2.3982–2.3990	.0008–.0015	3	.0040–.0080
	V6-171	.0011–.0019	.015	.015	.9448	2.2370–2.2378	.0006–.0016	2.2433–2.2441	.0008–.0015	—	.0040–.0080
1985	4-122	.0014–.0022	.010	.015	.9121	2.0462–2.0472	.0008–.0015	2.3982–2.3990	.0008–.0015	3	.0040–.0080
	4-140	.0014–.0022	.010	.015	.9121	2.0462–2.0472	.0008–.0015	2.3982–2.3990	.0008–.0015	3	.0040–.0080
	4-143②	.0016–.0024	.010	.010	—	2.087	—	2.598	—	3	.0008–.0020
	V6-171	.0011–.0019	.015	.015	.9448	2.2370–2.2378	.0006–.0016	2.2433–2.2441	.0008–.0015	—	.0040–.0080

①—Fit rings in tapered bores for clearance listed in tightest portion of ring travel.
②—Diesel engine.
③—Top, .016; second, .012.

continued

Valve Specifications

Year	Engine	Valve Lash		Valve Angles		Valve Spring Installed Height	Valve Spring Pressure Lbs. @ In.	Stem Clearance		Stem Diameter, Standard	
		Int.	Exh.	Seat	Face			Intake	Exhaust	Intake	Exhaust
1983–84	4-122	.035–.055①		45	44	1.49–1.55	149 @ 1.12	.0010–.0027	.0015–.0032	.3416–.3423	.3411–.3418
	4-135②	.012H	.012H	③	③	④	⑤	.0015–.0046	.0020–.0051	.3120–.3180	.3115–.3185
	4-140	.035–.055①		45	44	1.53–1.59	149 @ 1.12	.0010–.0027	.0015–.0032	.3416–.3423	.3411–.3418
	V6-171	.014C	.016C	45	44	1.58–1.61	144 @ 1.22	.0008–.0025	.0018–.0035	.3159–.3167	.3149–.3156
1985	4-122	.035–.055①		45	44	1.49–1.55	149 @ 1.12	.0010–.0027	.0015–.0032	.3416–.3423	.3411–.3418
	4-140	.035–.055①		45	44	1.49–1.55	149 @ 1.12	.0010–.0027	.0015–.0032	.3416–.3423	.3411–.3418
	4-143②	.010H	.010H	—	—	—	—	.0012–.0024	.0020–.0035	.3150	.3150
	V6-171	.014C	.016C	45	44	1.58–1.61	144 @ 1.22	.0008–.0025	.0018–.0035	.3159–.3167	.3149–.3156

①—Measured at camshaft with hydraulic lifter collapsed.
②—Diesel engine.
③—Intake, 45°; exhaust, 30°.
④—Inner spring, 1.488 inch; outer spring, 1.587 inch.
⑤—Inner spring, 28 @ 1.488; outer spring, 40 @ 1.587.

Engine Tightening Specifications★

★ Torque specifications are for clean and lightly lubricated threads only. Dry or dirty threads produce increased friction which prevents accurate measurement of tightness.

Year	Engine	Spark Plugs Ft. Lbs.	Cylinder Head Bolts Ft. Lbs.	Intake Manifold Ft. Lbs.	Exhaust Manifold Ft. Lbs.	Rocker Arm Shaft Bracket Ft. Lbs.	Rocker Arm Cover Ft. Lbs.	Connecting Rod Cap Bolts Ft. Lbs.	Main Bearing Cap Bolts Ft. Lbs.	Flywheel to Crank-shaft Ft. Lbs.	Vibration Damper or Pulley Ft. Lbs.
1983–84	4-122	5–10	①	14–21	②	—	6–8	③	①	56–64	100–120
	4-135④	⑦	80–85	12–17	17–20	—	2.2–3.3	50–54	80–85	95–137	253–286
	4-140	5–10	①	14–21	②	—	6–8	③	①	56–64	100–120
	V6-171	18–28	⑤	⑥	20–30	—	3–5	19–24	65–75	47–52	85–96
1985	4-122, 140	5–10	①	14–21	②	—	6–8	③	①	56–64	100–120
	4-143④⑧	⑦	⑨	11–14	11–14	25–28	4–5	33–34	55–61	94–101	123–137
	V6-171	14–18	⑤	⑥	20–30	—	3–5	19–24	65–75	47–52	85–96

①—Torque bolts in sequence in two steps: Step 1, 50–60 ft. lbs.; Step 2, 80–90 ft. lbs.
②—Torque nuts in sequence in two steps: Step 1, 5–7 ft. lbs.; Step 2, 16–23 ft. lbs.
③—Torque bolts in sequence in two steps: Step 1, 25–30 ft. lbs.; Step 2, 30–36 ft. lbs.
④—Diesel engine.
⑤—Torque bolts in sequence in three steps: Step 1, 29–40 ft. lbs.; Step 2, 40–51 ft. lbs.; Step 3, 70–85 ft. lbs.
⑥—Torque nuts in sequence in four steps after hand starting all nuts and snug-ging nuts 3 and 4: Step 1, 3–6 ft. lbs.; Step 2, 6–11 ft. lbs.; Step 3, 11–15 ft. lbs.; Step 4, 15–18 ft. lbs.
⑦—Glow plugs, 11–15 ft. lbs.
⑧—Turbocharged engine.
⑨—Cold engine, 76–83 ft. lbs.; hot engine 84–90 ft. lbs.

continued

Alternator Specifications

Year	Make or Model	Current Rating		Field Current @ 75°F.	
		Amperes	Volts	Amperes	Volts
1983–85	Orange①②	40	15	4	12
	Green①②	60	15	4	12

①—Color of identification tag.
②—Rear terminal alternator.

Starting Motor Specifications

Year	Starter Type	Ampere Draw Normal Load	Engine Cranking Speed R.P.M.	Minimum Stall Torque @ 5 Volts Ft. Lbs.	Maximum Head Amperes	No Load Ampere @ 12 Volts	Brushes		Spring Tension Ounces
							Length Inch	Wear Limit Inch	
1983–84	4″ Diameter/ gasoline engine	150–200	180–250	—	—	70	.500	.250	40
	4½″ Diameter/ gasoline engine	150–180	150–290	—	—	80	.500	.250	80
	Diesel engine	150–220	①	—	—	—	.669	.452	—
1985	4″ Diameter/ gasoline engine	150–200	180–250	—	—	80	.50	.25	80
	4½″ Diameter/ gasoline engine	150–180	150–290	—	—	80	.50	.25	80
	Diesel engine	②	150–220	—	—	③	.669	④	—

①—Less than 180 RPM.
②—Less than 500 amps.
③—Less than 50 amps.
④—Visible wear mark indicator.

Brake Specifications

Year	Model	Rear Drum I.D.	Wheel Cyl. Bore		Disc Brake Rotor					Master Cyl. I.D.
			Front Disc	Rear Drum	Nominal Thickness	Minimum Thickness	Thickness Variation (Parallelism)	Run Out (TIR)	Finish (microinch)	
1983–84	All	9.0	—	—	.870	.810	—	.003	15–125	2.600
1985	All	9.0	—	—	—	.810	—	.003	15–125	

continued

Drive Axle Specifications

Year	Ring Gear Diameter	Carrier Type	Ring Gear & Pinion Backlash Inch	Nominal Pinion Locating Shim, Inch	Pinion Bearing Preload				Differential Bearing Preload	Pinion Nut Torque Ft. Lbs.
					New Bearings With Seal Inch-Lbs.	Used Bearings With Seal Inch-Lbs.	New Bearings Less Seal Inch-Lbs.	Used Bearings Less Seal Inch-Lbs.		
1983–84	6¾"	Integral	.008–.015	—	—	8–14	16–29	—	.006	140
	7½"	Integral	.008–.015	—	—	8–14	16–29	—	.006	170
	①	Integral	.004–.010	—	—	15–35	15–35	—	.015	200
1985	7½"	Integral	.008–.015	—	—	8–14	16–29	—	.006	170
	8.8"	Integral	.008–.015	—	—	8–14	16–29	—	—	—
	①	Integral	.004–.010	—	—	15–35	15–35	—	.015	200

①—Front drive axle.

Cooling System & Capacity Data

Year	Model or Engine	Cooling Capacity Qts.		Radiator Cap Relief Pressure, Lbs.	Thermo. Opening Temp.	Fuel Tank Gals.	Engine Oil Refill Qts. ①	Transmission Oil			Transfer Case Pints	Rear Axle Oil Pints
		Less A/C	With A/C					4 Speed Pints	5 Speed Pints	Auto. Trans. Qts. ②		
1983–84	4-122	6.5	7.2	13	192	③	4①	3.0	3.0	⑦	—	⑧
	4-135⑤	10.0	10.7	13	—	③	5.5⑥	3.2	3.0	—	—	⑧
	4-140	6.5	7.2	13	192	③	5①	3.0	3.0	⑦	3.0	⑧
	V6-171	7.2	7.8	13	189	③④	4①	3.0	3.0	⑦	3.0	⑧⑨
1985	4-122	⑩	7.8	13	192	③	4①	—	3.0	—	—	⑧
	4-140	⑩	7.2	13	192	③	4①	—	3.0	—	3.0	⑧
	4-143⑤⑪	12	⑫	13	—	③④	6.8⑬	—	—	—	3.0	⑧⑨
	V6-171	7.2	7.8	13	—	③④	4①	—	3.0	—	3.0	⑧⑨

①—Add 1 qt. with filter change.

②—Approximate. Make final check with dipstick.

③—Ranger; all short wheelbase and long wheelbase with man. trans., 15.2 gals.; long wheelbase with auto. trans., 17.0 gals.; auxiliary tank, 13.0 gals.

④—Bronco II, 23.0 gals.

⑤—Diesel engine.

⑥—Add .9 qt. for primary filter replacement & .6 qt. for bypass filter replacement.

⑦—With C-3 transmission, 8.0 qts.; 4 × 2 models with C-5 transmission, 7.5 qts.; 4 × 4 models with C-5 transmission, 7.9 qts.

⑧—Ranger with 6¾ inch ring gear, 3.0 pts.; with 7½ inch ring gear, 5.0 pts.

⑨—Bronco II with 7½ inch ring gear, 5.5 pts.

⑩—Less extra cooling system, 6.5 qts.; w/extra cooling system, 7.2 qts.

⑪—Turbocharged engine.

⑫—Standard cooling system w/AC 13 qts.; extra cooling system w/AC 10.7 qts.

⑬—Includes oil filter change & cooler capacity.

Electrical Section

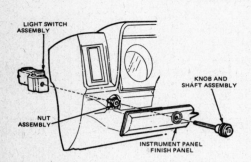

Fig. 1 Light switch replacement

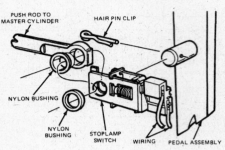

Fig. 2 Stop light switch replacement

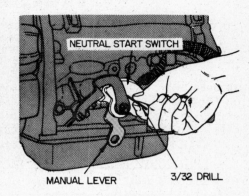

Fig. 3 Neutral safety switch adjustment. C5 automatic transmission

STARTER
REPLACE

EXC. DIESEL ENGINE

1. Disconnect battery ground cable.
2. Raise and support vehicle.
3. Disconnect starter cable from starter.
4. Remove starter motor attaching bolts, then disconnect ground cable and lower starter from vehicle.
5. Reverse procedure to install.

DIESEL ENGINE

4-135
1. Disconnect ground cables from both batteries.
2. Remove air intake hose between intake manifold and air cleaner.
3. Disconnect No. 1 glow plug relay from starter and position aside.
4. Disconnect starter cables, then remove starter motor attaching bolts and the starter motor.
5. Reverse procedure to install.

4-143
1. Disconnect battery ground cables from both battery assemblies.
2. Disconnect, then remove air intake hose between air cleaner and intake manifold.
3. Remove No. 1 glow plug relay from starter motor assembly, then position aside.
4. Mark, then disconnect starter motor solenoid electrical connectors.
5. Remove alternator reinforcement bracket attaching bolt.
6. Remove two starter motor attaching bolts, then the starter motor assembly from vehicle.
7. Reverse procedure to install.

IGNITION LOCK
REPLACE

1. Disconnect battery ground cable (two ground cables on diesel engines).
2. Remove steering column trim shroud, then disconnect electrical connector from key warning switch.
3. Turn lock cylinder to Run position and insert a ⅛ inch wire or pin into hole located on outer edge of lock cylinder housing. Depress retaining pin and remove lock cylinder.
4. To install, turn lock cylinder to Run position, depress retaining pin and insert assembly into housing.
5. Ensure cylinder is fully seated and aligned into interlocking washer, then turn key to Off position to extend cylinder retaining pin into cylinder housing.
6. Turn key to check for proper operation in all positions.
7. Connect key warning switch electrical connector, install steering column trim shroud and reconnect battery ground cable(s).

IGNITION SWITCH
REPLACE

1. Disconnect battery ground cable (two ground cables on diesel engines).
2. Turn lock cylinder key to Lock position.
3. On models equipped with tilt steering column, remove upper extension shroud by depressing top and bottom of shroud and releasing it from retaining plate on left side.
4. On all models, remove steering column trip shroud halves.
5. Disconnect electrical connector from ignition switch.
6. Drill out bolt heads from switch attaching bolts using a ⅛ inch drill, then remove bolts using an "Easy Out" or equivalent.

7. Disengage switch from actuator pin and remove switch from vehicle.
8. Reverse procedure to install. Turn lock cylinder to Run position before installing switch.

LIGHT SWITCH
REPLACE

1. Disconnect battery ground cable (two ground cables on diesel engines).
2. Pull light switch knob out to On position.
3. Depress shaft release button and remove knob and shaft assembly.
4. Remove instrument panel finish panel, **Fig. 1.**
5. Remove bezel nut, lower switch, disconnect electrical connector and remove switch.
6. Reverse procedure to install.

STOP LIGHT SWITCH
REPLACE

1. Disconnect battery ground cable (two ground cables on diesel engines).
2. Disconnect electrical connector from switch.
3. Remove hairpin retainer, then slide switch, push rod, nylon washers and bushings away from pedal and remove switch, **Fig. 2.**
4. Reverse procedure to install.

NEUTRAL SAFETY SWITCH
ADJUST

C5 UNITS

1. Loosen neutral safety switch attaching

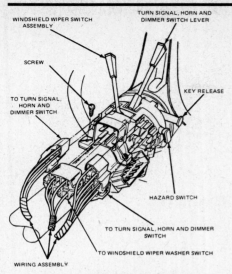

Fig. 4   Turn signal switch replacement

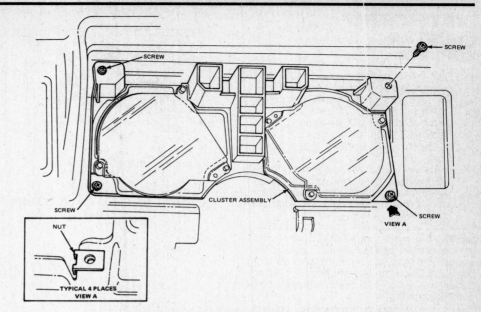

Fig. 5   Instrument cluster replacement

bolts, then position manual lever in Park position.

2. Insert a 3/32 inch drill into switch. Move switch as needed to allow drill to rest against case, **Fig. 3.**
3. Torque switch attaching bolts to 55-75 inch lbs., then remove drill from switch.

A4LD UNITS

1. Disconnect battery ground cable(s).
2. Disconnect neutral start switch electrical harness from switch.
3. Using a suitable tool, remove neutral start switch and O-ring.
4. Install new switch and O-ring.
5. Torque switch to 7–10 ft. lbs.
6. Connect neutral start switch electrical harness on to switch.
7. Connect battery ground cable(s) and check switch operation.

TURN SIGNAL SWITCH
REPLACE

1. Disconnect battery ground cable (two ground cables on diesel engines).
2. On models equipped with tilt steering column, remove upper extension shroud by depressing top and bottom of shroud and releasing it from retaining plate on left side.
3. On all models, remove steering column trim shroud halves.
4. Remove turn signal switch lever by grasping and using a twisting and pulling motion straight out from switch.
5. Peel back foam shield from turn signal switch, then disconnect electrical connectors from switch, **Fig. 4.**
6. Remove 2 turn signal switch attaching screws and the switch.
7. Reverse procedure to install.

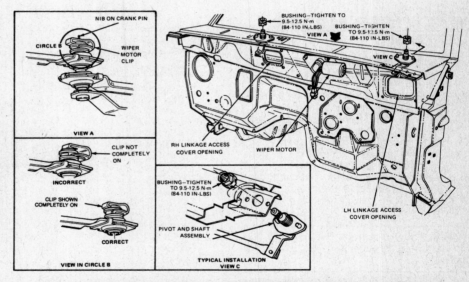

Fig. 6   W/S wiper motor retaining clip removal & W/S wiper transmission replacement

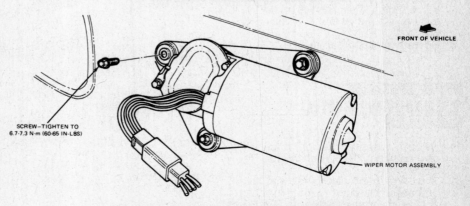

Fig. 7   W/S wiper motor replacement

INSTRUMENT CLUSTER
REPLACE

1. Disconnect battery ground cable (two ground cables on diesel engines).
2. Remove 2 steering column shroud attaching screws and the shroud.
3. Remove lower instrument panel trim.
4. Remove 8 instrument cluster trim cover attaching screws and the trim cover.
5. Remove 4 instrument cluster attaching screws, then pull cluster away slightly from panel and disconnect speedometer cable and all electrical connectors.

NOTE: If there is not sufficient clearance to disconnect speedometer cable from speedometer, it will be necessary to disconnect cable from transmission and route cable through cowl to reach speedometer quick disconnect.

6. Remove cluster from vehicle, **Fig. 5.**
7. Reverse procedure to install.

W/S WIPER MOTOR
REPLACE

1. Cycle windshield wipers until they are in straight up position, then turn ignition off.
2. Disconnect battery ground cable (two ground cables on diesel engines).
3. Remove right hand wiper arm and blade assembly and the pivot nut. Allow linkage to drop into cowl.
4. Remove linkage access cover from right hand side of dash panel.
5. Release wiper motor retaining clip, **Fig. 6,** then slide clip back until it clears nib on crank pin, and remove the clip.

NOTE: The wiper motor retaining clip can be reached through the access cover opening.

6. Remove wiper linkage from motor crank pin.
7. Disconnect electrical connector from wiper motor, then remove motor attaching screws and the motor, **Fig. 7.**
8. Reverse procedure to install.

W/S WIPER TRANSMISSION
REPLACE

1. Perform steps 1 through 6 as described under "W/S Wiper Motor, Replace."
2. Slide right hand pivot shaft and linkage assembly out through right hand access cover opening.
3. Remove left hand wiper arm and

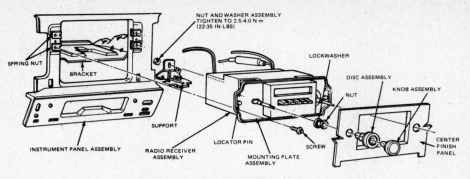

Fig. 8 Radio replacement

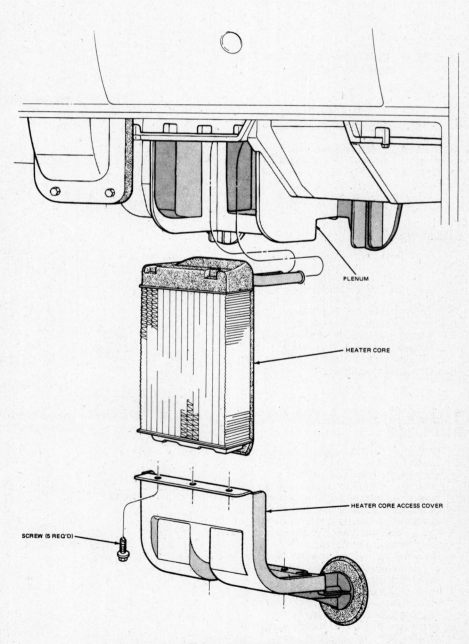

Fig. 9 Heater core replacement

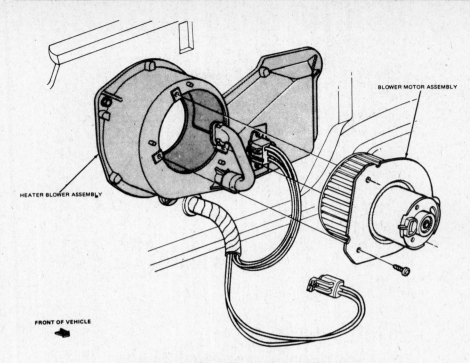

Fig. 10   Blower motor replacement

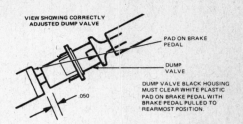

Fig. 11   Vacuum dump valve adjustment

blade assembly.

4. Remove left hand linkage access cover and pivot nut, then lower linkage and slide out through access cover opening, **Fig. 6.**
5. Reverse procedure to install.

W/S WIPER SWITCH
REPLACE

1. Disconnect battery ground cable (two ground cables on diesel engines).
2. Remove steering column trim shrouds, then disconnect electrical connector from switch.
3. Peel back foam shield, then remove wiper switch attaching screws and the switch.
4. Reverse procedure to install.

RADIO
REPLACE

1. Disconnect battery ground cable (two ground cables on diesel engines).
2. Remove control knobs and discs from radio shafts, **Fig. 8.**
3. Remove 2 steering column shroud attaching screws and the shroud.
4. Remove lower instrument panel trim.
5. Remove 8 instrument cluster trim cover attaching screws and the trim cover.
6. Remove 4 radio mounting plate attaching screws, then slide radio with bracket and mounting plate out of dash.
7. Disconnect all electrical connectors from radio, then remove rear support attaching nut.
8. Remove nuts, washers and mounting plate from radio shafts.
9. Remove radio from vehicle.
10. Reverse procedure to install.

HEATER CORE
REPLACE

1. Drain cooling system.
2. Disconnect hoses from heater core. Plug hoses and core openings to prevent leakage of residual coolant.
3. Remove 5 heater core access cover attaching screws and the cover, **Fig. 9.**
4. Remove heater core from passenger compartment.
5. Reverse procedure to install.

BLOWER MOTOR
REPLACE

1. Disconnect battery ground cable (two grounded cables on diesel engines).
2. Remove emission control module forward of blower motor, if equipped.
3. Disconnect electrical connector from blower motor.
4. Remove blower motor attaching screws and the blower motor, **Fig. 10.**
5. Reverse procedure to install.

SPEED CONTROL ADJUSTMENTS

ACTUATOR CABLE, ADJUST

1. Remove cable retaining clip, then disengage throttle positioner.
2. Set carburetor at hot idle.
3. Pull actuator cable to remove slack, then install cable retaining clip while maintaining light tension on cable.

VACUUM DUMP VALVE, ADJUST

1. Depress brake pedal firmly and hold in position.
2. Press in vacuum dump valve until valve collar meets retaining clip, **Fig. 11.**
3. Pull brake pedal firmly rearward to its normal position to allow valve to rachet backwards in retaining clip.
4. Ensure clearance between dump valve housing and white plastic pad on brake pedal is .050-.100 inch with brake pedal retracted to rearmost position.

4-122 & 4-140 Gasoline Engine Section

ENGINE MOUNTS
REPLACE

FRONT

1. Remove nuts from top of insulator brackets.
2. Raise and support vehicle, then lift engine until it clears mounts.
3. Remove attaching screws and mounts.
4. Reverse procedure to install. Refer to **Fig. 1** for torque specifications.

REAR

1. Raise and support vehicle.
2. Remove the two nuts attaching rear insulator to engine support, **Fig. 1.**
3. Using a suitable jack and wood block placed between engine and jack, raise transmission.
4. Remove bolts attaching mount to rear of engine and remove mount.
5. Reverse procedure to install. Torque bolts to 60–80 ft. lbs. and nuts to 71–94 ft. lbs.

ENGINE
REPLACE

EXCEPT 1985 4-140 EFI ENGINE

1. Raise hood, then mark location of hood hinges and remove hood.
2. Disconnect battery ground cable at engine and battery positive cable at battery.
3. Drain coolant from radiator, then remove air cleaner and duct assembly.
4. Remove upper and lower radiator hoses, engine fan, shroud and radiator.
5. Remove oil filler cap.
6. If equipped with air conditioning, remove compressor from mounting bracket and position it aside.
7. Disconnect wires from starter, alternator, ignition coil, water temperature sending unit, and oil pressure sending unit.
8. If equipped with automatic transmission, disconnect transmission kickdown rod.
9. Disconnect heater hoses at engine, and fuel line at fuel pump.
10. Disconnect power brake vacuum hose.
11. Remove engine mount nuts.
12. Raise vehicle, then drain oil from crankcase and remove starter motor.
13. Disconnect exhaust pipe from manifold.

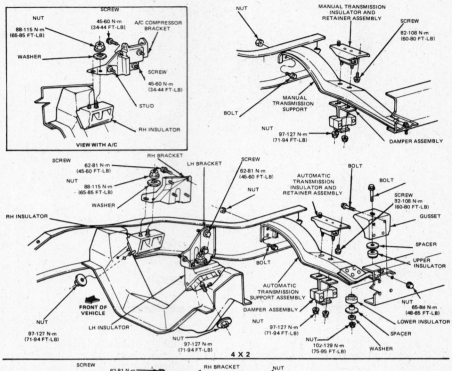

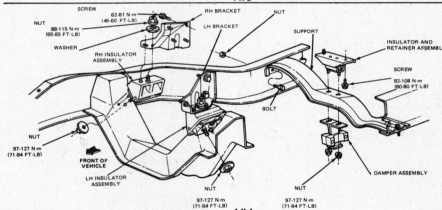

Fig. 1 Front & rear engine mounts

14. Remove dust cover on manual transmission vehicles, or inspection cover on automatic transmission vehicles.
15. On vehicles with manual transmission, remove flywheel housing cover lower bolts. On vehicles with automatic transmission, remove converter-to-flywheel bolts, then remove converter housing lower bolts.
16. On manual transmission vehicles, remove slave cylinder.
17. Lower vehicle, then support transmission using a floor jack.
18. Remove flywheel housing or converter housing bolts.
19. Using a suitable hoist, remove engine from vehicle.
20. Reverse procedure to install.

1985 4-140 EFI ENGINE

1. Raise hood, mark hood hinge locations, then remove hood.
2. Drain coolant from radiator.
3. Disconnect air cleaner outlet tube from throttle body, idle speed control hose and heat riser tube.
4. Disconnect battery cables.
5. Disconnect upper and lower radiator hoses from engine.
6. Remove radiator shroud attaching screws, radiator upper supports, then the shroud and fan assembly.
7. Remove radiator.
8. Remove oil filler cap.
9. Disconnect coil wire from coil.
10. Mark, then disconnect all electrical

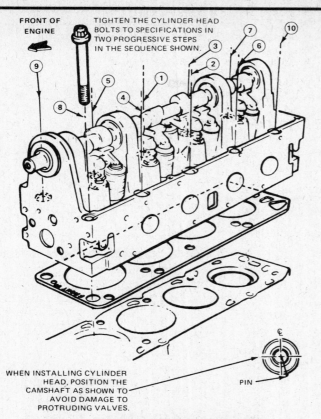

FRONT OF ENGINE

TIGHTEN THE CYLINDER HEAD BOLTS TO SPECIFICATIONS IN TWO PROGRESSIVE STEPS IN THE SEQUENCE SHOWN.

WHEN INSTALLING CYLINDER HEAD, POSITION THE CAMSHAFT AS SHOWN TO AVOID DAMAGE TO PROTRUDING VALVES.

PIN

Fig. 2   Cylinder head installation

FRONT OF ENGINE

TIGHTEN THE CYLINDER HEAD BOLTS TO SPECIFICATION IN TWO PROGRESSIVE STEPS IN THE SEQUENCE SHOWN

CAMSHAFT 6250

CYLINDER HEAD ASSEMBLY 6049

VIEW A

DOWEL 6A008 (2 PLACES)

GASKET 6051

CYLINDER BLOCK ASSEMBLY 6010

CAMSHAFT 90° TO PAN RAIL

14.0-14.5 mm (0.55-0.57 INCH)

CAMSHAFT 6250

30.9°
38.9°

VIEW A

SECTION B

NOTE: PRIOR TO CYLINDER HEAD INSTALLATION, CAMSHAFT MUST BE POSITIONED AS SHOWN TO PROTECT PROTRUDING VALVES

Fig. 3   Cylinder head bolt tightening sequence. 4-140 EFI engine

connectors and vacuum hoses from engine.
11. Disconnect accelerator cable and transmission kickdown rod, if equipped.
12. Remove A/C compressor from mounting bracket and position aside.

NOTE: Do not disconnect refrigerant lines from A/C compressor.

13. Disconnect power brake vacuum hose.
14. Disconnect two push connector fittings from engine fuel rail.
15. Disconnect heater hoses from engine.
16. Remove engine mount nuts.
17. Raise and support vehicle.
18. Drain engine oil from crankcase.
19. Remove starter motor.
20. Disconnect exhaust pipe from exhaust manifold.
21. Remove dust cover or torque converter inspection plate, if equipped.
22. On vehicles equipped with manual transmission, remove flywheel housing cover attaching bolts. On vehicles equipped with automatic transmission, remove torque converter to flywheel attaching bolts.
23. Lower vehicle.
24. Support transmission and flywheel or converter housing with a suitable jack.
25. Remove flywheel housing or converter housing upper attaching bolts.
26. Install suitable engine lifting equipment on to engine, then carefully raise

engine from vehicle.
27. Reverse procedure to install.

CYLINDER HEAD
REPLACE
REMOVAL

1. Disconnect battery ground cable.
2. Drain cooling system, then remove air cleaner assembly.
3. Remove heater hose to rocker arm cover retaining screw.
4. Remove distributor cap and spark plug wires, then the spark plugs.
5. Disconnect vacuum hoses as necessary.
6. Remove dipstick and rocker arm cover.
7. Remove intake manifold retaining bolts.
8. Remove alternator belt and alternator bracket-to-cylinder head bolts.
9. Remove upper radiator hose.
10. Remove timing belt cover. On vehicles with power steering, remove power steering pump bracket bolts.
11. Loosen cam idler retaining bolts, then position idler in the unloaded position and tighten bolts.
12. Remove timing belt.
13. Remove heated air intake pipe and exhaust manifold bolts.
14. Remove timing belt idler, the two bracket bolts and idler spring from cylinder head.
15. Disconnect oil pressure sending unit lead wire.
16. Remove cylinder head bolts and cylin-

der head.
17. Thoroughly clean all gasket surfaces, then blow out oil out of the cylinder head bolt block holes.

INSTALLATION

1. Position cylinder head gasket on to engine block.
2. Clean rocker arm cover (cam cover).
3. Using suitable contact cement, install rocker cover gasket on to rocker cover.
4. Install cylinder head attaching bolts and torque in sequence and to specifications, **Figs. 2 and 3.**
5. Connect oil sending unit electrical connector(s).
6. Install cam belt (timing belt) idler spring stop on to cylinder head.
7. Position cam belt idler on to cylinder head and install attaching bolts.
8. Install exhaust manifold attaching bolts and/or stud bolts.
9. Install heat air intake pipe to exhaust manifold.
10. Align distributor rotor with number one plug location in the distributor cap.
11. Align cam gear with pointer.
12. Align crank pulley (TDC) with pointer on cam belt cover.
13. Position cam belt on to cam and auxiliary pulleys.
14. Loosen idler retaining bolts, rotate engine and check timing alignment.
15. Adjust belt tensioner, then tighten bolts.
16. Install cam belt cover attaching bolts.
17. Install upper radiator hose on to

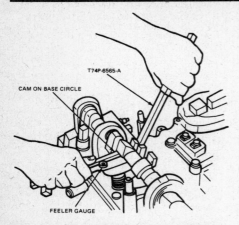

Fig. 4 Collapsing lash adjuster

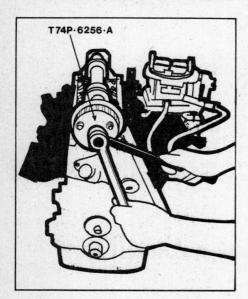

Fig. 7 Camshaft or auxiliary shaft sprocket removal

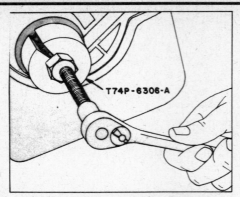

Fig. 5 Crankshaft sprocket removal

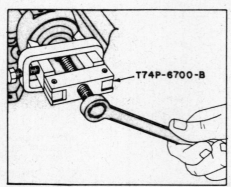

Fig. 8 Camshaft or auxiliary shaft seal removal

VALVE LIFT SPECS.

Engine	Year	Intake	Exhaust
4-122	1983–85	.390	.390
4-140	1983–84	.390	.390
4-140EFI	1985	.400	.400

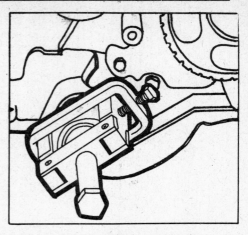

Fig. 6 Crankshaft front oil seal removal

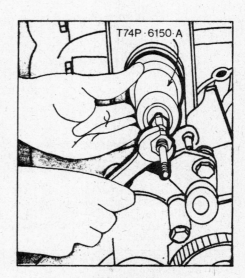

Fig. 9 Camshaft seal installation

engine and radiator assembly, then tighten retaining clamps.
18. Position alternator bracket on to cylinder head and install retainers.
19. Position drive belt on to pulley and adjust belt tension.
20. Position intake manifold to head and install attaching bolts.
21. Install rocker arm cover and attaching bolts.
22. Install spark plugs and dipstick.
23. Connect all vacuum hoses and spark plug wires.
24. Install air cleaner assembly.

VALVE ARRANGEMENT
FRONT TO REAR

All Engines . . . . E-I-E-I-E-I-E-I

F—14

VALVE GUIDES

Valve guides consist of holes bored in the cylinder head. For service the guides can be reamed oversize to accommodate valves with oversize stems of .015 inch and .030 inch.

VALVES
ADJUST

The valve lash on this engine cannot be adjusted due to the use of hydraulic valve lash adjusters. However, the valve train can be checked for wear as follows:
1. Crank engine to position camshaft with flat section of lobe facing rocker arm of valve being checked.
2. Collapse lash adjuster with tool T74P-6565A and insert correct size feeler gauge between rocker arm and camshaft lobe, **Fig. 4.** If clearance is not as listed in the "Valve Specifications"

chart in front of this chapter, remove rocker arm and check for wear and replace as necessary. If rocker arm is found satisfactory, check valve spring assembled height and adjust as needed. If valve spring assembled height is within specifications listed in the front of this chapter, remove lash adjuster and clean or replace as necessary.

ROCKER ARM SERVICE

1. Remove rocker arm cover.
2. Rotate camshaft until flat section of lobe faces rocker being removed.
3. Collapse lash adjuster and, if necessary, valve spring and slide rocker arm over lash adjuster, **Fig. 4.**
4. Reverse procedure to install.

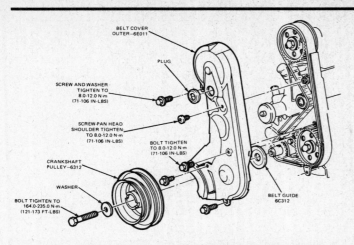

Fig. 10 Timing belt outer cover. Exploded view

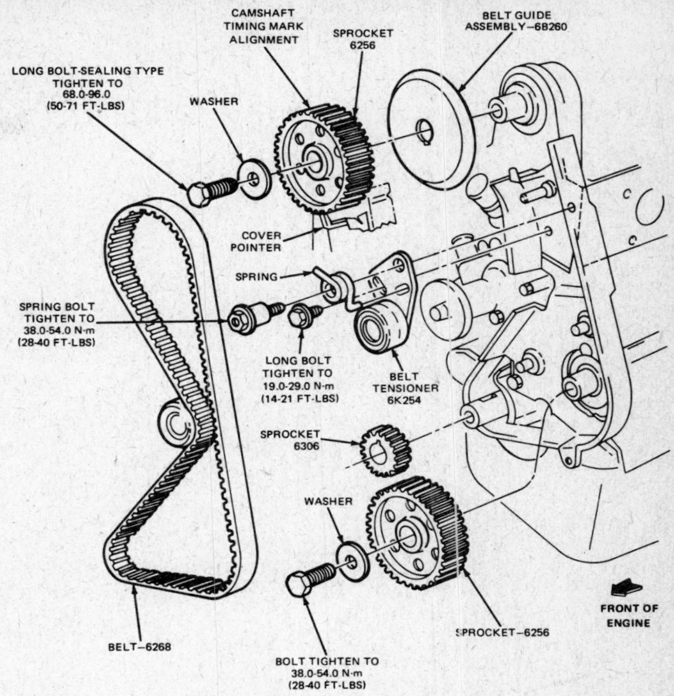

Fig. 11 Timing belt drive train

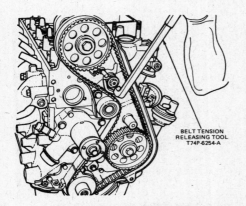

Fig. 12 Retracting belt tensioner

LASH ADJUSTERS
REPLACE

The hydraulic valve lash adjusters can be replaced after rocker arm removal.

FRONT ENGINE SEALS
REPLACE

CRANKSHAFT OIL SEAL

1. Remove crankshaft sprocket with tool T74P-6306-A, **Fig. 5.**
2. Remove crankshaft oil seal with tool A7082-1A, **Fig. 6.**
3. Install a new crankshaft oil seal with tool T74P-6150-A.
4. Install crankshaft sprocket with tool T74P-6306-A.

CAMSHAFT & AUXILIARY SHAFT OIL SEALS

1. Remove camshaft or auxiliary shaft sprocket with tool T74P-6256-A, **Fig. 7.**
2. Remove camshaft or auxiliary shaft seal with tool T74P-6700-B, **Fig. 8.**
3. Install a new oil seal with tool T74P-6150-A, **Fig. 9.**

4. Install camshaft or auxiliary shaft sprocket with tool T74P-6256-A with center arbor removed.

TIMING BELT
CHECKING BELT TIMING

1. Remove timing belt cover access plug, **Fig. 10.**
2. Rotate crankshaft in engine normal direction of rotation until TDC is reached. This is obtained by aligning the crankshaft pulley mark with the TC mark on the belt cover.

NOTE: Never rotate engine against normal rotation, as this may cause the timing belt to jump time.

3. While looking through the belt cover access hole, ensure the timing mark on the camshaft sprocket is aligned with the pointer on the inner belt cover.
4. Remove distributor cap to ensure the distributor rotor is pointed towards the distributor cap No. 1 firing position.
5. If belt timing is satisfactory, install distributor cap and belt cover access plug. If belt timing is unsatisfactory, refer to "Adjustment or Replacement" procedure.

ADJUSTMENT OR REPLACEMENT

1. Remove Thermactor pump drive belt, then the fan and water pump pulley.

2. Remove alternator drive belt, then drain cooling system and remove upper radiator hose.
3. Remove crankshaft pulley, then the thermostat housing and gasket.
4. On models equipped with power steering, disconnect power steering pump from bracket and position aside.
5. On all models, remove timing belt outer cover attaching bolts and the cover, **Fig. 10.**
6. Loosen belt tensioner adjustment bolt, **Fig. 11.**
7. Using tool, T74P-6254-A positioned on tension spring rollpin, retract tensioner, then tighten adjustment screw to hold tensioner in retracted position, **Fig. 12.**
8. Remove crankshaft pulley and belt guide, **Fig. 10.**
9. Remove timing belt and inspect for signs of wear and damage. Replace as necessary.
10. Refer to **Fig. 13,** for proper camshaft and crankshaft sprocket position.
11. Remove distributor cap, then set distributor rotor to No. 1 firing position by turning the auxiliary shaft as necessary.
12. Install timing belt on crankshaft sprocket, then working counterclockwise, position belt on auxiliary sprocket and camshaft sprocket. Ensure timing marks do not change position.
13. Align belt on sprockets, then loosen tensioner adjustment bolt to allow tensioner to move against the belt.
14. Remove spark plugs.

NOTE: Failure to remove spark plugs, may

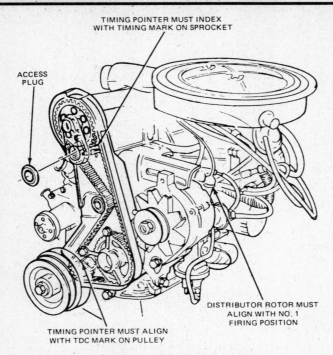

Fig. 13   Timing belt installation

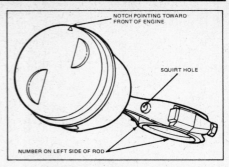

Fig. 14   Piston & rod

result in timing belt jumping time during next step.

15. Rotate engine in normal direction of rotation for two complete turns to remove slack from belt. Tighten tensioner adjustment and pivot bolts to specifications given in **Fig. 11**.
16. Recheck timing mark alignment, then install crankshaft pulley and belt guide.
17. Install timing belt cover, refer to **Fig. 10** for torque specifications. Install spark plugs.
18. Start engine and set ignition timing to specifications.

CAMSHAFT
REPLACE

1. Disconnect battery ground cable, then drain cooling system and remove air cleaner.
2. Disconnect ignition wires and position aside.
3. Disconnect any vacuum hoses interfering with camshaft removal.
4. Remove rocker arm cover, then remove alternator belt.
5. Remove alternator mounting bracket retaining bolts and position aside.
6. Remove upper radiator hose, then remove fan shroud retaining bolts and fan shroud.
7. Remove cam belt cover retaining bolts and cover.
8. If vehicle is equipped with power steering, remove power steering pump bracket.
9. Loosen idler cam retaining bolts, then position idler in the unloaded position

and tighten retaining bolts.
10. Remove timing belt from cam and auxiliary pulleys.
11. Remove rocker arms as described under "Rocker Arm Service", then remove gear and seal as described under "Front Engine Seals, Replace".
12. Remove camshaft rear retainer.
13. Raise and support vehicle.
14. Remove right and left engine support bolts and nuts, then position a suitable transmission jack under engine.
15. Place a block of wood on transmission jack, raise engine as high as possible and position blocks of wood between engine mounts and chassis bracket, then remove jack.
16. Carefully remove camshaft from front of head.
17. Reverse procedure to install.

PISTON & ROD
ASSEMBLE

Assemble rod to piston with arrow on top of piston facing front of engine, **Fig. 14**.

CRANKSHAFT OIL
SEAL

1. Remove oil pump retaining bolts if necessary.
2. Insert small sheet metal screws into seal and pull screws to remove seal.
3. Install new seal with tool T82L-6701-A, **Fig. 15**.

OIL PAN
REPLACE

1. Remove air cleaner assembly, engine oil dipstick and engine mount attaching nuts.
2. On models equipped with automatic transmission, disconnect transmission oil cooler lines from radiator.
3. On all models, remove fan shroud.
4. On models equipped with automatic transmission, remove radiator attaching bolts, then lift radiator up and wire it to the hood.
5. On all models, raise and support vehicle.
6. Drain engine oil, then remove starting motor.
7. Disconnect exhaust pipe to inlet pipe bracket from Thermactor check valve.
8. Remove transmission mount-to-crossmember attaching nuts.
9. On models equipped with automatic transmission, remove converter housing bellcrank, oil cooler lines and front crossmember.
10. On models equipped with manual transmission, disconnect right front lower shock absorber mount.
11. On all models, raise engine with a suitable jack, then place a 2½ inch block of wood under engine and remove jack.
12. On models equipped with automatic transmission, raise transmission slightly with a suitable jack.
13. On all models, remove oil pan attaching bolts and the oil pan.

NOTE: The oil pan must be removed out of the front of the engine compartment on models equipped with automatic transmission, and out of the rear of the engine compartment on models equipped with manual transmission.

14. Reverse procedure to install. Refer to **Fig. 16** for torque specifications.

OIL PUMP
REPLACE

1. Remove oil pan as described under "Oil Pan, Replace."
2. Remove oil pump and pick-up tube

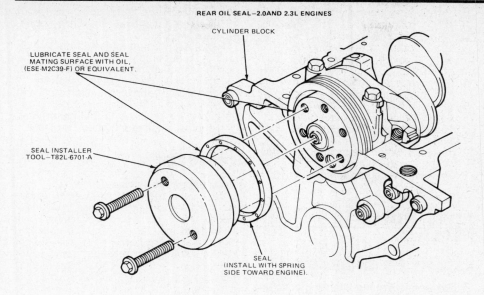

REAR OIL SEAL—2.0 AND 2.3L ENGINES

CYLINDER BLOCK

LUBRICATE SEAL AND SEAL MATING SURFACE WITH OIL, (ESE-M2C39-F) OR EQUIVALENT.

SEAL INSTALLER TOOL—T82L-6701-A

SEAL (INSTALL WITH SPRING SIDE TOWARD ENGINE).

NOTE: REAR FACE OF SEAL MUST BE WITHIN 0.127mm (0.005-INCH) OF THE REAR FACE OF THE BLOCK.

Fig. 15   Crankshaft rear oil seal replacement

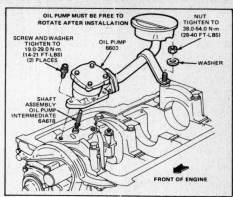

OIL PUMP MUST BE FREE TO ROTATE AFTER INSTALLATION

NUT TIGHTEN TO 38.0-54.0 N·m (28-40 FT-LBS)

SCREW AND WASHER TIGHTEN TO 19.0-29.0 N·m (14-21 FT-LBS) (2) PLACES

OIL PUMP 6600

WASHER

SHAFT ASSEMBLY OIL PUMP INTERMEDIATE 6A618

FRONT OF ENGINE

Fig. 17   Oil pump replacement

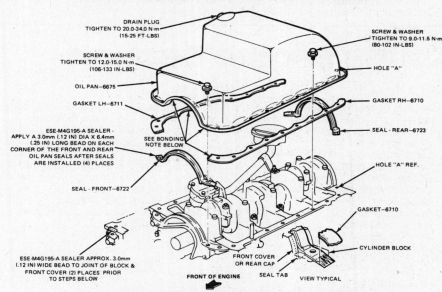

DRAIN PLUG TIGHTEN TO 20.0-34.0 N·m (15-25 FT-LBS)

SCREW & WASHER TIGHTEN TO 9.0-11.5 N·m (80-102 IN-LBS)

SCREW & WASHER TIGHTEN TO 12.0-15.0 N·m (106-133 IN-LBS)

OIL PAN—6675

GASKET LH—6711

HOLE "A"

GASKET RH—6710

SEAL - REAR—6723

ESE-M4G195-A SEALER - APPLY A 3.0mm (.12 IN) DIA X 6.4mm (.25 IN) LONG BEAD ON EACH CORNER OF THE FRONT AND REAR OIL PAN SEALS AFTER SEALS ARE INSTALLED (4) PLACES

SEE BONDING NOTE BELOW

HOLE "A" REF.

SEAL - FRONT—6722

GASKET—6710

CYLINDER BLOCK

ESE-M4G195-A SEALER APPROX. 3.0mm (.12 IN) WIDE BEAD TO JOINT OF BLOCK & FRONT COVER (2) PLACES PRIOR TO STEPS BELOW

FRONT COVER OR REAR CAP

SEAL TAB

VIEW TYPICAL

FRONT OF ENGINE

THERMAL BONDING INSTRUCTIONS - OIL PAN GASKETS TO BE BONDED SECURELY TO OIL PAN USING A THERMAL PROCESS MEETING THE REQUIREMENTS OF THE (ES-DOAE-6584-A OR EQUIVALENT) ADHESIVE COATING SPECIFICATION - IF NECESSARY IN PLACE OF THERMAL BONDING USE ADHESIVE (ESE-M2G52-A OR B OR EQUIVALENT) APPLY EVENLY TO OIL PAN FLANGE & TO PAN SIDE OF GASKETS - ALLOW ADHESIVE TO DRY PAST "WET" STAGE THEN INSTALL GASKETS TO OIL PAN.

1. APPLY SEALER AS NOTED ABOVE
2. INSTALL SEALS TO FRONT COVER & REAR BEARING CAP - PRESS SEAL TABS FIRMLY INTO BLOCK
3. INSTALL (2) GUIDE PINS
4. INSTALL OIL PAN OVER GUIDE PINS & SECURE WITH (4) BOLTS
5. INSTALL (18) BOLTS
6. TORQUE ALL BOLTS IN SEQUENCE CLOCKWISE FROM HOLE "A" AS NOTED ABOVE

Fig. 16   Oil pan replacement

NOTE: INNER TO OUTER ROTOR TIP CLEARANCE MUST NOT EXCEED 0.25mm (.012 IN) WITH FEELER GAUGE INSERTED 13mm (1/2") MINIMUM AND ROTORS REMOVED FROM PUMP HOUSING.

Fig. 18   Checking oil pump inner rotor tip clearance

assembly attaching bolts.
3. Remove oil pump and pick-up tube assembly from vehicle, **Fig. 17.**
4. Reverse procedure to install.

OIL PUMP REPAIRS

1. Inspect inside of pump housing, outer race and rotor for excessive wear or

scoring.
2. Inspect mating surface of pump cover for excessive wear, or scoring. Either of these conditions will necessitate replacement of pump.
3. Measure inner rotor tip clearance, **Fig. 18.**
4. Measure rotor end play, **Fig. 19.** Maximum end play is .004 inch.
5. Check driveshaft to housing bearing

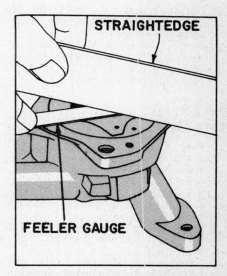

STRAIGHTEDGE

FEELER GAUGE

Fig. 19   Checking oil pump rotor end play

clearance. This measurement should be .0015–.0030 inch.

NOTE: Individual components of oil pump are not serviced. If any part of pump requires replacement, the entire pump assembly must be replaced.

6. Check relief valve spring tension. This should be 15.2–17.2 Lbs. @ 1.20 inches.
7. Inspect relief valve piston for scores and free operation in bore.

BELT TENSION DATA

	New Lbs.	Used Lbs.
A/C Compressor	170	150
A.I.R. Pump	70	50
Alternator	170	150
Power Steering Pump	170	150

WATER PUMP
REPLACE

1. Drain cooling system, then remove fan shroud attaching bolts and position shroud over fan.
2. Remove fan retaining bolts, then the fan and shroud assembly.
3. If equipped, remove A/C compressor and/or power steering pump drive belts.
4. Remove water pump pulley, then the vent tube to canister.
5. Remove heater hose to water pump, then the timing belt outer cover.
6. Remove lower radiator hose from water pump.
7. Remove water pump attaching bolts and the water pump.
8. Reverse procedure to install.

FUEL PUMP
REPLACE

EXCEPT EFI ENGINES

1. Loosen fuel pump attaching bolts one or two turns and apply hand force to pump to loosen gasket.
2. Rotate engine until fuel pump cam lobe is near its low position to reduce pressure on pump.
3. Disconnect fuel lines from pump.
4. Remove fuel pump attaching bolts and the pump. Remove and discard gasket.
5. Clean all gasket material from engine and fuel pump.
6. Install attaching bolts into fuel pump, then install new gasket over bolts.
7. Install bolts and torque alternately and evenly to 18 ft. lbs.
8. Connect fuel lines to fuel pump, then operate engine and check for leaks.

EFI ENGINES

High Pressure Pump

The high pressure fuel pump is frame mounted and can be accessed from under the vehicle. The fuel pump assembly is retained to the frame with three attaching bolts. Before removing the fuel pump, relieve fuel system pressure using either the tool on the fuel diagnostic valve or by opening the electrical circuit to the fuel pump and cranking the engine for a minimum of 20 seconds.

Low Pressure Pump

The low pressure fuel pump is mounted within the fuel tank and may require fuel tank removal for fuel pump service.

V6-171 Gasoline Engine Section

ENGINE MOUNTS
REPLACE

1. Remove fan shroud attaching screws, then support engine using a suitable jack and block of wood under oil pan.
2. Remove insulator-to-crossmember attaching nuts and washers, then raise engine until insulator stud clears crossmember.
3. Remove fuel pump shield-to-left side engine bracket attaching bolt, if necessary.
4. Remove mount-to-cylinder block attaching bolts and the mount, **Fig. 1.**
5. Reverse procedure to install. Refer to **Fig. 1** for torque specifications.

ENGINE
REPLACE

1. Disconnect battery ground cable.
2. Scribe hood hinge locations and remove hood from vehicle.
3. Remove air cleaner and intake duct assembly.
4. Disconnect upper and lower radiator hoses from radiator.
5. Remove fan shroud attaching bolts and position shroud over fan.
6. Remove radiator and fan shroud.
7. Remove alternator and bracket, and position aside. Disconnect alternator ground wire from engine.
8. If equipped, disconnect A/C compressor and/or power steering pump from mounting bracket and position aside.
9. Disconnect heater hoses from cylinder block and water pump.
10. Disconnect or remove Thermactor system components interfering with engine removal.
11. Disconnect ground wires from cylinder block.
12. Disconnect and plug fuel pump feed line at fuel pump.
13. Disconnect throttle cable linkage from carburetor and intake manifold.
14. Disconnect primary wires from ignition coil, then the brake booster vacuum line.
15. Disconnect oil pressure sender and engine coolant temperature sender electrical connections.
16. Raise and support vehicle.
17. Disconnect exhaust pipes from exhaust manifolds.

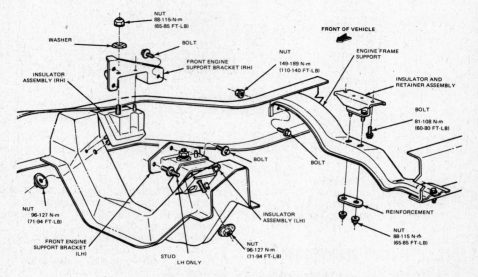

Fig. 1   Engine mounts

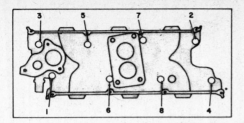

Fig. 2   Intake manifold bolt tightening sequence

18. Remove starter motor.
19. Remove engine front mount-to-cross-member attaching nuts or through bolts.
20. On vehicles equipped with automatic transmission, remove converter inspection cover, then disconnect flywheel from converter. Remove kickdown rod, then the converter housing-to-cylinder block attaching bolts and adapter plate-to-converter housing bolt. Lower vehicle.
21. On vehicles equipped with manual transmission, remove clutch linkage, then lower the vehicle.
22. On all models, attach suitable engine lifting equipment to brackets at exhaust manifolds and support transmission with a suitable jack, then carefully lift engine from vehicle.
23. Reverse procedure to install.

CYLINDER HEAD
REPLACE

1. Disconnect battery ground cable and drain cooling system.
2. Remove air cleaner, then disconnect throttle linkage from carburetor.
3. Remove distributor cap and wires as an assembly and disconnect distributor wiring harness.
4. Mark relationship of distributor rotor to housing for installation reference, and remove distributor from vehicle.
5. Remove radiator and bypass hoses from thermostat housing and intake

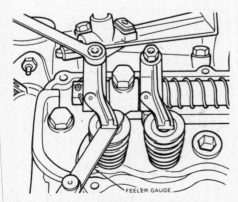

FEELER GAUGE

Fig. 4   Adjusting valve clearance

manifold.
6. Remove rocker arm covers and rocker arm shafts as described under "Rocker Arm Service."
7. Disconnect fuel line from carburetor and remove carburetor from vehicle.
8. Remove intake manifold.
9. Remove pushrods in order so they can be installed in their original positions.
10. Remove exhaust manifolds.
11. Remove cylinder head attaching bolts and the cylinder head.
12. Reverse procedure to install. Torque intake manifold attaching bolts to specifications in sequence shown in **Fig. 2**, and cylinder head attaching bolts to specifications in sequence shown in **Fig. 3**.

VALVE ARRANGEMENT
FRONT TO REAR

Right Bank . . . . I-E-I-E-I
Left Bank . . . . I-E-I-E-I

VALVE LIFT SPECS.

Engine Year		Intake	Exhaust
V6-171	1983–85	.3730	.3730

VALVE GUIDES

Valve guides consist of holes bored in the cylinder head. For service, the guides can be reamed oversize to accommodate valves with oversize stems of .008, .016 and .032 inch.

VALVES
ADJUST

1. Remove rocker arm cover as described in "Rocker Arm Service."
2. Rotate engine slightly until cylinder No. 5 intake valve just begins to open. This can be verified by placing a finger on intake valve rocker arm adjusting screw for cylinder No. 5 and feeling for movement while turning engine.
3. Adjust intake and exhaust valves on No. 1 cylinder to specifications by tightening or loosening adjusting screw as necessary, **Fig. 4**.
4. Adjust remaining valves in firing order by positioning cam according to chart, **Fig. 5**.

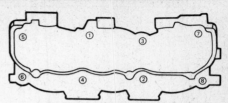

Fig. 3   Cylinder head bolt tightening sequence

NOTE: When checking valve clearance, insert feeler gauge between valve tip and rocker arm at front or rear of valve tip and move gauge in a forward or rearward motion parallel to the crankshaft centerline. If feeler gauge is inserted at outboard edge and moved perpendicular to crankshaft centerline, a false indication will be given, resulting in tight valve clearance.

ROCKER ARM SERVICE

1. Remove air cleaner assembly, then disconnect ignition wires from spark plugs.
2. Remove PCV valve and vacuum hose.
3. Remove carburetor choke air deflector shield.
4. Remove rocker arm cover attaching screws and reinforcement plates. Mark washers so they can be reinstalled in their original positions.
5. Drain transmission fluid, then remove level indicator tube and bracket from rocker arm cover.
6. On vehicles equipped with automatic transmission, disconnect kickdown linkage from carburetor.
7. On all models, move Thermactor air hose and wiring harness away from right side rocker arm cover, then remove engine oil fill cap.
8. Disconnect vacuum line from canister purge solenoid and the line between canister and solenoid.
9. On models equipped with power brakes, disconnect power brake booster hose.
10. On all models, remove rocker arm covers. It may be necessary to lightly tap covers with a plastic hammer to break seal.
11. Loosen rocker arm shaft attaching bolts in sequence two turns at a time, then remove bolts and the rocker arm and shaft assembly.

To adjust both valves for cylinder number	1	4	2	5	3	6
The intake valve must be opening for cylinder number	5	3	6	1	4	2

Fig. 5   Valve clearance adjustment chart

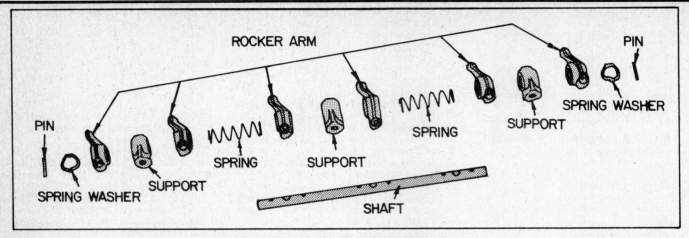

Fig. 6   Rocker arm shaft assembly

12. Disassemble rocker arm shaft assembly as shown in **Fig. 6.**
13. Reverse procedure to assemble and install. Refer to **Fig. 7** to install rocker arm cover reinforcement pieces.

LASH ADJUSTERS
REPLACE

The valve lash adjusters can be replaced after cylinder head removal.

ENGINE FRONT COVER
REPLACE

NOTE: The front cover oil seal can be replaced without removing the front cover, using tool No. 1175-AC or equivalent and a suitable slide hammer, **Fig. 8.**

1. Remove oil pan as described in "Oil Pan, Replace."
2. Drain cooling system, then remove radiator.
3. Remove alternator, Thermactor pump and drive belts.
4. Remove fan, then the water pump as described in "Water Pump, Replace."
5. Remove heater and radiator hoses, then the crankshaft pulley.
6. Remove front cover attaching bolts and the cover. It may be necessary to lightly tap covers with a plastic hammer to break seal.
7. Drive oil seal out of cover using tool No. T74P-6019-A or equivalent, **Fig. 9.**
8. Reverse procedure to install.

TIMING GEARS
REPLACE

1. Remove camshaft gear as described in "Camshaft, Replace."

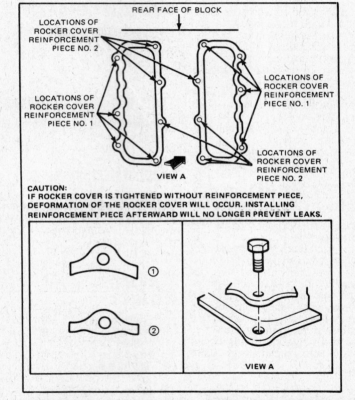

Fig. 7   Rocker arm cover reinforcement installation

2. Remove crankshaft gear using a suitable puller and a shaft protection sleeve.
3. Reverse procedure to install, ensuring marks on gears are properly aligned, **Fig. 10.**

CAMSHAFT
REPLACE

1. Disconnect battery ground cable, then drain engine oil.
2. Remove radiator, fan and spacer, drive belt and pulley.
3. Disconnect ignition wires from spark plugs.
4. Remove distributor cap and wires as an assembly, then disconnect distributor wiring harness and vacuum hose.
5. Mark relationship of distributor rotor to housing for installation reference, and remove distributor from vehicle.
6. Remove alternator and Thermactor pump.
7. Disconnect fuel lines, then remove fuel filter and carburetor.
8. Remove intake manifold.
9. Remove rocker arm covers and rocker

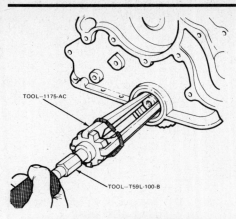

Fig. 8 Front cover oil seal removal with cover installed

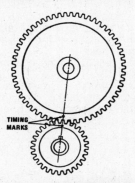

Fig. 10 Valve timing marks

arm shafts as described in "Rocker Arm Service."
10. Remove pushrods in order so they can be installed in their original positions.
11. Remove valve lash adjusters, then the oil pan as described in "Oil Pan, Replace."
12. Remove crankshaft damper, then the engine front cover and water pump as an assembly.
13. Remove camshaft gear attaching bolt and the gear.
14. Remove camshaft thrust plate, then carefully slide camshaft out of engine block.
15. Reverse procedure to install.

PISTON & ROD
ASSEMBLE

Assemble rod to piston with notches on top of piston facing front of engine, **Fig. 11**.

CRANKSHAFT OIL SEAL
REPLACE

1. Remove transmission assembly, and on models equipped with manual transmission, the clutch pressure plate and disc.
2. Remove flywheel, flywheel housing and rear plate.
3. Punch two holes in seal on opposite sides of crankshaft directly above bearing cap-to-cylinder block split line. Insert a sheet metal screw into each hole.
4. Remove oil seal by prying against screws with two screwdrivers.

NOTE: Use care to avoid scratching the crankshaft oil seal surface.

5. Clean oil seal groove in main bearing cap and cylinder block.
6. Reverse procedure to install. Apply suitable lubricant to new seal and install using tool No. T72C-6165 or equivalent.

OIL PAN
REPLACE

1. Disconnect battery ground cable.
2. Remove air cleaner assembly and fan shroud. Place shroud over fan.
3. Disconnect distributor cap with wires and position forward of dash panel. Remove distributor and cover bore opening.
4. Remove front engine mount-to-crossmember attaching nuts.
5. Remove engine oil dipstick tube.
6. Raise and support vehicle.
7. Drain engine oil.
8. On vehicles equipped with automatic transmission, remove transmission filler tube and plug pan hole.
9. On all models, remove oil filter, then disconnect exhaust pipes from exhaust manifolds.
10. Disconnect oil cooler bracket and lower cooler, if equipped.
11. Remove starter motor.
12. On vehicles equipped with automatic transmission, disconnect transmission oil cooler lines and position aside.
13. On all models, disconnect stabilizer bar and move forward.
14. Raise engine as high as possible using a suitable jack, then place wooden blocks between front engine mounts and crossmember. Lower engine to rest on wooden blocks and remove jack.
15. Remove oil pan attaching bolts and the oil pan.
16. Reverse procedure to install, using new oil pan gaskets.

OIL PUMP
REPLACE

1. Remove oil pan as described in "Oil Pan, Replace."
2. Remove oil pick-up screen and oil pump attaching bolts, then the oil pump and pump driveshaft.
3. Reverse procedure to install.

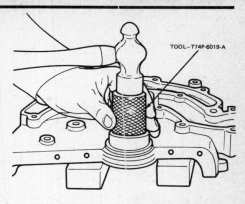

Fig. 9 Front cover oil seal removal with cover removed

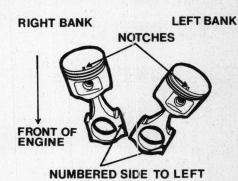

Fig. 11 Piston & rod assembly

OIL PUMP REPAIRS

1. Inspect inside of pump housing, outer race and rotor for excessive wear or scoring.
2. Inspect mating surface of pump cover for excessive wear or scoring. Either of these conditions will necessitate replacement of pump.
3. Measure inner rotor tip clearance, **Fig. 12.**
4. Measure rotor end play, **Fig. 13,** which should not exceed .004 inch.
5. Check driveshaft to housing bearing clearance. This measurement should be .0015–.0030 inch.
6. Measure relief valve spring tension, which should be 13.6–14.7 lbs. measured at a length of 1.39 inches.
7. Inspect relief valve piston for scores and ensure its free operation in bore.

NOTE: Individual oil pump components are not serviced. If any part of pump requires replacement, entire pump assembly must be replaced.

BELT TENSION DATA

	New Lbs.	Used Lbs.
1983–85 All	140	120

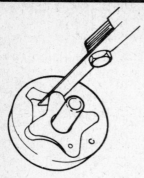

NOTE:
WITH ROTOR ASSEMBLY REMOVED FROM THE PUMP AND RESTING ON A FLAT SURFACE, THE INNER AND OUTER ROTOR TIP CLEARANCE MUST NOT EXCEED 0.30mm (0.012 IN) WITH FEELER GAUGE INSERTED 13mm (0.5 IN) MINIMUM.

Fig. 12 Measuring oil pump inner rotor tip clearance

FUEL PUMP
REPLACE

1. Loosen fuel pump attaching bolts one or two turns. Apply hand force to pump to loosen gasket.

2. Rotate engine until fuel pump cam lobe is near its low position to reduce pressure on pump.
3. Disconnect fuel lines from pump.
4. Remove fuel pump attaching bolts and the pump. Remove and discard gasket.
5. Clean all gasket material from engine and fuel pump.
6. Install attaching bolts into fuel pump, then install new gasket over bolts.
7. Install pump and torque alternately and evenly to 18 ft. lbs.
8. Connect fuel lines to pump, then operate engine and check for leaks.

WATER PUMP
REPLACE

1. Drain cooling system, then disconnect radiator lower hose and heater return hose from water inlet housing.
2. Remove fan and clutch assembly using tools No. T83T-6312-A and -B or equivalents.

NOTE: Fan and clutch assembly retaining nut has left hand threads and is removed by turning clockwise.

Fig. 13 Measuring oil pump rotor end play

3. All models equipped with A/C, remove alternator and mounting bracket.
4. On models less A/C, remove alternator drive belt.
5. On all models, remove water pump pulley.
6. Remove water pump attaching bolts, then the water pump, water inlet housing and thermostat from front cover.
7. Reverse procedure to install.

4-135 Diesel Engine Section

QUICK START & AFTERGLOW SYSTEM

This system improves cold engine starting performance. When ignition switch is turned On, a "Wait-to-Start" light illuminates on dash panel next to cold start knob. As this happens, relay No. 1 closes and full system voltage is applied to glow plugs. If engine coolant temperature is less than 86° F, relay No. 2 also closes. The control module extinguishes "Wait-to-Start" light after 3 seconds. If ignition is left on for approximately 3 more seconds without cranking engine, No. 1 relay opens, shutting off current to glow plugs to prevent overheating. However, if engine coolant temperature is below 86° F, relay No. 2 remains closed to apply limited voltage to plugs through glow plug resistor until ignition is turned Off.

During engine cranking, relay No. 1 is cycled by control module to provide alternate voltage to glow plugs between 4 and 12 volts with relay No. 2 closed, or between 0 and 12 volts with relay No. 2 open.

With engine running, alternator output signals cause control module to prevent No. 1 relay from cycling, and afterglow function takes over. If engine coolant temperature is below 86° F, limited voltage is applied to glow plugs through relay No. 2 and glow plug resistor. When clutch and neutral switches are closed or coolant temperature exceeds 86° F, relay No. 2 opens and all current to glow plugs is cut off.

FUEL INJECTION & GLOW PLUG SYSTEMS DIAGNOSIS
ENGINE CRANKS BUT WILL NOT START

1. Turn ignition switch to Run and check for voltage to fuel shut-off solenoid using a suitable 12 volt test lamp. If test lamp lights, proceed to step 2. If test lamp does not light, repair circuit as necessary.
2. Disconnect, then reconnect fuel shut-off solenoid electrical connector with ignition switch in Run. If solenoid clicks, proceed to step 3. If solenoid does not click, replace solenoid and repeat test.
3. Loosen one fuel injector nozzle line and crank engine. If there is no fuel flow while cranking engine, refer to "Poor Engine Performance" diagnosis. If fuel flow is observed, refer to "Glow Plug Control System" diagnosis.

ENGINE KNOCKS

1. Check all belt-driven components for looseness. If satisfactory, proceed to step 2. If any looseness is encoun-

tered, repair or replace component(s) as necessary.
2. Perform fuel system diagnostic procedures as described in "Poor Engine Performance" diagnosis. If fuel system is satisfactory, check engine main bearing clearances. If fuel system is malfunctioning, make necessary repairs and/or adjustments. If engine continues to knock, check main bearing clearances.

ENGINE MISSES

1. If engine misses only when cold, refer to "Glow Plug Control System" diagnosis.
2. If engine misses at operating temperature, refer to "Poor Engine Performance" diagnosis.

EXCESSIVE ENGINE SMOKE

1. If engine smokes only when cold, refer to "Glow Plug Control System" diagnosis.
2. If engine smokes at operating temperature, refer to "Poor Engine Performance" diagnosis.

POOR ENGINE PERFORMANCE

1. Ensure an adequate supply of fuel is available, and replenish as necessary. If fuel supply is sufficient, proceed to step 2.

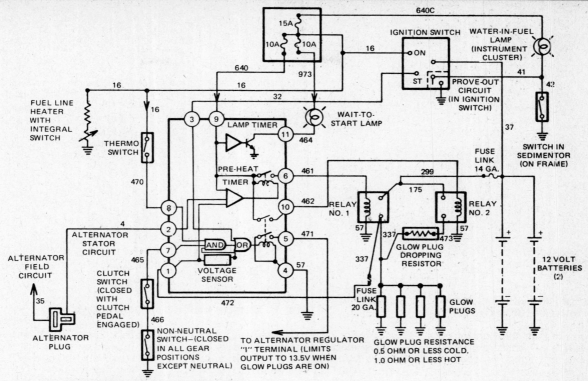

Fig. 1 Glow plug control system

GLOW PLUG CONTROL SYSTEM WIRE COLOR CODE

4 WHITE/BLACK STRIPE	462 PURPLE BASE
16 RED/LT GREEN STRIPE	464 BLACK/PINK STRIPE
32 RED/LT BLUE STRIPE	465 WHITE/LT BLUE STRIPE
35 ORANGE/LT BLUE STRIPE	466 PINK/ORANGE DOT
37 YELLOW BASE	470 PINK/BLACK DOT
41 BLACK/LT BLUE HASH	471 ORANGE/LT GREEN DOT
42 RED/WHITE DOT	472 YELLOW/BLACK DOT ③
57 BLACK BASE	473 LT GREEN/BLACK DOT ④
175 BLACK/YELLOW DOT	640 RED/YELLOW HASH
299 GREEN ①	687 GRAY/YELLOW STRIPE
337 ORANGE/WHITE STRIPE ②	973 RED BASE
461 ORANGE BASE	

① WITH ES-D5ZB-14A466-DA FUSE LINK (GREEN) AT STARTER SOLENOID END.
② BLACK/WHITE STRIPE AT ENGINE END.
③ WITH ES-D5ZB-14A466-AA FUSE LINK (BLUE) AT NO. 1 RELAY END.
④ BLACK AT ENGINE END.

CAUTION: WHEN CHECKING CONTROL MODULE CIRCUITS AT THE HARNESS CONNECTOR, INSERT TESTER PROBES INTO WIRING SIDE OF CONNECTOR CAVITIES. INSERTING PROBES INTO OPEN END OF CONNECTOR CAVITIES WILL DISTORT OR DAMAGE TERMINALS.

2. Check for fuel, oil and/or coolant leaks and restrictions in air cleaner, and replace or repair components as needed. If no leaks are evident and air cleaner is not restricted, proceed to step 3.
3. Inspect exhaust system for dents or other damage which could cause restrictions, and repair or replace components as necessary. If exhaust system is not restricted, proceed to step 4.
4. Disconnect fuel inlet line from injection pump and insert into a suitable container. Operate primer pump on top of fuel filter cover. If fuel flows freely from line, proceed to step 5. If there is no fuel flow, replace filter. If problem still exists, fuel tank(s) and/or fuel line(s) are faulty.
5. Examine fuel for contamination. If fuel is not contaminated, proceed to step 6. If there are contaminants in fuel, clean and/or repair fuel system components as necessary.
6. Disconnect and drain fuel line(s) from injection pump inlet and fuel tank(s).

Plug tank end of line(s) and pressurize to 20–25 psi, then apply a soap and water solution to all connections. If there are no bubbles, reconnect inlet line, bleed fuel system and proceed to step 7. If any bubbles are observed, repair leaking connection(s) and repeat leak test.
7. Ensure throttle lever contacts stop with accelerator pedal fully depressed. If lever contacts stop, proceed to step 8. If lever does not contact stop, adjust or replace throttle linkage as necessary.
8. Check engine idle speed with engine at normal operating temperature, transmission in Neutral and parking brake applied. Idle speed should be 780–830 RPM. If idle speed is within specifications, proceed to step 9, otherwise adjust as necessary.
9. Check ignition pump timing as described under "Injection Pump Timing," and adjust as necessary. If pump is properly timed, proceed to step 10.
10. Check fuel injection nozzles for dam-

age and ensure proper operation. If nozzles are satisfactory, proceed to step 11. If damaged or malfunctioning, clean, repair or replace as necessary.
11. Perform engine compression test. If compression is satisfactory, replace injection pump. If compression is low, inspect engine components to determine cause and repair or replace as necessary.

"WAIT-TO-START" LAMP

NOTE: Refer to **Fig. 1** when troubleshooting this system.

1. Turn ignition to Run position and observe "Wait" lamp. If lamp illuminates for 3 seconds and goes out, system is satisfactory; refer to "Glow Plug Control System" diagnosis. If lamp does not light, proceed to step 2. If lamp lights and remains lit, replace glow plug control module and recheck operation.
2. Connect a suitable jumper wire between connector terminal 11 and

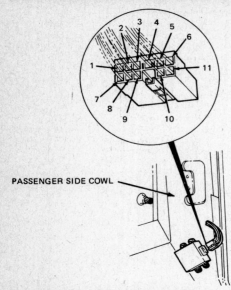

Fig. 2 Glow plug control system electrical connector location

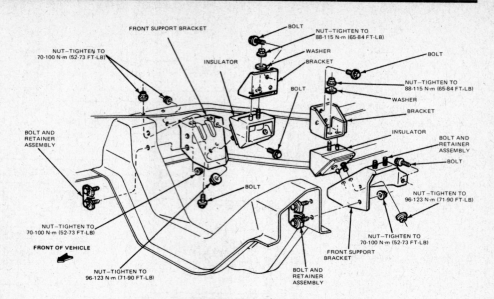

Fig. 3 Engine mount replacement

ground, **Fig. 2,** then turn ignition to Run position and observe "Wait" lamp. If lamp now lights, proceed to step 3. If lamp still does not light, inspect lamp bulb and its circuit and repair or replace as necessary.

3. Connect a suitable 12 volt test lamp between connector terminal 9 and ground, **Fig. 2,** then turn ignition to Run position and observe "Wait" lamp. If test lamp lights, replace glow plug control module and recheck operation. If test lamp does not light, repair or replace ignition switch or switch wiring as necessary and recheck operation.

GLOW PLUG CONTROL SYSTEM

NOTE: Refer to **Fig. 1** when troubleshooting this system.

1. Measure voltage at each glow plug lead with transmission in Neutral and ignition switch in Run position. Voltage at each lead should measure 11 volts for 6 seconds, then drop to 4.2–5.3 volts.

NOTE: If engine coolant temperature is higher than 86° F, connect jumper wire between coolant thermoswitch connector terminals.

2. If no voltage is recorded at any of the glow plugs, proceed to step 3. If voltmeter reads 11 volts for 6 seconds, then drops to zero, proceed to step 8. If voltage is satisfactory, remove jumper wire from coolant thermoswitch and proceed to step 15. If there is no voltage at 1, 2 or 3 glow plugs, replace glow plug harness and recheck voltage.

3. Disconnect glow plug harness from engine electrical harness and glow plugs, then connect a suitable self-powered test lamp between each glow plug terminal and harness connector. If test lamp lights, reconnect harness and proceed to step 4. If test lamp does not light, repair or replace glow plug harness as necessary and recheck.

4. Connect a suitable 12 volt test lamp between glow plug control module terminal 9 and ground. Observe test lamp with ignition in Run. If test lamp lights, proceed to step 5. If test lamp does not run, repair or replace ignition switch and switch wiring as necessary and recheck.

5. Connect a suitable 12 volt test lamp between glow plug control module terminal 6 and ground. Observe test lamp with ignition in Run. If test lamp lights for 6 seconds, proceed to step 6. If test lamp does not light, replace quick start control unit and recheck.

6. Connect a suitable 12 volt test lamp between No. 1 glow plug relay signal terminal and ground. Observe test lamp with ignition in Run. If test lamp lights for 6 seconds, proceed to step 7. If test lamp does not light, repair open or short in circuit 461 and recheck.

7. Measure voltage between No. 1 glow plug relay output terminal and ground with ignition in Run. If voltmeter reads 11 volts or more for 6 seconds, proceed to step 14. If voltage is less than 11 volts, replace No. 1 glow plug relay and recheck.

8. Connect a suitable 12 volt test lamp between glow plug control module terminal 10 and ground. Observe test lamp with ignition in Run. If test lamp does not light, proceed to step 9. If test lamp lights, proceed to step 10.

9. Check operation of clutch and neutral switches using a suitable self-powered test lamp. With transmission in gear and clutch pedal released, both switches should be closed (test lamp on). With transmission in Neutral and clutch pedal depressed, both switches should be open (test lamp off). If both switches operate satisfactorily, proceed to step 10, otherwise replace defective switch and recheck.

10. Connect a suitable 12 volt test lamp between No. 2 glow plug relay signal terminal and ground. Observe test lamp with transmission in Neutral and ignition in Run. If test lamp lights, proceed to step 11. If test lamp does not light, repair open or short in circuit 462 and recheck.

11. Connect a suitable 12 volt test lamp between No. 2 glow plug relay output terminal and ground. Observe test lamp with ignition in Run. If test lamp lights, proceed to step 12. If test lamp does not light, replace No. 2 glow plug relay and recheck.

12. Disconnect dropping resistor electrical connector and connect a suitable 12 volt test lamp between connector input terminal and ground. Observe test lamp with ignition in Run. If test lamp lights, proceed to step 13. If test lamp does not light, repair open or short in circuit 473 and recheck.

13. Measure resistance across dropping resistor connector terminals. If ohmmeter reads less than 1 ohm, reconnect dropping resistor and proceed to step 14. If resistance is 1 ohm or greater, replace dropping resistor and recheck.

14. Connect a suitable 12 volt test lamp between any glow plug terminal and ground. Observe test lamp with ignition in Run. If test lamp lights, repeat steps 1 and 2. If test lamp does not light, repair open or short in circuit 337 between No. 1 glow plug relay and glow plug harness and recheck.

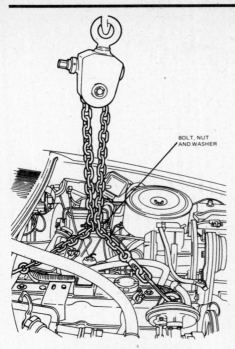

Fig. 4 Engine removal

BOLT, NUT AND WASHER

15. Disconnect glow plug leads and measure resistance between each glow plug terminal and ground. If ohmmeter reads less than 1 ohm, the glow plug system is operating satisfactorily; refer to "Poor Engine Performance" diagnosis. If resistance is 1 ohm or greater, replace defective glow plug(s) and recheck.

ENGINE MOUNTS
REPLACE

1. Remove nuts from top of insulator bracket, **Fig. 3**.
2. Raise and support vehicle.
3. Raise engine sufficiently to clear insulators.
4. Remove front support bracket attaching bolts and the bracket.
5. Remove insulator attaching nut and the insulator.
6. Reverse procedure to install.

ENGINE
REPLACE

1. Disconnect both battery ground cables from batteries and engine.
2. Scribe hood hinge locations and remove hood.
3. Drain cooling system.
4. Disconnect air intake hose from air cleaner and intake manifold, then the upper and lower radiator hoses from engine.
5. Remove engine cooling fan, then the radiator and fan shroud.
6. Disconnect radio ground strap, if equipped.
7. Disconnect No. 2 glow plug relay from dash and position aside with electrical connector attached.
8. Disconnect engine wiring harness from connector on left fender apron.

9. Disconnect starter cable from starter motor.
10. Disconnect accelerator cable and speed control cable, if equipped, from injector pump.
11. Disconnect cold start cable from injector pump.
12. On models equipped with A/C, discharge refrigerant from system, then disconnect A/C lines and position aside.
13. On models equipped with power steering, disconnect pressure and return lines from power steering pump.
14. On all models, disconnect vacuum fitting from vacuum pump and position fitting and hoses aside.
15. Disconnect and cap fuel return line at fuel heater and return line at air injection pump.
16. Disconnect heater hoses from engine, then loosen engine mount attaching nuts.
17. Raise and support vehicle.
18. Drain engine oil and remove primary oil filter.
19. Disconnect oil pressure sender hose from oil filter mounting adapter.
20. Disconnect exhaust pipe from manifold, then remove lower engine mount attaching nuts.
21. Remove transmission-to-engine attaching bolts, then lower vehicle.
22. Attach suitable lifting equipment to engine. Ensure bolt, nut and washer are installed as shown, **Fig. 4**.
23. Lift engine assembly from vehicle.
24. Reverse procedure to install.

CYLINDER HEAD
REPLACE

1. Disconnect ground cables from both batteries.
2. Mark hood hinge locations and remove hood.
3. Drain cooling system.
4. Disconnect breather hose from valve cover, then remove intake and breather hoses from air cleaner and intake manifold.
5. Remove heater hose bracket-to-valve cover and exhaust manifold attaching nuts.
6. Disconnect heater hoses from thermostat housing and water pump, and position heater hose tube assembly aside.
7. Remove vacuum pump support brace from cylinder head and vacuum pump bracket.
8. Remove alternator and vacuum pump drive belt.
9. Remove A/C compressor and/or power steering pump drive belt, if equipped.
10. Disconnect brake booster vacuum hose, then remove vacuum pump.
11. Disconnect exhaust pipe from exhaust manifold.
12. Disconnect coolant thermoswitch and temperature sender electrical connectors.
13. Remove fuel injection lines. Cap lines and fittings.

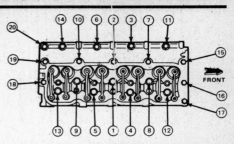

Fig. 5 Cylinder head bolt tightening sequence

FRONT

14. Disconnect alternator, glow plug harness and dropping resistor electrical connectors and position aside.
15. Disconnect fuel lines from both sides of fuel line heater.
16. Remove fuel filter from mounting bracket and position aside with outlet line connected.
17. Loosen lower No. 3 intake port nut and "Banjo" bolt on injection pump, then disconnect lower fuel return line from intake manifold stud and upper fuel return line.
18. If equipped with power steering, remove rear power steering pump bracket attaching bolt.
19. Remove upper radiator hose from engine, then loosen clamp on water pump-to-thermostat housing bypass hose.
20. If equipped with A/C, remove A/C compressor from mounting bracket and position aside with refrigerant lines attached.
21. Remove valve cover and rocker arm shaft.
22. Remove cylinder head attaching bolts and the cylinder head.
23. Reverse procedure to install. Torque cylinder head attaching bolts to specifications in sequence shown, **Fig. 5**.

CYLINDER SLEEVE
REPLACE
REMOVAL

1. Remove cylinder head as described in "Cylinder Head, Replace."
2. Remove oil pan as described in "Oil Pan, Replace."
3. Remove connecting rod bearing caps and bearings in order so they can be installed in their original positions.
4. Remove piston assemblies from cylinder block.

NOTE: To remove the pistons, it may be necessary to ridge ream top of cylinder sleeves.

5. Remove cylinder sleeves using tool No. 14-0316 or equivalent. Rotate crankshaft as necessary to avoid contact between connecting rod bearing journal and pilot screw on tool.

NOTE: When removing sleeve from cylinder No. 4, rear of engine must be raised to provide clearance at dash panel.

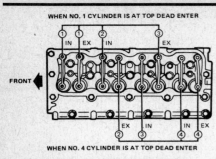

WHEN NO. 1 CYLINDER IS AT TOP DEAD ENTER

FRONT

WHEN NO. 4 CYLINDER IS AT TOP DEAD ENTER

Fig. 6   Valve adjustment sequence

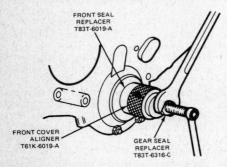

FRONT SEAL REPLACER T83T-6019-A

FRONT COVER ALIGNER T61K-6019-A

GEAR SEAL REPLACER T83T-6316-C

Fig. 8   Front oil seal installation

INSTALLATION

1. Remove scratches from cylinder bores using oil soaked emery cloth.
2. Lubricate cylinder bores and outside surface of cylinder sleeves with clean engine oil.
3. Install cylinder sleeves using tool No. 14-0317 or equivalent.

NOTE: Check turning torque on tool nut when sleeve is approximately halfway installed, and again when sleeve is almost seated in block. Torque should measure 13-37 ft. lbs. at both points.

4. Reverse steps 1 through 4 as described under "Removal" to complete installation.

VALVE ARRANGEMENT
FRONT TO REAR

I-E-I-E-I-E-I-E

VALVE LIFT SPECS.

Year	Intake	Exhaust
1983–84	.257	.257

VALVES
ADJUST

1. Run engine until normal operating temperature is reached, then remove valve cover.
2. Torque cylinder head attaching bolts

to specifications in sequence shown in **Fig. 5.**
3. Rotate crankshaft until cylinder No. 1 is at top dead center of compression stroke.
4. Check valve clearances in sequence, **Fig. 6,** using a suitable feeler gauge.
5. Adjust any valve clearances which do not meet specifications as follows:
   a. Loosen adjusting screw locknut.
   b. Rotate adjusting screw as necessary to bring clearance within specifications.
   c. Tighten locknut while holding adjusting screw in position.
   d. Recheck valve clearance.
6. Rotate crankshaft one complete revolution until cylinder No. 4 is at top dead center of compression stroke, then repeat steps 4 and 5.

FRONT OIL SEAL
REPLACE

1. Disconnect ground cables from both batteries.
2. Remove engine cooling fan and fan shroud.
3. Remove A/C compressor and/or power steering pump drive belt, if equipped.
4. Remove water pump and alternator drive belt.
5. Remove crankshaft pulley lock bolt using tool No. T83T-6316-D or equivalent.
6. Remove crankshaft pulley using a suitable puller.
7. Remove front oil seal using tool No. T72J-6700 or equivalent, **Fig. 7.**
8. Reverse procedure to install, using tools shown in **Fig. 8.**

TIMING GEAR CASE & TIMING GEARS
REPLACE

1. Disconnect ground cables from both batteries.
2. Remove engine cooling fan and fan shroud.
3. Drain cooling system and engine oil.
4. Remove A/C compressor and/or power steering pump drive belt, if equipped.
5. Remove alternator and vacuum pump drive belt.
6. Remove water pump as described in "Water Pump, Replace."
7. Remove crankshaft pulley lock bolt using tool No. T83T-6316-D or equivalent.
8. Remove timing gear case cover attaching bolts and the cover.
9. Remove oil pan as described in "Oil Pan, Replace."
10. Rotate crankhaft until timing gear marks are aligned, **Fig. 9.**
11. Remove camshaft gear and injection pump gear attaching bolts, washers and friction gears.

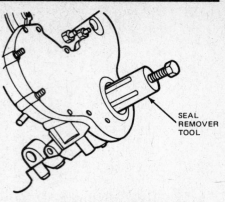

SEAL REMOVER TOOL

Fig. 7   Front oil seal removal

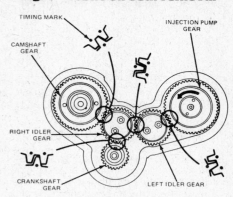

TIMING MARK

INJECTION PUMP GEAR

CAMSHAFT GEAR

RIGHT IDLER GEAR

CRANKSHAFT GEAR

LEFT IDLER GEAR

Fig. 9   Valve timing marks

12. Remove camshaft and injection pump gears using a suitable puller.
13. Remove idler gear attaching bolts, thrust plates and spindles, then the idler gears.

NOTE: Remove idler gears in order so they can be reinstalled in their original positions.

14. Disconnect injection pump from timing gear case and position aside.
15. Remove timing gear case attaching bolts and the case.

INSTALLATION

1. Clean timing gear case, water pump, oil pan and engine block mating surfaces.
2. Install timing gear case, using a new gasket, and torque attaching bolts to 15 ft. lbs.
3. Install timing gears so all timing marks are aligned, **Fig. 9,** in the following order; right idler gear, camshaft gear, left idler gear, injection pump gear.
4. Install all friction gears, washers, nuts and bolts on gears.
5. Remove front crankshaft oil seal from timing gear case front cover.
6. Install timing gear case cover, with a new gasket, using tool No. T61K-6019-A. Torque cover attaching bolts to 15 ft. lbs.
7. Install new front oil seal, **Fig. 8.**

Fig. 10 Piston & rod assembly

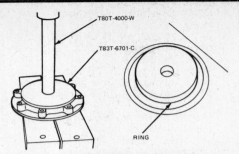

Fig. 11 Crankshaft rear oil seal installation

NOTE: INNER TO OUTER ROTOR TIP CLEARANCE MUST NOT EXCEED 0.305mm (0.012 INCH) WITH FEELER GAUGE INSERTED 12.7mm (1/2") MINIMUM AND ROTORS REMOVED FROM PUMP HOUSING.

Fig. 12 Measuring oil pump inner rotor tip clearance

8. Reverse steps 1 through 7 as described under "Removal" to complete installation.

CAMSHAFT
REPLACE

1. Remove engine from vehicle as described in "Engine, Replace."
2. Remove valve cover, rocker shaft assembly and pushrods.

NOTE: Remove pushrods so they can be reinstalled in their original positions.

3. Remove timing gear case cover and camshaft gear as described in "Timing Gear Case & Timing Gears, Replace."
4. Remove oil pan and oil pump from engine.
5. Remove camshaft thrust plate and the camshaft.

NOTE: Use care not to damage camshaft lobes during removal.

6. Reverse procedure to install.

PISTON & ROD ASSEMBLY

Assemble piston rod and install into cylinder block. Install with sub-combustion chamber on piston head toward intake manifold, **Fig. 10.**

CRANKSHAFT REAR OIL SEAL
REPLACE

1. Disconnect ground cables from both batteries.
2. Raise and support vehicle.
3. Remove transmission and clutch assemblies as described elsewhere in this chapter.
4. Remove flywheel, then the crankshaft rear cover assembly.
5. Remove oil seal from rear cover.
6. Reverse procedure to install, using tools shown in **Fig. 11.**

OIL PAN
REPLACE

1. Disconnect ground cables from both batteries.
2. Remove engine oil dipstick, then drain cooling system.
3. Disconnect air intake hose from intake manifold and air cleaner.
4. Remove engine cooling fan and fan shroud.
5. Disconnect radiator hoses, then remove radiator upper support brackets and the radiator and fan shroud.
6. Disconnect and cap fuel lines at fuel filter and return line at injection pump.
7. Remove fuel filter, then the filter mounting bracket.
8. Remove engine bracket-to-insulator attaching nuts.
9. Raise and support vehicle.
10. Loosen transmission insulator attaching bolts at rear of transmission.
11. Remove lower engine insulator attaching bolts, then drain engine oil.
12. Remove primary oil filter, then the bypass filter mounting bracket and hoses.
13. Lower vehicle.
14. Attach suitable lifting equipment to engine and raise engine until insulator studs clear insulators.
15. Slide engine forward and raise approximately 3 inches.
16. Install a 3 inch wooden block between each engine mount and bracket, then lower engine and remove engine lifting device.
17. Raise and support vehicle.
18. Remove oil pan attaching bolts and lower oil pan to rest on crossmember.
19. Disconnect oil pickup tube from oil pump and bearing cap and lay in oil pan.
20. Slide oil pan forward and up, and remove from vehicle.

NOTE: It may be necessary to move the A/C condenser forward to provide clearance for oil pan removal.

21. Reverse procedure to install. Apply a ⅛ inch bead of suitable sealer to split line between engine block and front cover along side rails and at ends of oil

pan seals which contact oil pan gaskets.

OIL PUMP
REPLACE

1. Remove oil pan as described in "Oil Pan, Replace."
2. Disconnect oil pump outlet tube from engine.
3. Remove oil pump set screw and the oil pump.
4. Reverse procedure to install.

NOTE: Apply teflon tape to oil pump set screw prior to installation.

OIL PUMP REPAIRS

NOTE: Individual oil pump components are not serviced. If any part of the pump requires replacement, the entire pump assembly must be replaced.

1. Inspect inside of pump housing, outer race and rotor for excessive wear or scoring.
2. Inspect pump cover mating surface for excessive wear or scoring.
3. Measure inner rotor tip clearance, **Fig. 12.**
4. Measure rotor end play, **Fig. 13,** which should be .0016–.0039 inch and must not exceed .0060 inch.
5. Measure driveshaft to bearing clearance, which must not exceed .0039 inch.
6. Inspect relief valve piston for scores and ensure its free operation in bore.

WATER PUMP
REPLACE

1. Disconnect ground cables from both batteries.

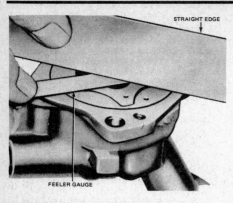

Fig. 13   Measuring oil pump rotor end play

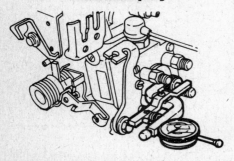

Fig. 15   Injection pump timing

2. Remove engine cooling fan and fan shroud.
3. Remove alternator and vacuum pump drive belt.
4. Remove A/C compressor and/or power steering pump drive belt, if equipped.
5. Drain cooling system, then disconnect hoses from water pump.
6. Remove water pump attaching bolts and the pump.
7. Reverse procedure to install.

BELT TENSION DATA

	New Lbs.	Used Lbs.
A/C Compressor	170	150
Alternator	140	120
Power Steering Pump	170	150
Vacuum Pump	110	90
Water Pump	140	120

INJECTION PUMP
REPLACE

REMOVAL

1. Disconnect ground cables from both batteries.
2. Remove engine cooling fan and fan shroud.
3. Remove A/C compressor and/or power steering pump drive belt and idler pulley, if equipped.

4. Remove injection pump drive gear cover and gasket.
5. Rotate crankshaft until injection pump drive gear keyway is at top dead center position.
6. Remove large nut and washer from pump drive gear. Use care to avoid dropping washer into timing gear case.
7. Disconnect air intake hose from intake manifold and air cleaner.
8. Disconnect throttle cable and speed control cable, if equipped.
9. Disconnect and cap fuel inlet line at injection pump.
10. Disconnect fuel shut-off solenoid electrical connector from injection pump.
11. Remove fuel injection lines. Cap lines and fittings.
12. Disconnect lower fuel return line from injection pump and fuel lines.
13. Loosen lower No. 3 intake port nut and remove fuel return line.
14. Remove injection pump attaching nuts and bolt, **Fig. 14.**
15. Disconnect cold start cable, then remove injection pump using a suitable puller.

NOTE: Use care to avoid dropping key into timing gear case when removing pump.

INSTALLATION

1. Connect cold start cable, then install injection pump in timing gear case, aligning key with keyway in drive gear in top dead center position.
2. Install injection pump attaching nuts and bolt and tighten sufficiently to draw pump into position.
3. Install pump drive gear washer and nut and torque to 40 ft. lbs.
4. Install injection pump gear cover with a new gasket.
5. Adjust pump timing as described under "Injection Pump Timing."
6. Install all fuel lines and clamps.
7. Connect fuel shut-off solenoid electrical connector.
8. Connect throttle cable and speed control cable, if equipped.
9. Bleed fuel system as follows:
   a. Loosen air vent plug on fuel filter.
   b. Operate priming pump on top of fuel filter adapter until clear, bubble-free fuel flows from vent plug.
   c. Close vent plug while holding priming plug in fully depressed position.
   d. Disconnect fuel return line from injection pump.
   e. Operate priming pump until fuel flows from return port on injection pump.
   f. Reconnect fuel return line to injection pump, then run engine and check for leaks.
10. Install air intake hose, drive belt and idler pulley.
11. Install engine cooling fan and fan shroud, then reconnect battery ground cables.

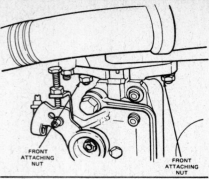

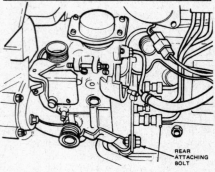

Fig. 14   Injection pump removal

INJECTION PUMP TIMING

1. Disconnect ground cables from both batteries.
2. Remove air intake hose from intake manifold and air cleaner.
3. Remove injection pump distributor head plug bolt and seal.
4. Install static timing gauge adapter (tool No. 14-0303 or equivalent) and a suitable dial indicator to injection pump, **Fig. 15.**

NOTE: Install dial indicator so pointer contacts injection pump plunger and gauge reads approximately .08 inch.

5. Align timing mark on crankshaft pulley with indicator on timing case cover, then rotate crankshaft slowly counterclockwise until dial indicator pointer stops moving.
6. Zero the dial indicator, then rotate crankshaft clockwise until crankshaft timing mark aligns with indicator pin. The dial indicator reading should be .0392–.0408 inch.
7. If reading is not within specifications, loosen injection pump nuts and bolt. Rotate pump counterclockwise past correct timing position, then rotate clockwise until timing is correct to eliminate gear backlash and repeat steps 5 and 6.
8. Remove dial indicator and adapter, then install injection pump distributor head plug.
9. Install air intake hose and reconnect battery ground cables.
10. Run engine and check for fuel leaks.

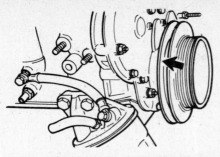

Fig. 16 Marking crankshaft pulley for idle speed adjustment

11. Adjust idle speed as described under "Idle Speed, Adjust."

INJECTION NOZZLE
REPLACE

1. Disconnect ground cables from both batteries.
2. Remove fuel injection lines. Cap lines and fittings.

3. Remove fuel return line and gaskets.
4. Remove fuel line heater clamp bolts and position heater aside.
5. Remove injection nozzles using a suitable socket.
6. Remove copper washer and steel gasket using tool No. T71-P-19703-C or equivalent.
7. Reverse procedure to install. Torque nozzles up to 47 ft. lbs.

NOTE: Install nozzle gaskets with blue side up, toward nozzle.

IDLE SPEED
ADJUST

1. Run engine until normal operating temperature is reached, then stop engine.
2. Wipe off crankshaft pulley and install reflective tape, **Fig. 16.**
3. Direct the light from photoelectric tachometer (part No. 99-0001 or equivalent) onto reflective tape and note RPM with engine running at idle.

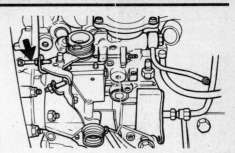

Fig. 17 Idle speed adjustment

4. If idle RPM is not within specifications listed on vehicle emissions decal, adjust idle speed as follows:
   a. Loosen idle speed adjusting bolt locknut, **Fig. 17.**
   b. Rotate bolt counterclockwise to decrease idle speed, or clockwise to increase idle speed.
   c. Tighten locknut when idle speed is within specifications.
   d. Depress accelerator several times to ensure engine speed returns to proper idle.

4-143 Turbocharged Diesel Engine Section

SUPER-QUICK GLOW PLUG SYSTEM

This system, **Fig. 1,** is used to enable the engine to start quickly when the engine is cold. This system consists of four glow plugs, control module, two relays, a glow plug resistor assembly, coolant temperature switch and connecting wiring. Relay power and feedback circuits are protected by fusible links in the wiring harness. The control module is protected by a separate 10A fuse in the fuse panel assembly.

The super-quick start system eliminates the waiting time to start the engine. When the ignition switch is turned to the ON position, relay No. 1 also closes and full system voltage is applied to the glow plugs. If the ignition switch is left in the ON position approximately three seconds more without cranking, the control module opens relay No. 1 and current to the plugs stops, preventing overheating. Relay No. 2 does not close until the engine is cranked.

When the engine is cranked, the control module cycles relay No. 1 intermittently allowing the glow plug voltage to alternate between 12 and 6 volts during cranking and with the No. 2 relay closed. After the engine starts, the alternator output signals the control module to stop the No. 1 relay cycling and the afterflow function takes place. If engine coolant temperature is below 86° F, the No. 2 relay remains closed. This applies reduced voltage (6–7.6 volts) to the glow plug resistor for approximately 30 seconds.

FUEL INJECTION & GLOW PLUG SYSTEMS DIAGNOSIS

ENGINE CRANKS BUT WILL NOT START

1. Turn ignition switch to RUN position. Using a 12 volt test lamp, ensure voltage is available at solenoid. If voltage is present proceed to step 2. If voltage is not present, repair circuit as necessary.
2. With ignition switch in RUN position, disconnect, then reconnect fuel shut-off electrical connector. If solenoid clicks, proceed to step 3. If solenoid does not click, replace fuel shut-off solenoid and repeat step 2.
3. Loosen one injector nozzle line nut and crank engine. If fuel discharges, proceed to "Glow Plug Control System". If fuel does not discharge, pro-

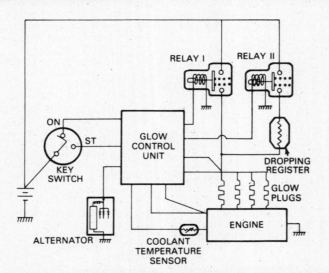

Fig. 1 Super-Quick start glow plug control system

ceed to "Engine Performance Diagnosis".

ENGINE KNOCKS

1. Check belt driven accessories for looseness. If belt tensions are correct, proceed to step 2. If belt tensions are incorrect, repair or replace component(s) as required.
2. Perform fuel system diagnostic procedures as described in "Engine Performance Diagnosis". If fuel system is satisfactory, check main bearing clearances. If fuel system is malfunctioning, conduct necessary repairs and/or adjustments. If engine continues to knock, check main bearing clearances.

ENGINE MISSES

1. If engine misses only when cold, proceed to "Glow Plug Control System".
2. If engine misses at operating temperature, check for air bubbles in fuel system lines. Repair fuel line leak(s) as required. If miss still occurs, proceed to "Engine Performance Diagnosis".

EXCESSIVE SMOKE

1. If engine smokes only when cold, proceed to "Glow Plug Control System".
2. If engine smokes at operating temperatures, proceed to "Engine Performance Diagnosis".

ENGINE PERFORMANCE DIAGNOSIS

1. With engine operating, visually check for fuel, engine oil and coolant leakage. Ensure air cleaner is properly installed. If no leakage is detected, proceed to step 2. If leakage is detected, repair and/or replace defective component(s) as required. If problem still exists, proceed to step 2.
2. Visually inspect exhaust system for dents or kinks which could cause restrictions. If system is satisfactory, proceed to step 3. If system is damaged, repair and/or replace exhaust system and/or component(s) as required.
3. Inspect fuel supply lines, return lines and hoses for damage. Check fuel line and hose fittings for tightness. If lines, hoses and fittings are satisfactory, proceed to step 4. If lines, hoses and/or fittings are damaged, repair and/or replace damaged component(s) as required. If problem still exists, proceed to step 4.
4. Using a suitable container, obtain a fuel sample. Using cetane tester included with dynamic timing meter 078-00116, check cetane value of fuel. Cetane value should be a minimum of 40. If satisfactory, proceed to step 5. If not satisfactory, use different fuel supply and proceed to step 5.

NOTE: Do not replace fuel pump because of a low cetane problem.

5. Install dynamic timing meter Rotunda model 078-00116 or equivalent, and check pump timing. If injection timing is satisfactory, proceed to step 6 and do not recheck timing in step 6. If injection timing is incorrect, do not reset timing at this time. Proceed to step 6 and recheck timing in step 6.
6. Ensure injection pump top lever contacts high speed stop during WOT. Ensure injection pump top lever contacts idle speed stop bolt. Ensure adjustment bead on T.V. cable is .008–.047 inch from threaded barrel at idle speed. If satisfactory, proceed to step 7. If not satisfactory, check and/or adjust throttle linkage as required, then proceed to step 7.
7. Disconnect fuel outlet hose from electric lift pump. Install adapter 5632 and pressure test kit 019-00002 or equivalent. Operate engine at idle speed. Pressure obtained should be 1–5.6 (s) psi. If pressure obtained is satisfactory, disconnect adapter 5632 and connect fuel hose. If pressure obtained is not satisfactory, repeat test.
8. Disconnect fuel outlet hose from fuel filter. Install adapter 5632 and pressure test kit 019-00002 or equivalent. Operate engine at idle speed. Vacuum reading obtained should be 5.7 inches Hg. Record reading. If vacuum is lower than vacuum specified, replace fuel filter and repeat test. If vacuum is the same or higher than vacuum specified, a restriction is in the fuel line from the fuel tank or fuel sender. Repair and/or replace component(s) as required. Proceed to step 9.
9. Remove oil filler cap, then install adapter 10325 and pressure test kit 019-00002 or equivalent. Disconnect and plug crankcase ventilation hose from air cleaner. Disconnect vacuum pump hose, and cap vacuum pump fitting. Operate engine at 3300 RPM. Pressure reading obtained should be 30 inches at normal engine operating temperature. If reading obtained is satisfactory, proceed to step 10. If reading obtained is not satisfactory, an internal engine problem exists.
10. Disconnect crankcase ventilation hose from turbocharger inlet duct. Install adapter 10326 and pressure test kit 019-00002 or equivalent. Operate engine at 3300 RPM. Pressure obtained should not exceed 4.8 inches.

NOTE: This reading also indicates turbocharger inlet pressure.

If reading is satisfactory, proceed to step 11. If reading is incorrect, replace air filter element and repeat test. If new element does not solve the problem, check for restrictions inside fender area or air cleaner opening.

11. Disconnect boost compensator hose from intake plenum chamber base. Install adapter 10396 and pressure test kit 019-00002 or equivalent.

NOTE: Ensure hose to altitude/boost compensator is reconnected to adapter 10396.

Using a suitable jack, raise and support rear of vehicle. With transmission in Drive and brakes applied, operate engine at a minimum of 2500 RPM.

NOTE: Do not operate engine under full load with brakes applied for longer than 30 seconds.

Pressure obtained should be 11.6 psi.

NOTE: After operating engine under full load, place transmission into Neutral and run engine at 1000 RPM for one minute to allow transmission to cool.

If pressure reading obtained is 11.6 psi, proceed to step 13. If pressure reading obtained is 10.6 psi, proceed to step 12. If pressure reading obtained exceeds 12.6 psi, replace turbocharger and repeat step 11.

12. Operate engine at idle speed. Check for air leaks at intake manifold in the following areas:
   a. Crossover pipe between turbo and intake plenum.
   b. Intake manifold at cylinder head.
   c. Pressure relief valve at base of intake plenum.
   If no leaks are detected, replace turbocharger and repeat step 11. If leaks are detected, repair or replace component(s) as required.
13. Disconnect fuel return line from base of lefthand fender apron chassis fitting. Install adapter 5663 and pressure test kit 019-00002 or equivalent. Operate engine at idle. Pressure reading obtained should be a maximum of 2 psi. If pressure obtained is as specified, proceed to step 14. If pressure reading obtained is not as specified, check fuel return line and fuel sender for kinks and/or restrictions, then repeat step 13.
14. Remove banjo bolt marked OUT from fuel return line on injection pump. Install adapter 10356 and pressure test kit 019-00002 or equivalent. Operate engine at the following RPM's and check pressure readings. Readings and RPM should be as follows:
   a. 800 RPM with engine at normal operating temperature. Pressure reading should be 400 psi.
   b. 4500 RPM. Pressure reading should be 116 psi.
   If readings are satisfactory, proceed to step 15. If readings are not as specified, replace injection pump. If performance problem still exists, proceed to step 15.
15. With dynamic timing meter installed, and engine at normal operating temperature, check injection timing. If

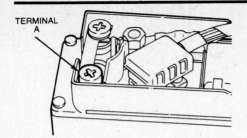

Fig. 2   Connecting voltmeter to terminal A of control module

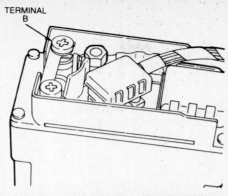

Fig. 3   Connecting voltmeter to terminal B of control module

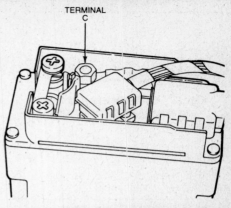

Fig. 4   Connecting voltmeter to terminal C of control module

injection timing obtained is correct proceed to step 16. If injection timing obtained is incorrect, adjust timing as required.

16. Check injection nozzle inlet for kinks or restrictions. Remove and test injection nozzles. If system is not satifactory, replace injection nozzles and/or injection nozzle inlet line(s) as required.

GLOW PLUG CONTROL SYSTEM

1. Connect positive lead of voltmeter on to glow plug. Connect negative lead to ground. With engine coolant temperature below 158° F., turn ignition switch to RUN position. Voltmeter should indicate battery voltage. If voltmeter indicates battery voltage, proceed to step 2. If battery voltage is not indicated, repeat step 1 and use another glow plug. If after using another glow plug, voltmeter indicates 12 volts, proceed to step 2. If no voltage is indicated, proceed to step 3.

2. Remove cover from glow plug module. Remove large connector from glow plug control module. Connect one lead of ohmmeter to ground. Probe each terminal of connector with other lead of ohmmeter. Ohmmeter should indicate .3–.6 ohms for each terminal. If ohmmeter readings are correct, proceed to step 3. If ohmmeter readings are incorrect, replace faulty glow plug(s) and repeat test step 2. If after replacing glow plug(s) and ohmmeter readings still are incorrect, replace wires and check system operation.

3. Remove cover from glow plug control module assembly. Connect negative lead of voltmeter to ground, then connect positive lead to terminal A, **Fig. 2**. Voltmeter should indicate battery voltage. If battery voltage is indicated, proceed to step 6. If battery voltage is not indicated, leave voltmeter connected to ground and proceed to step 4.

4. Connect voltmeter positive lead to terminal B, **Fig. 3**. Voltmeter should indicate battery voltage. If battery voltage is indicated, replace 80A fuse and check system operation. If battery voltage is not indicated, leave voltmeter connected to ground and proceed

to step 5.

5. Connect voltmeter positive lead to terminal C, **Fig. 4**. Voltmeter should indicate battery voltage. If battery voltage is indicated, replace glow plug control system module, then check system operation. If battery voltage is not indicated, repair open circuit in wire R between glow plug control module and starter motor assembly, then check system operation.

6. Disconnect small connector from glow plug control module. Connect a suitable ohmmeter between terminal 31 (brown colored) and ground. Ohmmeter reading obtained should be zero ohms. If zero ohms is obtained, proceed to step 7. If any other reading is obtained other than zero, repair brown wire between control module and ground. Check system operation.

7. Disconnect small connector from glow plug control module. Connect ohmmeter negative lead to ground. Connect positive lead to the N.T.C. terminal in the connector assembly. Compare ohmmeter readings obtained with the following specifications:

NOTE: Resistance should be within specifications depending on coolant temperature.

a. At a temperature of 32° F, ohmmeter reading obtained should be 2147–2747 ohms.

b. At a temperature of 68° F, ohmmeter reading obtained should be 930–1150 ohms.

c. At a temperature of 104° F, ohmmeter reading obtained should be 448–528 ohms.

d. At a temperature of 140° F, ohmmeter reading obtained should be 228.5–265.5 ohms.

e. At a temperature of 194° F, ohmmeter reading obtained should be 96–108 ohms.

f. At a temperature of 248° F, ohmmeter reading obtained should be 45–51 ohms.

If ohmmeter readings obtained at specified temperatures are correct, proceed to step 8. If ohmmeter

readings obtained are not as specified, check wire and replace temperature sensor assembly. Recheck system operation.

8. Disconnect small connector from glow plug control module. Connect negative lead of voltmeter to ground. Connect positive lead of voltmeter to terminal 15 in connector. Turn ignition switch to RUN position. Voltmeter should indicate battery voltage. If battery voltage is indicated, leave voltmeter connected to ground and proceed to step 9. If battery voltage is not obtained, service open circuit to GR/W wire at glow plug control module.

9. Connect voltmeter to terminal 50 in connector. Turn ignition switch to RUN position. Voltmeter should indicate that voltage is present. If voltage is obtained, replace glow plug control module and recheck system operation. If no voltage is obtained, service open circuit in BK/Y wire between glow plug control module and starter motor assembly and recheck system operation.

GLOW PLUG WAIT LAMP SYSTEM DIAGNOSIS

1. With engine coolant temperature below 150° F, turn ignition switch to RUN position. The wait lamp should light.

NOTE: The length of time the wait lamp is lit will depend on engine coolant temperature.

If wait lamp lights, wait lamp and connecting wiring is satisfactory. If wait lamp does not light, proceed to step 2.

2. With engine coolant temperature above 150° F, bypass control function by disconnecting the two temperature sensor wire electrical connectors located in the top water outlet connection.

NOTE: Bypassing the control function is necessary and should only be done for

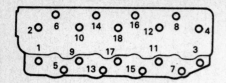

Fig. 5   Cylinder head bolt loosening sequence

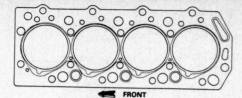

Fig. 6   Positioning cylinder head gasket on to engine block

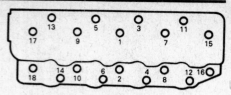

Fig. 7   Cylinder head bolt tightening sequence

diagnostic purposes. After completion of test, connect electrical connectors.

Turn ignition switch to RUN position. Wait lamp should light for approximately 10 seconds. If wait lamp lights the specified length of time, wait lamp and wiring is satisfactory. If not, proceed to step 3.

3. Remove plastic cover from glow plug control module. Disconnect small connector from glow plug connector module. Connect a suitable jumper wire to ground and pin LA1 in module connector. Turn ignition switch to RUN position. Wait lamp should light. If lamp lights, perform "Glow Plug Control System Diagnosis". If lamp does not light, repair or replace bulb and/or wiring harness as required.

ENGINE
REPLACE

1. Mark locations of hood hinges, then remove hood.
2. Disconnect battery ground cables from both battery assemblies.
3. Disconnect battery ground cables from engine.
4. Drain coolant system.
5. Disconnect crankcase breather hose from rocker cover.
6. Disconnect intake hose between air cleaner and turbocharger assembly.

NOTE: Cap turbocharger inlet using cap set T85T-9395-A or equivalent.

7. Remove A/C compressor and position aside. Do not disconnect refrigerant lines from compressor.
8. Disconnect heater hoses from inlet and outlet fittings on heater core.
9. Remove cooling fan assembly.
10. Disconnect radiator hoses, then remove radiator assembly.
11. Disconnect electrical connector from fuel conditioner.
12. Disconnect fuel supply line from fuel conditioner and fuel return line from injection pump.
13. Mark, then disconnect all necessary vacuum lines and electrical connectors from engine assembly.
14. Disconnect coolant overflow hose from filler neck.
15. Disconnect throttle cable and speed control cable, if equipped, from injec-

tion pump.
16. Disconnect starter motor cables, then remove starter motor assembly.
17. Using a suitable jack, raise vehicle slightly and remove righthand wheel, tire and inner fender.
18. Disconnect oil pressure switch electrical connector.
19. Disconnect cooler lines from oil filter adapter.
20. Raise and support vehicle.
21. Remove nut attaching engine insulators to engine support brackets.
22. Disconnect muffler inlet pipe from turbocharger exhaust outlet pipe.
23. Disconnect and cap power steering pump lines from pump assembly.
24. Disconnect clutch servo hydraulic line (red line) from clutch housing and position aside.
25. Remove transmission attaching bolts except the top two bolts.
26. Lower vehicle.
27. Attach suitable engine lifting equipment onto engine lifting eyes.
28. Remove top two transmission attaching bolts.
29. Carefully lift engine from vehicle.
30. Reverse procedure to install.

EXHAUST MANIFOLD
REPLACE

1. Disconnect battery ground cables from both battery assemblies.
2. Remove support brace from A/C compressor bracket and inlet fitting assembly.
3. Remove A/C compressor from mounting bracket and position aside.
4. Remove inlet fitting from intake manifold.
5. Remove air inlet tube from air cleaner to turbocharger inlet.
6. Remove wastegate actuator from turbocharger and mounting bracket.
7. Raise and support vehicle, then disconnect muffler inlet pipe from turbocharger exhaust fitting.
8. Lower vehicle.
9. Disconnect turbocharger oil feed line from cylinder head and turbocharger center housing.
10. Remove nuts attaching exhaust manifold to cylinder head, then the exhaust manifold and turbocharger as an assembly.
11. Remove turbocharger from exhaust manifold, if necessary.

12. Reverse procedure to install.

CYLINDER HEAD
REPLACE

1. Mark location of hood hinges, then remove hood.
2. Disconnect battery ground cables from both battery assemblies.
3. Drain cooling system.
4. Disconnect breather hose from rocker cover.
5. Remove heater hose clamp, then position heater hose aside.
6. Remove cooling fan and shroud assembly.
7. Remove accessory drive belts.
8. Remove upper front timing belt cover.
9. Loosen, then remove camshaft/injection pump timing belt from camshaft sprocket.
10. Remove inlet hose between air cleaner and turbocharger inlet.
11. Raise and support vehicle, then disconnect muffler inlet pipe from turbocharger exhaust fitting. Lower vehicle.
12. Remove fuel conditioner and bracket assembly.
13. Disconnect, then remove fuel lines between injection pump and nozzles. Cap all open lines and fittings.
14. Disconnect heater hose fitting from rear lefthand of cylinder head.
15. Remove A/C compressor and mounting bracket, then position aside.
16. Disconnect electrical leads from No. 2 and 3 glow plugs.
17. Disconnect coolant temperature switch electrical connector.
18. Remove intake and exhaust manifolds.
19. Remove rocker cover.
20. Loosen cylinder head bolts in sequence shown in **Fig. 5**.
21. Remove cylinder head and gasket.
22. Reverse procedure to install. During installation of cylinder head, note the following:
    a. Clean gasket mating surface on cylinder head and block.
    b. Position new gasket on to block as shown in **Fig. 6**.
    c. Position cylinder head on to engine block and install attaching bolts.
    d. Torque bolts in two steps.
    e. First, torque bolts in sequence shown in **Fig. 7** to 38–42 ft. lbs.

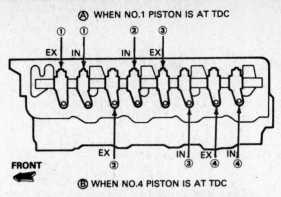

Fig. 8 Valve adjustment sequence

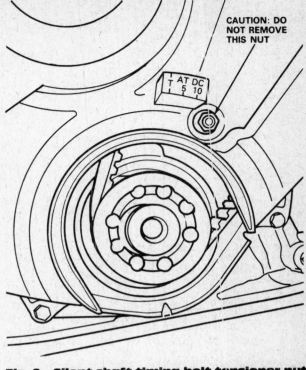

CAUTION: DO NOT REMOVE THIS NUT

Fig. 9 Silent shaft timing belt tensioner nut

f. Second, torque bolts in sequence shown to 76–83 ft. lbs.

VALVE ARRANGEMENT
FRONT TO REAR

E-I-E-I-E-I

VALVES
ADJUST

1. Start and operate engine until normal operating temperature is reached.
2. Remove rocker cover.
3. Rotate crankshaft until No. 1 piston is at TDC of compression stroke.
4. Using a suitable feeler gauge, check valve clearance in sequence shown in **Fig. 8**.
5. Valve clearance should be .010 inch.
6. To adjust valve clearance(s), proceed as follows:
   a. Loosen adjusting screw lock nut.
   b. Turn adjusting screw clockwise to reduce clearance or counterclockwise to increase valve clearance.
   c. Tighten lock nut while holding adjusting screw in position, then recheck valve clearance.
7. Rotate crankshaft 360° in direction of normal engine rotation until No. 4 piston is at TDC of compression stroke and repeat steps 4 through 6.

FRONT UPPER TIMING BELT
REPLACE

1. Disconnect battery ground cables from both battery assemblies.
2. Remove accessory drive belts.
3. Remove front upper timing belt cover attaching bolts.
4. Remove cover and gasket from engine.
5. Reverse procedure to install.

FRONT LOWER TIMING BELT COVER
REPLACE

1. Disconnect battery ground cables from both battery assemblies.
2. Remove cooling fan and fan shroud.
3. Remove accessory drive belts.
4. Remove four bolts attaching water pump pulley to water pump, then the pulley.
5. Remove crankshaft pulley.
6. Remove five bolts attaching timing cover to engine.

NOTE: Do not remove the nut shown in **Fig. 9**. This nut is for the silent shaft timing belt tensioner. Loosening this nut can alter belt tension.

7. Remove front lower timing belt cover from engine.
8. Reverse procedure to install.

CAMSHAFT
REPLACE

1. Disconnect battery ground cables from both battery assemblies.
2. Remove rocker cover attaching bolts, then the rocker cover assembly from engine.
3. Remove upper front timing belt cover as described previously.
4. Rotate crankshaft until No. 1 piston is at TDC of compression stroke.

5. Loosen camshaft/injection pump drive belt tensioner and remove timing belt from camshaft sprocket.
6. Remove camshaft sprocket bolt, then the camshaft sprocket.
7. Remove rocker shaft to cylinder head attaching bolts, one turn at a time starting from front of engine and working toward the rear.
8. Remove camshaft bearing caps and camshaft assembly from engine, **Fig. 10**.
9. Remove camshaft from engine.
10. Reverse procedure to install. During installation of camshaft, note the following:
    a. Ensure bearing caps are installed in their original positions.
    b. Coat sealing lip of camshaft seal with clean engine oil. Install seal using camshaft oil seal replacer T85T-6250-A or equivalent. Ensure seal installer is positioned with hole over spring pin on camshaft, **Fig. 11**.

TIMING BELT
ADJUST

INJECTION PUMP/CAMSHAFT

1. Remove timing belt upper cover as described previously.
2. Rotate engine until No. 1 piston is at TDC of compression stroke.

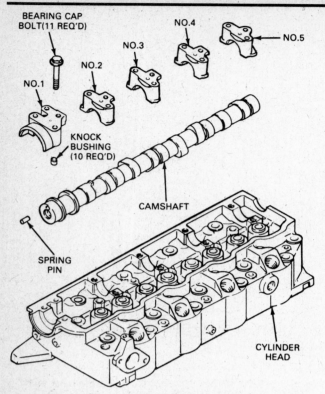

Fig. 10   Cylinder head & camshaft assembly

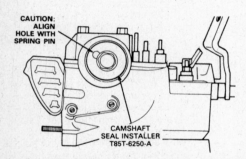

Fig. 11   Positioning seal installer with hole over spring pin on camshaft

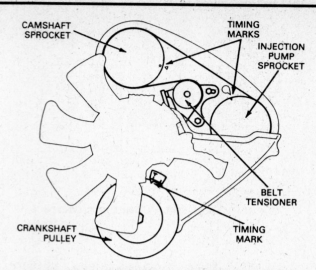

Fig. 12   Aligning injection pump sprocket & camshaft sprocket timing marks

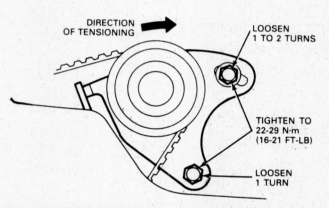

Fig. 13   Loosening top & bottom belt tensioner bolts

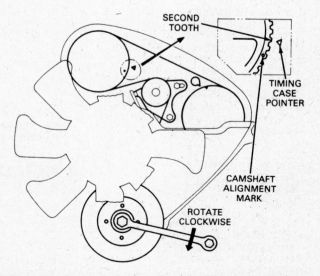

Fig. 14   Aligning pointer on timing cover with second tooth from alignment mark on camshaft sprocket

3. Check that crankshaft pulley, injection pump sprocket and camshaft sprocket are aligned properly with their timing marks, **Fig. 12.**
4. Loosen top belt tensioner bolt 1 to 2 turns, then loosen bottom bolt 1 complete turn, **Fig. 13.** This allows the tensioner spring to automatically adjust the timing belt tensioner.
5. Rotate crankshaft clockwise so alignment pointer on timing cover aligns with the second tooth from alignment mark on camshaft sprocket, **Fig. 14.**

NOTE: Rotate crankshaft smoothly by the specified amount (two camshaft sprocket teeth). Failure to do so will result in an incorrect belt tension and possible engine damage.

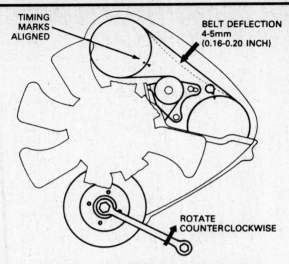

Fig. 15 Checking belt deflection

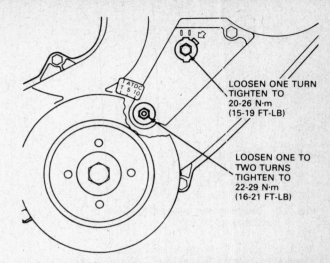

Fig. 17 Loosening top belt tensioner bolt 1 turn & bottom tensioner bolt 1–2 turns

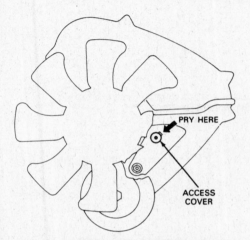

Fig. 16 Top belt tensioner bolt access cover

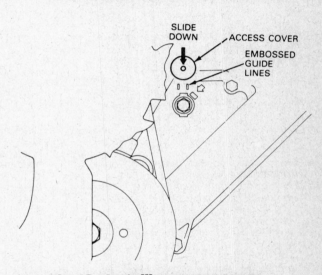

Fig. 18 Installing access cover

6. Tighten top belt tensioner bolt to 16–21 ft. lbs., then tighten bottom bolt also to 16–21 ft. lbs.

NOTE: Tighten the top bolt first. Tightening the bottom bolt first can cause tensioner to rotate and over-tension the timing belt.

7. Rotate crankshaft counterclockwise until timing marks are aligned, **Fig. 15**. Push belt downward halfway between injection pump sprocket and camshaft sprocket, then check deflection. If belt is properly tensioned, belt should deflect .16–.20 inches.

SILENT SHAFT

1. Rotate crankshaft until No. 1 piston is at TDC of compression stroke.
2. Remove access cover for top belt tensioner bolt by inserting a suitable screwdriver in slot shown in **Fig. 16** and prying outward.
3. Loosen top belt tensioner mounting bolt 1 complete turn. Then loosen bot-

tom bolt 1 to 2 turns, **Fig. 17**. This allows tensioner spring to automatically adjust belt tension.
4. Tighten bottom tensioner bolt to 16–21 ft. lbs., then tighten top bolt to 15–19 ft. lbs.

NOTE: Tighten the bottom bolt first. Tightening the top bolt first can cause the tensioner to rotate and over-tighten the timing belt.

5. Install access cover for top tensioner bolt by sliding downward along the two guide lines embossed on the front lower cover, **Fig. 18**.

INJECTION NOZZLES
REPLACE

1. Disconnect battery ground cables from both battery assemblies.
2. Mark, disconnect and cap injection

lines from injection nozzles and injection pump.
3. Disconnect, then remove fuel return pipe and gasket.
4. Remove injection nozzles from engine.
5. Reverse procedure to install.

INJECTION PUMP
REPLACE

1. Disconnect battery ground cables from both battery assemblies.
2. Remove radiator fan and shroud assembly.
3. Loosen, then remove accessory drive belts.
4. Rotate crankshaft in direction of normal engine rotation until No. 1 piston is at TDC of compression stroke.
5. Remove upper front timing cover as described previously.
6. Loosen, then remove timing belt from

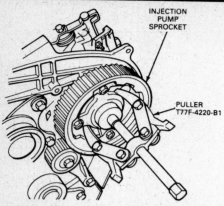

Fig. 19   Removing injection pump sprocket

injection pump sprocket as described previously.

7. Remove sprocket to injection pump attaching nut.
8. Using tool No. T77F-4220-B1 or equivalent, remove injection pump sprocket, **Fig. 19.**
9. Disconnect throttle and speed control cables, if equipped.
10. Disconnect coolant hoses from injection pump wax element.
11. Disconnect hoses from boost compensator and A/C throttle kicker.
12. Disconnect and cap fuel return line at return pipe on injection pump.
13. Disconnect chassis mounted fuel return line from injection pump assembly.
14. Disconnect and cap fuel supply line from fuel conditioner.
15. Disconnect, then remove fuel lines from injection pump and fuel nozzles. Cap all open lines and fittings.
16. Remove 2 nuts attaching injection pump to rear front case. Remove 2 injection pump bracket-to-engine bracket bolts and 2 engine bracket-to-engine block bolts, **Fig. 20.** Remove injection pump from engine assembly.
17. Reverse procedure to install.

INJECTION PUMP TIMING
ADJUST

1. Place transmission into Park.
2. Start and operate engine until normal operating temperature is reached.
3. Open cover on diagnostic connector, then connect adapter from dynamic timing meter tool No. 078-00116 or equivalent.
4. Check timing meter for RPM and injection timing.
5. Injection timing should be 5° at 1500 RPM.
6. If injection timing at specified RPM obtained is incorrect, proceed as follows:
   a. Turn ignition switch to OFF position.

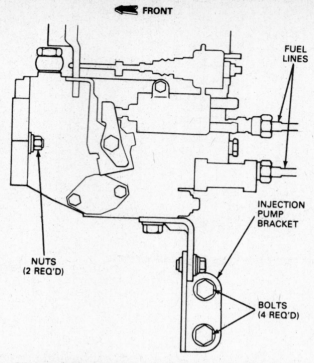

Fig. 20   Removing injection pump mounting nuts & attaching bracket bolts

b. Rotate engine until No. 1 cylinder is at TDC of compression stroke.
c. Remove injector pump distributor head plug bolt and sealing washer.
d. Install tools D84P-9000-D and 014-00420 or equivalents, into injection pump. The plunger portion of adapter D84P-9000-D must project into pump so it contacts the fuel injection pump plunger.
e. Install a suitable dial indicator into adapter D84P-9000-D. Ensure there is at least .100 inch preload on dial indicator.
f. Rotate crankshaft clockwise until dial indicator displays the lowest value, then set dial indicator to zero.
g. Continue rotating crankshaft clockwise until No. 1 piston is again at TDC of compression stroke. Install crankshaft holding tool T84P-6400-A or equivalent to secure crankshaft in position.
h. Dial indicator should read .0256 inch on timing belts with less than 10,000 miles of use, or .0248 inch on timing belts with more than 10,000 miles of use.
7. If injection pump timing obtained is not as specified, install adapter T84P-9000-B or equivalent on to injection pump.
8. Loosen injection pump mounting bolts and rotate tool clockwise to increase dial indicator reading or counterclockwise to decrease dial indicator reading.

9. Tighten injection pump rear mounting nuts first, then tighten injection pump front mounting nuts last.
10. Remove injection pump timing adapter and flywheel holding tool. Rotate engine 2 complete revolutions until No. 1 cylinder is at TDC of compression stroke. Check reading on dial indicator. If reading is correct, remove dial indicator and adapter and install distributor head plug and sealing washer. Torque bolt to 6–7 ft. lbs. If readings are incorrect, repeat steps 3 through 6.

PISTON & ROD ASSEMBLY

During removal of piston and rod assemblies, mark cylinder number on connecting rod and bearing cap to facilitate installation in their original positions. If oversize pistons are required, they must be installed in sets of four. Connecting rods have the letter "D" cast into them, **Fig. 21.** Pistons should be installed with the arrow on the top of the piston and the "D" on the connecting rod toward the front of the engine. Numbers marked on the connecting rod and bearing caps during disassembly, must be on the same side when installed into their cylinder bores. If a connecting rod is ever transposed from one block or cylinder to another, new bearings should be fitted and the connecting rod should be numbered to correspond with the new cylinder.

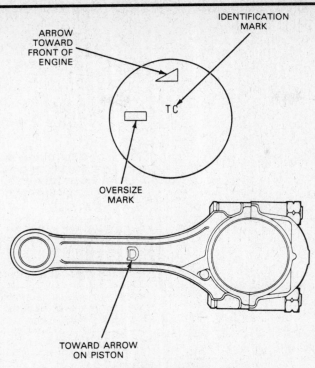

Fig. 21 Piston & rod assembly

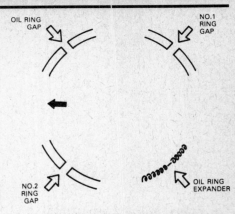

Fig. 22 Positioning piston ring end gaps approximately 90° apart

PISTONS, PINS & RINGS

Pistons and piston rings are available in standard size and oversizes of .010, .020, .030 and .040 inch.

During installation of piston rings on to pistons, position piston ring end gaps approximately 90° apart from each other as shown in **Fig. 22.**

MAIN & ROD BEARINGS

Main and rod bearings are available in standard size and undersizes of .010, .020 and .030 inch.

FRONT OIL SEAL
REPLACE

1. Disconnect battery ground cables from both battery assemblies.
2. Remove fan and fan shroud.
3. Remove accessory drive belts.
4. Remove crankshaft pulley, upper and lower timing belt covers and timing belt.
5. Remove crankshaft sprockets and timing plate.
6. Using a suitable punch, carefully punch a small hole in metal portion of seal. Insert tool No. T77L-9533-B or equivalent, then remove seal.
7. Reverse procedure to install. During installation of seal, use front seal

replacer tool T85T-6019-A or equivalent to properly install seal.

REAR OIL SEAL
REPLACE

1. Disconnect battery ground cables from both battery assemblies.
2. Raise and support vehicle.
3. Remove transmission from vehicle.
4. Remove clutch assembly.
5. Remove flywheel.
6. Drain oil from engine crankcase.
7. Loosen oil pan attaching bolts.
8. Remove 2 oil pan attaching bolts from rear seal retainer.
9. Remove five bolts attaching rear seal retainer to engine block.
10. Remove retainer and gasket.
11. Remove oil separator from rear seal retainer.
12. Reverse procedure to install. During installation of seal, note the following:
    a. Position seal retainer facing downward on a suitable press.

NOTE: Ensure lip on seal retainer is positioned on press plate with flange over the edge.

    b. Lubricate oil seal with clean engine oil and press seal into retainer (from back side of retainer) using rear seal replacer tool T85T-6701-A or equivalent.
    c. During installation of oil separator, ensure oil separator is installed into

seal retainer with drain hole at bottom.

WATER PUMP
REPLACE

1. Disconnect battery ground cables from both battery assemblies.
2. Remove cooling fan and shroud.
3. Loosen A/C compressor and power steering belt tensioner, then remove belt.
4. Remove belt tensioner.
5. Remove bolts attaching pulley to water pump, then the pulley.
6. Remove A/C compressor support bracket.
7. Drain cooling system.
8. Disconnect lower radiator hose from thermostat housing adapter.
9. Remove thermostat housing and thermostat.
10. Remove upper and lower front timing belt covers.
11. Remove water pump attaching bolts, then the water pump from engine block.
12. Reverse procedure to install.

OIL PAN
REPLACE

1. Disconnect battery ground cables from both battery assemblies.
2. Remove engine oil dipstick.
3. Remove cooling fan and fan shroud.
4. Drain cooling system and remove radiator.
5. Remove alternator drive belt.
6. Remove bolts attaching A/C compressor, then position compressor aside.
7. Raise and support vehicle.
8. Drain engine oil from crankcase.
9. Remove No. 1A crossmember.
10. Remove bolts attaching stabilizer bar brackets to frame, then lower stabilizer bar assembly.
11. Disconnect power steering lines from power steering pump.
12. Remove clamp securing power steer-

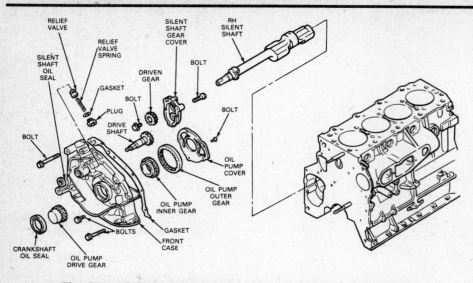

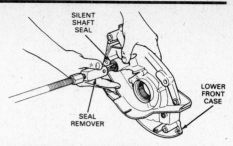

Fig. 24 Removing silent shaft reverse rotation drive gear oil seal from lower front case assembly

Fig. 23 Righthand silent shaft & oil pump assembly

ing line to crossmember, then position line aside.

13. Remove nuts attaching engine mounts to support brackets.
14. Position a suitable jack under transmission housing and raise engine assembly. Install wooden wedges between engine mounts and crossmember assemblies.
15. Loosen, then remove oil pan attaching bolts and allow oil pan to rest on crossmember.
16. Remove 2 bolts and 1 nut securing pick-up tube to engine and lower tube into oil pan.
17. Rotate crankshaft until crankshaft main bearing throws are parallel to bottom of engine, providing clearance to remove oil pan assembly.
18. Remove oil pan through the front by first raising pan up between engine and radiator support, then bring pan out through the bottom.
19. Reverse procedure to install. Torque oil pan attaching bolts to 4.5–5.5 ft. lbs.

RIGHTHAND SILENT SHAFT & OIL PUMP
REPLACE

1. Disconnect battery ground cables from both battery assemblies.
2. Remove cooling fan and shroud assembly.
3. Remove water pump pulley, crankshaft pulley, upper and lower timing belt covers, timing belts and crankshaft sprocket.
4. Loosen oil pan attaching bolts, then remove 6 front oil pan to front case bolts.
5. Remove pipe plug from righthand side of engine block. Insert a suitable screwdriver into hole to prevent righthand silent shaft from rotating.
6. Remove nut attaching silent shaft sprocket to drive gear, then the sprocket.
7. Remove bolts attaching front case to engine block, then the front case, **Fig. 23.**

8. Remove silent shaft reverse gear cover, silent shaft and gears from engine block. Remove oil pump cover.
9. Place alignment marks on oil pump gears, then remove pump gears.

NOTE: Do not use a sharp tool to place alignment marks on oil pump drive, inner or outer gears.

10. Using tool T85L-101-B or equivalent, remove silent shaft reverse rotation drive gear oil seal from lower front case assembly, **Fig. 24.**
11. Reverse procedure to install and note the following:
    a. Using a 21mm socket and hammer, install silent shaft oil seal into lower front case assembly.
    b. Install seal protector tool T85T-6571-A or equivalent, on to drive gear before installation.
    c. Install silent shaft reverse rotation gears with marks properly aligned as shown in **Fig. 25.**
    d. During installation of oil pump, ensure marks placed on pump gears during removal are correctly aligned.
    e. During installation of front cover, ensure correct length bolts are installed in their original locations as shown in **Fig. 26.**
    f. During installation of silent shaft sprocket, ensure "D" flat on silent

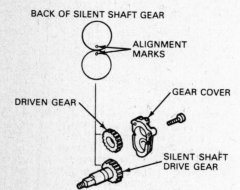

Fig. 25 Aligning silent shaft reverse rotation gear timing marks

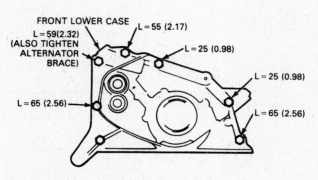

L = BOLT LENGTH mm (in.)

Fig. 26 Installing correct length front cover bolts into their original positions

Fig. 27 Aligning D flat on sprocket with D flat on shaft

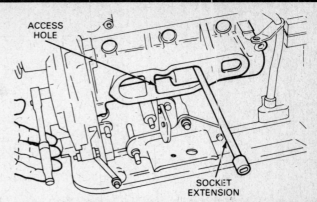

Fig. 28 Install extension to prevent silent shaft from turning

shaft sprocket aligns with "D" flat on shaft, **Fig. 27.**

UPPER FRONT CASE COVER & LEFTHAND SILENT SHAFT
REPLACE

1. Disconnect battery ground cables from both battery assemblies.
2. Remove cooling fan and shroud assembly.
3. Remove accessory drive belts.
4. Remove alternator and bracket, then position aside.
5. Remove water pump and crankshaft pulley.
6. Remove upper and lower timing belt covers, timing belts and injection

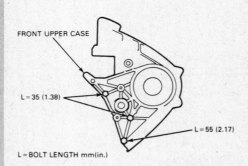

Fig. 29 Install correct length bolts into upper front cover

pump.
7. Remove access plate on lefthand side of engine, then insert a suitable socket extension tool into hole to prevent lefthand silent shaft from rotating, **Fig. 28.**
8. Remove bolt attaching sprocket to silent shaft, then the sprocket.
9. Remove bolts attaching front case to engine block, then the front case.
10. Remove silent shaft and silent shaft seal.
11. Reverse procedure to install and note the following:
   a. During installation of upper front cover, ensure correct length bolts are installed in their original locations as shown in **Fig. 29.**
   b. During installation of silent shaft, ensure "D" flat on silent shaft sprocket aligns with "D" flat in shaft, **Fig. 27.**

Clutch & Manual Transmission Section

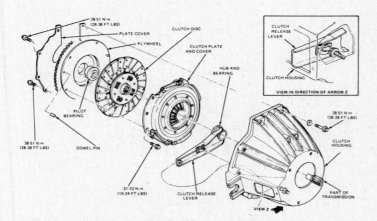

Fig. 1 Clutch housing. 4-122 & 4-140 engines

CLUTCH
REPLACE

EXCEPT 4-143 DIESEL ENGINE

1. Disconnect hydraulic clutch system master cylinder from clutch pedal.
2. Raise and support vehicle, then remove dust cover from clutch housing and disconnect hydraulic clutch linkage from housing and release lever. Remove starter.
3. Remove clutch housing to engine block bolts, noting direction of bolt installation, then mark alignment of driveshaft and companion flange and remove driveshaft, **Figs. 1, 2 and 3.**
4. Remove nuts which attach transmission and insulator to #2 crossmember support, **Fig. 4,** then raise transmission with suitable jack and remove #2 crossmember support. Lower transmission and clutch housing.
5. Remove release lever, and hub and bearing, then mark assembled posi-

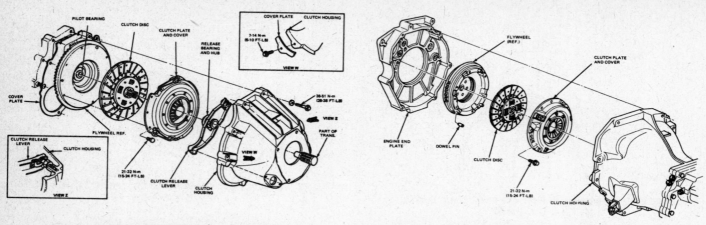

Fig. 2 Clutch housing. V6-171 engine

Fig. 3 Clutch housing. 4-135 diesel engine

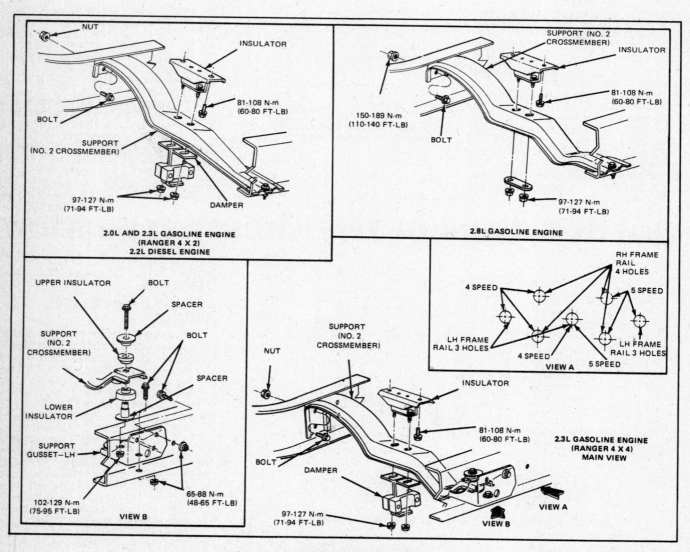

Fig. 4 Transmission rear support

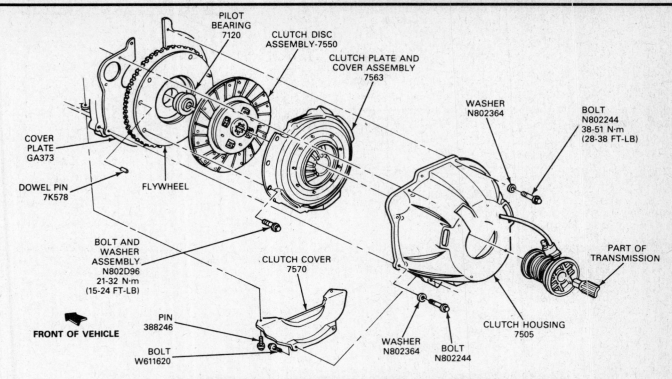

PILOT BEARING 7120

CLUTCH DISC ASSEMBLY-7550

CLUTCH PLATE AND COVER ASSEMBLY 7563

WASHER N802364

BOLT N802244 38-51 N·m (28-38 FT-LB)

COVER PLATE GA373

DOWEL PIN 7K578

FLYWHEEL

BOLT AND WASHER ASSEMBLY N802D96 21-32 N·m (15-24 FT-LB)

CLUTCH COVER 7570

PART OF TRANSMISSION

FRONT OF VEHICLE

PIN 388246

BOLT W611620

WASHER N802364

BOLT N802244

CLUTCH HOUSING 7505

Fig. 5 Clutch housing assembly. 4-143 turbocharged diesel engine

tion of pressure plate and cover to flywheel.

6. Loosen pressure plate and cover attaching bolts evenly until pressure plate springs are expanded, then remove bolts.

7. Remove pressure plate and cover assembly and clutch disc from flywheel.

8. Position clutch disc on flywheel so that tool D79T-7550-A or equivalent can enter clutch pilot bearing and align disc.

9. Align pressure plate and cover assembly to flywheel and position pressure plate and cover assembly on flywheel, aligning pressure plate and disc, then install assembly to flywheel retaining bolts. Torque bolts to 15–24 ft. lbs. and remove tool.

10. Position clutch release bearing and bearing hub on release lever and install release lever on release lever seat in flywheel housing, then coat release lever fingers and lever pivot ball with suitable lubricant and fill annular groove of release bearing hub with grease.

11. Raise transmission and clutch housing into position and install #2 crossmember support to frame, then install connecting nuts, bolts and washers and torque to specifications, **Fig. 4.**

12. Lower transmission and insulator into support, then install nuts and torque to 71–94 ft. lbs. Remove transmission jack.

13. Install driveshaft, aligning marks on driveshaft and companion flange, and torque bolts to 70–95 ft. lbs.

14. Install housing to engine block bolts in

same direction as removed and torque to 28–38 ft. lbs.

15. Install hydraulic clutch linkage, on housing in position with release lever, dust shield, and starter, then lower vehicle and check clutch for proper operation.

4-143 DIESEL ENGINE

1. Disconnect clutch hydraulic system master cylinder from clutch pedal and dash panel.

2. Raise and support vehicle.

3. Remove starter motor from engine.

4. Remove clutch housing to engine block attaching bolts, **Fig. 5.**

NOTE: Note direction in which the bolts are installed.

5. Mark driveshaft and companion flange for installation, then remove driveshaft.

6. Remove nuts attaching transmission and insulator to No. 2 crossmember support, **Fig. 6.**

7. Raise transmission slightly, then remove No. 2 crossmember support.

8. Lower transmission and clutch housing.

9. Mark assembled position of pressure plate and cover to the flywheel for installation.

10. Loosen pressure plate and cover attaching bolts evenly until pressure plate springs are completely expanded, then remove attaching bolts.

11. Remove pressure plate, cover assembly and clutch disc from flywheel.

These parts can be removed through the opening in the bottom of the clutch housing on models equipped with a dust cover.

12. Remove pilot bearing, if required.

13. Install pilot bearing, if removed.

14. Install clutch disc onto flywheel, then insert clutch alignment tool No. T74P-7137-K or equivalent into clutch pilot bearing hole. Ensure clutch disc is properly aligned on flywheel.

15. If installing original pressure plate and cover assembly, align marks made during removal and position pressure plate and cover assembly on to flywheel.

16. Install pressure plate attaching bolts and torque bolts to 15–25 ft. lbs.

17. Remove clutch disc alignment tool.

18. Raise transmission and clutch housing assembly into position, then install No. 2 crossmember support on to frame.

19. Lower transmission and insulator into crossmember support, and tighten attaching nuts.

20. Remove transmission jack.

21. Install driveshaft. Ensure marks made on driveshaft align properly with mark on companion flange. Tighten attaching nuts and bolts to 70–95 ft. lbs.

22. Install housing to engine block attaching bolts in correct position as removed. Torque attaching bolts to 28–38 ft. lbs.

23. Install starter motor on to engine.

24. Lower vehicle and connect clutch hydraulic system master cylinder to the clutch pedal and to the dash panel assembly. Check clutch for proper operation.

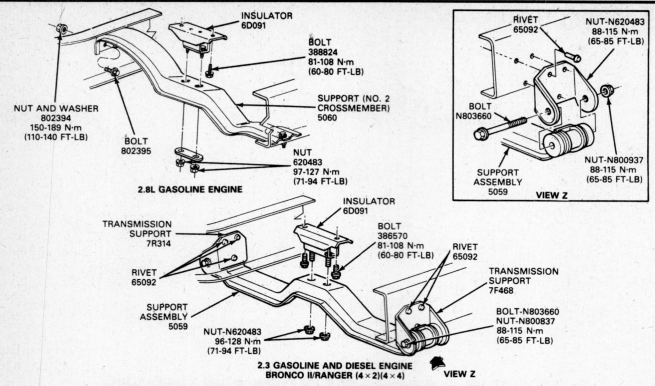

Fig. 6 **Transmission support installation. 4-143 turbocharged diesel engine**

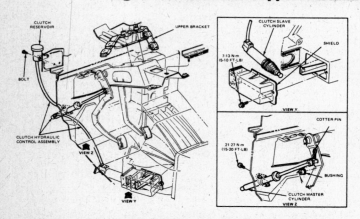

Fig. 7 **Hydraulic clutch system. 4-122 & 4-140 engines**

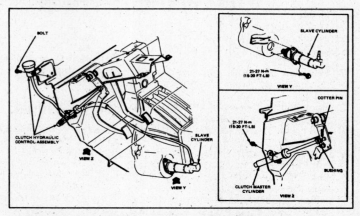

Fig. 8 **Hydraulic clutch system. V6-171 engine**

HYDRAULIC CLUTCH

The hydraulic clutch control system, **Figs. 7, 8, 9, and 10,** consists of a fluid reservoir, a master cylinder, a slave cylinder and connective tubing. The clutch master cylinder converts mechanical clutch pedal movement into hydraulic fluid movement. The slave cylinder converts hydraulic fluid movement to mechanical movement to activate the clutch release lever. The hydraulic clutch system locates the clutch pedal and provides automatic clutch adjustment. Adjustment of clutch pedal position or clutch linkage is not required.

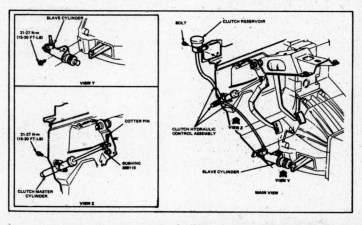

Fig. 9 **Hydraulic clutch system. 4-135 diesel engine**

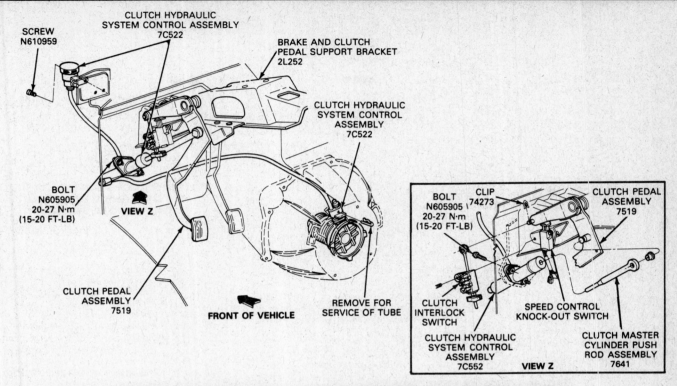

Fig. 10 Hydraulic clutch system. 4-143 turbocharged diesel engine

TRANSMISSION
REPLACE

1. Disconnect battery ground cable (both battery ground cables on diesel engine).
2. Place gearshift lever in neutral position then remove boot retainer screws.
3. Remove retainer cover to gearshift lever retainer attaching bolts then disconnect clutch master cylinder push rod from clutch pedal.
4. Pull gearshift lever assembly, shim and bushing straight up away from the gearshift lever retainer.
5. To avoid dirt entering shift tower opening in extension housing, cover with cloth.
6. Disconnect clutch hydraulic system master cylinder push rod from clutch pedal.
7. Raise and support vehicle.
8. Disconnect driveshaft at rear axle drive flange then pull driveshaft rearward and disconnect from transmission. Install suitable plug in extension housing to prevent lubricant leakage.
9. Remove clutch housing dust shield and slave cylinder and secure to the side.
10. Disconnect starter motor and back-up lamp switch wires.
11. Place suitable jack under engine using a block of wood between jack and engine to protect the oil pan.
12. Remove speedometer cable from extension housing.
13. On four-wheel drive vehicles, remove the transfer case as described in the "Transfer Case Section."
14. Remove starter motor and position a transmission jack under transmission.
15. Remove bolts, lockwasher and flat washer attaching transmission to the engine rear plate.
16. Remove nuts and bolts attaching transmission mount to crossmember.
17. Remove nuts attaching crossmember to frame side rails and remove crossmember.
18. Lower the jack then work clutch housing from locating dowels and slide transmission rearward until input shaft spline clears clutch disc.
19. Remove transmission from vehicle.
20. Reverse procedure to install.

Transfer Case Section

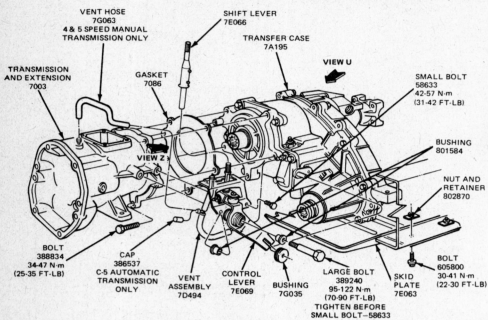

Fig. 1   Transfer case mounting

Fig. 2   Transfer case retaining bolt tightening sequence. Except 1985 models

Fig. 3   Transfer case retaining bolt tightening sequence. 1985 models

TRANSFER CASE
REPLACE

1. Raise and support vehicle.
2. Remove skid plate from frame, if equipped, then drain fluid from transfer case.
3. Disconnect four-wheel drive indicator switch electrical connector from transfer case.
4. Disconnect front driveshaft from axle input yoke.
5. Loosen clamp retaining front driveshaft boot to transfer case, then remove driveshaft and front boot assembly from transfer case front output shaft.
6. Disconnect rear driveshaft from transfer case output shaft yoke, then the speedometer driven gear from transfer case rear cover.
7. Disconnect vent hose from control lever, then remove shoulder bolt and the shifter to extension housing retaining bolt. Pull control lever out until bushing slides off shift lever pin. If necessary, remove shift lever from control lever, **Fig. 1.**
8. Remove heat shield from transfer case.
9. Support transfer case with a suitable

jack, then remove retaining bolts. Slide transfer case rearward and lower from vehicle.
10. Reverse procedure to install. Note the following:
   a. Torque transfer case retaining bolts to 25–35 ft. lbs. in sequence shown, **Figs. 2 and 3.**
   b. Torque heat shield retaining bolts to 27–37 ft. lbs.
   c. Torque shifter to extension housing retaining bolt to 31–42 ft. lbs. and shoulder bolt to 70–90 ft. lbs. The shifter retaining bolt must be tightened before the shoulder bolt.
   d. Torque speedometer driven gear attaching screw to 20–25 inch lbs., front and rear driveshaft retaining bolts to 12–15 ft. lbs., fill and drain plugs to 14–22 ft. lbs. and skid plate retaining bolts to 22–30 ft. lbs.
   e. Fill transfer case with 3 pints of Dexron II automatic transmission fluid, or equivalent.

SHIFT LEVER
REPLACE

NOTE: Removal of the shift ball is necessary only if the shift ball, boot, or lever is

being replaced. If not, remove the ball, boot and lever as an assembly.

1. Remove plastic insert from shift ball, then warm ball to approximately 140–180° F and knock ball off lever with a hammer and a block of wood.
2. Remove rubber boot and pan cover, then disconnect vent hose from control lever.
3. Unscrew shift lever from control lever, then remove shifter to extension housing retaining bolt and the shoulder bolt. Remove control lever and bushings.
4. Reverse procedure to install. Note the following:
   a. Torque shifter to extension housing retaining bolt to 31–42 ft. lbs. and shoulder bolt to 70–90 ft. lbs. The shifter retaining bolt must be tightened before the shoulder bolt.
   b. Torque shift lever to 27–37 ft. lbs.
   c. Install vent assembly so the white marking on housing is in line with notch in shifter. Position upper end of vent hose inside shift lever bolts.
   d. Install shift ball to the end of knurl on upper part of shift lever.

Rear Axle, Suspension & Brakes Section

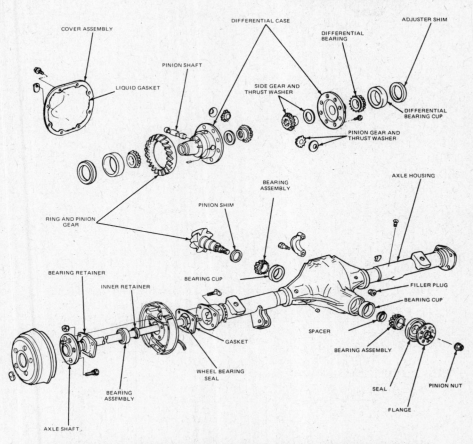

Fig. 1   Disassembled view of Ford 6¾ inch Ring Gear axle

6¾ INCH RING GEAR AXLE

DESCRIPTION

NOTE: This axle can be identified by the 8 cover bolts.

This rear axle, **Fig. 1,** is an integral design hypoid with the centerline of the pinion set below the centerline of the ring gear. The semi-floating axle shafts are retained in the housing by ball bearings and bearing retainers at axle ends.

The differential is mounted on two opposed tapered roller bearings which are retained in the housing by removable caps. Differential bearing preload and drive gear backlash is adjusted by nuts located behind each differential bearing cup.

The drive pinion assembly is mounted on two opposed tapered roller bearings. Pinion bearing preload is adjusted by a collapsible spacer on the pinion shaft. Pinion and ring gear tooth contact is adjusted by shims between the rear bearing cone and pinion gear.

REAR AXLE ASSEMBLY, REPLACE

1. Raise vehicle and support at rear frame members.
2. Drain lubricant from axle.
3. Mark driveshaft and pinion flange for proper reassembly. Disconnect driveshaft from pinion flange.
4. Remove wheels, brake drums and both axle shafts as outlined in "Axle Shaft & Oil Seal, Replace".
5. Remove vent tube hose, then remove vent tube from axle housing.
6. Remove bolt securing hydraulic brake T-fitting from axle housing, then carefully remove the hydraulic brake hose from retaining clip. Carefully wire rear brake backing plates, hydraulic brake system and parking brake cables as one unit out of the way.
7. Using a suitable jack, support rear axle. Remove U-bolts, shock absorber lower mounting and spring plates.
8. Lower axle housing and remove from vehicle.
9. Reverse procedure to install, noting the following torques: U-bolt nuts, 55–75 ft. lbs., shock absorber lower mounts, 40–60 ft. lbs., driveshaft-to-pinion flange bolts, 70–95 ft. lbs., rear axle shaft retainer plate nuts, 20–40 ft. lbs. and rear cover attaching bolts, 23–35 ft. lbs., except the ratio tag bolt which is torqued to 15–20 ft. lbs.

AXLE SHAFT & OIL SEAL, REPLACE

1. Remove wheel and tire assembly, then remove nuts attaching brake drum to axle shaft flange and remove brake drum.
2. Working through opening in axle shaft flange, remove nuts securing axle shaft bearing retainer.
3. Using a suitable puller, pull axle shaft from housing.
4. Remove brake backing plate and attach to frame side rail with a piece of wire.
5. Using a hook type puller, remove oil seal from housing.
6. Wipe all lubricant from oil seal area of axle housing, then install oil seal using tool No. T79P-1177-A.
7. Install gasket on housing flange, then install brake backing plate.
8. Carefully slide axle shaft into housing using care not to damage oil seal, then install bearing retainer attaching nuts and torque to 20 to 40 ft. lbs.
9. Install brake drum and retaining nuts, then install wheel and tire assembly.

REAR AXLE SHAFT BEARINGS, REPLACE

1. Remove axle shaft as described in "Axle Shaft & Oil Seal, Replace".
2. Loosen axle inner retainer ring by nicking deeply with a cold chisel in several places and slide off shaft.
3. Using a suitable press, remove bearing from axle.

NOTE: Do not ever attempt to use heat to make bearing removal easier, as it will weaken the axle shaft bearing journal area.

4. Position bearing retainer plate and bearing on axle, then using a suitable press, install bearing. Using the same tool, install bearing retainer ring.

NOTE: Do not press on the bearing and the retainer ring at the same time. They

5. Reinstall axle in axle housing. Ensure new seal is installed.

7½ INCH RING GEAR AXLE

DESCRIPTION

NOTE: This axle can be identified by the 10 cover bolts.

The gear set, **Fig. 2,** consists of a ring gear and an overhung drive pinion which is supported by two opposed tapered roller bearings. The differential case is a one-piece design with openings allowing assembly of the internal parts and lubricant flow. The differential pinion shaft is retained with a threaded bolt (lock) assembled to the case.

The roller type wheel bearings have no inner race, and the rollers directly contact the bearing journals of the axle shafts. The axle shafts do not use an inner and outer bearing retainer. Rather, they are held in the axle by means of C-locks. These C-locks also fit into a machined recess in the differential side gears within the differential case. There is no retainer bolt access hole in the axle shaft flange.

REAR AXLE ASSEMBLY, REPLACE

1. Raise vehicle and support at rear frame members.
2. Remove rear wheels and brake drums.
3. Drain rear axle lubricant by removing housing cover.
4. Remove axle shafts as described under "Axle Shafts, Seals & Bearings, Replace."
5. Remove 4 retaining nuts from each backing plate and wire the plates aside.
6. Disconnect rear axle housing vent.
7. Disconnect brake line from retaining clips on axle housing.
8. Remove hydraulic brake T-fitting from axle housing.
9. Mark driveshaft and axle flange for assembly reference, then disconnect shaft from flange.
10. Support axle with a suitable jack, then remove U-bolt nuts, U-bolts and plates.
11. Disconnect lower shock absorber studs from axle housing mounting brackets.
12. Lower axle housing and remove from vehicle.
13. Reverse procedure to install, noting the following torques: U-bolt nuts, 55—75 ft. lbs., shock absorber lower mounts, 40—60 ft. lbs., brake backing plate nuts, 20—40 ft. lbs., driveshaft-to-pinion flange bolts, 70—95 ft. lbs. and rear cover bolts, 25—35 ft. lbs., except ratio tag bolt, which is torqued to 15—24 ft. lbs.

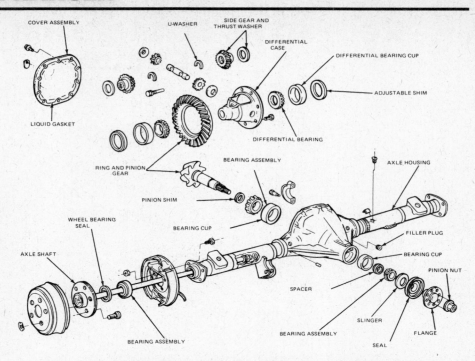

Fig. 2   Disassembled view of Ford 7½ inch Ring Gear Axle

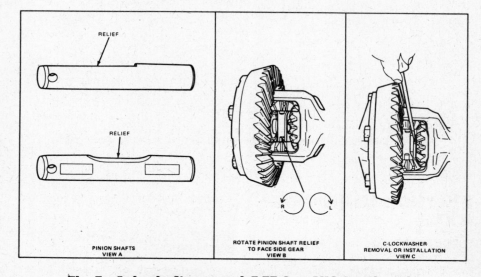

Fig. 3   Axle shaft removal. 3.73:1 or 4.10:1 ratio axle

AXLE SHAFTS, SEALS & BEARINGS, REPLACE

1. Raise and support vehicle.
2. Remove rear wheels and brake drums.
3. Drain rear axle lubricant by removing housing cover.
4. On models with 3.73:1 or 4.10:1 ratio axle, remove axle shafts as follows:
   a. Remove pinion shaft lock bolt, then rotate pinion shaft until relief in shaft faces either side gear, **Fig. 3,** and remove C-lockwasher from axle shaft.
   b. Rotate pinion shaft ½ turn until relief faces opposite side gear and remove C-lockwasher from axle shafts.
   c. Carefully slide shafts out of housing.
5. On all models except those with 3.73:1 or 4.10:1 ratio axle, remove axle shafts as follows:
   a. Remove differential pinion shaft lock bolt and the shaft.
   b. Push axle shafts inward toward center of vehicle and remove C-lockwashers from shafts, **Fig. 4.**
   c. Carefully slide axle shafts out of housing.
6. Remove seal and bearing using a suit-

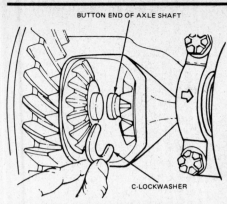

**Fig. 4   Axle shaft removal.
Except 3.73:1 or 4.10:1 ratio axle**

able hook-type puller.
7. Reverse procedure to install, noting the following:
   a. Apply suitable grease between lips of axle shaft seal.

b. Install seal and bearing using tool No. T78P-1225-A or equivalent.
c. Torque pinion shaft lock bolt to 15–22 ft. lbs.
d. Torque differential housing cover bolts to 25–35 ft. lbs., except the ratio tag bolt which is torqued to 15–24 ft. lbs.

8.8 INCH RING GEAR AXLE
DESCRIPTION

The gear set, **Fig. 5**, consists of an 8.8 inch diameter ring gear and an overhung drive pinion which is supported by two opposed tapered roller bearings. Pinion bearing preload is adjusted by the pinion nut and a collapsible spacer maintains correct seating of the inner race.

The housing assembly consists of a cast center section with two steel tube assemblies and a stamped rear cover.

The differential case is a one-piece design with two openings to allow for assembly of the internal components and lubricant flow. The differential pinion shaft is retained with a threaded bolt assembled to the case. The differential case assembly is mounted in the carrier between two opposed tapered roller bearings. The bearings are retained in the carrier by removable bearing caps.

REAR AXLE ASSEMBLY
REPLACE

1. Raise vehicle and support at rear frame members.
2. Remove rear wheels and brake assemblies.
3. Drain rear axle lubricant by removing housing cover.
4. Remove axle shafts as described under "Axle Shaft, Seals & Bearings, Replace".

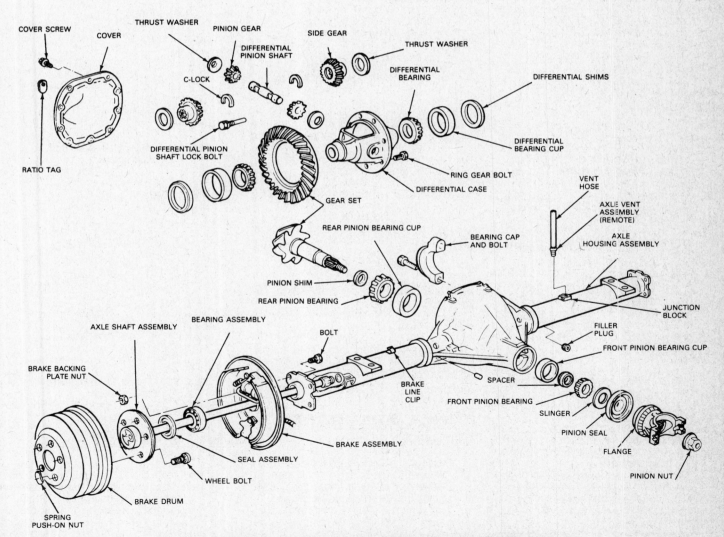

Fig. 5   Disassembled view of 8.8 inch rear axle assembly

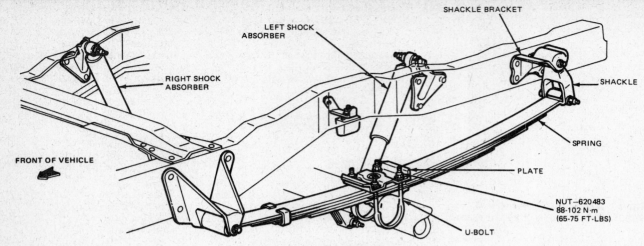

Fig. 6 Rear suspension

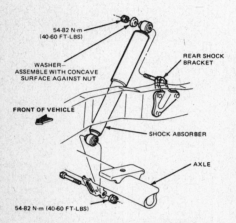

Fig. 7 Shock absorber replacement

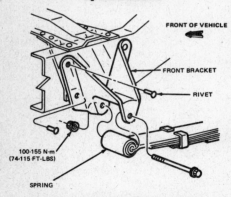

Fig. 9 Forward leaf spring mounting

taining line to the axle housing and carrier assembly.

8. Remove hydraulic brake junction block from axle housing assembly. Do not disconnect brake system lines.
9. Using a suitable jack, support rear axle housing, then remove U-bolt nuts.
10. Remove U-bolts and attaching plates from axle housing assembly.
11. Disconnect shock absorber lower bolts from the mounting brackets on axle housing assembly.
12. Remove axle housing assembly from vehicle.
13. Reverse procedure to install, noting the following torques: U-bolt nuts, 65–75 ft. lbs., shock absorber lower mounts, 40–60 ft. lbs., driveshaft-to-pinion flange bolts, 70–95 ft. lbs., rear cover bolts, 25–35 ft. lbs., except ratio tag bolt, which is torqued to 15–24 ft. lbs.

AXLE SHAFT, SEALS & BEARINGS
REPLACE

Refer to "Axle Shaft, Seals & Bearings, Replace" under 7½ Inch Ring Gear for service procedure.

SHOCK ABSORBER
REPLACE

1. Raise vehicle and support rear axle.
2. Remove lower attaching bolt and nut from shock absorber, then swing lower end free from mounting bracket.
3. Disconnect shock absorber from upper mounting, then remove shock from vehicle, **Figs. 6 and 7.**
4. Reverse procedure to install.

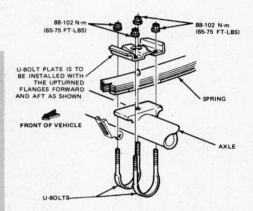

Fig. 8 Leaf spring U-bolt removal

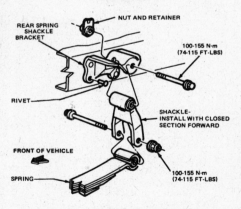

Fig. 10 Rear leaf spring mounting

LEAF SPRINGS
REPLACE

1. Raise rear of vehicle until weight is relieved from spring, with tires remaining in contact with floor.
2. Remove U-bolt nuts and the U-bolts, **Fig. 8.**
3. Remove spring-to-bracket attaching nut and bolt, **Fig. 9.**

5. Remove four retaining nuts from each backing plate, then wire backing plate to the underbody.
6. Disconnect vent hose from axle vent.

NOTE: The axle vent is secured to the housing assembly at the brake junction block.

7. Disconnect brake line from clips re-

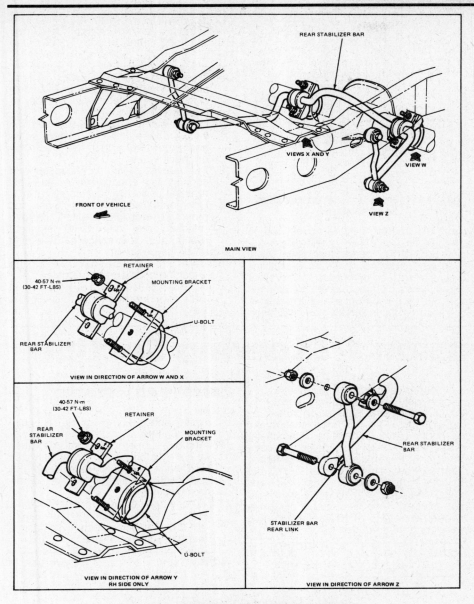

Fig. 11   Stabilizer bar replacement

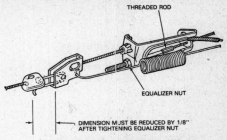

Fig. 12   Parking brake adjustment

4. Remove shackle-to-bracket attaching nuts and bolts, **Fig. 10,** then the spring and shackle assembly.
5. Reverse procedure to install.

STABILIZER BAR
REPLACE

1. Disconnect stabilizer bar from rear link, **Fig. 11.**
2. Remove mounting bracket U-bolt, then the mounting bracket, retainer and stabilizer bar.
3. Reverse procedure to install.

NOTE: The "UP" marking on the mounting bracket must be positioned as shown in **Fig. 11.**

BRAKES
ADJUST
REAR DRUM BRAKES

The rear brake shoes adjust automatically when the vehicle is driven forward and reverse and the brakes are applied several times sharply. Manual adjustment is required only when brake shoes are relined or replaced.

NOTE: When adjusting rear brake shoes, check parking brake cable for proper adjustment and be sure equalizer is operating properly.

1. With drums removed, clean areas where shoes contact backing plate, then apply suitable lubricant to these contact areas, being careful not to get lubricant on shoes.

2. Using brake shoe adjusting gauge or equivalent, adjust gauge to inside diameter of drum braking surface.
3. Reverse tool and adjust brake shoes until they touch gauge, being sure the gauge contact points on the shoes are parallel to vehicle with center line through center of axle. Holding automatic adjusting lever out of way, rotate adjustment screw. Oil screw threads with suitable lubricant if screw will not turn freely.
4. Install drums, drum retaining nuts, wheels and mounting nuts, then complete adjustment by applying brakes several times while driving vehicle in reverse and check brake operation by making several stops while driving forward.
5. Drum brakes may also be adjusted by raising vehicle enough to raise wheels off ground and turning adjusting screws through holes in brake backing plate.

PARKING BRAKE

NOTE: The following is a revised procedure.

1. Adjust parking brake with service brakes adjusted and drums cold.
2. Fully depress parking brake and measure distance between tension limiter bracket and strap hook, **Fig. 12.**
3. Tighten equalizer nut 6 full turns while holding threaded rod, then release and fully depress pedal 3 or 4 times.
4. Remeasure distance between tension limiter and strap hook. If measurement did not change by at least ⅛ inch from original measurement, tighten nut an additional 6 turns.
5. Release parking brake and check for rear wheel drag.

MASTER CYLINDER
REPLACE
WITH POWER BRAKES

1. With engine off, depress brake pedal to expel vacuum from brake booster system.
2. Disconnect hydraulic lines from master cylinder.
3. Remove brake booster to master cylinder retaining nuts and remove master cylinder from brake booster.
4. Reverse procedure to install and

bleed brake system, then refill master cylinder and bleed it.

LESS POWER BRAKES

1. Disconnect wires from stoplight switch inside cab below instrument panel.
2. Remove retaining nut, shoulder bolt and spacers which secure master cylinder push rod to brake pedal assembly, then remove stoplight switch from pedal.
3. Disconnect hydraulic brake lines from master cylinder, then remove master cylinder to dash panel retaining nuts, master cylinder, and boot from master cylinder push rod.
4. Reverse procedure to install and bleed brake system, then refill and bleed master cylinder.

BRAKE BOOSTER
REPLACE

NOTE: Make sure booster rubber reaction disc is properly installed as shown in **Fig.**

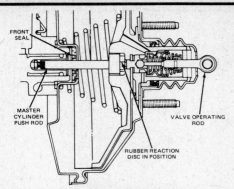

Fig. 13 Checking reaction disc installation

13 if the master cylinder push rod is removed or accidentally pulled out. A dislodged disc may cause excessive pedal travel and extreme operation sensitivity. The disc is black compared to the silver colored valve plunger that will be exposed after push rod and front seal are removed. The booster unit is serviced as an assembly and must be replaced if the reaction disc cannot be properly installed and aligned, or if it cannot be located within the unit itself.

1. Disconnect stoplight switch wiring, support master cylinder from underside, and remove master cylinder to booster retaining nuts.
2. Loosen clamp which secures manifold vacuum hose to booster check valve and remove hose, then remove booster check valve.
3. Pull master cylinder off booster and support far enough away to allow removal of booster assembly.
4. On models equipped with push rod mounted stoplight switch, remove retaining pin, then slide stoplight switch, push rod, spacer and bushing off brake pedal arm.
5. On all models, remove brake booster attaching bolts and the booster.
6. Reverse procedure to install, then start engine and check brake operation.

Front Suspension & Steering Section

DESCRIPTION

4 × 2

The twin I-beam suspension consists of coil springs, I-beam axle arms, radius arms, upper and lower ball joints, spindles, tie rods, shock absorbers and an optional stabilizer bar, **Fig. 1.**

4 × 4

The independent front suspension used on four wheel drive models is comprised of a two piece front driving axle assembly, two coil springs and two radius arms, **Fig. 2.** The front driving axle consists of two independent axle arm assemblies. One end of each axle arm assembly is mounted to the frame, with the opposite end supported by the coil spring and radius arm.

WHEEL ALIGNMENT

Front wheel alignment specifications and method of checking caster, camber and toe-in for Twin I-beam front axles on 4×2 models or independent front suspension on 4×4 models is determined with truck at normal operating height, provided front ride height is within specifications, and tires are inflated to specified cold pressure.

To determine riding height, measure distance between bottom of spring tower and top of axle, **Figs. 3 and 4.** Refer to "Wheel Alignment Specifications Chart" to determine alignment specifications for the particular riding height of truck. If riding height does not fall within specifications, it should be corrected by installing proper springs or by use of shims.

Alignment equipment indicates a true reading only when frame is horizontal. Measure left and right hand angle as shown in **Fig. 5.** If frame is not level (due to tire, spring or load differences), the caster angle reading must be modified to compensate for frame angles. If front is higher than rear, subtract amount of angle from reading. If front is lower than rear, add angle. Check frame angle with a spirit lever protractor and take frame angle measurement on flat area immediately adjacent to rear spring front hanger.

NOTE: Axles are not to be bent or twisted to correct caster or camber readings.

CAMBER ADJUSTMENT

4 × 2

1. Raise and support vehicle. Remove front wheels.
2. Remove upper ball joint nut, then remove cotter pin on lower ball stud and back nut down stud. Pop ball joint/camber adjuster taper assembly from mounting.
3. Wedge camber adjuster out of spindle with camber adjusting tool D81T-3010-B. Replace adjuster with desired camber adjuster, **Fig. 6.**

NOTE: Camber adjusters are available in 0°, ½°, 1° and 1½°. To increase camber

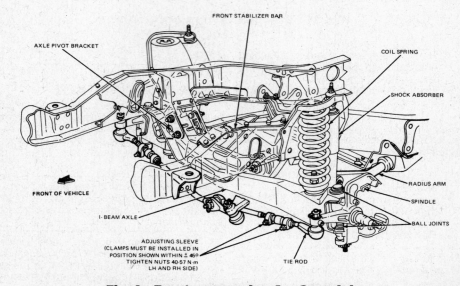

Fig. 1 Front suspension 4 × 2 models

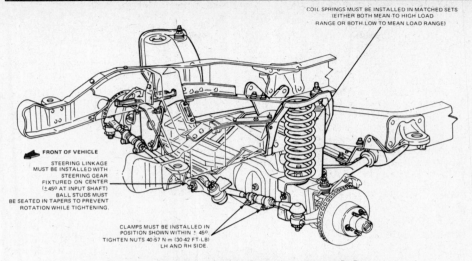

COIL SPRINGS MUST BE INSTALLED IN MATCHED SETS (EITHER BOTH MEAN-TO-HIGH LOAD RANGE OR BOTH LOW TO MEAN LOAD RANGE)

FRONT OF VEHICLE

STEERING LINKAGE MUST BE INSTALLED WITH STEERING GEAR FIXTURED ON CENTER (±45° AT INPUT SHAFT) BALL STUDS MUST BE SEATED IN TAPERS TO PREVENT ROTATION WHILE TIGHTENING.

CLAMPS MUST BE INSTALLED IN POSITION SHOWN WITHIN ± 45° TIGHTEN NUTS 40-57 N·m (30-42 FT·LB) LH AND RH SIDE.

Fig. 2   Front suspension. 4 × 4 models

RANGER (4x2)
BOTTOM OF SPRING TOWER TO TOP OF AXLE MEASURED AT CENTER OF JOUNCE STOP IN SIDE VIEW

Fig. 3   Ride height measurement at front end. 4 × 2 models

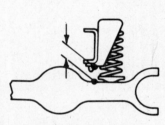

RANGER (4x4)
BOTTOM OF SPRING TOWER TO TOP OF AXLE MEASURED AT CENTER OF JOUNCE STOP IN SIDE VIEW

Fig. 4   Ride height measurement at front end. 4 × 4 models

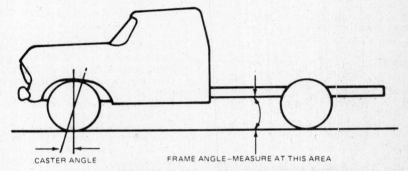

CASTER ANGLE   FRAME ANGLE—MEASURE AT THIS AREA

Fig. 5   Ride height measurement at frame

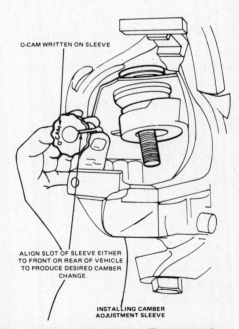

O-CAM WRITTEN ON SLEEVE

O-CAM

ALIGN SLOT OF SLEEVE EITHER TO FRONT OR REAR OF VEHICLE TO PRODUCE DESIRED CAMBER CHANGE.

INSTALLING CAMBER ADJUSTMENT SLEEVE

Fig. 6   Camber adjustment. 4 × 2 models

(more positive), align slot as follows: on driver's side, point slot to rear of vehicle. On passenger's side, point slot to front of vehicle. To decrease camber (more negative), align slot as follows: on driver's side point slot forward. On passenger's side, point slot rearward.

4. Remove lower ball joint stud nut and apply Locktite 242 to upper and lower ball joint studs. Hand start upper ball stud nut and torque lower ball stud nut to 35 ft. lbs. Torque upper ball stud nut to 85–110 ft. lbs. and finish torquing lower stud nut to 104–146 ft. lbs. Install cotter pin.

4 × 4
1. Raise and support vehicle. Remove front wheels.
2. Remove upper ball joint cotter pin and nut, then back off lower ball joint nut to end of stud.
3. Break spindle loose from ball joint studs, then remove camber adjuster sleeve from spindle using tool T64P-3590-F or equivalent, if necessary, **Fig. 7**.
4. Install camber adjuster on top ball joint stud with arrow pointing outboard for positive camber or inboard for negative camber.

NOTE: Zero camber bushings will not

have an arrow and may be turned in either direction as long as the lugs on the yoke engage the slots in the bushing.

5. Remove and discard lower ball joint stud nut, then install a new nut and torque to 40 ft. lbs.
6. Install new upper ball joint stud nut and torque to 85–100 ft. lbs. Continue to tighten nut until cotter pin hole lines up with castellation on nut, then install cotter pin. Retorque lower ball joint stud nut to 95–110 ft. lbs.

NOTE: The camber adjuster will be seated

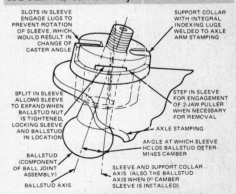

SLOTS IN SLEEVE ENGAGE LUGS TO PREVENT ROTATION OF SLEEVE, WHICH WOULD RESULT IN CHANGE OF CASTER ANGLE

SUPPORT COLLAR WITH INTEGRAL INDEXING LUGS WELDED TO AXLE ARM STAMPING

SPLIT IN SLEEVE ALLOWS SLEEVE TO EXPAND WHEN BALLSTUD NUT IS TIGHTENED, LOCKING SLEEVE AND BALLSTUD IN LOCATION

STEP IN SLEEVE FOR ENGAGEMENT OF 2-JAW PULLER WHEN NECESSARY FOR REMOVAL

AXLE STAMPING

ANGLE AT WHICH SLEEVE HOLDS BALLSTUD DETERMINES CAMBER

BALLSTUD (COMPONENT OF BALL JOINT ASSEMBLY)

BALLSTUD AXIS

SLEEVE AND SUPPORT COLLAR AXIS (ALSO THE BALLSTUD AXIS WHEN 0° CAMBER SLEEVE IS INSTALLED)

Fig. 7   Camber adjustment. 4 × 4 models

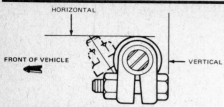

AFTER SETTING TOE, THE TWO CLAMP BOLTS/NUTS ON EACH ADJUSTING SLEEVE MUST BE POSITIONED WITHIN A LIMIT OF ± 45 DEGREES AS SHOWN WITH THE THREADED END OF THE BOLTS ON BOTH ADJUSTING SLEEVES POINTING TOWARDS THE FRONT OF THE VEHICLE.

Fig. 8   Toe-in adjustment

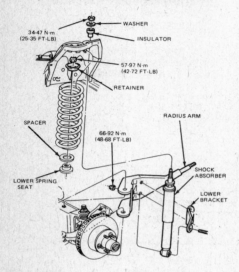

Fig. 10   Shock absorber replacement. 4 × 4 models

at a predetermined position during the tightening sequence. Do not attempt to change this position.

7. Reinstall wheels and lower vehicle.

CASTER ADJUSTMENT

Caster angle is non-adjustable on these vehicles.

TOE-IN, ADJUST

1. Loosen clamp bolts at each end of spindle connecting rod tube, then rotate the sleeve until correct toe alignment of 1/32 inch is obtained.
2. Center clamps between adjustment sleeve nibbs, then position bolts horizontally with clamps nuts positioned as shown in **Fig. 8**.
3. Recheck toe-in adjustment, then check that steering wheel spokes are properly positioned and adjust as necessary.

WHEEL BEARINGS
ADJUST

4 × 2

1. Raise and support front of vehicle.

2. Remove wheel cover, grease cap, cotter pin and locknut.
3. Loosen adjusting nut 3 turns, then rock wheel assembly in and out several times to push brake shoe and linings away from rotor.
4. Torque adjusting nut to 17–25 ft. lbs. while rotating wheel assembly.
5. Loosen adjusting nut ½ turn, then retorque to 10–15 inch lbs.
6. Install lock nut and cotter pin.
7. Ensure wheel assembly rotates smoothly, then reinstall grease cap and wheel cover and lower vehicle.

4 × 4

Manual Locking Hub

1. Raise and support front of vehicle.
2. Remove wheel and tire assembly.
3. Remove lug nut stud retainer washers, then the locking hub assembly.
4. Remove snap ring from end of spindle shaft.
5. Remove axle shaft spacer, needle thrust bearing and bearing spacer.
6. Remove outer wheel bearing locknut using a suitable spanner wrench.
7. Remove locknut washer from spindle.
8. Loosen inner wheel bearing locknut using a suitable spanner wrench, then torque locknut to 35 ft. lbs.
9. Loosen inner locknut ¼ turn, then install lockwasher on spindle. If necessary, rotate locknut slightly to align pin with closest hole in lockwasher.
10. Install outer bearing locknut and torque to 150 ft. lbs.
11. Install bearing thrust spacer, needle thrust bearing, axle shaft spacer and snap ring.
12. Install locking hub assembly and retainer washers, then the wheel and tire assembly.
13. Ensure wheel end play on spindle is .001–.003 inch.

Automatic Locking Hub

1. Perform steps 1 thru 5 as described under "Manual Locking Hub."
2. Remove cam assembly, thrust washer and needle thrust bearing from wheel bearing adjusting nut.
3. Loosen adjusting nut, then torque nut to 35 ft. lbs. while rotating hub and rotor assembly.
4. Back off adjusting nut ¼ turn, then torque nut to 16 inch lbs.
5. Align nearest hole in adjusting nut with center of spindle keyway slot. If necessary, advance nut to the next hole.
6. Install locknut needle bearing, thrust washer and cam assembly.
7. Install bearing thrust washer, needle thrust bearing, axle shaft spacer and snap ring.
8. Install locking hub assembly and retainer washers, then the wheel and tire assembly.
9. Ensure wheel end play on spindle is .001–.003 inch.

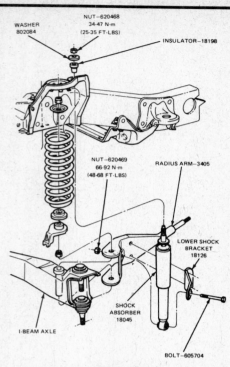

Fig. 9   Shock absorber replacement. 4 × 2 models

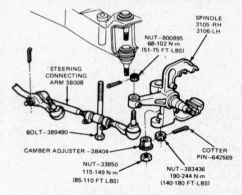

Fig. 11   Ball joint replacement. 4 × 2 models

SHOCK ABSORBER
REPLACE

1. Remove nut and washer from shock absorber at spring seat, **Figs. 9 and 10**.
2. Remove nut and bolt from shock absorber at radius arm and lower shock bracket. Slightly compress shock and remove.
3. Reverse procedure to install.

LOWER & UPPER BALL JOINTS
REPLACE

4 × 2

1. Remove spindle. Remove snap rings

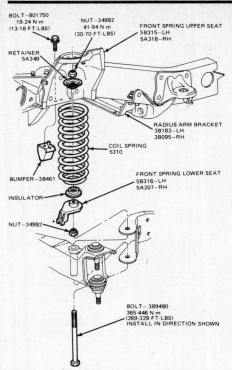

Fig. 12   Coil spring replacement. 4 × 2 models

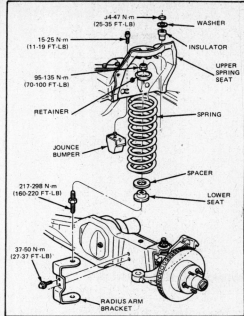

Fig. 13   Coil spring replacement. 4 × 4 models

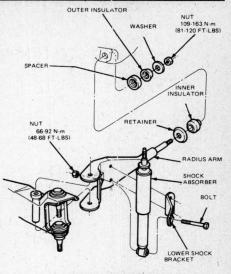

Fig. 14   Radius arm replacement. 4 × 2 models

from ball joints, **Fig. 11.**

2. Assemble C-Frame T74P-4635-C and receiving cup D81T-3010-A on upper ball joint. Turn forcing screw clockwise until ball joint is removed. Assemble C-Frame and cup on lower ball joint and turn forcing screw clockwise until ball joint is removed.

NOTE: Always remove upper ball joint first.

3. Reverse procedure to install. Install lower ball joint first using ball joint receiver cup D81T-3010-A5 and installation cup D81T-3010-A1 inside adapter cup D81T-3010-A4. Turn forcing screw until ball joint is seated. Install snap ring onto lower ball joint. Install upper ball joint in same manner.

4 × 4

Refer to the "Front Wheel Drive Section" in this chapter for ball joint replacement procedure.

COIL SPRING
REPLACE

4 × 2

1. Raise and support front of vehicle. Support axle.

2. Remove lower retainer nut and lower retainer, **Fig. 12.** Lower axle until it hangs unsupported.
3. Insert pry bar between axles and force appropriate I-beam axle down far enough to allow spring to be lifted over bolt in lower spring seat. Rotate spring until retainer on upper spring seat is cleared. Remove spring.

NOTE: The axle must be supported when replacing spring and not be permitted to hang by the brake hose. If the length of the brake hose is not sufficient to permit spring replacement, it will be necessary to remove the disc brake caliper. Do not suspend caliper by brake hose, if removed.

4. Reverse procedure to install. Install bolt in axle arm and tighten nut all the way down. Install top of spring into upper spring seat and rotate into position. Raise axle until spring is seated in lower spring upper seat. Install lower retainer and nut.

4 × 4

1. Raise and support front of vehicle. Support axle with a suitable jack so the spring is compressed.
2. Remove shock absorber to radius arm attaching bolt, then remove shock absorber from bracket.
3. Remove spring lower retainer attaching nut, then the retainer.
4. Lower axle until all spring tension is released, then remove spring by rotating upper coil out of tabs in upper spring seat, **Fig. 13.**
5. Remove spacer and seat from spring

and the stud from axle assembly, if necessary.

NOTE: The axle must be supported when replacing spring and not be permitted to hang by the brake hose. If the length of the brake hose is not sufficient to permit spring replacement, it will be necessary to remove the disc brake caliper. Do not suspend caliper by brake hose, if removed.

6. Reverse procedure to install.

RADIUS ARM
REPLACE

1. Raise and support front of vehicle. Support axle.
2. Disconnect lower end of shock absorber from shock lower bracket and remove front spring as described previously.
3. Loosen axle pivot bolt. Remove spring lower seat from radius arm. Remove nut and bolt from radius arm to axle and front bracket, **Figs. 14 and 15.**
4. Remove nut, rear washer and insulator from rear side of radius arm rear bracket and remove radius arm. Remove inner insulator and retainer from radius arm stud.
5. Reverse procedure to install.

RADIUS ARM INSULATORS
REPLACE

1. Loosen axle pivot bolt and upper shock absorber pivot bolt and compress shock.
2. Remove nut and washer attaching radius arm to radius arm bracket. Remove outer insulator and spacer,

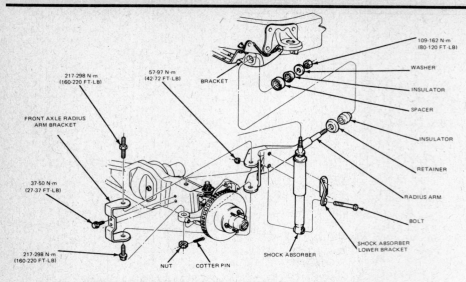

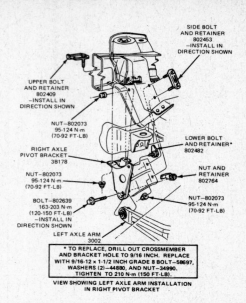

Fig. 15   Radius arm replacement. 4 × 4 models

Fig. 17   Right axle pivot bracket replacement. 4 × 4 models

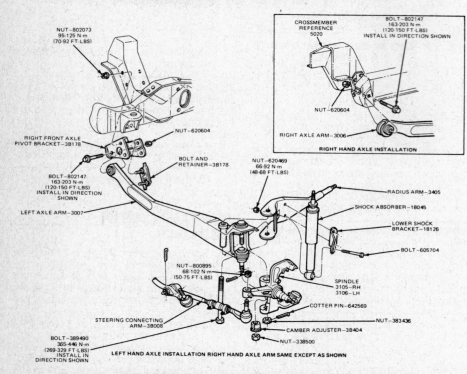

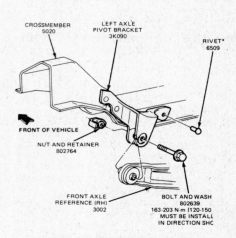

Fig. 16   Axle pivot bracket replacement. 4 × 2 models

Fig. 18   Left axle pivot bracket replacement. 4 × 4 models

Figs. 14 and 15.

3. Move radius arm and axle assembly forward out of radius arm bracket. Remove inner insulator and retainer.
4. Reverse procedure to install. Torque upper shock bolt to 25–35 ft. lbs. and axle pivot bolt and nut to 120–150 ft. lbs.

FRONT I-BEAM AXLE
REPLACE

1. Remove front wheel spindle and front spring.
2. Remove spring lower seat from radius arm and bolt and nut for radius arm to

front axle.

3. Remove axle-to-frame pivot bracket bolt and nut. Remove axle.
4. Reverse procedure to install.

AXLE PIVOT BRACKET
REPLACE

4 × 2

1. Remove front spring, radius arm, wheel spindle and I-beam.
2. Remove four attaching nuts and two

bolts and retainer assemblies. Remove axle pivot bracket, **Fig. 16.**

3. Reverse procedure to install. Position axle pivot bracket to frame and install forward and rearward bolts and retainer assemblies from inside of pivot bracket out through crossmember. Loosely install four nuts on outside of crossmember (two forward and two rearward). Torque nuts to 70–92 ft. lbs.

NOTE: Use nut N8802073-S2 or install one .20 inch thick hardened washer under each nut if a standard nut is used.

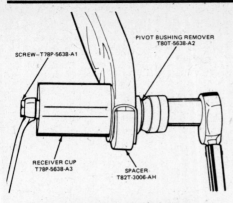

Fig. 19   Axle pivot bushing removal. 4 × 2 models

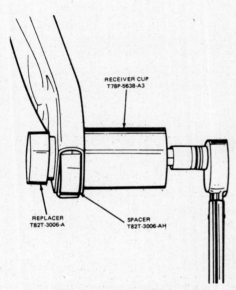

Fig. 20   Axle pivot bushing installation. 4 × 2 models

4 × 4

1. Remove coil spring and radius arm as described previously.
2. Remove front drive axle as described in the "Front Wheel Drive Section" of this chapter.
3. To remove right pivot bracket, remove upper bolt and retainer, then the side bolt and retainer, **Fig. 17**. Remove and discard lower bolt and retainer, then remove pivot bracket from crossmember.
4. To remove left pivot bracket, drill out rivets so that mounting holes in bracket and crossmember are 9/16 inch in diameter, then remove the bracket, **Fig. 18**.
5. Reverse procedure to install. Refer to **Figs. 17 and 18** for replacement hardware and torque specifications.

AXLE PIVOT BUSHING
REPLACE

4 × 2

1. Remove front coil spring as outlined in this chapter.
2. For left I-beam axle, remove axle pivot bolt and nut and pull left I-beam axle down until bushing is exposed. For right I-beam axle, entire right I-beam axle must be removed. Refer to "Front I-Beam Axle, Replace."
3. Install forcing screw T78P-5638-A1, bushing remover T80T-5638-A2, spacer T82T-3006-A4 and receiver cup T78P-5638-A3 onto pivot bushing. Turn forcing screw and remove pivot bushing, **Fig. 19**.
4. Reverse procedure to install. Refer to **Fig. 20**. Lower vehicle and with weight on suspension torque pivot bushing and nut to 120–150 ft. lbs.

4 × 4

Refer to the "Front Wheel Drive Section" in this chapter for axle pivot bushing replacement procedure.

FRONT STABILIZER BAR
REPLACE

1. Remove nuts and U-bolts retaining lower shock bracket/stabilizer bar bushing to radius arm. Remove retainers and stabilizer bar and bushings, **Fig. 21**.
2. Reverse procedure to install.

FRONT WHEEL SPINDLE
REPLACE

4 × 2

1. Raise and support front of vehicle. Remove front wheel, then the brake caliper assembly. Support caliper with a length of wire.
2. Remove dust cap, cotter pin, nut retainer, nut, washer, outer bearing and rotor from spindle.
3. Remove inner bearing cone and seal, then the brake dust shield. Discard the seal.
4. Disconnect steering linkage from spindle by removing cotter pin and nut.
5. Remove nut from upper ball joint stud, then the cotter pin and nut from lower ball joint stud.
6. Strike lower side of spindle to pop ball joints loose from spindle, **Fig. 22,** then remove the spindle.
7. Reverse procedure to install. Note the following:
   a. When installing ball joint stud nuts, coat studs with Loctite 242, or equivalent.
   b. Install lower ball joint stud nut first and torque to 30 ft. lbs., then install upper ball joint stud nut and torque

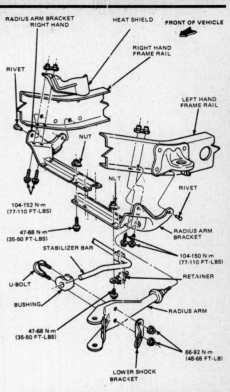

Fig. 21   Front stabilizer bar replacement

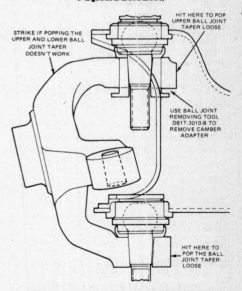

Fig. 22   Front wheel spindle replacement. 4 × 2 models

to 85–110 ft. lbs. Complete the tightening sequence by torquing lower ball joint stud nut to 104–106 ft. lbs.
   c. Torque steering linkage to spindle nut to 51–75 ft. lbs.

4 × 4

Refer to the "Front Wheel Drive Section" in this chapter for front wheel spindle replacement procedure.

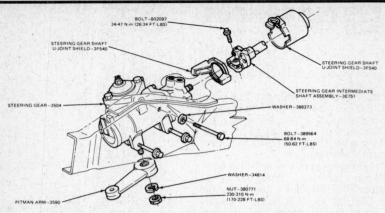

Fig. 23   Power steering gear replacement

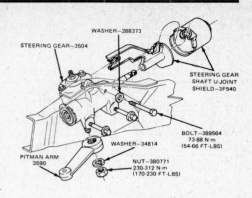

Fig. 24   Manual steering gear replacement

Wheel Alignment Specifications

Riding Height In Inches Fig. 3	Caster Angle Degrees①								
	2.95	3.15	3.35	3.55	3.75	3.95	4.15	4.35	4.55

1983—85 RANGER (4×2)

| Ranger | +5⅛°—+8° | +4⅝°—+7½° | +4°—+7° | +3½°—+6½° | +3°—+6° | +2⅜°—5⅜° | +1⅞°—+4⅞° | +1⅜°—+4¼° | +¾—+3¾° |

①—Side to side caster readings must be within 1½°, when vehicle riding height is within .12 inch side to side.

Riding Height In Inches Fig. 4	Caster Angle Degrees①									
	2.75	2.95	3.15	3.35	3.55	3.75	3.95	4.15	4.35	4.55

BRONCO II & 1983—85 RANGER (4×4)

| Ranger, Bronco II | +5⅜—+8⅛ | +4¾—+7⅝ | +4¼—+7 | +3¾—+6½ | +3⅛—+5⅞ | +2½—+5⅜ | +2—+4⅞ | +1½—+4⅜ | +1—+3⅞ | +1—+3⅜ |

①—Side to side caster readings must be within 1½°, when vehicle riding height is within .16 inch side to side.

Riding Height In Inches Fig. 3	Camber Angle Degrees①							
	2.75	2.95	3.15	3.35	3.55	3.75	3.95	4.15

1983—85 RANGER (4×2)

| Ranger | −1—−¾ | −1—−¼ | −1—+⅛ | −⅝—+⅝ | −⅛—+1⅛ | +⅜—+1⅝ | +⅞—+2⅛ | +1⅜—+2¾ |

①—Side to side camber readings must be within .7°, when truck frame to axle riding height is within .12 inch side to side.

Riding Height In Inches Fig. 4	Camber Angle Degrees①									
	2.75	2.95	3.15	3.35	3.55	3.75	3.95	4.15	4.35	4.55

BRONCO II & 1983—85 RANGER (4×4)

| Ranger, Bronco II | −1⅞—−⅜ | −1⅜—+⅛ | −⅞—+¾ | −⅜—+1⅛ | +⅛—+1¾ | +⅝—+2⅛ | +1⅛—+2⅝ | +1¾—+3⅛ | +2⅛—+3⅝ | +2¾—+4 |

①—Side to side camber readings must be within .7°, when truck frame to axle riding height is within .16 inch side to side.

POWER STEERING GEAR
REPLACE

1. Disconnect pressure and return lines from steering gear and plug openings to prevent entry of dirt.
2. Remove steering gear shaft U-joint shield from flex coupling, remove bolt securing flex coupling to steering gear, and disconnect flex coupling.
3. Raise and support vehicle and remove pitman arm using a suitable puller.
4. Support steering gear and remove gear attaching bolts.

5. Work steering gear free of flex coupling and remove gear from vehicle, **Fig. 23.**
6. Reverse procedure to install, making sure gear is centered with index flat on input shaft pointing down, and steering wheel spokes are in horizontal position.

MANUAL STEERING GEAR
REPLACE

1. Disconnect flex coupling shield from input shaft shield and slide it to upper part of intermediate shaft.
2. Remove bolt securing flex coupling to steering gear and remove steering gear input shaft shield.
3. Raise and support vehicle and remove pitman arm using a suitable puller.
4. Remove bolts securing gear to side rail and remove steering gear from vehicle, **Fig. 24.**
5. Reverse procedure to install, making sure gear is centered and flat on input shaft and is aligned with flat on flex coupling.

Front Wheel Drive Section

FRONT AXLE ASSEMBLY
REPLACE

1. Raise and support vehicle. Install jack stands under radius arm brackets.
2. Disconnect driveshaft from front axle yoke, then remove front wheels.
3. Remove disc brake calipers and position aside. Do not let caliper hang down on brake hose.
4. Disconnect steering linkage from spindle by removing the cotter pin and retaining nut.
5. Place a jack under axle arm assembly and compress the coil spring, then remove nut which retains bottom of spring to axle arm.
6. Lower axle until all spring tension is released, then remove the coil spring, spacer, seat and stud.

NOTE: The axle assembly must be supported when removing spring and not be permitted to hang by the brake hose. If the length of the brake hose is not sufficient to provide adequate clearance for spring removal, the disc brake caliper must be removed. If so, do not suspend caliper by brake hose.

7. Disconnect shock absorber from radius arm bracket, then remove the bracket and radius arm.
8. Remove pivot bolt securing right hand axle arm to crossmember.
9. Remove clamps from axle shaft slip yoke and axle shaft, then slide rubber boot over yoke.
10. Disconnect right driveshaft from slip yoke assembly, then lower jack and remove right axle arm assembly.
11. Position another jack under differential housing, then remove bolt securing left axle arm to crossmember and remove left axle arm assembly.
12. Reverse procedure to install. Note the following torques: pivot bracket bolts, 120–150 ft. lbs.; radius arm stud, 160–220 ft. lbs.; radius arm bracket bolts, 27–37 ft. lbs.; coil spring attaching nut, 70–100 ft. lbs.; shock absorber attaching nut, 42–72 ft. lbs.; ball joint attaching nut, 50–75 ft. lbs.; drive shaft to front axle yoke U-bolt nuts, 8–15 ft. lbs.

SPINDLE, SHAFT & JOINT ASSEMBLY
REPLACE

1. Raise and support vehicle. Remove front wheels.
2. Remove disc brake caliper, hub locks, wheel bearings and lock nuts, then the hub, rotor and outer wheel bearing cone, **Fig. 1.**
3. Remove and discard grease seal from rotor using tools 1175-AC and T50T-100-A, or equivalent.
4. Remove inner wheel bearing, then the inner and outer bearing cups using tool D78P-1225-B, or equivalent.
5. Remove spindle from steering knuckle attaching nuts, then break spindle loose from knuckle and remove splash shield.
6. Remove shaft and joint assembly from right side of vehicle by pulling assembly out of carrier.
7. Remove and discard clamp from shaft and joint assembly and the stub shaft on right side of carrier. Slide rubber boot onto stub shaft, then pull shaft and joint assembly from stub shaft splines.
8. Install spindle, on second step, in suitable soft jawed vise.
9. Remove oil seal and needle bearing from spindle using tools T50T-100-A and 1175-AC, or equivalent. Remove oil seal from shaft, if necessary.
10. Reverse procedure to install. Torque spindle to steering knuckle attaching nuts to 35–45 ft. lbs.

RIGHT HAND SLIP YOKE & STUB SHAFT ASSEMBLY, CARRIER, CARRIER OIL SEAL & BEARING
REPLACE

1. Disconnect driveshaft from yoke. Position driveshaft aside so it will not interfere with carrier removal.
2. Remove both spindles, **Fig. 1,** then the left and right shaft and U-joint assemblies as described previously.
3. Support carrier using a suitable jack, then remove carrier to support arm attaching bolts.
4. Remove carrier from support arm, then drain lubricant and remove carrier from vehicle.
5. Install carrier in suitable holding fixture, then rotate slip yoke and shaft assembly until open end of snap ring is exposed.
6. Remove snap ring, then the slip yoke and shaft assembly from carrier.
7. Remove oil seal and caged needle bearings simultaneously from carrier using tools T50T-100-A and D880L-100-A or equivalent. Discard seal and bearings.
8. Reverse procedure to install. Note the following:
   a. Clean mating surfaces of carrier and support arm. Apply a narrow bead of RTV sealant to mating surfaces.
   b. Install carrier attaching bolts hand tight, then torque in a clockwise or counterclockwise pattern to 40–50 ft. lbs.
   c. Torque carrier to axle arm shear bolt to 75–95 ft. lbs.
   d. Torque driveshaft to yoke U-bolt nuts to 8–15 ft. lbs.

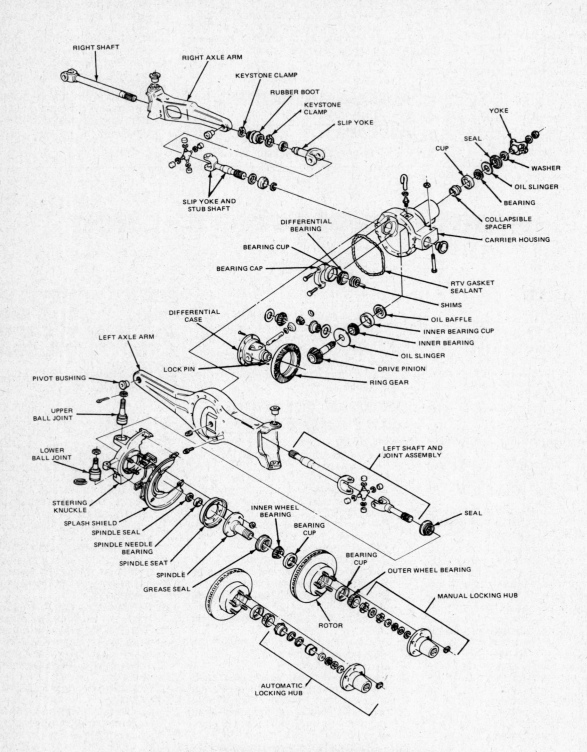

Fig. 1   Exploded view of front axle assembly

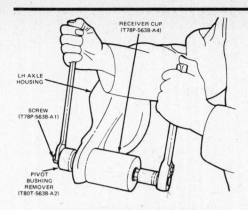

Fig. 2   Axle pivot bushing removal

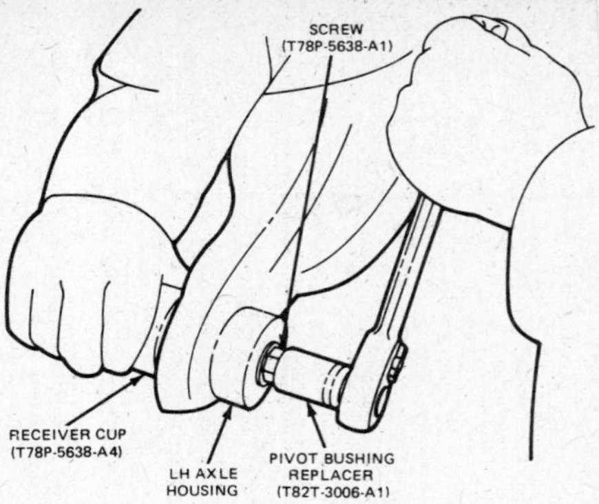

Fig. 3   Axle pivot bushing installation

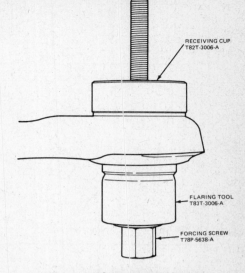

Fig. 4   Flaring axle pivot bushing

STEERING KNUCKLE & BALL JOINTS
REPLACE

1. Remove spindle, **Fig. 1,** then the shaft and joint assembly as described previously.
2. If tie rod has not been removed, remove cotter pin and nut and disconnect tie rod from steering arm.
3. Remove cotter pin and loosen nut on top ball joint stud. Loosen bottom nut inside knuckle, then remove top nut.
4. Break spindle loose from ball stud, then remove camber adjuster. Mark position of adjuster for assembly reference.
5. Install steering knuckle in suitable soft jawed vise, then remove snap ring from lower ball joint socket.
6. Press ball joints from steering knuckle using C-Frame D79T-3010-AA with tools D79T-3010-AE and T83T-3050-A, or equivalent.
7. Reverse procedure to install. The lower ball joint must be installed first. When installing ball joint stud nuts, first torque nut on lower stud to 40 ft. lbs., then torque nut on upper stud to 85–100 ft. lbs. Complete tightening sequence by torquing lower nut to 95–110 ft. lbs.

AXLE PIVOT BUSHING
REPLACE

1. Remove front axle assembly as described previously.
2. Remove pivot bushing from axle housing, **Fig. 2.**
3. Install bushing in axle housing, **Fig. 3,** then flare the bushing to prevent movement, **Fig. 4.** Complete installation by crimping bushing lip.

FRONT DRIVESHAFT
REPLACE

1. Remove nuts and U-bolts securing front driveshaft to front drive axle.

2. Remove U-joint assembly from axle yoke, then slide the splined yoke assembly out of transfer case front output shaft and remove driveshaft assembly.
3. Reverse procedure to install. Torque attaching nuts to 8–15 ft. lbs.

DIFFERENTIAL CARRIER
DISASSEMBLE

1. Remove left hand axle arm assembly as described previously.
2. Loosen carrier to axle arm retaining bolts, then drain fluid from differential.
3. Remove carrier retaining bolts, then the carrier.
4. Remove slip yoke and stub shaft as described previously, then install carrier in suitable holding fixture.
5. Clean gasket material from all mating surfaces, then remove bearing caps. Note location of markings on caps and carrier for assembly reference.
6. Remove differential case, then the bearing cups from carrier. Note which side of carrier bearing cups were removed from.
7. Support carrier with nose end up and hold end yoke with a suitable tool, then remove nut and washer from pinion shaft.
8. Remove end yoke using tool T65L-4851-B, or equivalent.

NOTE: The yoke must be replaced if the seal contact area shows any signs of wear.

9. Remove drive pinion, drive pinion oil seal, outer pinion bearing cone, oil slinger and collapsible spacer from carrier. Discard oil seal and collapsible spacer.
10. Remove inner pinion bearing cup, **Fig. 5,** then remove oil baffle from bearing cup bore.
11. Invert carrier, then remove outer pinion bearing cup, **Fig. 5.**

12. Remove differential case bearings and shims. Wire shims, bearing cup and cone together and note which side of case they were removed from.
13. Install differential case in suitable soft jawed vise. Remove ring gear attaching bolts, then the ring gear from case.

NOTE: Whenever the ring gear is removed, the ring gear attaching bolts must be replaced.

14. Remove inner pinion bearing cone and oil slinger from drive pinion using tool No. D81L-4220-A or equivalent.
15. Inspect all components for wear or damage and replace as necessary.

Total Differential Case End Play Check

1. Install ring gear onto differential case. Torque bolts alternately and evenly to 50–60 ft. lbs.
2. Clean trunnions on differential, then install master differential bearings onto case. Remove any burrs and nicks from hubs so bearings will rotate freely.
3. Install differential case into carrier, without drive pinion. Ensure that the case moves freely in the carrier.
4. Install suitable dial indicator on differential case flange. Position tip of indicator on a flat of one ring gear bolt.
5. Move differential case toward dial indicator as far as possible, then zero the indicator with force still applied. The dial indicator should have a minimum travel of .200 inch.
6. Move differential case away from dial indicator as far as possible and record reading. This reading indicates amount of shims needed behind differential side bearings to take up total

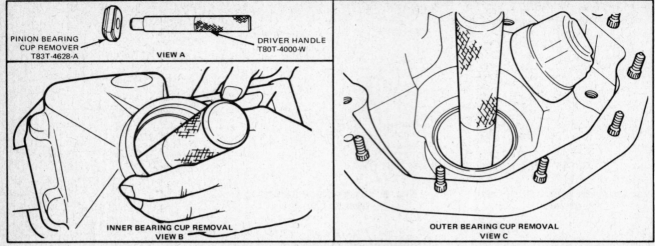

Fig. 5 Bearing cup removal

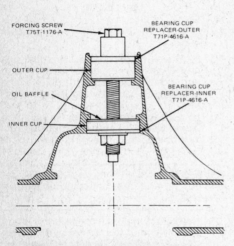

Fig. 6 Pinion bearing cup installation

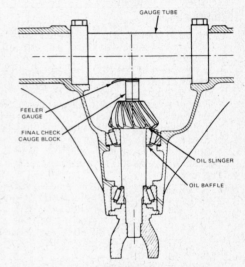

Fig. 7 Pinion depth check

clearance between differential bearing and case.

7. Remove differential case from carrier. Do not remove master differential bearings from case at this time.

Depth Gauge Check

1. Install oil baffle into inner bearing cup bore in carrier.
2. Install inner and outer pinion bearing cups in carrier, **Fig. 6**.
3. Position a new rear pinion bearing over aligning adapter T76P-4020-A1, then install into pinion bearing retainer assembly.
4. Install front pinion bearing into bearing cup in carrier. The old bearing may be reused, if serviceable. Assemble handle T76P-4020-A11 onto screw T76P-4020-A9 and hand tighten.
5. Install gauge tube T76P-4020-A7 into differential bearing bore, then install bearing caps and torque to 35–40 ft. lbs. Set bearing preload by torquing handle to 20–40 inch lbs.
6. Using a feeler gauge, measure dis-

tance between gauge tube and gauge block T76P-4020-A10.

7. If there are no markings on pinion gear, select an oil slinger with a thickness equal to the dimension measured in step 6. If pinion gear is marked with a "+" reading, this amount must be subtracted from the dimension measured in step 6. For example, if pinion is marked +2, use a slinger .002 inch thinner than measured. If pinion is marked with a "−" reading, this amount must be added to the measured dimension.

Measure thickness of oil slinger with a micrometer to verify correct size, then install slinger on pinion and press bearing onto pinion.

9. Apply lubricant C1AZ-19590-B, or equivalent, to ends of outer pinion bearing rollers, then install outer bearing cone in outer bearing cup.
10. Install drive pinion with inner bearing cone and oil slinger into carrier.

Drive Pinion Preload & Final Depth Checks

1. With pinion installed in carrier, install outer bearing cone and oil slinger.
2. Install end yoke, washer, deflector and slinger on pinion shaft using alignment tool T80T-4000-G and flange holder T78P-4851-A.
3. Install new pinion nut and tighten to a rotating torque of 10 inch lbs. Rotate pinion several times to seal bearing.
4. Install gauge tube T76P-4020-A7 in carrier, then install the bearing caps and torque to 35–40 ft. lbs.
5. Install final check gauge block T83T-4020-F58 on top of pinion button under gauge tube, **Fig. 7**. Press down on ends of gauge block to make sure it is level on pinion.
6. Measure clearance between gauge tube and final check block using a feeler gauge until a slight drag is felt. Clearance should be .020 inch added to the drive pinion etching, with a tolerance of ±.002 inch. For example, a pinion with an etching of "+2" will

have a .022 inch clearance and a .002 inch tolerance. Therefore, shims equalling .020–.024 inch would be required.

7. When drive pinion is set at correct depth, remove yoke using tools T78P-4851-A and T65L-4851-B. Remove yoke, nut and washer, and outer bearing cone.
8. Install a new collapsible spacer and outer bearing cone.
9. Apply lubricant C6AZ-19580-E, or equivalent, to drive pinion oil seal, then install the seal using tool T71T-3010-R. Make sure that garter spring remains in place.
10. Install yoke using tool T83T-4851. Torque nut to 175 ft. lbs.
11. Using an inch-pound torque wrench, check rotational torque of pinion. Rotational torque should be 15–35 inch lbs.

NOTE: If rotational torque is less than 15 inch lbs., tighten the pinion nut in small increments until 15–35 inch lbs. is

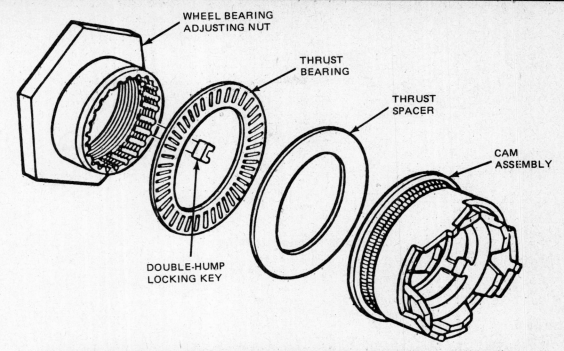

WHEEL BEARING
ADJUSTING NUT

THRUST
BEARING

THRUST
SPACER

CAM
ASSEMBLY

DOUBLE-HUMP
LOCKING KEY

Fig. 8   Exploded view of revised wheel bearing adjusting nut assembly

reached. Do not tighten nut more than 225 ft. lbs.

If reading is more than 35 inch lbs., the collapsible spacer has been compressed too far and must be replaced.

Differential Case, Service

1. Install differential case in suitable vise, then drive out lock pin which retains pinion mate shaft to case.
2. Remove drive pinion mate shaft using a suitable drift pin.
3. Rotate pinion mate gears and side gears until mate gears are exposed in windows of case, then remove mate gears and spherical washers.
4. Remove side gears and thrust washers, then install lock pin in case. Set lock pin in place by peening some metal of the case over pin.
5. Apply lubricant C1AZ-19590-B, or equivalent, to all gears and washers.
6. While holding side gears in position in case, install pinion mate gears and spherical washers. Rotate side gears and pinion mate gears until holes in washers and pinion mate gears line up with holes in case, then install pinion mate shaft into case. Ensure that lock pin hole in shaft lines up with lock pin holes in case.

ASSEMBLE

1. Install ring gear on differential case, using new bolts. Torque bolts alternately and evenly to 50–60 ft. lbs.
2. Position differential case in carrier. Move case away from drive pinion gear until it is seated against cross

bore face of carrier.
3. Install suitable dial indicator on differential so that indicator tip rests on a flat of one case bolt. Zero the dial indicator.
4. Force ring gear against pinion gear, then rock ring gear to make sure gear teeth are in contact. Move ring gear away from drive pinion gear, making sure indicator returns to zero. Repeat this procedure until reading is the same. This reading, minus .006 inch, indicates amount of shims needed between differential case and differential bearing on ring gear side.
5. Remove differential case from carrier, then the master bearings from case.
6. Install required shims, as determined in step 4, on ring gear hub of differential case.
7. Install bearing cone and bearing onto ring gear hub using tool T80T-4000-J.
8. To determine amount of shims needed on hub of drive pinion side of differential case, subtract reading obtained in step 4 from reading obtained in "Total Differential Case End Play" procedure, then add .003 inch to this amount.
9. Install required shims, as determined in step 8, on hub of drive pinion side of differential case.
10. Install bearing cone and bearing onto drive pinion hub using tool T80T-4000-J. Protect ring gear side bearing using step plate D80L-630-5, or equivalent.
11. Install bearing cone on pinion side of differential case. Protect ring gear bearing using tool T-53T-4621-C, or equivalent.
12. Install differential bearing cups on

bearing cones, then install differential case into carrier. If ring gear and drive pinion have alignment marks, the marks must be aligned during assembly.
13. Remove dial indicator and spreader from case, then install bearing caps and bolts. Make sure that markings on caps correspond, in both position and direction, to markings on carrier. Torque bolts to 35–40 ft. lbs.
14. Install suitable dial indicator on differential case and measure ring gear and pinion backlash at three equally spaced points on ring gear. Backlash must measure .004–.010 inch and cannot vary more than .003 inch between measuring points. If backlash is high, move ring gear closer to pinion by moving shims to ring gear side from opposite side. If backlash is low, move ring gear away from pinion by moving shims from ring gear side to opposite side.
15. Apply a narrow bead of RTV sealant on carrier mounting face support arm mating surfaces.

NOTE: Allow the sealant at least one hour curing time after the carrier is assembled to the axle arm before filling the differential with lubricant or operating vehicle.

16. Install differential assembly onto left hand axle arm, using two guide pins. Install bolts and torque to 40–50 ft. lbs. Torque one bolt, then the bolt directly opposite it. Torque remaining bolts in a clockwise or counterclockwise direction.
17. Install carrier shear bolt and nut. Torque to 75–95 ft. lbs.

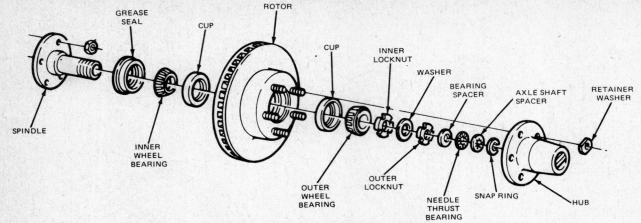

Fig. 9   Manual locking hub

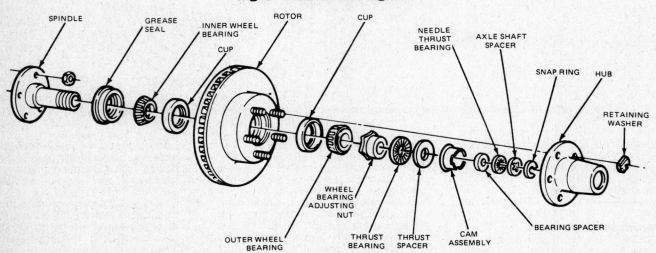

Fig. 10   Automatic locking hub

LOCKING HUB
REPLACE

SERVICE BULLETIN: Ranger and Bronco II 4×4 models built with front axle assembly No. E57A-3002-AFA (3.45 ratio) and E57A-3002-AGA (3.75 ratio) equipped with automatic locking hubs will now incorporate (as of January 1985) a new two piece wheel bearing spindle nut locking key and engagement cam retention system, **Fig. 8.**

This new retention system will replace the current integral one piece key/cam design.

To prevent damage to the spindle during removal, remove adjusting nut locking key from spindle keyway under adjusting nut prior to nut removal. A slight movement of the nut will loosen the locking key so that a magnet can be used for removal. During the front wheel bearing adjustment procedure, align the closest two holes in the wheel bearing adjusting nut with the center of the spindle keyway slot. Advance the nut to the next hole if required. To ensure prop-er wheel retention, install adjusting nut locking key in alignment with spindle key-way and insert into lock nut holes. The double humped portion must be complete-ly seated and flush with the lock nut as-sembly.

1. Raise and support vehicle.
2. Remove wheel and tire assembly.
3. Remove lug nug stud retainer washers, then the locking hub assembly, **Figs. 9 and 10.**
4. Reverse procedure to install.

FORD EXC. BRONCO II & 1983–85 RANGER

INDEX OF SERVICE OPERATIONS

NOTE: Refer to page 1 of this manual for vehicle manufacturer's special service tool suppliers.

General Engine Specifications

Year	Engine Code On Truck Rating Plate	Engine Model	Carb. Type	Bore & Stroke	Comp. Ratio	Horsepower @ R.P.M.	Torque Ft. Lbs. @ R.P.M.	Normal Oil Pressure Lbs.
1979	B	6-300[1]	1 Bore	4.00 × 3.98	[3]	[4]	[5]	40–60
	K	6-300[2]	1 Bore	4.00 × 3.98	[3]	[4]	[5]	40–60
	G	V8-302	2 Bore	4.00 × 3.00	8.4	[6]	[7]	40–60
	H	V8-351W	2 Bore	4.00 × 3.50	8.3	[8]	[9]	40–60
	H	V8-351M	2 Bore	4.00 × 3.50	8.0	[10]	[11]	40–65
	S	V8-400	2 Bore	4.00 × 4.00	8.0	[12]	[13]	50–75
	A	V8-460	2 Bore	4.36 × 3.85	8.0	[14]	[15]	40–65
	J	V8-460	2 Bore	4.36 × 3.85	8.0	[16]	[17]	40–65
1980	E	6-300	1 Bore	4.00 × 3.98	8.0	[18]	[19]	40–60
	F	V8-302	2 Bore	4.00 × 3.00	8.4	[20]	[21]	40–60
	G	V8-351M	2 Bore	4.00 × 3.50	8.0	[22]	[23]	50–75
	W	V8-351W	2 Bore	4.00 × 3.50	8.3	132 @ 3000	266 @ 1200	40–65
	Z	V8-400	2 Bore	4.00 × 4.00	8.0	[24]	[25]	50–75
	L	V8-460	4 Bore	4.36 × 3.85	8.0	212 @ 4000	339 @ 2400	40–65
1981	E	6-300	1 Bore	4.00 × 3.98	8.9	[26]	[27]	40–60
	D	V8-255	2 Bore	3.68 × 3.00	8.2	118 @ 3400	206 @ 2000	40–60
	F	V8-302	2 Bore	4.00 × 3.00	8.4	[28]	[29]	40–60
	G	V8-351	2 Bore	4.00 × 3.50	8.3	[30]	[31]	40–65
	Z	V8-400	2 Bore	4.00 × 4.00	8.0	153 @ 3200	296 @ 1600	50–75
	L	V8-460	4 Bore	4.36 × 3.85	8.0	212 @ 4000	339 @ 2400	40–65
1982	3	V6-232	2 Bore	3.81 × 3.39	8.7	109 @ 3600	184 @ 1600	40–60
	E	6-300	1 Bore	4.00 × 3.98	8.9	[32]	[33]	40–60
	D	V8-255	2 Bore	3.68 × 3.00	8.2	118 @ 3400	206 @ 2000	40–60
	F	V8-302	2 Bore	4.00 × 3.00	8.4	[34]	[35]	40–60
	W	V8-351	2 Bore	4.00 × 3.50	8.3	[30]	[31]	40–65
	Z	V8-400	2 Bore	4.00 × 4.00	8.0	153 @ 3200	296 @ 1600	50–75
	L	V8-460	4 Bore	4.36 × 3.85	8.0	212 @ 4000	339 @ 2400	40–65
1983	3	V6-232	2 Bore	3.81 × 3.39	8.7	109 @ 3600	184 @ 1600	40–60
	Y	6-300	1 Bore	4.00 × 3.98	8.4	[36]	[37]	40–60
	F	V8-302	2 Bore	4.00 × 3.00	8.4	139 @ 3400	250 @ 2000	40–60
	G	V8-351	2 Bore	4.00 × 3.50	8.3	[38]	[39]	40–65
	I	V8-420[40][41]	Fuel Inj.	4.00 × 4.18	19.7	161 @ 3300	307 @ 1800	40–60
	I	V8-420[40][42]	Fuel Inj.	4.00 × 4.18	19.7	146 @ 3300	278 @ 1800	40–60
	L	V8-460	4 Bore	4.36 × 3.85	8.0	202 @ 4000	331 @ 2200	40–65
1984	Y	6-300	1 Bore	4.00 × 3.98	8.4	[43]	[44]	40–60
	F	V8-302	2 Bore	4.00 × 3.00	8.4	[45]	[46]	40–60
	G	V8-351	2 Bore	4.00 × 3.50	8.3	[47]	[48]	40–65
	G	V8-351	4 Bore	4.00 × 3.50	8.3	210 @ 4000	305 @ 2800	40–65
	I	V8-420[40]	Fuel Inj.	4.00 × 4.18	20.7	—	—	40–60
	L	V8-460	4 Bore	4.36 × 3.85	8.0	[49]	[50]	40–65
1985	Y	6-300	1 Bore	4.00 × 3.98	8.4	[43]	[44]	40–60
	F	V8-302	2 Bore	4.00 × 3.00	8.4	[45]	[46]	40–60
	N	V8-302	Fuel Inj.	4.00 × 3.00	8.4	—	—	40–60
	G	V8-351	2 Bore	4.00 × 3.50	8.3	[47]	[48]	40–65
	H	V8-351	4 Bore	4.00 × 3.50	8.3	210 @ 4000	305 @ 2800	40–65
	I	V8-420[40]	Fuel Inj.	4.00 × 4.18	20.7	—	—	40–60
	L	V8-460	4 Bore	4.36 × 3.85	8.0	[49]	[50]	40–65

continued

GENERAL ENGINE SPECIFICATIONS—Continued

①—Heavy duty.

②—Light duty.

③—E-150-250 & F-150-250, 8.9; E-350 & F-350, 8.0.

④—E-100-150 & F-100-150, 117 @ 3000; E-250 & F-250 auto. trans., 116 @ 3200; E-250 & F-250 man. trans., 114 @ 3000; E-350 & F-350, 114 @ 3000.

⑤—E-100-150 & F-100-150, 243 @ 1600; E-250 & F-250 auto. trans., 247 @ 1000; E-250 & F-250 man. trans., 234 @ 1600; E-350 & F-350, 228 @ 1800.

⑥—Ranchero, 133 @ 3400; E-100-150 & F-100-150 exc. Calif., 135 @ 3400; E-100 Calif., 129 @ 3200; F-100 Calif., 132 @ 3200; E-150 & F-150 Calif., 137 @ 3400; E-250, 136 @ 3400.

⑦—Ranchero, 245 @ 1600; E-100-150 & F-100-150 exc. Calif., 243 @ 2000; E-100 Calif., 238 @ 3200; F-100 Calif., 240 @ 3200; E-150 & F-150 auto. trans. Calif., 245 @ 2000; F-150 man. trans. Calif., 243 @ 2000; E-250, 235 @ 2400.

⑧—E-100-150 exc. Calif., 135 @ 2800; E-150 Calif., 139 @ 3200; E-250 126 @ 2800; E-350, 143 @ 3200.

⑨—E-100-150 exc. Calif., 274 @ 1400; E-150 Calif., 269 @ 1200; E-250, 270 @ 1400; E-350, 272 @ 2000.

⑩—Bronco & F-150-250 exc. F-250 H.D. emissions, 137 @ 3400; F-100, 136 @ 3400; F-250 H.D. emissions & F-350, 140 @ 3600.

⑪—Bronco & F-100, 257 @ 1800; F-150-250 auto. trans. exc. F-250 H.D. emissions, 263 @ 1800; F-150-250 man. trans. exc. F-250 H.D. emissions, 242 @ 1600; F-250 H.D. emissions & F-350, 240 & 2000.

⑫—Exc. F-350, 149 & 3200; F-350, 153 @ 3200.

⑬—Exc. F-350, 300 @ 1400; F-350, 310 @ 2000.

⑭—E-250, 214 @ 3600; E-350, 217 @ 4000.

⑮—E-250, 362 @ 1800; E-350, 358 @ 2600.

⑯—F-150-250, 214 @ 3600; F-350, 217 @ 4000.

⑰—F-150-250, 362 @ 1800; F-350, 358 @ 2600.

⑱—Bronco & F-100-250 exc. Calif., 119 @ 3200; E-100-250 exc. Calif., 115 @ 3200; Bronco, F-100-250 & E-150-250 Calif., 116 @ 3200; E-350 & F-350, 118 @ 3200.

⑲—Bronco & F-150-250 exc. Calif., 243 @ 1200; E-150-250 exc. Calif., 241 @ 1200; Bronco, F-100-250 & E-150-250 Calif., 244 & 1200; E-350 & F-350, 238 @ 1200.

⑳—Bronco & F-100-250 exc. Calif., 137 @ 3600; E-100-250 exc. Calif., 138 @ 3600; Bronco, F-150 (4 × 4), F-250 & E-100-250, 136 @ 3600; F-100-150 (4 × 2), 133 @ 3400.

㉑—Bronco & F-100-250 exc. Calif., 239 @ 1800; E-100-250 exc. Calif., 242 @ 1800; Bronco, F-150 (4 × 4), F-250 & E-100-250 Calif., 235 @ 1800; F-100-150 (4 × 2), 235 @ 2000.

㉒—Bronco & F-150-250 exc. Calif., 138 @ 3400; Bronco & F-150-250 Calif., 135 @ 3200; E-250, 133 @ 3200; E-350 & F-350, 142 @ 3400.

㉓—Bronco & F-150-250 exc. Calif., 263 @ 2000; Bronco & F-150-250 Calif., 259 @ 1600; Bronco & E-250, 133 @ 3200; E-350 & F-350, 251 @ 2400.

㉔—F-250 (4 × 4), 136 @ 1200; E-250, @ 1200; E-350 & F-350, 153 @ 3200.

㉕—F-250 (4 × 4), 310 @ 1200; E-250, 309 @ 1200; E-350 & F-350, 296 @ 1600.

㉖—Bronco & F-150-250 exc. Calif., 122 @ 3000; E-100-250 exc. Calif., 119 @ 3000; F-150-250 E-100-250 & F-250 under 8500 lbs. Calif., 116 @ 3200; F-250 over 8500 lbs., E-350 & F-350, 118 @ 3200.

㉗—Bronco & F-100-250 exc. Calif., 255 @ 1400; E-100-250 exc. Calif., 253 @ 1200; F-100-250, E-100-250 & F-250 under 8500 lbs. Calif., 250 @ 1200; F-250 over 8500 lbs., E-350 & F-350, 238 @ 1200.

㉘—Bronco & F-100-250, 133 @ 3400; E-100-250 exc. Calif., 130 @ 3400; E-100-250 Calif., 132 @ 3600.

㉙—Bronco & F-100-250 exc. Calif., 233 @ 2000; E-150-250 exc. Calif., 230 @ 1400; Bronco, F-100-250 & E-100-250 Calif., 239 @ 1400.

㉚—E-150-250 exc. Calif., 144 @ 3200; E-250-350, 157 @ 3400; Bronco, F-150-250 & F-250 under 8500 lbs. exc. Calif., 136 @ 3000; Bronco, F-150-250, E-150-250 & F-250 under 8500 lbs. Calif., 139 & 3200; F-250 over 8500 lbs. & F-350, 142 @ 3400.

㉛—E-100-250 exc. Calif., 269 @ 1200; E-250-350, 271 @ 2400; Bronco, F-150-250 & F-250 under 8500 lbs. exc. Calif., 262 @ 1600; Bronco, F-150-250, E-150-250 & F-250 under 8500 lbs. Calif., 279 @ 1400; F-250 over 8500 lbs. & F-350, 251 @ 2400.

㉜—Bronco & F-100-250 & E-100-250 under 8500 lbs. exc. Calif., 119 @ 3000; F-100-250 under 8500 lbs. & E-100-250 Calif., 116 @ 3000; F-250 over 8500 lbs., F-350 & E-350, 117 @ 3200.

㉝—Bronco, F-100-250 & E-100-250 under 8500 lbs. exc. Calif., 253 @ 1200; F-100-250 under 8500 lbs. & E-100-250 Calif., 250 @ 1200; F-250 over 8500 lbs., F-350 & E-350, 234 @ 1200.

㉞—Bronco & F-100-250 exc. Calif., 132 @ 3400; E-100-250 exc. Calif., 131 @ 3600; Bronco, F-100-250 & E-100-250 Calif., 132 @ 3600.

㉟—Bronco & F-100-250 exc. Calif., 232 @ 1800; E-100-250 exc. Calif., 231 @ 1400; Bronco, F-100-250 & E-100-250 Calif., 239 @ 1400.

㊱—Exc. F-250 over 8500 lbs., F-350 & E-350, 120 @ 3200; F-250 over 8500 lbs., F-350 & E-350, 119 @ 3200.

㊲—Exc. F-250 over 8500 lbs., F-350 & E-350, 250 @ 1600; F-250 over 8500 lbs., F-350 & E-350 exc. Calif., 230 @ 2200; F-250 over 8500 lbs., F-350 & E-350 Calif., 220 @ 2200.

㊳—Bronco & F-150-250 under 8500 lbs., 139 @ 3200; F-250 over 8500 lbs. & F-350, 147 @ 3200; E-100-150 & E-250 van, 145 @ 3200; E-250 wagon & E-350, 150 @ 3200.

㊴—Bronco, F-150 & F-250 under 8500 lbs., 278 @ 1400; F-250 over 8500 lbs. & F-350, 276 @ 2000; E-100-150 & E-250 van, 270 @ 1400; E-250 wagon & E-350, 279 @ 2000.

㊵—Diesel engine.

㊶—Exc. High Alt.

㊷—High Alt.

㊸—120 @ 3000 or 125 @ 3200 depending on optional equipment, wheel base and/or emissions package.

㊹—260 @ 1400, 250 @ 1600, 245 @ 1600 or 235 @ 1200 depending on optional equipment, wheel base and/or emissions package.

㊺—145 @ 3400 or 150 @ 3600 depending on optional equipment, wheel base and/or emissions package.

㊻—250 @ 2200, 250 @ 2600 or 255 @ 1600 depending on optional equipment, wheel base and/or emissions package.

㊼—150 @ 3200, 160 @ 3200 or 165 @ 3200 depending on optional equipment, wheel base and/or emissions package.

㊽—280 @ 1800, 280 @ 2000 or 295 @ 2000 depending on optional equipment, wheel base and/or emissions package.

㊾—220 @ 4000 or 225 @ 4000 depending on optional equipment, wheel base and/or emissions package.

㊿—360 @ 2600 or 365 @ 2800 depending on optional equipment, wheel base and/or emissions package.

continued

Valve Specifications

Engine Model	Year	Valve Lash①		Valve Angles		Valve Springs		Valve Stem Clearance		Stem Diameter, Std.	
		Int.	Exh.	Seat	Face	Installed Height	Pressure Lbs. @ In.	Intake	Exhaust	Intake	Exhaust
V6-232	1982–83	.088–.189		45	44	1.74	215 @ 1.79	.0010–.0027	.0015–.0032	.3416–.3423	.3411–.3418
V8-255	1981–82	.123–.173		45	44	②	③	.0010–.0027	.0015–.0032	.3416–.3423	.3411–.3418
6-300	1979–84	.125–.175		45	44	⑤	⑥	.0010–.0027	.0010–.0027	.3416–.3423	.3416–.3423
6-300	1985	.125–.175		45	44	⑫	⑬	.0010–.0027	.0010–.0027	.3416–.3423	.3416–.3423
V8-302	1979–85	.096–.165		45	44	②	④	.0010–.0027	.0015–.0032	.3416–.3423	.3411–.3418
V8-351M	1979–81	.125		45	44	⑦	226 @ 1.39	.0010–.0027	.0015–.0032	.3416–.3423	.3411–.3418
V8-351W	1979–85	.123–.173		45	44	⑧	⑨	.0010–.0027	.0015–.0032	.3416–.3423	.3411–.3418
V8-400	1979–82	.175		45	44	⑦	226 @ 1.39	.0010–.0027	.0015–.0032	.3416–.3423	.3411–.3418
V8-420⑩	1983–85	—		⑪	⑪	—	60 @ 1.80	.0012–.0029	.0012–.0029	.3717–.3724	.3717–.3724
V8-460	1979–85	.100–.150		45	44	1¹³/₁₆	229 @ 1.33	.0010–.0027	.0010–.0027	.3416–.3423	.3416–.3423

①—On engines with hydraulic lifters, clearance specified is at valve stem tip with lifter collapsed.
②—Intake, 1¹¹/₁₆; exhaust, 1¹⁹/₃₂.
③—Intake, 202 @ 1.36; exhaust, 200 @ 1.20.
④—1979, intake, 202 @ 1.36; exhaust, 200 @ 1.20: 1980–85, intake, 204 @ 1.36; exhaust, 200 @ 1.20.
⑤—Intake, 1⁴⁵/₆₄; exhaust, 1³⁷/₆₄.
⑥—1979–83 intake, 197 @ 1.30; exhaust, 192 @ 1.18: 1984, intake, 170 @ 1.30; exhaust, 170 @ 1.18.
⑦—Intake, 1⁵³/₆₄; exhaust 1⁴⁵/₆₄.
⑧—Intake, 1²⁵/₃₂; exhaust, 1¹⁹/₃₂.
⑨—1979–83, intake, 200 @ 1.36; exhaust, 200 @ 1.20: 1984–85, intake, 200 @ 1.20; exhaust, 200 @ 1.20.
⑩—Diesel engine.
⑪—Intake, 30°; exhaust, 37.5°.
⑫—Intake, 1.64; exhaust, 1.47.
⑬—Intake, 175 @ 1.24; exhaust, 175 @ 1.07.

Piston, Pin, Ring, Crankshaft & Bearing Specifications

Year	Engine Model	Wristpin Diameter	Piston Clearance, Inch①	Ring End Gap, In. (Minimum)		Crank Pin Diameter, Inch	Rod Bearing Clearance, Inch	Main Bearing Journal Diameter, In.	Main Bearing Clearance, Inch	Shaft End Play
				Comp.	Oil					
1979–80	6-300	.9752	.0014–.0022	.010	.010	2.1228–2.1236	.0008–.0015	2.3982–2.3990	.0008–.0015	.004–.008
	V8-302	.9122	.0018–.0026	.010	②	2.1228–2.1236	.0008–.0015	2.2482–2.2490	③	.004–.008
	V8-351W	.9122	.0022–.0030	.010	②	2.3103–2.3111	.0008–.0015	2.9994–3.0002	.0008–.0015	.004–.008
	V8-351M	④	.0014–.0022	.010	⑤	2.3103–2.3111	.0008–.0015	2.9994–3.0002	.0008–.0015	.004–.008
	V8-400	④	.0014–.0022	.010	⑤	2.3103–2.3111	.0008–.0015	2.9994–3.0002	.0008–.0015	.004–.008
	V8-460	1.0401	⑥	.010	.010	2.4992–2.5000	.0008–.0015	2.9994–3.0002	.0008–.0015	.004–.008
1981	V8-255	.9122	.0018–.0026	.010	.010	2.1228–2.1236	.0008–.0015	2.2482–2.2490	③	.004–.008
	6-300	.9752	.0014–.0022	.010	.010	2.1228–2.1236	.0008–.0015	2.3982–2.3990	.0008–.0015	.004–.008
	V8-302	.9122	.0018–.0026	.010	.010	2.1228–2.1236	.0008–.0015	2.2482–2.2490	③	.004–.008
	V8-351W	.9122	.0022–.0030	.010	.010	2.3103–2.3111	.0008–.0015	2.9994–3.0002	.0008–.0015	.004–.008
	V8-351M	.9752	.0014–.0022	.010	.010	2.3103–2.3111	.0008–.0015	2.9994–3.0002	.0008–.0015	.004–.008
	V8-400	.9752	.0014–.0022	.010	.010	2.3103–2.3111	.0008–.0015	2.9994–3.0002	.0008–.0015	.004–.008
	V8-460	1.0401	.0022–.0030	.010	.010	2.4992–2.5000	.0008–.0015	2.9994–3.0002	.0008–.0015	.004–.008
1982	V6-232	.9122	.0014–.0022	.010	.015	2.3103–2.3111	.0010–.0014	2.5190–2.5198	.0010–.0014	.004–.008
	V8-255	.9122	.0018–.0026	.010	.010	2.1228–2.1236	.0008–.0015	2.2482–2.2490	③	.004–.008
	6-300	.9752	.0014–.0022	.010	.010	2.1228–2.1236	.0008–.0015	2.3982–2.3990	.0008–.0015	.004–.008
	V8-302	.9122	.0018–.0026	.010	.010	2.1228–2.1236	.0008–.0015	2.2482–2.2490	③	.004–.008
	V8-351W	.9122	.0018–.0026	.010	.010	2.3103–2.3111	.0008–.0015	2.9994–3.0002	.0008–.0015	.004–.008
	V8-351M	.9752	.0014–.0022	.010	.010	2.3103–2.3111	.0008–.0015	2.9994–3.0002	.0008–.0015	.004–.008
	V8-400	.9752	.0014–.0022	.010	.010	2.3103–2.3111	.0008–.0015	2.9994–3.0002	.0008–.0015	.004–.008
	V8-460	1.0401	.0022–.0030	.010	.010	2.4992–2.5000	.0008–.0015	2.9994–3.0002	.0008–.0015	.004–.008
1983	V6-232	.9122	.0014–.0022	.010	.015	2.3103–2.3111	.0010–.0014	2.5190–2.5198	.0010–.0014	.004–.008
	6-300	.9752	.0014–.0022	.010	.015	2.1228–2.1236	.0008–.0015	2.3982–2.3990	.0008–.0015	.004–.008
	V8-302	.9122	.0018–.0026	.010	.010	2.1228–2.1236	.0008–.0015	2.2482–2.2490	③	.004–.008
	V8-351W	.9122	.0018–.0026	.010	.010	2.3103–2.3111	.0008–.0015	2.9994–3.0002	.0008–.0015	.004–.008
	V8-420⑦	1.1100	.0055–.0065	⑧	.010	2.4980–2.4990	.0011–.0026	3.1228–3.1236	.0018–.0036	.002–.009
	V8-460	1.0401	.0022–.0030	.010	.010	2.4992–2.5000	.0008–.0015	2.9994–3.0002	.0008–.0015	.004–.008

continued

PISTON, PIN, RING, CRANKSHAFT & BEARING SPECIFICATIONS— Continued

Year	Engine Model	Wristpin Diameter	Piston Clearance, Inch①	Ring End Gap, In. (Minimum) Comp.	Ring End Gap, In. (Minimum) Oil	Crank Pin Diameter, Inch	Rod Bearing Clearance, Inch	Main Bearing Journal Diameter, In.	Main Bearing Clearance, Inch	Shaft End Play
1984	6-300	.9752	.0014–.0022	.010	.015	2.1228–2.1236	.0008–.0015	2.3982–2.3990	.0008–.0015	.004–.008
	V8-302	.9122	.0018–.0026	.010	.010	2.1228–2.1236	.0008–.0015	2.2482–2.2490	③	.004–.008
	V8-351W	.9122	.0018–.0026	.010	.010	2.3103–2.3111	.0008–.0015	2.9994–3.0002	.0008–.0015	.004–.008
	V8-420⑦	1.1100	.0055–.0065	⑧	.010	2.4980–2.4990	.0011–.0026	3.1228–3.1236	.0018–.0036	.002–.009
	V8-460	1.0401	.0022–.0030	.010	.010	2.4992–2.5000	.0008–.0015	2.9994–3.0002	.0008–.0015	.004–.008
1985	6-300	.9752	.0010–.0018	.010	.015	2.1228–2.1236	.0008–.0015	2.3982–2.3990	.0008–.0015	.004–.008
	V8-302	.9122	.0018–.0026	.010	.010	2.1228–2.1236	.0008–.0015	2.2482–2.2490	③	.004–.008
	V8-351W	.9122	.0018–.0026	.010	.010	2.3103–2.3111	.0008–.0015	2.9994–3.0002	.0008–.0015	.004–.008
	V8-420⑦	1.1100	.0055–.0065	⑧	.010	2.4980–2.4990	.0011–.0026	3.1228–3.1236	.0018–.0036	.002–.009
	V8-460	1.0401	.0022–.0030	.010	.010	2.4992–2.5000	.0008–.0015	2.9994–3.0002	.0008–.0015	.004–.008

①—Measured at bottom of skirt.
②—Exc. 1979, .010 inch; 1979, .015 inch.
③—No. 1, .0001–.0015 inch; others, .0005–.0015 inch.
④—1979, .9750 inch; 1980, .9752 inch.
⑤—.010 inch.
⑥—1979-80, .0022–.0030 inch.
⑦—Diesel engine.
⑧—Top, .014 inch; bottom, .060 inch.

Engine Tightening Specifications★

★Torque specifications are for clean and lightly lubricated threads only. Dry or dirty threads produce increased friction which prevents accurate measurement of tightness.

Year	Engine Model	Spark Plug Ft. Lbs.	Cylinder Head Ft. Lbs.	Intake Manifold Ft. Lbs.	Exhaust Manifold Ft. Lbs.	Rocker Shaft Support Ft. Lbs.	Rocker Cover Ft. Lbs.	Conn. Rod Cap Ft. Lbs.	Main Bearing Caps Ft. Lbs.	Flywheel To Crankshaft Ft. Lbs.	Damper or Pulley Ft. Lbs.
1979–80	6-300	①	②	22–32	28–33	③	4–7	40–45	60–70	75–85	70–90
	V8-302	10–15	65–72	23–25	18–24	④	3–5	19–24	60–70	75–85	70–90
	V8-351W	10–15	105–112	23–25	18–24	④	3–5	40–45	95–105	75–85	70–90
	V8-351M	10–15	95–105	⑤	18–24	⑥	3–5	40–45	95–105	75–85	70–90
	V8-400	10–15	95–105	⑤	18–24	⑥	3–5	40–45	95–105	75–85	70–90
	V8-460	⑦	130–140	22–32	28–33	⑥	5–6	40–45	95–105	75–85	70–90
1981	V8-255	10–15	65–72	23–25	18–24	⑥	3–5	19–24	60–70	75–85	70–90
	6-300	10–15	85	22–32	28–33	③	4–7	40–45	60–70	75–85	130–150
	V8-302	10–15	65–72	23–25	18–24	⑥	3–5	19–24	60–70	75–85	70–90
	V8-351W	10–15	105–112	23–25	18–24	⑥	3–5	40–45	95–105	75–85	70–90
	V8-351M	10–15	95–105	⑤	18–24	⑥	3–5	40–45	95–105	75–85	70–90
	V8-400	10–15	95–105	⑤	18–24	⑥	3–5	40–45	95–105	75–85	70–90
	V8-460	5–10	130–140	22–32	28–32	⑥	5–6	40–45	95–105	75–85	70–90
1982	V6-232	17–22	74	18	15–22	26	3–5	31–36	65–81	54–64	93–121
	V8-255	10–15	65–72	23–25	18–24	⑥	3–5	19–24	60–70	75–85	70–90
	6-300	10–15	85	22–32	22–32	③	4–7	40–45	60–70	75–85	130–150
	V8-302	10–15	65–72	23–25	18–24	⑥	3–5	19–24	60–70	75–85	70–90
	V8-351W	10–15	105–112	23–25	18–24	⑥	3–5	40–45	95–105	75–85	70–90
	V8-351M	10–15	95–105	⑤	18–24	⑥	3–5	40–45	95–105	75–85	70–90
	V8-400	10–15	95–105	⑤	18–24	⑥	3–5	40–45	95–105	75–85	70–90
	V8-460	5–10	130–140	22–32	28–32	⑥	5–6	40–45	95–105	75–85	70–90
1983	V6-232	17–22	74	18	15–22	26	3–5	31–36	65–81	54–64	93–121
	6-300	10–15	85	22–32	22–32	③	4–7	40–45	60–70	75–85	130–150
	V8-302	10–15	65–72	23–25	18–24	⑥	3–5	19–24	60–70	75–85	70–90
	V8-351W	10–15	105–112	23–25	18–24	⑥	3–5	45–50	95–105	75–85	70–90
	V8-420⑧	12⑨	80	24	30	⑩	6	46–51	95	47	90
	V8-460	5–10	130–140	22–32	28–32	⑥	5–6	40–45	95–105	75–85	70–90

continued

ENGINE TIGHTENING SPECIFICATIONS—Continued

★ Torque specifications are for clean and lightly lubricated threads only. Dry or dirty threads produce increased friction which prevents accurate measurement of tightness.

Year	Engine Model	Spark Plub Ft. Lbs.	Cylinder Head Ft. Lbs.	Intake Manifold Ft. Lbs.	Exhaust Manifold Ft. Lbs.	Rocker Shaft Support Ft. Lbs.	Rocker Cover Ft. Lbs.	Conn. Rod Cap Ft. Lbs.	Main Bearing Caps Ft. Lbs.	Flywheel To Crankshaft Ft. Lbs.	Damper or Pulley Ft. Lbs.
1984	6-300	10–15	85	22–32	22–32	③	4–7	40–45	60–70	75–85	130–150
	V8-302	10–15	65–72	23–25	18–24	⑥	3–5	19–24	60–70	75–85	70–90
	V8-351W	10–15	105–112	23–25	18–24	⑥	3–5	40–45	95–105	75–85	70–90
	V8-420⑧	12⑨	80	24	30	⑩	6	46–51	95	47	90
	V8-460	5–10	130–140	22–32	28–33	⑥	5–6	45–50	95–105	75–85	70–90
1985	6-300	10–15	70–85	22–32	22–32	③	70–105⑪	40–45	60–70	75–85	130–150
	V8-302	10–15	65–72	23–25	18–24	⑥	3–5	19–24	60–70	75–85	70–90
	V8-351W	10–15	105–112	23–25	18–24	⑥	3–5	40–45	95–105	75–85	70–90
	V8-420⑧	12⑨	80	24	30	⑩	6	48.5–53.5	95	47	90
	V8-460	5–10	130–140	22–32	28–33	⑥	5–6	45–50	95–105	75–85	70–90

①—1979, 15–25 ft. lbs.; 1980, 10–15 ft. lbs.
②—1979, 70–85 ft. lbs.; 1980, 85 ft. lbs.
③—1979 breakaway torque, 4.5–15 ft. lbs.; 1979–85 rocker arm stud nut torque, 17–23 ft. lbs. Refer to "Valves Adjust" procedure.
④—Rocker arm-to-cylinder head bolts, 18–25 ft. lbs.
⑤—⅜ inch bolts, 22–32 ft. lbs.; ⁵⁄₁₆ inch bolts, 19–25 ft. lbs.
⑥—Rocker arm-to-cylinder head bolts, 18–25 ft. lbs.
⑦—5–10 ft. lbs.
⑧—Diesel engine.
⑨—Glow plug.
⑩—Rocker arm to cylinder head bolts, 20 ft. lbs.
⑪—Inch lbs.

Alternator & Regulator Specifications

Year	Make or Model①	Current Rating		Field Current @ 75° F		Voltage Regulator	
		Amperes	Volts	Amperes	Volts	Part No.	Voltage @ 75° F
1979–80	Orange②	40	15	4.00	12	D9PF-AA	—
	Green②	60	15	4.00	12	D9PF-AA	—
	All③	70	15	4.00	12	D9PF-AA	—
	All③	100	15	4.00	12	D9PF-AA	—
1981–82	Orange②	40	15	4.00	12	④	—
	Green②	60	15	4.00	12	④	—
	Black③	70	15	4.00	12	④	—
	Red③	100	15	4.00	12	④	—
1983	Orange②	40	15	4.25	12	E2PF-AA	—
	Green②	60	15	4.25	12	E2PF-AA	—
	Green②	65	15	4.25	12	E2PF-AA	—
	Black③	70	15	4.00	12	E2PF-AA	—
	Red③	100	15	4.00	12	E2PF-AA	—
1984–85	Orange②	40	15	4.25	12	—	—
	Green②	60	15	4.25	12	—	—
	Black③	70	15	4.25	12	—	—
	Red③	100	15	4.25	12	—	—

①—Stamp color code.
②—Rear terminal alternator.
③—Side terminal alternator.
④—1981, D9PF-AA; 1982, E2PF-AA.

continued

Starting Motor Specifications

Year	Starter Type	Ampere Draw Normal Load	Engine Cranking Speed R.P.M.	Minimum Stall Torque @ 5 volts Ft. Lbs.	Maximum head Amperes	No Load Ampere @ 12 Volts	Brushes		
							Length Inch	Wear Limit Inch	Spring Tension Ounces
1979–85	Ford 4″ Diameter	150–200	180–250	—	—	70	.50	.25	40
	Ford 4½″ Diameter	150–180	150–290	—	—	80	.50	.25	①
1983–85	Delco Positive Engagement	430–530	170–230	—	—	120–200	.75	.24	50

①—1979–83, 80 ounces; 1984–85, 40 ounces.

Drive Axle Specifications

Year	Make & Ring Gear Diameter	Carrier Type	Ring, Gear & Pinion Backlash		Pinion Bearing Preload			Differential Bearing Preload	
			Method	Adjustment	Method	New Bearings Inch-Lbs.	Used Bearings Inch-Lbs.	New Bearings Inch	Used Bearings Inch
1979	Ford 9″	Removable	Threaded Adjuster	.008–.012	Collapsible Spacer	16–29	8–14	.008–.012	.005–.008
	Dana①	Integral	Shims	.004–.009	Shims	20–40	10–20	.015	.015
	Dana②	Integral	Shims	③	Shims	20–40	—	.015–.020	.015–.020
1980–82	Ford 9″	Removable	Threaded Adjuster	④	Collapsible Spacer	⑤	8–14	.008–.012	.005–.008
	Dana①	Integral	Shims	.004–.009	Shims	20–40	—	.015	.015
	Dana②	Integral	Shims	.005–.009	Shims	20–40	—	⑥	⑥
1983–85	Ford 8.8″	Integral	Shims	.008–.015	Collapsible Spacer	16–29	8–14	—	—
	Ford 9″	Removable	Threaded Adjuster	.008–.015	Collapsible Spacer	16–29	8–14	.008–.012	.005–.007
	Dana①	Integral	Shims	.004–.009	Shims	20–40	—	.015	.015
	Dana②	Integral	Shims	.005–.009	Shims	20–40	—	.010	.010
1985	Ford 10.25″	Integral	Shims	.0008–.0015	Collapsible Spacer	16–29	8–14	⑦	⑦

①—Rear drive axle.
②—Front drive axle.
③—Models 44-1F, 44-7F & 44-9F, .005–.009 inch; models 44-6CF-HD & 60-7F, .004–.009 inch.
④—1980–81, .008–.012 inch; 1982, .008–.015 inch.
⑤—1980, 17–27 inch lbs.; 1981–82, 16–29 inch lbs.
⑥—1980–81, .006 inch; 1982, .010 inch.
⑦—Slip fit plus .004 inch clearance on each side.

Wheel Alignment Specifications

For wheel alignment specifications on other models, refer to the "Front Suspension & Steering Section" of this chapter.

Year	Model	Caster Angle, Degrees		Camber Angle, Degrees				Toe-In Inch	Toe Out on Turns, Deg.	
		Limits	Desired	Limits		Desired			Outer Wheel	Inner Wheel
				Left	Right	Left	right			
1979	Ranchero	+3¼ to +4¾	+4	−¼ to +1¼	−½ to +1	+½	+¼	⅛	18.06	20

continued

Brake Specifications

Year	Model	Rear Drum I.D.	Wheel Cyl. Bore		Disc Brake Rotor					Master Cyl. I.D.
			Front Disc	Rear Drum	Nominal Thickness	Minimum Thickness	Thickness Variation (Parallelism)	Run Out (TIR)	Finish (Microinch)	
1979	E-100-150	11.031	2.875	.9375	1.185	1.120	.0007	.003	15–80	1.000
	E-250	12.000	2.180	1.0000	1.250	1.180	.0007	.003	15–80	1.062
	E-350	12.000	2.180	1.0602	1.250	1.180	①	②	15–80	1.062
	F-100-150	11.031	2.875	.9375	1.185	1.120	③	.003	15–80	1.000
	F-250④	12.000	2.875	1.0000	1.185	1.120	.0007	.003	15–80	1.062
	F-250⑤	12.000	2.180	1.0000	1.250	1.180	③	.003	15–80	1.062
	F-350	12.000	2.180	1.0620	1.250	1.180	①	②	15–80	1.062
	Bronco	11.031	2.875	.9375	1.185	1.120	.0007	.003	15–80	1.000
	Ranchero	11.031	3.100	.9375	1.180	1.120	.0005	.003	15–80	1.000
1980	E-100-150	11.031	2.875	.9375	1.185	1.120	.0007	.003	15–80	—
	E-250-350	12.000	—	⑬	1.250	1.180	.0007	②	15–80	—
	F-100-150	11.031	⑦	.9375	⑧	⑨	⑩	.003	15–80	—
	F-250④	12.000	2.875	.9375	1.185	1.120	.0007	.003	15–80	—
	F-250⑤	12.000	—	⑭	1.250	1.180	⑩	.003	15–80	—
	F-350	12.000	—	1.0620	1.250	1.180	.0007	.003	15–80	—
	Bronco	11.031	2.875	.9375	1.185	1.120	.0005	.003	15–80	—
1981–83	E-100-150	11.031	2.875	.9375	1.185	1.120	.0007	.003	15–80	⑮
	E-250-350	12.000	2.180	⑬	1.250	1.180	①	②	15–80	1.062
	F-100-150	⑫	⑦	.9375	⑧	⑨	①	⑪	15–80	1.000
	F-250④	12.000	2.875	.9375	1.185	1.120	.0007	.003	15–80	1.000
	F-250⑤	12.000	2.180	⑭	1.250	1.180	①	⑪	15–80	1.062
	F-350	12.000	2.180	1.0620	1.250	1.180	①	②	15–80	1.062
	Bronco	11.031	2.875	.9375	1.185	1.120	①	⑪	15–80	1.000
1984	E-150	12.000	2.875	—	1.185	1.120	.0007	.003	15–80	—
	E-250-350	12.000	—	—	1.250	1.180	①	②	15–80	—
	F-150	11.031	2.875	—	1.185	1.120	①	⑪	15–80	—
	F-250④	12.000	2.875	—	1.185	1.120	.0007	.003	15–80	—
	F-250⑤	12.000	—	—	1.250	1.180	①	⑪	15–80	—
	F-350	12.000	—	—	1.250	1.180	①	②	15–80	—
	Bronco	12.000	2.875	—	1.185	1.120	①	⑪	15–80	—
1985	E-150	11.031	—	—	1.190	1.120	.0007	.003	15–80	—
	E-250-350	12.000	—	—	1.250	1.180	①	⑯	15–80	—
	F-150	11.031	—	—	1.190	1.120	①	⑪	15–80	—
	F-250④	12.000	—	—	1.190	1.120	.0007	.003	15–80	—
	F-250⑤	12.000	—	—	1.250	1.180	①	⑪	15–80	—
	F-350	12.000	—	—	1.250	1.180	①	⑯	15–80	—
	Bronco	11.031	—	—	1.190	1.120	①	⑪	15–80	—

①—Integral hub & rotor, .0007 inch; separate hub & rotor, .0010 inch.
②—Integral hub and rotor, .0030 inch; separate hub & rotor, .0010 inch.
③—Exc. 1979 4 × 4 models, .0007 inch; 1979 4 × 4 models, .0050 inch.
④—4 × 2 models under 6900 lbs. GVW.
⑤—4 × 2 models over 6900 lbs. GVW & all 4 × 4 models.
⑥—Integral hub & rotor, .003 inch; 4 × 4 vehicles w/separate hub & rotor, .005 inch; E-350 & dual rear wheel F-350 w/separate hub & rotor, .010 inch.
⑦—Exc. F-100 under 4700 lbs. GVW with power brakes, 2.875 inches; F-100 under 4700 lbs. GVW with power brakes, 2.597 inches.
⑧—Exc. F-100 under 4700 lbs. GVW with power brakes, 1.185 inch; F-100 under 4700 lbs. GVW with power brakes, .980 inch.
⑨—Exc. F-100 under 4700 lbs. GVW with power brakes, 1.120 inch; F-100 under 4700 lbs. GVW with power brakes, .810 inch.
⑩—4 × 2 models, .0007 inch; 4 × 4 models, .0050 inch.
⑪—Integral hub & rotor, .003 inch; separate hub & rotor, .005 inch.
⑫—Exc. F-100 under 4700 lbs. GVW with power brakes, 11.031 inches; F-100 under 4700 lbs. GVW with power brakes, 10 inches.
⑬—E-250, .9375 inch; E-350, 1.062 inch.
⑭—Under 8500 lbs. GVW, .9375 inch; over 8500 lbs. GVW, 1.062 inch.
⑮—Exc. E-100 with manual brakes, 1.062 inch; E-100 with manual brakes, 1.000 inch.
⑯—Integral hub & rotor, .003 inch; 4 × 4 vehicles w/separate hub & rotor, .005 inch; E-350 & dual rear wheel F-350 w/separate hub & rotor, .010 inch.

continued

Cooling System & Capacity Data

Year	Model & Engine	Cooling Capacity, Qts.		Radiator Cap Relief Pressure, Lbs.	Thermo. Opening Temp.	Fuel Tank Gals.①	Engine Oil Refill Qts.②	Transmission Oil			Transfer Case Oil Pints	Rear Axle Oil Pints
		Less A/C	With A/C					3 Speed Pints	4 Speed Pints	Auto Trans Qts.③		
1979	E-100-350 6-300	15.0	20.0	13	—	④	5	3.5	4.5	11.9	—	㉝
	F-100-350 6-300	⑲	17.0	13	—	㉞	5	3.5	㉒	㉟㊱	⑨	㊲
	E-100-350 V8-302	㊳	17.5	13	—	④	5	3.5	4.5	11.9	—	㉝
	F-100-150 V8-302	㉖	18.0	13	—	19.2	5	3.5	㉒	10.0㊱	⑨	6.5
	Ranchero V8-302	14.3	14.6	16	196	26.0	4	—	—	㊴	—	5.0
	Bronco V8-351	㉗	22.0	13	—	25.0	5	—	7.0	13.2	⑨	6.5
	E-100-350 V8-351	㉘	㉘	13	—	④	5	3.5	4.5	11.9	—	㉝
	F-100-350 V8-351	㉙	18.0	13	—	㉞	5	3.5	㉒	13.2	⑨	㊲
	Ranchero V8-351	㉚	㉛	16	196	26.0	4	—	—	㊴	—	5.0
	Bronco V8-400	㉗	22.0	13	—	25.0	5	—	7.0	13.2	⑨	6.5
	F-100-350 V8-400	㉜	18.0	13	—	㉞	5	3.5	㉒	13.2	⑨	㊲
	Ranchero V8-400	16.5	16.5	16	196	26.0	4	—	—	11.0	—	5.0
	E-100-350 V8-460	28.0	28.0	13	—	④	5	3.5	4.5	11.9	—	㉝
	F-100-350 V8-460	24.0	24.0	13	—	㉞	5	3.5	㉒	—	⑨	㊲
1980	Bronco 6-300	㊵	14.0	13	—	25.0	5	—	7.0	13.4	6.5	6.5
	E-100-350 6-300	㊶	20.0	13	—	④	5	3.5	4.5	11.9	—	㉝
	F-100-350 6-300	㊵	14.0	13	—	㊷	5	3.5	㉒	㊸	6.5	㊹
	Bronco V8-302	㊺	14.0	13	—	25.0	5	—	7.0	13.4	6.5	6.5
	E-100-150 V8-302	㊻	㊼	13	—	④	5	3.5	4.5	11.9	—	6.5
	F-100-350 V8-302	㊵	14.0	13	—	㊷	5	3.5	㉒	㊸	6.5	㊹
	Bronco V8-351	㊺㊺	16.0	13	—	25.0	5	—	7.0	13.4	6.5	6.5
	E-100-350 V8-351	㊽	21.0	13	—	④	5	3.5	4.5	11.9	—	㉝
	F-100-350 V8-351	㊺㊺	16.0	13	—	㊷	5	3.5	㉒	13.2	6.5	㊹
	E-250-350 V8-400	㊾	21.0	13	—	④	5	3.5	4.5	11.9	—	㉝
	F-100-350 V8-400	㊿	16.0	13	—	㊷	5	3.5	㉒	13.4	6.5	㊹
	E-350 V8-460	28.0	28.0	13	—	④	5	3.5	4.5	11.9	—	㉝
1981	F-100 V8-255	㊺	14.0	13	—	㊷	5	3.5	㉒	52	—	㊹
	Bronco 6-300	㊵	14.0	13	—	25.0	5	—	㉒	13.4	7.0	6.5
	E-100-350 6-300	㊶	20.0	13	—	④	5	3.5	4.5	11.9	—	㉝
	F-100-350 6-300	㊵	14.0	13	—	㊷	5	3.5	㉒	52 53	54	㊹
	Bronco V8-302	㊺	14.0	13	—	25.0	5	—	㉒	13.4	7.0	6.5
	E-100-250 V8-302	㊻	㊼	13	—	④	5	3.5	4.5	11.9	—	㉝

continued

COOLING SYSTEM & CAPACITY DATA—Continued

Year	Model & Engine	Cooling Capacity, Qts. Less A/C	With A/C	Radiator Cap Relief Pressure, Lbs.	Thermo. Opening Temp.	Fuel Tank Gals.①	Engine Oil Refill Qts.②	Transmission Oil 3 Speed Pints	4 Speed Pints	Auto Trans Qts.③	Transfer Case Oil Pints	Rear Axle Oil Pints
1981 Cont'd	F-100-350 V8-302	㊺	14.0	13	—	㊷	5	3.5	㉒	㊵㊾	㊼	㊹
	Bronco V8-351	㊶	16.0	13	—	25.0	5	—	㉒	13.4	7.0	6.5
	E-100-350 V8-351	㊽	21.0	13	—	④	5	3.5	4.5	11.9	—	㉝
	F-150-350 V8-351	㊶	16.0	13	—	㊷	5	3.5	㉒	㊵㊾	㊼	㊹
	E-250-350 V8-400	㊾	21.0	13	—	④	5	3.5	4.5	11.9	—	㉝
	F-250-350 V8-400	㊿	16.0	13	—	㊷	5	3.5	㉒	㊵㊾	㊼	㊹
	E-350 V8-460	28.0	28.0	13	—	④	5	3.5	4.5	11.9	—	㉝
1982	F-100 V6-232	㊶	11.0	13	—	㊷	5	3.5	㉒	㉕	—	6.5
	F-100 V8-255	㊺	14.0	13	—	㊷	5	3.5	㉒	㉕	—	6.5
	Bronco 6-300	㊵	14.0	13	—	25.0	5	—	㉒	13.4	7.0	6.5
	E-100-350 6-300	㊶	20.0	13	—	④	5	3.5	㉒	11.9	—	㉔
	F-100-350 6-300	㊵	14.0	13	—	25.0	5	3.5	㉒	㉕	㊼	㉓
	Bronco V8-302	㊺	14.0	13	—	㊷	5	—	㉒	13.4	7.0	6.5
	E-100-250 V8-302	㊻	㊼	13	—	④	5	3.5	4.5	11.9	—	㉔
	F-100-350 V8-302	㊺	14.0	13	—	㊷	5	3.5	㉒	㉕	㊼	㉓
	Bronco V8-351	㊶	16.0	13	—	25.0	5	—	㉒	13.4	7.0	6.5
	E-100-350 V8-351	㊽	21.0	13	—	④	5	3.5	4.5	11.9	—	㉔
	F-150-350 V8-351	㊶	16.0	13	—	㊷	5	3.5	㉒	㉕	㊼	㉓
	E-250-350 V8-400	㊾	21.0	13	—	④	5	3.5	4.5	11.9	—	㉔
	F-250-350 V8-400	㊿	16.0	13	—	㊷	5	3.5	㉒	㉕	6.5	㉓
	E-350 V8-460	28.0	28.0	13	—	④	5	3.5	4.5	11.9	—	㉔
1983	F-100 V6-232	⑳	12.0	13	—	16.5	5	3.5	㉒	11.0	—	5.5
	Bronco 6-300	㊵	14.0	13	—	25.0	5	—	㉒	13.5	7.0	5.5
	E-100-350 6-300	15.0	20.0	13	—	④	5	3.5	4.5	11.8	—	⑱
	F-100-350 6-300	㊵	14.0	13	—	㊷	5	3.5	㉒	11.8	㊼	⑰
	Bronco V8-302	㊺	14.0	13	—	25.0	5	—	㉒	13.5	7.0	5.5
	E-100-350 V8-302	⑯	㊳	13	—	④	5	3.5	4.5	11.8	—	⑱
	F-100-250 V8-302	㊺	14.0	13	—	㊷	5	3.5	㉒	11.8㊾	㊼	⑰
	Bronco V8-351	㊶	16.0	13	—	25.0	5	—	㉒	13.5	7.0	5.5
	E-100-350 V8-351	⑭	⑬	13	—	④	5	3.5	4.5	11.8	—	⑱
	F-100-350 V8-351	㊶	16.0	13	—	㊷	5	3.5	㉒	11.8㊾	㊼	⑰
	F-250-350 V8-420㉑	31.0	31.0	13	—	㊷	9	3.5	㉒	11.8㊾	6.5	⑰
	E-250-350 V8-460	28.0	28.0	13	—	④	5	3.5	4.5	11.8	—	⑱
	F-250-350 V8-460	⑫	17.5	13	—	㊷	5	3.5	㉒	13.5	6.5	⑰

continued

COOLING SYSTEM & CAPACITY DATA—Continued

Year	Model & Engine	Cooling Capacity, Qts. Less A/C	Cooling Capacity, Qts. With A/C	Radiator Cap Relief Pressure, Lbs.	Thermo. Opening Temp.	Fuel Tank Gals.[1]	Engine Oil Refill Qts.[2]	Transmission Oil 3 Speed Pints	Transmission Oil 4 Speed Pints	Transmission Oil Auto Trans Qts.[3]	Transfer Case Oil Pints	Rear Axle Oil Pints
1984	Bronco 6-300	[40]	14.0	13	—	32.0	5	—	[22]	13.5	7.0	5.5
	E-150-350 6-300	15.0	17.5	13	—	[4]	5	3.5	4.5	11.8	—	[18]
	F-150-350 6-300	[40]	14.0	13	—	[42]	5	3.5	[22]	[11]	[54]	[17]
	Bronco V8-302	[45]	14.0	13	—	32.0	5	—	[22]	13.5	7.0	5.5
	E-150-350 V8-302	[46]	[10]	13	—	[4]	5	3.5	4.5	[51]	—	[18]
	F-150-250 V8-302	[45]	14.0	13	—	[42]	5	3.5	[22]	[15]	[54]	[17]
	Bronco V8-351	[55]	16.0	13	—	32.0	5	—	[22]	13.5	7.0	5.5
	E-150-350 V8-351	[14]	[13]	13	—	[4]	5	3.5	4.5	[51]	—	[18]
	F-150-350 V8-351	[55]	16.0	13	—	[42]	5	3.5	[22]	11.8[53]	[54]	[17]
	E-250-350 V8-420[21]	31.0	31.0	13	—	[4]	9	3.5	4.5	11.8	—	[17]
	F-250-350 V8-420[21]	31.0	31.0	13	—	[42]	9	3.5	[22]	11.8[53]	[54]	[17]
	E-250-350 V8-460	28.0	28.0	13	—	[4]	5	3.5	4.5	11.8	—	[18]
	F-250-350 V8-460	[12]	17.5	13	—	[42]	5	3.5	[22]	11.8[53]	[54]	[17]
1985	Bronco 6-300	[5]	[5]	13	—	32.0	5	—	[6]	13.5	9.0	5.5
	E-150-350 6-300	15.0	17.5	13	—	[4]	5	3.5	[6]	[51]	—	[8]
	F-150 & F-350 6-300	[5]	[5]	13	—	[42]	5	3.5	[6]	[15]	[7]	[8]
	Bronco V8-302	[45]	14.0	13	—	32.0	5	—	[6]	13.5	9.0	5.5
	E-150-350 V8-302	[46]	[10]	13	—	[4]	5	3.5	[6]	[51]	—	[8]
	F-150 & F-250 V8-302	[45]	14.0	13	—	[42]	5	3.5	[6]	[15]	[7]	[8]
	Bronco V8-351	[55]	15.0	13	—	32.0	5	—	[6]	13.5	9.0	5.5
	E-150-350 V8-351	[14]	[13]	13	—	[4]	5	3.5	[6]	[51]	—	[8]
	F-150 & F-350 V8-351	[55]	15.0	13	—	[42]	5	3.5	[6]	11.8[53]	[7]	[8]
	E & F-250-350 V8-420[21]	31.0	31.0	13	—	[4]	9	3.5	[6]	[51]	[7]	[8]
	Bronco V8-460	16.0	16.0	13	—	32.0	5	—	[6]	13.5	9.0	5.5
	E-250 & E-350 V8-460	28.0	28.0	13	—	[4]	5	3.5	[6]	[51]	—	[8]
	F-150 & F-350 V8-460	16.0	16.0	13	—	[42]	5	3.5	[6]	11.8[53]	[7]	[8]
	F-250 & F-350 V8-460	[12]	17.5	13	—	[42]	5	3.5	[6]	11.8[53]	[7]	[8]

[1]—Standard fuel tank.
[2]—Add 1 qt. with filter change.
[3]—Approximate: make final check with dipstick.
[4]—Exc. E-100-150 with 124" wheelbase, 22.1 gals.; E-100-150 with 124" wheelbase, 18 gals.
[5]—Manual trans., 13 qts.; auto. trans., 14 qts.
[6]—Ford overdrive trans., 4.5 pts.; New Process model 435 less extension, Warner model T-18 less extension & Warner model T-19, 6.5 pts.; New Process model 435 w/extension & Warner model T-18 w/extension, 7.0 pts.
[7]—Borg-Warner model 1345, 6.5 pts.; New Process Gear 208, 9 pts.
[8]—Dana model 60-3, 6.25 pts.; Dana model 61-1, 5.8 pts.; Dana model 70, 6.6 pts.; Dana model 70 HD, 7.4 pts.; Ford w/8.8 or 9 inch ring gear, 5.5 pts.; Ford w/10.25 inch ring gear, 7.5 pts.
[9]—Full time transfer case, 9 pts.; 2 speed part time transfer case, 4 pts.
[10]—Man. trans., 17.5 qts.; auto. trans., 18.5 qts.
[11]—C5 units, 11 qts.; C6 units, 11.8 qts.; 4 × 4 models, 13.5 qts.
[12]—Exc. models with man. trans. & heavy duty cooling, 17.5 qts.; models with man. trans. & heavy duty cooling, 16.5 qts.
[13]—Man. trans., 15 qts.; auto. trans., 21 qts.
[14]—Exc. models with super cooling, 20 qts.; models with super cooling, 21 qts.
[15]—C5 units, 11 qts.; C6 units, 11.8 qts.; automatic overdrive units, 12 qts.; 4 ×

continued

COOLING SYSTEM & CAPACITY DATA—Continued

4 models, 13.5 qts.

⑯—Models with man. trans. less super cooling, 12.5 qts.; models with auto. trans. less super cooling, 17.5 qts.; models with super cooling, 18.5 qts.

⑰—F-100-350, 5.5 pts.; F-250 exc. Ford standard axle, 6 pts.; F-250 with Ford standard axle, 5.5 pts.; F-350 with Dana model 70 axle, 6.5 pts.; F-350 with Dana model 70 HD axle, 7.4 pts.; other F-350 models, 6 pts.

⑱—E-150-350, 5.5 pts.; E-250 exc. Ford standard axle, 6 pts.; E-250 with Ford standard axle, 5.5 pts.; E-350 exc. Dana model 70 axle, 6 pts.; E-350 with Dana model 70 axle, 6.5 pts.

⑲—Man. trans., 13 qts.; auto. trans., 11 qts.

⑳—Exc. models with super cooling, 11 qts.; models with super cooling, 12 qts.

㉑—Diesel engine.

㉒—New Process model 435 with extension & Warner model T-18(-B), 7 pts; New Process model 435 less extension, 6.5 pts.; 4 speed overdrive units, 4.5 pts.

㉓—F-100-150, 6.5 pts.; F-250 exc. Dana model 60 axle, 6 pts.; F-250 with Dana model 60 axle, 5 pts.; F-350 with Dana model 70 axle, 6.5 pts.; F-350 with Dana model 70 HD axle, 7.4 pts.; F-350 with Dana model 61-1 axle, 6 pts.

㉔—Exc. models with dual rear wheels, 6 pts.; models with dual rear wheels, 6.5 pts.

㉕—C4 units, 9.6 qts.; C5 units, 11 qts.; C6 units, 11.9 qts.; automatic overdrive units, 12 qts.; 4 × 4 models, 14.4 qts.

㉖—Exc. models with auto. trans. & heavy duty cooling, 15 qts.; models with auto. trans. & heavy duty cooling, 18 qts.

㉗—Models with man. trans. & standard cooling, 20 qts.; models with super cooling, 24 qts.; other models, 22 qts.

㉘—Man. trans., 15 qts.; auto. trans., 20 qts.

㉙—Exc. F-150-350 with man. trans. & standard cooling & F-100-350 with super cooling, 17 qts.; F-150-350 with man. trans. & standard cooling, 15 qts.; F-100-350 with super cooling, 24 qts.

㉚—V8-351W engine, 15.4 qts.; V8-351M engine, 16.5 qts.

㉛—V8-351W engine, 15.7 qts.; V8-351M engine, 16.5 qts.

㉜—Exc. models with super cooling, 18 qts.; models with super cooling, 24 qts.

㉝—E-100-150 with Ford standard or Traction-Lok axle, 6.5 pts.; E-250 with Dana model 60-2, 61-1 or 61-2 axle, 6 pts.; other models, 7 pts.

㉞—F-250-350 4 × 2 crew cab & F-350 exc. styleside, 20.2 gals.; other models, 19 gals.

㉟—C4 units, 10 qts.; C6 units, 11.9 qts.

㊱—4 × 4 models, 13.2 qts.

㊲—F-100-150, 6.5 pts.; F-250 4 × 2 with Dana 60 axle & all F-350, 7 pts.; F-250 4 × 2 exc. Dana model 60 axle, 6 pts.

㊳—Man. trans., 15 qts.; auto. trans., 17.5 qts.

㊴—C4 units, 10 qts.; FMX units, 11 qts.

㊵—Exc. models with super cooling, 13 qts.; models with super cooling, 14 qts.

㊶—Exc. models with super cooling, 15 qts.; models with super cooling, 20 qts.

㊷—F-100-150 short wheelbase & F-250 short wheelbase super cab, 16.5 gals.; other models, 19 gals.

㊸—C4 units, 10 qts.; C6 units, 13.4 qts.

㊹—F-100-150, 6.5 pts.; F-250 exc. 4 × 2 with Dana model 61-2 axle, 5 pts.; F-250 with Dana model 61-2 axle, 6 pts.; F-350 exc. Dana 61-1 axle & 1981 F-350 with Dana 70 HD axle, 6.5 pts.; F-350 with Dana 61-1 axle & 1981 F-350 with Dana 70 HD axle, 6 pts.

㊺—Models with auto. trans. & heavy duty cooling & models with super cooling, 14 qts.; other models, 13 qts.

㊻—Models with man. trans. less super cooling, 15 qts.; models with auto. trans. less super cooling, 17.5 qts.; models with super cooling, 18.5 qts.

㊼—Exc. models with super cooling, 17.5 qts.; models with super cooling, 18.5 qts.

㊽—E-100-150 exc. super cooling & E-250-350 with standard cooling, 20 qts.; E-100-150 with super cooling & E-250-350 with heavy duty cooling, 21 qts.; E-250-350 with super cooling, 28 qts.

㊾—Models with standard cooling, 20 qts.; models with heavy duty cooling, 21 qts.; models with super cooling, 28 qts.

㊿—Models with man. trans. less super cooling, 15 qts.; models with auto. trans. and/or super cooling, 16 qts.

(51)—C6 units, 11.8 qts.; automatic overdrive units, 12 qts.

(52)—C4 units, 9.6 qts.; C6 units, 11.9 qts.; automatic overdrive units, 12 qts.

(53)—4 × 4 models, 13.4 qts.

(54)—Borg Warner model 1345, 6.5 pts.; New Process model 208, 7 pts.

(55)—Exc. models with super cooling, 15 qts.; models with super cooling, 16 qts.

(56)—Exc. models with super cooling, 10 qts.; models with super cooling, 11 qts.

Fig. 1   Ignition lock replacement. 1979 exc. Ranchero

STARTER
REPLACE

1. Disconnect battery ground cable.
2. Raise and support vehicle, if necessary.
3. Disconnect starter cable from starter motor.
4. On all models, remove starter motor attaching bolts and the starter motor.

NOTE: On some Ranchero models, it may be necessary to turn wheels to the left or right to provide clearance for starter removal.

5. Reverse procedure to install.

IGNITION LOCK
REPLACE

1979 EXC. RANCHERO

1. Disconnect battery ground cable.
2. Turn ignition key to accessory position.
3. Insert a suitable wire into retaining pin access hole, then turn lock cylinder counterclockwise out of ignition switch while depressing pin, **Fig. 1.**
4. Install lock in Accessory position. When cylinder is fully seated, turn key to Lock position.
5. Turn the key to check for proper operation in all positions, then reconnect battery ground cable.

1979 RANCHERO & 1980–85 ALL

1. Disconnect battery ground cable.
2. Remove steering wheel trim pad and steering wheel.
3. Shift transmission into Park on vehicles with automatic transmission, or into any gear on vehicles with manual transmission.
4. Insert a 1/8 inch diameter wire or small drift punch into retaining pin access slot and remove lock cylinder, **Figs. 2 and 3,** while depressing pin.

NOTE: The lock cylinder retaining pin is located adjacent to the hazard warning button on models with tilt steering column and inside the column near base of cylinder on models with fixed steering column.

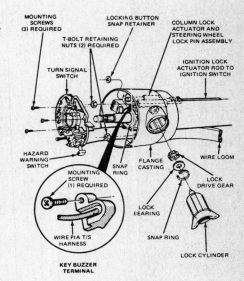

Fig. 2   Ignition lock replacement. Fixed steering column. 1979 Ranchero & 1980–85 all

5. To install, turn lock cylinder to On position and depress pin.
6. Install lock cylinder into housing. Turn ignition key to Off position after ensuring cylinder is fully seated and aligned into interlocking washer.
7. Turn the key to check for proper operation in all positions.
8. Install steering wheel and trim pad and reconnect battery ground cable.

IGNITION SWITCH
REPLACE

1979 EXC. RANCHERO

1. Remove ignition lock as previously described.
2. Remove switch-to-instrument panel attaching nut.
3. Disconnect electrical connector from switch and remove switch from vehicle.
4. Reverse procedure to install.

1979 RANCHERO & 1980–85 ALL

1. Disconnect battery ground cable.
2. On Ranchero models, remove instrument cluster as described under "Instrument Cluster, Replace."
3. On all models, remove steering column shroud and lower the steering column.
4. Disconnect electrical connector from switch, then remove 2 switch attach-

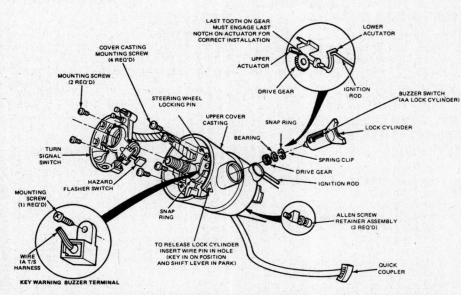

Fig. 3   Ignition lock replacement. Tilt steering column. 1979 Ranchero & 1980–85 all

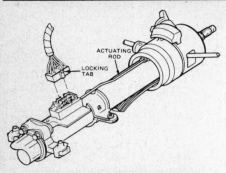

Fig. 4 Ignition switch replacement. 1979 Ranchero & 1980—85 all

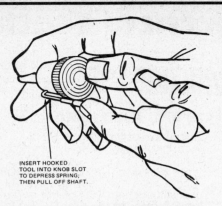

Fig. 5 Light switch & wiper switch knob removal. 1979 Ranchero

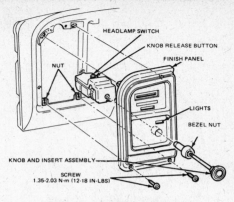

Fig. 6 Light switch replacement. 1979 exc. Ranchero & 1980—85 E-100—350

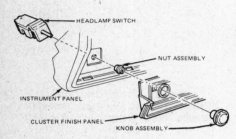

Fig. 7 Light switch replacement. 1980—85 F-100—350 & Bronco

ing nuts.
5. Lift switch up to disengage actuator rod, then remove switch from vehicle, **Fig. 4.**
6. Reverse procedure to install.

LIGHT SWITCH
REPLACE

1979 RANCHERO

1. Disconnect battery ground cable.
2. Remove light switch knob, **Fig. 5.**
3. Remove bezel nut using tool No. T65L-700-A or equivalent.
4. Disconnect electrical connector from switch and remove switch from vehicle.
5. Reverse procedure to install.

1979 EXC. RANCHERO & 1980—85 E-100—350

1. Disconnect battery ground cable.
2. Remove knob and shaft assembly by depressing release button on switch housing and pulling straight out.
3. Remove bezel or mounting nut from switch, **Fig. 6.**
4. Disconnect electrical connector from switch and remove switch from vehicle.
5. Reverse procedure to install.

1980—85 F-100—350 & BRONCO

1. Disconnect battery ground cable.
2. Remove knobs from headlight switch, windshield wiper switch and fog light switch (if equipped). Use a suitable hook tool to release each knob lock tab.
3. Remove steering column shroud, then the cluster finish panel assembly, **Fig. 7.**
4. Remove switch attaching nut, **Fig. 7.**
5. Disconnect electrical connector from switch and remove switch from vehicle.
6. Reverse procedure to install.

STOP LIGHT SWITCH
REPLACE

1979 F-100—350 & BRONCO LESS SPEED CONTROL

1. Disconnect battery ground cable.
2. Disconnect electrical connector from switch, then unscrew switch from retainer and remove from vehicle, **Fig. 8.**
3. Reverse procedure to install.

EXC. 1979 F-100—350 & BRONCO LESS SPEED CONTROL

1. Disconnect battery ground cable.
2. Disconnect electrical connector from switch, **Figs. 9 and 10.**
3. Remove hairpin retainer, then slide stop light switch, push rod, nylon washers and bushings away from pedal and remove the switch from vehicle.
4. Reverse procedure to install.

NOTE: Ensure stop light switch wires are of sufficient length to allow full travel of the brake pedal.

Fig. 8 Stop light switch replacement. 1979 F-100—350 & Bronco less speed control

NEUTRAL SAFETY SWITCH
REPLACE

1979 RANCHERO

1. Disconnect battery ground cable.
2. Place selector lever in Neutral.
3. Raise and support vehicle.
4. Remove shift rod-to-transmission manual lever attaching nut.
5. Lower vehicle and remove selector lever handle and dial housing.
6. Disconnect dial light and neutral safety switch electrical connectors from dash panel.

NOTE: On models equipped with FMX transmission, disconnect seat belt warning electrical connector.

7. Remove selector lever and housing assembly.
8. Remove pointer back-up shield attaching screws and the shield.
9. Remove neutral safety switch-to-selector lever housing attaching

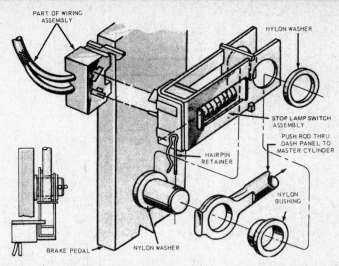

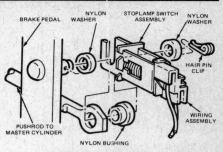

Fig. 10   Stop light switch replacement. 1980—83 E-100 w/manual brakes

Fig. 9   Stop light switch replacement. 1979—84 exc. 1979 F-100—350 & Bronco less speed control & 1980—83 E-100 w/manual brakes.

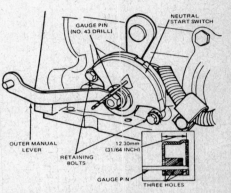

Fig. 12   Neutral safety switch replacement. 1979—85 exc. automatic overdrive transmission

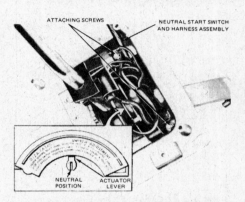

Fig. 11   Neutral safety switch replacement. 1979 Ranchero

screws.

10. Press neutral safety switch electrical connector inward and remove switch and connector assembly, **Fig. 11.**
11. To install switch, position switch and connector assembly on selector lever housing, then install attaching screws. Do not tighten screws at this time.

NOTE: Prior to installing switch and connector assembly, ensure selector lever is against neutral detent stop and actuator lever is properly aligned in neutral position.

12. Place selector lever in Park and hold against forward stop.
13. Slide neutral safety switch rearward as far as possible and tighten attaching screws while holding switch in position.
14. Install pointer back-up shield, then position selector lever and housing assembly on console and install attaching bolts.
15. Reconnect all electrical connectors, then install dial housing and shift lever handle and place selector in Drive.
16. Raise and support vehicle.

17. Install shift rod on transmission manual lever.
18. Check shift linkage adjustment, then lower vehicle and check operation of switch.

1979—85 EXC. AUTOMATIC OVERDRIVE TRANSMISSION

1. Disconnect battery ground cable.
2. Remove downshift linkage rod return spring from low-reverse servo cover.
3. Apply penetrating oil to outer lever attaching nut, then remove transmission downshift outer lever attaching nut and lever.
4. Remove neutral safety switch attaching bolts, then disconnect electrical connectors and remove switch from vehicle.
5. To install, position switch on transmission and secure with attaching bolts. Do not tighten bolts at this time.
6. Place transmission manual lever in neutral position, then insert a .091 inch gauge pin through gauge pin holes, **Fig. 12.**
7. Tighten switch attaching bolts, then remove gauge pin.
8. Install outer downshift lever and retaining nut.
9. Install downshift linkage rod return spring between lever and retaining clip on low-reverse servo cover.
10. Reconnect electrical connectors, then check operation of switch.

1981—85 W/AUTOMATIC OVERDRIVE TRANSMISSION

1. Disconnect battery ground cable.
2. Raise and support vehicle.
3. Disconnect electrical connector at neutral safety switch, lifting connector straight up.
4. Using suitable socket, remove neutral safety switch and O-ring seal.
5. Reverse procedure to install, installing new O-ring seal.

TURN SIGNAL SWITCH
REPLACE

1. Disconnect battery ground cable.
2. Remove horn switch, then the steering wheel.
3. Remove turn signal switch lever by unscrewing from steering column.
4. On 1979 Ranchero and 1981—85 F-100—350 and Bronco models, remove lower steering column shroud.
5. On 1981—85 E-100—350 models, remove upper and lower steering column shrouds.
6. On all models, disconnect electrical connector from turn signal switch and remove switch attaching screws.
7. On all models with tilt column and 1979—80 E-100—350, F-100—350 and Bronco with fixed column, remove wires and terminals from steering column electrical connector, after noting color code and location of each connector. Remove plastic cover sleeve, if equipped, from wiring harness, then lift switch assembly out through top of column.

NOTE: On 1981—85 E-100—350 models equipped with tilt column and automatic selector indicator light electrical connector from turn signal switch harness prior to removing the switch.

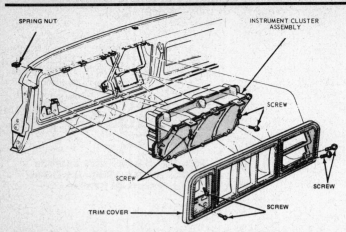

Fig. 13 Instrument cluster replacement. 1979 F-100—350 & Bronco

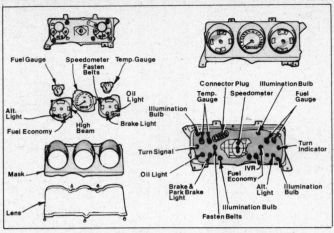

Fig. 14 Instrument cluster replacement. Ranchero w/standard cluster

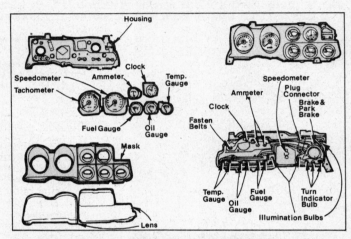

Fig. 15 Instrument cluster replacement. Ranchero w/performance cluster

8. On all models with fixed column, except 1979–80 E-100–350 F-100–350 and Bronco, remove switch assembly by lifting out of column while guiding connector plug through opening in shift socket.

NOTE: On 1981–85 E-100–350 models equipped with fixed column and automatic transmission, remove transmission selector indicator light assembly with turn signal switch.

9. Reverse procedure to install.

INSTRUMENT CLUSTER
REPLACE

1979 F-100—350 & BRONCO

1. Disconnect battery ground cable.
2. Remove radio control knobs, fuel gauge switch knob, heater control knobs and windshield wiper control knob, using a suitable hook tool to release each knob lock tab.
3. Remove light switch shaft and knob assembly.
4. Remove nut and washer from each radio control shaft, then slide bezel off over shafts.
5. Remove cluster trim cover attaching screws and the cover, **Fig. 13.**
6. Disconnect air conditioning duct, if equipped, and the illumination light from the bezel.
7. Remove 4 instrument cluster attaching screws, then disconnect speedometer cable and electrical connector from printed circuit and remove cluster from vehicle.
8. Reverse procedure to install.

RANCHERO

1. Disconnect battery ground cable.
2. Remove 3 upper and 4 lower instrument panel trim cover attaching screws and the trim cover.
3. On models equipped with standard cluster, remove 3 clock or cover attaching screws and the clock or cover.
4. On all models, remove 2 upper and 2 lower instrument cluster-to-instrument panel attaching screws.
5. Pull cluster back from panel and disconnect speedometer cable.
6. Disconnect cluster feed plug from printed circuit receptacle.
7. On models equipped with performance cluster, disconnect overlay harness connector.
8. On all models, remove cluster from vehicle, **Figs. 14 and 15.**
9. Reverse procedure to install.

E-100—350

1. Disconnect battery ground cable.
2. Remove steering column shroud.
3. On models equipped with tilt steering column, loosen column-to-band C support to provide sufficient clearance for cluster removal.

4. On all models, remove 7 instrument cluster-to-instrument panel attaching screws.
5. Pull cluster back from panel and disconnect speedometer cable.

NOTE: It may be necessary to disconnect speedometer cable from transmission to provide access to the quick disconnect on the cluster.

6. Disconnect electrical connector from printed circuit board and remove cluster from vehicle, **Fig. 16.**
7. Reverse procedure to install.

F-100—350 & BRONCO

1. Disconnect battery ground cable.
2. Remove wiper-washer knob, and on equipped 1980 models, the fuel gauge switch knob. Use a suitable hook tool to release each knob lock tab.
3. Remove light switch knob, windshield wiper switch knob and fog light switch knob, if equipped.
4. Remove steering column shroud, using care not to damage transmis-

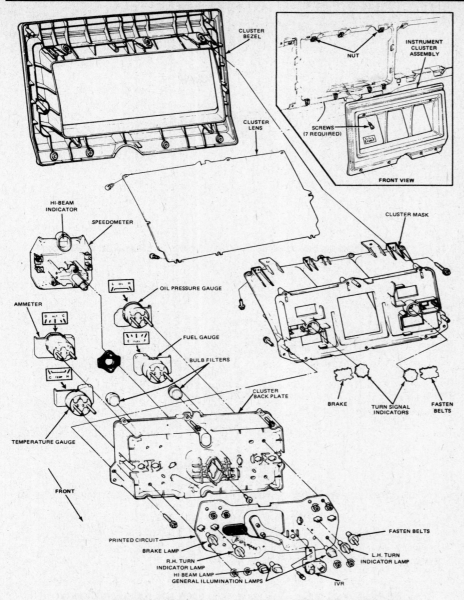

Fig. 16 Instrument cluster replacement. E-100—350

sion selector indicator cables on models equipped with automatic transmission.

5. On models equipped with automatic transmission, release shift lever indicator cable retaining clip(s), then remove cable loop from retainer pin. Remove cable bracket attaching screw and slide bracket out of slot in tube.

6. On all models, remove cluster finish panel and the 4 cluster attaching screws, **Fig. 17.**

7. Pull cluster back from panel and disconnect speedometer cable, printed circuit electrical connector and 4 × 4 indicator light electrical connector, if equipped.

8. Remove cluster from vehicle, **Fig. 17.**

9. Reverse procedure to install.

WIPER MOTOR
REPLACE

1979 F-100—350 & BRONCO

1. Disconnect battery ground cable.
2. Remove radio, if equipped, as described under "Radio, Replace."
3. Remove any engine components connected to lower wiper bracket bolt.
4. Remove wiper motor bracket attaching bolts.
5. Remove motor electrical connectors, then disconnect wiper arm linkage from motor shaft and remove motor from vehicle.
6. Reverse procedure to install.

RANCHERO

1. Disconnect battery ground cable.
2. Remove both wiper arm and blade assemblies.
3. Remove left cowl screen, then unfasten retaining clip from linkage drive arm and separate arm from motor output arm crankpin.
4. Disconnect electrical connectors from wiper motor on engine side of dash.
5. Remove wiper motor attaching bolts and the wiper motor.

NOTE: If output arm gets caught on dash while removing motor, hand turn arm clockwise to provide sufficient clearance.

6. Reverse procedure to install.

NOTE: Output arm must be in park position when installing motor.

E-100—350

1. Disconnect battery ground cable.
2. Remove fuse panel and bracket assembly.
3. Disconnect wiper motor electrical connectors from motor brush cap and gear box cover.
4. Remove both wiper arm and blade assemblies.
5. Remove outer air inlet cowl, then the motor drive arm-to-linkage mounting arm and pivot shaft assembly retaining clip.
6. Remove wiper motor attaching bolts and the wiper motor.
7. Reverse procedure to install.

1980—85 F-100—350 & BRONCO

1. Disconnect battery ground cable.
2. Remove both wiper arm and blade assemblies.
3. Remove cowl grille attaching screws and raise the grille slightly.
4. Disconnect washer nozzle hose, then remove cowl grille assembly.
5. Remove wiper linkage clip from motor output arm.
6. Disconnect wiper motor electrical connector.
7. Remove wiper motor attaching screws and the wiper motor.
8. Reverse procedure to install.

WIPER TRANSMISSION
REPLACE

1979 F-100—350 & BRONCO

1. Disconnect battery ground cable.
2. Remove both wiper arm and blade assemblies.
3. Disconnect speedometer cable from rear of instrument cluster.
4. Remove instrument cluster bezel.
5. Loosen 3 wiper motor bracket attach-

ing bolts.
6. Remove motor drive arm-to-link assembly retaining clip.
7. Remove left pivot and link assembly attaching bolts, working through cluster bezel opening.
8. Remove left pivot and link assembly through bottom of instrument panel.
9. Remove glove box assembly.
10. Remove right pivot and link assembly attaching bolts, then disconnect link from drive arm and remove pivot and link assembly.
11. Reverse procedure to install.

RANCHERO

1. Disconnect battery ground cable.
2. Remove both wiper arm and blade assemblies.
3. Remove 4 retaining pins from cowl left top vent screen, then the screen.
4. Remove drive arm-to-pivot retaining clip.
5. Remove 3 attaching screws from each pivot, then the pivot shaft and link assembly.
6. Reverse procedure to install.

1979—85 E-100—350 & 1980—85 F-100—350 & BRONCO

1. Disconnect battery ground cable.
2. Remove both wiper arm and blade assemblies.
3. Remove cowl grille attaching screws and raise the grille slightly.
4. Disconnect windshield washer fluid hose, then remove cowl grille.
5. Remove clip securing right and left linkage and the retaining clip from wiper motor arm.
6. Remove 3 pivot body-to-cowl panel attaching screws, then the arm and pivot shaft assembly.
7. Reverse procedure to install.

WIPER SWITCH
REPLACE

RANCHERO

1. Disconnect battery ground cable.
2. Remove wiper switch knob, **Fig. 5.**
3. Remove bezel nut, then disconnect electrical connector from switch and remove switch from vehicle.
4. Reverse procedure to install.

E-100—350

1. Disconnect battery ground cable.
2. Remove wiper switch knob.
3. Remove ignition switch bezel from finish panel.
4. Remove light switch knob and shaft assembly by depressing release button on switch housing and pulling straight out.
5. Remove 2 lower attaching screws from finish panel, then pry the 2 upper retainers away from instrument panel.

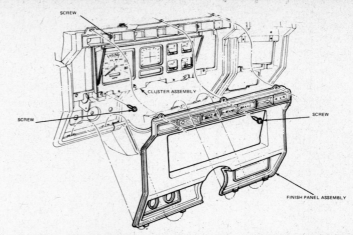

Fig. 17   Instrument cluster replacement. F-100—350 & Bronco

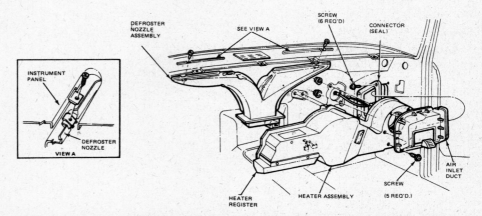

Fig. 18   Heater assembly removal. 1979 F-100—350 & Bronco less air conditioning

6. Disconnect wiper switch electrical connector, then remove switch attaching screws and the switch from vehicle.
7. Reverse procedure to install.

F-100—350 & BRONCO

1. Disconnect battery ground cable.
2. Remove wiper switch knob, bezel nut and bezel.
3. Pull switch down from under instrument panel, then disconnect electrical connector and remove switch from vehicle.
4. Reverse procedure to install.

RADIO
REPLACE

RANCHERO

1. Disconnect battery ground cable.
2. Remove knobs, discs, control shaft nuts and washers from radio.
3. Remove radio rear support-to-instrument panel attaching nut.

4. Remove radio rear support-to-radio attaching nut, then the rear support bracket.
5. On all models, lower radio, then disconnect power, speaker and antenna leads and remove radio from vehicle.
6. Reverse procedure to install.

E-100—350

1. Disconnect battery ground cable.
2. Remove heater, and if equipped, air conditioner control knobs.
3. Remove cigarette lighter, if equipped.
4. Remove radio knobs and discs from control shafts.
5. On models equipped with cigarette lighter, snap out name plate from right side of panel and remove the one accessible finish panel attaching bolt.
6. On all models, remove 5 finish panel attaching bolts and the finish panel.
7. Pry out cluster panel at two locations using a screwdriver.
8. Disconnect antenna and speaker leads from radio.
9. Remove 4 radio-to-instrument panel

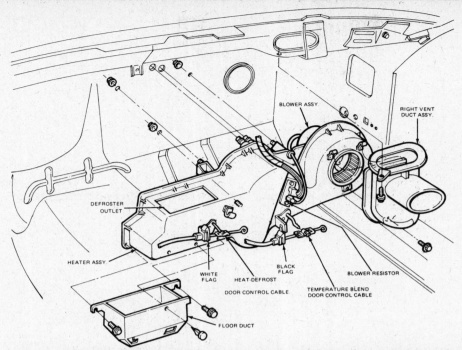

Fig. 19   Heater assembly removal. Ranchero less air conditioning

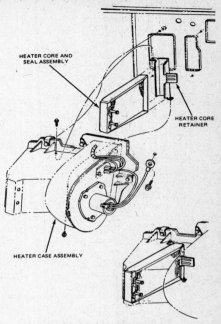

Fig. 21   Heater core replacement. E-100—350 less air conditioning

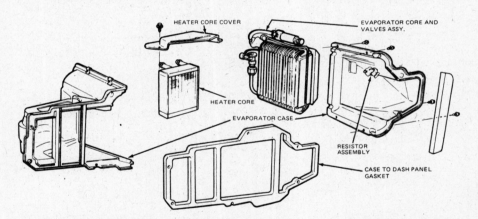

Fig. 20   Heater core replacement. Ranchero w/air conditioning

attaching screws and slide radio out of panel.
10. Disconnect power, speaker and antenna leads from radio and remove radio from vehicle.
11. Remove radio mounting plate and the radio rear support nut and washer.
12. Reverse procedure to install.

1979 F-100—350 & BRONCO

1. Disconnect battery ground cable.
2. Remove ash tray and bracket.
3. Disconnect power, speaker and antenna leads from radio.
4. Remove radio rear support attaching bolt from lower edge of instrument panel.
5. On models equipped with air conditioning, disconnect left air conditioner duct hose from plenum.

6. On all models, remove radio knobs and discs from control shafts.
7. Remove bezel retaining nuts and washers from control shafts, then slide bezel off over shafts.
8. Remove nuts and washers from control shafts, then slide radio out of instrument panel.
9. Reverse procedure to install.

1980—85 F-100—350 & BRONCO

1. Disconnect battery ground cable.
2. Remove radio knobs and discs from control shafts.
3. Remove cluster bezel attaching screws or nuts and the cluster bezel.
4. On 1982—85 models, remove radio mounting plate-to-instrument panel attaching screws and slide radio out of

panel.
5. On all models, disconnect power, speaker and antenna leads from radio.
6. Remove radio rear support attaching bolt from lower edge of instrument panel.
7. Remove nuts and washers from control shafts.
8. On 1982—85 models, remove radio front mounting plate.
9. On all models, remove radio from vehicle.
10. Reverse procedure to install.

HEATER CORE
REPLACE

1979 F-100—350 & BRONCO

Less Air Conditioning
1. Disconnect battery ground cable.
2. Disconnect temperature and air door Bowden cables from heater housing to prevent damage to cables.
3. Disconnect blower motor resistor electrical connectors.
4. Remove air inlet duct attaching screws and the duct, **Fig. 18,** then disconnect blower motor electrical connectors.
5. Drain cooling system, then disconnect hoses from heater core.
6. Remove 3 heater stud attaching nuts and the heater assembly, **Fig. 18.**
7. Remove gasket between heater hose ends and dash panel at heater core tubes.
8. Remove heater core cover and gasket, then the heater core and lower support from heater assembly.
9. Reverse procedure to install.

W/Air Conditioning

1. Disconnect battery ground cable.
2. Remove air cleaner and drain cooling system.
3. Disconnect hoses from heater core.
4. Remove air conditioner hose support bracket and cowl from engine compartment.
5. Remove insulation tape from expansion valve, then the cover plate and seal from evaporator housing at expansion valve.
6. Remove glove compartment liner and air conditioner duct.
7. Disconnect right hand cowl fresh air inlet vacuum hose from fresh air door vacuum motor.
8. Remove evaporator rear housing from bottom of instrument panel. Remove fresh air inlet tube from housing, then reinstall one upper nut to retain evaporator housing to dash.
9. Disconnect de-icing switch electrical connectors, then slide capillary tube out of evaporator core.
10. Remove 4 de-icing switch mounting plate attaching screws and the mounting plate.
11. Remove 4 plenum attaching screws and the plenum.
12. Install protective tape on "A" pillar inner cowl panel at lower right corner of instrument panel.
13. Remove "A" pillar-to-lower instrument panel attaching bolt, then lower center instrument panel brace, bolt and nut.
14. Move instrument panel rearward and reinstall "A" pillar bolt to hold panel in this position.
15. Remove 4 evaporator attaching screws, then move evaporator away from case and secure in a rearward and upward position.
16. Remove evaporator sealing grommet.
17. Remove 3 heater core attaching screws, 2 retaining plates and the heater core.
18. Reverse procedure to install.

RANCHERO

Less Air Conditioning

1. Disconnect battery ground cable.
2. Drain cooling system.
3. Remove heater assembly-to-dash retaining nuts.
4. Disconnect temperature and defroster cables from door crank arms.
5. Disconnect resistor and blower motor electrical connectors.
6. Remove glove compartment.
7. Remove right air duct control-to-instrument panel retaining bolts and nuts.
8. Remove right air duct retaining screws and the duct.
9. Remove heater assembly, **Fig. 19.**
10. Remove heater core cover, pad and heater core from heater assembly.
11. Reverse procedure to install.

W/Air Conditioning

1. Disconnect battery ground cable.
2. Drain cooling system, then disconnect hoses from heater core.

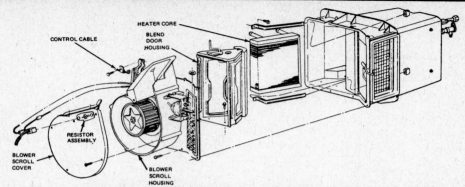

Fig. 22 Heater core replacement. E-100—350 w/air conditioning

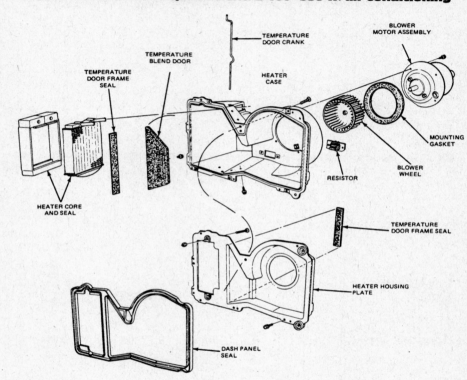

Fig. 23 Heater core replacement. 1980—85 F-100—350 & Bronco less air conditioning

3. Remove 4 heater core cover attaching screws and the cover, **Fig. 20.**
4. Press downward on heater core and tip toward front of vehicle to free seal from housing.
5. Lift heater core from case and remove from vehicle.
6. Reverse procedure to install.

E-100—350

Less Air Conditioning

1. Remove battery from vehicle.

NOTE: On models equipped with diesel engine, remove right hand battery.

2. Drain cooling system.
3. Disconnect resistor electrical connector, then the blower motor lead wire from wiring harness.
4. Remove ground wire attaching screw from dash.
5. Disconnect hoses from heater core, then remove plastic wrap securing hoses to heater assembly.
6. Remove 5 heater assembly attaching screws from passenger compartment, then lift heater assembly out of vehicle.
7. Remove seal and retainer from front of heater core case, then slide core and seal out of case, **Fig. 21.**
8. Reverse procedure to install.

W/Air Conditioning

1. Disconnect battery ground cable.
2. Disconnect electrical connector from resistor on front of air conditioner blower scroll cover.
3. Disconnect vacuum hose from outside-recirculated door vacuum motor.
4. Remove air conditioner blower cover

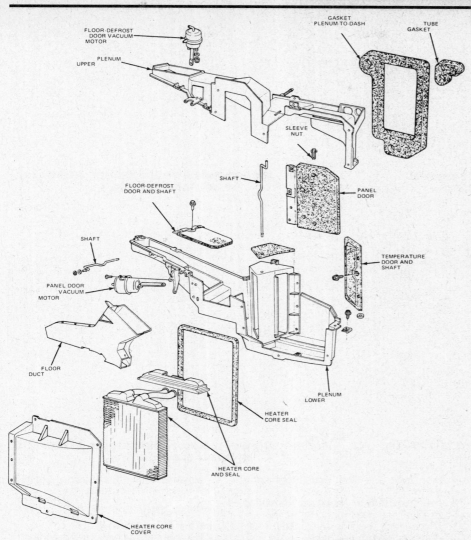

Fig. 24 Heater core replacement. 1980—85 F-100—350 & Bronco w/air conditioning

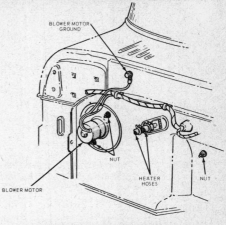

Fig. 25 Blower motor replacement. 1979 F-100—350 & Bronco less air conditioning

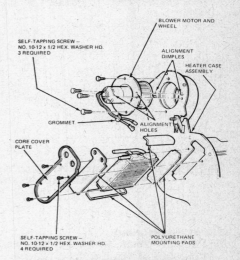

Fig. 26 Blower motor replacement. Ranchero less air conditioning

attaching screws and the cover.
5. Remove outside-recirculated door shaft push nut and washer.
6. Remove control cable attaching screw and slide cable over bracket.
7. Remove cable clip or wire loop from blend door shaft.
8. Remove 9 air conditioner blower motor housing attaching screws and the housing.
9. Remove 3 blend door housing attaching screws and the housing.
10. Drain cooling system, then disconnect hoses from heater core.
11. Remove 2 heater core retaining bracket attaching screws and the bracket.
12. Remove heater core and seal assembly, **Fig. 22.**
13. Reverse procedure to install.

1980—85 F-100—350 & BRONCO

Less Air Conditioning
1. Disconnect battery ground cable.
2. Disconnect cable from temperature

blend door and the mounting bracket from top of heater assembly.
3. Disconnect blower motor and resistor electrical connectors.
4. Disconnect and plug hoses from heater core.
5. Working under instrument panel, remove 2 nuts on 1980—81 models, or 3 nuts on 1982—85 models, attaching left side of heater assembly and right side of plenum to dash.
6. On 1980—81 models, remove screw attaching top center of heater assembly to dash.
7. On all models, remove 2 screws attaching right side of heater assembly to dash, then lift heater assembly out of vehicle.
8. Remove heater housing plate attaching screws, nut and bolt and the plate.
9. On 1980—82 models, remove 3 heater core frame attaching screws and the frame.
10. On all models, slide heater core and seal out of heater assembly, **Fig. 23.**

11. Reverse procedure to install.

W/Air Conditioning
1. Disconnect battery ground cable.
2. Disconnect and plug hoses from heater core.
3. Remove glove compartment liner.
4. Remove 8 heater core cover attaching screws and the cover.
5. Remove heater core from plenum, **Fig. 24.**
6. Reverse procedure to install.

BLOWER MOTOR
REPLACE

1979 F-100—350 & BRONCO

Less Air Conditioning
1. Remove heater assembly as described in steps 1 through 6 under "Heater Core, Replace," 1979 F-100—350 & Bronco less air conditioning.
2. Remove blower motor attaching screws and nuts and the blower

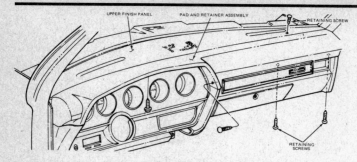

Fig. 27   Instrument panel pad removal. Ranchero w/air conditioning

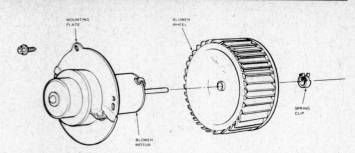

Fig. 28   Blower motor replacement. Ranchero w/air conditioning

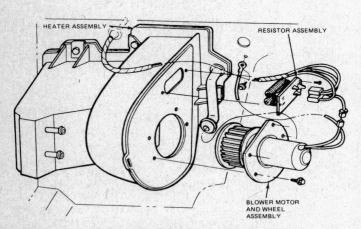

Fig. 29   Blower motor replacement. E-100—350 less air conditioning

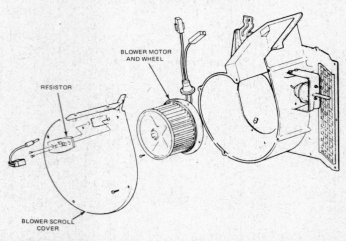

Fig. 30   Blower motor replacement. E-100—350 w/air conditioning

motor, **Fig. 25.**
3. Reverse procedure to install.

W/Air Conditioning
1. Perform steps 1 through 16 as described under "Heater Core, Replace," 1979 F-100—350 & Bronco with air conditioning.
2. Remove A/C-heat door, then the door arm support and pivot arm retainer.
3. Remove 2 blower motor attaching bolts and the blower motor.
4. Reverse procedure to install.

RANCHERO

Less Air Conditioning
1. Remove heater assembly as described in steps 1 through 9 under "Heater Core, Replace," Ranchero less air conditioning.
2. Remove 4 blower motor attaching screws and the blower motor, **Fig. 26.**
3. Reverse procedure to install.

W/Air Conditioning
1. Disconnect battery ground cable.
2. Remove instrument panel pad attaching screws and the pad from vehicle, **Fig. 27.**
3. Remove glove compartment, then the side cowl trim pad.
4. Remove instrument panel attachment from right side.
5. Remove one blower housing-to-dash attaching nut from engine compart-

ment and one from passenger compartment.
6. Remove blower housing mounting bracket and cowl top inner screw.
7. Disconnect outside-recirculation air door vacuum motor hose.
8. Disconnect blower motor electrical connector and remove ground wire screw.
9. Remove blower housing, then slide

blower motor from housing, **Fig. 28.**
10. Reverse procedure to install.

E-100—350

Less Air Conditioning
1. Disconnect battery ground cable.
2. Disconnect blower motor electrical connector, then remove ground wire screw from dash.
3. Disconnect cooling tube from blower

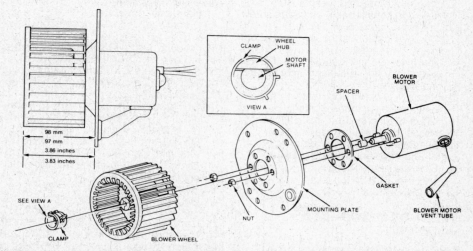

Fig. 31   Blower motor replacement. 1980—81 F-100—350 & Bronco less air conditioning

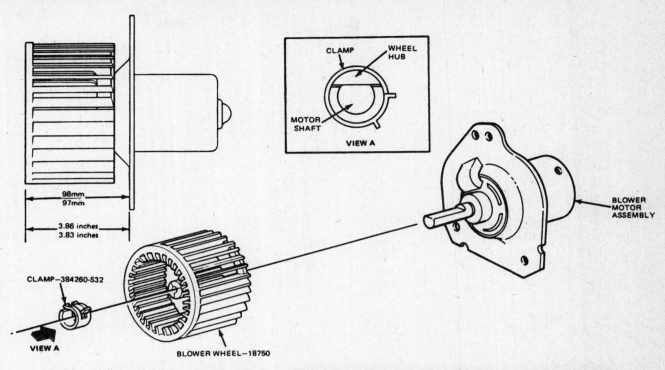

Fig. 32   Blower motor replacement. 1982—85 F-100—350 & Bronco less air conditioning

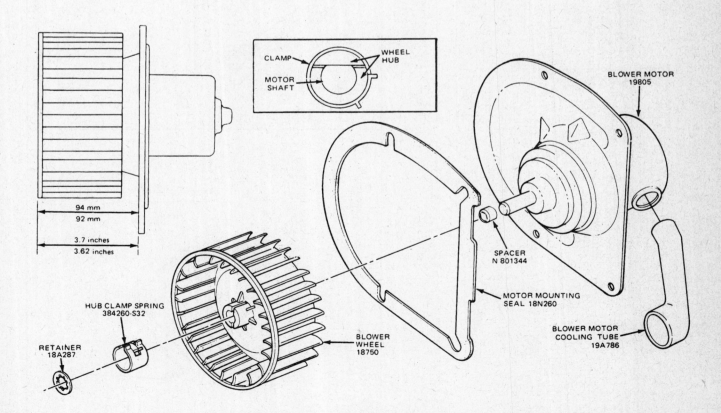

Fig. 33   Blower motor replacement. 1980—85 F-100—350 & Bronco w/air conditioning

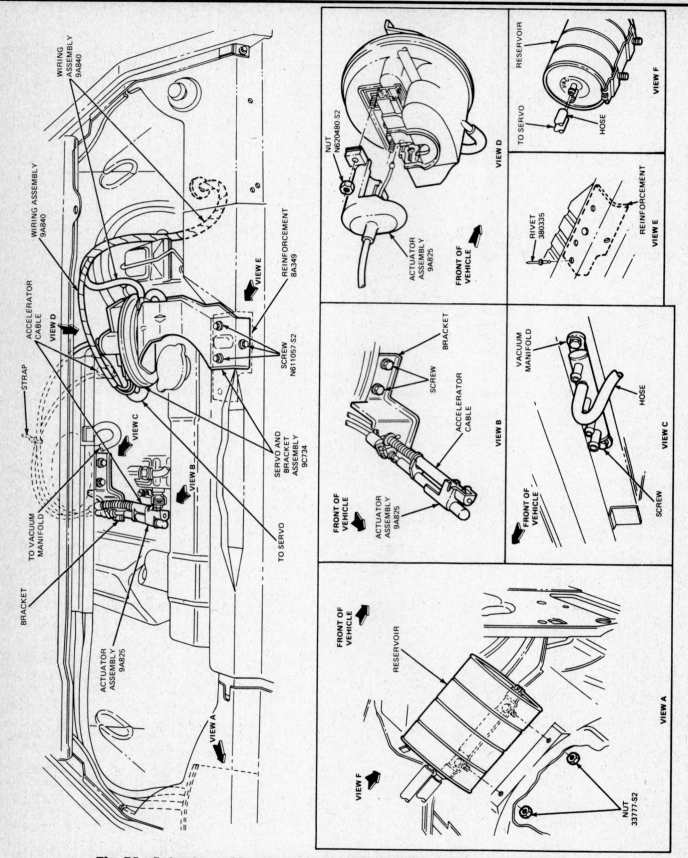

Fig. 34 Actuator cable adjustment. 1984–85 E-250–350 w/diesel engine

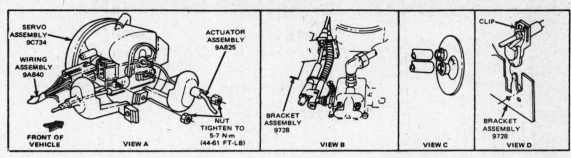

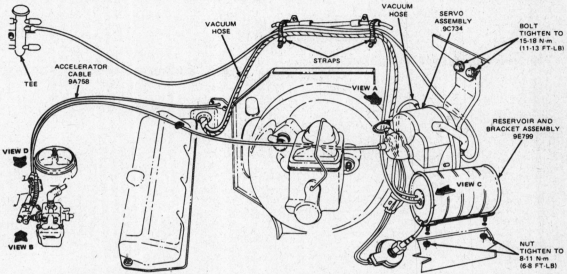

Fig. 35 Actuator cable adjustment. 1984—85 F-250—350 w/diesel engine

motor, if equipped.

4. Remove 4 blower motor attaching screws and the blower motor, **Fig. 29.**
5. Reverse procedure to install.

W/Air Conditioning

1. Disconnect battery ground cable.
2. Disconnect electrical connectors from resistor on front of blower scroll cover.
3. Remove blower scroll cover attaching screws and the scroll cover, **Fig. 30.**
4. Push wiring grommet out through hole in blower motor housing.
5. Remove 4 blower motor attaching screws and the blower motor.
6. Reverse procedure to install.

F-100—350 & BRONCO

1. Disconnect battery ground cable.
2. Disconnect blower motor electrical connector, and on 1980—81 models less air conditioning, remove ground wire screw.
3. On models equipped with air conditioning, disconnect air cooling tube from blower motor.
4. On all models, remove blower motor attaching screws and the blower motor, **Figs. 31, 32 and 33.**
5. Reverse procedure to install.

SPEED CONTROL ADJUSTMENTS
BEAD CHAIN, ADJUST
Exc. Ranchero

1. Adjust bead chain to obtain 1/16—1/4 inch (1979—81) or 1/16—1/8 inch (1982—85) actuator arm free travel with engine at hot idle. Make this adjustment to remove as much slack as possible from the bead chain without preventing carburetor from returning to idle.

NOTE: On models equipped with a solenoid anti-diesel valve, this adjustment must be performed with ignition switch in the Off position.

2. Cut off chain in excess of 4 beads.

Ranchero

1. Adjust bead chain to obtain 1/16—1/4 inch actuator arm free travel with engine at hot idle. Make this adjustment to remove as much slack as possible from the bead chain without preventing carburetor from returning to idle.

NOTE: On models equipped with a solenoid throttle positioner, perform this adjustment by opening throttle slightly with ignition switch in the On position.

VACUUM DUMP VALVE, ADJUST
1981—85 All

1. Slide vacuum dump valve forward in retaining clip. With valve plunger contacting brake pedal adapter and pedal in released position until 1/8 inch or less of white plunger is exposed.
2. Ensure brake pedal contacts stop in released position after making adjustment.

ACTUATOR CABLE, ADJUST
1984—85 Models W/Diesel Engine

1. Snap speed control actuator cable retainer over accelerator cable end fitting attached to throttle ball stud, **Figs. 34 and 35.**
2. Remove adjuster retainer clip, if equipped, from adjuster mounting tab.
3. Insert actuator cable adjuster mounting tab in accelerator cable support bracket slot.
4. Pull cable through adjuster until a slight tension is felt without opening throttle plate or increasing idle RPM.
5. Install adjuster retainer clip slowly until it engages, then push downward until locked in position.

Gasoline Engine Section

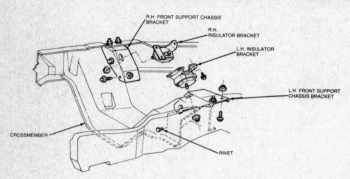

Fig. 1   Engine mounts. V6-232 engine

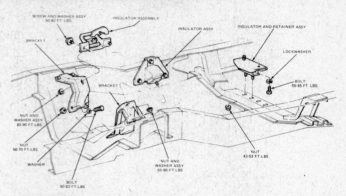

Fig. 2   Engine mounts. 1979—80 E-100—350 w/6-300 engine

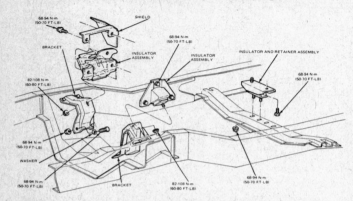

Fig. 3   Engine mounts. 1981—85 E-100—350 w/6-300 engine

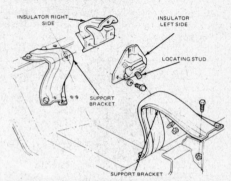

Fig. 4   Engine mounts. 1979 F-100—350 4 × 2 w/6-300 engine

ENGINE MOUNTS
REPLACE

V6-232

1. Remove fan shroud attaching bolts and position shroud over fan.
2. Raise and support vehicle.
3. Remove insulator-to-chassis bracket attaching nut and washer, **Fig. 1.**
4. Raise engine slightly, then remove 3 insulator-to-cylinder block attaching bolts and the insulator, **Fig. 1.**
5. Reverse procedure to install. Torque insulator-to-cylinder block attaching bolts to 60—80 ft. lbs. and insulator-to-chassis bracket nut to 50—70 ft. lbs.

6-300

E-100—350

1. Raise and support vehicle.
2. Remove front insulator-to-support bracket attaching nuts and washers from both insulators, **Figs. 2 and 3.**
3. Raise engine slightly using a block of wood placed under oil pan and a suitable jack.

4. Remove support bracket attaching bolts and the brackets, if necessary.
5. Remove insulator attaching bolts and the insulator.
6. Reverse procedure to install.

1980—85 Bronco & 1979—85 F-100—350

1. Remove insulator-to-support bracket attaching nut and washer.

NOTE: If only one insulator is being removed, loosen the opposite insulator at support bracket.

2. Raise engine slightly using a block of wood placed under oil pan and a suitable jack.
3. Remove insulator attaching bolts and the insulator, **Figs. 4 through 7.**
4. Reverse procedure to install.

V8-255, 302 & 351W
Ranchero

1. Remove fan shroud attaching screws.
2. Support engine using a block of wood placed under oil pan and a suitable jack.
3. Remove insulator-to-crossmember

through bolt and nut, then raise engine slightly and remove insulator and heat shield, if equipped, **Fig. 8.**
4. Reverse procedure to install.

E-100—350

1. Remove fan shroud attaching bolts and the insulator-to-support nuts.
2. Raise engine assembly and remove starter motor.
3. Remove insulator attaching bolts, then the alternator splash shield and insulator, **Fig. 9.**
4. Reverse procedure to install.

1979 F-100—150 & 1980—85 F-100—350 & Bronco

1. Remove fan shroud attaching bolts and position shroud over fan.
2. Remove insulator-to-chassis bracket attaching nut and washer.
3. Raise engine slightly, then remove insulator attaching bolts and the insulator, **Figs. 10 and 11.**

NOTE: When removing left hand insulator, the heat shield must also be removed.

4. Reverse procedure to install.

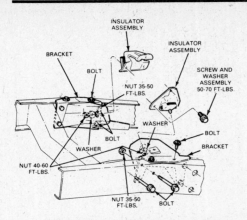

Fig. 5 Engine mounts. 1979 F-150—250 4 × 4 w/6-300 engine

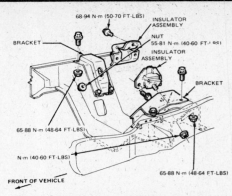

Fig. 6 Engine mounts. 1980 F-100—350 & Bronco w/6-300 engine

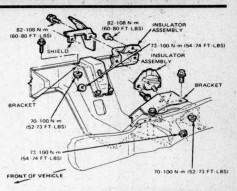

Fig. 7 Engine mounts. 1981—85 F-100—350 & Bronco w/6-300 engine

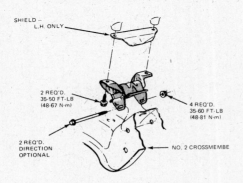

Fig. 8 Engine mounts. Ranchero w/V8-302, 351W engine

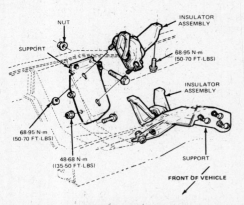

Fig. 9 Engine mounts. E-100—350 w/V8-302, 351W engine

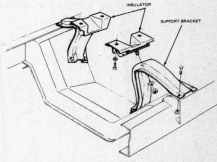

Fig. 10 Engine mounts. 1979 F-100—150 w/V8-302, 351W engine

V8-351M & 400

Ranchero
1. Remove fan shroud attaching bolts.
2. Remove insulator-to-support bracket through bolt and lock nut, **Fig. 12.**
3. Raise engine slightly using a block of wood placed under oil pan and a suitable jack.
4. Remove insulator attaching bolts, then

the insulator and heat shield, if equipped.
5. Reverse procedure to install.

1979—82 F-100—350 & Bronco
1. Remove fan shroud attaching bolts and position shroud over fan.
2. Remove insulator-to-chassis bracket attaching nut and washer, **Figs. 13, 14 and 15.**
3. Raise engine slightly, then remove

insulator attaching bolts and the insulator.
4. Reverse procedure to install.

1980—82 E-100—350
1. Remove fan shroud attaching bolts and the insulator-to-support nuts.
2. Raise engine slightly and remove starter motor.

NOTE: When raised, the engine and transmission assembly will pivot around the rear

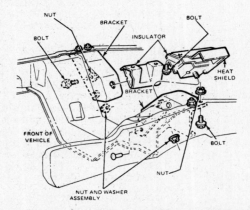

Fig. 11 Engine mounts. 1980—85 F-100—350 & Bronco w/V8-255, 302, 351W engine

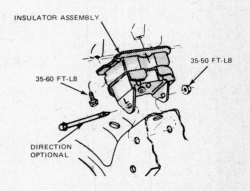

Fig. 12 Engine mounts. Ranchero w/V8-351M, 400 engine

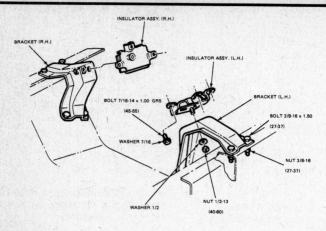

TORQUE SHOWN IN PARENTHESIS.

Fig. 13   Engine mounts. 1979 F-100—350 4 × 2 w/V8-351M, 400 engine

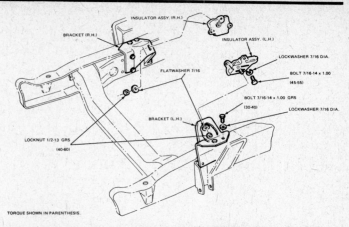

TORQUE SHOWN IN PARENTHESIS.

Fig. 14   Engine mounts. 1979 F-150—250 4 × 4 & Bronco w/V8-351M, 400 engine

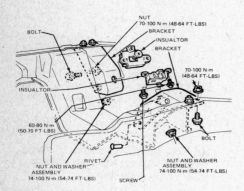

Fig. 15   Engine mounts. 1980—82 F-100—350 & Bronco w/V8-351M, 400 engine

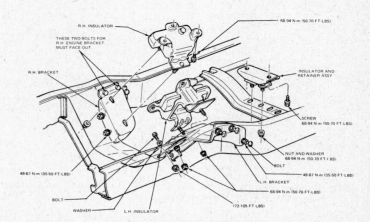

Fig. 16   Engine mounts. 1980—82 E-100—350 w/V8-351M, 400 engine

engine mount. The engine assembly must be lifted exactly two inches, measured from front mounts, and remain centered in the engine compartment. If the engine is lifted more than two inches, the A/C main and auxiliary lines will be damaged.

3. Remove insulator attaching bolts, then the alternator splash shield and insulator, **Fig. 16.**
4. Reverse procedure to install.

V8-460

1. Support engine using a block of wood placed under oil pan and a suitable jack.
2. Remove locknuts from support bracket-to-crossmember and side rail attaching bolts.
3. Remove support bracket-to-insulator through bolts, **Fig. 17.**
4. Raise engine until insulator clears bracket, then remove insulator and

bracket as an assembly.
5. Remove insulator-to-bracket attaching nuts and the insulator.
6. Reverse procedure to install.

ENGINE REPLACE

V6-232

1. Disconnect battery ground cable and drain cooling system.
2. On models equipped with an engine compartment light, disconnect electrical connector from light.
3. Mark hood hinge locations and remove hood.
4. Remove air cleaner assembly including air intake duct and heat tube.
5. Remove fan shroud attaching screws, then the fan and clutch assembly attaching bolts.
6. Remove fan and clutch assembly and

fan shroud from vehicle.
7. Loosen accessory drive belt idler, then remove drive belt and water pump pulley.
8. Disconnect upper and lower hoses from radiator.
9. Disconnect Thermactor hose from downstream air tube check valve, then remove air tube bracket attaching bolt from rear of right cylinder head.
10. Remove coil secondary wire from ignition coil.
11. On models equipped with power steering, disconnect steering pump from mounting bracket and position aside with hoses connected.
12. On models equipped with A/C, disconnect A/C compressor from mounting bracket and secure to right shock tower with hoses connected.
13. On all models, remove alternator attaching bolts and position alternator aside.
14. Disconnect hoses from heater core tubes.
15. On models equipped with speed control, disconnect servo chain from carburetor, then remove servo attaching bolts and the servo.

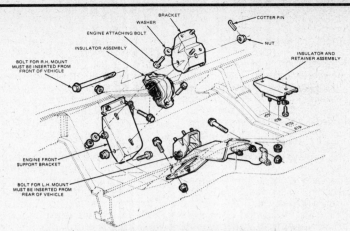

BRACKET
WASHER
ENGINE ATTACHING BOLT
COTTER PIN
INSULATOR ASSEMBLY
NUT
BOLT FOR R.H. MOUNT
MUST BE INSERTED FROM
FRONT OF VEHICLE
INSULATOR AND
RETAINER ASSEMBLY
ENGINE FRONT
SUPPORT BRACKET
BOLT FOR L.H. MOUNT
MUST BE INSERTED FROM
REAR OF VEHICLE

Fig. 17 Engine mounts. V8-460 engine

16. On all models, disconnect necessary vacuum hoses for engine removal.
17. Remove engine ground strap attaching screw from dash, then disconnect transmission linkage from carburetor.
18. Disconnect accelerator cable from carburetor, then remove cable routing bracket attaching bolts.
19. Disconnect electrical connectors necessary for engine removal.
20. Disconnect fuel inlet line and PCV hose from carburetor, then remove carburetor from vehicle.
21. Install engine lifting plate No. T75T-6000-A or equivalent over carburetor hold down studs, leaving EGR spacer and phenolic gasket in place. Tighten nuts securely.

NOTE: All studs must be used to secure the lifting plate to avoid damaging the intake manifold. When using the lifting plate, do not remove engine and transmission as an assembly.

22. Raise and support vehicle.
23. Drain engine oil, then disconnect and plug fuel inlet line from fuel pump.
24. Remove dust shield from transmission converter housing, if equipped.
25. Remove flex plate-to-torque converter attaching nuts.
26. Disconnect battery cable from starter motor, then remove starter attaching bolts and the starter.
27. Remove transmission oil cooler line routing clip.
28. Remove exhaust pipe-to-exhaust manifold attaching nuts.
29. Remove 4 transmission-to-engine lower attaching bolts.
30. Remove engine mount-to-crossmember attaching nuts, then lower the vehicle.
31. Support transmission using a suitable jack, then remove 2 upper transmission-to-engine attaching bolts.
32. Place a piece of ¼ inch plywood between radiator and engine to protect radiator.
33. Raise engine slightly, using a suitable lifting device, and carefully separate from transmission, then lift engine

from vehicle.
34. Reverse procedure to install.

6-300

E-100—350

1. Disconnect battery ground cable and drain cooling system.
2. Install protective seat covers, then remove hood cover and air cleaner assembly.
3. Remove front bumper, then the grille and lower gravel deflector as an assembly.
4. Disconnect radiator hose from engine, then remove alternator splash shield, if equipped, and the lower radiator hose from radiator.
5. On models equipped with automatic transmission, disconnect transmission oil cooler lines from radiator.
6. On all models, remove radiator and fan shroud, if equipped.
7. Disconnect heater hoses from engine.
8. Disconnect alternator from mounting bracket and position aside.
9. On models equipped with power steering, remove steering pump drive belt, then disconnect pump and support from mounting bracket and position aside.
10. On all models, disconnect and plug fuel line from fuel pump.
11. Disconnect distributor and sender unit wires and the brake booster hose from engine.
12. Disconnect electronic engine control harness from all sensors, if equipped.
13. Disconnect accelerator cable and remove bracket from engine.
14. On models equipped with automatic transmission, disconnect kickdown cable from bell crank.
15. On all models, remove exhaust manifold heat deflector, then the exhaust pipe-to-manifold attaching nuts.
16. Disconnect transmission vacuum line from intake manifold and junction.
17. Remove upper transmission-to-engine attaching bolts.
18. On models equipped with automatic transmission, remove transmission

dipstick tube support bolt from intake manifold.
19. On all models, raise and support vehicle.
20. Drain engine oil, then remove starter motor.
21. Remove flywheel inspection cover, then the 4 converter attaching nuts and front engine support nuts.
22. Remove oil filter, then the transmission-to-engine nuts.
23. Lower vehicle, then remove engine assembly using suitable lifting equipment.
24. Reverse procedure to install.

F-100—350 & Bronco

1. Disconnect battery ground cable, then drain cooling system and engine oil.
2. Mark hood hinge locations and remove hood.
3. Remove air cleaner assembly, then on 1979—85 models equipped with A/C, the A/C compressor and condenser.
4. Disconnect heater hose from water pump and coolant outlet housing.
5. Disconnect flexible fuel line from fuel pump, then remove radiator.
6. Remove cooling fan, viscous fan drive (if equipped), water pump pulley and fan drive belt.
7. Disconnect accelerator cable, and the choke cable on 1979—80 models, from carburetor and remove cable retracting spring.
8. On models equipped with power brakes, disconnect vacuum line from intake manifold.
9. On models equipped with automatic transmission, disconnect kickdown rod from bell crank.
10. On all models, disconnect exhaust manifold from exhaust pipe.
11. Disconnect battery ground cable and body ground strap from engine.
12. Disconnect electronic engine control harness from all sensors, if equipped.
13. Disconnect engine wiring harness from ignition coil and the coolant temperature and oil pressure sending units, and position harness aside.
14. Disconnect alternator from mounting bracket and position aside, leaving wires attached.
15. On models equipped with power steering, disconnect steering pump from mounting bracket and position aside, leaving lines attached.
16. On models equipped with an air compressor, bleed air system and disconnect pressure lines from compressor.
17. On all models, raise and support vehicle.
18. Remove starter motor, and on models equipped with automatic transmission, the fluid filler tube bracket.
19. Remove engine rear plate upper right bolt.
20. On models equipped with manual transmission, remove all flywheel housing lower attaching bolts and disconnect clutch retracting spring.
21. On models equipped with automatic transmission, remove converter housing access cover, then the fly-wheel-

to-converter nuts, and secure converter in housing. Disconnect transmission oil cooler lines from retaining clip on engine, then remove converter housing-to-engine lower attaching bolts.

22. Remove insulator-to-intermediate support bracket attaching nut from each engine front support.
23. Lower vehicle and support transmission using a suitable jack.
24. Remove remaining flywheel or converter housing-to-engine attaching bolts.
25. Raise engine slightly, using suitable lifting equipment, and carefully separate from transmission, then lift engine from vehicle.
26. Reverse procedure to install.

V8-255, 302 & 351W
Ranchero
1. Remove or disconnect any Thermactor system components that will interfere with engine removal.
2. Disconnect battery and alternator ground cables from cylinder block.
3. Drain cooling system and engine oil.
4. Mark hood hinge locations and remove hood.
5. Remove air cleaner and intake duct assembly.
6. Disconnect upper radiator hose from coolant outlet housing and lower hose from water pump.
7. On models equipped with automatic transmission, disconnect oil cooler lines from radiator.
8. On all models, remove fan shroud attaching bolts, then the radiator, fan, spacer, belt pulley and shroud.
9. Remove alternator mounting bolts and position alternator aside.
10. Disconnect electrical connector from oil pressure sending unit.
11. Disconnect and plug flexible fuel line at fuel tank, then remove accelerator cable from carburetor.
12. On models equipped with automatic transmission, disconnect throttle valve vacuum line from intake manifold. Disconnect manual shift rod, then the retracting spring from shift rod stud and transmission filler tube bracket from cylinder block.
13. On models equipped with A/C, remove A/C compressor.
14. On models equipped with power steering, disconnect steering pump bracket from cylinder head, then remove drive belt and position pump aside.
15. On models equipped with vacuum boosted power brakes, disconnect brake vacuum line from intake manifold.
16. On all models, disconnect heater hoses from water pump and intake manifold.
17. Disconnect electrical connector from coolant temperature sending unit.
18. Remove flywheel or converter housing-to-engine upper attaching bolts.
19. Disconnect primary wiring connector

from ignition coil and the wiring harness from left rocker arm cover.
20. Disconnect ground strap from cylinder block.
21. Raise and support vehicle.
22. Remove starter motor.
23. Disconnect exhaust pipes from exhaust manifolds, then the engine support insulators from frame brackets.
24. On models equipped with manual transmission, remove clutch equalizer bar attaching bolts and the equalizer, then the remaining flywheel housing attaching bolts.
25. On models equipped with automatic transmission, disconnect oil cooler lines from retainer, then remove converter housing inspection cover. Disconnect flywheel from converter and secure converter in housing, then remove remaining attaching bolts.
26. On all models, lower vehicle and support transmission with a suitable jack.
27. Raise engine slightly, using suitable lifting equipment, and carefully separate from transmission, then lift engine from vehicle.
28. Reverse procedure to install.

E-100—350
1. Remove engine cover, then disconnect battery cables and drain cooling system.
2. Remove grille assembly, including gravel deflector.
3. Remove upper grille support bracket, hood lock support and condenser upper mounting brackets, if equipped.
4. On models equipped with A/C, discharge refrigerant from system and remove condenser. Disconnect lines from A/C compressor and remove accelerator cable bracket.
5. On 1980—85 models, disconnect speed control linkage, if equipped.
6. On all models, disconnect heater hoses from engine and radiator hoses from radiator.
7. On 1983—85 models, disconnect heater hoses from heater core and water valve.
8. On all models equipped with automatic transmission, disconnect oil cooler lines from radiator.
9. Remove fan shroud, fan and radiator, then pivot alternator inward and disconnect electrical connectors from alternator.
10. Remove air cleaner, duct and valve assembly and exhaust manifold shroud, then the flex tube from exhaust manifold stove.
11. Disconnect throttle from carburetor, then remove accelerator cable bracket from engine.
12. Disconnect transmission shift rod, if equipped.
13. Disconnect fuel and choke lines, then remove carburetor and spacer.
14. On 1979—85 models, disconnect evaporative emission hoses from front of carburetor pad and/or top of PCV valve. Disconnect vacuum line from carburetor bowl vent and evaporative

canister line from vacuum harness. If equipped, also disconnect power brake booster vacuum line.
15. On all models, raise and support vehicle.
16. Drain engine oil and remove oil filter.
17. Disconnect exhaust pipes and exhaust heat control valve (if equipped) from exhaust manifolds.
18. Remove 2 transmission filler tube bracket attaching bolts from right cylinder head.
19. Remove engine mount attaching bolts and nuts, then the starter motor.
20. On models equipped with manual transmission, remove housing-to-engine attaching bolts.
21. On models equipped with automatic transmission, remove converter inspection cover attaching bolts. Remove 4 converter-to-flex plate nuts, 3 adapter plate-to-converter housing bolts and 4 converter housing-to-cylinder block lower bolts.
22. On all models, remove ground wire retaining bolt from cylinder block, then lower the vehicle and support transmission with a suitable jack.
23. On models equipped with power steering, remove steering pump drive belt and front bracket bolts.
24. On 1979 models, disconnect one vacuum line from rear of intake manifold.
25. On 1979—82 models, remove speed control servo (if equipped) and accelerator cable bracket from intake manifold and position aside.
26. On all models equipped with A/C, disconnect A/C compressor magnetic clutch lead wire.
27. On all models, install lifting bracket to intake manifold and remove 2 converter housing-to-cylinder block upper attaching bolts.
28. Support transmission with a suitable jack and attach lifting equipment to engine, then carefully move engine forward and lift from vehicle.
29. Reverse procedure to install.

F-100—250 & Bronco
1. Drain cooling system and engine oil.
2. On 1981—85 models, mark hood hinge locations and remove hood.
3. On all models, disconnect battery and ground cables from engine block.
4. Remove air cleaner and intake duct assembly, including carbon canister hose and crankcase ventilation hose.
5. Disconnect upper and lower hoses and transmission oil cooler lines (if equipped) from radiator.
6. On models equipped with A/C, discharge refrigerant from system, then remove A/C condenser and disconnect lines from compressor.
7. On all models, remove fan shroud attaching bolts and position shroud over fan.
8. Remove radiator, fan shroud, fan spacer, belts and pulley.
9. Remove alternator attaching bolts and swing alternator aside.
10. Disconnect electrical connector from oil pressure sending unit, then discon-

nect and plug flexible fuel line at fuel tank.

11. On 1979–85 models, disconnect vacuum hoses from evaporative canister.
12. On fuel injected models, disconnect chassis fuel line quick disconnects at fuel rail.
13. On all models, disconnect accelerator rod or cable from carburetor or throttle body.
14. Disconnect speed control linkages and transmission kickdown rod and remove rod retracting spring, if equipped.
15. Disconnect power brake booster vacuum hose, if equipped.
16. Disconnect heater hoses from water pump and intake manifold.
17. Disconnect electrical connector from coolant temperature sending unit.
18. Remove flywheel housing-to-engine upper attaching bolts.
19. Disconnect primary wire from ignition coil, then remove wiring harness from left rocker arm cover and position aside.
20. Disconnect ground strap from cylinder head.
21. Raise and support vehicle.
22. Remove starter motor.
23. Disconnect exhaust pipes and exhaust heat control valve (if equipped) from exhaust manifolds.
24. Disconnect engine support insulators from frame brackets.
25. On models equipped with automatic transmission, remove converter inspection plate and the converter-to-flywheel attaching bolts.
26. On all models, remove remaining flywheel housing-to-engine attaching bolts.
27. On models equipped with A/C, disconnect A/C compressor clutch electrical connector.
28. On all models, lower vehicle and support transmission with a suitable jack.
29. Install lifting brackets to intake manifold and attach suitable lifting equipment to engine.
30. Raise engine slightly and carefully separate from transmission, then lift engine from vehicle.
31. Reverse procedure to install.

V8-351M & 400

Ranchero
1. Remove or disconnect any Thermactor system components that will interfere with engine removal.
2. Disconnect battery cables and drain cooling system.
3. Mark hood hinge locations and remove hood.
4. Remove air cleaner and air intake tube assembly.
5. Disconnect upper radiator hose from engine, then the lower hose and transmission oil cooler lines (if equipped) from radiator.
6. Remove fan shroud attaching bolts and position shroud over fan.
7. Remove radiator, fan shroud, fan and spacer.

8. On models equipped with A/C, loosen idler pulley and remove A/C compressor drive belt.
9. On all models, remove alternator drive belt, power steering drive belt and water pump pulley.
10. Remove power steering pump mounting brackets and position pump aside.
11. On models equipped with A/C, remove A/C compressor.
12. Remove alternator and mounting bracket and position aside, then disconnect alternator ground wire from cylinder block.
13. Disconnect heater hoses from water pump and block, then remove ground wires from right cylinder head and cylinder block.
14. Disconnect and plug fuel line at fuel pump.
15. Disconnect vacuum lines from rear of intake manifold, then the vacuum control hoses and wires, if equipped.
16. Disconnect accelerator cable or linkage from carburetor and intake manifold.
17. Disconnect transmission downshift linkage and/or speed control cable, if equipped.
18. Disconnect electrical connectors from ignition coil, coolant temperature sending unit and oil pressure sending unit, then remove engine wiring harness from retaining clips and position aside.
19. Raise and support vehicle.
20. Disconnect exhaust pipes from exhaust manifolds, then remove exhaust heat control valve or exhaust manifold-to-pipe spacer.
21. Remove starter motor, then the engine front support through bolts and starter cable clamp from engine right front support.
22. Remove converter inspection cover, then disconnect flex plate from converter.
23. Remove downshift rod, then the 4 converter lower housing-to-engine bolts and adapter plate-to-converter housing bolt.
24. Lower vehicle, then remove 2 converter-to-housing upper bolts.
25. Attach lifting equipment to engine and support transmission with a suitable jack.
26. Raise engine slightly and carefully separate from transmission, then lift engine from vehicle.
27. Reverse procedure to install.

E-100–350, F-100–350 & Bronco
1. Drain cooling system and engine oil.
2. Disconnect battery and alternator ground cables from cylinder block.
3. Remove air cleaner and intake duct assembly, including carbon canister hose and crankcase ventilation hose.
4. Disconnect upper and lower hoses and transmission oil cooler lines (if equipped) from radiator.
5. Remove fan shroud attaching bolts and position shroud over fan.

6. Remove radiator, fan shroud, spacer, belts and pulley.
7. Disconnect electrical connectors from alternator, then loosen mounting bolts and swing alternator down.
8. Disconnect electrical connector from oil pressure sending unit, then disconnect and plug fuel line at fuel tank.
9. Disconnect accelerator rod or cable from carburetor.
10. Disconnect speed control cable and transmission kickdown rod and remove rod retracting spring, if equipped.
11. Disconnect heater hoses from water pump and intake manifold.
12. Disconnect electrical connector from coolant temperature sending unit.
13. On models equipped with A/C, unfasten A/C compressor and mounting brackets and position aside.
14. On all models, remove flywheel housing-to-engine upper attaching bolts.
15. Disconnect primary wire from ignition coil, then remove wiring harness from left rocker arm cover and position aside.
16. Disconnect ground strap from cylinder block.
17. Raise and support vehicle.
18. Remove starter motor.
19. Disconnect exhaust pipes from exhaust manifolds, then the engine support insulators from frame brackets.
20. On models equipped with automatic transmission, remove converter inspection plate, then the converter-to-flywheel attaching bolts.
21. On all models, remove remaining flywheel housing-to-engine attaching bolts.
22. Lower vehicle and support transmission with a suitable jack.
23. Install lifting brackets and attach suitable lifting equipment to engine.
24. Raise engine slightly and carefully separate from transmission, then lift engine from vehicle.
25. Reverse procedure to install.

V8-460

E-100–350
1. Remove engine cover, then disconnect battery cables and drain cooling system.
2. Remove grille assembly, including gravel deflector.
3. Remove upper grille support bracket, hood lock support and condenser upper mounting brackets.
4. On models equipped with A/C, discharge refrigerant from system and remove condenser. Disconnect lines from A/C compressor and remove accelerator cable bracket.
5. Disconnect heater hoses from engine.
6. Disconnect upper and lower radiator hoses and transmission oil cooler lines (if equipped) from radiator.
7. Remove fan shroud, fan and radiator, then pivot alternator inward and disconnect electrical connectors from alternator.
8. Remove air cleaner, duct and valve

assembly and exhaust manifold shroud, then the flex tube from exhaust manifold stove.
9. Disconnect throttle and transmission linkage from carburetor, then remove accelerator cable bracket from engine.
10. On models equipped with speed control, remove speed control servo vacuum line and cable.
11. On all models, disconnect fuel and choke lines, then remove carburetor and spacer.
12. Raise and support vehicle.
13. Drain engine oil and remove oil filter.
14. Disconnect exhaust pipes from exhaust manifolds.
15. Remove 2 transmission filler tube bracket attaching bolts from right cylinder head.
16. Remove engine mount attaching bolts and nuts, then the starter motor.
17. Remove converter inspection cover bolts, 4 converter-to-flex plate nuts, 3 adapter plate-to-converter housing bolts and 4 converter housing-to-cylinder block lower bolts.
18. Remove ground wire retaining bolt from cylinder block, then lower the vehicle.
19. On models equipped with power steering, remove steering pump drive belt and front bracket bolts.
20. On all models, disconnect one vacuum line from rear of intake manifold.
21. Disconnect engine wiring harness and position aside.
22. On models equipped with A/C, disconnect A/C compressor magnetic clutch electrical connector.
23. On all models, install lifting bracket to intake manifold and remove 2-converter housing-to-cylinder block upper attaching bolts.
24. Support transmission with a suitable jack and attach lifting equipment to engine, then carefully move engine forward and lift from vehicle.
25. Reverse procedure to install.

1979 F-150—350
1. Disconnect battery ground cable.
2. Mark hood hinge locations and remove hood.
3. Drain cooling system, then remove air cleaner and intake duct assembly.
4. Disconnect upper and lower radiator hoses from engine.
5. On models equipped with automatic transmission, disconnect oil cooler lines from radiator.
6. On all models, remove fan and fan shroud, then the radiator upper support and radiator.
7. On models equipped with A/C, proceed as follows:
   a. Isolate A/C compressor, then disconnect service valves and hoses from compressor.
   b. Remove compressor drive belt, then the compressor support bracket-to-water pump attaching bolt.
   c. Remove compressor mounting bracket attaching bolts, then unfas-

ten power steering pump.
   d. Disconnect compressor clutch electrical connector, then remove compressor, compressor mounting bracket and idler pulley.
8. On all models, disconnect and plug fuel inlet line at fuel pump.
9. Loosen alternator adjusting arm and mounting bolts, then remove drive belts and water pump pulley.
10. Remove alternator and mounting brackets and position aside, leaving wires attached.
11. Disconnect ground cable from right corner of cylinder block.
12. Disconnect heater hoses, then remove transmission fluid filler tube attaching bolt from right rocker arm cover and position tube aside.
13. Disconnect all vacuum lines from rear of intake manifold.
14. Disconnect speed control cable from carburetor and bracket, if equipped.
15. Disconnect accelerator and transmission rods from bell crank and position aside.
16. Disconnect engine wiring harness from dash and position aside.
17. Raise and support vehicle.
18. Disconnect exhaust pipes from exhaust manifolds, then remove starter motor.
19. Remove converter housing access cover, then the flywheel-to-converter attaching nuts and converter-to-engine lower rear cover plate attaching bolts.
20. Remove front engine mount through bolts.
21. Support transmission with a suitable jack, then lower vehicle.
22. Remove converter housing-to-cylinder block upper left attaching bolts.
23. Disconnect ignition coil electrical connector, then remove coil and bracket assembly from intake manifold.
24. Attach suitable lifting equipment to engine, then carefully lift engine assembly from vehicle.
25. Reverse procedure to install.

1983—1985 F-250—350
1. Drain cooling system and engine oil.
2. Mark hood hinge locations and remove hood.
3. Disconnect battery and ground cables from cylinder block.
4. Remove air cleaner and intake duct assembly, including carbon canister hose and crankcase ventilation hose.
5. Disconnect upper and lower radiator hoses and transmission oil cooler lines (if equipped) from radiator.
6. On models equipped with engine oil cooler, disconnect cooler lines from radiator.

NOTE: Do not disconnect engine oil cooler lines from fittings behind radiator.

7. On models equipped with A/C, discharge refrigerant from system, then remove A/C condenser and disconnect lines from compressor.
8. Remove fan shroud attaching bolts and position shroud over fan.

9. Remove radiator, fan shroud, fan spacer, belts and pulley.
10. Remove alternator mounting bolts and swing alternator aside.
11. Disconnect electrical connector from oil pressure sending unit, then disconnect and plug flexible fuel line at fuel tank.
12. Disconnect vacuum hoses from evaporative canister.
13. Disconnect accelerator cable from carburetor.
14. Disconnect speed control linkages and transmission kickdown rod and remove rod retaining spring, if equipped.
15. Disconnect power brake booster vacuum hose, if equipped.
16. Disconnect heater hoses from water pump and intake manifold.
17. Disconnect electrical connector from coolant temperature sending unit.
18. Remove flywheel housing-to-engine upper attaching bolts.
19. Disconnect primary wire from ignition coil, then remove wiring harness from left rocker arm cover and position aside.
20. Disconnect ground strap from cylinder head.
21. Raise and support vehicle.
22. Remove starter motor.
23. Disconnect exhaust pipes from exhaust manifolds, then the engine support insulators from frame brackets.
24. On models equipped with automatic transmission, remove converter inspection plate, then the converter-to-flywheel attaching bolts.
25. On models equipped with manual transmission, remove rear cover plate from flywheel housing, then the remaining flywheel housing-to-engine attaching bolts.
26. On models equipped with A/C, disconnect A/C compressor magnetic clutch electrical connector.
27. On all models, lower vehicle and support transmission with a suitable jack.
28. Install lifting brackets to intake manifold and attach suitable lifting equipment to engine.
29. Raise engine slightly and carefully separate from transmission, then lift engine from vehicle.
30. Reverse procedure to install.

CYLINDER HEAD
REPLACE

V8-460

1. Remove intake manifold and carburetor, then disconnect exhaust pipe from exhaust manifold.
2. Loosen air conditioner drive belt (if equipped), then loosen alternator bolts and remove the bolt attaching alternator bracket to cylinder head.
3. If equipped with air conditioning, shut off compressor service valves and remove valves and hoses from compressor then remove compressor and

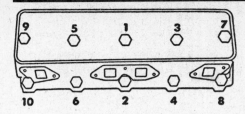

Fig. 18   Cylinder head tightening sequence. V8 engines

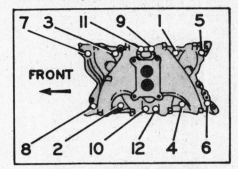

Fig. 21   Intake manifold tightening sequence. V8-351M & 400

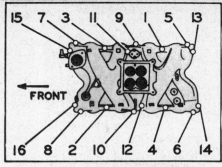

Fig. 19   Intake manifold tightening sequence. V8-460

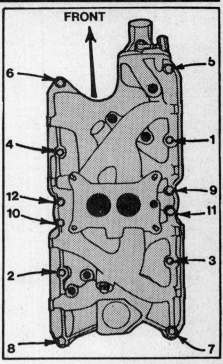

Fig. 20   Intake manifold tightening sequence. V8-255, 302 & V8-351W

place out of way. Remove compressor upper mounting bracket from cylinder head.

4. If not equipped with air conditioning, remove bolts attaching power steering reservoir bracket to left cylinder head and position reservoir and bracket out of the way.

5. Remove rocker arm covers, rocker arm bolts, rocker arms, oil deflectors, fulcrums and push rods.

NOTE: Keep all parts in sequence so that they can be reinstalled in their original locations.

6. Remove cylinder head bolts taking note as to the length of each bolt and remove the cylinder head.

NOTE: If necessary to loosen cylinder head gasket seal, pry at forward corners of cylinder head and against casting provided on cylinder block.

7. Install heads in the reverse order of removal and torque cylinder head bolts in three steps and in the sequence shown in **Fig. 18.** Final tightening should be to the torque listed in the Engine Tightening Table. Torque intake manifold bolts to torque spec given in Engine Tightening Table and in sequence shown in **Fig. 19.**

V8-255, 302, 351 & 400

1. Remove intake manifold and carburetor as an assembly.
2. Remove rocker arm covers.
3. If removing right cylinder head, perform the following steps:
   a. On models with V8-255, 302 and

351W engines, except Ranchero, loosen alternator and air pump mounting bracket and pivot alternator downward.

b. On Econoline models, remove ignition coil and air cleaner inlet duct from right cylinder head.

c. On models with V8-351M and 400 engines, remove air cleaner inlet duct and ground wire from right cylinder head.

4. If removing left cylinder head, perform the following steps:
   a. On models with V8-255, 302 and 351W engines and A/C, remove A/C compressor bracket attaching bolts.
   b. On models with V8-351M and 400 and all Ranchero models, unfasten power steering pump (if equipped), then remove pump drive belt and position pump aside. On models equipped with A/C, isolate and remove A/C compressor.
   c. On 1980–85 F series models with V8-255, 302 and 351W engines, remove oil dipstick and tube assembly and speed control bracket, if equipped.

5. Disconnect exhaust pipes from exhaust manifolds.

6. Loosen rocker arm studs or bolts and remove push rods in sequence so they may be installed in their original positions.

7. Remove exhaust valve stem caps, if equipped.

8. On Econoline models with V8-255, 302 and 351W engines, remove Thermactor air supply manifold and hose pump valve as an assembly.

9. On F series and Bronco models, disconnect Thermactor air supply hoses from check valves and plug the valves.

10. On all models, remove cylinder head attaching bolts and the cylinder head.

NOTE: On 1980–81 Econoline models with V8-351M and 400 engines, it may be necessary to remove forward bolt on left side of head as a unit with cylinder head, due to a lack of clearance with body flange.

11. Reverse procedure to install. Torque cylinder head attaching bolts to speci-

fications in sequence shown in **Fig. 18.** Torque intake manifold attaching bolts to specifications in sequence shown in **Figs. 20 and 21.**

6-300

1. Drain cooling system and remove air cleaner.
2. Remove PCV valve from rocker arm cover, then disconnect vent hose from intake manifold.
3. Remove carburetor fuel inlet line and distributor line.
4. Disconnect and tag all vacuum lines from carburetor.
5. On 1979 models, disconnect choke cable from carburetor and position cable and housing aside.
6. On all models, remove accelerator cable retracting spring and disconnect cable from carburetor.
7. On models equipped with automatic transmission, disconnect kickdown rod from carburetor.
8. On all models, disconnect upper radiator hose and heater hose from coolant outlet elbow.
9. Disconnect exhaust pipe from exhaust manifold and discard pipe gasket.
10. Remove ignition coil bracket attaching screws and position coil aside.
11. Remove rocker arm cover and loosen rocker arm stud nuts so rocker arms can be rotated to one side.
12. Remove rocker arms in order so they may be installed in their original position.
13. Disconnect ignition wires from spark

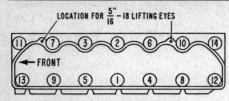

Fig. 22 Cylinder head tightening sequence. 6-300

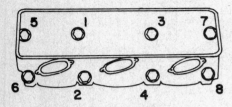

Fig. 24 Cylinder head tightening sequence. V6-232

plugs, then remove cylinder head attaching bolts.

14. Remove cylinder head, using suitable lifting equipment.
15. Reverse procedure to install. Tighten cylinder head bolts in 3 steps and in sequence shown in **Fig. 22** to torque listed in the Engine Tightening specifications. Torque intake and exhaust manifold bolts to specifications in sequence shown in **Fig. 23**.

V6-232

1. Disconnect battery ground cable, then drain cooling system.
2. Remove air cleaner, air intake duct and heat tube.
3. Loosen accessory drive belt idler and remove drive belt.
4. If left cylinder head is to be removed, proceed as follows:
   a. Remove oil filler cap.
   b. If equipped with power steering, remove pump bracket attaching bolts, then remove pump and bracket assembly and position pump aside with hoses attached.
   c. If equipped with A/C, remove compressor bracket attaching bolts, then position compressor and bracket assembly aside with refrigerant lines attached.
5. If right cylinder head is to be removed, proceed as follows:
   a. Remove Thermactor diverter valve and hose assembly.
   b. Remove accessory drive belt idler, then remove alternator.
   c. Remove Thermactor pump pulley, then remove Thermactor pump.
   d. Remove alternator mounting bracket.

NOTE: On models equipped with Tripminder, the fuel supply line from the fuel pump to the fuel sensor will have to be disconnected to gain access to the upper alternator bracket bolt.

e. Remove PCV valve.
6. Remove intake manifold and exhaust manifolds.
7. Remove rocker arm cover attaching screws, then loosen cover by using a putty knife under cover flange and remove cover. Do not use excess force when loosening rocker arm cover as cover may become damaged.
8. Loosen rocker arm fulcrum bolt enough to allow rocker arms to be rotated to one side, then remove push rods.

NOTE: Tag push rods so they can be installed in the same position.

9. Remove cylinder head attaching bolts, then remove cylinder head and gasket.
10. Reverse procedure to install. Apply a thin coating of pipe sealant D8AZ-19558-A or equivalent to the shorter cylinder head bolts which are installed on the exhaust manifold side of the cylinder head. Do not apply pipe sealant to long bolts which are installed on the intake manifold side of the cylinder head. Tighten cylinder head bolts in four steps to torque listed under Engine Tightening Specifications using sequence shown in **Fig. 24**. Loosen cylinder bolts approximately 2 to 3 turns, then retighten bolts in four steps to specified torque in sequence, **Fig. 24**. When installing intake manifold, tighten mounting bolts to torque specified under Engine Tightening specifications in sequence shown in **Fig. 25**.

NOTE: Before installing intake manifold, apply sealer to locations shown in **Fig. 26**.

INTAKE MANIFOLD
REPLACE

V6-232

1. Drain cooling system, then remove air cleaner with air intake duct and heat tube.
2. Disconnect accelerator cable and transmission linkage (if equipped) from carburetor.
3. Remove accelerator cable mounting bracket attaching bolts and position bracket aside.
4. On models equipped with speed control, disconnect chain from carburetor, then remove servo bracket assembly attaching nuts and position assembly aside.
5. On all models, disconnect bowl vent hose from carburetor.
6. Disconnect Thermactor air supply hose from check valve located on back of intake manifold.
7. Disconnect fuel inlet line from carburetor.
8. Disconnect upper radiator hose from thermostat housing and the coolant bypass hose from manifold.

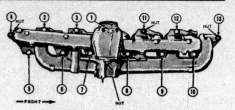

Fig. 23 Intake & exhaust manifold tightening sequence. 6-300

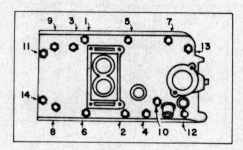

Fig. 25 Intake manifold tightening sequence. V6-232

9. Disconnect heater tube from intake manifold and remove tube support bracket attaching nut.
10. Disconnect all vacuum lines and electrical connectors necessary for intake manifold removal.
11. On models equipped with A/C, remove A/C compressor support bracket from intake manifold.
12. On 1982 models, loosen EGR tube at EGR valve adapter.
13. On 1983 models, remove EGR tube.
14. On all models, disconnect PCV line from carburetor.
15. Remove carburetor and discard phenolic gasket.
16. On 1982 models, remove carburetor hold-down studs from manifold.
17. On all models, remove 3 EGR spacer attaching screws from manifold.
18. Work EGR spacer loose from manifold with EGR adapter and valve attached, then remove spacer and discard gasket.

NOTE: On 1982 models, disconnect EGR tube from adapter prior to removing spacer.

19. Remove PCV line, then the intake manifold attaching bolts and intake manifold.

NOTE: It may be necessary to pry on front of manifold to break seal. If so, use care to prevent damage to machined surfaces.

20. Reverse procedure to install. Apply sealer to locations shown in **Fig. 26**. Torque manifold attaching bolts to specifications in sequence shown in **Fig. 25**.

6-300

1. Remove air cleaner.

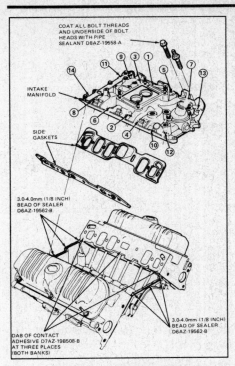

Fig. 26 Intake manifold installation. V6-232

2. On 1979 models, disconnect choke cable from carburetor.
3. On all models, disconnect accelerator cable or rod from carburetor and remove accelerator retracting spring.
4. On models equipped with automatic transmission, remove kickdown rod retracting spring and accelerator rod bellcrank assembly.
5. On all models, disconnect and tag fuel inlet line and all vacuum lines at carburetor.
6. Disconnect carburetor feedback solenoid connector at carburetor and the choke cap electric assist connector, if equipped.
7. Disconnect exhaust pipe from exhaust manifold.
8. Disconnect power brake vacuum line, if equipped.
9. Remove manifold attaching bolts and nuts and the intake and exhaust manifolds as an assembly.
10. Remove attaching nuts and separate intake and exhaust manifolds.
11. Reverse procedure to install. Torque manifold attaching bolts and nuts to specifications in sequence shown in **Fig. 23.**

SERVICE BULLETIN The following manifold installation procedure should be used to extend exhaust manifold service life:
1. Clean cylinder head and manifold mating surfaces.
2. Remove tube fittings from original manifold and install in replacement manifold, as needed.
3. Apply suitable graphite grease to exhaust manifold-to-intake manifold

---

mating surfaces.
4. Install 2 new bolts (part No. 374047-S) and a new stud (part No. 381733-S) into intake manifold.
5. Assemble intake manifold to exhaust manifold using lock washers and nuts. Tighten nuts finger tight only at this time.
6. Install a new intake manifold gasket. Do not install a combination intake/exhaust manifold gasket on a new exhaust manifold.
7. Apply suitable graphite grease to cylinder head-to-manifold mating surfaces.
8. Position manifold assemblies against cylinder head, ensuring intake manifold gaskets have not moved.
9. Install manifold attaching bolts and nuts and torque to specifications in sequence shown in **Fig. 23.**
10. Torque intake manifold-to-exhaust manifold attaching nuts to 22–32 ft. lbs.
11. Position a new gasket on exhaust pipe, then connect pipe to manifold and torque attaching bolts to 25–38 ft. lbs.

V8-255, 302 & 351W

1. Drain cooling system, then remove air cleaner with intake duct assembly and carnkcase ventilation hose.
2. Disconnect accelerator cable and speed control linkage (if equipped) from carburetor. Remove accelerator cable bracket, then disconnect kickdown rod from carburetor on models equipped with automatic transmission. Disconnect electric choke and carburetor solenoid electrical connectors, if equipped.
3. Disconnect high tension lead and wires from ignition coil.
4. Disconnect ignition wires from spark plugs, then remove wires and bracket assembly from rocker arm cover attaching stud.
5. Remove distributor cap and ignition wires as an assembly.
6. Disconnect fuel inlet line from carburetor.
7. Disconnect vacuum hoses from distributor, then remove distributor and disconnect evaporative hoses, if equipped.
8. Disconnect upper radiator hose from coolant outlet housing.
9. Disconnect electrical connector from coolant temperature sending unit, then remove heater hose from intake manifold.
10. Remove water pump bypass hose from coolant outlet housing, then disconnect crankcase vent hose from rocker arm cover.
11. Remove intake manifold attaching bolts, then the intake manifold and carburetor as an assembly.
12. Reverse procedure to install. Apply sealer as shown in **Fig. 27.** Torque manifold attaching bolts to specifications in sequence shown in **Fig. 20.**

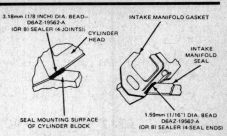

Fig. 27 Intake manifold installation. V8 engines

V8-351M & 400

1. Remove air cleaner and intake duct.
2. On models equipped with A/C, isolate and remove A/C compressor.
3. On all models, disconnect high tension lead and wires from ignition coil.
4. Disconnect ignition wires from spark plugs, then remove wires from brackets on rocker arm covers.
5. Remove distributor cap and ignition wires as an assembly.
6. Remove Thermactor bypass valve and hose from check valve.
7. Disconnect fuel inlet line from carburetor.
8. Disconnect heater hoses from retainers and position aside.
9. Remove ignition coil, vacuum solenoid valve and bracket, then disconnect crankcase emission hose from left rocker arm cover.
10. Disconnect vacuum lines from intake manifold and distributor.
11. Remove distributor hold-down bolt and the distributor.
12. Disconnect accelerator linkage and speed control cable (if equipped) from carburetor.
13. On models equipped with automatic transmission, disconnect transmission downshift linkage from carburetor.
14. On all models, remove carburetor, then the manifold attaching bolts and manifold.
15. Remove and discard manifold valley baffle and seals.
16. Reverse procedure to install. Apply sealer as shown in **Fig. 27.** Torque manifold attaching bolts to specifications in sequence shown in **Fig. 21.**

V8-460

1. Drain cooling system, then remove air cleaner and intake duct assembly.
2. Disconnect upper radiator hose from engine and the heater hose from intake manifold and water pump and position aside.
3. Loosen water pump bypass hose clamp at intake manifold.
4. Disconnect PCV valve hose from right rocker arm cover.
5. Disconnect and tag all vacuum lines at rear of intake manifold.
6. Disconnect ignition wires from spark plugs and position aside.

7. Disconnect high tension lead from ignition coil, then remove distributor cap and wires as an assembly.
8. Disconnect and tag all distributor vacuum lines at carburetor and vacuum control valve.
9. Disconnect accelerator linkage and transmission kickdown linkage (if equipped) from carburetor.
10. On models equipped with speed control, remove speed control linkage bracket from intake manifold and disconnect it from carburetor.
11. On all models, remove accelerator linkage cable attaching bolts and position linkage aside.
12. Disconnect fuel inlet line from carburetor.
13. Disconnect electrical connector from ignition coil battery terminal.
14. Disconnect engine temperature and oil pressure sending unit electrical connectors and any other connectors necessary for intake manifold removal.
15. Unfasten wiring harness from 3 retaining clips on left rocker arm cover and position harness aside.
16. Remove ignition coil and bracket assembly.
17. Remove intake manifold attaching bolts and nuts, then the intake manifold and carburetor as an assembly.
18. Reverse procedure to install. Apply sealer as shown in **Fig. 27.** Torque manifold attaching bolts to specifications shown in **Fig. 19.**

EXHAUST MANIFOLD
REPLACE

V6-232

Left Side
1. Disconnect battery ground cable.
2. Remove oil level dipstick tube support bracket.
3. On vehicles equipped with speed control, reposition air cleaner assembly and disconnect servo chain at carburetor, then remove servo bracket attaching bolts and nuts and position servo/bracket assembly aside.
4. On all models, disconnect electrical connector at exhaust gas oxygen sensor, if equipped.
5. Disconnect spark plug wires, then raise and support vehicle.
6. Remove exhaust pipe to manifold attaching nuts, then lower vehicle.
7. Remove exhaust manifold attaching bolts and the exhaust manifold.
8. Reverse procedure to install.

Right Side
1. Disconnect battery ground cable.
2. Remove air cleaner assembly and heat tube.
3. Disconnect thermactor hose from downstream air tube check valve.
4. Remove downstream air tube bracket attaching bolt at rear of right side cylinder head.
5. Disconnect coil secondary wire from

coil and the spark plug wires from spark plugs.
6. Remove spark plugs, then the outer heat shield.
7. Raise and support vehicle.
8. On vehicles equipped with automatic transmission, remove transmission dipstick tube.
9. Disconnect exhaust pipe at manifold.
10. Lower vehicle.
11. Remove exhaust manifold attaching bolts and the exhaust manifold, inner heat shroud and EGR tube as an assembly.
12. Reverse procedure to install.

6-300

Refer to "Intake Manifold, Replace".

V8-255, 302 & 351W EXC. RANCHERO

1. Disconnect battery ground cable.
2. Remove air cleaner and intake duct assembly including crankcase ventilation hose.
3. Remove bolts attaching air cleaner inlet duct, if equipped.
4. Disconnect exhaust pipes at manifolds.
5. Remove exhaust manifold heat shields with attaching bolts and flat washers, if equipped.
6. On 1980–85 models, remove oil dipstick tube assembly, speed control bracket and exhaust heat control valve from left side exhaust manifold, if equipped, then remove exhaust manifold.
7. Reverse procedure to install, torquing attaching bolts to specifications from centermost bolts outward.

RANCHERO W/V8-302 OR V8-351W

1. Disconnect battery ground cable.
2. When removing right side manifold, remove air cleaner and intake duct assembly, then disconnect automatic choke heat tubes.
3. Disconnect exhaust pipe from exhaust manifold, then remove attaching nuts, spark plug wires and spark plugs.
4. Disconnect exhaust gas oxygen sensor, if equipped.
5. Remove attaching bolts and washers, then the exhaust manifold.
6. Reverse procedure to install, torquing bolts to specifications from centermost bolts outward.

V8-351M & 400

1. Disconnect battery ground cable.
2. When removing right side manifold, remove air cleaner, intake duct and heat shield.
3. When removing left side manifold, remove oil filter.
4. On 1980–82 models, remove oil dipstick and tube assembly and speed control bracket from left side exhaust manifold, if equipped.

5. On vehicles equipped with column selector and automatic transmission, disconnect selector lever cross shaft.
6. On all models, disconnect exhaust pipe at manifold and remove spark plug heat shields.
7. Remove exhaust manifold attaching bolts and the exhaust manifold.
8. Reverse procedure to install, torquing attaching bolts to specifications from centermost bolts outward.

V8-460

1. Disconnect battery ground cable.
2. When removing right side exhaust manifold, remove air cleaner, intake duct assembly and heat shroud.
3. Remove spark plug wires as necessary.
4. Disconnect exhaust pipe at exhaust manifold.
5. Remove attaching bolts and washers, then the exhaust manifold, lifting bracket and spark plug wire heat shields.
6. Reverse procedure to install, torquing attaching bolts to specifications from centermost bolts outward.

VALVE ARRANGEMENT
FRONT TO REAR

6-300	E-I-E-I-E-I-E-I-E-I-E-I
V6-232 Right	I-E-I-E-I-E
V6-232 Left	E-I-E-I-E-I
V8-255, 302 Left Bank	E-I-E-I-E-I-E-I
V8-255, 302 Right Bank	I-E-I-E-I-E-I-E
V8-351, 400 Right Bank	I-E-I-E-I-E-I-E
V8-351, 400 Left Bank	E-I-E-I-E-I-E-I
V8-460 Left Bank	E-I-E-I-E-I-E-I
V8-460 Right Bank	I-E-I-E-I-E-I

VALVES
ADJUST

6-300

1. Crank engine with ignition Off, using an auxiliary starter switch.
2. Mark crankshaft damper at two locations, approximately 120° apart, so that, with the timing mark, the damper is divided into three equal sections.
3. Rotate crankshaft until No. 1 piston is on TDC of compression stroke.
4. Measure torque required to turn each stud nut in a counterclockwise direction (breakaway torque). Replace stud nuts where breakaway torque is not 4.5–15 ft. lbs.

NOTE: If breakaway torque is still not within specifications after replacing stud nut, the stud must be replaced.

5. Install stud nut and torque to 17–23 ft. lbs. with No. 1 piston at TDC of compression stroke. Using a suitable tool, **Fig. 28,** slowly apply pressure to bleed down lifter until plunger is completely

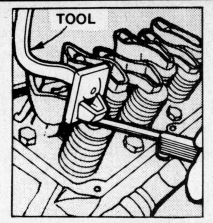

Fig. 28 Compressing valve lifter with tool to check clearance on engines with hydraulic valve lifters

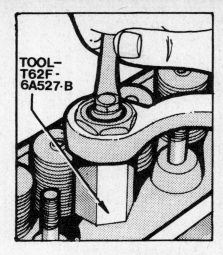

Fig. 29 Rocker arm stud removal. 6-300 & 1979 V8-302 & 351W

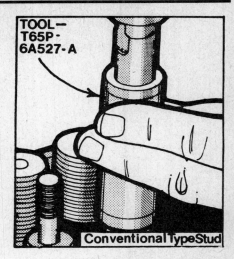

Fig. 30 Rocker arm stud installation. 6-300

bottomed. Hold lifter in this position and check clearance between rocker arm and valve. If clearance is not within specifications, install a longer or shorter push rod as needed.

6. On all models, repeat step 5 or 6 for remaining valves. Turn crankshaft 120° at a time in normal direction of rotation and adjust valves following engine firing order.

V6-232

A .060 inch longer or a .060 inch shorter push rod is available to compensate for dimensional changes in the valve train. If clearance is less than specified, the .060 inch shorter push rod should be used. If clearance is more than the maximum specified, the .060 inch longer push rod should be used.

Using an auxiliary starter switch crankshaft until No. 1 cylinder is at TDC compression stroke, compress valve lifter using tool T82C-6500-A or equivalent, **Fig. 30.** At this point, the following valves can be checked:

No. 1 Intake   No. 3 Intake
No. 1 Exhaust   No. 4 Exhaust
No. 2 Exhaust   No. 6 Intake

After clearance on these valves has been checked, rotate crankshaft until No. 5 cylinder is at TDC compression stroke (1 revolution of crankshaft), and then compress valve lifter using tool No. T82C-6500-A or equivalent, **Fig. 28,** and check the following valves:

No. 2 Intake   No. 5 Intake
No. 3 Exhaust   No. 5 Exhaust
No. 4 Intake   No. 6 Exhaust

V8 ENGINES

To provide a means to compensate for dimensional changes in the valve train and provide for valve adjustment, .060 inch shorter or longer push rods are available. If the valve clearance is less than the minimum, the .060 inch shorter push rod

should be used. If the clearance is more than the maximum, the longer push rod should be used. To check the valve clearance, proceed as follows:

1. Mark crankshaft pulley at three locations, with No. 1 location at TDC timing mark (end of compression stroke), location No. 2 one full turn (360°) clockwise from TDC and No. 3 location one quarter turn clockwise (90°) from position No. 2.
2. Turn crankshaft to number 1 location, then compress valve lifter using tool T71P-6513-A or equivalent, **Fig. 28,** and check the clearance on the following valves:

V8-255, 302, 460
No. 1 Intake   No. 1 Exhaust
No. 7 Intake   No. 5 Exhaust
No. 8 Intake   No. 4 Exhaust
V8-351 & 400
No. 1 Intake   No. 1 Exhaust
No. 4 Intake   No. 3 Exhaust
No. 8 Intake   No. 7 Exhaust

3. Turn crankshaft to number 2 location, then compress valve lifter using tool T71P-6513-A or equivalent, **Fig. 28,** and check the clearance on the following valves:

V8-255, 302, 460
No. 5 Intake   No. 2 Exhaust
No. 4 Intake   No. 6 Exhaust
V8-351 & 400
No. 3 Intake   No. 2 Exhaust
No. 7 Intake   No. 6 Exhaust

4. Turn crankshaft to number 3 location, then compress valve lifter using tool T71P-6513-A or equivalent, **Fig. 28,** and check the clearance on the following valves:

V8-255, 302, 460
No. 2 Intake   No. 7 Exhaust
No. 3 Intake   No. 3 Exhaust
No. 6 Intake   No. 8 Exhaust
V8-351 & 400
No. 2 Intake   No. 4 Exhaust
No. 5 Intake   No. 5 Exhaust
No. 6 Intake   No. 8 Exhaust

VALVE GUIDES

Valve guides in these engines are an integral part of the head and, therefore, cannot be removed. For service, guides can be reamed oversize to accommodate one of three service valves with oversize stems (.003″, .015″ and .030″).

Check the valve stem clearance of each valve (after cleaning) in its respective valve guide. If the clearance exceeds the service limits of .004″ of the intake or .005″ on the exhaust, ream the valve guides to accommodate the next oversize diameter valve.

ROCKER ARM STUD
6-300 & 1979 V8-302 & 351W

If necessary to replace a rocker arm stud, a rocker arm stud kit is available and contains a stud remover, a stud installer, and two reamers, one .006″ and the other .015″.

Rocker arm studs that are broken or have damaged threads may be replaced with standard studs. Loose studs in the head may be replaced with .006″, .010″ or .015″ oversize studs which are available for service.

When going from a standard size stud to a .015″ oversize stud, always use a .006″ reamer and a .010″ reamer before reaming is finished with a .015″ reamer.

If a stud is broken off flush with the stud boss, use an easy-out to remove the broken stud, following the instructions of the tool manufacturer.

Remove stud with tool T62F-6A527-B, **Fig. 29.** On 6-300, install new stud with tool T65P-6A527-A, **Fig. 30.** On 1979 V8-302 and V8-351W, install new stud with tool T69P-6049-D, **Fig. 31.**

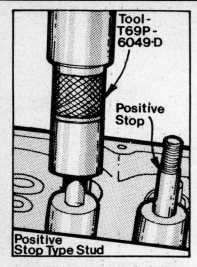

Fig. 31 Rocker arm stud Installation. 1979 V8-302 & 351W

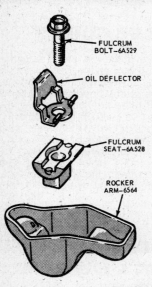

Fig. 34 Rocker arm assembly. V8-351M, 400 & 460

ROCKER ARM
REPLACE

1979—84 6-300

These engines use a rocker arm stud and nut. To disassemble, remove rocker arm nut, fulcrum seat and rocker arm, **Fig. 32.** Inspect condition of nut, **Fig. 33,** and replace if necessary.

ROCKER ARM & FULCRUM BOLT

V6-232, V8-255, 302, 351M, 351W, 400 & 460 & 1985 6-300

The rocker arm is supported by a ful-

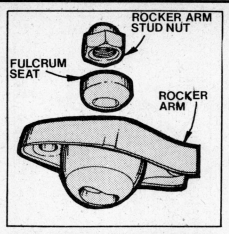

Fig. 32 Rocker arm assembly. 1979—84 6-300

crum bolt which fits through the fulcrum seat and threads into the cylinder head. To disassemble, remove the bolt, oil deflector, fulcrum seat and rocker arm, **Figs. 34 and 35.**

SERVICE BULLETIN 1981–82 models equipped with V8-255, 302 and 351W engines with low profile rocker arm fulcrums (part No. E1TZ-6A528-A) may experience excessive oil displacement when engine is operated for extended periods during high ambient temperatures. This problem may be corrected by replacing original rocker arm fulcrums with part No. D7AZ-6A528-A.

HYDRAULIC VALVE LIFTERS
REPLACE

6-300

1. Remove air cleaner and PCV valve.
2. On 1979–80 models, disconnect choke cable from carburetor.
3. On all models, disconnect accelerator and throttle cables from carburetor and remove retracting spring.
4. On 1985 models, remove fuel line between carburetor fuel filter and fuel pump.
5. On all models, remove coil bracket attaching bolt or "E" core assembly attaching nuts and place coil out of way.
6. Remove rocker arm cover.
7. Disconnect ignition wires from spark plugs and the secondary high tension wire from coil.
8. Remove distributor cap and ignition wires as an assembly.
9. Remove push rod cover.
10. Loosen rocker arm stud nuts or bolts until rocker arms can be disengaged from push rods.
11. Remove push rods and valve lifters in order so they can be installed in their

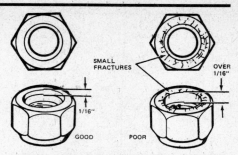

Fig. 33 Inspection of rocker arm stud nut

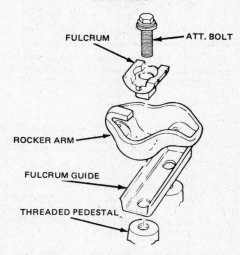

Fig. 35 Rocker arm assembly. V8-255, 302 & 351W & 1985 6-300

original positions. Use a suitable magnetic rod to remove lifters, **Fig. 36.**
12. Reverse procedure to install.

V6-232, V8-255, 302, 351, 400, & 460

1. Remove intake manifold.
2. Remove rocker arm covers. Loosen rocker arm stud nuts or bolts and rotate rocker arms to the side.
3. Remove push rods in sequence so they can be installed in their original bores.
4. Using a magnet, remove the lifters and place them in a numbered rack so they can be installed in their original bores. If lifters are stuck in their bores, it may be necessary to use a plier-type tool to remove them.
5. The internal parts of each lifter are matched sets. Do not intermix parts.

TIMING CASE COVER
V6-232

1. Disconnect battery ground cable, then drain cooling system.
2. Remove air cleaner assembly and air intake duct.

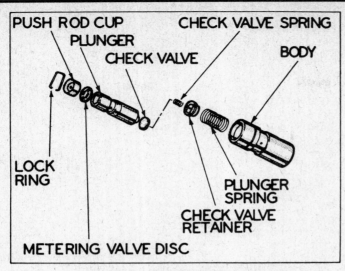

Fig. 36 Hydraulic valve lifter

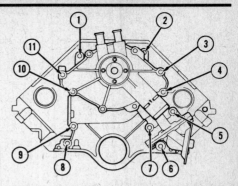

Fig. 37 Front cover attaching bolt location. V6-232

3. Remove fan shroud attaching screws and fan and clutch assembly attaching bolts.
4. Remove fan and clutch assembly and fan shroud.
5. Loosen accessory drive belt idler, then remove drive belt and water pump pulley.
6. On models equipped with power steering, remove steering pump bracket attaching bolts and position pump aside with hoses attached.
7. On models equipped with A/C, remove A/C compressor front support bracket.
8. On all models, disconnect coolant bypass hose and heater hose from water pump and the upper radiator hose from thermostat housing.
9. Disconnect coil wire from distributor cap, then remove cap with wires attached.
10. With cylinder No. 1 at TDC of compression stroke, mark position of rotor to distributor housing and position of distributor housing to front cover.
11. Remove distributor hold-down clamp, then lift distributor from front cover.
12. Raise and support vehicle.
13. Remove crankshaft damper using a suitable puller.
14. Remove fuel pump crash shield, if equipped.
15. Disconnect fuel outlet line from fuel pump.
16. Remove fuel pump attaching bolts and position pump aside with fuel line attached.
17. Remove oil filter, then disconnect lower radiator hose from water pump.
18. Remove oil pan as described under "Oil Pan, Replace".
19. Lower vehicle, then remove timing case cover attaching bolts, **Fig. 37.**

NOTE: Be sure to remove the cover attaching bolt located behind the oil filter adapter.

20. Remove ignition timing indicator, then

the timing case cover and water pump as an assembly.
21. Reverse procedure to install. Before installing bolt at location No. 10, **Fig. 37**, coat threads of bolt with pipe sealant D8AZ-19558-A or equivalent. Torque cover attaching bolts to 15—22 ft. lbs.

NOTE: If a replacement front cover is to be installed, the water pump, oil pump, oil filter adapter and intermediate shaft must be removed from the original front cover and reinstalled on the replacement cover. Also, it may be necessary to rotate crankshaft 180° from the No. 1 cylinder TDC location to position fuel pump eccentric for fuel pump installation. When installing distributor, No. 1 cylinder must be at TDC position and marks made during removal must be aligned.

6-300

1. Drain cooling system.
2. Remove shroud and radiator.
3. Remove alternator adjusting arm bolt, loosen drive belt and swing the adjusting arm aside.
4. Remove fan, drive belts, spacer and pulleys.
5. Remove vibration damper.
6. Remove the front oil pan and front cover attaching screw.
7. Remove timing case cover and discard gasket. Replace crankshaft oil seal with new one.
8. Reverse procedure to install.

V8-255, 302 & 351W

Ranchero

1. Drain cooling system, then remove carburetor air inlet tube.
2. Remove fan shroud attaching bolts and position shroud over fan.
3. Remove fan, spacer and shroud.
4. On models equipped with A/C, remove A/C compressor drive belt and idler pulley.

5. On models equipped with power steering, remove steering pump drive belt and the pump.
6. On all models, remove alternator drive belt and all brackets attached to water pump.
7. Remove water pump pulley, then disconnect hoses from water pump.
8. Drain engine oil, then remove crankshaft pulley and vibration damper.
9. Disconnect fuel outlet line from fuel pump, then remove fuel pump attaching bolts and position pump aside.
10. Remove oil level dipstick, then the timing case cover-to-oil pan attaching bolts.
11. Cut oil pan gasket flush with cylinder block face, then remove timing case cover and water pump as an assembly.
12. Reverse procedure to install. Apply RTV sealant to oil pan gasket surfaces.

E-100—350

1. Drain cooling system and, on 1981—85 models, remove radiator.
2. On models equipped with A/C, remove A/C idler pulley and bracket and compressor drive belt.
3. On all models, remove upper radiator hose, then the fan and shroud as an assembly.
4. Raise and support vehicle.
5. Remove alternator drive belt, then disconnect lower radiator hose from water pump.
6. Remove fuel pump, then lower vehicle.
7. Remove bypass hose, then the power steering pump drive belt (if equipped).
8. Remove pulley and disconnect heater hose from water pump.
9. On models equipped with A/C, remove A/C compressor upper bracket and (if equipped), the power steering pump mount from compressor and water pump.
10. On all models, remove crankshaft pulley and vibration damper.
11. Remove timing case cover-to-oil pan attaching bolts, then the timing case cover and water pump as an assembly.
12. Reverse procedure to install. Apply RTV sealant to oil pan-to-cylinder

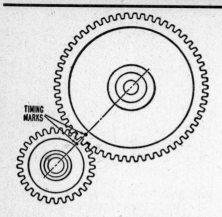

Fig. 38   Valve timing. 6-300

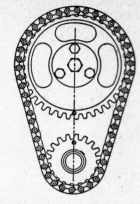

Fig. 39   Valve timing. Typical of V8 engines with timing chain

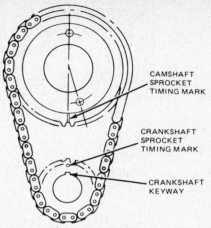

CAMSHAFT SPROCKET TIMING MARK

CRANKSHAFT SPROCKET TIMING MARK

CRANKSHAFT KEYWAY

Fig. 40   Timing marks aligned for correct valve timing. 1982 V6-232

block mating surface.

F-100—150 & Bronco
1. Drain cooling system, then remove fan shroud attaching bolts and position shroud over fan.
2. Disconnect hoses from water pump, then remove drive belts, fan, fan spacer and pulley.
3. Loosen alternator pivot bolt and the alternator adjusting arm-to-water pump attaching bolt.
4. Remove crankshaft pulley and vibration damper.
5. Disconnect fuel outlet line from fuel pump, then remove fuel pump attaching bolts and position pump aside.
6. On all models, remove timing case cover-to-oil pan attaching bolts.
7. Cut oil pan gasket flush with cylinder block face, then remove timing case cover and water pump as an assembly.
8. Reverse procedure to install. Apply RTV sealant to oil pan gasket surfaces.

V8-351M & 400
1. Drain cooling system and disconnect battery cables.
2. On Ranchero models, remove air inlet tube.
3. On all models, remove fan shroud attaching bolts and slide shroud rearward.
4. Remove fan and fan spacer from water pump shaft.
5. On models equipped with A/C, remove A/C compressor drive belt lower idler pulley and compressor mount-to-water pump bracket.
6. On all models, remove alternator drive belt, power steering pump drive belt (if equipped) and water pump pulley.
7. Remove alternator bracket and power steering pump bracket (if equipped) from water pump and position aside.
8. Disconnect heater hose and lower radiator hose from water pump.
9. Remove crankshaft pulley, vibration damper and timing pointer.
10. Remove timing case cover-to-cylinder block attaching bolts, then the timing

case cover and water pump as an assembly.
11. Reverse procedure to install. Apply suitable sealant to cylinder block and timing case cover gasket surfaces.

V8-460
1. Drain cooling system and engine oil.
2. Remove radiator shroud and fan, then disconnect radiator hoses from engine.
3. On models equipped with automatic transmission, disconnect oil cooler lines from radiator.
4. On all models, remove radiator upper support and radiator.
5. Loosen alternator mounting bolts and, on models equipped with A/C, the A/C compressor idler pulley.
6. Remove air pump (if equipped), drive belts and water pump pulley.
7. On models equipped with A/C, remove A/C compressor support from water pump.
8. On all models, remove crankshaft pulley, then the vibration damper and woodruff key.
9. Loosen bypass hose, then disconnect heater return tube from water pump.
10. Disconnect fuel lines from fuel pump, then remove pump. Plug open lines to prevent contamination.
11. Remove timing case cover attaching bolts, then the timing case cover and water pump as an assembly.
12. Reverse procedure to install. Apply suitable sealant to cylinder block and timing case cover gasket surfaces.

TIMING GEARS
6-300

CAUTION: When the crankshaft and camshaft lose their timing relationship through removal of timing gears, interference may occur between crankshaft and cam lobes. Therefore, to prevent possible damage to camshaft lobes, do not rotate crankshaft or camshaft without timing gears installed.

Camshaft Gear
1. With front cover removed, crank engine until timing gear marks are aligned as shown in **Fig. 38**.
2. Install gear puller and remove gear.
3. Be sure key and spacer are properly installed. Align keyway with key and install gear on camshaft.
4. Check backlash between crank and cam gear, using a dial indicator. Hold gear firmly against block while making check. Backlash should be between .002" and .004".

Crankshaft Gear
1. Remove timing gear case cover as previously described.
2. Remove gear using a suitable puller.
3. Remove key from crankshaft.
4. Reverse procedure to install. Ensure timing marks are aligned, **Fig. 38**.

TIMING CHAIN
V6-232, V8-255, 302, 351, 400 & 460

After removing the cover as outlined previously, remove the crankshaft front oil slinger, if equipped. On V6-232 engines, remove camshaft thrust button and spring from end of camshaft. Crank the engine until the timing marks are aligned as shown in **Figs. 39 and 40**. Remove camshaft sprocket retaining bolt, washer and fuel pump eccentric. Slide sprockets and chain forward and remove them as an assembly. Reverse the order of the foregoing procedure to install the chain and sprockets, being sure the timing marks are properly aligned.

CAMSHAFT
REPLACE

6-300
1. Disconnect battery ground cable.

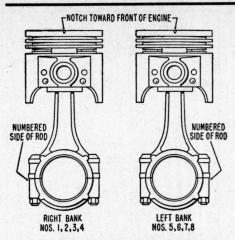

Fig. 41 Piston & rod assembly. V8-255, 302, 351, 400 & 460

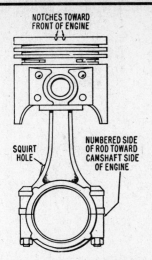

Fig. 42 Piston & rod assembly. 6-300

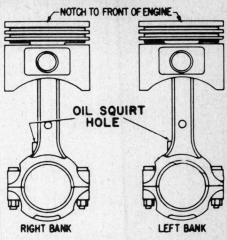

Fig 43 Piston & rod assembly. V6-232

2. Drain cooling system and oil pan.
3. Remove radiator, valve lifters & front cover.
4. Disconnect outlet lines at fuel pump and position fuel pump aside.
5. Remove distributor.
6. Rotate crankshaft to align timing marks, **Fig. 38.**
7. Remove camshaft thrust plate screws and the camshaft. Use caution not to damage the camshaft lobes when removing camshaft.
8. Reverse procedure to install.

V6-232

1. Remove radiator.
2. If equipped with air conditioning, remove condensor.
3. Remove grille, intake manifold and tappets, then remove front cover and timing chain.
4. Remove oil pan and remove camshaft

through front of engine, being careful not to damage bearing surfaces.
5. Reverse procedure to install.

V8 ENGINES

1. On Ranchero models with V8-302 and 351W engines, and all Econoline models except V8-351M and 400 engines, remove grille.
2. On all models, drain cooling system, then disconnect all lines and hoses from radiator and remove radiator.
3. Remove intake manifold, then the rocker arm covers.
4. Loosen rocker arms, then remove push rods and valve lifters in sequence.
5. Remove timing case cover and timing chain as previously described.
6. On models equipped with A/C, remove A/C condenser attaching bolts and position condenser aside.

7. On all models, remove camshaft thrust plate and carefully slide camshaft out through front of engine.
8. Reverse procedure to install.

PISTON & ROD
ASSEMBLE

Lubricate all parts with light engine oil. Position the connecting rod in the piston and push the pin into place, **Figs. 41, 42 and 43.** Insert new piston pin retainers (when used) by spiralling them into the piston with the fingers. Do not use pliers.

SERVICE BULLETIN Replacement pistons for the following 6-300 equipped vehicles have an increased ring land, which raises the top compression ring .035 inch: 1979–81 E & F-100–250 & Bronco except heavy duty. Before installing the new piston, the cylinder ridge must be removed to ensure that the top compression ring does not contact the ridge or deposits formed at the top of the cylinder bore. When removing the ridge, do not cut into the ring travel area more than 1/32 inch.

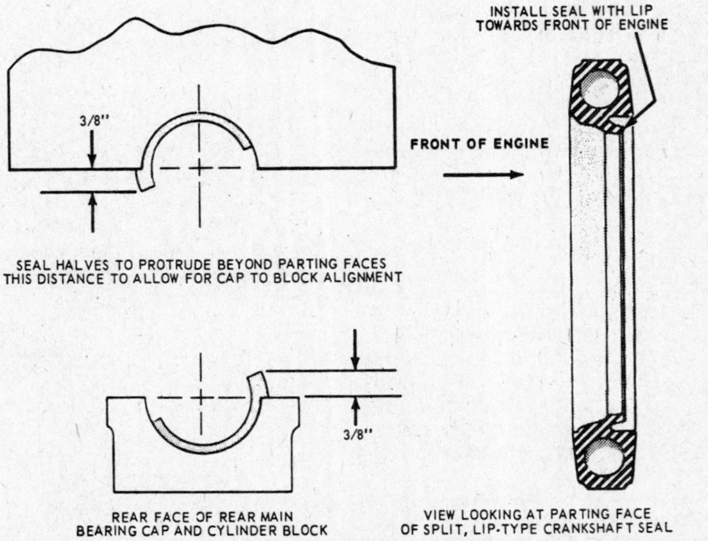

CRANKSHAFT REAR OIL SEAL
EXC. 6-300 & 1984–85 V8-302 & 351W

NOTE: Some 1985 V8-460 engines may use a one piece seal. Refer to "6-300 & 1984–85 V8-302 & 351W" for replacement procedure for one piece seal.

A new rubber split-lip rear crankshaft oil seal is released for service. This seal can be installed without removal of the crankshaft and also eliminates the necessity of seal installation tools.
1. Remove oil pan.
2. Remove rear main bearing cap.

Fig. 44 Crankshaft rear oil seal installation. All exc. 6-300 & 1984–85 V8-302 & 351W

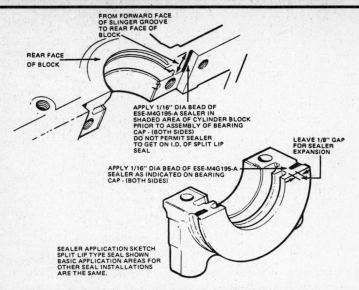

Fig. 45   Applying sealer to crankshaft rear oil seal. All exc. 6-300 & 1984—85 V8-302 & 351W

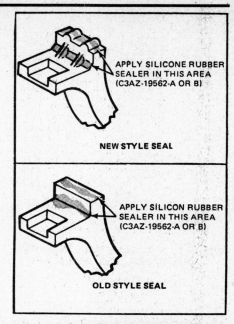

Fig. 46   Revised crankshaft rear oil seal

3. Loosen remaining bearing caps, allowing crankshaft to drop down about ⅟₃₂".
4. Remove old seals from both cylinder block and rear main bearing cap. Use a brass rod to drift upper half of seal from cylinder block groove. Rotate crankshaft while drifting to facilitate removal.
5. Carefully clean seal groove in block with a brush and solvent. Also clean seal groove in bearing cap. Remove the oil seal retaining pin from the bearing cap if so equipped. The pin is not used with the split-lip seal.
6. Dip seal halves in clean engine oil.
7. Carefully install upper seal half in its groove with undercut side of seal toward front of engine, **Fig. 44,** by rotating it on shaft journal of crankshaft until approximately ⅜" protrudes below the parting surface. Be sure no rubber has been shaved from outside diameter of seal by bottom edge of groove.

8. Retighten main bearing caps and torque to specifications.
9. Install lower seal in main bearing cap with undercut side of seal toward front of engine, and allow seal to protrude about ⅜" above parting surface to mate with upper seal upon cap installation.
10. Apply suitable sealer to parting faces of cap and block, **Fig. 45.** Install cap and torque to specifications.

NOTE: If difficulty is encountered in installing the upper half of the seal in position, lightly lap (sandpaper the side of the seal opposite the lip side using a medium grit paper). After sanding, the seal must be washed in solvent, then dipped in clean engine oil prior to installation.

SERVICE BULLETIN A revised crankshaft rear oil seal has been released for service. This new seal may be received when ordering an oil pan gasket kit and is installed in the same manner as described previously, **Fig. 46.**

6-300 & 1984—85 V8-302 & 351W

Removal

NOTE: If crankshaft rear oil seal replacement is the only operation being performed, it can be done in the vehicle. If the oil seal is being replaced in conjunction with a rear main bearing replacement, the engine must be removed from the vehicle. To replace the seal only, proceed as follows:

1. Remove starting motor.
2. Disconnect transmission from engine and slide it back. On manual shift transmission, remove clutch assem-

bly.
3. Remove flywheel and engine rear cover plate.
4. Use an awl to punch two holes in crankshaft rear oil seal. Punch holes on opposite sides of crankshaft and just above bearing cap-to-cylinder block split line. Insert a sheet metal screw in each hole.
5. Use two large screwdrivers or pry bars and pry against both screws at the same time to remove seal. It may be necessary to place small blocks of wood against cylinder block to provide a fulcrum point for pry bars. Use caution to avoid scratching or otherwise damaging crankshaft oil seal surfaces.

Installation
1. Clean oil seal recess in cylinder block

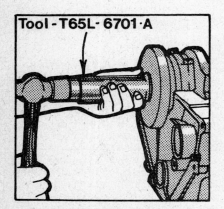

Fig. 47   Crankshaft rear oil seal installation. 6-300

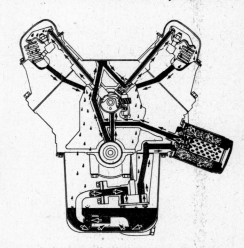

Engine oiling system. V8-302, 351, 400

and rear main bearing cap.

2. Coat new oil seal and crankshaft with a light film of engine oil.
3. Start seal in recess and install it until it is fully seated in seal recess, **Fig. 47.**
4. Be sure seal was not damaged during installation and reverse the procedure of removal to complete the operation.

OIL PAN
REPLACE

V6-232

1. Disconnect battery ground cable, then remove air cleaner.
2. Remove fan shroud attaching bolts and position shroud over fan.
3. Remove engine oil dipstick.
4. Raise and support vehicle.
5. Drain engine oil and remove oil filter.
6. Disconnect exhaust pipes from exhaust manifolds, then remove exhaust pipe-to-catalytic converter clamp and the exhaust pipe.
7. Disconnect shift linkage from transmission.
8. On models equipped with automatic transmission, disconnect oil cooler lines from radiator.
9. On all models, remove engine support-to-chassis brackets attaching nuts.
10. Raise engine assembly using a suitable jack and position wooden blocks between engine supports and chassis brackets, then lower engine to rest on blocks and remove jack.
11. Remove oil pan attaching bolts. Separate pick-up tube from oil pump and lay in oil pan, then remove oil pan from vehicle.
12. Reverse procedure to install.

6-300 EXC. ECONOLINE

1. Drain cooling system and engine oil.
2. Remove radiator.

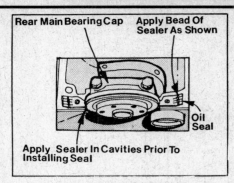

Rear Main Bearing Cap   Apply Bead Of Sealer As Shown

Oil Seal

Apply Sealer In Cavities Prior To Installing Seal

Fig. 48 Oil pan rear seal installation. 6-300

3. On 1981–85 F-100–250 California models, remove combination air bypass/air control valve from rear of engine.
4. On all models, raise and support vehicle.
5. Remove starter motor.
6. Remove engine front support insulator-to-support bracket attaching nuts and washers.
7. Raise front of engine using a suitable jack and wooden block. Position 1 inch wooden blocks between front support insulators and support brackets, then lower engine to rest on blocks and remove jack.
8. Remove oil pan and inlet tube attaching bolts.
9. Remove inlet tube and screen from oil pump and lay in oil pan, then remove oil pan from vehicle.
10. Reverse procedure to install, **Figs. 48 and 49.**

6-300 ECONOLINE

1. Remove engine cover, air cleaner and carburetor.
2. On vehicles equipped with air conditioning, discharge refrigerant system, then remove compressor.
3. Remove EGR valve if equipped, then

on E–250-HD and E–350 models disconnect thermactor check valve inlet hose and remove check valve.

4. Remove upper radiator hose, fan shroud and automatic transmission filler tube.
5. Remove nuts securing exhaust pipe to manifold.
6. Raise and support vehicle, then disconnect and plug fuel pump inlet hose. Remove alternator heat shield from engine support nuts.
7. Remove power steering return line clip from crossmember, then disconnect lower radiator hose and transmission cooler lines.
8. Remove starter, then raise engine and place 3 inch blocks under engine mounts. Remove oil pan dipstick tube from pan.
9. Remove oil pan bolts, then the pick-up screen and tube from oil pump. Remove the pan.
10. Reverse procedure to install, **Figs. 48 and 49.**

BRONCO V8-302 & 351W, EXC. 1980–85

1. Remove air cleaner and duct.
2. Remove oil level dipstick and tube.
3. Remove oil pan attaching bolts and remove oil pan.

ECONOLINE V8-255, 302 & 351W

1. Disconnect battery ground cable.
2. Remove engine cover and air cleaner, then drain cooling system.
3. On models equipped with power steering, remove steering pump drive belt, then unfasten pump and position aside.
4. On models equipped with A/C, unfasten A/C compressor and position aside.
5. On all models, disconnect upper radiator hose, then remove fan shroud attaching bolts, oil filler tube and oil dipstick-to-exhaust manifold attaching bolt.

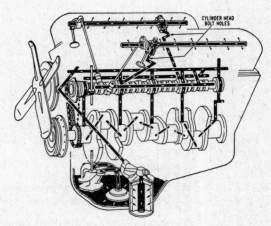

Engine oiling system. V8-460

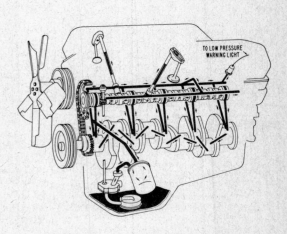

Engine oiling system. 6-300

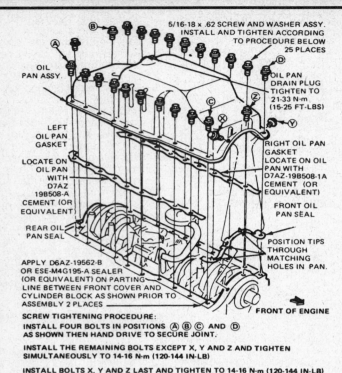

Fig. 49 Oil pan installation. 6-300 engine

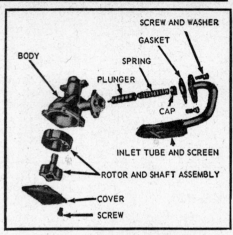

Fig. 50 Oil pump. 6-300

6. Raise and support vehicle.
7. Remove alternator splash shield, then disconnect lower radiator hose.
8. On models equipped with automatic transmission, disconnect oil cooler lines from radiator.
9. On all models, disconnect fuel line from fuel pump, then remove engine mount attaching nuts.
10. Drain engine oil, then remove dipstick tube from oil pan.
11. Disconnect exhaust pipes from exhaust manifolds.
12. On models equipped with automatic transmission, remove transmission oil dipstick and tube.
13. On all models, disconnect manual linkage from transmission, then remove center driveshaft support and driveshaft from transmission.
14. Raise engine and transmission assembly using a suitable jack and a wooden block. Position wooden blocks to support engine at uppermost position, then lower engine to rest on blocks.

NOTE: When raised, the engine and transmission assembly will pivot around the rear engine mount. The engine assembly must be lifted exactly four inches, measured from front mounts, and remain centered in the engine compartment.

15. Remove oil pan attaching bolts and lower the pan.
16. On all except 1981—85 models equipped with V8-351W engine, remove oil pump and pick-up tube

assembly and lay in oil pan.
17. On all models, remove oil pan from vehicle.
18. Reverse procedure to install.

F-100—350, & 1980—85 BRONCO V8-255, 302, 351W, 351M & 400 & 1979 ECONOLINE V8-351M & 400

1. Remove the oil level dipstick and tube, then remove the fan shroud attaching bolts and position shroud over the fan.
2. Remove engine mounts to chassis bracket retaining nuts.
3. If equipped with automatic transmission, disconnect the oil cooler line from the left side of the radiator.
4. On all vehicles equipped with V8-351M and 400 engines, remove starter.
5. Raise engine and place wooden blocks between the engine mounts and chassis brackets.
6. Drain the oil pan, then remove the oil pan attaching bolts and lower the oil pan onto the crossmember.
7. Remove the pickup tube attaching bolts then lower the pickup tube into the oil pan and remove the oil pan.
8. Reverse procedure to install.

RANCHERO V8-302, 351 & 400

1. Remove oil level dipstick.
2. Remove fan shroud attaching bolts

and position shroud over fan.
3. Raise and support vehicle.
4. Drain engine oil.
5. Lower or remove stabilizer bar as necessary.
6. Remove engine front support through bolts.
7. Raise engine using a suitable jack, then position wooden blocks between engine front supports and chassis brackets and lower engine to rest on blocks.
8. On models equipped with automatic transmission, disconnect oil cooler lines from radiator.
9. On all models, remove oil pan attaching bolts and lower the pan.
10. Remove pick-up tube and screen from oil pump, then remove oil pan from vehicle.
11. Reverse procedure to install.

1980—82 ECONOLINE V8-351M & 400

1. Perform steps 1 thru 8 as described under "Econoline V8-255, 302 & 351W."
2. Position suitable jack under oil pan and place 1¾ inch block of wood between pan and jack. Raise engine 2 inches.

NOTE: Do not raise engine more than 2 inches, as damage to the air conditioner system will result.

3. Position wood blocks under engine mounts, then lower engine onto mounts.
4. Remove oil pan from vehicle.
5. Reverse procedure to install.

1979 V8-460 EXCEPT ECONOLINE

1. Disconnect battery ground cable, then disconnect radiator shroud and place it over the fan.
2. Support vehicle on hoist and drain crankcase.
3. Remove engine support thru bolts,

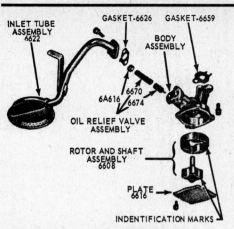

Fig. 51   Oil pump. V8-255, 302, 351W

then place a floor jack under front edge of oil pan with wood block between oil pan and jack.
4. Raise engine enough to place 1¼ inch wood blocks between insulators and brackets and remove floor jack.
5. Remove oil filter, then remove oil pan bolts and oil pan.

NOTE: It may be necessary to rotate crankshaft to obtain clearance between the crankshaft throws and oil pan.

6. Reverse procedure to install.

V8-460 1979 ECONOLINE & 1980—85 ALL

1. Remove engine cover, then disconnect battery ground cable and drain cooling system.
2. Remove air cleaner, then disconnect throttle and transmission linkages from carburetor.
3. Disconnect power brake vacuum line, if equipped.
4. Disconnect fuel line and choke lines, then remove air cleaner adapter from carburetor.
5. Disconnect upper and lower radiator hoses and transmission oil cooler lines (if equipped) from radiator.
6. Remove fan shroud, fan and radiator.
7. On models equipped with power steering, unfasten steering pump and position aside.
8. On all models, remove front engine mount through bolts, then the engine oil dipstick tube.
9. On models equipped with A/C, move refrigerant lines from rear of compressor downward to clear dash, or remove lines if necessary.
10. On all models, raise and support vehicle.
11. Drain engine oil and remove oil filter.
12. Remove muffler inlet pipe assembly, then disconnect manual and kickdown linkages from transmission.
13. Remove driveshaft and coupling shaft assembly, then the transmission dipstick tube.

14. Remove dipstick and tube from oil pan, then position a suitable jack and a wooden block under oil pan. Raise engine slightly until transmission contacts floor, then block engine in place at the mounts.

NOTE: The engine assembly must be raised exactly four inches and remain centered in the engine compartment to remove the oil pan.

15. Remove oil pan attaching bolts and lower the pan.
16. Remove oil pump and pick-up tube assembly and lay in oil pan, then slide oil pan rearward and remove from vehicle.
17. Reverse procedure to install.

OIL PUMP
REPLACE

6-300

1. After removing oil pan as outlined previously, unfasten and remove oil pump.
2. Prime pump with engine oil.
3. Coat a new pump gasket with oil-resistant sealer and place it on pump.
4. Install pump and oil pan.

V6-232

NOTE: On these engines the oil pump is contained within the front cover.

1. If necessary remove oil filter.
2. Remove oil pump cover attaching bolts and remove cover.
3. Lift pump gears off pocket in front cover.
4. Remove cover gasket. Discard gasket.
5. If necessary, remove pump gears from cover.
6. Reverse procedure to install. If gears have been removed, pack gear pocket with petroleum jelly. Do not use chassis lubricants.

V8 ENGINES

NOTE: On some models, the oil pump must be removed when removing the oil pan. These models are indicated in the "Oil Pan, Replace" procedures.

1. Remove oil pan as previously described.
2. Remove oil pump attaching bolts and the oil pump.
3. To install, prime pump with engine oil and apply sealant to gasket.
4. Insert distributor intermediate shaft, making sure that it is properly seated, then install oil pump.

NOTE: Do not force pump into place if it will not readily seat, as the intermediate shaft may be misaligned with distributor

Fig. 52   Oil pump assembly. 351M & 400

shaft. To align, rotate intermediate shaft until pump can be seated without applying force.

5. Install oil pan.

OIL PUMP
SERVICE

ROTOR TYPE PUMP

1. To disassemble, **Figs. 50, 51 and 52**, remove cover, inner rotor and shaft assembly and outer race. Remove staking marks at relief valve chamber cap. Insert a self-threading sheet metal screw of proper diameter into oil pressure relief valve chamber cap and pull cap out of chamber. Then remove spring and plunger.
2. To assemble, install pressure relief valve plunger, spring and a new cap. Stake cap in place. Install outer race, inner rotor and shaft.

NOTE: Be sure identification dimple mark on outer race is facing outward and on the same side as dimple on rotor. Inner rotor and shaft and outer race are furnished only as a unit. One part should not be replaced without replacing the other.

3. Install pump cover.

WATER PUMP
REPLACE

NOTE: All water pumps have a sealed bearing integral with the water pump shaft. The bearing requires no lubrication. A bleed hole in the pump housing allows water that may leak past the seal to be thrown out by the slinger. This is not a lubrication hole. If the pump is damaged and requires repair, replace it with a new pump or a rebuilt one.

V6-232

1. Drain cooling system.
2. Remove air cleaner and air intake duct.
3. Remove fan and clutch assembly and the fan shroud.
4. Loosen accessory drive idler, then remove drive belt and water pump pulley.
5. On models equipped with power steering, unfasten steering pump and position aside.
6. On models equipped with A/C, remove A/C compressor front support bracket.
7. On all models, disconnect heater hose and bypass hose from water pump.
8. Remove water pump attaching bolts and the water pump.
9. Reverse procedure to install.

SERVICE BULLETIN Prior to installing the No. 1 bolt, **Fig. 53**, sealant No. D8AZ-19554-A or equivalent must be applied to the bolt threads.

6-300

1. Drain cooling system, then remove alternator drive belt.
2. On models equipped with A/C, remove A/C compressor drive belt.
3. On all models, remove fan and water pump pulley.
4. Disconnect hoses from water pump.
5. Remove water pump attaching bolts and the water pump.
6. Reverse procedure to install.

V8-255, 302 & 351W

Ranchero

1. Drain cooling system and remove carburetor air inlet tube.
2. Remove fan shroud attaching bolts and position shroud over fan.
3. Remove fan, fan spacer and shroud.
4. On models equipped with A/C, remove A/C compressor drive belt and idler pulley bracket.
5. On all models, remove alternator drive belt, then the power steering pump (if equipped).
6. Remove all accessory brackets attached to water pump.
7. Remove water pump pulley, then disconnect all hoses from water pump.
8. Remove water pump attaching bolts and the water pump.
9. Reverse procedure to install.

E-100-350

1. Remove air cleaner and intake duct assembly, including crankcase ventilation hose.

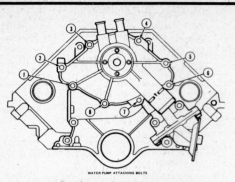

Fig. 53 Water pump installation. V6-232 engine

2. Drain cooling system, then remove radiator.
3. Remove drive belts, fan, spacer and water pump pulley.
4. Disconnect heater and bypass hoses from water pump.
5. Remove water pump attaching bolts and the water pump.
6. Reverse procedure to install.

F-100-350 & Bronco

1. Drain cooling system.
2. Remove fan shroud attaching bolts and position shroud over fan.
3. Disconnect lower radiator hose, heater hose and bypass hose from water pump.
4. Remove drive belts, fan, spacer, water pump pulley and fan shroud.
5. Loosen alternator pivot bolt and alternator adjusting arm-to-water pump attaching bolt.
6. Remove water pump attaching bolts and the water pump.
7. Reverse procedure to install.

V8-351M & 400

1. Disconnect battery ground cable, then drain cooling system.
2. On Ranchero models, remove carburetor air inlet tube.
3. On all models, remove fan shroud attaching bolts and slide shroud rearward.
4. Remove fan and fan spacer.
5. On models equipped with A/C, remove A/C compressor drive belt, lower idler pulley and compressor mount-to-water pump bracket.
6. On all models, remove alternator drive belt and power steering pump drive belt (if equipped).
7. Remove water pump pulley, then the alternator bracket from water pump.
8. On models equipped with power steering, unfasten steering pump bracket from water pump and position aside.
9. On all models, disconnect lower radiator hose and heater hose from water pump.
10. Remove water pump attaching bolts

and the water pump.
11. Reverse procedure to install.

V8-460

1. Drain cooling system, then remove fan shroud and fan.
2. On models equipped with power steering, loosen steering pump attaching bolts.
3. On models equipped with A/C, remove A/C compressor upper bracket, then the idler arm and bracket, compressor drive belt and power steering pump drive belt (if equipped).
4. On models equipped with Thermactor, remove Thermactor pump.
5. On all models, loosen alternator pivot bolt, then remove attaching bolts and spacer.
6. Remove alternator adjustment arm bolt, pivot bolt and drive belt, then the alternator and bracket as an assembly.
7. On all models equipped with power steering, remove steering pump attaching bolts and position pump aside.
8. On all models, disconnect lower radiator hose and heater hose from water pump.
9. Remove water pump attaching bolts and the water pump.
10. Reverse procedure to install.

FUEL PUMP
REPLACE

1. Loosen fuel line connections, then retighten hand tight. Do not disconnect lines at this time.
2. Loosen fuel pump attaching bolts one or two turns. Apply hand force to break pump free from gasket.
3. Rotate engine slightly until pump cam lobe is near lowest position.
4. Disconnect inlet and outlet lines and the vapor return line, if equipped, from pump.
5. Remove fuel pump attaching bolts and the pump. Remove and discard gasket.
6. Reverse procedure to install.

BELT TENSION DATA

		New Lbs.	Used Lbs.
1979–82	Exc. ¼ inch	65	50
	¼ inch	140	105
1983	V6-232 1	170	150
1983–85	Exc. Air Pump	140	120
	Air Pump Exc. 6-300 less A/C	110	90
	6-300 less A/C	70	50

Diesel Engine Section
V8-420, 6.9L Engine

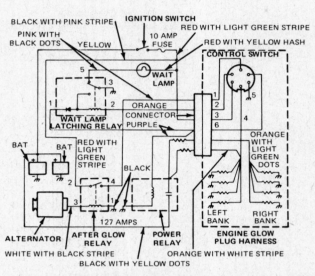

Fig. 1   Glow plug system wiring diagram. 1983

GLOW PLUG FAST START SYSTEM

The glow plug fast start system controls glow plug operation according to various operating conditions. When the ignition switch is turned on, the control switch is energized, which, in turn, energizes the power relay. The power relay contacts close and battery current is directed to the glow plugs. When the glow plugs reach a predetermined temperature, current to the plugs and the wait lamp is cut off. At this time, the engine can be started. After the engine is started, the glow plugs will cycle on and off for 40–90 seconds. This cycling of the glow plugs helps to eliminate start-up exhaust smoke.

A control switch, threaded into the cylinder head coolant jacket, senses engine coolant temperature. When restarting a warm engine, the glow plug system will not be activated unless the coolant temperature falls below normal operating temperature.

Refer to **Figs. 1 and 2** for troubleshooting the glow plug system.

ENGINE
REPLACE

E-250–350

1. Disconnect battery ground cables and remove engine cover.
2. Drain cooling system, then remove front bumper, grille assembly and gravel deflector.
3. On models equipped with speed control, unfasten speed control servo bracket and position aside.
4. On all models, scribe hood latch location, then remove latch and cable assembly from grille upper support bracket.
5. Remove upper grille support.
6. On models equipped with A/C, discharge refrigerant from system, then remove A/C condenser.
7. On all models, disconnect transmission oil cooler lines from oil cooler and radiator, then remove oil cooler with mounting brackets.
8. Disconnect radiator hoses from engine, then remove fan shroud, fan and radiator.

NOTE: The fan retaining nut has left hand threads.

9. Remove vacuum pump and drive belt, then disconnect vacuum line from transmission modulation pipe.
10. Remove alternator adjusting arm, adjusting arm bracket and drive belt,

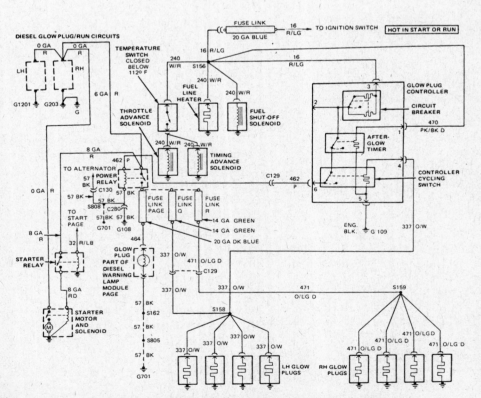

Fig. 2   Glow plug system wiring diagram. 1984–85

F–109

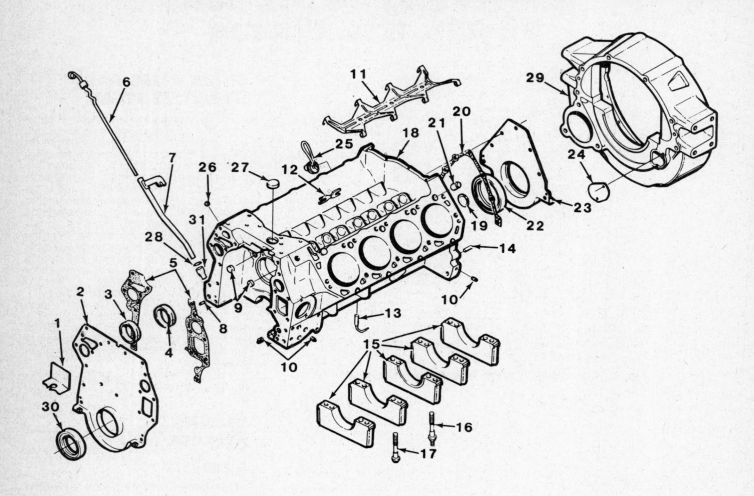

1. Timing Indicator
2. Front Cover
3. Bushing
4. Bushing
5. Front Cover Gaskets
6. Oil Level Gauge
7. Oil Level Gauge Tube, Upper
8. Dowel Pin
9. Cup Plug
10. Pipe Plug
11. Guide Retainer
12. Cam Follower Guide
13. Piston Cooling Tube
14. Dowel Pin
15. Bearing Cap
16. Bolt

17. Bolt
18. Crankcase with Plugs
19. Expansion Plugs
20. Rear Cover Gasket
21. Dowel Sleeve
22. Rear Oil Seal
23. Crankcase Rear Cover
24. Access Cover Plate
25. Block Heater
26. Ball 11/32''
27. Expansion Plug
28. "O" Ring
29. Flywheel Housing
30. Front Oil Seal
31. Oil Level Gauge Tube, Lower

Cylinder block assembly

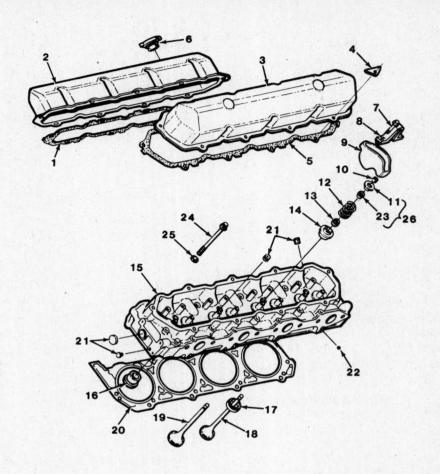

Cylinder head assembly

1. Valve Cover Gasket
2. Valve Cover (RH Side)
3. Valve Cover (LH Side)
4. Washer
5. Valve Cover Gasket
6. Closing Cap
7. Rocker Arm Bolt
8. Rocker Arm Post
9. Rocker Arm
10. Retainer Lock
11. Valve Spring Retainer
12. Valve Spring w/Damper
13. Valve Stem Seal (Intake Only)
14. Valve Rotator
15. Cylinder Head
16. Combustion Chamber Insert
17. Exhaust Valve Seat
18. Exhaust Valve
19. Intake Valve
20. Cylinder Head Gasket
21. Pipe Plug
22. Ball
23. Oil Shield
24. Cylinder Head Bolt
25. Washer
26. Spring Retainer Assembly

then pivot alternator inward toward engine.

11. Disconnect alternator electrical connectors from alternator and fuel line heater.
12. Disconnect water temperature sender electrical connector from left front of cylinder block.
13. Disconnect water temperature overheat lamp switch electrical connector from top front of left cylinder head.
14. Remove engine ground cables from bottom front of engine.
15. On models equipped with power steering, remove steering pump and bracket, then disconnect and plug return line from steering pump and position pump aside.
16. On models equipped with A/C, disconnect refrigerant lines from A/C compressor.
17. On all models, disconnect vacuum hose between injection pump and vacuum regulator valve and position aside.
18. Disconnect and cap fuel heater inlet line from fuel filter and fuel pump.
19. Remove air cleaner and intake duct and place a suitable cover over intake manifold opening.
20. Disconnect and cap fuel filter outlet line from fuel filter and injection pump, then cover the injection pump and fuel filter openings.
21. Remove fuel filter return line, then the fuel filter and bracket as an assembly.
22. On models equipped with A/C, loosen A/C compressor mounting bolts and rotate compressor toward engine.
23. On all models, disconnect and plug fuel inlet line at fuel pump.
24. Disconnect accelerator and speed control cables (if equipped) from injection pump and bracket on intake manifold and position aside. Remove cable bracket.
25. Disconnect engine wiring harnesses and position aside.
26. Remove transmission kickdown rod, then disconnect heater hose from water pump and right cylinder head.
27. On models equipped with A/C and/or auxiliary heater, remove hoses from bracket at left rear of engine.
28. On all models, disconnect oil pressure sender electrical connector from rear of engine.
29. Disconnect fuel return line from left rear of engine, then remove transmission oil dipstick tube attaching bolt from rear of right cylinder head.
30. Remove engine oil dipstick and tube.
31. Remove ground cable-to-cylinder block attaching bolt, then the 4 upper transmission-to-engine attaching bolts.
32. Raise and support vehicle.
33. Remove engine mount attaching nuts, then disconnect exhaust pipe from exhaust manifolds.
34. Remove converter inspection plate, then the 4 converter-to-flywheel attaching nuts.
35. Remove starter cable, then move fuel

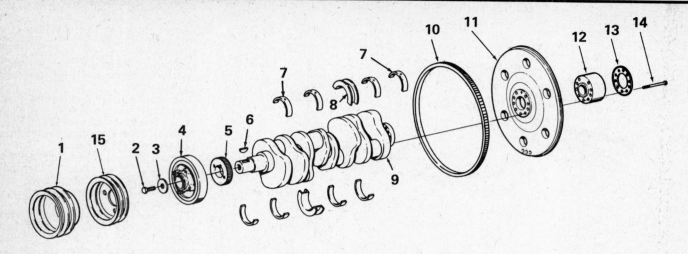

1. Pulley, Generator Drive
2. Screw
3. Crankshaft Washer
4. Vibration Damper
5. Crankshaft Gear
6. Woodruff Key
7. Bearing
8. Thrust Bearing
9. Crankshaft
10. Ring Gear
11. Flywheel
12. Flywheel Adapter
13. Reinforcement Ring
14. Bolt
15. Pulley, Crankshaft

Crankshaft assembly

line on No. 1 crossmember down and aside.
36. Lower vehicle and attach suitable lifting equipment to engine.
37. Support transmission with a suitable jack and remove remaining engine-to-transmission attaching bolts.
38. Separate engine from transmission, then raise engine high enough to clear No. 1 crossmember. Move engine forward and remove from vehicle.
39. Reverse procedure to install.

F-250—350

1. Disconnect battery ground cables and remove hood.
2. Drain cooling system, then remove air cleaner and intake duct assembly.
3. Place a suitable cover over intake manifold opening.
4. Remove fan shroud, then the fan and clutch assembly.

NOTE: The fan retaining nut has left hand threads.

5. Disconnect upper and lower hoses and the automatic transmission cooler lines from radiator.
6. Remove radiator.
7. If equipped, remove A/C compressor drive belt, then remove and position compressor on radiator upper support.

port.
8. Remove power steering pump drive belt and remove and position pump aside.
9. Disconnect fuel supply line heater and alternator wiring from alternator.
10. Remove oil pressure sender from firewall and lay sender on engine.
11. Disconnect accelerator cable and speed control cable, if equipped, from injection pump.
12. Remove accelerator cable bracket, with cables, from intake manifold and position aside.
13. If equipped, disconnect transmission kickdown rod from injection pump.
14. Disconnect main wiring harness connector from right side of engine.
15. Disconnect ground strap from rear of engine.
16. Disconnect fuel return hose from left rear of engine.
17. Remove two upper engine-to-transmission attaching bolts.
18. Disconnect heater hoses from water pump and right hand cylinder head.
19. Disconnect water temperature sender wiring from left front of cylinder block.
20. Disconnect water temperature overheat light switch from top front of left hand cylinder head.
21. Raise and support vehicle.
22. Disconnect battery ground cables

from lower front of engine and remove from vehicle.
23. Disconnect and plug fuel inlet line from supply pump.
24. Disconnect starter motor wiring.
25. Disconnect exhaust pipe from exhaust manifold.
26. Remove bolts attaching front engine mounts from front crossmember.
27. Remove flywheel cover, then the converter-to-flywheel attaching nuts.
28. Lower vehicle and support transmission with a suitable jack.
29. Attach suitable engine lifting equipment to engine and raise engine slightly to clear the front crossmember and pull engine forward. Move front of engine approximately 45 degrees toward the left side of engine compartment, then lift engine from vehicle.

NOTE: Use care not to damage the wiper motor when removing engine.

30. Reverse procedure to install.

INTAKE MANIFOLD
REPLACE

1. Disconnect battery ground cables.
2. On E-250—350 models, remove engine cover.
3. On all models, remove air cleaner and

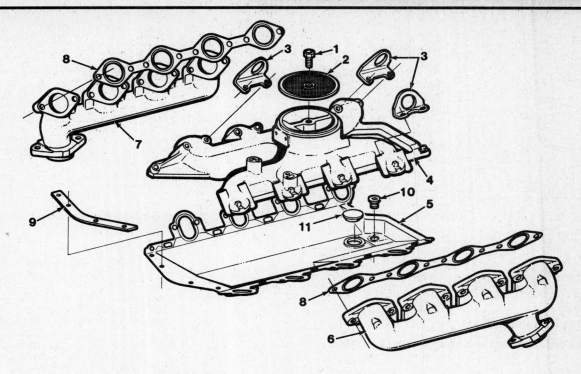

1. Stud
2. Guard
3. Lifting Bracket
4. Intake Manifold
5. Valley Pan and Gasket
6. L.H. Exhaust Manifold

7. R.H. Exhaust Manifold
8. Exhaust Manifold Gasket
9. Valley Pan Strap
10. Valley Pan Drain Plug
11. Valley Pan Closing Plug

Fig. 3   Manifold assemblies

place a suitable cover over intake manifold opening.
4. On E-250–350 models, disconnect fuel inlet and return lines from fuel filter, then remove fuel filter and bracket as an assembly.
5. On all models, remove injection pump as described under "Injection Pump, Replace."
6. On F-250–350 models, disconnect

fuel return lines from rear injection nozzles and remove return lines to fuel tank.
7. On all models, disconnect engine harness ground wire from rear left of cylinder head, then remove engine wiring harness from engine.
8. Remove intake manifold attaching bolts and the intake manifold, **Fig. 3**.
9. Reverse procedure to install. Torque

attaching bolts to specifications in sequence shown in **Fig. 4**.

EXHAUST MANIFOLD
REPLACE

E-250–350

1. Disconnect battery ground cables, then remove engine cover.
2. If removing right-hand manifold, proceed as follows:
   a. Remove fan shroud halves.
   b. Remove engine oil dipstick and tube and transmission filler tube and dipstick.
   c. Raise and support vehicle.
   d. Remove right-hand engine mount insulator-to-frame attaching nuts.
   e. Raise right side of engine slightly until fuel filter header touches body sheet metal, then install a wooden block between insulator and frame and lower engine to rest on block.
   f. Disconnect exhaust pipe from exhaust manifold, then lower vehicle.
   g. Bend back tabs on manifold attach-

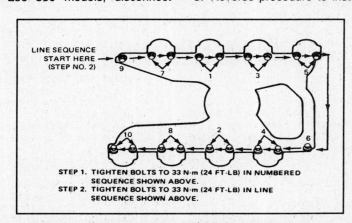

Fig. 4   Intake manifold tightening sequence

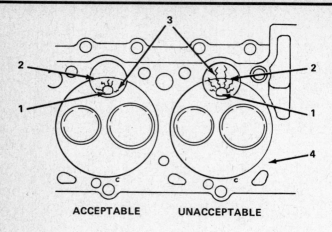

1. Throat of Pre-Combustion Chamber
2. Fire Ring Mark
3. Cracks
4. Cylinder Head (Bottom View)

Fig. 5   Pre-combustion chamber inspection

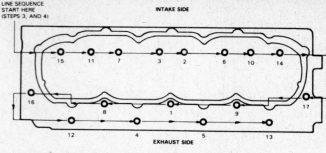

STEP 1: TORQUE BOLTS TO 40 LB. FT. IN NUMBERED SEQUENCE SHOWN ABOVE.
STEP 2: TORQUE BOLTS TO 70 LB. FT. IN NUMBERED SEQUENCE SHOWN ABOVE.
STEP 3: TORQUE BOLTS TO 80 LB. FT. IN LINE SEQUENCE SHOWN ABOVE.
STEP 4: REPEAT STEP 3.

Fig. 6   Cylinder head tightening sequence

ing bolts, then remove bolts and the manifold.
3. If removing left-hand manifold, proceed as follows:
   a. Raise and support vehicle.
   b. Disconnect exhaust pipe from exhaust manifold, then lower vehicle.
   c. Bend back tabs on manifold attaching bolts, then remove bolts and the manifold.
4. Reverse procedure to install.

F-250—350

1. Disconnect battery ground cables.
2. Raise and support vehicle.
3. Disconnect exhaust pipe from exhaust manifold.
4. If removing left manifold, bend tabs for manifold attaching bolts, then remove bolts and the manifold.
5. If removing right manifold, lower vehicle, then bend tabs for manifold attaching bolts and remove the attaching bolts and manifold.
6. Reverse procedure to install.

CYLINDER HEAD
REPLACE

NOTE: The procedure outlined below is for the right bank cylinder head. The left bank cylinder head is removed in a similar manner.

1. On E-250—350 models, remove engine cover.

2. On all models, disconnect battery ground cables, then drain cooling system.
3. Remove fan shroud halves, then the fan and clutch assembly.

NOTE: The fan retaining nut has left-hand threads.

4. Disconnect fuel supply line heater and alternator electrical connectors from alternator.
5. Remove alternator and vacuum pump.
6. On F-250—350 models, disconnect and plug fuel lines from fuel filter.
7. Remove alternator and vacuum pump mounting bracket, and on F-250—350 models, the fuel filter and bracket as an assembly.
8. Remove heater hose from cylinder head.
9. Remove injection pump as described under "Injection Pump, Replace."
10. Remove intake manifold as described under "Intake Manifold, Replace."
11. Raise and support vehicle.
12. Disconnect exhaust pipe from exhaust manifold.
13. Remove transmission filler tube attaching bolt, then lower vehicle and remove engine oil dipstick and tube.
14. Remove valve cover, rocker arms and push rods.
15. Remove injection nozzles and glow plugs.
16. Remove cylinder head attaching bolts.
17. On E-250—350 models, install suitable bar through rings on lifting eyes, then lift cylinder head from engine.

18. On F-250—350 models, attach hoist to lifting eyes and lift cylinder head from engine.

NOTE: Clean the pre-combustion chambers and inspect for cracks or burns. Some cracking and burning is acceptable, **Fig. 5.** When installed, the pre-combustion chambers may seat from .003 inch above to .001 inch below the cylinder head.

19. Reverse procedure to install. Torque cylinder head attaching bolts in sequence to specifications as shown in **Fig. 6.** Torque intake manifold attaching bolts in sequence, **Figs. 3 and 4,** to specifications.

ROCKER ARMS & PUSH RODS
REPLACE

1. Disconnect battery ground cables.
2. On E-250—350 models, remove fan shroud halves and the engine cover.
3. If working on right-hand cylinder bank on E-250—350 models, proceed as follows:
   a. Remove engine oil dipstick and tube assembly and the valve cover bracket.
   b. Remove transmission dipstick and filler tube.
   c. Raise and support vehicle.
   d. Remove right-hand engine mount insulator-to-frame attaching nuts.
   e. Raise right side of engine slightly until fuel filter header touches body sheet metal, then install a wooden block between insulator and frame and lower engine to rest on block.
   f. Lower vehicle.
4. On all models, remove valve cover attaching screws and the valve cover.
5. Remove rocker arm post mounting bolts.
6. Remove rocker arms and posts, and the pushrods in order so they may be installed in their original positions.
7. Reverse procedure to install. Install rocker arm post attaching bolts with

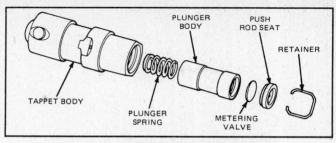

Fig. 7 Valve lifter, disassembled

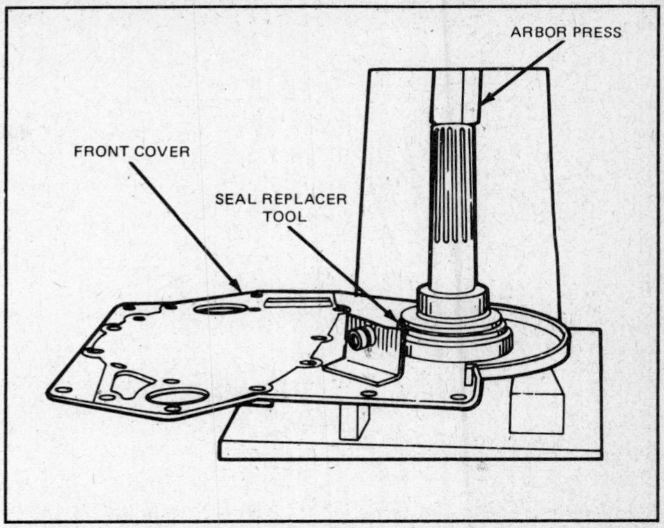

timing mark set at 11 o'clock position, as viewed from front of engine, and torque to 20 ft. lbs.

VALVE ARRANGEMENT
FRONT TO REAR

Left . . . . I-E-I-E-I-E-I-E
Right . . . . E-I-E-I-E-I-E-I

VALVE GUIDES
REPLACE

If valve guides are damaged, or are larger than specifications allow, install repair insert as follows:
1. Drill out valve guide, then ream the drilled bore to correct size for insert sleeve.
2. Chill insert in dry ice, then carefully press insert in place.
3. Finish insert with reamer to specified valve guide diameter.

NOTE: Re-face valve seat after valve guide has been reamed, then, using a suitable scraping tool, break the sharp corner at top of valve guide.

VALVE LIFTERS
REPLACE

1. Remove intake manifold as described under "Intake Manifold, Replace".
2. Remove crankcase Depression Regulator (CDR) tube and grommet from valley pan.
3. Remove valley pan strap and drain plug, then the valley pan.
4. Remove rocker arms and push rods as described under "Rocker Arms & Pushrods, Replace".
5. Remove guide retainer, then the guides and valve lifters.
6. Reverse procedure to install.

VALVE LIFTERS
SERVICE

1. Disassemble valve lifter, **Fig. 7,** then

clean all parts in solvent and wipe dry.
2. If any parts of lifter are worn or damaged, or plunger is not free in body, replace entire assembly.
3. Check that roller rotates freely and is not worn or damaged.
4. Lubricate all components with clean engine oil, then assemble as shown in **Fig. 7.**

TORSIONAL DAMPER
REPLACE

1. Disconnect battery ground cables.
2. Remove fan shroud, then the fan and clutch assembly.

NOTE: The fan retaining nut has left-hand threads.

3. Remove drive belts.
4. Raise and support vehicle.
5. Remove crankshaft pulley.
6. Remove damper-to-crankshaft attaching bolt, then the damper.
7. Reverse procedure to install.

ENGINE FRONT COVER
REPLACE

1. Disconnect battery ground cables, then drain cooling system.
2. Remove air cleaner. Install intake air opening cap, tool T83T-9424-A.
3. Remove fan shroud, then the fan and

clutch assembly.

NOTE: The fan retaining nut has left-hand threads.

4. Remove fuel injection pump, injection pump adapter and water pump.
5. Raise and support vehicle.
6. Remove torsional damper, then disconnect ground cables from front of engine.
7. Remove front cover-to-engine block and oil pan attaching bolts.
8. Lower vehicle.
9. Remove front cover-to-engine block attaching bolts, then the front cover.
10. Using tool T80T-4000-W, remove seal from front cover, **Fig. 8.**
11. Reverse procedure to install. Lubricate new oil seal with DOAZ-19584-A grease, or equivalent. Apply a bead of sealant to mating surface as shown in **Fig. 9.**

FRONT OIL SEAL
REPLACE

1. Remove torsional damper, then pry seal out of cover.
2. To install new seal on engines without three weldnuts on front cover, position seal into tool T83T-6700 and install over end of crankshaft. Install tool T83T-6316-B over installation tool and tighten nut against tool and washer to seat seal.
3. To install new seal on engines with three weldnuts on front cover, position seal in tool T83T-6700-A and install over end of crankshaft. Attach bridge to weldnuts and draw seal into front cover by turning center screw clockwise.

Fig. 8 Engine front cover seal replacement

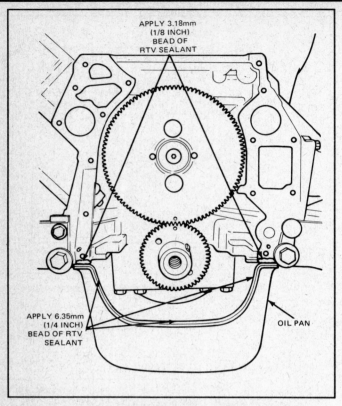

APPLY 3.18mm (1/8 INCH) BEAD OF RTV SEALANT

APPLY 6.35mm (1/4 INCH) BEAD OF RTV SEALANT

OIL PAN

Fig. 9   Engine front cover installation

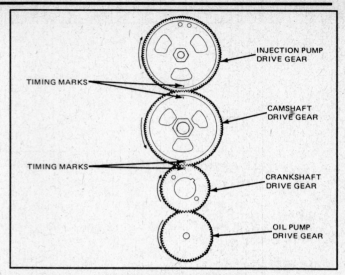

INJECTION PUMP DRIVE GEAR

TIMING MARKS

CAMSHAFT DRIVE GEAR

TIMING MARKS

CRANKSHAFT DRIVE GEAR

OIL PUMP DRIVE GEAR

Fig. 10   Timing gear alignment

NOTE: Prior to installation, lubricate oil seal with DOAZ-19584-A, or equivalent.

TIMING GEARS
REPLACE

1. Remove front cover.
2. Remove crankshaft drive gear, then the camshaft drive gear using tool T83T-6316-A.

NOTE: When removing crankshaft drive gear, use a breaker bar to prevent crankshaft rotation.

3. Reverse procedure to install. Align timing marks as shown in **Fig. 10.**

NOTE: The crankshaft drive gear may be heated in an oven to 300–350° F, to ease installation.

CAMSHAFT
REPLACE

1. Remove engine as described under "Engine, Replace".
2. Remove injection pump and adapter, intake manifold, valve lifters, engine front cover and fuel supply pump.
3. Remove camshaft drive gear, fuel supply pump cam, spacer and thrust plate from camshaft, **Fig. 11.**

4. Remove camshaft using tools T65L-6250-A and Rotunda 14-0314, or equivalent.
5. Reverse procedure to install. Lubricate camshaft lobes with DOAZ-19584-A grease, or equivalent, and the journals with clean engine oil.

PISTON & ROD ASSEMBLY

Assemble piston to rod so that connecting rod weight pad is installed on the opposite side of the piston as the relief pocket, **Fig. 12.** Install the piston into the cylinder so the piston relief pocket is on the camshaft side of the engine and the arrow on the piston top also faces the camshaft side of the engine, **Fig. 12.**

PISTON & RINGS

Pistons are available in standard sizes and oversize of .003 inch.

FLYWHEEL, ENGINE REAR COVER & OIL SEAL
REPLACE

1. Remove transmission, then the clutch and clutch housing.
2. Remove flywheel, then the rear cov-

er.
3. Using an arbor press and a 4⅛ inch spacer, remove oil seal.
4. Reverse procedure to install. Lubricate new oil seal with DOAZ-19584-A grease, or equivalent. Apply suitable sealant to sealing surfaces. Torque flywheel attaching bolts to specifications.

FLYWHEEL RING GEAR
REPLACE

1. Using a blow torch, heat ring gear on engine side of gear, then knock gear off of flywheel.
2. To install gear, heat it evenly until it expands enough to press onto flywheel.

NOTE: Do not allow temperature of ring gear to exceed 500° F.

OIL PAN & OIL PUMP
REPLACE

1. Disconnect battery ground cables, then remove engine oil and transmission oil dipsticks.
2. Remove air cleaner and install intake opening cover, tool T83T-9424-A.
3. Remove fan and clutch assembly.

NOTE: The fan retaining nut has left hand threads.

4. Drain cooling system, then disconnect lower radiator hose.
5. Disconnect return hose from power steering pump, then plug pump and hose to prevent contamination.
6. Disconnect fuel line heater connector and wiring harness from alternator.
7. Raise and support vehicle.

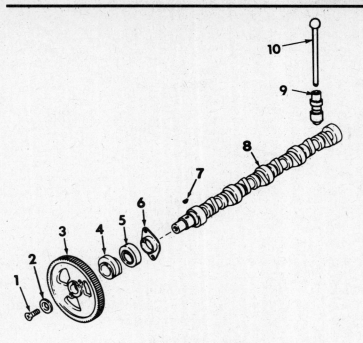

1. Camshaft Screw
2. Camshaft Washer
3. Camshaft Gear
4. Fuel Pump Cam
5. Thrust Flange Spacer
6. Thrust Flange
7. Woodruff Key
8. Camshaft
9. Cam Follower
10. Valve Push Rod

Fig. 11   Camshaft assembly

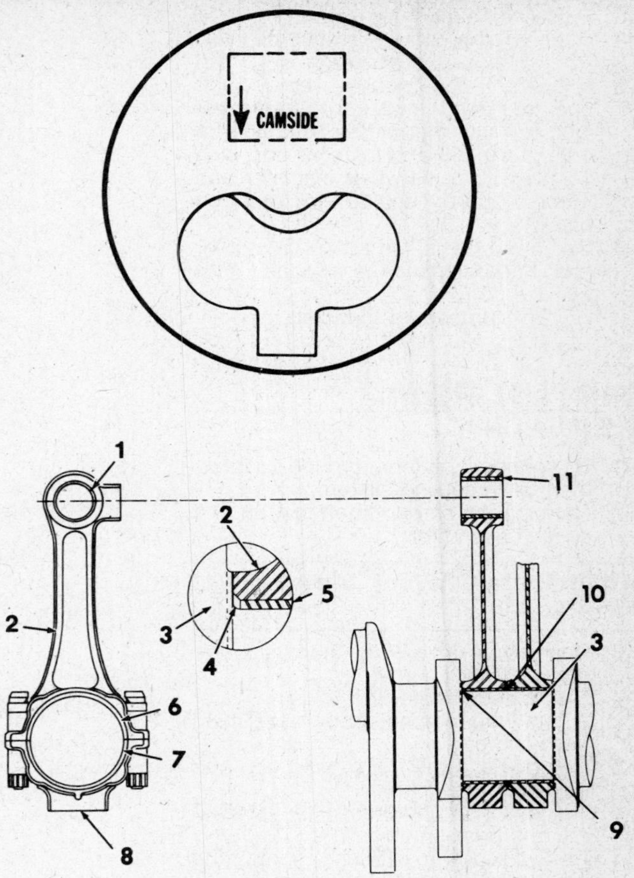

8. Disconnect, then plug transmission oil cooler lines from radiator, if equipped.
9. Disconnect and plug fuel pump inlet line, then drain crankcase and remove oil filter.
10. Remove transmission oil filler tube.
11. Disconnect exhaust pipe from exhaust manifolds and muffler flange, then remove the inlet pipe.
12. Remove upper inlet pipe mounting stud from right exhaust manifold.
13. Remove nuts and washers securing engine insulators to No. 1 crossmember, then lower vehicle.
14. Attach suitable engine lifting equipment to engine and raise engine until transmission housing contacts body.
15. Install wood blocks between engine insulators and crossmember. Use a 2¾ inch block on left side and a 2 inch block on right side. Lower engine to rest on the blocks.
16. Raise and support vehicle.
17. Remove flywheel inspection plate.
18. Position fuel pump inlet line at rear of No. 1 crossmember and, if equipped, position transmission oil cooler lines aside.
19. Remove oil pan attaching bolts, **Fig.**

13, then remove oil pump and pick-up tube, **Fig. 14,** from engine and lay in oil pan. Remove oil pan.

NOTE: The crankshaft may need to be rotated to reposition counterweights in order to remove oil pan.

20. Reverse procedure to install. Apply sealant to oil pan mating surface as shown in **Fig. 15.**

1. Split in Bushing
2. Connecting Rod
3. Crankshaft
4. Crankshaft Fillet
5. Bearing
6. Connecting Rod Bearing (Upper)
7. Connecting Rod Bearing (Lower)
8. Connecting Rod Bearing Cap
9. Large Chamfer Side
10. Small Chamfer Side
11. Bushing

Fig. 12   Piston & rod assembly

ENGINE OIL COOLER
REPLACE

1. Disconnect battery ground cables, then drain cooling system.
2. Remove fan shroud, then the fan and clutch assembly.

NOTE: The fan retaining nut has left hand threads.

3. Raise and support vehicle.
4. Drain engine oil and remove oil filter. Do not reinstall drain plug.
5. On F-250–350 models, remove left engine mount insulator-to-frame attaching nut, then raise left side of engine slightly and install a one inch wooden block between insulator and frame. Lower engine to rest on block.
6. On all models, remove oil cooler attaching bolts and the oil cooler, **Fig. 16.**
7. Reverse procedure to install.

WATER PUMP
REPLACE

1. Disconnect battery ground cables, then drain cooling system.
2. Remove fan shroud, then the fan and clutch assembly.

NOTE: The fan retaining nut has left-hand threads.

3. Remove all drive belts, then the water pump pulley.
4. Disconnect heater hose from water pump, then remove heater hose fitting from pump.
5. Remove alternator adjusting arm and adjusting arm bracket.
6. Remove A/C compressor and brackets and position aside.
7. Remove power steering pump and bracket and position aside.
8. Remove water pump attaching bolts, then the pump.
9. Reverse procedure to install. Apply RTV sealer to two top and two bottom bolts, **Fig. 17.** Apply suitable pipe sealant to heater hose fitting. Torque water pump attaching bolts to 14 ft. lbs.

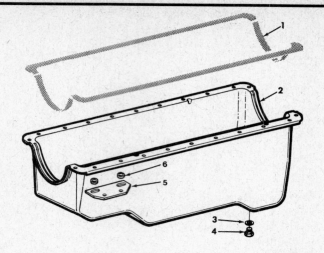

1. Oil Pan Gasket
2. Oil Pan
3. Washer
4. Drain Plug
5. Oil Pan Cover Mounting Bracket
6. Bracket Spacer

Fig. 13   Oil pan assembly

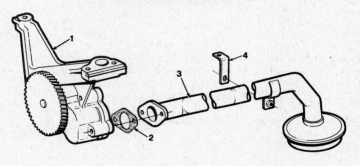

1. Oil Pump (With Gear)
2. Gasket
3. Oil Pick-Up Tube
4. Brace

Fig. 14   Oil pump, disassembled

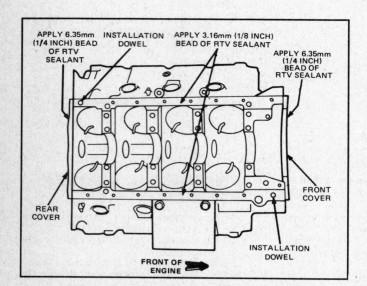

APPLY 6.35mm (1/4 INCH) BEAD OF RTV SEALANT
INSTALLATION DOWEL
APPLY 3.16mm (1/8 INCH) BEAD OF RTV SEALANT
APPLY 6.35mm (1/4 INCH) BEAD OF RTV SEALANT
FRONT COVER
REAR COVER
INSTALLATION DOWEL
FRONT OF ENGINE

Fig. 15   Sealing oil pan mating surface

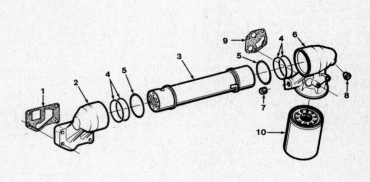

1. Front Manifold Gasket
2. Front Oil Cooler Adapter
3. Oil Cooler
4. "O" Ring
5. "O" Ring
6. Filter Header Assembly
7. Pipe Plug
8. Plug
9. Filter Header Gasket
10. Oil Filter

Fig. 16   Oil cooler, disassembled

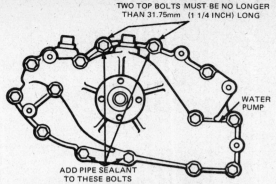

TWO TOP BOLTS MUST BE NO LONGER THAN 31.75mm (1 1/4 INCH) LONG

WATER PUMP

ADD PIPE SEALANT TO THESE BOLTS

Fig. 17   Water pump installation

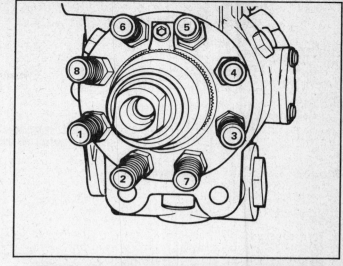

Fig. 18   Injection pump cylinder numbering sequence

FUEL SUPPLY PUMP
REPLACE

1. Loosen fuel line connections. Do not remove fuel lines at this time.
2. Loosen fuel pump attaching bolts one to two turns. Using hand force only, loosen fuel pump to break gasket free.
3. Rotate engine by tapping starter until fuel pump cam lobe is at low position. This will reduce spring tension against pump attaching bolts.
4. Disconnect fuel pump inlet, outlet and return lines.
5. Remove fuel pump attaching bolts, then the fuel pump. Remove and discard gasket.
6. Reverse procedure to install. Run engine and check all connections for leaks.

FUEL SUPPLY PUMP CAM, SPACER & THRUST PLATE
REPLACE

1. Remove camshaft drive gear, then the fuel supply pump as previously described.
2. Remove fuel pump cam and spacer using suitable puller.
3. Remove thrust plate attaching bolts, then the thrust plate.
4. Reverse procedure to install.

INJECTION PUMP
REPLACE

NOTE: Prior to removing any fuel lines, clean the exterior of lines with clean fuel oil or solvent to prevent contamination.

1. Disconnect battery ground cables.
2. On E-250–350 models, remove engine cover.
3. On all models, remove engine oil filler neck, then the injection pump-to-drive gear attaching bolts.

4. Disconnect electrical connectors from injection pump.
5. Disconnect accelerator cable and, if equipped, speed control cable from throttle lever.
6. Remove air cleaner and install intake opening cover, tool T83T-9424-A.
7. Remove accelerator cable bracket, with cables attached, and position aside.
8. Remove fuel filter to injection pump fuel line and cap fittings.
9. Remove and cap pump inlet elbow and fitting adapter.
10. Remove fuel return line from pump and cap fittings.

NOTE: It is not necessary to remove injection lines when removing injection pump. If lines are to be removed, loosen line fittings at pump before removing it from engine. Fuel lines must be removed in the following sequence, **Fig. 18**, 5-6-4-8-3-1-7-2, and installed in reverse order.

11. Remove injection lines from nozzles. Cap lines and nozzles.
12. Remove injection pump-to-adapter attaching nuts.
13. Loosen injection line retaining clips and injection nozzle fuel lines and cap all fittings.

NOTE: Do not install injection nozzle fuel lines until pump is installed in engine.

14. Remove injection pump, with nozzle lines attached, through passenger compartment on E-250–350 models, or from engine compartment on F-250–350 models.
15. Reverse procedure to install. Note the following:
    a. Install new O-rings on drive gear end of injection pump and pump fitting adapter.
    b. Torque pump adapter nuts to 14 ft. lbs.

   c. Torque nozzle connector nuts and pump outlet fitting nut to 22 ft. lbs.
   d. Install elbow in pump adapter and torque to a minimum of 6 ft. lbs., then tighten further to align elbow with fuel inlet line, if necessary. Do not exceed one full turn or 10 ft. lbs.
   e. Apply suitable pipe sealant to pump elbow threads and a 1/8 inch bead of RTV sealant to adapter housing mating surface.

INJECTION PUMP DRIVE GEAR & ADAPTER
REPLACE

1983

1. Disconnect battery ground cables, then remove air cleaner and install intake opening cover, tool T83T-9424-A.
2. On E-250–350 models, remove engine cover.
3. On all models, remove injection pump as described under "Injection Pump, Replace".
4. Remove injection pump adapter housing.
5. Crank engine until No. 1 cylinder is at TDC of compression stroke using one of the following methods:
   a. Remove right valve cover and observe No. 1 cylinder valve lever.
   b. Remove No. 1 cylinder glow plug and listen for escaping air while turning engine in normal direction of rotation.
   c. Using the timing quadrant and vibration damper, scribe a line to indicate TDC.

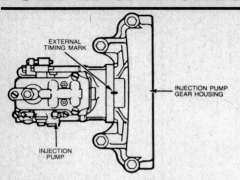

Fig. 19   Injection pump timing marks

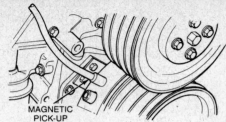

Fig. 20   Timing meter magnetic pickup installation

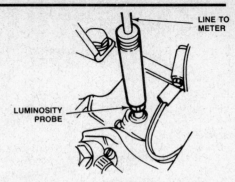

Fig. 21   Timing meter luminosity probe installation

6. With engine at TDC compression for No. 1 cylinder, gears with chamfers should be aligned and gears without chamfers should have the "Y" marks aligned.

NOTE: Injection pump and camshaft gears equipped with locating chamfers have one chamfer on the injection pump gear and two on the camshaft gear. Gears without chamfers are stamped with a "Y" on the face for proper alignment.

7. On gears with chamfers, scribe an alignment mark on front of injection pump gear where chamfer meshes with chamfer of camshaft gear, then remove gear.
8. On gears without chamfers, slide injection pump gear back so that top of camshaft gear is exposed when observed from top of front cover. Apply a small amount of paint to tip of a long screwdriver and mark top of camshaft teeth which mesh with injection pump gear. Also, scribe an alignment mark on front face of injection pump gear, then remove gear.
9. Reverse procedure to install. On gears with chamfers, position camshaft gear chamfers in the 12 o'clock position, then install injection pump gear so that its chamfer meshes with those on camshaft gear. On gears without chamfers, mark new gear as old gear was marked in reference to "Y" mark on old gear, then install gear with marks aligned.

1984—85

1. Perform steps 1 through 4 as described for 1983 models.
2. Using suitable tool, remove plugs, then turn engine over by hand to TDC of compression stroke of No. 1 piston.

NOTE: To determine that No. 1 piston is at TDC of compression stroke, position injection pump drive gear dowel at four o'clock position. The scribe line in vibration damper should be at TDC.

3. Draw a line on front of injection pump drive gear at six o'clock position where the one locating chamfer meshes between the two chamfers on the camshaft gear.
4. Remove injection pump drive gear.
5. Reverse procedure to install, noting the following:
   a. With drawn line on injection pump drive gear at six o'clock position, install gear and align all drive gear timing marks, **Fig. 10.**

CAUTION: Use extreme care to avoid disturbing injection pump drive gear after it is set in position.

INJECTION NOZZLE
REPLACE

NOTE: Prior to removing nozzle, clean exterior of nozzle assembly with clean fuel oil or solvent to prevent contamination.

1. Remove fuel line retaining clamp from nozzle line.
2. Disconnect fuel inlet and leak-off lines from nozzle assembly. Cap all openings.
3. Remove nozzle from head by turning counterclockwise.
4. Reverse procedure to install. Note the

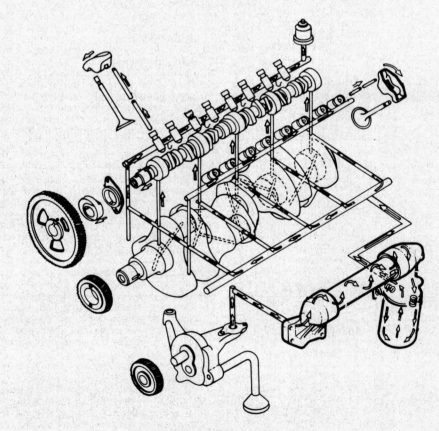

Engine oiling system

Fuel Cetane Value	Altitude	
	0-3000 Ft*	Above 3000 Ft*
38-42	6° ATDC	7° ATDC
43-46	5° ATDC	6° ATDC
47 or greater	4° ATDC	5° ATDC
*Installation or resetting tolerance for dynamic timing is ± 1°. Service limit is ± 2°.		

Fig. 22 Injection pump timing specifications. 1983—84

Fuel Cetane Value	Calibration	
	4-68J-ROD	4-68X-ROD
38-42	3.5° ATDC	4.5° ATDC
43-46	2.5° ATDC	3.5° ATDC
47 or greater	1.5° ATDC	2.5° ATDC
*Installation or resetting tolerance for dynamic timing is ± 1°. Service limit is ± 2°.		

Fig. 23 Injection pump timing specifications. 1985

following:
a. Install a new copper gasket on each nozzle assembly.
b. Apply suitable anti-seize compound to nozzle threads. Torque nozzle assembly to 33 ft. lbs.
c. Install two new O-rings in each fuel return tee.
d. Run engine and check for leaks. If necessary, purge air from high pressure fuel lines by loosening connector one half to one full turn and cranking engine until fuel, free of air bubbles, flows from connector.

INJECTION PUMP TIMING

LESS TIMING METER

1. Remove fast idle bracket and solenoid, if equipped, from injection pump.
2. Loosen 3 injection pump-to-mounting adapter attaching nuts using tool No. T83T-9000-B or equivalent.

3. Rotate injection pump, using tool No. T83T-9000-C or equivalent, to align timing marks on pump mounting flange and adapter, **Fig. 19,** to within .030 inch.
4. Remove rotating tool and torque pump attaching nuts to 14 ft. lbs.
5. Ensure timing marks are still aligned, then install fast idle bracket and solenoid, if equipped.

WITH TIMING METER 78-0100

1. Start engine and run until normal operating temperature is reached.

NOTE: Engine temperature must be stabilized between 192 and 212°F to ensure proper fuel ignition in the precombustion chambers. If temperature is less than 192°F, fuel ignition is delayed and the timing meter will record an inaccurate injection value.

2. Shut engine off, then install timing meter by inserting magnetic pickup into timing pointer probe hole, **Fig. 20.**

NOTE: Insert magnetic pickup until it almost touches vibration damper.

3. Remove No. 1 glow plug, then install luminosity probe, **Fig. 21,** and torque to 12 ft. lbs. Install photocell over probe.
4. Connect timing meter to battery and adjust offset on meter. Ensure wire leads are positioned away from drive belts.
5. Start and run engine with transmission in Neutral and rear wheels raised off ground.
6. Set engine speed to 1400 RPM, using tool No. 14-032 or equivalent, with all accessories off.
7. Observe injection timing on timing meter and compare to values listed in chart, **Figs. 22 and 23.** If timing is within specifications, proceed to step 13. If timing is not within specifications, proceed to step 8.

NOTE: Fuel cetane is a rating of a fuel's ability to ignite under compression ignition conditions. Fuels with high cetane values will ignite faster than fuels with low cetane values. A tester is supplied with timing meter to determine cetane value of fuel.

8. Shut engine off and note timing mark alignment.
9. Remove fast idle bracket and solenoid, if equipped, from injection pump.
10. Loosen 3 injection pump-to-mounting adapter attaching nuts using tool No. T83T-9000-B or equivalent.
11. Rotate injection pump, using tool T83T-9000-C or equivalent. Rotate pump clockwise (as viewed from front of engine) to retard, or counter-clockwise to advance timing.

NOTE: Each 2° of timing is equal to approximately .030 inch of timing mark movement.

12. Remove rotating tool and torque pump attaching nuts to 14 ft. lbs. Start engine and recheck timing. If timing is still not within specifications, repeat adjustment.
13. Shut engine off and remove timing meter, then install glow plug and torque to specifications.
14. Install fast idle bracket and solenoid, if equipped.

Clutch & Manual Transmission Section

HYDRAULIC CLUTCH RELEASE

1984—85

When the clutch pedal is depressed, fluid is forced from the master cylinder into a slave cylinder. The slave cylinder push rod moves the clutch release lever which in turn pivots on a trunnion in the flywheel housing, and forces the release bearing against the pressure plate release fingers.

When the clutch pedal is released, the master cylinder return spring and the release lever retracting spring force the fluid from the slave cylinder back to the master cylinder.

The fluid used in this system is the same as that used in the brake system. A bleeder fitting is installed on the slave cylinder and procedures for bleeding are the same as those for brakes. The master cylinder fluid level should be maintained at ½" below the top of the master cylinder reservoir.

CLUTCH PEDAL
ADJUST

1979—83 MODELS

NOTE: Clutch pedal total travel is not adjustable on these models.

1. Check clutch pedal free travel by measuring distance from clutch pedal pad to steering wheel rim, then depress clutch pedal until free travel is diminished and take a second measurement. If the difference between the two measurements is less than ¾ inches on 1979 vehicles or ½ inch on 1980—83 vehicles, the clutch linkage must be adjusted.
2. Loosen and back-off the two jam nuts several turns, then adjust the first jam nut until a free travel measurement of 1½ inches is obtained at the clutch pedal.
3. While holding the second jam nut, tighten the first jam nut against the second one.
4. Recheck free pedal travel and readjust as necessary.

1984—85 MODELS

No clutch linkage or pedal travel adjustments are required.

CLUTCH
REPLACE

1. On 1979—83 models, disconnect release lever retracting spring and

pushrod assembly from lever.
2. On 1984—85 models, remove clutch slave cylinder.
3. On all models, remove transmission as described under "Transmission, Replace."
4. On models not equipped with a clutch housing dust cover, remove starter motor and clutch housing.
5. On models equipped with a clutch housing dust cover, remove dust cover and the release lever from housing.
6. On all models, mark clutch assembly and flywheel for assembly reference.
7. Remove pressure plate and cover assembly and the clutch disc from flywheel.

NOTE: Loosen attaching bolts evenly to relieve spring tension without distorting cover.

8. Reverse procedure to install, noting the following:
   a. Apply a light coat of suitable lithium base grease to release lever fingers and lever trunnion, fulcrum or pivot ball. Do not grease the release lever pivot assembly on Econoline models.
   b. Fill release bearing hub annular groove with suitable grease.
   c. Adjust clutch pedal as described under "Clutch Pedal, Adjust."

TRANSMISSION
REPLACE

3 SPEED

E-100—350
1. Raise and support vehicle.
2. Drain transmission fluid by removing lower extension housing-to-transmission bolt.
3. Disconnect driveshaft from transmission and position aside.
4. Disconnect speedometer cable from extension housing and the gear shift rods from shift levers.
5. Raise transmission slightly, using a suitable jack, and remove 4 extension housing-to-insulator attaching bolts.
6. Remove 4 transmission-to-flywheel housing attaching bolts, then carefully lower transmission from vehicle.
7. Reverse procedure to install.

F-100—250
1. Raise and support vehicle.
2. Support engine with a suitable jack and a wooden block positioned under oil pan.
3. Drain transmission fluid by removing lower extension housing-to-transmis-

sion bolt.
4. Disconnect gearshift linkage and speedometer cable from transmission.
5. On 1981—85 models, disconnect back-up light electrical connector.
6. On all models, disconnect driveshaft from transmission and position aside.
7. Raise transmission and remove rear support, and on 1981—85 models, remove the insulator and retainer assembly.
8. Remove transmission-to-flywheel attaching bolts.
9. Slide transmission rearward until input shaft clears clutch housing, then carefully lower transmission from vehicle.

NOTE: Do not depress clutch pedal with transmission out of vehicle.

10. Reverse procedure to install.

Bronco
1. Shift transfer case into Neutral position, then remove fan shroud-to-radiator support attaching bolts.
2. Raise and support vehicle.
3. Support transfer case shield with a suitable jack, then remove shield attaching bolts and the shield.
4. Drain transmission and transfer case fluid by removing lower extension housing-to-transmission bolt.
5. Disconnect both driveshafts and the speedometer cable from transfer case.
6. Disconnect shift rods from shift levers.
7. Place 1st-reverse gear shift lever into 1st gear position, then insert a suitable tool to hold lever in place and prevent roller bearings from falling into transmission case.
8. Support transmission with a suitable jack, then remove 2 cotter pins, bolts, washers, plates and insulators securing crossmember to transfer case adapter.
9. Remove crossmember-to-frame side support attaching bolts.
10. Raise transmission and transfer case using a suitable jack, then remove crossmember upper insulators and the crossmember.
11. Roll back the transfer case shift linkage boot, then remove shift lever cap and shift lever assembly.
12. Remove 2 lower transmission-to-flywheel housing attaching bolts.
13. Position a suitable jack under transmission and secure with a safety chain.
14. Remove 2 upper transmission-to-flywheel housing attaching bolts, then move transmission and transfer case rearward and lower from vehicle.

15. Remove transmission-to-transfer case adapter attaching bolts, then slide transmission off transfer case.
16. Reverse procedure to install.

4 SPEED

WARNER UNITS

4 × 2 Models
1. Disconnect battery ground cable.
2. Remove floor mat and body floor pan cover, then the shift lever and boot assembly and the weather pad.
3. Raise and support vehicle.
4. Support transmission with a suitable jack and disconnect speedometer cable.
5. Disconnect back-up lamp switch electrical connector from back of gear shift lever housing.
6. Disconnect driveshaft or coupling shaft and clutch linkage from transmission and wire to one side.
7. On 1979–82 models equipped with model T-18 transmission, remove transmission rear support, and on 1981–82 models, the upper and lower absorbers.
8. On 1983–85 models equipped with model T-19B or T-19D transmission, remove transmission rear insulator and lower retainer, then the crossmember.
9. On all models, remove transmission attaching bolts, then slide transmission rearward and lower from vehicle.
10. Reverse procedure to install.

4 × 4 Models
1. Remove floor mat, then the access cover attaching screws from floor pan.
2. Place gearshift lever in Reverse, then remove access cover, insulator and dust cover.
3. Remove transfer case and transmission shift lever, shift ball and boot assemblies.
4. Raise and support vehicle.
5. Drain transmission fluid, then disconnect front and rear driveshafts from transfer case and wire to one side.
6. Remove retaining ring or cotter pins from shift link, then lift shift link from transfer case.
7. Remove speedometer cable from transfer case.
8. Support transfer case with a suitable jack, then remove transfer case attaching bolts and the transfer case.
9. Remove rear support-to-transmission attaching bolts.
10. Support transmission with a suitable jack and remove rear support bracket and brace.
11. Remove 4 transmission-to-bell housing attaching bolts, then lower transmission from vehicle.
12. Reverse procedure to install.

NEW PROCESS UNITS
1. Disconnect battery ground cable.
2. Remove transmission shift lever, ball and boot assembly.
3. On 4 × 4 models, remove transfer case shift lever, ball and boot assembly.
4. On all models, remove floor pan transmission cover.
5. On F-100–350 models, remove weather pad.

NOTE: It may be necessary to remove seat assembly to provide access for removal of the weather pad.

6. Remove gearshift lever and knob from housing. Use tool No. T37T-7220-A or equivalent to remove inner cap, then lift off spring seat, spring and lever.
7. On all models, disconnect back-up lamp switch electrical connector from gearshift housing cover.
8. Raise and support vehicle.
9. On 4 × 4 models, proceed as follows:
   a. Drain transfer case, then disconnect front driveshaft from case and wire to one side.
   b. Remove shift link cotter pin and the shift link.
   c. Remove speedometer cable from transfer case.
   d. Remove 3 support bracket-to-transfer case attaching bolts.
   e. Position suitable jack under transfer case, then remove mounting bolts and the transfer case.
10. On all models, position suitable jack under transmission, then remove rear support attaching bolts and the rear support.
11. On all models, remove transmission-to-clutch housing attaching bolts and lower transmission from vehicle.
12. Reverse procedure to install.

4 SPEED OVERDRIVE

EXC. SINGLE RAIL & TOP MOUNTED SHIFTER UNITS
1. Position a wooden block under clutch pedal to prevent it from being depressed.
2. Raise and support vehicle.
3. Mark relationship of driveshaft to flange, then disconnect driveshaft and slide off transmission output shaft. Install suitable seal installation tool into extension housing to prevent leakage.
4. Disconnect speedometer cable from extension housing.
5. Remove shift rod-to-shift lever retaining clips, flat washers and spring washers.
6. Remove shift control attaching bolts from extension housing and nuts from transmission case.
7. Remove crossmember support-to-extension housing attaching bolts from rear transmission support.
8. On 1979–81 models, support transmission with a suitable jack and remove extension housing-to-rear engine support attaching bolts.
9. On 1982–85 models, raise transmission, clutch and engine assembly high enough to relieve weight from No. 3 crossmember, then remove crossmember.

10. On all models, raise rear of engine high enough to relieve weight from crossmember, then remove crossmember.
11. Support transmission with a suitable jack and remove transmission-to-flywheel housing attaching bolts.
12. Slide transmission rearward until input shaft clears clutch housing, then carefully lower transmission from vehicle.

NOTE: Do not depress clutch pedal with transmission out of vehicle.

13. Reverse procedure to install.

SINGLE RAIL & TOP MOUNTED SHIFTER UNITS

4 × 2 Models
1. Disconnect battery ground cable.
2. Raise and support vehicle.
3. Mark relationship of driveshaft to flange, then disconnect driveshaft and slide off transmission output shaft. Install suitable seal installation tool into extension housing to prevent leakage.
4. Disconnect speedometer cable from extension housing.
5. On 1983–85 models, disconnect electrical connectors from back-up lamp switch and high gear switch (if equipped).
6. Remove shift lever, ball and boot as an assembly.
7. Support transmission with a suitable jack and remove extension housing-to-rear engine support attaching bolts.
8. Raise rear of engine high enough to relieve weight from crossmember, then remove crossmember.
9. Support transmission with a suitable jack and remove transmission-to-flywheel housing attaching bolts.
10. Slide transmission rearward until input shaft clears clutch housing, then carefully lower transmission from vehicle.

NOTE: Do not depress clutch pedal with transmission out of vehicle.

11. Reverse procedure to install.

4 × 4 Models
1. Disconnect battery ground cable.
2. Raise and support vehicle.
3. Drain lubricant from transmission and transfer case.
4. Disconnect 4-wheel drive indicator switch electrical connector from transfer case, and back-up lamp switch electrical connector from transmission.
5. Remove skid plate, if equipped, from frame.
6. Mark front and rear driveshafts for assembly reference, then disconnect driveshafts from transfer case and position aside.
7. Disconnect speedometer cable from transfer case.
8. On 1983–85 models, remove retaining clips and shift rod from transfer case control lever and shift lever.
9. On all models, disconnect vent hose

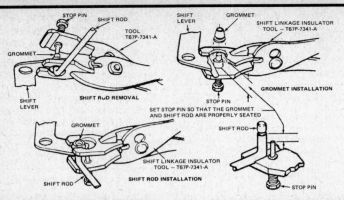

Fig. 1 Shift lever grommet & retainer ring replacement. 1979—81 E-100—350

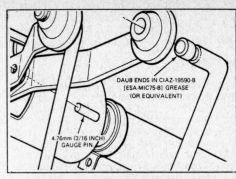

Fig. 2 Transmission linkage adjustment. 3 speed units

from transfer case.

10. On 1983–85 models, remove shift lever from transmission.

11. On all models, support transmission with a suitable jack and remove transmission housing-to-engine rear support bracket.

12. Raise rear of transmission to relieve weight from crossmember, then remove 2 nuts attaching upper gusset to frame on both sides of frame.

13. Remove left-hand gusset, then the transmission-to-crossmember support plate attaching bolts.

14. Raise transmission with a suitable jack, then remove support plate-to-crossmember attaching nuts and bolts. Remove support plate and right-hand gusset.

15. Remove crossmember attaching nuts and bolts and the crossmember.

16. Remove heat shield from transfer case.

17. On 1981–82 models, slightly lower transmission, then remove retaining clips and shift rod from transfer case control lever and the transfer case

shift lever.

18. On all models, support transfer case with a suitable jack and remove 6 transfer case-to-transmission adapter attaching bolts.

19. Slide transfer case rearward and remove from vehicle.

20. On 1981–82 models, remove 3 transmission shift lever attaching screws and the shift lever.

21. On all models, support transmission with a suitable jack and remove trans-

mission-to-flywheel housing attaching bolts.

22. Slide transmission rearward until input shaft clears clutch housing, then carefully lower transmission from vehicle. It may be necessary to lower engine to provide sufficient clearance.

NOTE: Do not depress clutch pedal with transmission out of vehicle.

23. Reverse procedure to install.

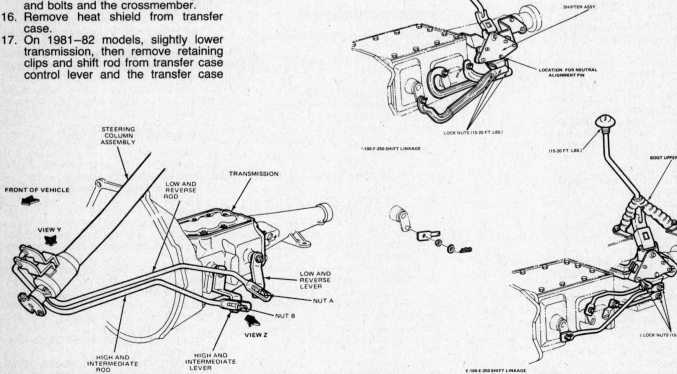

Fig. 3 Transmission linkage. 3 speed units. E-150—350 (others similar)

Fig. 4 Transmission linkage. 4 speed overdrive units

TRANSMISSION LINKAGE
ADJUST

3 SPEED

SERVICE BULLETIN 1979–81 Econoline models may experience problems with hard shifting, gear disengagement or incorrect shifting functions caused by worn, damaged or missing shift linkage components. This malfunction may be corrected by replacing plastic grommets in column mounted shift lever assembly and the retainer ring attaching adjusting stud to shifter levers, using tool shown in **Fig. 1.**

1. Install a ¾₆ inch diameter gauge pin through locating hole in steering column shift levers and plastic spacer, **Fig. 2.**

2. Loosen nuts "A" and "B," **Fig. 3,** and position shift levers in neutral detents.
3. Torque nuts "A" and "B" to 12–18 ft. lbs., ensuring there is no movement between stud and nut.
4. Remove gauge pin and check linkage for proper operation.

NOTE: Retaining rings and insulators must be replaced when adjusting transmission linkage. The rings and plastic grommets where shift rods are attached must also be replaced if excessive wear or looseness is observed.

4 SPEED OVERDRIVE

1. Disconnect 3 shift rods from shifter assembly, **Fig. 4.**
2. Insert a ¼ diameter gauge pin through alignment hole in shifter assembly,
ensuring levers are in neutral position.
3. Align 3rd–4th (forward) lever and 1st–2nd (rearward) lever in neutral (midway) position and rotate reverse (middle) lever counterclockwise to neutral position.
4. Rotate output shaft to ensure transmission is in neutral.
5. On 1979–81 models, attach slotted end of shift rods over slots of studs in shifter assembly. Install locknuts and torque to 15–20 ft. lbs.
6. On 1982–85 models, shift reverse lever clockwise to reverse position, then attach 1st–2nd and 3rd–4th shift rods to corresponding levers and torque locknuts to 15–20 ft. lbs. Rotate reverse lever back to neutral position, then install reverse shift rod and torque locknut to 15–20 ft. lbs.
7. On all models, remove gauge pin and check linkage for proper operation.

Transfer Case Section

TRANSFER CASE
REPLACE

1979 F-150—350 W/NEW PROCESS 203 TRANSFER CASE

1. Drain transfer case fluid by removing power take-off lower bolts and front output rear cover lower bolts.
2. Disconnect front axle shaft from transfer case flange.

3. Disconnect shift rods from transfer case.
4. Disconnect speedometer cable and lockout lamp switch electrical connector from transfer case rear output shaft housing.
5. Remove transfer case-to-transmission adapter attaching bolts, then disconnect rear axle driveshaft from transfer case flange.
6. On all models, support transfer case with a suitable jack.
7. Remove transfer case attaching nuts,
bolts, spacers and upper absorbers, then carefully lower transfer case from vehicle.
8. Reverse procedure to install.

1979 F-150—250 & BRONCO W/NEW PROCESS 205 TRANSFER CASE

1. Drain transfer case fluid, then disconnect front and rear driveshafts from transfer case.
2. Disconnect shift selector rod and speedometer cable from transfer case.
3. On all models, support transfer case with a suitable jack, then remove mounting bolts and carefully lower transfer case from vehicle.
4. Reverse procedure to install.

1980—85 MODELS W/BORG-WARNER 1345 TRANSFER CASE

1. Raise and support vehicle.
2. Drain transfer case fluid, then disconnect four-wheel drive indicator switch electrical connector from transfer case.
3. Remove skid plate from frame, if equipped.
4. Disconnect front and rear driveshafts from transfer case.
5. Disconnect speedometer driven gear from transfer case rear bearing retainer.
6. Remove transfer case control lever and shift lever retaining clips and shift rod.
7. Disconnect vent hose from transfer

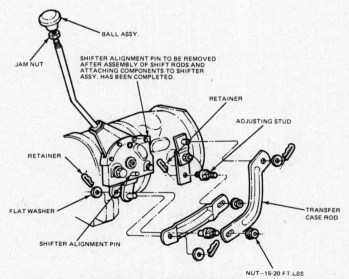

Fig. 1 Transfer case linkage adjustment.
1979 F-150—350 w/New Process 203 transfer case

BALL ASSY.

JAM NUT

SHIFTER ALIGNMENT PIN TO BE REMOVED AFTER ASSEMBLY OF SHIFT RODS AND ATTACHING COMPONENTS TO SHIFTER ASSY. HAS BEEN COMPLETED.

RETAINER

ADJUSTING STUD

RETAINER

FLAT WASHER

SHIFTER ALIGNMENT PIN

TRANSFER CASE ROD

NUT—15-20 FT. LBS.

8. Remove heat shield from engine mount bracket and transfer case.
9. Support transfer case with a suitable jack, then remove transfer case-to-transmission adapter attaching bolts.
10. Slide transfer case rearward until it clears transmission output shaft, then carefully lower transfer case from vehicle.
11. Reverse procedure to install.

1980—85 MODELS W/NEW PROCESS 208 TRANSFER CASE

1. Raise and support vehicle.

2. Drain transfer case fluid, then disconnect four-wheel drive indicator switch electrical connector from transfer case.
3. Disconnect speedometer driven gear from transfer case rear bearing retainer.
4. Remove transmission shift lever-to-transfer case attaching nut.
5. Remove skid plate, if equipped, from frame.
6. Remove heat shield from transfer case.
7. Support transfer case with a suitable jack, then disconnect front and rear driveshafts from output shaft yokes.
8. Remove transfer case-to-transmission adapter attaching bolts, then carefully lower transfer case from vehicle.
9. Reverse procedure to install.

TRANSFER CASE LINKAGE
ADJUST
1979 F-150—350 W/NEW PROCESS 203 TRANSFER CASE

1. Shift transfer case to Neutral, then remove 2 adjusting stud nuts, **Fig. 1**.
2. Insert a ¼ inch diameter gauge pin, 1¼ inches long, through shifter assembly.
3. Rotate bottom transfer case lever clockwise to forward position and place top lever in midway or neutral position.
4. Reposition shift rods and torque new adjusting stud nuts to 15–20 ft. lbs.
5. Remove gauge pin from shifter assembly.

Rear Axle, Suspension & Brakes Section

DANA/SPICER INTEGRAL HOUSING TYPE AXLE

This rear axle, **Fig. 1**, is a semi-floating type, while the axle shown in **Fig. 2** is of the full-floating type. The drive pinion of either axle is of the over-hung design, mounted on pre-loaded tapered roller bearings. Sealing of the pinion shaft is accomplished by a spring-loaded seal on the companion flange. The flange is splined and secured to the pinion shaft by a nut.

AXLE SHAFT, BEARING & OIL SEAL, REPLACE

Full-Floating Axle

1. Set parking brake and loosen axle shaft bolts.
2. Raise and support rear of vehicle so that axle is parallel with floor.
3. Remove axle shaft bolts.
4. Remove axle shaft and discard gasket.
5. Pry out locking wedge with screwdriver.
6. Raise wheel until weight is removed from wheel bearing.
7. Remove wheel bearing adjustment nut.
8. Remove outer bearing cone and pull wheel assembly from axle.
9. Drive inner bearing cone and seal out of wheel hub with brass drift.
10. Inspect bearings and races and replace if worn or damaged. Drive races from wheel hub with brass drift.
11. Lubricate bearing cone and roller assemblies and place inner assemblies into wheel hub. Install new hub inner seal.
12. Wrap spindle threads with tape, then slide wheel assembly onto axle housing spindle and remove tape.
13. Install outer wheel bearing and start adjuster nut. Lower wheel to ground.
14. While rotating wheel, torque adjusting nut to 120–140 ft. lbs. Back off the nut to obtain 0.001–0.010 inch end play (⅛–⅜ turn). If nut or locking wedge are damaged or do not allow for proper end play they should be replaced.
15. Position locking wedge in key way slot, making sure it is not bottomed against the shoulder of adjusting nut.
16. Install axle shaft and new flange gasket, then install retaining bolts and torque locking bolts to 40–50 ft. lbs.
17. Adjust brakes.
18. Remove supports and lower vehicle.

Semi-Floating Axle

1. Raise and support vehicle.

2. Remove wheel and brake drum.
3. Remove cover plate and discard gasket.
4. Remove differential pinion shaft lock screw and the shaft.
5. Remove "C" clip from button end of shaft by pushing inward on other end.
6. Pull shaft from axle tube. Do not rotate differential side gears.
7. Remove and discard oil seal from axle tube.
8. Pull bearing from axle tube.
9. Lubricate new bearing and install in axle tube.
10. Lubricate and install new oil seal.
11. Insert shaft into axle tube, making sure splines engage side gears, then install "C" clip and pull shaft outward until the clip locks.

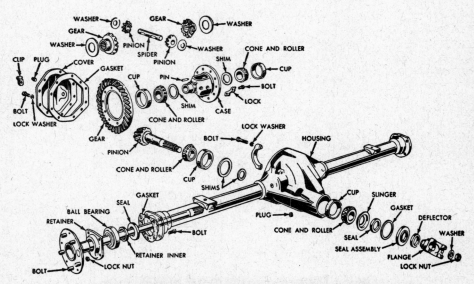

Fig. 1 Semi-floating integral housing hypoid rear axle

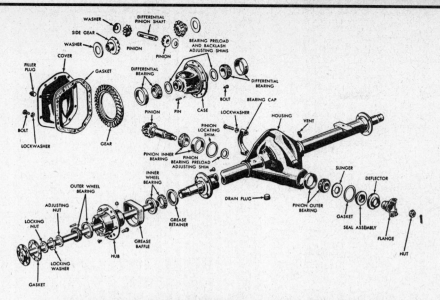

Fig. 2   Full-floating integral housing hypoid rear axle

12. Install pinion mate shaft, aligning lock pin holes, and pinion gear side washers.
13. Install new lock screw and torque to 8 ft. lbs. on 1979–81 models, or 20–25 ft. lbs. on 1982–85 models.
14. Install cover plate and gasket. Torque bolts to 30–40 ft. lbs.
15. Install wheel and drum assembly.
16. Remove supports and lower vehicle.

REAR AXLE ASSEMBLY, REPLACE

1. Raise vehicle from floor and support with stand jacks under frame side rails.

2. Remove rear wheels.
3. Split rear universal joint.
4. Disconnect parking brake cable from equalizer rod and unfasten brake cable brackets from frame crossmember.
5. Disconnect hydraulic brake line connection at rear axle housing.
6. Loosen and move shock absorbers out of the way.
7. While supporting axle housing with hydraulic jack, remove spring clips and lower axle assembly to the floor.
8. Reverse the foregoing procedure to install the rear axle assembly, being sure to bleed the brake system when the installation is completed.

FORD REMOVABLE CARRIER TYPE REAR AXLE

This rear axle, **Fig. 3,** is a banjo-housing hypoid in which the drive pinion is mounted 2¼″ below the centerline of the drive gear. The drive pinion is straddle-mounted in that two opposed tapered roller bearings support the pinion shaft at the front of the pinion gear and a straight roller bearing supports the pinion shaft at the rear of the pinion gear.

The pinion shaft and gear are assembled in the pinion retainer which is bolted to the carrier housing. Two carrier and differential cases are used to accommodate two bearing sizes. The right and left axle shafts are not interchangeable since the left shaft is shorter than the right.

AXLE SHAFT, BEARING & OIL SEAL, REPLACE

Removal, Units w/Ball Bearing
1. Remove wheel assembly.
2. Remove brake drum from flange.
3. Working through hole provided in axle shaft flange, remove nuts that secure wheel bearing retainer.
4. Pull axle shaft out of housing. If bearing is a tight fit in axle housing, use a slide hammer-type puller.
5. Remove brake backing plate and secure to frame rail.
6. If the axle shaft bearing is to be replaced, loosen the inner retainer by nicking it deeply with a chisel in several places. The bearing will then slide off easily.
7. Press bearing from axle shaft.
8. Inspect machined surface of axle shaft and housing for rough spots that would affect sealing action of the oil seal. Carefully remove any burrs or rough spots.

Installation
1. Press new bearing on shaft until it seats firmly against shoulder on shaft.
2. Press inner bearing retainer on shaft until it seats firmly against bearing.
3. If oil seal is to be replaced, use a hook-type tool to pull it out of housing. Wipe a small amount of oil resistant sealer on outer edge of seal before it is installed.

Removal, Units W/Roller Bearing
1. Remove wheel assembly.
2. Remove brake drum from flange.
3. Working through hole provided in axle flange, remove nuts securing wheel bearing retainer.
4. Pull axle shaft carefully from housing to prevent damage to outer seal rubber. Use a slide hammer type puller to remove tapered bearing cup from housing. Remove brake backing plate and secure to frame rail.
5. If the axle shaft bearing or seal is to be replaced, split the inner bearing retainer.

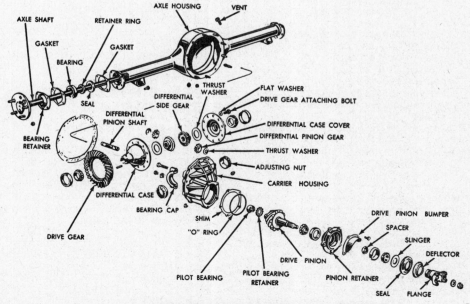

Fig. 3   Ford removable carrier rear axle

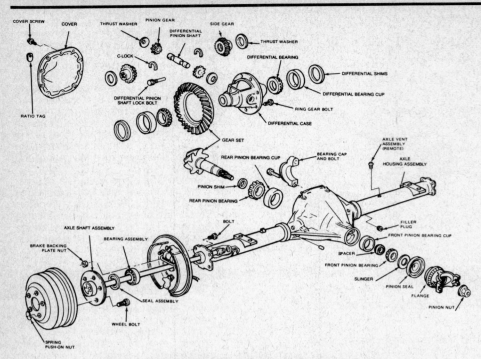

Fig. 4   Ford integral carrier type rear axle

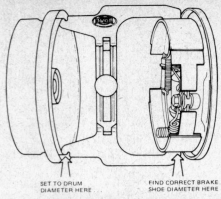

Fig. 5   Service brake adjustment

6. Press bearing from axle shaft.
7. Inspect machined surface of axle shaft and housing for rough spots that would affect sealing action of the oil seal. Carefully remove any burrs or rough spots.
8. Install outer retainer plate on axle shaft. Press lubricated seal and bearing onto shaft until firmly seated.

NOTE: Oil seal for rear drum brake equipped vehicles is different than that used on vehicles with rear disc brakes. Seals used with drum brakes have a gray metal colored outer rim, while seals used with disc brakes have a black or orange color.

9. Press new bearing retainer onto shaft until seated.

Installation
1. On 1978–84 models, place a new gasket on each side of brake carrier plate, and slide axle shaft into housing. On models with roller bearing, ensure outer seal is fully seated on bearing.
2. Start splines into differential side gear and push shaft in until bearing bottoms in housing.
3. Torque bearing retainer nuts to 50–75 ft. lbs. on 1979 models, or 20–40 ft. lbs. on 1980–85 models.

REAR AXLE ASSEMBLY, REPLACE

1. Raise and support vehicle.
2. Remove rear wheels and brake drums.
3. Remove rear wheel bearing retainer plate attaching nuts, then disconnect

axle shafts from axle housing.
4. Mark driveshaft end yoke and U-joint flange for assembly reference, then disconnect driveshaft from flange. Mark position of cups to flange and remove driveshaft from transmission extension housing. Install a suitable seal installation tool into housing to prevent leakage.
5. On Ranchero models, disconnect rear stabilizer bar, if equipped.
6. On all models, unfasten brake lines from retaining clips and disconnect vent tube, if equipped, from axle housing.
7. Remove brake backing plate assemblies from axle housing and wire aside.
8. Disconnect rear shock absorbers from lower mounts and position aside.
9. On all models except Ranchero, lower axle slightly to reduce spring tension, then remove spring clips, U-bolt nuts and spring seat caps from each rear spring and lower axle assembly from vehicle.
10. On Ranchero models, proceed as follows:
    a. Position suitable jack under axle housing to prevent housing from shifting when removing control arms.
    b. Disconnect lower control arms from axle housing and position arms downward.
    c. Disconnect upper control arms from axle housing and position arms upward.
    d. Lower axle slightly and remove coil springs and insulators, then remove axle assembly from vehicle.
11. On all models, reverse procedure to install.

FORD INTEGRAL CARRIER TYPE REAR AXLE

This rear axle, **Fig. 4,** is a hypoid gear design with the centerline of the pinion set below the centerline of the ring gear. The drive pinion is of the overhung design mounted on two opposed tapered roller bearings. Pinion bearing preload is adjusted by the pinion nut and a collapsible spacer maintains the seating of the inner race.

AXLE SHAFT, REPLACE

1. Raise and support vehicle, then remove rear wheel and brake drum.
2. Loosen rear housing cover screws and allow lubricant to drain, then remove cover.
3. Remove differential pinion shaft lock bolt and differential pinion shaft.
4. Move flanged end of axle shaft inward and remove C-lock from end of shaft.
5. Remove axle shaft from housing by pulling outward.
6. Reverse procedure to install. Apply locktite EOAZ-19554-B to pinion shaft lock bolt threads, then torque lock bolt to 15–30 ft. lbs.

OIL SEAL & WHEEL BEARING, REPLACE

1. Remove axle shaft as outlined in "Axle Shaft, Replace".
2. Insert tool T83T-1226-A for models with 8.8 inch ring gear, or tool T85T-1225-AH for models with 10.25 inch ring gear, and tool T50T-100-A into axle bore so tangs on tool engage bearing outer race. Remove bearing and seal as an assembly.
3. Install new bearing using tool T83T-1225-B on models with 8.8 inch ring gear, or tool T80T-4000-W on models with 10.25 inch ring gear, and new seal using tool T83T-1175-A on models with 8.8 inch ring gear, or tool T80T-4000-Y on models with 10.25 inch ring gear. Pack lips of seal with

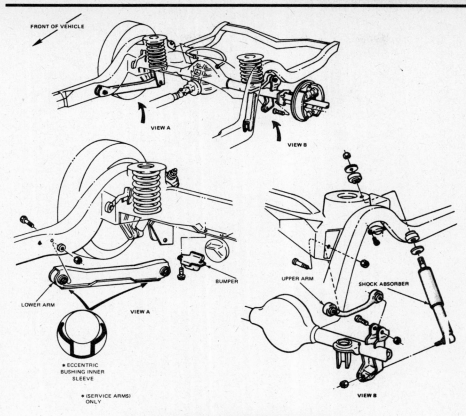

Fig. 6 Rear suspension. Ranchero

C1AZ-19590-B or equivalent.

4. Reinstall axle.

AXLE HOUSING, REPLACE

1. Remove four backing plate nuts from each side of axle and wire backing plate aside.
2. Remove vent hose from vent and vent from brake junction block on rear axle housing.
3. Remove brake line from clips on axle housing and remove brake junction block.

NOTE: Do not open brake lines when removing junction box.

4. Support rear axle housing on suitable jack and remove U-bolt nuts and plates.
5. Disconnect lower bolts on shock absorber mounting bracket and remove housing from vehicle.
6. Reverse procedure to install. Torque U-bolt nuts to 75–100 ft. lbs. on 1983 F-100–350 & Bronco; 75–105 ft. lbs. on 1983 E-100–150 and 1984–85 E-250; 75–115 ft. lbs. on 1984–85 models exc. F-250 4 × 2 chassis cab and E series; 150–180 ft. lbs. on 1983 E-250 and 1983–85 E-350; and 150–210 ft. lbs. on 1983 F-350 and 1984–85 F-250 4 × 2 chassis cab. Torque shock absorber lower bolts to 40–60 ft. lbs. on Econoline models, and 40–64 ft. lbs. on all other models. Torque backing brake attaching bolts to 20–

40 ft. lbs. on F-100–150 models, and 50–70 ft. lbs. on E-250 & F-250 models with 4050 lb. axle.

NOTE: No gaskets are required on brake backing plate.

SERVICE BRAKES
ADJUST

The hydraulic drum brakes are self-adjusting and require a manual adjustment only after brake shoes have been relined or replaced. The adjustment is made as follows:

1. Determine inside diameter of brake drum using brake adjustment gauge, **Fig. 5.**
2. Reverse tool and adjust brake shoes to fit the gauge. Hold automatic adjusting lever out of engagement while rotating adjusting screw to avoid damaging screw slots.

PARKING BRAKE
ADJUST

RANCHERO

1. Place transmission in Neutral with parking brake fully released.
2. Raise and support vehicle.
3. Tighten adjusting nut against cable equalizer to cause rear brakes to

drag.
4. Loosen adjusting nut until brakes are fully released, and ensure there is no drag.
5. Lower vehicle and check operation.

1979 EXC. RANCHERO

1. Depress parking brake pedal 2 notches.
2. Attach a suitable tension gauge to LH rear cable and adjust cable tension to 250 lbs. by tightening equalizer nut. Hold for 5 minutes and release pedal.
3. Back out equalizer nut until gauge registers zero pounds of tension.
4. Adjust cable tension to the following specifications: Except E series, 80 lbs.; E series except E-250–350 with Dana rear axle, 60 lbs.; E-250–350 with Dana rear axle, 65 lbs.
5. Remove gauge and release parking brake. If brake drag is noted on E-250–350 and F-250–350 models after brake adjustment, refer to NOTE following adjustment procedure for 1980–85 models.

1980–85

1. Depress parking brake pedal fully.
2. Tighten equilizer nut 2½ inches up rod while preventing tension limiter bracket from turning. Ensure cinch strap has slipped and less than 1⅜ inch remains.
3. Position parking brake pedal to fully released position, then tighten equalizer nut 6 full turns while preventing automatic adjuster from turning.
4. Depress parking brake pedal fully and measure cable tension. Cable tension should meet the following specifications: 1980 front cable with parking brake set in second notch, 120–160 lbs., and 1981–85 rear cable with parking brake fully applied, 350 lbs.
5. If cable tension is not within specifications, repeat step 3 and recheck.
6. Release parking brake and check for rear wheel drag.

NOTE: If brake drag is noted on 1979 & 1983–85 E-250–350 & F-250–350 models and 1980–82 E-250–350 models after brake adjustment, remove rear drums and measure clearance between parking brake lever and cam plate. This clearance should be .015 inch with brakes fully released. If clearance is not .015 inch, repeat cable adjustment procedure.

MASTER CYLINDER
REPLACE

LESS POWER BRAKES

Exc. Ranchero

1. Disconnect battery ground cable.
2. Disconnect stop lamp switch electrical connectors.
3. Remove retaining nut, shoulder bolt,

spacers and bushing securing master cylinder push rod to brake pedal.

4. Remove stop lamp switch from brake pedal.
5. Disconnect brake lines from master cylinder, then remove attaching screws or nuts and the master cylinder.
6. Remove boot from master cylinder push rod.
7. Reverse procedure to install.

Ranchero

1. Disconnect battery ground cable.
2. Disconnect stop lamp switch electrical connectors, then remove retaining pin and slide stop lamp switch off brake pedal.
3. Loosen master cylinder attaching nuts or bolts, then slide push rod and nylon bushings and washers off brake pedal pin.
4. Disconnect brake lines from master cylinder, then remove attaching screws or nuts and the master cylinder.
5. Reverse procedure to install.

POWER BRAKES

1. Depress brake pedal, with engine off, to release vacuum from power brake unit.
2. Disconnect brake lines from master cylinder.
3. Remove master cylinder-to-power brake unit attaching bolts, then lift master cylinder from mounting studs.
4. Reverse procedure to install.

POWER BRAKE UNIT
REPLACE

EXC. RANCHERO

1. Disconnect battery ground cable.
2. Disconnect stop lamp switch electrical connectors.
3. Support underside of master cylinder, then remove power brake unit-to-master cylinder attaching nuts.
4. Remove vacuum hose between manifold and power brake unit, or power brake unit check valve. Remove check valve, if equipped.
5. Separate power brake unit and master cylinder, leaving master cylinder supported far enough away to allow removal of power brake unit.
6. On models equipped with push rod mounted stop lamp switch, remove retaining pin, then slide switch, push rod, spacers and bushing off brake pedal pin.
7. On models equipped with brake pedal mounted stop lamp switch, remove attaching bolt, nut and plastic bushing, then disconnect power brake unit push rod from brake pedal.
8. Remove power brake unit attaching bolts and the power brake unit.
9. Reverse procedure to install.

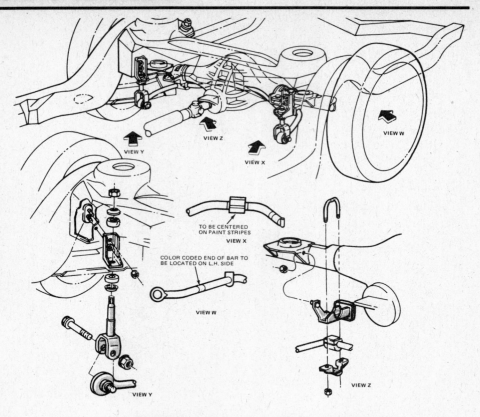

Fig. 7 Stabilizer bar replacement. Ranchero

RANCHERO

1. Disconnect battery ground cable.
2. Disconnect stop lamp switch electrical connectors.
3. Remove stop lamp switch retaining pin, then slide switch, push rod, spacers and bushing off brake pedal pin.
4. On models equipped with speed control, remove left cowl screen from engine compartment. Remove speed control servo attaching nuts and position servo aside.
5. Disconnect master cylinder from power brake unit and position aside. Do not disconnect brake lines.
6. Disconnect vacuum hose from power brake unit, then remove attaching nuts and the power brake unit.
7. Reverse procedure to install.

SHOCK ABSORBER
REPLACE

EXC. RANCHERO

1. Raise and support rear of vehicle to a point where weight is relieved from rear springs and tires are still in contact with floor.
2. Remove lower attaching nut and bolt from shock absorber and swing lower end free of mounting bracket.

3. Remove upper attaching nut and the shock absorber.
4. Reverse procedure to install.

RANCHERO

1. Raise and support vehicle.
2. Remove shock absorber attaching nut, washer and insulator from top of spring upper seat.
3. Compress shock absorber to clear hole in spring seat, then remove inner insulator and washer from upper attaching stud.
4. Remove lower attaching nut and the shock absorber.
5. Reverse procedure to install.

COIL SPRINGS
REPLACE

RANCHERO

1. Raise rear of vehicle and support at frame. Support axle with a suitable jack.
2. Disconnect shock absorbers from lower mountings.
3. Lower axle assembly and remove springs from vehicle, **Fig. 6**.

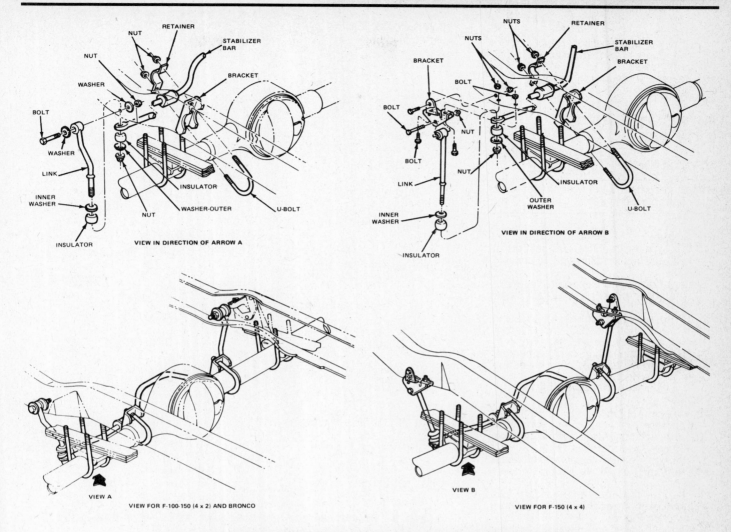

Fig. 8   Stabilizer bar replacement. 1981—85 F-100—150 & Bronco

4. Reverse procedure to install. Install an insulator between upper and lower seats and spring.

LEAF SPRING
REPLACE

E-100—350

1. Raise rear of vehicle and support at frame. Support axle with a suitable jack.
2. Disconnect shock absorbers from lower mountings.
3. Remove 2 U-bolts and the U-bolt plate.
4. On E-100—150 models, lower axle assembly and remove upper and lower rear shackle bolts, then pull rear shackle assembly from bracket and spring. Remove spring mounting nut and bolt, then lower spring assembly from vehicle.
5. On E-250—350 models, lower axle assembly and remove spring front bolt from hanger. Remove 2 attaching

bolts from rear of spring, then lower spring assembly from vehicle.
6. On all models, reverse procedure to install.

1979 F-100—250 4 × 2 & 1980—85 ALL EXC. E-100—350

1. Raise and support rear of vehicle to a point where weight is relieved from rear springs and tires are still in contact with floor.
2. Remove spring U-bolts, and if equipped, the auxiliary spring and spacer.
3. Remove spring-to-bracket attaching nut and bolt from front of spring.
4. Remove upper and lower shackle attaching nuts and bolts from rear of spring, then lower spring and shackle assembly from vehicle.
5. Reverse procedure to install.

1979 F-350

1. Raise and support rear of vehicle until

weight is relieved from rear springs and tires are still in contact with floor.
2. Remove spring U-bolts, spring spacer, and if equipped, the auxiliary spring and spacer.
3. Remove shackle-to-bracket attaching bolt and nut from rear of spring.
4. Remove spring-to-hanger attaching bolts and nut from front of spring, then lower spring and shackle assembly from vehicle.
5. Reverse procedure to install.

1979 BRONCO, F-150—250 4 × 4 & F-350 4 × 4

1. Raise rear of vehicle and support at frame. Support axle with a suitable jack.
2. Disconnect shock absorbers from lower mounts.
3. Remove spring U-bolts, axle spacer, U-bolt plate, and if equipped, the auxiliary spring and spacer.
4. Remove spring-to-frame attaching

nuts from front bracket and rear shackle.
5. Drive out spring attaching bolts, then lower spring and shackle assembly from vehicle.
6. Reverse procedure to install.

CONTROL ARMS
REPLACE

RANCHERO

NOTE: The upper and lower control arms must be replaced in pairs.

Upper Arm
1. Raise rear of vehicle and support at frame. Support axle with a suitable jack.
2. Lower axle and support axle under differential nose as well as under axle.
3. Remove upper arm-to-axle housing attaching nut and bolt, then disconnect arm from housing, **Fig. 6.**
4. Remove upper arm-to-crossmember attaching nut and bolt, then lower arm from vehicle.
5. Reverse procedure to install.

Lower Arm
1. Raise rear of vehicle and support at frame. Support axle with a suitable jack.
2. Lower axle and support axle under differential nose as well as under axle.
3. Remove pivot bolt and nut from axle bracket, then separate lower arm from bracket, **Fig. 6.**
4. Remove lower arm pivot bolt and nut from frame bracket.
5. Remove lower arm from vehicle.
6. Reverse procedure to install.

STABILIZER BAR
REPLACE

RANCHERO
1. Raise rear of vehicle and support at axle housing.
2. Remove stabilizer bar-to-rear link

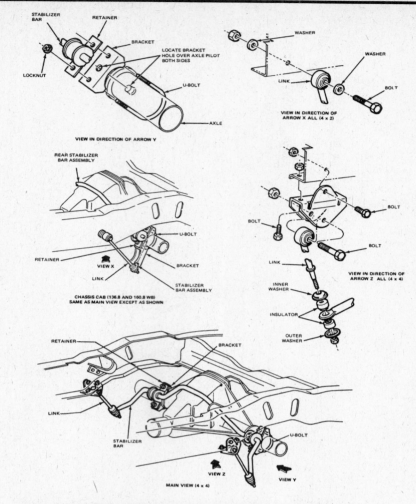

Fig. 9 Stabilizer bar replacement. 1981–85 F-250–350

attaching nuts and bolts from both sides, **Fig. 7.**
3. Remove 2 mounting bracket-to-U-bolt attaching nuts from each side of stabilizer.
4. Remove stabilizer bar from vehicle.
5. Reverse procedure to install.

1981–85 F-100–350 & BRONCO
1. Remove nut from lower end of stabiliz-er link, **Figs. 8 and 9.**
2. Remove outer washer and insulator, then disconnect stabilizer from link.
3. Remove inner insulators and wash-ers.
4. Remove stabilizer link attaching nuts and bolts, then disconnect link from frame.
5. Remove U-bolt, bracket and retainer attaching nuts, then the stabilizer bar from vehicle.
6. Reverse procedure to install.

Front Suspension & Steering Section

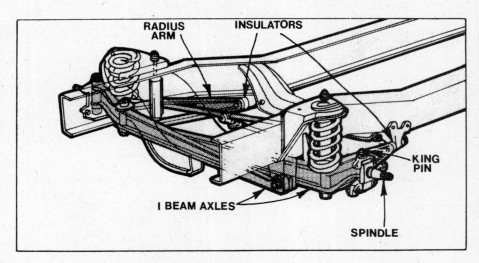

Fig. 1   Twin I-Beam front axle

Fig. 2   Spindle used with twin I Beam front axle. Typical

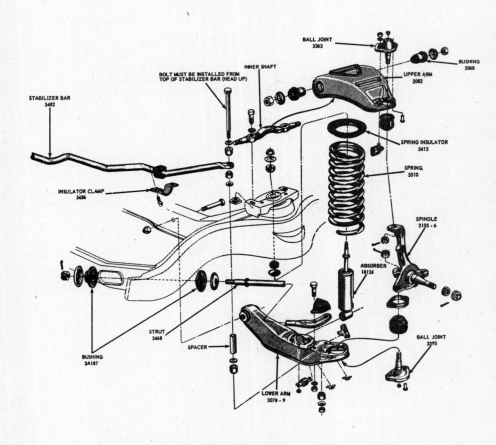

Fig. 3   Front suspension. Ranchero

DESCRIPTION

4 × 2

Twin I-Beam Axle

As illustrated in **Fig. 1** there are two I-beam axles, one for each front wheel. One end of each axle is attached to the spindle and a radius arm and the other end is attached to a frame bracket on the opposite side of the vehicle.

Each spindle is held in place on the axle by ball joints or a spindle bolt which pivots in bushings pressed in the upper and lower ends of the spindle, **Fig. 2**. On models equipped with spindle bolts, a thrust bearing is installed between the lower end of the axle and the spindle to support the load on the axle. On all models, a spindle arm is installed on each spindle for attachment to the steering linkage.

Ranchero

The front suspension, **Fig. 3**, is designed with the coil spring mounted on the lower control arm.

4 × 4

1980–85 Bronco & F-150

The independent front suspension on these vehicles is composed of a two piece front driving axle assembly, two coil springs and two radius arms, **Fig. 4**.

The front driving axle consists of two independent yoke and tube assemblies. One end of yoke and tube assembly is anchored to the frame. The other end of

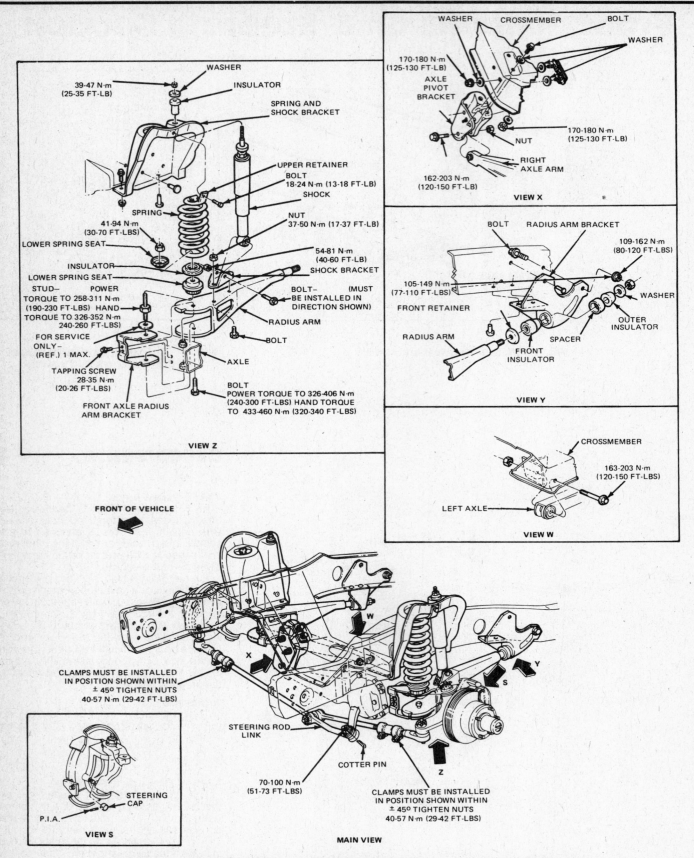

WASHER

39-47 N·m
(25-35 FT-LB)

INSULATOR

SPRING AND
SHOCK BRACKET

UPPER RETAINER

BOLT
18-24 N·m (13-18 FT-LB)
SHOCK

SPRING

41-94 N·m
(30-70 FT-LBS)

NUT
37-50 N·m (17-37 FT-LB)

LOWER SPRING SEAT

54-81 N·m
(40-60 FT-LB)
SHOCK BRACKET

INSULATOR

LOWER SPRING SEAT

STUD— POWER
TORQUE TO 258-311 N·m
(190-230 FT-LBS) HAND
TORQUE TO 326-352 N·m
240-260 FT-LBS)

BOLT— (MUST
BE INSTALLED IN
DIRECTION SHOWN)

RADIUS ARM

FOR SERVICE
ONLY—
(REF.) 1 MAX.

BOLT

TAPPING SCREW
28-35 N·m
(20-26 FT-LBS)

AXLE

FRONT AXLE RADIUS
ARM BRACKET

BOLT
POWER TORQUE TO 326-406 N·m
(240-300 FT-LBS) HAND TORQUE
TO 433-460 N·m (320-340 FT-LBS)

VIEW Z

WASHER   CROSSMEMBER   BOLT

WASHER

170-180 N·m
(125-130 FT-LB)
AXLE
PIVOT
BRACKET

170-180 N·m
(125-130 FT-LB)
NUT

RIGHT
AXLE ARM

162-203 N·m
(120-150 FT-LB)

VIEW X

BOLT   RADIUS ARM BRACKET

109-162 N·m
(80-120 FT-LBS)

105-149 N·m
(77-110 FT-LBS)

FRONT RETAINER

WASHER

RADIUS ARM

OUTER
INSULATOR

SPACER

FRONT
INSULATOR

VIEW Y

CROSSMEMBER

163-203 N·m
(120-150 FT-LBS)

LEFT AXLE

VIEW W

FRONT OF VEHICLE

CLAMPS MUST BE INSTALLED
IN POSITION SHOWN WITHIN
± 45° TIGHTEN NUTS
40-57 N·m (29-42 FT-LBS)

W

X

Y

S

Z

STEERING ROD
LINK

STEERING
CAP

P.I.A.

VIEW S

COTTER PIN

70-100 N·m
(51-73 FT-LBS)

CLAMPS MUST BE INSTALLED
IN POSITION SHOWN WITHIN
± 45° TIGHTEN NUTS
40-57 N·m (29-42 FT-LBS)

MAIN VIEW

**Fig. 4   Independent front suspension. Bronco & F-150 Four Wheel Drive.
1981–85 shown (similar to 1980)**

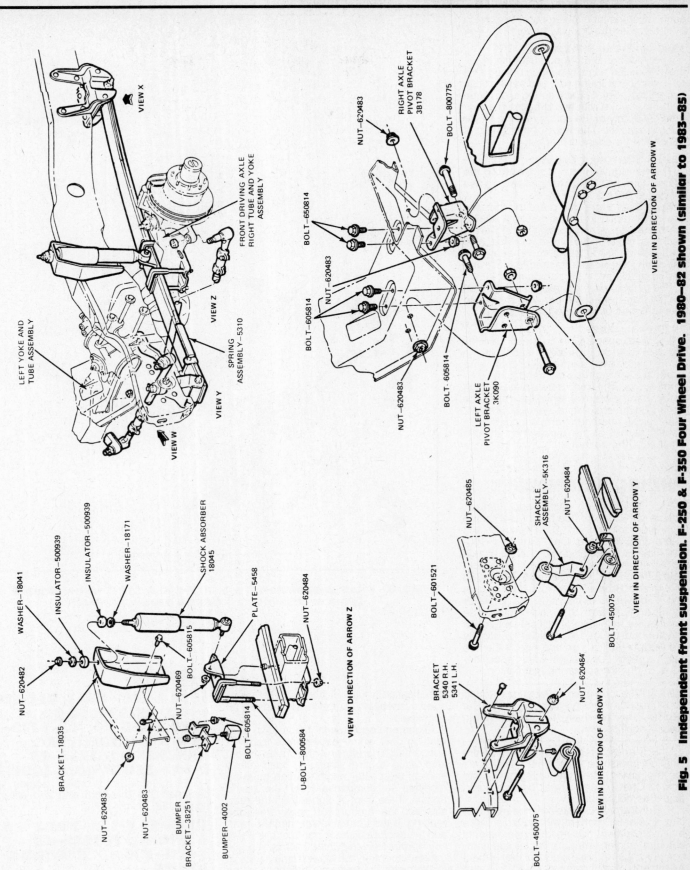

VIEW X

LEFT YOKE AND TUBE ASSEMBLY

VIEW Y

VIEW Z

FRONT DRIVING AXLE RIGHT TUBE AND YOKE ASSEMBLY

SPRING ASSEMBLY–5310

VIEW W

NUT–620483

RIGHT AXLE PIVOT BRACKET 3B178

BOLT–800775

BOLT–650814

NUT–620483

BOLT–605814

BOLT 605814

NUT–620483

LEFT AXLE PIVOT BRACKET 3K090

VIEW IN DIRECTION OF ARROW W

WASHER–18041

INSULATOR–500939

INSULATOR–500939

WASHER–18171

SHOCK ABSORBER 18045

PLATE–5458

NUT–620482

BRACKET–18035

NUT–620483

NUT–620483

BOLT–605815

NUT–620469

BUMPER BRACKET–3B251

BUMPER–4002

BOLT–605814

U-BOLT–800584

NUT–620484

VIEW IN DIRECTION OF ARROW Z

NUT–620485

BOLT–601521

SHACKLE ASSEMBLY–5K316

NUT–620484

BOLT–450075

VIEW IN DIRECTION OF ARROW Y

BRACKET 5340 R.H. 5341 L.H.

NUT–620484

BOLT–450075

VIEW IN DIRECTION OF ARROW X

Fig. 5   Independent front suspension. F-250 & F-350 Four Wheel Drive. 1980–82 shown (similar to 1983–85)

each yoke and tube assembly is supported by the coil spring and radius arm.

1980—85 F-250 & F-350

The independent front suspension on these vehicles has a two piece driving axle attached to the frame with two semi-elliptic leaf springs, **Fig. 5.** Each spring is clamped to the axle yoke with two U-bolts. The rear tube assembly of the spring rests in a rear hanger bracket. The front of the spring is attached to a shackle bracket.

1979 F-100, 150 & Bronco

The front driving axle is attached to the frame with two coil springs, two radius arms and a track bar, **Fig. 6.**

The radius arms clamp around the axle tube and attach to frame brackets behind the front axle. A coil spring is attached to each radius arm directly above the axle and extends to the frame spring seat. The shock absorbers are attached to the frame and to brackets on the radius arm.

The track bar is mounted to a bracket on the left frame side member and extends to the right side of the axle housing.

1979 F-250, 350

The front suspension on these vehicles consists of a driving axle attached to the frame with two semi-elliptic leaf type springs. Each spring is clamped to the axle with U-bolts. The front of the spring rests in a front hanger bracket, while the rear of the spring is attached to a shackle bracket. The shock absorbers are attached to a frame bracket at the top and to an axle bracket at the bottom.

WHEEL ALIGNMENT

Prior to checking caster and camber, ensure vehicle front ride height is within ⅛ inch side to side on 1979 models and 1980—85 E-100-350. On 1980—85 F-100-350 models, the left side ride height should be within 0—⅜ inch higher than the right side ride height. On 1980—85 F-150-350 (4×4) and Bronco, the front ride heights should be within ³⁄₁₆ inch side to side. Refer to **Figs. 7, 8 and 9.** If the vehicle ride heights are not within specifications, redistribute load on loaded vehicles or slightly load empty vehicles on one side. If the ride heights cannot be brought within specifications, verify correct spring installation.

NOTE: The ride height variations stated above are for checking purposes only. The vehicle does not have to operate within these specifications.

Check and correct as necessary all tire inflation pressures, then check front tires for the same size, ply rating and load range. Check front wheel bearings and adjust as necessary.

If all the above checks have been made, check wheel alignment with suitable alignment equipment. Using the ride heights obtained earlier, compare caster and camber readings to those listed in the "Wheel Alignment Specifications Chart". If the caster and camber angles exceed the

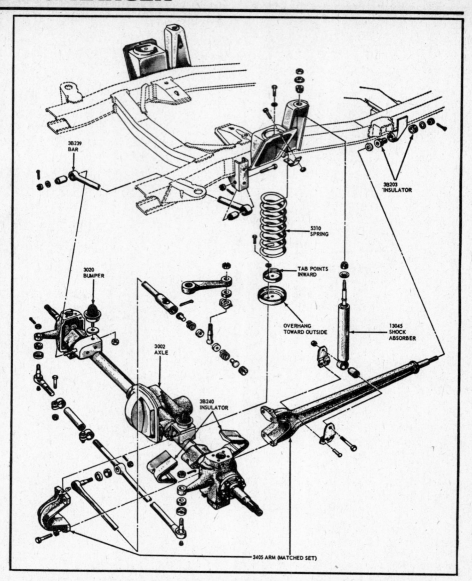

Fig. 6   Front suspension (Typical) F-100 & 150 4 wheel drive & Bronco. Less independent front suspension

specifications, inspect front end for damaged suspension components. Replace as necessary.

Alignment equipment indicates a true reading only when the vehicle's frame is horizontal. Therefore, if the frame is not level (due to tire, spring or load differences), the caster angle reading must be modified to compensate for the frame angles. If the front is higher than the rear, subtract the amount of angle from the reading. If the front is lower than the rear, add the angle. To check frame angle, use a spirit protractor, and take the frame angle measurement on the lower frame flange at the flat area immediately adjacent to the rear spring front hanger.

1979 F-100—150 & BRONCO 4 × 4, 1979 F-250 4 × 4, 1979 F-350 4 × 4 & 1979—85 4 × 2 MODELS EXC. RANCHERO & 1982—85 F-100—350 W/BALL JOINTS

The camber and caster angles are designed into the front end and are not adjustable.

1980—85 F-150—350 4 × 4 & BRONCO & 1982—85 F-100—350 4 × 2 W/BALL JOINTS

The caster angle on 1981—85 F-250—

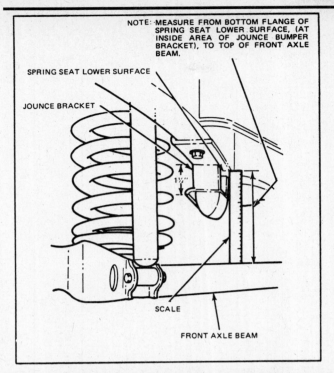

Fig. 7 Measuring riding height. 1979—85 E series

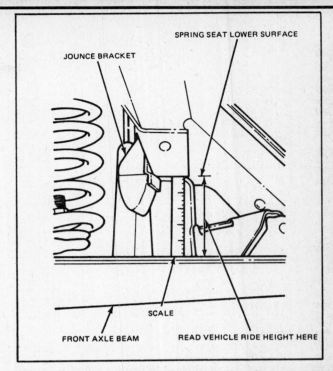

Fig. 8 Measuring riding height. 1979 F series

350 4 × 4 models with leaf spring front suspension can be adjusted by inserting a shim between the spring and axle. Shims are available in increments of 0°, 1° and 2°. The 0° shim is used to adjust side-to-side ride height when an angled shim is installed on the opposite side of the axle. On all other models, the caster angle is designed into the axle and is not adjustable.

The camber angle may be adjusted by means of mounting sleeves placed on the upper ball joint, **Figs. 10, 11 and 12.** Four sleeves are available in ½° camber increments to allow a 3° range of adjustment from −1½° to +1½°.

RANCHERO

Caster and camber can be adjusted by loosening the bolts that attach the upper suspension arm to the shaft at the frame side rail, and moving the arm assembly in or out in the elongated bolt holes. Since any movement of the arm affects both caster and camber, both factors should be balanced against one another when making the adjustment.

Install the tool with the pins in the frame holes and the hooks over the upper arm inner shaft. Tighten the hook nuts snug before loosening the upper arm inner shaft attaching bolts, **Fig. 13.**

Caster Adjust

1. Tighten the tool front hook nut or loosen the rear hook nut as required to increase caster to the desired angle.
2. To decrease caster, tighten the rear hook nut or loosen the front hook nut as required.

NOTE: The caster angle can be checked without tightening the inner shaft retaining bolts.

3. Check the camber angle to be sure it did not change during the caster adjustment and adjust if necessary.
4. Tighten the upper arm inner shaft retaining bolts and remove tool.

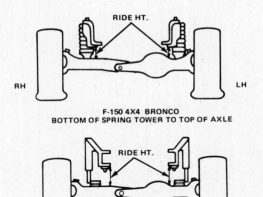

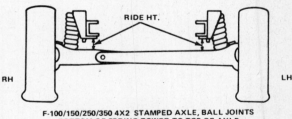

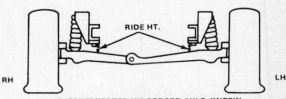

Fig. 9 Measuring riding height. 1980—85 F-100—350 & Bronco

1979–82 Wheel Alignment Specifications Chart

1979 E & F SERIES

Riding Height, Inches		3.00–3.25	3.50–3.75	4.00–4.25	4.25–4.50	4.75–5.00	5.25–5.50	Toe In
1979 E100, 150	Caster	—	+5¾° to +7¼°	+4½° to +5¾°	+4° to +5¼°	+2½° to +4°	+1½° to +2¾°	1/32
	Camber	—	−1½° to +¼°	−½° to +1¼°	0° to +1¾°	+1° to +2¾°	+2° to +3¾°	
1979 E250, 350	Caster	—	+8½° to +9¾°	+7⅛° to +8½°	+6½° to +7¾°	+5¼° to +6½°	+4° to +5½°	1/32
	Camber	—	−1½° to +¼°	−½° to +1¼°	0° to +1¾°	+1° to +2¾°	+2° to +3¾°	
1979 F100, 150, 250④	Caster	+7¾° to +9°	+6¼° to +7⅝°	+5⅛° to +6½°	+4½° to +5⅞°	+3¼° to +4⅝°	—	3/32
	Camber	−1½° to +⅛°	−¾° to +1°	0° to +1⅝°	+⅜° to +2°	+1¼° to +2¾°	—	
1979 F250①	Caster	+8⅜° to +7°	+5⅞° to +7⅛	+4½° to +5⅞°	+3⅞° to +5¼°	+2⅝° to +4°	—	3/32
	Camber	−1½° to +⅛°	+⅞° to −¾°	0° to +1⅝°	+⅜° to +2°	+1¼° to +2¾°	—	
1979 F250②③, 350	Caster	+8⅞° to +10⅜°	+7¾° to +9°	+6⅜° to 7¾°	+5¾° to +7⅛°	4½° to +5⅞°	—	3/32
	Camber	−1¾° to −¼°	−1⅛° to +½°	−¼° to +1¼°	0° to +1⅝°	+¾° to +2⅜°	—	

1980–82 E SERIES

Riding Height, Inches		3.25–3.50	3.50–3.75	4.00–4.25	4.25–4.50	4.50–4.75	5.00–5.25	5.25–5.50	Toe In
E100, 150	Camber	−1¾° to −¼°	−1½° to +¼°	−½° to +1¼°	0° to +1¾°	+½° to +2¼°	+1½° to +3¼°	+2° to +3¾°	⅛°
	Caster	+6¼° to +8°	+5¾° to +7¼°	+4½° to +5¾°	+4° to +5¼°	+3¼° to +4½°	+2° to +3¼°	+1½° to +2¾°	
E250, 350	Camber	−1¾° to −¼°	−1½° to +¼°	−½° to +1¼°	0° to +1¾°	+½° to +2¼°	+1½° to +3¼°	+2° to +3¾°	1/32°
	Caster	+9° to +10½°	+8½° to +9¾°	+7⅛° to +8½°	+6½° to +7¾°	+5¾° to +7°	+4⅝° to +6°	+4° to +5½°	

1980–82 F SERIES EXC. F-250/350 (4×4)

Riding Height, Inches		2.00–2.25	2.25–2.75	2.75–3.25	3.25–3.50	3.50–4.00	4.00–4.25	4.25–4.75	4.75–5.00	Toe In
F100, 150 (4×2)	Camber	—	−3°–−½°	−2°–+½°	−1¼°–+1¼°	−¼°–+2¼°	+½°–+3°	+1½°–+4°	—	3/32
	Caster	—	+6°–+10°	+5°–+9°	+4°–+8°	+3°–+7°	+2°–+6°	+1°–+5°	—	
F250/350 (4×2)	Camber	−2½°–0°	−1½°–+1°	+¾°–+1¾°	+¼°–+2¾°	+1°–+3½°	+2°–+4½°	—	—	⑤
	Caster	+5¾°–+9°	+4¾°–+8°	+3¾°–+7°	+2¾°–+6°	+1¾°–+5°	+¾°–+4°	—	—	
F150 Bronco (4×4)	Camber	—	—	−2½°–−¼°	−1¾°–+½°	−¾°–+1½°	0°–+2¼°	+1°–+3¼°	+1¾°–+4°	⑥
	Caster	—	—	+6°–+9°	+5°–+8°	+4° –+7°	+3°–+6°	+2°–+5°	+1°–+4°	

1980 F SERIES (4×4)

Riding Height, Inches		4.25–4.75	4.75–5.00	5.00–5.50	5.50–6.00	6.00–6.25	6.25–6.75	6.75–7.00	Toe In
F250-350 (4×4)	Camber	−4°–−1¼°	−2¾°–−0°	−1½°–+1¼°	−¼°–+2½°	+1°–+3¾°	+2¼°–+5°	—	2/32
	Caster	+3½°–+5¾°	+3¼°–+5½°	+3°–+5¼°	+2¾°–+5°	+2½°–+4¾°	+2¼°–+4½°	—	

1981–82 F SERIES (4×4)

Riding Height, Inches		4.25–4.75	4.75–5.00	5.00–5.50	5.50–6.00	6.00–6.25	6.25–6.75	6.75–7.00	Toe In
F250-350 (4×4)	Camber	—	−2¾°–−¼°	−1¾°–+¾°	−¾°–+1¾°	+¼°–+2¾°	+1¼°–+4°	+2½°–+5°	3/32
	Caster	—	+3°–+5°	+3⅛°–+5⅛°	+3⅛°–+5⅛°	+3¼°–+5¼°	+3⅜°–+5⅜°	+3½°–+5½°	

①—Regular Cab 7700-7900 GVW & Super Cab 6300-7800 GVW.
②—Super Cab 8100 GVW.
③—Super Cab with standard suspension.
④—6200-6800 GVW.
⑤—1980, 7/32; 1981, 3/32.
⑥—1980, 2/32; 1981, 3/32.

continued

1983–85 Wheel Alignment Specifications

Riding Height In Inches	Caster Angle Degrees①							
	4	4¼	4½	4¾	5	5¼	5½	5¾
1983–84 E-100 & 150								
E-100, 150	+4½–+6½	+4–+6	+3¼–+5¼	+2½–+4½	+2–+4	+1¼–+3¼	+¾–+2¾	+¼–+2¼

①—Side to side caster readings must be within 1½°, when vehicle riding height is within ⅛ inch side to side.

Riding Height In Inches	Caster Angle Degrees①							
	3.80	4.05	4.30	4.55	4.80	5.05	5.30	5.55
1985 E-150								
E-150	+7½–+9½	+7–+9	+6¼–+8¼	+5½–+7½	+5–+7	+4½–+6½	+3¾–+5¾	+3¼–+5¼

①—Side to side caster readings must be within 1½°, when vehicle riding height is within ⅛ inch side to side.

Riding Height In Inches	Caster Angle Degrees①							
	3.80	4.05	4.30	4.55	4.80	5.05	5.30	5.55
1983–85 E-250 & 350								
E-250, 350	+7½–+9½	+7–+9	+6¼–+8¼	+5½–+7½	+5–+7	+4½–+6½	+3¾–+5¾	+3¼–+5¼

①—Side to side caster readings must be within 1½°, when vehicle riding height is within ⅛ inch side to side.

Riding Height In Inches	Caster Angle Degrees①									
	3–3.2	3.2–3.4	3.4–3.6	3.6–3.8	3.8–4	4–4.2	4.2–4.4	4.4–4.6	4.6–4.8	4.8–5
1983–85 F-100 & 150 (4×2)										
F-100, 150	+5¼–+7¼	+5–+7	+4½–+6½	+4¼–+6¼	+3¾–+5¾	+3¼–+5¼	+2¾–+4¾	+2½–+4½	+2–+4	+1½–+3½

①—Side to side caster readings must be within 1½°, when truck frame to axle riding height is such that right hand side is from 0 to .4 inch less than left hand side.

Riding Height In Inches	Caster Angle Degrees①								
	2.4	2.6	2.8	3	3.2	3.4	3.6	3.8	4
1983 F-250 & 350 (4×2)									
F-250, 350	+6¼–+7¼	+5¾–+7¼	+5¼–+7¼	+4½–+6½	+4–+6	+3½–+5½	+3–+5	+3–+4½	+3–+4

①—Side to side caster readings must be within 1½°, when truck frame to axle riding height is such that right hand side is from 0–.2 inch less than left hand side.

continued

1983–85 Wheel Alignment Specifications— Continued

1984 F-250 & 350 (4×2)

Riding Height In Inches	Caster Angle Degrees①									
	2.4	2.6	2.8	3	3.2	3.4	3.6	3.8	4	4.2
F-250, 350	+5¼—+7¼	+5—+6¾	+4½—+6½	+4¼—+6¼	+3¾—+5¾	+3¼—+5¼	+2¾—+4¾	+2½—+4½	+2—+4	+1¼—+3¼

①—Side to side caster readings must be within 1½°, when truck frame to axle riding height is such that right hand side is from 0–.4 inch less than left hand side.

1985 F-250 & 350 (4×2)

Riding Height In Inches	Caster Angle Degrees①										
	2.1	2.5	2.9	3.3	3.7	4.1	4.5	4.9	5.3	5.7	6.1
F-250, 350	+5½—+7½	+5¼—+7	+4¾—+6½	+4½—+6¼	+4—+6	+3½—+5½	+3—+5	+2½—+4½	+2¼—+4½	+1¾—+3¾	+1¼—+3¼

①—Side to side caster readings must be within 1½°, when truck frame to axle riding height is such that right hand side is from 0–.4 inch less than left hand side.

1983–85 F-150 & Bronco (4×4)

Riding Height In Inches	Caster Angle Degrees①								
	3.2	3.4	3.6	3.8	4	4.2	4.4	4.6	4.8
F-150, Bronco	+6—+8	+5½—+7½	+5—+7	+4½—+6½	+4—+6	+3½—+5½	+3—+5	+2½—+4½	+2—+4

①—Side to side caster readings must be within 1½°, when vehicle riding height is within .16 inch side to side.

1983–85 F-250 & 350 (4×4)

Riding Height In Inches	Caster Angle Degrees①								
	5.2	5.4	5.6	5.8	6	6.2	6.4	6.6	6.8
F-250, 350	+3³⁄₁₆—+5⁵⁄₁₆	+3¹⁄₁₆—+5⁵⁄₁₆	+3⅜—+5⅝	+3³⁄₁₆—+5⁵⁄₁₆	+3¼—+5¼	+3³⁄₁₆—+5⁵⁄₁₆	+3⅜—+5⅝	+3⁷⁄₁₆—+5⁷⁄₁₆	+3½—+5½

①—Side to side caster readings must be within 1½°, when vehicle riding height is within .16 inch side to side.

continued

1983–85 Wheel Alignment Specifications—Continued

Riding Height In Inches	Camber Angle Degrees①							
	4	4¼	4½	4¾	5	5¼	5½	5¾
1983–84 E-100 & 150								
E-100, 150	−⅝–+⅝	0–+1¼	+⅜–+1⅝	+⅞–+2¼	+1⅜–+2⅝	+1⅞–+3¼	+2⅜–+3⅝	+2⅞–+4¼

①—Side to side camber readings must be within ⅝°, when vehicle riding height is within ⅛ inch side to side.

Riding Height In Inches	Camber Angle Degrees①							
	4.25	4.50	4.75	5.00	5.25	5.50	5.75	6.00
1985 E-150								
E-150	−¾–+½	−¼–+1⅛	+⅜–+1⅝	+⅞–+2⅛	+1⅜–+2⅝	+1¾–+3	+2¼–+3⅝	+2¾–+4

①—Side to side camber readings must be within ⅝°, when vehicle riding height is within ⅛ inch side to side.

Riding Height In Inches	Camber Angle Degrees①							
	3.9	4.15	4.4	4.65	4.9	5.15	5.4	5.65
1983–85 E-250 & 350								
E-250, 350	−⅝–+⅝	0–+1¼	+⅜–+1⅝	+⅞–+2¼	+1⅜–+2⅝	+1⅞–+3¼	+2⅜–+3⅝	+2⅞–+4¼

①—Side to side camber readings must be within ⅝°, when vehicle riding height is within ⅛ inch side to side.

Riding Height In Inches	Camber Angle Degrees①									
	3–3.2	3.2–3.4	3.4–3.6	3.6–3.8	3.8–4	4–4.2	4.2–4.4	4.4–4.6	4.6–4.8	4.8–5
1983–85 F-100 & 150 (4×2)										
F-100, 150	−1–+¼	−¾–+¾	−¼–+1¼	+¼–+1¾	+¾–+2	+1–+2½	+1½–+3	+2–+3½	+2½–+4	+3–+4½

①—Side to side camber readings must be within .7°, when truck frame to axle riding height is such that right hand side is from 0–.4 inch less than left hand side.

Riding Height In Inches	Camber Angle Degrees①									
	1.6	1.8	2	2.4	2.6	2.8	3	3.2	3.4	3.6
1983 F-250 & 350 (4×2)										
F-250, 350	−½–+½	−½–+¾	−¼–+⅞	+¼–+1½	+⅝–+1¾	+1–+2⅛	+1½–+2⅝	+2–+3¼	+2½–+3½	+2¾–+3½

①—Side to side camber readings must be within .7°, when truck frame to axle riding height is such that right hand side is from 0–.2 inch less than left hand side.

continued

1983–85 Wheel Alignment Specifications—Continued

Riding Height In Inches	Camber Angle Degrees①									
	3.1	3.3	3.5	3.7	3.9	4.1	4.3	4.5	4.7	4.9
1984 F-250 & 350 (4×2)										
F-250, 350	−1–+¼	−¾–+¾	−¼–+1¼	+¼–+1¾	+¾–+2¼	+1¼–+2¾	+1¾–+3¼	+2⅛–+3⅝	+2½–+4	+3–+4½

①—Side to side camber readings must be within .7°, when truck frame to axle riding height is such that right hand side is from 0–.2 inch less than left hand side.

Riding Height In Inches	Camber Angle Degrees①										
	2.1	2.5	2.9	3.3	3.7	4.1	4.5	4.9	5.3	5.7	6.1
1985 F-250 & 350 (4×2)											
F-250, 350	−1½–0	−1–+½	−½–+1	+0–+1½	+½–+2	+¾–+2¼	+1¼–+2½	+1¾–+3¼	+2¼–+3¾	+2¾–+4¼	+3¼–+4½

①—Side to side camber readings must be within .7°, when truck frame to axle riding height is such that right hand side is from 0–.2 inch less than left hand side.

Riding Height In Inches	Camber Angle Degrees①								
	3.1	3.3	3.5	3.7	3.9	4.1	4.3	4.5	4.7
1983–85 F-150 & Bronco (4×4)									
F-150, Bronco	−1⅝–−¼	−1–+¼	−⅝–+⅝	−¼–+1¼	+¼–+1⅝	+¾–+2¼	+1¼–+2⅝	+1⅝–+3¼	+2¼–+3½

①—Side to side camber readings must be within .7°, when truck frame to axle riding height is within 0–.16 inch of side to side.

Riding Height In Inches	Camber Angle Degrees①									
	5.1	5.3	5.5	5.7	5.9	6.1	6.3	6.5	6.7	6.9
1983–85 F-250 & 350 (4×4)										
F-250, 350	−1⅝–−¼	−1⅛–+¼	−⅝–+¾	−⅛–+1¼	+⅜–+1¾	+⅞–+2⅜	+1½–+2⅞	+2–+3½	+2½–+4	+3⅛–+4½

①—Side to side camber readings must be within .7°, when truck frame to axle riding height is within 0–.16 inch of side to side.

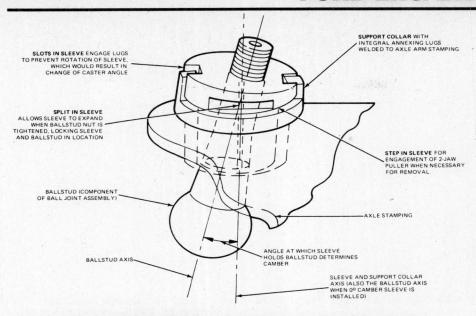

SLOTS IN SLEEVE ENGAGE LUGS TO PREVENT ROTATION OF SLEEVE, WHICH WOULD RESULT IN CHANGE OF CASTER ANGLE

SPLIT IN SLEEVE ALLOWS SLEEVE TO EXPAND WHEN BALLSTUD NUT IS TIGHTENED, LOCKING SLEEVE AND BALLSTUD IN LOCATION

BALLSTUD (COMPONENT OF BALL JOINT ASSEMBLY)

BALLSTUD AXIS

SUPPORT COLLAR WITH INTEGRAL ANNEXING LUGS WELDED TO AXLE ARM STAMPING

STEP IN SLEEVE FOR ENGAGEMENT OF 2-JAW PULLER WHEN NECESSARY FOR REMOVAL

AXLE STAMPING

ANGLE AT WHICH SLEEVE HOLDS BALLSTUD DETERMINES CAMBER

SLEEVE AND SUPPORT COLLAR AXIS (ALSO THE BALLSTUD AXIS WHEN 0° CAMBER SLEEVE IS INSTALLED)

Fig. 10 Camber adjustment. 1980—85 F-150—350 & Bronco

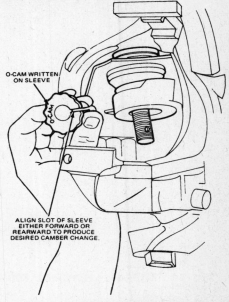

O-CAM WRITTEN ON SLEEVE

ALIGN SLOT OF SLEEVE EITHER FORWARD OR REARWARD TO PRODUCE DESIRED CAMBER CHANGE

Fig. 12 Camber adjustment. 1982—85 F-100—350 4 × 2 w/ball joints

Camber, Adjust

1. Install as previously outlined.
2. Loosen both inner shaft retaining bolts.
3. Tighten or loosen the hook nuts as necessary to increase or decrease camber.
4. Recheck caster angle.

TOE-IN, ADJUST

Check the steering wheel spoke position when the front wheels are in the straight-ahead position. If the spokes are not in the normal position, they can be adjusted while toe-in is being adjusted.

1. Loosen clamp bolts on each tie rod end sleeve.
2. Adjust toe-in. If steering wheel spokes are in their normal position, lengthen or shorten both rods equally to obtain correct toe-in. If spokes are not in nor-

mal position, make necessary rod adjustments to obtain correct toe-in and steering wheel spoke alignment.

WHEEL BEARINGS
ADJUST

4 × 2

Ranchero
1. With wheel rotating, torque adjusting nut to 17—25 ft. lbs.
2. Back off adjusting nut ½ turn and retorque nut to 10—15 inch lbs.
3. Place nut lock on nut so that castellations on lock are aligned with cotter pin hole in spindle and install cotter pin.
4. Check wheel rotation. If it rotates rough or noisily, clean or replace bearings.

E-100-350 & F-100-350
1. Remove wheel and tire assembly, disc brake caliper and pads, dustcap, locknut, adjusting nut, washer and cotter pin.
2. Tighten wheel adjusting nut to 22—25 ft. lbs. while rotating disc brake rotor in opposite direction.
3. Back off wheel retention nut ⅛ turn and install retainer and cotter pin without any additional movement of nut.
4. Reinstall dust cap, caliper, pads and tire and wheel assembly.

4 × 4

1979 Bronco, F-150, F-250 & F-350

NOTE: If vehicle is equipped with free running lock-out hubs, refer to "FRONT

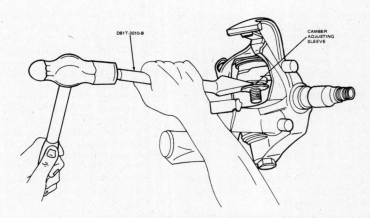

D81T-3010-B

CAMBER ADJUSTING SLEEVE

Fig. 11 Removing camber adjustment sleeve. 1982—85 F-100—350 4 × 2 w/ball joints

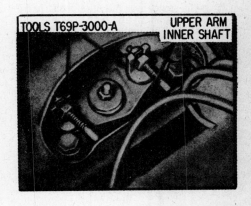

TOOLS T69P-3000-A   UPPER ARM INNER SHAFT

Fig. 13 Caster & camber adjustments. Ranchero

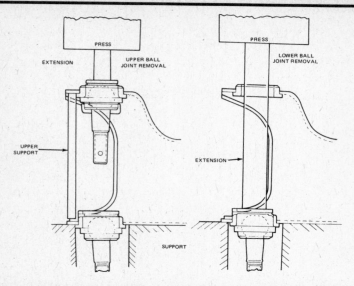

Fig. 14 Ball joint removal. 1981 F-100—350 w/stamped front axle

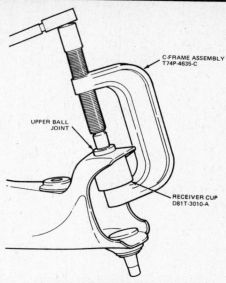

Fig. 15 Upper ball joint removal. 1982—83 F-100—350 & 1984—85 F-150 w/stamped front axle

WHEEL DRIVE" section for removal and installation

1. Raise vehicle and support with stands.
2. Back off brake adjustment, if necessary.
3. Remove grease cap and hub snap ring, then remove splined driving hub and pressure spring. This may require prying slightly.
4. Remove wheel bearing lock nut and lock ring.
5. Using tool T59T-1197-B and a torque wrench, torque bearing adjusting nut to 50 ft. lbs. while rotating wheel back and forth to seat bearings.
6. Back off adjusting nut ¼ turn, then assemble lock ring by turning nut to nearest notch for dowel pin installation.

NOTE: The dowel pin must seat in a lock ring hole for proper bearing adjustment and wheel retention.

7. Install outer lock nut and torque to 50—80 ft. lbs. Final end play of wheel when installed on spindle should be .001—.010 inch on all except 1979 F-250 with a Dana 44-9F axle, and .001—.006 inch on 1979 F-250 with a Dana 44-9F axle.
8. Install pressure spring, driving hub, snap ring and grease cap, then adjust brakes, if necessary.

1980 F-350, 1980—82 F-250, 1980—85 F-150 & Bronco & 1984—85 F-250 Exc. w/Dana 501FS Axle

NOTE: If vehicle is equipped with free running lock-out hubs, refer to "Front Wheel Drive Section" for removal and installation procedures.

1. Raise vehicle and support with

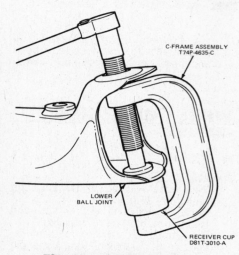

Fig. 16 Lower ball joint removal. 1982—83 F-100—350 & 1984—85 F-150 w/stamped front axle

stands.
2. Remove hub assembly, then, using tool No. T59T-1197-B and a torque wrench, torque bearing inner adjusting nut to 50 ft. lbs. while rotating wheel back and forth to seat bearings.
3. Back out adjusting nut ¼ turn on 1980 models, or ⅛ turn on 1981—85 models, and assemble lock tab and outer locknut.
4. Torque locknut to 50 ft. lbs. on 1980 models, or 150 ft. lbs. on 1981—85 models. Bend at least one tab into a slot on both the inner adjusting nut and outer locknut.
5. Final end play of wheel when installed on spindle should be .001—.006 inch.
6. Install hub assembly.

1981—85 F-350 & 1983—85 F-250 w/Dana 501FS Axle
1. Raise vehicle and support with

stands.
2. Remove hub assembly, then using front wheel bearing spanner, D78T-1197-A and torque wrench and tighten inner locknut to 50 ft. lbs. to seat bearing.
3. Back off inner locknut and retorque to 31—39 ft. lbs.
4. While rotating hub, back off locknut ⅜ turn.
5. Assemble lockwasher and outer locknut and torque to 65 ft. lbs. Bend at least one into a slot on both the inner adjusting nut and outer lock nut.
6. Final end play of the wheel when installed on spindle should be .001—.009 inch.
7. Install hub assembly.

WHEEL BEARINGS
REPLACE

4 × 2

1. Raise and support front of vehicle and remove front wheels.
2. Remove brake caliper and position aside, leaving brake lines attached.

NOTE: Do not allow weight of caliper to hang on brake lines.

3. Remove grease cap, cotter pin, locknut, adjusting nut and washer, then the outer bearing cone and roller.
4. Remove hub and rotor and discard grease retainer.
5. Remove inner bearing and roller.
6. Reverse procedure to install. Adjust bearings as described under "Wheel Bearings, Adjust".

4 × 4

1. Raise and support front of vehicle and

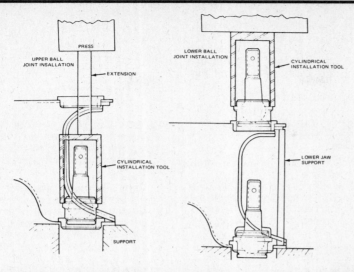

Fig. 17 Ball joint installation. 1981 F-100—350 w/stamped front axle

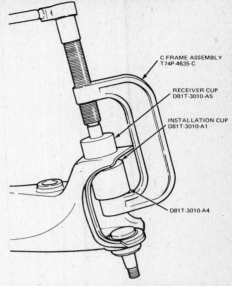

Fig. 18 Upper ball joint Installation. 1982—83 F-100—350 & 1984—85 F-150 w/stamped front axle

remove front wheels.
2. On models equipped with locking hubs, remove hubs as described in "Front Wheel Drive Section".
3. On 1979—81 models, remove front hub grease cap.
4. On 1979—81 models, remove driving hub snap ring, then the splined driving hub and pressure spring.
5. On all models, remove wheel bearing lock nut, lock ring and adjusting nut, then the hub and disc assembly.

NOTE: The outer bearing and roller assembly will slide out when the hub is removed.

6. Remove inner bearing and grease seal from wheel hub using a suitable driving tool on 1979—81 models or a puller on 1982—85 models.
7. Reverse procedure to install. Adjust bearings as described under "Wheel Bearings, Adjust".

BALL JOINTS
REPLACE

RANCHERO

Ford Motor Company recommends that new ball joints should not be installed on used control arms if ball joint replacement is required. Refer to "Control Arm, Replace" for procedure.

1981—83 F-100—350 & 1984—85 F-150 W/STAMPED FRONT AXLE

1. Raise and support front of vehicle and

remove front wheels.
2. Remove brake caliper and position aside, leaving brake lines attached.

NOTE: Do not allow weight of caliper to hang on brake lines.

3. Remove dust cap, cotter pin, nut retainer, nut washer and outer bearing, then the rotor from wheel spindle.
4. Remove inner bearing and seal, then the brake dust shield. Discard bearing seal.
5. Disconnect steering linkage from spindle and spindle arm by removing cotter pin and nut.
6. On 1983—85 models, remove tie rod end from spindle arm using tool No. 3290-C or equivalent.
7. On 1981—82 models, remove cotter pin from upper ball joint stud, then the nuts from upper and lower ball joint studs.
8. On 1983—85 models, remove cotter pins from upper and lower ball joint studs, then the nut from upper ball joint stud. Loosen lower nut to end of lower stud.
9. On all models, separate ball joint from spindle and remove spindle from vehicle.
10. On 1982—85 models, remove ball joint snap ring.
11. On all models, remove ball joints using tools shown in **Figs. 14, 15 and 16.**
12. Reverse procedure to install, using tools shown in **Figs. 17, 18 and 19.**

NOTE: On 1981 models, remove lower ball joint first and install last. On 1982—85 models, remove upper ball joint first and install last. Do not heat ball joint or axle to aid in removal or installation.

CHECKING BALL JOINTS FOR WEAR
RANCHERO & 1981—83 F-100—350 & 1984—85 F-150 W/STAMPED FRONT AXLE

1. Adjust front wheel bearings as described under "Wheel Bearings, Adjust".
2. Check lower ball joint by grasping lower edge of tire and moving wheel in and out while observing lower spindle arm and lower portion of axle jaw. If movement exceeds 1/4 inch on Ranchero models, or 1/32 inch on other models, **Fig. 20,** the lower ball joint must be replaced.
3. Check upper ball joint by grasping upper edge of tire and moving wheel in and out. If there is any movement between upper spindle arm and upper portion of axle jaw on Ranchero models, or movement exceeds 1/32 inch on other models, the upper ball joint must be replaced.

NOTE: On Ranchero models, the ball joint and control arm must be replaced as an assembly. Refer to "Control Arm, Replace".

CONTROL ARM
REPLACE

RANCHERO

Upper Arm
1. Raise and support front of vehicle and

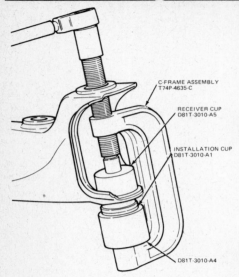

Fig. 19 Lower ball joint installation. 1982—83 F-100—350 & 1984—85 F-150 w/stamped front axle

remove front wheels.
2. Remove upper ball joint stud nut cotter pin, then loosen nut one or two turns. Do not remove nut at this time.
3. Install ball joint remover press, tool No. T57P-3006-B or equivalent, between upper and lower ball joint studs with adapter screw on top.
4. Turn adapter screw, using a suitable wrench, until tool places stud under compression. Tap spindle near upper stud to loosen stud in spindle, then remove tool and support lower control arm with a suitable jack.
5. Raise lower control arm to relieve tension from upper ball joint stud and remove stud nut.
6. Remove upper control arm attaching bolts and the upper control arm, **Fig. 3**.
7. Reverse procedure to install.

Lower Arm
1. Raise and support front of vehicle and remove front wheels.
2. Disconnect shock absorber lower mounting and push stock up to the retracted position.
3. Disconnect stabilizer bar link, if equipped, from lower control arm.
4. Remove cotter pin from lower ball joint stud nut.
5. Remove strut attaching bolts and the strut from lower control arm.
6. Loosen lower ball joint stud nut one or two turns. Do not remove nut at this time.
7. Install ball joint remover press, tool No. T57P-3006-B or equivalent, between upper and lower ball joint studs with adapter screw on top.
8. Turn adapter screw, using a suitable wrench, until tool places stud under compression. Tap spindle near lower stud to loosen stud in spindle, then support lower control arm with a suit-

able jack.
9. Remove ball joint stud nut, then lower the control arm from spindle.
10. Remove spring and insulator, then the lower control arm attaching nut and bolt and the lower control arm, **Fig. 3**.
11. Reverse procedure to install.

SHOCK ABSORBER
REPLACE

1. Disconnect shock absorber from upper mounting.
2. Disconnect shock absorber from lower mounting, then compress shock and remove from vehicle.
3. Reverse procedure to install.

COIL SPRING
REPLACE

RANCHERO

1. Raise and support front of vehicle.
2. Disconnect lower end of shock absorber from lower control arm, then support arm with a suitable jack.
3. Remove strut and jounce bumper-to-lower control arm attaching bolt and nut.
4. Disconnect sway bar, if equipped, from lower control arm.
5. Remove nut and bolt attaching inner end of lower control arm to crossmember.
6. Lower control arm slowly to relieve spring tension, then remove spring from vehicle, **Fig. 3**.
7. Reverse procedure to install.

NOTE: When installing, the end of the spring must be ½ inch or less from end of depression in control arm.

4 × 2 MODELS EXC. RANCHERO

1. Raise front of vehicle and support with stands. Support axle with a suitable jack.

NOTE: The axle must be supported when replacing spring and not be permitted to hang by brake hose. If length of brake hose is not sufficient to permit spring replacement, it will be necessary to remove the disc brake caliper. Do not suspend caliper by brake hose, if removed.

2. Disconnect shock absorber from lower mounting.
3. Remove spring upper retainer attaching bolts and the retainer.
4. Remove spring lower retainer attaching nut and the retainer.
5. Lower axle slowly and remove spring from vehicle.
6. Reverse procedure to install.

F-150 4 × 4 & BRONCO

1. Raise and support vehicle.

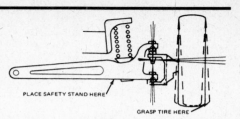

PLACE SAFETY STAND HERE

GRASP TIRE HERE

Fig. 20 Checking lower ball joint for wear. Ranchero & 1981—83 F-100—350 & 1984—85 F-150 w/stamped front axle

2. Remove shock absorber to lower bracket attaching bolt.
3. Remove spring lower retainer attaching nuts from inside coil spring.
4. Remove spring upper retainer attaching screw and the upper retainer.
5. Place jack stands under frame side rails and lower axle to relieve spring tension.

NOTE: The axle must be supported when replacing spring and not be permitted to hang by the brake hose. If the length of the brake hose is not sufficient to permit spring replacement, it will be necessary to remove the disc brake caliper. Do not suspend caliper by brake hose, if removed.

6. Remove spring and lower retainer.
7. Reverse procedure to install.

LEAF SPRING
REPLACE

F-250—350 4 × 4

1. Raise vehicle until weight is relieved from front spring with the front wheels still contacting floor. Support axle to prevent rotation.
2. Disconnect shock absorber lower end from U-bolt spacer, then remove U-bolts, cap and spacer.
3. Remove rear hanger bolt at rear of spring.
4. Remove front shackle bolt and remove spring.
5. Reverse procedure to install.

RADIUS ARM
REPLACE

4 × 2 MODELS EXC. RANCHERO

1. Remove coil spring as described under "Coil Spring, Replace".
2. Remove spring lower seat from radius arm.
3. Remove radius arm and stabilizer bracket (if equipped) attaching nut and bolt from axle.
4. On all except 1983—85 E-100—350 models, remove nut, rear washer, insulator and spacer from rear side of radius arm rear bracket.
5. On 1979—80 models, disconnect tie

rod end.
6. On all models, remove radius arm from vehicle.
7. Reverse procedure to install.

F-150 4 × 4 & BRONCO

1. Raise and support vehicle under frame side rails.
2. Remove shock absorber-to-lower bracket attaching bolt and nut and separate shock from radius arm.
3. Remove spring lower retainer attaching bolt(s) from inside coil spring.
4. On 1983–85 models, loosen axle pivot bolt.
5. On all models, remove radius arm-to-frame bracket attaching nut, then the radius arm rear insulator and spacer (if equipped).
6. On 1980–85 models, lower axle and slide it forward.

NOTE: The axle must be supported and not be permitted to hang by brake hose. If length of brake hose is not sufficient to provide adequate clearance, it will be necessary to remove the disc brake caliper. Do not suspend caliper by brake hose, if removed.

7. On 1979 models, remove radius arm cap attaching bolts, then the cap and insulator.
8. On 1980–85 models, remove axle-to-radius arm bracket attaching screws, then the radius arm-to-axle attaching bolt and stud.
9. On all models, move axle forward and remove radius arm from axle, then pull radius arm from frame bracket.
10. Reverse procedure to install.

STABILIZER BAR
REPLACE

RANCHERO

1. Raise front of vehicle and support under both front wheels.
2. Remove stabilizer bar attaching bolts and brackets, then the stabilizer bar, **Fig. 3.**
3. Reverse procedure to install, using new attaching bolts and nuts.

EXC. RANCHERO

1. Disconnect both ends of stabilizer bar from link assembly on I-beam bracket.
2. Remove stabilizer bar attaching bolts and the stabilizer bar.

NOTE: On 1980–85 F-150 4 × 4 and Bronco models, the coil spring must be removed to facilitate removal of the stabilizer bar mounting bracket.

3. Reverse procedure to install.

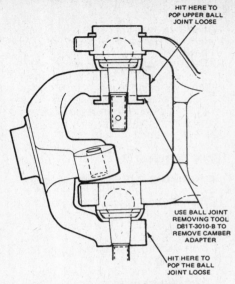

Fig. 21 Steering knuckle removal. 4 × 2 models exc. Ranchero

STEERING KNUCKLE
REPLACE

RANCHERO

1. Raise and support front of vehicle.
2. Remove caliper anchor plate from rotor and wire to one side.
3. Remove grease cap, cotter pin, nut lock, adjusting nut, washer and outer bearing and roller assembly, then slide hub and rotor off steering knuckle.
4. Remove caliper shield attaching bolts and the caliper shield.
5. Disconnect tie rod end from steering knuckle using tool No. 3290-C or equivalent.
6. Remove cotter pins from both ball joint stud nuts and loosen nuts one or two turns. Do not remove nuts at this time.
7. Install ball joint remover press, tool No. T57P-3006-B or equivalent, between upper and lower ball joints.
8. Turn adapter screw, using a suitable wrench, until tool places studs under compression. Hit spindle sharply with a hammer to break studs loose in spindle.
9. Support lower control arm using a suitable jack, then remove upper and lower ball joint stud nuts. Slowly lower jack and remove steering knuckle from vehicle, **Fig. 3.**
10. Reverse procedure to install.

4 × 2 MODELS EXC. RANCHERO

1. Raise and support front of vehicle.
2. Remove wheel and tire assembly, then unfasten brake caliper and position aside, leaving brake lines attached.

NOTE: Do not allow weight of caliper to hang on brake lines.

3. Remove dust cap, cotter pin, nut retainer, nut, washer and outer bearing, then slide hub off steering knuckle.
4. Remove inner bearing and seal and discard the seal.
5. Remove brake dust shield and caliper anchor plate, if equipped.
6. Disconnect steering linkage from knuckle.
7. On 1981–83 F-100–350 models with ball joints, remove cotter pins and nuts from upper and lower ball joint studs.
8. On 1984–85 F-150 models with ball joints, remove cotter pins from upper and lower ball joint studs. Remove nut from upper stud and loosen lower stud nut to end of stud.
9. On all models except 1981–85 with ball joints, remove lock pin nut and washer and the lock pin. Remove upper and lower steering knuckle pin plugs, then drive pin out from top of axle and remove steering knuckle and thrust bearing.
10. On 1981–85 models with ball joints, separate ball joints from steering knuckle, **Fig. 21,** and remove knuckle from vehicle.
11. Reverse procedure to install.

1979 4 × 4 MODELS EXC. F-250–350

1. Raise and support front of vehicle and remove front wheels.
2. On models equipped with locking hubs, remove hubs as described in "Front Wheel Drive Section".
3. On all models, remove brake caliper and the hub and rotor assembly. Position caliper aside, leaving brake lines attached.

NOTE: Do not allow weight of caliper to hang on brake lines.

4. Remove spindle from steering knuckle.
5. Remove axle shaft from axle housing.
6. Disconnect tie rod end from steering knuckle and remove knuckle housing.
7. Remove cotter pins and nuts from ball joint studs. Discard lower stud nut.
8. Remove steering knuckle from yoke.
9. Install knuckle in a vise and press out ball joints using a suitable tool.
10. Reverse procedure to install. Install new lower ball joint nut and torque to 70–90 ft. lbs. Torque upper ball joint stud nut to 100 ft. lbs.

1979 F-250–350 4 × 4

1. Raise and support front of vehicle and remove front wheels.
2. Remove brake caliper and the hub and rotor assembly. Position caliper aside, leaving brake lines attached.

NOTE: Do not allow weight of caliper to hang on brake lines.

3. Remove inner wheel bearing and seal.
4. Remove spindle from steering knuckle.
5. Remove axle shaft joint assembly and tie rod.
6. Remove 4 steering arm nuts. Loosen nuts alternately as arm is spring loaded.
7. Remove steering arm, compression spring and gasket. Discard gasket.
8. Remove 4 bearing cap attaching screws and the bearing cap.
9. Remove king pin tapered bushing and the steering knuckle from yoke.
10. Remove king pin from steering knuckle.
11. Reverse procedure to install.

1980—85 4 × 4 MODELS

1. Remove axle shaft and spindle from steering knuckle.
2. Disconnect tie rod from steering arm.
3. Remove upper ball joint nut and loosen lower ball joint nut. Strike upper ball joint stud to loosen ball joints.
4. Remove lower ball joint nut and remove knuckle from yoke tube.
5. Remove camber adjuster bushing from tube and yoke assembly.
6. Install knuckle into vise and press out ball joints using suitable tool.

NOTE: On some models, the lower ball joint is retained by a snap ring.

7. Reverse procedure to install. Install knuckle onto tube and yoke assembly, then install camber adjusting bushing with arrow pointing outward for "positive camber" or towards center of vehicle for "negative camber". Install new lower ball joint nut and torque both upper and lower ball joint nuts to 100 ft. lbs.

MANUAL STEERING GEAR
REPLACE

E-100—350 & 1980—85 F-100—350 4 × 2

1. Raise and support front of vehicle.
2. On 1983—85 F-100—350 models, unfasten flex coupling shield from steering gear input shaft shield and slide it up intermediate shaft.
3. On all models, disconnect flex coupling from steering shaft flange by removing 2 attaching nuts.
4. Disconnect drag link from Pitman arm using tool No. 3290-C.
5. Remove Pitman to sector shaft attaching nut and washer, then remove Pitman arm from gear sector shaft using tool No. T64P-3590-F.
6. While supporting steering gear, remove bolts and washer attaching gear assembly to frame side rail and lower gear assembly from vehicle.
7. Reverse procedure to install.

1979 F-100—350 4 × 2

1. Remove bolt attaching flex coupling to steering gear. Remove brake line bracket.
2. Raise and support front of vehicle, then disconnect Pitman arm from sector shaft using tool No. T64P-3590.
3. Remove steering gear to frame attaching bolts, then remove steering gear assembly.
4. Reverse procedure to install.

1979 BRONCO

Recirculating Ball Manual Steering Gear

1. Remove bolt attaching flex housing to coupling assembly shaft. Note alignment of bolt with groove in shaft.
2. Raise and support front of vehicle, then disconnect drag link from Pitman arm using tool No. 3290-C.
3. Remove Pitman arm nut and washer, then remove Pitman arm from sector shaft using tool No. T64P-3590-F.
4. Support steering gear, then remove steering gear to frame attaching bolts and lower steering gear assembly from vehicle.

1979 F-150 4 × 4 & BRONCO

Worm & Roller Manual Steering Gear

1. Raise and support front of vehicle, then remove Pitman arm attaching nut and washer.
2. Remove Pitman arm from sector shaft using tool No. T64P-3590-F.
3. Remove bolts attaching steering gear to frame side rail, then lower front of vehicle.
4. Remove flex coupling clamp bolt and nut. Loosen clamp from coupling at end of steering column and separate coupling from steering gear input shaft by pushing steering shaft toward steering column.
5. Remove flex coupling clamp from steering gear input shaft, then remove steering gear assembly from vehicle.

1979 F-250 & 350 4 × 4

1. Remove two bolts attaching steering shaft to steering gear and column shaft.
2. Remove fan shroud attaching bolts and position shroud to right hand side of engine compartment.
3. Raise and support front of vehicle, then remove pitman arm nut and washer.
4. Disengage steering shaft coupling from steering gear shaft.
5. Remove steering gear to frame attaching bolts and lower steering gear assembly from vehicle.

RANCHERO

1. Remove flex coupling bolts.
2. Remove Pitman arm nut and remove Pitman arm from sector shaft using a

puller.
3. On vehicles with manual transmission it may be necessary to disconnect the clutch linkage and on V8 models it may be necessary to lower the exhaust system.
4. Unfasten and remove steering gear.

POWER STEERING GEAR
REPLACE

EXC. 1979—82 E-100—350 & RANCHERO

1. Disconnect pressure and return lines from gear. Plug open lines and fittings to prevent contamination.
2. Disconnect brake line bracket attached to gear, if necessary.
3. Remove splash shield, if equipped, from flex coupling, then disconnect flex coupling from steering gear.
4. Raise and support vehicle.
5. Remove Pitman arm attaching nut and washer.
6. Remove Pitman arm from sector shaft using tool No. T64P-3590-F or equivalent.
7. Support steering gear, then remove attaching bolts and lower gear from vehicle.

NOTE: On models equipped with manual transmission, it may be necessary to remove clutch release lever retracting spring to provide clearance for gear removal.

1979—82 ECONOLINE & E-150—350

1. Disconnect pressure and return lines from gear and plug all open lines and fittings.
2. Raise and support vehicle, then remove drag link from Pitman arm.
3. Remove nuts securing flex coupling to steering column shaft assembly.
4. Support gear, then remove gear attaching bolts.
5. Remove flex coupling with pinch bolt, then the coupling from the gear.
6. Remove Pitman arm from sector shaft using tool T64-P3590-F, or equivalent.
7. Reverse procedure to install.

RANCHERO

These models use an integral power steering gear. Remove the gear assembly as follows:

1. Disconnect pressure and return lines from gear and plug openings to prevent entry of dirt.
2. Remove two bolts that secure flex coupling to the gear and to the column.
3. Raise vehicle and remove pitman arm with suitable puller.

4. If vehicle is equipped with synchro-mesh transmission, remove clutch release lever retracting spring to provide clearance to remove gear.
5. Support gear and remove three gear attaching bolts.

POWER STEERING PUMP
REPLACE
1979—85 E-100—350

1. Disconnect pressure and return lines

from pump.
2. Loosen belt tension adjusting bolt fully.
3. On models equipped with A/C, remove pump mounting bracket-to-A/C compressor mounting bracket attaching bolts.
4. On all models, remove pump and mounting brackets from vehicle.
5. Reverse procedure to install.

1979—85 F-100—350 & BRONCO

1. Disconnect return hose from pump

reservoir and drain steering pump fluid into a suitable container.
2. Remove pressure hose from pump.
3. On 1979 models, remove pump-to-mounting bracket attaching bolts, then disconnect pulley bolt and remove pump from vehicle.
4. On 1980—85 models, remove pump drive belt, then unfasten pump and adjusting bracket from support bracket. Remove pump pulley, then the pump attaching bolts and pump.
5. On all models, reverse procedure to install.

Front Wheel Drive Section

1979 4 × 4 SERVICE
FRONT AXLE ASSEMBLY, REPLACE

F-150 & Bronco & F-250 Exc. w/Dana 60-7F Axle

1. Raise front of vehicle and support with safety stands under radius arm brackets.
2. Remove front wheels, brake calipers, hub and rotor assemblies, dust shields, spindles, axle shafts and brake backing plates. Position brake calipers aside, leaving brake lines attached.

NOTE: Do not allow weight of caliper to hang on brake lines.

3. Remove brake line brackets from each end of axle, then disconnect brake lines from axle clips and position aside.
4. Disconnect steering linkage from steering knuckle and position aside.
5. Disconnect stabilizer bar from axle.
6. Disconnect front driveshaft from pinion companion flange and U-joint and position aside.
7. Lower vehicle and support axle with a suitable jack.
8. Remove radius arm-to-radius arm cap attaching bolts.

NOTE: Radius arms and caps are marked for assembly reference and must be installed in their original positions.

9. Remove rubber insulators, then roll axle assembly out from under vehicle, **Fig. 1.**
10. Reverse procedure to install.

F-250—350 w/Dana 60-7F Axle

1. Raise vehicle and support under front axle.
2. Remove front wheels, then unfasten brake caliper assemblies and position aside, leaving brake lines attached.

NOTE: Do not allow weight of calipers to

hang on brake lines.

3. Remove hub and rotor assemblies and axle shafts.
4. Disconnect both front shock absorbers from lower mountings.
5. Disconnect front driveshaft from pinion flange.
6. Support front axle using a suitable jack, then remove spring clip U-bolt nuts and spring seat.
7. Lower axle assembly and roll out from under vehicle, **Fig. 2.**
8. Reverse procedure to install.

AXLE SHAFT, REPLACE

F-150 & Bronco & F-250 Exc. w/Dana 60-7F Axle

1. Raise and support front of vehicle.
2. Remove locking hub, brake caliper and hub and rotor assembly. Position brake caliper aside, leaving brake lines attached.

NOTE: Do not allow weight of caliper to hang on brake lines.

3. Remove nuts attaching brake support bracket, dust shield and spindle to steering knuckle, then carefully separate spindle from knuckle.
4. Remove axle shaft assembly from axle housing, **Fig. 1.**
5. Reverse procedure to install.

F-250—350 w/Dana 60-7F Axle

1. Raise and support front of vehicle and remove wheel and tire assembly.
2. Remove brake caliper, hub and rotor assembly and inner wheel bearing and seal. Position caliper aside, leaving brake lines attached.

NOTE: Do not allow weight of caliper to hang on brake lines.

3. Remove spindle, then the axle shaft assembly, **Fig. 2.**
4. Reverse procedure to install.

DRIVE PINION SEAL, REPLACE

1. Raise front of vehicle. Position safety stands under frame side rails, then lower vehicle far enough to drop axle into rebound position to provide sufficient working clearance.
2. Scribe companion flange and U-joints for assembly reference, then remove driveshaft.
3. Remove pinion shaft nut while holding companion flange with a suitable tool.
4. Remove companion flange.
5. Remove pinion oil seal using a suitable puller and slide hammer.
6. Reverse procedure to install. Coat seating edge of new seal with suitable sealant and apply clean rear axle lubricant to inside of pinion flange.

NOTE: Do not apply sealant to sealing lip of seal.

1980—85 4 × 4 SERVICE
FRONT AXLE ASSEMBLY, REPLACE

F-150 & Bronco

1. Raise front of vehicle and support with safety stands under radius arm brackets.
2. On 1980 models, drain fluid from differential.
3. On all models, remove front tires and brake calipers. Position calipers aside, leaving brake lines attached.

NOTE: Do not allow weight of calipers to hang on brake lines.

4. On 1980 models, remove wheel hub and rotor assemblies, spindles, splash shields and axle shafts.

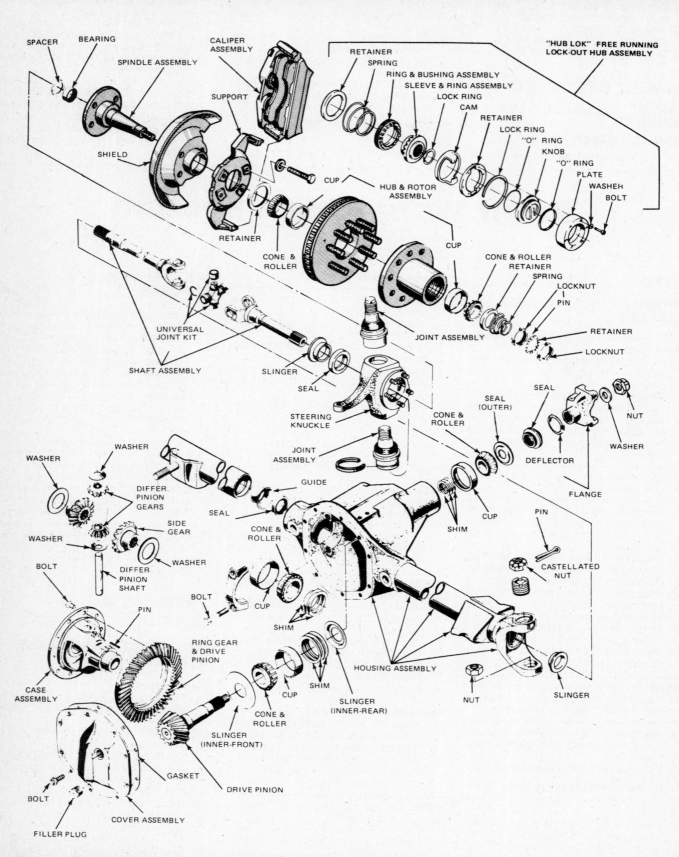

Fig. 1   Four wheel drive front axle assembly. 1979 F-150, Bronco & F-250 exc. w/Dana 60-7F axle

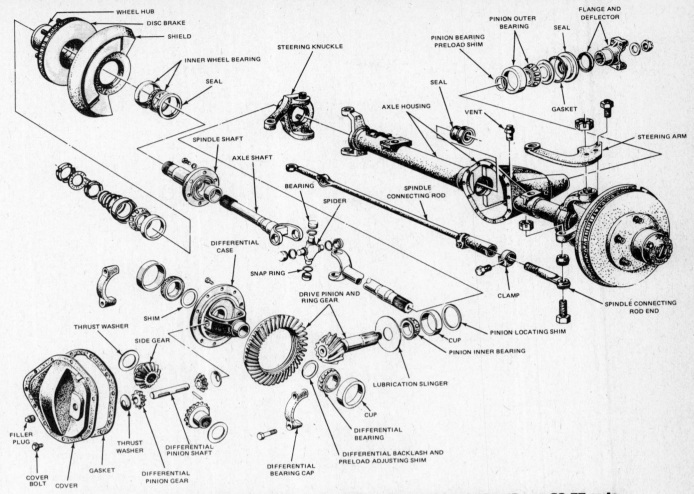

Fig. 2   Four wheel drive front axle assembly. 1979 F-250—350 w/Dana 60-7F axle

5. On all models, support axle arm assembly with a suitable jack and remove upper coil spring retainers. Carefully lower jack and remove coil springs, spring cushions and lower spring seats.

NOTE: The axle must be supported when removing springs and not be permitted to hang by brake hose. If length of brake hose is not sufficient to permit spring removal, it will be necessary to remove the disc brake caliper. Do not suspend caliper by brake hose, if removed.

6. Remove shock absorbers.
7. On 1980 models, remove upper and lower ball joint nuts and steering knuckle.
8. On all models, remove stud and spring seat from radius arm and axle arm, then the lower radius arm-to-axle arm attaching bolt.
9. Disconnect vent tube from left axle arm assembly on 1980 models, or from differential housing on 1981–85 models. Discard hose clamps.

NOTE: On 1981–85 models, remove vent fitting from differential housing and install a ⅛ inch pipe plug.

10. Remove right axle arm-to-crossmember pivot bolt.
11. On 1984–85 models, remove right axle shaft boot and discard boot clamps.
12. On all models, remove right drive axle assembly, and on 1981–85 models, slide axle shaft out of slip shaft.
13. Support differential housing with a suitable jack.
14. On 1980 models, remove differential retaining bolts.
15. On all models, remove left drive axle assembly attaching bolts and the axle assembly, **Fig. 3.**
16. Reverse procedure to install.

F-250—350
1. Raise and support front of vehicle.
2. On 1980 models, drain fluid from differential.
3. On all models, remove front tires and brake calipers. Position calipers aside, leaving brake lines attached.

NOTE: Do not allow weight of calipers to hang on brake lines.

4. On 1980 models, remove hub and rotor assemblies, spindles, splash shields and axle shafts.
5. On all models, support right axle assembly with a suitable jack and remove 2 U-bolts attaching shock absorber mounting plate and leaf spring to axle assembly.
6. On 1980 models, remove upper and lower ball joint nuts and steering knuckle.
7. On all models, disconnect vent tube, from left axle arm assembly on 1980 models, or from differential housing on 1981–85 models.

NOTE: On 1981–85 models, remove vent fitting from differential housing and install a ⅛ inch pipe plug.

8. Remove right axle assembly-to-crossmember pivot bolt and the axle assembly.
9. On 1984–85 models, remove right axle shaft boot and discard boot clamps.

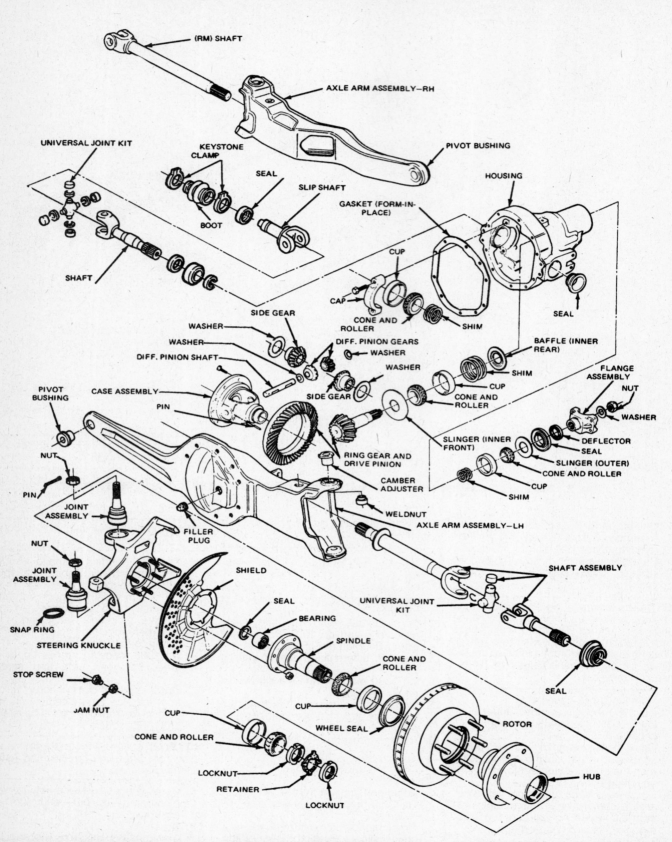

Fig. 3   Four wheel drive front axle assembly. 1980—85 F-150 & Bronco (similar to other 1980—85 models)

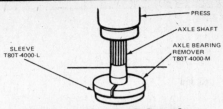

Fig. 4 Axle shaft bearing removal. 1980–82

10. On 1981–85 models, slide axle shaft out of slip shaft.
11. On all models, support left axle arm assembly with a suitable jack and remove 2 U-bolts attaching shock absorber mounting plate and leaf spring to axle assembly.
12. On 1980 models, remove steering knuckle from left axle arm assembly.
13. On all models, support differential housing with a suitable jack, then remove left axle assembly-to-cross-member pivot bolt and the axle assembly.
14. Reverse procedure to install.

AXLE SHAFT, REPLACE

1. Raise and support front of vehicle.
2. Remove front tire and brake caliper. Position caliper aside, leaving brake lines attached.

NOTE: Do not allow weight of caliper to hang on brake lines.

3. Remove spindle and brake splash shield, then the axle shaft, **Fig. 3**.

AXLE SHAFT BEARING, REPLACE

1980–82

1. Remove axle shaft as described under "Axle Shaft, Replace."
2. Remove 3 bearing retainer plate-to-carrier attaching bolts, then slide stud shaft and slip yoke out of housing.
3. Install axle shaft in a suitable vise and drill a ¼ inch hole ¾ through the bearing retainer.
4. Remove bearing retainer by breaking with a chisel positioned in drilled hole.
5. Press bearing from axle shaft, **Fig. 4.**
6. Remove seal and retainer plate from stub shaft. Discard seal.
7. Reverse procedure to install. Install bearing retainer and new seal onto shaft. Lubricate seal with wheel bearing grease. Install bearing onto axle with large radius on inner race facing yoke of axle. Press bearing, then the inner bearing retainer until fully seated, **Fig. 5.** Push seal and outer retainer away from bearing and fill with grease. Wrap a piece of tape around the space, then pull retainer and seal against bearing. This will force grease into bearing. Repeat until grease is visible on small end of rollers.

1983–85

1. Remove axle shaft as described under "Axle Shaft, Replace."
2. Remove carrier-to-cover support arm attaching screws, then separate carrier assembly from support arm and drain lubricant into a suitable container.
3. Install carrier assembly into a suitable holding fixture and rotate axle shaft until open side of snap ring is exposed.
4. Remove snap ring, then slide slip yoke and shaft assembly from housing.
5. Remove and discard right trunnion axle shaft seal from housing.
6. Remove axle shaft bearing.
7. Reverse procedure to install. Install bearing using tool No. T80T-4000-N or equivalent with bearing name and part number facing towards tool. Apply a light coat of suitable grease to new seal prior to installation.

FRONT WHEEL LOCKING HUB SERVICE

1979 F-150–350 & BRONCO W/INTERNAL TYPE MANUAL HUBS

Removal & Disassembly

1. Remove locking hub attaching screws and washers, **Fig. 6.**
2. Remove hub ring and knob, then the internal snap ring from groove on hub.
3. Remove cam body ring and clutch retainer, as an assembly, from hub.
4. Push axle shaft sleeve ring inward and pull axle out slightly with a bolt, then remove axle shaft snap ring.
5. Remove axle shaft sleeve ring, inner clutch ring, pressure spring and spring retainer ring.

Assembly & Installation

1. Apply suitable grease to hub inner spline, then install spring retainer ring with recessed side going in first.
2. Install coil spring, large end first, **Fig. 6.**
3. Lubricate, then install axle shaft sleeve and ring and inner clutch ring.
4. Install axle shaft snap ring. It may be necessary to push gear inward and pull axle shaft out slightly with a bolt to provide clearance.
5. Install actuating cam body ring into outer clutch retaining ring, then assemble into hub.
6. Install inner snap ring, then apply suitable grease to cam ears.
7. Apply suitable lubricant to actuating knob groove, then install outer O-ring.
8. Install actuating knob into hub ring and assemble to axle with knob in locked position.
9. Install 6 screws and washers and torque alternately and evenly to 30–

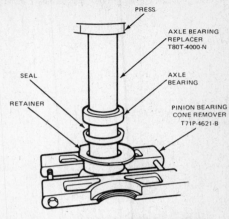

Fig. 5 Axle shaft bearing installation. 1980–82

35 inch lbs.

1980 F-250–350 & 1981 F-150–250 W/AUTOMATIC HUBS

Removal & Disassembly

1. Remove capscrews and cap assembly from spindle, **Fig. 7.**
2. Remove capscrew from end of axle shaft.
3. Remove lock ring from wheel hub groove.
4. Remove body assembly from spindle.

NOTE: If necessary, a puller may be used to remove body assembly.

5. Loosen screws in spindle locknut until heads are flush with edge of locknut, then remove locknut using tool No. T80T-4000-V or equivalent.

Assembly & Installation

1. On 1981 models, install slotted locknut, ensuring pin on inner bearing adjusting nut enters one of the slots.
2. On all models, install spindle locknut and torque to 15–20 ft. lbs. using tool No. T80T-4000-V or equivalent.
3. Install and tighten all setscrews, then push body down until friction shoes are on top of spindle outer locknut, **Fig. 7.**
4. Install capscrew into axle shaft and torque to 35–50 ft. lbs.
5. Install cap assembly and torque capscrews to 30–35 inch lbs.
6. Rotate dial from stop to stop to engage dialing mechanism with body spline.

1980–85 F-150–350 & BRONCO W/MANUAL HUBS

Removal & Disassembly

1. Remove cap assembly capscrews and the cap assembly, **Fig. 8.**
2. Remove snap ring from end of axle shaft.
3. Remove lock ring from wheel hub

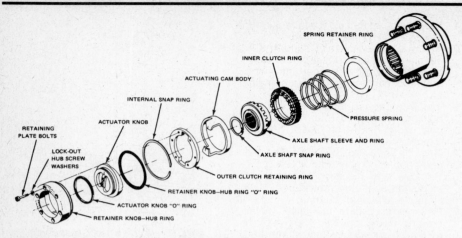

Fig. 6   Internal type manual front locking hub. 1979 F-150—350 & Bronco

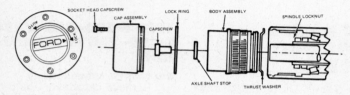

Fig. 7   Automatic front locking hub. 1980 F-250—350 & 1981 F-150—250

groove.
4. Remove body assembly from wheel hub.

NOTE: If necessary, a puller may be used to remove body assembly.

Assembly & Installation
1. Install body assembly onto wheel hub, **Fig. 8.**
2. Install lock ring into hub groove, then the snap ring onto axle shaft.
3. Install cap assembly and torque capscrews to 35—50 inch lbs.

1982—85 F-150—250 & BRONCO W/AUTOMATIC HUBS

Removal & Disassembly
1. Remove cap assembly capscrews and the cap assembly, **Fig. 9.**

NOTE: Avoid dropping ball bearing, bearing race and retainer when removing cap.

2. Remove rubber seal, then the seal bridge retainer from retainer ring space.
3. Remove retainer ring by closing ends with suitable pliers while pulling hub lock from wheel hub.
4. If wheel hub and spindle are to be removed, remove C-washer from stub shaft groove, splined spacer from shaft and the wheel bearing lock nuts and lock washer.

Assembly & Installation
1. Install wheel bearing locknut and lock washer. Torque locknut to 150 ft. lbs.
2. Install splined spacer and C-washer on axle shaft.
3. Install locking hub assembly into hub, ensuring large tangs are aligned with lock washer and splines align with hub and axle shaft splines, **Fig. 9.**
4. Install retainer ring by closing ends with suitable pliers while pushing locking hub assembly into wheel hub.
5. Install seal bridge retainer, narrow end first.
6. Install rubber seal, then the cap assembly. Torque capscrews alternately and evenly to 40—50 inch lbs.

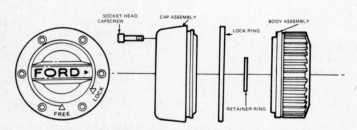

Fig. 8   Manual front locking hub. 1980—85 F-150—250 & Bronco

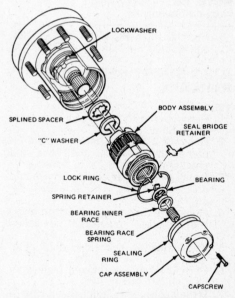

Fig. 9   Automatic front locking hub. 1980—85 F-150—350 & Bronco

AIR CONDITIONING

TABLE OF CONTENTS

A/C System Testing

INDEX

GENERAL PRECAUTIONS

The Freon refrigerant used is also known as R-12 or F-12. It is colorless and odorless both as a gas and a liquid. Since it boils (vaporizes) at −21.7° F., it will usually be in a vapor state when being handled in a repair shop. But if a portion of the liquid coolant should come in contact with the hands or face, note that its temperature momentarily will be at least 22° below zero.

Protective goggles should be worn when opening any refrigerant lines. If liquid coolant does touch the eyes, bathe the eyes quickly in cold water, then apply a bland disinfectant oil to the eyes. See an eye doctor.

When checking a system for leaks with a torch type leak detector, do not breathe the vapors coming from the flame. Do not discharge refrigerant in the area of a live flame. A poisonous phosgene gas is produced when R-12 or F-12 is burned. While the small amount of this gas produced by a leak detector is not harmful unless inhaled directly at the flame, the quantity of refrigerant released into the air when a system is purged can be extremely dangerous if allowed to come in contact with an open flame. Thus, when purging a system, be sure that the discharge hose is routed to a well ventilated place where no flame is present. Under these conditions the refrigerant will be quickly dissipated into the surrounding air.

Never allow the temperature of refrigerant drums to exceed 125° F. The resultant increase in temperature will cause a corresponding increase in pressure which may cause the safety plug to release or the drum to burst.

If it is necessary to heat a drum of refrigerant when charging a system, the drum should be placed in water that is no hotter than 125° F. Never use a blowtorch, or other open flame. If possible, a pressure release mechanism should be attached before the drum is heated.

When connecting and disconnecting service gauges on A/C system, ensure that gauge hand valves are fully closed and that compressor service valves, if equipped, are in the back-seated (fully counterclockwise) position. Do not disconnect gauge hoses from service port adapters, if used, while gauges are connected to A/C system. To disconnect hoses, always remove adapter from service port. Do not disconnect hoses from gauge manifold while connected to A/C system, as refrigerant will be rapidly discharged.

After disconnecting gauge lines, check the valve areas to be sure service valves are correctly seated and Schraeder valves, if used, are not leaking.

EXERCISE SYSTEM

An important fact most owners ignore is that A/C units must be used periodically. Manufacturers caution that when the air conditioner is not used regularly, particularly during cold months, it should be turned on for a few minutes once every two or three weeks while the engine is running. This keeps the system in good operating condition.

Checking out the system for the effects of disuse before the onset of summer is one of the most important aspects of A/C servicing.

First clean out the condenser core, mounted in all cases at the front of the radiator. All obstructions, such as leaves, bugs, and dirt, must be removed, as they will reduce heat transfer and impair the efficiency of the system. Make sure the space between the condenser and the radiator also is free of foreign matter.

Make certain the evaporator water drain is open. Certain systems have two evaporators, one in the engine compartment and one toward the rear of the vehicle. The evaporator cools and dehumidifies the air before it enters the passenger compartment; there, the refrigerant is changed from a liquid to a vapor. As the core cools the air, moisture condenses on it but is prevented from collecting in the evaporator by the water drain.

PERFORMANCE TEST

The system should be operated for at least 15 minutes to allow sufficient time for all parts to become completely stabilized. Determine if the system is fully charged by the use of test gauges and sight glass if one is installed on system. Head pressure will read from 180 psi to 220 psi or higher, depending upon ambient temperature and the type unit being tested. The sight glass should be free of bubbles if a glass is used in the system. Low side pressures should read approximately 15 psi to 30 psi, again depending on the ambient temperature and the unit being tested. It is not feasible to give a definite reading for all types of systems used, as the type control and component installation used on a particular system will directly influence the pressure readings on the high and low sides, **Fig. 1.**

The high side pressure will definitely be affected by the ambient or outside air temperature. A system that is operating normally will indicate a high side gauge reading between 150–170 psi with an 80°F ambient temperature. The same system will register 210–230 psi with an ambient temperature of 100°F. No two systems will register exactly the same, which requires that allowance for variations in head pressures must be considered. Following are the most important normal readings likely to be encountered during the season.

Ambient Temp.	High Side Pressure
80	150–170
90	175–195
95	185–205
100	210–230
105	230–250
110	250–270

RELATIVE TEMPERATURE OF HIGH AND LOW SIDES

The high side of the system should be uniformly hot to the touch throughout. A difference in temperature will indicate a partial blockage of liquid or gas at this point.

The low side of the system should be uniformly cool to the touch with no excessive sweating of the suction line or low side service valve. Excessive sweating or frosting of the low side service valve usually indicates an expansion valve is allowing an excessive amount of refrigerant into the evaporator.

EVAPORATOR OUTPUT

At this point, provided all other inspection tests have been performed, and components have been found to operate as they should, a rapid cooling down of the interior of the vehicle should result. The use of a thermometer is not necessary to determine evaporator output. Bringing all units to the correct operating specifications will insure that the evaporator performs as intended.

LEAK TEST

Testing the refrigerant system for leaks is one of the most important phases of troubleshooting. Several types of leak detectors are available that are suitable for detecting A/C system leaks. One or more of the following procedures will prove useful for detecting leaks and checking connections after service work has been performed. Prior to performing any leak test, prepare the vehicle as follows:

1. Attach a suitable gauge manifold to system and observe pressure readings.
2. If little or no pressure is indicated, the system must be partially charged.
3. If gauges indicate pressure, set engine to run at fast idle and operate system at maximum cooling for 10–15 minutes, then stop engine and perform leak tests.

Evaporator Pressure Gauge Reading	Evaporator Temperature F°	High Pressure Gauge Reading	Ambient Temperature
0	-21°	45	20°
0.6	-20°	55	30°
2.4	-15°	72	40°
4.5	-10°	86	50°
6.8	- 5°	105	60°
9.2	0°	126	70°
11.8	5°	140	75°
14.7	10°	160	80°
17.1	15°	185	90°
21.1	20°	195	95°
22.5	22°	220	100°
23.9	24°	240	105°
25.4	26°	260	110°
26.9	28°	275	115°
28.5	30°	290	120°
37.0	40°	305	125°
46.7	50°	325	130°
57.7	60°		
70.1	70°		
84.1	80°		
99.6	90°		
116.9	100°		
136.0	110°		
157.1	120°		
179.0	130°		

Fig. 1 A/C system pressure/temperature relationship (Typical). Equivalent to 1750 RPM (30 mph)

FLAME TYPE (HALIDE) LEAK DETECTORS

CAUTION: Avoid inhaling fumes produced by burning refrigerant when using flame-type detectors. Use caution when using detector near flammable materials such as interior trim components. Do not use flame-type detector where concentrations of combustible or explosive gasses, dusts or vapors may exist.

1. Light leak detector and adjust flame as low as possible to obtain maximum sensitivity.
2. Allow detector to warm until copper element is cherry-red. Flame should be almost colorless.
3. Test reaction plate sensitivity by passing end of sensor hose near an opened can of refrigerant. Flame should react violently, turning bright blue.
4. If flame does not change color, replace reaction plate following manufacturer's instructions.
5. Allow flame to clear, then slowly move sensor hose along areas suspected of leakage while observing flame.

NOTE: Position sensor hose under areas of suspected leakage, as R-12 refrigerant is heavier than air.

6. Move sensor hose under all lines, fittings and components. Insert hose into evaporator case, if possible, and check compressor shaft seal.
7. The presence of refrigerant will cause flame to change color as follows: Pale blue, no refrigerant; yellow-yellow/green, slight leak; bright blue-purple/blue, major leak or concentration of refrigerant.
8. If detector indicates a large leak or heavy concentration of refrigerant, ventilate area using a small fan in order to pinpoint leak.
9. Repair leaks as needed, evacuate and recharge system, then recheck system for leaks.

ELECTRONIC LEAK DETECTORS

The procedure for using an electronic leak detector is similar to the procedure for flame-type leak detectors, except that the presence of refrigerant is indicated by an

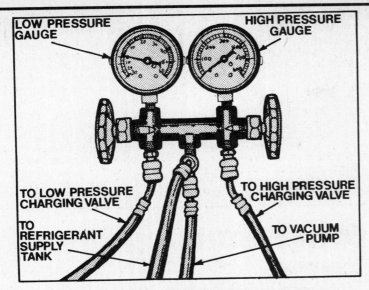

Fig. 2 Gauge manifold hose connections

audible tone or flashing light. Refer to operating instructions for unit being used, and observe the following procedures:

1. Move detector probe 1 inch per second along areas of suspected leakage.
2. Position probe under area to be tested as refrigerant is heavier than air.
3. Check gauge manifold, hoses and service ports for leakage.

FLUID LEAK DETECTORS

Apply leak detector solution around joints to be tested. A cluster of bubbles will form immediately if there is a leak. A white foam that forms after a short while will indicate an extremely small leak. In some confined areas such as sections of the evaporator and condenser, electronic leak detectors will be more useful.

DISCHARGING & EVACUATING SYSTEM

DISCHARGING

1. Ensure that all gauge manifold or charging station hand valves are closed and that compressor service valves, if equipped, are in the backseated (fully counterclockwise) position.
2. Connect compound (low) side gauge hose to the low (suction) side service port, and the high pressure gauge hose to the high (discharge) side port, **Fig. 2**, then open compressor service valves to mid-position, if equipped.

NOTE: Refer to "Charging Valve Location" chart in the "A/C System Servicing" section, for service port locations.

3. Insert gauge manifold center hose into

a suitable container that is vented to shop exhaust system.

4. If system is operational, set engine to run at fast idle and operate A/C system in maximum cooling position, with blower on high, for 10–15 minutes to return oil to compressor, then reduce idle and stop engine.
5. Slightly open low side control valve on manifold, and allow refrigerant to discharge slowly into container.

NOTE: Do not allow refrigerant to discharge rapidly. Too rapid purging will draw the system oil charge out with the refrigerant.

6. When system is nearly discharged, slightly open high side control valve on manifold to discharge remaining refrigerant from compressor and lines.
7. When system is completely discharged (gauges read zero), close high and low side control valves and measure amount of oil in discharge container.
8. If more than ½ ounce of refrigeration oil is trapped in container, perform "Oil Level Check," as outlined in the "A/C System Servicing" section.

NOTE: If addition of refrigeration oil is necessary, oil should be added prior to evacuating system.

EVACUATING SYSTEM WITH VACUUM PUMP

Vacuum pumps suitable for removing air and moisture from A/C systems are commercially available. The pump should be capable of drawing the system down to 28–29½ inches Hg at sea level. For each 1000 foot increase in altitude, this specification should be decreased by 1 inch Hg.

As an example, at 5000 feet elevation, only 23–24½ inches Hg can be obtained.

1. Connect suitable gauge manifold and discharge system as outlined previously.

NOTE: System must be completely discharged prior to evacuation. If pressurized refrigerant is allowed to enter vacuum pump, pump will be damaged.

2. Connect hose from gauge manifold center port to vacuum pump inlet.
3. Fully open both gauge manifold hand valves.
4. Operate vacuum pump while observing low side compound gauge. If system does not "pump-down" to 28–29½ inches Hg (at sea level) within approximately 5 minutes, recheck connections and leak test system.
5. Continue to operate vacuum pump for 15–30 minutes, longer if system was open for an extended period of time, then close both manifold valves and stop pump.
6. Check ability of system to hold vacuum. Watch low side compound gauge and ensure that reading does not rise at a rate faster than 1 inch Hg every 4–5 minutes.
7. If system fails to hold vacuum, recheck fittings and connections, and leak test system.
8. If system holds vacuum, charge system with refrigerant.

CHARGING THE SYSTEM

NOTE: Refer to "A/C Data Table" in the "A/C System Servicing" section, for refrigerant capacities.

CHARGING WITH 14 OZ. CANS

1. Connect a suitable refrigerant valve and can adapter, such as Motorcraft YT-280 or equivalent, to refrigerant can following manufacturer's instructions.
2. Ensure that valve on can adapter is closed, then connect hose from gauge manifold center port to adapter.
3. When can is connected, charge system according to procedure under "Charging From Drum." When can is empty, close valve and remove can. Connect new can, open valve and continue charging until correct weight of refrigerant has entered system. Note capacity of refrigerant cans. When specifications require the use of a portion of a can, weigh it to ensure proper amount of refrigerant is installed.

CHARGING FROM DRUM

1. With manifold gauge set valves closed to center hose, disconnect vacuum pump from manifold gauge set.

2. Connect center hose of manifold gauge set to refrigerant drum.
3. Purge air from center hose by loosening hose at manifold gauge set and open refrigerant drum valve. When refrigerant escapes from hose, tighten center hose connection at manifold gauge set.
4. On vehicles so equipped, disconnect wire harness connector at clutch cycling pressure switch. Install jumper wire across terminals of connector.
5. On all models, open manifold gauge set low side valve and allow refrigerant to enter system. Refrigerant can must be kept upright if vehicle low

pressure service gauge port is not on suction accumulator/drier or suction accumulator fitting.
6. When system stops drawing refrigerant in, start engine and set control lever to A/C position and blower switch to "HI" position to draw remaining refrigerant into system.
7. When specified weight of refrigerant is in system, close gauge set low pressure valve and refrigerant supply valve.
8. On vehicles so equipped, remove jumper wire from clutch cycling pressure switch connector and connect connector to pressure switch.
9. On all models, operate system until

pressures stabilize to check operation and system pressures.

NOTE: During charging, it may be necessary to use a high volume fan to blow air through the condenser in order to prevent excessive refrigerant system pressures or engine overheating.

10. When charging is complete and system operating pressures are normal, return compressor service valves, if equipped, to the back seated position, disconnect gauge manifold hoses from system and install protective caps over service fittings.

A/C System Servicing

INDEX

COMPRESSOR SERVICE VALVES

Most F100-350 and Bronco models are equipped with manual valves to isolate the compressor from the refrigerant system. These valves allow the compressor to be removed, or opened for oil level checks, without discharging the A/C system. Refrigerant system service access fittings, located on the manual valves, are also included on some models.

During normal system operation, the manual valves are in the back-seated (fully counterclockwise) position, **Fig. 1.** To isolate the compressor, the valves are rotated to the front-seated (fully clockwise) position, closing off the refrigerant line passage to the compressor. To allow refrigerant system service access, the valves are rotated to the mid-position, **Fig. 1,** which opens the service port while still allowing refrigerant to flow through the system.

NOTE: Manual compressor service valves should be in the back-seated (fully counterclockwise) position whenever service gauges are being connected or disconnected on the A/C system. Always install protective caps over manual valve stems and service ports, if equipped, after completing A/C service.

ISOLATING COMPRESSOR

1. Connect suitable gauge manifold to system and remove protective caps from manual valve stems.
2. Slightly open both service valves toward mid-position, then start engine and operate air conditioning.

a. On Tecumseh and York 2 cylinder compressors, slightly loosen oil sump filler plug.
b. On Ford FS-6 compressors, slightly loosen flare nut securing high (discharge) side manual valve to compressor.
3. Slowly rotate suction (low) side service valve clockwise toward front-seated position.
4. When suction (low) side gauge reads zero, stop engine, then rotate both low and high side valves to the fully clockwise (front-seated) position, **Fig. 1.**
5. Relieve internal compressor pressure as follows:

NOTE: A suitable face shield should be worn when relieving compressor pressure.

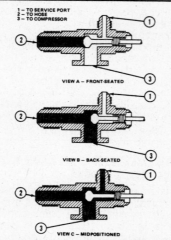

1 – TO SERVICE PORT
2 – TO HOSE
3 – TO COMPRESSOR

VIEW A – FRONT-SEATED

VIEW B – BACK-SEATED

VIEW C – MIDPOSITIONED

Fig. 1   Compressor service valves, cross-sectional view

PURGING COMPRESSOR

The compressor must be purged of air whenever it has been isolated from the system for service.
1. Install oil plugs or reconnect refrigerant lines and manual valves to compressor as needed.
2. Rotate low (suction) side manual valve counterclockwise to the back-seated position.
3. Loosen flare nut securing high (discharge) side manual valve to compressor just enough to allow refrigerant to force air from compressor.
4. When air is completely purged, tighten high side manual valve fitting, then back seat valve to complete installation.

OIL LEVEL CHECK

NOTE: Refer to "A/C Data Table" for oil level specifications.

TECUMSEH & YORK COMPRESSORS, EXC. TECUMSEH HR-980

NOTE: On models where compressor is mounted on an angle, reposition or remove compressor and check oil level in horizontal position.

1. Connect suitable gauge manifold to system, set engine to operate at fast idle and operate A/C in maximum cooling position, with blower on high, for 10–15 minutes, then lower idle

A/C Data Table

Year	Model	Refrigerant Capacity Lbs.	Refrigeration Oil: Viscosity	Refrigeration Oil: Total System Capacity Ounces	Refrigeration Oil: Compressor Oil Level Check Inches	Compressor Clutch Air Gap Inches
1979–82	E100-350①	3½	500	②	③	—
	E100-350④	4½	500	②	③	—
1979	Exc. E100-350	2¾	500	②	③	—
1980–81	Exc. E100-350	3½	500	②	③	—
1982–85	Bronco & F100-350	3½	500	10	⑤	.021–.036
1983–85	E100-350①	3½	500	10	⑤	.021–.036
	E100-350④	4¼	500	10	⑤	.021–.036
	Ranger	2½	500	10	⑤	⑥
1984–85	Bronco II	2½	500	10	⑤	⑥

①—Models less auxiliary (rear, overhead etc.) system.
②—Tecumseh comp., 11 oz.; York comp., 10 oz.
③—Tecumseh comp.: Horizontal mount, 7/8–1 5/8 in.; Vertical mount, 7/8–1 5/8 in. York comp.: Horizontal mount, 13/16–1 3/16 in.; Vertical mount, 7/8–1 5/8 in.
④—Models with auxiliary (rear, overhead etc.) system.
⑤—Note that "Oil Level Inches" can not be checked. Refer to total capacity and see text for checking procedure.
⑥—Exc. Tecumseh HR-980 compressor, .021–.036 inch; Tecumseh HR-980 compressor, .009–.041 inch.

Charging Valve Location

Year	Model	High Pressure Fitting	Low Pressure Fitting
1979	Exc. E100-350	Compressor Service Valve	Compressor Service Valve
1979–83	E100-350	Discharge Line At Condenser	Suction Line at Compressor
1980–85	Exc. E100-350	Discharge Line At Compressor	Accumulator
1984–85	E150-350	Compressor	Compressor

speed and stop engine.

2. On models with compressor service valves, isolate compressor as outlined. On models without service valves, discharge A/C system.
3. Slowly loosen, then remove oil filler plug.

NOTE: A suitable face shield should be worn when removing filler plug.

4. Insert clean dipstick, fabricated from flattened 1/8 inch rod, **Figs. 2 and 3,** through filler plug opening and measure oil level.

NOTE: Ensure that dipstick is bottomed in compressor sump. Rotate crankshaft as needed to provide clearance for dipstick. On York compressors, crankshaft keyway should face compressor head.

5. Add or remove oil, as needed, to bring oil level within specifications listed in "A/C Data Table."

NOTE: If other components are being replaced, refer to "Oil Charge."

6. Install filler plug and O-ring, then purge air from compressor or evacuate and recharge system, as needed.

FS-6, NIPPONDENSO 6E-171 & TECUMSEH HR-980 COMPRESSORS

Refer to "Oil Charge" for service procedures.

OIL CHARGE

OIL CHARGE—COMPONENT REPLACEMENT

Tecumseh & York Compressor Exc. Tecumseh HR-980

1. Discharge system as outlined, then repair or replace components as needed.

NOTE: If compressor is replaced, ensure that oil level in replacement compressor is the same as the oil level in the defective compressor.

2. Evacuate and recharge system, then operate air conditioning for approximately 10 minutes, or until pressure readings have stabilized.
3. Stop engine and perform "Oil Level Check."

FS-6, Nippondenso 6E-171 & Tecumseh HR-980 Compressors

If there are no signs of external oil leakage, use following procedure to add oil to system during component replacement.

1. Isolate compressor or discharge system, as needed, then remove defective component.
2. Add proper amount of new refrigeration oil for each replacement component as follows:
   a. If compressor is replaced or overhauled, add 6 ounces of oil to compressor prior to installation.

NOTE: A factory service replacement compressor contains 10 ounces of refrigeration oil. To ensure proper oil charge, drain 4 ounces of oil from compressor prior to installation.

   b. If accumulator is replaced, measure amount of oil remaining in defective accumulator, and add the same amount of oil to replacement accumulator plus 1 additional ounce.
   c. If condenser is replaced, add 1 ounce of oil to replacement condenser.
   d. If evaporator is replaced, add 3 ounces of oil to replacement evaporator.
3. Install replacement components, then evacuate and recharge system.

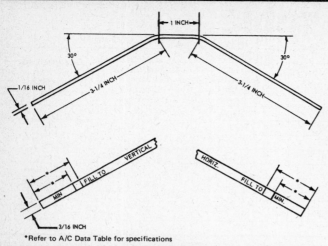

Fig. 2 Oil level dipstick fabrication. Tecumseh compressor exc. HR-980

*Refer to A/C Data Table for specifications

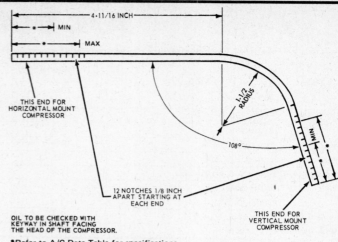

Fig. 3 Oil level dipstick fabrication. York compressor

*Refer to A/C Data Table for specifications

OIL CHARGE—LEAK CONDITION

Tecumseh & York Compressor, Exc. Tecumseh HR-980

Refer to "Oil Level Check" for service procedures.

FS-6, Nippondenso 6E-171 & Tecumseh HR-980 Compressors

1. If system is operational, set engine to run at fast idle and operate A/C in maximum cooling position, with blower on high, for 10 minutes.
2. Isolate compressor or discharge system, as required, then remove compressor and drain oil into a suitable container.
3. Measure amount of oil recovered from compressor and proceed as follows:
   a. If less than 3 ounces of oil are recovered from compressor, add 6 ounces of new refrigeration oil to compressor.
   b. If 3–6 ounces of oil are recovered, add the same amount of new refrigeration oil to compressor.
   c. If more than 6 ounces of oil are recovered, add only 6 ounces of new refrigeration oil to compressor.
4. Reinstall compressor, then evacuate and recharge system as needed.

VARIABLE SPEED FANS

INDEX

CAUTION: Do not operate engine until fan has first been inspected for cracks and/or separations. If a fan blade is found to be bent or damaged in any way, do not attempt to repair or reuse damaged part. Proper balance is essential in fan assembly operation. Balance cannot be assured once a fan assembly has been found to be bent or damaged and failure may occur during operation, creating an extremely dangerous condition. Always replace damaged fan assembly.

DESCRIPTION

The fan drive clutch, **Fig. 1**, is a fluid coupling containing silicone oil. Fan speed is regulated by the torque-carrying capacity of the silicone oil. The more silicone oil in the coupling, the greater the fan speed, and the less silicone oil, the slower the fan speed.

There are two types of fan drive clutches in use, one with a flat bi-metallic thermostatic spring, **Fig. 2**, and the second with a coiled bi-metallic thermostatic spring, **Fig. 3**.

The fan drive clutch with the flat bi-

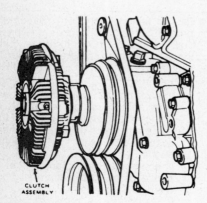

Fig. 1 Fan drive clutch assembly, 1984—85. 1979—83 similar

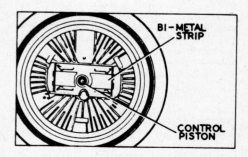

Fig. 2 Variable speed fan with flat bi-metallic thermostatic spring

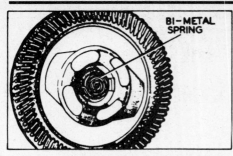

Fig. 3 Variable speed fan with coiled bi-metallic thermostatic spring

metallic spring works with a control piston on front of the fluid coupling to regulate the amount of silicone oil entering the coupling. The bi-metallic strip bows outward with an increase in ambient temperature and allows a piston to move outward. This piston opens a valve regulating the flow of silicone oil into the coupling from a reserve chamber. The silicone oil is returned to the observe chamber through a bleed hole when the valve is closed.

The second fan drive clutch uses a heat-sensitive, coiled bi-metallic spring connected to an opening plate which brings about similar results. Both units cause the fan speed to increase with a rise in temperature and to decrease as temperature decreases.

TROUBLESHOOTING
FAN DRIVE CLUTCH TEST

CAUTION: Do not operate the engine until the fan has been first checked for possible cracks and separations.

Run the engine at a fast idle speed (1000 RPM) until normal operating temperature is reached. This process can be speeded up by blocking off the front of the radiator with cardboard. Regardless of temperatures, the unit must be operated for at least five minutes immediately before being tested.

Stop the engine and, using a glove or a cloth to protect the hand, immediately check the effort required to turn the fan. If considerable effort is required, it can be assumed that the coupling is operating satisfactorily. If very little effort is required to turn the fan, it is an indication that the coupling is not operating properly and should be replaced.

If the clutch fan is the coiled bi-metallic spring type, it may be tested while the vehicle is being driven. To check, disconnect the bi-metal spring, **Fig. 4,** and rotate 90° counter-clockwise. This disables the temperature-controlled, free-wheeling feature and the clutch performs like a conventional fan. If this cures the overheating condition, replace the clutch fan.

FAN CLUTCH NOISE

Fan clutch noise can sometimes be noticed when clutch is engaged for maximum cooling. Clutch noise is also noticeable within the first few minutes after starting engine while clutch is redistributing the silicone fluid back to its normal, disengaged operating condition after settling for long periods of time (over night). However, continuous fan noise or an excessive roar indicates the clutch assembly is locked-up due to internal failure. This condition can be checked by attempting to manually rotate fan. If fan cannot be rotated manually or there is a rough, abrasive feel as fan is rotated, the clutch should be replaced.

LOOSENESS

Lateral movement can be observed at the fan blade tip under various temperature conditions because of the type bearing used. This movement should not exceed ¼ inch (6.5mm) as measured at the fan tip. If this lateral movement does not exceed specifications, there is no cause for replacement.

CLUTCH FLUID LEAK

Small fluid leaks do not generally affect the operation of the unit. These leaks generally occur around the area of the bearing assembly, but if the leaks appear to be excessive, engine overheating may occur. Check for clutch and fan free-wheeling by attempting to rotate fan and clutch assembly by hand five times. If no drag is felt, replace clutch.

FAN BLADE INSPECTION

Place fan on flat surface with leading edge facing down. If there is a clearance between fan blade touching surface and opposite blade of more than .090 inch (2mm), replace fan. (See caution at beginning of chapter.)

FAN SERVICE

CAUTION: To prevent silicone fluid from

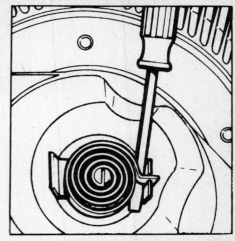

Fig. 4 Bi-metallic coiled spring removal

draining into fan drive bearing, do not store or place drive unit on bench with rear of shaft pointing downward.

The removal procedure for either type of fan clutch assembly is generally the same. Merely unfasten the unit from the water pump and remove the assembly from vehicle.

The type of unit shown in **Fig. 2** may be partially disassembled for inspection and cleaning. Take off the capscrews that hold the assembly together and separate the fan from the drive clutch. Next, remove the metal strip on the front by pushing one end of it toward the fan clutch body so it clears the retaining bracket, then push the strip to the side so that its opposite end will spring out of place. Now remove the small control piston underneath it.

Check the piston for free movement of the coupling device. If the piston sticks, clean it with emery cloth. If the bi-metal strip is damaged, replace the entire unit. These strips are not interchangeable.

When reassembling, install the control piston so that the projection on the end of it will contact the metal strip. Then install the metal strip with any identification number or letters facing the clutch. After reassembly, clean the clutch drive assembly with a cloth soaked in a suitable solvent. Avoid dipping the clutch assembly in any type liquid. Install the assembly in the reverse order of removal.

The coil spring type of fan clutch cannot be disassembled, serviced or repaired. If it does not function properly it must be replaced with a new unit.

ALTERNATOR SYSTEMS
Motorcraft Alternators

INDEX

DESCRIPTION

A charge indicator lamp or ammeter can be used in charging system.

If a charge indicator lamp is used in the charging system, **Figs. 1 through 4,** the system operation is as follows: when the ignition switch is turned ON, a small electrical current flows through the lamp filament (turning the lamp on) and through the alternator regulator to the alternator field. When the engine is started, the alternator field rotates and produces a voltage in the stator winding. When the voltage at the alternator stator terminal reaches about 3 volts, the regulator field relay closes. This puts the same voltage potential on both sides of the charge indicator lamp, causing it to go out. When the field relay has closed, current passes through the regulator A terminal and is metered to the alternator field.

If an ammeter is used in the charging system, **Figs. 2 and 4,** the regulator 1 terminal and the alternator stator terminal are not used. When the ignition switch is turned ON, the field relay closes and electrical current passes through the regulator A terminal and is metered to the alternator field. When the engine is started, the alternator field rotates, causing the alternator to operate.

All 1979–85 vehicles are equipped with new electronic voltage regulators, **Figs. 5 and 6.** These solid state regulators are used in conjunction with other new components in the charging system such as an alternator with a higher field current requirement, a warning indicator lamp shunt resistor (500 ohms) and a new wiring harness with a new regulator connector. When replacing system components, note the following precautions:

1. Always use the proper alternator in the system. If the 1979–85 alternator is installed on previous model systems, it will destroy the electro-mechanical regulator. If the older model alternator is used on the new system, it will have a reduced output.

2. Do not use an electro-mechanical regulator in the new system, as the wiring harness connector will not index properly with this type of regulator.

3. The new electronic regulators are color coded for proper installation. The black color coded unit is installed in systems equipped with a warning indicator lamp. The blue color coded regulator is installed in systems equipped with an ammeter.

4. The new systems use a 500 ohm resistor on the rear of the instrument cluster on vehicles equipped with a warning indicator lamp. Do not replace this resistor with the 15 ohm resistance wire used on previous systems.

On the new systems with an indicator lamp, closing the ignition switch energizes the warning lamp and turns on the regulator output stage. The alternator receives maximum field current and is ready to gen-

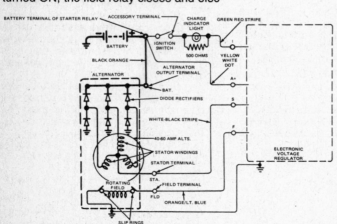

Fig. 1   Indicator light rear terminal alternator charging circuit

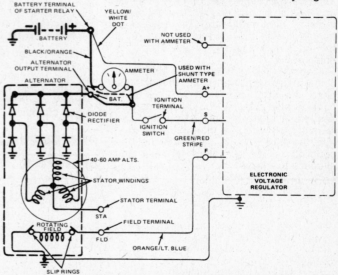

Fig. 2   Ammeter rear terminal alternator charging circuit

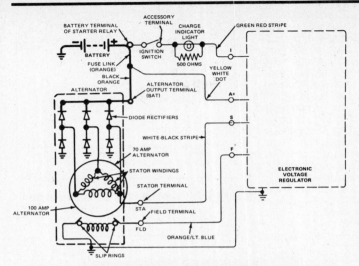

Fig. 3 Indicator light side terminal alternator charging circuit

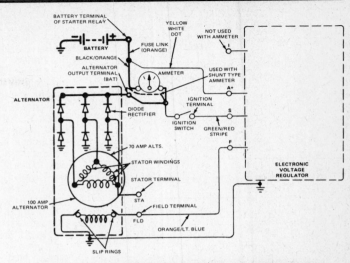

Fig. 4 Ammeter side terminal alternator charging circuit

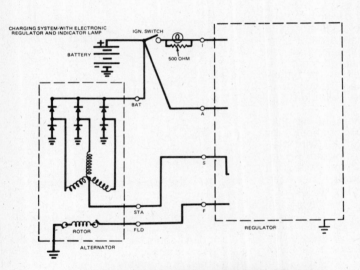

Fig. 5 Indicator light charging system w/electronic voltage regulator

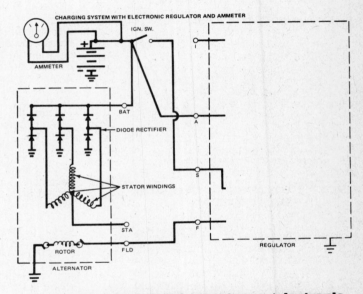

Fig. 6 Ammeter charging system w/electronic voltage regulator

erate an output voltage. As the alternator rotor speed increases, the output and stator terminal voltages increase from zero to the system regulation level determined by the regulator setting. When the ignition switch is turned off, the solid state relay circuit turns the output stage off, interrupting current flow through the regulator so there is not a current drain on the battery.

On vehicles equipped with an ammeter, the operating principle is similar.

NOTE: The ammeter indicates current flow into (charge) or out of (discharge) the vehicle battery.

SYSTEM TESTING

NOTE: The operations and in-vehicle test procedures for the side terminal alternator are same as for rear terminal alternator. However, the internal wiring, **Figs. 3 and 6,** and bench test procedures differ.

IN-VEHICLE VOLTMETER TEST

NOTE: Perform this test with all lights and electrical systems in the off position, parking brake applied, transmission in neutral

and a charged battery (at least 1,200 specific gravity).

1. Connect the negative lead of the voltmeter to the negative battery cable clamp (not bolt or nut).
2. Connect the positive lead of the voltmeter to the positive battery cable clamp (not bolt or nut).
3. Record the battery voltage reading shown on the voltmeter scale.
4. Connect the red lead of a tachometer to the distributor terminal of the coil and the black tachometer lead to a good ground.
5. Start and operate the engine at

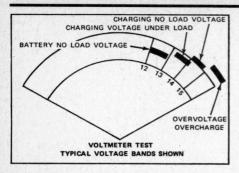

Fig. 7 Voltmeter test scale

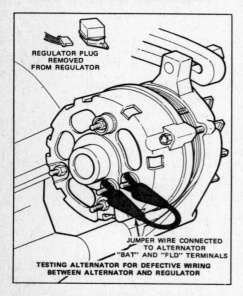

Fig. 9 Rear terminal alternator. Jumper wire connection

approximately 1500 rpm. With no other electrical load (foot off brake pedal and car doors closed), the voltmeter reading should increase but not exceed (2 volts) above the first recorded battery voltage reading. The reading should be taken when the voltmeter needle stops moving.

6. With the engine running, turn on the heater and/or air conditioner blower motor to high speed and headlights to high beam.

7. Increase the engine speed to 2000 rpm. The voltmeter should indicate a minimum reading of .05 volts above the battery voltage, **Fig. 7.**

NOTE: If the above tests indicate proper voltage readings, the charging system is operating normally. Proceed to "Test Results" if a problem still exists.

Test Results

1. If voltmeter reading indicates 2 volts over battery voltage (over voltage), proceed as follows:
   a. Stop the engine and check the ground connections between the regulator and alternator and/or reg-

ulator to engine. Clean and tighten connections securely and repeat the Voltmeter Test Procedures.
   b. If over voltage condition still exists, disconnect the regulator wiring plug from the regulator and repeat the Voltmeter Test Procedures.
   c. If over voltage still exists with the regulator wiring plug disconnected, repair the short in the wiring harness between the alternator and regulator. Then replace the regulator and connect the regulator wiring plug to the regulator and repeat the Voltmeter Test Procedures.

2. On 1979–85 units, if voltmeter does not indicate more than ½ volt above battery voltage, proceed as follows:
   a. Disconnect voltage regulator wire connector and connect an ohmmeter between wire connector F terminal and ground. Ohmmeter reading should indicate more than 3 ohms. If reading is less than 3 ohms, repair grounded field circuit and repeat Voltmeter Test procedure.
   b. If ohmmeter reading is more than 3 ohms, connect a jumper wire between voltage regulator wire connector terminals A and F, **Fig. 8,** then repeat Voltmeter Test procedure. If voltmeter reading is now more than ½ volt above battery voltage, the voltage regulator or wiring is defective. Refer to Regulator Test.
   c. If voltmeter still indicates less than ½ volt, disconnect jumper wire from voltage regulator wire connector and leave connector disconnected from regulator. Connect a jumper wire between alternator FLD and BAT terminals, **Figs. 9 and 10,** then repeat Voltmeter Test procedures.
   d. If voltmeter reading now indicates ½ volt or more above battery voltage, repair alternator to regulator wiring harness.
   e. If voltmeter still indicates less than ½ volt above battery voltage, stop engine and move voltmeter positive lead to alternator BAT terminal.
   f. If voltmeter now indicates battery voltage, the alternator should be removed, inspected and repaired. If zero volts is indicated, repair BAT terminal wiring.

FIELD CIRCUIT & ALTERNATOR TESTS

1. If the field circuit is satisfactory, disconnect the regulator wiring plug at the regulator and connect the jumper wire from the A to F terminals on the regulator wiring plug, **Fig. 8.**
2. Repeat the Voltmeter Test Procedures.
3. If the Voltmeter Test Procedures still indicate a problem of under voltage, remove the jumper wire at the regulator plug and leave the plug discon-

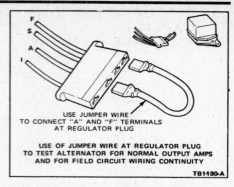

Fig. 8 Regulator plug. Jumper wire connection

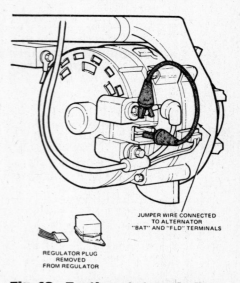

Fig. 10 Testing stator winding

nected from the regulator, **Figs. 9 and 10.** Connect a jumper wire to the FLD and BAT terminals on the alternator, **Figs. 9 and 10.**
4. Repeat the Voltmeter Test Procedures.
5. If the Voltmeter Tests are now satisfactory, repair the wiring harness from the alternator to the regulator. Then, remove the jumper wire at the alternator and connect the regulator wiring plug to the regulator.
6. Repeat the Voltmeter Test Procedures, to be sure the charging system is operating normally.
7. If the Voltmeter Test results still indicate under voltage, repair or replace the alternator. With the jumper wire removed, connect the wiring to the alternator and regulator.
8. Repeat the Voltmeter Test Procedures.

DIODE TEST

Test Procedure

1. Disconnect electric choke, if equipped.
2. Disconnect voltage regulator wiring connector.

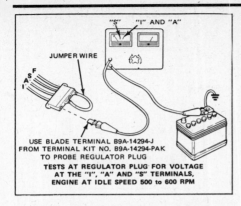

Fig. 11 Regulator plug voltage test

3. Connect a jumper wire between the "A" and "F" terminals of the voltage regulator wiring connector, **Fig. 8.**
4. Connect voltmeter to battery clamps. Then, start and idle engine.
5. Observe and note voltmeter reading.
6. Move the voltmeter positive lead to the alternator "S" terminal and note voltage reading.

Test Results

1. If voltmeter reading is within ½ of battery voltage, the diodes are satisfactory.
2. If voltmeter reading is approximately 1.5 volts, the alternator has a shorted negative diode or a grounded stator winding.
3. If voltmeter reading is approximately 1.5 volts less than battery voltage, the alternator has a shorted positive diode.
4. If voltage reading is approximately 1 to 1.5 volts less than ½ battery voltage, the alternator has an open positive diode.
5. If voltage reading is 1 to 1.5 volts above ½ battery voltage, the alternator has an open negative diode.
6. Reconnect electric choke into circuit after tests are completed, if equipped.

REGULATOR TESTS

EXC. 4-140 TURBOCHARGED DIESEL ENGINE

S Circuit Test—With Ammeter

1. Connect the positive lead of the voltmeter to the S terminal of the regulator wiring plug **Fig. 11.** Turn the ignition switch to the ON position. Do not start the engine.
2. The voltmeter reading should indicate battery voltage.
3. If there is no voltage reading, disconnect the positive voltmeter lead from the positive battery clamp and repair the S wire lead from the ignition switch to the regulator wiring plug.
4. Connect the positive voltmeter lead to the positive battery cable terminal and

repeat the Voltmeter Test Procedures.

S and I Circuit Test—With Indicator Light

1. Disconnect regulator wiring plug, then install a suitable jumper wire between connector "A" and "F" terminals, **Fig. 8.**
2. With the engine idling, connect the positive lead of the voltmeter to the S terminal and then to the I terminal of the regulator wiring plug, **Fig. 11.** The voltage of the S circuit should read approximately ½ of the I circuit.
3. If no voltage is present, repair the alternator or the wiring circuit at fault. Reconnect the positive voltmeter lead to the positive battery cable terminal and repeat the Voltmeter Test Procedures.
4. If the above tests are satisfactory, install a new regulator.
5. Then, remove the jumper wire from the regulator wiring plug and connect the wiring plug to the regulator. Repeat the Voltmeter Test Procedures.

4-140 TURBOCHARGED DIESEL ENGINE

Regulator I Circuit Test

1. Disconnect electrical connector from regulator.
2. Connect voltmeter negative lead to the battery ground terminal and the positive lead to the electrical connector terminal I. No voltage should be indicated with the ignition switch OFF. If voltage is present, service the I lead from the ignition switch to identify and eliminate the voltage source.
3. Turn the ignition switch to ON position. The voltmeter should indicate battery voltage at the connector terminal I. If there is no voltage reading, service the I lead from the ignition switch to the regulator for an open or grounded circuit.
4. If voltage readings obtained in steps 2 and 3 were normal, check the resistance value of the I circuit resistor. Conduct resistance check with the regulator wiring plug disconnected. Nominal value is 330 ohms for gauge systems. Replace resistor if value obtained is off by more than 50 ohms.

BENCH TESTS

RECTIFIER SHORT OR GROUNDED & STATOR GROUNDED TEST

Using a suitable ohmmeter, connect one probe to the alternator BAT terminal, **Fig. 12,** and the other probe to the STA terminal (rear blade terminal). Then, reverse the ohmmeter probes and repeat the test. A reading of about 60 ohms should be obtained in one direction and no needle movement with the probes reversed. A

Fig. 12 Testing diode trio

reading in both directions indicates a bad positive diode, a grounded positive diode plate or a grounded BAT terminal.

Perform the same test using the STA and GND (ground) terminals of the alternator. A reading in both directions indicates either a bad negative diode, a grounded stator winding, a grounded stator terminal, a grounded positive diode plate, or a grounded BAT terminal.

Infinite readings (no needle movement) in all four probe positions in the preceeding tests indicates an open STA terminal lead connection inside the alternator.

FIELD OPEN OR SHORT CIRCUIT TEST

Using a suitable ohmmeter, connect the alternator field terminal with one probe and the ground terminal with the other probe, **Fig. 13.** Then, spin the alternator pulley. The ohmmeter reading should be between 2.4 and 25 ohms on 1979–80 units, 2.4 and 100 ohms on 1981–85 units, and should fluctuate while the pulley is turning. An infinite reading (no meter movement) indicates an open brush lead, worn or stuck brushes, or a bad rotor assembly. An ohmmeter reading of less than 2.4 ohms indicates a grounded brush assembly, a grounded field terminal or a bad rotor.

DIODE TEST

To test one set of diodes, contact one probe of a suitable ohmmeter to the terminal bolt, **Figs. 14 and 15,** and contact each of the three stator lead terminals with the other probe. Reverse the probes and repeat the test. All diodes should show a low reading of about 60 ohms in one direction, and an infinite reading (no needle movement) with the probes reversed. Repeat the preceding tests for the other set of diodes except that the other terminal screw is used.

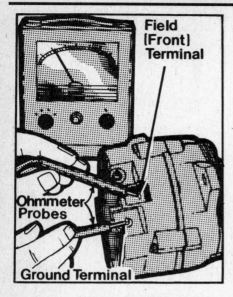

Fig. 13 Testing rectifier bridge diodes

If the meter readings are not as specified, replace the rectifier assembly.

STATOR COIL OPEN OR GROUNDED TEST

Disassemble stator from alternator, then set a suitable ohmmeter to read up to 1000 ohms. Connect ohmmeter probes to stator leads and to stator laminated core, ensuring probe makes good electrical connection with stator core. Ohmmeter should indicate an infinite reading (no meter movement). If meter does not indicate an infinite reading (needle movement), stator winding is shorted to core and must be replaced. Repeat test for each stator lead.

ROTOR OPEN OR SHORT CIRCUIT TEST

Disassemble the front housing and rotor from the rear housing and stator.

Contact each ohmmeter probe to a rotor slip ring. The meter reading should be 2.4 to 4.9 ohms on 1979–80 units, and 2.0 to 3.5 ohms on 1981–85 units. A higher reading indicates a damaged slip ring solder connection or a broken wire. A lower reading indicates a shorted wire or slip ring.

Contact one ohmmeter probe to a slip ring, and the other probe to the rotor shaft. The meter reading should be infinite (no deflection). A reading other than infinite indicates the rotor is shorted to the shaft. Inspect the slip ring soldered terminals to be sure they are not bent and touching the rotor shaft, or that excess solder is not grounding the rotor coil connections to the shaft. Replace the rotor if it is shorted and cannot be repaired.

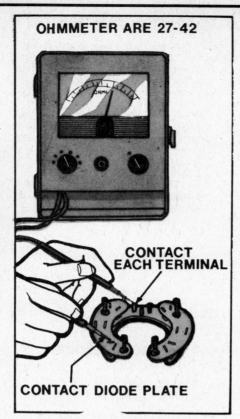

Fig. 14 Rear terminal diode test

REGULATOR ADJUSTMENTS
ELECTRONIC REGULATORS

These regulators are factory calibrated and sealed and no adjustment is possible. If regulator calibration values are not within specifications, the regulator must be replaced.

ALTERNATOR REPAIRS

REAR TERMINAL ALTERNATOR

NOTE: Use a 100 watt soldering iron.

1979–80 UNITS
Disassemble
1. Mark both end housings and the stator with a scribe mark for assembly, **Fig. 16.**
2. Remove the three housing through bolts.
3. Separate the front housing and rotor from the stator and rear housing.
4. Remove all the nuts and insulators from the rear housing, and the rear housing from the stator and rectifier assembly.

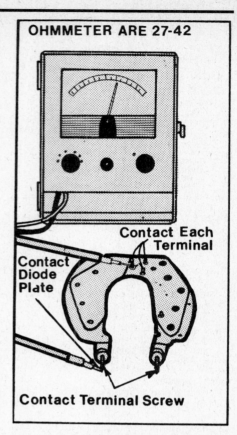

Fig. 15 Brush holder regulator installation

5. Remove the brush holder mounting screws, and the holder, brushes, brush springs, insulator and terminal.
6. If replacement is necessary, press the bearing from the rear housing, supporting the housing on the inner boss.
7. If the rectifier assembly is being replaced, unsolder the stator leads from the printed circuit board terminals, and separate the stator from the rectifier assembly.
8. Original production alternators will have one of two types of rectifier assembly circuit boards, **Fig. 17.** One has the circuit board spaced away from the diode plates with the diodes exposed. Another type is a single circuit board with built-in diodes.

If the alternator rectifier has an exposed diode circuit board, remove the screws from the rectifier by rotating the bolt heads ¼ turn clockwise to unlock them, and then remove the screws, **Fig. 17.** Push the stator terminal screw straight out on a rectifier with the diodes built into the circuit board, **Fig. 17.** Avoid turning the screw while removing to make certain that the straight knurl will engage the insulators when installing. Do not remove the grounded screw, **Fig. 18.**
9. Remove the drive pulley nut, **Fig. 19,** then pull the lockwasher, pulley, fan, fan spacer, front housing and rotor top from the rotor shaft.

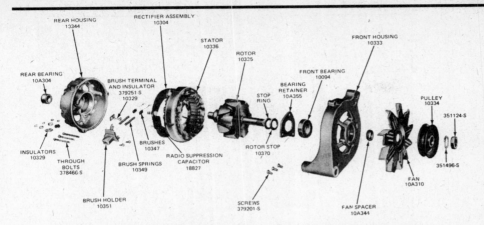

Fig. 16 Disassembled view of rear terminal alternator

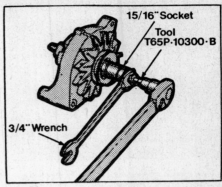

Fig. 19 Pulley removal (Typical)

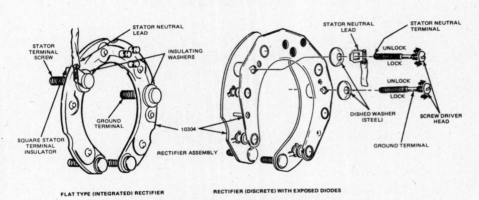

Fig. 17 Rectifier assembly

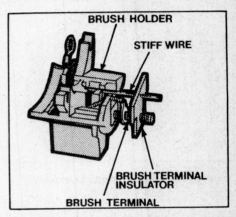

Fig. 20 Brush holder assembly

housing bearing boss (put pressure on the outer race only), and install the bearing retainer, **Fig. 16.**

3. If the stop ring on the rotor drive shaft was damaged, install a new stop ring. Push the new ring on the shaft and into the groove.

NOTE: Do not open the ring with snap ring pliers, as permanent damage will result.

4. Position the rotor stop on the drive shaft with the recessed side against the stop ring.
5. Position the front housing, fan spacer, fan, pulley and lock washer on the drive shaft and install the retaining nut. Torque the retaining nut, **Fig. 19,** to 60–100 ft. lbs.
6. If the rear housing bearing was removed, support the housing on the inner boss and press in a new bearing flush with the outer end surface.
7. Place the brush springs, brushes, brush terminal and terminal insulator in the brush holder, and hold the brushes in position by inserting a piece of stiff wire in the brush holder, **Fig. 20.**
8. Position the brush holder assembly in the rear housing and install the mounting screws. Position the brush leads in the brush holder, **Fig. 21.**
9. Wrap the three stator winding leads around the circuit board terminals and

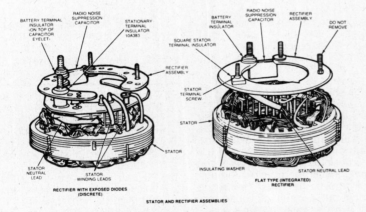

Fig. 18 Stator & rectifier assemblies

10. Remove the three screws that hold the front end bearing retainer, and remove the retainer. If the bearing is damaged or has lost its lubricant, support the housing close to the bearing boss and press out the old bearing from the housing.
11. Perform a diode test and a field open or short circuit test.

Assemble

NOTE: Refer to "Cleaning and Inspection" procedures before reassembly.

1. The rotor, stator and bearings must not be cleaned with solvent. Wipe these parts off with a clean cloth.
2. Press the front bearing in the front

Fig. 21 Brush lead positions (Typical)

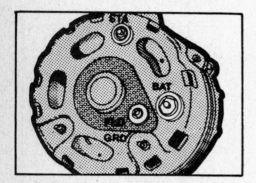

Fig. 23 Alternator terminal locations

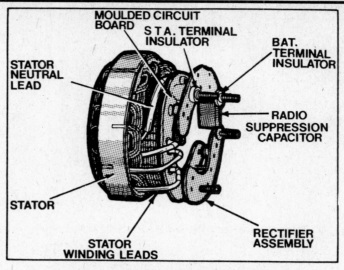

Fig. 22 Stator lead connections

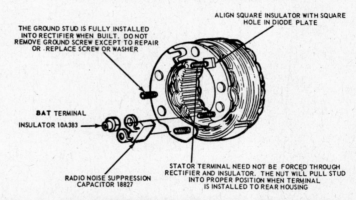

Fig. 24 Fiber-glass circuit board terminal insulators

solder them. Position the stator neutral lead eyelet on the stator terminal screw, and install the screw in the rectifier assembly, **Fig. 22.**

10. For a rectifier with the diodes exposed, insert the special screws through the wire lug, dished washers and circuit board, **Fig. 17.** Turn them ¼ turn counterclockwise to lock them. For single circuit boards with built-in diodes, insert the screws straight through the wire lug, insulating washer and rectifier into the insulator, **Fig. 18.**

NOTE: The dished washers are to be used only on the circuit board with exposed diodes, **Fig. 21.** If they are used on the single circuit board, a short circuit will occur. A flat insulating washer is to be used between the stator terminal and the board when a single circuit board is used, **Fig. 18.**

11. Position the radio noise suppression capacitor on the rectifier terminals. On the circuit board with exposed diodes, install the STA and BAT terminal insulators, **Fig. 23.** On the single circuit board, position the square stator terminal insulator in the square hole in the rectifier assembly, **Fig. 18.** Position the BAT terminal insulator, **Fig. 24.**

Position the stator and rectifier assembly in the rear housing. Make certain all terminal insulators are

seated properly in the recesses, **Fig. 22.** Position the STA (black), BAT (red) and FLD (orange) insulators on the terminal bolts, and install the retaining nuts, **Fig. 23.**

12. Wipe the rear end bearing surface of the rotor shaft with a clean, lint free rag.

13. Position the rear housing and stator assembly over the rotor and align the scribe marks made during disassembly. Seat the machined portion of the stator core into the step in both end housings. Install the housing through bolts. Remove the brush retracting wire, and put a daub of waterproof cement over the hole to seal it.

1981—85 UNITS

Disassemble

1. Mark both end housings and stator with a scribe mark for assembly, **Fig. 16.**
2. Remove three housing through bolts, then separate front housing and rotor assembly from stator and rear housing assembly.
3. Remove brush springs from rear housing holder, then the nuts, wash

ers and insulators from rear of rear housing terminals.

NOTE: Note color and location of insulators for reference during assembly.

4. Remove stator and rectifier assembly from rear housing, then the brush holder, brushes and brush terminal insulator from rear housing.
5. Support rear housing near boss, then remove rear housing bearing using a suitable press.
6. Place front housing in a suitable protective vise, then remove drive pulley nut, **Fig. 19,** from rotor shaft using tool No. T65P-10300-B or equivalent. Remove lockwasher, drive pulley, fan and fan spacer from rotor shaft.
7. Remove rotor from front housing, then the housing from vise.
8. Remove front bearing spacer from rotor shaft, then, if damaged, the stop ring.
9. Remove bearing retainer to front housing attaching screws, then the retainer.
10. Remove front housing bearing using a suitable press if necessary, ensuring

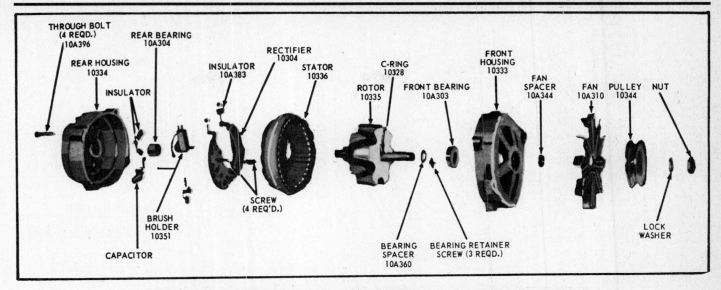

Fig. 25 Disassembled view of side terminal alternator (Typical)

housing is well supported when press is used.

11. Remove radio suppression capacitor and battery terminal insulator from rectifier assembly, **Fig. 18.**

NOTE: Use a 100 watt soldering iron.

12. Unsolder stator leads from rectifier assembly, then the terminals from the molded circuit board terminals. Using suitable needle nose pliers, pull stator lead terminals upwards from rectifier assembly, then clean excess solder from leads.

13. Disconnect neutral stator leads as follows:
    a. On flat type integrated rectifier units, press stator terminal screw from rectifier, ensuring it is not turned during removal, to prevent damage, **Fig. 17.**
    b. On exposed diode discrete rectifiers, remove stator terminal screw by rotating screw ¼ turn to unlock it from rectifier assembly, **Fig. 17.**

Assemble

NOTE: Refer to "Cleaning and Inspection" procedures before reassembly.

1. The rotor, stator and bearings must not be cleaned with solvent. Wipe these parts with a clean cloth.
2. Press front bearing into front housing bearing boss, ensuring pressure is applied only to race.
3. Position bearing retainer onto front housing, then insert attaching screws. Torque attaching screws to 25 to 40 inch lbs.
4. If removed, slide new stop ring over end of rotor shaft and into its groove. Do not use snap ring pliers.
5. Install rotor shaft bearing spacer with

recess against stop ring, then install front housing rotor and clamp housing into a suitable vise.

6. Install fan spacer, fan, drive pulley, lock washer and nut onto rotor shaft using tool No. T65P-10300-B or equivalent, then torque lock nut to 60 to 100 ft. lbs., **Fig. 19.**

7. Remove rotor and housing assembly from vise, then support rear housing near bearing boss to prevent damage during bearing installation. Install bearing using a suitable press.

8. Position brush wiring eyelet over brush terminal insulator, **Fig. 21.**

9. Install springs and brushes in brush holder, then apply pressure to holders against spring pressure by inserting a suitable piece of stiff wire through holder, **Fig. 21.**

10. Place brush holder in rear housing, then insert attaching screws. Torque attaching screws to 17 to 25 inch lbs.

NOTE: Press brush holder against housing while torquing screws, and ensure ground brush wiring eyelet is positioned under screw before torquing.

11. Connect stator neutral lead to rectifier as follows:
    a. On flat type integrated diode rectifier units, position stator terminal insulator and stator neutral lead on rectifier assembly, then insert attaching screw and press into position. Screw should be pressed in far enough to prevent movement.
    b. On rectifier with exposed diodes, position neutral lead and dished washer onto rectifier assembly, then insert terminal screw and lock into place by rotating it ¼ turn.

NOTE: If ground terminal was removed, use same procedures as in steps 11 a and b.

12. Wrap stator winding leads around rectifier assembly terminals, then solder into place using a 100 watt soldering iron and rosin core electrical solder.

13. Install radio suppression capacitor and battery terminal insulator onto rectifier, then insert insulator onto stator terminal screw.

14. Align rectifier assembly terminal screws with holes in rear housing, then insert stator rectifier assembly into rear housing, ensuring insulators are seated in recesses.

15. Install external insulators, washers and nuts on terminals, then torque attaching nuts as follows:
    a. Black insulator onto STA terminal, torque to 25 to 35 inch lbs.
    b. Red insulator onto BAT terminal, torque to 30 to 55 inch lbs.
    c. Orange insulator onto FLD terminal, torque to 25 to 35 inch lbs.

16. Clean surface of rotor shaft with clean lint free cloth, then position rear housing and stator assembly over rotor aligning scribe marks.

17. Seat stator core machined surfaces into both housing stops, then insert housing through bolts and torque to 35 to 60 inch lbs. Remove wire retaining brushes.

SIDE TERMINAL ALTERNATOR

Disassemble

NOTE: Use a 200 watt soldering iron.

1. Mark both end housings and the stator with a scribe mark for use during assembly, **Fig. 25.**

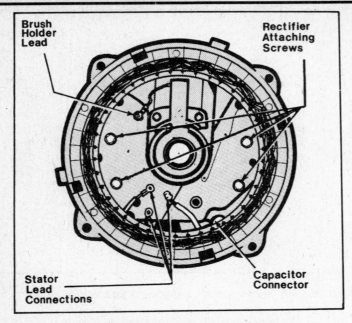

Fig. 26 Stator lead connections

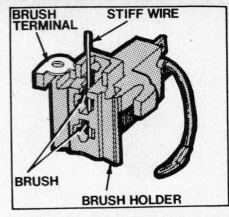

Fig. 27 Brush holder assembly

2. Remove the four housing through bolts, and separate the front housing and rotor from the rear housing and stator. Slots are provided in the front housing to aid in disassembly. Do not separate the rear housing from the stator at this time.
3. Remove the drive pulley nut, **Fig. 19.** Remove the lockwasher, pulley, fan and fan spacer from the rotor shaft.
4. Pull the rotor and shaft from the front housing, and remove the spacer from the rotor shaft, **Fig. 25.**
5. Remove three screws retaining the bearing to the front housing. If the bearing is damaged or has lost its lubricant, remove the bearing from the housing. To remove the bearing, support the housing close to the bearing boss and press the bearing from the housing.
6. Unsolder and disengage the three stator leads from the rectifier, **Fig. 26.**
7. Lift the stator from the rear housing.
8. Unsolder and disengage the brush holder lead from the rectifier.
9. Remove the screw attaching the capaciter lead to the rectifier.
10. Remove four screws attaching the rectifier to the rear housing, **Fig. 26.**
11. Remove the two terminal nuts and insulator from outside the housing, and remove the rectifier from the housing.
12. Remove two screws attaching the brush holder to the housing and remove the brushes and holder.
13. Remove sealing compound from rear housing and brush holder.
14. Remove one screw attaching the capacitor to the rear housing, and remove the capacitor.
15. If bearing replacement is necessary, support the rear housing close to the bearing boss and press the bearing

out of the housing from the inside.

Assemble

NOTE: Refer to "Cleaning and Inspection" procedures before reassembly.

1. If the front housing is being replaced, press the new bearing in the housing.

NOTE: Put pressure on the bearing outer race only, then install the bearing retaining screws and torque to 25 to 40 inch lbs.

2. Place the inner spacer on the rotor shaft, and insert the rotor shaft into the front housing and bearing.
3. Install the fan spacer, fan, pulley, lock washer and nut on the rotor shaft, **Fig. 19.**
4. If the rear bearing is being replaced, press a new bearing in from inside the housing until it is flush with the boss outer surface.
5. Position the brush terminal on the brush holder, **Fig. 27.** Install the springs and brushes in the brush holder, and insert a piece of stiff wire to hold the brushes in place, **Fig. 27.**
6. Position the brush holder in the rear housing and install the attaching screws. Push the brush holder toward the rotor shaft opening and tighten the brush holder attaching screws.
7. Position the capacitor to the rear housing and install the attaching screw.
8. Place the two cup shaped (rectifier) insulators on the bosses inside the housing. **Fig. 28.**
9. Place the insulator on the BAT (large) terminal of the rectifier, and position the rectifier in the rear housing. Place the outside insulator on the BAT terminal, and install the nuts on the BAT

and GRD terminals finger tight.
10. Install, but do not tighten, the four rectifier attaching screws.
11. Tighten the BAT and GRD terminal nuts on the outside of the rear housing, then tighten the four rectifier attaching screws.
12. Position the capacitor lead to the rectifier and install the attaching screw.
13. Press the brush holder lead on the rectifier pin and solder securely, **Fig. 26.**
14. Position the stator in the rear housing and align the scribe marks. Press the three stator leads on the rectifier pins and solder securely, **Fig. 26.**
15. Position the rotor and front housing into the stator and rear housing. Align the scribe marks and install the four through bolts. Tighten two opposing bolts and then the two remaining bolts.
16. Spin the fan and pulley to ensure nothing is binding within the alternator.
17. Remove the wire retracting the brushes, and place a daub of waterproof cement over the hole to seal it.

BRUSH REPLACEMENT
Removal
1. Mark both end housings and the stator with a scribe mark for use during assembly.
2. Remove the four housing through bolts, and separate the front housing and rotor from the rear housing and stator. Slots are provided in the front housing to aid in disassembly.

NOTE: Do not separate the rear housing and stator.

3. Unsolder and disengage the brush holder lead from the rectifier.
4. Remove the two brush holder attaching screws and lift the brush holder from the rear housing.
5. Remove the brushes from the brush holder.

Installation
1. Insert the brushes into the brush holder and position the terminal on the brush holder.

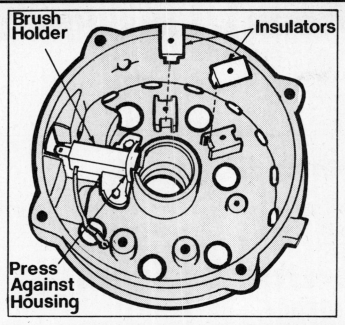

Fig. 28 Brush holder & rectifier insulators installed

through bolts. Partially tighten all four through bolts, then tighten two opposing bolts and the two remaining bolts.
10. Spin the fan and pulley to ensure nothing is binding within the alternator.
11. Remove the wire retracting the brushes in the brush holder, and place a daub of waterproof cement over the hole in the rear housing to seal it.

CLEANING & INSPECTION

NOTE: When rebuilding a high temperature alternator, use only high temperature rectifier assembly and bearings. If standard parts are used, alternator failure will occur.

1. The rotor, stator, and bearings must not be cleaned with solvent. Wipe these parts off with a clean cloth.
2. Rotate the front bearing on the drive end of the rotor drive shaft. Check for any scraping noise, looseness or roughness that will indicate that the bearing is excessively worn, and for excessive lubricant leakage. If any of these conditions exist, replace the bearing.
3. Inspect the rotor shaft at the rear bearing surface for roughness or severe chatter marks. Replace the rotor assembly if the shaft is not smooth.
4. Place the rear end bearing on the slip ring end of the shaft and rotate the bearing on the shaft. Make the same check for noise, looseness or roughness as was made for the front bearing. Inspect the rollers and cage for damage. Replace the bearing if these conditions exist, or if the lubricant is lost or contaminated.
5. Check the pulley and fan for excessive looseness on the rotor shaft. Replace any pulley or fan that is loose or bent out of shape. Check the rotor shaft for stripped or damaged threads. Inspect the hex hole in the end of the shaft for damage.
6. Check both the front and rear housing for cracks. Check the front housings for stripped threads in the mounting gear. Replace defective housings.
7. Check all wire leads on both the stator and rotor assemblies for loose soldered connections, and for burned insulation. Resolder poor connections. Replace parts that show burned insulation.
8. Check the slip rings for nicks and surface roughness. If the slip rings are badly damaged, the entire rotor will have to be replaced, as it is serviced as a complete assembly.
9. Replace any parts that are burned or cracked. Replace brushes and brush springs that are not to specification.

2. Depress the brushes and insert a 1½ inch piece of stiff wire, **Fig. 27,** to hold the brushes in the retracted position.
3. Position the brush holder to the rear housing, inserting the wire used to retract the brushes through the hole in the rear housing.
4. Install the brush holder attaching screws. Push the brush holder toward the rotor shaft opening and tighten the attaching screws.
5. Press the brush holder lead on the rectifier pin and solder securely.
6. Position the rotor and front housing into the stator and rear housing. Align the scribe marks and install the four through bolts. Tighten two opposing bolts and then the two remaining bolts.
7. Spin the fan and pulley to ensure nothing is binding within the alternator.
8. Remove the wire retracting the brushes, and place a daub of waterproof cement over the hole to seal it.

RECTIFIER REPLACEMENT
Removal
1. Mark both end housings and the stator with a scribe mark for use during assembly, **Fig. 25.**
2. Remove the four housing through bolts, and separate the front housing and rotor from the rear housing and stator. Slots are provided in the front housing to aid in disassembly.

NOTE: Do not separate the rear housing and stator at this time.

3. Unsolder and disengage the three stator leads from the rectifier, **Fig. 26.** Lift the stator from the rear housing.

4. Unsolder and disengage the brush holder lead from the rectifier.
5. Remove the screw attaching the capacitor lead to the rectifier.
6. Remove four screws attaching the rectifier to the rear housing, **Fig. 26.**
7. Remove two terminal nuts and insulator from outside the housing, and remove the rectifier from the housing.

Installation
1. Insert a piece of wire through the hole in the rear housing to hold the brushes in the retracted position.
2. Place the two cup-shaped (rectifier) insulators on the bosses inside the housing, **Fig. 28.**
3. Place the insulator on the BAT (large) terminal of the rectifier, and position the rectifier in the rear housing. Place the outside insulator on the BAT terminal, and install the nuts on the BAT and GRD terminals finger tight.
4. Install, but do not tighten, the four rectifier attaching screws.
5. Tighten the BAT and GRD terminal nuts on the outside of the rear housing, then tighten the four rectifier attaching screws.
6. Position the capacitor lead to the rectifier and install the attaching screw.
7. Press the brush holder lead on the rectifier pin and solder securely, **Fig. 26.**
8. Position the stator in the rear housing and align the scribe marks. Press the three stator leads on the rectifier pins and solder securely, **Fig. 26.**
9. Position the rotor and front housing into the stator and rear housing. Align the scribe marks and install the four

STARTER MOTORS & SWITCHES
TABLE OF CONTENTS

Delco-Remy Starters

NOTE: For service procedures on this starter, refer to "Delco-Remy Starters" section in "Chevrolet & GMC" chapter.

Ford Motorcraft Starters
INDEX

DESCRIPTION

This type starting motor, **Fig. 1,** is a four pole, series parallel unit with a positive engagement drive built into the starter. The drive mechanism is engaged with the flywheel by lever action before the motor is energized.

When the ignition switch is turned on to the start position, the starter relay is energized and supplies current to the motor. The current flows through one field coil and a set of contact points to ground. The magnetic field given off by the field coil pulls the movable pole, which is part of the lever, downward to its seat. When the pole is pulled down, the lever moves the drive assembly into the engine flywheel, **Fig. 2.**

When the movable pole is seated, it functions as a normal field pole and opens the contact points. With the points open, current flows through the starter field coils, energizing the starter. At the same time, current also flows through a holding coil to hold the movable pole in its seated position.

When the ignition switch is released from the start position, the starter relay opens the circuit to the starting motor. This allows the return spring to force the lever back, disengaging the drive from the flywheel and returning the movable pole to its normal position.

DIAGNOSIS

When diagnosing this starter motor, refer to **Fig. 3.**

IN-VEHICLE TESTING
ARMATURE & FIELD GROUNDED CIRCUIT TEST

1. Connect jumper lead to positive battery terminal.
2. Connect negative voltmeter lead to negative battery terminal.
3. Touch positive voltmeter lead to commutator and jumper wire to armature.
4. If voltmeter indicates voltage, armature windings are grounded.
5. Make connections as shown, **Fig. 4.** If voltmeter indicates voltage, field windings are grounded.

ARMATURE OPEN CIRCUIT TEST

An open circuit in the armature can sometimes be detected by examining commutator for signs of burning. A spot burned on the commutator is caused by an arc formed every time the commutator segment, connected to the open circuit winding, passes under a brush.

STARTER LOAD TEST

1. Connect test equipment as shown, **Fig. 5.**
2. Ensure that no current is flowing through ammeter and heavy duty carbon pile rheostat portion of circuit.
3. Disconnect push on connector "S" at starter relay and connect remote starter switch from positive battery terminal to "S" terminal of starter relay.
4. Crank engine with remote starter and determine exact reading on voltmeter.
5. Stop cranking engine, then reduce resistance of carbon pile until voltmeter indicates same reading as obtained while engine was cranked. Ammeter should read 150–200 amps on 4 inch diameter starter, or 150–180 amps on 4½ inch diameter starter.

STARTER NO-LOAD TEST

1. Connect test equipment as shown, **Fig. 6.**
2. Ensure that no current is flowing through ammeter, then determine exact reading on voltmeter.
3. Disconnect starter from battery, then reduce resistance of rheostat until voltmeter indicates same reading as while starter was running. Ammeter should read 70 amps on 4 inch diameter starter, or 80 amps on 4½ inch diameter starter.

STARTER OVERHAUL
DISASSEMBLY

1. Remove cover screw, cover, through bolts, starter drive end housing and starter drive plunger lever return

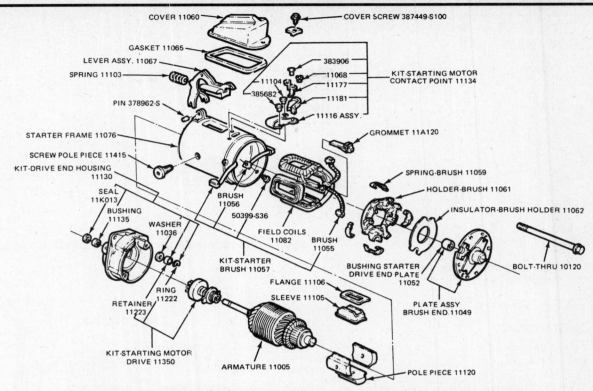

COVER 11060 **COVER SCREW 387449-S100**
GASKET 11065
LEVER ASSY. 11067
SPRING 11103
383906
11068
11104
11177
385682
11181
11116 ASSY.
KIT-STARTING MOTOR CONTACT POINT 11134
PIN 378962-S
GROMMET 11A120
STARTER FRAME 11076
SCREW POLE PIECE 11415
KIT-DRIVE END HOUSING 11130
SEAL 11K013
BUSHING 11135
WASHER 11036
SPRING-BRUSH 11059
HOLDER-BRUSH 11061
INSULATOR-BRUSH HOLDER 11062
BRUSH 11056
50399-S36
FIELD COILS 11082
BRUSH 11055
KIT-STARTER BRUSH 11057
BUSHING STARTER DRIVE END PLATE 11052
BOLT-THRU 10120
RING 11222
RETAINER 11223
FLANGE 11106
SLEEVE 11105
PLATE ASSY. BRUSH END 11049
KIT-STARTING MOTOR DRIVE 11350
ARMATURE 11005
POLE PIECE 11120

Fig. 1 Ford Motorcraft positive engagement starting motor (Typical)

spring.

2. Remove plunger lever retaining pin, then remove lever and armature.
3. Remove stop ring retainer from armature shaft, then remove stop ring and starter drive gear assembly.
4. Remove brush end plate and insulator assembly.
5. Remove brushes from brush holder, then remove brush holder. Note position of brush holder to end terminal.
6. Remove two screws retaining ground brushes to frame.
7. Bend up edges of sleeve inserted in frame, then remove sleeve and retainer.

8. Detach field coil ground wire from copper tab on frame.
9. Using tool No. 10044-A, remove three coil retaining screws, **Fig. 7.** Cut field coil connection at switch post lead and pole shoes and coils from frame.
10. Cut positive brush leads from field coils, as close to field connection as possible.

ASSEMBLY

1. Position pole pieces and coils in frame, then install retaining screws using tool No. 10044-A, **Fig. 7.** As pole shoes are tightened, strike frame several times with a soft faced mallet to seat and align pole shoes, then stake screws.
2. Install plunger coil sleeve and retainer, then bend tabs to retain coils to frame.

3. Position grommet on end terminal, then insert terminal and grommet into notch on frame.
4. Solder field coil to starter terminal post strap.

NOTE: Use 300 watt soldering iron and rosin core solder.

5. Check coils for continuity and grounds.
6. Position brushes to starter frame and install retaining screws.
7. Apply a thin coat of Lubriplate 777 or equivalent to armature shaft splines.
8. Install drive gear assembly on armature shaft, then install stop ring and stop ring retainer.
9. Install armature into starter frame.
10. Position starter drive gear plunger to frame and starter drive assembly, then

MOVABLE POLE SEATED BY MAGNETIC ATTRACTION OF ENERGIZED DRIVE COIL
FORKS MOVE DRIVE ASS'Y. INTO ENGAGEMENT
STOP COLLAR LIMITS TRAVEL (RETAINING CLIP)

Fig. 2 Starter drive engaged

CONDITION	POSSIBLE CAUSE	RESOLUTION
Engine will not crank — starter spins.	1. Starter motor. 2. Flywheel ring gear.	1. Remove starter, inspect for broken or worn starter drive components. Repair or replace as required. 2. Inspect ring gear teeth. Replace flywheel and ring gear if necessary.
Engine will not crank.	1. Loose or corroded battery cables. 2. Undercharged battery. 3. Burned fusible link in main wire feed to ignition switch. 4. Starter relay. 5. Loose or broken cables. 6. Loose or open wiring through neutral switch to relay. 7. Starter motor.	1. Clean and tighten cable connections. 2. Check battery. Charge or replace. 3. Check fusible link — correct wiring problem. 4. Replace starter relay. 5. Tighten or replace cable. 6. Repair, adjust or replace as required. 7. Repair or replace as required.
Engine cranks slowly.	1. Loose connections or corroded battery cables. 2. Undercharged battery. 3. Starter motor.	1. Clean and tighten cable connections. 2. Check battery. Charge or replace. 3. Repair or replace as required.

Fig. 3 Diagnosis chart

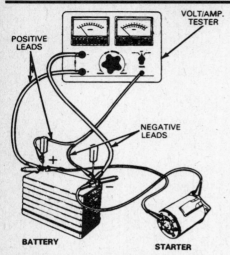

Fig. 4 Field grounded circuit test connections

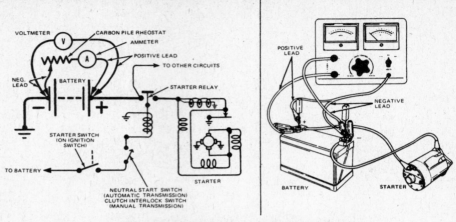

Fig. 5 Starter load test connections

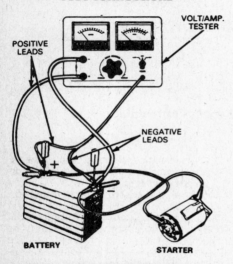

Fig. 6 Starter no-load test connections

install pivot assembly. Fill end housing bearing bore approximately ¼ full with grease, then position drive end housing to frame.

Install brush holder, then insert brushes into holder and install brush springs.

E: Ensure positive brush leads are erly positioned in slots on brush hold-

12. Install brush end plate. Ensure brush end plate insulator is properly positioned.
13. Install through bolts, then install starter drive plunger lever cover and tighten retaining screw.

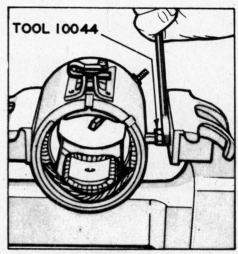

Fig. 7 Removing field coil pole shoe screws

Mitsubishi Starters

INDEX

DESCRIPTION

These starters are 12 volt units that have the solenoid mounted on the starter housing. The solenoid is energized when the starter relay contacts are closed causing the starter drive to engage with the flywheel ring gear, thereby starting the engine. An overrunning clutch in the drive protects the starter from excessive speeds once the engine starts. The current flows through the solenoid energizing coil until the solenoid plunger is at full travel, at which time the plunger closes a set of contacts that bypass the energizing coil, allowing the holding coil to keep the starter drive engaged and passing starting current to the starter.

TESTING

ARMATURE GROUNDED CIRCUIT TEST

NOTE: Perform this test after starter has been disassembled.

1. Touch one probe of circuit tester to commutator and the other probe to armature.
2. If less than infinite resistance is shown, replace armature.

ARMATURE OPEN CIRCUIT TEST

An open circuit in the armature can sometimes be detected by examining commutator for signs of burning. A spot burned on the commutator is caused by an arc formed every time a commutator segment connected to the open circuit winding passes under a brush.

BRUSH HOLDER GROUNDED CIRCUIT TEST

NOTE: Perform this test after starter has been disassembled.

1. Touch one probe of circuit tester to positive brush and other probe to brush holder.
2. If less than infinite resistance is shown, replace brush holder.

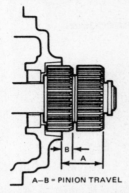

A—B = PINION TRAVEL

Fig. 1 Checking pinion travel. 4-134 engine

CHECKING DEPTH OF MICA SEGMENTS

NOTE: Perform this check after starter has been disassembled.

1. Check depth of mica between segments.
2. If depth is less than .0079 inch, increase to .0197–.0315 inch by repairing or replacing as necessary.

CHECKING PINION

4-134 Engine
1. Remove wire from M terminal on starter solenoid.
2. Connect positive lead of 12 volt source to terminal S and negative lead to starter motor body.

CAUTION: Do not apply power for more than 20 seconds continuously.

3. Measure pinion travel, **Fig. 1**. If pinion travel is less than .669 inch, repair or replace as necessary.

4-140 Engine
1. Remove wire from M terminal on starter solenoid.
2. Connect positive lead of 12 volt source to terminal S and negative lead to terminal M.
3. Set switch to "ON", causing pinion to move outward.

CAUTION: Do not apply power for more than 10 seconds continuously.

4. Lightly depress pinion, measuring length of depression. If this length is less than .008 inch, adjust number of gaskets at switch area as required.

FIELD GROUNDED CIRCUIT TEST

1. Check insulation between yoke and field terminal using circuit tester. Circuit tester should show infinite resistance.
2. Ensure that there is continuity between lead wires.

STARTER LOAD TEST

1. Connect test equipment as shown, **Fig. 2,** ensuring that there is no current flowing through ammeter and heavy duty carbon pile rheostat portion of circuit.
2. Disconnect push on connectors at starter solenoid and connect remote control starter switch from positive battery cable to S terminal of starter solenoid.
3. Crank engine with remote starter switch and determine exact reading on voltmeter.
4. Stop cranking engine, then reduce resistance of carbon pile until voltmeter indicates same reading as when engine was cranked. Ammeter should read less than 500 amps.

STARTER NO-LOAD TEST

NOTE: Perform this test on test bench after removing starter from vehicle.

1. Make test connections as shown, **Fig. 3.**
2. Ensure that no current is flowing through ammeter, then determine exact reading on voltmeter.
3. Disconnect starter from battery, then reduce resistance of rheostat until voltmeter indicates same reading as when motor was running. Ammeter should read less than 180 amps.

STARTER SOLENOID TESTS

4-134 ENGINE
1. Using circuit tester, check for continu-

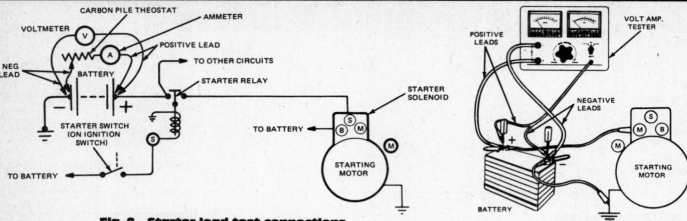

Fig. 2 Starter load test connections

Fig. 3 Starter no-load test connections

ity between S terminal and M terminal, and between S terminal and ground.
2. If there is no continuity in either case, replace solenoid.

4-140 ENGINE

Pull-In Test
1. Disconnect field coil wire from M terminal of solenoid.
2. Connect 12 volt battery between S terminal and M terminal.

CAUTION: Test must be performed in less than 10 seconds.

3. If pinion does not move outward, replace solenoid.

Hold-In Test
1. Disconnect field coil wire from M terminal of magnetic switch.
2. Connect 12 volt battery between S terminal and body.
3. If pinion moves inward, replace solenoid.

Return Test
1. Disconnect field coil wire from M terminal of magnetic switch.
2. Connect 12 volt battery between M terminal and body.

CAUTION: Test must be performed in less than 10 seconds.

3. Pull pinion outward and release. If pinion does not quickly return to its original position, replace solenoid.

TESTING ARMATURE FOR SHORT CIRCUIT

4-140 Engine
1. Place armature in growler.
2. Hold a thin steel blade parallel and just above armature while rotating armature slowly in growler.
3. If blade vibrates, replace armature.

TESTING OVERRUNNING CLUTCH

4-140 Engine
1. Hold clutch housing and rotate pinion.

Fig. 4 Exploded view of Mitsubishi starter. 4-134 engine

2. If pinion does not rotate clockwise or lock counterclockwise, replace overrunning clutch assembly.
3. Inspect pinion for wear or burrs, replacing overrunning clutch assembly as necessary.

STARTER OVERHAUL
4-134 ENGINE

1. Remove nut and washer from M terminal of starter solenoid and position field strap out of way.
2. Remove solenoid attaching screws, then the solenoid.

3. Remove through bolts and separate rear cover and armature assembly from starter drive assembly, **Fig. 4.**
4. Remove and discard gasket.
5. Remove rear housing to brush holder assembly attaching screws, then the housing, removing and discarding gasket.
6. Remove armature assembly from field coil assembly.
7. Remove end cap from center housing.
8. Remove C-clip and washer from driveshaft assembly.
9. Remove center housing to starter drive assembly attaching bolt, then the

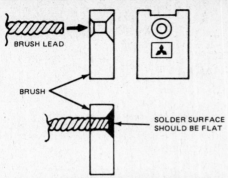

Fig. 5 Installing brush to brush lead wire

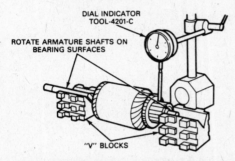

Fig. 7 Checking commutator for run-out

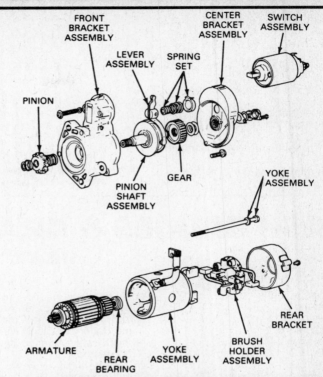

Fig. 6 Exploded view of Mitsubishi starter. 4-140 engine

center housing.

10. Using suitable tool with arbor press, remove bearings from armature assembly.

11. Clean, inspect, repair and replace parts as necessary.

12. If starter brushes measure less than .435 inch, replace them as follows:
    a. Remove brushes and brush lead wires from brush holder.
    b. Break brush to remove it from lead wire.
    c. Clean brush lead wire and position new brush on brush lead wire, through small taper side, **Fig. 5.**
    d. Solder brush and brush lead wire using rosin core solder and suitable soldering iron.

13. Using suitable tool and arbor press, install new armature assembly bearings.

14. Position center housing on starter drive assembly and install attaching bolt, torquing to 5–7 ft. lbs.

15. Install washer and C-clip on driveshaft assembly.

16. Install end cap on center housing.

17. Install armature assembly in field coil assembly, ensuring that brushes are correctly positioned on commutator.

18. Using new gasket, position rear housing and install bolts attaching housing to brush holder, torquing to 5–7 ft. lbs.

19. Using new gasket, position rear housing and armature assembly on starter drive housing, then install through bolts, torquing to 5–7 ft. lbs.

20. Position solenoid on starter and install

attaching screws, torquing to 5–7 ft. lbs.

21. Position strap on M terminal on solenoid and install nut and washer, torquing nut to 80–120 inch lbs.

4-140 ENGINE

1. Remove nut and washer from M terminal of starter solenoid and position field strap out of way.

2. Remove solenoid to starter attaching screws, then the solenoid.

3. Remove through bolts and screws, then the rear bracket, **Fig. 6.**

4. Slide brushes from brush holder by prying retaining springs back, then remove brush holder assembly.

5. Remove yoke assembly, then the armature.

6. Remove pinion shaft end cover from center cover.

7. Using feeler gauge, measure and record pinion shaft end play.

8. Remove retaining ring and washer from pinion shaft.

9. Remove center bracket, then the lever spring retainer and spring.

10. Remove adjusting washer and reduction gear.

11. Remove clutch shift lever and two lever holders.

12. Using suitable tool, press snap ring off stop ring.

13. Remove snap ring using screwdriver, then remove stop ring.

14. Remove pinion and spring from shaft,

then the overrunning clutch from front bracket.

15. Brush or blow clean field coils, armature assembly, brush holder, brushes, drive assembly, brush end plate assembly and drive end housing. Wash all other parts in suitable solvent.

16. Inspect armature windings for broken or burned insulation and unwelded or open connections.

17. Check armature for open circuits, shorts and grounds.

18. Check commutator for run-out, **Fig. 7.** If run-out exceeds .002 inch, or is rough, reface commutator. Remove only enough metal to provide a smooth, even surface.

19. Check plastic brush holder for cracks or broken mounting pads. Replace brushes if worn excessively.

20. Inspect field coils for burned or broken insulation and continuity.

21. Examine wear pattern on starter drive teeth. The pinion teeth must penetrate to a depth greater than ½ of the ring gear tooth depth to eliminate premature ring gear and starter drive failure. Replace starter drives and ring gears that have milled, pitted or broken teeth or show evidence of inadequate engagement.

22. Install overrunning clutch into front bracket.

23. Install pinion and spring onto pinion shaft. If end play measured during disassembly was greater than .020 inch, add adjusting washer(s) so that end play is less than .020 inch but not zero, **Fig. 8.**

24. Using suitable pliers, install snap ring onto pinion shaft.
25. Using suitable tool, pull stop ring over snap ring.
26. Install clutch shift lever holder and shift lever.
27. Install reduction gear, clutch shift lever spring and retainer.
28. Install center bracket, then the retaining washer and ring to retain pinion shaft.
29. Install pinion shaft end cover to center cover.
30. Install armature and yoke assembly.

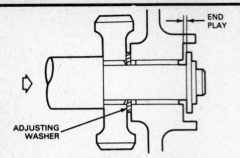

Fig. 8 Adjusting pinion and play. 4-140 engine

31. Slide brush retaining spring back, position brush holder assemblies and brushes in place and release retaining spring.
32. Position rear bracket to housing and install two through bolts and two retaining screws.
33. Position solenoid on starter and install attaching screws, torquing to 5–7 ft. lbs.
34. Position strap on M terminal and install nut washer, torquing nut to 80–120 inch lbs.

DASH GAUGES & GRAPHIC DISPLAYS
INDEX

DASH GAUGES

Gauge failures are often caused by defective wiring or grounds. The first step in locating trouble should be a thorough inspection of all wiring, terminals and printed circuits. If wiring is secured by clamps, check to see whether the insulation has been severed, thereby grounding the wire. In the case of a fuel gauge installation, rust may cause failure by corrosion at the ground connection of the tank unit.

The Constant Voltage Regulator (CVR) type indicator is a bimetal-resistance type system consisting of an Instrument Voltage Regulator (IVR), an indicator gauge, and a variable resistance sending unit. Current to the system is applied to the gauge terminals by the IVR, which maintains an average-pulsating value of 5 volts.

The indicator gauge consists of a pointer which is attached to a wire-wound bimetal strip. Current passing through the coil heats the bimetal strip, causing the pointer to move. As more current passes through the coil, heat increases, moving the pointer farther.

The circuit is completed through a sending unit which contains a variable resistor. When resistance is high, less current is allowed to pass through the gauge, and the pointer moves very little. As resistance decreases due to changing conditions in system being monitored, more current passes through gauge coil, causing pointer to move farther.

NOTE: Do not apply battery voltage to system or ground output terminals of IVR, as damage to system components or wiring circuits may result.

DASH GAUGE TEST

1. Disconnect battery ground cable and remove gauge from vehicle.
2. Connect ohmmeter between gauge terminals and read coil winding resistance.
3. An upward movement of ohmmeter needle from 10 ohms to 14 ohms is normal, as test current of ohmmeter causes a temperature rise in gauge coil windings.

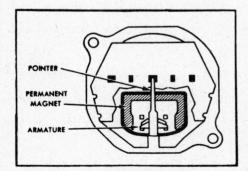

Fig. 1 Conventional type ammeter

4. If ohmmeter reads below 10 ohms or above 14 ohms, gauge is defective.

AMMETERS

The ammeter is an instrument used to indicate current flow into and out of the battery. When electrical accessories in the vehicle draw more current than the alternator can supply, current flows from the battery and the ammeter indicates a discharge (−) condition. When electrical loads of the vehicle are less than alternator output, current is available to charge the battery, and the ammeter indicates a charge (+) condition. If battery is fully charged, the voltage regulator reduces alternator output to meet only immediate vehicle electrical loads. When this happens, ammeter reads zero.

CONVENTIONAL AMMETER

A conventional ammeter must be connected between the battery and alternator in order to indicate current flow. This type ammeter, **Fig. 1**, consists of a frame to which a permanent magnet is attached. The frame also supports an armature and pointer assembly. Current in this system flows from the alternator through the ammeter, then to the battery or from the battery through the ammeter into the vehicle electrical system, depending on vehicle operating conditions.

When no current flows through the

ammeter, the magnet holds the pointer armature so that the pointer stands at the center of the dial. When current passes in either direction through the ammeter, the resulting magnetic field attracts the armature away from the effect of the permanent magnet, thus giving a reading proportional to the strength of the current flowing.

Troubleshooting

When the ammeter apparently fails to register correctly, there may be trouble in the wiring which connects the ammeter to the alternator and battery or in the alternator or battery itself.

To check the connections, first tighten the two terminal posts on the back of the ammeter. Then, following each wire from the ammeter, tighten all connections on the ignition switch, battery and alternator. Chafed, burned or broken insulation can be found by following each ammeter wire from end to end.

All wires with chafed, burned or broken insulation should be repaired or replaced. After this is done, and all connections are tightened, connect the battery cable and turn on the ignition switch. The needle should point slightly to the discharge (−) side.

Start the engine and run slightly above idling speed. The needle should move slowly to the charge side (+).

If the pointer does not move as indicated, the ammeter is out of order and should be replaced.

SHUNT TYPE AMMETER

The shunt type ammeter is actually a specifically calibrated voltmeter. It is connected to read voltage drop across a resistance wire (shunt) between the battery and alternator. The shunt is located either in the vehicle wiring or within the ammeter itself.

When voltage is higher at the alternator end of the shunt, the meter indicates a charge (+) condition. When voltage is higher at the battery end of the shunt, the meter indicates a discharge (−) condition. When voltage is equal at both ends of the shunt, the meter reads zero.

Troubleshooting

Ammeter accuracy can be determined by comparing reading with an ammeter of known accuracy.

1. With engine stopped and ignition switch in RUN position, switch on headlamps and heater fan. Meter should indicate a discharge (−) condition.
2. If ammeter pointer does not move, check ammeter terminals for proper connection and check for open circuit in wiring harness. If connections and wiring harness are satisfactory, ammeter is defective.
3. If ammeter indicates a charge (+) condition, wiring harness connections are reversed at ammeter.

ALTERNATOR INDICATOR LIGHT

When the ignition switch is in Start or Run position, battery current flows through the alternator warning indicator into regulator at terminal 1 and to ground through the indicator switch. The electronic control measures a low voltage at terminal A and closes the field switch. This applies battery voltage to the field through alternator terminal F. With current in the field and the rotor turning, alternator stator produces a voltage at terminals B and S.

A predetermined voltage at terminal S operates the electronic control to open indicator switch, which removes ground from alternator warning indicator.

Alternator current output is controlled by current in the field. Average field current depends on length of time field switch is closed. The electronic control closes field switch when voltage at terminal A is low and opens switch when voltage is high.

TROUBLESHOOTING

Exc. 4-140 Turbo Diesel Engine

1. If alternator indicator lamp does not light with ignition in On position and engine not running, check condition of indicator lamp bulb. If bulb is satisfactory, check for an open in circuit between ignition switch and regulator terminal (circuit 1).
2. If alternator indicator lamp does not light, disconnect electrical connector from regulator and connect a jumper wire between 1 terminal of regulator electrical connector and negative battery post cable clamp. With ignition turned to On position, indicator lamp should light.
3. If lamp does not light, check condition of indicator lamp bulb. If bulb is satisfactory, repair open in circuit between ignition switch and regulator or replace 500 ohm resistor (if equipped) across indicator lamp, as necessary.

VOLTMETER

The voltmeter is a gauge which measures the electrical flow from the battery to indicate whether the battery output is within tolerances. The voltmeter reading can range from 13.5–14.0 volts under normal operating conditions. If an undercharge or overcharge condition is indicated for an extended period, the battery and charging system should be checked.

TROUBLESHOOTING

To check voltmeter, turn key and headlights on with engine off. Pointer should move to 12.5 volts. If no needle movement is observed, check connections from battery to circuit breaker. If connections are tight and meter shows no movement, check wire continuity. If wire continuity is satisfactory, the meter is inoperative and must be replaced.

OIL PRESSURE INDICATOR LIGHT

Many trucks utilize a warning light on the instrument panel in place of the conventional dash indicating gauge to warn the driver when the oil pressure is dangerously low. The warning light is wired in series with the ignition switch and the engine unit—which is an oil pressure switch.

The oil pressure switch contains a diaphragm and a set of contacts. When the ignition switch is turned on, the warning light circuit is energized and the circuit is completed through the closed contacts in the pressure switch. When the engine is started, build-up of oil pressure compresses the diaphragm, opening the contacts, thereby breaking the circuit and putting out the light.

TROUBLESHOOTING

The oil pressure warning light should go on when the ignition is turned on. If it does not light, disconnect the wire from the engine unit and ground the wire to the frame or cylinder block. Then if the warning light still does not go on with the ignition switch on, replace the bulb.

If the warning light goes on when the wire is grounded to the frame or cylinder block, the engine unit should be checked for being loose or poorly grounded. If the unit is found to be tight and properly grounded, it should be removed and a new one installed. (The presence of sealing compound on the threads of the engine unit will cause a poor ground.)

If the warning light remains lit when it normally should be out, replace the engine unit before proceeding further to determine the cause for a low pressure indication.

The warning light will sometimes light up or flicker when the engine is idling, even though the oil pressure is adequate. However, the light should go out when the engine speed is increased.

TEMPERATURE INDICATOR LIGHT

A bimetal temperature switch located in the cylinder head control the operation of a temperature indicator light with a red lens. If the engine cooling system is not functioning properly and coolant temperature exceeds a predetermined value, the warning light will illuminate.

TROUBLESHOOTING

If the red light is not lit when the engine is being cranked, check for a burned out bulb, an open in the light circuit, or a defective ignition switch.

If the red light is lit when the engine is running, check the wiring between light and switch for a ground, defective temperature switch, or overheated cooling system.

NOTE: As a test circuit to check whether the red bulb is functioning properly, a wire which is connected to the ground terminal of the ignition switch is tapped into its circuit. When the ignition is in the "Start" (engine cranking) position, the ground terminal is grounded inside the switch and the red bulb will be lit. When the engine is started and the ignition switch is in the "On" position, the test circuit is opened and the bulb is then controlled by the temperature switch.

ELECTRICAL TEMPERATURE GAUGES

This temperature indicating system consists of a sending unit, located on the cylinder head, electrical temperature gauge and an instrument voltage regulator. As engine temperature increases or decreases, the resistance of the sending unit changes, in turn controlling current flow to the gauge. When engine temperature is low, the resistance of the sending unit is high, restricting current flow to the gauge, in turn indicating low engine temperature. As engine temperature increases, the resistance of the ending unit decreases, permitting an increased current flow to the gauge, resulting in an increased temperature reading.

TROUBLESHOOTING

A special tester is required to diagnose this type gauge. Follow instructions included with the tester.

ELECTRICAL OIL PRESSURE GAUGES

This oil pressure indicating system incorporates an instrument voltage regulator, electrical oil pressure gauge and a sending unit which are connected in series. The sending unit consists of a diaphragm, contact and a variable resistor. As oil pressure increases or decreases, the diaphragm actuated the contact on the variable resistor, in turn controlling current flow to the gauge. When oil pressure is low, the resistance of the variable resistor is high, restricting current flow to the gauge, in turn indicating low oil pressure. As oil pressure increases, the resistance of the variable resistor is lowered, permitting an increased current flow to the gauge, resulting in an increased gauge reading.

TROUBLESHOOTING

A special tester is required to diagnose this type gauge. Follow instructions included with the tester.

SPEEDOMETERS

The following material covers only that service on speedometers which is feasible to perform. Repairs on the units themselves are not included as they require special tools and extreme care when making repairs and adjustments that only an experienced speedometer mechanic should attempt.

The speedometer has two main parts—the speedometer head and the speedometer drive cable. When the speedometer fails to indicate speed or mileage, the cable or cable housing is probably broken.

SPEEDOMETER CABLE

Most cables are broken due to lack of

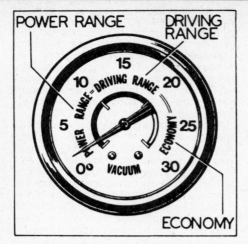

Fig. 2   Typical vacuum gauge

lubrication, or a sharp bend or kink in the housing.

A cable might break because of the speedometer head mechanism binds. In such cases, the speedometer head should be repaired or replaced before a new cable or housing is installed.

A "jumpy" pointer condition, together with a scraping noise, is due, in most instances, to a dry or kinked speedometer cable. The kinked cable rubs on the housing and winds up, slowing down the pointer. The cable then unwinds and the pointer "jumps."

To check for kinks, remove the cable, lay it on a flat surface and twist one end with the fingers. If it turns over smoothly the cable is not kinked. But if part of the cable flops over as it is twisted, the cable is kinked and should be replaced.

LUBRICATION

The speedometer cable should be lubricated with special cable lubricant. Fill the ferrule on the upper end of the housing with the cable lubricant. Insert the cable in the housing, starting at the upper end. Turn the cable around carefully while feeding it into the housing. Repeat filling the ferrule except for the last six inches of cable. Too much lubricant at this point may cause the lubricant to work into the speedometer head.

INSTALLING CABLE

During installation, if the cable sticks when inserted in the housing and will not go through, the housing is damaged inside or kinked. Be sure to check the housing from one end to the other. Straighten any sharp bends by relocating clamps or elbows. Replace housing if it is badly kinked or broken. Position the cable and housing so that they lead into the head as straight as possible.

Check the new cable for kinks before installing it. Use wide, sweeping, gradual curves where the cable comes out of the transmission and connects to the head so

the cable will not be damaged during installation.

Arrange the housing so it does not lean against the engine because heat from the engine may dry out the lubricant.

If inspection indicates that the cable and housing are in good condition, yet pointer action is erratic, check the speedometer head for possible binding.

The speedometer drive pinion should also be checked. If the pinion is dry or its teeth are stripped, the speedometer may not register properly.

VACUUM GAUGE

This gauge, **Fig. 2**, measures intake manifold vacuum. The intake manifold vacuum varies with engine operating conditions, carburetor adjustments, valve timing, ignition timing and general engine condition.

Since the optimum fuel economy is directly proportional to a properly functioning engine, a high vacuum reading on the gauge relates to fuel economy. Most gauges have colored sectors the green sector being the "Economy" range and the red the "Power" range. Therefore, the vehicle should be operated with gauge registering in the green sector or a high numerical number, **Fig. 2**, for maximum economy.

FUEL ECONOMY WARNING SYSTEM

This system actually monitors the engine vacuum just like the vacuum gauge, but all it registers is a low vacuum. The light on the instrument panel warns the vehicle operator when engine manifold vacuum drops below the economical limit. Switch operation is similar to that of the oil pressure indicating light, except that the switch opens when vacuum , rather than oil pressure, is applied.

TROUBLESHOOTING

Fuel Economy Warning Light

The fuel economy warning light should go on when the ignition is turned on. If it does not light, disconnect the wire from the fuel economy vacuum switch connector and ground the wire to the frame or cylinder block. If the warning light still does not go on, check for burned out indicating bulb or an open in the harness between the vacuum switch and instrument panel. If the warning light goes on, circuit is functioning and the vacuum switch should be checked for proper ground. Remove and clean the mounting bracket screws and the mounting surfaces.

If system still does not operate, perform the following:

With the electrical connector and vacuum tube disconnected from the switch, connect a self-powered test light to the switch electrical connector and to the vacuum gauge mountng bracket. Attach a vacuum pump to gauge. If the following conditions are not met the switch has to be

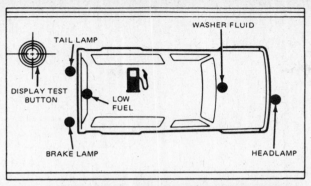

Fig. 3   Graphic display warning system display. 1984—85 Bronco II & Ranger

replaced:
1. With vacuum applied test light should be "Off".
2. With no vacuum to the vacuum switch test light should be "On".

If the warning light remains lit when it normally should be out, check vacuum hose to vacuum switch for damage or plugged condition.

ELECTRIC CLOCKS

Regulation of electric clocks is accomplished automatically by resetting the time. If the clock is running fast, the action of turning the hands back to correct the time will automatically cause the clock to run slightly slower. If the clock is running slow, the action of turning the hands forward to correct the time will automatically cause the clock to run slightly faster (10 to 15 seconds daily).

A lock-out feature prevents the clock regulator mechanism from being reset more than once per wind cycle, regardless of the number of times the time is reset. After the clock rewinds, if the time is then reset, automatic regulation will take place. If a clock varies over 10 minutes per day, it will never adjust properly and must be repaired or replaced.

WINDING CLOCK WHEN CONNECTING BATTERY OR CLOCK WIRING

The clock requires special attention when reconnecting a battery that has been disconnected for any reason, a clock that has been disconnected, or when replacing a blown clock fuse. It is very important that the initial wind be fully made. The procedure is as follows:
1. Make sure that all other instruments and lights are turned off.
2. Connect positive cable to battery.
3. Before connecting the negative cable, press the terminal to its post on the battery. Immediately afterward, strike the terminal against the battery post to see if there is a spark. If there is a

spark, allow the clock to run down until it stops ticking, and repeat as above until there is no spark. Then immediately make the permanent connection before the clock can again run down. The clock will run down in approximately two minutes.
4. Reset clock after all connections have been made. The foregoing procedure should also be followed when reconnecting the clock after it has been disconnected, or if it has stopped because of a blown fuse. Be sure to disconnect battery before installing a new fuse.

TROUBLESHOOTING

If clock does not run, check for blown "clock" fuse. If fuse is blown, check for short in wiring. If fuse is not blown, check for open circuit.

With an electric clock, the most frequent cause of clock fuse blowing is voltage at the clock which will prevent a complete wind and allow clock contacts to remain closed. This may be caused by any of the following: discharged battery, corrosion on contact surface of battery terminals, loose connections at battery terminals, at junction block, at fuse clips, or at terminal connection of clock. Therefore, if in reconnecting battery or clock it is noted that the clock is not ticking, always check for blown fuse, or examine the circuits at the points indicated above to determine and correct the cause.

GRAPHIC DISPLAY WARNING SYSTEM

The graphic display warning system, **Fig. 3,** consists of a warning module equipped with 5 light-emitting diodes (LED). The module is mounted on the console and alerts the driver of the following conditions: low washer fluid, taillight failure, brake light failure, low beam headlight failure, low fuel level.

The wiring harness used with this system use special resistance wire. Do not

alter wire lengths or replace bulbs with any type other than original equipment, as the system will not function properly.

TROUBLESHOOTING

NOTE: The following precautions must be taken when performing any diagnosis:
a. Check condition of system fuse before proceeding.
b. All tests must be performed with ignition switch in Run position.
c. Ambient temperature must be 60–80°F to provide accurate test results.
d. All voltage measurements must be made using a suitable digital voltmeter. Do not touch voltmeter probes with fingers.
e. Refer to system wiring diagram, **Figs. 4 and 5,** when performing tests. The harness connectors, **Fig. 6,** are located at front of console.

Taillight LED Illuminates or Gives False Indication
1. Measure voltage between terminals 14 and 102 with ignition switch in Run position and headlight switch On.
2. Voltage should measure .48 volt or more.
3. If voltage is not within specifications, check condition of bulbs and replace as necessary. If bulbs are satisfactory, check circuits for an open or short and repair as necessary.
4. If voltage is within specifications, but taillight LED remains lit, replace graphic display module.

Headlight LED Illuminates or Gives False Indication
1. Measure voltage between terminals 13 and 108 with ignition switch in Run position and headlight switch On.
2. Voltage should measure .47 volt or more.
3. If voltage is not within specifications, check condition of bulbs and replace as necessary. If bulbs are satisfactory, check circuits for an open or short and repair as necessary.
4. If voltage is within specifications, but headlight LED remains lit, replace graphic display module.

Brake Light LED Illuminates or Gives False Indication
1. Measure voltage between terminals 9 and 104 with ignition switch in Run position.
2. Voltage should measure .19 volt or more.
3. If voltage is not within specifications, check condition of left brake light bulb and replace as necessary. If bulb is satisfactory, check circuits for an open or short and repair as necessary.
4. If voltage is within specifications, but brake light LED remains lit, proceed to step 5.
5. Measure voltage between terminals 5 and 105 with ignition switch in Run

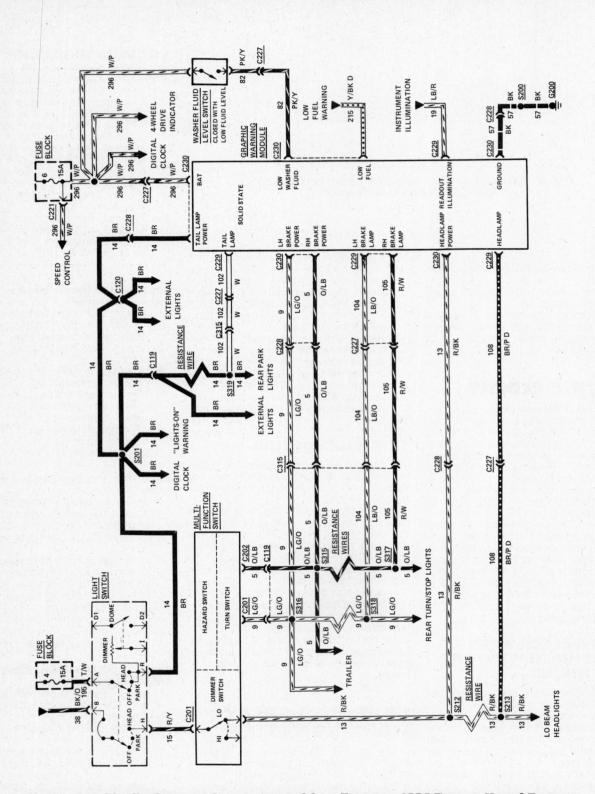

Fig. 4 Graphic display warning system wiring diagram. 1984 Bronco II and Ranger

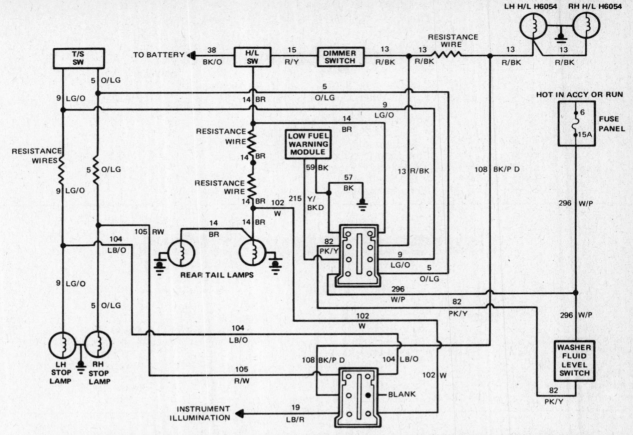

Fig. 5 Graphic display warning system wiring diagram. 1985 Bronco II & Ranger

position.
6. Voltage should measure .19 volt or more.
7. If voltage is not within specifications, check condition of right brake light bulb and replace as necessary. If bulb is satisfactory, check circuits for an open or short and repair as necessary.
8. If voltage is within specifications, but brake light LED remains lit, replace graphic display module.

Low Fuel LED Illuminates or Gives False Indication
1. Measure voltage between terminals 57 and 215 with ignition switch in Accessory or Run position and fuel level low enough to illuminate LED.
2. Voltage should be 10.5–13.5 volts.
3. If voltage is not within specifications, check circuits for an open or short and repair as necessary.

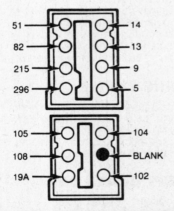

Fig. 6 Graphic display warning system electrical connectors. 1984–85 Bronco II & Ranger

Washer Fluid LED Illuminates or Gives False Indication
1. Measure voltage between terminals 82 and 57 with ignition switch in Accessory or Run position and washer fluid level low enough to illuminate LED.
2. Voltage should be 10.5–13.5 volts.
3. If voltage is not within specifications, check circuits for an open or short and repair as necessary.

No LED's Will Illuminate
1. Measure voltage between terminals 57 and 296 with ignition switch in Accessory or Run position.
2. Voltage should be 10.5–13.5 volts.
3. If voltage is not within specifications, check circuits for an open or short and repair as necessary.

One or More LED's Will Not Illuminate
1. Replace defective LED indicator(s) located in console.

DISC BRAKES

TABLE OF CONTENTS

General Information

INDEX

TROUBLESHOOTING

EXCESSIVE PEDAL TRAVEL

1. Worn brake lining.
2. Shoe and lining knock back after cornering or rough road travel.
3. Piston and shoe and lining assembly not properly seated or positioned.
4. Air leak or insufficient fluid in system or caliper.
5. Loose wheel bearing adjustment.
6. Damaged or worn caliper piston seal.
7. Improper booster push rod adjustment.
8. Shoe out of flat more than .005".
9. Rear brake automatic adjusters inoperative.
10. Improperly ground rear brake shoe and lining assemblies.

BRAKE ROUGHNESS OR CHATTER; PEDAL PUMPING

1. Excessive lateral run-out of rotor.
2. Rotor excessively out of parallel.

EXCESSIVE PEDAL EFFORT

1. Frozen or seized pistons.
2. Brake fluid, oil or grease on linings.
3. Shoe and lining worn below specifications.
4. Proportioning valve malfunction.
5. Booster inoperative.
6. Leaking booster vacuum check valve.

PULL, UNEVEN OR GRABBING BRAKES

1. Frozen or seized pistons.
2. Brake fluid, oil or grease on linings.
3. Caliper out of alignment with rotor.
4. Loose caliper attachment.
5. Unequalized front tire pressure.
6. Incorrect front end alignment.
7. Lining protruding beyond end of shoe.

BRAKE RATTLE

1. Excessive clearance between shoe and caliper or between shoe and splash shield.
2. Shoe hold-down clips missing or improperly positioned.

HEAVY BRAKE DRAG

1. Frozen or seized pistons.
2. Operator riding brake pedal.
3. Incomplete brake pedal return due to linkage interference.
4. Faulty booster check valve holding pressure in hydraulic system.
5. Residual pressure in front brake hydraulic system.

CALIPER BRAKE FLUID LEAK

1. Damaged or worn caliper piston seal.
2. Scores in cylinder bore.
3. Corrosion build-up in cylinder bore or on piston surface.
4. Metal clip in seal groove.

NO BRAKING EFFECT WHEN PEDAL IS DEPRESSED

1. Piston and shoe and lining assembly not properly seated or positioned.
2. Air leak or insufficient fluid in system or caliper.
3. Damaged or worn caliper piston seal.
4. Bleeder screw open.
5. Air in hydraulic system or improper bleeding.

REAR BRAKES LOCKING ON APPLICATION

On brake system equipped with a proportioning or rear pressure regulator valve, should the valve malfunction, rear brakes may receive excess pressure, resulting in wheel lock-up.

SERVICE PRECAUTIONS

BRAKE LINES & LININGS

Remove one of the front wheels and inspect the brake disc, caliper and linings. (The wheel bearings should be inspected at this time and repacked if necessary).

Do not get any oil or grease on the linings. It is recommended that both front wheel sets be replaced whenever a respective shoe and lining is worn or damaged. Inspect and, if necessary, replace rear brake linings also.

If the caliper is cracked or fluid leakage through the casting is evident, it must be replaced as a unit.

BRAKE ROUGHNESS

The most common cause of brake chatter on disc brakes is a variation in thickness of the disc. If roughness or vibration is encountered during highway operation or if pedal pumping is experienced at low speeds, the disc may have excessive thickness variation. To check for this condition, measure the disc at 12 points with a micrometer at a radius approximately one inch from edge of disc. If thickness measurements vary more than specifications allow, the disc should be replaced with a new one.

Excessive lateral runout of braking disc may cause a "knocking back" of the pistons, possibly creating increased pedal travel and vibration when brakes are applied.

Before checking the runout, wheel bearings should be adjusted. Be sure to make the adjustment according to the recommendations given in the individual truck chapters.

BRAKE DISC SERVICE

Servicing of disc brakes is extremely critical due to the close tolerances required in machining the brake disc to insure proper brake operation.

The maintenance of these close controls on the friction surfaces is necessary to prevent brake roughness. In addition, the surface finish must be non-directional and maintained at a micro-inch finish. This close control of the rubbing surface finish is necessary to avoid pulls and erratic performance and promote long lining life and

equal lining wear of both left and right brakes.

In light of the foregoing remarks, refinishing of the rubbing surfaces should not be attempted unless precision equipment, capable of measuring in micro-inches (millionths of an inch) is available.

To check runout of a disc, mount a dial indicator on a convenient part (steering knuckle, tie rod, disc brake caliper housing) so that the plunger of the dial indicator contacts the disc at a point one inch from the outer edge. If the total indicated runout exceeds specifications, install a new disc.

GENERAL PRECAUTIONS

1. Grease or any other foreign material must be kept off the caliper, surfaces of the disc and external surfaces of the hub, during service procedures. Handling the brake disc and caliper should be done in a way to avoid deformation of the disc and nicking or scratching brake linings.
2. If inspection reveals rubber piston seals are worn or damaged, they should be replaced immediately.
3. During removal and installation of a wheel assembly, exercise care so as not to interfere with or damage the caliper splash shield, the bleeder screw or the transfer tube, (if equipped).
4. Front wheel bearings should be adjusted to specifications.
5. Be sure vehicle is centered on hoist before servicing any of the front end components to avoid bending or damaging the disc splash shield on full right or left wheel turns.
6. Before the vehicle is moved after any brake service work, be sure to obtain a firm brake pedal.
7. The assembly bolts of the two caliper housings (if equipped) should not be disturbed unless the caliper requires service.

INSPECTION OF CALIPER

Should it become necessary to remove the caliper for installation of new parts, clean all parts in alcohol, wipe dry using lint-free cloths. Using an air hose, blow out drilled passages and bores. Check dust boots for punctures or tears. If punctures or tears are evident, new boots should be installed upon reassembly.

Inspect piston bores in both housings for scoring or pitting. Bores that show light scratches or corrosion can usually be cleaned with crocus cloth. However, bores that have deep scratches or scoring may be honed, provided the diameter of the bore is not increased more than .002". If the bore does not clean up within this specification, a new caliper housing should be installed (black stains on the bore walls are caused by piston seals and will do no harm).

When using a hone, be sure to install the hone baffle before honing bore. The baffle is used to protect the hone stones from damage. Use extreme care in cleaning the caliper after honing. Remove all dust and grit by flushing the caliper with alcohol. Wipe dry with clean lint-less cloth and then clean a second time in the same manner.

BLEEDING DISC BRAKES

The disc brake hydraulic system can be bled manually or with pressure bleeding equipment. On vehicles with disc brakes the brake pedal will require more pumping and frequent checking of fluid level in master cylinder during bleeding operation.

Never use brake fluid that has been drained from hydraulic system when bleeding the brakes. Be sure the disc brake pistons are returned to their normal positions and that the shoe and lining assemblies are properly seated. Before driving the vehicle, check brake operation to be sure that a firm pedal has been obtained.

Ford Single Piston Sliding Caliper, Exc. 1983—85 Ranger & 1984—85 Bronco II
INDEX

DESCRIPTION

The single piston sliding caliper assembly is made up of a sliding caliper housing assembly and spindle. On 2-wheel drive models, the supporting member and steering arm are cast as one piece and are combined with a wheel spindle stem to form an integral spindle assembly. On 4-wheel drive models, an integral caliper support and steering knuckle assembly contains a bolted-on spindle and dust shield.

The ends of the inner shoe and lining assembly are within the spindle assembly. An anti-rattle clip is positioned between the shoe and spindle assembly at the bottom of the caliper. The outer shoe flange bearing rests against the shoe locating and torque surfaces on the caliper housing.

The caliper is positioned either on the spindle or knuckle assembly against machined surfaces at the top end. The caliper and spindle assembly is retained by a caliper support key and spring, while a key retaining screw prevents the key from sliding out of the spindle assembly.

A square section seal fitted into a groove in the caliper cylinder bore, and a rubber boot seal the piston and caliper bore.

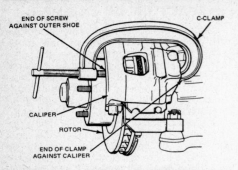

Fig. 1   Bottoming caliper piston in cylinder bore

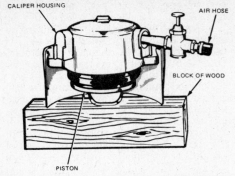

Fig. 2   Removing caliper piston

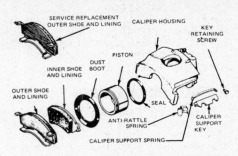

Fig. 3   Exploded view of disc brake caliper assembly

Torque from the inner shoe is transferred directly to the spindle or knuckle assembly, while torque from the outer shoe is transferred through the caliper to the spindle or knuckle assembly.

CALIPER REMOVAL

1. Remove a portion of brake fluid from master cylinder disc brake reservoir.
2. Raise and support vehicle and remove wheel and tire assembly.
3. Install eight inch C-clamp on caliper, **Fig. 1,** and tighten clamp to bottom piston in cylinder bore, then remove clamp.

NOTE: Do not use screwdriver or other edged tool to pry piston from rotor.

4. Remove key retaining screw, then using hammer and drift, drive out caliper support key and caliper support spring.
5. Remove caliper by pushing it downward against spindle assembly and rotating upper end upward and out of spindle assembly.
6. Disconnect hydraulic line from caliper.

BRAKE SHOE REMOVAL

1. Remove caliper as previously described.

NOTE: If caliper is not being serviced, it is not necessary to disconnect hydraulic line from caliper.

2. Remove outer shoe from caliper, tapping shoe as necessary to loosen shoe flange.
3. Remove inner shoe, then the anti-rattle clip from lower end of shoe.

BRAKE SHOE INSTALLATION

1. Place new anti-rattle clip on lower end of inner shoe, ensuring tabs on clip are properly positioned and that clip is fully seated.
2. Place inner shoe and anti-rattle clip in shoe abutment with anti-rattle clip tab against shoe abutment and looped spring away from rotor, then compress anti-rattle clip and slide upper end of shoe into position.
3. Ensure caliper position is fully bottomed in cylinder bore.

NOTE: Replacement outer shoe differs from original equipment. The replacement shoe has tabs on flange at lower edge of shoe and distance between upper tabs and lower flange is reduced to provide a slip-on interference fit.

4. Position outer shoe on caliper and press shoe tabs into place.
5. Install caliper.

DISASSEMBLING CALIPER

1. Remove plug from caliper inlet port and drain fluid from caliper housing.
2. Position caliper on block of wood, **Fig. 2.**
3. Slowly and carefully apply low pressure air to caliper inlet port until piston pops out.
4. If piston is jammed or cocked and will not pop out, release air pressure and tap sharply on end of piston with soft hammer or plastic or rubber mallet to straighten piston, then apply air pressure again to remove piston.
5. Remove boot from piston and seal from caliper cylinder bore, **Fig. 3.**

ASSEMBLING CALIPER

1. Lubricate piston seal with clean brake fluid and position seal in groove in cylinder bore.
2. Coat outside of piston and both beads of dust boot with clean brake fluid, then insert piston through dust boot until boot is around closed end of piston.
3. Hold piston and dust boot directly above caliper cylinder bore and use fingers to work bead of dust boot into groove near top of cylinder bore.
4. One bead is seated in groove, press straight down on piston until piston bottoms in bore.

NOTE: Ensure piston is not cocked in bore.

CALIPER INSTALLATION

1. Position caliper on spindle assembly by pivoting caliper around support upper mounting surface, being careful not to tear or cut boot as boot slips over inner shoe.
2. Using brake adjusting tool or screwdriver, hold upper machined surface of caliper against surface of support assembly and install new caliper support spring and new caliper support key.
3. Using suitable mallet, drive key and spring assembly into position, then install key retaining screw and torque to 14–20 ft. lbs.
4. Connect hydraulic line to caliper.
5. Install wheel and tire assembly and lower vehicle to ground, then fill master cylinder as necessary with suitable brake fluid.
6. Firmly depress brake pedal several times to seat linings on rotor.
7. Bleed brakes.

Ford Single Piston Sliding Caliper, 1983–85 Ranger & 1984–85 Bronco II

INDEX

DESCRIPTION

The caliper assembly consists of a pin slider caliper housing, inner and outer shoe and lining assemblies and a single piston. The assembly slides on two pins which also secure the caliper to the spindle.

The caliper housing contains a piston which has a molded rubber boot on its outer end which is pressed into a cylinder bore groove to prevent cylinder contamination. Also installed in the housing is a rubber piston seal located in the cylinder bore to provide sealing between cylinder and piston.

The outer shoe and lining assemblies are secured to the caliper by spring clips riveted to the shoe surfaces and two rectangular torque buttons on each shoe. The inner shoe and lining assemblies use a replaceable finger anti-rattle clip.

FRONT CALIPER & LINING REMOVAL

1. Remove and discard portion of brake fluid from larger master cylinder reservoir to avoid fluid overflow when caliper piston is depressed.
2. Raise and support vehicle, then remove front wheel and tire assemblies.
3. Working on either side of vehicle, place an eight-inch C-clamp or equivalent on caliper and tighten clamp to bottom caliper piston in cylinder bore, then remove clamp.

NOTE: Do not use screwdriver or similar tool to pry piston away from rotor.

4. On 1983–84 models, three types of caliper pins are used: a single tang type, a double tang type, and a split-shell type. The pin removal process depends on bolt head direction of installed pin.

NOTE: Always remove upper caliper pin first.

5. On 1983–84 models, if bolt head is on outside of caliper, proceed as follows:
   a. Tap caliper pin bolt on inner side of caliper until there is a gap between outer bolt head and caliper pin.
   b. Using suitable cutter, remove bolt head from bolt.
   c. Using screwdriver, depress tab on bolt head end of upper caliper pin, then tap on pin with hammer until tab is depressed by V-slot.
   d. Using ½ inch or smaller punch placed against end of caliper pin, drive pin out of caliper toward inside of vehicle.

NOTE: Do not use screwdriver or other edged tool to drive out pin.

6. On 1983–84 models, if nut end of bolt is on outside of caliper, proceed as follows:
   a. Remove nut from bolt.
   b. Using screwdriver, depress lead tang on end of upper caliper pin, then tap pin with hammer until lead tang is depressed by V-slot.
   c. Using ½ inch or smaller punch placed against end of caliper pin, drive pin out of caliper toward inside of vehicle.

NOTE: Do not use screwdriver or other edged tool to drive out pin.

7. On all 1985 models, proceed as follows:
   a. Clean all excess dirt from area around pin tabs.
   b. Tap upper caliper pin towards inboard side until pin tabs just touch spindle face.
   c. Insert a screwdriver into slot provided behind pin tabs on inboard side of pin.
   d. Compress outboard end of pin with needle nose pliers, while simultaneously prying with screwdriver until tabs slip into spindle groove.
   e. Position one end of a ⁷⁄₁₆ inch

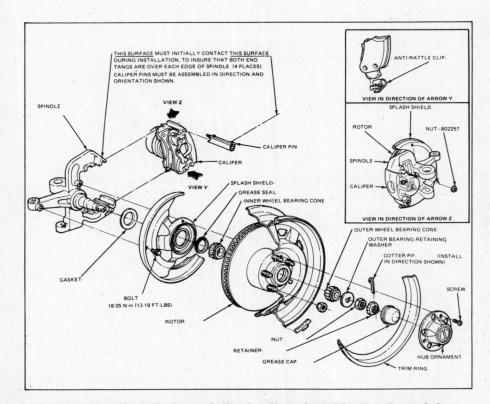

Fig. 1 Exploded view of disc brake assembly. 4 × 2 models

punch against end of caliper pin and drive caliper pin out of caliper slide groove.

8. On all models, remove lower caliper pin using procedure in step 5, 6 or 7, as applicable.
9. Remove caliper from rotor, then the brake hose from caliper, **Figs. 1 and 2.**
10. Remove outer lining, then the anti-rattle clips and inner lining.

FRONT CALIPER & LINING INSTALLATION

1. Place new anti-rattle clip on lower end of inner shoe, being sure tabs on clip are properly positioned and clip is fully seated.
2. Place inner shoe and anti-rattle clip in shoe abutment with anti-rattle clip tab against shoe abutment and loop type spring away from rotor. Compress anti-rattle clip and slide upper end of shoe into position.
3. Install outer shoe, being sure torque buttons on shoe spring clip are firmly seated in matching holes in caliper.
4. On 1983–84 models, clean mounting surfaces of caliper and, using suitable lubricant, lubricate caliper grooves, then install new caliper pins. Pin must be installed with lead tang in first, bolt head facing outward. Place lead tang in V-slot mounting surface and drive into caliper until drive tang is flush with caliper assembly, then install nut and torque to 32–47 ft. lbs.
5. On 1985 models, clean caliper mounting surfaces, then apply suitable lubricant to caliper grooves and install caliper on spindle. Position pin with pin retention tabs adjacent to spindle groove. Tap pin on outboard end with a hammer until tabs contact spindle face. Repeat procedure for lower pin.

NOTE: Do not install bolt and nut with new pins.

6. On all models, install brake hose on caliper.
7. Repeat steps 3–10 of removal procedure and steps 1–6 of installation procedure on opposite side of vehicle.
8. Bleed brakes, then install wheel and tire assemblies and torque nuts to 85–115 ft. lbs.
9. Lower vehicle, check brake fluid level and replenish as necessary, then check brakes for proper operation.

FRONT CALIPER OVERHAUL

1. Remove caliper assembly as described in caliper and lining removal.
2. Placing cloth over piston to prevent damage to piston, apply air pressure to fluid port in caliper with suitable tool to remove piston. If piston is seized

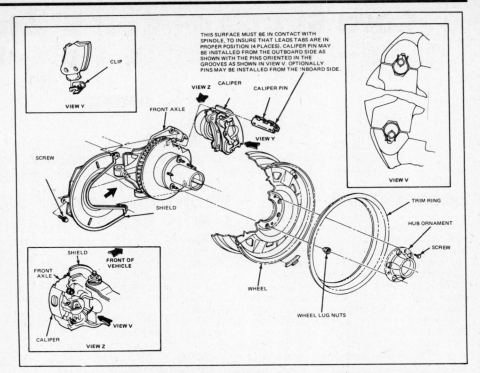

Fig. 2   Exploded view of disc brake assembly. 4 × 4 models

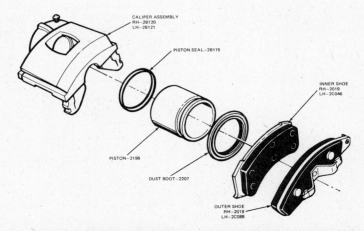

Fig. 3   Exploded view of disc brake caliper assembly

and cannot be forced from caliper, tap lightly around piston while applying air pressure.

CAUTION: Piston may develop considerable force from pressure build-up.

3. Remove dust boot from caliper assembly, then remove and discard rubber piston seal of cylinder, **Fig. 3.**
4. Using suitable solvent, clean all metal parts, then clean out and dry grooves and passageways with compressed air.
5. Check cylinder bore and piston for damage or excessive wear and re-

place piston if it is pitted, scored, or corroded, or the plating is worn away.
6. Apply film of clean brake fluid on new caliper piston seal and install it in cylinder bore, being sure seal does not become twisted but is firmly seated in groove.
7. Install new dust boot by setting flange squarely in outer groove of caliper bore.
8. Coat piston with brake fluid and install in cylinder bore, spreading dust boot over piston as it is installed, seating dust boot in piston groove.
9. Install caliper as described in front caliper and lining installation.

Ford (Dayton) Dual Piston Sliding Caliper

INDEX

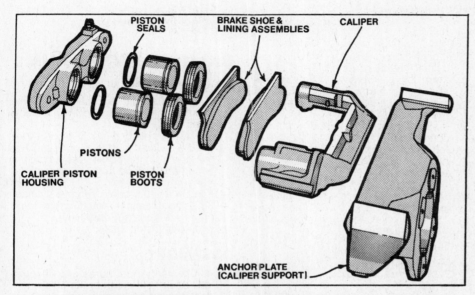

Fig. 1   Exploded view of disc brake caliper assembly. 1979–80

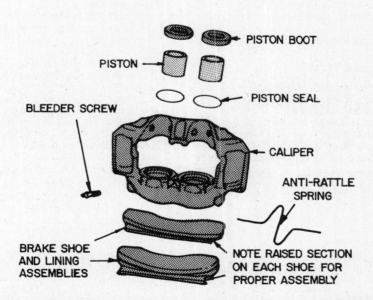

Fig. 2   Exploded view of disc brake caliper assembly. 1981–85

DESCRIPTION

1979–80

This disc brake, **Fig. 1,** is of the sliding caliper design with two pistons on one side of the rotor. The caliper which slides on the anchor plate is retained by a key and spring. A key retaining screw maintains the key and spring in proper position. Two brake shoes and lining assemblies, one on each side of the rotor, are used and are not identical. The brake shoes slide on the caliper bridge and one anti-rattle clip is used on both shoes. The cylinder housing contains the two pistons. The pistons and caliper bores are protected by boot seals fitted to a piston groove and attached to the cylinder housing. The cylinder assembly is attached to the caliper with cap screws and washers. The anchor plate and shield are bolted to the spindle.

1981–85

This disc brake, **Fig. 2,** is of the sliding caliper design with two pistons on one side of the rotor. The caliper, which slides on the support assembly, is retained by a key and spring. A key retaining screw holds the key and spring in position. Each caliper contains one brake shoe and lining assembly on each side of the rotor. The shoes, which slide on the caliper bridge, are not identical. One anti-rattle clip is used on both shoes. The caliper contains two pistons. The pistons and cylinder bores are protected by boot seals fitted to a groove in the piston and a groove in the cylinder housing.

BRAKE SHOE & LINING
REPLACE

REMOVAL

1. To avoid fluid overflow when pistons are pushed into caliper, remove some brake fluid from master cylinder.
2. Raise vehicle and remove wheel assembly.
3. Remove key retaining screw then, using a brass drift and hammer, drive out the key and spring.
4. Remove caliper and its support by

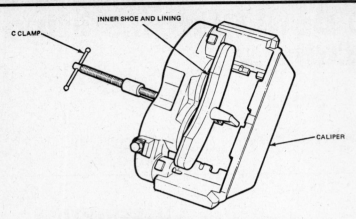

Fig. 3   Bottoming caliper pistons

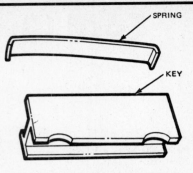

Fig. 4   Caliper spring & key

rotating the key and spring end out and away from the rotor. Slide opposite end of caliper clear of the slide in the support and off the rotor. Place caliper on tie rod or axle.

NOTE: Do not allow the brake hose to support weight of caliper, as this can damage the hose.

5. Remove caliper brake shoe anti-rattle spring and inner and outer shoe and lining assemblies.
6. Clean and inspect caliper assembly. Thoroughly clean areas of caliper and support that contact during the sliding action of the caliper.

INSTALLATION

1. Place used inner lining and shoe assembly over the pistons, then place a C-clamp on the caliper housing midway between the two pistons over the lining and shoe assembly, **Fig. 3.** Tighten the clamp until pistons are bottomed in caliper, then remove C-clamp and lining and shoe assembly.
2. Install the new inner and outer shoe and lining assemblies, and the anti-rattle spring.
3. Position caliper rail into the slide on the support and rotate the caliper onto rotor.
4. Position the key and spring, **Fig. 4,** then install the sub-assembly between the caliper and support. Note that the spring is between the key and caliper and that spring tangs overlap the ends of the key.

5. If necessary use a screwdriver to hold caliper against support assembly, then using a hammer, drive the key and spring into position aligning the correct notch with the existing hole in the support.
6. Install the key to support retaining screw and torque to 12–20 ft. lbs.
7. Install wheel assembly and lower vehicle. Check brake fluid level and add as necessary with heavy duty brake fluid.
8. Depress brake pedal several times to seat linings on rotor. Do not move vehicle until a firm brake pedal has been obtained.

CALIPER
REPLACE

REMOVAL

1. Perform steps 1 to 5 outlined under "Brake Shoe & Lining, Replace" removal procedure.
2. Disconnect flexible hose from caliper.
3. Remove caliper assembly.

INSTALLATION

1. Perform steps 1 and 2 outlined under "Brake Shoe & Lining, Replace" installation procedure.
2. Connect flexible hose to caliper.
3. Perform steps 3 to 6 outlined under "Brake Shoe & Lining, Replace" installation procedure, then after bleeding brakes, proceed with the remainder of the procedure.

CALIPER OVERHAUL
DISASSEMBLY

1. Drain brake fluid from caliper.
2. Remove brake shoe and lining assemblies.
3. To remove pistons, apply air pressure to the caliper fluid port to ease the pistons from the bores. Use a block of wood and a shop towel to protect pistons from damage.
4. On 1979–80 models, remove cylinder housing to caliper attaching bolts and separate housing from caliper.
5. Remove piston seals.

ASSEMBLY

1. Lubricate cylinder bores and new piston seals with clean brake fluid.
2. Install piston seals in cylinder bore grooves.
3. Lubricate dust boot retaining lips with clean brake fluid and install retaining lips in the boot retaining grooves in the cylinder bores.
4. Lubricate piston with clean brake fluid and insert pistons into dust boots. Start pistons into cylinders until located beyond the piston seals.
5. Place a block of wood over one piston and press piston into cylinder using caution not to damage the piston seals or piston. Press the second piston into the bore.
6. On 1979–80 models, place piston housing on caliper and install and torque mounting bolts to 155–185 ft. lbs.

DRUM BRAKES

TABLE OF CONTENTS

General Information

INDEX

SERVICE PRECAUTIONS

When working on or around brake assemblies, care must be taken to prevent breathing asbestos dust, as many manufacturers incorporate asbestos fibers in the production of brake linings. During routine service operations, the amount of asbestos dust from brake lining wear is at a low level due to a chemical breakdown during use, and a few precautions will minimize exposure.

CAUTION: Do not sand or grind brake linings unless suitable local exhaust ventilation equipment is used to prevent excessive asbestos exposure.

1. Wear a suitable respirator approved for asbestos dust use during all repair procedures.
2. When cleaning brake dust from brake parts, use a vacuum cleaner with a highly efficient filter system. If a suitable vacuum cleaner is not available, use a water soaked rag.

NOTE: Do not use compressed air or dry brush to clean brake parts.

3. Keep work area clean, using same equipment as for cleaning brake parts.
4. Properly dispose of rags and vacuum cleaner bags by placing them in plastic bags.
5. Do not smoke or eat while working on brake systems.

GENERAL INSPECTION

BRAKE DRUMS

Any time the brake drums are removed for brake service, the braking surface diameter should be checked with a suitable brake drum micrometer at several points to determine if they are within the safe oversize limit stamped on the brake drum outer surface. If the braking surface diameter exceeds specifications, the drum must be replaced. If the braking surface diameter is within specifications, drums should be cleaned and inspected for cracks, scores, deep grooves, taper, out of round and heat spotting. If drums are cracked or heat spotted, they must be replaced. Minor scores should be removed with sandpaper. Grooves and large scores can only be removed by machining with special equipment, as long as the braking surface is within specifications stamped on brake drum outer surface. Any brake drum sufficiently out of round to cause vehicle vibration or noise while braking, or showing taper should also be machined, removing only enough stock to true up the brake drum.

After a brake drum is machined, wipe the braking surface diameter with a cloth soaked in denatured alcohol. If one brake drum is machined, the other should also be machined to the same diameter to maintain equal braking forces.

BRAKE LININGS & SPRINGS

Inspect brake linings for excessive wear, damage, oil, grease or brake fluid contamination. If any of the above conditions exists, brake linings should be replaced. Do not attempt to replace only one set of brake shoes; they should be replaced as an axle set only to maintain equal braking forces. Examine brake shoe webbing, hold down and return springs for signs of over-heating indicated by a slight blue color. If any component exhibits signs of overheating, replace hold down and return springs with new ones. Overheated springs lose their pull and could cause brake linings to wear out prematurely. Inspect all springs for sags, bends and external damage, and replace as necessary.

Inspect hold down retainers and pins for bends, rust and corrosion. If any of the above conditions exist, replace retainers and pins.

BACKING PLATE

Inspect backing plate shoe contact surface for grooves that may restrict shoe movement and cannot be removed by lightly sanding with emery cloth or other suitable abrasive. If backing plate exhibits above condition, it should be replaced. Also inspect for signs of cracks, warpage and excessive rust, indicating need for replacement.

ADJUSTER MECHANISM

Inspect all components for rust, corrosion, bends and fatigue. Replace as necessary. On adjuster mechanism equipped with adjuster cable, inspect cable for kinks, fraying or elongation of eyelet and replace as necessary.

PARKING BRAKE CABLE

Inspect parking brake cable end for kinks, fraying and elongation, and replace as necessary. Use a small hose clamp to compress clamp where it enters backing plate to remove.

Exc. E-250, 350 & F-250, 350

INDEX

REMOVAL

1. Raise and support vehicle.
2. Remove hub cap, then the wheel and tire as an assembly.
3. On vehicles with full-floating axles, remove brake drum as follows:
   a. Loosen rear brake shoe adjustment screw.
   b. Remove rear axle retaining bolts and lock washers, axle shaft, and gasket.
   c. Remove wheel bearing lock nut, lock washer, and adjusting nut.
   d. Remove hub and drum from axle.
   e. Remove brake drum to hub retaining screws, bolts, or bolts and nuts, then remove brake drum from hub.
4. On vehicles with semi-floating axles, remove brake drum as follows:
   a. Remove brake drum retaining nuts.
   b. Remove brake drum. If brake lining is dragging on brake drum, back off brake adjustment by rotating adjustment screw.
5. Install suitable clamp over ends of wheel cylinder.
6. Contract brake shoes as follows:
   a. Disengage adjusting lever from adjusting screw by pulling backward on adjusting lever, **Fig. 1.**
   b. Move outboard side of adjusting screw upward and back off pivot nut as far as it will go.
7. Pull adjusting lever, cable, and automatic adjuster spring down and toward rear to unhook pivot hook from large hole in secondary shoe web.

NOTE: Do not pry pivot hook out of hole.

8. Remove automatic adjuster spring and adjusting lever.
9. Using suitable tool, remove secondary shoe to anchor spring, then the primary shoe to anchor spring.
10. Unhook cable anchor and remove anchor pin plate, if equipped.
11. Remove cable guide from secondary shoe.
12. Remove shoe hold down springs, shoes, adjusting screw, pivot nut, and socket.

NOTE: Note color and position of each hold down spring for proper assembly.

13. On rear brakes, remove parking brake link and spring, then disconnect parking brake cable from parking brake lever.
14. Remove rear brake secondary shoe and disassemble parking brake lever from shoe by removing retaining clip and spring washer.

INSTALLATION

1. Assemble parking brake lever on secondary shoe and secure with spring washer and retaining clip.
2. Apply light coating of suitable lubricant at points where brake shoes contact backing plate.
3. Position brake shoes on backing plate, then install hold down spring pins, springs, and cups.
4. On rear brakes, install parking brake link, spring, and washer, then connect parking brake cable to parking brake lever.
5. Install anchor pin plate, if equipped, then place cable anchor over anchor pin with crimped side facing backing plate.
6. Install primary shoe to anchor spring.
7. Install cable guide on secondary shoe web with flanged holes fitted into hole in secondary shoe web, then thread cable around cable guide groove.

NOTE: Ensure that cable is positioned in groove and not between guide and shoe web.

8. Install secondary shoe to anchor spring.

NOTE: Ensure that all parts lay flat on anchor pin.

9. Remove clamp from wheel cylinder.
10. Apply suitable lubricant to threads and socket end of adjusting screw, turn adjusting screw into adjusting pivot nut to end of threads and back off ½ turn, then place adjusting socket on screw and install assembly between shoe ends with adjusting screw closer to secondary shoe.

NOTE: Socket end of each adjusting screw is stamped "R" or "L" to indicate use on right or left side of vehicle. Adjusting pivot nuts can be identified by number of lines machined around body of nut. Two lines indicate right-hand nut and one line indicates left-hand nut.

11. Hook cable hook into hole in adjusting lever from outboard plate side.

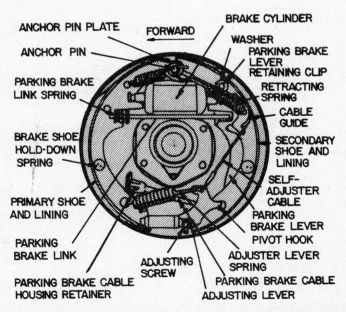

Fig. 1 Drum brake assembly. Exc. E-250, 350 & F-250, 350

NOTE: Adjusting levers are stamped "R" or "L" to indicate use on right- or left-hand brake assembly.

12. Place hooked end of adjuster spring in large hole in primary shoe web and connect looped end of spring to adjuster lever hole.
13. Pull adjuster lever, cable, and automatic adjuster spring down toward rear to engage pivot hook in large hole in secondary shoe web, then ensure that adjusting mechanism works properly.
14. On vehicles with full-floating axles, install brake drums as follows:

a. Place brake drum on hub and install attaching screws, bolts, or bolts and nuts.
b. Place hub and drum as an assembly on axle and start adjusting nut.
c. Adjust wheel bearing nut and install wheel bearing lock washer and lock nut. Refer to individual truck chapter for procedure.
d. Install new gasket and the bolts and lock washers.
e. Install wheel and tire assembly.
f. Adjust brakes. Refer to individual truck chapter for correct adjustment procedure.
15. On vehicles with semi-floating axles,

install brake drums as follows:
a. Adjust brakes. Refer to individual truck chapter for correct adjustment procedure.
b. Install drum.
c. Install brake drum retaining nuts and tighten securely.
d. Install wheel on axle shaft flange studs against drum, and tighten retaining nuts.
16. If any hydraulic connections have been opened, bleed brake system.
17. Check master cylinder fluid lever, filling as necessary.
18. Check brake pedal for proper feel and return.
19. Lower vehicle and road test.

E-250, 350 & F-250, 350

INDEX

REMOVAL

1. Raise and support vehicle.
2. Remove hub cap, then the wheel and tire assembly.
3. On vehicles with full-floating axles, remove brake drums as follows:
a. Loosen rear brake shoe adjustment screw.
b. Remove rear axle retaining bolts and lock washers, axle shaft, and gasket.
c. Remove wheel bearing lock nut, lock washer, and adjusting nut.
d. Remove hub and drum from axle.
e. Remove brake drum-to-hub retaining screws, bolts, or bolts and nuts, then remove brake drum from

hub.
4. On vehicles with semi-floating axles, remove brake drums as follows:
a. Remove brake drum retaining nuts.
b. Remove brake drum. If brake lining is dragging on brake drum, back off brake adjustment by rotating adjusting screw.
5. Remove parking brake lever assembly retaining nut from behind backing plate and remove parking brake lever assembly.
6. Remove adjusting cable assembly from anchor pin, cable guide, and adjusting lever, **Fig. 1.**
7. Remove brake shoe retracting springs.

8. Remove brake shoe hold down springs.
9. Remove brake shoes and adjusting screw assembly.
10. Disassemble adjusting screw assembly.

INSTALLATION

1. Clean ledge pads on backing plate, sanding lightly to bare metal.
2. Apply suitable lubricant to retracting and hold down spring contacts on brake shoes and backing plate.
3. Apply suitable lubricant to threads and socket end of adjusting screw.
4. Install upper retracting spring on primary and secondary shoes and position shoe assembly on backing plate with wheel cylinder push rods in shoe slots.
5. Install brake shoe hold down springs.
6. Install brake shoe adjustment screw assembly with the slot in the head of adjustment screw facing primary shoe, lower retracting spring, adjusting lever spring, and adjusting lever assembly, and connect adjusting cable to adjusting lever.

NOTE: Socket end of each adjusting screw is stamped "R" or "L" to indicate use on right or left side of vehicle. Adjusting pivot nuts can be identified by number of lines machined around body of nut. Two lines indicate right-hand nut and one line indicates left-hand nut.

7. Position cable in cable guide and install cable anchor fitting on the anchor pin.
8. Install parking brake assembly in anchor pin and secure with retaining nut behind backing plate.

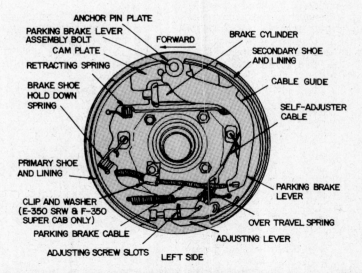

ANCHOR PIN PLATE
PARKING BRAKE LEVER ASSEMBLY BOLT
CAM PLATE
RETRACTING SPRING
BRAKE SHOE HOLD DOWN SPRING
PRIMARY SHOE AND LINING
CLIP AND WASHER (E-350 SRW & F-350 SUPER CAB ONLY)
PARKING BRAKE CABLE
ADJUSTING SCREW SLOTS
LEFT SIDE
FORWARD
BRAKE CYLINDER
SECONDARY SHOE AND LINING
CABLE GUIDE
SELF-ADJUSTER CABLE
PARKING BRAKE LEVER
OVER TRAVEL SPRING
ADJUSTING LEVER

Fig. 1   Drum brake assembly. Exc. E-250, 350 & F-250, 350

9. On vehicles with full-floating axles, install brake drums as follows:
   a. Place brake drum on hub and install attaching screws, bolts, or bolts and nuts.
   b. Place hub and drum as an assembly on axle and start adjusting nut.
   c. Adjust wheel bearing nut and install wheel bearing lock washer and lock nut. Refer to individual truck chapter for procedure.

   d. Install new gasket and the bolts and lock washers.
   e. Install wheel and tire assembly.
   f. Adjust brakes. Refer to individual truck chapter for correct adjustment procedure.
10. On vehicles with semi-floating axles, install brake drums as follows:
    a. Adjust brakes. Refer to individual truck chapter for correct adjustment procedure.
    b. Install drum.

   c. Install brake drum retaining nuts and tighten securely.
   d. Install wheel on axle shaft flange studs against drum, and tighten retaining nuts.
11. If any hydraulic connections have been opened, bleed brake system.
12. Check master cylinder fluid level, filling as necessary.
13. Check brake pedal for proper feel and return.
14. Lower vehicle and road test.

UNIVERSAL JOINTS

INDEX

SERVICE NOTES

Before disassembling any universal joint, examine the assembly carefully and note the position of the grease fitting (if used). Also, be sure to mark the yokes with relation to the propeller shaft so they may be reassembled in the same relative position. Failure to observe these precautions may produce rough vehicle operation which results in rapid wear and failure of parts, and place an unbalanced load on transmission, engine and rear axle.

When universal joints are disassembled for lubrication or inspection, and the old parts are to be reinstalled, special care must be exercised to avoid damage to universal joint spider or cross and bearing cups.

NOTE: Some driveshafts use an injected nylon retainer on the universal joint bearings. When service is necessary, pressing the bearings out will sheer the nylon retainer, **Fig. 1.** Replacement with the conventional steel snap ring type is then necessary, **Fig. 2.**

CROSS & ROLLER TYPE

Figs. 3 and 4 illustrate typical examples of universal joints of this type. They all operate on the same principle and similar service and replacement procedures may be applied to all.

SERVICING WITHOUT UNIVERSAL JOINT REPLACEMENT TOOL

Disassembly

1. Remove snap rings (or retainer plates) that retain bearings in yoke and drive shaft.
2. Place U-joint in a vise.
3. Select a wrench socket with an outside diameter slightly smaller than the U-joint bearings. Select another wrench socket with an inside diameter slightly larger than the U-joint bearings.
4. Place the sockets at opposite bearings in the yoke so that the smaller socket becomes a bearing pusher and the larger socket becomes a bearing receiver when the vise jaws come together, **Fig. 5.** Close vise jaws until both bearings are free of yoke and remove bearings from the cross or spider.
5. If bearings will not come all the way out, close vise until bearing in receiver socket protrudes from yoke as much as possible without using excessive force. Then remove from vise and place that portion of bearing which protrudes from yoke between vise jaws. Tighten vise to hold bearing and drive yoke off with a soft hammer.
6. To remove opposite bearing from yoke, replace in vise with pusher socket on exposed cross journal with receiver socket over bearing cup. Then tighten vise jaws to press bearing back through yoke into receiving socket.
7. Remove yoke from drive shaft and again place protruding portion of bearing between vise jaws. Then tighten vise to hold bearing while driving yoke off bearing with soft hammer.

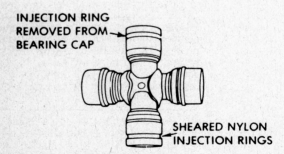

Fig. 1 Production type universal joints which use nylon injection rings in place of snap rings

INJECTION RING REMOVED FROM BEARING CAP

SHEARED NYLON INJECTION RINGS

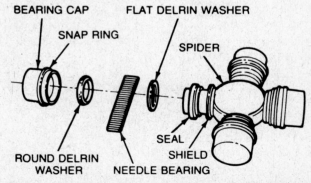

Fig. 2 Service type universal joint (internal snap ring type)

BEARING CAP

SNAP RING

FLAT DELRIN WASHER

SPIDER

ROUND DELRIN WASHER

NEEDLE BEARING

SEAL

SHIELD

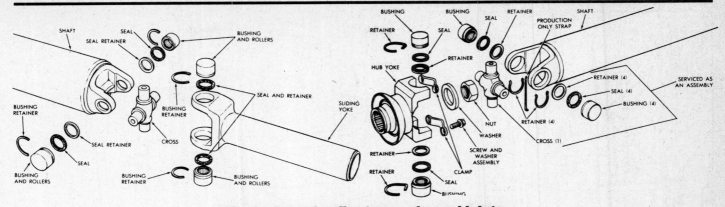

Fig. 3   Cross & roller type universal joints

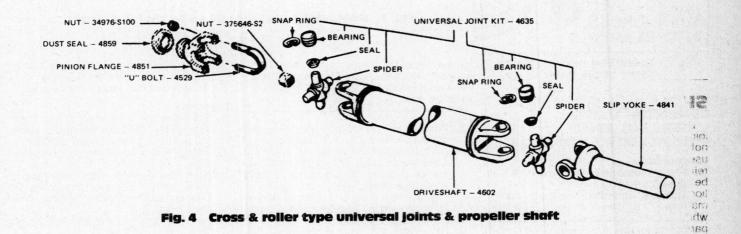

Fig. 4   Cross & roller type universal joints & propeller shaft

Fig. 5   Removing bearings from yoke using a small socket as a driver & large socket as a receiver

8. Turn spider or cross ¼ turn and use the same procedure to press bearings out of drive shaft.

Assembly

1. If old parts are to be reassembled, pack bearing cups with universal joint grease. Do not fill cups completely or use excessive amounts as over-lubrication may damage seals during reassembly. Use new seals.
2. If new parts are being installed, check new bearings for adequate grease before assembling.
3. With the pusher (smaller) socket, press one bearing part way into drive shaft. Position spider into the partially installed bearing. Place second bearing into drive shaft. Fasten drive shaft in vise so that bearings are in contact with faces of vise jaws, **Fig. 6**. Some spiders are provided with locating lugs which must face toward drive shaft when installed.
4. Press bearings all the way into position and install snap rings or retainer plates.
5. Install bearings in yoke in same manner. When installation is completed, check U-joint for binding or roughness. If free movement is impeded, correct the condition before installation in vehicle.

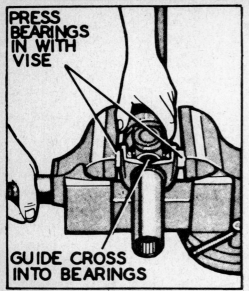

PRESS BEARINGS IN WITH VISE

GUIDE CROSS INTO BEARINGS

Fig. 6   Installing bearings into drive shaft yoke

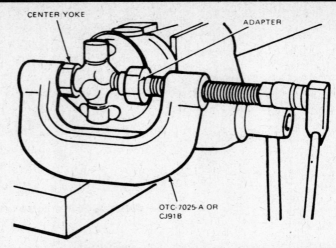

CENTER YOKE   ADAPTER

OTC-7025-A OR CJ91B

Fig. 7   Removing bearing caps using tool & adapter

SERVICING USING UNIVERSAL JOINT REPLACEMENT TOOL

Disassembly

1. Place driveshaft in a vise using care to avoid damaging it.
2. Remove bearing retaining snap rings.

NOTE: Some universal joints use injected nylon retainers in place of snap rings. During servicing, the snap rings supplied with the replacement universal joint assembly must be used.

3. Position tool on shaft and press bearing out of yoke, **Fig. 7.** If bearing cannot be pressed all the way out, remove it using vise grips or channel lock pliers or position driveshaft as shown and strike center yoke with hammer, **Fig. 8.** Mark yoke and shaft to make sure they will be reassembled in their same relative positions.
4. Reposition tool so that it presses on the spider in order to press other bearing from opposite side of flange.
5. If used, remove flange from spider.

Assembly

1. Start new bearing into yoke, then position spider into yoke and press bearing until it is ¼ inch below surface.
2. Remove tool and install a new snap ring.
3. Start new bearing in opposite side of yoke, then install tool and press on bearing until opposite bearing contacts snap ring.
4. Remove tool and install remaining snap ring.

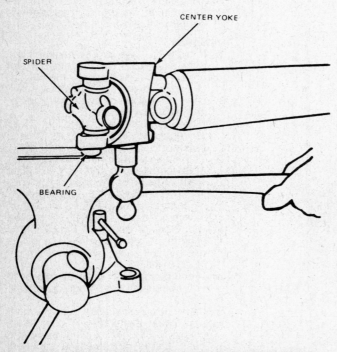

CENTER YOKE

SPIDER

BEARING

Fig. 8   Removing bearing cap by holding cap in vise & striking center yoke with hammer

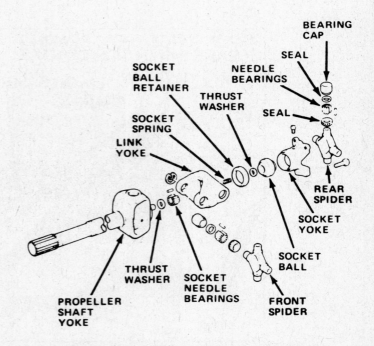

SOCKET BALL RETAINER

SOCKET SPRING

LINK YOKE

THRUST WASHER

BEARING CAP

SEAL

NEEDLE BEARINGS

SEAL

REAR SPIDER

SOCKET YOKE

SOCKET BALL

FRONT SPIDER

PROPELLER SHAFT YOKE

THRUST WASHER

SOCKET NEEDLE BEARINGS

Fig. 9   Double cardan universal joint exploded view

DOUBLE CARDAN TYPE

The double cardan type joint, **Fig. 9,** incorporates two universal joints, a centering socket yoke, and center yoke at one end of the shaft. A single universal joint is used at the other end.

DISASSEMBLY

1. Remove all bearing cap retainers.
2. Mark bearing caps, spiders, propeller shaft yoke, link yoke and socket yoke for assembly alignment reference, **Fig. 9.**
3. Remove bearing caps attaching from spider to propeller shaft yoke as follows:
   a. Use a ⅝ inch socket to drive the bearing cap and a 1¹⁄₁₆ inch socket to receive the opposite bearing cap as it is driven out.
   b. Place ⅝ inch socket on one bearing cap and 1¹⁄₁₆ inch socket on opposite bearing.
   c. Position assembly in vise so vise jaws bear directly against sockets.
   d. Tighten vise to press first bearing cap out of link yoke.
   e. Loosen vise, reposition sockets and press opposite bearing cap out of link yoke.
4. Disengage propeller shaft yoke from link yoke.
5. Remove bearing caps attaching front spider to propeller shaft as described in step 3 above.
6. Remove front spider from yoke.
7. Remove bearing caps attaching rear spider to link yoke as outlined in step 3 above and remove spider and socket yoke from link yoke.
8. Clean all parts in solvent and wipe dry. Inspect assembly for damage or wear. If any component is worn or damaged, the entire assembly must be replaced.

ASSEMBLY

NOTE: When assembling universal joint, make sure to align spiders and yokes according to marks made during disassembly.

1. Lubricate all bearings and contact surfaces with lithium base chassis grease.
2. Install bearing caps on yoke ends of rear spider and secure caps with tape, **Fig. 9.**
3. Assemble socket yoke and rear spider.
4. Position rear spider in link yoke and install bearing caps. Press caps into yoke using ⅝ inch socket until bearing cap retainer grooves are exposed.
5. Install rear spider-to-link yoke bearing cap retainers.
6. Position front spider in propeller shaft yoke and install bearing caps. Press caps into yoke using a ⅝ inch socket until bearing cap retainer grooves are exposed.
7. Install front spider-to-propeller shaft yoke bearing cap retainers.
8. Install thrust washer and socket spring in ball socket bearing bore, if removed.
9. Install thrust washer on ball socket bearing boss (located on propeller shaft yoke), if removed.
10. Align ball socket bearing boss on propeller shaft yoke with ball socket bearing bore and insert boss into bore.
11. Align front spider with link yoke bearing cap bores and install bearing caps. Press caps into yoke using a ⅝ inch socket until bearing cap retainer grooves are exposed.
12. Install front spider-to-link yoke bearing cap retainers.

MANUAL TRANSMISSIONS

NOTE: See individual truck chapters for procedures on removing the transmission and adjusting the gearshift linkage.

TABLE OF CONTENTS

Tremec 3 Speed Manual Transmission

INDEX

DISASSEMBLE

1. Remove transmission cover, **Fig. 1.**
2. Remove extension housing. To prevent mainshaft from following housing (with resultant loss of needle bearings) tap end of mainshaft while withdrawing housing.
3. Remove front bearing retainer.
4. Remove filler plug from right side of case. Then working through plug opening, drive roll pin out of case and countershaft with small punch, **Fig. 2.**
5. Hold counter gear with a hook and, with a dummy shaft, push countershaft out rear of case until counter gear can be lowered to bottom of case, **Fig. 3.**
6. Pull main drive gear forward until gear contacts case, then remove large snap ring.

NOTE: On some models, it is necessary to move gear forward to provide clearance when removing mainshaft assembly. On other models, the drive gear is removed from front of case.

7. Remove snap ring and slide speedometer drive gear off mainshaft. Remove lock ball from shaft.
8. Remove snap ring and remove mainshaft rear bearing from shaft and case, **Fig. 4.**
9. Place both shift levers in neutral (central) position.
10. Remove set screw that retains detent springs and plugs in case. Remove one spring and plug, **Fig. 5.**
11. Remove low-reverse set screw and slide shift rail out through rear of case.
12. Rotate low-reverse shift fork upward and lift it from case.
13. Remove 2-3 set screw and rotate 2-3 shift rail 90 degrees with pliers.
14. Lift interlock plug from case with a magnet rod, **Fig. 5.**
15. Tap inner end of 2-3 shift rail to remove expansion plug from front of case. Remove shift rail.
16. Remove 2-3 detent plug and spring from detent bore.
17. Rotate 2-3 shift fork upward and lift from case.

18. Lift mainshaft assembly out through top of case.
19. On some transmissions, push main drive gear into case until bearing is free of bore, then lift gear and bearing through top of case.
20. Working through front bearing opening, drive reverse idler gear shaft out through rear of case with a drift, **Fig. 6.**
21. Lift reverse idler gear and two thrust washers from case.
22. Lift counter gear and thrust washers from case, **Fig. 7.** Be careful not to allow dummy shaft and needle bearings to fall out of gear.
23. Remove countershaft-to-case retaining pin and any needle bearings that may have fallen into case.
24. Unfasten and lift shift levers off shafts. Slide each lever and shaft out of case. Discard O-ring seal from each shaft, **Fig. 8.**
25. Remove snap ring from front end of mainshaft and remove synchronizers, gears and related parts, **Fig. 9.**
26. If main drive gear is to be disassembled, refer to **Fig. 10.**

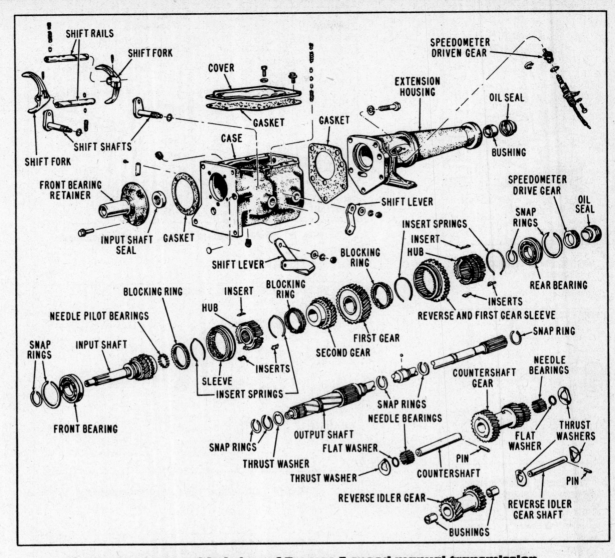

Fig. 1   Disassembled view of Tremec 3 speed manual transmission

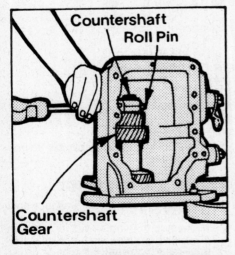

Fig. 2   Removing countershaft roll pin

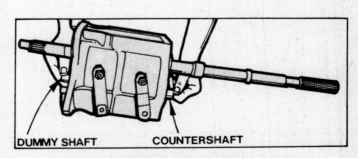

Fig. 3   Removing countershaft

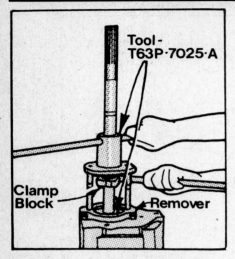

Fig. 4   Removing mainshaft bearing

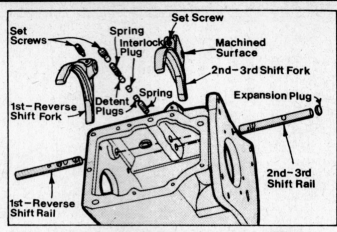

Fig. 5   Shift rods & forks, disassembled

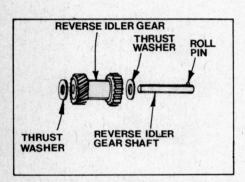

Fig. 6   Reverse idler gear, disassembled

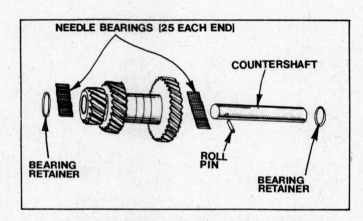

Fig. 7   Countergear, disassembled

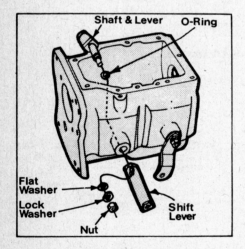

Fig. 8   Shift lever & related components

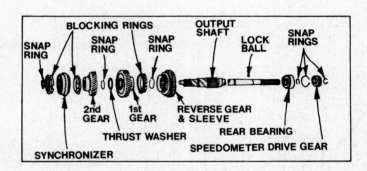

Fig. 9   Mainshaft components

ASSEMBLE

COUNTER GEAR

1. Coat bore at each end of counter gear with grease.
2. Hold appropriate dummy shaft in gear and install 25 needle bearings and a retainer washer in each end of gear, **Fig. 7.**
3. Install counter gear, thrust washers and countershaft in case.
4. Place transmission case in vertical position and check end play with a feeler gauge as shown in **Fig. 11.** If end play exceeds .018", replace thrust washers as required to obtain .004–.018" end play.
5. Once end play has been established, remove countershaft with dummy shaft.
6. Allow counter gear assembly to remain in case.

REVERSE IDLER GEAR

1. Install idler gear, thrust washers and shaft in case.
2. Make sure that thrust washer with flat side is at the web end, and that the spur gear is toward the rear of case, **Fig. 6.**
3. Check reverse idler gear end play in

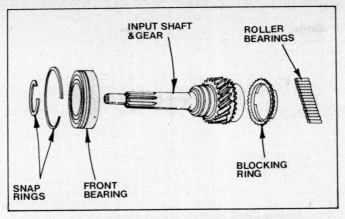

Fig. 10   Main drive gear, disassembled

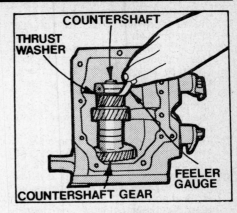

Fig. 11   Checking countergear end-play

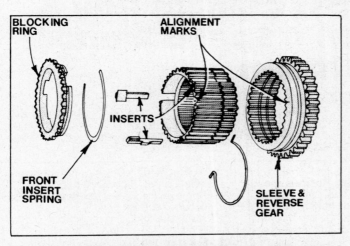

Fig. 12   Low—reverse synchronizer, disassembled

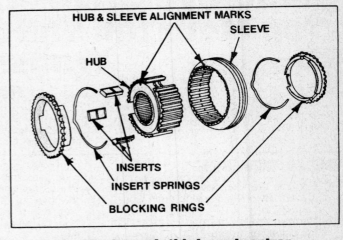

Fig. 13   Second—third synchronizer, disassembled

same manner and to the same clearance as the counter gear. If end play is within limits of .004–.018" leave gear in case.

LOW—REVERSE SYNCHRONIZER

1. Install an insert spring, **Fig. 12**, in groove of low—reverse synchronizer hub. Make sure spring covers all insert grooves.
2. Start hub in sleeve, making sure that alignment marks are properly indexed.
3. Position three inserts in hub, making sure that small end is over spring and that shoulder is on inside of hub.
4. Slide sleeve and reverse gear onto hub until detent is engaged.
5. Install other insert spring in front of hub to hold inserts against hub.

SECOND—THIRD SYNCHRONIZER

1. Install one insert spring, **Fig. 13**, into a groove of synchronizer hub, making sure that all three insert slots are fully covered.

2. With alignment marks on hub and sleeve aligned, start hub into sleeve.
3. Place three inserts on top of retaining spring and push assembly together.
4. Install remaining insert spring so that spring ends cover same slots as do other spring. Do not stagger springs.
5. Place a synchronizer blocking ring in each end of sleeve.

MAIN DRIVE LINE

1. Lubricate mainshaft splines and machined surfaces with transmission lube.
2. Slide low—reverse synchronizer, **Fig. 9**, onto mainshaft with teeth end of gear facing toward rear of shaft. Secure in place with snap ring.
3. Coat tapered machined surface of low gear with grease. Place blocking ring on greased surface.
4. Slide low gear onto mainshaft with blocking ring toward rear of shaft. Rotate gear as necessary to engage the three notches in blocking ring with synchronizer inserts. Secure low gear with thrust washer and snap ring.
5. Coat tapered machined surface of 2nd gear with grease and slide blocking

ring onto it. Slide 2nd gear with blocking ring and 2-3 synchronizer onto mainshaft. Tapered machined surface of 2nd gear must be toward front of shaft. Make sure that notches in blocking ring engage synchronizer inserts. Secure synchronizer with snap ring.
6. Install new O-ring on each of two shift lever shafts, **Fig. 8**. Lubricate shafts with transmission lube and install them in case. Secure each lever on its shaft with a flat washer, lock washer and nut.
7. Coat bore of main drive gear shaft with thick coat of grease. Install 15 needle bearings in gear pocket, **Fig. 10**.
8. Position drive gear assembly into case.
9. Place a detent spring and plug in case, **Fig. 5**. Place 2-3 shift fork in synchronizer groove. Rotate fork into position and install 2-3 shift rail. It will be necessary to depress detent plug to enter rail in bore. Move rail inward until detent plug engages center (neutral) notch. Secure fork to shaft with set screw.
10. Install interlock plug in case. If 2-3 shift rail is in neutral position, top of interlock will be slightly lower than surface

of low–reverse shift rail bore.

11. Place low–reverse shift fork in groove of synchronizer. Rotate fork into position and install low-reverse shift rail. Move rail inward until center (neutral) notch is aligned with detent bore. Secure fork to shaft with set screw.
12. Install remaining detent plug and spring. Secure spring with slotted head set screw. Turn set screw in until head is flush with case.
13. Install new expansion plug in case.
14. Install drive gear through front of case with bearing in place on shaft.
15. Position new front bearing retainer gasket on case. Place bearing retainer on case, making sure oil return groove is at the bottom. Install and tighten attaching screws to 30–36 ft-lbs.

16. Install large snap ring on mainshaft rear bearing. Place bearing on mainshaft with snap ring end toward rear of shaft. Press bearing into place and secure with snap ring.
17. Hold speedometer drive gear lock ball in detent and slide gear into place. Secure gear with snap ring.

FINAL ASSEMBLY

1. Place transmission in vertical position. Working through drain hole in bottom of case, align bore of counter gear and thrust washers with bore of case, using a screwdriver.
2. Working through rear of case, push dummy shaft out with countershaft. Before countershaft is completely in-

serted, make sure the hole that accommodates roll pin is aligned with hole in case.
3. Working through lubricant filler hole, install roll pin, **Fig. 2,** in case and countershaft.
4. Install filler and drain plugs, making sure magnetic plug is installed in bottom of case.
5. Install extension housing with new gasket and torque attaching cap screws to 42–50 ft-lbs.
6. Place transmission in gear, pour lubricant over entire gear train while rotating input and output shafts.
7. Install cover with new gasket and torque attaching screws to 20–25 ft-lbs. Coat gasket and cover screws with sealer.

Ford Overdrive (Except Single Rail & Top Mounted Shifter) 4 Speed Manual Transmission

INDEX

DISASSEMBLE

1. Remove the lower extension housing to case attaching screw to drain lubricant.
2. Remove cover attaching screws and the cover from case.
3. Remove the long spring retaining detent plug in case, then, using a magnet, remove detent plug.
4. Remove extension housing to case screws and the extension housing.
5. Remove input shaft bearing retainer attaching screws and slide retainer from input shaft.
6. Support countershaft gear with a wire hook. Working from front of case, push countershaft out rear of case with a dummy shaft. Lower countershaft gear to bottom of case and remove the wire hook.
7. Remove set screw from first and second speed shift fork, then slide first and second speed shift rail out rear of case, **Fig. 1.**
8. With a magnet, remove interlock detent from between the first and second and the third and overdrive shift rails.
9. Shift transmission into overdrive position. Remove set screw from the third and overdrive shift fork. Remove the side detent bolt, detent plug and spring. Rotate the third and overdrive speed shift rail 90 degrees and tap rail out front of case with a suitable punch and hammer.
10. With a magnet, remove interlock plug from top of case.
11. Remove snap ring securing speedom-

eter drive gear to output shaft, then slide gear from shaft. Remove speedometer gear drive ball.
12. Remove output shaft bearing retaining snap ring and the snap ring from outside diameter of output shaft bearing.
13. Remove output shaft bearing.
14. Remove input shaft bearing retaining snap ring and the snap ring from outside diameter of input shaft bearing.
15. Remove input shaft bearing from shaft and case, then the input shaft and blocking from front of case.
16. Position output shaft to right side of case and remove shift forks, **Fig. 2.**
17. Lift output shaft assembly from case, **Fig. 3,** support the thrust washer and first speed gear to prevent the washer and gear from sliding from shaft.
18. Remove reverse shift gear fork set screw, rotate reverse shift rail 90 degrees, **Fig. 4,** slide shift rail out rear of case and lift the reverse shift fork from case.
19. With a magnet, remove reverse detent plug and spring with a magnet.
20. Remove reverse idler gear shaft with a dummy shaft and lower reverse idler gear to bottom of case, **Fig. 5.**
21. Lift countershaft gear and thrust washers from bottom of case, using caution not to drop bearings or the dummy shaft from countershaft gear.
22. Lift reverse idler gear shaft from case, using caution not to drop bearings or the dummy shaft from reverse idler gear.
23. Remove snap ring from front of output shaft and slide the third and overdrive

synchronizer, blocking and gear from output shaft, **Fig. 6.**
24. Remove the next snap ring and the second speed gear thrust washer, gear and blocking ring from output shaft.
25. Remove the next snap ring and the first speed gear thrust washer, gear and blocking ring from rear of output shaft.

SUB-ASSEMBLY SERVICE

CAM & SHAFT SEALS

NOTE: To facilitate reassembly, note position of cams and shafts assemblies and levers before removal from transmission case.

1. Remove three shift levers, **Fig. 7.**
2. Remove three cams and shafts from inside of case.
3. Remove O-ring from each cam and shaft.
4. Dip new O-rings into gear lubricant and install them on cam and shafts.
5. Slide each cam and shaft into its respective bore in case.
6. Secure each shift lever.

SYNCHRONIZERS

1. Place alignment marks between hub and sleeve. Push synchronizer hub from sleeve, **Fig. 8.**
2. Separate inserts and springs from hubs. Do not mix parts from one synchronizer to another.

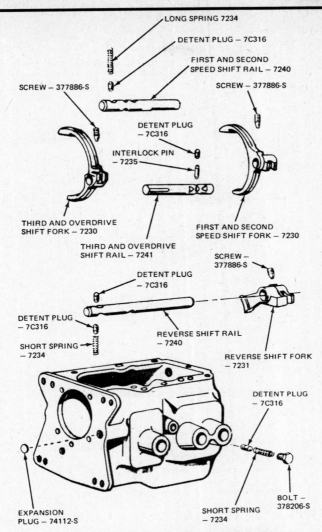

LONG SPRING 7234

DETENT PLUG – 7C316

FIRST AND SECOND SPEED SHIFT RAIL – 7240

SCREW – 377886-S

SCREW – 377886-S

DETENT PLUG – 7C316

INTERLOCK PIN – 7235

THIRD AND OVERDRIVE SHIFT FORK – 7230

FIRST AND SECOND SPEED SHIFT FORK – 7230

THIRD AND OVERDRIVE SHIFT RAIL – 7241

SCREW – 377886-S

DETENT PLUG – 7C316

DETENT PLUG – 7C316

REVERSE SHIFT RAIL – 7240

SHORT SPRING – 7234

REVERSE SHIFT FORK – 7231

DETENT PLUG – 7C316

EXPANSION PLUG – 74112-S

SHORT SPRING – 7234

BOLT – 378206-S

Fig. 1 Ford overdrive (Except Single Rail & Top Mounted Shifter) 4 speed manual transmission

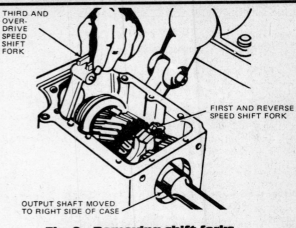

THIRD AND OVERDRIVE SPEED SHIFT FORK

FIRST AND REVERSE SPEED SHIFT FORK

OUTPUT SHAFT MOVED TO RIGHT SIDE OF CASE

Fig. 2 Removing shift forks

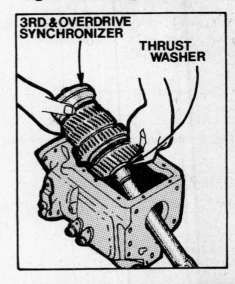

3RD & OVERDRIVE SYNCHRONIZER

THRUST WASHER

Fig. 3 Removing output shaft assembly

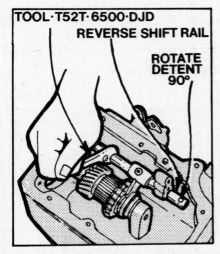

TOOL·T52T·6500·DJD REVERSE SHIFT RAIL

ROTATE DETENT 90°

Fig. 4 Removing reverse shift rail

3. Position hub in sleeve, being sure that alignment marks are properly indexed.
4. Place three inserts into hub. Install insert springs, making sure that irregular surface (hump) is seated in one of inserts. Do not stagger springs.

COUNTERSHAFT GEAR BEARINGS

1. With unit disassembled, coat bore in each end of countergear with grease, **Fig. 9.**
2. Hold a suitable dummy shaft in gear and insert 21 rollers and a retainer washer in each end of gear.

REVERSE IDLER GEAR BEARINGS

1. With unit disassembled, **Fig. 10,** coat bore at each end of gear with grease.
2. Hold a suitable dummy shaft in gear and insert 22 rollers and retainer washer at each end of gear.

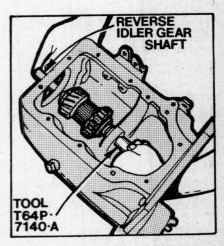

REVERSE IDLER GEAR SHAFT

TOOL T64P· 7140·A

Fig. 5 Removing reverse idler gear shaft

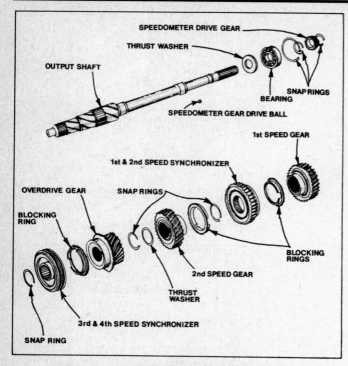

Fig. 6   Output shaft disassembled

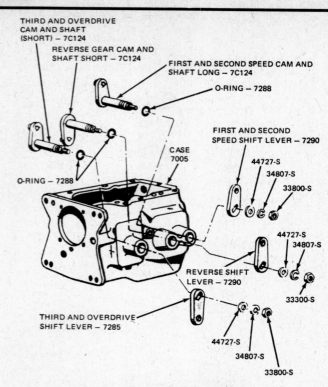

Fig. 7   Cams, shafts & levers

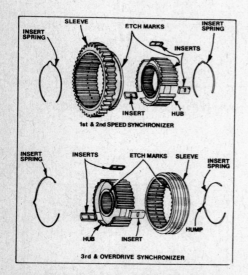

Fig. 8   Synchronizer assemblies

3. Install sliding gear on reverse idler gear, making sure that shift fork groove is toward front.

INPUT SHAFT SEAL

1. Remove seal from input shaft bearing retainer.
2. Lubricate sealing surface and install new seal.

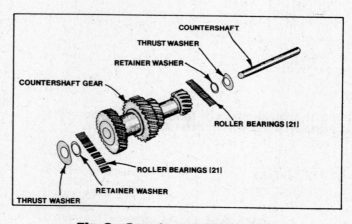

Fig. 9   Countergear assembly

ASSEMBLE

1. Lubricate countershaft gear thrust surfaces and position a thrust washer at each end of case. Place countershaft gear, dummy shaft and roller bearings in the case.
2. Place case in the vertical position, align gear bore and thrust washers with case bores and install countershaft.
3. Place case in the horizontal position and, with a feeler gauge, check countershaft gear end play which should be .004–.018 inch. If not, replace thrust washers.
4. Reinstall dummy shaft in countershaft gear and place gear at bottom of

case.
5. Lubricate reverse idler gear thrust surfaces and place the two thrust washers in position. Install reverse idler gear, sliding gear, dummy shaft and roller bearings in place, ensuring the sliding gear shift fork groove is facing toward front of case. Align gear bore and thrust washers with case bores and install the reverse idler shaft.
6. With a feeler gauge, check reverse idler gear end play which should be .004–.018 inch. If not, replace thrust washers. If end play is within limits, do not remove gear and shaft.
7. Install reverse gear shift rail detent spring and detent plug into case. Holding reverse shift fork in place on the

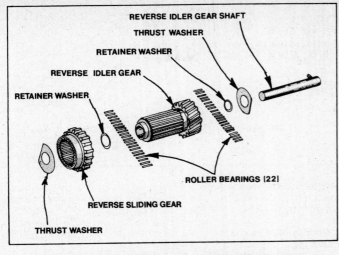

Fig. 10 Reverse idler gear & components

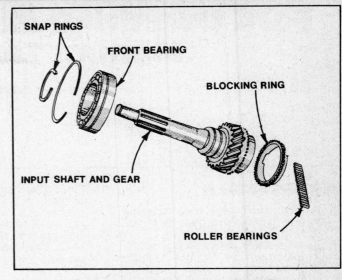

Fig. 11 Input shaft assembly

reverse idler sliding gear, install the shift rail from rear of case. Install shift rail to fork set screw.

8. Place first and second speed synchronizer onto output shaft with shift fork groove facing toward rear of shaft. The synchronizer hub is installed with the teeth end of the gear facing toward rear of output shaft.

9. Place blocking ring on second speed gear, then slide the gear onto front of output shaft, ensuring synchronizer inserts engage the blocker ring notches.

10. Install second speed gear thrust washer and snap ring.

11. Slide overdrive gear onto shaft with coned surface facing toward front of output shaft, then install blocking ring on gear.

12. Slide third and overdrive gear synchronizer onto shaft, ensuring synchronizer inserts engage blocking ring notches and the thrust surface is facing toward overdrive gear.

13. Install snap ring at front of output shaft.

14. Place blocking ring on first speed gear, then slide first speed gear onto rear of output shaft, ensuring synchronizer inserts engage blocking ring notches.

15. Install the heavy thrust washer at rear of output shaft.

16. Support thrust washer and first speed gear to prevent washer and gear from sliding off shaft and lower assembly into case, **Fig. 3.**

17. Install first and second speed shift fork and the third and overdrive speed shift fork, rotating forks into place.

18. Install detent spring and plug into reverse shift rail, then place rail in neutral position.

19. Lubricate third and overdrive shift rail interlock pin and install in shift rail.

20. Align third and overdrive shift fork with shift rail bores and slide shift rail into position, ensuring the three detents are facing toward outside of case. Place front synchronizer into neutral position and install the third and overdrive shift fork set screw. Place synchronizer in neutral position and install the third and overdrive shift rail detent plug, spring and bolt into left side of case. Install detent plug into case bore.

21. Align first and second speed shift fork with case bores and slide shift rail into place, then install set screw.

22. Lubricate input gear bore and install 15 roller bearings into bore.

NOTE: Apply a thin coat of lubricant since a heavy application may plug the lubricant holes and restrict lubrication of the bearings.

23. Place front blocking ring in the third and overdrive synchronizer.

24. Place a dummy bearing on rear of output shaft to support and align shaft in case.

25. Install input shaft gear into case, ensuring output shaft pilot enters roller bearings in input gear pocket.

26. Place input shaft bearing on input shaft and press bearing onto shaft and into case bore, **Fig. 11.**

27. Install input shaft and bearing snap rings, **Fig. 11.**

28. Place new gasket on input shaft bearing retainer, apply sealer to attaching bolts and install and torque attaching bolts to 19–25 ft. lbs.

29. Remove dummy bearing from output shaft and install output shaft bearing onto shaft and press into case bore.

NOTE: Before pressing bearing onto output shaft, ensure the bearing is aligned with the case bore and the countershaft is not interfering with the output shaft assembly.

30. Install output shaft and bearing snap rings.

31. Place transmission in the vertical position. Align countershaft gear bore and thrust washers with case bore and install countershaft.

32. Install extension housing on case with a new gasket, apply sealer to attaching screws and install and torque to 42–50 ft. lbs.

33. Install filler plug.

34. Pour transmission lubricant over gear train while rotating input shaft.

35. Place each shift fork in all positions to ensure proper operation.

36. Install remaining detent plug in case and the long spring to secure detent plug.

37. Install cover with a new gasket, apply sealer to attaching screws and install and torque attaching screws to 20–25 ft. lbs.

38. Apply sealer to the third and overdrive shift rail plug bore and install new expansion plug.

Ford Overdrive (Single Rail) 4 Speed Manual Transmission

INDEX

DISASSEMBLE

1. Remove transmission cover retaining screws, and remove cover and gasket, **Fig. 1.**
2. Remove screw, detent spring and detent plug from case, **Fig. 2.** A magnetic rod may have to be used to remove spring and detent plug.
3. Drive roll pin from shifter shaft, **Fig. 3,** then remove back-up light switch, snap ring and dust cover from rear of extension housing.
4. Remove shifter shaft from turret assembly, **Fig. 4,** then remove extension housing retaining screws, and extension housing and gasket.
5. Remove speedometer gear retaining snap ring, then slide speedometer gear off shaft and remove drive ball.
6. Remove output shaft bearing to shaft retaining snap ring, then using two screwdrivers, pry out bearing, **Fig. 5.**
7. From front of case, push countershaft out of rear of case with a dummy shaft. Lower countershaft to bottom of case.
8. Remove input shaft bearing retainer bolts, then slide retainer and gasket off input shaft.
9. Remove input shaft bearing to shaft retaining snap ring, then remove input shaft bearing from input shaft and transmission case.
10. Remove input shaft, blocking ring and roller bearings from case.
11. Remove overdrive shift pawl, gear selector interlock plate and 1–2 gearshift selector arm plate.
12. Remove roll pin from 3rd-overdrive shift fork, **Fig. 6,** then remove 3rd overdrive shift rail, **Fig. 7.**
13. Remove first, second and third overdrive speed shift fork.
14. Lift countershaft gear and thrust washers from case. Use care to avoid dropping the bearings or dummy shaft from counter-shaft gear.
15. Remove snap ring from front of output shaft, then slide third and overdrive synchronizer blocking ring and gear off the shaft.
16. Remove the next snap ring and thrust washer, first speed gear and blocking ring from rear of shaft.
17. Lift countershaft gear thrust washers and roller bearings from case. Use care to avoid dropping the bearings or dummy shaft from countershaft gear.
18. From front of case, drive the reverse gear shaft out of case.
19. Remove reverse idler gear, thrust washers and roller bearings. Use care to avoid dropping bearing.
20. Remove retaining clip, reverse gearshift relay lever and reverse gear selector fork pivot pin.
21. Remove overdrive shift control link assembly, then remove shift shaft seal from rear of case.
22. Remove expansion plug from front of case.

ASSEMBLE

1. Reverse disassembly procedure to assemble.
2. The transmission mainshaft bearing rollers, extension housing bushing, reverse idler bearing rollers and counter-shaft gear bearing rollers must be lubricated with ESW-M1C109-A or equivalent at each location. The low gear and 2nd and overdrive gear journals are to be lubricated with ESP-M2C83-G transmission oil or equivalent. All other internal components of the transmission are to be lubricated with ESP-M2C83-C transmission oil or equivalent.
3. The intermediate and high rail welch plug must be seated firmly and must not protrude above the front face of case, nor must it be recessed more than .06 inch below front face of case.
4. The end play of the 1st, 2nd and overdrive gears after their assembly on the output shaft must be checked using a suitable gauge and must meet the following specifications:

a. With 1st gear thrust washer clamped against the shoulder on the output shaft, the 1st gear end play should be .005–.024 inch.
b. 2nd gear end play should be .003–.021 inch.
c. Overdrive gear end play should be .009–.023 inch.
d. Countershaft gear end play after its assembly into case between thrust washers must be .004–.018.

NOTE: If dimensions are not within specifications, replace components as necessary.

5. When gearshift selector arm plate is firmly seated in the first-second shift fork plate slot, the transmission shifter shaft must pass freely through the first-second shift fork shifter shaft bore without indication of binding.
6. Torque specifications for the bolts or parts are as follows:

Bolt or Part	Torque (Ft. Lbs.)
Back-up Lamp Switch	8–12
Bearing Retainer	11–25
Case Access Cover	20–25
Detent Bolt	10–15
Extension Housing	42–50
Filler Plug	10–20
Reverse Gear Fork Pivot Pin	15–25
Turret Assembly	8–12

Fig. 2 Removing detent plug, spring & screw

Fig. 3 Removing shifter shaft roll pin

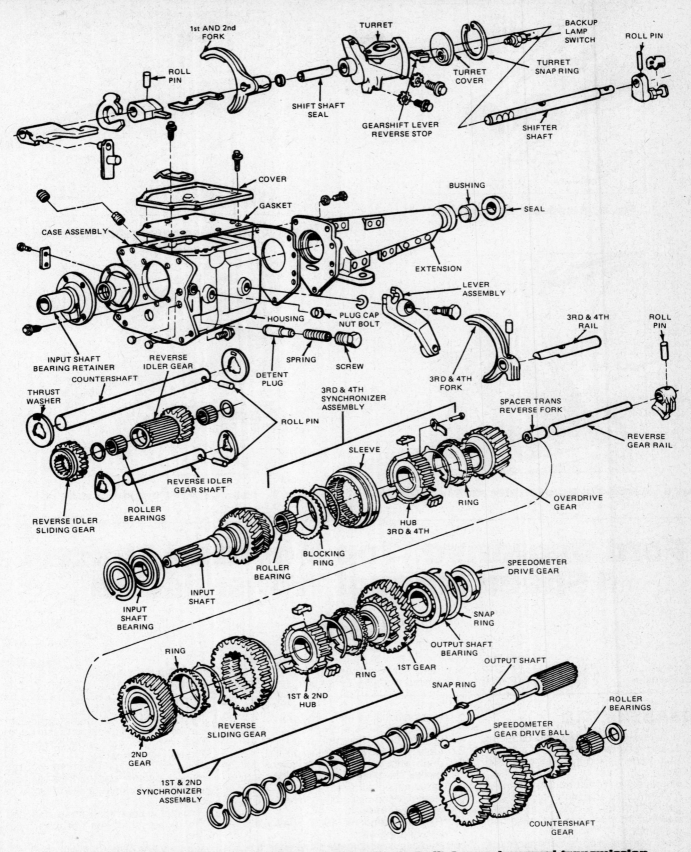

Fig. 1   Disassembled view of Ford Overdrive (Single Rail) 4 speed manual transmission

Fig. 4 Removing shifter shaft

Fig. 5 Removing output shaft bearing

Fig. 6 Removing 3rd-overdrive shift fork roll pin

Fig. 7 Removing 3rd-overdrive shift rail

Ford Overdrive (Top Mounted Shifter) 4 Speed Manual Transmission

INDEX

DISASSEMBLE

1. Unscrew gearshift housing cap, **Fig. 1,** and remove shift lever.
2. Shift transmission into 2nd gear, **Fig. 2.**
3. Remove 6 gearshift housing-to-transmission case attaching bolts and the gearshift housing. Clean all gasket material from housing and case mating surfaces.
4. Shift transmission synchronizer assemblies into neutral position.
5. Place a suitable container under extension housing, then remove 5 extension housing-to-transmission case attaching bolts. Separate housing from case and allow transmission fluid to drain into container, then clean all gasket material from housing and case mating surfaces.
6. Remove and discard shipping seal, if equipped, from shaft.
7. Remove speedometer drive gear snap ring and the gear.
8. Remove speedometer drive gear lock ball from output shaft.
9. Drive roll pin out of 3rd-4th shift fork.
10. Position a ⅜ inch diameter rod against 3rd-4th shift rail in transmission case, then tap on rod and remove rail through front of case.
11. Push countershaft out of rear of case using a dummy shaft at front of case. Lower countershaft gear to bottom of case.
12. Remove output shaft snap ring and the output shaft rear bearing snap ring.
13. Remove and discard output shaft rear bearing, **Fig. 3.**
14. Remove input shaft bearing retainer

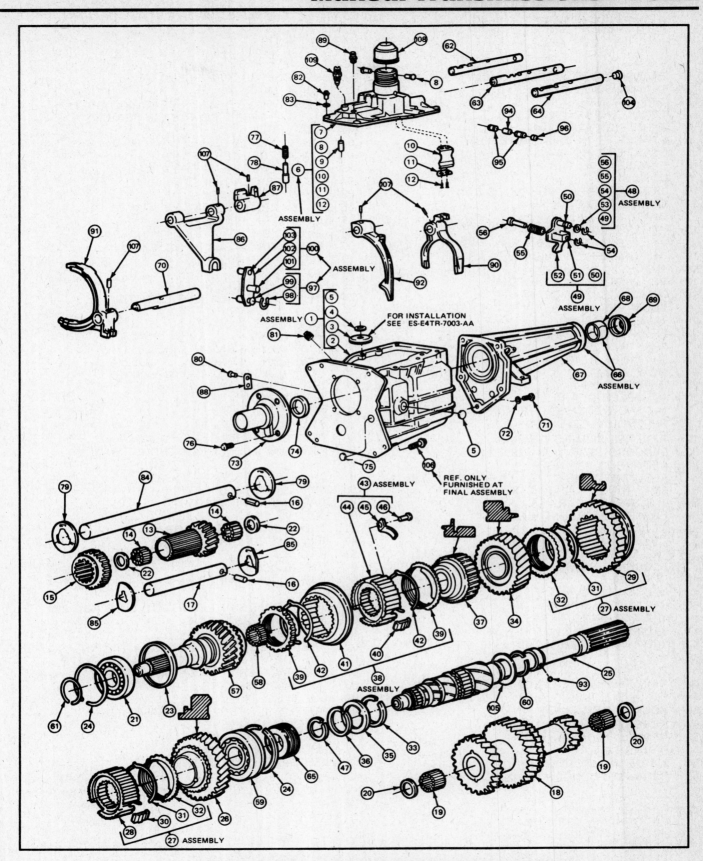

Fig. 1   Disassembled view of Ford Overdrive (Top Mounted Shifter) 4 speed manual transmission (Part 1 of 2)

1	TRANSMISSION CASE ASSEMBLY	56	REVERSE ROCKER PLUNGER
2	TRANSMISSION CASE	57	INPUT SHAFT
3	CHIP MAGNET	58	INPUT SHAFT ROLLER BEARINGS (15)
4	SPRING PUSH-ON NUT	59	OUTPUT SHAFT REAR BALL BEARING
5	EXPANSION CUP PLUG	60	SNAP RING
6	GEARSHIFT HOUSING ASSEMBLY	61	SNAP RING
7	GEARSHIFT HOUSING	62	1ST-2ND SHIFTER RAIL
8	GEARSHIFT LEVER PIN	63	3RD-OVERDRIVE SHIFTER RAIL
9	DOWEL	64	REVERSE GEAR SHIFTER RAIL
10	3RD-OVERDRIVE SHIFT BIAS SPRING	65	SPEEDOMETER DRIVE GEAR
11	SPRING RETAINER PLATE	66	EXTENSION HOUSING ASSEMBLY
12	RIVET	67	EXTENSION HOUSING
13	REVERSE IDLER GEAR	68	EXTENSION HOUSING BUSHING
14	IDLER SHAFT ROLLER BEARINGS (44)	69	EXTENSION HOUSING OIL SEAL
15	REVERSE IDLER SLIDING GEAR	70	3RD-4TH SHIFT RAIL
16	PIN	71	BOLT
17	REVERSE IDLER GEAR SHAFT	72	7/16 EXT. TOOTH WASHER
18	COUNTERSHAFT GEAR	73	INPUT SHAFT BEARING RETAINER
19	COUNTERSHAFT GEAR ROLLER BEARINGS (42)	74	INPUT SHAFT OIL SEAL
20	7/8 FLATWASHER	75	EXPANSION PLUG
21	FRONT INPUT SHAFT BALL BEARING	76	BOLT
22	3/4 FLATWASHER	77	SHIFTER INTERLOCK SPRING
23	RETAINER RING	78	MESHLOCK PLUNGER
24	SNAP RING	79	COUNTERSHAFT THRUST WASHER
25	OUTPUT SHAFT	80	DRIVE SCREW
26	1ST SPEED GEAR	81	FILLER PLUG
27	1ST-2ND GEAR SYNCHRONIZER ASSEMBLY	82	BOLT
28	1ST-2ND CLUTCH HUB	83	EXT. TOOTH WASHER
29	REVERSE SLIDING GEAR	84	COUNTERSHAFT
30	SYNCHRONIZER HUB INSERT	85	REVERSE IDLER GEAR THRUST WASHER
31	RETAINING SPRING	86	3RD-OVERDRIVE SHIFT PAWL
32	BLOCKING RING	87	3RD-OVERDRIVE SHIFT GATE
33	SNAP RING	88	SERVICE IDENTIFICATION TAG
34	2ND SPEED GEAR	89	BACK-UP LAMP SWITCH
35	LOW GEAR THRUST WASHER	90	1ST-2ND GEARSHIFT FORK
36	RETAINING RING	91	3RD-4TH GEARSHIFT FORK
37	OVERDRIVE GEAR	92	REVERSE GEARSHIFT FORK
38	3RD-4TH GEAR SYNCHRONIZER ASSEMBLY	93	BALL
39	BLOCKING RING	94	INTERLOCK PIN
40	HUB INSERT	95	INTERLOCK PLUNGER
41	CLUTCH SLEEVE	96	PLUG
42	RETAINING SPRING	97	OVERDRIVE SHIFT CONTROL LINK AND PIN
43	3RD-4TH SPEED HUB	98	RETAINING EXT. RING
44	3RD-4TH GEAR CLUTCH HUB	99	FINGER PIN
45	3RD-4TH SYNCHRONIZER HUB SPRING	100	OVERDRIVE SHIFT CONTROL LINK PIN ASSEMBLY
46	RIVET	101	OVERDRIVE SHIFT CONTROL LINK SHAFT
47	SNAP RING	102	OVERDRIVE SHIFT CONTROL LINK
48	REVERSE ROCKER ARM ASSEMBLY	103	SHIFT CONTROL FINGER PIN
49	PIN AND HOUSING ARM	104	CUP PLUG
50	ROCKER ARM PIVOT PIN	105	OUTPUT SHAFT THRUST WASHER
51	REVERSE PLUNGER HOUSING	106	SCREW AND WASHER
52	REVERSE ROCKER ARM	107	PIN
53	O-RING SEAL	108	HOUSING CAP
54	3/8 RETAINING EXT. RING	109	4TH GEAR SENSING SWITCH
55	REVERSE PLUNGER SPRING		

Fig. 1 Disassembled view of Ford Overdrive (Top Mounted Shifter) 4 speed manual transmission (Part 2 of 2)

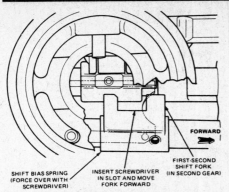

Fig. 2   Positioning 1st—2nd shift fork into 2nd gear

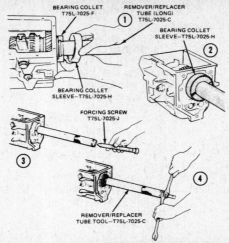

Fig. 3   Output shaft rear bearing removal. 4 × 2 models (4 × 4 models similar)

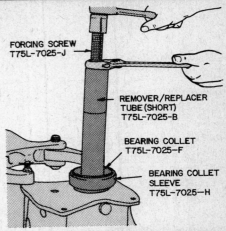

Fig. 4   Input shaft front bearing removal

attaching bolts and the retainer. Clean all gasket material from retainer and case mating surfaces.

15. Remove snap ring retaining front input shaft ball bearing, then the snap ring and retainer from the bearing.
16. Remove and discard front input shaft bearing, **Fig. 4.**
17. Rotate input shaft until flats on synchronizer teeth align with teeth on countershaft gear, then remove input shaft from case. Use care to avoid dropping needle bearings from rear of input shaft.
18. Mark 3rd-4th blocking ring for assembly reference, then remove ring from rear of input shaft.
19. Remove 3rd-4th shift fork from intermediate and high clutch sleeve.
20. Remove output shaft and geartrain assembly from transmission case.
21. Lift countershaft gear, with dummy shaft inside, from bottom of transmission case. Use care to avoid dropping needle bearings from gear.
22. Remove countershaft nylon thrust washers from each end of case.
23. Remove reverse idler bronze thrust washers, reverse idler gear, reverse idler sliding gear, two flat washers and idler shaft needle bearings from transmission case.
24. Remove 3rd-4th roll pin from bottom of case.
25. Remove overdrive shift control link and pin assembly from case.

SUB-ASSEMBLY SERVICE

GEARSHIFT HOUSING ASSEMBLY

Disassemble
1. Position gearshift housing in a suitable vise, then drive out roll pins retaining 3rd-overdrive shift pawl and shift gate, **Fig. 5.** Use care to avoid striking bias spring when removing shift gate roll pin.
2. Slide 3rd-overdrive shift pawl to front of housing, then insert a punch into exposed roll pin hole in rail and rotate

rail 90°.
3. Pry plugs out of housing using a suitable screwdriver. Discard the plugs.
4. Drive 3rd-overdrive shift rail out of housing and remove interlock pin from rail.
5. Remove 3rd-overdrive shift pawl and shift gate from housing.
6. Remove interlock plungers from housing through rear 3rd-overdrive rail bore.
7. Drive out roll pin retaining 1st-2nd shift fork to rail. Use care to avoid driving pin into inner wall of housing.
8. Slide 1st-2nd shift fork to front of case, then insert a punch into exposed roll pin hole and rotate rail 90°.
9. Drive 1st-2nd shift fork out of housing, while covering plunger and spring bore to prevent spring from popping out.
10. Remove 1st-2nd shift fork from housing.
11. Slide reverse fork and rail assembly forward to reverse position, then drive out reverse fork roll pin.
12. Slide reverse fork rearward, then insert a punch into exposed roll pin hole and rotate 90°.
13. Drive reverse rail out of housing, while covering plunger and spring bore to prevent spring from popping out.
14. Remove reverse fork from housing.
15. Remove meshlock plungers and interlock springs from housing bores.
16. Remove C-clip retaining reverse rocker arm assembly to housing.
17. Push shift bias spring outward enough to provide sufficient clearance to remove reverse rocker arm assembly, then remove assembly from housing.

NOTE: Do not disassemble reverse rocker arm assembly.

18. Remove back-up lamp switch and gasket from housing, as required.

Assemble

NOTE: Prior to assembly, apply suitable lubricant to all shift rails.

1. Install back-up lamp switch, if previously removed, in housing.
2. Lubricate reverse rocker arm assembly O-ring and shaft with suitable lubricant.
3. Move shift bias spring outward enough to provide sufficient clearance to install reverse rocker arm assembly and install the assembly.
4. Install C-clip retaining reverse rocker arm assembly to housing.
5. Install interlock springs and meshlock plungers in housing bores.
6. Position reverse shift rail in housing, ensuring detent slots in rail are inserted into housing first with slots facing meshlock plunger.
7. Install reverse shift fork to engage reverse rocker arm assembly with fork pad facing inside. Slide rail through fork bore and up to meshlock plunger.
8. Drive meshlock plunger into bore, then push rail forward until it blocks plunger. Remove punch and push rail through bore.
9. Align holes in fork and rail and install roll pin.
10. Repeat steps 5 thru 8 for 1st-2nd shift rail.
11. Ensure 1st-2nd and reverse shift forks are in neutral position, then install interlock plungers through 3rd-overdrive bore in rear of housing.
12. Position 3rd-overdrive shift rail in housing, ensuring detent slots are inserted into housing first with slots facing meshlock plunger.
13. Install 3rd-overdrive shift gate into housing so slot on gate faces down and small tab is rearward in housing. Slide rail forward until it is just through the gate.
14. Install interlock pin in rear of 3rd-overdrive shift rail.
15. Install 3rd-overdrive shift pawl in housing with slot on reverse rail side of

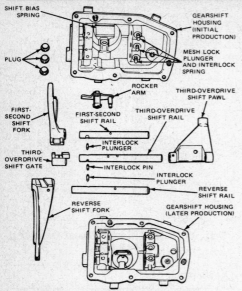

Fig. 5 Gearshift housing assembly

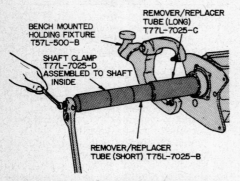

Fig. 6 Input shaft front bearing installation

housing. Slide rail through pawl up to plunger.
16. Drive meshlock plunger into bore using a suitable punch. Push rail forward until it blocks plunger, then remove punch and push rail through bore.
17. Align roll pin holes in pawl, gate and rail and install roll pins.
18. Apply sealant No. EOAZ-19554-B or equivalent to outside diameter of shift rail cup plugs, then drive plugs into bores in rear of housing.
19. Place gearshift housing in 2nd gear for installation.

OUTPUT SHAFT & GEARTRAIN

Disassemble
1. Remove snap ring from front of output shaft, **Fig. 1**.
2. Remove 3rd-4th synchronizer assembly and overdrive gear from shaft.
3. Remove snap ring, 2nd gear thrust washer, 2nd gear and blocking ring from shaft.
4. Remove snap ring, then press 1st-2nd

synchronizer assembly off shaft.

Assemble
1. Apply suitable lubricant to 1st gear journal, then press 1st-2nd synchronizer assembly onto front of output shaft, ensuring shift fork groove is facing toward rear of shaft.
2. Install 1st speed gear and blocking ring on rear of shaft.
3. Install snap ring in front of 1st-2nd synchronizer assembly.
4. Position blocking ring on 2nd gear, then apply suitable lubricant to 2nd gear journal on shaft.
5. Install 2nd speed gear and blocking ring on front of shaft, ensuring inserts in synchronizer engage notches in blocking ring.
6. Install 2nd gear thrust washer and snap ring, then apply suitable lubricant to overdrive gear journal on shaft.
7. Install overdrive gear on shaft with coned synchronizer surface facing forward.
8. Install blocking ring on overdrive gear, then slide 3rd-4th synchronizer assembly onto shaft. Ensure synchronizer inserts engage notches in blocking ring and small thrust surface faces forward.
9. Install snap ring on front of shaft.

SYNCHRONIZERS

Disassemble
1. Scribe alignment marks on synchronizer hub and sleeve for assembly reference.
2. Push synchronizer hubs from sleeves, **Fig. 1**.
3. Remove inserts and insert springs from hubs.

Assemble
1. Position hubs in sleeves, ensuring scribe marks are properly aligned.
2. Install inserts and insert springs, ensuring tab is located in a common insert rotating in opposite directions. Do not stagger springs.

ASSEMBLE
1. Install overdrive shift control link and pin assembly into case, ensuring square shouldered pin is positioned toward bottom of case.
2. Apply suitable lubricant to reverse idler bronze thrust washers, then install washers in case, aligning tabs on washers with slots in case.
3. Apply suitable lubricant to reverse idler gear shaft needle bearings, then install two rows of 22 bearings in reverse idler gear. Retain bearings with a washer on each end of gear.
4. Install reverse idler sliding gear onto reverse idler gear, ensuring grooved portion of gear faces front of transmission gear.
5. Lower reverse idler gear and sliding gear into case.
6. Install reverse idler gear shaft through sliding gear and reverse idler gear

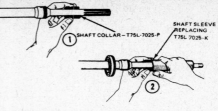

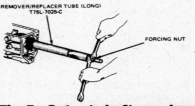

Fig. 7 Output shaft rear bearing installation. 4 × 2 models (4 × 4 models similar)

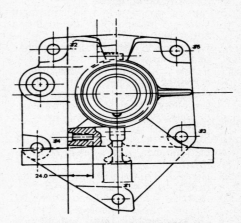

Fig. 8 Extension housing attaching bolt tightening sequence

assembly and thrust washers. Ensure roll pin in end of shaft faces rear of case.
7. Apply suitable lubricant to countershaft nylon thrust washers, then install washers in case.
8. Apply suitable lubricant to countershaft needle bearings, then install two rows of 21 bearings into countershaft gear. Install dummy shaft No. T64P-7111-A or equivalent into countershaft gear, then install washers on each end of gear to retain bearings.
9. Lower countershaft to bottom of case.

NOTE: The countershaft gear must be at bottom of case with countershaft removed to provide sufficient clearance to install input shaft and output shaft and geartrain assembly.

10. Position rear of output shaft and geartrain through rear bearing bore in case and tilt assembly until it can be installed in case.
11. Install 3rd-4th shift fork with slot facing down. Align fork pads with 3rd-4th synchronizer assembly and slotted groove with overdrive shift control link

and pin assembly.

12. Install 15 needle bearings into input shaft bearing bore. Apply suitable lubricant to bearings.
13. Install blocking ring in intermediate and high clutch hub and sleeve on output shaft and geartrain.
14. Install input shaft, then move shaft into position on output shaft and geartrain. Align slots in blocking ring with inserts on sleeve.
15. Install input shaft front bearing, **Fig. 6**, then the bearing retaining ring and snap rings.
16. Apply suitable sealer to transmission case and input bearing retainer mating surfaces, then position retainer on case, with slot in retainer facing bottom of case. Apply suitable sealer to retainer attaching bolts, then install bolts and torque to 12–16 ft. lbs.
17. Install output shaft rear bearing, **Fig.**

7, then the bearing snap rings.
18. Install speedometer drive gear lock ball, then the speedometer drive gear and snap ring.
19. Lift countershaft gear assembly, with dummy shaft inside, into position in case.
20. Position countershaft in rear of case, then drive countershaft into case while removing dummy shaft.
21. Apply suitable sealer to extension housing mating surface. Install extension housing attaching bolts and tighten all at least two full turns. Torque bolts to 42–50 ft. lbs. in sequence shown in **Fig. 8.**
22. Install 3rd-4th shift rail through front of case, then drive roll pin through shift fork.
23. Drive welch plug into 3rd-4th shift rail bore in case. Ensure plug does not protrude above front face of case, or

recess more than .006 inch below front face of case.
24. Place transmission and gearshift housing assembly in 2nd gear position, ensuring reverse idler gear is positioned rearward.
25. Install gearshift housing assembly on transmission case. Torque attaching bolts to 18–22 ft. lbs.

NOTE: When the gearshift housing is properly installed, the 3rd-overdrive shift pawl engages the rounded portion of the overdrive shift control link and pin assembly, the reverse fork engages the reverse idler sliding gear and the 1st-2nd shift fork engages the 1st-2nd synchronizer assembly.

26. Install transmission shift lever.
27. Remove fill plug, then add 4.5 pints of suitable transmission fluid to case and reinstall fill plug.

New Process 435 4 Speed Manual Transmission

NOTE: For service procedures on this transmission, refer to the New Process 435 4 Speed Manual Transmission section in the Dodge & Plymouth chapter.

Toyo Kogyo (Models W/Diesel Engine) 4 Speed Manual Transmission

INDEX

DISASSEMBLE

1. Drain lubricant from transmission, **Fig. 1**, then remove fork and release bearing from clutch housing.
2. Remove 6 front cover attaching bolts, then the front cover, shim and gasket.
3. Remove front cover oil seal, **Fig. 2**, then the input shaft snap ring.
4. Remove outer snap ring from input shaft bearing.
5. Remove input shaft bearing, **Figs. 3 and 4.**
6. Remove 8 extension housing-to-transmission case attaching bolts, then slide housing off mainshaft with control lever end laid down and to the left as far as possible.
7. Remove control lever end attaching bolt, then the control lever end and rod from extension housing.
8. Remove speedometer driven gear assembly from extension housing.
9. Remove back-up lamp and neutral sensing switches from extension housing.
10. On models equipped with speed control, remove speed control sensor

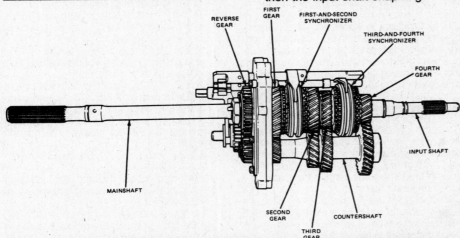

Fig. 1 Gears & shaft components. Toyo Kogyo (Models W/Diesel Engine) 4 speed manual transmission

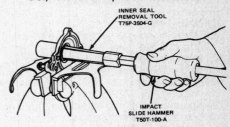

Fig. 2 Front cover oil seal removal

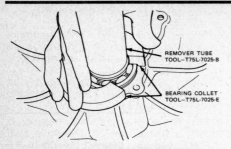

Fig. 3 Input shaft bearing removal tool installation

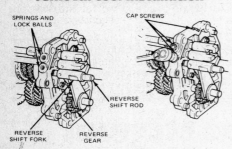

Fig. 6 Shift lock ball & spring removal

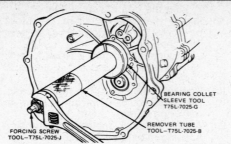

Fig. 4 Input shaft bearing removal

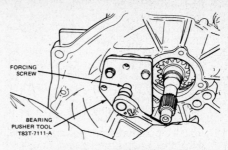

Fig. 5 Countershaft & front bearing removal

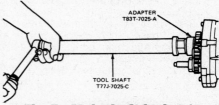

Fig. 7 Mainshaft locknut removal

retaining bolt, then the speed sensor and speedometer drive gear.

11. On models less speed control, remove speedometer drive gear snap ring, then the drive gear and lock ball.

12. On all models, separate bearing housing from transmission case, **Fig. 5,** then remove countershaft gear assembly and bearing housing from case.

13. Remove 3 spring cap screws, springs and balls, **Fig. 6.**

NOTE: Personal injury may result if case is not used when removing the spring-loaded lower ball.

14. Remove reverse shift rod and shift fork assembly, and reverse gear from bearing housing.

15. Drive out shift fork roll pins, then remove shift forks and rods. Mark shift forks so they can be installed in their original positions.

16. Remove lower reverse shift rod locking bolt and spring and the interlock pins from bearing housing.

17. Bend down tab on mainshaft lockwasher, then lock transmission synchronizers into any 2 gears and remove mainshaft locknut, **Fig. 7.**

18. Remove reverse gear and key from mainshaft.

19. Remove counter reverse gear snap ring and the gear.

20. Remove 5 bearing cover attaching bolts, then the bearing cover and reverse idler gear shaft from bearing housing.

21. Tap mainshaft and countershaft out of bearing housing using a soft-faced hammer.

22. Remove input shaft and roller bearing from mainshaft, **Fig. 8.**

23. Remove rear countershaft bearing from bearing housing using tool T77J-7025-B or equivalent.

24. Remove rear mainshaft bearing from bearing housing using tools T77F-4222-A and T77J-7025-B or equivalents.

25. Remove thrust washer, first gear, sleeve and synchronizer ring from rear of mainshaft, **Fig. 8.**

26. Remove mainshaft snap ring.

27. Remove 3rd–4th clutch hub, sleeve, synchronizer ring and 3rd gear from front of mainshaft using a suitable press and tool No. T71P-4621-B or equivalent.

28. Remove 1st–2nd clutch hub, sleeve and 2nd gear from rear of mainshaft using a suitable press and tool No. T71P-4621-B or equivalent.

29. Press front bearing out of countershaft, **Fig. 9.**

CLEANING & INSPECTION

CLEANING

Wash all parts except the ball bearings and seal, in suitable solvent. Brush all foreign matter from the parts. Be careful not to damage any parts. Do not clean, wash or soak transmission seals in cleaning solvent. Dry all parts with compressed air.

Rotate bearings in a cleaning solvent until all lubricant is removed. Hold bearing assembly to prevent it from rotating and dry with compressed air. Lubricate bearings with approved transmission lubricant and wrap in a clean, lint-free cloth or paper until ready for use.

INSPECTION

Inspect transmission case and housing for cracks, worn or damaged bores, damaged threads, or any other damage that could affect the operation of the transmission. Inspect machined mating surfaces for burrs, nicks or damage.

Inspect front face of case for small nicks or burrs that could cause misalignment of transmission with flywheel housing. Remove all small nicks or burrs with a fine stone. Inspect bell housing for cracks. Ensure machined mating surfaces are free

from burrs, nicks or other damage.

Check condition of shift covers, forks, shift rails and shafts. Inspect ball bearings for cracks or deformations and replace any roller bearings that are broken, worn or rough

ASSEMBLE

1. Assemble 1st-2nd and 3rd-4th clutch hub assemblies by installing clutch hub and synchronizer into sleeve, positioning 3 keys into clutch hub slots, and placing springs onto hub, **Fig. 10.**

NOTE: Open end of springs must be inserted into hub holes in direction shown in **Fig. 10** to maintain equal spring tension on each key.

2. Install 3rd gear and synchronizer ring onto front of mainshaft.

3. Press 3rd-4th clutch hub assembly onto mainshaft, **Fig. 11,** in direction shown in **Fig. 12.**

4. Install snap ring on mainshaft.

5. Install 2nd gear and synchronizer ring onto rear of mainshaft.

6. Press 1st-2nd clutch hub assembly onto mainshaft, **Fig. 13,** in direction shown in **Fig. 12.**

7. Install synchronizer ring, 1st gear with sleeve and thrust washer onto mainshaft.

8. Install input shaft and bearing onto mainshaft.

9. Measure countershaft rear bearing and mainshaft bearing clearances as follows:

   a. Measure bearing bore depth "A," **Figs. 14 and 15,** using a suitable depth micrometer.

   b. Measure bearing height "B," **Figs. 14 and 15.**

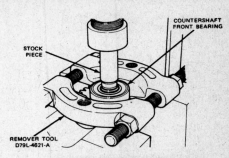

Fig. 9   Countershaft front bearing removal

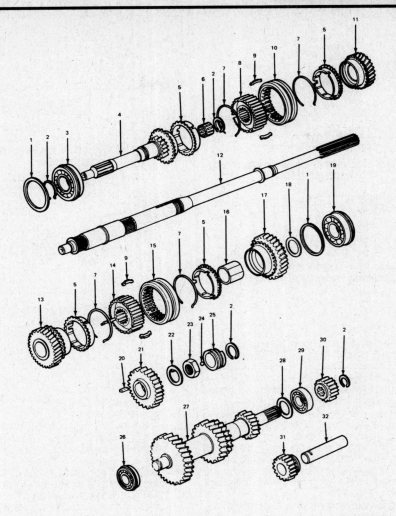

1. ADJUSTING SHIM
2. SNAP RING
3. INPUT BEARING
4. INPUT SHAFT
5. SYNCHRONIZER RING
6. NEEDLE BEARING (CAGED)
7. SYNCHRONIZER KEY SPRING
8. 3RD-AND-4TH CLUTCH HUB

9. SYNCHRONIZER KEY
10. CLUTCH HUB SLEEVE
11. 3RD GEAR
12. MAINSHAFT
13. 2ND GEAR
14. 1ST-AND-2ND CLUTCH HUB
15. CLUTCH HUB SLEEVE
16. GEAR SLEEVE

17. 1ST GEAR
18. THRUST WASHER
19. BALL BEARING
20. KEY
21. REVERSE GEAR
22. LOCK WASHER
23. LOCK NUT
24. LOCKING BALL

25. SPEEDOMETER DRIVE GEAR
26. BALL BEARING
27. COUNTERSHAFT
28. ADJUSTING SHIM
29. BALL BEARING
30. COUNTER REVERSE GEAR
31. REVERSE IDLE GEAR
32. SHAFT

Fig. 8   Exploded view of shafts & gears

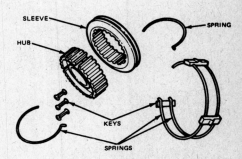

Fig. 10   Clutch assembly

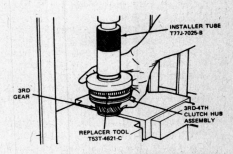

Fig. 11   3rd-4th clutch hub assembly installation

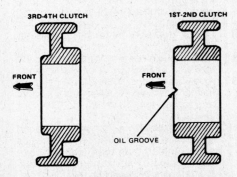

Fig. 12   Clutch hub assembly position

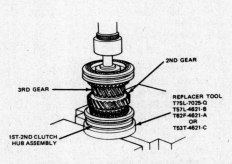

Fig. 13   1st-2nd clutch hub assembly installation

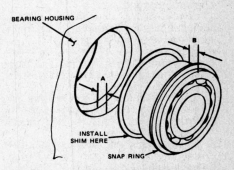

Fig. 14   Measuring countershaft rear bearing clearance

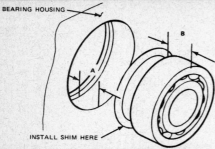

Fig. 15 Measuring mainshaft bearing clearance

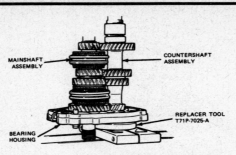

Fig. 16 Countershaft assembly installation

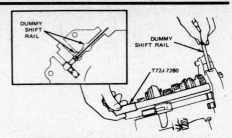

Fig. 17 Shift fork interlock pin installation

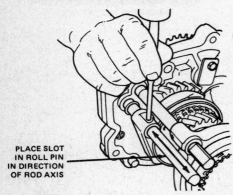

Fig. 18 Shift fork pin installation

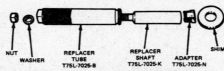

Fig. 19 Input shaft front bearing installation tools

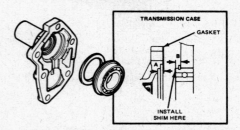

Fig. 20 Front cover clearance adjustment

c. The difference between measurements "A" and "B" should be less than .0039 inch.
d. Select shims needed to bring bearing clearances within specifications. Shims are available in thicknesses of .0039 and .0118 inch.

10. Place selected shim on countershaft rear bearing and press into bearing housing using tool No. T77J-7025-B or equivalent.
11. Place selected shim on mainshaft bearing and press into bearing housing using tool No. T77J-7025-K or equivalent.
12. Press front bearing onto countershaft using tool No. T71P-7025-A or equivalent.
13. Position countershaft and mainshaft assemblies on bearing housing with gears meshed.

NOTE: Ensure mainshaft thrust washer is installed at rear of 1st gear.

14. Hold mainshaft in position and press countershaft assembly into bearing housing, **Fig. 16.**
15. Install bearing cover and reverse idler gear shaft onto bearing housing. Ensure cover is fully seated in idler gear shaft groove.
16. Install mainshaft reverse gear with key, then install and hand tighten mainshaft locknut.
17. Install countershaft reverse gear and

snap ring, then lock transmission in any 2 gears.

NOTE: Mainshaft and countershaft reverse gears must be installed with chamfer on gear teeth facing rearward.

18. Install short spring and ball into bearing housing reverse bore. Hold ball down with a suitable tool and install reverse shift rod and shift lever assembly with reverse idle gear.
19. Install shift fork rods and interlock pins, **Fig. 17.**
20. Assemble shift forks to clutch sleeves, then align roll pin holes of each shift fork and rod and install new roll pins as shown in **Fig. 18.**
21. Install balls, springs and spring cap screws.
22. Apply suitable sealer to both bearing housing mating surfaces, then temporarily install housing to transmission case using 1 upper and 2 lower bolts only. Tighten attaching bolts to position countershaft front bearing in bore.

NOTE: It may be necessary to remove plugs from bell housing shift rod bores to align shift rods. When reinstalling plugs, a suitable silicone sealer must be used.

23. Torque mainshaft locknut to 116–174 ft. lbs., then bend up a tab on lockwasher.
24. On models equipped with speed control, install speedometer drive gear and speed sensor.
25. On models less speed control, install speedometer drive gear, lock ball and snap ring.
26. On all models, position outer snap ring on mainshaft, then install input shaft front bearing using tools shown in **Fig. 19.** Tighten nut on forcing screw until

bearing outer snap ring is fully seated against housing.
27. Install input shaft snap ring.
28. Attach speedometer driven gear assembly to extension housing with bolt and lock nut.
29. Install shift control lever through openings in front of extension housing.
30. Connect control lever end to control lever and torque attaching bolt to 20–25 ft. lbs.
31. Install back-up lamp and neutral sensing switches to extension housing and torque to 20–25 ft. lbs.
32. Remove 4 bolts which were temporarily installed to hold bearing housing in place.
33. Apply suitable sealer to bearing housing and extension housing mating surfaces, then install extension housing with control lever laid down and as far to the left as possible. Torque attaching bolts to 41–59 ft. lbs. and ensure proper operation of control rod.
34. Install gearshift lever retainer and gasket and torque attaching bolts to 41–59 ft. lbs.
35. Install gearshift lever, if previously removed.
36. Install new oil seal in front cover using tool No. T71P-7050-A or equivalent.
37. Apply transmission fluid to oil seal lip inside front cover, then install cover and torque attaching bolts to 41–59 ft. lbs.
38. Measure clearance between bearing outer race and front cover. Clearance must be less than .004 inch and can be adjusted by adding a shim of .006 or .012 inch as needed, **Fig. 20.**
39. Install release bearing and fork.

Toyo Kogyo (Models W/Gasoline Engine) 4 Speed Manual Transmission

INDEX

DISASSEMBLE

1. Remove bell housing-to-transmission case attaching nuts, then the bell housing and gasket.
2. Remove drain plug and drain lubricant from transmission, **Fig. 1.** If necessary, clean metal filings from plug and reinstall.
3. Place transmission in neutral.
4. Remove 4 gearshift lever retainer-to-extension housing attaching bolts, then the retainer and gasket.
5. Remove 6 bolts attaching extension housing to transmission case.
6. Raise control lever to the left and slide toward rear of transmission.
7. Slide extension housing off transmission being careful not to damage the oil seal.

NOTE: If necessary remove gearshift control lever end and control by removing attaching bolt. If required also remove back-up lamp switch from extension housing.

8. Remove anti-spill seal from output shaft and discard, seal is not necessary for reassembly.
9. Remove snap ring from speedometer drive gear. Slide drive gear off mainshaft and remove lock ball.
10. Evenly loosen 14 bolts securing transmission case cover to transmission case and remove cover and gasket.
11. Remove 3 spring cap bolts. Remove detent springs and balls from trans-

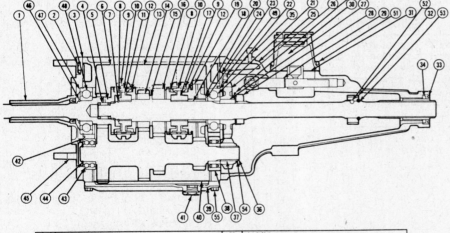

1	Clutch Adapter Plate	28	Lock Nut
2	Flange Bolt	29	Control Rod
3	Gasket	30	Control Case
4	Needle Bearing	33	Oil Seal
5	Main Drive Gear	34	Anti-Spill Seal
6	Transmission Case	35	Breather
7	Snap Ring	36	Counter Shaft Gear
8	Synchronizer Ring	37	Counter Reverse Gear
9	Clutch Hub Sleeve	38	Needle Bearing
10	Synchronizer Key	39	Under Cover
11	Clutch Hub 3rd-4th	40	Gasket
12	Synchronizer Spring	41	Magnet Plug
13	I.D. Tag	42	Adjust Shim
14	3rd-Gear	43	Ball Bearing
15	Main Shaft	44	Retaining Ring
16	2nd-Gear	45	Stud
17	Clutch Hub 1st-2nd	46	Retaining Ring
18	Gear Sleeve	47	Adjust Shim
19	1st Gear	48	Ball Bearing
20	Thrust Washer	49	Washer and Bolt
21	Ball Bearing	50	Lock Washer
22	Gasket	51	Bolt
23	Adjust Shim	52	Steel Ball
24	Bearing Stopper	53	Retaining Ring
25	Extension Housing	54	Retaining Ring
26	Reverse Gear	55	Bolt
27	Key		

Fig. 1 Sectional view of Toyo Kogyo (Models W/Gasoline Engine) 4 speed manual transmission

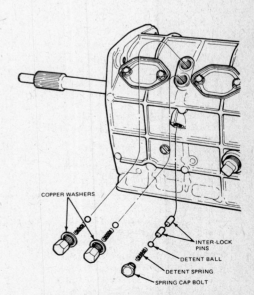

COPPER WASHERS

INTER-LOCK PINS

DETENT BALL

DETENT SPRING

SPRING CAP BOLT

Fig. 2 Detent spring & ball removal

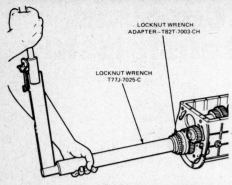

Fig. 3 Removing or installing locknut

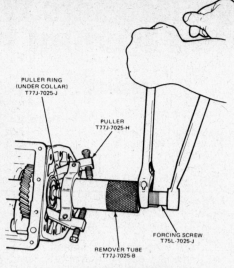

Fig. 4 Countershaft rear bearing removal

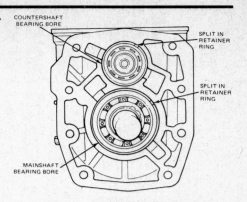

Fig. 5 Positioning of the retainer ring for removal

mission using a magnet, **Fig. 2.**

12. Remove 4 blind covers-to-transmission case attaching bolts, and remove blind covers and gasket.

13. Slide reverse shift fork shaft assembly and idler gear out of transmission case.

14. Shift transmission into 4th gear. With a small drift, drive roll pin from 3rd and 4th fork assembly. Slide 3rd-4th shift fork shaft out of transmission case.

15. Remove roll pin from 1st-2nd shift fork. Slide shift fork out of transmission case. Remove inter-lock pins, **Fig. 2.**

16. Reinstall reverse idler gear then install tool No. T77J-7025-E between 4th speed synchronizer ring and synchromesh gear on mainshaft, and shift transmission into 2nd gear.

17. Fold back ends of lockwasher then remove locknut and washer, slide reverse idler gear off mainshaft, **Fig. 3.**

18. Remove key from mainshaft then remove reverse idler gear.

19. Remove snap ring from end of countershaft, and slide reverse gear off countershaft.

20. Remove 4 bearing retainer attaching bolts then remove bearing retainer together with reverse idler gear shaft.

21. Remove countershaft rear bearing using a suitable puller, **Fig. 4.**

NOTE: The retainer ring may need to be turned to position the split in the retainer ring midway between the recessed areas, before the puller is installed, **Fig. 5.** This will reduce the possibility of the retainer ring becoming distorted as the bearing is removed.

22. Turn forcing screw clockwise to remove bearing.

23. Remove mainshaft rear bearing using suitable puller, **Fig. 6.** Turn forcing screw clockwise to remove bearing.

24. Remove shim and spacer from behind mainshaft rear bearing.

25. Remove 4 studs and bolts attaching front cover to case and remove front cover. Save shim on inside of the cover.

26. Remove snap ring from input shaft.

27. Remove mainshaft drive gear bearing using suitable puller, **Fig. 6.** Turn forcing screw clockwise to remove bearing.

28. Rotate both shift forks so that main gear train will fall to bottom of case. Remove shift forks. Rotate input shaft so that one of two flats on input shaft face upward, **Fig. 7.**

29. Remove snap ring from front of countershaft.

30. Install tool No. T77J-7025-E between 1st gear on countershaft and rear of case, **Fig. 8.**

31. Install tools No. T75L-7025-J, T82T-7003-BH and T77J-7025-N, **Fig. 8.**

32. Turn forcing screw clockwise until countershaft contacts tool No. T77J-7025-E.

33. Remove countershaft front bearing using suitable puller. Turn forcing screw clockwise.

34. Remove shim from behind counter-

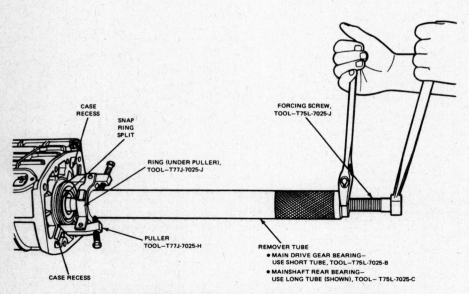

Fig. 6 Mainshaft rear bearing & mainshaft drive gear bearing removal

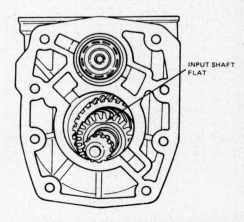

Fig. 7 Positioning input shaft flats

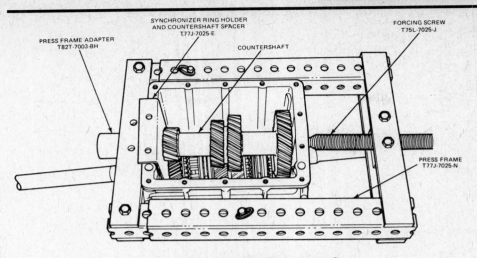

Fig. 8 Countershaft removal

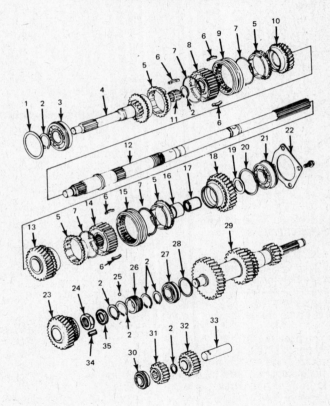

Fig. 9 Exploded view of shafts & gears

1. SHIM	19. THRUST WASHER
2. SNAP RING	20. SHIM
3. MAIN DRIVE SHAFT BEARING	21. MAIN SHAFT FRONT BEARING
4. MAIN DRIVE SHAFT GEAR	22. BEARING COVER
5. SYNCHRONIZER RING	23. REVERSE GEAR
6. SYNCHRONIZER KEY	24. MAIN SHAFT LOCK NUT
7. SYNCHRONIZER KEY SPRING	25. LOCK BALL
8. 3RD-AND-4TH CLUTCH HUB	26. SPEEDOMETER DRIVE GEAR
9. CLUTCH SLEEVE	27. COUNTER SHAFT
10. 3RD GEAR	FRONT BEARING
11. CAGED BEARING	28. SHIM
12. MAIN SHAFT	29. COUNTER SHAFT
13. 2ND GEAR	30. COUNTER SHAFT REAR BEARING
14. 1ST-AND-2ND CLUTCH HUB	31. COUNTER REVERSE GEAR
15. CLUTCH SLEEVE	32. REVERSE IDLER GEAR
16. FIRST GEAR SLEEVE	33. IDLER GEAR SHAFT
17. BUSHING	34. KEY
18. 1ST GEAR	35. LOCKWASHER

shaft front bearing.

35. Remove input shaft from transmission case then remove synchronizer ring and caged bearing from main driveshaft.
36. Remove countershaft from transmission case.
37. Remove inner race of countershaft center bearing from countershaft, using suitable press.
38. Remove mainshaft and gear assembly from transmission case.
39. Remove snap rings from front of mainshaft. Slide clutch hubs, sleeve assembly synchronizer ring, gears and thrust washer from mainshaft, **Fig. 9.**
40. Remove thrust washer, 1st gear and sleeve and the 1st- and clutch hub and sleeve from mainshaft. Remove bushing from 1st gear using a suitable press.

NOTE: Do not mix the synchronizer rings.

CLEANING & INSPECTION

CLEANING

Wash all parts, except the ball bearings and seal, in suitable solvent. Brush all foreign matter from the parts. Be careful not to damage any parts. Do not clean, wash or soak transmission seals in cleaning solvent. Dry all parts with compressed air.

Rotate the bearings in a cleaning solvent until all lubricant is removed. Hold the bearing assembly to prevent it from rotating and dry it with compressed air. Lubricate the bearings with approved transmission lubricant and wrap them in a clean, lint-free cloth or paper, until ready for use.

INSPECTION

Inspect the transmission case and housing for cracks, worn or damaged bores, damaged threads, or any other damage that could affect the operation of the transmission. Inspect the machined mating surfaces for burrs, nicks or damage.

Inspect the front face of the case for small nicks or burrs that could cause misalignment of the transmission with the flywheel housing. Remove all small nicks or burrs with a fine stone. Inspect the bell housing for cracks. Make sure the machined mating surfaces are free from burrs, nicks or other damage.

Check the condition of the shift covers, forks, shift rails and shafts. Inspect the ball bearings for cracks or deformations and replace any roller bearings that are broken, worn or rough.

Check mainshaft and countershaft thrust play by measuring bearing bore depths in transmission case using a suitable depth micrometer. Measure mainshaft rear bearing and countershaft front bearing heights and compare these measurements with

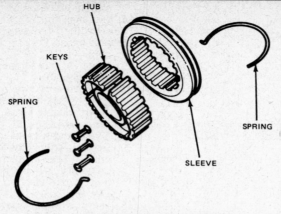

Fig. 10   Synchronizer mechanism

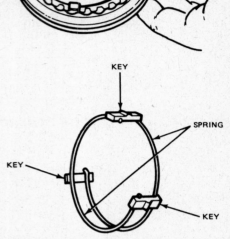

Fig. 11   Key spring installation

3RD & 4TH CLUTCH

1ST & 2ND CLUTCH

FRONT

Fig. 12   Clutch hub assembly direction

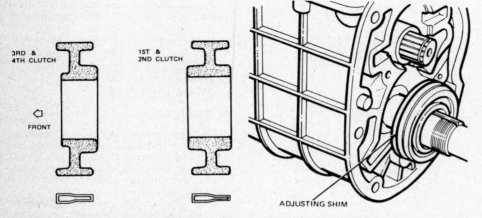

ADJUSTING SHIM

Fig. 13   Mainshaft thrust play adjusting shim

bearing bore depths. The difference between these measurements indicates the thickness of the required shim to be used during assembly. Both mainshaft and countershaft thrust play should be .0000–.0039 inch. Adjusting shims are available in .0039 and .0118 inch sizes.

Check main driveshaft bearing clearance by measuring bearing bore depth in clutch adapter using a suitable depth micrometer positioned on second step of plate. The difference between this measurement and the measured height of the bearing indicates bearing clearance which must be .0000–.0039 inch. Select a shim for use during reassembly which will bring clearance within specifications.

ASSEMBLE

1. Assemble 1st-2nd synchromesh mechanism by installing clutch hub to sleeve, placing 3 synchronizer keys into clutch hub keys slots and installing key springs to clutch hub, **Fig. 10.**

NOTE: When installing key springs, the open end of the spring should be kept 120°

apart, **Fig. 11.** This will keep the spring tension on each key uniform.

2. Assemble 3rd-4th synchromesh mechanisms in the same manner as step 1.
3. Place synchronizer ring on 3rd gear and slide 3rd gear to front of mainshaft with synchronizer ring toward front.
4. Slide 3rd-4th clutch hub and sleeve assembly to front of mainshaft, making sure that three synchronizer keys are engaged with notches in synchronizer ring.

NOTE: The direction of the 3rd-4th clutch hub and assembly should be as shown in **Fig. 12.**

5. Install snap ring in front of mainshaft then place synchronizer ring on 2nd gear and slide second gear to mainshaft with synchronizer ring toward rear of shaft.
6. Slide 1st-2nd clutch hub and sleeve assembly to mainshaft with oil grooves of clutch hub toward front of mainshaft. Make sure that 3 synchronizer keys in synchromesh mechanism engage with notches in second

synchronizer ring.
7. Insert 1st gear sleeve in mainshaft then press bushing in 1st gear using a suitable press adapter.
8. Place synchronizer ring on 1st gear and slide 1st gear onto mainshaft with ring facing front of shaft then rotate gear as necessary to engage 3 notches in ring with keys.
9. Install original thrust washer on mainshaft and position mainshaft and gears assembly in case.
10. Position caged bearing in front end of mainshaft.
11. Place synchronizer ring on 4th gear input shaft, and install input shaft to front end of mainshaft that 3 keys engage notches in ring.
12. Position 1st-2nd shift fork and 3rd-4th shift fork in groove of clutch hub and sleeve.
13. Using suitable press install inner race of countershaft rear bearing onto countershaft.
14. Position countershaft gear in case, making sure that gear engages each gear of mainshaft assembly.
15. Install correct shim in mainshaft rear bearing bore, **Fig. 13** as selected in the "Inspection procedure."
16. Position main drive gear bearing and mainshaft rear bearing into proper bearing bores. Be sure synchronizer and shifter forks have not been moved out of position.
17. Press both main drive gear and rear mainshaft bearings into case using suitable press until both bearings are seated properly, **Fig. 14.** Install main drive gear bearing snap ring.

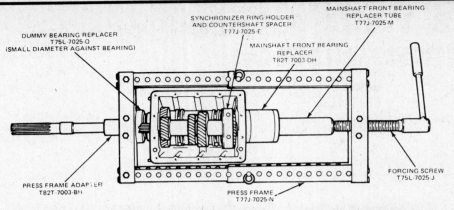

Fig. 14 Main drive gear & mainshaft rear bearing installation

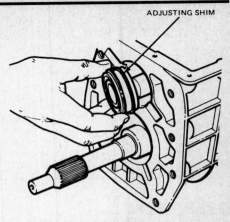

Fig. 15 Placing shim in countershaft front bearing bore

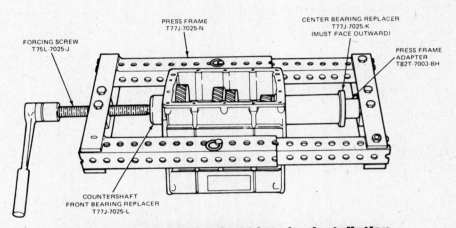

Fig. 16 Countershaft front bearing installation

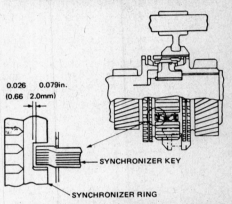

Fig. 17 Checking synchronizer key clearance

18. Place shim in countershaft front bearing bore, **Fig. 15.**
19. Position countershaft front and rear bearings in bores and install suitable tools, **Fig. 16.** Turn forcing screw until bearing is properly seated. Install snap ring to secure countershaft front bearing.
20. Install bearing retainer together with reverse idler gear shaft to transmission case. Tighten the four attaching bolts.
21. Slide counter reverse gear onto countershaft with chamfer to rear then install snap ring.
22. Install key on mainshaft.
23. Slide reverse gear and lockwasher onto mainshaft. Install new locknut and hand tighten.
24. Shift into 2nd gear and reverse gear to lock rotation of mainshaft. Torque locknut to 145–203 ft. lbs., **Fig. 3.**
25. Place 3rd-4th clutch sleeve in 3rd gear using tool No. T77J-7025-E.
26. Check clearance between synchronizer key and exposed edge of synchronizer ring with feeler gauge, **Fig. 17.** If measurement is greater than 0.079 inch, change thrust washer between mainshaft rear bearing and first gear. Check clearance again; if within specifications, bend tab of lockwasher.

NOTE: Thrust washers are available in the following thicknesses: .098, .138 and .118 inch.

27. From rear of case install 1st-2nd shift fork shaft assembly then install roll pin. Stake roll pin to secure shift fork to fork shaft.
28. Insert inter-lock pin into transmission.
29. From rear of case install 3rd-4th shift fork shaft assembly, then install roll pin and stake to secure shift fork to fork shaft. Place transmission in neutral.
30. Use the preceding two steps to install the reverse fork shaft assembly and reverse idler gear.
31. Position 3 detent balls and springs into case. Place copper washers on top 2 bolts and install 3 spring cap bolts, then install 2 blind covers and gaskets and torque the attaching bolts to 23–34 ft. lbs.
32. Install lock ball, speedometer drive gear, and snap ring onto mainshaft.
33. Apply a thin coat of liquid gasket No. E2AZ-19562-A or equivalent to extension housing and transmission case mating surfaces.
34. Position extension housing with gear-

shift control lever end laid down to left as far as it will go, tighten the four attaching bolts.

NOTE: The 2 lower attaching bolts must be coated with a suitable locking compound prior to installation.

35. If removed, insert speedometer driven gear assembly to extension housing and secure it with bolt.
36. Check to ensure gearshift control lever operates properly.
37. Install transmission case cover gasket and cover with drain plug to rear. Install and torque the 14 attaching bolts to 23–34 ft. lbs.
38. Position gasket and gearshift lever retainer to extension housing, and tighten the 4 attaching bolts.
39. Install shim (selected in "Inspection") on second step of clutch adapter plate, then coat adapter plate with liquid gasket No. E2AZ-19562-A or equivalent. Install adapter plate to transmission case and tighten the 4 attaching bolts and studs.
40. Remove filler plug and fill transmission with 3.0 pints of suitable lubricant. Reinstall plug and torque to 18–29 ft. lbs.

Warner T-18 & T-18A 4 Speed Manual Transmission

INDEX

DISASSEMBLE

1. Remove gear shift housing from transmission, **Figs. 1 and 2,** then the parking brake drum, with the transmission locked in two gears remove U-joint flange and oil seal.
2. Remove speedometer driven gear and bearing assembly.
3. Remove output shaft bearing retainer and speedometer drive gear and spacer, then remove output bearing retainer studs from case.
4. Remove output shaft bearing snap ring, then using suitable tool remove bearing.
5. Remove countershaft and idler shaft retainer and power take-off cover.
6. Remove input shaft bearing snap ring and bearing.
7. Remove oil baffle.
8. Remove roll pin from reverse gear shifter arm shaft, then remove shaft from shifter and lift shifter from case.
9. Remove output shaft and gear assembly from case.
10. Using a dummy shaft, drive countershaft out from front of transmission.

NOTE: Keep dummy shaft in contact with countershaft to avoid dropping rollers.

11. Remove input shaft and synchronizer blocking ring, then using a suitable puller remove idler shaft.
12. Remove idler gear and countershaft

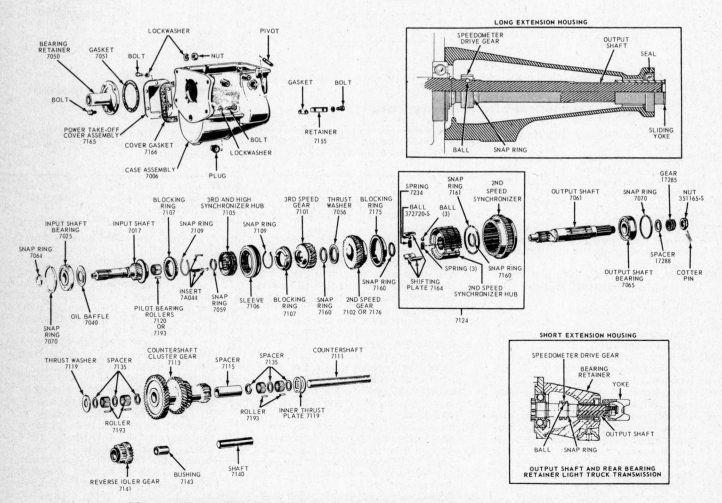

Fig. 1   Disassembled view of Warner T-18 & T-18A 4 speed transmission

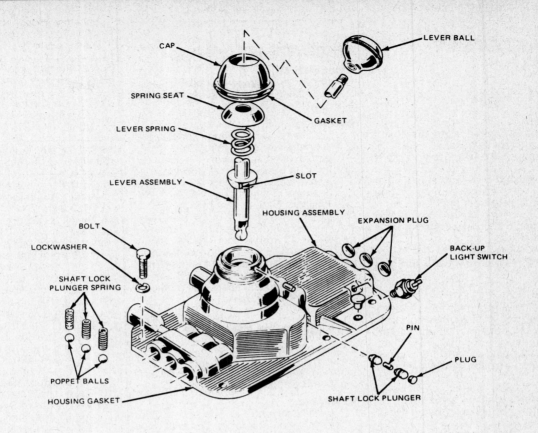

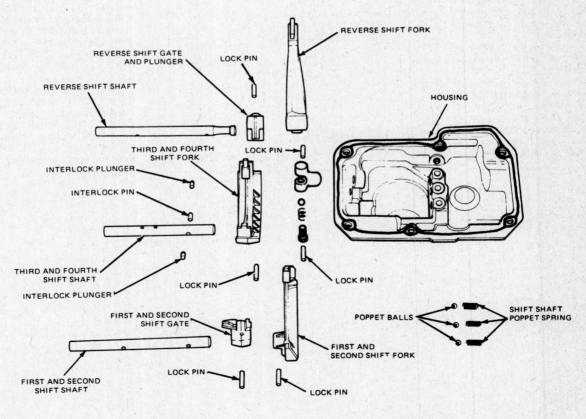

Fig. 2   Disassembled view of gear shift housing

gear, use care not to lose rollers.

SUB-ASSEMBLY SERVICE

OUTPUT SHAFT

Disassemble

1. Remove 3-4 speed synchronizer hub snap ring from output shaft. Slide synchronizer assembly and 3rd gear from shaft.
2. Press reverse gear from output shaft.
3. Remove 1st speed gear snap ring, then slide gear from shaft.
4. Remove 1st-2nd speed synchronizer snap ring, then slide synchronizer from shaft.
5. Remove snap ring from rear of 2nd speed gear, then remove gear and thrust washer.

Assemble

1. Install 2nd speed gear thrust washer and snap ring on shaft, then hold shaft in vertical position and install 2nd speed gear.
2. Install snap ring at rear of 2nd speed gear, then position blocking ring on gear.
3. Press 1st-2nd speed synchronizer onto shaft and install snap ring.
4. Install 1st speed gear and snap ring on shaft.
5. Press reverse gear onto shaft, then remove shaft from press and install 3rd speed gear and synchronizer blocking ring.
6. Install snap ring with openings staggered at both ends 3rd-4th speed synchronizer hub.
7. Place inserts into synchronizer sleeve and position sleeve on hub.
8. Slide synchronizer assembly onto output shaft and install snap ring at front of synchronizer assembly.

NOTE: Slots in blocking ring must be aligned with synchronizer inserts.

COUNTERSHAFT GEAR

Disassemble

Remove dummy shaft, pilot bearing rollers, bearing spacers and center spacer from countershaft gear.

Assemble

1. Position long bearing spacer into countershaft gear bore, then insert dummy shaft in spacer.
2. Position gear in vertical position, then install spacer and place 22 pilot roller bearings in gear bore.
3. Position bearing spacer on top of rollers, then install 2 more roller bearings and another bearing spacer.
4. Place a large washer against end of countershaft gear to prevent rollers from dropping out then turn assembly over.
5. Install rollers and spacers in other end of countershaft gear.

REVERSE IDLER GEAR

Disassemble

Remove snap ring from end of gear, then remove bearing rollers thrust washers, bearing spacer and bushing.

Assemble

1. Install snap ring in one end of idler gear, then set gear on end with snap ring on bottom.
2. Position thrust washer and bushing in gear bore, then install 37 bearing rollers between bushing and gear bore.
3. Install spacer on top of rollers then install 37 more bearing rollers.
4. Place remaining thrust washer on rollers and install snap ring.

ASSEMBLE

1. Lubricate all parts with transmission oil, then position countershaft gear assembly in case.
2. Position idler gear assembly in case, then install idler shaft and shifter arm.

NOTE: Position idler shaft so that slot at rear will engage retainer.

3. Drive countershaft in through rear of case forcing dummy shaft out through front.

NOTE: Position countershaft so that slot at rear will engage retainer.

4. Install thrust washers as necessary to obtain countershaft end play of .006 to .020 inch.
5. Install countershaft and idler shaft retainer.
6. Position oil baffle and input shaft pilot rollers so that baffle will not rub on bearing race, then position input shaft in case and install blocking ring.
7. Install output shaft assembly in case.
8. Using a suitable tool drive input shaft bearing onto shaft then install thickest select fit snap ring that will fit on bearing. Snap ring is available in thicknesses of, .117–.119, .120–122, .123–.125 and .127–.129 inch. Install input shaft snap ring.
9. Install output shaft bearing.
10. Install input shaft bearing retainer without gasket and tighten bolts only enough to bottom retainer on bearing snap ring. Measure distance between retainer and case and select a gasket that will seal and also prevent end play retainer and snap ring. Gaskets are available in thicknesses of, .008–.011, .0135–.0165, .018–.022 and .0225–.0275 inch. Install gasket and tighten bolts.
11. Position speedometer drive gear and spacer, then install output shaft bearing retainer and gasket.
12. Install brake drum then lubricate extension housing bushing, seal and U joint flange with ball joint grease.
13. Install U joint flange and tighten bolt.

Warner T-19B & T-19D 4 Speed Manual Transmission

INDEX

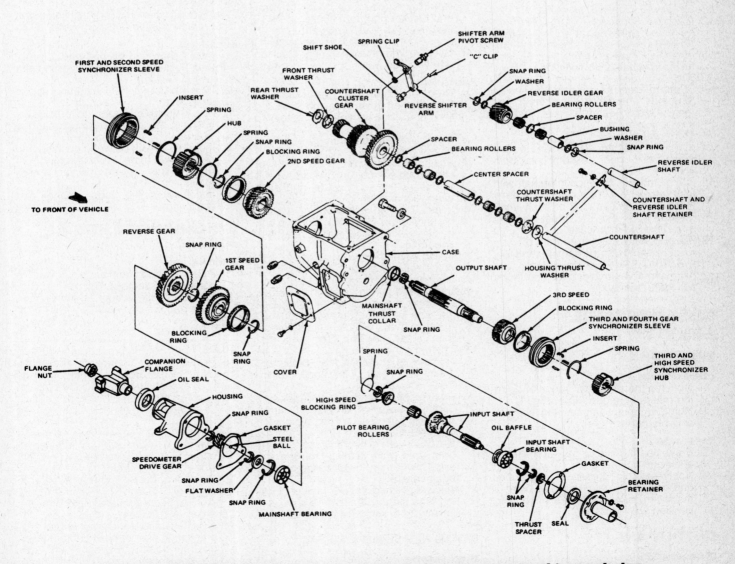

Fig. 1   Disassembled view of Warner T-19B & T-19D 4 speed manual transmission

DISASSEMBLE

1. Remove fill plug and drain lubricant from transmission.
2. Remove gearshift housing attaching bolts and the housing.
3. Lock transmission in any two gears and remove U-joint flange and output oil seal.
4. Remove speedometer driven gear and bearing assembly.
5. Remove output shaft rear bearing retainer or extension housing and gasket, **Fig. 1.**
6. Remove speedometer drive gear snap ring, then the drive gear and ball, if equipped.
7. Remove output shaft bearing snap rings from shaft and bearing, then the bearing spacer.
8. Remove output shaft bearing, **Fig. 2.**
9. Remove input shaft bearing retainer and gasket, then the bearing snap rings from shaft and bearing.
10. Remove input shaft bearing using suitable tool.
11. Remove input shaft oil baffle.
12. Remove spring clip or roll pin from reverse shifter arm pivot screw. Remove pivot screw, then pry shifter arm and shoe assembly out of case using a suitable screwdriver.
13. On 1983 models, remove input shaft, synchronizer blocking ring and needle bearings, then the output shaft and gear assemblies from case. Remove retainer attaching bolts and retainer from rear of case.
14. On 1984–85 models, remove output shaft and gear assemblies from case.
15. On all models, drive countershaft with cluster gear out of case, using dummy shaft No. T83T-7111-B or equivalent. Ensure front and rear thrust washers are removed from case.
16. Remove idler shaft from front of case using a suitable slide hammer and tool No. T50T-7140-C or equivalent.
17. Remove reverse idler gear and thrust washers from case.

SUB-ASSEMBLY SERVICE

INPUT SHAFT

Disassemble

1. Remove thrust spacer and pilot bearing rollers from gear bore, **Fig. 1.**
2. Remove input shaft bearing using a suitable puller.

Assemble

1. Press bearing and oil baffle onto input shaft and against gear.
2. Apply suitable grease to gear bore and position 17 pilot rollers in bore.
3. Install thrust spacer in bore and hold in position with grease.

OUTPUT SHAFT

Disassemble

1. Remove snap ring, 3rd–4th synchro-

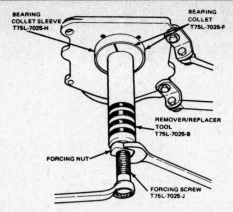

Fig. 2 Output shaft bearing removal

nizer assembly, blocking ring and 3rd gear from output shaft, **Fig. 1.**
2. Remove reverse gear from shaft using an arbor press or suitable puller.
3. Remove 1st gear snap ring, 1st gear and blocker ring from shaft.
4. Remove 1st–2nd synchronizer snap ring and the synchronizer assembly.
5. Remove 2nd gear snap ring, blocking ring and 2nd gear.

Assemble

1. Position output shaft vertically with front of shaft downward and slide 2nd gear onto shaft with gear cone toward rear.
2. Install snap ring on output shaft at rear of 2nd gear.
3. Position blocking ring in 1st–2nd synchronizer assembly next to side of hub with counterbore. Ensure ring slots align with insert.
4. Install 1st–2nd synchronizer assembly on shaft while holding blocking ring in place, and secure assembly with snap ring.
5. Install second blocking ring into synchronizer assembly, ensuring ring slots are aligned with inserts.
6. Install 1st gear and snap ring on shaft, ensuring coned portion of gear faces 1st–2nd synchronizer assembly.
7. Install output shaft in a suitable press, then press reverse gear and rear bearing cone onto shaft.
8. Remove output shaft from press and install 3rd gear with cone toward front.
9. Position blocking ring in 3rd–4th synchronizer assembly on side with larger diameter hub. Ensure ring slots align with inserts.
10. Slide 3rd–4th synchronizer assembly onto shaft while holding blocking ring in position, then install thrust bearing against race.
11. Apply suitable grease to face of blocking ring, then install ring on shaft and into 3rd–4th synchronizer assembly.

COUNTERSHAFT GEAR

Disassemble

1. Remove dummy shaft and bearing

rollers from countershaft gear, **Fig. 1.**
2. Remove bearing spacers and center spacer from gear.

Assemble

1. Slide long bearing spacer into countershaft gear bore, then insert well-greased dummy shaft into spacer.
2. Install one bearing spacer, then 22 pilot rollers in gear bore, while holding gear in a vertical position.
3. Install second spacer, then the remaining 22 rollers and spacer.
4. Apply suitable grease to face of large thrust washer, then hold washer against face of countershaft gear and invert assembly. Install rollers, spacers and thrust washer in opposite end of gear.

REVERSE IDLER GEAR

Disassemble

1. Remove snap ring, idler gear bearing rollers and thrust washer from reverse idler gear, **Fig. 1.**
2. Remove bearing spacer, bushing and remaining snap ring from gear.

Assemble

1. Install snap ring on one end of gear, then position gear vertically with snap ring at bottom.
2. Install thrust washer into gear on top of snap ring.
3. Apply suitable grease to outside of bushing, then install bushing on top of washer.
4. Install 37 rollers between bushing and gear bore. Install spacer on top of rollers, then insert remaining 37 rollers.
5. Install remaining thrust washer and snap ring.

SYNCHRONIZER HUB & SLEEVE

Disassemble

1. Remove spring from each side of synchronizer assembly, **Fig. 1.**
2. Remove 3 inserts from assembly, then slide hub out of sleeve.

Assemble

NOTE: The following procedure applies to the 1st–2nd synchronizer assembly. Assembly of the 3rd–4th synchronizer is identical except that the two grooves on the chamfered portion of the clutch sleeve can be assembled in either direction on the hub.

1. Install 1st–2nd clutch hub into sleeve, ensuring hub counterbore is on same side as sleeve chamfer.
2. Position 3 inserts into hub slots.
3. Hook end of spring under an insert, then position spring around hub and under each insert.
4. Invert assembly and hook end of second spring over opposite end of insert used for hooking first spring.
5. Position spring around hub and under each insert, in opposite direction of

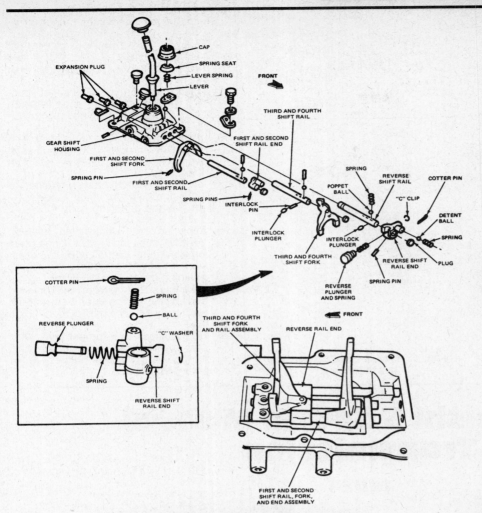

Fig. 3 Gearshift housing assembly

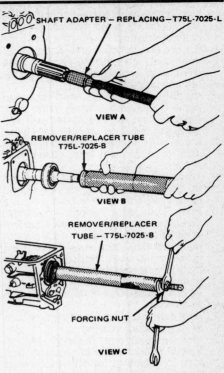

Fig. 4 Output shaft bearing installation

12. Install expansion plugs into 3 shift rail openings at each end of housing.
13. Install gearshift lever, spring, spring seat and lever housing cap.

ASSEMBLE

NOTE: Lubricate components with transmission fluid prior to assembly.

1. Insert countershaft, small end first, into bore at rear of case. Slide shaft in just enough to position rear countershaft steel thrust washer on shaft and against case. Hold washer in place with a small amount of grease.
2. Insert small end of shaft into front countershaft bore just enough to hold steel thrust washer in position, then install the thrust washer. Use reverse idler shaft as a temporary holding tool.

NOTE: Ensure notch in thrust washers are aligned with boss at each end of case.

3. Position countershaft cluster gear assembly in case. Use care to avoid losing any rollers.
4. Slide out reverse idler shaft and countershaft gear dummy shaft by installing countershaft from rear. Maintain contact between shaft ends to avoid losing rollers. Do not drive countershaft completely into case at this time.
5. Install reverse idler gear assembly and idler shaft into case, ensuring shift

---

first spring.

GEARSHIFT HOUSING

Disassemble

NOTE: All shafts must be in neutral position prior to disassembly.

1. Remove gearshift lever housing cap, then lift shift lever out of housing, **Fig. 3.**
2. Remove spring pins from shift forks and shift rail ends.
3. Remove expansion plugs from ends of housing.
4. Drive shift rails out of housing while covering holes in housing with one hand to prevent springs and balls from popping out.
5. Remove shift rail end and forks, then the two shaft interlock plungers and pin from housing.
6. Remove C-washer, cotter pin, spring and ball from reverse shift rail end.

Assemble

1. Slide notched end of 1st–2nd shift rail through rear bore of housing.
2. Install 1st–2nd shift fork onto shift rail,

ensuring 3 poppet notches face top of housing. Do not slide shaft into front end bore at this time.
3. Slide 1st–2nd shift rail end into rail, then install poppet spring and ball in hole in front end of cover.
4. Depress ball and spring and slide rail into bore over ball.
5. Drive a spring pin through hole in 1st–2nd shift rail end and into hole in rail.
6. Secure shift fork to rail with a spring pin, then slide rail to neutral position.
7. Install interlock plunger into housing, ensuring end of plunger is in side notch of 1st–2nd shift rail.
8. Install 3rd–4th shift rail in same manner as described for 1st–2nd rail in preceding steps.
9. Install reverse plunger and spring in reverse shift rail end and secure with a C-washer in plunger groove.
10. Install ball, spring and cotter pin into reverse shift rail end.
11. Install reverse shift rail, rail end, and poppet spring and ball into housing. Secure shift rail end to rail with a spring pin, then slide rail to neutral position.

fork groove is not toward front of case. Do not drive shaft completely into case at this time.

6. Ensure countershaft and reverse idler gear shaft are properly aligned, then drive shafts into position and install retainer and bolt.
7. Install output shaft assembly into case. Tilt assembly slightly to the right, then position reverse shifter arm and shoe assembly on reverse idler gear.
8. Install pivot screw through hole in left side of case and into shifter arm hole.
9. Install spring clip to secure shifter arm to pivot screw, then center output shaft assembly in case bore.
10. Slide input shaft through front bore, ensuring flats on shaft face upward. When past countershaft, rotate input shaft so flats face downward, then guide input shaft onto output shaft. Install input shaft oil baffle.
11. Install dummy bearing No. T75L-7025-Q or equivalent on transmission input shaft.
12. Install snap ring in groove in outer race of output shaft bearing.
13. Install output shaft bearing, **Fig. 4.** Install spacer washer against rear face of bearing, then position snap

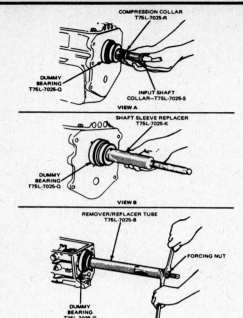

Fig. 5   Input shaft bearing installation

ring behind washer in output shaft. Remove dummy bearing from input shaft.

14. Insert input shaft bearing, **Fig. 5,** and secure with thickest snap rings that will fit on bearing.
15. Install input shaft bearing thrust spacer, retainer gasket and retainer. Torque retainer attaching bolts to 15–25 ft. lbs.
16. Install speedometer drive gear and spacer, if equipped, on output shaft over lock ball. Secure drive gear with snap ring.
17. Install output shaft bearing retainer, or extension housing, using a new gasket. Torque attaching bolts to 34–45 ft. lbs.
18. Apply suitable lubricant to retainer, bushing, seal and U-joint flange, then install U-joint flange. Lock transmission in any two gears and torque retaining nut to 75–115 ft. lbs.
19. Install gearshift housing, with housing and lever in 2nd gear, on transmission and torque attaching bolts to 25–35 ft. lbs.
20. Fill transmission to proper level, then add an additional ½ pint of lubricant through speedometer cable hole in extension housing.

Mitsubishi 5 Speed Manual Transmission

INDEX

DISASSEMBLE

1. Remove nuts attaching clutch housing to transmission, then the housing, **Fig. 1.**
2. Remove clutch slave cylinder from input shaft.
3. Remove backup lamp switch and shift indicator switch from transmission.
4. Drain fluid from transmission, if necessary.
5. Remove pan attaching bolts from transmission. Remove gasket from transmission to pan gasket surface.
6. Remove bolts attaching cover to transfer case adapter.
7. Remove detent spring and ball from adapter.
8. Remove three shift gate roll pin access plugs.
9. Using a suitable punch and hammer, drive roll pins from the shift gates.
10. Working from the right side of the adapter, remove bolt spring and neutral return plunger. Note that the plunger has a slot in the center for the detent ball.
11. Working from the left side of the adapt-

er, remove bolt, spring and neutral return plunger.
12. Remove gate selector from shift gates. Move the lever to the rear as far as it will go. This will allow clearance to remove the adapter from case.
13. Remove bolts retaining transfer case adapter to the transmission case assembly.

NOTE: There are three different bolt sizes (35mm, 55mm and 110 mm) used to retain the case to the adapter assembly. Mark bolt holes accordingly for installation.

14. Remove adapter from case assembly. Ensure shift gates do not bind in the adapter during removal. Rotate gates on the rails as required. Remove and discard gasket.
15. Identify each shift rail and gate, then remove gates from the rails.
16. Working from inside the case, drive out the roll pins retaining the 1–2 and 3–4 shift forks to the rails. Drive out the overdrive-reverse shift fork roll pin.

NOTE: The roll pin in the switch actuator

does not need to be removed for transmission disassembly.

17. Remove set screw from top of the case, then the poppet spring and steel ball. Remove two bolts on the side of the case. Remove two poppet springs and two steel balls.
18. Remove overdrive-reverse shift rail and the 3–4 shift rail from case. Remove the overdrive-reverse shift fork.

NOTE: When the two shift rails are removed, the interlock pins can be driven from case assembly.

19. Unstake locknuts on the mainshaft.
20. Double engage the transmission in two gears to lock the transmission.
21. Remove and discard countershaft locknut.
22. Remove mainshaft locknut.
23. Pull rear bearing from mainshaft using tools, T77J-7025-B, T84T-7025-B, T77J-7025-H and T77J-7025-J or equivalents. Remove and discard bearing.

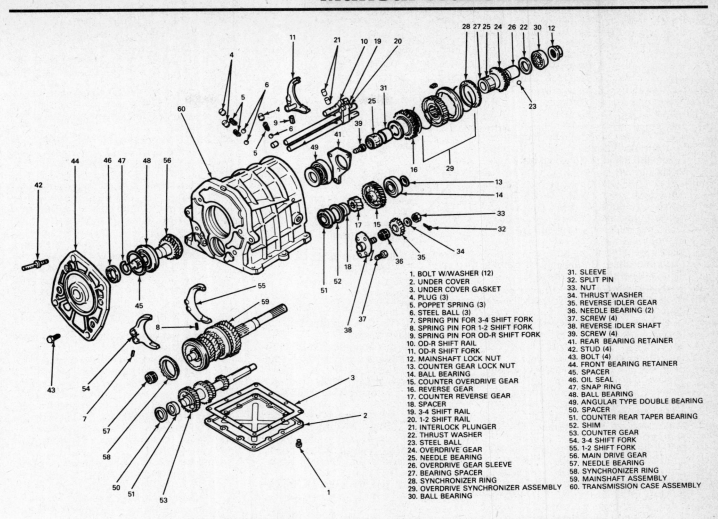

Fig. 1   Disassembled view of Mitsubishi 5 speed manual transmission

1. BOLT W/WASHER (12)
2. UNDER COVER
3. UNDER COVER GASKET
4. PLUG (3)
5. POPPET SPRING (3)
6. STEEL BALL (3)
7. SPRING PIN FOR 3-4 SHIFT FORK
8. SPRING PIN FOR 1-2 SHIFT FORK
9. SPRING PIN FOR OD-R SHIFT FORK
10. OD-R SHIFT RAIL
11. OD-R SHIFT FORK
12. MAINSHAFT LOCK NUT
13. COUNTER GEAR LOCK NUT
14. BALL BEARING
15. COUNTER OVERDRIVE GEAR
16. REVERSE GEAR
17. COUNTER REVERSE GEAR
18. SPACER
19. 3-4 SHIFT RAIL
20. 1-2 SHIFT RAIL
21. INTERLOCK PLUNGER
22. THRUST WASHER
23. STEEL BALL
24. OVERDRIVE GEAR
25. NEEDLE BEARING
26. OVERDRIVE GEAR SLEEVE
27. BEARING SPACER
28. SYNCHRONIZER RING
29. OVERDRIVE SYNCHRONIZER ASSEMBLY
30. BALL BEARING

31. SLEEVE
32. SPLIT PIN
33. NUT
34. THRUST WASHER
35. REVERSE IDLER GEAR
36. NEEDLE BEARING (2)
37. SCREW (4)
38. REVERSE IDLER SHAFT
39. SCREW (4)
41. REAR BEARING RETAINER
42. STUD (4)
43. BOLT (4)
44. FRONT BEARING RETAINER
45. SPACER
46. OIL SEAL
47. SNAP RING
48. BALL BEARING
49. ANGULAR TYPE DOUBLE BEARING
50. SPACER
51. COUNTER REAR TAPER BEARING
52. SHIM
53. COUNTER GEAR
54. 3-4 SHIFT FORK
55. 1-2 SHIFT FORK
56. MAIN DRIVE GEAR
57. NEEDLE BEARING
58. SYNCHRONIZER RING
59. MAINSHAFT ASSEMBLY
60. TRANSMISSION CASE ASSEMBLY

24. Remove spacer and lock ball from mainshaft.
25. Remove counter-overdrive gear and ball bearing from countershaft. While removing the gear, remove 1–2 shift rail from the case.
26. Remove 1–2 and 3–4 shift forks from the case.
27. Remove overdrive gear, needle bearing, spacer and synchronizer ring from the mainshaft.
28. Remove overdrive synchronizer sleeve from the synchronizer hub on the mainshaft.
29. Using suitable tools, pull overdrive synchronizer hub and overdrive gear bearing sleeve from mainshaft.
30. Slide reverse gear and needle bearing assembly from mainshaft.
31. Slide counter-reverse gear and spacer from the countershaft.
32. Remove cotter pin and nut from reverse idler gear shaft. Remove thrust washer, reverse idler gear and two sets of needle bearings from the shaft.
33. Remove Allen head bolts attaching

mainshaft rear bearing retainer to the case assembly. Remove retainer.
34. Remove Allen head bolts attaching reverse idler gearshaft assembly to the case assembly.
35. Pull reverse idler gearshaft assembly from case.
36. Remove four studs attaching input shaft front bearing retainer to the case assembly. Remove bolts attaching retainer to case.
37. Remove input shaft front bearing retainer from case. Remove selective shim from inside input shaft from bearing retainer.
38. Remove small selective snap ring retaining input shaft to the bearing.
39. Remove large snap ring retaining input shaft bearing to the case.
40. Remove bearing from input shaft. Remove and discard bearing.
41. Rotate input shaft so flats on shaft face the countershaft, then remove input shaft.

NOTE: The mainshaft may have to be pulled to the rear of the case. Remove the

small caged needle bearing from the inside of the input gear.

42. Remove snap ring from mainshaft outer bearing race.
43. Remove outer mainshaft bearing race, ball bearing and bearing sleeve from case.

NOTE: The inner race of the front bearing will remain on the mainshaft.

44. Remove countershaft front spacer and bearing race.
45. Remove countershaft from case.

NOTE: The mainshaft assembly may have to be moved slightly to the side to allow clearance for countershaft removal.

46. Remove mainshaft assembly from case assembly.

ASSEMBLE

1. Install mainshaft assembly into case.

2. Install 1–2 and 3–4 shift forks into their synchronizer sleeves. The roll pin bosses on the forks must face each other.
3. Install countershaft into the case.

NOTE: It may be necessary to move the mainshaft to one side in order for the countershaft to be easily inserted.

4. Install correct size selective snap ring in front of the input shaft bearing. Select the thickest snap ring that will fit in the groove.
5. Install small caged needle bearing inside input gear. Install synchronizer ring on to input shaft. Check clearance between ring and gear. If clearance is less than .009 inch, replace ring and/or input shaft.
6. Install synchronizer ring and input shaft into case. Rotate input shaft so flats on shaft face countershaft.

NOTE: It may be necessary to gently tap the input shaft into position.

7. Install a new snap ring on to outer bearing race. The longer portion of the race must be installed in the case.
8. Slide outer ball bearing on to mainshaft. Using a suitable tool, press bearing into position on mainshaft. When pressed into position, all gears and shafts must rotate freely.
9. If removed, drive a new seal into input shaft front bearing retainer.
10. Install large snap ring retaining input shaft bearing to the case.
11. Check input shaft front bearing retainer to bearing clearance as follows:
    a. With retainer selective shim removed, use a suitable depth micrometer to measure the distance between the top machined surface to the spacer surface. Record the reading.
    b. Bottom the input shaft bearing so the snap ring is flush against the case.
    c. Using a depth micrometer, measure distance from the top of the outer front bearing race to the machined surface of the case.
    d. Subtract the distance of the bearing to case from the retainer dimensions. This will give the required maximum selective shim size to obtain a .000–.004 inch clearance.
    e. Measure, then install the appropriate size selective shim in the front bearing retainer.
12. Install countershaft front outer bearing race and non-selective spacer. Install the countershaft rear outer bearing race.
13. Install a new gasket between the front bearing retainer and case. Position the retainer on to the case (with selective shim installed). Install the four bolts and four studs. Torque to 22–30 ft. lbs.
14. Check and adjust countershaft endplay as follows:

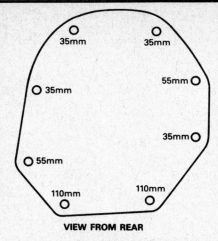

Fig. 2   Adapter bolt hole pattern

a. Place transmission so rear of mainshaft and countershaft face upward. Install countershaft rear selective spacer.
b. Force the countershaft downward so it bottoms against the front bearing retainer.
c. Place a straight edge across the rear countershaft selective spacer in the case.
d. Try to turn the spacer. If the spacer turns lightly, replace the spacer with the next larger size. Install a spacer so the clearance between the spacer and straight edge is .000–.002 inch.
15. Install rear bearing retainer into case. Torque Allen head bolts to 11–16 ft. lbs.

NOTE: Ensure spacer installed does not fall out of position when installing the rear bearing retainer.

16. Position reverse idler gear shaft assembly on to case. Install the Allen head bolts. Install reverse idler gear shaft remover tool, T85T-7140-A on to the shaft and drive assembly into position. Torque Allen head bolts to 11–16 ft. lbs.
17. Install two caged needle bearings, reverse idler gear and thrust washer on to idler shaft. The boss on the idler gear should face away from the transmission. Install locknut and torque to 15–42 ft. lbs. If required, turn nut to the next hole and install cotter pin.
18. Install spacers and counter-reverse gear on to mainshaft.
19. Using a suitable tool, press reverse gear sleeve on to mainshaft.
20. Install caged needle bearing and reverse gear on to mainshaft.
21. Assemble overdrive synchronizer hub and sleeve as follows:
    a. Install hub into sleeve. The recessed boss on the sleeve must face the front of the transmission. The large boss on the hub must face the front of the transmission.
    b. When installing hub into the sleeve and three keys, ensure that the single tooth between the two spacers will touch the key. Install springs so open ends do not face each other.
22. Install overdrive synchronizer on to mainshaft. The recessed boss of the sleeve must face the front of the transmission.
23. Press sleeve of overdrive gear on to mainshaft.
24. Install ring on overdrive synchronizer.
25. Slide small spacer, caged needle bearing and overdrive gear on to mainshaft. Check clearance between overdrive gear and synchronizer ring. If clearance is less than .009 inch, replace ring and/or overdrive gear.
26. Install counter-overdrive gear and ball bearing on to countershaft along with the 1–2 shift rail. Seat bearing into position. Ensure the rail engages the forks.
27. Install lock ball and spacer on to mainshaft.
28. Place rear bearing over mainshaft and press bearing into position.
29. Install new locknuts on to countershaft and mainshaft assemblies. Double engage transmission into two gears, then torque mainshaft locknut to 180–195 ft. lbs. Torque countershaft locknut to 115–137 ft. lbs. Disengage transmission.
30. Stake locknuts on mainshaft and countershaft.
31. Install and interlock plunger into bore between 1–2 and 3–4 shift rails. Position 1–2 shift rail so that flats for the poppet ball, spring and interlock plunger are in correct position. Ensure roll pin holes for the shift forks are aligned properly.
32. Install overdrive-reverse shift fork on to synchronizer sleeve. Slide 3–4 shift rail through the overdrive-reverse shift fork into the case and into the 3–4 shift fork inside the case. Position the shift rail flats to accept the poppet balls and interlock plunger. Insert the interlock plunger into the bore between the 3–4 shift rail and overdrive-reverse shift rail. Ensure roll pin holes in the fork are aligned.
33. Insert the overdrive-reverse shift rail so it engages the forks in the case. Ensure roll pin holes in the fork are aligned.
34. Insert poppet ball and spring into 1–2 (upper) bore in case. The small end of the spring should be installed toward the ball. Install the set screw and tighten until screw head is .24 inch below the top of the bore.
35. Insert a poppet spring and poppet ball into 3–4 and overdrive-reverse bore (side two bores in the case). The small end of the spring faces toward the ball. Install and tighten the bolts.
36. Install roll pins into shift forks. If removed, install switch actuator and roll pin.
37. Install shift gates on to appropriate

shift rails. Move the 1–2 gate to the rear of the rail.

38. Position a new gasket between the transmission case and transfer case adapter. Ensure selector arm is out of the gates and the change shifter is at the rear of the adapter. Position adapter on to case. Ensure shift gates clear the adapter assembly. Ensure shift rails and rear bearings align with adapter bores.
39. Install the three sizes of bolts (35mm, 55mm and 110mm) into their appropriate holes in the adapter, **Fig. 2.** Torque bolts to 11–16 ft. lbs.
40. Install neutral return plungers, springs

and bolts into adapter assembly. The longer plunger with the slot for the detent ball is installed on the right side of the adapter.

41. Position shift gates so roll pin holes in the gates and rails align. Install roll pins through the access holes. Install access hole plugs.
42. Position pan and new gasket on to case. Install bolts and torque to 11–16 ft. lbs. Do not over torque the bolts. Install drain plug and torque to 25–32 ft. lbs.
43. Insert plunger detent ball and spring into hole above the neutral return plunger in the adapter case.

44. Ensure the stopper bracket assembly on the cover for the transfer case adapter moves smoothly. Position a new gasket on to the adapter and install housing cover. Torque attaching bolts to 11–16 ft. lbs.
45. Install backup lamp switch and shift indicator light switch into adapter.
46. Fill transmission assembly with suitable lubricant, then install and torque fill plug to 22–25 ft. lbs.
47. Position clutch slave cylinder on to input shaft. Position clutch housing on to transmission case and tighten nuts.

Toyo Kogyo 5 Speed Overdrive Manual Transmission (Models W/Diesel Engine)

INDEX

DISASSEMBLE

1. Drain transmission lubricant, then remove fork and release bearing from transmission case, **Fig. 1.**
2. Remove 6 front cover attaching bolts, then the front cover, shim and gasket.
3. Remove front cover oil seal, **Fig. 2,** then the input shaft snap ring.
4. Remove gearshift lever, if installed. Remove 4 gearshift lever retainer attaching bolts, then the retainer and gasket from extension housing.
5. Remove outer snap ring from input shaft bearing.
6. Remove input shaft bearing, **Figs. 3 and 4.**
7. Remove 8 extension housing-to-transmission case attaching bolts, then slide housing off output shaft with

control lever end laid down and to the left as far as possible.

8. Remove control lever end attaching bolt, then the control lever end and rod from extension housing.
9. Remove speedometer driven gear assembly from extension housing.
10. Remove back-up lamp and neutral sensing switches from extension housing.
11. Remove grommet from end of output shaft, then the speedometer drive gear snap ring, speedometer drive gear and lock ball.
12. Remove countershaft, with front bearing, from transmission case, **Fig. 5.**
13. Remove and discard 1st-2nd shift fork roll pin and shift rail snap ring.
14. Remove upper cap bolt, spring and detent ball, **Fig. 6,** then the 1st-2nd shift rail and fork. Note position of shift

fork, rail and detent slots for assembly reference.

15. Remove and discard 3rd-4th shift fork roll pin and shift rail snap ring.
16. Remove middle cap bolt, spring and detent ball, **Fig. 6,** then the 3rd-4th shift fork, rail and interlock pin. Note position of shift rail and detent slots for assembly reference.
17. Remove 5th-reverse shift rail snap ring and washer, then the lower cap bolt and outer spring and detent ball, **Fig. 6.**
18. Remove 5th-reverse shift fork roll pin, then the inner detent ball and spring from lower bore, **Fig. 6.**
19. Pry intermediate housing away from bearing housing, then remove gear and bearing assembly from the intermediate housing.
20. Secure gear train and bearing housing assembly in a suitable soft-jawed vise, then remove 5th-reverse shift rail and

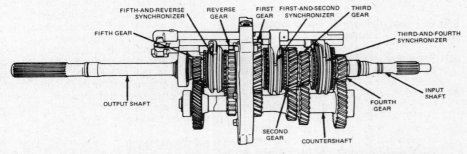

Fig. 1 Gears & shaft components. Toyo Kogyo 5 speed overdrive manual transmission

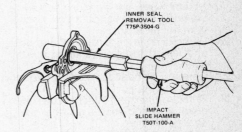

Fig. 2 Front cover oil seal removal

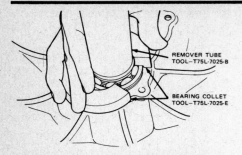

Fig. 3   Input shaft bearing removal tool installation

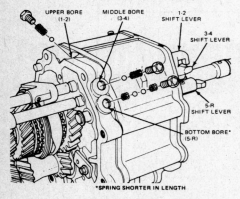

Fig. 6   Shift lock ball & spring removal

interlock pin. Note position of shift fork, rail and detent slots for assembly reference.
21. Remove and discard output shaft rear bearing, **Fig. 7.**

NOTE: It may be necessary to hold shaft protectors in place with putty when removing bearing.

22. Remove countershaft rear bearing snap ring, then remove and discard the bearing, **Fig. 8.**
23. Remove retaining ring, thrust washer and lock ball from output shaft.
24. Remove counter 5th gear, sleeve and reverse gear from countershaft.
25. Remove 5th gear and 5th-reverse synchronizer ring from output shaft.
26. Bend down tab on mainshaft lock-washer, then lock transmission into reverse and any forward gear and remove and discard output shaft (mainshaft) locknut, **Fig. 9.**
27. Remove 5th-reverse synchronizer assembly, reverse gear, caged needle bearing, sleeve and thrust washer from output shaft.
28. Remove snap ring, reverse idler gear and keyed thrust washer from idler shaft.
29. Remove 5 bearing cover attaching bolts and the cover.
30. Remove idler shaft attaching bolt, then drive plate and shaft assembly out of bearing housing.
31. Tap output shaft and countershaft out of bearing housing using a suitable soft-faced hammer.

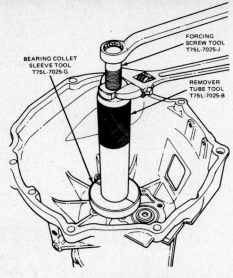

Fig. 4   Input shaft bearing removal

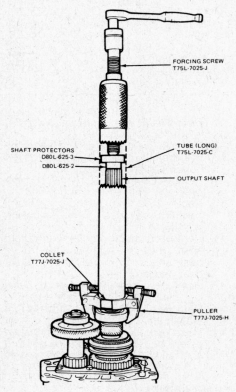

Fig. 7   Output shaft rear bearing removal

32. Separate input shaft, caged needle bearing and synchronizer from output shaft.
33. Remove rear countershaft bearing from bearing housing using tool No. T77J-7025-B or equivalent.
34. Remove rear output shaft bearing from bearing housing using tools T77F-4222-A and T77J-7025-B or equivalents.
35. Remove thrust washer, 1st gear,

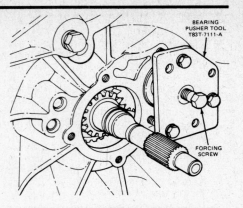

Fig. 5   Countershaft & front bearing removal

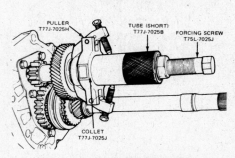

Fig. 8   Countershaft rear bearing removal

sleeve and synchronizer ring from rear of output shaft, **Fig. 10.**
36. Remove 3rd-4th hub, sleeve, synchronizer ring and 3rd gear from front of output shaft using a suitable press and tool No. T71P-4621-B or equivalent.
37. Remove 1st-2nd hub, sleeve, synchronizer ring and 2nd gear from rear of output shaft using a suitable press and tool No. T71P-4621-B or equivalent.
38. Press front bearing out of countershaft, **Fig. 11.**

CLEANING & INSPECTION
CLEANING

Wash all parts except the ball bearings and seal, in suitable solvent. Brush all foreign matter from the parts. Be careful not to damage any parts. Do not clean, wash or soak transmission seals in cleaning solvent. Dry all parts with compressed air.

Rotate bearings in a cleaning solvent until all lubricant is removed. Hold bearing assembly to prevent it from rotating and dry with compressed air. Lubricate bearings with approved transmission lubricant and wrap in a clean, lint-free cloth or paper until ready for use.

INSPECTION

Inspect the transmission case and housing for cracks, worn or damaged bores,

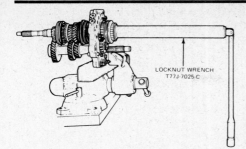

Fig. 9 Mainshaft locknut removal & installation

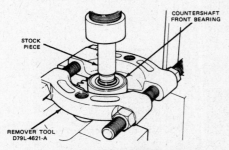

Fig. 11 Countershaft front bearing removal

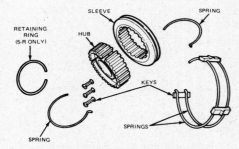

Fig. 12 Clutch assembly

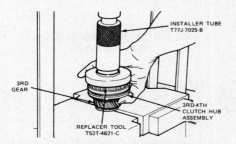

Fig. 13 3rd-4th clutch hub assembly installation

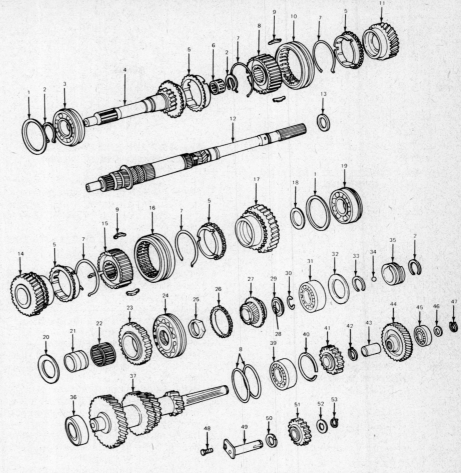

1. ADJUSTING SHIM
2. SNAP RING
3. INPUT BEARING
4. INPUT SHAFT AND FOURTH GEAR
5. SYNCHRONIZER RING
6. CAGED NEEDLE BEARING
7. SYNCHRONIZER KEY SPRING
8. THIRD-AND-FOURTH HUB
9. SYNCHRONIZER KEY
10. HUB SLEEVE
11. THIRD GEAR
12. OUTPUT SHAFT
13. GROMMET
14. SECOND GEAR
15. FIRST-AND-SECOND HUB
16. HUB SLEEVE
17. FIRST GEAR
18. THRUST WASHER
19. BALL BEARING (IN BEARING HOUSING)
20. THRUST WASHER
21. SLEEVE
22. CAGED NEEDLE BEARING
23. REVERSE GEAR
24. FIFTH-AND-REVERSE SYNCHRONIZER
25. LOCKNUT
26. SYNCHRONIZER
27. FIFTH GEAR
28. LOCK BALL
29. THRUST WASHER
30. RETAINING RING
31. OUTPUT BEARING
32. THRUST WASHER
33. RETAINING RING
34. LOCK BALL
35. SPEEDOMETER DRIVE GEAR
36. COUNTERSHAFT FRONT BEARING
37. COUNTERSHAFT
38. ADJUSTING SHIMS
39. BALL BEARING (IN BEARING HOUSING)
40. RETAINING RING
41. COUNTERSHAFT REVERSE GEAR
42. SNAP RING
43. SLEEVE
44. COUNTERSHAFT FIFTH GEAR
45. COUNTERSHAFT REAR BEARING
46. THRUST WASHER
47. SNAP RING
48. BOLT
49. IDLER SHAFT AND RETAINER
50. KEYED THRUST WASHER
51. REVERSE IDLER GEAR
52. THRUST WASHER
53. SNAP RING

Fig. 10 Exploded view of shafts & gears

damaged threads, or any other damage that could affect the operation of the transmission. Inspect machined mating surfaces for burrs, nicks or damage.

Inspect front face of case for small nicks or burrs that could cause misalignment of transmission with flywheel housing. Remove all small nicks or burrs with a fine stone. Inspect bell housing for cracks. Ensure machined mating surfaces are free from burrs, nicks or other damage.

Check condition of shift covers, forks, shift rails and shafts. Inspect ball bearings for cracks or deformations and replace any roller bearings that are broken, worn or rough.

ASSEMBLE

1. Assemble 1st-2nd, 3rd-4th and 5th-reverse clutch hub assemblies by installing keys in hub, positioning sleeve over hub and keys, and placing springs onto hub, **Fig. 12.**

NOTE: Open end of springs must be inserted into hub holes in direction shown in **Fig. 12** to maintain equal spring tension on each key.

2. Install retaining ring in 5th-reverse assembly.
3. Install 3rd gear and synchronizer ring onto front of mainshaft.
4. Press 3rd-4th clutch hub assembly onto mainshaft, **Fig. 13,** in direction shown in **Fig. 14.**
5. Install snap ring on mainshaft.
6. Install 2nd gear and synchronizer ring onto rear of mainshaft.
7. Press 1st-2nd clutch hub assembly onto mainshaft, **Fig. 15,** in direction shown in **Fig. 14.**
8. Install synchronizer ring, 1st gear with sleeve, and thrust washer onto mainshaft.
9. Install input shaft and bearing onto mainshaft.
10. Measure countershaft rear bearing and mainshaft bearing clearances as follows:
   a. Measure bearing bore depth "A", **Figs. 16 and 17,** using a suitable depth micrometer.

F—233

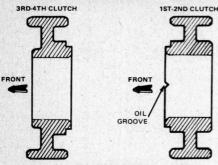

Fig. 14 Clutch hub assembly position

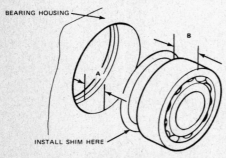

Fig. 17 Measuring mainshaft bearing clearance

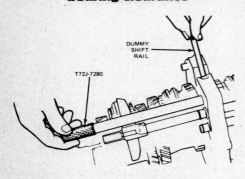

Fig. 19 Shift fork rod interlock pin installation

b. Measure bearing height "B", **Figs. 16 and 17.**

c. The difference between measurements "A" and "B" should be less than .0039 inch.

d. Select shims needed to bring bearing clearances within specifications. Shims are available in thicknesses of .0039 and .0118 inch.

11. Place selected shim on countershaft rear bearing and press into bearing housing using tool No. T77J-7025-B or equivalent.

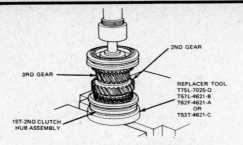

Fig. 15 1st-2nd clutch hub assembly installation

12. Place selected shim on mainshaft bearing and press into bearing housing using tool No. T77J-7025-K or equivalent.

13. Press front bearing onto countershaft using tool No. T71P-7025-A or equivalent.

14. Position countershaft and mainshaft assemblies on bearing housing with gears meshed.

NOTE: Ensure mainshaft thrust washer is installed at rear of 1st gear.

15. Hold mainshaft in position and press countershaft assembly into bearing housing, **Fig. 18.**

16. Install bearing cover and reverse idler gear shaft onto bearing housing. Ensure cover is fully seated in idler gear shaft groove.

17. Install thrust washer, sleeve, caged needle bearing and reverse gear onto output shaft (mainshaft).

18. Install reverse gear onto countershaft with offset toward bearing housing.

19. Install keyed thrust washer with tab in bearing housing groove.

20. Install reverse idler gear with offset toward bearing housing.

21. Ensure reverse gears are properly meshed, then install spacer and snap ring on idler shaft.

22. Install 5th-reverse clutch hub assembly on output shaft.

23. Lock transmission in reverse and any forward gear, then install a new output shaft locknut and torque to 94–152 ft. lbs., **Fig. 9.** Bend up tab on locknut.

24. Install 5th-reverse synchronizer ring and gear on mainshaft, ensuring grooves in synchronizer rings are aligned with keys in hub.

25. Install sleeves and counter 5th gear on countershaft.

26. Install lock ball in output shaft.

27. Install thrust washer and retaining ring on output shaft. Ensure slot in washer is aligned with lock ball in output shaft.

28. Install output shaft bearing using tool No. T75L-7025-Q or equivalent, then the thrust washer and retaining ring.

29. Install countershaft rear bearing using tool No. T75L-7025-Q or equivalent, then the thrust washer and retaining ring.

30. Place all synchronizers in neutral position, then install inner spring and

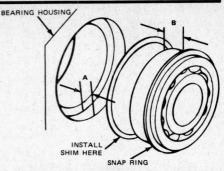

Fig. 16 Measuring countershaft rear bearing clearance

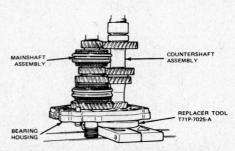

Fig. 18 Countershaft assembly installation

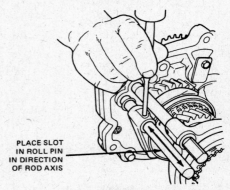

Fig. 20 Shift fork roll pin installation

detent ball in lower bore.

31. Install 5th-reverse shift rail using tool No. T75L-7025-Q or equivalent, then slide interlock pin through upper bore, **Fig. 19.**

32. Install 3rd-4th shift rail, then the interlock pin and 1st-2nd shift rail, **Fig. 19.**

33. Assemble 1st-2nd and 3rd-4th shift forks to sleeves, then align roll pin holes of each shift fork and install new roll pins as shown in **Fig. 20.**

34. Install detent balls, springs and spring cap screws.

35. Install snap rings on 1st-2nd and 3rd-4th shift rails, and the snap ring and washer on 5th-reverse shift rail.

36. Apply suitable sealer to transmission case and bearing housing mating surfaces, and position case on housing.

37. Position shift lever gates on shift rails and install new roll pins.

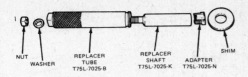

Fig. 21   Input shaft front bearing installation tools

38. Install lock ball in output shaft and position speedometer drive gear over ball.
39. Install snap ring and grommet on end of output shaft.
40. Apply suitable sealer to extension housing and intermediate housing mating surfaces, then install extension housing with control lever laid down and as far to the left as possible.

Torque attaching bolts to 6–9 ft. lbs.

NOTE: It may be necessary to remove plugs from transmission case shift rod bores to align shift rods. When reinstalling plugs, a suitable silicone must be used.

41. Position outer snap ring on input shaft front bearing, then install bearing using tools shown in **Fig. 21.** Tighten nut on forcing screw until bearing outer snap ring is fully seated.
42. Install input shaft snap ring.
43. Measure clearance between bearing outer race and front cover. This clearance must be less than .004 inch and can be adjusted by adding a shim of .006 or .012 inch as needed, **Fig. 22.**
44. Install new oil seal in front cover using tool No. T71P-7050-A or equivalent.
45. Install shim in front cover recess.
46. Apply transmission fluid to oil seal lip inside front cover, then install cover and tighten attaching bolts.
47. Connect control lever end to control

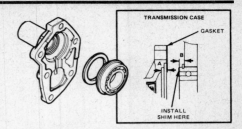

Fig. 22   Front cover clearance adjustment

lever and torque attaching bolt to 20–25 ft. lbs.
48. Install back-up lamp and neutral sensing switches to extension housing and torque to 20–25 ft. lbs.
49. Install gearshift lever retainer and gasket and torque attaching bolts to 20–27 ft. lbs.
50. Install gearshift lever if previously removed.
51. Install release bearing and fork.

Toyo Kogyo 5 Speed Overdrive Manual Transmission (Models W/Gasoline Engine)

INDEX

DISASSEMBLE

1. Remove bell housing-to-transmission case attaching nuts, then the bell housing and gasket.
2. Remove drain plug and drain lubricant from transmission. If necessary, clean metal filings from drain plug and reinstall.
3. Place transmission in neutral, then remove speedometer sleeve and driven gear assembly from extension housing.
4. Remove 3 bolts and 4 nuts securing extension housing to transmission case. Lift control lever to the left and slide rearward, then remove extension housing. Use care to avoid damaging oil seal.
5. Remove control lever and rod through opening in front end of extension housing.
6. Remove back-up lamp switch from extension housing, if necessary.
7. Remove and discard anti-spill seal from mainshaft.

NOTE: A replacement anti-spill seal is not necessary for assembly.

8. Remove speedometer drive gear snap ring, then the drive gear and lock ball.
9. Evenly loosen transmission case cover attaching bolts, then remove the

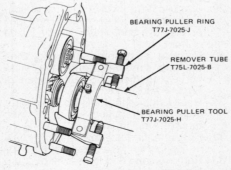

Fig. 1   Mainshaft rear bearing removal

cover and gasket.
10. Mark shift rails and forks for assembly reference, then drive roll pins out of shift rod ends and remove the rod ends.
11. Separate transmission case and bearing housing by prying with a screwdriver, then slide bearing housing off mainshaft.
12. Remove mainshaft rear bearing snap ring and washer, then the rear bearing, **Fig. 1.**
13. Remove snap ring from rear end of countershaft, then the countershaft bearing, **Fig. 2.**
14. Remove counter 5th gear and spacer from rear of countershaft.
15. Remove center housing complete with reverse idler gear and 2 spacers from transmission case. Remove cap screw and idler gear shaft from center housing.
16. Remove 3 spring cap bolts, detent springs and balls, **Fig. 3.**
17. Remove 4 blind cover-to-transmission case attaching bolts, then the blind covers and gaskets.

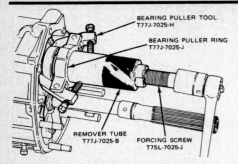

Fig. 2 Countershaft rear bearing removal

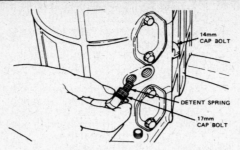

Fig. 3 Detent spring & ball removal

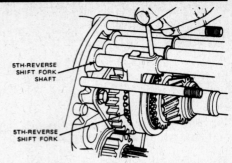

Fig. 4 5th-reverse shift fork removal

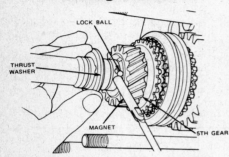

Fig. 5 5th gear removal

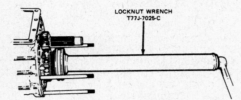

Fig. 6 Removing or installing locknut

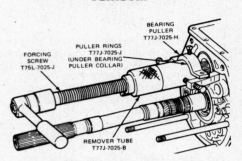

Fig. 7 Countershaft center bearing removal

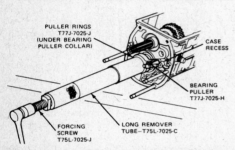

Fig. 8 Mainshaft center bearing removal

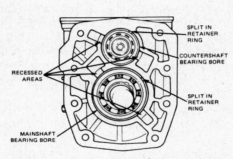

Fig. 9 Positioning retainer ring for removal

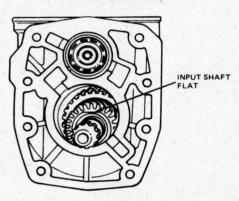

Fig. 10 Positioning input shaft flats

18. Remove 5th-reverse shift fork roll pin, then slide shift fork shaft out of transmission case, **Fig. 4.**
19. Shift transmission into 4th gear, then drive out 3rd-4th shift fork roll pin and slide shift fork shaft out of transmission case.
20. Remove 1st-2nd shift fork roll pin, then slide shift fork shaft out of transmission case.
21. Remove both interlock pins.
22. Remove 5th gear snap ring, then the thrust washer, lock ball, 5th gear and synchronizer ring from rear of mainshaft, **Fig. 5.**
23. Install tool No. T77J-7025-E between 4th speed synchronizer ring and synchromesh gear on mainshaft and shift transmission into 2nd gear.
24. Fold back end of lockwasher, then remove mainshaft locknut, **Fig. 6.**
25. Remove reverse gear and clutch hub assembly from mainshaft and the counter reverse gear from countershaft.
26. Remove mainshaft center bearing cover attaching bolts and the cover.

27. Remove countershaft center bearing, **Fig. 7,** then the mainshaft center bearing, **Fig. 8.**

NOTE: It may be necessary to rotate the retainer ring to align the spit in ring midway between recessed areas, **Fig. 9.** This will protect the retainer ring during bearing removal.

28. Remove mainshaft rear bearing shim and spacer.
29. Remove 4 front cover-to-case attaching bolts and studs, then the front cover. Remove and retain shim on inside of front cover.
30. Remove input shaft snap ring, then the input shaft bearing in same manner as countershaft center bearing, **Figs. 7 and 9.**
31. Rotate both shift forks so main gear train falls to bottom of case, then remove the shift forks.
32. Rotate input shaft so one of two flats on input shaft faces upward, **Fig. 10.**
33. Remove snap ring from front of countershaft.
34. Install tools shown in **Fig. 11** and press countershaft until it contacts

synchronizer ring holder and countershaft spacer.
35. Remove countershaft front bearing in same manner as countershaft center bearing, **Figs. 7 and 9.**
36. Remove shim from behind countershaft front bearing.
37. Remove countershaft, then the input shaft from transmission case.
38. Remove synchronizer ring and bearing from mainshaft.
39. Remove mainshaft and gear assembly from transmission case.
40. Remove countershaft center bearing inner race, **Fig. 12.**
41. Remove 1st gear, 1st-2nd synchronizer ring and snap ring from mainshaft.
42. Install tool No. T71P-4621-B between 2nd and 3rd gears and press mainshaft out of 3rd gear and 3rd-4th clutch hub sleeve.

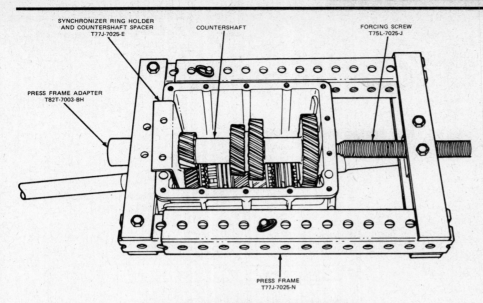

Fig. 11 Countershaft removal

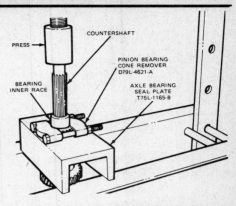

Fig. 12 Countershaft bearing inner race removal

43. Press 1st-2nd clutch hub and sleeve assembly and 1st gear sleeve from mainshaft, **Fig. 13**.

CLEANING & INSPECTION

CLEANING

Wash all parts, except the ball bearings and seal, in suitable solvent. Brush all foreign matter from the parts. Be careful not to damage any parts. Do not clean, wash or soak transmission seals in cleaning solvent. Dry all parts with compressed air.

Rotate the bearings in a cleaning solvent until all lubricant is removed. Hold the bearing assembly to prevent it from rotating and dry it with compressed air. Lubricate the bearings with approved transmission lubricant and wrap them in a clean, lint-free cloth or paper, until ready for use.

INSPECTION

Inspect the transmission case and housing for cracks, worn or damaged bores, damaged threads, or any other damage that could affect the operation of the transmission. Inspect the machined mating surfaces for burrs, nicks or damage.

Inspect the front face of the case for small nicks or burrs that could cause misalignment of the transmission with the flywheel housing. Remove all small nicks or burrs with a fine stone. Inspect the bell housing for cracks. Make sure the machined mating surfaces are free from burrs, nicks or other damage.

Check the condition of the shift covers, forks, shift rails and shafts. Inspect the ball bearings for cracks or deformations and replace any roller bearings that are broken, worn or rough.

Check mainshaft and countershaft thrust play by measuring bearing bore depths in transmission case using a suitable depth micrometer. Measure mainshaft rear bearing and countershaft front bearing heights and compare these measurements with bearing bore depths. The difference between these measurements indicates

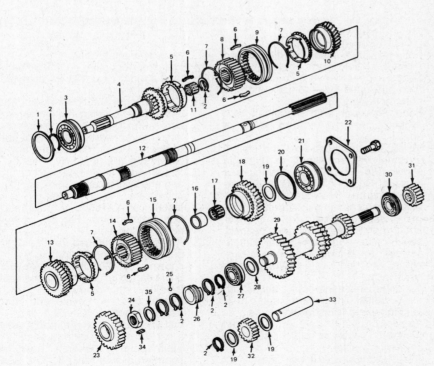

1. SHIM
2. SNAP RING
3. MAIN DRIVESHAFT BEARING
4. MAIN DRIVESHAFT GEAR
5. SYNCHRONIZER RING
6. SYNCHRONIZER KEY
7. SYNCHRONIZER KEY SPRING
8. 3RD-AND-4TH CLUTCH HUB
9. CLUTCH SLEEVE
10. 3RD GEAR
11. CAGED BEARING
12. MAINSHAFT

13. 2ND GEAR
14. 1ST-AND-2ND CLUTCH HUB
15. CLUTCH SLEEVE
16. 1ST GEAR SLEEVE
17. BEARING
18. 1ST GEAR
19. THRUST WASHER
20. SHIM
21. MAINSHAFT FRONT BEARING
22. BEARING COVER
23. REVERSE GEAR
24. MAINSHAFT LOCK NUT

25. LOCK BALL
26. SPEEDOMETER DRIVE GEAR
27. COUNTERSHAFT FRONT BEARING
28. SHIM
29. COUNTERSHAFT
30. COUNTERSHAFT REAR BEARING
31. COUNTER REVERSE GEAR
32. REVERSE IDLER GEAR
33. IDLER GEAR SHAFT
34. KEY
35. LOCKWASHER

Fig. 13 Exploded view of shafts & gears

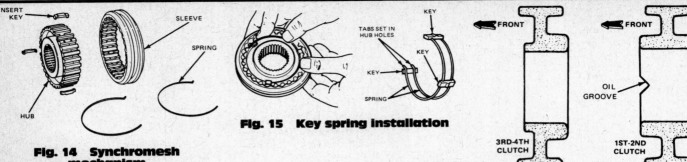

Fig. 14 Synchromesh mechanism

Fig. 15 Key spring installation

Fig. 16 Clutch hub assembly direction

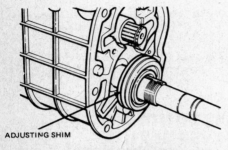

Fig. 17 Mainshaft thrust play adjusting shim

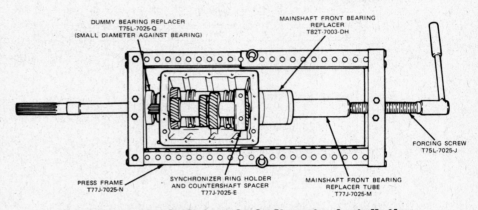

Fig. 18 Input shaft & mainshaft center installation

the thickness of the required shim to be used during assembly. Both mainshaft and countershaft thrust play should be .0000–.0039 inch. Adjusting shims are available in .0039 and .0118 inch sizes.

Check main driveshaft bearing clearance by measuring bearing bore depth in clutch adapter using a suitable depth micrometer positioned on second step of plate. The difference between this measurement and the measured height of the bearing indicates bearing clearance which must be .0000–.0039 inch. Select a shim for use during reassembly which will bring clearance within specifications.

ASSEMBLE

1. Assemble 1st-2nd and 3rd-4th synchromesh mechanisms by installing clutch hub into sleeve, positioning 3 synchronizer keys into clutch hub key slots, and placing springs onto hub, **Fig. 14.**

NOTE: Open end of springs must be inserted into hub holes in direction shown in **Fig. 15** to maintain an equal spring tension on each key.

2. Install synchronizer ring on 2nd gear, then slide 2nd gear on mainshaft with synchronizer ring toward rear of shaft.
3. Install 1st-2nd clutch hub and sleeve assembly on mainshaft with oil grooves on clutch hub toward front of mainshaft, **Fig. 16.** Ensure 3 synchronizer keys engage notches in second synchronizer ring.
4. Press 2nd gear and 1st-2nd clutch

hub and sleeve assembly into position using a suitable press adapter.
5. Slide 1st gear sleeve onto mainshaft, then assemble synchronizer ring and roller bearing to 3rd gear.
6. Slide 3rd gear onto mainshaft with synchronizer ring toward front of shaft.
7. Install 3rd-4th clutch hub and sleeve assembly on mainshaft in direction shown, **Fig. 16,** using a suitable press and tool No. T77J-7025-B or equivalent. Ensure 3 synchronizer keys engage notches in synchronizer ring.
8. Install snap ring onto front of mainshaft, then slide on 1st gear bearing, synchronizer ring and 1st gear. Rotate 1st gear to engage 3 notches in synchronizer ring with synchronizer keys.
9. Slide thrust washer onto mainshaft, then install mainshaft and gear assembly into transmission case.
10. Position 1st-2nd and 3rd-4th shift forks in groove of clutch hub and sleeve assembly.
11. Slide synchronizer ring onto input shaft, then install input shaft to front end of mainshaft. Ensure 3 synchronizer keys in 3rd-4th synchromesh mechanism engage notches in synchronizer ring.
12. Install countershaft rear bearing inner race onto countershaft using a suitable press.
13. Install countershaft gear in case, ensuring countershaft gear engages

each mainshaft gear.
14. Install correct shim on mainshaft center bearing, **Fig. 17,** as selected in "Inspection."
15. Position input shaft bearing and mainshaft center bearing in their respective bores, ensuring synchronizer and shift forks have not been moved out of position. Press both bearings into place, **Fig. 18,** until fully seated.
16. Install input shaft bearing snap ring and ensure free operation of both synchronizers.
17. Install correct shim in countershaft front bearing bore, **Fig. 19,** as selected in "Inspection."
18. Position countershaft front and center bearings in bores and install tools shown, **Fig. 20.** Turn forcing screw until bearing is fully seated, then install front bearing snap ring.
19. Install bearing cover and torque attaching bolts to 41–59 ft. lbs.
20. Install reverse idler gear and shaft with a spacer on each side of shaft.
21. Slide counter reverse gear, with chamfered side forward, and spacer onto countershaft.
22. Install thrust washer, reverse gear, caged roller bearings and clutch hub assembly onto mainshaft.
23. Install and hand tighten a new mainshaft locknut.
24. Shift transmission into 2nd and reverse gears to lock mainshaft, then torque locknut to 115–172 ft. lbs., **Fig. 6,** and stake locknut into mainshaft

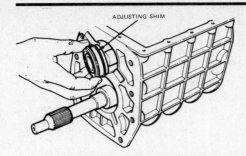

Fig. 19 Placing shim in countershaft front bearing bore

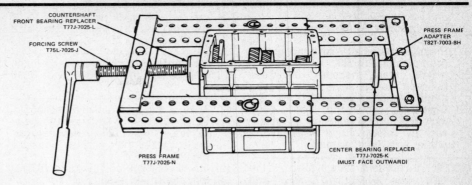

Fig. 20 Countershaft front bearing installation

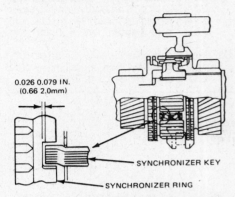

Fig. 21 Checking synchronizer key clearance

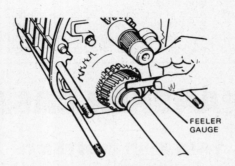

Fig. 22 Checking 5th gear clearance

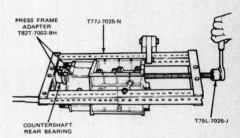

Fig. 23 Countershaft rear bearing installation

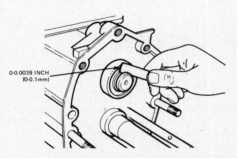

Fig. 24 Checking countershaft rear bearing clearance

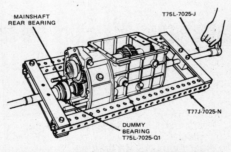

Fig. 25 Mainshaft rear bearing installation

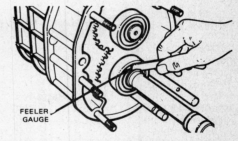

Fig. 26 Checking mainshaft rear bearing clearance

keyway.

25. Install 3rd-4th clutch sleeve in 3rd gear using synchronizer ring holder and spacer (tool No. T77J-7025-C or equivalent).
26. If new synchronizers have been installed, measure clearance between synchronizer key and exposed edge of synchronizer ring using a suitable feeler gauge, **Fig. 21**. If clearance is greater than .079 inch, change thrust washer between mainshaft center bearing and 1st gear, then recheck. If clearance is now within specifications, bend tab of lockwasher.

NOTE: Thrust washers are available in the following thicknesses: .098, .118 and .138 inch.

27. Install synchronizer ring on 5th gear,

then slide 5th gear onto mainshaft with synchronizer ring toward front of shaft. Rotate 5th gear to engage 3 notches in synchronizer ring with keys in reverse clutch and hub.

28. Install thrust washer and lock ball onto rear of 5th gear and secure thrust washer with snap ring.
29. Measure clearance between 5th gear thrust washer and snap ring, **Fig. 22.** Clearance should be .0039–.0118 inch and can be adjusted as necessary by selecting and installing the proper size thrust washer.

NOTE: Thrust washers are available in the following thicknesses: .2362, .2441, .2520, .2559, .2598, .2638, .2677, .2756 and .2835 inch.

30. Slide 1st-2nd shift fork shaft into trans-

mission case, then connect shift fork to shaft using a new roll pin and install interlock pin.
31. Shift synchronizer hub into 5th gear, then position 5th-reverse shift fork on clutch hub. Slide shift fork shaft into case and connect fork to shaft using a new roll pin.
32. Install 2 blind covers and gaskets, and torque attaching bolts to 23–34 ft. lbs.
33. Install 3 detent balls, springs and cap bolts into transmission case.
34. Apply a thin coat of liquid gasket No. E2AZ-19562-A or equivalent to center housing and transmission case mating surfaces, then position center housing on case.
35. Align reverse idler gear shaft boss with center housing attaching bolt boss, then install idler shaft capscrew

and torque to 41–59 ft. lbs.

36. Install counter 5th gear onto countershaft.
37. Press countershaft rear bearing onto countershaft, **Fig. 23**.
38. Install, then measure clearance between countershaft rear bearing thrust washer and snap ring, **Fig. 24**. Clearance should be .0000–.0059 inch and can be adjusted as necessary by selecting and installing the proper size thrust washer.

NOTE: Thrust washers are available in the following sizes: .0748, .0787, .0827 and .0866 inch.

39. Remove filler plugs, then press mainshaft rear bearing into place, **Fig. 25**.
40. Install, then measure clearance between mainshaft rear bearing thrust washer and snap ring, **Fig. 26**. Clearance should be .0000–.0039 inch and

can be adjusted as necessary by selecting and installing the proper size thrust washer.

NOTE: Thrust washers are available in the following sizes: .0787, .0846 and .0906 inch.

41. Apply a thin coat of liquid gasket No. E2AZ-19562-A or equivalent to bearing housing and center housing mating surfaces, then position housings together.
42. Install shift fork shaft ends onto shift fork shafts and secure with roll pins.
43. Install lock ball, speedometer drive gear and snap ring onto mainshaft.
44. Install control lever and rod in extension housing.
45. Apply a thin coat of liquid gasket No. E2AZ-19562-A or equivalent to bearing housing and extension housing mating surfaces. Position housings

together with gearshift control lever end laid down to the left as far as possible. Install attaching bolts and nuts and torque to 60–80 ft. lbs.
46. Install speedometer driven gear assembly into extension housing and secure with attaching bolt.
47. Ensure proper operation of gearshift control lever, then install transmission case cover gasket, with drain plug at rear. Install 14 cover attaching bolts and torque to 23–34 ft. lbs.
48. Install correct shim, as selected in the "Inspection", on second step of front cover.
49. Apply a thin coat of liquid gasket No. E2AZ-19562-A or equivalent to front cover mating surface, then install front cover and tighten the 4 bolts and studs.
50. Fill transmission with 3 pints of suitable lubricant, then install filler plug and torque to 18–29 ft. lbs.

TRANSFER CASES

TABLE OF CONTENTS

Borg Warner Transfer Cases

INDEX

MODEL 1345

DISASSEMBLY

SERVICE BULLETIN On some 1980–82 Ford vehicles, a transfer case vibration may be noticed in two or four wheel drive between 35–55 mph.

To determine if the vibration is caused by the transfer case, raise and support vehicle, then disconnect both driveshafts from transfer case flanges. Run transfer case up to speed to confirm the transfer case is the cause. If the vibration remains the same, the transfer case may have an imbalanced lock plate. If a substantial difference in vibration is noted, the transfer case most likely is not at fault.

The transfer case vibration is serviced by replacing the one long-legged locking plate with two new short-legged locking

plates.

1. Drain fluid by removing filler plug from case.
2. Remove both output shaft yoke nuts, then the front and rear output yoke, **Fig. 1**.
3. Remove 4-wheel drive indicator switch.
4. Remove case bolts and separate cover from case using a screwdriver.
5. Remove magnetic chip collector from bottom of case half.
6. Remove shift collar hub from the rear output shaft, then compress shift fork spring and remove the upper and lower spring retainers from shaft, **Fig. 2**.
7. Lift out 4-wheel drive lockup fork and shift collar as a complete assembly.
8. Remove snap ring and thrust washer from front output shaft, then lift the chain, drive and driven sprockets ver-

tically from the output shafts.
9. Remove front output shaft from case.
10. Remove oil pump attaching screws, then the oil pump rear cover, pick-up tube, filter and pump body, 2 pump pins, pump spring and oil pump front cover from rear output shaft.
11. Remove snap ring securing the bearing retainer inside case, then lift the rear output shaft while tapping on the bearing retainer with a soft mallet. Remove the rear output shaft and bearing retainer from case.

NOTE: When the retainer is removed, 2 dowel pins will fall into the case.

12. Remove rear output shaft from bearing retainer and then, if necessary, press needle bearing assembly from bearing retainer.

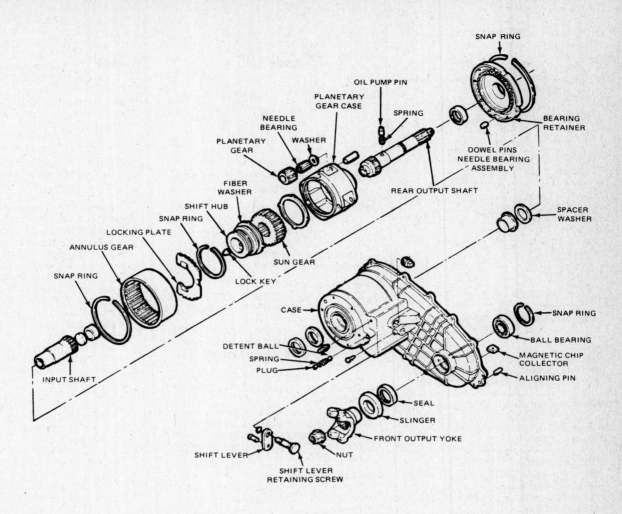

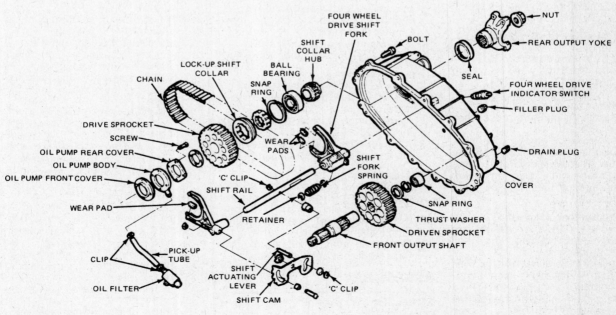

Fig. 1 Borg Warner 1345 transfer case exploded view

Fig. 2   Removal of spring retainers

13. Remove C-clip securing shift cam to shift actuating lever, then the shift lever retaining screw and shift lever.

NOTE: When removing the shift lever, the shift cam will disengage from shift lever shaft and may release the detent ball and spring from case.

14. Remove planetary gear set, shift rail, shift cam, input shaft and shift forks as an assembly, **Fig. 3.**
15. Remove spacer washer from bottom of case.
16. Drive out plug from the detent spring bore using a drift.

SUB-ASSEMBLY SERVICE

Planetary Gear Set Disassembly

1. Slide input shaft rearward from gear set, **Fig. 4.**
2. Remove snap ring, shift hub and planetary gear case from annulus gear.
3. Release locking plate from hub, then remove shift hub snap ring and T-shaped lock key. Remove shift hub.
4. Remove outer fiber washer, sun gear and inner fiber washer. Rotate inner fiber washer slightly upon removal to allow positioning tabs to clear planetary gears.

Planetary Gear Set Assembly

1. Place a new inner fiber washer into planetary gear housing and then install sun gear.
2. Coat a new outer fiber washer with vaseline or equivalent, then install washer on hub.
3. Place hub in planetary gear cage and install T-shaped lock key and snap ring.
4. Install locking plate on shift hub with dished side facing toward planetary

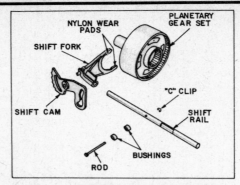

Fig. 3   Components of shifter mechanism

gear set.
5. Lower planetary assembly into annulus gear. Be sure the tabs on locking plate engage annulus gear teeth, then install the snap ring.

Cover, Disassembly

1. Remove snap ring retaining rear output shaft ball bearing assembly in the cover.
2. Turn cover over and remove the rear output shaft seal using seal remover 1175-AG and slide hammer T50T-100-A.
3. Remove speedometer drive gear.
4. Press rear output shaft ball bearing from cover.
5. Remove speedometer gear adapter.
6. Remove front output shaft inner needle bearing from cover using seal remover OTC 33864 and slide hammer T50T-100-A.

Cover, Assembly

1. Press a new needle bearing into cover using tool T80T-7127-B.
2. Press a new ball bearing assembly into cover, then install snap ring.
3. Turn the cover and install the speedometer drive gear.
4. Install a new output shaft seal.
5. Install speedometer gear adapter.

Case, Disassembly

1. Remove snap ring retaining front output shaft ball bearing assembly in case.
2. Remove output shaft seal and both input shaft seals.
3. Press out the front output shaft bearing and input shaft bushing from case.

Case, Assembly

1. Press a new input shaft bushing into case, making sure that the lug is in downward position.
2. Install a new output shaft ball bearing, then install snap ring.
3. Press both input shaft seals into case, then the front output shaft seal.

ASSEMBLY

NOTE: Before assembly, lubricate all parts with ATF meeting Ford specification ESP-M2C138-CJ or Dexron II, Series D or equivalent.

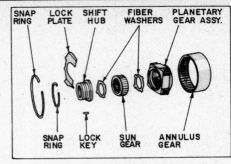

Fig. 4   Planetary gear set exploded view

1. Assemble planetary gear set, shift rail, shift cam, input shaft and shift fork together as a unit, making sure that the boss on the shift cam is installed toward the case. Install spacer washer on the input shaft.
2. Place rear output shaft into planetary gear set, making sure shift cam engages shift fork actuating pin.
3. Position case on its side and install rear output shaft and planetary gear set.
4. Install shift rail in case, then the outer roller bushing into guide in case.
5. Remove rear output shaft and position the shift fork in neutral position.
6. Place shift control lever shaft through the cam and install the clip ring. Be sure that the shift control lever is facing downward and is parallel to the front face of case.
7. Check shift fork and planetary gear engagement. The unit should operate freely.
8. Press new needle bearing into bearing retainer using tool T80T-7127-C if the bearing was removed during disassembly.
9. Insert output shaft through bearing retainer.
10. Insert rear output shaft pilot into input shaft rear bushing. Align dowel holes and lower the bearing into position.
11. Install dowel pins, then the snap ring retaining the bearing retainer in the case.
12. Insert detent ball and spring into detent bore in case. Coat seal plug with RTV sealer or equivalent and drive plug into case until the lip of the plug is $1/32$ inch below the surface of the case. Peen the case over the plug in 2 places.
13. Install oil pump front cover over the output shaft with the flanged side facing downward. The word "Top" must be facing the top of the transfer case.
14. Install oil pump spring and 2 pump pins with flat side facing outward in the output shaft. Push in both pins to install the oil pump body, pickup tube and filter.
15. Place oil pump rear cover on output shaft with the flanged side facing outward. The word "Top" must be positioned toward the top of case. Apply

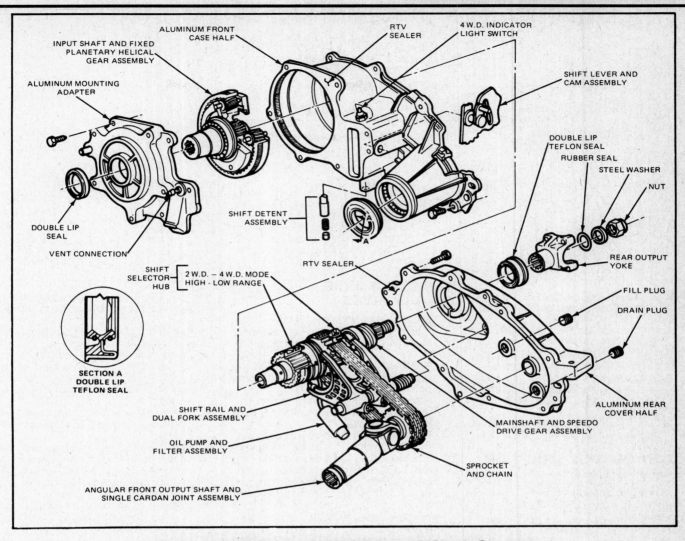

Fig. 5 Exploded view of Borg-Warner 1350 transfer case

Loctite or equivalent to oil pump bolts, then install in pump cover and torque to 3–3.3 ft. lbs.

16. Install thrust washer onto rear output shaft next to oil pump.
17. Place drive sprocket onto front output shaft, then install snap ring and thrust washer.
18. Install chain onto the drive and driven sprockets, then lower the unit into position in case.
19. Engage 4-wheel drive shift fork on shift collar, then slide shift fork over shift shaft and shift collar over rear output shaft. Be sure that the nylon wear pads are installed on shift fork tips and the tapered portion of the shift collar is facing rearward.
20. Push 4-wheel drive shift spring downward and install upper spring retainer. Then push spring upward and install lower retainer.
21. Install shift collar hub on rear output shaft.
22. Apply RTV sealer or equivalent to case mounting surface, then lower the cover over rear output shaft while aligning shift rail with the blind hole in cover. Also be sure the front output shaft is fully seated in its support bearing. Install and torque bolts to 40–45 ft. lbs. Allow 1 hour curing time for gasket material prior to operating vehicle.
23. Install 4-wheel drive indicator switch and torque to 8–12 ft. lbs.
24. Press oil slinger onto the front yoke, then install front and rear output shaft yokes. Coat the nuts with Loctite or equivalent and torque to 100–130 ft. lbs.
25. Refill transfer case with 6 pts. of ATF. Torque level and drain plugs to 6–14 ft. lbs. Torque fill plug to 15–25 ft. lbs.
26. Install transfer case into vehicle, then start engine and check transfer case for correct operation. Stop engine and check fluid level. Fluid should drip from level hole. If fluid flows out in a stream, the pump may not be operating properly.

MODEL 1350
SHIFT LEVER, REPLACE

NOTE: Removal of the shift ball is necessary only if the shift ball, boot, or lever is being replaced. If not, remove the ball, boot and lever as an assembly.

1. Remove plastic insert from shift ball, then warm ball to approximately 140–180° F and knock ball off lever with a hammer and a block of wood.
2. Remove rubber boot and pan cover, then disconnect vent hose from control lever.
3. Unscrew shift lever from control lever, then remove shifter to extension housing retaining bolts and the shoulder bolt. Remove control lever and bushings.
4. Reverse procedure to install. Note the following:
   a. Torque shifter to extension housing retaining bolt to 31–42 ft. lbs. and shoulder bolt to 70–90 ft. lbs. The shifter retaining bolt must be

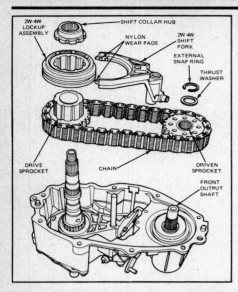

Fig. 6 Shift collar hub & 2W-4W lock-up & shift fork assemblies

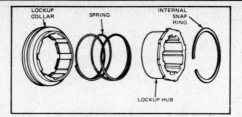

Fig. 7 2W-4W lock-up assembly

a. Apply lubricant C1AZ-19590-B, or equivalent, to oil seal.
b. Install oil seal using tools T83T-7065-B and T80T-4000-W, or equivalent.
c. Torque output shaft yoke retaining nut to 100–130 ft. lbs. and rear driveshaft retaining bolts to 12–15 ft. lbs.

TRANSFER CASE, DISASSEMBLE

1. Drain lubricant from transfer case, then remove four-wheel indicator switch and the breather vent plug, **Fig. 5.**
2. Remove rear output yoke, then the front case to rear cover attaching bolts.
3. Separate front case from rear cover, then remove all gasket material from mating surfaces.
4. If speedometer drive gear or ball bearing assembly is to be replaced, remove output shaft oil seal. The seal can be removed from inside of rear cover with a brass drift and hammer, or from outside by bending and pulling the oil seal lip. Discard oil seal, then remove speedometer drive gear assembly.
5. Remove rear output shaft ball bearing snap ring, then the bearing using tools T83T-7025-B and T50T-100-A, or equivalent.
6. Remove front output shaft caged needle bearing from rear cover using tools D80L-100-S and T50T-100-A, or equivalent.
7. Remove 2W-4W shift fork spring from rear cover.
8. Remove shift collar hub from output shaft, then the 2W-4W lock-up assembly and shift fork as an assembly, **Fig. 6.**
9. Remove shift fork from lock-up assembly, **Fig. 6.** If necessary, remove external clip, then roller bushing assembly from shift fork.
10. Remove internal snap ring from lock-up collar, then remove lock-up hub and spring from collar, **Fig. 7.**
11. Remove snap ring and thrust washer retaining drive sprocket to front output shaft, then remove chain, driven sprocket and drive sprocket as an assembly, **Fig. 6.** Remove magnet from front case, **Fig. 8.**
12. Remove output shaft and oil pump as an assembly.
13. Remove shift rail, high-low range shift

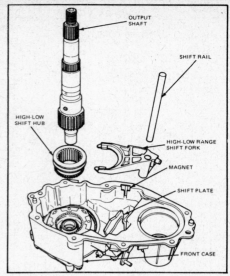

Fig. 8 High-low shift assembly, output shaft & collector magnet

fork and high-low shift hub from front case, **Fig. 8.**
14. Invert front case and remove mounting adapter retaining bolts, then remove mounting adapter, input shaft and planetary gearset as an assembly, **Fig. 9.**
15. Press ring gear from front case. Note position of ring gear for assembly reference.
16. Remove planetary gearset and input shaft from mounting adapter by expanding large snap ring under adapter and prying under gearset with screwdrivers, **Fig. 9.**
17. Remove oil seal from mounting adapter using tools 1175-AC and T50T-100-A, or equivalent.
18. Remove internal snap ring from planetary carrier, then remove planetary gearset from input shaft assembly, **Fig. 9.**
19. Remove external snap ring from input shaft, then install input shaft assembly in suitable press and remove ball bearing using tool D79L-4621-A.
20. Remove thrust washer, thrust plate and sun gear from input shaft, **Fig. 9.**
21. Place shift lever in "TWO WHEEL HIGH" (2WH) position, then make an alignment mark on outside of front case at the shift lever.
22. Remove set screws from front case and shift cam, then invert front case and remove external clip.
23. Remove shift lever from front case and shift cam. Remove O-ring from second groove in shift lever shaft.
24. Remove detent plunger and compression spring from inside of front case.
25. Remove internal snap ring and ball bearing retainer from front case. Remove bearing from retainer using tools T83T-7025-B and T80T-4000-W.
26. Remove front output shaft and U-joint assembly from front case. Remove oil seal, then the internal snap ring and

---

tightened before the shoulder bolt.
b. Torque shift lever to 27–37 ft. lbs.
c. Install vent assembly so the white marking on housing is in line with notch in shifter. Position upper end of vent hose inside shift lever bolts.
d. Install shift ball to the end of knurl on upper part of shift lever.

FRONT OUTPUT SHAFT OIL SEAL, REPLACE

1. Raise and support vehicle.
2. Remove front driveshaft from axle input yoke.
3. Loosen clamp retaining front driveshaft boot to transfer case, then remove driveshaft and boot assembly from front output shaft.
4. Drain fluid from transfer case, then remove oil seal using tools 1175-AC and T50T-100-A.
5. Reverse procedure to install. Note the following:
a. Apply lubricant C1A-19590-B, or equivalent to oil seal and front output shaft female spline.
b. Install oil seal using tools T83T-7065-B and T80T-4000-W, or equivalent.
c. Torque front driveshaft retaining bolts to 12–15 ft. lbs. and the drain and fill plugs to 14–22 ft. lbs.

REAR OUTPUT SHAFT OIL SEAL, REPLACE

1. Raise and support vehicle.
2. Remove rear driveshaft from transfer case output shaft yoke and position aside.
3. Remove output shaft yoke, then the oil seal using tools 1175-AC and T50T-100-A.
4. Reverse procedure to install. Note the following:

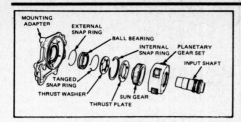

Fig. 9 Mounting adapter assembly

ball bearing from case, **Fig. 10.**

27. Install front output shaft and U-joint assembly in a soft jawed vise, then remove internal snap rings which retain bearings in shaft.
28. Press bearing out of front output shaft using tool T74P-4635-C, or equivalent. Reposition tool on spider and remove opposite bearing. Repeat procedure for remaining bearings.

TRANSFER CASE, ASSEMBLE

NOTE: Prior to assembly, lubricate all transfer case components with Dexron II automatic transmission fluid, or equivalent.

1. Install output shaft in a soft jawed vise, then install a new bearing into end of shaft ear.
2. Install spider into bearing. Press bearing below snap ring groove using tool T74P-4625-C. Remove tool and install a new internal snap ring in groove.
3. Install a new bearing into opposite end of shaft ear. Press bearing until opposite bearing contacts snap ring. Remove tool and install a new internal snap ring in groove.
4. Reposition output shaft in vise and install remaining two bearings. Check U-joint for free movement. If there is any binding, tap ears of both shafts to relieve the bind.
5. Install ball bearing into front output shaft case bore using tools T83T-7024-B and T80T-4000-W, then install internal snap ring. Make sure bearing is not cocked in the bore.
6. Install front output oil seal in front case bore.
7. Install ring gear in front case, using a suitable press.
8. Install ball bearing, then the internal snap ring into bearing retainer bore, **Fig. 10.**
9. Install front output shaft and U-joint assembly through front case seal, then install the ball bearing and retainer assembly and internal snap ring. The clip on bearing retainer must align with slot in front case, **Fig. 10.**
10. Install compression spring and detent plunger into bore from inside of case.
11. Install a new O-ring into second groove of shift lever shaft.
12. Install shift cam in front case with "2WH" detent position over the detent plunger. While holding shift cam in

position, push shift lever shaft into front case to engage shift cam, using alignment mark made during disassembly.
13. Install external clip on end of shift lever shaft.
14. Install two set screws in front case and shift cam. Torque screws to 5–7 ft. lbs.

NOTE: The set screw in the front case must be in first groove of shift lever shaft, and not bottomed against the shaft. Also, check that the shift lever can be moved to all positions.

15. Install sun gear, thrust plate, thrust washer, ball bearing and external snap ring onto input shaft, **Fig. 9.**
16. Install planetary gearset onto sun gear and input shaft assembly, then the internal snap ring on planetary carrier, **Fig. 9.**
17. Install oil seal, then the tanged snap ring into mounting adapter.
18. Install input shaft and planetary gearset in mounting adapter. Push the assembly into adapter until it is fully seated and the snap ring engages.
19. Apply a bead of RTV sealant to front case mating surface, then install mounting adapter on front case. Torque bolts to 35–40 ft. lbs.
20. Install high-low shift hub into planetary gearset. Position high-low shift fork into inside track of shift cam and groove of the high-low shift hub, **Fig. 8.** Ensure that nylon wear pads are installed on shift fork and dot on pad lines up with fork hole.
21. Install shift rail through high-low fork until rail is fully seated in front case bore, **Fig. 8.**
22. Install oil pump cover with "TOP" marking facing front of front case. Install pump pins, flats facing up, with spring between pins, then install assembly in oil pump bore in output shaft.
23. Install oil pump body and pickup tube over shaft, then install oil pump rear body with "TOP REAR" marking facing rear of front case.
24. Install oil pump retainer and attaching bolts. Torque bolts, while rotating output shaft, to 36–40 inch lbs.
25. Install output shaft and oil pump assembly in input shaft. Ensure that external splines of output shaft engage internal splines of high-low shift hub and that the oil pump retainer and oil filter leg are in the groove and notch of front case.
26. Install collector magnet in front case, **Fig. 8.**
27. Install chain, drive sprocket and driven sprocket assembly over shafts. Install thrust washer on front output shaft, then the external snap ring over thrust washer.
28. Assemble 2W-4W lockup assembly, then install 2W-4W shift fork to 2W-4W lockup assembly, **Fig. 6.** Ensure nylon wear pads are installed on shift fork and dot on pad lines up with fork

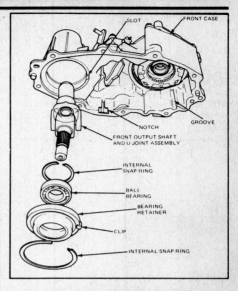

Fig. 10 Front output shaft assembly

hole.
29. Install 2W-4W lockup collar and hub assembly over output shaft and into shift rail. Install shaft, bushing and external clip on 2W-4W lockup fork.
30. Install shift collar hub on output shaft, then install caged needle bearing into rear cover using tools T83T-7127-A and T80T-4000-W, or equivalent.
31. Install ball bearing in rear cover bore using tools T83T-7025-B and T80T-4000-W, or equivalent. Make sure that bearing is not cocked in bore, then install snap ring to retain bearing in rear cover.
32. Install speedometer drive gear assembly into rear cover so that round end of speedometer gear clip faces the inside of rear cover.
33. Install oil seal in rear cover using tools T83T-7065-B and T80T-4000-W, or equivalent.
34. Install 2W-4W shift fork spring on inside boss of rear cover.
35. Apply a bead of silicone rubber sealant D6AZ-19562-A, or equivalent, to front case mating surface.
36. Position transfer case shift lever in "4H" detent, then install front case on rear cover, making sure the 2W-4W shift fork spring engages shift rail. Install attaching bolts, starting with rear cover bolts, and torque to 35–40 ft. lbs.
37. Install rear yoke on output shaft with rubber seal, washer and nut. Torque nut to 120–150 ft. lbs.
38. Install four-wheel drive indicator switch and torque to 8–12 ft. lbs.
39. Install breather plug and torque to 6–14 ft. lbs.
40. Install drain plug and torque to 14–22 ft. lbs.
41. Fill transfer case with 3 pints of Dexron II automatic transmission fluid, or equivalent, then install fill plug and torque to 14–22 ft. lbs.

New Process Transfer Cases

MODEL 203

NOTE: For service procedures on this transfer case, refer to "Dodge & Plymouth" chapter.

MODEL 205

NOTE: For service procedures on this transfer case, refer to "Dodge & Plymouth" chapter.

MODEL 208

NOTE: For service procedures on this transfer case, refer to "Dodge & Plymouth" chapter. Due to vehicle applications, there may be minor differences in repair procedures. See **Figs. 1 and 2.**

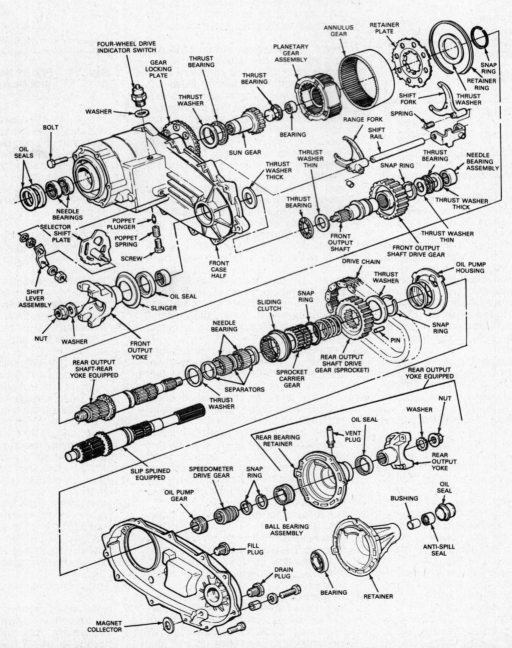

Fig. 1   Exploded view of New Process model 208 transfer case. 1983–85 models

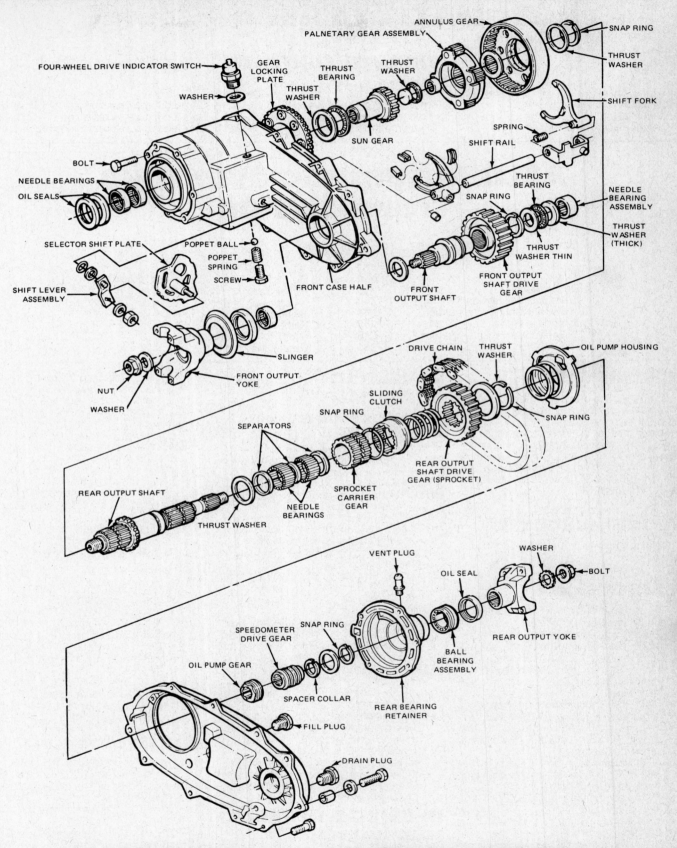

Fig. 2 Exploded view of New Process model 208 transfer case. 1980—82 models

AUTOMATIC TRANSMISSIONS

TABLE OF CONTENTS

A4LD Automatic Overdrive Transmission

INDEX

DESCRIPTION

The A4LD is a 4 speed automatic overdrive transmission and is a derivative of the C3 automatic transmission.

This transmission incorporates the use of electronic controls integrated in the onboard EEC-IV system. These controls operate a piston/plate clutch in the torque converter that eliminates torque converter slip when applied.

TROUBLESHOOTING

Refer to **Fig. 1** for troubleshooting procedures.

MAINTENANCE

The automatic transmission fluid level should be checked as follows:
1. Place transmission in Park, then allow engine to idle with foot brake applied and vehicle on a level surface.
2. Clean all dirt from the transmission dipstick cap, before removing from the filler tube.
3. With the transmission at operating temperature (between 150–170° F), the dip stick should be hot to the touch. Fluid level should be within the cross hatched area.
4. With transmission cold (between 70–95° F), fluid level should be between the middle and top holes.
5. When adding fluid, use DEXRON II or equivalent

NOTE: The use of a fluid other than that specified, could result in transmission malfunction and/or failure.

IN-VEHICLE ADJUSTMENTS

MANUAL LINKAGE ADJUSTMENT

1. Position transmission selector control lever in Drive (D) position, then loosen trunnion bolt, **Fig. 2.**

NOTE: Do not use the overdrive position.

2. Ensure that the shift lever detent pawl is held against the rearward Drive (D) detent stop during the linkage adjustment procedure.
3. Position transmission manual lever into Drive (D) range by moving bellcrank lever completely rearward, then forward four detents.
4. With the transmission selector lever and manual lever in (D) position, apply light forward pressure to the shifter control lower arm while tightening trunnion bolt to 13–23 ft. lbs. Forward pressure on the shifter lower arm will ensure correct positioning within the drive detent.
5. After adjustment, check for correct Park engagement. Control lever must move to the right when engaged in Park detent. Check transmission control lever in all detent positions with the engine operating, to ensure correct detent/transmission action. Readjust, if necessary.

IN-VEHICLE REPAIRS

SELECTOR HOUSING, REPLACE

1. Loosen trunnion bolt and remove trunnion from shift control arm grommet.
2. Remove shifter handle by grasping the handle firmly with the shifter in Drive position, then pulling straight upward.
3. Remove attaching screws, disconnect electrical connectors and remove bezel assembly. On 4×4 models, remove transfer case shift boot to housing attaching bolts.
4. Remove selector housing to floor pan attaching bolts, then the selector housing.
5. Reverse procedure to install.

CONTROL VALVE BODY, REPLACE

1. Disconnect battery ground cable.
2. Raise and support vehicle.
3. Loosen pan attaching bolts and drain fluid from transmission.
4. Remove pan and gasket.
5. Remove filter screen and gasket.
6. Remove rear servo cover and gasket.
7. Remove control valve body attaching bolts, then the valve body.
8. Reverse procedure to install. Torque pan attaching bolts to 12–17 ft. lbs.

REAR SERVO, REPLACE

1. Disconnect battery ground cable.
2. Starting from rear of pan and working toward front, loosen bolts and allow fluid to drain.
3. Remove all pan attaching bolts and pan.
4. Remove oil filter screen and gasket.
5. Remove rear servo cover, servo and gasket.
6. Reverse procedure to install.

CONDITION	POSSIBLE SOURCE	RESOLUTION

Converter clutch does not engage.	1. Converter clutch solenoid not being energized electrically.
	  a. Wires to solenoid shorted or open circuit.
	  b. Transmission case connector not seated.
	  c. Open or short circuit inside of solenoid.
	  d. Malfunctioning engine coolant temperature sensor.
	  e. Malfunctioning throttle position sensor.
	  f. Malfunctioning manifold absolute pressure sensor.
	  g. Brake switch that provides signal to processor not hooked up or malfunctioning.
	  h. Malfunctioning EEC-IV processor.
		1.
		
		Perform EEC-IV diagnostic check — key on — engine off.
		Perform EEC-IV diagnostic check engine running.
		Run diagnostic check on processor.

	2. Converter clutch solenoid is energized electrically but foreign material on hydraulic part of solenoid valve prevents valve closure.	2. Remove transmission oil pan. Remove valve body. Remove solenoid. Check operation of solenoid. **NOTE:** Remove any foreign material or contamination.
	3. Converter clutch shuttle valve stuck in unlock position (against plug) or too high a load spring.	3. Remove valve body. Check operation of converter clutch shuttle valve. Remove any contamination. Spring load is approximately 17.80 N (4.0 lb.) at 13 mm (.512 in.).
	4. Converter clutch shift valve stuck in downshift position (up against 4-3 T.D. sleeve assembly).	4. Remove valve body. Check operation of converter clutch shift valve. Remove any contamination. Make sure valve moves freely. **NOTE:** 2.3L use a modulator spring and a shift spring; 2.8L just use a modulator spring.
	5. Internal problems in torque converter prevent lockup piston from coming on.	5. Remove transmission. Replace converter.
Converter clutch always engaged even at zero road speed. (Symptoms: engine will only run in "N" and "P" selector positions. Vehicle can only be driven away from standing start if engine rpm is brought up high and selector dropped into O.D. (D) position.)	1. Converter clutch shift valve stuck in lock position (away from 4-3 T.D. valve sleeve).	1. Remove transmission valve body. Check to see that converter clutch shift valve moves freely. **NOTE:** 2.3L use a modulator spring and a shift spring; 2.8L just use a modulator spring.
	2. Converter clutch shuttle valve stuck in locked position (away from plug).	2. Remove valve body. Check converter clutch shuttle valve for freeness of movement.
	3. Lockup piston in torque converter will not disengage.	3. Remove transmission. Replace converter.

Fig. 1   A4LD automatic overdrive transmission troubleshooting chart (Part 1 of 12)

CONDITION	POSSIBLE SOURCE	RESOLUTION
Converter clutch will not disengage on a coast down. (Symptoms: vibration on a coast down.)	1. Malfunctioning throttle position sensor (should unlock at closed throttle). 2. Converter clutch solenoid sticking.	1. Perform EEC-IV diagnostic check — key on — engine off. 2. Remove valve body. Check operation of solenoid. Remove if required.
Slow initial engagement.	1. Improper fluid level. 2. Damaged or improperly adjusted manual linkage. 3. Contaminated fluid. 4. Improper clutch and band application, or low main control pressure.	1. Perform fluid level check. 2. Service or adjust manual linkage. 3. Perform fluid condition check. 4. Perform control pressure test.
Rough initial engagement in either forward or reverse.	1. Improper fluid level. 2. High engine idle. 3. Automatic choke on (warm temp). 4. Looseness in the driveshaft, U-joints or engine mounts. 5. Improper clutch or band application, or oil control pressure. 6. Sticking or dirty valve body. 7. Converter clutch not disengaging.	1. Perform fluid level check. 2. Adjust idle to specification. 3. Disengage choke. 4. Service as required. 5. Perform control pressure test. 6. Clean, service or replace valve body. 7. Check converter clutch engagement/disengagement.
Harsh engagements (warm engine).	1. Improper fluid level. 2. Engine curb idle too high. 3. Valve body bolts loose/too tight. 4. Valve body dirty/sticking valves.	1. Perform fluid level check. 2. Check engine curb idle. 3. Tighten to specification. 4. Determine source of contamination. Service as required.
No/delayed forward engagement (reverse OK).	1. Improper fluid level. 2. Manual linkage misadjusted/damaged. 3. Low main control pressure (leakage). Forward clutch stator support seal rings leaking. 4. Forward clutch assembly burnt/damaged/leaking. Check ball in cylinder/leaking piston seal rings. 5. Valve body bolts loose/too tight. 6. Valve body dirty/sticking valves. 7. Transmission filter plugged. 8. Pump damaged, leaking.	1. Perform fluid level check. 2. Check and adjust or service as required. 3. Control pressure test, note results. 4. Perform air pressure test. 5. Tighten to specification. 6. Determine source of contamination. Service as required. 7. Replace filter. 8. Visually inspect pump gear. Replace pump if necessary.

Fig. 1   A4LD automatic overdrive transmission troubleshooting chart (Part 2 of 12)

CONDITION	POSSIBLE SOURCE	RESOLUTION
No/delayed reverse engagement (forward OK).	1. Improper fluid level.	1. Perform fluid level check.
	2. Manual linkage misadjusted/ damaged.	2. Check and adjust or service as required.
	3. Low main control pressure in reverse.	3. Control pressure test.
	4. Reverse clutch assembly burnt/ worn/leaking. Check ball in piston/ leaking piston seal rings.	4. Perform air pressure test.
	5. Valve body bolts loose/too tight.	5. Tighten to specification.
	6. Valve body dirty/sticking valves.	6. Determine source of contamination. Service as required.
	7. Transmission filter plugged.	7. Replace filter.
	8. Pump damaged.	8. Visually inspect pump gears. Replace pump if necessary.
	9. Low pressure servo piston seal cut/ leaking.	9. Perform air pressure test. Check and replace piston seal. Check and replace low reverse board.
No engagement or drive in forward (any position) or reverse.	1. Improper fluid level.	1. Perform fluid level check.
	2. Low main control pressure.	2. Control pressure test.
	3. Mechanical damage.	3. Check splines on turbine, input shaft and O/D carrier, O/D one-way clutch, center shaft, forward clutch, forward carrier and output shaft. Replace if necessary.
No engagement/drive in Ⓓ, D or 1 — (2 OK).	1. Manual linkage misadjusted.	1. Adjust manual linkage.
	2. Rear one-way clutch damaged.	2. Replace rear one-way clutch.
		3. Clean transmission and valve body.
Vehicle creeping in neutral.	1. Forward clutch failing to disengage.	1. Clean transmission.
No/delayed reverse engagement and/ or no engine braking in manual low (1).	1. Improper fluid level.	1. Perform fluid level check.
	2. Linkage out of adjustment.	2. Service or adjust linkage.
	3. Low reverse servo piston seal leaking.	3. Check and replace piston seal.
	4. Low reverse band burnt or worn.	4. Perform air pressure test.
	5. Overdrive clutch, overdrive one-way clutch damaged.	5. Replace as required.
	6. Polished, glazed band or drum.	6. Service or replace as required.
	7. Rear one-way clutch damaged.	7. Replace.
	8. End play clearance too tight.	8. Check and correct transmission end play clearance.

Fig. 1   A4LD automatic overdrive transmission troubleshooting chart (Part 3 of 12)

CONDITION	POSSIBLE SOURCE	RESOLUTION
No engine braking in manual second gear.	1. Intermediate band out of adjustment.	1. Adjust intermediate band.
	2. Improper band or clutch application, or oil pressure control system.	2. Perform control pressure test.
	3. Intermediate servo leaking.	3. Perform air pressure test of intermediate servo for leakage. Service as required.
	4. O/D clutch, O/D one-way clutch damaged.	4. Replace as required.
	5. Glazed band.	5. Service or replace as required.
Forward engagement slips/shudders/chatters.	1. Improper fluid level.	1. Perform fluid level check.
	2. Manual linkage misadjusted/damaged.	2. Check and adjust or service as required.
	3. Low main control pressure.	3. Control pressure test.
	4. Valve body bolts loose/too tight.	4. Tighten to specification.
	5. Valve body dirty/sticking valves.	5. Determine source of contamination. Service as required.
	6. O.D./forward clutch piston ball — check not seating/leaking.	6. Replace O.D./forward clutch piston. Service transmission as required.
	7. O.D./forward clutch piston seals cut/worn.	7. Replace seal and service clutch as required.
	8. O.D. one-way clutch damaged.	8. Replace as required.
	9. Rear one-way clutch damaged.	9. Determine cause of condition. Service as required.
Reverse shudder/chatters/slips.	1. Improper fluid level.	1. Perform fluid level check.
	2. Low main control pressure in reverse.	2. Control pressure test.
	3. Low-reverse servo leaking.	3. Air pressure test. Visually inspect seal rings and piston bore.
	4. O.D. and/or rear one-way clutch damaged.	4. Determine cause of condition. Service as required.
	5. O.D. and/or reverse-high clutch drum bushing damaged.	5. Determine cause of condition. Service as required.
	6. O.D. and/or reverse-high clutch support seal rings/ring grooves worn/damaged.	6. Determine cause of condition. Service as required.
	7. O.D. and/or reverse-high clutch piston seals cut/worn.	7. Determine cause of condition. Service as required.
	8. Low-reverse servo piston damaged/worn.	8. Service as required.
	9. Low-reverse band out of adjustment or damaged.	9. Adjust, inspect low-reverse band.
	10. Looseness in the driveshaft, U-joints or engine mounts.	10. Service as required.
	11. Servo piston/seals or bores damaged.	11. Perform air pressure check.

Fig. 1   A4LD automatic overdrive transmission troubleshooting chart (Part 4 of 12)

CONDITION	POSSIBLE SOURCE	RESOLUTION
No drive, slips or chatters in first gear in Ⓓ or D. All other gears normal.	1. Damaged or worn O/D or rear one-way clutch.	1. Service or replace.
No drive, slips or chatters in second gear.	1. Intermediate band out of adjustment.	1. Adjust intermediate band.
	2. Improper band or clutch application, or control pressure.	2. Perform control pressure test.
	3. Damaged or worn intermediate servo piston and/or internal leaks.	3. Perform air pressure test.
	4. Dirty or sticking valve body.	4. Clean, service or replace valve body.
	5. Polished, glazed intermediate band or drum.	5. Replace or service as required.
Starts up in 2nd or 3rd.	1. Improper band and/or clutch application, or oil pressure control system.	1. Perform control pressure test.
	2. Damaged or worn governor. Sticking governor.	2. Perform governor check. Replace or service governor, clean screen, check oil seals on collector body.
	3. Valve body loose.	3. Tighten to specification.
	4. Dirty or sticking valve body.	4. Clean, service or replace valve body.
	5. Cross leaks between valve body and case mating surface.	5. Service or replace valve body and/ or case as required.
Shift points incorrect.	1. Improper fluid level.	1. Perform fluid level check.
	2. Vacuum line damaged, clogged or leaks.	2. Perform vacuum supply test.
	3. Improper operation of EGR system.	3. Service or replace as required.
	4. Improper speedometer gear installed.	4. Replace gear.
	5. Improper clutch or band application, or oil pressure control system.	5. Perform shift test and control pressure test.
	6. Damaged or worn governor.	6. Service or replace governor — clean screen.
	7. Vacuum diaphragm bent, sticking or leaks.	7. Service or replace as required.
	8. Dirty or sticking valve body.	8. Clean, service or replace valve body.

Fig. 1   A4LD automatic overdrive transmission troubleshooting chart (Part 5 of 12)

CONDITION	POSSIBLE SOURCE	RESOLUTION
All upshifts harsh/delayed or no upshifts.	1. Improper fluid level.	1. Perform fluid level check.
	2. Manual linkage misadjusted/ damaged.	2. Check and adjust or service as required.
	3. Governor sticking.	3. Perform governor test. Service as required.
	4. Main control pressure too high.	4. Control pressure test. Service as required.
	5. Valve body bolts loose/too tight.	5. Tighten to specification.
	6. Valve body dirty/sticking valves.	6. Determine source of contamination. Service as required.
	7. Vacuum leak to diaphragm unit.	7. Perform vacuum supply and diaphragm test. Check vacuum lines to diaphragm unit. Service as required.
	8. Vacuum diaphragm bent, sticking, leaks.	8. Check diaphragm unit. Service as required.
Mushy/early all upshifts pile up/ upshifts.	1. Low main control pressure.	1. Control pressure test. Note results.
	2. Valve body bolts loose/too tight.	2. Tighten to specification.
	3. Valve body or throttle control valve sticking.	3. Determine source of contamination. Service as required.
	4. Governor valve sticking.	4. Perform governor test. Repair as required.
	5. Kickdown linkage misadjusted/ sticking/damaged.	5. Adjust linkage. Service as required.
No 1-2 upshift.	1. Improper fluid level.	1. Perform fluid level check.
	2. Kickdown linkage misadjusted.	2. Adjust linkage.
	3. Manual linkage misadjusted/ damaged.	3. Check and adjust or service as required.
	4. Governor valve sticking.	4. Perform governor test. Service as required.
	5. Intermediate band out of adjustment.	5. Adjust intermediate band.
	6. Vacuum leak to diaphragm unit.	6. Check vacuum lines to diaphragm. Service as required.
	7. Vacuum diaphragm bent, sticking, leaks.	7. Check diaphragm unit. Service as necessary.
	8. Valve body bolts loose/too tight.	8. Tighten to specification.
	9. Valve body dirty/sticking valves.	9. Determine source of contamination. Service as required.
	10. Intermediate band and/or servo assembly burnt.	10. Perform air pressure test.

Fig. 1   A4LD automatic overdrive transmission troubleshooting chart (Part 6 of 12)

CONDITION	POSSIBLE SOURCE	RESOLUTION
Rough/harsh/delayed 1-2 upshift.	1. Improper fluid level.	1. Perform fluid level check.
	2. Poor engine performance.	2. Tune engine.
	3. Kickdown linkage misadjusted.	3. Adjust linkage.
	4. Intermediate band out of adjustment.	4. Adjust intermediate band.
	5. Main control pressure too high.	5. Control pressure test. Note results.
	6. Governor valve sticking.	6. Perform governor test. Service as required.
	7. Damaged intermediate servo.	7. Air pressure check intermediate servo.
	8. Engine vacuum leak.	8. Check engine vacuum lines. Check vacuum diaphragm unit. Perform vacuum supply and diaphragm test. Service as necessary.
	9. Valve body bolts loose/too tight.	9. Tighten to specifications.
	10. Valve body dirty/sticking valves.	10. Determine source of contamination. Service as required.
	11. Vacuum leak to diaphragm unit.	11. Check vacuum lines to diaphragm unit. Service as required.
	12. Vacuum diaphragm bent, sticking, leaks.	12. Check diaphragm unit. Service as necessary.
Mushy/early/soft/slipping 1-2 upshift.	1. Improper fluid level.	1. Perform fluid level check.
	2. Incorrect engine performance.	2. Tune and adjust engine idle as required.
	3. Kickdown linkage misadjusted.	3. Adjust linkage.
	4. Intermediate band out of adjustment.	4. Adjust intermediate band.
	5. Low main control pressure.	5. Control pressure test. Note results.
	6. Valve body bolts loose/too tight.	6. Tighten to specification.
	7. Valve body dirty/sticking valves.	7. Determine source of contamination. Service as required.
	8. Governor valve sticking.	8. Perform governor test. Service as required.
	9. Damaged intermediate servo or band.	9. Perform air pressure test. Service as required.
	10. Polished, glazed band or drum.	10. Service or replace as required.

Fig. 1   A4LD automatic overdrive transmission troubleshooting chart (Part 7 of 12)

FORD—Automatic Transmissions

CONDITION	POSSIBLE SOURCE	RESOLUTION
No 2-3 upshift.	1. Low fliud level.	1. Perform fluid level check.
	2. Kickdown linkage misadjusted.	2. Adjust linkage.
	3. Low main control pressure to reverse-high clutch.	3. Control pressure test. Note results.
	4. Valve body bolts loose/too tight.	4. Tighten to specification.
	5. Valve body dirty/sticking valves.	5. Determine source of contamination, then service as required.
	6. Reverse-high clutch assembly burnt/worn.	6. Determine cause of condition. Service as required.
Harsh/delayed 2-3 upshift.	1. Incorrect engine performance.	1. Check engine tuneup.
	2. Engine vacuum leak.	2. Check engine vacuum lines. Check vacuum diaphragm unit. Perform vacuum supply and diaphragm test. Service as necessary.
	3. Kickdown linkage misadjusted.	3. Adjust linkage.
	4. Damaged or worn intermediate servo release and reverse-high clutch piston check ball.	4. Air pressure test the intermediate servo. Apply and release the reverse-high clutch piston check ball. Service as required.
	5. Valve body bolts loose/too tight.	5. Tighten to specification.
	6. Valve body dirty/sticking valves.	6. Determine source of condition. Service as required.
	7. Vacuum diaphragm bent, sticking, leaks.	7. Check diaphragm. Replace as necessary.
Soft/early/mushy 2-3 upshift.	1. Kickdown linkage misadjusted.	1. Adjust linkage.
	2. Valve body bolts loose/too tight.	2. Tighten to specification.
	3. Valve body dirty/sticking valves.	3. Determine source of contamination. Service as required.
	4. Vacuum diaphragm bent, sticking, leaks.	4. Check diaphragm. Replace as necessary.
Erratic shifts.	1. Poor engine performance.	1. Check engine tuneup.
	2. Valve body bolts loose/too tight.	2. Tighten to specification.
	3. Valve body dirty/sticking valves.	3. Air pressure test, note results. Determine source of contamination. Service as required.
	4. Governor valve stuck.	4. Perform governor test. Service as required.
	5. Output shaft collector body seal rings damaged.	5. Service as required.

Fig. 1   A4LD automatic overdrive transmission troubleshooting chart (Part 8 of 12)

CONDITION	POSSIBLE SOURCE	RESOLUTION
Shifts 1-3 in Ⓓ or D.	1. Intermediate band out of adjustment.	1. Adjust band.
	2. Damaged intermediate servo and/or internal leaks.	2. Perform air pressure test. Service front servo and/or internal leaks.
	3. Improper band or clutch application, or oil pressure control system.	3. Perform control pressure test.
	4. Polished glazed band or drum.	4. Service or replace band or drum.
	5. Dirty/sticky valve body, or governor.	5. Clean, service or replace valve body or governor.
	6. Governor valve stuck.	6. Perform governor test. Service as required.
Engine over-speeds on 2-3 shift.	1. Kickdown linkage out of adjustment.	1. Service or adjust kickdown linkage.
	2. Improper band or clutch application, or oil pressure control system.	2. Perform control pressure test.
	3. Damaged or worn reverse high clutch and/or intermediate servo piston.	3. Perform air pressure test. Service as required.
	4. Intermediate servo piston seals cut, leaking.	4. Replace seals. Check for leaks.
	5. Dirty or sticking valve body.	5. Clean, service or replace valve body.
Rough/shudder 3-1 shift at closed throttle in D.	1. Incorrect engine idle or performance.	1. Tune, and adjust engine idle.
	2. Improper kickdown linkage adjustment.	2. Service or adjust kickdown linkage.
	3. Improper clutch or band application or oil pressure control system.	3. Perform control pressure test.
	4. Improper governor operation.	4. Perform governor test. Service as required.
	5. Dirty or sticking valve body.	5. Clean, service or replace valve body.
No 3-4 upshift.	1. Kickdown linkage misadjusted.	1. Adjust linkage.
	2. O.D. servo damaged, leaking.	2. Check and replace O.D. piston, seal.
	3. Polished, glazed O.D. band or drum.	3. Service or replace O.D. band or drum.
	4. Dirty or sticking valve body.	4. Clean, service or replace valve body. Check 3-4 shift valve.
Slipping 4th gear.	1. O.D. servo damaged, leaking.	1. Check and replace O.D. piston seal.
	2. Polished, glazed O.D. band or drum.	2. Service or replace O.D. band or drum.
Engine stall speed exceeded in Ⓓ, D or R.	1. Vacuum system.	1. Check and service vacuum system.
	2. Low main control pressure.	2. Control pressure test. Check and clean valve body. Replace valve body gasket. Check and service pump.

Fig. 1   A4LD automatic overdrive transmission troubleshooting chart (Part 9 of 12)

CONDITION	POSSIBLE SOURCE	RESOLUTION
Engine stall speed exceeded in R. OK in Ⓓ, D, 2 and 1.	1. Low/reverse servo/band damaged. 2. Reverse and high clutch damaged.	1. Check engine braking in 1. If not OK, check, service or replace low/reverse servo and band. 2. If low/reverse servo OK, check and repair reverse and high clutch.
Engine stall speed exceeded in Ⓓ or D, OK in R.	1. O.D. one-way clutch or rear one-way clutch damaged.	1. Check engine stall speeds in 2 and 1. If OK, repair O.D. or rear one-way clutches. Clean transmission.
At moderate acceleration shift into 2nd gear is above 27 MPH.	1. Vacuum system. 2. Main control pressure. 3. Governor damaged or worn. 4. Dirty or sticking valve body.	1. Check and service hoses, vacuum diaphragm. 2. Control pressure test. 3. Check governor and connector body oil seals. Replace if required. 4. Check 1/2 shift valve, clean or replace valve body.
Kickdown shift speeds low (too early) or shifts too late.	1. Kickdown linkage misadjusted. 2. Main control pressure. 3. Governor damaged or worn.	1. Adjust linkage. 2. Control pressure test. 3. Check governor and connector body oil seals.
No kickdown into 2nd gear between 50-70 mph in Ⓓ or D.	1. Kickdown linkage misadjusted. 2. Main control pressure. 3. Dirty or sticking valve body.	1. Adjust linkage. 2. Control pressure test. 3. Check kickdown valve, clean or replace valve body.
No shift to 2nd gear with accelerator 3/4 depressed at 30 mph in Ⓓ or D.	1. Main control pressure. 2. Governor damaged or worn. 3. Dirty or sticking valve body.	1. Control pressure test. 2. Check governor. 3. Clean or replace valve body.
When moving selector from Ⓓ/D to manual 1, at 55 mph with accelerator released, no braking felt from downshift to 2nd gear.	1. Main control pressure. 2. Intermediate band out of adjustment. 3. Overdrive clutch damaged.	1. Control pressure test. 2. Adjust band. Check intermediate servo. 3. Check and service O.D. clutch.
When moving selector from Ⓓ/D to manual 1, at 55 mph with accelerator released, shift into 1st gear occurs over 45 mph.	1. Main control pressure. 2. Dirty, sticking valve body. 3. Governor damaged or worn. 4. Kickdown linkage misadjusted.	1. Control pressure test. 2. Check and clean valve body. 3. Check and service governor. 4. Check and adjust kickdown linkage.
When moving selector from Ⓓ/D to manual 1, at 55 mph with accelerator released, shift into 1st gear occurs under 15 mph.	1. Main control pressure. 2. Dirty, sticking valve body. 3. Low/reverse servo damaged. 4. Governor damaged or worn. 5. Overdrive clutch damaged.	1. Control pressure test. 2. Check and clean valve body. 3. Check and service as required. 4. Check and service governor. 5. Check and service O.D. clutch.

Fig. 1   A4LD automatic overdrive transmission troubleshooting chart (Part 10 of 12)

CONDITION	POSSIBLE SOURCE	RESOLUTION
No forced downshifts.	1. Kickdown linkage out of adjustment.	1. Service or adjust linkage.
	2. Damaged internal kickdown linkage.	2. Service internal kickdown linkage.
	3. Improper clutch or band application, or oil pressure control system.	3. Perform control pressure test.
	4. Dirty or sticking governor.	4. Service or replace governor, clean screen.
	5. Dirty or sticking valve body.	5. Clean, service, or replace valve body.
Engine over-speeds on 3-2 downshift.	1. Linkage out of adjustment.	1. Service or adjust linkage.
	2. Intermediate band out of adjustment.	2. Adjust intermediate band.
	3. Improper band or clutch application, and one-way clutch, or oil pressure control system.	3. Perform control pressure test service clutch.
	4. Damaged or worn intermediate servo.	4. Air pressure test check the intermediate servo. Service servo and/or seals.
	5. Polished, glazed band or drum.	5. Service or replace as required.
	6. Dirty or sticking valve body.	6. Clean, service or replace valve body.
Shift efforts high.	1. Manual shaft linkage damaged/misadjusted.	1. Check and adjust or service as required.
	2. Inner manual lever nut loose.	2. Tighten nut to specification.
	3. Manual lever retainer pin damaged.	3. Adjust linkage and install pin.
Transmission overheats.	1. Improper fluid level.	1. Perform fluid level check.
	2. Incorrect engine idle, or performance.	2. Tune, or adjust engine idle.
	3. Improper clutch or band application, or oil pressure control system.	3. Perform control pressure test.
	4. Restriction in cooler or lines.	4. Service restriction.
	5. Seized converter one-way clutch.	5. Replace one-way clutch.
	6. Dirty or sticking valve body.	6. Clean, service or replace valve body.
Transmission leaks.	1. Case breather vent.	1. Check the vent for free breathing. Repair as required.
	2. Leakage at gasket, seals, etc.	2. Remove all traces of lube on exposed surfaces of transmission. Check the vent for free breathing. Operate transmission at normal temperatures and perform fluid leakage check. Service as required.

Fig. 1   A4LD automatic overdrive transmission troubleshooting chart (Part 11 of 12)

CONDITION	POSSIBLE SOURCE	RESOLUTION
Poor vehicle acceleration.	1. Poor engine performance.	1. Check engine tuneup.
	2. Torque converter one-way clutch locked up.	2. Replace torque converter.
Transmission noisy — valve resonance. **NOTE:** Gauges may aggravate any hydraulic resonance. Remove gauge and check for resonance level.	1. Improper fluid level.	1. Perform fluid level check.
	2. Linkage out of adjustment.	2. Service or adjust linkage.
	3. Improper band or clutch application, or oil pressure control system.	3. Perform control pressure test.
	4. Cooler lines grounding.	4. Free up cooler lines.
	5. Dirty or sticking valve body.	5. Clean, service or replace valve body.
	6. Internal leakage or pump cavitation.	6. Service as required.

Fig. 1 A4LD automatic overdrive transmission troubleshooting chart (Part 12 of 12)

EXTENSION HOUSING, REPLACE

1. Disconnect battery ground cable.
2. Raise and support vehicle.
3. Remove drive shaft.
4. Support transmission with a suitable jack.
5. Disconnect speedometer cable from extension housing.
6. Remove rear support-to-crossmember attaching bolts or nuts.
7. Remove extension housing attaching bolts, then the extension housing.
8. Reverse procedure to install. Torque extension housing attaching bolts to 27–39 ft. lbs.

GOVERNOR, REPLACE

1. Remove extension housing as described previously.
2. Remove governor body to oil collector body attaching bolts.
3. Remove governor body, valve, spring and weight from collector body.
4. Reverse procedure to install.

TRANSMISSION REPLACE

1. Disconnect battery ground cable.
2. Raise and support vehicle.
3. Loosen pan attaching bolts and allow fluid to drain.
4. Remove converter access cover and adapter plate attaching bolts from lower end of converter housing.
5. Remove four flywheel to converter attaching nuts.

NOTE: On belt driven overhead camshaft engines, never turn crankshaft backwards.

6. Remove driveshaft and install extension housing oil seal replacer tool.
7. Disconnect speedometer cable from extension housing.
8. Disconnect shift rod from transmission

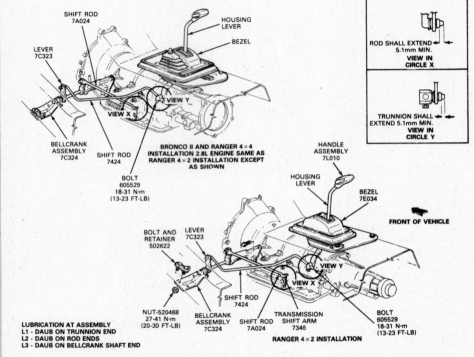

Fig. 2 Shift control linkage adjustment. A4LD automatic overdrive transmission

manual lever.
9. Remove starter to converter housing attaching bolts, then position starter aside.
10. Disconnect neutral start switch electrical connectors from switch assembly.
11. Remove vacuum line from transmission vacuum modulator.
12. Position a suitable jack under transmission and raise slightly.
13. Remove engine rear support-to-crossmember attaching bolts.
14. Remove crossmember-to-frame side support attaching bolts, then the crossmember insulator and support damper.
15. Lower jack and allow transmission to hang.
16. Position a suitable jack under engine assembly and raise engine to gain access to the upper two converter housing-to-engine attaching bolts.
17. Disconnect oil cooler lines from transmission. Cap all openings.
18. Remove lower converter housing-to-engine attaching bolts.
19. Remove transmission filler tube.
20. Secure transmission to jack using a suitable safety chain.
21. Remove two upper converter housing-to-engine attaching bolts.
22. Remove transmission from vehicle.
23. Reverse procedure to install.

C3 Automatic Transmission

INDEX

DESCRIPTION

The main control incorporates a manually selective first and second gear range. The transmission features a drive range that provides for fully automatic upshifts and downshifts, and manually selected low and second gears.

The transmission consists essentially of a torque converter, a compound planetary gear train, two multiple disc clutches, a one-way clutch and a hydraulic control system, **Fig. 1.**

For all normal driving the selector lever is moved to the green dot under "Drive" on the selector quadrant on the steering column or on the floor console. As the throttle is advanced from the idle position, the transmission will upshift automatically to intermediate gear and then to high.

With the throttle closed the transmission will downshift automatically as the car speed drops to about 10 mph. With the throttle open at any position up to the detent, the downshifts will come in automatically at speeds above 10 mph and in proportion to throttle opening. This prevents engine lugging on steep hill climbing, for example.

When the selector lever is moved to "L" with the transmission in high, the transmission will downshift to intermediate or to low depending on the road speed. At speeds above 25 mph, the downshift will be from high to intermediate. At speeds below 25 mph, the downshift will be from high to low. With the selector lever in the "L" position the transmission cannot upshift.

TROUBLESHOOTING GUIDE

The items to check for each trouble symptom are arranged in a logical sequence that should be followed for quickest results.

ROUGH INITIAL ENGAGEMENT IN D1 OR D2

1. Engine idle speed.
2. Vacuum diaphragm unit or tubes restricted, leaking or maladjusted.
3. Check control pressure.
4. Pressure regulator.
5. Valve body.
6. Forward clutch.

1–2 OR 2–3 SHIFT POINTS ERRATIC

1. Check fluid level.
2. Vacuum diaphragm unit or tubes restricted, leaking or maladjusted.
3. Intermediate servo.
4. Manual linkage adjustment.
5. Governor.
6. Check control pressure.
7. Valve body.
8. Make air pressure check.

ROUGH 1–2 UPSHIFTS

1. Vacuum diaphragm unit or tubes restricted, leaking or maladjusted.
2. Intermediate servo.
3. Intermediate band.
4. Check control pressure.
5. Valve body.
6. Pressure regulator.

ROUGH 2–3 UPSHIFTS

1. Vacuum diaphragm unit or tubes restricted, leaking or maladjusted.
2. Intermediate servo.
3. Check control pressure.
4. Pressure regulator.
5. Intermediate band.
6. Valve body.

7. Make air pressure check.
8. Reverse-high clutch.
9. Reverse-high clutch piston air bleed valve.

DRAGGED OUT 1–2 SHIFT

1. Check fluid level.
2. Vacuum diaphragm unit or tubes restricted, leaking or maladjusted.
3. Intermediate servo.
4. Check control pressure.
5. Intermediate band.
6. Valve body.
7. Pressure regulator.
8. Make air pressure check.
9. Leakage in hydraulic system.

ENGINE OVERSPEEDS ON 2–3 SHIFT

1. Manual linkage.
2. Check fluid level.
3. Vacuum diaphragm unit or tubes restricted, leaking or maladjusted.
4. Reverse servo.
5. Check control pressure.
6. Valve body.
7. Pressure regulator.
8. Intermediate band.
9. Reverse-high clutch.
10. Reverse-high clutch piston air bleed valve.

NO 1–2 OR 2–3 SHIFT

1. Manual linkage.
2. Downshift linkage, including inner lever position.
3. Vacuum diaphragm unit or tubes restricted, leaking or maladjusted.
4. Governor.
5. Check control pressure.
6. Valve body.
7. Intermediate band.
8. Intermediate servo.

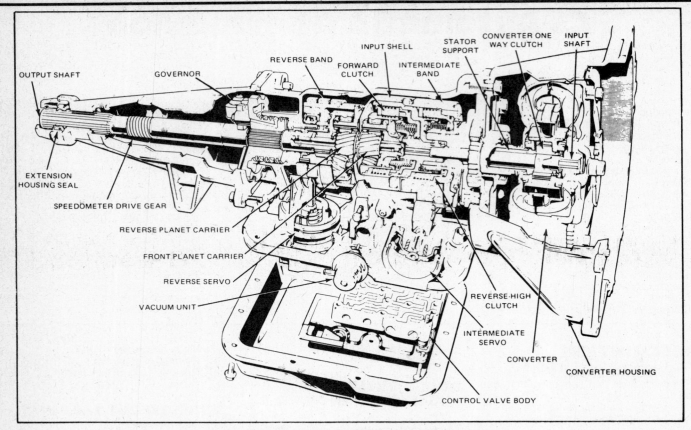

Fig. 1 Sectional View of C3 automatic transmission

9. Reverse-high clutch.
10. Reverse-high clutch piston air bleed valve.

NO 3—1 SHIFT IN D1 OR 3—2 SHIFT IN D2

1. Governor.
2. Valve body.

NO FORCED DOWNSHIFTS

1. Downshift linkage, including inner lever position.
2. Valve body.
3. Vacuum diaphragm unit or tubes restricted, leaking or maladjusted.

RUNAWAY ENGINE ON FORCED 3—2 DOWNSHIFT

1. Check control pressure.
2. Intermediate servo.
3. Intermediate band.
4. Pressure regulator.
5. Valve body.
6. Vacuum diaphragm unit or tubes restricted, leaking or maladjusted.
7. Leakage in hydraulic system.

ROUGH 3—2 OR 3—1 SHIFT AT CLOSED THROTTLE

1. Engine idle speed.
2. Vacuum diaphragm unit or tubes restricted, leaking or maladjusted.

3. Intermediate servo.
4. Valve body.
5. Pressure regulator.

SHIFTS 1—3 IN D1 AND D2

1. Intermediate band.
2. Intermediate servo.
3. Vacuum diaphragm unit or tubes restricted, leaking or maladjusted.
4. Valve body.
5. Governor.
6. Make air pressure check.

NO ENGINE BRAKING IN 1ST GEAR—MANUAL LOW

1. Manual linkage.
2. Reverse band.
3. Reverse servo.
4. Valve body.
5. Governor.
6. Make air pressure check.

SLIPS OR CHATTERS IN 1ST GEAR—D1

1. Check fluid level.
2. Vacuum diaphragm unit or tubes restricted, leaking or maladjusted.
3. Check control pressure.
4. Press regulator.
5. Valve body.
6. Forward clutch.
7. Leakage in hydraulic system.
8. Planetary one-way clutch.

SLIPS OR CHATTERS IN 2ND GEAR

1. Check fluid level.
2. Vacuum diaphragm unit or tubes restricted, leaking or maladjusted.
3. Intermediate servo.
4. Intermediate band.
5. Check control pressure.
6. Pressure regulator.
7. Valve body.
8. Make air pressure check.
9. Forward clutch.
10. Leakage in hydraulic system.

SLIPS OR CHATTERS IN R

1. Check fluid level.
2. Vacuum diaphragm unit or tubes restricted, leaking or maladjusted.
3. Reverse band.
4. Check control pressure.
5. Reverse servo.
6. Pressure regulator.
7. Valve body.
8. Make air pressure check.
9. Reverse-high clutch.
10. Leakage in hydraulic system.
11. Reverse-high piston air bleed valve.

NO DRIVE IN D1 ONLY

1. Check fluid level.
2. Manual linkage.
3. Check control pressure.
4. Valve body.

5. Make air pressure check.
6. Planetary one-way clutch.

NO DRIVE IN D2 ONLY

1. Check fluid level.
2. Manual linkage.
3. Check control pressure.
4. Intermediate servo.
5. Valve body.
6. Make air pressure check.
7. Leakage in hydraulic system.
8. Planetary one-way clutch

NO DRIVE IN L ONLY

1. Check fluid level.
2. Manual linkage.
3. Check control pressure.
4. Valve body.
5. Reverse servo.
6. Make air pressure check.
7. Leakage in hydraulic system.
8. Planetary one-way clutch.

NO DRIVE IN R ONLY

1. Check fluid level.
2. Manual linkage.
3. Reverse band.
4. Check control pressure.
5. Reverse servo.
6. Valve body.
7. Make air pressure check.
8. Reverse-high clutch.
9. Leakage in hydraulic system.
10. Reverse-high clutch piston air bleed valve.

NO DRIVE IN ANY SELECTOR POSITION

1. Check fluid level.
2. Manual linkage.
3. Check control pressure.
4. Pressure regulator.
5. Valve body.
6. Make air pressure check.
7. Leakage in hydraulic system.
8. Front pump.

LOCKUP IN D1 ONLY

1. Reverse-high clutch.
2. Parking linkage.
3. Leakage in hydraulic system.

LOCKUP IN D2 ONLY

1. Reverse band.
2. Reverse servo.
3. Reverse-high clutch.
4. Parking linkage.
5. Leakage in hydraulic system.
6. Planetary one-way clutch.

LOCKUP IN L ONLY

1. Intermediate band.
2. Intermediate servo.
3. Reverse-high clutch.
4. Parking linkage.
5. Leakage in hydraulic system.

LOCKUP IN R ONLY

1. Intermediate band.
2. Intermediate servo.
3. Forward clutch.
4. Parking linkage.
5. Leakage in hydraulic system.

PARKING LOCK BINDS OR DOES NOT HOLD

1. Manual linkage.
2. Parking linkage.

MAXIMUM SPEED TOO LOW, POOR ACCELERATION

1. Engine performance.
2. Brakes bind.
3. Converter one-way clutch.

NOISY IN N OR P

1. Check fluid level.
2. Pressure regulator.
3. Front pump.
4. Planetary assembly.

NOISY IN ALL GEARS

1. Check fluid level.
2. Pressure regulator.
3. Planetary assembly.
4. Forward clutch.
5. Front pump.
6. Planetary one-way clutch.

TRUCK MOVES FORWARD IN N

1. Manual linkage.
2. Forward clutch.

MAINTENANCE
CHECKING OIL LEVEL

1. Make sure car is on a level floor.
2. Apply parking brake firmly.
3. Run engine at normal idle speed. If transmission fluid is cold, run engine at a fast idle until fluid reaches normal operating temperature. When fluid is warm, slow engine to normal idle speed.
4. Shift selector lever through all positions, then place lever at "P". Do not shut down engine during fluid level checks.
5. Clean all dirt from dipstick cap before removing dipstick from filler tube.
6. Pull dipstick out of tube, wipe it clean and push it all the way back in tube.
7. Pull dipstick out of tube again and check fluid level. If necessary, add enough fluid to raise the level to the "F" mark on dipstick. Do not overfill.

DRAIN & REFILL

NOTE: The Ford Motor Company recommends the use of an automatic transmission fluid with Qualification No. M2C-33F, type F, for 1979 models and M2C-138-CJ or Dexron II for 1980–85 models (on container). The recommended fluid is said to have a greater coefficient of friction and greater ability to handle maximum engine torques without band or clutch slippage.

Normal maintenance and lubrication requirements do not necessitate periodic fluid changes. If a major failure has occurred in the transmission, it will have to be removed for service. At this time the converter and transmission cooler must be thoroughly flushed to remove any foreign matter.

When filling a dry transmission and converter, add five quarts of fluid. Start engine, shift the selector lever through all ranges and place in a R position. Check fluid level and add enough to raise the level in the transmission to the "F" (full) mark on the dipstick.

When a partial drain and refill is required due to front band adjustment or minor repair, proceed as follows:

1. Loosen and remove all but two oil pan bolts and drop one edge of the pan to drain the oil.
2. Remove and clean pan and screen.
3. Place a new gasket on pan and install pan and screen.
4. Add three quarts of fluid to transmission.
5. Run engine at idle speed for about two minutes.
6. Check oil level and add oil as necessary.
7. Run engine at a fast idle until it reaches normal operating temperature.
8. Shift selector lever through all ranges and then place it in R position.
9. Add fluid as required to bring the level to the full mark.

IN-VEHICLE ADJUSTMENTS
SHIFT LINKAGE, ADJUST

1. Place transmission selector control lever into Drive (D) position, then loosen trunnion bolt, **Fig. 2.**

NOTE: Ensure shift lever detent pawl is held against the rearward Drive (D) detent stop during shift linkage adjustment.

2. Place transmission manual lever into Drive (D) range by moving bellcrank lever completely rearward, then forward three detents.
3. With transmission selector lever and manual lever in Drive (D) position, apply a light forward pressure onto the shifter control lower arm while tightening the trunnion bolt. Torque bolt to 13–23 ft. lbs.

NOTE: Forward pressure on shifter lower arm will ensure correct positioning within the Drive (D) detent.

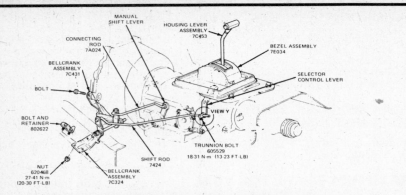

Fig. 2 Shift linkage adjustment (Typical)

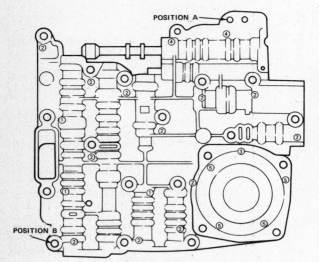

Fig. 3 Valve body bolt hole location

Position	Bolt Size Metric	Length in Millimeters	Length in Inches
1	M6 x 45	45mm	1.772
2	M6 x 40	40.1mm	1.578
3	M6 x 35	35mm	1.378
4	M6 x 30	29mm	1.141
5	M6 x 20	20mm	.787

Position	Quantity	Torque N·m	Torque Ft-Lb
1	3	8-11	6-8
2	12	8-11	6-8
3	1	8-11	6-8
4	2	8-11	6-8
5	4	9.5-13.5	7-10

FRONT BAND, ADJUST

1. Remove downshift rod from transmission downshift lever.
2. Clean area around band adjusting screw, then remove and discard locknut.
3. Install a new locknut onto adjusting screw.
4. Using tool kit T71P-7737-A or equivalent, tighten adjusting screw until tool handle "clicks".

NOTE: The tool kit is a preset torque wrench that clicks and breaks when the torque on the adjusting screw reaches 10 ft. lbs.

5. Back off adjusting screw 1½ turns on 1979 models or 2 turns on 1980–85 models, then holding the adjusting screw from turning, torque adjusting screw locknut to 35–45 ft. lbs.
6. Install downshift rod onto transmission downshift lever.

IN-VEHICLE REPAIRS

VALVE BODY, REPLACE

1. Disconnect battery ground cable.
2. Raise and support vehicle.
3. Loosen oil pan attaching bolts and drain fluid from transmission.
4. Remove oil pan and gasket.
5. Remove filter screen and gasket.
6. Remove rear servo cover and gasket.
7. Remove valve body attaching bolts, then the valve body from transmission.
8. Reverse procedure to install. During installation of valve body, proceed as follows:
   a. Insert the correct length bolts finger tight in holes A and B to position valve body correctly on case, **Fig. 3.**
   b. Insert all remaining bolts, except the filter screen bolts, and tighten to specifications given in **Fig. 3.**

REAR SERVO, REPLACE

1. Disconnect battery ground cable.
2. Raise and support vehicle.
3. Loosen oil pan attaching bolts and drain fluid from transmission.
4. Remove oil pan and gasket.
5. Remove oil filter screen and gasket.
6. Remove servo attaching bolts, then the rear servo cover, servo and gasket.
7. Reverse procedure to install.

EXTENSION HOUSING, REPLACE

1. Disconnect battery ground cable.
2. Raise and support vehicle.
3. Remove propeller shaft from vehicle.
4. Position a suitable jack under transmission.
5. Disconnect speedometer cable from extension housing.
6. Remove rear support to crossmember bolts or nuts.
7. Raise transmission slightly, then remove rear support assembly from extension housing.
8. Loosen extension housing to transmission case attaching bolts and allow fluid to drain.
9. Remove extension housing from transmission case.
10. Reverse procedure to install. Torque extension housing to transmission case attaching bolts to 27–39 ft. lbs.

GOVERNOR, REPLACE

1. Disconnect battery ground cable.
2. Remove extension housing as described under "Extension Housing, Replace."
3. Remove governor body to oil collector body attaching bolts, then the governor.
4. Reverse procedure to install.

TRANSMISSION
REPLACE
EXCEPT RANGER & BRONCO II

1. Raise and support vehicle.
2. Place a drain pan under transmission oil pan, then, starting at rear, loosen attaching bolts and drain fluid from transmission. Leave two bolts in front and reinstall two bolts on rear of oil pan to temporarily hold it in place.
3. Remove converter drain plug access cover and adapter plate bolts from lower end of converter housing.
4. Remove converter-to-flywheel attaching nuts. Place a wrench on crankshaft pulley attaching bolt to rotate converter to gain access to nuts.

NOTE: Do not turn engine backwards on belt driven overhead camshaft engines.

5. Rotate converter to gain access to converter drain plug, then remove the plug. After fluid has drained from converter, reinstall drain plug and torque to 20–30 ft. lbs.
6. Remove driveshaft, then install extension housing seal replacer tool in extension housing.
7. Remove speedometer cable from extension housing, then disconnect shift rod from transmission manual

lever and the downshift rod from transmission downshift lever.

8. Remove starter-to-converter housing attaching bolts and position starter motor aside.
9. Disconnect neutral start switch wires from the switch, then remove vacuum line from transmission vacuum modulator.
10. Position a suitable transmission jack under transmission and raise it slightly, then remove engine rear support-to-crossmember attaching bolts.
11. Remove crossmember-to-frame side support attaching bolts, then the crossmember insulator and support and damper.
12. Lower the transmission jack, then position a suitable jack under front of engine and raise engine to gain access to the two upper converter housing-to-engine attaching bolts.
13. Disconnect oil cooler lines from transmission. Plug all openings to prevent contamination.
14. Remove lower converter housing-to-engine attaching bolts, then the transmission filler tube.
15. Install a safety chain to hold transmission on jack, then remove two upper converter housing-to-engine attaching bolts.
16. Move transmission rearward and lower it from vehicle.
17. Reverse procedure to install. Note the following torques: converter housing to engine bolts, 28–38 ft. lbs.; filler tube bolt, 28–38 ft. lbs.; crossmember-to-frame side rail bolts, 20–30 ft. lbs.; rear engine-to-crossmember bolt, 60–80 ft. lbs.; starter bolts, 15–20 ft. lbs.; flywheel-to-converter nuts, 20–34 ft. lbs.; converter drain plug access cover and adapter plate bolts, 12–16 ft. lbs.; companion flange bolts, 70–95 ft. lbs.

RANGER & BRONCO II

1. Disconnect battery ground cable.
2. Raise and support vehicle.
3. Place a suitable fluid drain pan under transmission oil pan.
4. Starting from the rear of the pan and working toward the front, loosen transmission fluid pan attaching bolts and allow fluid to drain.
5. Remove all transmission fluid pan attaching bolts except two front bolts. After all transmission fluid has drained, temporarily install two pan rear bolts.
6. Remove converter drain plug access cover and adapter plate attaching bolts from lower end of the converter housing.
7. Remove four flywheel to converter attaching nuts. Crank engine to turn converter to gain access to the converter nuts.
8. Remove converter drain plug and drain fluid from converter. After all the fluid has drained, install plug and torque to 20–30 ft. lbs.
9. Remove drive shaft from transmission and install seal protector tool onto transmission extension housing.
10. Disconnect speedometer cable from extension housing.
11. Disconnect shift rod from transmission manual lever. Disconnect downshift rod from transmission downshift lever.
12. Remove starter-to-converter housing attaching bolts and position starter aside.
13. Disconnect neutral start switch electrical connectors from switch.
14. Disconnect vacuum line from transmission vacuum modulator.
15. Position a suitable jack under transmission and raise transmission assembly slightly.
16. Remove engine rear support-to-crossmember attaching bolts.
17. Remove engine rear support-to-crossmember attaching bolts.
18. Remove crossmember insulator, support and damper.
19. Lower jack supporting transmission and allow transmission to hang.
20. Position a suitable jack onto front of engine, then raise engine to gain access to the 2 upper converter housing-to-engine attaching bolts.
21. Disconnect and cap oil cooler lines from transmission.
22. Remove lower converter housing-to-engine attaching bolts.
23. Remove transmission oil filler tube.
24. Secure transmission to the jack with a safety chain.
25. Remove two upper coverter housing-to-engine attaching bolts. Move transmission rearward and downward and remove from vehicle.
26. Reverse procedure to install.

NOTE: During installation of transmission, do not allow transmission to get into a converter down position as this will cause the converter to move forward and disengage from the pump gear. The converter must rest against the flywheel. This indicates that the converter pilot is not binding in the engine crankshaft.

C4 Automatic Transmission

INDEX

DESCRIPTION

The main control incorporates a manually selective first and second gear range. The transmission features a drive range that provides for fully automatic upshifts and downshifts, and manually selected low and second gears.

The transmission consists essentially of a torque converter, a compound planetary gear train, two multiple disc clutches, a one-way clutch and a hydraulic control system, **Fig. 1.**

For all normal driving the selector lever is moved to the green dot under "Drive" on the selector quadrant on the steering column or on the floor console. As the throttle is advanced from the idle position, the transmission will upshift automatically to intermediate gear and then to high.

With the throttle closed the transmission will downshift automatically as the vehicle speed drops to about 10 mph. With the throttle open at any position up to the detent, the downshifts will come in automatically at speeds above 10 mph and in proportion to throttle opening. This prevents engine lugging on steep hill climbing, for example.

When the selector lever is moved to "L" with the transmission in high, the transmission will downshift to intermediate or to low depending on the road speed. At speed above 25 mph, the downshift will be from high to intermediate. At speeds below 25 mph, the downshift will be from high to low. With the selector lever in the "L" position the transmission cannot upshift.

TROUBLESHOOTING GUIDE

The items to check for each trouble symptom are arranged in a logical sequence that should be followed for quickest results.

ROUGH INITIAL ENGAGEMENT IN D1 OR D2

1. Engine idle speed.
2. Vacuum diaphragm unit or tubes restricted, leaking or maladjusted.
3. Check control pressure.
4. Pressure regulator.
5. Valve body.
6. Forward clutch.

1–2 OR 2–3 SHIFT POINTS ERRATIC

1. Check fluid level.
2. Vacuum diaphragm unit or tubes restricted, leaking or maladjusted.
3. Intermediate servo.
4. Manual linkage adjustment.
5. Governor.
6. Check control pressure.
7. Valve body.
8. Make air pressure check.

ROUGH 1–2 UPSHIFTS

1. Vacuum diaphragm unit or tubes restricted, leaking or maladjusted.
2. Intermediate servo.
3. Intermediate band.
4. Check control pressure.
5. Valve body.
6. Pressure regulator.

ROUGH 2–3 UPSHIFTS

1. Vacuum diaphragm unit or tubes restricted, leaking or maladjusted.
2. Intermediate servo.
3. Check control pressure.
4. Pressure regulator.
5. Intermediate band.
6. Valve body.
7. Make air pressure check.
8. Reverse-high clutch.
9. Reverse-high clutch piston air bleed valve.

DRAGGED OUT 1–2 SHIFT

1. Check fluid level.
2. Vacuum diaphragm unit or tubes restricted, leaking or maladjusted.
3. Intermediate servo.
4. Check control pressure.
5. Intermediate band.
6. Valve body.
7. Pressure regulator.
8. Make air pressure check.
9. Leakage in hydraulic system.

ENGINE OVERSPEEDS ON 2–3 SHIFT

1. Manual linkage.
2. Check fluid level.
3. Vacuum diaphragm unit or tubes restricted, leaking or maladjusted.
4. Reverse servo.

5. Check control pressure.
6. Valve body.
7. Pressure regulator.
8. Intermediate band.
9. Reverse-high clutch.
10. Reverse-high clutch piston air bleed valve.

NO 1–2 OR 2–3 SHIFT

1. Manual linkage.
2. Downshift linkage, including inner lever position.
3. Vacuum diaphragm unit or tubes restricted, leaking or maladjusted.
4. Governor.
5. Check control pressure.
6. Valve body.
7. Intermediate band.
8. Intermediate servo.
9. Reverse-high clutch.
10. Reverse-high clutch piston air bleed valve.

NO 3–1 SHIFT IN D1 OR 3–2 SHIFT IN D2

1. Governor.
2. Valve body.

NO FORCED DOWNSHIFTS

1. Downshift linkage, including inner lever position.
2. Valve body.
3. Vacuum diaphragm unit or tubes restricted, leaking or maladjusted.

RUNAWAY ENGINE ON FORCED 3–2 DOWNSHIFT

1. Check control pressure.
2. Intermediate servo.
3. Intermediate band.
4. Pressure regulator.
5. Valve body.
6. Vacuum diaphragm unit or tubes restricted, leaking or maladjusted.
7. Leakage in hydraulic system.

ROUGH 3–2 OR 3–1 SHIFT AT CLOSED THROTTLE

1. Engine idle speed.
2. Vacuum diaphragm unit or tubes restricted, leaking or maladjusted.
3. Intermediate servo.
4. Valve body.
5. Pressure regulator.

SHIFTS 1–3 IN D1 & D2

1. Intermediate band.
2. Intermediate servo.
3. Vacuum diaphragm unit or tubes restricted, leaking or maladjusted.
4. Valve body.
5. Governor.
6. Make air pressure check.

NO ENGINE BRAKING IN 1ST GEAR—MANUAL LOW

1. Manual linkage.
2. Reverse band.

3. Reverse servo.
4. Valve body.
5. Governor.
6. Make air pressure check.

SLIPS OR CHATTERS IN 1ST GEAR—D1

1. Check fluid level.
2. Vacuum diaphragm unit or tubes restricted, leaking or maladjusted.
3. Check control pressure.
4. Press regulator.
5. Valve body.
6. Forward clutch.
7. Leakage in hydraulic system.
8. Planetary one-way clutch.

SLIPS OR CHATTERS IN 2ND GEAR

1. Check fluid level.
2. Vacuum diaphragm unit or tubes restricted, leaking or maladjusted.
3. Intermediate servo.
4. Intermediate band.
5. Check control pressure.
6. Pressure regulator.
7. Valve body.
8. Make air pressure check.
9. Forward clutch.
10. Leakage in hydraulic system.

SLIPS OR CHATTERS IN R

1. Check fluid level.
2. Vacuum diaphragm unit or tubes restricted, leaking or maladjusted.
3. Reverse band.
4. Check control pressure.
5. Reverse servo.
6. Pressure regulator.
7. Valve body.
8. Make air pressure check.
9. Reverse-high clutch.
10. Leakage in hydraulic system.
11. Reverse-high piston air bleed valve.

NO DRIVE IN D1 ONLY

1. Check fluid level.
2. Manual linkage.
3. Check control pressure.
4. Valve body.
5. Make air pressure check.
6. Planetary one-way clutch.

NO DRIVE IN D2 ONLY

1. Check fluid level.
2. Manual linkage.
3. Check control pressure.
4. Intermediate servo.
5. Valve body.
6. Make air pressure check.
7. Leakage in hydraulic system.
8. Planetary one-way clutch.

NO DRIVE IN L ONLY

1. Check fluid level.
2. Manual linkage.
3. Check control pressure.
4. Valve body.
5. Reverse servo.

6. Make air pressure check.
7. Leakage in hydraulic system.
8. Planetary one-way clutch.

NO DRIVE IN R ONLY

1. Check fluid level.
2. Manual linkage.
3. Reverse band.
4. Check control pressure.
5. Reverse servo.
6. Valve body.
7. Make air pressure check.
8. Reverse-high clutch.
9. Leakage in hydraulic system.
10. Reverse-high clutch piston air bleed valve.

NO DRIVE IN ANY SELECTOR POSITION

1. Check fluid level.
2. Manual linkage.
3. Check control pressure.
4. Pressure regulator.
5. Valve body.
6. Make air pressure check.
7. Leakage in hydraulic system.
8. Front pump.

LOCKUP IN D1 ONLY

1. Reverse-high clutch.
2. Parking linkage.
3. Leakage in hydraulic system.

LOCKUP IN D2 ONLY

1. Reverse band.
2. Reverse servo.
3. Reverse-high clutch.
4. Parking linkage.
5. Leakage in hydraulic system.
6. Planetary one-way clutch.

LOCKUP IN L ONLY

1. Intermediate band.
2. Intermediate servo.
3. Reverse-high clutch.
4. Parking linkage.
5. Leakage in hydraulic system.

LOCKUP IN R ONLY

1. Intermediate band.
2. Intermediate servo.
3. Forward clutch.
4. Parking linkage.
5. Leakage in hydraulic system.

PARKING LOCK BINDS OR DOES NOT HOLD

1. Manual linkage.
2. Parking linkage.

MAXIMUM SPEED TOO LOW, POOR ACCELERATION

1. Engine performance.
2. Brakes bind.
3. Converter one-way clutch.

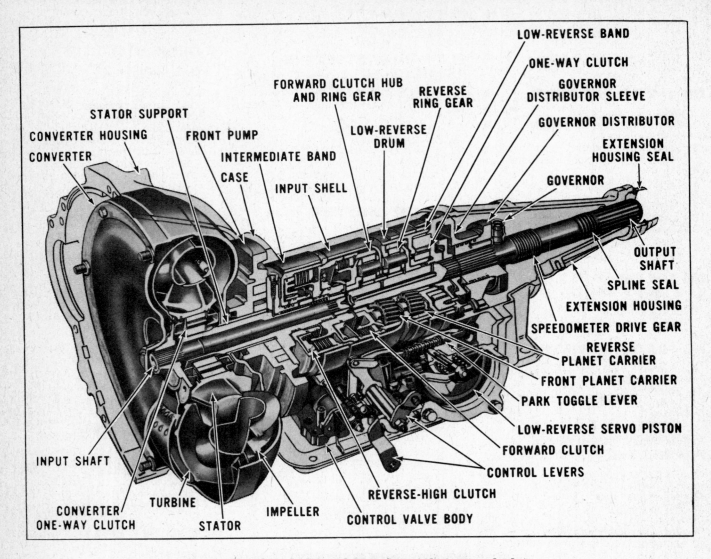

Fig. 1 Sectional view of C4 automatic transmission

NOISY IN N OR P

1. Check fluid level.
2. Pressure regulator.
3. Front pump.
4. Plantetary assembly.

NOISY IN ALL GEARS

1. Check fluid level.
2. Pressure regulator.
3. Planetary assembly.
4. Forward clutch.
5. Front pump.
6. Planetary one-way clutch.

TRUCK MOVES FORWARD IN N

1. Manual linkage.
2. Forward clutch.

MAINTENANCE
CHECKING OIL LEVEL

1. Make sure vehicle is on a level floor.
2. Apply parking brake firmly.
3. Run engine at normal idle speed. If transmission fluid is cold, run engine at a fast idle until fluid reaches normal operating temperature. When fluid is warm, slow engine to normal idle speed.
4. Shift selector lever through all positions, then place lever at "P". Do not shut down engine during fluid level checks.
5. Clean all dirt from dipstick cap before removing dipstick from filler tube.
6. Pull dipstick out of tube, wipe it clean and push it all the way back in tube.
7. Pull dipstick out of tube again and

check fluid level. If necessary, add enough fluid to raise the level to the "F" mark on dipstick. Do not overfill.

DRAIN & REFILL

NOTE: The Ford Motor Company recommends the use of an automatic transmission fluid with Qualification No. M2C-33F, type F, for 1979 models and M2C-138-CJ or Dexron II for 1980–81 models (on container). The recommended fluid is said to have a greater coefficient of friction and greater ability to handle maximum engine torques without band or clutch slippage.

Normal maintenance and lubrication requirements do not necessitate periodic fluid changes. If a major failure has occurred in the transmission, it will have to be removed for service. At this time the

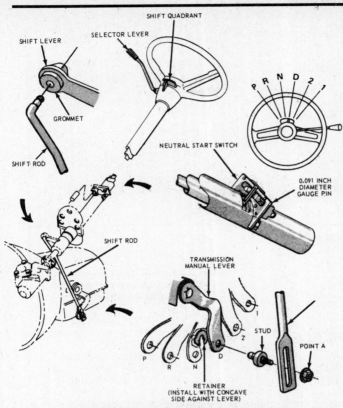

Fig. 2   Shift linkage adjustment. F-100 through 350 except 4 × 4

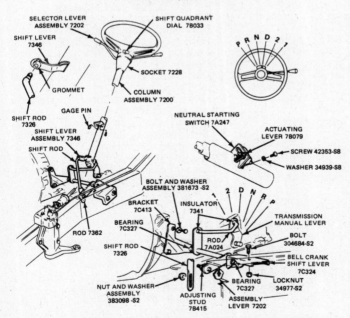

Fig. 3   Shift linkage adjustment. F-150 4 × 4

converter and transmission cooler must be thoroughly flushed to remove any foreign matter.

When filling a dry transmission and converter, install five quarts of fluid. Start engine, shift the selector lever through all ranges and place it a R position. Check fluid level and add enough to raise the level in the transmission to the "F" (full) mark on the dipstick.

When a partial drain and refill is required due to front band adjustment or minor repair, proceed as follows:

1. Loosen and remove all but two oil pan bolts and drop one edge of the pan to drain the oil.
2. Remove and clean pan and screen.

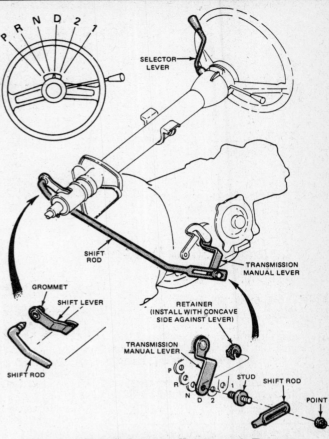

Fig. 4   Shift linkage adjustment. Bronco

3. Place a new gasket on pan and install pan and screen.
4. Add three quarts of fluid to transmission.
5. Run engine at idle speed for about two minutes.
6. Check oil level and add oil as necessary.
7. Run engine at a fast idle until it reaches normal operating temperature.
8. Shift selector lever through all ranges and then place it in R position.
9. Add fluid as required to bring the level to the full mark.

IN-VEHICLE ADJUSTMENTS

SHIFT LINKAGE, ADJUST

1. Disconnect battery ground cable.
2. Place transmission selector lever on steering column into Drive (D) position. Secure selector lever in this position.
3. Loosen shift for adjusting nut at point A, **Figs. 2 through 5.**
4. Place transmission manual lever into Drive (D) position by moving lever completely rearward, then forward 2 detents.
5. With selector lever and transmission

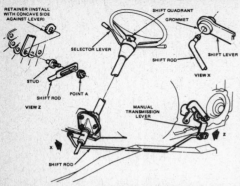

Fig. 5 Shift linkage adjustment. E-100 through 350

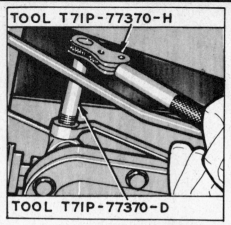

Fig. 6 Intermediate band adjustment

Fig. 7 Low-reverse band adjustment

lever in (D) position, torque nut at point A to 12—18 ft. lbs.

THROTTLE LINKAGE, ADJUST

1. Rotate throttle to wide open position.
2. Insert a .060 inch feeler gauge between throttle lever and adjusting screw.
3. Rotate transmission kickdown lever until lever engages transmission internal stop.

NOTE: Do not use kickdown rod to rotate transmission lever.

4. Rotate adjusting screw until contact is made between adjusting screw and .060 inch feeler gauge, then tighten locknut.
5. Remove .060 inch feeler gauge.

INTERMEDIATE BAND, ADJUST

1. Loosen lock nut several turns.
2. With tool shown in **Fig. 6** tighten adjusting screw until tool handle clicks. This tool is a pre-set torque wrench which clicks and overruns when the torque on the adjusting screw reaches 10 ft-lbs.
3. Back off adjusting screw exactly 1¾ turns.
4. Hold adjusting screw from turning and tighten lock nut.

REAR BAND

1. Loosen lock nut several turns.
2. Tighten adjusting screw until tool handle clicks, **Fig. 7.** Tool shown is a pre-set torque wrench which clicks and overruns when the torque on the adjusting screw reaches 10 ft-lbs.
3. Back off adjusting screw exactly 3 full turns.
4. Hold adjusting screw from turning and tighten lock nut.

IN-VEHICLES REPAIRS
VALVE BODY, REPLACE

1. Disconnect battery ground cable.
2. Raise and support vehicle.
3. Remove fluid filler tube from oil pan and drain fluid from transmission.
4. Remove oil pan attaching bolts, pan and gasket.
5. Place transmission manual lever into Park (P) position, then remove 2 bolts securing detent spring to valve body and transmission case.
6. Remove remaining valve body to case attaching bolts, then the valve body from transmission.
7. Reverse procedure to install. Torque valve body to transmission case attaching bolts to 80—120 inch lbs.

INTERMEDIATE SERVO, REPLACE

1. Disconnect battery ground cable.
2. Raise and support vehicle.
3. Disconnect and cap forward transmission fluid cooler line.
4. Remove 4 servo cover to transmission case bolts.
5. Disconnect vacuum line from transmission, then remove servo cover, gasket, piston and piston return spring.
6. Reverse procedure to install. Torque intermediate servo to transmission case bolts to 16—22 ft. lbs.

LOW-REVERSE SERVO, REPLACE

1. Disconnect battery ground cable.
2. Raise and support vehicle.
3. Loosen reverse band adjusting screw locknut. Torque reverse band adjusting screw to 10 ft. lbs.
4. Remove 4 servo cover to transmission case attaching bolts. Remove vent tube retaining clip, servo cover and seal from transmission case.

5. Remove servo piston from transmission case.
6. Reverse procedure to install. Torque low-reverse servo cover to transmission case bolts to 12—20 ft. lbs.

EXTENSION HOUSING, REPLACE
E-100, 150, F-100—250 Models
1. Disconnect battery ground cable.
2. Raise and support vehicle.
3. Remove propeller shaft from vehicle.
4. Position a suitable jack under transmission.
5. Disconnect speedometer cable from extension housing.
6. Remove crossmember to extension housing attaching bolts.
7. Loosen extension housing to transmission case attaching bolts and drain fluid from transmission.
8. Remove 6 extension housing to transmission case attaching bolts, then the extension housing and gasket.
9. Reverse procedure to install. Torque extension housing to transmission case attaching bolts to 28—40 ft. lbs.

GOVERNOR, REPLACE
E-100, 150, F100—250 Models
1. Disconnect battery ground cable.
2. Raise and support vehicle.
3. Remove extension housing as described under "Extension Housing, Replace".
4. Remove governor housing to governor distributor attaching bolts.
5. Remove governor housing from distributor.
6. Reverse procedure to install. Torque governor housing to governor distributor bolts to 80—120 inch lbs.

Bronco Models
1. Disconnect battery ground cable.
2. Remove fan shroud from radiator.

3. Raise and support vehicle.
4. Remove transfer case shield, if equipped.
5. Remove drain plug from transfer case and drain lubricant.
6. Disconnect front and rear driveshafts from transfer case assembly and position aside.
7. Disconnect speedometer cable from transfer case assembly.
8. Disconnect shift rod from transfer case shift lever bracket.
9. Remove bolts, washers, plates and insulators securing crossmember to transfer case adapter.
10. Remove crossmember to frame side support attaching bolts.
11. Position a suitable jack under transmission and transfer case assemblies.
12. Raise transmission and transfer case assembly slightly, then remove 4 bolts securing left side support bracket to frame. Remove side support bracket, crossmember and upper crossmember insulators from vehicle.
13. Remove bolts securing shift lever bracket to transfer case adapter. Allow assembly to hang by the shift lever.
14. Remove transfer case to transmission case attaching bolts. Remove transfer case from vehicle.
15. Remove governor housing to governor distributor attaching bolts. Remove governor housing from distributor.
16. Reverse procedure to install.

TRANSMISSION
REPLACE

EXC. BRONCO, ECONOLINE & RANCHERO

1. Drain transmission and converter.
2. Remove drive shaft.
3. Disconnect oil cooler lines from transmission.
4. Remove downshift lever return spring from low-reverse servo cover.
5. Disconnect shift rods from transmission levers.
6. Disconnect neutral start switch wiring harness and back-up wires at connectors, then retaining clips and retainer.
7. Remove speedometer gear from extension housing.
8. Remove four converter-to-flywheel

bolts.
9. Remove starter.
10. Disconnect vacuum line from diaphragm unit.
11. Support transmission with a jack.
12. Remove crossmember from under extension housing.
13. Remove transmission-to-engine bolts.
14. Move transmission away from engine, then lower and remove transmission from under truck.
15. Reverse procedure to install.

BRONCO

1. Remove fan shroud and raise vehicle.
2. Remove transfer case shield, if used, and drain transmission, converter and transfer case.
3. Disconnect rear drive shaft from transfer case and remove front drive shaft from vehicle.
4. Disconnect exhaust system and position aside.
5. Remove speedometer gear from transfer case.
6. Disconnect oil cooler lines, shift linkage and neutral start switch wires from transmission.
7. Remove starter.
8. Disconnect vacuum lines from modulator and retaining clip.
9. Remove crossmember-to-transfer case adapter and crossmember-to-frame side support attaching bolts.
10. Raise transmission and transfer case with a suitable jack and remove left side support bracket-to-frame bolts, side support bracket, crossmember and upper crossmember insulators.
11. Raise transmission and transfer case slightly and disconnect shift rod and shift lever bracket from transfer case.
12. Remove converter housing to engine bolts, slide transmission and transfer case rearward and lower assembly from vehicle.
13. Remove transfer case adapter to transmission bolts and slide transmission from transfer case.
14. Reverse procedure to install.

ECONOLINE

1. Working from inside the truck, remove engine cover and disconnect neutral start switch wires.
2. On V8 units, remove air cleaner heat

tube flex hose.
3. Remove upper converter housing-to-engine bolts.
4. On V8, disconnect exhaust pipe from manifold.
5. Raise vehicle and drain transmission and converter.
6. Remove converter cover and remove converter-to-flywheel bolts.
7. Disconnect drive shaft.
8. Remove transmission filler tube.
9. Remove starter.
10. Install suitable engine support bar.
11. Disconnect vacuum and cooler lines, shift linkage and speedometer cable.
12. Support transmission with suitable jack and remove crossmember.
13. Remove remaining converter housing-to-engine bolts and lower transmission away from vehicle.
14. Reverse procedure to install.

RANCHERO

1. Disconnect neutral safety switch wires in engine compartment.
2. Raise vehicle and remove converter cover at low front side of converter housing.
3. Drain converter.
4. Remove propeller shaft.
5. Remove vacuum line hose from transmission vacuum unit. Disconnect vacuum line from clip.
6. Remove two extension housing to crossmember bolts.
7. Remove speedometer cable from extension housing.
8. Disconnect exhaust pipe from manifold.
9. Remove parking brake cable from equalizer lever.
10. Loosen transmission oil pan bolts and drain oil at one corner of pan.
11. Disconnect cooler lines from the transmission.
12. Remove the manual and kick down linkage rods from transmission shift levers.
13. Where necessary, disconnect the neutral start switch wires.
14. Remove starter.
15. Remove fluid.
16. Remove four converter-to-flywheel nuts.
17. Support transmission with jack.
18. Remove crossmember.
19. Remove converter housing-to-engine bolts.
20. Lower transmission and remove from vehicle.

C5 Automatic Transmission

INDEX

DESCRIPTION

The C5 transmission, **Fig. 1,** is a fully automatic transmission with three speeds and one reverse. It consists of a welded torque converter assembly, a two unit planetary gear train, and a hydraulic system to control gear selection and automatic shift. The 12-inch torque converter, used with larger displacement engine, has a converter clutch. The planetary gear train is a Simpson design with two gear sets in series and a common sun gear. It is the same gear train used in model C4 with minor changes. Two friction clutches and two bands are used to control the gear operation.

The torque converter is coupled to the engine crankshaft, and transmits engine power into the gear train. The output shaft drives the rear wheels through a conventional driveshaft and rear axle. Gear reductions needed to match the engine to the axle take place in the planetary gear train and in the torque converter.

The C5 transmission is closest in resemblance to the C4 which it replaced in production.

Some major differences from the C4 transmission are in the hydraulic system. Several new valves are incorporated along with a new timing valve body. Also the converter relief valve is moved from the reactor support (in the pump assembly) to the timing valve body. Thus, C4 oil pump assemblies must not be used to service the C5. The C5 12 inch converter with the converter clutch is also different than the C4 conventional converter.

In general, C4 special tools will service the C5. One new seal protector tool is needed to install the reverse and high clutch piston. The tool number is T82L-77404-A.

TROUBLESHOOTING GUIDE

SLOW INITIAL ENGAGEMENT

1. Improper fluid level.
2. Damaged or improperly adjusted linkage.
3. Contaminated fluid.
4. Improper clutch and band application or low main control pressure.

ROUGH INITIAL ENGAGEMENT IN EITHER FORWARD OR REVERSE

1. Improper fluid level.
2. High engine idle.
3. Automatic choke on (warm temp.).
4. Looseness in the driveshaft U-joint or engine mount.
5. Incorrect linkage adjustment.
6. Improper clutch or band application, or oil control pressure.

NO OR DELAYED FORWARD ENGAGEMENT

1. Improper fluid level.
2. Manual linkage, misadjusted or damaged.
3. Low main control pressure.
4. Valve body bolts, loose or too tight.
5. Valve body, dirty or sticking valve.
6. Forward clutch assembly burnt or damaged.
7. Forward clutch assembly piston seals worn or cut.
8. Forward clutch assembly cylinder ball check not seating.
9. Forward clutch assembly stator support seal ring grooves, damaged or worn.

NO OR DELAYED REVERSE ENGAGEMENT

1. Improper fluid level.
2. Low main control pressure in reverse.
3. Manual linkage misadjusted or damaged.
4. Valve body, dirty or sticking valve.
5. Valve body bolts loose or too tight.
6. Reverse clutch assembly, burnt or worn.
7. Reverse clutch assembly piston seals, worn or cut.
8. Reverse clutch assembly piston ball not seating.
9. Reverse clutch assembly stator support seal rings or ring grooves, worn or damaged.

NO OR DELAYED REVERSE ENGAGEMENT AND/OR NO ENGINE BRAKING IN MANUAL LOW (1)

1. Low reverse band or servo piston burnt or worn.
2. Low reverse servo seal worn or cut.
3. Low reverse servo bore damaged.
4. Low reverse servo piston sticking in bore.
5. Low reverse band, line pressure low.
6. Low reverse bands out of adjust-

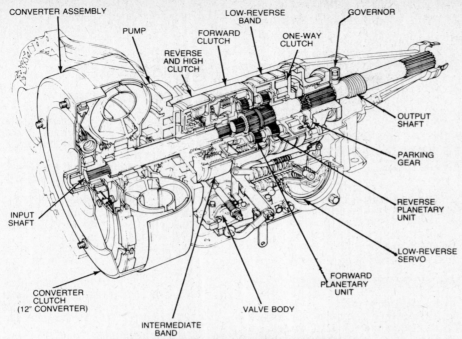

CONVERTER ASSEMBLY

PUMP

FORWARD CLUTCH

REVERSE AND HIGH CLUTCH

LOW-REVERSE BAND

ONE-WAY CLUTCH

GOVERNOR

OUTPUT SHAFT

PARKING GEAR

REVERSE PLANETARY UNIT

LOW-REVERSE SERVO

FORWARD PLANETARY UNIT

VALVE BODY

INTERMEDIATE BAND

CONVERTER CLUTCH (12" CONVERTER)

INPUT SHAFT

Fig. 1 C5 automatic transmission

ment.

7. Polished or glazed band or drum.

NO ENGINE BRAKING IN MANUAL SECOND GEAR

1. Improper fluid level.
2. Linkage out of adjustment.
3. Intermediate band out of adjustment.
4. Improper band or clutch application, or oil pressure control system.
5. Intermediated servo leaking.
6. Polished or glazed band or drum.

NO OR DELAYED ENGAGEMENT FORWARD AND REVERSE

1. Pump gear damaged (no engagement).
2. Output shaft broken (no engagement only).
3. Turbine shaft or input shaft broken (no engagement only).

FORWARD ENGAGEMENT SLIP, SHUDDERS OR CHATTERS

1. Improper fluid level.
2. Manual linkage misadjusted or damaged.
3. Low main control pressure.
4. Valve body bolts, loose or too tight.
5. Valve body dirty or sticking valve.
6. Forward clutch piston ball check not sealing.
7. Forward clutch piston seal cut or worn.
8. Contamination blocking forward clutch feed hole.
9. Low (planetary) one way clutch damaged.

REVERSE ENGAGEMENT SLIP, SHUDDERS OR CHATTERS

1. Improper fluid level.
2. Low main control pressure in reverse.
3. Reverse servo or servo bore damaged.
4. Low (planetary) one-way clutch damaged.
5. Reverse clutch drum bushing damaged.
6. Reverse clutch stator support seal rings or ring grooves worn or damaged.
7. Reverse clutch piston seal cut or worn.
8. Reverse band out of adjustment or damaged.
9. Looseness in the driveshaft U-joints or engine mounts.

NO DRIVE, SLIPS OR CHATTERS IN FIRST GEAR "D"

1. Damaged or worn one-way clutch.

NO DRIVE, SLIPS OR CHATTERS IN SECOND

1. Improper fluid level.
2. Damaged or improperly adjusted linkage.
3. Intermediated band out of adjustment.
4. Improper band or clutch application, or oil pressure control.
5. Damaged or worn servo and/or internal leaks.
6. Dirty or sticking valve body.
7. Polished or glazed intermediate band

or drum.

START UP IN SECOND OR THIRD

1. Improper fluid level.
2. Damaged or improperly adjusted linkage.
3. Improper band and/or clutch application, or oil pressure control system.
4. Damaged or worn governor, governor sticking.
5. Valve body loose.
6. Dirty or sticking valve body.
7. Cross leaks between valve body and case mating surface.

SHIFT POINTS INCORRECT

1. Improper fluid level.
2. Improper vacuum hose routing or leaks.
3. Improper operation of EGR system.
4. Throttle out of adjustment.
5. Improper clutch or band application, or oil pressure control system.
6. Damaged or worn governor.
7. Dirty or sticking valve body.

ALL UPSHIFTS HARSH, DELAYED OR NO UPSHIFTS

1. Improper fluid level.
2. Manual linkage misadjusted or damaged.
3. Governor sticking.
4. Main control pressure too high.
5. Valve body bolts loose or too tight.
6. Valve body dirty or valves sticking.
7. Vacuum leak to diaphragm unit.

ALL UPSHIFTS EARLY OR SLUGGISH

1. Improper fluid level.
2. Low main control pressure.
3. Valve body loose or too tight.
4. Valve body valve sticking.
5. Governor valve sticking.

NO LOW TO SECOND UPSHIFT

1. Improper fluid level.
2. Manual linkage misadjusted or damaged.
3. Governor valve sticking.
4. Valve body bolts loose or too tight.
5. Valve body dirty or sticking valves.
6. Intermediate clutch or band and/or servo assembly burnt.
7. Intermediate piston seals worn or cut.
8. Intermediate piston not positioned properly.
9. Intermediate clutch improper stack up.
10. Low line pressure in intermediate clutch or band.

ROUGH, HARSH, OR DELAYED UPSHIFT LOW TO SECOND

1. Governor valve sticking.

2. Improper fluid level.
3. Poor engine performance.
4. Main control pressure too high.
5. Valve body bolts loose or too tight.
6. Valve body dirty or valves sticking.
7. Intermediate band out of adjustment.
8. Damaged intermediate servo.
9. Engine vacuum leak.

EARLY, SOFT OR SLIPPING LOW TO SECOND UPSHIFT

1. Improper fluid level.
2. Low main control.
3. Valve body bolts loose or too tight.
4. Valve body dirty or valves sticking.
5. Governor valve sticking.
6. Incorrect engine performance.
7. Intermediate band out of adjustment.
8. Damaged intermediate servo or band.
9. Polished or glazed band or drum.

NO SECOND TO THIRD UPSHIFT

1. Low fluid level.
2. Low main control pressure to direct clutch.
3. Valve body bolts too loose or too tight.
4. Valve body dirty or valves sticking.
5. Converter damper hub weld broken.

HARSH OR DELAYED SECOND TO THIRD UPSHIFT

1. Low fluid level.
2. Valve body bolts loose or too tight.
3. Valve body dirty or valves sticking.
4. Damaged or worn intermediate servo release and high clutch piston check ball.
5. Incorrect engine performance.
6. Engine vacuum leak.

EARLY OR SOFT SECOND TO THIRD UPSHIFT

1. Improper fluid level.
2. Valve body bolts loose or too tight.
3. Valve body dirty or valves sticking.

ERRATIC SHIFTS

1. Improper fluid level.
2. Throttle linkage binding or sticking.
3. Valve body bolts loose or too tight.
4. Valve body dirty or valves sticking.
5. Governor valve sticking.
6. Output shaft collector body seal rings (large cast iron) worn or cut.

SHIFTS FROM LOW TO THIRD IN "D"

1. Improper fluid level.
2. Intermediate band out of adjustment.
3. Damaged intermediate servo and/or internal leaks.
4. Polished or glazed band or drum.
5. Improper band or clutch application, or oil pressure control system.
6. Valve body dirty or valves sticking.

ENGINE OVER SPEEDS ON SECOND TO THIRD UPSHIFT

1. Improper fluid level.
2. Linkage out of adjustment.
3. Improper band or clutch application, or oil pressure control system.
4. Damaged or worn high clutch and/or intermediate servo.
5. Valve body dirty or valves sticking.

ROUGH OR SHUDDER THIRD TO LOW SHIFT AT CLOSED THROTTLE

1. Improper fluid level.
2. Incorrect engine idle or performance.
3. Improper linkage adjustment.
4. Improper clutch or band application, or oil pressure control system.
5. Improper governor operation.
6. Valve body dirty or valves sticking.

NO FORCED DOWNSHIFT

1. Improper fluid level.
2. Kickdown linkage out of adjustment.
3. Damaged internal kickdown linkage.
4. Damaged or misadjusted (short) throttle linkage.
5. Valve body dirty or valves sticking.
6. Dirty or sticking governor.

ENGINE OVER SPEEDS ON THIRD TO SECOND SHIFT

1. Improper fluid level.
2. Linkage out of adjustment.
3. Intermediate band out of adjustment.
4. Improper band or clutch application, or oil pressure control system.
5. Damaged or worn intermediate servo.
6. Polished or glazed band or drum.
7. Valve body dirty or valves sticking.

SHIFT EFFORTS HIGH

1. Manual shift linkage damaged or misadjusted.
2. Inner manual lever nut loose.
3. Manual lever retainer pin damaged.

NO START IN "P"

1. Manual linkage misadjusted.
2. Plug connector for the neutral start switch does not fit properly.
3. Neutral start switch plunger travel, inadequate.

NO START IN "P" & "N"

1. Plug connector for the neutral start switch does not fit properly.

TRANSMISSION OVERHEATS

1. Improper fluid level.
2. Incorrect engine idle or performance.
3. Improper band or clutch application, or oil pressure control system.

4. Restriction in cooler or lines.
5. Seized converter one-way clutch.
6. Valve body dirty or valves sticking.

MAINTENANCE

CHECKING OIL LEVEL

1. With engine idling, foot brake applied and vehicle on level surface, move selector lever through each range, pausing in each position.
2. Place selector in Park and apply parking brake. Leave engine running during fluid level check.
3. Clean dirt from transmission fluid dipstick cap and remove dipstick. Wipe dipstick and push back into tube making sure it is fully seated.
4. Pull dipstick out and check fluid level. With transmission at operating temperature, fluid level should be between arrows. With transmission cool, fluid level should read between inner holes. Use only Type H fluid, Ford spec. ESP M2C166-H. Do not overfill.
5. Insert dipstick, making sure it is fully seated.

NOTE: If transmission fluid is at operating temperature, the fluid level on the dipstick should be between the arrows. If fluid level is checked at room temperature, the fluid level on the dipstick should be between the middle and top holes.

DRAIN & REFILL

NOTE: Normal maintenance and lubrication requirements do not necessitate periodic fluid changes. If a major failure has occurred in the transmission, it will have to be removed for service. At this time, the converter, transmission cooler and cooler lines must be thoroughly flushed to remove any foreign matter.

If vehicle is operated under continuous or severe conditions, the transmission and torque converter should be drained and refilled every 20,000 miles.

When a partial drain and refill is required due to an in-vehicle repair operation, proceed as follows:
1. On all except Ranger models, disconnect fluid filler tube from transmission oil pan and drain fluid.
2. On Ranger models, loosen oil pan bolts and lower one edge of pan to drain fluid.
3. Remove and clean pan and screen.
4. Place new gasket on pan and install pan and screen. Torque bolts to 12–16 ft. lbs.
5. Connect filler tube to pan and tighten fitting.
6. Add three quarts of fluid to transmission through the filler tube.
7. Check oil level and add fluid as necessary.

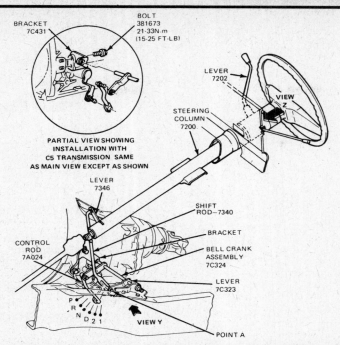

Fig. 2   Shift linkage adjustment. Except Ranger & Bronco II

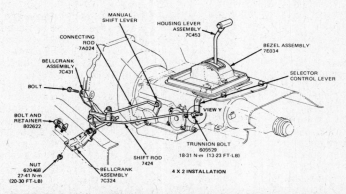

Fig. 3   Shift linkage adjustment. Ranger & Bronco II 4 × 2 models

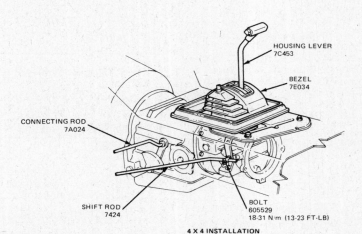

Fig. 4   Shift linkage adjustment. Ranger & Bronco II 4 × 4 models

IN-VEHICLE ADJUSTMENTS

SHIFT LINKAGE

Except Ranger & Bronco II
1. Disconnect battery ground cable.
2. Place transmission selector lever on steering column in Drive (D) position. Secure selector lever in this position.
3. Loosen shift rod adjusting nut at point A, **Fig. 2.**
4. Place transmission shift lever into Drive (D) position by moving lever completely rearward, then forward 2 detents.
5. With selector lever and transmission manual lever in (D) position, torque nut at point A to 12–18 ft. lbs.

Ranger & Bronco II
1. Disconnect battery ground cable.
2. Position transmission selector lever in Drive (D) position, then loosen trunnion bolt, **Figs. 3 and 4.**
3. Position transmission manual lever into Drive (D) position by moving bell-crank lever completely rearward, then forward 3 detents.
4. With transmission selector lever and manual lever in Drive (D) position, apply a light forward pressure onto shifter control lower arm and torque trunnion bolt to 13–23 ft. lbs.

KICKDOWN ROD

1. Install a suitable weight onto transmission kickdown lever.
2. Rotate throttle to wide open throttle position.
3. Insert a .060 inch feeler gauge between throttle lever and adjusting screw.
4. Rotate adjusting screw until contact is made between screw and feeler gauge, then tighten locknut.
5. Remove feeler gauge.
6. After removing feeler gauge a gap of .010 inch on all except Ranger and Bronco II models is acceptable. On Ranger and Bronco II models, a gap of .001–.008 inch is acceptable.
7. Remove weight from kickdown lever.

INTERMEDIATE BAND

1. Clean all dirt from the band adjusting screw area. Remove and discard the locknut.
2. Install a new locknut on the adjusting screw.
3. Tighten adjusting screw using Band Adjusting Ratchet T71P-77370-H and Socket T71P-77370-D or equivalent, **Fig. 5.** Tool T71P-77370-H or equivalent, is a pre-set torque wrench which will click when the torque on the adjusting screw reaches 10 ft. lbs.
4. Back off adjusting screw exactly 4¼ turns.
5. Hold the adjusting screw from turning and tighten locknut to 40 ft. lbs.

Fig. 5   Intermediate band adjustment

LOW REVERSE BAND

1. Clean all dirt from the band adjusting screw area. Remove and discard the locknut.
2. Install a new locknut on the adjusting screw.
3. Tighten adjusting screw using Band Adjusting Ratchet T71P-77370-H and Socket T71P-77370-D or equivalent, **Fig. 6**. Tool T71P-77370-H or equivalent, is a pre-set torque wrench which will click when the torque on the adjusting screw reaches 10 ft. lbs.
4. Back off adjusting screw exactly three full turns. Hold adjusting screw from turning and tighten locknut to 40 ft. lbs.

NEUTRAL START SWITCH

1. Loosen neutral start switch attaching bolts.
2. On all except 1983–85 models, proceed as follows:
   a. Set manual lever in park position, then insert a 3/32 inch drill bit through switch hole.
   b. Move switch as necessary to allow drill bit to fully seat, then torque switch attaching bolts to 8 ft. lbs.
   c. Remove drill bit.
3. On 1983–85 models:
   a. Set manual lever in neutral position, then insert a No. 43 drill bit into the three switch holes.
   b. Move switch as necessary to allow drill bit to fully seat, then torque switch attaching bolts to 65 inch lbs.
   c. Remove drill bit.

IN-VEHICLE REPAIRS
EXTENSION HOUSING SEAL REPLACEMENT

1. Raise and support vehicle.

2. Remove the driveshaft.
3. Remove extension housing seal using Seal Remover T74P-77248-A and Slide Hammer T50T-100-A or equivalent.
4. Reverse procedure to install using Seal Installer T61L-7657-A or equivalent.

EXTENSION HOUSING, REPLACE

4 × 2 Models
1. Raise vehicle and remove driveshaft.
2. Using suitable jack, support transmission.
3. Remove speedometer cable from extension housing.
4. Remove engine rear support to crossmember nuts.
5. Raise transmission and remove rear support bolts. Remove crossmember.
6. Loosen extension housing bolts and let transmission drain.
7. Remove the six extension housing bolts and vacuum tube clip and remove extension housing.
8. Reverse procedure to install, noting the following torques: extension housing bolts, 28–40 ft. lbs.; crossmember nuts, 35–50 ft. lbs.; rear support bolts, 25–35 ft. lbs.

4 × 4 Models
1. Disconnect battery ground cable.
2. Remove transfer case assembly from vehicle.
3. Position a suitable jack under transmission assembly.
4. Remove engine rear support to crossmember nuts.
5. Raise transmission slightly, then remove rear support to body bracket attaching bolts.
6. Loosen extension housing attaching bolts and allow transmission fluid to drain.
7. Remove extension housing bolts, extension housing and vacuum tube clip.
8. Disconnect transmission vent fitting line.
9. Reverse procedure to install. Torque extension housing to transmission case bolts to 28–40 ft. lbs. Torque crossmember attaching nuts to 75–95 ft. lbs. Torque engine rear support to crossmember attaching nuts to 71–94 ft. lbs.

GOVERNOR, REPLACE

1. Refer to "Extension Housing, Replace" and remove extension housing.
2. Remove bolts holding governor housing to governor distributor.
3. Slide governor away from distributor body and off output shaft.
4. Reverse procedure to install. Torque

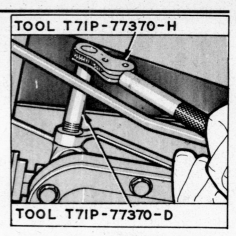

Fig. 6   Low-reverse band adjustment

governor bolts to 80–120 inch lbs.

LOW-REVERSE SERVO, REPLACE

1. Raise and support vehicle.
2. Loosen low-reverse band adjusting screw lock nut. Torque band adjusting screw to 10 ft. lbs. to prevent band strut from falling when reverse servo piston assembly is removed.
3. Disengage neutral switch harness from clips on servo cover.
4. Remove servo cover bolts, servo cover, and seal from case.
5. Remove servo piston from case. If seal is bad, piston must be replaced.
6. Install piston in case. Install cover with new seal. Use two 5/16-18 × 1¼ bolts to position cover against case. Install two cover bolts, remove two locating bolts and install remaining bolts. Torque to 12–20 ft. lbs.
7. Position neutral switch harness in clips.
8. Adjust low-reverse band.

NOTE: If band cannot be adjusted properly, low-reverse band struts are not in position. Remove oil pan and valve body. Position struts and install valve body and pan. Adjust band.

9. Lower vehicle and check transmission fluid level.

TRANSMISSION
REPLACE

1. On 4 × 4 models, remove filler tube-to-valve cover bracket attaching bolt.
2. On all models, raise and support vehicle.
3. Position a drain pan under transmission oil pan, then, starting at rear, loosen attaching bolts and drain fluid from transmission. Leave 2 bolts in

front and reinstall 2 bolts in rear of oil pan to temporarily hold it in place.

4. Remove converter drain plug access cover from lower end of converter housing.

5. Remove converter-to-flywheel attaching nuts. Rotate converter to gain access to nuts using a suitable wrench on crankshaft pulley attaching bolt.

6. Rotate converter to gain access to converter drain plug, then remove the plug to drain converter. After fluid has been drained, reinstall plug.

7. On 4 × 2 models, mark relationship between rear driveshaft yoke and axle flange, then disconnect driveshaft from rear axle and slide shaft rearward from transmission. Install a suitable seal installation tool in extension housing to prevent fluid leakage.

8. On all models, disconnect starter cables, then remove starter motor from vehicle.

9. Disconnect neutral start switch electrical connector.

10. Remove rear engine mount-to-crossmember attaching nuts.

11. Remove 2 crossmember-to-frame attaching bolts, then the right and left gussets.

12. Remove 2 rear engine mount-to-extension housing attaching bolts.

13. Disconnect manual and downshift linkage rods from transmission control levers.

14. On 4 × 4 models, disconnect vacuum hose from vacuum diaphragm unit and remove from retaining clip.

15. On all models, remove 2 bellcrank bracket-to-converter housing attaching bolts.

16. On 4 × 4 models, remove transfer case.

17. On all models, raise transmission using a suitable jack, then remove rear engine mount and crossmember.

18. Lower transmission and disconnect oil cooler lines from transmission.

19. Disconnect speedometer cable from extension housing.

20. On 4 × 2 models, remove filler tube-to-cylinder block attaching bolt, then the filler tube with dipstick.

21. On all models, install a safety chain to secure transmission to jack, then remove converter housing-to-cylinder block attaching bolts.

22. Move transmission and converter assembly away from engine, then lower assembly and remove from vehicle.

23. Reverse procedure to install. Torque converter housing-to-engine attaching bolts to 22–32 ft. lbs. and converter-to-flywheel attaching nuts to 20–34 ft. lbs.

NOTE: Ensure converter rests squarely against flywheel, indicating converter pilot is not binding in crankshaft.

C6 Automatic Transmission

INDEX

DESCRIPTION

As shown in **Fig. 1,** the transmission consists essentially of a torque converter, a compound planetary gear train controlled by one band, three disc clutches and a one-way clutch, and a hydraulic control system.

TROUBLESHOOTING GUIDE

NO DRIVE IN FORWARD SPEEDS

1. Manual linkage adjustment.
2. Check control pressure.
3. Valve body.
4. Make air pressure check.
5. Forward clutch.
6. Leakage in hydraulic system.

ROUGH INITIAL ENGAGEMENT IN D, D1, D2 OR 2

1. Engine idle speed too high.
2. Vacuum diaphragm unit or tubes restricted, leaking or maladjusted.
3. Check control pressure.
4. Valve body.
5. Forward clutch.

1–2 OR 2–3 SHIFT POINTS INCORRECT OR ERRATIC

1. Check fluid level.
2. Vacuum diaphragm unit or tubes restricted, leaking or maladjusted.
3. Downshift linkage, including inner lever position.
4. Manual linkage adjustment.

5. Governor defective.
6. Check control pressure.
7. Valve body.
8. Make air pressure check.

ROUGH 1–2 UPSHIFTS

1. Vacuum diaphragm unit or tubes restricted, leaking or maladjusted.
2. Intermediate servo.
3. Intermediate band.
4. Check control pressure.
5. Valve body.

ROUGH 2–3 SHIFTS

1. Vacuum diaphragm or tubes restricted leaking or maladjusted.
2. Intermediate servo.
3. Check control pressure.
4. Intermediate band.
5. Valve body.
6. Make air pressure check.
7. Reverse-high clutch.
8. Reverse-high clutch piston air bleed valve.

DRAGGED OUT 1–2 SHIFT

1. Check fluid level.
2. Vacuum diaphragm unit or tubes restricted, leaking or maladjusted.
3. Intermediate servo.
4. Check control pressure.
5. Intermediate band.
6. Valve body.
7. Make air pressure check.
8. Leakage in hydraulic system.

ENGINE OVERSPEEDS ON 2–3 SHIFT

1. Manual linkage adjustment.
2. Check fluid level.

3. Vacuum diaphragm unit or tubes restricted, leaking or maladjusted.
4. Intermediate servo.
5. Check control pressure.
6. Valve body.
7. Intermediate band.
8. Reverse-high clutch.
9. Reverse-high clutch piston air bleed valve.

NO 1–2 OR 2–3 SHIFT

1. Manual linkage adjustment.
2. Downshift linkage including inner lever position.
3. Vacuum diaphragm unit or tubes restricted, leaking or maladjusted.
4. Governor.
5. Check control pressure.
6. Valve body.
7. Intermediate band.
8. Intermediate servo.
9. Reverse-high clutch.
10. Leakage in hydraulic system.

NO 3–1 SHIFT IN D1, 2 OR 3–2 SHIFT IN D2 OR D

1. Governor.
2. Valve body.

NO FORCED DOWNSHIFTS

1. Downshift linkage, including inner lever position.
2. Check control pressure.
3. Valve body.

RUNAWAY ENGINE ON FORCED 3–2 SHIFT

1. Check control pressure.
2. Intermediate servo.
3. Intermediate band.

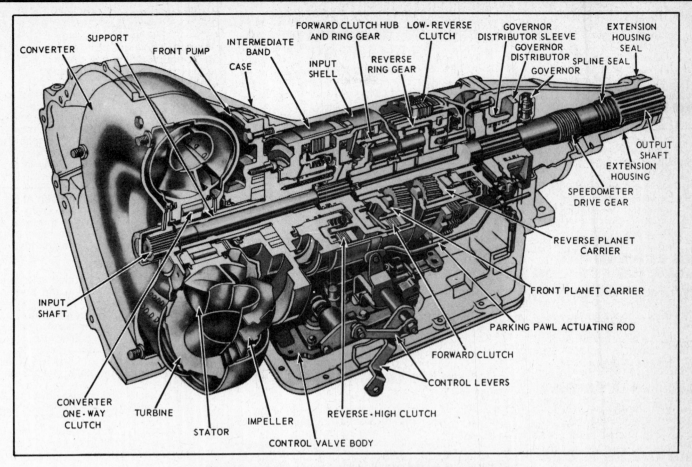

Fig. 1 C6 dual range automatic transmission

4. Valve body.
5. Vacuum diaphragm unit or tubes restricted, leaking or maladjusted.
6. Leakage in hydraulic system.

ROUGH 3—2 SHIFT OR 3—1 SHIFT AT CLOSED THROTTLE

1. Engine idle speed.
2. Vacuum diaphragm unit or tubes restricted, leaking or maladjusted.
3. Intermediate servo.
4. Check control pressure.
5. Valve body.

SHIFTS 1—3 IN D, D1, 2, D2

1. Intermediate band.
2. Intermediate servo.
3. Valve body.
4. Governor.
5. Make air pressure check.

NO ENGINE BRAKING IN 1ST GEAR—MANUAL LOW RANGE

1. Manual linkage adjustment.
2. Low-reverse clutch.
3. Valve body.
4. Governor.

5. Make air pressure check.
6. Leakage in hydraulic system.

CREEPS EXCESSIVELY

1. Engine idle speed too high.

SLIPS OR CHATTERS IN 1ST GEAR, D1

1. Check fluid level.
2. Vacuum diaphragm unit or tubes restricted, leaking or maladjusted.
3. Check control pressure.
4. Valve body.
5. Forward clutch.
6. Leakage in hydraulic system.
7. Planetary one-way clutch.

SLIPS OR CHATTERS IN 2ND GEAR

1. Check fluid level.
2. Vacuum diaphragm unit or tubes restricted, leaking or maladjusted.
3. Intermediate servo.
4. Intermediate band.
5. Check control pressure.
6. Valve body.
7. Make air pressure check.
8. Forward clutch.
9. Leakage in hydraulic system.

SLIPS OR CHATTERS IN REVERSE

1. Check fluid level.
2. Vacuum diaphragm unit or tubes restricted, leaking or maladjusted.
3. Manual linkage adjustment.
4. Low-reverse clutch.
5. Check control pressure.
6. Valve body.
7. Make air pressure check.
8. Reverse-high clutch.
9. Leakage in hydraulic system.
10. Reverse-high clutch piston air bleed valve.

NO DRIVE IN D1 OR 2

1. Manual linkage adjustment.
2. Check control pressure.
3. Valve body.
4. Planetary one-way clutch.

NO DRIVE IN D, D2

1. Check fluid level.
2. Manual linkage adjustment.
3. Check control pressure.
4. Intermediate servo.
5. Valve body.
6. Make air pressure check.
7. Leakage in hydraulic system.

NO DRIVE IN L OR 1

1. Check fluid level.
2. Check control pressure.
3. Valve body.
4. Make air pressure check.
5. Leakage in hydraulic system.

NO DRIVE IN R ONLY

1. Check fluid level.
2. Manual linkage adjustment.
3. Low-reverse clutch.
4. Check control pressure.
5. Valve body.
6. Make air pressure check.
7. Reverse-high clutch.
8. Leakage in hydraulic system.
9. Reverse-high clutch piston air bleed valve.

NO DRIVE IN ANY SELECTOR POSITION

1. Check fluid level.
2. Manual linkage adjustment.
3. Check control pressure.
4. Valve body.
5. Make air pressure check.
6. Leakage in hydraulic system.
7. Front pump.

LOCKUP IN D1 OR 2

1. Valve body.
2. Parking linkage.
3. Leakage in hydraulic system.

LOCKUP IN D2 OR D

1. Low-reverse clutch.
2. Valve body.
3. Reverse-high clutch.
4. Parking linkage.
5. Leakage in hydraulic system.
6. Planetary one-way clutch.

LOCKUP IN L OR 1

1. Valve body.
2. Parking linkage.
3. Leakage in hydraulic system.

LOCKUP IN R ONLY

1. Valve body.
2. Forward clutch.
3. Parking linkage.
4. Leakage in hydraulic system.

PARKING LOCK BINDS OR DOES NOT HOLD

1. Manual linkage adjustment.
2. Parking linkage.

TRANSMISSION OVERHEATS

1. Oil cooler and connections.
2. Valve body.
3. Vacuum diaphragm unit or tubes restricted, leaking or maladjusted.
4. Check control pressure.
5. Converter one-way clutch.

6. Converter pressure check valves.

MAXIMUM SPEED TOO LOW, POOR ACCELERATION

1. Engine performance.
2. Car brakes.
3. Forward clutch.

TRANSMISSION NOISY IN N & P

1. Check fluid level.
2. Valve body.
3. Front pump.

NOISY IN 1ST, 2ND, 3RD OR REVERSE

1. Check fluid level.
2. Valve body.
3. Planetary assembly.
4. Forward clutch.
5. Reverse-high clutch.
6. Planetary one-way clutch.

VEHICLE MOVES FORWARD IN N

1. Manual linkage adjustment.
2. Forward clutch.

FLUID LEAK

1. Check fluid level.
2. Converter drain plugs.
3. Oil pan gasket, filler tube or seal.
4. Oil cooler and connections.
5. Manual or downshift lever shaft seal.
6. ⅛" pipe plugs in case.
7. Extension housing-to-case gasket.
8. Extension housing rear oil seal.
9. Speedometer driven gear adapter seal.
10. Vacuum diaphragm unit or tubes.
11. Intermediate servo.
12. Engine rear oil seal.

MAINTENANCE

CHECKING OIL LEVEL

1. Make sure vehicle is on a level floor.
2. Apply parking brake firmly.
3. Run engine at normal idle speed. If transmission fluid is cold, run engine at a fast idle until fluid reaches normal operating temperature. When fluid is warm, slow engine to normal idle speed.
4. Shift selector lever through all positions, then place lever at "P." Do not shut down engine during fluid level checks.
5. Clean all dirt from dipstick cap before removing dipstick from filler tube.
6. Pull dipstick out of tube, wipe it clean and push it all the way back in tube.
7. Pull dipstick out of tube again and check fluid level. If necessary, add enough fluid to raise the level to the "F" mark on dipstick. Do not overfill.

DRAIN & REFILL

NOTE: The Ford Motor Company recom-

mends the use of an automatic transmission fluid M2C-138-CJ or Dexron II for 1979–85 models (on container). The recommended fluid is said to have a greater coefficient of friction and greater ability to handle maximum engine torques without band or clutch slippage.

Normal maintenance and lubrication requirements do not necessitate periodic fluid changes. If a major failure has occurred in the transmission, it will have to be removed for service. At this time the converter and transmission cooler must be thoroughly flushed to remove any foreign matter.

1. To drain the fluid, loosen pan attaching bolts and allow fluid to drain.
2. After fluid has drained to the level of the pan flange, remove pan bolts working from rear and both sides of pan to allow it to drop and drain slowly.
3. When fluid has stopped draining, remove and clean pan and screen. Discard pan gasket.
4. Using a new gasket, install pan.
5. Add 3 quarts of recommended fluid to transmission through filler tube.
6. Run engine at idle speed for 2 minutes, and then run it at a fast idle until it reaches normal operating temperature.
7. Shift selector lever through all positions, place it at "P" and check fluid level.
8. If necessary, add enough fluid to transmission to bring it to the "F" mark on the dipstick.

IN-VEHICLE ADJUSTMENTS

SHIFT LINKAGE, ADJUST

1. Disconnect battery ground cable.
2. Place transmission selector lever on steering column into Drive (D) position. Secure lever in this position.
3. Loosen shift rod adjusting nut at point A, **Figs. 2 through 6.**
4. Place transmission manual lever into Drive (D) position by moving lever completely rearward, then forward 2 detents.
5. With selector lever and transmission manual lever in Drive (D) position, tighten nut at point A to 12–18 ft. lbs.

NEUTRAL START SWITCH, ADJUST

1. Apply parking brake.
2. Loosen 2 switch attaching bolts.
3. Position transmission selector lever into Neutral. Rotate switch, then insert a ³⁄₃₂ inch drill shank end into gauge pin holes of switch.
4. Completely seat drill shank end into hole, then tighten switch attaching bolts.
5. Remove drill shank end from switch.

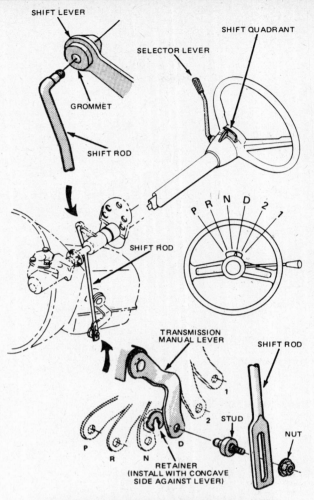

Fig. 2   Shift linkage adjustment. 1979 F-100-350 models

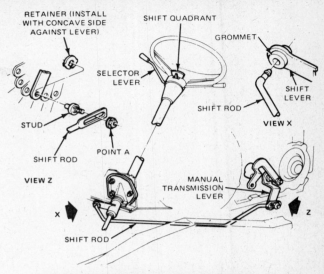

Fig. 3   Shift linkage adjustment. 1979 E-100-350 models

INTERMEDIATE BAND, ADJUST

NOTE: When making the intermediate band adjustment, the lock nut must be discarded and a new one installed each time the band is adjusted.

1. Raise truck on hoist and support on suitable jack stands.
2. Loosen the locknut on the adjusting screw several turns.
3. Torque the screw to 10 ft. lbs., or until the adjuster wrench overruns.
4. Back the screw off exactly 1½ turns.
5. Hold the adjustment and torque the lock-nut to the 35–45 ft. lbs. on all except 1980–85 vehicles, 22–29 ft.

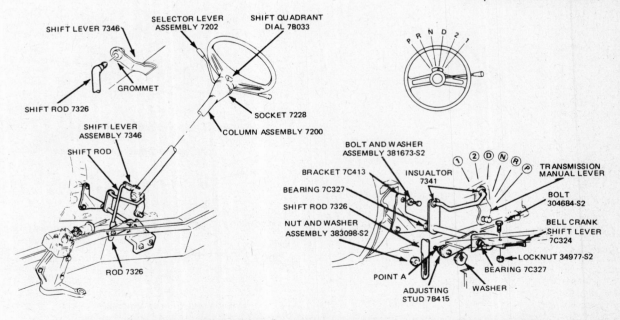

Fig. 4   Shift linkage adjustment. 1979 Bronco, F-150-250 4 × 4 models

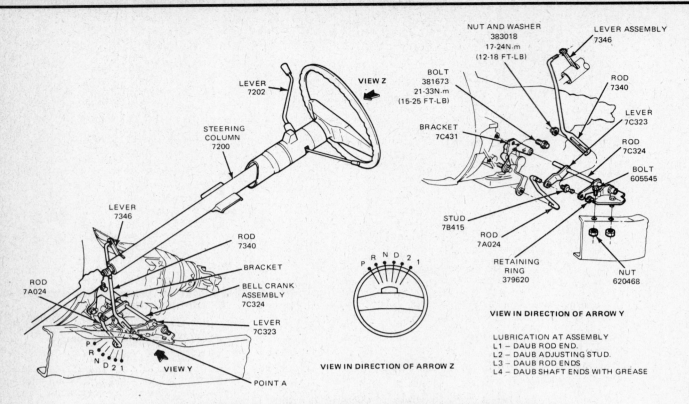

Fig. 5   Shift linkage adjustment. Bronco, F-100-350 models

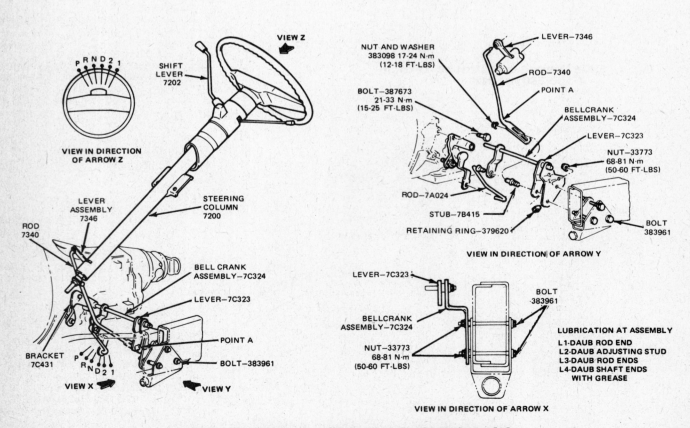

Fig. 6   Shift linkage adjustment. E-100-350 models

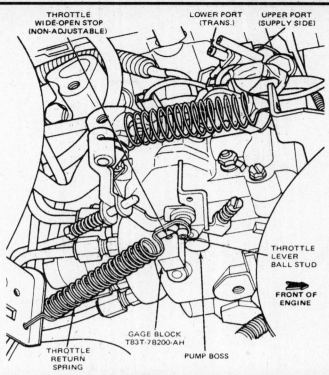

THROTTLE
WIDE-OPEN STOP
(NON-ADJUSTABLE)

LOWER PORT
(TRANS.)

UPPER PORT
(SUPPLY SIDE)

THROTTLE
LEVER
BALL STUD

FRONT OF
ENGINE

GAGE BLOCK
T83T-7B200-AH

PUMP BOSS

THROTTLE
RETURN
SPRING

Fig. 7   VRV gauge block installation. V8-420 6.9L diesel engine

lbs. on 1980 vehicles, 40 ft. lbs. on 1981 vehicles, or 35–40 ft. lbs. on 1982–85 vehicles.

VACUUM REGULATOR VALVE, ADJUST
Models With V8-420 Diesel Engine
1. Disconnect 2 port vacuum connector from VRV located on left side of fuel injection pump.
2. Disconnect throttle cable from throttle lever located on right side of fuel injection pump.
3. Remove throttle return spring. Install one end of spring over throttle lever ball stud and other end of spring over throttle cable support bracket. Insert gage block T83T-7B200-AH or equivalent, **Fig. 7,** between pump and throttle wide open stop.
4. Install a suitable vacuum pump onto upper port of VRV (vacuum supply side).
5. Install a vacuum gauge to lower port of VRV marked TRANS.
6. Apply and maintain 20 inches of vacuum to VRV. Vacuum gauge should indicate 7 inches of vacuum. If gauge does not indicate specified amount, proceed as follows:
   a. Loosen the 3 adjustment screws attaching VRV to the fuel injection pump.
   b. Rotate VRV until correct vacuum reading on gauge is obtained.
   c. Torque adjustment screws to 75–90 inch lbs.

NOTE: If correct vacuum reading cannot be obtained, replace VRV.

IN-VEHICLE REPAIRS
OIL PAN & CONTROL VALVE
Removal
1. Raise truck on hoist or jack stands.
2. Loosen and remove all but two oil pan bolts from front of case and drop rear edge of pan to drain fluid. Remove and clean pan and screen.
3. Unfasten and remove valve body.

Installation
1. Position valve body to case, making sure that selector and downshift levers are engaged, then install and torque attaching bolts to 95–125 inch lbs.
2. Using a new pan gasket, secure pan to case and torque bolts to 12–16 ft. lbs.
3. Lower truck and fill transmission to correct level with specified fluid.

INTERMEDIATE SERVO
Removal
1. Raise truck and remove engine rear support-to-extension housing bolts.
2. Raise transmission high enough to relieve weight from support.
3. Remove support (1 bolt).
4. Lower transmission.
5. Disconnect muffler inlet pipe from exhaust manifolds and let pipe hang free.
6. Place drain pan beneath servo.
7. Remove servo cover-to-case bolts.
8. Loosen band adjusting screw locknut.
9. Remove servo cover, piston, spring and gasket from case, screwing band

adjusting screw inward as piston is removed. This insures that there will be enough tension on the band to keep the struts properly engaged in the band end notches while the piston is removed.

Replacing Seal
1. Apply air pressure to port in servo cover to remove piston and stem.
2. Remove seals from piston.
3. Remove seal from cover.
4. Dip new seals in transmission fluid.
5. Install seals in piston and cover.
6. Dip piston in transmission fluid and install in cover.

Installation
1. Position new gasket on servo cover and spring on piston stem.
2. Insert piston stem in case. Secure cover with bolts, taking care to back off band adjusting screw while tightening cover bolts. Make sure that vent tube retaining clip is in place.
3. Connect muffler inlet pipe to exhaust manifolds.
4. Raise transmission high enough to install engine rear support. Secure support to extension housing. Lower transmission as required to install support-to-crossmember bolt.
5. Remove jack and adjust band.
6. Lower truck and replenish fluid as required.

EXTENSION HOUSING & GOVERNOR
Removal
1. Raise truck and drain transmission.
2. Disconnect drive shaft from rear axle flange and remove from transmission.

NOTE: On 4 × 4 models, the transfer case must be removed.

3. Disconnect speedometer cable from extension housing.
4. Remove two nuts that secure engine rear mount to crossmember.
5. Raise transmission with a jack just high enough to relieve weight from crossmember. Remove crossmember.
6. Remove engine rear support.
7. Lower transmission to permit access to extension housing bolts. Remove bolts and slide housing off output shaft.
8. Disconnect governor from distributor (4 bolts) and slide governor off output shaft.

Installation
1. Secure governor to distributor flange.
2. Position new gasket on transmission.
3. Secure extension housing to case.
4. Secure engine rear support to case.
5. Install crossmember.
6. Lower transmission and remove jack. Then install and torque engine rear support-to-extension housing bolts.
7. Install speedometer cable and install drive shaft.
8. Replenish transmission fluid.

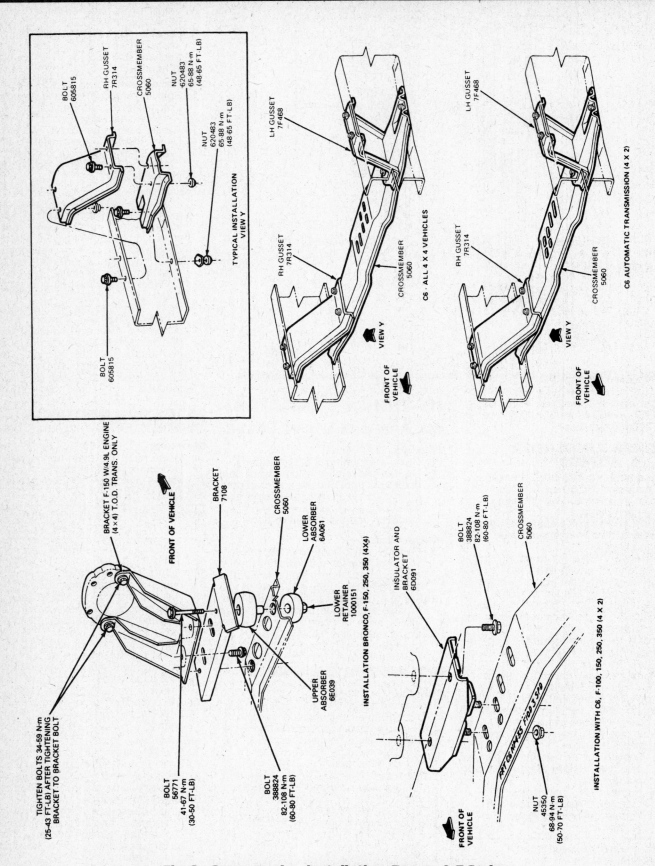

Fig. 8   Crossmember installation. Bronco & F Series

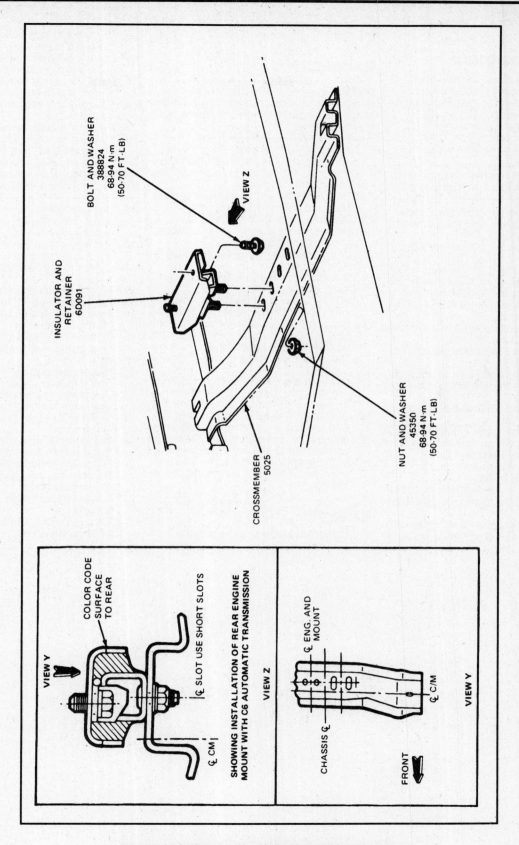

Fig. 9 Crossmember installation. E Series

FORD—Automatic Transmissions

TRANSMISSION
REPLACE

F150-350 & BRONCO

1. Drive vehicle onto a suitable hoist.
2. Disconnect battery ground cable.
3. Remove 2 upper converter housing to engine attaching bolts.
4. Raise and support vehicle.
5. Loosen transmission pan drain plug and drain fluid from transmission.

NOTE: If pan does not have a drain plug, loosen pan bolts and allow fluid to drain.

6. Remove converter drain plug access cover from lower end of converter housing.
7. Remove converter to flywheel attaching bolts and/or nuts.
8. On 4 × 2 models, disconnect driveshaft from axle and slide driveshaft rearward from transmission. Install a suitable seal tool into transmission extension housing.
9. Disconnect speedometer cable from extension housing.
10. Disconnect and cap transmission fluid cooler lines.
11. Disconnect downshift and manual linkage rods from transmission levers.
12. Disconnect vacuum line from vacuum diaphragm.
13. Remove starter motor from vehicle.
14. On 4 × 4 models, remove transfer case assembly from vehicle.
15. Remove 2 engine rear support to insulator attaching bolts.
16. Position a suitable jack under transmission, then raise transmission slightly.
17. Remove crossmembers from vehicle.
18. Remove remaining converter housing to engine attaching bolts.
19. Lower transmission from vehicle.
20. Reverse procedure to install.

RANCHERO

NOTE: On models with the neutral safety switch wire harness connected at the dash panel, disconnect the harness before raising the vehicle.

1. Working from engine compartment, remove the two bolts retaining the fan shroud to the radiator. Disconnect the battery ground cable.
2. Raise vehicle and drain transmission and converter.
3. Remove drive shaft and starter.
4. Remove four converter to flywheel attaching points.
5. Disconnect parking brake front cable from equalizer.
6. Disconnect speedometer cable and transmission linkage.
7. Where necessary, disconnect muffler inlet pipes from exhaust manifold.
8. Support the transmission with a suitable jack, remove parking brake rear cables from the equalizer and remove the crossmember and rear engine support.
9. Lower transmission and remove oil cooler lines, vacuum line and transmission oil filler tube.
10. Secure the transmission to the jack with the chain, remove the converter housing to cylinder block bolts and carefully move the transmission away from the engine, at the same time lowering it to clear the underside of the vehicle.

E150-350

1. Disconnect battery ground cable.
2. Working from inside of vehicle, remove engine compartment cover.
3. Disconnect neutral start switch electrical connectors.
4. On V8 engine models, remove flex hose from air cleaner heat tube.
5. Remove upper converter housing to engine attaching bolts.
6. Remove bolt securing oil filler tube to engine.
7. Raise and support vehicle.
8. Loosen transmission pan drain plug and drain fluid from transmission.

NOTE: If pan does not have a drain plug, loosen pan bolts and allow fluid to drain.

9. Remove converter drain plug access cover from lower end of converter housing.
10. Remove converter to flywheel attaching bolts and/or nuts.
11. Disconnect driveshaft from transmission.
12. Remove transmission fluid filler tube.
13. Remove starter motor from vehicle.
14. Position a suitable jack under transmission assembly.
15. Position a suitable engine support bar onto frame and engine oil pan flanges.
16. Disconnect and cap transmission fluid cooler lines.
17. Disconnect speedometer cable from extension housing.
18. Disconnect vacuum line from vacuum diaphragm.
19. Disconnect downshift and manual linkage from transmission levers.
20. Remove crossmembers from vehicle.
21. Remove remaining converter housing to flywheel bolts.
22. Lower transmission assembly from vehicle.
23. Reverse procedure to install, referring to **Figs. 8 and 9.**

FMX Automatic Transmission

INDEX

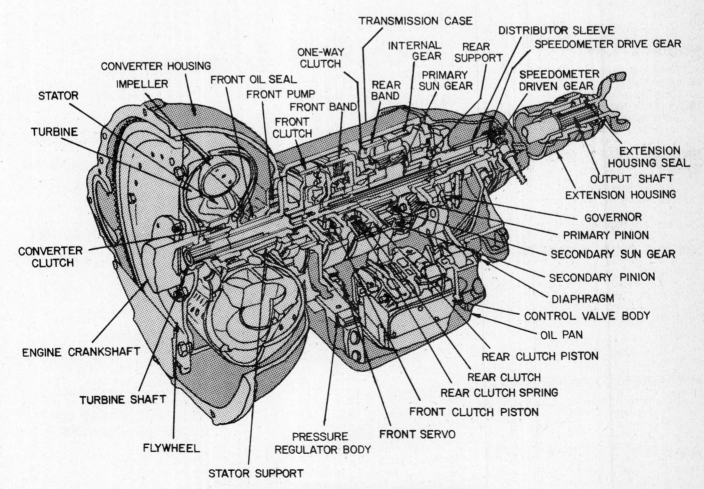

Fig. 1   FMX automatic transmission

DESCRIPTION

This transmission, **Fig. 1,** is a three speed unit which provides automatic upshifts and downshifts. First and second gears may be selected manually. This unit consists of a torque converter, planetary gear train, multiple disc clutches and hydraulic control system.

TROUBLESHOOTING GUIDE

ROUGH INITIAL ENGAGEMENT

1. Idle speed.
2. Vacuum unit or tubes.
3. Front band.
4. Check control pressure.
5. Pressure regulator.
6. Valve body.

SHIFT POINTS HIGH, LOW OR ERRATIC

1. Fluid level.
2. Vacuum unit or tubes.
3. Manual linkage.
4. Governor.
5. Check control pressure.
6. Valve body.
7. Downshift linkage.

ROUGH 2—3 SHIFT

1. Manual linkage.
2. Front band.
3. Vacuum unit or tubes.
4. Pressure regulator.
5. Valve body.
6. Front servo.

ENGINE OVERSPEEDS, 2—3 SHIFT

1. Vacuum unit or tubes.
2. Front band.
3. Valve body.
4. Pressure regulator.

NO 1—2 OR 2—3 SHIFTS

1. Governor.
2. Valve body.
3. Manual linkage.
4. Rear clutch.
5. Front band.
6. Front servo.
7. Leakage in hydraulic system.
8. Pressure regulator.

NO FORCED DOWNSHIFTS

1. Downshift linkage.
2. Check control pressure.
3. Valve body.

ROUGH 3—2 OR 3—1 SHIFTS

1. Engine idle speed.
2. Vacuum unit or tubes.
3. Valve body.

SLIPS OR CHATTERS IN 2ND

1. Fluid level.
2. Vacuum unit or tubes.
3. Front band.
4. Check control pressure.
5. Pressure regulator.
6. Valve body.
7. Front servo.
8. Front clutch.
9. Leakage in hydraulic system.

SLIPS OR CHATTERS IN 1ST

1. Fluid level.
2. Vacuum unit or tubes.
3. Check control pressure.
4. Pressure regulator.
5. Valve body.
6. Front clutch.
7. Leakage in hydraulic system.
8. Fluid distributor sleeve in output shaft.
9. Planetary one-way clutch.

SLIPS OR CHATTERS IN REVERSE

1. Fluid level.
2. Rear band.
3. Check control pressure.
4. Pressure regulator.
5. Valve body.
6. Rear servo.
7. Rear clutch.
8. Vacuum unit or tubes.
9. Leakage in hydraulic system.
10. Fluid distributor sleeve in output shaft.

NO DRIVE IN D OR D2

1. Valve body.
2. Make air pressure check.
3. Manual linkage.
4. Front clutch.
5. Leak in hydraulic system.
6. Fluid distributor sleeve in output shaft.

NO DRIVE IN D1

1. Manual linkage.
2. Valve body.
3. Planetary one-way clutch.

NO DRIVE IN L

1. Manual linkage.
2. Front clutch.
3. Valve body.
4. Make air pressure check.
5. Leak in hydraulic system.
6. Fluid distributor sleeve in output shaft.

NO DRIVE IN R

1. Rear band.
2. Rear servo.
3. Valve body.
4. Make air pressure check.
5. Rear clutch.
6. Leak in hydraulic system.
7. Fluid distributor sleeve in output shaft.

NO DRIVE IN ANY RANGE

1. Fluid level.
2. Manual linkage.
3. Check control pressure.
4. Pressure regulator.
5. Valve body.
6. Make air pressure check.
7. Leak in hydraulic system.

LOCKUP IN D OR D1

1. Manual linkage.
2. Rear servo.
3. Front servo.
4. Rear clutch.
5. Parking linkage.
6. Leak in hydraulic system.

LOCKUP IN D2

1. Manual linkage.
2. Rear band.
3. Rear servo.
4. Rear clutch.
5. Parking linkage.
6. Leak in hydraulic system.
7. Planetary one-way clutch.

LOCKUP IN R

1. Front band.
2. Front servo.
3. Front clutch.
4. Parking linkage.
5. Leak in hydraulic system.

LOCKUP IN L

1. Front band.
2. Pressure regulator.
3. Valve body.
4. Rear clutch.
5. Parking linkage.
6. Leak in hydraulic system.

PARKING LOCK BINDS OR WON'T HOLD

1. Manual linkage.
2. Parking linkage.

UNABLE TO PUSH START

1. Fluid level.
2. Manual linkage.
3. Pressure regulator.
4. Valve body.
5. Rear pump.
6. Leak in hydraulic system.

TRANSMISSION OVERHEATS

1. Oil cooler and connections.
2. Pressure regulator.
3. Converter one-way clutch.

ENGINE RUNAWAY ON FORCED DOWNSHIFT

1. Front band.
2. Pressure regulator.
3. Valve body.
4. Front servo.
5. Vacuum unit or tubes.

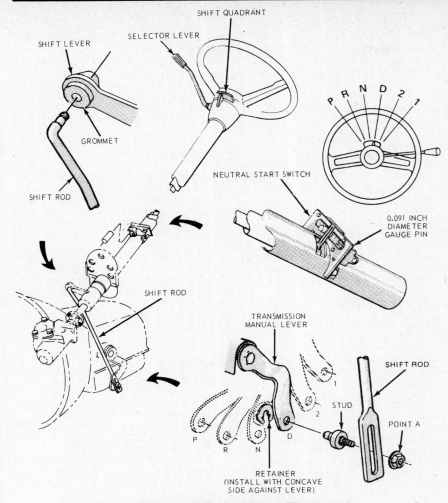

Fig. 2 Shift linkage adjustment

6. Leak in hydraulic system.

MAXIMUM SPEED BELOW NORMAL, ACCELERATION POOR

1. Converter one-way clutch.

NO 3—1 DOWNSHIFT

1. Engine idle speed.
2. Vacuum unit or tubes.
3. Valve body.

NOISE IN NEUTRAL

1. Pressure regulator.
2. Front clutch.
3. Front pump.

NOISE IN 1—2—3 OR R

1. Pressure regulator.
2. Planetary assembly.
3. Front clutch.
4. Rear clutch.
5. Front pump.

NOISE IN REVERSE

1. Pressure regulator.
2. Front pump.

NOISE ON COAST IN NEUTRAL

1. Rear pump.

MAINTENANCE

ADDING FLUID

The fluid level in the transmission should be checked at 1000-mile intervals. Make sure that the vehicle is standing level, and firmly apply the parking brake.

Run the engine at normal idle speed. If the transmission fluid is cold, run the engine at fast idle speed until the fluid reaches normal operating temperature. When the fluid is warm, slow the engine down to normal idle speed, shift the transmission through all ranges and then place the lever or button at P.

Clean all dirt from the transmission fluid dipstick cap before removing the dipstick from the filler tube. Pull the dipstick out of the tube, wipe it clean and push it all the way back into the tube.

Pull the dipstick out again and check the fluid level. If necessary, add enough Type F Automatic Transmission Fluid to the transmission to raise the fluid level to the F (full mark) on the dipstick.

CHANGING FLUID

The transmission fluid should be changed at 24,000-mile intervals. The procedure for changing fluid is as follows:

1. Remove cover from lower front side of converter housing.
2. Remove one of the converter drain plugs. Then rotate the converter 180° and remove the other plug. Do not attempt to turn the converter with a wrench on the converter stud nuts as there is danger of stripping threads as well as skinning your knuckles on the bell housing.
3. When all fluid has drained, remove and clean the oil pan and screen.
4. Using a new pan gasket, install screen and pan.
5. Connect filler tube to oil pan and tighten fitting securely.
6. Install both converter drain plugs.
7. Install converter housing cover.
8. Add 5 quarts of automatic transmission fluid.
9. Run engine at idle speed for about 2 minutes; then add the additional quantity of oil required for the particular transmission being serviced.
10. Run engine at a fast idle until it reaches normal operating temperature.
11. Shift the transmission through all positions, then place it at P and check fluid level. If necessary, add enough fluid to bring the level to the F mark on the dipstick.

IN-VEHICLE ADJUSTMENTS

SHIFT LINKAGE, ADJUST

1. Place transmission selector lever on steering column into Drive (D) position. Secure lever in this position.
2. Loosen shift rod adjusting nut at point A, **Fig. 2.**
3. Place manual lever on transmission into Drive (D) position by moving lever completely rearward, then forward 2 detents.
4. With selector lever and manual lever in Drive (D) position, tighten nut at point A to 12—18 ft. lbs.

FRONT BAND, ADJUST

1. Drain fluid from transmission, remove and clean oil pan and screen.
2. Loosen front servo adjusting screw locknut.
3. Pull back on actuating rod and insert a ¼ inch spacer between adjusting screw and servo piston stem.

FORD—Automatic Transmissions

4. Tighten adjusting screw to 10 inch-lbs. torque. Remove spacer and tighten adjusting screw an additional ¾ turn. Hold adjusting screw stationary and tighten locknut securely.
5. Install oil pan with new gasket and add fluid to transmission.

REAR BAND, ADJUST

1. Loosen rear bank adjusting screw locknut. A special tool is required to gain access in limited space.
2. Tighten adjusting screw until special tool clicks. It is preset to overrun when torque reaches 10 ft. lbs.
3. Back off adjusting screw 1½ turns.

CAUTION: Severe damage may result if the adjusting screw is not backed off exactly 1½ turns.

4. Hold adjusting screw stationary and tighten locknut securely.

IN-VEHICLE REPAIRS
OIL PRESSURE REGULATOR

Remove oil pan and screen. Maintain constant pressure on spring retainer to prevent damage to springs and remove retainer from bosses on oil pressure regulator body. Remove springs and pilots. Remove the three pipes. Unfasten and remove the oil pressure regulator from the transmission case.

CONTROL VALVE

To remove the assembly, loosen the adjustment on the front and rear bands 5 or 6 turns. Loosen front servo attaching screws. Remove cap screws and washers which attach control valve to case. Align throttle and manual levers to permit removal of control valve. Disengage front servo tubes from control valve and lift valve assembly from case.

FRONT & REAR SERVOS

To remove the front servo, remove the cap screw which holds it to the case. Hold the actuating lever strut with one hand and lift the servo from the case.

To remove the rear servo, take out the attaching cap screws. Then hold the anchor strut and lift the servo from the case.

EXTENSION HOUSING SEAL

After removing the drive shaft and telescopic shield, the seal may be pulled out of the extension housing.

Before installing the new seal, inspect the sealing surface of the universal joint yoke for scores. If scores are evident, replace the yoke. Inspect the counterbore in the housing for burrs. Polish all burrs with crocus cloth.

To install the new seal, position it in the bore of the extension housing with the felt side of the seal to the rear. The seal may be driven into the housing with a special tool designed for the purpose.

OIL DISTRIBUTOR
With Bolted Distributor & Sleeve

After removing the extension case remove the spacer from the transmission output shaft and slide the distributor toward the rear of the transmission. Note that the tube spacer is located in the center tube.

Remove the three tubes and spacer from the distributor. Remove the screws which attach the distributor to the sleeve and separate these parts.

Inspect the distributor and sleeve for burrs on the mating surfaces and obstructed fluid passages. Check the fit of the tubes in the distributor. Inspect the distributor sleeve for wear and scores in the sleeve bore.

To assemble, align the distributor and sleeve and install the cap screws. Install the tubes in the distributor with the spacer installed on the center tube.

With One Piece Distributor & Sleeve

After removing the extension housing, remove the distributor drive gear snap ring. Remove distributor gear, taking care not to lose the gear drive ball. Remove distributor sleeve and pipes from the transmission. Inspect the 4 seal rings on the output shaft for wear or breakage, and replace if necessary. Inspect the distributor sleeve for wear and the tubes for proper alignment and fit into the distributor sleeve.

With tubes installed in the distributor sleeve, install distributor on output shaft (chamfer forward) sliding the distributor over the seal rings and at the same time guiding tubes into the case. Install speedometer drive ball and gear and install snap ring.

GOVERNOR

Remove the governor inspection cover from the extension housing. Rotate the drive shaft to bring the governor body in line with the inspection hole. Remove the two screws which attach the governor body to the counterweight, and remove the body.

Remove the valve from the new governor body. Lubricate the valve with automatic transmission fluid. Install the valve in the body, making sure the valve moves freely in the bore. Install the body in the counterweight making sure the fluid passages in the counterweight and body are aligned.

TRANSMISSION
REPLACE

1. Drive vehicle onto a suitable hoist.
2. Disconnect battery ground cable.
3. Remove converter access hole covers.
4. Raise and support vehicle.
5. Loosen transmission pan attaching bolts, and allow fluid to drain.
6. Remove converter housing to flywheel attaching bolts.
7. Remove starter from vehicle.
8. Disconnect and cap transmission oil cooler lines.
9. Disconnect manual and throttle linkages from transmission.
10. Disconnect speedometer cable from extension housing.
11. Position a suitable jack under transmission assembly.
12. Remove crossmembers from vehicle.
13. Lower engine from vehicle.
14. Reverse procedure to install.

Ford Automatic Overdrive Transmission

INDEX

DESCRIPTION

This unit is a 4-speed automatic transmission incorporating an integral overdrive feature. With selector lever in 1 position, the transmission will start and remain in first gear until the selector lever is moved to another position. In 3 position, the transmission will automatically shift through 1-2-3 range, but will not engage overdrive. In D position, the transmission will automatically select the appropriate time to shift into overdrive (4th gear). The design of the transmission features a split torque path in third gear, where 40% of the engine torque is transmitted hydraulically through the torque converter and 60% is transmitted mechanically through solid connections (direct drive input shaft) to the driveshaft. When transmission is in overdrive (4th gear), 100% of engine torque is transmitted through the direct drive input shaft.

The transmission consists essentially of a torque converter assembly, compound planetary gear train and an hydraulic control system, **Fig. 1.** For gear control the transmission has four friction clutches, two one-way roller clutches and two bands. Overdrive is accomplished by the addition of a band to lock the reverse sun gear while driving the planet carrier. The torque con-

verter operation is similar to other types of automatic transmission, but has an added damper assembly and input shaft for 3rd gear and overdrive. The direct drive input shaft couples the engine directly to the direct clutch. This shaft is driven by the torque converter cover through the damper assembly which cushions engine shock to the transmission.

TROUBLESHOOTING GUIDE

ROUGH INITIAL ENGAGEMENT IN FORWARD OR REVERSE

1. Improper fluid level.
2. High engine idle.
3. Loose driveshaft, engine mounts or U-joints.
4. Sticking or dirty valve body.
5. Improper clutch or band application, or low oil control pressure.

SLOW INITIAL ENGAGEMENT

1. Improper fluid level.

2. Damaged or improperly adjusted linkage.
3. Contaminated fluid.
4. Low main control pressure or improper clutch and band application.

HARSH ENGAGEMENTS WITH WARM ENGINE

1. Improper fluid level.
2. Damaged or improperly adjusted linkage.
3. High engine idle.
4. Sticking or dirty valve body.

SLOW FORWARD ENGAGEMENT

1. Improper fluid level.
2. Damaged or improperly adjusted linkage.
3. Low main control pressure.
4. Sticking or dirty valve body.
5. Blocked filter.
6. Damaged pump.

SLOW REVERSE ENGAGEMENT

1. Improper fluid level.
2. Damaged or improperly adjusted link-

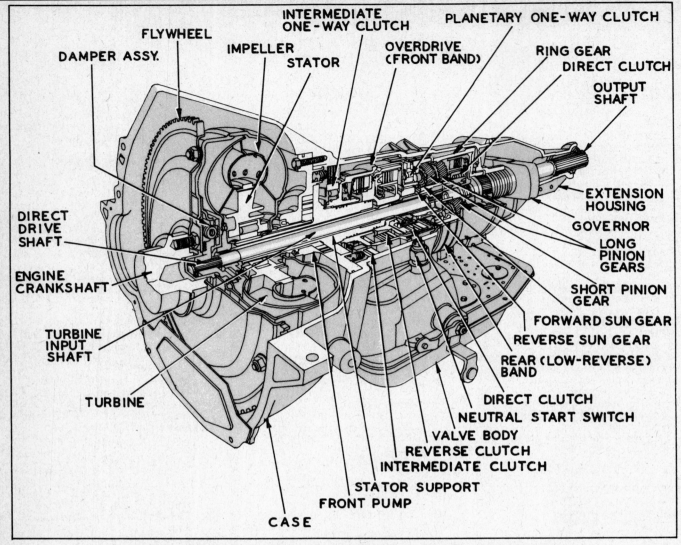

Fig. 1   Sectional view of Ford automatic overdrive transmission

age.
3. Low main control pressure.
4. Damaged forward clutch assembly.
5. Sticking or dirty valve body.
6. Blocked filter.
7. Damaged pump.

NO ENGINE BRAKING IN MANUAL LOW

1. Improper fluid level.
2. Damaged or improperly adjusted linkage.
3. Damaged low reverse servo piston band.
4. Damaged planetary low one-way clutch.

NO ENGINE BRAKING IN MANUAL 2ND

1. Improper fluid level.
2. Damaged or improperly adjusted linkage.
3. Improper clutch or band application.

4. Improper control system pressure.
5. Leaking intermediate servo.
6. Damaged intermediate one-way clutch.

SLIPS OR CHATTERS IN DRIVE

1. Improper fluid level.
2. Improper throttle valve rod adjustment.
3. Damaged or improperly adjusted linkage.
4. Low main control pressure.
5. Sticking or dirty valve body.
6. Open forward clutch check valve.
7. Damaged forward clutch piston seal.
8. Blocked forward clutch feed hole.
9. Damaged planetary low one-way clutch.

SLIPS OR CHATTERS IN REVERSE

1. Improper fluid level.

2. Low main control pressure in reverse.
3. Damaged reverse servo bore.
4. Damaged planetary low one-way clutch.
5. Damaged reverse clutch drum bushing.
6. Worn reverse clutch stator support seal rings or grooves.
7. Reverse clutch piston seal.
8. Reverse band adjustment.
9. Loosen driveshaft, engine mounts or U-joints.

NO DRIVE OR SLIPS OR CHATTERS IN D2

1. Improper fluid level.
2. Damaged or improperly adjusted linkage.
3. Intermediate friction or one-way clutch.
4. Blocked intermediate bleed hole or bleed hole not at 12 o'clock position.
5. Sticking or dirty valve body.

6. Damaged or worn servo.

NO DRIVE OR SLIPS OR CHATTERS IN D1

1. Damaged planetary low one-way clutch.

STARTS IN 2ND OR 3RD

1. Improper fluid level.
2. Damaged or improperly adjusted linkage.
3. Improper clutch or band application.
4. Improper control system pressure.
5. Sticking governor valve.
6. Sticking or dirty valve body.
7. Leaking valve body mating surface.

IMPROPER SHIFT POINTS

1. Improper fluid level.
2. Damaged or improperly adjusted linkage.
3. Improper speedometer gear installed.
4. Improper clutch or band application.
5. Improper control system pressure.
6. Damaged or worn governor.
7. Sticking or dirty valve body.

HARSH, DELAYED OR NO UPSHIFTS

1. Improper fluid level.
2. Damaged or improperly adjusted linkage.
3. Governor sticking.
4. High main control pressure.
5. Sticking or dirty valve body.

ALL UPSHIFTS EARLY

1. Improper fluid level.
2. Damaged or improperly adjusted linkage.
3. Low main control pressure.
4. Sticking throttle control valve or valve body.
5. Sticking governor valve.

NO 1-2 UPSHIFTS

1. Improper fluid level.
2. Damaged or improperly adjusted linkage.
3. Low main control pressure to intermediate friction clutch.
4. Sticking, leaking or bent diaphragm unit.
5. Sticking or dirty valve body.
6. Burnt intermediate clutch, band or servo.

EARLY OR SLIPPING UPSHIFT IN 1-2

1. Improper fluid level.
2. Improperly tuned engine.
3. Damaged or improperly adjusted linkage.
4. High main control pressure.
5. Sticking governor valve.

NO 2-3 UPSHIFT

1. Improper fluid level.

2. Damaged or improperly adjusted linkage.
3. Low main control pressure to direct clutch.
4. Sticking or dirty valve body.
5. Burnt or worn direct clutch.
6. Broken weld on converter damper hub.

EARLY OR SLIPPING 2-3 UPSHIFT

1. Improper fluid level.
2. Improperly tuned engine.
3. Damaged or improperly adjusted linkage.
4. Cut or worn 2-3 accumulator piston seals.
5. Plugged 2-3 accumulator piston drain hole.
6. Damaged accumulator.
7. Dirty or sticking valve body.
8. Leaking vacuum diaphragm.

NO 3-4 UPSHIFT

1. Low fluid level.
2. Damaged or improperly adjusted linkage.
3. Low pressure to overdrive band servo.
4. Sticking or dirty valve body.
5. Burnt or worn overdrive band assembly.
6. Blocked case passage.
7. Broken converter damper hub.

EARLY OR SLIPPING 3-4

1. Improper fluid level.
2. Damaged or improperly adjusted linkage.
3. Low main control pressure to overdrive band servo.
4. Sticking or dirty valve body.
5. Burnt overdrive band assembly.
6. Damaged or glazed reverse clutch drum or overdrive band.

ERRATIC SHIFTS

1. Improper fluid level.
2. Improperly tuned engine.
3. Damaged or improperly adjusted linkage.
4. Dirty or sticking valve body.
5. Sticking governor valve.
6. Damaged output shaft collector body seal rings.

SHIFTS 1-3 IN D

1. Improper fluid level.
2. Damaged or burnt intermediate friction clutch.
3. Damaged intermediate one-way clutch.
4. Improper control system pressure or clutch application.
5. Sticking or dirty valve body.
6. Sticking governor valve.

LATE 2-3 SHIFTING

1. Improper fluid level.
2. Damaged or improperly adjusted linkage.

age.
3. Improper control system pressure or clutch application.
4. Damaged or worn high clutch or intermediate servo.
5. Sticking or dirty valve body.
6. Broken converter damper hub.

SHIFT HUNTING 3-4 OR 4-3

1. Improperly tuned engine.
2. Damaged or improperly adjusted linkage.

NO FORCED DOWNSHIFTS

1. Improper fluid level.
2. Damaged or improperly adjusted linkage.
3. Improper control system pressure or clutch application.
4. Sticking or dirty valve body.
5. Sticking or dirty governor.

3-1 SHIFT AT CLOSED THROTTLE IN D

1. Improper fluid level.
2. Improperly tuned engine.
3. Damaged or improperly adjusted linkage.
4. Improper control system pressure or clutch application.
5. Improper governor operation.
6. Sticking or dirty valve body.

HARSH OR SLIPPING 4-2 OR 3-1 SHIFT

1. Improper fluid level.
2. Improperly tuned engine.
3. Damaged or improperly adjusted linkage.
4. Improper application of intermediate friction and one-way clutch.
5. Sticking or dirty valve body.

HIGH SHIFT EFFORT

1. Damaged or improperly adjusted linkage.
2. Loose manual lever nut.
3. Damaged manual lever retainer pin.

TRANSMISSION OVERHEATS

1. Improper fluid level.
2. Improperly tuned engine.
3. Improper control system pressure or clutch application.
4. Restricted cooler or lines.
5. Seized converter one-way clutch.
6. Sticking or dirty valve body.

CLUNK OR SQUAWK IN 1-2 OR 2-3

1. Blocked intermediate bleed hole or bleed hole not at 12 o'clock position.
2. Misaligned anti-clunk spring.

HARSH DOWNSHIFT COASTING CLUNK

1. Improperly seated anti-clunk spring.

2. Damaged or improperly adjusted linkage.

POOR VEHICLE ACCELERATION

1. Improperly tuned engine.
2. Seized torque converter one-way clutch.

SLIPPING SHIFT FOLLOWED BY SUDDEN ENGAGEMENT

1. Throttle valve linkage set too short.

TRANSMISSION NOISY (VALVE RESONANCE)

1. Improper fluid level.
2. Damaged or improperly adjusted linkage.
3. Improper control system pressure or clutch application.
4. Cooler lines contacting frame, floor pan or other components.
5. Sticking or dirty valve body.
6. Internal leakage or pump cavitation.

TRANSMISSION NOISY (OTHER THAN VALVE RESONANCE)

1. Improper fluid level.
2. Damaged or improperly adjusted linkage.
3. Contaminated fluid.
4. Loose converter to flywheel housing bolts or nuts.
5. Loose or worn speedometer driven gear.
6. Damaged or worn extension housing bushing seal or driveshaft.
7. Damaged or worn front or rear planetary and/or one-way clutch.

THROTTLE VALVE LINKAGE DIAGNOSIS

Refer to the following for TV linkage conditions and subsequent shift troubles.

T.V. CONTROL LINKAGE ADJUSTED TOO SHORT

1. Early or soft up-shifts.
2. Harsh light throttle shift into and out of overdrive.
3. No forced downshift at proper speeds.

T.V. LINKAGE ADJUSTED TOO LONG

1. Harsh idle engagement after engine warm up.
2. Clunking when throttle is released after heavy acceleration.
3. Harsh coasting downshifts out of overdrive.

INTERFERENCE PREVENTING RETURN OF T.V. CONTROL ROD

1. Delayed or harsh upshifts.

2. Harsh idle engagement.

BINDING GROMMETS PREVENTING T.V. LINKAGE RETURN

1. Delayed or harsh upshifts.
2. Harsh idle engagement.

T.V. CONTROL ROD DISCONNECTED

1. Delayed or harsh upshifts.
2. Harsh idle engagement.

CLAMPING BOLT ON TRUNNION AT LOWER END OF T.V. CONTROL ROD LOOSE

1. Delayed or harsh upshifts.
2. Harsh idle engagement.

LINKAGE LEVER RETURN SPRING BROKEN OR DISCONNECTED

1. Delayed or harsh upshifts.
2. Harsh idle engagements.

MAINTENANCE
CHECKING OIL LEVEL

1. With transmission at operating temperature, park vehicle on level surface.
2. Operate engine at idle speed with parking brake applied and move selector lever through each detent position. Return selector lever to Park.
3. With engine idling, remove dipstick and check fluid level. Fluid level should be between arrows on dipstick.
4. Add fluid as necessary to bring fluid to proper level. Use only fluid meeting Ford Qualification No. M2C-138-CJ or Dexron II.

DRAIN & REFILL

1. Raise the vehicle and place a drain pan under the transmission.
2. Loosen the pan attaching bolts and drain the fluid.
3. Remove and clean the pan discarding the filter, filter gasket, oil pan gasket, and valve body gasket.
4. Install new gaskets and the pan.
5. Add three quarts of fluid to the transmission through the filler tube.
6. Run the engine and move the selector lever through the detents checking the fluid level as described above.

IN-VEHICLE ADJUSTMENTS
SHIFT LINKAGE, ADJUST

1. Place transmission selector lever on

steering column into D (Overdrive) position. Secure lever in this position.
2. Loosen shift rod adjusting nut at point A, **Figs. 2 and 3.**
3. Place manual lever on transmission into D (Overdrive) position by moving lever completely rearward, then forward 2 detents.
4. With selector lever and transmission manual lever in D (Overdrive) position, torque adjusting nut at point "A" to 12–18 ft. lbs.

T.V. CONTROL ROD LINKAGE, ADJUST

V8 ENGINE

Adjustment At Carburetor

1. Ensure engine idle speed is set to specification.
2. Disconnect fast idle cam from carburetor so throttle lever is at its idle stop.
3. Turn adjusting on linkage lever completely counterclockwise.
4. Turn adjusting screw clockwise until a .005 feeler gauge can be installed with minimum friction, **Fig. 4.**
5. Turn adjusting screw an additional 4 turns.

Adjustment At Transmission

1. Ensure engine idle speed is set to specification.
2. Disconnect fast idle cam from carburetor so throttle lever is at its idle stop.
3. Position linkage lever screw at approximately the midpoint.
4. Raise and support vehicle.
5. Using a suitable tool, loosen bolt on sliding trunnion block on T.V. control rod assembly, **Fig. 5.**
6. Push up on the lower end of the control rod, **Fig. 5,** to ensure linkage lever at carburetor is firmly against the throttle lever.
7. Push T.V. control lever on the transmission up against internal stop, then tighten bolt on trunnion block, **Fig. 5.**

T.V. CONTROL CABLE, ADJUST

6 Cylinder Engines & 1985 V8-302 With Fuel Injection

On 1985 V8-302 fuel injected engine, proceed directly to step 6. On 6 cylinder engines, the ISC plunger must first be retracted before adjusting T.V. cable. To retract ISC plunger, follow steps 1 through 5.

1. Working inside of engine compartment, locate Self Test Connector and Self Test Input Connector. These two connectors are next to each other, **Fig. 6.**
2. Connect a jumper wire between the Self Test Input Connector and the Signal Return (ground) of the Self Test Connector, **Figs. 7 and 8.**
3. Turn ignition key to Run position but do not start engine.
4. Ensure that ISC plunger retracts, **Fig. 9.** Wait approximately 10 seconds for plunger to fully retract.

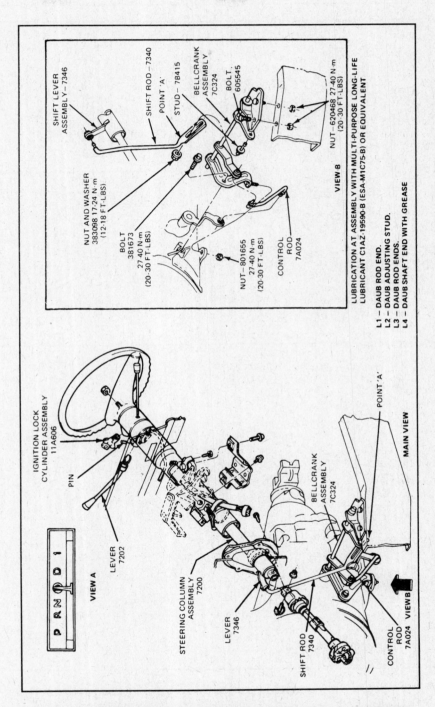

Fig. 2 Shift linkage adjustment. F-150-250 4 × 2 models

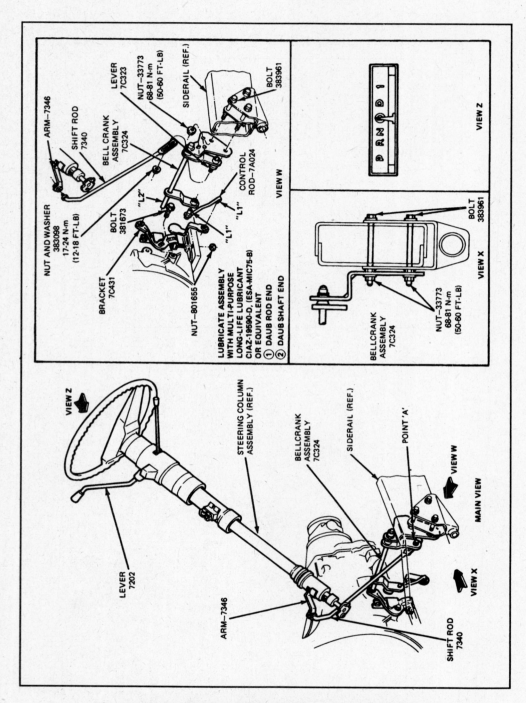

Fig. 3 Shift linkage adjustment. E-150-250 models

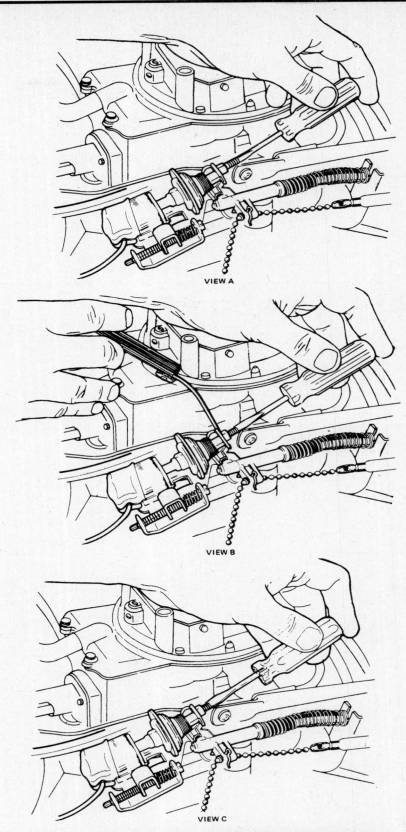

Fig. 4 Throttle valve control linkage adjustment

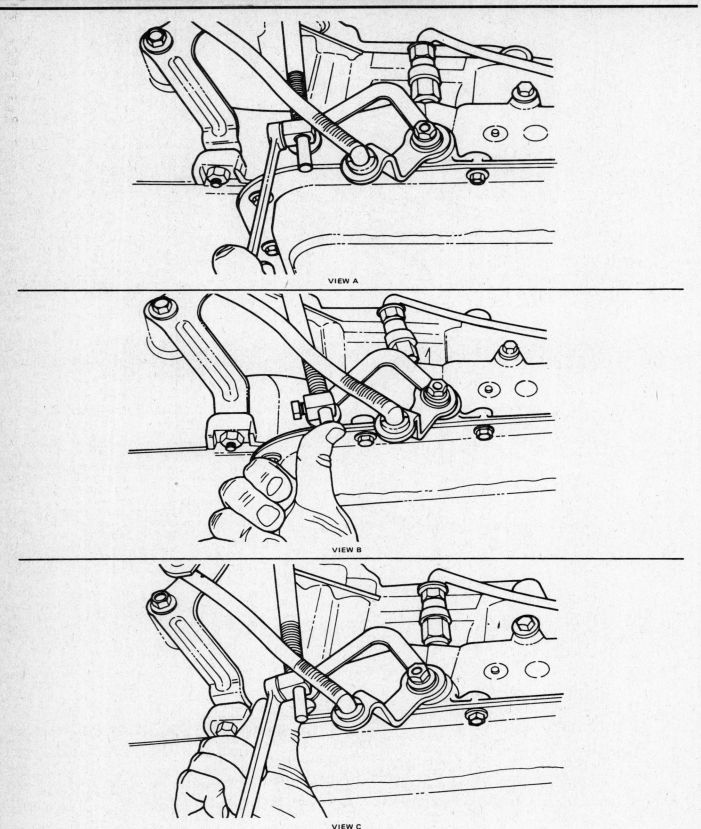

VIEW A

VIEW B

VIEW C

Fig. 5 Transmission linkage adjustment

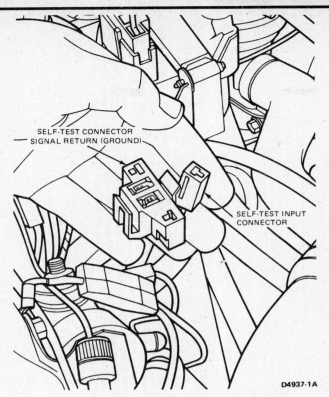

Fig. 6   Self test connector location

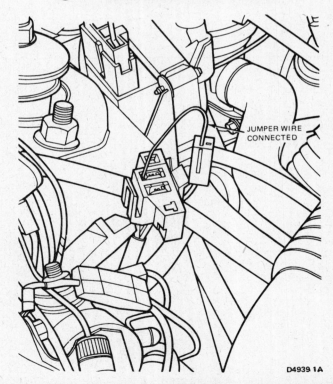

Fig. 7   Connecting jumper wires between self test connectors

5. Shut off key, remove jumper wire and remove air cleaner.
6. Apply parking brake and place selector lever in "N".
7. Ensure that throttle lever is at idle stop. If not, check for binding or inter-ference in throttle system, do not attempt to adjust idle stop.
8. Ensure that cable routing is free of sharp bends or pressure points and that cable operates freely. Lubricate T.V. lever ball stud with suitable lubri-cant as necessary.
9. Unlock locking tab at end by pushing up from below, then pry up the rest of the way to free cable, **Figs. 10 and 11.**
10. Install retention spring on T.V. control lever to hold lever in idle position. If suitable single spring is not available, two V8 T.V. return springs may be used. Attach retention spring(s) to transmission T.V. lever and hook rear end of spring to transmission case, **Fig. 12.**
11. On 6 cylinder engine, de-cam carbure-tor, **Fig. 13.** The carburetor throttle lever must be in the anti-diesel idle position. Ensure that take up spring properly tensions cable and that there is no binding or sticking in sliding ad-justing mechanism. If spring is loose or bottomed out, check for bent cable brackets.
12. Press down on locking key until flush, **Fig. 14.**
13. Remove retention springs from trans-mission T.V. lever.

T.V. CONTROL PRESSURE, ADJUST

1. Ensure engine idle speed is set to specification.
2. Connect a 0–100 psi pressure gauge with adapter fitting D80L-77001 or equivalent onto transmission T.V. port., **Fig. 15.**
3. Operate engine until normal operating temperature is obtained and throttle lever is off of fast idle.
4. Apply parking brake, place transmis-sion selector lever into Neutral and remove air cleaner assembly from car-buretor.
5. With engine idling in Neutral, insert a 1/16 inch drill bit, T.V. control pressure gauge block or fabricated block be-tween carburetor throttle lever and ad-justing screw on T.V. linkage lever at carburetor, **Figs. 16 and 17.**
6. The T.V. pressure should be 35 psi. If not, turn adjusting screw inward to raise T.V. pressure or outward to low-er T.V. pressure.

IN-VEHICLE REPAIRS
CONTROL VALVE BODY

1. Raise and support vehicle, drain transmission fluid, then remove trans-mission pan, gasket and filter.
2. Remove detent spring attaching bolt, then the spring.
3. Remove valve body to case attaching bolts, then the valve body.
4. Reverse procedure to install. Use suit-able guide pins to align valve body to case.

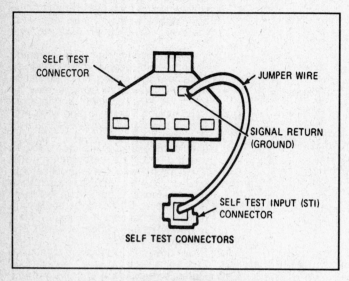

Fig. 8   Connecting self test connector ground circuit

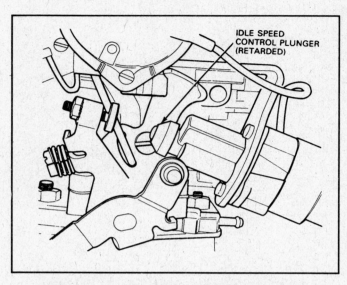

Fig. 9   ISC plunger in retracted position

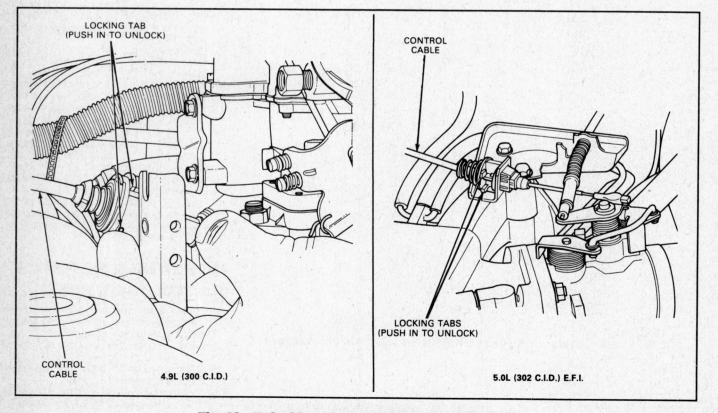

Fig. 10   Unlocking T.V. control cable locking tab

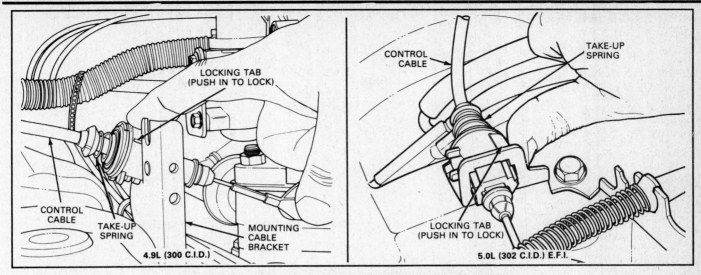

Fig. 11   Prying up T.V. control cable locking tab

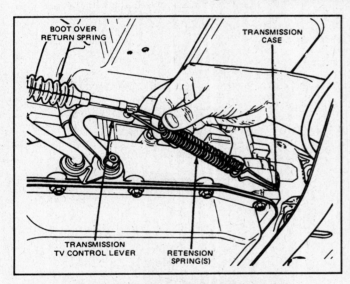

Fig. 12   T.V. lever retention spring

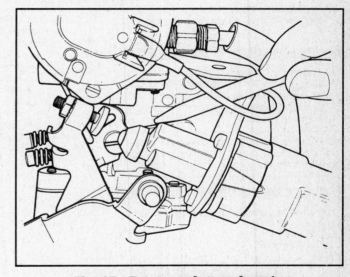

Fig. 13   De-camming carburetor

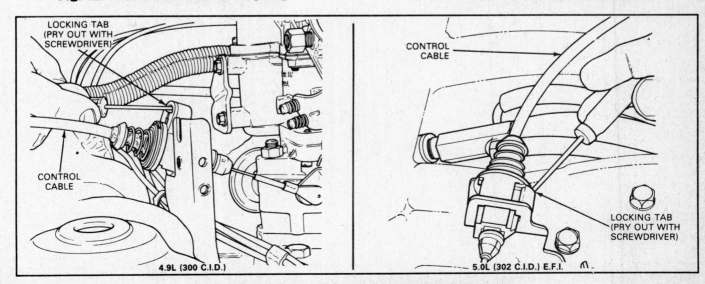

Fig. 14   Installing T.V. control cable locking tab

OVERDRIVE SERVO ASSEMBLY

1. Remove valve body as previously described.
2. Compress overdrive servo piston cover with a suitable tool, then remove snap ring retainer.
3. Apply compressed air to servo piston release passage and remove the overdrive servo piston cover and spring. Remove piston from cover, then the rubber seal from piston and cover.
4. Install new servo piston and cover seals on the servo piston and cover.
5. Lubricate all seals, piston and piston bore with transmission fluid.
6. Install servo piston into cover, then the return spring into servo piston.
7. Install overdrive piston assembly into overdrive servo bore.
8. Compress overdrive piston using suitable tool, then install snap ring retainer.
9. Install valve body, filter, pan and gasket. Refill transmission to proper fluid level.

REVERSE SERVO ASSEMBLY

1. Refer to "Overdrive Servo Assembly" procedure for replacement. Apply compressed air to the servo piston release passage to remove servo piston from case.

NOTE: Reverse servo piston is under spring pressure. Use caution when removing servo piston cover.

3-4 ACCUMULATOR PISTON

1. Remove valve body as previously de-

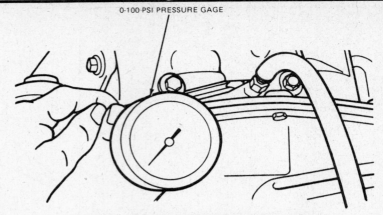

Fig. 15   Install 0-100 pressure gauge

scribed.
2. Compress 3-4 accumulator piston cover, then remove snap ring retainer.
3. Release cover slowly, then remove piston cover, return spring and piston. Some models do not use a spring.
4. Remove seal from 3-4 accumulator cover and piston and inspect for damage and wear.
5. Install new seals on 3-4 accumulator cover, if necessary. Lubricate cover pocket of case with transmission fluid.
6. Install 3-4 accumulator piston and return spring into case, then the cover.

7. Compress cover using suitable tool, then install snap ring. Ensure cover is reseated snugly against snap ring.
8. Install valve body, filter, pan and gasket. Refill transmission pan to proper fluid level.

2-3 ACCUMULATOR PISTON

1. Refer to "3-4 Accumulator Piston" procedure for replacement.

EXTENSION HOUSING

1. Raise and support vehicle.
2. Disconnect parking brake cable from equalizer, if necessary.

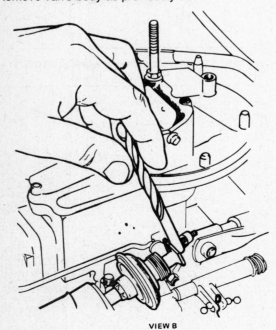

Fig. 16   Install ¹⁄₁₆ drill bit between carburetor throttle lever & adjusting screw

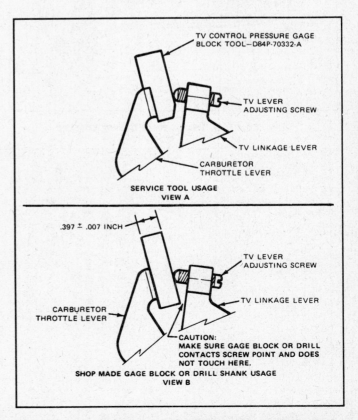

Fig. 17   T.V. control pressure gauge block tool

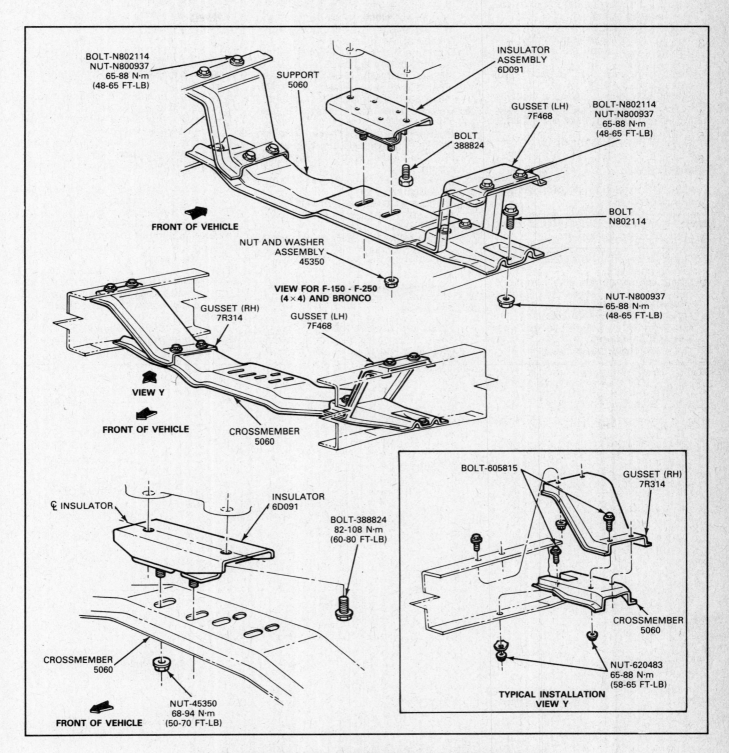

Fig. 18 Crossmember installation. F-150-250 & Bronco

3. Disconnect drive shaft from rear axle flange, then remove drive shaft from transmission.
4. Disconnect speedometer cable from extension housing.
5. Remove engine rear support to extension housing attaching bolts.
6. Support transmission with suitable jack and raise transmission enough to remove weight from rear engine support.
7. Remove engine rear support from crossmember, then lower transmission and remove extension housing attaching bolts. Slide extension housing from output shaft and allow fluid to drain.
8. Reverse procedure to install.

GOVERNOR

1. Remove extension housing as described above.

NOTE: If governor body only is being removed, proceed to step 4.

2. Remove governor to output shaft retaining snap ring.
3. Remove governor assembly from output shaft using suitable tool. Remove governor driveball.
4. Remove governor to counterweight attaching screws. Remove governor from counterweight.
5. Reverse procedure to install.

INTERNAL & EXTERNAL SHIFT LINKAGE

1. Raise and support vehicle.
2. Drain transmission fluid from pan, then remove pan and gasket.
3. Disconnect shift rod at transmission manual lever, then the throttle valve linkage at transmission.
4. Disconnect inner throttle lever spring. Remove detent spring.
5. Hold outer throttle lever, then loosen outer throttle lever attaching nut. Remove attaching nut and lock washer.
6. Remove outer throttle lever seal, then the manual lever roll pin.
7. Remove outer manual lever attaching bolt, then the outer manual lever.
8. Remove inner throttle lever and spring.
9. Remove inner manual lever and park pawl actuating rod.
10. Remove manual lever oil seal.
11. Reverse procedure to install. Adjust transmission manual linkage and throttle linkage as outlined previously.

TRANSMISSION
REPLACE

1. Raise and support vehicle.
2. Drain transmission fluid from pan. After fluid is drained, install pan.
3. Remove converter drain plug access cover from lower end of converter housing. Rotate engine to gain access to converter drain plug. Remove drain plug, drain fluid from converter, then replace drain plug.
4. Remove converter to flywheel attaching nuts, then the driveshaft from vehicle.
5. Disconnect battery cable from starter motor, then remove starter motor. Disconnect neutral start switch electrical connector.
6. Remove rear mount to crossmember bolts and crossmember to frame bolts.
7. Remove engine rear support to extension housing bolts.
8. Disconnect manual linkage from transmission, then remove bolts securing bellcrank bracket to converter housing.
9. Raise transmission with suitable jack and remove crossmember.
10. Lower transmission slightly and disconnect oil cooler lines and speedometer cable from transmission.
11. Remove filler tube and dipstick from transmission.
12. With transmission secured to jack, remove converter housing to cylinder block attaching bolts. Move transmission and converter assembly rearward, then lower transmission and remove from under vehicle.
13. Reverse procedure to install, referring to **Fig. 18**.

GENERAL MOTORS CORP.

SECTION INDEX

CHEVROLET ASTRO VAN & GMC SAFARI VAN

INDEX OF SERVICE OPERATIONS

NOTE: Refer to page 1 of this manual for vehicle manufacturer's special service tool suppliers.

General Engine Specifications

Year	Engine Model	Carb. Type	Bore & Stroke	Comp. Ratio	Net Horsepower @ R.P.M.	Torque Ft. Lbs. @ R.P.M.	Normal Oil Press. Lbs.
1985	4-151/2.5L	T.B.I.①	4.00 × 3.00	9.0	92 @ 4400	134 @ 2800	45
	V6-262/4.3L	4 Bore	4.00 × 3.48	9.3	145 @ 4000	225 @ 2400	50

①—Throttle body fuel injection.

Valve Specifications

Year	Engine	Valve Lash Int.	Valve Lash Exh.	Valve Angles Seat	Valve Angles Face	Valve Spring Installed Height	Valve Spring Pressure Lbs. @ In.	Stem Clearance Intake	Stem Clearance Exhaust	Stem Diameter Intake	Stem Diameter Exhaust
1985	4-151	Hydraulic①		②	45	1.69	151 @ 1.25	.0010–.0027	③	.3418–.3425	.3418–.3425
	V6-262	1 Turn④		46	45	1.72	200 @ 1.25	.0010–.0027	.0010–.0027	—	—

①—No adjustment.
②—Intake, 46°; exhaust, 45°.
③—Top, .0010–.0027; bottom, .0020– .0037.
④—Turn rocker arm stud nut until all lash is eliminated, then tighten nut the additional turns listed.

Pistons, Pins, Rings, Crankshaft & Bearings Specifications

Year	Engine	Piston Clearance	Ring End Gap① Comp.	Ring End Gap① Oil	Wrist Pin Diameter	Rod Bearings Shaft Diameter	Rod Bearings Bearing Clearance	Main Bearings Shaft Diameter	Main Bearings Bearing Clearance	Main Bearings Thrust Bearing No.	Shaft End Play
1985	4-151	②	.010	.015	.9400	2.000	.0005–.0026	2.300	.0005–.0022	5	.0035–.0085
	V6-262	.0007–.0017	.010	.015	.9271	2.2487–2.2497	.0020–.0030	③	④	4	.0020–.0060

①—Fit rings in tapered bores for clearance listed in tightest portion of ring travel.
②—Top, .0025–.0033; bottom, .0017–.0041.
③—Front, 2.4484–2.4493; intermediate, 2.4481–2.4490; rear, 2.4479–2.4488.
④—Front, .0010–.0015; intermediate, .0010–.0020; rear, .0025–.0030.

Engine Tightening Specifications★

★ Torque specifications are for clean and lightly lubricated threads only. Dry or dirty threads produce increased friction which prevents accurate measurement of tightness.

Year	Engine	Spark Plugs Ft. Lbs.	Cylinder Head Bolts Ft. Lbs.	Intake Manifold Ft. Lbs.	Exhaust Manifold Ft. Lbs.	Rocker Arm Shaft Bracket Ft. Lbs.	Rocker Arm Cover Ft. Lbs.	Connecting Rod Cap Bolts Ft. Lbs.	Main Bearing Cap Bolts Ft. Lbs.	Flywheel to Crankshaft Ft. Lbs.	Vibration Damper or Pulley Ft. Lbs.
1985	4-151	7–15	92	29	44	20①	6	32	70	44	160
	V6-262	22	65	30	20	—	4	45	70	65	60

①—Rocker arm bolt.

continued

Alternator Specifications

Year	Model	Field Current @ 80° F 12 volts	Rated Hot Output Amperes	Cold Output	
				Amperes @ 2000 RPM	Amperes @ 7000 RPM
1985	1100206	4.5–5	37	60	56
	1100217	4.5–5	51	81	78
	1100250	4.5–5	51	81	78
	1100259	4.5–5	51	81	78
	1100287	4.5–5	37	60	56
	1105492	4.5–5	56	103	94
	1105507	4.5–5	56	103	94
	1105582	4.5–5	56	103	94

Starting Motor Specifications

Year	Engine	Starter Model	Brush Spring Tension ①	Free Speed Test		
				Amperes	Volts	R.P.M.
1985	4-151	1998450	—	50–75	10	6000–11900
	V6-262	1998441	—	70–110	10	6500–10700

①—Minimum.
②—Includes solenoid.

Wheel Alignment Specifications

Year & Model	Caster Deg.	Camber Deg.	Toe In. Deg.
1985 All	+2.2 to +3.2	+.44 to +1.44	+.10 to +.20

Brake Specifications

Year	Model	Rear Drum I.D.	Wheel Cyl. Bore		Disc Brake Rotor					Master Cyl I.D.
			Front Disc	Rear Drum	Nominal Thickness	Minimum Thickness	Thickness Variation (Parallelism)	Run Out (TIR)	Finish (microinch)	
1985	All	9.5	2.94	.812	—	.980	.0005	.004	—	①

①—Manual brakes, 1.00; power brakes, 1.25.

continued

Drive Axle Specifications

Year	Model	Carrier Type	Ring Gear & Pinion Backlash		Pinion Bearing Preload			Differential Bearing Preload		
			Method	Adjustment	Method	New Bearings Inch-Lbs.	Used Bearings Inch-Lbs.	Method	New Bearings Inch-Lbs.	Used Bearings Inch-Lbs.
1985	All	Integral	Shim	.005–.009	Collapsible spacer	24–32①	8–12①	Shim	②	②

①—Measured with torque wrench at pinnion flange nut.
②—Slip fit plus .004 inch clearance on each side.

Cooling System & Capacity Data

Year	Model or Engine	Cooling Capacity, Qts.		Radiator Cap Relief Pressure, Lbs.	Thermo. Opening Temp.	Fuel Tank Gals.	Engine Oil Refill Qts.	Transmission Oil				Rear Axle Oil Pints
		Less A/C	With A/C					4 Speed Pints	5 Speed Pints	Auto. Trans.①	Trans. Case Pints	
1985	4-151	10.0	10.0	15	195	17	3②	2.4	4.1	④	—	4
	V6-262	13.5	13.5	15	195	17	4③	2.4	—	④	—	4

①—Approximate; make final check with dipstick.
②—With or without filter.
③—Add one quart with filter change.
④—Total, 11½ qts.; pan only, 5 qts.

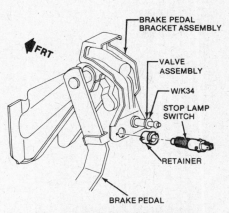

Fig. 1 Stop lamp switch replacement

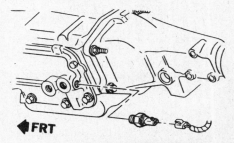

Fig. 3 Back-up light switch replacement. Manual transmission

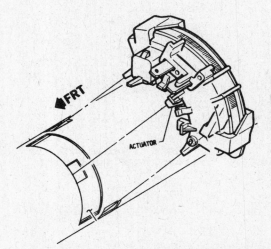

Fig. 2 Neutral start/back-up light switch replacement. Automatic transmission

INSTALLATION PROCEDURE

1. PLACE GEAR SELECTOR IN NEUTRAL.

2. ALIGN ACTUATOR ON SWITCH WITH HOLE IN SHIFT TUBE.

3. POSITION REARWARD PORTION OF SWITCH (CONNECTOR SIDE) TO FIT INTO CUTOUT IN LOWER JACKET.

4. PUSH DOWN ON FRONT OF SWITCH: THE TWO TANGS ON HOUSING BACK WILL SNAP INTO PLACE IN RECTANGULAR HOLES IN JACKET.

5. ADJUST SWITCH BY MOVING GEAR SELECTOR TO PARK. THE MAIN HOUSING AND THE HOUSING BACK SHOULD RATCHET, PROVIDING PROPER SWITCH ADJUSTMENT.

READJUSTMENT PROCEDURE

1. WITH SWITCH INSTALLED, MOVE THE HOUSING ALL THE WAY TOWARD "LOW GEAR" POSITION.

2. REPEAT STEP 5.

4. Adjust stop lamp switch by bringing brake pedal to normal position.

NOTE: Electrical contact should be made when the brake pedal is now depressed .53 inch from its fully released position. If adjustment is necessary, the switch may be pulled or rotated in the clip.

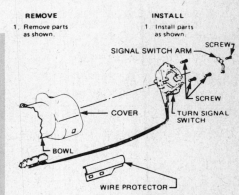

Fig. 4 Turn signal switch replacement

STARTER
REPLACE

1. Disconnect battery ground cable.
2. Raise and support vehicle.
3. Remove starter braces, shields and any other components necessary to gain access to starter mounting bolts.
4. Remove starter motor-to-engine attaching bolts.
5. Lower starter from engine, then disconnect solenoid wires and battery cable and remove starter from vehicle.
6. Reverse procedure to install.

STOP LAMP SWITCH
REPLACE

1. Disconnect electrical connector from switch by reaching up under right side of instrument panel at brake pedal support.
2. Pull switch from mounting bracket, **Fig. 1,** and remove from vehicle.
3. To install new switch, depress brake pedal and push switch into clip until shoulder on switch bottoms out against clip.

NEUTRAL START & BACK-UP LIGHT SWITCH
REPLACE

Refer to **Fig. 2** when replacing the combination neutral start/back-up light switch on automatic transmission vehicles and **Fig. 3** when replacing the back-up light switch on manual transmission vehicles.

STEERING WHEEL
REPLACE

1. Disconnect battery ground cable.
2. Remove steering wheel shroud attaching screws, if equipped, from underside of steering wheel.
3. Remove cap or lift steering wheel shroud and horn contact lead assembly from steering wheel.
4. Remove snap ring, then the steering wheel nut.
5. Remove steering wheel using puller J-1859 or equivalent.
6. Reverse procedure to install.

TURN SIGNAL SWITCH
REPLACE

1. Disconnect battery ground cable.
2. Remove steering wheel as described under "Steering Wheel, Replace."
3. Refer to **Fig. 4** to replace turn signal switch.

IGNITION LOCK
REPLACE

1. Remove turn signal switch as described under "Turn Signal Switch, Replace."
2. Turn lock cylinder to Run position and remove key warning buzzer switch, if equipped.
3. Remove retaining screw and the lock cylinder, **Figs. 5 and 6.**
4. Reverse procedure to install.

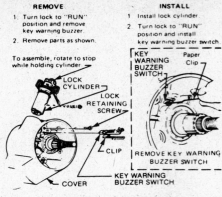

REMOVE
1. Turn lock to "RUN" position
2. Remove parts as shown.

To assemble, rotate to stop while holding cylinder.

INSTALL
1. Install lock cylinder.
2. Turn lock to "RUN" position

LOCK CYLINDER
LOCK RETAINING SCREW
HOUSING

Fig. 5 Ignition lock replacement. Exc. tilt column

REMOVE
1. Turn lock to "RUN" position and remove key warning buzzer.
2. Remove parts as shown.

To assemble, rotate to stop while holding cylinder.

INSTALL
1. Install lock cylinder
2. Turn lock to "RUN" position and install key warning buzzer switch.

LOCK CYLINDER
LOCK RETAINING SCREW
CLIP
COVER
KEY WARNING BUZZER SWITCH

KEY WARNING BUZZER SWITCH
Paper Clip
REMOVE KEY WARNING BUZZER SWITCH

Fig. 6 Ignition lock replacement. Tilt column

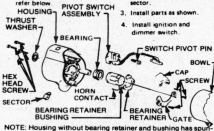

REMOVE
1. Remove ignition and dimmer switch.
2. Remove parts as shown.
3. For KEY RELEASE refer below.

INSTALL
1. For KEY RELEASE refer below.
2. Assemble rack so that first rack tooth engages between first and second tooth of sector.
3. Install parts as shown.
4. Install ignition and dimmer switch.

THRUST WASHER
HOUSING
PIVOT SWITCH ASSEMBLY
BEARING
SWITCH PIVOT PIN
BOWL
HEX HEAD SCREW
SECTOR
HORN CONTACT
BEARING RETAINER BUSHING
BEARING RETAINER
CAP SCREW
GATE

NOTE: Housing without bearing retainer and bushing has spun-in bearing. If repair is necessary, complete housing assembly replacement is necessary.

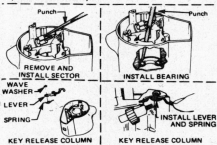

Punch
REMOVE AND INSTALL SECTOR
Punch
INSTALL BEARING

WAVE WASHER
LEVER
SPRING
KEY RELEASE COLUMN

INSTALL LEVER AND SPRING
KEY RELEASE COLUMN

Fig. 7 W/S wiper switch replacement. Exc. tilt column

scribed under "Turn Signal Switch, Replace."
2. Refer to **Figs. 9 and 10** to replace ignition and dimmer switches.

INSTRUMENT CLUSTER
REPLACE
1. Disconnect battery ground cable.
2. Remove steering column lower trim plate.
3. Remove instrument cluster trim plate attaching screws and allow panel to hang to left side by wiring.
4. Remove A/C control assembly attaching screws and position assembly to one side.
5. Remove alarm assembly, then the instrument panel cluster trim panel.

6. Remove instrument panel-to-cluster attaching screws.
7. Disconnect speedometer cable and all electrical connectors from rear of cluster, then remove cluster, **Fig. 11** from vehicle.
8. Reverse procedure to install.

NOTE: Turn lock cylinder to Run position prior to installation.

W/S WIPER SWITCH
REPLACE
1. Remove ignition lock as described under "Ignition Lock, Replace."
2. Refer to **Figs. 7 and 8** to replace wiper switch.

IGNITION & DIMMER SWITCHES
REPLACE
1. Remove turn signal switch as de-

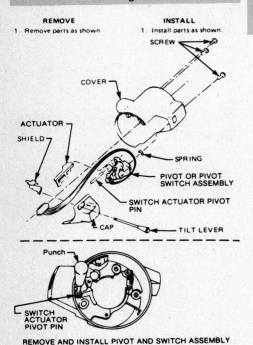

REMOVE
1. Remove parts as shown

INSTALL
1. Install parts as shown.

SCREW
COVER
ACTUATOR
SHIELD
SPRING
PIVOT OR PIVOT SWITCH ASSEMBLY
SWITCH ACTUATOR PIVOT PIN
CAP
TILT LEVER

Punch
SWITCH ACTUATOR PIVOT PIN
REMOVE AND INSTALL PIVOT AND SWITCH ASSEMBLY

Fig. 8 W/S wiper switch replacement. Tilt column

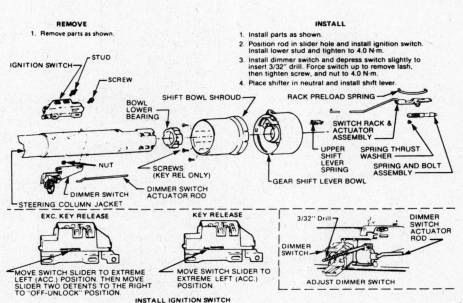

REMOVE
1. Remove parts as shown.

IGNITION SWITCH
STUD
SCREW
BOWL LOWER BEARING
SHIFT BOWL SHROUD
NUT
SCREWS (KEY REL ONLY)
DIMMER SWITCH
DIMMER SWITCH ACTUATOR ROD
STEERING COLUMN JACKET
GEAR SHIFT LEVER BOWL
UPPER SHIFT LEVER SPRING
RACK PRELOAD SPRING
SWITCH RACK & ACTUATOR ASSEMBLY
SPRING THRUST WASHER
SPRING AND BOLT ASSEMBLY

INSTALL
1. Install parts as shown.
2. Position rod in slider hole and install ignition switch. Install lower stud and tighten to 4.0 N·m.
3. Install dimmer switch and depress switch slightly to insert 3/32 drill. Force switch up to remove lash, then tighten screw, and nut to 4.0 N·m.
4. Place shifter in neutral and install shift lever.

EXC. KEY RELEASE
MOVE SWITCH SLIDER TO EXTREME LEFT (ACC.) POSITION. THEN MOVE SLIDER TWO DETENTS TO THE RIGHT TO "OFF-UNLOCK" POSITION.

KEY RELEASE
MOVE SWITCH SLIDER TO EXTREME LEFT (ACC.) POSITION.

INSTALL IGNITION SWITCH

3/32" Drill
DIMMER SWITCH
DIMMER SWITCH ACTUATOR ROD
ADJUST DIMMER SWITCH

Fig. 9 Ignition & dimmer switch replacement. Exc. tilt column

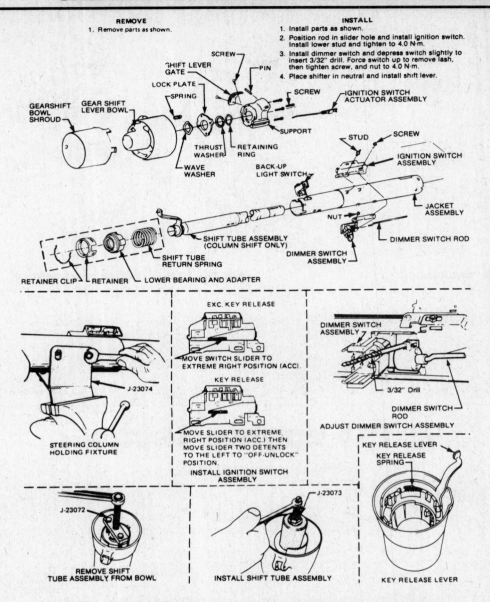

Fig. 10 Ignition & dimmer switch replacement. Tilt column

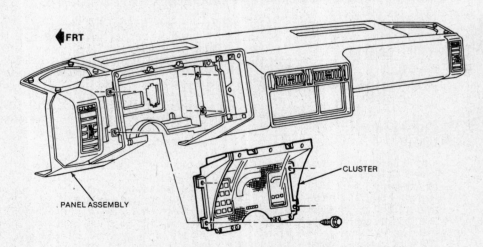

Fig. 11 Instrument cluster replacement

RADIO
REPLACE

1. Disconnect battery ground cable.
2. Refer to **Fig. 12** to replace radio assembly.

BLOWER MOTOR
REPLACE

1. Disconnect battery ground cable.
2. Disconnect electrical connectors from blower motor, then remove coolant overflow bottle.
3. Remove windshield washer fluid bottle attaching bolts and position bottle aside.
4. Remove blower motor attaching screws and the blower motor, **Fig. 13**.

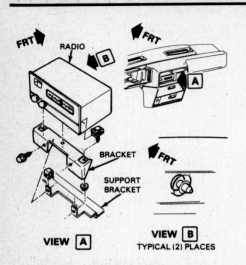

Fig. 12   Radio replacement

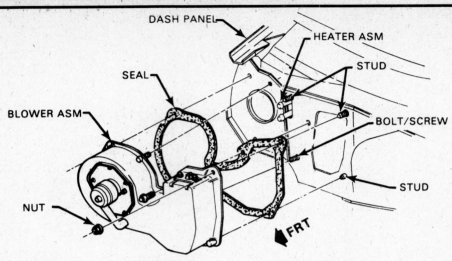

Fig. 13   Blower motor replacement

5. Reverse procedure to install.

HEATER CORE
REPLACE

1. Disconnect battery ground cable.

2. Drain cooling system, then remove coolant overflow bottle.
3. Remove windshield washer fluid bottle attaching bolts and position bottle aside.
4. Disconnect heater core hose from core and plug tubes to prevent con-

tamination.
5. Remove core cover attaching screws and the cover.
6. Remove attaching screws from rear of heater core.
7. Remove heater core from vehicle.
8. Reverse procedure to install.

4-151 Engine Section

ENGINE
REPLACE

1. Disconnect battery ground cable.
2. Drain cooling system, then remove engine cover.
3. Remove headlamp bezel and grille, then the radiator lower close-out panel and radiator support brace.
4. Remove lower tie bar and the cross brace.
5. Remove hood latch mechanism, then the upper core support.
6. Disconnect coolant hoses from radiator, then remove radiator filler panels.
7. Remove radiator and fan shroud as an assembly.
8. Disconnect engine harness from bulkhead connector.
9. Disconnect electrical connector from ECM and pull through bulkhead.
10. Disconnect heater hoses from heater core and plug heater core tubes to prevent contamination.
11. Disconnect accelerator cable, then the battery ground cable from cylinder head.
12. Disconnect canister purge hose, then remove air cleaner and air cleaner adapter.
13. Raise and support vehicle.

14. Disconnect exhaust pipe from exhaust manifold.
15. Disconnect wiring harness from transmission and frame and the starter wires from starter motor.
16. Remove starter motor, then the flywheel shield.
17. Disconnect fuel lines from fuel pump.
18. Remove engine mount through bolts.
19. Lower vehicle, then remove oil filler neck and thermostat outlet.
20. Install engine lifting device and support transmission with a suitable jack, then remove engine from vehicle.
21. Reverse procedure to install.

ENGINE MOUNTS
REPLACE

Refer to **Fig. 1** to replace engine mounts.

CYLINDER HEAD
REPLACE

1. Disconnect battery ground cable.
2. Remove air cleaner assembly, then drain cooling system.
3. Unfasten A/C compressor, if equipped, and position to one side, leaving refrigerant lines connected.
4. Disconnect PCV hose, then remove EGR valve.
5. Disconnect spark plug wires from

valve cover.
6. Disconnect vacuum line hold-down from thermostat.
7. Disconnect vacuum hoses from throttle body and the lines from studs on intake manifold.
8. Remove valve cover, then disconnect electrical connectors from throttle body.
9. Disconnect accelerator, throttle valve and, if equipped, cruise control cables.
10. Remove alternator brace, then disconnect bypass and heater hoses from intake manifold.
11. Disconnect spark plug wires from plugs, then remove A/C compressor bracket, if equipped.
12. Disconnect exhaust pipe from exhaust manifold, then remove A/C line hold-down, if equipped.
13. Remove alternator, then disconnect upper radiator hose.
14. Disconnect fuel line bracket from fuel filter, then remove engine oil dipstick tube.
15. Disconnect fuel and vacuum lines near fuel filter, then remove cylinder head attaching bolts.
16. Disconnect wiring harness bracket from rear of cylinder head.
17. Disconnect coil bracket from cylinder head, then remove push rods.
18. Remove brace between intake manifold and block.
19. Remove cylinder head with intake and

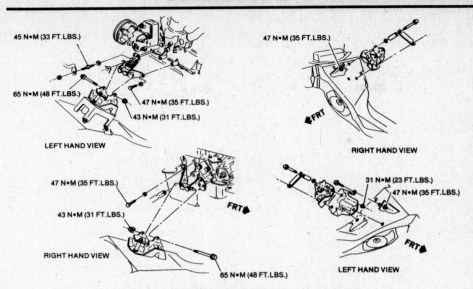

Fig. 1 Engine mount replacement

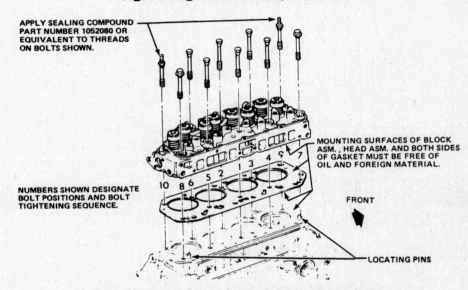

APPLY SEALING COMPOUND PART NUMBER 1052080 OR EQUIVALENT TO THREADS ON BOLTS SHOWN.

MOUNTING SURFACES OF BLOCK ASM., HEAD ASM. AND BOTH SIDES OF GASKET MUST BE FREE OF OIL AND FOREIGN MATERIAL.

NUMBERS SHOWN DESIGNATE BOLT POSITIONS AND BOLT TIGHTENING SEQUENCE.

FRONT

LOCATING PINS

Fig. 2 Cylinder head bolt tightening sequence

1	34 N·m (25 LB. FT.)
2	50 N·m (37 LB. FT.)
3	38 N·m (28 LB. FT.)

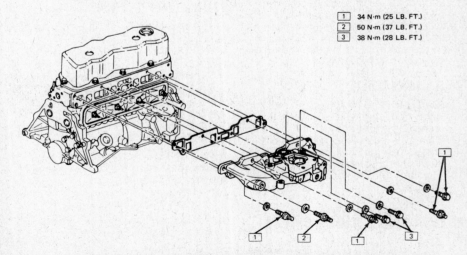

Fig. 3 Intake manifold bolt tightening sequence

exhaust manifolds as an assembly.
20. Remove intake and exhaust manifolds from cylinder head, if necessary.
21. Reverse procedure to install. Torque cylinder head attaching bolts to specifications in sequence shown, **Fig. 2.**

INTAKE MANIFOLD
REPLACE

1. Disconnect battery ground cable.
2. Remove air cleaner assembly, then disconnect all wires necessary for intake manifold removal.
3. Disconnect accelerator and throttle valve cables from bellcrank.
4. Disconnect fuel and vacuum lines from throttle body and manifold.
5. Drain cooling system, then disconnect bypass hose from intake manifold.
6. Remove alternator rear adjusting bracket, then disconnect alternator brace and position to one side.
7. Disconnect cruise control cable, if equipped.
8. Disconnect remaining vacuum hoses necessary for intake manifold removal.
9. Disconnect vacuum line hold-down from thermostat.
10. Disconnect heater hose and coil from intake manifold.
11. Remove intake manifold attaching bolts and the intake manifold.
12. Reverse procedure to install. Torque intake manifold attaching bolts to specifications in sequence shown, **Fig. 3.**

EXHAUST MANIFOLD
REPLACE

1. Disconnect battery ground cable.
2. On models equipped with A/C, unfasten A/C compressor and position aside, then remove rear compressor adjusting bracket.
3. Raise and support vehicle.
4. Disconnect exhaust pipe from exhaust manifold, then lower vehicle.
5. Remove air cleaner assembly, then disconnect electrical connector from oxygen sensor.
6. Remove exhaust manifold attaching bolts and the exhaust manifold.
7. Reverse procedure to install. Torque exhaust manifold attaching bolts to specifications in sequence shown, **Fig. 4.**

ROCKER ARMS & PUSH RODS
REPLACE

1. Disconnect battery ground cable.
2. Remove air cleaner assembly, then disconnect PCV hose.
3. Remove EGR valve, then disconnect spark plug wires from valve cover.
4. Disconnect vacuum lines from studs on intake manifold.

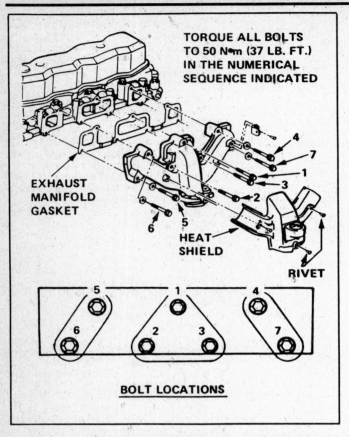

TORQUE ALL BOLTS TO 50 N·m (37 LB. FT.) IN THE NUMERICAL SEQUENCE INDICATED

EXHAUST MANIFOLD GASKET

HEAT SHIELD

RIVET

BOLT LOCATIONS

Fig. 4 Exhaust manifold bolt tightening sequence

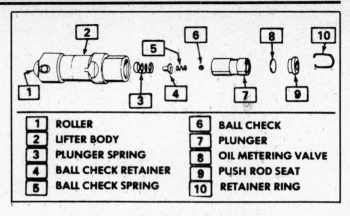

1	ROLLER	6	BALL CHECK
2	LIFTER BODY	7	PLUNGER
3	PLUNGER SPRING	8	OIL METERING VALVE
4	BALL CHECK RETAINER	9	PUSH ROD SEAT
5	BALL CHECK SPRING	10	RETAINER RING

Fig. 5 Hydraulic valve lifter

5. Remove valve cover attaching bolts and the valve cover.
6. Remove rocker arm bolt and ball, then the rocker arm(s) and push rod(s).

NOTE: If only push rods are being replaced, loosen rocker bolt and swing arm away from push rod, then remove push rod through hole in cylinder head.

7. Reverse procedure to install.

VALVE ARRANGEMENT
FRONT TO REAR
I-E-I-E-E-I-E-I

VALVE LIFT SPECS.

Year	Intake	Exhaust
1985	.398	.398

VALVE TIMING
INTAKE OPENS BEFORE TDC

Year	Degrees
1985	33

VALVE LIFTER
SERVICE

Failure of a hydraulic valve lifter, **Fig. 5**, is generally caused by an inadequate oil supply or dirt. An air leak at the intake side of the oil pump or too much oil in the engine will cause air bubbles in the oil supply to the lifters causing them to collapse. This is a probable cause of trouble if several lifters fail to function, but air in the oil is an unlikely cause of failure of a single unit.

Valve lifters can be removed after removing rocker arm cover and push rod cover. Loosen rocker arm stud nut and rotate rocker arm so that push rod can be removed, then remove valve lifter.

DISASSEMBLY

1. Depress plunger with a push rod, then remove push rod seat retainer, **Fig. 5**, using a suitable screwdriver.
2. Remove push rod seat, metering valve, plunger, ball check valve assembly and plunger spring.
3. Pry ball retainer loose from plunger and remove ball check valve and spring.

CLEANING & INSPECTION

1. Clean all lifter components in suitable solvent.
2. Inspect all parts for wear or damage. If

any one component is worn or damaged, the entire assembly must be replaced.
3. If lifter body wall is worn, inspect cylinder block lifter bore.
4. If bottom of lifter is worn, inspect camshaft lobe.
5. If push rod seat is worn, inspect push rod.

ASSEMBLY

1. Position check ball on small hole in bottom of plunger, then install spring and ball retainer.
2. Install plunger spring over ball retainer, then slide lifter body over spring and plunger. Ensure oil holes in lifter body and plunger are aligned.
3. Fill assembly with SAE 10 oil, then depress plunger with a 1/8 inch drift pin. Insert a 1/16 inch drift pin through both oil holes to hold plunger down against spring tension.
4. Remove the 1/8 inch drift pin and refill assembly with SAE 10 oil, then install metering valve and push rod seat.
5. Install push rod seat retainer, then push down on push rod seat and remove 1/16 inch drift pin from oil holes.

NOISE DIAGNOSIS

Momentary Noise When Engine Is Started

Condition normal. Oil drains from lifters which are holding valves open when engine is not running.

Intermittent Noise at Idle, Disappears As Engine Speed Is Increased
1. Dirt in lifter.
2. Pitted check ball.

Noise At Slow Idle Or With Hot Oil; Quiet With Cold Oil Or Increased Engine Speed
1. Excessive lifter leak down, lifter should be replaced.

Noise At Idle, Becomes Louder As Engine Speed Increased To 1500 RPM
1. Excessive valve stem to guide clearance.

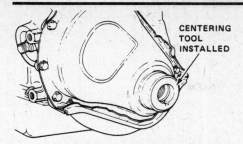

Fig. 6   Engine front cover installation

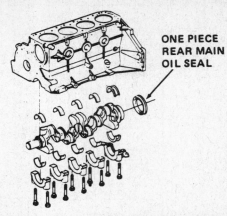

Fig. 7   Rear main seal removal

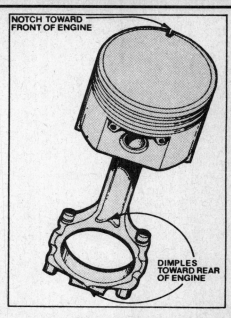

Fig. 8   Piston & rod assembly

2. Off square valve spring.
3. Scuffed or worn valve tip/rocker arm pad.
4. Excessive valve seat or face runout.
5. Damper spring clicking on rotator.

Valves Noisy At All Speeds
1. Rotate crankshaft until piston of affected cylinder is at TDC of firing stroke.
2. Hold rocker arm against valve spring and check for valve lash by moving push rod up and down.
3. If no lash is present, check for dirt in lifter or pitted check ball.
4. If valve lash is present, inspect push rod and rocker arm for excessive wear and replace as needed.
5. If valve lash is present, and push rod and rocker arm are satisfactory, lifter should be replaced.

Quiet At Low Speeds, Noisy At High Speeds
1. Incorrect oil level, oil foaming.
2. Clogged oil pump screen, bent pan or oil pump pickup.
3. Incorrect oil pressure.

CAMSHAFT
REPLACE

REMOVAL
1. Disconnect battery ground cable.
2. Remove alternator and alternator bracket.
3. Remove brace between intake manifold and block.
4. Drain cooling system, then disconnect lower radiator and heater hoses.
5. Remove oil sender, then the wiring harness brackets from push rod side cover.
6. Remove push rod side cover attaching nuts and the side cover.
7. On models equipped with power steering, remove power steering reservoir fan shroud.
8. On all models, remove upper fan shroud.
9. Remove power steering pump drive belt and/or A/C compressor drive belt as equipped.
10. Remove fan and pulley, crankshaft pulley and crankshaft flange.
11. Remove front cover attaching bolts and the front cover.

12. Remove distributor cap and distributor.
13. Remove oil pump drive shaft and cover, then the air cleaner assembly and EGR valve.
14. Disconnect vacuum lines from intake manifold and thermostat housing.
15. Disconnect spark plug wires from valve cover.
16. Remove valve cover, then the push rods, lifter guides and lifters.
17. On models equipped with automatic transmission, disconnect transmission cooler lines from radiator.
18. On all models, disconnect hoses from radiator and remove radiator from vehicle.
19. Remove cam thrust plate bolts.
20. On models equipped with A/C, remove A/C condenser baffles, then unfasten compressor, raise and block in position.
21. On all models, remove headlamp bezel, then the grille and bumper filler panel.
22. Carefully remove camshaft from engine.

INSTALLATION
1. Lubricate camshaft journals with suitable engine oil supplement.
2. Slide camshaft into engine block, using care to avoid damaging bearings or cam.
3. Rotate crankshaft and camshaft until valve timing marks on gear teeth are aligned, then install camshaft thrust plate-to-block attaching screws and torque to 75 inch lbs.
4. Slide hub onto crankshaft with keyway in hub and key on crankshaft aligned, then install center bolt and torque to 160 ft. lbs.
5. Install valve lifters, push rods, push rod side cover, oil pump shaft and gear assembly.
6. Rotate crankshaft 360° to firing position of No. 1 cylinder, then install distributor in original position, aligning shaft so rotor arm points toward No. 1 cylinder spark plug contact.
7. Pivot rocker arms over push rods,

then torque rocker arm bolt to specifications with lifters on base circle of camshaft.
8. Install water pump pulley and fan assembly, A/C condenser (if equipped) and radiator.
9. Refill cooling system and crankcase.

ENGINE FRONT COVER
REPLACE

1. Disconnect battery ground cable.
2. On models equipped with power steering, remove power steering pump fan shroud.
3. On all models, remove upper fan shroud, then the fan and pulley.
4. Loosen drive belts, then remove alternator, alternator brackets, brace and front bracket.
5. Remove crankshaft pulley, then the hub bolt and hub.
6. Disconnect lower radiator hose clamp at water pump.
7. Remove front cover attaching bolts and the front cover.
8. Reverse procedure to install, noting the following:
   a. Apply a continuous bead of RTV sealant on cover prior to installation.
   b. Install front cover with centering tool No. J-34995 positioned in seal, **Fig. 6.**

FRONT OIL SEAL
REPLACE

1. Disconnect battery ground cable.
2. Remove all drive belts.
3. Remove center bolt, then slide hub and pulleys from shaft.

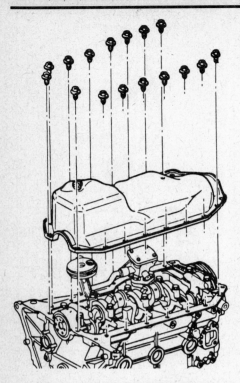

Fig. 9 Oil pan replacement

4. Pry seal out of front cover using a suitable screwdriver.
5. Reverse procedure to install, using tool No. J-23042 to drive seal into position.

REAR MAIN OIL SEAL
REPLACE

1. Remove transmission as described elsewhere in this manual.
2. On models equipped with manual transmission, remove flywheel, pressure plate and disc.
3. On models equipped with automatic transmission, remove flex plate.
4. On all models, remove seal, **Fig. 7**, using a suitable screwdriver.
5. Install new seal using tool No. J-34924 or equivalent.

TIMING GEARS

When necessary to install a new camshaft gear, the camshaft will have to be removed as the gear is press fit on the camshaft. The camshaft is held in place by a thrust plate which is retained to the engine by two capscrews, accessible through the two holes in the gear web.

To remove gear, use an arbor press and a suitable sleeve to properly support gear on its steel hub.

Before installing gear, assemble thrust plate and gear spacer ring, then press gear onto shaft until it bottoms against spacer ring. The thrust plate end clearance should be .0015–.0050 inch. If clearance is less

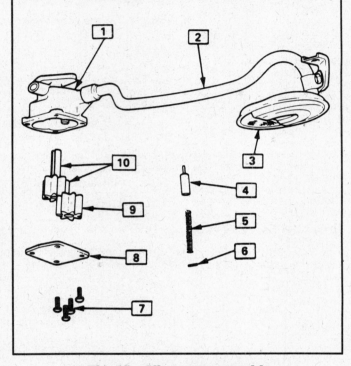

1	PUMP BODY	6	SPRING RETAINER
2	PICKUP TUBE	7	COVER SCREWS
3	PICKUP SCREW ASSEMBLY	8	COVER
4	PRESSURE REGULATOR VALVE	9	IDLER GEAR
5	PRESSURE REGULATOR SPRING	10	DRIVE GEAR AND SHAFT

Fig. 10 Oil pump assembly

than .0015 inch, the thrust plate must be replaced.

The crankshaft gear can be removed using a puller and two bolts in the tapped holes of the gear.

PISTONS & RODS
ASSEMBLE

Assemble piston to rod with notch on piston facing toward front of engine and the raised notch side of rod at bearing end facing toward rear of engine, **Fig. 8**.

PISTONS & RINGS

Pistons and rings are available in standard size and oversizes of .005, .010, .020 and .030 inch.

MAIN & ROD BEARINGS

Main and rod bearings are available in standard size and undersizes of .001, .002 and .010 inch.

OIL PAN
REPLACE

1. Disconnect battery ground cable.
2. Raise and support vehicle.
3. Drain oil pan, then remove strut rods.
4. Remove torque converter cover attaching bolts.
5. Disconnect exhaust pipe from catalytic converter.
6. Disconnect starter brace from engine

block, then remove starter motor.

7. On models equipped with automatic transmission, disconnect transmission oil cooler lines from oil pan.
8. On all models, remove oil pan attaching bolts and the oil pan, **Fig. 9.**
9. Reverse procedure to install, noting the following:
   a. Prior to installation, ensure sealing surfaces on pan, cylinder block and front cover are clean and free of oil.
   b. If reinstalling old pan, ensure all RTV has been removed, paying particular attention to the blind attaching holes.
   c. With clean sealing surfaces, apply a ⅛ inch bead of RTV sealant to entire oil pan sealing flange.

OIL PUMP SERVICE
REMOVAL

1. Remove oil pan as previously described.

2. Remove oil pump attaching bolts, then the pump and screen as an assembly.

DISASSEMBLY

1. Remove 4 pump cover attaching screws, then the cover, idler gear, drive gear and shaft, **Fig. 10.**
2. Remove pressure regulator valve and valve components.

NOTE: Do not remove the oil pickup tube in relation to the pump body or screen.

INSPECTION

Inspect oil pump components. Should any of the following conditions be found, the pump assembly should be replaced.
1. Inspect pump body for cracks or excessive wear.
2. Inspect pump gears for damage, cracks or excessive wear.
3. Check shaft for looseness in housing.
4. Check interior of cover for wear that would allow oil to leak past ends of

gears.
5. Inspect oil pickup screen and relief grommet for damage. Also, remove any debris from screen.
6. Ensure proper fit of valve plunger in body.

ASSEMBLY

1. Position drive gear and shaft in pump body, then install idler gear with smooth side of gear toward cover.
2. Install pump cover and torque attaching screws to 105 inch lbs., then ensure shaft turns freely.
3. Install regulator valve plunger, spring, retainer and pin.

WATER PUMP
REPLACE

1. Disconnect battery ground cable.
2. Drain cooling system.
3. Remove water pump attaching bolts and the water pump.
4. Reverse procedure to install.

V6-262 Engine Section

ENGINE
REPLACE

1. Disconnect battery ground cable.
2. Drain cooling system.
3. Raise and support vehicle.
4. Disconnect exhaust pipe from exhaust manifold.
5. Disconnect strut rods from flywheel inspection cover, then remove flywheel cover.
6. Remove torque converter attaching bolts.
7. Disconnect starter wires from starter, then remove starter motor from vehicle.
8. Remove oil filter, then disconnect electrical connectors from transmission and frame.
9. On models equipped with automatic transmission, disconnect lower transmission cooler line from radiator.
10. On all models, disconnect lower engine oil cooler lines from radiator.
11. Remove lower fan shroud attaching bolts, then the engine mount thru bolts.
12. Remove bell housing attaching bolts, then lower vehicle.
13. Remove headlamp bezel and grille, then the radiator lower close-out panel.
14. Remove radiator support brace, then the core support cross brace.
15. Remove lower tie bar, then the hood latch mechanism.
16. Unfasten master cylinder and position aside.

17. Remove upper fan shroud, then the upper core support.
18. Disconnect remaining hoses and lines from radiator, then remove radiator from vehicle.
19. On models equipped with A/C, discharge refrigerant from A/C system.
20. On all models, remove radiator filler panels, then the engine cover.
21. On models equipped with A/C, remove brace from back of A/C compressor, then disconnect refrigerant hose from accumulator and remove compressor and bracket.
22. On models equipped with power steering, remove power steering pump.
23. On all models, disconnect all vacuum hoses necessary for engine removal.
24. Disconnect engine harness at bulkhead, then remove right kick panel.
25. Disconnect electrical connector from ESC module and push connector through bulkhead.
26. Remove distributor cap, then, if equipped, the A/C accumulator.
27. Disconnect fuel line from carburetor, then remove diverter valve.
28. Disconnect transmission oil dipstick tube.
29. Disconnect heater hoses from heater core and plug heater core tubes to prevent contamination.
30. Remove horn assembly, then the air injection system check valves.
31. Install engine lifting device and support transmission with a suitable jack, then remove engine from vehicle.

32. Reverse procedure to install.

ENGINE MOUNTS
REPLACE

FRONT

1. Remove mount retaining bolt from below frame mounting bracket.
2. Raise front of engine, then remove mount attaching bolts and the mount, **Fig. 1.** Check for interference between rear of engine and cowl panel.

NOTE: Raise engine only enough to provide sufficient clearance for mount removal.

3. Reverse procedure to install.

REAR

1. Support transmission to relieve weight from rear mounts.
2. Remove crossmember-to-mount attaching nuts.
3. Remove mount attaching bolts, then raise transmission and remove mount, **Fig. 1.**
4. Reverse procedure to install.

NOTE: Align mount to crossmember when lowering transmission into position.

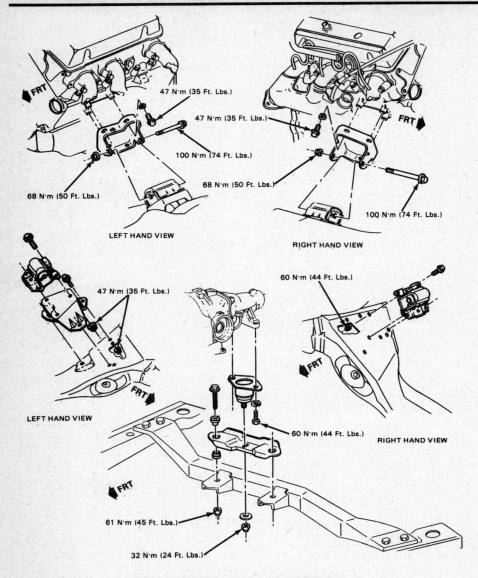

Fig. 1 Engine mount replacement

Left-hand view / Right-hand view callouts:
- 47 N·m (35 Ft. Lbs.)
- 47 N·m (35 Ft. Lbs.)
- 100 N·m (74 Ft. Lbs.)
- 68 N·m (50 Ft. Lbs.)
- 68 N·m (50 Ft. Lbs.)
- 100 N·m (74 Ft. Lbs.)

LEFT HAND VIEW / RIGHT HAND VIEW

- 47 N·m (35 Ft. Lbs.)
- 60 N·m (44 Ft. Lbs.)
- 60 N·m (44 Ft. Lbs.)
- 61 N·m (45 Ft. Lbs.)
- 32 N·m (24 Ft. Lbs.)

LEFT HAND VIEW / RIGHT HAND VIEW

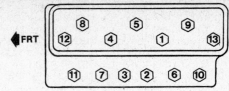

Fig. 2 Cylinder head bolt tightening sequence

3. Raise and support vehicle.
4. Disconnect exhaust pipe from exhaust manifold.
5. Disconnect air injection hoses and exhaust manifold from cylinder head, then lower vehicle.
6. On models equipped with power steering, remove power steering pump.
7. On models equipped with A/C, remove A/C compressor idler pulley and compressor mounting bracket.
8. On all models, disconnect spark plug wires from cylinder head and remove spark plugs.
9. Remove cylinder head attaching bolts and the cylinder head.
10. Reverse procedure to install, noting the following:
    a. On engines using a steel gasket, apply a suitable sealant to both sides of gasket.
    b. On engines using a steel asbestos gasket, do not use any sealant on gasket.
    c. Apply suitable sealant to cylinder head bolt threads prior to installation.
    d. Torque cylinder head attaching bolts to specifications in sequence shown, **Fig. 2.**

INTAKE MANIFOLD
REPLACE

1. Disconnect battery ground cable.
2. Remove engine cover and air cleaner, then drain cooling system.
3. Remove distributor cap and spark plug wires.
4. Disconnect ESC electrical connector, then remove distributor.
5. Remove detent and accelerator cables, then the A/C compressor rear brace, if equipped.
6. Remove transmission and engine oil filler tubes at alternator brace.
7. On models equipped with A/C, remove A/C idler pulley from alternator brace.
8. On all models, remove alternator brace, then disconnect fuel line from carburetor.
9. Disconnect necessary vacuum lines and electrical connectors from carburetor.
10. Remove air injection hoses and brackets from manifold.
11. Disconnect heater hose from manifold, then remove manifold attaching bolts and the manifold.

CYLINDER HEAD
REPLACE

RIGHT SIDE

1. Remove intake manifold as described under "Intake Manifold, Replace."
2. Raise and support vehicle.
3. Disconnect exhaust pipe from exhaust manifold, then lower vehicle.
4. Remove spark plug wires, PCV hose and oil filler tube.
5. Disconnect air injection pipe and electrical connector from rear of cylinder head.
6. Remove engine ground wire from rear of cylinder head.
7. Remove valve cover, then the spark plugs.
8. Remove alternator lower mounting bolt, then remove alternator and position aside.
9. Remove push rods, then the cylinder head attaching bolts and cylinder head.
10. Reverse procedure to install, noting the following:
    a. On engine using a steel gasket, apply a suitable sealant to both sides of gasket.
    b. On engines using a steel asbestos gasket, do not use any sealant on gasket.
    c. Apply suitable sealant to cylinder head bolt threads prior to installation.
    d. Torque cylinder head attaching bolts to specifications in sequence shown, **Fig. 2.**

LEFT SIDE

1. Remove intake manifold as described under "Intake Manifold, Replace."
2. Disconnect electrical harness from valve cover, then remove the valve cover and push rods.

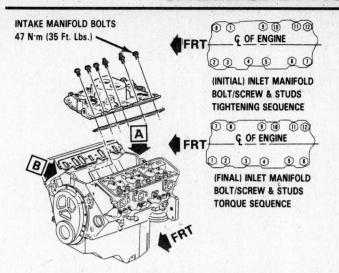

INTAKE MANIFOLD BOLTS
47 N·m (35 Ft. Lbs.)

FRT

Ⅽ OF ENGINE

(INITIAL) INLET MANIFOLD
BOLT/SCREW & STUDS
TIGHTENING SEQUENCE

A

FRT

Ⅽ OF ENGINE

(FINAL) INLET MANIFOLD
BOLT/SCREW & STUDS
TORQUE SEQUENCE

B

FRT

FRT

① 27 N·m (20 Ft. Lbs.)
② 35 N·m (26 Ft. Lbs.)

FRT

Fig. 3   Intake manifold bolt tightening sequence

Fig. 4   Exhaust manifold replacement

12. Reverse procedure to install, noting the following:
   a. Remove all traces of old sealant from cylinder head, block and manifold.
   b. Install gaskets on cylinder heads and apply a 3/16 inch bead of RTV sealant to front and rear ridges of cylinder case. Extend sealant 1/2 inch up each cylinder head to seal and retain side gaskets.
   c. Apply suitable sealant at water passages.
   d. Torque manifold attaching bolts to specifications in sequence shown, **Fig. 3.**

EXHAUST MANIFOLD
REPLACE

RIGHT SIDE

1. Disconnect battery ground cable.
2. Raise and support vehicle.
3. Disconnect exhaust pipe from manifold, then lower vehicle.
4. Remove engine cover, then disconnect air injection hose from check valve.
5. Remove exhaust manifold attaching bolts, then disconnect air injection hose from diverter valve and remove exhaust manifold, **Fig. 4.**
6. Reverse procedure to install.

LEFT SIDE

1. Disconnect battery ground cable.
2. Raise and support vehicle.
3. Disconnect exhaust pipe from manifold.
4. Disconnect air injection hose bracket from cylinder head.
5. Remove manifold attaching bolts and the manifold, **Fig. 4.**
6. Reverse procedure to install.

ROCKER ARMS & PUSHRODS
REPLACE

1. Disconnect battery ground cable.
2. Remove engine cover and the air cleaner assembly.
3. To remove right side valve cover, proceed as follows:
   a. Disconnect air injection hoses from diverter valve.
   b. Disconnect diverter valve bracket from intake manifold.
   c. Remove engine and transmission oil filler tubes from alternator bracket.
   d. Remove PCV valve, then disconnect air injection hoses from rear of right cylinder head and position aside.
   e. Remove distributor cap and wires, then the valve cover attaching bolts and valve cover.
4. To remove left side valve cover, proceed as follows:
   a. Disconnect vacuum pipe from carburetor.
   b. Disconnect electrical harness from valve cover, then remove valve cover attaching bolts.
   c. Disconnect detent and accelerator cables from carburetor.
   d. Remove detent and accelerator cable bracket from intake manifold.
   e. Remove valve cover.
5. Remove rocker arm nuts and balls, then the rocker arms and push rods, **Fig. 5.**

VALVES
ADJUST

1. Remove valve covers as described under "Rocker Arms & Pushrods, Replace."

2. Crank engine until mark on torsional damper is aligned with "0" mark on timing tab fastened to crankcase front cover. Ensure engine is at No. 1 cylinder firing position by placing fingers on No. 1 cylinder valves as mark on damper approaches "0" mark on timing tab. If valves are not moving, engine is in the No. 1 cylinder firing position. If valves are moving, engine is in the No. 4 cylinder firing position and should be rotated one revolution to the No. 1 position.
3. With engine in No. 1 cylinder firing position, adjust the following valves: exhaust, 1, 5 and 6; intake, 1, 2 and 3. To adjust valves, back off adjusting nut until lash is felt at push rod, then tighten nut until all lash is removed. This can be determined by rotating push rod while turning adjusting nut, **Fig. 6.** When all lash is removed, turn adjusting nut in one full turn to center lifter plunger.
4. Crank engine one full revolution until mark on torsional damper and "0" mark on timing tab are aligned. This is the No. 4 cylinder firing position. With engine in this position, adjust the following valves: exhaust, 2, 3 and 4; intake, 4, 5 and 6.
5. Install valve covers and related components, then start engine and check timing and idle speed.

VALVE ARRANGEMENT
FRONT TO REAR

Right .... E-I-I-E-I-E
Left .... E-I-E-I-I-E

VALVE LIFT SPECS.

Year	Intake	Exhaust
1985	.357	.390

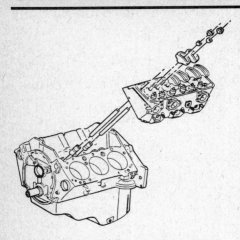

Fig. 5   Rocker arm & push rod replacement

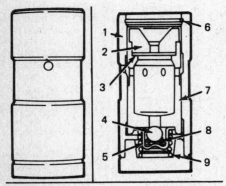

I. Lifter Body	6. Push Rod Seat
2. Push Rod Seat	Retainer
3. Metering Valve	7. Plunger
4. Check Ball	8. Check Ball Spring
5. Check Ball Retainer	9. Plunger Spring

Fig. 7   Sectional view of hydraulic valve lifter

VALVE TIMING
INTAKE OPENS BEFORE TDC

Year	Degrees
1985	22

VALVE LIFTERS
REPLACE

1. Remove intake manifold as described under "Intake Manifold, Replace."
2. Remove valve cover, spark plug, rocker arm and push rods on cylinder(s) to be serviced.
3. Install air line adapter No. J-23590 or equivalent to spark plug port and apply compressed air to hold valves in place.

4. Compress valve spring, then remove valve and valve components.
5. Remove valve lifter.
6. Reverse procedure to install. Coat foot of valve lifters with Molykote or equivalent. Following installation, adjust valves as described under "Valves, Adjust."

VALVE LIFTERS
SERVICE

DISASSEMBLY

1. Depress plunger with a push rod, then remove push rod seat retainer, Fig. 7, using a suitable screwdriver.
2. Remove push rod seat, metering valve, plunger, ball check valve assembly and plunger spring.
3. Pry ball retainer loose from plunger and remove ball check valve and spring.

CLEANING & INSPECTION

1. Clean all lifter components in suitable solvent.
2. Inspect all parts for wear or damage. If any one component is worn or damaged, the entire assembly must be replaced.
3. If lifter body wall is worn, inspect cylinder block lifter bore.
4. If bottom of lifter is worn, inspect camshaft lobe.
5. If push rod seat is worn, inspect push rod.

ASSEMBLY

1. Position check ball on small hole in bottom of plunger, then install spring and ball retainer.
2. Install plunger spring over ball retainer, then slide lifter body over spring and plunger. Ensure oil holes in lifter body and plunger are aligned.
3. Fill assembly with SAE 10 oil, then depress plunger with a 1/8 inch drift pin. Insert a 1/16 inch drift pin through both oil holes to hold plunger down against spring tension.
4. Remove the 1/8 inch drift pin and refill assembly with SAE 10 oil, then install metering valve and push rod seat.
5. Install push rod seat retainer, then push down on push rod seat and remove 1/16 inch drift pin from oil holes.

ROCKER ARM STUDS

Rocker arm studs that have damaged threads or are loose in cylinder head should be replaced with oversize studs. Studs are available in oversizes of .003 and .013 inch and can be installed after reaming holes as follows:
1. Remove stud using tool No. J-5802-1 or equivalent with a nut and flat washer placed over the tool.

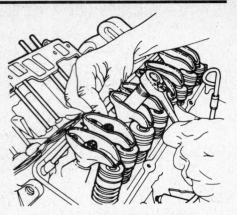

Fig. 6   Valve adjustment

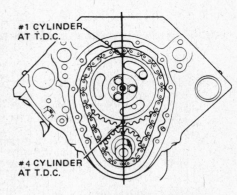

#1 CYLINDER AT T.D.C.

#4 CYLINDER AT T.D.C.

Fig. 8   Valve timing marks

2. Ream hole for oversize stud using tool No. J-5715 for .003 inch oversize or tool No. J-6036 for .013 inch oversize.
3. Apply suitable axle lubricant to press-fit area of stud, then install new stud using tool No. J-6880 or equivalent.

CAMSHAFT
REPLACE

1. Disconnect battery ground cable.
2. Remove engine cover and air cleaner, then drain cooling system.
3. Remove distributor, then the carburetor.
4. On models equipped with A/C, remove A/C compressor rear brace.
5. On all models, remove transmission and engine oil filler tubes from alternator bracket.
6. Disconnect A/C idler pulley, if equipped.
7. Unfasten alternator adjusting bracket and position aside.
8. Remove diverter valve bracket, then disconnect air injection hoses from diverter valve.
9. Remove intake manifold attaching bolts and the intake manifold.
10. Remove upper fan shroud, then the power steering pump, if equipped.

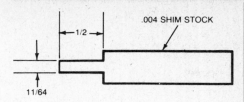

Fig. 9 Rear main oil seal installation tool

11. Remove air injection pump and bracket, then the fan and pulley.
12. Remove water pump, torsional damper and engine front cover.
13. Align timing marks, **Fig. 8,** then remove timing chain and camshaft gear.
14. Remove fuel pump, then disconnect engine and transmission cooler lines, as equipped.
15. Remove lower fan shroud, then disconnect brake master cylinder from power brake unit.
16. Remove valve lifters, then carefully remove camshaft using two $5/16 \times 18 \times 4$ inch bolts installed in camshaft bolt holes.
17. Reverse procedure to install. When installing camshaft, align marks on camshaft and crankshaft sprockets, **Fig. 9.**

ENGINE FRONT COVER
REPLACE

REMOVAL

1. Remove drive belts and pulley.
2. Raise and support vehicle.
3. Remove crankshaft pulley, then the damper retaining bolt.
4. Remove torsional damper using tool No. J-23523-1 or equivalent.
5. Remove water pump as described under "Water Pump, Replace."
6. Remove front cover attaching bolts, then the front cover and gasket. Discard gasket.

INSTALLATION

1. Clean gasket surface on front cover and block.
2. Remove any excess gasket material protruding at oil pan-to-engine block junction using a suitable cutting tool.
3. Apply a 1/8 inch bead of RTV sealant to joint formed at oil pan and block.
4. Apply suitable gasket sealant to gasket and place in position on cover.
5. install cover-to-oil pan seal, then lightly coat bottom of seal with clean engine oil.
6. Position cover over crankshaft end, then loosely install cover-to-block attaching screws.
7. Tighten attaching screws alternately and evenly while pressing down on

cover so dowels in block align with holes in cover.

NOTE: Do not force cover over dowels so that cover flange or holes are distorted.

8. Install remaining screws and torque to 7 ft. lbs.
9. Install torsional damper and water pump.

FRONT OIL SEAL
REPLACE

1. Remove torsional damper as described in steps 1 through 4 under "Engine Front Cover, Replace."
2. Pry seal out of front cover using a suitable screwdriver.
3. Drive new seal into position using tool No. J-23042 or equivalent.

REAR MAIN OIL SEAL
REPLACE

1. Remove oil pan and oil pump as described under "Oil Pan, Replace," and "Oil Pump, Service."
2. Remove rear main bearing cap, then pry seal out of cap using a suitable screwdriver.
3. Remove upper half of seal using a small hammer and punch to tap seal far enough until it may be removed with pliers.
4. Clean all sealant and debris from cylinder case bearing cap and crankshaft using a suitable non-abrasive cleaner.
5. Apply clean engine oil to seal lips and bead, keeping seal mating ends dry.
6. Position tip of fabricated tool, **Fig. 9,** between crankshaft and seal seat in cylinder case.
7. Insert seal between crankshaft and tip of tool so seal bead contacts tip of tool. Ensure oil seal lip is positioned toward front of engine.
8. Roll seal around crankshaft using tool to protect seal from sharp corner of seal seat surface in cylinder case.

NOTE: Installation tool must remain in place until seal is properly positioned with both ends flush with block.

9. Remove installation tool, being careful not to disturb seal.
10. Install seal half in bearing cap, using installation tool to feed seal into cap.
11. Apply sealant to bearing cap and case mating surfaces, then install bearing cap.

NOTE: Avoid getting any sealant on seal split line.

12. Install rear main bearing cap and torque to 11 ft. lbs. Tap end of crankshaft rearward, then forward to align thrust surfaces, then retorque bearing cap to specifications.

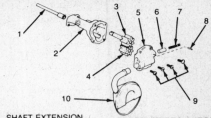

1. SHAFT EXTENSION
2. PUMP BODY
3. DRIVE GEAR AND SHAFT
4. IDLER GEAR
5. PUMP COVER
6. PRESSURE REGULATOR VALVE
7. PRESSURE REGULATOR SPRING
8. RETAINING PIN
9. SCREWS
10. PICKUP SCREEN AND PIPE

Fig. 10 Exploded view of oil pump

MAIN & ROD BEARINGS

Main bearings are available in standard size and undersizes of .001, .002, .009, .010 and .020 inch. Connecting rod bearings are available in standard size and .001 and .002 inch undersize for use with new and used standard size crankshafts and .010 and .020 inch undersize for use with reconditioned crankshafts.

OIL PAN
REPLACE

1. Disconnect battery ground cable.
2. Raise and support vehicle.
3. Drain oil pan, then disconnect exhaust pipes from exhaust manifolds.
4. Disconnect engine struts from inspection cover, then remove inspection cover.
5. Unfasten starter motor and position aside.
6. Remove engine mount trim bolts, then raise and support engine using a suitable jack.
7. Remove oil pan attaching bolts and the oil pan.
8. Reverse procedure to install, using new seals and gaskets.

OIL PUMP SERVICE
REMOVAL

1. Remove oil pan as previously described.
2. Remove pump-to-rear main bearing cap bolt, then the pump and extension shaft, **Fig. 10.**

DISASSEMBLY

1. Remove pump cover attaching bolts and the pump cover, **Fig. 10.**
2. Mark drive and idler gear teeth for assembly reference, then remove idler and drive gear and shaft from pump body.
3. Remove pin, spring and pressure regulator valve from pump cover.
4. If pickup tube and screen assembly

are to be replaced, mount pump cover in a soft-jawed vise and remove pick-up tube from cover.

NOTE: Do not remove screen from pickup tube, as these components are serviced as an assembly.

INSPECTION

1. Inspect pump body and cover for excessive wear or cracks.
2. Inspect pump gears for damage or excessive wear.

NOTE: If pump body or gears are damaged or worn, the entire oil pump assembly must be replaced.

3. Check drive gear shaft for looseness in pump body.
4. Inspect interior of cover for wear that would allow oil to leak past ends of gears.
5. Inspect pickup tube, screen and relief grommet for damage.
6. Check pressure regulator valve for fit in pump cover.

ASSEMBLY

1. If pickup tube and screen were removed, apply suitable sealant to end of tube, then mount pump cover in a soft-jawed vise and tap tube into position with a rubber mallet and tool No. J-8369.

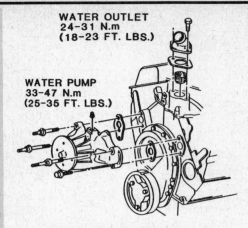

WATER OUTLET
24-31 N.m
(18-23 FT. LBS.)

WATER PUMP
33-47 N.m
(25-35 FT. LBS.)

Fig. 11 Water pump replacement

2. Install pressure regulator valve, spring and pin.
3. Install drive gear and shaft in pump body.
4. Install idler gear in pump body with smooth side of gear towards pump cover opening.
5. Install pump cover and torque attaching screws to 7 ft. lbs.
6. Rotate pump drive shaft by hand to ensure smooth operation.

INSTALLATION

1. Position pump and extension shaft in

rear main bearing cap, aligning slot on top of extension shaft with drive tang on lower end of distributor drive shaft.
2. Install pump-to-rear main bearing cap bolt and torque to 65 ft. lbs.
3. Install oil pan as previously described.

WATER PUMP
REPLACE

1. Disconnect battery ground cable.
2. Drain cooling system, then disconnect heater hose from pump.
3. Remove water pump attaching bolts and the water pump, **Fig. 11.**
4. Reverse procedure to install, using suitable pipe sealant on bolt threads.

FUEL PUMP
REPLACE

1. Disconnect fuel inlet line, outlet line and vapor return hose, if equipped, from fuel pump.
2. Remove fuel pump attaching bolts, then the fuel pump, push rod, gasket and mounting plate.
3. Reverse procedure to install. Following installation, start engine and check for leaks.

NOTE: If it is difficult to start fuel outlet line fitting, disconnect upper end of line from carburetor and tighten fitting while holding fuel pump nut with a wrench.

Clutch & Manual Transmission Section

CLUTCH
ADJUST

These models are equipped with a hydraulic clutch. No adjustment of the clutch pedal or linkage is provided.

CLUTCH
REPLACE

1. Disconnect battery ground cable.
2. Raise and support vehicle.
3. Remove slave cylinder attaching bolts from bell housing.
4. Remove transmission as described under "Transmission, Replace."
5. Remove bell housing, then slide clutch fork from ball stud.

NOTE: Ball stud is threaded in housing and can be easily removed, if necessary.

6. Install tool No. J-33169, **Fig. 1,** to support clutch assembly.

NOTE: Look for "X" mark on flywheel and on clutch cover, or white painted letter on clutch cover. If marks are not evident, mark

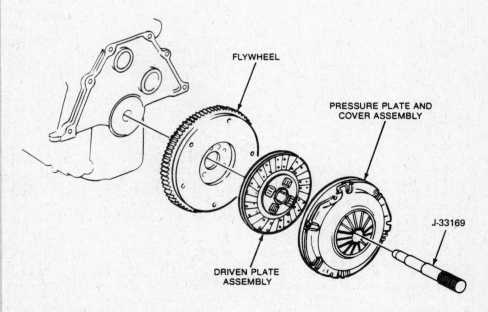

FLYWHEEL

PRESSURE PLATE AND COVER ASSEMBLY

J-33169

DRIVEN PLATE ASSEMBLY

Fig. 1 Clutch assembly

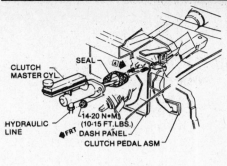

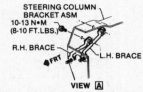

Fig. 2 Clutch master cylinder replacement

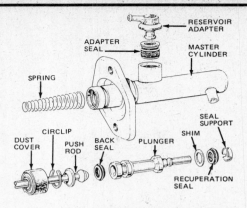

Fig. 3 Exploded view of clutch master cylinder

defective.

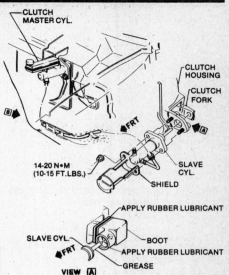

Fig. 4 Clutch slave cylinder replacement

flywheel and clutch cover for proper alignment during assembly.

7. Loosen clutch-to-flywheel attaching bolts evenly, one at a time, until spring pressure is released, then remove bolts, clutch and pressure plate assembly, **Fig. 1.**
8. Clean pressure plate and flywheel mating surfaces and inspect flywheel for defects. Replace or repair as necessary.
9. Reverse procedure to install.

CLUTCH MASTER CYLINDER
SERVICE

REMOVAL

1. Disconnect battery ground cable.
2. Remove hush panel from passenger compartment, then disconnect push rod from clutch pedal.
3. Disconnect slave cylinder hydraulic line from master cylinder.
4. Remove master cylinder retaining nuts and the master cylinder, **Fig. 2.**

DISASSEMBLY

1. Remove rubber dust cover from cylinder, **Fig. 3.**
2. Remove snap ring and push rod, then shake out plunger and spring assembly.
3. Remove reservoir adapter and seal.
4. Remove spring, seal support, recuperation seal and shim from plunger.

INSPECTION

1. Replace seals and clean all components in clean brake fluid.
2. Inspect cylinder bore for visible scores and ridges end ensure it is smooth to the touch. Replace master cylinder if

ASSEMBLY

1. Install back seal, shim, recuperation seal, seal support and spring on plunger.
2. Apply clean brake fluid to seals and cylinder bore, then carefully slide plunger assembly into master cylinder bore.
3. Position push rod into plunger, then depress plunger and install snap ring.
4. Apply suitable grease to inside of rubber dust cover, then install the dust cover.
5. Install reservoir adapter seal, then press in the adapter.

INSTALLATION

1. Install master cylinder assembly and torque retaining nuts to 10–15 ft. lbs.
2. Connect push rod to clutch pedal and install retaining clip.
3. Install hush panel, then connect slave cylinder hydraulic line to master cylinder.
4. Fill master cylinder reservoir with new brake fluid, then bleed system as described under "Clutch System, Bleed."

CLUTCH SLAVE CYLINDER SERVICE
REMOVAL

1. Disconnect battery ground cable.
2. Raise and support vehicle.
3. Disconnect hydraulic line from slave cylinder.
4. Remove slave cylinder attaching nuts and the slave cylinder, **Fig. 4.**

DISASSEMBLY

1. Remove push rod and rubber dust cover from slave cylinder, **Fig. 5.**
2. Remove snap ring, then shake out plunger and spring assembly.
3. Remove seal from plunger, using care to avoid damaging plunger surfaces.

INSPECTION

1. Replace seal and clean all components in clean brake fluid.
2. Inspect cylinder bore for visible scores and ridges and ensure it is smooth to the touch. Replace slave cylinder if defective.

ASSEMBLY

1. Install seal and spring on plunger.
2. Lubricate seal and cylinder bore with clean brake fluid, then slide plunger and spring assembly into cylinder bore.
3. Depress plunger and install snap ring.
4. Apply suitable grease to inside of rubber dust cover, then install the dust cover and push rod.

INSTALLATION

1. Connect hydraulic line to slave cylinder, then fill reservoir with new brake fluid and bleed system as described under "Clutch System, Bleed."
2. Install slave cylinder to bell housing and torque retaining nuts to 10–15 ft. lbs.

CLUTCH SYSTEM
BLEED

NOTE: When refilling or bleeding system, use only new brake fluid conforming to

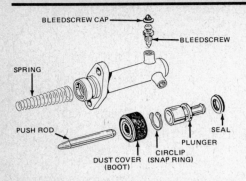

Fig. 5 Exploded view of clutch slave cylinder

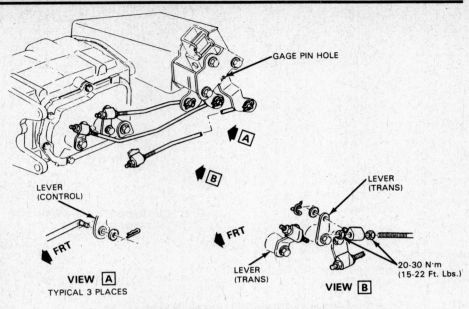

Fig. 6 4-speed shift linkage adjustment

DOT 3 specifications. Never use fluid which has been bled from a system to fill the reservoir, as it may be aerated or otherwise contaminated.

1. Fill master cylinder reservoir with new brake fluid.
2. Raise and support vehicle.
3. Remove slave cylinder attaching bolts and hold cylinder at a 45° angle with bleeder at highest point.
4. Fully depress clutch pedal and open bleeder valve, then close bleeder and release clutch pedal.
5. Repeat sequence until all air is evacuated from system.
6. Check and refill master cylinder reservoir as needed to prevent air from entering system.

TRANSMISSION
REPLACE
4 SPEED

1. Disconnect battery ground cable.
2. Raise and support vehicle.
3. Drain transmission fluid, then remove propeller shaft.
4. Disconnect speedometer cable and electrical connectors from transmission.
5. Disconnect shift linkage from shifter.
6. Remove shifter support attaching bolts from transmission.
7. Remove transmission mount attaching bolts.
8. Support transmission and remove crossmember attaching bolts and the crossmember.
9. Remove transmission attaching bolts and the transmission.
10. Reverse procedure to install.

NOTE: Apply a light coating of high temperature grease to main drive gear bearing retainer and splined portion of transmission drive gear shaft to ensure free movement of clutch and transmission components during installation.

5 SPEED

1. Disconnect battery ground cable.
2. Remove shift lever boot attaching screws and slide boot up shift lever, then remove shift lever from vehicle.
3. Raise and support vehicle.
4. Remove propeller shaft, then disconnect speedometer cable and all electrical connectors from transmission.
5. Support transmission and remove transmission mount attaching bolts.
6. Remove crossmember attaching bolts and the crossmember.
7. Remove transmission support braces.
8. Remove transmission-to-engine attaching bolts and the transmission.
9. Reverse procedure to install.

4-SPEED SHIFT LINKAGE
ADJUST

Transmission and shifter levers must be in Neutral position at time of rod assembly. A ¼ inch gage pin must fit freely into gage pin hole when levers are positioned as outlined above, **Fig. 6.**

Rear Axle, Suspension & Brake Section

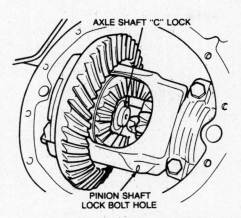

Fig. 1   Removing differential pinion shaft

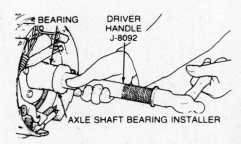

Fig. 4   Axle shaft bearing installation

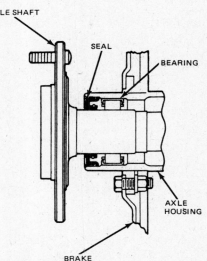

Fig. 2   Cross-sectional view of axle shaft & seal

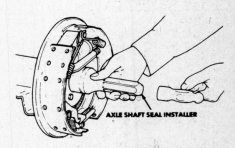

Fig. 3   Axle shaft bearing removal

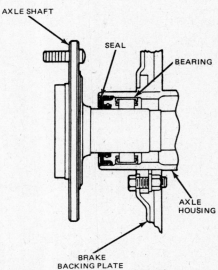

Fig. 5   Axle shaft seal installation

AXLE SHAFT
REPLACE

1. Raise and support rear of vehicle, then remove wheel and brake drum on side axle is to be replaced.
2. Loosen carrier cover attaching bolts and allow lubricant to drain, then remove the bolts and carrier cover.
3. Remove rear axle pinion shaft lock screw and the pinion shaft, **Fig. 1.**
4. Push flanged end of axle shaft toward center of vehicle, then remove "C" lock from button end of shaft.
5. Remove axle shaft from housing, using care to avoid damaging seal, **Fig. 2.**
6. Reverse procedure to install, noting the following:
   a. Torque new pinion shaft lock screw to 25 ft. lbs.
   b. Torque carrier cover attaching bolts to 20 ft. lbs.
   c. Fill axle to bring lubricant level within ⅜ inch of filler hole.

WHEEL BEARING & AXLE SEAL
REPLACE

1. Remove axle shaft as described under "Axle Shaft, Replace."
2. Remove axle seal by prying behind seal steel case with a suitable pry bar. Use care to avoid damaging axle housing.
3. Remove axle bearing using a suitable slide hammer, **Fig. 3.**
4. Lubricate new bearing with gear lubricant, then install bearing in axle housing with tool No. J-34974 until bearing is seated in housing, **Fig. 4.**
5. Apply suitable gear lubricant to seal lips, then position seal on tool No. J-33782 and install in axle housing, tapping into place until seal is flush with housing, **Fig. 5.**

AXLE ASSEMBLY
REPLACE

NOTE: Construction of the axle assembly is such that service operations may be performed with the housing installed in the vehicle or with the housing removed and installed in a holding fixture. The following procedure is necessary only when the housing requires replacement.

1. Raise vehicle and place jack stands under frame side rails.
2. Position a suitable jack under rear axle housing and raise slightly to support axle assembly.
3. Disconnect shock absorbers from anchor plates.
4. Scribe reference marks between drive shaft and pinion flange for assembly reference, then disconnect drive shaft and position aside.
5. Remove brake lines from axle housing, then disconnect brake lines from backing plate.
6. Remove U-bolts and anchor plates.
7. Remove vent hose from axle housing, then lower axle and remove from vehicle.
8. Reverse procedure to install. Torque shock absorber nuts to 76 ft. lbs. and U-bolt nuts to 52 ft. lbs.

SHOCK ABSORBER
REPLACE

1. Raise vehicle and place jack stands under frame side rails.
2. Position a suitable jack under rear axle housing and raise slightly to support axle assembly.
3. Disconnect shock absorber from upper mounting, **Fig. 6.**
4. Disconnect shock absorber from lower mounting, then remove from vehicle.
5. Reverse procedure to install. Torque retaining nuts to 76 ft. lbs.

LEAF SPRING ASSEMBLY
REPLACE

1. Raise vehicle and place jack stands under frame side rails to relieve spring load. Support axle assembly.
2. Remove wheel and tire assembly.
3. Loosen, but do not remove, spring-to-shackle and shackle-to-body retaining nut, **Fig. 7**.
4. Disconnect shock absorber at lower mounting.
5. Remove U-bolt retaining nuts, spring retainer and spring plate, then lower axle.

NOTE: Do not allow weight of axle to hang on brake hoses. Always support axle and body separately.

6. Remove nuts, washers and retainer from front spring hanger.
7. Slide spring forward to gain access to spring-to-shackle bolt through rear bumper bracket, then remove nut, washer, bolt and spring assembly, **Fig. 8**.
8. If necessary, drill out rivets and remove leaf spring eye, **Fig. 9**.
9. Reverse procedure to install. If eye assembly was removed, replace rivets with 10mm bolts and nuts.

SHACKLE
REPLACE

1. Raise vehicle and place jack stands under frame side rails to relieve spring load. Support axle assembly.
2. Remove bumper brace, bumper bracket-to-frame bolts and the bumper.
3. Remove shackle attaching bolts and the shackle, **Fig. 7**.
4. If necessary, press center sleeve and bushing out of shackle.
5. Reverse procedure to install. Press in new center sleeve and bushing, if removed.

DRUM BRAKE ADJUSTMENTS

These brakes have self adjusting shoe mechanisms that ensure correct lining-to-drum clearances at all times. The automatic adjusters operate only when brakes are applied as vehicle is moving rearward.

Although the brakes are self-adjusting, an initial adjustment is necessary after brake shoes have been relined or replaced, or when length of star wheel adjuster has been changed during some other service operation.

Frequent usage of an automatic transmission forward range to halt reverse vehicle motion may prevent automatic adjusters from functioning, thereby inducing low pedal heights. Should low pedal heights be encountered, it is recommended that nu-

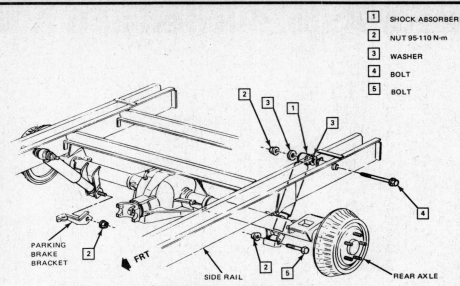

1	SHOCK ABSORBER
2	NUT 95-110 N·m
3	WASHER
4	BOLT
5	BOLT

Fig. 6   Shock absorber replacement

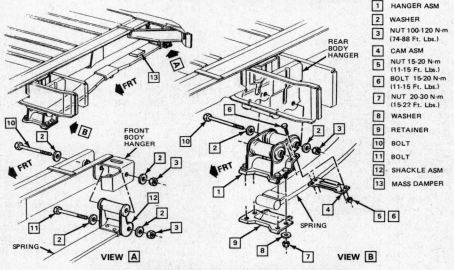

1	HANGER ASM
2	WASHER
3	NUT 100-120 N·m (74-88 Ft. Lbs.)
4	CAM ASM
5	NUT 15-20 N·m (11-15 Ft. Lbs.)
6	BOLT 15-20 N·m (11-15 Ft. Lbs.)
7	NUT 20-30 N·m (15-22 Ft. Lbs.)
8	WASHER
9	RETAINER
10	BOLT
11	BOLT
12	SHACKLE ASM
13	MASS DAMPER

Fig. 7   Leaf spring & shackle mounting

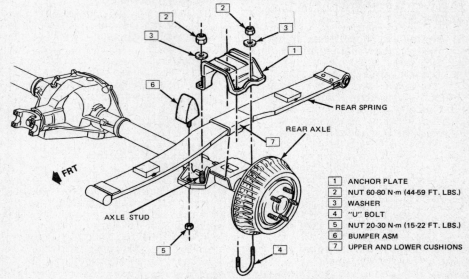

1	ANCHOR PLATE
2	NUT 60-80 N·m (44-59 FT. LBS.)
3	WASHER
4	"U" BOLT
5	NUT 20-30 N·m (15-22 FT. LBS.)
6	BUMPER ASM
7	UPPER AND LOWER CUSHIONS

Fig. 8   Leaf spring removal

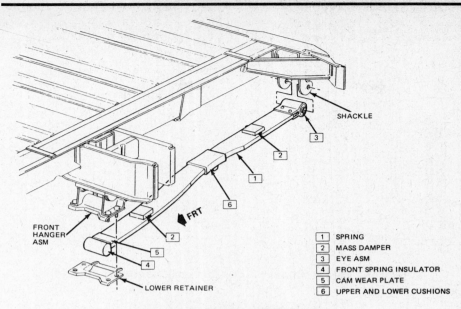

Fig. 9 Leaf spring assembly

1	SPRING
2	MASS DAMPER
3	EYE ASM
4	FRONT SPRING INSULATOR
5	CAM WEAR PLATE
6	UPPER AND LOWER CUSHIONS

merous forward and reverse stops be made until satisfactory pedal height is obtained.

NOTE: If a low pedal height condition cannot be corrected by making numerous reverse stops (provided hydraulic system is free of air), the self-adjusting mechanism is not functioning. Therefore it will be necessary to remove brake drum, clean, free up and lubricate adjusting mechanism, then adjust brakes as follows, being sure parking brake is fully released.

ADJUSTMENTS

Upon initial adjustment, a lanced area in the brake backing plate must be removed prior to adjusting brakes. To remove lanced area, knock out with a suitable hammer and punch, then remove brake drum to clear any metal particles caught inside the brake compartment. Install brake drum and proceed with adjustment. After adjustment is complete, install brake adjustment hole cover to prevent entry of water and dirt.

1. Turn brake adjusting screw to expand shoes until wheel can just be turned by hand.
2. Using a suitable tool to hold actuator from adjuster, back off adjuster 24 notches. If shoes still drag, back off one or two additional notches.

NOTE: Brakes should be free of drag when adjuster has been backed off approximately 12 notches. Heavy drag at this point indicates tight parking brake cables.

3. Install adjusting hole cover on brake backing plate.

4. Check parking brake adjustment.

PARKING BRAKE
ADJUST

1. Depress parking brake pedal exactly 2 clicks.
2. Raise and support vehicle.
3. Tighten adjusting nut until left rear wheel can just be turned rearward, but cannot be turned forward.
4. Release parking brake and ensure both rear wheels turn freely in either direction with no brake drag, then lower vehicle.

NOTE: To avoid brake drag, the parking brake cable must not be tightened excessively.

MASTER CYLINDER
REPLACE

1. Disconnect hydraulic brake lines from master cylinder.
2. Remove master cylinder retaining nuts and the master cylinder.
3. Reverse procedure to install. Torque master cylinder retaining nuts to 22–33 ft. lbs. and hydraulic line nuts to 120–180 inch lbs.

POWER BRAKE UNIT
REPLACE

1. Disconnect master cylinder from power brake unit.
2. Disconnect power brake unit push rod from brake pedal.
3. Remove power brake unit retaining nuts and the power brake unit.
4. Reverse procedure to install. Torque master cylinder retaining nuts to 22–33 ft. lbs.

Front Suspension & Steering Section

WHEEL ALIGNMENT
CASTER & CAMBER, ADJUST

NOTE: Before checking and adjusting caster and camber angles, jounce front bumper at least three times, then allow vehicle to return to normal height to prevent false readings.

Caster and camber adjustments are made by shims inserted between upper control arm shaft and frame bracket, **Fig. 1.** Add, subtract or transfer shims as noted below.

To adjust caster and/or camber, loosen upper control arm shaft-to-frame nuts, then add or subtract shims as necessary and retorque nuts to 96 ft. lbs. After adjustment, the shim pack should have at least two threads of bolt exposed beyond the nut. The difference between front and rear shim packs must not exceed .040 inch.

When adjusting caster, transfer shims from front to rear or rear to front. The transfer of one shim from rear to front bolt will decrease positive caster.

When adjusting camber, change shims equally at both front and rear of shaft. Adding an equal number of shims at front and rear will decrease positive camber.

NOTE: When performing either caster or camber adjustment, always tighten nut on thinner shim pack first to improve shaft-to-frame clamping force and torque retention.

TOE-IN, ADJUST

To adjust toe-in, loosen clamp bolts at each end of steering tie rod adjusting sleeves. With steering wheel in straight ahead position, turn tie rod adjusting sleeves to obtain proper adjustment. After adjustment, check that number of threads showing on each end of sleeve are equal and that the tie rod end stud lines up with steering knuckle. Position tie rod clamps and sleeves as shown in **Fig. 2,** then torque nuts to 14 ft. lbs.

WHEEL BEARINGS
ADJUST

1. Raise and support front of vehicle.
2. While rotating wheel assembly in forward direction, torque spindle nut to fully seat the bearings.
3. Back off spindle nut until just loose, then tighten nut finger tight.
4. Loosen nut until either hole in spindle aligns with a spindle nut slot, then install new cotter pin.
5. Measure hub end play, which should measure .001–.005 inch.

UPPER CONTROL ARM
REPLACE

1. Remove retaining nuts and shims, **Fig. 3.** Note location of shims for assembly reference.
2. Raise vehicle and support lower control arm with suitable jack stands.

NOTE: Jack must be positioned between coil spring seat and ball joint of lower control arm to obtain maximum leverage against coil spring pressure.

3. Remove front wheel, then loosen upper ball joint from steering knuckle as described under "Upper Ball Joint, Replace."
4. Support hub assembly to prevent damage to brake line when removing control arm.
5. Remove control arm attaching bolts and the control arm, **Fig. 3.**
6. Reverse procedure to install. Torque control arm retaining nuts to 66 ft. lbs.

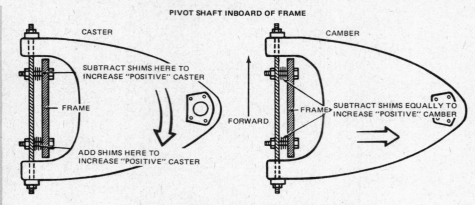

Fig. 1   Caster & camber adjustment

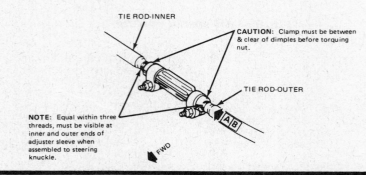

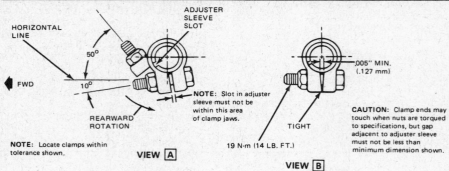

Fig. 2   Tie rod clamp & sleeve positioning

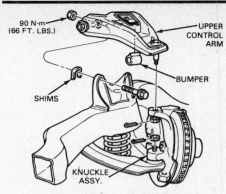

Fig. 3 Upper control arm replacement

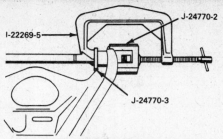

Fig. 4 Upper control arm bushing removal

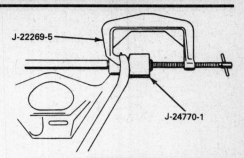

Fig. 5 Upper control arm bushing installation

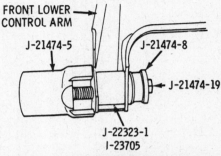

Fig. 7 Lower control arm front bushing removal

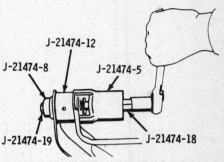

Fig. 8 Lower control arm rear bushing removal

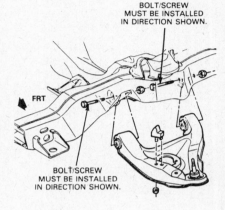

SUGGESTED ASSEMBLY SEQUENCE
INSTALL THE FRONT LEG OF THE LOWER CONTROL ARM INTO THE CROSSMEMBER PRIOR TO INSTALLING THE REAR LEG IN THE FRAME BRACKET.

Fig. 6 Lower control arm replacement

UPPER CONTROL ARM BUSHING
REPLACE

1. Remove upper control arm as previously described.
2. Remove nuts from end of pivot shaft, then press bushings out of control arm, **Fig. 4.**
3. Position pivot shaft in control arm and press new bushings into control arm and over pivot shaft, **Fig. 5.**

NOTE: Both bushings must be installed .48–.52 inch from face of control arm to bushing outer sleeve.

4. Install pivot shaft retaining nuts and torque to 85 ft. lbs.

LOWER CONTROL ARM
REPLACE

1. Remove coil spring as described

under "Coil Spring, Replace."
2. Remove lower ball joint stud, then guide control arm through opening in splash shield and remove from vehicle, **Fig. 6.**
3. Reverse procedure to install.

LOWER CONTROL ARM BUSHINGS
REPLACE

1. Drive bushing flare down flush with rubber of front bushing, then remove front and rear bushings from control arm, **Figs. 7 and 8.**
2. Install front bushing, **Fig. 9,** then flare the bushing, **Fig. 10.**
3. Install rear bushing, **Fig. 11,** then the lower control arm.

COIL SPRING
REPLACE

1. Raise and support vehicle.
2. Remove the 2 shock absorber screws and push shock up through control arm and into spring.
3. Support vehicle so control arms hang free.
4. Secure tool No. J-23028 to a suitable jack and position tool to cradle inner bushings, **Fig. 12.**
5. Remove stabilizer-to-lower control arm attachment.
6. Raise jack to relieve tension from lower control arm pivot bolts, then install a chain around spring and through control arm.

7. Remove attaching nuts and bolts, then slowly lower jack and control arm and remove spring.

NOTE: Do not apply force to lower control arm and ball joint to remove spring. Proper maneuvering of spring will allow for easy removal.

8. Reverse procedure to install. Refer to **Figs. 7 and 13** for proper assembly of coil spring and pivot ball.

UPPER BALL JOINT
REPLACE

1. Raise vehicle and support lower control arm with suitable jack stands.

NOTE: Jack must be positioned between coil spring seat and ball joint of lower control arm to obtain maximum leverage against coil spring pressure.

2. Remove wheel and tire assembly, then the cotter pin and stud nut from ball joint.
3. Break stud loose from steering knuckle using tool No. J-23742 or equivalent. Apply pressure on stud by expanding tool until stud breaks free.
4. With control arm in raised position, drill rivets 1/4 inch deep with a 1/8 inch drill, then drill off rivet heads with a 1/2 inch drill.
5. Punch out rivets, then remove ball joints.
6. Reverse procedure to install. Replace rivets with attaching bolts and nuts. Torque retaining nuts to 8 ft. lbs. and the stud nut to 52 ft. lbs.

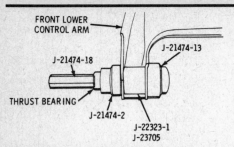

Fig. 9   Lower control arm front bushing installation

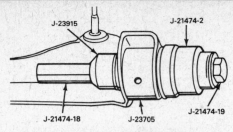

Fig. 10   Flaring lower control arm front bushing

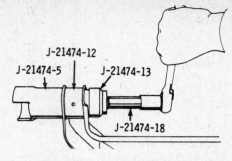

Fig. 11   Lower control arm rear bushing installation

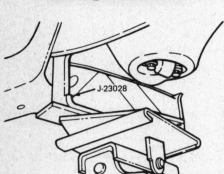

Fig. 12   Coil spring removal

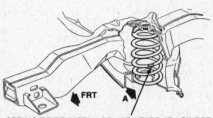

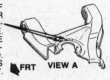

SPRING TO BE INSTALLED WITH TAPE AT LOWEST POSITION. BOTTOM OF SPRING IS COILED HELICAL, AND THE TOP IS COILED FLAT WITH A GRIPPER NOTCH NEAR END OF SPRING COIL.

AFTER ASSEMBLY, END OF SPRING COIL MUST COVER ALL OR PART OF ONE INSPECTION DRAIN HOLE. THE OTHER HOLE MUST BE PARTLY EXPOSED OR COMPLETELY UNCOVERED. ROTATE SPRING AS NECESSARY.

Fig. 13   Coil spring installation

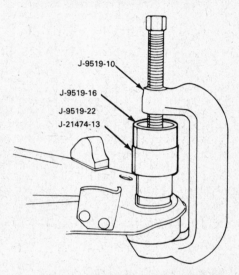

Fig. 14   Lower ball joint removal

LOWER BALL JOINT
REPLACE

1. Raise vehicle and support with jack stands under frame side rails.
2. Remove wheel and tire assembly, then support control arm spring seat with a suitable jack.
3. Remove cotter pin and stud nut, then break ball joint loose from steering knuckle using tool No. J-23742 or equivalent.

NOTE: Inspect and clean the tapered hole in steering knuckle. If hole is out of round or damaged in any way, the steering knuckle must be replaced.

4. Guide lower control arm out of opening in splash shield, then position a wooden brake backing plate block between frame and upper control arm to block knuckle assembly out of the way.
5. Remove grease fittings, then press ball joint out of lower control arm, **Fig. 14.**
6. Reverse procedure to install. Refer to **Fig. 15** and torque stud nut to 81 ft. lbs.

SHOCK ABSORBER
REPLACE

1. Raise and support vehicle.
2. Hold shock upper stem from turning with a suitable wrench and remove nut, retainer and grommet.
3. Remove lower shock pivot bolts and

the shock, **Fig. 16.**
4. Reverse procedure to install. Torque upper attaching nut to 15 ft. lbs. and lower attaching bolts to 18 ft. lbs.

STEERING KNUCKLE
REPLACE

1. Raise front of vehicle and support with jack stands under front lift points, then remove wheel and tire assembly.

NOTE: Do not support vehicle under lower control arm at this time, as spring tension will aid in breaking ball joint studs loose from steering knuckle.

2. Remove brake caliper, then the brake and hub assembly.
3. Remove splash shield-to-steering knuckle attaching bolts.
4. Remove tie rod end from steering knuckle using tool No. J-6227 or equivalent.
5. If steering knuckle is to be replaced, remove knuckle seal.
6. Remove ball joint studs from steering knuckle using tool No. J-23742 or equivalent.
7. Position a suitable jack under lower control arm near spring seat and raise jack until it just supports control arm.

NOTE: Jack must remain in position under control arm during removal and installation to hold spring and control arm in position.

8. Raise upper control arm to disengage upper ball joint stud from knuckle.
9. Remove steering knuckle from lower ball joint stud, **Fig. 17.**
10. After removal, inspect and clean tapered hole in steering knuckle. If hole is out of round or damaged in any way, then knuckle must be replaced.
11. Reverse procedure to install. Torque splash shield attaching bolts to 10 ft. lbs. and tie rod end to 33 ft. lbs.

STABILIZER BAR
REPLACE

1. Raise and support front of vehicle.
2. Remove nuts from both sides to disconnect linkage, then remove retainers, grommets and spacer.
3. Remove bracket-to-frame or body bolts, then the stabilizer bar, rubber bushings and brackets, **Fig. 18.**
4. Reverse procedure to install, noting the following:
   a. Install stabilizer bar so identification stamping appears on right side

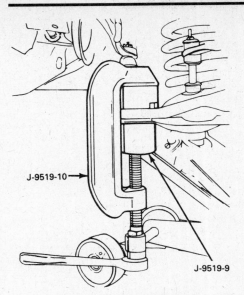

Fig. 15 Lower ball joint installation

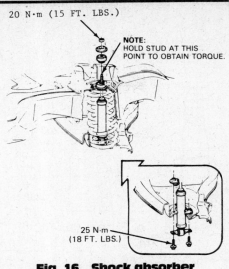

20 N·m (15 FT. LBS.)

NOTE: HOLD STUD AT THIS POINT TO OBTAIN TORQUE.

25 N·m (18 FT. LBS.)

Fig. 16 Shock absorber replacement

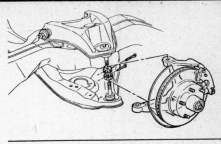

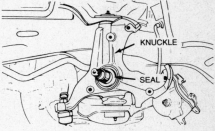

KNUCKLE

SEAL

Fig. 17 Steering knuckle replacement

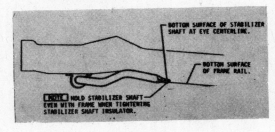

BOTTOM SURFACE OF STABILIZER SHAFT AT EYE CENTERLINE.

BOTTOM SURFACE OF FRAME RAIL.

NOTE: HOLD STABILIZER SHAFT EVEN WITH FRAME WHEN TIGHTENING STABILIZER SHAFT INSULATOR.

17 N·m (13 FT. LBS.)

INSTALL STABILIZER SHAFT INSULATOR WITH SLIT TOWARD FRONT OF VEHICLE AS SHOWN.

30 N·m (22 FT. LBS.)

STABILIZER SHAFT

Fig. 18 Stabilizer bar replacement

③ ROCK WHEEL IN AND OUT AT TOP AND BOTTOM.

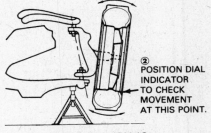

② POSITION DIAL INDICATOR TO CHECK MOVEMENT AT THIS POINT.

① SUPPORT L. C. ARM AS FAR OUTBOARD AS POSSIBLE.

Fig. 19 Checking upper ball joint

---

of vehicle.

b. Position rubber bushings squarely in brackets with slit in bushings facing front of vehicle.

c. Torque stabilizer bar retaining nuts to 13 ft. lbs. and bracket bolts to 22 ft. lbs. with weight of vehicle resting on wheels.

BALL JOINT INSPECTION

NOTE: Prior to inspecting ball joints, ensure wheel bearings are properly adjusted.

UPPER BALL JOINT

1. Raise vehicle and position jack stands under right and left lower control arms near each lower ball joint.
2. Position dial indicator against wheel rim, **Fig. 19.**
3. Shake wheel and observe gauge. Horizontal deflection should not exceed .125 inch.
4. If reading exceeds specification, or if ball stud had been disconnected from knuckle assembly and any looseness is evident, or if stud can be turned by hand, replace ball joint.

LOWER BALL JOINT

The lower ball joint is equipped with a visual wear indicator, **Fig. 20.** Check ball joint with vehicle weight resting on wheels.

STEERING GEAR
REPLACE

1. Disconnect battery ground cable.
2. On models equipped with power steering, disconnect pressure and return lines from steering gear housing, then plug hose ends and gear housing ports to prevent contamination.

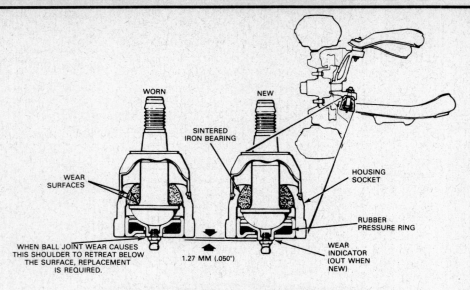

Fig. 20   Lower ball joint wear indicators

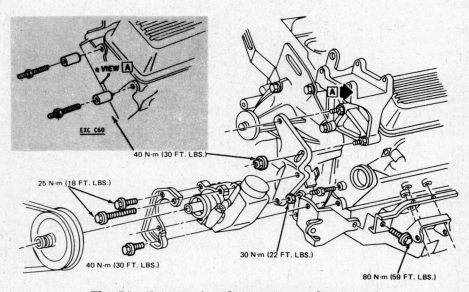

Fig. 21   Power steering pump replacement

3. On all models, remove pinch bolt from intermediate shaft.
4. Remove pitman arm nut and washer from pitman shaft, then mark relationship between shaft and arm for assembly reference.
5. Remove pitman arm using tool No. J-6632 or equivalent.
6. Remove steering gear attaching bolts and the steering gear.
7. Reverse procedure to install. Torque steering gear attaching bolts to 70 ft. lbs., intermediate shaft pinch bolt to 30 ft. lbs. and pitman shaft nut to 180 ft. lbs. on power steering gear or 177 ft. lbs. on manual steering gear.

POWER STEERING PUMP
REPLACE

1. Disconnect battery ground cable.
2. Disconnect return line, then the pressure line from steering gear. Plug hose ends and gear housing ports to prevent contamination.
3. Disconnect drive belt from power steering pump, then remove pump attaching bolts and the pump, **Fig. 21**.
4. Reverse procedure to install.

CHEVROLET S/T 10 & GMC S/T 15

INDEX OF SERVICE OPERATIONS

NOTE: Refer to page 1 of this manual for vehicle manufacturer's special service tool suppliers.

General Engine Specifications

Year	Engine Model	Carb. Type	Bore & Stroke	Comp. Ratio	Net Horsepower @ R.P.M.	Torque Ft. Lbs. @ R.P.M.	Normal Oil Press. Lbs.
1982	4-119/1.9L	2 Bore	3.43 × 3.23	8.4	82 @ 4600	101 @ 3000	57
	V6-173/2.8L	2 Bore	3.50 × 3.00	8.5	110 @ 4800	145 @ 2400	30—50②
1983	4-119/1.9L	2 Bore	3.42 × 3.23	8.4	82 @ 4600	101 @ 3000	57
	4-121/2.0L	2 Bore	3.50 × 3.15	9.3	83 @ 4600	108 @ 2400	45③
	V6-173/2.8L	2 Bore	3.50 × 3.00	8.5	110 @ 4800	145 @ 2100	30—50②
1984	4-119/1.9L	2 Bore	3.42 × 3.23	8.4	82 @ 4600	101 @ 3000	57
	4-121/2.0L	2 Bore	3.50 × 3.15	9.3	83 @ 4600	108 @ 2400	45③
	4-137/2.2L①	Fuel Inj.	3.46 × 3.62	21.0	62 @ 4300	96 @ 2200	60
	V6-173/2.8L	2 Bore	2.99 × 3.50	8.5	110 @ 4800	145 @ 2100	30—50②
1985	4-119/1.9L	2 Bore	3.43 × 3.23	8.4	82 @ 4600	101 @ 3000	57
	4-137/2.2L①	Fuel inj.	3.46 × 3.62	21.0	62 @ 4300	96 @ 2200	60
	4-151/2.5L	Fuel inj.	4.00 × 3.0	9.0	92 @ 4400	134 @ 2800	37.5
	V6-173/2.8L	2 Bore	2.99 × 3.50	8.5	115 @ 4800	150 @ 2100	30—50②

①—Diesel engine.   ②—At 2000 RPM.   ③—At 2200 RPM.

Alternator & Regulator Specifications

Year	Model	Alternator Field Current @ 80°F. 12 volts	Cold Output @ 14 volts Amperes @ 2000 R.P.M.	Cold Output @ 14 volts Amperes @ 5000 R.P.M.	Rated Hot Output Amperes	Regulator Type
1982	1100140	4.0—5	22	33	37	Integral
	1100146	4.0—5	32	60	63	Integral
	1100201	4.0—5	22	33	37	Integral
	1100202	4.0—5	32	60	63	Integral
1983—84	1100204	4.0—5	22	33	37	Integral
	1100207	4.5—5	38	70②	66	Integral
	1100209	4.5—5	51	81②	78	Integral
	1100227	4.0—5	22	33	37	Integral
	1100249	4.5—5	38	70②	66	Integral
	1100273	4.5—5	51	81②	78	Integral
	1100275	—	—	—	66	Integral
	1100276	—	—	—	78	Integral
	1105185	4.0—5	22	33	37	Integral
1984	1105370①	4.5—5	51	81②	78	Integral
1985	1100207①	4.5—5	38	70②	66	Integral
	1100250③	4.5—5	51	81②	78	Integral
	1105368③	4.5—5	51	81②	78	Integral
	1105370①③	4.5—5	51	81②	78	Integral
	1105492③	4.5—5	56	103②	94	Integral
	1105504	4.5—5	38	70②	66	Integral
	1105516	4.5—5	38	70②	66	Integral
	1105575	4.5—5	37	60②	56	Integral
	1105621	—	—	—	66	Integral
	1105623	—	—	—	78	Integral
	1105624	—	—	—	56	Integral
	1105627	—	—	—	78	Integral
	1105633	—	—	—	56	Integral
	1105635	—	—	—	66	Integral
	1105647③	—	—	—	78	Integral

①—Alternator used on diesel engine models.   ②—At 7000 RPM.   ③—Service replacement part.

continued

Starter Motor Specifications

Year	Engine	Starter Model	Brush Spring Tension Oz.[1]	Free Speed Test		
				Amperes	Volts	R.P.M.
1982	4-119	94241705	56.5	—	—	—
	V6-173	1109535	—	50–80[2]	10.6	7500–11400
1983–84	4-119	94241705	56.5	—	—	—
	4-121	1109561	—	50–75	9.0	6000–11900
	V6-173	1109535	—	45–70	9.0	7000–11900
1984–85	4-137[3]	—	—	120[2]	11.5	4000[4]
1985	4-119	—	56.5	—	—	—
	4-151	1998431	—	50–75	10	6000–11,900
	4-151	1998482	—	50–75	10	6000–11,900
	V6-173	1998427	—	50–75	10	6000–11,900

①—Minimum.
②—Includes solenoid.
③—Diesel engine.
④—Minimum speed.

Pistons, Pins, Rings, Crankshaft & Bearings Specifications

Year	Engine	Piston Clearance	Ring End Gap[1]		Wrist Pin Diameter	Rod Bearings		Main Bearings		Thrust Bearing No.	Shaft End Play
			Comp.	Oil		Shaft Diameter	Bearing Clearance	Shaft Diameter	Bearing Clearance		
1982	4-119	.0018–.0026	②	.008	⑥	1.929	.0007–.0030	2.205	.0008–.0025	3	.002–.009
	V6-173	.0017–.0027	.010	.020	.9054	1.9983–1.9993	.0014–.0035	2.4937–2.4946	.0017–.0030	3	.002–.007
1983–84	4-121	.0006–.016	.010	.020	.9054	1.9983–1.9993	.0010–.0031	③	④	4	.002–.008
1983–85	4-119	.0018–.0026	.014	.008	⑥	1.929	.0007–.0030	2.205	.0008–.0025	3	.002–.009
	V6-173	.0007–.0017	.010	.020	.9054	1.9983–1.9993	.0014–.0037	⑤	.0016–.0032	3	.002–.007
1984–85	4-137⑦	.0014–.0022	.008	.008	1.0630	2.0835–2.0839	.0016–.0047	2.3591–2.3594	.0011–.0033	3	.0039–.011
1985	4-151	.0014–.0022	.010	.015	.938	2.000	.0005–.0026	2.300	.0005–.0022	5	.0035–.0085

①—Fit rings in tapered bores for clearance listed in tightest portion of ring travel.
②—Top ring, .012 inch; second ring, .008 inch.
③—Nos. 1, 2, 3, 4; 2.4945–2.4954. No. 5; 2.4937–2.4946.
④—Nos. 1, 2, 3, 4; .0006–.0018. No. 5; .0014–.0027.
⑤—Nos. 1, 2, 4; 2.4937–2.4946. No. 3; 2.4930–2.4941.
⑥—Piston pin clearance is correct when pin is snug fit into piston and piston rotates smoothly.
⑦—Diesel engine.

Valve Specifications

Year	Engine	Valve Lash		Valve Angles		Valve Spring Installed Height	Valve Spring Pressure Lbs. @ In.	Stem Clearance		Stem Diameter	
		Int.	Exh.	Seat	Face			Intake	Exhaust	Intake	Exhaust
1982–83	4-119	.006C	.010C	45	45	①	②	.0009–.0022	.0015–.0031	.3102④	.3091④
1982–85	V6-173	1½ Turn③		46	45	1.57	195 @ 1.181	.0010–.0027	.0010–.0027	.3410–.3420	.3410–.3420
1983–84	4-121	1½ Turn③		46	45	1.60	182 @ 1.33	.0011–.0026	.0014–.003	—	—
1984–85	4-119	.006C	.010C	45	45	⑤	55 @ 1.614	.0009–.0022	.0015–.0031	.3102④	.3091④
	4-137⑧	.016C	.016C	45	45	⑥	⑦	.0015–.0027	.0025–.0037	.3140	.3140
1985	4-151	Hydraulic⑨		46	45	1.66	1 @ 1.254	.0010–.0027	⑩	.3418–.3425	.3418–.3425

continued

VALVE SPECIFICATIONS—Continued

①—Valve spring free length, inner 1.7835 inch; outer 1.8465 inch.
②—Valve spring tension, inner 18–21 @ 1.516; outer 32–37 @ 1.614
③—Turn rocker arm stud nut until all lash is eliminated, then tighten nut the additional turn listed.
④—Minimum diameter.
⑤—Valve spring free length, 1.894.
⑥—Valve spring free length: inner, 1.887 inch; outer, 1.864 inch.
⑦—Valve spring tension: inner, 12–14 @ 1.456; outer, 43–49 @ 1.5354.
⑧—Diesel engine.
⑨—Not adjustable.
⑩—Top, .0010–.0027 inch; Bottom, .0020–.0037 inch.

Engine Tightening Specifications★

★ Torque specifications are for clean and lightly lubricated threads only. Dry or dirty threads produce increased friction which prevents accurate measurement of tightness.

Year	Engine	Spark Plugs Ft. Lbs.	Cylinder Head Bolts Ft. Lbs.	Intake Manifold Ft. Lbs.	Exhaust Manifold Ft. Lbs.	Rocker Arm Shaft Bracket Ft. Lbs.	Rocker Arm Cover Ft. Lbs.	Connecting Rod Cap Bolts Ft. Lbs.	Main Bearing Cap Bolts Ft. Lbs.	Flywheel to Crankshaft Ft. Lbs.	Vibration Damper or Pulley Ft. Lbs.
1982–85	4-119	18–22	72	16	16	16	4	43	72	76	87
1982	V6-173	7–15	65–75	20–25	22–28	43–49①	6–9	34–40	63–74	45–55	66–84
1983–84	4-121	7–19	65–75	22–29	19–29	43–49①	3	34–42	63–77	45–59	66–88
1983–85	V6-173	7–15	55–77	13–25	20–30	43–53①	6–12	34–44	63–83	45–59	48–55
1984–85	4-137②	—	③	10–17	10–17	9–17	9–13	58–65	116–130	70	124–151
1985	4-151	7–15	92	④	37	20	6	32	70	44	160

①—Rocker arm stud.
②—Diesel engine.
③—Torque to 40–47 ft. lbs., then retorque new bolts to 54–61 ft. lbs. or used bolts to 61–69 ft. lbs.
④—Lower rear, upper center (2) & upper & lower front, 25 ft. lbs.; upper rear, 37 ft. lbs.; lower center (2), 28 ft. lbs.

Wheel Alignment Specifications

Year	Truck Model	Caster Deg.	Camber Deg.	Toe-In (Inches)	King Pin Angle Deg.
1982–85	S/T-10, 15	+1.5° to +2.5°	+.3° to +1.3°	①	—

①—Toe-in, +15°.

Brake Specifications

Year	Model	Rear Drum I.D.	Wheel Cyl. Bore		Disc Brake Rotor					
			Front Disc	Rear Drum	Nominal Thickness	Minimum Thickness	Thickness Variation (Parallelism)	Run Out (TIR)	Finish (microinch)	Master Cyl. I.D.
1982–84	All	9.45	—	.874	—	.978	.0005	.004	30–80	.945①
1985	All	9.45	—	—	—	.978	.0005	.004	30–80	.945①

①—Piston diameter.
②—Exc. power brakes, .875 inch; Power brakes, .750 inch.

continued

Drive Axle Specifications

Year	Model	Carrier Type	Ring Gear & Pinion Backlash		Pinion Bearing Preload			Differential Bearing Preload		
			Method	Adjustment	Method	New Bearings Inch-Lbs.	Used Bearings Inch-Lbs.	Method	New Bearings Inch-Lbs.	Used Bearings Inch-Lbs.
1982–85	All③	Integral	Shim	.005–.009	Spacer	24–32①	8–12①	Shim	②	②
1983–85	All④	Split	Sleeve	.005–.007	Spacer	15–25①	—	—	—	—

①—Measured with torque wrench at pinion flange nut.
②—Slip fit plus .004 inch preload on each side.
③—Rear axle.
④—Front axle (four wheel drive).

Cooling System & Capacity Data

Year	Model or Engine	Cooling Capacity, Qts.		Radiator Cap Relief Pressure, Lbs.	Thermo. Opening Temp.	Fuel Tank Gals.	Engine Oil Refill Qts.	Transmission Oil				Rear Axle Oil Pints
		Less A/C	With A/C					4 Speed Pints	5 Speed Pints	Auto. Trans.②	Trans. Case Pints	
1982	4-119	9.4	9.5	15	180°	13	4①	⑦	⑦	⑥	—	3.5
	V6-173	12.0	12.0	15	195°	13⑧	4①	⑦	⑦	⑥	—	3.5
1983	4-119	9.3	9.5	15	180°	③⑧	4①	⑦	⑦	⑥	4.5	3.5⑤
	4-121	9.5	9.6	15	195°	③⑧	4①	⑦	⑦	⑥	4.5	3.5⑤
	V6-173	12.0	12.0	15	195°	③⑧	4①	⑦	⑦	⑥	4.5	3.5⑤
1984	4-119	9.5	9.5	15	180°	③⑧	4①	⑦	⑦	⑥	4.5	3.5⑤
	4-121	9.5	9.5	15	195°	③⑧	4①	⑦	⑦	⑥	4.5	3.5⑤
	4-137④	11.5	12.0	15	180°	14⑧	5.5①	⑦	⑦	⑥	4.5	3.5⑤
	V6-173	12.0	12.0	15	195°	③⑧	4①	⑦	⑦	⑥	4.5	3.5⑤
1985	4-119	9.5	9.5	15	180°	13⑧	4①	⑨	4.1	⑥	4.5	3.5⑤
	4-137④	11.5	12	15	180°	14⑧	5.5①	⑨	4.1	—	4.5	3.5⑤
	4-151	12	12	15	—	③⑧	3①	⑨	4.1	⑥	4.5	3.5⑤
	V6-173	12	12	15	195°	③⑧	4①	⑨	4.1	⑥	4.5	3.5⑤

①—Additional oil may be required with filter change.
②—Approximate, make final check with dipstick.
③—All models exc. Blazer & Jimmy, 13.0; Blazer & Jimmy, 13.5.
④—Diesel engine.
⑤—Front drive axle, 2.6 pts.
⑥—THM 200C—total 9.5 qts., pan only, 3.5 qts.; THM 7004R—total 11.5 qts., pan only, 5 qts.
⑦—Fill to bottom of oil filler plug.
⑧—Optional tank 20 gals.
⑨—77mm trans., 4.5 pts.; 77.5mm trans., 4.8 pts.

Electrical Section

STARTER
REPLACE

4-119

1. Disconnect battery ground cable.
2. Disconnect EGR pipe from EGR valve and exhaust manifold, then remove.
3. Disconnect starter solenoid wiring.
4. Remove starter mounting bolts and nuts.
5. Remove starter motor assembly.
6. Reverse procedure to install.

4-121, 4-151 & V6-173

NOTE: Upon removal of starter, note if any shims are used. If shims are used, they should be reinstalled in their original location during replacement.

If starter is noisy during cranking, remove one .015 inch double shim or add one .015 inch single shim to the outer bolt. If starter makes a high pitched whine after firing, add .015 inch double shims until noise ceases.

1. Disconnect battery ground cable.
2. Raise and support front of vehicle.
3. Remove any shields or braces blocking access to the starter.
4. Remove starter mounting bolts, then allow starter to drop down.
5. Remove solenoid wiring and battery cable, then the starter assembly.
6. Reverse procedure to install.

4-137 DIESEL

1. Disconnect battery ground cable.
2. Disconnect starter motor wiring.
3. Remove starter mounting bolts and nuts.
4. Remove starter motor assembly.
5. Reverse procedure to install.

IGNITION LOCK
REPLACE

1. Disconnect battery ground cable.
2. Remove steering wheel. Refer to "Horn Sounder and Steering Wheel, Replace."
3. Remove turn signal switch. Refer to "Turn Signal Switch, Replace."
4. Place ignition switch in "Run" position, then remove lock cylinder retaining screw and lock cylinder.
5. To install, rotate lock cylinder to stop while holding housing, **Fig. 1.** Align cylinder key with keyway in housing, then push lock cylinder assembly into housing until fully seated.
6. Install lock cylinder retaining screw, turn signal switch and steering wheel.

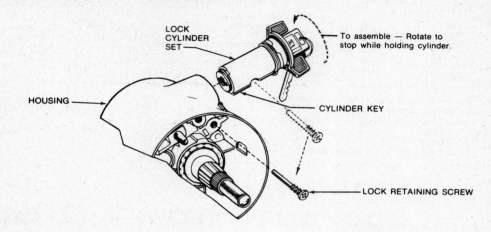

LOCK CYLINDER SET

To assemble — Rotate to stop while holding cylinder.

HOUSING

CYLINDER KEY

LOCK RETAINING SCREW

Fig. 1   Ignition lock removal & installation

IGNITION & DIMMER SWITCHES
REPLACE

1. Disconnect battery ground cable.
2. Remove lower instrument panel trim and nuts securing steering column bracket, then lower column just enough to gain access to switches.

NOTE: Use care when lowering steering column to prevent damage to column assembly. It may be necessary to remove bracket from column to gain access to switches.

3. Rotate ignition lock to the "ACC" position on models with key release lever, or to the "Off" unlocked position on models less release lever.
4. If lock cylinder has been removed, pull actuator rod back to stop, then, on models without key release lever, push rod down to second detent.
5. Remove nut and screw securing dimmer switch, disconnect electrical connector, then disengage and remove dimmer switch, **Figs. 2 and 3.**

NOTE: If ignition switch is not being replaced, proceed to step 10.

6. Remove stud screw securing ignition switch, disconnect electrical connector, then disengage and remove switch.
7. Position slider on replacement switch in "ACC" position for models with key release, or in "Off" unlocked position for models less key release as shown in **Figs. 2 and 3.**
8. Mount ignition switch over actuator rod and install stud screw finger tight.
9. Apply slight rearward pressure to switch body, ensuring that switch remains in proper detented position, then torque screw to 35 inch lbs. to secure adjustment.
10. Depress dimmer switch plunger slightly and insert 3/32 inch drill or rod to lock plunger to switch body, **Figs. 2 and 3.**
11. Engage actuator rod in switch and install retaining nut and screw finger tight.
12. Apply slight rearward pressure to switch to take up slack, then torque mounting nut and screw to 35 inch lbs.
13. Connect electrical connectors to ignition and dimmer switches, align steering column and bracket on mounting studs and torque retaining nuts to 20 ft. lbs.
14. Reverse remaining procedure to complete installation and ensure that switches operate properly in all positions.

LIGHT SWITCH
REPLACE

1982–83

1. Disconnect battery ground cable.
2. Pull headlight switch knob to "On" position.
3. Reach up under instrument panel and depress headlight switch shaft retainer button while gently pulling on switch control shaft knob to remove control shaft.
4. Remove three headlight switch trim plate retaining screws, then the trim plate.
5. Using a suitable large bladed screwdriver, remove switch ferrule nut.
6. Working behind instrument panel, remove switch wiring connector, then the switch.

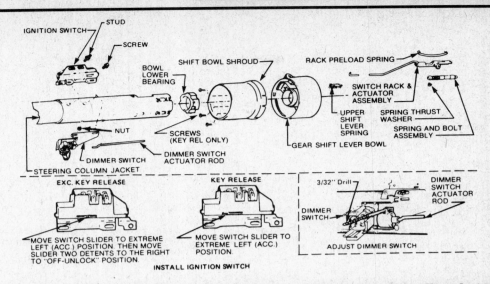

Fig. 2   Ignition & dimmer switch removal & installation. Exc. tilt column

7. Reverse procedure to install.

1984—85
1. Disconnect battery ground cable and remove hush panel over fuse box.
2. Remove screws securing hood release handle, then the lower steering column cover.
3. Remove cruise control module and delay wiper switch knob and locknut, if equipped.
4. Pull light switch to full on position, depress retainer on frame of switch, then remove shaft and knob assembly.
5. Disconnect parking brake release cable, depress tabs on release handle and remove cable assembly.
6. Remove headlamp switch bezel and retaining nut.
7. Disconnect electrical connector and remove headlamp switch.
8. Reverse procedure to install.

STOP LIGHT SWITCH
REPLACE

1. Disconnect battery ground cable.
2. Disconnect wiring connector from brake light switch located on brake pedal bracket.
3. Pull switch from mounting bracket.
4. Depress brake pedal, then push new switch into clip until shoulder bottoms out, **Fig. 4.**
5. Pull brake pedal rearward against pedal stop to adjust switch. Switch is properly adjusted when brake lights operate when brake pedal is depressed .53 inch from normal position. If further adjustment of switch is necessary, switch can be rotated or pulled in clip.

CLUTCH START SWITCH
REPLACE

1. Refer to **Fig. 5** for procedure.

NEUTRAL START & BACK-UP LIGHT SWITCH
REPLACE

NOTE: The following procedure applies to automatic transmission equipped models only. On vehicles with manual transmission, a transmission mounted back-up light switch is used.

1. Disconnect battery ground cable.
2. Place gear selector in "Neutral" position.
3. Remove screws securing switch to steering column, then the switch.
4. Disconnect wiring connectors. Connect wiring connectors to new switch.
5. Insert .096 inch gage pin into switch gage hole to a depth of $\frac{3}{8}$ inch, **Fig. 6.**

NOTE: The switch is fixed in neutral position by a plastic shear pin installed during production.

6. Position the switch on the steering column. Ensure switch carrier tang is inserted in shift tube slot, then install switch retaining screws and tighten.
7. Remove gage pin, then place gear selector in "Park" position to shear plastic pin.
8. Return gear selector to "Neutral" position and attempt to insert a .089 inch gage pin in gage hole. Pin should enter freely.
9. If gage pin does not enter gage hole freely, switch should be reset.
10. Connect battery ground cable and check switch operation.

NEUTRAL START MECHANICAL LOCKOUT

Actuation of the ignition switch is prevented by a mechanical lockout system, **Figs. 7 and 8,** which prevents the lock cylinder from rotating when the selector lever is out of Park or Neutral. When the selector lever is in Park or Neutral, the slots in the bowl plate and the finger on the actuator rod align, allowing the finger to pass through the bowl plate in turn actuating the ignition switch. If the selector lever is in any position other than Park or Neutral, the finger contacts the bowl plate when the lock cylinder is rotated, thereby preventing full travel of the lock cylinder.

HORN SOUNDER & STEERING WHEEL
REPLACE

1. Disconnect battery ground cable.
2. Remove steering wheel trim pad retaining screws from underside of steering wheel spokes, then lift off trim pad and remove wiring connector.
3. Remove snap ring and nut from steering shaft.
4. Remove steering wheel using puller J-2927.
5. Reverse procedure to install.

TURN SIGNAL SWITCH
REPLACE

1. Disconnect battery ground cable.
2. Remove steering wheel as outlined under "Horn Sounder and Steering Wheel, Replace" procedure.
3. Using a screwdriver, pry cover from housing.
4. Using lock plate compressing tool J-23653, compress lock plate and pry retaining ring from groove on shaft, **Fig. 9.** Slowly release lock plate compressing tool, remove tool and lock plate from shaft end.
5. Slide canceling cam and upper bearing preload spring from end of shaft.

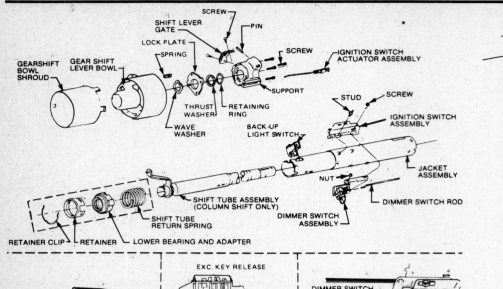

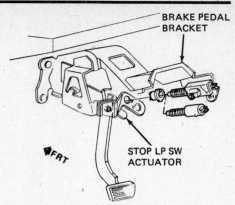

Fig. 4 Stop light switch installation

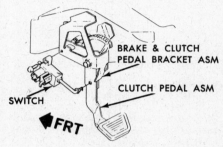

Fig. 5 Clutch start switch installation

Fig. 3 Ignition & dimmer switch removal & installation. Tilt column

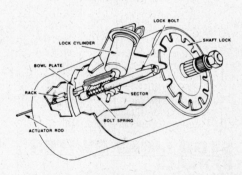

Fig. 7 Mechanical lockout. Exc. tilt column

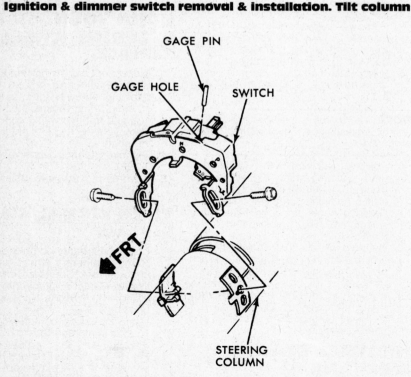

Fig. 6 Neutral start & back-up light switch installation

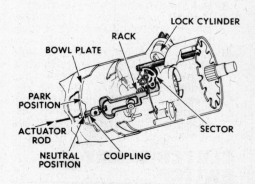

Fig. 8 Mechanical lockout. Tilt column

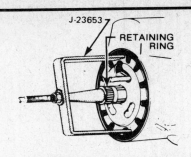

Fig. 9 Compressing lock plate

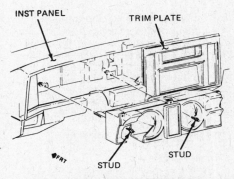

Fig. 10 Instrument cluster removal

6. Remove turn signal (multi-function) lever.
7. Remove hazard warning knob retaining screw, button, spring and knob.
8. Remove pivot arm.
9. Wrap upper part of electrical connector with tape to prevent snagging of wires during switch removal.
10. Remove switch retaining screws and pull switch up from column, guiding wire harness through column.
11. Reverse procedure to install.

INSTRUMENT CLUSTER
REPLACE

1. Disconnect battery ground cable.
2. Remove five instrument cluster trim plate retaining screws, then trim plate.
3. Lift off instrument cluster face plate and lens.
4. Disconnect speedometer cable.
5. Disconnect electrical connector from instrument cluster, then remove cluster, **Fig. 10.**
6. Reverse procedure to install.

W/S WIPER SWITCH
REPLACE

1. Remove turn signal switch. Refer to "Turn Signal Switch, Replace" procedure.
2. Refer to **Figs. 11 and 12** for wiper switch replacement.

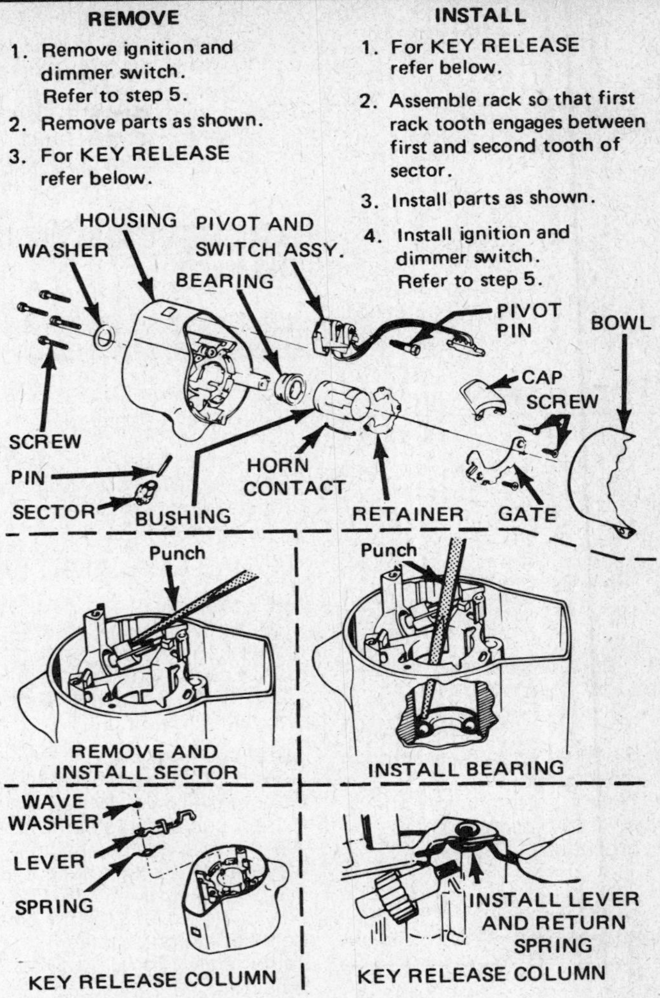

REMOVE

1. Remove ignition and dimmer switch. Refer to step 5.
2. Remove parts as shown.
3. For KEY RELEASE refer below.

INSTALL

1. For KEY RELEASE refer below.
2. Assemble rack so that first rack tooth engages between first and second tooth of sector.
3. Install parts as shown.
4. Install ignition and dimmer switch. Refer to step 5.

Fig. 11 W/S wiper switch removal. Exc. tilt column

W/S WIPER MOTOR
REPLACE

1. Disconnect battery ground cable.
2. Remove windshield wiper arms.
3. Remove cowl vent and grille.
4. Loosen, but do not remove transmission drive link to motor crank arm attaching nuts, then disconnect drive link from motor crank arm.
5. Disconnect motor electrical connector and remove attaching bolts.
6. Remove motor by rotating up and outward.
7. Reverse procedure to install. Torque motor attaching bolts to 49 to 75 inch lbs.

W/S WIPER TRANSMISSION
REPLACE

1. Disconnect battery ground cable.
2. Remove windshield wiper arms.
3. Remove cowl vent and grille.
4. Remove motor assembly to wiper linkage retaining nut.

5. Remove screws securing wiper linkage to cowl panel and lift out linkage.
6. Reverse procedure to install. Torque all attaching fasteners to 49 to 80 inch lbs.

RADIO
REPLACE

1. Disconnect battery ground cable.
2. Remove screws securing center instrument panel bezel, then the bezel.
3. Remove four screws securing radio bracket, then pull radio outward.
4. Disconnect radio electrical connectors, then unplug antenna lead and remove radio.
5. Reverse procedure to install.

BLOWER MOTOR
REPLACE

1. Disconnect battery ground cable.
2. On models equipped with A/C, remove vacuum tank.

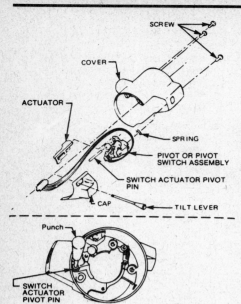

Fig. 12 W/S wiper switch removal. Tilt column

3. On all models, remove blower motor electrical connections.
4. Remove blower motor flange attaching screws, then blower motor.
5. Reverse procedure to install.

HEATER CORE
REPLACE

1. Disconnect battery ground cable.
2. Drain radiator coolant.

3. Disconnect heater hoses at heater core and plug core tubes.
4. Working inside vehicle, remove core cover.
5. Remove four heater core retaining screws, then heater core.
6. Reverse procedure to install.

SPEED CONTROLS
ADJUST

BRAKE RELEASE SWITCH & VACUUM RELEASE VALVE

With brake or clutch pedal depressed, push valve or switch fully into tubular clip until seated. Pull brake or clutch pedal rearward until pedal is against stop. Valve or switch will travel in tubular clip to provide proper adjustment.

SERVO LINKAGE, ADJUST

1982 Models

With carburetor throttle completely closed (ignition "Off" and fast idle cam off), loosen cable adjustment jam nuts. Position cable so chain is almost tight (some slack), and tighten jam nuts.

1983—84 Models

With carburetor throttle completely closed (ignition "Off" and fast idle cam off), loosen cable adjustment jam nuts. On 4-122 models, position cable so cable sleeve at carburetor is tight but not holding throttle open. On 4-119 and V6-173 models, position cable so a 1.0 mm clearance exists between throttle lever stud and end of cable slot. On all models, tighten jam nuts.

1985 Models

Ensure that throttle is completely closed,

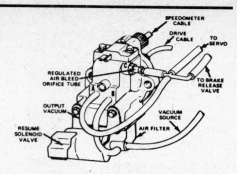

Fig. 13 Cruise control transducer assembly

ignition and fast idle cam, if equipped, off. With cable properly secured and connected at throttle lever end, install cable in bracket at servo. Pull on cable just enough to remove slack, then connect cable to hole in servo actuator that will provide approximately .15 inch slack in cable. Do not stretch cable to make connection at servo, as engine will not return to idle.

CRUISE SPEED, ADJUST

1982 Models

The cruise speed adjustment is made at the transducer, **Fig. 13,** as follows: If vehicle cruises below engagement speed, loosen regulated air bleed orifice tube locknut, **Fig. 13,** and turn orifice tube outward. If cruising speed is higher than engagement speed, turn orifice tube inward. Turning the orifice tube 90° (¼ turn) changes the engagement-cruising speed difference one MPH. After adjustment is completed, tighten locknut.

1983—85 Models

There is no provision for adjusting cruise speed on these models.

4-119 Gasoline Engine Section

ENGINE
REPLACE

NOTE: The following is a revised procedure.

1. Disconnect battery ground cable.
2. Scribe reference marks in the hood hinge area, then remove hood.
3. Drain cooling system, then remove radiator hoses, overflow hose, transmission cooler lines (if equipped), upper radiator shroud and radiator.
4. Remove cooling fan, then disconnect heater hoses.
5. Remove air cleaner assembly.
6. Identify, then disconnect vacuum hoses from engine.
7. Disconnect necessary engine wiring from bulkhead.
8. Disconnect throttle linkage as neces-

sary, then remove distributor cap.
9. Raise and support vehicle.
10. Remove converter to exhaust pipe bolts, then disconnect exhaust pipe at manifold.
11. Remove strut rods at bellhousing (if equipped).
12. Remove flywheel cover bolts, then cover.
13. On models equipped with automatic transmission, remove torque converter bolts.
14. Disconnect shield at rear of catalytic converter, then remove converter hanger.
15. Remove lower radiator fan shroud.
16. Disconnect fuel lines from fuel pump.
17. Remove two outer bolts from front air deflector.
18. Remove left side body mount bolts, then raise body using suitable lifting equipment.

19. Remove bellhousing bolts, then lower body to frame.
20. Remove motor mount through bolts, then lower vehicle.
21. If equipped with A/C or power steering, disconnect A/C compressor and/or power steering pump.
22. Install suitable lifting device on engine.
23. Support transmission with suitable jack.
24. Remove engine assembly.
25. Reverse procedure to install.

ENGINE MOUNTS
REPLACE

FRONT

1. Disconnect battery ground cable.

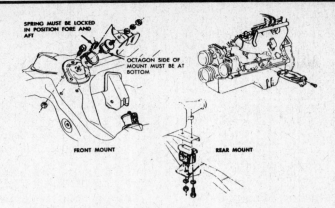

Fig. 1   Engine mount

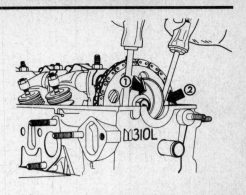

Fig. 2   Depressing adjusting lock lever

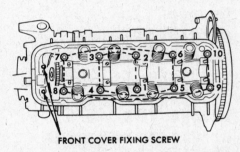

Fig. 3   Cylinder head hold-down bolt torque sequence

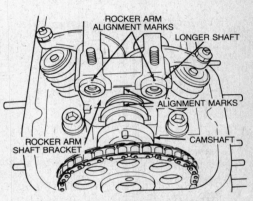

Fig. 4   Rocker arm shaft installation

2. Remove air cleaner duct and upper fan shroud.
3. Remove engine mount nuts and retaining wire.
4. With vehicle raised, raise engine to take weight off mounts.
5. Remove engine mount to engine bracket.
6. Remove engine mount using tool J-25510, or equivalent, **Fig. 1.**
7. Reverse procedure to install.

REAR

1. Disconnect battery ground cable.
2. Remove mount nut and bolts.
3. Support, and slightly raise, transmission at extension housing and remove engine mount, **Fig. 1.**
4. Reverse procedure to install.

CYLINDER HEAD
REPLACE

1. Remove cam cover.
2. Remove EGR pipe clamp at rear of cylinder head.
3. Raise and support vehicle.
4. Disconnect exhaust pipe at manifold.
5. Lower vehicle, drain cooling system and disconnect heater hoses.
6. Remove A/C compressor and/or power steering pump, and position aside.
7. Disconnect accelerator linkage and fuel line at carburetor, all necessary electrical connections, spark plug

wires and necessary vacuum lines.
8. Rotate crankshaft until No. 4 cylinder is in firing position. Remove distributor cap and mark rotor to housing relationship, then remove distributor.
9. Remove fuel pump.
10. Lock shoe on timing chain automatic adjuster in fully retracted position by depressing the adjuster lock lever with a screwdriver or equivalent in direction as indicated, **Fig. 2.**
11. Remove timing sprocket to camshaft bolt. Remove sprocket and fuel pump drive cam from the camshaft. Do not remove the sprocket from the chain.
12. Disconnect AIR hose and check valve at air manifold.
13. Remove cylinder head to timing cover bolts.
14. Remove cylinder head bolts using tool J-24239-01, or equivalent. Remove outer bolts first.
15. With an assistant, remove cylinder head, intake and exhaust manifold as an assembly.
16. Clean all gasket material from cylinder head and block surfaces.

NOTE: Gasket surfaces on both head and block must be clean of all foreign matter and free of nicks or heavy scratches. Cylinder bolt threads in the block and threads on the bolts must be cleaned, as dirt will affect bolt torque.

17. Reverse procedure to install and tighten head bolts to specifications in sequence, **Fig. 3.**

INTAKE MANIFOLD
REPLACE

1. Drain engine cooling system.

NOTE: Before removing intake manifold, check that the cooling system is completely drained. Any coolant left in the engine will flow into the cylinder when the manifold is removed.

2. Remove air cleaner assembly.
3. Disconnect radiator upper hose from intake manifold.

4. Disconnect vacuum hose from manifold.
5. Disconnect heater hoses from manifold and from connector under the dashboard.
6. Disconnect accelerator control cable from carburetor.
7. Disconnect distributor vacuum hose from distributor and the thermo-unit wiring at the connector.
8. Disconnect automatic choke and solenoid wiring at connectors.
9. Disconnect PCV hose from the rocker arm cover.
10. Disconnect oil level gage guide tube fixing bolt at the intake manifold.
11. Disconnect the EGR pipe from the EGR valve adapter and the AIR vacuum hose from the 3-way joint.
12. Remove EGR valve and adapter.
13. Remove the eight attaching nuts and remove the intake manifold.
14. Using a new gasket, reverse procedure to install.

EXHAUST MANIFOLD
REPLACE

1. Disconnect battery ground cable.
2. Raise and support vehicle.
3. Disconnect exhaust pipe from exhaust manifold.
4. Disconnect E.G.R pipe at exhaust manifold.

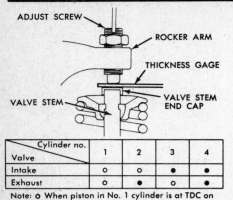

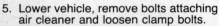

Note: o When piston in No. 1 cylinder is at TDC on compression stroke.
● When piston in No. 4 cylinder is at TDC on compression stroke.

Fig. 5   Valve adjustment

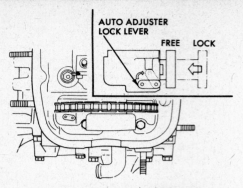

Fig. 6   Locking timing chain adapter

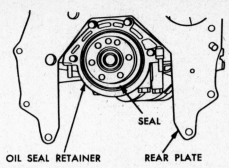

Fig. 7   Rear main oil seal

5. Lower vehicle, remove bolts attaching air cleaner and loosen clamp bolts.
6. Raise air cleaner slightly, then remove air cleaner hot air inlet hose.
7. If equipped with A/C or power steering, remove A/C compressor and/or power steering pump.
8. Remove the four attaching bolts and remove the manifold cover.
9. Remove the seven mounting nuts from the manifold and remove the exhaust manifold.
10. Using a new gasket, reverse procedure to install. Torque manifold stud nuts to 16 ft. lbs. in a sequence beginning with the inner nuts and working outward.

ROCKER ARMS & SHAFTS
REMOVAL

1. Remove cam cover.
2. Alternately loosen rocker arm shaft bracket nuts and remove nuts from brackets.
3. Remove springs from rocker arm shaft, then the rocker arm brackets and arms, keeping components in order.

INSTALLATION

1. Lubricate rocker arms, shafts and valve stems with engine oil.
2. Install the longer rocker shaft on the exhaust valve side and the shorter rocker shaft on the intake valve side, **Fig. 4,** with the aligning marks facing front.
3. Install rocker arm shaft brackets and rocker arms on the rocker arm shafts with the cylinder number on the upper face of the brackets facing toward front of engine.
4. Align the mark on the No. 1 rocker arm

shaft bracket with the mark on the rocker arm shafts.
5. The exhaust side rocker arm shaft should project a greater distance from the face of the No. 1 rocker shaft bracket outer face than the intake side rocker arm shaft when the rocker arm shaft stud holes are aligned with the rocker arm shaft bracket stud holes.
6. Position rocker arm shaft springs between rocker arm shaft bracket and rocker arm.
7. Ensure punch mark on rocker arm shaft is facing upward. Install rocker arm shaft bracket assembly onto cylinder head studs. Align mark on camshaft with mark on No. 1 rocker arm shaft bracket.
8. Torque rocker arm shaft stud nuts to 16 ft. lbs.

NOTE: Hold the rocker arm springs in position while torquing the stud nuts to prevent spring damage.

9. Adjust valves and install cam cover.

VALVES
ADJUST

1. Before adjusting valve clearances, check the rocker arm shaft bracket nuts for looseness and retighten as necessary.
2. Bring either No. 1 or No. 4 piston to top dead center on the compression stroke by turning the crankshaft to align timing mark on crankshaft pulley with pointer.
3. Hold crankshaft in above position and adjust clearance of the valves indicated, **Fig. 5,** to specifications. Take measurement at the clearance between rocker arm and valve stem.
4. Turn crankshaft one full turn and adjust clearance of remaining valves to specifications.

VALVE ARRANGEMENT
FRONT TO REAR

E-I-I-E-E-I-I-E

VALVE TIMING
INTAKE OPENS BEFORE TDC

Year	Degrees
1982–85	21

CAMSHAFT
REPLACE
REMOVAL

1. Remove cam cover.
2. Rotate camshaft until No. 4 cylinder is in firing position. Remove distributor cap and mark rotor to housing position, then remove distributor.
3. Remove the fuel pump.
4. Lock the shoe on timing chain automatic adjuster in fully retracted position by depressing the adjuster lock lever with a screwdriver or equivalent in direction as indicated, **Figs. 2 and 6.** After locking the automatic adjuster, check that the chain is loose.
5. Remove timing sprocket to camshaft bolt. Remove sprocket and fuel pump drive cam from camshaft. Do not remove sprocket from chain.
6. Remove rocker arm, shaft and bracket assembly.
7. Remove camshaft assembly.

INSTALLATION

1. Lubricate camshaft and journals of cylinder head with engine oil.
2. Install camshaft assembly.
3. Install rocker arm, shaft and bracket assembly.
4. Align mark on the No. 1 rocker arm shaft bracket with the mark on the camshaft. Also, ensure that the crank-

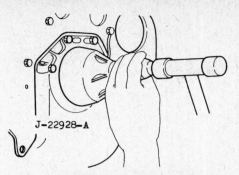

Fig. 8 Installing rear main oil seal

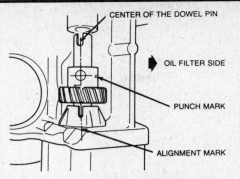

Fig. 9 Oil pump alignment

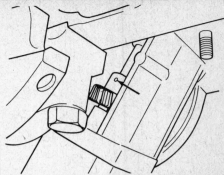

Fig. 10 Checking alignment

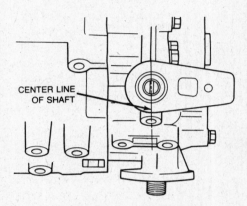

Fig. 11 Oil pump shaft alignment

shaft pulley groove is aligned with TDC mark on front cover.
5. Assemble timing sprocket to camshaft by aligning sprocket with pin on camshaft. Use caution not to remove chain from sprocket.
6. Install fuel pump drive cam and sprocket retaining bolt and washer. Remove the half-moon seal at front of head, then torque retaining bolt to 60 ft. lbs. Then install the half-moon seal in cylinder head.
7. Install distributor.
8. Release lock by depressing shoe on timing chain automatic adjuster and check timing chain for proper tension.
9. Check that distributor rotor and mark on distributor housing are aligned with No. 4 piston firing position in distributor cap, then install distributor. Timing mark on crank pulley should also be aligned with TDC mark on front cover.
10. Install distributor cap.
11. Install cam cover.

REAR MAIN SEAL

1. Remove starter motor and position aside.
2. Remove transmission.
3. On vehicles equipped with manual transmission, remove clutch cover and pressure plate assembly, then the flywheel and flywheel cover.

4. On vehicles equipped with automatic transmission, remove flex plate.
5. Pry seal from retainer, **Fig. 7**.
6. Install new seal using tool J-22928-A, **Fig. 8**. Prior to installation, fill clearance between lips of seal with suitable grease and lubricate seal lip with clean engine oil.

FRONT OIL SEAL
REPLACE

1. Disconnect battery ground cable and drain cooling system.
2. Disconnect radiator hoses and remove radiator assembly.
3. Remove drive belts and engine fan.
4. Remove crankshaft pulley center bolt and the pulley and balancer assembly.
5. Pry seal from timing cover with a suitable screwdriver.
6. Install new seal with tool J-26587.

FRONT COVER
REPLACE

REMOVAL

1. Disconnect battery ground cable.
2. Remove oil pan as described under "Oil Pan, Replace".
3. Remove cylinder head.
4. Remove oil pickup tube from oil pump.
5. Remove harmonic balancer and the AIR pump drive belt.
6. On air conditioned vehicles, remove A/C compressor and position aside. Remove compressor mounting brackets.
7. On models equipped with power steering, remove power steering pump and bracket and position aside.
8. Remove distributor assembly.
9. Remove front cover attaching bolts and the front cover.

INSTALLATION

1. Install new gasket onto cylinder block.

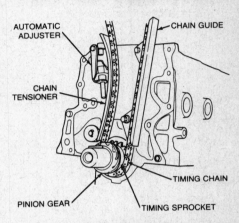

Fig. 12 Timing chain removal

2. Align oil pump drive gear punch mark with oil filter side of cover, **Fig. 9**, then align the center of dowel pin with alignment mark on oil pump case.
3. Rotate crankshaft until Nos. 1 and 4 cylinders are at top dead center.
4. Install front cover by engaging pinion gear with oil pump drive gear on crankshaft.
5. Check that punch mark on oil pump drive gear is turned to the rear, viewed through the clearance between front cover and cylinder block, **Fig. 10**.
6. Check that slit at the end of oil pump shaft is parallel with front face of cylinder block and is offset forward, **Fig. 11**.
7. Install front cover and tighten front cover bolts.
8. Reverse steps 1 thru 7 under "Front Cover, Replace".
9. Check engine timing.
10. Check for leaks.

TIMING CHAIN
REPLACE

1. Remove front cover assembly. Refer to steps under "Front Cover, Replace" procedure.
2. Lock automatic adjuster shoe in fully retracted position.
3. Remove timing chain from crankshaft sprocket, **Fig. 12**.

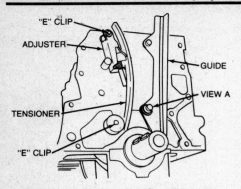

Fig. 13 Timing chain guide, tensioner and adjuster

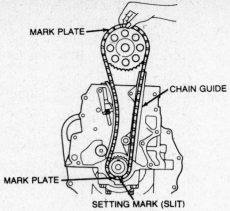

Fig. 14 Timing chain alignment

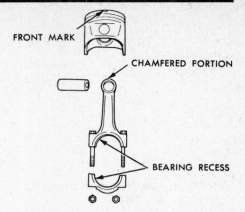

Fig. 15 Piston and connecting rod assembly

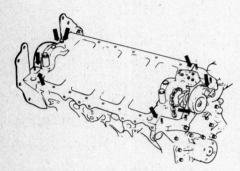

Fig. 16 Sealer locations on oil pan gasket surface

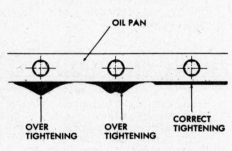

Fig. 17 Oil pan gasket installation

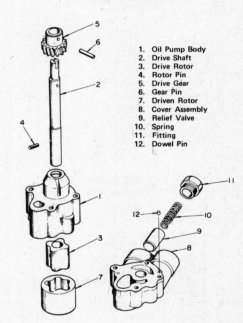

1. Oil Pump Body
2. Drive Shaft
3. Drive Rotor
4. Rotor Pin
5. Drive Gear
6. Gear Pin
7. Driven Rotor
8. Cover Assembly
9. Relief Valve
10. Spring
11. Fitting
12. Dowel Pin

Fig. 18 Oil pump assembly

4. Remove "E" clip and the chain adjuster and tensioner, **Fig. 13.** Inspect components for wear or damage. Also, inspect chain guide and oil jet. View "A", **Fig. 13.**
5. Install timing sprocket and pinion gear with groove side toward front cover. Align key grooves with key on crankshaft, then drive into position with tool J-26587.
6. Turn crankshaft so key is turned toward cylinder head side with Nos. 1 and 4 pistons at top dead center.
7. Install timing chain by aligning mark plate on chain with the mark on crankshaft timing sprocket. The side of the chain with mark plate is located on the front side and the side of chain with the most links between mark plates is located on the chain guide side, **Fig. 14.**
8. Install the camshaft timing sprocket so marked side of sprocket faces forward and the triangular mark aligns with the chain mark plate.

NOTE: Keep the timing chain engaged with camshaft timing sprocket until the camshaft timing sprocket is installed on camshaft.

9. Install automatic chain adjuster, then release lock by depressing the adjusting shoe.
10. Install front cover assembly as outlined previously.

PISTONS & RODS

Assemble piston to rod so the mark on the piston is facing toward front of engine, **Fig. 15,** and the face of the connecting rod with the cylinder number mark is facing toward the starter side of the engine.

Pistons are available in oversizes of .020 and .030 inch.

OIL PAN
REPLACE

REMOVAL

1. Remove engine as outlined under "Engine, Replace".
2. Remove nuts and bolts attaching oil pan to cylinder block and remove oil pan.

3. Remove oil level gage guide tube from the intake manifold and oil pan.

INSTALLATION

1. Apply a thin coat of Permatex No. 2, or equivalent, to locations indicated by arrows, **Fig. 16.**
2. Install new oil pan gasket aligning holes and install oil pan on cylinder block.
3. Install nuts and bolts and torque evenly to 4 ft. lbs.

NOTE: Check edge of gasket to check proper positioning. If projection of gasket edge beyond the oil pan flange is uneven, remove and reinstall, **Fig. 17.**

4. Install engine into vehicle as outlined under "Engine, Replace".

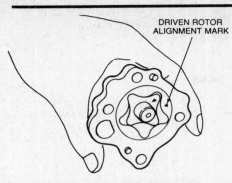

Fig. 19   Aligning drive and driven rotors

OIL PUMP

REMOVAL

1. Remove cam cover, distributor assembly and oil pan.
2. Remove bolt securing oil pick-up tube to engine block and the tube from the oil pump.
3. Remove oil pump mounting bolts, then the oil pump.
4. Remove rubber hose and relief valve assembly from the pump.

SERVICE

1. Measure clearance between drive rotor and driven rotor with a feeler gauge, **Fig. 18.** If clearance is greater than .0079 inch, replace oil pump assembly.
2. Measure clearance between driven rotor and inner wall of pump body, **Fig. 18.** If clearance is greater than .0098 inch, replace oil pump assembly.
3. Measure clearance between drive rotor, driven rotor and oil pump cover with a feeler gauge and a straight edge, **Fig. 18.** If clearance is greater than .0079 inch, replace oil pump assembly.
4. Determine clearance between drive shaft and drive shaft hole in pump cover. Measure the inside diameter of the shaft hole in the cover and the diameter of the drive shaft. Subtract the drive shaft diameter from the inside diameter of the shaft hole. If the clearance is greater than .0098 inch, replace oil pump.
5. Inspect components for wear or damage.

INSTALLATION

1. Align mark on camshaft with mark on No. 1 rocker arm shaft bracket. Align notch on crankshaft pulley with "O" mark on front cover. When these two sets of marks are properly aligned, No. 4 piston is at top dead center, compression stroke.
2. Install driven rotor with alignment mark aligned with mark on drive rotor. **Fig. 19.**
3. Engage oil pump drive gear with pinion gear on crankshaft so alignment mark on drive gear is turned rearward and approximately 20° from the crankshaft in a clock-wise direction, **Fig. 20.**
4. Ensure oil pump drive gear is turned rearward as viewed from clearance between front cover and cylinder block and the slit at the end of the oil pump drive shaft is parallel with the front face of the cylinder block and is offset forward as viewed through the distributor fitting hole, **Fig. 11.**
5. Install oil pump cover and mounting bolts.
6. Install relief valve assembly and rubber hose on cover.
7. Connect oil pick-up tube to rubber hose and secure tube to cylinder block.
8. Install oil pan and cam cover.
9. Install distributor so boss on shaft is fitted into slit at end of oil pump drive shaft.
10. Refill engine oil and check for leaks.

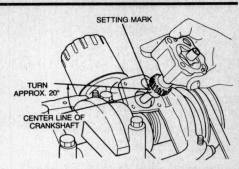

Fig. 20   Oil pump installation

WATER PUMP
REPLACE

1. Disconnect battery ground cable.
2. Remove lower cover.
3. Drain cooling system.
4. On models less A/C, remove engine fan.
5. On models with A/C:
   a. Remove air pump and alternator mounting bolts and the fan and air pump drive belt.
   b. Remove engine fan and pulley assembly.
   c. Remove fan set plate and fan pulley.
6. On all models, remove water pump attaching bolts and the water pump.
7. Reverse procedure to install.

FUEL PUMP
REPLACE

1. Disconnect battery ground cable.
2. Remove distributor.
3. Disconnect fuel pump inlet and outlet hoses.
4. Remove engine lift hook.
5. Remove fuel pump and gasket.
6. Reverse procedure to install.

NOTE: Rotate camshaft to "down stroke" position before installing pump. Lubricate rod with engine oil.

7. Adjust timing and check for leaks.

4-121 Gasoline Engine Section

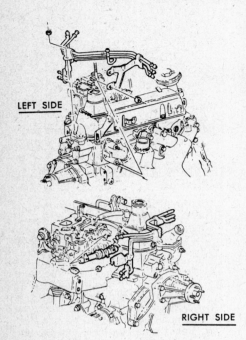

LEFT SIDE

RIGHT SIDE

Fig. 1 Fuel vapor canister harness

ENGINE, REPLACE

1. Disconnect battery cables.
2. Scribe alignment marks on hood and hood hinge, then remove hood.
3. Drain cooling system, then remove radiator hoses from radiator.
4. Remove upper fan shroud, then the radiator and fan.
5. Disconnect heater hoses from engine.
6. Disconnect wiring harness at bulkhead, then remove air cleaner.
7. Disconnect accelerator cable from carburetor, then the fuel line from frame.
8. Disconnect battery ground cable from engine block, then remove the ground strap from bulkhead.
9. Raise and support vehicle.
10. Remove clutch bell crank, then disconnect exhaust pipe from manifold.
11. Remove motor mount through bolt, left hand body mount bolts and left air dam bolts.
12. Raise body to gain access to upper bell housing bolts, then remove the bolts.
13. Lower body, then remove flywheel dust shield.
14. Lower vehicle and support transmission with suitable jack.
15. If equipped, disconnect power steering pump and/or A/C compressor and position aside.

16. Install suitable lifting device, then remove engine from vehicle.
17. Reverse procedure to install.

ENGINE MOUNTS
REPLACE

1. Disconnect battery ground cable.
2. Remove upper fan shroud.
3. Raise and support vehicle.
4. Remove engine mount through bolt. On left mount, remove mount-to-engine upper bracket attaching nuts.
5. Raise front of engine and remove mount-to-engine attaching bolts, then the mount.

NOTE: Raise engine only enough to provide sufficient clearance to remove mount. Check for interference between rear of engine and cowl panel which could cause damage to the distributor or EGR.

6. Reverse procedure to install. Torque mount-to-engine attaching bolts to 29–39 ft. lbs. and mount-to-frame bolt to 35–47 ft. lbs.

CYLINDER HEAD
REPLACE

1. Disconnect battery ground cable.
2. Remove air cleaner and drain cooling system.
3. Raise and support vehicle.
4. Disconnect exhaust pipe from exhaust manifold, then lower vehicle.
5. Disconnect accelerator linkage and any necessary wires and vacuum lines.
6. Remove fuel vapor canister harness lines, **Fig. 1.**
7. Remove distributor cap and distributor. Mark position of distributor for reference during installation.
8. Remove rocker arm cover, then the rocker arms and push rods.
9. Remove radiator and heater hoses.
10. Remove upper fan shroud, then the fan.
11. Remove air management valve, then the air pump and upper AIR bracket.
12. Remove fuel line from fuel pump.
13. Remove cylinder head attaching bolts, then the cylinder head. Disconnect wires from rear of head.
14. Reverse procedure to install. Coat cylinder head gasket and bolts with suitable sealant and install bolts finger tight. Torque bolts to specifications in sequence shown in **Fig. 2.**

INTAKE MANIFOLD
REPLACE

1. Disconnect battery ground cable.
2. Remove air cleaner and distributor cap.

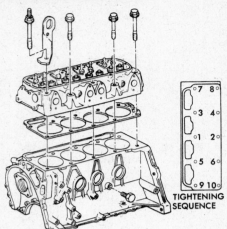

TIGHTENING SEQUENCE

Fig. 2 Cylinder head bolt tightening sequence

3. Raise and support vehicle.
4. Remove middle right bell housing-to-engine block attaching bolt, then move wiring harness aside.
5. Remove distributor hold down nut and clamp, then disconnect primary wires from coil.
6. Remove fuel pump attaching bolts and position pump aside, then lower vehicle.
7. Disconnect accelerator cable, fuel inlet line and any necessary wires and vacuum lines.
8. Remove carburetor, then drain cooling system.
9. Disconnect fuel vapor canister harness lines, **Fig. 1.**
10. Disconnect hoses and wires from manifold.
11. Remove intake manifold attaching bolts, then the manifold.
12. Reverse procedure to install. Clean mating surface and install a new gasket. Torque bolts to specifications.

EXHAUST MANIFOLD
REPLACE

1. Disconnect battery ground cable.
2. Remove air cleaner.
3. Raise and support vehicle.
4. Remove exhaust pipe from manifold.
5. Remove AIR hose and pipe bracket bolt, then the dipstick tube bracket.
6. Remove fuel vapor canister harness pipes, **Fig. 1.**
7. Remove exhaust manifold attaching bolts, then the manifold.
8. Reverse procedure to install. Torque attaching bolts to specifications.

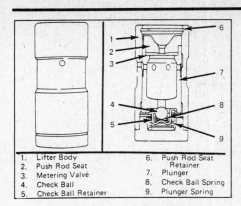

1. Lifter Body	6. Push Rod Seat Retainer
2. Push Rod Seat	7. Plunger
3. Metering Valve	8. Check Ball Spring
4. Check Ball	9. Plunger Spring
5. Check Ball Retainer	

Fig. 3 Sectional view of hydraulic valve lifter

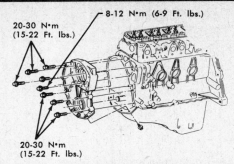

Fig. 4 Engine front cover replacement

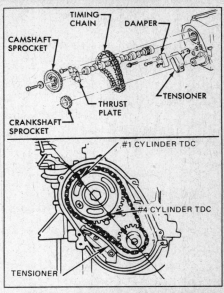

Fig. 5 Valve timing marks

NOTE: If exhaust manifold is being replaced, remove AIR manifold and exhaust manifold seal.

ROCKER ARM STUDS

Rocker arm studs that have stress cracks or damaged threads should be replaced. If threads in cylinder head are damaged, the head can be retapped and a helical type insert installed. When installing a new rocker arm stud, torque stud to 43–49 ft. lbs.

VALVES
ADJUST

1. Crank engine until mark on crankshaft pulley is aligned with "O" mark on timing tab. Check to ensure engine is in the No. 1 cylinder firing position by placing fingers on No. 1 cylinder rocker arms as mark on pulley comes near "O" mark on timing tab. If valves are not moving, the engine is in the No. 1 firing position. If valves are moving, engine is on No. 4 cylinder firing position and should be rotated one revolution to reach the No. 1 cylinder firing position.
2. With engine in No. 1 cylinder firing position, adjust the following valves: exhaust, 1 and 3: intake 1 and 2. To adjust valves, back off adjusting nut until lash is felt at push rod, then tighten nut until all lash is removed. This can be determined by rotating push rod while tightening adjusting nut. When all lash has been removed, turn adjusting nut in an additional 1½ turns.
3. Crank one full revolution until mark on crankshaft pulley and "O" mark are aligned. This is the No. 4 cylinder firing position. With engine in this position, adjust the following valves: exhaust, 2 and 4: intake 3 and 4.
4. Install rocker arm cover, then start engine and check timing and idle speed.

VALVE ARRANGEMENT

E-I-I-E-E-I-I-E

CAMSHAFT LIFT SPECS.

Year	Intake	Exhaust
1983–84	.26	.26

VALVE TIMING
INTAKE OPENS BEFORE TDC

Year	Degrees
1983–84	14

VALVE GUIDES

Valve guides are an integral part of the cylinder head and are not removable. If valve stem clearance becomes excessive, the valve stem guide should be reamed to the next oversize and the appropriate oversize valves installed. Valves are available in .003, .006 and .012 inch oversizes.

VALVE LIFTERS
REPLACE

1. Remove rocker arm cover and push rod.
2. Remove rocker arm studs and push rod guide.
3. Using tool J-29834, or equivalent, remove valve lifter.
4. Reverse procedure to install. Coat foot of valve lifters with Molykote, or equivalent. Following installation, adjust valve as described under "Valves, Adjust".

VALVE LIFTERS
SERVICE

DISASSEMBLY

1. Depress plunger with a push rod, then remove push rod seat retainer using a small screwdriver, **Fig. 3.**
2. Remove push rod seat, metering valve, plunger, ball check valve assembly and plunger spring.
3. Pry ball retainer loose from plunger and remove ball check valve and spring.

CLEANING & INSPECTION

1. Clean all parts in suitable solvent.
2. Inspect all lifter components for wear or damage. If any one part is worn or damaged, that entire assembly must be replaced.
3. If lifter body wall is worn, inspect cylinder block lifter bore.
4. If bottom of lifter is worn, inspect camshaft lobe.
5. If push rod seat is worn, inspect push rod.

ASSEMBLY

1. Position check ball on small hole in bottom of plunger, then install spring and ball retainer.
2. Install plunger spring over ball retainer, then slide lifter body over spring and plunger. Make sure oil holes in lifter body and plunger are aligned.
3. Fill assembly with SAE 10 oil, then depress plunger with a ⅛ inch drift pin. Insert a 1/16 inch drift pin through both oil holes to hold plunger down against spring tension.
4. Remove the ⅛ inch drift pin and refill assembly with SAE 10 oil, then install the metering valve and push rod seat.
5. Install push rod seat retainer, then push down on the push rod seat and remove the 1/16 inch drift pin from oil holes.

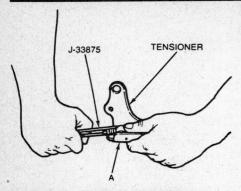

Fig. 6 Compressing timing chain tensioner spring

TIMING CHAIN TENSIONER
REPLACE

1. Remove engine front cover as previously described.
2. Remove tensioner attaching bolts, then the tensioner.
3. To install tensioner, position tangs of tool J-33875 under tensioner sliding blocks, then pull tool to compress tensioner spring.
4. While compressing tensioner spring, insert a cotter pin or other suitable tool into hole "A", **Fig. 6,** to hold spring in the compressed position. Remove tool J-33875 from tensioner.
5. Install tensioner on engine, then remove cotter pin holding spring in the compressed position.

CAMSHAFT
REPLACE

1. Remove rocker arm cover, then the timing chain and camshaft sprocket as previously described.
2. Drain cooling system, then remove radiator.
3. Mark position of rotor to distributor body for assembly reference.
4. Raise and support vehicle.
5. Remove fuel pump, then the distributor hold down nut and clamp.
6. Lower vehicle, then remove distributor.
7. Remove rocker arm studs and push rod guides.
8. Remove valve lifter, then the camshaft.
9. Reverse procedure to install. Align timing marks on crankshaft and camshaft sprockets, **Fig. 5.**

PISTONS & RODS
ASSEMBLE

Install piston to rod with notch and hole on piston facing toward front of engine, **Fig. 7.**

MAIN & ROD BEARINGS

Main bearings are available in standard size and undersizes of .016 and .032 inch. Connecting rod bearings are available in standard size and undersizes of .005 and .010 inch.

OIL PAN
REPLACE

4 × 2

1. Remove engine as described under "Engine, Replace".
2. Drain engine oil, then remove oil pan

ENGINE FRONT COVER
REPLACE

1. Disconnect battery ground cable.
2. Drain cooling system.
3. Remove upper fan shroud, accessory drive belts, fan and pulley.
4. Remove radiator and heater hoses.
5. Remove water pump as described under "Water Pump, Replace."
6. Remove crankshaft pulley retaining bolts, then the pulley.
7. Remove crankshaft hub using tool J-24420, or equivalent.
8. Remove front cover attaching bolts, then the front cover, **Fig. 4.**
9. Reverse procedure to install. Apply a continuous bead of sealant 1052357, or equivalent to front cover sealing surface and 1052366, or equivalent to oil pan surface of front cover.

TIMING CHAIN
REPLACE

1. Remove engine front cover as previously described.
2. Align timing marks on camshaft and crankshaft sprockets, then remove timing chain tensioner as described under "Timing Chain Tensioner, Replace".
3. Remove camshaft sprocket and timing chain, **Fig. 5.**
4. If crankshaft sprocket is to be replaced, remove sprocket using a suitable puller.
5. Reverse procedure to install. Note the following:
   a. Lubricate thrust surface of sprockets with Molykote, or equivalent.
   b. Align timing marks on sprockets.
   c. Align dowel in camshaft with dowel hole in camshaft sprocket.
   d. Lubricate timing chain with clean engine oil.
   e. Torque camshaft sprocket attaching bolts to 66–88 ft. lbs.

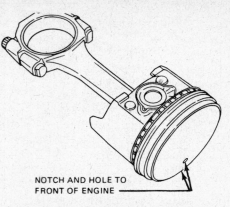

NOTCH AND HOLE TO FRONT OF ENGINE —

Fig. 7 Piston & rod assembly

attaching bolts and the oil pan.
3. Reverse procedure to install. Also, refer to step 12 under 4 × 4 oil pan replacement procedure.

4 × 4

1. Disconnect battery ground cable.
2. Remove starter motor front brace bolt.
3. Remove engine mount through bolts.
4. Raise and support vehicle.
5. Remove splash shield, then the brake and fuel line clip retaining bolts.
6. Remove crossmember attaching bolts, then the crossmember.
7. Drain crankcase, then remove starter motor and position aside.
8. Disconnect steering damper from frame.
9. Mark location of pitman arm, then disconnect pitman arm and steering gear from frame.
10. Disconnect front axle from frame, then the front propeller shaft from front differential. Slide differential forward.
11. Remove oil pan attaching bolts, then raise engine slightly and remove the oil pan.
12. Reverse procedure to install. Note the following:
    a. Apply a thin coat of RTV sealant to both ends of new rear oil pan seal prior to installing seal in rear main bearing cap. The sealant must not extend beyond tabs of seal.
    b. Apply a continuous bead of RTV sealant on oil pan side rails. The bead of sealant should circle inboard at each bolt hole location.
    c. Do not apply sealant to rear oil pan seal mating surface.
    d. Apply RTV sealant to oil pan-to-front cover mating surface. This sealant must meet the two side rail beads.
    e. Torque oil pan-to-cover bolts to 6–9 ft. lbs., oil pan-to-side rail bolts to 4–9 ft. lbs. and oil pan-to-rear rail bolts to 11–17 ft. lbs. All bolts must be torqued before sealant dries.

OIL PUMP SERVICE
REMOVAL

1. Drain crankcase, then remove oil pan as previously described.

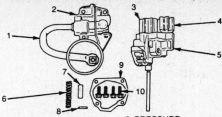

1. PICK UP TUBE AND SCREEN.
2. PUMP COVER.
3. DRIVE GEAR AND SHAFT.
4. IDLER GEAR.
5. PUMP BODY.
6. PRESSURE REGULATOR SPRING.
7. PRESSURE REGULATOR VALVE.
8. RETAINING PIN.
9. GASKET.
10. ATTACHING BOLTS.

Fig. 8 Oil pump assembly

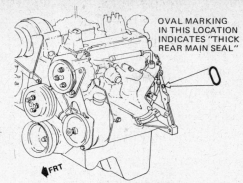

OVAL MARKING IN THIS LOCATION INDICATES "THICK REAR MAIN SEAL"

Fig. 9 Rear main oil seal installation. 1983 & early production 1984

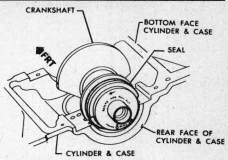

CRANKSHAFT
BOTTOM FACE CYLINDER & CASE
SEAL
REAR FACE OF CYLINDER & CASE
CYLINDER & CASE

CAUTION RETAINER SPRING SIDE OF SEAL MUST FACE TOWARD FRONT OF CYLINDER & CASE.

Fig. 10 Rear main seal identification stamping

2. Remove pump to rear main bearing attaching bolt, then remove pump and extension shaft.

DISASSEMBLE

1. Remove four pump cover to body attaching bolts, then remove cover, idler and drive gears and shaft, **Fig. 8.**

NOTE: Place alignment marks on oil pump drive and idler gear teeth so they can be installed in the same position.

2. Remove pressure regulator valve retaining pin, spring and the valve from pump body.

INSPECTION

Inspect pump components and should any of the following conditions exist, the oil pump assembly should be replaced.
1. Inspect pump body, gears and cover for cracks or excessive wear.
2. Check drive gear shaft for looseness in housing.
3. Check inside of pump cover for wear that would allow oil to leak past ends of gears.
4. Check oil pickup screen assembly for damage to screen or pickup tube.
5. Check pressure regulator valve for fit in pump body.

ASSEMBLE

1. Install a replacement pickup screen and tube assembly, if removed. Position pump in a soft jawed vise then apply sealer to end of tube and tap into position using tool No. J8369 and a plastic hammer. Use care not to damage inlet screen and tube assembly when installing on pump housing.
2. Place pressure regulator valve, spring and retaining pin into pump body, then install drive gear and shaft.
3. Install idler gear into pump body, then the pump cover gasket, **Fig. 8.**
4. Install pump cover and cover retaining bolts, then torque bolts to 6–9 ft. lbs.

INSTALLATION

1. Align oil pump extension shaft to distributor drive gear socket and pump housing with dowels on cap, then install shaft retainer and pump assembly.
2. Install oil pump assembly retaining bolt to rear main bearing cap and torque bolt to 26–38 ft. lbs.
3. Install oil pan as previously described.

REAR MAIN BEARING OIL SEAL
REPLACE

SERVICE BULLETIN A new, one piece, rear crankshaft oil seal has been introduced for 1984 4-121 engines. As this new seal has been proven effective in correcting rear main seal oil leaks, this seal should be used to replace the two piece seal on 1983 4-121 engines. Use of the two piece seal should be discontinued when servicing these engines.

Early production 4-121 engines installed in 1984 vehicles were assembled with a thin, one piece rear main oil seal, service P/N 14081761, which is also suitable for installation in 4-121 engines used in 1983 vehicles. Beginning with December 1983 production, 4-121 engines are equipped with a thick one piece seal, service P/N 14085829. As these seals are not interchangeable, 4-121 engines installed in 1984 vehicles must be inspected for an identification mark stamped on the left rear engine block boss, **Fig. 9.** Engines without an oval stamping in this area must be serviced with the thin, one piece seal, while engines with an oval stamping in this area must be serviced with the thick seal. Service replacement procedures for the two types of rear main oil seals are outlined below.

1983 & EARLY PRODUCTION 1984

1. Drain cooling and lubrication systems,

then remove engine assembly.
2. Install engine in suitable engine stand in inverted position, then remove oil pan and oil pump.
3. Remove timing chain. Refer to "Timing Chain, Replace" for procedure.
4. Rotate crankshaft to horizontal position, then remove connecting rod bearing nuts, caps and bearings.

NOTE: Keep nuts, caps and bearings in order so they can be installed in their original positions.

5. Remove main bearing bolts, caps and bearings, then the crankshaft.

NOTE: Keep bolts, caps and bearings in order so they can be installed in their original positions.

6. Remove old seal and sealant from cylinder block grooves and rear main cap grooves.
7. Clean excess sealant from crankshaft using suitable solvent.
8. Apply a light coating of sealant 1052357 or equivalent to outside diameter of seal included in kit 14081761.
9. Place seal tool assembly on rear area of crankshaft, then position tool so arrow points towards cylinders and crankcase, **Fig. 10.**
10. Install crankshaft in engine with tool installed, then remove tool and discard.
11. Lightly lubricate crankshaft journals.
12. Seal rear main bearing split-line surface with sealant 1052357 or equivalent, then install rear main bearing and cap.
13. Install remaining main bearings, caps and bolts. Torque to specifications.
14. Install connecting rod bearings, caps and bolts. Torque to specifications.
15. Install oil pump.
16. Install timing chain.
17. Install oil pan, then the engine assembly.

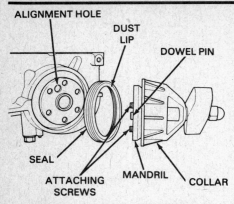

Fig. 11 Rear main oil seal installation. Late production 1984

ALIGNMENT HOLE
DUST LIP
DOWEL PIN
SEAL
ATTACHING SCREWS
MANDRIL
COLLAR

5. Lubricate seal lip and bore contact surface with engine oil, then slide seal onto mandril of J-34686 until dust lip is bottomed against collar of tool, **Fig. 11.**
6. Align dowel pin on tool with dowel pin hole in crankshaft, then mount tool on shaft and tighten bolts hand tight (2–4 ft. lbs.).
7. Rotate "T" handle of tool clockwise to press seal into place, turning handle until collar is tight against case to ensure that seal is seated.
8. Rotate "T" handle of tool counter-clockwise to stop to set collar in proper position for next repair, then remove tool from crankshaft.
9. Inspect seal ensuring that seal is seated squarely in bore.
10. Reverse remaining procedure to complete installation.

LATE PRODUCTION 1984

1. Disconnect battery ground cable, raise and support vehicle, and place suitable support under engine.
2. Remove transmission assembly, clutch assembly if equipped, and flywheel or flex plate.
3. Insert screwdriver or suitable puller through dust lip of seal and pull seal from cavity, taking care not to mar crankshaft.
4. Inspect seal bore and crankshaft surface for nicks, burrs and excessive wear, and correct as needed.

WATER PUMP
REPLACE

1. Disconnect battery ground cable.
2. Remove accessory drive belts.
3. Remove upper fan shroud, then drain cooling system.
4. Remove radiator and heater hoses.
5. Remove water pump attaching bolts, then the water pump, **Fig. 12.**
6. Reverse procedure to install. Apply a narrow bead of sealant 10523357, or equivalent to sealing surfaces. Torque attaching bolts to 15–22 ft. lbs.

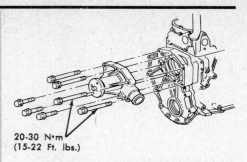

20-30 N·m (15-22 Ft. lbs.)

Fig. 12 Water pump replacement

BELT TENSION DATA

	New Lbs.	Used Lbs.
Air Cond.	145	65–100
Alternator	130	50–80
Power Steer.	130	50–80
Air Pump	130	50–80

FUEL PUMP
REPLACE

1. Disconnect battery ground cable.
2. Remove distributor, then disconnect inlet and outlet lines from fuel pump.
3. Remove engine lift hook, then the fuel pump attaching bolts and fuel pump.
4. Reverse procedure to install. Install pump with camshaft on down stroke.
5. Adjust timing and check for fuel leaks.

4-151 Gasoline Engine Section

ENGINE
REPLACE

1. Disconnect battery ground cable, mark position of hood hinges and remove hood.
2. Disconnect power steering reservoir from fan shroud, then remove upper shroud and fan.
3. Drain coolant, then disconnect radiator hoses and overflow hose from radiator.
4. Disconnect transmission cooling lines from radiator, if equipped, then plug lines.
5. Remove radiator.
6. Remove A/C compressor and power steering pump from brackets and secure aside.
7. Remove air cleaner and disconnect fuel line bracket by filter.
8. Disconnect fuel lines and vacuum hoses, accelerator cable, and TV and cruise control cables, as equipped, then secure aside.

CAUTION: To reduce risk of fire and injury, it is necessary to allow fuel system pressure to bleed off prior to disconnecting lines.

9. Disconnect heater hoses from engine.
10. Disconnect electrical connector to oxygen sensor and other engine mounted components, release engine harness from retainers and secure harness aside.
11. Raise and support vehicle.
12. On 2 wheel drive models, disconnect strut rods.
13. On 4 wheel drive models, proceed as follows:
    a. Remove clips securing brake lines to crossmember, then the crossmember.
    b. Disconnect transmission cooler lines at flywheel cover, if equipped.
    c. Disconnect propeller shaft at front axle.
14. On all models, disconnect exhaust pipe at converter hanger and manifold, and secure aside.
15. Remove flywheel cover and drive belt splash shield, as equipped.
16. Remove starter motor.
17. Remove bolts securing torque converter to flex plate if equipped.
18. Remove 2 outer (left side) air dam bolts and the lower fan shroud.

19. Remove left body mount bolts, then position suitable jacks under body.
20. Carefully raise body and insert suitable block of wood between body and frame.
21. Remove upper bell housing to engine bolts, then lower body onto block of wood.
22. Remove remaining bell housing to engine bolts and motor mount through bolts, then lower vehicle.
23. Place suitable support under transmission and attach suitable lifting equipment to engine.
24. Raise engine and disconnect remaining wires, wire loom brackets at side cover and rear of head, and ground straps.
25. Separate engine from transmission and remove engine assembly from vehicle.
26. Reverse procedure to install.

ENGINE MOUNTS
REPLACE

FRONT MOUNTS

1. Disconnect battery ground cable, then

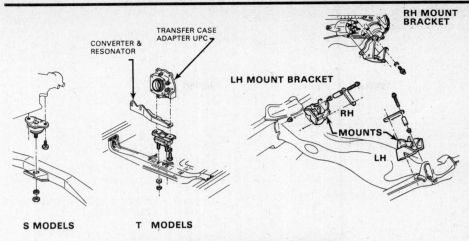

Fig. 1 Engine mount installation

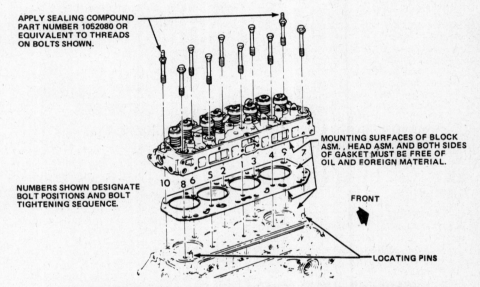

APPLY SEALING COMPOUND PART NUMBER 1052080 OR EQUIVALENT TO THREADS ON BOLTS SHOWN.

MOUNTING SURFACES OF BLOCK ASM., HEAD ASM. AND BOTH SIDES OF GASKET MUST BE FREE OF OIL AND FOREIGN MATERIAL.

NUMBERS SHOWN DESIGNATE BOLT POSITIONS AND BOLT TIGHTENING SEQUENCE.

FRONT

LOCATING PINS

Fig. 2 Cylinder head installation & bolt torque sequence

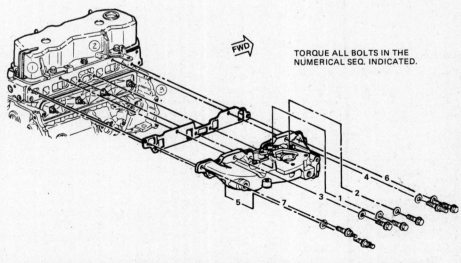

FWD

TORQUE ALL BOLTS IN THE NUMERICAL SEQ. INDICATED.

Fig. 3 Intake manifold installation & bolt torque sequence

raise and support vehicle.
2. Remove mount center bolt(s), then raise and support engine to take weight off mount.
3. Remove mount retaining nuts from underside of crossmember, then remove mount, bolts and spacers, **Fig. 1.**
4. Reverse procedure to install.

REAR MOUNT

1. Raise and support vehicle.
2. Remove nut(s) securing mount to crossmember, **Fig. 1,** then raise and support rear of transmission to take weight off mount.
3. Remove bolts securing mount to transmission tail housing, then the mount.
4. Reverse procedure to install ensuring that converter bracket, if equipped, is properly positioned.

CYLINDER HEAD
REPLACE

1. Disconnect battery ground cable, drain cooling system and remove air cleaner.
2. Remove A/C compressor, if equipped, and secure aside.
3. Disconnect wires from spark plugs and disconnect PCV hose and plug wires from rocker cover.
4. Remove EGR valve.
5. Disconnect vacuum line hold down at thermostat housing and vacuum hoses from throttle body and studs on intake manifold.
6. Remove bolts securing rocker cover and the cover.
7. Disconnect necessary electrical connectors and harness clips, and secure wiring harness aside.
8. Disconnect accelerator, TV and cruise control cables, as equipped, from throttle levers and brackets.
9. Disconnect bypass and heater hoses from intake manifold, and remove upper radiator hose.
10. Remove alternator brace and A/C compressor bracket, disconnect A/C line hold down, then remove alternator and secure aside.
11. Disconnect exhaust pipe from manifold.
12. Disconnect fuel line bracket near filter and remove dipstick tube.
13. Disconnect fuel and vacuum hoses at fuel filter.

CAUTION: To avoid possibility of fire or injury, allow fuel system pressure to bleed off before servicing fuel system components.

14. Remove cylinder head bolts, noting position for installation.
15. Disconnect harness bracket and ground from rear of head and remove coil bracket.
16. Remove brace between engine block and intake manifold.

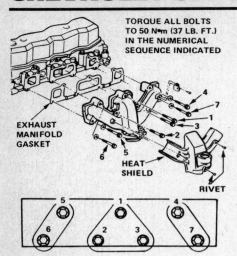

TORQUE ALL BOLTS TO 50 N·m (37 LB. FT.) IN THE NUMERICAL SEQUENCE INDICATED

EXHAUST MANIFOLD GASKET

HEAT SHIELD

RIVET

BOLT LOCATIONS

Fig. 4   Exhaust manifold installation & bolt torque sequence

17. Remove rocker arms and pushrods, keeping components in order for assembly.
18. Remove cylinder head as an assembly with intake and exhaust manifolds.
19. Thoroughly clean gasket from head and block mating surfaces.
20. Install new head gasket, then the cylinder head, ensuring that both gasket and head are seated over dowel pins in block.
21. Clean threads of head bolts, coat threads with suitable sealing compound, then install head bolts finger tight.
22. Gradually torque head bolts to specified torque in sequence shown in **Fig. 2,** then reverse remaining steps to complete installation.

INTAKE MANIFOLD
REPLACE

1. Disconnect battery ground cable,

drain cooling system and remove air cleaner.
2. Disconnect necessary electrical connectors from injector assembly, sensors and solenoids.
3. Disconnect accelerator, TV and cruise control cables, as equipped.
4. Disconnect fuel and vacuum pipes at injector and manifold.

CAUTION: To prevent possibility of fire or injury, allow fuel system pressure to bleed off before servicing fuel system components.

5. Disconnect bypass and heater hoses from manifold.
6. Remove alternator rear adjusting bracket, then disconnect alternator brace and position aside.
7. Disconnect necessary vacuum hoses and remove vacuum pipe from brace at thermostat housing.
8. Disconnect coil from manifold.
9. Remove manifold retaining bolts then the manifold and gasket.
10. Ensure that manifold and cylinder head mating surfaces are clean, position new gasket and manifold on head, then install retaining bolts hand tight.
11. Torque intake manifold bolts to specifications in sequence shown in **Fig. 3.**
12. Reverse remaining procedure to complete installation.

EXHAUST MANIFOLD
REPLACE

1. Disconnect battery ground cable.
2. Release A/C compressor belt tension, remove compressor from bracket and secure aside, then remove rear adjusting bracket.
3. Raise and support vehicle, disconnect exhaust pipe from manifold, then lower vehicle.
4. Remove air cleaner and disconnect electrical connector to oxygen sensor.
5. Remove exhaust manifold bolts and the manifold.

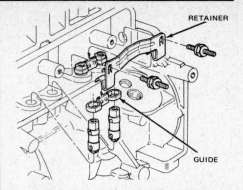

RETAINER

GUIDE

Fig. 5   Lifter & guide plate installation

6. Position new gasket and manifold on cylinder head, then install bolts hand tight.
7. Torque exhaust manifold bolts to specifications in sequence shown in **Fig. 4.**
8. Reverse remaining procedure to complete installation.

HYDRAULIC ROLLER VALVE LIFTERS
LIFTERS, REPLACE

1. Remove rocker and side covers.
2. Loosen rocker arms and remove pushrods, noting position for installation.
3. Remove guide plate and clamp, **Fig. 5,** then the lifter.
4. Reverse procedure to install, torquing side cover nuts to 90 inch lbs.

SERVICE
Disassembly

1. Depress pushrod seat with push rod, remove seat retainer, **Fig. 6,** then slowly release spring tension.
2. Remove pushrod seat and metering valve.
3. Invert lifter and tap on flat surface to remove plunger.

NOTE: If plunger cannot be removed, clean with suitable solvent and repeat step 3. Tool BT-6438 or equivalent can also be used to remove plunger.

4. Remove ball check valve assembly using small screwdriver.
5. Remove plunger spring from lifter body.
6. Clean lifter components in suitable solvent, keeping components for each lifter separate.

Inspection

1. Inspect lifter body for internal and external wear and scuffing, and inspect bottom for wear grooves and flat spots.
2. Inspect roller for free operation, flat spots and pitting. Replace lifter if roller

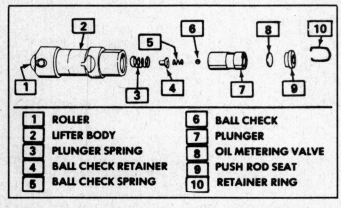

1	ROLLER	**6**	BALL CHECK
2	LIFTER BODY	**7**	PLUNGER
3	PLUNGER SPRING	**8**	OIL METERING VALVE
4	BALL CHECK RETAINER	**9**	PUSH ROD SEAT
5	BALL CHECK SPRING	**10**	RETAINER RING

Fig. 6   Hydraulic roller lifter exploded view

is worn, pitted, or if roller cannot be freed-up.
3. Inspect push rod seat, and replace lifter and push rod if seat is scored or excessively worn.
4. Inspect check ball and replace lifter if ball is pitted or scored.

NOTE: Do not attempt to recondition lifter assembly by interchanging components from other lifters. If components are damaged or worn, lifter assembly should be replaced.

Assembly

NOTE: Ensure that lifter components are kept clean during assembly, as small particles of dirt or lint can cause lifter to fail.

1. Position check ball on small hole in bottom of plunger.
2. Install check ball spring and retainer, **Fig. 6,** over check ball, then press retainer into position in plunger with small screwdriver.
3. Install plunger spring over check ball retainer, align oil holes in lifter body with plunger, then slide body over spring and plunger.
4. Fill lifter with SAE 10 engine oil and proceed as follows:
   a. Using a ⅛ inch drift, press plunger into lifter body until oil holes in plunger and body are aligned.
   b. Insert 1/16 inch pin through oil holes to lock plunger into body.
   c. Remove ⅛ inch drift and fill lifter with SAE 10 engine oil.
5. Install metering valve, push rod seat and seat retainer.
6. Depress push rod seat to relieve spring tension, then remove 1/16 inch pin holding plunger.

NOISE DIAGNOSIS

Momentary Noise When Engine Is Started

Condition normal. Oil drains from lifters which are holding valves open when engine is not running.

Intermittent Noise At Idle, Disappears As Engine Speed Is Increased

1. Dirt in lifter.
2. Pitted check ball.

Noise At Slow Idle Or With Hot Oil; Quiet With Cold Oil Or Increased Engine Speed

1. Excessive lifter leak down, lifter should be replaced.

Noise At Idle, Becomes Louder As Engine Speed Increased To 1500 RPM

1. Excessive valve stem to guide clearance.
2. Off square valve spring.
3. Scuffed or worn valve tip/rocker arm pad.
4. Excessive valve seat or face runout.
5. Damper spring clicking on rotator.

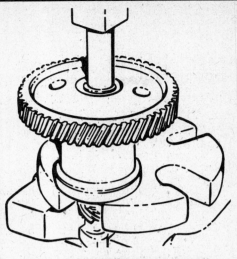

Fig. 7 Camshaft timing gear removal

Valves Noisy At All Speeds

1. Rotate crankshaft until piston of affected cylinder is at TDC of firing stroke.
2. Hold rocker arm against valve spring and check for valve lash by moving push rod up and down.
3. If no lash is present, check for dirt in lifter or pitted check ball.
4. If valve lash is present, inspect push rod and rocker arm for excessive wear and replace as needed.
5. If valve lash is present, and push rod and rocker arm are satisfactory, lifter should be replaced.

Quiet At Low Speeds, Noisy At High Speeds

1. Incorrect oil level, oil foaming.
2. Clogged oil pump screen, bent pan or oil pump pickup.
3. Incorrect oil pressure.

VALVE GUIDES

Measure valve stem diameter in 3 places, top, center and bottom, noting that exhaust valve stems are approximately .001 inch larger at top of stem than at the bottom. Measure valve guide bore with suitable gauge and compare with valve stem diameter to obtain clearance. If clearance is not within specifications, replace valves and/or ream valve guide bores as needed. Valves are available in standard size and .003 inch and .005 inch oversize.

VALVE ARRANGEMENT

I-E-I-E-E-I-E-I

VALVE LIFT SPECS

CAMSHAFT LOBE LIFT (INCH)

Year	Engine	Intake	Exhaust
1985	4-151	.398	.398

ROCKER ARM RATIO

Year	Engine	Intake	Exhaust
1985	4-151	1.175:1	1.175:1

CAMSHAFT & TIMING GEARS
REPLACE
REMOVAL

1. Disconnect battery ground cable and drain cooling system.
2. Remove side cover as outlined.
3. Disconnect power steering reservoir and set aside, then remove upper fan shroud, drive belts, fan and pulley.
4. Remove crankshaft pulley and hub.
5. Remove front cover.
6. Rotate crankshaft until timing marks on crank and camshaft timing gears are aligned.
7. Remove distributor cap and plug wire assembly, mark position of rotor and distributor body, disconnect electrical connectors and remove distributor.
8. Remove oil pump driveshaft cover and driveshaft.
9. Remove air cleaner and EGR valve.
10. Disconnect vacuum hoses at intake manifold and thermostat housing, then remove rocker cover.
11. Remove valve lifters as outlined.
12. Disconnect hoses and transmission cooler lines from radiator, as equipped, plug cooler lines, then remove radiator.
12. On models equipped with A/C, proceed as follows:
   a. Remove A/C condenser baffles.
   b. Remove condenser mounting bolts, raise condenser to provide clearance for camshaft removal and block in position.

NOTE: Care must be taken not to bend or twist condenser fittings when repositioning condenser.

13. On all models, remove headlamp bezel, grille and bumper filler panel.
14. Remove bolts securing camshaft thrust plate, then withdraw camshaft from engine, taking care not to damage cam bearings.
15. Inspect timing gear on crankshaft and replace as needed.

CAMSHAFT DISASSEMBLY

1. Position adapter J-971 or equivalent on suitable press.
2. Insert camshaft through adapter with timing gear facing up, **Fig. 7.**
3. Secure adapter in press, then press shaft out of gear using suitable spacer.

NOTE: Align thrust plate so that plate is not damaged by woodruff key as camshaft is pressed out of gear.

CAMSHAFT ASSEMBLY

1. Support rear of front camshaft journal

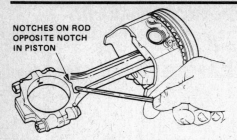

Fig. 8 Piston & connecting rod assembly

in press using suitable adapters.
2. Install gear spacer ring and thrust plate/retainer over end of camshaft, then seat woodruff key in shaft keyway.
3. Mount timing gear on shaft ensuring that keyway is aligned with woodruff key, then press gear onto shaft until it bottoms against spacer ring.
4. Measure clearance between thrust plate and front camshaft journal. If clearance is not .0015–.005 inch, thrust plate should be replaced.

INSTALLATION

1. Coat camshaft journals and lobes with suitable assembly lubricant.
2. Insert camshaft into bearing bores, taking care not to damage bearings.
3. Rotate crankshaft and/or camshaft as needed to ensure that stamped timing marks are aligned when camshaft is fully seated in block.
4. Install thrust plate/retainer bolts, and torque bolts to 75 inch lbs.
5. Align and install front cover assembly as outlined in "Front Cover, Replace."
6. Reverse remaining procedure to complete installation.

NOTE: With cam and crankshaft timing gear marks aligned, engine should be in number 4 cylinder firing position and distributor can be indexed to marks made during removal procedure. However, if crankshaft is rotated during reassembly, rotate crankshaft until engine is in firing position for number 1 cylinder, with timing mark on balancer indexed at TDC on timing pad, then install distributor with body in original position but with rotor arm pointing toward number 1 cylinder spark plug contact in cap.

PISTON & ROD
ASSEMBLY

There are 2 notches in the piston crown. When assembling pistons onto connecting rods, position rod so that raised notch side of rod at bearing end, **Fig. 8,** is opposite notch in piston crown. Install piston and rod assemblies in engine block with notches in piston crowns facing front of engine. After installation, check connecting rod side

clearance. If clearance is not .006–.022 inch, connecting rod should be replaced.

SIDE COVER
REPLACE

1. Disconnect battery ground cable and drain cooling system.
2. Remove alternator and bracket and secure alternator aside.
3. Remove brace between intake and exhaust manifold.
4. Disconnect lower radiator and heater hoses.
5. Remove oil pressure sending unit and disconnect wiring harness brackets from side cover.
6. Remove side cover retaining nuts and the cover.
7. Ensure that old sealant is removed from cover and block mating surfaces, then apply a continuous bead of RTV sealant, 3/16 inch wide, to cover sealing surface.
8. Install side cover and torque retaining nuts to 90 inch lbs., then reverse remaining procedure to complete installation.

FRONT COVER
REPLACE

1. Disconnect battery ground cable.
2. Disconnect power steering pump reservoir from fan shroud and position aside.
3. Release drive belt tension, then remove upper fan shroud, fan and water pump pulley.
4. Remove alternator, brackets, brace and front bracket.
5. Remove crankshaft pulley, hub bolt and the hub.
6. Loosen lower radiator hose clamp at water pump and reposition as needed.
7. Remove front cover bolts and the front cover.
8. Thoroughly clean front cover and block sealing surfaces, then apply a continuous bead of RTV sealer, 3/16 inch wide, to cover sealing surface and oil pan joint.
9. Position centering tool J-34995 or equivalent in front cover seal, mount front cover on block, **Fig. 9,** then install and partially tighten 2 oil pan to front cover bolts.
10. Torque front cover to engine block bolts to 90 inch lbs. and oil pan to front cover bolts to 75 inch lbs., then remove centering tool.
11. Reverse remaining procedure to complete installation.

FRONT OIL SEAL
REPLACE

1. Remove drive belts.
2. Remove center bolt, then slide hub and pulleys off crankshaft.

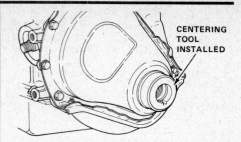

Fig. 9 Engine front cover installation

3. Carefully pry seal from front cover, taking care not to damage or distort cover.
4. Install seal with helical lip toward rear of engine, using J-23042 or equivalent to seat seal in cover.
5. Coat seal lip with clean engine oil, then reverse remaining procedure to complete installation.

REAR MAIN BEARING OIL SEAL
REPLACE

1. Raise and support vehicle and place suitable supports under engine.
2. Remove transmission assembly.
3. Remove clutch and pressure plate, if equipped, then the flywheel or flex plate.
4. Pry seal from bore with suitable tool, taking care not to mar crankshaft.
5. Thoroughly clean seal bore in block, inspect bore and crankshaft surface for nicks, burrs and wear, and correct as needed.
6. Apply light coat of clean engine oil to inner and outer surfaces of seal, install seal using J-34924 or equivalent, then reverse remaining procedure to complete installation.

OIL PAN
REPLACE

TWO WHEEL DRIVE MODELS

1. Disconnect battery ground cable, raise and support vehicle, and drain oil pan.
2. Remove strut rods.
3. Disconnect exhaust pipe at converter bracket and manifold and secure aside.
4. Remove flywheel dust cover.
5. Disconnect starter brace from engine block and remove starter motor.
6. Disconnect transmission cooler lines, if equipped, and plug lines and open fittings.
7. Remove oil pan bolts and the oil pan.
8. Thoroughly clean oil pan and block mating surfaces, ensuring that sealer is removed from pan bolt holes.

9. Apply a continuous bead of RTV sealer, ³⁄₁₆ inch wide, to entire pan sealing surface.
10. Install oil pan, torque retaining bolts to 75 inch lbs. and reverse remaining procedure to complete installation.

FOUR WHEEL DRIVE MODELS

1. Disconnect battery ground cable.
2. Disconnect power steering pump reservoir from upper fan shroud, secure reservoir aside and remove upper shroud.
3. Remove dipstick.
4. Raise and support vehicle and drain oil pan.
5. Disconnect brake line clips from crossmember and remove crossmember.
6. Disconnect cooler lines from transmission, if equipped, then plug lines and open fittings.
7. Disconnect exhaust pipe from manifold.
8. Disconnect catalytic converter hanger, removing one bolt and loosening the other.
9. Remove flywheel cover and driveshaft splash shield.
10. Mark position of idler arm for installation, then remove idler arm retaining bolts.
11. Remove steering gear retaining bolts, then pull gear and linkage forward.
12. Remove differential housing bolts at bracket on right side and at frame on left side, then move housing forward.
13. Remove starter motor bolts, position starter aside and loosen brace.
14. Disconnect front propeller shaft at drive pinion, **Fig. 10.**
15. Remove motor mount through bolts and oil pan retaining bolts.
16. Raise engine to provide clearance, then remove oil pan.
17. Clean pan and block sealing surfaces, ensuring that sealer is removed from pan bolt holes.
18. Apply continuous bead of RTV sealer, ³⁄₁₆ inch wide, to entire sealing surface of pan.
19. Raise engine, position pan on block and secure with bolts, then lower engine.
20. Install remaining pan bolts and torque to 75 inch lbs., then reverse remaining procedure to complete installation.

OIL PUMP SERVICE

REMOVAL

1. Remove oil pan as outlined.
2. Remove bolts securing pump to block and the oil pump and screen assembly.

DISASSEMBLY

1. Remove 4 cover retaining bolts and the cover, **Fig. 10.**
2. Mark position of drive gear and rotor to ensure proper assembly.

1 PUMP BODY	**6** SPRING RETAINER
2 PICKUP TUBE	**7** COVER SCREWS
3 PICKUP SCREW ASSEMBLY	**8** COVER
4 PRESSURE REGULATOR VALVE	**9** IDLER GEAR
5 PRESSURE REGULATOR SPRING	**10** DRIVE GEAR AND SHAFT

Fig. 10   Oil pump exploded view

3. Remove drive gear and rotor from body.
4. Remove pin, spring and pressure regulator valve.

NOTE: Do not remove oil pump pickup and screen assembly. If pickup tube is loose, or if tube or screen are damaged or clogged, oil pump should be replaced.

INSPECTION

1. Inspect pump body for cracks, scoring and excessive wear.
2. Inspect gears for cracks, excessive wear and damage, and check shaft for looseness in housing.
3. Inspect inside of cover for wear and scoring that would allow oil to leak past ends of gears.
4. Check fit of relief valve in bore, checking for looseness or binding.

5. If any components are damaged or excessively worn, or if pickup assembly is loose or damaged, oil pump assembly should be replaced.

ASSEMBLY

1. Insert drive gear shaft through pump housing bore, align matching marks and install idler gear with smooth side toward cover.
2. Install cover and torque retaining screws to 105 inch lbs., then ensure that pump shaft rotates freely.
3. Install regulator valve plunger and spring, compress spring and secure assembly with retaining pin.

INSTALLATION

1. Prime pump with engine oil or pack with petroleum jelly.
2. Align slot in pump shaft with tang on drive shaft.

3. Install pump on block, positioning flange over oil pump driveshaft lower bushing, and torque mounting bolts to 22 ft. lbs.
4. Reinstall oil pan as outlined.

WATER PUMP
REPLACE

1. Disconnect battery ground cable and drain cooling system.
2. Disconnect power steering pump reservoir from upper fan shroud and remove upper shroud.
3. Remove necessary drive belts, fan and pulley.
4. Disconnect radiator and heater hose and position aside.
5. Remove bolts securing pump and the pump.
6. Thoroughly clean old sealant from block sealing surface, retaining bolts and bolt holes.
7. Apply a continuous bead of RTV sealer, ⅛ inch wide, to pump sealing surface and apply suitable sealer to retaining bolt threads.
8. Install pump, torque retaining bolts to 15 ft. lbs., then reverse remaining procedure to complete installation.

BELT TENSION DATA

	New Lbs.	Used Lbs.
Air Cond.	169	90
Alternator①	169	145
Alternator②	90	67
Power Steer.	146	67
Vac. Pump	146	67

①With A/C. ②Less A/C.

FUEL PUMP
REPLACE

1. Allow fuel system pressure to bleed off through orifice in pressure regulator, disconnect battery ground cable, then raise and support vehicle.
2. Drain fuel tank, support tank and remove bolts securing tank retaining straps, lower tank enough to disconnect ground and harness connectors, then remove tank from under vehicle.
3. Turn fuel sender unit cam lock ring counterclockwise, then lift sending unit/pump assembly from tank.
4. Pull fuel pump up into hose while pulling out from bottom and remove pump from sending unit.
5. Reverse procedure to install, using new O-ring when installing sending unit in tank.

V6-173 Gasoline Engine Section

ENGINE
REPLACE

4 × 2

NOTE: The following is a revised procedure.

1. Disconnect battery ground cable.
2. Scribe reference marks in the hood hinge area, then remove hood.
3. Drain cooling system, then remove radiator hoses, overflow hose, transmission cooler lines (if equipped), upper radiator shroud and radiator.
4. Remove cooling fan, then disconnect heater hoses.
5. Remove air cleaner assembly.
6. Identify, then disconnect vacuum hoses from engine.
7. Disconnect necessary engine wiring from bulkhead.
8. Disconnect throttle linkage as necessary, then remove distributor cap.
9. Raise and support vehicle.
10. Remove converter to exhaust pipe bolts, then disconnect exhaust pipes at manifolds.
11. Remove strut rods at bellhousing (if equipped).
12. Remove flywheel cover bolts, then cover.
13. On models equipped with automatic transmission, remove torque converter bolts.
14. Disconnect shield at rear of catalytic converter, then remove converter hanger.
15. Remove lower radiator fan shroud.
16. Disconnect fuel lines from fuel pump.
17. Remove two outer bolts from front air deflector.
18. Remove left side body mount bolts, then raise body using suitable lifting equipment.
19. Remove bellhousing bolts, then lower body to frame.
20. Remove motor mount through bolts, then lower vehicle.
21. If equipped with A/C or power steering, disconnect A/C compressor and/or power steering pump.
22. Install suitable lifting device on engine.
23. Support transmission with suitable jack.
24. Remove engine assembly.
25. Reverse procedure to install.

4 × 4

Man. Trans.

NOTE: The following is a revised procedure.

1. Disconnect battery ground cable.
2. Scribe reference marks in hood hinge area, then disconnect under hood light and remove hood.
3. Remove air cleaner assembly.
4. Drain cooling system, then remove radiator hoses, overflow hose, upper fan shroud, radiator, cooling fan and fan clutch.
5. Remove A/C compressor (if equipped) and position aside.
6. Remove power steering pump (if equipped) and position aside.
7. Disconnect fuel lines from fuel pump.
8. Identify, then disconnect vacuum hoses from engine.
9. Disconnect throttle linkage as necessary, then remove heater hoses.
10. Disconnect engine wiring harness at bulkhead connector, then the ground strap at bulkhead.
11. On 1982–83 models, disconnect clutch cable, then remove clutch cross shaft. On 1984–85 models, remove hydraulic clutch slave cylinder and position aside.
12. On all models, remove lower radiator fan shroud.
13. Disconnect battery ground cable from engine, then the main feed wire from bulkhead.
14. Remove distributor cap, then the AIR system diverter valve.
15. Remove console cover, shifter boot, transfer case shifter, transmission shift lever and shifter.
16. Raise and support vehicle, then remove front and rear skid plates and front splash shield.
17. Drain transmission and transfer case, then remove rear driveshaft.
18. Disconnect speedometer cable, then the front driveshaft from transfer case.
19. Disconnect shift linkage and vacuum hoses from transfer case.
20. Disconnect parking brake cable, then remove rear mount.
21. Remove catalytic converter bracket, then support transfer case.
22. Remove transfer case to transmission retaining bolts, then the transfer case.
23. Remove transmission crossmember, then disconnect back-up light switch wire and clip.
24. Remove transmission to bell housing retaining bolts, then the transmission.
25. Remove clutch release bearing and inspection cover from bell housing.
26. Remove left hand body mount bolts, then loosen radiator support to frame mount bolt.
27. Raise left side of body using suitable lifting equipment, then install a block of wood between frame and body.
28. On 1982–83 models, disconnect remaining clutch linkage.

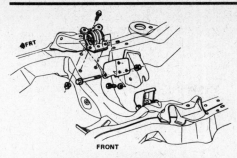

Fig. 1 Engine mount installation

29. On all models, remove bell housing to engine block retaining bolts, then the bell housing.
30. Disconnect exhaust pipes from manifolds, then from the catalytic converter.
31. Remove starter motor.
32. Remove motor mount through bolts.
33. Lower vehicle.
34. Install suitable lifting device on engine.
35. Remove engine assembly.
36. Reverse procedure to install.

Auto. Trans.

NOTE: The following is a revised procedure.

1. Disconnect battery ground cable.
2. Scribe reference marks in the hood hinge area, then disconnect under hood light and remove hood.
3. Raise and support vehicle.
4. Remove front end air dam end bolts.
5. Remove body mount bolts as necessary to enable body to be raised to gain access to top transmission mounting bolts.
6. Remove top transmission mounting bolts, then lower body.
7. Remove remaining transmission mounting bolts, then the second crossmember.
8. Disconnect exhaust pipes at manifolds, then the catalytic converter hanger.
9. Disconnect front driveshaft from differential.
10. Remove torque converter cover bolts, then the cover.
11. Disconnect transmission cooler lines from clips on engine.
12. Remove motor mount through bolts.
13. Remove torque converter to flex plate bolts.
14. Remove front splash shield, then the lower radiator fan shroud mounting bolts.
15. Lower vehicle.
16. Drain cooling system, then remove upper fan shroud, radiator hoses, transmission cooler lines at radiator, radiator and cooling fan.
17. Remove air cleaner assembly.
18. Remove A/C compressor (if equipped) and position aside.
19. Remove power steering pump (if equipped) and position aside.

20. Disconnect fuel lines from fuel pump.
21. Identify, then disconnect all necessary vacuum lines, wires and emission hoses.
22. Disconnect throttle linkage as necessary.
23. Disconnect engine wiring harness at bulkhead.
24. Disconnect heater hoses at engine.
25. Support transmission with suitable jack.
26. Install suitable lifting device on engine.
27. Remove engine assembly.
28. Reverse procedure to install.

ENGINE MOUNTS
REPLACE

1. Disconnect battery ground cable.
2. Remove top half of fan shroud.
3. Raise and support vehicle.
4. Remove mount through bolt, then raise front of engine and remove mount, **Fig. 1.**

NOTE: Do not raise engine any more than is needed to provide sufficient clearance. Also, check for interference between rear of engine and cowl panel which could damage the distributor.

5. Reverse procedure to install.

CYLINDER HEAD
REPLACE

1. Remove intake manifold.
2. Raise and support vehicle.
3. Drain engine block.
4. Disconnect exhaust pipe.
5. If removing left cylinder head, remove dipstick tube attachment.
6. Lower vehicle.
7. If removing right cylinder head, remove alternator bracket.
8. Loosen rocker arm retaining nuts until push rods can be removed.
9. Remove push rods.

NOTE: Keep push rods in order so they can be installed in their original positions.

10. Remove head bolts and cylinder head.

NOTE: The gasket surfaces on both head and cylinder case deck must be clean of any foreign matter and free of nicks or heavy scratches. Cylinder bolt threads in the case and threads on the cylinder head bolts must be clean. Dirt will affect bolt torque.

11. Reverse procedure to install.

NOTE: Coat cylinder head bolt threads with sealer, #1052080 or equivalent, and install bolts. Torque bolts in proper sequence to specifications, **Fig. 2.**

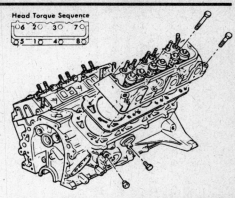

Fig. 2 Cylinder head installation

INTAKE MANIFOLD
REPLACE

1. Disconnect battery ground cable.
2. Remove air cleaner.
3. Drain coolant.
4. Remove wires and hoses at carburetor.
5. Disconnect linkages and fuel line at carburetor.
6. Disconnect linkages and cables.
7. Remove Air Management hose.
8. Disconnect Emission Canister hoses. Remove pipe bracket (front valve cover).
9. Remove left valve cover.
10. Remove Air Management bracket.
11. Remove right valve cover.
12. Remove upper radiator hose.
13. Disconnect heater hose. Remove A/C belt and rotate A/C compressor.
14. Disconnect coolant switches.
15. Remove manifold bolts and nuts.
16. Remove manifold. Discard manifold gaskets and remove loose RTV from front and rear ridges of cylinder case.
17. Reverse procedure to install.

NOTE: Ensure that no oil or water is present on surface when new RTV is applied. Place a (3/16") bead of RTV, #1052366 or equivalent, on each ridge. Install manifold retaining bolts and nuts and torque in the sequence shown in **Fig. 3** to 23 ft. lbs.

EXHAUST MANIFOLDS
REPLACE

1. Disconnect battery ground cable.
2. Raise and support vehicle, then disconnect exhaust pipe.
3. If removing left manifold, remove rear manifold bolts and nut, then lower vehicle. Disconnect air management hoses and wires, remove power steering bracket, if equipped, and remove manifold.
4. If removing right manifold, lower vehicle, remove manifold attaching bolts, disconnect air management hose and remove manifold.
5. Reverse procedure to install.

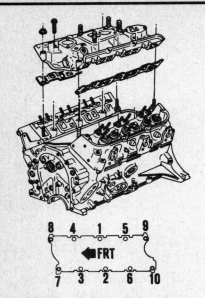

Fig. 3 Intake manifold

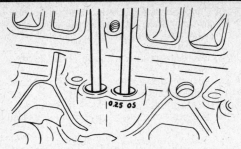

Fig. 4 Oversize valve lifter marking

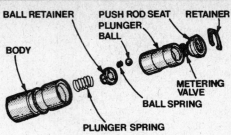

Fig. 5 Hydraulic valve lifter

NOTE: Clean mating surfaces on manifold and head, then install manifold in position and torque manifold bolts to 25 ft. lbs.

ROCKER ARM STUDS

Rocker arm studs that are cracked or have damaged threads can be replaced. If threads in cylinder head are damaged or stripped, the head can be retapped and a helical type insert added. When installing a new rocker arm stud, torque stud to 43 to 53 ft. lbs.

VALVES
ADJUST

1. Crank engine until mark on torsional damper is aligned with TDC mark on timing tab. Check to ensure engine is in the No. 1 cylinder firing position by placing fingers on No. 1 cylinder rocker arms as mark on damper comes near TDC mark on timing tab. If valves are not moving, the engine is in the No. 1 firing position. If valves move as damper mark nears TDC mark on timing tab, engine is in the No. 4 cylinder firing position and should be rotated one revolution to reach the No. 1 cylinder firing position.
2. With engine in the No. 1 cylinder firing position, adjust the following valves: Exhaust- 1, 2, 3; Intake- 1, 5, 6. To adjust valves, back off adjusting nut until lash is felt at push rod, then tighten adjusting nut until all lash is removed. This can be determined by rotating the push rod while tightening the adjusting nut. When all lash has been eliminated, turn adjusting nut the additional number of turns listed in the Valve Specifications.

3. Crank engine one revolution until mark on torsional damper and TDC mark are again aligned. This is the No. 4 cylinder firing position. With engine in this position, the following valve can be adjusted: Exhaust- 4, 5 & 6; Intake- 2, 3 & 4.
4. Install rocker arm covers, then start engine and check timing and idle speed.

VALVE GUIDES

Valve guides are an integral part of the cylinder head and are not removable. If valve stem clearance becomes excessive, the valve stem guide should be reamed to the next oversize and the appropriate oversize valves installed. Valves are available in .0035″, .0155″ and .0305″ oversizes.

VALVE LIFTERS

NOTE: Some engines will be equipped with both standard and .25 mm. oversize valve lifters. The cylinder case will be marked where the oversize valve lifters are installed with a daub of white paint and .25 mm. O.S. will be stamped on the valve lifter boss, **Fig. 4.**

Failure of a hydraulic valve lifter, **Fig. 5,** is generally caused by an inadequate oil supply or dirt. An air leak at the intake side of the oil pump or too much oil in the engine will cause air bubbles in the oil supply to the lifters causing them to collapse. This is a probable cause of trouble if several lifters fail to function, but air in oil is an unlikely cause of failure of a single unit.

Valve lifters can be removed after removing rocker arm covers, intake manifold, rocker arm nuts, rocker arm balls, rocker arms and push rods.

VALVE ARRANGEMENT

E-I-I-E-I-E

VALVE TIMING
INTAKE OPENS BEFORE TDC

Engine	Year	Degrees
V6-173	1982–85	7°

CAMSHAFT LIFT SPECS.

Engine	Year	Intake	Exhaust
V6-173	all	.231	.262

CAMSHAFT
REPLACE

1. Remove valve lifters and engine front cover as described previously.
2. Remove fuel pump and push rod.
3. Remove timing chain and sprocket as described under "Timing Chain, Replace".
4. Withdraw camshaft from engine, using care not to damage camshaft bearings.
5. Reverse procedure to install. When installing timing chain, align valve timing marks as shown in **Fig. 6.**

NOTE: Whenever new camshaft is installed, coat lobes with GM Engine Oil Supplement or equivalent. It is also recommended that valve lifters be replaced to ensure durability of camshaft lobes and lifter feet.

TIMING CHAIN
REPLACE

1. Remove front cover as described under "Front Cover, Replace".
2. Place No. 1 piston at top dead center with marks on camshaft and crankshaft sprockets aligned, **Fig. 6.**
3. Remove camshaft sprocket bolts, then remove sprocket and timing chain. If sprocket does not come off easily, tap lower edge of sprocket with a plastic mallet.

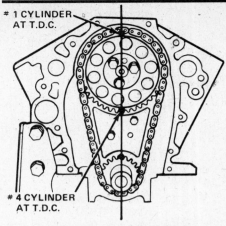

Fig. 6   Valve timing marks

#1 CYLINDER AT T.D.C.

#4 CYLINDER AT T.D.C.

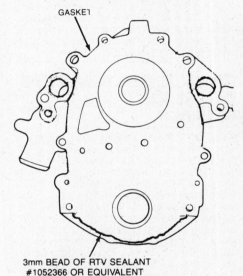

GASKET

3mm BEAD OF RTV SEALANT #1052366 OR EQUIVALENT

Fig. 8   Engine front cover sealant application. 1984 models

4. Install timing chain on camshaft sprocket. Hold sprocket vertically with chain hanging down and align marks on camshaft and crankshaft sprockets.
5. Align dowel pin hole in sprocket with dowel pin on camshaft, then install sprocket on camshaft.
6. Using camshaft sprocket attaching bolts, draw sprocket on camshaft. Torque bolts to 15 to 20 ft. lbs.
7. Lubricate timing chain with engine oil, then install front cover as outlined previously.

FRONT COVER
REPLACE

1. Remove water pump as described under "Water Pump, Replace".
2. If equipped, remove A/C compressor and bracket and position aside.
3. Remove torsional damper, then disconnect lower radiator hose from front cover and the heater hose from water pump.

4. Remove remaining front cover attaching bolts and stud, then the front cover.
5. Reverse procedure to install. On 1982–83 models, clean engine block and front cover mating surfaces of oil, water and old gasket sealer. Apply RTV and anaerobic sealer as shown in **Fig. 7**. On 1984 models, clean engine block and front cover mating surfaces of oil, water and old gasket. Install new gasket and apply RTV sealant as shown in **Fig. 8**.

NOTE: On 1982 models, torque M8 × 1.25 bolts to 13–18 ft. lbs. and M10 × 1.5 bolts to 20–30 ft. lbs. On 1983–84 models, torque front cover bolts to 13–22 ft. lbs. and front cover studs to 19–24 ft. lbs.

PISTONS & RODS
ASSEMBLE

Assemble pistons to connecting rods as shown in **Fig. 9**.

OIL PAN
REPLACE

4 × 2

1. Disconnect battery ground cable.
2. Remove engine as described under "Engine, Replace".
3. Remove oil pan.
4. Reverse procedure to install.

NOTE: Before installing oil pan, thoroughly clean all sealing surfaces, then apply a ⅛ inch bead of RTV sealant, or equivalent, to the entire oil pan sealing flange.

4 × 4

1. Disconnect battery ground cable and remove dipstick.
2. Raise and support vehicle.
3. Remove drive belt splash shield, front axle shield and transfer case shield.
4. Disconnect brake line clips from No. 2 crossmember.
5. On models equipped with automatic transmission, remove catalytic converter hanger bolts, then disconnect exhaust pipe clamp from converter.
6. On models equipped with automatic transmission, disconnect exhaust pipes from manifolds, then slide exhaust rearward.
7. On all models, disconnect front driveshaft from axle drive pinion.
8. Disconnect engine braces from flywheel cover and loosen braces at the block.
9. Remove flywheel cover.
10. Remove starter motor retaining bolts and position starter aside.
11. Disconnect steering shock absorber from frame bracket, then remove steering gear bolts.

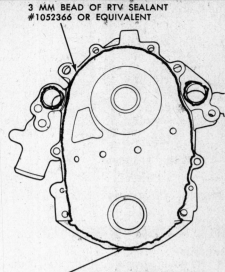

3 MM BEAD OF RTV SEALANT #1052366 OR EQUIVALENT

2 MM DIAMETER BEAD OF ANAEROBIC SEALANT #1052357 OR EQUIVALENT

Fig. 7   Engine front cover sealant application. 1982–83 models

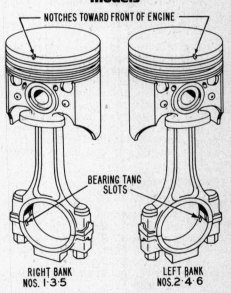

NOTCHES TOWARD FRONT OF ENGINE

BEARING TANG SLOTS

RIGHT BANK NOS. 1·3·5

LEFT BANK NOS. 2·4·6

Fig. 9   Piston and rod assembly

12. Mark position of idler arm for reference during installation, then remove attaching bolts.
13. Pull steering gear and linkage forward, then remove differential housing attaching bolts and move the housing forward.
14. Remove motor mount bolts, then drain oil pan and remove oil pan bolts.
15. Install suitable engine lifting equipment, raise engine and remove oil pan.
16. Reverse procedure to install.

NOTE: Before installing oil pan, thoroughly clean all sealing surfaces, then apply a ⅛ inch bead of RTV sealant, or equivalent to entire oil pan sealing flange.

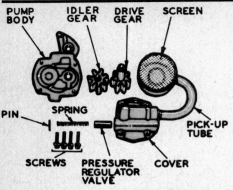

Fig. 10 Oil pump disassembled

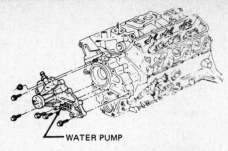

Fig. 11 Water pump removal

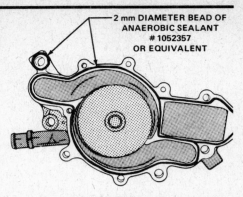

Fig. 12 Water pump sealer application

OIL PUMP SERVICE

Removal
1. Remove oil pan as described under "Oil Pan, Replace".
2. Remove pump to rear main bearing cap bolt and remove pump and extension shaft.

Disassembly
1. Remove pump cover attaching bolts and pump cover, **Fig. 10**.
2. Mark drive and idler gear teeth so they can be installed in the same position, then remove idler and drive gear and shaft from pump body.
3. Remove pin, spring and pressure regulator valve from pump cover.
4. If pick-up tube and screen assembly are to be replaced, mount pump cover in a soft jawed vise and remove pick-up tube from cover. Do not remove screen from pick-up tube, these components are serviced as an assembly.

INSPECTION
1. Inspect pump body and cover for excessive wear and cracks.
2. Inspect pump gear for damage or excessive wear. If pump gears are damaged or worn, the entire pump assembly must be replaced.
3. Check drive gear shaft for looseness in pump body.
4. Inspect pump cover for wear that would allow oil to leak past gear teeth.
5. Inspect pick-up tube and screen assembly for damage.
6. Check pressure regulator valve for fit in pump cover.

ASSEMBLY
1. If pick-up tube and screen were removed, apply sealer to end of pick-up tube, then mount pump cover in a soft jawed vise and using tool No. J-8369, tap pick-up tube into position using a plastic mallet.

NOTE: Whenever the pick-up tube and screen assembly have been removed, a new pick-up tube and screen assembly should be installed. Use care when installing pick-up tube and screen assembly so

that tube does not twist, shear or collapse. Loss of a press fit condition could result in an air leak and a loss of oil pressure.

2. Install pressure regulator valve, spring and pin, **Fig. 10**.
3. Install drive gear and shaft in pump body.
4. Align marks made during disassembly, then install idler gear.
5. Install pump cover gasket, cover and attaching bolts. Torque bolts to 6 to 9 ft. lbs.
6. Rotate pump drive shaft by hand and check pump for smooth operation.

INSTALLATION
1. Assemble pump and extension shaft with retainer to rear main bearing cap, aligning top end of hexagon extension shaft with hexagon socket on lower end of distributor shaft.
2. Install pump to rear main bearing cap bolt.
3. Install oil pan as described under Oil Pan, Replace.

FUEL PUMP
REPLACE
1. Disconnect battery ground cable.
2. Disconnect inlet and outlet hoses from fuel pump.
3. Remove fuel pump attaching bolts, then the fuel pump and gasket.
4. Reverse procedure to install.

NOTE: Before installing pump, rotate camshaft to "down stroke" position. Also, when installation is completed, start engine and check for fuel leaks.

WATER PUMP
REPLACE
1. Disconnect battery ground cable.
2. Drain cooling system then remove the fan and the heater hose and drive belts from the pump.
3. Remove water pump attaching bolts and nut, then the pump, **Fig. 11**.
4. Reverse procedure to install. Torque M6 × 1.0 bolts to 6–9 ft. lbs., M8 × 1.25 bolts to 13–18 ft. lbs. and on 1982 models, M10 × 1.5 bolts to 20–30 ft. lbs.

NOTE: Prior to installing water pump, thoroughly clean sealing surfaces, then apply a 3/32 inch bead of sealant 1052357, or equivalent, to the pump sealing surface, **Fig. 12**. Also, coat bolt threads with sealant 1052080, or equivalent.

REAR MAIN BEARING OIL SEAL
REPLACE

SERVICE BULLETIN When rear main oil seal replacement is required on 1982–84 models with V6-173 engines, the existing seal should be replaced with the thin, one piece, lip type seal used on early production engines installed in 1985 models. This seal, available as kit P/N 14081761, should be used to replace the rope type seal used on early production engines and the two piece rubber seal released for service on 1982–84 models, both for oil leak correction and during engine service. In addition, a redesigned crankshaft has been recommended for use on 1982–84 engines where installation of the one piece seal alone does not correct oil leakage at the rear main seal. This new crankshaft, P/N 14089826, has had the knurling removed from the rear seal area to improve sealing and oil retention.

On V6-173 engines installed in 1985 models, early production engines use the lip seal designated for service on 1982–84 engines (P/N 14081761, thin seal), while late production engines have been modified to use a thicker lip type seal. Models that use the thin type rear seal require engine and crankshaft removal for seal replacement, while later production 1985 models do not require that the crankshaft be removed for seal replacement.

1982–84 & Early Production 1985 (Thin Seal)
1. Remove engine as outlined previously.
2. Remove clutch assembly, if equipped, and flywheel or flex plate, drain engine oil and mount engine in suitable holding fixture.
3. Remove crankshaft as follows:
   a. Remove spark plugs, crankshaft pulley and damper.

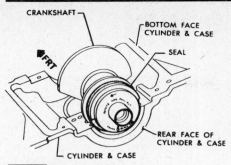

CAUTION RETAINER SPRING SIDE OF SEAL MUST FACE TOWARD FRONT OF CYLINDER & CASE.

Fig. 13   Rear main oil seal installation. 1982–84 & early production 1985 (thin seal)

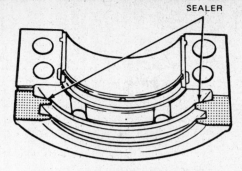

Fig. 14   Sealing rear main bearing cap

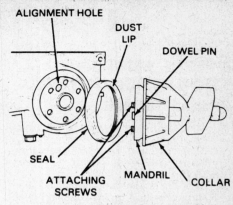

Fig. 15   Rear main oil seal installation. Late production 1985 (thick seal)

b. Remove oil pan and oil pump.
c. Remove water pump, front cover, camshaft sprocket and timing chain, referring to "Timing Chain, Replace" procedure.
d. Note position of connecting rod caps, remove caps and place in order for assembly, then push pistons to tops of bores, taking care not to mar crankshaft.
e. Note installation position of main bearing caps, loosen main bearing bolts and remove main caps, keeping them in order for assembly.
f. Lift crankshaft from block and set aside, taking care not to damage bearing surfaces.
4. Remove old oil seal and clean all sealant and foreign material from seal groove, engine case and bearing cap, and crankshaft sealing surface.
5. Inspect seal groove and crankshaft for wear, nicks, burrs and machining defects, and repair as needed.
6. Leaving seal on installation tool, coat outer diameter of seal with anaerobic sealer such as Loctite 515 or equivalent.
7. Push seal and tool assembly onto crankshaft as far as it will go, positioning tool so that arrow points toward cylinder case as shown in **Fig. 13.**
8. Ensure that main bearings in block are properly positioned and lubricated, then set crankshaft into engine, aligning oil seal with case groove.
9. Lightly lubricate crankshaft journals, and ensure that bearing shells are properly installed in main caps and that rear main cap sealing surfaces

are clean and free from oil.
10. Apply a 1–2mm bead of anaerobic sealer (Loctite 515 or equivalent) to rear main cap as shown in **Fig. 14,** install cap and torque retaining bolts to specifications.

NOTE: It is important that cap joint be properly sealed to prevent oil leakage. Do not substitute RTV sealer for the specified anaerobic sealer, and do not apply an excessive amount of sealer to the cap, as this will cause oil leaks.

11. Install remaining main bearing caps and torque to specifications.
12. Ensure that connecting rod bearings are properly seated in rods and caps, lightly lubricate bearings and crankpin journals, then reconnect rods to crankpins, install caps and torque cap nuts to specifications.
13. Complete engine reassembly and installation as outlined in appropriate service procedures.

Late Production 1985 (Thick Seal)

NOTE: Engines with this type rear main oil seal can be identified by the date code stamping located on the horizontal pad above the left upper water pump bolt.

1. Raise and support vehicle.
2. Support engine as needed, then remove transmission.
3. Remove clutch and pressure plate, if equipped, then remove flywheel or flex plate.

4. Insert screwdriver through seal lip and pry seal from bore, taking care not to damage crankshaft.
5. Clean seal bore and crankshaft, then inspect for burrs, nicks and wear, and repair as needed.
6. Lightly lubricate replacement seal lip, mount seal on installer J-34686 or equivalent, **Fig. 15,** and seat dust lip of seal squarely against collar.
7. Lubricate outer diameter of seal, align dowel pin of tool with dowel pin hole in crankshaft, mount tool on crankshaft and torque retaining bolts to 2–5 ft. lbs.
8. Rotate "T" handle of tool clockwise, pressing seal into bore until collar is tight against engine case to ensure that seal is fully seated.
9. Rotate "T" handle of tool counterclockwise to stop, then remove tool and ensure that seal is seated squarely in bore.
10. Reverse remaining procedure to complete installation.

BELT TENSION DATA

	New Lbs.	Used Lbs.
Air Cond.— 1982–85	146	67
Air/Vac. Pump— 1982–85	135	67
Alternator— 1982–85	146	67
Power Steering— 1982–85	135	67

DIESEL ENGINE TROUBLESHOOTING

HARD STARTING

1. Check fuel level and replenish if necessary.
2. Check notched line on injection pump flange and reset timing as necessary.
3. Check to ensure fuel is reaching injection nozzles. If fuel is reaching injectors:
   a. Check connections of fuse, glow plugs, Q.O.S. controller and glow plug relays.
   b. Check fuel spray pattern and ensure injection starting pressure is 1493 p.s.i.
   c. Ensure valve clearances are satisfactory. Refer to specifications.
   d. Check compression pressure in each cylinder. Standard value should be 441 p.s.i.
   e. Ensure proper installation of timing belt and camshaft.
4. If fuel is not reaching injectors:
   a. Check for air in fuel filter.
   b. Check if air is being drawn into fuel line through leakage in the pipe joints.
   c. Check operation of fuel cut out solenoid.
   d. Check fuel filter for restrictions.
   e. Check fuel pipes for restrictions.
   f. Check delivery valve for possible sticking.
5. Replace or readjust setting of injection pump.

ENGINE IDLING ROUGH

1. Check if idle speed is within specifications.
2. Ensure accelerator control cable is not binding or twisting.
3. Check accelerator lever setting for looseness.
4. Check for air or water in fuel filter.
5. On models with A/C, check that Fast Idle Control Device (FICD) is operating properly.
6. Check for proper alignment on injection pump flange.
7. Check engine mounting for cracks or looseness.
8. Check fuel spray valve pattern and ensure injection starting pressure is 1493 p.s.i.
9. Ensure valve clearances are satisfactory. Refer to specifications.
10. Check compression pressure in each cylinder. Standard value should be 441 p.s.i.
11. Ensure proper installation of timing belt and camshaft.
12. Check delivery valve for sticking.
13. Replace or readjust setting of injection pump.

LACK OF POWER

1. Check intake system for restrictions.
2. Ensure accelerator control cable is not twisted or binding.
3. Check seals on full load adjustment bolt and maximum speed stop bolt.
4. Ensure accelerator control lever is in contact with maximum speed stop bolt.
5. Check exhaust system for restrictions.
6. Ensure all air has been removed from fuel filter.
7. Check fuel lines to ensure all connections are secure and no lines are collapsed.
8. Check fuel tank breather for restrictions.
9. Check fuel quality.
10. Check notched line on injection pump flange, and reset timing as necessary.
11. Check fuel spray pattern and ensure injection starting pressure is 1493 p.s.i.
12. Ensure valve clearances are satisfactory. Refer to specifications.
13. Check compression pressure in each cylinder. Standard value should be 441 p.s.i.
14. Check delivery valve for sticking.
15. Replace or readjust setting of injection pump.

EXCESSIVE EXHAUST SMOKE

1. Ensure engine is thoroughly warmed up.
2. Check intake system for restrictions.
3. Ensure all air and water has been removed from fuel filter.
4. Check seal on full load adjust bolt.
5. Check exhaust system for restrictions.
6. Check fuel quality.
7. Check notched line on injection pump flange, and reset timing as necessary.
8. Check fuel spray pattern and ensure injection starting pressure is 1493 p.s.i.
9. Ensure valve clearances are satisfactory. Refer to specifications.
10. Check compression pressure in each cylinder. Standard value should be 441 p.s.i.
11. Ensure proper installation of timing belt and camshaft.
12. Check delivery valve for sticking.
13. Check condition of valve guides and seals.
14. Replace or readjust setting of injection pump.

ENGINE OVERHEATING

1. Check coolant level in radiator.
2. Check condition of coolant for contamination, anti-freeze concentration and leakage of oil into coolant.
3. Check hoses and clamps for signs of leakage.
4. Check water pump and thermostat housing for leakage.
5. Check cylinder head gasket for leakage.
6. Check fan belt tension. Belt deflection should not exceed .4 inch.
7. Check fan clutch operation.
8. Check radiator cap operation.
9. Check thermostat operation. Thermostat opening temperature is approximately 192° F.
10. Check notched line on injection pump flange, and reset timing as necessary.
11. Check fuel spray pattern and ensure injector starting pressure is 1493 p.s.i.
12. Check water pump impeller condition.
13. Check combustion chambers for excessive combustion deposits.
14. Replace or readjust setting of injection pump.

ENGINE KNOCKING

1. Ensure engine has been thoroughly warmed up.
2. Check injection timing.
3. Check fuel spray pattern, and ensure injection starting pressure is 1493 p.s.i.
4. Check compression pressure in each cylinder. Standard value should be 441 p.s.i.
5. Ensure proper quality of fuel is being used.
6. Replace or readjust setting of injection pump.

NOISE INDICATING ABNORMAL LEAKAGE

1. Check exhaust system for loose connections or leakage.
2. Ensure proper installation of nozzles and glow plugs.
3. Check for damaged cylinder head gasket.
4. Ensure valve clearances are satisfactory. Refer to specifications.
5. Check compression pressure in each cylinder. Standard value should be 441 p.s.i.

CONTINUOUS NOISE

1. Check fan belt tension. Deflection of fan belt should be no more than .4 inch.
2. Ensure cooling fan is secure.
3. Check water pump bearing for wear and damage.

4. Check operation of alternator and vacuum pump.
5. Ensure valve clearances are satisfactory. Refer to specifications.

SLAPPING NOISE

1. Ensure valve clearances are satisfactory. Refer to specifications.
2. Check rocker arms for damage.
3. Check to ensure flywheel bolts are secure.
4. Check crankshaft and thrust bearing for wear and/or damage.
5. Check main bearing oil clearances.
6. Check connecting rod bearing and bushing oil clearances.
7. Ensure clearance between pistons and cylinder walls is satisfactory. Refer to specifications.

EXCESSIVE OIL CONSUMPTION

1. If oil is leaking:
   a. Check oil level.
   b. Ensure drain plug is secure.
   c. Check oil pipes for leakage.
   d. Check oil seal retainer and oil filter gasket for leakage.
   e. Check cylinder head cover, oil pan and oil pump for leakage.
   f. Check cylinder head gasket for leakage.
   g. Check oil seal for leakage.
2. If oil is burning:
   a. Ensure proper quality of oil is being used.
   b. Check valve stem oil seals.
   c. Check valve guides and valve stems for wear and damage.
   d. Check for damaged cylinder head gasket.
   e. Ensure proper setting of piston rings.
   f. Check piston rings for wear and damage.
   g. Check cylinder walls for wear and damage.

EXCESSIVE FUEL CONSUMPTION

1. Check air cleaner for restrictions.
2. Check full load adjustment bolt seal for leakage.
3. Check fuel pipes for leakage.
4. Check exhaust system for restrictions.
5. Ensure idle speed is within specifications.
6. Ensure proper quality of fuel.
7. Check injection timing.
8. Check fuel spray pattern, and ensure injection starting pressure is 1493 p.s.i.
9. Ensure valve clearances are satisfactory. Refer to specifications.
10. Check compression pressure in each cylinder. Standard value should be 441 p.s.i.
11. Check delivery valve for sticking.
12. Replace or readjust setting of injection pump.

GLOW PLUG SYSTEM ELECTRICAL DIAGNOSIS
COLD ENGINE

With a normally operating Q.O.S. (Quick On System) with coolant temperature below 140° F. and ignition turned to "On" position, glow plug indicator turns on for about 3.5 seconds and No. 1 relay (quick pre-heat) turns on for a few seconds, then off. When ignition switch is turned to "Start" position, glow plug indicator and No. 2 relay (constant heat) will go on and remain on until ignition is returned to "On" position.

IGNITION IN "ON" (PRE-HEAT) POSITION

Relay No. 1 And Glow Indicator Are Both Inoperative
1. Starter circuit fuse is burnt out or fusible link wire is open.
2. Starter wire circuit is open or not properly connected.
3. Controller is defective or not properly connected.
4. Starter switch is inoperative.

Relay No. 1 Inoperative
1. Relay No. 1 is open.
2. Relay coil in relay No. 1 is open.
3. Controller to No. 1 relay circuitry is open or not properly connected.
4. Grounding circuit for No. 1 relay is open or not properly connected.
5. Controller is inoperative.
6. Circuit from controller to signal feed wire of sensing resistor is open or not properly connected.
7. Terminals of sensing resistor are not connected.
8. Main terminal of No. 1 relay is not connected.
9. Main contact is open in No. 1 relay.
10. Terminals in quick preheat circuit are not connected.
11. Engine harness ground is not properly connected.
12. Quick preheating wiring is not properly connected or circuit is open.

Glow Indicator Light Inoperative
1. Light bulb is burnt out.

Relay No. 1 Turns Off Within 2 Seconds
1. Controller is damaged.
2. One or more glow plugs are defective.
3. Wiring at connector is poorly connected.

Relay No. 1 Will Not Turn Off After A Few Seconds
1. Controller is damaged.

Relay No. 1 Operates When Coolant Temperature Is Above 140° F.
1. Thermostat switch is inoperative.
2. Circuit has a short.

IGNITION IN "START" (CONSTANT HEAT) POSITION

Relay No. 2 And Glow Indicator Inoperative
1. Starter switch "R" circuit is not properly connected or open.

Relay No. 2 Inoperative
1. Relay No. 2 terminals are not connected.
2. Circuit between R terminal and No. 2 relay is not properly connected or open.
3. No. 2 relay coil is open.

Glow Indicator Light Inoperative
1. Controller is damaged.

WARM ENGINE

With a normally operating Q.O.S. (Quick On System) with coolant temperature above 140° F. and ignition turned to "On" position, glow plug indicator turns on for about .3 second, then off. When ignition switch is turned to "Start" position, glow plug indicator and No. 2 relay (constant heat) turn on and remain on until ignition switch is returned to "On" position.

IGNITION IN "ON" POSITION

Glow Plug Light Remains On For 3.5 Seconds And Causes Relay No. 1 To Turn On
1. Thermo-switch circuit is not properly connected or open.
2. Thermostat switch is inoperative.

IGNITION IN "START" POSITION

Relay No. 2 And Glow Plug Indicator Inoperative
1. Starter switch "R" terminal not properly connected or open.

Relay No. 2 Inoperative
1. Relay No. 2 terminals not connected.
2. Circuit between "R" terminal and No. 2 relay not properly connected or open.
3. No. 2 relay coil is open.

Glow Indicator Light Inoperative
1. Controller damaged.

DIESEL ENGINE ELECTRICAL DIAGNOSIS & TESTING
CONTROLLER

The controller in this system, **Fig. 1,** has four functions. As engine coolant temperature changes, it controls the glow plug relay. For determining glow plug heating requirements, it monitors differences between sensing resistance and glow plug resistance. It controls rapid preheat circuit to 1652° F. of glow plug temperature and, during pre-heat cycle, controls glow plug pre-heat indicator lamp (3.5 sec.). Refer to **Fig. 2** for wiring connections.

DROPPING RESISTOR

During stabilized heating, this fixed value resistor is used to lower voltage of glow plugs. Check dropping resistor by performing continuity check across the terminals. Replace resistor if no continuity is found. Refer to **Fig. 3.**

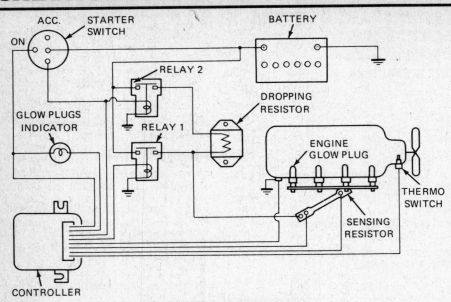

Fig. 1   Glow plug system

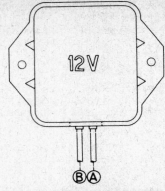

Fig. 3   Dropping resistor test connections

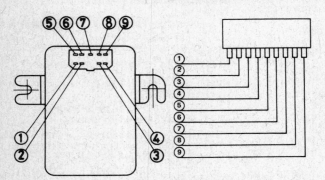

Position to which connector terminal is connected

1. Starter switch (ON position)
2. Sensing resistor
3. Thermo switch
4. Starter switch (ST position)
5. Sensing resistor
6. Glow plug relay No. 1
7. Ground
8. Glow indicator lamp
9. Not used

Fig. 2   Controller wiring connections

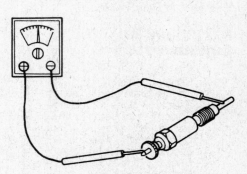

Fig. 4   Testing glow plug

GLOW PLUGS

The glow plugs used in this system are the fast warm up type. Check glow plugs by performing continuity test across plug terminals and body. If no continuity is found, heater wire is damaged and glow plug should be replaced. Refer to **Fig. 4.**

GLOW PLUG RELAY NO. 1

This is the main relay for stabilized heating circuit and rapid pre-heat cycle. Check glow relay by performing continuity test across terminals C and D while battery voltage is applied to terminals A and B. If no continuity is found, replace glow plug relay. Refer to **Fig. 5.**

GLOW PLUG RELAY NO. 2

During starting, this relay is used to provide stabilized heating. To check this relay use same procedure as for glow plug relay No. 1.

FUSIBLE LINKS

These two in-line fusible links are used to protect the glow plug electrical wiring. To check fusible links, perform continuity check across terminals. If no continuity is found, fusible link should be replaced. Refer to **Fig. 6.**

SENSING RESISTOR

Used in series with the glow plugs, this shunt type sensing resistor causes a small voltage drop which is monitored by the controller.

THERMO SWITCH

This thermo switch is used to provide a ground circuit to controller circuitry when engine temperature is above 140° F. To check thermo switch, perform continuity check across terminal and body while end of thermal switch is submerged in water. Gradually bring temperature of water to 140° F. Replace thermal switch if continuity is not found at this temperature. Refer to **Fig. 7.**

ENGINE
REPLACE

1. Disconnect battery ground cable.
2. Disconnect exhaust pipe from manifold.
3. Disconnect power steering reservoir from upper fan shroud and position aside, then remove upper shroud.
4. Drain cooling system and disconnect hoses from radiator.
5. Remove radiator and cooling fan, then lower fan shroud.
6. Disconnect heater hoses from engine, then PCV valve at cylinder head cover.
7. Disconnect positive cable from battery, and remove air cleaner and bracket.
8. If equipped with air conditioning, evacuate system and remove manifold at compressor.
9. If equipped with power steering, disconnect power steering pump.
10. Disconnect necessary vacuum hoses, wiring, fuel hoses and throttle linkage.
11. Remove starter.
12. Scribe alignment marks in hood hinge area, then remove hood.
13. Remove shifter assembly, then raise and support vehicle.
14. Remove right side motor mount through bolt, **Fig. 8,** then disconnect lower clutch cable.
15. Disconnect clutch bellcrank at frame.
16. Disconnect back-up light switch wires and speedometer cable and position aside.
17. Remove driveshaft and transmission mount nut, then support transmission.
18. Remove transmission crossmember, then transmission to bellhousing mounting bolts.
19. Remove transmission, then engine to bellhousing mounting bolts.

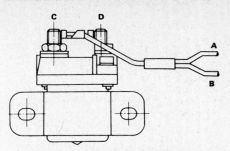

Fig. 5   Glow plug relay test connections

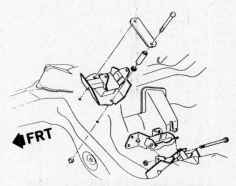

Fig. 8   4-137 engine mounts

20. Remove bellhousing, then lower vehicle.
21. Disconnect upper clutch cable, then remove bellcrank.
22. Install suitable engine lifting device.
23. Remove left side motor mount through bolt, **Fig. 8,** then disconnect battery ground cable at engine block.
24. Remove engine.
25. Reverse procedure to install.

CYLINDER HEAD
REPLACE

1. Disconnect battery ground cable.
2. Remove rocker arms and pushrods. Refer to "Rocker Arms, Replace."
3. Drain radiator coolant, then disconnect radiator hose from cylinder head.
4. Remove heater tube.
5. Disconnect exhaust pipe from manifold, then remove vacuum pump.
6. If equipped with air conditioning, remove A/C compressor and bracket and position aside.
7. Disconnect heater hose and bracket.
8. Disconnect PCV hose and position aside, then the oil dipstick and dipstick tube.
9. Disconnect necessary electrical wiring from engine and accessories.
10. Disconnect injection lines.

NOTE: Cover all open injection lines to prevent entry of dirt.

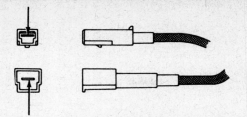

Fig. 6   Fusible link connections

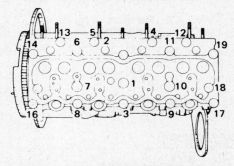

Fig. 9   Cylinder head tightening sequence

11. Disconnect breather pipe and the oil jet pipe.
12. Disconnect fuel return hose.
13. Remove cylinder head bolts, then the cylinder head.
14. Position new gasket on engine block with "TOP" side of gasket facing up.
15. Apply engine oil to sealing faces and threads of cylinder head bolts, then install cylinder head and bolts. Torque bolts in sequence shown in **Fig. 9** to values given in specifications at beginning of chapter.

ROCKER ARM COVER
REPLACE

1. Disconnect battery ground cable.
2. Remove PCV valve from rocker arm cover.
3. Remove air cleaner assembly.
4. Disconnect PCV hose.
5. Remove rocker arm cover bolts, then the cover.
6. Reverse procedure to install. Torque rocker arm cover bolts to value given in specifications at beginning of chapter.

EXHAUST MANIFOLD
REPLACE

1. Disconnect battery ground cable.
2. Disconnect PCV valve from rocker arm cover.
3. Remove air cleaner assembly.
4. Disconnect exhaust pipe from manifold.
5. Remove exhaust manifold retaining nuts and washers, then the manifold, **Fig. 10.**

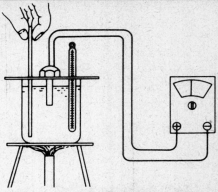

Fig. 7   Testing Thermo switch

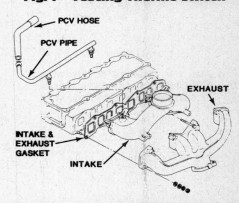

Fig. 10   Exhaust & intake manifold removal

NOTE: If exhaust manifold gasket replacement is required, the intake manifold must be removed. Refer to "Intake Manifold, Replace" for procedure.

6. Reverse procedure to install. Torque exhaust manifold nuts to value given in specifications at beginning of chapter.

INTAKE MANIFOLD
REPLACE

1. Disconnect battery ground cable.
2. Remove air cleaner assembly.
3. Disconnect heater pipe bracket, then the PCV pipe hose, **Fig. 10.**
4. Disconnect clips and wires from intake manifold.
5. Remove intake manifold retaining bolts, then the manifold.

NOTE: If intake manifold gasket replacement is required, the exhaust manifold must be removed. Refer to "Exhaust Manifold, Replace" for procedure.

6. Reverse procedure to install. Torque intake manifold bolts to values given in specifications at beginning of chapter.

ROCKER ARMS
REPLACE

1. Disconnect battery ground cable.

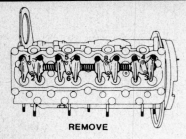

REMOVE

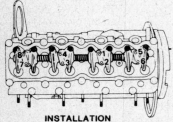

INSTALLATION

Fig. 11   Rocker arm shaft assembly mounting bolts removal & installation

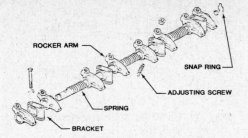

ROCKER ARM
SNAP RING
ADJUSTING SCREW
SPRING
BRACKET

Fig. 12   Rocker arm shaft assembly

12. Install rocker arm cover.

VALVES
ADJUST

1. Rotate crankshaft until cylinder No. 1 is at T.D.C.
2. Remove rocker arm cover. Refer to "Rocker Arm Cover, Replace."
3. Ensure rocker arm bracket bolts are torqued to specifications.
4. Adjust cylinder No. 1 intake and exhaust, cylinder No. 2 intake and cylinder No. 3 exhaust to specifications.
5. Rotate crankshaft one revolution and adjust remaining valves to specifications.
6. Install rocker arm cover.

VALVE TIMING
INTAKE OPENS BEFORE TDC

Engine	Degrees
4-137	16

VALVE GUIDE
REPLACE

1. Using tool J-26512, drive out valve guide from lower face of cylinder head, **Fig. 13.**
2. Apply engine oil to outer circumference of valve guide. Using tool J-26512, drive guide into position from upper face of cylinder head, **Fig. 14.**

NOTE: Always replace valve guides and valve as a set.

CRANKSHAFT PULLEY
REPLACE

1. Disconnect battery ground cable.
2. Loosen accessory drive belts.
3. Remove crankshaft pulley retaining bolts, then the pulley.
4. Reverse procedure to install.

Fig. 13   Valve guide removal

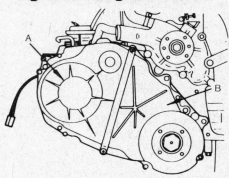

A   B

Fig. 15   Timing pulley housing upper & lower covers

TIMING PULLEY HOUSING COVER
REPLACE

UPPER

1. Disconnect battery ground cable.
2. If equipped with power steering, remove P/S pump reservoir.
3. Remove upper fan shroud and cooling fan.
4. Loosen accessory drive belts, then remove fan drive pulley.
5. Remove timing pulley housing upper cover, **Fig. 15,** view A.
6. Reverse procedure to install.

LOWER

1. Remove timing pulley housing upper cover as described above.
2. Remove alternator belt.
3. Align crankshaft pulley TDC mark with pointer, **Fig. 16,** then remove crankshaft pulley. Refer to "Crankshaft Pulley, Replace."
4. Remove timing pulley housing lower cover, **Fig. 15,** view B.
5. Reverse procedure to install.

TIMING BELT
REPLACE

1. Disconnect battery ground cable.
2. Remove timing pulley housing covers. Refer to "Timing Pulley Housing Cover, Replace" for procedure.

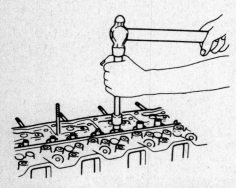

Fig. 14   Valve guide installation

2. Remove rocker arm cover. Refer to "Rocker Arm Cover, Replace."
3. Loosen rocker arm shaft assembly bracket bolts in sequence shown in **Fig. 11.**
4. Remove rocker arm shaft assembly and pushrods.
5. Mark rocker arms and push rods to ensure they are reinstalled in the same position.
6. Remove snap ring, then the rocker arms, springs and brackets, **Fig. 12.**
7. Apply clean engine oil to rocker arm shaft, rocker arms, springs and brackets.
8. Assemble rocker arm shaft assembly, **Fig. 12.**

NOTE: When assembling rocker arm shaft assembly, position brackets with "F" mark facing front of engine.

9. Install push rods, then rocker arm shaft bracket.
10. Torque rocker arm shaft retaining bolts in sequence shown in **Fig. 11** to values given in specifications at beginning of chapter.
11. Adjust valves. Refer to "Valves, Adjust" for procedure.

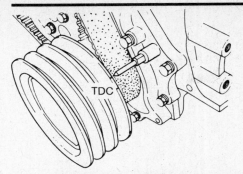

Fig. 16 Crankshaft pulley at TDC

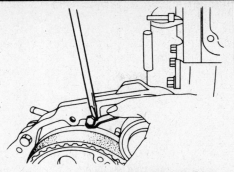

Fig. 17 Belt tensioner spring removal

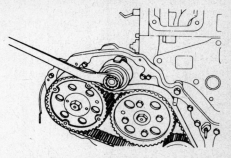

Fig. 18 Belt tensioner pulley nut removal

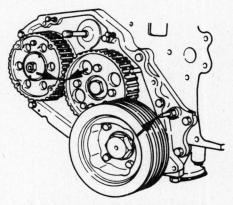

Fig. 19 Pulley alignment

3. Remove injection pump timing pulley flange retaining bolts.
4. Remove tension spring, **Fig. 17.**

NOTE: When removing tension spring, use care to avoid distorting spring.

5. Remove tension pulley nut, **Fig. 18,** then the pulley and tension center.
6. Remove timing belt.

NOTE: Avoid twisting or kinking belt. Keep the belt free of water, oil, dust and other foreign material.

7. Ensure crankshaft pulley TDC mark is still aligned with timing pointer, **Fig. 16.**
8. Rotate injection pump timing pulley and camshaft timing pulley as necessary to bring them into alignment, **Fig. 19.**
9. Install timing belt over crankshaft timing pulley, then the camshaft timing pulley and the injection timing pulley.
10. Install tension center and tension pulley. Ensure tension center end is in proper contact with two pins on timing pulley housing, **Fig. 20.**
11. Loosely install tension pulley nut, then install tension pulley spring.
12. Semi-tighten tension pulley nut.
13. Rotate crankshaft two complete revolutions in normal direction of rotation to seat timing belt, then rotate an additional 90° beyond TDC to settle injection pump, **Fig. 21.**

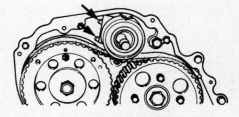

Fig. 20 Belt tensioner installation

NOTE: Do not attempt to rotate crankshaft in opposite direction of normal crankshaft rotation.

14. Loosen tension pulley nut, allowing the tension pulley assembly to take up belt slack. Torque tension pulley nut to 78–95 ft. lbs.
15. Install injection pump pulley flange. The hole in the flange outer circumference should be aligned with injection pump timing mark.
16. Again rotate engine in normal direction of rotation and bring cylinder No. 1 to TDC on compression stroke. Check injection pump and camshaft pulley alignment marks to ensure proper installation, **Fig. 22.**
17. Check timing belt tension between crankshaft and injection pump pulley with tool J-29771, **Fig. 23.** Tension should be 213–356 psi.
18. Install upper and lower timing pulley housing covers.
19. Install crankshaft pulley and drive belts.

TIMING PULLEY HOUSING
REPLACE
REMOVAL

1. Disconnect battery ground cable.
2. Drain radiator coolant, then remove radiator hoses and radiator.
3. Remove timing pulley housing covers. Refer to "Timing Pulley Housing Cover, Replace" for procedure.
4. Remove timing belt. Refer to "Timing Belt, Replace" for procedure.
5. Install a 6mm bolt through injection pump pulley hole into threaded hole in

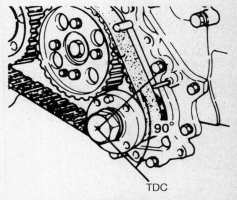

Fig. 21 Crankshaft hub positioning

timing pulley housing to prevent pulley from turning, then remove injection pump pulley nut.
6. Remove injection pump pulley using puller J-22888-D, **Fig. 24.**
7. Remove camshaft pulley retaining bolt.
8. Remove camshaft pulley and center assembly using puller J-22888-D, **Fig. 25.**
9. Remove camshaft center assembly oil seal.
10. Remove crankshaft hub bolt, then crankshaft pulley hub and pulley using puller J-24420-A.

NOTE: If crankshaft front seal requires replacement, it may be replaced at this time.

11. Disconnect fuel shut-off solenoid and vacuum line.
12. Remove injection lines.
13. Disconnect fuel and return lines.
14. Disconnect throttle return spring, then remove injection pump bracket to injection pump mounting bolts.
15. Remove timing pulley housing bolts, then remove housing and injection pump as an assembly.

INSTALLATION

1. Clean timing pulley housing and engine block mounting surfaces, then install new gasket.
2. Position timing pulley housing on engine block and install bolts. Torque bolts to 10–17 ft. lbs.

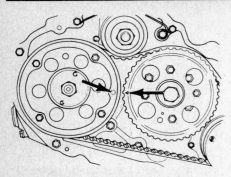

Fig. 22   Injection pump & camshaft pulley alignment

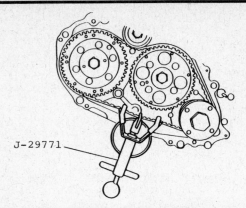

Fig. 23   Measuring belt tension

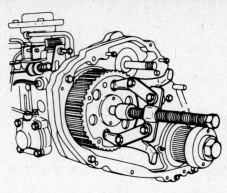

Fig. 24   Injection pump pulley removal

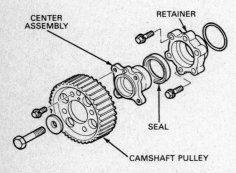

Fig. 25   Camshaft pulley and center assembly

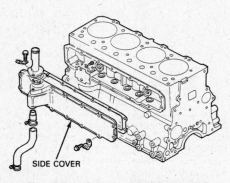

Fig. 26   Side cover removal

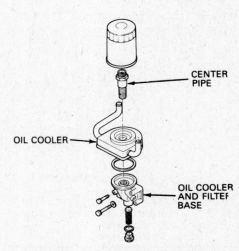

Fig. 27   Oil cooler assembly

3. Install crankshaft front seal using tool J-24250.
4. Install new camshaft seal using tool J-24254, then install oil seal retainer.
5. Install injection pump mounting bracket bolts.
6. Install all removed wires and hoses.
7. Install crankshaft pulley hub and pulley using tool J-26587, then install hub bolt and torque to specifications at beginning of chapter.
8. Install camshaft pulley and center assembly, then install retaining bolt. Torque retaining bolt to 42–52 ft. lbs.
9. Remove injection pump pulley locking bolt.
10. Install timing belt.
11. Install timing pulley cover.
12. Install crankshaft pulley.
13. Install radiator and hoses.
14. Refill cooling system and connect battery ground cable.

ENGINE SIDE COVER
REPLACE

1. Disconnect battery ground cable.
2. Remove injection pump lines and cap all open lines to prevent entry of dirt.
3. Disconnect crankcase breather hoses.
4. Disconnect dipstick tube bracket from dipstick, then remove dipstick.
5. Disconnect bus bar input lead.
6. Remove oil filter.
7. Remove side cover bolts, then the side cover, **Fig. 26.**
8. Reverse procedure to install.

REAR MAIN OIL SEAL
REPLACE

1. Remove transmission.
2. Remove clutch assembly and flywheel.
3. Remove rear main bearing oil seal using a suitable screwdriver.
4. Apply clean engine oil to lipped portion and fitting face of new seal.
5. Install new seal using tool J-29818.
6. Install flywheel and clutch assembly.
7. Install transmission.

OIL COOLER
REPLACE

1. Disconnect battery ground cable.
2. Disconnect cooler hoses, **Fig. 27.**
3. Remove oil filter and center pipe.
4. Remove oil cooler.

NOTE: If oil cooler and filter base are to be removed, raise and support vehicle to gain access to retaining bolts.

5. Reverse procedure to install.

CAMSHAFT
REPLACE

1. Remove engine assembly. Refer to "Engine, Replace" for procedure.
2. Remove rocker arm cover. Refer to "Rocker Arm Cover, Replace" for procedure.
3. Remove rocker arm shaft. Refer to "Rocker Arms, Replace" for procedure.
4. Remove timing belt. Refer to "Timing Belt, Replace" for procedure.
5. Remove camshaft gear and hub, then the oil seal retainer.
6. Remove oil pan and oil pump. Refer to "Crankcase And Oil Pump, Replace" for procedure.
7. Carefully withdraw camshaft from engine block to avoid damaging camshaft bearings.

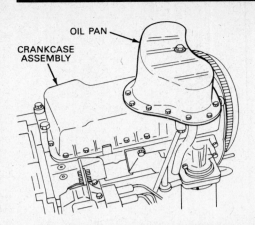

Fig. 28 Oil pan & crankcase assembly

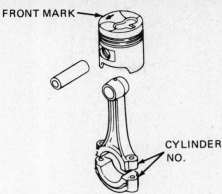

Fig. 29 Piston & connecting rod assembly

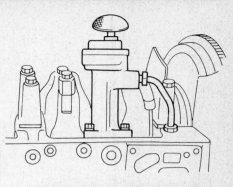

Fig. 30 Oil pump assembly

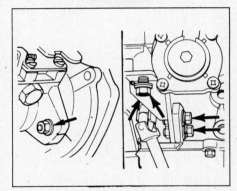

Fig. 31 Injection pump bracket bolts

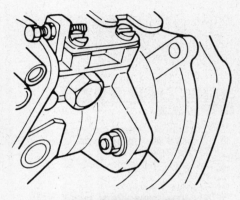

Fig. 32 Injection pump alignment

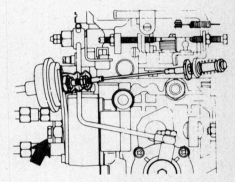

Fig. 33 Injection pump distributor head screw location

8. Remove valve lifters.
9. Reverse procedure to install.

OIL PAN
REPLACE

1. Disconnect battery ground cable.
2. Raise and support vehicle.
3. Drain crankcase, then remove oil pan bolts and oil pan, **Fig. 28.**
4. Reverse procedure to install. Torque oil pan mounting bolts to 2–4 ft. lbs.

VALVE LIFTERS
REPLACE

To replace valve lifters, the camshaft must be removed. Refer to "Camshaft, Replace."

PISTON & ROD ASSEMBLE

Assemble piston to rod so combustion chamber on piston head is positioned on side of connecting rod with cylinder No.

stamp, **Fig. 29.**
Install piston and rod assembly in cylinder with arrow on piston head facing front of engine.

CRANKCASE & OIL PUMP
REPLACE

1. Remove engine. Refer to "Engine, Replace."
2. Disconnect crankcase end of PCV hose.
3. Remove dipstick tube, then the oil pan, **Fig. 28.**
4. Remove crankcase retaining bolts, then the crankcase.
5. Remove oil pump sleeve nut, retaining bolts and pump, **Fig. 30.**
6. Reverse procedure to install.

INJECTION PUMP
REPLACE

1. Disconnect battery ground cable.
2. Remove timing belt. Refer to "Timing Belt, Replace."
3. Remove injection pump pulley using tool J-22888-D, **Fig. 24.**

4. Remove fuel input and return lines.
5. Remove injection pump electrical wiring, then the throttle cable.
6. Remove injection lines, then the throttle return spring.
7. Raise and support vehicle.
8. Remove injection pump bracket bolts, **Fig. 31,** then lower vehicle.

NOTE: If injection pump bracket is removed, injection timing must be reset. Refer to "Injection Pump Timing" for procedure.

9. Remove injection pump.
10. Reverse procedure to install.

INJECTION PUMP TIMING

1. Ensure notched line on injection pump flange is aligned with notched line on injection pump front bracket, **Fig. 32.**
2. Rotate crankshaft in normal direction of rotation until cylinder No. 1 is at TDC compression stroke, **Fig. 16.**
3. Remove upper radiator fan shroud.
4. Remove timing pulley housing upper cover. Refer to "Timing Pulley Housing Cover, Replace" for procedure.
5. Check timing belt for proper tension,

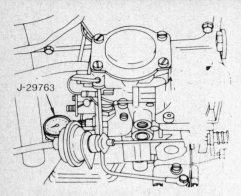

Fig. 34 Static timing gauge installed

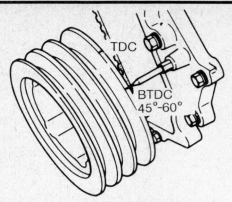

Fig. 35 Crankshaft pulley alignment

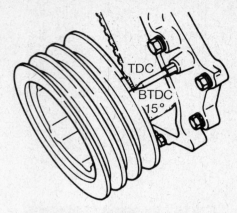

Fig. 36 Crankshaft pulley at 15° BTDC

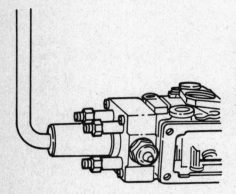

Fig. 37 High pressure plug removal

then check timing mark alignment, **Fig. 19.**

NOTE: If timing marks are not properly aligned, timing belt must be removed and reinstalled properly.

6. Remove injection pump lines, then the distributor head screw and washer, **Fig. 33.**
7. Install static timing gauge J-29763 in distributor head screw threaded hole. Set gauge lift approximately .004 inch from the plunger, **Fig. 34.**
8. Rotate crankshaft to bring cylinder No. 1 to a point 45–60 degrees BTDC, **Fig. 35.** Calibrate dial on gauge to zero. Rotate crankshaft slightly in either direction to ensure gauge needle is stable.
9. Rotate crankshaft in normal direction of rotation until timing pointer is aligned with 13° BTDC mark for California models or 15° BTDC for non-California models, **Fig. 36,** then observe dial indicator.
10. If indicator reading is not .020 inch, maintain crankshaft position, loosen injection pump flange nuts and rotate pump, as needed, until indicator reading is .020 inch.
11. Tighten pump flange nuts, recheck indicator reading and readjust as needed.

12. Remove dial gauge, reinstall distributor head and screw, and reinstall remaining components in reverse order of removal.

INJECTION NOZZLE
REPLACE

1. Disconnect battery ground cable.
2. Remove fuel return pipe at injection nozzle.
3. Disconnect injection line at injection nozzle.
4. Remove nozzle.
5. Reverse procedure to install.

INJECTION PUMP ON VEHICLE SERVICE
FUEL INLET & RETURN PIPE GASKETS, REPLACE

1. Disconnect battery ground cable.
2. If equipped with air conditioning, remove A/C belt, then compressor and position aside.
3. If removing fuel inlet hose, disconnect hose, then remove fuel inlet pipe and gaskets. If removing fuel return hose, disconnect hose, then remove fuel return pipe and gaskets.
4. Replace gaskets, then reverse procedure to install.

TACHOMETER PLUG O-RING, REPLACE

1. Disconnect battery ground cable.
2. If equipped with air conditioning, remove A/C belt, then compressor and position aside.
3. Remove "Tach" plug and replace O-ring.
4. Reverse procedure to install. Torque "Tach" plug to 8 ft. lbs.

HIGH PRESSURE PLUG O-RING, REPLACE

1. Disconnect battery ground cable.

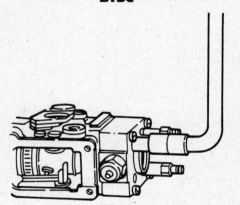

Fig. 38 Delivery valve removal

2. If equipped with air conditioning, remove A/C belt, then compressor and position aside.
3. Remove fuel injection lines as an assembly.
4. Remove high pressure plug using tool J-33309, **Fig. 37.** Remove O-ring.
5. Reverse procedure to install. Torque high pressure plug to 50 ft. lbs.

DELIVERY VALVE HOLDER GASKET, REPLACE

1. Disconnect battery ground cable.
2. If equipped with air conditioning, remove A/C belt, then compressor and position aside.
3. Remove fuel injection lines as an assembly.
4. Using a suitable 14mm wrench, remove delivery valve holder(s), **Fig. 38.**
5. Remove delivery valve and seat assembly. The delivery valve and seat assembly are match ground and should not be interchanged with other delivery valve and seat assemblies.

NOTE: The letters A, B, C, & D are engraved on each cylinder of the distributor head. Remove each delivery valve in proper sequence to ensure correct assembly.

6. Remove delivery valve gasket.
7. Reverse procedure to install. Torque delivery valve holder(s) to 28 ft. lbs.

MAXIMUM FUEL ADJUSTMENT SCREW/LOAD SCREW O-RING, REPLACE

1. Disconnect battery ground cable.
2. If equipped with air conditioning, remove A/C belt, then compressor and position aside.
3. Remove fuel return hose and pipe.
4. Remove staking wire, then disconnect accelerator cable.
5. Install an M8 × 1 jam nut against adjusting screw locknut. Tighten the two nuts together to preserve adjust-ment.
6. Remove full load adjusting screw, then O-ring.
7. Install new O-ring.
8. Reverse procedure to install. Torque full load adjusting screw lock nut to 6 ft. lbs. and remove jam nut.

Clutch & Manual Transmission Section

CLUTCH
ADJUST

1982—83

1. Clutch is adjusted by lifting clutch pedal up to allow mechanism to adjust cable. Depress pedal several times to set pawl into mesh with detent teeth.
2. Check clutch linkage for lost motion caused by loose or worn swivels, deflection of mounting brackets or damaged cordon shaft.

1984—85

These models are equipped with a hydraulic clutch. No adjustment of the clutch pedal or linkage is provided.

CLUTCH
REPLACE

1. On 1984—85 models, remove slave cylinder mounting bolts and position cylinder aside. On 1982—83 models, disconnect clutch fork cable.
2. On all models, remove transmission assembly as outlined under "Transmission, Replace."
3. On models equipped with 4 speed (77mm) or 5 speed, remove bell housing.

NOTE: On models equipped with 4 speed (77mm) or 5 speed, it may be necessary to remove left body mounting bolts, loosen radiator support bolt and raise the cab to gain access to upper bell housing mounting bolts. After cab is raised, a suitable block of wood should be installed between frame and cab for support.

4. Slide clutch fork from ball stud and remove fork from dust boot.
5. Install tool J-33169 for 4-121, 151 and V6-173 engines or tool J-33034 for 4-119 and 4-137 engines to support clutch assembly.

NOTE: Look for "X" mark on flywheel and on clutch cover or white painted letter on clutch cover. If marks are not evident, mark flywheel and clutch cover for proper alignment during assembly.

6. Loosen clutch-to-flywheel attaching bolts evenly, one turn at a time, until spring pressure is released. Then remove bolts, clutch and pressure plate assembly.
7. Clean pressure plate and flywheel mating surfaces and inspect flywheel for defects. Replace or repair as needed.
8. Reverse procedure to install.

CLUTCH MASTER CYLINDER
REPLACE

1984—85

Removal
1. Remove sound absorbing panel from upper left side foot well.
2. Disconnect master cylinder push rod from clutch pedal.
3. Remove master cylinder retaining nuts, **Fig. 1.**
4. Disconnect reservoir hose and slave cylinder hydraulic line from master cylinder.
5. Remove clutch master cylinder.

Installation
1. Position master cylinder at front of dash, then install retaining nuts and torque to 10—15 ft. lbs., **Fig. 1.**
2. Connect master cylinder push rod to clutch pedal and install retaining clip.
3. Install sound absorbing panel.
4. Connect reservoir hose and slave cylinder hydraulic line to master cylinder.
5. Bleed system.

CLUTCH SLAVE CYLINDER
REPLACE

1984—85

Removal
1. Raise and support vehicle.
2. Disconnect hydraulic line from slave cylinder, **Fig. 2.**
3. Remove slave cylinder retaining nuts, then the slave cylinder.

Installation
1. Connect hydraulic line to slave cylinder, **Fig. 2.**
2. Bleed system.
3. Position slave cylinder on bell housing, then install retaining nuts and torque to 10—15 ft. lbs.

CLUTCH SYSTEM
BLEED

1984—85

NOTE: When refilling or bleeding system, use only new brake fluid conforming to DOT 3 or DOT 4 specifications.

1. Raise and support vehicle.
2. Remove slave cylinder retaining nuts, then the slave cylinder.
3. While holding slave cylinder at approximately 45 degrees with bleeder at highest point, have an assistant depress clutch pedal while opening bleeder valve.
4. With clutch pedal held at end of stroke, close bleeder valve and release clutch pedal.
5. Repeat steps 3 and 4 until all air has been expelled from system.

NOTE: While bleeding clutch system, constantly check master cylinder reservoir fluid level and replenish as necessary to prevent master cylinder running out of fluid.

TRANSMISSION
REPLACE

4 SPEED (77MM) & 5 SPEED

NOTE: On four wheel drive models, prior to removing transmission, transfer case must be removed. Refer to Transfer Case Section for procedures.

1. Disconnect battery ground cable.
2. Remove attaching screws and slide shift lever boot up shift lever.
3. With transmission in neutral, remove shift lever.
4. Raise and support vehicle.

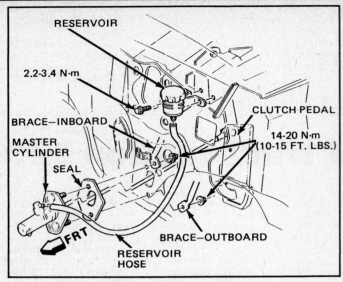

Fig. 1   Clutch master cylinder

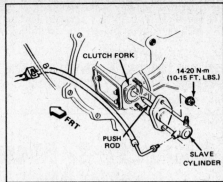

Fig. 2   Clutch slave cylinder

5. Remove propeller shaft.
6. Disconnect speedometer cable and electrical connectors at transmission.
7. On 1984–85 models, disconnect slave cylinder from transmission. On 1982–83 models, disconnect clutch cable at transmission.
8. Support transmission and remove transmission mount attaching bolts.
9. Remove catalytic converter hanger.
10. Remove crossmember attaching bolts and crossmember.
11. Remove dust cover bolts.
12. Remove transmission-to-bell housing attaching bolts and the transmission.
13. Reverse procedure to install.

4-SPEED (77.5MM)

1. Disconnect battery ground cable.

2. Remove upper starter motor retaining nut.
3. Remove attaching screws and slide shift lever boot up shift lever.
4. Remove shift lever attaching bolts at transmission.
5. Disconnect electrical connection and clip at transmission shift tower.
6. Raise and support vehicle.
7. Remove propeller shaft.
8. Disconnect exhaust pipe at manifold.
9. Disconnect speedometer cable and electrical connector at transmission.
10. On 1984–85 models, disconnect slave cylinder from transmission. On 1982–83 models, disconnect clutch cable at transmission.
11. With transmission supported, remove transmission mount attaching bolts.
12. Remove catalytic converter hanger.

13. Remove crossmember attaching bolts and crossmember.
14. Remove lower dust cover bolts.
15. Remove lower starter motor attaching bolt.
16. Remove transmission-to-engine mounting bolts and the transmission.

NOTE: It may be necessary to remove left body mounting bolts, loosen radiator support bolt and raise the cab to gain access to upper transmission mounting bolts. After cab is raised, a suitable block of wood should be installed between frame and cab for support.

17. Reverse procedure to install.

SHIFT LINKAGE
ADJUST

The shift mechanism does not require adjustment and may be serviced independently of the transmission.

Transfer Case Section

SHIFT LEVER
REPLACE

REMOVAL

1. Disconnect battery ground cable.
2. Remove console, then shift boot.
3. Loosen shift lever jam nut, then unscrew shift lever.
4. Remove transfer case selector switch.
5. Raise and support vehicle.
6. Disconnect shift rod at shifter assembly, then remove pivot and adjusting bolt, Fig. 1.
7. Remove shifter.

INSTALLATION

1. Position shifter at bracket, then install

pivot and adjusting bolt, Fig. 1.
2. Connect shift rod, then adjust shift linkage.
3. Lower vehicle.
4. Install shift lever on shifter, then screw lever down until pawl just clears bracket, then tighten shift lever an additional 1½ turns and tighten jam nut.
5. Install selector switch, shift boot and console.
6. Install battery ground cable.

SHIFT LINKAGE
ADJUST

1. Loosen small bolt and washer (A) and pivot bolt (B), Fig. 2.
2. Position transfer case shift lever at 4 Hi position.

3. Remove console, then pull shift boot up shift lever.
4. Install a 8mm gage pin or ⁵⁄₁₆ inch drill bit through shifter into bracket (C), Fig. 2.
5. Install a suitable bolt at the transfer case lever to lock transfer case in 4 Hi, Fig. 3.
6. Torque small bolt and washer (A) to 25–35 ft. lbs., then pivot bolt (B) to 88–103 ft. lbs., Fig. 2.
7. Remove bolt installed at transfer case lever, then gage pin or drill bit from shifter and bracket.
8. Place shift boot in proper position, then install console.

SELECTOR SWITCH
REPLACE

1. Disconnect battery ground cable.

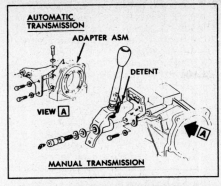

Fig. 1 Shifter & shift lever mounting

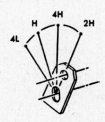

Fig. 3 Transfer case shift lever positioning

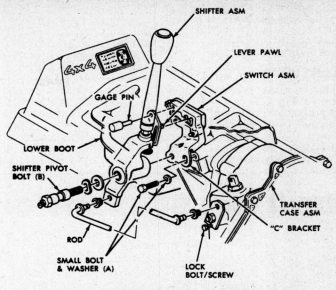

Fig. 2 Transfer case shift linkage

2. Remove console, then disconnect console wiring harness.
3. Remove shifter boot retaining screws and slide boot up shift lever.
4. Remove switch attaching screw, then the switch and harness, **Fig. 2**.
5. Position new switch on mounting bracket and install attaching screw.

NOTE: Ensure shift lever assembly pawl is on the switch contact carrier.

6. Route wiring as shown in **Fig. 4**.
7. Place shifter boot in proper position, then install retaining screws.
8. Connect console wiring harness, then install console.
9. Connect battery ground cable.

TRANSFER CASE
REPLACE
REMOVAL
1. Position transfer case shift lever at 4 Hi.
2. Disconnect battery ground cable.
3. Raise and support vehicle and remove skid plate, then drain transfer case.
4. Scribe reference marks on transfer case front output shaft yoke and drive shaft, then disconnect front drive shaft from transfer case.

5. Scribe reference marks on rear axle yoke and drive shaft, then remove rear drive shaft.
6. Disconnect vacuum harness and speedometer cable from transfer case, then remove shift lever.
7. Remove catalytic converter hanger bolts, then raise transmission and transfer case assembly and remove transmission mount attaching bolts and the mount.
8. Remove catalytic converter hanger, then lower transmission and transfer case assembly.
9. Support transfer case with a suitable jack, then remove transfer case attaching bolts.

NOTE: On models equipped with automatic transmission, remove shift lever bracket

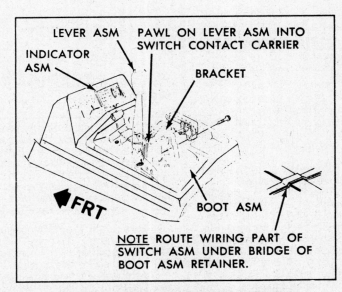

Fig. 4 Selector switch installation

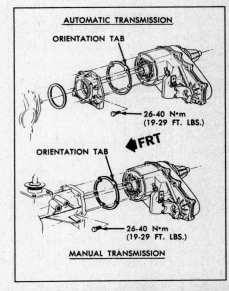

Fig. 5 Transfer case installation

mounting bolts, **Fig. 1,** to gain access to upper left side transfer case mounting bolt.

10. Remove transfer case.

INSTALLATION

1. Position new gasket on transfer case as shown in **Fig. 5.**
2. Position transfer case near end of transmission, then align transfer case input shaft splines with transmission splines and slide transfer case forward until seated against transmission.

3. Install transfer case attaching bolts. Torque bolts to 19–29 ft. lbs.

NOTE: On models equipped with automatic transmission, install shift lever bracket mounting bracket bolts.

4. Raise transmission and transfer case assembly with a suitable jack, then install mount and catalytic converter hanger bracket. Lower transmission and transfer case assembly.
5. Install transmission mount attaching bolts and torque to 25 ft. lbs.

6. Install and tighten catalytic converter hanger bolts at converter.
7. Install shift lever to transfer case, then connect vacuum harness and speedometer cable.
8. Install front and rear drive shafts. Ensure reference marks are aligned prior to assembly.
9. Fill transfer case with suitable lubricant.
10. Install skid plate, then lower vehicle.
11. Connect battery ground cable.
12. Road test vehicle. Ensure vehicle shifts and operates in all ranges.

Rear Axle, Suspension & Brake Section

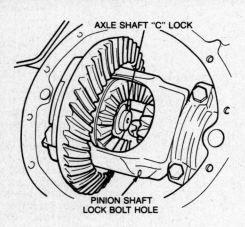

Fig. 1   **Removing differential pinion shaft.**

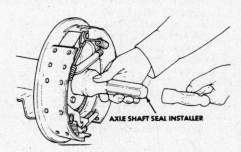

Fig. 2   **Axle shaft bearing removal**

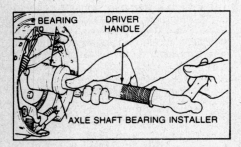

Fig. 3   **Axle shaft bearing installation**

AXLE SHAFT
REPLACE

1. Raise and support rear of vehicle, then remove wheel and brake drum on side axle is to be replaced.
2. Loosen carrier cover bolts and allow lubricant to drain, then remove bolts and carrier cover.
3. Remove rear axle pinion shaft lock screw, then the pinion shaft, **Fig. 1.** Discard the lock screw.
4. Push flanged end of axle shaft toward center of vehicle, then remove "C" lock from button end of shaft.

5. Withdraw axle shaft from housing using caution not to damage seal.
6. Reverse procedure to install, noting the following: torque new pinion shaft lock screw to 20 ft. lbs. on 1982 models or 25 ft. lbs. on 1983–85 models. Torque carrier cover bolts to 20 ft. lbs. on all models.

WHEEL BEARING & AXLE SEAL
REPLACE

1. Remove axle shaft as described under "Axle Shaft, Replace."
2. Remove axle seal by prying behind seal steel case with a suitable pry bar. Use caution to avoid damaging axle housing.
3. Using a suitable puller and slide hammer, remove axle bearing, **Fig. 2.**
4. Lubricate new bearing with gear lubricant, then install bearing in axle housing with tool J-23765 or equivalent until bearing is seated in housing, **Fig. 3.**
5. Lubricate seal lips with gear lubricant, then position seal on tool J-23771 or equivalent and install in axle housing, tapping into place until seal is flush with axle housing, **Fig. 4.**
6. Reinstall axle shaft.

Fig. 4   **Axle shaft seal installation**

AXLE ASSEMBLY
REPLACE

NOTE: Construction of the axle assembly is such that service operations may be performed with the housing installed in the vehicle or with the housing removed and installed in a holding fixture. The following procedure is necessary only when the housing requires replacement.

1. Raise vehicle and place jack stands under frame side rails. Position a suitable jack under the rear axle housing and raise slightly to support axle assembly.
2. Disconnect shock absorbers from anchor plates.

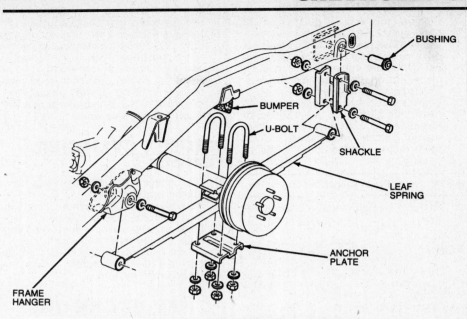

Fig. 5   Rear suspension (left side)

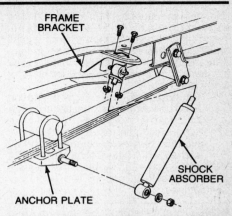

Fig. 6   Shock absorber mounting

3. Scribe reference marks between drive shaft and pinion flange for use during reassembly, then disconnect drive shaft and position aside.
4. Disconnect brake lines from junction block, then remove junction block attaching bolt and junction block and position aside.
5. Remove rear wheels, drums, axles and backing plates.
6. Remove U-bolts and anchor plates, **Fig. 5.**
7. Lower rear axle assembly, then remove lower spring shackle bolts.
8. Remove rear axle assembly.
9. Reverse procedure to install. Torque shock absorber nut to 70 ft. lbs., U-bolt nuts to 85 ft. lbs. and lower spring shackle bolts to 88 ft. lbs.

SHOCK ABSORBER
REPLACE

1. Raise vehicle and place jack stands under frame side rails. Position a suitable jack under the rear axle housing and raise slightly to support axle assembly.
2. Disconnect shock absorber from upper mounting location, **Fig. 6.**
3. Disconnect shock absorber attaching nut from spring anchor plate.
4. Remove shock absorber.
5. Reverse procedure to install. Torque upper mount to 15 ft. lbs. and lower mount nut to 50 ft. lbs.

LEAF SPRING ASSEMBLY
REMOVAL

1. Raise vehicle and place jack stands under frame side rails to relieve spring load. Support axle assembly.
2. Loosen, but do not remove, spring to shackle attaching nut, **Fig. 5.**
3. Remove U-bolt attaching nuts, then the U-bolts. Rotate anchor plate on shock absorber lower mount to clear the leaf spring assembly.
4. Remove shackle to frame attaching nut and bolt.

NOTE: After removal of shackle to frame attaching nut and bolt, spring is free to rotate on front hanger bolt. Use suitable restraining device to prevent rotation.

5. Remove front spring hanger nut and bolt, then the spring.

BUSHING, REPLACE

1. Straighten or remove bushing flares.
2. Place spring in suitable press and press out bushing.
3. Press in new bushing using suitable tool that presses on steel outer shell of bushing.
4. Flare bushing outer sleeve to spring.

INSTALL

1. Clean axle spring pad, then position spring at front hanger and install through bolt and nut. Do not tighten nut at this time.
2. Position spring shackle at rear mount and install through bolt and nut. Do not tighten at this time.

NOTE: Prior to installing rear mount through bolt and nut, ensure shackle is loosely attached to spring rear eye, open end of shackle is facing forward and axle is in position above spring.

3. Position axle spring pad onto spring, ensuring spring center bolt head is seated in spring pad seat pilot hole.
4. Rotate anchor plate on shock absorber to bring anchor plate into proper position, then install U-bolts and nuts. Using a diagonal tightening sequence, tighten U-bolt nuts snugly.
5. Lower vehicle so suspension components are supporting vehicle, then torque U-bolt nuts to 85 ft. lbs. and spring mounting nuts to 88 ft. lbs.

DRUM BRAKE ADJUSTMENTS

These brakes have self adjusting shoe mechanisms that ensure correct lining-to-drum clearances at all times. The automatic adjusters operate only when brakes are applied as vehicle is moving rearward.

Although the brakes are self-adjusting, an initial adjustment is necessary after brake shoes have been relined or replaced, or when length of star wheel adjuster has been changed during some other service operation.

Frequent usage of an automatic transmission forward range to halt reverse vehicle motion may prevent automatic adjusters from functioning, thereby inducing low pedal heights. Should low pedal heights be encountered, it is recommended that numerous forward and reverse stops be made until satisfactory pedal height is obtained.

NOTE: If a low pedal height condition cannot be corrected by making numerous reverse stops (provided hydraulic system is free of air), the self-adjusting mechanism is not functioning. Therefore it will be necessary to remove brake drum, clean, free up and lubricate adjusting mechanism. Then adjust brakes as follows, being sure parking brake is fully released.

ADJUSTMENTS

Upon initial adjustment, a lanced area in the brake backing plate must be removed prior to adjusting brakes. To remove lanced area, knock out with a suitable hammer and punch, then remove brake drum to clear any metal particles caught inside the brake compartment. Install brake drum and proceed with adjustment. After adjustment is complete, install brake adjustment hole cover to prevent entry of water and dirt.

1. Turn brake adjusting screw to expand shoes until wheel can just be turned by hand.
2. Using a suitable tool to hold actuator lever off adjuster, back adjuster off 30 notches on 1982–84 models or 24 notches on 1985 models. If shoes still drag, back off one or two additional notches.

NOTE: Brakes should be free of drag when adjuster has been backed off approximately 12 notches. Heavy drag at this point indicates tight parking brake cables.

3. Install adjusting hole cover on brake drum or backing plate.
4. Check parking brake adjustment.

PARKING BRAKE
ADJUST

1982–84

1. Depress parking brake pedal 10 clicks on all models except two-wheel drive pickup. On two-wheel drive pickup, depress parking brake pedal 8 clicks.
2. Raise and support vehicle.

3. Place a cable tension gauge on right hand side cable on all except two-wheel drive pickup. On two-wheel drive pickup, place tension gauge on left hand side cable. On all models, place tension gauge as close as possible to cable equalizer.
4. Tighten or loosen adjusting nut as necessary to provide 140–150 lbs. of tension on all except two-wheel drive pickup. On two-wheel drive pickup, adjust nut to provide 200–220 lbs. of tension.

NOTE: Do not over adjust parking brake.

5. Remove tension gauge and lower vehicle.

1985

1. Block front wheels, ensure that brake pedal is fully released, then raise and support rear of vehicle.
2. Loosen adjusting nut at rear cable equalizer until rear wheels spin freely and ensure that cables do not bind or stick over operating range.

NOTE: On Pickup models with intermediate cable bracket, remove bracket before performing any parking brake adjustments.

3. Depress parking brake pedal 2 clicks on 2 wheel drive models or 3 clicks on 4 wheel drive models.
4. Tighten equalizer adjusting nut until rear wheels will not rotate forward

without applying excessive force.
5. Loosen adjusting nut until moderate drag is felt when rotating wheels forward, ensuring that drag at each wheel is approximately equal.
6. Reinstall cable guide, if removed, release parking brake pedal, and ensure that little or no brake drag is felt when rotating rear wheels.

MASTER CYLINDER
REPLACE

1. Disconnect hydraulic brake lines from master cylinder.
2. Remove two master cylinder attaching nuts, then the master cylinder.
3. Install master cylinder and attaching nuts. Torque nuts to 22–33 ft. lbs.
4. Attach hydraulic brake lines. Torque nuts to 120–180 inch lbs.
5. Bleed brake system.

POWER BRAKE UNIT
REPLACE

1. Disconnect master cylinder assembly and vacuum hose from power brake unit.
2. Disconnect power brake unit push rod from brake pedal.
3. Remove power brake unit attaching nuts from inside of vehicle.
4. Remove power brake unit.
5. Reverse procedure to install. Torque power brake unit attaching nuts and master cylinder attaching nuts to 22–33 ft. lbs.

Front Suspension & Steering Section

WHEEL ALIGNMENT

NOTE: Before checking or adjusting caster and camber angles, jounce vehicle at least 3 times to prevent false geometric readings.

4 × 2

Caster and camber adjustments are made by shims inserted between upper control arm shaft and frame bracket, **Fig. 1.** Add, subtract, or transfer shims to change readings as noted below.

To adjust caster and/or camber, loosen upper control arm shaft to frame nuts, then add or subtract shims as necessary and torque upper control arm shaft to frame nuts to 45 ft. lbs. After adjustment, the shim pack should have at least two threads of bolt exposed beyond the nut. The difference between front and rear shim packs must not exceed 0.40 inches.

Caster, Adjust

Transfer shims from front to rear, or rear to front. The transfer of one shim from rear

to front bolt will decrease positive caster.

Camber, Adjust

Change shims at both front and rear of shaft. Adding an equal amount of shims at both front and rear locations will decrease positive camber.

4 × 4

NOTE: Before checking or adjusting caster and camber angles, jounce vehicle at least 3 times to prevent false geometric readings.

Caster and camber adjustments are made by cam mounted upper control arm attaching bolts.

To adjust caster and/or camber, loosen upper control arm to frame attaching bolt nut, then rotate cam by turning bolt head. When proper alignment settings are established, torque upper control arm to frame attaching bolt nut to 70 ft. lbs.

Caster, Adjust

To increase positive caster, move front cam lobe inward and rear cam lobe outward.

Camber, Adjust

To increase positive camber, move both front and rear cam lobes inward.

TOE-IN
ADJUST

To adjust, loosen clamp bolts at each end of steering tie rod adjustable sleeves. With steering wheel in straight ahead position, turn tie rod adjusting sleeves to obtain proper adjustment. After adjusting, check that number of threads showing on each end of sleeve are equal and that the tie rod end housings are at the right angles to steering arm. Position tie rod clamps and sleeves, **Fig. 2,** and torque nuts to 15 ft. lbs.

WHEEL BEARINGS
ADJUST

4 × 2

1. Raise and support front of vehicle.

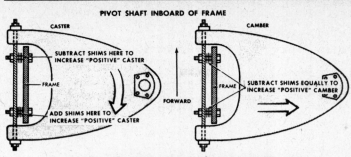

Fig. 1 Caster and camber adjustment. 4 × 2 models

Tie rod and sleeve positioning figure:

Fig. 2 Tie rod clamp and sleeve positioning

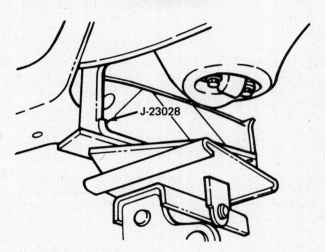

Fig. 3 Removing spring with adapter J-23028. 4 × 2 models

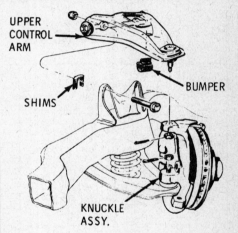

Fig. 4 Upper control arm replacement. 4 × 2 models

2. Remove hub dust cover, then the cotter pin.
3. While rotating wheel assembly in forward direction, torque spindle nut to 12 ft. lbs. to fully seat the bearings.
4. Loosen nut to the "just loose" position, then tighten the spindle nut finger tight.
5. If either spindle hole does not line up with a spindle nut slot, back off spindle nut not more than ½ nut flat.
6. Install new cotter pin, then measure hub end play. End play should be .001–.005 inches when properly adjusted.
7. Install hub dust cover and lower vehicle.

4 × 4

These vehicles use sealed front wheel bearings which require no lubrication or adjustment.

COIL SPRING
REPLACE

4 × 2

1. Raise and support vehicle.
2. Remove the two shock absorber screws and push shock up through control arm and into spring.
3. Support vehicle so that control arms hang free.
4. Place Tool J-23028, or equivalent, into position cradling the inner bushings, **Fig. 3.** Tool should be secured to a suitable jack.
5. Remove stabilizer to lower control arm attachment.
6. Raise the jack to remove tension on lower control arm pivot bolts, then install a chain around spring and through control arm and remove the nuts and bolts.
7. Lower control arm by slowly lowering jack.
8. With all pressure removed from spring, remove safety chain and spring.

NOTE: Do not apply force to lower control arm and ball joint to remove spring. Proper maneuvering of spring will allow for easy removal.

9. Reverse procedure to install, noting the following:
   a. Ensure that coil spring is installed with flat coiled end with gripper notch on top and the lower coil covering all or part of one drain hole in lower control arm and with other hole exposed.
   b. Install both lower control arm bolts from front to rear to ensure adequate steering linkage clearance.
   c. Torque stabilizer link nuts to 13 ft. lbs., lower vehicle and torque lower control arm bolt nuts to 65 ft. lbs. after suspension had been weighted.

UPPER CONTROL ARM
REPLACE

4 × 2

1. Remove retaining nuts and shims from control arm, **Fig. 4.** Note location of shims for assembly reference.
2. Raise and support vehicle. Support lower control arm using a suitable jack.

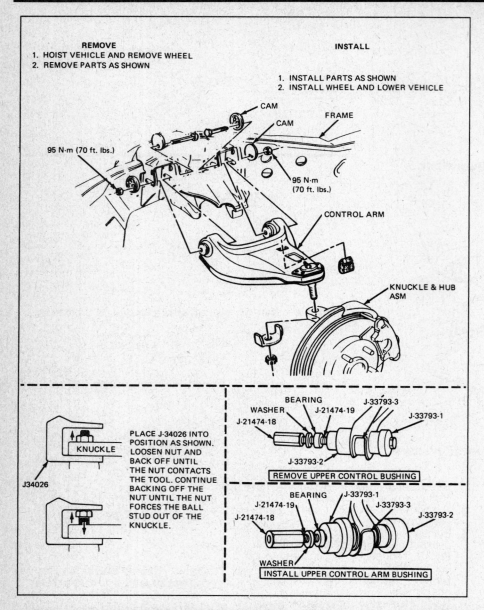

Fig. 5   Upper control arm & bushing replacement. 4 × 4 models

NOTE: Jack must be positioned between coil spring seat and ball joint of lower control arm to obtain maximum leverage against coil spring pressure.

3. Remove front wheel, then loosen upper ball joint from steering knuckle as described under "Upper Ball Joint, Replace".
4. Support hub assembly to prevent damage to brake line when removing control arm.
5. Remove upper control arm attaching bolts, then the control arm.
6. Reverse procedure to install. Torque retaining nuts to 45 ft. lbs.

4 × 4

1. Raise vehicle and support at frame,

raise lower control arm to relieve spring tension, placing jack as far outboard on lower control arm as possible.
2. Remove front wheel.
3. Remove and install control arm as shown in **Fig. 5**, supporting spindle to prevent damaging brake hoses.

UPPER CONTROL ARM BUSHING
REPLACE

4 × 2

1. Remove upper control arm as described previously.

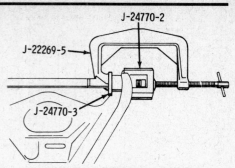

Fig. 6   Upper control arm bushing removal. 4 × 2 models

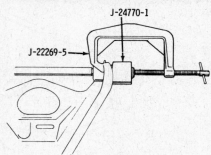

Fig. 7   Upper control arm bushing installation. 4 × 2 models

2. Remove nuts from end of pivot shaft, then remove bushings, **Fig. 6**.
3. Install bushings by installing pivot shaft in control arm and pressing new bushings into control arm, **Fig. 7**. Torque pivot shaft nuts to 85 ft. lbs. with weight of vehicle resting on wheels.

NOTE: Both bushings must be installed .48–.52 inch from face of control arm to bushing outer sleeve.

4 × 4

Refer to **Fig. 5** for upper control arm bushing replacement procedure on four-wheel drive vehicles.

LOWER CONTROL ARM
REPLACE

4 × 2

1. Remove coil spring as described previously.
2. Remove lower ball joint stud, then remove lower control arm through opening in splash shield.
3. Reverse procedure to install.

4 × 4

Refer to **Fig. 8** for lower control arm replacement procedure on four-wheel drive vehicles.

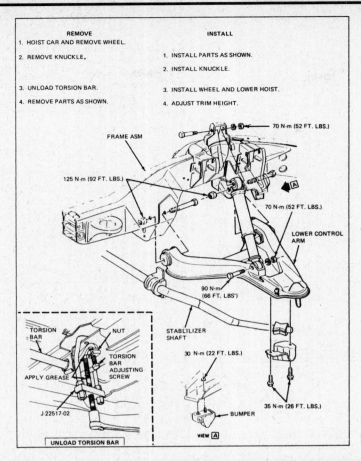

REMOVE
1. HOIST CAR AND REMOVE WHEEL.
2. REMOVE KNUCKLE.
3. UNLOAD TORSION BAR.
4. REMOVE PARTS AS SHOWN.

INSTALL
1. INSTALL PARTS AS SHOWN.
2. INSTALL KNUCKLE.
3. INSTALL WHEEL AND LOWER HOIST.
4. ADJUST TRIM HEIGHT.

Fig. 8   Lower control arm replacement. 4 × 4 models

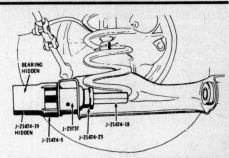

Fig. 9   Lower control arm front bushing removal. 4 × 2 models

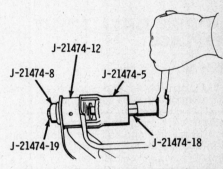

Fig. 10   Lower control arm rear bushing removal. 4 × 2 models

LOWER CONTROL ARM BUSHINGS
REPLACE

4 × 2

1. Drive bushing flare down flush with rubber of front bushing, then remove front and rear bushings from control arm, **Figs. 9 and 10.**

2. Install front bushing, **Fig. 11,** then flare the bushing, **Fig. 12.**
3. Install rear bushings, **Fig. 13,** then the lower control arm as described previously.

4 × 4

Refer to **Fig. 14** for lower control arm bushing replacement procedure on four-wheel drive vehicles.

LOWER BALL JOINT
REPLACE

4 × 2

1. Raise vehicle and support with jack stands under frame side rails.
2. Remove front wheel, then support control arm spring seat with a suitable jack.
3. Remove cotter pin and stud nut, then break ball joint loose from steering knuckle using tool J-23742, or equivalent.

NOTE: Inspect and clean the tapered hole in steering knuckle. If hole is out of round, or damaged in any way, the steering knuckle must be replaced.

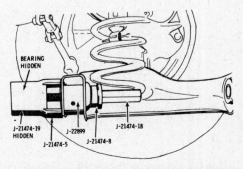

Fig. 11   Lower control arm front bushing installation. 4 × 2 models

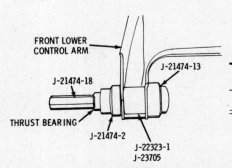

Fig. 12   Flaring lower control arm front bushing. 4 × 2 models

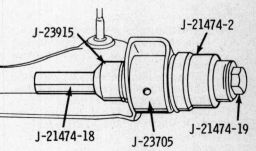

Fig. 13   Lower control arm rear bushing installation. 4 × 2 models

4. Guide lower control arm out of opening in splash shield, then position a wooden brake backing plate block between frame and upper control arm to block knuckle assembly out of the way.
5. Remove grease fittings, then press ball joint from lower control arm.
6. Reverse procedure to install. Torque stud nut to 90 ft. lbs.

4 × 4

Refer to **Fig. 15** for lower ball joint replacement procedure on four-wheel drive vehicles.

UPPER BALL JOINT
REPLACE

4 × 2

1. Raise vehicle and support at lower control arm with suitable jacks.

NOTE: Jack must be positioned between coil spring seat and ball joint of lower control arm to obtain maximum leverage against coil spring pressure.

2. Remove wheel, then remove cotter pin and stud nut from ball joint.
3. Break stud loose from steering knuckle using tool J-23742, or equivalent. Support knuckle assembly to avoid damaging brake line.
4. With control arm in raised position, drill rivets ¼ inch deep with a ⅛ inch drill, then drill off rivet heads with a ½ inch drill.
5. Punch out rivets, then remove ball joint.
6. Reverse procedure to install. Replace rivets with attaching bolts and nuts. Torque attaching nuts to 8 ft. lbs. and the stud nut to 65 ft. lbs.

4 × 4

Refer to **Fig. 15** for upper ball joint replacement procedure on four-wheel drive vehicles.

SHOCK ABSORBER
REPLACE

4 × 2

1. Raise and support vehicle.
2. Hold shock upper stem from turning with a suitable wrench and remove nut, retainer and grommet.
3. Remove lower shock pivot bolts, then remove shock absorber from vehicle.
4. Reverse procedure to install. Torque upper attaching nut to 8 ft. lbs. and lower attaching bolts to 20 ft. lbs.

4 × 4

Refer to **Fig. 16** for shock absorber replacement procedure on four-wheel drive vehicles.

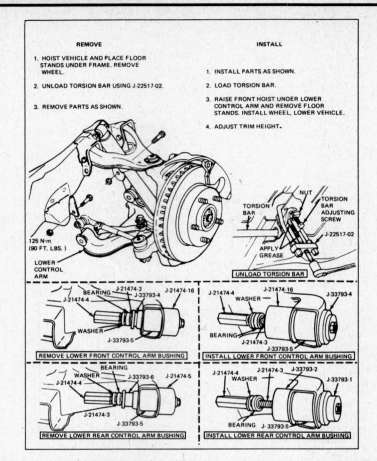

Fig. 14   Lower control arm bushing replacement. 4 × 4 models

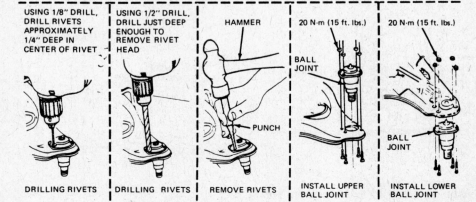

Fig. 15   Ball joint replacement. 4 × 4 models

REMOVE

1. HOIST VEHICLE
2. REMOVE PARTS AS SHOWN

INSTALL

1. INSTALL PARTS AS SHOWN.
2. LOWER VEHICLE

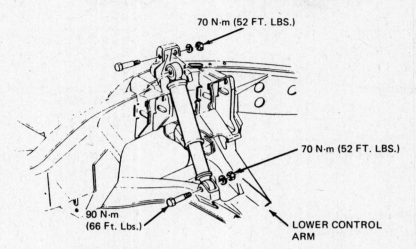

70 N·m (52 FT. LBS.)

70 N·m (52 FT. LBS.)

90 N·m (66 Ft. Lbs.)

LOWER CONTROL ARM

Fig. 16 Shock absorber replacement. 4 × 4 models

STEERING KNUCKLE
REPLACE

4 × 2

1. Raise and support front of vehicle, then support lower control arm with suitable jack.

NOTE: Jack must be positioned between coil spring seat and ball joint of lower control arm to obtain maximum leverage against coil spring pressure.

2. Remove brake caliper, then the hub and rotor assembly.
3. Remove splash shield to steering knuckle attaching bolts.
4. Remove tie rod end from steering knuckle using tool J-6627, or equivalent.
5. If steering knuckle is to be replaced, remove knuckle seal.
6. Remove ball joint studs from steering knuckle using tool J-23742 or equivalent.
7. Raise upper control arm to disengage upper ball joint stud from knuckle.
8. Remove knuckle from lower ball joint stud.
9. After removal, inspect tapered holes. If holes are out of round, or deformation or damage is observed, replace steering knuckle.
10. Reverse procedure to install. Torque splash shield attaching bolts to 10 ft. lbs. When installing tie rod end, install tool J-29193 and torque to 15 ft. lbs., then remove tool and torque to 40 ft. lbs.

4 × 4

Refer to **Fig. 17** for steering knuckle replacement procedure on four-wheel drive vehicles.

STABILIZER BAR
REPLACE

4 × 2

1. Raise and support front of vehicle.
2. Remove stabilizer link bolt nuts from both sides, then pull link bolt from linkage and remove retainers, grommets and spacers, **Fig. 18.**
3. Remove stabilizer bracket to frame or body attaching bolts, then the stabilizer bar, bushings and brackets.
4. Reverse procedure to install, noting the following: install stabilizer bar so the identification stamping appears on

REMOVE
1. REMOVE PARTS AS SHOWN.

INSTALL
1. INSTALL PARTS AS SHOWN.

DO NOT BACK OFF NUT TO INSTALL NEW COTTER PIN.

68 N·m (50 ft. lbs.)

KNUCKLE

KNUCKLE SEAL

235 N·m (174 FT. LBS.)

HUB AND BEARING ASSEMBLY

105 N·m (78 FT. LBS.)   48 N·m (35 ft. lbs.)   113 N·m (83 ft. lbs.)

J-28712

INSTALL DRIVE AXLE COVER

J-34026
KNUCKLE
J-34026

PLACE J-34026 INTO POSITION AS SHOWN. LOOSEN NUT AND BACK OFF UNTIL THE NUT CONTACTS THE TOOL. CONTINUE BACKING OFF THE NUT UNTIL THE NUT FORCES THE BALL STUD OUT OF THE KNUCKLE.

DISCONNECT BALL JOINT

TIE ROD END
J-24319

REMOVE TIE ROD END

HAMMER
J-28574
KNUCKLE

INSTALL KNUCKLE SEAL

Fig. 17 Steering knuckle replacement. 4 × 4 models

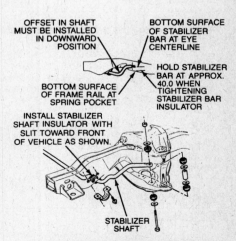

OFFSET IN SHAFT MUST BE INSTALLED IN DOWNWARD POSITION

BOTTOM SURFACE OF STABILIZER BAR AT EYE CENTERLINE

BOTTOM SURFACE OF FRAME RAIL AT SPRING POCKET

HOLD STABILIZER BAR AT APPROX. 40.0 WHEN TIGHTENING STABILIZER BAR INSULATOR

INSTALL STABILIZER SHAFT INSULATOR WITH SLIT TOWARD FRONT OF VEHICLE AS SHOWN.

STABILIZER SHAFT

Fig. 18 Stabilizer bar replacement. 4 × 2 models

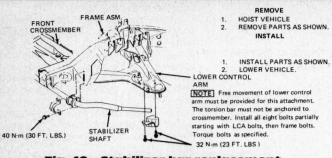

REMOVE
1. HOIST VEHICLE
2. REMOVE PARTS AS SHOWN.
INSTALL

1. INSTALL PARTS AS SHOWN.
2. LOWER VEHICLE.

NOTE Free movement of lower control arm must be provided for this attachment. The torsion bar must not be anchored to crossmember. Install all eight bolts partially starting with LCA bolts, then frame bolts. Torque bolts as specified.

Fig. 19 Stabilizer bar replacement. 1983 4 × 4 models

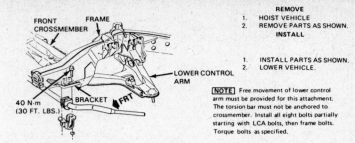

REMOVE
1. HOIST VEHICLE
2. REMOVE PARTS AS SHOWN.
INSTALL

1. INSTALL PARTS AS SHOWN.
2. LOWER VEHICLE.

NOTE Free movement of lower control arm must be provided for this attachment. The torsion bar must not be anchored to crossmember. Install all eight bolts partially starting with LCA bolts, then frame bolts. Torque bolts as specified.

Fig. 20 Stabilizer bar replacement. 1984 4 × 4 models

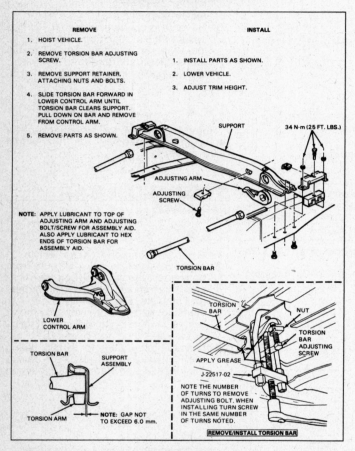

REMOVE
1. HOIST VEHICLE.
2. REMOVE TORSION BAR ADJUSTING SCREW.
3. REMOVE SUPPORT RETAINER, ATTACHING NUTS AND BOLTS.
4. SLIDE TORSION BAR FORWARD IN LOWER CONTROL ARM UNTIL TORSION BAR CLEARS SUPPORT. PULL DOWN ON BAR AND REMOVE FROM CONTROL ARM.
5. REMOVE PARTS AS SHOWN.

INSTALL
1. INSTALL PARTS AS SHOWN.
2. LOWER VEHICLE.
3. ADJUST TRIM HEIGHT.

NOTE: APPLY LUBRICANT TO TOP OF ADJUSTING ARM AND ADJUSTING BOLT/SCREW FOR ASSEMBLY AID. ALSO APPLY LUBRICANT TO HEX ENDS OF TORSION BAR FOR ASSEMBLY AID.

Fig. 21 Torsion bar replacement. 4 × 4 models

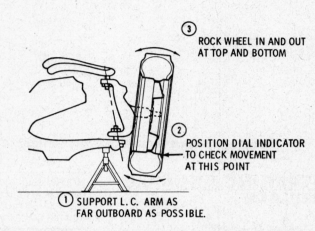

Fig. 22 Checking upper ball joint. 4 × 2 models

the right side of vehicle. Position the rubber bushings squarely in the brackets with the slit facing the front of vehicle. Torque link nuts to 13 ft. lbs. and bracket bolts to 24 ft. lbs.

4 × 4

Refer to **Figs. 19 and 20** for stabilizer bar replacement procedure on four-wheel drive vehicles.

TORSION BAR
REPLACE

4 × 4

Refer to **Fig. 21** for torsion bar replacement procedure on four-wheel drive vehicles.

BALL JOINT INSPECTION

4 × 2

Upper Ball Joint

NOTE: Before checking ball joints, wheel bearings must be properly adjusted.

1. Raise vehicle and position floor stands under right and left lower control arms near each lower ball joint.
2. Position dial indicator against wheel rim, **Fig. 22.**
3. Shake wheel, **Fig. 22,** and read gauge. Horizontal deflection should not exceed .125 in.
4. If reading exceeds .125 in., or if ball stud has been disconnected from knuckle assembly and any looseness is detected or stud is loose, replace ball joint.

Lower Ball Joint

The lower ball joint has a visual wear indicator, **Fig. 23.** To check, vehicle weight must rest on wheels to properly load ball joints.

4 × 4

Refer to **Fig. 24** for ball joint inspection procedure on four-wheel drive vehicles.

STEERING GEAR
REPLACE

1. On models equipped with power steering, disconnect pressure and return hoses from steering gear housing, then plug hose ends and gear housing ports to prevent entry of dirt.

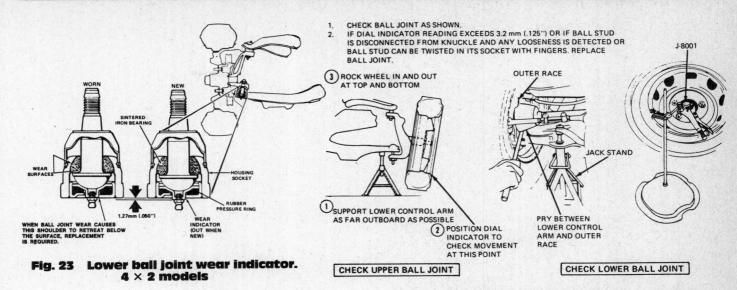

1. CHECK BALL JOINT AS SHOWN.
2. IF DIAL INDICATOR READING EXCEEDS 3.2 mm (.125") OR IF BALL STUD IS DISCONNECTED FROM KNUCKLE AND ANY LOOSENESS IS DETECTED OR BALL STUD CAN BE TWISTED IN ITS SOCKET WITH FINGERS, REPLACE BALL JOINT.

3. ROCK WHEEL IN AND OUT AT TOP AND BOTTOM

WORN   NEW
SINTERED IRON BEARING
WEAR SURFACES
HOUSING SOCKET
1.27mm (.050")
RUBBER PRESSURE RING
WHEN BALL JOINT WEAR CAUSES THIS SHOULDER TO RETREAT BELOW THE SURFACE, REPLACEMENT IS REQUIRED.
WEAR INDICATOR (OUT WHEN NEW)

OUTER RACE
J-8001
JACK STAND

1. SUPPORT LOWER CONTROL ARM AS FAR OUTBOARD AS POSSIBLE
2. POSITION DIAL INDICATOR TO CHECK MOVEMENT AT THIS POINT

PRY BETWEEN LOWER CONTROL ARM AND OUTER RACE

CHECK UPPER BALL JOINT   CHECK LOWER BALL JOINT

Fig. 23   Lower ball joint wear indicator. 4 × 2 models

Fig. 24   Checking ball joints. 4 × 4 models

2. Disconnect battery ground cable and remove coupling shield if so equipped.
3. Remove retaining nuts, lock washers and bolts at steering coupling to steering shaft flange.
4. Remove pitman arm nut and washer from pitman shaft and mark relation of arm position to shaft, then remove pitman arm with Tool J-6632, or equivalent.
5. Remove screws securing steering gear to frame and remove gear from vehicle.
6. Reverse procedure to install.

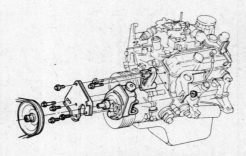

Fig. 25   Power steering pump assembly mounting

POWER STEERING PUMP
REPLACE

1. Disconnect pressure and return hoses from power steering pump or steering gear housing, then secure ends in raised position to prevent oil drainage. Cap all open lines and fittings.
2. Remove power steering pump belt, then power steering pump attaching bolts.
3. Remove power steering pump assembly, **Fig. 25**.

Front Wheel Drive Section

DESCRIPTION

The front suspension is independent with torsion bars attached to the lower control arms. The front differential is mounted to the frame, with universal joints mounted on the inner and outer ends of the axle shafts. The front axle utilizes a center disconnect system which makes shifting in or out of four-wheel drive possible at any vehicle speed. When the transfer case is shifted, a vacuum diaphragm locks or unlocks the center disconnect. This system replaces automatic-locking front hubs.

TUBE & SHAFT ASSEMBLY
REPLACE

REMOVAL

Fig. 1
1. Disconnect battery ground cable.
2. Disconnect shift cable from vacuum actuator. Disengage locking spring, then push actuator diaphragm in to release cable, **Fig. 2**.
3. Unlock steering wheel so linkage is free to move.

4. Raise vehicle and place jack stands under frame side rails.
5. Remove front wheels, drive belt shield and the axle skid plate, if equipped.
6. Support right hand lower control arm with a suitable jack, then disconnect right upper ball joint and remove support so that control arm hangs free.
7. Disconnect right hand drive axle shaft from tube assembly, **Fig. 3**. Insert a drift through opening in top of brake caliper and into corresponding vane of brake rotor to prevent axle from turning.
8. Disconnect four-wheel drive indicator light electrical connector from switch.

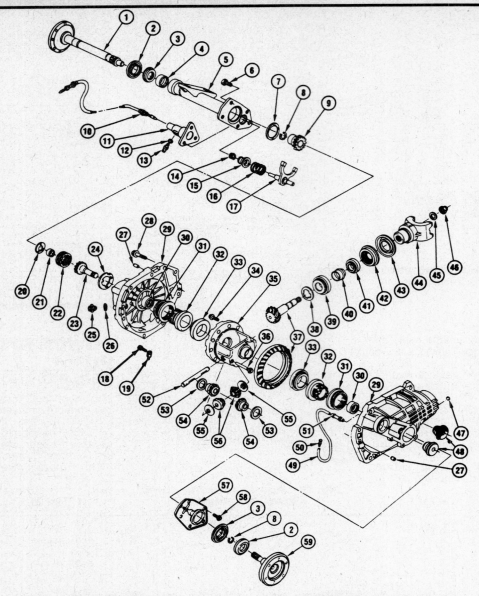

1. SHAFT, Differential Output — Right Hand (Including #2, 8)
2. DEFLECTOR, Differential Output Shaft
3. SEAL, Differential Output Shaft Tube
4. BEARING, Differential Output Shaft Tube
5. TUBE, Differential Carrier Output Shaft
6. BOLT, Tube to Carrier
7. WASHER, Carrier Thrust
8. RING, Shaft Retainer
9. CONNECTOR, Differential Carrier
10. CABLE, Differential Lock
11. HOUSING, Differential Shifter Cable
12. GASKET, Four Wheel Drive Indicator Switch
13. SWITCH, Four Wheel Drive Indicator
14. SPRING, Differential Shifter
15. SEAL, Differential Shifter
16. SPRING, Differential Shifter
17. SHAFT, w/Fork, Differential Shifter
18. BOLT, Hex Flange Head (M6 x 1 x 14)
19. LOCK, Differential Adjuster
20. WASHER, Differential Output Shaft Thrust
21. BEARING, Differential Output Shaft Pilot
22. SLEEVE, Differential
23. SHAFT, Differential Output — Left Hand
24. WASHER, Differential Thrust
25. PLUG, Differential Carrier (M20 x 1.5)
26. WASHER, Differential Carrier Plug
27. PIN, Differential Carrier Alignment
28. BOLT, Differential Carrier (10 Required)
29. CARRIER, Differential (Including #27, 28, 47, 51) (Carrier halves not serviced separately)

30. BEARING, Differential Output Shaft
31. INSERT, Differential Carrier Bearing Adjuster
32. SLEEVE, Differential Carrier Bearing Adjuster
33. BEARING, Differential Side
34. BOLT, Hypoid Drive Gear to Case
35. CASE, Differential
36. SCREW, Differential Pinion Shaft Lock
37. GEAR KIT, Ring and Pinion (Gear Kits also Include #34, 40)
38. SHIM KIT
39. BEARING, Pinion Inner
40. SPACER, Pinion Bearing
41. BEARING, Pinion Outer
42. SEAL, Differential Carrier Pinion
43. DEFLECTOR, Differential Carrier Flange
44. FLANGE, Prop Shaft Pinion (Including #43)
45. WASHER, Prop Shaft Pinion Flange
46. NUT, Prop Shaft Pinion Flange
47. PLUG, Cup Expansion (3/8")
48. BUSHING, Differential Carrier
49. HOSE, Bulk (5/16" ID)
50. VENTILATOR, Front Axle
51. CONNECTOR, Front Axle Vent Hose
52. SHAFT, Differential Pinion
53. WASHER, Differential Side Gear Thrust
54. GEAR, Differential Side
55. WASHER, Differential Carrier Pinion Thrust
56. GEAR, Differential Pinion
57. COVER, Differential Carrier
58. BOLT, Differential Carrier Cover
59. SHAFT, Differential (Including #2, 8)

Fig. 1   Exploded view of front drive axle

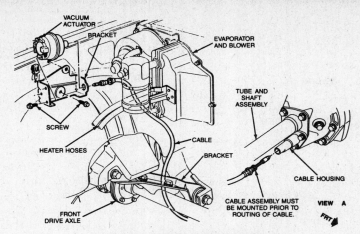

Fig. 2 Vacuum actuator

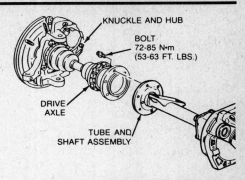

Fig. 3 Drive axle & tube assembly

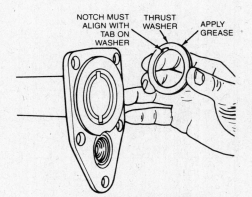

Fig. 4 Thrust washer installation

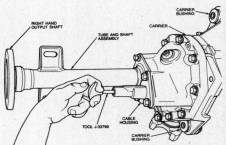

Fig. 5 Checking operation of four-wheel drive mechanism

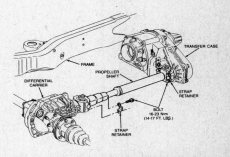

Fig. 6 Front propeller shaft

9. Remove the three shift cable and switch housing-to-carrier attaching bolts and pull housing out to gain access to cable locking spring. Do not remove cable coupling nut unless cable is being replaced.
10. Disconnect shift cable from fork shaft by lifting spring over slot in shift fork.
11. Remove tube bracket bolts from frame and tube assembly attaching bolts from carrier.
12. Remove tube assembly from axle. Use care not to allow sleeve, thrust washers, connector and output shaft to fall from carrier or be damaged when removing tube.

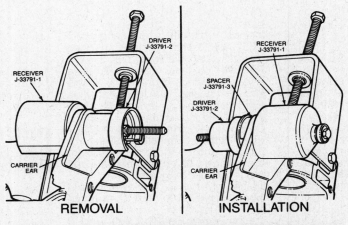

Fig. 7 Differential carrier bushing replacement

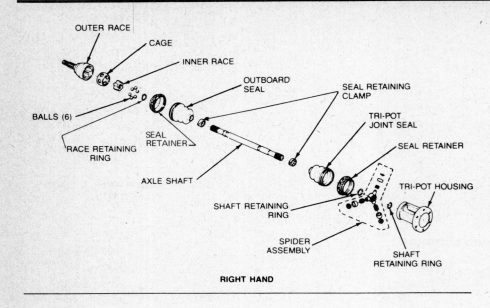

RIGHT HAND

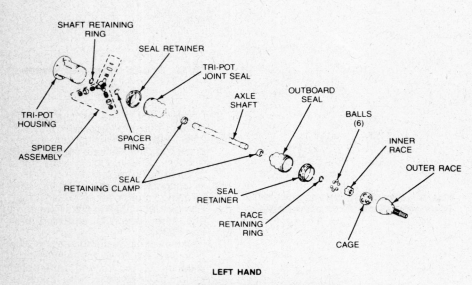

LEFT HAND

Fig. 8   Exploded view of front axle

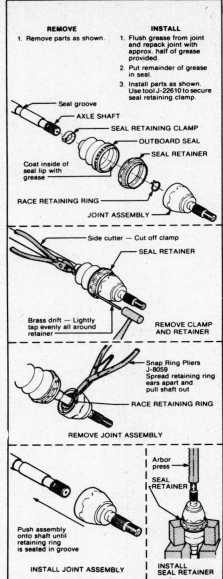

Fig. 9   Outer constant velocity joint seal removal & installation

INSTALLATION

1. Install sleeve, thrust washers, connector and output shaft in carrier. The thrust washer notch must align with tab on washer, **Fig. 4.**
2. Coat the tube to carrier mating surface with Locktite 514 sealant or equivalent.
3. Install tube and shaft assembly to carrier using only one bolt installed finger tight at the one o'clock position. Pull assembly down, then install cable and switch housing and four remaining bolts. Torque bolts to 30–40 ft. lbs.
4. Install the two tube to frame attaching bolts and torque to 45–60 ft. lbs.
5. Check four-wheel drive mechanism

for proper operation by inserting tool J-33799 into shift fork and checking for rotation of axle shaft, **Fig. 5.**
6. Remove tool and install shift cable switch housing, then guide cable through housing into fork shaft hole and push cable in by sliding cable through into fork shaft hole.
7. Connect four wheel drive indicator light electrical connector to switch.
8. Support and raise right hand lower control arm using a suitable jack and connect upper ball joint.
9. Install right hand drive axle to axle tube. Install one bolt first, then rotate axle to install five remaining bolts. Torque bolts to 53–63 ft. lbs.
10. Install front axle skid plate, if

equipped, drive belt shield and front wheels. Torque skid plate bolts to 20–28 ft. lbs.
11. Connect shift cable to vacuum actuator by pushing cable end into actuator shaft hole.

DIFFERENTIAL CARRIER
REPLACE

1. Raise vehicle and place jack stands under frame side rails.
2. Remove tube and shaft assembly as described under "Tube & Shaft Assembly, Replace".

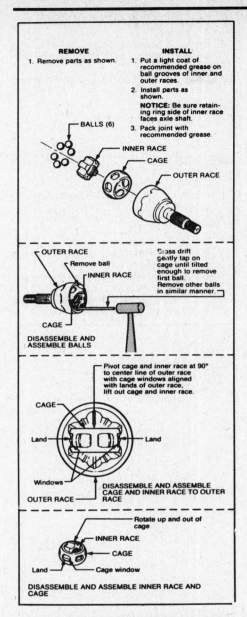

Fig. 10 Outer constant velocity joint disassembly & assembly

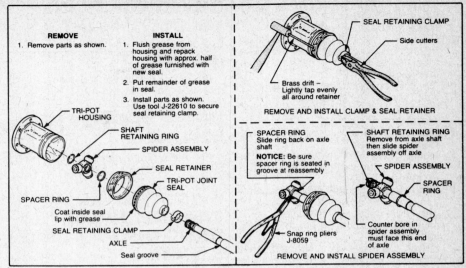

Fig. 11 Inner tri-pot seal removal & installation

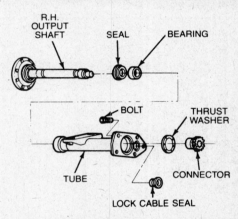

Fig. 12 Right hand output shaft & tube

3. Remove steering stabilizer to frame attaching bolt.
4. Mark position of steering idler arm for reference during installation, then remove idler arm-to-frame attaching bolts.
5. Push steering linkage towards front of vehicle, then remove axle vent hose from carrier fitting.
6. Disconnect left hand drive axle shaft from carrier. When removing bolts, insert a drift through opening in top of brake caliper and into corresponding vane of brake rotor to prevent axle from turning.
7. Disconnect front propeller shaft, **Fig. 6.**
8. Remove carrier-to-frame attaching bolts, then the carrier.

9. Reverse procedure to install. Torque carrier-to-frame attaching bolts to 60–74 ft. lbs. and axle shaft-to-carrier bolts to 53–63 ft. lbs.

DIFFERENTIAL CARRIER BUSHING
REPLACE

1. Remove tube and shaft assembly as described under "Tube & Shaft Assembly, Replace".
2. Remove differential carrier as described under "Differential Carrier, Replace".
3. Remove bushing from carrier ear using tool J-33791, **Fig. 7.**
4. Install new bushing using tool J-33791, **Fig. 7.** Ensure tool J-33791-3 is positioned properly between bush-

ing and carrier ear to prevent bushing from being pressed in too far.

DIFFERENTIAL OUTPUT SHAFT PILOT BEARING
REPLACE

1. Remove bearing using tool J-34011.
2. Install new bearing using tool J-33842.

SHIFT CABLE
REPLACE

1. Remove shift cable from vacuum actuator by disengaging locking spring and pushing actuator diaphragm in to release cable. Compress cable lock-

ing fingers with pliers, then remove cable from bracket.

2. Raise and support vehicle.
3. Remove switch housing mounting bolts and pull housing away from axle tube flange to gain access to cable locking spring.
4. Disconnect cable from shaft fork by lifting spring over slot in shift fork, then unscrew cable from housing and remove from vehicle.
5. Install cable following proper routing, **Fig. 2.**
6. Install cable and switch housing to carrier. Torque mounting bolts to 30–40 ft. lbs.
7. Slide cable through switch housing into fork shaft hole and push cable in. The cable will snap in place automatically. Torque coupling nut to 71–106 inch lbs.
8. Lower vehicle, then connect shift cable to vacuum actuator by pressing cable into bracket hole. The cable will snap in place automatically.
9. Check cable for proper operation.

OUTER CONSTANT VELOCITY JOINT & SEAL
REPLACE

For removal and installation procedures, refer to **Figs. 8, 9, and 10.**

INNER TRI-POT SEAL
REPLACE

For removal and installation procedures, refer to **Fig. 11.**

DIFFERENTIAL CARRIER RIGHT HAND OUTPUT SHAFT & TUBE
DISASSEMBLE

1. Remove output shaft from tube by tap-

ping inside of flange with a rubber mallet, **Fig. 12.**
2. Pry tube seal from tube, then remove bearing from tube using tool J-29369-2.
3. Drive differential shift cable housing seal out of tube using a suitable punch.

ASSEMBLE

1. Install output shaft tube bearing using tool J-33844. When bearing is properly installed, the tool will be flush with tube.
2. Install tube seal using tool J-33893. Flange of seal must be flush with tube outer surface.
3. Install output shaft into tube by tapping flange with a rubber mallet.
4. Install differential shift cable housing seal using tool J-33799.

CHEVROLET & GMC EXC. S/T 10-15, ASTRO VAN & SAFARI VAN

INDEX OF SERVICE OPERATIONS

NOTE: Refer to page 1 of this manual for vehicle manufacturer's special service tool suppliers.

General Engine Specifications

Year	Engine Model	Carb. Type	Bore & Stroke	Comp. Ratio	Horsepower @ R.P.M. ①	Torque Ft. Lbs. @ R.P.M. ②	Normal Oil Pressure Lbs.
1979	V6-200⑯	2 Bore	3.50 × 3.48	8.2	94 @ 4000	154 @ 2000	34–39
	V6-231⑯	2 Bore	3.80 × 3.40	8.0	115 @ 3800	190 @ 2000	37
	6-250⑩	2 Bore	3.87 × 3.53	8.3	130 @ 4000	210 @ 2000	40–60
	6-250⑫	2 Bore	3.87 × 3.53	8.3	125 @ 4000	205 @ 2000	40–60
	6-250⑭	2 Bore	3.87 × 3.53	8.3	130 @ 4000	205 @ 2000	40–60
	6-292⑮	1 Bore	3.87 × 4.12	7.8	115 @ 3400	215 @ 1600	40–60
	V8-267	2 Bore	3.50 × 3.48	8.5	125 @ 3800	215 @ 2400	40
	V8-305⑰	2 Bore	3.74 × 3.48	8.4	140 @ 4000	240 @ 2000	45
	V8-305⑯㉒	4 Bore	3.74 × 3.48	8.4	160 @ 4000	235 @ 2400	45
	V8-305⑯㉓	4 Bore	3.74 × 3.48	8.4	155 @ 4000	225 @ 2400	45
	V8-350⑯	4 Bore	4.00 × 3.48	8.2	165 @ 3800	260 @ 2400	45
	V8-350⑤⑰	4 Bore	4.00 × 3.48	8.2	165 @ 3600	270 @ 2000	45
	V8-350⑥⑰	4 Bore	4.00 × 3.48	8.2	155 @ 3600	260 @ 2000	45
	V8-350⑦	—	4.057 × 3.385	22.5	125 @ 3600	225 @ 1600	35
	V8-350⑧⑰	4 Bore	4.00 × 3.48	8.3	165 @ 3800	255 @ 2800	45
	V8-400⑩	4 Bore	4.125 × 3.75	8.2	185 @ 3600	300 @ 2400	40
	V8-400⑪	4 Bore	4.125 × 3.75	8.2	170 @ 3600	305 @ 1600	40
	V8-400⑧	4 Bore	4.125 × 3.75	8.3	180 @ 3600	310 @ 2400	40
	V8-454⑬	4 Bore	4.25 × 4.00	7.6	205 @ 3600	335 @ 2800	40
1980	V6-229	2 Bore	3.736 × 3.48	8.6	115 @ 4000	175 @ 2000	45
	V6-231	2 Bore	3.80 × 3.4	8.0	110 @ 3800	190 @ 1600	37
	6-250	2 Bore	3.876 × 3.53	8.25	130 @ 4000	210 @ 2000	40–60
	V8-267	2 Bore	3.50 × 3.48	8.3	120 @ 3600	215 @ 2000	45
	6-292⑮	1 Bore	3.876 × 4.12	7.8	115 @ 3400	215 @ 1600	50
	V8-305㉓	4 Bore	3.74 × 3.48	8.6	155 @ 4000	230 @ 2400	45
	V8-305㉒	4 Bore	3.74 × 3.48	8.6	155 @ 4000	240 @ 1600	45
	V8-350	4 Bore	4.00 × 3.48	8.5	—	—	45
	V8-350⑦	—	4.057 × 3.385	22.5	125 @ 3600	225 @ 1600	35
	V8-400	4 Bore	4.125 × 3.750	8.5	—	—	40
	V8-454	4 Bore	4.25 × 4.00	7.6	225 @ 4000	365 @ 2400	40–55
1981	V6-229㉒	2 Bore	3.736 × 3.48	8.6	110 @ 4200	170 @ 2000	45
	V6-231㉓	2 Bore	3.80 × 3.40	8.0	110 @ 3800	190 @ 1600	37
	6-250⑩	2 Bore	3.88 × 3.53	8.3	115 @ 3600	200 @ 2000	40–60
	6-250⑪	2 Bore	3.88 × 3.53	8.3	105 @ 3600	195 @ 1600	40–60
	6-292⑮	1 Bore	3.88 × 4.12	7.8	115 @ 3400	215 @ 1600	40–60
	V8-267㉒	2 Bore	3.50 × 3.48	8.3	115 @ 4000	200 @ 2400	45
	V8-305⑯㉒	4 Bore	3.74 × 3.48	8.6	145 @ 3800	240 @ 2400	45
	V8-305⑩	4 Bore	3.74 × 3.48	9.2	165 @ 4400	240 @ 2000	45
	V8-350⑦㉒	—	4.057 × 3.385	22.5	125 @ 3600	225 @ 1600	35
	V8-350⑦㉓	—	4.057 × 3.385	22.5	105 @ 3200	200 @ 1600	35
	V8-350⑩	4 Bore	4.00 × 3.48	8.2	165 @ 3800	275 @ 1600	45
	V8-350⑪	4 Bore	4.00 × 3.48	8.2	150 @ 3600	255 @ 1600	45
	V8-350⑧㉒	4 Bore	4.00 × 3.48	8.3	165 @ 3800	255 @ 2800	45
	V8-350⑧㉓	4 Bore	4.00 × 3.48	8.3	155 @ 4000	240 @ 2800	45
	V8-454⑧	4 Bore	4.25 × 4.00	7.9	210 @ 3800	340 @ 2800	40
1982	V6-229㉒	2 Bore	3.74 × 3.48	8.6	110 @ 4200	170 @ 2000	50
	V6-231㉓	2 Bore	3.8 × 3.4	8.0	110 @ 3800	190 @ 1600	37
	6-250⑩	2 Bore	3.88 × 3.53	8.3	120 @ 3600	200 @ 2000	40–60
	6-250⑪	2 Bore	3.88 × 3.53	8.3	110 @ 3600	195 @ 2000	40–60
	6-292⑮	1 Bore	3.88 × 4.12	7.8	115 @ 3400	215 @ 1600	40–60
	V8-267㉒	2 Bore	3.50 × 3.48	8.3	115 @ 4000	205 @ 2400	45
	V8-305⑯	4 Bore	3.74 × 3.48	8.6	150 @ 3800	240 @ 2400	45
	V8-305⑰⑲㉒	4 Bore	3.74 × 3.48	9.2	160 @ 4400	235 @ 2000	45

continued

GENERAL ENGINE SPECIFICATIONS—Continued

Year	Engine Model	Carb. Type	Bore & Stroke	Comp. Ratio	Horsepower @ R.P.M. [1]	Torque Ft. Lbs. @ R.P.M. [2]	Normal Oil Pressure Lbs.
	V8-305[17][20][23]	4 Bore	3.74 × 3.48	9.2	165 @ 4400	240 @ 2000	45
	V8-305[17][23]	4 Bore	3.74 × 3.48	8.6	155 @ 4000	245 @ 1600	45
	V8-350[9]	4 Bore	4.0 × 3.48	8.2	165 @ 3800	275 @ 1600	45
	V8-350[18][22]	4 Bore	4.0 × 3.48	8.3	160 @ 3800	250 @ 2800	45
	V8-350[18][23]	4 Bore	4.0 × 3.48	8.3	155 @ 4000	240 @ 2800	45
	V8-379[3][7]	—	3.98 × 3.80	21.5	130 @ 3600	240 @ 2000	35
	V8-379[4][7]	—	3.98 × 3.80	21.5	135 @ 3600	240 @ 2000	35
	V8-454	4 Bore	4.25 × 4.00	7.9	210 @ 3800	340 @ 2800	40
1983	V6-229[16][22]	2 Bore	3.74 × 3.48	8.6	110 @ 4200	170 @ 2000	50
	V6-231[16][23]	2 Bore	3.80 × 3.40	8.0	110 @ 3800	190 @ 1600	37
	6-250[10]	2 Bore	3.88 × 3.53	8.3	120 @ 3600	200 @ 2000	40–60
	6-250[11]	2 Bore	3.88 × 3.53	8.3	110 @ 3600	195 @ 2000	40–60
	6-292[8]	1 Bore	3.88 × 4.12	7.8	115 @ 3400	215 @ 1600	40–60
	V8-305[16]	4 Bore	3.74 × 3.48	8.6	150 @ 3800	240 @ 2400	45
	V8-305[20][22]	4 Bore	3.74 × 3.48	9.2	165 @ 4400	240 @ 2000	45
	V8-305[19][22]	4 Bore	3.74 × 3.48	9.2	160 @ 4400	235 @ 2000	45
	V8-305[3][23]	4 Bore	3.74 × 3.48	8.6	155 @ 4000	245 @ 1600	45
	V8-350[3][9]	4 Bore	4.00 × 3.48	8.2	165 @ 3800	275 @ 1600	45
	V8-350[8][18][22]	4 Bore	4.00 × 3.48	8.3	160 @ 3800	250 @ 2800	45
	V8-350[8][18][23]	4 Bore	4.00 × 3.48	8.3	155 @ 4000	240 @ 2800	45
	V8-350[7][16]	—	4.057 × 3.385	22.1	105 @ 3200	200 @ 1600	35
	V8-379[3][7][9]	—	3.98 × 3.80	21.3	130 @ 3600	240 @ 2000	35
	V8-379[4][7][18]	—	3.98 × 3.80	21.3	135 @ 3600	240 @ 2000	35
	V8-454[8]	4 Bore	4.25 × 4.00	7.9	230 @ 3800	360 @ 2800	40
1984	V6-229[16][22]	2 Bore	3.74 × 3.48	8.6	110 @ 4000	190 @ 1600	50–65
	V6-231[16][23]	2 Bore	3.80 × 3.40	8.0	110 @ 3800	190 @ 1600	50–65
	6-250[10]	2 Bore	3.88 × 3.53	8.3	115 @ 3600	200 @ 2000	40–60
	6-250[11]	2 Bore	3.88 × 3.53	8.3	110 @ 3600	200 @ 1600	40–60
	6-292[8]	1 Bore	3.88 × 4.12	7.8	115 @ 3600	215 @ 1600	40–60
	V8-305[16]	4 Bore	3.74 × 3.48	8.6	150 @ 4000	240 @ 2400	50–65
	V8-305[10]	4 Bore	3.74 × 3.48	9.2	160 @ 4400	235 @ 2000	45
	V8-305[3][23]	4 Bore	3.74 × 3.48	8.6	155 @ 4000	245 @ 1600	45
	V8-350[3][9]	4 Bore	4.00 × 3.48	8.2	165 @ 3800	275 @ 1600	45
	V8-350[8][18][22]	4 Bore	4.00 × 3.48	8.3	160 @ 3800	250 @ 2800	45
	V8-350[8][18][23]	4 Bore	4.00 × 3.48	8.3	155 @ 4000	240 @ 2800	45
	V8-350[7][16]	—	4.057 × 3.385	22.1	105 @ 3200	200 @ 1600	35
	V8-379[3][7][9]	—	3.98 × 3.80	21.3	130 @ 3600	240 @ 2000	35
	V8-379[4][7][18]	—	3.98 × 3.80	21.3	135 @ 3600	240 @ 2000	35
	V8-454[8]	4 Bore	4.25 × 4.00	7.9	230 @ 3800	360 @ 2800	40
1985	V6-262[16]	[21]	4.00 × 3.48	9.3	130 @ 3600	210 @ 2000	35
	V6-262[17]	4 Bore	4.00 × 3.48	9.3	[24]	[25]	50
	6-292[8][22]	1 Bore	3.88 × 4.12	7.8	115 @ 4000	210 @ 800	50
	6-292[8][23]	1 Bore	3.88 × 4.12	7.8	115 @ 3600	215 @ 1600	50
	V8-305[16]	4 Bore	3.74 × 3.48	8.6	150 @ 4000	240 @ 2400	50–65
	V8-305[17][22]	4 Bore	3.74 × 3.48	9.2	160 @ 4400	235 @ 2000	45
	V8-305[17][23]	4 Bore	3.74 × 3.48	8.6	155 @ 4000	245 @ 1600	45
	V8-350[3]	4 Bore	4.00 × 3.48	8.2	165 @ 3800	275 @ 1600	45
	V8-350[8][22]	4 Bore	4.00 × 3.48	8.3	185 @ 4000	285 @ 2400	45
	V8-350[8][23]	4 Bore	4.00 × 3.48	8.3	155 @ 4000	240 @ 2800	45
	V8-379[3][7]	—	3.98 × 3.82	21.3	130 @ 3600	240 @ 2000	35
	V8-379[4][7]	—	3.98 × 3.82	21.3	148 @ 3600	246 @ 2000	35
	V8-454[8][22]	4 Bore	4.25 × 4.00	7.9	240 @ 3800	375 @ 3200	40
	V8-454[8][23]	4 Bore	4.25 × 4.00	7.9	230 @ 3800	360 @ 2800	40

continued

GENERAL ENGINE SPECIFICATIONS—Continued

①—Horsepower ratings may vary slightly depending on model application.
②—Torque ratings may vary slightly depending on model application.
③—Except heavy duty emissions.
④—Heavy duty emissions.
⑤—Light & medium duty emissions (G.V.W.R. 8500 lbs. or under) except Calif. & high altitude.
⑥—California light & medium duty emissions (G.V.W.R. 8500 lbs. or under) & high altitude emissions (G.V.W.R. 6000 lbs. or under).
⑦—Diesel engine.
⑧—Heavy duty emissions (G.V.W.R. 8501 lbs. or above).
⑨—Except C6P heavy duty chassis.
⑩—Light duty emissions (G.V.W.R. 8500 lbs. or under) except Calif.
⑪—California light & medium duty emissions (G.V.W.R. 8500 lbs. or under).
⑫—California Series 10/1500 light duty emissions (G.V.W.R. 6000 lbs. or under.)
⑬—Light & medium duty emissions (G.V.W.R. 8500 lbs. or under).
⑭—California Series 20/2500 & 30/3500 light & medium duty emissions
(G.V.W.R. 8500 lbs. or under).
⑮—P-10/1500–30/3500 & C, K-30/3500.
⑯—Caballero & El Camino.
⑰—Except Caballero & El Camino.
⑱—With C6P heavy duty chassis.
⑲—All models except C-10/1500.
⑳—C-10/1500.
㉑—Electronic fuel injection.
㉒—Except Calif.
㉓—California.
㉔—C & K models, 155 @ 4000; G models, 145 & 4000.
㉕—C & K models, 230 @ 2400; G models, 225 @ 2400.

Alternator Specifications

Year	Model ①	Field Current @ 80° F. 12 Volts	Rated Hot Output Amperes	Year	Model ①	Field Current @ 80° F. 12 Volts	Rated Hot Output Amperes
1979–80	1101016	4–4.5	80		1103161	4–4.5	37
	1101028	4–4.5	80		1103162	4–4.5	37
	1102394	4–4.5	37	1982	1101044	4.0–4.5	70
	1102480	4–4.5	61		1101066	4.0–4.5	70
	1102485	4–4.5	37		1101071	4.0–4.5	70
	1102486	4–4.5	61		1103043	4.0–4.5	42
	1102491	4–4.5	37		1103044	4.0–4.5	63
	1102841	4–4.5	42		1103085	4.0–4.5	55
	1102886	4–4.5	61		1103088	4.0–4.5	55
	1102887	4–4.5	42		1103091	4.0–4.5	63
	1102888	4–4.5	61		1103092	4.0–4.5	55
	1102889	4–4.5	37		1103118	4.0–4.5	37
1980	1101044	4–4.5	70		1103169	4.0–4.5	63
	1101066	4–4.5	70	1983–84	1100200	4.0–4.5	78
	1101071	4–4.5	70		1100203	4.0–5.0	37
	1103043	4–4.5	42		1100204	4.0–5.0	37
	1103044	4–4.5	63		1100207	4.5–5.0	66
	1103085	4–4.5	55		1100208	4.5–5.0	66
	1103088	4–4.5	55		1100209	4.5–5.0	66
	1103091	4–4.5	63		1100217	4.5–5.0	78
	1103092	4–4.5	55		1100225	4.0–5.0	37
	1103100	4–4.5	55		1100226	4.0–5.0	37
	1103118	4–4.5	37		1100228	4.0–5.0	37
	1103161	4–4.5	37		1100229	4.0–5.0	42
	1103162	4–4.5	37		1100230	4.0–5.0	42
	1103169	4–4.5	63		1100231	4.0–5.0	42
1981–82	1101016	4–4.5	80		1100237	4.5–5.0	55
	1101028	4–4.5	80		1100239	4.5–5.0	55
	1102394	4–4.5	37		1100241	4.5–5.0	66
	1102480	4–4.5	61		1100242	4.5–5.0	66
	1102485	4–4.5	42		1100247	4.5–5.0	63
	1102486	4–4.5	61		1100259	4.5–5.0	78
	1102491	4–4.5	37		1100263	4.5–5.0	78
	1102841	4–4.5	42		1100264	4.5–5.0	78
	1102886	4–4.5	61		1100270	4.5–5.0	78
	1102887	4–4.5	42		1100293	4.0–4.6	85
	1102888	4–4.5	61		1100297	4.0–5.0	42
	1102889	4–4.5	37		1100300	4.5–5.0	63

continued

ALTERNATOR SPECIFICATIONS—Continued

Year	Model ①	Field Current @ 80° F. 12 Volts	Rated Hot Output Amperes	Year	Model ①	Field Current @ 80° F. 12 Volts	Rated Hot Output Amperes
	1101063	4.4–4.9	80		1100231	4.0–5.0	42
	1101064	4.4–4.9	80		1100237	4.5–5.0	56
	1105022	4.5–5.0	78		1100241	4.5–5.0	66
	1105025	4.5–5.0	63		1100242	4.5–5.0	66
	1105041	4.5–5.0	78		1100246	4.5–5.0	66
1985	1100204	4.0–5.0	37		1100259	4.5–5.0	78
	1100207	4.5–5.0	66		1100293	4.0–4.6	85
	1100208	4.5–5.0	66		1101063	4.4–4.9	80
	1100209	4.5–5.0	66		1101064	4.4–4.9	80
	1100217	4.5–5.0	78		1105521	4.5–5.0	78
	1100223	4.0–4.6	37		1105523	4.5–5.0	56
	1100225	4.0–5.0	37		1105652	—	78
	1100229	4.0–5.0	42				

①—Part number.

Starting Motor Specifications

Year	Engine	Starter Model	Free Speed Test		
			Amperes ②	Volts	R.P.M.
1979	V6-200③⑥	1109056	50–80	10.6	7500–11400
	V6-231③	1109061	60–85	9	6800–10300
	6-250④	1108778	50–80	9	5500–10500
	6-250⑤	1108779	50–80	9	5500–10500
	6-292	1108780	50–80	9	3500–6000
	V8-267③	1109524	45–70	9	7000–11900
	V8-305③	1109056	50–80	10.6	7500–11400
	V8-305	1109056	50–80	9	5500–10500
	V8-305⑤	1109798	50–80	9	5500–10500
	V8-350③⑥	1109052	65–95	10.6	7500–10500
	V8-350③⑦	1109059	65–95	10.6	7500–10500
	V8-350	1109052	65–95	9	7500–10500
	V8-350⑧	1109213	40–140	9	8000–13000
	V8-400	1108776	65–95	9	7500–10500
	V8-454	1108776	65–95	9	7500–10500
1980	V6-229③⑥	1109524	50–80	10.6	7500–11400
	V6-231③	1109061	60–85	9	6800–10300
	6-250④	1108778	50–80	9	5500–10500
	6-250⑤	1108779	50–80	9	5500–10500
	6-292	1108780	50–80	9	3500–6000
	V8-267, 305③	1109524	50–80	10.6	7500–11400
	V8-305	1109056	50–80	9	5500–10500
	V8-305⑤	1109798	50–80	9	5500–10500
	V8-350③⑦	1109061	65–95	10.6	7500–10500
	V8-350	1109052	65–95	9	7500–10500
	V8-350⑧	1109216	100–230	9	8000–14000
	V8-400	1108776	65–95	9	7500–10500
	V8-454	1108776	65–95	9	7500–10500
1981	V6-229③⑥	1109524	50–80	10.6	7500–11400
	V6-231③	1109061	60–85	9	6800–10300
	6-250④	1108778	50–80	9	5500–10500
	6-250⑤	1108779	50–80	9	5500–10500
	6-292	1108780	50–80	9	3500–6000

continued

Year	Engine	Starter Model	Free Speed Test		
			Amperes ②	Volts	R.P.M.
	V8-267, 305③	1109524	50–80	10.6	7500–11400
	V8-305	1109056	50–80	9	5500–10500
	V8-305⑤	1109798	50–80	9	5500–10500
	V8-350	1109052	65–95	9	7500–10500
	V8-350⑧	1109216	100–230	9	8000–14000
	V8-454	1108776	65–95	9	7500–10500
1982	V6-229③	1109534	50–80	10.6	7500–11400
	V6-231③	1998236①	60–85	9	6800–10300
	6-250④	1108778	50–80	9	5500–10500
	6-250⑤	1108779	50–80	9	5500–10500
	6-292	1108780	50–80	9	3500–6000
	V8-267, 305③	1109534	50–80	10.6	7500–11400
	V8-305	1109056	50–80	9	5500–10500
	V8-305⑤	1109798	50–80	9	5500–10500
	V8-350	1109052	65–95	9	7500–10500
	V8-379⑧	1109219	—	—	
	V8-454	1108776	65–95	9	7500–10500
1983	V6-229③	1109534	50–80	10.6	7500–11400
	V6-231③	1998236①	60–85	9	6800–10300
	6-250⑨	1998244①	60–85	10	6800–10300
	6-250⑩	1998396①	70–110	10	6500–10700
	6-292⑪⑫	1998244①	60–85	10	6800–10300
	6-292⑩	1998396①	70–110	10	6500–10700
	V8-305③	1109534	45–70	10	7000–11900
	V8-305⑫	1109535	45–70	10	7000–11900
	V8-305⑩	1998396①	70–110	10	6500–10700
	V8-305⑤	1998244①	65–95	10	7500–10500
	V8-350⑪⑫	1998241①	65–95	10	7500–10500
	V8-350⑤	1998244①	65–95	10	7500–10500
	V8-350⑩	1998396①	70–110	10	6500–10700
	V8-350③⑧	1998554①	140–160	10	4400–6300
	V8-379⑧⑨⑩⑪	1109563	120–210	10	9000–13400
	V8-454⑪⑫	1998243①	65–95	10	7500–10500
	V8-454⑩	1998397①	70–110	10	6500–10700
1984	V6-229③	1998452①	50–75	10	6000–11900
	V6-231③	1998236①	60–85	9	6800–10300
	6-250⑨	1998437①	60–90	10	6500–10500
	6-250⑦⑩	1998437①	60–90	10	6500–10500
	6-250⑥⑩	1998438①	70–110	10	6500–10700
	6-292⑫	1998437①	60–90	10	6500–10500
	6-292⑦⑩	1998437①	60–90	10	6500–10700
	6-292⑥⑩	1998438①	70–110	10	6500–10700
	6-292⑪	1998437①	60–90	10	6500–10500
	V8-305③	1998430①	50–75	10	6000–11900
	V8-305⑫	1998427①	50–75	10	6000–11900
	V8-305⑦⑩	1998427①	50–75	10	6000–11900
	V8-305⑥⑩	1998438①	70–110	10	6500–10700
	V8-305⑤	1998439①	70–110	10	6500–10700
	V8-350⑨	1998439①	70–110	10	6500–10700
	V8-350⑦⑩	1998439①	70–110	10	6500–10700
	V8-350⑥⑩	1998438①	70–110	10	6500–10700
	V8-350⑪	1998444①	—	—	—
	V8-350③⑧	1998554①	160–240	10	4400–6300
	V8-379⑧⑨⑩⑪	—	—	—	—

G–94

continued

STARTING MOTOR SPECIFICATIONS—Continued

Year	Engine	Starter Model	Free Speed Test Amperes ②	Volts	R.P.M.
	V8-454⑪⑫	1998441①	70–110	10	6500–10700
	V8-454⑥⑩	1998443①	70–110	10	6500–10700
	V8-454⑦⑩	1998441①	70–110	10	6500–10700
1985	V6-262③	1998435①	50–75	10	6000–11900
	V6-262⑤⑩⑫	—	—	—	—
	6-292⑫	1998437①	60–90	10	6500–10500
	6-292⑦⑩	1998437①	60–90	10	6500–10500
	6-292⑪	1998437①	60–90	10	6500–10500
	6-292⑥⑩	1998438①	70–110	10	6500–10700
	V8-305③	1998435①	50–75	10	6000–11900
	V8-305⑫	1998427①	50–75	10	6000–11900
	V8-305⑦⑩	1998427①	50–75	10	6000–11900
	V8-305⑥⑩	1998438①	70–110	10	6500–10700
	V8-305⑤	1998439①	70–110	10	6500–10700
	V8-350⑥⑩	1998438①	70–110	10	6500–10700
	V8-350⑦⑩	1998439①	70–110	10	6500–10700
	V8-350⑨	1998439①	70–110	10	6500–10700
	V8-379⑧⑨⑩⑪	—	—	—	—
	V8-454⑪⑫	1998441①	70–110	10	6500–10700
	V8-454⑦⑩	1998441①	70–110	10	6500–10700
	V8-454⑥⑩	1998443①	70–110	10	6500–10700

①—Part No.
②—Includes solenoid.
③—Caballero & El Camino.
④—C, K-10.
⑤—G series.
⑥—With auto. trans.
⑦—With manual trans.
⑧—Diesel engine.
⑨—C & G series.
⑩—K series.
⑪—P series.
⑫—C series.

Valve Specifications

Engine	Year	Valve Lash Int.	Valve Lash Exh.	Valve Angles Seat	Valve Angles Face	Valve Springs Installed Height	Valve Springs Pressure Lbs. @ In.	Valve Stem Clearance Intake	Valve Stem Clearance Exhaust	Stem Diameter, Std. Intake	Stem Diameter, Std. Exhaust
V6-200	1979	1 Turn①		46	45	1.70	200 @ 1.25	.0010–.0027	.0010–.0027	.3410–.3417	.3410–.3417
V6-229	1980–84	1 Turn①		46	45	1.70	200 @ 1.25	.0010–.0027	.0010–.0027	.3410–.3417	.3410–.3417
V6-231	1979–81	Hydraulic②		45	45	1.727	③	.0015–.0035	.0015–.0032	.3401–.3412	.3405–.3412
V6-231	1982	Hydraulic②		45	45	1.727	220 @ 1.34	.0015–.0035	.0015–.0032	.3401–.3412	.3405–.3412
V6-231	1983–84	Hydraulic②		45	45	1.727	182 @ 1.34	.0015–.0035	.0015–.0032	.3401–.3412	.3405–.3412
6-250	1979–80	1 Turn①		46	45	1.66	172 @ 1.26	.0010–.0027	.0015–.0032	.3410–.3417	.3410–.3417
6-250	1981–84	1 Turn①		46	45	1.66	175 @ 1.26	.0010–.0027	.0015–.0032	.3410–.3417	.3410–.3417
V6-262	1985	1 Turn①		46	45	1.70	200 @ 1.25	.0010–.0027	.0010–.0027	.3410–.3417	.3410–.3417
V8-267	1979–82	1 Turn①		46	45	1.70	200 @ 1.25	.0010–.0027	.0010–.0027	.3410–.3417	.3410–.3417
6-292	1979–85	1 Turn①		46	46	1.66	175 @ 1.26	.0010–.0027	.0015–.0032	.3410–.3417	.3410–.3417
V8-305	1979–85	1 Turn①		46	45	1.70	200 @ 1.25	.0010–.0027	.0010–.0027	.3410–.3417	.3410–.3417
V8-350	1979–85	1 Turn①		46	45	1.70	200 @ 1.25	.0010–.0027	.0010–.0027	.3410–.3417	.3410–.3417
V8-350④	1979–81	Hydraulic②		⑦	⑧	1.670	151 @ 1.30	.0010–.0027	.0015–.0032	.3425–.3432	.3420–.3427
V8-350④	1983–84	Hydraulic②		⑦	⑧	1.670	210 @ 1.22	.0010–.0027	.0015–.0032	.3425–.3432	.3420–.3427
V8-379④	1982–85	Hydraulic②		46	45	1.811	230 @ 1.38	.0010–.0027	.0010–.0027	—	—
V8-400	1979–80	1 Turn①		46	45	⑤	⑥	.0010–.0027	.0010–.0027	.3410–.3417	.3410–.3417
V8-454	1979	1 Turn①		46	45	1.88	300 @ 1.38	.0010–.0027	.0012–.0029	.3715–.3722	.3715–.3722
V8-454	1980–85	1 Turn①		46	45	1.80	220 @ 1.40	.0010–.0027	.0012–.0029	.3715–.3722	.3715–.3722

①—Turn rocker arm stud nut until all lash is eliminated, then tighten nut the additional turns listed.
②—No adjustment.
③—Intake, 164 @ 1.34; exhaust, 182 @ 1.34.
④—Diesel engine.
⑤—Intake, 1.70; exhaust, 1.61.
⑥—Intake, 200 @ 1.25; exhaust, 200 @ 1.16.
⑦—Intake, 45°; exhaust, 31°.
⑧—Intake, 44°; exhaust, 30°.

Pistons, Pins, Rings, Crankshaft & Bearings Specifications

Engine	Year	Piston Clearance	Ring End Gap①		Piston Pin Diam.	Rod Bearings		Main Bearings			Shaft End Play
			Comp.	Oil		Shaft Diameter	Bearing Clearance	Shaft Diameter	Bearing Clearance	Thrust Bearing No.	
V6-200	1979	.0007–.0017	.010	.015	.9271	2.0986–2.0998	.0013–.0035	②	③	4	.002–.006
V6-229	1980–84	.0007–.0017	.010	.015	.9271	2.0986–2.0998	.0013–.0035	②	③	4	.002–.006
V6-231	1979–84	.0008–.0020	.013	.015	.9392	2.2487–2.2495	.0005–.0026	2.4995	.0003–.0018	2	.003–.009
6-250	1979–84	.0010–.0020	.010	.015	.9271	1.999–2.000	.0010–.0026	2.2979–2.2994	⑤	7	.002–.006
V6-262	1985	.0007–.0017	.010	.015	.9271	2.2487–2.2497	.0013–.0035	②	③	5	.002–.006
V8-267	1979–82	.0007–.0017	.010	.015	.9271	2.0986–2.0998	.0013–.0035	②	③	5	.002–.006
6-292	1979–85	.0026–.0036	.010	.015	.9271	2.099–2.100	.0010–.0026	2.2979–2.2994	⑤	7	.002–.006
V8-305	1979–85	.0007–.0017	.010	.015	.9271	2.0986–2.0998	.0013–.0035	②	③	5	.002–.006
V8-350⑥	1979–85	.0007–.0017	.010	.015	.9271	2.0986–2.0998	.0013–.0035	②	③	5	.002–.006
V8-350⑭	1979–81	.005–.006	.015	.015	1.0951	2.1238–2.1248	.0005–.0026	2.9993–3.0003	⑮	3	.0035–.0135
V8-350⑭	1983–84	.0035–.0045	④	.015	1.0951	2.1238–2.1248	.0005–.0026	2.9993–3.0003	⑧	3	.0035–.0135
V8-379⑭	1982–85	.004–.005	⑨	.009	1.2205	2.398–2.399	.0017–.0039	2.949–2.950	⑬	3	.0019–.0070
V8-400	1979–80	.0014–.0024	.010	.015	.9271	2.0988–2.0998	.0013–.0035	⑦	③	5	.002–.006
V8-454	1979	.0014–.0024	.010	.015	.9896	2.1985–2.1995	.0009–.0025	⑩	⑪	5	.006–.010
V8-454	1980–85	.0030–.0040	.010	.015	.9896	2.199–2.200	.0009–.0025	⑫	⑪	5	.006–.010

①—Fit rings in tapered bores to clearance listed in tightest portion of ring travel.
②—Front, 2.4484–2.4493 inch; intermediate, 2.4481–2.4490 inch; rear, 2.4479–2.4488 inch.
③—Front, .0008–.0020 inch; intermediate, .0011–.0023 inch; rear, .0017–.0032 inch.
④—Top compression ring, .019; 2nd compression ring, .013.
⑤—Nos. 1, 2, 3, 4, 5, 6—.0010–.0024 inch; No. 7, .0016–.0035 inch.
⑥—Caballero, El Camino & Series 10–30 & 1500–3500.
⑦—Nos. 1, 2, 3, 4—2.6484–2.6493 inch; No. 5, 2.6479–2.6488 inch.
⑧—No. 1, 2, 3, 4: .0005–.0021; No. 5: .0020–.0035.
⑨—Top compression ring, .011; 2nd compression ring, .029.
⑩—No. 1, 2.7485–2.7494 inch; Nos. 2, 3, 4—2.7481–2.7490 inch; No. 5, 2.7478–2.7488 inch.
⑪—Nos. 1, 2, 3, 4—.0013–.0025 inch; No. 5, .0024–.0040 inch.
⑫—Nos. 1, 2, 3, 4—2.7481–2.7490 inch; No. 5, 2.7476–2.7486 inch.
⑬—No. 1, 2, 3, 4: .0017–.0032; No. 5: .0022–.0037.
⑭—Diesel engine.
⑮—No. 1, 2, 3, 4: .0005–.0021; No. 5: .0015–.0031.

Engine Tightening Specifications

Engine	Year	Spark Plug Ft. Lbs.	Cylinder Head Bolts Ft. Lbs.	Intake Manifold Ft. Lbs.	Exhaust Manifold Ft. Lbs.	Rocker Arm Stud Ft. Lbs.	Rocker Arm Cover Ft. Lbs.	Connecting Rod Cap Bolts Ft. Lbs.	Main Bearing Cap Bolts Ft. Lbs.	Flywheel to Crankshaft Ft. Lbs.	Vibration Damper or Pulley Ft. Lbs.
V6-200	1979	22	65	30	20	—	45①	45	70	60	60
V6-229	1980–84	22	65	30	20	—	45①	45	70	60	60
V6-231	1979–84	15	80	45	25	30②	4	40	100	60	225
6-250	1979–84	17–27	95⑥	—	30	—	45①	35	65	60	—
V6-262	1985	22	65	30	20	—	45①	45	70	60	60
V8-267	1979–82	22	65	30	20	—	45①	45	70	60	60
6-292	1979–85	17–27	95⑥	40	45	—	45①	40	65	110	60
V8-305③	1979–85	22	65	30	20	—	45①	45	70	60	60
V8-305④	1979–82	17–27	65	30	20	—	45①	45	80	60	60
V8-305④	1983–85	22	65	30	20	—	45①	45	70	60	60
V8-350③	1979	22	65	30	20⑦	—	45①	45	70	60	60
V8-350④	1979–82	17–27	65	30	20⑦	—	45①	45	80⑩	60	60
V8-350④	1983–85	22	65	30	20	—	45①	45	70	60	60
V8-350⑭	1979	12⑨	130⑧	40⑧	25	25⑪	15①	42	120	60	200–310
V8-350⑭	1980–81	12⑨	130⑧	40⑧	25	28⑪	15①	42	120	60	200–310
V8-350⑭	1983–84	12⑨	130⑧	40⑧	25	28⑪	⑫	42	120	60	200–310
V8-379⑭	1982–83	10⑨	⑤	31	22	34②	17	48	⑬	—	151
V8-379⑭	1984–85	10⑨	⑤	31	25	41②	17	48	⑬	—	151
V8-400	1979–80	17–27	65	30	20	—	45①	45	80⑩	60	60
V8-454	1979–85	17–27	80	30	20	50	50①	50	110	65	85

continued

ENGINE TIGHTENING SPECIFICATIONS—Continued

①—Inch Lbs.
②—Rocker arm shaft.
③—Caballero & El Camino.
④—Series 10–30 & 15–3500.
⑤—Torque bolts in sequence in three steps: Step 1, 20 ft. lbs.; Step 2, 50 ft. lbs.; Step 3, turn each bolt an additional ¼ turn.
⑥—Torque left hand front bolt to 85 ft. lbs.
⑦—Inside bolts, 30 ft. lbs.
⑧—Clean & dip entire bolt in engine oil before tightening to obtain a correct specified torque reading.
⑨—Glow plugs.
⑩—Intermediate (2, 3, 4) outer bolts, 70 ft. lbs.
⑪—Rocker arm pivot bolt.
⑫—Fully driven, seated & not stripped.
⑬—Inner, 111 ft. lbs.; outer, 100 ft. lbs.
⑭—Diesel Engine.

Wheel Alignment Specifications

Year	Model	Caster Deg.	Camber Deg.	Toe-In Inch
CABALLERO & EL CAMINO				
1979–85	Man. Steer.	+½ to +1½	0 to +1	¹⁄₁₆–³⁄₁₆
	Power Steer.	+2½ to +3½	0 to +1	¹⁄₁₆–³⁄₁₆
SERIES 10 THRU 30 & 1500 THRU 3500				
1979–80	C, P	①	+.2	³⁄₁₆
	G-10, 20/1500, 2500	①	+.5	³⁄₁₆
	G-30/3500	①	+.2	³⁄₁₆
	K-10, 20/1500, 3500	①	+1②	0
	K-30/3500	①	+.5②	0
	Motor Home (32)	①	+.2	⁵⁄₁₆
1981	C, P	①	+.2	³⁄₁₆
	G-10, 20/1500, 2500	①	+.5	³⁄₁₆
	G-30/3500	①	+.2	³⁄₁₆
	K-10, 20/1500, 2500	①	+1②	³⁄₁₆
	K-30/3500	①	+.5②	³⁄₁₆
	Motor Home (32)	①	+.2	⁵⁄₁₆
1982–84	C-10/1500	①	+.7	³⁄₁₆
	C-20, 30/2500, 3500	①	+.2	³⁄₁₆
	G-10, 20/1500, 2500	①	+.5	³⁄₁₆
	G-30/3500	①	+.2	³⁄₁₆
	K-10, 20/1500, 2500	①	+1②	³⁄₁₆
	K-30/3500	①	+.5②	³⁄₁₆
	P	①	+.2	³⁄₁₆
	Motor Home (32)	①	+.2	⁵⁄₁₆
1985	C-10/1500	①	+.70	.18
	C-20, 30/2500, 3500	①	+.25	.36
	G-10, 20/2500, 3500	①	+.50	.18
	G-30/3500	①	+.25	.18
	K-10, 20, 30/1500, 2500, 3500	①	+1.5②	0
	P-20, 30/2500, 3500	①	+.25	.18
	Motor Home (32)	①	+.25	.25

①—Refer to Front Suspension & Steering section of this chapter.
②—No adjustment provision.

Brake Specifications

Year	Model	Rear Drum I.D.	Wheel Cyl. Bore		Disc Brake Rotor				Master Cyl. I.D.	
			Front Disc	Rear Drum	Nominal Thickness	Minimum Thickness	Thickness Variation (Parallelism)	Run Out (TIR)	Manual Brakes	Power Brakes
1979–80	C10/1500②	③	2.940	④	1.280	1.215	.0005	.004	1.00	1.125
	G10/1500	③	2.940	④	1.280	1.215	.0005	.004	1.00	1.125
	C10/1500⑤	11.15	2.940	937	1.280	1.215	.0005	.004	—	1.125
	C10/1500⑥⑦	11.15	2.940	.937	1.280	1.215	.0005	.004	—	1.125
	P10/1500	11.15	2.940	.937	1.280	1.215	.0005	.004	—	1.125
	K10/1500⑦	11.15	2.940	.937	1.280	1.215	.0005	.004	—	1.125
	C10/1500⑧⑨	11.00	2.940	1.00	1.280	1.215	.0005	.004	—	1.125
	K10/1500②⑧	11.00	2.940	1.00	1.280	1.215	.0005	.004	—	1.125
	G10/1500⑩	11.00	2.940	1.00	1.280	1.215	.0005	.004	—	1.125
	C10/1500②⑪	③	2.940	④	1.280	1.215	.0005	.004	—	1.125
	C, K20/2500②⑤⑥	⑫	2.940	⑬	1.280	1.215	.0005	.004	—	⑭
	P20/2500	⑫	2.940	⑬	1.280	1.215	.0005	.004	—	⑭
	C20/2500②⑮	13.00	2.940	1.062	1.280	1.215	.0005	.004	—	1.250
	G20/2500⑩	11.15	2.940	1.00	1.280	1.215	.0005	.004	—	1.125
	C30/3500②⑤	13.00	⑯	⑰	⑱	⑲	.0005	.004	—	⑳
	C30/3500⑮	13.00	3.380	1.187	1.530	1.465	.0005	.004	—	1.312
	K30/3500②⑤	13.00	3.380	1.187	1.530	1.465	.0005	.004	—	1.312
	G30/3500⑩	⑫	2.940	⑬	1.280	1.215	.0005	.004	—	⑭
	G30/3500㉑㉒	13.00	2.940	1.062	1.280	1.215	.0005	.004	—	1.250
	G30/3500㉑㉓	13.00	3.380	1.187	1.530	1.465	.0005	.004	—	1.312
	P30/3500㉔㉕	13.00	⑯	⑰	⑱	⑲	.0005	.004	—	⑳
	P30/3500㉔㉖	—	3.380	3.380㉗	1.530	1.465	.0005	.004	—	1.336
	P30/3500㉕㉘	13.00	3.380	1.187	1.530	1.465	.0005	.004	—	1.312
	P30/3500㉖㉘	—	3.380	3.380㉗	1.530	1.465	.0005	.004	—	1.336
1979–85	①	9.50	2.50	.750	1.030	.965	.0005	.004	—	.940
1981–82	C10/1500②	③	2.940	1.00	㉚	㊳	.0005	.004	1.00	1.125
	C10/1500②⑪	③	2.940	④	1.280	1.215	.0005	.004	—	1.125
	G10/1500	③	2.940	④	1.280	1.215	.0005	.004	1.00	1.125
	K10/1500②	11.15	2.940	.937	1.280	1.215	.0005	.004	—	1.125
	C, K10/1500⑥⑧	11.15	2.940	.937	1.280	1.215	.0005	.004	—	1.125
	G20/2500⑩	11.15	2.940	.937	1.280	1.215	.0005	.004	—	1.125
	C, K20/2500②	⑫	㉛	⑬	1.280	1.215	.0005	.004	—	⑭
	P20/2500	⑫	㉛	⑬	1.280	1.215	.0005	.004	—	⑭
	C, K20/2500⑤⑥	13.00	3.150	1.062	1.280	1.215	.0005	.004	—	1.250
	C20/2500②⑮	13.00	3.150	1.062	1.280	1.215	.0005	.004	—	1.250
	G30/3500⑩	13.00	3.150	1.062	1.280	1.215	.0005	.004	—	1.250
	G30/3500㉑㉒	13.00	3.150	1.062	1.280	1.215	.0005	.004	—	1.250
	G30/3500㉑㉓	13.00	3.380	1.190	1.530㉟	1.465	.0005	.004	—	1.340㊲
	C, K30/3500②⑤	13.00	3.380	1.190	1.530㉟	1.465	.0005	.004	—	1.340㊲
	P30/3500㉔㉕	13.00	㉜	㉝	⑱㊱	⑲	.0005	.004	—	㉞㊳
	P30/3500㉔㉖	—	3.380	3.380㉗	1.530㉟	1.465	.0005	.004	—	1.336
	P30/3500㉕㉘	13.00	3.380	1.190	1.530㉟	1.465	.0005	.004	—	1.340㊲
	P30/3500㉖㉘	—	3.380	3.380㉗	1.530㉟	1.465	.0005	.004	—	1.336
1983–85	C10/1500②	③	2.940	④	㉚	㊴	.0005	.004	1.00	1.125
	C10/1500②⑪	③	2.940	④	㉚	㊴	.0005	.004	—	1.250
	K10/1500②	11.15	2.940	.937	1.280	1.215	.0005	.004	—	1.125
	K10/1500②⑪	11.15	2.940	.937	1.280	1.215	.0005	.004	—	1.250
	C, K10/1500⑥	11.15	2.940	.937	1.280	1.215	.0005	.004	—	1.125
	C, K10/1500⑥⑪	11.15	2.940	.937	1.280	1.215	.0005	.004	—	1.250
	K10/1500⑧	11.15	2.940	.937	1.280	1.215	.0005	.004	—	1.125

continued

BRAKE SPECIFICATIONS—Continued

Year	Model	Rear Drum I.D.	Wheel Cyl. Bore		Disc Brake Rotor				Master Cyl. I.D.	
			Front Disc	Rear Drum	Nominal Thickness	Minimum Thickness	Thickness Variation (Parallelism)	Run Out (TIR)	Manual Brakes	Power Brakes
1983—85	K10/1500[8][11]	11.15	2.940	.937	1.280	1.215	.0005	.004	—	1.250
	G10/1500[40]	[3]	2.940	[4]	1.280	1.215	.0005	.004	1.00	1.125
	G10/1500[41]	[3]	2.940	[4]	1.280	1.215	.0005	.004	—	1.125
	G20/2500[10]	11.15	2.940	.937	1.280	1.215	.0005	.004	—	1.125
	G20/2500[10][11]	11.15	2.940	.937	1.280	1.215	.0005	.004	—	1.250
	C, K20/2500[2][42]	11.15	2.940	1.00	1.280	1.215	.0005	.004	—	1.125
	C, K20/2500[2][11][42]	11.15	2.940	.937	1.280	1.215	.0005	.004	—	1.250
	C, K20/2500[2][43]	13.00	3.150	1.062	1.280	1.215	.0005	.004	—	1.250
	C20/2500[5]	13.00	3.150	1.062	1.280	1.215	.0005	.004	—	1.250
	C20/2500[2][15]	13.00	3.150	1.062	1.280	1.215	.005	.004	—	1.250
	C, K20/2500[6]	13.00	3.150	1.062	1.280	1.215	.0005	.004	—	1.250
	P20/2500	[12]	[31]	[13]	1.280	1.215	.0005	.004	—	[14]
	P20/2500[11][44]	11.15	2.940	.937	1.280	1.215	.0005	.004	—	1.250
	P20/2500[11][29]	13.00	3.150	1.062	1.280	1.215	.0005	.004	—	1.250
	G30/3500[2][5]	13.00	3.380	1.190	1.530	1.465	.0005	.004	—	1.312
	G30/3500[10]	13.00	3.150	1.062	1.280	1.215	.0005	.004	—	1.250
	G30/3500[21][22]	13.00	3.150	1.062	1.280	1.215	.0005	.004	—	1.250
	G30/3500[23]	13.00	3.380	1.190	1.530	1.465	.0005	.004	—	1.336
	P30/3500[24][25]	13.00	[32]	[33]	[18]	[19]	.0005	.004	—	[20]
	P30/3500[24][26]	—	3.380	3.380[27]	1.530	1.465	.0005	.004	—	1.336
	P30/3500[25][28]	13.00	3.380	1.190	1.530	1.465	.0005	.004	—	1.312
	P30/3500[26][28]	—	3.380	3.380[27]	1.530	1.465	.0005	.004	—	1.336

①—Caballero & El Camino.
②—Pickup.
③—Exc. heavy duty power brakes, 11.00; Heavy duty power brakes, 11.15.
④—Exc. heavy duty power brakes, 1.060; Heavy duty power brakes, .937.
⑤—Chassis cab.
⑥—Suburban.
⑦—With V-8 engine.
⑧—Blazer & Jimmy.
⑨—Suburban with 6 cylinder engine.
⑩—Sportvan, Rally, Vandura & Chevy van.
⑪—With diesel engine.
⑫—Exc. heavy duty power brakes, 11.15; Heavy duty power brakes, 13.00.
⑬—Exc. heavy duty power brakes, 1.00; Heavy duty power brakes, 1.062.
⑭—Exc. heavy duty power brakes, 1.125; Heavy duty power brakes, 1.250.
⑮—Bonus & Crew cab.
⑯—Exc. heavy duty power brakes, 2.940; Heavy duty power brakes, 3.380.
⑰—Exc. heavy duty power brakes, 1.062; Heavy duty power brakes, 1.187.
⑱—Exc. heavy duty power brakes, 1.280; Heavy duty power brakes, 1.530.
⑲—Exc. heavy duty power brakes, 1.215; Heavy duty power brakes, 1.465.
⑳—Exc. heavy duty power brakes, 1.250; Heavy duty power brakes, 1.312.
㉑—Cutaway & Hi-cube van.
㉒—Single rear wheels.
㉓—Dual rear wheels.
㉔—Exc. motor home chassis.
㉕—Less 4-wheel disc brakes.
㉖—With 4-wheel disc brakes.
㉗—Rear caliper.
㉘—Motor home chassis.
㉙—Gross vehicle weight rating, 8600 lbs.
㉚—Exc. heavy duty power brakes, 1.040; Heavy duty power brakes, 1.280.
㉛—Exc. heavy duty power brakes, 2.940; Heavy duty power brakes, 3.150.
㉜—Exc. heavy duty power brakes, 3.150; Heavy duty power brakes, 3.380.
㉝—Exc. heavy duty power brakes, 1.062; Heavy duty power brakes, 1.190.
㉞—Exc. heavy duty power brakes, 1.250; Heavy duty power brakes, 1.340
㉟—1982 models, 1.540.
㊱—1982 models with heavy duty power brakes, 1.540.
㊲—1982 models, 1.310.
㊳—1982 models with heavy duty power brakes, 1.312.
㊴—Exc. heavy duty power brakes, .965; Heavy duty power brakes, 1.215.
㊵—Van & Vandura.
㊶—Sportvan & Rally.
㊷—Less C6P heavy duty chassis.
㊸—With C6P heavy duty chassis.
㊹—Gross vehicle weight rating, 6800 lbs.

Drive Axle Specifications

Year	Make & Application	Ring Gear Size	Carrier Type	Ring Gear & Pinion Backlash		Pinion Bearing Preload			Differential Bearing Preload		
				Method	Adjustment	Method	New Bearings Inch-Lbs.	Used Bearings Inch-Lbs.	Method	New Bearings Inch-Lbs.	Used Bearings Inch-Lbs.
1979–80	Chevrolet (1)	7½	Integral	Shims	.005–.008	Spacer	20–25	10–15	Shims	(3)	(3)
	Chevrolet (5)(21)	8½	Integral	Shims	.005–.008	Spacer	20–25	10–15	Shims	(3)	(3)
	Chevrolet (4)(5)	8⅞	Integral	Shims	.005–.008	Spacer	20–25	10–15	Shims	(3)	(3)
	Spicer (6)(7)	8½	Integral	Shims	.005–.010	Shims	20–40	10–20	Shims	.015(8)	.015(8)
	Chevrolet (6)(7)	8½	Integral	Shims	.005–.008	Spacer	20–25	10–15	Shims	(3)	(3)
	Spicer (6)(9)	9¾	Integral	Shims	.004–.009	Shims	20–40	10–20	Shims	.015(8)	.015(8)
	Chevrolet (10)(11)	10½	Integral	Adj. Nut	.005–.008	Spacer	25–35	5–15	Adj. Nut	(12)	(13)
	Chevrolet (14)	10½	Integral	Adj. Nut	.005–.008	Spacer	25–35	5–15	Adj. Nut	(12)	(13)
	Spicer (15)	9¾	Integral	Shims	.004–.009	Shims	20–40	10–20	Shims	.015(8)	.015(8)
	Spicer (16)	10½	Integral	Shims	.004–.009	Shims	20–40	10–20	Shims	.006(8)	.006(8)
	Chevrolet (17)	12¼	Integral	Adj. Nut	.005–.008	—	—	—	Adj. Nut	(18)	(18)
1981	Chevrolet (1)	7½	Integral	Shims	.005–.008	Spacer	20–25	10–15	Shims	(3)	(3)
	Chevrolet (5)(22)	8½	Integral	Shims	.005–.008	Spacer	20–25	10–15	Shims	(3)	(3)
	Chevrolet (4)(5)	8⅞	Integral	Shims	.005–.008	Spacer	20–25	10–15	Shims	(3)	(3)
	Chevrolet (6)(7)	8½	Integral	Shims	.005–.008	Spacer	20–25	10–15	Shims	(3)	(3)
	Spicer (6)(9)	9¾	Integral	Shims	.004–.009	Shims	20–40	10–20	Shims	.015(8)	.015(8)
	Chevrolet (23)(24)	9½	Integral	Shims	.005–.008	Spacer	20–25	10–15	Adj. Nut	(2)	(2)
	Chevrolet (11)(14)(19)	10½	Integral	Adj. Nut	.005–.008	Spacer	25–35	5–15	Adj. Nut	(12)	(13)
	Spicer (15)	9¾	Integral	Shims	.004–.009	Shims	20–40	10–20	Shims	.015(8)	.015(8)
	Spicer (16)	10½	Integral	Shims	.004–.009	Shims	20–40	10–20	Shims	.006(8)	.006(8)
	Chevrolet (17)	12¼	Integral	Adj. Nut	.005–.008	—	—	—	Adj. Nut	(18)	(18)
1982	Chevrolet (1)	7½	Integral	Shims	.005–.009	Spacer	24–32	8–12	Shims	(3)	(3)
	Chevrolet (5)(22)	8½	Integral	Shims	.005–.008	Spacer	20–25	10–15	Shims	(3)	(3)
	Chevrolet (4)(5)	8⅞	Integral	Shims	.005–.008	Spacer	20–25	10–15	Shims	(3)	(3)
	Chevrolet (6)(7)	8½	Integral	Shims	.005–.008	Spacer	20–25	10–15	Shims	(3)	(3)
	Spicer (6)(9)	9¾	Integral	Shims	.004–.009	Shims	20–40	10–20	Shims	.015(8)	.015(8)
	Chevrolet (23)(24)	9½	Integral	Shims	.005–.008	Spacer	20–25	10–15	Adj. Nut	(2)	(2)
	Chevrolet (11)(14)(19)	10½	Integral	Adj. Nut	.005–.008	Spacer	25–35	5–15	Adj. Nut	(12)	(13)
	Spicer (15)	9¾	Integral	Shims	.004–.009	Shims	20–40	10–20	Shims	.015(8)	.015(8)
	Spicer (16)	10½	Integral	Shims	.004–.009	Shims	20–40	10–20	Shims	.006(8)	.006(8)
	Timken (17)	12	Removeable	Adj. Ring	.010	Spacer	5–15	—	Adj. Nut	(20)	(20)

continued

DRIVE AXLE SPECIFICATIONS—Continued

Year	Make & Application	Ring Gear Size	Carrier Type	Ring Gear & Pinion Backlash		Pinion Bearing Preload			Differential Bearing Preload		
				Method	Adjustment	Method	New Bearings Inch-Lbs.	Used Bearings Inch-Lbs.	Method	New Bearings Inch-Lbs.	Used Bearings Inch-Lbs.
1983–85	Chevrolet ①	7½	Integral	Shims	.005–.009	Spacer	24–32	8–12	Shims	③	③
	Chevrolet ⑤㉒	8½	Integral	Shims	.005–.008	Spacer	20–25	10–15	Shims	③	③
	Chevrolet ⑥⑦	8½	Integral	Shims	.005–.008	Spacer	20–25	10–15	Shims	③	③
	Spicer ⑥⑨	9¾	Integral	Shims	.004–.009	Shims	20–40	10–20	Shims	.015⑧	.015⑧
	Chevrolet ㉓㉔	9½	Integral	Shims	.005–.008	Spacer	20–25	10–15	Adj. Nut	②	②
	Chevrolet ⑪⑭⑲	10½	Integral	Adj. Nut	.005–.008	Spacer	25–35	5–15	Adj. Nut	⑫	⑬
	Spicer⑮	9¾	Integral	Shims	.004–.009	Shims	20–40	10–20	Shims	.015⑧	.015⑧
	Spicer⑯	10½	Integral	Shims	.004–.009	Shims	20–40	10–20	Shims	.006⑧	.006⑧
	Timken⑰	12	Removeable	Adj. Ring	.010	Spacer	5–15	—	Adj. Nut	⑳	⑳

①—Caballero & El Camino.
②—Tighten adjusting nut until it contacts bearing, then tighten an additional 3 slots.
③—Slip fit plus .004 inch clearance on each side.
④—Series 10/1500.
⑤—G20/2500.
⑥—Front axle.
⑦—K10–20/1500–2500.
⑧—Inch.
⑨—K30/3500.
⑩—C, K, P20/2500.

⑪—C, G, K30/3500 less dual rear wheels.
⑫—Tighten adjusting nut until it contacts bearing, then tighten an additional 3 slots.
⑬—Tighten adjusting nut until it contacts bearing, then tighten an additional 2 slots.
⑭—P30/3500 exc. 5.43 & 6.17 rear axle ratio.
⑮—G30/3500 with dual rear wheels.
⑯—C, G, K30/3500 with dual rear wheels.
⑰—P30/3500 with 5.43 & 6.17 rear axle

ratio.
⑱—Tighten adjusting nut until it contacts bearing, then tighten an additional 1–2 notches.
⑲—C20/2500 Bonus & Crew cab.
⑳—Tighten adjusting nut to obtain zero end play, then tighten nut one additional notch.
㉑—C, G10/1500.
㉒—C, G, K10/1500.
㉓—K, P20/2500.
㉔—C20/2500 exc. Bonus & Crew cab.

Cooling System & Capacity Data

Year	Model	Engine	Cooling Capacity, Qts.		Radiator Cap Relief Pressure, Lbs.	Thermo. Opening Temp.	Fuel Tank Gals.	Engine Oil Refill Qts.①	Transmission Oil			Transfer Case Pints	Rear Axle Oil Pints
			Less A/C	With A/C					3 Speed Pints	4 Speed Pints	Auto Trans. Qts.㉒		
1979	②	V6-200	18.5	18.5	15	195	17.7	4㉓	3	—	10	—	3.5
		V6-231	15.5	15.5	15	195	17.7	4㉓	—	—	10	—	3.5
		V8-267	21	21	15	195	17.7	4	—	3	10	—	3.5
		V8-305	19	19	15	195	17.7	4	—	3	10	—	3.5
		V8-350	19.5	19.5	15	195	17.7	4	—	—	10	—	3.5
	C10/1500	6-250	14.8	15.6	15	195	③④	4	3	8	⑥	—	⑧
		V8-305	17.6	17.6	15	195	③④	4	3	8	⑥	—	⑧
		V8-350	17.6	18.4	15	195	③④	4	3	8	⑥	—	⑧
		V8-350㉔	18	18	15	195	—	7㉓	—	—	⑥	—	⑧
		V8-454	22.8	24.4	15	195	⑪	6	—	—	⑥	—	⑧
	G10/1500	6-250	16.8	17.2	15	195	21	4	⑤	—	10	—	⑧
		V8-305	19.6	20.4	15	195	21	4	⑤	—	10	—	⑧
		V8-350	20	20.4	15	195	21	4	⑤	—	10	—	⑧
	K10/1500	6-250	14.8	15.6	15	195	③④	4	3	8	⑥	⑨	3.5⑩
		V8-305	17.6	17.6	15	195	③④	4	3	8	⑥	⑨	3.5⑩
		V8-350	17.6	18.4	15	195	③④	4	3	8	⑥	⑨	3.5⑩
		V8-400	18.4	20.4	15	195	③④	4	—	—	⑥	⑨	3.5⑩
	P10/1500	6-292	13.6	—	15	195	21	5	3	8	⑥	—	3.5

continued

COOLING SYSTEM & CAPACITY DATA—Continued

Year	Model	Engine	Cooling Capacity, Qts. Less A/C	With A/C	Radiator Cap Relief Pressure, Lbs.	Thermo. Opening Temp.	Fuel Tank Gals.	Engine Oil Refill Qts.①	Transmission Oil 3 Speed Pints	4 Speed Pints	Auto Trans. Qts. ㉒	Transfer Case Pints	Rear Axle Oil Pints
	C20/2500	6-250	14.8	15.6	15	195	⑪	4	3	8	⑥	—	5.4
		V8-305	17.6	18	15	195	⑪	4	3	8	⑥	—	5.4
		V8-350	17.6	18.4	15	195	⑪	4	—	8	⑥	—	5.4
		V8-454	22.8	24.8	15	195	⑪	6	—	8	⑥	—	5.4
	G20/2500	6-250	17.2	—	15	195	21	4	⑤	—	10	—	⑧
		V8-350	20	20.4	15	195	21	4	⑤	—	10	—	⑧
		V8-400	20	20	15	195	21	4	—	—	10	—	⑧
	K20/2500	V8-350	17.6	18.4	15	195	⑪	4	3	8	⑥	⑨	5.4⑩
		V8-400	18.4	20.4	15	195	⑪	4	—	—	⑥	⑨	5.4⑩
	P20/2500	6-292	13.6	—	15	195	31	5	3	8	⑥	—	5.4
		V8-350	⑬	—	15	195	31	4	3	8	⑥	—	5.4
	C30/3500	6-292	14.8	—	15	195	20	5	—	8	⑥	—	⑭
		V8-350	17.6	18.4	15	195	20	4	—	8	⑥	—	⑭
		V8-454	22.8	24.8	15	195	20	6	—	8	⑥	—	⑭
	G30/3500	6-250	17.2	—	15	195	21	4	⑤	—	10	—	⑮
		V8-350	20	20.4	15	195	21	4	⑤	—	10	—	⑮
		V8-400	20	20.4	15	195	21	4	—	—	10	—	⑮
	K30/3500	6-292	14.8	—	15	195	20	5	—	8	⑥	⑨	⑩⑭
		V8-350	17.6	18.4	15	195	20	4	—	8	⑥	⑨	⑩⑭
		V8-400	18.4	20.4	15	195	20	4	—	—	⑥	⑨	⑩⑭
	P30/3500⑯	6-292	13.6	—	15	195	31	5	—	8	⑥	—	⑰
		V8-350	17.2	—	15	195	31	4	—	8	⑥	—	⑰
		V8-454	24.8	—	15	195	31	㉕	—	—	⑥	—	⑰
	P30/3500⑱	V8-350	20	20	15	195	40	4	—	—	⑥	—	⑰
		V8-454	24.8	24.8	15	195	40	6	—	—	⑥	—	⑰
1980	②	V6-229	18.5	18.5	15	195	17.7	4㉓	3	—	㉖	—	3.5
		V6-231	15.5	15.5	15	195	17.7	4㉓	—	—	㉖	—	3.5
		V8-267	21	21	15	195	17.7	4	—	—	㉖	—	3.5
		V8-305	19	19	15	195	17.7	4	—	3	㉖	—	3.5
	C10/1500	6-250	14.4	14.4	15	195	③④	4	⑤	8	⑥	—	⑧
		V8-305	17.2	17.2	15	195	③④	4	⑤	8	⑥	—	⑧
		V8-350	17.2	17.2	15	195	③④	4	⑤	8	⑥	—	⑧
		V8-350㉔	18	19.6	15	195	—	7㉓	—	—	⑥	—	⑧
	G10/1500	6-250	14.4	14.8	15	195	22	4	⑤	—	10	—	⑧
		V8-305	16.8	17.2	15	195	22	4	⑤	—	10	—	⑧
		V8-350	17.2	17.2	15	195	22	4	⑤	—	10	—	⑧
	K10/1500	6-250	14.4	14.4	15	195	③④	4	⑤	8	⑥	⑨	3.5⑩
		V8-305	17.2	17.2	15	195	③④	4	⑤	8	⑥	⑨	3.5⑩
		V8-350	17.2	17.2	15	195	③④	4	⑤	8	⑥	⑨	3.5⑩
		V8-400	18.4	20.4	15	195	③④	4	—	—	⑥	⑨	3.5⑩
	P10/1500	6-292	13.6	—	15	195	21	5	3	8	⑥	—	3.5
	C20/2500	6-250	14.4	14.4	15	195	⑪	4	3	8	⑥	—	5.4
		6-292	15.2	15.2	15	195	⑪	5	—	8	⑥	—	5.4
		V8-305	17.2	17.2	15	195	⑪	4	3	8	⑥	—	5.4
		V8-350	17.2	17.2	15	195	⑪	4	—	8	⑥	—	5.4
		V8-454	21.6	24.8	15	195	⑪	6	—	8	⑥	—	5.4
	G20/2500	6-250	17.2	—	15	195	22	4	⑤	—	10	—	⑧
		V8-350	20	20.4	15	195	22	4	⑤	—	10	—	⑧
		V8-400	20	20	15	195	22	4	—	—	10	—	⑧
	K20/2500	6-292	15.2	15.2	15	195	⑪	5	—	8	⑥	⑨	5.4⑩
		V8-350	17.6	18.4	15	195	⑪	4	3	8	⑥	⑨	5.4⑩
		V8-400	18.4	20.4	15	195	⑪	4	—	—	⑥	⑨	5.4⑩

continued

COOLING SYSTEM & CAPACITY DATA—Continued

Year	Model	Engine	Cooling Capacity, Qts. Less A/C	Cooling Capacity, Qts. With A/C	Radiator Cap Relief Pressure, Lbs.	Thermo. Opening Temp.	Fuel Tank Gals.	Engine Oil Refill Qts. [1]	Transmission Oil 3 Speed Pints	Transmission Oil 4 Speed Pints	Transmission Oil Auto Trans. Qts. [22]	Transfer Case Pints	Rear Axle Oil Pints
	P20/2500	6-292	13.6	—	15	195	31	5	3	8	[6]	—	5.4
		V8-350	[13]	—	15	195	31	4	3	8	[6]	—	5.4
	C30/3500	6-292	15.2	15.2	15	195	20	5	—	8	[6]	—	[14]
		V8-350	17.2	17.2	15	195	20	4	—	8	[6]	—	[14]
		V8-454	21.6	24.8	15	195	20	6	—	8	[6]	—	[14]
	G30/3500	6-250	17.2	—	15	195	22	4	[5]	—	10	—	[15]
		V8-350	20	20.4	15	195	22	4	[5]	—	10	—	[15]
		V8-400	20	20.4	15	195	22	4	—	—	10	—	[15]
	K30/3500	6-292	14.8	—	15	195	20	5	—	8	[6]	[9]	[10][14]
		V8-350	17.6	18.4	15	195	20	4	—	8	[6]	[9]	[10][14]
		V8-400	18.4	20.4	15	195	20	4	—	—	[6]	[9]	[10][14]
	P30/3500[16]	6-292	13.6	—	15	195	31	5	—	8	[6]	—	[17]
		V8-350	17.2	—	15	195	31	4	—	8	[6]	—	[17]
		V8-454	24.8	—	15	195	31	[25]	—	—	[6]	—	[17]
	P30/3500[18]	V8-350	20	20	15	195	40	4	—	—	[6]	—	[17]
		V8-454	24.8	24.8	15	195	40	6	—	—	[6]	—	[17]
1981	[2]	V6-229	18.5	18.5	15	195	17.7	4[23]	3.5	—	[26]	—	3
		V6-231	15.5	15.5	15	195	17.7	4[23]	—	—	[26]	—	3
		V8-267	21	21	15	195	17.7	4	—	—	[26]	—	3
		V8-305	19	19	15	195	17.7	4	—	3.5	[26]	—	3
	C10/1500	6-250	14.4	14.4	15	195	[3][4]	4	[5]	8	[6]	—	[8]
		V8-305	17.2	17.2	15	195	[3][4]	4	[5]	8	[6]	—	[8]
		V8-350	17.2	17.2	15	195	[3][4]	4	[5]	8	[6]	—	[8]
		V8-350[24]	18	19.6	15	195	—	7[23]	—	—	[6]	—	[8]
	G10/1500	6-250	14.4	14.8	15	195	22	4	[5]	—	[6]	—	[8]
		V8-305	16.8	17.2	15	195	22	4	[5]	—	[6]	—	[8]
		V8-350	17.2	17.2	15	195	22	4	[5]	—	[6]	—	[8]
	K10/1500	6-250	14.4	14.4	15	195	[3][4]	4	[5]	8	[6]	[9]	[8][10]
		V8-305	17.2	17.2	15	195	[3][4]	4	[5]	8	[6]	[9]	[8][10]
		V8-350	17.2	17.2	15	195	[3][4]	4	—	8	[6]	[9]	[8][10]
	C20/2500	6-250	14.4	14.4	15	195	[11]	4	[5]	8	[6]	—	5.4
		6-292	15.2	15.2	15	195	[11]	5	—	8	[6]	—	5.4
		V8-305	17.2	17.2	15	195	[11]	4	[5]	8	[6]	—	5.4
		V8-350	17.2	17.2	15	195	[11]	4	—	8	[6]	—	5.4
		V8-454	21.6	24.8	15	195	[11]	6	—	8	[6]	—	5.4
	G20/2500	6-250	14.4	14.8	15	195	22	4	[5]	—	[6]	—	[8]
		V8-305	16.8	17.2	15	195	22	4	[5]	—	[6]	—	[8]
		V8-350	17.2	17.2	15	195	22	4	[5]	—	[6]	—	[8]
	K20/2500	6-292	15.2	15.2	15	195	[11]	5	—	8	[6]	[9]	5.4[10]
		V8-350	17.2	17.2	15	195	[11]	4	—	8	[6]	[9]	5.4[10]
	P20/2500	6-292	14	—	15	195	31	5	[5]	8	[6]	—	5.4
		V8-350	15.6	—	15	195	31	4	[5]	8	[6]	—	5.4
	C30/3500	6-292	15.2	15.2	15	195	20	5	—	8	[6]	—	[14]
		V8-350	17.2	17.2	15	195	20	4	—	8	[6]	—	[14]
		V8-454	21.6	24.8	15	195	20	6	—	8	[6]	—	[14]
	G30/3500	V8-350	17.2	17.6	15	195	22	4	[5]	—	[6]	—	[15]
	K30/3500	6-292	15.2	15.2	15	195	20	5	—	8	[6]	[9]	[10][14]
		V8-350	17.2	17.2	15	195	20	4	—	8	[6]	[9]	[10][14]
		V8-454	21.6	24.8	15	195	20	5	—	8	[6]	[9]	[10][14]
	P30/3500[16]	6-292	14	—	15	195	31	5	—	8	[6]	—	[17]
		V8-350	15.6	—	15	195	31	4	—	8	[6]	—	[17]

continued

Year	Model	Engine	Cooling Capacity, Qts. Less A/C	With A/C	Radiator Cap Relief Pressure, Lbs.	Thermo. Opening Temp.	Fuel Tank Gals.	Engine Oil Refill Qts.[1]	Transmission Oil 3 Speed Pints	4 Speed Pints	Auto Trans. Qts.[22]	Transfer Case Pints	Rear Axle Oil Pints
	P30/3500[18]	V8-350	19.2	—	15	195	40	4	—	—	[6]	—	[17]
		V8-454	24.4	—	15	195	40	6	—	—	[6]	—	[17]
1982	[2]	V6-229	15	15	15	195	17.7	4[23]	—	—	[27]	—	3
		V6-231	12	12	15	195	17.7	4[23]	—	—	[27]	—	3
		V8-267	18.6	18.6	15	195	17.7	4	—	—	[27]	—	3
		V8-305	16.3	16.3	15	195	17.7	4	—	—	[27]	—	3
	C10/1500	6-250	14.4	14.4	15	195	[3][4]	4	3	8	[12]	—	[8]
		V8-305	17.2	17.2	15	195	[3][4]	4	3	8	[12]	—	[8]
		V8-350	17.2	17.2	15	195	[3][4]	4	—	—	[12]	—	[8]
		V8-379[24]	25.2	25.2	15	195	[7]	7[23]	—	8	[12]	—	[8]
	G10/1500	6-250	14.4	14.8	15	195	22	4	3	—	[12]	—	[8]
		V8-305	16.8	17.2	15	195	22	4	3	—	[12]	—	[8]
		V8-350	17.2	17.2	15	195	22	4	3	—	[12]	—	[8]
	K10/1500	6-250	14.4	14.4	15	195	[3][4]	4	3	8	[12]	[9]	[8][10]
		V8-305	17.2	17.2	15	195	[3][4]	4	3	8	[12]	[9]	[8][10]
		V8-350	17.2	17.2	15	195	[3][4]	4	—	—	[12]	[9]	[8][10]
		V8-379[24]	25.2	25.2	15	195	[7]	7[23]	—	8	[12]	[9]	[8][10]
	C20/2500	6-250	14.4	14.4	15	195	[11]	4	3	8	[12]	—	5.4
		6-292	15.2	15.2	15	195	[11]	5	3	8	[12]	—	5.4
		V8-305	17.2	17.2	15	195	[11]	4	3	8	[12]	—	5.4
		V8-350	14.4	14.4	15	195	[11]	4	—	—	[12]	—	5.4
		V8-379[24]	25.2	25.2	15	195	[19]	7[23]	—	8	[12]	—	5.4
		V8-454	21.6	24.4	15	195	[11]	6	—	8	[12]	—	5.4
	G20/2500	6-250	14.4	14.8	15	195	22	4	3	—	[12]	—	[8]
		V8-305	16.8	17.2	15	195	22	4	3	—	[12]	—	[8]
		V8-350	17.2	17.2	15	195	22	4	3	—	[12]	—	[8]
	K20/2500	6-292	15.2	15.2	15	195	[11]	5	3	8	[12]	[9]	5.4[10]
		V8-350	17.2	17.2	15	195	[11]	4	—	—	[12]	[9]	5.4[10]
		V8-379[24]	—	—	15	195	[19]	7[23]	—	8	[12]	[9]	5.4[10]
	P20/2500	6-292	14	—	15	195	40	5	—	8	—	—	5.4
		V8-350	15.6	—	15	195	40	4	—	8	[12]	—	5.4
		V8-379[24]	—	—	15	195	40	7[23]	—	8	[12]	—	5.4
	C30/3500	6-292	15.2	15.2	15	195	20	5	—	8	—	—	[14]
		V8-350	17.2	17.2	15	195	20	4	—	8	[12]	—	[14]
		V8-379[24]	25.2	25.2	15	195	20	7[23]	—	8	[12]	—	[14]
		V8-454	21.6	24.4	15	195	20	6	—	8	[12]	—	[14]
	G30/3500	6-250	14.4	14.8	15	195	22	4	3	—	[12]	—	[15]
		V8-350	17.2	17.2	15	195	22	4	3	—	[12]	—	[15]
	K30/3500	6-292	15.2	15.2	15	195	20	5	—	8	—	[9]	[10][14]
		V8-350	17.2	17.2	15	195	20	4	—	8	[12]	[9]	[10][14]
		V8-379[24]	25.2	24.8	15	195	20	7[23]	—	8	[12]	[9]	[10][14]
		V8-454	21.6	24.4	15	195	20	6	—	8	[12]	[9]	[10][14]
	P30/3500[16]	6-292	14	—	15	195	40	5	—	8	—	—	[21]
		V8-350	15.6	—	15	195	40	4	—	8	[12]	—	[21]
	P30/3500[18]	V8-350	19.2	—	15	195	40	5	—	—	[12]	—	[21]
		V8-454	24.4	—	15	195	40	6	—	—	[12]	—	[21]
1983–84	[2]	V6-229	15	15	15	195	17.7	4[23]	—	—	[27]	—	3
		V6-231	12	12	15	195	17.7	4[23]	—	—	[27]	—	3
		V8-305	16.3	16.3	15	195	17.7	4	—	—	[27]	—	3
		V8-350[24]	18.3	18.3	15	195	22	7[23]	—	—	[27]	—	3

continued

COOLING SYSTEM & CAPACITY DATA—Continued

Year	Model	Engine	Cooling Capacity, Qts.		Radiator Cap Relief Pressure, Lbs.	Thermo. Opening Temp.	Fuel Tank Gals.	Engine Oil Refill Qts.①	Transmission Oil			Transfer Case Pints	Rear Axle Oil Pints
			Less A/C	With A/C					3 Speed Pints	4 Speed Pints	Auto Trans. Qts. ㉒		
	C10/1500	6-250	14.4	14.4	15	195	③④	4	3	8⑳	⑫	—	4.2
		V8-305	17.2	17.2	15	195	③④	4	3	8⑳	⑫	—	4.2
		V8-350	17.2	17.2	15	195	③④	4	—	8⑳	⑫	—	4.2
		V8-379㉔	24.8	24.8	15	195	⑦	7㉓	—	8⑳	⑫	—	4.2
	G10/1500	6-250	14.4	14.8	15	195	22	4	3	8⑳	⑫	—	4.2
		V8-305	16.8	17.2	15	195	22	4	3	8⑳	⑫	—	4.2
		V8-350	16.8	16.8	15	195	22	4	—	—	⑫	—	4.2
	K10/1500	6-250	14.4	14.4	15	195	③④	4	3	8⑳	⑫	⑨	4.2⑩
		V8-305	17.2	17.2	15	195	③④	4	3	8⑳	⑫	⑨	4.2⑩
		V8-350	17.2	17.2	15	195	③④	4	—	8⑳	⑫	⑨	4.2⑩
		V8-379㉔	24.8	24.8	15	195	⑦	7㉓	—	8⑳	⑫	⑨	4.2⑩
	C20/2500	6-250	14.4	14.4	15	195	⑪	4	—	8	⑫	—	5.4
		6-292	15.2	15.6	15	195	⑪	5	—	8	⑫	—	5.4
		V8-305	17.2	17.2	15	195	⑪	4	—	8	⑫	—	5.4
		V8-350	17.2	17.2	15	195	⑪	4	—	8	⑫	—	5.4
		V8-379㉔	24.8	24.8	15	195	⑲	7㉓	—	8⑳	⑫	—	5.4
		V8-454	21.6	24.8	15	195	⑪	6	—	8	⑫	—	5.4
	G20/25	6-250	14.4	14.8	15	195	22	4	3	8	⑫	—	4.2
		V8-305	16.8	17.2	15	195	22	4	—	8	⑫	—	4.2
		V8-350	16.8	16.8	15	195	22	4	—	—	⑫	—	4.2
		V8-379㉔	25.2	25.2	15	195	22	7㉓	—	8	⑫	—	4.2
	K20/2500	6-292	15.2	15.6	15	195	⑪	5	—	8	⑫	⑨	5.4⑩
		V8-350	17.2	17.2	15	195	⑪	4	—	8	⑫	⑨	5.4⑩
		V8-379㉔	24.8	24.8	15	195	⑲	7㉓	—	8⑳	⑫	⑨	5.4⑩
	P20/2500	6-292	14	—	15	195	40	5	—	8	—	—	5.4
		V8-350	15.6	—	15	195	40	4	—	8	⑫	—	5.4
		V8-379㉔	24.8	—	15	195	40	7㉓	—	8	⑫	—	5.4
	C30/3500	6-292	15.2	15.6	15	195	20	5	—	8	⑫	—	⑭
		V8-350	17.2	17.2	15	195	20	4	—	8	⑫	—	⑭
		V8-379㉔	24.8	25.2	15	195	20	7㉓	—	8	⑫	—	⑭
	G30/3500	6-250	14.4	14.8	15	195	22	4	3	—	⑫	—	⑮
		V8-350	17.2	16.8	15	195	22	4	—	8	⑫	—	⑮
		V8-379㉔	24.8	24.8	15	195	22	7㉓	—	8	⑫	—	⑮
	K30/3500	6-292	15.2	15.6	15	195	20	5	—	8	⑫	⑨	⑩⑭
		V8-350	17.2	17.2	15	195	20	4	—	8	⑫	⑨	⑩⑭
		V8-379㉔	24.8	25.2	15	195	20	7㉓	—	8	⑫	⑨	⑩⑭
		V8-454	21.6	24.8	15	195	20	6	—	8	⑫	⑨	⑩⑭
	P30/3500⑯	6-292	14.0	—	15	195	40	5	—	8	⑫	—	㉑
		V8-350	15.6	—	15	195	40	4	—	8	⑫	—	㉑
		V8-379㉔	24.8	—	15	195	40	7㉓	—	8	⑫	—	㉑
	P30/3500⑱	V8-379㉔	27.6	—	15	195	40	7㉓	—	—	⑫	—	㉑
		V8-454	22.8	—	15	195	40	6	—	—	⑫	—	㉑
1985	②	V6-262	13.1	13.1	15	195	17.7	4㉓	—	—	㉗	—	3.5
		V8-305	15.6	15.6	15	195	17.7	5㉓	—	—	㉗	—	3.5
	C10/1500	V6-262	13.6	13.6	15	195	③④	5㉓	3	8⑳	⑫	—	4.2
		V8-305	17.2	17.2	15	195	③④	5㉓	3	8⑳	⑫	—	4.2
		V8-350	17.2	17.2	15	195	③④	5㉓	—	8⑳	⑫	—	4.2
		V8-379㉔	24.8	24.8	15	195	⑦	7㉓	—	8⑳	⑫	—	4.2
	G10/1500	V6-262	13.6	13.6	15	195	22	5㉓	3	—	⑫	—	4.2
		V8-305	16.8	16.8	15	195	22	5㉓	3	8⑳	⑫	—	4.2
		V8-350	16.8	16.8	15	195	22	5㉓	—	—	⑫	—	4.2

continued

COOLING SYSTEM & CAPACITY DATA—Continued

Year	Model	Engine	Cooling Capacity, Qts.		Radiator Cap Relief Pressure, Lbs.	Thermo. Opening Temp.	Fuel Tank Gals.	Engine Oil Refill Qts.①	Transmission Oil			Transfer Case Pints	Rear Axle Oil Pints
			Less A/C	With A/C					3 Speed Pints	4 Speed Pints	Auto Trans. Qts.㉒		
	K10/1500	V6-262	13.6	13.6	15	195	③④	5㉓	—	8⑳	⑫	⑨	4.2⑩
		V8-305	17.2	17.2	15	195	③④	5㉓	—	8⑳	⑫	⑨	4.2⑩
		V8-350	17.2	17.2	15	195	③④	5㉓	—	8⑳	⑫	⑨	4.2⑩
		V8-379㉔	24.8	24.8	15	195	⑦	7㉓	—	8⑳	⑫	⑨	4.2⑩
	C20/2500	V6-262	13.6	13.6	15	195	⑪	5㉓	—	8	⑫	—	5.4
		6-292	15.2	15.6	15	195	⑪	6㉓	—	8	⑫	—	5.4
		V8-305	17.2	17.2	15	195	⑪	5㉓	—	8	⑫	—	5.4
		V8-350	17.2	17.2	15	195	⑪	5㉓	—	8	⑫	—	5.4
		V8-379㉔	24.8	24.8	15	195	⑲	7㉓	—	8	⑫	—	5.4
		V8-454	21.6	24.8	15	195	⑪	7㉓	—	8	⑫	—	5.4
	G20/2500	V6-262	13.6	13.6	15	195	22	5㉓	3	—	⑫	—	4.2
		V8-305	16.8	17.2	15	195	22	5㉓	—	8⑳	⑫	—	4.2
		V8-350	16.8	17.2	15	195	22	5㉓	—	—	⑫	—	4.2
		V8-379㉔	25.2	25.2	15	195	22	7㉓	—	8⑳	⑫	—	4.2
	K20/2500	6-292	15.2	15.6	15	195	⑪	6㉓	—	8⑳	⑫	⑨	5.4⑩
		V8-350	17.2	17.2	15	195	⑪	5㉓	—	8⑳	⑫	⑨	5.4⑩
		V8-379㉔	24.8	24.8	15	195	⑲	7㉓	—	8⑳	⑫	⑨	5.4⑩
	P20/2500	6-292	14.0	14.0	15	195	40	5㉓	—	8	⑫	—	5.4
		V8-350	16.0	16.0	15	195	40	5㉓	—	8	⑫	—	5.4
		V8-379㉔	24.8	—	15	195	40	7㉓	—	8	⑫	—	5.4
	C30/3500	6-292	15.2	15.6	15	195	20	6㉓	—	8	⑫	—	⑭
		V8-350	17.2	17.2	15	195	20	5㉓	—	8	⑫	—	⑭
		V8-379㉔	24.8	24.8	15	195	20	7㉓	—	8	⑫	—	⑭
		V8-454	21.6	21.6	15	195	20	7㉓	—	8	⑫	—	⑭
	G30/3500	V6-262	13.6	13.6	15	195	22	5㉓	—	—	⑫	—	⑮
		V8-350	17.2	17.2	15	195	22	5㉓	—	—	⑫	—	⑮
		V8-379㉔	24.8	24.8	15	195	22	7㉓	—	—	⑫	—	⑮
	K30/3500	6-292	15.2	15.2	15	195	20	6㉓	—	8	⑫	⑨	⑩⑭
		V8-350	17.2	17.2	15	195	20	6㉓	—	8	⑫	⑨	⑩⑭
		V8-379㉔	24.8	24.8	15	195	20	7㉓	—	8	⑫	⑨	⑩⑭
		V8-454	21.6	24.8	15	195	20	7㉓	—	8	⑫	⑨	⑩⑭
	P30/3500⑯	6-292	14.0	14.0	15	195	40	5㉓	—	8	⑫	—	㉑
		V8-350	16.0	16.0	15	195	40	5㉓	—	8	⑫	—	㉑
		V8-379㉔	24.8	—	15	195	40	7㉓	—	8	⑫	—	㉑
	P30/3500⑱	V8-379	28.0	—	15	195	40	7㉓	—	—	⑫	—	㉑
		V8-454	22.8	—	15	195	40	7㉓	—	—	⑫	—	㉑

①—Add one quart with filter change.
②—Caballero & El Camino.
③—Exc. Suburban, Jimmy & Blazer, 20 gals; Suburban, Jimmy & Blazer, 25 gals.
④—Chassis cab, 16 gals.
⑤—Exc. Muncie 3 pints; Muncie, 4 pints.
⑥—THM 350, 10 qts.; THM 400, 475, 11 qts.
⑦—Exc. Suburban, Jimmy & Blazer, 20 gals.; Suburban, Jimmy & Blazer, 27 gals.
⑧—With 8½" ring gear, 4.2; with 8⅞" ring gear, 3.5.
⑨—New Process 203, 8.2 pints; New Process 205, 5.2 pints; New Process 208, 10 pints.
⑩—Front axle, 5.0.
⑪—Exc. Suburban, 20 gals; Suburban, 25 gals.
⑫—THM 350C, 10 qts.; THM 400, 11 qts.; THM 700-R4, 11.5 qts.; THM 475, 9.5 qts.
⑬—Exc. heavy duty cooling 16.8; heavy duty cooling, 17.2.
⑭—Less dual rear wheels, 5.4; with dual rear wheels 7.2.
⑮—Less dual rear wheels, 5.4; with dual rear wheels and 9¾" ring gear, 6.0; with dual rear wheels and 10½" ring gear, 7.2.
⑯—Exc. motor home.
⑰—With 10½" ring gear, 5.4; with 12¼" ring gear, 14.0.
⑱—Motor home.
⑲—Exc. Suburban, 20 gals.; Suburban, 27 gals.
⑳—With overdrive, 7.5 pints.
㉑—With 10½" ring gear, 5.4; with 12" ring gear, 14.0.
㉒—Approximate. Make final check with dipstick.
㉓—Includes filter.
㉔—Diesel engine.
㉕—Exc Step van, 6 qts; Step van, 4 qts.
㉖—THM 200, 5 qts.; THM 350, 10 qts.
㉗—THM 200C, 9.5 qts.; THM 200-4R, 11 qts.; THM 250C, 10.5 qts.; THM 350C, 10 qts.; THM 700-R4, 11.5 qts.

STARTER
REPLACE

SERVICE BULLETIN Starter whining or a no-start condition on 1982–83 vehicles equipped with V8-379 diesel engines, may be due to insufficient flywheel ring gear to starter pinion clearance. To correct the above mentioned complaint, proceed as follows:

1. Disconnect battery ground cable, then raise and suppport vehicle.
2. Remove flywheel inspection cover and inspect flywheel teeth for damage. If teeth are excessively worn, replace flywheel.
3. Loosen both starter mounting bolts, then remove outside bolt and shim pack.
4. Measure shim pack thickness. If shim pack is less than .120 inch thick, add shims until total thickness is as stated above. If shim pack is already .120 inch thick, add an additional .040 inch shim to pack. Shim pack thickness should not exceed .160 inch.
5. Reposition shims, install outside mounting bolt, then torque both bolts to 30–40 ft. lbs.
6. Install flywheel inspection cover, then lower vehicle and reconnect battery ground cable.

1. Disconnect battery ground cable.
2. Raise and support vehicle.
3. Remove starter to engine brace and heat shields, if equipped.
4. Remove starter mounting bolts and lower starter. Note position of shims, if used.
5. Disconnect wires from solenoids, then remove starter from vehicle.
6. Reverse procedure to install.

HORN SOUNDER & STEERING WHEEL
REPLACE

CABALLERO & EL CAMINO

NOTE: Scribe alignment marks on steering wheel and shaft to ensure correct installation.

Standard Wheel
1. Disconnect battery ground cable.
2. Remove attaching screws on underside of steering wheel.
3. Lifting steering wheel shroud and pull horn wires from cancelling cam tower.
4. Remove steering wheel retaining nut, washer and snap ring.

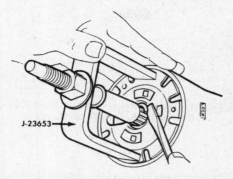

Fig. 1   Lock plate retaining ring removal. Caballero, El Camino and C & K models

5. Using a suitable puller, remove steering wheel.
6. Reverse procedure to install.

Cushioned Rim Wheel
1. Disconnect battery ground cable.
2. Pry off horn button cap.
3. Remove three spacer screws, spacer, plate and belleville spring.
4. Remove steering wheel retaining nut, washer and snap ring.
5. Using a suitable puller, remove steering wheel.
6. Reverse procedure to install.

SERIES 10–30/1500–3500

NOTE: Scribe alignment marks on steering wheel and shaft to ensure correct installation.

C & K Models
1. Disconnect battery ground cable.
2. Remove horn button cap.
3. Remove snap ring and steering wheel retaining nut.
4. Using a suitable puller, remove steering wheel.
5. Reverse procedure to install, ensuring that turn signal switch is in neutral position.

G & P Models
1. Disconnect battery ground cable.
2. Remove horn button or shroud, then the receiving cup, belleville spring and bushing.
3. Remove snap ring and steering wheel retaining nut.
4. Using a suitable puller, remove steering wheel.
5. Reverse procedure to install, ensuring that turn signal switch is in neutral position.

TURN SIGNAL SWITCH
REPLACE

CABALLERO, EL CAMINO & C & K MODELS

1. Disconnect battery cable, then remove steering wheel and column to instrument panel trim cover.
2. On models with telescoping column, remove bumper spacer and snap ring retainer. On all other models, remove cover from lockplate.
3. Using a suitable tool, compress lock plate (horn contact carrier on tilt models) and remove snap ring ("C" ring on tilt models), **Fig. 1.**
4. Remove lock plate, cancelling cam, upper bearing preload spring, thrust washer and signal lever.
5. Remove turn signal lever or actuating arm screw, if equipped, or on models with column mounted wiper switch, pull lever straight out of detent. Depress hazard warning button, then unscrew button.
6. Pull connector from bracket and wrap upper part of connector with tape to prevent snagging the wires during removal. On Tilt models, position shifter housing in "Low" position. Remove harness cover.
7. Remove retaining screws and remove switch, **Fig. 2.**
8. Reverse procedure to install.

G & P MODELS

1. Remove steering wheel as outlined previously.
2. Remove cancelling cam and spring, then the instrument panel trim plate, if equipped.
3. Disconnect turn signal switch wiring harness at half moon connector.
4. Pry wiring harness protector from column retaining slots, **Fig. 3.**
5. Mark location of each wire in half moon connector, then disconnect wires from connector using tool J-22727 or equivalent, **Fig. 4.**
6. Remove turn signal lever screw and lever.
7. Push hazard warning knob inward, then unscrew knob from plunger.
8. On tilt column models:
   a. If equipped with automatic transmission, remove PRNDL dial screws, then the dial and indicator needle. Remove cap and dial bulb from housing cover.
   b. Unscrew, then remove tilt release lever.
   c. Using tool J-22708 or equivalent,

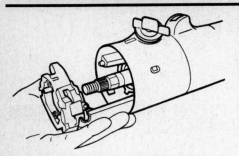

Fig. 2 Turn signal switch replacement. Caballero, El Camino and C & K models

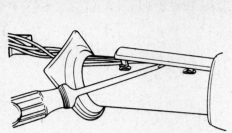

Fig. 3 Removing wiring harness protector. G & P models

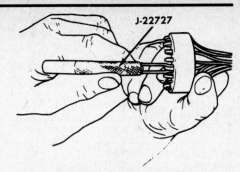

Fig. 4 Removing wires from connector. G & P models

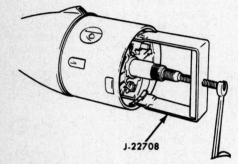

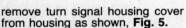

Fig. 5 Removing turn signal housing cover. G & P models

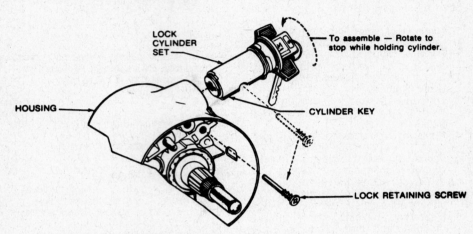

Fig. 6 Ignition lock installation. Exc. G & P models

remove turn signal housing cover from housing as shown, **Fig. 5.**

9. Remove turn signal switch mounting screws, then carefully remove switch assembly from column by guiding wiring harness through opening in shift lever housing.
10. Reverse procedure to install.

IGNITION LOCK
REPLACE

G & P MODELS

1. Disconnect battery ground cable.
2. Position lock cylinder in "ACC" position.
3. Insert a stiff wire into hole in cylinder face, then depress plunger while turning ignition key counterclockwise.
4. Remove lock cylinder from vehicle.
5. Reverse procedure to install.

EXC. G & P MODELS

1. Remove steering wheel as outlined previously.
2. Remove turn signal switch as outlined in "Turn Signal Switch, Replace" procedure.
3. Place ignition switch in "Run" position, then remove lock cylinder retaining screw and lock cylinder.
4. To install, rotate lock cylinder to stop, while holding housing as shown, **Fig. 6.** Align cylinder key with keyway in housing, then push lock cylinder

assembly into housing until fully seated.
5. Install lock cylinder retaining screw. Torque screw to 40 inch lbs. for standard columns, or 22 inch lbs. for adjustable columns.
6. Install buzzer switch, turn signal switch and steering wheel.

IGNITION SWITCH
REPLACE

CABALLERO, EL CAMINO & C & K MODELS

The ignition switch is mounted on top of the mast jacket inside the brake pedal support and is actuated by a rod and rack assembly.
1. Disconnect battery ground cable.
2. Disconnect and lower steering column.

NOTE: On some models, it may be necessary to remove the upper column mounting bracket if it hinders servicing of switch. Use extreme care when lowering steering column to prevent damage to column assembly. Only lower steering column a sufficient distance to perform ignition switch service.

3. On Caballero or El Camino, rotate

ignition lock to "Off" unlocked position.
4. On C & K models, rotate ignition lock to "Off" locked position.
5. If lock cylinder has been removed, pull switch actuator rod up to stop, then push rod down to second (Caballero or El Camino) or first (C & K models) detent as shown, **Fig. 7.**
6. Remove column mounted dimmer switch, if equipped, then remove switch retaining screws and switch.
7. Reverse procedure to install, noting the following:
   a. Place gear shift lever in neutral.
   b. Place lock cylinder and switch in positions noted in Steps 3 & 4.
   c. Fit actuator rod into hole in switch slider and secure switch with retaining screws, ensuring switch does not move out of detent.
   d. Install and adjust dimmer switch, if equipped, as outlined in "Column Mounted Dimmer Switch, Replace" procedure.
   e. Torque retaining screws to 35 inch lbs., then check switch operation.

G & P MODELS

1. Disconnect battery ground cable.
2. Remove ignition lock as outlined previously.
3. Remove metallic nut from ignition switch.

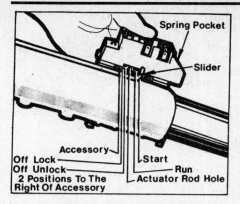

Fig. 7   Positioning ignition switch

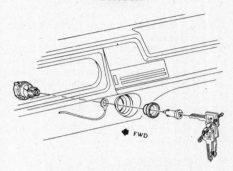

Fig. 8   Ignition switch replacement. G & P models

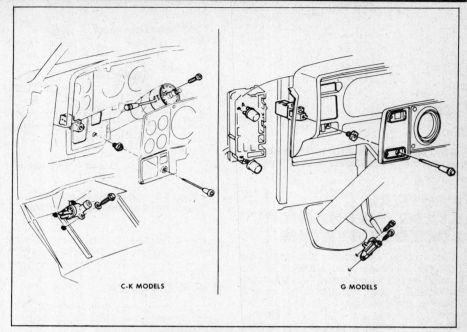

Fig. 9   Headlamp switch. C, G & K models

4. Pull ignition switch away from instrument panel, then using a screwdriver or equivalent, unsnap locking tangs from theft resistant connector.
5. Remove ignition switch.
6. To install, snap connector onto switch, position grounding ring, **Fig. 8,** then install ignition switch and metallic nut.
7. Install ignition lock, then connect battery ground cable.

LIGHT SWITCH
REPLACE

C & K MODELS

1. Disconnect battery ground cable.
2. Reaching behind instrument cluster, depress shaft retaining button and remove switch knob and rod.
3. Remove left side instrument cluster bezel screws, then pull outward on bezel and hold switch retaining nut with wrench, **Fig. 9.**
4. Disconnect wiring connector, then rotate switch counterclockwise and remove from vehicle.
5. Reverse procedure to install.

G MODELS

1. Disconnect battery ground cable.

2. Reaching from behind instrument panel, depress shaft retaining button and remove switch knob and shaft.
3. Remove switch retaining nut from front of instrument panel, **Fig. 9,** then push switch from panel opening, disconnect wiring connector and remove from vehicle.
4. Reverse procedure to install.

CABALLERO & EL CAMINO

1. Disconnect battery ground cable.
2. Remove instrument panel bezel.
3. Pull switch knob to "On" position.
4. Remove three screws attaching windshield wiper/light switch mounting plate to cluster and pull assembly rearward.
5. Depress shaft retainer button on switch and pull knob and shaft assembly from switch, **Fig. 10.**
6. Remove ferrule nut and switch assembly from mounting plate.
7. Reverse procedure to install.

STOP LIGHT SWITCH
REPLACE

1. Disconnect wiring connector at switch.
2. Remove retaining nut, if equipped, then unscrew switch from mounting bracket.
3. To install, depress brake pedal and push new switch into clip until shoulder bottoms out.
4. Plug connector onto switch and check operation. Electrical contact should be made when pedal is depressed .500 inch (exc. C, G, K & P models), .700 inch (G & P models) or 1.125 inch (C & K models) from its fully released position.

COLUMN MOUNTED DIMMER SWITCH
REPLACE

1. Disconnect battery ground cable.
2. Remove instrument panel lower trim and on models with A/C, remove A/C duct extension at column.
3. Disconnect shift indicator from column and remove toe-plate cover screws.
4. Remove two nuts from instrument panel support bracket studs and lower steering column, resting steering wheel on front seat.
5. Remove dimmer switch retaining screws and the switch. Tape actuator rod to column and separate switch from rod.
6. Reverse procedure to install. To adjust switch, depress dimmer switch slightly and install a 3/32 inch twist drill to lock the switch to the body, **Fig. 11.** Force switch upward to remove lash between switch and pivot. Torque switch retaining screw to 35 inch lbs. and remove tape from actuator rod. Remove twist drill and check for proper operation.

FLOOR MOUNTED DIMMER SWITCH
REPLACE

1. Disconnect battery ground cable.
2. Fold back carpeting in area of switch, then disconnect electrical connector from switch.
3. Remove switch retaining screws and the switch.
4. Reverse procedure to install.

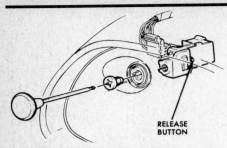

Fig. 10   Headlamp switch knob removal. Caballero & El Camino

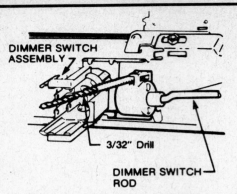

Fig. 11   Column mounted dimmer switch installation

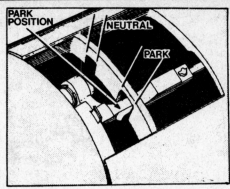

Fig. 12   Mechanical neutral start system, shown in Park position

NEUTRAL START/MECHANICAL LOCKOUT SYSTEM

On some automatic transmission equipped vehicles, the actuation of the ignition switch is prevented by a mechanical lockout system, **Fig. 12,** which prevents the lock cylinder from rotating when the selector lever is out of Park or Neutral. When the selector lever is in Park or Neutral, the slots in the bowl plate and the finger on the actuator rod align, allowing the finger to pass through the bowl plate, in turn actuating the ignition switch, **Fig. 12.** If the selector lever is in any position other than Park or Neutral, the finger contacts the bowl plate when the lock cylinder is rotated, thereby preventing full travel of the lock cylinder.

NEUTRAL START SWITCH
REPLACE

NOTE: On some automatic transmission equipped vehicles, the back up light switch is integral with the neutral start switch.

C & K MODELS

1. Disconnect battery ground cable.
2. Disconnect electrical connector at switch.
3. Remove switch mounting screws, then the switch.
4. Position shift lever in neutral gate notch.
5. Insert a .098 inch gauge pin into switch gauge hole as shown, **Fig. 13,** then assemble switch to column by inserting carrier tang into shift tube slot.
6. Install switch mounting screws into retainers.

NOTE: If retainers strip, they must be replaced.

7. Remove gauge pin, then position shift lever into Park to shear internal plastic pin in switch.
8. Return shift lever to neutral gate notch, then ensure switch gauge hole will accept .080 inch gauge pin. If not, loosen mounting screws, then rotate switch on column until .098 inch gauge pin can be reinserted into gauge hole.
9. Reconnect electrical connector and battery ground cable.

G & P MODELS

1. Raise and support vehicle, then disconnect battery ground cable.
2. Disconnect electrical harness from switch.
3. Remove switch to mounting bracket retaining bolts and the switch, **Fig. 13.**
4. Loosely install new switch to mounting bracket, then align .093–.097 inch hole in transmission lever with hole in switch assembly. Insert pin to hold in

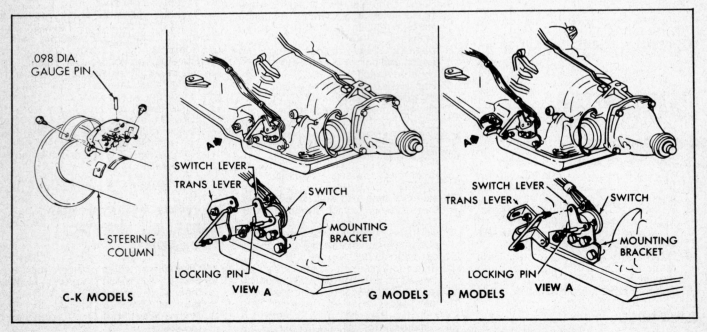

Fig. 13   Neutral start switch replacement. Series 10–30/1500–3500

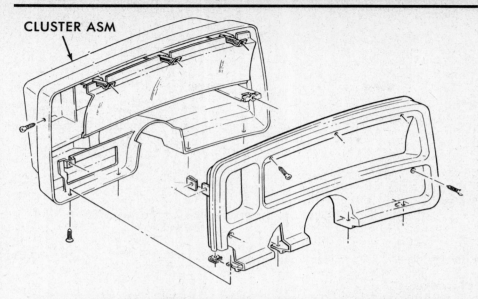

CLUSTER ASM

Fig. 14 Instrument cluster bezel removal. 1979—84 Caballero & El Camino

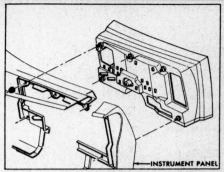

INSTRUMENT PANEL

Fig. 15 Instrument cluster removal. 1982—85 Caballero & El Camino

neutral position, **Fig. 13.**

5. Set transmission lever in neutral position by moving lever counterclockwise to L1 detent, then move clockwise three detents.
6. Install rod into transmission and switch levers and secure with clips.
7. Tighten switch retaining bolts, lower vehicle and check switch for proper operation.

BACK-UP LIGHT SWITCH
REPLACE

MANUAL TRANSMISSION MODELS

Column Mounted Type
1. Disconnect battery ground cable.
2. Disconnect switch wiring harness.
3. Remove switch retaining screws and switch.
4. Assemble new switch onto column, then install retaining screws.
5. Reconnect battery ground cable, then check switch for proper operation.

Transmission Mounted Type
1. Disconnect battery ground cable.
2. Raise and support vehicle.
3. Disconnect switch wiring harness, then remove switch from transmission.
4. Reverse procedure to install, then check switch for proper operation.

MODELS WITH NEUTRAL START/MECHANICAL LOCKOUT

1. Disconnect battery ground cable.

2. Disconnect wiring harness connectors at switch.
3. Remove switch retaining screws and switch from mast jacket.
4. Place gear selector in neutral, then align actuator on new switch with hole in shift tube.
5. Position connector side of switch into cutout in lower jacket, then push down on front of switch until tangs snap into holes in jacket. Install retaining screws.
6. Reconnect wiring harness connectors, then place shift lever in Park.
7. Reconnect battery ground cable, then check switch for proper operation.

INSTRUMENT CLUSTER
REPLACE

CABALLERO & EL CAMINO

1979—81
1. Disconnect battery ground cable.
2. Remove clock set stem knob, if equipped.
3. Remove instrument bezel retaining screws, **Fig. 14.**
4. Pull bezel from panel slightly and disconnect rear defogger switch, if equipped.
5. Remove bezel, **Fig. 14.**
6. Remove two screws at transmission selector indicator and lower indicator assembly to disconnect cable.
7. Remove three screws at windshield wiper/light switch mounting plate and pull assembly rearward for access to lower left cluster attaching bolt and nut.
8. Remove nuts attaching cluster to instrument panel.

9. Pull cluster rearward and disconnect the speedometer cable and all wiring and cables.
10. Remove cluster from vehicle.
11. Reverse procedure to install.

1982—85
1. Disconnect battery ground cable.
2. Remove radio knobs and clock set stem knob.
3. Remove instrument bezel retaining screws, **Fig. 14.**
4. Pull bezel rearward slightly and disconnect the rear defogger switch and remote control mirror control, if equipped.
5. Remove bezel, **Fig. 14.**
6. Remove speedometer retaining screws, pull speedometer from cluster slightly, disconnect speedometer cable and remove speedometer.
7. Remove fuel gauge or tachometer retaining screws, disconnect electrical connectors and remove fuel gauge or tachometer.
8. Remove clock or voltmeter retaining screws, disconnect electrical connectors and remove clock or voltmeter.
9. Disconnect transmission shift indicator cable from steering column.
10. Disconnect all wiring connectors and remove cluster case, **Fig. 15.**
11. Reverse procedure to install.

C & K MODELS
1. Disconnect battery ground cable.
2. Remove headlight switch knob as outlined in "Light Switch, Replace" procedure.
3. Remove radio control knobs.
4. Remove steering column cover, if necessary.
5. Remove the eight instrument panel bezel attaching screws, **Fig. 16,** then the bezel.
6. Working from behind instrument cluster, disconnect speedometer cable.
7. Disconnect all lines and electrical connectors that will interfere with cluster removal.
8. Remove instrument cluster attaching screws, **Fig. 16,** then the instrument cluster.
9. Reverse procedure to install.

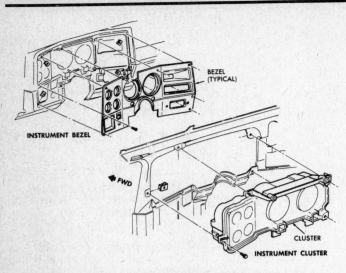

Fig. 16 Instrument bezel & cluster removal. C & K models

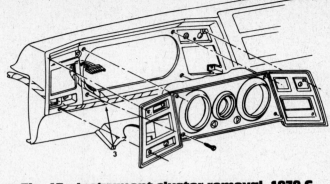

Fig. 17 Instrument cluster removal. 1979 G models

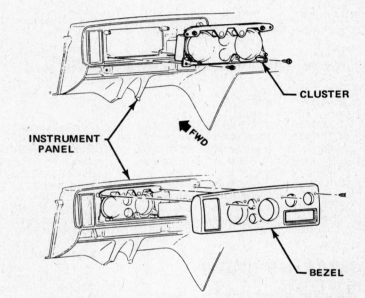

Fig. 18 Instrument bezel & cluster removal. 1980—85 G models

G MODELS

1979
1. Disconnect battery ground cable.
2. Working from behind instrument cluster, disconnect speedometer cable.
3. Disconnect instrument panel harness connector from printed circuit.
4. Disconnect oil pressure line from gauge, if equipped.
5. Remove the two lower instrument panel to cluster stud attaching nuts.
6. Remove instrument cluster retaining screws, **Fig. 17,** then pull top of cluster outward and remove from vehicle.
7. Reverse procedure to install.

1980—85
1. Disconnect battery ground cable.
2. Working from behind instrument cluster, disconnect speedometer cable.
3. Remove clock set stem knob, if equipped.
4. Remove instrument cluster bezel attaching screws, then the bezel, **Fig. 18.**
5. Remove two lower cluster attaching screws, then pull top of cluster outward.
6. Disconnect instrument panel harness connector from printed circuit, then remove cluster from vehicle.
7. Reverse procedure to install.

WIPER MOTOR
REPLACE

C & K MODELS
1. Ensure that wiper motor is in Park position, then disconnect battery ground cable.
2. Disconnect electrical connector from wiper motor and hoses from washer pump.
3. Loosen wiper drive rod attaching screws, then remove drive rod from motor crank arm.
4. Remove wiper motor to dash panel attaching screws, then the wiper motor.
5. Reverse procedure to install.

G MODELS
1. Ensure that wiper motor is in Park position, then disconnect battery ground cable.
2. Remove wiper arms from wiper transmission linkage.
3. Remove cowl panel cover attaching screws, then the cowl panel cover.
4. Loosen transmission linkage to motor crank arm retaining nuts, then disconnect linkage from crank arm.
5. Disconnect wiper motor electrical connector, then remove left dash defroster duct flex hose to gain access to wiper motor retaining screws.
6. Remove left heater duct to engine cover shroud attaching screw, then pull heater duct downward and out of vehicle.
7. Disconnect hoses from washer pump.
8. Remove wiper motor retaining screws, then the wiper motor.
9. Reverse procedure to install.

CABALLERO & EL CAMINO
1. Raise hood and remove cowl screen or grille.
2. Disconnect wiring and washer hoses.
3. Reaching through cowl opening, loosen transmission drive link attaching nuts to motor crankarm.
4. Disconnect drive link from motor crankarm.
5. Remove motor attaching screws.
6. Remove motor while guiding crankarm through hole.
7. Reverse procedure to install.

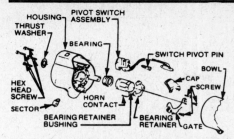

Fig. 19 Windshield wiper switch replacement. 1983—85 Caballero & El Camino with standard column

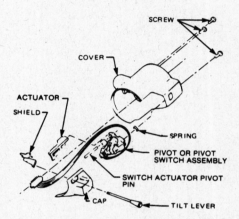

Fig. 20 Windshield wiper switch replacement. 1983—85 Caballero & El Camino with tilt steering column

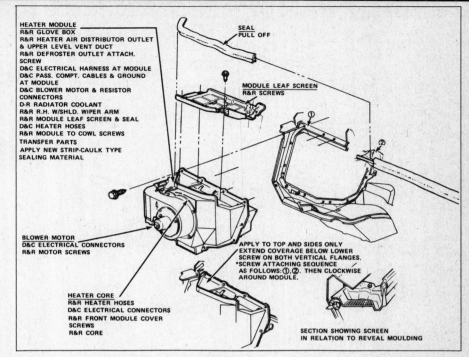

HEATER MODULE
R&R GLOVE BOX
R&R HEATER AIR DISTRIBUTOR OUTLET
& UPPER LEVEL VENT DUCT
R&R DEFROSTER OUTLET ATTACH.
SCREW
D&C ELECTRICAL HARNESS AT MODULE
D&C PASS. COMPT. CABLES & GROUND
AT MODULE
D&C BLOWER MOTOR & RESISTOR
CONNECTORS
D-R RADIATOR COOLANT
R&R R.H. W/SHLD. WIPER ARM
R&R MODULE LEAF SCREEN & SEAL
D&C HEATER HOSES
R&R MODULE TO COWL SCREWS
TRANSFER PARTS
APPLY NEW STRIP-CAULK TYPE
SEALING MATERIAL

SEAL
PULL OFF

MODULE LEAF SCREEN
R&R SCREWS

BLOWER MOTOR
D&C ELECTRICAL CONNECTORS
R&R MOTOR SCREWS

APPLY TO TOP AND SIDES ONLY
EXTEND COVERAGE BELOW LOWER
SCREW ON BOTH VERTICAL FLANGES.
*SCREW ATTACHING SEQUENCE
AS FOLLOWS:①,②. THEN CLOCKWISE
AROUND MODULE.

HEATER CORE
R&R HEATER HOSES
D&C ELECTRICAL CONNECTORS
R&R FRONT MODULE COVER
SCREWS
R&R CORE

SECTION SHOWING SCREEN
IN RELATION TO REVEAL MOULDING

Fig. 21 Blower motor & heater core (less A/C). Caballero & El Camino

WIPER TRANSMISSION
REPLACE

C & K MODELS

1. Remove wiper arms from pivot shafts.
2. Remove cowl ventilator grille, if necessary.
3. Working from plenum access hole, remove connector link to motor drive arm retaining nuts and washers.
4. Remove transmission pivot shaft assembly to windshield frame attaching screws.
5. Remove wiper linkage and transmission assembly from vehicle.
6. Reverse procedure to install.

G MODELS

1. Remove wiper arms from pivot shafts.
2. Remove ventilator grille to cowl attaching screws, then the ventilator grille.
3. Working from center of cowl, remove link rod to motor drive attaching nuts, then disconnect link rods from pins.
4. Remove transmission pivot shaft assembly to cowl retaining screws.

5. Remove transmission pivot shaft assembly with link rods through opening in plenum chamber.
6. Reverse procedure to install.

CABALLERO & EL CAMINO

1. Raise hood and remove cowl vent screen.
2. Remove wiper arms from pivot shafts.
3. Loosen drive link to motor crank arm attaching nuts, then disconnect transmission drive link from crank arm.
4. Remove transmission to body attaching screws.
5. Remove transmission and linkage through opening in cowl.
6. Reverse procedure to install.

WINDSHIELD WIPER/WASHER SWITCH
REPLACE

CABALLERO & EL CAMINO

1979—82
1. Disconnect battery ground cable.
2. Remove instrument panel bezel.
3. Remove screws securing wiper switch mounting plate to cluster and pull assembly rearward.
4. Disconnect electrical connector and remove wiper switch.
5. Reverse procedure to install.

1983—85
1. Disconnect battery ground cable.
2. Remove turn signal switch, ignition lock, ignition switch and dimmer switch as outlined previously.
3. Remove parts, then the switch as shown, **Figs. 19 and 20.**
4. Reverse procedure to install.

C & K MODELS

1. Disconnect battery ground cable.
2. Remove instrument panel bezel screws, then the bezel.
3. Remove switch to instrument panel attaching screws, then pull switch assembly outward and disconnect electrical connector.
4. Remove wiper/washer switch.
5. Reverse procedure to install.

G MODELS

1. Disconnect battery ground cable.
2. Working from behind left side of instrument panel, disconnect electrical connector from switch, then remove switch to bezel mounting screws.
3. Remove wiper/washer switch.
4. Reverse procedure to install, ensuring that ground wires are attached properly to switch.

RADIO
REPLACE

NOTE: When installing radio, be sure to adjust antenna trimmer for peak reception.

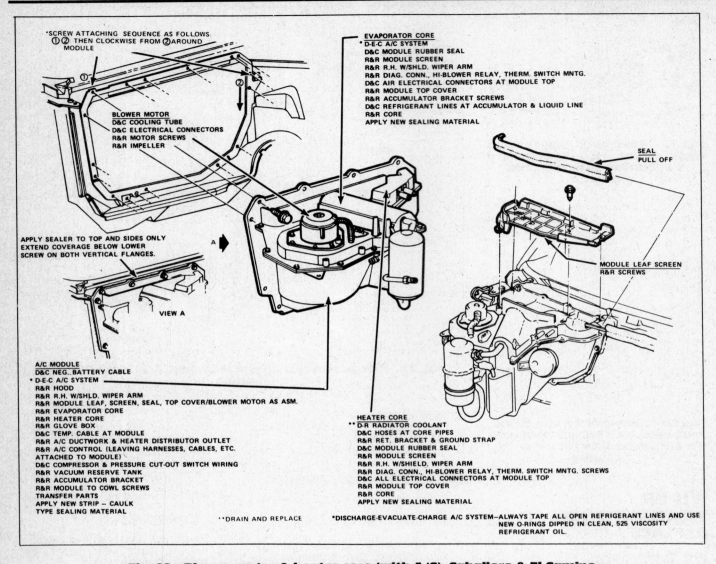

*SCREW ATTACHING SEQUENCE AS FOLLOWS:
①② THEN CLOCKWISE FROM ② AROUND MODULE

BLOWER MOTOR
D&C COOLING TUBE
D&C ELECTRICAL CONNECTORS
R&R MOTOR SCREWS
R&R IMPELLER

APPLY SEALER TO TOP AND SIDES ONLY
EXTEND COVERAGE BELOW LOWER
SCREW ON BOTH VERTICAL FLANGES.

VIEW A

EVAPORATOR CORE
*D-E-C A/C SYSTEM
D&C MODULE RUBBER SEAL
R&R MODULE SCREEN
R&R R.H. W/SHLD. WIPER ARM
R&R DIAG. CONN., HI-BLOWER RELAY, THERM. SWITCH MNTG.
D&C AIR ELECTRICAL CONNECTORS AT MODULE TOP
R&R MODULE TOP COVER
R&R ACCUMULATOR BRACKET SCREWS
D&C REFRIGERANT LINES AT ACCUMULATOR & LIQUID LINE
R&R CORE
APPLY NEW SEALING MATERIAL

SEAL
PULL OFF

MODULE LEAF SCREEN
R&R SCREWS

A/C MODULE
D&C NEG. BATTERY CABLE
*D-E-C A/C SYSTEM
R&R HOOD
R&R R.H. W/SHLD. WIPER ARM
R&R MODULE LEAF, SCREEN, SEAL, TOP COVER/BLOWER MOTOR AS ASM.
R&R EVAPORATOR CORE
R&R HEATER CORE
R&R GLOVE BOX
D&C TEMP. CABLE AT MODULE
R&R A/C DUCTWORK & HEATER DISTRIBUTOR OUTLET
R&R A/C CONTROL (LEAVING HARNESSES, CABLES, ETC. ATTACHED TO MODULE)
D&C COMPRESSOR & PRESSURE CUT-OUT SWITCH WIRING
R&R VACUUM RESERVE TANK
R&R ACCUMULATOR BRACKET
R&R MODULE TO COWL SCREWS
TRANSFER PARTS
APPLY NEW STRIP – CAULK
TYPE SEALING MATERIAL

HEATER CORE
**D-R RADIATOR COOLANT
D&C HOSES AT CORE PIPES
R&R RET. BRACKET & GROUND STRAP
D&C MODULE RUBBER SEAL
R&R MODULE SCREEN
R&R R.H. W/SHIELD. WIPER ARM
R&R DIAG. CONN., HI-BLOWER RELAY, THERM. SWITCH MNTG. SCREWS
D&C ALL ELECTRICAL CONNECTORS AT MODULE TOP
R&R MODULE TOP COVER
R&R CORE
APPLY NEW SEALING MATERIAL

**DRAIN AND REPLACE

*DISCHARGE-EVACUATE-CHARGE A/C SYSTEM—ALWAYS TAPE ALL OPEN REFRIGERANT LINES AND USE NEW O-RINGS DIPPED IN CLEAN, 525 VISCOSITY REFRIGERANT OIL.

Fig. 22 Blower motor & heater core (with A/C). Caballero & El Camino

CABALLERO & EL CAMINO

1. Disconnect battery ground cable.
2. Remove control knobs from control shafts.
3. Remove trim plate attaching screws and trim plate.
4. Disconnect antenna lead and wire connector from radio.
5. Remove stud nut at right side of bracket attachment.
6. Remove control shaft nuts and washers.
7. Remove instrument panel bracket screws and bracket.
8. Remove radio through opening in instrument panel.
9. Reverse procedure to install.

C & K MODELS

1. Disconnect battery ground cable.
2. Remove radio control knobs and bezels.
3. Remove nuts and washers from control shafts.
4. On AM radio equipped vehicles, remove radio support bracket stud nut and washer.
5. On AM-FM equipped vehicles, remove radio support bracket to instrument panel attaching screws.
6. Lift upward on rear edge of radio, then push radio forward until control shafts clear instrument panel.
7. Disconnect power feed, speaker and antenna lead, then remove radio.
8. Reverse procedure to install.

G MODELS

1. Disconnect battery ground cable.
2. Remove engine cover.
3. Remove air cleaner cover and filter element.

NOTE: On some models, it may be necessary to remove the air cleaner stud to gain sufficient clearance to remove radio.

4. Remove control knobs, washers and retaining nuts from control shafts.

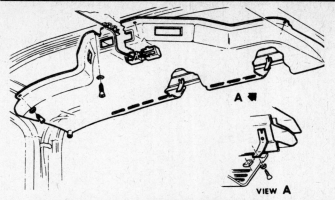

Fig. 23 Rear duct assembly. C, G, K models with overhead system

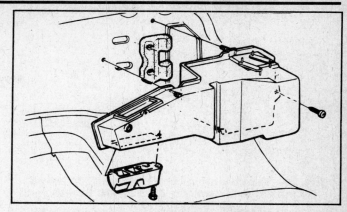

Fig. 24 Heater distributor assembly. C & K models

5. Remove mounting bracket retaining screw, then the bracket.
6. Push radio forward, then lower assembly until electrical connector and antenna lead can be disconnected.
7. Remove radio from vehicle.
8. Reverse procedure to install.

BLOWER MOTOR
REPLACE

CABALLERO & EL CAMINO

1. Disconnect battery ground cable.
2. Disconnect blower motor lead wire.
3. If equipped with A/C, disconnect cooling tube from motor.
4. Remove blower motor attaching screws, then the blower motor, **Figs. 21 and 22.**
5. Reverse procedure to install.

C, G & K MODELS

Exc. Overhead Type System
1. Disconnect battery ground cable.

NOTE: On some G model vehicles, it may be necessary to remove the battery, coolant recovery tank and power antenna, if equipped, to gain access to the blower motor.

2. On G models equipped with A/C and diesel engine, proceed as follows:
   a. Remove parking lamp assembly, then the coolant recovery tank.
   b. Remove retaining screws, then the blower insulation through the hood opening.
3. On all models, disconnect blower motor electrical connections.
4. If equipped with A/C, remove blower motor cooling tube.
5. Remove blower motor attaching screws, then pry blower motor from case.
6. Reverse procedure to install.

Overhead Type System
1. Disconnect battery ground cable.
2. Remove rear duct drain tube, duct to header bracket and roof panel screws, then rear duct assembly, **Fig. 23.**

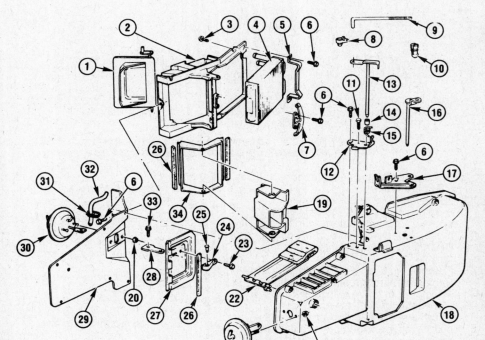

1. BAFFLE
2. TEMPERATURE VALVE HOUSING
3. SCREW
4. HEATER CORE
5. MOUNTING STRAP
6. SCREW
7. CLAMP
8. CONNECTOR
9. DIVERTER VALVE LINK
10. CONNECTOR
11. SCREW
12. DIVERTER VALVE ADJ. BRACKET
13. PIVOT SHAFT
14. SPACER
15. SPRING
16. PIVOT SHAFT
17. CABLE ADJ. BRACKET
18. CASE
19. BI-LEVEL VALVE
20. NUT
21. DEFROSTER VALVE VACUUM ACTUATOR
22. DEFROSTER VALVE
23. SCREW
24. LINK
25. PIN
26. SEAL
27. DIVERTER VALVE
28. CONNECTOR
29. FRONT CASE PLATE
30. AIR DIST. VACUUM ACTUATOR
31. GROMMET
32. HOSE
33. SCREW
34. SLAVE VALVE YOKE

Fig. 25 A/C & heater assembly. C & K models

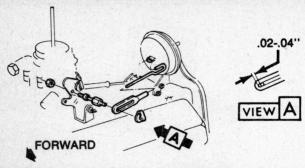

Fig. 26 Servo unit rod adjustment. 1979–83 Caballero & El Camino & 1979–80 Series 10–30/1500–3500

3. Disconnect blower motor harness lead and ground wire.
4. While supporting lower case to prevent damage to motor or case assemblies, remove case mounting screws, then lower case from vehicle roof.
5. Remove motor retaining strap, then lift motor and cage assembly from case. Remove cages by removing shaft retaining nuts.
6. Reverse procedure to install. When installing cages on motor shaft, tension springs must be installed on motor shafts. Cages should be mounted so leading edges of blades face lower evaporator case (thin edge first). After installing blower assembly in case, check to ensure there is no interference with rotating cages.

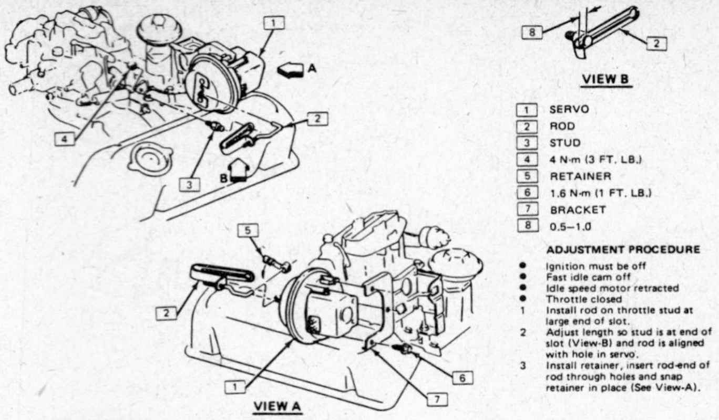

HEATER CORE
REPLACE

C & K MODELS

Less A/C
1. Disconnect battery ground cable, then drain cooling system.
2. Disconnect heater hoses at core, then plug core tubes to prevent coolant spillage.
3. Working from engine compartment, remove distributor duct stud attaching nuts.
4. Remove glove box and door assembly.
5. Disconnect air-defrost and temperature door cables.
6. Remove floor outlet, then the defroster duct to heater distributor duct attaching screw.
7. Remove heater distributor to dash panel attaching screws, **Fig. 24**.
8. Pull distributor rearward, then disconnect all harnesses that will interfere with distributor removal.
9. Remove heater distributor from vehicle.
10. Remove heater core retaining straps, then the heater core.
11. Reverse procedure to install.

With A/C
1. Disconnect battery ground cable, then drain cooling system.

Fig. 27 Servo unit rod adjustment. 1984 Caballero & El Camino with V6-231 engine

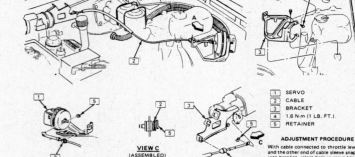

Fig. 28 Servo unit cable adjustment. 1984 Caballero & El Camino with V6-229 engine

2. Disconnect heater hoses at core and plug core tubes.
3. Remove glove box assembly.
4. Remove screws at center duct to selector duct/instrument panel. Remove center upper and lower ducts.
5. Disconnect bowden cable at temperature door.
6. Remove nuts at selector duct studs (projecting through firewall). Remove selector duct to firewall screw.
7. Draw selector duct assembly rearward so core tubes clear firewall. Lower assembly sufficiently to remove vacuum lines and harness connections.
8. Remove selector duct assembly. Disconnect core mounting straps and remove core, **Fig. 25**.
9. Reverse procedure to install.

CABALLERO & EL CAMINO

Less A/C
1. Disconnect battery ground cable, then drain cooling system.
2. Disconnect hoses from heater core, then plug outlets to prevent coolant spillage.
3. Disconnect wire connectors, then remove front module cover attaching screws and cover.
4. Remove heater core from module,

Fig. 21.
5. Reverse procedure to install.

With A/C
1. Disconnect battery ground cable, then drain cooling system.
2. Disconnect heater hoses at core.
3. Remove retaining bracket and ground strap.
4. Remove module rubber seal and module screen, **Fig. 22.**
5. Remove right hand wiper arm.
6. Remove high blower relay and thermostatic switch mounting screws.
7. Disconnect wire connector at top of module, then remove module top cover.
8. Remove heater core from module.
9. Reverse procedure to install.

G MODELS

Less A/C
1. Disconnect battery ground cable.
2. Remove coolant recovery tank, and place to side.
3. After placing suitable drain pan under vehicle, disconnect heater hoses at core, plug hose ends, and allow core to drain.
4. Remove heater air distributor duct to air distributor case retaining screws.

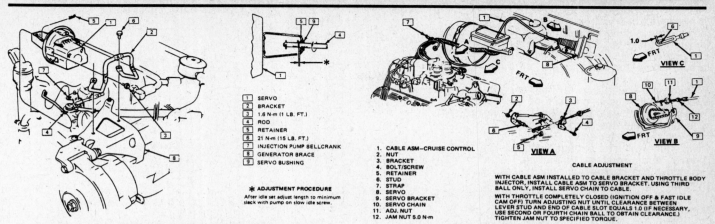

1	SERVO
2	BRACKET
3	1.6 N·m (1 LB. FT.)
4	ROD
5	RETAINER
6	21 N·m (15 LB. FT.)
7	INJECTION PUMP BELLCRANK
8	GENERATOR BRACE
9	SERVO BUSHING

★ ADJUSTMENT PROCEDURE
After idle set adjust length to minimum slack with pump on slow idle screw.

Fig. 29 Servo unit rod adjustment. 1984 Caballero & El Camino with V8-350 diesel engine

1.	CABLE ASM—CRUISE CONTROL
2.	NUT
3.	BRACKET
4.	BOLT/SCREW
5.	RETAINER
6.	STUD
7.	STRAP
8.	SERVO
9.	SERVO BRACKET
10.	SERVO CHAIN
11.	ADJ. NUT
12.	JAM NUT 5.0 N·m

CABLE ADJUSTMENT

WITH CABLE ASM INSTALLED TO CABLE BRACKET AND THROTTLE BODY INJECTOR, INSTALL CABLE ASM TO SERVO BRACKET. USING THIRD BALL ONLY, INSTALL SERVO CHAIN TO CABLE.

WITH THROTTLE COMPLETELY CLOSED (IGNITION OFF & FAST IDLE CAM OFF) TURN ADJUSTING NUT UNTIL CLEARANCE BETWEEN LEVER STUD AND END OF CABLE SLOT EQUALS 1.0 (IF NECESSARY, USE SECOND OR FOURTH CHAIN BALL TO OBTAIN CLEARANCE.) TIGHTEN JAM NUT TO SPECIFIED TORQUE.

Fig. 30 Servo unit cable adjustment. 1985 Caballero & El Camino with V6-262 engine

5. Remove engine housing cover.
6. Remove upper (at windshield) and all lower instrument panel retaining screws. Remove right lower instrument panel support bracket.
7. Lower steering column. Raise right side of instrument panel, and place on suitable support.
8. Remove air distributor case to defroster duct retaining screw. Remove 2 air distributor to heater case retaining screws.
9. Disconnect temperature door cable. Fold cable away from work area to provide access.
10. Remove air distributor case retaining nuts in engine compartment. Remove retainer screw in vehicle interior.
11. Remove core and case from vehicle as assembly by tilting case assembly rearward at top. Lift case assembly up at same time, until core tubes clear openings in dash.
12. Remove core retaining strap screws and core.
13. Reverse procedure to install, replacing sealer where needed.

With A/C

1. Disconnect battery ground cable, then remove engine cover.
2. Remove steering column support bolts at instrument panel, then lower column.
3. Remove instrument panel upper and lower mounting screws, and radio bracket attaching screws.
4. Raise right side of instrument panel and place on suitable support. Remove right lower instrument panel support bracket.
5. Remove vacuum actuator at recirculating air door.
6. Disconnect vacuum hoses and temperature cable at air distributor case. Remove heater distributor duct.
7. Remove both defroster duct to firewall screws below windshield.
8. Drain cooling system. Remove heater hoses at core connections and plug core tubes.

9. Remove 3 nuts retaining heater core case to firewall, then remove screw at lower right corner of case.
10. Remove distributor assembly from vehicle.
11. Expose screws holding case halves together by removing gasket.
12. Remove temperature cable support bracket, and remove screws to separate case parts.
13. Remove heater core.
14. Reverse procedure to install.

SPEED CONTROLS
ADJUST

CABALLERO & EL CAMINO

1979—83

Servo Unit Adjustment

Adjust the bead chain cable or rod so that it is as tight as possible without holding the throttle open when the carburetor is set at its lowest idle throttle position. The cable is adjusted by turning the hex portion of servo. The bead chain or cable is adjusted so there is 1/16 inch of lost motion in servo cable. The rod is adjusted by turning link onto rod. With rod hooked through tab, on power unit, turn link onto rod until dimension in **Fig. 26** is obtained, then install link and retainer. This adjustment should be made with ignition off and fast idle cam in off position with throttle completely closed.

When connecting the bead chain or cable (engine stopped) manually set the fast idle cam at its lowest step and connect the chain so that it does not hold the idle screw off the cam. If the chain needs to be cut, cut it three beads beyond the bead that pulls the linkage.

Regulator Unit Adjustment

To remove any difference between engagement and cruising speed, one adjustment is possible. However, no adjustment should be made until the following items have been checked or serviced.
1. Bead chain or cable properly adjusted.

2. All hoses in good condition, properly attached, not leaking, pinched or cracked.
3. Regulator air filter cleaned and properly oiled.
4. Electric and vacuum switches properly adjusted.

Engagement-Cruising Speed Zeroing

If the cruising speed is lower than the engagement speed, loosen the orifice tube locknut and turn the tube outward; if higher turn the tube inward. Each 1/4 turn will alter the engagement-cruising speed difference one mph. Tighten locknut after adjustment and check the system operation at 50 mph.

Brake Release Switch

The electric brake switch is actuated when the brake pedal is depressed .38—.64 inch. The vacuum release switch is actuated when brake pedal is moved 5/16 inch on all units.

1984—85

Brake Release Switches

The brake electric and vacuum release switches are both mounted on the brake pedal support bracket and are self-adjusting. If either switch is replaced, pull brake pedal rearward against stop until audible clicks are no longer heard. Release brake pedal, then repeat operation. Release switches are now adjusted.

Servo Unit Adjustment

Refer to **Figs. 27 through 31** for servo unit adjustments.

SERIES 10—30/1500—3500

1979—80

Servo Unit Adjustment

With throttle closed and ignition and fast idle cam off, adjust linkage length by turning link onto rod until dimension shown in **Fig. 26** is obtained. Reinstall link and link retainer.

Engagement-Cruising Speed Zeroing

The only transducer adjustment possible

is engagement-cruising speed zeroing. No adjustment should be performed unless the servo unit and brake release switches are properly adjusted and all vacuum lines are checked for kinks, leaks or punctures.

If cruising speed is lower than engagement speed, loosen orifice tube locknut and turn tube counterclockwise. If cruising speed is greater than engagement speed, turn orifice tube clockwise. Each ¼ turn of orifice tube will alter engagement-cruising speed approximately one mph. After adjustment is completed, tighten locknut and test system at 55 mph.

Brake Release Switches

The brake release electrical switch should be adjusted so that the switch contacts are open when the brake pedal is depressed .38–.64 inch.

The brake release vacuum switch should be adjusted so that the valve plunger clears the pedal arm when the arm is moved 1.17–1.36 (less Hydro-Boost) or 1.23–1.49 (with Hydro-Boost) inch.

1981–82

Power Unit Adjustment

With air conditioner off and idle speed solenoid disconnected (if equipped), set curb hot idle speed to 500 RPM, then shut engine off. Unsnap swivel from ball stud, then hold chain taught. Center of swivel should extend ⅛ inch beyond center of ball stud. If not, remove swivel and chain assembly retainer, then position chain into swivel cavities which will give adjustment stated above. Reinstall retainer.

Engagement-Cruising Speed Zeroing

The only transducer adjustment possible is engagement-cruising speed zeroing. No adjustment should be performed unless the servo unit and brake release switches are properly adjusted and all vacuum lines are checked for kinks, leaks or punctures.

If cruising speed is lower than engagement speed, loosen orifice tube locknut and turn tube counterclockwise. If cruising speed is greater than engagement speed, turn orifice tube clockwise. Each ¼ turn of orifice tube will alter engagement-cruising speed approximately one mph. After adjustment is completed, tighten locknut and test system at 50 mph.

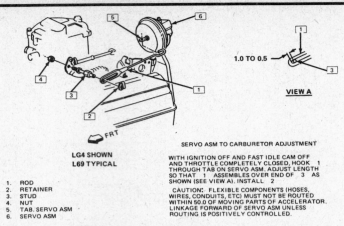

1. ROD
2. RETAINER
3. STUD
4. NUT
5. TAB. SERVO ASM
6. SERVO ASM

LG4 SHOWN
L69 TYPICAL

SERVO ASM TO CARBURETOR ADJUSTMENT

WITH IGNITION OFF AND FAST IDLE CAM OFF AND THROTTLE COMPLETELY CLOSED, HOOK 1 THROUGH TAB ON SERVO ASM. ADJUST LENGTH SO THAT 1 ASSEMBLES OVER END OF 3 AS SHOWN (SEE VIEW A). INSTALL 2

CAUTION: FLEXIBLE COMPONENTS (HOSES, WIRES, CONDUITS, ETC) MUST NOT BE ROUTED WITHIN 50.0 OF MOVING PARTS OF ACCELERATOR. LINKAGE FORWARD OF SERVO ASM UNLESS ROUTING IS POSITIVELY CONTROLLED.

Fig. 31   Servo unit rod adjustment. 1985 Caballero & El Camino with V8-305 engine

Brake Release Switch & Valve

With brake pedal fully depressed, push switch and valve fully forward against bracket or arm. Pull pedal rearward with a force of 15–20 lbs. to automatically adjust switch and valve.

Clutch Release Switch & Valve

With clutch pedal at rest, push switch and valve assembly forward against bracket or arm. Pull pedal rearward with a force of 15–20 lbs. to automatically adjust switch and valve.

1983–84

Servo Unit Adjustment

To adjust servo on six cylinder engines, use second (6-292) or third (6-250) ball on servo chain. With throttle closed and ignition and fast idle off, adjust cable jam nuts until .040 inch clearance exists between lever pin and cable assembly end slots. Tighten jam nuts.

To adjust servo on V8 gasoline engines, close throttle, then with ignition and fast idle off, adjust rod assembly length to give .007–.015 inch clearance between rod and stud.

To adjust servo on V8 diesel engines, position idle screw against stop, then with engine off, assemble lower end of rod link to throttle lever and upper end to hole closest servo which will provide .040 inch slack minimum.

Engagement-Cruising Speed Zeroing

There is no provision for engagement-cruising speed zeroing. If cruising speed is too high or low, check vacuum hoses for improper routing, restrictions or leaks and servo linkage for proper adjustment. If cruising speed is still too high or low, replace the electronic controller.

1985

Servo Unit Adjustment

To adjust servo on V6 and V8 gasoline engines, close throttle, then with ignition and fast idle off, adjust rod assembly length to give .020–.040 (Exc. C and K models with V8 engine) or .007–.015 (C and K models with V8 engine) inch clearance between rod and stud.

To adjust servo on G models with diesel engines, use third ball on servo chain. With ignition off, adjust cable jam nuts until cable sleeve at throttle lever is tight, without holding throttle open. To adjust servo on C and K models with diesel engines, position idle screw against stop, then with ignition off, assemble lower end of rod link to throttle lever and upper end to hole closest servo which will provide .040 inch slack maximum.

Engagement-Cruising Speed Zeroing

There is no provision for engagement-cruising speed zeroing. If cruising speed is too high or low, check vacuum hoses for improper routing, restrictions or leaks and servo linkage for proper adjustment. If cruising speed remains too high or low, replace the electronic controller.

Gasoline Engine Section

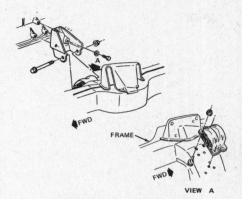

Fig. 1   Engine mount replacement. Caballero & El Camino with 6-250 engine

ENGINE MOUNTS
REPLACE

CABALLERO & EL CAMINO

6-250
1. Remove nut, washer and engine mount through-bolt.
2. Raise engine to release weight from mount.
3. Remove bracket-to-mount bolt, then remove mount.
4. Install new mount on bracket.
5. Lower engine, install through-bolt and tighten all mount bolts, **Fig. 1**.

V6-200
1. Remove mount retaining bolt from below frame mounting bracket, **Fig. 2**.
2. Raise front of engine and remove mount to engine bolts and remove mount.

NOTE: Right hand mount may be removed by loosening through bolt. It is not necessary to remove it. Raise engine only enough to provide sufficient clearance for mount removal. Check for interference between rear of engine and cowl panel.

3. Reverse procedure to install.

V6-231
1. Raise and support front of vehicle.
2. Support engine at front edge of oil pan, then remove mount to engine attaching bolts.
3. Raise engine slightly, then remove mount to mount bracket retaining bolt and nut. Remove mount from vehicle.

4. Reverse procedure to install.

V6-229, 262 & All V8 Engines
1. Remove mount retaining bolt from below frame mounting bracket, **Fig. 3**.
2. Raise front of engine and remove mount to engine bolts and mount. On models equipped with V6 engine, the right hand mount may be removed by loosening the through bolt.

NOTE: Raise engine only enough to provide sufficient clearance for mount removal. Check for interference between rear of engine and cowl panel which could result in distributor damage.

3. Reverse procedure to install.

SERIES 10—30/1500—3500

L-6 Engines
1. Remove engine mount through bolt, **Figs. 4 and 5**.
2. Raise engine, then remove mount to frame bracket attaching bolts and mount.

NOTE: Raise engine only enough to gain sufficient clearance for removal. Check for interference between rear of engine and cowl panel.

3. Install new engine mount to frame bracket, then install and tighten attaching bolts.
4. Install engine mount through bolt and torque bolt to 30 ft. lbs.

V-8 Engines
1. Working from below frame mounting bracket, remove engine mount through bolt, **Figs. 6 and 7**.
2. Raise engine, then remove mount to engine attaching bolts and mount.

NOTE: Raise engine only enough to gain sufficient clearance for removal. Check for interference between rear of engine and cowl panel.

3. Install new engine mount to engine, then tighten attaching bolts.
4. Install and tighten engine mount through bolt.

ENGINE
REPLACE

CABALLERO & EL CAMINO

1. Disconnect battery ground cable and remove air cleaner.
2. Mark position of hinges for reassem-

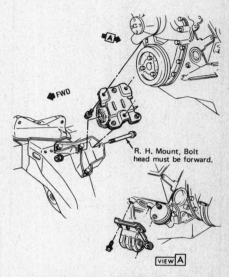

R. H. Mount, Bolt head must be forward.

Fig. 2   Engine mount replacement. Caballero & El Camino with V6-200 engine

bly, then remove hood.
3. Drain cooling system, remove radiator hoses, and disconnect heater hoses from engine.
4. On models with A/C, disconnect electrical connector from compressor clutch and ground wire from bracket, remove compressor and secure aside.
5. On V6-231 engines, remove fan blade, pulleys and shroud. On all other engines, remove fan shroud and radiator.

NOTE: On models with automatic transmission, disconnect and plug cooler lines.

6. Remove power steering pump retaining bolts, if equipped, and secure pump aside.
7. Disconnect accelerator linkage at throttle lever and bracket. Disconnect vacuum hoses to body mounted accessories and fuel hoses at fuel pump, then plug fuel hoses.
8. Disconnect battery and chassis ground straps from engine.
9. Disconnect electrical connectors from alternator, distributor or remote mounted coil and all engine mounted switches and accessories.
10. Remove engine harness from retaining clips and secure aside.
11. Raise and support vehicle and drain crankcase.
12. Disconnect exhaust pipes and AIR pipe from manifolds, and remove front exhaust and cruise control brackets, if equipped.

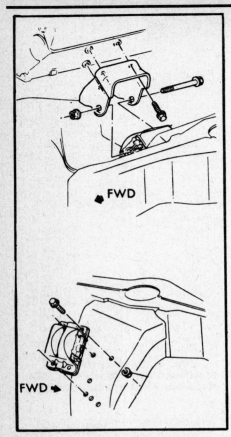

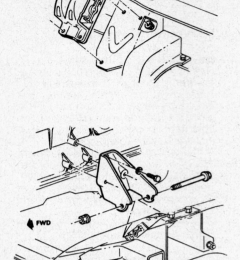

Fig. 4 Engine mount replacement. C, K & P models with in-line 6 cylinder engine

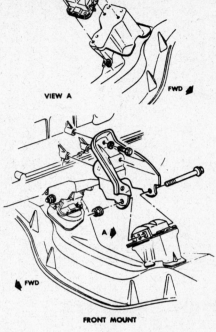

Fig. 5 Engine mount replacement. G models with in-line 6 cylinder engine

Fig. 3 Engine mount replacement. Caballero & El Camino with V6-229, 262 and all V-8 engines

13. Disconnect electrical connectors and battery cable from starter, or remove starter.
14. Remove flywheel shield and remove bolts securing torque converter to flex plate, if equipped.

NOTE: Mark position of converter in relation to flex plate for reassembly.

15. Remove motor mount through bolts and bolts securing bell housing to engine.
16. Lower vehicle and support transmission with suitable floor jack.
17. Attach suitable lifting equipment to engine lifting brackets, raise engine and transmission, and remove motor mount to engine brackets.
18. Separate engine and transmission while supporting transmission with jack.

NOTE: On automatic transmission models, ensure converter remains with transmission during engine removal and is properly seated prior to engine installation.

19. Lift and remove engine after disconnecting any remaining harness connectors.
20. Reverse procedure to install.

SERIES 10—30/1500—3500

L-6 ENGINES

C & K Models

1. Disconnect battery ground cable, then drain cooling system.
2. Remove air cleaner.
3. Disconnect accelerator cable and detent cable (automatic transmission models) from carburetor throttle lever.
4. Disconnect all engine wiring that will interfere with engine removal.
5. Disconnect radiator hoses from radiator and heater hoses from engine.

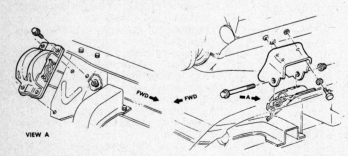

Fig. 6 Engine mount replacement. C, K & P models with V-8 engines

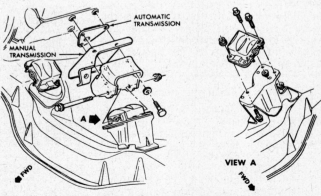

Fig. 7 Engine mount replacement. G models with V-8 engines

6. Remove radiator attaching bolts, then the radiator.
7. Remove fan and water pump pulley, then disconnect fuel line from fuel pump.
8. Remove hood.
9. Raise and support vehicle, then remove starter motor.
10. Remove flywheel or torque converter splash shield.
11. Disconnect exhaust pipe from exhaust manifold and wire pipe aside.
12. Remove engine mount through bolts.
13. On automatic transmission equipped vehicles, remove torque converter to flex plate attaching bolts.
14. On K models, remove strut rods at motor mounts.
15. Support transmission, then remove bell housing to engine retaining bolts.
16. Lower vehicle.
17. Attach a suitable engine lifting device and remove engine from vehicle.
18. Reverse procedure to install.

G Models
1. Disconnect battery ground cable, then drain cooling system.
2. Remove engine cover and air cleaner assembly.
3. Evacuate A/C system, then remove A/C compressor, if equipped.
4. Disconnect accelerator linkage, then remove carburetor mounting bolts and carburetor.
5. Remove grille and grille cross brace.
6. Remove windshield washer reservoir and A/C vacuum reservoir, if equipped.
7. Disconnect hoses from radiator.
8. On automatic transmission equipped vehicles, disconnect cooling lines from radiator.
9. If equipped with A/C, remove A/C condenser to radiator support attaching bolts, then position condenser aside.
10. Remove radiator to radiator support attaching brackets, then the radiator.
11. Disconnect heater hoses from engine.
12. Disconnect all wiring that will interfere with engine removal.
13. Raise and support vehicle.
14. Disconnect fuel line from fuel pump, then drain crankcase.
15. Remove propeller shaft, then plug transmission housing to prevent fluid leakage.
16. Disconnect exhaust pipe from exhaust manifold.
17. Disconnect shift linkage and speedometer cable from transmission.
18. Remove transmission mount retaining bolts.
19. On manual transmission equipped vehicles, disconnect clutch linkage, then remove clutch cross shaft.
20. Remove engine mount through bolts, then lower vehicle.
21. Attach a suitable engine lifting device, then raise engine and remove right hand engine mount from engine.
22. Remove engine/transmission assembly.
23. Reverse procedure to install.

V6-ENGINES

C & K Models
1. Disconnect battery ground cable, then drain cooling system.
2. Remove air cleaner assembly.
3. Remove accessory drive belts, then the fan and water pump pulley.
4. Disconnect all hoses from engine.
5. If equipped with automatic transmission, disconnect cooling lines from radiator.
6. Remove radiator and fan shroud.
7. Disconnect accelerator linkage and detent cable (automatic transmission models) from carburetor throttle lever.
8. If equipped with A/C, remove A/C compressor from mounting bracket and position aside. Do not disconnect lines from compressor.
9. Remove power steering pump, if equipped, and position aside.
10. Disconnect wiring harness from engine, then the fuel line from fuel pump.
11. Disconnect vacuum lines from intake manifold, then raise and support vehicle.
12. Drain crankcase, then disconnect exhaust pipes from exhaust manifolds.
13. On K models with automatic transmission, remove strut rods from motor mounts.
14. Remove flywheel or converter splash shield, then disconnect wiring along right pan rail.
15. Disconnect starter wiring and remove starter.
16. Disconnect wiring from gas gauge.
17. If equipped with automatic transmission, remove converter to flex plate attaching bolts.
18. Support transmission with a suitable transmission jack, then remove bell housing to engine attaching bolts.
19. Remove lower engine mount bracket to frame attaching bolts, then lower vehicle.
20. Remove hood.
21. Attach a suitable engine lifting device and remove engine from vehicle.
22. Reverse procedure to install.

G Models
1. Disconnect battery ground cable, then remove glove box.
2. Remove engine cover, then drain cooling system.
3. Remove outside air duct and power steering reservoir bracket, if applicable.
4. Disconnect hood release cable, then remove upper fan shroud bolts and overflow hoses.
5. Disconnect transmission cooler lines, then remove radiator.
6. Remove upper fan shroud, then the fan and pulley.
7. Remove air cleaner assembly, then the cruise control servo, if equipped.
8. Disconnect brake vacuum line, cables and fuel line from carburetor.
9. Remove carburetor and distributor cap, then disconnect AIR hoses from diverter valve. Remove diverter valve.

10. Disconnect coolant hoses, PCV valve, and all vacuum hoses and electrical harnesses that will interfere with engine removal.
11. Discharge A/C system, if equipped, then remove compressor brace and position compressor aside.
12. Remove upper oil dipstick, oil filler and transmission dipstick tubes, then disconnect accelerator cable at dipstick.
13. Disconnect fuel hoses from fuel pump, then remove power steering pump, if equipped, and position aside.
14. If equipped with A/C, remove idler pulley.
15. Remove headlamp bezels, grille and upper radiator support, then the lower fan shroud and filler panel.
16. Remove hood latch support.
17. If equipped with A/C, disconnect lines, then remove condenser from vehicle.
18. Raise and support vehicle, then drain crankcase.
19. Disconnect exhaust pipe from manifolds.
20. Disconnect strut rods at flywheel cover, then remove cover.
21. Disconnect starter electrical wires, then remove attaching bolts and starter.
22. On automatic transmission equipped vehicles, remove flex plate to torque converter attaching bolts.
23. On all vehicles, remove transmission to engine attaching bolts, then the motor mount through bolts.
24. Lower vehicle, then support transmission with suitable jack.
25. Attach suitable engine lifting device, then remove engine from vehicle.
26. Reverse procedure to install.

V-8 ENGINES EXC. V8-454

C & K Models
1. Disconnect battery ground cable, then drain cooling system.
2. Remove air cleaner assembly.
3. Remove accessory drive belts, then the fan and water pump pulley.
4. Disconnect all hoses from engine.
5. If equipped with automatic transmission, disconnect cooling lines from radiator.
6. Remove radiator and fan shroud.
7. Disconnect accelerator linkage and detent cable (automatic transmission models) from carburetor throttle lever.
8. If equipped with A/C, remove A/C compressor from mounting bracket and position aside. Do not disconnect lines from compressor.
9. Remove power steering pump, if equipped, and position aside.
10. Disconnect wiring harness from engine, then the fuel line from fuel pump.
11. Disconnect vacuum lines from intake manifold, then raise and support vehicle.
12. Drain crankcase, then disconnect exhaust pipes from exhaust manifolds.
13. On K models with automatic transmission, remove strut rods from motor mounts.

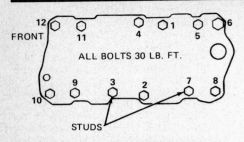

Fig. 8 Intake manifold tightening sequence. V6-200 & 229

14. Remove flywheel or converter splash shield, then disconnect wiring along right pan rail.
15. Disconnect starter wiring and remove starter.
16. Disconnect wiring from gas gauge.
17. If equipped with automatic transmission, remove converter to flex plate attaching bolts.
18. Support transmission with a suitable transmission jack, then remove bell housing to engine attaching bolts.
19. Remove lower engine mount bracket to frame attaching bolts, then lower vehicle.
20. Remove hood.
21. Attach a suitable engine lifting device and remove engine from vehicle.
22. Reverse procedure to install.

G Models
1. Disconnect battery ground cable, then drain cooling system.
2. Remove coolant reservoir, then the grille, upper radiator support and lower grille valence.
3. Disconnect hoses from radiator.
4. If equipped with automatic transmission, disconnect cooling lines from radiator.
5. If equipped with A/C, evacuate system, then remove A/C condenser and vacuum reservoir.
6. Remove washer reservoir and bracket.
7. Remove radiator to radiator support mounting brackets, then the radiator and shroud.
8. Remove power steering pump, if equipped, and position aside.
9. Remove engine cover.
10. Remove air cleaner stove pipe.
11. Disconnect accelerator cable from carburetor, then remove carburetor mounting bolts and the carburetor.
12. Disconnect engine wiring harness from firewall connection.
13. Disconnect heater hoses from engine, then remove thermostat housing.
14. Remove oil filler pipe.
15. If equipped with cruise control, remove servo, servo bracket and transducer.
16. Raise and support vehicle.
17. Disconnect exhaust pipes from exhaust manifolds.
18. Remove propeller shaft, then plug transmission housing to prevent fluid leakage.

19. Disconnect shift linkage and speedometer cable from transmission.
20. Disconnect fuel line from fuel pump, then remove transmission mount retaining bolts.
21. Remove engine mount bracket to frame retaining bolts, then drain crankcase.
22. Remove engine mount through bolts, then raise engine slightly and remove engine mounts.
23. Position a piece of wood between oil pan and front crossmember, then lower vehicle.
24. Attach a suitable engine lifting device, then remove engine/transmission assembly.
25. Reverse procedure to install.

V8-454
1. Remove hood.
2. Disconnect battery ground cable, then remove air cleaner.
3. Drain cooling system.
4. Disconnect radiator and heater hoses, then remove radiator and fan shroud.
5. Disconnect wires at starter solenoid, alternator, TRC speed switch, TRC solenoid, temperature and oil pressure switches, and the distributor.
6. Disconnect accelerator linkage from intake manifold.
7. Disconnect fuel line from fuel pump and fuel vapor hose from vapor storage canister, if applicable.
8. Disconnect brake booster vacuum line from intake manifold, if equipped.
9. Remove power steering pump and A/C compressor, if equipped. Do not disconnect hoses from pump or compressor.
10. Raise and support vehicle, then drain crankcase.
11. Disconnect exhaust pipes from manifolds and converter bracket from transmission mount, if equipped.
12. Disconnect wires, then remove starter motor.
13. Remove flywheel splash shield or converter housing cover.
14. On automatic transmission equipped vehicles, remove converter to flex plate attaching bolts.
15. Lower vehicle, then attach a suitable engine lifting device.
16. Remove engine mount through bolts, then the bell housing to engine attaching bolts.
17. Support transmission, then disconnect motor mounts from engine brackets.
18. Remove engine from vehicle.
19. Reverse procedure to install.

INTAKE MANIFOLD
REPLACE

6-250, 292

NOTE: On some 6-250 engines, the intake manifold is an integral part of the cylinder head. The procedure outlined below applies to engines with non-integrated cylinder heads. The exhaust manifold is re-

Fig. 9 Intake manifold tightening sequence. V6-231

moved together with the intake manifold. Refer to "Exhaust Manifold, Replace" procedure for removal of exhaust manifold on integrated cylinder heads.

1. Disconnect battery ground cable, then remove air cleaner assembly.
2. Disconnect throttle controls at bellcrank, then remove throttle control spring.
3. Disconnect fuel and vacuum lines at carburetor and crankcase ventilation hose at valve cover.
4. Disconnect vapor hose at canister.
5. Disconnect exhaust pipe at manifold flange, then remove manifold attaching bolts and clamps and the manifold assembly.
6. Remove bolts and nut at center of assembly, then separate manifolds.
7. Reverse procedure to install using new gasket. Torque bolts to specification, working from center of cylinder head outward.

V6-200, 231

1. Disconnect battery ground cable.
2. Drain cooling system, then remove air cleaner.
3. Disconnect upper radiator and heater hose at manifold.
4. Disconnect accelerator, downshift or throttle valve cables at carburetor.
5. Disconnect brake booster vacuum line from manifold, if applicable.
6. Disconnect fuel line from carburetor.
7. Disconnect all remaining vacuum hoses and electrical connections that will interfere with manifold removal.
8. On V6-231 engines, remove distributor cap and rotor to gain access to left side torx bolt.
9. On V6-200 engines, remove distributor.
10. Remove A/C compressor and alternator mounting brackets, if applicable.
11. Remove spark plug wires, if necessary, then the accelerator linkage springs.
12. Remove intake manifold attaching bolts, then the intake manifold.
13. Reverse procedure to install using new gasket(s) and seals. Coat seal surface with RTV sealant. Torque manifold bolts to specification in sequence shown in **Figs. 8 and 9.**

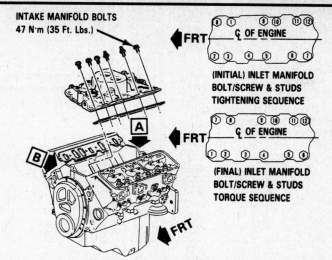

INTAKE MANIFOLD BOLTS
47 N·m (35 Ft. Lbs.)

FRT — ₵ OF ENGINE

(INITIAL) INLET MANIFOLD
BOLT/SCREW & STUDS
TIGHTENING SEQUENCE

FRT — ₵ OF ENGINE

(FINAL) INLET MANIFOLD
BOLT/SCREW & STUDS
TORQUE SEQUENCE

FRT

Fig. 10   Intake manifold tightening sequence. V6-262

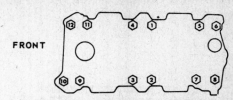

FRONT

Fig. 11   Intake manifold tightening sequence. V8-267, 305, 350 & 400

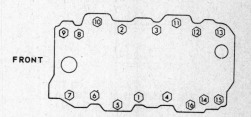

FRONT

Fig. 12   Intake manifold tightening sequence. V8-454

V6-229

1. Disconnect battery ground cable.
2. Remove air cleaner, then drain cooling system.
3. Remove AIR crossover hose, if applicable.
4. Remove alternator upper mounting bracket.
5. Disconnect all vacuum hoses and electrical connections that will interfere with manifold removal.
6. Disconnect fuel line and linkage from carburetor.
7. Disconnect spark plug wires, if necessary, then remove distributor.
8. If equipped with A/C, remove compressor and mounting bracket and position aside.
9. Remove attaching bolts, then the EGR valve.
10. Remove intake manifold attaching bolts, then the intake manifold.
11. Reverse procedure to install, using new gaskets and seals. Coat front and rear ridges of cylinder case with a 3/16 inch bead of RTV sealant. Extend bead 1/2 inch up each cylinder head to retain side gaskets, then seal around all water passages. Torque manifold bolts to specification in sequence shown in **Fig. 8.**

V6-262

Caballero & El Camino

1. Disconnect battery ground cable.
2. Remove air cleaner, then drain cooling system.
3. Disconnect heater and radiator hoses, then remove upper alternator bracket.
4. Disconnect all remaining hoses and electrical connections that will interfere with manifold removal.
5. Disconnect fuel line at TBI unit.
6. Disconnect accelerator and T.V. cables, if applicable.
7. Disconnect spark plug wires, if necessary, then remove distributor.
8. Remove ignition coil.
9. If equipped with A/C, remove com-

pressor bracket and position compressor aside.
10. Remove intake manifold attaching bolts, then the intake manifold.
11. Reverse procedure to install, using new gaskets and seals. Coat front and rear ridges of cylinder case with a 3/16 inch bead of RTV sealant. Extend bead 1/2 inch up each cylinder head to retain side gaskets, then seal around all water passages. Torque manifold bolts to specification in sequence shown in **Fig. 10.**

Series 10–30/1500–3500

1. Disconnect battery ground cable.
2. On G models, remove engine cover.
3. On all models, remove air cleaner, then drain cooling system.
4. Remove distributor cap and wires, then disconnect ESC connector, if applicable.
5. Remove distributor.
6. Disconnect detent and accelerator cables.
7. If equipped with A/C, remove rear compressor brace.
8. Remove transmission and engine oil filler tubes from alternator brace.
9. If equipped with A/C, remove idler pulley.
10. Remove alternator brace, then disconnect fuel line from carburetor.
11. Disconnect all vacuum hoses and electrical connections from carburetor.
12. Remove AIR hoses and brackets, then disconnect heater hose from intake manifold and remove carburetor.
13. Remove intake manifold attaching bolts, then the intake manifold.
14. Reverse procedure to install, using new gaskets and seals. Coat front and rear ridges of cylinder case with a 3/16 inch bead of RTV sealant. Extend bead 1/2 inch up each cylinder head to retain side gaskets, then seal around all water passages. Torque manifold bolts to specification in sequence shown in **Fig. 10.**

V-8 ENGINES EXC. V8-454

Caballero & El Camino

1. Disconnect battery ground cable, then drain cooling system.
2. Remove air cleaner.
3. If applicable, disconnect C3 wiring harness and position aside.
4. Remove heater and radiator hoses, then the upper alternator bracket.
5. Disconnect all vacuum hoses and electrical connections that will interfere with manifold removal.
6. Disconnect accelerator linkage, cables and fuel line from carburetor.
7. If necessary, remove spark plug wires from right cylinder head.
8. Remove distributor.
9. Remove carburetor, if necessary.
10. If equipped with A/C, remove compressor brace and bracket, then position compressor aside.
11. Remove intake manifold attaching bolts, then the intake manifold.
12. Reverse procedure to install, using new gaskets and seals. Coat front and rear ridges of cylinder case with a 3/16 inch bead of RTV sealant. Extend bead 1/2 inch up each cylinder head to retain side gaskets, then seal around all water passages. Torque manifold bolts to specification in sequence shown in **Fig. 11.**

Series 10–30/1500–3500

1. Disconnect battery ground cable, then drain cooling system.
2. Remove air cleaner.
3. On G models, remove engine cover.
4. Remove AIR crossover hose, if applicable.
5. Disconnect heater and radiator hoses, then remove upper alternator bracket.
6. Disconnect all vacuum hoses and electrical connections that will interfere with manifold removal.

Fig. 13 **Exhaust manifold tightening sequence. 1979 6-250**

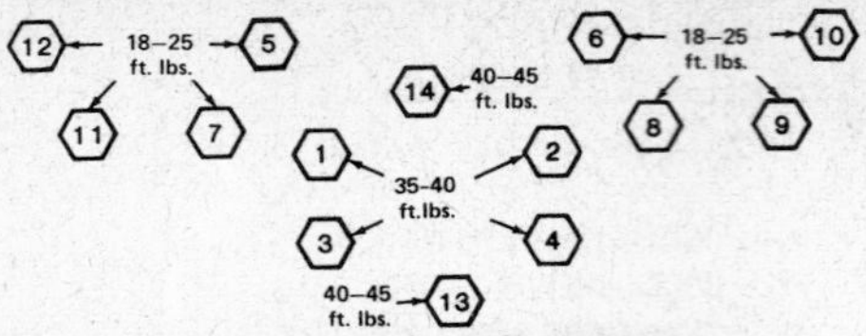

Fig. 14 **Exhaust manifold tightening sequence. 1980—84 6-250**

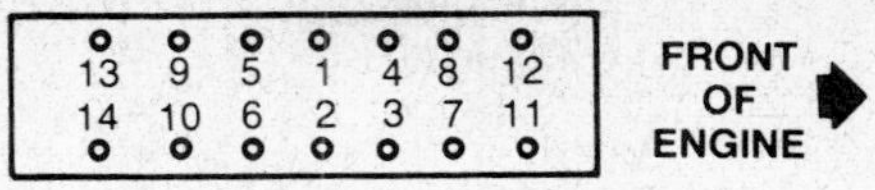

Fig. 15 **Cylinder head tightening sequence. 6-250 & 292**

FRONT OF ENGINE

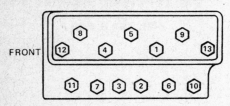

Fig. 16 **Cylinder head tightening sequence. V6-200, 229 & 262**

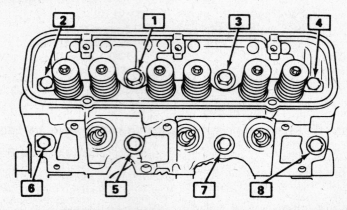

Fig. 17 **Cylinder head tightening sequence. 1979—83 V6-231**

7. Disconnect fuel line, linkage and cables from carburetor.
8. Remove spark plug wires, if necessary.
9. Remove distributor.
10. If equipped with A/C, remove compressor and bracket and position aside.
11. Remove carburetor, if necessary.
12. Remove intake manifold attaching bolts, then the intake manifold.
13. Reverse procedure to install, using new gaskets and seals. Coat front and rear ridges of cylinder case with a 3/16 inch bead of RTV sealant. Extend bead 1/2 inch up each cylinder head to retain side gaskets, then seal around all water passages. Torque manifold bolts to specification in sequence shown in **Fig. 11.**

V8-454

1. Disconnect battery ground cable, then drain cooling system.
2. Remove air cleaner.
3. Disconnect upper radiator and heater hoses at manifold and bypass hose at water pump.
4. Disconnect fuel line, accelerator linkage and cables from carburetor.
5. Remove distributor.
6. If equipped with A/C, remove compressor and front bracket and position aside.
7. Remove alternator upper mounting bracket.
8. Remove rear A/C bracket, if equipped.
9. Remove intake manifold attaching bolts, then the intake manifold.
10. Reverse procedure to install, using new gaskets and seals. Torque manifold bolts to specification in sequence shown in **Fig. 12.**

EXHAUST MANIFOLD
REPLACE

6-250 WITH INTEGRATED CYLINDER HEAD

1. Disconnect battery ground cable, then

remove air cleaner.
2. Remove power steering and/or AIR pump brackets, if equipped.
3. If equipped with Pulsair, remove pipes as necessary.
4. Raise and support vehicle, then disconnect exhaust pipe from manifold and, if equipped, the converter bracket from transmission mount.
5. Lower vehicle and, if applicable, remove rear heat shield and accelerator cable bracket.
6. Remove exhaust manifold attaching bolts, then the exhaust manifold.
7. Reverse procedure to install, using new gasket. Torque bolts to specification in sequence shown in **Figs. 13 and 14.**

V-6 ENGINES
CABALLERO & EL CAMINO
V6-200, 229

1. Disconnect battery ground cable, then remove air cleaner.
2. If removing right side manifold, disconnect heat stove pipe.
3. Remove spark plug wires and heatshield, if necessary, then raise and support vehicle.
4. Disconnect exhaust pipe from manifold, then lower vehicle.
5. If removing right side manifold, disconnect EFE valve vacuum hose, if equipped, then remove oil dipstick tube retainer, if necessary.
6. If removing left side manifold, remove A/C compressor and power steering pump brackets, if equipped.
7. Remove exhaust manifold attaching bolts, then the exhaust manifold.
8. Reverse procedure to install, using new gasket.

V6-231

1. Raise and support vehicle.
2. Disconnect crossover pipe from manifolds.
3. Disconnect EFE pipe from manifold, if applicable.
4. Remove exhaust manifold attaching bolts, then the exhaust manifold.
5. Reverse procedure to install, using new gasket.

V6-262

1. Disconnect battery ground cable, then raise and support vehicle.
2. If removing right side manifold, proceed as follows:
   a. Disconnect exhaust pipe from manifold, then lower vehicle.
   b. Disconnect air management valve bracket and AIR hoses.
   c. Disconnect AIR pipes from converter, cylinder head and manifold.
   d. Disconnect spark plug wires, then remove exhaust manifold attaching bolts and manifold.
3. If removing left side manifold, proceed as follows:
   a. Disconnect exhaust pipe from manifold, then remove A/C compressor, if equipped, and position aside.
   b. xemove power steering pump, if equipped, then the rear A/C compressor adjusting brace, if applicable.
   c. If equipped, remove rear power steering pump adjusting brace.
   d. Disconnect spark plug wires, then remove exhaust manifold attaching bolts and manifold.
4. Reverse procedure to install, using new gasket.

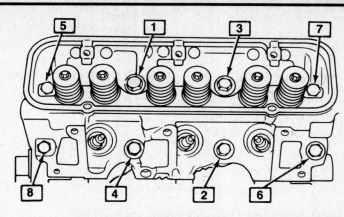

Fig. 17A Cylinder head tightening sequence. 1984 V6-231

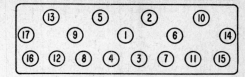

Fig. 18 Cylinder head tightening sequence. V8-267, 305, 350 & 400

CYLINDER HEAD
REPLACE

6-250, 292

1. Remove necessary access covers depending on vehicle being serviced.
2. Drain cooling system and remove air cleaner and air compressor.
3. Disconnect choke cable, accelerator pedal rod at bellcrank on manifold, and fuel and vacuum lines at carburetor.
4. Disconnect exhaust pipe at manifold flange, then remove manifolds and carburetor as an assembly.
5. Disconnect wire harness from temperature sending unit and coil, leaving harness clear of clips in rocker arm cover.
6. Disconnect radiator hose at water outlet housing and battery ground strap at cylinder head.
7. Remove spark plugs and ignition coil.
8. Remove rocker arm cover. Back off rocker arm nuts, pivot rocker arms to clear push rods and remove push rods.
9. Unfasten and remove cylinder head.
10. Reverse removal procedure to install and tighten head bolts to the specified torque and in the sequence shown in **Fig. 15.**

V6-200, 229

1. Drain cooling system and engine block.
2. Remove intake and exhaust manifolds.
3. Remove alternator lower mounting bolt and position alternator aside.
4. If equipped with A/C, remove compressor and forward mounting bracket and position aside.
5. Remove rocker arm cover, rocker arms and push rods.

NOTE: Keep rocker arm, rocker arm balls and push rods in order so they can be installed in the same position.

6. Remove cylinder head bolts and cylinder head.
7. Reverse procedure to install. Tighten cylinder head and intake manifold bolts in sequence shown in **Figs. 8 and 16.**

V6-231

1. Drain coolant and disconnect battery.
2. Remove intake manifold.

SERIES 10—30/1500—3500

V6-262

1. Disconnect battery ground cable, then raise and support vehicle.
2. If removing right side manifold, proceed as follows:
   a. Disconnect exhaust pipe from manifold, then lower vehicle.
   b. On G models, remove engine cover.
   c. On all models, disconnect AIR hose from check valve.
   d. Remove exhaust manifold attaching bolts, disconnect AIR pipe from diverter valve, then remove manifold.
3. If removing left side manifold:
   a. Disconnect exhaust pipe from manifold and AIR pipe from cylinder head.
   b. Remove exhaust manifold attaching bolts, then the exhaust manifold.
4. Reverse procedure to install, using new gaskets.

V-8 ENGINES

1979—84 Caballero & El Camino

1. Disconnect battery ground cable, then remove air cleaner.
2. If removing right side manifold, disconnect heat stove pipe.
3. Remove spark plug wires and heatshield, if necessary, then raise and support vehicle.
4. Disconnect exhaust pipe from manifold, then lower vehicle.
5. If removing right side manifold, disconnect EFE vacuum hose and all emission components that will interfere with manifold removal.
6. If removing left side manifold, remove A/C compressor and power steering pump brackets, if equipped.
7. Remove exhaust manifold attaching bolts, then the exhaust manifold.
8. Reverse procedure to install, using new gasket.

1985 Caballero & El Camino

1. Disconnect battery ground cable, then raise and support vehicle.
2. If removing right side manifold, proceed as follows:
   a. Disconnect exhaust pipe from manifold, then lower vehicle.
   b. Remove air cleaner, then disconnect spark plug wires.
   c. Disconnect vacuum hose from EFE valve.
   d. Disconnect AIR hose, loosen alternator drive belt, then remove lower alternator bracket and AIR valve.
   e. Disconnect converter AIR pipe from rear of manifold.
   f. Remove exhaust manifold attaching bolts, then the exhaust manifold.
3. If removing left side manifold:
   a. Disconnect exhaust pipe from manifold and electrical connector from oxygen sensor, if applicable.
   b. Lower vehicle, then disconnect AIR hose.
   c. Remove power steering pump, then loosen front A/C compressor bracket, if equipped, from cylinder head.
   d. Remove rear A/C compressor bracket, if equipped, then position compressor aside.
   e. Remove lower power steering pump adjusting bracket, if equipped.
   f. Remove wire loom holder from valve cover.
   g. Remove exhaust manifold attaching bolts, then the exhaust manifold.
4. Reverse procedure to install, using new gasket.

Series 10—30/1500—3500

1. Remove air cleaner and carburetor heat stove pipe.
2. Remove spark plugs and spark plug wiring heatshields.
3. Disconnect exhaust pipe from manifold, then remove manifold attaching bolts and the manifold.
4. Reverse procedure to install, using new gasket.

3. When removing right cylinder head, remove Delcotron and/or A/C compressor with mounting bracket and move out of the way. Do not disconnect hoses from A/C compressor.
4. When removing left cylinder head, remove oil dipstick, power steering pump and move out of the way with hoses attached.
5. Disconnect exhaust manifold from head to be removed.
6. Remove rocker arm shaft and lift out push rods.
8. Remove cylinder head.
9. Reverse procedure to install and tighten bolts gradually and evenly in the sequence shown in **Figs. 17 and 17A.**

NOTE: When installing intake manifold, refer to **Fig. 9** for bolt tightening sequence.

V6-262

Caballero & El Camino
1. Remove intake manifold.
2. Remove alternator lower mounting bolt, then position alternator aside.
3. Remove exhaust manifold.
4. Remove rocker arm cover, rocker arms and push rods.
5. Drain coolant from cylinder block, then remove diverter valve, if equipped.
6. Remove cylinder head attaching bolts, then the cylinder head.

NOTE: Before installing cylinder head, check gasket surfaces on both head and block for nicks or heavy scratches. Bolt threads in block and threads on head bolts must be clean as dirt will affect bolt torque.

7. On engines using steel gasket, coat both sides of gasket using suitable sealer. On engines equipped with steel/asbestos type gasket, no sealer should be used.
8. Place gasket in position over dowel pins, then carefully lower cylinder head into place.
9. Coat threads of cylinder head bolts with suitable sealer, then install bolts finger-tight.
10. Tighten each bolt a little at a time in sequence shown in **Fig. 16** until specified torque is reached.
11. Install intake manifold, then torque bolts to specification in sequence shown in **Fig. 10.**
12. Install exhaust manifold.
13. Install valve train, then adjust valves as outlined in "Valves, Adjust" procedure.

Series 10–30/1500–3500
1. Remove intake manifold.
2. Raise and support vehicle, then disconnect exhaust pipe from manifold.
3. Lower vehicle, then disconnect AIR hose from check valve.
4. If removing right side cylinder head, proceed as follows:
   a. Remove exhaust manifold, then

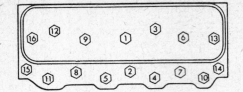

Fig. 19 Cylinder head tightening sequence V8-454

disconnect AIR pipe at cylinder head and diverter valve.
   b. Disconnect oil filler tube and PCV valve.
   c. Disconnect wiring harness, then remove valve cover.
   d. Remove alternator mounting bolt, then disconnect spark plug wires and remove spark plugs.
   e. Remove rocker arms and push rods.
   f. Remove cylinder head attaching bolts, then the cylinder head.
5. If removing left side cylinder head:
   a. Remove exhaust manifold, then disconnect power steering pump and A/C compressor, if equipped, and position aside.
   b. Remove valve cover, then disconnect spark plug wires and remove spark plugs.
   c. Remove rocker arms and push rods.
   d. Remove cylinder head attaching bolts, then the cylinder head.

NOTE: Before installing cylinder head, check gasket surfaces on both head and block for nicks or heavy scratches. Bolt threads in block and threads on head bolts must be clean as dirt will affect bolt torque.

6. On engines using steel gasket, coat both sides of gasket using suitable sealer. On engines equipped with steel/asbestos type gasket, no sealer should be used.
7. Place gasket in position over dowel pins, then carefully lower cylinder head into place.
8. Coat threads of cylinder head bolts with suitable sealer, then install bolts finger-tight.
9. Tighten each bolt a little at a time in sequence shown in **Fig. 16** until specified torque is reached.
10. Install intake manifold, then torque bolts to specification in sequence shown in **Fig. 10.**
11. Install exhaust manifold.
12. Install valve train, then adjust valves as outlined in "Valves, Adjust" procedure.

V8-267, 305, 350, 400 & 454

1. Remove intake and exhaust manifolds and A/C compressor, if equipped.
2. Remove valve mechanism.
3. Drain coolant from block.
4. Unfasten and remove cylinder head.

Installation

The gasket surfaces on both head and block must be clean of any foreign material and free of nicks or heavy scratches. Cylinder bolt threads in the block and threads on the head bolts must be clean as dirt will affect bolt torque.

1. On engines using a steel gasket, coat both sides of a new gasket with a good sealer. One method of applying the sealer that will assure the proper coat is with the use of a paint roller. Too much sealer may hold the gasket away from the head or block.

CAUTION: Use no sealer on engines using a composition steel asbestos gasket.

2. Place gasket in position over the dowel pins with the head up.
3. Carefully guide cylinder head into place over dowel pins and gasket.
4. Coat threads of cylinder head bolts with sealing compound and install bolts finger tight.
5. Tighten each bolt a little at a time in the sequence shown in **Figs. 18 and 19** until the specified torque is reached.
6. Install and tighten intake manifold bolts in sequence shown in **Figs. 11 and 12.**
7. Install and adjust valve mechanism as outlined further on.

VALVE ARRANGEMENT
FRONT TO REAR

6-250, 292	E-I-I-E-E-I-I-E-E-I-I-E
V6-231	E-I-I-E-I-E
V6-262	
Left Side	E-I-E-I-I-E
Right Side	E-I-I-E-I-E
V8-267, 305, 350, 400	E-I-I-E-E-I-I-E
V8-454	E-I-E-I-E-I-E-I

VALVES
ADJUST
6-250, 292, V6-200, 229, 262, V8-267, 305, 350, 400 & 454

1. Start engine and allow to reach normal operating temperature, then shut engine off.
2. With engine in position to fire No. 1 cylinder, adjust the following valves: V6-200, 229 and 262, Exhaust Nos. 1, 5 and 6; Intake Nos. 1, 2 and 3. 6-250 and 292, Exhaust Nos. 1, 3 and 5; Intake Nos. 1, 2 and 4. V-8 engines, Exhaust Nos. 1, 3, 4 and 8; Intake Nos. 1, 2, 5 and 7.

NOTE: To properly adjust valves, tighten adjusting nut until all lash is eliminated, then tighten nut the additional turns specified in the Valve Specifications Chart.

3. Turn crankshaft one complete revolution, which will bring engine in position

Fig. 20 Valve rotator & retaining components

to fire cylinders 4(V-6) or 6(Inline 6 and V-8). With engine in this position, adjust the following valves: V6-200, 229 and 262, Exhaust Nos. 2, 3 and 4; Intake Nos. 4, 5 and 6. 6-250 and 292, Exhaust Nos. 2, 4 and 6; Intake Nos. 3, 5 and 6. V8 engines, Exhaust Nos. 2, 5, 6 and 7; Intake Nos. 3, 4, 6 and 8.

The following procedure, performed with the engine running should be done only in case readjustment is required.
1. After engine has been warmed to operating temperature, remove valve cover and install a new valve cover gasket.
2. With engine running at idle speed, back off valve rocker arm nut until rocker arm starts to clatter.
3. Turn rocker arm nut down slowly until the clatter just stops. This is the zero lash position.
4. Turn nut down ¼ additional turn and pause 10 seconds until engine runs smoothly. Repeat additional ¼ turns, pausing 10 seconds each time, until nut has been turned down the number of turns listed in the Valve Specifications Chart from the zero lash position.

CAUTION: This preload adjustment must be done slowly to allow the lifter to adjust itself to prevent the possibility of interference between the intake valve head and top of piston, which might result in internal damage and/or bent push rods. Noisy lifters should be replaced.

VALVE ROTATORS

The parts involved in the rotating mechanism, **Fig. 20,** are a special spring seat retainer, a pair of flat half-moon keys, a close fitting cap located on the valve stem and a specially constructed valve stem.

In order to accommodate valve expansion, the valve lash must be maintained. When camshaft rotation causes this lash or clearance to be taken up, the cap on the valve stem causes the valve keys to raise the spring retainer, removing the load on the valve springs from the valve before the valve is moved from its seat. A clearance of .002–.004″ should be maintained between the end face of the valve stem and cap. This is the distance the spring retainer is moved before the valve is moved. The slow valve rotating motion is caused by the vibration of the valve, the flowing of exhaust gases around the valve head, and a slight rotating motion imparted to the valve by the valve spring.

Whenever valve work is being done, a check for clearance should be made by holding the assembled valve and rotating mechanism in the hands. With one hand, press down on the valve cap and turn the valve with the other hand. If the valve turns readily, it indicates that there is clearance present.

A special gauge is available to check this clearance. If the gauge indicates no clearance, grind off the end of the valve stem. If the clearance is too great, grind off the open end of the valve cap.

VALVE GUIDES

Valve guides in these engines are an integral part of the head and, therefore, cannot be removed. For service, guide holes can be reamed oversize to accommodate one of several service valves with oversize stems.

Check the valve stem clearance of each valve (after cleaning) in its respective valve guide. If the clearance exceeds the service limits of .004″ on the intake or .005″ on the exhaust, ream the valve guide to accommodate the next oversize diameter valve stem.

Select the reamer for the smallest oversize which will provide a clean straight bore through the valve guide. After reaming, a new seat should be cut into the head to assure perfect seating of the new valve.

ROCKER ARM SERVICE
V6-231

A nylon retainer is used to retain the rocker arm. Break them below their heads with a chisel or pry out with channel locks, **Fig. 21.** Production rocker arms can be installed in any sequence since the arms are identical.

Replacement rocker arms for all engines are identified with a stamping, right (R) and left (L), **Fig. 22** and must be installed as shown in **Fig. 23.**

ROCKER ARM STUDS
REPLACE
Exc. V6-231

Rocker arm studs that have damaged threads may be replaced with standard

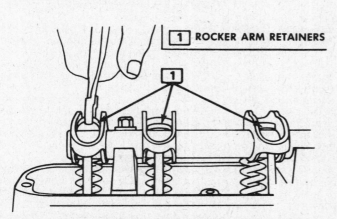

Fig. 21 Removing rocker arm nylon retainer. V6-231

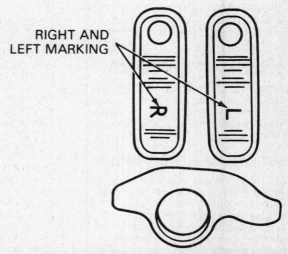

RIGHT AND LEFT MARKING

Fig. 22 Service rocker arm identification. V6-231

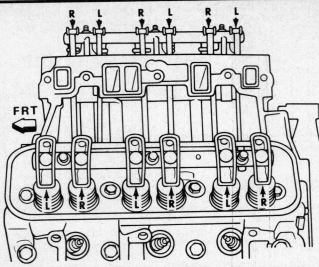

Fig. 23   Service rocker arm installation. V6-231

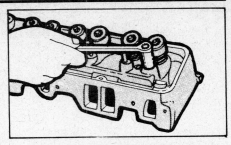

Fig. 24   Rocker arm stud removal. 6-250, 292, V6-200, 229, 262, V8-267, 305, 350, 400 & 454

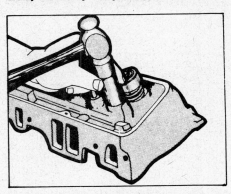

Fig. 25   Rocker arm stud installation. 6-250, 292, V6-200, 229, 262, V8-267, 305 & 400

studs. Loose studs should be replaced with .003" or .013" oversize studs which are available for replacement.

Remove the old stud by placing a suitable spacer over the stud, **Fig. 24.** Install a nut and flat washer on the stud and pull out the stud by turning the nut. After reaming the hole for an oversize stud, coat the press-fit area of the new stud with rear axle lubricant. Install the stud by driving it in until it protrudes from the head the same distance as the other studs, **Fig. 25.**

NOTE: On V8-454, the rocker arm studs are threaded into the cylinder head. Coat threads on cylinder head end of stud before assembling to head.

PUSH RODS

NOTE: When a replacement push rod has a paint stripe at one end, this painted end must be installed in contact with the rocker arm. To provide durability a hardened insert is incorporated in the rocker arm end of these push rods.

HYDRAULIC LIFTERS

The hydraulic valve lifters, **Fig. 26,** are simple in design. Readjustments are not necessary and servicing them requires that care and cleanliness be exercised in the handling of parts.

DISASSEMBLE & ASSEMBLE

1. Hold plunger down with push rod and, using a small screw driver or awl, remove plunger retainer.
2. Remove parts from lifter body.
3. Clean all parts and inspect for damage. If any parts are damaged, the entire lifter assembly should be replaced. The inertia valve in the plunger for

rocker arm lubrication should move when the plunger is shaken.
4. To reassemble, invert plunger and set ball into hole in plunger. Place ball check valve retainer over ball and on plunger. Place check valve retainer spring over retainer. Assemble body over plunger assembly. Turn assembly over and install push rod seat. Compress plunger with push rod and install retainer.
5. Compress plunger to open oil holes and fill plunger with engine oil. Work plunger up and down and refill.

TIMING CASE COVER
REPLACE

6-250, 292

1. Remove radiator.
2. Remove vibration damper.
3. Remove the two oil pan to front cover attaching screws.
4. Remove front cover to cylinder block attaching screws.
5. On 6-250 engines, pull cover slightly forward, then using a sharp knife, cut oil pan front seal flush with cylinder block at both sides of cover.
6. Remove cover and attached portion of oil pan front seal.
7. Pry oil seal out of cover with a large screwdriver. Install new seal with open side of seal inside of cover and drive or press seal into place.
8. Clean gasket surfaces.
9. On 6-250 engines, cut tabs from new oil pan front seal, then install seal on cover, pressing tips into cover holes.
10. Apply a ⅛ inch bead of RTV sealant to the joint formed at oil pan and cylinder block.
11. Install a suitable centering tool over end of crankshaft.
12. Coat gasket with light grease and position on cover.

13. Apply a ⅛ inch bead of RTV sealer at joint of oil pan and cover.
14. Install cover over centering tool, **Fig. 27,** and install cover screws, tightening them to 6 to 8 ft. lbs. It is important that the centering tool be used to align the cover so the vibration damper installation will not damage the seal. Position seal evenly around damper hub surface.

V6-200, 229, 262, V8-267, 305, 350, 400 & 454

1. Remove vibration damper and water pump.
2. Remove cover retaining screws and cover.
3. Clean gasket surface of block and timing case cover.
4. Remove any excess oil pan gasket material that may be protruding at the oil pan to engine block junction.
5. Apply a thin bead of RTV #1052366 sealer or equivalent to the joint formed at oil pan and block.
6. Coat new gasket with sealer and position it on cover, then install cover to oil pan seal on cover and coat bottom of seal with engine oil.
7. Position cover on engine and loosely install the upper bolts.
8. Tighten screws alternately and evenly while pressing downward on cover so that dowels are aligned with holes in cover. Do not force cover over dowels as cover can be distorted.
9. Install remaining cover screws, vibration damper and water pump.

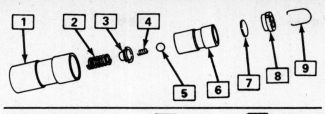

1 LIFTER BODY   **5** BALL CHECK   **6** PLUNGER
2 PLUNGER SPRING   **7** OIL METERING VALVE
3 BALL CHECK RETAINER   **8** PUSH ROD SEAT
4 BALL CHECK SPRING   **9** RETAINER RING

Fig. 26 Hydraulic valve lifter (Typical)

REMOVE BOLTS MARKED ➡ FOR COMPLETE REMOVAL

SEAL THREADS

FUEL PUMP MUST BE REMOVED

Fig. 28 Timing case cover installation. V6-231

V6-231

1. Drain cooling system and remove radiator.
2. Remove fan, pulleys and belts.
3. Remove crankshaft pulley and reinforcement.
4. If equipped with power steering, remove any pump bracket bolts attached to timing chain cover and loosen and remove any other bolts necessary that will allow pump and brackets to be moved out of the way.
5. Remove fuel pump.
6. Remove alternator and brackets.
7. Remove distributor cap and pull spark plug wire retainers off brackets on rocker arm cover. Swing distributor cap with wires attached out of the way. Disconnect distributor primary lead.
8. Remove distributor. If chain and sprockets are not to be disturbed, note position of distributor rotor for installation in the same position.
9. Loosen and slide clamp on thermostat bypass hose rearward.
10. Remove bolts attaching chain cover to block.

11. Remove two oil pan-to-chain cover bolts and remove cover.
12. Reverse procedure to install, noting data shown in **Fig. 28.**

NOTE: Remove the oil pump cover and pack the space around the oil pump gears completely with vaseline. There must be no air space left inside the pump. Reinstall the cover using a new gasket. This step is very important as the oil pump may lose its prime whenever the pump, pump cover or timing chain cover is disturbed. If the pump is not packed it may not pump oil as soon as the engine is started.

TIMING GEARS
REPLACE

6-250 & 292

When necessary to install a new camshaft gear, the camshaft will have to be removed as the gear is a pressed fit on the shaft. The camshaft is held in position by a thrust plate which is fastened to the crankcase by two capscrews which are accessible through two holes in the gear web.

Use an arbor press to remove the gear and when doing so, a suitable sleeve, **Fig. 29,** should be employed to support the gear properly on its steel hub.

Before installing a new gear, assemble a new thrust plate on the shaft and press the gear on just far enough so that the thrust plate has practically no clearance, yet is free to turn. The correct clearance is from .001" to .005". **Fig. 30.**

The crankshaft gear can be removed by utilizing the two tapped holes in conjunction with a gear puller.

When the timing gears are installed, be sure the punch-marks on both gears are in mesh, **Fig. 31.** Backlash between the gears should be from .004" to .006", **Fig. 32.** Check the run-out of the gears, **Fig. 33,** and if the camshaft gear run-out exceeds .004" or the crank gear run-out is in excess of .003", remove the gear (or gears) and examine for burrs, dirt or some other fault which may cause the run-out. If these conditions are not the cause, replace the gear (or gears).

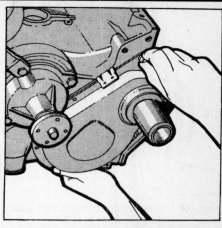

Fig. 27 Timing case cover installation. 6-250 & 292

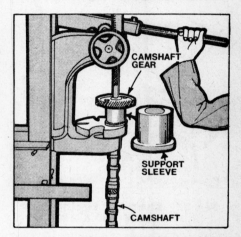

CAMSHAFT GEAR

SUPPORT SLEEVE

CAMSHAFT

Fig. 29 Camshaft gear removal. 6-250 & 292

TIMING CHAIN
REPLACE

V6-200, 229, 262, V8-267, 305, 350, 400 & 454

1. Remove timing case cover as outlined previously.
2. Remove crankshaft oil slinger.
3. Crank engine until "O" marks on sprockets are in alignment, **Fig. 34.**
4. Remove three camshaft-to-sprocket bolts.
5. Remove camshaft sprocket and timing chain together. Sprocket is a light press fit on camshaft for approximately ⅛". If sprocket does not come off easily, a light blow with a plastic hammer on the lower edge of the sprocket should dislodge it.
6. If crankshaft sprocket is to be replaced, remove it with a suitable gear puller. Install new sprocket, aligning key and keyway.
7. Install chain onto camshaft sprocket. Hold sprocket with chain hanging vertically, then align marks on sprockets as shown, **Fig. 34.**

Fig. 30 Checking camshaft end play. 6-250 & 292

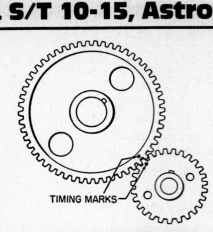

Fig. 31 Valve timing marks. 6-250 & 292

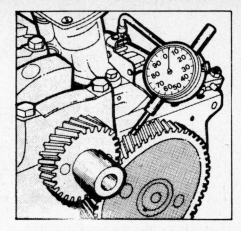

Fig. 32 Checking timing gear backlash. 6-250 & 292

Fig. 33 Checking timing gear runout. 6-250 & 292

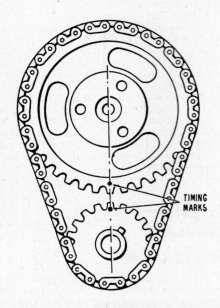

Fig. 34 Valve timing marks. V6-200, 229, 262, V8-267, 305, 350, 400 & 454

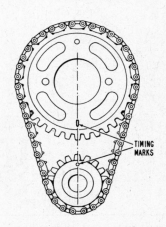

Fig. 35 Valve timing marks. V6-231

NOTE: The valve timing marks shown in **Fig. 34**, do not indicate TDC compression stroke for No. 1 cylinder, which is used during distributor installation. If distributor was removed, install timing chain and sprockets, aligning timing marks, **Fig. 34**, then rotate engine until No. 1 cylinder is on compression and camshaft timing mark is 180° from valve timing position shown in **Fig. 34**. Install distributor.

8. Align dowel in camshaft with dowel hole in sprocket and install sprocket on camshaft. Do not attempt to drive sprocket on camshaft as welch plug at rear of engine can be dislodged.
9. Draw sprocket onto camshaft, using the three mounting bolts. Tighten to 20 ft. lbs. torque.
10. Lubricate timing chain and install cover.

V6-231

1. With the timing case cover removed as outlined previously, temporarily install the vibration damper bolt and washer in end of crankshaft.

2. Turn crankshaft so sprockets are positioned as shown in **Fig. 35**. Use a sharp rap on a wrench handle to start the vibration damper bolt out, without disturbing the position of the sprockets.
3. Remove oil slinger.
4. Remove camshaft sprocket retaining bolt.
5. Use two large screwdrivers to alternately pry the camshaft sprocket then the crankshaft sprocket forward until the camshaft sprocket is free. Then remove camshaft sprocket and chain, and the crankshaft sprocket.
6. To install, assemble chain on sprockets and slide sprockets on their respective shafts with the "O" marks on the sprockets lined up as shown, **Fig. 35**.
7. Complete the installation in the reverse order of removal. Torque sprocket bolts to 22 ft. lbs.

CAMSHAFT
REPLACE

6-250 & 292

It is recommended that the engine be removed from the vehicle for camshaft removal. Remove valve train components, engine front cover, fuel pump and distributor. Remove camshaft thrust plate screws and pull camshaft from cylinder block.

V6-200, 229, 262, V8-267, 305, 350, 400 & 454

NOTE: Depending on vehicle and engine application, the grille, radiator and condenser (if equipped) must be removed to facilitate camshaft removal.

1. Remove intake manifold as outlined previously.
2. Remove valve lifters.
3. Remove timing case cover and timing chain as outlined previously.
4. Install two 5/16-18 × 4 inch bolts into camshaft bolt holes, then pull camshaft out of cylinder block.

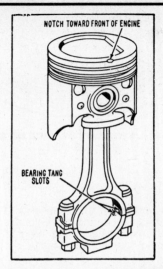

Fig. 36 Piston & rod assembly. 6-250

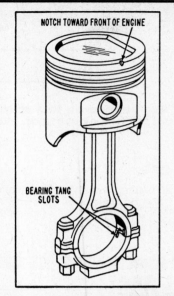

Fig. 37 Piston & rod assembly. 6-292

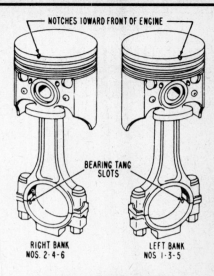

Fig. 38 Piston and rod assembly. V6-200, 229 & 262

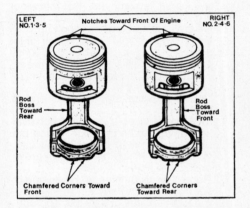

Fig. 39 Piston & rod assembly. V6-231

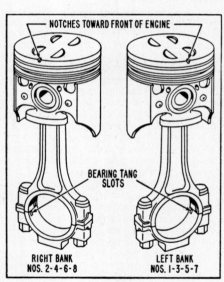

Fig. 40 Piston & rod assembly. V8-267, 305, 350 & 400

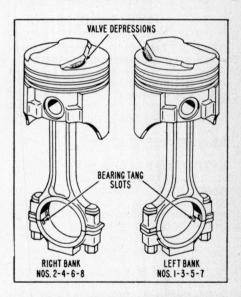

Fig. 41 Piston & rod assembly. V8-454

5. Reverse procedure to install.

V6-231

NOTE: If engine is in the vehicle, the radiator, grille and A/C components will have to be removed. If engine is out, proceed as follows:

1. To remove camshaft, remove intake manifold, rocker arm shaft assemblies, push rods and valve lifters.
2. Remove timing chain and sprockets.
3. Slide camshaft out of engine, using care not to mar the bearing surfaces.
4. Reverse procedure to install.

PISTON & ROD
ASSEMBLE

Assemble pistons to connecting rods as shown in **Figs. 36 through 41.**

PISTONS
EXC. V6-231

A .001″ oversize piston is available for service use so that proper clearances can be obtained for slightly worn cylinder bores requiring only light honing. In addition, oversizes of .020″, .030″ and .040″ are available. If the cylinders have less than .005″ taper or wear, they can be reconditioned with a hone and fitted with the .001″ oversize piston.

V6-231

Pistons are available in standard sizes and oversizes of .005, .010 and .030 inch.

ROD BEARINGS

6-250, 292, V6-200, 229, 262, V8-267, 305, 350, 400 & 454

Connecting rod bearing inserts are available in standard size and undersizes of .001″, .002″, .010″ and .020″. The bearings can be replaced without removing the rod assembly by removing the cap and replacing the upper and lower halves of the bearing.

V6-231

Rod bearings are available in standard

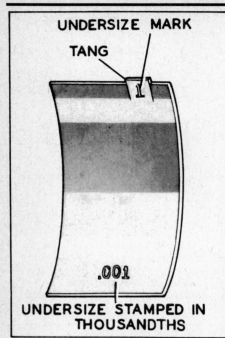

Fig. 42 Location of main & rod bearing undersize markings. V6-231

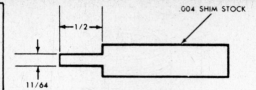

Fig. 43 Fabricated seal starting tool for helix type seal. Exc. V6-231

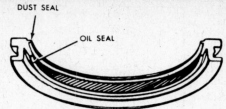

Fig. 44 Crankshaft rear oil seal. Exc. V6-231

V6-231

Main bearings are available in standard sizes and undersizes of .001, .002, and .010 inch. Refer to **Fig. 42** for undersize markings.

CRANKSHAFT REAR OIL SEAL
REPLACE

Exc. V6-231

NOTE: These engines are equipped with helix type rear seal. A seal starting tool, **Fig. 43,** must be used to prevent the upper seal half from coming into contact with the sharp edge of the block.

When necessary to correct an oil leak due to a defective seal, always replace the upper and lower seal halves as a unit, **Fig. 44.** When installing either half, lubricate the lip portion only with engine oil, keeping oil off the parting line surface as this is treated with glue. Always clean crankshaft surface before installing a new seal.
1. To replace the lower seal, remove seal from groove in bearing cap, using a small screwdriver.
2. Insert new seal and roll it in place with finger and thumb.
3. To replace the upper seal (with engine in car) use a small hammer and tap a brass pin punch on one end of the seal until it protrudes far enough to be removed with pliers.
4. Position tip of tool, **Fig. 43,** between crankshaft and seal seat in cylinder block.
5. Position seal between crankshaft and tip of tool with seal bead contacting tip of tool. Ensure oil seal lip is facing toward front of engine.
6. Roll seal around crankshaft, using tool as a "Shoehorn" to protect seal bead from sharp corner of seal seat surface in cylinder block.

NOTE: Tool must remain in position until seal is properly seated with both ends flush with block.

7. Remove tool, using care not to dislodge seal.
8. Install new seal into bearing cap with tool as outlined previously.
9. Install bearing cap with sealant applied to the cap to case interface. Do

sizes and undersizes of .001, .002 and .010 inch. Refer to **Fig. 42,** for undersize markings on bearing.

MAIN BEARINGS
6-250, 292

NOTE: The rear main bearing journal has no oil hole drilling. To remove the upper bearing half (bearing half with oil hole) proceed as follows after cap is removed:
1. Use a small drift punch and hammer to start the bearing rotating out of the block.
2. Use a pair of pliers (tape jaws) to hold the bearing thrust surface to the oil slinger and rotate the crankshaft to pull the bearing out.
3. To install, start the bearing (side not notched) into side of block by hand, then use pliers as before to turn bearing half into place.
4. The last ¼" movement may be done by holding just the slinger with the pliers or tap in place with a drift punch.

Main bearings are available in standard and undersizes of .001, .002, .009, .010 and .020 inch.

V6-200, 229, 262, V8-267, 305, 350, 400 & 454

Shell type bearings are used, and if worn excessively, should be replaced. No attempt should be made to shim, file or otherwise take up worn bearings.

Main bearings are available in standard and undersizes of .001, .002, .009, .010 and .020 inch.

not apply sealant to seal ends. Torque rear main bearing cap bolts to specifications as listed in the "Engine Tightening Specification Chart".

V6-231

Since the braided fabric seal used on these engines can be replaced only when the crankshaft is removed, the following repair procedure is recommended.
1. Remove oil pan and bearing cap.
2. Drive end of old seal gently into groove, using a suitable tool, until packed tight. This may vary between ¼ and ¾ inch depending on amount of pack required.
3. Repeat previous step for other end of seal.
4. Measure and note amount that seal was driven up on one side. Using the old seal removed from bearing cap, cut a length of seal the amount previously noted plus ¹⁄₁₆ inch.
5. Repeat previous step for other side of seal.
6. Pack cut lengths of seal into appropriate side of seal groove. A guide tool, J-21526-1, and packing tool, J-21526-2, may be used since these tools have been machined to provide a built-in stop.
7. Install new seal in bearing cap.

OIL PAN
REPLACE

6-250, 292

Exc. 1979—84 G Models
1. Disconnect battery ground cable.
2. Raise and support vehicle. Drain oil pan and remove starter.
3. Remove flywheel splash shield or converter underpan, as applicable.
4. Remove front engine mount through bolts, raise front of engine and reinstall bolts, then lower engine.
5. Remove oil pan bolts and oil pan.
6. Reverse procedure to install.

1979—84 G Models
1. Disconnect battery ground cable. Remove engine cover.
2. Remove air cleaner and studs. Remove fan shroud and radiator upper support brackets.

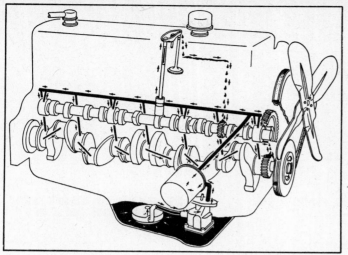

Engine oiling system. 6-250 & 292

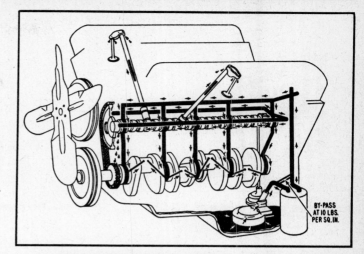

BY-PASS AT 10 LBS. PER SQ. IN.

Engine oiling system. V8-267, 305, 350 & 400

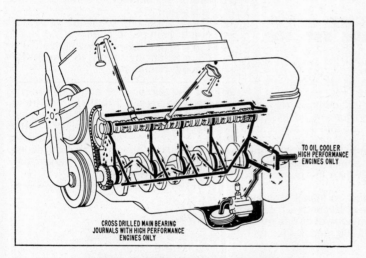

TO OIL COOLER HIGH PERFORMANCE ENGINES ONLY

CROSS DRILLED MAIN BEARING JOURNALS WITH HIGH PERFORMANCE ENGINES ONLY

Engine oiling system. V8-454

3. Raise and support vehicle.
4. On models equipped with a manual transmission:
   a. Disconnect clutch cross shaft from motor mount bracket.
   b. Remove transmission to bell housing upper bolt.
   c. Remove transmission rear mount bolts and install two $7/16 \times 3$ inch bolts.
   d. Raise transmission and install 2 inch block between mount and crossmember.
5. On all models, remove starter and drain oil.
6. Remove front engine mount through bolts, raise engine and install wood blocks between engine mounts and crossmember brackets.
7. Remove flywheel splash shield or converter cover, as applicable.
8. Remove oil pan bolts and lower pan.
9. Reverse procedure to install.

V6-200, 229, 262, V8-267, 305, 350 & 400

1979—84

1. Drain engine oil and remove dipstick and tube.
2. If equipped, remove exhaust crossover pipe.
3. With automatic transmission, remove converter housing under pan.
4. Remove starter brace and inboard bolt and swing starter aside.
5. On K models, remove strut rods, if equipped.
6. On 1980—84 El Camino and Caballero with V6-229, remove upper half of fan shroud. Loosen left engine front mount through bolt and remove right bolt. Raise engine and reinstall bolt. Do not tighten.
7. Remove oil pan and discard gaskets and seals.
8. Reverse procedure to install.

1985

Caballero & El Camino

1. Disconnect battery ground cable, then remove air cleaner.
2. Remove upper fan shroud.
3. Raise and support vehicle, then drain oil pan.
4. On V-8 engines, disconnect AIR pipes from converter and exhaust manifold.
5. Remove exhaust crossover pipe, if equipped.
6. Remove starter and flywheel cover.
7. Disconnect transmission cooler lines at oil pan.
8. On V-8 engines, remove engine mount through bolts. On V-6 engines, loosen right bolt and remove left through bolt.
9. Remove oil pan attaching bolts, then lower oil pan.

NOTE: If crankshaft counterweights are blocking oil pan removal, turn crankshaft as necessary to facilitate removal.

10. Raise engine and reinstall engine mount through bolts to provide necessary clearance, then remove oil pan.
11. Reverse procedure to install.

Series 10—30/1500—3500

1. Drain oil pan.
2. Raise and support vehicle, then remove exhaust crossover pipe.
3. On vehicles equipped with automatic transmission, remove converter housing under pan.
4. If equipped with V-6 engine, remove strut rods at flywheel cover, then remove starter.
5. On K models with automatic transmission, remove strut rods at motor mounts.
6. Remove oil pan attaching bolts, then the oil pan.
7. Reverse procedure to install.

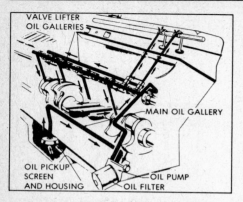

Engine oiling system. V6-231

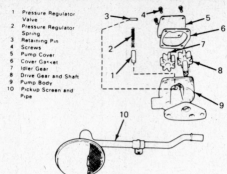

1. Pressure Regulator Valve
2. Pressure Regulator Spring
3. Retaining Pin
4. Screws
5. Pump Cover
6. Cover Gasket
7. Idler Gear
8. Drive Gear and Shaft
9. Pump Body
10. Pickup Screen and Pipe

Fig. 45   Oil pump. 6-250 & 292

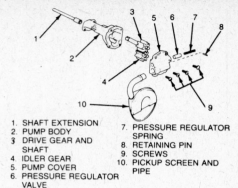

1. SHAFT EXTENSION
2. PUMP BODY
3. DRIVE GEAR AND SHAFT
4. IDLER GEAR
5. PUMP COVER
6. PRESSURE REGULATOR VALVE
7. PRESSURE REGULATOR SPRING
8. RETAINING PIN
9. SCREWS
10. PICKUP SCREEN AND PIPE

Fig. 46   Oil pump. V6-200, 229, 262, V8-267, 305, 350 & 400

V6-231

1. Support vehicle on hoist and drain oil.
2. Remove flywheel cover and exhaust crossover pipe, then raise engine.
3. Remove oil pan bolts and allow pan to drop.

NOTE: To remove oil pan, front wheels must be turned to the left, also the crankshaft may have to be turned to provide clearance.

4. Reverse procedure to install.

NOTE: Some 1981–84 engines use R.T.V. silicone sealer instead of a cork gasket for oil pan to crankcase sealing. When replacing the oil pan or sealing material on these engines, either R.T.V. sealer or a cork gasket can be used during reassembly. If R.T.V. sealer is used, the pan rail and block sealing surfaces should be cleaned thoroughly and a ¼ inch bead of sealant applied evenly to the pan rail, avoiding any breaks or gaps in the sealer during application.

V8-454

1. Disconnect battery ground cable.
2. Loosen fan shroud, then remove air cleaner assembly.
3. Remove distributor cap.
4. Raise and support vehicle, then drain oil pan.
5. On manual transmission equipped vehicles, remove starter.
6. Remove torque converter or clutch cover as applicable.
7. Remove oil filter.
8. If equipped with oil pressure gauge, disconnect oil pressure line from side of cylinder block to prevent damaging line.
9. Remove engine mount through bolts, then raise engine.
10. Remove oil pan attaching bolts, then the oil pan.
11. Reverse procedure to install.

OIL PUMP
REPLACE & SERVICE

6-250, 292, V6-200, 229, 262, V8-267, 305, 350, 400 & 454

Oil Pump, Replace
1. Remove oil pan as described previously.
2. On 6-250 and 6-292 engines, remove the two flange mounting bolts, then the pickup pipe bolt and oil pump assembly.
3. On all except 6-250 and 6-292 engines, remove pump to rear main bearing cap bolt, then the pump and extension shaft.
4. Reverse procedure to install. Ensure that bottom edge of oil pump screen is parallel to bottom edge of oil pan rails, on all except 6-250 and 6-292 engines.

Oil Pump Service
1. Remove oil pump as described previously.
2. Remove pump cover screws and pump cover, **Figs. 45 through 47.** On 6-250 and 292 engines, remove pump cover gasket.
3. Mark gear teeth so they can be reassembled with same teeth indexing, then remove drive gear, idler gear and shaft.
4. Remove pressure regulator valve retaining pin, pressure regulator valve and related parts.
5. If pickup screen and pipe require replacement, mount pump in a soft-jawed vise and extract pipe from pump.
6. Wash all parts in cleaning solvent and dry with compressed air.
7. Inspect pump body and cover for cracks and excessive wear.
8. Inspect pump gears for damage or excessive wear.
9. Check drive gear shaft for looseness in pump body.
10. Inspect inside of pump cover for wear that would allow oil to leak past the ends of the gears.
11. Inspect pickup screen and pipe assembly for damage to screen, pipe or relief grommet.
12. Check pressure regulator valve for proper fit in pump housing.
13. Reverse procedure to assemble. Turn drive shaft by hand to check for smooth operation.

NOTE: The pump gears and body are not serviced separately. If the pump gears or body are damaged or worn, the pump assembly should be replaced. Also, if the pick-up screen was removed, it should be replaced with a new one as loss of the press fit condition could result in an air leak and loss of oil pressure.

V6-231

Removal & Disassembly
1. Remove oil filter.
2. Disconnect wire from oil pressure indicator switch in filter by-pass valve cap (if so equipped).
3. Remove screws attaching oil pump cover to timing chain cover. Remove cover and slide out pump gears. Replace any parts not serviceable.
4. Remove oil pressure relief valve cap, spring and valve, **Fig. 48.**
5. Check relief valve in its bore in cover. Valve should have no more clearance than an easy slip fit. If any perceptible side shake can be felt, the valve and/or cover should be replaced.
6. The filter by-pass valve should be flat and free of nicks and scratches.

Assembly & Installation
1. Lubricate and install pressure relief valve and spring in bore of pump cover. Install cap and gasket. Torque cap to 30–35 ft. lbs.
2. Install pump gears and shaft in pump body section of timing chain cover to check gear end clearance. Check clearance as shown in **Fig. 49.** If clearance is less than .0020", check timing chain cover for evidence of wear.

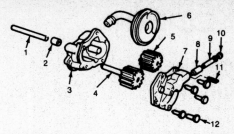

1. Shaft Extension
2. Shaft Coupling
3. Pump Body
4. Drive Gear and Shaft
5. Idler Gear
6. Pickup Screen and Pipe
7. Pump Cover
8. Pressure Regulator Valve
9. Pressure Regulator Spring
10. Washer
11. Retaining Pin
12. Screws

Fig. 47   Oil pump. V8-454

1 CHECK CLEARANCE BETWEEN GEAR TEETH AND SIDE WALL, CLEARANCE SHOULD BE BETWEEN .002" & .005"

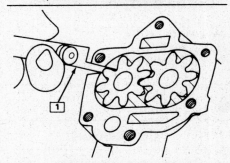

Fig. 50   Checking oil pump side clearance. V6-231

3. Check oil pump side clearance as shown in **Fig. 50**. Clearance should be .002–.005 inch. If clearance is not as specified, measure gears and pocket to determine which is at fault, **Figs. 51 and 52**.
4. Check oil pump cover for wear with straight edge and feeler gauge. If clearance is greater than .001 inch, replace cover.
5. If clearances are as specified, remove gears and pack gear pocket with vaseline.
6. Reinstall gears so vaseline is forced into every cavity of gear pocket and between teeth of gears. Unless pump is packed with vaseline, it may not prime itself when engine is started.

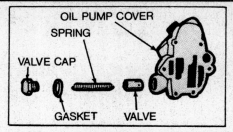

Fig. 48   Oil pump cover & bypass valve. V6-231

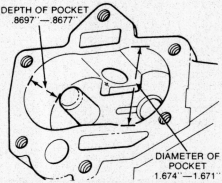

DEPTH OF POCKET .8697"—.8677"

DIAMETER OF POCKET 1.674"—1.671"

Fig. 51   Checking oil pump gear pocket for wear. V6-231

7. Install cover and tighten screws alternately and evenly. Final tightening is 10–15 ft-lbs. torque. Install filter on nipple.

WATER PUMP
REPLACE

EXCEPT V6-231

1. Drain cooling system.
2. Remove fan belt and fan.
3. Disconnect all hoses from water pump.
4. Remove alternator upper and lower mounting braces, if necessary.
5. Remove pump attaching bolts and remove water pump. On 6-250 engines, pull pump straight out of block to prevent damage to impeller.
6. Reverse procedure to install.

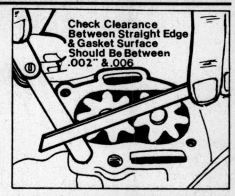

Check Clearance Between Straight Edge & Gasket Surface Should Be Between .002" & .006"

Fig. 49   Checking clearance between oil pump gear & housing gasket surface. V6-231

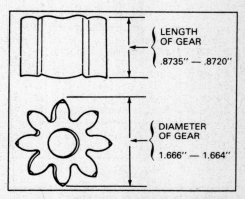

LENGTH OF GEAR .8735"—.8720"

DIAMETER OF GEAR 1.666"—1.664"

Fig. 52   Checking oil pump gears for wear. V6-231

V6-231

1. Disconnect battery ground cable, then drain cooling system.
2. Remove drive belts, then remove fan and pulley from water pump shaft hub.

NOTE: On some models, it may be necessary to remove the alternator upper and lower mounting braces, and if equipped, the lower power steering pump brace.

3. Disconnect radiator hose and heater hose from water pump fittings.
4. Remove bolts attaching water pump to timing case cover, then remove water pump assembly.
5. Reverse procedure to install.

V8-350 Diesel Engine Section

INDEX OF SERVICE OPERATIONS

DIESEL ENGINE DIAGNOSIS

Condition	Possible Cause	Correction
ENGINE WILL NOT CRANK	1. Loose or corroded battery cables	1. Check connections at battery, engine block and starter solenoid.
	2. Discharged batteries	2. Check charging system.
	3. Starter inoperative	3. Check starting system.
ENGINE CRANKS SLOWLY—WILL NOT START (Minimum Engine Crank Speed—100 RPM)	1. Battery cable connections loose or corroded	1. Check connections at battery, engine block and starter.
	2. Batteries undercharged.	2. Check charging system.
	3. Wrong engine oil	3. Drain and refill with recommended oil.
ENGINE CRANKS NORMALLY—WILL NOT START	1. Incorrect starting procedure.	1. Use recommended starting procedure.
	2. Incorrect or contaminated fuel	2. Flush fuel system and install correct fuel.
	3. No fuel to nozzles	3. Loosen injection line at a nozzle. Do not disconnect. Use care to direct fuel away from sources of ignition. Wipe connection to be sure it is dry. Crank 5 seconds. Fuel should flow from injection line. Tighten connection. If fuel does not flow, check fuel solenoid operation as follows: Connect a 12 volt test lamp from wire at injection pump solenoid to ground. Turn ignition to "On". Lamp should light. If lamp does not light, check wiring to solenoid.
	4. No fuel to injection pump	4. Remove line at inlet to injection pump fuel filter. Connect hose from line to metal container. Crank engine. If no fuel is discharged, test the fuel supply pump. If lamp does not light, check wiring to solenoid. If the pump is OK, check the injection pump fuel filter and replace if plugged. If filter and inlet line to injection pump are OK, replace injection pump.

DIESEL ENGINE DIAGNOSIS—Continued

Condition	Possible Cause	Correction
ENGINE CRANKS NORMALLY— WILL NOT START (Continued)	5. Plugged fuel return system	5. Disconnect fuel return line at injection pump and route hose to a metal container. Connect a hose to the injection pump connection and route it to the metal container. Crank the engine; if engine starts and runs, correct restriction in fuel return system.
	6. Pump timing incorrect	6. Make certain that pump timing mark is aligned with mark on adapter.
	7. Glow plug control system inoperative	7. Refer to Glow Plug System Trouble-Shooting & Diagnosis.
	8. Glow plugs inoperative	8. Refer to Glow Plug System Trouble-Shooting & Diagnosis.
	9. Internal engine problems	9. Correct as necessary.
	10. No voltage to fuel solenoid	10. Connect a 12 volt test lamp from injection pump solenoid to ground. Turn ignition to "On"; lamp should light. If lamp lights, remove test lamp and connect and disconnect solenoid connector and listen for solenoid operation. If solenoid does not operate, remove injection pump for repairs. If lamp does not light, refer to Glow Plug System Trouble-Shooting & Diagnosis.
	11. Restricted fuel tank filter.	11. Remove fuel tank and check filter.
ENGINE STARTS BUT WILL NOT CONTINUE TO RUN AT IDLE	1. No fuel in tank	1. Install correct fuel in tank.
	2. Incorrect or contaminated fuel	2. Flush fuel system and install correct fuel.
	3. Limited fuel to injection pump	3. Test the fuel supply pump. Replace as necessary.
	4. Fuel solenoid disengaged with ignition switch in the "ON" position	4. Connect a 12 volt test lamp from wire at injection pump solenoid to ground. Turn ignition to "ON". Lamp should light. Turn ignition to "START". Lamp should light. If lamp does not light in both positions, check wiring to solenoid.
	5. Restricted fuel return system	5. Disconnect fuel return to a metal container. Connect a hose to injection pump connection and route to metal container. Crank engine; if engine starts and runs, correct restriction in fuel system.
	6. Fast idle solenoid inoperative	6. With engine cold, start car; solenoid should move to support injection pump lever in "Fast idle position" for about 5 seconds. If solenoid does not move, refer to Electrical System Diagnosis.
	7. Low idle incorrectly adjusted	7. Adjust idle screw to specification.
	8. Pump timing incorrect.	8. Make certain that timing mark, on injection pump, is aligned with mark on adapter.
	9. Glow plug control system malfunction	9. Refer to Glow Plug System Trouble-Shooting & Diagnosis.
	10. Injection pump malfunction	10. Install replacement pump.
	11. Internal engine problems	11. Correct as necessary.
ENGINE STARTS, IDLES ROUGH, WITHOUT ABNORMAL NOISE OR SMOKE	1. Low idle incorrectly adjusted	1. Adjust idle screw to specification
	2. Injection line leaks	2. Wipe off injection lines and connections. Run engine and check for leaks. Correct leaks.
	3. Restricted fuel return system	3. Disconnect fuel return line at injection pump and route hose to a metal container. Connect a hose to the injection pump container. Crank the engine; if engine starts and runs, correct restriction in fuel return system.

DIESEL ENGINE DIAGNOSIS—Continued

Condition	Possible Cause	Correction
ENGINE STARTS, IDLES ROUGH, WITHOUT ABNORMAL NOISE OR SMOKE, continued	4. Incorrect or contaminated fuel	4. Flush fuel system and install correct fuel.
	5. Nozzle(s) inoperative	5. With engine running, loosen injection line fitting at each nozzle in turn. Use care to direct fuel away from sources of ignition. Each nozzle should contribute to rough running. If nozzle is found that does not change idle quality, it should be replaced.
	6. Internal fuel leak at nozzle(s)	6. Disconnect fuel return system from nozzles on one bank at a time. With the engine running, observe the normal fuel seepage at the nozzles. Replace any nozzle with excessive fuel leakage.
	7. Fuel supply pump malfunctions	7. Test the fuel supply pump. Replace if necessary.
	8. Uneven fuel distribution to cylinders	8. Install new or reconditioned nozzles, one at a time, until condition is corrected as indicated by normal idle.
ENGINE STARTS AND IDLES ROUGH WITH EXCESSIVE NOISE AND/OR SMOKE	1. Injection pump timing incorrect	1. Be sure timing mark on injection pump is aligned with mark on adapter.
	2. Nozzle(s) inoperative	2. With engine running, crank injection line at each nozzle, one at a time. Use care to direct fuel away from sources of ignition. Each nozzle should contribute to rough running. If a nozzle is found that does not affect idle quality or changes noise and/or smoke, it should be replaced.
	3. High pressure lines incorrectly installed	3. Check routing of each line. Correct as required.
ENGINE MISFIRES BUT IDLES CORRECTLY	1. Plugged fuel filter	1. Replace filter.
	2. Incorrect injection pump timing	2. Be sure that timing mark on injection pump and adapter are aligned.
	3. Incorrect or contaminated fuel	3. Flush fuel system and install correct fuel.
ENGINE WILL NOT RETURN TO IDLE	1. External linkage misadjustment or failure	1. Reset linkage or replace as required.
	2. Internal injection pump malfunction	2. Install replacement injection pump.
FUEL LEAKS ON GROUND—NO ENGINE MALFUNCTION	1. Loose or broken fuel line or connection	1. Examine complete fuel system, including tank, supply, injection and return system. Determine source and cause of leak and repair.
	2. Internal injection pump failure	2. Install replacement injection pump.
SIGNIFICANT LOSS OF POWER	1. Incorrect or contaminated fuel	1. Flush fuel system and install correct fuel.
	2. Pinched or otherwise restricted return system	2. Examine system for restriction and correct as required.
	3. Plugged fuel tank vent	3. Remove fuel cap. If "hissing" noise is heard, vent is plugged and should be cleaned.
	4. Restricted fuel supply	4. Examine fuel supply system to determine cause of restriction. Repair as required.
	5. Plugged fuel filter	5. Remove and replace filter.
	6. External compression leaks	6. Check for compression leaks at all nozzles and glow plugs, using "Leak-Tec" or equivalent. If leak is found, tighten nozzle clamp or glow plug. If leak persists at a nozzle, remove it and reinstall with a new carbon stop seal and compression seal.
	7. Plugged nozzle(s)	7. Remove nozzles, check for plugging and have repaired or replaced.

DIESEL ENGINE DIAGNOSIS—Continued

Condition	Possible Cause	Correction
SIGNIFICANT LOSS OF POWER (continued)	8. Internal engine problem	8. Correct as necessary.
	9. EGR malfunction	9. Correct as necessary
NOISE—"RAP" FROM ONE OR MORE CYLINDERS	1. Air in fuel system	1. Check for leaks and correct.
	2. Air in high pressure line(s)	2. Crack line at nozzle(s) and bleed air at each cylinder determined to be causing noise. Use care to direct fuel away from sources of ignition and be sure to carefully retighten lines.
	3. Nozzle(s) sticking open or with very low blowoff pressure	3. Replace the nozzle(s) causing the problem.
	4. Internal engine problem	4. Correct as necessary.
NOISE—SIGNIFICANT OVERALL COMBUSTION NOISE INCREASE WITH EXCESSIVE BLACK SMOKE	1. Timing not set to specification	1. Align timing marks on adapter and injection pump.
	2. Internal engine problem	2. Check for presence of oil in the air crossover. If present, determine cause and correct.
	3. Injection pump housing pressure out of specifications.	3. Check housing pressure. If incorrect, replace fuel return line connector assembly.
	4. Internal injection pump problem	4. Replace pump.
	5. EGR malfunction	5. Correct as necessary.
NOISE—INTERNAL OR EXTERNAL	1. Fuel supply pump, alternator, water pump, valve train, vacuum pump, bearings, etc.	1. Inspect and correct as necessary.
ENGINE OVERHEATS	1. Coolant system leak or oil cooler system leak	1. Check for leaks and correct as required.
	2. Belt failure or slippage	2. Replace or adjust as required.
	3. Thermostat malfunction, head gasket failure or internal engine problem	3. Inspect and correct as necessary.
INSTRUMENT PANEL OIL WARNING LAMP "ON" AT IDLE	1. Oil cooler or oil cooler line restricted	1. Remove restriction in cooler or cooler line.
	2. Internal engine problem	2. Correct as necessary.
ENGINE WILL NOT SHUT OFF WITH KEY	1. Injection pump solenoid does not drop out	1. Refer to electrical diagnosis. If problem is determined to be internal with the injection pump, replace the injection pump.
	2. Injection pump solenoid return spring failed	2. Replace injection pump.

NOTE: With engine at idle, pinch the fuel return line at the injection pump to shut off engine.

DESCRIPTION

ENGINE CONSTRUCTION

The Oldsmobile four stroke cycle diesel V8-350 engine is basically the same in construction as the Oldsmobile gasoline V8-350 engine. The cylinders are numbered 1, 3, 5, 7 on the left bank and 2, 4, 6, 8 on the right bank. The firing order is 1-8-4-3-6-5-7-2. The major differences between the diesel and gasoline versions is in the cylinder heads, combustion chamber, fuel distribution system, air intake manifold and method of ignition. The cylinder block, crankshaft, main bearings, connecting rods, pistons and pins are of heavy construction due to the high compression ratio required to ignite the diesel fuel. The diesel fuel is ignited when the heat developed in the combustion chamber during the compression stroke reaches a certain temperature.

The valve train operates the same as in the gasoline engine, but are of special design and material for diesel operation. The stainless steel pre-chamber inserts in the cylinder head combustion chambers are serviced separately from the cylinder head. With the cylinder head removed, these pre-chamber inserts can be driven from the cylinder head after removing the glow plugs or injection nozzles.

On 1979–80 models and 1981 models except California, the glow plugs are threaded into the cylinder head and the injection nozzles are retained by a bolt and clamp. On 1981 California and all 1983–84 models, the glow plugs and the injection nozzles are both threaded into the cylinder head. The injection nozzles are spring loaded and calibrated to open at a specified fuel pressure.

FUEL SYSTEM

The fuel injection pump is mounted on top of the engine and is gear driven by the camshaft and rotates at camshaft speed. This high pressure rotary pump injects a metered amount of fuel to each cylinder to the proper time. Eight high pressure fuel delivery pipes from the injection pump to the injection nozzles, **Figs. 1 and 2,** are the same length to prevent any difference in timing from cylinder to cylinder. The fuel injection pump provides the required timing advance under all operating conditions.

Engine speed is controlled by a rotary fuel metering valve, **Fig. 3.** When the accelerator is depressed, the throttle cable opens the metering valve and allows more fuel to be delivered to the engine. The injection pump also incorporates a low pressure transfer pump to deliver fuel to the fuel line to the high pressure pump, **Fig. 3.**

The fuel filter is located between the mechanical fuel pump and the injection pump. The diaphragm type mechanical fuel pump is mounted on the right side of the engine and is driven by a cam on the crankshaft. The fuel tank at the rear of the vehicle is connected by fuel pipes to the mechanical fuel pump. Excess fuel returns from the fuel injection pump and injection nozzles to the fuel tank through pipes and hoses.

NOTE: Injection nozzles used on 1981 California models and all 1983–84 models do not use a fuel return line.

WATER IN FUEL SYSTEM

This system is available on some 1980 and all 1981 and 1983–84 models. These

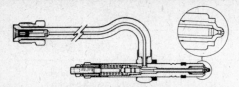

Fig. 1 Fuel injection nozzle. 1979–80 & 1981 exc. Calif.

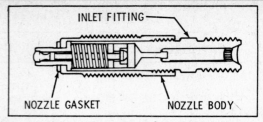

Fig. 2 Fuel injection nozzle. 1981 Calif. & all 1983–84

vehicles have a "Water in Fuel" light mounted in the instrument panel. The "Water in Fuel" light has a bulb check feature and should light for 2 to 2½ seconds when the ignition is turned on. If not, the bulb is burned out or there is an open in the wiring circuit. When there is water in the fuel, the light will come back on and remain on after a 15 to 20 second delay.

A water sensing probe, mounted on the fuel sender, actuates the instrument panel light when it is partially covered with water. About 1 to 2½ gallons of water must be present in the fuel tank to cause the sensor light to activate.

If the "Water in Fuel" lamp goes on while the vehicle is being driven, the fuel system should be checked for water. If the lamp goes on immediately after refueling and before the vehicle is moved, there is a large quantity of water in the tank and should be removed immediately.

The water may be removed from the tank with a pump or by siphoning. The pump or siphon hose should be connected to the quarter inch fuel return hose (the smaller of the two hoses), located under the hood near the fuel pump. Refer to "Purging Water From Fuel Tank" procedure.

FUEL HEATER

This cold weather device is installed on some 1981 and 1983–84 vehicles. This thermostatically controlled fuel heater reduces the possibility of wax plugging the filter when temperatures are below 20°F. Battery voltage is directed to the heater whenever the ignition is in the "Run" position.

The heater consists of a strip spiral wound around the fuel pipe and a bimetal thermal switch which closes and completes the circuit when fuel temperatures are approximately 20°F. When fuel temperatures reach 50°F. the thermal switch opens and deactivates the circuit.

The fuel tank filter sock is equipped with a bypass valve which opens when the filter is covered with wax, allowing fuel to flow to the heater.

HOUSING PRESSURE COLD ADVANCE (HPCA)

This feature is used on all 1981 and 1983–84 engines and advances the injection timing 3° during cold operation. This circuit is actuated by a temperature switch calibrated to open the circuit at 125° F. Below the switching point, housing pressure is decreased from 10 to 0 psi which advances the injection timing 3°. Above the

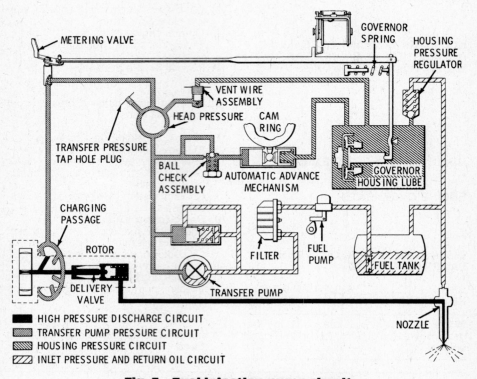

HIGH PRESSURE DISCHARGE CIRCUIT
TRANSFER PUMP PRESSURE CIRCUIT
HOUSING PRESSURE CIRCUIT
INLET PRESSURE AND RETURN OIL CIRCUIT

Fig. 3 Fuel injection pump circuit

switching point, the switch opens, deenergizing the solenoid and the housing pressure is returned to 10 psi. The fast idle solenoid is energized by the same switch and closes when the temperature falls below 95° F.

HOUSING PRESSURE ALTITUDE ADVANCE (HPAA)

Used on 1984 engines, the HPAA is used to meet emission standards at both low and high altitudes. Altitude compensation is achieved through timing changes and EGR modification and is controlled by an altitude sensitive switch.

Timing is controlled by two pressure regulators, the Housing Pressure Cold Advance, located in the injection pump, and the Housing Pressure Altitude Advance solenoid in the fuel return line.

The HPAA solenoid regulates housing pressure according to altitude. When the solenoid is activated, the glass check ball seats, regulating pressure at its calibrated

value. When the solenoid is de-activated, the check ball moves off its seat, opening the fuel return line and preventing pressure regulation. It is possible for both the HPCA and the HPAA to regulate housing pressure at the same time. Likewise, it is also possible to have just the HPCA or the HPAA regulate pressure singularly. The HPCA must be energized and not regulating to allow the HPAA solenoid to regulate at its calibrated value.

ENGINE LUBRICATION SYSTEM

NOTE: On 1979–80 engines, the recommended diesel engine oil designation is SE/CC. On 1981 engines, the recommended diesel engine oil is SF/CC, SF/CD or SE/CC. On 1983–84 engines, the recommended diesel engine oil is SF/SC or SF/CD, it is also recommended that the oil be a fuel saving product.

The diesel engine lubrication system is basically the same as the gasoline engine.

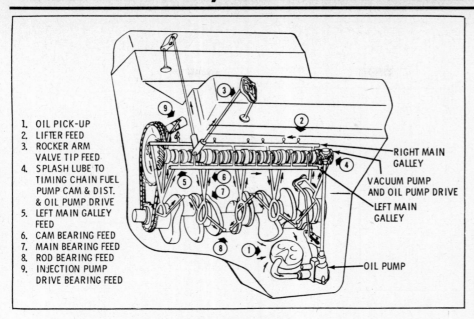

1. OIL PICK-UP
2. LIFTER FEED
3. ROCKER ARM VALVE TIP FEED
4. SPLASH LUBE TO TIMING CHAIN FUEL PUMP CAM & DIST. & OIL PUMP DRIVE
5. LEFT MAIN GALLEY FEED
6. CAM BEARING FEED
7. MAIN BEARING FEED
8. ROD BEARING FEED
9. INJECTION PUMP DRIVE BEARING FEED

RIGHT MAIN GALLEY

VACUUM PUMP AND OIL PUMP DRIVE

LEFT MAIN GALLEY

OIL PUMP

Fig. 4   Engine lubricating system

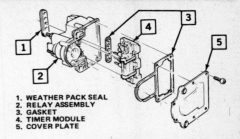

1. WEATHER PACK SEAL
2. RELAY ASSEMBLY
3. GASKET
4. TIMER MODULE
5. COVER PLATE

Fig. 5   Glow plug control module. 1984

The fuel injection pump driven gear is lubricated by oil directed through a passage from the top of the camshaft bearing, **Fig. 4.** An angled passage in the shaft portion of the driven gear directs the oil to the rear driven gear bearing. At the front of the right oil gallery, a small orifice sprays oil to lubricate the fuel pump eccentric cam on the crankshaft and timing chain.

ENGINE COOLING SYSTEM

The diesel engine cooling system is the same as the gasoline engine except the radiator incorporates two oil coolers. One cooler is used to cool the transmission fluid and the other cooler is used to cool the engine oil.

ENGINE ELECTRICAL SYSTEM

1979—81 & 1983

Eight glow plugs are used to pre-heat the pre-chamber to aid in starting. The type 1 glow plugs are 12 volt heaters and are activated when the ignition switch is turned to the "Run" position. The type 1 system uses steady current applied to 12 volt glow plugs. The type 2 system uses 6 volt glow plugs with a controlled pulsating current applied to them for starting. The type 2 glow plug system uses an electromechanical controller for glow plug temperature, pre-glow time, wait/start lights and after glow time. The 6 and 12 volt plugs are not interchangeable and can be identified by the wire connector spade. The 6 volt glow plugs have a $\frac{5}{16}$ inch wire connector spade, while the 12 volt plugs have a $\frac{1}{4}$ inch wide spade. The glow plug remains activated for a short time after starting then is automatically turned "Off." Two 12 volt batteries, connected in parallel, are re-

quired for the higher electrical load due to the glow plugs and starting motor. The diesel starter motor is larger than the gasoline starter motor. It is designed to crank the engine at least the 100 RPM required for starting. An alternator supplies charging current to both batteries at the same time and there are no switches or relays in the charging circuit.

1984

A new glow plug system is used for 1984 diesel engines. A self-limiting feature regulates maximum temperature, while the glow plugs are programmed to shut off automatically should the vehicle not be started within the specified time period.

System Components

The glow plug control module, **Fig. 5,** is an integral assembly that includes the timer functions, lamp switch and glow plug relay. The control module serves the following functions:

1. Controls wait lamp operation, which varies according to system voltage and/or ambient temperature.
2. Controls system shutdown timing depending on voltage and ambient temperature.
3. An overvoltage function that protects the glow plugs from failure, should higher than normal voltages be incurred.
4. A thermal cutout function that disengages the glow plug system when module temperatures are greater than 113°F.
5. A power relay function that switches the voltage applied to the glow plugs.
6. A quick reset function that permits the module to recycle quickly, after initial shutdown time.

This control module can only be used

with glow plugs that regulate their own temperature. The new glow plugs used have positive temperature coefficient properties, which mean they have low resistance values at low temperatures and high resistance values at high temperatures. The new plugs offer a fast temperature rise similar to past fixed resistance plugs, plus improved and simpler glow plug control.

System Operation

The glow plug control circuit, **Fig. 6,** operates the glow plug system in three steps: pre-glow, after-glow and off. During pre-glow, the circuit activates the wait lamp and heats the glow plugs until they are sufficiently warm to start the engine. During after-glow, the circuit deactivates the wait lamp, but continues to apply power to the glow plugs. During the Off cycle, the circuit removes power from the glow plugs and keeps it off until the engine is restarted.

As stated previously, the glow plug control module controls all circuit functions. The thermal controls open the pre-glow and after-glow switches to end the respective cycles, and are responsive to engine temperature. When the system is energized with the engine cold, both switches are in the "Cold" position. As time passes, current flow heats the thermal controls, moving both switches toward their "HOT" position. The time needed for each switch to reach its "HOT" position is dependent upon how cold the engine and control module were when the system was first energized. As the pre-glow switch reaches the "HOT" position, the wait lamp deactivates and the engine may now be started. The control module continues to operate, whether the engine is started or not, since the after-glow switch has not yet reached its "HOT" position. Current flow continues to heat the thermal control. When the thermal control reaches full temperature, the after-glow switch moves to "HOT", opening the path to ground from the coil of the glow plug relay. This allows current flow to bypass the coil of the reset relay. With the path to ground now open, current must flow to bypass the coil of the reset relay. With the path to ground now open, current must flow to ground through the reset relay coil. The glow plug relay de-energizes, removing power to the glow plugs. The reset relay now energizes, opening the contact of the relay and locking off the thermal

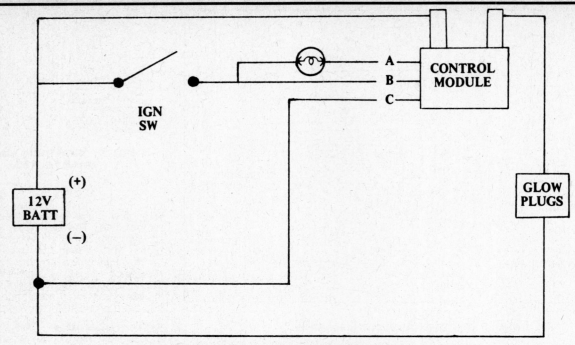

Fig. 6   Glow plug control circuit schematic. 1984

controls. When the ignition switch is turned off, the reset relay contact closes, and the glow plug module is ready to repeat the cycle. If the engine is above 140°F. when restarted, the thermal controls will be "HOT", energizing the reset relay and preventing glow plug operation.

The over-voltage protector protects the glow plugs should battery voltage rise above 14 volts. When the protector senses over 14 volts, it opens the circuit to the glow plug relay coil and prevents current from flowing to the glow plugs. After a short time, the protector closes the circuit. If battery voltage is still above 14 volts, it will reopen the circuit again. The protector continues to cycle in this way as long as the over-voltage condition exists and as long as glow plug operation is needed.

GLOW PLUG SYSTEM TROUBLESHOOTING & DIAGNOSIS

1984

Refer to wiring diagram, **Fig. 7,** then use the following procedures for troubleshooting and diagnosis of glow plug system.

NOTE: When troubleshooting system, the glow plug controller must be operated with engine below 122°F. If it is necessary to remove or test glow plug controller, ensure that battery ground cable is disconnected, since damage to electrical components may result.

No Wait Lamp-Engine Cold
1. With ignition switch in "RUN" position and engine off, check wait lamp oper-ation. Wait lamp should be on. If not, proceed to next step.
2. Check gauge fuse. If fuse is blown, re-place fuse and repeat step 1. If fuse is good, check pink and pink/black wires between ignition switch and S203 for opens.
3. Disconnect connector of glow plug controller. Connect a jumper wire at connector pin A(dark blue wire) to ground. If wait lamp does not go on, check for burned out bulb. If bulb is not burned out, check for opens in dark blue wire between controller connec-tor and wait lamp, and also in pink/black wire between wait lamp and S203. If wires are not open, proceed to next step.
4. Connect one end of test lamp BT-7905 or equivalent to red wire terminal of glow plug relay and other end to ground, then touch lead to glow plug controller connector pin C(black wire). If wait lamp comes on, replace glow plug controller.

Wait Lamp Stays On More Than 15 Seconds
1. With ignition switch "OFF", check bat-tery voltage. Charge battery if voltage is below 10.5 volts.
2. Connect one end of test lamp BT-7905 or equivalent to ground, and the other lead to red wire post of glow plug relay. Turn ignition switch "ON", then touch test lead to green wire post of relay. If test lamp comes on, the glow plug relay should operate. If relay operates, replace controller. If relay does not operate, proceed to next step.
3. Check diesel fuse. If fuse is good, sep-arate connector at glow plug control-ler. Connect test light between pins B(pink/black wire) and C(black wire) at harness connector. Turn ignition switch to "RUN" and observe test lamp. If test lamp does not come on, check continuity of pink/black wires. If test lamp comes on proceed to next step.
4. Check continuity (less than 75 ohms) between pins B and C at controller. If no continuity is evident, remove glow plug controller, disconnect glow plug relay and replace thermal controller.

Engine Does Not Start—Wait Lamp OK
1. Ensure that cranking speed is greater than 100 RPM. If not, check battery voltage and charge battery if neces-sary.
2. With ignition switch in "RUN", use test lamp mentioned previously and check for voltage at pink wire of injection pump fuel solenoid. If no voltage is evident, repair wire. If voltage is present, proceed to next step.
3. Turn ignition switch "OFF". Using a self-powered test lamp, check for con-tinuity from fuel control solenoid to ground. If no continuity exists, replace solenoid.
4. Connect one end of test lamp BT-7905 or equivalent to ground, and the other end to red wire post of glow plug relay. With ignition switch "ON", touch test lead to green wire post of relay. Test lamp should come on and relay should operate.
5. If relay operates, turn ignition switch "OFF", then disconnect glow plug har-ness connectors at glow plugs. Con-nect self-powered test lamp between green wire post of relay and ground. At

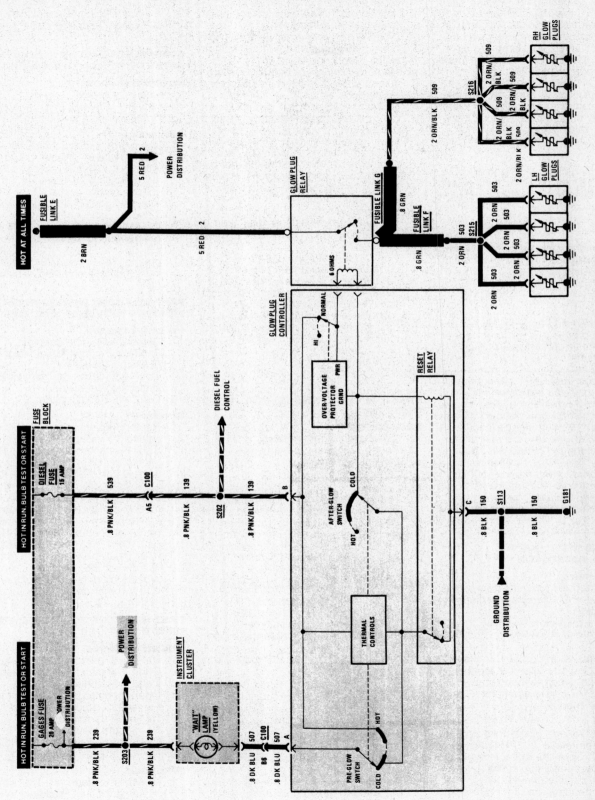

Fig. 7 Glow plug system wiring diagram. 1984

each glow plug, momentarily connect harness connector to glow plug spade terminal. Observe test lamp. If lamp comes on, glow plug and harness lead are OK. If test lamp does not come on, ground harness connector and observe test lamp. If test lamp comes on, replace glow plug. If test lamp does not come on, replace harness connector.

6. If glow plug relay does not operate, remove controller and relay. Check for continuity of both parts. Replace controller or relay as necessary.

1983

Refer to wiring diagram, **Fig. 8 and Fig. 9 through 15,** for troubleshooting and diagnosis procedures for the 1983 glow plug system.

1980–81

Refer to wiring diagram, **Fig. 16, and Figs. 17 through 21,** for troubleshooting and diagnosis procedures for the 1980–81 glow plug system.

1979

Refer to wiring diagram, **Fig. 22,** and use the following procedures for troubleshooting and diagnosis procedures for the 1979 glow plug system.

NOTE: Unless specified, testing is performed with a 12 volt voltmeter. Measurements should be made to a good engine ground. Grounding signals should be less than 1.5 volts. 12 volt signals should be 10.5–12.5 volts unless otherwise stated. Measurements are obtained with the ignition switch in the "On" position within a time period prior to emergency shut-down (2–5 minutes) after the engine is "On". Check battery voltage before testing. Charge batteries if voltage is less than 12.4 with ignition "Off".

GLOW PLUGS "OFF" DURING PREGLOW & AFTERGLOW

Possible Causes
1. Open 940 or 941 circuits from relays.
2. Open 2X or 2Y circuits from junction block relays.
3. Defective relay or relays.
4. Open 901 circuit between module and relays.
5. Open module ground at 150 circuit.
6. Open 3 circuit to relays or module.
7. Faulty 935 circuit to thermistor.
8. Open 925 circuit to alternator.
9. Defective module.

Diagnosis
1. Measure voltage of the following circuits at the relays: 2, 3, 150, 901, 940 and 941. Note the voltage readings. The voltage readings for the 2, 3, 940 and 941 circuits should be 12 volts. Voltage reading for the 150 circuit should be 9 volts. Voltage reading for the 901 circuit should be zero volts.
2. If circuits 2, 3, and 901 are satisfactory and circuits 940 and 941 are not,

replace defective relay.
3. If circuits 2 and 3 are not satisfactory, repair open circuit or fusible link.
4. If circuit 901 is not satisfactory, measure voltage at module.
5. If circuit 150 is not satisfactory (right bank glow plugs not functioning), repair ground circuit.
6. Measure voltage of 940 and 941 circuits at glow plugs. If not satisfactory, repair open circuit.
7. Measure voltage of 901 circuit at module. If voltage is satisfactory, replace open relays. If voltage is not satisfactory, measure voltage of 3 and 150 circuits at module. Reading of circuit 3 should be 12 volts and reading of circuit 150 should be zero volts. If readings are not within specifications, repair open circuits.
8. Measure voltage of 25 circuit at module. Voltage should be less than 3 volts. If not, repair open circuit to alternator.
9. Replace the thermistor in the 935 circuit with a milliammeter placed on 0–1ma range. The reading should be .3–.5ma. If the reading is within specifications, leave milliammeter in place and recheck 901 circuit. If 901 circuit is now satisfactory, check thermistor as follows: check resistance of the thermistor. Resistance should be 2000–5000 ohms at 60°–80° F.
10. If 901 circuit is unsatisfactory at this time, replace module.

PREGLOW OKAY, TIME PERIOD INCORRECT

Possible Causes
1. Open circuit to thermistor.
2. Faulty 935 circuit to thermistor.
3. Defective thermistor.
4. Defective module.

Diagnosis
1. Replace the thermistor in the 935 circuit with a milliammeter placed on the 0–1ma range. Reading should be .3–.5ma. If satisfactory, check thermistor resistance. Resistance should be 2000–5000 ohms at 60°–80° F. If satisfactory, replace module.

PREGLOW OKAY, AFTERGLOW TIME PERIOD INCORRECT

Possible Causes
1. Defective module.
2. Defective 906A circuit to module from starter solenoid.
3. Defective 925 circuit to module from alternator.

Diagnosis
1. Check voltage of 906A circuit at module while cranking engine. Voltage should be 8–12 volts. Then, check the voltage with ignition key in "Run" position. Voltage should be zero volts. If voltages are not within specifications, repair circuit.
2. On vehicles equipped with an alternator warning lamp, ensure that lamp is "On" before cranking engine and the lamp is "Off" after the engine starts. On vehicles equipped with a voltmeter or on vehicle equipped with an alter-

nator warning lamp that checked satisfactory, check the voltage of the 925 circuit at the module with the engine running. Voltage should be 14–15 volts. If not, repair 25 circuit to alternator.

GLOW PLUGS REMAIN ACTIVATED AFTER REQUIRED TIME PERIOD

Possible Causes
1. Defective relays.
2. Faulty 901 circuit.
3. Defective module.

Diagnosis
1. Check 901 circuit voltage with ignition "On." Voltage should be zero and after 2–5 minutes, voltage should be 12 volts without cranking engine. If voltages are satisfactory, replace relays if circuits 940 and 941 check at 12 volts.
2. If 901 circuit is not satisfactory, remove module and recheck 901 circuit for 12 volts. If no voltage is present, repair open 901 circuit. If a 12 volt reading is obtained, replace module.

FAST IDLE "ON" WITH HIGH ENGINE TEMPERATURE &/OR A/C "OFF"

Possible Causes
1. Defective fast idle solenoid.
2. Faulty 951 circuit to solenoid.
3. Defective module.
4. Open 935 circuit to thermistor.
5. Defective thermistor.
6. Defective A/C controller.

Diagnosis
1. Remove solenoid connector, replace solenoid if it does not retract.
2. Check voltage at 951 circuits. Reading should be 12 volts. If not, disconnect module and recheck reading. If still not 12 volts, repair faulty 951 circuit.
3. If 951 circuit reads zero volts with module connected but 12 volts disconnected, apply a short to ground at 935 circuit at module. Recheck 951 with A/C "Off." If satisfactory, repair open 935 circuit to thermistor. If not, check voltage at 66 circuit. If zero volts, replace module. If no volts with A/C "Off", repair defective A/C controller switch.

FAST IDLE "OFF" WITH COLD ENGINE OR A/C "ON"

Possible Causes
1. Defective fast idle solenoid.
2. Open 139 circuit feed to solenoid.
3. Defective module.
4. Open module ground 150 circuit.
5. Faulty 935 circuit to thermistor.
6. Defective thermistor.
7. No module feed, 3 circuit.
8. Open or faulty 66 circuit to A/C clutch.
9. No A/C voltage at feed point.

Diagnosis
1. Measure voltage at 139 circuit on solenoid. If not satisfactory, repair open 139 circuit. If voltage is satisfactory, measure 951 circuit. Reading should be zero volts. If within specifications, remove solenoid connector

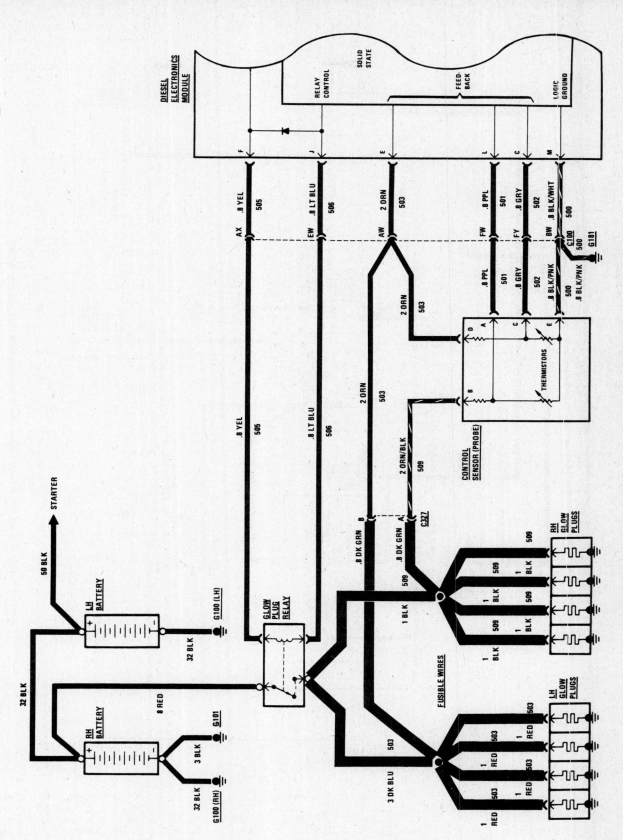

Fig. 8 (Part 1 of 2). Glow plug system wiring diagram. 1983

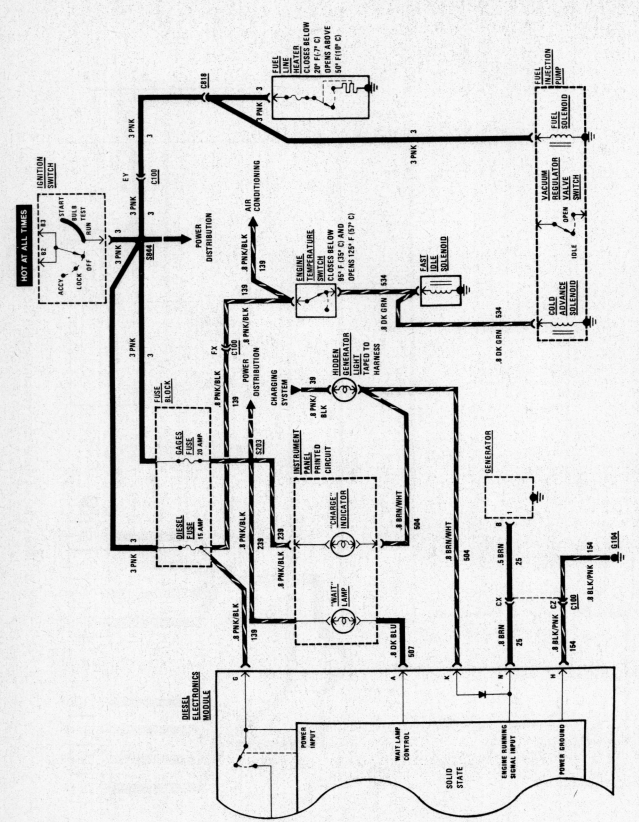

Fig. 8 (Part 2 of 2). Glow plug system wiring diagram. 1983

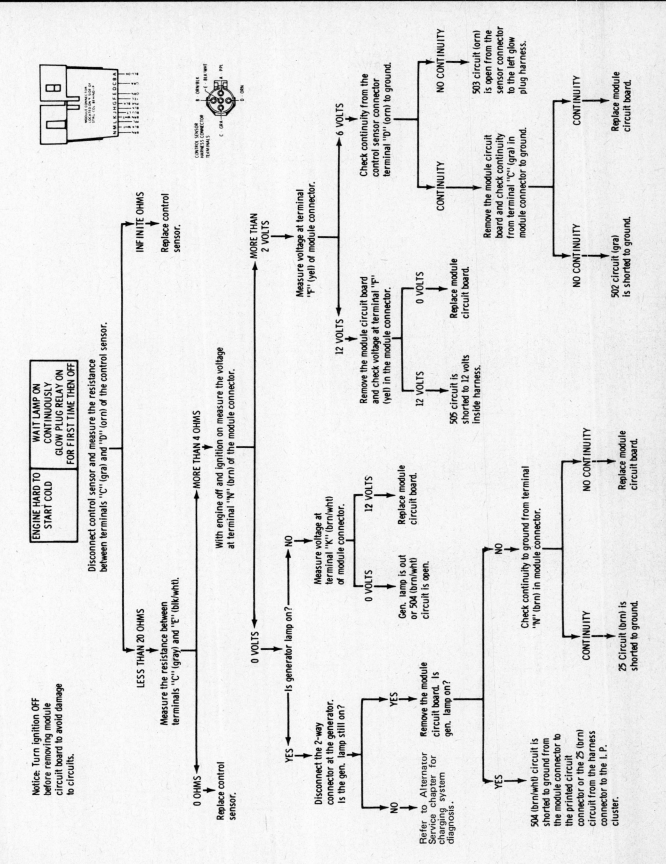

Fig. 9 Glow plug system diagnosis chart. 1983

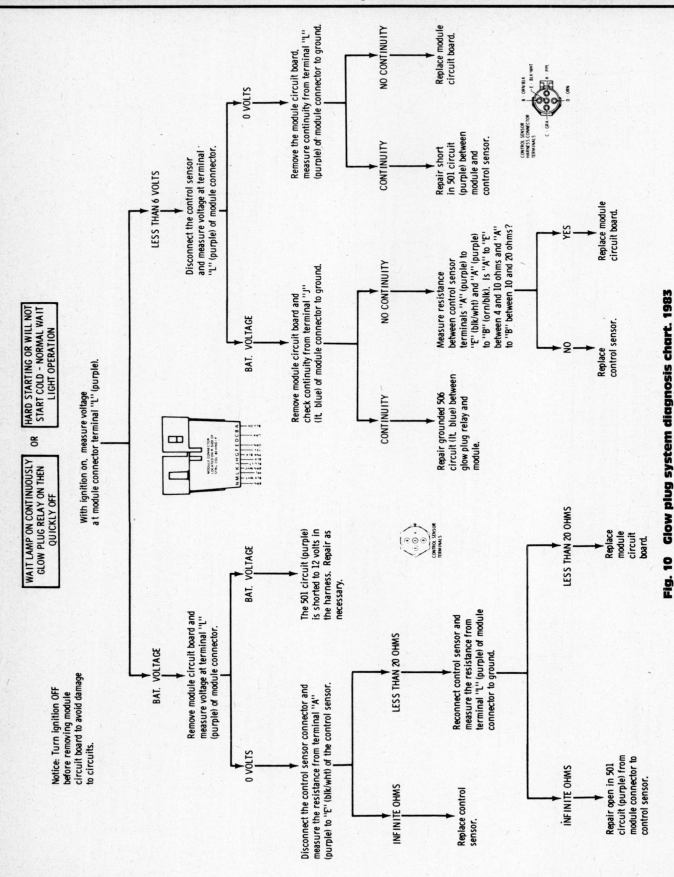

Fig. 10 Glow plug system diagnosis chart. 1983

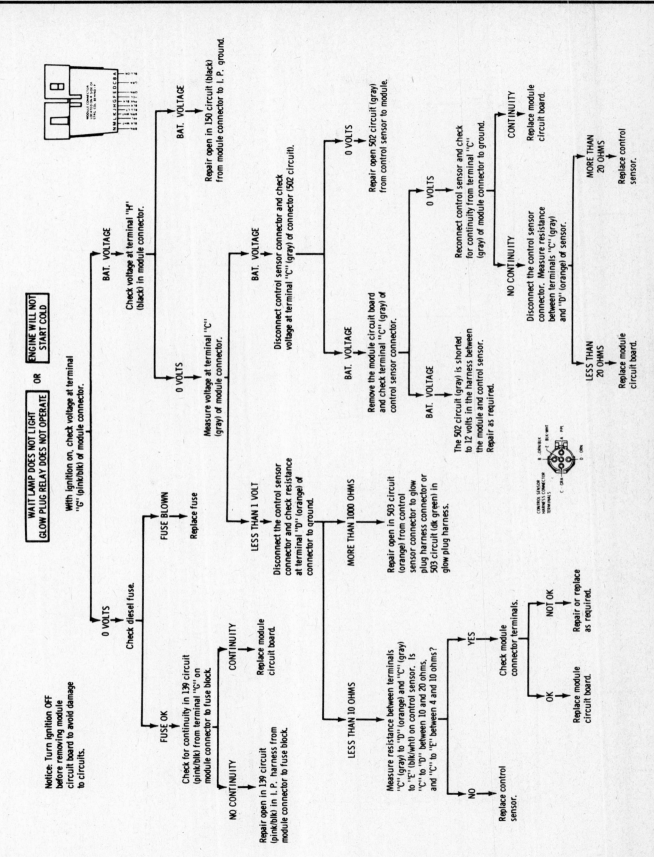

Fig. 11 Glow plug system diagnosis chart. 1983

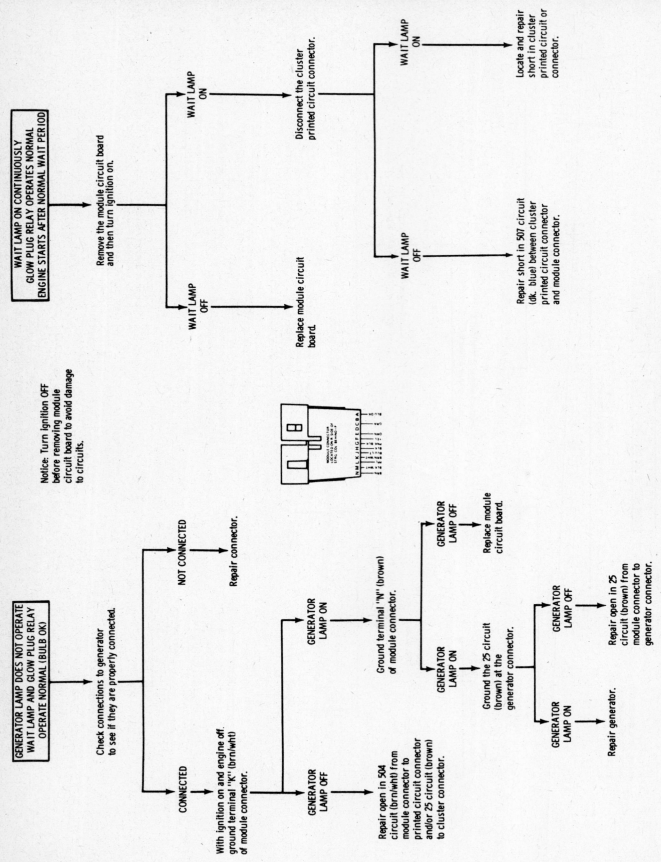

Fig. 12 Glow plug system diagnosis chart. 1983

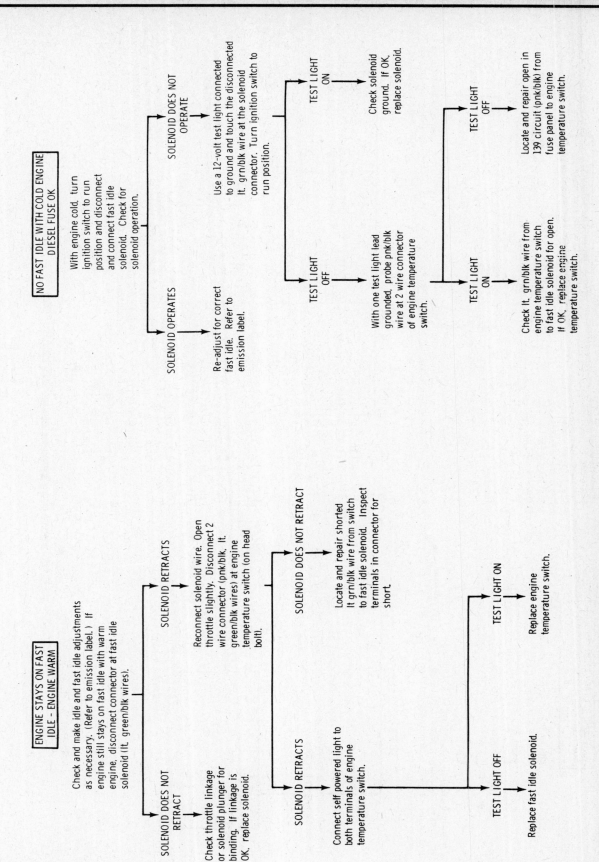

NO FAST IDLE WITH COLD ENGINE DIESEL FUSE OK

With engine cold, turn ignition switch to run position and disconnect and connect fast idle solenoid. Check for solenoid operation.

SOLENOID DOES NOT OPERATE

Use a 12-volt test light connected to ground and touch the disconnected lt. grn/blk wire at the solenoid connector. Turn ignition switch to run position.

TEST LIGHT ON

Check solenoid ground. If OK, replace solenoid.

TEST LIGHT OFF

With one test light lead grounded, probe pnk/blk wire at 2 wire connector of engine temperature switch.

TEST LIGHT OFF

Locate and repair open in 139 circuit (pnk/blk) from fuse panel to engine temperature switch.

TEST LIGHT ON

Check lt. grn/blk wire from engine temperature switch to fast idle solenoid for open. If OK, replace engine temperature switch.

SOLENOID OPERATES

Re-adjust for correct fast idle. Refer to emission label.

ENGINE STAYS ON FAST IDLE – ENGINE WARM

Check and make idle and fast idle adjustments as necessary. (Refer to emission label.) If engine still stays on fast idle with warm engine, disconnect connector at fast idle solenoid (lt. green/blk wires).

SOLENOID RETRACTS

Reconnect solenoid wire. Open throttle slightly. Disconnect 2 wire connector (pnk/blk, lt. green/blk wires) at engine temperature switch (on head bolt).

SOLENOID DOES NOT RETRACT

Locate and repair shorted lt grn/blk wire from switch to fast idle solenoid. Inspect terminals in connector for short.

SOLENOID RETRACTS

Connect self powered light to both terminals of engine temperature switch.

TEST LIGHT ON

Replace engine temperature switch.

TEST LIGHT OFF

Replace fast idle solenoid.

SOLENOID DOES NOT RETRACT

Check throttle linkage or solenoid plunger for binding. If linkage is OK, replace solenoid.

Fig. 13 Glow plug system diagnosis chart. 1983

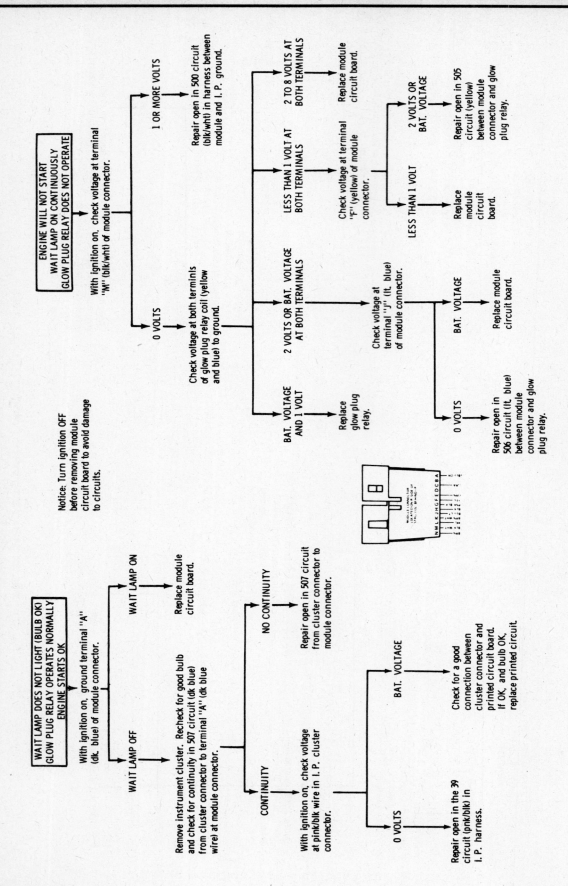

ENGINE WILL NOT START
WAIT LAMP ON CONTINUOUSLY
GLOW PLUG RELAY DOES NOT OPERATE

With ignition on, check voltage at terminal "M" (blk/wht) of module connector.

1 OR MORE VOLTS

Repair open in 500 circuit (blk/wht) in harness between module and I. P. ground.

0 VOLTS

Check voltage at both terminls of glow plug relay coil (yellow and blue) to ground.

2 TO 8 VOLTS AT BOTH TERMINALS

Replace module circuit board.

LESS THAN 1 VOLT AT BOTH TERMINALS

Check voltage at terminal "F" (yellow) of module connector.

2 VOLTS OR BAT. VOLTAGE

Repair open in 505 circuit (yellow) between module connector and glow plug relay.

LESS THAN 1 VOLT

Replace module circuit board.

2 VOLTS OR BAT. VOLTAGE AT BOTH TERMINALS

Check voltage at terminal "J" (lt. blue) of module connector.

BAT. VOLTAGE

Replace module circuit board.

0 VOLTS

Repair open in 506 circuit (lt. blue) between module connector and glow plug relay.

BAT. VOLTAGE AND 1 VOLT

Replace glow plug relay.

Notice: Turn ignition OFF before removing module circuit board to avoid damage to circuits.

WAIT LAMP DOES NOT LIGHT (BULB OK)
GLOW PLUG RELAY OPERATES NORMALLY
ENGINE STARTS OK

With ignition on, ground terminal "A" (dk. blue) of module connector.

WAIT LAMP ON

Replace module circuit board.

WAIT LAMP OFF

Remove instrument cluster. Recheck for good bulb and check for continuity in 507 circuit (dk blue) from cluster connector to terminal "A" (dk blue wire) at module connector.

NO CONTINUITY

Repair open in 507 circuit from cluster connector to module connector.

CONTINUITY

With ignition on, check voltage at pink/blk wire in I.P. cluster connector.

BAT. VOLTAGE

Check for a good connection between cluster connector and printed circuit board. If OK, and bulb OK, replace printed circuit.

0 VOLTS

Repair open in the 39 circuit (pnk/blk) in I.P. harness.

Fig. 14   Glow plug system diagnosis chart, 1983

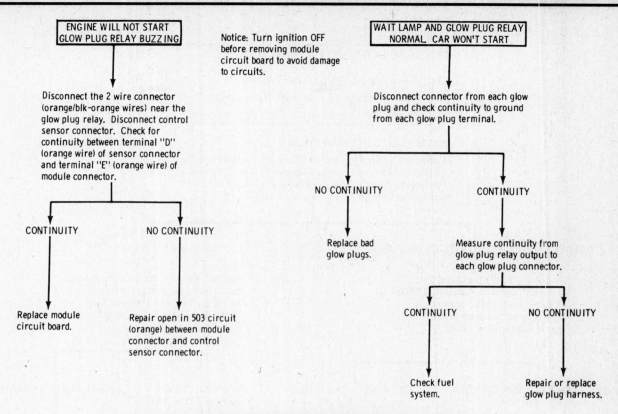

ENGINE WILL NOT START GLOW PLUG RELAY BUZZING

Notice: Turn ignition OFF before removing module circuit board to avoid damage to circuits.

WAIT LAMP AND GLOW PLUG RELAY NORMAL, CAR WON'T START

Disconnect the 2 wire connector (orange/blk-orange wires) near the glow plug relay. Disconnect control sensor connector. Check for continuity between terminal "D" (orange wire) of sensor connector and terminal "E" (orange wire) of module connector.

Disconnect connector from each glow plug and check continuity to ground from each glow plug terminal.

CONTINUITY

NO CONTINUITY

NO CONTINUITY

CONTINUITY

Replace module circuit board.

Repair open in 503 circuit (orange) between module connector and control sensor connector.

Replace bad glow plugs.

Measure continuity from glow plug relay output to each glow plug connector.

CONTINUITY

NO CONTINUITY

Check fuel system.

Repair or replace glow plug harness.

Fig. 15   Glow plug system diagnosis chart. 1983

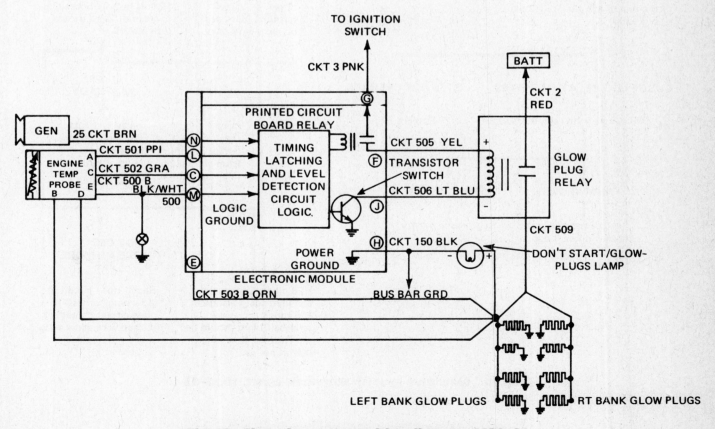

Fig. 16   Glow plug system wiring diagram. 1980—81

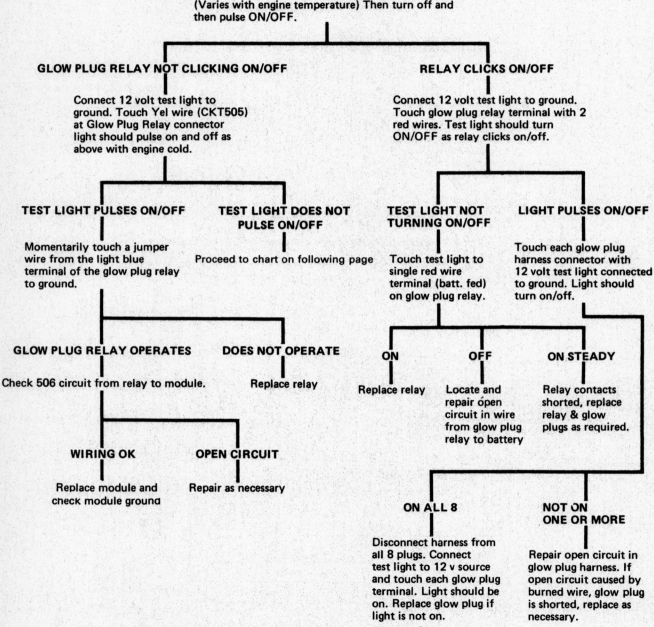

ENGINE DOES NOT START-COLD

1. Fuel system checked and is OK.
2. Battery voltage 12.4 or more (Ignition OFF)
3. Engine cranking speed OK (100 RPM or more)

WITH IGNITION SW IN "RUN"

Listen for Glow Plug Relay clicking with cold engine. Relay should come on for approximately 6 seconds. (Varies with engine temperature) Then turn off and then pulse ON/OFF.

GLOW PLUG RELAY NOT CLICKING ON/OFF

Connect 12 volt test light to ground. Touch Yel wire (CKT505) at Glow Plug Relay connector light should pulse on and off as above with engine cold.

TEST LIGHT PULSES ON/OFF

Momentarily touch a jumper wire from the light blue terminal of the glow plug relay to ground.

TEST LIGHT DOES NOT PULSE ON/OFF

Proceed to chart on following page

GLOW PLUG RELAY OPERATES

Check 506 circuit from relay to module.

DOES NOT OPERATE

Replace relay

WIRING OK

Replace module and check module ground

OPEN CIRCUIT

Repair as necessary

RELAY CLICKS ON/OFF

Connect 12 volt test light to ground. Touch glow plug relay terminal with 2 red wires. Test light should turn ON/OFF as relay clicks on/off.

TEST LIGHT NOT TURNING ON/OFF

Touch test light to single red wire terminal (batt. fed) on glow plug relay.

LIGHT PULSES ON/OFF

Touch each glow plug harness connector with 12 volt test light connected to ground. Light should turn on/off.

ON

Replace relay

OFF

Locate and repair open circuit in wire from glow plug relay to battery

ON STEADY

Relay contacts shorted, replace relay & glow plugs as required.

ON ALL 8

Disconnect harness from all 8 plugs. Connect test light to 12 v source and touch each glow plug terminal. Light should be on. Replace glow plug if light is not on.

NOT ON ONE OR MORE

Repair open circuit in glow plug harness. If open circuit caused by burned wire, glow plug is shorted, replace as necessary.

Fig. 17   Glow plug system diagnosis chart. 1980—81

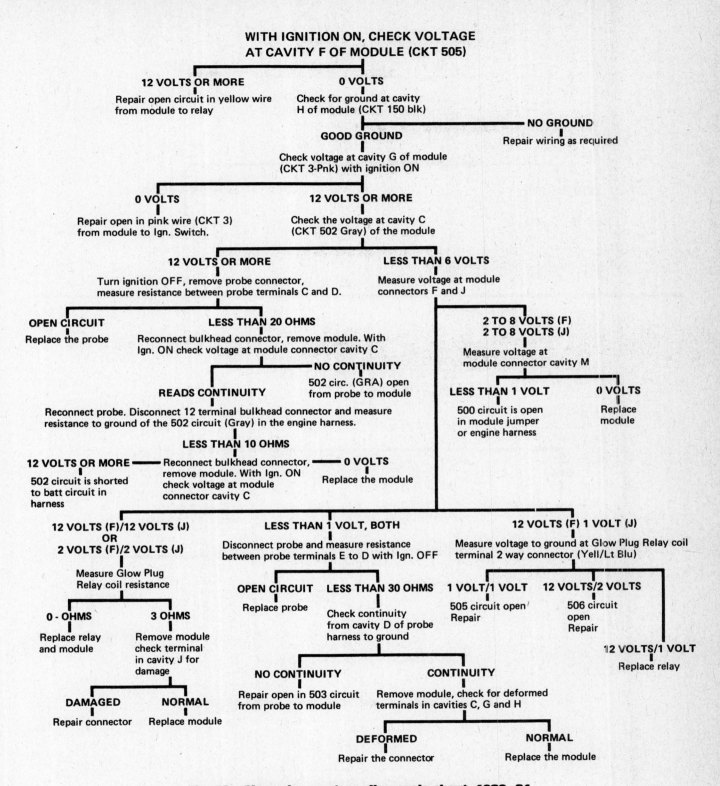

Fig. 18   Glow plug system diagnosis chart. 1980—81

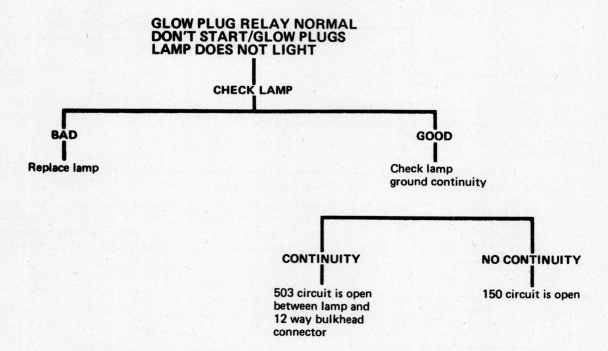

GLOW PLUG RELAY BUZZING

Disconnect the 12 way bulkhead connector. Check the continuity of the 503 circuit in the module connector to the glow plug relay.

CONTINUITY

Replace the module

NO CONTINUITY

503 circuit is open in the module jumper Repair as required

GLOW PLUG RELAY NORMAL DON'T START/GLOW PLUGS LAMP DOES NOT LIGHT

CHECK LAMP

BAD

Replace lamp

GOOD

Check lamp ground continuity

CONTINUITY

503 circuit is open between lamp and 12 way bulkhead connector

NO CONTINUITY

150 circuit is open

Fig. 19 Glow plug system diagnosis chart. 1980—81

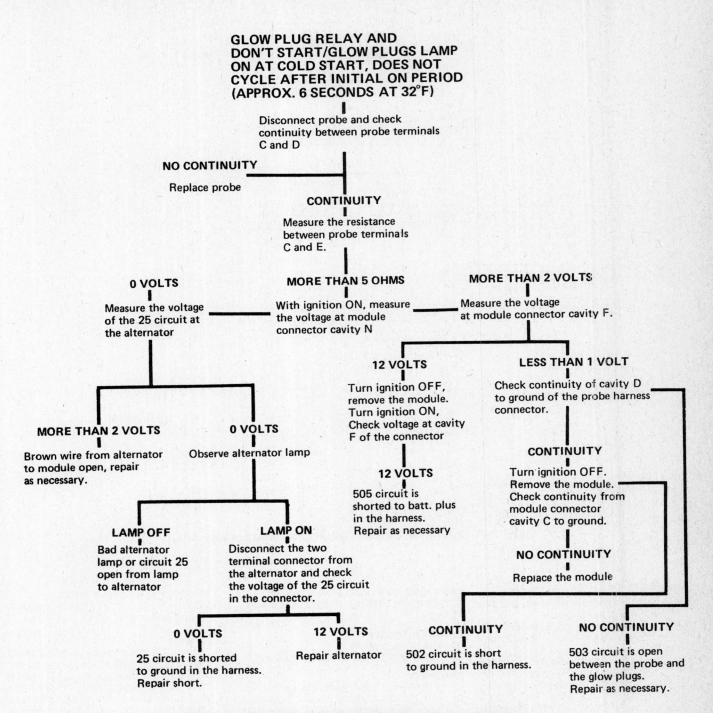

GLOW PLUG RELAY AND DON'T START/GLOW PLUGS LAMP ON AT COLD START, DOES NOT CYCLE AFTER INITIAL ON PERIOD (APPROX. 6 SECONDS AT 32°F)

Disconnect probe and check continuity between probe terminals C and D

NO CONTINUITY

Replace probe

CONTINUITY

Measure the resistance between probe terminals C and E.

0 VOLTS

Measure the voltage of the 25 circuit at the alternator

MORE THAN 5 OHMS

With ignition ON, measure the voltage at module connector cavity N

MORE THAN 2 VOLTS

Measure the voltage at module connector cavity F.

MORE THAN 2 VOLTS

Brown wire from alternator to module open, repair as necessary.

0 VOLTS

Observe alternator lamp

12 VOLTS

Turn ignition OFF, remove the module. Turn ignition ON, Check voltage at cavity F of the connector

12 VOLTS

505 circuit is shorted to batt. plus in the harness. Repair as necessary

LESS THAN 1 VOLT

Check continuity of cavity D to ground of the probe harness connector.

CONTINUITY

Turn ignition OFF. Remove the module. Check continuity from module connector cavity C to ground.

NO CONTINUITY

Replace the module

LAMP OFF

Bad alternator lamp or circuit 25 open from lamp to alternator

LAMP ON

Disconnect the two terminal connector from the alternator and check the voltage of the 25 circuit in the connector.

0 VOLTS

25 circuit is shorted to ground in the harness. Repair short.

12 VOLTS

Repair alternator

CONTINUITY

502 circuit is short to ground in the harness.

NO CONTINUITY

503 circuit is open between the probe and the glow plugs. Repair as necessary.

Fig. 20   Glow plug system diagnosis chart. 1980—81

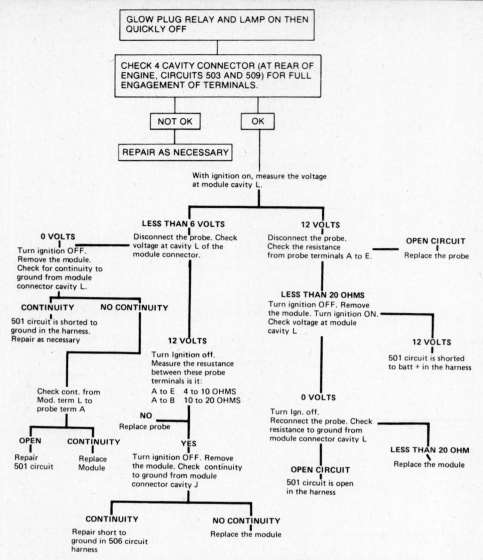

Fig. 21   Glow plug system diagnosis chart. 1980—81

and apply 12 volts to one side of solenoid and ground the other side. If defective, replace solenoid.

2. If circuit 951 is not zero volts, recheck at module. If satisfactory, repair open circuit.

3. If circuit 951 is not zero volts at module, check 3 circuit, 150 circuit, and 66 circuit at module. Repair if not as follows: 3 circuit, 12 volts; 150 circuit, zero volts; 66 circuit, 12 volts (A/C on). If satisfactory, replace module.

4. If solenoid is activated with A/C "On", but inactive with A/C off and engine cold, check 935 circuit to thermistor. If 935 circuit voltage is present (0.3–0.5 volts), check thermistor. If thermistor is satisfactory, replace module. Repair 935 circuit or thermistor for defects.

5. If 66 circuit voltage is zero volts with A/C "On", repair open circuit to A/C feed.

FAST IDLE NOT "ON" FOR 5 SEC. AFTER EACH ENGINE START WITH A/C "OFF"

Possible Causes
1. Defective module.
2. Open 906 circuit to starter solenoid.

Diagnosis
1. If solenoid does operate when tested with jumper lead, but does not operate after each start with engine hot and A/C "Off", check 906A circuit at module with ignition switch in "Crank" position. If reading is 12 volts, replace module. If no reading is obtained, repair open 906A circuit.

NO VOLTAGE AT PUMP SOLENOID WITH IGNITION "ON"

Possible Causes
1. Defective ignition switch.

2. No voltage at ignition switch.
3. Open circuit 3 from ignition switch to pump solenoid.

Diagnosis
1. Check 3A circuit voltage at solenoid. The reading should be 12 volts with ignition "On". If not, check 3C circuit at left bank glow plug relay. If satisfactory, repair fault in 3A circuit from bulkhead connector to solenoid. If not satisfactory at relay also, check instrument cluster gauges or tell-tale lamps for proper operation. If satisfactory, repair open circuit in 3 circuit from ignition switch to bulkhead connector.

2. If instrument cluster is not satisfactory, check headlamps, and if satisfactory, repair open circuit in 3 circuit from starter to ignition switch or replace ignition switch, if circuit 2 is satisfacto-

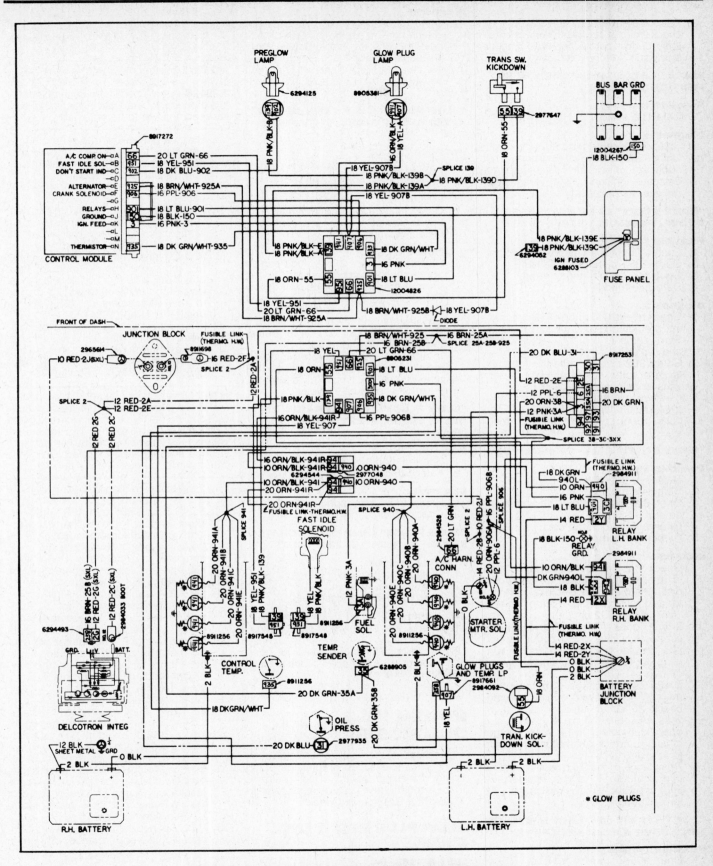

Fig. 22   Glow plug system wiring diagram. 1979

ry.

3. If circuit 2 and ignition are satisfactory, check 2 circuit at relays. If not satisfactory, check connections at junction block and battery voltage.

VOLTAGE AT PUMP SOLENOID WITH IGNITION "OFF"

Possible Causes
1. Defective switch.

Diagnosis
1. Check voltage at pump 3A circuit with ignition switch "Off". If zero volts is not obtained, check for maladjusted or defective ignition switch. Readjust or replace, as necessary.

"DON'T START" LAMP NOT "ON" DURING PREGLOW, RELAYS "ON"

Possible Causes
1. Faulty "Don't Start" lamp.
2. Open 139A circuit feed to lamp.
3. Open 902 circuit feed to lamp.
4. Defective module.

Diagnosis
1. Check relays 940 and 941 circuits during preglow. If satisfactory but "Don't Start" lamp is not "On", check bulb and replace if necessary.
2. Check 902 circuit at module, if reading is zero volts, check at bulb. If zero volts at bulb, repair open circuit.
3. If relays are satisfactory during preglow and 902 circuit voltage is not zero volts during preglow, replace module.

"DON'T START" LAMP REMAINS "ON"

Possible Causes
1. Defective 902 circuit.
2. Defective module.
3. Open 925 circuit to module from alternator.
4. Open alternator lamp circuit.
5. Defective alternator.

Diagnosis
1. Check 902 circuit voltage during start of afterglow. If reading is zero volts, disconnect module electrical connector and recheck bulb. If lamp remains "On", repair 902 circuit.
2. If lamp goes "Out" with module disconnected, check 25 circuit during afterglow at module with engine running. If 14 volts are obtained, replace module.
3. If 925 circuit voltage is not approximately 14 volts with engine running, check 25 circuit at alternator. If 14 volts are obtained, repair 925 circuit open to module. If 14 volts are not obtained, check alternator lamp bulb for correct type.
4. Resistance of the 25 circuit should be approximately 10 ohms between the alternator and ignition switch with the ignition switch "Off".

"DON'T START" LAMP NOT RECYCLED "ON" AFTER A NO START CRANK

Possible Causes
1. Open 906A circuit to module.
2. Defective module.

Diagnosis
1. Check 906A circuit voltage at module when cranking engine. Voltage should be 8–12 volts. If voltage is within specifications, replace module. If zero volts are obtained, repair open 906A circuit between starter solenoid and module.

"GLOW PLUGS" LAMP REMAINS "ON" AFTER ENGINE START, GLOW PLUGS "ON"

Possible Causes
1. Faulty 907 circuit to "Glow Plugs" lamp.
2. Shorted glow plug temperature switch.
3. Glow plug temperature switch improperly calibrated.
4. Defective alternator.

Diagnosis
1. Disconnect the "Glow plugs-engine temperature switch", located at the front of the intake manifold. If "Glow Plugs" lamp goes "Out", with glow plugs still "On" in normal afterglow period, replace temperature switch. If lamp remains "On", check for defective 907 circuit and repair.
2. If lamp remains "On" with no defect indicated in the 907 circuit, check voltage of the 25 circuit at alternator. Reading should be 14 volts.

"GLOW PLUGS" LAMP REMAINS "ON" AFTER ENGINE START, GLOW PLUGS "OFF"

Possible Causes
1. Shorted diode.
2. Faulty 25 circuit.

Diagnosis
1. Replace diode in module harness.
2. Check 25 circuit for defect.

"GLOW PLUGS" LAMP "OFF" IGNITION SWITCH IN "RUN", ENGINE "OFF"

Possible Causes
1. Glow plugs not "On".
2. Faulty diode.
3. Defective "Glow Plugs" bulb.

Diagnosis
1. Check for defective "Glow Plugs" bulb.
2. If bulb is satisfactory, check for open diode or open 907 or 25 circuit to alternator.

ROUGH IDLE DIAGNOSIS

Check for mechanical malfunctions such as incorrect idle speed or injection pump timing, or leaking nozzles or high pressure lines. If rough idle is still evident, refer to "Glow Plug Resistance Check".

GLOW PLUG RESISTANCE CHECK

1981 & 1983–84
1. Using multi-meter J-29125 (1981 and 1983) or J-29125A (1984), set left selector switch to "OHMS", right selector switch to 200 ohms and center slide switch to "D.C. LO".

NOTE: If another ohmmeter is used, different values will result. Tools J-29125 and J-29125A were used in the development of this procedure. Their use is required if similar readings are to be obtained.

2. Start engine, allow it to reach normal operating temperature, then disconnect all feed wires from glow plugs. Turn heater to "On" position.
3. Disconnect alternator two wire connector.
4. Using tachometer J-26925, or equivalent, adjust idle speed screw to obtain worst engine idle roughness condition. Do not exceed 900 RPM.
5. Allow engine to run at worst idle speed for approximately one minute, then attach an alligator clip to black test lead of meter. Ground black test lead to fast idle solenoid (1983–84) or engine lift strap (1981).
6. Write down the engine firing order on a piece of paper, then with engine idling, probe each glow plug terminal and record the resistance values on each cylinder in the firing sequence.

NOTE: If vehicle is equipped with an electric cooling fan, record resistance values with cooling fan inoperative. Do not disconnect cooling fan circuitry. The resistance values are dependent on the temperature in each cylinder, and therefore, can indicate cylinder output.

7. If a resistance reading on any cylinder is 1.3–1.4 ohms for 1984 vehicles, or 1.2–1.3 for 1981 and 1983 vehicles, check engine for a mechanical problem. Make a compression check of the lowest reading cylinder and the cylinders which fire before and after. Correct cause of low compression before proceeding to fuel system.
8. On 1984 vehicles, install glow plug luminosity probe, from tool J-33075, into cylinder with lowest resistance value. Observe combustion light flashes of probe. The flashes will usually be erratic and in sequence with the misfire. If not, move to the next lowest reading cylinder, until the misfire is found.
9. On all vehicles, observe the results of all glow plug resistance readings, looking for differences between cylinders. Rough engines will normally have a difference of .4 ohms or more between cylinders in the firing sequence. To correct rough engine idle, it will be ncessary to raise or lower the resistance values on one or more of the offending cylinders by replacing the injection nozzles.
10. Remove nozzle from the cylinder(s) affecting idle performance. Determine the pop off pressure of the nozzle and check the nozzle for leakage and spray pattern. Refer to tool manufac-

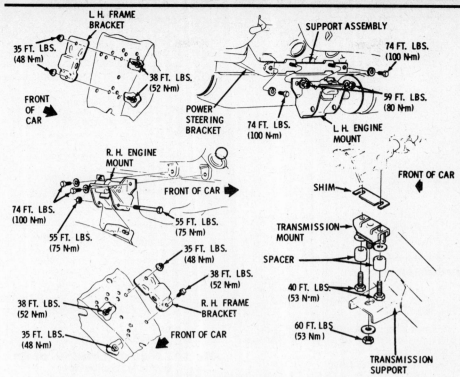

Fig. 23 Engine & transmission mount replacement (Typical). V8-350 diesel engine

turer for proper testing procedures. Install nozzles with higher pop off pressures to lower resistance values, and nozzles with lower pop off pressures to raise values. A change of 30 psi nozzle pressure will result in a .1 ohm difference in resistance. Use new nozzles on new vehicles and broken in nozzles on vehicles with 1500 or more miles, if possible.

NOTE: Whenever a nozzle is cleaned or replaced, crank the engine and watch for air bubbles at the nozzle inlet before connecting the injection pipe. If bubbles are evident, clean or replace the nozzle.

11. Connect injection pipe, restart engine and check idle quality. If idle quality is still not acceptable, repeat steps 6 through 10.
12. After making additional nozzle changes, check idle quality again.
13. If problem moves from cylinder to cylinder and resistance values do not change as nozzles are changed, the injection pump may be defective.

NOTE: Always recheck cylinder at same engine RPM. Sometimes cylinder readings may not indicate that an improvement has been made, even though the engine may idle better. A nozzle with a tip leak can allow more fuel than required into a cylinder, raising the glow plug resistance value. This will steal fuel from the next nozzle in the firing order and will result in that glow plug having a lower resistance value. If this is evident, remove and check the nozzle with the high reading. If it is leaking, it may be responsible for the rough idle. If low readings are evident on a glow plug and it does not change with a nozzle change, switch glow plugs between the good and bad cylinder. If the reading of each cylinder is not the same as before the switch, then the glow plug cannot be used for rough idle diagnosis.

WATER IN FUEL SYSTEM DIAGNOSIS

WATER IN FUEL LAMP DOES NOT GO ON

If the likelihood of water in the fuel tank exists and the Water In Fuel lamp is off, siphon the fuel tank to check for water by connecting a pump to the fuel return line. If at least 3 gallons of water are siphoned from the tank, proceed as follows:

1. Disconnect Water In Fuel electrical lead at fuel tank and ground the lead. If lamp does not go on, proceed to step 4. If it does, check for at least 8 volts at the electrical lead. If no voltage is present, replace the Water In Tank light bulb.
2. Ground the Water In Tank electrical lead. If lamp does not go on, check for open circuit in wiring.
3. Remove fuel level sender and Water in Fuel detector unit from fuel tank.
4. Check connections to "Water In Fuel". If satisfactory, check detector unit as follows:
   a. Remove detector from fuel sender unit.
   b. Connect the detector to a bulb and power source. The lamp should go on when the detector probe is lowered into the container of water ⅜ inch or less. Make sure water is grounded to negative side of battery.

WATER IN FUEL LAMP STAYS ON

Under this condition, siphon the tank to check for water by connecting a pump to the fuel line. If no water is present, proceed as follows:

1. Disconnect the Water In Fuel electrical lead near the fuel tank. If lamp does not go off, proceed to step 2. If lamp goes off, remove fuel level sender and check detector as described previously under "Water In Fuel Lamp Does Not Go On".
2. Check for short circuit in wire between the "Water In Fuel" connection at the fuel tank and the dash indicator lamp.

ENGINE MOUNTS
REPLACE

1. Raise and support vehicle.
2. Support engine, then remove engine mount through bolts.
3. Raise engine slightly, then remove engine mount attaching bolts as shown, **Fig. 23.**
4. Reverse procedure to install, torquing bolts to specifications.

ENGINE
REPLACE

1. Disconnect ground cable from batteries and drain cooling system.
2. Remove air cleaner.
3. Scribe hood hinge locations and remove hood.
4. Disconnect ground wires at inner fender and the engine ground strap at right cylinder head.
5. Disconnect radiator hoses, oil cooler lines, heater hoses, vacuum hoses, power steering hoses from gear, A/C attached, fuel pump hose from fuel pump and the wiring.
6. Remove hairpin clip from bellcrank.
7. Remove throttle and throttle valve cables from intake manifold brackets and position cables aside.
8. Remove upper radiator support and the radiator.
9. Raise and support vehicle.
10. Disconnect exhaust pipes from exhaust manifold.
11. Remove torque converter cover and the three bolts securing torque converter to flywheel.
12. Remove engine mount bolts or nuts.
13. Remove three engine to transmission bolts on the right side.
14. Disconnect starter wiring and remove starter.
15. Lower vehicle.

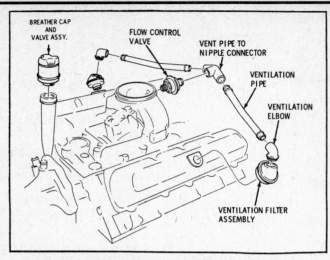

Fig. 24   Crankcase ventilation system

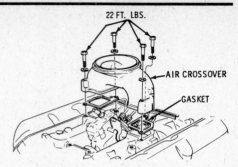

Fig. 25   Air crossover installation

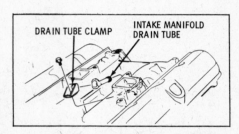

Fig. 27   Intake manifold drain tube installation

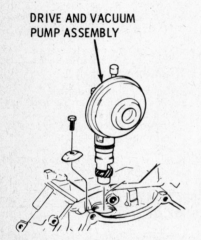

Fig. 26   Vacuum pump & oil pump drive assembly

16. Attach suitable engine lifting equipment to engine. Support transmission with a suitable jack.
17. Remove the three engine to transmission bolts on the left side.
18. Remove engine from vehicle.
19. Reverse procedure to install.

EXHAUST MANIFOLD
REPLACE

LEFT SIDE

1. Remove air cleaner and cover carburetor.
2. Remove lower generator bracket.
3. Raise and support vehicle.
4. Remove crossover or exhaust pipe.
5. Lower vehicle, then remove exhaust manifold from above.
6. Reverse procedure to install, torquing bolts to 25 ft. lbs.

RIGHT SIDE

1. Raise and support vehicle.
2. Remove crossover pipe and/or exhaust pipe as necessary.
3. On 1983–84 vehicles, remove right front wheel.
4. Remove exhaust manifold.
5. Reverse procedure to install, torquing attaching bolts to 25 ft. lbs.

INTAKE MANIFOLD
REPLACE

1. Disconnect ground cables from batteries.
2. Remove air cleaner assembly.
3. Drain cooling system, then disconnect upper radiator hose and thermostat bypass hose from water pump outlet. Disconnect heater hose and vacuum hose from water control valve.
4. Remove breather pipes from valve covers and air crossover, **Fig. 24.**
5. Remove air crossover and cap intake manifold, **Fig. 25.**
6. Disconnect throttle rod and return spring. If equipped with Cruise Control, remove servo.
7. Remove hairpin clip from bellcrank and disconnect the cables. Remove throttle and throttle valve cables from intake manifold brackets and position cables aside.
8. Disconnect wiring as necessary.
9. Disconnect or remove alternator and A/C compressor as necessary.
10. Disconnect fuel line from fuel pump and filter and remove fuel filter and bracket.
11. Disconnect lines from injector nozzles and remove injection pump. Cap all open fuel lines and fittings.
12. Disconnect vacuum lines at vacuum pump. Remove vacuum pump, if equipped with A/C, or oil pump drive assembly, if less A/C, **Fig. 26.**
14. Remove intake manifold drain tube, **Fig. 27.**

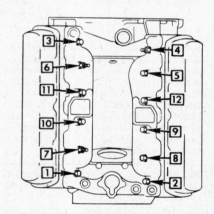

Fig. 28   Intake manifold tightening sequence

15. Remove intake manifold bolts and the intake manifold.
16. Remove adapter seal and injection pump adapter.
17. Reverse procedure to install. Torque intake manifold bolts in sequence, **Fig. 28,** to specifications.

CYLINDER HEAD
REPLACE

NOTE: If a cylinder head is being removed to correct a head gasket problem on these engines, a few checks should be made to ensure the cause of the condition is corrected. The checks are as follows:

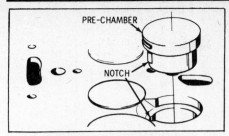

Fig. 29   Pre-chamber installation

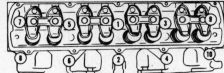

Fig. 30   Cylinder head tightening sequence

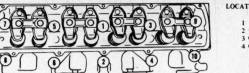

LOCATION NUMBER	PART NUMBER	SIZE
1	22510580	1/2 - 13 x 3.10
2	22510582	1/2-13 x 3.10 stud end
3	22510579	1/2 - 13 x 4.30
4	22510585	1/2 - 13 x 4.30 stud end

Fig. 31   Cylinder head bolt identification

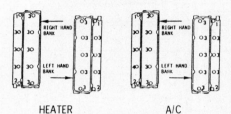

HEATER   A/C

Fig. 32   Cylinder head bolt locations

a. Cylinder head warpage. If any cylinder head is warped more than .010 inch, it should be replaced. Resurfacing is not recommended.

b. Cylinder head to cylinder block dowel pin interference. With the head properly positioned on the block, without the head gasket installed, run a .005 inch feeler gauge around the perimeter of the area where the head and block meet. There should be zero clearance, thus ensuring the head is flush with the block and no dowel pin interference exists.

c. Prechamber location. The cylinder head prechambers must not be recessed into the cylinder head or protrude out of the cylinder head by more than .004 inch as this will affect head gasket sealing.

d. Head gasket sealing bead. Ensure the head gasket sealing bead goes around all core holes in the block and head. If the sealing bead crosses a raised, depressed or stamped area, the raised area should be filed and the depressed or stamped area filled with RTV sealer and assembled before the RTV sealer cures.

e. Cylinder head cracks. Minor surface cracks in the cylinder head valve port area between the intake and exhaust ports are considered a normal condition and does not warrant replacement of the heads.

1. Remove intake manifold as outlined previously.
2. Remove valve cover. It may be necessary to remove any interfering accessory brackets.
3. Disconnect glow plug wiring.
4. If right side head is to be removed, remove ground strap from head.
5. Remove rocker arm bolts, pivots, rocker arms and push rod. Note locations of valve train components so they can be installed in original loca-

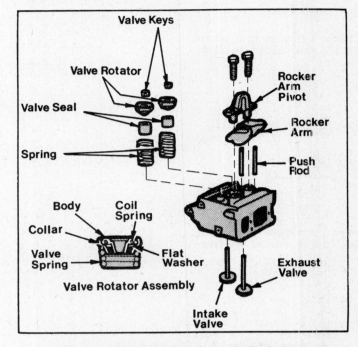

Fig. 33   Cylinder head exploded view

tions.
6. Remove fuel return lines from injection nozzles.
7. Remove exhaust manifold.
8. Remove engine block drain plug on side of block that cylinder head is being removed.
9. Remove cylinder head bolts, then cylinder head.
10. If necessary to remove pre-chamber, remove glow plug and injection nozzle, then tap out pre-chamber with a suitable drift, **Fig. 29.**
11. Reverse procedure to install. Do not use any sealing compound on cylinder head gasket. Torque cylinder head bolts in sequence, **Fig. 30,** to 100 ft. lbs., then 130 ft. lbs.

SERVICE BULLETIN New head bolts with increased torque capacity were introduced into production during March 1980 and are now available, **Fig. 31.**

When replacing a cylinder head, it is recommended new head bolts be used if they have not already been installed in the engine. When installing later production model head bolts, be sure to clean and oil the threads. Before installation of the cylinder head ensure bolt holes are tapped deep enough into the block. Blow out any chips or liquid in the bolt holes. Then position cylinder head on cylinder block without

the cylinder head gasket. Install bolt and tighten by hand until bolt head contacts the cylinder head. This will indicate that the holes are tapped deep enough into the block, allowing for proper torque. For cylinder head bolt location, refer to **Fig. 32.**

A new designed head gasket went into production in March 1981, and is available for service replacement. It can be identified by the use of blue print O sealer instead of orange. This gasket is of the slotted and shim design.

No sealer should be used on the gasket during installation. Also the prechamber shield on the cylinder head gasket must be installed towards the cylinder head.

ROCKER ARMS

NOTE: This engine uses valve rotators, **Fig. 33.** The rotator operates on a sprag clutch principle utilizing the collapsing action of a coil spring to give rotation to the rotor body which turns the valve.

SERVICE BULLETIN Some 1979–83 V8-350 diesel engines may experience valve train ticking noise and/or exhaust backfire. This condition may be caused by premature wear of the rocker arm pivots. Two types of rocker arm pivots were used on these engines. Type 1 pivot assem-

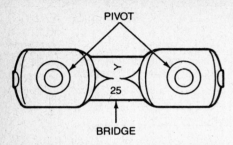

Fig. 34   Type 1 rocker arm pivot. 1979—83 V8-350 diesel engine

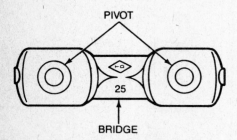

Fig. 35   Type 2 rocker arm pivot. 1979—83 V8-350 diesel engine

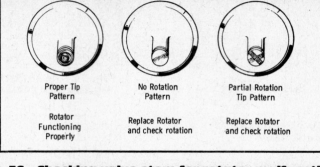

Fig. 36   Checking valve stem for rotator malfunction

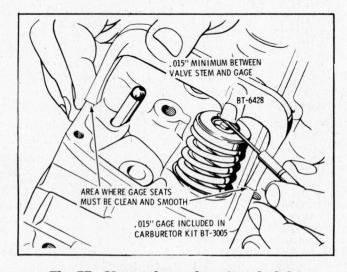

Fig. 37   Measuring valve stem height

blies, **Fig. 34,** are the only ones showing premature wear. It is therefore recommended that only Type 2 pivot assemblies, **Fig. 35,** be used when servicing the engine for the above mentioned condition.

1. Remove valve cover.
2. Remove flanged bolts, rocker arm pivot and rocker arms, **Fig. 33.**
3. When installing rocker arm assemblies, lubricate wear surfaces with suitable lubricant. Torque flanged bolts to 25 ft. lbs. on 1979—80 models and 28 ft. lbs on 1981 and 1983—84 models.

VALVE ROTATORS

The rotator operates on a Sprag clutch principle utilizing the collapsing action of coil spring to give rotation to the rotor body which turns the valve, **Fig. 33.**

To check rotator action, draw a line across rotator body and down the collar. Operate engine at 1500 rpm. Rotator body should move around collar. Rotator action can be in either direction. Replace rotator if no movement is noted.

When servicing valves, valve stem tips should be checked for improper wear pattern which could indicate a defective valve rotator, **Fig. 36.**

VALVE ARRANGEMENT

V8-350 Diesel . . . . I-E-I-E-I-E-I

VALVE LIFT SPECS.

Engine	Year	Intake	Exhaust
V8-350 Diesel	1979—84	.375	.376

VALVE TIMING
INTAKE OPENS BEFORE TDC

Engine	Year	Degrees
V8-350 Diesel	1979—84	16

VALVES
REPLACE

Whenever a new valve is installed or after grinding valves, it is necessary to measure the valve stem height with the special tool as shown in **Fig. 37.**

There should be at least .015 inch clearance between the gauge and end of valve stem. If clearance is less than .015 inch, remove valve and grind end of valve stem as required.

Check valve rotator height, **Fig. 38.** If valve stem end is less than .005 inch above rotator, the valve is too short and a new valve must be installed.

VALVE GUIDES

Valve stem guides are not replaceable, due to being cast in place. If valve guide bores are worn excessively, they can be reamed oversize.

If a standard valve guide bore is being reamed, use a .003" or .005" oversize reamer. For the .010" oversize valve guide bore, use a .013" oversize reamer. If too large a reamer is used and the spiraling is removed, it is possible that the valve will not receive the proper lubrication.

NOTE: Occasionally a valve guide will be oversize as manufactured. These are marked on the cylinder head as shown in **Fig. 39.** If no markings are present, the guide bores are standard. If oversize markings are present, any valve replacement will require an oversize valve. Service valves are available in standard diameters as well as .003", .005", .010" and .013" oversize.

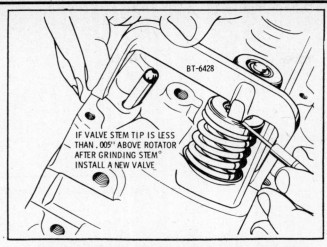

Fig. 38   Measuring valve rotator height

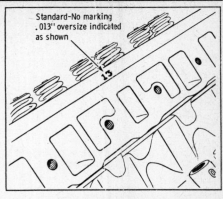

Fig. 39   Valve guide bore marking

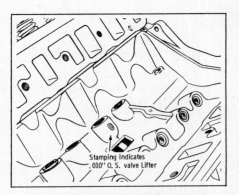

Fig. 40   Oversize valve lifter bore marking

VALVE LIFTERS
REPLACE

NOTE: Some engines have both standard and .010 inch oversize valve lifters. The .010 inch oversize valve lifters are etched with a "0" on the side of the lifter. Also, the cylinder block will be marked if an oversize lifter is used, **Fig. 40.**

NOTE: 1981 and 1983–84 engines are equipped with roller lifters. These are the same internally as in the past. However, the lifter can not be "leak down" tested at this time as a tester adapter is not available. On this type lifter, a guide holds the lifters from rotating, **Fig. 41.** A spring steel retainer holds the guide in place.

1. Remove intake manifold as outlined previously.
2. Remove valve covers, rocker arm assemblies and push rods. On 1981 and 1983–84 models, remove the lifter retainer and lifter guides. Note location of valve train components so they can be installed in original position.
3. Remove valve lifters.
4. Reverse procedure to install.

VALVE LIFTERS
SERVICE

1. Remove valve lifters, refer to "Valve lifters, Replace".
2. Using a small screwdriver, remove retainer ring, **Figs. 42 and 43.**
3. Remove pushrod seat, oil metering valve, plunger and plunger spring.
4. Remove check ball retainer from plunger, then remove ball and spring.
5. Clean parts in a suitable solvent.

NOTE: Do not interchange parts between lifters. If any parts are worn, replace lifter.

6. Inspect all parts for nicks, burrs or scoring. If any parts are defective, replace lifter.
7. On 1981 and 1983–84 roller lifters, inspect roller. It should rotate freely, but without excessive play, also check for missing or broken needle bearing. If any parts are defective, replace lifter.
8. Apply a coating of light engine oil to all lifter surfaces.
9. Install ball check spring and retainer into plunger. Ensure retainer flange is pressed tight against bottom of recess in plunger.
10. Install plunger spring over check retainer.
11. Hold plunger with spring up and insert in lifter body. Hold plunger vertically to prevent cocking spring.
12. Submerge lifter assembly in clean diesel fuel or kerosene, then install oil metering valve and push rod seat into lifter and install retaining ring.

VALVE LIFTER BLEED DOWN

If the intake manifold has been removed and if any rocker arms have been removed or loosened, it will be necessary to remove those lifters, disassemble them, drain the oil from them and reassemble. Refer to "Valve Lifters, Service".

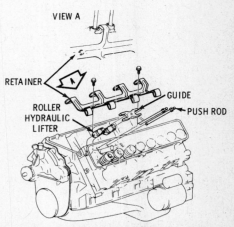

Fig. 41   Valve lifters & guide. 1981 & 1983–84

If the intake manifold has not been removed, but rocker arms have been loosened or removed, the valve lifters must be bled down to prevent possible valve to piston interference by using the following procedure;

1. Prior to installing rocker arms, rotate crankshaft pulley to a position 32° BTDC (before top dead center). This is approximately 2 inches counterclockwise from 0° pointer.
2. If the right side valve cover was removed only, remove cylinder No. 1 glow plug and determine if No. 1 piston is in the correct position. This can be determined by compression pressure.
3. If the left side valve cover was removed only, rotate crankshaft until No. 5 cylinder intake valve push rod is .28 inch above the No. 5 cylinder exhaust valve push rod.
4. If removed, install cylinder No. 5 pivot and rocker arms. Alternately torque the bolts until the intake valve begins to open and stop tightening.

NOTE: When torquing rocker arms, use only hand wrenches to prevent engine damage.

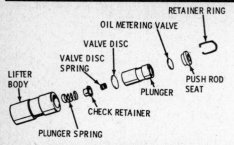

Fig. 42   Valve lifter exploded view. 1979—80

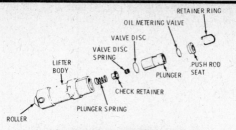

Fig. 43   Valve lifter exploded view. 1981 & 1983—84

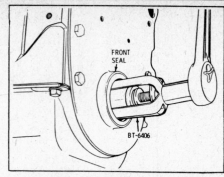

Fig. 44   Front oil seal removal

Fig. 45   Modifying tool for front seal installation

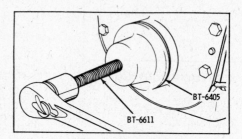

Fig. 46   Front oil seal installation

Fig. 47   Dowel pin chamfer

5. Install remaining rocker arms except No. 3 exhaust valve. Torque bolt to 25 ft. lbs. on 1979—80 models and 28 ft. lbs on 1981 and 1983—84 models.
6. If removed, install No. 3 exhaust rocker arm and pivot, but do not torque beyond the point that the valve would be fully opened. This is indicated by a strong resistance while turning the pivot retaining bolt. Going beyond this point would bend the push rod.

NOTE: While performing step 6, torque bolt slowly allowing the lifter to bleed down.

7. Finish torquing No. 5 rocker arm pivot bolt slowly, allowing valve lifter to bleed down. Do not torque beyond the point that the valve would be fully opened. This is indicated by a strong resistance while turning the pivot retaining bolt. Going beyond this point would bend the push rod.
8. Do not turn the crankshaft for at least 45 minutes while lifters bleed down.

NOTE: Do not rotate the engine until the valve lifters have bled down, otherwise engine damage might occur.

FRONT OIL SEAL
REPLACE

1. Disconnect ground cables from batteries.

ENGINE FRONT COVER
REPLACE

1. Disconnect ground cables from batteries.
2. Drain cooling system and disconnect radiator hoses and bypass hose.
3. Remove all drive belts, fan and pulley, crankshaft pulley and harmonic balancer, and accessory brackets.
4. Remove front cover to block attaching bolts, then remove front cover, timing indicator and water pump assembly.
5. Remove front cover alignment dowel pins. It may be necessary to grind a flat on the dowel pins to provide a rough surface for gripping.
6. Grind a chamfer on one end of each dowel pin, **Fig. 47.**
7. Cut excess material from front end of oil pan gasket on each side of cylinder block.
8. Trim approximately ⅛ inch from each end of new front pan seal, **Fig. 48.**

2. Remove accessory drive belts.
3. Remove crankshaft pulley and harmonic balancer.
4. Using tool BT-6406, remove front oil seal, **Fig. 44.**
5. Apply suitable sealer to outside diameter of new oil seal.
6. File .020 inch from flange of tool No. BT-6405 **Fig. 45,** to prevent tool from contacting oil slinger before seal is properly seated in front cover.
7. Using tool BT-6611 and BT-6405, install new oil seal, **Fig. 46.**
8. Install harmonic balancer and crankshaft pulley.
9. Install and tension accessory drive belts.

9. Install new front cover gasket and apply suitable sealer to gasket around coolant holes.
10. Apply RTV sealer to mating surfaces of cylinder block, oil pan and front cover.
11. Place front cover on cylinder block and press downward to compress seal. Rotate cover right and left and guide oil pan seal into cavity with a small screwdriver.
12. Apply engine oil to bolts.
13. Install two bolts finger tight to retain cover.
14. Install the two dowel pins, chamfered end first.
15. Install timing indicator and water pump and torque bolts as shown in **Fig. 49.**
16. Install harmonic balancer and crankshaft pulley.
17. Install accessory brackets.
18. Install fan and pulley and drive belts.
19. Connect radiator hoses and bypass hose.
20. Connect ground cables to batteries.

TIMING CHAIN & GEARS
REPLACE

1. Remove front cover as outlined previously.
2. Remove oil slinger, cam gear, crank gear and timing chain.
3. Remove fuel pump eccentric from crankshaft, if necessary.
4. Install key in crankshaft, if removed.
5. Install fuel pump eccentric, if removed.
6. Install cam gear, crank gear and timing chain with timing marks aligned, **Fig. 50.**

NOTE: With the timing marks aligned in **Fig. 50,** No. 6 cylinder is in the firing posi-

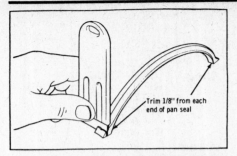

Fig. 48 Trimming oil pan seal

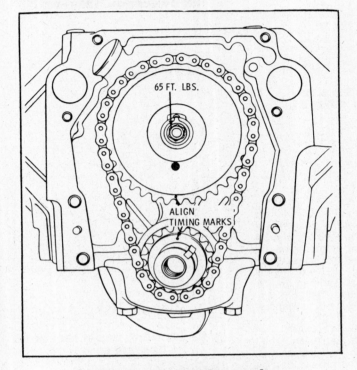

Fig. 50 Valve timing marks

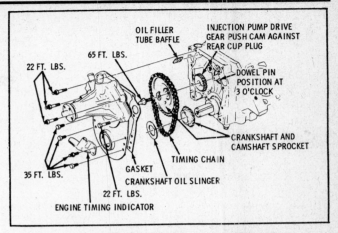

Fig. 49 Engine front cover installation

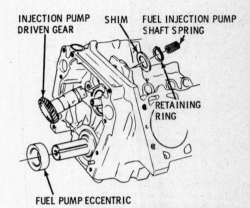

Fig. 51 Fuel injection pump driven gear installation

tion. To place No. 1 cylinder in the firing position, rotate crankshaft one complete revolution. This will bring the camshaft gear mark to top and No. 1 cylinder will be in the firing position.

7. Install oil slinger.
8. Install front cover.

NOTE: Whenever timing chain and gears are replaced, it will be necessary to retime the engine. Refer to "Injection Pump Timing" procedure.

CAMSHAFT & INJECTION PUMP DRIVE & DRIVEN GEARS

1. Disconnect ground cables from batteries.
2. Drain cooling system.
3. Remove radiator upper baffle.
4. Disconnect upper radiator hose at water outlet and hose support clamp.
5. Disconnect cooler lines at radiator.
6. Remove fan shroud and radiator.
7. Remove intake manifold as outlined previously.
8. Remove engine front cover as outlined previously.
9. Remove valve covers.
10. Remove rocker arm bolts, pivots, rocker arms and push rod. Note valve train component locations to install components in original locations.
11. If equipped with A/C, discharge refrigerant system and remove condenser.
12. On all models, remove timing chain and gears as outlined previously.
13. Position camshaft dowel pin at 3 o'clock position.
14. While holding the camshaft rearward and rocking the injection pump driven gear slide, slide the injection pump drive gear from camshaft.
15. Remove injection pump adapter, snap

ring, selective washer, injection pump driven gear and spring, **Fig. 51.**
16. Slide camshaft from front of engine.
17. Reverse procedure to install. Check injection pump driven gear end play. If end play is not .002–.006 inch, replace selective washer, **Fig. 51.** Selective washers are available from .080 to .115 inch in increments of .003 inch.

PISTON & ROD ASSEMBLE

1983–84

Install piston and rod assembly so that notch at top of piston is facing toward front of engine, **Fig. 52.**

1979–81

Assemble piston to rod and install into cylinder block. The piston is installed with the valve depression facing toward the crankshaft. Also, there are two different pistons used in this engine. In cylinder numbers 1, 2, 3 and 4, the large valve depression faces the front of the engine, **Fig. 53.** In cylinder numbers 5, 6, 7 and 8 the large valve depression faces the rear of

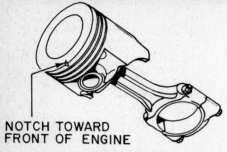

NOTCH TOWARD
FRONT OF ENGINE

**Fig. 52 Piston & rod
installation. 1983—84**

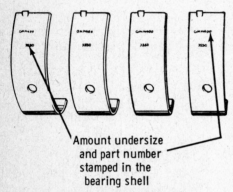

Amount undersize
and part number
stamped in the
bearing shell

**Fig. 55 Main bearing
identification. 1979—81**

LARGE VALVE DEPRESSION FACES FRONT
OF ENGINE ON #2 & #4, REAR ON
#5 & #7
PISTON AND CONNECTING
ROD. INSTALL IN
CYLINDER BORES
#2, #4, #5 & #7

42 FT. LBS.

CONNECTING ROD BEARING
CONNECTING
ROD CAP

PISTON AND CONNECTING
ROD. INSTALL IN
CYLINDER BORES
#1 #3 #6, & #8
LARGE VALVE DEPRESSION
FACES FRONT OF ENGINE
ON #1 & #3, REAR OF
ENGINE ON #6 & # 8

**Fig. 53 Piston & rod
installation. 1979—81**

AMOUNT
UNDERSIZE
STAMPED AT
THIS END
(.0005, etc.)
OR ON TANG
WITH A
LETTER
STAMP,
A = .0005,
B = .0010,
C = .0015.

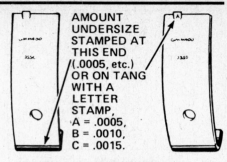

**Fig. 54 Main bearing
identification. 1983—84**

REAR MAIN OIL
SEAL GROOVE

TOOL BT-6433

PACK SEAL
INTO GROOVE

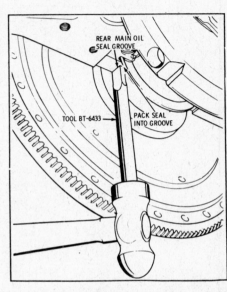

**Fig. 56 Packing upper rear main
bearing seal**

the engine, **Fig. 53.** The pistons are interchangeable between cylinder numbers 1, 3, 6 and 8 and 2, 4, 5 and 7.

PISTONS, RINGS & PINS

SERVICE BULLETIN Some V8-350 diesel engines may exhibit excessive oil consumption, low compression and/or excessive blowby. These conditions may be caused by stuck or frozen piston rings. To correct the above mentioned problem, proceed as follows:
1. With engine warm, remove all glow plugs from cylinders.
2. Using top engine cleaner Part No. 1050002 or equivalent, divide contents of can equally into each cylinder. Allow engine to soak for 24 hours.
3. Crank engine with glow plugs removed to expel excess cleaner.
4. Install glow plugs and start engine.

Pistons are available in standard sizes and oversizes of .010 and .030".
Rings are available in standard sizes and oversizes of .010 and .030".

MAIN & ROD BEARINGS

Main bearing inserts are available in standard sizes and undersizes of .0005,

.0010 and .0015 inch. On 1983—84 models, a letter stamped on the bearing tang identifies the size of the bearing, **Fig. 54.** The undersize is also stamped on the bearing insert on the other side of the insert tang, **Fig. 54.** On 1979—81 models, the amount of undersize and part number is stamped on the bearing shell, **Fig. 55.**

Rod bearings are available in standard sizes and an undersize of .010 inch.

SERVICE BULLETIN Beginning in the 1981 model year, a ¼ inch longer main bearing cap bolt entered production. The new part number is 22511818, replacing 392190. All 1981 and newer diesel engine main bearing bolt holes have a ¼ inch deeper tap and ¼ inch longer counter bore.

REAR CRANKSHAFT SEAL SERVICE

Since the braided fabric seal used on these engines can be replaced only when the crankshaft is removed, the following repair procedure is recommended.
1. Remove oil pan and bearing cap.
2. Drive end of old seal gently into groove, using a suitable tool, until packed tight. This may vary between ¼ and ¾ inch depending on amount of pack required.
3. Repeat previous step for other end of seal.
4. Measure and note amount that seal was driven up on one side. Using the old seal removed from bearing cap, cut a length of seal the amount previously noted plus 1/16 inch.

5. Repeat previous step for other side of seal.
6. Pack cut lengths of seal into appropriate side of seal groove. A packing tool, BT-6433, **Fig. 56,** may be used since the tool has been machined to provide a built-in stop. Use tool BT-6436 to trim the seal flush with block, **Fig. 57.**
7. Install new seal in lower bearing cap.

OIL PAN
REPLACE

1. Disconnect battery ground cables.
2. Remove oil pump drive and vacuum pump.
3. Remove fan shroud attaching screws and pull upward from clips.
4. Raise and support vehicle. Drain oil pan.
5. Disconnect exhaust and crossover pipes, then remove oil cooler lines from filter base.

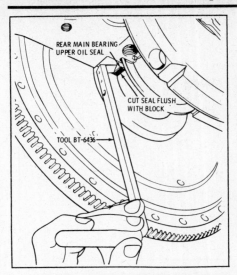

Fig. 57 Trimming upper rear main bearing seal

6. Remove flywheel cover and the starter motor.
7. Remove both engine mount through bolts and raise engine with suitable equipment.
8. Loosen the right-hand engine mount and remove the left-hand engine mount.
9. Remove oil pan attaching bolts and the oil pan.
10. Reverse procedure to install. Torque oil pan attaching bolts to 10 ft. lbs.

OIL PUMP
REPLACE & SERVICE

REPLACEMENT

1. Remove oil pan as outlined previously.
2. Remove oil pump to rear main bearing cap attaching bolts, **Fig. 58.**
3. Remove oil pump and drive shaft ex-

tension.
4. Reverse procedure to install. Torque attaching bolts to 35 ft. lbs.

SERVICE
Disassembly
1. Remove oil pump drive shaft extension, **Fig. 59.** Do not attempt to remove washers from drive shaft extension. The drive shaft extension and washers is serviced as an assembly.
2. Remove cotter pin, spring and pressure regulator valve.

NOTE: Apply pressure on pressure regulator bore before removing cotter pin since the spring is under pressure.

3. Remove oil pump cover attaching screws and the oil pump cover and gasket.
4. Remove drive gear and idler gear from pump body.

Inspection
1. Check gears for scoring or other damage, replace if necessary.
2. Proper end clearance is .0005–.0075 inch.
3. Check pressure regulator valve, valve spring and bore for damage. Proper bore to valve clearance is .0025–.0050 inch.
4. Check extension shaft ends for wear, **Fig. 60.**

Assembly
1. Install gears and shaft in oil pump body.
2. Check gear end clearance by placing a straight edge over the gears and measure the clearance between the straight edge and gasket surface. If end clearance is excessive, check for scores in cover that would bring the clearance over specified limits.
3. Install cover and torque attaching screws to 8 ft. lbs.
4. Install pressure regulator valve, closed end first, into bore, then the valve spring and cotter pin.

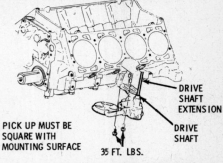

Fig. 58 Oil pump installation

WATER PUMP
REPLACE

1. Disconnect ground cables from batteries.
2. Drain cooling system.
3. Loosen drive belts and remove fan and pulley assembly.
4. Disconnect all hoses from water pump.
5. Remove alternator bracket, then the power steering pump and air conditioning compressor brackets, if equipped.
6. Remove water pump attaching screws and the water pump.
7. Reverse procedure to install.

MECHANICAL FUEL PUMP
REPLACE

SERVICE BULLETIN Some diesel engines may exhibit a condition of hard cold starts. If this condition exists, check the fuel pump housing for a crack in the area where the fuel line is connected to the fuel pump, which may allow air to enter the system. The cracked fuel pump housing could be caused by the fuel line vibrating.

To correct this condition, remove the right hand thermostat housing bolt and install stud, part No. 6270979. Disconnect fuel line at the fuel pump and install clip, part No. 343463 onto fuel line as shown in **Fig. 61.** Install washer face nut, part No. 10008001. Replace the fuel pump and connect the fuel line.

1. Disconnect fuel lines from pump.
2. Remove fuel pump mounting bolts and the fuel pump.

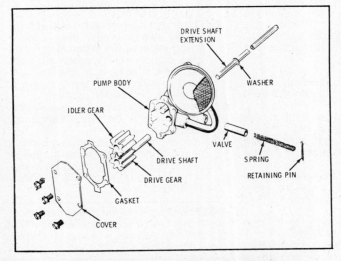

Fig. 59 Oil pump disassembled

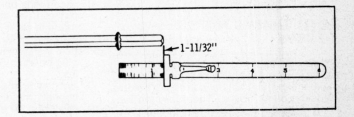

Fig. 60 Oil pump driveshaft extension

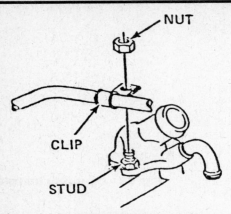

Fig. 61 Installing fuel line stud & clip assembly

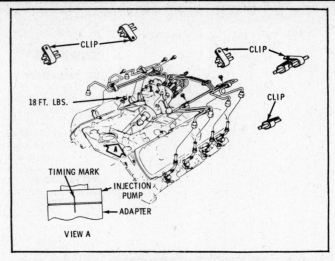

Fig. 62 Fuel injection pump timing marks

3. Remove all gasket material from the pump and block gasket surfaces. Apply sealer to both sides of new gasket.
4. Position gasket on pump flange and hold pump in position against its mounting surface. Make sure rocker arm is riding on crankshaft eccentric.
5. Press pump tight against its mounting. Install retaining screws and tighten them alternately.
6. Connect fuel lines. Then operate engine and check for leaks.

NOTE: Before installing the pump, it is good practice to crank the engine so that the nose of the crankshaft eccentric is out of the way of the fuel pump rocker arm when the pump is installed. In this way there will be the least amount of tension on the rocker arm, thereby easing the installation of the pump.

INJECTION PUMP TIMING

LESS TIMING METER

1. The mark on the injection pump adapter must be aligned with the mark on the injection pump flange, **Fig. 62.**
2. To adjust:
   a. Loosen the injection pump retaining nuts with tool J-26987.
   b. Align the mark on the injection pump flange with the mark on the injection pump adapter, **Fig. 62.**
   c. Torque injection pump retaining nuts to 18 ft. lbs.

WITH TIMING METER J-33075

NOTE: Certain engine malfunctions can cause inaccurate timing readings. Engine malfunctions should be corrected before adjusting pump timing. The marks on the pump and pump adapter will normally be aligned within .030 inch.

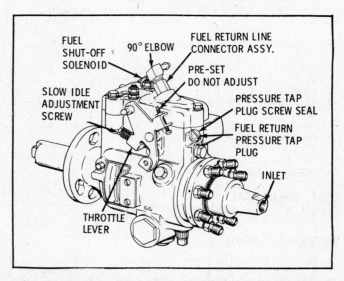

Fig. 63 Fuel injection pump connections. 1979–80

1. Place transmission in Park, apply parking brake and block drive wheels.
2. Start engine and allow to reach normal operating temperature.
3. Shut engine off.
4. Remove air cleaner assembly, install cover J-26996-1 then disconnect EGR valve hose.
5. Clean dirt from engine probe holder and crankshaft balancer rim.
6. Clean lens on both ends of glow plug probe. Look through probe to ensure that it is clean.
7. Remove glow plug from No. 3 cylinder. Insert glow plug probe into glow plug opening and torque probe to 8 ft. lbs.
8. Set timing meter selector to B, then connect meter battery leads.
9. Disconnect generator two lead connector, then start engine and adjust idle speed to specifications.

10. Observe timing meter, wait approximately two minutes, then observe timing meter again. When meter stabilizes, compare timing reading to specifications. If timing is as specified, proceed to step 16. If timing is not as specified, proceed to next step.
11. Turn engine off and note relative position of marks on pump flange and adapter.
12. Loosen nuts or bolts holding pump to adapter, then rotate pump to the left (advance) or right (retard) as necessary. Torque retaining nuts or bolts to 18 ft. lbs.

NOTE: Move pump gradually when adjusting timing. On V8 engines, the width of the adapter timing mark is equal to approximately 1 degree.

13. Start engine and recheck timing.

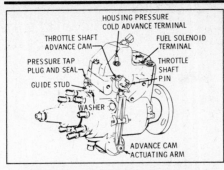

Fig. 64 Fuel injection pump housing right side view. 1981 & 1983—84

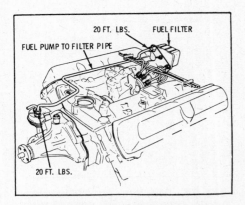

Fig. 66 Fuel filter & lines

Reset timing, if necessary.

14. On V8 engines, adjust pump rod, then reset curb and fast idle speeds.
15. Disconnect timing meter and install removed glow plug. Torque glow plug to 12 ft. lbs.
16. Connect generator two lead connector, install air cleaner assembly and reconnect EGR valve hose.

SERVICE BULLETIN The timing marks on the injection pump and adapter should be close to being lined up after timing the engine. If they are not, and the engine still exhibits poor performance, the timing may still be incorrect. A misfiring cylinder can result in incorrect timing. When this occurs, it is necessary that timing be checked in an alternate cylinder. Timing can be checked in cylinders 2 or 3. If a difference exists between cylinders, try both positions to determine which timing performs best.

If the engine continues to run poorly and excessive exhaust smoke is evident, check the housing pressure cold advance (1981–84) for proper operation. If the advance is operating properly, a stuck or frozen injection pump advance piston may be at fault. This piston is used on 1980–84 vehicles and can be checked by pushing in on the bottom of the face cam lever on the right side of the injection pump. If the piston is free, the timing will retard and cause the engine to run roughly. If no change is evident, the piston is sticking and must be repaired.

FUEL INJECTION PUMP HOUSING FUEL PRESSURE CHECK

1. With engine thoroughly warmed up, remove air crossover and install screened covers, tool J-26996-2 or equivalent.
2. Remove fuel return pressure tap plug or torque screw, **Figs. 63, 64 and 65.** If equipped with torque screw, add a second nut to the lock nut and back out screw to avoid disturbing the adjustment.
3. Remove the seal from the pressure tap plug or torque screw and place seal on pressure tap adapter J-29382. Screw pressure tap adapter into pressure tap hole in pump, then screw adapter J-28526 into J-29382 adapter.
4. Attach a suitable low pressure gauge to J-28526 adapter.
5. Connect magnetic pick-up tachometer, tool J-26925, to engine.
6. With engine running at 1000 RPM in park, check fuel pressure. Pressure should be 8—12 PSI with no more than 2 PSI fluctuation.

NOTE: If vehicle is equipped with Housing Pressure Cold Advance (HPCA) and housing pressure is zero, disconnect electrical connector from housing pressure cold advance terminal, **Figs. 64 and 65.** If pressure remains zero, remove injection pump cover and check advance solenoid operation. If binding or not operating, free up or replace parts as necessary. If pressure is normal after electrical lead is disconnected, check for proper operation of temperature switch located on the cylinder head bolt.

7. If fuel pressure is too low, replace the fuel return line connector assembly. If fuel pressure is too high, the fuel return system may be restricted. Remove the fuel return line at the injection pump, then install a fitting and short piece of hose to discharge the return line fuel into a suitable container.
8. Recheck fuel injection pump housing fuel pressure. If fuel pressure is lower than in previous step, correct fuel restriction in fuel return line. If pressure is still too high, replace fuel return line connector assembly.

NOTE: Whenever the fuel return line connector assembly is replaced, the injection pump timing should be checked and reset as necessary. Refer to "Injection Pump Timing".

9. Recheck fuel injection pump housing fuel pressure. If still too high, remove injection pump for repair.
10. Remove tachometer, pressure gauge and adapters.
11. Install new pressure tap plug screw seal on the pressure tap plug or torque screw and replace in pump.

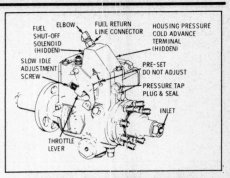

Fig. 65 Fuel injection pump housing left side view. 1981 & 1983—84

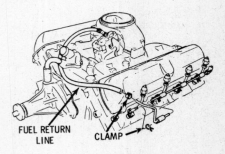

L. H. SIDE OF ENGINE

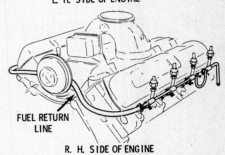

R. H. SIDE OF ENGINE

Fig. 67 Fuel return lines. 1979—80 & 1981 exc. Calif.

12. Remove screened covers and install crossover.

INJECTION PUMP
REPLACE

REMOVAL

1. Disconnect battery ground cables and remove air cleaner assembly.
2. Remove crankcase ventilation filters and pipes from valve covers and air crossover, **Fig. 24.**
3. Remove air crossover, then install screened covers J-26996-2 or equivalent.
4. Disconnect throttle rod and throttle return spring.
5. Remove bellcrank.
6. Remove throttle and T.V. detent cables from intake manifold brackets and position aside.

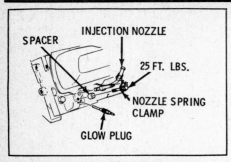

Fig. 68 Injection nozzle installation. 1979—80 & 1981 exc. Calif.

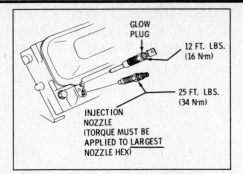

Fig. 69 Injection nozzle installation. 1981 Calif. & all 1983—84

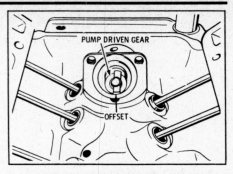

Fig. 70 Offset on fuel injection pump driven gear

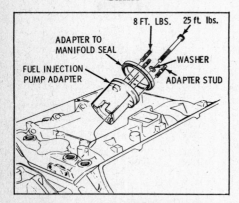

Fig. 71 Fuel injection pump adapter installation

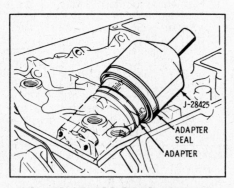

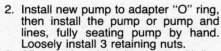

Fig. 72 Fuel injection pump adapter seal installation

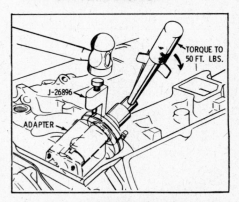

Fig. 73 Marking fuel injection pump adapter with new timing mark

7. Remove fuel lines to fuel filter, then the fuel filter and bracket, **Fig. 66.** If equipped with A/C, remove rear compressor base.
8. Disconnect fuel return line from injection pump.
9. To remove injection pump only:
   a. Disconnect injection line clips,
   b. Disconnect injection lines from injection pump and plug all open lines.
   c. Reposition injection lines to gain access for pump removal.
   d. Using tool J-26987, remove 3 pump retaining nuts, then remove pump.
10. To remove injection pump with injection lines attached:
   a. On 1979—80 and 1981 models except California, slide clamp from fuel return lines at injector nozzles, **Fig. 67,** and remove fuel return lines from each bank.
   b. On all models, disconnect injection pump lines at injector nozzles, **Figs. 68 and 69.** It is necessary to use two wrenches.
   c. Remove three nuts retaining injection pump with tool J-26987.
   d. Remove injection pump and lines. Cap all lines and fittings.

INSTALLATION

1. With cylinder No. 1 at T.D.C., align offset tang on pump drive shaft with pump driven gear, **Fig. 70.**

2. Install new pump to adapter "O" ring, then install the pump or pump and lines, fully seating pump by hand. Loosely install 3 retaining nuts.
3. Align mark on injection pump with line on adapter, **Fig. 62,** then torque retaining nuts to 18 ft. lbs.
4. To install injection pump with injection lines attached:
   a. Connect injector lines at injector nozzles. Using a back up wrench on upper nozzle hex, torque line nuts to 25 ft. lbs., **Figs. 68 and 69.**
   b. On 1979—80 and 1981 except California, install fuel return lines to injectors on each bank, **Fig. 67.**
5. To install injection pump only:
   a. Position injector lines in proper position and connect injector lines to injection pump. Torque line nuts to 25 ft. lbs.
   b. Install injection line clips.
6. Connect fuel return line to injection pump.
7. Install fuel filter and bracket, then install fuel line. Return to **Fig. 66,** for torque specifications.
8. Install throttle and T.V. detent cables. Adjust T.V. cable.
9. Install bellcrank, then install throttle rod and throttle return spring. If equipped with A/C, install rear compressor brace.
10. Remove screened covers, then install air crossover.
11. Install crankcase ventilation filters and

pipes to valve covers and air crossover, **Fig. 24.**
12. Install air cleaner assembly. Connect battery ground cables.
13. Start engine and allow to idle for several minutes. Turn ignition "Off", for approximately two minutes, then restart to allow air to bleed off within pump.

INJECTION PUMP ADAPTER, ADAPTER SEAL & NEW TIMING MARK

ADAPTER SEAL, REPLACE

1. Remove injection pump. Refer to "Injection Pump, Replace".
2. Using a suitable probe, pry out adapter seal.

NOTE: When prying out adapter seal, use caution not to nick or gouge adapter.

3. Loosen bolts securing adapter to engine block, **Fig. 71.**
4. Lubricate new adapter seal inside and outside diameter with chassis lube.
5. Using seal installer J-28425, install seal on adapter, **Fig. 72.**
6. Remove seal installer tool and inspect seal for proper installation.
7. Torque adapter bolts to 25 ft. lbs.

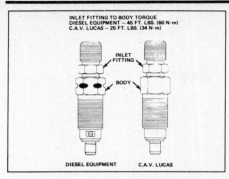

Fig. 74 Injection nozzle identification

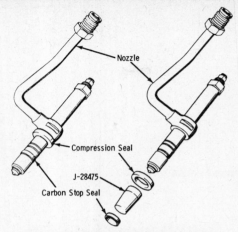

Fig. 75 Injection nozzle seal installation

FERRULE TYPE   FLARE TYPE

LINE   LINE

GRAY NUT   BLACK NUT

SEALING RING   NEW FLARE

SHOULDERED SEAT   CONE SHAPE SEAT

NOZZLE   NOZZLE

Fig. 76 Injection nozzle connections. 1979

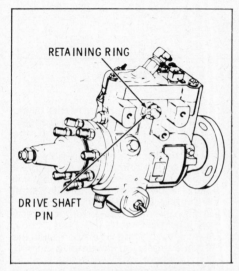

Fig. 77 Throttle shaft retention. 1979

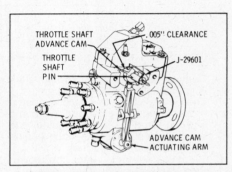

Fig. 78 Injection pump with tool J-29601 installed

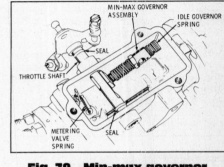

Fig. 79 Min-max governor removal

8. Refer to "Marking Injection Pump Adapter" for remaining procedure.

ADAPTER, REPLACE

1. Remove injection pump. Refer to "Injection Pump, Replace".
2. Remove bolts securing adapter into engine block, **Fig. 71.** Then remove adapter.
3. Install replacement adapter in engine block and install bolts. Do not tighten.
4. Refer to "Adapter Seal, Replace" steps 4 through 8, for remaining procedure.

MARKING INJECTION PUMP ADAPTER

1. Using a suitable file, remove original timing mark from adapter. Do not remove timing mark from injection pump.
2. With cylinder No. 1 approaching TDC, align timing mark on balancer with zero mark on indicator. The injection

pump driven gear should be slightly offset to the right when cylinder No. 1 is at TDC, **Fig. 70.**
3. Install timing tool J-26896, into pump adapter, **Fig. 73.** Using a suitable torque wrench, torque tool towards cylinder No. 1 to 50 ft. lbs. While holding torque steady, mark pump adapter, **Fig. 73.** Remove tool.
4. Reinstall injection pump. Refer to "Injection Pump, Replace".

INJECTION NOZZLE
REPLACE

1981 CALIF. MODELS & 1983–84 ALL

SERVICE BULLETIN Injection nozzle body leaks may be corrected by loosening the inlet fitting and retorquing to 45 ft. lbs. on DED type injection nozzles, and 25 ft. lbs. on CAV type injection nozzles, **Fig. 74.** In the event this does not correct the leak, remove the inlet fitting. Using a piece of crocus cloth, press and rotate the end of the inlet fitting against the crocus cloth back and forth about six times. After polishing has been performed, flush inlet fit-

ting using diesel fuel and install fitting onto pump.

1. Remove fuel lines, using a backup wrench on upper injection nozzle hex.
2. Remove nozzle by applying torque to largest nozzle hex, **Fig. 69.**
3. Cap nozzle and lines to prevent entry of dirt. Also remove copper gasket from cylinder head if gasket did not remain with nozzle.
4. Reverse procedure to install. Torque nozzle to 25 ft. lbs. When tightening nozzle, torque must be applied to largest nozzle hex. Torque fuel line to 25 ft. lbs. using a backup wrench on upper injection nozzle hex.

1979–80 MODELS & 1981 EXC. CALIF.

1. Remove fuel line from injector nozzle.
2. Remove fuel line clamps from all nozzles on bank where nozzle is being removed. Remove fuel return line from nozzle being replaced.
3. Remove nozzle hold down clamp and spacer, **Fig. 68,** then the nozzle with tool J-26952.

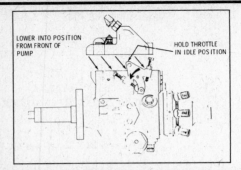

Fig. 80 Installing injection pump cover

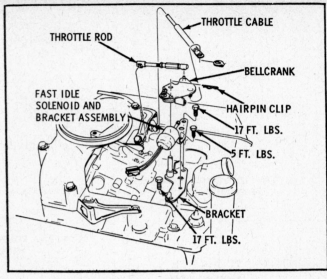

Fig. 81 Throttle linkage

4. Cap nozzle inlet line and tip of nozzle.
5. Reverse procedure to install. Install new seals on injection nozzles, **Fig. 75**. Torque nozzle hold down clamp bolt to 25 ft. lbs.

NOTE: 1979 diesel engines use two different types of connections to attach the high pressure fuel lines to the injection nozzles. Before replacing an injection nozzle or high pressure fuel line, it is necessary to determine which type of connection is used, either the "Flare Type" or "Ferrule Type", **Fig. 76**. Also, check the replacement part to ensure that the proper connection is used.

THROTTLE SHAFT SEAL
REPLACE

1. Disconnect battery ground cables, then remove the air cleaner and crossover, and install screened covers, J-26996-2 or equivalent.
2. Disconnect injection pump fuel solenoid wire and fuel return line. On 1981 and 1983–84 models, disconnect housing pressure cold advance (HPCA) wires, **Fig. 64**.
3. On 1979–80 models, remove the transmission vacuum regulator valve. On 1981 and 1983–84 models, scribe a line on the vacuum regulator valve and pump body to aid in reassembly, and remove the vacuum regulator. Refer to "Transmission Vacuum Regulator Valve, Replace".
4. Remove the throttle rod, return spring and throttle cable bracket.
5. On 1979 models, drive the throttle shaft drive pin out of shaft, then remove the shaft retaining ring and fiber washer, **Fig. 77**. On 1980–81 and 1983–84 models, position tool J-29601 over throttle shaft with tool slots engaging pin. Place the tool spring clip over the throttle shaft advance cam and tighten the wing nut, **Fig. 78**. Without loosening the wing nut, pull tool from throttle shaft. This will maintain proper alignment during reassembly. Drive pin from throttle shaft, loosen the clamp screw and remove the throt-

tle shaft advance cam and fiber washer.
6. Remove any burrs on throttle shaft with shaft still installed in pump.
7. Thoroughly clean the injection pump cover, the upper portion of the pump and the throttle shaft and guide stud area. Place shop towels in the engine valley to catch spilled fuel.
8. Remove injection pump top cover, then remove screws from cover.

NOTE: When the injection pump top cover is removed, extreme care must be taken to keep foreign materials out of the pump. If any objects are dropped in the injection pump, they must be removed before the engine is started to prevent engine or injection pump damage.

9. Note position of metering valve spring over top of guide stud. This position must be duplicated exactly during reassembly.
10. Remove guide stud and washer, **Fig. 64**. Note part location prior to removal.
11. Rotate min-max governor assembly upwards to provide clearance, then remove from throttle shaft, **Fig. 79**.
12. Remove throttle shaft assembly and examine shaft for unusual wear or damage. Replace if necessary.

NOTE: When removing throttle shaft assembly, it may be necessary to loosen the injection pump mounting nuts and rotate pump slightly to provide clearance for shaft removal.

13. Examine pump housing bushings for unusual wear or damage. If wear is evident, the pump should be removed and sent to manufacturer for repairs.
14. Remove throttle shaft seals. Do not attempt to cut seals to remove, as nicks in the seat will cause fuel leakage.

15. Install replacement shaft seals taking care not to cut seals on shaft edges. Apply chassis lube lightly to the seals.
16. Slide the throttle shaft assembly carefully into the pump body to the point the min-max governor assembly will slide back onto the throttle shaft assembly, **Fig. 79**.
17. Rotate the min-max governor assembly downward into the pump body, then while holding in position, slide the throttle shaft and governor assembly into position.
18. On 1979 models, install new fiber washer, throttle shaft retaining ring and throttle shaft drive pin, **Fig. 77**. On 1980–81 and 1983–84 models, install new mylar washer, throttle shaft advance cam (do not tighten screw at this time) and throttle shaft drive pin. Align the throttle shaft advance cam so tool J-29601 can be reinstalled over the throttle shaft, pin in the slots and the spring clip over the advance cam, **Fig. 78**. Insert a .005 inch feeler gauge between the mylar washer on the throttle shaft and the pump housing. Squeeze the cam and throttle shaft together and tighten the cam screw. Torque to 30 in. lbs. Secure with suitable locking compound.
19. Install guide stud with new washer, **Fig. 64**. Ensure the metering valve spring upper extension rides on top of the guide stud. Torque guide stud to 85 in. lbs. Do not overtorque.
20. Hold throttle in idle position.
21. Install new pump cover seal. Ensure the securing screws are not in the cover and position the cover approximately ¼ inch forward and ⅛ inch above the pump.
22. Move cover rearward and downward into proper position, using caution not to cut the seal, then install pump cover screws, **Fig. 80**. Torque screws to 35 in. lbs.

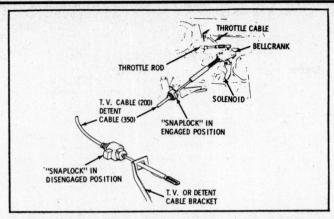

Fig. 82 Throttle valve or detent cable adjustment

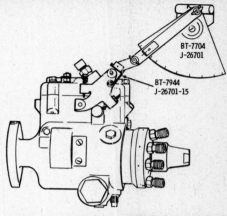

Fig. 83 Transmission vacuum regulator valve adjustment. 1979—83 Turbo Hydra-Matic 350

NOTE: Use caution not to drop and lose flat washer and internal lock washer with each screw. Flat washers must be against pump cover.

23. On 1979–80 models, install vacuum regulator valve. On 1981 and 1983–84 models, install vacuum regulator valve aligning marks made previously.
24. Connect battery ground cables.
25. Turn ignition to "Run" position. Touch pink solenoid wire to the injection pump solenoid terminal. A clicking noise should be heard indicating the fuel solenoid is operating. If clicking noise is heard, proceed to step 28. If no clicking noise is heard, the solenoid linkage may be jammed in a wide open position and the engine must not be started. Proceed to step 26.
26. Remove injection pump top cover, then ground the solenoid lead opposite the hot lead and connect the pink wire. With ignition switch in the "Run" position, the solenoid should move the linkage. If not, replace the solenoid.

NOTE: The minimum voltage across the solenoid terminals must be 12 volts.

27. Reinstall cover and repeat step 25.
28. Install throttle cable bracket and throttle rod, then install throttle cable and return spring. Connect solenoid wire and on 1981 and 1983–84 models housing pressure cold advance (HPCA) wire.
29. Install fuel return line. Ensure the timing mark on the pump is aligned with the adapter timing mark. Also ensure the injection pump retaining bolts are tight.
30. Start engine and check for leaks.

NOTE: If engine roughness is observed, it may be due to air in the pump. To purge air, let engine idle for several minutes. It may be necessary to shut engine down for several minutes to allow air bubbles to rise to top of pump where they will be purged.

31. Remove intake manifold screens, then reinstall air crossover and air cleaner.

TRANSMISSION VACUUM REGULATOR VALVE
REPLACE

1. Note location of the valve vacuum hoses, then disconnect the vacuum hoses.
2. Remove the two valve attaching bolts and the valve.
3. Reverse procedure to install.
4. Adjust vacuum valve. Refer to "Transmission Vacuum Regulator Valve, Adjust".

THROTTLE ROD
ADJUST

1. If equipped with Cruise Control, remove clip from Cruise Control rod, then the rod from bellcrank.
2. Remove throttle valve cable from bellcrank, **Fig. 81.**
3. Loosen the throttle rod locknut and shorten the rod several turns.
4. Rotate the bellcrank to the full throttle stop, then lengthen the throttle rod until the injection pump lever contacts the injection pump full throttle stop. Release the bellcrank.
5. Tighten the throttle rod locknut.
6. Connect the throttle valve cable and Cruise Control rod, if equipped, to bellcrank.

THROTTLE VALVE OR DETENT CABLE
ADJUST

1. Remove throttle rod from bellcrank, **Fig. 82.**
2. Push snap lock to disengaged position.

3. Rotate bellcrank to full throttle stop position and push in snap lock until flush with cable end fitting. Release bellcrank.
4. Connect the throttle rod.

TRANSMISSION VACUUM REGULATOR VALVE
ADJUST

1. Remove air crossover, then install screen covers J26996-2.
2. Remove throttle rod from throttle lever, then loosen transmission regulator vacuum valve injection pump bolts.
3. Install carburetor angle gauge adapter, J-26701-15 on injection pump throttle lever, then place angle gauge, J-26701 on adapter, **Fig. 83.**
4. Rotate throttle lever to wide open position and set angle gauge to zero degrees.
5. Center bubble in level, then set angle gauge to 49 degrees on 1979 units, 50 degrees on 1980 units and 58 degrees on 1981–84 units.
6. Rotate throttle lever so level bubble is centered.
7. Attach a suitable vacuum pump to center port of vacuum regulator valve, then install a vacuum gauge to outside port of vacuum regulator valve. Apply 18–22 inches of vacuum.
8. Rotate vacuum regulator valve clockwise to obtain 10.6 inches of vacuum on 1983–84 models, 8½ to 9 inches of vacuum on 1979 and 1981 models and 7 to 8 inches of vacuum on 1980 models.
9. Tighten vacuum regulator to injection pump retaining bolts, then remove vacuum gauge and pump.
10. Install throttle rod to bellcrank, then remove screened covers and install air crossover and air cleaner.

1. REMOVE AND INSTALL

REMOVE

1. Remove hose from pump inlet.
2. Remove bolt and bracket holding pump to engine block.
3. Remove pump.

INSTALL

1. Insert pump in engine, making sure the gears on the pump mesh with the gears on the engine cam shaft.
2. Rotate the pump into position so the bracket and bolt can be installed.
3. Install vacuum hose.

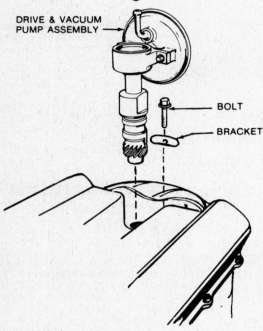

VACUUM HOSE

DRIVE & VACUUM PUMP ASSEMBLY

BOLT

BRACKET

Removing assembly from engine.

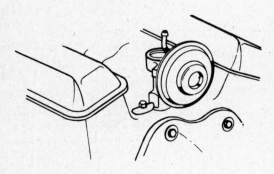

View showing assembly from rear of engine.

2. DISASSEMBLE AND ASSEMBLE

CAUTION: *Take extreme care when clamping the vacuum pump in vise.*

DISASSEMBLE

1. Remove hex head tapping screws.
2. Remove "O" Ring Seal.

ASSEMBLE

1. Install "O" Ring Seal in cavity of drive assembly.
2. Connect drive assembly to vacuum pump with hex head tapping screws.

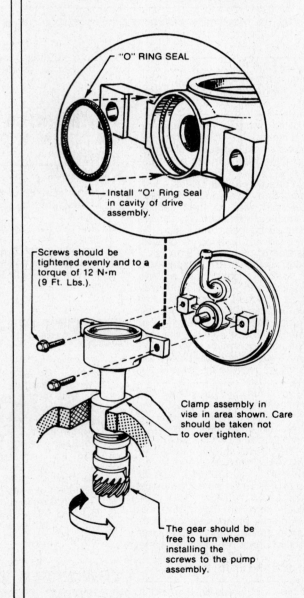

"O" RING SEAL

Install "O" Ring Seal in cavity of drive assembly.

Screws should be tightened evenly and to a torque of 12 N·m (9 Ft. Lbs.).

Clamp assembly in vise in area shown. Care should be taken not to over tighten.

The gear should be free to turn when installing the screws to the pump assembly.

Fig. 84   Vacuum Pump service

PURGING WATER FROM FUEL TANK

1980—84 MODELS WITH WATER IN FUEL DETECTOR

Single Tank Models

Water in the fuel tank may be purged by siphoning or using a pump. The pump or siphon hose should be connected to the ¼ inch fuel return hose (smaller of the two hoses) under the hood near the fuel pump. Purging should continue until all water is removed from the fuel tank. Also, remove fuel filler cap while purging, and replace cap when completed.

CAUTION: Use all safety precautions while handling the fuel/water mixture.

Dual Tank Models

Water in the dual fuel tanks is purged in much the same way as single tank models, except that the fuel selector control should be switched to the main tank position. Siphoning should continue until all water is removed from the main tank. Place ignition switch in the "On" position, and move the fuel selector control to the auxiliary position. Turn ignition "Off" and continue to siphon water from auxiliary tank until all water is removed.

NOTE: Auxiliary tank must be siphoned within twenty minutes. If water cannot be siphoned within twenty minutes, cycle ignition switch "Run" and back to "Off" to obtain another twenty minute siphon period.

When siphoning water from tanks, fuel filler caps should be removed and reinstalled when siphoning is completed.

CAUTION: Use all safety precautions while handling the fuel/water mixture.

VACUUM PUMPS

NOTE: On engines equipped with gear driven type vacuum pump, do not operate engine unless vacuum pump and drive assembly are installed, as the drive gear of the vacuum pump also drives the engine lubricating oil pump.

On these engines, a vacuum pump is required to provide vacuum for accessory operation. The vacuum pump may be either gear driven or belt driven, depending on vehicle application. The gear driven pump has a drive gear located at the lower end of the shaft which meshes with a gear on the engine camshaft. This vacuum pump drive gear also drives the engine lubricating oil pump. The belt driven pump has a pulley attached to the lower end of the shaft and is driven by an accessory belt.

When servicing the vacuum pump, refer to **Fig. 84** for service procedures.

V8-379 Diesel Engine Section

INDEX OF SERVICE OPERATIONS

DESCRIPTION

The V8-379 (6.2L) diesel engine is similar in many ways to gasoline engines, but major differences are evident in the cylinder heads, combustion chambers, fuel distribution system, intake manifold and method of ignition. The cylinder block, crankshaft, main bearings, connecting rods, pistons and wrist pins are all heavy duty designs, due to the higher compression ratios inherent in diesel engines. Intake and exhaust valves are of special alloy material to combat the higher internal operating temperatures. Steel alloy prechamber inserts are installed in the combustion chambers and are serviced separately from the cylinder head. Glow plugs and injector nozzles are threaded into the cylinder head. The injector nozzles are spring loaded and designed to open at specifically calibrated fuel pressures. The intake manifold is always open to atmospheric pressures, therefore no vacuum supply is available. A vacuum pump is therefore installed to supply vacuum to vacuum dependent components (Cruise Control, A/C, Power Brakes, etc.). The main bearing caps are 4 bolt design to provide rigid crankshaft support, while minimizing stress. Roller hydraulic lifters are used to minimize wear on the forged steel camshaft. A block heater is used to aid starting in cold climates.

LUBRICATION SYSTEM

The gear-type oil pump is attached to the bottom side of the rear main bearing cap and is driven by the camshaft through an intermediate shaft. Oil flows through the pump outlet tube to the cooler located in the radiator. From the cooler, the oil then flows through a cartridge type oil filter. A bypass valve is incorporated into the system to prevent oil starvation should the filter become clogged. From the oil filter, oil then flows through the drilled galleries in the cylinder block.

A second bypass valve is incorporated into the oil cooler system, should the cooler become clogged.

GLOW PLUG CONTROL SYSTEM

The glow plug control system consists of a thermal controller, a glow plug relay, 6 volt glow plugs and a glow plug warning lamp.

The thermal controller is mounted in the water passage at the rear of the engine. Glow plug operation is controlled by thermostatic elements within the controller which open or close the ground circuit to the glow plug relay as necessary. The relay is located on the left inner fender panel and provides current to the glow plugs as long as the thermal controller completes the ground circuit. The 6 volt

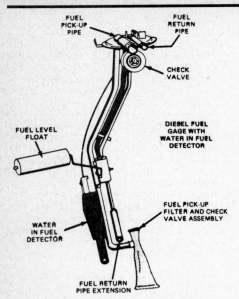

Fig. 1   Water in fuel detector, filter and pickup tube assembly

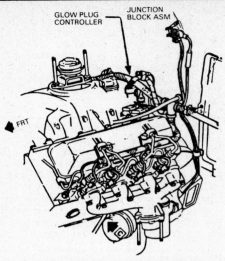

Fig. 2   Glow plug controller. Early 1982 models

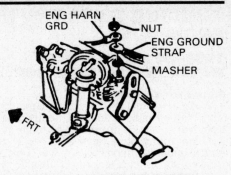

Fig. 3   Ground connections. Early 1982 models.

glow plugs which are operated at electrical system voltage (12 volts), are designed to burn continuously and are pulsed on and off by the glow plug relay in response to messages received by the controller. The glow plug warning lamp, mounted in the instrument cluster, is wired across the glow plugs and is illuminated whenever the glow plugs are heating.

FUEL SYSTEM

Components

The fuel system components consist of a fuel tank with water sensor and screen filter, a primary fuel filter, a mechanical fuel pump, a secondary fuel filter, a fuel line heater, and an injection pump, lines and injector nozzles.

System Operation

Fuel is routed from the fuel tank through the primary fuel filter and to the camshaft driven mechanical fuel pump. It then flows through the fuel line heater, which prevents fuel waxing, to the secondary fuel filter, which again strains contaminants from the fuel. The fuel is then directed to the high pressure rotary vane type injection pump. The injection pump meters and pressurizes the fuel, then directs it through the equal length high pressure lines to the injector nozzles.

Water In Fuel Warning System

The fuel tank is equipped with a filter and water in fuel detector, **Fig. 1.** The filter prevents water from entering the pickup tube, allowing it instead to lay at the bottom of the fuel tank, below the tube. When the water level reaches a point where it may enter the fuel system, the detector activates a warning lamp on the dash panel, alerting the driver. A siphoning system starting at the tank and going to the rear spring hanger (C & K models) or to the midpoint of the right frame rail (G models),

allows the driver to attach a hose to the shut-off valve and drain the system.

ELECTRICAL SYSTEM DIAGNOSIS

SERVICE BULLETIN On early 1982 vehicles, the engine wiring harness connector at the glow plug controller, **Fig. 2,** has an open hole at the No. 2 pin connection. Accumulated moisture and dirt in this hole may cause controller malfunction. If the engine is hard to start, or has burned glow plugs, remove the connector and clean the pin area on the controller and connector, then reconnect the connector. Apply a small amount of RTV sealant, or equivalent, over the No. 2 pin hole to prevent further contamination. Check operation of controller. If the controller does not cycle and/or the pins are excessively corroded, the controller must be replaced.

Also note that the wires from pins 5 and 6 are ground wires, and that the ground connection is at the rear of the right hand head on a stud which also grounds the body. Ensure that this ground connection, **Fig. 3,** is secure.

Refer to **Figs. 4 through 7** for electrical diagnostic procedures.

GLOW PLUG RESISTANCE CHECK

1982

1. Use Kent-Moore High Impedence Digital Multimeter (J-29125) for resistance measurements.
2. Select scales as follows: LH switch to "OHMS", RH switch to full counterclockwise, "200 OHMS", slide center switch to left "DC.LO."
3. Start engine, turn on heater and allow engine to warm up. Remove all feed

wires from glow plugs.
4. Turn engine idle speed screw on side of injector pump to worst engine idle roughness. Do not exceed 900 RPM. Allow engine to run for a minimum of one minutes.
5. Attach alligator clip to black test lead of multimeter and grounded to engine lift strap on left hand side of intake manifold.
6. Probe each glow plug terminal and record resistance values on each cylinder in firing sequence (1-8-7-2-6-5-4-3) with engine idling. Readings should be between 1.8 and 3.4 OHMS.

NOTE: If these readings are not obtained, turn engine off for several minutes and recheck glow plugs. Resistance should be .7–.9 OHMS. Readings of 1.2–1.3 OHMS would indicate an engine mechanical problem.

ENGINE MOUNTS
REPLACE

1. Raise and support vehicle.
2. Support engine, then working from below frame mounting bracket, remove engine mount retaining bolt.
3. Raise engine slightly, then remove mount to engine retaining bolts and mount.
4. Reverse procedure to install.

ENGINE
REPLACE

EXC. VAN

1. Disconnect batteries and raise vehicle.
2. Remove transmission dust cover and disconnect torque converter and exhaust.
3. Disconnect wires from starter and remove starter.
4. Remove transmission bell housing bolts and motor mount bolts.
5. Disconnect block heaters, then remove wiring harness, transmission

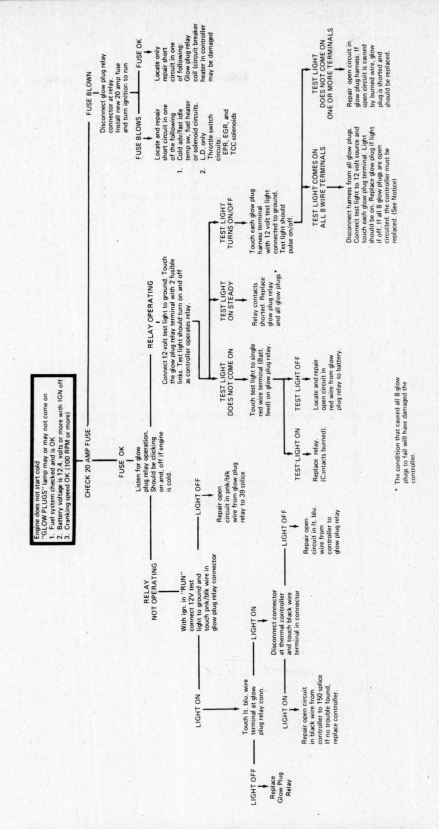

Fig. 4 Electrical system diagnosis (Part 1 of 5). 1982—84

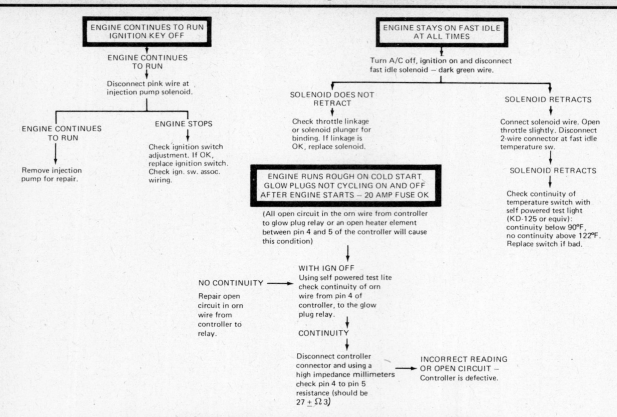

Fig. 4   Electrical system diagnosis (Part 2 of 5). 1982—84

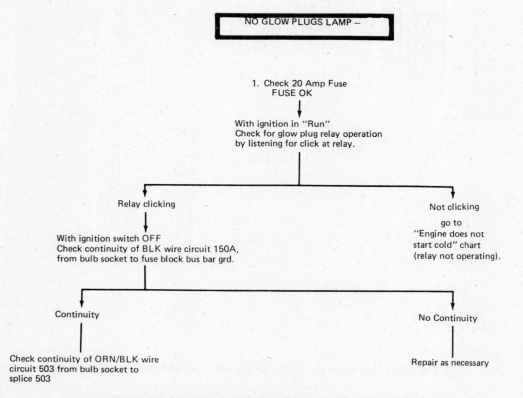

Fig. 4   Electrical system diagnosis (Part 3 of 5). 1982—84

THERMAL CONTROLLER CHECK

With connector removed from controller
the controller heater circuits may be
checked using a high impedance
ohmeter. However, this check will not determine
shorted switches within the controller.

Pin 3 – Pin 2   .40 to .75 Ω Pin 5 – Pin 1   130 Ω ± 10%

Pin 4 – Pin 5   27 Ω ± 3 Ω Pin 2 – Pin 6   Continuity ("O" ohms)

GLOW PLUGS LAMP
CYCLES ON AND OFF
WARM ENGINE

This condition can be caused by an open circuit
in 25 circuit from gen telltale output to pin 1 of
the controller, or by generator output failure —

Fig. 4   Electrical system diagnosis (Part 4 of 5). 1982—84

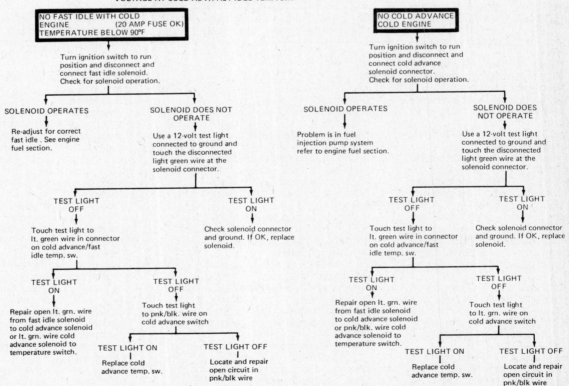

IF NEITHER FAST IDLE OR COLD ADVANCE SOLENOIDS OPERATE, CHECK FOR
VOLTAGE AT COLD ADV/FAST IDLE TEMP. SW.

Fig. 4   Electrical system diagnosis (Part 5 of 5). 1982—84

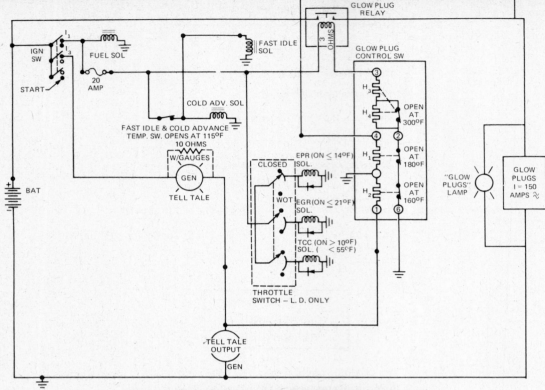

Fig. 5   Glow plug wiring schematic. 1982—84

cooler lines and front battery cable clamp at oil pan.
6. Disconnect fuel return lines and oil cooler lines from engine and remove lower fan shroud bolts and lower vehicle.
7. Scribe hood hinge locations and remove hood.
8. Drain cooling system, remove air cleaner with resonator attached and primary filter from cowling.
9. Disconnect ground cable at alternator bracket and remove alternator wires and clips.
10. Disconnect TPS, EGR-EPR and fuel cut-off at injection pump.
11. Remove harness from clips at rocker covers and disconnect glow plugs.
12. Disconnect EGR-EPR solenoids, glow plugs, controller and temperature sender. Move harness aside.
13. Disconnect ground strap from left side.
14. Remove fan, upper radiator hoses from engine, fan shroud, power steering pump and belt, and power steering reservoir.
15. Disconnect vacuum at cruise servo and accelerator cable at injection pump.
16. Disconnect heater hose and lower radiator hose from engine and oil cooler lines from radiator.
17. Disconnect heater hose and overflow at radiator, automatic transmission cooler lines, upper radiator cover and radiator.
18. Remove detent cable.

19. Support transmission and remove engine.
20. Reverse procedure to install.

NOTE: If fuel filters were removed, they must be filled with clean diesel fuel.

VAN

1. Disconnect batteries.
2. Remove headlight bezels, then the grille.
3. Remove bumper, then the lower valence.
4. Remove hood latch assembly.
5. Remove coolant recovery bottle and upper fan shroud.
6. Remove upper tie bar, then engine cover.
7. If vehicle is equipped with A/C, discharge system, then disconnect A/C condenser inlet and outlet lines and remove condenser.
8. Disconnect low coolant sensor wire and drain radiator.
9. Disconnect transmission and engine oil cooler lines from radiator.
10. Remove radiator upper and lower hose, then remove radiator and fan assembly.
11. Remove fuel injection pump. Refer to "Injection Pump, Replace."
12. Raise and support vehicle.
13. Disconnect exhaust pipes from manifolds.
14. Remove inspection cover, then re-

move torque converter to flex plate bolts.
15. Remove motor mount through bolt nuts.
16. Disconnect block heater electrical connector from heating element and the ground wire from block.
17. Remove bellhousing-to-cylinder case attaching bolts.
18. Disconnect starter wiring, then remove starter.
19. Lower vehicle.
20. If equipped with cruise control, remove cruise control transducer.
21. If equipped with A/C, disconnect A/C compressor suction and discharge lines, then remove rear compressor brace, brackets and compressor.
22. Remove power steering pump and position aside.
23. Remove oil filler tube upper bracket.
24. Remove glow plug relay, then disconnect oil pressure sender and loom.
25. Remove air cleaner resonator and bracket.
26. Remove transmission filler tube bracket nut and position bracket aside.
27. Disconnect radiator, heater and by-pass hoses at air crossover.
28. Remove generator upper bracket.
29. Remove coolant crossover.
30. Disconnect fuel lines from fuel pump.
31. Install engine lifting adapter J-33888 or equivalent.
32. Position suitable engine lifting device and connect to engine lifting adapter. Remove engine.
33. Reverse procedure to install.

Connect an ammeter in series (induction type meter may also be used)* with DK red or orange wire leading from the Glow Plug Relay to the LH bank of glow plugs. Operate the system and note the ammeter reading. Repeat the procedure for the red or orange wire leading from the Glow Plug Relay to the RH bank of glow plugs. Operate the system and note the reading.

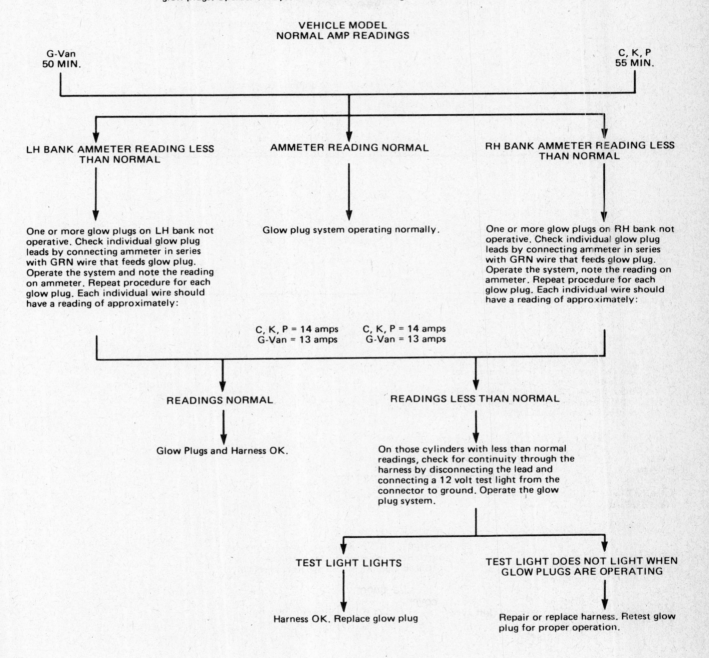

VEHICLE MODEL
NORMAL AMP READINGS

G-Van
50 MIN.

C, K, P
55 MIN.

LH BANK AMMETER READING LESS THAN NORMAL

AMMETER READING NORMAL

RH BANK AMMETER READING LESS THAN NORMAL

One or more glow plugs on LH bank not operative. Check individual glow plug leads by connecting ammeter in series with GRN wire that feeds glow plug. Operate the system and note the reading on ammeter. Repeat procedure for each glow plug. Each individual wire should have a reading of approximately:

Glow plug system operating normally.

One or more glow plugs on RH bank not operative. Check individual glow plug leads by connecting ammeter in series with GRN wire that feeds glow plug. Operate the system, note the reading on ammeter. Repeat procedure for each glow plug. Each individual wire should have a reading of approximately:

C, K, P = 14 amps
G-Van = 13 amps

C, K, P = 14 amps
G-Van = 13 amps

READINGS NORMAL

READINGS LESS THAN NORMAL

Glow Plugs and Harness OK.

On those cylinders with less than normal readings, check for continuity through the harness by disconnecting the lead and connecting a 12 volt test light from the connector to ground. Operate the glow plug system.

TEST LIGHT LIGHTS

TEST LIGHT DOES NOT LIGHT WHEN GLOW PLUGS ARE OPERATING

Harness OK. Replace glow plug

Repair or replace harness. Retest glow plug for proper operation.

*If using an in line ammeter read both banks at once. Do not cut wire.

(Snap-on meter MT552, VAT-40, or equivalent)

Fig. 6   Electrical system diagnosis (Part 1 of 3). 1985

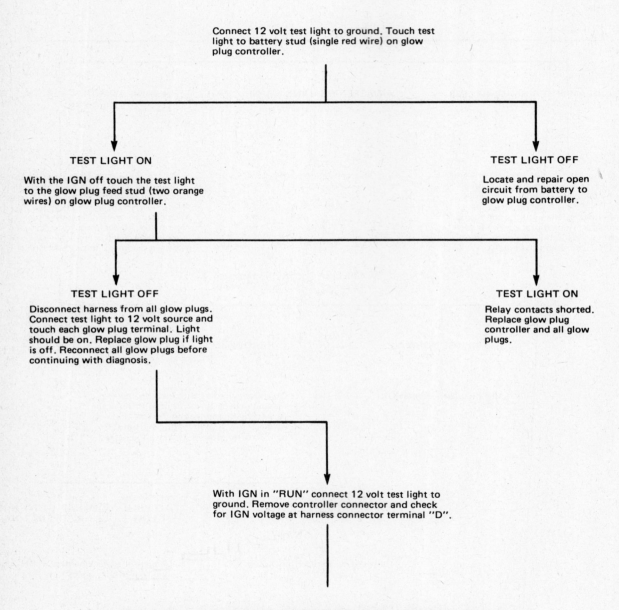

Engine does not start cold — "GLOW PLUGS" lamp may or may not come on
1. Fuel system checked and is OK.
2. Battery voltage is 12.4 volts or more with IGN off.
3. Cranking speed OK (100 RPM or more).
4. Reference electronic glow plug system figure for wiring harness terminal identification.

Connect 12 volt test light to ground. Touch test light to battery stud (single red wire) on glow plug controller.

TEST LIGHT ON

With the IGN off touch the test light to the glow plug feed stud (two orange wires) on glow plug controller.

TEST LIGHT OFF

Locate and repair open circuit from battery to glow plug controller.

TEST LIGHT OFF

Disconnect harness from all glow plugs. Connect test light to 12 volt source and touch each glow plug terminal. Light should be on. Replace glow plug if light is off. Reconnect all glow plugs before continuing with diagnosis.

TEST LIGHT ON

Relay contacts shorted. Replace glow plug controller and all glow plugs.

With IGN in "RUN" connect 12 volt test light to ground. Remove controller connector and check for IGN voltage at harness connector terminal "D".

Fig. 6 Electrical system diagnosis (Part 2 of 3). 1985

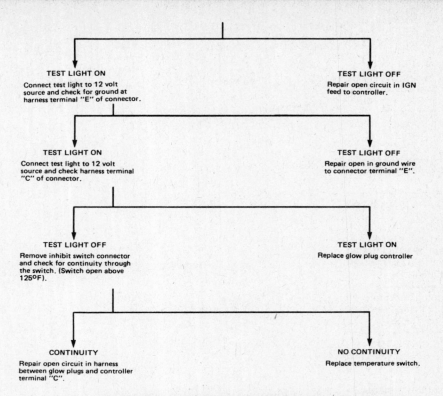

TEST LIGHT ON
Connect test light to 12 volt source and check for ground at harness terminal "E" of connector.

TEST LIGHT OFF
Repair open circuit in IGN feed to controller.

TEST LIGHT ON
Connect test light to 12 volt source and check harness terminal "C" of connector.

TEST LIGHT OFF
Repair open in ground wire to connector terminal "E".

TEST LIGHT OFF
Remove inhibit switch connector and check for continuity through the switch. (Switch open above 125°F).

TEST LIGHT ON
Replace glow plug controller

CONTINUITY
Repair open circuit in harness between glow plugs and controller terminal "C".

NO CONTINUITY
Replace temperature switch.

Fig. 6   Electrical system diagnosis (Part 3 of 3). 1985

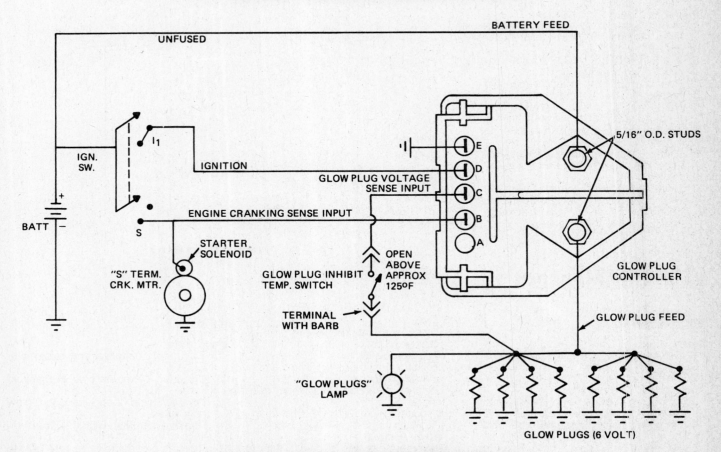

Fig. 7   Glow plug wiring schematic. 1985

INTAKE MANIFOLD
REPLACE

EXC. VAN

1. Disconnect batteries, remove air cleaner, crankcase ventilator tubes, secondary filter lines and secondary filter and adapter, if equipped.
2. Loosen vacuum pump bolts and rotate pump for access to manifold bolts. Remove bolts.

NOTE: Injection line clips are retained by same bolts.

3. Remove EGR/EPR valve bracket and A/C bracket, if equipped.
4. Remove intake manifold.
5. Reverse procedure to install. Refer to **Fig. 8** for bolt torque and tightening sequence. Refer to **Figs. 9 through 13** for fuel line installation.

NOTE: Gasket has opening for EGR on light duty application and insert to cover opening for heavy duty applications.

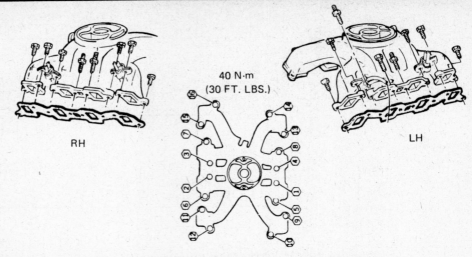

RH

40 N·m (30 FT. LBS.)

LH

Fig. 8 Intake manifold tightening sequence

VAN

1. Disconnect batteries, then remove engine cover.
2. Remove air cleaner assembly.
3. Remove EGR/EPR switches.
4. Remove crankcase depression regulator valve hoses from intake manifold.
5. If equipped with A/C, remove rear compressor bracket.
6. Remove fuel filter to intake manifold bracket.
7. Remove vacuum pump. After removal, place a rag or cover over hole to prevent foreign material from entering engine.
8. Remove intake manifold bolts and fuel line clips, then remove intake manifold.
9. Reverse procedure to install. Refer to **Fig. 8** for bolt torque and tightening sequence. Refer to **Figs. 9 through 13** for fuel line installation.

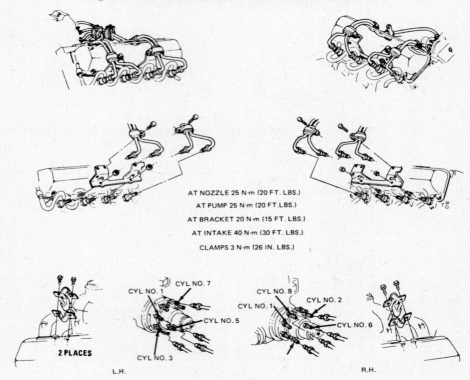

AT NOZZLE 25 N·m (20 FT. LBS.)
AT PUMP 25 N·m (20 FT. LBS.)
AT BRACKET 20 N·m (15 FT. LBS.)
AT INTAKE 40 N·m (30 FT. LBS.)
CLAMPS 3 N·m (26 IN. LBS.)

CYL NO. 7
CYL NO. 1
CYL NO. 5
CYL NO. 3
2 PLACES
L.H.

CYL NO. 8
CYL NO. 1
CYL NO. 2
CYL NO. 6
R.H.

Fig. 9 Fuel injection lines

EXHAUST MANIFOLD
REPLACE

EXC. VAN

Right Side
1. Disconnect batteries and raise vehicle.
2. Disconnect exhaust pipe from manifold and lower vehicle.
3. Disconnect glow plug wires and remove air cleaner duct bracket.
4. Remove glow plugs and manifold bolts.
5. Reverse procedure to install. Refer to **Fig. 14** for bolt locations and torque.

Left Side
1. Disconnect batteries.
2. Remove dipstick tube bracket nut, then the dipstick tube.
3. Disconnect glow plug wires, then remove glow plugs.
4. Remove manifold bolts, then raise vehicle.
5. Disconnect exhaust pipe from manifold, then remove manifold from bottom of vehicle.
6. Reverse procedure to install. Refer to **Fig. 14** for bolt location and torque.

VAN

Right Side
1. Disconnect batteries and raise vehicle.
2. Disconnect exhaust pipe at manifold flange.
3. Lower vehicle, then disconnect glow plug wires.
4. Remove manifold bolts, then the manifold.
5. Reverse procedure to install. Refer to **Fig. 14** for bolt locations and torque.

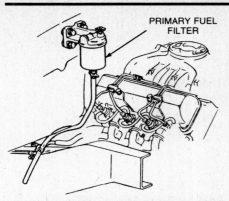

Fig. 10   Primary fuel filter. 1982

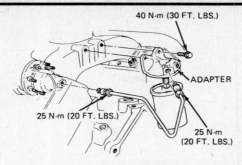

Fig. 11   Secondary fuel filter. 1982

Fig. 14 for bolt locations and torque.

CYLINDER HEAD
REPLACE

SERVICE BULLETIN Whenever removing a cylinder head on 1982–83 models, the original head bolts should be discarded and new bolts (part No. 14077193) installed. These new type bolts are standard equipment on 1984 and later production engines.

EXC. VAN

SERVICE BULLETIN External coolant loss from the rear lower corner of the left cylinder head and front lower corner of the right cylinder head is the result of a sealing condition around the core cleanout hole in the cylinder head. This condition can be corrected by installing a brass plug kit (part No. 14077197), consisting of two brass plugs and one driver. To install plugs, remove cylinder head as outlined below, then proceed as follows:
1. Clean inside edge of plug hole, **Fig. 14A**, with a wire brush and suitable solvent.
2. Apply suitable sealant to sides of brass plug and hole.
3. Install plug slowly and squarely using

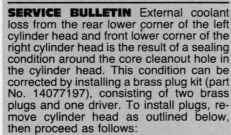

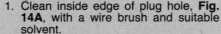

Fig. 12   Fuel filter. 1983–85 exc. vans

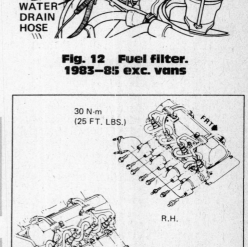

Fig. 14   Exhaust manifold bolt location

an arbor press and plug driver, until plug is flush with head surface. If the plug deforms or pulls away from side of hole, lightly tap sides of plug to move back into contact with side of hole while sealant is still wet.
4. Remove all old sealant from cylinder head bolt holes in block using an M12 × 1.75 tap.
5. Clean block mating surfaces and remove any sheared brass or excessive sealant from cylinder head.
6. Install cylinder head as outlined below.

1. Remove injection lines, then the intake manifold and rocker arm covers.
2. Drain coolant, remove dipstick tube and disconnect ground wire at cowl.
3. Raise vehicle, disconnect exhaust manifold, and lower vehicle.
4. Remove A/C compressor (if equipped).
5. Remove generator and disconnect glow plug wires. Remove rocker arm assemblies.

NOTE: Mark rocker arms and push rods so they can be reinstalled in same location.

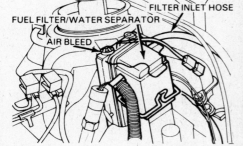

Fig. 13   Fuel filter. 1983–85 vans

Left Side
1. Disconnect batteries and raise vehicle.
2. Disconnect glow plug wires, then lower vehicle.
3. Disconnect exhaust pipe at manifold flange.
4. Remove manifold bolts, then the manifold.
5. Reverse procedure to install. Refer to

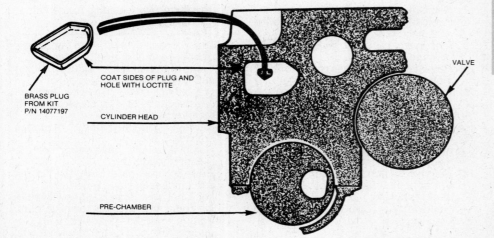

Fig. 14A   Installing brass plug into cylinder head

6. Disconnect radiator, bypass, heater hoses and ground strap.
7. Remove thermostat housing/cross-over at cylinder head.
8. Remove cylinder head bolts and cylinder head.
9. Reverse procedure to install. Do not use any sealer on cylinder head gasket. Coat cylinder head bolts with sealing compound 1052080, or equivalent. Torque cylinder head bolts in sequence, **Fig. 15**, a little at a time, until torque is reached. Refer to "Engine Tightening Specifications" chart.

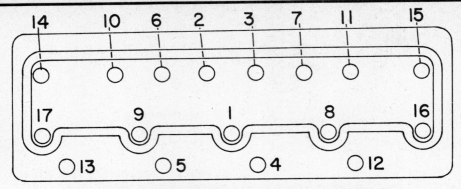

Fig. 15 Cylinder head bolt tightening sequence

VAN

Right Side

1. Remove intake manifold. Refer to "Intake Manifold, Replace."
2. Remove injection lines.
3. If equipped with cruise control, remove cruise control transducer.
4. If equipped with A/C, remove upper fan shroud and A/C compressor belt.
5. Raise vehicle, then disconnect exhaust pipe at manifold flange.
6. If equipped with A/C, remove A/C compressor brace from exhaust manifold.
7. Disconnect glow plug wires and lower vehicle.
8. If equipped with A/C, discharge system, disconnect A/C compressor suction and discharge lines, then remove A/C compressor from brackets and remove.
9. Loosen dipstick tube front bracket and remove from stud.
10. Remove upper bracket from oil fill tube.
11. Remove wire loom bracket, rocker cover bolts and rocker cover.
12. Remove rocker arm assemblies, then remove push rods.

NOTE: Prior to removing push rods, mark upper end as an aid during reassembly. Failure to identify push rods could result in incorrect installation, leading to premature wear or damage.

13. Drain cooling system, then remove air cleaner resonator and bracket.
14. Remove transmission fill tube bracket nut and position tube aside.
15. Disconnect heater, radiator and bypass hoses at coolant crossover, then remove crossover.
16. Remove generator upper bracket.
17. Remove cylinder head bolts.
18. Remove transmission dipstick at rear of head and remove tube.
19. Remove cylinder head.
20. Reverse procedure to install. Do not use any sealer on cylinder head gasket. Coat cylinder head bolts with sealing compound 1052080, or equivalent. Torque cylinder head bolts in sequence, **Fig. 15,** a little at a time, until torque is reached. Refer to "Engine Tightening Specifications" chart.

Left Side

1. Remove intake manifold. Refer to "Intake Manifold, Replace."

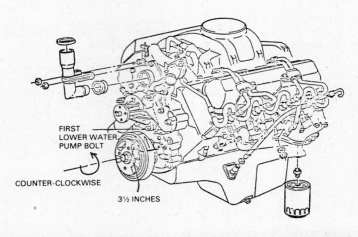

Fig. 16 Positioning engine for rocker arm shaft installation

2. Remove fuel injection lines from injection pump.
3. If equipped with cruise control, remove cruise control transducer.
4. If equipped with A/C, remove upper fan shroud and A/C compressor belt.
5. Raise vehicle, then disconnect exhaust pipe at manifold flange.
6. If equipped with A/C, remove A/C compressor brace from exhaust manifold.
7. Remove exhaust manifold.
8. Remove power steering pump lower adjusting bolts.
9. Disconnect glow plug wiring and temperature switch.
10. Remove injection lines from nozzles, then cap all openings. Lower vehicle.
11. If equipped with A/C, discharge system, disconnect A/C compressor suction and discharge lines, then remove A/C compressor.
12. Remove power steering pump upper attaching bolt and position pump aside.
13. Remove stud from dipstick tube front bracket, then remove oil filler tube upper bracket.
14. Remove glow plug controller and bracket, then remove glow plug relay.
15. Disconnect T.V. cable.
16. Disconnect oil pressure switch and

loom, then remove loom bracket.
17. Remove vacuum line clip attaching bolt from head.
18. Remove rocker cover bolts, then disconnect fuel return line bracket.
19. Remove rocker cover, then remove rocker arm assemblies and push rods.

NOTE: Prior to removing push rods, mark upper end as an aid during reassembly. Failure to identify push rods could result in incorrect installation, leading to premature wear or damage.

20. Drain cooling system, then remove air cleaner resonator and bracket.
21. Remove transmission fill tube bracket nut, then position tube aside.
22. Disconnect heater, radiator and bypass hoses at coolant crossover, then remove crossover.
23. Remove generator upper mounting bracket.
24. Remove cylinder head bolts, then the cylinder head.
25. Reverse procedure to install. Do not use any sealer on cylinder head gasket. Coat cylinder head bolts with sealing compound 1052080 or equivalent. Torque cylinder head bolts in sequence, **Fig. 15,** a little at a time, until torque is reached. Refer to "Engine Tightening Specifications" chart.

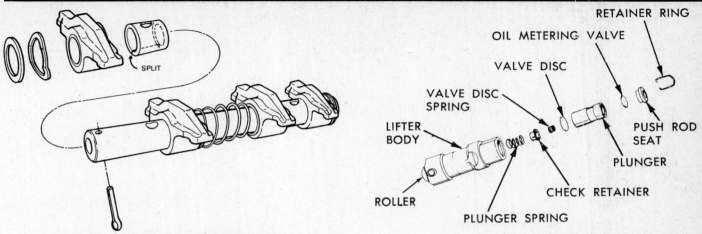

Fig. 17 Rocker arm shaft assembly

Fig. 18 Valve lifter

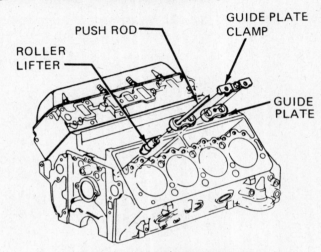

Fig. 19 Valve lifter removal

ROCKER ARMS & PUSH RODS
REPLACE

1. Remove valve cover.
2. Remove rocker arm and shaft. Remove cotter pin, and remove rocker arms from shaft.
3. Remove push rods and mark upper end for reinstallation.

NOTE: Failure to identify push rods could result in incorrect installation, leading to premature wear or damage.

4. Before installing rocker arm shafts, align TDC mark on engine with mark on engine balancer, then rotate crankshaft 3½ inches counterclockwise, or to first lower water pump bolt, **Fig. 16.** This will position engine so that all valves are closed. Torque rocker arm shaft bolts to specifications.

NOTE: The rocker arm shaft must be installed with the split in the ring around the shaft at bottom, **Fig. 17.**

VALVE ARRANGEMENT

V8-379 Diesel . . . . I-E-I-E-I-E-I-E

VALVE TIMING
INTAKE OPENS BEFORE TDC

V8-379 Diesel   13 Degrees

VALVE GUIDES

The valve guides are an integral part of the cylinder head and are not replaceable. Check valve stem to guide clearance and compare to specifications. If clearance is excessive, ream valve guides using tool set J-7049 and install oversize valves.

VALVE LIFTERS
REPLACE

Roller hydraulic lifters are used to re-duce friction between valve lifter and cam-shaft lobe. Guides keep the lifters from rotating on the camshaft lobes, **Figs. 18 and 19.**

EXC. VAN

1. Remove rocker arm covers and rocker arms.
2. Remove guide clamps and guide plates.
3. Remove valve lifters through access hole in cylinder head using Tool J-29834 and a magnet.
4. Reverse procedure to install.

NOTE: Crankshaft must be manually rotated 720° after assembly of lifter guide plate clamp to insure free movement of lifters.

VAN

1. Remove cylinder head as described under "Cylinder Head, Replace."
2. Remove valve guide clamps and guide plates.
3. Remove valve lifters through holes in cylinder head.
4. Reverse procedure to install.

CRANKSHAFT PULLEY
REPLACE

1. Disconnect batteries.
2. On van models, remove upper fan shroud. On all models, remove generator belt.
3. Remove power steering belt.
4. If equipped with A/C, remove A/C compressor belt.
5. On van models, raise vehicle.
6. Remove crankshaft pulley.
7. Reverse procedure to install.

TORSIONAL DAMPER
REPLACE

1. Disconnect batteries, then remove

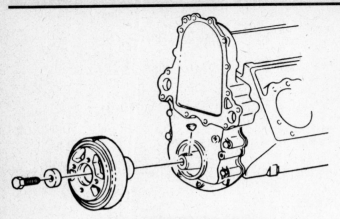

Fig. 20   Torsional damper

crankshaft pulley as described under "Crankshaft Pulley, Replace".
2. Remove torsional damper using Tool J-23523 and suitable pilot.
3. Reverse procedure to install. Torque bolt to 150 ft. lbs. on 1982–84 models, or 200 ft. lbs. on 1985 models, **Fig. 20.**

WATER PUMP
REPLACE

1. Disconnect batteries.
2. Remove fan and fan shroud and drain radiator.
3. Remove A/C hose bracket nuts (if equipped). Remove oil fill tube generator pivot bolt and generator belt.
4. Remove generator lower bracket, power steering pump and belt and A/C belt.
5. Disconnect by-pass hose and lower radiator hose. Remove water pump plate and water pump, **Fig. 21.**
6. Reverse procedure to install.

NOTE: Before installing attaching bolts, apply anaerobic sealer 1052357 or equivalent to sealing surface as shown, **Fig. 21.** Sealer should be wet to touch before installing bolts. Torque attaching bolts as shown.

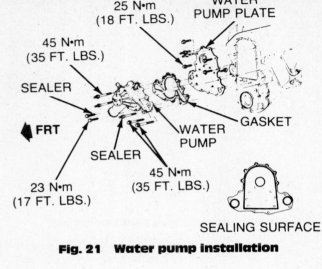

Fig. 21   Water pump installation

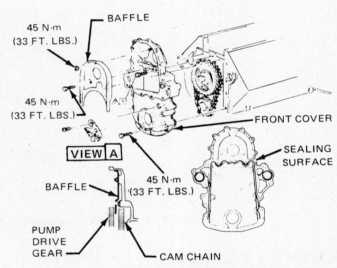

Fig. 22   Front cover installation

ENGINE FRONT COVER
REPLACE

1. Drain engine block and remove water pump.
2. Align marks on pump gear and camshaft gear, then scribe mark aligning injection pump flange and front cover.
3. Remove crank pulley, torsional damper, front cover to oil pan bolts, fuel return line clips and injection pump driven gear.
4. Remove injection pump retaining nuts from front cover.
5. Remove baffle, remaining cover bolts and front cover.

6. Reverse procedure to install. Apply a bead of sealant around sealing surface as shown in **Fig. 22.** Use sealant #1052357 or equivalent. Use RTV sealant around bottom portion of front cover which attaches to oil pan. Make sure scribe marks on injection pump and front cover are aligned and marks on cam gear and pump gear are aligned. Torque pump gear attaching bolts to 20 ft. lbs., **Fig. 23.**

FRONT OIL SEAL
REPLACE

1. Remove front cover and pry seal out of cover.
2. Install new seal using Tool J-22102.

TIMING CHAIN & GEARS
REPLACE

1. Remove front cover.
2. Remove camshaft and injection pump gears.
3. Remove cam sprocket, chain and crank sprocket.
4. Reverse procedure to install. Install cam sprocket and crank sprocket so that timing marks are aligned. Next, rotate crankshaft 360° so that camshaft gear and injection pump gear timing marks will align. Torque cam gear bolt to 65 ft. lbs. on 1982–83 models, or 77 ft. lbs. on 1984–85 models, **Fig. 24.**

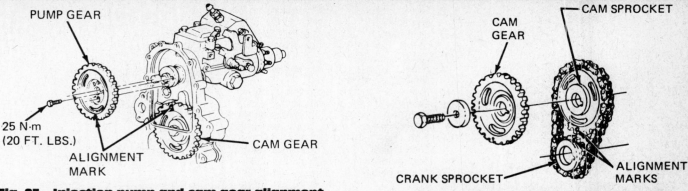

Fig. 23   Injection pump and cam gear alignment

Fig. 24   Timing chain alignment marks

CAMSHAFT REPLACE
EXC. VAN

1. Disconnect batteries, raise vehicle and drain radiator and block.
2. Disconnect exhaust pipe from engine and remove fan shroud attaching bolts.
3. Lower vehicle and remove radiator, fan, vacuum pump and intake manifold.
4. Remove injector pump lines. Cap injector nozzles and identify lines for installation.
5. Remove water pump and injection pump gear.
6. Scribe a mark on front cover and injection pump flange for realignment. Remove injection pump from front cover.
7. Remove power steering pump, generator and (if equipped) A/C compressor.
8. Remove rocker arm covers, rocker arm shaft assemblies and push rods.

NOTE: Mark valve train locations so parts may be reinstalled in original location.

9. Remove thermostat housing/crossover from cylinder head, then the cylinder head.
10. Remove valve lifter clamps, guide plates and valve lifters.

NOTE: Mark location of parts so they can be reinstalled in same position.

11. Remove front cover, timing chain, fuel pump and cam retainer plate. Remove A/C condenser (if equipped).
12. Remove camshaft.
13. Reverse procedure to install. Camshaft retainer plate should be torqued to 20 ft. lbs.

VAN

1. Disconnect batteries, then remove headlight bezels, grille and front bumper.
2. Remove lower valence panel and hood latch mechanism.
3. Remove coolant recovery bottle, then the upper tie bar.

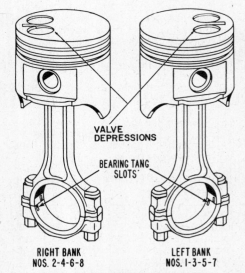

Fig. 25   Piston and rod assembly

VALVE DEPRESSIONS

BEARING TANG SLOTS

RIGHT BANK NOS. 2-4-6-8

LEFT BANK NOS. 1-3-5-7

4. On models equipped with A/C, disconnect refrigerant lines and remove condenser.
5. On all models, disconnect low coolant sensor electrical connector.
6. Disconnect all hoses and lines from radiator, then remove radiator and fan assembly.
7. On 1984–85 models, remove oil pump drive unit.
8. On all models, remove cylinder heads, then the alternator lower bracket.
9. Remove water pump, crankshaft pulleys and torsional damper.
10. Remove timing cover plate and water pump.
11. Rotate crankshaft to align timing marks, then remove injection pump driven gear and inner baffle.
12. Mark relationship between injection pump and front cover for assembly reference, then remove front cover, fuel pump and valve lifters.
13. Remove injection pump drive gear, timing chain and crankshaft gear.
14. Remove camshaft retainer plate and the camshaft.
15. Reverse procedure to install. Torque camshaft retainer plate bolts to 20 ft. lbs.

PISTON & ROD ASSEMBLY

Assemble piston to rod and install into cylinder block. Install with depression on top of piston toward outside of engine, **Fig. 25**. Install connecting rod bearing with tang slots positioned on side opposite camshaft.

PISTON & RINGS

Pistons are available in standard sizes and oversize of .030 inch. Rings are available in standard sizes and oversize of .030 inch.

MAIN & ROD BEARINGS

Main bearings are available in standard sizes and undersizes of .005 and .010 inch. Rod bearings are available in standard sizes and undersizes of .010 inch and .020 inch.

CRANKSHAFT REAR OIL SEAL SERVICE

Since the seal can be replaced only when the crankshaft is removed, the following repair procedure is recommended.

1. Remove oil pan, oil pump and bearing cap.
2. Drive end of old seal into groove using suitable packing tool approximately ¼ inch. Do this on both sides of seal, **Fig. 26.**
3. Measure and note amount that seal was driven up on one side. Using old seal removed from bearing cap, cut a length of seal the length previously noted plus ¹⁄₁₆ inch. Do this for both sides of seal.
4. Pack cut lengths of seal into appropriate side of seal groove. Use packing tool J-33154-2 and guide tool J-33154-1 since these tools are machined with a built-in stop, **Fig. 26.**

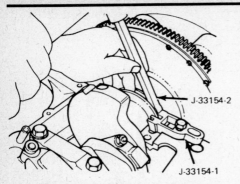

Fig. 26   Installation of guide tool

5. Apply Loctite 496 or equivalent, and install new rope seal in lower bearing cap. Cut ends of seal flush with cap, using tool J-33153, **Fig. 27**.

OIL PAN
REPLACE

EXC. VAN

1. Disconnect batteries and raise vehicle.
2. Drain oil and remove transmission dust cover, oil pan bolts and engine mount through bolt (left side).
3. Raise engine and remove oil pan.
4. Reverse procedure to install. Torque oil pan bolts to 6 ft. lbs., **Fig. 28**.

VAN

1. Disconnect batteries and remove engine cover.

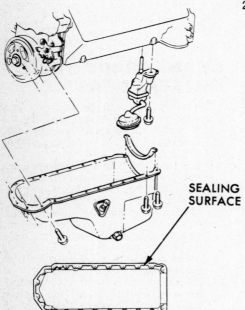

Fig. 28   Oil pan installation

2. Remove engine and transmission oil dipsticks and tubes.
3. Disconnect T.V. cable at injection pump rod and remove upper routing clips if used.
4. Remove upper bellhousing to engine retaining bolts.
5. Remove vacuum pump assembly.
6. Raise and support vehicle.
7. Remove driveshaft, then disconnect speedometer cable from transmission.
8. Disconnect torque converter clutch connector from transmission.
9. Disconnect transmission shift linkage.
10. Disconnect transmission cooler lines from transmission.
11. Remove transmission flex plate inspection cover, then remove torque converter to flex plate retaining bolts.
12. Support transmission with a suitable jack.
13. Remove transmission mount, then remove crossmember.
14. Remove transmission to engine block retaining bolts, then remove transmission.
15. Remove flex plate.
16. Drain oil into a suitable container.
17. Disconnect engine oil cooler lines from engine block.
18. Remove starter.
19. Remove oil bolts, then lower pan from engine block.

NOTE: It may be necessary to gain additional clearance. This may be obtained by rotating the crankshaft so number one and two crankshaft throws are up, providing additional lower clearance.

20. Remove oil pump retaining bolt and allow oil pump assembly to fall into oil pan.
21. Remove oil pan.
22. Reverse procedure to install. Torque oil pan bolts to 6 ft. lbs., **Fig. 28**.

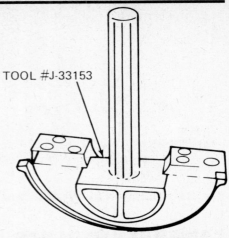

TOOL #J-33153

Fig. 27   Installing new seal (lower half)

OIL PUMP
REPLACE & SERVICE

REMOVAL

1. Remove oil pan as outlined previously.
2. Remove oil pump to rear main bearing cap attaching bolts and remove pump and extension shaft.

SERVICE
Disassembly

1. Remove pump cover attaching screws and pump cover.
2. Remove drive gear and idler gear and shaft from pump body.

NOTE: Mark gear teeth so that they can be reassembled with same teeth indexing.

3. Remove retaining pin, pressure regulator valve and related parts.

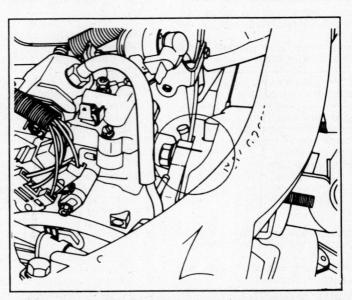

Fig. 29   Front cover to injection pump timing mark

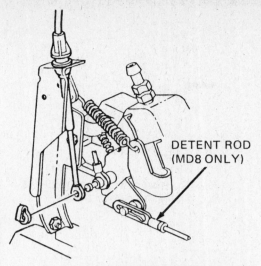

Fig. 30 Accelerator linkage

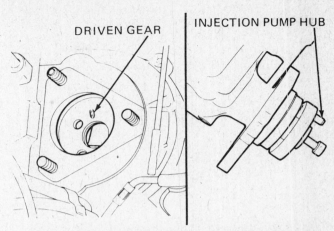

Fig. 31 Injection pump locating pin

Inspection

1. Inspect pump body and pump gears for damage or excessive wear. If either pump body or pump gears are damaged or worn, entire oil pump assembly must be replaced.
2. Check pressure regulator valve for fit and drive gear shaft for looseness in pump body.

Assembly

1. Install pressure regulator valve and related parts.

NOTE: Install idler gear with smooth side of gears toward pump cover opening.

2. Install gears and shaft in oil pump body.

3. Install pump cover.

INSTALLATION

1. Reverse removal procedures to install. Align hex on lower end of vacuum pump drive shaft with hex on top of pump drive extension shaft. Install oil pump to bearing cap bolts and torque to 67 ft. lbs.

INJECTION PUMP TIMING

1. Check marks on top of engine front cover and injection pump flange.

These marks must be aligned for engine to be properly timed, **Fig. 29**.
2. To adjust:
   a. Loosen three pump retaining nuts.
   b. Align mark on front cover with mark on injection pump. Torque nuts to 30 ft. lbs.
   c. Adjust throttle rod.

INJECTION PUMP REPLACE

SERVICE BULLETIN 1982—85 V8-379 diesel engines used in California have been timed with a microwave process.

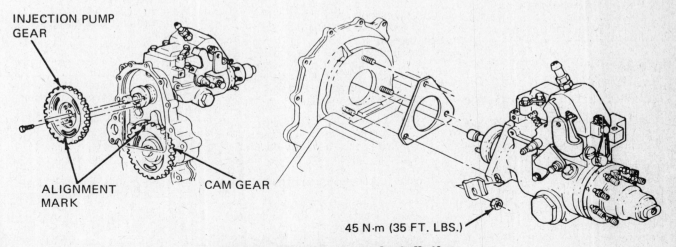

Fig. 32 Injection pump installation

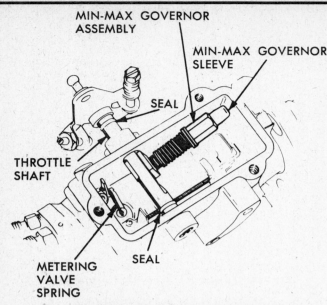

Fig. 33 Injection pump cover removed

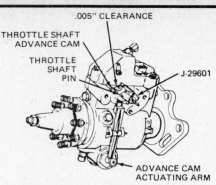

Fig. 34 Installing tool J-29601 onto injection pump

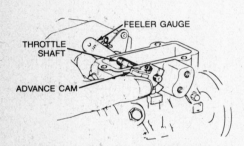

Fig. 35 Adjusting throttle shaft advance cam

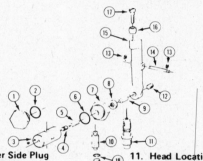

1. Power Side Plug
2. "O" Ring Seal
3. Piston Assembly
4. Servo Advance Valve
5. Mechanical Light Load
6. "O" Ring Seal
7. Spring Side Plug
8. Washer
9. Servo Advance Plunger
10. Cam Advance Pin
11. Head Locating Screw
12. Servo Advance Adjusting Screw (DO NOT ADJUST)
13. Retaining Ring
14. Rocker Lever Pin
15. Rocker Lever
16. Roller
17. Screw
18. "O" Ring
19. Cam Advance Pin Hole Plug

Fig. 36 Automatic advance group

After timing with the microwave, an additional timing mark consisting of two half circles is stamped over the pump flange/housing interface. This mark is in addition to the factory scribed marks shown in **Fig. 29.**

Whenever replacing the injection pump, ensure that the half circles align to form a complete circle. Any deviation in timing will result in the two half circles not matching. If a new injection pump is being installed, use the conventional timing marks.

EXC. VAN

Removal

1. Disconnect batteries and remove fan and fan shroud.
2. Remove intake manifold and fuel lines.
3. Disconnect accelerator cable at injection pump. On models equipped with 700-4R auto. trans. also disconnect detent cable, **Fig. 30.**
4. Disconnect fuel return line and remove wires and hoses from injection pump.
5. Remove fuel line from pump.
6. Remove A/C hose retainer bracket, if equipped.

7. Remove oil fill tube and PCV or CDRV vent hose assembly.
8. Scribe a mark on front cover and pump for alignment at reinstallation.

NOTE: In order to gain access to injection pump retaining bolts through oil filler neck, it will be necessary to rotate engine.

9. Remove front cover to injection pump attaching nuts and remove pump. Cap all open lines and nozzles.

Installation

1. Install new gasket. Align locating pin on pump hub with slot in injection pump gear, **Fig. 31.** Align scribe mark on front cover and pump and torque attaching nuts to 35 ft. lbs., **Figs. 29 and 32.**
2. Install pump-driven gear to pump and torque bolts to 20 ft. lbs.
3. Install oil fill tube and PCV vent hose assembly. Install A/C hose retainer bracket (if equipped).
4. Install fuel line at pump and torque to 20 ft. lbs.
5. Connect fuel return line, accelerator cable, injection lines and necessary wires and hoses.
6. Install intake manifold, fan shroud and fan. Connect batteries.

VAN

Removal

1. Remove intake manifold. Refer to "Intake Manifold, Replace".
2. Rotate air cleaner snorkel up to gain clearance.
3. Remove hood latch, then the windshield washer bottle.
4. Remove upper fan shroud.
5. Remove oil fill tube and grommet.
6. Working through oil fill tube hole, remove injection pump drive gear bolts.

NOTE: It may be necessary to rotate engine to gain access to injection pump drive gear bolts.

7. Remove fuel filter, bracket and injection pump feed line.
8. Disconnect wire looms from injection lines.
9. Disconnect fuel injection lines from brackets, then remove engine oil dipstick.
10. Disconnect injection pump electrical connectors.
11. Disconnect T.V. cable (if equipped).
12. Disconnect throttle cable.

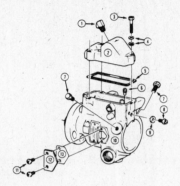

1. Return Line Connector
2. Cover, Governor Control
3. Screw
4. Lockwasher or Plain Washer
5. Governor Cover Gasket
6. Vent Screw Assembly
7. Head Locking Screw
8. Pressure Tap Screw
9. Seal
10. Housing
11. Screw
12. Timing Line Cover
13. Timing Line Cover Gasket

Fig. 37   Side housing and drive group

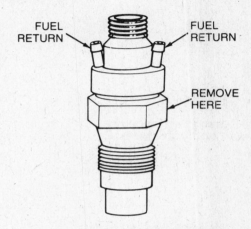

FUEL RETURN

FUEL RETURN

REMOVE HERE

Fig. 38   Injection nozzle

13. Disconnect injection lines 2, 4, 5, 6, 7 and 8.
14. Raise and support vehicle.
15. Disconnect injection lines 1 and 3.
16. Cap injectors and lines to prevent entry of dirt.
17. Identify injection lines at pump and remove. Cap line and pump openings.
18. Disconnect fuel return line.
19. Scribe a mark on front cover and pump flange to aid during reassembly.
20. Remove injection pump retaining bolts, then remove injection pump.

Installation

1. Install new gasket. Align locating pin on pump hub with slot in injection pump gear, **Fig. 31.** Align scribe mark on front cover and pump flange, then torque attaching nuts to 35 ft. lbs., **Figs. 29 and 32.**
2. Install pump driven gear into injection pump and torque bolts to 20 ft. lbs.
3. Reverse remaining removal procedure to install.

INJECTION PUMP ON-TRUCK SERVICE

PUMP COVER SEAL AND/OR GUIDE STUD SEAL, REPLACE

1. Disconnect battery ground cables.
2. Remove air cleaner and intake, then install protective screens J-29664.

3. Disconnect injection pump fuel solenoid and housing pressure cold advance electrical leads, then the fuel return pipe.
4. Remove fast idle solenoid upper attaching bolt, then loosen lower bolt and position solenoid aside.
5. Clean injection pump cover, upper portion of pump and guide stud area.
6. Remove injection pump cover attaching screws and cover. Ensure that no dirt or foreign material enters pump, since damage to pump or engine may result.
7. Observe metering valve spring to top of guide position, **Fig. 33,** to aid reassembly.
8. Remove guide stud and washer, noting location of parts.
9. Install guide stud and new washer ensuring that upper extension of metering valve spring is positioned over guide stud. Torque guide stud to 85 inch lbs.
10. Hold throttle in idle position, then install new seal onto pump cover. Install cover onto injection pump, then torque cover attaching screws to 33 inch lbs.
11. Reconnect battery ground cables.
12. Turn ignition switch to "Run" position, then momentarily connect pink wire to solenoid. A clicking noise should be heard whenever wire contacts solenoid. If clicking noise is evident, connect fuel solenoid and housing pressure cold advance electrical leads and proceed to Step 14. If clicking noise is not evident, proceed to next step.
13. Remove cover. With ignition switch in

"Run" position, ground solenoid lead and connect pink wire. The solenoid should activate and move the linkage. If solenoid does not activate, replace it. Repeat Steps 11 and 12.
14. Reinstall fuel return pipe, throttle cable and return springs, then reposition fast idle solenoid.
15. Start engine and check for leaks.

NOTE: Engine may idle roughly due to air in the injection system. Allowing engine to idle for several moments will usually purge system of air. If not, shut engine off and allow air bubbles to rise to the top of the injection pump, then restart engine.

16. Remove intake manifold screens, then reinstall intake and air cleaner.

THROTTLE SHAFT SEAL, REPLACE

1. Disconnect battery ground cables.
2. Remove air cleaner and intake, then install protective screens J-29664.
3. Disconnect injection pump fuel solenoid and housing pressure cold advance electrical leads, then the fuel return pipe.
4. Mark position of TPS swtich or vacuum regulator valve to aid in reassembly, then remove throttle rod and return springs.
5. Loosen, then position fast idle solenoid aside.
6. Remove throttle cable bracket.
7. Install tool J-29601 over throttle shaft, with slots of tool engaging shaft pin, **Fig. 34.** Position spring clip over throttle shaft advance cam, then tighten wingnut. Pull tool off throttle shaft without loosening wingnut, to provide

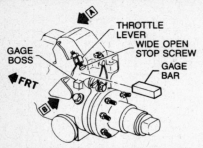

Fig. 39 Installing vacuum regulator valve gauge bar

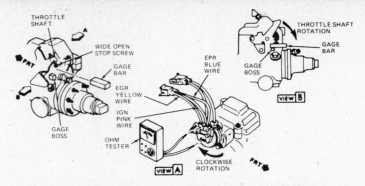

Fig. 40 Throttle position switch adjustment. All 1982 & 1983—85 with light duty emissions

proper alignment for reassembly. Loosen face cam screw.

8. Drive pin from throttle shaft, then remove throttle shaft advance cam and fiber washer. Remove any burrs from shaft.

9. Clean injection pump cover, upper portion of pump, throttle shaft and guide stud area.

10. Remove injection pump cover attaching screws and cover. Ensure that no dirt or foreign material enters pump, since damage to pump or engine may result.

11. Observe metering valve spring to top of guide position, **Fig. 33,** to aid reassembly.

12. Remove guide stud and washer, noting location of parts.

13. Rotate min-max governor assembly, **Fig. 33,** then remove from throttle shaft.

NOTE: If idle governor spring becomes disengaged from throttle block, reinstall spring with tightly wound coils facing toward throttle block.

14. Remove throttle shaft assembly and examine for wear or damage. Replace if necessary.

15. Examine pump housing throttle shaft bushings. If bushings are worn or show signs of leakage, remove pump and send to authorized Stanadyne distributor for bushing replacement.

16. Remove seals from throttle shaft. Do not cut seals from shaft, since nicks in seal seat can cause leakage.

17. Coat new seals with chassis grease or equivalent, and install seals onto throttle shaft.

18. Slide throttle shaft into pump housing until min-max governor assembly can be installed onto throttle shaft.

19. Rotate min-max governor assembly downward, hold in this position, then slide throttle shaft and governor into position.

20. Install new washer, throttle shaft advance cam and a new throttle shaft drive pin. Do not tighten cam screw at

this time.

21. Align throttle shaft advance cam so tool J-29601 can be installed as outlined in Step 7.

22. Insert a .005 inch feeler gauge between throttle shaft white washer and pump housing, then squeeze throttle shaft and torque cam screw to 30 inch lbs, **Fig. 35.** Apply Locktite 290 or equivalent to secure screw, then remove tool.

23. Install guide stud and new washer, ensuring that upper extension of metering valve spring is positioned over guide stud. Torque guide stud to 85 inch lbs.

24. Hold throttle in idle position, then install new seal onto pump cover. Install cover onto injection pump, then torque attaching screws to 33 inch lbs.

25. Install vacuum regulator valve or TPS switch, then reconnect battery ground cables.

26. Turn ignition switch to "Run" position, then momentarily connect pink wire to solenoid. A clicking noise should be heard whenever wire contacts solenoid. If clicking noise is evident, connect fuel solenoid and housing pressure cold advance electrical leads and proceed to Step 28. If clicking noise is not evident, proceed to next step.

27. Remove cover. With ignition switch in "Run" position, ground solenoid lead and connect pink wire. The solenoid should activate and move the linkage. If solenoid does not activate, replace it. Repeat steps 26 and 27.

28. Reinstall throttle cable bracket, detent cable and fast idle solenoid.

29. Reinstall throttle cable and return springs.

30. Ensure that timing marks on injection pump and housing are aligned, then tighten attaching nuts. Reconnect fuel return line.

31. Start engine and check for leaks.

NOTE: Engine may idle roughly due to air in the injection system. Allowing engine to idle for several moments will usually purge system of air. If not, shut engine off and

allow air bubbles to rise to the top of the injection pump, then restart engine.

32. Remove intake manifold screens, then reinstall intake and air cleaner.

INJECTION PUMP OFF-TRUCK SERVICE

ADVANCE PIN HOLE PLUG SEAL, REPLACE

1. Loosen advance pin hole plug seal by tapping with hammer.
2. Remove plug and seal, **Fig. 36.**
3. Reverse procedure to install. Torque plug to 75–100 inch. lbs.

AUTO ADVANCE SEALS, REPLACE

1. Remove advance pin hole plug.
2. Remove spring side advance piston hold plug, plug, piston, spring and slide washer.
3. Remove power side advance piston hole plug, plug, piston, and slide washer, **Fig. 36.**
4. Disassemble both plugs and pistons.
5. Reverse procedure to install. Torque plugs to 20 ft. lbs.

HYDRAULIC HEAD SEAL-O-RING, REPLACE

Removal
1. Remove throttle shaft and seals.
2. Remove metering valve, **Fig. 33.**
3. Remove housing vent screw assembly, **Fig. 37.**
4. Remove advance pin hole plug and advance pin, **Fig. 36.**
5. Remove head locating screws and seal.
6. Remove hydraulic head assembly and O-ring.

Installation
1. Install hydraulic head seal and place

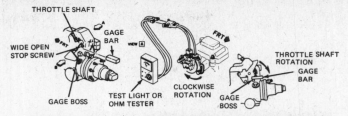

Fig. 41   Throttle position switch adjustment. 1983—85 with heavy duty emissions

head assembly into pump housing.
2. Install two head locking screws finger-tight and turn pump upside down.
3. Install head-locating screw and torque to 15—18 ft. lbs., **Fig. 36.**
4. Torque head-locking screws to 15—18 ft. lbs.
5. Install advance pin and advance pin plug.
6. Turn pump so cover opening is up, and install metering valve.
7. Install throttle shaft, seals and pump cover.

INJECTION NOZZLE
REPLACE

NOTE: The fuel injection nozzles used on 1983—85 vehicles have a different thread pitch size than on 1982 vehicles. Also, the injection nozzles used on 1983—85 vans are shorter than those used on other models. If replacement becomes necessary, make certain the correct nozzle is used.

1. Disconnect batteries, fuel return clip, fuel return hose and fuel injection line.
2. Remove injection nozzle by applying torque to largest nozzle hex with tool J-29873, **Fig. 38.**
3. Reverse procedure to install. Torque nozzle to 50 ft. lbs. Torque fuel injection line to 20 ft. lbs.

TRANSMISSION VACUUM REGULATOR VALVE
ADJUST

1. Attach vacuum regulator valve to injection pump.

NOTE: Vacuum regulator valve should be attached snugly without being overtightened.

2. Attach vacuum gauge to outboard vacuum nipple (1982) or bottom vacuum nipple (1983—84).
3. Attach vacuum source to inboard vacuum nipple (1982) or top vacuum nipple (1983—84), then apply 9.7 ± .7 PSI vacuum to nipple.
4. Open stop screw on throttle lever to fully open position, then insert vacuum regulator gage bar between gage boss on pump and stop screw, **Fig. 39.**
5. Rotate and hold throttle shaft against gage bar, then slowly rotate regulator body clockwise until vacuum gauge reads 5.6 ± .3 PSI (1982) or 3.9 ± .3 PSI (1983—84). Hold body in this position, then torque mounting screws to 4 ft. lbs.
6. Allow throttle shaft to return to idle position, then repeat Step 5. Readjust valve if necessary.

THROTTLE POSITION SWITCH
ADJUST

1. Place throttle position switch on fuel injector pump with throttle lever in closed position.

NOTE: Throttle position switch should be attached snugly. Do not tighten.

2. Attach continuity meter across terminals or wires as shown, **Figs. 40 and 41.**
3. Turn stop screw on throttle shaft to wide open position and insert "switch closed" gage block between gage boss on injection pump and stop screw.
4. Rotate and hold throttle lever against gage block.
5. Rotate throttle switch clockwise (facing throttle switch) until continuity just occurs across terminals or wires. Hold switch body in this position and tighten mounting screws.

NOTE: Switch point must be set only while rotating switch body in clockwise direction.

6. Check by allowing throttle lever to return to idle position. Remove "switch closed" gage bar and install "switch open" gage bar. Rotate throttle lever against it. There should be no continuity between terminals or wires.

Clutch & Manual Transmission Section

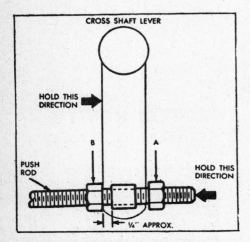

Fig. 1   Clutch pedal free travel adjustment. 1979–85 G models

CLUTCH PEDAL
ADJUST

G MODELS

1. Disconnect clutch fork return spring at fork.
2. Loosen nut "A", **Fig. 1,** and back off from swivel about ½".
3. Hold clutch fork push rod against fork to move clutch release bearing against clutch fingers (push rod will slide through swivel at cross-shaft).
4. Adjust nut "B" to obtain ³⁄₁₆ to ¼" clearance between nut "B" and swivel.
5. Release push rod, connect return spring and tighten nut "A" to lock swivel against nut "B".
6. Check free pedal travel which should be 1¼ to 1½ inch.

1979–84 C & K MODELS AND 1979–85 P MODELS EXCEPT 157″ WHEEL BASE P30/3500 & MOTOR HOME

1. Disconnect return spring at clutch fork.
2. Position clutch lever firmly against rubber bumper on brake pedal bracket.
3. Push outer end of fork rearward until release bearing lightly contacts pressure plate.
4. Loosen locknut and adjust rod length so that swivel slips freely into gauge hole, **Fig. 2.** Increase length until all lash is removed from linkage.
5. Reinstall rod into lower hole on lever. Install two washers and cotter pin. Tighten locknut without changing rod length.

6. Reinstall return spring and check pedal travel. Pedal travel should be 1⅜ to 1⅝ inch on C-K models; and 1¼ to 1½ inch on P models.

157 INCH WHEEL BASE P30/3500

1. Disconnect return spring from clutch fork.
2. Loosen nut "G" at swivel, **Fig. 2.**
3. Move clutch fork rod against fork to eliminate play between release bearing and clutch.
4. Position clutch lever against rubber stop on brake pedal bracket.
5. Rotate fork rod until a clearance of ¼ to ⁵⁄₁₆ inch is obtained between shoulder fork rod and the adjustment nut.
6. Tighten nut "G" against swivel and install return spring.
7. Check free pedal clearance at pedal. Pedal clearance should be 1⅜ to 1⅝ inch.

1979–81 EL CAMINO & CABALLERO

1. Disconnect return spring at clutch fork.
2. Rotate clutch lever and shaft assembly until pedal is against rubber bumper on dash brace.
3. Push outer end of clutch fork rearward until throwout bearing lightly contacts pressure plate fingers.
4. Install push rod in gauge hole and increase length until all lash is removed, **Fig. 3.**
5. Remove swivel or rod from gauge hole and insert into lower hole on lever. Install retainer and tighten lock nut using care not to change rod length.
6. Install return spring and check clutch pedal free travel. Free travel should be ¾ to 1⁵⁄₁₆ in.

CLUTCH
REPLACE

CABALLERO & EL CAMINO

1. Remove transmission as outlined in "Transmission, Replace" procedure.
2. Disconnect clutch fork push rod and return spring.
3. Remove flywheel housing.
4. Slide clutch fork from ball stud and remove fork from dust boot.

NOTE: Look for "X" mark on flywheel and clutch cover. If no marks are present, scribe marks on flywheel and cover to aid reassembly.

5. Loosen clutch to flywheel attaching bolts evenly one turn at a time until

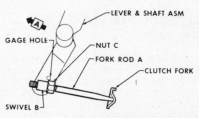

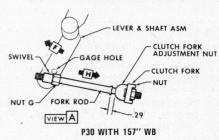

Fig. 2   Clutch pedal adjustment. 1979–85 C-K-P models

spring pressure is released.
6. Remove attaching bolts and clutch assembly.
7. Reverse procedure to install.

SERIES 10-30/1500–3500

1. Remove transmission as outlined in "Transmission, Replace" procedure.
2. On all 1979–84 models and 1985 G and P models, disconnect clutch fork push rod and return spring. On 1985 C and K models, remove slave cylinder from flywheel housing.
3. Remove flywheel housing.

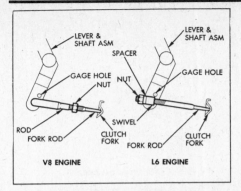

Fig. 3   Clutch pedal adjustment. 1979—81 Caballero & El Camino

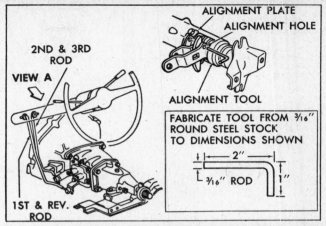

Fig. 4   Three speed column shift linkage adjustment. 1979—81 Caballero & El Camino

4. Press clutch fork away from ball mounting, then remove clutch fork, retainer and throwout bearing.
5. Support clutch assembly with suitable tool, then scribe alignment marks on flywheel and clutch cover.
6. Loosen clutch to flywheel attaching bolts evenly one turn at a time until spring pressure is released.

NOTE: On coil spring type pressure plates, it may be helpful to install ⅜ inch spacers between clutch levers and cover.

7. Remove support tool, then the attaching bolts and clutch assembly.
8. Reverse procedure to install.

TRANSMISSION
REPLACE

Caballero & El Camino

NOTE: It may be necessary to disconnect the catalytic converter to provide adequate clearance for transmission removal.

1. Disconnect battery ground cable.
2. Remove shift lever knob and, on four speed models, the spring and "T" handle.
3. Raise and support vehicle.
4. Disconnect speedometer cable and TCS wiring at transmission.
5. Remove propeller shaft.
6. Remove transmission mount to crossmember bolts and the crossmember to frame bolts.
7. Remove shift lever attaching bolts and shift levers from transmission. Disconnect back drive rod at bell housing crank on floor shift models.
8. On floor shift models, remove bolts attaching shift control assembly to support on transmission. Carefully pull unit downward until shift lever clears rubber boot and remove assembly from vehicle.
9. On all models, remove transmission to clutch housing upper retaining bolts and install guide pins in holes and

remove the lower retaining bolts.
10. Slide transmission rearward until clutch drive gear clears the clutch assembly and remove transmission from vehicle.
11. Reverse procedure to install.

Series 10—30/ 1500—3500
EXC. K MODELS

1. Raise and support vehicle, then drain transmission lubricant.
2. Disconnect speedometer cable, then remove shift controls from transmission.
3. On some 4-speed models, remove gearshift lever boot, retainer and gearshift lever. Place cloth over transmission opening to prevent dirty entry.
4. Disconnect parking brake lever and controls, if necessary, then the backup light switch wiring.
5. Disconnect propeller shaft from transmission, then the exhaust pipes from exhaust manifolds, if necessary.
6. Support transmission with a suitable jack.
7. Remove any lines or brackets that will interfere with transmission removal.
8. Remove transmission mount and rear crossmember, if applicable.
9. Remove transmission to clutch housing attaching bolts.
10. Slide transmission rearward, lower and remove from vehicle.
11. Reverse procedure to install.

K MODELS
3-SPEED UNITS

1. Raise and support vehicle.
2. Drain transfer case and transmission, then disconnect speedometer cable.
3. Remove propeller shafts.
4. Remove shift lever control assembly to adapter attaching bolt, then the shift lever rod to transfer case connector link.
5. Remove transfer case to engine sup-

port strut.
6. Support transfer case, then remove transfer case to adapter attaching bolts and the transfer case.
7. Disconnect shift linkage from transmission, then support rear of engine and remove adapter mount bolts.
8. Remove the top two transmission to clutch housing attaching screws, then install guide pins in holes.
9. Remove the two lower transmission to clutch housing attaching screws.
10. Slide transmission and adapter assembly rearward and remove from vehicle.
11. Separate adapter from transmission.
12. Reverse procedure to install.

4-SPEED UNITS
1979—81 Models

1. Remove transfer case shift lever boot retainer.
2. Remove transmission shift lever boot, retainer and shift lever.
3. Remove carpeting or floor mat from cab.
4. Remove heater distributor duct center floor outlet, if necessary.
5. Remove center console, if equipped.
6. Remove transmission floor cover, then disconnect shift lever rod assembly from transfer case connecting link.
7. Remove shift lever control attaching bolt and shift lever from adapter.
8. Raise and support vehicle, then drain transfer case and transmission.
9. Disconnect speedometer cable and propeller shafts.
10. Remove transmission mount to crossmember attaching bolts.
11. Support transmission and transfer case, then remove crossmember.
12. Remove exhaust crossover pipe, if equipped.
13. Remove upper transmission to clutch housing attaching bolts, then install guide pins in holes.
14. Remove lower transmission to clutch housing attaching bolts.
15. Slide transmission rearward, lower, then remove transmission/transfer

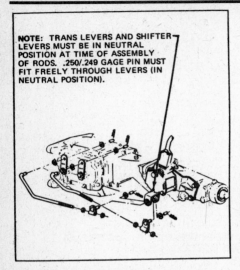

NOTE: TRANS LEVERS AND SHIFTER LEVERS MUST BE IN NEUTRAL POSITION AT TIME OF ASSEMBLY OF RODS. .250/.249 GAGE PIN MUST FIT FREELY THROUGH LEVERS (IN NEUTRAL POSITION).

Fig. 5 Three speed floor shift linkage adjustment. 1979—81 Caballero & El Camino

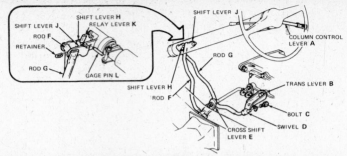

Fig. 6 Three speed column shift linkage adjustment. C & K models

case assembly.
16. Separate transfer case from transmission.
17. Reverse procedure to install.

1982 Models
1. Remove transmission shift lever boot, retainer and shift lever.
2. On vehicles equipped with New Process 208 transfer case, raise and support vehicle, then disconnect transfer case shift lever from control rod. Lower vehicle.
3. On vehicles equipped with New Process 205 transfer case, remove transfer case shift lever boot retainer.
4. On all vehicles, remove floor mat or carpeting, then the center console, if equipped.
5. Remove transmission floor cover.
6. On vehicles equipped with New Process 205 transfer case, disconnect shift lever rod assembly from connecting link, then remove shift lever to adapter attaching bolt.
7. Raise and support vehicle, then drain transmission and transfer case.
8. Disconnect speedometer cable and propeller shafts.
9. Support transfer case, then remove transfer case to adapter attaching bolts and the transfer case.
10. Remove transmission mount attaching bolts, then support transmission and remove crossmember.
11. Remove upper transmission to clutch housing attaching bolts, then install guide pins in holes.
12. Slide transmission rearward, then lower and remove from vehicle. Remove adapter.
13. Reverse procedure to install.

1983—85 Exc. 117 mm. Transmission
1. Raise and support vehicle, then drain transmission and transfer case.
2. Disconnect propeller shafts and speedometer cables.

3. Disconnect shift lever from transfer case.
4. Support transfer case, then remove transfer case to adapter attaching bolts and the transfer case.
5. Remove all lines and brackets that will interfere with transmission removal.
6. Remove attaching bolts, then remove crossmember.
7. Remove upper transmission to clutch housing attaching bolts, then install guide pins in holes.
8. Remove lower bolts, then slide transmission rearward and remove from vehicle.
9. Remove adapter from transmission.
10. Reverse procedure to install.

1983—85 117 mm. Transmission
1. Remove transmission shift lever boot, retainer and shift lever.
2. Raise and support vehicle, then drain transfer case and transmission.
3. Disconnect speedometer cable and propeller shafts.
4. Support transfer case, then remove transfer case to adapter attaching bolts and the transfer case.
5. Disconnect exhaust pipes from manifolds, then remove transmission mount to crossmember attaching bolts.
6. Support transmission, then remove crossmember.
7. Remove upper transmission to clutch housing attaching bolts, then install guide pins in holes.
8. Remove lower bolts, slide transmission rearward and remove from vehicle.
9. Remove adapter from transmission.
10. Reverse procedure to install.

3-SPEED SHIFT LINKAGE
ADJUST

CABALLERO & EL CAMINO

Column Shift
1. Place shift lever in "Reverse" position and ignition switch in "Lock".
2. Raise vehicle on a hoist.
3. Loosen shift control rod swivel lock nuts. Pull down slightly on 1/R rod attached to column lever to remove

any slack and then tighten clevis lock nut at transmission lever, **Fig. 4.**
4. Unlock ignition switch and shift column lever to "Neutral". Position column lower levers in "Neutral", align gauge holes in levers and insert gauge pin.
5. Support rod and swivel to prevent movement and tighten 2–3 shift control rod lock nut.
6. Remove alignment tool from column lower levers and check operation. Then place column lever in "Reverse" and check interlock control.

Floor Shift
1. Place ignition switch in "Off" position and raise vehicle.
2. Loosen lock nuts at shift rod swivels, **Fig. 5.** The rods should pass freely through the swivels.
3. Place transmission shift levers in neutral position.
4. Move shift control lever into the neutral detent position, align control assembly levers and insert gage pin into lever alignment slot.
5. Tighten lock nuts at shift rod swivels and remove gage pin.
6. Place transmission control lever in reverse position and the ignition switch in "Lock" position. Loosen lock nut at back-drive control rod swivel, then pull rod downward slightly to remove slack in the column mechanism, then tighten the lock nut.
7. Check interlock control. The ignition switch should move freely to and from the "Lock" position.
8. Check transmission shift operation and if satisfactory, lower vehicle.

SERIES 10—30/1500—3500

Column Shift
1. Position transmission lever B (C & K models) or C (G & P models) clockwise to forward detent, **Figs. 6 and 7,** then turn ignition switch to "LOCK".
2. Remove column lash by rotating lever J (C & K models) or L (G & P models) downward and tightening bolt C (C & K models) or M (G & P models).
3. Turn ignition switch to "UNLOCK", then position transmission levers in Neutral.

NOTE: To position levers in Neutral, move levers B and E (C & K models) or B and C

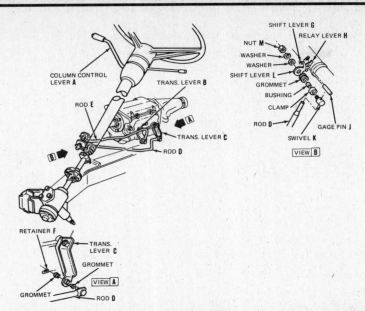

Fig. 7   Three speed column shift linkage adjustment. G & P models

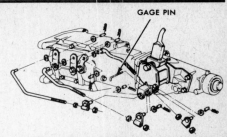

Fig. 8   Four speed floor shift linkage adjustment. 1979–81 Caballero & El Camino

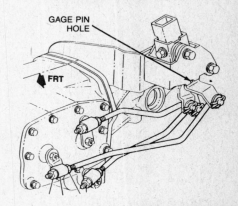

Fig. 9   Four speed shift linkage adjustment. Series 10–30/1500–3500

(G & P models) to forward detent, then turn counterclockwise one detent, **Figs. 6 and 7.**

4. Align gage pin holes in levers H, J and K (C & K models) or G, H, and L (G & P models), then insert gage pin.
5. Repeat Step 2 for rod F (C & K models) or E (G & P models) and levers E and H (C & K models) or B and G (G & P) models).
6. Remove gage pin.
7. Place column lever in Reverse and check interlock control. Ignition should lock only when in Reverse.

4-SPEED SHIFT LINKAGE
ADJUST

CABALLERO & EL CAMINO

Refer to **Fig. 8,** then follow the same procedure as outlined under "3-Speed Floor Shift Linkage, Adjust".

SERIES 10–30/1500–3500

Transmission and shifter levers must be in Neutral position at time of rod assembly. A .250 inch gage pin must fit freely into gage pin hole when shifter levers are positioned as outlined above, **Fig. 9.**

SERVICE BULLETIN Some 1982–83 C, K and P models equipped with V8-379 diesel engine and four speed 117 mm. transmission may exhibit hard shifting, bearing or gear noise, or improper clutch operation. The above mentioned complaints may be caused by the transmission top cover protruding beyond the front face of the transmission, resulting in transmission to engine misalignment. If the vehicle exhibits any of the complaints noted, proceed as follows:
1. Raise and support vehicle.
2. Using a .005 inch feeler gauge or shim, check for gaps between transmission and clutch housing.

3. If a gap or separation is noted, check for interference between top cover and clutch housing. If interference exists, proceed to next step.
4. Loosen, but do not remove, transmission to clutch housing attaching bolts.
5. Remove transmission top cover, then grind excess material from forward side of cover until proper transmission to clutch housing clearance is obtained. Deburr ground edges.
6. Wash cover with suitable solvent, then torque transmission to clutch housing attaching bolts to 100 ft. lbs.
7. Install reworked top cover, using a new gasket.
8. Torque top cover attaching bolts to 20 ft. lbs., then lower vehicle.

Transfer Case Section

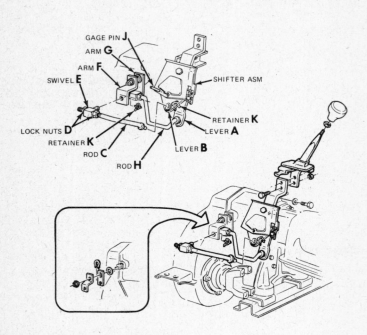

Fig. 1   Transfer case shift linkage adjustment. New Process Model 203

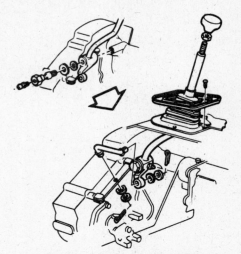

Fig. 2   Transfer case shift linkage. New Process Model 205

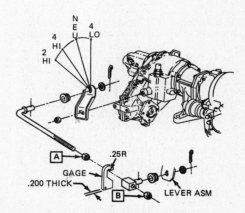

Fig. 3   Transfer case shift linkage adjustment. New Process Model 208

TRANSFER CASE
REPLACE

NEW PROCESS MODEL 203 & 205

1. Raise and support vehicle.
2. Drain transfer case, then disconnect speedometer cable, back up light switch connector and TCS switch, if equipped.
3. Remove skid plate and crossmember supports, if necessary.
4. Disconnect front and rear propeller shafts from case and position aside.
5. Disconnect shift lever rod from shift rail link.
6. On full-time units, disconnect shift levers from transfer case.
7. Support transfer case, then remove case to adapter attaching bolts.
8. Slide transfer case rearward until input shaft clears adapter and remove from vehicle.
9. Reverse procedure to install.

NEW PROCESS MODEL 208

1. Place transfer case shift lever in 4H position.
2. Raise and support vehicle, then drain transfer case.
3. Remove cotter pin from shift lever swivel.
4. Scribe alignment marks on front and rear output shaft yokes and propeller shafts to aid reassembly.
5. Disconnect speedometer cable and indicator switch wiring.
6. Disconnect propeller shafts from yokes.
7. Disconnect parking brake cable guide from right frame rail pivot, if necessary.
8. On automatic transmission equipped vehicles, disconnect engine strut rod from transfer case.
9. Support transfer case, then remove case to adapter attaching bolts.
10. Slide transfer case rearward until free of transmission output shaft and remove from vehicle. Remove gasket from adapter housing.
11. Reverse procedure to install using new gasket on adapter housing.

TRANSFER CASE LINKAGE
ADJUST

NEW PROCESS MODEL 203

1. Align gage holes in levers (A) and (B) with gage hole in shifter assembly, then insert gage pin (J), **Fig. 1.**
2. Position arms (F) and (G) in neutral position by placing arms straight down.
3. With swivel (E) and lock nuts (D) loosely assembled to rod (C), rotate swivel until ends of rod simultaneously enter lever (B) and arm (F).
4. Lock in position using retainers (K).
5. Tighten lock nuts against swivel ensuring that position of arm (F) does not

change.

6. Repeat Steps 3 through 5 for rod (H), lever (A) and arm (G).
7. Remove gage pin.

NEW PROCESS MODEL 205

The control linkage for New Process Model 205 transfer cases is shown in **Fig.**

2. Inspect linkage system periodically for freedom of operation, proper engagement or loose attaching bolts. Adjust, clean and tighten as necessary.

NEW PROCESS MODEL 208

1. Position transfer case shift lever in 4 Hi detent.

2. Push lower shifter lever forward to 4 Hi stop, then install rod swivel into shift lever hole.
3. Install .200 inch gage behind swivel as shown, **Fig. 3.**
4. With shifter against 4 Hi stop, tighten rod nut (A) until it contacts gage.
5. Remove gage, then push swivel rearward against nut (A) and tighten nut (B).

Rear Axle, Suspension & Brakes Section

CHEVROLET SALISBURY TYPE SEMI-FLOATING AXLE

In these rear axles, **Figs. 1 and 2,** the rear axle housing and differential carrier are cast into an integral assembly. The drive pinion assembly is mounted in two opposed tapered roller bearings. The pinion bearings are preloaded by a spacer behind the front bearing. The pinion is positioned by a washer between the head of the pinion and the rear bearing.

The differential is supported in the carrier by two tapered roller side bearings. These bearings are preloaded by spacers located between the bearings and carrier housing. The differential assembly is positioned for proper ring gear and pinion backlash by varying these spacers. The differ-

ential case houses two side gears in mesh with two pinions mounted on a pinion shaft which is held in place by a lock pin. The side gears and pinions are backed by thrust washers.

AXLE HOUSING, REPLACE

Caballero & El Camino

1. Raise vehicle and support at frame rails, then raise and support rear axle with suitable jack.
2. Disconnect shock absorbers from lower mountings.
3. Remove propeller shaft.
4. Disconnect upper control arms from axle housing attachments.
5. Disconnect brake line from axle housing junction block.
6. Disconnect parking brake cable, then the lower control arms from axle housing.

7. Lower axle slowly until spring tension is relieved, then roll axle housing out from underneath vehicle.
8. Reverse procedure to install.

Series 10–30/1500–3500

Construction of the axle assembly is such that service operations may be performed with the housing installed in the vehicle or with the housing removed and installed in a holding fixture. The following procedure is necessary only when the housing requires replacement.

1. Raise vehicle and place stand jacks under frame side rails.
2. Remove rear wheels and drums.
3. Support rear axle assembly with a suitable jack so that tension is relieved in springs and tie rod, if equipped.
4. Disconnect tie rod at axle housing bracket, if equipped.
5. Remove trunnion bearing "U" bolts from rear yoke, split universal joint, position propeller shaft to one side and tie it to frame side rail.
6. Remove axle "U" bolt nuts and allow shock absorbers to hang freely so that they do not interfere with axle. On K Series trucks, remove spacer from axle housing.
7. Disconnect hydraulic brake hose at connector on axle housing.
8. Remove brake drum and disconnect parking brake cable at lever and at flange plate.
9. Lower axle and remove from vehicle.
10. Reverse foregoing procedure to install axle assembly.

AXLE SHAFT, REPLACE

1. Raise vehicle and remove wheel and brake drum.
2. Drain lube from carrier and remove cover.
3. Remove differential pinion shaft lock screw and remove differential pinion shaft, **Fig. 3.**
4. Pull flanged end of axle shaft toward center of vehicle and remove "C" lock from button end of shaft.
5. Remove axle shaft from housing, being careful not to damage seal.

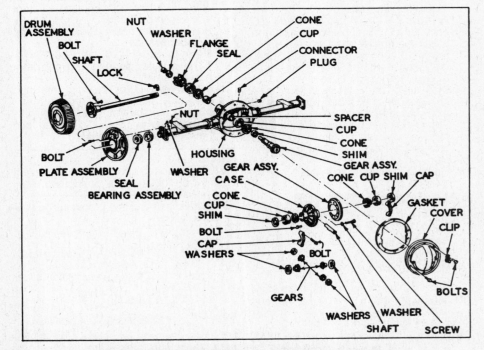

Fig. 1 Salisbury type semi-floating rear axle

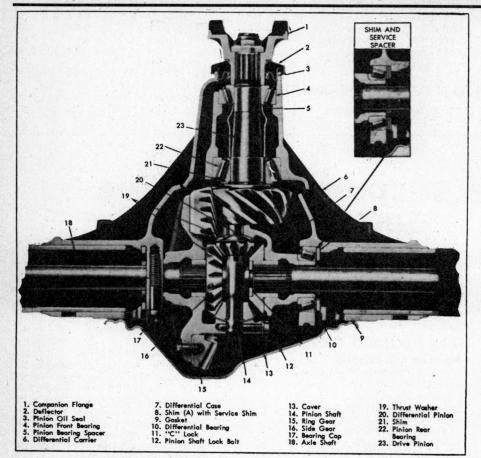

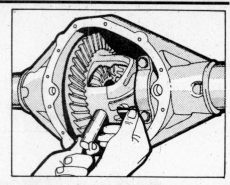

SHIM AND SERVICE SPACER

Fig. 3   Removing differential pinion shaft

Fig. 2   Semi floating rear axle of 3300 and 3500 lbs. rated capacity

1. Companion Flange	7. Differential Case	13. Cover	19. Thrust Washer
2. Deflector	8. Shim (A) with Service Shim	14. Pinion Shaft	20. Differential Pinion
3. Pinion Oil Seal	9. Gasket	15. Ring Gear	21. Shim
4. Pinion Front Bearing	10. Differential Bearing	16. Side Gear	22. Pinion Rear Bearing
5. Pinion Bearing Spacer	11. "C" Lock	17. Bearing Cap	23. Drive Pinion
6. Differential Carrier	12. Pinion Shaft Lock Bolt	18. Axle Shaft	

6. Reverse foregoing procedure to install the axle shaft.

WHEEL BEARING/OIL SEAL, REPLACE

1. Remove axle shaft as previously described.
2. Use a suitable puller to remove bearing and oil seal.
3. Lubricate wheel bearing and cavity between seal lips with wheel bearing lubricant before installation.
4. Reverse procedure to install.

CHEVROLET FULL FLOATING AXLES

The straddle mounted drive pinion is supported at the front by two opposed tapered roller bearings. The pinion gear roller bearing consists of an outer race and roller assembly and a precision ground diameter on the pinion pilot functions as an inner race.

On units with 10½ inch ring gear, **Fig. 4**, side bearing preload and ring gear to pinion backlash are controlled by side bearing adjusting rings threaded into the carrier. Pinion depth is controlled by a shim located between the pinion bearing retainer assembly and axle housing.

AXLE HOUSING, REPLACE

1. Raise and support vehicle, then remove rear wheels.
2. Remove the two trunnion bearing "U" bolts, then split universal joint and position propeller shaft aside.
3. Remove hub and drum assembly, then disconnect parking brake cable at lever and flange plate.
4. Disconnect brake hose at axle connector, then the shock absorbers at axle brackets.
5. Support axle housing with a suitable jack, remove spring plate "U" bolts and remove axle housing from vehicle.
6. Reverse procedure to install.

AXLE SHAFT, REPLACE

1. Remove bolts that attach axle shaft flange to wheel hub.
2. Tap on flange with a rawhide mallet to loosen axle shaft, then remove axle shaft by twisting shaft with locking pliers.
3. Thoroughly clean both axle shaft flange and end of wheel hub. Any lubricant on these surfaces tends to loosen axle shaft flange bolts.
4. Place a new gasket over axle shaft and position axle shaft in housing so that shaft splines enter differential side

gear. Position gasket so that holes are in alignment and install flange-to-hub attaching bolts. Torque bolts to 115 ft. lbs.

WHEEL BEARINGS, REPLACE

Hub & Drum, Remove

1. Remove wheel and axle shaft.
2. Disengage tang of nut lock from slot or flat of lock nut, then remove lock nut from housing tube, using appropriate tool, **Fig. 5.**
3. Disengage tang of nut lock from slot or flat of adjusting nut and remove nut lock from housing tube.
4. Use appropriate tool, **Fig. 5,** to remove adjusting nut from housing tube. Remove thrust washer from housing tube.
5. Pull hub and drum straight off axle housing.

Bearing & Cup, Replace

1. Using a hammer and suitable drift, drive inner bearing, cup and seal from hub assembly.
2. Remove outer bearing snap ring using suitable pliers.
3. Using tools J-24426 and J-8092, **Fig. 6,** drive outer bearing and cup from hub assembly.
4. Install new outer bearing into hub assembly.
5. Install outer bearing cup using tools mentioned in Step 3. Drive cup beyond snap ring groove.

NOTE: Install outer bearing cup with tool J-8092 positioned upside down to prevent chamfer on tool from damaging cup.

6. Install snap ring into groove using suitable pliers.
7. Using tool J-24426, drive cup against snap ring.
8. Install inner bearing cup using tools J-24427 and J-8092. Drive cup into position until it seats against shoulder of hub bore.
9. Install new oil seal.

WHEEL BEARINGS, ADJUST

Before checking wheel bearing adjustment, make sure brakes are fully released and do not drag. Check bearing play by

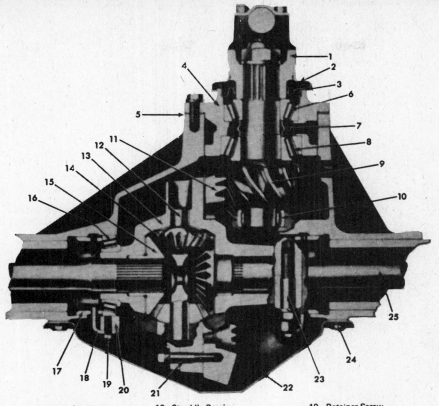

Fig. 5   Removing bearing adjusting nut lock nut

1. Companion Flange
2. Oil Deflector
3. Oil Seal
4. Bearing Retainer
5. Shim
6. Pinion Front Bearing
7. Collapsible Spacer
8. Pinion Rear Bearing
9. Drive Pinion
10. Straddle Bearing
11. Ring Gear
12. Differential Spider
13. Differential Case
14. Differential Pinion
15. Differential Side Gear
16. Side Bearing
17. Side Bearing Adjusting Nut
18. Adjusting Nut Retainer
19. Retainer Screw
20. Bearing Cap
21. Case-to-Ring Gear Bolt
22. Differential Cover
23. Bearing Cap Bolt
24. Cover Screw
25. Axle Shaft

Fig. 4   Full floating rear axle

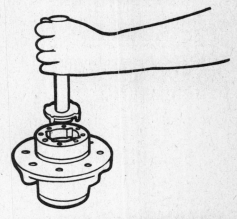

Fig. 6   Removing outer bearing and cup

grasping tire at top and pulling back and forth or by using a pry bar under tire. If bearings are properly adjusted, movement of brake drum in relation to brake flange plate will be barely noticeable and wheel will turn freely. If movement is excessive, adjust bearings as follows:

1. Remove axle shaft, then raise vehicle until wheel is free to rotate.
2. Disengage retainer tang and remove retainer from axle housing tube.
3. Tighten adjusting nut to 50 ft. lbs. while rotating hub assembly. Ensure that bearing cones are seated and in contact with spindle shoulder.
4. Back off adjusting nut until just loose.
5. Insert key into adjusting nut slot, if equipped. Install snap ring to retain key in position.
6. Lower vehicle, then install axle shaft.

GMC SINGLE SPEED AXLE

This axle, **Fig. 7**, is a full floating type and enables removal of the axle shafts without removing the truck load or raising

the rear axle. The drive pinion is straddle mounted and supported at the rear end by a straight roller bearing and at the front end by a double row ball bearing.

AXLE HOUSING, REPLACE

Refer to "Chevrolet Full Floating Axles" for axle housing replacement procedures, since procedures are identical for both axles.

AXLE SHAFT, REPLACE

1. Remove hub cap retaining cap screws and hub cap.
2. Install a slide hammer adapter into tapped hole in axle flange.
3. Attach slide hammer onto adapter and remove axle shaft from housing, **Fig. 8.**
4. Reverse procedure to install. Lubricate small end of axle shaft and install into housing using a new gasket. Torque axle flange cap screws on 15 ft. lbs.

WHEEL BEARINGS, REPLACE

1. Remove wheel and axle shaft.

2. Disengage tang of retainer from slot or flat of locknut, then remove locknut from housing tube, **Fig. 5.**
3. Disengage tang of retainer from slot or flat of adjusting nut, then remove retainer.
4. Using tool shown in **Fig. 5,** remove adjusting nut from housing tube. Remove thrust washer.
5. Pull hub and drum assembly off axle housing. Remove oil seal and discard.
6. Using a suitable steel bar and an arbor press, press inner bearing cup from hub.
7. Using a suitable pliers, remove outer bearing retaining ring, **Fig. 9.**
8. Using an old axle shaft or equivalent, drive on axle shaft spacer to remove outer bearing assembly from hub.
9. Position axle shaft spacer and outer bearing into hub, ensuring that larger side of bearing faces outer end of hub.
10. Position outer bearing cup into hub with thin edge facing toward outer end of hub, then press cup into hub.
11. Install retaining ring, then press cup into contact with ring.
12. Drive inner bearing cup into hub, then install new oil seal.
13. Reverse Steps 1 through 5 to com-

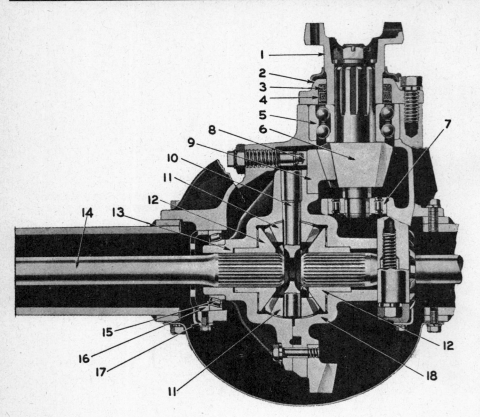

Fig. 8   Removing axle shaft. GMC single speed axle

1. Universal Joint Yoke
2. Pinion Bearing Retainer and Oil Seal
3. Oil Seal Packing
4. Oil Seal
5. Front Pinion Bearing
6. Drive Pinion
7. Rear Pinion Bearing
8. Ring Gear Thrust Pad
9. Ring Gear
10. Differential Spider
11. Differential Pinion (Spider) Gear
12. Differential Side Gear
13. Differential Case—Left Half
14. Axle Shaft
15. Differential Bearing
16. Differential Bearing Adjusting Nut
17. Adjusting Nut Lock
18. Differential Case—Right Half

Fig. 7   GMC single speed rear axle of 11,000 lbs. rated capacity

Fig. 9   Removing bearing retainer ring

---

plete installation, then adjust wheel bearings as outlined in "Wheel Bearing, Adjust" procedure.

WHEEL BEARINGS, ADJUST

1. Raise and support rear axle.
2. Remove axle shaft as outlined previously. Release brakes.
3. Disengage retainer tang from locknut, then remove locknut and retainer from axle housing tube.
4. Torque inner adjusting nut to 50 ft. lbs. while rotating wheel, then back off nut ⅛ of a turn.
5. Install retainer so that short tang engages nearest slot on adjusting nut.
6. Install outer locknut and torque to 250 ft. lbs., then bend long tang of retainer into slot of outer nut.

SPICER AXLES

These axles, **Figs. 10 and 11,** are similar to Salisbury type units. They are different, however, in that the axle shafts are full floating and the drive pinion incorporates two shim packs. The inner shim pack controls pinion depth, while the outer pack controls pinion bearing preload.

SERVICE

Refer to "Chevrolet Full Floating Axles" for axle housing and shaft replacement, hub and drum components and wheel bearing service, since procedures are identical for both types of axles.

TIMKEN (ROCKWELL) AXLE

This axle, **Fig. 12,** employs a heavy duty hypoid drive pinion and ring gear. The differential and gear assembly is mounted on tapered roller bearings. The straddle mounted pinion has two tapered roller bearings in front of the pinion teeth which take the forward and reverse thrust, while a third bearing behind the pinion teeth carries the radial load.

AXLE HOUSING, REPLACE

Refer to "Chevrolet Full Floating Axles" for axle housing replacement procedures, since procedures are identical for both axles.

AXLE SHAFT, REPLACE

1. Remove hub cap, then install slide hammer adapter into tapped hole in axle flange.
2. Attach slide hammer onto adapter, then remove axle shaft from housing.
3. Install axle shaft, ensuring that flange and hub splines align.
4. Install new gasket, position flange to hub, then install attaching bolts and tighten to specifications.

WHEEL BEARINGS, ADJUST

1. Remove axle shaft as outlined previously.
2. Raise and support vehicle.
3. Disengage retainer tang from locknut, then remove locknut and retainer from axle housing tube.
4. While rotating wheel, torque inner adjusting nut to 50 ft. lbs., then back off nut ⅛ of a turn.
5. Install retainer so that short tang engages nearest slot on adjusting nut.
6. Install outer locknut and torque to 250

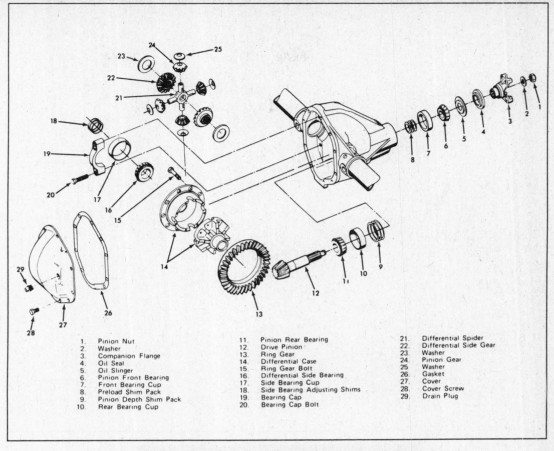

1.	Pinion Nut	11.	Pinion Rear Bearing	21.	Differential Spider
2.	Washer	12.	Drive Pinion	22.	Differential Side Gear
3.	Companion Flange	13.	Ring Gear	23.	Washer
4.	Oil Seal	14.	Differential Case	24.	Pinion Gear
5.	Oil Slinger	15.	Ring Gear Bolt	25.	Washer
6.	Pinion Front Bearing	16.	Differential Side Bearing	26.	Gasket
7.	Front Bearing Cup	17.	Side Bearing Cup	27.	Cover
8.	Preload Shim Pack	18.	Side Bearing Adjusting Shims	28.	Cover Screw
9.	Pinion Depth Shim Pack	19.	Bearing Cap	29.	Drain Plug
10.	Rear Bearing Cup	20.	Bearing Cap Bolt		

Fig. 10   Spicer axle with 10½ inch ring gear

ft. lbs., then bend long tang of retainer into slot of outer nut.

SHOCK ABSORBER
REPLACE

CABALLERO & EL CAMINO
1. Raise and support vehicle, then the rear axle.
2. Remove retaining bolts, then disconnect shock absorber from upper mounting bracket.
3. Disconnect shock absorber from lower mounting bracket.
4. Remove shock absorber from vehicle.
5. Reverse procedure to install.

SERIES 10–30/1500–3500
1. Raise and support vehicle, then the rear axle.
2. On models equipped with air lift shock absorbers, bleed air from lines, then disconnect line from shock.
3. Remove upper retaining nut or bolt, then the lower retaining bolt, nut and washer.
4. Remove shock absorber from vehicle.
5. Reverse procedure to install.

COIL SPRING
REPLACE

CABALLERO & EL CAMINO
1. Support vehicle at frame and rear axle.
2. Disconnect shock absorbers at lower mountings.
3. Disconnect upper control arms from axle housing.
4. If equipped with a stabilizer bar, disconnect bar from either right or left hand side of control arm.
5. Remove brake hose support bolt and support without disconnecting the brake lines.
6. Lower axle until it reaches end of its travel and using a suitable tool, pry lower pigtail over retainer on axle bracket. Remove spring and insulator.
7. Reverse procedure to install. Springs must be installed with an insulator between upper seat and spring and positioned properly, **Fig. 13.**

LEAF SPRING & BUSHING
REPLACE

SERIES 10–30/1500–3500
1. Raise and support vehicle and allow

axle to hang freely.
2. Loosen, but do not remove, spring to shackle retaining nut.
3. Remove shackle to spring hanger retaining nut and bolt.
4. Remove spring to front hanger retaining nut and bolt.
5. Remove "U" bolt retaining nuts, then the "U" bolt and spring plate.
6. Remove leaf spring from vehicle.
7. To replace bushing, position spring on an arbor press and press bushing from spring using a suitable rod or pipe.

NOTE: On some vehicles equipped with heavy duty leaf springs, the front bushing is staked in place. Before attempting to remove these bushings, the staked locations must be straightened with a suitable drift. After installation of bushing, restake bushing in three equally spaced locations.

8. Reverse procedure to install, installing "U" bolts as follows:
   a. Install four attaching nuts uniformly on "U" bolts to retain and position anchor plate in proper position.
   b. Torque four nuts to 18 ft. lbs. in diagonal sequence.
   c. Torque four nuts to specifications in diagonal sequence, **Fig. 14.**

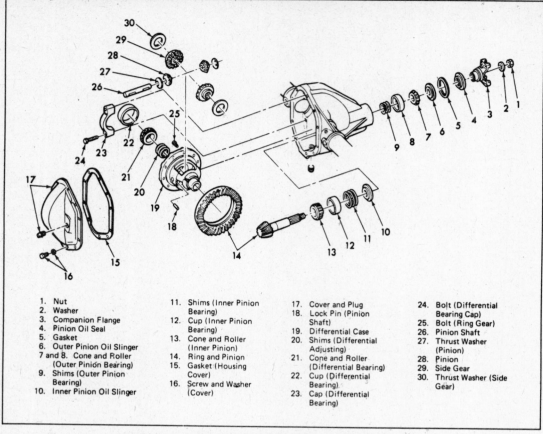

1. Nut
2. Washer
3. Companion Flange
4. Pinion Oil Seal
5. Gasket
6. Outer Pinion Oil Slinger
7 and 8. Cone and Roller (Outer Pinion Bearing)
9. Shims (Outer Pinion Bearing)
10. Inner Pinion Oil Slinger

11. Shims (Inner Pinion Bearing)
12. Cup (Inner Pinion Bearing)
13. Cone and Roller (Inner Pinion)
14. Ring and Pinion
15. Gasket (Housing Cover)
16. Screw and Washer (Cover)

17. Cover and Plug
18. Lock Pin (Pinion Shaft)
19. Differential Case
20. Shims (Differential Adjusting)
21. Cone and Roller (Differential Bearing)
22. Cup (Differential Bearing)
23. Cap (Differential Bearing)

24. Bolt (Differential Bearing Cap)
25. Bolt (Ring Gear)
26. Pinion Shaft
27. Thrust Washer (Pinion)
28. Pinion
29. Side Gear
30. Thrust Washer (Side Gear)

Fig. 11   Spicer axle with 9¾ inch ring gear

CONTROL ARM
REPLACE

CABALLERO & EL CAMINO

1. Raise and support vehicle.
2. Support nose of axle housing with suitable jack to prevent assembly from twisting when control arm is removed.
3. If lower control arm is being replaced, remove stabilizer bar attaching bolts, if equipped.
4. Remove control arm to chassis and control arm to axle housing retaining bolts, then the control arm.
5. Reverse procedure to install. Lower vehicle to floor, then torque retaining bolts as follows:
   a. On 1979–83 vehicles, torque front bolts to 70 ft. lbs. and rear bolts to 73 ft. lbs.
   b. On 1984–85 vehicles, torque front bolts to 92 ft. lbs. and rear bolts to 70 ft. lbs.

STABILIZER BAR
REPLACE

CABALLERO & EL CAMINO

1. Raise and support vehicle, then the rear axle.

2. Remove stabilizer bar to lower control arm attaching bolts, then the stabilizer bar, **Fig. 15.**
3. Reverse procedure to install. Use spacer shims, if needed, placed equally on each side of stabilizer bar. Tighten attaching bolts with vehicle at curb height.

SERIES 10–30/1500–3500

1. Raise and support vehicle, then the rear axle.
2. Remove link bolt to frame attaching nut, washer and grommet at each side of vehicle. Remove link bolts.
3. Remove support bracket to anchor plate attaching screws, then withdraw stabilizer bar and remove from vehicle.
4. Reverse procedure to install. Ensure that parking brake cable is positioned over stabilizer bar.

MASTER CYLINDER
REPLACE

1. Disconnect and plug brake lines from master cylinder.
2. Remove attaching nuts, then the master cylinder.
3. Reverse procedure to install.

POWER BRAKE UNIT
REPLACE

CABALLERO & EL CAMINO

Exc. Hydro-Boost

1. Remove vacuum hose from check valve and master cylinder retaining nuts.
2. Pull master cylinder forward so it clears mounting studs and move to one side. Support cylinder to avoid stress on hydraulic lines.
3. Remove power unit to dash nuts.
4. Remove brake pedal push rod retainer and disconnect push rod from pin.
5. Remove power brake unit from vehicle.
6. Reverse procedure to install.

Hydro-Boost

NOTE: Pump brake pedal several times with engine off to deplete accumulator of fluid.

1. Remove two nuts attaching master cylinder to booster, then move master cylinder away from booster with brake lines attached.
2. Remove three hydraulic lines from booster. Plug and cap all lines and outlets.
3. Remove retainer and washer securing booster push rod to brake pedal

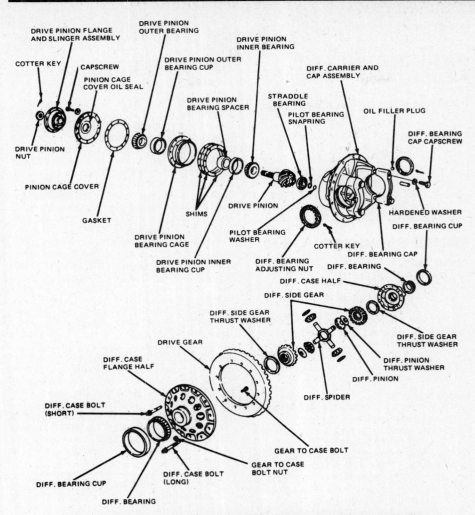

Fig. 12 Timken (Rockwell) axle with 12 inch ring gear

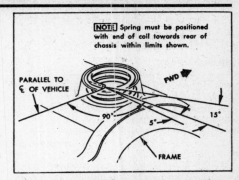

Fig. 13 Coil spring installation

arm.
4. Remove four nuts attaching booster unit to dash panel.
5. From engine compartment, loosen booster from dash panel and move booster push rod inboard until it disconnects from brake pedal arm. Remove spring washer from brake pedal arm.
6. Remove booster unit from vehicle.
7. Reverse procedure to install. To purge system, disconnect feed wire from injection pump. Fill power steering pump reservoir, then crank engine for several seconds and recheck power steering pump fluid level. Connect injection pump feed wire and start engine, then cycle steering wheel from stop to stop twice and stop engine. Discharge accumulator by depressing brake pedal several times, then check fluid level. Start engine, then turn steering wheel from stop to stop and turn engine off. Check fluid level and add fluid as necessary. If foaming occurs, stop engine and wait approximately one hour for foam to dissipate, then recheck fluid level.

SERIES 10–30/1500–3500
Exc. Hydro-Boost
1. Remove master cylinder attaching nuts and position master cylinder aside. Do not disconnect brake lines from cylinder.
2. Disconnect power brake unit push rod from brake pedal.

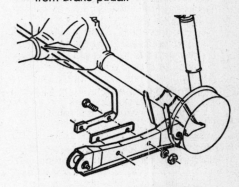

Fig. 15 Stabilizer bar replacement. Caballero & El Camino

Year	Model	Bolts Located Above Axle①	Bolts Located Below Axle①
1979–81	C & K	140	140
	G10-20/1500-2500	120	120
	G30/3500	150	150
1979–85	P10-20/1500-2500	140	140
	P30/3500	②	②
1982–83	C & K	148	170
	G10-20/1500-2500	125	177
	G30/3500	177	177
1984–85	C & K	125	147
	G	114	151

①—Ft. lbs.
②—¾ inch bolt, 200 ft. lbs.; exc. ¾ inch bolt, 170 ft. lbs.

Fig. 14 "U" bolt nuts torque chart

3. Remove attaching nuts, then the power brake unit.
4. Reverse procedure to install.

Hydro-Boost

NOTE: Before disconnecting lines from power unit, depress and release brake pedal several times to allow pressure to discharge from accumulator.

1. On P30 motor home, raise and support vehicle.
2. On all vehicles, remove master cylinder to power brake unit attaching nuts, then position master cylinder aside. Do not disconnect brake lines from master cylinder.
3. Disconnect hydraulic lines from power brake unit. Plug all lines and ports to prevent fluid loss and dirt entry.
4. On all models except P30 motor home, remove pedal push rod cotter pin and washer, then disconnect push rod from brake pedal (C and K models) or pivot lever (G and P models). Lower steering column (C and K models) or remove support brackets (P models). Remove power brake unit bracket to dash panel or support bracket attaching nuts, then the power brake unit.
5. On P30 motor home, remove operating lever to vertical brake rod cotter pin, nut, bolt and washers. Remove power brake unit linkage bracket to front and rear support bracket attaching nuts, washers and bolts, then remove power brake unit from vehicle. Remove operating lever to pedal rod cotter pin, nut, washer and bolt. Remove brake pedal rod lever nut and bolt, then the lever, sleeve and bushing.
6. Reverse procedure to install, then bleed hydraulic system as follows:
   a. Fill power steering reservoir to proper level and allow vehicle to sit for approximately two minutes.
   b. Start engine and allow to run for several minutes, then shut engine off. Correct fluid level as necessary. Do this several times until fluid level becomes constant.
   c. Raise and support front of vehicle, then turn wheels lock to lock. Shut engine off and add fluid as necessary.
   d. Lower vehicle, then start engine and depress brake pedal several times while turning steering wheel lock to lock.
   e. Shut engine off, then depress brake pedal 4 to 5 times to allow accumulator to deplete.
   f. Check reservoir and refill as required.

NOTE: If fluid is extremely foamy, allow vehicle to sit for several minutes, then repeat procedure above.

PARKING BRAKE
ADJUST

CABALLERO & EL CAMINO

1. Raise and support rear of vehicle.
2. Apply parking brake two clicks.
3. Tighten adjusting nut until left rear wheel can just be rotated rearward, but is locked when forward rotation is attempted.
4. Release parking brake and check to ensure that rear wheels rotate freely in either direction with no brake drag.

SERIES 10–30/1500–3500

Pedal Type
1. Raise and support rear of vehicle.
2. Loosen equilizer adjusting nut, then apply parking brake four clicks from fully released position.
3. Tighten equilizer nut until moderate drag is felt when rear wheels are rotated forward.
4. Release parking brake and rotate rear wheels. No drag should be present.
5. Lower vehicle.

Lever Type
1. Turn parking brake lever adjusting knob fully counterclockwise.
2. Apply parking brake, then raise and support rear of vehicle.
3. Loosen nut at intermediate cable equalizer, then adjust nut to give light drag at rear wheels.
4. Fine tune adjustment with adjusting knob on parking brake lever.
5. Release parking brake lever and rotate rear wheels. No drag should be present.
6. Lower vehicle.

Propeller Shaft Type
1. Raise and support rear of vehicle.
2. Remove cotter and clevis pins connecting pull rod and relay lever.
3. Rotate brake drum to bring access holes in alignment with adjusting screw.
4. Expand shoes by rotating adjusting screws with a screwdriver. Continue adjustment until shoes are tight against drum and drum cannot be rotated by hand. Back off adjustment ten notches and check drum for free rotation.
5. Ensure parking brake lever is in fully released position.
6. Take up slack in brake linkage by pulling rearward on cable just enough to overcome spring tension. Adjust clevis of pull rod or front cable to align with hole in relay levers, then insert clevis and cotter pins. Tighten clevis lock-

nut.
7. Install new metal plug in drum, then lower vehicle.

SERVICE BRAKES
ADJUST

These brakes, have self-adjusting shoe mechanisms that assure correct lining-to-drum clearances at all times. The automatic adjusters operate only when the brakes are applied as the car is moving rearward or when the car comes to an uphill stop.

Although the brakes are self-adjusting, an initial adjustment is necessary after the brake shoes have been relined or replaced, or when the length of the adjusting screw has been changed during some other service operation.

Frequent usage of an automatic transmission forward range to halt reverse vehicle motion may prevent the automatic adjusters from functioning, thereby inducing low pedal heights. Should low pedal heights be encountered, it is recommended that numerous forward and reverse stops be made until satisfactory pedal height is obtained.

NOTE: If a low pedal condition cannot be corrected by making numerous reverse stops (provided the hydraulic system is free of air) it indicates that the self-adjusting mechanism is not functioning. Therefore it will be necessary to remove the brake drum, clean, free up and lubricate the adjusting mechanism. Then adjust the brakes, being sure the parking brake is fully released.

1. Using a suitable punch, knock out lanced area in backing plate or drum. If drum is installed on vehicle when this is done, remove drum and clean brake compartment of all metal.

NOTE: When adjustment is completed, a new hole cover must be installed in the backing plate.

2. Using suitable tool, turn brake adjusting screw to expand brake shoes at each wheel until wheel can just be turned by hand. Drag should be equal on all wheels.
3. Back off adjusting screw at each wheel 30 notches.
4. If shoe still drags slightly on drum, back off adjusting screw an additional one or two notches.
5. When adjusting screw has been backed off approximately 12 notches, brakes should be free of drag. Heavy drag at this point indicates tight parking brake cables.
6. Install adjusting hole cover in brake backing place.
7. Check parking brake for proper adjustment.

Front Suspension & Steering Section

NOTE: On 1979 G-Series and all 1980–85 models, steering linkage relay rod assemblies will use crimped nuts. Whenever a crimped nut is loosened or removed, it must be replaced with a prevailing torque nut, Fig. 1.

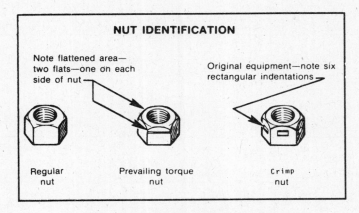

NUT IDENTIFICATION

Note flattened area—two flats—one on each side of nut

Original equipment—note six rectangular indentations

Regular nut

Prevailing torque nut

Crimp nut

Fig. 1   Crimp nut identification

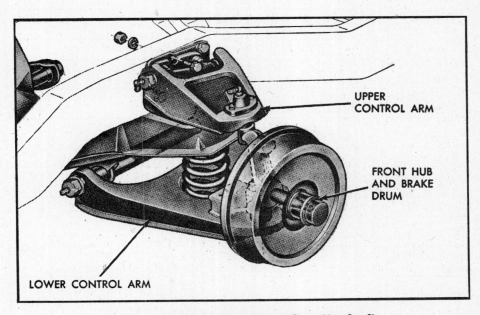

UPPER CONTROL ARM

FRONT HUB AND BRAKE DRUM

LOWER CONTROL ARM

Fig. 2   Coil spring suspension. (typical)

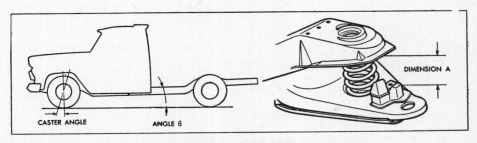

CASTER ANGLE

ANGLE B

DIMENSION A

Fig. 3   Caster-camber adjustment

COIL SPRING SUSPENSION

This suspension, **Fig. 2,** consists of upper and lower control arms pivoting on steel threaded bushings on upper and lower control arm shafts which are bolted to the front suspension crossmember and bracket assembly. These control arms are connected to the steering knuckle through pivoting ball joints. A coil spring is located between the lower control arm and a formed seat in the suspension crossmember, thus the lower control arm is the load-carrying member. The double-acting shock absorbers are also attached to the lower control arms and connect with the frame to the rear of the suspension on the upper end.

WHEEL ALIGNMENT

EXCEPT CABALLERO & EL CAMINO

Caster and camber adjustments are made by means of shims located between upper control arm shaft and mounting bracket attached to suspension crossmember. A series of convex and concave spacers with flat opposite sides are used. These spacers allow a positive cross shaft-to-bracket attachment regardless of the number of shims used. Shims may be changed at either front or rear to vary caster, or at both points to vary camber.

Caster

1. Measure frame angle at "B", **Fig. 3.**
2. Check caster on alignment machine.
3. Using frame angle measurement and measured caster angle, determine actual (corrected) caster angle as follows:
   a. Subtract a "down in rear" frame angle from a positive caster angle reading, **Fig. 4 (A).**
   b. Add an "up in rear" frame angle to a positive caster angle reading, Fig. 4 (B).
   c. Add a "down in rear" frame angle to a negative caster angle reading, **Fig. 4 (C).**
   d. Subtract an "up in rear" frame angle from a negative caster angle reading, **Fig. 4 (D).**
4. Measure dimension "A" Fig. 3.
5. Using dimension "A", and Caster Specification Chart, **Figs. 5 through 7,** find the recommended caster angle.
6. The frame corrected angle should correspond to the recommended angle on the chart within plus or minus ¼ degree. Make necessary changes to bring caster angle within limits.

Camber

1. Determine camber angle using suitable equipment.

2. Add or subtract shims from both front and rear bolts to adjust camber as required.

Toe-In

Toe-in can be increased or decreased by changing the length of the tie rods. A threaded sleeve is provided for this purpose. When tie rods are mounted ahead of the steering knuckle, decrease the length to increase toe-in. When tie rods are mounted behind the steering knuckle, increase the length to increase toe-in.

CABALLERO & EL CAMINO

Caster and camber adjustments are made by means of shims between the upper control arm inner support shaft and the support bracket attached to the frame. Shims may be added, subtracted or transferred to change the readings as follows.

Caster, Adjust

Transfer shims from front to rear or rear to front. The transfer of one shim to the front bolt from the rear bolt will decrease positive caster. One shim (1/32") transferred from the rear bolt to the front bolt will change caster about 1/2 degree.

Camber, Adjust

Change shims at both the front and rear of the shaft. Adding an equal number of shims at both front and rear of the support shaft will decrease positive camber. One shim (1/32") at each location will move camber approximately 1/5 degree.

Toe-In

Toe-in can be increased or decreased by changing the length of the tie rods. A threaded sleeve is provided for this purpose. When tie rods are mounted ahead of the steering knuckle, decrease the length to increase toe-in. When tie rods are mounted behind the steering knuckle, increase the length to increase toe-in.

COIL SPRINGS, REPLACE

1. Raise front of vehicle and place jack stands under frame, allowing control arms to hang free.
2. Disconnect shock absorber and stabilizer bar from lower control arm.
3. Install tool J-23028 or similar tool onto a suitable jack, **Fig. 8,** place jack under cross-shaft so cross-shaft seats in grooves of tool.
4. Place a safety chain through coil spring and lower control arm, then raise jack, relieving tension from coil spring.
5. Remove cross-shaft to crossmember "U" bolts, lower jack slowly and remove spring.
6. Reverse procedure to install.

BALL JOINT INSPECTION

UPPER BALL JOINT

1979 Caballero & El Camino

The upper ball joint is spring loaded internally to keep the bearing in position under vehicle loads and to provide wear take-up. Any looseness indicates a worn condition requiring replacement of ball

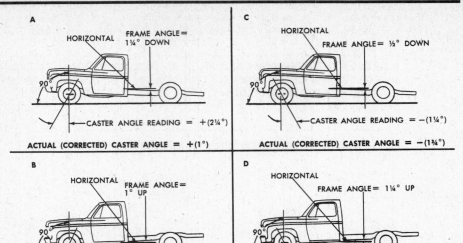

Fig. 4 Determining actual (corrected) caster angle

MODELS	2½"	2¾"	3"	3¼"	3½"	3¾"	4"	4¼"	4½"	4¾"	5"	
(mm)	63.5	69.8	76.2	82.5	89.0	95.2	102.0	107.9	114.3	121.6	127.0	
C10	2.4°	2.1°	1.8°	1.5°	1.2°	1.0°	0.7°	0.5°	0.2°	0.1°	0.3°	
C20, 30	1.5°	1.2°	0.9°	0.6°	0.3°	0.1°	0°	-0.1°	-0.7°	-1.0°	-1.2°	
K10,20,30	(8°) (NO ADJUSTMENT PROVISION)											
(mm)	1½"	1¾"	2"	2¼"	2½"	2¾"	3"	3¼"	3½"	3¾"	4"	4¼"
	38.0	44.4	51.0	57.1	63.5	69.8	76.2	82.5	89.0	95.2	102.0	107.9
G10, 20	3.5°	3.3°	3.1°	2.9°	2.7°		2.4°	2.2°	2.1°	1.9°	1.8°	1.6°
G30	2.8°	2.5°	2.2°	1.9°	1.6°		1.0°	.7°	.5°	.2°	0°	-0.2°
(mm)	2½"	2¾"	3"	3¼"	3½"	3¾"	4"	4¼"	4½"	4¾"	5"	
	63.5	69.8	76.2	82.5	89.6	95.2	102.0	107.9	114.3	120.6	127.0	
P10	2.3°	2.0°	1.7°	1.5°	1.2°	0.9°	0.6°	0.4°	0.1°	-0.1°	-0.3°	
(mm)	2"	2¼"	2½"	2¾"	3"	3¼"	3½"	3¾"	4"	4¼"	4½"	4¾"
	51.0	57.1	63.5	69.8	76.2	82.5	89.0	95.2	102.0	107.9	114.3	120.6
*P20, 30	2.9°	2.6°	2.3°	2.0°	1.7°	1.4°	1.2°	0.9°	0.6°	0.4°	0.2°	0.1°
* Add .3 degrees on vehicles equipped with Hydro - Boost												
Subtract .4 degrees on vehicles with dual rear wheels												
MOTOR HOME (32)	2½"	2¾"	3"	3¼"	3½"	3¾"	4"	4¼"	4½"	4¾"	5"	
(mm)	63.5	69.8	76.2	82.5	89.0	95.2	102.0	107.9	114.3	120.6	127.0	
	5.5°	5.3°	5.0°	4.7°	4.4°	4.1°	3.8°	3.6°	3.3°	3.1°	2.9°	

Fig. 5 Caster specification chart. 1979–81 exc. Caballero & El Camino

joint assembly.

1. Raise front of vehicle, supporting front suspension under each lower control arm between suspension spring pocket and ball joint
2. Grasp wheel at top and bottom and shake top of wheel in an in and out motion.
3. Observe for any movement of steering knuckle relative to control arm.

1979–85 Exc. Caballero & El Camino

The upper ball joint is spring loaded in its socket. This minimizes looseness at this point and compensates for normal wear. If

upper stud has any perceptible lateral shake, or if it can be manually twisted in its socket, the upper ball joint should be replaced.

1980–85 Caballero & El Camino

1. Ensure that wheel bearings are properly adjusted.
2. Raise vehicle and position supporting devices under lower control arms as near as possible to lower ball joints, ensuring that vehicle is stable and does not rock on supporting devices.
3. Position dial indicator against wheel rim, **Fig. 9.**

MODELS (mm)	2½" 63.5	2¾" 69.8	3" 76.2	3¼" 82.5	3½" 89.0	3¾" 95.2	4" 102.0	4¼" 107.9	4½" 114.3	4¾" 121.6	5" 127.0
C10	3.6°	3.4°	3.1°	2.8°	2.6°	2.4°	2.0°	1.8°	1.5°	1.2°	1.0°
C20, 30	1.5°	1.2°	0.9°	0.6°	0.3°	0.1°	0°	-0.1°	-0.7°	-1.0°	-1.2°
K10,20,30	(8°) (NO ADJUSTMENT PROVISION)										

(mm)	1½" 38.0	1¾" 44.4	2" 51.0	2¼" 57.1	2½" 63.5	2¾" 69.8	3" 76.2	3¼" 82.5	3½" 89.0	3¾" 95.2	4" 102.0	4¼" 107.9
G10, 20	3.5'	3.3'	3.1'	2.9'	2.7'		2.4'	2.2'	2.1'	1.9'	1.8'	1.6'
G30	2.8'	2.5'	2.2'	1.9'	1.6'		1.0'	.7'	.5'	.2'	0'	-0.2'

(mm)	2½" 63.5	2¾" 69.8	3" 76.2	3¼" 82.5	3½" 89.6	3¾" 95.2	4" 102.0	4¼" 107.9	4½" 114.3	4¾" 120.6	5" 127.0
P10	2.3°	2.0°	1.7°	1.5°	1.2°	0.9°	0.6°	0.4°	0.1°	-0.1°	-0.3°

(mm)	2" 51.0	2¼" 57.1	2½" 63.5	2¾" 69.8	3" 76.2	3¼" 82.5	3½" 89.0	3¾" 95.2	4" 102.0	4¼" 107.9	4½" 114.3	4¾" 120.6
*P20, 30	2.9°	2.6°	2.3°	2.0°	1.7°	1.4°	1.2°	0.9°	0.6°	0.4°	0.2°	0.1°

* Add .3 degrees on vehicles equipped with Hydro - Boost
Subtract .4 degrees on vehicles with dual rear wheels

MOTOR HOME (32) (mm)	2½" 63.5	2¾" 69.8	3" 76.2	3¼" 82.5	3½" 89.0	3¾" 95.2	4" 102.0	4¼" 107.9	4½" 114.3	4¾" 120.6	5" 127.0
	5.5°	5.3°	5.0°	4.7°	4.4°	4.1°	3.8°	3.6°	3.3°	3.1°	2.9°

Fig. 6 Caster specification chart. 1982–84 exc. Caballero & El Camino

4. Grasp front wheel and push in on bottom of tire while pulling out at top and read gauge, then reverse push pull procedure.
5. If dial indicator reading exceeds .125 inch or if ball stud has been disconnected from knuckle assembly and any looseness is detected or the stud can be manually twisted in its socket, replace ball joint.

LOWER BALL JOINT

NOTE: Lower ball joints are a loose fit when not connected to the steering knuckle. Wear may be checked without disassembling the ball stud as follows:

1. Support weight of control arms at wheel hub and drum.
2. Measure distance between tip of ball stud and tip of grease fitting below ball joint, **Fig. 10.**
3. Move support to control arm to allow wheel hub and drum to hang free. Measure distance as in Step 2. If difference in measurements exceeds 1/16 inch for Caballero and El Camino and 3/32 inch for all other models, ball joint is worn and should be replaced.

NOTE: Caballero and El Camino models have lower ball joints that incorporate wear indicators. Refer to **Fig. 11** to check for wear.

BALL JOINT, REPLACE

Upper

1. Raise vehicle, then support lower control arm with suitable jack.
2. Remove cotter pin from upper ball stud, then loosen stud nut approximately two turns.
3. Separate ball joint from steering knuckle using suitable tool, then remove stud nut.
4. Center punch rivet heads, then drill out rivets and remove ball joint from control arm.
5. Reverse procedure to install. Torque stud nut to 50 ft. lbs. on 10 Series, 90 ft. lbs. on 20 and 30 Series, and 65 ft. lbs. on Caballero and El Camino.

Dimension "A"	2½"	2¾"	3"	3¼"	3½"	3¾"	4"	4¼"	4½"	4¾"	5"	5¼"	5½"	5¾"	6"
C10	3.65°	3.45°	3.15°	2.85°	2.60°	2.35°	2.05°	1.75°	1.50°	1.25°	1.00°	.75°	.05°	.25°	0°
C20, 30	1.507°	1.224°	.928°	.612°	.328°	.114°	-.011°	-.152°	-.746°	-.999°	-1.246°	-1.440°	-1.638°	-1.849°	
K10, 20, 30	8° (No adjustment provision)														

Dimension "A"	1½"	1¾"	2"	2¼"	2½"	2¾"	3"	3¼"	3½"	3¾"	4"	4¼"	4½"
G10, 20	3.417°	3.217°	3.00°	2.85°	2.667°	2.48°	2.33°	2.15°	2.00°	1.80°	1.687°	1.53°	1.40°
G30	3.094°	2.967°	2.667°	2.367°	2.100°	1.833°	1.500°	1.233°	.967°	.700°	.450°	.200°	-.033°

Dimension "A"	2"	2¼"	2½"	2¾"	3"	3¼"	3½"	3¾"	4"	4¼"	4½"	4¾"	5"	5¼"	5½"	5¾"
P20, 30①	2.950°	2.583°	2.266°	2.000°	1.733°	1.433°	1.166°	.933°	.633°	.400°	.166°	-.100°				
P20, 30②	2.516°	2.183°	1.866°	1.600°	1.316°	1.050°	.800°	.516°	.266°	0°	-.216°	-.433°				
P30③	3.233°	2.933°	2.600°	2.350°	2.066°	1.766°	1.500°	1.233°	.983°	.700°	.450°	.200°	-.066°	-.316°	-.533°	-.733°

Dimension "A"	2½"	2¾"	3"	3¼"	3½"	3¾"	4"	4¼"	4½"	4¾"	5"	5¼"	5½"	5¾"	6"
Motor Home	5.533°	5.283°	5.000°	4.716°	4.400°	4.133°	3.833°	3.566°	3.333°	3.100°	2.866°	2.633°	2.400°	2.200°	2.000°

①—With single rear wheels, less hydro-boost.　②—With dual rear wheels, less hydro-boost.　③—With hydro-boost.

Fig. 7 Caster specification chart. 1985 exc. Caballero & El Camino

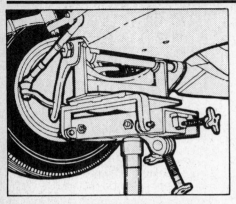

Fig. 8 Coil spring removal. (typical)

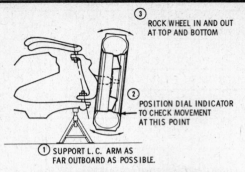

③ ROCK WHEEL IN AND OUT AT TOP AND BOTTOM

② POSITION DIAL INDICATOR TO CHECK MOVEMENT AT THIS POINT

① SUPPORT L.C. ARM AS FAR OUTBOARD AS POSSIBLE.

Fig. 9 Checking upper ball joint. 1980—85 Caballero & El Camino

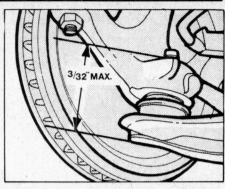

3/32" MAX.

Fig. 10 Checking lower ball joint for wear

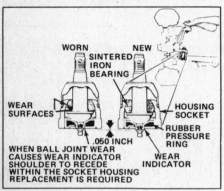

WORN   NEW

SINTERED IRON BEARING

WEAR SURFACES

HOUSING SOCKET

RUBBER PRESSURE RING

.050 INCH

WEAR INDICATOR

WHEN BALL JOINT WEAR CAUSES WEAR INDICATOR SHOULDER TO RECEDE WITHIN THE SOCKET HOUSING REPLACEMENT IS REQUIRED

Fig. 11 Lower ball joint wear indicator

NOTE: If cotter pin does not align with stud nut, tighten nut an additional amount until cotter pin can be installed. Never loosen stud nut when installing cotter pin.

Lower
1. Raise and support front of vehicle.
2. Support lower control arm with a suitable jack, then remove wheel and tire.
3. Remove cotter pin from lower ball stud, then loosen stud nut approximately two turns.
4. Separate ball joint from steering knuckle using suitable tool, then remove stud nut.
5. Lift knuckle assembly from ball stud, then position knuckle aside to allow clearance for joint removal.
6. Press ball joint from control arm using suitable tool, **Fig. 12.**
7. Press new joint into control arm by reversing removal tool.
8. Install ball joint to steering knuckle.
9. Install stud nut. Torque stud nut to 90 ft. lbs. on 10—30 Series and 1980—85 Caballero & El Camino or 83 ft. lbs. on 1979 Caballero and El Camino. Install cotter pin.

NOTE: If cotter pin does not align with stud nut, tighten nut an additional amount until cotter pin can be installed. Never loosen stud nut when installing cotter pin.

10. Install wheel and tire assembly, then lower vehicle.

WHEEL BEARINGS, ADJUST
1. While rotating wheel forward, torque spindle nut to 12 ft. lbs.
2. Back off nut until "just loose" then hand tighten nut and back it off again until either hole in spindle lines up with hole in nut.

NOTE: Do not back off nut more than ½ flat.

3. Install new cotter pin. With wheel bearing properly adjusted, there will be .001—.005 inch end play.

WHEEL BEARINGS, REPLACE
1. Raise and support vehicle, then remove wheel and tire assembly.
2. Remove hub cap and cotter pin.
3. Remove brake caliper. Do not allow caliper to hang from brake hose.
4. Remove retaining nut, then the hub and disc assembly.
5. Remove outer wheel bearing.
6. To remove inner bearing, pry out grease seal, then remove seal and inner bearing.
7. Reverse procedure to install, then adjust wheel bearings as previously described.

SHOCK ABSORBER, REPLACE
1. Raise and support vehicle.
2. Remove wheel and tire assembly.
3. Remove upper retaining nuts or bolts.
4. Remove lower retaining bolts, then the shock absorber.
5. Reverse procedure to install.

MANUAL STEERING GEAR
REPLACE
1. Place front wheels in straight ahead position.
2. On C-K and Caballero and El Camino

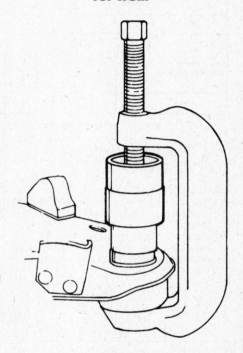

Fig. 12 Pressing lower ball joint from control arm

models, remove flexible coupling to steering shaft bolts. On P models, remove lower universal joint pinch bolts and mark position of universal yoke to wormshaft.
3. On all models, mark position of pitman arm to pitman shaft and remove pitman shaft nut or pinch bolt, then pitman arm from shaft with a puller.
4. Unfasten steering gear and remove.
5. On C-K models, remove flexible coupling pinch bolt, then flexible coupling from steering gear wormshaft.
6. Reverse procedure to install.

POWER STEERING GEAR
REPLACE

To remove gear assembly, disconnect

pressure and return hoses from gear housing and cap both hoses and steering gear outlets to prevent foreign material from entering system, then follow procedure as outlined under "Manual Steering Gear, Replace."

POWER STEERING PUMP
REPLACE

1. Disconnect hoses at power steering pump, then plug pump ports and hoses to prevent dirt entry.
2. Loosen pump adjusting bolt and remove pump drive belt.
3. Remove pump to support bracket retaining bolts, then the pump.
4. Reverse procedure to install.

Front Wheel Drive Section

DESCRIPTION

The front axles on these vehicles, **Figs. 1 and 2,** are hypoid gear units equipped with steering knuckles retained by either ball joints (K10–20/1500–2500) or king pins (K30/3500). The axle shafts drive the front wheels through yoke and trunnion type universal joints.

AXLE HOUSING
REPLACE

1. Disconnect propeller shaft from differential.
2. Raise front of vehicle, then support behind front springs.
3. Disconnect drag link or connecting rod from steering arm.
4. Remove brake calipers. Do not allow calipers to hang from brake hose.
5. Disconnect shock absorbers from spring clamp plate or axle bracket.
6. Disconnect axle vent tube clip from differential housing.
7. Remove "U" bolts, then separate leaf springs from axle housing.
8. Roll axle housing assembly out from underneath vehicle.
9. Reverse procedure to install.

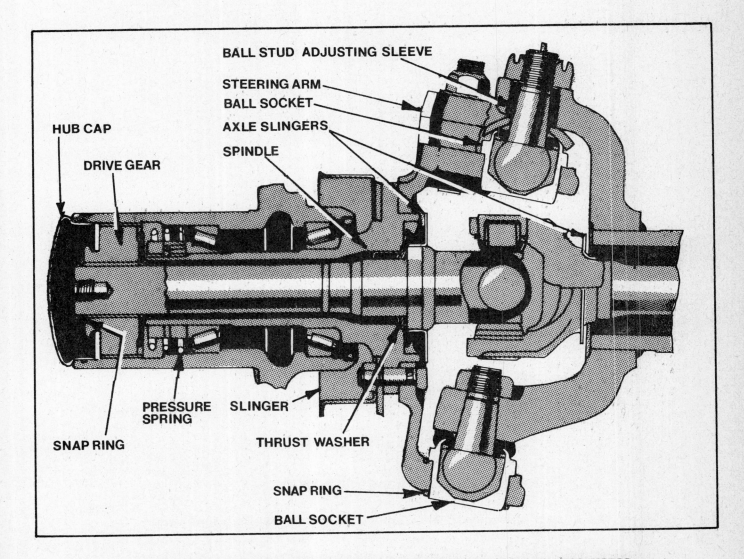

Fig. 1   Sectional view of front driving axle. 1979–85 K10/K1500, K20/K2500

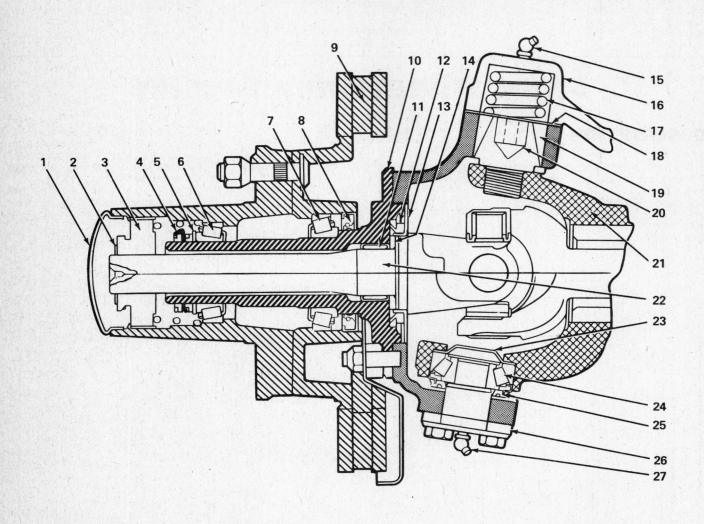

1. HUB CAP	11. SPINDLE BEARING	24. LOWER BEARING
2. SNAP RING	12. SEAL	25. SEAL
3. HUB DRIVE GEAR	13. DEFLECTOR	26. BEARING CAP
4. ADJUSTING NUT ASM	14. SPACER	27. LUBE FITTING
LOCK NUT	15. LUBE FITTING	
LOCK TANG	16. UPPER BEARING CAP	
ADJUSTING NUT	17. PRESSURE SPRING	
5. WASHER	18. GASKET	
6. OUTER WHEEL BEARING	19. BUSHING, KING-PIN	
7. INNER WHEEL BEARING	20. KING-PIN	
8. SEAL	21. YOKE	
9. HUB-AND-DISC ASM	22. OUTER AXLE SHAFT	
10. SPINDLE	23. GREASE RETAINER	

Fig. 2   Sectional view of front driving axle. 1979—85 K30/K3500 series

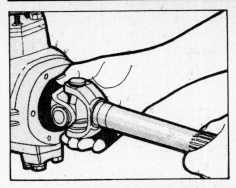

Fig. 3   Removing & installing axle shaft and U-joint

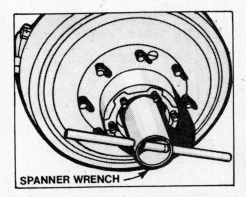

SPANNER WRENCH

Fig. 4   Adjusting wheel bearing

AXLE SHAFT
REPLACE

1. Raise and support vehicle.
2. Remove wheel and tire assembly.
3. Remove brake caliper and position aside. Do not allow caliper to hang from brake hose.
4. Remove hub lock mechanism, then the gears and snap rings.
5. Remove rotor.
6. Remove inner bearing and seal.
7. Remove spindle and backing plate.
8. Withdraw axle shaft from housing, **Fig. 3**.
9. Reverse procedure to install, then adjust wheel bearings as outlined under "Wheel Bearings, Adjust".

AXLE JOINT REPAIRS

1. Remove lock rings from trunnion bearings.
2. Support shaft yoke in a suitable vise.
3. With a brass drift and a hammer, tap on one end of trunnion bearing to drive the opposite bearing from yoke. Then, support other side of yoke and drive out remaining bearing.
4. Remove trunnion. Inspect and replace bearings if necessary, then lubricate with wheel bearing grease.
5. Replace trunnion and press bearings into yoke and over trunnion hubs far

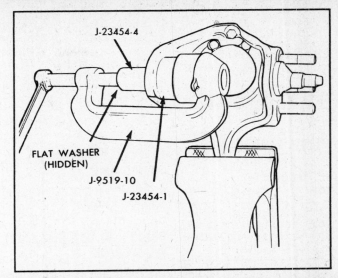

Fig. 5   Pressing lower ball joint from steering knuckle

enough to install lock rings.
6. Gently tap yoke to seat bearings against lock rings.

BALL JOINT ADJUSTMENT

Ball joint adjustment is generally required only when excessive play exists in steering, tires wear irregularly, or tie rods continually loosen. If any of the above mentioned complaints are evident, proceed as follows:
1. Raise vehicle and support with jack stands placed just inside front springs.
2. Disconnect drag link or connecting rod, then the tie rod to permit independent movement of each steering knuckle.
3. Attach a spring scale to tie rod mounting hole of steering knuckle.
4. With wheel in straight ahead position, measure the force required to keep knuckle assembly turning after initial breakaway. The force required should not exceed 25 lbs. If force required exceeds specifications, proceed to next step.
5. Remove upper ball stud nut, then loosen adjusting sleeve as required. Retighten ball stud nut, then recheck turning effort.

WHEEL BEARINGS
ADJUST

EXC. HUBS W/MONROE AUTO. TYPE LOCKING HUB

1. Remove dust cap or locking hub, lockwasher and outer locknut.
2. Using suitable spanner wrench, torque inner adjusting nut to 50 ft. lbs. Back off adjusting

nut and retorque to 35 ft. lbs. while rotating hub, **Fig. 4**.
3. Back off adjusting nut ⅜ of a turn.
4. On K10-20/1500-2500 vehicles, proceed as follows:
   a. On 1979-80 models, assemble adjusting nut lock by aligning nearest hole in lock with adjusting nut pin. Install outer locknut and torque to 80 ft. lbs.
   b. On 1981-85 models, assemble drag sleeve retainer washer over the axle shaft and against bearing adjusting nut. The tang on the inside diameter of this washer is assembled in the keyway of the spindle. Assemble and tighten outer locknut to 160-205 ft. lbs.
5. On K30/3500 vehicles, proceed as follows:
   a. On 1979-81 models, assemble lockwasher and locknut, then torque locknut to 65 ft. lbs. Bend one ear of lockwasher at least 30° over inner adjusting nut, and the other ear at least 60° over outer locknut.
   b. On 1982-85 models, assemble drag sleeve retainer washer over axle shaft and against bearing adjusting nut. The tang on the inside diameter of this washer is assembled in the keyway of the spindle. Assemble and tighten outer locknut to 160-205 ft. lbs.
6. On all vehicles, check to ensure that all hub assemblies have .001-.010 inch end play.
7. Install dust cap or locking hub.

HUBS W/MONROE AUTO. TYPE LOCKING HUB

1. Remove locking hub assembly.
2. Torque lock nut to 70 ft. lbs. while rotating hub and disc assembly.
3. Back off locknut, then retorque to 25 ft. lbs. while rotating hub and disc.

4. Back off locknut to align nearest slot, then install locknut key.
5. Measure end play. End play should be .001–.010 inch.
6. Reinstall locking hub assembly.

STEERING KNUCKLE
REPLACE

1979—85 WITH BALL JOINTS

1. Remove hub and spindle.
2. Disconnect tie rod from steering arm.

CAUTION: If steering arm is removed from knuckle, discard the self-locking nuts and replace with new ones during installation. Tighten nuts to 90 ft. lbs.

3. Remove cotter pin from upper ball joint stud nut, and remove retaining nuts from both ball joints.
4. Separate stud from yoke using suitable ball joint fork at lower joint and repeat at upper joint is required.

CAUTION: Do not remove upper ball joint adjusting sleeve from yoke unless ball joint is being replaced. If it is necessary to loosen the sleeve to remove the knuckle, only loosen the sleeve two threads. The non-hardened threads in the yoke can be easily damaged by the adjusting sleeve.

5. Reverse procedure to install.
6. Torque lower ball joint to 70 ft. lbs., adjusting sleeve to 50 ft. lbs., and upper ball joint to 100 ft. lbs. Tighten tie-rod nut to 45 ft. lbs.

1979—85 WITH KING PINS

1. Remove hub and spindle.
2. Remove upper king pin cap by alternately loosening nuts to unload the compression spring. Withdraw the spring and gasket.
3. Remove the lower bearing cap and king pin.
4. Remove upper king pin tapered bushing and knuckle from yoke. Remove felt king pin seal.
5. Remove upper king pin from yoke using a large breaker bar.
6. Drive lower king pin bearing cup, cone, grease retainer, and seal through bottom of knuckle using suitable tool.
7. Reverse procedure to install.
8. Torque upper king pin to 500–600 ft. lbs., and upper and lower bearing cap nuts to 70–90 ft. lbs.

BALL JOINT
REPLACE

1. Remove steering knuckle as previously described.
2. Remove lower ball joint snap ring.

NOTE: The lower ball joint must be removed before servicing the upper joint.

3. Using a suitable "C" clamp and service tools as shown, **Fig. 5,** press lower ball joint from steering knuckle.
4. Press upper joint from steering knuckle in the same manner as stated in Step 3.
5. Reverse procedure to install.

KING PIN
REPLACE

Follow the procedure under "Steering Knuckle, Replace" for king pin service.

HUB & BEARING
REPLACE

1. Raise and support vehicle.
2. Remove dust cap, if equipped.
3. Remove locking hub as outlined under "Locking Hub Service".
4. Remove disc brake caliper and position aside. Do not allow caliper to hang from brake hose.
5. Remove wheel bearing outer locknut, lock ring and wheel bearing inner adjusting nut.
6. Remove hub and disc assembly, and outer wheel bearing.
7. Remove oil seal, inner wheel bearing and inner and outer bearing cups using a suitable drift.
8. Reverse procedure to install. Adjust wheel bearings as outlined under "Wheel Bearings, Adjust" procedure.

LOCKING HUB SERVICE
WARNER AUTO. LOCKING HUB

Description

The Automatic Locking Hub, shown in **Fig. 6,** engages or disengages to lock the front axle shaft to the hub of the front wheel. Engagement occurs whenever the vehicle is operated in 4WD. Disengagement occurs whenever 2WD has been selected and the vehicle is moving rearward. Disengagement will not occur when the vehicle is moved rearward if 4WD is selected and the hub has already been engaged.

Before disassembling a unit for a complaint of abnormal noise, note the following:

a. To obtain all-wheel drive, the transfer case lever must be placed in 4L or 4H, at which time the hublocks will automatically engage.
b. To unlock the hubs, shift the transfer case lever to 2H, then slowly reverse the vehicle direction approximately 10 feet.
c. An incomplete shift from 2WD to 4WD, or disengagement of only one hublock may cause an abnormal sound from the

front axle. Shift to 4WD to stop the noise, then unlock the hubs as previously stated.

Removal

1. Remove 5 screws retaining the cover to outer clutch housing.
2. Remove cover, seal, seal bridge and bearing components.
3. Compress the wire retaining ring and remove the remaining components from the hub.

Disassembly

1. Remove snap ring from groove in hub sleeve, then turn clutch gear until it falls into engagement with the outer clutch housing. Lift and tilt the drag sleeve to unlock the tangs of the brake band from window of inner cage, then remove the drag sleeve and brake assembly.

NOTE: The brake band must never be removed from the drag sleeve. The spring tension of the brake band can be changed if the coils are over-expanded and could affect hub operation.

2. Remove snap ring from groove in outer clutch housing, then pry plastic outer cage free from inner cage while inner cage is being removed.
3. Pry plastic outer cage tabs free from groove in outer clutch housing, then remove outer cage.
4. Remove clutch sleeve and attached components from outer clutch housing.
5. Compress return spring and hold the spring with clamps, then position the assembly in a vise so that the vise holds both ends of the clutch sleeve. Remove retaining spring.
6. Remove clamps holding the return spring, then slowly open the vise to permit the release of the return spring in a safe manner. Remove retainer seat, spring and spring support washers from the hub sleeve.
7. Remove C-ring from clutch sleeve. It is necessary to position sleeve assembly so that the C-ring ends are aligned with legs of cam follower, allowing removal between the legs.
8. Remove conical spring from between cam follower and clutch gear, then separate cam follower from clutch gear. Do not pry the legs of the cam follower apart.

Assembly & Installation

1. Install tangs of cam follower over flats of clutch gear, then compress conical spring and position with large diameter located against clutch gear.
2. Position clutch gear assembly over splines of hub sleeve. The teeth of the cam follower should be located at the end of the hub sleeve with no splines, and the clutch gear and spring should slide freely over splines of hub sleeve.
3. Install C-ring into groove of hub sleeve, then install a spring retainer over each end of return spring.
4. Position one end of return spring with

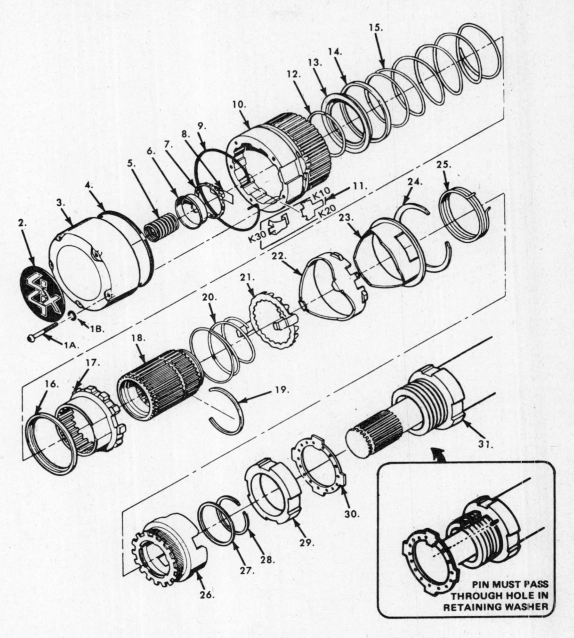

Fig. 6   Exploded view of Warner automatic locking hub

1A. Machine Screw	11. (K10-20) Seal Bridge-Retainer
1B. O-Ring Seal	(K30) Assembly Aid-Retainer
2. Cover Plate	12. Retaining Ring
3. Cover	13. Spring Support Washer
4. Sealing Ring	14. Spring Retainer
5. Bearing Race Spring	15. Return Spring
6. Bearing Inner Race	16. Spring Retainer
7. Bearing	17. Clutch Gear
8. Bearing Retainer Clip	18. Hub Sleeve
9. Wire Retaining Ring	19. "C" Type Retaining Ring
10. Outer Clutch Housing	20. Conical Spring

21. Cam Follower
22. Outer Cage
23. Inner Cage
24. Snap Ring
25. Brake Band
26. Drag Sleeve and Detent
27. Small Spacer
28. Retaining Ring
29. Lock Nut
30. Drag Sleeve Retainer Washer
31. Adjusting Nut, Wheel Bearing

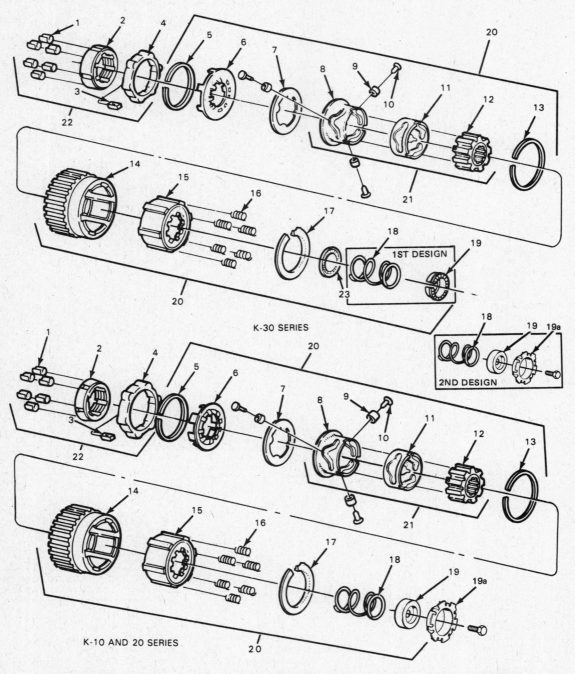

K-30 SERIES

1ST DESIGN

2ND DESIGN

K-10 AND 20 SERIES

1 Spiral Pin	9 Roller-Cam Follower	17 Ring Gear Spring Retainer
2 Lock Nut	10 Rim-Cam Follower	18 Drive Gear Spring
3 Key	11 Camlock	19 Drive Shaft Spring Retainer
4 Cage	12 Drive Gear	19a Bearing
5 Inboard Retaining Ring	13 Gear Seat Retaining Ring	20 Autolok Assembly
6 Spindle Lock Weldment	14 Adapter	21 Cam Lock Assembly
7 Thrust Bearing	15 Ring Gear	22 Cage and Nut Assembly
8 Tri Cam	16 Ring Gear Spring	23 Spring Retainer K-30 Series Only

Fig. 7   Exploded view of Monroe automatic locking hub

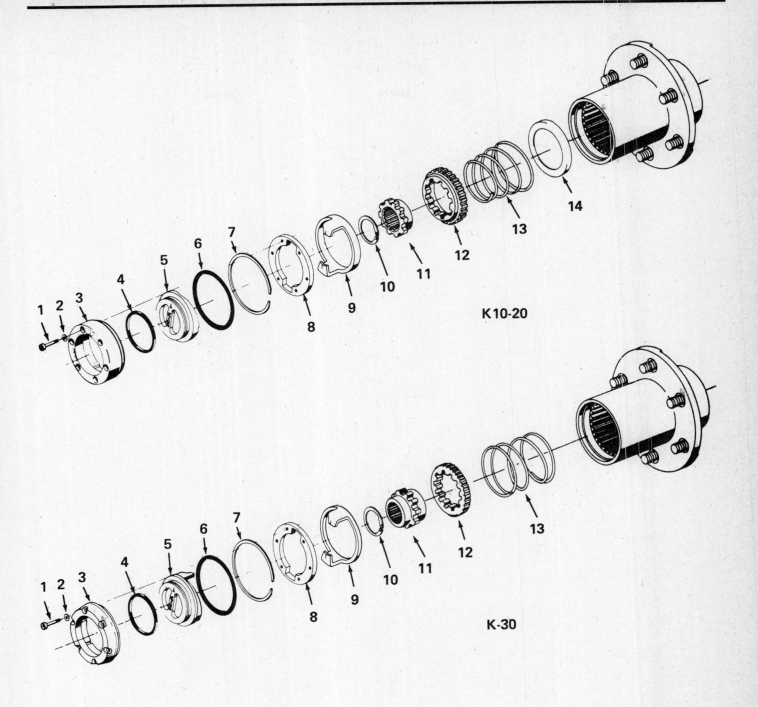

K 10-20

K-30

1. RETAINING PLATE BOLTS
2. WASHER
3. HUB RING RETAINING KNOB
4. ACTUATOR KNOB "O" RING
5. ACTUATOR KNOB
6. "O" RING
7. INTERNAL SNAP RING
8. OUTER CLUTCH RETAINING RING
9. ACTUATING CAM BODY
10. AXLE SHAFT SNAP RING
11. AXLE SHAFT SLEEVE AND RING
12. INNER CLUTCH RING
13. PRESSURE SPRING
14. SPRING RETAINER PLATE

Fig. 8 Exploded view of Spicer manual locking hub

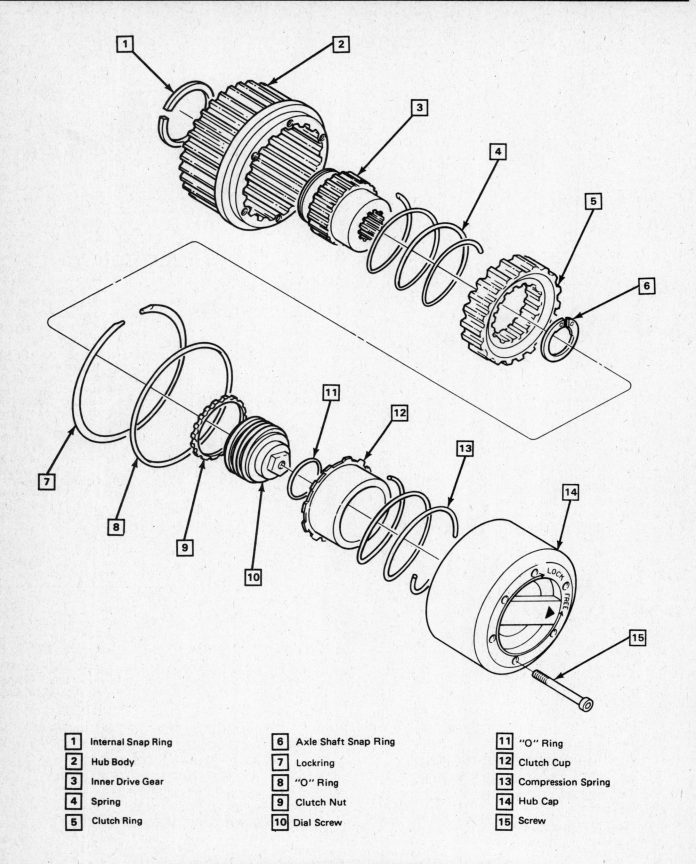

1 Internal Snap Ring	**6** Axle Shaft Snap Ring	**11** "O" Ring
2 Hub Body	**7** Lockring	**12** Clutch Cup
3 Inner Drive Gear	**8** "O" Ring	**13** Compression Spring
4 Spring	**9** Clutch Nut	**14** Hub Cap
5 Clutch Ring	**10** Dial Screw	**15** Screw

Fig. 9 Exploded view of Warner manual locking hub

retainer against shoulder of clutch gear, then place support washer on end of the return spring. Compress return spring and install retainer ring into groove of hub sleeve.

5. Place assembled components into outer housing. The cam follower should be positioned with legs facing outward.
6. Install 3 of the cover screws into 3 holes of the outer clutch housing. These screws will support the component to permit the clutch hub to drop down so that the tangs of the brake band can be assembled.
7. Carefully install the plastic outer cage into outer clutch housing with ramps facing toward cam follower. The small external tabs of the plastic cage should be located in wide groove of outer clutch housing.
8. Install steel inner cage into the outer cage, aligning tab of outer cage with window of the inner cage, then install retaining ring into groove of outer clutch housing above outer cage.
9. The brake band and drag are serviced as a complete assembly. Install one of the 2 tangs of the brake band on each side of the lug of the outer cage, located in the window of the steel inner cage. It will be necessary to tilt these parts to engage the tangs in this position as the drag sleeve is positioned against the face of the cam follower.
10. Remove the 3 screws and rest the end of the hub sleeve on a suitable support, then install washer and snap ring above drag sleeve.

NOTE: The following steps may be completed as the hub is installed into vehicle.

11. Install wire retaining ring into groove of unsplined end of clutch housing. The tangs of retainer ring should point away from splined end of clutch housing.
12. Hold the tangs together and install the 2 bent down tabs of seal bridge over tangs. The seal bridge holds the wire retainer ring in a clamped position in groove of outer clutch housing. Install O-ring into groove of outer clutch housing and over the seal bridge.
13. Lubricate and install the bearing over the inner race. The steel ball bearing should be visible when the bearing is properly installed.
14. Install bearing retainer clip into hole in outer race, then install bearing and retainer assembly in end of hub sleeve. Install seal ring over outer clutch housing.
15. Install bearing race spring into bore of cover, then install cover and spring assembly. Align holes in cover to holes in outer clutch housing and install 5 screws.
16. Install O-ring over seal bridge to prevent it from dislodging during handling prior to the hub bearing being installed into the vehicle.
17. The hub and attached parts should turn freely after installation. The 5 cov-

er screws must be loosened to install the hub into the vehicle. After installation, torque the cover screws to 40—50 inch lbs.

MONROE AUTO. LOCKING HUB

Description

This automatic locking hub, **Fig. 7**, when placed in four wheel drive, directs power to the front wheels. The front axle turns the axle shaft, activating the tri-cam mechanism, which then moves the drive gear outward into engagement with the ring gear.

When two wheel drive is selected, disengagement is accomplished by the reverse movement of the wheels, which causes the drive gear and tri-cam to rotate to the disengaged position, moving the drive gear out of mesh with the ring gear.

Removal

1. Remove tire and wheel assembly, hubcap and hublock.
2. Remove spring retainer, then the loose spring.
3. Carefully pull hublock assembly from wheel.

NOTE: If hublock assembly will not slide out freely, rotate wheel to facilitate removal.

Disassembly

1. Position hublock assembly with plastic bearing side facing downward.
2. Pry inboard spring from assembly, then remove spindle lock, thrust bearing and tri-cam assembly.
3. Clean adapter housing assembly. If any part of this assembly is worn, replace as necessary.
4. Slide ring gear from adapter housing, then remove the six ring gear springs.
5. Remove ring gear spring retainer.

Assembly

1. Install ring gear spring retainer.
2. Position the six ring gear springs into adapter housing.
3. Grease outside surface of ring gear, then install into adapter housing. Ensure that gear teeth are closest to springs.
4. Insert and install ring gear retaining ring. Ensure that the ring gear springs are properly seated in adapter housing.
5. Grease tri-cam assembly, then install into adapter housing.
6. Install thrust bearing, spindle lock and inboard snap ring. Rotate spindle lock tangs in both directions to check for free movement.

Installation

1. Install hub lock by first sliding hub onto axle shaft spline, then guide hub into wheel hub spline. When hub lock bottoms out, rotate entire wheel while pressing inward on hub until hub lock tangs engage wheel bearing locknut. Allow hub lock to seat itself.

NOTE: Hub lock should not protrude more than ⅜ inch from face of wheel hub.

2. Install spring, then unlock hub lock by rotating wheel hub while applying force to drive gear spring.
3. Install spring retainer and spring.
4. Install hub cap.

SPICER MANUAL LOCKING HUB DESCRIPTION

As shown in **Fig. 8**, the splines on the inside diameter of the axle shaft sleeve and ring assembly mesh with the axle shaft splines. The assembly is retained on the axle shaft with a snap ring. The splines on the outside diameter of the inner clutch ring assembly mesh with the wheel hub splines. Therefore, when the actuator knob is turned towards the "L" position, the actuating cam body is forced outward towards the hub end, allowing the inner clutch to be forced under spring tension towards the axle shaft sleeve and ring assembly until the inner clutch assembly teeth are engaged in the axle shaft sleeve and ring assembly teeth, locking the axle and hub.

Operation

When the transfer case is shifted into the position for driving the front axle, turn the actuating knob so that it is aligned with the letter L. If the clutch teeth do not engage with the knob turned to this position, the clutch teeth are butted and a slight movement of the wheel in either direction will complete the lock. The front axle will now drive the wheel.

When the transfer case is to be shifted into the position for driving the rear axle only, turn the actuating knob so that it is aligned with the letter F. This will disengage the clutch teeth and thus unlock the wheel hub from the axle shaft. The wheel will now turn free on the axle.

CAUTION: Be certain that the transfer case is shifted into two-wheel drive position before disengaging the Hub-Lok.

Removal

1. Position actuator knob in "LOCK", then raise and support vehicle.

NOTE: Rotate tire to ensure engagement of hub lock.

2. Remove retaining plate attaching bolts, then the retaining plate, actuating knob and O-rings.
3. Remove internal snap ring, outer clutch retaining ring, actuating cam body, outer clutch gear and pressure spring, **Fig. 8**.
4. Remove axle shaft snap ring, then the inner clutch ring.
5. Remove spring retainer plate, if equipped.

Installation

1. Install spring retainer plate, if equipped, over spindle nuts and against wheel bearing outer cup. Ensure that flanged side of plate faces toward wheel bearing.

2. Install inner clutch ring onto axle shaft, press ring inward, then install snap ring.
3. Install pressure spring with larger side facing inward.
4. Install outer clutch gear, actuating cam body, outer clutch retaining ring and the internal snap ring. Ensure that actuating cams face outward.
5. Install O-ring, actuating knob, actuating knob O-ring and the retaining plate.
6. Install retaining plate attaching bolts and torque to 38 inch lbs.

WARNER MANUAL LOCKING HUB

Description

Turning the locking hub clutch control to the "L" or "4" position connects the wheel hubs to the axle shafts. Therefore, when the transfer case is driving the front axle and the locking hubs are in the "L" or "4" position, the wheels are driven by the axle shafts. When the transfer case is not driving the front axle, the locking hub clutch controls are turned to the "F" or "2" position to disconnect the wheel hubs from the axle shafts. The wheels now rotate freely, but the axle shafts remain stationary.

On any vehicle equipped with manually operated locking hubs, extreme care must be taken to ensure the locking hub dials are fully engaged or disengaged, to prevent possible damage to the locking hubs.

If the locking hubs are not properly maintained, full engagement of the control dials may become impossible due to excessive dirt and dust. Any time the vehicle is driven through water deep enough to cover the hubs, the locking hubs should be removed and cleaned, then lubricated thoroughly.

These hubs are serviced as an assembly or subassembly only (hub body or hub clutch assembly only). Do not attempt to disassemble these units. If an entire hub or subassembly is defective, replace the entire assembly or subassembly. The hubs may be removed for cleaning and inspection purposes and for periodic lubrication only.

Removal

1. Remove socket head screws, axle hub retaining ring and axle shaft retaining ring.
2. Remove hub clutch assembly, **Fig. 9.**
3. Clean and inspect all components. Replace as necessary.

Installation

1. Lubricate all hub components.
2. Install hub clutch, axle hub retaining ring and axle shaft retaining ring.
3. Install new O-ring in hub body and position in clutch.
4. Install socket head screws and torque to 30 inch lbs.
5. Raise and support front of vehicle, then set control dial to "FREE" position and rotate wheels. If wheels drag,

check hub installation.
6. Lower vehicle.

LEAF SPRINGS & BUSHINGS
REPLACE

1. Raise and support vehicle.
2. Support axle with suitable jack.
3. Remove spring shackle upper retaining bolt.
4. Remove eye bolt.
5. Remove spring to axle housing "U" bolt nuts, then the spring, lower plate and spring pads.
6. To replace bushings, position spring on a suitable press and press bushings from spring using suitable tools. Install bushings in same manner, ensuring that bushings protrude an equal amount at each side of spring.
7. Reverse procedure to install. Torque "U" bolt nuts to 150 ft. lbs.

STABILIZER BAR
REPLACE

1. Raise and support vehicle.
2. Remove stabilizer bar attaching bolts and nuts at frame locations.
3. Remove brackets and bushings at leaf spring anchor plates.
4. Remove stabilizer bar from vehicle.
5. Reverse procedure to install.

AIR CONDITIONING

TABLE OF CONTENTS

A/C System Testing

INDEX

GENERAL PRECAUTIONS

The Freon refrigerant used is also known as R-12 or F-12. It is colorless and odorless both as a gas and a liquid. Since it boils (vaporizes) at −21.7° F., it will usually be in a vapor state when being handled in a repair shop. But if a portion of the liquid coolant should come in contact with the hands or face, note that its temperature momentarily will be at least 22° below zero.

Protective goggles should be worn when opening any refrigerant lines. If liquid coolant does touch the eyes, bathe the eyes quickly in cold water, then apply a bland disinfectant oil to the eyes. See an eye doctor.

When checking a system for leaks with a torch type leak detector, do not breathe the vapors coming from the flame. Do not discharge refrigerant in the area of a live flame. A poisonous phosgene gas is produced when R-12 or F-12 is burned. While the small amount of this gas produced by a leak detector is not harmful unless inhaled directly at the flame, the quantity of refrigerant released into the air when a system is purged can be extremely dangerous if allowed to come in contact with an open flame. Thus, when purging a system, be sure that the discharge hose is routed to a well ventilated place where no flame is present. Under these conditions the refrigerant will be quickly dissipated into the surrounding air.

Never allow the temperature of refrigerant drums to exceed 125° F. The resultant increase in temperature will cause a corresponding increase in pressure which may cause the safety plug to release or the drum to burst.

If it is necessary to heat a drum of refrigerant when charging a system, the drum should be placed in water that is no hotter than 125° F. Never use a blowtorch, or other open flame. If possible, a pressure release mechanism should be attached before the drum is heated.

When connecting and disconnecting service gauges on A/C system, ensure that gauge hand valves are fully closed and that compressor service valves, if equipped, are in the back-seated (fully counterclockwise) position. Do not disconnect gauge hoses from service port adapters, if used, while gauges are connected to A/C system. To disconnect hoses, always remove adapter from service port. Do not disconnect hoses from gauge manifold while connected to A/C system, as refrigerant will be rapidly discharged.

After disconnecting gauge lines, check the valve areas to be sure service valves are correctly seated and Schraeder valves, if used, are not leaking.

EXERCISE SYSTEM

An important fact most owners ignore is that A/C units must be used periodically. Manufacturers caution that when the air conditioner is not used regularly, particularly during cold months, it should be turned on for a few minutes once every two or three weeks while the engine is running. This keeps the system in good operating condition.

Checking out the system for the effects of disuse before the onset of summer is one of the most important aspects of A/C servicing.

First clean out the condenser core, mounted in all cases at the front of the radiator. All obstructions, such as leaves, bugs, and dirt, must be removed, as they will reduce heat transfer and impair the efficiency of the system. Make sure the space between the condenser and the radiator also is free of foreign matter.

Make certain the evaporator water drain is open. Certain systems have two evaporators, one in the engine compartment and one toward the rear of the vehicle. The evaporator cools and dehumidifies the air before it enters the passenger compartment; there, the refrigerant is changed from a liquid to a vapor. As the core cools the air, moisture condenses on it but is prevented from collecting in the evaporator by the water drain.

PERFORMANCE TEST

The system should be operated for at least 15 minutes to allow sufficient time for all parts to become completely stabilized. Determine if the system is fully charged by the use of test gauges and sight glass if one is installed on system. Head pressure will read from 180 psi to 220 psi or higher, depending upon ambient temperature and the type unit being tested. The sight glass should be free of bubbles if a glass is used in the system. Low side pressures should read approximately 15 psi to 30 psi, again depending on the ambient temperature and the unit being tested. It is not feasible to give a definite reading for all types of systems used, as the type control and component installation used on a particular system will directly influence the pressure readings on the high and low sides, **Fig. 1.**

The high side pressure will definitely be affected by the ambient or outside air temperature. A system that is operating normally will indicate a high side gauge reading between 150–170 psi with an 80°F ambient temperature. The same system will register 210–230 psi with an ambient temperature of 100°F. No two systems will register exactly the same, which requires that allowance for variations in head pressures must be considered. Following are the most important normal readings likely to be encountered during the season.

Ambient Temp.	High Side Pressure
80	150–170
90	175–195
95	185–205
100	210–230
105	230–250
110	250–270

RELATIVE TEMPERATURE OF HIGH AND LOW SIDES

The high side of the system should be uniformly hot to the touch throughout. A difference in temperature will indicate a partial blockage of liquid or gas at this point.

The low side of the system should be uniformly cool to the touch with no excessive sweating of the suction line or low side service valve. Excessive sweating or frosting of the low side service valve usually indicates an expansion valve is allowing an excessive amount of refrigerant into the evaporator.

EVAPORATOR OUTPUT

At this point, provided all other inspection tests have been performed, and components have been found to operate as they should, a rapid cooling down of the interior of the vehicle should result. The use of a thermometer is not necessary to determine evaporator output. Bringing all units to the correct operating specifications will insure that the evaporator performs as intended.

LEAK TEST

Testing the refrigerant system for leaks is one of the most important phases of troubleshooting. Several types of leak detectors are available that are suitable for detecting A/C system leaks. One or more of the following procedures will prove useful for detecting leaks and checking connections after service work has been performed. Prior to performing any leak test, prepare the vehicle as follows:

Evaporator Pressure Gauge Reading	Evaporator Temperature F°	High Pressure Gauge Reading	Ambient Temperature
0	-21°	45	20°
0.6	-20°	55	30°
2.4	-15°	72	40°
4.5	-10°	86	50°
6.8	- 5°	105	60°
9.2	0°	126	70°
11.8	5°	140	75°
14.7	10°	160	80°
17.1	15°	185	90°
21.1	20°	195	95°
22.5	22°	220	100°
23.9	24°	240	105°
25.4	26°	260	110°
26.9	28°	275	115°
28.5	30°	290	120°
37.0	40°	305	125°
46.7	50°	325	130°
57.7	60°		
70.1	70°		
84.1	80°		
99.6	90°		
116.9	100°		
136.0	110°		
157.1	120°		
179.0	130°		

Fig. 1   A/C system pressure/temperature relationship (Typical). Equivalent to 1750 RPM (30 mph)

1. Attach a suitable gauge manifold to system and observe pressure readings.
2. If little or no pressure is indicated, the system must be partially charged.
3. If gauges indicate pressure, set engine to run at fast idle and operate system at maximum cooling for 10–15 minutes, then stop engine and perform leak tests.

FLAME TYPE (HALIDE) LEAK DETECTORS

CAUTION: Avoid inhaling fumes produced by burning refrigerant when using flame-type detectors. Use caution when using detector near flammable materials such as interior trim components. Do not use flame-type detector where concentrations of combustible or explosive gasses, dusts or vapors may exist.

1. Light leak detector and adjust flame as low as possible to obtain maximum sensitivity.
2. Allow detector to warm until copper element is cherry-red. Flame should be almost colorless.
3. Test reaction plate sensitivity by passing end of sensor hose near an

opened can of refrigerant. Flame should react violently, turning bright blue.
4. If flame does not change color, replace reaction plate following manufacturer's instructions.
5. Allow flame to clear, then slowly move sensor hose along areas suspected of leakage while observing flame.

NOTE: Position sensor hose under areas of suspected leakage, as R-12 refrigerant is heavier than air.

6. Move sensor hose under all lines, fittings and components. Insert hose into evaporator case, if possible, and check compressor shaft seal.
7. The presence of refrigerant will cause flame to change color as follows: Pale blue, no refrigerant; yellow-yellow/green, slight leak; bright blue-purple/blue, major leak or concentration of refrigerant.
8. If detector indicates a large leak or heavy concentration of refrigerant, ventilate area using a small fan in order to pinpoint leak.
9. Repair leaks as needed, evacuate and recharge system, then recheck system for leaks.

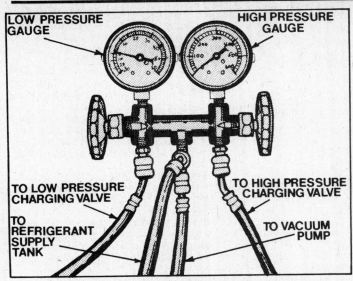

Fig. 2 Gauge manifold hose connections

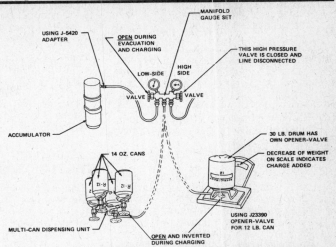

Fig. 3 A/C system charging. Chevrolet & GMC with C.C.O.T. system

ELECTRONIC LEAK DETECTORS

The procedure for using an electronic leak detector is similar to the procedure for flame-type leak detectors, except that the presence of refrigerant is indicated by an audible tone or flashing light. Refer to operating instructions for unit being used, and observe the following procedures:

1. Move detector probe 1 inch per second along areas of suspected leakage.
2. Position probe under area to be tested as refrigerant is heavier than air.
3. Check gauge manifold, hoses and service ports for leakage.

FLUID LEAK DETECTORS

Apply leak detector solution around joints to be tested. A cluster of bubbles will form immediately if there is a leak. A white foam that forms after a short while will indicate an extremely small leak. In some confined areas such as sections of the evaporator and condenser, electronic leak detectors will be more useful.

DISCHARGING & EVACUATING SYSTEM

DISCHARGING

1. Ensure that all gauge manifold or charging station hand valves are closed.
2. Connect compound (low) side gauge hose to the low (suction) side service port, and the high pressure gauge hose to the high (discharge) side port, **Fig. 2.**

NOTE: Refer to "Charging Valve Location" in the "A/C System Servicing" section for service port locations.

3. If charging station is being used, disconnect hose from vacuum pump inlet and ensure that vacuum valve is open.
4. Insert charging station vacuum hose or gauge manifold center hose into a suitable container that is vented to shop exhaust system.
5. If system is operational, set engine to run at fast idle and operate A/C system in maximum cooling position, with blower on high, for 10–15 minutes to return oil to compressor, then reduce idle and stop engine.
6. Slightly open low side control valve on manifold or charging station, and allow refrigerant to discharge slowly into container.

NOTE: Do not allow refrigerant to discharge rapidly. Too rapid purging will draw the system oil charge out with the refrigerant.

7. When system is nearly discharged, slightly open high side control valve on manifold to discharge remaining refrigerant from compressor and lines.
8. When system is completely discharged (gauges read zero), close high and low side control valves and measure amount of oil in discharge container.
9. If more than ½ ounce of refrigerant oil is trapped in container, perform "Oil Level Check" as outlined in the "A/C System Servicing" section.

NOTE: If addition of refrigeration oil is necessary, oil should be added prior to evacuating system.

EVACUATING SYSTEM WITH VACUUM PUMP

Vacuum pumps suitable for removing air and moisture from A/C systems are commercially available. The pump should be capable of drawing the system down to 28–29½ inches Hg at sea level. For each 1000 foot increase in altitude, this specification should be decreased by 1 inch Hg. As an example, at 5000 feet elevation, only 23–24½ inches Hg can be obtained.

1. Connect suitable gauge manifold and discharge system as outlined previously.

NOTE: System must be completely discharged prior to evacuation. If pressurized refrigerant is allowed to enter vacuum pump, pump will be damaged.

2. Connect hose from gauge manifold center port to vacuum pump inlet.
3. Fully open both gauge manifold hand valves.
4. Operate vacuum pump while observing low side compound gauge. If system does not "pump-down" to 28–29½ inches Hg (at sea level) within approximately 5 minutes, recheck connections and leak test system.
5. Continue to operate vacuum pump for 15–30 minutes, longer if system was open for an extended period of time, then close both manifold valves and stop pump.
6. Check ability of system to hold vacuum. Watch low side compound gauge and ensure that reading does not rise at a rate faster than 1 inch Hg every 4–5 minutes.
7. If system fails to hold vacuum, recheck fittings and connections, and leak test system.
8. If system holds vacuum, charge system with refrigerant.

EVACUATING SYSTEM WITH CHARGING STATION

A vacuum pump is built into the charging station that is constructed to withstand repeated and prolonged use without damage. Complete moisture removal from the A/C system is possible only with a pump of this type.

1. Connect charging station and discharge system as outlined previously.

NOTE: System must be completely discharged prior to evacuation. If pressurized refrigerant is allowed to enter vacuum pump, pump will be damaged.

2. Reconnect vacuum hose to vacuum pump and ensure that vacuum control valve is closed.
3. Fully open low pressure control valve only.
4. Connect station to a suitable voltage source and operate vacuum pump.
5. Slowly open vacuum control valve and observe low side compound gauge. If system does not "pump down" to 28–29½ inches Hg (at sea level) within approximately 5 minutes, recheck connections and leak test system.
6. Continue to operate vacuum pump for 15–30 minutes, longer if system was open for an extended period of time, then close all control valves and stop pump.
7. Check ability of system to hold vacuum. Watch low side compound gauge and ensure that reading does not rise at a rate faster than 1 inch Hg every 4–5 minutes.
8. If system fails to hold vacuum, recheck fittings and connections, and leak test system.

9. If system holds vacuum, charge system with refrigerant.

CHARGING THE SYSTEM

Refer to A/C Data Table in the "A/C System Servicing" section for refrigerant capacities.

J 23500-01 CHARGING STATION METHOD

Use instructions provided with charging station with the following exceptions:
1. Do not connect high pressure line to A/C system.
2. Always keep high pressure valve closed on charging station.
3. Perform all evacuation and charging through low-side pressure service fitting.

Use of these procedures will prevent charging station from being accidentally exposed to high-side system pressure.

DISPOSABLE CAN OR REFRIGERANT DRUM METHOD

NOTE: If R-12 drum is used, place on scale and note total weight before charging. During charging, watch scale to determine amount of R-12 used. If 14 ounce R-12 cans are used, close tapping valve, then attach cans following instructions included with manifold adaptor.

1. Start engine and allow to warm up (choke off, normal idle). Set A/C control lever to OFF.
2. With R-12 drum or cans inverted, open R-12 supply valve and allow 1 lb. of liquid R-12 to flow into system through low-side service fitting, **Fig. 3.**
3. When 1 lb. of refrigerant has entered system, engage compressor by setting A/C lever to NORM and blower switch to HI to draw in remainder of charge. Cooling the condenser with a large fan will speed up charging procedure by maintaining condenser temperature below charging cylinder temperature.
4. Close refrigerant supply valve and run engine for 30 seconds to clear lines and gauges.
5. With engine running, remove charging low-side hose adapter from accumulator service fitting. Unscrew rapidly to avoid excessive refrigerant loss.
6. Replace protective cap on accumulator fitting and turn engine off.
7. Check system for leaks.
8. Start engine and check for proper system operation.

A/C System Servicing

INDEX

OIL LEVEL CHECK

NOTE: Refer to "A/C Data Table" for oil level specifications.

The Frigidaire/Delco Air axial 6 cylinder and radial 4 cylinder compressors must be removed from vehicle and drained to check the oil level. Refer to "Oil Charge" for service procedures.

OIL CHARGE

Compressor oil level need only be checked when there is evidence of major oil loss from the system as in the case of a broken hose or severely leaking fitting, defective compressor seal or collision damage to the system.

OIL CHARGE—COMPONENT REPLACEMENT

If there are no external signs of oil leakage from the A/C system, maintain the proper system oil charge by adding new refrigeration oil during component replacement as follows:
1. Discharge system as outlined, then measure amount of oil collected in discharge container.

NOTE: If more than ½ ounce of oil is collected when discharging system, an equal amount of new refrigeration oil must be added to the system.

2. Remove defective components. Drain and measure oil remaining in compressor or accumulator, if removed.
3. Add the proper amount of oil to each replacement component as follows:
   a. If accumulator is being replaced, add the same amount of oil that was drained from the defective accumulator plus 1 additional ounce on 1979–80 models or 2 additional ounces on 1981–85 models.
   b. If compressor is replaced, add the same amount of oil that was drained from defective compressor plus 1 additional ounce.
   c. If condenser is replaced, add 1 ounce of oil to replacement condenser.
   d. If evaporator is replaced, add 3 ounces of oil to replacement evaporator.
   e. If receiver/drier is replaced, add 1 ounce of oil to replacement receiver/drier.

OIL LEVEL CHECK—LEAK CONDITION

If external oil leakage is evident, check compressor oil level using the following procedures.

Exc. 1979 Models With A-6 Axial Compressor
1. Discharge system as outlined, then measure amount of oil collected in discharge container.

NOTE: If more than ½ ounce of oil is collected when discharging system, an equal

A/C Data Table

Year	Model	Refrigerant Capacity Lbs.	Refrigeration Oil				Compressor Clutch Air Gap Inches
			Viscosity	Total System Capacity Ounces	Compressor Oil Level Check Inches		

Year	Model	Refrigerant Capacity Lbs.	Viscosity	Total System Capacity Ounces	Compressor Oil Level Check Inches	Compressor Clutch Air Gap Inches
CHEVROLET & GMC						
1979	Blazer & Jimmy	3¾	525	①	②	③
	C & K Series④	3¾	525	①	②	③
	C & K Series⑤	5⅓	525	①	②	③
	G Series④	3	525	①	②	③
	G Series⑤	5⅓	525	①	②	③
1979–80	Caballero & El Camino	3¾	525	①	②	③
1980–83	Blazer & Jimmy exc. S-10/15	3¾	525	①	②	③
	C & K Series④	3¾	525	①	②	③
	C & K Series⑤	5⅓	525	①	②	③
	G Series④	3	525	①	②	③
	G Series⑤	5	525	①	②	③
1981–82	Caballero & El Camino	3¼	525	①	②	③
1982–85	S & T-10/15	2½	525	6	②	.020–.040
1983	Caballero & El Camino	3¼	525	⑥	②	⑦
	S10 Blazer & S15 Jimmy	2½	525	6	②	.020–.040
1984–85	Blazer & Jimmy Exc. S-10/15	3	525	①	②	③
	C & K Series④	3	525	①	②	③
	C & K Series⑤	5⅓	525	①	②	③
	G Series④	3	525	①	②	③
	G Series⑤	4½	525	①	②	③

①—A-6 axial 6 cyl., comp. 10 oz.; R-4 radial 4 cyl. comp., 6 oz.
②—Note that "Oil Level Inches" can not be checked. Refer to total capacity and see text for checking procedure.
③—A-6 axial 6 cyl. comp., .022–.057 in.; R-4 radial 4 cyl. comp., .020–.040 in.
④—Models less auxiliary (rear, overhead etc.) system.
⑤—Models with auxiliary (rear, overhead etc.) system.
⑥—DA-6 axial 6 cyl. comp., 8 oz.; R-4 radial 4 cyl. comp., 6 oz.
⑦—DA-6 axial 6 cyl. comp., .015–.025 in.; R-4 radial 4 cyl. comp., .020–.040 in.

amount of new refrigeration oil must be added to the system.

2. On models with A-6 axial compressor, proceed as follows:
   a. Remove compressor and accumulator, drain oil from components into a suitable container and measure amount of oil recovered.
   b. If 4 ounces of oil or more are recovered, add the same amount of new refrigeration oil to system.
   c. If less than 4 ounces of oil are recovered, add 6 ounces of new refrigeration oil to system.
3. On models with R-4 radial compressor, proceed as follows:
   a. Remove accumulator, drain oil remaining in accumulator into a suitable container and measure amount of oil recovered.

NOTE: The R-4 radial compressor does not have an oil sump, therefore it is unnecessary to drain this compressor to check system oil level.

   b. If the amount of oil recovered is 2 ounces or more for 1979–80 models, or 3 ounces or more for 1981–85 models, add the same amount of new refrigeration oil to system.
   c. If less than 2 ounces of oil are recovered on 1979–80 models, add 2 ounces of new refrigeration oil to system.
   d. If less than 3 ounces of oil are recovered on 1981–85 models, add 3 ounces of new refrigeration oil to system.
4. On models with DA-6 axial compressors, proceed as follows:
   a. Remove accumulator, drain oil into suitable container, then measure amount of oil recovered.
   b. If amount of oil recovered is less than 3 ounces, add 3 ounces of new refrigeration oil to system.
   c. If amount of oil recovered is more than 3 ounces, add the same amount of new refrigeration oil to system.
5. Add refrigeration oil, as needed, to compressor sump or accumulator, reinstall components, then evacuate and recharge system.

1979 Models With A-6 Axial Compressor
1. If A/C system is operational, set engine to run at normal curb idle speed and operate system in maximum cooling position, with blower on high, for 10 minutes in order to return oil to compressor.
2. Stop engine and discharge system as outlined, then measure amount of oil collected in discharge container.

NOTE: If more than ½ ounce of oil is collected when discharging system, an equal amount of new refrigeration oil must be added to system.

3. Remove compressor from vehicle and place compressor in a horizontal position with drain plug downward.
4. Remove drain plug and drain compressor into a suitable container by tipping compressor back and forth while rotating shaft.
5. Measure oil recovered from compressor, then proceed as follows:
   a. If system was operational and the amount of oil recovered is 4

ounces or more, add the same amount of new refrigeration oil to system.

b. If system was operational and less than 4 ounces of oil are recovered, add 6 ounces of new refrigeration oil to system.

c. If system was not operational, the amount of oil recovered is 1½ ounces or more, and there is little evidence of leakage, add the same amount of new refrigeration oil to

system.

d. If system was not operational and less than 1½ ounces of oil are recovered, add 6 ounces of new refrigeration oil to system.

6. Add new refrigeration oil, as needed, to compressor sump, reinstall compressor, then evacuate and recharge system.

NOTE: Raise rear of compressor when adding oil, to prevent oil from flowing out

through suction and discharge ports.

CHARGING VALVE LOCATION

The high pressure fitting is located either in the high pressure vapor line or muffler, while the low pressure fitting is located on the accumulator.

VARIABLE SPEED FANS

INDEX

CAUTION: Do not operate engine until fan has first been inspected for cracks and/or separations. If a fan blade is found to be bent or damaged in any way, do not attempt to repair or reuse damaged part. Proper balance is essential in fan assembly operation. Balance cannot be assured once a fan assembly has been found to be bent or damaged and failure may occur during operation, creating an extremely dangerous condition. Always replace damaged fan assembly.

DESCRIPTION

The fan drive clutch, **Fig. 1,** is a fluid coupling containing silicone oil. Fan speed is regulated by the torque-carrying capacity of the silicone oil. The more silicone oil in the coupling, the greater the fan speed, and the less silicone oil, the slower the fan speed.

There are two types of fan drive clutches in use, one with a flat bi-metallic thermo-

static spring, **Fig. 2,** and the second with a coiled bi-metallic thermostatic spring, **Fig. 3.**

The fan drive clutch with the flat bi-metallic spring works with a control piston on front of the fluid coupling to regulate the amount of silicone oil entering the coupling. The bi-metallic strip bows outward with an increase in ambient temperature and allows a piston to move outward. This piston opens a valve regulating the flow of silicone oil into the coupling from a reserve chamber. The silicone oil is returned to the reserve chamber through a bleed hole when the valve is closed.

The second fan drive clutch uses a heat-sensitive, coiled bi-metallic spring connected to an opening plate which brings about similar results. Both units cause the fan speed to increase with a rise in temperature and to decrease as temperature decreases.

TROUBLESHOOTING
FAN DRIVE CLUTCH TEST

CAUTION: Do not operate the engine until the fan has been first checked for possible cracks and separations.

Run the engine at a fast idle speed (1000 RPM) until normal operating temperature is reached. This process can be speeded up by blocking off the front of the radiator with cardboard. Regardless of temperatures, the unit must be operated for at least five minutes immediately before being tested.

Stop the engine and, using a glove or a cloth to protect the hand, immediately check the effort required to turn the fan. If considerable effort is required, it can be assumed that the coupling is operating satisfactorily. If very little effort is required to turn the fan, it is an indication that the

coupling is not operating properly and should be replaced.

If the clutch fan is the coiled bi-metallic spring type, it may be tested while the vehicle is being driven. To check, disconnect the bi-metal spring, **Fig. 4,** and rotate 90° counter-clockwise. This disables the temperature-controlled, free-wheeling feature and the clutch performs like a conventional fan. If this cures the overheating condition, replace the clutch fan.

FAN CLUTCH NOISE

Fan clutch noise can sometimes be noticed when clutch is engaged for maximum cooling. Clutch noise is also noticeable within the first few minutes after starting engine while clutch is redistributing the silicone fluid back to its normal, disengaged operating condition after settling for long periods of time (over night). However, continuous fan noise or an excessive roar indicates the clutch assembly is locked-up due to internal failure. This condition can be checked by attempting to manually rotate fan. If fan cannot be rotated manually or there is a rough, abrasive feel as fan is rotated, the clutch should be replaced.

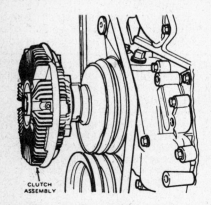

Fig. 1 Fan drive clutch assembly, 1984—85. 1979—83 similar

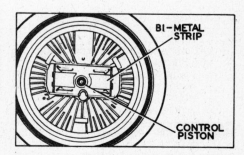

Fig. 2 Variable speed fan with flat bi-metallic thermostatic spring

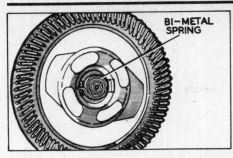

Fig. 3 Variable speed fan with coiled bi-metallic thermostatic spring

FAN LOOSENESS

Lateral movement can be observed at the fan blade tip under various temperature conditions because of the type bearing used. This movement should not exceed ¼ inch (6.5mm) as measured at the fan tip. If this lateral movement does not exceed specifications, there is no cause for replacement.

CLUTCH FLUID LEAK

Small fluid leaks do not generally affect the operation of the unit. These leaks generally occur around the area of the bearing assembly, but if the leaks appear to be excessive, engine overheating may occur. Check for clutch and fan free-wheeling by attempting to rotate fan and clutch assembly by hand five times. If no drag is felt, replace clutch.

FAN BLADE INSPECTION

Place fan on flat surface with leading edge facing down. If there is a clearance between fan blade touching surface and opposite blade of more than .090 inch (2mm), replace fan. (See caution at beginning of chapter.)

FAN SERVICE

CAUTION: To prevent silicone fluid from draining into fan drive bearing, do not store or place drive unit on bench with rear of shaft pointing downward.

The removal procedure for either type of fan clutch assembly is generally the same. Merely unfasten the unit from the water pump and remove the assembly from vehicle.

The type of unit shown in **Fig. 2,** may be partially disassembled for inspection and cleaning. Remove capscrews that hold the assembly together and separate the fan from the drive clutch. Next, remove metal strip on front of clutch assembly by pushing one end of it toward the fan clutch body so it clears the retaining bracket. Push the strip to the side so that its opposite end will spring out of place. Now remove the small control piston underneath it.

Check the piston for free movement of the coupling device. If piston sticks, clean it with emery cloth. If the bi-metal strip is damaged, replace the entire unit. These strips are not interchangeable.

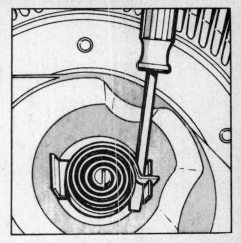

Fig. 4 Bi-metallic coiled spring removal

When reassembling, install the control piston so that the projection on the end of it will contact the metal strip. Next install metal strip with any identification number or letters facing the clutch. After reassembly, clean the clutch drive assembly with a cloth soaked in a suitable solvent. Avoid dipping the clutch assembly in any type liquid. Install the assembly in the reverse order of removal.

The coil spring type fan clutch cannot be disassembled, serviced or repaired. If it does not function properly, it must be replaced with a new unit.

ALTERNATOR SYSTEMS
Delcotron 10, 12, 15 & 27 SI (Type 100) Integral Charging Systems

INDEX

DESCRIPTION

These units, **Figs. 1, 2, 3 and 4,** feature a solid state regulator mounted inside the alternator slip ring end frame along with the brush holder assembly. All regulator components are enclosed in a solid mold with no need or provision for adjustment of the regulator. A rectifier bridge, containing six diodes and connected to the stator windings, changes A.C. voltage to D.C. voltage which is available at the output terminal. Generator field current is supplied through a diode trio which is also connected to the stator windings. The diodes and rectifiers are protected by a capacitor which is also mounted in the end frame.

NOTE: Some units incorporate a resistor in the warning indicator circuit, **Fig. 5**

Some alternators used on diesel engines are equipped with an R terminal for the tachometer. On these units, if the alternator pulley is to be replaced, a pulley of the same diameter as the one removed must be installed, or tachometer may provide inaccurate readings.

No maintenance or adjustments of any kind are required on this unit.

TROUBLESHOOTING
UNDERCHARGED BATTERY

NOTE: Before checking for the above mentioned condition, perform the following preliminary checks:

1. Ensure that accessories have not

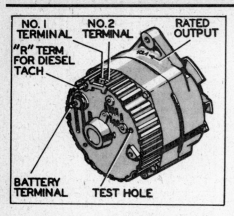

Fig. 1 Delcotron type 10 SI alternator

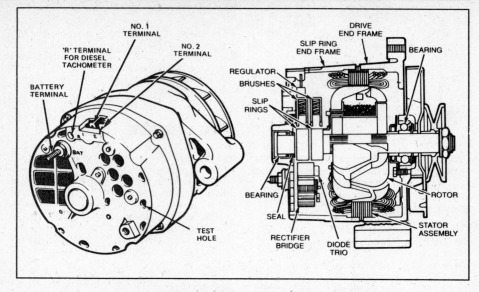

Fig. 2 Crossectional view of 12 SI alternator

been left on for extended periods, causing undercharged condition.

2. Check alternator drive belt for proper tension.
3. Check battery for internal defects.
4. Check all wiring connections for corrosion or looseness. Repair or replace as necessary.
5. With ignition switch On and alternator leads connected, connect voltmeter from:
   a. Alternator "BAT" terminal and ground.
   b. Alternator No. 1 terminal and ground.
   c. Alternator No. 2 terminal and ground.
6. If reading in step 5 is zero volts, check for open between voltmeter connection and battery.

1. Disconnect battery ground cable.
2. Disconnect wire at "BAT" terminal of alternator, connect ammeter, positive lead to "BAT" terminal and negative lead to wire.
3. Connect battery ground cable.
4. Turn on all accessories, then connect a carbon pile regulator across battery.
5. Operate engine at moderate speed, adjust carbon pile regulator to obtain maximum current output.
6. If ammeter reading is within 10 amps

of rated output, alternator is not at fault.

NOTE: Alternator rated output is stamped on alternator frame.

7. If ammeter reading is not within 10 amps of rated output, ground field winding by inserting screwdriver in end frame hole, contacting tab, **Fig. 6.**

NOTE: Do not insert screwdriver deeper than one inch, as tab is usually located within ¾ inch of casing surface.

8. If reading is within 10 amps of rated output, check field winding, diode trio, rectifier bridge and voltage regulator. If reading is not within limits, check field winding, diode trio, rectifier bridge

and stator.

9. Turn off all accessories and disconnect ammeter and carbon pile regulator.

OVERCHARGED BATTERY

1. Remove alternator from vehicle and separate end frames as outlined under "Alternator Disassembly."
2. Check field winding. If shorted, replace rotor and test regulator.

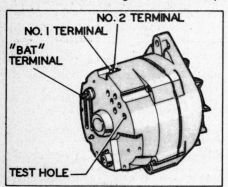

Fig. 3 Delcotron type 15 SI alternator

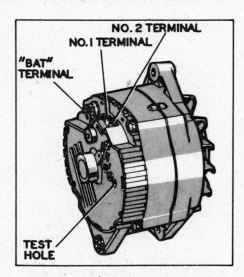

Fig. 4 Delcotron type 27 SI alternator

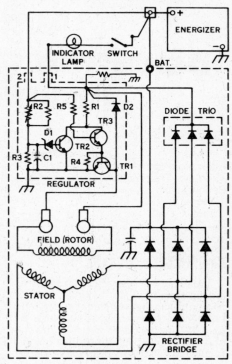

Fig. 5 Wiring diagram of charging circuit. 1979–85 vehicles

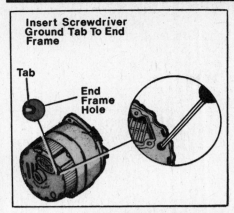

Fig. 6 Grounding field windings

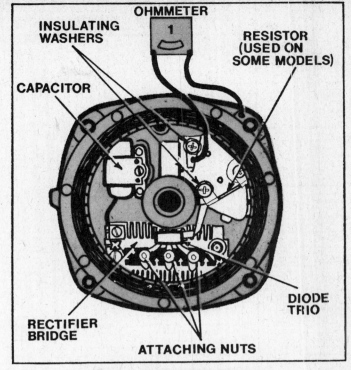

Fig. 7 Testing brush clip

3. Connect ohmmeter from brush clip to end frame, set meter on low scale and note reading, **Fig. 7.**
4. Reverse leads, if both readings are zero, remove screw from brush clip and inspect sleeve and insulator.
5. If sleeve and insulator are in good condition, then regulator is at fault and must be replaced.

ALTERNATOR NOISE

Alternator noise may be caused by a loose drive pulley, loose mounting bolts, worn or dirty bearings, defective diodes or a defective stator. Inspect all components and replace as necessary.

CHARGING SYSTEM DIAGNOSIS

For charging system diagnosis, refer to "Charging System Diagnosis Chart," **Fig. 8.**

TRANSISTORIZED VOLTAGE REGULATOR TEST

On-Car Test

1. Connect a suitable voltmeter and fast charger to battery, **Fig. 9.**
2. Turn ignition on and slowly increase charge rate, while observing voltmeter and generator warning light.
3. The generator warning light should dim when voltmeter reads 13.5–16.0 volts. If light does not dim at specified voltage, replace voltage regulator.

Off-Car Test

1. Connect a suitable voltmeter, fast charger and test light to regulator, **Fig. 10.** Test light should be illuminated.
2. Turn charger on and slowly increase charge rate, while observing voltmeter and test light.
3. The test light should go out when voltmeter reads 13.5–16.0 volts. If light does not go out, replace voltage regulator.

ALTERNATOR DISASSEMBLY

NOTE: When pressing bearings or seals from end frames, support frames from inside.

1. Scribe mark across end frames and stator ring so parts can be installed in same position.
2. Remove four through bolts, then using screw driver in stator slot, pry end frames apart, **Fig. 11.**

NOTE: Brushes may fall from holders and become contaminated with bearing grease; if so, they must be cleaned prior to assembly.

3. Place tape over slip ring end frame bearing and shaft at slip ring end.
4. Remove nut, washer, pulley, fan and collar from rotor shaft, then slide drive end frame from shaft.
5. Remove bearing, retainer and seal from drive end frame.
6. Remove attaching bolts, then pry stator from slip ring end frame.
7. On units except 27 SI, remove ground screw and battery terminal stud nut from rectifier bridge, then remove rectifier bridge, terminal stud and insulating washer from end frame. On 27 SI units, remove two ground screws, connector strap screw and battey stud nut, then remove rectifier bridge, connector, terminal stud and insulating washers from end frame.

NOTE: On diesel engine alternators equipped with R terminal for tachometer, the R terminal nut and jumper strap must be removed before removing the rectifier bridge and battery terminal.

8. Remove resistor (if equipped), brush holder and regulator.
9. Remove bearing and seal from slip ring end-frame.

BENCH TESTS
ROTOR & SLIP RING

NOTE: Ohmmeter must be at low scale setting during this test.

1. Inspect rotor for wear or damage.
2. Check rotor for opens as follows:
   a. Connect ohmmeter leads to slip rings as shown, **Fig. 12.**
   b. Ohmmeter should read 2.4–3.0 ohms for 1979–81 units, or 2.4–3.5 ohms for 1982–85 units.
   c. If readings are below 2.4 ohms, windings are shorted.
   d. If readings are above specified values, excessive resistance exists in windings.
3. Check rotor for grounds as follows:
   a. Connect one ohmmeter lead to rotor shaft and other lead to slip rings, **Fig. 12.**
   b. Ohmmeter should read infinity.
4. If rotor shows signs of wear or damage; or resistance values are not within specification, replace rotor.

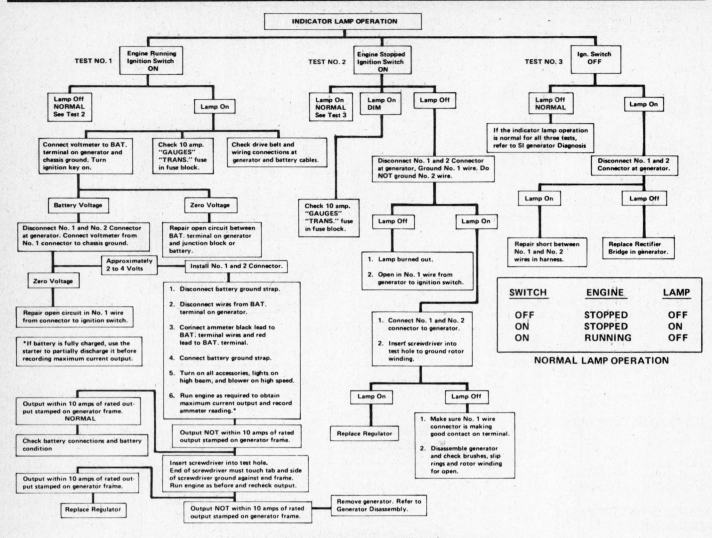

Fig. 8 Charging system diagnosis chart

STATOR WINDING

1. Inspect stator for discolored windings, loose connections and damage.
2. Connect an ohmmeter from stator lead to frame. If any reading is obtained windings are grounded. **Fig. 13.**
3. On 10 SI units, connect ohmmeter between stator leads. If reading is infinite when connected between each pair of leads, an open circuit exists in windings. The stator windings on 12 SI, 15 SI and 27 SI units cannot be checked for open circuits.

NOTE: Shorted windings are difficult to locate without special equipment. If other tests indicate normal, but rated alternator output cannot be obtained, the windings are probably shorted.

DIODE TRIO

1. With diode unit removed, connect an

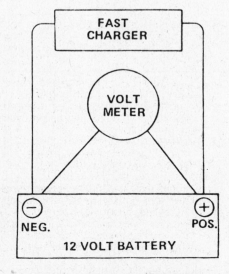

Fig. 9 On-car voltage regulator test

ohmmeter to the single connector and to one of the three connectors, **Fig. 14.**
2. Observe the reading. Reverse ohmmeter leads.
3. Reading should be high with one connection and low with the other. If both readings are the same, unit must be replaced.
4. Repeat procedure between the single connector and each of the other two connectors.

NOTE: There are two diode units differing in appearance. These are completely interchangeable.

RECTIFIER BRIDGE

1. Connect ohmmeter to the grounded heat sink and one of the three terminals, **Fig. 15.**
2. Observe the reading then reverse leads.
3. Reading should be high with one con-

nection and low with the other. If both readings are the same, unit must be replaced.

4. Repeat test for each of the other terminals.

ALTERNATOR ASSEMBLY

NOTE: When pressing bearings or seals, end frames must be supported from inside.

1. Lightly lubricate seal and position on slip ring end frame with lip facing toward rotor, **Fig. 11.**
2. Press seal part way into housing.
3. On 10 SI, 12 SI and 27 SI units, position bearing and end plug on slip ring end frame, then press bearing and plug in until flush with end frame. On 15 SI units, refer to **Fig. 16** when installing slip ring end frame bearing.
4. Place regulator in end frame, install

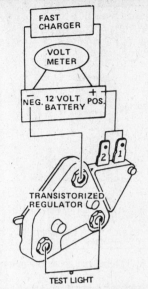

Fig. 10 Off-car voltage regulator test

brushes and springs in brush holder, use pin to hold brushes in compressed position.

NOTE: Insulating washers are installed under two of the attaching screws, **Fig. 17.**

5. On units except 27 SI, install insulating washer, battery terminal stud, rectifier bridge and ground screw, then secure bridge to stud with nut and tighten ground screw and nut. On 27 SI units, install rectifier bridge to end frame using two ground screws, then install terminal, insulators and connector and tighten screw and nut.
6. On diesel engine alternators equipped with R terminal for tachometer, install plastic insulating washer on R terminal stud, then position terminal stud into end frame. Install fiber insulating washer, jumper strap and nut on R terminal stud. Position jumper strap on rectifier bridge, then tighten R terminal stud.

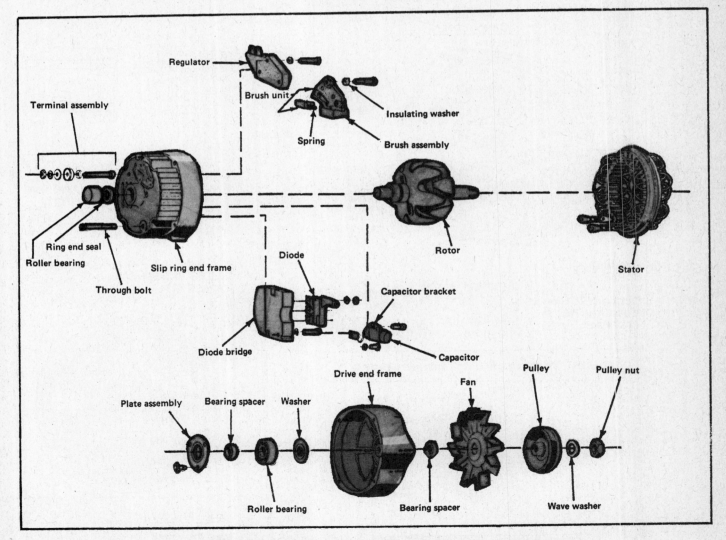

Fig. 11 Disassembled view of typical Delcotron type alternator

Fig. 12   Rotor & slip ring testing

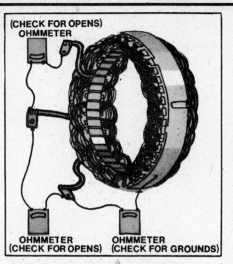

Fig. 13   Testing stator winding

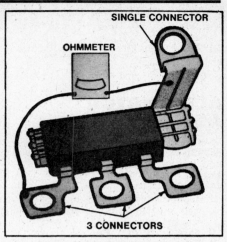

Fig. 14   Testing diode trio

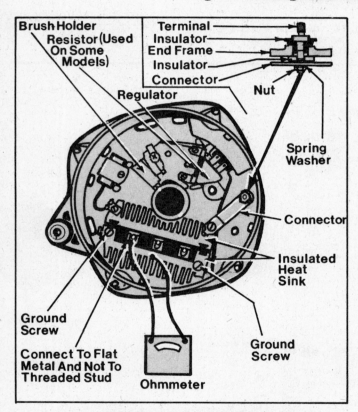

Fig. 15   Testing rectifier bridge diodes

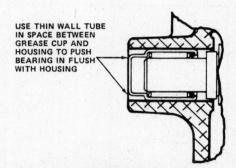

Fig. 16   Installing slip ring end frame bearing. 15 SI units

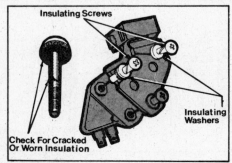

Fig. 17   Brush holder & regulator installation

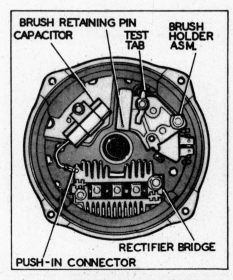

Fig. 18   Slip ring end frame. 15 SI units

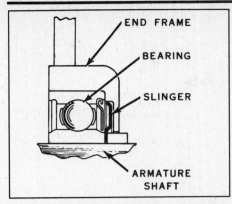

Fig. 19 Drive end frame bearing & slinger installed. 1979—82 10 SI & 27 SI units

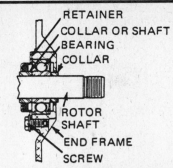

Fig. 20 Drive end frame bearing. 1979—82 15 SI & early production 1983—85 15 SI & 27 SI units

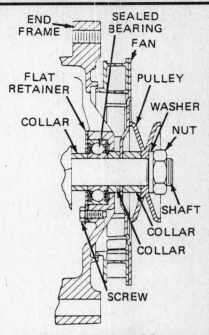

Fig. 21 Drive end frame bearing. All 1983—85 10 SI & 12 SI units & late production 1983—85 15 SI & 27 SI units

7. Install diode trio, ensuring current only flows one way through single connector.
8. Install capacitor.

NOTE: On 15 SI units, the capacitor lead uses a push clip connector to attach the rectifier bridge instead of a screw, **Fig. 18.**

9. Install stator, check the three leads for continuity, ensure stator is not grounded against case or holder.
10. On 1979—82 10 SI and 27 SI units, position slinger on drive end frame, then press ball bearing into end frame, **Fig. 19.** On 1979—82 and early production 1983—85 15 SI and 27 SI units, refer to **Fig. 20** when installing drive end bearing. On late production 1983—85 15 SI and 27 SI units and all 1983—85 10 SI and 12 SI units, refer to **Fig. 21.**
11. Fill seal cavity ¼ full with special alternator lubricant, then install retainer.

NOTE: On units equipped with sealed bearing, **Fig. 21,** no lubricant is required.

12. Install rotor in drive end frame, then install collar, fan, pulley, washer and nut.
13. Align scribe marks on end frames and stator plate, install through bolts and remove brush retaining pins.

STARTER MOTORS & SWITCHES

TABLE OF CONTENTS

Delco-Remy Starters

INDEX

DESCRIPTION

The Delco-Remy starter, **Figs. 1 through 4,** has the solenoid shift lever mechanism and the solenoid plunger enclosed in the drive housing to protect them from exposure to road dirt, icing conditions and splash. They have an extruded field frame and an overrunning clutch type drive. The overrunning clutch is operated by a solenoid switch mounted to a flange on the drive housing. The diesel starters, 25MT and 27MT, have a center bearing.

The solenoid, **Fig. 5,** is attached to the drive end housing by two screws. The cover can be removed to inspect the contacts and contact disc, but the switch is serviced as an assembly only.

Most motors of this type have graphite and oil impregnated bronze bearings which ordinarily require no added lubrication except at time of overhaul when a few drops of light engine oil should be placed on each bearing before reassembly.

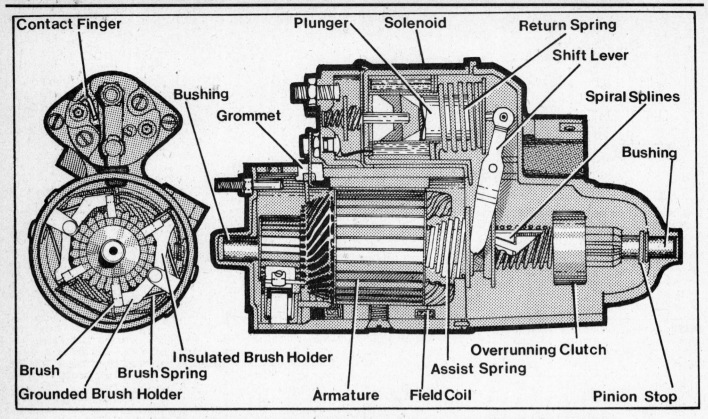

Fig. 1   Delco Remy 5MT & 10MT standard duty starter. 1984 shown, others similar

DIAGNOSIS

When diagnosing Delco-Remy starters refer to **Fig. 6.**

IN-VEHICLE TESTING

FREE SPEED CHECK

With the circuit connected as shown in **Fig. 7,** use a tachometer to measure armature revolutions per minute. Failure of the motor to perform to specifications may be due to tight or dry bearings, or high resistance connections.

PINION CLEARANCE

There is no provision for adjusting pinion clearance on this type motor. When the shift lever mechanism is correctly assembled, the pinion clearance should fall within the limits of .010 to .140". When the clearance is not within these limits, it may indicate excessive wear of the solenoid linkage or shift lever yoke buttons.

Pinion clearance should be checked after the motor has been disassembled and reassembled. To check, disconnect motor field coil connector from solenoid terminal and insulate end. Connect one battery lead to solenoid switch terminal and the other lead to the solenoid frame, **Fig. 8.** Using a jumper lead connected to the solenoid motor terminal, momentarily flash the lead to the solenoid frame. This

will shift the pinion into the cranking position until the battery is disconnected.

After energizing the solenoid with the clutch shifted toward the pinion stop retainer, push the pinion back toward the commutator end as far as possible to take up any slack movement; then check the clearance with feeler gauge, **Fig. 9.**

STARTER OVERHAUL

1. Remove screw from field coil connector and the solenoid mounting screws.
2. Rotate solenoid 90° and remove together with plunger return spring.
3. Remove two through bolts, then the commutator end frame, the insulator if

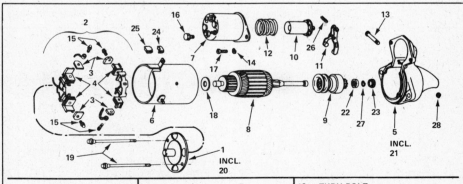

1. FRAME—COMMUTATOR END	10. PLUNGER	19. THRU BOLT
2. BRUSH AND HOLDER PKG.	11. SHIFT LEVER	20. BUSHING—COMMUTATOR END
3. BRUSH	12. PLUNGER RETURN SPRINGER	21. BUSHING—DRIVE END
4. BRUSH HOLDER	13. SHIFT LEVER SHAFT	22. PINION STOP COLLAR
5. HOUSING—DRIVE END	14. LOCK WASHER	23. THRUST COLLAR
6. FRAME AND FIELD ASM.	15. SCREW—BRUSH ATTACHING	24. GROMMET
7. SOLENOID SWITCH	16. SCREW—FIELD LEAD TO SWITCH	25. GROMMET
8. ARMATURE	17. SCREW—SWITCH ATTACHING	26. PLUNGER PIN
9. DRIVE ASM.	18. WASHER—BRAKE	27. PINION STOP RETAINER RING
		28. LEVER SHAFT RETAINING RING

Fig. 2   Disassembled view of Delco-Remy 5MT series starting motor

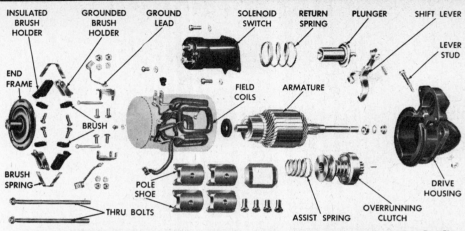

Fig. 3 Disassembled view of 10MT series starting motor (Typical)

equipped, and the washer.

4. On diesel starters, proceed as follows:
   a. Remove shift lever pivot bolt.
   b. Remove center bearing screws, if equipped, then the drive gear housing from armature shaft.
   c. Remove shift lever and plunger assembly from starter clutch.

5. On all models, remove overrunning clutch from armature shaft as follows:
   a. Remove thrust washer or collar from armature shaft, **Fig. 10.**
   b. Slide suitable deep socket or piece of pipe over shaft against retainer and tap retainer off snap ring.
   c. Remove snap ring from groove in shaft. If snap ring is distorted, use new snap ring during reassembly.
   d. Remove retainer and clutch assembly, then the fiber washer and center bearing on diesel starters, from the armature shaft.
   e. Disassemble shift lever and plunger by removing roll pin.

6. On 5MT starter, proceed as follows:
   a. Remove brush holder from brush support.
   b. Remove screw from brush holder and separate brush and holder.
   c. Inspect brush holder for wear or damage.
   d. Replaces brushes and/or holders as necessary.

7. Except on 5MT starter, proceed as follows:
   a. Remove brush holder pivot pin which positions one insulated and one grounded brush.
   b. Remove brush spring.
   c. Replace brushes as necessary.

8. Clean all starter motor parts, but do not use grease dissolving solvents on the overrunning clutch, armature or field coils.

9. Inspect armature commutator, shaft and bushings, overrunning clutch pinion, brushes and springs for discoloration, damage or wear, replacing as necessary.

10. Check fit of armature shaft in bushing in drive housing. If shaft does not fit snugly in bushing, replace bushing.

11. Inspect armature commutator. If commutator is rough, it should be turned

down. Do not undercut or turn less than 1.650 inch O. D. Do not turn out of round commutators. Inspect points where armature conductors join commutator bars to ensure good connection.

12. Check armature for short circuits by placing on growler and holding hacksaw blade over armature core while armature is rotated. If saw blade vibrates, armature is shorted.

13. Using test lamp, place one lead on shunt coil terminal and connect other lead to ground brush. If test lamp does not light, replace field coil.

14. Using test lamp, place one lead on series coil terminal and other lead on insulated brush. If lamp does not light, repair or replace series coil as necessary.

15. On starters equipped with shunt coil, proceed as follows:
   a. Separate series and shunt coil strap terminals and do not let strap terminals touch case or other ground.
   b. Using test lamp, place one lead on grounded brush holder and other lead on either insulated brush. If lamp lights, repair or replace series coil as necessary.

16. Check current draw of solenoid winding as follows:

NOTE: If solenoid is not removed from starter motor, the connector strap terminals must be removed from terminal on solenoid before making these tests. Complete tests in a minimum time to prevent overheating of solenoid.

   a. Connect ammeter in series with 12 volt battery and "switch" terminal on solenoid. Connect voltmeter to "switch" terminal and ground. Connect carbon pile across battery. Adjust voltage to 10 volts. Ammeter should read 14.5–16.5 amperes.
   b. Ground solenoid motor terminal, then adjust voltage to 10 volts and note ammeter reading. Ammeter should read 41–47 amperes.

NOTE: Current draw readings above specifications indicate shorted turns or a ground in the windings of the solenoid. If this occurs, the solenoid should be re-

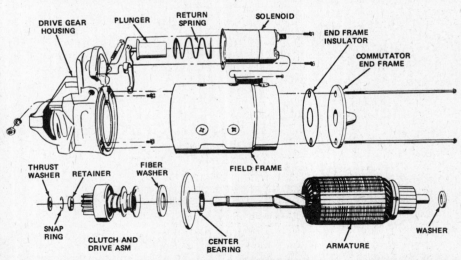

Fig. 4 Disassembled view of Delco-Remy 25MT & 27MT series starting motor

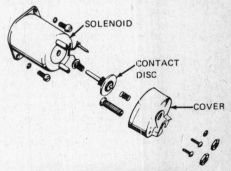

Fig. 5 Solenoid contact assembly

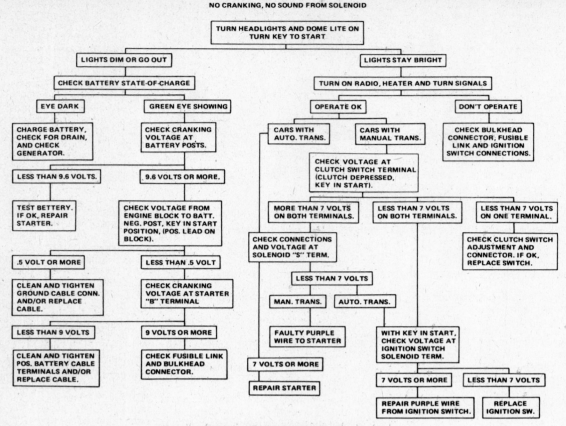

Fig. 6   Diagnosis chart (Part 1 of 2)

placed. Current draw readings below specification indicate excessive resistance. No reading indicates an open circuit. Check connections, then replace solenoid as necessary.

17. Assemble armature and clutch as follows:
   a. Lubricate drive end of armature shaft with suitable lubricant.
   b. On diesel starters, install center bearing with bearing toward armature winding, then install fiber washer on armature shaft.
   c. On all models, slide clutch assembly onto armature shaft with pinion away from armature.
   d. Slide retainer onto shaft with cupped side facing end of shaft.
   e. Install snap ring into groove on armature shaft, then the thrust washer onto the shaft.
   f. Position retainer and thrust washer with snap ring in between, then, using two pliers, grip retainer and thrust washer or collar and squeeze until snap ring is forced into retainer and is held firmly in groove in armature shaft.
18. Lubricate drive gear housing bushing with suitable lubricant.
19. Engage shift lever yoke with clutch and slide complete assembly into drive gear housing.

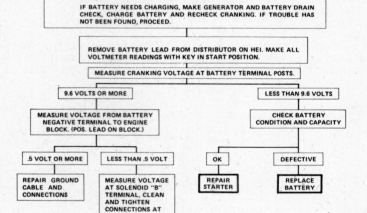

Fig. 6   Diagnosis chart (Part 2 of 2)

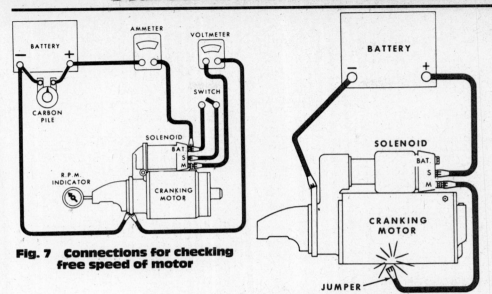

Fig. 7 **Connections for checking free speed of motor**

Fig. 8 **Connections for checking pinion clearance**

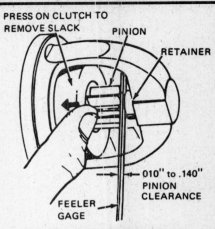

Fig. 9 **Checking pinion clearance**

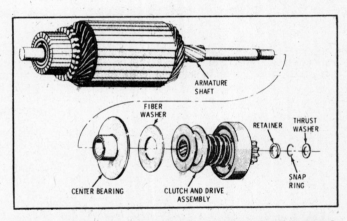

Fig. 10 **View of armature and overrunning clutch**

20. Install center bearing screws, if equipped, and the shift lever pivot bolt, tightening securely.
21. Install solenoid assembly, applying suitable sealant to solenoid flange where field frame contacts flange.
22. Position field frame against gear housing on alignment pin, being careful not to damage brushes.
23. Lubricate commutator end frame bushing with suitable lubricant.
24. Install washer on armature shaft and slide end frame onto shaft, then install and tighten through bolts.
25. Connect field coil connector to solenoid terminal, then check pinion clearance.

Hitachi Starters

INDEX

DIAGNOSIS

When diagnosing Hitachi starters, refer to **Figs. 1** and **2**.

STARTER OVERHAUL
DIESEL STARTER

Disassembly
1. Disconnect lead wire at solenoid, **Fig.**

3.
2. Remove through bolts, then separate starter housing, armature, and brush assembly from solenoid and drive gear assembly.
3. Using suitable pliers, remove four brushes and pull out brush holder from armature.
4. Tap housing with plastic mallet to separate armature from housing.
5. Remove two screws from drive housing and separate drive housing from

solenoid.
6. Remove two pinion gears, then the overrunning clutch and retainer.
7. Remove return spring from solenoid.
8. Remove steel ball from overrunning clutch.

Inspection
1. Inspect parts for wear or damage, replacing as necessary.
2. Ensure that commutator run-out does not exceed .002 inch.

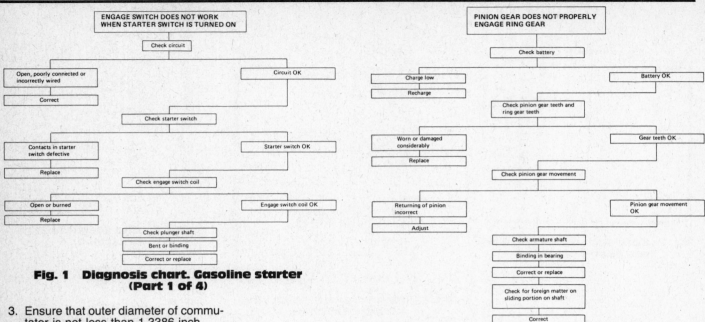

Fig. 1   Diagnosis chart. Gasoline starter (Part 1 of 4)

Fig. 1   Diagnosis chart. Gasoline starter (Part 2 of 4)

3. Ensure that outer diameter of commutator is not less than 1.3386 inch.
4. Ensure that depth of segment mica is not less than .0079 inch.
5. Touch one lead of circuit tester to commutator segment and other lead to armature core. If there is continuity, replace armature.
6. Connect leads of circuit tester across

two segments of armature. If there is no continuity, replace armature.
7. Touch one lead of circuit tester to field

winding end or brush and other lead to bare surface of yoke body. If there is continuity, replace yoke assembly.
8. Touch one lead of circuit tester to "C" terminal lead wire and other lead to brush. If there is no continuity, replace yoke.
9. Check length of brushes, replacing any brush less than .374 inch long.
10. Touch one lead of circuit tester to brush holder plate and other lead to positive brush holder. There should be no continuity.
11. Ensure that pinion rotates smoothly clockwise and locks counterclockwise.

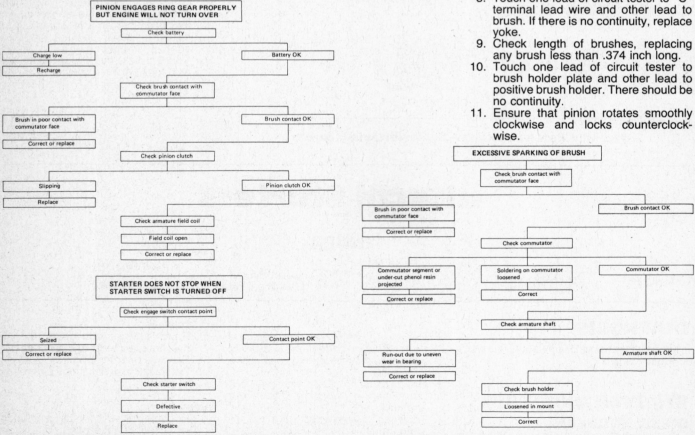

Fig. 1   Diagnosis chart. Gasoline starter (Part 3 of 4)

Fig. 1   Diagnosis chart. Gasoline starter (Part 4 of 4)

Complaint	Faulty parts	Cause	Correction
Pinion does not jump out when starter switch is turned on	Wiring	Circuit open, battery or switch terminals loosened, or poor connections at connector	Correct and retighten
	Starter switch	Current not flowing due to poor contact	Correct or replace
	Starter	1. Helical splines on pinion shaft damaged preventing smooth movement of pinion	Correct or replace
		2. Torsion spring or shift lever broken	Replace
	Solenoid	Plunger operation sluggish, coil open or shorted	Correct or replace
	Battery	Under-charged	Recharge
Pinion engages ring gear but starter does not turn over	Wiring	1. Cable connecting solenoid to battery broken 2. Lead wire between solenoid and motor poorly connected.	Correct, retighten or replace
	Starter	1. Incorrectly installed.	Remove and reinstall correctly
		2. Brushes worn beyond limit	Replace
		3. Commutator face fouled	Correct
		4. Armature or field coil(s) shorted	Replace
		5. Brushes not properly connected to field coils	Correct
		6. Ball bearing locked	Replace
	Solenoid	Contact points defective	Replace
Motor operates before pinion engages ring gear	Starter	1. Torsion spring weakened or shift lever distorted	Replace
		2. Pinion shaft sticking or binding	Replace
		3. Pinion gear teeth worn	Correct
		4. Pinion setting incorrect	Replace
	Engine	Ring gear worn	Replace
Pinion engages ring gear and motor operates but power is not carried to engine	Starter	1. Clutch defective	Replace
		2. Reduction gear broken	Replace
Motor continues to spin even when starter switch is turned off after engine starting.	Starter switch	Contact point returning action poor	Replace
	Solenoid	Contact point returning action poor	Replace

Fig. 2   Diagosis chart. Diesel starter

Assembly

1. Reverse disassembly procedure to assemble.
2. Check difference between point to which pinion is extended and point to which pinion can be pulled out with fingers, **Fig. 4.** If pinion gap is not within specifications, adjust with .0196 or .0314 inch shim.

GASOLINE STARTER

1. Disconnect field lead from "M" terminal of solenoid, **Fig. 4.**
2. Remove solenoid attaching bolts and separate plunger shaft from shift lever, **Fig. 5.**
3. Pry off dust cover and remove snap ring washer.
4. Remove the two through bolts.
5. Remove two screws and rear cover assembly, **Fig. 6.**
6. Raise brush springs and pull out brushes, then remove brush holder assembly, **Fig. 7.**
7. Separate yoke assembly and gear case.
8. Remove armature and shift lever.
9. Remove drive assembly retainer and snap ring.
10. If field coils are to be removed, remove the four pole shoe retaining screws.
11. Check commutator surface for roughness or burning. Turn commutator down on a lathe if necessary to clean up. The commutator can be turned down to a minimum of 1.497 in. diameter.
12. Measure undercut of insulator from surface of commutator. Depth should be from .0197 to .0315 inch.
13. Check insulation between commutator coils and core using a growler. If growler light turns on, the coils are poorly insulated and should be repaired, if possible, or the armature replaced.
14. Rotate armature slowly on growler while holding strip of steel over each segment. If strip of steel is pulled or vibrates, the coils are shorted and the armature should be repaired, if possible, or replaced, **Fig. 8.**
15. Make a continuity test between the commutator segments using the growler. If growler light does not come on when tester leads are connected across the segments, the coils are open and the armature should be replaced.

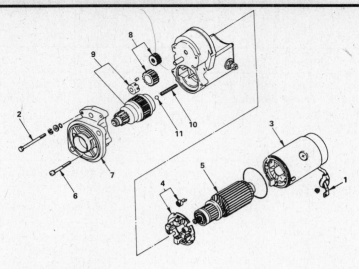

Disassembly order

▲ 1. Lead wire
▲ 2. Through bolt
▲ 3. Yoke
▲ 4. Brush and brush holder
▲ 5. Armature
▲ 6. Screw

   7. Drive side housing
▲ 8. Two pinions
   9. Overrunning clutch and retainer
▲10. Return spring
▲11. Steel ball

▲See disassembly procedures for details.

Fig. 3 Hitachi diesel starter, disassembled

repaired if possible or replaced, **Fig. 9.**

16. Using a pair of "V" blocks and a dial indicator, check armature shaft for runout. If runout exceeds .0031 in., correct or replace the armature, **Fig. 10.**
17. Check shaft and bearings for wear. Maximum allowable clearance between shaft and bearings is .0079 in.
18. With an ohmmeter check resistance between the field coils and yoke. Insulation resistance should be 1 ohm or more. If poor insulation is noted, remove the pole shoes one at a time to locate grounded parts and correct as necessary.
19. Check brushes for wear, cracks or broken lead and replace if found to be

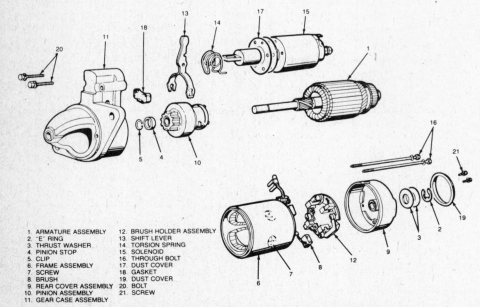

1. ARMATURE ASSEMBLY	12. BRUSH HOLDER ASSEMBLY	
2. "E" RING	13. SHIFT LEVER	
3. THRUST WASHER	14. TORSION SPRING	
4. PINION STOP	15. SOLENOID	
5. CLIP	16. THROUGH BOLT	
6. FRAME ASSEMBLY	17. DUST COVER	
7. SCREW	18. GASKET	
8. BRUSH	19. DUST COVER	
9. REAR COVER ASSEMBLY	20. BOLT	
10. PINION ASSEMBLY	21. SCREW	
11. GEAR CASE ASSEMBLY		

Fig. 4 Hitachi gasoline starter, disassembled

STARTER SOLENOID

Fig. 5 Solenoid removal, Hitachi gasoline starter

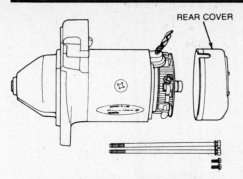

Fig. 6   Rear cover removal

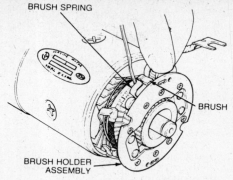

Fig. 7   Removing brush holder assembly

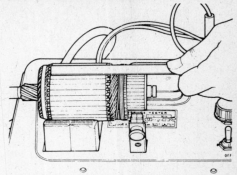

Fig. 8   Using a growler to test armature for shorts

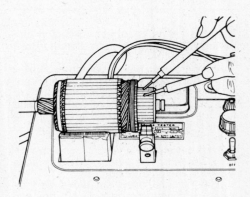

Fig. 9   Using a growler to test armature for opens

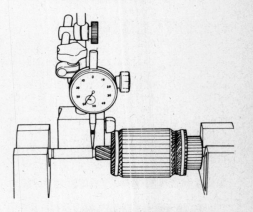

Fig. 10   Checking armature shaft for runout

dress with an oil stone if necessary.

23. Make a continuity test between the "C" and "M" terminals and between the "C" terminal and ground using a circuit tester. If an open circuit is indicated, replace solenoid.

24. The solenoid is satisfactory when the plunger is pulled in as 12 volts is applied between terminals "C" and "M" and returns smoothly as power is cut off.

25. Inspect pinion gear for wear, clutch for slipping and sliding surface in pinion. Replace pinion and clutch assembly, if necessary.

26. Reverse procedure to assemble, noting the following:
    a. Apply lubricant to the bearings and sliding surfaces.
    b. Set shift lever on lever guide of pinion assembly as the armature is being installed. Do not turn armature after installation since shift lever may become dislodged from the lever guide.
    c. Install dust cover and yoke assembly to gear case by aligning the groove in the yoke with corresponding projection.
    d. When installing brush and retainer assembly, do not scratch commutator surface.
    e. Install adjustment plate and torsion spring to solenoid, then assemble

defective. Minimum usable brush length is .472 inch.

20. Inspect brush springs for rusting, distortion, weakening or breakage and replace as necessary. Spring tension should be 3.53 lbs.

21. Clean brush holder to remove carbon and check for insulation between insulated brush holder and plate using an ohmmeter. If poor insulation is indicated, replace brush holder assembly.

22. Remove cover and check solenoid points for fouling or roughness and

plunger over shift lever with torsion spring in intermediate groove of shift lever and install the two retaining bolts.

f. Apply 12 volts between the "C" and "M" terminals and measure clearance between end of pinion and the retainer. Clearance should be from .011 to .098 inch. To adjust clearance, the solenoid must be removed to replace adjustment plates.

DASH GAUGES & GRAPHIC DISPLAYS

INDEX

DASH GAUGES

Gauge failures are often caused by defective wiring or grounds. The first step in locating trouble should be a thorough inspection of all wiring, terminals and printed circuits. If wiring is secured by clamps, check to see whether the insulation has been severed, thereby grounding the wire. In the case of a fuel gauge installation, rust may cause failure by corrosion at the ground connection of the tank unit.

VARIABLE VOLTAGE TYPE

The variable voltage type dash gauge consists of two magnetic coils to which battery voltage is applied. The coils act on the gauge pointer and pull in opposite directions. One coil is grounded directly to the chassis, while the other coil is grounded through a variable resistor within the sending unit. Resistance through the sending unit determines current flow through its coil, and therefore pointer position.

When resistance is high in the sending unit, less current is allowed to flow through its coil, causing the gauge pointer to move toward the directly grounded coil. When resistance in the sending unit decreases, more current is allowed to pass through its coil, increasing the magnetic field. The gauge pointer is then attracted toward the coil which is grounded through the sending unit.

A special tester is required to diagnose this type gauge. Follow instructions included with the tester.

AMMETERS

The ammeter is an instrument used to indicate current flow into and out of the battery. When electrical accessories in the vehicle draw more current than the alternator can supply, current flows from the battery and the ammeter indicates a discharge (−) condition. When electrical loads of the vehicle are less than alternator output, current is available to charge the battery, and the ammeter indicates a charge (+) condition. If battery is fully charged, the voltage regulator reduces

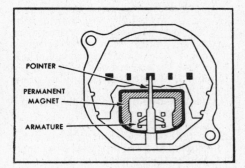

Fig. 1 Conventional type ammeter

alternator output to meet only immediate vehicle electrical loads. When this happens, the ammeter reads zero.

A conventional ammeter must be connected between the battery and alternator in order to indicate current flow. This type ammeter, **Fig. 1,** consists of a frame to which a permanent magnet is attached. The frame also supports an armature and pointer assembly. Current in this system flows from the alternator through the ammeter, then to the battery or from the battery through the ammeter into the vehicle electrical system, depending on vehicle operating conditions.

When no current flows through the ammeter, the magnet holds the pointer armature so that the pointer stands at the center of the dial. When current passes in either direction through the ammeter, the resulting magnetic field attracts the armature away from the effect of the permanent magnet, thus giving a reading proportional to the strength of the current flowing.

TROUBLESHOOTING

When the ammeter apparently fails to register correctly, there may be trouble in the wiring which connects the ammeter to the alternator and battery or in the alternator or battery itself.

To check the connections, first tighten the two terminal posts on the back of the ammeter. Then, following each wire from the ammeter, tighten all connections on the ignition switch, battery and alternator.

Chafed, burned or broken insulation can be found by following each ammeter wire from end to end.

All wires with chafed, burned or broken insulation should be repaired or replaced. After this is done, and all connections are tightened, connect the battery cable and turn on the ignition switch. The needle should point slightly to the discharge (−) side.

Start the engine and run slightly above idling speed. The needle should move slowly to the charge side (+).

If the pointer does not move as indicated, the ammeter is out of order and should be replaced.

ALTERNATOR INDICATOR LIGHT

DELCOTRON SI INTEGRAL CHARGING SYSTEM

This system features an integral solid state regulator mounted inside the alternator slip ring end frame. The alternator indicator lamp is installed in the field wire circuit connected between the ignition "Ign." terminal and alternator No. 1 terminal, **Fig. 2.** The resistance provided by the alternator warning light circuit is needed to protect the diode trio. The alternator indicator lamp should light when the ignition switch is turned on before engine is started. If lamp does not light, either lamp is burned out or indicator lamp wiring has an open circuit. After engine is started, the indicator lamp should be out at all times. If indicator lamp comes on, alternator belt may be loose, alternator or regulator may be defective, charging circuit may be defective or fuse may be blown.

Troubleshooting
1. Switch Off, lamp On:
   a. Disconnect electrical connector from alternator terminals 1 and 2.
   b. If indicator light remains lit, repair short circuit between leads.
   c. If indicator light goes out, replace alternator rectifier bridge.
2. Switch On, lamp Off, engine not running:
   a. Perform tests described in step 1.

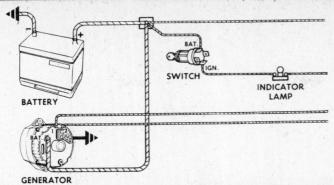

Fig. 2   Charge indicator lamp wiring system. Delco S1 type charging system

b. If problem still exists, there may be an open circuit.
c. To locate open circuit, check for blown fuse or fusible link, burned out bulb, defective bulb socket or an open in No. 1 lead circuit between alternator and ignition switch.
d. If no faults are found, check charging system for proper operation.
3. Switch On, lamp On, engine running:
a. On models so equipped, check condition of fuse between indicator light and ignition switch and fuse in A/C circuit.
b. Check charging system for proper operation.

VOLTMETER

The voltmeter is a gauge which measures the electrical flow from the battery to indicate whether the battery output is within tolerances. The voltmeter reading can range from 13.5–14.0 volts under normal operating conditions. If an undercharge or overcharge condition is indicated for an extended period, the battery and charging system should be checked.

TROUBLESHOOTING

To check voltmeter, turn key and headlights on with engine off. Pointer should move to 12.5 volts. If no needle movement is observed, check connections from battery to circuit breaker. If connections are tight and meter shows no movement, check wire continuity. If wire continuity is satisfactory, the meter is inoperative and must be replaced.

OIL PRESSURE INDICATOR LIGHT

Many trucks utilize a warning light on the instrument panel in place of the conventional dash indicating gauge to warn the driver when the oil pressure is dangerously low. The warning light is wired in series with the ignition switch and the engine unit—which is an oil pressure switch.

The oil pressure switch contains a diaphragm and a set of contacts. When the ignition switch is turned on, the warning light circuit is energized and the circuit is completed through the closed contacts in the pressure switch. When the engine is started, build-up of oil pressure compresses the diaphragm, opening the contacts, thereby breaking the circuit and putting out the light.

TROUBLESHOOTING

NOTE: On some models, the oil pressure indicator light also serves as the electric choke defect indicator. If Oil or Eng. indicator light does not light, check to ensure electric choke is not disconnected at carburetor. Also check for defect in electric choke heater, blown gauge fuse or defect in lamp or wiring circuit. If indicator light stays on with engine running possible causes are: oil pressure is low, switch to indicator light wiring has an open circuit, oil pressure switch wire connector has disconnected or on some models, gauge or radio fuse has blown.

The oil pressure warning light should go on when the ignition is turned on. If it does not light, disconnect the wire from the engine unit and ground the wire to the frame or cylinder block. Then if the warning light still does not go on with the ignition switch on, replace the bulb.

If the warning light goes on when the wire is grounded to the frame or cylinder block, the engine unit should be checked for being loose or poorly grounded. If the unit is found to be tight and properly grounded, it should be removed and a new one installed. (The presence of sealing compound on the threads of the engine unit will cause a poor ground.)

If the warning light remains lit when it normally should be out, replace the engine unit before proceeding further to determine the cause for a low pressure indication.

The warning light will sometimes light up or flicker when the engine is idling, even though the oil pressure is adequate. However, the light should go out when the engine speed is increased.

TEMPERATURE INDICATOR LIGHT

A bimetal temperature switch located in the cylinder head controls the operation of a temperature indicator light with a red lens. If the engine cooling system is not functioning properly and coolant temperature exceeds a predetermined value, the warning light will illuminate.

TROUBLESHOOTING

If the red light is not lit when the engine is being cranked, check for a burned out bulb, an open in the light circuit, or a defective ignition switch.

If the red light is lit when the engine is running, check the wiring between light and switch for a ground, defective temperature switch, or overheated cooling system.

NOTE: As a test circuit to check whether the red bulb is functioning properly, a wire which is connected to the ground terminal of the ignition switch is tapped into its circuit. When the ignition is in the "Start" (engine cranking) position, the ground terminal is grounded inside the switch and the red bulb will be lit. When the engine is started and the ignition switch is in the "On" position, the test circuit is opened and the bulb is then controlled by the temperature switch.

SPEEDOMETERS

The following material covers only that service on speedometers which is feasible to perform. Repairs on the units themselves are not included as they require special tools and extreme care when making repairs and adjustments that only an experienced speedometer technician should attempt.

The speedometer has two main parts—the speedometer head and the speedometer drive cable. When the speedometer fails to indicate speed or mileage, the cable or cable housing is probably broken.

SPEEDOMETER CABLE

Most cables are broken due to lack of lubrication, or a sharp bend or kink in the housing.

A cable might break because of the speedometer head mechanism binds. In such cases, the speedometer head should be repaired or replaced before a new cable or housing is installed.

A "jumpy" pointer condition, together with a scraping noise, is due, in most instances, to a dry or kinked speedometer cable. The kinked cable rubs on the housing and winds up, slowing down the pointer. The cable then unwinds and the pointer "jumps."

To check for kinks, remove the cable, lay it on a flat surface and twist one end with the fingers. If it turns over smoothly the cable is not kinked. But if part of the cable

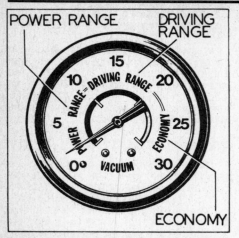

Fig. 3   Typical vacuum gauge

flops over as it is twisted, the cable is kinked and should be replaced.

LUBRICATION

The speedometer cable should be lubricated with special cable lubricant. Fill the ferrule on the upper end of the housing with the cable lubricant. Insert the cable in the housing, starting at the upper end. Turn the cable around carefully while feeding it into the housing. Repeat filling the ferrule except for the last six inches of cable. Too much lubricant at this point may cause the lubricant to work into the speedometer head.

INSTALLING CABLE

During installation, if the cable sticks when inserted in the housing and will not go through, the housing is damaged inside or kinked. Be sure to check the housing from one end to the other. Straighten any sharp bends by relocating clamps or elbows. Replace housing if it is badly kinked or broken. Position the cable and housing so that they lead into the head as straight as possible.

Check the new cable for kinks before installing it. Use wide, sweeping, gradual curves where the cable comes out of the transmission and connects to the head so the cable will not be damaged during installation.

Arrange the housing so it does not lean against the engine because heat from the engine may dry out the lubricant.

If inspection indicates that the cable and housing are in good condition, yet pointer action is erratic, check the speedometer head for possible binding.

The speedometer drive pinion should also be checked. If the pinion is dry or its teeth are stripped, the speedometer may not register properly.

VACUUM GAUGE

This gauge, **Fig. 3,** measures intake manifold vacuum. The intake manifold vacuum varies with engine operating condi-

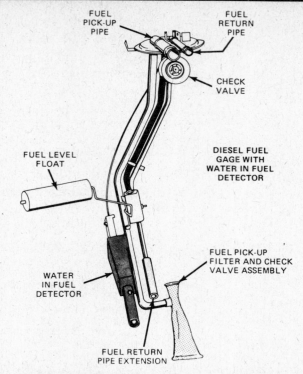

Fig. 4   Water in fuel detector & tank purge procedure. 1979–84

tions, carburetor adjustments, valve timing, ignition timing and general engine condition.

Since the optimum fuel economy is directly proportional to a properly functioning engine, a high vacuum reading on the gauge relates to fuel economy. Most gauges have colored sectors, the green sector being the "Economy" range and the red the "Power" range. Therefore, the vehicle should be operated with gauge registering in the green sector or a high numerical number, **Fig. 3,** for maximum economy.

FUEL ECONOMY WARNING SYSTEM

This system actually monitors the engine vacuum just like the vacuum gauge, but all it registers is a low vacuum. The light on the instrument panel warns the vehicle operator when engine manifold vacuum drops below the economical limit. Switch operation is similar to that of the oil pressure indicating light, except that the switch opens when vacuum , rather than oil pressure, is applied.

TROUBLESHOOTING

Fuel Economy Warning Light

The fuel economy warning light should go on when the ignition is turned on. If it does not light, disconnect the wire from the fuel economy vacuum switch connector and ground the wire to the frame or cylinder block. If the warning light still does not go on, check for burned out indicating bulb or an open in the harness between the

vacuum switch and instrument panel. If the warning light goes on, circuit is functioning and the vacuum switch should be checked for proper ground. Remove and clean the mounting bracket screws and the mounting surfaces.

If system still does not operate, perform the following:

With the electrical connector and vacuum tube disconnected from the switch, connect a self-powered test light to the switch electrical connector and to the vacuum gauge mountng bracket. Attach a vacuum pump to gauge. If the following conditions are not met, the switch has to be replaced:

1. With vacuum applied, test light should be "Off".
2. With no vacuum to the vacuum switch, test light should be "On".

If the warning light remains lit when it normally should be out, check vacuum hose to vacuum switch for damage or plugged condition.

ELECTRIC CLOCKS

Regulation of electric clocks is accomplished automatically by resetting the time. If the clock is running fast, the action of turning the hands back to correct the time will automatically cause the clock to run slightly slower. If the clock is running slow, the action of turning the hands forward to correct the time will automatically cause the clock to run slightly faster (10 to 15 seconds day).

A lock-out feature prevents the clock regulator mechanism from being reset

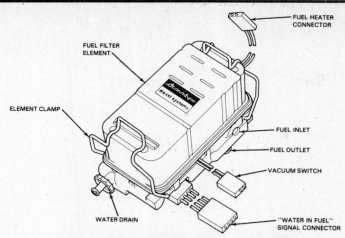

Fig. 5   Water in fuel detector. 1985

more than once per wind cycle, regardless of the number of times the time is reset. After the clock rewinds, if the time is then reset, automatic regulation will take place. If a clock varies over 10 minutes per day, it will never adjust properly and must be repaired or replaced.

WINDING CLOCK WHEN CONNECTING BATTERY OR CLOCK WIRING

The clock requires special attention when reconnecting a battery that has been disconnected for any reason, a clock that has been disconnected, or when replacing a blown clock fuse. It is very important that the initial wind be fully made. The procedure is as follows:

1. Make sure that all other instruments and lights are turned off.
2. Connect positive cable to battery.
3. Before connecting the negative cable, press the terminal to its post on the battery. Immediately afterward, strike the terminal against the battery post to see if there is a spark. If there is a spark, allow the clock to run down until it stops ticking, and repeat as above until there is no spark. Then immediately make the permanent connection before the clock can again run down. The clock will run down in approximately two minutes.
4. Reset clock after all connections have been made. The foregoing procedure should also be followed when reconnecting the clock after it has been disconnected, or if it has stopped because of a blown fuse. Be sure to disconnect battery before installing a new fuse.

TROUBLESHOOTING

If clock does not run, check for blown "clock" fuse. If fuse is blown, check for short in wiring. If fuse is not blown, check for open circuit.

With an electric clock, the most frequent cause of clock fuse blowing is voltage at the clock which will prevent a complete wind and allow clock contacts to remain closed. This may be caused by any of the following: discharged battery, corrosion on contact surface of battery terminals, loose connections at battery terminals, at junction block, at fuse clips, or at terminal connection of clock. Therefore, if in reconnecting battery or clock it is noted that the clock is not ticking, always check for blown fuse, or examine the circuits at the points indicated above to determine and correct the cause.

WATER IN FUEL INDICATOR
DESCRIPTION & OPERATION

1979–84
The Water In Fuel warning system employs an electronic water detector mounted inside the fuel tank on the fuel gauge sending unit. The detector provides a warning when 1–2½ gallons of water are present in the fuel tank by lighting a warning lamp on the instrument panel. The sending unit assembly also contains a provision for siphoning off water in the fuel tank through the fuel return line, **Fig. 4.**

The Water In Fuel lamp will come on for 2–5 seconds each time ignition is switched to Run position to ensure lamp is operating. If water is present in fuel, the lamp will come on after a 15–20 second delay and remain on.

1985
The Water In Fuel warning system employs a fuel detector integral with the fuel filter and fuel heater, **Fig. 5,** and mounted on the engine. When more than 2.2 ounces of water has collected in the

filter, the Water In Fuel lamp on the instrument panel will light. After the light comes on, the filter should be drained as soon as possible and must be drained within 2 hours of operation.

TROUBLESHOOTING

1979–84
1. If warning indicator fails to light during bulb check, proceed as follows:
   a. Disconnect electrical connector from fuel gauge sensing unit.
   b. Ground yellow/black wire in connector, then turn ignition to Run position.
   c. If indicator lamp lights, remove fuel gauge tank unit and check yellow wire for opens. Also, check connections to Water In Fuel detector and mounting screws. If connections and attachments are satisfactory, replace detector.
   d. If indicator lamp fails to light, check indicator lamp bulb. If bulb is satisfactory, check for open in yellow wire between lamp socket and sending unit and repair as necessary.
2. If warning indicator is lit at all times, proceed as follows:
   a. Disconnect electrical connector from fuel gauge sending unit, then turn ignition to Run position.
   b. If light remains lit, repair short to ground in yellow/black wire between sender and warning lamp.
   c. If light goes out, drain water from fuel tank, then recheck circuit. If lamp remains on with harness connected to sending unit, wiring to water detector or the detector itself is at fault.

1985
1. If warning lamp lights intermittently, drain water from fuel filter.
2. If warning lamp remains lit with engine running and ambient temperature above 32° F, drain fuel filter immediately. If lamp remains lit, replace filter.
3. If warning lamp remains lit with engine running and ambient temperature 32° F or below, drain fuel filter immediately. If water is frozen and cannot be drained, open air bleed to check for fuel pressure. If no fuel pressure is present, replace filter.
4. If warning lamp lights at high speed or under heavy acceleration, the fuel filter is plugged and must be replaced.
5. If warning lamp remains lit and engine stalls and will not restart after initial start-up, then fuel filter or fuel lines may be plugged. Repair or replace as necessary.
6. If warning lamp remains lit and engine stalls and will not restart immediately after refueling, a large quantity of water has likely been pumped into the fuel tank and the tank should be purged.

DISC BRAKES

TABLE OF CONTENTS

General Information

INDEX

TROUBLESHOOTING

EXCESSIVE PEDAL TRAVEL

1. Worn brake lining.
2. Shoe and lining knock back after cornering or rough road travel.
3. Piston and shoe and lining assembly not properly seated or positioned.
4. Air leak or insufficient fluid in system or caliper.
5. Loose wheel bearing adjustment.
6. Damaged or worn caliper piston seal.
7. Improper booster push rod adjustment.
8. Shoe out of flat more than .005".
9. Rear brake automatic adjusters inoperative.
10. Improperly ground rear brake shoe and lining assemblies.

BRAKE ROUGHNESS OR CHATTER; PEDAL PUMPING

1. Excessive lateral run-out of rotor.
2. Rotor excessively out of parallel.

EXCESSIVE PEDAL EFFORT

1. Frozen or seized pistons.
2. Brake fluid, oil or grease on linings.
3. Shoe and lining worn below specifications.
4. Proportioning valve malfunction.
5. Booster inoperative.
6. Leaking booster vacuum check valve.

PULL, UNEVEN OR GRABBING BRAKES

1. Frozen or seized pistons.
2. Brake fluid, oil or grease on linings.
3. Caliper out of alignment with rotor.
4. Loose caliper attachment.
5. Unequalized front tire pressure.
6. Incorrect front end alignment.
7. Lining protruding beyond end of shoe.

BRAKE RATTLE

1. Excessive clearance between shoe and caliper or between shoe and splash shield.
2. Shoe hold-down clips missing or improperly positioned.

HEAVY BRAKE DRAG

1. Frozen or seized pistons.
2. Operator riding brake pedal.
3. Incomplete brake pedal return due to linkage interference.
4. Faulty booster check valve holding pressure in hydraulic system.
5. Residual pressure in front brake hydraulic system.

CALIPER BRAKE FLUID LEAK

1. Damaged or worn caliper piston seal.
2. Scores in cylinder bore.

3. Corrosion build-up in cylinder bore or on piston surface.
4. Metal clip in seal groove.

NO BRAKING EFFECT WHEN PEDAL IS DEPRESSED

1. Piston and shoe and lining assembly not properly seated or positioned.
2. Air leak or insufficient fluid in system or caliper.
3. Damaged or worn caliper piston seal.
4. Bleeder screw open.
5. Air in hydraulic system or improper bleeding.

REAR BRAKES LOCKING ON APPLICATION

On brake system equipped with a proportioning or rear pressure regulator valve, should the valve malfunction, rear brakes may receive excess pressure, resulting in wheel lock-up.

SERVICE PRECAUTIONS

BRAKE LINES & LININGS

Remove one of the front wheels and inspect the brake disc, caliper and linings. (The wheel bearings should be inspected at this time and repacked if necessary).

Do not get any oil or grease on the linings. It is recommended that both front wheel sets be replaced whenever a respective shoe and lining is worn or damaged. Inspect and, if necessary, replace rear brake linings also.

If the caliper is cracked or fluid leakage through the casting is evident, it must be replaced as a unit.

BRAKE ROUGHNESS

The most common cause of brake chatter on disc brakes is a variation in thickness of the disc. If roughness or vibration is encountered during highway operation or if pedal pumping is experienced at low speeds, the disc may have excessive thickness variation. To check for this condition, measure the disc at 12 points with a micrometer at a radius approximately one inch from edge of disc. If thickness measurements vary more than specifications allow, the disc should be replaced with a new one.

Excessive lateral runout of braking disc may cause a "knocking back" of the pistons, possibly creating increased pedal travel and vibration when brakes are applied.

Before checking the runout, wheel bearings should be adjusted. Be sure to make the adjustment according to the recommendations given in the individual truck chapters.

BRAKE DISC SERVICE

Servicing of disc brakes is extremely critical due to the close tolerances required in machining the brake disc to insure proper brake operation.

The maintenance of these close controls on the friction surfaces is necessary to prevent brake roughness. In addition, the surface finish must be non-directional and maintained at a micro-inch finish. This close control of the rubbing surface finish is necessary to avoid pulls and erratic performance and promote long lining life and equal lining wear of both left and right brakes.

In light of the foregoing remarks, refinishing of the rubbing surfaces should not be attempted unless precision equipment, capable of measuring in micro-inches is available.

To check runout of a disc, mount a dial indicator on a convenient part (steering knuckle, tie rod, disc brake caliper housing) so that the plunger of the dial indicator contacts the disc at a point one inch from the outer edge. If the total indicated runout exceeds specifications, install a new disc.

GENERAL PRECAUTIONS

1. Grease or any other foreign material must be kept off the caliper, surfaces of the disc and external surfaces of the hub, during service procedures. Handling the brake disc and caliper should be done in a way to avoid deformation of the disc and nicking or scratching brake linings.
2. If inspection reveals rubber piston seals are worn or damaged, they should be replaced immediately.
3. During removal and installation of a wheel assembly, exercise care so as not to interfere with or damage the caliper splash shield, the bleeder screw or the transfer tube (if equipped).
4. Front wheel bearings should be adjusted to specifications.
5. Be sure vehicle is centered on hoist before servicing any of the front end components to avoid bending or damaging the disc splash shield on full right or left wheel turns.
6. Before the vehicle is moved after any brake service work, be sure to obtain a firm brake pedal.
7. The assembly bolts of the two caliper housings (if equipped) should not be disturbed unless the caliper requires service.

INSPECTION OF CALIPER

Should it become necessary to remove the caliper for installation of new parts, clean all parts in alcohol, wipe dry using lint-free cloths. Using an air hose, blow out drilled passages and bores. Check dust boots for punctures or tears. If punctures or tears are evident, new boots should be installed upon reassembly.

Inspect piston bores in both housings for scoring or pitting. Bores that show light scratches or corrosion can usually be cleaned with crocus cloth. However, bores that have deep scratches or scoring may be honed, provided the diameter of the bore is not increased more than .002". If the bore does not clean up within this specification, a new caliper housing should be installed (black stains on the bore walls are caused by piston seals and will do no harm).

When using a hone, be sure to install the hone baffle before honing bore. The baffle is used to protect the hone stones from damage. Use extreme care in cleaning the caliper after honing. Remove all dust and grit by flushing the caliper with alcohol. Wipe dry with clean lint-less cloth and then clean a second time in the same manner.

BLEEDING DISC BRAKES

The disc brake hydraulic system can be bled manually or with pressure bleeding equipment. On vehicles with disc brakes the brake pedal will require more pumping and frequent checking of fluid level in master cylinder during bleeding operation.

Never use brake fluid that has been drained from hydraulic system when bleeding the brakes. Be sure the disc brake pistons are returned to their normal positions and that the shoe and lining assemblies are properly seated. Before driving the vehicle, check brake operation to be sure that a firm pedal has been obtained.

Delco-Moraine Single Piston Caliper

INDEX

DESCRIPTION

The caliper assembly, **Fig. 1,** slides on its mounting bolts. Upon brake application, fluid pressure against the piston forces the inboard shoe and lining assembly against the inboard side of the disc. This action causes the caliper assembly to slide until the outboard lining comes into contact with the disc. As pressure builds up, the linings are pressed against the disc with increased force.

CALIPER REMOVAL

1. Siphon enough brake fluid out of the master cylinder to bring fluid level to ⅓ full to avoid fluid overflow when the caliper piston is pushed back into its bore.
2. Raise vehicle and remove front wheels.
3. Using a "C" clamp, as illustrated in **Fig. 2,** push piston back into its bore.
4. Remove two mounting bolts and lift caliper away from disc.

BRAKE SHOE REMOVAL

1. Remove caliper assembly as outlined above.
2. Remove inboard shoe. Dislodge outboard shoe and position caliper on the front suspension so the brake hose will not support the weight of the caliper.
3. Remove shoe support spring from piston.
4. Remove two sleeves from inboard ears of the caliper.
5. Remove four rubber bushings from the grooves in each of the caliper ears.

BRAKE SHOE INSTALLATION

1. Lubricate new sleeves, rubber bushings, bushing grooves and mounting bolt ends with Delco Silicone Lube or its equivalent.
2. Install new bushings and sleeves in caliper ears.

NOTE: Position the sleeve so that the end toward the shoe is flush with the machined surface of the ear.

3. Install shoe support spring in piston cavity, **Fig. 3.**
4. Position inboard shoe in caliper so spring ends centrally contact shoe edge. Initially, this will place the shoe on an angle. Push upper edge of shoe down until shoe is flat against caliper. When properly seated, spring ends will not extend past shoe more than .100".
5. Position outboard shoe in caliper with shoe ears over caliper ears and tab at bottom of shoe engaged in caliper cutout.
6. With shoes installed, lift caliper and rest bottom edge of outboard lining on outer edge of brake disc to be sure

there is no clearance between outboard shoe tab and caliper abutment.
7. Using a ¼" × 1" × 2½" metal bar to bridge caliper cutout, clamp outboard shoe to caliper with a "C" clamp.
8. Bend both ears of outboard shoe over caliper until clearance between shoe ear and caliper (measured at both the edge and side of the caliper) is .005" or less, **Fig. 4.**
9. Remove "C" clamp and install caliper.

DISASSEMBLING CALIPER

1. Remove caliper as outlined above.
2. Disconnect hose from steel line, remove U-shaped retainer and withdraw hose from frame support bracket.
3. After cleaning outside of caliper, remove brake hose and discard copper gasket.
4. Drain brake fluid from caliper.
5. Pad caliper interior with clean shop towels and use compressed air to remove piston, **Fig. 5.**

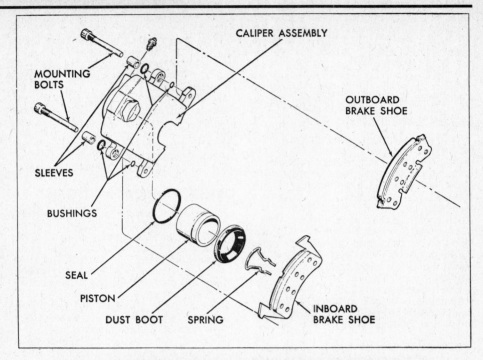

Fig. 1 Exploded view of disc brake caliper assembly

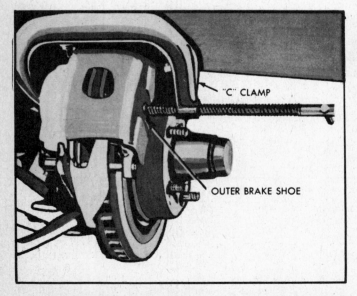

Fig. 2 Compressing piston & shoes with C-clamp

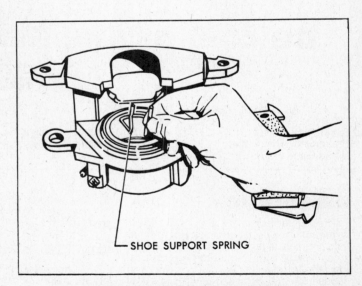

Fig. 3 Installing support spring

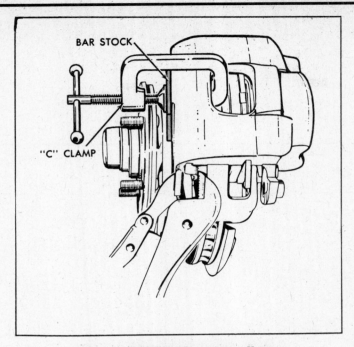

Fig. 4   Fitting shoe to caliper

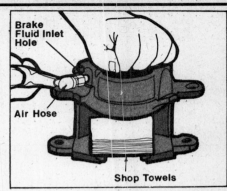

Fig. 5   Removing piston from caliper

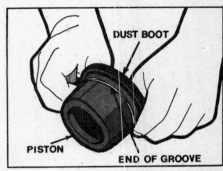

Fig. 6   Installing boot to piston

NOTE: Use just enough air pressure to ease piston out of bore. Do not blow piston out of bore.

CAUTION: Do not place fingers in front of piston in an attempt to catch or protect it when applying compressed air. This could result in serious injury.

6. Carefully pry dust boot out of bore.
7. Using a small piece of wood or plastic, remove piston seal from bore.

NOTE: Do not use a metal tool of any kind to remove seal as it may damage bore.

8. Remove bleeder valve.

ASSEMBLING CALIPER

1. Lubricate caliper piston bore and new piston seal with clean brake fluid. Position seal in bore groove.
2. Lubricate piston with clean brake fluid and assemble a new boot into the groove in the piston so the fold faces the open end of the piston, **Fig. 6.**
3. Using care not to unseat the seal, insert piston into bore and force the piston to the bottom of the bore.
4. Position dust boot in caliper counterbore and install, **Fig. 7.**

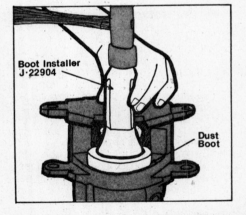

Fig. 7   Installing boot to caliper.

NOTE: Check the boot installation to be sure the retaining ring moulded into the boot is not bent and that the boot is installed below the caliper face and evenly all around. If the boot is not fully installed, dirt and moisture may enter the bore and cause corrosion.

5. Install the brake hose in the caliper using a new copper gasket.
6. Install shoes and re-install caliper assembly.

CALIPER INSTALLATION

1. Position caliper over disc, lining up holes in caliper with holes in mounting bracket. If brake hose was not disconnected during removal, be sure not to kink it during installation.
2. Start mounting bolts through sleeves in inboard caliper ears and the mounting bracket, making sure ends of bolts pass under ears on inboard shoe.

NOTE: Right and left calipers must not be interchanged.

3. Push mounting bolts through to engage holes in the outboard ears. Then thread mounting bolts into bracket.
4. Torque mounting bolts to 30–40 ft. lbs.
5. If brake hose was removed, reconnect it and bleed the calipers.
6. Replace front wheels, lower vehicle and add brake fluid to master cylinder to bring level to ¼″ from top.

NOTE: Before moving vehicle, pump brake pedal several times to be sure it is firm. Do not move vehicle until a firm pedal is obtained.

Bendix Single Piston Sliding Caliper

INDEX

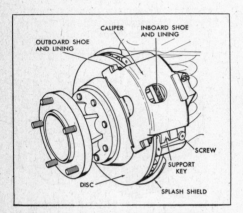

Fig. 1   Disc brake assembly

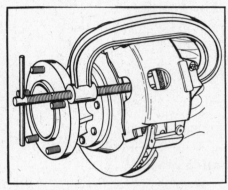

Fig. 2   Bottoming position in bore

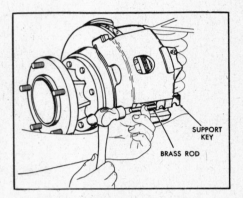

Fig. 3   Removing caliper support key

DESCRIPTION

The Bendix single piston sliding caliper disc brake is standard equipment on some truck applications, while on other trucks it is used only in Hydro-Boost power brake applications with both front disc brakes and 4-wheel disc brakes.

NOTE: On 4-wheel disc brakes, the front & rear systems are identical.

The sliding caliper attaches to and slides on the steering knuckle. The caliper assembly is held in place with a support key and spring **Fig. 1.** A screw prevents the key from sliding on the steering knuckle. The linings are riveted to the brake shoes. The inboard and outboard brake shoes are not interchangeable.

CALIPER REMOVAL

1. Siphon two-thirds of brake fluid from master cylinder reservoir serving front disc brakes.
2. Raise vehicle, support on jackstands and remove front wheels.
3. Bottom the caliper piston in bore. Insert a screwdriver between inboard shoe and piston, then pry piston back into bore. The piston can also be bottomed in the bore with a large "C" clamp, **Fig. 2.**
4. Remove support key retaining screw.
5. Drive caliper support key and spring from steering knuckle with a suitable drift and hammer, **Fig. 3.**

6. Lift caliper from anchor plate and off rotor, **Fig. 4.** Hang caliper from coil spring with wire. Do not allow caliper to hang from brake hose.
7. Remove inboard brake shoe from steering knuckle, then the anti-rattle spring from the brake shoe.
8. Remove outboard brake shoe from caliper. It may be necessary to loosen the brake shoe with a hammer to permit shoe removal.

CALIPER DISASSEMBLY

1. Drain brake fluid from caliper.
2. Position caliper with shop cloths, **Fig. 5,** and apply compressed air to fluid inlet port to ease piston from bore.

NOTE: Do not attempt to catch piston or to protect it when applying compressed air, since personal injury is possible.

3. Remove boot from piston, then the piston seal from bore, **Fig. 6.** Use wooden or plastic tool to remove piston seal since metal tools may damage piston.
4. Remove bleeder screw.

CALIPER ASSEMBLY

1. Coat square cut piston seal with clean

brake fluid, then install seal into piston bore. Work seal into groove with clean fingers.
2. Install and torque bleeder screw to 100 inch lbs.
3. Lubricate boot and tool J-24548 with clean brake fluid, then place dust seal on tool, allowing ¼ inch of tool to extend past small lip of boot, **Fig. 7.**
4. Place dust seal and tool over piston bore, then work large lip of boot into seal groove, **Fig. 8.** Ensure dust seal is fully seated.
5. Lubricate caliper piston and insert through tool. Center piston in bore and use a hammer handle to apply pressure to install piston halfway into bore, **Fig. 8.**
6. Remove tool J-24548 and seat small lip of boot in caliper piston groove, then bottom piston in bore.

BRAKE SHOE & LINING
REPLACE

The procedures to remove & install the brake shoe and lining assemblies are outlined under "Caliper Removal" and "Caliper Installation". It is not necessary to disconnect the brake hose, however, use caution not to twist or kink hose.

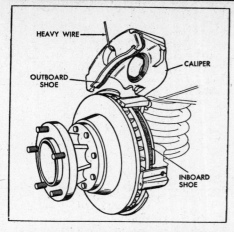

Fig. 4 Removing caliper from disc

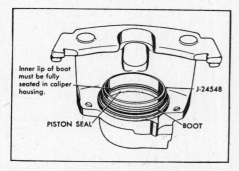

Fig. 7 Installing caliper piston boot

CALIPER INSTALLATION

1. Clean and lubricate sliding surfaces of

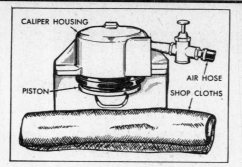

Fig. 5 Removing caliper piston

caliper and the anchor plate with Delco Silicone Lube, P/N 5459912, or equivalent.
2. Install inboard brake shoe anti-rattle spring on brake shoe rear flange, and ensure looped section of clip is facing away from rotor.
3. Install inboard brake shoe in steering knuckle.
4. Install outboard brake shoe in caliper. Ensure the shoe flange is seated fully into outboard arms of caliper. It may be necessary to use a "C" clamp to seat the shoe.
5. Place caliper assembly over rotor and position in steering knuckle. Ensure dust boot is not torn or mispositioned by inboard brake shoe during caliper installation.
6. Align caliper with steering knuckle abutment surfaces, then insert support key and spring between abutment surfaces at the trailing end of caliper and steering knuckle. With a hammer and brass drift, drive caliper support

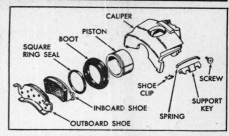

Fig. 6 Exploded view of disc brake caliper assembly

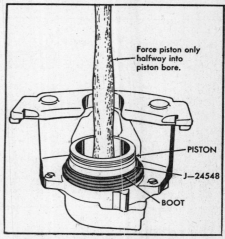

Fig. 8 Installing piston in caliper

key and spring into position, then install and torque support key retaining screw to 12–18 ft. lbs.
7. Refill master cylinder to within one inch of rim. Press brake pedal several times to seat shoes.
8. Install front wheels and lower vehicle.

DRUM BRAKES

TABLE OF CONTENTS

General Information

INDEX

SERVICE PRECAUTIONS

When working on or around brake assemblies, care must be taken to prevent breathing asbestos dust, as many manufacturers incorporate asbestos fibers in the production of brake linings. During routine service operations, the amount of asbestos dust from brake lining wear is at a low level due to a chemical breakdown during use, and a few precautions will minimize exposure.

CAUTION: Do not sand or grind brake linings unless suitable local exhaust ventilation equipment is used to prevent excessive asbestos exposure.

1. Wear a suitable respirator approved for asbestos dust use during all repair procedures.
2. When cleaning brake dust from brake parts, use a vacuum cleaner with a highly efficient filter system. If a suitable vacuum cleaner is not available, use a water soaked rag.

NOTE: Do not use compressed air or dry brush to clean brake parts.

3. Keep work area clean, using same equipment as for cleaning brake parts.
4. Properly dispose of rags and vacuum cleaner bags by placing them in plastic bags.
5. Do not smoke or eat while working on brake systems.

GENERAL INSPECTION
BRAKE DRUMS

Any time the brake drums are removed for brake service, the braking surface diameter should be checked with a suitable brake drum micrometer at several points to determine if they are within the safe oversize limit stamped on the brake drum outer surface. If the braking surface diameter exceeds specifications, the drum must be replaced. If the braking surface diameter is within specifications, drums should be cleaned and inspected for cracks, scores, deep grooves, taper, out of round and heat spotting. If drums are cracked or heat spotted, they must be replaced. Minor scores should be removed with sandpaper. Grooves and large scores can only be removed by machining with special equipment, as long as the braking surface is within specifications stamped on brake drum outer surface. Any brake drum sufficiently out of round to cause vehicle vibration or noise while braking, or showing taper should also be machined, removing only enough stock to true up the brake drum.

After a brake drum is machined, wipe the braking surface diameter with a cloth soaked in denatured alcohol. If one brake drum is machined, the other should also be machined to the same diameter to maintain equal braking forces.

BRAKE LININGS & SPRINGS

Inspect brake linings for excessive wear, damage, oil, grease or brake fluid contamination. If any of the above conditions exists, brake linings should be replaced. Do not attempt to replace only one set of brake shoes; they should be replaced as an axle set only to maintain equal braking forces. Examine brake shoe webbing, hold down and return springs for signs of overheating indicated by a slight blue color. If any component exhibits signs of overheating, replace hold down and return springs with new ones. Overheated springs lose their pull and could cause brake linings to wear out prematurely. Inspect all springs for sags, bends and external damage, and replace as necessary.

Inspect hold down retainers and pins for bends, rust and corrosion. If any of the above conditions exist, replace retainers and pins.

BACKING PLATE

Inspect backing plate shoe contact surface for grooves that may restrict shoe movement and cannot be removed by lightly sanding with emery cloth or other suitable abrasive. If backing plate exhibits above condition, it should be replaced. Also inspect for signs of cracks, warpage and excessive rust, indicating need for replacement.

ADJUSTER MECHANISM

Inspect all components for rust, corrosion, bends and fatigue. Replace as necessary. On adjuster mechanism equipped with adjuster cable, inspect cable for kinks, fraying or elongation of eyelet and replace as necessary.

PARKING BRAKE CABLE

Inspect parking brake cable end for kinks, fraying and elongation, and replace as necessary. Use a small hose clamp to compress clamp where it enters backing plate to remove.

Exc. 1982–84 S/T 10-15

INDEX

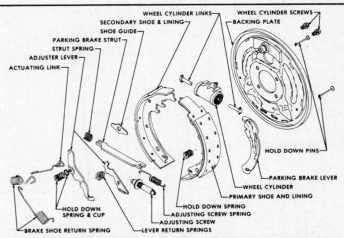

Fig. 1 Exploded view of drum brake assembly. Exc. Caballero, El Camino & 1985 S/T 10-15

REMOVAL

1. Raise and support vehicle, then remove tire and wheel assembly.
2. Remove brake drum. If brake lining is dragging on brake drum, back off brake adjustment by rotating adjustment screw. Refer to individual truck chapter for procedure.

NOTE: If brake drum is rusted or corroded to axle flange and cannot be removed, lightly tap axle flange to drum mounting surface with a suitable hammer.

3. Using brake spring pliers or equivalent, unhook primary and secondary return springs, **Figs. 1 and 2.**

NOTE: Observe location of brake parts being removed to aid during installation.

4. Remove brake hold down springs with suitable tool.
5. Lift actuating lever, then unhook actuator link from anchor pin and remove.
6. Remove actuating lever(s) and return spring.
7. Spread shoes apart and remove parking brake strut and spring.
8. Disconnect parking brake cable from lever, then remove brake shoes from backing plate.
9. Separate brake shoes by removing adjusting screw and spring, then unhook parking brake lever from shoe assembly.
10. Clean dirt from brake drum, backing plate and all other components.

CAUTION: Do not use compressed air or dry brush to clean brake parts. Many brake parts contain asbestos fibers which, if inhaled, can cause serious injury. Clean brake parts with a water soaked rag or a suitable vacuum cleaner to minimize airborne dust.

INSPECTION

1. Inspect components for damage and unusual wear. Replace as necessary.
2. Inspect wheel cylinders. Boots which are torn, cut or heat damaged indicate need for wheel cylinder replacement. On all models except Caballero, El Camino and 1985 S/T 10-15, remove wheel cylinder links. On Caballero, El Camino and 1985 S/T 10-15 models, use a small screwdriver to pry center hole of boot away from piston. If fluid spills from center hole, cup leakage is indicated and wheel cylinder should be replaced. On all models, light fluid coatings on piston within cylinder is considered normal.
3. Inspect backing plate for evidence of axle seal leakage. If leakage exists, refer to individual car chapters for axle seal replacement procedures.
4. Inspect backing plate attaching bolts, and ensure they are tight.
5. Using fine emery cloth or other suitable abrasive, clean rust and dirt from shoe contact surface on backing plate.

INSTALLATION

1. Lubricate parking brake lever fulcrum with suitable brake lube, then attach lever to brake shoe. Ensure lever operates smoothly.
2. Connect brake shoes with adjusting screw spring, then position adjusting screw.

NOTE: Ensure adjusting screw star wheel does not contact adjusting screw spring after installation, and also ensure right hand thread adjusting screw is installed on left side of vehicle and left hand thread adjusting screw is installed on right side of vehicle. When brake shoe installation is completed, ensure starwheel lines up with adjusting hole in backing plate.

3. Lightly lubricate backing plate shoe contact surfaces with suitable brake lube, then the area where parking brake cable contacts backing plate.
4. Install brake shoes on backing plate while engaging wheel cylinder links (if equipped) with shoe webbing. Connect parking brake cable to parking brake lever.

NOTE: The primary shoe (short lining) faces towards front of vehicle.

5. Install actuating levers, actuating link

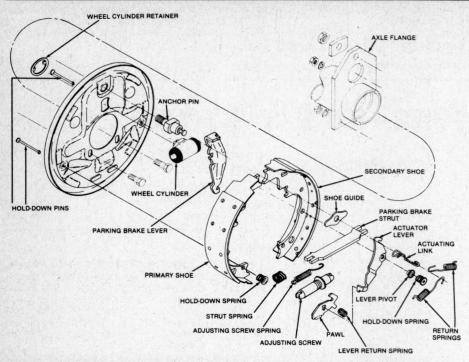

WHEEL CYLINDER RETAINER

AXLE FLANGE

ANCHOR PIN

SECONDARY SHOE

WHEEL CYLINDER

SHOE GUIDE

HOLD-DOWN PINS

PARKING BRAKE STRUT

PARKING BRAKE LEVER

ACTUATOR LEVER

ACTUATING LINK

PRIMARY SHOE

HOLD-DOWN SPRING

STRUT SPRING

ADJUSTING SCREW SPRING

LEVER PIVOT

ADJUSTING SCREW

PAWL

HOLD-DOWN SPRING

LEVER RETURN SPRING

RETURN SPRINGS

Fig. 2 Exploded view of drum brake assembly. Caballero, El Camino & 1985 S/T 10-15

Fig. 3 Measuring brake drum inside diameter

and return spring, **Figs. 1 and 2.**

6. Install hold down springs with suitable tool.

7. Install primary and secondary shoe return springs using brake spring pliers or equivalent.

8. Using suitable brake drum to shoe gauge, **Fig. 3,** measure brake drum inside diameter. Adjust brake shoes to dimension obtained on outside portion of gauge, **Fig. 4.**

9. Install brake drum, wheel and tire assembly.

10. If any hydraulic connections have been opened, bleed brake system.

11. Adjust parking brake. Refer to individual truck chapters for procedures.

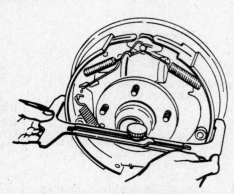

Fig. 4 Adjusting brake shoes to brake drum inside diameter

12. Inspect all hydraulic lines and connections for leakage, and repair as necessary.

13. Check master cylinder fluid level and replenish as necessary.

14. Check brake pedal for proper feel and return.

15. Lower vehicle and road test.

NOTE: Do not severely apply brakes immediately after installation of new brake linings or permanent damage may occur to linings, and/or brake drums may become scored. Brakes must be used moderately during first several hundred miles of operation to ensure proper burnishing of linings.

INDEX

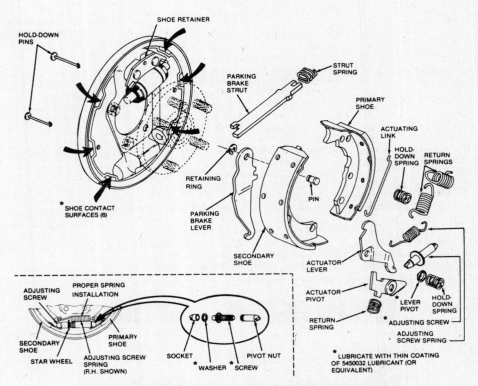

Fig. 1   Exploded view of drum brake assembly

REMOVAL

1. Raise and support rear of vehicle, then remove tire and wheel assembly.
2. Remove brake drum. If brake lining is dragging on brake drum, back off brake adjustment by rotating adjustment screw.

NOTE: If brake drum is rusted or corroded to axle flange and cannot be removed, lightly tap axle flange to drum mounting surface with a suitable hammer.

3. Using brake spring pliers or equivalent, unhook primary and secondary return springs, **Fig. 1.**
4. Remove hold down springs with suitable tool, then lift off lever pivot.
5. Remove hold down pins, then lift actuator lever and remove actuator link.
6. Remove actuator lever, pivot and return spring.
7. Spread shoes apart and remove parking brake strut and spring.
8. With brake shoes spread, disconnect parking brake spring from lever, then lift brake shoes, adjusting screw and spring from backing plate.
9. Note position of adjusting screw and spring, then remove from shoe assemblies.
10. Remove parking brake lever from secondary shoe.
11. Clean dirt from brake drum, backing plate and all other components.

CAUTION: Do not use compressed air or dry brush to clean brake parts. Many brake parts contain asbestos fibers which, if inhaled, can cause serious injury. Clean brake parts with a water soaked rag or a suitable vacuum cleaner to minimize airborne dust.

INSPECTION

1. Inspect components for damage or unusual wear. Replace as necessary.
2. Inspect backing plate attaching bolts, and ensure they are tight.
3. Inspect wheel cylinders. Excessive fluid indicates cup leakage and need for wheel cylinder replacement.

NOTE: A slight amount of fluid is always present and is considered normal, acting as a lubricant for the cylinder pistons.

4. Check adjuster screw operation. If satisfactory, lightly lubricate adjusting screw and washer with suitable brake lube. If operation is unsatisfactory, replace.
5. Using fine emery cloth or other suitable abrasive, clean rust and dirt from shoe contact surfaces on backing plate, **Fig. 1.**

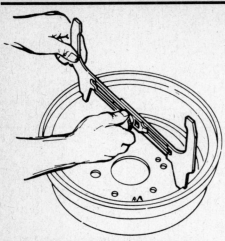

Fig. 2   Measuring brake drum inside diameter

INSTALLATION

1. Lightly lubricate backing plate shoe contact surfaces with suitable brake lube.
2. Install parking brake lever on secondary shoe.
3. Connect primary and secondary brake shoes with adjusting screw spring, then position adjusting screw in same position from which it was removed.

NOTE: Ensure adjusting screw spring

starwheel does not contact adjusting screw spring after installation, and also ensure right hand thread adjusting screw is installed on left side of vehicle and left hand thread adjusting screw is installed on right side of vehicle.

4. Spread brake shoes apart to clear axle flange, then install parking brake cable on lever. Position brake assembly on backing plate.
5. Spread brake shoes slightly, then install parking brake strut and spring. Spring end of strut engages the primary shoe, while the other end engages the parking brake lever and secondary shoe.
6. Install actuator lever, pivot and return spring, then hook actuating link in shoe retainer.
7. Lift actuator lever and hook actuating link to lever.
8. Install hold down pins, lever pivot and hold down springs.
9. Install primary and secondary return springs using suitable brake spring pliers.
10. Using suitable brake drum to shoe gauge, **Fig. 2,** measure brake drum inside diameter. Adjust brake shoes to dimension obtained on outside portion of gauge, **Fig. 3.**
11. Install brake drum, tire and wheel assembly.
12. If any hydraulic connections have been opened, bleed brake system.
13. Adjust parking brake. Refer to individual truck chapters for procedures.

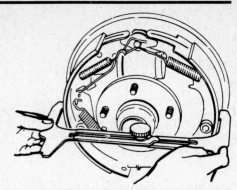

Fig. 3   Adjusting brake shoes to brake drum inside diameter

14. Inspect all hydraulic lines and connections for leakage, and repair as necessary.
15. Check master cylinder fluid level, and replenish as necessary.
16. Check brake pedal for proper feel and return.
17. Lower vehicle and road test.

NOTE: Do not severely apply brakes immediately after installation of new brake linings or permanent damage may occur to linings, and/or brake drums may become scored. Brakes must be used moderately during first several hundred miles of operation to ensure proper burnishing of linings.

UNIVERSAL JOINTS

INDEX

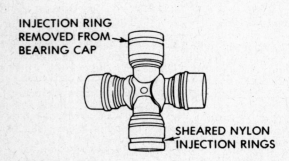

Fig. 1   Production type universal joints which use nylon injection rings in place of snap rings

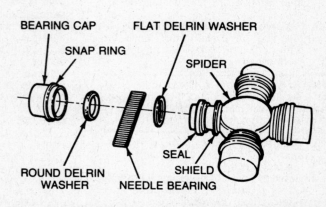

Fig. 2   Service type universal joints (internal snap ring type)

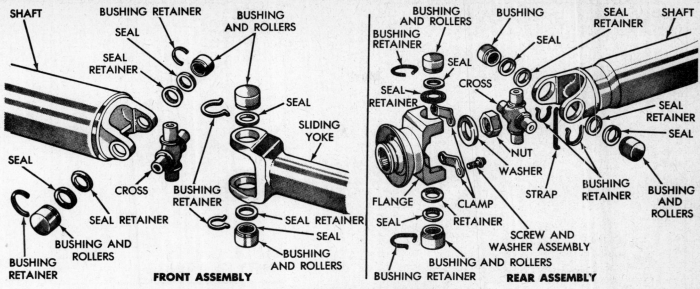

Fig. 3   Cross & roller type universal joints

SERVICE NOTES

Before disassembling any universal joint, examine the assembly carefully and note the position of the grease fitting (if used). Also, be sure to mark the yokes with relation to the propeller shaft so they may be reassembled in the same relative position. Failure to observe these precautions may produce rough vehicle operation which results in rapid wear and failure of parts, and place an unbalanced load on transmission, engine and rear axle.

When universal joints are disassembled for lubrication or inspection, and the old parts are to be reinstalled, special care must be exercised to avoid damage to universal joint spider or cross and bearing cups.

NOTE: Some driveshafts use an injected nylon retainer on the universal joint bearings. When service is necessary, pressing the bearings out will sheer the nylon retainer, **Fig. 1**. Replacement with the conventional steel snap ring type is then necessary, **Fig. 2**

CROSS & ROLLER TYPE

Figs. 3 and 4 illustrate typical examples of universal joints of this type. They all operate on the same principle and similar service and replacement procedures may be applied to all.

SERVICING WITHOUT UNIVERSAL JOINT REPLACEMENT TOOL

Disassembly

1. Remove snap rings (or retainer plates) that retain bearings in yoke and drive shaft.
2. Place U-joint in a vise.
3. Select a wrench socket with an outside diameter slightly smaller than the U-joint bearings. Select another wrench socket with an inside diameter slightly larger than the U-joint bearings.
4. Place the sockets at opposite bearings in the yoke so that the smaller socket becomes a bearing pusher and the larger socket becomes a bearing

receiver when the vise jaws come together, **Fig. 5**. Close vise jaws until both bearings are free of yoke and remove bearings from the cross or spider.

5. If bearings will not come all the way out, close vise until bearing in receiver socket protrudes from yoke as much as possible without using excessive force. Then remove from vise and place that portion of bearing which protrudes from yoke between vise jaws. Tighten vise to hold bearing and drive yoke off with a soft hammer.
6. To remove opposite bearing from yoke, replace in vise with pusher socket on exposed cross journal with receiver socket over bearing cup. Then tighten vise jaws to press bearing back through yoke into receiving socket.
7. Remove yoke from drive shaft and again place protruding portion of bearing between vise jaws. Then tighten vise to hold bearing while driving yoke off bearing with soft hammer.
8. Turn spider or cross ¼ turn and use the same procedure to press bearings

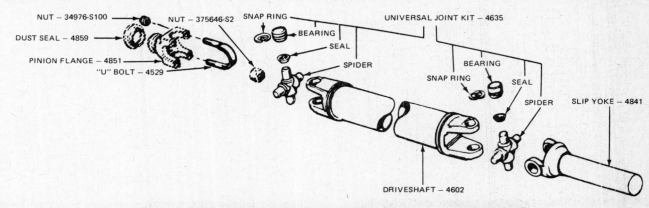

Fig. 4   Cross & roller type universal joints & propeller shaft

Fig. 5   Removing bearings from yoke using a small socket as a driver & large socket as a receiver

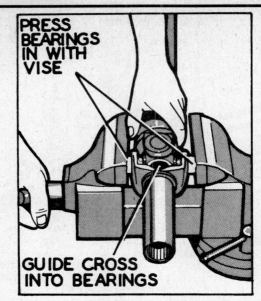

Fig. 6   Installing bearings into drive shaft yoke

out of drive shaft.

Assembly

1. If old parts are to be reassembled, pack bearing cups with universal joint grease. Do not fill cups completely or use excessive amounts as over-lubrication may damage seals during reassembly. Use new seals.
2. If new parts are being installed, check new bearings for adequate grease before assembling.
3. With the pusher (smaller) socket, press one bearing part way into drive shaft. Position spider into the partially installed bearing. Place second bearing into drive shaft. Fasten drive shaft in vise so that bearings are in contact with faces of vise jaws, **Fig. 6.** Some

spiders are provided with locating lugs which must face toward drive shaft when installed.

4. Press bearings all the way into position and install snap rings or retainer plates.
5. Install bearings in yoke in same manner. When installation is completed, check U-joint for binding or rough-

ness. If free movement is impeded, correct the condition before installation in vehicle.

SERVICING USING UNIVERSAL JOINT REPLACEMENT TOOL

Disassembly

1. Place driveshaft in a vise using care to avoid damaging it.

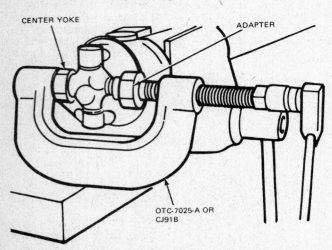

Fig. 7   Removing bearing caps using tool & adapter

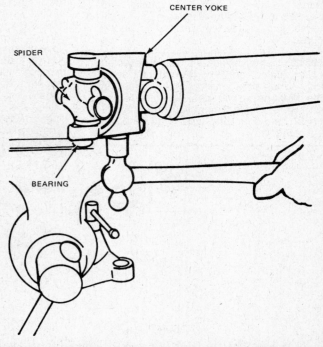

Fig. 8   Removing bearing cap by holding cap in vise & striking center yoke with hammer

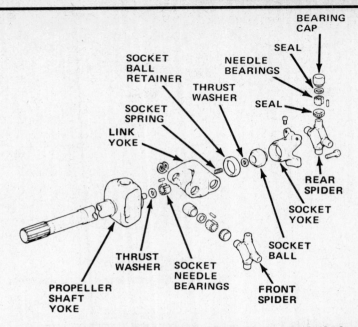

Fig. 9   Double cardan universal joint exploded view

2. Remove bearing retaining snap rings.

NOTE: Some universal joints use injected nylon retainers in place of snap rings. During servicing, the snap rings supplied with the replacement universal joint assembly must be used.

3. Position tool on shaft and press bearing out of yoke, **Fig. 7.** If bearing cannot be pressed all the way out, remove it using vise grips or channel lock pliers or position driveshaft as shown and strike center yoke with hammer, **Fig. 8.** Mark yoke and shaft to make sure they will be reassembled in their same relative positions.
4. Reposition tool so that it presses on the spider in order to press other bearing from opposite side of flange.
5. If used, remove flange from spider.

Assembly
1. Start new bearing into yoke, then position spider into yoke and press bearing until it is ¼ inch below surface.
2. Remove tool and install a new snap ring.
3. Start new bearing in opposite side of yoke, then install tool and press on bearing until opposite bearing contacts snap ring.
4. Remove tool and install remaining snap ring.

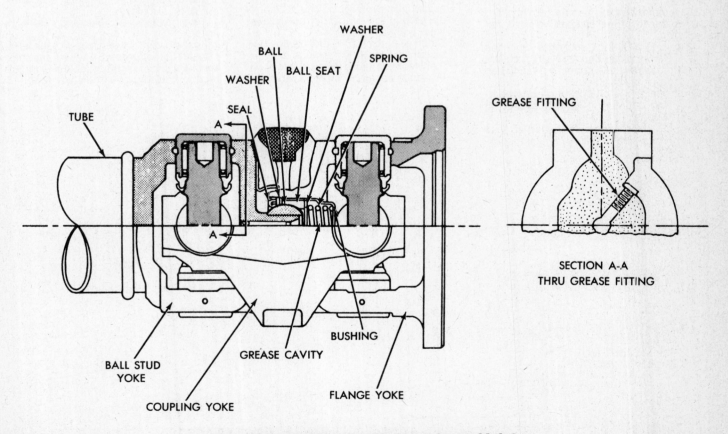

Fig. 10   Constant velocity (CV) universal joint

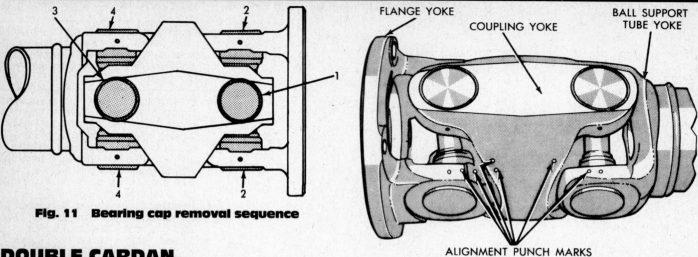

Fig. 11 Bearing cap removal sequence

Fig. 12 Alignment punch marks

DOUBLE CARDAN TYPE

The double cardan type joint, **Fig. 9**, incorporates two universal joints, a centering socket yoke, and center yoke at one end of the shaft. A single universal joint is used at the other end.

DISASSEMBLY

1. Remove all bearing cap retainers.
2. Mark bearing caps, spiders, propeller shaft yoke, link yoke and socket yoke for assembly alignment reference, **Fig. 9.**
3. Remove bearing caps attaching from spider to propeller shaft yoke as follows:
   a. Use a ⅝ inch socket to drive the bearing cap and a 1¹/₁₆ inch socket to receive the opposite bearing cap as it is driven out.
   b. Place ⅝ inch socket on one bearing cap and 1¹/₁₆ inch socket on opposite bearing.
   c. Position assembly in vise so vise jaws bear directly against sockets.
   d. Tighten vise to press first bearing cap out of link yoke.
   e. Loosen vise, reposition sockets and press opposite bearing cap out of link yoke.
4. Disengage propeller shaft yoke from link yoke.
5. Remove bearing caps attaching front spider to propeller shaft as described in step 3 above.
6. Remove front spider from yoke.
7. Remove bearing caps attaching rear spider to link yoke as outlined in step 3 above and remove spider and socket yoke from link yoke.
8. Clean all parts in solvent and wipe dry. Inspect assembly for damage or wear. If any component is worn or damaged, the entire assembly must be replaced.

ASSEMBLY

NOTE: When assembling universal joint, make sure to align spiders and yokes according to marks made during disassembly.

1. Lubricate all bearings and contact surfaces with lithium base chassis grease.
2. Install bearing caps on yoke ends of rear spider and secure caps with tape, **Fig. 9.**
3. Assemble socket yoke and rear spider.
4. Position rear spider in link yoke and install bearing caps. Press caps into yoke using ⅝ inch socket until bearing cap retainer grooves are exposed.

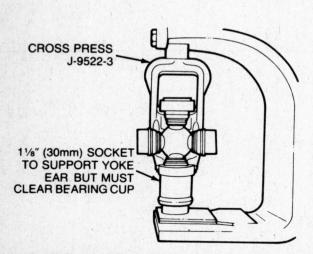

Fig. 13 Cross press being used in place of socket

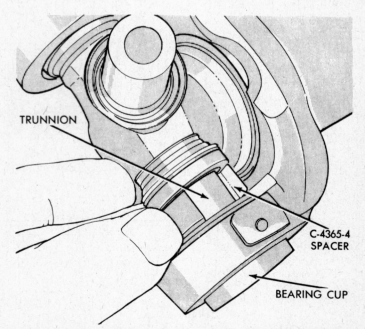

Fig. 14 Using spacer to completely drive out bearing

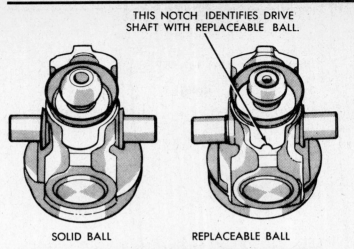

THIS NOTCH IDENTIFIES DRIVE SHAFT WITH REPLACEABLE BALL.

SOLID BALL   REPLACEABLE BALL

Fig. 15   Solid ball & replaceable balls. Notch identifies driveshaft with replaceable ball

WASHER (LARGE OD)   3-BALL SEATS

SEAL   WASHER (SMALL OD)

REPLACEABLE BALL

SPRING

Fig. 16   Ball & seat exploded view

5. Install rear spider-to-link yoke bearing cap retainers.
6. Position front spider in propeller shaft yoke and install bearing caps. Press caps into yoke using a ⅝ inch socket until bearing cap retainer grooves are exposed.
7. Install front spider-to-propeller shaft yoke bearing cap retainers.
8. Install thrust washer and socket spring in ball socket bearing bore, if removed.
9. Install thrust washer on ball socket bearing boss (located on propeller shaft yoke), if removed.
10. Align ball socket bearing boss on propeller shaft yoke with ball socket bearing bore and insert boss into bore.
11. Align front spider with link yoke bearing cap bores and install bearing caps. Press caps into yoke using a ⅝ inch socket until bearing cap retainer grooves are exposed.
12. Install front spider-to-link yoke bearing cap retainers.

CONSTANT VELOCITY TYPE

This type of universal joint, **Fig. 10**, consists of two conventional cross and roller joints connected with a special link yoke. Because the two joint angles are the same, even though the usual universal joint fluctuation is present within the unit, the acceleration of the front joint (within the yoke) is always neutralized by the deceleration of the rear joint (within the yoke) and vice versa. The end result is the front and rear propeller shafts always turn at a constant velocity.

DISASSEMBLY
Constant Velocity Joint

NOTE: To disassemble the constant velocity joint, the bearings should be removed in sequence shown in **Fig. 11**. This method requires the least amount of work.

1. Mark all yokes before disassembly as shown in **Fig. 12**, so that they can be reassembled in their original relationship to maintain driveshaft balance.

NOTE: The following procedure can be performed in a vise. A cross press tool, **Fig. 13**, can be used in place of the socket used to drive the bearings.

2. Support the driveshaft horizontally in line with the base plate of a press. Place rear end of coupling yoke over a 1⅛ inch socket to accept the bearing. Place a socket slightly smaller than the bearing, on the opposite side of the spider.
3. Press bearing cup out of coupling yoke ear. If bearing cup is not completely removed, insert spacer C-4365-4 or equivalent, **Fig. 14**, and complete removal of bearing cup.

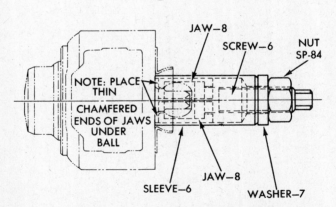

JAW—8

SCREW—6   NUT SP-84

NOTE: PLACE THIN CHAMFERED ENDS OF JAWS UNDER BALL

SLEEVE—6   JAW—8   WASHER—7

Fig. 17   Removing centering ball

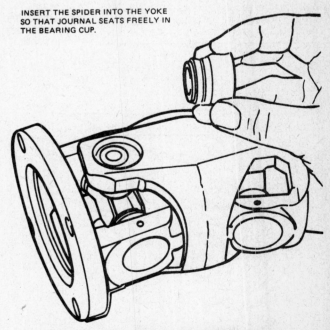

INSERT THE SPIDER INTO THE YOKE SO THAT JOURNAL SEATS FREELY IN THE BEARING CUP.

Fig. 18   Inserting cross into yoke

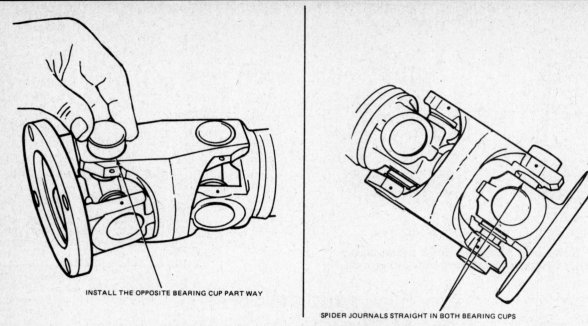

INSTALL THE OPPOSITE BEARING CUP PART WAY

SPIDER JOURNALS STRAIGHT IN BOTH BEARING CUPS

Fig. 19 Aligning bearing cups & journals

4. Rotate driveshaft 180° and shear the opposite retaining ring, and press the bearing cup out of the coupling yoke as described previously, using spacer C-4365-4 or equivalent.
5. Disengage cross trunnions, still attached to flange yoke, from coupling yoke. Pull flange yoke and cross from centering ball on ball support tube yoke. The ball socket is part of the flange yoke.

NOTE: The ball on some joints is not replaceable. The joints with a replaceable ball can be recognized as shown in **Fig. 15.** Do not attempt to remove solid ball, as removal tool may be damaged.

6. Pry seal from ball cavity, then remove washers, spring and shoes, **Fig. 16.**

Ball Socket
1. To remove ball, separate universal joint between coupling yoke and flange yoke by pressing out trunnion bearing in coupling yoke. Pull flange yoke and cross with ball socket from centering ball as a unit.
2. Clean and inspect ball seat insert bushing for wear. If worn, replace flange yoke and cross assembly.
3. Pry seal from ball cavity, then remove washers, spring and ball seats.
4. Clean and inspect centering ball surface, seal, ball seats, spring and washer. If parts are worn or broken,

replace with a service kit.
5. Remove centering ball as shown in **Fig. 17,** using components of tool C-4365 or equivalent. Install components as shown, and draw ball off ball stud.

ASSEMBLY
Ball Socket & Constant Velocity Joint

NOTE: During assembly, make sure that marks made during disassembly, **Fig. 12,** are aligned to maintain balance.

1. To install centering ball onto stud, use

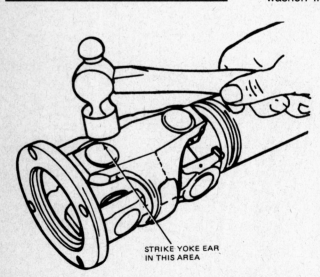

STRIKE YOKE EAR IN THIS AREA

Fig. 20 Relieving binding condition at point A

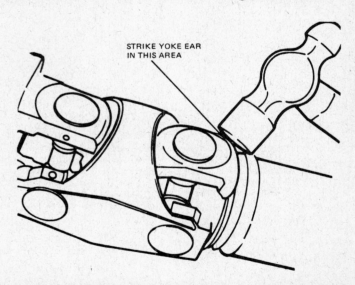

STRIKE YOKE EAR IN THIS AREA

Fig. 21 Relieving binding condition at point B

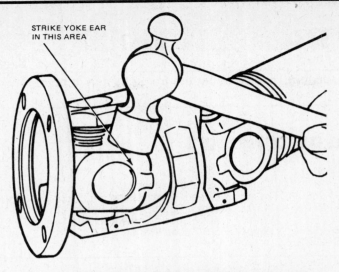

Fig. 22   Relieving binding condition at point C

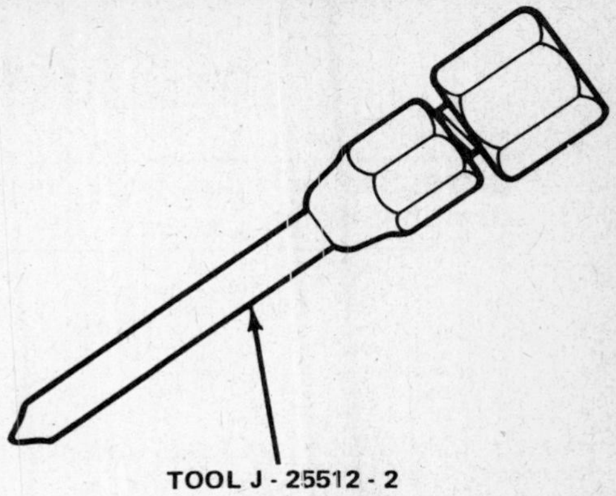

TOOL J - 25512 - 2

Fig. 23   Lubrication fitting adapter

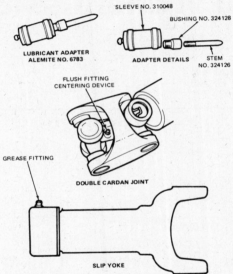

Fig. 24   Lubrication fitting adapter & fitting location

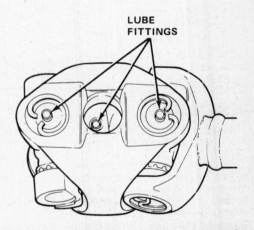

Fig. 25   Lubrication fitting locations

tool C-4365 or equivalent, and drive ball until it can be seen that ball has seated firmly against shoulder at base of stud.

2. To install cross assembly, install one bearing cup part way into one side of yoke and turn this yoke to the bottom. Insert cross into yoke so that the trunnion seats into bearing, **Fig. 18.** Install opposite bearing cup part way, **Fig. 19.** Make sure that both cross journals are started straight into both bearing cups.

3. Press bearing cups, while moving cross to ensure free movement of trunnions in bearing. If any binding is felt, stop pressing and check needle bearings to make sure that needle bearings have not been trapped under the ends of the cross journals.

4. As soon as one of the retaining ring grooves clears the inside of yoke, stop pressing and install retaining ring.

5. Continue to press until opposite retaining ring can be snapped into place. If difficulty is encountered, strike the yoke firmly in locations shown in **Figs. 20, 21 and 22,** to spring the yoke ears slightly.

6. Relube center ball and socket, and assemble other half universal joint, if disassembled.

LUBRICATION

Lubrication of the constant velocity joints should not be overlooked during the regular service intervals recommended by the manufacturer. During lubrication, use only the type of lubricant recommended by the manufacturer. This lubricant is usually lithium type chassis grease.

Lubrication fitting adapters and locations of the lubrication fittings are shown in **Figs. 23, 24 and 25.**

MANUAL TRANSMISSIONS

NOTE: See individual truck chapters for procedures on removing the transmission and adjusting the gearshift linkage.

TABLE OF CONTENTS

Muncie 3 Speed Manual Transmission

INDEX

DISASSEMBLE

1. Remove side cover, **Fig. 1.**
2. Remove clutch gear retainer and gasket.
3. Remove clutch gear bearing-to-gear stem snap ring, then remove bearing by pulling outward on clutch gear until a screwdriver can be inserted between large snap ring and case to complete removal. The bearing is slip fit on the gear and into the case bore.
4. Remove extension to case attaching bolts.
5. Rotate extension to left until groove in extension housing flange lines up with reverse idler shaft. Using a drift, drive reverse idler shaft out of gear and case.
6. Remove clutch gear, mainshaft and extension assembly together through rear case opening. Remove reverse idler gear from case.
7. Remove clutch gear from mainshaft.
8. Expand snap ring in extension housing, tap on end of mainshaft and remove extension from mainshaft.

ASSEMBLE

1. Load double row of roller bearings and thrust washers into each end of countergear. Use heavy grease to hold them in place.
2. Place countergear in case and install countergear shaft and woodruff key from rear of case.

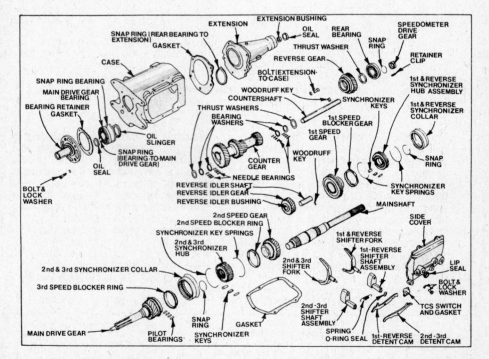

Fig. 1   Disassembled view of Muncie 3 speed manual transmission

NOTE: Be sure countershaft picks up both thrust washers and that the tangs are aligned in the notches in the case.

3. Position reverse idler in case.
4. Expand snap ring in extension housing and assemble mainshaft and extension.
5. Load rollers into clutch gear bore and assemble 3rd gear blocker ring onto gear with clutching teeth toward gear.
6. Install clutch gear assembly onto mainshaft. Do not install bearing over gear stem as yet.

NOTE: Be sure notches in blocker ring align with keys in the synchronizer assembly.

7. Place gasket on rear of case, and assemble the entire mainshaft-extension to the case as a unit.

NOTE: Be sure clutch gear engages the teeth of the countergear anti-lash plate and that the oil slinger is in place on the clutch gear.

8. Rotate extension and install reverse idler shaft and Woodruff key. Install extension-to-case bolts.
9. With large snap ring on bearing, install clutch gear bearing onto stem of gear and into case bore. Install small snap ring.
10. Install clutch gear bearing retainer with oil return hole at bottom.
11. Install side cover.

Saginaw 3 Speed Manual Transmission

INDEX

DISASSEMBLY
TRANSMISSION

1. Drain lubricant.
2. Remove side cover and gasket, **Fig. 1.**
3. Remove front bearing retainer.
4. Remove front bearing snap ring, pull main drive gear out of case as far as possible and remove bearing.
5. Remove rear bearing retainer-to-case bolts.
6. Remove reverse idler shaft-to-gear "E" ring, **Fig. 2.**
7. From front of case, remove rear bearing retainer and mainshaft assembly.
8. Remove main drive gear, 14 needle rollers and 3rd speed gear blocking ring from mainshaft.
9. Expand snap ring and remove rear bearing retainer, **Fig. 3.**
10. Remove countershaft through rear of case, **Fig. 4,** and remove two tanged thrust washers.
11. Use a long brass drift or punch and drive reverse idler shaft and key through rear of case.
12. Remove reverse idler gear tanged thrust washer.

MAINSHAFT

1. Referring to **Fig. 5,** remove 2–3 synchronizer sleeve.
2. Remove rear bearing snap ring.
3. Using a ram or arbor press, remove rear bearing, spring washer, thrust washer and reverse gear.
4. Remove speedometer drive gear.
5. Remove first speed synchronizer snap ring. Support first gear on a press and remove first gear and its synchronizer.
6. Remove 2–3 synchronizer snap ring and press off synchronizer and second speed gear.

SYNCHRONIZERS

NOTE: The synchronizer hubs and sliding sleeves are a selected assembly and should be kept together as originally assembled. The keys and springs may be replaced if worn or broken.

1. Mark hub and sleeve so they can be reassembled in same position.
2. Remove sleeve from hub.
3. Remove keys and springs from hub.
4. Place three keys and two springs in position (one on each side of hub) so all three keys are engaged by both springs, **Fig. 6.** The tanged end of each synchronizer spring should be installed in different key cavities on either side of hub. Slide sleeve onto hub, aligning marks made before disassembly.

NOTE: A chamfer around outside of synchronizer hub splines identifies end that must be opposite shift fork slot in sleeve, **Fig. 7.**

ASSEMBLY
MAINSHAFT

1. Install second speed gear and synchronizer on mainshaft. Using a ram or arbor press, press 2–3 synchronizer (with chamfer toward rear) onto mainshaft, **Fig. 8.**
2. Install first speed gear and synchronizer on mainshaft, **Fig. 9,** and install snap ring. Make certain notches in blocking ring align with keys.
3. Install rear bearing retainer. Spread spring washer and rear bearing. Grooves on bearing must be toward reverse gear.
4. Install speedometer drive gear on mainshaft. Press gear until its rear face is 6 inches from rear bearing, **Fig. 10.**
5. Install 2–3 synchronizer sleeve.

TRANSMISSION

1. Install countergear-to-case thrust washers. Install countergear into case from rear. Make certain woodruff key is in place. Note that antirattle gear is riveted to countergear in four places and is not serviced separately, **Fig. 11.**
2. Install reverse idler gear tanged steel thrust washer. Install idler gear, shaft and woodruff key. Reverse idler gear snap ring will be installed after installation of mainshaft.
3. Install rear bearing retainer. Spread snap ring in retainer to allow snap ring to drop around rear bearing. Press on end of mainshaft until snap ring engages groove in rear bearing.
4. Install 14 needle rollers in main drive gear pocket, using grease to hold them in place. Assemble third gear. Pilot main drive gear and blocking ring over front of mainshaft. Make certain notches in blocking ring align with keys in 2–3 synchronizer.
5. Install rear bearing retainer-to-case gasket.
6. Install rear bearing retainer and mainshaft assembly into case. Torque bearing retainer-to-case bolts to 35–

1.	Snap Ring	24.	Bearing Retainer Bolts and Washers (4)	46.	Thrust Washer
2.	Synchronizer Ring	25.	Front Bearing Retainer	47.	Countergear Shaft
3.	2-3 Synchronizer Sleeve	26.	Bearing Retainer Gasket	48.	Countergear Shaft Key
4.	Synchronizer Key Spring	27.	Bearing Retainer Oil Seal	49.	Idler Shaft Key
5.	Synchronizer Hub and Keys	28.	Snap Ring	50.	Reverse Idler Shaft
6.	Synchronizer Key Spring	29.	Bearing Snap Ring	51.	Snap Ring
7.	Synchronizer Ring	30.	Front Bearing	52.	Reverse Idler Gear
8.	Second Gear	31.	Drive Gear	53.	Side Cover Gasket
9.	Main Shaft	32.	Pilot Bearings	54.	2-3 Shift Fork
10.	First Gear	33.	Case	55.	1-Rev Shift Fork
11.	Synchronizer Ring	34.	Extension to Case Gasket	56.	2-3 Shifter Shaft
12.	Synchronizer Key Spring	35.	Rear Bearing to Extension Retaining Ring	57.	Retaining "E" Ring
13.	Synchronizer Hub and Keys	36.	Rear Extension	58.	1-Rev Shifter Shaft with "O" Ring
14.	Synchronizer Key Spring	37.	Extension to Case Retaining Bolts and Washers	59.	2-3 Detent Cam
15.	1-2 Synchronizer Sleeve	38.	Rear Extension Bushing	60.	Detent Cam Spring
16.	Snap Ring	39.	Rear Seal	61.	1-Rev Detent Cam
17.	Reverse Gear	40.	Thrust Washer	62.	Shift Cover
18.	Thrust Washer	41.	Spacer	63.	TCS Switch and Gasket
19.	Waved Washer	42.	Countergear Shaft Bearings	64.	Shifter Shaft Seal
20.	Rear Bearing	43.	Countergear	65.	Shifter Shaft Seal
21.	Snap Ring	44.	Countergear Shaft Bearings	66.	Shift Cover Bolts and Washers
22.	Speedometer Gear Clip	45.	Spacer		
23.	Speedometer Drive Gear				

Fig. 1   Disassembled view of Saginaw 3 speed manual transmission

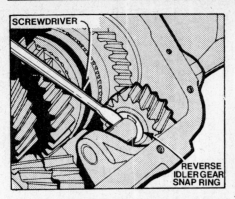

Fig. 2 Removing reverse idler "E" ring

Fig. 3 Removing rear bearing retainer after spring snap ring

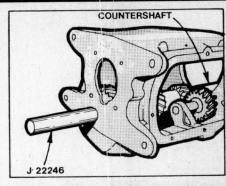

Fig. 4 Removing countershaft, using alignment arbor to hold needle bearings in place

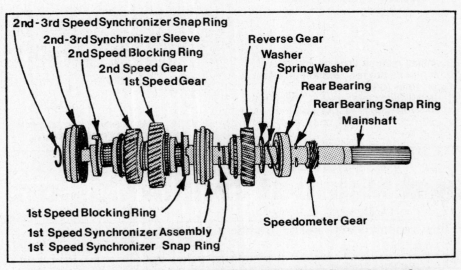

Fig. 5 Mainshaft & related parts assembled loosely to show location of parts

2nd - 3rd Speed Synchronizer Snap Ring
2nd-3rd Synchronizer Sleeve
2nd Speed Blocking Ring
2nd Speed Gear
1st Speed Gear

Reverse Gear
Washer
Spring Washer
Rear Bearing
Rear Bearing Snap Ring
Mainshaft

1st Speed Blocking Ring
1st Speed Synchronizer Assembly
1st Speed Synchronizer Snap Ring

Speedometer Gear

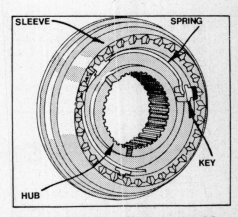

Fig. 6 Synchronizer assembly

SLEEVE   SPRING   KEY   HUB

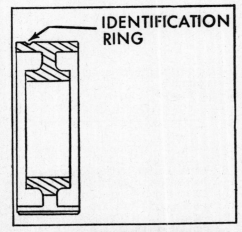

Fig. 7 Identification chamfer around synchronizer hub

IDENTIFICATION RING

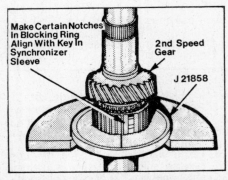

Fig. 8 Installing second speed gear

Make Certain Notches In Blocking Ring Align With Key In Synchronizer Sleeve

2nd Speed Gear

J·21858

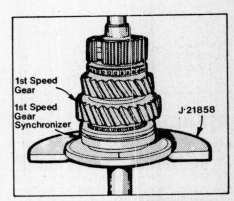

Fig. 9 Installing first speed gear

1st Speed Gear
1st Speed Gear Synchronizer

J·21858

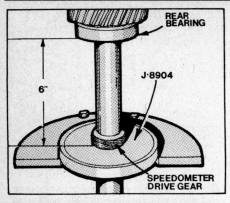

Fig. 10 Installing speedometer drive gear (6" from bearing)

Fig. 11 Anti-rattle gear is riveted to countergear

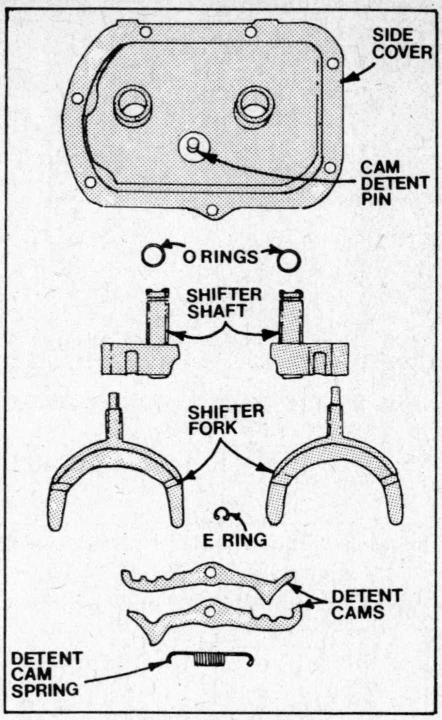

Fig. 12 Disassembled view of side cover assembly

55 ft. lbs. torque.
7. Install bearing on main drive gear. Outer snap ring groove must be toward front of gear. Install snap ring.
8. Install front bearing retainer and gasket.

9. Install reverse idler gear "E" ring.
10. If repairs are required to the side cover, refer to **Fig. 12**.
11. Install side cover gasket. Place transmission gears in neutral and install side cover. Install bolts and tighten evenly.

Tremec 3 Speed Manual Transmission

NOTE: For service procedures on this transmission, refer to Tremec 3 Speed Manual Transmission section in the Ford Chapter.

Isuzu M-150 (77.5mm) 4 Speed Manual Transmission

INDEX

DISASSEMBLE

1. Disconnect retaining springs from bearing side and remove bearing, boot, and clutch fork, **Figs. 1 and 2**.
2. Drain transmission, then remove bearing retainer bolts, retainer, gasket, and ball stud, **Fig. 3**.
3. Remove speedometer driven gear, back-up light switch, shift cover retaining bolts, shift cover, and gasket.
4. Remove rear extension retaining bolts, rear extension, and gasket.
5. Remove speedometer driven gear from mainshaft, **Fig. 4**.
6. Using suitable tool, drive pin from reverse shift block while supporting shaft end with bar or block of wood.
7. Remove reverse block retaining bolts and remove reverse shifter shaft, shift block, shift fork, and reverse gear as an assembly, **Fig. 5**.
8. Remove retaining ring from drive gear shaft bearing outer race, then remove retaining ring from countershaft front bearing outer race, **Fig. 6**.
9. Remove center support assembly from transmission case, being careful not to hit front end of drive gear shaft while removing transmission case.

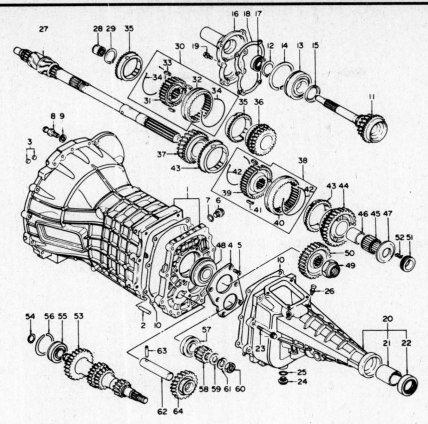

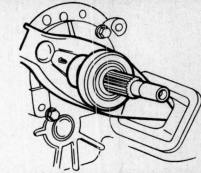

Fig. 2 Removing clutch fork & bearing

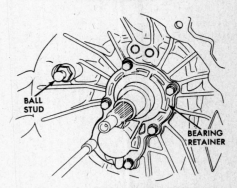

Fig. 3 Removing bearing retainer

1. Transmission case and center support	17. Oil seal	33. Insert
2. Dowel	18. Gasket	34. Spring
3. Plug	19. Bolt and spring washer	35. Blocker ring
4. Rear bearing retainer	20. Extension housing	36. 3rd gear
5. Screw	21. Bushing	37. 2nd gear
6. Oil filler plug	22. Rear oil seal	38. 1st/2nd synchronizer
7. Gasket	23. Bolt, plain washer and spring washer	39. Clutch hub
8. Ball stud	24. Oil drain plug	40. Sleeve
9. Washer	25. Gasket	41. Insert
10. Gasket	26. Ventilator	42. Spring
11. Drive gear shaft	27. Mainshaft	43. Blocker ring
12. Retaining ring	28. Needle roller bearing	44. 1st gear
13. Bearing	29. Retaining ring	45. Needle roller bearing
14. Retaining ring	30. 3rd/4th sychronizer	46. Bearing collar
15. Spacer	31. Clutch hub	47. Thrust washer
16. Front bearing retainer	32. Sleeve	48. Bearing

49. Nut	
50. Reverse gear	
51. Speedometer drive gear	
52. Clip	
53. Counter shaft	
54. Retaining ring	
55. Bearing	
56. Retaining ring	
57. Bearing	
58. Reverse gear	
59. Plain washer	
60. Nut	
61. Spring washer	
62. Reverse idler shaft	
63. Spring pin	
64. Reverse idler gear	

Fig. 1 Disassembled view of Isuzu M-150 (77.5mm) 4 speed manual transmission

10. Using suitable tool, drive pins from 1st/2nd & 3rd/4th shift forks while supporting ends of shafts with bar or block of wood, **Fig. 7.**
11. Loosen retaining bolts and remove plate, gasket, and springs.
12. Place the three shifter shafts in neutral position and remove reverse shifter shaft, 1st/2nd shifter shaft, and 3rd/4th shifter shaft in that order, being careful not to lose interlock pins or detent balls.
13. Remove three detent balls, two interlock pins, and shift forks.
14. Engage synchronizers to prevent rotation of mainshaft and temporarily install transmission case to center support.

15. Using suitable tool, raise staking on mainshaft rear nut and remove nut, then remove reverse gear from mainshaft, **Fig. 8.**
16. Remove nut, spring washer, plain washer, and reverse gear from countershaft, then remove case from center support.
17. Place synchronizers in neutral positions, then remove rear bearing retainer from center support, **Fig. 9.**
18. Slide rear bearing outer race rearward by moving countershaft fore and aft and, using suitable tool, remove outer race, **Fig. 10.**
19. Remove countershaft and drive gear shaft, then remove 4th blocker ring and needle roller bearing.

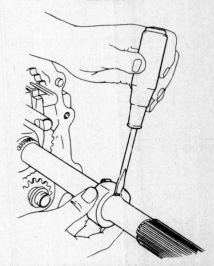

Fig. 4 Removing speedometer driven gear

UNIT INSPECTION & OVERHAUL

1. Thoroughly wash transmission case inside and out with suitable solvent, then inspect case for cracks.
2. Check front and rear faces for burrs and correct if necessary.
3. Inspect all main drive gear and countergear roller bearings and replace as required, then inspect countershaft and reverse idler shaft together and replace if necessary. Replace all worn

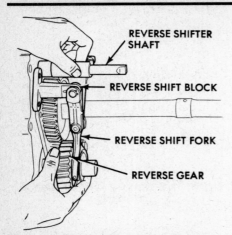

Fig. 5 Removing reverse shifter assembly

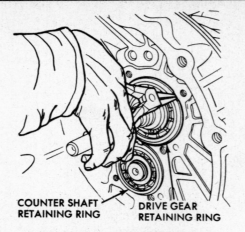

Fig. 6 Removing drive gear retaining ring

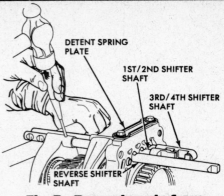

Fig. 7 Removing pin from shifter shafts

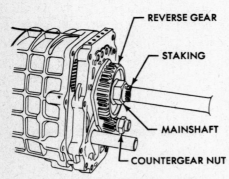

Fig. 8 Removing reverse gear

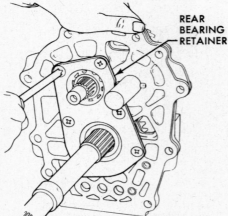

Fig. 9 Removing rear bearing retainer

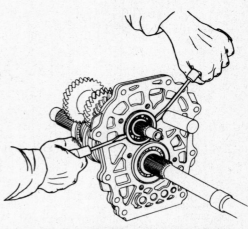

Fig. 10 Removing countershaft outer race

spacers.

4. Wash front and rear ball bearings in suitable solvent and blow out bearings with compressed air.

NOTE: Do not allow bearings to spin. Turn them slowly by hand. Spinning bearings may damage race and balls.

5. Lubricate bearings and check for roughness by slowly turning race by hand.
6. Inspect all gears for excessive wear, chips, or cracks and replace if damaged or worn.
7. Check oil seal contact area on drive gear shaft and replace gear if pitted, rusted, or cracked.
8. Inspect interlock levers for cracking at detent and clearance notches at either end of levers.
9. Inspect shift forks for wear and inspect fork shaft bores in shift lever.

SUB-ASSEMBLY SERVICE
MAINSHAFT

1. Using tool J-22912-01 or equivalent at rear face of second gear on mainshaft,

remove mainshaft from center support using an arbor press, then remove 2nd gear, 1st/2nd synchronizer, 1st and 2nd blocker rings, 1st gear needle roller bearing, bearing collar, and thrust washer. Remove mainshaft rear bearing from center support, **Fig. 11.**
2. Remove snap ring from front of mainshaft. Set blocks to rear face of 3rd gear and remove mainshaft using an arbor press, then remove 3rd gear, 3rd blocker ring, and 3rd/4th synchronizer.
3. Install 3rd gear and 3rd gear blocker ring to front of mainshaft.
4. Install 3rd/4th synchronizer assembly to mainshaft using arbor press. Plates should be fitted against parts, so that force will be exerted on boss of synchronizer hub.
5. Install retaining ring to front of mainshaft, then install 2nd gear and 2nd blocker ring to rear of mainshaft.
6. Install 1st/2nd synchronizer assembly to mainshaft using arbor press. Plates should be fitted against parts, so that force will be exerted on boss of synchronizer hub.

7. Install 1st gear bearing collar to mainshaft using tool J-8853-011 or equivalent, and an arbor press. Install 1st blocker ring, needle roller bearing, and 1st gear, then install thrust washer with oil grooves turned toward gear.
8. Install reverse idler shaft into center support with suitable tool, after making certain spring pin is fitted to shaft.

SYNCHRONIZER KEYS & SPRINGS

NOTE: Synchronizer hubs and sliding sleeves are a selected assembly and should be kept together as originally assembled, but the keys and springs may be replaced if worn or broken.

1. Mark relation of hub and sleeve for reassembly reference.
2. Push hub from sliding sleeve, allowing keys to fall free and simplifying spring removal.
3. Place keys in position and hold in place while sliding sleeve onto hub, aligning reference marks.
4. Place the two springs in position on either side of hub so that all three keys are engaged by both springs.

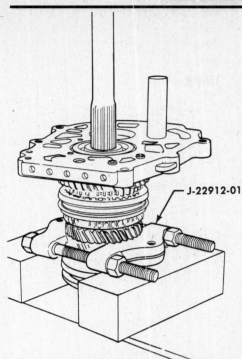

Fig. 11 Removing mainshaft from center support

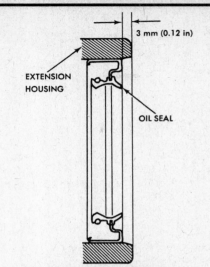

3 mm (0.12 in)

EXTENSION HOUSING

OIL SEAL

Fig. 12 Installing rear extension seal

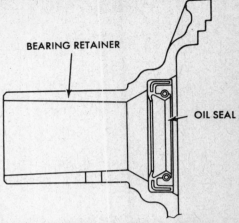

BEARING RETAINER

OIL SEAL

Fig. 13 Installing front bearing retainer seal

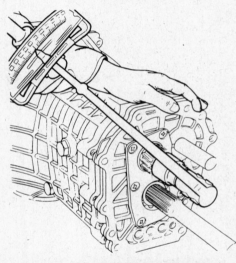

Fig. 15 Torquing countergear nut

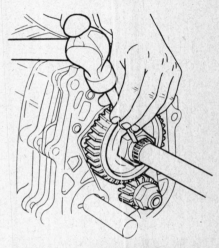

Fig. 16 Staking nut on mainshaft

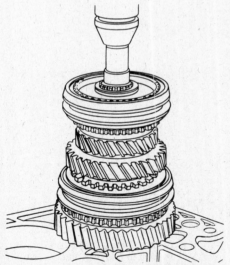

Fig. 14 Installing mainshaft to center support

DRIVE GEAR SHAFT BEARING

1. Remove retaining ring from drive gear shaft, then remove bearing using an arbor press.
2. Ensure that spacer is fitted to shaft.
3. Using suitable tool and arbor press, install bearing to shaft so that snap ring groove is turned away from gear.
4. Install retaining ring to shaft.

COUNTERGEAR SHAFT

1. Remove retaining ring from countershaft.
2. Remove bearing using suitable press.
3. Using suitable tool and press, install bearing to shaft so that snap ring groove is turned away from gear.
4. Install retaining ring to shaft.

REAR BEARING INNER RACE

1. Remove inner race using press.
2. Using suitable tool and press, install bearing inner race to shaft so that flanged face of race is turned toward gears.

EXTENSION OIL SEAL

1. Remove oil seal by prying outward with suitable tool.
2. Apply thin coat of suitable sealer to

outer circumference of oil seal and install into housing using tool J-33035 and a hammer so that its face is recessed from rear end of housing by .12 in., **Fig. 12**.

FRONT BEARING RETAINER OIL SEAL

1. Remove oil seal by prying outward.
2. Drive new oil seal into retainer using tool J-26540, **Fig. 13**.

ASSEMBLE

1. Being sure snap ring is fitted to mainshaft rear bearing, install bearing into center support with snap ring side turned rearward.
2. Using an arbor press, install mainshaft into bearing which has been fitted into center support. When installing mainshaft, care should be taken so as not to damage reverse block dowels fitted to center support, **Fig. 14**.
3. Install 4th blocker ring, needle roller bearing, and drive gear shaft.
4. Install countershaft to center support,

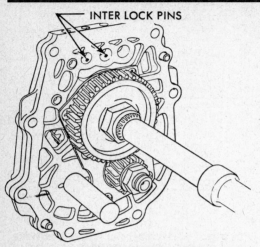

Fig. 17   Installing interlock pins

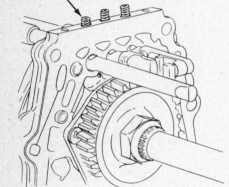

Fig. 20   Installing detent balls

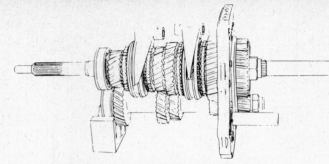

Fig. 18   Installing shift forks

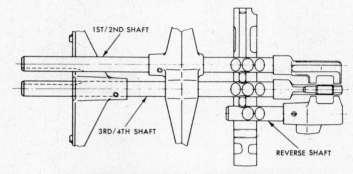

Fig. 19   Installing shifter shafts

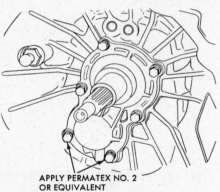
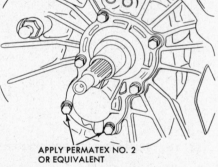

Fig. 21   Installing front bearing retainer

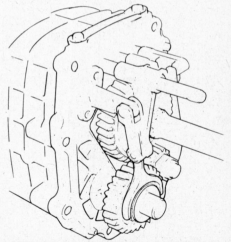

Fig. 22   Installing reverse shift block front bearing retainer

then install rear bearing outer race to countershaft from rear side of center support.

5. Install bearing retainer to center support. Clean threaded hole in center support, apply suitable sealer to screw threads, install screws, and torque to 15 ft. lbs.

6. Engage synchronizers in lock and place center support in transmission case temporarily.

7. Install reverse gear, washer, and spring washer to rear end of countershaft and torque nut to 80 ft. lbs., Fig. 15. Install reverse gear so that teeth with rounded edges are turned rearward.

8. Install reverse gear to mainshaft with rounded teeth turned rearward and torque nut to 95 ft. lbs., then stake nut to mainshaft, Fig. 16.

9. Remove case from center support.

10. Lubricate and install two interlock pins to center support, Fig. 17.

11. Noting direction of installation, install shift fork to synchronizers, Fig. 18.

12. Install 3rd/4th shifter shaft to center support and shift fork, then bring shaft into neutral position. Install 1st/2nd

shifter shaft and reverse shifter shaft to center support, Fig. 19.

13. Supporting end of shaft with piece of wood, drive spring pin to 1st/2nd and 3rd/4th shift forks.

14. Install three detent balls and springs into holes in center support, then install gasket and plate and torque bolts to 15 ft. lbs. The reverse spring is shorter than the others, Fig. 20.

15. Install gasket to transmission case and install center support by aligning it with dowels on case. Avoid hitting support or case during installation.

16. Install retaining rings to drive gear shaft and countershaft bearing outer races.

17. Assemble reverse shift block, reverse block, and reverse shift fork using pins and snap rings.

18. Install shift block assembly to reverse

shift fork, then insert shift fork into groove in reverse idler gear. Install gear to idler shaft and reverse shift block to shifter shaft, Fig. 21.

19. Tighten reverse block retaining bolts.

20. Secure reverse shift block to shifter shaft by driving spring pin with suitable tool.

21. Insert clip end into hole in mainshaft and install speedometer driven gear.

22. Install gasket to center support, then install extension housing to support by aligning it with dowels and torque bolts to 30 ft. lbs.

23. Install back-up light switch.

24. Install gasket to upper face of exten-

25. Install speedometer driven gear and ball stud.
26. Install gasket to transmission case, then install front bearing retainer, **Fig. 22.** Apply suitable sealer to bolt threads on lower side before installation and torque bolts to 15 ft. lbs.
27. Install bearing, boot, and clutch fork.
28. Install gearshift lever to shifter cover temporarily and check for smooth and correct operation.

Muncie CH & SM-465 4 Speed Manual Transmission

INDEX

DISASSEMBLE

1. Mount transmission in suitable holding fixture and remove transmission cover. If required, insert two 5/16 × 18 screws in cover flange threaded holes and turn evenly to raise cover dowel pins from case.

NOTE: Move reverse shifter fork so that reverse idler gear is partially engaged before attempting to remove cover. Forks must be positioned so rear edge of the slot in the reverse fork is in line with the front edge of the slot in the forward forks as viewed through tower opening.

2. Place transmission in two gears at once to lock gears and remove universal joint flange nut, universal joint from flange and brake drum assembly.
3. Remove parking brake and brake flange plate assembly on models so equipped.
4. Remove rear bearing retainer and gasket, **Fig. 1.**
5. Slide speedometer drive gear off mainshaft.
6. Remove clutch gear bearing retainer and gasket.
7. Remove countergear front bearing cap and gasket.
8. Pry countergear front bearing out by inserting screw drivers into groove at cast slots in case.
9. Remove countergear rear bearing retaining rings from shaft and bearing. With a suitable tool remove countergear rear bearings. This will allow countergear assembly to rest on bottom of case.
10. Remove clutch gear bearing outer race to case retaining ring.
11. Remove clutch gear and bearing by tapping gently on bottom side of clutch gear shaft and prying directly opposite against the case and bearing snap ring groove at the same time. Remove 4th gear synchronizer ring.

CAUTION: Index cut out section of clutch gear in down position with countergear to obtain clearance for removing clutch gear.

12. Remove rear mainshaft bearing snap ring and using a suitable tool remove bearing from case. Slide 1st speed gear thrust washer off mainshaft.
13. Raise rear of mainshaft assembly and push rearward in case bore, then swing front end up and lift from case. Remove synchronizer cone from shaft.
14. Slide reverse idler gear rearward and move countergear rearward until front end is free of case, then lift to remove from case.
15. To remove reverse idler gear, drive reverse idler gear shaft out of case from front to rear using a drift. Remove reverse idler gear from case.

SUB-ASSEMBLY SERVICE

CLUTCH GEAR, DISASSEMBLE

1. Removing mainshaft pilot bearing rollers from clutch gear and remove roller retainer. Do not remove snap ring on inside of clutch gear.
2. Remove snap ring securing bearing on stem of clutch gear.
3. Using an arbor press, press gear and shaft out of bearing, **Fig. 2.**

CLUTCH GEAR, INSPECT

1. Wash all components in cleaning solvent.
2. Inspect roller bearings for pits and galling.
3. Inspect bearing diameter in shaft recess for galling.
4. Inspect gear teeth for excessive wear.
5. Inspect clutch shaft pilot for excessive wear.
6. Re-oil bearing, then rotate clutch gear bearing slowly and check for roughness.

CLUTCH GEAR, ASSEMBLE

1. Press bearing and new oil slinger onto clutch gear shaft, **Fig. 3.** Slinger should be located flush with bearing shoulder on clutch gear, **Fig. 4.**
2. Install snap ring to secure bearing on clutch gear shaft.
3. Install bearing retainer ring in groove on O.D. of bearing.

CAUTION: Bearing must turn freely after it is installed on shaft.

4. Install snap ring on I.D. of mainshaft pilot bearing bore in clutch gear.
5. Apply a small amount of grease to bearing surface in shaft recess, install transmission mainshaft pilot roller bearings and install retainer.

NOTE: This roller bearing retainer holds bearings in position and in final transmission assembly is pushed forward into recess by mainshaft pilot.

MAINSHAFT, DISASSEMBLE

1. Remove first speed gear.
2. Remove snap ring in front of 3rd-4th synchronizer assembly.
3. Remove reverse driven gear.
4. Press behind 2nd speed gear to remove 3rd-4th synchronizer assembly, 3rd speed gear and 2nd speed gear along with 3rd gear bushing and thrust washer, **Fig. 5.**
5. Remove 2nd speed synchronizer ring and keys.
6. Support 2nd speed synchronizer hub at front face and press mainshaft through removing 1st speed gear bushing and 2nd speed synchronizer hub.
7. Split 2nd speed gear bushing with chisel and remove bushing from shaft.

CAUTION: Exercise care not to damage mainshaft.

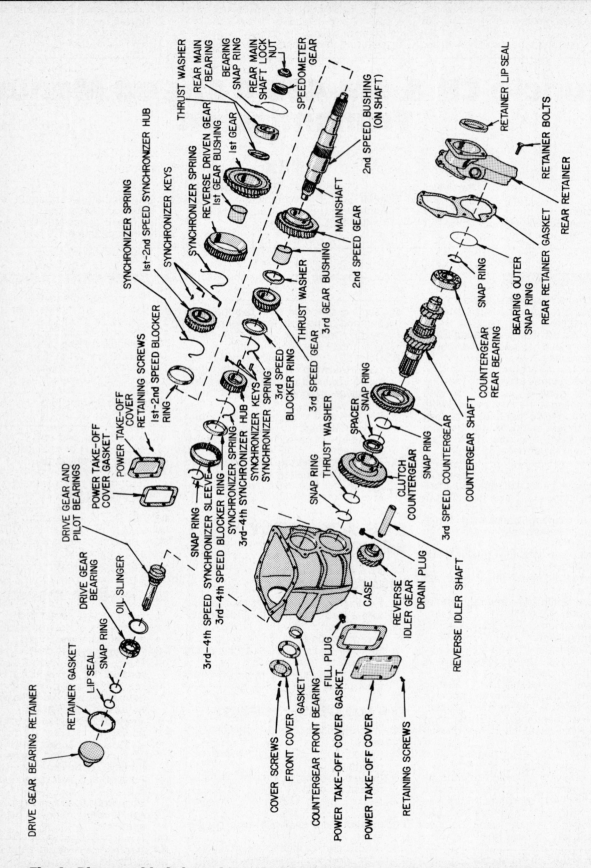

Fig. 1   Disassembled view of Muncie CH & SM-465 4 speed manual transmission

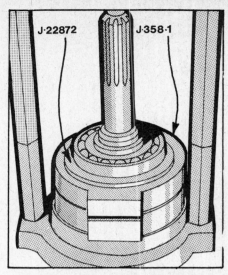

Fig. 2   Removing clutch gear bearing

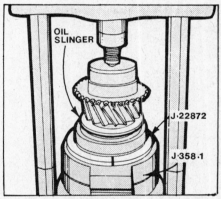

Fig. 3   Replacing clutch gear bearing

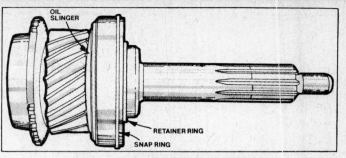

Fig. 4   Clutch gear assembly

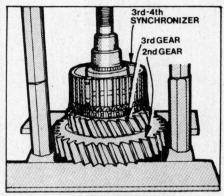

Fig. 5   Disassembly of mainshaft

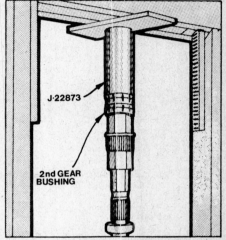

Fig. 6   Installing 2nd speed gear bushing

MAINSHAFT, INSPECT

1. Wash all components in cleaning solvent.
2. Inspect mainshaft for scoring or excessive wear at thrust surfaces or splines.
3. Inspect clutch hub and clutch sleeve for excessive wear and make sure sleeve slides freely on clutch hub. Also check fit of clutch hub on mainshaft splines.

NOTE: 3rd and 4th speed clutch sleeve should slide freely on 3rd and 4th speed clutch hub but clutch hub should be snug fit on shaft splines.

4. Inspect 3rd speed gear thrust surfaces for excessive scoring and inspect 3rd speed gear mainshaft bushing for excessive wear.

NOTE: 3rd speed gear must be a running fit on mainshaft bushing and mainshaft bushing should be a press fit on shaft.

5. Check 2nd speed thrust washer for excessive scoring.

6. Inspect 2nd speed gear for excessive wear at thrust surface. Check synchronizer springs for looseness or breakage.
7. Inspect 2nd speed gear synchronizing ring for excessive wear.
8. Inspect bronze synchronizer cone on 2nd speed gear for excessive wear or damage. Also inspect clutch gear synchronizer cone and 3rd speed gear synchronizer cone for excessive wear or damage.

NOTE: 1st and reverse sliding gear must be sliding fit on synchronizer hub and must not have excessive radial and circumferential play. If sliding gear is not free on hub, inspect for burrs which may have rolled up on front ends of half-tooth internal splines and remove by honing.

9. Inspect all gear teeth for excessive wear.

MAINSHAFT, ASSEMBLE

1. Press 2nd speed bushing onto mainshaft until it bottoms against shoulder, **Fig. 6.**

CAUTION: 1st, 2nd and 3rd speed gear bushings are sintered iron. Exercise care when installing.

2. Press 1st and 2nd speed synchronizer hub onto mainshaft until it bottoms against shoulder with annulus toward rear of shaft.
3. Install 1st and 2nd synchronizer keys

and springs.
4. Press 1st speed gear bushing onto mainshaft until it bottoms against hub, **Fig. 7.**
5. Install synchronizer blocking ring and 2nd speed gear onto mainshaft and against synchronizer hub. Index synchronizer key slots with keys in synchronizer hub.
6. Install 3rd speed gear thrust washer onto mainshaft with tang or thrust washer in slot on shaft and against 2nd speed gear bushing. Then press 3rd speed gear bushing onto mainshaft until it bottoms against thrust washer, **Fig. 8.**
7. Install 3rd speed gear synchronizer blocker ring and 3rd speed gear onto mainshaft, against 3rd speed gear thrust washer.
8. Index synchronizer ring key slots with synchronizer assembly keys and drive 3rd and 4th synchronizer assembly onto mainshaft and against 3rd speed gear bushing with thrust face toward 3rd speed gear. Retain synchronizer assembly with snap ring, **Fig. 9.**
9. Install reverse driver gear with fork groove toward rear.
10. Install 1st speed gear onto mainshaft and against 1st and 2nd synchronizer hub. Install 1st speed gear thrust washer.

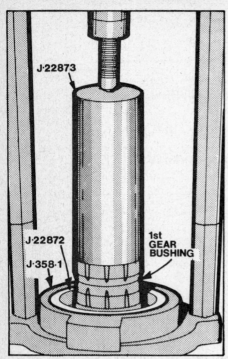

Fig. 7   Installing 1st speed gear bushing

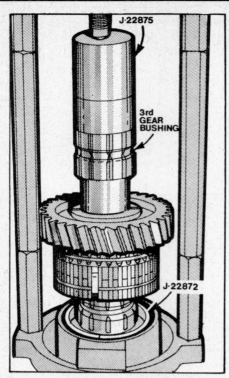

Fig. 8   Installing 3rd speed gear bushing

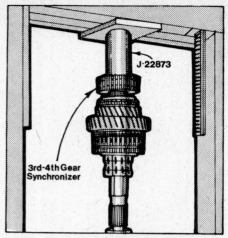

Fig. 9   Installing 3rd & 4th gear synchronizer

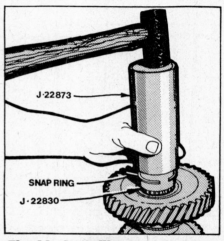

Fig. 11   Installing countergear snap ring

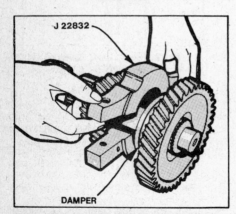

Fig. 10   Positioning tool J-22832 on to countershaft

COUNTERSHAFT, DISASSEMBLE

NOTE: As of 1980, a change was incorporated into the Muncie 4-speed transmission. This change consists of elimination of 1 spacer and 2 snap rings and includes a part called spacerclutch countergear, part No. 14020811. The new spacer may also be used on earlier transmissions and should reduce possibility of 3rd speed countergear becoming loose and overrunning retaining ring.

1. Remove front countergear snap ring and thrust washer. Discard snap ring.
2. Install Tool J-22832 on countershaft, open side to damper, **Fig. 10.** Support assembly in arbor press and press countershaft out of clutch countergear assembly.
3. Remove clutch countergear rear retaining ring. Discard snap ring.
4. Remove 3rd speed countergear snap ring. Discard snap ring.
5. Position assembly on an arbor press and press shaft from 3rd speed countergear.

COUNTERSHAFT, ASSEMBLE

1. Position 3rd speed countergear and shaft in arbor press and press gear onto shaft.

NOTE: Install gear with marked surface toward front of shaft.

2. Install new 3rd speed countergear snap ring.
3. Install new clutch countergear rear snap ring as follows: Install Tool J-22830, on end of shaft and position snap ring on tool. Using Tool J-22873, push down on snap ring until it engages groove on shaft. Using snap ring pliers, carefully expand ring until it just slides onto splines, then push ring down on shaft until it engages groove on shaft, **Fig. 11.**
4. Position clutch countergear on shaft and press countergear onto shaft against snap ring, **Fig. 12.**
5. Install clutch countergear thrust washer and front snap ring.

ASSEMBLE

1. Lower countergear into case until it rests on bottom.
2. Place reverse idler gear in transmission case with gear teeth toward the front. Install idler gear shaft from rear to front, being careful to have slot in end of shaft facing down. Shaft slot face must be at least flush with case.
3. Install mainshaft assembly into case with rear of shaft protruding out rear bearing hole in case. Position Tool J-22874-5 in clutch gear case opening and engaging front mainshaft. Rotate case onto front end, **Fig. 13.**

NOTE: Install 1st speed gear thrust washer on shaft if not previously installed.

4. Install snap ring on bearing O.D. and position rear mainshaft bearing on shaft. Using Tool J-22874-1 drive bearing onto shaft and into case. Align tangs on snap ring with lube slot of case and slot in tool before driving

Fig. 12   Installing clutch countergear

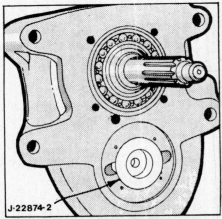

Fig. 14   Countergear front support tool

bearing. Rotate case and remove Tool J-22874-5, **Fig. 13.**

5. Install synchronizer cone on pilot end of mainshaft and slide rearward to clutch hub.

CAUTION: Make sure three cut-out sections of 4th speed synchronizer cone align

with three clutch keys in clutch assembly.

6. Install snap ring on clutch gear bearing O.D. Index cut-out portion of clutch gear teeth to obtain clearance over countershaft drive gear teeth and install clutch gear assembly into case. Raise mainshaft to get clutch gear started and tap bearing outer race with plastic tip hammer.
7. Install clutch gear bearing retainer using a new gasket. Tighten bolts to 15–18 ft. lbs.
8. Install Tool J-22874-2 in countergear front bearing opening in case to support countergear and rotate case onto front end, **Fig. 14.**
9. Install snap ring on countergear rear bearing O.D., position bearing on countergear and using Tool J-22874-1, drive bearing into place. Rotate case and install snap ring on countershaft at rear bearing, then remove tool, **Fig. 15.**
10. Tap countergear front bearing assembly into case.
11. Install countergear front bearing cap and gasket.
12. Slide speedometer drive gear over mainshaft to bearing.
13. Install rear bearing retainer and new gasket. Be sure snap ring ends are in Wube slot and cut-out in bearing retainer. Install bolts and tighten to 15–18 ft. lbs. Install brake backing plate on models equipped with propeller shaft brake.
14. Install parking brake drum and/or universal joint flange.

NOTE: Apply light coat of oil to seal surface.

15. Lock transmission in two gears at once. Install universal joint flange locknut and tighten to 90–120 ft. lbs.
16. Move all transmission gears to neutral except the reverse idler gear which should be engaged approximately ⅜ of an inch (leading edge of reverse idler gear taper lines up with front edge of 1st speed gear). Install cover assembly. Shifting forks must slide into their proper positions on clutch

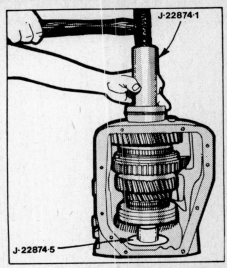

Fig. 13   Installing mainshaft rear bearing

Fig. 15   Installing countergear rear bearing

sleeves and reverse idler gear. Forks must be positioned as in removal.
17. Install cover bolts and tighten to 20–25 ft. lbs.

Saginaw 4 Speed Manual Transmission

INDEX

DISASSEMBLE

1. Remove side cover assembly and shift forks, **Fig. 1.** Remove damper assembly which is bolted to extension housing.
2. Remove clutch gear bearing retainer.
3. Remove clutch gear bearing to gear

stem snap ring, then remove bearing by pulling clutch gear outward until a screwdriver can be inserted between large snap ring and case to complete removal, **Fig. 2.** Do not remove clutch gear. The bearing is a slip fit on the gear and into the case bore.

4. Remove extension to case bolts and

remove clutch gear, mainshaft and extension assembly through rear case opening. Remove clutch gear and blocker ring from mainshaft.

5. Expand extension housing to rear mainshaft bearing snap ring and remove extension, **Fig. 3.**
6. Using a dummy shaft, drive counter-

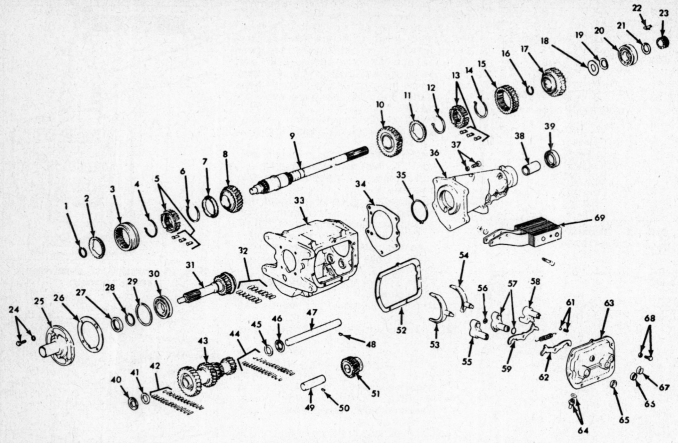

1. Snap ring, Hub to Shaft	24. Bearing Retainer Bolts and Washers (4)	47. Countergear Shaft
2. Synchronizer Ring	25. Front Bearing Retainer	48. Countergear Shaft Key
3. 3-4 Synchronizer Sleeve	26. Bearing Retainer Gasket	49. Reverse Idler Shaft
4. Synchronizer Key Spring	27. Bearing Retainer Oil Seal	50. Idler Shaft Key
5. Synchronizer Hub and Keys	28. Snap Ring	51. Reverse Idler Gear
6. Synchronizer Key Spring	29. Bearing Snap Ring	52. Side Cover Gasket
7. Synchronizer Ring	30. Front Bearing	53. 3-4 Shift Fork
8. Third Gear	31. Drive Gear	54. 1-2 Shift Fork
9. Main Shaft	32. Pilot Bearings	55. 3-4 Shifter Shaft
10. Second Gear	33. Case	56. Retaining "E" Ring
11. Synchronizer Ring	34. Extension to Case Gasket	57. 1-2 Shifter Shaft with "O" Rings
12. Synchronizer Key Spring	35. Rear Bearing to Extension Retaining Ring	58. Reverse Shifter Shaft
13. Synchronizer Hub and Keys	36. Rear Extension	59. 3-4 Detent Cam
14. Synchronizer Key Spring	37. Extension to Case Retaining Bolts and Washers	60. Detent Cam Spring
15. 1-2 Synchronizer Sleeve & Rev. Gear	38. Rear Extension Bushing	61. Reverse Detent Ball & Spring
16. Snap Ring, Hub to Shaft	39. Rear Seal	62. 1-2 Detent Cam
17. First Gear	40. Thrust Washer	63. Shift Cover
18. Thrust Washer	41. Spacer	64. TCS Switch and Gasket
19. Waved Washer	42. Countergear Shaft Roller Bearings	65. Shifter Shaft Seal
20. Ring Bearing	43. Countergear	66. Shifter Shaft Seal
21. Snap Ring, Bearing to Shaft	44. Countergear Shaft Roller Bearings	67. Shift Cover Bolts and Washers
22. Speedometer Gear Clip	45. Spacer	68. Shift Cover Attaching Bolts and Lock Washers
23. Speedometer Drive Gear	46. Thrust Washer	69. Damper Assembly

Fig. 1 Disassembled view of Saginaw 4 speed manual transmission

shaft and woodruff key out through rear of case, **Fig. 4.** Dummy shaft will hold roller bearings in position within countergear bore. Remove countergear.

7. Remove reverse idler gear stop ring and, using a long drift, drive idler shaft and woodruff key out through rear of case.

SUB-ASSEMBLY SERVICE

DISASSEMBLE MAINSHAFT

1. Remove snap ring and press 3-4 syn-

chronizer clutch assembly, 3rd speed blocker ring and 3rd gear off mainshaft, **Fig. 5.**

2. Depress speedometer gear retaining clip and remove gear.

3. Remove rear bearing to mainshaft snap ring, **Fig. 6,** support 1st gear with press plates and press on rear of mainshaft to remove 1st speed gear, thrust, washer, spring washer and rear bearing, **Fig. 7.**

4. Remove 1-2 sliding clutch hub snap ring, **Fig. 8,** support 2nd speed gear and press clutch assembly, 2nd speed blocker ring and gear from mainshaft.

CLUTCH KEYS & SPRINGS

NOTE: The clutch hubs and sleeves are a selected assembly and should be kept together as originally assembled, but the keys and springs may be replaced separately.

1. Mark hub and sleeve so they can be matched upon reassembly.

2. Push hub from sliding sleeve and remove keys and springs.

3. Install the three keys and two springs so all three keys are engaged by both springs. The tanged end of each spring should be installed into different

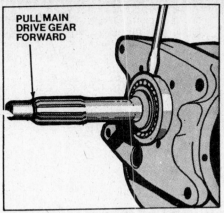

Fig. 2 Removing clutch gear bearing

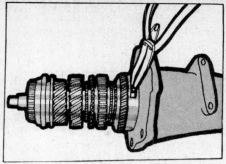

Fig. 3 Removing extension housing

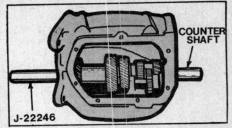

Fig. 4 Removing countershaft

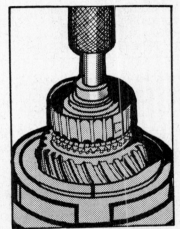

Fig. 5 Removing 3—4 synchronizer assembly

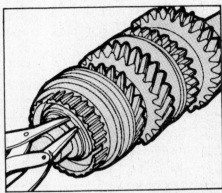

Fig. 6 Removing rear bearing to mainshaft snap ring

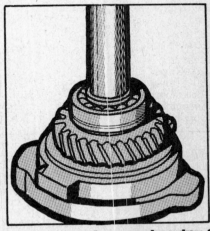

Fig. 7 Removing rear bearing & first speed gear

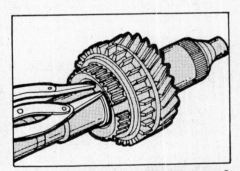

Fig. 8 Removing first & second synchronizer snap ring

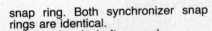

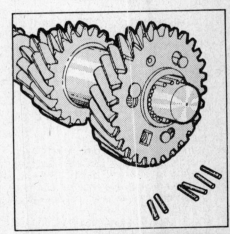

Fig. 9 Loading roller bearings into countergear

1. Install 3rd speed gear with clutching teeth upward.
2. Install blocker ring with clutching teeth downward over cone of gear. All blocker rings in this unit are identical.
3. Install 3—4 synchronizer assembly with fork slot downward and press it onto mainshaft until it bottoms. Be sure the notches of the blocker ring align with the keys of the synchronizer assembly.
4. Install synchronizer hub to mainshaft

snap ring. Both synchronizer snap rings are identical.

With rear of mainshaft upward:
5. Install 2nd speed gear with clutching teeth upward.
6. Install a blocker ring with clutching teeth downward over cone of gear.
7. Press 1—2 synchronizer assembly onto mainshaft with fork slot downward. Be sure notches in blocker ring align with keys of synchronizer assembly.
8. Install synchronizer hub snap ring.
9. Install a blocker ring with notches downward so they align with the synchronizer keys.
10. Install 1st gear with clutching teeth downward. Install 1st gear thrust washer and spring washer.
11. Press rear bearing onto mainshaft. Install snap ring.
12. Install speedometer drive gear and clip.

ASSEMBLE

1. Load a row of roller bearings and a thrust washer at each end of the countergear, **Fig. 9.** Use heavy grease to hold them in place.
2. Install countergear through case rear opening with a tanged thrust washer at each end and install countershaft and woodruff key from rear of case. Be sure countershaft picks up both thrust washers and that the tangs are

aligned with their notches in the case.
3. Install reverse idler gear, shaft and woodruff key from rear of case.
4. Expand extension housing snap ring and assemble extension housing over mainshaft.
5. Load roller bearings into clutch gear bore, using heavy grease to hold them in place, place blocker ring on gear cone with teeth toward gear, and install gear and ring onto mainshaft. Do not install clutch gear bearing at this time. Be sure notches in blocker

ring align with synchronizer keys.
6. Using new gasket, install mainshaft and extension assembly through rear opening in case. Use sealing cement on bottom bolt.
7. Install large outer snap ring on clutch

gear bearing and install bearing onto gear and into case bore. Install gear stem snap ring and bearing retainer.

NOTE: The retainer oil hole should be at the bottom.

8. With transmission in neutral, install cover assembly. Be sure the shift forks are properly aligned in their grooves in the synchronizer sleeves before attempting to tighten cover bolts.

Warner 83mm 4 Speed Manual Transmission

INDEX

DISASSEMBLE

1. Position transmission in 2nd gear, then remove side cover, gasket and both shift forks, **Fig. 1.**
2. Remove reverse shifter lock pin, **Fig. 2,** pull shifter shaft outward, disengaging lever from reverse gear.
3. Remove extension housing bolts and tap housing with a mallet to loosen, then pull extension housing rearward until idler shaft clears idler gear. Turn housing to left thereby freeing reverse shift fork from collar and remove housing.
4. Remove snap ring, then slide speedometer gear from mainshaft, remove second speedometer gear snap ring, **Fig. 3.**
5. Remove reverse gear from mainshaft, then slide rear reverse idler gear from rear bearing retainer, **Fig. 4.**
6. Remove lock bolt from rear bearing retainer and drive locating pin from bearing retainer into case.
7. Rotate rear bearing retainer counterclockwise, providing access to rear of countershaft.
8. From front of case, using a dummy shaft, tap countershaft and key out the rear of case, **Fig. 5.**
9. Using a mallet, tap rear bearing retainer rearward, and remove mainshaft through rear of transmission.
10. Remove bearing rollers and washer from main drive gear bore.
11. Remove front reverse idler gear and thrust washer from case.
12. Remove fourth gear synchronizing ring from main drive gear.
13. Remove main drive gear bearing retainer from case, remove snap ring and washer from main drive gear, then press gear from bearing, **Fig. 6.**
14. Tap drive gear bearing from case, remove countergear assembly and 2 washers. Drive locating pin from case.

NOTE: It is not necessary to remove countershaft and main gear assemblies if only main drive gear bearing is to be replaced. This is accomplished by using tools J-22912 and J-8433-1, **Fig. 7.**

SUB-ASSEMBLY SERVICE

DISASSEMBLE MAINSHAFT

1. From rear of mainshaft, remove snap ring and slide rear bearing retainer from mainshaft, **Fig. 8.**
2. Remove rear bearing snap ring and washer.
3. From front of mainshaft, remove snap ring, then remove 3–4 synchronizer assembly and 3rd gear, **Fig. 1.**
4. Support forward face of 2nd gear and press mainshaft from rear, then remove the rear bearing, thrust washer, 1st gear and bushing, 1–2 synchronizer and 2nd gear.

DISASSEMBLE COUNTERGEAR

Remove dummy shaft, bearings rollers, spacers and tubular spacer, **Fig. 9.**

DISASSEMBLE SIDE COVER

1. Remove forks from shifter shafts, **Fig. 10.**

NOTE: Forks are identical and are interchangeable.

2. Slowly push shifter shafts into side cover until detent balls fall from cover, then remove shifter shafts.

NOTE: The 3–4 shifter shaft has a detent.

3. Remove interlock sleeve, poppet spring and lock pin.
4. Replace shifter shaft seals if necessary.

REVERSE IDLER SHAFT, REPLACE

1. Remove thrust washer, use punch to drive welch plug and pin into idler shaft, **Fig. 11,** until idler shaft can be removed.
2. Position idler shaft in extension housing.
3. Align hole in shaft with hole in extension housing, drive in pin and install welch plug with sealer.

REVERSE SHIFTER & SEAL, REPLACE

1. Remove shifter fork, tap shaft into extension housing until detent ball falls from housing, then remove shaft and detent spring.
2. Remove "O" ring and discard.
3. Install detent spring, then position "O" ring on shaft.
4. Position ball on spring, then while pressing ball downward, slide shaft into place and rotate shaft until ball is seated.
5. Install shift fork.

EXTENSION HOUSING SEAL & BUSHING, REPLACE

1. Pry out oil seal, then drive out bushing, **Fig. 12.**
2. Press in new bushing using tool No. J-21465-17 and J-8092.
3. Coat bushing and seal with transmission oil, then using tool No. J-21359 install oil seal, **Fig. 13.**

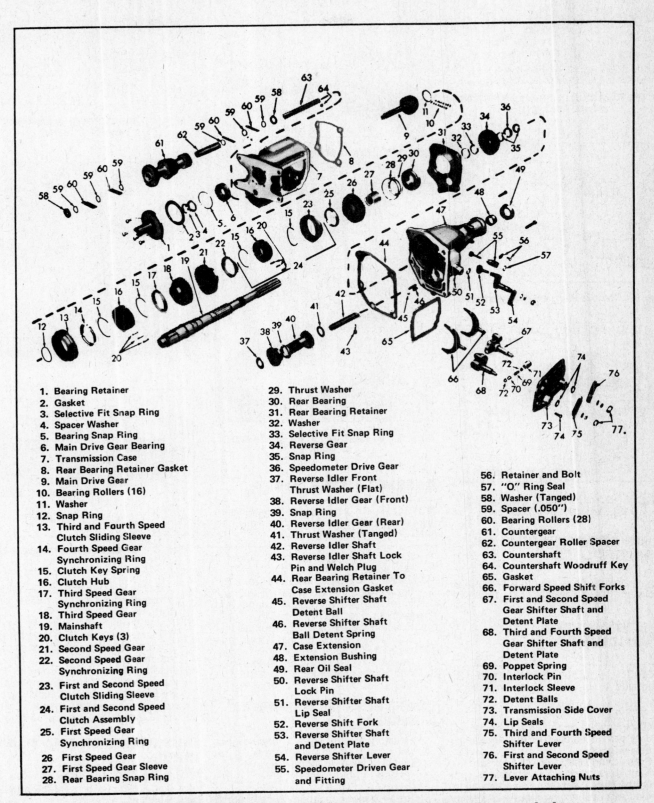

1. Bearing Retainer
2. Gasket
3. Selective Fit Snap Ring
4. Spacer Washer
5. Bearing Snap Ring
6. Main Drive Gear Bearing
7. Transmission Case
8. Rear Bearing Retainer Gasket
9. Main Drive Gear
10. Bearing Rollers (16)
11. Washer
12. Snap Ring
13. Third and Fourth Speed Clutch Sliding Sleeve
14. Fourth Speed Gear Synchronizing Ring
15. Clutch Key Spring
16. Clutch Hub
17. Third Speed Gear Synchronizing Ring
18. Third Speed Gear
19. Mainshaft
20. Clutch Keys (3)
21. Second Speed Gear
22. Second Speed Gear Synchronizing Ring
23. First and Second Speed Clutch Sliding Sleeve
24. First and Second Speed Clutch Assembly
25. First Speed Gear Synchronizing Ring
26. First Speed Gear
27. First Speed Gear Sleeve
28. Rear Bearing Snap Ring

29. Thrust Washer
30. Rear Bearing
31. Rear Bearing Retainer
32. Washer
33. Selective Fit Snap Ring
34. Reverse Gear
35. Snap Ring
36. Speedometer Drive Gear
37. Reverse Idler Front Thrust Washer (Flat)
38. Reverse Idler Gear (Front)
39. Snap Ring
40. Reverse Idler Gear (Rear)
41. Thrust Washer (Tanged)
42. Reverse Idler Shaft
43. Reverse Idler Shaft Lock Pin and Welch Plug
44. Rear Bearing Retainer To Case Extension Gasket
45. Reverse Shifter Shaft Detent Ball
46. Reverse Shifter Shaft Ball Detent Spring
47. Case Extension
48. Extension Bushing
49. Rear Oil Seal
50. Reverse Shifter Shaft Lock Pin
51. Reverse Shifter Shaft Lip Seal
52. Reverse Shift Fork
53. Reverse Shifter Shaft and Detent Plate
54. Reverse Shifter Lever
55. Speedometer Driven Gear and Fitting

56. Retainer and Bolt
57. "O" Ring Seal
58. Washer (Tanged)
59. Spacer (.050'')
60. Bearing Rollers (28)
61. Countergear
62. Countergear Roller Spacer
63. Countershaft
64. Countershaft Woodruff Key
65. Gasket
66. Forward Speed Shift Forks
67. First and Second Speed Gear Shifter Shaft and Detent Plate
68. Third and Fourth Speed Gear Shifter Shaft and Detent Plate
69. Poppet Spring
70. Interlock Pin
71. Interlock Sleeve
72. Detent Balls
73. Transmission Side Cover
74. Lip Seals
75. Third and Fourth Speed Shifter Lever
76. First and Second Speed Shifter Lever
77. Lever Attaching Nuts

Fig. 1   Disassembled view of Warner 83mm 4 speed manual transmission

Fig. 2   Removing reverse shifter shaft lock pin

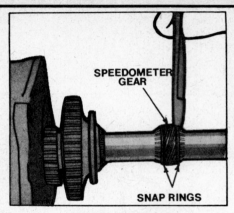

Fig. 3   Speedometer gear & snap rings

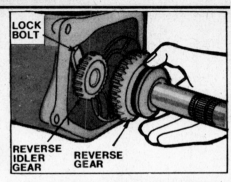

Fig. 4   Removing & installing reverse gear

Fig. 5   Removing countershaft

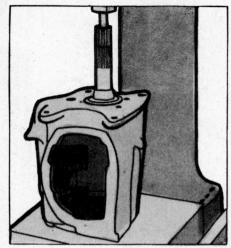

Fig. 6   Pressing drive gear from bearing

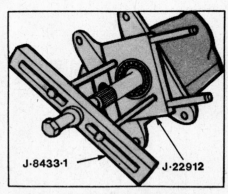

Fig. 7   Main drive gear bearing removal

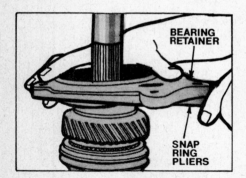

Fig. 8   Removing & installing rear bearing retainer

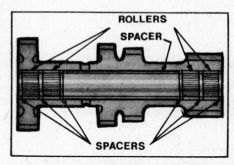

Fig. 9   Countergear assembly

DRIVE GEAR BEARING OIL SEAL, REPLACE

Pry seal with screw driver. Position seal in bore and tap in with flat plate, **Fig. 14.**

SYNCHRONIZERS, OVERHAUL

NOTE: The synchronizer clutch hub and sliding sleeve are replaced as an assembly.

1. Mark clutch hub and sliding sleeve so they can be installed in the same position, **Fig. 15.**
2. Press clutch hub from sliding sleeve, remove clutch keys and springs.
3. Install clutch keys and springs, align marks, install sliding sleeve on clutch hub.

ASSEMBLE SIDE COVER

NOTE: When assembling transmission always use new gaskets, oil seals and snap rings.

1. Install seals in shifter shaft bores, if removed.
2. Install 3–4 shifter shaft in bore, position in neutral, then install detent ball, interlock sleeve, poppet spring and lock pin, **Fig. 10.**
3. Position detent ball in other end of interlock sleeve, depress ball and install 1–2 shifter shaft.
4. Position 1–2 shifter shaft in 2nd gear and install shift forks.

COUNTERGEAR ASSEMBLE & INSTALL

1. Position dummy shaft in countergear bore and install tubular spacer.
2. Install spacer in bore. Using heavy grease to hold rollers in place, install 28 rollers, **Fig. 9.**
3. Install second spacer, 28 additional rollers and third spacer.

4. Install rollers and spacers in other end of countergear using above procedure.
5. Install thrust washers in each end of transmission case with tangs inserted in case recesses, using grease to hold washers in place.
6. Insert countershaft through rear of case, in turn forcing dummy shaft out through front of case. Install woodruff key on countershaft, then tap countershaft until flush with rear of case.

COUNTERGEAR END PLAY CHECK

Attach dial indicator, **Fig. 16,** then check end play. If end play is greater than .025 in. new selective thrust washers must be installed.

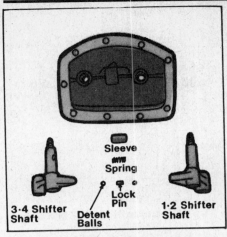

Fig. 10   Side cover assembly

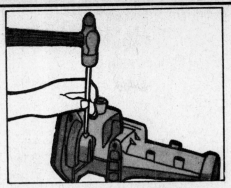

Fig. 11   Removing roll pin from reverse idler shaft

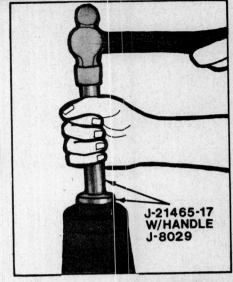

Fig. 12   Removing & installing extension housing bushing

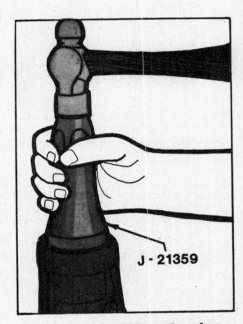

Fig. 13   Installing extension housing oil seal

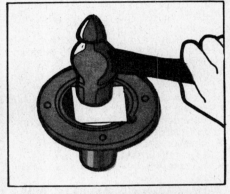

Fig. 14   Installing drive gear bearing retainer oil seal

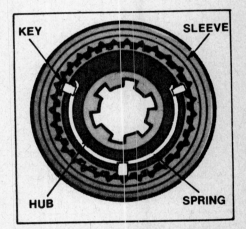

Fig. 15   Synchronizer assembly

ASSEMBLE MAINSHAFT

1. From rear of mainshaft, install 2nd gear with hub facing rearward.
2. Position synchronizing rings on 1–2 synchronizer, then install synchronizer on mainshaft with hub facing forward.
3. Press 1st gear bushing on mainshaft until 2nd gear, 1–2 synchronizer and bushing are against mainshaft shoulder, **Fig. 17.**
4. Install 1st gear and inner race with gear hub facing front, then press rear

bearing on mainshaft with snap ring groove facing front, **Fig. 18.**
5. Install spacer and selective thickness snap ring.

NOTE: Use the thickest snap ring that will fit in mainshaft groove.

6. Install 3rd gear with hub facing front and the 3rd gear synchronizing ring with notches facing front.
7. Install 3rd and 4th gear clutch assembly with the taper facing front.

NOTE: Ensure that keys in hub mate with notches in 3rd gear synchronizing ring.

8. Install selective thickness snap ring. Use thickness snap ring that will fit mainshaft groove.
9. Install locating pin in rear bearing retainer. Place bearing retainer over rear of mainshaft; spread retainer snap ring and align with groove in rear bearing, **Fig. 18.**
10. Using heavy grease, install 16 rollers and flat washer into main drive gear bore, **Fig. 19.**
11. Position 4th gear synchronizer ring on 3–4 synchronizer, aligning ring

notches with hub keys.
12. Install front drive gear on main shaft.

ASSEMBLE

1. Install drain plug in transmission case.
2. Install thrust washer and front section of reverse idler gear with hub facing rear and position gasket on rear of transmission case.
3. Position synchronizers in neutral and install mainshaft in case. Install retain-

Fig. 16 Countergear end-play check

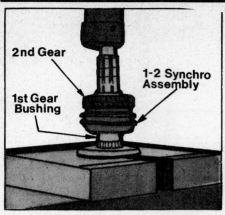

Fig. 17 Installing 2nd gear, 1—2 synchronizer assembly & 1st gear bushing

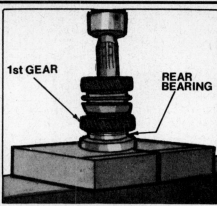

Fig. 18 Installing 1st gear & rear bearing

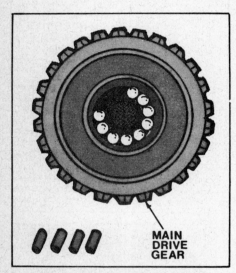

Fig. 19 Installing bearing rollers into main drive gear bore

er locating pin and torque retainer lock bolt to 25 ft. lbs.

4. Tap main drive gear bearing into case. Using suitable tool, pull drive gear shaft forward, and tap bearing again until bearing bottoms on main drive gear and the washer and snap ring

can be installed on main gear drive shaft, **Fig. 20.**

5. Install main drive gear bearing retainer and gasket, apply sealer to bolts and torque to 18 ft. lbs.

6. Install rear reverse idler gear, engaging splines with front section.

7. Install reverse sliding gear with hub facing rear, **Fig. 4,** then install the speedometer gear and two snap rings on mainshaft, **Fig. 3.**

8. Position gasket on rear bearing retainer and, install thrust washer on reverse idler shaft in extension housing.

9. Rotate reverse shifter shaft until fork is in full forward position. With synchronizer sleeves in neutral, slide extension housing over mainshaft. Guide reverse idler shaft into reverse idler gears, engaging fork on collar, then position shifter shaft in neutral.

10. Rotate reverse shifter shaft clockwise and push extension housing forward, aligning rear bearing retainer locating pin with extension housing. Apply sealer to bolts and torque long bolts to 40 ft. lbs., short bolts to 25 ft. lbs.

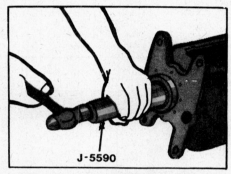

Fig. 20 Installing drive gear bearing

11. Install reverse shifter shaft lock pin.

12. Shift transmission into 2nd gear. The front synchronizer sleeve should be in neutral and the rear sleeve in forward position to engage 2nd gear synchronizer teeth.

13. Position slide cover and gasket to transmission case and index shift forks to shift collars, then install and torque side cover bolts to 18 ft. lbs.

New Process A-833 4 Speed Overdrive Manual Transmission

NOTE: For service procedures on this transmission, refer to New Process A-833 4 Speed Overdrive Manual Transmission section in the Dodge & Plymouth chapter.

Warner T-4C 4 Speed Manual Transmission

INDEX

DISASSEMBLE

1. Drain transmission lubricant and thoroughly clean outside of transmission assembly, **Fig. 1**.
2. Remove roll pin that attaches offset lever to shift rail, **Fig. 2**.
3. Remove retaining bolts from extension housing, then separate extension housing from transmission case and remove housing and offset lever as an assembly.
4. Remove detent ball and spring from offset lever, then remove roll pin from extension housing or offset lever, **Fig. 3**.
5. Remove attaching bolts from transmission shift cover and remove the shift cover.
6. Remove clip which retains reverse lever to reverse lever pivot bolt, then remove the bolt and remove reverse lever and fork as an assembly, **Fig. 4**.
7. Scribe position of front bearing cap to transmission case, then remove front bearing cap bolts and bearing cap.
8. Remove snap rings from front drive gear bearing, then, using appropriate tools, **Fig. 5**, remove the front bearing.
9. Remove snap rings from rear bearing and mainshaft, then, using appropriate tools, **Fig. 6**, remove the bearing.

NOTE: New front and rear bearings must be installed when assembling the transmission.

10. Remove drive gear from mainshaft and transmission case, then remove mainshaft from transmission case.
11. Remove roll pin retaining reverse idler gear shaft from transmission case and remove idler gear and shaft from case, **Fig. 7**.
12. Using loading tool J-26624, remove countershaft from rear of case, then remove countershaft gear and loading tool as an assembly from the case together with the thrust washers.

SUB-ASSEMBLY SERVICE

MAINSHAFT, DISASSEMBLE

1. Scribe alignment mark on third-fourth synchronizer hub and sleeve for reference during assembly, then remove snap ring and remove third-fourth synchronizer assembly from mainshaft, **Fig. 8**.
2. Slide third gear off mainshaft, then remove snap ring from second gear and remove tabbed thrust washer, second gear and blocker ring from mainshaft, **Fig. 9**.
3. Remove first gear thrust washer and roll pin from mainshaft, then remove first gear and blocker ring from mainshaft.
4. Scribe alignment mark on first-second gear synchronizer hub and sleeve for reference during assembly, then remove synchronizer springs and

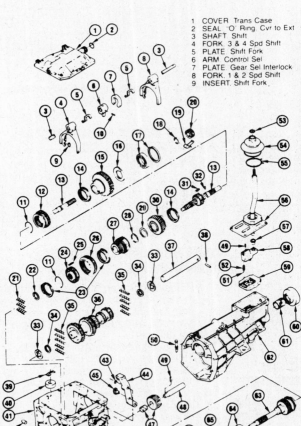

1 COVER, Trans Case
2 SEAL, "O" Ring, Cvr to Ext
3 SHAFT, Shift
4 FORK, 3 & 4 Spd Shift
5 PLATE, Shift Fork
6 ARM, Control Sel
7 PLATE, Gear Sel Interlock
8 FORK, 1 & 2 Spd Shift
9 INSERT, Shift Fork
10 PIN, Roll
11 SPRING, Syn
12 GEAR, Rev Sliding
13 SHAFT, W 1 & 2 Spd Syn
14 RING, 1 & 2 Syn Blocking
15 GEAR, 1st
16 WASHER, 1st Spd Gear Thrust
17 BEARING, Main Shaft, W Snap Ring
18 RING, Rr Brg-to Output Shf Ret
19 CLIP, Speedo Drive Gear
20 GEAR, Speedo Drive
21 ROLLER, Main Shaft
22 RING, Syn Ret
23 RING, 3 & 4 Syn Blocking
24 HUB, 3 & 4 Syn
25 KEY, 3 & 4 Syn
26 SLEEVE, 3 & 4 Syn
27 GEAR, 3rd
28 RING, 2nd Spd Gr Thr Wa Ret
29 WASHER, 2nd Spd Thrust
30 GEAR, 2nd
31 KEY, 1 & 2 Syn
32 PIN, 1st Spd Gr Thr Wa Ret
33 WASHER, Counter Gear Thrust
34 SPACER, Counter Gear Rir
35 ROLLER, Counter Gear
36 GEAR, Counter
37 SHAFT, Counter Gear
38 PIN, Roll
39 NUT, Spring
40 MAGNET
41 CASE
42 PLUG, Fill & Drain
43 RING, Rev Rly Lvr Ret
44 LEVER, Rev Relay
45 FORK, Rev Shift Lvr
46 PIN, Rev Shift Lvr Pivot
47 GEAR, Rev Idler, W Bushing
48 SHAFT, Rev Idler Gear
49 PIN, Spr
50 VENTILATOR, Ext
51 BALL, Steel
52 SPRING, Detent
53 RETAINER, Cont Lvr Boot
54 BOOT, Cont Lvr
55 RETAINER, Cont Lvr Boot
56 CONTROL, Trans Lvr & Hsg
57 SLEEVE, Shift Lvr Damper
58 LEVER, Offset Shift
59 PLATE, Detent & Guide
60 SEAL, Ext Rear Oil
61 BUSHING, Extension Housing
62 HOUSING, Extension
63 GEAR, Main Drive
64 BEARING, Main Drive Gear, W Snap Ring
65 RING, Main Dr Gr Brg to Shf Ret
66 SEAL, Main Drive Gear Brg Oil
67 RETAINER, Main Drive Gear Brg

Fig. 1 Disassembled view of Warner T-4C 4 speed manual transmission

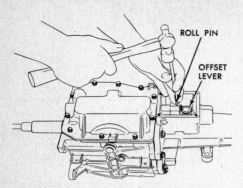

Fig. 2 Removing offset lever roll pin

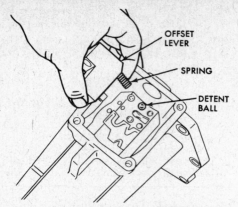

Fig. 3 Removing detent ball & spring

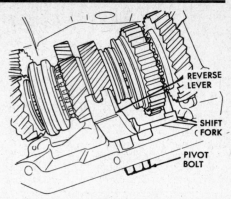

Fig. 4 Removing reverse lever & shift fork

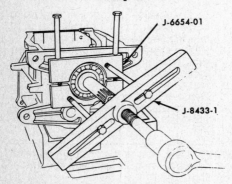

Fig. 5 Removing front bearing

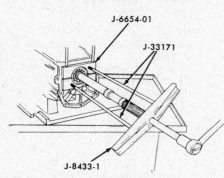

Fig. 6 Removing rear bearing

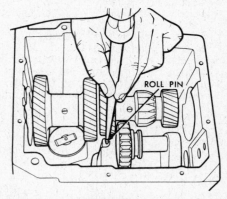

Fig. 7 Removing reverse idler gear shaft

keys from first-second sleeve and remove sleeve from shaft.

NOTE: The first-second hub and mainshaft are assembled as a unit and no attempt must be made to separate them.

5. Remove loading tool, roller bearings, spacers and thrust washers from the countershaft gear.

DRIVE GEAR, DISASSEMBLE

1. Remove roller bearings from cavity of drive gear and wash parts in a suitable cleaning solvent.
2. Inspect gear teeth and drive shaft pilot for wear.

CLEANING & INSPECTION

1. Thoroughly wash transmission using a suitable cleaning solvent and inspect the case for cracks.
2. Clean magnetic disc at bottom of transmission case and check front and rear faces of case for burrs. Dress any burrs off with a fine mill file.
3. Inspect all drive gear and countergear bearing rollers and replace as necessary.
4. Inspect countershaft and reverse idler shaft and all spacers and replace as necessary.
5. Inspect all gears for wear or damage and replace as necessary.

SYNCHRONIZER KEYS & SPRINGS, REPLACE

NOTE: The synchronizer hubs and sliding sleeves are a selected assembly and must be kept together as originally assembled, however, the keys and springs may be replaced if worn or broken.

1. Mark relation of hub and sleeve for reference during assembly.
2. Push sliding sleeve from hub and remove keys and springs.
3. Install sliding sleeve on hub, aligning the marks made previously.
4. Place a blocker ring on side of hub and sleeve and install keys and a spring. Then place blocker ring on opposite side of hub and sleeve and install remaining spring.

EXTENSION HOUSING OIL SEAL & BUSHING, REPLACE

1. Pry seal out with screwdriver, then drive bushing out of housing using tools J-8092 and J-23062-14, or equivalent.
2. Install new bushing in housing using same tools as for removal.
3. Coat outer edge of new seal with suitable sealing cement, then install seal using Tool J-21426, or equivalent and coat inside edge of seal with transmission lubricant.

DRIVE GEAR BEARING RETAINER OIL SEAL, REPLACE

1. Pry seal out with screwdriver.
2. Using Tool J-23096, or equivalent, install new seal into retainer until it bottoms out, then coat inner edge of seal with transmission lubricant.

TRANSMISSION COVER, DISASSEMBLE

1. Place selector arm plates and shift rail in neutral position, then rotate shift rail until selector arm disengages from selector arm plates and roll pin is accessible.
2. Remove selector arm roll pin, **Fig. 10,** then remove shift rail, shift forks, selector arm plates, selector arm, interlock plate and roll pin.
3. Pry out shift cover to extension housing O-ring with a screwdriver.
4. Remove nylon inserts and selector arm plates from shift forks, noting their position for reference during assembly.

TRANSMISSION COVER, ASSEMBLE

1. Install nylon inserts and selector arm plates in shift forks, then install shift

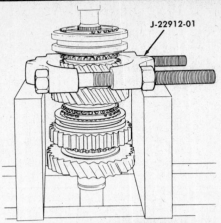

Fig. 8   Removing 3rd—4th synchronizer assembly

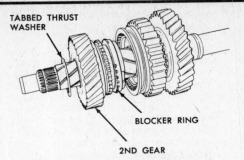

Fig. 9   Removing 2nd gear

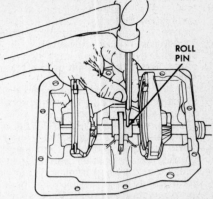

Fig. 10   Removing selector arm roll pin

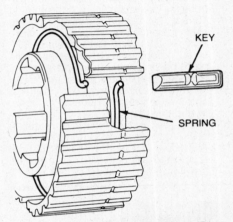

Fig. 11   Installing synchronizer spring

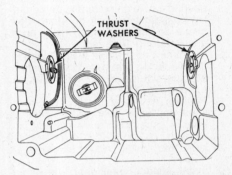

Fig. 12   Installing countershaft thrust washers

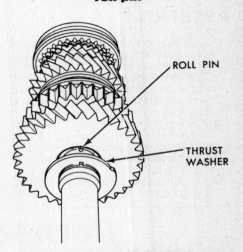

Fig. 13   Installing 1st gear thrust washer

rail plug after coating edges with suitable sealer.

2. Coat shift rail and rail bores with light weight grease and install shift rail in cover so that it is flush with inside edge of cover.

3. Install first-second shift fork in cover with fork offset facing rear of cover and push shift rail through fork.

NOTE: The first-second shift fork is the larger of the two forks.

4. Install selector arm and C-shaped interlock plate in cover and insert shift rail through arm.

NOTE: The widest part of interlock plate must face away from cover, and the selector arm roll pin hole must face downward and toward rear of cover.

5. Position third-fourth shift fork in cover with fork offset facing rear of cover.

NOTE: Third-fourth shift fork selector arm plate must be under first-second shift fork selector arm plate.

6. Push shift rail through third-fourth shift fork and into front bore in cover, then rotate shift rail until selector arm plate at forward end of rail faces away from, but is parallel to cover.

7. Align roll pin holes in selector arm and shift rail and install roll pin.

NOTE: Roll pin must be flush with surface of selector arm to prevent pin and selector arm from contacting each other during shifts.

8. Install a new shift cover to extension housing seal and coat the seal with transmission lubricant.

DRIVE GEAR, ASSEMBLE

Coat roller bearings and drive gear bearing bore with suitable lightweight grease and install roller bearings into bore of drive gear.

MAINSHAFT, ASSEMBLE

1. Coat mainshaft and gear bores with transmission lubricant, then install first-second synchronizer sleeve on mainshaft, aligning marks made during disassembly.

2. Install synchronizer keys and springs into the first-second synchronizer sleeve. Engage tang end of springs into same synchronizer key, but position open ends of springs so that they face away from each other, **Fig. 11.**

3. Place blocking ring on first gear and install gear and ring on mainshaft.

NOTE: Ensure that synchronizer keys engage notches in first gear blocking ring.

4. Install first gear roll pin in mainshaft, then place blocking ring on second gear and install gear and ring on mainshaft, ensuring synchronizer keys engage notches in second gear blocking ring.

5. Install second gear thrust washer and snap ring, ensuring that thrust washer tab is engaged in mainshaft notch.

6. Check second gear end play using a feeler gage. End play should be .004—.014 inch. If end play exceeds .014 inch, replace thrust washer and snap ring and inspect synchronizer hub for excessive wear.

7. Place blocking ring on third gear and install gear and ring on mainshaft, then install third-fourth synchronizer sleeve on hub, aligning marks made during disassembly.

8. Install synchronizer keys and springs in third-fourth synchronizer sleeve. Engage tang end of each spring in same key, but position open ends of springs so that they face away from

9. Install third-fourth synchronizer assembly on mainshaft with machined groove in hub facing forward, then install snap ring on mainshaft, ensuring that synchronizer keys are engaged in notches in third gear blocker ring.

10. On 1982 models, measure third-fourth synchronizer end play following procedure in step No. 6 above.

11. On all models, install Tool J-26624, or equivalent, into countershaft gear, then, using a suitable lightweight grease, lubricate roller bearings and install into bores at front and rear of countershaft gear. Install roller bearing retainers on Tool J-26624.

ASSEMBLE

1. Coat countershaft gear thrust washers with suitable grease and install washers in case, **Fig. 12.**

2. Position countershaft gear in case and install countershaft from rear of case, ensuring that thrust washers remain in place.

3. Position reverse idler gear in case with shift lever groove facing rear of case and install reverse idler shaft from rear of case, then install roll pin in shaft and center pin in shaft.

4. Install mainshaft assembly into case, being careful not to change position of

synchronizer assemblies.

5. Install fourth gear blocking ring in third-fourth synchronizer sleeve, ensuring that synchronizer keys engage in notches in blocker ring, then install drive gear into case and engage with mainshaft.

6. Position mainshaft first gear against rear of case, then start new front bearing onto drive gear. Align bearing with bearing bore in case and drive bearing onto drive gear and into case using Tool J-25234, or equivalent, then install front bearing snap rings.

7. Apply a ⅛ inch bead of RTV sealant #732, or equivalent on case mating surface of front bearing cap and install bearing cap aligning marks made during disassembly. Apply non-hardening sealer on attaching bolts, install bolts, and torque to 15 ft. lbs.

8. Install first gear thrust washer with oil groove facing first gear on mainshaft, aligning slot in washer with first gear roll pin, **Fig. 13.**

9. Position new rear bearing on mainshaft and align bearing with bearing bore in case, then drive bearing into case using Tool J-25234, or equivalent, and install rear bearing snap rings.

10. Install speedometer gear and retaining clip on mainshaft.

11. Apply non-hardening sealer to threads of reverse lever pivot bolt and start bolt into case. Engage reverse lever fork in reverse idler gear and reverse lever

on pivot bolt, tighten bolt to 20 ft. lbs., and install retaining clip.

12. While rotating drive gear and mainshaft gears, check if blocker rings stick on gears. Rings can be released by carefully prying them off the cones.

13. Apply a ⅛ inch bead of RTV sealant #732, or equivalent, on cover mating surface of transmission, then place reverse lever in neutral and position cover on case.

14. Align cover to case by installing two dowel type bolts first, then install remaining cover bolts and torque to 10 ft. lbs.

NOTE: The offset lever to shift rail roll pin hole must be in a vertical position after cover installation.

15. Apply a ⅛ inch bead of RTV sealant #732, or equivalent on extension housing to transmission case mating surface, then place extension housing over mainshaft in a position where shift rail is in shift cover opening.

16. Install detent spring in offset lever and place ball in neutral guide plate detent position. Apply pressure on offset lever, slide offset lever onto shift rail and seat extension housing to transmission case.

17. Install extension housing retaining bolts and torque to 25 ft. lbs.

18. Align hole in offset lever and shift rail and install roll pin, then fill transmission to proper level with lubricant.

Warner T-5 5 Speed Manual Transmission

INDEX

DISASSEMBLE

1. Drain transmission and thoroughly clean exterior of transmission case.

2. Using suitable tools remove roll pin attaching offset lever to shift rail, **Fig. 1.**

3. Remove extension housing to transmission case bolts and remove housing and offset lever as an assembly.

NOTE: Do not attempt to remove offset lever while extension housing is still bolted in place. The lever has a positioning lug engaged in the housing detent plate which prevents moving the lever far enough for removal.

4. Remove detent ball and spring from

offset lever and remove roll pin from extension housing or offset lever, **Fig. 2.**

5. Remove plastic funnel, thrust bearing race, and thrust bearing from rear of countershaft. These parts may be found inside extension housing.

6. Remove bolts attaching transmission cover and shift fork assembly and remove cover. Two of the transmission cover attaching bolts are alignment type dowel bolts. Note location of these bolts for assembly reference.

7. Using suitable tools, drive roll pin from fifth gearshift fork while supporting end of shaft with a block of wood.

8. Remove fifth synchronizer gear snap ring, shift fork, fifth gear synchronizer

sleeve, blocking ring, and fifth speed driven gear from rear of countershaft.

9. Remove snap ring from fifth speed driven gear.

10. Mark bearing cap and case for assembly reference, **Fig. 3.**

11. Remove front bearing cap bolts and cap, then remove front bearing race and end play shims from front bearing cap, **Fig. 4.**

12. Turn drive gear until flat surface faces countershaft and remove drive gear from transmission case.

13. Remove reverse lever "C" clip and pivot bolt, **Fig. 5.**

14. Remove mainshaft rear bearing race, tilt mainshaft assembly upward, and remove assembly from transmission case, **Fig. 6.**

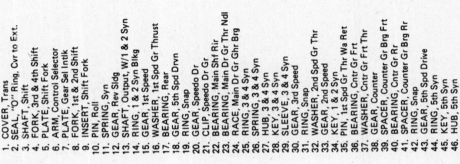

47. SPRING, 5th Syn
48. SLEEVE, 5th Syn
49. RETAINER, 5th Syn Key
50. RACE, 5th Syn Thr Brg Frt
51. BEARING, 5th Syn Ndl Thr
52. RACE, 5th Syn Thr Brg Rr
53. RING, Snap
54. FUNNEL, Trans Oiling
55. NUT, Magnet
56. MAGNET
57. CASE, Trans
58. PLUG, Fill & Drain
59. SPRING, Rev Lock
60. FORK, Rev Shift
61. ROLLER, Fork
62. PIN, Rev Fork
63. PIN, Shift Rail
64. ROLLER, Rail pin
65. RAIL, 5th & Rev Shft
66. INSERT, Shift Fork
67. PIN, Roll
68. FORK, 5th Shift
69. LEVER, 5th & Rev Relay
70. RING, Rev, Relay Lever Ret
71. SHAFT, Rev Idler Gr
72. GEAR, Rev Idler (Incl Bshg)
73. PIN, 5th Spd Shft Lvr Piv
74. VENTILATOR, Ext
75. BALL, Steel
76. SPRING, Detent
77. RETAINER, Cont Lvr Boot
78. BOOT, Cont Lvr
79. RETAINER, Cont Lvr Boot Lwr
80. CONTROL, Trans Lvr & Hsg
81. SLEEVE, Shift Lvr Dmpr
82. LEVER, Offset Shift
83. PLATE, Detent & Guide
84. SEAL, Ext Rr Oil
85. BUSHING, Extension Housing
86. HOUSING, Extension
87. GEAR, Main Drive
88. BEARING, Front
89. SHIM, Brg Adj
90. RETAINER, Drive Gr Brg
91. SEAL, Drive Gr Brg Oil

1. COVER, Trans
2. SEAL, "O" Ring, Cvr to Ext.
3. SHAFT, Shift
4. FORK, 3rd & 4th Shift
5. PLATE, Shift Fork
6. ARM, Control Selector
7. PLATE, Gear Sel Intlk
8. FORK, 1st & 2nd Shift
9. INSERT, Shift Fork
10. PIN, Roll
11. SPRING, Syn
12. GEAR, Rev Sldg
13. SHAFT, Output, W/1 & 2 Syn
14. RING, 1 & 2 Syn Blkg
15. GEAR, 1st Speed
16. WASHER, 1st Spd Gr Thrust
17. BEARING, Rear
18. GEAR, 5th Spd Drvn
19. RING, Snap
20. CLIP, Speedo Dr Gr
21. GEAR, Speedo Dr
22. BEARING, Main Shf Rir
23. BEARING, Main Dr Gr Thr Ndl
24. RACE, Main Dr Gr Ghr Brg
25. RING, 3 & 4 Syn
26. SPRING, 3 & 4 Syn
27. HUB, 3 & 4 Syn
28. KEY, 3 & 4 Syn
29. SLEEVE, 3 & 4 Syn
30. GEAR, 3rd Speed
31. RING, Snap
32. WASHER, 2nd Spd Gr Thr
33. GEAR, 2nd Speed
34. KEY, 1 & 2 Syn
35. PIN, 1st Spd Gr Thr Wa Ret
36. BEARING, Cntr Gr Frt
37. WASHER, Cntr Gr Frt Thr
38. GEAR, Counter
39. SPACER, Counter Gr Brg Frt
40. BEARING, Cntr Gr Rr
41. SPACER, Counter Gr Brg Rr
42. RING, Snap
43. GEAR, 5th Spd Drive
44. RING, Snap
45. KEY, 5th Syn
46. HUB, 5th Syn

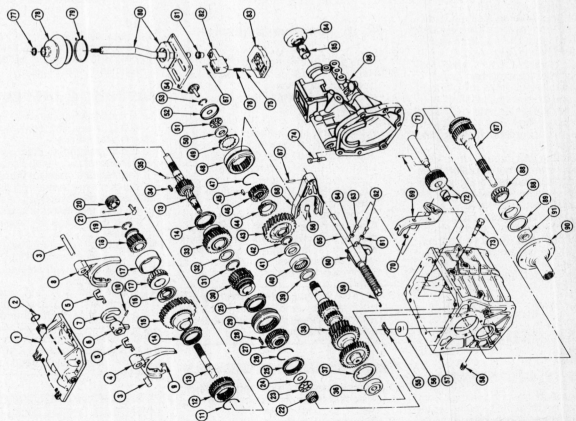

Fig. 1 Disassembled view of Warner T-5 5 speed manual transmission

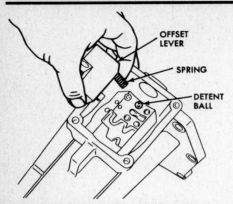

Fig. 2   Removing detent ball & spring

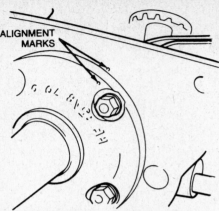

Fig. 3   Marking bearing cap to case alignment

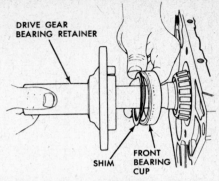

Fig. 4   Removing bearing cap & shims

Fig. 5   Removing reverse lever retaining clip

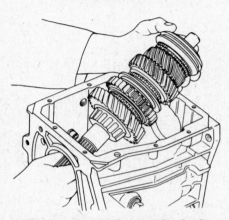

Fig. 6   Removing mainshaft

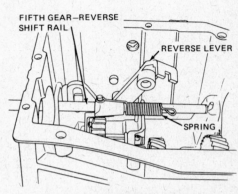

Fig. 7   Removing 5th gear reverse shift rail

15. Unhook overcenter link spring from front of transmission case.
16. Turn fifth gear-reverse shift rail to disengage rail from reverse lever assembly, then remove shift rail from rear of transmission case, **Fig. 7.**
17. Remove reverse lever and fork assembly from transmission case.
18. Using suitable tool, drive roll pin from forward end of reverse idler shaft, then remove rubber O-ring and gear from transmission case.
19. Remove rear countershaft snap ring and spacer.
20. Insert suitable tool through drive gear opening in front of transmission case and, using arbor press, carefully press countershaft rearward to remove rear countershaft bearing, **Fig. 8.**
21. Move countershaft assembly rearward, tilt countershaft upward, and remove from case. Remove countershaft front thrust washer and rear bearing spacer.
22. Remove countershaft front bearing from transmission case, using arbor press.

SUB-ASSEMBLY SERVICE

MAINSHAFT, DISASSEMBLE

1. Remove thrust bearing washer from front end of mainshaft, then scribe alignment mark on third-fourth synchronizer hub and sleeve for refer-

ence during assembly.
2. Remove third-fourth synchronizer blocking ring, sleeve, hub and third gear as an assembly from mainshaft, **Fig. 9.**
3. Remove snap ring, tabbed thrust washer and second gear from mainshaft, then remove fifth gear using Tool J-22912-01 and arbor press, and slide rear bearing off mainshaft.
4. Remove first gear thrust washer, roll pin, first gear and synchronizer ring from mainshaft.
5. Scribe mark on first-second synchronizer hub and sleeve for reference during assembly, then remove synchronizer spring and keys from first-reverse sliding gear and remove gear from mainshaft hub.

NOTE: The first-second-reverse hub and mainshaft are assembled and machined as a matched set and no attempt should be made to separate them.

DRIVE GEAR, DISASSEMBLE

1. Remove bearing race, thrust bearing and roller bearings from cavity of drive gear.
2. Remove bearing from drive gear using Tool J-22912-01 and arbor press, **Fig.**

10.
3. Wash parts in suitable cleaning solvent, then inspect gear teeth and drive pilot shaft for wear or damage and replace as necessary.

CLEANING & INSPECTION

1. Thoroughly wash transmission using a suitable cleaning solvent and inspect case for cracks.
2. Clean magnetic disc at bottom of transmission case and check front and rear faces of case for burrs. Dress any burrs off with a fine mill file.
3. Inspect all drive gear bearing rollers, reverse idler shaft and all spacers for wear or damage and replace as necessary.
4. Inspect all gears for wear or damage and replace as necessary.
5. Check that clutch sleeves slide freely on their hubs.
6. Wash front and rear bearings thoroughly with a suitable cleaning solvent and dry them with compressed air.

NOTE: When drying bearings, slowly turn them by hand. To avoid damaging race and balls, do not allow bearings to spin.

SYNCHRONIZER KEYS & SPRINGS, REPLACE

NOTE: The synchronizer hubs and sliding

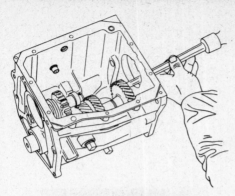

Fig. 8   Removing rear countershaft bearing

sleeves are a selected assembly and must be kept together as originally assembled, however, the keys and springs may be replaced if worn or broken.

1. Mark relation of hub and sleeve for reference during assembly.
2. Push sliding sleeve from hub and remove keys and springs.
3. Place a blocker ring on side of hub and sleeve and install keys and a spring, then place blocker ring on opposite side of hub and sleeve and install remaining spring.

EXTENSION HOUSING OIL SEAL & BUSHING, REPLACE

1. Pry seal out with screwdriver, then drive bushing out of housing using tools J-8092 and J-23062-14, or equivalent.
2. Install new bushing in housing using same tools as for removal.
3. Coat outer edge of new seal with suitable sealing cement, then install seal using Tool J-21426, or equivalent and coat inside edge of seal with transmission lubricant.

DRIVE GEAR BEARING RETAINER OIL SEAL, REPLACE

1. Pry seal out with screwdriver.
2. Using Tool J-23096, or equivalent, install new seal into retainer until it bottoms out, then coat inner edge of seal with transmission lubricant.

TRANSMISSION COVER, DISASSEMBLE

1. Place selector arm plates and shift rail in neutral position, then rotate shift rail until selector arm disengages from selector arm plates and roll pin is accessible.
2. Remove selector arm roll pin, **Fig. 11**, then remove shift rail, shift forks, selector arm plates, selector arm, interlock plate and roll pin.
3. Pry out shift cover to extension housing O-ring with a screwdriver.
4. Remove nylon inserts and selector arm plates from shift forks, noting their position for reference during assembly.

TRANSMISSION COVER, ASSEMBLE

1. Install nylon inserts and selector arm plates in shift forks, then install shift rail plug after coating edges with suitable sealer.
2. Coat shift rail and rail bores with light weight grease and install shift rail in cover so that it is flush with inside edge of cover.
3. Install first-second shift fork in cover with fork offset facing rear of cover and push shift rail through fork.

NOTE: The first-second shift fork is the larger of the two forks.

4. Install selector arm and C-shaped interlock plate in cover and insert shift rail through arm.

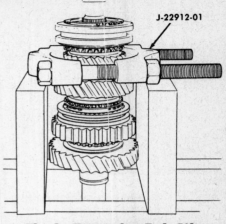

Fig. 9   Removing 3rd—4th synchronizer

NOTE: The widest part of interlock plate must face away from cover, and the selector arm roll pin hole must face downward and toward rear of cover.

5. Position third-fourth shift fork in cover with fork offset facing rear of cover.

NOTE: Third-fourth shift fork selector arm plate must be under first-second shift fork selector arm plate.

6. Push shift rail through third-fourth shift fork and into front bore in cover, then rotate shift rail until selector arm plate at forward end of rail faces away from, but is parallel to cover.
7. Align roll pin holes in selector arm and shift rail and install roll pin.

NOTE: Roll pin must be flush with surface of selector arm to prevent pin and selector arm from contacting each other during shifts.

8. Install a new shift cover to extension housing seal and coat the seal with transmission lubricant.

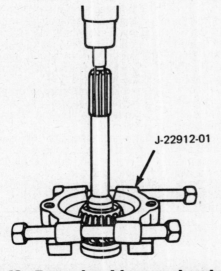

Fig. 10   Removing drive gear bearing

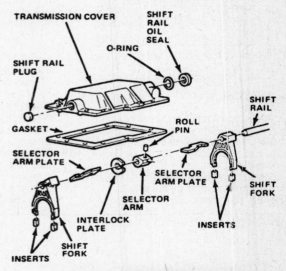

Fig. 11   Transmission cover

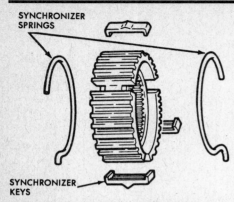

Fig. 12 Installing synchronizer keys & springs

DRIVE GEAR, ASSEMBLE

1. Using Tool J-22912-01 and an arbor press, install bearing on drive gear.
2. Coat roller bearings and drive gear bearing bore with grease and install roller bearings into bore of drive gear.
3. Install thrust bearing and race in drive gear.

MAINSHAFT, ASSEMBLE

1. Coat mainshaft and gear bores with transmission lubricant, then install first-second synchronizer sleeve on hub, aligning marks made during disassembly.
2. Install first-second synchronizer keys and springs, **Fig. 12**.
3. Install blocker ring, second gear, tabbed thrust washer and second gear retaining snap ring on mainshaft, ensuring that washer tab is properly seated in mainshaft notch, **Fig. 13**.
4. Install blocker ring and first gear on mainshaft, then install first gear roll pin and thrust washer.
5. Install rear bearing on mainshaft, then install fifth speed gear on mainshaft using Tool J-22912-01 and arbor press and install snap ring.
6. Install third gear, third-fourth synchronizer assembly and thrust bearing on mainshaft.

NOTE: Synchronizer hub offset must face forward.

ASSEMBLE

1. Coat countershaft front bearing bore with Loctite 601, or equivalent, then install front countershaft bearing flush with facing of case using an arbor press.
2. Coat countershaft tabbed thrust washer with grease and install washer so that tab engages depression in case.

3. Tip transmission on end and install countershaft in front bearing bore.
4. Install countershaft rear bearing spacer, then coat countershaft rear bearing with grease and install bearing using tool J-29895 or equivalent.

NOTE: When correctly installed, the bearing will extend .125 inch beyond the case surface.

5. Position reverse idler gear in case with shift lever groove facing rear of case, then install reverse idler shaft from rear of case and install roll pin in idler shaft.
6. Install mainshaft and rear mainshaft bearing race in transmission case, then install drive gear in case and engage in third-fourth synchronizer sleeve and blocker ring.
7. Install front bearing race and temporarily install front bearing cap.

NOTE: Do not install shims in front bearing cap at this time.

8. Install fifth speed-reverse lever, pivot bolt and retaining clip, ensuring that reverse lever fork is engaged in reverse idler gear.

NOTE: Coat bolt threads with non-hardening sealer before installing.

9. Install countershaft rear bearing spacer and snap ring, then install fifth speed gear on countershaft.
10. Insert fifth speed-reverse rail in rear of case and install in to reverse fifth speed lever, then connect spring to front of case.

NOTE: To simplify engagement with lever, rotate rail during installation.

11. Position fifth gear shift fork on fifth gear synchronizer assembly, then install synchronizer on countershaft and shift fork on shift rail, ensuring that roll pin hole in shift fork and shift rail are aligned.
12. Support fifth gear shift rail and fork on a block of wood and install roll pin.
13. Install thrust race against fifth speed synchronizer hub and install snap ring, then install thrust bearing against race on countershaft and coat bearing and race with petroleum jelly.
14. Install lipped thrust race over needle-type thrust bearing, then install plastic funnel into hole in end of countershaft gear.
15. Temporarily install extension housing and attaching bolts, then turn transmission case on end and mount a dial indicator on extension housing. Check end play of mainshaft and re-

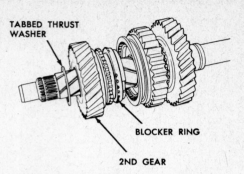

Fig. 13 Install second gear & thrust washer

record reading. Mainshaft bearings must have a preload of .001–.005 inch. To set preload, use a shim pack measuring .001–.005 inch greater than reading of dial indicator.
16. Remove front bearing cap and race, install shims and reinstall bearing race.
17. Apply a ⅛ inch bead of RTV sealant #732, or equivalent, on case mating surface of front bearing cap, then install bearing cap, referring to alignment marks made during disassembly, and torque bolts to 15 ft. lbs.
18. Remove extension housing, then move shift forks on transmission cover and synchronizer sleeves inside transmission to the neutral position.
19. Apply a ⅛ inch bead of RTV sealant #732, or equivalent, to cover mating surface of transmission, then lower cover onto case while aligning shift forks and synchronizer sleeves. Center cover and install the two dowel bolts, then install remaining bolts and torque to 10 ft. lbs.

NOTE: The offset lever to shift rail roll pin hole must be in a vertical position after cover installation.

20. Apply a ⅛ inch bead of RTV sealant #732, or equivalent on extension housing to transmission case mating surface, then install extension housing over mainshaft and shift rail until shift rail just enters shift cover opening.
21. Install detent spring into offset lever and place steel ball into neutral guide plate detent.
22. Position offset lever on steel ball and apply pressure to offset lever and to extension housing against transmission case.
23. Install extension housing and bolts and torque bolts to 25 ft. lbs., then install and align roll pin in offset lever and shift rail.
24. Fill transmission to proper level with lubricant.

TRANSFER CASES

INDEX

MODEL 203

NOTE: For service procedures on this transfer case, refer to "Dodge & Plymouth" chapter.

MODEL 205

NOTE: For service procedures on this transfer case, refer to "Dodge & Plymouth" chapter. Due to vehicle applications, there may be minor differences in repair procedures. See **Fig. 1.**

MODEL 207

DISASSEMBLY

1. Remove fill and drain plugs and front yoke. Discard yoke seal washer and nut.
2. Turn transfer case on end and support

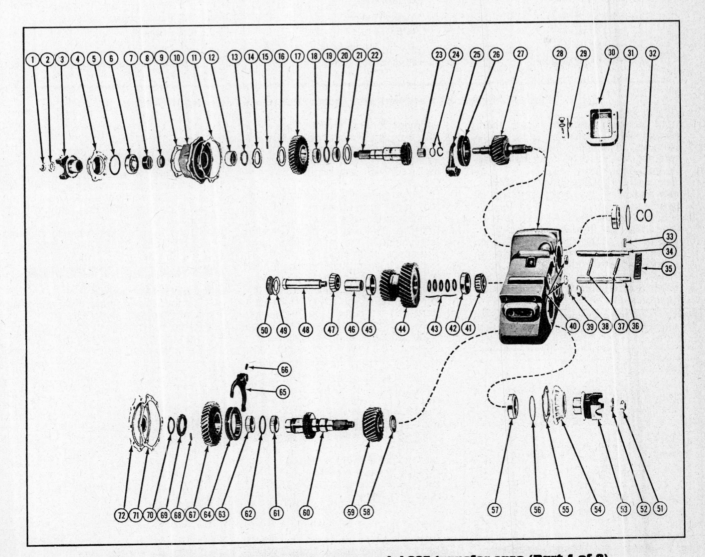

Fig. 1   Exploded view of New Process model 205 transfer case (Part 1 of 2)

1. Rear Output Shaft Locknut
2. Washer
3. Yoke
4. Bearing Retainer and Seal Assembly
5. Snap Ring
6. Bearing
7. Speedometer Gear
8. Spacer
9. Gasket
10. Housing
11. Gasket
12. Bearing
13. Snap Ring
14. Thrust Washer
15. Thrust Washer Lock Pin
16. Thrust Washer (Tanged)
17. Low Speed Gear
18. Needle Bearings
19. Spacer
20. Needle Bearings
21. Tanged Washer
22. Rear Output Shaft
23. Needle Bearings
24. Washer and Retainer

25. Shift Fork
26. Sliding Clutch
27. Input Shaft
28. Transfer Case
29. Poppet Plug, Spring and Ball
30. P.T.O. Gasket and Cover
31. Input Shaft Bearing and Snap Ring
32. Snap Ring and Rubber 'O' Ring
33. Shift Link Clevis Pin
34. Range Shift Rail
35. Shift Rail Connector Link
36. Front Wheel Drive Shift Rail
37. Interlock Pins
38. Rear Idler Lock Nut
39. Washer
40. Shift Rail Seals
41. Idler Shaft Bearing
42. Bearing Cup
43. Shims
44. Idler Gear
45. Bearing Cup
46. Spacer
47. Idler Shaft Bearing
48. Idler Shaft

49. Cover Gasket
50. Rear Cover
51. Front Output Shaft Locknut
52. Washer
53. Yoke
54. Bearing Retainer and Seal
55. Gasket
56. Snap Ring
57. Front Bearing
58. Thrust Washer
59. Front Wheel High Gear
60. Front Output Shaft
61. Needle Bearings
62. Spacer
63. Needle Bearing
64. Sliding Clutch Gear
65. Shift Fork
66. Roll Pin
67. Front Output Low Gear
68. Thrust Washer Lock Pin
69. Thrust Washer
70. Snap Ring
71. Rear Cover Gasket
72. Rear Cover and Bearing

Fig. 1 Exploded view of New Process model 205 transfer case (Part 2 of 2)

front case on wooden blocks, then shift to "4 Lo" position.

3. Remove extension housing, then remove and discard mainshaft rear bearing snap ring.
4. Remove rear retainer and pump housing, **Fig. 2.** Discard pump housing seal.
5. Remove speedometer drive gear and the pump gear from mainshaft.
6. Remove rear case attaching bolts and separate rear case from front case by prying with screwdrivers at slots provided in case ends.
7. Remove front output shaft and chain as an assembly.

NOTE: Raise the mainshaft slightly to provide clearance for removing the output shaft, **Fig. 3.**

8. Lift mode fork rail until it clears range fork, then rotate mode fork and rail and remove from case, **Fig. 4.**
9. Remove mainshaft, then the planetary assembly with range fork from case, **Fig. 5.**
10. Remove planetary thrust washer, input gear, thrust bearing and front thrust washer from case, **Fig. 6.**
11. Remove shift sector detent spring, retaining bolt, the shift sector, shaft and spacer from case, **Fig. 7.**
12. Remove locking plate from case, **Fig. 8.**
13. Remove inner gear pilot bearing using tool J-29369-1 and a slide hammer.
14. Remove front output shaft seal, input shaft seal and rear extension seal using a brass drift or screwdriver.
15. Remove the two front input shaft

caged roller bearings from case using tool J-33841 and J-8092, **Fig. 9.**
16. Remove front output shaft rear bearing using tool J-29369-2 with J-33367 or a slide hammer, **Fig. 10.**
17. Remove rear mainshaft bearing from rear retainer, then remove front output shaft bearing snap ring and the bearing.
18. Remove extension housing bushing using tools J-33839 and J-8092.

SUB-ASSEMBLY SERVICE

Mainshaft Disassembly

1. Remove speedometer gear and pump gear from mainshaft, **Fig. 11.**
2. Remove synchronizer hub snap ring, then the synchronizer hub.
3. Remove drive sprocket, then, using

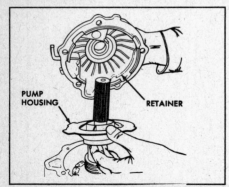

Fig. 2 Pump housing & retainer removal

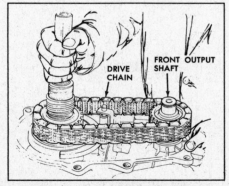

Fig. 3 Front output shaft & chain replacement

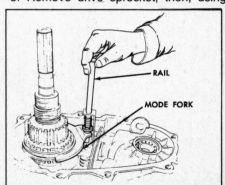

Fig. 4 Mode fork & rail replacement

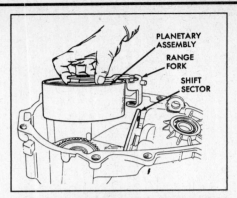

Fig. 5 Planetary gear assembly & range fork replacement

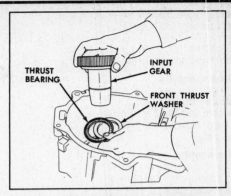

Fig. 6 Input gear replacement

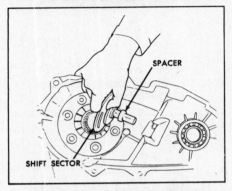

Fig. 7 Shift sector removal

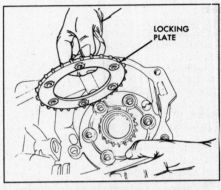

Fig. 8 Locking plate removal

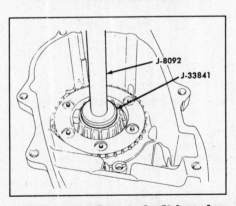

Fig. 9 Front input shaft bearing removal

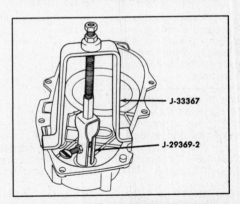

Fig. 10 Front output shaft rear bearing removal

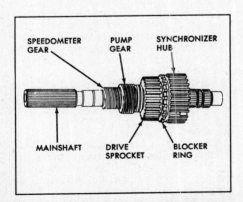

Fig. 11 Mainshaft components

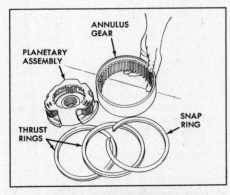

Fig. 12 Planetary gear assembly

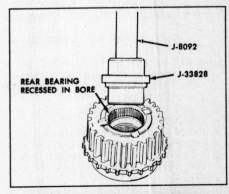

Fig. 13 Drive sprocket rear bearing installation

tools J-33826 and J-8092, remove the two caged roller bearings from sprocket.

4. Remove synchronizer keys and retaining rings from synchronizer hub.

Planetary Gear Disassembly

1. Remove snap ring, then remove and discard outer thrust ring, **Fig. 12.**
2. Separate planetary assembly from annulus gear, then remove and discard inner thrust ring.

Planetary Gear Assembly

1. Install a new inner thrust ring on planetary assembly, then install planetary assembly into annulus gear.
2. Install a new outer thrust ring and the snap ring in the planetary gear.

Mainshaft Assembly

1. Install front drive sprocket bearing using tools J-33828 and J-8092 until tool bottoms out and bearing is flush with front surface.
2. Reverse tool on J-8092 and install rear bearing into sprocket until tool bottoms out and bearing is recessed in bore, **Fig. 13.**
3. Install thrust washer, drive sprocket, blocker ring and synchronizer hub on mainshaft.
4. Install hub with a new snap ring on mainshaft.
5. Install pump gear and speedometer gear on mainshaft.

ASSEMBLY

NOTE: All bearings used in the transfer case must be properly aligned to avoid blocking the oil passages. After installing bearings, check their position to make sure that oil passages are clear.

1. Install lock plate in case. Coat case and lock plate surfaces around bolt holes with Loctite 515, or equivalent. Install attaching bolts and torque to 20–30 ft. lbs.
2. Install input shaft roller bearings into case using tool J-33830 and J-8092, **Fig. 14.**
3. Install front output shaft rear bearing using tools J-33832 and J-8092.
4. Install front output shaft front bearing using tools J-33833 and J-8092.
5. Install front output shaft bearing snap ring, then install the seal using tool J-33834.
6. Install input shaft seal using tool J-33831.
7. Install spacer on shift sector shaft, then install sector and shift lever in case. Torque shift lever retaining nut to 15–20 ft. lbs.
8. Install shift sector detent spring and retaining bolt.
9. Install pilot bearing into input gear using tools J-33829 and J-8029.
10. Install input gear front thrust washer, thrust bearing and input gear in case, **Fig. 6.**
11. Install planetary gear thrust washer on input gear and range fork on planetary assembly, then install planetary as-

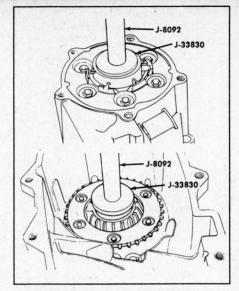

Fig. 14   Input shaft bearing installation

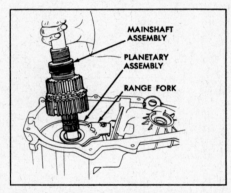

Fig. 15   Mainshaft installation

sembly into case, **Fig. 5.**

12. Install mainshaft into case, ensuring that thrust washer is aligned with input gear and planetary assembly, **Fig. 15.**
13. Install mode fork on synchronizer sleeve so that it is aligned with range fork, then slide mode fork down through range fork until rail is seated in bore of case, **Fig. 4.**
14. Position drive chain around front output shaft and drive sprocket, then install front output shaft in case, **Fig. 3.**
15. Install magnet into pocket in case.
16. Apply a ⅛ inch bead of Loctite 515 or equivalent to front case mating surface, then position rear case on front case dowel pins. Install case bolts and torque to 20–25 ft. lbs., then install two bolts and washers into the dowel pin holes.
17. Install output bearing into rear retainer using tools J-33833 and J-8092.
18. Install seal in pump housing using tool J-33835, then apply petroleum jelly to pump housing tabs and install housing in rear retainer.

19. Apply a ⅛ inch bead of Loctite 515 or equivalent to mating surface of rear retainer, then install retainer onto case. Torque bolts to 15–20 ft. lbs.
20. Install a new snap ring on mainshaft, then install bushing in extension housing using tools J-33826 and J-8092.
21. Install a new extension housing seal using tool J-33843.
22. Apply a ⅛ inch bead of Loctite 515 or equivalent to mating surface of extension housing, then install housing onto case. Torque bolts to 20–25 ft. lbs.
23. Install front yoke on output shaft using a new seal washer and nut. Torque nut to 90–130 ft. lbs.
24. Install drain and fill plugs and torque to 30–40 ft. lbs.

MODEL 208

NOTE: For service procedures on this transfer case, refer to "Dodge & Plymouth chapter. Due to vehicle applications, there may be minor differences in repair procedures. See Fig. 16.

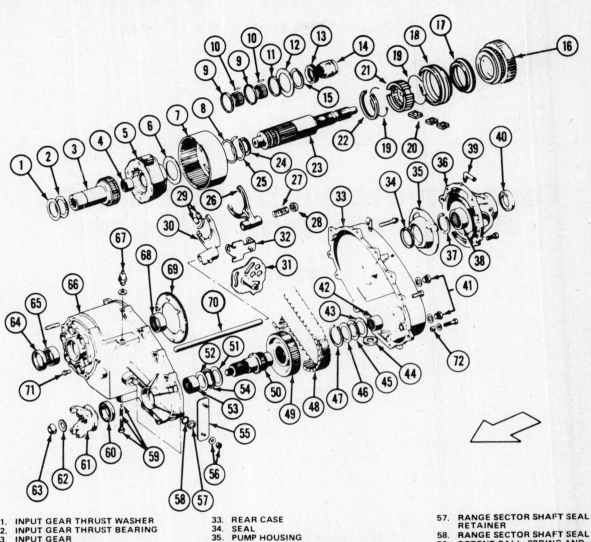

Fig. 16 Exploded view of New Process model 208 transfer case

1. INPUT GEAR THRUST WASHER
2. INPUT GEAR THRUST BEARING
3. INPUT GEAR
4. MAINSHAFT PILOT BEARING
5. PLANETARY ASSEMBLY
6. PLANETARY THRUST WASHER
7. ANNULUS GEAR
8. ANNULUS GEAR THRUST WASHER
9. NEEDLE BEARING SPACERS
10. MAINSHAFT NEEDLE BEARINGS (120)
11. NEEDLE BEARING SPACER
12. SPACER WASHER
13. OIL PUMP GEAR
14. SPEEDOMETER GEAR
15. DRIVE SPROCKET SNAP RING
16. DRIVE SPROCKET
17. BLOCKER RING
18. SYNCHRONIZER SLEEVE
19. SYNCHRONIZER SPRING
20. SYNCHRONIZER KEY
21. SYNCHRONIZER HUB
22. SYNCHRONIZER HUB SNAP RING
23. MAINSHAFT
24. MAINSHAFT THRUST BEARING
25. INTERNAL GEAR SNAP RING
26. MODE FORK
27. SPRING
28. SPRING RETAINER
29. RANGE FORK PADS
30. RANGE FORK
31. RANGE SECTOR
32. MODE FORK BRACKET

33. REAR CASE
34. SEAL
35. PUMP HOUSING
36. REAR RETAINER
37. BEARING SNAP RING
38. REAR OUTPUT BEARING
39. VENT TUBE
40. REAR SEAL
41. DRAIN AND FILL PLUGS
42. FRONT OUTPUT SHAFT REAR BEARING
43. FRONT OUTPUT SHAFT REAR THRUST BEARING RACE (THICK)
44. CASE MAGNET
45. FRONT OUTPUT SHAFT REAR THRUST BEARING
46. FRONT OUTPUT SHAFT REAR THRUST BEARING RACE (THIN)
47. DRIVEN SPROCKET RETAINING RING
48. DRIVE CHAIN
49. DRIVEN SPROCKET
50. FRONT OUTPUT SHAFT
51. FRONT OUTPUT SHAFT FRONT THRUST BEARING RACE (THIN)
52. FRONT OUTPUT SHAFT FRONT THRUST BEARING RACE (THICK)
53. FRONT OUTPUT SHAFT FRONT BEARING
54. FRONT OUTPUT SHAFT FRONT THRUST BEARING
55. OPERATING LEVER
56. WASHER AND LOCKNUT

57. RANGE SECTOR SHAFT SEAL RETAINER
58. RANGE SECTOR SHAFT SEAL
59. DETENT BALL, SPRING AND RETAINER BOLT
60. FRONT SEAL
61. FRONT YOKE
62. YOKE SEAL WASHER
63. YOKE NUT
64. INPUT GEAR OIL SEAL
65. INPUT GEAR FRONT BEARING
66. FRONT CASE
67. LOCK MODE INDICATOR SWITCH AND WASHER
68. INPUT GEAR REAR BEARING
69. LOCKPLATE
70. SHIFTER FORK SHAFT
71. LOCKPLATE BOLTS
72. CASE ALIGNMENT DOWELS

AUTOMATIC TRANSMISSIONS

TABLE OF CONTENTS

Turbo Hydra-Matic 200 & 200C Automatic Transmission

INDEX

DESCRIPTION

The Turbo Hydra-Matic 200 transmission, **Fig. 1,** is fully automatic and consists of a three element torque converter and a compound planetary gear set. Three multiple disc clutches, a roller clutch and a band provide the required friction elements to obtain the desired function of the planetary gear set.

The Turbo Hydra-Matic 200C incorporates a converter clutch assembly consisting of a three element torque converter, and a converter clutch, **Fig. 2.** The converter clutch is splined to the turbine assembly and when operated, applies against the converter cover providing a mechanical direct drive coupling of the engine to the planetary gears. When the converter clutch is released, the assembly operates as a normal torque converter. The converter clutch is applied only when transmission is in third gear, vehicle speed is above 30 mph, engine coolant temperature is above 130° F, engine vacuum is above 3 in. Hg. and brake pedal is released.

TROUBLESHOOTING GUIDE

NO DRIVE IN DRIVE RANGE

1. Low oil level.
2. Manual linkage maladjusted.
3. Low oil pressure due to:
   a. Restricted or plugged oil screen.
   b. Oil screen gasket improperly installed.
   c. Oil pump pressure regulator.
   d. Pump drive gear tangs damaged by converter.
   e. Case porosity in intake bore.
4. Forward clutch malfunctioning due to:
   a. Forward clutch not applying due to cracked piston, damaged or missing seals, burned clutch plates, snap ring not in groove.
   b. Forward clutch seal rings damaged or missing on turbine shaft, leaking feed circuits due to damaged or mispositioned gasket.
   c. Clutch housing check ball stuck or missing.
   d. Cup plug leaking or missing from rear of turbine shaft in clutch apply passage.
   e. Incorrect forward clutch piston assembly or incorrect number of clutch plates.
5. Roller clutch malfunctioning due to missing rollers or springs or possibly galled rollers.

OIL PRESSURE HIGH OR LOW

1. Throttle valve cable maladjusted, binding, disconnected or broken.
2. Throttle lever and bracket improperly installed, disconnected or binding.
3. Throttle valve shift valve, throttle valve or plunger binding.
4. Pressure regulator valve and spring malfunctioning due to:
   a. Binding valve.
   b. Incorrect spring.
   c. Oil pressure control orifice in pump cover plugged, causing high oil pressure.

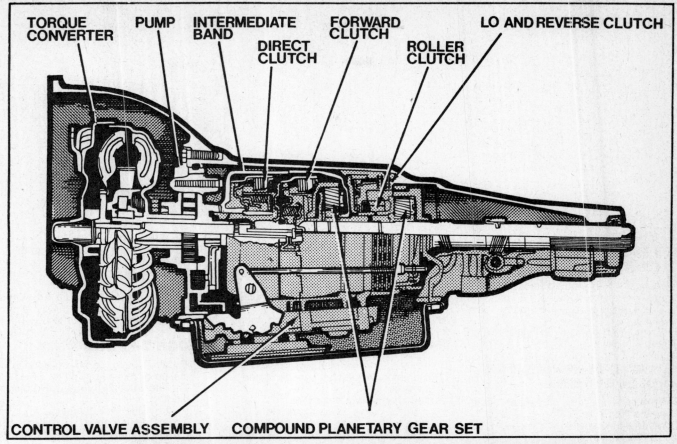

TORQUE CONVERTER — PUMP — INTERMEDIATE BAND — DIRECT CLUTCH — FORWARD CLUTCH — ROLLER CLUTCH — LO AND REVERSE CLUTCH

CONTROL VALVE ASSEMBLY — COMPOUND PLANETARY GEAR SET

Fig. 1 Sectional view of Turbo Hydra-Matic 200 & 200C automatic transmission

d. Pressure regulator bore plug leaking.
5. Manual valve disconnected.
6. Intermediate boost valve binding, causing oil pressures to be incorrect in 2nd and low ranges.
7. Orifice in spacer plate at end of intermediate boost valve plugged.
8. Reserve boost valve binding, causing pressure to be incorrect in reverse only.
9. Orifice in spacer plate at end of reverse boost valve plugged.

1–2 SHIFT AT FULL THROTTLE ONLY

1. Throttle valve cable maladjusted, binding, disconnected or broken.
2. Throttle lever and bracket assembly binding or disconnected.
3. Throttle valve exhaust ball lifter or number 5 check ball binding, mispositioned or disconnected.

NOTE: If number 5 ball is fully seated, it will cause full throttle valve pressure regardless of throttle valve position.

4. Throttle valve and plunger binding.
5. Valve body gaskets leaking, damaged or incorrectly installed.
6. Porous control valve assembly.

FIRST SPEED ONLY, NO 1–2 SHIFT

1. Due to governor and governor feed passages:
   a. Plugged governor oil feed orifice in spacer plate.
   b. Plugged orifice in spacer plate that feeds governor oil to the shift valves.
   c. Balls missing in governor assembly.
   d. Governor cover O-ring missing or leaking. If governor cover O-ring leaks, an external oil leak will be present and there will be no upshift.
   e. Governor shaft seal missing or damaged.
   f. Governor driven gear stripped.
   g. Governor weights binding.
   h. Governor assembly missing.
2. Control valve assembly 1–2 shift valve or 1–2 throttle valve stuck in downshift position.
3. Porosity in case channels or undrilled 2nd speed feed holes.
4. Excessive leakage between case bore and intermediate band apply ring.
5. Intermediate band anchor pin missing or disconnected from band.
6. Missing or broken intermediate band.
7. Due to intermediate servo assembly:
   a. Servo to cover oil seal ring damage or missing.
   b. Porous servo cover or piston.
   c. Incorrect intermediate band apply pin.
   d. Incorrect cover and piston.

1ST & 2ND ONLY, NO 2–3 SHIFT

1. 2–3 shift valve or 2–3 throttle valve stuck in downshift position.
2. Direct clutch feed orifice in spacer plate plugged.
3. Valve body gaskets leaking, damaged or incorrectly installed.
4. Porosity between case passages.
5. Pump passages plugged or leaking.
6. Pump gasket incorrectly installed.
7. Rear seal on pump cover leaking or missing.
8. Direct clutch oil seals missing or damaged.
9. Direct clutch piston or housing cracked.
10. Direct clutch plates damaged or missing.
11. Direct clutch backing plate snap ring out of groove.
12. Intermediate servo to case oil seal broken or missing on intermediate servo piston.
13. Intermediate servo exhaust hole in case between servo piston seals plugged or undrilled.

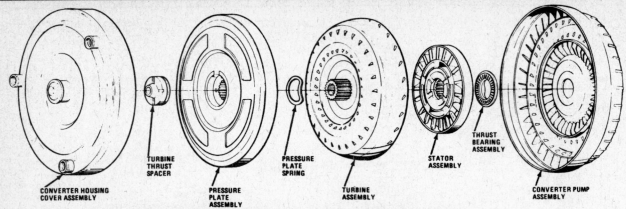

CONVERTER HOUSING COVER ASSEMBLY — **TURBINE THRUST SPACER** — **PRESSURE PLATE ASSEMBLY** — **PRESSURE PLATE SPRING** — **TURBINE ASSEMBLY** — **STATOR ASSEMBLY** — **THRUST BEARING ASSEMBLY** — **CONVERTER PUMP ASSEMBLY**

Fig. 2   Torque converter clutch. 200C transmission

MOVES FORWARD IN NEUTRAL

1. Manual linkage maladjusted.
2. Forward clutch does not release.
3. Cross leakage between pump passages.
4. Cross leakage to forward clutch through clutch passages.

NO DRIVE IN REVERSE OR SLIPS IN REVERSE

1. Throttle valve cable binding or maladjusted.
2. Manual linkage maladjusted.
3. Throttle valve binding.
4. Reverse boost valve binding in bore.
5. Low overrun clutch valve binding in bore.
6. Reverse clutch piston cracked, broken or has missing seals.
7. Reverse clutch plates burned.
8. Reverse clutch has incorrect selective spacer ring.
9. Porosity in passages to direct clutch.
10. Pump to case gasket improperly installed or missing.
11. Pump passages cross leaking or restricted.
12. Pump cover seals damaged or missing.
13. Direct clutch piston or housing cracked.
14. Direct clutch piston seals cut or missing.
15. Direct clutch housing ball check, stuck, leaking or missing.
16. Direct clutch plates burned.
17. Incorrect direct clutch piston.
18. Direct clutch orifices plugged in spacer plate.
19. Intermediate servo to case seal cut or missing.

SLIPS 1—2 SHIFT

1. Aerated oil due to low level.
2. 2nd speed feed orifice in spacer plate partially blocked.
3. Improperly installed or missing spacer plate gasket.
4. 1—2 accumulator valve stuck, causing low 1—2 accumulator pressure.

5. Weak or missing 1—2 accumulator valve spring.
6. 1—2 accumulator piston seal leaking or spring missing or broken.
7. Leakage between 1—2 accumulator piston and pin.
8. Incorrect intermediate band apply pin.
9. Excessive leakage between intermediate band apply pin and case.
10. Porous intermediate servo piston.
11. Servo cover to servo seal damaged or missing.
12. Incorrect servo and cover.
13. Throttle valve cable improperly adjusted.
14. Shift throttle valve or throttle valve binding.
15. Intermediate band worn or burned.
16. Case porosity in 2nd clutch passages.

ROUGH 1—2 SHIFT

1. Throttle valve cable improperly adjusted or binding.
2. Throttle valve or plunger binding.
3. Shift throttle or 1—2 accumulator valve binding.
4. Incorrect intermediate servo pin.
5. Intermediate servo piston to case seal damaged or missing.
6. 1—2 accumulator oil ring damaged piston stuck, bore damaged or spring broken or missing.

SLIPS 2—3 SHIFT

1. Low oil level.
2. Throttle valve cable improperly adjusted.
3. Throttle valve binding.
4. Direct clutch orifice in spacer plate partially blocked.
5. Spacer plate gaskets improperly installed or missing.
6. Intermediate servo to case seal damaged.
7. Porous direct clutch feed passages in case.
8. Pump to case gasket improperly installed or missing.
9. Pump passages cross feeding, leaking or restricted.

10. Pump cover oil seal rings damaged or missing.
11. Direct clutch piston or housing cracked.
12. Direct clutch piston seals cut or missing.
13. Direct clutch plates burned.

ROUGH 2—3 SHIFT

1. Throttle valve cable improperly installed or missing.
2. Throttle valve or throttle valve plunger binding.
3. Shift throttle valve binding.
4. Intermediate servo exhaust hole undrilled or plugged between intermediate servo piston seals.
5. Direct clutch exhaust valve number 4 check ball missing or improperly installed.

NO ENGINE BRAKING IN 2ND SPEED

1. Intermediate boost valve binding in valve body.
2. Intermediate-Reverse number 3 check ball improperly installed or missing.
3. Shift throttle valve number 3 check ball improperly installed or missing.
4. Intermediate servo to cover seal missing or damaged.
5. Intermediate band off anchor pin, broken or burned.

NO ENGINE BRAKING IN 1ST SPEED

1. Low overrun clutch valve binding in valve body.

NOTE: The following conditions will also cause no reverse.

2. Low-reverse clutch piston seals broken or missing.
3. Porosity in low-reverse piston or housing.
4. Low-reverse clutch housing snap ring out of case.
5. Cup plug or rubber seal missing or damaged between case and low-

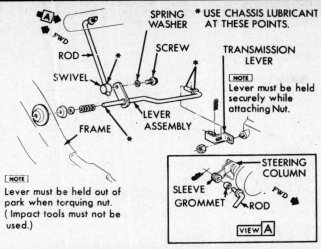

SPRING WASHER
* USE CHASSIS LUBRICANT AT THESE POINTS.
ROD
SCREW
SWIVEL
TRANSMISSION LEVER
NOTE
Lever must be held securely while attaching Nut.
LEVER ASSEMBLY
FRAME

NOTE
Lever must be held out of park when torquing nut. (Impact tools must not be used.)

STEERING COLUMN
SLEEVE
GROMMET
ROD
FWD
VIEW A

Fig. 3 Shift linkage adjustment. Except S-10 & S-15 models

reverse clutch housing.

NO PART THROTTLE DOWNSHIFT

1. Throttle plunger bushing passages obstructed.
2. 2–3 throttle valve bushing passages obstructed.
3. Valve body gaskets improperly installed or damaged.
4. Spacer plate hole obstructed or undrilled.
5. Throttle valve cable maladjusted.
6. Throttle valve or shift throttle valve binding.

LOW OR HIGH SHIFT POINTS

1. Throttle valve cable binding or disconnected.
2. Throttle valve or shift throttle valve binding.
3. Number 1 throttle shift check ball improperly installed or missing.
4. Throttle valve plunger, 1–2 or 2–3 throttle valves binding.
5. Valve body gaskets improperly installed or missing.
6. Pressure regulator valve binding.
7. Throttle valve exhaust number 5 check ball and lifter, improperly installed, disconnected or missing.
8. Throttle lever binding, disconnected or loose at valve body mounting bolt or not positioned at the throttle valve plunger bushing pin locator.
9. Governor shaft to cover seal broken or missing.
10. Governor cover O-rings broken or missing.

NOTE: Outer ring will leak externally and the inner ring will leak internally.

11. Case porosity.

WILL NOT HOLD IN PARK

1. Manual linkage maladjusted.

2. Parking pawl binding in case.
3. Actuator rod or plunger damaged.
4. Parking pawl damaged.
5. Parking bracket loose or damaged.
6. Detent lever nut loose.
7. Detent lever hole worn or damaged.
8. Detent roller to valve body bolt loose.
9. Detent roller or pin damaged, incorrectly installed or missing.

CONVERTER CLUTCH APPLIED IN ALL RANGES, ENGINE STALLS WHEN TRANSMISSION IS PUT IN GEAR (T.H.M. 200C)

1. Converter clutch valve in pump sticking in apply position.

CONVERTER CLUTCH APPLIES ERRATICALLY (T.H.M. 200C)

1. Vacuum switch malfunction.
2. Release orifice at pump blocked or restricted.
3. Damaged turbine shaft O-ring.
4. Converter malfunctioning, clutch pressure plate warped.
5. O-ring damaged at solenoid.
6. Solenoid bolts loose.

CONVERTER CLUTCH APPLIES AT A VERY LOW OR HIGH 3RD SPEED GEAR (T.H.M. 200C)

1. Governor switch malfunction.
2. Governor malfunction.
3. High line pressure.
4. Converter clutch valve sticking or binding.
5. Solenoid inoperative or shorted to case.

MAINTENANCE

To check fluid, drive vehicle for at least

15 minutes to bring fluid to operating temperature (200° F). With vehicle on a level surface, engine idling in Park and parking brake applied, the level on the dipstick should be at the "F" mark. To bring the fluid level from the ADD mark to the FULL mark requires 1 pint of fluid. If vehicle cannot be driven sufficiently to bring fluid to operating temperature, the level on the dipstick should be between the two dimples on the dipstick with fluid temperature at 70° F.

If additional fluid is required, use only Dexron or Dexron II automatic transmission fluid.

NOTE: An early change to a darker color from the usual red color and or a strong odor that is usually associated with overheated fluid is normal and should not be considered as a positive sign of required maintenance or unit failure.

CAUTION: When adding fluid, do not over-fill, as foaming and loss of fluid through the vent may occur as the fluid heats up. Also, if fluid level is too low, complete loss of drive may occur especially when cold, which can cause transmission failure.

Every 100,000 miles, the oil should be drained, the oil pan removed, the screen cleaned and fresh fluid added. For vehicles subjected to more severe use such as heavy city traffic especially in hot weather, prolonged periods of idling or towing, this maintenance should be performed every 15,000 miles.

DRAINING BOTTOM PAN

1. Remove front and side oil pan attaching bolts, then loosen the rear oil pan attaching bolts.
2. Carefully pry oil pan loose and allow fluid to drain into a suitable container.
3. Remove the oil pan and gasket, then remove the screen attaching bolts and remove screen.
4. Thoroughly clean oil screen and oil pan with solvent.
5. Install oil screen using a new gasket and torque attaching bolts to 6–10 ft. lbs., then install oil pan using a new gasket and torque attaching bolts to 10–13 bolts.
6. Add 3½ quarts of fluid, then with engine idling and parking brake applied, move selector lever through each range and return selector lever to PARK.
7. Check fluid level and add fluid as required to bring level between the two dimples on the dipstick.

ADDING FLUID TO DRY TRANSMISSION AND CONVERTER

1. Add 5 quarts of fluid on 1979–85 vehicles.
2. With transmission in PARK and parking brake applied, start the engine and

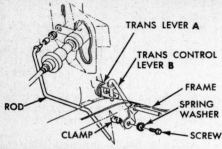

Fig. 4 Shift linkage adjustment. S-10 & S-15 models

place carburetor on fast idle cam.
3. Move shifter lever through each range, then with transmission in PARK, add additional fluid as required to bring the level between the two dimples on the dipstick.

IN-VEHICLE ADJUSTMENTS

SHIFT LINKAGE, ADJUST

Except S-10 & S-15 Models
1. Position shift lever assembly into Neutral.
2. Insert pin and lock nut onto fork with shift lever in Neutral, **Fig. 3**.
3. Move rod until rod hole aligns with shifter assembly pin and install rod onto pin.
4. Install washer and retaining clip.

S-10 & S-15 Models
1. Position the steering column shift lever in neutral gate notch.
2. Set transmission lever (A) in neutral detent, **Fig. 4**.
3. Assemble clamp spring washer and screw to transmission control lever (B) and control rod, **Fig. 4**.
4. Hold clamp flush against transmission control lever (B) and finger tighten clamping screw against rod. No force should be exerted in either direction on the rod or transmission control lever (B) while tightening the clamping screw.
5. Tighten screw securely.

T.V. CABLE, ADJUST

Gasoline Engine
1. Depress and hold metal readjust tab. Move slider back through fitting in direction away from throttle body until slider stops against fitting, **Fig. 5**.
2. Release metal readjust tab.
3. Open carburetor lever to "full throttle stop" position to automatically adjust cable and release carburetor lever.
4. Check cable for proper operation. If sticking or binding occurs, proceed with the following:
   a. Remove the oil pan and inspect the throttle lever and bracket assembly.

NOTE: Check that the T.V. exhaust valve

lifter rod is not distorted and not binding in the control valve assembly or spacer plate.
   b. T.V. exhaust check ball must move up and down as the lifter does. Also ensure lifter spring holds the lifter rod up against the bottom of the control valve assembly.
   c. Make sure T.V. plunger is not stuck. Inspect transmission for correct throttle lever to cable link, **Fig. 6**.

Diesel Engine
1. On vehicles equipped with cruise control, remove cruise control rod.
2. Disconnect T.V. cable from throttle assembly, then loosen lock nut on pump rod and shorten several turns.
3. Rotate lever assembly to full throttle stop and hold in this position.
4. Adjust pump rod until injection pump lever contacts full throttle stop.
5. Release the lever assembly and tighten pump rod lock nut, then remove pump rod from the lever assembly.
6. Reconnect T.V. cable to throttle assembly, then depress and hold metal readjust tab. Move slider back through fitting in direction away from lever assembly until slider stops against fitting.
7. Release the readjust tab, then rotate lever assembly to full throttle stop and release the lever.
8. Reconnect pump rod and, if equipped, the cruise control throttle rod.
9. On vehicles equipped with cruise control, adjust the servo throttle rod to minimum slack position, then install clip into the servo bail in first free hole closest to the bellcrank.

IN-VEHICLE REPAIRS

VALVE BODY ASSEMBLY
1. Drain transmission fluid, then remove oil pan and screen.
2. Remove detent cable retaining bolt and disconnect cable.
3. Remove throttle lever and bracket assembly. Use care to avoid bending throttle lever link.
4. Remove detent roller and spring assembly.
5. Support valve body and remove retaining bolts, then while holding manual valve, remove valve assembly, spacer plate and gaskets as an assembly to prevent dropping the five check balls.

NOTE: After removing valve body assembly, the intermediate band anchor pin, and reverse cup plug may be removed.

6. To install, control valve reverse removal procedure and torque all valve body bolts to 8 ft. lbs.

CAUTION: Ensure that intermediate band anchor pin is located on intermediate band

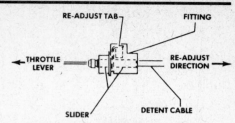

Fig. 5 T.V. cable adjustment

prior to installation of valve body, as damage to transmission may result.

GOVERNOR
1. Disconnect battery ground cable and remove air cleaner.
2. If necessary, on vehicles with air conditioning, remove the five heater core cover screws, then disconnect the electrical connectors and position heater core aside.
3. Disconnect exhaust pipe and allow to hang down.
4. Support transmission, then remove transmission rear support bolts and propeller shaft and lower transmission until enough clearance is obtained to remove governor.
5. Remove governor retainer ring and cover, then remove governor and washer.

NOTE: If governor to case washer falls into transmission, use a small magnet to remove it. If it cannot be easily removed, replace the washer with a new one.

6. To install governor, reverse removal procedure.

CAUTION: Do not attempt to hammer governor assembly into case, as damage to governor, case or cover may result.

PRESSURE REGULATOR VALVE
1. Drain transmission fluid, then remove oil pan and screen.
2. Using a small screwdriver or tool J-24684, **Fig. 7**, compress regulator spring.
3. Remove retaining ring and slowly release spring tension.
4. Remove pressure regulator bore plug, valve, spring and guide.
5. To assemble, install pressure regulator spring, guide and valve with stem end first and bore plug with hole side out.
6. Using a small screwdriver or tool J-24684, **Fig. 7**, compress regulator spring and install retaining ring.

TRANSMISSION
REPLACE

EXCEPT S-10 & S-15
1. Disconnect battery ground cable and

Fig. 6 Throttle lever to cable link

Fig. 7 Removing or installing pressure regulator

detent cable from bracket and carburetor.

2. On models equipped with air conditioning, remove heater core cover from heater assembly.
3. Raise and support vehicle, then disconnect drive shaft from transmission.
4. Disconnect speedometer cable from transmission.
5. Disconnect and cap fluid lines from transmission.
6. Disconnect shift control linkage from transmission.
7. Position a suitable jack under transmission, then remove rear transmission support bolts.
8. Remove nuts attaching catalytic converter to rear support.
9. Disconnect exhaust pipe from exhaust manifold, then remove exhaust pipe, catalytic converter and bracket as an assembly.
10. Remove torque converter cover bolts, then the cover.
11. Remove torque converter to flexplate attaching bolts.
12. Lower transmission slightly, then remove transmission to engine mounting bolts.
13. Raise transmission to original position and place a suitable jack under engine.
14. Remove transmission from vehicle.
15. Reverse procedure to install.

S-10 & S-15 MODELS

1. Open hood and place fender covers on both fenders.

2. Remove air cleaner assembly.
3. Disconnect T.V. cable at its upper end.
4. On vehicles equipped with 4-119 engine, remove starter motor upper retaining nut.
5. Raise and support vehicle.
6. Remove propeller shaft.
7. Disconnect speedometer cable at the transmission.
8. Disconnect shift linkage at transmission.
9. Disconnect all electrical leads at the transmission and any clips that retain the leads to the transmission case.
10. If equipped, remove transmission support brace attaching bolts at converter cover.
11. Remove converter cover and mark flywheel and torque converter to maintain original balance.
12. Remove exhaust crossover pipe and catalytic converter attaching bolts and remove as an assembly from vehicle.
13. Remove torque converter cover, then mark relationship between flywheel and torque converter for reference during installation.
14. Remove torque converter to flywheel bolts and/or nuts.
15. Disconnect the catalytic converter support bracket.
16. Position a transmission jack under the transmission and raise the transmission slightly.
17. Remove transmission support to transmission mount bolt and transmission support to frame bolts (and insulators if used).

18. Slide the transmission support rearward.
19. Lower the transmission to gain access to the oil cooler lines and T.V. cable attachments.
20. Disconnect the oil cooler lines and T.V. cable. Cap all openings.
21. Support engine with a suitable tool and remove the transmission to the engine bolts.
22. Disconnect the transmission assembly, being careful not to damage any cables, lines or linkage.
23. Install torque converter holding tool J-21366 and remove the transmission assembly from the vehicle.
24. To install, reverse the removal procedure, and note the following:
   a. Before installing the flex plate to converter bolts, make certain that the weld nuts on the converter are flush with the flex plate and the converter rotates freely by hand in this position.
   b. Hand start the bolts and tighten finger tight, then torque to 35 ft. lbs. This will ensure proper converter alignment. Install new oil filler tube before installing tube.

Turbo Hydra-Matic 200-4R Automatic Transmission

INDEX

DESCRIPTION

This transmission is a fully automatic unit consisting primarily of a three-element hydraulic torque converter with a converter clutch, a compound planetary gear set and an overdrive unit, **Fig. 1.** Five multiple-disc clutches and a band provide the friction elements required to obtain the desired function of the compound planetary gear set and the overdrive unit.

The torque converter couples the engine to the overdrive unit and planetary gears through oil and provides torque multiplication. The combination of the compound planetary gear set and the overdrive unit provides four forward ratios and one reverse. Fully automatic changing of the gear ratios is determined by vehicle speed and engine torque.

The hydraulic system in this transmission is pressurized by a variable capacity vane type pump to provide the working pressure required to operate the friction elements and automatic controls.

TROUBLESHOOTING

NO DRIVE

1. Low fluid level.
2. Manual linkage maladjusted.
3. Low fluid pressure.
   a. Plugged or restricted oil filter.
   b. Cut or missing oil filter O-ring seals.
   c. Faulty pressure regulator valve.
   d. Damaged pump rotor tangs.
   e. Porosity in oil filter to pump intake bore.
4. Springs missing in overdrive unit roller clutch.
5. Overdrive unit roller galled or missing.
6. Forward clutch.

a. Forward clutch does not apply—piston cracked, seals missing, damaged; clutch plates burned; snap ring out of groove.
b. Missing or damaged forward clutch oil seal rings; leak in feed circuits; pump to case gasket improperly positioned or damaged.
c. Stuck or missing clutch housing ball check.
d. Cup plug leaking or missing in the rear of the forward clutch shaft in the clutch apply passage.
7. Lo and reverse roller clutch springs missing.
8. Lo and reverse roller clutch rollers galled or missing.

HIGH OR LOW OIL PRESSURE

1. Throttle valve cable misadjusted, binding, unhooked, broken, or wrong link.
2. Damaged or leaking throttle valve assembly.
   a. Throttle lever and bracket assembly binding, unhooked or improperly positioned.
   b. Binding throttle valve or plunger valve.
3. Pressure regulator valve binding.
4. Throttle valve boost valve.
   a. Valve binding.
   b. Wrong valve (causing low oil pressure only)
5. Reverse boost valve binding.
6. Manual valve unhooked or improperly positioned.
7. Pressure relief valve ball missing or spring damaged.
8. Pump.
   a. Slide stuck.
   b. Slide seal damaged or missing.
   c. Decrease air bleed orifice missing or damaged causing high oil pressure.

sure.
d. Decrease air bleed orifice plugged causing low oil pressure.
9. Throttle valve limit valve binding.
10. Line bias valve binding in open position causing high oil pressure.
11. Line bias valve binding in closed position causing high oil pressure.
12. Incorrect orifices or passages in control valve assembly spacer plate or case.

1-2 SHIFT ONLY AT FULL THROTTLE

1. Throttle valve cable binding, unhooked, broken, or improperly adjusted.
2. Throttle lever and bracket assembly binding or unhooked.
3. Throttle valve exhaust ball lifter or #5 ball binding, improperly positioned, or unhooked.
4. #5 ball sealed causing full throttle valve pressure regardless of throttle valve position.
5. Throttle valve and plunger binding.
6. Control valve body gaskets leaking, damaged, or incorrectly installed.
7. Porous case assembly.

NO 1-2 SHIFT

1. Governor and governor feed passages.
   a. Plugged governor oil feed orifice in spacer plate.
   b. Governor balls missing in governor assembly.
   c. Missing or leaking inner governor assembly.
   d. Governor shaft seal missing or damaged.
   e. Stripped governor driven gear.
   f. Governor weights binding on pin.
   g. Governor driven gear not engaged with governor shaft.

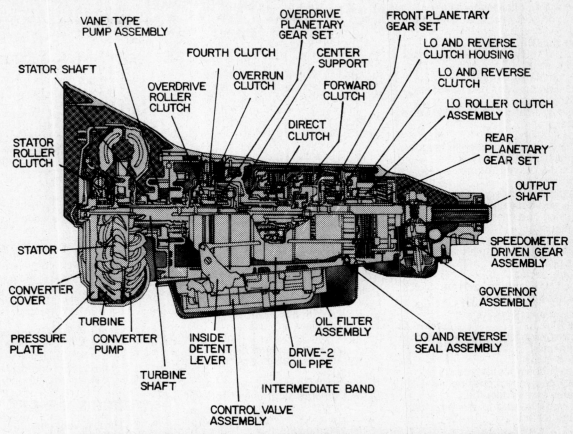

Fig. 1 Sectional view of Turbo Hydra-Matic 200-4R automatic transmission

2. Control valve assembly.
   a. 1-2 shift, Lo 1st/Detent, or 1-2 throttle valve stuck in downshift position.
   b. Spacer plate gaskets improperly positioned.
3. Case
   a. Case channels porous or 2nd oil feed hole undrilled.
   b. Excessive leakage between case bore and intermediate band apply rings.
   c. Intermediate band anchor pin missing or unhooked from band.
   d. Broken or missing band.
4. Intermediate servo assembly.
   a. Missing servo cover oil seal.
   b. Porosity in serve; cover, inner piston, or outer piston.
   c. Incorrect intermediate band apply pin.
   d. Incorrect usage of cover and piston.
5. 1-2 accumulator.
   a. Loose 1-2 accumulator housing bolts.
   b. Damaged 1-2 accumulator housing face.

c. Missing or damaged accumulator plate.

NO 2-3 SHIFT

1. Control valve assembly and spacer plate.
   a. 2-3 shift valve or 2-3 throttle valve stuck in the downshift position.
   b. Leaking, damaged or incorrectly installed valve body gaskets.
   c. Reverse/3rd check ball not seating, damaged or missing.
2. Case channels porous.
3. Center support.
   a. Plugged or undrilled center support.
   b. Damaged steel oil seal rings on center support.
4. Direct clutch.
   a. Inner oil seal ring on piston damaged or missing.
   b. Center oil seal ring on direct clutch hub damaged or missing.
   c. Check ball and/or retainer damaged or missing from direct clutch piston.
   d. Damaged or missing direct clutch

piston or housing.
   e. Damaged or missing direct clutch plates.
   f. Direct clutch backing plate snap ring not in groove.
   g. Release spring guide improperly located, preventing piston check ball from seating in retainer.
5. Intermediate servo assembly (third clutch accumulator oil passages).
   a. Broken or missing servo to case oil seal ring on intermediate servo piston.
   b. Intermediate servo and/or capsule missing or damaged.
   c. Plugged or undrilled exhaust hole in case between servo piston seal rings.
   d. Bleed orifice cup plug missing from intermediate servo pocket in case.

NO MOVEMENT IN R OR SLIPS IN R

1. Binding or improperly adjusted throttle valve cable.
2. Improperly adjusted manual linkage.

3. Binding throttle valve.
4. Throttle valve limit valve binding.
5. Binding line bias valve.
6. Reverse boost valve binding in pressure regulator bore.
7. Reverse/3rd or Lo/Reverse check ball missing or seat in spacer plate damaged.
8. Reverse clutch.
   a. Cracked piston, or missing inner or outer seals.
   b. Clutch plates burned.
   c. Missing or damaged reverse oil seal in case.
   d. Missing clutch plate or valve plate.
9. Center support.
   a. Loose or missing center support attaching bolts.
   b. Blocked or undrilled passages.
   c. Porosity.
10. Direct clutch housing.
    a. Cracked housing or piston.
    b. Missing or damaged inner or outer piston seal.
    c. Missing or damaged check ball in either the direct clutch housing or the piston.
    d. Plates burned.
11. Plugged Lo/Reverse overrun clutch orifice in spacer plate.

DRIVE IN NEUTRAL

1. Manual linkage improperly adjusted or disconnected.
2. Forward clutch.
   a. Clutch does not release.
   b. Sticking exhaust check ball.
   c. Plates burned together.
3. Case cross leaking to forward clutch passage (D4).

SLIPPING 1-2 SHIFT

1. Low fluid level.
2. Spacer plate gaskets damaged or incorrectly installed.
3. Accumulator valve.
   a. Valve sticking in valve body causing low 1-2 accumulator pressure.
   b. Weak or missing spring.
4. 1-2 accumulator piston.
   a. Leaking seal, broken or missing spring.
   b. Leak between piston and pin.
   c. Binding 1-2 accumulator piston.
   d. Damaged 1-2 accumulator piston bore.
5. Intermediate band apply pin.
   a. Incorrect selection of apply pin.
   b. Excessive leakage between apply pin and case.
   c. Apply pin feed hole not completely drilled.
6. Intermediate servo assembly.
   a. Porosity in piston.
   b. Damaged or missing cover to servo oil seal ring.
   c. Leak between servo apply pin and case.
7. Improperly adjusted throttle valve cable.
8. Throttle valve binding, causing low throttle valve pressure.
9. Binding throttle valve limit valve.

10. Line bias valve sticking, causing low line pressure.
11. Worn or burned intermediate band.
12. Case porosity in 2nd clutch passage.

ROUGH 1-2 SHIFT

1. Throttle valve cable binding or improperly adjusted.
2. Binding throttle valve to throttle valve plunger.
3. Binding throttle valve limit valve.
4. Binding accumulator valve.
5. Binding line bias valve.
6. Intermediate servo assembly.
   a. Incorrect selection apply pin.
   b. Damaged or missing servo piston to case oil seal ring.
   c. Bleed cup plug missing in case.
7. 1-2 accumulator.
   a. Oil ring damaged.
   b. Piston stuck.
   c. Broken or missing spring.
   d. Damaged bore.
8. 1-2 shift check ball #8 missing or sticking.

SLIPPING 2-3 SHIFT

1. Low fluid level.
2. Improperly adjusted throttle valve cable.
3. Binding throttle valve.
4. Spacer plate and gaskets.
   a. Direct clutch orifice partially blocked in spacer plate.
   b. Gaskets out of position or damaged.
5. Intermediate servo assembly.
   a. Damaged or missing servo to case oil seal ring.
   b. Damaged piston or servo bore.
   c. Intermediate servo orifice bleed cup plug in case missing.
   d. Case porous in the servo bore area.
6. Direct clutch feed.
   a. Direct clutch feed channels porous.
   b. Loose case to support bolts causing leakage.
   c. Cracked direct clutch piston or housing.
   d. Cut or missing piston seals.
   e. Burned direct clutch plates.
   f. Check ball in piston and/or housing missing, damaged, or leaking.
   g. Check ball capsule damaged.
   h. Release spring guide improperly located preventing check ball from seating in piston.
7. Center support.
   a. Channels cross feeding, leaking, or restricted.
   b. Damaged or missing oil seal rings.

ROUGH 2-3 SHIFT

1. Missing or improperly positioned throttle valve cable.
2. Throttle valve and plunger.
   a. Throttle valve plunger binding.
   b. Throttle valve binding.
3. Throttle valve limit valve binding.
4. Intermediate servo assembly exhaust

hole undrilled or plugged between intermediate servo piston seals, preventing intermediate servo piston from completing its stroke.
5. 3-2 exhaust check ball #4 missing or improperly positioned.
6. 3rd accumulator check ball #2 missing or improperly positioned.

SLIPPING 3-4 SHIFT

1. Low fluid level.
2. Control valve assembly and spacer plate.
   a. Gaskets of space plate damaged or incorrectly installed.
   b. Accumulator valve sticking causing low 3-4 accumulator pressure.
   c. Weak or missing accumulator valve spring.
3. 3-4 accumulator.
   a. Piston stuck.
   b. Damaged bore or oil ring.
4. Center support porosity.
5. Loose center support attaching bolts.
6. Fourth clutch piston surface or seals damaged.
7. Improper clutch plate usage.
8. Burned fourth clutch plate.
9. Case.
   a. Porosity.
   b. 1-2 accumulator housing bolts loose.
   c. 3-4 accumulator piston seal damaged.
   d. 3-4 accumulator leaking between the piston and pin.
   e. 3-4 accumulator bore damaged.

ROUGH 3-4 SHIFT

1. Throttle valve cable improperly positioned or missing.
2. Throttle valve and plunger.
   a. Throttle valve plunger binding.
   b. Throttle valve binding.
3. Throttle valve limit valve binding.
4. 3-4 accumulator.
   a. Piston stuck.
   b. Bore damaged.
5. Fourth clutch piston binding.

NO CONVERTER CLUTCH APPLICATION

1. Electrical problem.
   a. 12 volts not being supplied to clutch solenoid.
   b. Defective solenoid.
   c. Damaged electrical connector.
   d. Defective pressure switch.
   e. Wire grounded.
2. Converter clutch shift valve or throttle valve stuck.
3. Pump Assembly.
   a. Plugged converter signal oil orifice in pump.
   b. Damaged or missing solenoid O-ring.
   c. Orificed cup plug missing in oil cooler passage in pump.
   d. Damaged or improperly positioned pump to case gasket.
   e. Converter clutch application valve stuck.

f. Cup plug missing from application passage.

ROUGH CONVERTER CLUTCH APPLICATION

1. Damaged converter clutch pressure plate.
2. Damaged or missing check ball in end of turbine shaft.

CONVERTER CLUTCH DOES NOT RELEASE

1. Converter clutch apply valve stuck.
2. Damaged converter.
3. Missing cup plug in pump release passage.
4. Missing or damaged turbine shaft end seal.
5. Hole not drilled through turbine shaft.

FIRST, SECOND & THIRD SPEED ONLY, NO 3-4 SHIFT

1. Control valve assembly and spacer plate.
   a. 3-4 shift valve or 3-4 throttle valve stuck.
   b. Plugged spacer plate orifice.
2. Center support.
   a. Plugged or undrilled oil passages.
   b. Loose or missing center support attaching bolts.
   c. Cracked or damaged fourth clutch piston.
   d. Damaged, missing or improperly assembled fourth clutch piston seals.
   e. Improper plate usage.
   f. Burned fourth clutch plates.
   g. Binding overrun clutch plates.
3. Case porosity.
4. Orificed cup plug missing in 3-4 accumulator passage in case.
5. Leakage between accumulator piston and pin.
6. 3-4 accumulator bore damaged.

NO ENGINE BRAKING IN L1

1. Improperly adjusted manual linkage.
2. D-3 orifice in space plate plugged.
3. Control valve body gaskets leaking, damaged, or incorrectly installed.
4. D-2 oil pipe leaking or out of position.
5. L1 overrun clutch valve binding in valve body.
6. L1/Detent check ball #10 improperly positioned or missing.
7. L1/Detent check ball #9 improperly positioned or missing.
8. PT/D-3 check ball #3 improperly positioned or missing.
9. Turbine shaft and overrun clutch. No manual 3rd or 2nd should also be a complaint with the following:
   a. Plugged or undrilled D-3 oil passage in turbine shaft.
   b. D-3 oil passage not drilled through in overrun clutch hub.
   c. Missing or damaged oil seals in the overrun clutch piston.
   d. Burned overrun clutches.
   e. Overrun clutch backing plate snap

ring out of groove.
10. Case porosity.
11. L1/Reverse clutch assembly. No reverse should also be a complaint with any of the following conditions:
   a. Broken or missing piston seals.
   b. Clutch housing snap ring out of case.
   c. Cracked/porous piston or housing.
   d. Missing or damaged cup plug or rubber seal between case and L1/Reverse clutch housing.

NO ENGINE BRAKING IN L2

1. Manual linkage improperly adjusted.
2. Valve body gaskets leaking, damaged, or improperly installed.
3. Leaking or out of position D-2 oil pipe.
4. Plugged D-3 orifice in spacer plate.
5. PT/D-3 check ball #3 improperly positioned or missing.
6. Porous case.
7. Missing or damaged intermediate servo cover to case oil seal ring.
8. Intermediate band off anchor pin.
9. Broken or burned intermediate band.
10. D-3 oil passage not drilled through in overrun clutch hub.
11. Missing or damaged oil seals in the overrun clutch piston.
12. Undrilled or plugged D-3 oil hole in turbine shaft.
13. Burned overrun clutches.
14. Overrun clutch backing plate snap ring out of groove.

NO ENGINE BRAKING IN D

1. Manual linkage improperly adjusted.
2. Plugged D-3 orifice in spacer plate.
3. Leaking, damaged, or incorrectly installed valve body gaskets.
4. PT/D-3 check ball #3 improperly positioned or missing.
5. Undrilled or plugged D-3 oil passage in turbine shaft.
6. D-3 oil hole not drilled through in overrun clutch hub.
7. Missing or damaged oil seals in the overrun clutch piston.
8. Burned overrun clutches.
9. Overrun clutch backing plate snap ring out of groove.

LOW OR HIGH SHIFT POINT

1. Binding or improperly adjusted throttle valve cable.
2. Throttle valve limit valve binding.
3. Throttle valve binding.
4. Throttle valve modulator upshift valve binding.

MAINTENANCE

OIL LEVEL CHECK

To check fluid, drive vehicle for at least 15 minutes to bring fluid to operating temperature (200°F). With vehicle on a level surface and engine idling in Park and parking brake applied, the level on the dipstick should be at the "F" mark. To bring the fluid level from the ADD mark to the FULL

mark requires 1 pint of fluid. If vehicle cannot be driven sufficiently to bring fluid to operating temperature, the level on the dipstick should be between the two dimples on the dipstick with fluid temperature at 70°F.

If additional fluid is required, use only Dexron II automatic transmission fluid.

NOTE: An early change to a darker color from the usual red color and/or a strong odor that is usually associated with overheated fluid is normal and should not be considered as a positive sign of required maintenance of unit failure.

CAUTION: When adding fluid, do not overfill, as foaming and loss of fluid through the vent may occur as the fluid heats up. Also, if fluid level is too low, complete loss of drive may occur especially when cold, which can cause transmission failure.

Every 100,000 miles, the oil should be drained, the oil pan removed, the screen cleaned and fresh fluid added. For vehicles subjected to more severe use such as heavy city traffic especially in hot weather, prolonged periods of idling or towing, this maintenance should be performed every 15,000 miles.

DRAINING BOTTOM PAN

1. Remove front and side oil pan attaching bolts, then loosen the rear oil pan attaching bolts.
2. Carefully pry oil pan loose and allow fluid to drain into a suitable container.
3. Remove the oil pan and gasket, then remove the screen attaching bolts and remove screen.
4. Thoroughly clean oil screen and oil pan with solvent.
5. Install oil screen using a new gasket, then install oil pan using a new gasket and torque attaching bolts to 10–13 ft. lbs.
6. Add approximately 3 quarts of fluid, then with engine idling and parking brake applied, move selector lever through each range and return selector lever to PARK.
7. Check fluid level and add fluid as required to bring level between the two dimples on the dipstick.

IN-VEHICLE ADJUSTMENTS

THROTTLE VALVE LINKAGE, ADJUST

Models Equipped With Diesel Engine

1. Remove cruise control rod on vehicles equipped with cruise control.
2. Disconnect throttle valve linkage from throttle assembly.
3. Loosen lock nut on pump rod, then shorten rod by rotating several turns.

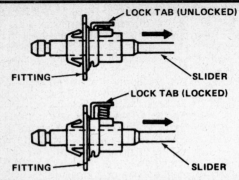

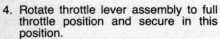

Fig. 2   Self adjusting throttle valve linkage

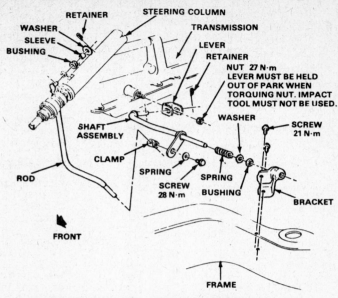

Fig. 3   Column mounted shift linkage adjustment

4. Rotate throttle lever assembly to full throttle position and secure in this position.
5. Lengthen pump rod by rotating in opposite direction as described in step 3 until injection pump lever contacts full throttle stop.
6. Release throttle lever assembly and tighten pump rod lock nut.
7. Disconnect pump rod from throttle lever assembly.
8. Connect throttle valve linkage to throttle assembly.
9. Depress metal locking tab on upper end of cable and hold in this position.
10. Position slider through fitting and away from lever assembly until slider contacts metal fitting.
11. Release metal tab, then rotate throttle lever assembly to full throttle position and release.
12. Connect pump rod to lever assembly, then connect cruise control throttle rod, if equipped.
13. On models equipped with cruise control, adjust servo throttle rod until minimum amount of slack is present. Install clip into first hole closest to bellcrank that is within servo ball.

Models Equipped With Gasoline Engine, Manual Type Linkage
1. With engine static, disconnect throttle valve linkage retaining lock.
2. Rotate throttle lever to wide open position and hold in this position.
3. Connect throttle valve linkage retaining lock.

Self Adjusting Linkage, All Models
1. With engine static, depress locking tab and move slider rearward through fitting until slider contacts fitting, **Fig. 2.**
2. Release locking tab, then move carburetor throttle lever to wide open position and release.
3. Check cable for sticking or binding, then test vehicle for proper operation.
4. If transmission does not shift properly, raise and support vehicle and remove transmission oil pan. Inspect throttle lever and bracket assembly on valve body for damage. Check to ensure

that throttle valve exhaust valve rod is not worn or damaged. Check to ensure that lifter spring holds lifter rod against bottom of valve body and that throttle valve plunger is not sticking.

MANUAL LINKAGE, ADJUST
Column Mounted
1. Position transmission shift lever in Neutral.
2. Position transmission manual valve lever in Neutral detent.
3. With clamp spring washer and screw assembled into equalizer lever and control rod, hold clamp against equalizer lever, then snug tighten clamp screw against control rod, **Fig. 3.**

Console Mounted
1. Position console shift lever in Park position.
2. Position transmission in manual valve lever in Park detent.
3. Position pin, **Fig. 4,** until pin fits loosely in transmission lever, then tighten attaching nut.

IN VEHICLE REPAIRS
INTERMEDIATE SERVO, REPLACE
1. Remove intermediate servo cover retaining ring, using a small screwdriver.
2. Remove servo cover and discard seal ring.
3. Remove servo piston and band apply pin assembly.
4. Reverse procedure to install.

SPEEDOMETER DRIVEN GEAR, REPLACE
1. Disconnect speedometer cable.
2. Remove bolt, retainer, speedometer driven gear and the O-ring seal.
3. Reverse procedure to install.

REAR OIL SEAL, REPLACE
1. Remove propeller shaft.
2. Pry seal from extension housing with a suitable tool.
3. Drive new oil seal into extension housing, using a suitable tool.
4. Install propeller shaft.

VALVE BODY, REPLACE
1. Drain transmission oil pan.
2. Remove oil pan and filter.
3. Remove screw and washer securing T.V. cable to transmission and disconnect the cable.
4. Remove throttle lever and bracket assembly. Use caution not to bend throttle lever link.
5. Disconnect electrical connectors at the 4-3 pressure switch and the 4th clutch pressure switch.
6. Remove solenoid attaching bolts, clips and solenoid assembly.
7. Remove manual detent roller and spring assembly.
8. Remove valve body retaining bolts while supporting valve body. Secure manual valve and remove valve body. Use caution not to lose the three check balls.
9. Reverse procedure to install. Torque valve body bolts to 12 ft. lbs.

1-2 & 3-4 ACCUMULATOR, REPLACE

1. Remove valve body.
2. While supporting 1-2 accumulator housing, remove housing retaining bolts. Then, remove housing and gasket.
3. Support valve body spacer plate, gaskets and accumulator plate to prevent loss of the eight check balls and the 3-4 accumulator spring piston and pin located in the case. Remove remaining retaining bolt on accumulator plate.

NOTE: The intermediate band anchor pin may become dislodged after removing spacer plate and gaskets.

4. Reverse procedure to install.

GOVERNOR, REPLACE

1. Drain transmission oil pan.
2. Remove oil pan and filter.
3. Remove governor attaching bolts, cover and gasket. The governor may come out with the cover. Also, it may be necessary to rotate output shaft counterclockwise while removing governor.
4. Reverse procedure to install.

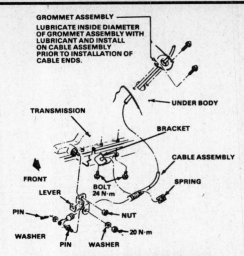

GROMMET ASSEMBLY

LUBRICATE INSIDE DIAMETER OF GROMMET ASSEMBLY WITH LUBRICANT AND INSTALL ON CABLE ASSEMBLY PRIOR TO INSTALLATION OF CABLE ENDS.

UNDER BODY
TRANSMISSION
BRACKET
CABLE ASSEMBLY
FRONT
SPRING
LEVER
BOLT 24 N·m
PIN
NUT
20 N·m
WASHER
PIN   WASHER

Fig. 4 Console mounted shift linkage adjustment

TRANSMISSION
REPLACE

1. Disconnect battery ground cable and remove air cleaner.
2. Disconnect throttle valve cable.
3. Remove transmission oil lever dipstick. Remove upper bolt on dipstick tube.

4. Raise and support vehicle.
5. Mark driveshaft and companion flange for reference during installation, then remove driveshaft.
6. Disconnect speedometer cable and manual shift linkage from transmission.
7. Disconnect torque converter clutch solenoid electrical connector.
8. Remove flywheel under cover. Mark flywheel and converter for reference during installation. Remove three flywheel to converter attaching bolts.
9. Remove catalytic converter support bracket bolts and the tunnel strap.
10. Remove transmission crossmember to transmission mount bolts. Remove transmission crossmember to frame bolts.
11. Support transmission with suitable jack, then move crossmember rearward.
12. Lower transmission slightly and disconnect throttle valve cable and oil cooler lines.
13. Support engine with suitable jack, then remove engine to transmission mounting bolts.
14. Lower jack and remove transmission from vehicle. Use caution not to drop torque converter as transmission is removed. Install suitable converter holding tool to secure converter.
15. Reverse procedure to install.

GM Turbo Hydra-Matic 250, 250C, 350 & 350C

INDEX

DESCRIPTION

The Turbo Hydra-Matic 250, 350, **Figs. 1 and 2,** are fully automatic three speed transmissions consisting of a three element torque converter and a compound planetary gear set. The Turbo Hydra-Matic 250C and 350C, also incorporate a torque converter clutch, **Fig. 3.** The Turbo Hydra-Matic 350 transmission has four multiple-disc clutches, two roller clutches and a band to provide the required friction elements to obtain the desired function of the planetary gear set. The Turbo Hydra-Matic 250 transmission uses an adjustable intermediate band in place of the intermediate clutch found in the Turbo Hydra-Matic 350. Also, the Turbo Hydra-Matic 250 has three multiple-disc clutches and one roller clutch.

The friction elements couple the engine to the planetary gears through oil pressure, providing three forward speeds and one reverse.

The three element torque converter is of welded construction and is serviced as an assembly. The unit consists of a pump or

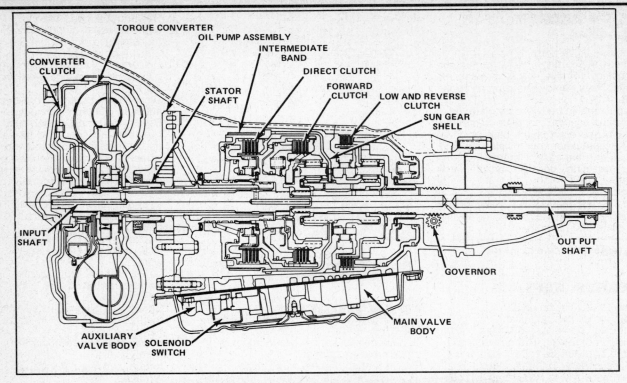

Fig. 1   Sectional view of Turbo Hydra-Matic 250C transmission

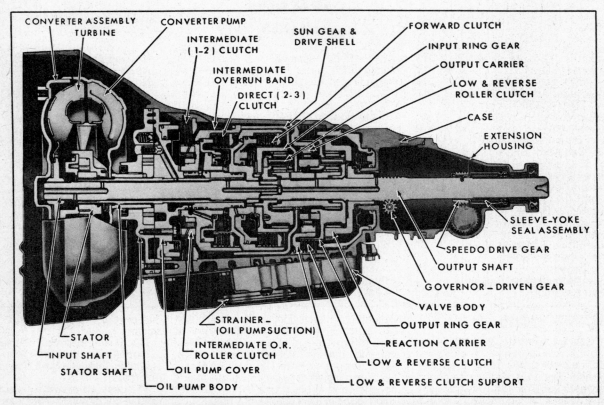

Fig. 2   Sectional view of Turbo Hydra-Matic 350 transmission

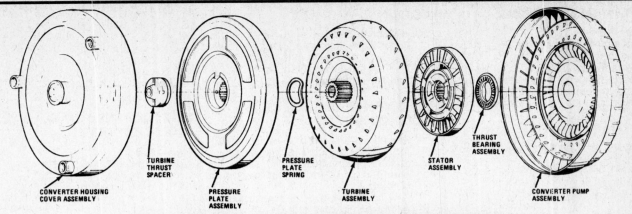

Fig. 3 Torque converter clutch 250C & 350C transmission

driving member, a turbine or driven member and a stator assembly. When required, the torque converter supplements the gears by multiplying engine torque.

On the Turbo Hydra-Matic 250C and 350C, the converter clutch assembly consists of a three element torque converter, with the addition a converter clutch, **Fig. 3.** The converter clutch is splined to the turbine assembly and when operated, applies against the converter cover providing a mechanical direct drive coupling of the engine to the planetary gears. When the converter clutch is released, the assembly operates as a normal torque converter. The converter clutch is applied only when transmission is in third gear, vehicle speed is above 30 mph, engine coolant temperature is above 130°F, engine vacuum is above 3 in. Hg. and brake pedal is released.

TROUBLESHOOTING GUIDE

NO DRIVE IN DRIVE RANGE

1. Low oil level (check for leaks).
2. Manual control linkage improperly adjusted.
3. Low oil pressure due to blocked strainer, defective pressure regulator, pump assembly or pump drive gear. See that tangs have not been damaged by converter. Check case for porosity in intake bore.
4. Check control valve assembly to be sure manual valve has not been disconnected from inner lever.
5. Forward clutch may be stuck or damaged. Check pump feed circuits to forward clutch, including clutch drum ball check.
6. Roller clutch assembly broken or damaged.

OIL PRESSURE HIGH OR LOW

High Pressure:
1. Vacuum line or fittings leaking.
2. Vacuum modulator.
3. Modulator valve.

4. Pressure regulator.
5. Oil pump.

Low Pressure:
1. Vacuum line or fittings obstructed.
2. Vacuum modulator.
3. Modulator valve.
4. Pressure regulator.
5. Governor.
6. Oil pump.

1–2 SHIFT AT FULL THROTTLE ONLY

1. Detent valve may be sticking or linkage may be misadjusted.
2. Vacuum line or fittings leaking.
3. Control valve body gaskets leaking, damaged or incorrectly installed. Detent valve train or 1–2 valve stuck.
4. Check case for porosity.

FIRST SPEED ONLY, NO 1–2 SHIFT

T.H.M. 250 & 350
1. Governor valve may be sticking.
2. Driven gear in governor assembly loose, worn or damaged. If driven gear shows damage, check output shaft drive gear for nicks or rough finish.
3. Control valve governor feed channel blocked or gaskets leaking. 1–2 shift valve train stuck closed.
4. Check case for blocked governor feed channels or for scored governor bore which will allow cross pressure leak. Check case for porosity.
5. Intermediate clutch or seals damaged.
6. Intermediate roller clutch damaged.

T.H.M. 250
1. Intermediate servo piston seals damaged, missing or installed improperly.
2. Intermediate band improperly adjusted.
3. Intermediate servo apply rod broken.

1ST & 2ND ONLY, NO 2–3 SHIFT

1. Control valve 2–3 shift train stuck.

Valve body gaskets leaking, damaged or improperly installed.
2. Pump hub-to-direct clutch oil seal rings broken or missing.
3. Direct clutch piston seals damaged. Piston ball check stuck or missing.

NO FIRST SPEED

T.H.M. 250
1. Intermediate band adjusted too tightly.
2. 1–2 shift valve stuck in upshift position.

T.H.M. 350
1. Excessive number of clutch plates in intermediate clutch pack.
2. Incorrect intermediate clutch piston.

MOVES FORWARD IN NEUTRAL

1. Manual linkage misadjusted.
2. Forward clutch not releasing.

NO MOVEMENT IN REVERSE OR SLIPS IN REVERSE

1. Low oil level.
2. Manual linkage misadjusted.
3. Modulator valve stuck.
4. Modulator and reverse boost valve stuck.
5. Pump hub-to-direct clutch oil seal rings broken or missing.
6. Direct clutch piston seal cut or missing.
7. Low and reverse clutch piston seal cut or missing.
8. Number 1 check ball missing.
9. Control valve body gaskets leaking or damaged.
10. 2–3 valve train stuck in upshifted position.
11. 1–2 valve train stuck in upshifted position.
12. Intermediate servo piston or pin stuck so intermediate overrun band is applied.
13. Low and reverse clutch piston out or seal damaged.
14. Direct clutch plates burned—may be caused by stuck ball check in piston.
15. Forward clutch not releasing.

SLIPS IN ALL RANGES

1. Low oil level.
2. Vacuum modulator valve defective or sticking.
3. Filter assembly plugged or leaking.
4. Pressure regulator valve stuck.
5. Pump to case gasket damaged.
6. Check case for cross leaks or porosity.
7. Forward clutch slipping.

SLIPS 1—2 SHIFT

T.H.M. 250 & 350
1. Low oil level.
2. Vacuum modulator assembly defective.
3. Modulator valve sticking.
4. Pump pressure regulator valve defective.
5. 2—3 accumulator oil ring damaged or missing. 1—2 accumulator oil ring damaged or missing. Case bore damaged.
6. Pump to case gasket mispositioned or damaged.
7. Check for case porosity.
8. Intermediate clutch piston seals damaged. Clutch plates burned.

T.H.M. 250
1. Intermediate servo piston seals damaged or missing.
2. Burned intermediate band.

T.H.M. 350
1. 2—3 accumulator oil ring damaged or missing.

ROUGH 1—2 SHIFT

T.H.M. 250 & 350
1. Vacuum modulator, check for loose fittings, restrictions in line or defective modulator assembly.
2. Modulator valve stuck.
3. Valve body regulator or boost valve stuck.
4. Pump to case gasket mispositioned or damaged.
5. Check case for porosity.
6. Check 1—2 accumulator assembly for damaged oil rings, stuck piston, broken or missing spring, or damaged case bore.

T.H.M. 250
1. Intermediate band improperly adjusted.
2. Improper or broken servo spring.

T.H.M. 350
1. Burned intermediate clutch plates.
2. Improper number of intermediate clutch plates.

SLIPS 2—3 SHIFT

1. Low oil level.
2. Modulator valve or vacuum modulator assembly defective.
3. Pump pressure regulator valve or boost valve; pump to case gasket mispositioned.
4. Check case for porosity.
5. Direct clutch piston seals or ball check leaking.

ROUGH 2—3 SHIFT

1. High oil pressure. Vacuum leak, modulator valve sticking or pressure regulator or boost valve inoperative.
2. 2—3 accumulator piston stuck, spring broken or missing.

NO ENGINE BRAKING IN SECOND SPEED

1. Intermediate servo or 2—3 accumulator oil rings or bores leaking or accumulator piston stuck.
2. Intermediate overrun band burned or broken.
3. Low oil pressure: Pressure regulator and/or boost valve stuck.

NO ENGINE BRAKING IN 1ST SPEED

1. Manual low control valve assembly stuck.
2. Low oil pressure: Pressure regulator and/or boost valve stuck.
3. Low and reverse clutch piston inner seal damaged.

NO PART THROTTLE DOWNSHIFT

1. Oil pressure: Vacuum modulator assembly, modulator valve or pressure regulator valve train malfunctioning.
2. Detent valve and linkage sticking, disconnected or broken.
3. 2—3 shift valve stuck.

NO DETENT DOWNSHIFTS

1. 2—3 valve stuck.
2. Detent valve and linkage sticking, disconnected or broken.

LOW OR HIGH SHIFT POINTS

1. Oil pressure: Check engine vacuum at transmission end of modulator pipe.
2. Vacuum modulator assembly vacuum line connections at engine and transmission, modulator valve, pressure regulator valve train.
3. Check governor for sticking valve, restricted or leaking feed holes, damaged pipes or plugged feed line.
4. Detent valve stuck open.
5. 1—2 or 2—3 valve train sticking.
6. Check case for porosity.

WON'T HOLD IN PARK

1. Manual linkage misadjusted.
2. Parking brake lever and actuator assembly defective.
3. Parking pawl broken or inoperative.

BURNED FORWARD CLUTCH PLATES

1. Check ball in clutch drum damaged, stuck or missing.
2. Clutch piston cracked, seals damaged or missing.
3. Low line pressure.
4. Pump cover oil seal rings missing, broken or undersize; ring groove oversize.
5. Transmission case valve body face not flat or porosity between channels.

BURNED INTERMEDIATE CLUTCH PLATES

T.H.M. 350
1. Intermediate clutch piston seals damaged or missing.
2. Low line pressure.
3. Transmission case valve body face not flat or porosity between channels.

BURNED INTERMEDIATE BAND

T.H.M. 250
1. Intermediate servo piston seals damaged or missing.
2. Low line pressure.
3. Transmission case valve body face not flat or porosity between channels.

BURNED DIRECT CLUTCH PLATES

1. Restricted orifice in vacuum line to modulator.
2. Check ball in clutch drum damaged, stuck or missing.
3. Defective modulator.
4. Clutch piston cracked, seals damaged or missing.
5. Transmission case valve body face not flat or porosity between channels.

NOISY TRANSMISSION

NOTE: Before checking transmission for noise, ensure noise is not coming from water pump, alternator or any belt driven accessory.

Park, Neutral & All Driving Ranges
1. Low fluid level.
2. Plugged or restricted screen.
3. Damaged screen to valve body gasket.
4. Porosity in valve body intake area.
5. Transmission fluid contaminated with water.
6. Porosity at transmission case intake port.
7. Improperly installed case to pump gasket.
8. Pump gears are damaged.
9. Driving gear assembled backwards.
10. Crescent interference in pump.
11. Damaged or worn oil pump seals.
12. Loose converter to flywheel bolts.
13. Damaged converter.

1st, 2nd And/Or Reverse Gear
1. Planetary gears or thrust bearings damaged.
2. Damaged input or output ring gear.

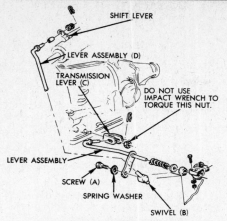

Fig. 4 Column shift linkage adjustment. 1979—81 C & K models

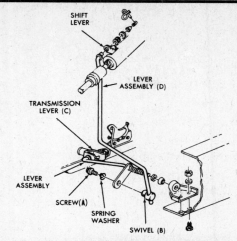

Fig. 5 Column shift linkage adjustment. 1979—81 P models

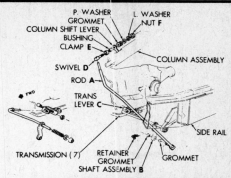

Fig. 6 Column shift linkage adjustment. 1979—81 G models

Acceleration In Any Gear

1. Transmission case or transmission oil cooler lines contacting underbody.
2. Broken or loose engine mounts.

Squeal At Low Vehicle Speed

1. Speedometer driven gear shaft seal requires lubrication or replacement.

CONVERTER CLUTCH APPLIED IN ALL RANGES; ENGINE STALLS WHEN TRANSMISSION IS PUT IN GEAR

T.H.M. 250C & 350C

1. Converter clutch valve in pump sticking in apply position.

CONVERTER CLUTCH APPLIES ERRATICALLY

T.H.M. 250C & 350C

1. Vacuum switch malfunction.
2. Release orifice at pump blocked or restricted.
3. Damaged turbine shaft O-ring.
4. Converter malfunctioning, clutch pressure plate warped.
5. O-ring damaged at solenoid.
6. Solenoid bolts loose.

CONVERTER CLUTCH APPLIES AT A VERY LOW OR HIGH 3RD SPEED GEAR

T.H.M. 250C & 350C

1. Governor switch malfunction.
2. Governor malfunction.
3. High line pressure
4. Converter clutch valve sticking or binding.
5. Solenoid inoperative or shorted to case.

MAINTENANCE

Fluid should be checked every 6,000 miles with engine idling, selector lever in neutral position, parking brake set and transmission at operating temperature. Use only General Motors Dexron transmission fluid when adding oil. Do not overfill.

Every 100,000 miles drain transmission oil sump. After replacing sump, add approximately 5½ pints fluid. Check fluid and add as necessary to bring level to full mark on dipstick with engine at operating temperature.

NOTE: An early change to a darker color from the usual red color and or a strong odor that is usually associated with overheated fluid is normal, and should not be treated as a positive sign of needed maintenance or unit failure.

The normal maintenance schedule for drain and refill of this type fluid remains unchanged under normal service at 100,000 miles. If vehicle is operated under severe conditions, such as frequent trailer towing, fluid should be changed at the following intervals: all 1979—85 with Heavy Duty Emissions and/or diesel engine, 12,000 miles; 1979—85 with Light Duty Emissions, 15,000 miles.

IN-VEHICLE ADJUSTMENTS

SHIFT LINKAGE, ADJUST

1979—81 C, K & P Models

1. Remove screw (A) and spring washer from swivel (B), **Figs. 4 and 5.**
2. Place transmission lever (C) into Neutral position by moving lever counterclockwise to L1 detent, then clockwise 3 detent positions to Neutral.
3. Place transmission selector lever into Neutral.
4. Assemble swivel, spring washer and screw onto shift lever assembly. Tighten screw to 20 ft. lbs.

1979—81 G Models

1. Move transmission lever (C) counterclockwise to L1 detent, then clockwise 3 detent positions to Neutral or obtain Neutral by moving transmission lever (C) clockwise to the Park detent, then counterclockwise 2 detent positions to Neutral, **Fig. 6.**
2. Position column shift lever into Neutral.
3. Connect rod (A) to shaft assembly (B).
4. Slide swivel (D) and clamp (E) onto rod (A).
5. Hold column lever against Neutral stop Park position side.
6. Tighten nut (F) to 18 ft. lbs.

1982—85 C, G & K Models

1. Position transmission shift lever into Neutral by moving shift lever (A) clockwise to the Park detent, then counterclockwise 2 detents to Neutral, **Fig. 7.**
2. Position column shift lever into Neutral.
3. Connect rod (C) to transmission shaft assembly (B).
4. Align column shift lever with transmission shaft assembly (B), then slide swivel and clamp onto rod (C).
5. Hold column lever against Neutral stop Park position side.
6. Tighten nut to 20 ft. lbs.

Console Shift 1979—81 Caballero & El Camino

1. Loosen swivel screw so rod is free to move in swivel, **Fig. 8.**
2. Place transmission control lever in Drive and loosen pin in transmission, so it moves in slot.
3. Move transmission lever counterclockwise to L1 detent, then 3 detents clockwise to Drive position. Tighten nut on transmission lever to 20 ft. lbs.
4. Place transmission control lever in Park and ignition switch in the lock position and pull lightly against lock stop, then tighten swivel screw to 20 ft. lbs.

Column Shift 1979—81 Caballero & El Camino

1. Place transmission lever into Neutral by moving lever counterclockwise to L1 detent, then clockwise 3 detent

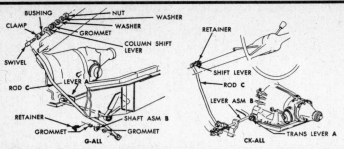

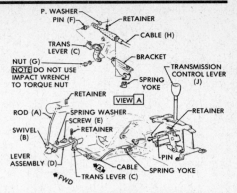

Fig. 7 Column shift linkage adjustment. 1982—85 C, G & K models

Fig. 8 Console shift adjustment. 1979—81 Caballero & El Camino

positions to Neutral.

2. Place selector lever in Neutral as determined by mechanical stop on steering column. Do not use indicator as reference.
3. Assemble swivel, spring washer and screw to lever assembly, then tighten screw to 20 ft. lbs, **Fig. 9.**

Column Shift 1982—85 Caballero & El Camino

1. Position steering column shift lever into Neutral.
2. Position transmission lever into Neutral.
3. Assemble clamp spring and screw onto equalizer lever and control rod, **Fig. 10.**
4. Hold clamp flush against equalizer lever and finger tighten clamping screw against rod.

NOTE: No force should be exerted in either direction on rod or equalizer lever while tightening clamping screw.

5. Torque screw to 20 ft. lbs.

T.V. OR DETENT CABLE, ADJUST

1979—81 C, G, K & P Models

1. Push up on bottom end of snap lock, then disconnect detent cable, **Figs. 11 and 12.**
2. With snap lock disconnected, cable installed onto support bracket and connected to transmission lever, position carburetor to wide open throttle.
3. With carburetor lever in wide open

throttle position, push snap lock downward until snap lock top is flush with cable.

1979—85 CABALLERO, EL CAMINO & 1982—85 C, G, K & P MODELS

Diesel Engine Models

1. Remove cruise control rod on vehicles equipped with cruise control.
2. Disconnect throttle valve linkage from throttle assembly.
3. Loosen lock nut on pump rod, then shorten rod by rotating several turns.
4. Rotate throttle lever assembly to full throttle position and secure in this position.
5. Lengthen pump rod by rotating in opposite direction as described in step 3 until injection pump lever contacts full throttle stop.
6. Release throttle lever assembly and tighten pump rod lock nut.
7. Disconnect pump rod from throttle lever assembly.
8. Connect throttle valve linkage to throttle assembly.

9. Depress metal locking tab on upper end of cable and hold in this position.
10. Position slider through fitting and away from lever assembly until slider contacts metal fitting.
11. Release metal tab, then rotate throttle lever assembly to full throttle position and release.
12. Connect pump rod to lever assembly, then connect cruise control throttle rod, if equipped.
13. On models equipped with cruise control, adjust servo throttle rod until minimum amount of slack is present. Install clip into first hole closest to bellcrank that is within servo bail.

Gasoline Engine Models

1. With engine off, depress locking tab and move slider rearward through fitting until slider contacts fitting, **Fig. 13.**
2. Release locking tab, then move carbu-

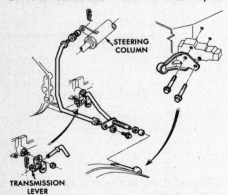

Fig. 9 Column shift linkage adjustment. 1979—81 Caballero & El Camino

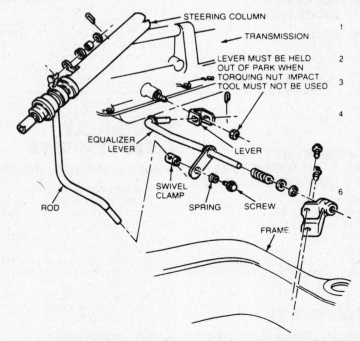

Fig. 10 Column shift linkage adjustments. 1982—85 Caballero & El Camino models

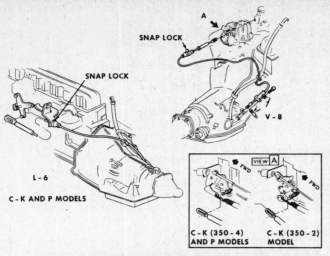

Fig. 11 Detent cable adjustment. C, K & P models

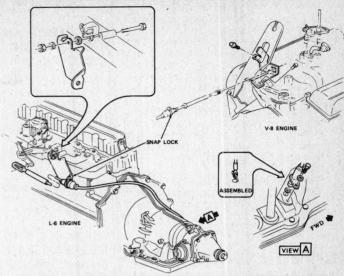

Fig. 12 Detent cable adjustment. G models

retor throttle lever to wide open position and release.
3. Check cable for sticking or binding, then test vehicle for proper operation.
4. If transmission does not shift properly, raise and support vehicle and remove transmission oil pan. Inspect throttle lever and bracket assembly on valve body for damage. Check to ensure that throttle valve exhaust valve rod is not worn or damaged. Check to ensure that lifter spring holds lifter rod against bottom of valve body and that throttle valve plunger is not sticking.

INTERMEDIATE BAND, ADJUST

Turbo Hydra-Matic 250

Since the Turbo Hydra-Matic 250 transmission uses an intermediate band instead of a clutch (used in the Turbo Hydra-Matic 350 transmission) to control the operation of the planetary gear sets, it is necessary to adjust the intermediate band as follows:
1. Loosen adjusting screw lock nut, located on case right side, ½ turn.
2. Torque adjusting screw to 30 inch pounds, then back off screw 3 turns.
3. Torque adjusting screw lock nut to 15 foot pounds while holding adjusting screw in position.

T.H.M. 250C & 350C TORQUE CONVERTER CLUTCH SWITCH ADJUSTMENTS

Low Vacuum Switch
1. Disconnect vacuum and electrical connectors from low vacuum switch, **Fig. 14.**
2. Connect a suitable test light to either terminal of vacuum switch. Connect a suitable jumper cable from the other terminal to a good ground.
3. Connect remaining lead of test light to power side of removed vacuum switch connector.
4. Attach suitable vacuum pump to vacuum port of switch.
5. Turn ignition on, then actuate vacuum pump. On V6-231 engines, test light should remain off until vacuum pump gauge reads 5.5–6.5 in. Hg. On V8-350 gas engines, test light should remain off until vacuum gauge reads 7.5–8.5 in. Hg. On V8-350 diesel engines, test light should remain off until vacuum gauge reads 5–6 in. Hg.

6. Decrease vacuum slowly. Light should remain on until vacuum drops to .3–1.3 in. Hg. on V6-231, 1.5–2.5 in. Hg. on V8-350 gas engines and 3.5–4.5 in. Hg. on V8-350 diesel engines. Decreasing vacuum beyond above values should cause light to go out.
7. If above results cannot be obtained, switch is defective and must be replaced.
8. The point at which light comes on and the point at which light goes out must have at least 4 in. of vacuum difference.

High Vacuum Switch

NOTE: The high vacuum switch must be adjusted anytime the throttle rod, transmission vacuum valve and high idle speed adjustments are changed.

1. Disconnect high vacuum switch electrical connector, **Fig. 14.**
2. Connect the leads of a suitable test light across the terminals of the high vacuum switch.
3. Energize fast idle solenoid by disconnecting pink and green wire from cool-

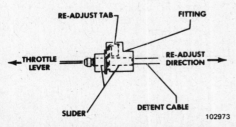

Fig. 13 Self adjusting T.V. cable. Gasoline engine models

IF AIR CLEANER IS REMOVED WHEN MAKING SWITCH ADJUSTMENT, THE EGR SOLENOID PORT TO THE EGR VALVE MUST BE PLUGGED TO PREVENT A VACUUM LEAK AT THE EGR SOLENOID.

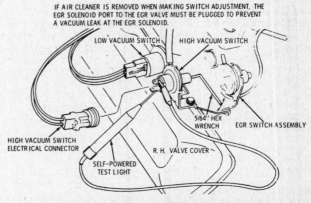

Fig. 14 Vacuum switch location

GENERAL MOTORS—Automatic Transmissions

ant switch and operate engine at high idle speed, then remove cap from back of high vacuum switch.

4. Before adjustment is performed, the test light must be on, indicating that the switch contacts are closed. If test light is off, close the switch contacts by turning switch adjusting screw clockwise until contacts close.

5. Adjust vacuum switch by turning adjusting screw counterclockwise until switch contact just opens and test light goes off. Turn adjusting screw counterclockwise an additional 1/8—3/16 turn.

6. Reinstall cap on back of vacuum switch and reconnect high vacuum switch and coolant switch electrical connectors.

IN-VEHICLE REPAIRS
VALVE BODY ASSEMBLY

1. Remove oil pan and strainer.
2. Remove retaining pin to disconnect downshift actuating lever bracket, remove valve body attaching bolts and detent roller and spring assembly.
3. Remove valve body assembly while disconnecting manual control valve link from range selector inner lever.

CAUTION: Do not drop valve.

4. Remove manual valve and link from valve body assembly.
5. Reverse procedure to install.

GOVERNOR

1. Where necessary, remove shift linkage and transmission to crossmember bolts.
2. Raise transmission with jack and remove crossmember. Lower transmission enough to remove governor.
3. Remove governor cover retainer and cover.
4. Remove governor.

INTERMEDIATE CLUTCH ACCUMULATOR PISTON ASSEMBLY

1. Remove two oil pan bolts adjacent to accumulator piston cover, install compressor on oil pan lip and retain with these two bolts.
2. Compress intermediate clutch accumulator piston cover and remove retaining ring piston cover and O ring from case.
3. Remove spring and intermediate

clutch accumulator piston.

VACUUM MODULATOR & MODULATOR VALVE ASSEMBLY

1. Disconnect vacuum hose from modulator stem and remove vacuum modulator screw and retainer.
2. Remove modulator and its O ring.
3. Remove modulator valve from case.

EXTENSION HOUSING OIL SEAL

1. Remove propeller shaft.
2. Pry out lip seal with screwdriver or small chisel.

MANUAL SHAFT, RANGE SELECTOR INNER LEVER & PARKING LINKAGE ASSEMBLIES

1. remove oil pan and strainer.
2. Remove manual shaft to case retainer and unthread jam nut holding range selector inner lever to manual shaft.
3. Remove jam nut and remove manual shaft from range selector inner lever and case. Do not remove manual shaft lip seal unless replacement is required.
4. Disconnect parking pawl actuating rod from range selector inner lever and remove bolt from case.
5. Remove bolts and parking lock bracket.
6. Remove pawl disengaging spring.
7. If necessary to replace pawl or shaft, clean up bore in case and remove shaft retaining plug, shaft and pawl.

TRANSMISSION
REPLACE

4 × 2 MODELS

1. Disconnect battery ground cable.
2. Remove air cleaner assembly from engine.
3. Disconnect T.V. or detent cable from throttle lever.
4. Remove transmission oil dipstick tube.
5. Raise and support vehicle.
6. Disconnect propeller shaft and shift linkage from transmission.
7. Disconnect speedometer cable and electrical connectors from transmission.
8. Remove transmission braces and flywheel cover.

9. Mark flywheel and torque converter for installation.
10. Remove torque converter to flywheel bolts and/or nuts.
11. Remove catalytic converter support bracket, if equipped.
12. Remove transmission mount attaching bolts.
13. Position a suitable jack under transmission fluid pan, then raise transmission slightly.
14. Remove transmission crossmember to frame attaching bolts, then slide crossmember rearward from vehicle.
15. Lower transmission, then disconnect fluid cooler lines, T.V. or detent cable from transmission.
16. Position a suitable jack under engine, then remove transmission to engine attaching bolts.
17. Carefully separate transmission from engine.
18. Install torque converter holding tool No. J-21366 or equivalent, and remove transmission from vehicle.
19. Reverse procedure to install.

4 × 4 MODELS

1. Disconnect battery ground cable.
2. Remove air cleaner assembly from engine.
3. Disconnect T.V. or detent cable at upper end.
4. Remove transfer case shift lever knob and boot.
5. Raise and support vehicle.
6. Remove propeller shafts from vehicle.
7. Disconnect speedometer cable.
8. Disconnect electrical connectors from transmission and transfer case.
9. Disconnect shift linkage assemblies from transmission and transfer case.
10. Remove transmission support strut rods and flywheel cover.
11. Mark torque converter and flywheel for installation.
12. Remove torque converter to flywheel attaching bolts and/or nuts.
13. Disconnect transmission fluid cooler lines from transmission.
14. Position a suitable jack under transmission and transfer case assemblies.
15. Remove transfer case to frame bracket attaching bolts.
16. Remove crossmember mounting bolts, then the crossmember from vehicle.
17. Remove transmission to engine attaching bolts.
18. Carefully separate transmission and transfer case assembly from engine and remove from vehicle.
19. Reverse procedure to install.

Turbo Hydra-Matic 400 & 475 Automatic Transmission

INDEX

DESCRIPTION

This transmission, **Fig. 1,** is a fully automatic unit consisting primarily of a three-element hydraulic torque converter and a compound planetary gear set. Three multiple-disc clutches, two one-way clutches, and two bands provide the friction elements required to obtain the desired functions of the planetary gear set.

NOTE: The two one-way clutches mentioned above consist of two roller clutches.

The torque converter, the multiple-disc clutches and the one-way clutches couple the engine to the planetary gears through oil pressure, providing three forward speeds and reverse. The torque converter, when required, supplements the gears by multiplying engine torque.

TORQUE CONVERTER

The torque converter is of welded construction and is serviced as an assembly. The unit is made up of two vaned sections, or halves, that face each other in an oil-filled housing. The pump half of the converter is connected to the engine and the turbine half is connected to the transmission.

When the engine makes the converter pump revolve, it sends oil against the turbine, making it revolve also. The oil then returns in a circular flow back to the converter pump, continuing this flow as long as the engine is running.

STATOR

The convertor also has a smaller vaned section, called a stator, that funnels the oil back to the converter pump through smaller openings, at increased speed. The speeded up oil directs additional force to the engine-driven converter pump, thereby multiplying engine torque. In other words, without the stator, the unit is nothing more than a fluid coupling.

TROUBLESHOOTING GUIDE

OIL PRESSURE HIGH

1. Vacuum line or fittings clogged or leaking.
2. Improper engine vacuum.
3. Vacuum leak in vacuum operated accessory.
4. Vacuum modulator.
5. Modulator valve.
6. Water in modulator.
7. Pressure regulator.
8. Oil pump.
9. Governor.
10. Malfunction in detent downshift system. Check for shorted detent wiring, detent solenoid stuck open, detent feed orifice in spacer plate blocked or restricted, loose detent solenoid, damaged detent valve bore plug or detent regulator valve pin too short.

OIL PRESSURE LOW

1. Low oil level.
2. Defective vacuum modulator.
3. Filter blocked or restricted, or incorrect filter assembly.
4. O-ring seal on intake pipe and/or grommet omitted or damaged.
5. Split or leaking oil intake pipe.
6. Malfunction in oil pump. Check for stuck pressure regulator and/or boost valve, weak pressure regulator valve spring, insufficient spacers in pressure regulator, excessive gear clearance, gears damaged, worn or incorrectly installed, pump cover-to-body gasket mispositioned, defective or mismatched pump body-to-pump cover.
7. Internal circuit leakage.
8. Case porosity.
9. Intermediate clutch cup plug leaking or mispositioned.
10. Low-reverse check ball mispositioned or missing. This will cause no reverse and no overrun braking in low range.

NO DRIVE IN DRIVE RANGE

1. Low oil level (check for leaks).
2. Manual control linkage not adjusted properly.
3. Low oil pressure. Check for blocked strainer, defective pressure regulator, pump assembly or pump drive gear. See that tangs have not been damaged by converter.
4. Check control valve assembly to see if manual valve has been disconnected from manual lever pin.
5. Forward clutch may be stuck or damaged. Check pump feed circuits to forward clutch, including clutch drum ball check.
6. Roller clutch assembled incorrectly.

1-2 SHIFT AT FULL THROTTLE ONLY

1. Detent switch may be sticking or defective.
2. Detent solenoid may be stuck open, loose or have leaking gasket.
3. Control valve assembly may be leaking, damaged or incorrectly installed.
4. Third-to-second shift valve stuck.
5. Case porosity.

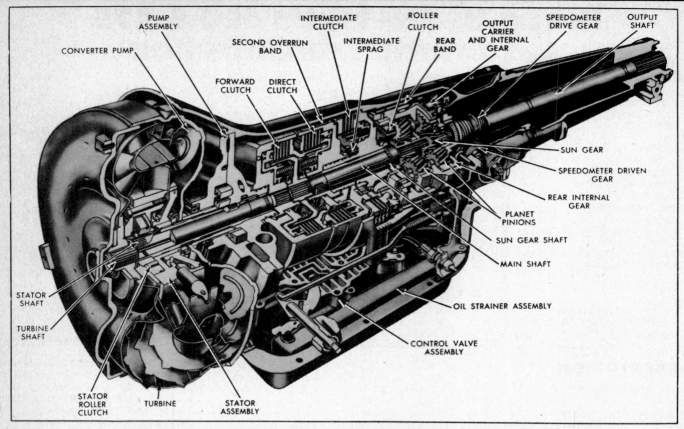

Fig. 1 Cutaway view of Turbo Hydra-Matic 400 & 475 automatic transmission

1ST SPEED ONLY—NO 1-2 SHIFT

1. Governor valve may be sticking.
2. Driven gear in governor assembly loose, worn or damaged.
3. The 1-2 shift valve in control valve assembly stuck closed. Check governor feed channels for blocks, leaks, and position. Also check control valve body gaskets for leaks and damage.
4. Intermediate clutch plug in case may be leaking or blown out.
5. Check for porosity between channels and for blocked governor feed channels in case.
6. Center support oil rings missing, or damaged. Orifice plug missing.
7. Intermediate clutch piston seals missing, incorrectly installed or damaged.

NO 2-3 SHIFT—1ST & 2ND ONLY

1. Detent solenoid may be stuck open.
2. Detent switch may not be properly adjusted.
3. Control valve assembly may be stuck, leaking, damaged, or incorrectly installed.
4. Control valve body gaskets leaking, damaged or incorrectly installed.
5. Check direct clutch case center support for broken, leaking or missing oil rings.
6. Check clutch piston seals and piston ball check in clutch assembly.

MOVES FORWARD IN NEUTRAL

1. Manual control linkage improperly adjusted.
2. Manual valve disconnected or broken.
3. Inside detent lever pin broken.
4. Transmission oil pressure leaking into forward clutch apply passage.
5. Burned forward clutch plates.
6. Forward clutch does not release.

NO MOVEMENT IN REVERSE OR SLIPS IN REVERSE

1. Check oil level.
2. Manual control linkage improperly adjusted.
3. Vacuum modulator assembly may be defective.
4. Vacuum modulator valve sticking.
5. Strainer may be restricted or leaking at intake.
6. Regulator or boost valve in pump assembly may be sticking.
7. Low oil pressure.
8. Rear servo and accumulator may have damaged or missing servo piston seal ring.
9. Reverse band burned out or damaged. Determine that apply pin or anchor pins engage properly.
10. Direct clutch may be damaged or may have stuck ball check in piston.
11. Forward clutch does not release.
12. Low-reverse ball check missing from case.
13. Control valve body malfunctioning. Check for leaking, damaged or incorrectly installed gaskets, 2-3 shift valve stuck open, or restricted reverse feed passage.

SLIPS IN ALL RANGES & ON STARTS

1. Check oil level.
2. Vacuum modulator defective.
3. Modulator valve sticking.
4. Strainer assembly plugged or leaking at neck.
5. Pump assembly regulator or boost valve sticking.
6. Leaks from damaged gaskets or cross leaks from porosity of case.
7. Forward and direct clutches burned.
8. Low oil pressure.

SLIPS 1-2 SHIFT

1. Incorrect oil level.
2. Vacuum modulator valve sticking.
3. Vacuum modulator defective.

4. Pump pressure regulator valve defective.
5. Porosity between channels in case.
6. Control valve assembly.
7. Pump-to-case gasket may be mispositioned.
8. Intermediate clutch plug in case may be missing or leaking excessively.
9. Intermediate clutch piston seal missing or damaged.
10. Intermediate clutch plates burned.
11. Front or rear accumulator oil ring may be damaged.
12. Leak in center support feed circuit, excessive leak between center support tower and bushing, blocked center support orifice bleed plug hole, center support bolt not properly seated.
13. Raised ridge around case center support bolt not allowing control valve assembly to seat properly.
14. Low oil pressure.

SLIPS 2—3 SHIFT

1. Items 1 through 6 under Slips 1-2 Shift will also cause 2-3 shift slips.
2. Direct clutch plates burned.
3. Oil seal rings on direct clutch may be damaged permitting excessive leaking between tower and bushing.

ROUGH 1—2 SHIFT

1. Modulator valve sticking.
2. Modulator assembly defective.
3. Pump pressure regulator or boost valve stuck or inoperative.
4. Control valve assembly loosened from case, damaged or mounted with wrong gaskets.
5. Intermediate clutch ball missing or not sealing.
6. Porosity between channels in case.
7. Rear servo accumulator assembly may have oil rings damaged, stuck piston, broken or missing spring or damaged bore.

ROUGH 2—3 SHIFT

1. Items 1, 2 and 3 under Rough 1-2 Shift will also cause rough 2-3 shift.
2. Front servo accumulator spring broken or missing. Accumulator piston may be sticking.

NO ENGINE BRAKING IN SECOND SPEED

1. Front servo or accumulator oil rings may be leaking.
2. Front band may be broken or burned out.
3. Front band not engaged on anchor pin and/or servo pin.

NO ENGINE BRAKING IN LOW RANGE

1. Low-reverse check ball may be missing from control valve assembly.
2. Rear servo may have damaged oil seal ring, bore or piston; leaking, apply pressure.

3. Rear band broken, burned out or not engaged on anchor pins or servo pin.

NO PART THROTTLE DOWNSHIFTS

1. Vacuum modulator assembly.
2. Modulator valve.
3. Regulator valve train.
4. Control valve assembly has stuck 3-2 valve or broken spring.

NO DETENT DOWNSHIFTS

1. Detent switch needs fuse, connections tightened or adjustment.
2. Detent solenoid may be inoperative.
3. Detent valve train in control valve assembly malfunctioning.

LOW OR HIGH SHIFT POINTS

1. Oil pressure. Check vacuum modulator assembly, vacuum line connections, modulator valve, and pressure regulator valve train.
2. Governor may have sticking valve or feed holes that are leaking, plugged or damaged.
3. Detent solenoid may be stuck open or loose.
4. Control valve assembly. Check detent, 3-2, and 1-2 shift valve trains, and check spacer plate gaskets for positioning.
5. Check case for porosity, missing or leaking intermediate plug.

WON'T HOLD IN PARK

1. Manual control linkage improperly adjusted.
2. Internal linkage defective; check for chamfer on actuator rod sleeve.
3. Parking pawl broken or inoperative.
4. Parking pawl return spring missing, broken or incorrectly installed.

NOISY TRANSMISSION

1. Pump noises caused by high or low oil level.
2. Cavitation due to plugged strainer, porosity in intake circuit or water in oil.
3. Pump gears may be damaged.
4. Gear noise in low gear of Drive Range - transmission grounded to body.
5. Defective planetary gear set.
6. Clutch noises during application can be worn or burned clutch plates.

FORWARD CLUTCH PLATES BURNED

1. Check ball in clutch housing damaged, stuck or missing.
2. Clutch piston cracked, seals damaged or missing.
3. Low line pressure.
4. Manual valve mispositioned.
5. Restricted oil feed to forward clutch.
6. Pump cover oil seal rings missing, broken or undersize; ring groove oversize.

size.
7. Case valve body face not flat or porosity between channels.
8. Manual valve bent and center land not properly ground.

INTERMEDIATE CLUTCH PLATES BURNED

1. Constant bleed orifice in center support missing.
2. Rear accumulator piston oil ring damaged or missing.
3. 1-2 accumulator valve stuck in control valve assembly.
4. Intermediate clutch piston seal damaged or missing.
5. Center support bolt loose.
6. Low line pressure.
7. Intermediate clutch plug in case missing.
8. Case valve body face not flat or porosity between channels.
9. Manual valve bent and center land not ground properly.

DIRECT CLUTCH PLATES BURNED

1. Restricted orifice in vacuum line to modulator.
2. Check ball in direct clutch piston damaged, stuck or missing.
3. Defective modulator bellows.
4. Center support bolt loose.
5. Center support oil rings or grooves damaged or missing.
6. Clutch piston seals damaged or missing.
7. Front and rear servo pistons and seals damaged.
8. Manual valve bent and center land not cleaned up.
9. Case valve body face not flat or porosity between channels.
10. Intermediate sprag clutch installed backwards.
11. 3-2 valve, 3-2 spring or 3-2 spacer pin installed in wrong location in 3-2 valve bore.

MAINTENANCE
CHECKING & ADDING FLUID

Fluid level should be checked at every engine oil change. The full ("F") and "ADD" marks on the transmission dipstick are one pint apart and determine the correct fluid level at normal operating temperature (180°F.). Careful attention to transmission oil temperature is necessary as proper fluid level at low operating temperatures will be below the "ADD" mark on the dipstick. Proper fluid level at higher operating temperatures will rise above the "F" mark.

Fluid level must always be checked with the car on a level surface, and with the engine running to make certain the converter is full. To determine proper fluid level, proceed as follows:
1. Operate engine at a fast idle for about 1½ minutes with selector lever in park ("P") position.

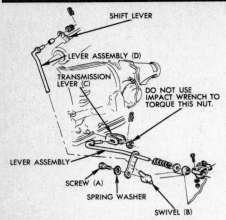

Fig. 2   Column shift linkage adjustment. 1979–81 C & K models

2. Reduce engine speed to slow idle and check fluid level.
3. With engine running, add fluid as required to bring it to the proper level.

NOTE: An early change to a darker color from the usual red color and or a strong odor that is usually associated with overheated fluid is normal, and should not be treated as a positive sign of needed maintenance or unit failure.

On 1979–85 vehicles, the drain interval is 100,000 miles under normal service and 15,000 miles under severe operating conditions on Light Duty Emissions vehicles, or 12,000 miles on diesel and/or Heavy Duty Emissions vehicles.

CAUTION: Do not overfill as foaming might occur when the fluid heats up. If fluid level is too low, especially when cold, complete loss of drive may result after quick stops. Extremely low fluid level will result in damage to transmission.

CHANGING FLUID

1. Raise vehicle and support with suitable jack stands.
2. Place drain pan under transmission oil pan, then remove oil pan attaching bolts from front and side of pan.
3. Loosen rear and side pan attaching bolts approximately four turns, then pry oil pan loose with a screwdriver and allow fluid to drain.
4. Remove remaining bolts and separate oil pan from transmission.
5. Drain remaining fluid from pan, then clean pan with a suitable solvent and thoroughly dry with compressed air.
6. On 1979–81 vehicles, remove oil filter assembly and the O-ring from intake pipe. Install new O-ring and filter and torque filter retaining bolt to 10 ft. lbs., then install a new strainer-to-valve body gasket, strainer and two screws.
7. On 1982–85 vehicles, remove screen/filter-to-body bolts, then the screen/filter and gasket. Clean screen in sol-

vent and dry with compressed air. If applicable, paper or felt filter should be replaced. Install screen/filter assembly using a new O-ring and torque attaching bolt to 10 ft. lbs.
8. Install oil pan with a new gasket. Torque attaching bolts to 12 ft. lbs.
9. Lower vehicle and add 5 pints of Dexron II or equivalent transmission fluid through filler tube.
10. With transmission in Park, start engine and run at idle.
11. Move transmission through each gear range and return to Park position, then recheck fluid level. Add additional fluid to bring level to ¼ inch below add mark on dipstick on 1979–81 vehicles, or between dimples on dipstick on 1982–85 vehicles.

ADDING FLUID TO FILL DRY TRANSMISSION & CONVERTER

1. Add 9 pints of transmission fluid through filler tube.
2. Operate engine at high idle and move transmission lever through each gear range.
3. After 1–3 minutes of idle operation with transmission in Park, recheck fluid level. Add additional fluid to bring level to ⅜ inch below add mark on dipstick on 1979–82 vehicles or between dimples on dipstick on 1982–85 vehicles.

IN-VEHICLE ADJUSTMENTS
SHIFT LINKAGE, ADJUST
1979–81 C, K & P Models
1. Loosen shift rod clamp nut.
2. Remove screw (A) and spring washer from swivel (B), **Figs. 2 and 3.**
3. Place transmission lever (C) into Neutral by moving lever counterclockwise to L1 detent, then clockwise 3 detent positions to Neutral.
4. Position transmission selector lever into Neutral as determined by mechanical stop in steering column assembly.

NOTE: Do not use indicator pointer as a reference to position transmission selector lever into Neutral.

5. Assemble swivel, spring washer and screw to lever assembly (D). Tighten screw to 20 ft. lbs.

1982–85 C, G & K Models
1. Loosen shift rod clamp nut.
2. Place transmission lever (A) into Neutral by moving lever (A) clockwise to the Park detent, then counterclockwise 2 detent positions into Neutral.
3. Place column shift lever rod (C) into Neutral, **Fig. 4.**

NOTE: Do not use indicator pointer as a reference to position transmission selector lever into Neutral.

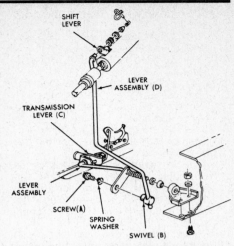

Fig. 3   Column shift linkage adjustment. 1979–81 P models

4. Connect rod (C) onto transmission shaft lever assembly (B).
5. Slide swivel and clamp onto rod (C).
6. Hold column lever against Neutral stop Park position side.
7. Tighten nut to 20 ft. lbs.

DOWNSHIFT SWITCH
C, G, K & P Models
Install switch as shown in **Fig. 5.** After installing switch, press switch plunger as far forward as possible. This switch will then adjust itself the first time the accelerator pedal is pushed to the floor.

IN VEHICLE REPAIRS
PRESSURE REGULATOR VALVE

NOTE: A solid type pressure regulator valve must be used only in a pump cover with a "Squared Off" (machined) pressure regulator boss, **Fig. 6.** A pressure regulator valve with oil holes and an orifice cup plug may be used with either type pump.

1. Remove bottom pan and strainer.
2. Using a screwdriver or steel rod, compress regulator boost valve bushing against pressure regulator spring.

CAUTION: Pressure regulator spring is under extreme pressure and will force valve bushing out of bore when snap ring is removed if valve bushing is not held securely.

3. Continue to exert pressure on valve bushing and remove snap ring. Gradually release pressure on valve bushing until spring force is exhausted.
4. Carefully remove regulator boost valve bushing and valve, and pressure regulator spring. Be careful not to drop parts as they will fall out if they are not held.
5. Remove pressure regulator valve and

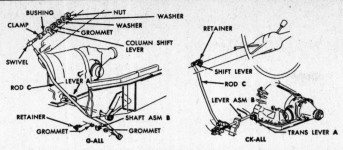

Fig. 4 Column shift linkage adjustment. 1982–85 C, G & K models

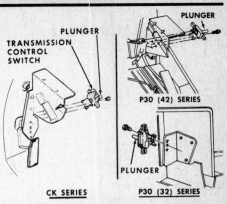

Fig. 5 Detent switch location

spring retainer. Remove spacers if present.
6. Reverse procedure to install.

CONTROL VALVE BODY

1. Remove bottom pan and strainer.
2. Disconnect pressure switch lead wire.
3. Remove control valve body attaching screws and detent roller spring assembly. Do not remove solenoid attaching screws.
4. Remove control valve body and governor pipes. If care is used in removing control valve body, the six check balls will stay in place above spacer plate.
5. Remove governor pipes and manual valve from control valve body.
6. Reverse procedure to install.

GOVERNOR

1. Remove governor cover and discard gasket.
2. Withdraw governor from case.
3. Reverse procedure to install, using a new gasket.

MODULATOR & MODULATOR VALVE

1. Remove modulator attaching screw and retainer.
2. Remove modulator assembly from case and discard O-ring seal.
3. Remove modulator valve from case.
4. Reverse procedure to install, using a new O-ring seal.

PARKING LINKAGE

1. Remove bottom pan and oil strainer.
2. Unthread jam nut holding detent lever to manual shaft.
3. Remove manual shaft retaining pin from case.
4. Remove manual shaft and jam nut from case.
5. Remove O-ring seal from manual shaft.
6. Remove parking actuator rod and detent lever assembly.
7. Remove parking pawl bracket, pawl return spring and pawl shaft retainer.
8. Remove parking pawl shaft, O-ring seal and parking pawl.
9. Reverse procedure to install, using new seals and gasket.

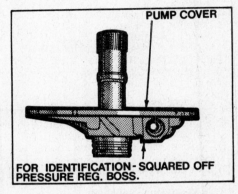

FOR IDENTIFICATION - SQUARED OFF PRESSURE REG. BOSS.

Fig. 6 Solid type pressure regulator

REAR SEAL

1. Remove propeller shaft.
2. Pry out seal with screwdriver.
3. Install new seal with a suitable seal driver.
4. Install propeller shaft.

TRANSMISSION
REPLACE

C, G & P 4 × 2 MODELS

1. Disconnect battery ground cable.
2. Remove air cleaner assembly.
3. Remove transmission fluid dipstick tube.
4. Raise and support vehicle.
5. Remove drive shaft from vehicle.
6. Disconnect speedometer cable and electrical connectors from transmission.
7. Disconnect shift linkage assembly from transmission.
8. Remove transmission support braces and flywheel cover.
9. Mark position of torque converter and flywheel for installation.
10. Remove torque converter to flywheel attaching bolts and/or nuts.
11. Disconnect catalytic converter support bracket, if equipped from transmission.
12. Remove transmission mount attaching bolts.

13. Position a suitable jack under transmission fluid pan, then raise transmission slightly.
14. Remove transmission crossmember to frame attaching bolts, then slide crossmember rearward and out of vehicle.
15. Lower transmission.
16. Disconnect and cap transmission fluid cooler lines.
17. Position a suitable jack under engine, then remove transmission to engine attaching bolts.
18. Carefully separate transmission from engine. Install torque converter holding tool No. J-21366 and remove transmission from vehicle.
19. Reverse procedure to install.

K 4 × 4 MODELS

1. Disconnect battery ground cable.
2. Remove air cleaner assembly.
3. Remove transfer case shift lever knob and boot.
4. Raise and support vehicle.
5. Remove drive shafts from vehicle.
6. Disconnect speedometer cable and electrical connectors from transmission.
7. Disconnect shift linkage assembly from transfer case.
8. Remove transmission support strut rods and flywheel cover. Mark position of torque converter and flywheel for installation.
9. Remove torque converter to flywheel attaching bolts/and or nuts.
10. Disconnect and cap transmission fluid cooler lines.
11. Position a suitable jack under transmission and transfer case assembly.
12. Position a suitable jack under engine.
13. Remove transfer case to frame bracket attaching bolts.
14. Remove mounting bolts and crossmember assembly from vehicle.
15. Remove transmission to engine attaching bolts, then carefully separate transmission from engine.
16. Remove transmission from vehicle.
17. Reverse procedure to install.

Turbo Hydra-Matic 700-R4 Automatic Transmission

INDEX

DESCRIPTION

The model 700-R4 **Fig. 1,** is fully automatic transmission consisting of a 3-element hydraulic torque converter with the addition of a converter clutch.

Also two planetary gear sets, five multiple-disc type clutches, two roller or one-way clutches and a band are used which provide the friction elements to produce four forward speeds, the last of which is overdrive.

The torque converter, through oil, couples the engine power to the gear sets and hydraulically provides additional torque multiplication when required. Also, through the converter clutch, **Fig. 2,** the converter drive and driven members operate as one unit when applied, providing mechanical drive from the engine through the transmission.

The gear ratio changes are fully automatic in relation to the vehicle speed and engine torque. Vehicle speed and engine torque are directed to the transmission providing the proper gear ratio for maximum efficiency and performance at all throttle openings.

A hydraulic system pressurized by a variable capacity vane type pump provides the operating pressure required for the operation of the friction elements and automatic controls.

TROUBLESHOOTING GUIDE

OIL PRESSURE HIGH OR LOW

1. Pump assembly pressure regulator valve binding, dirty or damaged spring.
2. T.V. and reverse boost plug and bushing are dirty, sticking, damaged or incorrectly assembled.
3. Pump assembly pressure relief ball not seated or damaged.
4. Pump assembly slide sticking.
5. Pump assembly not regulating.
6. Excess rotor clearance in pump assembly.
7. Manual valve not engaged or damaged.
8. T.V. exhaust valve binding or damaged.
9. Throttle lever and bracket assembly, misassembled, binding, damaged or check valve missing.
10. Valve body throttle valve or plunger sticking.
11. Valve body T.V. limit valve sticking.
12. Throttle link, not engaged, damaged, incorrect, burr on upper end or hanging on T.V. sleeve.
13. Filter, restricted, has missing "O" ring or hole in intake pipe.

HIGH OR LOW SHIFT POINTS

1. T.V. cable binding or not adjusted properly.
2. Improper external linkage travel.
3. Binding throttle valve or plunger.
4. T.V. modulator up or down valve sticking.
5. Valve body gaskets or spacer plate mispositioned or damaged.
6. T.V. limit valve sticking.
7. Pump assembly, sticking pressure regulator valve, T.V. boost valve.
8. Pump slide sticking.

FIRST SPEED ONLY—NO UPSHIFT

1. Sticking governor valve.
2. Governor driven gear is damaged.
3. Governor driven gear retainer pin missing.
4. Nicks or burrs on output shaft.
5. Correct governor retainer pin in case (longer or shorter).
6. Burrs on governor sleeve.
7. Burrs on governor case.
8. Governor weights and springs damaged.
9. 1-2 Shaft valve sticking.
10. Valve body gaskets or spacer plate are mispositioned.
11. Valve body pad—porosity and or damaged lands.
12. Restricted or damaged governor screen.
13. 2-4 Servo apply passages, servo apply pin and pin hole in case, restricted or damaged.
14. Damaged or missing servo piston seals.
15. 2-4 Band assembly burned, band anchor pin not engaged.
16. 2-4 Band assembly apply end broken.

SLIPS IN FIRST GEAR

1. Forward clutch plates burned.
2. Porosity—forward clutch piston.
3. Forward clutch seals, cut or damaged.
4. Damaged forward clutch housing.
5. Forward clutch internal leak.
6. Forward clutch housing check ball damage.
7. Low oil or oil pressure.
8. Accumulator valve sticking.
9. Valve body lands or interconnected passages damaged.
10. Valve body gasket, spacer plate damaged or mispositioned.
11. Binding internal T.V. linkage.
12. 1-2 Accumulator piston assembly, piston or bore porous.
13. 1-2 Accumulator piston assembly seals, cut or damaged.
14. Leak between piston and pin.
15. Missing or broken accumulator spring.

1-2 FULL THROTTLE SHIFTS ONLY

1. T.V. Cable not connected.
2. T.V. Cable too long or short.
3. Throttle lever bracket assembly misassembled or binding.

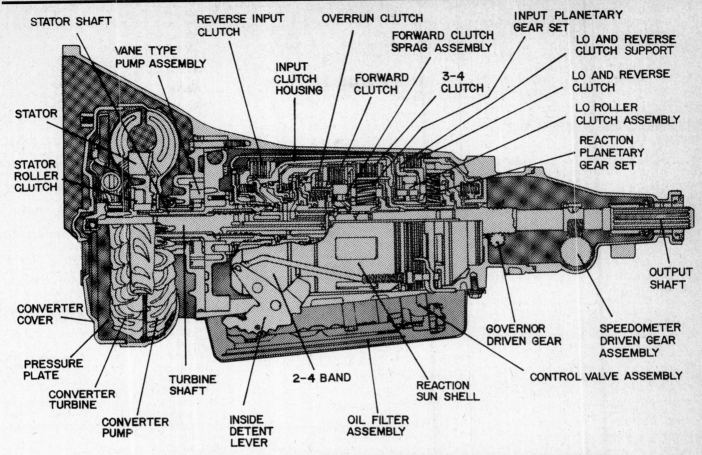

Fig. 1 Sectional view of Turbo Hydra-Matic 700-R4 automatic transmission

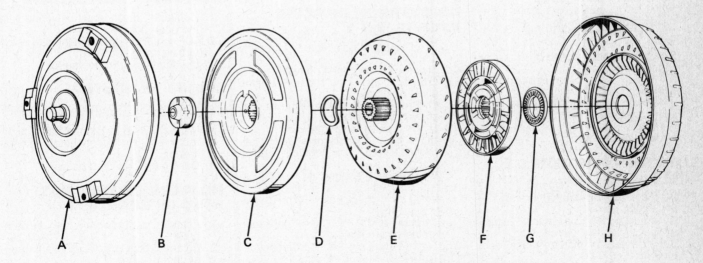

A HOUSING COVER ASSEMBLY, CONVERTER
B SPACER, TURBINE THRUST
C PRESSURE PLATE ASSEMBLY
D SPRING, PRESSURE PLATE

E TURBINE ASSEMBLY
F STATOR ASSEMBLY
G THRUST BEARING ASSEMBLY
H CONVERTER PUMP ASSEMBLY

*THE TORQUE CONVERTER CLUTCH ASSEMBLY CANNOT BE DISASSEMBLED. SHOWN HERE FOR INFORMATION ONLY. SEE SECTION 7A FOR MORE INFORMATION.

Fig. 2 Lockup torque converter

4. Missing exhaust check valve.
5. Throttle link not connected, burr on upper end or hanging on T.V. sleeve.
6. Throttle valve or plunger hanging or sticking in full open position.
7. Inter connected passages—pump, case or valve body restricted or damaged.

SLIPPING OR ROUGH 1-2 SHIFT

1. Throttle lever and bracket assembly, damaged or incorrectly installed.
2. Throttle valve or bushing, sticking.
3. Sticking 1-2 shift valve train.
4. Valve body gasket or spacer plate, mispositioned.
5. Sticking line bias valve.
6. Sticking accumulator valve.
7. Sticking T.V. limit valve.
8. Incorrect 2-4 servo apply pin.
9. 2-4 Servo oil seal rings or seals, damaged.
10. 2-4 Servo bores, damaged.
11. 2-4 Servo oil passages, restricted or missing.
12. 2nd Accumulator piston seal, damaged.
13. Accumulator spring, missing.
14. 2nd Accumulator bores, damaged.
15. 2nd Accumulator piston, porous.
16. 2nd Accumulator oil passages, restricted or missing.
17. Burned 2-4 band.

SLIPPING OR ROUGH 2-3 SHIFT

1. 2-3 Shift valve train, sticking.
2. Accumulator valve sticking.
3. Valve body gasket or spacer plate mispositioned.
4. Throttle valve sticking.
5. T.V. Limit valve sticking.
6. 3-4 Clutch plates burned or excessive clutch plate travel.
7. 3-4 Piston seals, cut or damaged.
8. 3-4 Piston porosity.
9. 3-4 Piston exhaust ball open.
10. Apply passages restricted.
11. 3-4 Clutch check ball capsule, damaged or misassembled.

SLIPPING OR ROUGH 3-4 SHIFT

1. 3-4 Accumulator spring, missing.
2. 3-4 Piston porosity.
3. Accumulator feed passages, restricted.
4. 3-4 Accumulator piston oil seal ring, broken.
5. Accumulator case bore damaged.
6. Servo band apply incorrect.
7. Servo piston seals damaged or missing.
8. Servo piston bores damaged.
9. Servo piston porosity.
10. 3-4 Clutch burned. (Refer to 2-3 slip for other clutch diagnosis.)
11. 2-4 Band burned.
12. Valve body 2-3 shift valve train, sticking.

13. Accumulator valve sticking.
14. Valve body gaskets or spacer plate mispositioned.
15. Valve body throttle valve sticking.
16. T.V. limit valve sticking.

NO REVERSE OR SLIPS IN REVERSE

1. Forward clutch will not release.
2. Manual linkage improperly adjusted.
3. Pump assembly reverse boost plug, sticking.
4. Valve body gaskets or saucer plate mispositioned.
5. Lo reverse clutch piston seals cut or damaged.
6. Lo reverse clutch apply passages restricted or missing.
7. Lo reverse clutch plates burned.
8. Lo reverse clutch cover plate loose or cover plate gasket damaged.
9. Reverse input clutch plates burned.
10. Reverse input clutch piston seals cut or damaged.
11. Reverse input clutch apply passage restricted or missing.
12. Reverse input clutch housing exhaust ball and capsule, damaged.

NO PART THROTTLE DOWNSHIFTS

1. Binding external or internal linkage.
2. Valve body T.V. modulator downshift valve binding.
3. Valve body throttle valve binding.
4. Valve body throttle valve bushing, feed hole restricted or missing.
5. Valve body check ball #3 mispositioned.

NO OVERRUN BRAKING MANUAL 3-2-1

1. External manual linkage not properly adjusted.
2. Overrun clutch plates burned.
3. Overrun clutch inner or outer piston seals damaged.
4. Overrun clutch piston exhaust ball sticking or missing.
5. Overrun clutch piston porosity.
6. Valve body gaskets or spacer plate mispositioned or orifice holes plugged.
7. Valve body 4-3 sequence valve sticking.
8. Valve body check balls 3, 9 or 10 mispositioned.
9. Turbine shaft oil feed passages restricted or missing.
10. Turbine shaft oil seal ring damaged.
11. Turbine shaft plug missing.

NO CONVERTER CLUTCH APPLY

1. 12 Volts not being supplied to the transmission.
2. Defective transmission outside electrical connector.
3. Defective inside electrical connectors, wiring harness, solenoid.
4. Defective electrical ground inside

transmission.
5. Defective pressure switch or improper connection.
6. Solenoid not grounded.
7. Valve body converter clutch shift or throttle valve sticking.
8. Valve body casting or spacer plate in converter clutch valve area are mispositioned or damaged.
9. Converter clutch apply valve, stuck or installed backwards.
10. Pump assembly signal oil orifice, restricted or missing.
11. Pump assembly "O" ring on solenoid damaged or missing.
12. Pump to case gasket, damaged or mispositioned.
13. Pump assembly cup plug missing from apply passage.
14. Pump assembly orifice plug missing from the cooler input passage.
15. High or uneven bolt torque on cover to body.
16. Converter clutch stop valve or retainer ring not installed properly.

CONVERTER SHUDDER

1. Converter clutch pressure plate damaged.
2. Check ball on end of turbine shaft damaged.
3. Sticking converter clutch shift valve in valve body.
4. Sticking converter clutch apply valve in valve body.
5. Restricted converter clutch apply passage.
6. Low oil or oil pressure.
7. Engine not tuned properly.

NO CONVERTER RELEASE

1. Converter clutch apply valve stuck in the open position.
2. "O" ring or check ball in the end of the turbine shaft damaged.
3. Internal converter damaged.

DRIVES IN NEUTRAL

1. Forward clutch burned or not releasing.
2. Manual linkage or manual valve incorrectly set, or disconnected internal linkage.
3. Case interconnected passage.

NO PARK OR WILL NOT HOLD IN PARK

1. Actuator rod assembly bent or damaged.
2. Actuator rod spring, binding or improper crimp.
3. Parking lock pawl return spring, damaged or not assembled properly.
4. Actuator rod is not attached to inside detent lever.
5. Parking brake bracket damaged or bolts not torqued.
6. Inside detent lever nut, not torqued.
7. Detent roller improperly installed or damaged.
8. Parking lock pawl, binding or damaged.

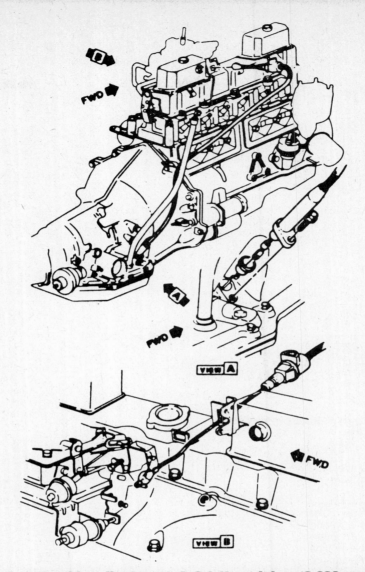

Fig. 3   T.V. cable adjustment. C, G & K models w/6-292 engine

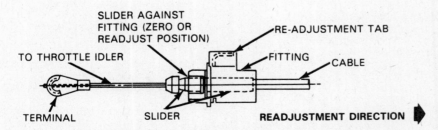

Fig. 4   Self adjusting T.V. cable. Gasoline engine models

9. Parking lock pawl interference with the lo reverse piston.

NOTE: Be careful to always check oil level, T.V. cable and oil pressure following each trouble shooting procedure.

MAINTENANCE
ADDING OIL

To check fluid, drive vehicle for at least 15 minutes to bring fluid to operating temperature (190°–200° F.). With vehicle on a level surface and engine idling in Park and parking brake applied, the level on the dipstick should be at the Full Hot mark. To bring the fluid level from the ADD mark to the FULL mark requires one pint of fluid. If vehicle cannot be driven sufficiently to bring fluid to operating temperature, the level on the dipstick should be between the two dimples on the dipstick with fluid tem-

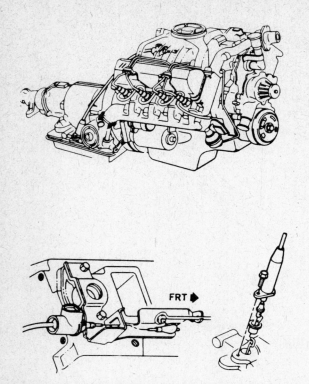

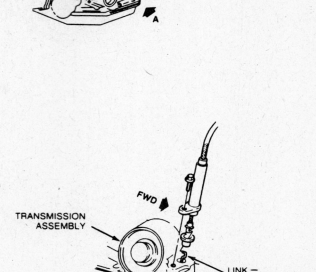

Fig. 5 T.V. cable adjustment. Models w/diesel engine

perature at 65°–85° F.

If additional fluid is required, use only Dexron II automatic transmission fluid.

NOTE: An early change to a darker color from the usual red color and or a strong odor that is usually associated with overheated fluid is normal and should not be considered as a positive sign of required maintenance or unit failure.

CAUTION: When adding fluid, do not over fill, as foaming and loss of fluid through the vent may occur as the fluid heats up. Also, if fluid level is too low, complete loss of drive may occur especially when cold, which can cause transmission failure.

Every 100,000 miles, the oil should be drained, the oil pan removed, the screen cleaned and fresh fluid added. For vehicles subjected to more severe use such as heavy city traffic especially in hot weather, prolonged periods of idling or towing, this maintenance should be performed every 15,000 miles.

CHANGING OIL

1. Raise vehicle and position drain pan under transmission pan.
2. Loosen rear and side pan attaching bolts approximately four turns.
3. Carefully pry transmission pan loose with a screwdriver and allow fluid to

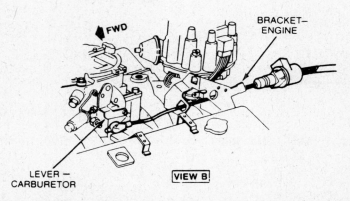

Fig. 6 T.V. cable adjustment. C, G & K models w/V6 and V8 gasoline engines

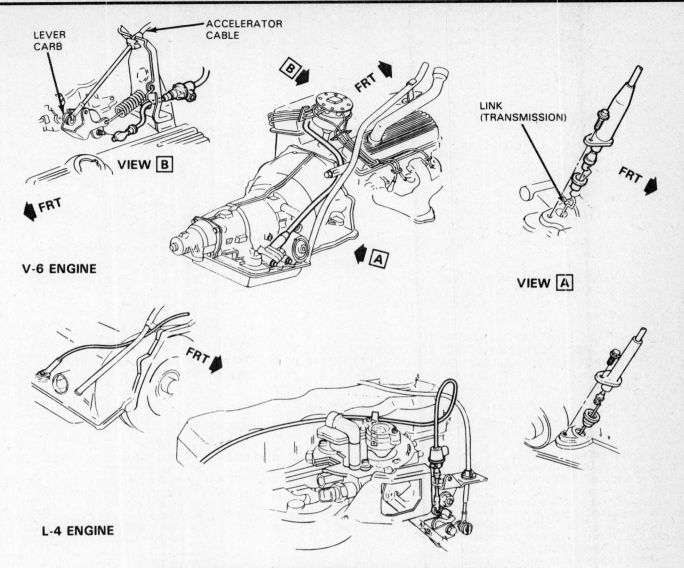

Fig. 7   T.V. cable adjustment. M Vans, S/T 10 & 15 series

drain.

4. Remove pan attaching bolts, pan and pan gasket.
5. Drain remaining fluid from pan, then clean pan with solvent and dry with compressed air.
6. Remove transmission screen. Remove O-ring seal from intake pipe or case bore.
7. Thoroughly clean screen assembly with solvent and dry with compressed air.
8. Install O-ring on intake pipe, then install screen retainer.
9. Install gasket on pan, then install pan and torque attaching bolts to 12 ft. lbs.
10. Lower vehicle and add approximately 5 qts. of Dexron II type transmission fluid through filler tube.
11. Start engine and operate at idle speed, then move selector lever through each range.
12. Place transmission in Park position and check fluid level.

IN-VEHICLE ADJUSTMENTS
T.V. CABLE, ADJUST
Gasoline Engine
1. Depress and hold metal readjust tab. Move slider back through fitting in direction away from throttle body until slider stops against fitting, **Figs. 3, 4, 6 and 7.**
2. Release metal readjust tab.
3. Open carburetor lever to full throttle stop position to automatically adjust cable, and release carburetor lever.
4. Check cable for proper operation. If

Fig. 8   Throttle lever to cable link

sticking or binding occurs, proceed as follows:
a. Remove oil pan and inspect throttle lever and bracket assembly.

NOTE: Check that the T.V. exhaust valve lifter rod is not distorted and not binding in the control valve assembly or spacer plate.

b. T.V. exhaust check ball must move up and down as the lifter does. Also ensure lifter spring holds the lifter rod up against the bottom of control valve assembly.
c. Ensure T.V. plunger is not stuck. Inspect transmission for correct throttle lever to cable link, **Fig. 8.**

Diesel Engine
1. On vehicles equipped cruise control, remove cruise control rod.
2. Disconnect T.V. cable from throttle assembly, then loosen lock nut on pump rod and shorten several turns.
3. Turn lever assembly to full throttle

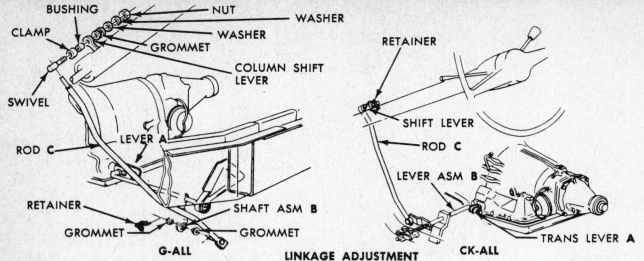

G-ALL

CK-ALL

LINKAGE ADJUSTMENT

1. SET TRANS LEVER (A) IN "NEUTRAL" POSITION BY MOVING TRANS LEVER (A) CLOCKWISE TO THE "PARK" DETENT THEN COUNTERCLOCKWISE TWO DETENTS TO "NEUTRAL".

2. SET THE COLUMN SHIFT LEVER IN "NEUTRAL" GATE NOTCH. THIS IS OBTAINED BY ROTATING UNTIL SHIFT LEVER DROPS INTO "NEUTRAL" GATE NOTCH. [NOTE] DO NOT USE INDICATOR POINTER AS A REFERENCE TO POSITION THE SHIFT LEVER.

3. ATTACH ROD (C) TO TRANS SHAFT ASM (B) AS SHOWN.

4. SLIDE SWIVEL AND CLAMP ONTO ROD (C) ALIGN WITH COLUMN SHIFT LEVER AND COMPLETE ATTACHMENT.

5. HOLD COLUMN LEVER AGAINST NEUTRAL STOP "PARK POSITION SIDE".

6. TIGHTEN NUT USING RECOMMENDED TORQUE.

Fig. 9   Shift linkage adjustment. C, G & K models

stop and hold in this position.
4. Adjust pump rod until injection pump lever contacts full throttle stop.
5. Release lever assembly and tighten pump rod lock nut, then remove pump rod from lever assembly.
6. Connect T.V. cable to throttle assembly, then depress and hold metal readjusting tab. Move slider back through fitting in direction away from lever assembly until slider stops against fitting, **Fig. 5.**
7. Release readjust tab, then rotate lever assembly to full throttle stop and release the lever.
8. Connect pump rod and, if equipped, the cruise control throttle rod.
9. On vehicles equipped with cruise control, adjust servo throttle rod to minimum slack position. Install clip into servo ball in first free hole closest to the bellcrank.

MANUAL LINKAGE ADJUSTMENT
C, G & K Series
1. Position transmission lever (A), **Fig. 9,** in neutral position by moving lever clockwise to the park detent, then counterclockwise two detents to neutral.
2. Place column shift lever in neutral gate notch by rotating lever until it drops into neutral gate notch.

NOTE: Do not use indicator pointer as a reference to position shift lever.

3. Attach rod (C), **Fig. 9,** to transmission shaft assembly.
4. Slide swivel and clamp onto rod, (C), **Fig. 9,** then attach to column shift lever.
5. Hold column shift lever against neutral stop, park position side, then tighten attaching nuts.

M Series
1. Position transmission lever (J), **Fig. 10,** to neutral position by one of the following methods:
   a. Obtain neutral position by moving transmission lever counterclockwise to "L1" detent, then three detent positions to neutral.
   b. Obtain neutral position by moving transmission lever clockwise to the park detent, then counterclockwise two detents to neutral.
2. Place column shift lever in neutral gate notch by rotating lever until it drops into neutral gate notch.

NOTE: Do not use indicator pointer as a reference to position shift lever.

3. Attach rod to column shift lever.
4. Slide swivel (A), retainer (B), spacer (C), washer (D), and insulator (E), onto rod (K), then align with lever (H), and complete attachment, **Fig. 10,** Torque nut (F) to 9–12 ft. lbs.

S Series
1. Place steering column shift lever in neutral gate notch.

2. Place transmission lever (A), **Fig. 11,** in neutral detent.
3. Install clamp spring washer and screw on transmission control lever (B), **Fig. 11,** and control rod.
4. Hold clamp flush against transmission control lever (B), **Fig. 11,** then finger tighten clamping screw against rod.

NOTE: No force should be exerted in either direction on the rod or transmission control lever (B), **Fig. 11,** while tightening the clamping screw.

Tighten control rod attaching screw.

IN VEHICLE REPAIRS
SERVO ASSEMBLY, REPLACE
1. Disconnect battery ground cable, then raise and support vehicle.
2. Install tool No. J-29714, then remove 2-4 servo cover retaining ring using a small screwdriver.
3. Remove servo cover and O-ring using suitable tool.
4. Remove fourth gear apply piston and O-ring, then the second servo piston assembly.
5. Remove inner servo piston assembly oil seal and spring.
6. Reverse procedure to install.

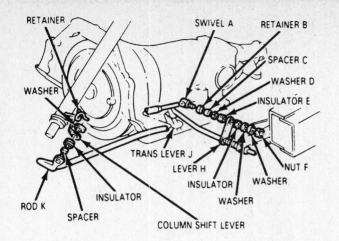

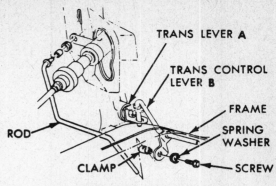

TRANSMISSION CONTROL LINKAGE ADJUSTMENT

1. STEERING COLUMN ATTACHMENT TO BODY MUST BE COMPLETE AND ALL BODY BOLT/SCREWS MUST BE SECURED BEFORE ADJUSTING TRANS CONTROL LINKAGE.

2. SET TRANS LEVER (J) IN "NEUTRAL" POSITION BY ONE OF THE FOLLOWING OPTIONAL METHODS.

    A. OBTAIN "NEUTRAL" POSITION BY MOVING TRANS LEVER (J) COUNTER-CLOCKWISE TO "L1" DETENT, THEN CLOCKWISE THREE DETENT POSITIONS TO "NEUTRAL" OR OBTAIN

    B. "NEUTRAL" POSITION BY MOVING TRANS LEVER (J) CLOCKWISE TO THE "PARK" DETENT THEN COUNTER-CLOCKWISE TWO DETENTS TO "NEUTRAL".

3. SET THE COLUMN SHIFT LEVER IN "NEUTRAL" GATE NOTCH. THIS IS OBTAINED BY ROTATING UNTIL SHIFT LEVER DROPS INTO "NEUTRAL" GATE NOTCH. NOTE DO NOT USE INDICATOR POINTER AS A REFERENCE TO POSITION THE SHIFT LEVER.

4. ATTACH ROD (K) TO COLUMN SHIFT LEVER AS SHOWN.

5. SLIDE SWIVEL (A), RETAINER (B), SPACER (C), WASHER (D) AND IN-SULATOR (E) ONTO ROD (K) ALIGN WITH LEVER (H) AND COMPLETE ATTACHMENT.

6. TIGHTEN NUT (F) USING RECOMMENDED TORQUE 12-17 N·m (9-12 Ft. Lbs.)

Fig. 10   Shift linkage adjustment. M Vans

ADJUSTMENT PROCEDURE

1. POSITION THE STEERING COLUMN SHIFT LEVER IN NEUTRAL GATE NOTCH.

2. SET TRANS LEVER (A) IN NEUTRAL DETENT.

3. ASSEMBLE CLAMP SPRING WASHER AND SCREW TO TRANS CONTROL LEVER (B) & CONTROL ROD.

4. HOLD CLAMP FLUSH AGAINST TRANS CONTROL LEVER (B) & FINGER TIGHTEN CLAMPING SCREW AGAINST ROD.
NO FORCE SHOULD BE EXERTED IN EITHER DIRECTION ON THE ROD OR TRANS CONTROL LEVER (B) WHILE TIGHTENING THE CLAMPING SCREW.

5. TIGHTEN SCREW TO SPECIFIED TORQUE.

Fig. 11   Shift linkage adjustment. S/T 10 & 15

5. Reverse procedure to install. Torque bolts to 8 ft. lbs. and replenish fluid. alignment.

TRANSMISSION
REPLACE

C, G, M, S-10 & S-15 4 × 2 MODELS

1. Disconnect battery ground cable.
2. Remove air cleaner assembly.
3. Disconnect T.V. cable at its upper end.
4. On vehicles equipped with 4-119 engine, remove starter motor upper retaining nut.
5. Raise and support vehicle.
6. Remove propeller shaft from vehicle.
7. Disconnect speedometer cable, shift linkage assembly and electrical connectors from transmission.
8. Remove transmission support brace attaching bolts from converter cover, if equipped.
9. Remove converter cover, then mark flywheel and torque converter for installation.
10. Remove exhaust crossover pipe and catalytic converter attaching bolts from vehicle.
11. Remove torque converter to flywheel bolts and/or nuts.
12. Disconnect catalytic converter support bracket.

SPEEDOMETER DRIVEN GEAR, REPLACE

1. Disconnect speedometer cable.
2. Remove retainer bolt, retainer, speedometer driven gear, and O-ring seal.
3. Reverse procedure to install, using new O-ring and adjusting fluid level.

REAR OIL SEAL, REPLACE

1. Remove driveshaft, and tunnel strap, if equipped.
2. Using suitable tool, pry out lip oil seal.
3. Coat outer casting of new oil seal with suitable sealer and drive into place with installer J-21426.
4. Install tunnel strap if used, then install driveshaft.

GOVERNOR, REPLACE

1. Raise and support vehicle.

2. Remove governor cover from case using extreme care not to damage cover. If cover is damaged, it must be replaced.
3. Remove governor.
4. Reverse procedure to install and check fluid level.

CONTROL VALVE ASSEMBLY, REPLACE

1. Drain and remove oil pan and remove filter and gasket.
2. Disconnect electrical connectors at valve body.
3. Remove detent spring and roller assembly from valve body and remove valve body to case bolts.
4. Remove valve body assembly while disconnecting manual control valve link from range selector inner lever and removing throttle lever bracket from T.V. link.

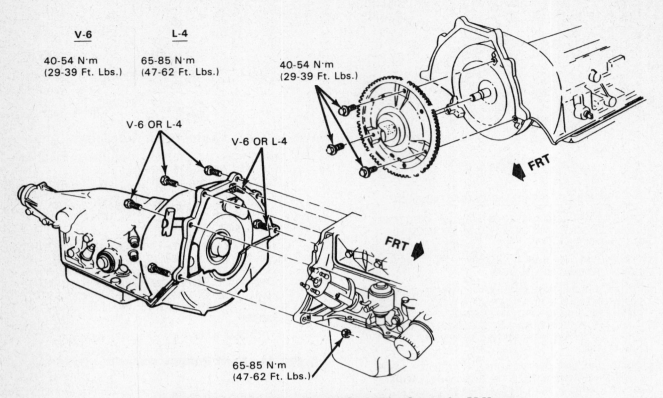

V-6 40-54 N·m (29-39 Ft. Lbs.)

L-4 65-85 N·m (47-62 Ft. Lbs.)

40-54 N·m (29-39 Ft. Lbs.)

V-6 OR L-4

V-6 OR L-4

FRT

FRT

65-85 N·m (47-62 Ft. Lbs.)

Fig. 12 Transmission-to-engine attachments. M Vans

13. Position a suitable jack under transmission and raise transmission slightly.
14. Remove transmission crossmember to transmission mount bolt.
15. Remove transmission crossmember to frame bolts and/or insulators, if equipped.
16. Slide crossmember rearward and remove from vehicle.
17. Lower transmission.
18. Disconnect and cap transmission fluid cooler lines.
19. Disconnect T.V. cable from transmission.
20. Position a suitable jack under engine, then remove transmission to engine attaching bolts.
21. Carefully separate transmission from engine. Install torque converter holding tool No. J-21366.
22. Remove transmission from vehicle.
23. To install transmission, reverse removal procedure and note the following:
   a. Before installing torque converter to flywheel bolts, ensure weld nuts on torque converter are flush with flywheel and torque converter rotates freely by hand in this position.
   b. Hand start, then finger tighten the bolts. Torque bolts to specifica-

tions shown in **Figs. 12 through 15.** This will ensure proper torque converter alignment.
   c. Install a new oil filler tube seal onto tube.
   d. Torque the remaining nuts and bolts to specifications shown in **Figs. 12 through 15.**

K, S/T 10 & S/T 15 4 × 4 MODELS

1. Disconnect battery ground cable.
2. Remove air cleaner assembly.
3. Disconnect T.V. cable at its upper end.
4. Remove transfer case shift lever knob and boot.
5. Raise and support vehicle.
6. Remove skid plate, then drain lubricant from transfer case.
7. Place an alignment mark between transfer case front output shaft yoke and propeller shaft. Disconnect front propeller shaft from transfer case.
8. Place an alignment mark between rear axle yoke and propeller shaft. Remove rear propeller shaft.
9. Disconnect speedometer cable, shift linkage assembly and electrical connectors from transmission. Remove

catalytic converter hanger, if necessary.
10. Disconnect shift linkage from transfer case assembly.
11. Remove transmission support strut rods and flywheel cover. Mark flywheel and torque converter for installation.
12. Remove torque converter to flywheel attaching bolts and/or nuts.
13. Disconnect and cap transmission fluid cooler lines.
14. Position a suitable jack under transmission and transfer case assembly.
15. Remove transfer case to frame bracket bolts. Remove mounting bolts and crossmember from vehicle.
16. Remove transmission to engine attaching bolts.
17. Carefully separate transmission from engine and remove from vehicle.

NOTE: In order to remove the upper left transfer case attaching bolts, it is necessary to remove the shift lever bracket mounting bolts from the transfer case adapter.

18. Reverse procedure to install. Refer to **Figs. 12 through 15** for torque specifications.

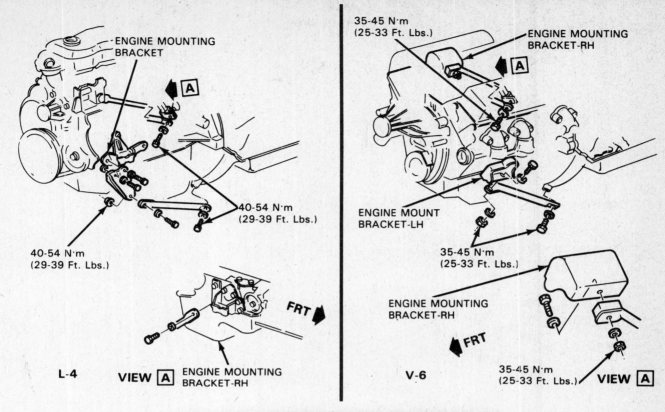

Fig. 13   Transmission support braces. M Vans

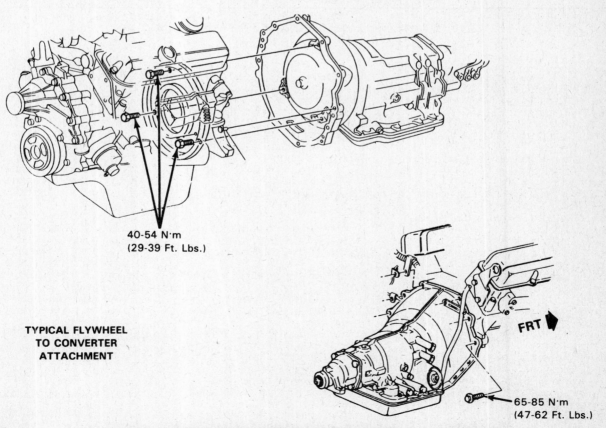

Fig. 14   Transmission-to-engine attachments. S/T 10 & 15

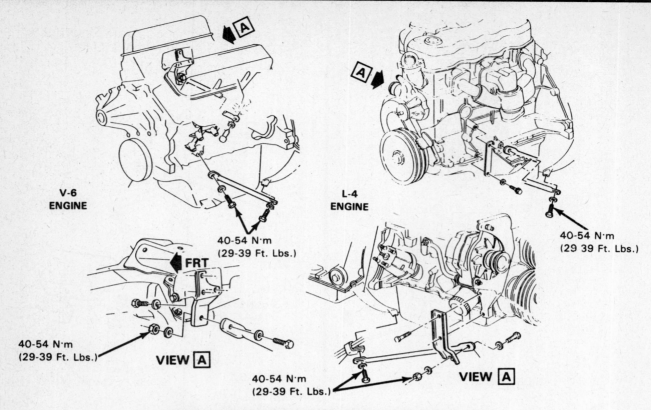

V-6
ENGINE

L-4
ENGINE

40-54 N·m
(29-39 Ft. Lbs.)

40-54 N·m
(29 39 Ft. Lbs.)

FRT

40-54 N·m
(29-39 Ft. Lbs.)

VIEW A

40-54 N·m
(29-39 Ft. Lbs.)

VIEW A

Fig. 15   Transmission support braces. S/T 10 & 15